MW01493226

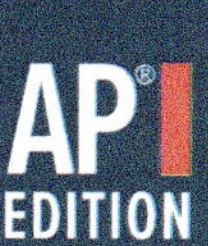

TEACHER WRAPAROUND EDITION

AMERICAN HISTORY

Connecting with the Past | SIXTEENTH EDITION

ALAN BRINKLEY
Columbia University

AP CONTRIBUTORS

JOHN IRISH
Carroll Senior High School

MICHAEL FLAMM
Ohio Wesleyan University

MARK KLOPFENSTEIN
Palmer Ridge High School

Cover Credits: Front Cover: Tetra Images/Getty Images, (bkgd)whitemay/E+/Getty Images; Back Cover: McGraw Hill

mheducation.com/prek-12

Send all inquiries to:
McGraw Hill
8787 Orion Place
Columbus, OH 43240

ISBN 978-1-26-624021-8
MHID 1-26-624021-7

Printed in the United States of America.

2 3 4 5 6 7 8 9 10 11 12 13 MER 31 30 29 28 27 26 25 24 23 22

ABOUT THE AUTHORS

Alan Brinkley (1949–2019) was the Allan Nevins Professor of History at Columbia University. He served as university provost at Columbia from 2003 to 2009. He authored works such as *Voices of Protest: Huey Long, Father Coughlin, and the Great Depression,* which won the 1983 National Book Award; *The Unfinished Nation: A Concise History of the American People*; *The End of Reform: New Deal Liberalism in Recession and War*; *Liberalism and Its Discontents*; *Franklin D. Roosevelt*; and *The Publisher: Henry Luce and His American Century.* He served as board chair of the National Humanities Center, board chair of the Century Foundation, and a trustee of Oxford University Press. He was also a member of the Academy of Arts and Sciences. In 1998–1999 he was the Harmsworth Professor of History at Oxford University, and in 2011–2012 the Pitt Professor at the University of Cambridge. He won the Joseph R. Levenson Memorial Teaching Award at Harvard and the Great Teacher Award at Columbia. He was educated at Princeton and Harvard.

John Irish is a teacher of AP United States History, American Studies, and Special Topics in Humanities at Carroll Senior High School in Southlake, Texas. He is a nationally certified consultant in AP U.S. History and AP European History for the Southwestern Region of the College Board. He is the co-author of *Historical Thinking Skills: A Workbook for World History.*

Michael Flamm is Professor of U.S. History at Ohio Wesleyan University. He is the author of *How 1954 Changed History* (2020), *In the Heat of the Summer: The New York Riots of the 1964 and the War on Crime* (2017), and *Law and Order: Street Crime, Civil Unrest, and the Crisis of Liberalism in the 1960s* (2005)

Mark Klopfenstein is the Social Studies Department Chair at Palmer Ridge High School in Monument, Colorado, in the Lewis Palmer School District, where he has taught since 2014. He has taught Advanced Placement United States History since 1991 and has served at all levels in the AP United States History reading from Reader to Exam Leader since 2001. He previously taught for 25 years at Blue Valley High School in Overland Park, Kansas, where he won the 2004 Discourse Challenge sponsored by Educational Testing Service and Hewlett-Packard. He has received undergraduate degrees from the University of Kansas and Kansas State University, and earned a Master's Degree in History from the University of Missouri-Kansas City.

CONTENTS

SURRENDER OF CORNWALLIS.

CONTENTS

CONTENTS

CONTENTS

CONTENTS

Library of Congress (cwpb.01402)

CONTENTS

CONTENTS

CONTENTS

CONTENTS

CONTENTS

PREFACE

DESIGNED FOR AP SUCCESS

Developed in collaboration with veteran AP teachers and College Board consultants, the Teacher Wraparound Edition for the 16th edition of *American History: Connecting with the Past* provides solid guidance and innovative strategies fully aligned to the AP U.S. History framework. This engaging teacher resource was mindfully created to support student mastery of the skills needed to achieve course and Exam success.

The Teacher Wraparound Edition effectively supports the planning and delivering of lessons and assessments by providing discussion topics, activities, and writing prompts in the side and bottom margins alongside the corresponding reduced-size pages of the Student Edition. This complementary placement aids teachers by connecting activities directly to the content at the point of use. AP Exam Practice and Tips throughout the book help students fully prepare for exam day.

The margin content in the Teacher Wraparound Edition addresses Key Concepts, Historical Developments, Historical Thinking Skills, and Reasoning Processes contextualized within Themes and Units from the AP U.S. History framework. This content provides students with frequent opportunities to engage with historical primary and secondary sources, historical analysis, and historical argumentation.

AP EXAM PREPARATION AND PRACTICE

The 16th edition of *American History: Connecting with the Past* provides students with exam prep support for the AP U.S. History Exam.

Student Edition

- Exam Practice features cover content at each chapter and unit level.
- A full AP Practice Exam at the end of the Student Edition has been designed to mirror the actual AP U.S. History Exam.

Digital Course

- Question banks include AP-style Multiple Choice, Short Answer, Document-Based, and Long Essay questions.
- Unit Reviews revisit and reinforce students' content knowledge and skill mastery.
- Two complete AP Practice Exams that can be administered in print or online provide more opportunities for practice.

5 Steps to a 5: AP U.S. History

- Hundreds of practice exercises are provided with thorough answer explanations.
- 5 Minutes to a 5 feature includes 180 questions and activities to reinforce the most vital course material.
- 3 full-length practice tests reflect the latest exam requirements and are accompanied by rubrics and overviews of essay sections and/or free-response questions.

PLAN YOUR LESSONS WITH PACING GUIDES AND AP KEY CONCEPTS

The Teacher Wraparound Edition contains Unit and Chapter level **Pacing Guides,** and **AP Key Concepts** are provided to help plan your instruction for each Unit and Chapter.

UNIT OPENER SUPPORT

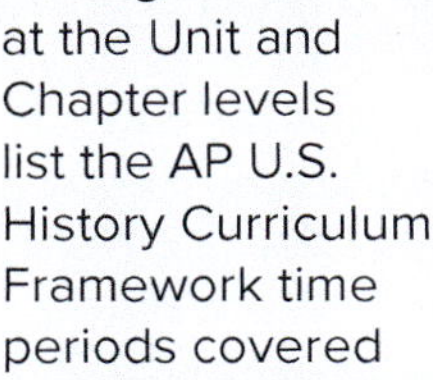

Pacing Guides at the Unit and Chapter levels list the AP U.S. History Curriculum Framework time periods covered in each unit and chapter, along with recommended instruction time for each.

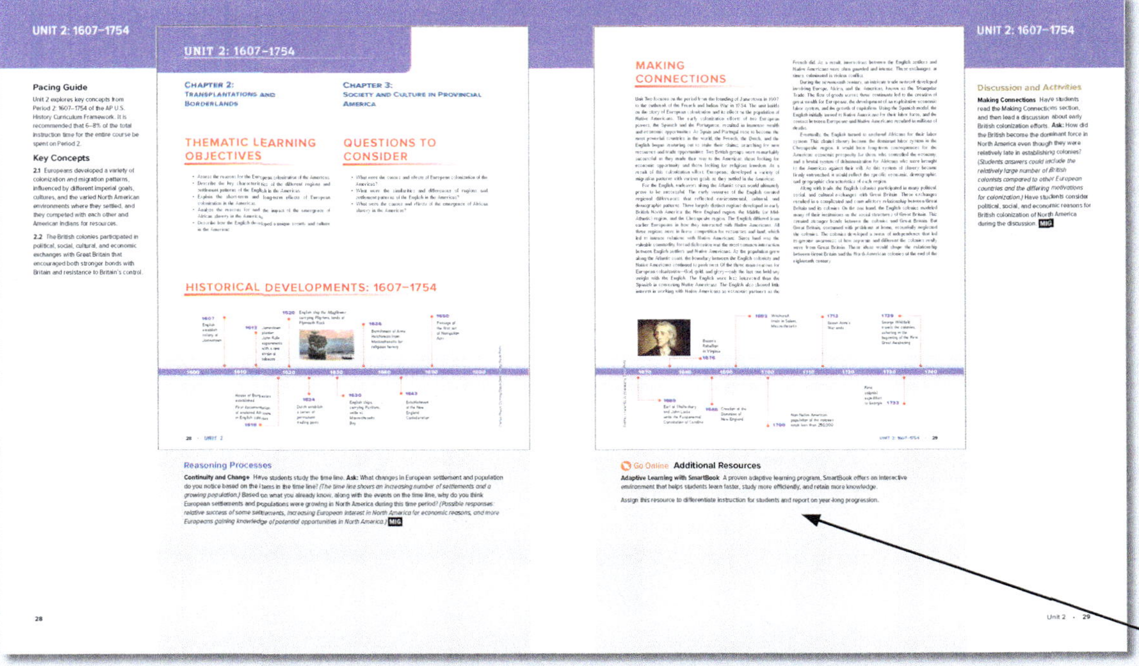

The **Go Online** features in the Unit and Chapter Openers provide information about the digital resources that enhance instruction and enrich the content of the Student Edition.

CHAPTER OPENER SUPPORT

Key Concepts at the Unit and Chapter levels list the concepts from the AP U.S. History Framework covered in the content of each unit and chapter.

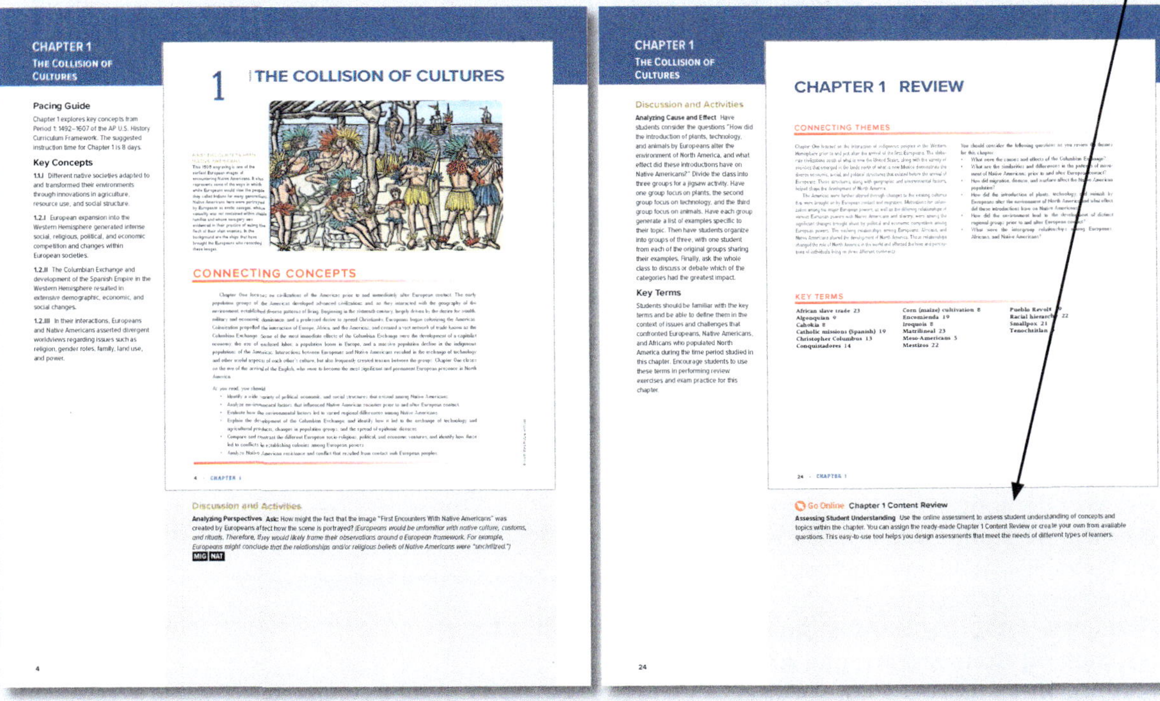

HOW TO USE YOUR *AMERICAN HISTORY* AP TEACHER EDITION

DELIVER MEANINGFUL HISTORICAL THINKING SKILLS AND REASONING PROCESSES PRACTICE

Each chapter of the Teacher Wraparound Edition contains a variety of activities to accompany the Student Edition content utilizing **Historical Thinking Skills** and **Reasoning Processes**, along with **Discussion and Activities**. Badges at the end of activities identify the AP U.S. History course themes that apply to the activity.

Reasoning Processes activities challenge students to dive deep into the content and put what they are learning into a larger historical context, making connections between past and present events and predicting what the future may hold. Many of these activities require students to draw upon prior knowledge and content they have studied in previous chapters. Reasoning Processes activities focus on **Comparing and Contrasting, Causation,** and **Continuity and Change.**

Historical Thinking Skills activities call on students to draw conclusions and form opinions about historical events and to think about, discuss, and write about their thoughts and interpretations. The activities encourage critical thinking skills and active debate. This feature includes such activities as **Argumentation, Sourcing and Situation,** and **Contextualization.**

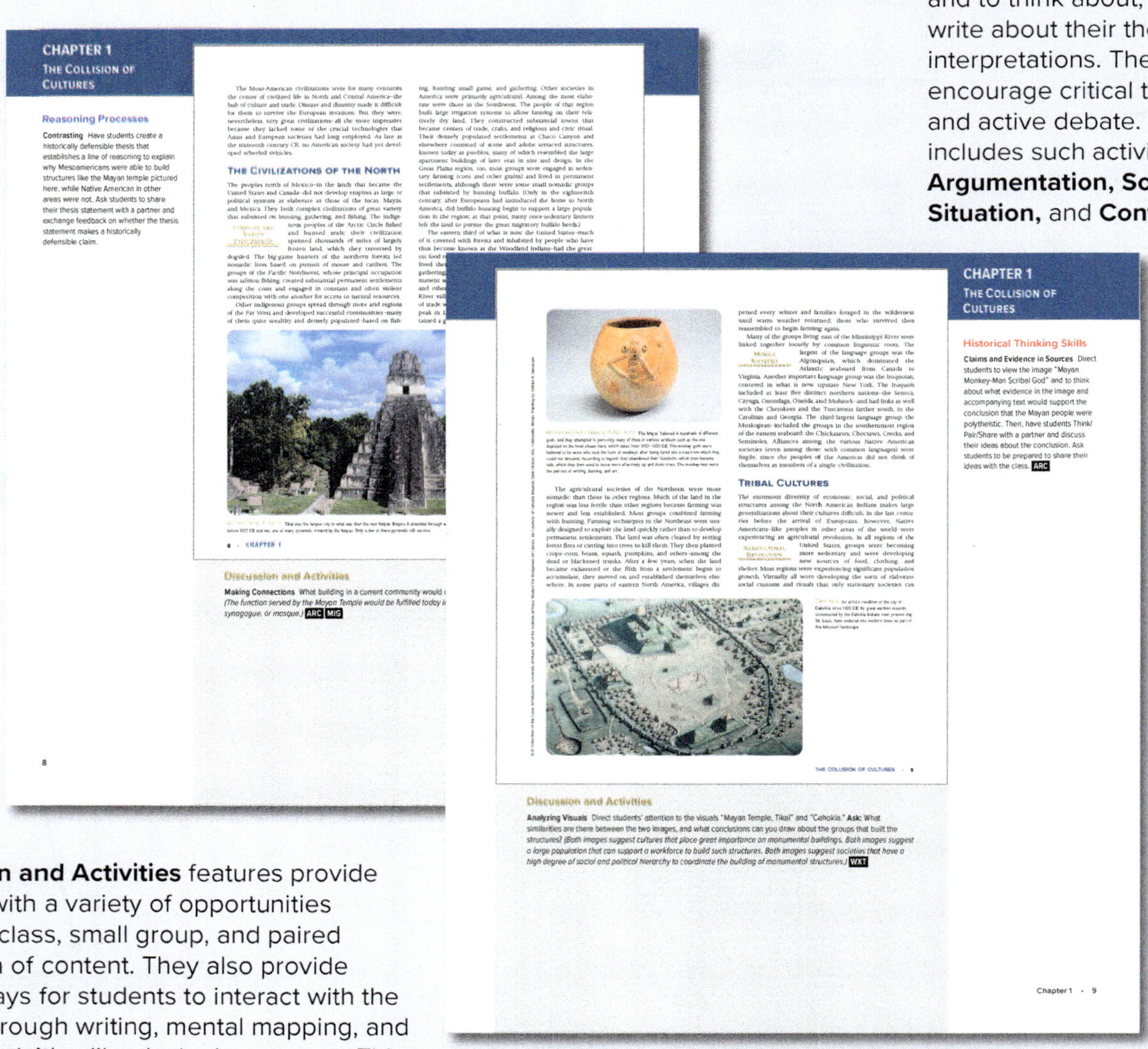

Discussion and Activities features provide students with a variety of opportunities for whole class, small group, and paired discussion of content. They also provide several ways for students to interact with the content through writing, mental mapping, and creative activities like designing posters. This feature includes such activities as **Analyzing Visuals, Making Connections,** and **Analyzing Points of View.**

PREPARE YOUR STUDENTS FOR THE AP EXAM

AP Exam Tips and additional AP Exam Practice to help your students succeed on the AP Exam.

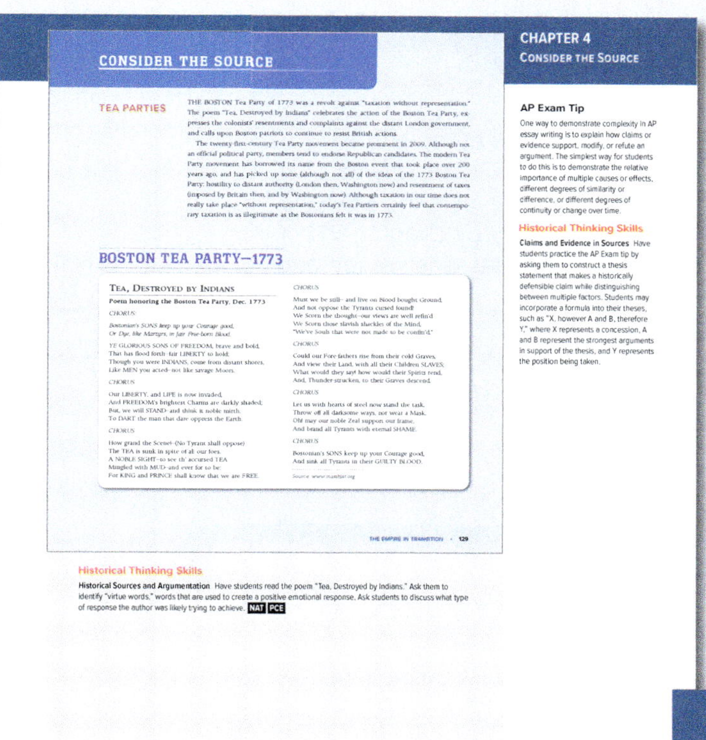

CONSIDER THE SOURCE

TEA PARTIES

THE BOSTON Tea Party of 1773 was a revolt against "taxation without representation." The poem "Tea, Destroyed by Indians" celebrates the action of the Boston Tea Party, expresses the colonists' resentments and complaints against the distant London government, and calls upon Boston patriots to continue to resist British actions.

The twenty-first-century Tea Party movement became prominent in 2009. Although not an official political party, members tend to endorse Republican candidates. The modern Tea Party movement has borrowed its name from the Boston event that took place over 200 years ago, and has picked up some (although not all) of the ideas of the 1773 Boston Tea Party: hostility to distant authority (London then, Washington now) and resentment of taxes (imposed by Britain then, and by Washington now). Although taxation in our time does not really take place "without representation," today's Tea Partiers certainly feel that contemporary taxation is as illegitimate as the Bostonians felt it was in 1773.

BOSTON TEA PARTY—1773

TEA, DESTROYED BY INDIANS

Poem honoring the Boston Tea Party, Dec. 1773

CHORUS:

Bostonian's SONS keep up your Courage good,
Or Dye, like Martyrs, in fair Free-born Blood.

YE GLORIOUS SONS OF FREEDOM, brave and bold,
That has flood forth–fair LIBERTY to hold;
Though you were INDIANS, come from distant shores,
Like MEN you acted–not like savage Moors.

CHORUS

Our LIBERTY, and LIFE is now invaded,
And FREEDOM's brightest Charms are darkly shaded;
But, we will STAND–and think it noble mirth,
To DART the man that dare oppress the Earth.

CHORUS

How grand the Scene!–(No Tyrant shall oppose)
The TEA is sunk in spite of all our foes.
A NOBLE SIGHT–to see th' accursed TEA
Mingled with MUD–and ever for to be;
For KING and PRINCE shall know that we are FREE.

CHORUS

Must we be still– and live on Blood bought Ground,
And not oppose the Tyrants cursed found?
We Scorn the thought–our views are well refin'd
We Scorn those slavish shackles of the Mind,
"We've Souls that were not made to be confin'd."

CHORUS

Could our Fore-fathers rise from their cold Graves,
And view their Land, with all their Children SLAVES;
What would they say! how would their Spirits rend,
And, Thunder-strucken, to their Graves descend.

CHORUS

Let us with hearts of steel now stand the task,
Throw off all darksome ways, nor wear a Mask.
Oh! may our noble Zeal support our frame,
And brand all Tyrants with eternal SHAME.

CHORUS

Bostonian's SONS keep up your Courage good,
And sink all Tyrants in their GUILTY BLOOD.

Source: www.mainhist.org

THE EMPIRE IN TRANSITION • 129

CHAPTER 4
CONSIDER THE SOURCE

AP Exam Tip

One way to demonstrate complexity in AP essay writing is to explain how claims or evidence support, modify, or refute an argument. The simplest way for students to do this is to demonstrate the relative importance of multiple causes or effects, different degrees of similarity or difference, or different degrees of continuity or change over time.

Historical Thinking Skills

Claims and Evidence in Sources Have students practice the AP Exam tip by asking them to construct a thesis statement that makes a historically defensible claim while distinguishing between multiple factors. Students may incorporate a formula into their theses, such as "X, however A and B, therefore Y," where X represents a concession, A and B represent the strongest arguments in support of the thesis, and Y represents the position being taken.

Historical Thinking Skills

Historical Sources and Argumentation Have students read the poem "Tea, Destroyed by Indians." Ask them to identify "virtue words," words that are used to create a positive emotional response. Ask students to discuss what type of response the author was likely trying to achieve. NAT PCE

Chapter 4 • 129

AP Exam Tips are provided throughout the Teacher Wraparound Edition to help teachers provide students with information about the AP Exam, the expectations they will face, and suggestions on how to approach a variety of exam questions. Following these tips are either Historical Thinking Skills or Reasoning Processes activities to help students practice the tip.

Additional **AP Exam Practice** questions are provided to offer more practice opportunities to ensure student readiness for the AP Exam. These allow students to familiarize themselves with the format of the AP Exam and to allow them a chance to answer AP Exam-style questions.

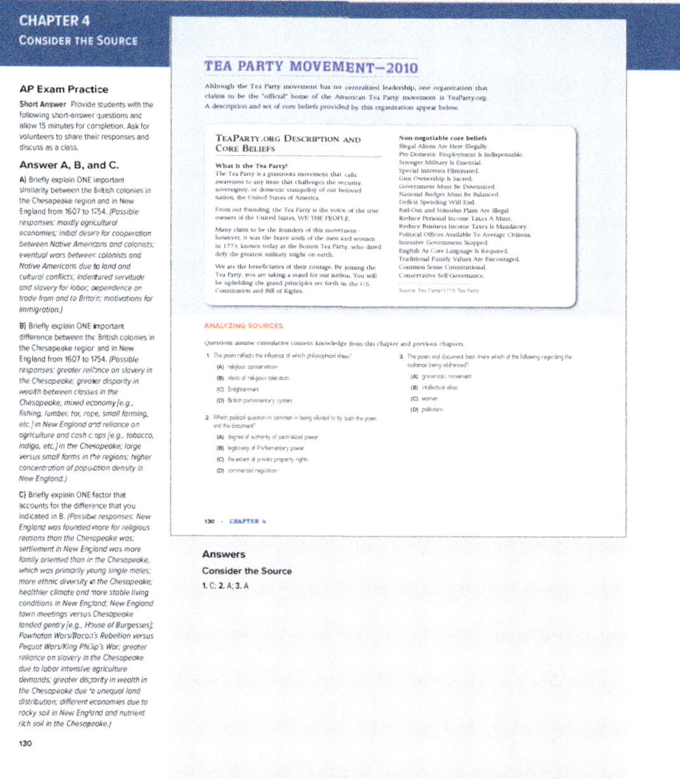

CHAPTER 4
CONSIDER THE SOURCE

AP Exam Practice

Short Answer Provide students with the following short-answer questions and allow 15 minutes for completion. Ask for volunteers to share their responses and discuss as a class.

Answer A, B, and C.

A) Briefly explain ONE important similarity between the British colonies in the Chesapeake region and in New England from 1607 to 1754. *(Possible responses: mostly agricultural economies; initial desire for cooperation between Native Americans and colonists; eventual wars between colonists and Native Americans due to land and cultural conflicts; indentured servitude and slavery for labor; dependence on trade from and to Britain; motivations for immigration.)*

B) Briefly explain ONE important difference between the British colonies in the Chesapeake region and in New England from 1607 to 1754. *(Possible responses: greater reliance on slavery in the Chesapeake; greater disparity in wealth between classes in the Chesapeake, mixed economy [e.g., fishing, lumber, tar, rope, small farming, etc.] in New England and reliance on agriculture and cash crops [e.g., tobacco, indigo, etc.] in the Chesapeake; large versus small farms in the regions; higher concentration of population density in New England.)*

C) Briefly explain ONE factor that accounts for the difference that you indicated in B. *(Possible responses: New England was founded more for religious reasons than the Chesapeake was; settlement in New England was more family oriented than in the Chesapeake, which was primarily young single males; more ethnic diversity in the Chesapeake; healthier climate and more stable living conditions in New England; New England town meetings versus Chesapeake landed gentry [e.g., House of Burgesses]; Powhatan Wars/Bacon's Rebellion versus Pequot Wars/King Philip's War; greater reliance on slavery in the Chesapeake due to labor intensive agriculture demands; greater disparity in wealth in the Chesapeake due to unequal land distribution; different economies due to rocky soil in New England and nutrient rich soil in the Chesapeake.)*

130

TEA PARTY MOVEMENT—2010

Although the Tea Party movement has no centralized leadership, one organization that claims to be the "official" home of the American Tea Party movement is TeaParty.org. A description and set of core beliefs provided by this organization appear below.

TEAPARTY.ORG DESCRIPTION AND CORE BELIEFS

What Is the Tea Party?
The Tea Party is a grassroots movement that calls awareness to any issue that challenges the security, sovereignty, or domestic tranquility of our beloved nation, the United States of America.

From our founding, the Tea Party is the voice of the true owners of the United States, WE THE PEOPLE.

Many claim to be the founders of this movement–however, it was the brave souls of the men and women in 1773, known today as the Boston Tea Party, who dared defy the greatest military might on earth.

We are the beneficiaries of their courage. By joining the Tea Party, you are taking a stand for our nation. You will be upholding the grand principles set forth in the U.S. Constitution and Bill of Rights.

Non-negotiable core beliefs
Illegal Aliens Are Here Illegally.
Pro-Domestic Employment Is Indispensable.
Stronger Military Is Essential.
Special Interests Eliminated.
Gun Ownership Is Sacred.
Government Must Be Downsized.
National Budget Must Be Balanced.
Deficit Spending Will End.
Bail-Out and Stimulus Plans Are Illegal.
Reduce Personal Income Taxes A Must.
Reduce Business Income Taxes Is Mandatory.
Political Offices Available To Average Citizens.
Intrusive Government Stopped.
English As Core Language Is Required.
Traditional Family Values Are Encouraged.
Common Sense Constitutional.
Conservative Self-Governance.

Source: Tea Party/1773 Tea Party

ANALYZING SOURCES

Questions assume cumulative content knowledge from this chapter and previous chapters.

1. The poem reflects the influence of which philosophical ideas?
   (A) religious conservatism
   (B) ideals of religious toleration
   (C) Enlightenment
   (D) British parliamentary system
2. Which political question in common is being alluded to by both the poem and the document?
   (A) degree of authority of centralized power
   (B) legitimacy of Parliamentary power
   (C) the extent of private property rights
   (D) commercial regulation
3. The poem and document best share which of the following regarding the audience being addressed?
   (A) grassroots movement
   (B) intellectual elites
   (C) women
   (D) politicians

130 • CHAPTER 4

Answers

Consider the Source

1. C; 2. A; 3. A

PROVIDE CHAPTER REVIEWS AND CHAPTER AP EXAM PRACTICE

Teacher wraparound material to support your students as they review chapter material. Answers and suggested answers for all AP Exam practice questions to assist with grading.

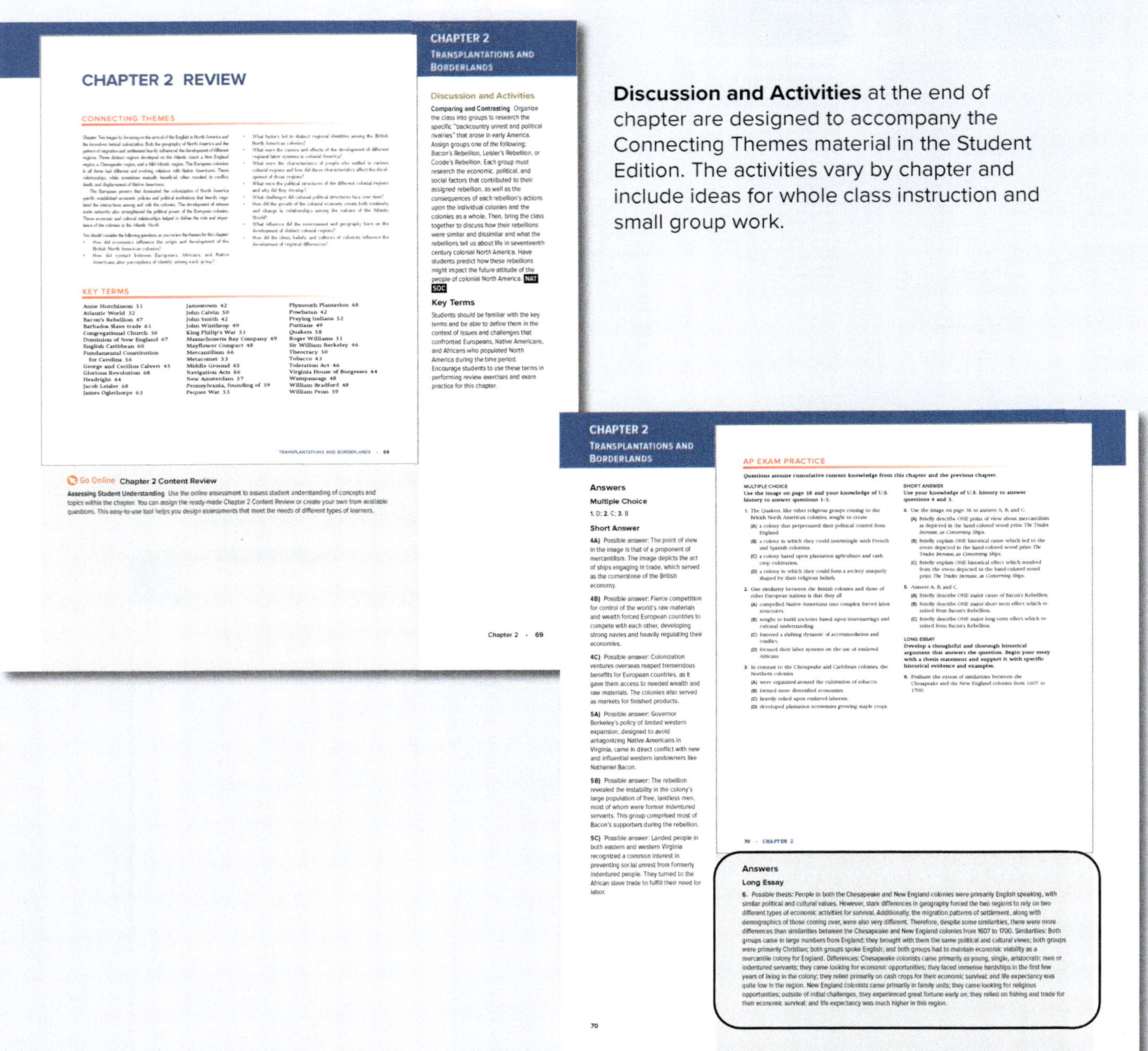

Discussion and Activities at the end of chapter are designed to accompany the Connecting Themes material in the Student Edition. The activities vary by chapter and include ideas for whole class instruction and small group work.

Answers are provided for all questions in the Student Edition. The short-answer question answers and long-essay thesis answers are meant to provide teachers with an indication of what to look for in student responses.

REINFORCE WITH UNIT AP EXAM PRACTICE

Prepare your students for the AP Exam with Multiple Choice, Short Answer, and Long Essay Practice questions based on the unit material.

Discussion and Activities have students review the **Questions to Consider** posed at the beginning of the unit and discuss as a class to review key concepts and demonstrate what they've learned in the unit.

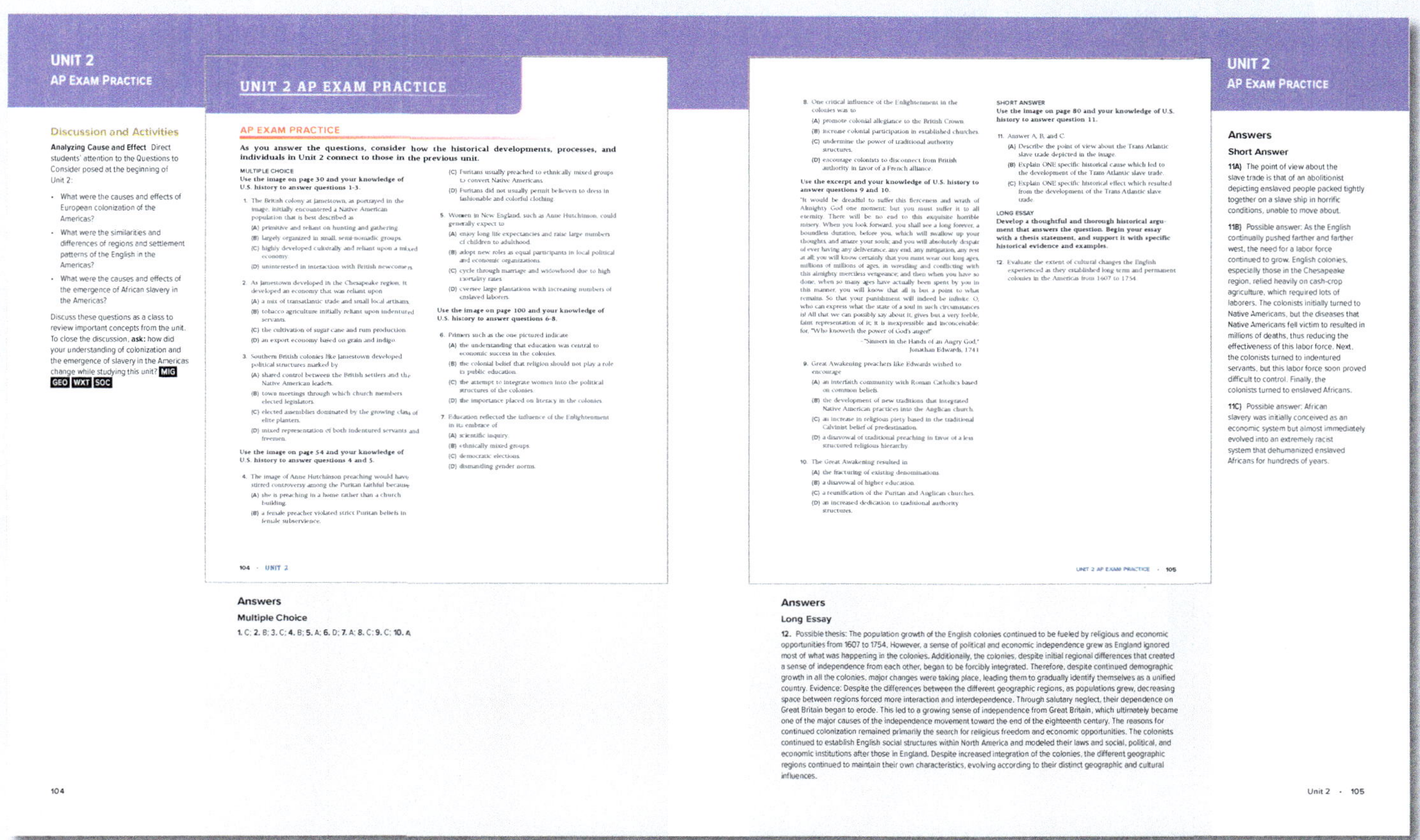

Answers are provided at point of use for all Multiple Choice, Short Answer, and Long Essay questions to assign with grading. There are possible answers for provided for all Short Answer questions and a possible thesis for the Long Essay question in each Unit.

HOW TO USE YOUR DIGITAL RESOURCES

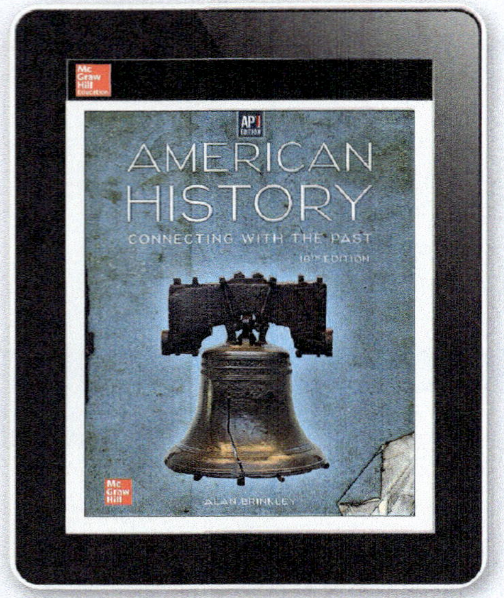

The **Teacher Edition eBook** includes activities and discussion prompts, questions reflecting the AP U.S. History Exam, and pacing guides from the print edition in a digital format. The Teacher Edition eBook provides a convenient, searchable way to access all content from the *American History* Teacher Wraparound Edition.

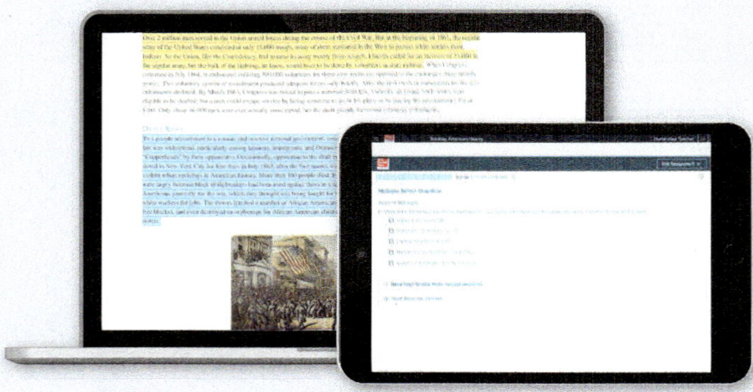

SmartBook® is an assignable, adaptive study tool that features personalized learning with self-guided tools that assess proficiency and knowledge, track which topics have been mastered, and identify areas that need more study. *SmartBook®* delivers meaningful practice with guidance and instant feedback and recharges learning with personalized recommendations, and it allows teachers to assign material at the topic and subtopic level.

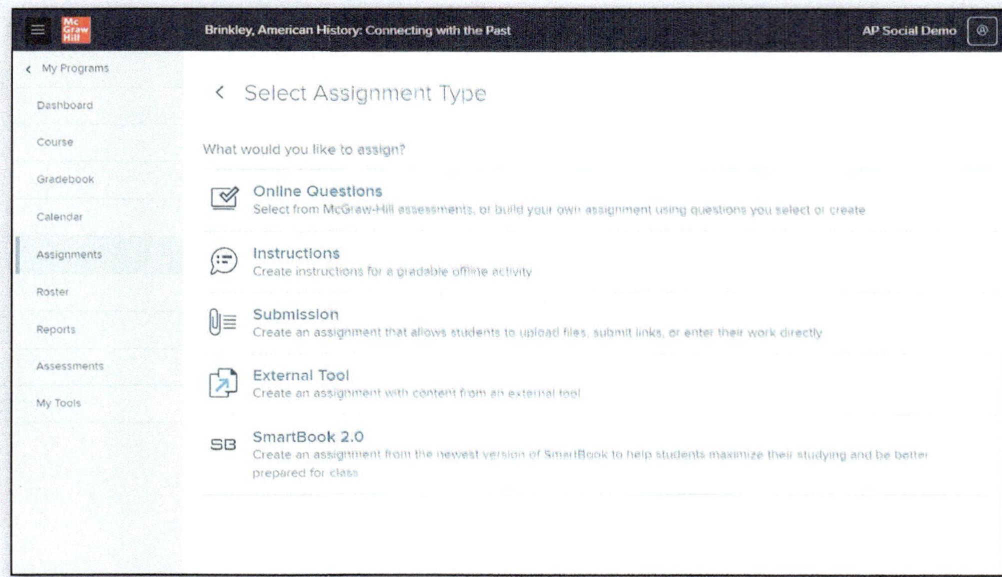

The **Assignments** page of the digital course allows teachers to select premade assessments, or build their own, and assign them to students. Teachers can also customize instructions for a gradable offline activity, create assignments that allow students to upload files, submit links or enter their work directly, and create assignments using content from an external tool. Teachers can generate assignments from the SmartBook to help students focus on discrete topics to maximize their studying and be better prepared for class.

McGraw Hill

PERFORMANCE ASSESSMENT STRATEGIES: PROJECT-BASED LEARNING

In response to the growing demand for accountability in the classroom, educators must use multiple assessment measures to accurately gauge student performance. In addition to quizzes, tests, essay exams, and standardized tests, assessment incorporates a variety of performance-based measures, such as project-based learning.

Project-based learning is a way of teaching and learning in which students apply and acquire knowledge, and develop skills by investigating complex questions or challenges over an extended period of time. Students use their creativity and collaboration skills to communicate their ideas. These activities help students become aware of diverse audiences for their work. Project-based learning includes individual products, group products, or a combination of both.

Teachers may allow students to choose the type of project to complete so that the project is more meaningful to them.

What Are Some Typical Performance-Based Assessments?

There are many kinds of performance-based assessments. They all challenge students to create products that demonstrate what they know and their ability to apply it.

Writing

Performance-based writing assessments challenge students to apply their knowledge of social studies in a variety of contexts. Writing activities are most often completed by an individual rather than by a group.

Journals: Students write from the perspective of a historical character or a citizen of a particular historical era.

Letters: Students write a letter from one historical figure to another or from a historical figure to a family member or another audience.

Position Papers or Editorials: Students explain a controversial issue and present their own opinion and recommendations, supported with strong evidence and convincing reasons.

News Articles: Students write a variety of stories from the perspective of a reporter living in a particular historical time period. This could also involve writing letters to the editor.

Biographies and Autobiographies: Students write about historical figures either from the third person point of view (biography) or from the first person (autobiography).

Creative Stories: Students integrate historical events into a piece of fiction, incorporating the customs, language, and geography of the period.

Poems and Songs: Students follow the conventions of a particular type of song or poem as they tell about a historical event or person.

Research Reports: Students synthesize information from a variety of sources into a well-developed research report.

Oral Presentations

Oral presentations allow students to demonstrate their social studies literacy before an audience. Oral presentations are often group efforts, although this need not be the case.

Simulations: Students hold simulations, or reenactments, of actual events, such as trials, acts of civil disobedience, battles, speeches, and so forth.

Debates: Students debate opposing viewpoints of a historical policy or issue. Students can debate from a contemporary perspective or in a role in which they assume a viewpoint held by a historical character.

Interviews: Students conduct a mock interview of a historical character or bystander.

Oral Reports: Students present the results of research efforts in a lively oral report. This report may be accompanied by visuals.

Visual Presentations

Visual presentations allow students to demonstrate their social studies understandings in a variety of visual formats. Visual presentations can be either group or individual projects.

Models: Students make models to demonstrate or represent a process, place, event, battle, artifact, or custom.

Museum Exhibit: Students create a rich display of material around a topic. Typical displays might include models, illustrations, photographs, videos, writings, and audiotaped explanations.

Graphs or Charts: Students analyze and represent historical data in a line graph, bar graph, table, or other chart format.

Drawings: Students represent or interpret a historical event or period through illustration, including political cartoons.

Posters and Murals: Posters and murals may include maps, time lines, diagrams, illustrations, photographs, collages, and written explanations that reflect students' understandings of historical information.

Quilts: Students sew or draw a design for a patchwork quilt that shows a variety of perspectives, events, or issues related to a key topic.

Videos: Students film a video to show historical fiction or to preserve a simulation of a historical event.

Multimedia Presentations or Slide Shows: Students create a computer-generated multimedia presentation containing historical information and analysis.

How Are Performance Assessments Scored?

Visual presentations allow students to demonstrate their social studies understandings in a variety of visual formats. Visual presentations can be either group or individual projects.

Scoring Rubrics: A scoring rubric is a set of guidelines for assessing the quality of a process and/or product. It establishes criteria used to distinguish acceptable responses from unacceptable ones, generally along a scale from excellent to poor. Rubrics clearly outline expectations for behaviors and outcomes. Rubrics may be used as guidelines as the students prepare their products. They are also commonly used for selfassessment.

Models of Excellent Work: Teacher-selected models of excellent work concretely illustrate expectations and help students set goals for their own projects.

PERFORMANCE ASSESSMENT STRATEGIES: PROJECT-BASED LEARNING

Student Self-Assessment: Students can assess themselves using a variety of methods. Students can rank their work in relation to the model, use a scoring rubric, and write their own goals. Students can then evaluate how well they have met the goals they set for themselves. Regardless of which method or methods students use, they should be encouraged to evaluate their behaviors and processes, as well as the finished product.

Peer or Audience Assessment: Many of the performance tasks target an audience other than the classroom teacher. If possible, an audience of peers should give feedback to the student or group. Have the class create rubrics for specific projects together.

Observation: As students carry out their performance tasks, you may want to formally observe students at work. Start by developing a checklist, identifying all the specific behaviors and understandings you expect students to demonstrate. Then observe students as they carry out performance tasks, and check off the behaviors as you observe them.

Interviews: As a form of ongoing assessment, you may want to conduct interviews with students, asking them to analyze, explain, and assess their participation in performance tasks.

ABOUT THE AP UNITED STATES HISTORY COURSE

Course Themes and Structure

This Advanced Placement course replicates a college-level introductory United States history survey course. The course provides students with the knowledge and skills necessary for more specialized courses in American history. Students that complete the AP course should understand the chronological framework of United States history and how events and trends are related to one another. Additionally, students should acquire critical thinking skills, including analyzing primary and secondary sources, developing and supporting a thesis or argument with historical evidence, and understanding the major interpretive frameworks that historians use to interpret the past.

The College Board and the Educational Testing Service, which administer the AP Exam, survey more than 100 college and university instructors across the country to keep abreast of content covered in introductory college survey courses. A Test Development Committee, which consists of three college or university professors and three high school teachers, uses this information to create an examination that reflects the experience most undergraduate students receive. The test is administered in early May. Thousands of AP high school teachers and college and university professors, who serve as AP Exam Readers, score the AP United States History (APUSH) Exam. These teachers gather for a fun-filled, action-packed week in early June, receive training in scoring the exams, and spend the remainder of the week reading and scoring student essays.

The College Board introduced eight themes to help prepare students for the AP Exam. These include the following (1) American and National Identity, (2) Work, Exchange, and Technology, (3) Geography and the Environment, (4) Migration and Settlement, (5) Politics and Power, (6) America in the World, (7) American and Regional Culture, and (8) Social Structures. Student familiarity with these themes is essential for scoring well on the exam since they provide the basis for both multiple-choice and essay questions. Below is a brief description of each. A fuller discussion of these themes is available on the AP Central website.

Themes

American and National Identity: This theme focuses on Americans' sense of what being an American means, what America symbolizes, the group identities of Americans, and how and why identities developed and changed over time. In exploring this theme, students will examine ideas about democracy, individualism, constitutionalism, citizenship, and foreign policy in relation to national identity, interactions among different groups, and the expression of these ideas in social, political, and economic contexts.

Work, Exchange, and Technology: This theme focuses on the development of the agricultural, commercial, and manufacturing elements of the American economy and attendant labor systems along with the important role of technological development. In exploring this theme, students will examine the ways the government has interacted with the economic system and the results of that interaction. Students will also evaluate the relationship between business and labor in various time periods and examine how work has affected all classes of society, racial and ethnic groups, and men and women.

Geography and the Environment: This theme focuses on the effects of geographic factors and natural and human-made environments on communities' social, political, and economic development. In exploring this theme, students will examine the competition for and management of natural resources, the development of environmental policies, and Americans' evolving perceptions of their environment.

Migration and Settlement: This theme focuses on the emigration and immigration of people within and to the United States. In exploring this theme, students will examine demographics, changing migration patterns, and how various groups adapted to or changed the social and physical environment.

Politics and Power: This theme focuses on the impact of social and political groups on American society and government. In exploring this theme, students will examine how political beliefs and institutions have changed throughout various time periods.

America in the World: This theme focuses on the interactions between nations during the colonial period and the impact of the United States on world affairs throughout various time periods. In exploring this theme, students will examine the competition for territory and resources and the economic, political, and social influence of the United States on the world.

American and Regional Culture: This theme focuses on the development of a variety of cultures in the United States along with the impact of cultures on government and the economy. In exploring this theme, students will evaluate the influence of culture on continuity and change in the United States at the national, state, and local levels.

Social Structures: This theme focuses on the development and growth of social systems. In exploring this theme, students will consider how and why social systems develop and the social, economic, and political impact of these systems.

ABOUT THE AP UNITED STATES HISTORY COURSE

Historical Thinking Skills and Reasoning Processes

The AP U.S. History course and exam also emphasizes the development and use of historical thinking skills and reasoning processes designed by the College Board. Students must respond to exam questions using particular historical thinking skills and reasoning processes, including:

Developments and Processes: Historical thinking requires students to explain historical events and processes. Students must analyze cause/effect relationships, examine historical trends, and recognize connections to support an argument of change or continuity. As the course progresses, students should become proficient in analyzing multi-causation and multi-effect, evaluating their relative significance and making distinctions between causation, correlation, and historical contingency.

Contextualization: Historical thinking requires students to analyze historical events and developments using context. Students should use the circumstances that create the setting for a historical event, development, or process to understand historical situations and how events relates to a broader situation or process.

Sourcing and Situation: Historical thinking requires students to analyze primary and secondary sources. Students must identify and explain the author's relevance, place and time, purpose, audience, main idea, point of view, and historical situation. Critical for the AP Exam, students must draw conclusions and inferences from sources to support their argument.

Claims and Evidence in Sources: Historical thinking involves the ability to describe and evaluate evidence from a variety of primary sources. Students must identify the argument within the source and realize the importance of the claim and supporting examples and evidence provided. The ability to explain how claims and evidence change, support, or refute an argument is essential for success on the AP Exam.

Making Connections: Historical thinking requires students to make connections among events within and across time periods. Students should also make connections by comparing and contrasting historical developments, including from different time periods, geographic regions, and societies.

Argumentation: Historical thinking requires students to frame and/or answer a question and construct an argument supporting a position. Such arguments require students to create an analytical thesis, relevant historical evidence, and analysis of how and why that evidence supports the thesis. Students should also describe, analyze, and evaluate contradictory evidence or arguments of other historians.

SAMPLE SYLLABUS ADVANCED PLACEMENT UNITED STATES HISTORY

Planning Your Syllabus for Advanced Placement United States History

Advanced Placement U.S. History is a survey course of American History, focusing on the time from pre-colonial America to the present. The course will focus on the skills requisite to success in the academic world, including critical thinking, writing, analysis, discussion, and debate. Below are notes about the structuring of units and following are suggested pacing guides to allow for the full coverage of the course material.

Unit 1: Period 1: 1491–1607
The Invasions of North America
4–6% of course content

This introductory unit sets the foundation for the interaction of Americans, Europeans, and Africans. Key focus should be placed upon the pre-contact lives on all three continents, with an additional geographic and climate focus on North America.

Chapter 1 provides students with an introduction to these concepts as well as the complexity presented by such interactions. The European beliefs translated strongly into the colonial systems developed by such countries, and the multiplicity of contacts led to a variety of responses by Native Americans to European contacts. An introduction to multiple labor and social systems will also challenge students to practice advanced thinking at an early stage in the course.

This unit should also include an introduction to the basic skills of the class, including the Historical Thinking Skills and Reasoning Processes. Additionally, the course themes will assist students in understanding the complex nature of the topics.

Unit 2: Period 2: 1607–1754
European Expansion and Colonial Development
6–8% of course content

The second unit will move students into more familiar territory with the British colonization of the Atlantic seaboard. Chapter 2 details the expansion of the European powers into the mainland of North America and discusses the conflicts that understandably arose with the Native Americans who already occupied those areas. This chapter correlates with Topics 2.2 through 2.5 from the College Board Course and Exam Description (CED). Spanish expansion into California and European expansion into the Caribbean continues the focus on labor systems, including the development of plantation agriculture that generated enormous wealth through the labor of enslaved Africans. The concept of Middle Ground allows students a more sophisticated framework to evaluate the interactions between Europeans and Native Americans.

Chapter 3 advances the chronological development of the colonies, with significant focus on the demographic changes as the colonies developed. This is also the chapter that introduces the differences between indentured servitude and slavery, correlating to CED Topic 2.6. The development of an increasingly distinct American culture moved the colonial population further from their English roots, while increasing economic prosperity allowed colonists to purchase English products and engage in transatlantic print culture. European intellectual and religious trends spread to the colonies. These topics reflect CED Topic 2.7.

For skill development, students should begin course specific writing assignments. Short Answer questions provide an opportunity to practice writing at an introductory level.

Unit 3: Period 3: 1754–1800
The American Revolutions
10–17% of course content

Chapter 4 covers the Seven Years' War and the events leading to the American Revolution. The involvement of the American colonies in the string of Anglo-French conflicts and the resultant change in British policies present complexity for students. This also aligns with Topics 3.2 and 3.3 in the CED.

Chapter 5 covers the war and the creation of new American governments, and as such opens discussions of the underpinnings of our political systems. The American Revolution is perhaps the most familiar content for many students, and thus provides an opportunity to introduce many primary source documents. This aligns to CED Topics 3.4 through 3.7.

Chapter 6 rounds out the unit with the construction of the Constitution and its implementation in the first two presidential administrations. The immense challenges faced by Presidents George Washington and John Adams marked the solidification of American independence. The same topics are included in the CED in topics 3.8 through 3.12. Finally, the fall of the Federalist party was the first incarnation of American political party politics.

Unit 4: Period 4: 1800–1848
Forming an American Identity
10–17% of course content

Unit Four contains a variety of loosely connected topics detailing America's development through the Early Republic, Era of Good Feelings, Jacksonian Era, and Second Great Awakening. At this point in the course, students should also be introduced and gain familiarity with the writing components of the Long Essay and Document-Based Questions.

Chapter 7 covers the Jefferson Administration and the War of 1812, aligning with topic 4.2 of the CED. The devolution of political parties and subsequent rise of the Second Party System should be traced through much of this unit. Chapter 8 presents material with which students may have less familiarity, the Era of Good Feelings and surge of post-war nationalism but provides the opportunity to move students to more complex modes of thinking about national identity. Chapter 9 focuses on Jackson and the many areas of political disagreement during his presidency, aligning with Topics 4.7 and 4.8 in the CED. Chapter 10, the Market Revolution, is another area about which students may have less previous knowledge but provides an excellent starting point to economic history and the history of technology. Chapter 11 discusses the institution of slavery and its economic role in the Southern and American economies, and the subsequent development of social structures around and supporting the institution. Finally, Chapter 12 mixes more common information on the reform movements of the era with perhaps lesser-known information on cultural development and aligns with Topics 4.9 through 4.11 in the CED.

SAMPLE SYLLABUS ADVANCED PLACEMENT UNITED STATES HISTORY

Unit 5: Period 5: 1844–1877
Contesting the American Identity
10–17% of course content

This unit contains some of the most familiar material to many students as well as some of the perhaps least familiar. Careful consideration should be given to ensuring that enough time is allotted to teach the complexities of Reconstruction, as few students have the level of understanding of that time period compared to the war itself. Chapter 13 covers the territory of the escalating conflict over the expansion of slavery through territorial acquisition as well as sympathetic legislation and court decisions. This aligns with topics 5.2 through 5.6 of the CED.

Chapter 14 deals with secession and the war itself, and students may be less familiar with more complicated aspects of the war such as wartime diplomacy and its importance. These topics are covered in 5.7 through 5.9 of the CED, and teachers have latitude in choosing on which of the overwhelming number of battles they prefer to focus. Reconstruction from its beginnings through abandonment are in Chapter 16, and this is the unit topic that traditionally is the least familiar to all students and thus may require some additional consideration when planning the unit.

Unit 6: Period 6: 1865–1898
The Long Gilded Age
10–17% of course content

This unit bears some similarity to Unit 4, both in terms of the variety of topics covered as well as the newness of some of the material for students. The unit contains four main topics. Chapter 16 covers the post-civil war movement of Americans west and the resulting clashes with the Native Americans who lived in those areas. The imagery of the west as "frontier," the conflicts between multiple groups and exacerbation by population increase and shifting policies toward Native American nations allow students to continue the discussion about American identity and assimilation and covers Topics 6.2 and 6.3 in the CED. Chapter 17 is about industry and the transformative changes occurring in the American economy and their impacts on all aspects of American life. Questions of wealth and labor resonate through much of American history, and they are central to the Gilded Age. Chapter 18 focuses on the many changes in American society in the era, from the migration and immigration that brings more people to the cities, to the economic movement that elevates more to the middle class and the resulting changes wrought with the expansion of leisure time. Students may find some of this material novel in the appearance of topics such as consumer culture as topics of historical inquiry. This covers Topics 6.8 through 6.10 in the CED. Finally, Chapter 19 discusses the politics of the Gilded Age, including local through national politics and the rising agrarian tide of political activity. In a similar fashion to Unit 4, this unit presents multiple opportunities for students to connect historical trends across time periods and enhance understanding of both continuities and changes in history.

Unit 7: Period 7: 1890–1945
Redefining America
10–17% of course content

This unit contains an enormous amount of material and many opportunities to break topics into smaller units, either chronologically or thematically (such as foreign and domestic issues). The unit contains six major topics: Progressivism, the 1920s, Great Depression and New Deal, Imperialism, World War I and Interwar Diplomacy, and World War II. At this stage, all classes will be firmly in the second half of the school year and should be using all three forms of writing in class in order to be well-prepared for the AP Exam.

Chapter 20 covers imperialism and the United States' movement into spreading abroad on an enduring basis. Covered in the CED in Topics 7.2 and 7.3, the Spanish-American War and the resulting movement to become an empire challenges students to encounter the questions resulting from such moves, especially around the nature of citizenship. Chapter 21 covers the Progressives, the movement to save the industrializing country from its own excesses, and to ameliorate the worsening conditions in rapidly expanding cities. Chapter 22 on World War I raise important and difficult questions about wartime responsibilities and rights as well as the conflicts that persisted after the war. This is covered in the CED in Topics 7.5 and 7.6. Chapter 23 continues into the 1920s and details all of the cultural clashes that consumed the decade, with the conflict between traditional and modern beliefs manifesting in many different aspects of American society. Additionally, the explosion of artistic production led to the development of a new culture centered in cities. Chapter 24 covers the Great Depression and chapter 25 details the New Deal, including its limits and enduring legacies. Many students may have familiarity with the New Deal agencies, so ideally class lessons can build upon this existing knowledge to move students toward the larger questions about the roles of individuals and government and the relationship between them. These are also in Topics 7.9 and 7.10 in the CED. Finally, Chapter 26 covers interwar diplomacy, and Chapter 27 covers World War II, topics which challenge classes to engage in the larger questions surrounding the changes in American foreign policy from isolation to intervention. The human tragedy encompassed in the wars of the twentieth century is difficult but important to convey.

Unit 8: Period 8: 1945–1980
America Moves to Center Stage
10–17% of course content

Unit 8 possesses a large amount of content and many may want to subdivide into smaller increments in some class settings. Chapter 28 covers the early Cold War, a topic largely unfamiliar to many students. The domestic aspects of this time period are largely found in Chapter 29 and may commonly be taught together. These reflect the content in CED topics 8.2 through 8.5 and allow for multiple pathways of organization. Chapter 30 details the first post-war waves of rights movements, particularly those among African Americans and women, and may be added to other topics or may stand alone. The CED focuses on these events in Topic 8.6. Chapter 31, the Later Cold War, and Chapter 32, Turbulent Times, focus on the extraordinary upheaval of the 1960s and 1970s, and students may be less familiar with the history of the era than they think. Placing these within the larger context of the Cold War should assist in student understanding. These events and trends are found in the CED in Topics 8.14 through 8.16. Additionally, with the Advanced Placement Exam approaching, students should be perfecting their writing skills as measured on the exam.

Unit 9: Period 9: 1980–Present
Redefining the American Dream
4–6% of course content

This unit presents critical information about our recent past, and well-organized units earlier in the year should leave sufficient time to cover these events and trends with students. Chapter 33 details the ascendancy of President Reagan and the success of the Modern Conservative movement as well as the end of the Cold War. Covered in the CED in topics 9.2 and 9.3, these are crucial to students contextualizing our politics and society today. Chapter 34 notes economic changes and events that progress even closer to our current world, and those before 2003 may appear on the AP US History exam.

Syllabus Notes:

1. This syllabus is used for a full-year course.
2. An important decision is where to place the semester break; this is prepared for a school year that has more days in the first semester, and thus includes the first six units in the first semester.

Unit One Lessons

Day 1: Intro Lecture to North America, Europe, Africa
Day 2: The Concept of 1491
Day 3: The Atlantic World and the Trade of Enslaved Africans *Primary source analysis* – maps and charts of the Trans-Atlantic Slave trade as accessed on www.slavevoyages.org
Day 4: The Regions of North America and Cultural Difference "The Columbian Exchange"
Day 5: Spanish Expansion
Day 6: French Expansion
Day 7: English Expansion

Unit Two Lessons

Day 1: Intro Lecture to European Expansion
Day 2: Comparison of Colonies
Day 3: The Chesapeake Colonies *primary sources:* "The Starving Time," John Smith; "The Laws of Virginia, 1610–1611"
Day 4: New England's Colonies *primary sources:* "A Model of Christian Charity," John Winthrop; "Before the Birth of one of her Children," Anne Bradstreet
Day 5: Discussion: The Puritans – Theology and Democracy Discussion questions: To what extent were the Puritans theocratic? To what extent were they democratic?
Day 6: The Middle Colonies *primary sources:* "Model of Government," William Penn, Maryland Act of Toleration
Day 7: Growing Pains in the British Colonies
Day 8: Bacon's Rebellion and the Emergence of Racially based Slavery
Day 9: The Role of Women in the Colonies
Day 10: Lecture/Discussion: Challenges of growth – the Salem Witch Trials
Day 11: Comparing Indentured Servitude and Slavery
Day 12: The Great Awakening
Day 13: The Great Awakening *continued* *primary source:* "Sinners in the Hands of an Angry God," Jonathan Edwards
Day 14: Discussion: Religious Freedom in the Colonies *Discussion Question:* To what extent did religious freedom exist in the British North American colonies?

Unit Three Lessons

Day 1: Intro Lecture to the Age of American Revolutions
Day 2: Seven Years' War
Day 3: Lecture – Timeline of events leading to the Revolution
Day 4: The American Mindset *primary source:* Ben Franklin's testimony before the House of Commons
Day 5: Events Leading to the Revolution
Day 6: Primary Source Analysis – *Common Sense* vs. *The Declaration of Independence*
Day 7: Battles of the American Revolution
Day 8: For the Enslaved, Native Americans, and Women – truly a Revolution?
Day 9: The Critical Period
Day 10: Discussion – Challenges of the Early Republic *Alien and Sedition Acts, Kentucky and Virginia Resolves* (documents from 1977 DBQ)
Day 11: The Constitution
Day 12: Alexander Hamilton – Evil Genius or Misunderstood Patriot?
Day 13: Foreign Policy in the Early Republic
Days 14–16: The Presidency of John Adams
Day 17: Discussion – To what extent was the Revolution a revolution? Students must identify (and defend) three main causes of the Revolution and two main outcomes. (Historical Causation)

Unit Four Lessons

Day 1: Intro Lecture to Forming the American Identity – Expansion of democracy and the expulsion of Indians, expansion of slavery, and stirring of reform
Day 2: Jefferson's presidency
Day 3: Lewis and Clark expedition *primary sources:* excerpts from the journals / Mandan Indians/ maps of exploration
Day 4: Era of Good Feelings
Day 5: Discussion – Monroe's Presidency Discussion Question: To What extent was Monroe's Presidency an "Era of Good Feelings"? (Use documents from 2002 Form B DBQ)

SAMPLE SYLLABUS ADVANCED PLACEMENT UNITED STATES HISTORY

Day 6: Market Revolution
Day 7: Issues of Jackson's presidency
Day 8: Evaluating Jackson through the lens of Indian Removal
Day 9: Forming the American Identity *primary source:* "Democracy in America," Tocqueville
Day 10: Discussion Enslavement and Resistance
Day 11: Life under Slavery
Day 12: Intro to Reformer Party
Day 13: The Fight for Gender Rights *primary sources:* The Declaration of Sentiments, The Lowell girls
Day 14: Reformer Party

Unit Five Lessons

Day 1: The Breakdown of Compromise
Day 2: Manifest Destiny and James K. Polk *primary source:* "The Great Nation of Futurity," John O'Sullivan
Day 3: The expansion of slavery
Day 4: The Mexican War
Day 5: The Events Leading to the Civil War
Day 6: The Events Leading to the Civil War *continued* *primary sources:* excerpts from *Dred Scott* decision, Lincoln-Douglas debates
Day 7: Discussion – Was compromise possible in 1860, or had the war become inevitable? (Students must use documents from 2005 form B DBQ to support their position.)
Day 8: The Underpinnings of the Civil War
Day 9: The Military Aspects of the Civil War
Day 10: The Military Aspects of the Civil War *continued*
Day 11: Lecture: Civil War Homefront *primary sources:* Lincoln's letter to Horace Greeley ("My Paramount Object"), The Emancipation Proclamations (preliminary and final)
Day 12: Lecture: Civil War Homefront *continued* *primary sources:* The Gettysburg Address, Lincoln's Second Inaugural address
Day 13: Reading day: Documents from the Draft Riots
Day 14: Socratic Seminar : The New York Draft Riots
Day 15: Intro to Reconstruction
Day 16: Reconstruction: April 1865
Day 17: Reading day: *primary sources*: 13th, 14th, 15th Amendments, Sharecroppers Contract, Mississippi Black Code.
Day 18: Fishbowl Discussion: Was Reconstruction a limited success or a total failure?

Unit Six Lessons

Day 1: The Long Gilded Age – Industrialization, Expansion, Immigration, Urbanization, Migration
Day 2: The Creation of Wealth in the post-Civil War United States
Day 3: Wealth in the Gilded Age
Day 4: New Technologies of the Gilded Age
Day 5: American Labor History and Changes in Approaches to Work
Day 6: Expanding westward
Day 7: The Taking of Indian land
Day 8: Primary Source Reading/Discussion: *primary sources:* excerpts from: *A Century of Dishonor,* two accounts of the Wounded Knee Massacre, Turner thesis, Rolvaag *Giants in the Earth*
Day 9: Graded Discussion: Although the economic development of the Trans-Mississippi West is popularly associated with hardy individualism, it was in fact largely dependent on the federal government and driven by major industry. Assess the validity of this statement with specific reference to western economic activities in the nineteenth century. (slightly altered 1991 FRQ)
Day 10: Politics of the Gilded Age
Day 11: Ranking the Presidents of the Gilded Age
Day 12: Immigration in the Gilded Age – Waves of Immigration
Day 13: Introduction to Chicago development *(Note: If relevant, you may want to select a city in your state during the Gilded Age instead of Chicago for the next several lessons.)*
Day 14: Mapping the growth of Chicago Students will analyze the connections between Chicago and the greater history of America using maps found in the digital collections of the Newberry Library
Day 15: Video clips – *Chicago, City of the Century*
Day 16: Project workday – Chicago documentary
Day 17: Viewing of class documentary

Unit Seven Lessons

Day 1: America in the Twentieth Century – the view forward from 1890 and backwards from 1945
Day 2: Quiz – Lecture – Intro to the Progressive Era
Day 3: Progressives and Populists – Comparing and Contrasting the Omaha Platform and the 1912 Platform of the Progressive Party

Day 4: Working in *The Jungle* *primary sources:* Upton Sinclair, Thomas Nast, Jacob Riis, and Lewis Hine
Day 5: Development of Labor Unions
Day 6: The Progressive Era Presidents
Day 7: Spotlight – Hull House and Chicago – Jane Addams
Day 8: World War I in the U.S.
Day 9: Intro to Global Expansion
Day 10: The War in the Philippines
Day 11: Treaty of Versailles; Wilson's 14 Points Discussion Question: To what extent did the United States achieve the objectives that led it to enter the First World War? (2000 FRQ)
Day 12: The Roaring 20s
Day 13: The Harlem Renaissance
Day 14: The Closing of America – Immigration changes, Scopes Trial, and the rise of the KKK in the 1920s
Day 15: Graded Discussion – Did the Women's Movement die in the 1920s?
Day 16: The Great Depression
Day 17: The New Deal and FDR
Day 18: Fishbowl Discussion: "The depression of the 1890's delayed reform; the depression of the 1930's stimulated it." To what extent and in what ways do you agree or disagree with this statement?" (1972 FRQ)
Day 19: Quiz / Lecture – U.S. in World War II
Day 20: Comparing World War II Propaganda *primary sources:* "Triumph of the Will" vs. "In Der Fuhrer's Face", WWII propaganda posters, United We Stand magazine campaign
Day 21: World War II at Home
Day 22: Discussion: Was World War II really the "Good War? – roles of women, African Americans, Mexican Americans
Day 23: Japanese Internment and the suppression of rights in wartime
Day 24: The Holocaust – viewing of Frontline *"The Memory of the Camps"*

Unit Eight Lessons

Day 1: America Moves to the Center Stage
Day 2: America in the Post-war World
Day 3: Timeline of Cold War events, 1945–1960 – Truman Doctrine, Marshall Plan
Day 4: The Politics of Fear – McCarthyism in 1950s America
Day 5: The Cold War at Home
Day 6: The Major Events of the Civil Rights Movement – from *Plessy v. Ferguson* to *Brown v. Board of Education*
Day 7: Compare/Contrast Discussion: "Compare the goals and strategies of black reform movements in the period 1890–1910 to the goals and strategies of black reform movements in the period 1950–1970." (1982 FRQ)
Day 8: Primary Source Analysis: excerpts from: *Letter from a Birmingham Jail*, SNCC Statement of Purpose, *I Have a Dream* speech, *Black Power*, Platform of Black Panther party
Day 9: The presidencies of JFK and LBJ
Day 10: Fishbowl Discussion: "In what ways did the Great Society resemble the New Deal in its origins, goals, and social and political legacy? Cite specific programs and policies in support of your arguments." (1992 FRQ)
Day 11: Graded Discussion: "In what ways did the administrations of Presidents Eisenhower, Kennedy, and Johnson maintain the policy of containment of communism developed during the Truman administration?" (1969 FRQ)
Day 12: The Vietnam War
Day 13: The Rise of the Anti-War movement
Day 14: The Historical Significance of 1968
Day 15: The Women's Movement
Day 16: Backlash against the Feminist Movement
Day 17: Nixon, Ford, Carter
Day 18: The Rise and Fall of Richard Nixon
Day 19: The Rise of the Modern Conservative Movement
Day 20: The Sunbelt
Day 21: The Ford and Carter Presidencies

Unit Nine Lessons

Day 1: The Rise of Ronald Reagan
Day 2: The changing of Presidential electoral images
Day 3: Foreign policy in the 1980s–2000
Day 4: Implementation of the New Conservatism – The Reagan Administration's response to the emerging HIV/AIDS crisis
Day 5: The New Democrats and Bill Clinton
Day 6: The Election of 2000 and the Presidency of George W. Bush
Day 7: The September 11th Attacks and the War on Terror

ABOUT THE AP UNITED STATES HISTORY EXAM

There are four sections to the Advanced Placement United States History Examination: a multiple-choice section, a short-answer section, a document-based question, and a long essay.

Section	Question Type	Number of Questions	Timing	Percentage of Total Exam Score
I	Part A: Multiple choice questions	55 Questions	55 Minutes	40%
	Part B: Short-answer questions	4 Questions	50 Minutes	20%
II	Part A: Document-based question	1 Question	55 Minutes	25%
	Part B: Long essay question	1 Question (chosen from three options)	35 Minutes	15%

Breakdown of Coverage by Periods

Nine distinct time periods make up the AP U.S. History course. Students should reflect on why historians view each period as a turning point in U.S. history. Below is a breakdown of course coverage and exam emphasis for each of the time periods.

Table 1: Breakdown of the AP United States History Exam

Time periods	Approximate Percentage of Instructional Time	Approximate Percentage of Coverage on the AP U.S. History Exam
1491–1607	5%	5%
1607–1754	10%	45%
1754–1800	12%	
1800–1848	10%	
1844–1877	13%	
1865–1898	13%	45%
1890–1945	17%	
1945–1980	15%	
1980–present	5%	5%

ABOUT THE AP UNITED STATES HISTORY EXAM

Understanding the Format

Multiple-Choice Questions

There are 55 multiple-choice questions with four answer choices (A-D). Only one answer choice is correct for each question, and there is no penalty for guessing incorrectly. Students have 55 minutes to complete the section. The multiple-choice questions are stimulus-based, with a primary or secondary source followed by one to five questions based on the stimulus. Multiple-choice questions may include information from Period 1 through Period 9.

Short-Answer Questions

The short-answer section examines the historical developments or processes of specific time periods. Students are required to answer three short answer questions. Students have forty minutes to write the three answers (roughly 13 minutes for each question). Two short-answer questions offer an element of choice to allow students to write about what they know best. All short answer questions will test students' use of historical thinking skills and reasoning processes. Students will respond to a primary or secondary source using historical examples in their reasoning for two short-answer questions. There is a finite space for student answers, and content outside the designated answer area will not receive credit. Student responses must be complete sentences (bulleted answers will not receive credit), but a thesis statement is not required. Short-answer questions may include information from Period 1 through Period 9. Students must follow all directions and explicitly answer the question.

Document-Based Question (DBQ)

The DBQ requires students to analyze and interpret primary source documents. Students must use the documents, and outside information, to support a well-developed thesis statement that directly answers the question, takes a position, establishes categories, and gives direction to those categories. Thesis statements that restate the prompt as a statement will not receive credit. Students have 60 minutes to read associated documents and write an answer to the question. The DBQ only addresses historical content within the time frames of Period 2 through Period 8 and is scored on a 0-7 scale using an analytic rubric.

The key elements of the rubric are:

0–1 point Thesis statement.

0–1 point Contextualization: Explicitly connects historical phenomena to broader historical events.

0–2 points Analysis of documents as follows:

- **0–1 point** Use evidence to develop an argument that demonstrates a deep understanding of the question and makes connections across time periods and themes.
- **0–1 point** Examines the following for at least **three** of the documents:
  - Intended audience
  - Purpose
  - Historical context
  - The author's point of view

0–2 points Use the content from at least six documents to develop an argument that addresses the question.

0–1 point Uses outside evidence not included in the documents to develop an argument.

Long Essay

Students must choose one of three long essay questions to answer. Each long essay question utilizes the same reasoning process combined with historical developments or processes in different time periods: 1491-1800, 1800-1898, or 1890-2001. The long essay question measures the student's ability to use historical thinking skills and reasoning processes in thesis development, presenting a historical argument, and evaluating evidence to support an argument.

UNIT 1: 1491–1607

Pacing Guide

Unit 1 explores key concepts from Period 1: 1491–1607 of the AP U.S. History Curriculum Framework. It is recommended that 4–6% of the total instruction time for the entire course be spent on Period 1.

Key Concepts

1.1 As native populations migrated and settled across the vast expanse of North America over time, they developed distinct and increasingly complex societies by adapting to and transforming their diverse environments.

1.2 Contact among Europeans, Native Americans, and Africans resulted in the Columbian Exchange and significant social, cultural, and political changes on both sides of the Atlantic Ocean.

UNIT 1: 1491–1607

CHAPTER 1: THE COLLISION OF CULTURES

THEMATIC LEARNING OBJECTIVES

- Describe the regional differences among Native Americans before the arrival of Europeans.
- Compare and contrast the Americas before and after the arrival of Europeans.
- Identify the causes and effects of Spanish and Portuguese colonization of the Americas.
- Explain the reasons for the emergence of slavery in the Americas.
- Analyze the trans-Atlantic exchanges which took place in the Americas.

QUESTIONS TO CONSIDER

- What were the similarities and differences between Native American groups in North America?
- What were the major effects of the Columbian Exchange?
- What were the major reasons Europeans turned to enslaved African laborers in the Americas?

HISTORICAL DEVELOPMENTS: 1491–1607

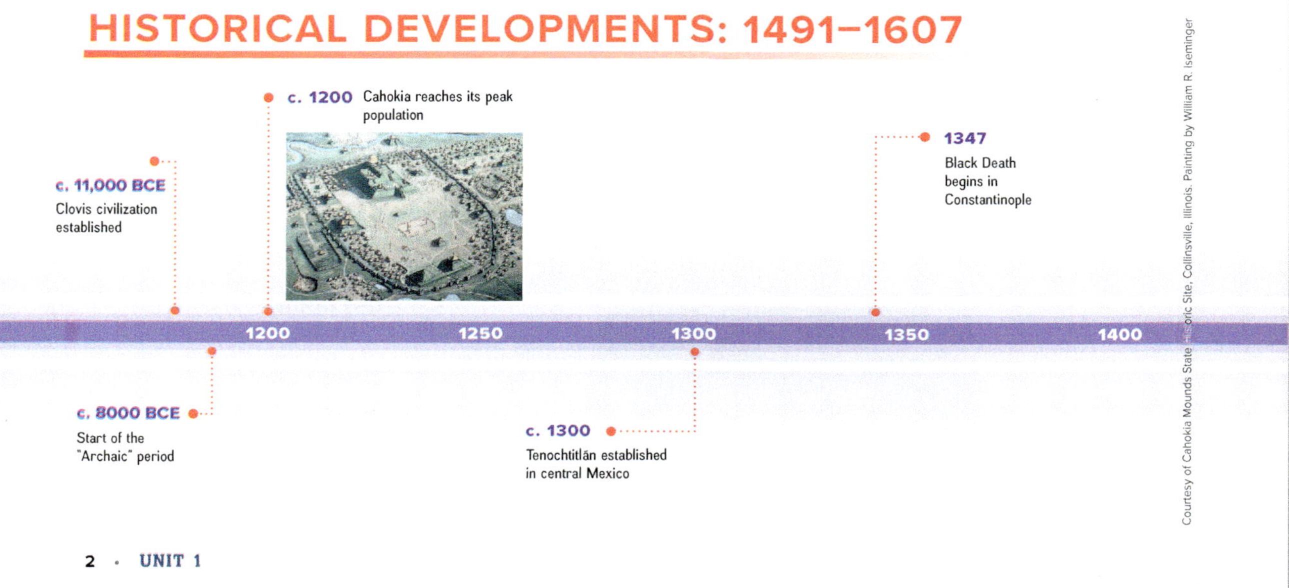

c. 11,000 BCE Clovis civilization established
c. 8000 BCE Start of the "Archaic" period
c. 1200 Cahokia reaches its peak population
c. 1300 Tenochtitlán established in central Mexico
1347 Black Death begins in Constantinople
1200
1250
1300
1350
1400

Courtesy of Cahokia Mounds State Historic Site, Collinsville, Illinois. Painting by William R. Iseminger

Historical Thinking Skills

Making Connections Have students study the time line. **Ask**: What events in the time line show the development of European exploration? *(The time line shows a progression from the arrival of Europeans in 1488, to the military conquest of Mexico in 1518, to the establishment of permanent settlements in 1565 and 1609.)* **MIG**

MAKING CONNECTIONS

Unit One focuses on the period prior to the arrival of the English in North America in 1607. The unit begins with the arrival of Paleolithic hunter-gatherers, who began migrating to the Americas from Asia around 14,000 years ago. These migrant groups quickly spread across the continent, creating diverse and sophisticated societies that were heavily dependent on their environment for survival.

Geography influenced the unique characteristics of societies across the Americas. The development of agricultural techniques based on the environment, in addition to hunting, gathering, and fishing, provided the stable food supplies necessary for the growth of complex societies. A variety of economic, social, and political structures developed among these societies. While some groups led nomadic lives, others established permanent settlements with thriving cities and large trading networks. Social customs, rituals, and religion became as important to the early societies of the Americas as it was to most other cultures around the world.

As the societies of the Americas were growing and developing, other societies halfway across the globe were beginning to take an interest in exploring different parts of the world. Europeans were generally unaware of the existence of the Americas before the fifteenth century. But as European interaction with other parts of the world increased, European monarchs saw the potential to enrich their country's dominance and prestige through exploration. Consequently, the great trans-Atlantic exchange began among continents, cumulating in what became known as the Columbian Exchange.

The Columbian Exchange had both positive and negative effects for all involved. Spain and Portugal took the early leads in the race for resources half-way across the globe. God, gold, and glory were leading incentives for these European powers to pursue exploration and colonization. Religion would play a major role in colonization, whether through the spread of Christianity or the pursuit of religious freedom. The great wealth and raw materials that exploration and colonization could provide also drove European colonization. Both Spain and Portugal gained influence during the fifteenth century and would become powerful countries through colonization.

The Columbian Exchange also became a vast network of interactions between the Americas, Europe, and Africa, and its presence shaped subsequent development of each of these continents. Likely the most significant effect of the Columbian Exchange was the emergence of enslaved labor in the Americas. On all three continents groups engaged in warfare, often over scarce resources. Individuals captured during warfare often became enslaved laborers who met the ever-increasing European demand for an extensive labor force in its colonies.

The cycle of warfare and enslavement did not begin with Europeans. The African slave trade began long before European exploration and colonization, but the market for enslaved laborers grew dramatically during the sixteenth century. The Spanish began enslaving Native Americans, and the English, at least initially, relied on indentured servitude. Europeans eventually turned to Africa for enslaved laborers.

European colonization of the Americas began with Spain and Portugal, but these two countries would quickly give way to a new group of explorers whose impact would long surpass that of any other European group: the English. In 1607 the English would establish their first permanent settlement at Jamestown, thus ushering in a major paradigm shift in the development of North America.

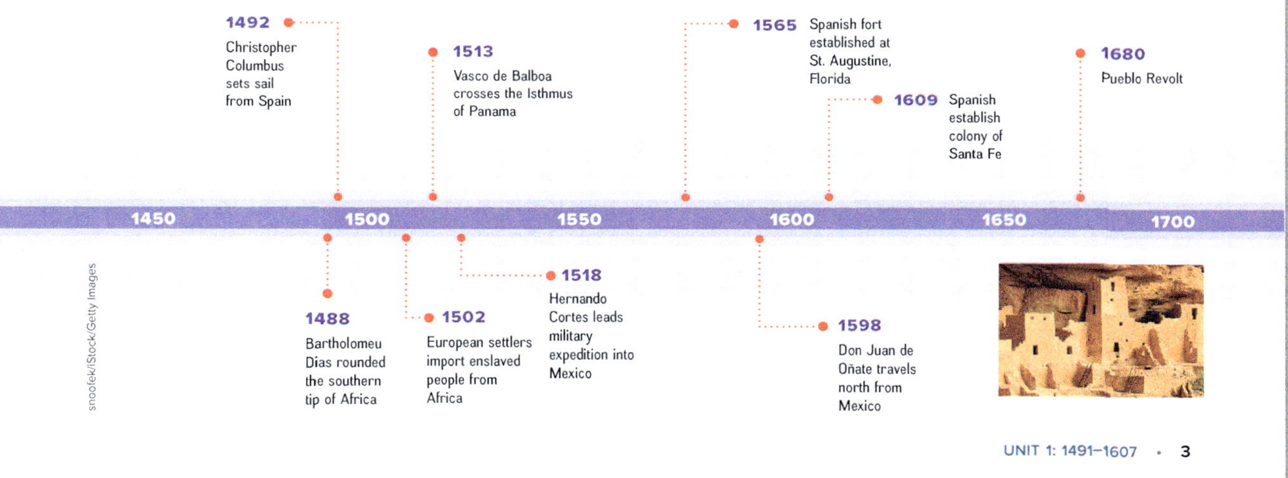
1492 Christopher Columbus sets sail from Spain
1513 Vasco de Balboa crosses the Isthmus of Panama
1565 Spanish fort established at St. Augustine, Florida
1609 Spanish establish colony of Santa Fe
1680 Pueblo Revolt
1450
1500
1550
1600
1650
1700
1488 Bartholomeu Dias rounded the southern tip of Africa
1502 European settlers import enslaved people from Africa
1518 Hernando Cortes leads military expedition into Mexico
1598 Don Juan de Oñate travels north from Mexico

snoofek/iStock/Getty Images

Discussion and Activities

Contextualization After students read the Making Connections section, lead a discussion about the impact of geography on early migrants to the Americas.
Ask: What geographic factors allowed some migrants to establish complex societies, while other migrant groups remained nomadic? Use the discussion to create a T-chart, or two-column graphic organizer, to separate the factors that led to permanent settlements versus nomadic lifestyles. **GEO**

Go Online Additional Resources

Adaptive Learning with SmartBook A proven adaptive learning program, SmartBook offers an interactive environment that helps students learn faster, study more efficiently, and retain more knowledge.

Assign this resource to differentiate instruction for students and report on year-long progression.

CHAPTER 1
THE COLLISION OF CULTURES

Pacing Guide

Chapter 1 explores key concepts from Period 1: 1492–1607 of the AP U.S. History Curriculum Framework. The suggested instruction time for Chapter 1 is 8 days.

Key Concepts

1.1.I Different native societies adapted to and transformed their environments through innovations in agriculture, resource use, and social structure.

1.2.I European expansion into the Western Hemisphere generated intense social, religious, political, and economic competition and changes within European societies.

1.2.II The Columbian Exchange and development of the Spanish Empire in the Western Hemisphere resulted in extensive demographic, economic, and social changes.

1.2.III In their interactions, Europeans and Native Americans asserted divergent worldviews regarding issues such as religion, gender roles, family, land use, and power.

1 THE COLLISION OF CULTURES

FIRST ENCOUNTERS WITH NATIVE AMERICANS
This 1505 engraving is one of the earliest European images of encountering Native Americans. It also represents some of the ways in which white Europeans would view the people they called Indians for many generations. Native Americans here were portrayed by Europeans as exotic savages, whose sexuality was not contained within stable families and whose savagery was evidenced in their practice of eating the flesh of their slain enemies. In the background are the ships that have brought the Europeans who recorded these images.

CONNECTING CONCEPTS

Chapter One focuses on civilizations of the Americas prior to and immediately after European contact. The early population groups of the Americas developed advanced civilizations and, as they interacted with the geography of the environment, established diverse patterns of living. Beginning in the sixteenth century, largely driven by the desire for wealth, military and economic dominance, and a professed desire to spread Christianity, Europeans began colonizing the Americas. Colonization propelled the interaction of Europe, Africa, and the Americas, and created a vast network of trade known as the Columbian Exchange. Some of the most immediate effects of the Columbian Exchange were the development of a capitalist economy, the use of enslaved labor, a population boom in Europe, and a massive population decline in the indigenous populations of the Americas. Interactions between Europeans and Native Americans resulted in the exchange of technology and other useful aspects of each other's culture, but also frequently created tension between the groups. Chapter One closes on the eve of the arrival of the English, who were to become the most significant and permanent European presence in North America.

As you read, you should:

- Identify a wide variety of political, economic, and social structures that existed among Native Americans.
- Analyze environmental factors that influenced Native American societies prior to and after European contact.
- Evaluate how the environmental factors led to varied regional differences among Native Americans.
- Explain the development of the Columbian Exchange, and identify how it led to the exchange of technology and agricultural products, changes in population groups, and the spread of epidemic diseases.
- Compare and contrast the different European socio-religious, political, and economic ventures, and identify how these led to conflicts in establishing colonies among European powers.
- Analyze Native American resistance and conflict that resulted from contact with European peoples.

Discussion and Activities

Analyzing Perspectives Ask: How might the fact that the image "First Encounters With Native Americans" was created by Europeans affect how the scene is portrayed? *(Europeans would be unfamiliar with native culture, customs, and rituals. Therefore, they would likely frame their observations around a European framework. For example, Europeans might conclude that the relationships and/or religious beliefs of Native Americans were "uncivilized.")* **MIG** **NAT**

AMERICA BEFORE COLUMBUS

We still know relatively little about the first peoples in the Americas. What we do know comes from scattered archaeological discoveries–new evidence from artifacts that have survived over many millennia.

THE PEOPLES OF THE PRECONTACT AMERICAS

For many decades, scholars believed that all early migrations into the Americas came from humans crossing an ancient land bridge over the Bering Strait into what is now Alaska, approximately 11,000 years ago. These migrants then traveled from the glacial north, through an unfrozen corridor between two great ice sheets, until they reached the nonglacial lands to the south. The migrations were probably a result of the development of new stone tools–spears and other hunting implements–with which migrating people could pursue the large animals that regularly crossed between Asia and North America. All of these land-based migrants are thought to have come from a Mongolian stock related to that of modern-day Siberia. They are known to scholars as the "Clovis" people, named for a town in New Mexico.

THE "CLOVIS" PEOPLE

The Clovis people established one of the first civilizations in the Americas. Archaeologists believe that they lived about 13,000 years ago. They were among the first people to make tools and to eat other animals. The Clovis are believed to have migrated from Siberia across the Bering land bridge into Alaska. From there, they moved southward to warmer regions, including New Mexico.

More recent archaeological evidence, however, suggests that not all the early migrants came across the Bering Strait. Some migrants from Asia appear to have settled as far south as Chile and Peru even before people began moving into North America by land. This suggests that these first South Americans may have come not by land but by sea, using boats. Other discoveries on other continents made clear that migrants had traveled by water much earlier to populate Japan, Australia, and other areas of the Pacific. Those discoveries suggest that migrants were capable of making long ocean voyages–long enough to bring them to the American coasts.

ARCHAEOLOGISTS AND POPULATION DIVERSITY

This new evidence suggests that the early population of the Americas was much more diverse and more scattered than scholars used to believe. Some people came to the Americas from farther south in Asia than Mongolia–perhaps Polynesia and Japan. Recent DNA evidence has identified what may have been yet another population group that, unlike most other American groups, does not seem to have Asian genetic markers. Thus it is also possible that, thousands of years before Columbus, there may have been some migration from Europe or Africa. Most Native Americans in the Americas today share relatively similar genetic characteristics, and those characteristics link them to modern Siberians and Mongolians. But that does not prove that Mongolian migrants were the only immigrants to the Americas. It suggests, rather, that Mongolian migrants eventually came to dominate and perhaps eliminate earlier population groups.

The "Archaic" period is a scholarly term for the history of humans in America during a period of about 5,000 years beginning around 8000 BCE. In the first part of this period, most humans continued to support themselves through hunting and gathering, using the same stone tools that earlier Americans had brought with them from Asia. Some of the largest animals that the earliest humans in America once hunted became extinct during the Archaic period. But archaic people continued to hunt with spears in the area later known as the Great Plains of North America who, then as centuries later, pursued bison (also known as buffalo). Bows and arrows were unknown in most of North America until 400–500 CE.

THE "ARCHAIC" PERIOD

Later in the Archaic period, population groups also began to develop new tools to perform work. Among them were nets and hooks for fishing, traps for smaller animals, and baskets for gathering berries, nuts, seeds, and other plants. Later, some groups began to farm. Through much of the Americas, the most important farm crop was corn, but many agricultural communities also grew other crops such as beans and squash. In agricultural areas, the first sedentary settlements slowly began to form, creating the basis for larger civilizations.

THE GROWTH OF CIVILIZATIONS: THE SOUTH

The most elaborate early civilizations emerged south of what is now the United States–in South and Central America and in what is now Mexico. In Peru, the Incas created the largest empire in the Americas. They began as a small tribe in the mountainous region of Cuzco, in the early fifteenth century–spurred by a powerful leader, Pachacuti (whose name meant "world shaker"). His empire stretched along almost 2,000 miles of western South America. It was an empire created as much by persuasion as by force. Pachacuti's agents fanned out around the region and explained the benefits of the empire to people in the areas the Incas hoped to control. Most local leaders eventually allied themselves with the Incas. The empire was sustained by innovative administrative systems and by the creation of a large network of paved roads.

Another great civilization emerged from the so-called Meso-Americans, the peoples of what is now Mexico and much of Central America. Organized societies emerged in these regions as early as 10,000 BCE, and the first truly complex society in the Americas–of the Olmec people–began in approximately 1000 BCE. A more sophisticated culture emerged beginning around 800 CE in parts of Central America and in the Yucatán peninsula of Mexico, in an area known as Maya. Mayan civilization developed a written language, a

Reasoning Processes

Continuity and Change After students read "The Peoples of the Precontact Americas," **ask:** What was one continuity in how the peoples of precontact America fed themselves? *(Native Americans largely fed themselves through hunting and gathering throughout the time period.)* **GEO** **MIG**

Go Online AP Exam Preparation

AP Exam Practice Use the online assessment to help prepare students for the AP Exam. You can assign the ready-made AP-style short answer questions, document-based questions, and multiple-choice questions assessing concepts, themes, and skills from Period 1 and AP style long-essay questions organized in sets of 3 questions from various time periods. You can also create your own tests from available questions. This easy-to-use tool helps you design assessments that meet the needs of different types of learners.

Historical Thinking Skills

Contextualization Have students examine the map on North American Migrations, then divide the class into small groups to discuss reasons for the southward migration of precontact Americans. **Ask**: What advantages might people who settled in Mesoamerica have enjoyed? **WXT** **MIG** **GEO**

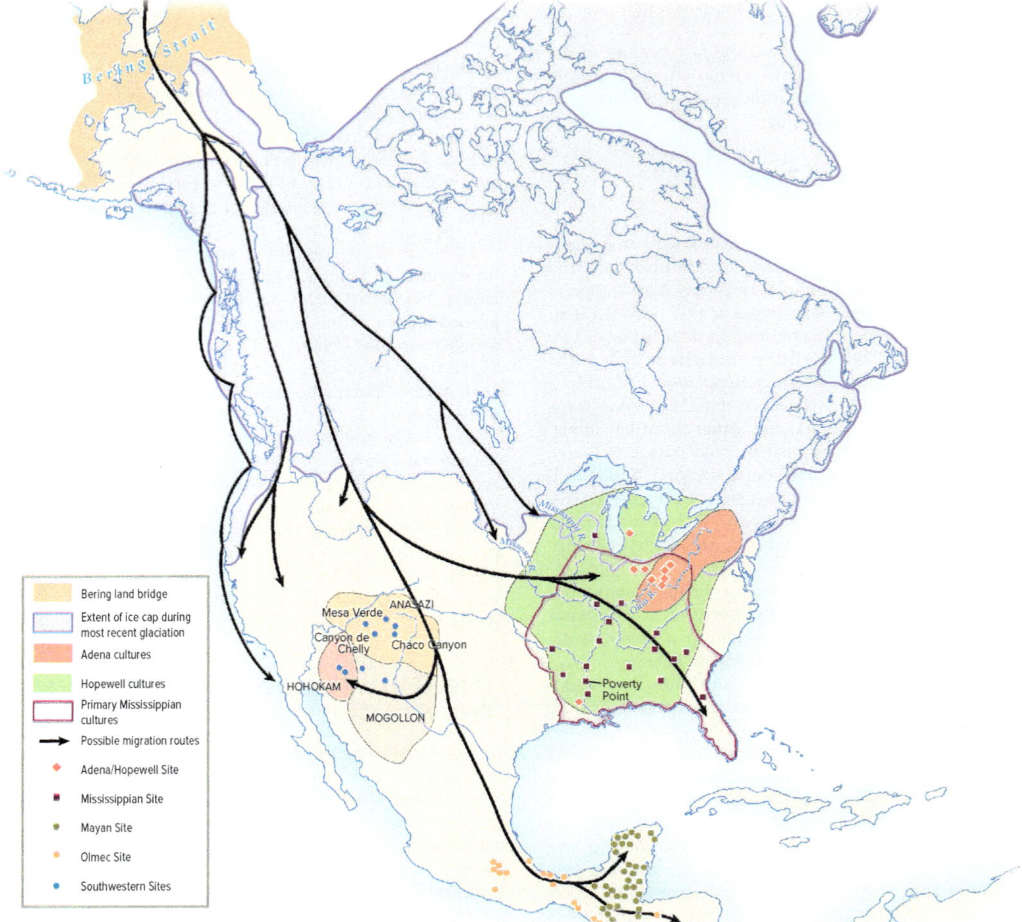

NORTH AMERICAN MIGRATIONS This map tracks some of the early migrations into, and within, North America in the centuries preceding contact with Europe. The map shows the now-vanished land bridge between Siberia and Alaska over which thousands, perhaps millions, of migrating people passed into the Americas. It also shows the locations of some of the earliest settlements in North America.

What role did the extended glacial field in what is now Canada have on residential patterns in the ancient American world?

numerical system similar to the Arabic, an accurate calendar, an advanced agricultural system, and important trade routes into other areas of the continents.

Gradually, the societies of the Mayan regions were followed by other Meso-American tribes. They became known collectively (and somewhat inaccurately) as the Aztec. They called themselves Mexica, a name that eventually came to describe people of a number of different tribes. In about 1300 CE, the Mexica established a city, which they named Tenochtitlán, on a large island in a lake in central Mexico, the site of present-day Mexico City. The Mexica soon incorporated the peoples of other tribes into their society as well. It became by far the greatest city ever created in the Americas to that point, with a population as high as 100,000 by 1500, connected to water supplies from across the region by aqueducts. The residents of Tenochtitlán also created large and impressive public buildings, schools that all male children attended, an organized military, a medical system, and an

Answers

North American Migrations

The extended glacial field in what is now Canada channeled migrants to North America southward in search of food and warmer climates.

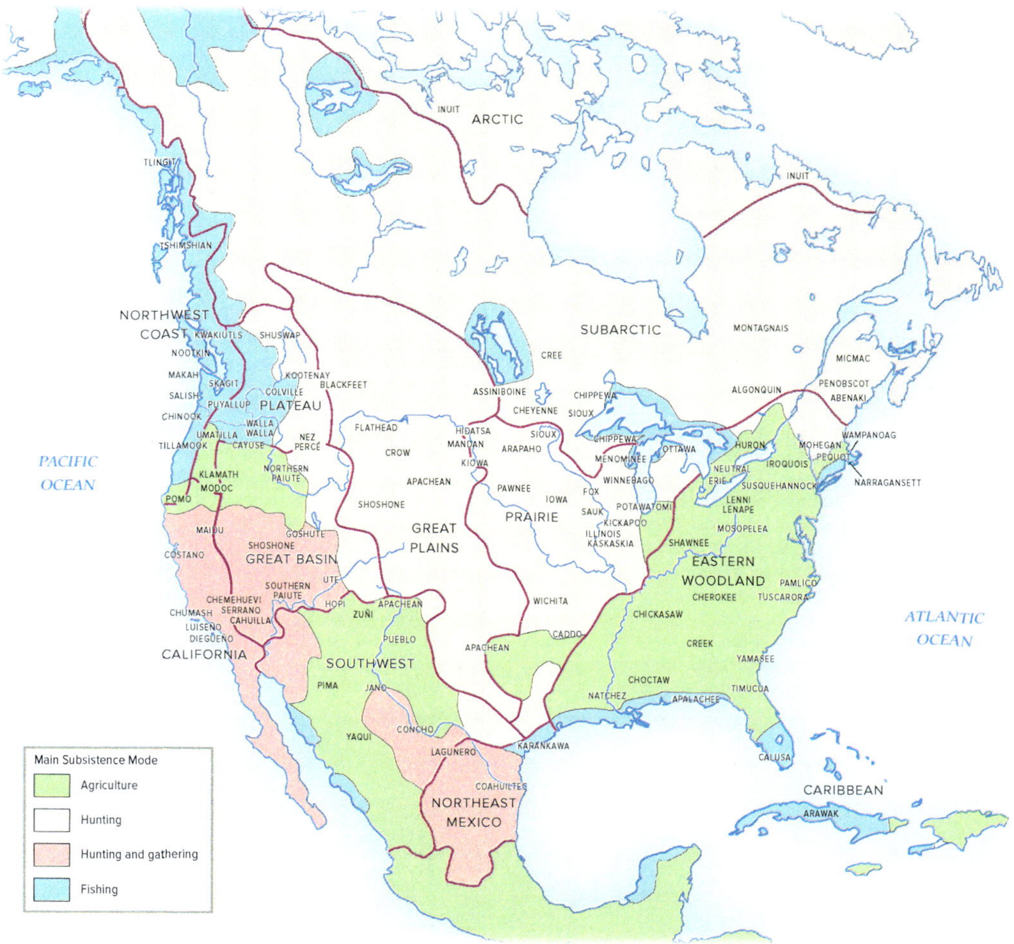

HOW THE EARLY NORTH AMERICANS LIVED This map shows the various ways in which indigenous groups of North America supported themselves before the arrival of European civilization. Like most precommercial peoples, the Native Americans survived largely on the resources available in their immediate surroundings. Note, for example, the reliance on the products of the sea among the groups along the northern coastlines of the continent, and the way in which groups in relatively inhospitable climates in the North—where agriculture was difficult—relied on hunting large game. Most Native Americans were farmers.

What different kinds of farming would have emerged in the very different climates of the agricultural regions shown on this map?

enslaved workforce drawn from conquered tribes. They gradually established their dominance over almost all of central Mexico, and beyond, through a system of tribute (a heavy tax paid in crops, cloth, or animals) enforced by military power. The peoples ruled by the Mexica maintained a significant element of independence nevertheless, and many of them always considered the Mexica to be tyrannical rulers, but too powerful to resist.

Like other Meso-American societies, the Mexica developed a religion based on a belief in human sacrifice. Unlike earlier societies in the Americas, whose sacrifices to the gods emphasized blood-letting and other mostly nonfatal techniques, the Mexica also believed that the gods could be satisfied by being fed the living hearts of humans. As a result, they sacrificed people—largely prisoners captured in combat—on a scale unknown in other American civilizations.

AP Exam Practice

Short Answer Provide students with the following short-answer questions and allow 15 minutes for completion. Ask for volunteers to share their responses and discuss as a class.

Answer A, B, and C.

A) Briefly explain ONE important similarity between the Clovis people and other early migrants to North America. *(Possible answer: Most groups hunted game animals using stone tools.)*

B) Briefly explain ONE important difference between the Clovis people and other early migrants to North America. *(Possible answer: The Clovis people came across the Bering Strait corridor on foot, while other groups may have arrived farther south by boat.)*

C) Briefly explain ONE important reason for the difference cited in B. *(Possible answer: Some groups had access to boat-building technology, while others had easier access to the Bering Land Bridge.)*

Answers

How the Early North Americans Lived

Native Americans with easier access to fresh water, such as rivers and lakes, would have been better able to establish a farming lifestyle, growing crops such as corn, beans, and squash. Native American groups without access to reliable sources of fresh water would more likely rely on hunting and gathering.

Reasoning Processes

Contrasting Have students create a historically defensible thesis that establishes a line of reasoning to explain why Mesoamericans were able to build structures like the Mayan temple pictured here, while Native American in other areas were not. Ask students to share their thesis statement with a partner and exchange feedback on whether the thesis statement makes a historically defensible claim.

The Meso-American civilizations were for many centuries the center of civilized life in North and Central America–the hub of culture and trade. Disease and disunity made it difficult for them to survive the European invasions. But they were, nevertheless, very great civilizations–all the more impressive because they lacked some of the crucial technologies that Asian and European societies had long employed. As late as the sixteenth century CE, no American society had yet developed wheeled vehicles.

The Civilizations of the North

The peoples north of Mexico–in the lands that became the United States and Canada–did not develop empires as large or political systems as elaborate as those of the Incas, Mayas, and Mexica. They built complex civilizations of great variety that subsisted on hunting, gathering, and fishing. The indigenous peoples of the Arctic Circle fished and hunted seals; their civilization spanned thousands of miles of largely frozen land, which they traversed by dogsled. The big-game hunters of the northern forests led nomadic lives based on pursuit of moose and caribou. The groups of the Pacific Northwest, whose principal occupation was salmon fishing, created substantial permanent settlements along the coast and engaged in constant and often violent competition with one another for access to natural resources.

COMPLEX AND VARIED CIVILIZATIONS

Other indigenous groups spread through more arid regions of the Far West and developed successful communities–many of them quite wealthy and densely populated–based on fishing, hunting small game, and gathering. Other societies in America were primarily agricultural. Among the most elaborate were those in the Southwest. The people of that region built large irrigation systems to allow farming on their relatively dry land. They constructed substantial towns that became centers of trade, crafts, and religious and civic ritual. Their densely populated settlements at Chaco Canyon and elsewhere consisted of stone and adobe terraced structures, known today as pueblos, many of which resembled the large apartment buildings of later eras in size and design. In the Great Plains region, too, most groups were engaged in sedentary farming (corn and other grains) and lived in permanent settlements, although there were some small nomadic groups that subsisted by hunting buffalo. (Only in the eighteenth century, after Europeans had introduced the horse to North America, did buffalo hunting begin to support a large population in the region; at that point, many once-sedentary farmers left the land to pursue the great migratory buffalo herds.)

The eastern third of what is now the United States–much of it covered with forests and inhabited by people who have thus become known as the Woodland Indians–had the greatest food resources of any region of the continent. Many groups lived there, and most of them engaged in farming, hunting, gathering, and fishing. In the South there were substantial permanent settlements and large trading networks based on corn and other grains grown in the rich lands of the Mississippi River valley. Among the major cities that emerged as a result of trade was Cahokia (near present-day St. Louis), which at its peak in 1200 CE had a population of about 10,000 and contained a great complex of large earthen mounds.

MAYAN TEMPLE, TIKAL Tikal was the largest city in what was then the vast Mayan Empire. It extended through what is now Mexico, Guatemala, and Belize. The temple shown here was built before 800 CE and was one of many pyramids created by the Mayas. Only a few of these pyramids still survive.

Discussion and Activities

Making Connections What building in a current community would carry out the same function as the Mayan Temple? *(The function served by the Mayan Temple would be fulfilled today in a modern house of worship, such as a church, synagogue, or mosque.)* ARC MIG

MAYAN MONKEY-MAN SCRIBAL GOD The Mayas believed in hundreds of different gods, and they attempted to personify many of them in various artifacts such as the one depicted on the bowl shown here, which dates from 900–1100 CE. The monkey gods were believed to be twins who took the form of monkeys after being lured into a tree from which they could not descend. According to legend, they abandoned their loincloths, which then became tails, which they then used to move more effectively up and down trees. The monkey-men were the patrons of writing, dancing, and art.

The agricultural societies of the Northeast were more nomadic than those in other regions. Much of the land in the region was less fertile than other regions because farming was newer and less established. Most groups combined farming with hunting. Farming techniques in the Northeast were usually designed to exploit the land quickly rather than to develop permanent settlements. The land was often cleared by setting forest fires or cutting into trees to kill them. They then planted crops—corn, beans, squash, pumpkins, and others—among the dead or blackened trunks. After a few years, when the land became exhausted or the filth from a settlement began to accumulate, they moved on and established themselves elsewhere. In some parts of eastern North America, villages dispersed every winter and families foraged in the wilderness until warm weather returned; those who survived then reassembled to begin farming again.

Many of the groups living east of the Mississippi River were linked together loosely by common linguistic roots. The largest of the language groups was the Algonquian, which dominated the Atlantic seaboard from Canada to Virginia. Another important language group was the Iroquoian, centered in what is now upstate New York. The Iroquois included at least five distinct northern nations—the Seneca, Cayuga, Onondaga, Oneida, and Mohawk—and had links as well with the Cherokees and the Tuscaroras farther south, in the Carolinas and Georgia. The third-largest language group—the Muskogean—included the groups in the southernmost region of the eastern seaboard: the Chickasaws, Choctaws, Creeks, and Seminoles. Alliances among the various Native American societies (even among those with common languages) were fragile, since the peoples of the Americas did not think of themselves as members of a single civilization.

MOBILE SOCIETIES

TRIBAL CULTURES

The enormous diversity of economic, social, and political structures among the North American Indians makes large generalizations about their cultures difficult. In the last centuries before the arrival of Europeans, however, Native Americans—like peoples in other areas of the world—were experiencing an agricultural revolution. In all regions of the United States, groups were becoming more sedentary and were developing new sources of food, clothing, and shelter. Most regions were experiencing significant population growth. Virtually all were developing the sorts of elaborate social customs and rituals that only stationary societies can

AGRICULTURAL REVOLUTION

CAHOKIA An artist's rendition of the city of Cahokia circa 1100 CE. Its great earthen mounds, constructed by the Cahokia Indians near present-day St. Louis, have endured into modern times as part of the Missouri landscape.

Historical Thinking Skills

Claims and Evidence in Sources Direct students to view the image "Mayan Monkey-Man Scribal God" and to think about what evidence in the image and accompanying text would support the conclusion that the Mayan people were polytheistic. Then, have students Think/Pair/Share with a partner and discuss their ideas about the conclusion. Ask students to be prepared to share their ideas with the class. **ARC**

Discussion and Activities

Analyzing Visuals Direct students' attention to the visuals "Mayan Temple, Tikal" and "Cahokia." **Ask:** What similarities are there between the two images, and what conclusions can you draw about the groups that built the structures? *(Both images suggest cultures that place great importance on monumental buildings. Both images suggest a large population that can support a workforce to build such structures. Both images suggest societies that have a high degree of social and political hierarchy to coordinate the building of monumental structures.)* **WXT**

Historical Thinking Skills

Historical Significance and Argumentation Have students read the section "Commerce and Nationalism." In a short paragraph, ask students to explain which of the two changes identified that created incentives for the beginning of European exploration was more important, and why they think so. **WXT** **MIG**

produce. Religion was as important to Native American society as it was to most other cultures, and it was usually closely bound up with the natural world on which the various groups depended. Native Americans worshiped many gods, whom they associated with crops, game, forests, rivers, and other elements of nature. Some groups created elaborate, brightly colored totems as part of their religious ritual; most staged large festivals on such important occasions as harvests or major hunts.

As in other parts of the world, the societies of North America tended to divide tasks according to gender. All groups assigned women the jobs of caring for children, preparing meals, and gathering certain foods. But the allocation of other tasks varied from one society to another. Some groups (notably the Pueblos of the Southwest) reserved farming tasks almost entirely for men. Among others (including the Algonquins, the Iroquois, and the Muskogees), women tended the fields, while men engaged in hunting, warfare, or clearing land. Iroquois women and children were often left alone for extended periods while men were away hunting or fighting battles. As a result, women tended to control the social and economic organization of the settlements and played powerful roles within families.

EUROPE LOOKS WESTWARD

Europeans were almost entirely unaware of the existence of the Americas before the fifteenth century. A few early wanderers–Leif Eriksson, an eleventh-century Norse seaman, and perhaps others–had glimpsed parts of the Americas and had demonstrated that Europeans were capable of crossing the ocean to reach it. But even if their discoveries had become common knowledge (and they had not), there would have been little incentive for others to follow. Europe in the Middle Ages (roughly 500–1500 CE) was not an adventurous civilization. Divided into innumerable small duchies and kingdoms, Europe had an overwhelmingly provincial outlook. Subsistence agriculture predominated, and commerce was limited; few merchants looked beyond the boundaries of their own regions. The Roman Catholic Church exercised a measure of spiritual authority over most of the continent, and the Holy Roman Empire provided at least a nominal political center. Even so, real power was widely dispersed; only rarely could a single leader launch a great venture. Gradually, however, conditions in Europe changed so that by the late fifteenth century, interest in overseas exploration had grown.

COMMERCE AND NATIONALISM

Two important and related changes provided the first incentive for Europeans to look toward new lands. One was a result of the significant population growth in fifteenth-century Europe. The Black Death, a catastrophic epidemic of the bubonic plague that began in Constantinople in 1347, had decimated Europe, killing (according to some estimates) more than a third of the people of the continent and debilitating its already-limited economy. But a century and a half later, the population had rebounded. With that growth came a rise in land values, a reawakening of commerce, and a general increase in prosperity. Affluent landlords became eager to purchase goods from distant regions, and a new merchant class emerged to meet their demand. As trade increased, and as advances in navigation and shipbuilding made long-distance sea travel more feasible, interest in developing new markets, finding new products, and opening new trade routes rapidly increased.

A REAWAKENING OF COMMERCE

Paralleling the rise of commerce in Europe, and in part responsible for it, was the rise of new governments that were more united and powerful than the feeble political entities of the feudal past. In the western areas of Europe, the authority of the distant pope and the even more distant Holy Roman Emperor was necessarily weak. As a result, strong new monarchs emerged and created centralized nation-states, with national courts, national armies, and–perhaps most important–national tax systems. As these ambitious kings and queens consolidated their power and increased their wealth, they became eager to enhance the commercial growth of their nations.

CENTRALIZED NATION-STATES

Ever since the early fourteenth century, when Marco Polo and other adventurers had returned from Asia bearing exotic goods (spices, fabrics, dyes) and exotic tales, Europeans who hoped for commercial glory had dreamed of trade with the East. For two centuries, that trade had been limited by the difficulties of the long, arduous overland journey to the Asian courts. But in the fourteenth century, as the maritime capabilities of several western European societies increased and as Muslim societies seized control of the eastern routes to Asia, there began to be serious talk of finding a faster, safer sea route to Asia. Such dreams found a receptive audience in the courts of the new monarchs. By the late fifteenth century, some of them were ready to finance daring voyages of exploration.

The first to do so were the Portuguese. They were the preeminent maritime power in the fifteenth century, in large part because of the work of one man, Prince Henry the Navigator. Henry's own principal interest was not in finding a sea route to Asia, but in exploring the western coast of Africa. He dreamed of establishing a Christian empire there to aid in his country's wars against the Moors of northern Africa; and he hoped to find new stores of gold. The explorations he began did not fulfill his own hopes, but they ultimately led farther than he had dreamed. Some of Henry's mariners went as far south as Cape Verde, on Africa's west coast. In 1488 (eight years after Henry's death), Bartholomeu Dias rounded the southern tip of Africa (the Cape of Good Hope); and in 1497–1498 Vasco da Gama proceeded all the way around the cape to India. In 1500, the next fleet bound for India, under the command of Pedro Cabral, was blown westward off its southerly course and happened upon the coast of Brazil. But by then another man, in the service of another country, had already encountered the New World.

PRINCE HENRY THE NAVIGATOR

Discussion and Activities

Speculating How might European exploration of the Americas have been different if Europe and Asia had been better connected by land transportation? *(Europeans would likely have placed less emphasis on sea-going navigation and exploration, possibly delaying exploration and colonization of the Americas.)* **MIG** **GEO**

WHY DO HISTORIANS SO OFTEN DIFFER?

Early in the twentieth century, when the professional study of history was still relatively new, many historians believed that questions about the past could be answered with the same certainty and precision that questions in more-scientific fields could be answered. By sifting through available records, using precise methods of research and analysis, and producing careful, closely argued accounts of the past, they believed they could create definitive histories that would survive without controversy. Scholars who adhered to this view believed that real knowledge can be derived only from direct, scientific observation of clear "facts". They were known as "positivists."

A vigorous debate continues to this day over whether historical research can or should be truly objective. Almost no historian any longer accepts the "positivist" claim that history could ever be an exact science. Disagreement about the past is, in fact, at the heart of the effort to understand history. Critics of contemporary historical scholarship often denounce the way historians are constantly revising earlier interpretations. Some denounce the act of interpretation itself. History, they claim, is "what happened," and historians should "stick to the facts."

Historians, however, continue to differ with one another both because the "facts" are seldom as straightforward as their critics claim and because facts by themselves mean almost nothing without an effort to assign meaning to them. Some historical "facts," of course, are not in dispute. Everyone agrees, for example, that the Japanese bombed Pearl Harbor on December 7, 1941, and that Abraham Lincoln was elected president in 1860. But many other "facts" are much harder to determine—among them, for example, the questions of how large the American population was before the arrival of Columbus or how many enslaved people resisted slavery? This sounds like a reasonably straightforward question, but it is almost impossible to answer with any certainty—because the records of resistance are spotty and the definition of "resistance" is a matter of considerable dispute.

GEORGE BANCROFT

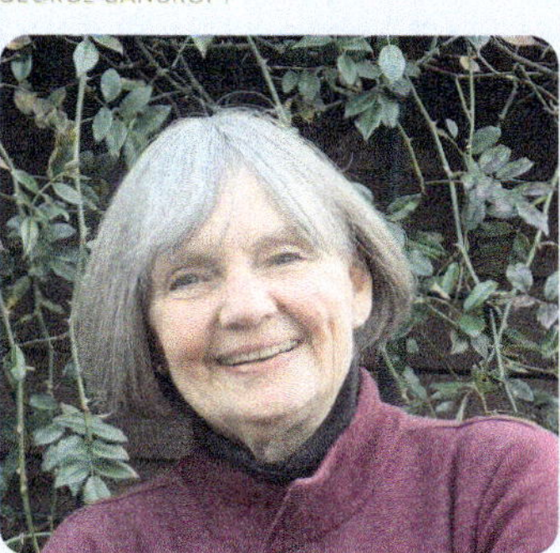

PAULINE MAIER

Even when a set of facts is clear and straightforward, historians disagree—sometimes quite radically—over what they mean. Those disagreements can be the result of political and ideological disagreements. Some of the most vigorous debates in recent decades have been between scholars who believe that economic interests and class divisions are the key to understanding the past, and those who believe that ideas and culture are at least as important as material interests. Whites and people of color, men and women, people from the American South and people from the North, young people and older people: these and many other points of difference find their way into scholarly disagreements. Debates can also occur over differences in methodology—between those who believe that quantitative studies can answer important historical questions and those who believe that other methods come closer to the truth.

Most of all historical interpretation changes in response to the time in which it is written. Historians may strive to be "objective" in their work, but no one can be entirely free from the assumptions and concerns of the present. In the 1950s, the omnipresent shadow of the Cold War had a profound effect on the way most historians viewed the past. In the 1960s, concerns about racial justice and disillusionment with the Vietnam War altered the way many historians viewed the past. Those events introduced a much more critical tone to scholarship and turned the attention of scholars away from politics and government and toward the study of society and culture.

Many areas of scholarship in recent decades are embroiled in a profound debate over whether there is such a thing as "truth." The world, some scholars argue, is simply a series of "narratives" constructed by people who view life in very different and often highly personal ways. "Truth" does not really exist. Everything is a product of interpretation. Not many historians embrace such radical ideas; most would agree that interpretations, to be of any value, must rest on a solid foundation of observable facts. But historians do recognize that even the most compelling facts are subject to many different interpretations and that the process of understanding the past is a forever continuing—and forever contested—process.

HISTORICAL THINKING SKILLS

1. **Identifying** Identify three arguments made regarding the issue of historical objectivity.
2. **Analyzing Perspectives** Explain at least two factors that influence historians when they are writing a historical account.
3. **Developing Arguments** Take a position on the following statement: There is value to differing historical interpretations of "events." Provide examples to support your position.

Historical Thinking Skills

Distinguishing Fact From Opinion Have students read the Debating the Past feature, "Why Do Historians So Often Differ?" **Ask:** What impact does political ideology have on the study of history? What other factors might affect historical interpretation? *(Political ideology may influence how generally agreed upon facts are interpreted. Economic ideology and racial and class differences might also affect interpretation.)*

Answers

Debating the Past

1. First, historians often disagree about the objectivity of facts. Second, when historians do agree about the objectivity of facts, they often disagree about what those facts mean. Third, historians may disagree about how objective facts are acquired.
2. First, the time in which history is written can influence the interpretation and writing of history. Second, the nature of "truth" is difficult to ascertain and varies from the way individuals construct their view of life.
3. The discipline of history does use objective "facts," but the interpretation and meaning of those facts is subjective, which means the historian's craft is individualized. The individualization of historical scholarship allows for differing opinions, which creates a complex and nuanced interpretation of the past.

Historical Thinking Skills

Historical Developments and Argumentation Have students read the Debating the Past feature "The American Population Before Columbus." Remind students of their answers to the Debating the Past Historical Thinking Skills activity. Ask them to consider how one of the factors they identified might apply to the debate over Native American populations. *(Political ideology or racial or ethnic identification may lead some to support higher or lower population numbers.)*

DEBATING THE PAST

THE AMERICAN POPULATION BEFORE COLUMBUS

No one knows how many people lived in the Americas in the centuries before Columbus. But scholars and other researchers have spent more than a century and have written many thousands of pages debating the question nevertheless. Interest in this question survives, despite the near impossibility of answering it. The debate over the pre-Columbian population is closely connected to the much larger debate over the consequences of European settlement of the Western Hemisphere.

Throughout the nineteenth century, Native Americans spoke often of the great days before Columbus when there were many more people in their communities. They drew from their own rich tradition of oral history handed down through storytelling from one generation to another. The painter and ethnographer George Catlin spent much time among Native Americans in the 1830s painting portraits of a race that he feared was "fast passing to extinction". He listened to these oral legends and estimated that there had been 16 million Native Americans in North America before the Europeans came. Other white Americans dismissed such claims as preposterous, insisting that Native American civilization was far too primitive to have been able to sustain so large a population.

In 1928, James Mooney, an ethnologist at the Smithsonian Institution, drew from early accounts of soldiers and missionaries in the sixteenth century. He came up with the implausibly precise figure of 1.15 million Native Americans who lived north of Mexico in the early sixteenth century. That was a larger figure than nineteenth-century writers had suggested, but still much smaller than the Native American themselves claimed. A few years later, the anthropologist Alfred Kroeber used many of Mooney's methods and come up with an estimate of the population of the entire Western Hemisphere—considerably larger than Mooney's, but much lower than Catlin's. He concluded in 1934 that there were 8.4 million people in the Americas in 1492, half in North America and half in the Caribbean and South America.

These low early estimates reflected an assumption that the arrival of the Europeans did not much reduce the indigenous population. But in the 1960s and 1970s, scholars discovered that the early Native American groups had been catastrophically decimated by European plagues not long after the arrival of Columbus—meaning that the numbers Europeans observed even in the late 1500s were already dramatically smaller than the numbers in 1492. Drawing on early work by anthropologists and others who discovered evidence of widespread deaths by disease, historians William McNeill in 1976 and Alfred Crosby a decade later, as well as other scholars, produced powerful accounts of the near extinction of some groups and the dramatic depopulation of others in a pestilential catastrophe with few parallels in history. Almost all scholars now accept that much, perhaps most, of the indigenous population was wiped out by disease—smallpox, measles, tuberculosis, and other plagues imported from Europe.

Henry Dobyns, an anthropologist who was one of the earliest scholars to challenge the early, low estimates, claimed in 1966 that in 1492 there were between 10 and 12 million people north of Mexico and between 90 and 112 million in all of the Americas. No subsequent scholar has made so high a claim, but most estimates that followed have been much closer to Dobyns's than to Kroeber's. The geographer William M. Denevan, for example, argued in 1976 that the American population in 1492 was around 55 million and that the population north of Mexico was under 4 million. Those are among the lowest of modern estimates, but still dramatically higher than the nineteenth-century numbers.

The vehemence with which scholars have debated these figures is not just because it is very difficult to determine population size. It is also because the debate over the population is part of the debate over whether the arrival of Columbus—and the millions of Europeans who followed him—was a great advance in the history of civilization or an unparalleled catastrophe that exterminated a large and flourishing indigenous population. How to balance the many achievements of European civilization in the Americas after 1492 against the terrible destruction of indigenous peoples that accompanied it is, in the end, less a historical question, perhaps, than a moral one.

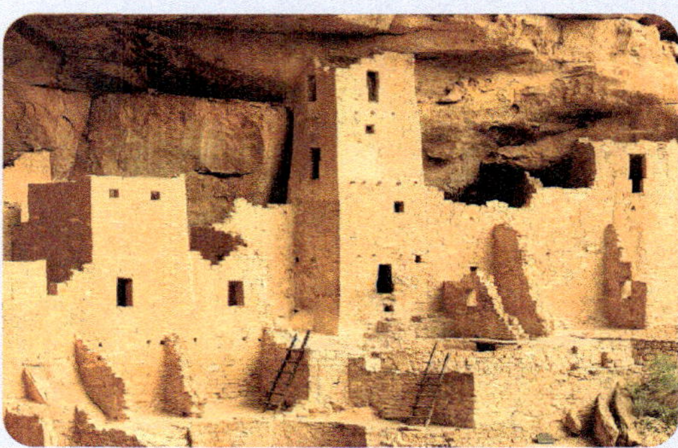

PUEBLO VILLAGE

HISTORICAL THINKING SKILLS

1. **Assessing Credibility** Identify at least two historical estimates of the pre-Columbian population and the methods used to make them. For each estimate, provide one problem with the method used, which might lead to a questioning of the estimate.
2. **Evaluating Significance** Identify a discovery, which can be viewed as a turning point, or significant event, in the debate over the pre-Columbian population. How did this discovery change the debate?
3. **Evaluating Evidence** Identify and explain one reason why the debate over the population of Native Americans before the arrival of Columbus constitutes a significant question.
4. **Developing Arguments** Take a position on the following statement: "The arrival of Columbus to the Western World was a great event." Provide examples to support your position.

Answers

Debating the Past

1. George Catlin estimated that 16 million Native Americans lived in North America before the arrival of Europeans, which was dismissed by some historians as being much too large. The problem with using oral legends is that they often romanticize the past with inaccurate information. James Mooney used early accounts from missionaries and soldiers in the sixteenth century to estimate the Native American population to be 1.15 million, which reflects the questionable belief that Europeans did not reduce the population of Native Americans by much.
2. During the 1960s and 1970s, scholars discovered that Native Americans had been decimated by European plagues not long after the arrival of Columbus. This means that their numbers in the late 1500s were already significantly reduced from the numbers in 1492.
3. The ongoing debate over population estimates centers on the significance of the arrival of Europeans and arguments as to whether this was a great advance in the history of civilization or an unparalleled catastrophe.
4. Arguments in support should mention population increases in Europe, the introduction of new foods, access to natural resources and minerals, and the advent of world-wide capitalism. Arguments against should focus on the negative impact on Native Americans in the decimation of their populations, forced removal from lands, and the displacement of their culture.

CHRISTOPHER COLUMBUS

Christopher Columbus, who was born and reared in Genoa, Italy, obtained most of his early seafaring experience in the service of the Portuguese. As a young man, he became intrigued with the possibility, already under discussion in many seafaring circles, of reaching Asia by going not east but west. Columbus's hopes rested on several basic misconceptions. He believed that the world was far smaller than it actually is.

IROQUOIS WOMEN This 1734 French engraving shows Iroquois women at work in a settlement somewhere in what is now upstate New York. In the foreground, women are cooking. Others are working in the fields. Men spent much of their time hunting and fighting battles, leaving the women to govern and dominate the internal lives of the villages. Property in Iroquois society was inherited through the mother, and women occupied positions of great authority.

Library of Congress

Columbus also believed that the Asian continent extended farther eastward than it actually does. He assumed, therefore, that the Atlantic was narrow enough to be crossed on a relatively brief voyage. It did not occur to him that anything lay to the west between Europe and Asia.

Columbus failed to win support for his plan in Portugal, so he turned to Spain. The Spaniards were not yet as advanced a maritime people as the Portuguese, but they were at least as energetic and ambitious. And in the fifteenth century, the marriage of Spain's two most powerful regional rulers, Ferdinand of Aragon and Isabella of Castile, had produced the strongest monarchy in Europe. Like other young monarchies, Spain soon grew eager to demonstrate its strength by sponsoring new commercial ventures.

Columbus appealed to Queen Isabella for support for his proposed westward voyage. In 1492, Isabella agreed to Columbus's request. Commanding ninety men and three ships–the *Niña*, the *Pinta*, and the *Santa Maria*–Columbus left Spain in August 1492 and sailed west into the Atlantic on what he thought was a straight course for Japan. Ten weeks later, he sighted land and assumed he had reached his target.

COLUMBUS'S FIRST VOYAGE

In fact, he had landed on an island in the Bahamas. When he pushed on and encountered Cuba, he assumed he had reached China. He returned to Spain in triumph, bringing with him several captured indigenous people as evidence of his achievement. (He called the indigenous people "Indians" because he believed they were from the East Indies in the Pacific.)

But Columbus had not, of course, encountered the court of the great khan in China or the fabled wealth of the Indies. A year later, therefore, he tried again, this time with a much larger expedition. As before, he headed into the Caribbean, discovering several other islands and leaving a small and short-lived colony on Hispaniola. On a third voyage, in 1498, he finally reached the mainland and cruised along the northern coast of South America. When he passed the mouth of the Orinoco River (in present-day Venezuela), he concluded for the first time that what he had discovered was not an island off the coast of China, as he had assumed, but a separate continent; such a large freshwater stream, he realized, could emerge only from a large body of land. Still, he remained convinced that Asia was only a short distance away. And although he failed in his efforts to sail around the northeastern coast of South America to the Indies (he was blocked by the Isthmus of Panama), he returned to Spain believing that he had explored at least the fringes of the Far East. He continued to believe that for the rest of his life.

Columbus's celebrated accomplishments made him a popular hero for a time, but he later died in obscurity. When Europeans at last gave a name to the New World, they ignored him. The distinction went instead to a Florentine merchant, Amerigo Vespucci, a member of a later Portuguese expedition to the New World who wrote a series of vivid descriptions of the lands he had visited and who recognized the Americas as new continents.

Columbus has been celebrated for centuries as the "Admiral of the Ocean Sea" and as a representative of the new, secular, scientific impulses of Renaissance Europe. But Columbus was also a deeply religious man, even something of a mystic. His voyages were inspired as much by his conviction that he was fulfilling a divine mission as by his interest in geography and trade. A strong believer in biblical prophecies, he came to see himself as a man destined to advance the coming of the millennium. "God made me the messenger of the new heaven and the new earth," Columbus wrote near the end of his life, "and he showed me the spot where to find it." A similar combination of worldly and religious passions lay behind many subsequent efforts at exploration and settlement of the Americas.

RELIGIOUS MOTIVES FOR EXPLORATION

AP Exam Practice

Short Answer Provide students with the following short-answer questions and allow 15 minutes for completion. Ask for volunteers to share their responses and discuss as a class.

Answer A, B, and C.

A) Briefly explain the central reason for Columbus's expeditions to the Americas. *(Columbus believed he would reach the East Indies by sailing west; he thought that a new trade route would lead to great wealth.)*

B) Briefly explain ONE effect of Columbus's expeditions to the Americas. *(Possible answers: Columbus's expeditions led to further European exploration of the Americas. His expeditions brought back indigenous enslaved people to Europe. Columbus experienced temporary fame in Europe but then faded into obscurity during his lifetime.)*

C) Briefly explain ONE additional reason for Columbus's expeditions to the Americas as described in question A. *(Possible response: Existing trade with Asia was profitable, but it was limited by the logistics of overland travel.)*

Historical Thinking Skills

Drawing Conclusions Have students read the section "Columbus's First Voyage." **Ask:** Why did Columbus conclude that he and his crew had reached Asia? *(He had no knowledge of landmasses between Europe and Asia. He may have been influenced by his desire to reach Asia.)* **GEO** **MIG**

Reasoning Processes

Continuity and Change Have students read the section "Ferdinand Magellan." As a class or in small groups, have students discuss ways in which the expeditions of Balboa and Magellan built on Columbus's expeditions, and in what ways they marked a departure from those expeditions. **MIG** **GEO**

THE ALGONQUIAN VILLAGE OF SECOTON (C. 1585), BY JOHN WHITE John White created this illustration of life in an Algonquian village along the coast of North Carolina. It shows the diversified agriculture practiced by the Native Americans: squash, tobacco, and three varieties of corn. The hunters shown in nearby woods suggest another element of the Native American economy. At bottom right, Native Americans perform a religious ritual, which White described as "strange gestures and songs."

Partly as a result of Columbus's initiative, Spain began to devote greater resources and energy to maritime exploration and gradually replaced Portugal as the leading seafaring nation. The Spaniard Vasco de Balboa fought his way across the Isthmus of Panama in 1513. He became the first known European to gaze westward upon the great ocean that separated the Americas from China and the Indies. Seeking access

FERDINAND MAGELLAN

to that ocean, Ferdinand Magellan, a Portuguese in the employ of the Spanish, found the strait that now bears his name at the southern end of South America. He struggled through the stormy narrows and into the ocean (so calm by contrast that he christened it the "Pacific"), then proceeded to the Philippines. There Magellan died in a conflict, but his expedition went on to complete the first known circumnavigation of the globe (1519–1522). By 1550, Spaniards had explored the coasts of North America as far north as Oregon in the west and Labrador in the east, as well as some of the interior regions of the continent.

CHRISTOPHER COLUMBUS This oil painting by Frederick Kemmelmeyer (1801/1805), First Landing of Christopher Columbus, depicts Columbus and his crew in a somewhat idealized fashion. The artist's perspective shows the Europeans as larger and more powerful than the indigenous peoples they encounter.

THE CONQUISTADORES

In time, Spanish explorers stopped thinking of the Americas simply as an obstacle to their search for a route to the East. They began instead to consider it a possible source of wealth rivaling and even surpassing the original Indies. On the basis of Columbus's discoveries, the Spanish claimed for themselves the whole of the Americas, except for a piece of it (today's Brazil) that was reserved by a papal decree for the Portuguese. By the mid-sixteenth century, the Spanish were well on their way to establishing a substantial American empire.

The first Spanish colonists, whom Columbus brought on his second voyage, settled on the islands of the Caribbean, where they tried to enslave the indigenous people and find gold. They had little luck in either effort. But then, in 1518, Hernando Cortés led a small military expedition of about 600 men into Mexico. Cortés had been a Spanish government official in Cuba for fourteen years and to that point had achieved little success. But when he heard stories of

CORTÉS CONQUERS THE AZTECS

great treasures in Mexico, he decided to go in search of them. He met strong and resourceful resistance from the Aztecs and their powerful emperor, Montezuma. But Cortés and his army had, unknowingly, unleashed an assault on the Aztecs far more devastating than military attack: they had exposed the Aztecs to smallpox during an early and relatively peaceful visit to Tenochtitlán. A smallpox epidemic decimated the population and made it possible for the Spanish to triumph in

Discussion and Activities

Identifying Bias Have students view the image "Christopher Columbus." In small groups, have students create a KWL chart to identify what they know about European attitudes toward Native Americans in the fifteenth and sixteenth centuries, what they want to know, and what they learned from viewing the image. Extend the activity by discussing the KWL charts as a class. Ask students to identify in bias they noticed in the image. **NAT** **MIG** **PCE**

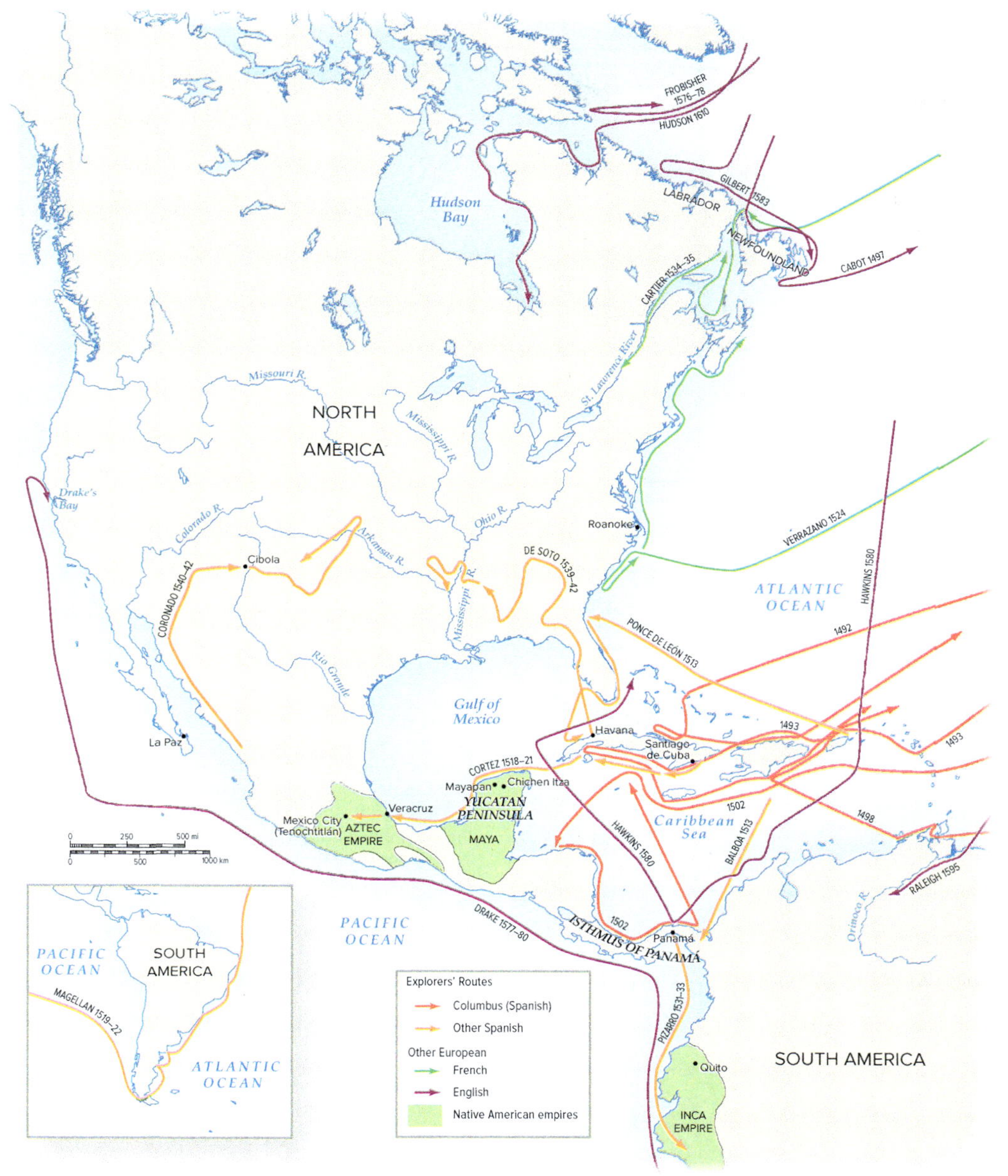

EUROPEAN EXPLORATION AND CONQUEST, 1492–1583 This map shows the many voyages of exploration and conquest of North America launched by Europeans in the late fifteenth and sixteenth centuries. Note how Columbus and the Spanish explorers who followed him tended to move quickly into the lands of Mexico, the Caribbean, and Central and South America, while the English and French explored the northern territories of North America.

What factors might have led these various nations to explore and colonize these different areas of the New World?

Historical Thinking Skills

Analyzing Visuals Ask students to review the map, "European Exploration and Conquest, 1492–1583." Then ask students to explain how to use the map to identify where each European country explored and colonized. *(The countries are distinguished by color on the map, and the various countries' explorations are indicated by different-colored arrows.)* **MIG**

Answers

European Exploration and Conquest, 1492–1583

Nations may have explored and colonized different areas of the New World due to their different economic goals. For example, Spanish exploration and colonization were largely driven by a desire to acquire precious metals, while the English were more motivated by a desire to establish permanent settlements.

Historical Thinking Skills

Evaluating Evidence Have students view the image "The Mexicans Strike Back." Ask them to look for features of the image that would confirm that it was created by Native Americans. *(The image portrays Native Americans in color, while the Spanish are black and white. The image depicts Native Americans advancing, while the Spanish have retreated and all appear to be leaning backward, away from the advancing Native Americans.)* **ARC**

THE MEXICANS STRIKE BACK In this vivid scene from the Duran Codex, Mexican artists illustrate a rare moment in which Mexican warriors gained the upper hand over the Spanish invaders. Driven back, the Spanish have taken refuge in a room in the royal palace in Tenochtitlán while brightly attired Mexican warriors besiege them. Although the Mexicans gained a temporary advantage in this battle, the drawing illustrates one of the reasons for their inability to withstand the Spanish in the longer term. The Spanish soldiers are armed with rifles and crossbows, while the Mexican warriors carry only spears and shields.

their second attempt at conquest. The Spanish believed that the epidemic was a vindication of their efforts. When the Christians were exhausted from war, one follower of Cortés said at the time, "God saw fit to send the Indians smallpox." Through his ruthless suppression of the surviving Aztecs, Cortés established a lasting reputation as the most brutal of the Spanish *conquistadores* (conquerors).

PIZARRO IN PERU A European artist depicted Pizarro's arrival on the coast of Peru in the early 1530s, where he was greeted by crowds of hostile Native Americans. By 1538, Pizarro had conquered the empire of the Incas.

The news that silver was to be found in Mexico attracted the attention of other Spaniards. From the island colonies and from Spain itself, a wave of conquistadores descended on the mainland in search of fortune. Francisco Pizarro, who conquered Peru (1532–1538) and revealed to Europeans the wealth of the Incas, opened the way for other advances into South America. His onetime deputy Hernando de Soto, in a futile search for gold, silver, and jewels, led several expeditions (1539–1541) through Florida west into the continent and became the first European known to have crossed the Mississippi River. Francisco Coronado traveled north from Mexico (1540–1542) into what is now New Mexico in a similarly fruitless search for gold and jewels; in the process, he helped open the Southwest of what is now the United States to Spanish settlement.

The story of the Spanish warriors is one of great military daring and achievement. It is also a story of great brutality and greed—a story that would be repeated time and again over centuries of European conquest of the Americas. The conquistadores in some areas almost exterminated the indigenous populations through a combination of warfare and disease.

BRUTALITY AND GREED

Discussion and Activities

Comparison and Argumentation Have students read the section "The Conquistadors." As a class or in small groups, have students consider the evidence relating to the motivations of the conquistadors. Which motive seems more compelling—religion or wealth? Why? Make sure students provide evidence for their arguments. **ARC** **WXT**

DE SOTO IN NORTH AMERICA This gruesome drawing portrays Spanish troops under Hernando de Soto massacring a group of Native Americans in what is now Alabama, in the winter of 1540–1541. De Soto had been governor of Cuba, but in 1539 he sailed to Florida with 600 troops and for the next several years traveled through large areas of what would later become the southern United States until he died of fever in 1542. Here, as elsewhere, his troops dealt with the Native Americans they encountered along the way with unrestrained brutality.

SPANISH AMERICA

Lured by dreams of treasure, Spanish explorers, conquistadores, and colonists established a vast empire for Spain in the Americas. The history of the Spanish Empire spanned three distinct periods. The first was the age of discovery and exploration–beginning with Columbus and continuing through the first two decades of the sixteenth century. The second was the age of the conquest, in which Spanish military forces (aided by the diseases they unleashed) established their dominion over the lands once ruled by Native Americans. The third phase began in the 1570s, when new Spanish laws–the Ordinances of Discovery–banned the most brutal military conquests. From that point on, the Spanish expanded their presence in the Americas through colonization.

ORDINANCES OF DISCOVERY

The first Spaniards to arrive in the Americas, the conquistadores, had been interested in only one thing: getting rich. And in that they were fabulously successful. For 300 years, beginning in the sixteenth century, the mines in Spanish America yielded more than ten times as much gold and silver as the rest of the world's mines put together. These riches made Spain the wealthiest and most powerful nation for a time.

After the first wave of conquest, however, most Spanish settlers in America came for other reasons. Many went in hopes of creating a profitable agricultural economy. Unlike the conquistadores, who left little but destruction behind them, these settlers helped establish elements of European civilization in the Americas that permanently altered both the landscape and the social structure.

Another important force for colonization was the Catholic Church. Ferdinand and Isabella, in establishing Spain's claim to most of the Americas from Mexico south, bowed to the wishes of the Church and established the requirement that Catholicism be the only religion of the new territories. Spain abided by that condition. Although the Spanish founded commercial and military centers in the sixteenth century, another common form of settlement by the early seventeenth century was the Catholic mission. Missions had commercial lives. But their primary purpose, at least at first, was converting Native Americans to Catholicism. There were usually military garrisons connected to the missions, to protect the Europeans from attacks. *Presidios* (military bases) often grew up nearby to provide additional protection.

AP Exam Practice

Short Answer Provide students with the following short-answer questions and allow 15 minutes for completion. Ask for volunteers to share their responses and discuss as a class.

Answer A, B, and C.

A) Briefly explain one primary motive for Spanish exploration of the New World. *(Possible answer: Spanish explorers came in search of precious metals.)*

B) Briefly explain a second motive for Spanish exploration of the New World. *(Possible answer: Spanish explorers came to convert Native Americans to Catholicism.)*

C) Briefly explain how these motives led to the conflict depicted in the image "De Soto in North America." *(Spanish conquistadors sometimes used violence to subdue Native Americans who did not convert to Catholicism or cooperate with the search for precious metals.)*

Discussion and Activities

Analyzing Change Have students read the section "Ordinances of Discovery." Ask them to consider how the reasons for Spanish colonization changed after the first wave. Ask students to place events of Spanish colonization on a time line and assign a reason or motive to each event. Use the time line as a basis for a whole class or small group discussion. **ARC** **WXT** **MIG**

AP Exam Practice

Short Answer Provide students with the following short-answer questions and allow 15 minutes for completion. Ask for volunteers to share their responses and discuss as a class.

Answer A, B, and C.

A) Briefly explain ONE reason for Spanish settlement in New Spain. *(One reason for the settlement of New Spain was in order to found missions to facilitate the conversion of Native Americans to Catholicism.)*

B) Briefly explain ONE reason for Spanish settlement in New Granada. *(One reason for the settlement of New Granada was for the extraction of precious metals.)*

C) Briefly explain ONE difference between the reasons for settlement in the two areas. *(Possible answer: One reason for the difference was the relative lack of precious metals in New Spain.)*

SPANISH AMERICA From the time of Columbus's initial voyage in 1492 until the mid-nineteenth century, Spain was the dominant colonial power in the Americas. From the southern regions of South America to the northern regions of the Pacific Northwest, Spain controlled one of the world's largest empires. Note how much of the Spanish Empire was simply grafted upon the earlier empires of indigenous peoples—the Incas in what is today Chile and Peru, and the Aztecs across much of the rest of South America, Mexico, and the Southwest of what is now the United States.

What characteristics of Spanish colonization would account for Spain's preference for already-settled regions?

18 · CHAPTER 1

Answers

Spanish America

Spanish settlers wanted to settle in regions where people already lived because they wanted to use indigenous laborers in their mines and on their farms.

Indeed, after the era of the conquistadores came to a close in the 1540s, the missionary impulse became one of the most important motives for European emigration to America. Priests or friars accompanied almost all colonizing ventures. Through their zealous work, the gospel of the Catholic Church ultimately extended throughout South and Central America, Mexico, and into the South and Southwest of the present United States.

CATHOLIC MISSIONS

NORTHERN OUTPOSTS

The Spanish fort established in 1565 at St. Augustine, Florida, became the first permanent European settlement in what is now the United States. It served as a military outpost, an administrative center for Franciscan missionaries, and a headquarters for unsuccessful campaigns against Native Americans that were ultimately abandoned. But it did not mark the beginning of a substantial effort at colonization in the region.

ST. AUGUSTINE

A more substantial colonizing venture began thirty years later in the Southwest. In 1598, Don Juan de Oñate traveled north from Mexico with a party of 500 men. He claimed for Spain some of the lands of the Pueblo Indians that Coronado had passed through over fifty years before. The Spanish migrants established a colony in what is now New Mexico, modeled roughly on those the Spanish had created farther south. Oñate distributed *encomiendas* to the Spanish settlers. They were licenses to exact labor and tribute from the Native Americans in specific areas (a system first used in dealing with the Moors in Spain). The Spanish demanded tribute from the local Native Americans (and at times commandeered them as laborers). Spanish colonists founded Santa Fe in 1609.

Oñate's harsh treatment of the Native Americans (who greatly outnumbered the small Spanish population) threatened the stability of the new colony and led to his removal as governor in 1606. Over time, relations between the Spanish and the Pueblos improved. Substantial numbers of Pueblos converted to Christianity under the influence of Spanish missionaries. Others entered into important trading relationships with the Spanish. The colony remained precarious nevertheless because of the danger from Apache and Navajo raiders, who threatened the Spanish and Pueblos alike. Even so, the New Mexico settlement continued to grow. By 1680, there were over 2,000 Spanish colonists living among about 30,000 Pueblos. The economic heart of the colony was not the gold and precious metals the early Spanish explorers had tried in vain to find. It was cattle and sheep, raised on the *ranchos* that stretched out around the small towns Spanish settlers established.

In 1680, the colony was nearly destroyed when the Pueblos rose in revolt. In the 1660s and 1670s, the Spanish priests and the colonial government, which was closely tied to the missionaries, launched efforts to suppress tribal rituals that Europeans considered incompatible with Christianity. The discontent among the Pueblos at this suppression survived for decades. More important as a cause of the Pueblo revolt of 1680, however, was a major drought and a series of raids by neighboring Apache groups. The instability these events produced sparked the uprising. A Native American religious leader named Pope led an uprising that killed hundreds of European settlers (including twenty-one priests), captured Santa Fe, and drove the Spanish temporarily from the region. But twelve years later the Spanish returned, resumed seizing Pueblo lands, and crushed a last revolt in 1696.

PUEBLO REVOLT OF 1680

Spanish exploitation of the Pueblos did not end. But after the revolts, many Spanish colonists realized that they could not prosper in New Mexico if they remained constantly in conflict with a Native American that greatly outnumbered them. They tried to solve the problem in two ways. On the one hand, the Spanish intensified their assimilation efforts by baptizing Native American children at birth and enforcing observance of Catholic rituals. On the other hand, they now permitted the Pueblos to own land. They stopped commandeering Native American labor, they replaced the encomienda system with a less demanding and oppressive one, and they tacitly tolerated the practice of tribal religious rituals.

These efforts were at least partially successful. After a while, there was significant intermarriage between Europeans and Native Americans. Increasingly, the Pueblos came to consider the Spanish their allies in the continuing battles with the Apaches and Navajos. By 1750, the Spanish population had grown modestly to about 4,000. The Pueblo population had declined (through disease, war, and migration) to about 13,000, less than half what it had been in 1680. New Mexico had by then become a reasonably stable, but still weak and isolated, outpost of the Spanish Empire.

THE EMPIRE AT HIGH TIDE

By the end of the sixteenth century, the Spanish Empire had become one of the largest in the history of the world. It included the islands of the Caribbean and the coastal areas of South America that had been the first targets of the Spanish expeditions. It extended to Mexico and southern North America, where a second wave of colonizers had established outposts. Most of all, the empire spread southward and westward into the vast landmass of South America–the areas that are now Chile, Argentina, and Peru. In 1580, when the Spanish and Portuguese monarchies temporarily united, Brazil came under Spanish jurisdiction as well.

SPAIN'S VAST EMPIRE

It was, however, a colonial empire very different from the one the English would establish in North America beginning in the early seventeenth century. The earliest Spanish ventures in the New World had been largely independent of the throne. But by the end of the sixteenth century, the monarchy had extended its authority directly into the governance of local communities. Colonists had few opportunities to establish political institutions independent of Spain. There was also a significant economic difference between the Spanish Empire and the later British one. The Spanish were far more successful than the British would be in extracting great surface wealth–gold and silver–from their American colonies. But they concentrated less energy on making agriculture and commerce

Reasoning Processes

Causation Have students read the section "Northern Outposts." Ask them to write a paragraph identifying reasons for the Pueblo Revolt. Ask students to share their paragraphs with the class. **ARC** **WXT** **MIG**

Discussion and Activities

Comparing After students read the section "Northern Outposts," have them work in small groups to create Venn diagrams comparing Spanish settlements in Florida and New Mexico. **GEO** **MIG**

Historical Thinking Skills

Argumentation Have students read the section "The Empire at High Tide." Ask students to write a thesis statement that clearly identifies an argument as to why the Spanish were more successful at extracting precious metals from their colonies in the New World than the British were. Ask for volunteers to share with the class, while the class provides feedback as to the clarity and effectiveness of the thesis statement. PCE WXT

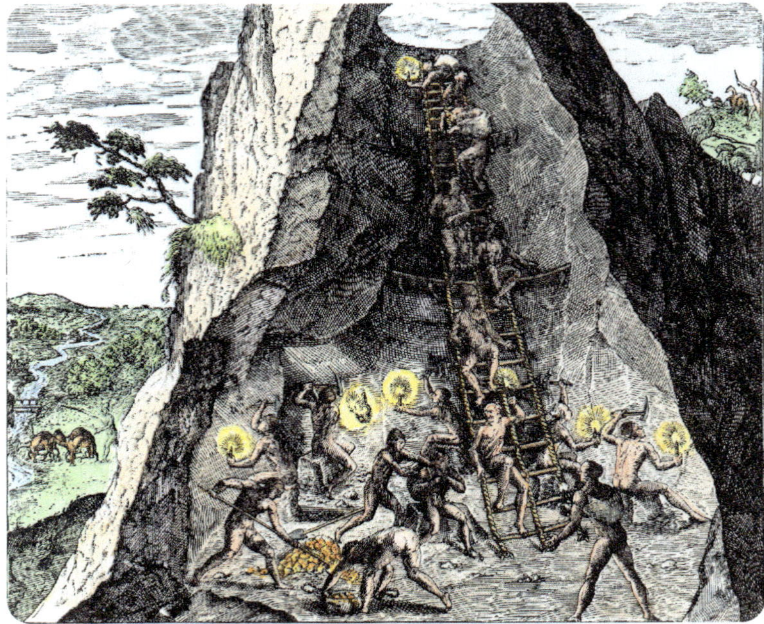

GOLD IN THE AMERICAS Spanish conquistadors and settlers were wildly successful in their acquisition of gold in the Americas. For three hundred years, beginning in the sixteenth century, mines in America produced more than ten times as much gold and silver as the rest of the world's production put together. This image shows how the Spaniards enslaved Native Americans to do the hard work of mining gold.

© North Wind Picture Archives/Alamy

profitable in their colonies. The strict commercial policies of the Spanish government (policies that the British Empire was never strong enough to impose on their colonies to the north) made things worse. To enforce the collection of duties and to provide protection against pirates, the government established rigid and restrictive regulations that required all trade with the colonies to go through a single Spanish port and only a few colonial ports, in fleets making but two voyages a year. The system stifled economic development of the Spanish areas of the Americas.

RIGID ROYAL CONTROL

There was also an important difference between the character of the population in the Spanish Empire and that of the colonies to the north. Almost from the beginning, the English, Dutch, and French colonies in North America concentrated on establishing permanent settlements and family life. The Europeans in North America reproduced rapidly after their first difficult years and in time came to outnumber the Native Americans. The Spanish, by contrast, ruled their empire but did not people it. In the first century of settlement, fewer than 250,000 settlers in the Spanish colonies were from Spain itself or from any other European country. Only about 200,000 more arrived in the first half of the seventeenth century. Some additional settlers came from various outposts of Spanish civilization in the Atlantic–the Azores, the Cape Verde Islands, and elsewhere; but even with these other sources, the number of European settlers in Spanish America remained very small relative to the indigenous population. Despite the ravages of disease and war, the vast majority of the population of the Spanish Empire continued to consist of indigenous peoples. The Spanish, in other words, imposed a small ruling class upon a much larger existing population; they did not create a self-contained European society in the New World as the English would attempt to do in North America.

A COLLISION OF CULTURES

BIOLOGICAL AND CULTURAL EXCHANGES

The lines separating the races in the Spanish Empire gradually grew less distinct than they would be in the English colonies to the north. European and Native American cultures never entirely merged in the Spanish colonies. Indeed, significant differences remain today between European and Native American cultures throughout South and Central America.

Europeans would not have been exploring the Americas at all without their early contacts with Native Americans. From them, they first learned of the rich deposits of gold and silver. After that, the history of the Americas became one of increasing levels of exchanges–some beneficial, some catastrophic–among different peoples and cultures.

INCREASING LEVELS OF EXCHANGE

The first and most profound result of this exchange was the importation of European diseases to the Americas. It would be difficult to exaggerate the consequences of the exposure of

Discussion and Activities

Analyzing Continuity After students have read the section "The Empire at High Tide," ask them as a class or in small groups to discuss how Spain was able to maintain control of its New World empire throughout the sixteenth and seventeenth centuries. PCE WXT

Native Americans to such illnesses as influenza, measles, chicken pox, mumps, typhus, and above all smallpox–diseases to which Europeans had over time developed at least a partial immunity but to which Native Americans were tragically vulnerable. Millions died.

Indigenous groups inhabiting some of the large Caribbean islands and some areas of Mexico were virtually extinct within fifty years of their first contact with Europeans. On Hispaniola–where the Dominican Republic and Haiti are today and where Columbus landed and established a small, short-lived colony in the 1490s–the indigenous population quickly declined from approximately 1 million to about 500. In the Mayan areas of Mexico, as much as 95 percent of the population perished within a few years of their first contact with the Spanish. Some groups fared better than others; some of the groups north of Mexico, whose contact with European settlers came later and less intimately, were spared the worst of the epidemics. But most areas of the Americas experienced a demographic catastrophe at least as grave as, and in many places far worse than, the Black Death that had killed at least a third of the population of Europe two centuries before.

DEMOGRAPHIC CATASTROPHE

The decimation of indigenous populations in the southern regions of the Americas was not, however, purely a result of this inadvertent exposure to infection. It was also a result of the conquistadores' deliberate policy of subjugation and extermination. Their brutality was in part a reflection of the ruthlessness with which Europeans waged war in all parts of the world. It was also a result of their conviction that the indigenous peoples were "savages"–uncivilized peoples whom they considered somehow not fully human.

DELIBERATE SUBJUGATION AND EXTERMINATION

Not all aspects of the exchange were so disastrous to Native Americans. The Europeans introduced important new crops to America (among them sugar and bananas), domestic livestock (cattle, pigs, and sheep), and perhaps most significantly the horse, which had disappeared from the Western Hemisphere in the Ice Age and now returned aboard Spanish ships in the sixteenth century. The Europeans imported these things for their own use. But Native Americans soon learned to cultivate the new crops, and European livestock proliferated rapidly and spread widely. In the past, most Native American societies had possessed no domesticated animals other than dogs. The horse, in particular, became central to the lives of many Native Americans and transformed their societies.

The exchange was at least as important (and far more beneficial) to the Europeans. In both North and South America, the arriving Europeans learned new agricultural techniques from Native Americans, techniques often better adapted to the character of the new land than those they had brought with them from Europe. They discovered new crops, above all maize (corn), which became an important staple among the settlers. Columbus took corn back to Europe from his first trip to America, and it soon spread through much of Europe as well. Such American foods as squash, pumpkins, beans, sweet potatoes, tomatoes, peppers, and potatoes also found their way back to Europe and in the process revolutionized European agriculture. Agricultural discoveries ultimately proved more important to the future of Europe than the gold and silver the conquistadores valued so highly.

NEW CROPS AND AGRICULTURAL TECHNIQUES

In South America, Central America, and Mexico, societies emerged in which Europeans and Native Americans lived in intimate, if unequal, contact with one another. As a result, some Native Americans adopted features of European civilization. Many Native Americans gradually came to learn Spanish or Portuguese, but in the process they created a range of dialects, combining the European languages with their own. European missionaries–through both persuasion and coercion–spread Catholicism through most areas of the Spanish Empire. But Native Americans tended to connect the new creed with features of their old religions, creating a hybrid of faiths that were, while essentially Christian, nevertheless distinctively American.

Colonial officials were expected to take their wives with them to America, but among the ordinary settlers–the majority–European men outnumbered European women by at least ten to one. Not surprisingly, therefore, the Spanish immigrants had substantial sexual contact with Native American women. Intermarriage became frequent,

SMALLPOX AMONG THE NATIVE AMERICANS Far more devastating to the Native Americans than the military ventures of Europeans were deadly diseases carried to the Americas by invaders from the Europe. Native Americans had developed no immunity to the infectious diseases of Europe, and they died by the hundreds of thousands from such epidemics as measles, influenza, and (as depicted here by a European artist) smallpox.

AP Exam Practice

Short Answer Provide students with the following short-answer questions and allow 15 minutes for completion. Ask for volunteers to share their responses and discuss as a class.

Answer A, B, and C.

A) Briefly explain ONE way in which the Columbian Exchange benefited the New World. *(The Columbian Exchange brought useful new plants and animals to the New World, such as sugar, cattle, and pigs.)*

B) Briefly explain ONE way in which the Columbian Exchange was detrimental to the New World. *(The Columbian Exchange caused a catastrophic population decline as result of new diseases like smallpox.)*

C) Briefly explain ONE way in which the Columbian Exchange benefited Europe. *(The Columbian Exchange brought useful food crops to Europe, such as potatoes.)*

Discussion and Activities

Analyzing Change Have students read the section "Biological and Cultural Exchanges." In pairs or small groups, ask them to create a T-chart comparing the benefits of the cultural exchanges discussed for Europeans and Native Americans. As a class, discuss the lists and rank the benefits by order of impact. Complete the discussion by asking students to predict which continent would eventually be changed more dramatically by these exchanges. **GEO** **WXT** **MIG**

Reasoning Processes

Comparison and Argumentation Have students read the sections "Ghana and Mali" and "Benin, Congo, and Songhay." Ask them to complete a Venn Diagram to identify similarities and differences between the two regions. Have them circle those differences that might have made one region more vulnerable to the European slave trade compared to the other. **MIG** **ARC** **SOC**

and before long the population of the colonies came to be dominated (numerically, at least) by people of mixed race, or *mestizos*. Through much of the Spanish Empire an elaborate racial hierarchy developed, with the Spanish at the top, Native Americans at the bottom, and multiracial people in between. Racial categories, however, were much more fluid than the Spanish wanted to believe and did not long remain fixed. Over time, the wealth and influence of a family often came to define its place in the "racial" hierarchy more decisively than race itself. Eventually, a successful or powerful person could become "Spanish" regardless of his or her actual ancestry.

A COMPLEX RACIAL HIERARCHY

Native Americans were the principal labor source for the Europeans. Virtually all the commercial, agricultural, and mining enterprises of the Spanish and Portuguese colonists depended on an Native American workforce. Different labor systems emerged in different areas of the Spanish Empire. In some places, Native Americans were sold into slavery. More often, colonists used a wage system closely related, but not identical, to slavery, by which Native Americans were forced to work in the mines and on the plantations for fixed periods, unable to leave without the consent of their employers. Such systems survived in some areas of the South American mainland for many centuries. So great was the need for Native American labor that European settlers were less interested in acquiring land than they were in gaining control over Native American villages, which could become a source of labor.

VARIED LABOR SYSTEMS

Even so, the Native American population could not meet all the labor needs of the colonists–particularly since the population had declined (and in some places virtually vanished) because of disease and war. As early as 1502, therefore, European settlers began importing enslaved people from Africa.

AFRICA AND AMERICA

Most of the African men and women who were forcibly taken to the Americas came from a large region in west Africa below the Sahara Desert, known as Guinea. It was the home of a wide variety of peoples and cultures. Since over half of all the new arrivals in the New World between 1500 and 1800 were Africans, those cultures greatly affected the character of American civilization. Europeans and white Americans came to portray African society as primitive and uncivilized (in part to justify the enslavement of Africa's people). But most Africans were civilized peoples with well-developed economies and political systems.

Humans began settling in west Africa at least 10,000 years ago. By the fifteenth century CE, they had developed extensive civilizations and complex political systems. The residents of upper Guinea had substantial commercial contact with the Mediterranean world–trading ivory, gold, and enslaved people for finished goods. Largely as a result, they became early converts to Islam. After the collapse of the ancient kingdom of Ghana around 1100 CE, the even larger empire of Mali emerged and survived well into the fifteenth century. Its great city, Timbuktu, became renowned as a trading center and a seat of education.

GHANA AND MALI

Africans farther south were more isolated from Europe and the Mediterranean. They were also more politically fragmented. The central social unit in much of the south was the village, which usually consisted of members of an extended family group. Some groups of villages united in small kingdoms–among them Benin, Congo, and Songhay. But no large empires emerged in the south comparable to the Ghana and Mali kingdoms farther north. Nevertheless, these southern societies also developed extensive trade–in woven fabrics, ceramics, and wooden and iron goods, as well as crops and livestock–both among themselves and, to a lesser degree, with the outside world.

BENIN, CONGO AND SONGHAY

The African civilizations naturally developed economies that reflected the climates and resources of their lands. In upper Guinea, fishing and rice cultivation, supplemented by the extensive trade with Mediterranean lands, were the foundation of the economy. Farther south, Africans grew wheat and other food crops, raised livestock, and fished. There were some nomadic societies in the interior, which subsisted largely on hunting and gathering and developed less elaborate social systems. But most Africans were sedentary people, linked by elaborate political, economic, and familial relationships.

SCULPTURE OF DJENNÉ Many of the Africans forcibly taken from their homes to America in the seventeenth and eighteenth centuries were natives of Mali, the seat of an ancient east African civilization. This terra cotta sculpture, discovered in the 1940s, dates from between 600 and 900 years ago. It portrays a prisoner who most likely represented an African enslaved by the Malis.

Discussion and Activities

Identifying Cause and Effect Have students read the section "Varied Labor Systems." Then in pairs or small groups, have them discuss reasons why the native population was insufficient to meet Spanish demands for labor. **WXT** **MIG**

Like many Native American societies, but unlike those in Europe, African societies tended to be matrilineal–which means that people traced their heredity through, and inherited property from, their mothers rather than their fathers. When a couple married, the husband left his own family to join the family of his wife. Like most other peoples, Africans divided work by gender, but the nature of that division varied greatly from place to place. Women played a major role, often the dominant role, in trade; in many areas they were the principal farmers (while the men hunted, fished, and raised livestock); and everywhere, they managed child care and food preparation. Most societies also divided political power by gender, with men choosing leaders and systems for managing what they defined as male affairs and women choosing parallel leaders to handle female matters. Tribal chiefs generally were men (although in some places there was a female counterpart), but the position customarily passed down not to the chief's son but to the son of the chief's eldest sister. African societies, in short, were characterized by a greater degree of sexual equality than those of most other parts of the world at the time.

MATRILINEAL SOCIETIES

In those areas of west Africa where indigenous religions had survived the spread of Islam (which included most of the lands south of the empire of Mali), people worshiped many gods, whom they associated with various aspects of the natural world and whose spirits they believed lived in trees, rocks, forests, and streams. Most Africans also developed forms of ancestor worship and took great care in tracing family lineage; the most revered priests (who were often also important social and political leaders as well) were generally the oldest people in the tribe.

African societies had elaborate systems of social ranks (or hierarchies). Small elites of priests and nobles stood at the top. Most people belonged to a large middle group of farmers, traders, crafts workers, and others. At the bottom of society were enslaved people–men and women who were put into bondage after being captured in wars or because of criminal behavior or unpaid debts. Slavery in Africa was not usually permanent; people were generally placed in bondage for a fixed period and in the meantime retained certain legal protections (including the right to marry). Their children, moreover, did not inherit their parents' condition of bondage.

The African slave trade began long before the European migration to the New World. As early as the eighth century CE, west Africans began selling enslaved people to traders from the Mediterranean. They were responding to a demand from affluent families who wanted enslaved people as domestic servants. They were also responding to more-general labor shortages in some areas of Europe and North Africa. When Portuguese sailors began exploring the coast of Africa in the fifteenth century, they too bought enslaved people–usually criminals and people captured in war–and took them back to Portugal, where there was a small but steady demand. By the 1500s, people from the Guinea region had moved into much of sub-Saharan Africa and traded gold, ivory, pepper, and many other precious commodities.

In the sixteenth century, however, the market for enslaved people grew dramatically as a result of the rising European demand for sugarcane. The small areas of sugar cultivation in the Mediterranean were proving inadequate, and production soon moved to the island of Madeira off the African coast, which became a Portuguese colony. Not long after that, it moved to the Caribbean islands and Brazil. Sugar was a labor-intensive crop, and the demand for enslaved laborers in these new areas increased rapidly. European slave traders responded to that demand by increasing the enslavement of people from along the coast of west Africa (and from some areas of east Africa as well). As the demand increased, African kingdoms warred with one another in an effort to capture potential enslaved people to exchange for European goods. At first the slave traders were overwhelmingly Portuguese and, to a lesser extent, Spanish. By the seventeenth century, the Dutch had won control of most of the slave market. In the eighteenth century, the English dominated it. (Despite some false claims, Jews were never significantly involved in the slave trade.) By 1700, slavery had begun to spread well beyond its original locations in the Caribbean and South America and into the English colonies to the north.

GROWTH OF THE AFRICAN SLAVE TRADE

Historical Thinking Skills

Comparing and Contrasting Have students read the section "Africa and America." Then have them create a Venn Diagram and complete it using examples of how African and American cultures were similar and different. **ARC** **SOC**

Discussion and Activities

Identifying Cause and Effect After students have read the section "Africa and America," as a class or in small groups, ask them to discuss how the cultivation of sugar led to the growth of African slavery in the New World. **WXT** **GEO**

Discussion and Activities

Analyzing Cause and Effect Have students consider the questions "How did the introduction of plants, technology, and animals by Europeans alter the environment of North America, and what effect did these introductions have on Native Americans?" Divide the class into three groups for a jigsaw activity. Have one group focus on plants, the second group focus on technology, and the third group focus on animals. Have each group generate a list of examples specific to their topic. Then have students organize into groups of three, with one student from each of the original groups sharing their examples. Finally, ask the whole class to discuss or debate which of the categories had the greatest impact.

Key Terms

Students should be familiar with the key terms and be able to define them in the context of issues and challenges that confronted Europeans, Native Americans, and Africans who populated North America during the time period studied in this chapter. Encourage students to use these terms in performing review exercises and exam practice for this chapter.

CHAPTER 1 REVIEW

CONNECTING THEMES

Chapter One focused on the interaction of indigenous peoples in the Western Hemisphere prior to and just after the arrival of the first Europeans. The elaborate civilizations south of what is now the United States, along with the variety of societies that emerged in the lands north of what is now Mexico demonstrate the diverse economic, social, and political structures that existed before the arrival of Europeans. These structures, along with geographic and environmental factors, helped shape the development of North America.

The Americas were further altered through changes to the existing cultures that were brought on by European contact and migration. Motivations for colonization among the major European powers, as well as the differing relationships of various European powers with Native Americans and slavery, were among the significant changes brought about by political and economic competition among European powers. The evolving relationships among Europeans, Africans, and Native Americans altered the development of North America. These relationships changed the role of North America in the world and affected the lives and perceptions of individuals living on three different continents.

You should consider the following questions as you review the themes for this chapter.

- What were the causes and effects of the Columbian Exchange?
- What are the similarities and differences in the patterns of movement of Native Americans prior to and after European contact?
- How did migration, disease, and warfare affect the Native American population?
- How did the introduction of plants, technology, and animals by Europeans alter the environment of North America and what effect did these introductions have on Native Americans?
- How did the environment lead to the development of distinct regional groups prior to and after European contact?
- What were the intergroup relationships among Europeans, Africans, and Native Americans?

KEY TERMS

African slave trade 23
Algonquian 9
Cahokia 8
Catholic missions (Spanish) 19
Christopher Columbus 13
Conquistadores 14
Corn (maize) cultivation 8
Encomienda 19
Iroquois 8
Matrilineal 23
Meso-Americans 5
Mestizos 22
Pueblo Revolt 19
Racial hierarchy 22
Smallpox 21
Tenochtitlan 6

Go Online **Chapter 1 Content Review**

Assessing Student Understanding Use the online assessment to assess student understanding of concepts and topics within the chapter. You can assign the ready-made Chapter 1 Content Review or create your own from available questions. This easy-to-use tool helps you design assessments that meet the needs of different types of learners.

AP EXAM PRACTICE

MULTIPLE CHOICE

Use the image of the Algonquian village on page 14 and your knowledge of U.S. history to answer questions 1–3.

1. The illustration indicates which quality of Native American societies as encountered by the Europeans?
   (A) complex societies supported by mixed economic activities
   (B) mobile communities that largely existed as hunter-gatherer societies
   (C) significant reliance on the natural environment to build agricultural societies
   (D) maritime societies that thrived on transatlantic trade networks
2. The illustration portrayed Native American societies in a way that would most likely encourage which goal of English expansion?
   (A) to conquer diverse peoples and establish an American empire
   (B) to establish enduring links for trade in goods such as furs
   (C) to establish North American colonies for English settlement
   (D) to establish small outposts for transatlantic trade
3. The introduction of which of the following would have likely most impacted the village in the illustration?
   (A) enslaved African laborers
   (B) horses for agricultural use
   (C) corn and other European crops
   (D) smallpox and other diseases

SHORT ANSWER

Use your knowledge of U.S. history to answer questions 4 and 5.

4. Use the painting, *First Landing of Christopher Columbus*, to answer A, B, and C.
   (A) Briefly describe ONE point of view about Christopher Columbus as depicted in the painting.
   (B) Briefly explain ONE historical cause that led to the event depicted in the painting.
   (C) Briefly explain ONE historical effect that resulted from the event depicted in the painting.
5. Answer A, B, and C.
   (A) Briefly describe ONE major difference between Native American and European culture.
   (B) Briefly describe ONE major similarity between Native American and European culture.
   (C) Briefly explain ONE historical change in either Native American or European culture which happened as a result of interaction with each other.

LONG ESSAY

Develop a thoughtful and thorough historical argument that answers the question. Begin your essay with a thesis statement, and support it with specific historical evidence and examples.

6. Evaluate the extent of cultural changes in the lives of Native Americans from the late fifteenth to the early seventeenth century.

Answers

Multiple Choice

1. A; **2.** C; **3.** D

Short Answer

4A) The point of view in the painting is that of a European. The image generally presents Europeans from an idealized and nonthreatening perspective. The Europeans are presented as larger and more powerful than the Native Americans they encounter.

4B) Possible answer: The event depicted in the painting is that of European colonization/exploration. One cause that led to European colonization/exploration was the desire to spread Christianity. The image contains a religious figure in the back of the group carrying a cross.

4C) Possible answer: The event depicted in the painting is that of European colonization/exploration. One effect that resulted from European colonization/exploration was the spread of diseases, such as smallpox, which led to widespread death among the Native American populations.

5A) Possible answer: Many Europeans practiced a monotheistic religious belief, as many followed Christianity. Many Native American cultures practiced a polytheistic religious belief, as they worshiped many different gods and spirits in nature.

5B) Possible answer: Both Europeans and Native Americans engaged in warfare with each other. Europeans often engaged in warfare over political boundaries, while Native Americans often engaged in warfare over hunting grounds.

5C) Possible answer: The introduction of horses into certain Native American groups, such as the Lakota, led to more mobile lifestyles and certain advantages in hunting.

Answers

Long Essay

6. Possible thesis: With the arrival of Europeans, Native Americans experienced significant changes in many areas of their lives despite some cultural continuities. Continuities: They continued to build large settlements, as with the Mound Builders and the Pueblo, and large cities, like Cahokia. They continued to organize politically, as with the Iroquois League of Nations. They also continued to fight over land with each other, as with the Iroquois and Huron during the Beaver Wars. Changes: The introduction of European diseases decimated some Native American populations. They developed a new-found sense of rebellion and independence by occasionally rebelling against the Europeans, as with the Pueblo Revolt. As more and more Europeans arrived, this led to the displacement of Native Americans. The introduction of horses changed the lifestyles and ways of hunting for many Native American groups. The introduction of new foods, such as apples, bananas, coffee, and rice, led to a more diverse diet. Native Americans developed new trade networks with Europeans, such as the French. In addition, the introduction of the encomienda system by the Spanish enslaved thousands of Native Americans.

Discussion and Activities

Argumentation Direct students' attention to the Questions to Consider posed at the beginning of Unit 1:

- What were the similarities and differences between Native American groups in North America?
- What were the major effects of the Columbian Exchange?
- What were the major reasons Europeans turned to enslaved African laborers in the Americas?

Discuss these questions as a class to review important concepts from the unit. To close the discussion, **ask:** What evidence from Chapter 1 would be useful in answering the questions?
GEO **WXT** **MIG** **ARC**

UNIT 1 AP EXAM PRACTICE

AP EXAM PRACTICE

As you answer the questions, consider how the historical developments, processes, and individuals in Unit 1 connect to those in previous units.

MULTIPLE CHOICE

Use the excerpt below and your knowledge of U.S. history to answer questions 1-3.

". . . on the said 18th day of the month of December, 1681, for the judicial proceedings and inquiry which must be made in this new reduction and pacification and in order to learn of all the motives, reasons, circumstances, designs, and other supports which the treacherous apostate rebels against the royal crown of his Majesty had and may have at present for the conspiracy, alliance, and rebellion which they executed, apostatizing from the holy faith, forsaking royal obedience, burning images and temples, killing atrociously priests, soldiers, women, and children, taking possession of all the things pertaining to divine worship, of haciendas, and of everything in the kingdom that they could, returning to the blind idolatry and superstitions of their ancient days, his lordship caused to appear before him an Indian of the Tegua nation who said his name is Juan, that he is a native of the pueblo of Tesuque, and is married."

–Spanish colonial government record of judicial proceedings regarding Pueblo Indian revolt, 1681

1. The excerpt describes which issue as being deeply troubling for Native Americans regarding the colonizing efforts of the Spanish in the sixteenth and seventeenth centuries?
   (A) intermarriage between Native Americans and Europeans
   (B) suppression of Native American beliefs and culture
   (C) introduction by the Europeans of new agricultural techniques
   (D) the gender roles and beliefs of the Europeans

2. What significantly influenced the Pueblo revolt of 1680?
   (A) Spanish abolition of Pueblo political structures
   (B) Spanish interference in the Pueblo trade with Navajo and Apache
   (C) hardship caused by drought and raids by rival Native American groups
   (D) Pueblo anger at the Spanish refusal to allow for conversions to Christianity

3. In the wake of the Pueblo revolt, how did the Spanish achieve greater colonial stability?
   (A) increased efforts at cultural negotiation and accommodation
   (B) replacement of the indigenous population with an enslaved labor force
   (C) ending attempts to convert the Pueblo Indians to Christianity
   (D) abandoning unsuccessful attempts at colonizing the American Southwest

Use the image on page 21 and your knowledge of U.S. history to answer questions 4-8.

4. What impact did disease have on the interactions between the Spanish and indigenous populations?
   (A) Illness made it easier for the Spaniards to conquer indigenous societies.
   (B) Illness convinced indigenous peoples to abandon their lands.
   (C) Illness led indigenous populations to convert to Christianity.
   (D) Illness led the Spanish to regard indigenous peoples with more respect.

5. Which elements of European life, as introduced by the Columbian Exchange, did Native Americans most rapidly integrate into their lives?
   (A) gender roles
   (B) European rivalries
   (C) religions
   (D) food and animals

6. What impact did the Columbian Exchange have on European nations?
   (A) The influx of new goods led to a series of military conflicts over markets.
   (B) New foods led to healthier diets and population growth.
   (C) Native American religions found a significant number of European converts.
   (D) Disease led to massive European pandemics.

Answers

Multiple Choice

1. B; **2.** C; **3.** A; **4.** A; **5.** D; **6.** B; **7.** A; **8.** D; **9.** B; **10.** C

7. The societies formed in Central America generally differed from those farther north in that the Central American societies were more commonly
   (A) larger societies that supported advanced cultural and political structures.
   (B) geographically isolated and thus had no contact with other civilizations.
   (C) smaller societies that were less technologically and socially developed.
   (D) decentralized and thus less vulnerable to European invasion.

8. Unlike those in Central America and the American Southwest, Native American societies on the Atlantic seaboard were generally supported by
   (A) transatlantic commercial trade.
   (B) tobacco cultivation.
   (C) maize cultivation.
   (D) mixed agricultural and hunter-gatherer systems.

Use the excerpt below and your knowledge of U.S. history to answer questions 9 and 10.

"The Spaniards first set Sail to America, not for the Honour of God, or as Persons moved and merited thereunto by servent Zeal to the True Faith, nor to promote the Salvation of their Neighbours, nor to serve the King, as they falsely boast and pretend to do, but in truth, only stimulated and goaded on by insatiable Avarice and Ambition, that they might for ever Domineer, Command, and Tyrannize over the West- Indians, whose Kingdoms they hoped to divide and distribute among themselves."

—Bartolome de las Casas, *A Brief Account of the Destruction of the Indies*, 1552

9. According to Las Casas, how did the Spanish diverge from their original stated goals?
   (A) The Spanish sought little interaction with the indigenous societies they encountered.
   (B) The Spanish were not truly interested in religious conversion of the Native Americans.
   (C) The Spanish were mainly interested in trade partnerships with Native American societies.
   (D) The Spanish frequently withdrew from locations to avoid military conflicts.

10. As a result of the way in which they treated Native Americans, the Spanish increasingly
   (A) relied on Native American political and social structures.
   (B) sought to integrate Native Americans into leadership positions in Spanish colonies.
   (C) engaged in the Transatlantic slave trade to build an enslaved labor force.
   (D) sought alliances with other European colonies to conquer powerful Native American nations.

SHORT ANSWER

Use the images "The Mexicans Strike Back" and "De Soto in North America" from pages 16-17 and your knowledge of U.S. history to answer question 11.

11. Answer A, B, and C.
   (A) Briefly describe ONE major difference in the images: "The Mexicans Strike Back" and "De Soto in North America."
   (B) Briefly describe ONE major similarity in the images: "The Mexicans Strike Back" and "De Soto in North America."
   (C) Briefly explain ONE effect which resulted from European colonization of the Americas.

LONG ESSAY

Develop a thoughtful and thorough historical argument that answers the question. Begin your essay with a thesis statement, and support it with specific historical evidence and examples.

12. Evaluate the extent of similarities between African and Native American societies.

Answers

Short Answer

11A) Possible answer: Both images show Europeans involved in armed conflict with the Native American population. One major difference between the two images is that "The Mexicans Strike Back" shows them fighting back with weapons, while "De Soto in North America" shows the Native Americans being overpowered by the Spanish and not fighting back.

11B) Possible answer: Both images show Europeans involved in armed conflict with the Native American population. One major similarity is that they both depict the military force with which the Europeans engaged with the Native Americans. Force was often used in these interactions.

11C) Possible answer: The most significant effect of European colonization was the widespread decimation of Native American populations due to their lack of antibodies to fend off European diseases. The reported number of Native Americans killed off by these deadly epidemics vary widely, but it is generally accepted that millions were killed as a result of colonization.

Answers

Long Essay

12. Possible thesis: The way that enslaved Africans and Native Americans arrived in the Americas was very different. Africans were brought by force, while Native Americans followed food sources across geographic land bridges. However, both groups had similar cultural values and maintained political hierarchies within their societies. Therefore, each group had both societal differences and similarities. Differences: Africans were brought by force to America, largely to supply enslaved labor. Native Americans migrated to the Americas thousands of years ago, typically following the food supply over the Bering Land Bridge. Similarities: The societies and economies of both groups reflected the climate and resources available to them, and most engaged in hunting and gathering. Both societies tended to be matrilineal, and both societies had specific gender expectations. They also tended to worship many gods, whom they associated with the natural world, and had elaborate systems of social ranking. Both groups engaged in warfare and enslaved their captives.

Pacing Guide

Unit 2 explores key concepts from Period 2: 1607–1754 of the AP U.S. History Curriculum Framework. It is recommended that 6–8% of the total instruction time for the entire course be spent on Period 2.

Key Concepts

2.1 Europeans developed a variety of colonization and migration patterns, influenced by different imperial goals, cultures, and the varied North American environments where they settled, and they competed with each other and American Indians for resources.

2.2 The British colonies participated in political, social, cultural, and economic exchanges with Great Britain that encouraged both stronger bonds with Britain and resistance to Britain's control.

UNIT 2: 1607–1754

CHAPTER 2: TRANSPLANTATIONS AND BORDERLANDS

CHAPTER 3: SOCIETY AND CULTURE IN PROVINCIAL AMERICA

THEMATIC LEARNING OBJECTIVES

- Assess the reasons for the European colonization of the Americas.
- Describe the key characteristics of the different regions and settlement patterns of the English in the Americas.
- Explain the short-term and long-term effects of European colonization in the Americas.
- Analyze the reasons for and the impact of the emergence of African slavery in the Americas.
- Describe how the English developed a unique society and culture in the Americas.

QUESTIONS TO CONSIDER

- What were the causes and effects of European colonization of the Americas?
- What were the similarities and differences of regions and settlement patterns of the English in the Americas?
- What were the causes and effects of the emergence of African slavery in the Americas?

HISTORICAL DEVELOPMENTS: 1607–1754

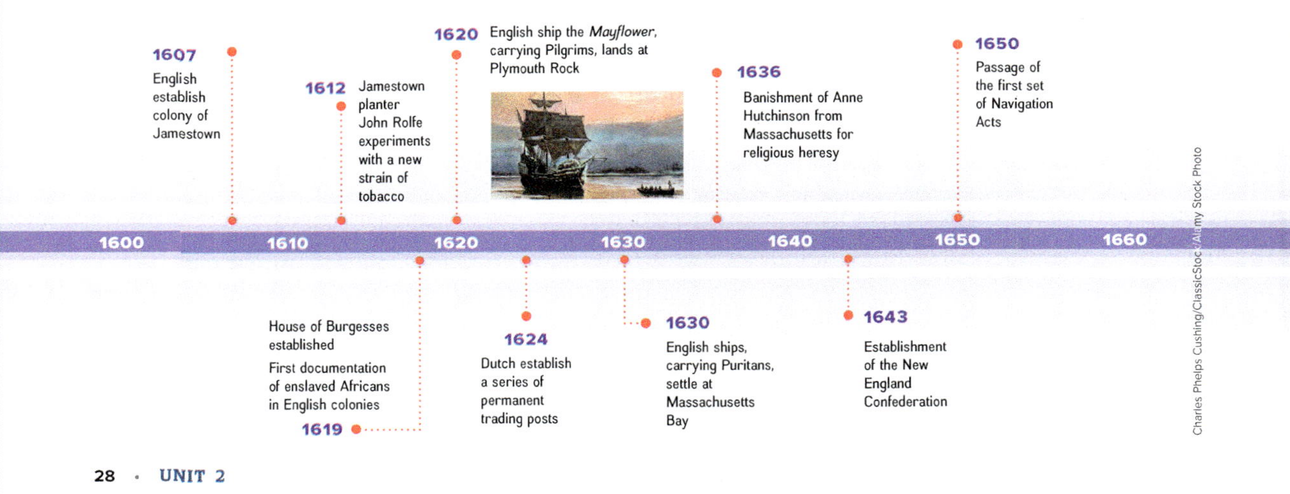
1607
English establish colony of Jamestown
1612
Jamestown planter John Rolfe experiments with a new strain of tobacco
1620
English ship the *Mayflower*, carrying Pilgrims, lands at Plymouth Rock
1636
Banishment of Anne Hutchinson from Massachusetts for religious heresy
1650
Passage of the first set of Navigation Acts
1600
1610
1620
1630
1640
1650
1660
House of Burgesses established
First documentation of enslaved Africans in English colonies
1619
1624
Dutch establish a series of permanent trading posts
1630
English ships, carrying Puritans, settle at Massachusetts Bay
1643
Establishment of the New England Confederation
Charles Phelps Cushing/ClassicStock/Alamy Stock Photo

Reasoning Processes

Continuity and Change Have students study the time line. **Ask:** What changes in European settlement and population do you notice based on the items in the time line? *(The time line shows an increasing number of settlements and a growing population.)* Based on what you already know, along with the events on the time line, why do you think European settlements and populations were growing in North America during this time period? *(Possible responses: relative success of some settlements, increasing European interest in North America for economic reasons, and more Europeans gaining knowledge of potential opportunities in North America.)* **MIG**

MAKING CONNECTIONS

Unit Two focuses on the period from the founding of Jamestown in 1607 to the outbreak of the French and Indian War in 1754. The unit builds on the story of European colonization and its effect on the population of Native Americans. The early colonization efforts of two European powers, the Spanish and the Portuguese, resulted in immense wealth and economic opportunities. As Spain and Portugal rose to become the most powerful countries in the world, the French, the Dutch, and the English began venturing out to stake their claims, searching for new resources and trade opportunities. Two British groups were remarkably successful as they made their way to the Americas: those looking for economic opportunity and those looking for religious freedom. As a result of this colonization effort, Europeans developed a variety of migration patterns with various goals as they settled in the Americas.

For the English, endeavors along the Atlantic coast would ultimately prove to be successful. The early ventures of the English created regional differences that reflected environmental, cultural, and demographic patterns. Three largely distinct regions developed in early British North America: the New England region, the Middle (or Mid-Atlantic) region, and the Chesapeake region. The English differed from earlier Europeans in how they interacted with Native Americans. All three regions were in fierce competition for resources and land, which led to intense relations with Native Americans. Since land was the valuable commodity, forced dislocation was the most common interaction between English settlers and Native Americans. As the population grew along the Atlantic coast, the boundary between the English colonists and Native Americans continued to push west. Of the three main reasons for European colonization—God, gold, and glory—only the last one held any weight with the English. The English were less interested than the Spanish in converting Native Americans. The English also showed little interest in working with Native Americans as economic partners as the French did. As a result, interactions between the English settlers and Native Americans were often guarded and intense. These exchanges. at times, culminated in violent conflict.

During the seventeenth century, an intricate trade network developed involving Europe, Africa, and the Americas, known as the Triangular Trade. The flow of goods across three continents led to the creation of great wealth for Europeans, the development of an exploitative economic labor system, and the growth of capitalism. Using the Spanish model, the English initially turned to Native Americans for their labor force, and the contact between Europeans and Native Americans resulted in millions of deaths.

Eventually, the English turned to enslaved Africans for their labor system. This chattel slavery became the dominant labor system in the Chesapeake region. It would have long-term consequences for the Americas: economic prosperity for those who controlled the economy, and a brutal system of dehumanization for Africans who were brought to the Americas against their will. As this system of slavery became firmly entrenched, it would reflect the specific economic, demographic, and geographic characteristics of each region.

Along with trade, the English colonies participated in many political, social, and cultural exchanges with Great Britain. These exchanges resulted in a complicated and contradictory relationship between Great Britain and its colonies. On the one hand, the English colonies modeled many of their institutions on the social structures of Great Britain. This created stronger bonds between the colonies and Great Britain. But Great Britain, consumed with problems at home, essentially neglected the colonies. The colonies developed a sense of independence that led to greater awareness of how separate and different the colonies really were from Great Britain. These ideas would shape the relationship between Great Britain and the North American colonies at the end of the eighteenth century.

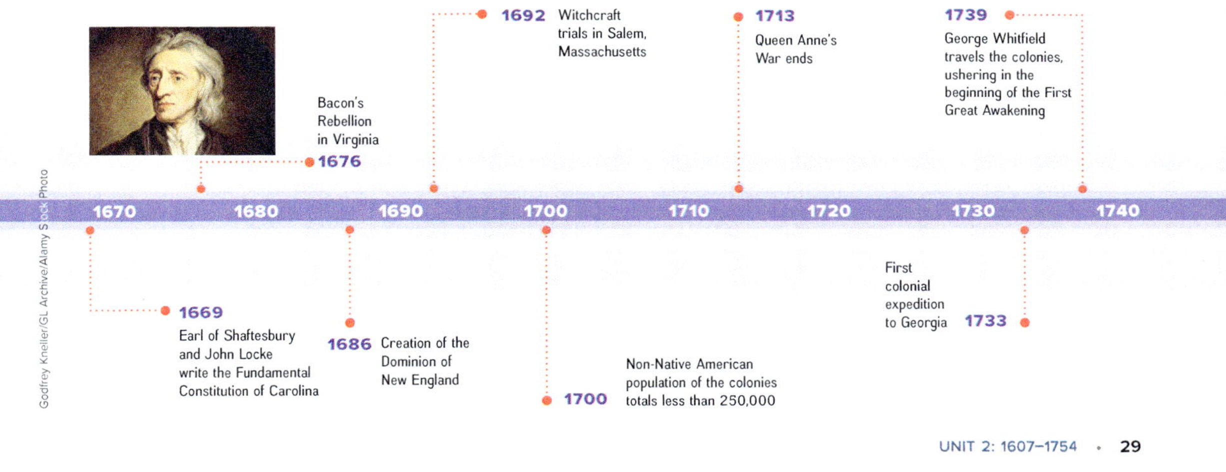
1692 Witchcraft trials in Salem, Massachusetts
1713 Queen Anne's War ends
1739 George Whitfield travels the colonies, ushering in the beginning of the First Great Awakening
Bacon's Rebellion in Virginia 1676
1670
1680
1690
1700
1710
1720
1730
1740
1669 Earl of Shaftesbury and John Locke write the Fundamental Constitution of Carolina
1686 Creation of the Dominion of New England
1700 Non-Native American population of the colonies totals less than 250,000
First colonial expedition to Georgia 1733

Godfrey Kneller/GL Archive/Alamy Stock Photo

Discussion and Activities

Making Connections Have students read the Making Connections section, and then lead a discussion about early British colonization efforts. **Ask:** How did the British become the dominant force in North America even though they were relatively late in establishing colonies? *(Students answers could include the relatively large number of British colonists compared to other European countries and the differing motivations for colonization.)* Have students consider political, social, and economic reasons for British colonization of North America during the discussion. **MIG**

Go Online Additional Resources

Adaptive Learning with SmartBook A proven adaptive learning program, SmartBook offers an interactive environment that helps students learn faster, study more efficiently, and retain more knowledge.

Assign this resource to differentiate instruction for students and report on year-long progression.

Pacing Guide

Chapter 2 explores key concepts from Period 2: 1607–1754 of the AP U.S. History Curriculum Framework. The suggested instruction time for Chapter 2 is 7 days.

Key Concepts

2.1.I Spanish, French, Dutch, and British colonizers had different economic and imperial goals involving land and labor that shaped the social and political development of their colonies as well as their relationships with native populations.

2.1.II In the 17th century, early British colonies developed along the Atlantic coast, with regional differences that reflected various environmental, economic, cultural, and demographic factors.

2.1.III Competition over resources between European rivals and American Indians encouraged industry and trade and led to conflict in the Americas.

2 TRANSPLANTATIONS AND BORDERLANDS

THE FORT AT JAMESTOWN
The Jamestown settlement was beset with difficulties from its first days, and it was many decades before it became a stable and successful town. In the early days, the colonists suffered from the climate, the lack of food, and the spread of disease. They also struggled with growing hostility with neighboring Native Americans. This painting, made almost 150 years after the colony at Jamestown was first settled, conveys a cooperative relationship between the Native Americans and the Europeans who are seen here engaging in trade.

CONNECTING CONCEPTS

Chapter Two begins by focusing on the arrival of the English in North America. Early English colonists to North America came primarily for two reasons: economic and religious opportunities. Economic motivations largely drove colonization efforts in the Chesapeake region while religious incentives dominated the colonization of New England. Colonists were attracted by the ideas of social mobility, economic prosperity, religious freedom, and improved living conditions.

As more European colonists arrived, colonial North America began to form a culture of its own as geography and the colonists' migration patterns helped shape the subsequent evolution of different regions. The Chesapeake region became increasingly populated by the wealthy and by male indentured servants seeking riches in the Americas, while the New England colonies were largely populated by Pilgrims and Puritans seeking religious freedom. The middle colonies attracted a broad range of European migrants and supported a flourishing export economy. These mid-Atlantic colonies boasted societies with great cultural, ethnic, and religious diversity. In most instances, North American colonies experienced both accommodation and conflict with Native Americans.

Chapter Two concludes with the British closing ranks on the North American colonies, as the Crown attempted to exercise greater control by reorganizing and implementing new laws, known collectively as the Navigation Acts, which governed their economic interactions. To enforce these acts the English government established the Dominion of New England. But it came to an end when England experienced a change in dynasty with the Glorious Revolution, which led to further drifting between Britain and her North American colonies.

Discussion and Activities

Analyzing Visuals Direct students' attention to the image "The Fort at Jamestown." **Ask:** Who is the intended audience for this image? *(Europeans)* What do you think the artist's goals were? *(to demonstrate a cooperative relationship between Native Americans and Europeans)* To which theme of this chapter does this image relate, and why? *(settlement and social structures; depicts both the Jamestown settlement and interactions with Native Americans)* Is there a bias in this image? If so, what is it, and against whom is it directed? *(The image is biased; it depicts an idyllic representation of these relationships in a pristine and well-organized settlement.)* **MIG**

As you read, you should:

- Compare and contrast the way that different colonies and regional identities developed throughout North America as a result of differing motives for settlement, geographic and environmental factors, and ethnic and religious differences.
- Identify various labor systems that developed in the different colonial regions as colonists worked to make a livelihood and economies developed.
- Analyze how increasing distrust between the British colonies and the home country intensified over time, leading to periodic attempts by Great Britain to increase imperial control over the colonies.
- Compare and contrast the ways that Spanish colonization in the Southwest differed greatly from British settlement on the Atlantic coast.
- Explain why significant clashes between Native Americans and European colonizers continued throughout the colonial period.
- Identify the reasons why the growth of the American economy led to ever-strengthening ties and increased interdependence throughout the Atlantic World.

THE ARRIVAL OF THE ENGLISH

England's first documented contact with the New World came only five years after Spain's. In 1497, John Cabot (like Columbus, a native of Genoa) sailed to the northeastern coast of North America on an expedition sponsored by King Henry VII. Other English navigators continued Cabot's unsuccessful search for a northwest passage through the New World to the Orient. They explored other areas of North America during the sixteenth century.

JOHN CABOT

But even though England claimed dominion over the lands its explorers surveyed, nearly a century passed before the English made any serious efforts to establish colonies there. Like other European nations, England had to experience an internal transformation before it could begin settling new lands. That transformation occurred in the sixteenth century.

THE COMMERCIAL INCENTIVE

Part of the attraction of the Americas to the English was its newness, its contrast to their own troubled land. America seemed a place where human settlement could start anew, where a perfect society could be created without the flaws and inequities of Europe. Such dreams began to emerge in England only a few years after Columbus's voyages. They found classic expression in Sir Thomas More's *Utopia* (published in Latin in 1516, translated into English thirty-five years later), which described a mythical and nearly perfect society on an imaginary island supposedly discovered by a companion of Amerigo Vespucci in the waters of the New World.

More's picture of an ideal community was, among other things, a comment on the social and economic ills of the England of his own time. The people of Tudor England suffered from frequent and costly European wars,

THE ENCLOSURE MOVEMENT

from almost constant religious strife, and above all from a harsh economic transformation of the countryside. Because the worldwide demand for wool was growing rapidly, many landowners were finding it profitable to convert their land from fields for crops to pastures for sheep. The result was a significant growth in the wool trade. But that meant land worked at one time by agricultural serfs and later by rent-paying tenant farmers was steadily enclosed for sheep runs and taken away from the farmers. Thousands of evicted tenants roamed the countryside in gangs, begging from (and at times robbing) the more fortunate householders through whose communities they passed.

The government passed various laws designed to halt enclosures, relieve the worthy poor, and compel the able-bodied or "sturdy beggars" to work. Such laws had little effect. The enclosure movement continued unabated, and few of the dislocated farmers could find reemployment in raising sheep or manufacturing wool. By removing land from cultivation, the enclosure movement also limited England's ability to feed its rising population, which grew from 3 million in 1485 to 4 million in 1603. Because of both the dislocation of farmers and the restriction of the food supply, therefore, England had a serious problem of surplus population.

Amid this growing distress, a rising class of merchant capitalists was prospering from the expansion of foreign trade. At first, England had exported little except raw wool; but new merchant capitalists helped create a domestic

Reasoning Processes

Identifying Cause and Effect After students read "The Arrival of the English," discuss how the political environment in Europe led to the exploration and colonization of North America. Have students brainstorm, from prior knowledge, other historical developments in U.S. history that were driven by similar political environments

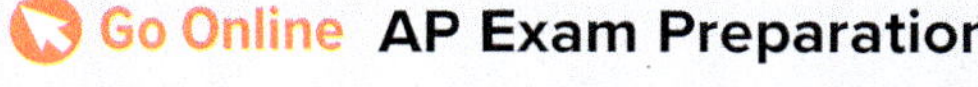

Go Online AP Exam Preparation

AP Exam Practice Use the online assessment to help prepare students for the AP Exam. You can assign the ready-made AP-style short answer questions, document-based questions, and multiple-choice questions assessing concepts, themes, and skills from Period 2 and AP style long-essay questions organized in sets of 3 questions from various time periods. You can also create your own tests from available questions. This easy-to-use tool helps you design assessments that meet the needs of different types of learners.

AP Exam Tip

Students often lose points on the AP U.S. History Exam because they use information that is outside the time period of the prompt of a question. Periodization is the skill of understanding the chronological limits of a time period.

Reasoning Processes

Periodization To practice the skill of periodization, have students review the time line in the Unit 2 Opener. Ask students why 1607 would mark the beginning of the colonization period. At the end of the chapter, you may choose to have students come back to the time line and ask them what event they think would mark the end of the colonization period and why.

AMERICA IN THE WORLD

The Atlantic Context of Early American History

Most Americans understand that in the twenty-first century our nation has become intimately bound up with the rest of the world—that we live in a time that is often called the "age of globalization." But globalization long preceded our own time, and historians have recently come to recognize that the "New World" of seventeenth- and eighteenth-century America was part of a vast network of connections that has become known as the "Atlantic World."

The idea of an "Atlantic World" rests in part on the obvious connections between western Europe and the Spanish, British, French, and Dutch colonies in North and South America. The massive European emigration to the Americas beginning in the sixteenth century, the defeat and devastation of indigenous populations, the creation of European agricultural and urban settlements, and the imposition of imperial regulations on trade, commerce, landowning, and political life—all of these forces reveal the influence of Old World, or European, imperialism on the history of the New World.

Although some Europeans traveled to the New World to escape oppression or to search for adventure, the great majority of European emigrants were in search of economic opportunity. Not surprisingly, therefore, the European settlements in the Americas were almost from the start connected to Europe through the growth of commerce between them. The commercial relationship between America and Europe was responsible not just for the growth of trade, but also for the increases in migration over time—as the demand for labor in the New World drew more and more settlers from the Old World. Commerce was also the principal reason for the rise of slavery in the Americas, and for the growth of the slave trade between European America and Africa. The Atlantic World, in other words, included not just Europe and the Americas, but Africa as well.

Religion was another force binding together the Atlantic World. The vast majority of people of European descent were Christians, and most of them maintained important religious ties to Europe. Catholics, of course, were part of a hierarchical church based in Rome and maintained close ties with the Vatican. But the Protestant faiths that predominated in North America were linked to their European counterparts as well. New religious ideas and movements spread back and forth across the Atlantic with astonishing speed. Great revivals that began in Europe moved quickly to America. The "Great Awakening" of the mid-eighteenth century, for example, began in Britain and traveled to America in large part through the efforts of the English evangelist George Whitefield. American evangelists later carried religious ideas from the New World back to Europe.

The early history of European America was also closely bound up with the intellectual life of Europe. The Enlightenment—the cluster of ideas that emerged in Europe in the seventeenth and eighteenth centuries emphasizing the power of human reason—moved quickly to the Americas, producing considerable intellectual ferment throughout the New World, but particularly in the British colonies in North America and the Caribbean. Many of the ideas that lay behind the American Revolution were products of British and French philosophy that had traveled across the Atlantic. The reinterpretation of those ideas by Americans to help justify their drive to independence—by, among others, Thomas Paine—moved back across the Atlantic to Europe and helped to inspire the French Revolution. Scientific and technological knowledge—another product of the Enlightenment—moved rapidly back and forth across the Atlantic. Americans borrowed industrial technology from Britain. Europe acquired much of its early knowledge of electricity from experiments done in America. But the

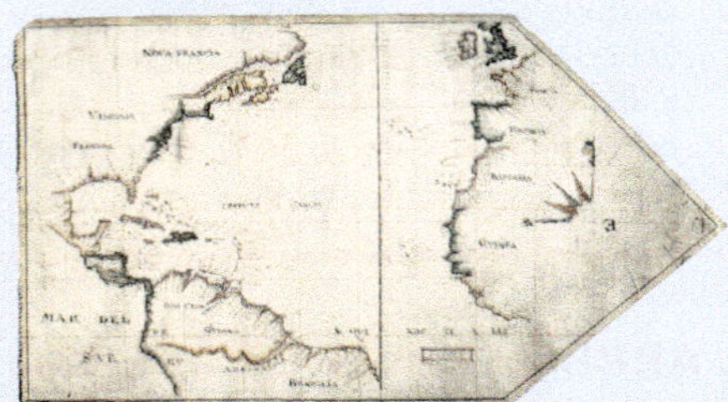

Enlightenment was only one part of the continuing intellectual connections within the Atlantic World, connections that spread artistic, scholarly, and political ideas widely through the lands bordering the ocean.

Instead of thinking of the early history of what became the United States simply as the story of the growth of thirteen small colonies along the Atlantic seaboard of North America, the idea of the "Atlantic World" encourages us to think of early American history as a vast pattern of exchanges and interactions—trade, migration, religious and intellectual exchange, and many other relationships—among all the societies bordering the Atlantic: western Europe, western Africa, the Caribbean, and North and South America.

HISTORICAL THINKING SKILLS

1. **Explaining Historical Concepts** Explain what it means when historians talk about an Atlantic World.
2. **Evaluating Evidence** Analyze the reasons why historians began studying the idea of an Atlantic World?
3. **Evaluating Historical Significance** Does studying American history in an Atlantic World context broaden or distort our understanding of American history?

Answers

America in the World: The Atlantic Context of Early American History

1. The idea of an "Atlantic World" rests in part on the noticeable connections between Europe and the Americas. Those connections and interactions helped shape all facets of subsequent developments in multiple continents, all connected to the Atlantic Ocean.
2. The idea stemmed from the recognition that Europe, the Americas, and Africa were becoming more interdependent on each other, and as more and more interaction occurred, all three continents were dramatically shaped and reshaped by those exchanges.
3. Thinking of the early history of the United States only in terms of the growth of the 13 original colonies is a narrow focus and does not give the entire picture. Instead, historians have broadened this view by framing the history as including a vast pattern of exchanges and interactions among all societies bordering the Atlantic Ocean.

cloth industry that allowed them to begin marketing finished goods at home and abroad. At first, most exporters did business almost entirely as individuals. In time, however, some merchants joined forces and formed chartered companies. Each such enterprise operated on the basis of a charter acquired from the monarch, which gave the company a monopoly for trading in a particular region. Among the first of these were the Muscovy Company (1555), the Levant Company (1581), the Barbary Company (1585), the Guinea Company (1588), and the East India Company (1600). Investors in these companies often made fantastic profits from the exchange of English manufactures, especially woolens, for exotic goods; and they felt a powerful urge to continue the expansion of their profitable trade.

CHARTERED COMPANIES

Central to this drive was the emergence of a new concept of economic life known as mercantilism, which was gaining favor throughout Europe. Mercantilism rested on the assumption that the nation as a whole, not the individuals within it, was the principal actor in the economy. The goal of economic activity should be to increase the nation's total wealth. Mercantilists believed that the world's wealth was finite. One person or nation could grow rich only at the expense of another. A nation's economic health depended, therefore, on extracting as much wealth as possible from foreign lands and exporting as little wealth as possible from home.

The principles of mercantilism guided the economic policies of virtually all the European nation-states in the sixteenth and seventeenth centuries. Mercantilism greatly enhanced the position of the new merchant capitalists, whose overseas ventures were thought to benefit the entire nation and to be worthy of government assistance. It also increased competition among nations. Every European state was trying to find markets for its exports while trying to limit its imports. One result was the increased attractiveness of acquiring colonies, which could become the source of goods that a country might otherwise have to buy from other nations.

MERCANTILISM

In England, the mercantilistic program thrived at first on the basis of the flourishing wool trade with the European continent and, particularly, with the great cloth market in Antwerp. Beginning in the 1550s, however, that glutted market collapsed, and English merchants found themselves obliged to look elsewhere for overseas trade. The establishment of colonies seemed to be a ready answer to that and other problems. Richard Hakluyt, an Oxford clergyman and the outstanding English propagandist for colonization, argued that colonies would not only create new markets for English goods, but they would also help alleviate poverty and unemployment by siphoning off the surplus population. For the poor who remained in England "idly to the annoy of the whole state," there would be new work as a result of the prosperity the colonies would create. Perhaps most important, colonial commerce would allow England to acquire products from its own new territories for which the nation had previously been dependent on foreign rivals– products such as lumber, naval stores, and, above all, silver and gold.

RICHARD HAKLUYT'S ARGUMENT FOR COLONIES

THE RELIGIOUS INCENTIVE

In addition to these economic motives for colonization, there were religious ones, rooted in the events of the European and English Reformations. The Protestant Reformation began in Germany in 1517, when Martin Luther openly challenged some of the basic practices and beliefs of the Roman Catholic Church–until then, the supreme religious authority and also one of the strongest political authorities throughout western Europe. Luther, an Augustinian monk and ordained priest, challenged the Catholic belief that salvation could be achieved through good works or through loyalty (or payments) to the Church itself. He denied the Church's claim that God communicated to the world through the pope and the clergy. The Bible, not the church, was the authentic voice of God, Luther claimed, and salvation was to be found not through "works" or through the formal practice of religion, but through faith alone. Luther's challenge quickly won him a wide following among ordinary men and women in northern Europe. He himself insisted that he was not revolting against the Church, that his purpose was to reform it from within. But when the pope excommunicated him in 1520, Luther defied him and began to lead his followers out of the Catholic Church entirely. A schism within European Christianity had begun that was never to be healed.

As the spirit of the Reformation spread rapidly throughout Europe, other dissidents began offering alternatives to orthodox Catholicism. The French theologian John Calvin was, after Luther, the most influential reformer and went even further than Luther had in rejecting the Catholic belief that human institutions could affect an individual's prospects for salvation. Calvin introduced the doctrine of predestination. God "elected" some people to be saved and condemned others to damnation; each person's destiny was determined before birth, and no one could change that predetermined fate. But while individuals could not alter their destinies, they could strive to know them. Calvinists believed that the way people led their lives might reveal to them their chances of salvation. A wicked or useless existence would be a sign of damnation; saintliness, diligence, and success could be signs of grace. Calvinism created anxieties among its followers, to be sure; but it also produced a strong incentive to lead virtuous, productive lives. The new creed spread rapidly throughout northern Europe and produced (among other groups) the Huguenots in France and the Puritans in England.

DOCTRINE OF PREDESTINATION

The English Reformation was very different from the Protestant Reformation. It occurred more because of a political dispute between the king and the pope than as a result of doctrinal revolts. In 1529, King Henry VIII became angered by the pope's refusal to grant him a divorce from his Spanish wife

Discussion and Activities

Distinguishing Fact From Opinion Have students read the section "Richard Hakluyt's Argument for Colonies." Then ask them to create a T-chart, or two-column graphic organizer, titled "Arguments for Colonies" with the headings "Fact" and "Opinion." Have students write examples of each on their chart. Then have the class discuss which column's examples would have been more compelling for prospective colonists. **MIG**

Discussion and Activities

Understanding Change As a class, discuss mercantilism as an incentive for colonization and the ways in which it influenced and changed colonial economic systems. Again as a class, create a list of pros and cons of mercantilism, and ask students for modern examples of mercantilism. **WXT**

CHAPTER 2

TRANSPLANTATIONS AND BORDERLANDS

AP Exam Practice

Short Answer Provide students with the following short-answer questions and allow 15 minutes for completion. Ask for volunteers to share their responses, and discuss as a class.

Answer A, B, and C.

A) Briefly explain ONE reason for the development of trade between Europe and Africa in the fifteenth century. *(Europeans were in search of spices and luxury items, and trade with Asia was difficult.)*

B) Briefly explain ONE system of trade that developed. *(Europeans delivered cloth and other manufactured goods to northern Africa, and then camels carried the cargoes across the Sahara to cities such as Timbuktu, Gao, and Djenné. There they loaded gold, ivory, and kola nuts for return to the Mediterranean. Africans also traded with Asia to obtain cloth, porcelain, and spices.)*

C) Briefly explain ONE consequence of the development of this trade. *(By the end of the century, Europeans had begun the trade in enslaved Africans.)*

EUROPE AND WEST AFRICA IN THE FIFTEENTH CENTURY Exploration of North and South America was in part an outgrowth of earlier European trade in the Eastern Hemisphere. Europeans delivered cloth and other manufactures to northern Africa; then camels carried the cargoes across the Sahara to cities such as Timbuktu, Gao, and Djenné. There they loaded gold, ivory, and kola nuts for return to the Mediterranean. Africans also traded with Asia to obtain cloth, porcelain, and spices.

What areas of trade were most important to the early interaction between Africa and the Americas?

Answers

Europe and West Africa in the Fifteenth Century

The textile, gold, and silver trades were important to early interactions between Africa and Europe and would impact the colonization of the Americas.

Reasoning Processes

Cause and Effect After students have read the section "The Religious Incentive," ask them to create a flow chart connecting religious issues in England to England's colonization of North America. *(For example: Protestant Reformation > creation of Church of England > division between Anglicans and Puritans > Puritan Separatists seeking refuge outside of England.)* Then ask students to speculate about whether colonization would have happened in the absence of any of those steps. **SOC**

(who had failed to bear him the son he desperately wanted). In response, he broke England's ties with the Catholic Church and established himself as the head of the Christian faith in his country. He made relatively few other changes in English Christianity, however, and after his death the survival of Protestantism remained in doubt for a time. When Henry's Catholic daughter Mary ascended the throne, she quickly restored England's allegiance to Rome and harshly persecuted those who refused to return to the Catholic fold. Many Protestants were executed (the origin of the queen's enduring nickname, "Bloody Mary"); others fled to the European continent, where they came into contact with the most radical ideas of the Reformation. Mary died in 1558, and her half-sister, Elizabeth, became England's sovereign. Elizabeth once again severed the nation's connection with the Catholic Church (and, along with it, an alliance with Spain that Mary had forged).

THE ENGLISH REFORMATION

The Church of England, as the official religion was now known, satisfied the political objectives of the queen, but it failed to satisfy the religious desires of many English Christians. Catholics continued to assert allegiance to the pope. More important, many Protestants believed that the "reformation" did not create enough changes in theology. The most ardent Protestants became known as "Puritans," because they hoped to "purify" the church.

JOHN CALVIN Next to Martin Luther, John Calvin was the most important figure of the European Reformation. His belief in predestination was central to the Puritan faith of early New England.

Some Puritans took genuinely radical positions. They were known as Separatists, and they were determined to worship as they pleased in their own independent congregations. That flew in the face of English law—which outlawed unauthorized religious meetings, required all subjects to attend regular Anglican services, and levied taxes to support the established church. The radicalism of the Separatists was visible in their rejection of prevailing assumptions about the proper religious roles of women. Many Separatist sects, perhaps most prominently the Quakers, permitted women to serve as preachers, which would have been impossible in the established church.

PURITAN SEPARATISTS

Most Puritans resisted separatism. Still, their demands were by no means modest. They wanted to simplify Anglican forms of worship. They wanted to reduce the power of the bishops, who were appointed by the Crown and who were, in many cases, openly corrupt and highly extravagant. Perhaps above all they wanted to reform the local clergy, many of them greedy, uneducated men with little interest in (or knowledge of) theology.

Puritan discontent, already festering, grew rapidly after the death of Elizabeth, the last of the Tudors, and the accession to the throne of James I, a Scotsman and the first of the Stuarts, in 1603. James believed kings ruled by divine right, and he felt no obligation to compromise with his opponents. He quickly antagonized the Puritans, a group that included most of the rising businessmen, by resorting to arbitrary taxation, by favoring English Catholics in granting charters and other favors, and by supporting "high church" forms of ceremony. By the early seventeenth century, some religious nonconformists were beginning to look for places of refuge outside the kingdom. Along with the other economic and social incentives for colonization, such religious discontent helped turn England's gaze to distant lands.

PURITAN DISCONTENT

THE ENGLISH IN IRELAND

England's first experience with colonization came not in the Americas, but in a land separated from Britain only by a narrow stretch of sea: Ireland. The English had long laid claim to the island and had for many years maintained small settlements in the area around Dublin. Only in the second half of the sixteenth century, however, did serious efforts at large-scale colonization begin. During the 1560s and 1570s, would-be colonists moved through Ireland, capturing territory and attempting to subdue the Irish population. In the process they developed many of the assumptions that would guide later English colonists in America.

The most important of these assumptions was that the native population of Ireland—approximately 1 million people, loyal to the Catholic Church, with their own language (Gaelic) and their own culture—was a collection of wild,

Discussion and Activities

Contextualization After students have read the section "The Religious Incentive," ask them to write a letter to King James I advising him on his relationship with English Puritans. Ask students to address what economic, political, social, or religious factors he should take into consideration and what course of action he should ultimately take. **WXT** **MIG**

Historical Thinking Skills

Historical Evidence and Argumentation Have students read the feature "Mercantilism and Colonial Commerce." The feature asserts that "Naval power became an integral part of the mercantilist idea." Ask students to create a recruiting poster for the Royal Navy, keeping in mind what they have already learned about economic, political, and religious conditions in England at the time. **SOC** **MIG** **WXT**

AMERICA IN THE WORLD

MERCANTILISM AND COLONIAL COMMERCE

For more than two centuries, the economic life of Europe and its growing colonial possessions (the North American colonies among them) was shaped by a theory known as mercantilism. The actual application of mercantilism differed from country to country and empire to empire. But virtually all versions of mercantilism shared a belief in the economic importance of colonies to the health of the colonizing nations. As a result, mercantilism helped spur the growth of European empires around the world.

The Trades Increase

AS concerning SHIPS, It is that which everyone knoweth and can say: They are our *Weapons*; They are our *Armaments*; They are our *Strength*; They are our *Pleasures*; They are our *Defence*; They are our *Profit*. The *Subject* by them is made rich, the *Kingdom* through them, strong. The *Prince* in them is mighty, in a word: By them in manner, we live, the Kingdom is, the King Reigneth.

—From an English Pamphlet [*circa* 1681].

MERCANTILISM "The Trades Increase, as Concerning Ships" is a hand-colored wood print depicting the vibrant state of late-seventeenth-century British mercantilism. The extended caption beneath the print acknowledges how British trade stands as a cornerstone of the British economy and a primary source of strength for the monarchy.

In one sense, mercantilism was a highly nationalist, as opposed to a global, theory. It rested on the conviction that the nation (not the individual) was at the center of economic life and that each nation should work to maximize its own share of the finite wealth for which all nations were competing. A gain for France, mercantilism taught, was in effect a loss for Britain or Spain. Thus, it encouraged each nation to work for itself and to attempt to weaken its rivals. But mercantilism was also a global force. What made it so was not the modern notion of the value of international economic growth but, rather, the belief that each nation must search for its own sources of trade and raw materials around the world. Every European state was trying to find markets for its exports, which would bring wealth into the nation, while trying to limit imports, which would transfer wealth to others. (Most of these central mercantilist tenets would eventually be overturned in Adam Smith's 1776 tract, *The Wealth of Nations*, which instead advocated free trade among nations and individual self-interest over national largesse as the route to increasing global—and thus national—wealth.)

In a mercantilist economy, colonies were critical to a nation's economic well-being. They served both as providers of raw materials and as markets for finished goods. Colonies, mercantilism taught, should trade only with their mother nation, and the direction of wealth should flow only in one direction, toward the center of the empire. Naval power became an integral part of the mercantilist idea. Only by controlling the sea lanes between the colonies and the homeland could a nation preserve its favorable balance of trade.

Despite the common assumptions underlying all forms of mercantilism, the system took many different forms, often depending on whether colonial merchants or state bureaucrats drove the economic discussion. In England, Spain, and the Netherlands, mercantilism was closely identified with the emerging middle class, who stood to profit personally from the increased trade. (Hence the term "mercantilism," from merchant.) In France and Germany, on the other hand, state officials rather than private citizens laid more of the groundwork for mercantilism principles. In France, mercantilism was often known as "Colbertism," after its primary proponent, Jean-Baptiste Colbert, foreign minister under Louis XIV. In Germany, the theory was known as "cameralism," for the *Kammer*, or royal treasury.

In its early years, mercantilism was closely associated with "bullionism," which is the theory that only gold and silver defined a nation's wealth. As such, the early Spanish colonies of the New World, in particular, emphasized the procurement of gold, silver, and other precious metals for the mother nation. (English colonies such as Jamestown were founded in part with the same intention, but they were much less successful at finding precious metals.) But even when gold and silver were scarce, colonies could still provide other important resources for the imperial capitals—for example, fur, timber, sugar, tobacco, and enslaved people.

The theory of mercantilism taught that wealth creation was a zero-sum game: there was a fixed amount of wealth in the world, and any wealth a nation acquired was, in effect, taken away from some other nation. As a result, mercantilists believed that nations should heavily regulate the economic affairs of their colonies. One good example of this was England's passage of the Navigation Acts in the 1660s, laws that sharply restricted colonial trade with anyone else but England. But England was not alone in passing such

Discussion and Activities

Analyzing Visuals Have students examine the image and read the caption directly under it. Ask them as a class to brainstorm ways in which the image and words of the caption are consistent or inconsistent. *(For example, the image shows a walled city, but the caption talks about ships, not walls, as being the primary line of defense.)*

restrictions. Spain took equally definitive control over its colonial economies, passing similarly intensive regulation and insisting until 1720 that all colonial trade pass through the port of Seville.

Still, naval vessels could not be everywhere at once. And despite the many laws restricting colonial economies to their home nations, many colonial merchants around the world struck up trade with their nonaffiliated neighbors when possible. The French, Spanish, and Dutch West Indies in particular became the site of a thriving intercolonial trade that was not, for all intent and purposes, legal according to mercantilist doctrine. Indeed, so many traders from so many countries violated mercantile laws in the eighteenth century, and so many of them amassed great profits in the process, the mercantilist system gradually began to unravel. By the time of the American Revolution, in part a result of the colonists' resistance to mercantilist policies, the patterns of global trade were already moving toward the less-regulated trading patterns of the modern capitalist world.

HISTORICAL THINKING SKILLS

1. **Evaluating Historical Significance** Evaluate the effect that mercantilism had on colonial economies.
2. **Drawing Conclusions** Analyze how mercantilism contributed to power rivalries among the European nations.
3. **Evaluating Historical Significance** Mercantilism as a nation's driving economic force has largely given way to economic globalization—that is, the increased interdependence of nations' economies. Why do you think this is so?

Private Collection / © Mallett Gallery, London, UK / The Bridgeman Art Library

ELIZABETH I This is the Kitchener Portrait of Queen Elizabeth I (1533–1603) painted by an unknown artist in the English style. In this portrait, the artist conveys Elizabeth as she was seen by many of her contemporaries: a strong, confident ruler, richly dressed, presiding over an ambitious, increasingly prosperous, and expansionist state.

vicious, and ignorant "savages." The Irish lived in ways the English considered crude and wasteful ("like beasts"), and they fought back against the intruders with a ferocity that the English considered barbaric. Such people could not be tamed, the English concluded. They certainly could not be assimilated into English society. They must, therefore, be suppressed, isolated, and if necessary destroyed. Eventually, they might be "civilized," but only after they were thoroughly subordinated.

SUBJUGATION OF IRELAND

Whatever barbarities the Irish people may have inflicted on the colonizers, the English more than matched them in return. Sir Humphrey Gilbert, who was later to establish the first British colony in the New World (an unsuccessful venture in Newfoundland), served for a time as governor of one Irish district and suppressed rebellions with extraordinary viciousness. Gilbert was an educated and supposedly civilized man. But he considered the Irish people less than human and therefore not entitled to whatever decencies civilized people reserved for their treatment of one another. As a result, he managed to justify, both to himself and to others, such atrocities as beheading Irish soldiers after they were killed in battle. Gilbert himself, Sir Walter Raleigh, Sir Richard Grenville, and others active in Ireland in the mid-sixteenth century derived from their experi-

Discussion and Activities

Comparing and Contrasting After reading the feature "Mercantilism and Colonial Commerce," ask students to create a Venn diagram comparing mercantilism with the economy of the United States today. Then ask them to write a journal entry considering how their daily lives might be different if mercantilism was still practiced. **WXT**

Answers

America in the World

1. Mercantilism was highly nationalistic as opposed to global. It rested on the belief that the nation, not the individual, was at the center of economic life. Colonies were viewed as critical to a nation's well-being; they provided raw materials and served as markets for finished goods.
2. Mercantilism was based on the idea that there was a finite amount of wealth in the world, so each nation should work to maximize its own share of the wealth for which all nations were competing. Only by controlling the sea lanes between the colonies and the homeland could a nation preserve its favorable balance of trade.
3. It was impossible for a country to regulate every part of its trade network. Despite the fact that many laws restricted colonial economies to their home nations, many colonial merchants around the world struck up trade with their non-affiliated neighbors when possible. So, many traders violated mercantile laws, amassing great profits, and so this system gradually began to unravel.

Historical Thinking Skills

Analyzing Points of View After students have read the section "The English in Ireland," ask them to think about the question "How could both the English and Irish consider the other to be barbarians?" Have students pair up, with each student in a pair choosing to represent either the English or the Irish, and then draft a 30-second elevator pitch to their partner to make their case.

THE DOCKS OF BRISTOL, ENGLAND By the eighteenth century, when this scene was painted, Bristol had become one of the principal English ports serving the so-called triangular trade among the American colonies, the West Indies, and Africa. The lucrativeness of that trade is evident in the bustle and obvious prosperity of the town. Even earlier, however, Bristol was an important port of embarkation for the thousands of English settlers migrating to the New World.

Docks and Quay. English School (18th Century). City of Bristol Museum and Art Gallery/The Bridgeman Art Library, London

ences there an outlook they would take to America, where they made similarly vicious efforts to subdue and subjugate the Native Americans.

The Irish experience led the English to another important (and related) assumption about colonization: that English settlements in distant lands must retain a rigid separation from a Native American populations. In Ireland, English colonizers established what they called "plantations," transplantations of English society in a foreign land. Unlike the Spanish in America, the English in Ireland did not try simply to rule a subdued Irish population; they tried to build a separate society, peopled with emigrants from England itself. The new society would exist within a "pale of settlement," an area physically separated from the Irish. That concept, too, they would take with them to the New World, even though in Ireland, as later in America, the separation of peoples and the preservation of "pure" English culture proved impossible.

THE PLANTATION MODEL

The French and the Dutch in America

English settlers in North America, unlike those in Ireland, would encounter not only Native Americans but also other Europeans who were, like them, driven by mercantilist ideas to establish economic outposts abroad. To the south and southwest was the Spanish Empire. Spanish ships continued to threaten English settlements along the coast for years. But except for Mexico and scattered outposts such as those in Florida and New Mexico, the Spanish made little serious effort to colonize North America.

England's more formidable North American rivals in the early sixteenth century were the French. France founded its first permanent settlement in America at Quebec in 1608, less than a year after the English started their first colony at Jamestown. The French colony's population grew very slowly. Few French Catholics felt any inclination to leave

38 · CHAPTER 2

Discussion and Activities

Analyzing Visuals Have students view the image "The Docks of Bristol England." Then ask them to make a web diagram (a diagram with a central bubble showing the main idea, with several smaller bubbles coming out from the center showing details) including all the details they can extract about the social, economic, and religious life of the town. *(Possible responses: Trade is a prominent activity; it is a port city; there are numerous storefronts; there are well-dressed townspeople conversing; there are townspeople doing manual labor; there are churches, etc.)* SOC WXT their homeland, and French Protestants who might have wished to emigrate were excluded from the colony. The French, however, exercised an influence in the New World disproportionate to their numbers, largely because of their relationships with Native Americans. Unlike the English, who for many years hugged the coastline and traded with the Native Americans of the interior through intermediaries, the French forged close, direct ties with Native Americans deep inside the continent. French Jesuit missionaries were among the first to penetrate Native American societies, and they established some of the first contacts between the two peoples. More important still were the *coureurs de bois*–adventurous fur traders and trappers–who also moved far into the wilderness and developed an extensive trade that became one of the underpinnings of the French colonial economy.

COUREURS DE BOIS

The fur trade was, in fact, more a Native American than a French enterprise. The *coureurs de bois* were, in many ways, little more than agents for the Algonquins and the Hurons, who were the principal fur traders among the Native Americans of the region and from whom the French purchased their pelts. The French traders were able to function only to the degree that they could form partnerships with the Native Americans. Successful partnerships often resulted from their ability to become part of Native American society. Fur traders often lived among Native Americans and married Native American women. The fur trade helped open the way for the other elements of the French presence in North America–the agricultural estates (or *seigneuries*) along the St. Lawrence River, the development of trade and military centers at Quebec and Montreal, and the creation of an alliance with the Algonquins and others–that enabled the French to compete with the more numerous British in the contest for control of North America. That alliance also brought the French into conflict with the Iroquois, the Algonquins' ancient enemies, who assumed the central role in the English fur trade. An early result of these tensions was a 1609 attack led by Samuel de Champlain, the founder of Quebec, on a band of Mohawks, apparently at the instigation of his Algonquin trading partners.

The Dutch, too, were establishing a presence in North America. The Netherlands had won its independence from Spain in the early seventeenth century and had become one of the leading trading nations of the world. Its merchant fleet was larger than England's, and its traders were active not only in Europe but also in Africa, Asia, and–increasingly–America. In 1609, an English explorer in the employ of the Dutch, Henry Hudson, sailed up the river that was to be named for him in what is now New York State. Because the river was so wide, he believed for a time that he had found the long-sought water route through the continent to the Pacific. He was wrong, of course, but his explorations led to a Dutch claim on territory in America and to the establishment of a permanent Dutch presence in the New World.

HENRY HUDSON

For more than a decade after Hudson's voyage, the Dutch maintained an active trade in furs in and around present-day New York. In 1624, the Dutch West India Company established a series of permanent trading posts on the Hudson, Delaware, and

NEW AMSTERDAM

THE "RESTITUTION" OF NEW AMSTERDAM This is a detail from an elaborate engraving created to celebrate the "Restitutio" (or return) of New Amsterdam to the Dutch in 1673. England had captured New Amsterdam in 1664 and made claim to the entire province of New Netherland. But in 1672, war broke out between England and the Netherlands, and the Dutch recaptured their lost province. In celebration of that event, this heroic picture of the Dutch fleet in New York was created for sale in the Netherlands. Early in 1674, at the conclusion of the war, the Dutch returned the colony to England.

Reasoning Processes

Comparing and Contrasting After students read the section "The French and the Dutch in America," ask them to construct a Janus figure comparing the attributes of French or Dutch settlers in America to the English. (A Janus figure is an outline drawing of a human figure divided down the middle, with one set of attributes on one side and another set on the other side.) As an incentive, have students get together in pairs, then groups of four, then groups of eight, and so on until you bring the whole class together to select the most informative and creative Janus figure. **MIG** **WXT** **SOC**

Discussion and Activities

Analyzing Visuals Have students view the image "The 'Restitution' of New Amsterdam." Tell them to compare this image of New Amsterdam with the image of the British town on the previous page. **Ask**: In what ways are the images similar? *(Possible responses: Both show port cities; both feature ships; both were created to promote their respective countries' accomplishments.)* **SOC** **WXT**

Historical Thinking Skills

Predicting Have students read the section "The Spanish Armada." Lead the class in a discussion of the scenario, "What would have happened to colonization in North America if the Spanish Armada had been victorious?" *(Possible responses: If England had been occupied, no colonization could have taken place. If England survived but suffered a naval defeat, English colonization likely would have been delayed, giving an opportunity to other European powers like France and the Netherlands to establish stronger colonies first. Potentially, there might not have been a United States as we know it.)*

Connecticut Rivers. The company actively encouraged settlement of the region–not just from Holland itself, but also from such other parts of northern Europe as Germany, Sweden, and Finland. It transported whole families to the Americas and granted vast feudal estates to landlords (known as "patroons") on condition that they bring still more immigrants to America. The result was the colony of New Netherland and its principal town, New Amsterdam, on Manhattan Island. Its population, diverse as it was, remained relatively small; the colony was only loosely united, with chronically weak leadership.

The First English Settlements

The first enduring English settlement in the New World was established at Jamestown, in Virginia, in 1607. But for nearly thirty years before that, English merchants and adventurers had been engaged in a series of failed efforts to create colonies in America. Through much of the sixteenth century, the English had mixed feelings about the New World. They knew of its existence, and they were intrigued by its possibilities. Under the leadership of Elizabeth I, they were developing a powerful sense of nationalism that encouraged dreams of expansion. At the same time, however, England was leery of Spain, which remained the dominant force in America and, it seemed, the dominant naval power in Europe.

THE SPANISH ARMADA

But much changed in the 1570s and 1580s. English "sea dogs" such as Sir Francis Drake staged successful raids on Spanish merchant ships and built confidence in England's ability to challenge Spanish sea power. More important was the attempted invasion of England in 1588. Philip II, the powerful Spanish king, had recently united his nation with Portugal. He was now determined to end England's challenges to Spanish commercial supremacy and to bring the English back into the Catholic Church. He assembled one of the largest military fleets in the history of warfare–known to history as the "Spanish Armada"–to carry his troops across the English Channel and into England itself. Philip's bold venture turned into a fiasco when the smaller English fleet dispersed the Armada and, in a single stroke, ended Spain's domination of the Atlantic. The English now felt much freer to establish themselves in the New World.

The pioneers of English colonization were Sir Humphrey Gilbert and his half-brother Sir Walter Raleigh–both friends of Queen Elizabeth and both veterans of the earlier colonial efforts in Ireland. In 1578, Gilbert obtained from Elizabeth a patent granting him the exclusive right for six years "to inhabit and possess at his choice all remote and heathen lands not in the actual possession of any Christian prince."

GILBERT'S EXPEDITION TO NEWFOUNDLAND

After numerous setbacks, Gilbert led an expedition to Newfoundland in 1583 and took possession of it in the queen's name. He proceeded southward along the coast, looking for a good place to build a military outpost that might eventually grow into a profitable colony. But a storm sank his ship, and he was lost at sea.

Roanoke

Raleigh was undeterred by Gilbert's misfortune. The next year, he secured from Elizabeth a six-year grant similar to Gilbert's and sent a small group of men on an expedition to explore the North American coast. They returned with two captive Native Americans and glowing reports of what they had seen. They were particularly enthusiastic about an island Native Americans called Roanoke and about the area of the mainland just beyond it (in what is now North Carolina). Raleigh asked the queen for permission to name the entire region "Virginia" in honor of Elizabeth, "the Virgin Queen." But while Elizabeth granted the permission, she did not offer the financial assistance Raleigh had hoped his flattery would produce. So he turned to private investors to finance another expedition.

THE FIRST ROANOKE COLONY

In 1585 Raleigh recruited his cousin, Sir Richard Grenville, to lead a group of men (most of them from the English plantations in Ireland) to Roanoke to establish a colony. Grenville deposited the settlers on the island, remained long enough to antagonize the Native Americans by razing a village as retaliation for a minor theft, and returned to England. The following spring, Sir Francis Drake unexpectedly arrived in Roanoke. With supplies and reinforcements from England long overdue, the beleaguered colonists boarded Drake's ships and left.

Raleigh tried again in 1587, sending an expedition carrying ninety-one men, seventeen women (two of them pregnant), and nine children–the nucleus, he hoped, of a viable "plantation." The settlers landed on Roanoke and attempted to take up where the first group of colonists had left off. (Shortly after arriving, one of the women–the daughter of the commander of the expedition, John White–gave birth to a daughter, Virginia Dare, the first American-born child of English parents.) White returned to England after several weeks (leaving his daughter and granddaughter behind) in search of supplies and additional settlers; he hoped to return in a few months. But the hostilities with Spain intervened, and White did not return to the island for three years. When he did, in 1590, he found the island deserted, with no clue to the settlers' fate other than the cryptic inscription "Croatoan" carved on a post. Some historians have argued that the colonists were slaughtered by Native Americans in retaliation for Grenville's hostilities. Others have contended that they left their settlement and joined Native American society, ultimately becoming entirely assimilated. But no conclusive solution to the mystery of the "Lost Colony" has ever been found.

The Roanoke mystery marked the end of Sir Walter Raleigh's involvement in English colonization of the New World. In 1603, when James I succeeded Elizabeth to the throne, Raleigh was accused of plotting against the king, stripped of his monopoly, and imprisoned for more than a decade. Finally (after being released for one last ill-fated maritime expedition), he was executed by the king in 1618. No

Discussion and Activities

Contextualization Have students read the section "The First Roanoke Colony." Then ask them to write a paragraph explaining why Roanoke was important, even though it only lasted a brief time.

ROANOKE A drawing by one of the English colonists in the ill-fated Roanoke expedition of 1585 became the basis for this engraving by Theodor de Bry, published in England in 1590. A small European ship carrying settlers approaches the island of Roanoke, at left. The wreckage of several larger vessels farther out to sea and the presence of Native American settlements on the mainland and on Roanoke itself suggest some of the perils the settlers encountered.

later colonizer would receive grants of land in the New World as vast or undefined as those Raleigh and Gilbert had acquired. But despite the discouraging example of these early experiences, the colonizing impulse remained alive.

In the first years of the seventeenth century, a group of London merchants to whom Raleigh had assigned his charter rights decided to renew the attempt at colonization in Virginia. A rival group of merchants, from Plymouth and other West Country towns, were also interested in American ventures and were sponsoring voyages of exploration farther north, up to Newfoundland, where West Country fishermen had been going for many years. In 1606 James I issued a new charter, which divided America between the two groups. The London group got the exclusive right to colonize in the south, and the Plymouth merchants received the same right in the north. Through their efforts, the first enduring English colonies were planted in America.

NEW COLONIAL CHARTERS

THE EARLY CHESAPEAKE

Once James I had issued his 1606 charters, the London Company moved quickly and decisively to launch a colonizing expedition headed for Virginia. A party of 144 men aboard three ships, the *Godspeed*, the *Discovery*, and the *Susan Constant*, set sail for America in 1607.

COLONISTS AND NATIVE AMERICANS

Only 104 men survived the journey. They reached the American coast in the spring of 1607, sailed into the Chesapeake and up a river they named the James, establishing their colony, Jamestown, on a peninsula. They chose this setting because they believed it would provide security from the Native Americans. But they chose poorly: the site was low and swampy and surrounded by thick woods. The results could hardly have been more disastrous. The colonists were vulnerable to local

Historical Thinking Skills

Historical Evidence and Argumentation Have students study the image "Roanoke." Then ask them to think about whether the image was intended to promote or discourage immigration to America. Have students pair up and share their conclusions and reasoning. **MIG**

Historical Thinking Skills

Making Connections Have students review the image "Roanoke." As a class or in small groups, ask them to brainstorm reasons that settlers might keep coming to America despite the hazards portrayed in the image. **Ask:** How do those hazards compare to the challenges of relocating to a new city or country today? **MIG**

Reasoning Processes

Causation Have students read the section "The Starving Time." Then have them work in small groups to create a list of reasons why settlers would continue to come to Jamestown when so many of them were dying. Ask the groups to rank the reasons on their lists in order of importance, and prepare to share with the class. **MIG**

diseases, particularly malaria, which was especially virulent along the marshes.

EARLY PROBLEMS

Other problems were to a large degree of the colonists' own making. They focused less on growing food and building community than on a futile search for gold. Community building was impossible because they had brought no women, and had no real households or real stakes in their settlement.

That the colonies survived at all was a result of the neighboring Native Americans teaching the colonists how to live in their new land. The Native Americans showed the colonists their agricultural technologies, which were better adapted to the soil and climate of Virginia than the agricultural traditions the English settlers had brought with them. The Native Americans were settled farmers whose villages were surrounded by neatly ordered fields on which they grew a variety of crops including beans, pumpkins, and above all maize (corn), which was easy to cultivate and generated large yields. The English also learned the advantages of growing beans alongside corn to enrich the soil. And they also began to combine foods they grew with food they hunted and fished. From the Native Americans, the English learned how to build canoes, which were good for navigating the local streams. Without what they learned from the Native Americans, the early settlers would not have survived. Despite this help, the settlers often expressed hostilities toward the Native Americans believing that English civilization was superior to that of these "savages."

Jamestown remained a tiny colony for more than a decade. The Native Americans were far more powerful than the English for years. Coastal Virginia had numerous tribes: the Algonquins, Sioux, and Iroquois, which were all part of the Powhatan Confederacy, named after the great chief who controlled a large area near the coasts. What the English called Virginia, the Native Americans called Tsenacommacah.

Within a few months of settling in Virginia, only 38 men of the original 144 were alive, the rest killed by disease and famine. These men owed their survival to the help provided by the Native Americans and to the leadership of Captain John Smith, who at age 27 was already a famous world traveler. Smith imposed work and order on the settlement and created a shaky relationship with the Native Americans (sometimes negotiating for food and at other times stealing it).

REORGANIZATION AND EXPANSION

As Jamestown struggled to survive, the London Company (now renamed the Virginia Company) was already dreaming of bigger things. In 1609, it obtained a new charter from the king, which increased its power and enlarged its territory. It offered stock in the company to planters who were willing to migrate at their own expense. And it provided free passage to Virginia for poorer people who would agree to serve the company for seven years. In the spring of 1609, two years after the first arrival of the English, a fleet of nine vessels was dispatched to Jamestown with approximately 600 people, including some women and children.

THE STARVING TIME

Nevertheless, disaster followed. One of the Virginia-bound ships was lost at sea in a hurricane. Another ran aground in the Bermuda Islands and was unable to sail again for months. Many of the new settlers succumbed to fevers before winter came. The winter of 1609–1610 was especially severe, a period known as the "starving time." By then the Native Americans realized that the colonists were a threat to their civilization and stopped them from moving farther inland. Barricaded within a small palisade and unable to hunt or cultivate food, the colonists lived on what they could find: "dogs, cats, rats, snakes, toadstools, horsehides," and even "the corpses of dead men," as one survivor recalled. When the migrants who had run aground in

THE ENGLISH COME TO THE AMERICAS
Jamestown was the first English settlement in the Americas. Supported by the London Company, it was established in 1607.

Discussion and Activities

Speculating After students read the section "Early Problems," ask the class to identify ways in which Native Americans helped the Jamestown settlers to survive. Then **ask:** why Native Americans initially seemed willing to assist the English settlers. *(Possible responses: The English were few in number, and weren't seen as a threat. Native Americans hoped to trade with the English for weapons with which to fight their neighbors.)* Discuss student responses as a class. **MIG** **PCE**

Bermuda finally arrived in Jamestown the following May, they found only 60 emaciated people still alive. The new arrivals took the survivors onto their ship and sailed for England. But as the refugees proceeded down the James, they met an English ship coming up the river–part of a fleet bringing supplies and the colonies' first governor, Lord De La Warr. The departing settlers agreed to return to Jamestown. New relief expeditions soon began to arrive and the fort began to thrive.

New settlements began lining the river above and below Jamestown. There settlers discovered tobacco, which was for them a new crop that was already popular among the Spanish colonies to the south. In 1612, the Jamestown planter John Rolfe began cultivating the crop in Virginia. Soon other planters in the area followed. Tobacco was the first profitable crop in the new colony for the settlers, and it encouraged tobacco planters to move farther inland deeper into Native American farmlands.

De La Warr's Harsh Discipline

De La Warr and his successors (Sir Thomas Dale and Sir Thomas Gates) imposed a harsh and rigid discipline on the colony: they organized settlers into work gangs, and they sentenced offenders to be flogged, hanged, or broken on the wheel. But this communal system of labor did not function effectively for long. Settlers often evaded work. Governor Dale soon concluded that the colony would fare better if the colonists had personal incentives to work. He began to permit the private ownership and cultivation of land. Landowners would repay the company with part-time work and contributions of grain to its storehouses.

Under the leadership of these first, harsh governors, Virginia was not always a happy place. But it survived and even expanded. New settlements began lining the river above and below Jamestown. The expansion was partly a result of the order and discipline the governors at times managed to impose. It was partly a product of increased military assaults on the local Native American groups, which provided protection for the new settlements. But it also occurred because the colonists had at last discovered a marketable crop: tobacco.

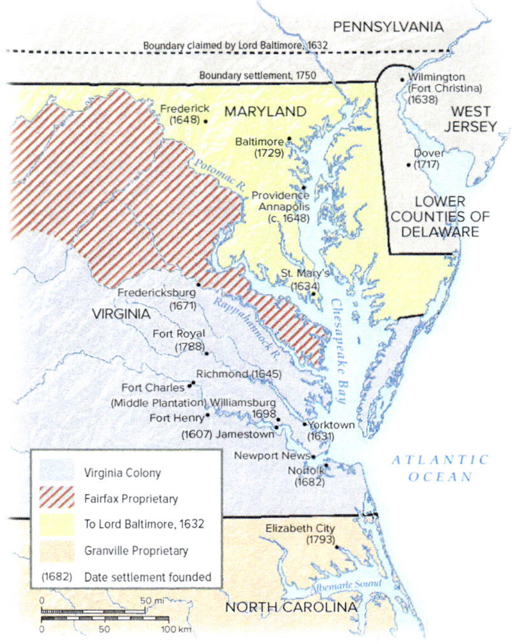

THE GROWTH OF THE CHESAPEAKE, 1607–1750 This map shows the political forms of European settlement in the region of the Chesapeake Bay in the seventeenth and early eighteenth centuries. Note the several different kinds of colonial enterprises: the royal colony of Virginia, controlled directly by the English Crown after the failure of the early commercial enterprises there; and the proprietary regions of Maryland, northern Virginia, and North Carolina, which were under the control of powerful English aristocrats.

Did these political differences have any significant effect on the economic activities of the various Chesapeake colonies?

TOBACCO

Europeans had become aware of tobacco soon after Columbus's first return from the West Indies, where he had seen the indigenous Cubans smoking small cigars *(tabacos)*, which they inserted in the nostril. By the early seventeenth century, tobacco from the Spanish colonies was already in wide use in Europe. Some critics denounced it as a poisonous weed, the cause of many diseases. King James I himself led the attack with "A Counterblaste to Tobacco" (1604), in which he urged his people not to imitate "the barbarous and beastly manners of the wild, godless, and slavish Indians, especially in so vile and stinking a custom." Other critics were concerned because England's tobacco purchases from the Spanish colonies meant a drain of English gold to the Spanish importers. Still, the demand for tobacco soared.

Emergence of the Tobacco Economy

Then in 1612, the Jamestown planter John Rolfe began to experiment in Virginia with a harsh strain of tobacco that local Native Americans had been growing for years. He produced crops of high quality and found ready buyers in England. Tobacco cultivation quickly spread up and down the James. The character of this tobacco economy–its profitability, its uncertainty, its land and labor demands–transformed Chesapeake society in fundamental ways.

Of most immediate importance was that tobacco cultivation required territorial expansion. Tobacco growers needed large areas of farmland to grow their crops; and because tobacco exhausted the soil after only a few years, the demand for land increased even more. English farmers began establishing plantations deeper and deeper in the interior, moving from the center of European settlement at Jamestown into the territory the Native Americans considered their own.

EXPANSION

Even the discovery of tobacco cultivation was not enough to help the Virginia Company. By 1616, there were still no prof-

Reasoning Processes

Analyzing Change Have students read the section "De La Warr's Harsh Discipline." Ask them to think about how De La Warr's decision to allow private ownership of land was a departure from mercantilist policies. Then have students write a thesis statement that identifies a significant change. Ask students to share and discuss their theses with a partner.

Answers

The Growth of the Chesapeake, 1607–1750

All the Chesapeake colonies quickly adopted a tobacco-based economy, regardless of political differences.

Reasoning Processes

Periodization Have students read the section "The Headright System." The text describes two important events that occurred in Virginia in 1619. **Ask:** Which event would you expect to have a greater impact on the development of America, the introduction of an elected assembly or the introduction of African slavery? Have students write a thesis statement taking a position. Then ask them to share their theses and receive feedback from the class. **WXT** **SOC** **PCE**

its, only land and debts. Nevertheless, the promoters continued to hope that the tobacco trade would allow them finally to turn the corner. In 1618, they launched a last great campaign to attract settlers and make the colony profitable.

Part of that campaign was an effort to recruit new settlers and workers to the colony. The company called it the "headright" system. Headrights were fifty-acre grants of land, which new settlers could acquire in a variety of ways. Those who already lived in the colony received 100 acres apiece. Each new settler received a single headright for himself or herself. This system encouraged family groups to migrate together, since the more family members traveled to America, the larger the landholding the family would receive. In addition, anyone (new settler or old) who paid for the passage of other immigrants to Virginia would receive an additional headright for each new arrival–thus, the company hoped, inducing the prosperous to import new laborers to America. Some colonists were able to assemble sizable plantations with the combined headrights they received for their families and their servants. In return, they contributed a small quitrent (one shilling a year for each headright) to the company.

THE HEADRIGHT SYSTEM

The company added other incentives as well. To diversify the colonial economy, it transported ironworkers and other skilled craftsmen to Virginia. In 1619, it sent 100 Englishwomen to the colony (which was still overwhelmingly male) to become the wives of male colonists. (The women were purchased for 120 pounds of tobacco. Their status was somewhere between indentured servants and free people, depending on the goodwill–or lack of it–of their husbands.) The company promised the colonists the full rights of Englishmen (as provided in the original charter of 1606), an end to the strict and arbitrary rule of the communal years, and even a share in self-government. On July 30, 1619, in the Jamestown church, delegates from the various communities met as the House of Burgesses. It was the first meeting of an elected legislature within what was to become the United States.

TOBACCO PLANT This 1622 woodcut, later hand-colored, represents the tobacco plant cultivated by English settlers in Virginia in the early seventeenth century after John Rolfe introduced it to the colonists. On the right is an image of a man smoking the plant through a very large pipe.

A month later, another event in Virginia established a very different but no less momentous precedent. As John Rolfe recorded, in August a Dutch ship brought the first enslaved Africans to the English colonies. Some colonists may have thought of them as indentured servants to be held for a term of years and then freed, like the white indentured servants with whom the planters were already familiar. For a time, moreover, the use of black labor remained limited. Although enslaved Africans trickled steadily into the colony, planters continued to prefer European indentured servants until at least the 1670s, when white servants began to become scarce and expensive. But 1619 marked a first step toward the enslavement of Africans within what was to be the American republic.

The expansion of the colony was able to proceed only because of effective suppression of local Native Americans who resisted the expanding English presence. For two years, Sir Thomas Dale led unrelenting assaults against the Powhatan Indians and in the process kidnapped the great chief Powhatan's daughter Pocahontas. When Powhatan refused to ransom her, she converted to Christianity and in 1614 married John Rolfe. (Pocahontas accompanied her husband back to England, where, as a Christian convert and a gracious woman, she stirred interest in projects to "civilize" the Native Americans. She died while abroad.) At that point, Powhatan ceased his attacks on the English in the face of overwhelming odds. But after his death several years later, his brother, Opechancanough, became head of the native confederacy. Recognizing that the position of this confederacy was rapidly deteriorating, he resumed the effort to defend tribal lands from European encroachments. On a March morning in 1622, Native Americans called on the white settlements as if to offer goods for sale, then suddenly attacked. Not until 347 colonists of both sexes and all ages lay dead or dying were the Native American warriors finally forced to retreat. The surviving English struck back mercilessly at the Native Americans and turned back the threat for a time. Only after Opechancanough failed in another uprising in 1644 did the Powhatans finally cease to challenge the eastern regions of the colony.

SUPPRESSION OF THE POWHATAN INDIANS

By then the Virginia Company in London was defunct. The company had poured all its funds into its profitless Jamestown venture and, in the aftermath of the 1622 Native American uprising, faced imminent bankruptcy. In 1624, James I revoked the company's charter, and the colony came under the control of the Crown. It would remain so until 1776.

DEMISE OF THE VIRGINIA COMPANY

Discussion and Activities

Analyzing Change Have students read the section "Suppression of the Powhatan Indians." Then ask them to refer back to the section "Early Problems" and create a time line showing interactions between English settlers in Virginia and the Powhatan Indians. Ask students to circle those events that represent a change in the relationship between the two groups. Then have them write a paragraph explaining possible reasons for those changes. *(Possible responses: the growing English population, growing demand by the English for more land, violent clashes between the groups, etc.)* **PCE** **MIG** **SOC**

Exchanges of Agricultural Technology

The hostility of the early English settlers toward their Native American neighbors was in part a result of their conviction that their own civilization was greatly superior to that of the Native Americans–and above all that they were more technologically advanced. The English, after all, had great oceangoing vessels, muskets and other advanced implements of weaponry, and many other tools that the Native Americans had not developed. Indeed, when John Smith and other early Jamestown residents grew frustrated at their inability to find gold and other precious commodities, they often blamed their failure on the backwardness of the Native Americans.

AGRICULTURAL TECHNIQUES

Yet the survival of Jamestown was, in the end, largely a result of agricultural technologies developed by Native Americans and borrowed from them by the English. Native American agricultural practices were far better adapted to the soil and climate of Virginia than were the agricultural traditions the English settlers brought with them. The American Indians of Virginia had built successful farms with neatly ordered fields in which grew a variety of crops, some previously unknown to the English. Some Native American farmlands stretched over hundreds of acres and supported substantial populations.

The English settlers did not adopt all the Native American agricultural techniques. Native Americans cleared fields not, as the English did, by cutting down and uprooting all the trees. Instead, they killed trees in place by "girdling" them (that is, making deep incisions around the base) in the areas in which they planted or by setting fire to their roots; and they planted crops not in long, straight rows, but in curving patterns around the dead tree trunks. But in other respects, the English learned a great deal from the Native Americans about how to grow food in North America. In particular, they quickly recognized the great value of corn, which proved to be easier to cultivate and to produce much greater yields than any of the European grains the English had known at home. Corn was also attractive to the settlers because its stalks could be a source of sugar and because it spoiled less easily than other grains. The English also learned the advantages of growing beans alongside corn to enrich the soil.

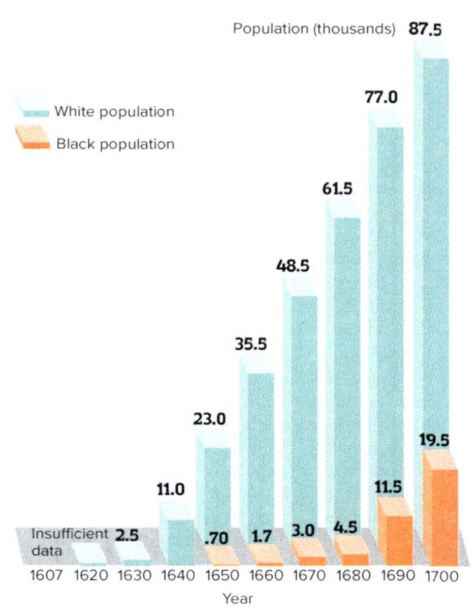

THE NON-INDIAN POPULATION OF THE CHESAPEAKE, 1607–1700 This graph shows the rapid growth of the population of the Chesapeake during its first century of European settlement. Note the dramatic increases in the first half of the century and the somewhat slower increase in the later decades. If the enslaved population were not counted in the last two decades of the century, the non-Indian population would not have grown at all.

What impact did the growth of African slavery have on the rate of immigration by Europeans?

Maryland and the Calverts

Maryland was founded under circumstances very different from those of Virginia, but it nonetheless developed in ways markedly similar to those of its neighbor to the south. The new colony was the dream of George Calvert, the first Lord Baltimore, a recent convert to Catholicism and a shrewd businessman. Calvert envisioned establishing a colony both as a great speculative venture in real estate and as a retreat for English Catholics, many of whom felt oppressed by the Anglican establishment at home. He died before he could receive a charter from the king. But in 1632, his son Cecilius, the second Lord Baltimore, received a charter remarkable not only for the extent of the territory it granted him–an area that encompassed parts of what are now Pennsylvania, Delaware, and Virginia, in addition to present-day Maryland–but also for the powers it bestowed on him. He and his heirs were to hold their province as "true and absolute lords and proprietaries," and were to acknowledge the sovereignty of the king only by paying an annual fee to the Crown.

PROPRIETARY RULE

Lord Baltimore named one of his brothers, Leonard Calvert, governor and sent him with another brother to oversee the settlement of the province. In March 1634, two ships–the *Ark* and the *Dove*–bearing 200 to 300 passengers entered the Potomac River and turned into one of its eastern tributaries. On a high and dry bluff, these first arrivals laid out the village of St. Mary's (named, diplomatically, for the queen). The neighboring Native Americans, who were more worried about rival groups in the region than they were about the new arrivals, befriended the settlers, provided them with temporary shelter, sold them land, and supplied them with corn. Unlike the Virginians, the early Marylanders experienced no assaults by Native Americans, no plagues, no starving time.

The Calverts had invested heavily in their American possessions, and they needed to attract many settlers to make the

Reasoning Processes

Comparing and Contrasting Have students read the section "Proprietary Rule." Then have them think about how the establishment of the Maryland Colony was similar to or different from earlier English colonies in the Americas. Have students create a chart with examples from the text showing similarities and differences. **MIG** **SOC** **PCE**

Answers

The Non-Indian Population of the Chesapeake, 1607–1700

It appears that the growth rate of the white population slowed down as the population of enslaved people increased. This may have been due to a decreased demand for labor from white indentured servants.

Discussion and Activities

Analyzing Visuals Have students study the image "The Maryland Proprietor, c. 1670." Then ask them to think about what the painting suggests about childhood and family life among the British aristocracy. Have students share their ideas with a partner. Then ask for volunteers to share their insights with the entire class. **SOC**

effort profitable. As a result, they had to encourage the immigration of Protestants as well as their fellow English Catholics, who were both relatively few in number (about 2 percent of the population of England) and generally reluctant to emigrate. The Protestant settlers (mostly Anglicans) outnumbered the Catholics from the start, and the Calverts quickly realized that Catholics would always be a minority in the colony. They prudently adopted a policy of religious toleration. To appease the non-Catholic majority, Calvert appointed a Protestant as governor in 1648. A year later, he sent from England the draft of an "Act Concerning Religion," or the Toleration Act, which assured freedom of worship to all Christians.

RELIGIOUS TOLERATION

Nevertheless, politics in Maryland remained plagued for years by tensions between the Catholic minority (which included the proprietor) and the Protestant majority. Zealous Jesuits and crusading Puritans frightened and antagonized their opponents with their efforts to establish the dominance of their own religion. At one point, the Protestant majority barred Catholics from voting and repealed the Toleration Act. There was frequent violence, and in 1655 a civil war temporarily unseated the proprietary government and replaced it with one dominated by Protestants.

By 1640, a severe labor shortage in the colony had forced a change in the land grant procedure; and Maryland, like Virginia, adopted a "headright" system—a grant of 100 acres to each male settler, another 100 for his wife and each servant, and 50 for each of his children. Like Virginia, Maryland became a center of tobacco cultivation; and as in Virginia, planters worked their land with the aid, first, of indentured servants imported from England and then, beginning late in the seventeenth century, with enslaved Africans.

THE MARYLAND PROPRIETOR, C. 1670 In a detail of a portrait by the court painter to King Charles II, the young Cecilius Calvert reaches for a map of Maryland. His grandfather and namesake, the second Lord Baltimore (1606–1675), holds it out to him. George Calvert, the father of the elder Cecilius, began negotiations to win a royal charter for Maryland; his son completed them in 1632 and became the first proprietor of the colony. He published the map shown here in 1635 as part of an effort to attract settlers to the colony. By the time this portrait was painted, Lord Baltimore's son, Charles, was governor of Maryland. The boy Cecilius, the heir apparent, died in 1681 before he could assume his title.

TURBULENT VIRGINIA

By the mid-seventeenth century, the Virginia colony had survived its early disasters. Both its population and the complexity and profitability of its economy were increasing. It was also growing more politically contentious, as emerging factions within the province began to compete for the favor of the government. Perhaps the most important dispute involved policy toward the Native Americans. As settlement moved west, farther into Native American lands, border conflicts grew increasingly frequent. Much of the tension within English Virginia in the late seventeenth century revolved around how to respond to those conflicts.

VIRGINIA'S WESTWARD EXPANSION

Sir William Berkeley arrived in Virginia in 1642 at the age of thirty-six, having been appointed governor by King Charles I. With but one interruption, he remained in control of the government until the 1670s. Berkeley was a popular governor at first as he sent explorers across the Blue Ridge Mountains to open up the western interior of Virginia. He organized the force that put down the 1644 Indian uprising. The defeated Powhatan Confederacy ceded a large area of land to the English. In return, Berkeley agreed to prohibit white settlement west of a line he negotiated with the tribes.

This attempt to protect Native American territory—like many such attempts later in American history—was a failure from the start, largely because of the rapid growth of the Virginia population. Oliver Cromwell's victory in 1649 in the English Civil War and the flight of many of his defeated opponents to the colony contributed to what was already a substantial population increase. Between 1640 and 1650, Virginia's population doubled from 8,000 to 16,000. By 1660, it had more than doubled again, to 40,000. As the choice lands along the tidewater became scarce, new arrivals and indentured servants completing their terms or escaping from their contract holders pressed westward into the piedmont. By 1652, English settlers had established three counties in the territory promised to the Native Americans. Unsurprisingly, there were frequent clashes between Native Americans and settlers.

By the 1660s, Berkeley had gradually become an autocrat in the colony. When the first burgesses were elected in 1619, all men aged seventeen or older were entitled to vote. By 1670, the vote was restricted to landowners, and elections were rare. The

BERKELEY'S AUTOCRATIC RULE

Historical Thinking Skills

Analyzing Cause and Effect Have students read the section "Virginia's Westward Expansion." Ask them to construct a flow chart (a chart showing a sequence of events, with arrows placed between each event) showing the impact of political turmoil in England leading to clashes with Native Americans in Virginia. *(Possible entries: Cromwell's forces win the English Civil War > Defeated opponents emigrate to Virginia > Virginia's population increases rapidly > New settlements are formed in areas promised to Native Americans > Clashes erupt between the two groups)* As a possible extension activity, have students keep their flow charts and add to them as they encounter other examples of tension between the settlers and Native Americans. **MIG** **PCE**

same burgesses, loyal and subservient to the governor, remained in office year after year. Each county continued to have only two representatives, even though some of the new counties of the interior contained many more people than the older ones of the tidewater area. Thus the more recent settlers in the "backcountry" were underrepresented or (if living in areas not yet formally organized as counties) not represented.

Representation in the backcountry was not the only source of turbulence in Virginia. The system of indentured servants also played a role. By the 1670s, many young men had finished their term as indentures and found themselves without a home or money. Many of them moved around the colony working, begging, or stealing. They would soon become a factor in what became known as Bacon's Rebellion.

BACON'S REBELLION

In 1676, backcountry unrest and political rivalries combined to create a major conflict. Nathaniel Bacon, a wealthy young graduate of Cambridge University, arrived in Virginia in 1673. He purchased a substantial farm in the west and won a seat on the governor's council. He established himself, in other words, as a member of the backcountry gentry.

But the new and influential western landowners were soon squabbling with the leaders of the tidewater region in the east. They disagreed on many issues but, above all, on policies toward the Native Americans. The backcountry settlements were in constant danger of attack from Native Americans, because many of them had been established on lands reserved for the Native American nations by treaty. White settlers in western Virginia had long resented the governor's attempts to hold the line of settlement steady so as to avoid antagonizing the Native Americans.

BACKCOUNTRY GRIEVANCES

Bacon, an aristocratic man with great political ambitions, had additional reasons for unhappiness with Berkeley. He resented his exclusion from the inner circle of the governor's council (the so-called Green Spring group, whose members enjoyed special access to patronage). Bacon also fumed about Berkeley's refusal to allow him a piece of the Native American fur trade. He was developing grievances that made him a natural leader of an opposing faction.

Bloody events thrust him into that role. In 1675, some Doeg Indians—angry about the European intrusions into their lands—raided a western plantation and killed a white servant. Bands of local settlers struck back angrily and haphazardly, attacking not only the small Doeg tribe but the powerful Susquehannock as well. The Native Americans responded with more raids on plantations and killed many more white settlers. As the fighting escalated, Bacon and other concerned landholders—unhappy with the governor's cautious response to their demand for help—defied Berkeley and struck out on their own against the Native Americans. Berkeley proclaimed him and his men rebels. At that point, what had started as an unauthorized assault on the Native Americans became a military challenge to the colonial government, a conflict known as Bacon's Rebellion. It was the largest and most powerful insurrection against established authority in the history of the colonies, one that would not be surpassed until the Revolution.

Twice, Bacon led his army east to Jamestown. The first time, he won a temporary pardon from the governor; the second time, after the governor reneged on the agreement, he burned the city and drove the governor into exile. In the midst of widespread social turmoil throughout the colony, Bacon stood on the verge of taking command of Virginia. Instead, he died suddenly of dysentery; and Berkeley, his position bolstered by the arrival of British troops, soon managed to regain control. In 1677, the Native Americans (aware of their inability to defeat the white forces militarily) reluctantly signed a new treaty that opened additional lands to white settlement.

Bacon's Rebellion was significant for several reasons. It was part of the continuing struggle to define the boundary between Native American and white lands in Virginia; it showed how unwilling the English settlers were to abide by earlier agreements with Native Americans, and how unwilling Native Americans were to tolerate further white movement into their territory. It revealed the bitterness of the competition between eastern and western landowners. But it also revealed something that Bacon himself had never intended to unleash: the potential for instability in the colony's large population of free, landless men. These men—most of them former indentured servants, propertyless, unemployed, with no real prospects—had formed the bulk of Bacon's constituency during the rebellion. They had become a large, unstable, floating population eager above all for access to land. Bacon had for a time maintained his popularity among them by exploiting their hatred of Native Americans. Gradually, however, he found himself unintentionally leading a movement that reflected the animosity of these landless men toward the landed gentry of which Bacon himself was a part.

SIGNIFICANCE OF BACON'S REBELLION

One result was that landed people in both eastern and western Virginia began to recognize a common interest in preventing social unrest from the former indentures. That was one of several reasons that they turned increasingly to the African slave trade to fulfill their need for labor. Enslaved Africans might pose dangers too, but the events of 1676 persuaded many colonists that the perils of importing a large white subordinate class were even greater.

THE GROWTH OF NEW ENGLAND

The first enduring settlement in New England—the second in English America—resulted from the discontent of a congregation of Puritan Separatists in England. For years, Separatists had been periodically imprisoned and even executed for defying the government and the Church of England; some of them, as a result, began to contemplate leaving England permanently in search of freedom to worship as they wished—even though Puritans did not believe in religious freedom for all others.

RELIGIOUS REPRESSION

Historical Thinking Skills

Causation Have students read the section "Bacon's Rebellion." Ask them to brainstorm examples of what they have learned about the early history of the Virginia Colony. Have students create a web diagram or chart to organize the reasons for Bacon's Rebellion into categories, such as "Social," "Political," "Religious," and "Economic." Ask students to write a short paragraph explaining which of these categories was most responsible for Bacon's Rebellion. Their paragraphs could be used as an exit ticket at the end of class. PCE MIG SOC WXT

Discussion and Activities

Argumentation After reading the section "Bacon's Rebellion," have students create a poster that encourages indentured servants to either stay peaceful and loyal to the royal governor or to continue to rebel. Advise students to consider the type of incentives that might influence indentured servants. WXT

Discussion and Activities

Making Connections Have students read the section "The Mayflower Compact." Ask them to recall the ideas of the Columbian Exchange from Chapter 1. Lead a class or small group discussion focusing on how the Plymouth settlers benefited from plants and animals from both the Old and New Worlds. MIG

PLYMOUTH PLANTATION

It was illegal to leave England without the consent of the king. In 1608, however, a congregation of Separatists from the hamlet of Scrooby began emigrating quietly, a few at a time, to Leyden, Holland, where they could worship without interference. They were, however, barred from the Dutch craft guilds and had to work at unskilled and poorly paid jobs. They were also troubled by the effects of the tolerant atmosphere of Dutch society, which threatened their dream of a close-knit Christian community. As a result, some of the Separatists decided to move again, this time across the Atlantic, where they hoped to create the kind of community they wanted and where they could spread "the gospel of the Kingdom of Christ in those remote parts of the world."

Leaders of the Scrooby group obtained permission from the Virginia Company to settle in British America. From the king, they received informal assurances that he would "not molest them, provided they carried themselves peaceably." (This was a historic concession by the Crown, for it opened British America to settlement not only by the Scrooby group but by other dissenting Protestants as well.) Several English merchants agreed to advance the necessary funds in exchange for a share in the profits of the settlement at the end of seven years.

The migrating Puritans "knew they were pilgrims" even before they left Holland, their leader and historian, William Bradford, later wrote. In September 1620 they left the port of Plymouth, on the English coast, in the *Mayflower* with thirty-five "saints" (Puritan Separatists) and sixty-seven "strangers" (people who were not full members of the Puritan church) aboard. By the time they sighted land in November, it was too late in the year to go on. Their original destination was probably the mouth of the Hudson River, in what is now New York. But they found themselves instead on Cape Cod. After exploring the region for a while, they chose a site for their settlement just north of the cape, an area Captain John Smith had named "Plymouth" (after the English port from which the Puritans had sailed) during an exploratory journey some years before. Plymouth lay outside the London Company's territory, and the settlers realized they had no legal basis for settling there. As a result, forty-one male passengers signed a document, the Mayflower Compact, which established a civil government and proclaimed their allegiance to the king. Then, on December 21, 1620, the immigrants, called Pilgrims, stepped ashore at Plymouth Rock.

THE MAYFLOWER COMPACT

They settled on cleared land that had once been a Native American village until, three years earlier, a mysterious epidemic–known as "the plague" and probably brought by earlier European explorers–had swept through the region and substantially depopulated it. The Pilgrims' first winter was a difficult one; half the colonists perished from malnutrition, disease, and exposure. Still, the colony survived.

Bradford became the governor at Plymouth, an office he would hold for more than twenty years. Despite the death of his wife, and many other losses, he managed his plantation for many years.

Like the Spanish and Portuguese colonists in the southern regions of the Americas, the Pilgrims (and other future English colonists) brought more to the New World than people and ideas. They also made profound changes in the natural landscape of New England. A smallpox epidemic caused by English carriers almost eliminated the Native American population in the areas around Plymouth in the early 1630s. The English demand for furs, animal skins, and meat greatly depleted the number of wild animals in the areas around Plymouth, one reason colonists worked so hard to develop stocks of domestic animals such as horses, cattle, sheep, and hogs. The Pilgrims and later English settlers also introduced new crops (wheat, barley, oats, and others), while incorporating many native foods (among them corn, potatoes, and peas) into their own diets–and eventually exporting them back to England and the rest of Europe. Gradually, colonial society imposed a European pattern onto the American landscape, as the settlers fenced in pastures, meadows, orchards, and fields for cultivation.

The Pilgrims' experience with the Native Americans was, for a time, very different from the experiences of the early English settlers farther south. That was in part because the remaining Native Americans in the region–their numbers thinned by disease–were significantly weaker than their southern neighbors and realized they had to get along with the Europeans. In the end, the survival and growth of the colony depended crucially on the assistance they received from Native Americans. Important Native American friends–Squanto and Samoset, among others–showed them how to gather seafood, cultivate corn, and hunt local animals. Squanto, a Pawtuxet who earlier in his life had been captured by an English explorer and taken to Europe, spoke English and was particularly helpful to the settlers in forming an alliance with the local Wampanoags, under Chief Massasoit. After the first harvest, in 1621, the settlers marked the alliance by inviting the Native Americans to join them in an October festival, the first Thanksgiving.

RELATIONS WITH THE NATIVE AMERICANS

But the good relationship between the settlers and the local Native Americans did not last. Thirteen years after the Pilgrims' arrival, a devastating smallpox epidemic–a result of contact with English settlers–wiped out much of the Native American population around Plymouth.

The Pilgrims could not hope to create rich farms on the sandy, marshy soil, and their early fishing efforts produced no profits. In 1622 the military officer Miles Standish, one of the leaders of the colony, established a semi-military regime to impose discipline on the settlers. Eventually the Pilgrims began to grow enough corn and other crops to provide them with a modest trading surplus. They also developed a small fur trade with the Abenaki Indians of Maine. From time to time new colonists arrived from England, and in a decade the population reached 300.

The people of "Plymouth Plantation," as they called their settlement, chose William Bradford again and again to be their governor. As early as 1621, he persuaded the Council for New England (the successor to the old Plymouth Company, which had

WILLIAM BRADFORD

Historical Thinking Skills

Evaluating Evidence Have students review the section "The Mayflower Compact." Ask them to consider how the Plymouth settlement was illegal. Then ask students to consider whether the colony should have been established and whether the Mayflower Compact was sufficient to make it legal. Divide students into pairs, and assign a position to each partner for a brief debate. MIG PCE charter rights to the territory) to give them legal permission to live there. He ended the communal labor plan Standish had helped create, distributed land among the families, and thus, as he explained it, made "all hands very industrious." He and a group of fellow "undertakers" took over the colony's debt to its original financiers in England and, with earnings from the fur trade, finally paid it off–even though the financiers had repeatedly cheated them and had failed to send them promised supplies.

The Pilgrims were always a poor community. As late as the 1640s, they had only one plow among them. But they clung to the belief that God had put them in the New World to live as a truly Christian community; and they were content to live their lives in what they considered godly ways.

At times, they spoke of serving as a model for other Christians. Governor Bradford wrote in retrospect: "As one small candle may light a thousand, so the light here kindled hath shone to many, yea in some sort to our whole nation." But the Pilgrims were less committed to grand designs, less concerned about how they were viewed by others, than were the Puritans who settled the larger and more ambitious English colonies to their north.

THE PURITAN EXPERIMENT

Turbulent events in England in the 1620s (combined with the example of the Plymouth colony) created strong interest in colonization among other groups of Puritans. King James I had been creating serious tensions for years between himself and Parliament through his effort to claim the divine right of kings and by his harsh, repressive policies toward the Puritans. The situation worsened after his death in 1625, when he was succeeded by his son, Charles I. By favoring Roman Catholicism and trying to destroy religious nonconformity, Charles I started the nation down the road that in the 1640s would lead to civil war. The Puritans were particular targets of Charles's policies. Some were imprisoned for their beliefs, and many began to consider the climate of England intolerable. The king's disbanding of Parliament in 1629 (it was not to be recalled until 1640) ensured that there would be no political solution to the Puritans' problems.

In the midst of this political and social turmoil, a group of Puritan merchants began organizing a new enterprise designed to take advantage of opportunities in America. At first their interest was largely an economic one. They obtained a grant of land in New England for most of the area now comprising Massachusetts and New Hampshire; they acquired a charter from Charles I (who was evidently unaware that they were Puritans) allowing them to create the Massachusetts Bay Company and to establish a colony in the New World; and they bought equipment and supplies from a defunct fishing and trading company that had attempted (and failed) to establish a profitable enterprise in North America earlier. In 1629, they were ready to dispatch a substantial group of settlers to New England.

MASSACHUSETTS BAY COMPANY

Among the members of the Massachusetts Bay Company, however, were a number of Puritans who saw the enterprise as something more than a business venture. They began to consider emigrating themselves and creating a haven for Puritans in New England. Members of this faction met secretly in Cambridge in the summer of 1629 and agreed to buy out the other investors and move en masse to America.

As governor, the new owners of the company chose John Winthrop, an affluent, university-educated gentleman with a deep piety and a forceful character. Winthrop had been instrumental in organizing the migration, and he commanded the expedition that sailed for New England in 1630: seventeen ships and 1,000 people (who were, unlike the earlier migrants to Virginia, mostly family groups). It was the largest single migration of its kind in the seventeenth century. Winthrop carried with him the charter of the Massachusetts Bay Company, which meant that the colonists would be responsible to no company officials in England, only to themselves.

JOHN WINTHROP

The Massachusetts migration quickly produced several different new settlements. The port of Boston, at the mouth of the Charles River, became the company's headquarters and the colony's capital. But in the course of the next decade, colonists moved into a number of other new towns in eastern Massachusetts: Charlestown, Newtown (later renamed Cambridge), Roxbury, Dorchester, Watertown, Ipswich, Concord, Sudbury, and others.

COLONIAL CURRENCY This seal was created in 1690 by the Massachusetts Bay Company to validate the paper "bills of credit" with which colonists conducted many financial transactions. Paper money met considerable resistance at first. Many people doubted its value and would not accept it, preferring instead the Spanish silver coins that were in wide circulation. Gradually, however, a shortage of silver required increasing reliance on this and other paper devices. The seal shows a Native American saying "Come over and help us," which represents the English belief in the superiority of white European society.

Reasoning Processes

Comparison Have students read the sections "Massachusetts Bay Company" and "John Winthrop." Ask them to create a Venn diagram and populate it with examples of how the Massachusetts Bay Company was similar to or different from the Plymouth Colony. When complete, ask students to evaluate whether the two were more similar or different. **MIG** **SOC** **PCE**

Discussion and Activities

Explaining Significance Have students review the sections "Massachusetts Bay Company" and "John Winthrop." **Ask:** Why was it important that the leadership of the Massachusetts Bay Company brought its charter to the New World with them? *(Having the charter physically with them in the New World meant that it was more difficult for the Crown to revoke the charter, thus giving the Company more autonomy.)* **PCE**

AP Exam Practice

Short Answer Provide students with the following short-answer questions and allow 15 minutes for completion. Ask for volunteers to share their responses and discuss as a class.

Answer A, B, and C

A) Briefly explain ONE significant similarity between the founding of the Plymouth Colony and the Massachusetts Bay Colony. *(Possible answer: Both were founded primarily to provide refuge for religious minorities.)*

B) Briefly explain ONE significant difference between the founding of the Plymouth Colony and the Massachusetts Bay Colony. *(Possible responses: Plymouth was founded by Separatists, while Massachusetts Bay was founded by Puritans. Massachusetts Bay was much larger and better supplied than Plymouth.)*

C) Briefly explain ONE important reason for the similarity listed in A. *(Both Separatists and Puritans faced discrimination and limits to their worship in England.)*

The Massachusetts Bay Company soon transformed itself into a colonial government. According to the original company charter, the eight stockholders (or "freemen") were to meet as a general court to choose officers and adopt rules for the corporation. But eventually the definition of "freemen" changed to include all male citizens, not just the stockholders. John Winthrop dominated colonial politics just as he had dominated the original corporation, but after 1634 he and most other officers of the colony had to face election each year.

THE CONGREGATIONAL CHURCH

Unlike the Separatist founders of Plymouth, the founders of Massachusetts had no intention of breaking from the Church of England. Yet, if they continued to feel any real attachment to the Anglican establishment, they gave little sign of it. In every town, the community church had (in the words of the prominent minister John Cotton) "complete liberty to stand alone," unlike churches in the highly centralized Anglican structure in England. Each congregation chose its own minister and regulated its own affairs. In both Plymouth and Massachusetts, this form of parish organization eventually became known as the Congregational Church.

PORTRAIT OF A BOSTON WOMAN Anne Pollard, a member of the original Winthrop expedition to Boston, was 100 years old when this portrait was painted in 1721. In 1643, thirteen years after her arrival in Massachusetts, she married a Boston innkeeper with whom she had 13 children. After her husband's death in 1679, she continued to manage the tavern on her own. When she died in 1725, at the age of 104, she left 130 direct descendants. The artist who painted this early portrait is unknown, but is assumed to be an American working in the primitive style common in New England before the arrival in 1729 of the first academically trained portraitists from England.

The Puritans, although nominally members of the Anglican Church, were in fact worshipers of a very different faith. They did not accept the authority of either the Roman Catholic hierarchy or the Church of England. They did not follow traditional ceremonial worship and did not receive sacraments from priests. They learned, instead, from reading the Bible and from listening to ministers who spoke from their own knowledge and belief, not from the orthodoxies of traditional institutional faith. They accepted the doctrines of John Calvin's vision that everyone was destined at birth for either salvation or damnation—that nothing in people's earthly life could change their fate after death. But living a good and productive life might be a sign of salvation. Puritans not only sought salvation. They also sought freedom—not the kind of freedom Americans understand today, but the right to worship without interference from England or from established churches. That did not mean that they were free to behave as they liked; the community expected obedience to authority. But authority was based largely within the community itself and monitored by its members. It did not come from England or from centralized institutions in America.

The Massachusetts Puritans were not grim or joyless, as many observers would later portray them. They were, however, serious and pious. They strove to lead useful, conscientious lives of thrift and hard work, and they honored material success as evidence of God's favor. "We here enjoy God and Jesus Christ," Winthrop wrote to his wife soon after his arrival; "is this not enough?" He and the other Massachusetts founders believed they were founding a holy commonwealth—a "city upon a hill"—that could serve as a model for the rest of the New World.

A THEOCRATIC SOCIETY

If Massachusetts was to become a beacon to other emigrants, it had first to maintain its own "holiness." Ministers had no formal political power, but they exerted great influence on church members, who were the only people who could vote or hold office. The government in turn protected the ministers, taxed the people (members and nonmembers alike) to support the church, and enforced the law requiring attendance at services. Dissidents had no more freedom of worship in America than the Puritans themselves had had in England. Colonial Massachusetts was in many ways a "theocracy," a society in which the line between the church and the state was hard to see.

Like other new settlements, the Massachusetts Bay colony had early difficulties. During their first winter, an unusually severe one, nearly a third of the colonists died; others left in the spring. But more rapidly than Jamestown or Plymouth, the colony grew and prospered. The Pilgrims and neighboring Native Americans helped with food and advice. Affluent incoming settlers brought needed tools and other goods, which they exchanged for the cattle, corn, and other produce

Historical Thinking Skills

Argumentation Have students read the section "A Theocratic Society." Ask them to craft an argument as to why Massachusetts Bay could be considered theocratic even though religious leaders had no direct political authority. Have students write a short paragraph explaining their argument. *(Possible responses: Political and religious leaders were often the same people; ministers were protected by the government; people were taxed to support the church, etc.)* This could be done as an exit ticket.

of the established colonists and Native Americans. The large number of family groups in the colony (in sharp contrast to the early years at Jamestown) helped ensure a feeling of commitment to the community and a sense of order among the settlers. It also allowed the population to reproduce itself more rapidly. The strong religious and political hierarchy ensured a measure of social stability.

THE EXPANSION OF NEW ENGLAND

As the population grew, more and more people arrived in Massachusetts who were not Puritan "saints" and hence could not vote. Newcomers had a choice of conforming to the religious practices of the colony or leaving. Many left, helping to begin a process that would spread settlement throughout present-day New England and beyond.

GROWING RELIGIOUS DISSENT

The Connecticut Valley, about 100 miles west of the edge of European settlement around Boston, began attracting English families as early as the 1630s. The valley appealed in particular to Thomas Hooker, a minister of Newtown (Cambridge), who defied the Massachusetts government in 1635 and led his congregation through the wilds to establish the town of Hartford. Four years later, the people of Hartford and of two other towns established a colonial government of their own and adopted a constitution known as the Fundamental Orders of Connecticut.

Another Connecticut colony, the project of a Puritan minister and a wealthy merchant from England, grew up around New Haven on the Connecticut coast. It reflected impatience with what its founders considered increasing religious laxity in Massachusetts. The Fundamental Articles of New Haven (1639) established a religious government even stricter than that in Boston. New Haven remained independent until 1662, when a royal charter combined it with Hartford to create the colony of Connecticut.

Rhode Island had its origins in the religious and political dissent of Roger Williams, an engaging but controversial young minister who lived for a time in Salem, Massachusetts. Even John Winthrop, who considered Williams a heretic, called him a "sweet and amiable" man, and William Bradford described him as "a man godly and zealous." But he was, Bradford added, "very unsettled in judgment." Williams, a confirmed Separatist, argued that the Massachusetts church should abandon all allegiance to the Church of England. More disturbing to the clergy, he called for a complete separation of church and state–to protect the church from the corruption of the secular world. The colonial government, alarmed at this challenge to its spiritual authority, banished him. During the bitter winter of 1635–1636, Williams took refuge with Narragansett tribesmen; the following spring he bought a tract of land from them and, with a few followers, created the town of Providence on it. Other communities of dissidents followed him to what became Rhode Island, and in 1644 Williams obtained a charter from Parliament permitting him to establish a government. Rhode Island's government gave no support to the church and allowed "liberty in religious concernments." For a time, it was the only colony in which members of all faiths (including Jews) could worship without interference.

ROGER WILLIAMS

An even greater challenge to the established order in Massachusetts Bay emerged in the person of Anne Hutchinson, an intelligent and charismatic woman from a substantial Boston family. Hutchinson had come to Massachusetts with her husband in 1634. She antagonized the leaders of the colony by arguing vehemently that the members of the Massachusetts clergy who were not among the "elect"–that is, had not undergone a conversion experience–had no right to spiritual office. Over time, she claimed that many clergy–among them her own uninspiring minister–were among the non-elect and had no right to exercise authority over their congregations. She eventually charged that all the ministers in Massachusetts–save community leader John Cotton and her own brother-in-law–were not among the elect. Alongside such teachings (which her critics called "Antinomianism," from the Greek word meaning "hostile to the law"), Hutchinson also created alarm by affronting prevailing assumptions about the proper role of women in Puritan society. She was not a retiring, deferential wife and mother, but a powerful religious figure in her own right.

ANNE HUTCHINSON

Hutchinson developed a large following among women, to whom she offered an active role in religious affairs. She also attracted support from merchants, young men, and dissidents of many sorts who resented the oppressive character of the colonial government. As her influence grew, the Massachusetts leadership mobilized to stop her. Hutchinson's followers were numerous and influential enough to prevent Winthrop's reelection as governor in 1636, but the next year he returned to office and put her on trial for heresy. Hutchinson embarrassed her accusers by displaying a remarkable knowledge of theology; but because she continued to defy clerical authority (and because she claimed she had herself communicated directly with the Holy Spirit–a violation of the Puritan belief that the age of such revelations had passed), she was convicted of sedition and banished as "a woman not fit for our society." Her unorthodox views had challenged both religious belief and social order in Puritan Massachusetts. With her family and some of her followers, she moved to Rhode Island and then into New Netherland (later New York), where in 1643 she died during Native American uprising.

Alarmed by Hutchinson's heresy, male clergy began to restrict further the already-limited public activities of women within congregations. As a result, many of Hutchinson's followers began to migrate out of Massachusetts Bay, especially to New Hampshire and Maine.

Colonies had been established there in 1629 when two English proprietors, Captain John Mason and Sir Ferdinando Gorges, had received a grant from the Council for New England and divided it along the Piscataqua River to create two separate provinces. But despite their lav-

NEW HAMPSHIRE AND MAINE

Reasoning Processes

Comparing and Contrasting Have students read the sections "Roger Williams" and "Anne Hutchinson." Ask them to create a Janus figure (a Janus figure is an outline drawing of a human figure divided down the middle, with one set of attributes on one side and another set on the other side) showing the teachings of Roger Williams on one side and the teachings of Anne Hutchinson on the other. Then ask students to discuss why colonial leaders may have viewed Anne Hutchinson as a greater threat than Roger Williams. *(Possible responses: Hutchinson was a woman taking a leadership role; Hutchinson claimed that most religious leaders were unfit for office; Hutchinson claimed to have direct communication with God.)* **SOC**

Discussion and Activities

Historical Evidence and Argumentation Have students review the section "Growing Religious Dissent." Then ask them to discuss why dissenters in Connecticut might have been able to exercise more autonomy than those in other areas. *(Connecticut at the time was essentially the frontier, far away from sources of colonial control in Boston.)* **SOC**

Discussion and Activities

Evaluating Evidence Have students read the section "Importance of Native American Assistance." Based on this and their previous knowledge, ask students to brainstorm a list of ways that Native Americans helped early English colonies survive or thrive. Have them discuss in small groups the relative importance of these assistance efforts and create a ranked list. Ask the groups to share their lists, and discuss any differences as a class. **WXT** **MIG** **SOC** **GEO**

THE GROWTH OF NEW ENGLAND, 1620–1750 The European settlement of New England, as this map reveals, traces its origins primarily to two small settlements on the Atlantic coast. The first was the Pilgrim settlement at Plymouth, which began in 1620 and spread out through Cape Cod, southern Massachusetts, and the islands of Martha's Vineyard and Nantucket. The second, much larger settlement began in Boston in 1630 and spread rapidly through western Massachusetts, north into New Hampshire and Maine, and south into Connecticut.

Why did the settlers of Massachusetts Bay expand more rapidly and expansively than those of Plymouth?

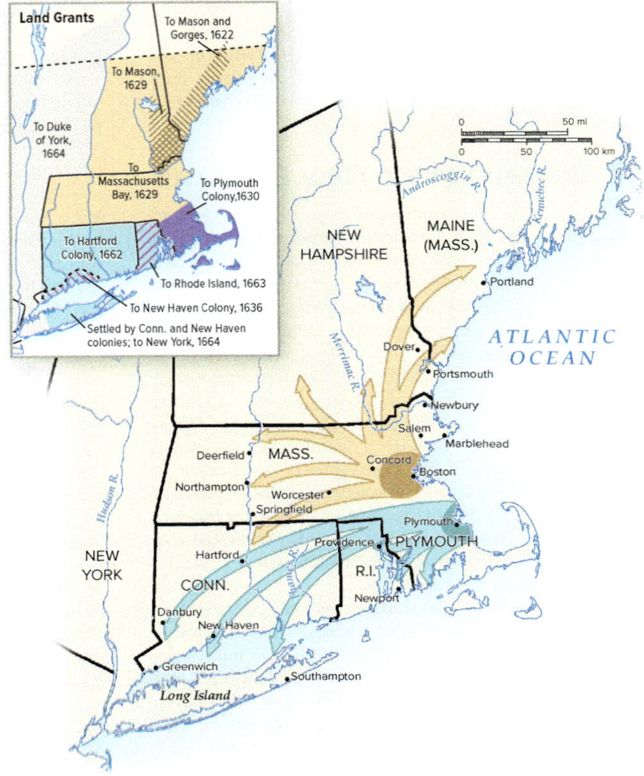

ish promotional efforts, few settlers had moved into these northern regions until the religious disruptions in Massachusetts Bay. In 1639, John Wheelwright, a disciple of Anne Hutchinson, led some of his fellow dissenters to Exeter, New Hampshire. Other groups—of both dissenting and orthodox Puritans—soon followed. New Hampshire became a separate colony in 1679. Maine remained a part of Massachusetts until 1820.

SETTLERS AND NATIVE AMERICANS

By the mid-1630s, the Native American population, small to begin with, had been almost extinguished by the European epidemics. The surviving Native Americans sold much of their land to the English (a great boost to settlement, since much of it had already been cleared). Some Native Americans—known as "praying Indians"—even converted to Christianity and joined Puritan communities.

Native Americans provided crucial assistance to the early settlers. Settlers learned about vital local food crops: corn, beans, pumpkins, and potatoes from Native Americans. They also learned such crucial agricultural techniques as annual burning for fertilization and planting beans to replenish soil. Native Americans also served as important trading partners to settlers, particularly in the creation of the thriving North American fur trade. They were an important market for such manufactured goods as iron pots, blankets, metal-tipped arrows, eventually guns and rifles, and (often tragically) alcohol. Indeed, commerce with the Native Americans was responsible for the creation of some of the first great fortunes in British North America and for the emergence of wealthy families who would exercise influence in the colonies (and later the nation) for many generations.

IMPORTANCE OF NATIVE AMERICAN ASSISTANCE

But as in other areas of white settlement, there were also conflicts; and the early peaceful relations between settlers and

Answers

The Growth of New England, 1620–1750.

Massachusetts Bay was founded by a much larger, much better supplied group of settlers.

Native Americans did not last. Tensions soon developed as a result of the white colonists' continuing appetite for land. The expanding demand for land was also a result of a change in the colonists' agrarian economy. As wild animals began to disappear from overhunting, colonists began to concentrate more and more on raising domesticated animals. As the herds expanded, so did the colonists' need for new land. As a result, the colonists moved steadily into territories such as the Connecticut Valley where they came into conflict with Native Americans who were more numerous and more powerful than those along the Massachusetts coast.

SHIFTING ATTITUDES

The character of those conflicts–and the brutality with which white settlers assaulted their Native American foes–changed Puritan attitudes toward the Native Americans. At first, many white New Englanders had looked at the Native Americans with a slightly condescending admiration. Before long, however, they came to view them primarily as "heathens" and "savages," and hence as a constant threat to the existence of a godly community in the New World. Some Puritans believed the solution to the "problem" was to "civilize" the Native Americans by converting them to Christianity and European ways, and some English missionaries had modest success in producing converts. One such missionary, John Eliot, even translated the Bible into an Algonquian language. Other Puritans, however, envisioned a harsher "solution": displacing or, if that failed, exterminating the Native Americans.

To the Native Americans, the threat from the English was very direct. European settlers were penetrating deeper and deeper into the interior, seizing land, clearing forests, driving away much of the wild game on which the tribes depended for food. English farmers often let their livestock run wild, and the animals frequently destroyed Native Americans' crops. Land and food shortages exacerbated the drastic Native American population decline that had begun as a result of epidemic diseases. There had been more than 100,000 Native Americans in New England at the beginning of the seventeenth century; by 1675, only 10,000 remained. This decline drove some Native Americans to alcoholism and others to conversion to Christianity. But it drove others to war.

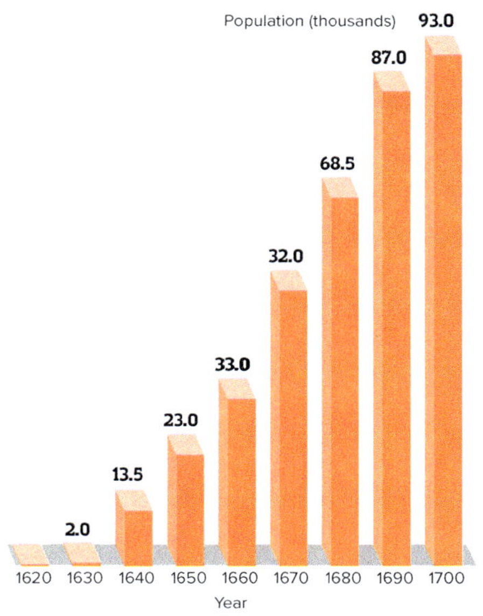

THE NON-INDIAN POPULATION OF NEW ENGLAND, 1620–1700 As in the Chesapeake colonies, the European population of New England grew very rapidly after settlement began in 1620. The most rapid rate of growth, unsurprisingly, came in the first thirty years, when even a modest wave of immigraton could double or triple the small existing population. But the largest numbers of new immigrants arrived between 1650 and 1680.

What events in England in those years might have led to increased emigration to America in that period?

THE PEQUOT WAR, KING PHILIP'S WAR, AND THE TECHNOLOGY OF BATTLE

THE PEQUOT WAR

The first major conflict came in 1637, when hostilities broke out between English settlers in the Connecticut Valley and the Pequot Indians of the region as a result of competition over trade with the Dutch in New Netherland and friction over land. In what became known as the Pequot War, English settlers allied with the Mohegan and Narragansett Indians (rivals of the Pequots). The greatest savagery in the conflict was the work of the English. In the bloodiest act of the war, white raiders under Captain John Mason marched against a palisaded Pequot stronghold and set it afire. Hundreds of Pequots either burned to death in the flaming stockade or were killed as they attempted to escape. Those who survived were hunted down, captured, enslaved, and sold. The Pequot tribe was almost wiped out.

KING PHILIP'S WAR

The most prolonged and deadly encounter between white settlers and Native Americans in the seventeenth century began in 1675, a conflict that the English would remember for generations as King Philip's War. As in the earlier Pequot War in Connecticut, a Native American tribe–in this case the Wampanoags, under the leadership of a chieftain known to the white settlers as King Philip and among his own people as Metacomet–rose up to resist the English. The Wampanoags had not always been hostile to the settlers; indeed, Metacomet's grandfather had once forged an alliance with the English, and Metacomet himself was well acquainted with the colonists. But by the 1670s, he had become convinced that only armed resistance could protect the Wampanoag from English incursions into their lands and, more immediately, from the efforts by the colonial governments to impose English law on them. (A court in Plymouth had recently tried and hanged several Wampanoags for murdering a member of their own tribe.)

For three years, the Native Americans–well organized and armed with guns–terrorized a string of Massachusetts towns,

Reasoning Processes

Change Over Time Have students read the section "Shifting Attitudes." **Ask:** How did the attitudes of the settlers toward Native Americans change during the seventeenth century? What do you think most accounts for these changes? How did these changes impact the Native American population? Have students discuss as a class or in small groups. **MIG** **PCE**

Answers

The Non-Indian Population of New England, 1620–1700

The largest influx of immigrants was the result of the English Civil War.

Reasoning Processes

Comparing After students have read the sections "The Pequot War" and "King Philip's War," ask them to create a bisected Venn Diagram comparing similarities and differences in the causes of the two wars above the line and similarities and differences in effects of the two wars below the line. **MIG** **WXT** **PCE**

ANNE HUTCHINSON PREACHING IN HER HOUSE IN BOSTON Anne Hutchinson was alarming to many of Boston's religious leaders not only because she openly challenged the authority of the clergy, but also because she implicitly challenged norms of female behavior in Puritan society.

destroying twenty of them and causing the deaths of as many as a thousand people (including at least one-sixteenth of the white males in the colony). The war greatly weakened both the society and economy of Massachusetts. But, in 1676, the white settlers fought back and gradually prevailed. They received critical aid from the Mohawks, longtime rivals of the Wampanoags, and guides, spies, and soldiers recruited from among the so-called praying Indians (Christian converts) of the region. While white militiamen attacked Native American villages and destroyed food supplies, a group of Mohawks ambushed, shot, and killed Metacomet, then bore his severed head to Boston to present to the colonial leaders. After that, the fragile alliance that Metacomet had managed to forge among local groups collapsed. Europeans were soon able to crush the uprising. Some Wampanoag leaders were executed; others were sold into slavery in the West Indies. The Wampanoags and their allies, their populations depleted and their natural resources reduced, were now powerless to resist the English.

Yet these victories by the white colonists did not end the danger to their settlements. Other Native Americans in other groups survived and were still capable of attacking English settlements. The New England settlers also faced competition from the Native Americans and also from the Dutch and the French, who claimed the territory on which some of the outlying settlements were established. The French, in particular, posed a constant threat to the English through their alliance with the Algonquins. In later years, the French would join forces with Native Americans in their attacks on the New England frontier.

The character of the Pequot War, King Philip's War, and many other conflicts between Native Americans and settlers in the years that followed was crucially affected by earlier exchanges of technology between the English and the tribes.

FLINTLOCK MUSKET

In particular, the Native Americans made effective use of a new weapon introduced to New England by Miles Standish and others: the flintlock rifle. It replaced the earlier staple of colonial musketry, the matchlock rifle, which proved too heavy, cumbersome, and inaccurate to be useful in the kind of combat characteristic of Anglo-Indian struggles. The matchlock had to be steadied on a fixed object and ignited with a match before firing; the flintlock could be held up without support and fired without a match. (Native Americans using bows and arrows often outmatched settlers using the clumsy matchlocks.)

Many English settlers were slow to give up their cumbersome matchlocks for the lighter flintlocks. But the Native Americans recognized the advantages of the newer rifles right away and began purchasing them in large quantities as part of their regular trade with the colonists. Despite rules forbidding colonists to instruct Native Americans on how to use and repair the weapons, the Native Americans learned to handle the rifles, and even to repair them, very effectively on their own. They even built

A PEQUOT VILLAGE DESTROYED An English artist drew this view of a fortified Pequot village in Connecticut surrounded by English soldiers and their allies from other tribes during the Pequot War in 1637. The invaders massacred more than 600 residents of the settlement.

Discussion and Activities

Analyzing Visuals Have students examine the image "A Pequot Village Destroyed." Ask them to speculate on the significance of the small mounds surrounding the village. *(The crosses on top of each mound suggest that they are graves.)* Ask students to discuss the point of view of the artist. Does the image seem sympathetic to one side over the other? **PCE** **SOC**

a substantial forge for shaping and repairing rifle parts. In King Philip's War, the very high casualties on both sides were a result of the use of these more advanced rifles.

Native Americans also used more traditional military technologies in their conflicts with the English—especially the construction of forts. The Narragansetts, allies of the Wampanoags in King Philip's War, built an enormous fort in the Great Swamp of Rhode Island in 1675, which became the site of one of the bloodiest battles of the war before English attackers burned it down. After that, a band of Narragansetts set out to build a large stone fort, with the help of a Narragansett who had learned masonry while working with the English. When English soldiers discovered the stone fort in 1676, after the end of King Philip's War, they killed most of its occupants and destroyed it. In the end, the technological skills of the Native Americans (both those they borrowed from the English and those they drew from their own traditions) proved no match for the overwhelming advantages of the English settlers in both numbers and firepower.

THE RESTORATION COLONIES

By the end of the 1630s, English settlers had established six significant colonies in the New World: Virginia, Massachusetts, Maryland, Connecticut, Rhode Island, and New Hampshire. (Maine remained officially part of Massachusetts until after the American Revolution.) But for nearly thirty years after Lord Baltimore received the charter for Maryland in 1632, the English government launched no additional colonial ventures. It was preoccupied with troubles of its own at home.

THE ENGLISH CIVIL WAR

ORIGINS

England's problems had begun during the rule of James I, who attracted widespread opposition before he died in 1625. James, however, did not openly challenge Parliament. His son, Charles I, was not so prudent. He dissolved Parliament in 1629 and began ruling as an absolute monarch, steadily alienating a growing number of his subjects—especially the members of the powerful Puritan community. Finally, desperately in need of money, Charles called Parliament back into session and asked it to levy new taxes. But he antagonized the members by dismissing them again twice in two years. In 1642, some of them organized a military challenge to the king, thus launching the English Civil War.

The conflict between the Cavaliers (the supporters of the king) and the Roundheads (the forces of Parliament, who were mostly Puritans) lasted seven years. Finally, in 1649, the Roundheads defeated the king's forces, captured Charles himself, and—in an action that horrified not only much of continental Europe at the time but also future generations of English men and women—beheaded the monarch. To replace him, they elevated the stern Roundhead leader Oliver Cromwell to the position of "protector," from which he ruled for the next nine years. When Cromwell died in 1658, his son and heir proved unable to maintain his authority. Two years later, King Charles II, son of the beheaded monarch, returned from exile and claimed the throne.

Charles II faced some of the same problems as his father, mostly because of the belief held by many that secretly he was a Roman Catholic. The king supported religious toleration, which, to the dismay of many Protestants, allowed Catholicism in England once again. The Parliament refused to agree, and prudently Charles did not fight them for the right of Catholics to worship openly. He did, however, make a private agreement with Louis XIV of France that he would become Catholic, which he did only on his deathbed. His son James II continued to face many of the same difficulties.

NEW PROPRIETARY COLONIES

Among the many results of the Stuart Restoration—the return of Charles II, a member of the Stuart royal family—was the resumption of colonization in America. Charles II quickly began to reward faithful courtiers with grants of land in the New World; and in the twenty-five years of his reign, he issued charters for four additional colonies: Carolina, New York, New Jersey, and Pennsylvania. The new colonies were all proprietary ventures (modeled on Maryland rather than on Virginia and Massachusetts), thus exposing an important change in the nature of American settlement. No longer were private companies interested in launching colonies, realizing at last that there were no quick profits to be had in the New World. The goal of the new colonies was not so much quick commercial success as permanent settlements that would provide proprietors with land and power.

THE CAROLINAS

Carolina (a name derived from the Latinate form of "Charles") was, like Maryland, carved in part from the original Virginia grant. Charles II awarded the territory to a group of eight court favorites, all prominent politicians already active in colonial affairs. In successive charters issued in 1663 and 1665, the eight proprietors received joint title to a vast territory stretching south to the Florida peninsula and west to the Pacific Ocean. Like Lord Baltimore, they received almost kingly powers over their grant.

Also like Lord Baltimore, they expected to profit as landlords and land speculators. They reserved large estates for themselves, and they proposed to sell or give away the rest in smaller tracts (using a headright system similar to those in Virginia and Maryland) and to collect annual payments ("quitrents") from the settlers. Although committed Anglicans themselves, they welcomed any settlers they could get. The charter of the colony guaranteed religious freedom to everyone who would worship as a Christian. The proprietors also promised a measure of political freedom; laws were to be made by a representative assembly. With these incentives, they hoped to attract settlers from the existing American colonies and thus to avoid the expense of financing expeditions from England.

INCENTIVES FOR SETTLEMENT

Reasoning Processes

Analyzing Change After students have read the section "Flintlock Musket," ask them to make a chart with examples of new technologies that favored either the English or the Native Americans in the Pequot War and King Philip's War. Ask students to write a brief argument of a few sentences explaining why those changes tended to favor one side over the other. **WXT**

Discussion and Activities

Making Connections Have students read the section "The English Civil War." Ask them to discuss how the English Civil War and its aftermath impacted English colonization. *(Colonization slowed down during the war, as the nation's focus and energy were fixed on the political and religious conflict in England. After the war, Restoration monarchs, particularly Charles II, used patronage to reward supporters with proprietorships in America.)* **MIG** **PCE** **WOR**

Discussion and Activities

Analyzing Visuals Have students examine the map "Charles Town, South Carolina." **Ask:** How did the Native American mapmaker use geometry to describe the nature of the different settlements? *(The more permanent English settlement is represented with straight lines and right angles, while the Native American settlements are represented by circles.)* Which settlement does the map suggest is most permanent? **MIG**

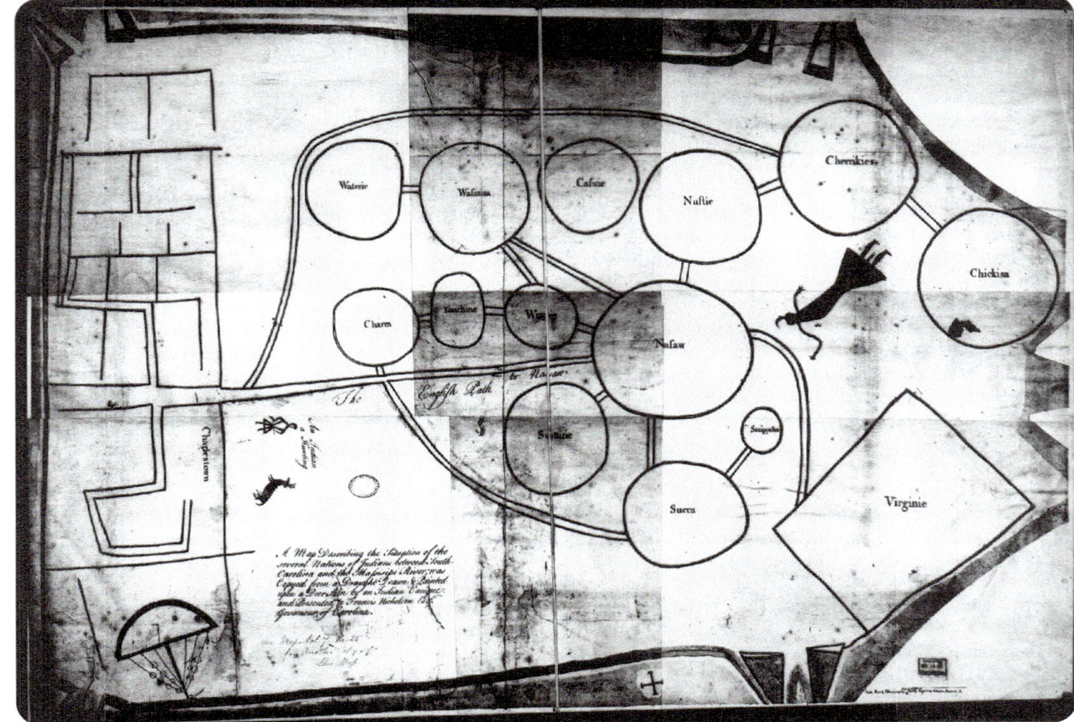

CHARLES TOWN, SOUTH CAROLINA This map, drawn on deerskin by a Native American around 1730, illustrates the close juxtaposition of the ordered English settlement in Charles Town, South Carolina, seen on the left, and the more fluid Native American settlements near the town, on the right. It also illustrates the way in which southeastern Native Americans understood political relations as a series of linked circles.

Their initial efforts failed dismally, and some of the original proprietors gave up. But one man–Anthony Ashley Cooper, soon to become the Earl of Shaftesbury–persisted. Cooper convinced his partners to finance migrations to Carolina from England. In the spring of 1670, the first of these expeditions–a party of 300–set out from England. Only 100 people survived the difficult voyage; those who did established a settlement in the Port Royal area of the Carolina coast. Ten years later they founded a city at the junction of the Ashley and Cooper Rivers, which in 1690 became the colonial capital. They called it Charles Town. (It was later renamed Charleston.)

The Earl of Shaftesbury, troubled by the instability in England, wanted a planned and well-ordered community. With the aid of the English philosopher John Locke, he drew up the Fundamental Constitution for Carolina in 1669, which created an elaborate system of land distribution and an elaborately designed social order. In fact, however, Carolina developed along lines quite different from the utopian vision of Shaftesbury and Locke. For one thing, the colony was never united in anything more than name. The northern and southern regions remained socially and economically distinct from one another. The northern settlers were mainly backwoods farmers, isolated from the outside world, scratching out a meager existence through subsistence agriculture. They developed no important aristocracy and for many years imported virtually no enslaved Africans. In the south, fertile lands and the good harbor at Charles Town promoted a prosperous economy and an aristocratic society. Settlements grew up rapidly along the Ashley and Cooper Rivers, and colonists established a flourishing trade in corn, lumber, cattle, pork, and (beginning in the 1690s) rice–which was to become the colony's principal commercial crop. Traders from the interior used Charles Town to market furs and hides they had acquired from Native American trading partners; some also marketed enslaved Native Americans, generally captured by rival Native American groups and sold to the white traders.

FUNDAMENTAL CONSTITUTION FOR CAROLINA

Southern Carolina very early developed close ties to the large (and now overpopulated) English colony on the island of Barbados. For many years, Barbados was Carolina's most important trading partner. During the first ten years of settle-

Historical Thinking Skills

Argumentation After students have read the section "Incentives for Settlement," ask them to write a thesis that makes a historically defensible claim as to why the Carolina colony failed to attract significant settlements despite the incentives offered by the proprietors. *(Despite the incentives offered, many prospective immigrants did not have the resources necessary to pay their passage to the New World.)*

ment, most of the new settlers in Carolina were Barbadians, some of whom arrived with large groups of enslaved Africans and established themselves quickly as substantial landlords. African slavery had taken root on Barbados earlier than in any of the mainland colonies; and the white Caribbean migrants—tough, uncompromising profit seekers—established a similar slave-based plantation society in Carolina. The proprietors, four of whom had a financial interest in the African slave trade, also encouraged the use of enslaved African laborers.

For several decades, Carolina remained one of the most unstable English colonies in America. There were tensions between the small farmers of the Albemarle region in the north and the wealthy planters in the south. There were conflicts between the rich Barbadians in southern Carolina and the smaller landowners around them. After Lord Shaftesbury's death, the proprietors proved unable to establish order, and in 1719 the colonists seized control of the colony from them. Ten years later, the king divided the region into two royal colonies, North and South Carolina.

NORTH AND SOUTH CAROLINA

NEW NETHERLAND, NEW YORK, AND NEW JERSEY

In 1664, one year after he issued the Carolina charter, Charles II granted to his brother James, the Duke of York, all the territory lying between the Connecticut and Delaware Rivers. But much of the territory included in the grant was already claimed by the Dutch, who had established substantial settlements at New Amsterdam and other strategic points beginning in 1624.

The growing conflict between the English and the Dutch in America was part of a larger commercial rivalry between the two nations throughout the world. But the English particularly resented the Dutch presence in America, because it served as a wedge between the northern and southern English colonies and because it provided bases for Dutch smugglers evading English customs laws. And so in 1664, an English fleet under the command of Richard Nicolls sailed into the lightly defended port of New Amsterdam and extracted a surrender from its unpopular Dutch governor, Peter Stuyvesant, who had failed to mobilize resistance to the invasion. Under the Articles of Capitulation, the Dutch colony surrendered to the British in return for assurances that the Dutch settlers would not be displaced. In 1673, the Dutch briefly reconquered New Amsterdam. But they lost it for good in 1674.

CAPTURE OF NEW AMSTERDAM

James, the Duke of York, his title to New Netherland now clear, renamed the colony New York and prepared to govern a colony of extraordinary diversity. New York contained not only Dutch and English, but Scandinavians, Germans, French,

NEW AMSTERDAM The small Dutch settlement on Manhattan Island, known before 1664 as New Amsterdam, fell to the English in 1664. This painting shows buildings clustered at the southern tip of the island, which remained the center of what would become New York City until the nineteenth century.

Reasoning Processes

Comparing and Contrasting Have students read the section "North and South Carolina." Ask them to create a Venn diagram that shows examples of commonalities (in the overlapping section of the diagram) and differences between the two regions. **ARC** **PCE** **SOC**

Discussion and Activities

Analyzing Visuals Have students examine the painting "New Amsterdam." Ask them to consider why this settlement would have been so appealing to both the Dutch and the British, and discuss as a class or in small groups. *(There was an excellent port, as well as access to the interior via the Hudson River. Both England and the Netherlands were wealthy trading nations, so these advantages would have been appealing.)* **GEO**

Discussion and Activities

Explaining Significance After students have read the section "New Netherland, New York, and New Jersey," **ask:** Why was it important for England to eliminate the Dutch presence in New Netherland? How did the decision to allow Dutch settlers to remain impact the development of New York? Ask students to speculate how New York might have been different if the Dutch settlers had been displaced. **PCE** **SOC**

enslaved Africans (forcibly brought by the Dutch West India Company), and members of several different Native American nations. There were, of course, many different religious faiths among these groups. James made no effort to impose his own Roman Catholicism on the colony. Like other proprietors before him, he remained in England and delegated powers to a governor and a council. But he provided for no representative assembly in New York perhaps because a parliament had executed his own father, Charles I. The laws did, however, establish local governments and guarantee religious toleration. Nevertheless, there were immediate tensions over the distribution of power in the colony. The great Dutch "patroons" (large landowners) survived with their economic and political power largely intact. James granted large estates as well to some of his own political supporters in an effort to create a class of influential landowners loyal to him. Power in the colony thus remained widely and unequally dispersed–among wealthy English landlords, Dutch patroons, fur traders (who forged important alliances with the Iroquois), and the Duke of York's political appointees. Like Carolina, New York would for many years be a highly fractious society.

It was also a growing and generally prosperous colony. By 1685, when the Duke of York ascended the English throne as James II, New York contained approximately 30,000 people, about four times as many as when James had received his grant twenty years before. Most of them still lived within the Hudson Valley, close to the river itself, with the largest settlement at its mouth, in the town of New York (formerly New Amsterdam).

ESTABLISHMENT OF NEW JERSEY

Originally, James's claims in America extended south of the Hudson to the Delaware Valley and beyond. But shortly after receiving his charter, James gave a large portion of that land to a pair of political allies, Sir John Berkeley and Sir George Carteret, both of whom were also Carolina proprietors. Carteret named the territory New Jersey, after the island in the English Channel on which he had been born. In 1702, after nearly a decade of political squabbling and economic profitlessness, the proprietors ceded control of the territory back to the Crown and New Jersey became a royal colony.

Like New York (from which much of the population had come), New Jersey was a place of enormous ethnic and religious diversity. But unlike New York, New Jersey developed no important class of large landowners; most of its residents remained small farmers. Nor did New Jersey (which, unlike New York, had no natural harbor) produce any single major city.

THE QUAKER COLONIES

THE SOCIETY OF FRIENDS

Pennsylvania, like Massachusetts, was born out of the efforts of dissenting English Protestants to find a home for their own religion and their own distinctive social order. The Society of Friends (also known as "Quakers") originated in mid-seventeenth-century England and grew into an important force as a result of the preachings of George Fox, a Nottingham shoemaker, and Margaret Fell. Their followers came to be known as Quakers because Fox urged them to "tremble at the name of the Lord." Unlike the Puritans, Quakers rejected the concepts of predestination and original sin. All people had divinity within themselves (an "Inner Light," which could guide them along the path of righteousness), and all who cultivated that divinity could attain salvation. Also unlike the Puritans, Quakers granted women a position within the church generally equal to that of men. Women and men alike could become preachers and define church doctrine, an equality symbolized by the longtime partnership between Fox and Fell.

Of all the Protestant sectarians of the time, the Quakers were the most anarchistic and democratic. They had no church government, only periodic meetings of representatives from congregations. They had no paid clergy, and in their worship they spoke up one by one as the spirit moved them. Disregarding distinctions of gender and class, they addressed one another with the terms "thee" and "thou," words then commonly used in other parts of English society only in speaking to servants and social inferiors. And as confirmed pacifists, they refused to fight in wars. The Quakers were unpopular enough in England as a result of these beliefs and practices. They increased their unpopularity by occasionally breaking up other religious groups at worship. Many were jailed.

A QUAKER MEETING Egbert van Heemskerck the Elder (c. 1635–1704) was a painter from Haarlem, in the Netherlands, who worked in England from about 1675 until his death. His subject matter, familiar to the Dutch but new to English viewers of his time, features ordinary people in comic or everyday scenes. In this undated oil painting, van Heemskerck shows a gathering of Quakers. Because the Society of Friends, as the Quakers were formally known, believed that all people were equal in the eyes of God, they appointed no ministers and imposed no formal structure on their religious services.

Discussion and Activities

Comparing and Contrasting Have students read the section "The Society of Friends." Ask them to create a Venn diagram identifying similarities and differences between Quakerism and other Protestant sects. Ask students to speculate how those differences might have manifested in the development of Pennsylvania, founded on Quaker principles. **SOC**

As a result, like the Puritans before them, the Quakers looked to America for asylum. A few went to New England. But except in Rhode Island, they were greeted there with fines, whippings, and banishment; three men and a woman who refused to leave were put to death. Others migrated to northern Carolina, where they became the fastest-growing religious community in the region. They were soon influential in colonial politics. But many Quakers wanted a colony of their own. As a despised sect, they had little chance of getting the necessary royal grant without the aid of someone influential at court. But fortunately for Fox and his followers, a number of wealthy and prominent men had become attracted to the faith. One of them was William Penn–the son of an admiral in the Royal Navy who was a landlord of valuable Irish estates. He had received the gentleman's education expected of a person of his standing, but he resisted his father in moving to untraditional religions. Converted to the doctrine of the Inner Light, the younger Penn became an evangelist for Quakerism. With George Fox, he visited the European continent and found Quakers there who, like Quakers in England, longed to emigrate to the New World. He set out to find a place for them to go.

WILLIAM PENN

Penn turned his attention first to New Jersey and soon became an owner and proprietor of part of the colony. But in 1681, after the death of his father, Penn inherited his father's Irish lands and also his father's claim to a large debt from the king. Charles II, short of cash, paid the debt with a grant of territory between New York and Maryland–an area larger than England and Wales combined and which (unknown to him) contained more valuable soil and minerals than any other province of English America. Penn would have virtually total authority within the province. At the king's insistence, the territory was named Pennsylvania, after Penn's late father.

Like most proprietors, Penn wanted Pennsylvania to be profitable for him and his family. And so he set out to attract settlers from throughout Europe through informative and honest advertising in several languages. Pennsylvania soon became the best known of all the colonies among ordinary people in England and on the European continent, and also the most cosmopolitan. Settlers flocked to the province from throughout Europe, joining several hundred Swedes and Finns who had been living in a small trading colony–New Sweden–established in 1638 at the mouth of the Delaware River. But the colony was never profitable for Penn and his descendants. Indeed, Penn himself, near the end of his life, was imprisoned in England for debt and died in poverty in 1718.

Penn was more than a mere real estate promoter, however, and he sought to create in Pennsylvania what he called a holy experiment. In 1682, he sailed to America and supervised the laying out of a city between the Delaware and Schuylkill Rivers, which he named Philadelphia ("Brotherly Love"). With its rectangular streets, like those of Charles Town, Philadelphia helped set the pattern for most later cities in America. Penn believed, as had Roger Williams, that the land belonged to the Native American nations, and he was careful to see that they were reimbursed for it, as well as to see that they were not debauched by the fur traders' alcohol. The Native Americans, who respected Penn, had no major conflicts with Penn's colony during his lifetime. More than any other English colony, Pennsylvania prospered from the outset (even if its proprietor did not), because of Penn's successful recruitment of emigrants, his thoughtful planning, and the region's mild climate and fertile soil.

PENNSYLVANIA FOUNDED

Penn maintained good relations with the Native Americans owing to his religious beliefs. Quakerism was against participation in war or violence of any kind and held that all people, whatever their background, were capable of becoming Christian. Penn worked to respect Native Americans and their culture. He recognized Native American claims to the land in the province and was usually scrupulous in reimbursing them for their land. In later years, however, the relationships between the English residents of Pennsylvania and the Native Americans were not always peaceful.

By the late 1690s, some residents of Pennsylvania were beginning to resist the nearly absolute power of the proprietor. Southern residents in particular complained that the government in Philadelphia was unresponsive to their needs. As a result, a substantial opposition emerged to challenge Penn. Pressure from these groups grew to the point that in 1701, shortly before he departed for England for the last time, Penn agreed to a Charter of Liberties for the colony. The charter established a representative assembly (consisting, alone among the English colonies, of only one house), which greatly limited the authority of the proprietor. The charter also permitted "the lower counties" of the colony to establish their own representative assembly. The three counties did so in 1703 and, as a result, became a separate colony: Delaware–although until the American Revolution, it had the same governor as Pennsylvania.

CHARTER OF LIBERTIES

BORDERLANDS AND MIDDLE GROUNDS

The English colonies along the Atlantic seaboard of North America eventually united, expanded, and became the beginnings of a great nation. But in the seventeenth and early eighteenth centuries, they were small, frail settlements surrounded by other, competing societies. The British Empire in North America was, in fact, much smaller and weaker than the great Spanish Empire to the south, and not clearly stronger than the enormous French Empire to the north.

The continuing contest for control of North America, and the complex interactions among the diverse peoples populating the continent, were most clearly visible in areas around the borders of English settlement–the Caribbean and along the northern, southern, and western borders of the coastal colonies.

Historical Thinking Skills

Explaining Historical Developments Ask students to brainstorm a list of reasons why William Penn wanted to create a colony in America. In pairs or small groups, have them discuss the importance of each reason and rank them in order of importance. Then ask students to write a thesis statement that makes a historically defensible claim in response to the question: What were the most important reasons for the establishment of Pennsylvania? *(Possible responses: as a Quaker haven; a desire for profit; to establish peaceful relations with Native Americans, etc.)* **SOC** **WXT** **PCE**

Discussion and Activities

Analyzing Change Ask students to think about the government of Pennsylvania and how it evolved from a strong proprietorship to a colony with an autonomous assembly. Have students write a letter to William Penn advising him on how to best govern Pennsylvania. **PCE**

Reasoning Processes

Causation Have students read the section "Imperial Conflict." Then ask them to consider and discuss why colonists in the Caribbean largely turned to cultivation of sugar, rather than tobacco or cotton. *(Caribbean colonies depended on trade, and sugar was in high demand. It was also easily transportable in the form of molasses or rum.)* **WXT** **GEO** **WOR**

MAKING MOLASSES IN BARBADOS Enslaved Africans, who constituted the vast majority of the population of the flourishing sugar-producing island of Barbados, work here in a sugar mill grinding sugarcane and then boiling it to produce refined sugar, molasses, and—after a later distillation process not pictured here—rum.

THE CARIBBEAN ISLANDS

THE ENGLISH CARIBBEAN

Throughout the first half of the seventeenth century, the most important destination for English immigrants was not the mainland, but rather the islands of the Caribbean and the northern way station of Bermuda. More than half the English migrants to the New World in those years settled on these islands. The island societies had close ties to English North America from the beginning and influenced the development of the mainland colonies in several ways. But they were also surrounded by, and sometimes imperiled by, outposts of the Spanish Empire.

IMPERIAL CONFLICT

Before the arrival of Europeans, most of the Caribbean islands had substantial indigenous populations–the Arawaks, the Caribs, and the Ciboney. But beginning with Christopher Columbus's first visit in 1492, and accelerating after the Spanish established their first colony on Hispaniola in 1496, the indigenous population was all but wiped out by European epidemics. The indigenous populations were never a significant factor in European settlement of the Caribbean. Indeed, by the time significant European settlement of the islands began, many were almost entirely deserted.

The Spanish Empire claimed title to all the islands in the Caribbean, but there was substantial Spanish settlement only on the largest of them: Cuba, Hispaniola, and Puerto Rico. English, French, and Dutch traders began settling on some of the smaller islands early in the sixteenth century, although these weak colonies were always vulnerable to Spanish attack. After Spain and the Netherlands went to war in 1621 (distracting the Spanish navy and leaving the English in the Caribbean relatively unmolested), the pace of English colonization increased. By midcentury, there were several substantial English settlements on the islands, the most important of them on Antigua, St. Kitts, Jamaica, and Barbados. Even so, through the seventeenth century, the English settlements in the Caribbean were the targets of almost constant attacks and invasions by the Spanish, the Portuguese, the French, the Dutch, and the remaining indigenous people of the region. The world of the Caribbean was a violent and turbulent place.

The Caribbean colonies built their economies on raising crops for export. In the early years, English settlers experimented unsuccessfully with tobacco and cotton. But they soon discovered that the most lucrative crop was sugar, for which there was a substantial and growing market in Europe. Sugarcane could also be distilled into rum, for which there was a booming market abroad. Within a decade of the introduction of sugar cultivation to the West Indies, planters were devoting almost all of their land to sugarcane. In their appetite for more land for sugarcane, they cut down forests and destroyed the natural habitats of many animals, which greatly reduced the amount of land available for growing food.

Discussion and Activities

Analyzing Visuals Have students examine the image "Making Molasses in Barbados." Ask them to make a T-chart to compile information about what is visible in the image about the production of molasses and what is not pictured. *(Pictured: grinding sugarcane, boiling the juice. Not pictured: growing sugarcane, distilling rum)* Ask students to speculate about which of these activities would be the most labor-intensive. **WXT**

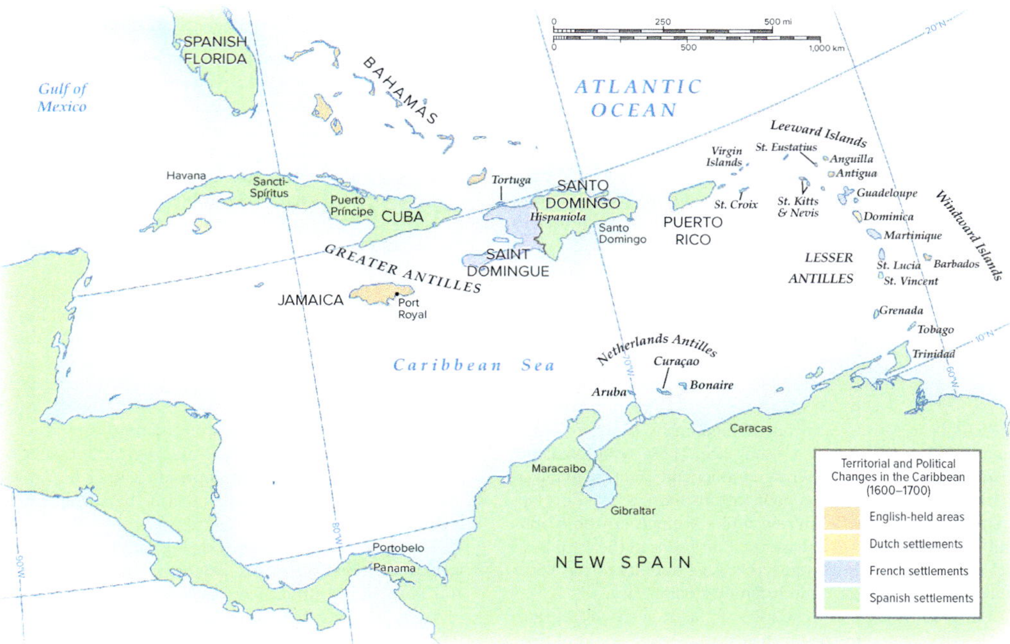

THE SEVENTEENTH-CENTURY CARIBBEAN At the same time that European powers were expanding their colonial presence on the mainland of the American continents, they were also establishing colonies in the islands of the Caribbean. In some cases, these islands were even more important to the Atlantic economy than many of the mainland possessions, particularly the large, heavily populated sugar-growing islands (among them Jamaica and Barbados), in which the majority of the population consisted of enslaved Africans.

What role did the Caribbean islands play in the spread of slavery in North America?

Because sugar was a labor-intensive crop, and because the remnant of the indigenous population was too small to provide a workforce, English planters soon found it necessary to import laborers. As in the Chesapeake, they began by bringing indentured servants from England. But the arduous work discouraged white laborers; many found it impossible to adapt to the harsh tropical climate so different from that of England. By midcentury, therefore, the English planters in the Caribbean (like the Spanish colonists who preceded them) were relying more and more on an enslaved African workforce, which soon substantially outnumbered them.

SUGAR AND SLAVERY

On Barbados and other islands where a flourishing sugar economy developed, the English planters were a tough, aggressive, and ambitious breed. Some of them grew enormously wealthy; and since their livelihoods depended on their workforces, they expanded and solidified the system of African slavery there remarkably quickly. By the late seventeenth century, there were four times as many enslaved Africans as there were white settlers. By then the West Indies had ceased to be an attractive destination for ordinary English immigrants; most now went to the colonies on the North American mainland instead.

SLAVERY IN THE CARIBBEAN

SLAVE REVOLTS

A small, mostly wealthy white population and a large enslaved African population made for a potentially explosive combination. As in other English colonies in the New World in which enslaved Africans came to outnumber Europeans, white settlers in the Caribbean grew fearful of slave revolts. They had good reason, for there were at least seven major slave revolts in the islands, more than the English colonies of North America experienced in their entire history as slave societies. As a result, white planters monitored enslaved laborers closely and often harshly. Beginning in the 1660s, all the islands enacted legal codes to regulate relations between slaveholders and enslaved people and to give white people absolute authority over enslaved Africans. A slaveholder could even murder an enslaved person with virtual impunity.

Discussion and Activities

Analyzing Points of View After students have read the section "Sugar and Slavery," ask them to think about the various sources of labor available to Caribbean sugar producers. *(indigenous persons, indentured servants, free laborers, enslaved persons)* Then ask students to consider the environmental damaged that sugar production caused. Instruct students to write a brief summary of the costs of sugar cultivation. **WXT** **GEO** **SOC**

Answers

The Seventeenth-Century Caribbean

Sugar was a highly profitable and very labor-intensive crop. Plantation owners believed the enslaved Africans were the cheapest and most reliable source of labor available. The harsh climate and difficult working conditions led to high mortality among the work force, necessitating the constant replenishment of the supply of enslaved Africans.

Historical Thinking Skills

Evaluating Evidence Have students read the section "Unstable Societies." Ask them to make a list of factors that contributed to instability and then rank their lists in order of importance. Have students then write a thesis statement that makes a historically defensible claim about what the most important causes of societal instability in the Caribbean were. Have them share their thesis with a partner, and have the partners give feedback to each other. SOC WXT GEO

There was little either in the law or in the character of the economy to compel planters to pay much attention to the welfare of their workers. Many white slaveholders concluded that it was cheaper to buy enslaved people periodically than to protect the well-being of those they already owned, and it was not uncommon for slaveholders to work enslaved people to death. Few enslaved Africans survived more than a decade in the brutal Caribbean working environment–they either were sold to planters in North America or died. White settlers and laborers, who were subjected to far less brutal conditions than enslaved Africans, often succumbed to the harsh climate; most died before the age of forty–often from tropical diseases to which they had no immunity.

Establishing a stable society and culture was extremely difficult for people living in such harsh and even deadly conditions. Many of the white settlers were principally interested in getting rich and had no long-term commitment to the islands.

UNSTABLE SOCIETIES

Those who could returned to England with their fortunes and left their estates in the hands of overseers. A large proportion of the European settlers were single men, many of whom either died or left the islands at a young age. Those who remained, many of them common white farmers and laborers living in extreme poverty, were too poor to contribute to the development of the society. With few white women on the islands and little with interracial marriage, Europeans in the Caribbean lacked many of the institutions that gave stability to the North American settlements: church, family, community.

Enslaved Africans in the Caribbean faced even greater difficulties, of course, but they managed to create a world of their own despite the hardships. They started families (although many of them were broken up by death or the slave trade); they sustained African religious and social traditions (and showed little interest in Christianity); and within the rigidly controlled world of the sugar plantations, they established patterns of resistance.

The Caribbean settlements were connected to the North American colonies in many ways. They were an important part

CONNECTION TO BRITISH NORTH AMERICA

of the Atlantic trading world in which many Americans became involved–a source of sugar and rum and a market for goods made in the mainland colonies and in England. They were the principal source of enslaved Africans for the mainland colonies; well over half the enslaved people in North America came from the islands, not directly from Africa. And because Caribbean planters established an elaborate plantation system earlier than planters in North America, they provided models that many mainland people consciously or unconsciously copied. In the American South, too, planters grew wealthy at the expense of poor whites and, above all, of enslaved Africans.

THE SOUTHWESTERN BORDERLANDS

By the end of the seventeenth century, the Spanish Empire had established only a small presence in the regions that became the United States. In Mexico and regions farther south, however, the Spanish had established a sophisticated and impressive empire. Their capital, Mexico City, was the most dazzling metropolis in the Americas. The Spanish residents, numbering well over a million, enjoyed much greater prosperity than all but a few English settlers in North America.

The principal Spanish colonies north of Mexico–Florida, Texas, New Mexico, Arizona, and California–attracted religious

SPAIN'S NORTHERN COLONIES

minorities, Catholic missionaries, independent ranchers fleeing the heavy hand of imperial authority, and Spanish troops defending the northern flank of the empire. These colonies remained weak and peripheral parts of the great empire to their south.

New Mexico was the most prosperous and populous of these Spanish outposts. Once the Spanish quelled the Pueblo revolt there in 1680, they worked effectively with the Native Americans of the region to develop a flourishing agriculture. By the early nineteenth century, New Mexico had a non-Indian population of over 10,000–the largest European settlement west of the Mississippi and north of Mexico–and it was steadily expanding through the region. But New Mexico was prosperous only when compared to other borderlands. Its residents were far less successful than the Spanish in Mexico and other more densely settled regions.

The Spanish began to colonize California once they realized that other Europeans–among them English merchants and French and Russian trappers–were beginning to estab-

CALIFORNIA

lish a presence in the region. Formal Spanish settlement of California began in the 1760s, when the governor of Baja California was ordered to create outposts of the empire farther north. Soon a string of missions, forts (or *presidios*), and trading communities were springing up along the Pacific coast, beginning with San Diego and Monterey in 1769 and eventually San Francisco (1776), Los Angeles (1781), and Santa Barbara (1786). As in other areas of European settlement, the arrival of the Spanish in California (and the diseases they imported) had a devastating effect on the Native American population. Approximately 65,000 at the time of the first Spanish settlements, by 1820 it had declined by two-thirds. As the new settlements spread, however, the Spanish insisted that the remaining Native Americans convert to Catholicism. That explains the centrality of missions in almost all the major Spanish outposts in California. But the Spanish colonists were also intent on creating a prosperous agricultural economy, and they forced Native Americans to help them do so. The Native Americans had no choice but to accede to the demands of the Spanish, although there were frequent revolts by Native Americans against the harsh conditions imposed upon them. Already decimated by disease, the Native American populations of the area declined further as a result of malnutrition and overwork at the hands of the Spanish missions.

In the late seventeenth and early eighteenth centuries, the Spanish considered the greatest threat to the northern borders of their empire to be the growing ambitions of the French. In

Discussion and Activities

Comparing and Contrasting Have students read the sections "Spain's Northern Colonies" and "California." Ask them as a class to compile a list of similarities and differences between the Spanish colonies in New Mexico and California. Ask students to discuss which were more prominent, the similarities of the differences. SOC WXT GEO the 1680s, French explorers traveled down the Mississippi Valley to the mouth of the river and claimed the lands they had traversed for their king, Louis XIV. They called the territory Louisiana. Fearful of French incursions farther west, and unsettled by the nomadic Native Americans driven into the territory by the French, the Spanish began to fortify their claim to Texas by establishing new forts, missions, and settlements there, including San Fernando (later San Antonio) in 1731. The region that is now Arizona was also becoming increasingly tied to the Spanish Empire. Northern Arizona was a part of the New Mexico colony and was governed from Santa Fe. The rest of Arizona (from Phoenix south) was controlled by the Mexican region of Sonora. As in California, much of the impetus for these settlements came from Catholic missionaries (in this case Jesuits), eager to convert the Native Americans to Catholicism. But the missionary project met with little success. Unlike the sedentary Pueblos around Santa Fe, the Arizona Native Americans were nomadic peoples, unlikely to settle down or to Christianize, frequently at war with rival groups, and—like Native Americans elsewhere—tragically vulnerable to smallpox, measles, and other imported diseases. As in California, epidemics reduced the Native American population of Arizona by two-thirds in the early eighteenth century.

Although peripheral to the great Spanish Empire to the south, the Spanish colonies in the Southwest nevertheless helped create enduring societies very unlike those being established by the English along the Atlantic seaboard. The Spanish colonies were committed not to displacing the Native American populations but, rather, to enlisting them. They sought to convert them to Catholicism, to recruit them (sometimes forcibly) as agricultural workers, and to cultivate them as trading partners. The Spanish did not consider the Native Americans to be their equals, certainly, and they did not treat them very well. But neither did they consider them merely as obstacles to their own designs, as many English settlers along the Atlantic seaboard did.

IMPORTANCE OF THE SPANISH BORDERLANDS

THE SOUTHEASTERN BORDERLANDS

A more direct challenge to English ambitions in North America was the Spanish presence in the southeastern areas of what is now the United States. After the establishment of the Spanish claim to Florida in the 1560s, missionaries and traders began moving northward into Georgia and westward into what is now known as the panhandle. Some ambitious Spaniards began to dream of expanding their empire still farther north, into what became the Carolinas, and perhaps beyond. The founding of Jamestown in 1607 replaced those dreams with fears. The English colonies, they believed, could threaten their existing settlements in Florida and Georgia. As a result, the Spanish built forts in both regions to defend themselves against the slowly increasing English presence there. Throughout the eighteenth century, the area between the Carolinas and Florida was the site of continuing tension, and frequent conflict, between the Spanish and the English—and, to a lesser degree, between the Spanish and the French, who were threatening their northwestern borders with settlements in Louisiana and in what is now Alabama.

There was no formal war between England and Spain in these years, but that did not dampen the hostilities in the Southeast. English pirates continually harassed the Spanish settlements and, in 1668, sacked St. Augustine. Both sides in this conflict sought to make use of the Native Americans. The English encouraged Native Americans in Florida to rise up against the Spanish missions. The Spanish, for their part, offered freedom to enslaved Africans held by Carolina settlers if they agreed to convert to Catholicism. About 100 enslaved Africans accepted the offer, and the Spanish later organized some of them into a military regiment to defend the northern border of New Spain. The English correctly viewed the Spanish recruitment of enslaved people as an effort to undermine their economy. By the early eighteenth century, the constant fighting in the region had driven almost all the Spanish settlers out of Florida. The Spanish presence became almost entirely confined to St. Augustine on the Atlantic coast to Pensacola on the Gulf Coast, and to the modest colonies that surrounded the forts there. Because they were so few and so weak, they came to rely—far more than most British did—on Native Americans and Africans and intermarried frequently with them.

HOSTILITIES IN THE SOUTHEAST

Eventually, after more than a century of conflict in the southeastern borderlands, the English prevailed—acquiring Florida in the aftermath of the Seven Years' War (known in America as the French and Indian War) and rapidly populating it with settlers from their colonies to the north. Before that point, however, protecting the southern boundary of the British Empire in North America was a continual concern to the English and contributed in crucial ways to the founding of the colony of Georgia.

THE FOUNDING OF GEORGIA

Georgia was unique in its origins. Its founders were a group of unpaid trustees led by General James Oglethorpe, a member of Parliament and military hero. They were interested in economic success, but they were driven primarily by military and philanthropic motives. They wanted to erect a military barrier against the Spanish lands on the southern border of English America, and they wanted to provide a refuge for the impoverished, a place where English men and women without prospects at home could begin anew.

JAMES OGLETHORPE'S VISION

The need for a military buffer between South Carolina and the Spanish settlements in Florida was particularly urgent in the first years of the eighteenth century. In a 1676 treaty, Spain had recognized England's title to lands already occupied by English settlers. But conflict between the two colonizing powers had continued. In 1686, a force of Native Americans and Creoles from Florida, directed by Spanish agents, attacked

Discussion and Activities

Explaining Significance Have students read the section "Importance of the Spanish Borderlands." Ask them to discuss why the Spanish borderlands were important to the Spanish empire in the Americas. Have students speculate about how the empire might have been different if this area was not Spanish controlled. **GEO** **WOR**

Reasoning Processes

Comparing and Contrasting Have students read the section "The Southeastern Borderlands." Then have them compare the Southeastern borderlands in this section to the Southwestern borderlands students read about previously. Ask them to write a thesis statement that makes a claim as to which region was more important to Spain. **GEO**

AP Exam Tip

When answering the short-answer questions, students must respond directly to each part of the prompt with a historically defensible claim. The claim then must be supported with specific, relevant evidence.

Historical Thinking Skills

Make a Historically Defensible Claim Have students practice the skill by responding to the following short-answer questions:

A) Briefly explain ONE important motive for English colonization in the Americas. *(Land, economic opportunity, religious freedom, political freedom)*

B) Briefly explain ONE important motive for Spanish colonization in the Americas. *(Land, economic opportunity, political freedom)*

C) Briefly explain ONE important difference in the motives for English and Spanish colonization. *(Few Spanish settlers came to the New World seeking religious liberty.)*

DEBATING THE PAST

NATIVE AMERICANS AND THE "MIDDLE GROUND"

For many generations, historians chronicling the westward movement of European settlement in North America incorporated Native Americans into the story largely as weak and inconvenient obstacles swept aside by the inevitable progress of "civilization." Native Americans were presented either as murderous savages or as relatively docile allies of white people, but rarely as important actors of their own. Francis Parkman, the great nineteenth-century American historian, described Native Americans as a civilization "crushed" and "scorned" by the march of European powers in the New World. Many subsequent historians departed little from his assessment.

Challenges to this traditional view have come from many more-recent historians—among them, Gary Nash in *Red, White, and Black* (1974) and Ramón Gutiérrez in *When Jesus Came, the Corn Mothers Went Away* (1991). They, and other scholars, rejected the optimistic, progressive view of white triumph over adversity and presented, instead, a picture of conquest that affected both the conqueror and the conquered and did not bring to an end their influence on one another.

A new, more recent view of the relationship between the peoples of the Old and New Worlds sees Native Americans and Euro-Americans as uneasy partners in the shaping of a new society in which, for a time at least, both were a vital part. In *The Middle Ground* (1991), Richard White examined the culture of the Great Lakes region in the eighteenth century, in which Algonquin Indians created complex trading and political relationships with French, English, and American settlers and travelers in the region. In this "borderland" between the growing European settlements in the East and the still largely intact Native American civilizations farther west, a new kind of hybrid society emerged in which many cultures intermingled. In *Into the American Woods* (1999), James Merrell examined the world of negotiators and go-betweens along the western Pennsylvania frontier in the seventeenth and eighteenth centuries. Like White, he emphasized the complicated blend of European and Native American diplomatic rituals that allowed both groups to conduct business, make treaties, and keep the peace.

Daniel Richter extended the idea of a "middle ground" further in *The Ordeal of the Longhouse* (1992) and *Facing East from Indian Country* (2001). Richter demonstrates that the Iroquois Confederacy was an active participant in the power relationships in the Hudson River basin. In his later book, he tells the story of European colonization from the Native American perspective, revealing how western myths of "first contact" such as the story of John Smith and Pocahontas look entirely different when seen through the eyes of Native Americans, who remained in many ways the more powerful of the two societies in the seventeenth century.

How did these important collaborations collapse? What happened to the "middle ground"? Over time, the delicate partnerships along the frontiers of white settlement gave way to the sheer numbers of Europeans (and, in some places, Africans) who moved westward. Joyce Chaplin in *Subject Matter* (2001) argued as well that Old World Americans at first admired the Native Americans as a kind of natural nobility until European diseases ravaged them, helping strengthen the Europeans' sense of superiority that had been a part of their view of Native Americans from the beginning. In *The Name of War* (1998), Jill Lepore described how the violence of King Philip's War in seventeenth-century New England helped transform English views of the Native American nations both because of the white victory and because of their success in turning this victory into a rationale for the moral superiority of Europeans by portraying the Native Americans as brutal, uncivilized people. (In reality, the Europeans had used as much "savagery" against the Native Americans as the Native Americans had used against them.) As the pressures of white settlement grew, as the Native American populations weakened as a result of disease and war, and as the relationship between Native American nations and the European settlers grew increasingly unequal, the cultural "middle ground" that for many decades characterized much of the contact between the Old and New Worlds gradually disappeared. By the time historians began seriously chronicling this story in the late nineteenth century, the Native American nations had indeed become the defeated, helpless "obstacles" that they portrayed. But for generations before, the relationship between white Americans and Native Americans was a much less unequal one than it would later become.

TRADING PARTNERS *Ralph Hamor Visits Powhatan with a Proposal* is an etching by Theodor de Bry (1528–1598) showing how Europeans and Native Americans sometimes made economic deals for mutual gain.

HISTORICAL THINKING SKILLS

Questions assume cumulative content knowledge from this chapter and previous chapters.

1. **Identifying Historical Developments** Identify two historical views regarding the relationship between Native Americans and the European settlers.
2. **Explaining Historical Concepts** Explain what it means when historians talk about a "middle ground."
3. **Developing Arguments** If you were writing a history of European settlement in North America, which event would you consider the most significant turning point in the relationship between Native Americans and European settlers? Explain.

Answers

Debating the Past

1. First, Francis Parkman described Native Americans as a civilization "crushed" and "scorned" by the march of European powers in the New World. Second, Gary Nash challenged the traditional view by rejecting the optimistic view of European triumph over adversity and presented, instead, a picture of conquest that affected both the conquerors and the conquered.
2. Richard White captured the phrase in his book where he views the relationship between peoples of the Old and New Worlds as uneasy partners in the shaping of a new society in which, for a time at least, both were a vital part. In this "borderland" between the growing European settlements in the East and the still largely intact Native American civilizations farther west, a new kind of hybrid society emerged in which many cultures intermingled.
3. Possible response: A significant turning point was King Philips's War, in which the technological skills of the Native Americans proved no match for the overwhelming advantages of the English settlers in both numbers and firepower. It has been argued that the conclusion of this war marked the beginning of the development of an American identity, as the colonists largely fought this war without any European help.

and destroyed an outlying South Carolina settlement south of the treaty line. And when hostilities broke out again between Spain and England in 1701 (known in England as Queen Anne's War and on the Continent as the War of the Spanish Succession), the fighting renewed in America as well.

Oglethorpe, a veteran of Queen Anne's War, was keenly aware of the military advantages of an English colony south of the Carolinas. Yet his interest in settlement rested even more on his philanthropic commitments. As head of a parliamentary committee investigating English prisons, he had grown appalled by the plight of honest debtors dying in confinement. Such prisoners, and other poor people in danger of succumbing to a similar fate, could, he believed, become the farmer-soldiers of the new colony in America.

In 1732, King George II granted Oglethorpe and his fellow trustees control of the land between the Savannah and Altamaha Rivers. Their colonization policies reflected the vital military purposes of the colony. They limited the size of landholdings to make the settlement compact and easier to defend against Spanish and Native American attacks. They excluded Africans, free or enslaved; Oglethorpe feared slave labor would produce internal revolts and that disaffected enslaved people might turn to the Spanish as allies. The trustees prohibited rum (both because Oglethorpe disapproved of it on moral grounds and because the trustees feared its effects on the Native Americans). They strictly regulated trade with the Native Americans, again to limit the possibility of wartime insurrection. They also excluded Catholics for fear they might collude with their coreligionists in the Spanish colonies to the south.

GEORGIA'S MILITARY RATIONALE

Oglethorpe himself led the first colonial expedition to Georgia, which built a fortified town at the mouth of the Savannah River in 1733 and later constructed additional forts south of the Altamaha. In the end, only a few debtors were released from jail and sent to Georgia. Instead, the trustees brought hundreds of impoverished tradesmen and artisans from England and Scotland and many religious refugees from Switzerland and Germany. Among the immigrants was a small group of Jews. English settlers made up a lower proportion of the European population of Georgia than of any other English colony.

The strict rules governing life in the new colony stifled its early development and ensured the failure of Oglethorpe's vision. Settlers in Georgia—many of whom were engaged in labor-intensive agriculture—needed a workforce as much as those in other southern colonies. Almost from the start they began demanding the right to buy enslaved Africans. Some opposed the restrictions on the size of individual property holdings. Many resented the nearly absolute political power of Oglethorpe and the trustees. As a result, newcomers to the region generally preferred to settle in South Carolina, where there were fewer restrictive laws.

Oglethorpe (whom some residents of Georgia began calling "our perpetual dictator") at first bitterly resisted the demands of

GENERAL JAMES OGLETHORPE Oglethorpe was one of the founders of the English colony of Georgia. He and his followers established the colony to stand as a military buffer between South Carolina and the Spanish settlements in Florida. They also wanted a refuge for British men and women without economic prospects in England.

the settlers for social and political reform. Over time, however, he wearied of the conflict in the colony and grew frustrated at its failure to grow. He also suffered military disappointments, such as a 1740 assault on the Spanish outpost at St. Augustine, Florida, which ended in failure. Oglethorpe, now disillusioned with his American venture, began to loosen his grip. Even before the 1740 defeat, the trustees had removed the limitation on individual landholdings. In 1750, they removed the ban on slavery. A year later they ended the prohibition of rum and returned control of the colony to the king, who immediately permitted the summoning of a representative assembly. Georgia continued to grow more slowly than the other southern colonies, but in other ways it now developed along lines roughly similar to those of South Carolina. By 1770, there were over 20,000 non-Indian residents of the colony, nearly half of them enslaved Africans.

TRANSFORMATION OF GEORGIA

MIDDLE GROUNDS

The struggle for the North American continent was, of course, not just one among competing European empires. It was also a contest between the new European immigrants and the Native American populations.

In some parts of the British Empire—Virginia and New England, for example—English settlers quickly established their dominance, subjugating and displacing most Native Americans until they had established societies that were dominated almost entirely by Europeans. But elsewhere the balance of power remained far more precarious. Along the western

CONFLICT AND ACCOMMODATION

Historical Thinking Skills

Evaluating Arguments After students read the section "The Founding of Georgia," ask them to identify a significant claim that the text makes concerning the founding of the Georgia colony. Then ask students to identify evidence from the text that supports the claim. **GEO** **MIG** **SOC** **ARC**

Discussion and Activities

Speculating After students read the section "The Founding of Georgia," ask them to consider how life in the Georgia colony may have been different from life in other English colonies based on the reasons for settlement and the immigrants who settled there. Have students pair up to share their thoughts. Afterward, bring the class together and have each pair share an example that they discussed. **SOC** **WXT**

Reasoning Processes

Continuity and Change After students read the section "Middle Grounds," ask them to create a time line that includes events between English settlers and Native Americans. Have them circle events on their time line that indicate a change over time. Then have students evaluate whether relations between the English settlers and Native Americans were characterized more by continuity or change. **MIG** **PCE**

borders of English settlement, in particular, Europeans and Native Americans lived together in regions in which neither side was able to establish clear dominance. In these "middle grounds," as they have been called, the two populations–despite frequent conflicts–carved out ways of living together, with each side making concessions to the other. Here the Europeans found themselves obliged to adapt to Native American expectations at least as much as the Native Americans had to adapt to European ones.

To the Native Americans, the European migrants were both menacing and appealing. The Native Americans feared the power of these strange people: their guns, their rifles, their forts. But they also wanted the French and British settlers to behave like "fathers"–to help them mediate their own internal disputes, to offer them gifts, to help them moderate their conflicts. Europeans came from a world in which the formal institutional and military power of a nation or empire governed relationships between societies. But Native Americans had no understanding of the modern notion of a "nation" and thought much more in terms of ceremony and kinship. Gradually, Europeans learned to fulfill at least some of their expectations.

In the seventeenth century, before many English settlers had entered the interior of the continent, the French were particularly adept at creating mutually beneficial relationships with the Native Americans. They welcomed the chance to form close relationships with–even to marry within–the Native American communities. They also recognized the importance of treating tribal chiefs with respect and channeling gifts and tributes through them. But by the mid-eighteenth century, French influence in the interior was in decline, and British settlers gradually became the dominant European group in the "middle grounds." It took the British a considerable time to learn the lessons the French had long ago absorbed–that simple commands and raw force were much less effective in creating a workable relationship with the tribes than were gifts and ceremonies and mediation. Eventually they did so, and in large western regions–especially those around the Great Lakes–they established a precarious peace with the Native American nations that lasted for several decades.

MUTUALLY BENEFICIAL RELATIONS

But as the British and (after 1776) American presence in the region grew, the balance of power between Europeans and Native Americans shifted. Newer settlers had difficulty adapting to the complex rituals of gift-giving and mediation that the earlier migrants had developed. The stability of the relationship between the Native Americans and white settlers deteriorated. By the early nineteenth century, the "middle grounds" had collapsed, replaced by a European world in which Native Americans were ruthlessly subjugated and eventually removed. Nevertheless, it is important to recognize that for a considerable period of early American history, the story of the relationship between white settlers and Native Americans was not simply a story of conquest and subjugation, but also–in some regions–a story of a difficult but stable accommodation and mutual adaptation. The Native Americans were not simply victims in the story of the growth of European settlement in North America. They were also important actors, sometimes obstructing and sometimes facilitating the development of the new societies.

THE SHIFTING BALANCE

THE EVOLUTION OF THE BRITISH EMPIRE

The English colonies in America had originated as separate projects, and for the most part they grew up independent of one another. But by the mid-seventeenth century, the growing commercial success of the colonial ventures was producing pressure in England for a more rational, uniform structure to the empire.

THE DRIVE FOR REORGANIZATION

Imperial reorganization, many people in England claimed, would increase the profitability of the colonies and the power of the English government to supervise them. Above all, it would contribute to the success of the mercantile system, the foundation of the English economy. Colonies would provide a market for England's manufactured goods and a source for raw materials it could not produce at home, thus increasing the total wealth of the nation. But for the new possessions truly to promote mercantilist goals, England would have to exclude foreigners (as Spain had done) from its colonial trade. According to mercantilist theory, any wealth flowing to another nation could come only at the expense of England itself. Hence the British government sought to monopolize trade relations with its colonies.

MERCANTILISM

In theory, the mercantile system offered benefits to the colonies as well by providing them with a ready market for the raw materials they produced and a source for the manufactured goods they did not. But some colonial goods were not suitable for export to England, which produced wheat, flour, and fish and had no interest in obtaining them from America. Colonists also found it more profitable at times to trade with the Spanish, French, or Dutch even in goods that England did import. Thus, a considerable trade soon developed between the English colonies and non-English markets.

For a time, the English government made no serious efforts to restrict this challenge to the principles of mercantilism. But London began passing laws to regulate colonial trade. During Oliver Cromwell's "Protectorate," in 1650 and 1651, Parliament passed laws to keep Dutch ships out of the English colonies. After the Restoration, the government of Charles II adopted three Navigation Acts designed to regulate colonial commerce even more strictly. The first of them, in 1660, closed the colonies to all trade except that carried in English ships. This law also required the colonists to export certain items, among them tobacco, only to England or English possessions. The second act, in 1663, provided that all goods being shipped from Europe to the colonies had to pass through England on the way; that would make it possible for England to tax them. The third act, in 1673, was a response to

THE NAVIGATION ACTS

Discussion and Activities

Analyzing Cause and Effect Have students read the section "Mercantilism." Ask them to create a T-chart listing motives for mercantilism on one side and effects of mercantilism on the other. Then have students discuss whether mercantilism had the effects the British government intended. Ask them to conclude by writing a short paragraph explaining why mercantilism either did or did not produce the intended results. **WXT** **PCE** **WOR**

Historical Thinking Skills

Argumentation After students have read the section "The Navigation Acts," ask them to brainstorm a list of advantages and disadvantages that the acts presented to the colonists. Have students pair up to divide the list. Give pairs a few minutes to develop a 30-second "elevator pitch" designed to persuade each other that the Navigation Acts were either good for or bad for the colonies. **PCE** **WXT** **WOR**

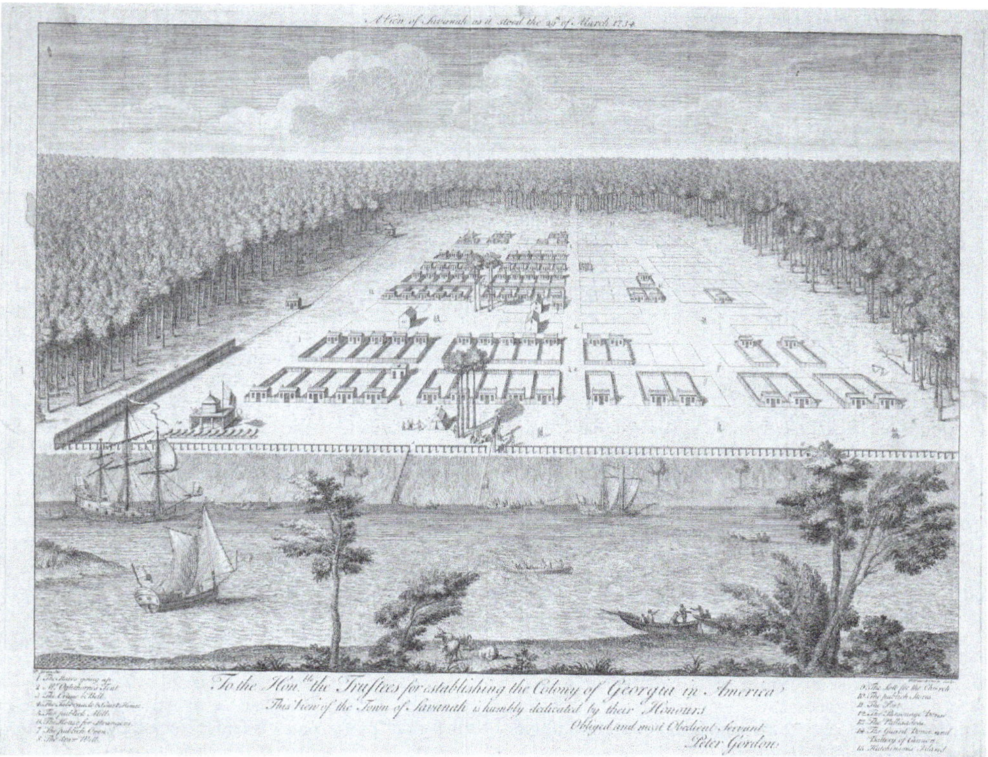

SAVANNAH IN 1734 This early view of the English settlement at Savannah by an English artist shows the intensely orderly character of Georgia in the early moments of European settlement there. As the colony grew, its residents gradually abandoned the rigid plan created by Georgia's founders.

Smith Collection/Gado/Archive Photos/Getty Images

the widespread evasion of the first two laws by the colonial shippers, who frequently left port claiming to be heading for another English colony but then sailed to a foreign port. It imposed duties on the coastal trade among the English colonies, and it provided for the appointment of customs officials to enforce the Navigation Acts. These acts formed the legal basis of England's mercantile system in America for a century.

The system created by the Navigation Acts had obvious advantages for England. But it had some advantages for the colonists as well. By restricting all trade to British ships, the laws encouraged the colonists (who were themselves legally British subjects) to create an important shipbuilding industry of their own. And because the English wanted to import as many goods as possible from their own colonies (as opposed to importing them from rival nations), they encouraged—and at times subsidized—the development of American production of goods they needed, among them iron, silk, and lumber. Despite the bitter complaints the laws provoked in America in the late seventeenth century, and the bitter conflicts they would help to provoke decades later, the system of the Navigation Acts served the interests of the British and the Americans alike reasonably well through most of the eighteenth century.

THE DOMINION OF NEW ENGLAND

Enforcement of the Navigation Acts required not only the stationing of customs officials in America, but also the establishment of an agency in England to oversee colonial affairs. In 1679, Charles II attempted to increase his control over Massachusetts (which behaved at times as if its leaders considered it an independent nation) by stripping the colony of its authority over New Hampshire and chartering a separate, royal colony there whose governor he would himself appoint. Five years later, after the Massachusetts General Court defied instructions from Parliament to enforce the Navigation Acts, Charles revoked the Massachusetts corporate charter and made it a royal colony.

Discussion and Activities

Analyzing Visuals Have students examine the image "Savannah in 1734," then compare it to the map "Charles Town, South Carolina." What similarities and differences can they identify? *(Similarities: Both show very orderly English settlements, and both indicate the English settlement is a port. Differences: no Native American settlement is indicated on the Savannah image.)* Ask students to discuss what might account for the difference. *(Possible response: The English artist may not have thought it important to portray Native American activity.)* **PCE** **MIG**

Historical Thinking Skills

Argumentation After students have read the section "The Dominion of New England," ask them to think about the reasons for the creation of the Dominion and its effectiveness. Have students write a short letter to King Charles II advising him on whether to maintain or disband the Dominion of New England, making sure to include specific examples and evidence in support of their argument. PCE ARC

Charles II's brother and successor, James II, who came to the throne in 1685, went much further. In 1686, he created a single Dominion of New England, which combined the government of Massachusetts with the governments of the rest of the New England colonies and, in 1688, with those of New York and New Jersey as well. He eliminated the existing assemblies within the new Dominion and appointed a single governor, Sir Edmund Andros, to supervise the entire region from Boston. Andros was an able administrator but a stern and tactless man; his rigid enforcement of the Navigation Acts, his brusque dismissal of the colonists' claims to the "rights of Englishmen," and his crude and arbitrary tactics made him highly unpopular. He was particularly despised in Massachusetts, where he tried to strengthen the Anglican Church.

SIR EDMUND ANDROS

THE "GLORIOUS REVOLUTION"

James II, unlike his father, was openly Catholic. Not only that, he made powerful enemies as he appointed his fellow Catholics to high offices. The restoration of Catholicism led to fears among Protestants that the pope would soon overtake England and that the king would defer to him. At the same time, James II tried to control Parliament and the courts to make himself an absolute monarch. By 1688, the opposition to the king was so great that the Parliament voted to force James II from the throne. James didn't resist giving up the crown, remembering his grandfather's execution. He eventually left the country and spent the rest of his life in France. His daughter, Mary II, and her husband, William of Orange of the Netherlands–both Protestants–replaced James II to reign jointly. No Catholic monarch has reigned since. This bloodless coup came to be known as the "Glorious Revolution."

When Bostonians heard of the overthrow of James II, they moved quickly to unseat his unpopular viceroy in New England. Andros managed to escape an angry mob, but he was arrested and imprisoned as he sought to flee the city dressed as a woman. The new sovereigns in England chose not to contest the toppling of Andros and quickly acquiesced in what the colonists had, in effect, already done: abolishing the Dominion of New England and restoring separate colonial governments. They did not, however, accede to all the colonists' desires. In 1691, they combined Massachusetts with Plymouth and made it a royal colony. The new charter restored the General Court (Massachusetts's legislature), but it gave the Crown the right to appoint the governor. It also replaced church membership with property ownership as the basis for voting and officeholding and required the Puritan leaders of the colony to tolerate Anglican worship.

END OF THE DOMINION

Andros had been governing New York through a lieutenant governor, Captain Francis Nicholson, who enjoyed the support of the wealthy merchants and fur traders of the province–the same groups who had dominated the colony for years. Other, less favored colonists–farmers, mechanics, small traders, and shopkeepers–had a long accumulation of grievances against both Nicholson and his allies. The leader of the New York dissidents was Jacob Leisler, a German immigrant and a prosperous merchant who had married into a prominent Dutch family but had never won acceptance as one of the colony's ruling class. Much like Nathaniel Bacon in Virginia, the ambitious Leisler resented his exclusion and eagerly grasped the opportunity to challenge the colonial elite. In May 1689, when news of the Glorious Revolution in England and the fall of Andros in Boston reached New York, Leisler raised a militia, captured the city fort, drove Nicholson into exile, and proclaimed himself the new head of government in New York. For two years, he tried in vain to stabilize his power in the colony amid fierce factional rivalry. In 1691, when William and Mary appointed a new governor, Leisler briefly resisted this challenge to his authority. Although he soon yielded, his hesitation allowed his many political enemies to charge him with treason. He and one of his sons-in-law were hanged, drawn, and quartered. Fierce rivalry between what became known as the "Leislerians" and the "anti-Leislerians" dominated the politics of New York for many years thereafter.

In Maryland, many people erroneously assumed when they heard news of the Glorious Revolution that their proprietor, the Catholic Lord Baltimore, who was living in England, had sided with the Catholic James II and opposed William and Mary. So in 1689, an old opponent of the proprietor's government, John Coode, started a new revolt, which drove out Lord Baltimore's officials in the name of Protestantism. Through an elected convention, his supporters chose a committee to run the government and petitioned the Crown for a charter as a royal colony. In 1691, William and Mary complied, stripping the proprietor of his authority. The colonial assembly established the Church of England as the colony's official religion and forbade Catholics to hold public office, to vote, or even to practice their religion in public. Maryland became a proprietary colony again in 1715, but only after the fifth Lord Baltimore joined the Anglican Church.

JOHN COODE'S REBELLION

As a result of the Glorious Revolution, the colonies revived their representative assemblies and successfully thwarted the plan for colonial unification. In the process, they legitimized the idea that the colonists had some rights within the empire, that the English government needed to consider their views in making policies that affected them. But the Glorious Revolution in America was not, as many Americans would later come to believe, a clear demonstration of American resolve to govern itself or a clear victory for colonial self-rule. In New York and Maryland, in particular, the uprisings had more to do with local factional and religious divisions than with any larger vision of the nature of the empire. And while the insurgencies did succeed in eliminating the short-lived Dominion of New England, their ultimate results were governments that increased the Crown's potential authority in many ways. As the first century of English settlement in America came to its end and as colonists celebrated their victories over arbitrary British rule, they were becoming more a part of the imperial system than ever before.

Discussion and Activities

Comparing and Contrasting Have students read the section "The 'Glorious Revolution.'" Ask them to create a Venn diagram comparing the Glorious Revolution to the English Civil War. Discuss as a class which event had a greater impact on English colonization. PCE SOC MIG

CHAPTER 2 REVIEW

CONNECTING THEMES

Chapter Two began by focusing on the arrival of the English in North America and the incentives behind colonization. Both the geography of North America and the pattern of migration and settlement heavily influenced the development of different regions. Three distinct regions developed on the Atlantic coast: a New England region, a Chesapeake region, and a Mid-Atlantic region. The European colonists in all three had different and evolving relations with Native Americans. These relationships, while sometimes mutually beneficial, often resulted in conflict, death, and displacement of Native Americans.

The European powers that dominated the colonization of North America quickly established economic policies and political institutions that heavily regulated the interactions among and with the colonies. The development of intense trade networks also strengthened the political power of the European colonies. These economic and cultural relationships helped to define the role and importance of the colonies in the Atlantic World.

You should consider the following questions as you review the themes for this chapter:

- How did economics influence the origin and development of the British North American colonies?
- How did contact between Europeans, Africans, and Native Americans alter perceptions of identity among each group?
- What factors led to distinct regional identities among the British North American colonies?
- What were the causes and effects of the development of different regional labor systems in colonial America?
- What were the characteristics of people who settled in various colonial regions and how did these characteristics affect the development of those regions?
- What were the political structures of the different colonial regions and why did they develop?
- What challenges did colonial political structures face over time?
- How did the growth of the colonial economy create both continuity and change in relationships among the nations of the Atlantic World?
- What influence did the environment and geography have on the development of distinct colonial regions?
- How did the ideas, beliefs, and cultures of colonists influence the development of regional differences?

KEY TERMS

Anne Hutchinson 51
Atlantic World 32
Bacon's Rebellion 47
Barbados Slave trade 61
Congregational Church 50
Dominion of New England 67
English Caribbean 60
Fundamental Constitution for Carolina 56
George and Cecilius Calvert 45
Glorious Revolution 68
Headright 44
Jacob Leisler 68
James Oglethorpe 63
Jamestown 42
John Calvin 50
John Smith 42
John Winthrop 49
King Philip's War 53
Massachusetts Bay Company 49
Mayflower Compact 48
Mercantilism 66
Metacomet 53
Middle Ground 65
Navigation Acts 66
New Amsterdam 57
Pennsylvania, founding of 59
Pequot War 53
Plymouth Plantation 48
Powhatan 42
Praying Indians 52
Puritans 49
Quakers 58
Roger Williams 51
Sir William Berkeley 46
Theocracy 50
Tobacco 43
Toleration Act 46
Virginia House of Burgesses 44
Wampanoags 48
William Bradford 48
William Penn 59

Discussion and Activities

Comparing and Contrasting Organize the class into groups to research the specific "backcountry unrest and political rivalries" that arose in early America. Assign groups one of the following: Bacon's Rebellion, Leisler's Rebellion, or Coode's Rebellion. Each group must research the economic, political, and social factors that contributed to their assigned rebellion, as well as the consequences of each rebellion's actions upon the individual colonies and the colonies as a whole. Then, bring the class together to discuss how their rebellions were similar and dissimilar and what the rebellions tell us about life in seventeenth century colonial North America. Have students predict how these rebellions might impact the future attitude of the people of colonial North America. **NAT** **SOC**

Key Terms

Students should be familiar with the key terms and be able to define them in the context of issues and challenges that confronted Europeans, Native Americans, and Africans who populated North America during the time period. Encourage students to use these terms in performing review exercises and exam practice for this chapter.

Go Online Chapter 2 Content Review

Assessing Student Understanding Use the online assessment to assess student understanding of concepts and topics within the chapter. You can assign the ready-made Chapter 2 Content Review or create your own from available questions. This easy-to-use tool helps you design assessments that meet the needs of different types of learners.

CHAPTER 2
TRANSPLANTATIONS AND BORDERLANDS

Answers

Multiple Choice

1. D; **2.** C; **3.** B

Short Answer

4A) Possible answer: The point of view in the image is that of a proponent of mercantilism. The image depicts the act of ships engaging in trade, which served as the cornerstone of the British economy.

4B) Possible answer: Fierce competition for control of the world's raw materials and wealth forced European countries to compete with each other, developing strong navies and heavily regulating their economies.

4C) Possible answer: Colonization ventures overseas reaped tremendous benefits for European countries, as it gave them access to needed wealth and raw materials. The colonies also served as markets for finished products.

5A) Possible answer: Governor Berkeley's policy of limited western expansion, designed to avoid antagonizing Native Americans in Virginia, came in direct conflict with new and influential western landowners like Nathaniel Bacon.

5B) Possible answer: The rebellion revealed the instability in the colony's large population of free, landless men, most of whom were former indentured servants. This group comprised most of Bacon's supporters during the rebellion.

5C) Possible answer: Landed people in both eastern and western Virginia recognized a common interest in preventing social unrest from formerly indentured people. They turned to the African slave trade to fulfill their need for labor.

AP EXAM PRACTICE

Questions assume cumulative content knowledge from this chapter and the previous chapter.

MULTIPLE CHOICE

Use the image on page 58 and your knowledge of U.S. history to answer questions 1-3.

1. The Quakers, like other religious groups who came to the British North American colonies, sought to create
   (A) a colony that perpetuated their political control from England.
   (B) a colony in which they could intermingle with French and Spanish colonists.
   (C) a colony based upon plantation agriculture and cash crop cultivation.
   (D) a colony in which they could form a society uniquely shaped by their religious beliefs.

2. One similarity between the British colonies and those of other European nations is that they all
   (A) compelled Native Americans into complex forced labor structures.
   (B) sought to build societies based upon intermarriage and cultural understanding.
   (C) fostered a shifting dynamic of accommodation and conflict.
   (D) focused their labor systems on the use of enslaved Africans.

3. In contrast to the Chesapeake and Caribbean colonies, the Northern colonies
   (A) were organized around the cultivation of tobacco.
   (B) formed more diversified economies.
   (C) heavily relied upon enslaved laborers.
   (D) developed plantation economies growing staple crops.

SHORT ANSWER

Use your knowledge of U.S. history to answer questions 4 and 5.

4. Use the image on page 36 to answer A, B, and C.
   (A) Briefly describe ONE point of view about mercantilism as depicted in the hand-colored wood print *The Trades Increase, as Concerning Ships.*
   (B) Briefly explain ONE historical cause that led to the event depicted in the hand-colored wood print *The Trades Increase, as Concerning Ships.*
   (C) Briefly explain ONE historical effect which resulted from the event depicted in the hand-colored wood print *The Trades Increase, as Concerning Ships.*

5. Answer A, B, and C.
   (A) Briefly describe ONE major cause of Bacon's Rebellion.
   (B) Briefly describe ONE major short-term effect which resulted from Bacon's Rebellion.
   (C) Briefly describe ONE major long-term effect which resulted from Bacon's Rebellion.

LONG ESSAY

Develop a thoughtful and thorough historical argument that addresses the statement below. Begin your essay with a thesis statement, and support it with specific historical evidence and examples.

6. Evaluate the extent of similarities between the Chesapeake and the New England colonies from 1607 to 1700.

Answers

Long Essay

6. Possible thesis: People in both the Chesapeake and New England colonies were primarily English speaking with similar political and cultural values. However, stark differences in geography forced the two regions to rely on two different types of economic activities for survival. Additionally, the migration patterns of settlement, along with demographics of those coming over, were also very different. Therefore, despite some similarities, there were more differences than similarities between the Chesapeake and New England colonies from 1607 to 1700. Similarities: Both groups came in large numbers from England; they brought with them the same political and cultural views; both groups were primarily Christian; both groups spoke English; and both groups had to maintain economic viability as a mercantile colony for England. Differences: Chesapeake colonists came primarily as young, single, aristocratic men or indentured servants; they came looking for economic opportunities; they faced immense hardships in the first few years of living in the colony; they relied primarily on cash crops for their economic survival; and life expectancy was quite low in the region. New England colonists came primarily in family units; they came looking for religious opportunities; outside of initial challenges, they experienced great fortune early on; they relied on fishing and trade for their economic survival; and life expectancy was much higher in this region.

3 SOCIETY AND CULTURE IN PROVINCIAL AMERICA

LIFE IN THE AMERICAN COLONIES
This colored engraving shows the domestic life of Americans during the eighteenth century. Depicted are family members at work in their cozy surroundings. Their industriousness is shown to be a singular virtue of the era.

CONNECTING CONCEPTS

Chapter Three describes the development of colonial society in the seventeenth and eighteenth centuries. The rapidly expanding population of colonial British North America contained various religious, social, and ethnic groups. This diverse population drove the development of a variety of cultural and social entities.

A large proportion of the population in the Chesapeake were indentured servants. However, the indentured servant system failed to provide an adequate supply of labor and by the beginning of the seventeenth century all the British colonies participated in varying degrees in the Atlantic slave trade. Towns in New England had smaller populations of enslaved people than the Chesapeake and colonies further south, where large numbers of enslaved people lived.

In the early eighteenth century, English immigration declined while non-English European immigration continued and increased. As the population grew and diversified, the roles of women changed and a variety of family structures arose in different colonies. The diversity of the population led to a significant degree of pluralism and intellectual exchange, which resulted in two interrelated phenomena: the First Great Awakening and the Enlightenment. Colonies also became more anglicized and developed independent political communities based on English models. The growing colonial resistance to British rule drew heavily on local experiences of self-government, an evolving sense of liberty, philosophical principles of the Enlightenment, a growing sense of diversity, and perceived corruption in the British system. All of these factors cumulated in an increasing and evolving sense of independence within British North America.

Pacing Guide

Chapter 3 explores key concepts from Period 2: 1607–1754 of the AP U.S. History Curriculum Framework. The suggested instruction time for Chapter 3 is 7 days.

Key Concepts

2.2.I Transatlantic commercial, religious, philosophical, and political exchanges led residents of the British colonies to evolve in their political and cultural attitudes as they became increasingly tied to Britain and one another.

2.2.II Like other European empires in the Americas that participated in the Atlantic slave trade, the English colonies developed a system of slavery that reflected the specific economic, demographic, and geographic characteristics of those colonies.

Discussion and Activities

Analyzing Visuals Have students view the image "Life in the American Colonies." Ask them to construct a two-column chart with the headings "Political" and "Social." Have students work in pairs or small groups to compile examples from the image that suggest social and political factors that impacted family life in the American colonies. Ask students to update their charts as the read through the chapter. **NAT** **ARC**

Discussion and Activities

Predicting After they read the section "Immigration and Natural Increase," ask students to discuss with a partner why English settlers of different classes migrated to North America. Have each pair construct a three-column KWL chart listing what they know, what they want to know, and what they learned about population growth in the American colonies in each column. Ask students to add to their charts as they continue through the chapter.

As you read, you should:

- Analyze the economic and geographic conditions, as well as perceptions of racial superiority, that led to the institutionalization of slavery in the British North American colonies.
- Compare and contrast the distinct regional identities developed throughout the British North American colonies, which resulted from motives for settlement, geographic and environmental factors, and ethnic and religious differences.
- Evaluate the similarities and differences of the roles of women throughout the different colonial regions.
- Analyze how the regional differences between the colonies diminished over time, and a more unified colonial culture began to emerge.
- Identify how science, technology, and education systems led to expanding social networks and greater economic development.

THE COLONIAL POPULATION

IMMIGRATION AND NATURAL INCREASE

Not until long after the beginning of European colonization did Europeans and Africans in North America outnumber the Native American population. But after uncertain beginnings at Jamestown and Plymouth, the nonnative population grew rapidly and substantially, through continued immigration, forced migration of enslaved Africans, and through natural increase, until by the late seventeenth century Europeans and Africans became the dominant population groups along the Atlantic coast.

A few of the early English settlers were members of the upper classes–usually the younger sons of the lesser gentry, men who stood to inherit no land at home and aspired to establish estates for themselves in America. For the most part, however, the early English population was very unaristocratic. It included some members of the emerging middle class, businessmen who migrated to America for religious or commercial reasons, or (like John Winthrop) both. But the dominant element was English laborers. Some came independently. The religious dissenters who formed the bulk of the population of early New England, for example, were men and women of modest means who arranged their own passage, brought their families with them, and established themselves immediately on their own land. But in the Chesapeake, at least three-fourths of the immigrants in the seventeenth century arrived as indentured servants.

INDENTURED SERVITUDE

ORIGINS

The system of temporary servitude in the Americas developed out of existing practices in England. Young men and women bound themselves to a contract holder for a fixed term of servitude (usually four to five years). In return they received passage to America, food, and shelter. Upon completion of their terms of service, male indentures were supposed to receive such benefits as clothing, tools, and occasionally land; in reality, however, many left service without anything, unprepared and unequipped to begin earning a living on their own. Roughly one-fourth of the indentures in the Chesapeake were women, most of whom worked as domestic servants. Because men greatly outnumbered women in the region in the seventeenth century, women could reasonably expect to marry when their terms of servitude expired. Male domestic servants, however, usually had no such options.

Most indentured servants came to the colonies voluntarily, but not all. Beginning as early as 1617, the English government occasionally dumped shiploads of convicts in America to be sold into servitude, although some criminals, according to Captain John Smith, "did chuse to be hanged ere they would go thither, and were." The government also sent prisoners taken in battles with the Scots and the Irish in the 1650s, as well as other groups deemed undesirable: orphans, vagrants, paupers, and those who were "lewd and dangerous." Other forced migrants were neither dangerous nor indigent but were simply victims of kidnapping, or "impressment," by aggressive and unscrupulous investors and promoters.

It was not difficult to understand why the system of indentured servitude proved so appealing to colonial employers–particularly once it became clear, as it quickly did, that the Native American population could not easily be transformed into a servile workforce. The indenture system provided a means of coping with the severe

Go Online AP Exam Preparation

AP Exam Practice Use the online assessment to help prepare students for the AP Exam. You can assign the ready-made AP-style short answer questions, document-based questions, and multiple-choice questions assessing concepts, themes, and skills from Period 2 and AP style long-essay questions organized in sets of 3 questions from various time periods. You can also create your own tests from available questions. This easy-to-use tool helps you design assessments that meet the needs of different types of learners.

NORTH AMERICA IN 1700 This map reveals how tiny a proportion of North America was settled by Europeans in 1700, nearly a century after the first English settlements began there. The largest area of settlement was the thin fringe of colonies along the northern Atlantic seaboard. There were additional scattered settlements, almost all of them tiny, in eastern Canada, along the southern Atlantic coast, in the Mississippi Valley, and in the Southwest.

What accounted for the isolated colonies in noncoastal areas of North America?

labor shortage in the colonies. In the Chesapeake, the headright system (by which settlers received additional land grants for every servant they imported) offered another incentive. For the servants themselves, the attractions were not always so clear. Those who came voluntarily often did so to escape troubles in England; others came in the hope of establishing themselves on land or in trades of their own when their terms of service expired. Yet the reality often differed sharply from the hope.

Some former indentures managed to establish themselves successfully as farmers, tradespeople, or artisans. Others (mostly males) found themselves without land, without employment, without families, and without prospects. A large floating population of young single men traveled restlessly from place to place, often in groups, in search of work or land and were a potential (and at times actual) source of social unrest, particularly in the Chesapeake. Even free laborers who found employment or land and settled down with families often did not stay put for very long. The phenomenon of families simply pulling up stakes and moving to another, more promising location every several years was one of the most prominent characteristics of the colonial population.

REALITIES OF INDENTURED SERVITUDE

Indentured servitude remained an important source of population growth well into the eighteenth century, but beginning in the 1670s the flow began to decline substantially. A decrease in the English birth rate and an increase in English prosperity reduced the pressures on many men and women who might otherwise have considered emigrating. After 1700, those who did travel to America as indentured servants generally avoided the southern colonies, where working conditions were arduous and prospects for advancement were slim, and took advantage of the better opportunities in the mid-Atlantic colonies, especially Pennsylvania and New York. In the Chesapeake, landowners themselves began to find the indenture system less attractive, in part because they were troubled by the instability that former servants created or threatened to create. That was one reason for the increasing centrality of African slavery in the southern agricultural economy.

BIRTH AND DEATH

At first, new arrivals in most colonies, whatever their background or status, could anticipate great hardship: inadequate food, frequent epidemics, and in an appalling number of cases,

Reasoning Processes

Comparing After students read the section "Indentured Servitude," ask them to construct a 3-part Venn diagram comparing conditions for indentured servants in New England, the Chesapeake region, and the South. **SOC** **WXT** **ARC**

Answers

North America in 1700

The isolation of the colonies in non-coastal areas was largely the result of the lack of roads connecting those areas.

Discussion and Activities

Analyzing Visuals Have students examine the image of the auction advertisement. Ask them to read the text of the ad and make a list of what stands out to them and why. Have students share their lists with the class or in small groups. *(Possible responses: People are advertised for sale along with various supplies; the term of indenture offered was four years.)* **WXT** **SOC**

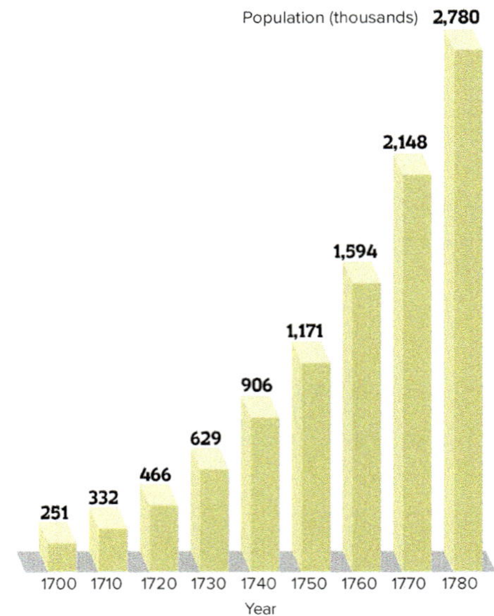

THE NON-INDIAN POPULATION OF NORTH AMERICA, 1700–1780 The European population of North America grew much more dramatically in the eighteenth century than it had in the seventeenth, exceeding 2 million by 1770. But unlike in the seventeenth century, the most important reason for this expansion was natural increase (children born in America), replacing immigration from Europe.

Why was the natural increase so much larger than in the past?

early death. Gradually, however, conditions improved enough to allow the non-Indian population to begin to expand. By the end of the seventeenth century, the non-Indian population in the English colonies of North America had grown to over a quarter of a million, of whom about 25 percent were Africans.

Although immigration remained for a time the greatest source of population increase, marked improvement in the reproduction rate began in New England and the mid-Atlantic colonies in the second half of the seventeenth century. After the 1650s, natural increase became the most important source of population. The New England population more than quadrupled through reproduction alone in the second half of the seventeenth century. This was less a result of unusual fertility (families in New England and in other regions were probably equally fertile) than of exceptional longevity. Indeed, the average life spans of residents of some areas of New England were nearly equal to those of people in the twentieth century. In the first generation of American-born colonists, according to one study, men who survived infancy lived to an average age of seventy-one, women to seventy. The next generation's life expectancy declined somewhat–to sixty-five for men who survived infancy–but remained at least ten years higher than the English equivalent and approximately twenty years higher than life expectancy in the South. Scholars disagree on the reasons for these remarkable life spans, but contributing factors probably included the cool climate and the relatively disease-free environment it produced, clean water (a stark contrast to England in these years), and the absence of large population centers that might breed epidemics.

EXCEPTIONAL LONGEVITY IN NEW ENGLAND

Conditions improved much more slowly in the South. The mortality rates for the white population in the Chesapeake region remained markedly higher than those elsewhere until the mid-eighteenth century (and the mortality rates for Africans higher still). Throughout the seventeenth century, the average life expectancy for white men in the region was just over forty years and, for white women, slightly less. One in four children died in infancy, and fully half died before the age of twenty. The high death rate among adults meant that only about a third of all marriages lasted more than ten years; thus those children who survived infancy often lost one or both of their parents before reaching maturity. Widows, widowers, and orphans formed a substantial proportion of the white population of the Chesapeake. The continuing ravages

P O S T S C

To the SOUTH-CAROLINA GAZETTE,

TO BE SOLD, on board the *George-Town* Galley, *Thomas Crosthwaite* Mafter, lying at *Frankland's* Wharff, fundry *Englifh SERVANTS*, Men and Women, well recommended, amongft whom are Tradefmen, Hufbandmen, &c. indented for *Four Years.* Likewife fundry *Englifh* Provifions, and a parcel of new iron-bound fizable Water-Cafks, handy for the *Weft-India* Trade; fundry old Sails, fome fmall Carriage Guns, Pipes, Earthen Ware, Cheefe, &c.

Whereas the Subfcriber intends to depart this Province early in the next Spring, he defires all Perfons indebted to him, or the Hon. *Benjamin Whitaker*, Efq; to difcharge, or, at leaft, fettle their refpective Debts to his Satisfaction, on or before the firft Day of *January* next: And thofe who have any Demands on the Subfcriber or the faid Mr. *Whitaker*, are requefted to bring them in, that they may be fatisfied by

WILLIAM GEORGE FREEMAN.

SERVANTS FOR SALE The South-Carolina Gazette of Charles Town ran this advertisement in November 1749 to announce the arrival of a group of English "indentures"—men and women who had accepted passage to America in exchange for their agreement to sell themselves as servants for a fixed period of years once they arrived. Indentures were the most common form of labor in most of the colonies during much of the seventeenth century, but by 1749 the system was already beginning to die out—replaced in the South by the enslavement of Africans.

Answers

The Non-Indian Population of North America, 1700–1780

Conditions were improving, leading to higher birth rates and lower death and infant mortality rates.

of disease (particularly malaria) and the prevalence of salt-contaminated water kept the death rate high in the South; only after the settlers developed immunity to the local diseases (a slow process known as "seasoning") did life expectancy increase significantly. Population growth was substantial in the region, but largely as a result of immigration.

Natural increases in the population, wherever they occurred, were largely a result of a steady improvement in the sex ratio through the seventeenth century. In the early years of settlement, more than three-quarters of the white population of the Chesapeake consisted of men. And even in New England, which from the beginning had attracted more families (and thus more women) than the southern colonies, 60 percent of the white inhabitants in 1650 were male. Gradually, however, more women began to arrive in the colonies; and increasing birth rates, which of course produced roughly equal numbers of males and females, contributed to shifting the sex ratio as well. Not until well into the eighteenth century did the ratio begin to match that in England (where women were a slight majority), but by the late seventeenth century, the proportion of males to females in all the colonies was becoming more balanced.

MORE-BALANCED SEX RATIO

MEDICINE IN THE COLONIES

The very high death rates of women who bore children illustrate the primitive nature of medical knowledge and practice in the colonies. Seventeenth- and eighteenth-century physicians had little or no understanding of infection and sterilization. As a result, many people died from infections contracted during childbirth or surgery from dirty instruments or dirty hands. Because communities were unaware of bacteria, many were plagued with infectious diseases transmitted by garbage or unclean water.

One result of the limited extent of medical knowledge was that it was relatively easy for people to enter the medical field, even without professional training. The biggest beneficiaries of this ease of access were women, who established themselves in considerable numbers as midwives. Midwives assisted women in childbirth, but they also dispensed other medical advice—usually urging their patients to use herbs or other natural remedies. Midwives were popular because they were usually friends and neighbors of the people they treated, unlike physicians, who were few and therefore not often well known to their patients. Male doctors felt threatened by the midwives and struggled continually to drive them from the field, although they did not make substantial progress in doing so until the nineteenth century.

MIDWIVES

Midwives and doctors alike practiced medicine on the basis of the prevailing assumptions of their time, most of them derived from the theory of "humoralism" popularized by the second-century Roman physician Galen. Galen argued that the human body was governed by four "humors" that were lodged in four bodily fluids: yellow bile (or "choler"), black bile ("melancholy"), blood, and phlegm. In a healthy body, the four humors existed in balance. Illness represented an imbalance and suggested the need for removing from the body the excesses of whatever fluid was causing the imbalance. That was the rationale that lay behind the principal medical techniques of the seventeenth century: purging, expulsion, and bleeding. Bleeding was the most extreme of the treatments (and the most destructive), and it was practiced mostly by male physicians. Midwives preferred more homeopathic treatments and favored "pukes" and laxatives. The great majority of early Americans, however, had little contact with physicians, or even midwives, and sought instead to deal with illness on their own, confident that their abilities were equal to those of educated physicians—which, given the state of medical knowledge, was often true.

That seventeenth-century medicine rested so much on ideas produced 1,400 years before is evidence of how little support there was for the scientific method—which rests on experimentation and observation rather than on inherited faiths—in England and America at the time. Bleeding, for example, had been in use for hundreds of years, during which time there had been no evidence that it helped people recover from illness; indeed, if anyone had chosen to look for it, there was considerable evidence that bleeding could do great harm. But what would seem in later eras to be the simple process of testing scientific assumptions was not yet a common part of Western thought. Only with the birth of the Enlightenment in the late seventeenth century—with its faith in human reason and its belief in the capacity of individuals and societies to create better lives—would the scientific method begin to find acceptance.

WOMEN AND FAMILIES IN THE CHESAPEAKE

The importance of reproduction in the labor-scarce society of seventeenth-century America had particularly significant effects on women. The high sex ratio meant that few women remained unmarried for long. The average European woman in America married for the first time at twenty or twenty-one years of age, considerably earlier than in England; in some areas of the Chesapeake, the average bride was three to four years younger. In the Chesapeake, the most important factor affecting women and families remained, until at least the mid-eighteenth century, the extraordinarily high mortality rate. Under those circumstances, the traditional male-centered family structure of England—by which husbands and fathers exercised firm, even dictatorial control over the lives of their wives and children—was difficult to maintain. Because so few families remained intact for long, rigid patterns of male authority were constantly undermined. Standards of sexual behavior were also more flexible in the South than they were in England or other parts of America. Because of the large numbers of indentured servants

MALE AUTHORITY UNDERMINED

Historical Thinking Skills

Argumentation Have students read the section "More-Balanced Sex Ratio." Ask them to think about the reasons that there were fewer women than men in the English colonies during the seventeenth century. Ask students to make a poster or design a social media campaign to encourage women in England to emigrate to America. Remind them that their images and text should communicate specific reasons for women to emigrate. **MIG** **WXT** **SOC**

Discussion and Activities

Making Connections Have students read the section "Medicine in the Colonies." The text indicates that many medicines and procedures may actually have been harmful to patients. Ask students to brainstorm as a class practices today that are widely used but not necessarily proven to work or approved for use by the government. *(Possible responses: unregulated supplements, memory aids, magnets, etc.)* **WXT**

Historical Thinking Skills

Argumentation After students read the section "Women and Families in the Chesapeake," have them create a short paragraph arguing why women in the Chesapeake region had more freedom, authority, and autonomy than women in other regions. Remind students to include a thesis that makes a historically defensible claim supported by at least one specific example. **SOC** **PCE**

who were forbidden to marry until their terms of service expired, premarital sexual relationships were frequent. Female servants who became pregnant before the expiration of their terms could expect harsh treatment: heavy fines, whippings if no one could pay the fines, an extra year or two of service added to their contract, and the loss of their children after weaning. Bastard children were themselves bound out as indentures at a very early age. On the other hand, a woman whose term of service expired before the birth of her child or whose partner was able to buy her remaining time from her contract holder might expect to marry quickly. Over a third of Chesapeake marriages occurred with the bride already pregnant.

Women in the Chesapeake could anticipate a life consumed with childbearing. The average wife became pregnant every two years. Those who lived long enough bore an average of eight children apiece (up to five of whom typically died in infancy or early childhood). Since childbirth was one of the most frequent causes of female death, relatively few women survived to see all their children grow to maturity.

For all the hardships women encountered in the seventeenth-century South, they also enjoyed more power and a greater level of freedom than women in other parts of America (or than southern women in later years). Because men were plentiful and women scarce, females had considerable latitude in choosing husbands. (They also often had no fathers or other male relatives nearby trying to control their choices.) Because women generally married at a much younger age than men, they often outlived their husbands (even though female life expectancy was somewhat shorter than male). Widows were often left with several children and with responsibility for managing a farm or plantation, a circumstance of enormous hardship but one that also gave them significant economic power.

GREATER INDEPENDENCE IN THE SOUTH

Widows seldom remained unmarried for long, however. Those who had no grown sons to work the tobacco farms and plantations had particular need for male assistance, and marriage was the surest way to secure it. Since many widows married men who were themselves widowers, complex combinations of households were frequent. With numerous stepchildren, half brothers, and half sisters living together in a single household, women often had to play the role of peacemaker–a role that may have further enhanced their authority within the family.

By the early eighteenth century, the character of the Chesapeake population was beginning to change, and with it the nature of the typical family. Life expectancy was increasing; indentured servitude was in decline; and natural reproduction was becoming the principal source of white population increase. The sex ratio was becoming more equal. One result of these changes was that life for white people in the region became less perilous and less arduous. Another result was that women lost some of the power that their small numbers had once given them. As families grew more stable, traditional patterns of male authority revived. By the mid-eighteenth century, southern families were becoming highly "patriarchal," that is, dominated by the male head of the family.

REVIVAL OF PATRIARCHY

GUIDE TO THE SEASONS Among their many purposes, almanacs sought to help farmers predict weather and plan for the demands of changing seasons. This illustration, part of a "calendar" of farming images, shows a man and a woman tending fields in July, in preparation for the coming harvest.

Discussion and Activities

Analyzing Visuals Have students examine the image "Guide to the Seasons." Ask them to think about why a farmers' almanac would include images like this one. Have students share their thoughts with a partner. *(Many farmers were likely illiterate.)* **SOC**

Women and Families in New England

In New England, where many more immigrants arrived with family members and where death rates declined quickly, family structure was much more stable than it was in the Chesapeake and hence much more traditional. Because the sex ratio was reasonably balanced, most men could expect to marry.

Women, however, remained in the minority; and as in the Chesapeake, they married young, began producing children early, and continued to do so well into their thirties. In contrast to the South, however, northern children were more likely to survive (the average family raised six to eight children to maturity), and families were more likely to remain intact. Fewer New England women became widows, and those who did generally lost their husbands later in life. Hence women were less often cast in roles independent of their husbands. Young women, moreover, had less control over the conditions of marriage, both because there were fewer unmarried men vying for them and because their fathers were more often alive and able to exercise control over their choice of husbands.

Among other things, increased longevity meant that, unlike in the Chesapeake (where three-fourths of all children lost at least one parent before the age of twenty-one), white parents in New England usually lived to see their children and even their grandchildren grow to maturity. Still, the lives of most New England women were nearly as consumed by childbearing and child rearing as those of women in the Chesapeake.

LIFE SPANS

Even women who lived into their sixties spent the majority of their mature years with young children in the home. The longer lives in New England also meant that parents continued to control their children far longer than did parents in the South. Although they were less likely than parents in England to "arrange" marriages for their children, few sons and daughters could choose spouses entirely independent of their parents' wishes. Men usually depended on their fathers for land–generally a prerequisite for beginning families of their own. Women needed dowries from their parents if they were to attract desirable husbands. Stricter parental supervision of children meant, too, that fewer women became pregnant before marriage than in the South (although even in Puritan New England the premarital pregnancy rate was not insubstantial–as high as 20 percent in some communities).

Puritanism placed a high value on the family, which was the principal economic and religious unit within every community.

THE PATRIARCHAL PURITAN FAMILY

At the same time, however, Puritanism reinforced the idea of nearly absolute male authority and the assumption of female weakness and inferiority. Women were expected to be modest and submissive. Such popular girls' names as Prudence, Patience, Chastity, and Comfort suggest something about Puritan expectations of female behavior. A wife was expected to devote herself to serving the needs of her husband and household.

The Beginnings of Slavery in British America

Almost from the beginning of European settlement in North America, there was a demand for enslaved Africans to supplement the always-scarce southern labor supply. The demand grew rapidly once tobacco cultivation became a staple of the Chesapeake economy. But the supply of enslaved laborers was limited during much of the seventeenth century, because the Atlantic slave trade did not at first serve the English colonies in America. Portuguese slavers, who had dominated the trade since the sixteenth century, shipped captive men and women from the west coast of Africa to the new European colonies in South America and the Caribbean. Gradually, Dutch and French navigators joined the slave trade. But a substantial commerce in enslaved people grew up within the Americas, particularly between the Caribbean islands and the southern colonies of British America. By the late seventeenth century, the supply of enslaved laborers in North America was becoming plentiful.

As the commerce in enslaved people grew more extensive and sophisticated, it also grew more horrible. Before it ended in the nineteenth century, it was responsible for the forced immigration of as many as 11 million Africans to the New World. (Until the late eighteenth century, the number of enslaved Africans to the Americas was higher than that of Europeans.)

THE MIDDLE PASSAGE

Native African chieftains captured members of enemy tribes in battle, tied them together in long lines, or "coffles," and sold them in the flourishing slave marts on the African coast. Then, after some haggling on the docks between the European traders and the African suppliers, the terrified victims were packed into the dark, filthy holds of ships for the horrors of the "middle passage"–the journey to America.

For weeks, sometimes even months, the African prisoners remained chained in the bowels of the slave ships. Conditions varied from one ship to another. Some captains took care to see that their potentially valuable cargo remained reasonably healthy. Others accepted the deaths of numerous Africans as inevitable and tried to cram as many as possible into their ships to ensure that enough would survive to yield a profit at journey's end. On such ships, the African prisoners were sometimes packed together in such close quarters that they were unable to stand, hardly able to breathe. Some ships supplied them with only minimal food and water. Women were often victims of rape and other sexual abuse. Those who died en route were simply thrown overboard. Upon arrival in the New World, enslaved Africans were auctioned off to white landowners and transported, frightened and bewildered, to their new homes.

The first enslaved Africans arrived in English North America before 1620, and as English seamen began to establish themselves in the slave trade, the flow of Africans to the colonies gradually increased. But North America was always a much less important market for enslaved Africans than were other

Reasoning Processes

Comparing Have students read the section "Women and Families in New England." Ask them to create a Venn diagram comparing conditions for women in New England and the Chesapeake. Have students discuss as a class or in small groups which region they would have preferred to live in as a seventeenth century woman. **SOC** **ARC**

Historical Thinking Skills

Evaluating Evidence Have students read the section "The Middle Passage." Divide students into small groups, and ask them to develop an argument for slave ship captains to treat enslaved Africans well during the Middle Passage. *(Possible responses: Well-fed and treated enslaved persons would arrive healthier and therefore bring higher prices at auction. Fewer would die during the passage.)* **WXT** **MIG** **WOR**

AP Exam Tip

For document-based questions, the AP Exam will require students to analyze the sources and situation of a document. Students will be asked to identify a source's point of view, purpose, historical situation, and/or audience.

Historical Thinking Skills

Sourcing and Situation To practice the skill, instruct students to choose one of the authors identified in the feature "The Origins of Slavery." Ask students to identify either a purpose or audience. (Students will not have enough information yet to evaluate the author's point of view or the historical situation of the document.) **WOR**

DEBATING THE PAST

THE ORIGINS OF SLAVERY

The debate among historians over how and why white Americans created a system of slave labor in the seventeenth century—and how and why they determined that people of African descent and no others should populate that system—has been a long and unusually heated one. At its center is the question of whether slavery was a result of white racism or whether slavery created racism.

In 1950, Oscar and Mary Handlin published an influential article, "Origins of the Southern Labor System," comparing slavery to other systems of "unfreedom" in the colonies. What differentiated slavery from other conditions of servitude, they argued, was that it was restricted to people of African descent, it was permanent, and it passed from one generation to the next. The unique characteristics of slavery, the Handlins maintained, were part of an effort by colonial legislatures to increase the available labor force. White laborers needed an incentive to come to America; black laborers, forcibly imported from Africa, did not. The distinction between the conditions of white workers and the conditions of black workers was, therefore, based on legal and economic motives, not on racism. Racism emerged to justify slavery; it did not cause slavery.

Winthrop D. Jordan was one of a number of historians who later challenged the Handlins' thesis and argued that white racism, more than economic interests, produced African slavery. In *White Over Black* (1968) and other works, Jordan argued that Europeans had long viewed people of color—and black Africans in particular—as inferior beings appropriate for serving whites. Those attitudes migrated with white Europeans to the New World, and white racism shaped the treatment of Africans in America—and the nature of the slave labor system—from the beginning.

George Fredrickson echoed Jordan's emphasis on the importance of racism as an independent factor reinforcing slavery; but unlike Jordan, he argued that racism did not precede slavery. "The treatment of blacks," he wrote, "engendered a cultural and psycho-social racism that after a certain point took on a life of its own. . . . Racism, although the child of slavery, not only outlived its parent but grew stronger and more independent after slavery's demise."

In *Black Majority* (1974), a study of seventeenth-century South Carolina, Peter Wood moved the debate away from racism and back toward social and economic conditions. Wood demonstrated that black people and white people often worked together on relatively equal terms in the early years of settlement. But as rice cultivation expanded, finding white laborers willing to do the arduous work became more difficult. The forcible importation of enslaved Africans and the creation of a system of permanent bondage was a response to a growing demand for labor and to fears among white people that without slavery a black labor force would be difficult to control.

Edmund Morgan argued similarly in *American Slavery, American Freedom* (1975) that the southern labor system was at first relatively flexible and later grew more rigid. In colonial Virginia, he claimed, white settlers did not at first intend to create a system of permanent bondage. But as the tobacco economy grew and created a high demand for cheap labor, white landowners began to feel uneasy about their dependence on a large group of dependent white workers, since such workers were difficult to recruit and control. Thus slavery was less a result of racism than of the desire of white landowners to find a reliable and stable labor force.

In *The Making of New World Slavery* (1996), Robin Blackburn argued that while race was a factor in allowing white people to justify to themselves the enslavement of Africans, the real reasons for slavery were hardheaded economic decisions by ambitious entrepreneurs, who realized early on that a slave-labor system in the labor-intensive agricultural world of the American South and the Caribbean was more profitable than a free-labor system. Slavery served the interests of a powerful combination of groups: planters, merchants, governments, industrialists, and consumers.

Race may have been a rationale for slavery, allowing planters and traders to justify to themselves the terrible human costs of the system. But the most important reason for the system was not just racism, but the pursuit of profit—and the success of the system in producing it. Blackburn concluded that slavery was not an antiquated remnant of an older world but, rather, a recognizably modern labor system that, however ugly, served the needs of an emerging market economy.

HISTORICAL THINKING SKILLS

1. **Identifying Historical Developments** Identify three differing historical arguments regarding how and why American colonists created a slave labor system.
2. **Analyzing Points of View** Describe the point of view in the image "London's Virginia" about the tobacco industry, which developed in the Chesapeake during the 17th century.
3. **Developing Arguments** With which historian's interpretation do you most agree? Explain why, supporting your argument with historical evidence.

Answers

Debating the Past

1. Possible responses: First, the Handlins argued that African slavery was part of an effort to increase the available labor force. Second, Jordan argued that the system of African slavery that developed in the Americas was a direct result of long-held European opinions that people of color were inferior to whites. Third, Morgan argued that at first, the southern labor system was relatively flexible but later grew more rigid; as the tobacco economy grew, landowners grew less and less confident in the ability to control white workers, and they turned more toward enslaved labor.
2. The image presents the point of view of a Virginia planter. While the presence of enslaved Africans is displayed in the image, the focus of the image is on how the tobacco economy allowed landowners to have leisure time and led to immense wealth in the colony.
3. Answers will vary. Students who point to the Handlins' position may focus on the fact that the struggling economy drove colonists to look for ways to provide financial and economic accountability to Europe. Students who point to the positions of Jordan and Fredrickson would focus on the long history of racism in Europe.

parts of the New World, especially the Caribbean islands and Brazil, whose labor-intensive sugar economies created an especially large demand for enslaved laborers. Less than 5 percent of enslaved Africans imported to the Americas went directly to the English colonies on the mainland. Most enslaved people who ended up in what became the United States spent time first in the West Indies. Not until the 1670s did traders bring enslaved Africans directly from Africa to North America. Even then, however, the flow remained small for a time, mainly because a single group, the Royal African Company of England, maintained a monopoly on trade in the mainland colonies and managed as a result to keep prices high and supplies low.

A turning point in the history of the African population in North America came in the mid-1690s, when the Royal African Company's monopoly was finally broken. With the trade now opened to English and colonial merchants on a competitive basis, prices fell and the number of enslaved Africans arriving in North America rapidly increased. By the end of the seventeenth century, only about one in ten of the residents of the colonies were Africans (about 25,000 in all). But because enslaved Africans were so heavily concentrated in a few southern colonies, they were already beginning to outnumber Europeans in some areas. The high ratio of men to women among enslaved Africans (there were perhaps two males to one female in most areas) retarded the natural increase of the population. But in the Chesapeake at least, more new enslaved people were being born by 1700 than were being imported from Africa. In South Carolina, by contrast, the difficult conditions of rice cultivation—and the high death rates of those who worked in the rice fields—ensured that the black population would barely be able to sustain itself through natural increase until much later.

GROWING ENSLAVED POPULATION

Between 1700 and 1760, the number of Africans in the colonies increased tenfold to about a quarter of a million. A relatively small number (16,000 in 1763) lived in New England; there were slightly more (29,000) in the middle colonies. The vast majority, however, continued to live in the South. By then the flow of free white laborers to that region had all but stopped, and enslaved Africans had become securely established as the basis of the southern workforce.

It was not entirely clear at first that the status of African laborers in America would be fundamentally different from that of white indentured servants. In the rugged conditions of the seventeenth-century South, it was often difficult for Europeans and Africans to maintain strictly separate roles. In some areas—South Carolina, for example, where the number of African laborers swelled more quickly than anywhere else—Black and white people lived and worked together. Some Black laborers were treated much like white servants, and some were freed after a fixed term of servitude. A few Africans themselves became land owners and some apparently became slaveholders themselves.

UNCERTAIN STATUS

By the early eighteenth century, however, a rigid distinction had become established between black people and white people. Contract holders were contractually obliged to free white servants after a fixed term of servitude. There was no such necessity to free enslaved laborers, and the assumption slowly spread that enslaved Africans would remain in service permanently. Another incentive for making the status of enslaved Africans rigid was that the children of enslaved people provided white landowners with a self-perpetuating labor force.

White assumptions about the inferiority of people of color contributed to the growing rigidity of the system. Such assumptions came naturally to the English settlers. They had already defined themselves as a superior race in their relations with the Native American population (and earlier in their relations with the Irish). The idea of subordinating a supposedly inferior race was, therefore, already established in the English imagination by the time substantial numbers of Africans appeared in America.

In the early eighteenth century, colonial assemblies began to pass "slave codes," limiting the rights of enslaved people in law and ensuring almost absolute authority to slaveholders. One factor, and one factor only, determined whether a person was subject to the slave codes: skin color. In contrast to the colonial societies of Spanish America, where biracial and multiracial people had a different (and higher) status than pure Africans, English America recognized no such distinctions. Any African ancestry was enough to classify a person as black.

SLAVE CODES

CHANGING SOURCES OF EUROPEAN IMMIGRATION

By the early eighteenth century, the flow of immigrants from England itself began to decline substantially—a result of better economic conditions there and of new government restrictions on emigration in the face of massive depopulation in some regions of the country. But as English immigration declined, French, German, Swiss, Irish, Welsh, Scottish, and Scandinavian immigration continued and increased.

The earliest, although not the most numerous, of these non-English European immigrants were the French Calvinists, or Huguenots. A royal proclamation, the Edict of Nantes of 1598, had allowed them to become practically a state within the state in Roman Catholic France. In 1685, however, the French government revoked the edict. Soon after that, Huguenots began leaving the country. About 300,000 left France in the following decades. A small proportion of them traveled to the English colonies in North America. Many German Protestants suffered similarly from the arbitrary religious policies of their rulers; and all Germans, Catholics as well as Protestants, suffered from the devastating wars with King Louis XIV of France (the "Sun King"). The Rhineland of southwestern Germany, the area known as the Palatinate, experienced particular hardships. Because it was close to France, its people were particularly exposed to slaughter and ruin at the hands of invaders. The unusually cold winter of

HUGUENOTS AND PENNSYLVANIA DUTCH

Reasoning Processes

Analyzing Change Have students read the sections "Growing Enslaved Population," "Uncertain Status," and "Slave Codes." In small groups, ask students to make time lines based on the reading and their prior knowledge of events, issues, or developments related to the treatment of enslaved persons. Have students circle items that represent a change in treatment. Then ask the groups to discuss reasons for those changes. **WXT** **SOC**

Discussion and Activities

Analyzing Cause and Effect Have students read the section "Growing Enslaved Population." In small groups, ask students to make a list of reasons for the rapidly growing enslaved population during the eighteenth century. After discussion, have students rank their lists of reasons in order of importance, and debate these rankings as a class. **WXT** **SOC** **WOR**

Reasoning Processes

Analyzing Change After students read the section "Huguenots and Pennsylvania Dutch," ask them to think about how the arrival of these new groups of settlers represented a change over time. Have students share their thoughts with a partner. **MIG** **SOC** **WOR**

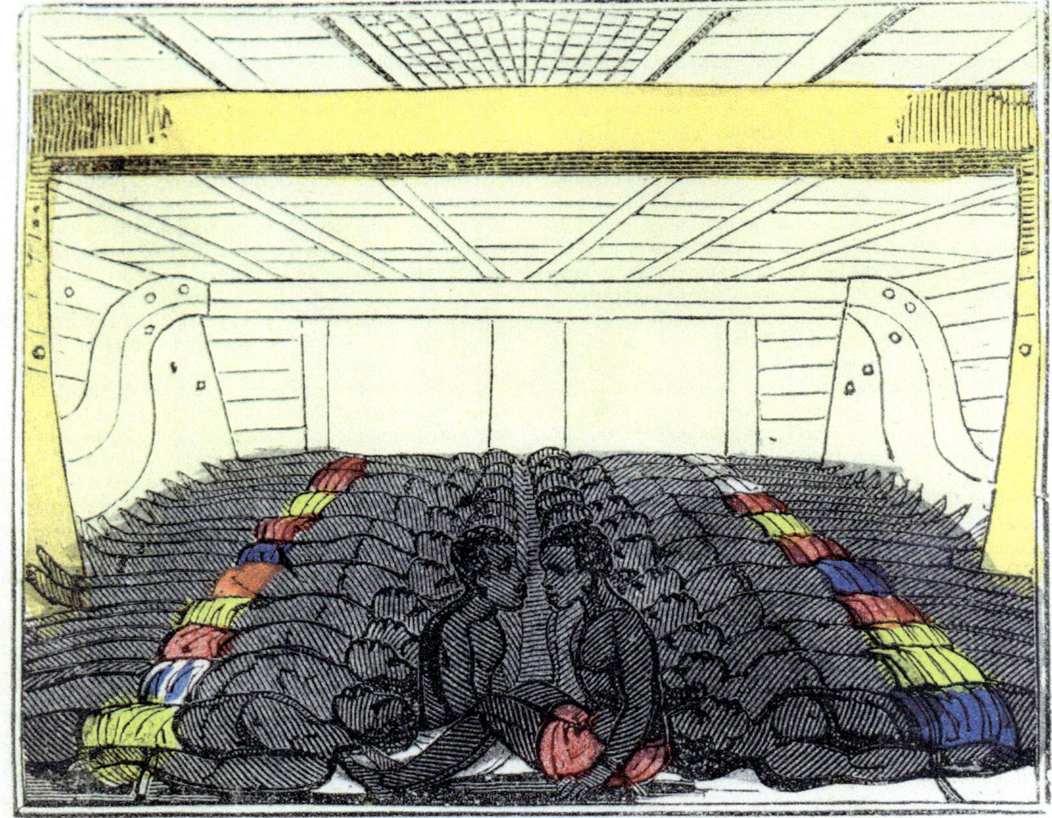

AFRICAN SLAVE TRADE This image is from a plate from British author Amelia Opie's poem *Black Slaves in the Hold of the Slave Ship: or How to Make Sugar*, published in London in 1826. Opie's poem depicts the life of an African man who was captured by slave traders and chronicles his journey to the West Indies on a slave ship and his enforced work on the sugar plantations there. Enslaved people were packed like cargo for the long ocean voyage.

1708–1709 dealt a final blow to the precarious economy of the region. More than 12,000 Palatinate Germans sought refuge in England, and approximately 3,000 of them soon found their way to America. They arrived in New York and tried at first to make homes in the Mohawk Valley, only to be ousted by the powerful landlords of the region. Some of the Germans moved farther up the Mohawk, out of reach of the patroons; but most made their way to Pennsylvania, where they received a warm welcome (and where they ultimately became known to English settlers as the "Pennsylvania Dutch," a corruption of their own word for "German": "Deutsch"). The Quaker colony became the most common destination for Germans, who came to America in growing numbers. (Among them were Moravians and Mennonites, with religious views similar in many ways to those of the Quakers.) Many German Protestants went to North Carolina as well, especially after the founding of New Bern in 1710 by a company of 600 German-speaking Swiss.

The most numerous of the newcomers were the Scots-Irish–Scottish Presbyterians who had settled in northern Ireland (in the province of Ulster) in the early seventeenth century. The Ulster colonists had prospered for a time despite the barren soil and the constant, never wholly successful, struggle to suppress the Catholic natives. But in the first years of the eighteenth century, Parliament prohibited Ulster from exporting to England the woolens and other products that had become the basis of the northern Irish economy; at the same

Discussion and Activities

Analyzing Points of View Have students view the image "African Slave Trade." Ask them to evaluate the image in terms of the artist's point of view. Do they think the artist was supportive of the trade in enslaved Africans or opposed to it? Why do they think so? *(The artist was likely opposed to the trade. The image depicts the tremendous overcrowding and lack of ventilation common on slave ships.)* **WXT** **SOC**

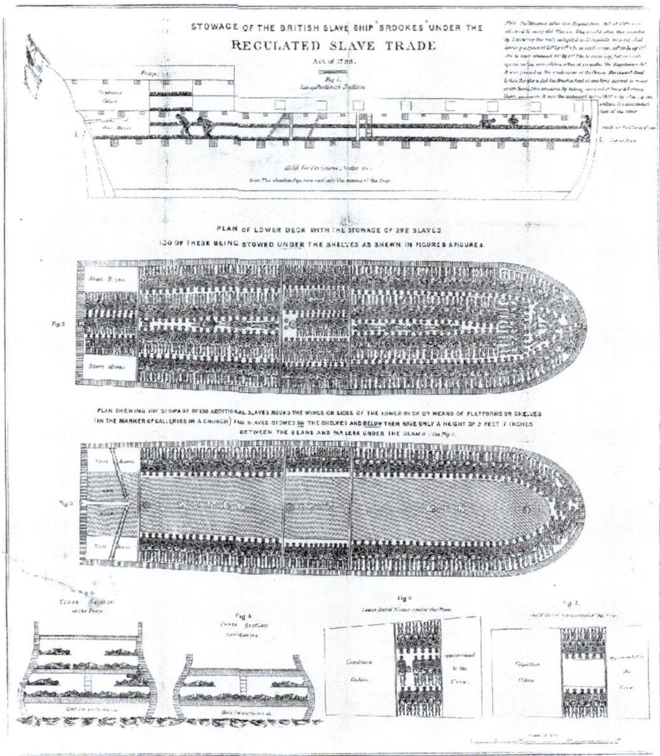

THE SLAVE SHIP *BROOKES* The British slave ship *Brookes* provided this plan of its "stowage" of enslaved people to conform to 1798 legislation from Parliament. It illustrates vividly the terrible conditions under which enslaved people were shipped from Africa to the Americas—human beings squeezed into every available space like cargo for the long, dangerous passage during which many Africans died.

time, the English government virtually outlawed the practice of the Presbyterian religion in Ulster and insisted on conformity with the Anglican Church. After 1710, moreover, the long-term leases of many Scots-Irish expired; English landlords doubled and even tripled the rents. Thousands of tenants embarked for America.

SCOTS-IRISH

Often coldly received at the colonial ports, many of the Scots-Irish pushed out to the edges of European settlement. There they occupied land without much regard for who actually claimed to own it, whether absentee whites, Native Americans, or the colonial governments. They were as ruthless in their displacement and suppression of the Native Americans as they had been with the native Irish Catholics.

Immigrants from Scotland and southern Ireland added other elements to the colonial population in the eighteenth century. Scottish Highlanders, some of them Roman Catholics who had been defeated in rebellions in 1715 and 1745, immigrated into several colonies, North Carolina above all. Presbyterian Lowlanders, faced in Scotland with high rents in the country and unemployment in the towns, left for America in large numbers shortly before the American Revolution, joining earlier groups of Scots, who had arrived in the late seventeenth century. They became a significant influence in New Jersey and Pennsylvania and helped establish Presbyterianism as an important religion in those colonies. The Catholic Irish migrated steadily over a long period, and by the time of the Revolution they were almost as numerous as the Scots, although less conspicuous. Many of them had by then abandoned their Roman Catholic religion and with it much of their ethnic identity.

Continuing immigration and natural increase contributed to a rapid population growth in the colonies in the eighteenth century. In 1700, the non-Indian population of the colonies totaled less than 250,000; by 1775, it was over 2 million—a nearly tenfold increase. Throughout the colonial period, the non-Indian population nearly doubled every twenty-five years.

Historical Thinking Skills

Analyzing Points of View Have students examine the image "The Slave Ship *Brookes*," then compare it to the image on the previous page. Ask students to discuss how the two images are similar or different in purpose and in effect. *(Possible responses: The second image was produced by the shipping company to comply with a legal requirement, while the first image was created to illustrate a poem that was likely intended to oppose the slave trade. Both images illustrate extremely crowded, unhealthy conditions aboard slave ships.)* **WXT** **SOC**

Reasoning Processes

Comparing and Contrasting After students read the section "The Scots-Irish," have them create a Venn diagram comparing the Scots-Irish with the Huguenots and Pennsylvania Dutch. Ask students to evaluate which was more prevalent, the similarities or the differences between the groups. **MIG** **SOC** **ARC**

Historical Thinking Skills

Argumentation Have students read the section "Tobacco." Ask them to write a thesis statement making a historically defensible claim about why the dependence on tobacco cultivation in the Chesapeake led to economic booms and busts. Have students share their theses with a partner or with the class for feedback. **WXT**

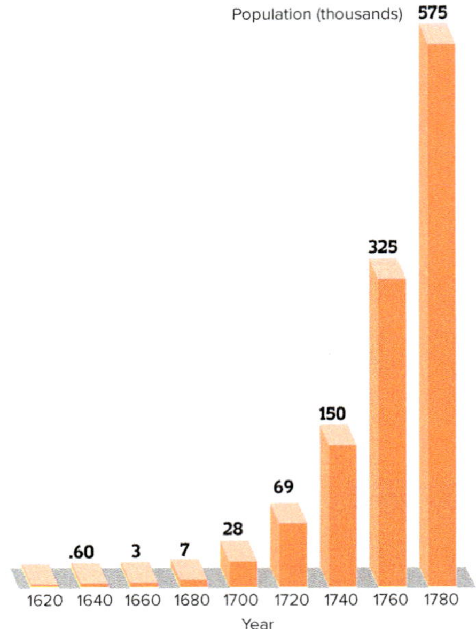

THE AFRICAN POPULATION OF THE BRITISH COLONIES, 1620–1780 From tiny beginnings in the seventeenth century, the African population of the British colonies grew rapidly in the eighteenth century. The growth of slavery was a result of both supply (a readily available enslaved population in the Caribbean islands) and demand (the growth of tobacco, rice, and cotton cultivation in larger areas of the South). The enslaved population in the colonies also increased naturally in this period at a far greater rate than in the past, largely because living conditions improved.

Why did slaveholders invest in better conditions for enslaved people?

THE "PENNSYLVANIA DUTCH" This folk-art painted dish illustrates the traditional dress of the Pennsylvania Dutch. The Pennsylvania Dutch were, in fact, German immigrants, known to their neighbors as "Dutch" because that was how their native word for their nationality ("Deutsch") sounded to most English speakers.

THE COLONIAL ECONOMIES

To those who remained in Europe, and even to some who settled in North America, the English colonies often appeared so small and isolated as to seem virtually at the end of the world. But from the beginning, almost all the English colonies were commercial ventures and were tied in crucial ways to other economies. They developed substantial trade with the native population of North America, with the French settlers to the north and, to a lesser extent, with Spanish colonists to the south and west. And over time they developed an even more substantial trade within the growing Atlantic economy of the sixteenth and seventeenth centuries, of which they became a critical part.

American colonists engaged in a wide range of economic pursuits. But except for a few areas in the West where the small white populations subsisted largely on the fur and skin trade with the Native Americans, farming dominated all areas of European and African settlement throughout the seventeenth and eighteenth centuries. Some farmers engaged in simple subsistence agriculture; but whenever possible, American farmers attempted to grow crops for the local, intercolonial, and export markets.

THE SOUTHERN ECONOMY

In the Chesapeake region, tobacco quickly became the basis of the economy. A strong European demand for the crop enabled some planters to grow enormously wealthy and at times allowed the region as a whole to prosper. But production frequently exceeded demand, and as a result the price of tobacco periodically suffered severe declines. The first major bust in the tobacco economy occurred in 1640, and the boom-and-bust pattern continued throughout the colonial period and beyond. Growing more tobacco only made the problem of overproduction worse, but Chesapeake farmers never understood that. Those planters who could afford to do so expanded their landholdings, enlarged their fields, and acquired additional enslaved laborers. After 1700, tobacco plantations with several dozen enslaved people or more were common.

TOBACCO

The staple of the economies of South Carolina and Georgia was rice. By building dams and dikes along the many tidal rivers, farmers managed to create rice paddies that could be flooded and then drained. Rice cultivation was arduous work, performed standing knee-deep in the mud of malarial swamps under a blazing sun, surrounded by insects. It was a task so difficult and unhealthful that white laborers generally refused

Answers

The African Population of the British Colonies, 1620–1780

Many slaveholders believed that better food and living conditions would lead to a self-sustaining population of enslaved persons, which would be cheaper in the long run than continued importation of large numbers of enslaved Africans. Also, if enslaved persons lived longer, they were more likely to have children who could be kept to work or sold for revenue.

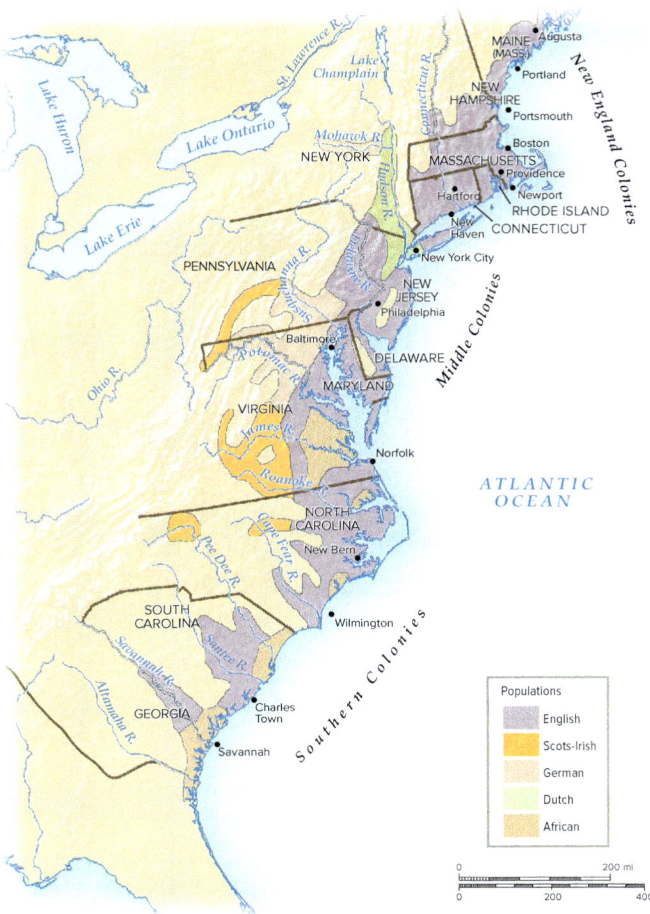

POPULATION DISTRIBUTION OF COLONIAL AMERICA, 1760 Even though the entire Atlantic seaboard of what is now the United States had become a series of British colonies by 1760, the population consisted of people from many nations. As this map reveals, English settlers dominated most of the regions of North America. But note the large areas of German settlement in the western Chesapeake and Pennsylvania; the swath of Dutch settlement in New York and New Jersey; the Scots-Irish areas in the western regions of the South; and the large areas in which Africans were becoming the majority of the population, even if subjugated by the white minority.

What aspects of the history of these colonies help explain their ethnic composition?

to perform it. As a result, planters in South Carolina and Georgia were even more dependent than those elsewhere on enslaved Africans. It was not only because enslaved Africans could be compelled to perform difficult work that planters found them so valuable. It was also because they showed from the beginning a greater resistance to malaria and other local diseases (although the impact of disease on African laborers was by no means inconsiderable). They also proved more adept at the basic agricultural tasks required, in part because some of them had come from rice-producing regions of western Africa.

In the early 1740s, another staple crop contributed to the South Carolina economy: indigo. Eliza Lucas, a young Antiguan woman who managed her family's North American plantations, experimented with cultivating the West Indian plant (which was the source of a blue dye in great demand in Europe) on the mainland. She discovered that it could grow on the high ground of South Carolina, which was unsuitable for rice planting, and that its harvest came while the rice was still growing. Indigo became an important complement to rice and a popular import in England.

INDIGO

Because of the South's early dependence on large-scale cash crops, the southern colonies developed less of a commercial or industrial economy than the colonies of the North. The trading in tobacco and rice was handled largely by merchants based in London and, later, in the northern colonies. Few cities of more than modest size developed in the South.

Discussion and Activities

Making Connections Have students read the section "Indigo." Ask them what products they may still use that utilize the dye from the indigo plant. *(Indigo is the color used to dye blue jeans.)* WXT

Answers

Population Distribution of Colonial America, 1760

English settlers arrived first and settled around ports and along the coast. Later groups of immigrants had to move farther inland in search of land or other economic opportunities. Some groups, such as the Scots-Irish, may have also preferred being farther away from sources of colonial control. MIG SOC PCE

Reasoning Processes

Speculating Have students read the section "More Diverse Economy in the North." Ask them to identify the main reason that the Northern economy diversified more than the Southern economy did. *(There was limited agriculture in the North, so they were forced to diversify.)* Ask students to speculate how the different levels of diversification might have impacted daily life in the North and South. **ARC** **WXT**

PREPARING TOBACCO This 1790 engraving is designed to illustrate the African origins of the enslaved workers who processed tobacco in Virginia. Their "primitive" costumes seemed to the artist, a French visitor to America, to be in keeping with the crude processes they had created for drying, rolling, and sorting tobacco.

NORTHERN ECONOMIC AND TECHNOLOGICAL LIFE

In the North, agriculture was the single most important part of the economy. But unlike in the South, the northern colonies were less dominated by farming. The northern economy was more diverse than the economy in the South in part because conditions for farming were less favorable there. In northern New England, in particular, colder weather and hard, rocky soil made it difficult for colonists to develop the kind of large-scale commercial farming system that southerners were creating. Conditions for agriculture were better in southern New England and the middle colonies, where the soil was fertile and the weather more temperate. New York, Pennsylvania, and the Connecticut River valley were the chief suppliers of wheat to much of New England and to parts of the South. Even there, however, a substantial commercial economy emerged alongside the agricultural one.

MORE DIVERSE ECONOMY IN THE NORTH

Almost every colonist engaged in a certain amount of industry at home. Occasionally these home industries provided families with surplus goods they could trade or sell. Beyond these domestic efforts, craftsmen and artisans established themselves in colonial towns as cobblers, blacksmiths, riflemakers, cabinetmakers, silversmiths, and printers. In some areas, entrepreneurs harnessed water power to run small mills for grinding grain, processing cloth, or milling lumber. And in several places, large-scale shipbuilding operations began to flourish.

The first effort to establish a significant metals industry in the colonies was an ironworks established in Saugus, Massachusetts, in the 1640s after iron ore deposits had been discovered in the region. Iron technology was already advancing rapidly in England, and the colonists attempted to transfer those skills to America. The Saugus works used water power to drive a bellows, which controlled the heat in a charcoal furnace. As the ore melted, it trickled down into molds or was taken in the form of simple "sow bars" to a forge to be shaped into such marketable objects as plows, hoes, axes, pots, and other tools. The Saugus works was a technological success; indeed, it could boast technological capabilities equal to those of any ironworks in Europe at the time. But it was a financial failure. It began operations in 1646; in 1668, its financial problems forced it to close its doors.

SAUGUS IRONWORKS

Metalworks, however, gradually became an important part of the colonial economy. The largest industrial enterprise

Discussion and Activities

Analyzing Visuals Ask students to examine the image "Preparing Tobacco." After they read the section "More Diverse Economy in the North," ask students to evaluate whether the tobacco processing depicted in the image is more agriculture or more industry. Ask them to think about why it may be difficult to make clear distinctions. **WXT**

COMMERCE IN NEW ENGLAND This late-eighteenth-century painting of the home, wharves, countinghouse, and fleet of a prosperous New England fisherman gives some indication of how commerce was expanding even in such relatively small places as Duxbury, Massachusetts. The owner, Joshua Winsor, was active in the mackerel and cod fishing industry. The painting—evidently an effort to celebrate Winsor's great material success and record it for posterity—was by his son-in-law, Dr. Rufus Hathaway.

anywhere in English North America was the ironworks of the German ironmaster Peter Hasenclever in northern New Jersey. Founded in 1764 with British capital, it employed several hundred laborers, many of them imported from ironworks in Germany. There were other, smaller ironmaking enterprises in every northern colony (with particular concentrations in Massachusetts, New Jersey, and Pennsylvania), and there were ironworks as well in several southern colonies. Even so, these and other growing industries did not become the basis for the kind of explosive industrial growth that Great Britain experienced in the late eighteenth century—in part because English parliamentary regulations such as the Iron Act of 1750 restricted metal processing in the colonies. Similar prohibitions limited the manufacture of woolens, hats, and other goods. But the biggest obstacles to industrialization in America were an inadequate labor supply, a small domestic market, and inadequate transportation facilities and energy supplies.

More important than manufacturing were industries that exploited the natural resources of the continent. By the mid-seventeenth century, the flourishing fur trade of earlier years was in decline. Taking its place were lumbering, mining, and fishing, particularly in the waters off the New England coast. These industries provided commodities that could be exported to England in exchange for manufactured goods. And they helped produce the most distinctive feature of the northern economy: a thriving commercial class.

EXTRACTIVE INDUSTRIES

THE EXTENT AND LIMITS OF TECHNOLOGY

Despite the technological progress that was occurring in some parts of America in the seventeenth and eighteenth centuries, much of colonial society was conspicuously lacking in even very basic technologies. Up to half the farmers in the colonies were so primitively equipped that they did not even own a plow. Substantial numbers of households owned no pots or kettles for cooking. And only about half the households in the

Historical Thinking Skills

Evaluating Evidence Have students examine the image "Commerce in New England." Ask them what evidence from the image demonstrates a change over time in the New England economy. *(Possible response: Although the New England economy had always relied on trade and fishing, the image provides evidence of a growing commercial scale of these activities.)* WXT

Discussion and Activities

Analyzing Perspectives After students read the section "Northern Economic and Technological Life," **ask:** Why would Great Britain limit colonial manufacturing but not colonial extractive industries? Discuss as a class or in small groups. *(In keeping with the goals of mercantilism, Britain wanted to keep as much of the more profitable manufacturing under their control, while extracted raw materials like lumber and cotton from the colonies were needed by British manufacturers.)* WXT PCE WOR

Historical Thinking Skills

Analyzing Points of View After students read the section "The Extent and Limits of Technology," ask them to develop a list of basic tools and technologies many settlers lived without. Have students develop that list into a short paragraph from the point of view of early settlers lacking basic tools and technologies, describing the impact of that lack on their daily lives. Ask students to conclude with a brief argument speculating why or how the myth of self-sufficiency developed. **SOC** **WXT**

colonies owned guns or rifles–with rural people almost as unlikely to have firearms as urban people. The relatively low levels of ownership of these and other elementary tools was not because such things were difficult to make, but because most Americans remained too poor or too isolated to be able to afford them. Many households had few if any candles, because they were unable to afford candle molds or tallow (wax), or because they had no access to commercially produced candles. In the early eighteenth century, very few farmers owned wagons. Most made do with two-wheeled carts, which could be hauled by hand (or by horse) around the farm but which were not very efficient for transporting crops to market. The most commonly owned tool on American farms was the axe, which suggests how much time most farmers had to spend clearing land. But throughout the colonies, the ability of people to acquire manufactured implements lagged far behind the capacity to produce them.

MYTH OF SELF-SUFFICIENCY

Even so, few colonists were self-sufficient in the late seventeenth and early eighteenth centuries. The popular image of early American households is of people who had little connection to the market, who grew their own food, made their own clothes, and bought little from anyone else. In fact, relatively few colonial families owned spinning wheels or looms, which suggests that most people purchased whatever yarn and cloth they needed, or could afford, from merchants. Most farmers who grew grain took it to centralized facilities for processing.

THE RISE OF COLONIAL COMMERCE

SHORTAGE OF CURRENCY

Perhaps the most remarkable feature of colonial commerce in the seventeenth century was that it was able to survive. American merchants faced such bewildering and intimidating obstacles, and lacked so many basic institutions of trade, they managed to stay afloat only with great difficulty. There was, first, no commonly accepted medium of exchange. The colonies had almost no specie (gold or silver coins). They experimented at times with different forms of paper currency–tobacco certificates, for example, which were secured by tobacco stored in warehouses; or land certificates, secured by property. Such paper was not, however, acceptable as payment for any goods from abroad, and it was in any case ultimately outlawed by Parliament. For many years, colonial merchants had to rely on a haphazard barter system or on crude money substitutes such as beaver skins.

A second obstacle was the near impossibility of imposing order on their trade. In the fragmented, jerry-built commercial world of colonial America, no merchants could be certain that the goods they sold would be produced in sufficient quantity; nor could they be certain of finding adequate markets for them. Few channels of information existed to inform traders of what they could expect in foreign ports; vessels sometimes stayed at sea for several years, journeying from one market to another, trading one commodity for another, attempting to find some way to turn a profit. Engaged in this chaotic commerce, moreover, were an enormous number of small, fiercely competitive companies, which made the problem of stabilizing the system even more acute.

TRIANGULAR TRADE

Despite these and other problems, commerce in the colonies not only survived but grew. There was an elaborate coastal trade, through which the colonies did business with one another and sold goods to the West Indies–among them rum, agricultural products, meat, and fish. The mainland colonies bought sugar, molasses, and enslaved people from the Caribbean markets in return. There was also an expanding transatlantic trade, which linked the North American colonies in an intricate network of commerce with England, continental Europe, and the west coast of Africa. This commerce has often been described, somewhat inaccurately, as the "triangular trade," suggesting a neat process: merchants carried rum and other goods from New England to Africa; exchanged their merchandise for enslaved people, whom they then transported to the West Indies (hence the term "middle passage" for the dreaded journey–it was the second of the three legs of the voyage); and then exchanged enslaved people for sugar and molasses, which they shipped back to New England to be distilled into rum. In fact, the system was almost never so simple. The "triangular" trade in rum, enslaved people, and sugar was in fact part of a maze of highly diverse trade routes: between the northern and southern colonies, America and England, America and Africa, the West Indies and Europe, and other combinations.

EMERGING MERCHANT CLASS

Out of this complex and highly risky trade emerged a group of adventurous entrepreneurs who by the mid-eighteenth century were beginning to constitute a distinct merchant class. Concentrated in the port cities of the North (above all, Boston, New York, and Philadelphia), they enjoyed protection from foreign competition within the English colonies–the British Navigation Acts had excluded all non-British ships from the colonial carrying trade. They had access to a market in England for such American products as furs, timber, and ships. That did not, however, satisfy all their commercial needs. Many colonial products–fish, flour, wheat, and meat, all of which England could produce for itself–needed markets outside the British Empire. Ignoring laws restricting colonial trade to England and its possessions, many merchants developed markets in the French, Spanish, and Dutch West Indies, where prices were often higher than in the British colonies. The profits from this illegal commerce enabled the colonies to import the manufactured goods they needed from Europe.

THE RISE OF CONSUMERISM

Among relatively affluent residents of the colonies, the growing prosperity and commercialism of British America created both new appetites and new opportunities. The result was a growing preoccupation with the consumption of material goods–and of the association of possessions with social status.

Discussion and Activities

Argumentation Have students read the section "The Rise of Colonial Commerce." Ask them to list and rank the obstacles that colonial traders had to overcome. Have students write a thesis that makes a claim about which of the barriers was the most difficult to overcome. **WXT** **WOR**

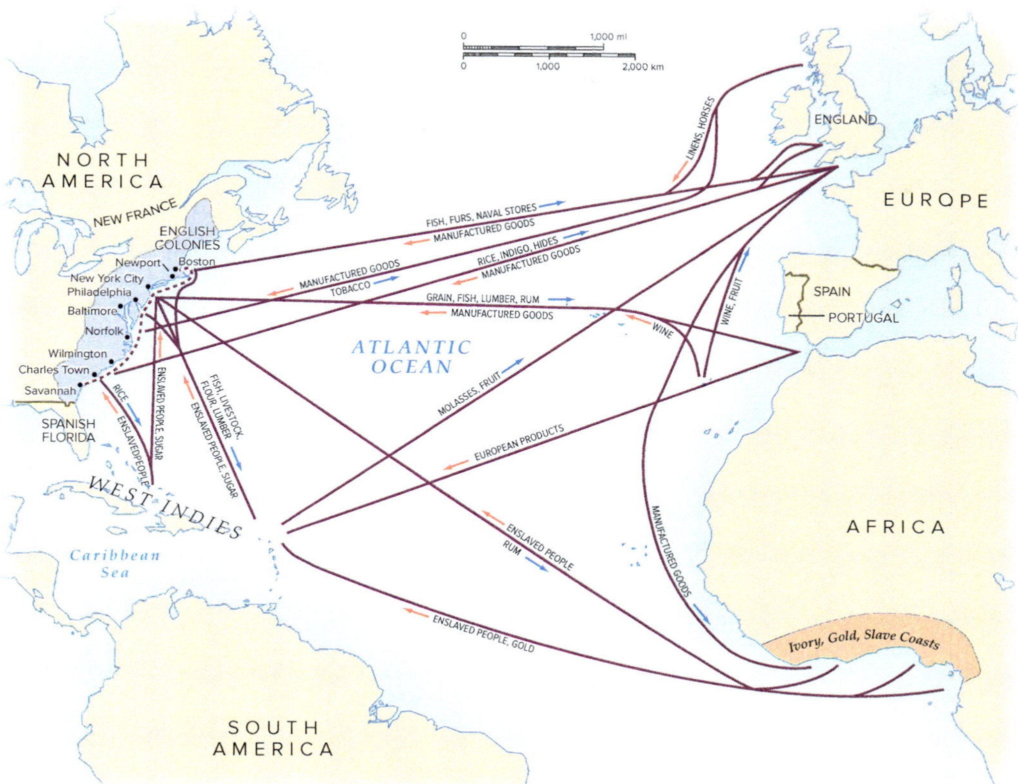

THE "TRIANGULAR TRADE" This map illustrates the complex pattern of trade that fueled the colonial American economy in the seventeenth and eighteenth centuries. A simple explanation of this trade is that the American colonies exported raw materials (agricultural products, furs, and others) to Britain and Europe and imported manufactured goods in return. But while that explanation is accurate, it is not complete, largely because the Atlantic trade was not a simple exchange between America and Europe but, rather, a complex network of exchanges involving the Caribbean, Africa, and the Mediterranean. Note the important exchanges between the North American mainland and the Caribbean islands; the important trade between the American colonies and Africa; and the wide range of European and Mediterranean markets in which Americans were active. Not shown on this map, but also very important to colonial commerce, was a large coastal trade among the various regions of British North America.

Why did the major ports of trade emerge almost entirely in the northern colonies?

The growth of eighteenth-century consumerism was partly a result of the increasing division of American societies by class. As the difference between the upper and lower classes became more glaring, people of means became more intent on demonstrating their own membership in the upper ranks of society. The ability to purchase and display consumer goods was an important way of doing so, particularly for affluent people in cities and towns. But the growth of consumerism was also a product of the early stages of the industrial revolution. Although there was relatively little industry in America in the eighteenth century, England and Europe were making rapid advances and producing more and more affordable goods for affluent Americans to buy. The new manufacturing was dependent, of course, on customers for its products. In an increasingly commercial society, therefore, there were many people committed to promoting the purchase of consumer goods as a positive social good. Consumption also grew because of an increasing tendency among colonists to take on debt to finance purchases and because of the willingness of some merchants to offer credit.

GROWING CONSUMERISM

To facilitate the new consumer appetites, merchants and traders began advertising their goods in journals and newspapers. Agents of urban merchants–the first traveling

Discussion and Activities

Making Connections Have students read the section "Growing Consumerism." As a class or in small groups, ask students to compare eighteenth-century consumerism with twenty-first century consumerism using a Venn diagram. Ask them to evaluate whether consumerism in the two time periods was/is more similar or different. **SOC** **WXT**

Answers

The "Triangular Trade"

The northern colonies were centers of manufacturing, trade, and shipbuilding.

Historical Thinking Skills

Making Connections Have students read the section "Social Mobility." Divide students into small groups and ask them to identify reasons why there was greater social mobility in America than in England. Then ask them to discuss whether the United States today remains a country with great social mobility. **SOC**

TEA PARTY IN THE TIME OF GEORGE I This painting by an unknown artist dates from the 1720s and shows a prosperous Virginian posing with a fashionable and expensive tea service, some of it from China. His eagerness to display his possessions in this way is a sign of the growing interest in the badges of refinement among colonial Americans of means in the eighteenth century.

salesmen—fanned out through the countryside, attempting to interest wealthy landowners and planters in luxury goods. George and Martha Washington, for example, spent considerable time and money ordering elegant furnishings for their home at Mount Vernon, goods that were shipped to them mostly from England and Europe.

SOCIAL CONSEQUENCES

Things that had once been considered expensive luxuries gradually became commonplace necessities—among them tea, household linens, glassware, manufactured cutlery, crockery, and furniture, and many others. Another result of consumerism was the association of material goods—of the quality of a person's home and possessions and clothing, for example—with virtue and "refinement." The ideal of the cultivated "gentleman" and the gracious "lady" became increasingly powerful throughout the colonies in the eighteenth century. That meant striving to become educated and "refined"—"gentlemanly" or "ladylike" in speech and behavior. Americans read books on manners and fashion. They bought magazines about London society. They also commissioned portraits of themselves and their families, devoted large portions of their homes to entertainment, built shelves and cases in which they could display fashionable possessions, constructed formal gardens, and lavished attention on their wardrobes and hairstyles.

The growing importance of consumption and refinement was visible in public spaces as well. Eighteenth-century cities—in America as in England and Europe—began to plan their growth to ensure that there would be elegant and gracious public squares, parks, and boulevards. In the past, social interaction in American communities had largely been between neighbors and relatives, or at most among members of church congregations. Now that a wider "society" was emerging within cities, it became important to create not just private but also public stages for social display.

PATTERNS OF SOCIETY

SOCIAL MOBILITY

Although there were sharp social distinctions in the colonies, the deeply entrenched class system of England failed to reproduce itself in America. In England, land was scarce and the population large. The relatively small number of people who owned property had power over the great majority who did not; the imbalance between land and population became a foundation of the English economy and the cornerstone of its class system.

In early America, the opposite was true. Land was abundant, and people were scarce. Aristocracies emerged in America, to be sure. But they tended to rely less on landownership than on control of a substantial workforce, and they were generally less secure and less powerful than their English counterparts. Far more than in England, there were opportunities in America for social mobility—both up and down.

THE PLANTATION

The plantation defined a distinctive way of life for many white and black southerners that would survive, in varying forms, until the Civil War. The first plantations emerged in the early settlements of Virginia and Maryland, once tobacco became the economic basis of the Chesapeake.

Some plantations were enormous—much like some of the great estates of England. The Maryland plantation of Charles Carroll of Carrollton, reputedly the wealthiest man in the colonies, covered 40,000 acres and contained 285 enslaved people. On the whole, however, seventeenth-century colonial plantations were rough and relatively small estates. In the early days in Virginia, most plantations were crude clearings where landowners and indentured servants worked side by side in conditions so rugged that death was an everyday occurrence. Even in later years, when the death rate declined and the landholdings became more established, plantation workforces seldom exceeded thirty people.

Discussion and Activities

Analyzing Visuals Have students examine the image "Tea Party in the Time of George I." Then ask them to review the section "Growing Consumerism" and identify examples of consumerism in the image. *(Clothing of fine fabric, possibly silk, porcelain china tea cups, silver tea service, etc.)*

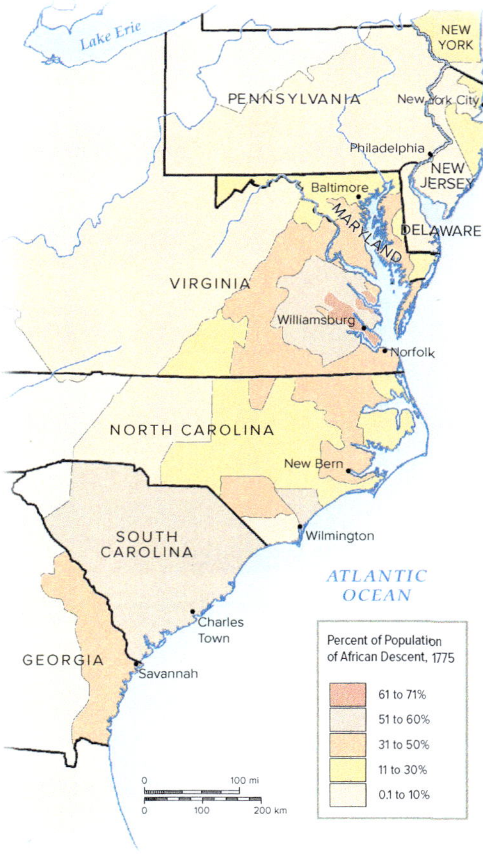

POPULATION OF AFRICAN DESCENT AS A PROPORTION OF TOTAL POPULATION, C. 1775 This map illustrates the parts of the colonies in which enslaved people made up a large proportion of the population—in some areas, a majority. The densest African population was in Tidewater Virginia, but there were black majorities as well in South Carolina and parts of North Carolina. The enslaved population was smallest in the western regions of the southern colonies and in the area north of the Chesapeake, although there remained a significant African population in parts of New Jersey and New York (some enslaved, some free).

Why did certain areas of the South have a higher percentage of enslaved people?

The economy of the plantation, like all agricultural economies, was precarious. In good years, successful growers could earn great profits and expand their operations. But since they could not control their markets, even the largest planters were constantly at risk. When prices for their crops fell—as tobacco prices did, for example, in the 1660s—they faced ruin.

VAGARIES OF THE PLANTATION ECONOMY

Because plantations were sometimes far from cities and towns—which were relatively few in the South—they tended to become self-contained communities. Residents lived in close proximity to one another in a cluster of buildings that included the "great house" of the planter (a house that was usually far from great), the service buildings, the barns, and the cabins of the enslaved people. Wealthier planters often created something approaching a full town on their plantations, with a school (for white children only), a chapel, and a large population. Smaller planters lived more modestly, but still in a relatively self-sufficient world. In some parts of the South, for example, the region around Charleston, South Carolina, planters often divided their time between the city and their nearby plantations.

On the larger plantations, the presence of a substantial enslaved workforce altered not only the economic but also the family lives of the planter class. The wives of plantation owners, unlike the wives of small farmers, could rely on servants to perform ordinary household chores. They could thus devote more time to their husbands and children than people in poorer parts of colonial society. But there were also frequent sexual liaisons between their husbands or sons and black women of the slave community. Southern white women generally learned to pretend not to notice these relationships, but they were almost certainly a source of anxiety and resentment. Black women, naturally, had even greater cause to resent such liaisons.

Southern society was highly stratified. Within given areas, great landowners controlled not only the lives of those who worked on their own plantations. Wealthy planters also shaped the livelihoods of small farmers, who could not effectively compete with the wealthy planters and thus depended on them to market crops and receive credit. Small farmers, working modest plots of land with few or no enslaved laborers to help them, formed the majority of the southern agrarian population, but it was the planters who dominated the southern agrarian economy. Most landowners lived in rough cabins or houses, with servants and enslaved people nearby. Few landowners lived in anything resembling aristocratic splendor.

STRATIFIED SOUTHERN SOCIETY

PLANTATION SLAVERY

Enslaved Africans, of course, lived very differently than white planters. On the smaller farms with fewer enslaved people, there was not always a rigid social separation between white people and enslaved people. But by the mid-eighteenth century, over three-fourths of all African Americans lived on plantations with at least ten enslaved people; nearly half lived in communities of fifty enslaved people or more. In these larger establishments, enslaved people developed a society and culture of their own—influenced by slaveholders, to be sure, but also partly independent of them.

Although slaveholders seldom encouraged formal marriages among enslaved people, Africans themselves developed an

Reasoning Processes

Comparing After students read the section "The Plantation," have them create a T-chart with columns titled "Small Plantations" and "Large Plantations." Have students write information about each type of plantation in the appropriate column. Use the T-charts as the basis for a class discussion about similarities and differences between different types of plantations. **WXT** **SOC**

Answers

Population of African Descent as a Proportion of Total Population, c. 1775

Regions that could support large-scale cultivation of cash crops like tobacco and cotton tended to have higher concentrations of enslaved persons.

AP Exam Practice

Short Answer Provide students with the following short-answer questions and allow 15 minutes for completion. Ask for volunteers to share their responses and discuss as a class.

Answer A, B, and C.

A) For ONE of the regions of colonial America listed below, briefly describe the development of slavery as a labor system in that region.

- New England
- The South

(Possible answer: Slavery first developed in Virginia and Massachusetts due to a growing shortage of indentured servants and a fear that former indentured servants may attempt to change the status quo [e.g., Bacon's Rebellion]. In New England, enslaved people were primarily used as house servants and as field hands on the small farms that were scattered across the region. There was no need for large numbers of enslaved people, as most farms were no more than 100 acres.)

B) Briefly explain ONE piece of historical evidence to support your claim in Part A. *(Possible answer: The growing season was shorter in New England than it was in the South, and therefore, enslaved people often learned a trade in order to continue working through the non-growing season. Many of these enslaved people became blacksmiths, tailors, or domestic servants. In the South, enslaved people were largely used almost year-round for intensive field work. Large plantations grew tobacco, rice, and indigo, all crops that required a significant amount of arduous labor. White people would often not seek that type of work, so it became more efficient to bring in African forced labor.)*

C) Compare one region's development of slavery to the development of slavery in one other region. *(Possible answer: Slavery existed in South Carolina from the beginning of the colony, but in Virginia, slavery evolved out of indentured servitude and the growth of the Atlantic slave trade by English and New England merchants.)*

MULBERRY PLANTATION, 1770 This painting of a rice plantation in South Carolina is unusual in placing the slave quarters in the forefront of the picture. The steep roofs of the cabins, which were built by enslaved people, reflected African architectural styles. The high roofs helped keep the cabins cool by allowing the heat to rise into the rafters. The slaveholder's house and adjacent chapel, built in conventional European style, are in the background.

elaborate family structure. This became possible beginning in the eighteenth century as a result of the increased life expectancy of enslaved people, the gradual equalization of the sex ratio, and the growth of the population through natural increase. Enslaved people attempted to construct nuclear families, and they managed at times to build stable households, even to work together growing their own food in gardens provided by their slaveholders. But such efforts were in constant jeopardy. Any family member could be sold at any time to another planter, even to one in another colony. As a result, the black family developed in ways different from its white counterpart. Africans placed special emphasis on extended kinship networks, even creating surrogate "relatives" for those who were separated from their own families. They adapted themselves, in short, to difficult conditions over which they had limited control.

Enslaved Africans also developed languages of their own. In South Carolina, for example, the early enslaved Africans communicated with one another in Gullah, a hybrid of English and African tongues, which enabled them to engage in conversations slaveholders could not understand. There emerged, too, a distinctive religion, which blended Christianity with African folklore.

SLAVE CULTURE

Nevertheless, slave society was heavily tied to white society. African house servants, for example, at times lived in what was, by the standards of slavery, great luxury; but they were also isolated from their own community and under constant surveillance from whites. Enslaved women were often subjected to unwanted sexual advances from slaveholders and overseers and hence to bearing children. These children were rarely recognized by their white fathers but generally accepted as members of the slave community. On a few plantations, enslaved Africans may have received kindness and even affection and displayed genuine devotion in return, but on most they encountered physical brutality and occasionally even sadism, against which they were powerless.

There were occasional acts of individual resistance by enslaved people against slaveholders, and at least twice during the colonial period there were actual slave rebellions. In the most important such revolt, the so-called Stono Rebellion in South Carolina in 1739, about 100 enslaved people rose up, seized weapons, killed several white people, and attempted to escape south to Florida. The white community quickly crushed the uprising and executed most participants. The most frequent form of resistance was simply running away, but for most enslaved people that provided no real solution either. There was nowhere to go.

STONO REBELLION

Most enslaved people, male and female, worked as field hands (with women also shouldering the additional burdens of

Discussion and Activities

Analyzing Visuals Have students examine the image "Mulberry Plantation, 1770." Ask them to think about how the image portrays the living quarters for enslaved people. Have students share with a partner what the image illustrates about the lives of enslaved people, and what it leaves out. *(Possible answer: It tells something about the physical living quarters inhabited by enslaved people on this plantation. It does not tell anything about living conditions on other plantations. It also does not tell anything about the treatment of enslaved people by their slaveholders, nor about the work performed by enslaved people.)* WXT SOC cooking and child rearing). On the larger plantations that aspired to genuine self-sufficiency, some enslaved people learned trades and crafts: blacksmithing, carpentry, shoemaking, spinning, weaving, sewing, midwifery, and others. These skilled craftsmen and craftswomen were at times hired out to other planters. Some set up their own establishments in towns or cities and shared their profits with slaveholders. On occasion, they were able to buy their freedom. There was a small free black population living in southern cities by the time of the Revolution.

THE PURITAN COMMUNITY

A very different form of community emerged in Puritan New England, but one that was also distinctively American. The characteristic social unit in New England was not the isolated farm, but the town. Each new settlement drew up a "covenant" among its members, binding all residents in a religious and social commitment to unity and harmony. Some such settlements consisted of people who had emigrated to America together (occasionally entire Puritan congregations who had traveled to the New World as a group).

PATTERNS OF SETTLEMENT

The structure of the towns reflected the spirit of the covenant. Colonists laid out a village, with houses and a meetinghouse arranged around a central pasture, or "common." They also divided up the outlying fields and woodlands of the town among the residents; the size and location of a family's field depended on the family's numbers, wealth, and social station. But wherever their lands might lie, families generally lived in the village with their neighbors close by, reinforcing the strong sense of community.

Once established, a town was generally able to run its own affairs with little interference from the colonial government. Residents held a yearly "town meeting" to decide important questions and to choose a group of "selectmen," who governed until the next meeting. Only adult males were permitted to participate

PURITAN DEMOCRACY

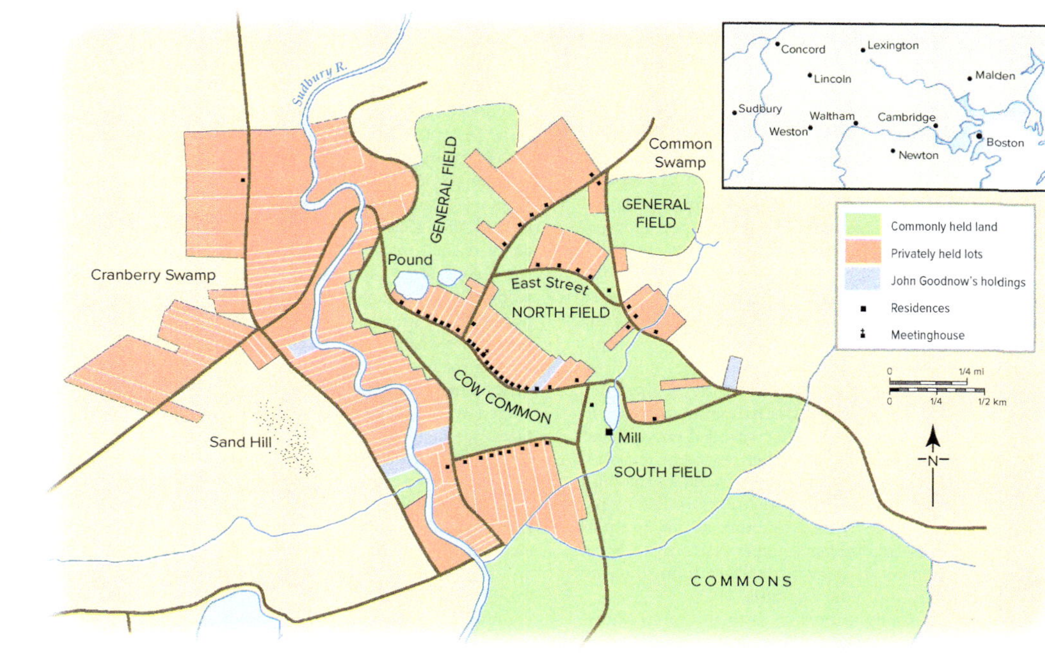

THE NEW ENGLAND TOWN: SUDBURY, MASSACHUSETTS, 17TH CENTURY Just as the plantation was a characteristic social form in the southern colonies, the town was the most common social unit in New England. This map shows the organization of Sudbury, Massachusetts, a town west of Boston, in the early years in the seventeenth century. Note the location of the houses, which are grouped mostly together around a shared pasture (or "commons") and near the church. Note, too, the outlying fields, which were divided among residents of the town, even though they were often not connected to the land on which they lived. The gray areas of the map illustrate the holdings of a single resident of Sudbury, John Goodnow, whose house was on the common, but whose lands were scattered over a number of areas of Sudbury.

What aspects of New England life might help explain the clustering of residences at the center of the town?

Discussion and Activities

Making Connections Have students examine the map "The New England Town: Sudbury, Massachusetts, 17th Century." Ask them to think about how the layout of the town and the surrounding fields might contribute to a strong sense of community. *(Families lived and worked side-by-side; families shared use of common lands.)* Then ask how the arrangement of the towns and surrounding fields might create stresses. *(Disagreements could arise over the use of the common areas; living in close proximity for extended periods might limit personal privacy.)* **GEO** **SOC**

Answers

The New England Town: Sudbury, Massachusetts, 17th Century

Residences would tend to cluster near the meeting house, which was the religious and political center of the town.

Reasoning Processes

Analyzing Change After students read the section "The Puritan Community," have them write a short paragraph describing changes that took place in the Puritan community over the course of the seventeenth century. Ask students to conclude with an evaluation of how well these communities remained true to their founding ideals. **SOC**

in the meeting. But even among them, important social distinctions remained, the most crucial of which was membership in the church. Only those residents who could give evidence of grace, of being among the elect (the "visible saints") confident of salvation as a result of a conversion experience, were admitted to full membership. Residents who had not experienced "conversion" could participate in the church through what was known as the "halfway covenant."

The English system of primogeniture–the passing of all inherited property to the firstborn son–did not take root in New England. Instead, a father divided his lands among all his sons. His control of this inheritance was one of the most effective means of exercising power over the male members of his family. Often a son would reach his late twenties before his father would allow him to move into his own household and work his own land. Even then, sons would usually continue to live in close proximity to their fathers. Young women were generally more mobile than their brothers, since they did not stand to inherit land; their dowries and their inheritances consisted instead of movable objects (furniture, household goods, occasionally money or precious objects) and thus did not tie them to a particular place.

As the years passed and the communities grew, the tight-knit social structure of the Puritans experienced strains. This was partly because of the increasing commercialization of New England society. But it was also a result of other pressures that developed even within purely agricultural communities, pressures that were a result primarily of population growth.

As towns grew larger, residents tended to cultivate lands farther and farther from the community center. Some farmers moved out of the town center to be nearer their lands and thus began to find themselves far away from the church. Outlying residents would often apply for permission to build a church of their own, which was usually the first step toward creation of a new town. Such applications were frequently the occasion for bitter quarrels between the original townspeople and those who proposed to break away.

POPULATION PRESSURE

The dispersion of communities was a result of the practice of distributing land through the patriarchal family structure. In the first generations, fathers generally controlled enough land to satisfy the needs of all their sons. After several generations, however, when such lands were being subdivided for the third or fourth time, there was often too little to go around, particularly in communities surrounded by other towns, with no room to expand outward, forcing younger residents to break off and move elsewhere–at times far away–to form towns of their own where land was more plentiful.

Even within the family, economic necessity often undermined the patriarchal model to which most Puritans, in theory at least, subscribed. It was not only the sons who needed their fathers (as a source of land and wealth); fathers needed their sons, as well as their wives and daughters, as a source of labor to keep the farm and the household functioning. Thus, while in theory men had nearly dictatorial control over their wives and children, in reality relationships were contractual, with the authority of husbands and fathers limited by economic necessity (and, of course, bonds of affection).

GENERATIONAL INTERDEPENDENCE

THE WITCHCRAFT PHENOMENON

By the late seventeenth century, growth and diversity had begun to undermine the cohesiveness of many New England communities. At times, such tensions could produce bizarre and disastrous events. One example was the widespread hysteria in the 1680s and 1690s over supposed witchcraft in New England.

The most famous outbreak (although by no means the only one) was in Salem, Massachusetts, where adolescent girls began to exhibit strange behavior and leveled accusations of witchcraft against several West Indian servants steeped in voodoo lore. The hysteria they produced spread throughout the town, and before it was over, hundreds of people (most of them women) were accused of witchcraft. As the crisis in Salem grew, accusations shifted from marginal women like the West Indians to prominent and substantial people. Nineteen residents of Salem were put to death before the trials ended in 1692; the girls who had been the original accusers later recanted and admitted that they had made up the story.

SALEM WITCH TRIALS

The Salem experience was only one of many. Accusations of witchcraft spread through many New England towns in the early 1690s (and indeed had emerged periodically in Puritan society for many years before). Research into the background of accused witches reveals that most were middle-aged women, often widowed, with few or no children. Many accused witches were of low social position, were often involved in domestic conflicts, had frequently been accused of other crimes, and were considered abrasive by their neighbors. Others were women who, through inheritance or enterprise, had come into possession of substantial land and property on their own and hence also challenged the gender norms of the community. Puritan society had little tolerance for "independent" women. That so many "witches" were women who were not securely lodged within a male-dominated family structure (and that many seemed openly to defy the passive, submissive norms society had created for them) suggests that tensions over gender roles played a substantial role in generating the crisis.

Above all, however, the witchcraft controversies were a reflection of the highly religious character of these societies. New Englanders believed in the power of Satan and his ability to assert his power in the world. Belief in witchcraft was not a marginal superstition, rejected by the mainstream. It was a common feature of Puritan religious conviction.

CITIES

To call the commercial centers that emerged along the Atlantic coast in the eighteenth century "cities" would be to strain the modern definition of that word. Even the largest colonial community was scarcely bigger than a modern small town. Yet, by

Discussion and Activities

Making Generalizations Have students read the section "The Witchcraft Phenomenon." Ask them to create a list of the attributes of the accused witches. Discuss which of these attributes seem to have been generally true of those accused of witchcraft. **SOC**

Historical Thinking Skills

Making Connections Have students read the section "Growth of Colonial Cities." Ask them to consider what features the largest colonial cities shared in common. Discuss as a class or in small groups. *(They were ports; they were centers of trade; many immigrants continued to arrive and stay in these cities.)* GEO SOC WXT

SALEM WITCH TRIALS In his painting The Trial of George Jacobs, Fifth August 1692, Tompkins Harrison Matteson (1813–1884) depicts the trial of George Jacobs, who was accused by his granddaughter of practicing witchcraft. At his trial, Jacobs failed to recite the Lord's Prayer—a failure that was interpreted as evidence of his status as sorcerer. He was found guilty and hanged on August 19, 1692.

the standards of the eighteenth century, cities did indeed exist in America. By the 1770s the two largest ports–Philadelphia and New York–had populations of 28,000 and 25,000, respectively, which made them larger than most English urban centers. Boston (16,000), Charles Town (later Charleston), South Carolina (12,000), and Newport, Rhode Island (11,000), were also substantial communities by the standards of the day.

GROWTH OF COLONIAL CITIES

Colonial cities served as trading centers for the farmers of their regions and as marts for international trade. Their leaders were generally merchants who had acquired substantial estates. Disparities of wealth were features of almost all communities in America, but in cities they seemed particularly glaring. Moving beside the wealthy merchants were numerous minor tradesmen, workers, and indigents who lived in crowded and often filthy conditions. More than in any other area of colonial life (except, of course, in the relationship between slaveholders and enslaved people), social distinctions were real and visible in urban areas.

Cities were also the centers of much of what industry there was in the colonies, such as ironworks and distilleries for turning imported molasses into exportable rum. And they were the locations of the most advanced schools, the most sophisticated cultural activities, and shops where imported goods could be bought. In addition, they were communities with peculiarly urban social problems: crime, vice, pollution, epidemics, traffic. Unlike smaller towns, cities were required to establish elaborate governments. They set up constables' offices and fire departments. They developed systems for supporting the urban poor, whose numbers grew steadily and became especially large in times of economic crisis.

COMMERCIAL AND CULTURAL IMPORTANCE

Cities were also particularly vulnerable to fluctuations in trade. When a market for a particular product became glutted and prices fell, the effects on merchants and other residents could be severe. In the countryside, the impact of economic instability was generally more muted than in cities. Farmers

Discussion and Activities

Analyzing Visuals Have students examine the image "Salem Witch Trials." Ask them to think about why the image might focus on a male accused of witchcraft when most of the accused were women. Have students pair up and share their thoughts. SOC

Reasoning Processes

Identifying Cause and Effect Have students read the section "Inequality." Ask them to organize reasons for inequality into a two-column chart with headings for social and economic factors. Use the charts as the basis for a class discussion about inequality. As part of the discussion, ask students to predict whether these inequalities were likely to increase or decrease as the colonies grew. **SOC** **WXT**

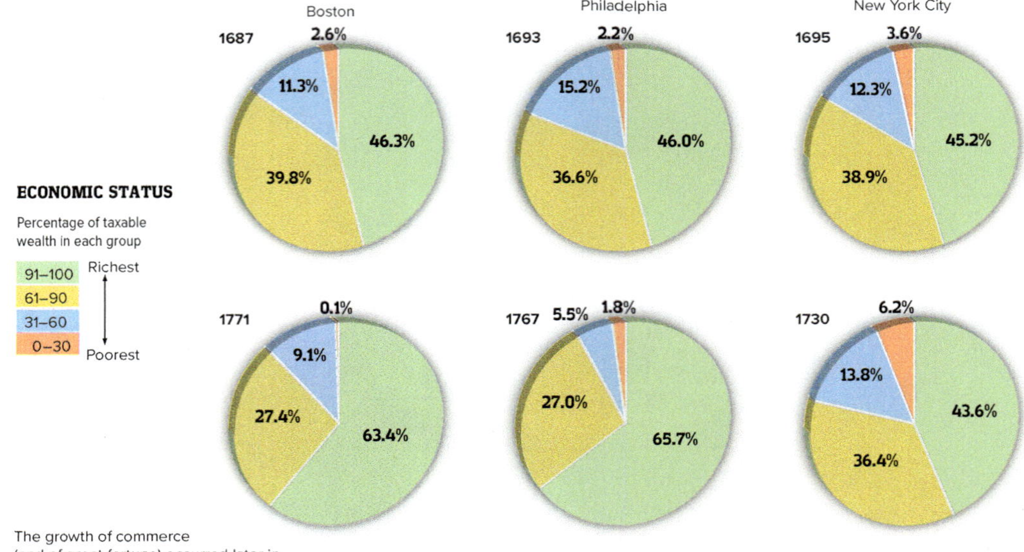

WEALTH DISTRIBUTION IN COLONIAL CITIES, 1687–1771 Although the gap between rich and poor in colonial America was not as large as it would become in the nineteenth and twentieth centuries, the rise of commerce in the early eighteenth century did produce increasing inequality. This chart shows the distribution of wealth in three important commercial cities—Boston, Philadelphia, and New York. The upper pie charts show the distribution of wealth in the late seventeenth century, and the lower charts show how that distribution had changed by the mid- or late eighteenth century. Note the heavy concentration of wealth in the top 10 percent of the population in the seventeenth century, and the even heavier concentration of wealth in Boston and Philadelphia in the eighteenth century. In New York, by contrast, wealth distribution became slightly more equal between 1695 and 1730, because of the breaking up of the great Dutch estates once the colony came under the control of the British. In later years, New York would show the same pattern of growing inequality that Boston and Philadelphia experienced.

What aspects of colonial commerce helped concentrate so much wealth in the hands of a relatively small group?

were still somewhat independent from the larger world of the markets.

Of particular importance for the political future of the colonies, cities became places where new ideas could circulate and be discussed. Because there were printers, it was possible to have regular newspapers. Books and other publications from abroad introduced new intellectual influences. And the taverns and coffeehouses of cities provided forums in which people could gather and debate the issues of the day. It was not surprising that when the revolutionary crisis began to build in the 1760s and 1770s, it was first visible in the cities.

INEQUALITY

New England, for all its belief in community and liberty, was far from an egalitarian society. "Some must be rich and some poor," John Winthrop wrote early in the seventeenth century, and his prediction perhaps exceeded his expectations. Wealthy families and socially distinguished ones (which were usually the same people) had privileges and rights that were not available to poor citizens. Elites were called "ladies" and "gentleman," while people in the lower levels of society were known as "goodman" or "goodwife." Elites were given the best seats in their churches and had the most influence over the parish. Men had more power than women. Servants had few rights. The church itself taught that inequality reflected God's intention.

In cities, such economic stratification was significant—although, unlike in later eras, the ranks of the richest were the largest group in the population and, in Boston in the eighteenth century, the majority. That was partly because wealthy people were more likely than poor people to move to cities and participate in commerce. In the agricultural countryside, many fewer people accumulated significant wealth.

AWAKENINGS AND ENLIGHTENMENTS

Two powerful forces were competing in American intellectual life in the eighteenth century. One was the traditional outlook of the sixteenth and seventeenth centuries, with its emphasis on a personal God, intimately involved with the world, keep-

Answers

Wealth Distribution in Colonial Cities, 1687–1771

The colonial economy was based on trade, and the merchants and traders made larger profits than colonial farmers or industrial workers.

ing watch over individual lives. The other was the new spirit of the Enlightenment, a movement sweeping both Europe and America, which stressed the importance of science and human reason. The old views supported such phenomena as the belief in witchcraft, and they placed great value on a stern moral code in which intellect was less important than faith. The Enlightenment, by contrast, suggested that people had substantial control over their own lives and the course of their societies, that the world could be explained and therefore could be structured along rational scientific lines. Much of the intellectual climate of colonial America (and long after) was shaped by the tension between these two impulses.

THE PATTERN OF RELIGIONS

Religious toleration flourished in many parts of America to a degree unmatched in any European nation, not because Americans deliberately sought to produce it but because conditions virtually required it. Settlers in America brought with them so many different religious practices that it proved difficult to impose a single religious code on any large area.

ROOTS OF RELIGIOUS TOLERATION

The Church of England was established as the official faith in Virginia, Maryland, New York, the Carolinas, and Georgia. But with few exceptions, the laws establishing the Church of England as the official colonial religion were largely ignored. Even in New England, where the Puritans had originally believed that they were all part of a single faith, there was a growing tendency in the eighteenth century for different congregations to affiliate with different denominations, especially Congregationalism and Presbyterianism. In parts of New York and New Jersey, Dutch settlers had established their own Calvinist denomination, Dutch Reformed, which survived after the colonies became part of the British Empire. American Baptists (considered to have been introduced to Americans by Roger Williams) developed a great variety of sects. All Baptists shared the belief that rebaptism, usually by total immersion, was necessary when believers reached maturity. But while some Baptists remained Calvinists (believers in predestination), others came to believe in salvation by free will.

Protestants extended toleration to one another more readily than they did to Roman Catholics. Many Protestants in America, like many in England, feared and hated the pope. New Englanders, in particular, viewed their Catholic neighbors in New France (Canada) not only as commercial and military rivals but also as dangerous agents of Rome. In most of the English colonies, however, Roman Catholics were too few to cause serious conflict. They were most numerous in Maryland, and even there they numbered no more than 3,000. Perhaps for that reason they suffered their worst persecution in that colony. After the overthrow of the original proprietors in 1691, Catholics in Maryland not only lost their political rights but also were forbidden to hold religious services except in private houses.

ANTI-CATHOLICISM

Jewish people in provincial America totaled no more than about 2,000 at any time. The largest community lived in New York City. Smaller groups settled in Newport and Charles Town, and there were scattered Jewish families in all the colonies. Nowhere could they vote or hold office. Only in Rhode Island could they practice their religion openly.

SINNERS IN HELL, 1744 This mid-eighteenth-century religious image illustrates both the fears and prejudices of many colonial Christians. The idyllic city of Sion, in the center of the drawing, is threatened on all sides by forces of evil, which include images not just of Satan and sin, but also of some of the perceived enemies of Protestants—the Catholic Church (symbolized by the image of the pope) and Islam (symbolized by Turks).

By the beginning of the eighteenth century, some Americans were growing troubled by the apparent decline in religious piety in their society. The movement of the population westward and the wide scattering of settlements had caused many communities to lose touch with organized religion. The rise of commercial prosperity created a secular outlook in urban areas. The progress of science and free thought in Europe–and the importation of Enlightenment ideas to America–caused at least some colonists to doubt traditional religious beliefs.

Discussion and Activities

Explaining Historical Concepts Have students read the sections "Roots of Religious Toleration" and "Anti-Catholicism." Ask them to write a journal entry from the point of view of a Catholic immigrant explaining why they chose to come to the Americas and the treatment they received once they arrived. **SOC**

Historical Thinking Skills

Determining Context Have students examine the image "Sinners in Hell." In small groups, ask students to discuss what the purpose of the image might have been. *(Possible answer: The purpose of the image was likely to encourage the people of the colonies to remain faithful to the Church and obedient to their leaders in order to avoid eternal punishment.)* **SOC**

AP Exam Tip

Essays on the AP Exam will require students to place their arguments into a broader historical context. Students can demonstrate that skill by linking their arguments to developments immediately before or after the time period of the prompt, or by describing how other themes within the time period of the prompt affect their argument.

Historical Thinking Skills

Contextualization To practice this tip, ask students to read the feature "The Witchcraft Trials," then create a list of specific facts they already know about the political, economic, social, or cultural development of the colonies that might have influenced the trials. Then have students write a short paragraph explaining how those factors might have contributed to the witchcraft hysteria. *(Possible responses: Most accused witches were relatively independent women; many colonists strongly believed in supernatural forces; there were disputes over political and religious leadership that may have led to accusations.)* **PCE** **SOC**

DEBATING THE PAST

THE WITCHCRAFT TRIALS

The witchcraft trials of the 1690s—which began in Salem, Massachusetts, and spread to other areas of New England—have been the stuff of popular legend for centuries. They have also engaged the interest of generations of historians, who have tried to explain why these seventeenth-century Americans became so committed to the belief that some of their own neighbors were agents of Satan. Although there have been many explanations of the witchcraft phenomenon, some of the most important in recent decades have focused on the central place of women in the story.

Through the first half of the twentieth century, most historians dismissed the witchcraft trials as "hysteria," prompted by the intolerance and rigidity of Puritan society. This interpretation informed perhaps the most prominent popular portrayal of witchcraft in the twentieth century: Arthur Miller's play *The Crucible*, first produced in 1953, which was clearly an effort to use the Salem trials as a comment on the great anticommunist frenzy of his own time. But at almost the same time, the renowned scholar of Puritanism Perry Miller argued in a series of important studies that belief in witchcraft was not a product of hysteria or intolerance but, rather, a widely shared part of the religious worldview of the seventeenth century. To the Puritans, witchcraft seemed not only plausible, but scientifically rational as well.

A new wave of interpretation of witchcraft began in the 1970s, with the publication of *Salem Possessed* (1976), by Paul Boyer and Stephen Nissenbaum. Their examination of the town records of Salem in the 1690s led them to conclude that the witchcraft controversy there was a product of class tensions between the poor, marginal residents of one part of Salem and the wealthy, privileged residents of another. These social tensions, which could not find easy expression on their own terms, led some poor Salemites to lash out at their rich neighbors by charging them, or their servants, with witchcraft. A few years later, John Demos, in *Entertaining Satan* (1983), examined witchcraft accusations in a larger area of New England and similarly portrayed them as products of displaced anger about social and economic grievances that could not be expressed otherwise. Demos provided a far more complex picture of the nature of these grievances than had Boyer and Nissenbaum but, like them, saw witchcraft as a symptom of a persistent set of social and psychological tensions.

At about the same time, however, a number of scholars were beginning to look at witchcraft through the scholarly lens of gender. Carol Karlsen's *The Devil in the Shape of a Woman* (1987) demonstrated through intensive scrutiny of records across New England that a disproportionate number of those accused of witchcraft were property-owning widows or unmarried women—in other words, women who did not fit comfortably into the normal pattern of male-dominated families. Karlsen concluded that such women were vulnerable to these accusations because they seemed threatening to people (including many women) who were accustomed to women as subordinate members of the community.

Mary Beth Norton's *In the Devil's Snare* (2002) placed the witchcraft trials in the context of other events of their time—particularly in the terrifying upheavals and dislocations that the Indian wars of the late seventeenth century created in Puritan communities. In the face of this crisis, in which refugees from King William's War were fleeing towns destroyed by the Native Americans and flooding Salem and other eastern towns, fear and social instability helped create a more-than-normal readiness to connect aberrant behavior (such as the actions of unusually independent or eccentric women) to supernatural causes. The result was a wave of witchcraft accusations that ultimately led to the execution of at least twenty people, mostly women.

The Wonders of the Invisible World:
Being an Account of the
TRYALS
OF
Several Witches,
Lately Excuted in
NEW-ENGLAND:
And of several remarkable Curiosities therein Occurring.
Together with,
I. Observations upon the Nature, the Number, and the Operations of the Devils.
II. A short Narrative of a late outrage committed by a knot of Witches in *Swede-Land*, very much resembling, and so far explaining, that under which *New-England* has laboured.
III. Some Councels directing a due Improvement of the Terrible things lately done by the unusual and amazing Range of *Evil-Spirits* in *New-England*.
IV. A brief Discourse upon those *Temptations* which are the more ordinary Devices of Satan.
By COTTON MATHER.
Published by the Special Command of his EXCELLENCY the Governour of the Province of the *Massachusetts-Bay* in *New-England*.
Printed first, at *Bostun* in *New-England*; and Reprinted at *London*, for *John Dunton*, at the *Raven* in the *Poultry*. 1693.

HISTORICAL THINKING SKILLS

Questions assume cumulative content knowledge from this chapter and previous chapters.

1. **Identifying Historical Developments** Briefly describe how historical interpretations of the witchcraft trials of the New England colonies in the seventeenth century have changed over time. Identify the different scholarly "lenses" through which the historical phenomenon [i.e., the witchcraft trials] has been viewed.
2. **Evaluating Evidence** Briefly describe the historical context that gave way to the economic interpretation of the Salem witchcraft trials.
3. **Developing Arguments** With which historical interpretation do you tend to agree? Explain why, using historical evidence.

Answers

Debating the Past

1. Originally, historians viewed the witchcraft trials though the lens of religion. The intolerance of Puritan society drove this interpretation. Later, historians started viewing the witchcraft trials through the lens of economics. Class tensions, which developed as the population grew and changed, drove the accusations. And finally, some historians view the witchcraft trials through the lens of gender. As most of the accused women were property-owning widows or unmarried women, these accusations were in reaction to individuals who were not conforming to the gender norms of New England society at the time.
2. At this time, Salem was becoming a very prosperous trade community. Newer arrivals were more interested in Salem's location for economic development rather than for religious Puritan reasons. Tensions developed between different social and economic classes in the town. According to some historians, these tensions manifested themselves in the witchcraft trials.
3. Answers will vary. Supporters of Miller's interpretation should focus on the intolerant communities that developed out of the Puritan and Pilgrim migrations. Supporters of Boyer, Nissenbaum, and Demos's interpretations should focus on the economic changes that were taking place within the Salem community. Support of Karlsen and Norton's interpretations should focus on the gender changes that were taking place within the New England communities.

Concerns about weakening piety surfaced as early as the 1660s in New England, where the Puritan oligarchy warned of a decline in the power of the church. Sabbath after Sabbath, ministers preached sermons of despair (known as "jeremiads"), deploring the signs of waning piety. By the standards of other societies or other eras, the Puritan faith remained remarkably strong. But New Englanders measured their faith by their own standards, and to them the "declension" of religious piety seemed a serious problem.

JEREMIADS

THE GREAT AWAKENING

By the early eighteenth century, concerns about declining piety and growing secularism were emerging in other regions and among members of other faiths. The result was the first major American revival: the Great Awakening.

The Great Awakening began in earnest in the 1730s, reached its climax in the 1740s, and brought a new spirit of religious fervor to the colonies. The revival had particular appeal to women (who constituted the majority of converts) and to younger sons of the third or fourth generation of settlers–those who stood to inherit the least land and who faced the most uncertain futures. The rhetoric of the revival emphasized the potential for every person to break away from the constraints of the past and start anew in his or her relationship with God. Such beliefs may have reflected the desires of many people to break away from their families or communities and start a new life.

Powerful evangelists from England helped spread the revival. John and Charles Wesley, the founders of Methodism, visited Georgia and other colonies in the 1730s. George Whitefield, a powerful open-air preacher and for a time an associate of the Wesleys, made several evangelizing tours through the colonies and drew tremendous crowds. But the outstanding preacher of the Great Awakening was the New England Congregationalist Jonathan Edwards, a deeply orthodox Puritan but a highly original theologian. From his pulpit in Northampton, Massachusetts, Edwards attacked the new doctrines of easy salvation for all. He preached anew the traditional Puritan ideas of the absolute sovereignty of God, predestination, and salvation by God's grace alone. His vivid descriptions of hell could terrify his listeners.

The Great Awakening led to the division of congregations between "New Light" revivalists and "Old Light" traditionalists. It also affected areas of society outside the churches. Some of the revivalists denounced book learning as a hindrance to salvation, and some communities repudiated secular education. But other evangelists saw education as a means of furthering religion, and they founded or led schools for the training of New Light ministers.

OLD LIGHTS AND NEW LIGHTS

THE ENLIGHTENMENT

The Great Awakening caused one great upheaval in the culture of the colonies. The Enlightenment, a very different–and in many ways competing–phenomenon, caused another.

The Enlightenment was largely the product of some of the great scientific and intellectual discoveries in seventeenth-century Europe. As scientists and other thinkers discovered natural laws that they believed regulated the workings of nature, they came to celebrate the power of human reason and scientific inquiry. Enlightenment thinkers argued that reason, not just faith, could create progress and advance knowledge. They argued that humans had a moral sense on which they could rely to tell the difference between right and wrong–that they did not need always to turn to God for guidance in making decisions. They insisted that men and women could, through the power of their own reason, move civilization to ever-greater heights.

In celebrating reason, the Enlightenment slowly helped undermine the power of traditional authority–something the Great Awakening did as well. But unlike the Great Awakening, the Enlightenment encouraged men and women to look to themselves–not to God–for guidance as to how to live their lives and to shape society. Enlightenment thought, with its emphasis on human rationality, encouraged a new emphasis on education and a heightened interest in politics and government (for through governments, the believers in reason argued, society had its best chance of bettering itself). Most Enlightenment figures did not challenge religion and insisted that rational inquiry would support, not undermine, Christianity. But they challenged the notion of some religious groups that the answer to all questions about human society should, or could, come directly from God.

TRADITIONAL AUTHORITY CHALLENGED

In the early seventeenth century, Enlightenment ideas in America were largely borrowed from abroad–from such earlier giants as Francis Bacon and John Locke, and from more contemporary Enlightenment thinkers in England and Scotland. Few Americans had yet made important contributions of their own to the new age of science and reason. Later, however, such Americans as Benjamin Franklin, Thomas Jefferson, Thomas Paine, and James Madison made their own contributions to the Enlightenment tradition.

EDUCATION

Even before Enlightenment ideas became common in America, colonists had placed a high value on education, despite the difficulties they confronted in gaining access to it. Some families tried to teach their children to read and write at home, although the heavy burden of work in most agricultural households limited the time available for schooling. In Massachusetts, a 1647 law required every town to support a public school, and while many communities failed to comply, a modest network of educational establishments emerged as a result. Elsewhere, the Quakers and other sects operated church schools. And in some communities, widows or unmarried women conducted "dame schools" by holding private classes in their homes. In cities, master craftsmen set up evening schools for their apprentices; at least a hundred such schools appeared between 1723 and 1770.

Reasoning Processes

Analyzing Cause and Effect Have students read the section "The Great Awakening." Ask them to construct a two-column chart listing causes and effects of this revival. When completed, ask students to write summary statements explaining what they believe to be the most important cause and the most important effect of the Great Awakening. This can used as an exit ticket or as the basis for a short class discussion. **SOC**

Discussion and Activities

Comparing and Contrasting After students read the section "The Great Enlightenment," **ask**: what were the effects of the Great Awakening as compared to the effects of the Enlightenment on the American colonies? Have students write a summary statement explaining whether the similarities or differences were greater and what they believe to be the most important similarity and the most important difference. Ask students to create a thesis statement making a historically defensible claim about which of the events had a greater impact on the colonies. **SOC**

CHAPTER 3
Patterns of Popular Culture

Historical Thinking Skills

Explaining Significance Have students read the feature "Colonial Almanacs." Ask them to write a short paragraph explaining the importance of these publications to colonial life. *(Possible answers: Colonists gained practical knowledge and information about events in the colonies; almanacs created large audiences sharing the same experience; almanacs give us information about what colonists thought important or funny.)*

Colonial Almanacs

Books were scarce and expensive in colonial America, and many families owned only one: the Bible. But starting very early in the life of the English colonies, men and women had another important source of information: almanacs, the most popular nonreligious literature in early America.

Almanacs first appeared in America in 1638 or 1639 when printers in Cambridge, Massachusetts, began publishing the *Philomath Almanac,* which combined an elaborate calendar of religious holidays with information about astronomy, astrology, and other popular interests. By the 1680s, the *Farmer's Almanac,* a heavily illustrated publication that added medical advice, practical wisdom, navigational information, and humor, began to rival the *Philomath.* Through a combination of superstition, popular folklore, and astronomical (and astrological) devices, the *Farmer's Almanac* also predicted weather patterns throughout the year, crop yields, and many other things. Almanac predictions were notoriously unreliable, but many people relied on them nevertheless.

By 1700, there were dozens, perhaps hundreds, of almanacs circulating throughout the colonies and even in the sparsely settled lands to the west and north. The most popular almanacs sold tens of thousands of copies every year. Most families had at least one, and many had several. "It is easy to prove," one almanac writer claimed in the mid-eighteenth century, "that no book we read (except the Bible) is so much valued and so serviceable to the community." America was a multilingual society, and although most almanacs were in English, some appeared in French, Dutch, Hebrew, Norwegian, Spanish, German, and various Indian languages. For five years just after the Revolution, Benjamin Banneker of Maryland was the only African American almanac writer, publishing a book that occasionally included harsh commentary on slavery and the slave trade.

The best-known almanac in the colonies in the years before the American Revolution was *Poor Richard's Almanack,* published in Philadelphia by Benjamin Franklin under the pseudonym Richard Saunders. "I endeavor'd to make it both entertaining and useful," Franklin later wrote in his autobiography. "And observing that it was generally read, . . . I consider'd it as a proper vehicle for conveying instruction among the common people, who bought scarcely any other books." In issue after issue, Franklin accompanied his calendars, astronomical information, and other standard almanac fare with "proverbial sentences, chiefly such as inculcated industry and frugality." Poor Richard's many sayings became among the most familiar passages in America. Franklin was among many writers who used the almanac to promote the new scientific discoveries of his time and to try to discredit what he considered the backward superstitions standing in the way of knowledge.

Almanacs were the only widely read publications in America that contained popular humor, and they are one of the best sources today for understanding what early Americans considered funny. Not unlike later generations, they delighted in humor that ridiculed the high and mighty (aristocrats, lawyers, clergymen, politicians), made fun of relationships between men and women, and expressed stereotypes about racial and ethnic groups. In the 1760s and 1770s, almanac humor was often used to disguise political ideas, in the way it ridiculed British officials and American Tories. During the war itself, humorous anecdotes about military officers and political leaders reflected the uneasy views of Americans about the long and difficult struggle.

During and after the Revolution, much almanac humor consisted of admiring anecdotes about the man who was by then perhaps the most famous and beloved man in America—Poor Richard himself, Benjamin Franklin. Much less reverential, and probably funnier to readers, was the often-ribald ethnic and racial humor in almanacs. In *Beer's Almanac* of 1801, an Irishman boasted that he had owned a large estate in Ireland before leaving for America. Why, he was asked, had he left it to come to the United States? "Ah," he replied, "It was indeed under a small encumbrance; for another man's land lay right a top of it."

Almanacs remained enormously popular throughout the nineteenth century, and some are still published today. But they had their greatest influence in the early years of European settlement when, for thousands of Americans, they were virtually the only source of printed information available. "A good Almanac," the printer Isaac Briggs wrote in 1798, in a preface to one of his own, "is, like iron, far more valuable (although much less valued) than gold, if we estimate its value by its absolute usefulness to the common purposes of life."

II Mon. April hath xxx days.

Kind Katharine to her husband kiss'd these words,
"Mine own sweet *Will,* how dearly I love thee!"
If true (quoth Will) the World no such affords.
And that its true I durst his warrant be;
For ne'er heard I of Woman good or ill,
But always loved best, her own sweet Will.

POOR RICHARD'S ALMANACK This page from a 1757 edition of Poor Richard's Almanack illustrates the wide range of material that almanacs presented to their readers—an uplifting poem, a calendar of holidays and weather predictions, and such scattered pieces of advice and wisdom as "A rich rogue is like a fat hog, who never does good till as dead as a log."

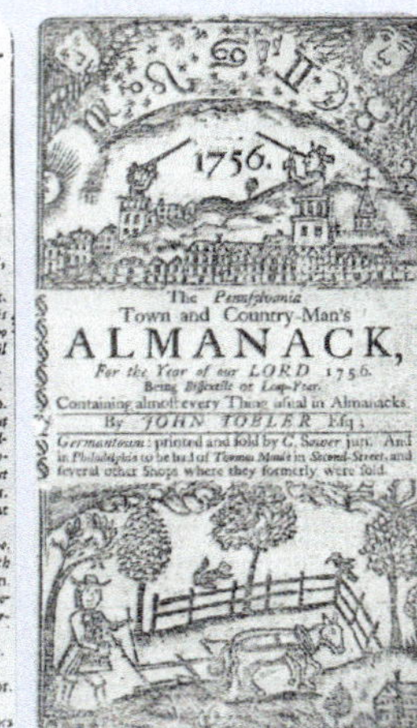

TOWN AND COUNTRY-MAN'S ALMANACK As the population of colonial cities and towns grew, almanacs—originally targeted mainly at farmers—began to make explicit appeal to townspeople as well.

HISTORICAL THINKING SKILLS

1. **Identifying Historical Context** Briefly describe why almanacs were so popular, and explain what that tells us about life in colonial America.
2. **Identifying Evidence** Identify the ways that science was used and promoted in the early almanacs.
3. **Explaining Historical Developments** Explain the connections between high literacy rates and the coming American Revolution.

Answers

Patterns of Popular Culture

1. Outside of the Bible, local almanacs were the only source of reading material in much of colonial America. America was much more intellectual and literate than what might be thought. The literacy rate of white Americans was much higher than that of their European counterparts.
2. Franklin wanted to make his almanac both entertaining and useful. It served as a source of valuable instruction to the common people, who rarely had other reading options. It contained new scientific discoveries, and it was a platform for Franklin to discredit what he considered backward superstitions standing in the way of knowledge.
3. The American colonies developed a very important trans-Atlantic print culture. As the population was highly literate compared to Europe, more and more reading material became available to colonists. Some of the reading material that was finding its way to the colonies promoted Enlightenment political ideas, like those of John Locke and his social contract theory. These materials would serve as source material for much of the justification by colonists for the American Revolution.

Only a relatively small number of children received education beyond the primary level; but white male Americans, at least, achieved a high degree of literacy. By the time of the Revolution, well over half of all white men could read and write, a rate substantially higher than in most European countries. The large number of colonists who could read helped create a market for the first widely circulated publications in America other than the Bible: almanacs (see "Patterns of Popular Culture," above). The literacy rate of women lagged behind that of men until the nineteenth century; and while opportunities for education beyond primary school were scarce for males, they were almost nonexistent for females. Nevertheless, in their early years colonial girls often received the same home-based education as boys, and their literacy rate too was substantially higher than that of their European counterparts. Enslaved Africans had virtually no access to education. Occasionally slaveholders would teach enslaved children to read and write, but they had few real incentives to do so. Indeed, as the slave system became firmly entrenched, strong social (and ultimately legal) sanctions developed to discourage any efforts to promote literacy among enslaved populations, lest it encourage enslaved people to question their station. Native Americans, too, remained largely outside the white educational system—to a large degree by choice; Native Americans preferred to educate their children in their own way. But some white missionaries and philanthropists established schools for Native Americans and helped create a small but significant population literate in spoken and written English.

HIGH WHITE LITERACY RATES

Nowhere was the intermingling of the influences of traditional religiosity and the new spirit of the Enlightenment clearer than in the colleges and universities that grew up in colonial America. Of the six colleges in operation by 1763, all but two were founded by religious groups primarily for the training of preachers. Yet in almost all, the influences of the new scientific, rational approach to knowledge could be felt. Harvard, the first American college, was established in 1636 by the General Court (legislature) of Massachusetts at the behest of Puritan theologians, who wanted to create a training center for ministers. The college was named for a Charlestown minister, John Harvard, who had died and left his library and half his estate to the college. Decades later, in 1693, William and Mary College (named for the English king and queen) was established in Williamsburg, Virginia, by Anglicans; like Harvard, it was conceived as an academy to train clergymen. In 1701, conservative Congregationalists, dissatisfied with what they considered the growing religious liberalism of Harvard, founded Yale (named for one of its first benefactors, Elihu Yale) in New Haven, Connecticut. Out of the Great Awakening emerged the College of New Jersey, founded in 1746 and known later as Princeton (after the town in which it is located). One of its first presidents was Jonathan Edwards.

Despite the religious basis of these colleges, students at most of them could derive something of a secular education from the curricula, which included not only theology, but logic, ethics, physics, geometry, astronomy, rhetoric, Latin, Hebrew, and Greek as well. From the beginning, Harvard attempted not only to provide an educated ministry but also to "advance learning and perpetuate it to posterity." Members of the Harvard faculty made strenuous efforts to desseminate new scientific ideas—particularly the ideas of Copernican astronomy—to a larger public, often publishing their ideas in popular almanacs. By doing so, they hoped to stamp out popular belief in astrology, which they considered pagan superstition.

LIBERAL CURRICULA

King's College, founded in New York in 1754 and later renamed Columbia, was even more devoted to the spread of secular knowledge. Although it was founded in part by the Anglican Trinity Church in New York, it had no theological faculty and was interdenominational from the start. The Academy and College of Philadelphia, which became the University of Pennsylvania, was a completely secular institution, founded in 1755 by a group of laymen under the inspiration of Benjamin Franklin. It offered courses in utilitarian subjects—mechanics, chemistry, agriculture, government, commerce, and modern languages—as well as in the liberal arts. It also became the site of the first medical school in British America, founded in 1765.

GEORGE WHITEFIELD Whitefield succeeded John Wesley as leader of the Calvinist Methodists in Oxford, England. Like Wesley, he was a major force in promoting religious revivalism in both England and America. He made his first missionary journey to the New World in 1738 and returned in the mid-1740s for a celebrated journey through the colonies that helped spark the Great Awakening.

Reasoning Processes

Identifying Cause and Effect After students read the section "Education," ask them to think about ways that the Great Awakening and the Enlightenment led to the creation of institutions of higher learning in the colonies. Have students then discuss to what extent the early American institutions of higher learning are carrying out their original goals today. **SOC**

Discussion and Activities

Making Connections After students read the section "Education," hold a class discussion about what "liberal" meant in the eighteenth century in relation to education to what is commonly meant by the term today. **SOC**

CHAPTER 3

SOCIETY AND CULTURE IN PROVINCIAL AMERICA

Historical Thinking Skills

Determining Context Have students examine the image "A 'Dame School' Primer." Ask students to write a short paragraph explaining why New England schools would emphasize moral and religious instruction so heavily. *(Communities were dominated by religious leaders; instruction on morals would promote obedience to religious and political leaders; colonists sincerely believed in the need for religious instruction in order to win salvation.)* **SOC** **ARC**

THE SPREAD OF SCIENCE

The clearest indication of the spreading influence of the Enlightenment in America was an increasing interest in scientific knowledge. Most of the early colleges established chairs in the natural sciences and introduced some of the advanced scientific theories of Europe, including Copernican astronomy and Newtonian physics, to their students.

But the most vigorous promotion of science in these years occurred outside the colleges, through the private efforts of amateurs and the activities of scientific societies. Leading merchants, planters, and even theologians became corresponding members of the Royal Society of London, the leading English scientific organization. Benjamin Franklin, the most celebrated amateur scientist in America, won international fame through his experimental proof of the nature of lightning and electricity and his invention of the lightning rod. His 1752 demonstration, using a kite, of his theory that lightning and electricity were the same was widely celebrated in the colonies.

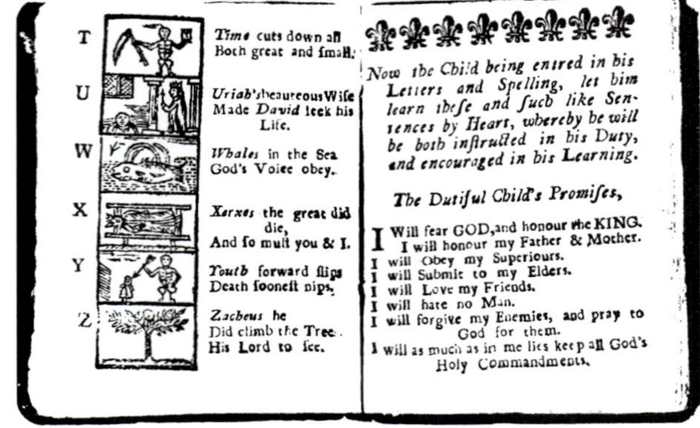

T Time cuts down all
Both great and small.

U Uriah's beauteous Wife
Made David seek his
Life.

W Whales in the Sea
God's Voice obey.

X Xerxes the great did
die,
And so must you & I.

Y Youth forward slips
Death soonest nips.

Z Zacheus he
Did climb the Tree
His Lord to see.

Now the Child being entred in his Letters and Spelling, let him learn these and such like Sentences by Heart, whereby he will be both instructed in his Duty, and encouraged in his Learning.

The Dutiful Child's Promises,

I Will fear GOD, and honour the KING.
I will honour my Father & Mother.
I will Obey my Superiours.
I will Submit to my Elders.
I will Love my Friends.
I will hate no Man.
I will forgive my Enemies, and pray to God for them.
I will as much as in me lies keep all God's Holy Commandments.

A "DAME SCHOOL" PRIMER More than the residents of any other region of North America (and far more than those of most of Europe), the New England colonists strove to educate their children and achieved perhaps the highest level of literacy in the world. Throughout the region, young children attended institutions known as "dame schools" (because the teachers were almost always women) and learned from primers like this one. Puritan education emphasized both basic skills (the alphabet and reading) and moral and religious precepts, as this sample page suggests.

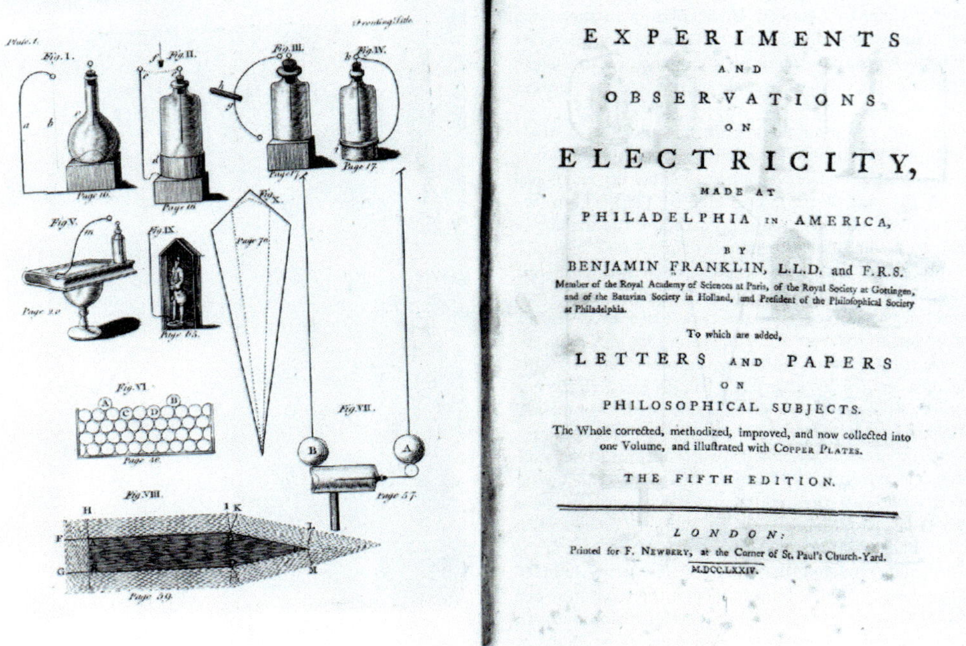

EXPERIMENTS
AND
OBSERVATIONS
ON
ELECTRICITY,
MADE AT
PHILADELPHIA IN AMERICA,
BY
BENJAMIN FRANKLIN, L.L.D. and F.R.S.
Member of the Royal Academy of Sciences at Paris, of the Royal Society at Gottingen, and of the Batavian Society in Holland, and President of the Philosophical Society at Philadelphia.

To which are added,
LETTERS AND PAPERS
ON
PHILOSOPHICAL SUBJECTS.

The Whole corrected, methodized, improved, and now collected into one Volume, and illustrated with COPPER PLATES.

THE FIFTH EDITION.

LONDON:
Printed for F. NEWBERY, at the Corner of St. Paul's Church-Yard.
M.DCC.LXXIV.

BENJAMIN FRANKLIN ON ELECTRICITY The discovery of electricity was one of the great scientific events of the eighteenth century, even though large-scale practical use of electrical energy emerged much later. Benjamin Franklin was one of the first Americans, and certainly the most famous one, to experiment with electricity. This is the frontispiece for a book, originally published in 1750 in Philadelphia, that describes his "experiments and observations." The pages shown here are from the London edition, which appeared in 1774.

Discussion and Activities

Analyzing Visuals Have students examine the image "Benjamin Franklin on Electricity." Discuss with the class how publication of scientific treatises such as this one might have impacted relations between England and its colonies. *(Recognition of American scientific achievements might lead to greater respect for the colonies generally. Individual scientists like Franklin gained notoriety that might enhance his later political standing.)* **WOR** **SOC**

The high value that influential Americans were beginning to place on scientific knowledge was clearly demonstrated by the most daring and controversial scientific experiment of the eighteenth century: inoculation against smallpox. The Puritan theologian Cotton Mather heard, reportedly from an enslaved man he named Onesimus, of the practice of deliberately infecting people with mild cases of smallpox in order to immunize them against the deadly disease. He learned, too, that experiments in inoculation were being conducted, with some success, in England. Mather was not, certainly, a wholly committed scientist. He continued to believe that disease was a punishment for sin. Yet, despite strong opposition from many of his neighbors, he urged inoculation on his fellow Bostonians during an epidemic in the 1720s. The results confirmed the effectiveness of the technique. Other theologians (including Jonathan Edwards) took up the cause, along with many physicians. By the mid-eighteenth century, inoculation had become a common medical procedure in America.

Smallpox Inoculation

Concepts of Law and Politics

In seventeenth- and eighteenth-century law and politics, as in other parts of their lives, Americans of European descent believed that they were re-creating in the Americas the practices and institutions of the Europe. But as in other areas, they managed to create something very different.

Changes in the law in America resulted in part from the scarcity of English-trained lawyers, who were almost unknown in the colonies until after 1700. Not until well into the eighteenth century did authorities in England try to impose the common law and the statutes of the realm upon the provinces. By then, it was already too late. Although the American legal system adopted most of the essential elements of the English system, including such ancient rights as trial by jury, significant differences had already become well established. Pleading and court procedures were simpler in America than in England, and punishments were different. Instead of the gallows or prison, colonists more commonly resorted to the whipping post, the branding iron, the stocks, and (for "gossipy" women) the ducking stool. In a labor-scarce society, it was not in the interests of communities to execute or incarcerate potential workers. Crimes were redefined. In England, a printed attack on a public official, whether true or false, was considered libelous. In the 1734–1735 trial of the New York publisher John Peter Zenger, who was powerfully defended by the Philadelphia lawyer Andrew Hamilton, the courts ruled that criticisms of the government were not libelous if factually true—a verdict that removed some restrictions on the freedom of the press: there was a subtle but decisive transformation in legal philosophy. Some colonists came to think of law as a reflection of the divine will; others saw it as a result of the natural order. In neither case did they consider it an expression of the power of an earthly sovereign.

Colonial Legal System

© Fotosearch/Getty Images

PUNISHMENT IN NEW ENGLAND New England communities prescribed a wide range of punishments for misconduct and crime in the seventeenth and eighteenth centuries. Among the more common punishments were public humiliations—placing offenders in stocks, forcing them to wear badges of shame, or, as in this woodcut, publicly ducking them in a stream or pond to create both discomfort and embarrassment.

Even more significant for the future of the relationship between the colonies and England were important differences between the American and British political systems. Because the royal government was so far away, Americans created a group of institutions of their own that gave them—in reality, if not in theory—a large measure of self-government. In most colonies, local communities grew accustomed to running their own affairs with minimal interference from higher authorities. Communities also expected to maintain strict control over their delegates to the colonial assemblies, and those assemblies came to exercise many of the powers that Parliament exercised in England (even though in theory Parliament remained the ultimate authority in America). Provincial governors appointed by the Crown had broad powers on paper, but in fact their influence was sharply limited. They lacked control over appointments and contracts; such influence resided largely in England or with local colonial leaders. They could never be certain of their tenure in office; because governorships were patronage appointments, a governor could be removed any time his patron in England lost favor. And in many cases, governors were not even familiar with the colonies they were meant to govern. Some governors were native-born Americans, but most were Englishmen who came to the colonies for the first time to assume their offices. The result of all this was that the focus of politics in the colonies became a local one. The provincial governments became accustomed to acting more or less independently of Parliament, and a set of assumptions and expectations about the rights of the colonists began to take hold in America that policymakers in England did not share. These differences caused few problems before the 1760s, because the British did little to exert the authority they believed they possessed. But when, beginning in 1763, the English government began attempting to tighten its control over the American colonies, a great imperial crisis developed.

Colonial Governments

Discussion and Activities

Making Connections After students read the section "The Spread of Science," ask them to construct a two-column chart comparing eighteenth-century efforts to encourage inoculation against smallpox to twenty-first century efforts to encourage vaccinations. Discuss with the class how those efforts in different time periods were/are similar and different. SOC WXT

Reasoning Processes

Analyzing Change Have students read the section "Concepts of Law and Politics." Ask them to brainstorm examples of how the legal system had changed in America by the late eighteenth century and how it stayed the same. Have students use the information collected to write a thesis statement that makes a historically defensible claim about whether the American legal system was characterized more by continuity or change over time. SOC

Discussion and Activities

Making Connections Have students read the "Connecting Themes" section. Ask them to think about how colonial Americans could both practice slavery and subscribe to the values of the Second Great Awakening and the Enlightenment at the same time. Then have students pair up to share their thoughts. Conclude by bringing the class together to identify and discuss examples of seeming contradictions in contemporary society. **NAT** **ARC**

Key Terms

Students should be familiar with the key terms and be able to define them in the context of the development of colonial society in the seventeenth and eighteenth centuries. Encourage students to use these terms in performing review exercises and exam practice for this chapter.

CHAPTER 3 REVIEW

CONNECTING THEMES

Chapter Three covered the growing population and development of society and culture of colonial British North America. Early focus was on the growth of the family and how the familial social structure evolved and developed unique characteristics based on the region. Family life in the Chesapeake was different, in some significant ways, from family life in New England. The development of slavery and slave culture in North America was also explored; slavery grew to exist in all parts of colonial North America and all parts benefited, economically, from that institution of exploitation. Both the family and slavery were woven deeply into the social fabric of colonial North America.

Two other important cultural movements heavily influenced ideas and beliefs in colonial North America: the First Great Awakening and the Enlightenment. Both movements were critical in furthering the idea of an American identity and encouraged the challenging of authority, which loosened the bonds within the colonies and allowed the beginning of an American independence movement to emerge and grow. Although the idea of independence from England remained years away in colonial North America, the seeds planted in the minds of the colonists, partly through the ideas of the First Great Awakening and the Enlightenment, would eventually bloom into full political revolution.

You should consider the following questions as you review the themes for this chapter:

- What were the factors that led to the development of distinct colonial regional identities?
- What were the various roles of colonial women within different regions of colonial North America and how did those differences help shape the identities of women in these regions?
- How did technology, science, and education affect the development of culture within colonial North America?
- What were the causes and effects of the growth of the institution of slavery?
- How did free and forced migration affect the development of cultural, economic, and social systems?
- What was the impact of cooperation and conflict between different social groups on the formation of early colonial governments?
- How did the growth of the colonial economy create both continuity and change in relationships among the nations of the Atlantic World?
- How did the ideas, beliefs, and cultures of colonists influence the development of regional differences in colonial North America?

KEY TERMS

Cotton Mather 101
Covenant 91
Enlightenment ideals 95
George Whitefield 97
Great Awakening 97
Gullah 90
Huguenots 79
Indentured servitude 72
Jeremiad 97
John and Charles Wesley 97
John Locke 97
John Peter Zenger 101
Jonathan Edwards 97
Middle Passage 77
Primogeniture 92
Saugus ironworks 84
Scots-Irish 81
Slave codes 79
Stono Rebellion 90
Triangular Trade 86

 Go Online **Chapter 3 Content Review**

Assessing Student Understanding Use the online assessment to assess student understanding of concepts and topics within the chapter. You can assign the ready-made Chapter 3 Content Review or create your own from available questions. This easy-to-use tool helps you design assessments that meet the needs of different types of learners.

AP EXAM PRACTICE

Questions assume cumulative content knowledge from this chapter and previous chapters.

MULTIPLE CHOICE

Use the image on page 90 and your knowledge of U.S. history to answer questions 1–3.

1. The use of African-style architecture for living quarters is an example of
   (A) continuing cultural practices as a means of resistance.
   (B) British recognition of African architectural achievements.
   (C) persuading enslaved workers to remain in the colonies.
   (D) incorporating African traditions into white colonial society.

2. The British colonies increasingly depended on an enslaved labor force because
   (A) they wished to build a political culture that blended English and African traditions.
   (B) they wished to limit their dependence on plantations and economically diversify.
   (C) they valued the religious diversity that enslaved Africans brought to the colonies.
   (D) they found indentured servants difficult to hire and increasingly problematic to control.

3. In contrast to other colonial regions, the fact that enslaved laborers constituted a majority of the population in areas of South Carolina allowed them to
   (A) achieve higher political office.
   (B) retain more cultural autonomy.
   (C) integrate within the Puritan church.
   (D) negotiate more permissive legal guidelines.

SHORT ANSWER

Use your knowledge of U.S. history to answer questions 4 and 5.

4. Use the map on page 87 to answer A, B, and C.
   (A) Briefly describe ONE specific cause that led to the development of the Triangular Trade.
   (B) Briefly explain ONE specific short-term effect of the development of the Triangular Trade.
   (C) Briefly explain ONE specific long-term effect of the Triangular Trade.

5. Answer A, B, and C.
   (A) Briefly describe ONE specific historical difference between the First Great Awakening and the Enlightenment.
   (B) Briefly describe ONE specific historical similarity between the First Great Awakening and the Enlightenment.
   (C) Briefly explain ONE specific effect of either the First Great Awakening or the Enlightenment.

LONG ESSAY

Develop a thoughtful and thorough historical argument that addresses the statement below. Begin your essay with a thesis statement, and support it with specific historical evidence and examples.

6. Evaluate the extent of changes in the development of an American identity in the colonies from 1650 to 1750.

Answers

Multiple Choice

1. A; **2.** D; **3.** B

Short Answer

4A) Possible answer: As European powers engaged in American colonization, a vast network of trade developed. These European powers needed raw materials and new markets.

4B) Possible answer: European powers noticed a return on their investment for overseas colonies, as wealth was readily available.

4C) Possible answer: For people living in Europe, one effect was population growth, but for people living in the Americas, the result was widespread death and disease.

5A) Possible answer: The First Great Awakening resulted in increased church attendance and was driven largely by religious figures. The Enlightenment resulted in a decrease in church attendance and was driven largely by secular figures.

5B) Possible answer: Both the First Great Awakening and the Enlightenment led to a loosening of political bonds in the colonies by challenging traditional authorities, which ultimately served as one of the causes for the American independence movement.

5C) Possible answer: The infiltration of Enlightenment ideas led to increased interest in science and learning in the colonies. It also fundamentally changed the direction of curriculum in universities, as they moved from institutions primarily designed to train young boys for the ministry to a more general humanities focus.

Answers

Long Essay

6. Possible thesis: By 1750, most colonists still viewed themselves as British in many respects. However, the colonies began to experience great change with regard to the development of an American identity. First, the colonies were moving away from much of their religious foundations, which loosened the bonds of authority. Second, the country transformed from a society reliant on indentured servants to one that was dependent on slavery. The ideas of independence and exploitation went hand-in-hand with the development of an American identity. The colonies grew further and further apart from their theological ties to each other, and the First Great Awakening was an attempt to pull the colonists back to God. The Enlightenment was designed to provide the colonists with a sense of safety in ideas without an overreliance on the Bible. Despite the fact that most of the early colonies were very different in terms of geography, economics, politics, and culture, as they moved closer and closer to the eighteenth century, these differences began to melt away and a sense of the "American" began to take hold. Still, the colonies remained British in most respects, including language, culture, and political values. The population continued to grow as the colonies served as outlets to individuals looking for economic opportunities and political and religious freedom.

Discussion and Activities

Analyzing Cause and Effect Direct students' attention to the Questions to Consider posed at the beginning of Unit 2:

- What were the causes and effects of European colonization of the Americas?
- What were the similarities and differences of regions and settlement patterns of the English in the Americas?
- What were the causes and effects of the emergence of African slavery in the Americas?

Discuss these questions as a class to review important concepts from the unit. To close the discussion, **ask:** How did your understanding of colonization and the emergence of slavery in the Americas change while studying this unit? **MIG** **GEO** **WXT** **SOC**

UNIT 2 AP EXAM PRACTICE

AP EXAM PRACTICE

As you answer the questions, consider how the historical developments, processes, and individuals in Unit 2 connect to those in the previous unit.

MULTIPLE CHOICE

Use the image on page 30 and your knowledge of U.S. history to answer questions 1-3.

1. The British colony at Jamestown, as portrayed in the image, initially encountered a Native American population that is best described as
   (A) primitive and reliant on hunting and gathering.
   (B) largely organized in small, semi-nomadic groups.
   (C) highly developed culturally and reliant upon a mixed economy.
   (D) uninterested in interaction with British newcomers.

2. As Jamestown developed in the Chesapeake region, it developed an economy that was reliant upon
   (A) a mix of transatlantic trade and small local artisans.
   (B) tobacco agriculture initially reliant upon indentured servants.
   (C) the cultivation of sugarcane and rum production.
   (D) an export economy based on grain and indigo.

3. Southern British colonies like Jamestown developed political structures marked by
   (A) shared control between the British settlers and the Native American leaders.
   (B) town meetings through which church members elected legislators.
   (C) elected assemblies dominated by the growing class of elite planters.
   (D) mixed representation of both indentured servants and freemen.

Use the image on page 54 and your knowledge of U.S. history to answer questions 4 and 5.

4. The image of Anne Hutchinson preaching would have stirred controversy among the Puritan faithful because
   (A) she is preaching in a home rather than a church building.
   (B) a female preacher violated strict Puritan beliefs in female subservience.
   (C) Puritans usually preached to ethnically mixed groups to convert Native Americans.
   (D) Puritans did not usually permit believers to dress in fashionable and colorful clothing.

5. Women in New England, such as Anne Hutchinson, could generally expect to
   (A) enjoy long life expectancies and raise large numbers of children to adulthood.
   (B) adopt new roles as equal participants in local political and economic organizations.
   (C) cycle through marriage and widowhood due to high mortality rates.
   (D) oversee large plantations with increasing numbers of enslaved laborers.

Use the image on page 100 and your knowledge of U.S. history to answer questions 6-8.

6. Primers such as the one pictured indicate
   (A) the understanding that education was central to economic success in the colonies.
   (B) the colonial belief that religion should not play a role in public education.
   (C) the attempt to integrate women into the political structures of the colonies.
   (D) the importance placed on literacy in the colonies.

7. Education reflected the influence of the Enlightenment in its embrace of
   (A) scientific inquiry.
   (B) ethnically mixed groups.
   (C) democratic elections.
   (D) dismantling gender norms.

Answers

Multiple Choice

1. C; **2.** B; **3.** C; **4.** B; **5.** A; **6.** D; **7.** A; **8.** C; **9.** C; **10.** A

UNIT 2
AP Exam Practice

8. One critical influence of the Enlightenment in the colonies was to
   (A) promote colonial allegiance to the British Crown.
   (B) increase colonial participation in established churches.
   (C) undermine the power of traditional authority structures.
   (D) encourage colonists to disconnect from British authority in favor of a French alliance.

Use the excerpt and your knowledge of U.S. history to answer questions 9 and 10.

"It would be dreadful to suffer this fierceness and wrath of Almighty God one moment; but you must suffer it to all eternity. There will be no end to this exquisite horrible misery. When you look forward, you shall see a long forever, a boundless duration, before you, which will swallow up your thoughts, and amaze your souls; and you will absolutely despair of ever having any deliverance, any end, any mitigation, any rest at all; you will know certainly that you must wear out long ages, millions of millions of ages, in wrestling and conflicting with this almighty merciless vengeance; and then when you have so done, when so many ages have actually been spent by you in this manner, you will know that all is but a point to what remains. So that your punishment will indeed be infinite. O, who can express what the state of a soul in such circumstances is! All that we can possibly say about it, gives but a very feeble, faint representation of it; it is inexpressible and inconceivable: for, "Who knoweth the power of God's anger?"

—"Sinners in the Hands of an Angry God," Jonathan Edwards, 1741

9. Great Awakening preachers like Edwards wished to encourage
   (A) an interfaith community with Roman Catholics based on common beliefs.
   (B) the development of new traditions that integrated Native American practices into the Anglican church.
   (C) an increase in religious piety based in the traditional Calvinist belief of predestination.
   (D) a disavowal of traditional preaching in favor of a less structured religious hierarchy.

10. The Great Awakening resulted in
   (A) the fracturing of existing denominations.
   (B) a disavowal of higher education.
   (C) a reunification of the Puritan and Anglican churches.
   (D) an increased dedication to traditional authority structures.

SHORT ANSWER

Use the image on page 80 and your knowledge of U.S. history to answer question 11.

11. Answer A, B, and C.
   (A) Describe the point of view about the transatlantic slave trade depicted in the image.
   (B) Explain ONE specific historical cause that led to the development of the transatlantic slave trade.
   (C) Explain ONE specific historical effect that resulted from the development of the transatlantic slave trade.

LONG ESSAY

Develop a thoughtful and thorough historical argument that addresses the statement below. Begin your essay with a thesis statement, and support it with specific historical evidence and examples.

12. Evaluate the extent of cultural changes the English experienced as they established long-term and permanent colonies in the Americas from 1607 to 1754.

Answers

Short Answer

11A) The point of view is that of an abolitionist depicting enslaved people packed tightly together on a slave ship in horrific conditions, unable to move about.

11B) Possible answer: As the English continually pushed farther and farther west, the need for a labor force continued to grow. English colonies, especially those in the Chesapeake region, relied heavily on cash-crop agriculture, which required lots of laborers. The colonists initially turned to Native Americans, but European introduced diseases resulted in millions of deaths, thus reducing the Native American labor force. Next, the colonists turned to indentured servants, but this labor force soon proved difficult to control. Finally, the colonists turned to enslaved Africans.

11C) Possible answer: The slave trade was initially conceived as an economic system but almost immediately evolved into a racist system that dehumanized enslaved Africans.

Answers

Long Essay

12. Possible thesis: The population growth of the English colonies continued to be fueled by religious and economic opportunities from 1607 to 1754. However, a sense of political and economic independence grew as England ignored most of what was happening in the colonies. Additionally, the colonies, despite initial regional differences that created a sense of independence from each other, began to be forcibly integrated. Therefore, despite continued demographic growth in all the colonies, major changes were taking place, leading them to gradually identify themselves as a unified country. Evidence: Despite the differences between the different geographic regions, as populations grew, decreasing space between regions forced more interaction and interdependence. Through salutary neglect, their dependence on Great Britain began to erode. This led to a growing sense of independence from Great Britain, which ultimately became one of the major causes of the independence movement toward the end of the eighteenth century. The reasons for continued colonization remained primarily the search for religious freedom and economic opportunities. The colonists continued to establish English social structures within North America and modeled their laws and social, political, and economic institutions after those in England. Despite increased integration of the colonies, the different geographic regions continued to maintain their own characteristics, evolving according to their distinct geographic and cultural influences.

Pacing Guide

Unit 3 explores key concepts from Period 3: 1754–1800 of the AP U.S. History Curriculum Framework. It is recommended that 10–17% of the total instruction time for the entire course be spent on Period 3.

Key Concepts

3.1 British attempts to assert tighter control over its North American colonies and the colonial resolve to pursue self-government led to a colonial independence movement and the Revolutionary War.

3.2 The American Revolution's democratic and republican ideals inspired new experiments with different forms of government.

3.3 Migration within North America and competition over resources, boundaries, and trade intensified conflicts among peoples and nations.

UNIT 3: 1754–1800

Chapter 4: The Empire in Transition

Chapter 5: The American Revolution

Chapter 6: The Constitution and the New Republic

THEMATIC LEARNING OBJECTIVES

- Analyze the causes that led to the American Revolution.
- Compare and contrast the advantages and disadvantages each side had at the start of the American Revolution.
- Explain the steps the Americans went through to establish a democracy and ratify the Constitution.
- Evaluate the importance of the Enlightenment to the establishment of the United States.
- Assess the different foreign policy goals established in the presidencies of Washington, Adams, and Jefferson.
- Analyze how westward migration affected relationships with Native Americans and foreign powers.

QUESTIONS TO CONSIDER

- What were the major causes that led to the independence movement in the North American colonies?
- What were the major factors that led to the ratification of the U.S. Constitution?
- What were the major domestic and foreign challenges the newly independent country faced?

HISTORICAL DEVELOPMENTS: 1754–1800

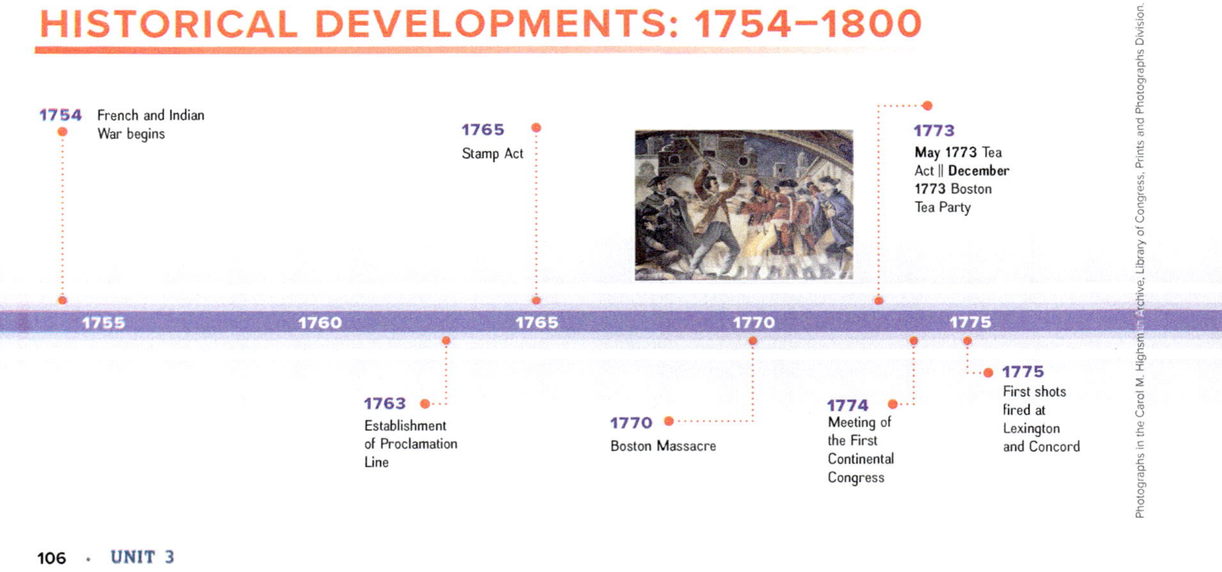
1754 French and Indian War begins
1765 Stamp Act
1773 May 1773 Tea Act || December 1773 Boston Tea Party
1755
1760
1765
1770
1775
1763 Establishment of Proclamation Line
1770 Boston Massacre
1774 Meeting of the First Continental Congress
1775 First shots fired at Lexington and Concord
Photographs in the Carol M. Highsmith Archive, Library of Congress, Prints and Photographs Division.

Reasoning Processes

Causation Have students examine the time line. **Ask:** Based on the time line and what you already know, which events appear to be causes of the Declaration of Independence, and which events appear to be effects of the document? *(Causes: Stamp Act, Boston Massacre, Tea Act, Publication of "Common Sense." Effects: Articles of Confederation, Constitutional Convention.)*

MAKING CONNECTIONS

Unit Three focuses on the transition of the American colonies from British control through the Declaration of Independence and finally to the establishment of the United States. The first permanent English settlement in North America was in the Chesapeake at Jamestown in 1607. The next wave of immigration across the Atlantic began in the 1620s and 1630s with the arrival of the Pilgrims and Puritans in New England. While these diverse groups settled in different places for a variety of reasons, they were all English and shared important cultural connections.

Competition over resources and land among the different European powers, as well as between British colonists and Native Americans, came to a head in 1754 with the outbreak of the French and Indian War in the Ohio River Valley. The clash between France and Britain over control of the territory was part of a major international conflict, known in Europe as the Seven Years War. In North America, the fighting led to the departure of French forces, but victory brought mixed results for Britain. On one hand, the removal of France meant that the British could continue expansion in North America with little resistance from European powers. On the other, expansion meant continued conflict with Native Americans, who could mount significant resistance against colonists and Great Britain.

Above all, the cost of the French and Indian War was enormous for Great Britain. The war debt forced the British to shift the focus of their tax policy, leading to more aggressive and consistent enforcement of the Navigation Acts. For the first time, taxes were imposed on the colonies to raise revenue rather than to regulate trade. The British colonists in North America objected to this new policy, claiming that the British Parliament lacked the constitutional authority to implement it. New taxes and continued resistance by Native Americans began to unite the colonies through shared issues and in opposition to British rule.

The American Revolution began in 1775 and led to the successful overthrow of British authority. Now the dependent colonies had to transition to independent states as part of a new country. The original national constitution, the Articles of Confederation, was ratified in 1777. It was an important first step, but the Articles had significant flaws, which led to a major political debate between the Federalists and Antifederalists over a new constitution for the United States. After ratification of the Constitution in 1788, the two factions evolved into political parties. These political parties, in different forms, dominated state and national politics in the 1790s.

The new nation also found that independence brought additional challenges. Being part of the British Empire had provided certain advantages. Now the United States had to fend for itself in a dangerous world where most European powers—including Great Britain—were not willing to grant the young republic immediate status on the world stage. But it was in 1800 that the United States truly faced the first real test of its new democracy. In that year, a bitterly contested election led to the peaceful transition of power from Federalist John Adams of Massachusetts to Democratic-Republican Thomas Jefferson of Virginia.

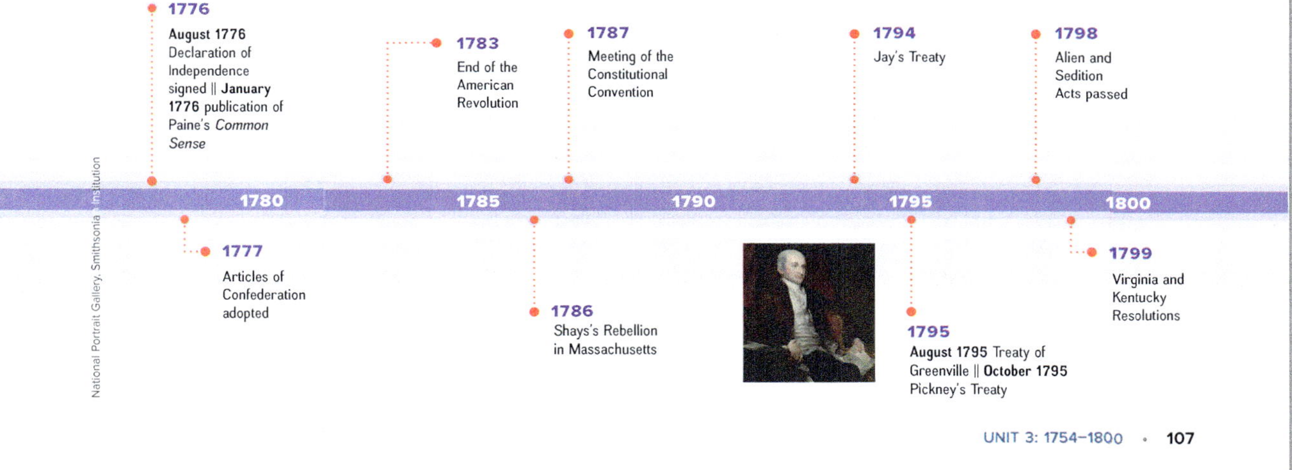
1776
August 1776 Declaration of Independence signed || January 1776 publication of Paine's *Common Sense*
1783
End of the American Revolution
1787
Meeting of the Constitutional Convention
1794
Jay's Treaty
1798
Alien and Sedition Acts passed
1780
1785
1790
1795
1800
1777
Articles of Confederation adopted
1786
Shays's Rebellion in Massachusetts
1795
August 1795 Treaty of Greenville || October 1795 Pickney's Treaty
1799
Virginia and Kentucky Resolutions
National Portrait Gallery, Smithsonian Institution

Reasoning Processes

Change Over Time Have students read the section "Making Connections." Ask them to create a two-column chart listing ways that British colonial policy stayed the same following the French and Indian War and ways that it changed following the war. Have students add to their charts as they learn more about this conflict and its aftermath through Unit 3. **NAT** **WOR**

Go Online Additional Resources

Adaptive Learning with SmartBook A proven adaptive learning program, SmartBook offers an interactive environment that helps students learn faster, study more efficiently, and retain more knowledge.

Assign this resource to differentiate instruction for students and report on year-long progression.

Pacing Guide

Chapter 4 explores key concepts from Period 3: 1754–1800 of the AP U.S. History Curriculum Framework. The suggested instruction time for Chapter 4 is 6 days.

Key Concepts

3.1.I The competition among the British, French, and American Indians for economic and political advantage in North America culminated in the Seven Years' War (the French and Indian War), in which Britain defeated France and allied American Indians.

3.1.II The desire of many colonists to assert ideals of self-government in the face of renewed British imperial efforts led to a colonial independence movement and war with Britain.

4 THE EMPIRE IN TRANSITION

TOPPLING GEORGE III
In the immediate aftermath of the Declaration of Independence, patriots in New York pulled down a statue of King George III from its pedestal in the center of the city. Among those pulling down the statue were a number of African Americans—both free and enslaved. This print is a French illustration of the event, with captions in both French and German.

CONNECTING CONCEPTS

Chapter Four begins by exploring the tenuous relationship that developed between Great Britain and its North American colonies. At first Great Britain, preoccupied with events in Europe, largely left the British colonies to govern themselves. The colonists continued to clash over land and resources with Native Americans, which sometimes resulted in warfare. Yet both English and French settlers developed complicated economic relationships with Native American groups, which in turn led to shifting alliances and future conflicts.

At the same time, the colonists developed an increased sense of political and economic autonomy with regard to Great Britain. This growing sense of independence was based more on sentiment than well developed political and economic ideas. The onset of the French and Indian War, part of the Seven Years' War, brought to the forefront colonial noncompliance with the mercantile system and the British perception of how the colonies should conduct themselves. As the war raged in North America, both colonists and Native Americans had to choose sides.

The outcome of the French and Indian War had two major consequences. First, the French abandoned any territorial claims in North America. Second, the British assumed an enormous war debt and began to assert a more aggressive political and economic policy toward its North American colonies. In opposition, the colonists drew heavily on Enlightenment ideas to oppose this new assertion of British power and control. The end of British neglect, coupled with an evolved sense of colonial independence, set the stage for the beginning of the American Revolution.

The Library of Congress (ppmsca-17521)

Discussion and Activities

Analyzing Visuals Have students examine the image "Toppling George III." Ask them to think about the symbolic meaning of the action portrayed. *(Toppling the statue of the king symbolizes the end of British rule.)* Have students write a short journal entry from the point of view of a New York resident who witnessed the scene. **SOC** **PCE**

As you read, you should:

- Identify the ways Native Americans continuously adjusted their alliances with European powers during the eighteenth century.
- Analyze the ways the British attempted to assert control over the colonies which led to violent resistance.
- Evaluate how the Enlightenment and the First Great Awakening led to new experiments in democratic and republican forms of government which led to increasing questioning of imperial authority.

LOOSENING TIES

After the Glorious Revolution of 1688 in England and the collapse of the Dominion of New England in America, the English government (which became the British government after 1707, when a union of England and Scotland created Great Britain) made no serious or sustained effort to tighten its control over the colonies for over seventy years. During those years, an increasing number of colonies were brought under the direct control of the king. New Jersey in 1702, North and South Carolina in 1729, Georgia in 1754–all became royal colonies, bringing the total to eight; in all of them, the king had the power to appoint the governors and other colonial officials. During those years, Parliament also passed new laws supplementing the original Navigation Acts and strengthening the mercantilist program–laws restricting colonial manufactures, prohibiting paper currency, and regulating trade. On the whole, however, the British government remained uncertain and divided about the extent to which it ought to interfere in colonial affairs. The colonies were left, within broad limits, to go their separate ways.

A Tradition of Neglect

In the fifty years after the Glorious Revolution, the British Parliament established a growing supremacy over the king. During the reigns of George I (1714–1727) and George II (1727–1760), both of whom were German born and unaccustomed to English ways, the prime minister and his cabinet ministers began to become the nation's real executives. They held their positions not by the king's favor but by their ability to control a majority in Parliament.

Growing Power of Parliament

These parliamentary leaders were less inclined than the seventeenth-century monarchs had been to try to tighten imperial organization. They depended heavily on the support of the great merchants and landholders, most of whom feared that any such experiments would require large expenditures, increase taxes, and diminish the profits they were earning from the colonial trade. The first of the modern prime ministers, Robert Walpole, deliberately refrained from strict enforcement of the Navigation Acts, believing that relaxed trading restrictions would stimulate commerce.

Meanwhile, the day-to-day administration of colonial affairs remained decentralized and inefficient. There was no colonial office in London. The nearest equivalent was the Board of Trade and Plantations, established in 1696–a mere advisory body that had little role in any actual decisions. Real authority rested in the Privy Council (the central administrative agency for the government as a whole), the admiralty, and the treasury. But those agencies were responsible for administering laws at home as well as overseas; none could concentrate on colonial affairs. To complicate matters further, there was considerable overlapping and confusion of authority among the departments.

Decentralized Colonial Administration

Few of the London officials, moreover, had ever visited America; few knew very much about conditions there. What information they did gather came in large part from agents sent to England by the colonial assemblies to lobby for American interests. These agents, naturally, did nothing to encourage interference with colonial affairs. (The best known of them, Benjamin Franklin, represented not only his own colony, Pennsylvania, but also Georgia, New Jersey, and Massachusetts.)

It was not only the weakness of administrative authority in London and the policy of neglect that weakened England's hold on the colonies. It was also the character of the royal officials in America–among them the governors, the collectors of customs, and naval officers. Some of these officeholders were able and intelligent; most were not. Appointments generally came as the result of bribery or favoritism, not as a reward for merit. Many appointees remained in England and, with part of their salaries, hired substitutes to take their places in America. Such deputies received paltry wages and thus faced great temptations to augment their incomes with bribes. Few resisted the temptation. Customs collectors, for example, routinely waived duties on goods when merchants paid

Historical Thinking Skills

Understanding Change Have students read the section "Growing Power of Parliament." Ask them to think about how Parliament increased its power relative to the king. Then ask students to share with a partner why they think the increasingly powerful Parliament would have been reluctant to strictly enforce mercantilist trade laws. *(Parliament depended upon support from wealthy merchants and traders whose income could be hurt by strict enforcement.)* **PCE** **WXT**

Go Online AP Exam Preparation

AP Exam Practice Use the online assessment to help prepare students for the AP Exam. You can assign the ready-made AP-style short-answer questions, document-based questions, and multiple-choice questions assessing concepts, themes, and skills from Period 3 and AP style long-essay questions organized in sets of 3 questions from various time periods. You can also create your own tests from available questions. This easy-to-use tool helps you design assessments that meet the needs of different types of learners.

Historical Thinking Skills

Speculating Have students read the section "Powerful Colonial Legislatures." Ask them to consider the reasons why colonial legislatures had a great degree of autonomy. Have students consider additional reasons why the legislatures might have had a great deal of independence from England. *(The distance of the colonies from England made enforcement of British laws difficult.)* **PCE** **WOR**

them to do so. Even honest and well-paid officials usually found it expedient, if they wanted to get along with their neighbors, to yield to the colonists' resistance to trade restrictions.

Resistance to imperial authority centered in the colonial legislatures. By the 1750s, the American assemblies had claimed the right to levy taxes, make appropriations, approve appointments, and pass laws for their respective colonies. Their legislation was subject to veto by the governor or the Privy Council. But the assemblies had leverage over the governor through their control of the colonial budget, and they could circumvent the Privy Council by repassing disallowed laws in slightly altered form. The assemblies came to look upon themselves as little parliaments, each practically as sovereign within its colony as Parliament itself was in England.

POWERFUL COLONIAL LEGISLATURES

THE COLONIES DIVIDED

Despite their frequent resistance to the authority of London, the colonists continued to think of themselves as loyal English subjects. In many respects, in fact, they felt stronger ties to England than they did to one another. "Fire and water," an English traveler wrote, "are not more heterogeneous than the different colonies in North America." New Englanders and Virginians viewed each other as something close to foreigners. A Connecticut man denounced the merchants of New York for their "frauds and unfair practices," while a New Yorker condemned Connecticut because of the "low craft and cunning so incident to the people of that country." Only an accident of geography, it seemed, connected these disparate societies to one another.

Yet, for all their differences, the colonies could scarcely avoid forging connections with one another. The growth of the colonial population produced an almost continuous line of settlement along the seacoast and led to the gradual construction of roads and the rise of intercolonial trade. The colonial postal service helped increase communication. In 1691, it had operated only from Massachusetts to New York and Pennsylvania. In 1711, it extended to New Hampshire in the North; in 1732, to Virginia in the South; and ultimately, all the way to Georgia.

AN APPEAL FOR COLONIAL UNITY This sketch, one of the first American editorial cartoons, appeared in Benjamin Franklin's Philadelphia newspaper, the *Pennsylvania Gazette*, on May 9, 1754. It was meant to illustrate the need for intercolonial unity and, in particular, for the adoption of Franklin's Albany Plan.

Still, the colonists were loath to cooperate even when, in 1754, they faced a common threat from their old rivals, the French, and France's Native American allies. A conference of colonial leaders—with delegates from Pennsylvania, Maryland, New York, and New England—was meeting in Albany in that year to negotiate a treaty with the Iroquois, as the British government had advised the colonists to do. The delegates stayed on to talk about forming a colonial federation for defense against Native Americans. Benjamin Franklin proposed, and the delegates tentatively approved, a plan by which Parliament would set up in America "one general government" for all the colonies (except Georgia and Nova Scotia). Each colony would "retain its present constitution," but would grant to the new general government such powers as the authority to govern all relations with Native Americans. The central government would have a "president general" appointed and paid by the king (just as colonial governors were) and a legislature (a "grand council") elected by the colonial assemblies.

ALBANY PLAN

War with the French and the Native Americans was already beginning when this Albany Plan was presented to the colonial assemblies. None approved it. "Everyone cries, a union is necessary," Franklin wrote to the Massachusetts governor, "but when they come to the manner and form of the union, their weak noodles are perfectly distracted."

THE STRUGGLE FOR THE CONTINENT

In the late 1750s and early 1760s, a great war raged through North America, changing forever the balance of power both on the continent and throughout much of the world. The war in America was part of a titanic struggle between England and France for dominance in world trade and naval power. The British victory in that struggle, known in Europe as the Seven Years' War, rearranged global power and cemented England's role as the world's great commercial and imperial nation. It also cemented its control of most of the settled regions of North America.

In America, however, the conflict was the final stage in a long battle among the three principal powers in northeastern North America: the English, the French, and the Iroquois. For more than a century prior to the conflict known in America as the French and Indian War, these three groups had maintained an uneasy balance of power. The events of the 1750s upset that balance, produced a prolonged and open conflict, and established a precarious dominance for the English societies throughout the region.

AN UNEASY BALANCE OF POWER

Reasoning Processes

Comparing Have students read the section "The Colonies Divided." Ask them to create a two-column chart listing factors that began to unify the colonies by the late eighteenth century and factors that began to divide them. Use students' charts as the basis for a discussion about which set of factors was more compelling, and why. **SOC** **PCE** **ARC**

The French and Indian War was important to the English colonists in America for another reason as well. By bringing the Americans into closer contact with British authority than ever before, it raised to the surface some of the underlying tensions in the colonial relationship.

NEW FRANCE AND THE IROQUOIS NATION

The French and the English had coexisted peacefully in North America for nearly a century. But by the 1750s, religious and commercial tensions began to produce new conflicts. The crisis began in part because of the expansion of the French presence in America in the late seventeenth century—a result of Louis XIV's search for national unity and increased world power. The lucrative fur trade drew immigrant French peasants deeper into the wilderness, while missionary zeal drew large numbers of French Jesuits into the interior in search of potential converts. The bottomlands of the Mississippi River valley attracted French farmers discouraged by the short growing season in Canada.

NEW SOURCES OF CONFLICT

By the mid-seventeenth century, the French Empire in America comprised a vast territory. Louis Joliet and Father Jacques Marquette, French explorers of the 1670s, journeyed together by canoe from Green Bay on Lake Michigan as far south as the junction of the Arkansas and Mississippi Rivers. A year later, René-Robert Cavelier, Sieur de La Salle, began the explorations that in 1682 took him to the delta of the Mississippi, where he claimed the surrounding country for France and named it Louisiana in the king's honor. Subsequent traders and missionaries wandered to the southwest as far as the Rio Grande; and the explorer Pierre Gaultier de Varennes, Sieur de La Vérendrye, pushed westward in 1743 from Lake Superior to a point within sight of the Rocky Mountains. The French had by then revealed the outlines of, and laid claim to, almost the whole continental interior.

To secure their hold on these enormous claims, they founded a string of widely separated communities, fortresses, missions, and trading posts. Fort Louisbourg, on Cape Breton Island, guarded the approach to the Gulf of St. Lawrence. Would-be feudal lords established large estates *(seigneuries)* along the banks of the St. Lawrence River; and on a high bluff above the river stood the fortified city of Quebec, the center of the French Empire in America. To the south was Montreal, and to the west Sault Sainte Marie and Detroit. On the lower Mississippi emerged plantations much like those in the southern colonies of English America, worked by enslaved Africans and owned by "Creoles" (white immigrants of French descent). New Orleans, founded in 1718 to service the French plantation economy, soon was as big as some of the larger cities of the Atlantic seaboard; Biloxi and Mobile to the east completed the string of French settlement.

FRANCE'S NORTH AMERICAN EMPIRE

But the French were not, of course, alone in the continental interior. They shared their territories with a large and powerful Native American population in regions now often labeled the "middle grounds." The relations between the French and Native Americans were crucial to the shaping of the French empire. They also shared the interior with a growing number of English traders and settlers, who had been moving beyond the confines of the colonial boundaries in the East. Both the French and the English were aware that the battle for control of North America would be determined in part by which group could best win the allegiance of Native American nations—as trading partners and, at times, as military allies. The Native Americans, for their part, were principally concerned with protecting their independence. Whatever alignments they formed with the European societies growing up around them were generally marriages of convenience, determined by which group offered the most attractive terms.

The English—with their more advanced commercial economy—could usually offer the Native Americans better and more plentiful goods. But the French offered something that was often more important: tolerance. Unlike the English settlers, most of whom tried to impose their own social norms on the Native Americans they encountered, the French settlers in the interior generally adjusted their own behavior to Native American patterns. French fur traders frequently married Native American women and adopted Native American customs. Jesuit missionaries interacted comfortably with Native Americans and converted them to Catholicism by the thousands without challenging most of their social customs. By the mid-eighteenth century, therefore, the French had better and closer relations with most of the groups of the interior than did the English.

The most powerful Native American group, however, had a different relationship with the French. The Iroquois Confederacy—the five Native American nations (Mohawk, Seneca, Cayuga, Onondaga, and Oneida) that had formed a defensive alliance in the fifteenth century—had been the most powerful tribal presence in the Northeast since the 1640s, when they had fought—and won—a bitter war against the Hurons. Once their major competitors were largely gone from the region, the Iroquois forged an important commercial relationship with the English and Dutch along the eastern seaboard—although they continued to trade with the French as well. Indeed, the key to the success of the Iroquois in maintaining their independence was that they avoided too close a relationship with either group and astutely played the French and the English against each other. As a result, they managed to maintain an uneasy balance of power in the Great Lakes region and beyond.

THE IROQUOIS CONFEDERACY

The principal area of conflict among these many groups was the Ohio Valley. The French claimed it. Several competing Native American nations (many of them refugees from lands farther east, driven into the valley by the English expansion) lived there. English settlement was expanding into it. And the Iroquois were trying to establish a presence there as traders. With so many competing groups jostling for influence, the Ohio Valley quickly became a potential battleground.

Reasoning Processes

Comparing Have students read the section "France's North American Empire." Ask them to create a Venn diagram comparing French and English relations with Native Americans. **SOC** **PCE**

Discussion and Activities

Have students read the section "The Iroquois Confederacy." Ask them to list the factors that led to the Confederacy becoming an important power. *(Possible responses: The Confederacy had created an alliance bringing together five powerful nations; they avoided aligning too closely with any European nation; they maintained trade relations with England, Holland, and France.)* Ask students to predict whether the Iroquois Confederacy would be able to maintain its independence going forward from this point. **WXT** **PCE**

Historical Thinking Skills

Contextualization Have students read the section "European Seeds of Conflict." As a class or in small groups, discuss how conflicts in Europe led to conflicts in the American colonies. **WOR** **PCE**

ANGLO-FRENCH CONFLICTS

As long as England and France remained at peace in Europe, and as long as the precarious balance in the North American interior survived, the tensions among the English, French, and Iroquois remained mild. But after the Glorious Revolution in England, the English throne passed to one of Louis XIV's principal enemies, William III, who was also the stadholder (chief magistrate) of the Netherlands and who had long opposed French expansionism. William's successor, Queen Anne (the daughter of James II), ascended the throne in 1702 and carried on the struggle against France and its new ally, Spain. The result was a series of Anglo-French wars that continued intermittently in Europe for nearly eighty years.

EUROPEAN SEEDS OF CONFLICT

The wars had important repercussions in America. King William's War (1689–1697) produced a few, indecisive clashes between the English and French in northern New England. Queen Anne's War, which began in 1701 and continued for nearly twelve years, generated substantial conflicts: border fighting with the Spaniards in the South as well as with the French and their Native American allies in the North. The Treaty of Utrecht, which brought the conflict to a close in 1713, transferred substantial areas of French territory in North America to the English, including Acadia (Nova Scotia) and Newfoundland. Two decades later, European rivalries led to still more conflicts in America. Disputes over British trading rights in the Spanish colonies produced a war between England and Spain and led to clashes between the British in Georgia and the Spaniards in Florida. (It was in the context of this conflict that the last English colony in America, Georgia, was founded in 1733.) The Anglo-Spanish conflict soon merged with a much larger European war, in which England and France lined up on opposite sides of a territorial dispute between Frederick the Great of Prussia and Maria Theresa of Austria. The English colonists in America were soon drawn into the struggle, which they called King George's War; and between 1744 and 1748, they engaged in a series of conflicts with the French. New Englanders captured the French bastion at Louisbourg on Cape Breton Island; but the peace treaty that finally ended the conflict forced them (in bitter disappointment) to abandon it.

THE SIEGE OF LOUISBOURG, 1758 The fortress of Louisbourg, on Cape Breton Island in Nova Scotia, was one of the principal French outposts in eastern Canada during the French and Indian War. It took a British fleet of 157 ships nearly two months to force the French garrison to surrender. "We had not had our Batteries against the Town above a Week," wrote a British soldier after the victory, "tho we were ashore Seven Weeks; the Badness of the Country prevented our Approaches. It was necessary to make Roads for the Cannon, which was a great Labour, and some Loss of Men; but the spirits the Army was in is capable of doing any Thing."

Discussion and Activities

Analyzing Perspectives Have students examine the image "The Siege of Louisbourg, 1758." Ask students to speculate whether the painting was created by a French or British artist, and why. Have students write a short paragraph making their arguments. *(Possible response: Likely British, since the scene portrayed is the site of a British victory, and only French ships appear to have been damaged. Also, the artist has painted in the trajectories of British cannonballs that are damaging French ships.)* **WOR** **PCE**

In the aftermath of King George's War, relations among the English, French, and Iroquois in North America quickly deteriorated. The Iroquois (in what in retrospect appears a major blunder) began to grant trading concessions in the interior to English merchants. In the context of the already tense Anglo-French relationship in America, the decision to side with the British set in motion a chain of events disastrous for the Iroquois Confederacy. The French feared that the English were using the concessions as a first step toward expansion into French lands (which to some extent they were). They began in 1749 to construct new fortresses in the Ohio Valley. The English interpreted the French activity as a threat to their western settlements. They protested and began making military preparations and building fortresses of their own. The balance of power that the Iroquois had striven to maintain for so long rapidly disintegrated, and the five Native American nations allied themselves with the British and assumed an essentially passive role in the conflict that followed.

For the next five years, tensions between the English and the French increased. In the summer of 1754, the governor of Virginia sent a militia force (under the command of an inexperienced young colonel, George Washington) into the Ohio Valley to challenge French expansion. Washington built a crude stockade (Fort Necessity) not far from the larger French outpost, Fort Duquesne, on the site of what is now Pittsburgh. After the Virginians staged an unsuccessful attack on a French detachment, the French countered with an assault on Fort Necessity, trapping Washington and his soldiers inside. After a third of them died in the fighting, Washington surrendered.

FORT NECESSITY

That clash marked the beginning of what became the French and Indian War, the American part of the much larger Seven Years' War that spread through Europe at the same time. It was the climactic event in the long Anglo-French struggle for empire.

THE GREAT WAR FOR THE EMPIRE

The French and Indian War lasted nearly nine years, and it proceeded in three distinct phases. The first phase lasted from the Fort Necessity debacle in 1754 until the expansion of the war to Europe in 1756. It was primarily a North American conflict, which the English colonists managed largely on their own.

The British provided modest assistance during this period, but they provided it so ineptly that it had little impact on the struggle. The British fleet failed to prevent the landing of large French reinforcements in Canada; and the newly appointed commander in chief of the British army in America, General Edward Braddock, failed miserably in a major effort in the summer of 1755 to retake the crucial site at the forks of the Ohio River where Washington had lost the battle at Fort Necessity. A French and Native American ambush a few miles from the fort left Braddock dead and his remaining forces in disarray.

BRADDOCK DEFEATED

The local colonial forces, meanwhile, were preoccupied with defending themselves against raids on their western settlements by the Native Americans of the Ohio Valley. Virtually all of the groups (except the Iroquois) were now allied with the French, having interpreted the defeat of the Virginians at Fort Duquesne as evidence of British weakness. Even the Iroquois, who were nominally allied with the British, remained fearful of antagonizing the French. They engaged in few hostilities and launched no offensive into Canada, even though they had, under heavy English pressure, declared war on the French. By late 1755, many English settlers along the frontier had withdrawn to the east of the Allegheny Mountains to escape the hostilities.

The second phase of the struggle began in 1756, when the governments of France and England formally opened hostilities and a truly international conflict (the Seven Years' War) began. In Europe, the war was marked by a realignment within the complex system of alliances. France allied with its former enemy, Austria; England joined France's former ally, Prussia. The fighting now spread to the West Indies, India, and Europe. But the principal struggle remained the one in North America, where so far England had suffered nothing but frustration and defeat.

Beginning in 1757, William Pitt, the English secretary of state (and future prime minister), began to transform the war effort in America by bringing it for the first time fully under British control. Pitt himself began planning military strategy for the North American conflict, appointing military commanders, and issuing orders to the colonists. Military recruitment had slowed dramatically in America after the defeat of Braddock. To replenish the army, British commanders began forcibly enlisting colonists (a practice known as "impressment"). Officers also began to seize supplies and equipment from local farmers and tradesmen and compelled colonists to offer shelter to British troops—all generally without compensation. The Americans had long ago become accustomed to running their own affairs and had been fighting for over two years without much assistance or direction from the British. They resented these new impositions and firmly resisted them—at times, as in a 1757 riot in New York City, violently. By early 1758, the friction between the British authorities and the colonists was threatening to bring the war effort to a halt.

WILLIAM PITT TAKES CHARGE

Beginning in 1758, therefore, Pitt initiated the third and final phase of the war by relaxing many of the policies that Americans found oppressive. He agreed to reimburse the colonists for all supplies requisitioned by the army. He returned control over military recruitment to the colonial assemblies (which resulted in an immediate and dramatic increase in enlistments). And he dispatched large numbers of additional troops to America.

Finally, the tide of battle began to turn in England's favor. The French had always been outnumbered by the British colonists; after 1756, the French colonies suffered as well from a series of poor harvests. As a result, they were unable to sustain their early military successes. By mid-1758, the British regulars

Discussion and Activities

Speculating Have students read the section "Braddock Defeated." Ask them to create a list of British actions at the beginning of the French and Indian War and discuss in small groups what England could have done differently. PCE WOR

Discussion and Activities

Analyzing Change Have students read the section "William Pitt Takes Charge." Ask them to refer back to the lists they created for the previous section ("Braddock Defeated") and identify which English actions or policies Pitt modified. Then discuss as a class how Pitt's decisions changed the direction of the war. PCE WOR

Historical Thinking Skills

Contextualization Have students examine the image "The Seven Years' War." **Ask:** Why would French citizens have celebrated the end of the Seven Years' War? *(Although France lost considerable territory in the New World, the end of hostilities meant that France no longer had to support the costs of a global war.)* **PCE**

AMERICA IN THE WORLD

THE FIRST GLOBAL WAR

The French and Indian War in North America was only a small part of a much larger conflict. Known in Europe as the Seven Years' War it was one of the longest, most widespread, and most important wars in modern history. "Ministers in this country, where every part of the World affects us, in some way or another, should consider the whole Globe," the Duke of Newcastle wrote in Britain in 1758, reflecting the international achievements and war aims of the British in the mid-eighteenth century. Two centuries later, Winston Churchill, the former British prime minister, wrote of the Seven Years' War as the first "World War."

In North America, the war was a result of tensions along the frontiers of the British Empire, but a larger war resulted from conflicts among the great powers in Europe. It began in the 1750s with what historians have called a "diplomatic revolution." Well-established alliances between Britain and the Austro-Hungarian Empire, and between France and Prussia, collapsed, replaced by new alliances that set Britain and Prussia against France and Austria. The instability that these changing alliances produced helped speed the European nations toward war. The one thing that did not change was the continuing rivalry between Britain and France.

The Austrian-British alliance collapsed because Austria suffered a series of significant defeats at the hands of the Prussians. To the British government, these failures suggested that the Austro-Hungarian Empire was now too weak to help Britain balance French power. As a result, Britain sought new partnerships with the rising powers of northern Germany, Austria's enemies. Seeking protection from the power of their former British allies, the Austrians allied with France. Russia, concerned about the Austro-Hungarian Empire's possible dominance in central Europe, allied with Britain and Prussia.

The tensions that these complicated realignments created eventually led to war (just as the complicated alliances in Europe in the early twentieth century helped produce World War I). The European part of the war was a result of the continuing conflict between Prussia and Austria and the effect of those wars on the allies of both. The Seven Years' War soon spread across much of the world, engaging not only most of the great powers in Europe, from England to Russia, but also the emerging colonial world—India, West Africa, the Caribbean, and the Philippines—as the powerful British navy worked to strip France, and eventually Spain, of their valuable colonial holdings.

Like most modern conflicts, the Seven Years' War was a struggle for economic power. Colonial possessions, many European nations believed, were critical to their future wealth, well worth fighting for. The war's outcome affected not only the future of America, but also the distribution of power through much of the world. It destroyed the French navy and much of the French Empire, and it elevated Great Britain to undisputed preeminence among colonial powers—especially when, at the conclusion of the war, India and all of eastern North America fell firmly under English control. The war also reorganized the balance of power in Europe, with Britain now preeminent among the great powers and Prussia (later to become the core of modern Germany) rapidly rising in wealth and military power.

The Seven Years' War was not only one of the first great colonial wars; it was also one of the last great wars of religion. It extended the dominance of Protestantism in Europe. In what is now Canada, the war replaced French with British rule and thus Catholic with Protestant rule. The Vatican, no longer a military power itself, had relied on the great Catholic empires—Spain, France, and Austria-Hungary—as bulwarks of the Vatican's power and influence. The shift of power toward Protestant governments in Europe and North America weakened the Catholic Church and reduced its geopolitical influence.

THE SEVEN YEARS' WAR was one of the first great colonial conflicts. This etching shows a fireworks display at the Hôtel de Ville in Paris on February 10,1763, to celebrate the end of the hostilities.

The conclusion of the Seven Years' War strengthened Britain and Germany and weakened France. But it did not provide any lasting solution to the rivalries among the great colonial powers. In North America, a dozen years after the end of the war, the American Revolution—the origins of which were in many ways a direct result of the Seven Years' War—stripped the British Empire of one of its most important and valuable colonial appendages. By the time the American Revolution came to an end, the French Revolution had sparked another lengthy period of war, culminating in the Napoleonic Wars of the early nineteenth century, which once again redrew the map of Europe and, for a while, the world.

HISTORICAL THINKING SKILLS

1. **Analyzing Change** Analyze the factors that led to the French and Indian War in North America.
2. **Making Connections** Analyze the effect the war's outcome had on the European colonies in North America.
3. **Assessing Credibility** Evaluate the claim that the Seven Years' War is "one of the most important wars in modern history."

Answers

America in the World: The First Global War

1. The balance of power in Europe was mimicked in North America, as the different European powers vied for power on the continent. An initial border dispute between France and England developed into a full-blown war, sucking in countries from around the world. Economics played a major role, as the territory fought after was rich in natural resources. This war would also determine the subsequent history of North America.
2. Both Great Britain and France suffered costly losses, and important military leaders were killed on both sides. But ultimately the victory for the British turned out to be both positive and negative. A positive effect saw the elimination of the French from the continent. A negative effect saw the British colonies slide farther away from Britain, thus sowing the seeds of the American Revolution.
3. The subsequent history of the North American colonies were greatly affected by the war. Not only did Britain lose one of its most important young military minds in General Wolfe, who would have been in charge during the American Revolution (probably leading to very different results), but the confidence that the colonies gained from the war was enough to encourage them as they contemplated their relationship with Great Britain.

(who did the bulk of the fighting) and the colonial militias were seizing one French stronghold after another. Two brilliant English generals, Jeffrey Amherst and James Wolfe, captured the fortress at Louisbourg in July 1758; a few months later Fort Duquesne fell without a fight. The next year, at the end of a siege of Quebec, supposedly impregnable atop its towering cliff, the army of General James Wolfe struggled up a hidden ravine under cover of darkness, surprised the larger forces of the Marquis de Montcalm, and defeated them in a battle in which both commanders died. The dramatic fall of Quebec on September 13, 1759, marked the beginning of the end of the American phase of the war. A year later, in September 1760, the French army formally surrendered to Amherst in Montreal.

SIEGE OF QUEBEC

Not all aspects of the struggle were as romantic as Wolfe's dramatic assault on Quebec. The British resorted at times to such brutal military expedients as population dispersal. In Nova Scotia, for example, they uprooted several thousand French inhabitants, whom they suspected of disloyalty, and scattered them throughout the English colonies. (Some of these Acadians eventually made their way to Louisiana, where they became the ancestors of the present-day Cajuns.) Elsewhere, English and colonial troops inflicted even worse atrocities on the Native American allies of the French–for example, offering "scalp bounties" to those who could bring back evidence of having killed a Native American. The French and their Native American allies retaliated, and hundreds of families along the English frontier perished in brutal raids on their settlements.

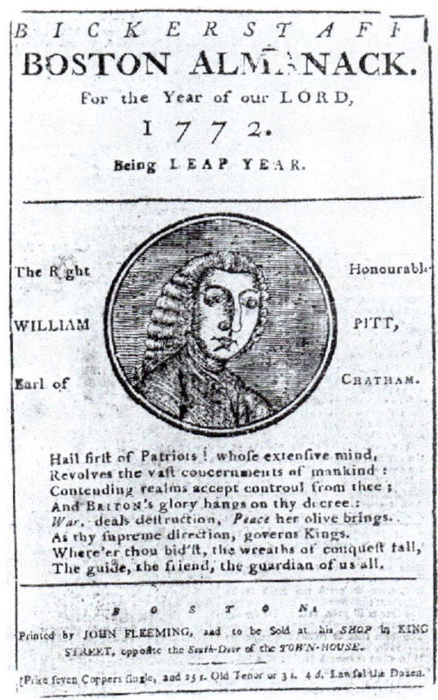

BICKERSTAFF'S
BOSTON ALMANACK.
For the Year of our LORD,
1772.
Being LEAP YEAR.

The Right Honourable WILLIAM PITT, Earl of CHATHAM.

Hail first of Patriots! whose extensive mind,
Revolves the vast concernments of mankind:
Contending realms accept controul from thee;
And BRITON's glory hangs on thy decree:
War, death destruction, Peace her olive brings.
As thy supreme direction, governs Kings.
Where'er thou bid'st, the wreaths of conquest fall,
The guide, the friend, the guardian of us all.

BOSTON:
Printed by JOHN FLEEMING, and to be Sold at his SHOP in KING STREET, opposite the South-Door of the TOWN-HOUSE.
[Price seven Coppers single, and 25 s. Old Tenor or 3 s. 4 d. Lawful the Dozen.]

WILLIAM PITT THE ELDER This dedication on the cover of the Bickerstaff *Boston Almanac* in 1772 honors the British statesman who voiced his support for the American colonialists in the years leading to the Revolution.

Peace finally came after the accession of George III to the British throne and the resignation of Pitt, who, unlike the new king, wanted to continue hostilities. The British achieved most of Pitt's aims nevertheless in the Peace of Paris, signed in 1763. Under its terms, the French ceded to Great Britain some of their West Indian islands and most of their colonies in India. They also transferred Canada and all other French territory east of the Mississippi, except New Orleans, to Great Britain. They ceded New Orleans and their claims west of the Mississippi to Spain, thus surrendering all title to the mainland of North America.

PEACE OF PARIS

The French and Indian War had profound effects on the British Empire and the American colonies. It greatly expanded England's territorial claims in the Americas. At the same time, it greatly enlarged Britain's debt; financing the vast war had been a major drain on the treasury. It also generated substantial resentment toward the Americans among British leaders, many of whom were contemptuous of the colonists for what they considered American military ineptitude during the war. They were angry as well that the colonists had made so few financial contributions to a struggle waged largely for American benefit; they were particularly bitter that some colonial merchants had been selling food and other goods to the French in the West Indies throughout the conflict. All these factors combined to persuade many English leaders that a major reorganization of the empire, giving London increased authority over the colonies, would be necessary in the aftermath of the war.

The war had an equally profound but very different effect on the American colonists. It forced them, for the first time, to act in concert against a common foe. The friction of 1756–1757 over British requisition and impressment policies, and the 1758 return of authority to the colonial assemblies, established an important precedent in the minds of the colonists: it seemed to confirm the illegitimacy of English interference in local affairs. For thousands of Americans–the men who served in the colonial armed forces–the war was an important socializing experience. The colonial troops, unlike the British regiments, generally viewed themselves as part of a "people's army." The relationship of soldiers to their units was, the soldiers believed, in some measure voluntary; their army was a communal, not a coercive or hierarchical, organization. The contrast with the British regulars, whom the colonists widely resented for their arrogance and arbitrary use of power, was striking; and in later years, the memory of that contrast helped to shape the American response to British imperial policies.

CONSEQUENCES OF THE SEVEN YEARS' WAR

For the Native Americans of the Ohio Valley, the third major party in the French and Indian War, the British victory was disastrous. The Native American nations that had allied themselves with the French had earned the enmity of the victorious English. The Iroquois Confederacy, which had allied with Britain, fared only slightly better. English officials saw the passivity of the Iroquois during the war (a result of their effort

Reasoning Processes

Change Over Time Have students reread the section "William Pitt Takes Charge," and then read "Siege of Quebec." Then ask them to create a time line of events in the French and Indian War. Have students circle the three events they think are most responsible for turning the tide of the war in favor of the British. Use the time lines as the basis for a class discussion. **WOR** **PCE**

Discussion and Activities

Analyzing Cause and Effect Have students read the sections "Peace of Paris" and "Consequences of the Seven Years' War." Ask them to create a list of divisions that were exposed by the war between the colonists and the English government. Discuss as a class what caused those divisions, and speculate on how the two sides are going to address those divisions as students continue to read the chapter. **SOC** **WXT** **PCE**

CHAPTER 4

The Empire in Transition

Discussion and Activities

Analyzing Visuals Have students examine the map "The Seven Years' War." Ask why so many of the battles took place on the seas or along waterways. *(In the absence of roads, rivers were critical to movement in the interior of the continent. Many sea battles indicate the importance of controlling trade routes with strong navies.)* **WOR** **PCE**

THE SEVEN YEARS' WAR After Washington's surrender and Braddock's defeat in the Pennsylvania backcountry, the British and French waged their final contest for supremacy in North America in northern New York and New France. But the rivalry for empire between France and Britain was worldwide, with naval superiority providing the needed edge to Britain.

to hedge their bets and avoid antagonizing the French) as evidence of duplicity. In the aftermath of the peace settlement, the Iroquois alliance with the British quickly unraveled, and the Iroquois Confederacy itself began to crumble from within. The Iroquois nations would continue to contest the English for control of the Ohio Valley for another fifty years; but increasingly divided and increasingly outnumbered, they would seldom again be in a position to deal with their white rivals on terms of military or political equality.

THE NEW IMPERIALISM

With the treaty of 1763, England found itself at peace for the first time in more than fifty years. But saddled with enormous debts and responsible for vast new lands in the Americas, the imperial government could not long avoid expanding its involvement in its colonies.

Burdens of Empire

The experience of the French and Indian War suggested that such increased involvement would not be easy to achieve. Not only had the colonists proved so resistant to British control that Pitt had been forced to relax his policies in 1758, but the colonial assemblies had continued after that to respond to British needs slowly and grudgingly. Unwilling to be taxed by Parliament to support the war effort, the colonists were generally reluctant to tax themselves as well. Defiance of imperial trade regulations and other British demands continued, and even increased, through the last years of the war.

The problems of managing the empire became more difficult after 1763 because of a basic shift in Britain's imperial design. In the past, the English had viewed their colonial empire primarily in terms of trade; they had opposed acquisition of territory for its own sake. But by the mid-eigh-

Commercial versus Territorial Imperialists

Historical Thinking Skills

Comparing and Contrasting After students read the section "Consequences of the Seven Years' War," ask them to create a T-chart identifying ways in which Native American groups benefitted or suffered as a result of the Seven Years' War. Then have students evaluate which was more prevalent and write a thesis statement that makes a historically defensible claim about whether the war benefitted or harmed Native Americans. **SOC** **PCE**

teenth century, a growing number of English and American leaders (including William Pitt and Benjamin Franklin) were beginning to argue that land itself was of value to the empire—because of the population it could support, the taxes it could produce, and the imperial splendor it would confer. The debate between the old commercial imperialists and the new territorial ones came to a head at the conclusion of the French and Indian War. The mercantilists wanted England to return Canada to France in exchange for Guadeloupe, the most commercially valuable of the French "sugar islands" in the West Indies. The territorialists, however, prevailed. The acquisition of the French territories in North America was a victory for, among others, Benjamin Franklin, who had long argued that the American people would need these vast spaces to accommodate their rapid and, he believed, limitless growth.

With the territorial annexations of 1763, the area of the British Empire was suddenly twice as great as it had been, and the problems of governing it were thus considerably more

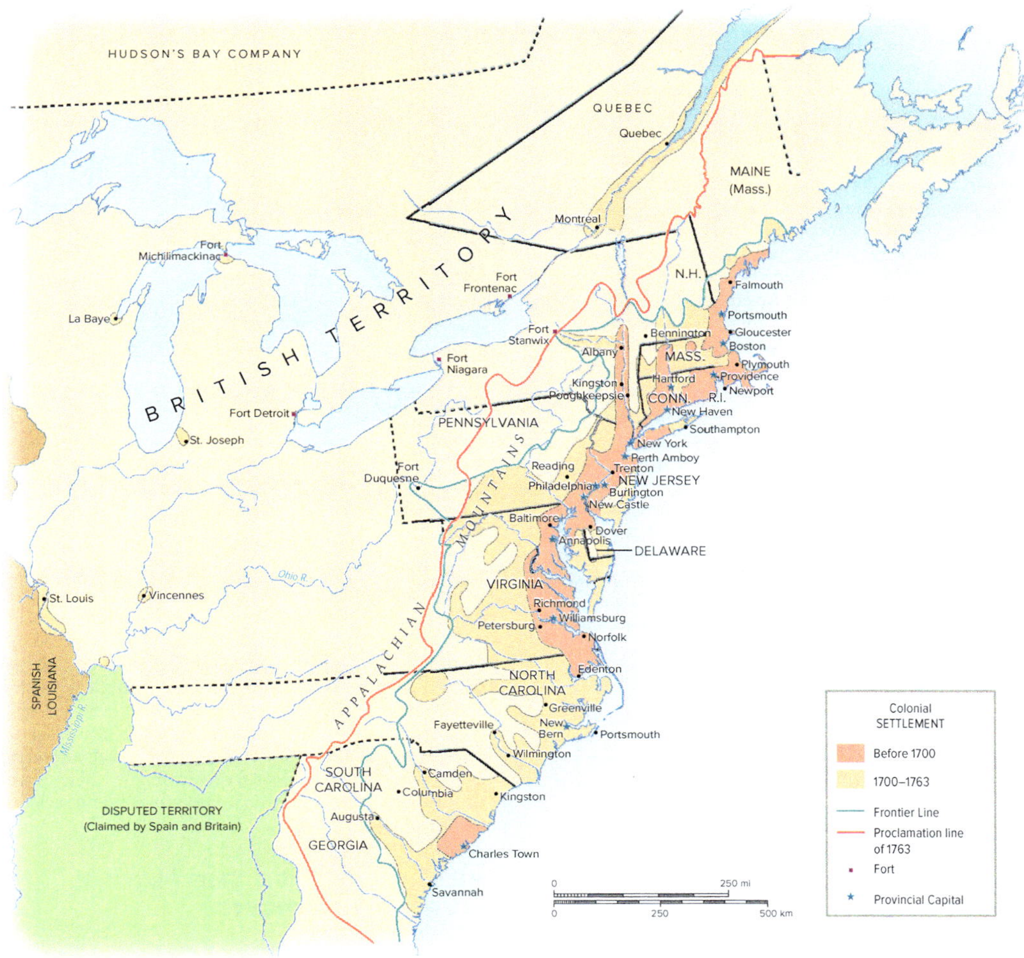

THE THIRTEEN COLONIES IN 1763 This map is a close-up of the thirteen colonies at the end of the Seven Years' War. It shows the line of settlement established by the Proclamation of 1763 (the red line), as well as the extent of actual settlement in that year (the blue line). Note that in the middle colonies (North Carolina, Virginia, Maryland, and southern Pennsylvania), settlement had already reached the red line—and in one small area of western Pennsylvania moved beyond it—by the time of the Proclamation of 1763. Note also the string of forts established beyond the Proclamation line.

How do the forts help to explain the efforts of the British to restrict settlement? And how does the extent of actual settlement help explain why it was so difficult for the British to enforce their restrictions?

Discussion and Activities

Analyzing Visuals Have students examine the map "The Thirteen Colonies in 1763." Ask them to identify any patterns of settlement and how those patterns changed from 1700 to 1763. *(In 1700, most settlement was along the coast, which provided relatively easy access to trade with Britain. By 1763, settlement had extended much farther inland, mostly along rivers that gave settlers a mode of travel in the absence of roads, along with access to goods from the coastal cities.)* **MIG** **WXT**

Answers

The Thirteen Colonies in 1763

The British forts could not offer any protection to colonists who settled beyond them. By 1763, settlement was so extensive, and much of the frontier line was so rugged, that it was virtually impossible to monitor colonists' movements.

Historical Thinking Skills

Argumentation After students read the section "Burdens of Empire," ask them to compile a list of new challenges faced by Britain following the end of the Seven Years' War. *(Disagreements over emphasis on trade or acquiring territory; strained relations with American colonists; debt taken on during the war.)* Have students write a short paragraph making a claim about which of those challenges was the greatest, and why. **PCE** **WXT** **WOR**

complex. Some British officials argued that the empire should restrain rapid settlement in the western territories. To allow Europeans to move into the new lands too quickly, they warned, would run the risk of stirring up costly conflicts with Native Americans. Restricting settlement would also keep the land available for hunting and trapping.

Many colonists wanted to see the new territories opened for immediate development, but they disagreed among themselves about who should control the western lands. Colonial governments made fervent, and often conflicting, claims of jurisdiction. Other colonists argued that control should remain in England, and that the territories should be considered entirely new colonies, unlinked to the existing settlements. There were, in short, a host of problems and pressures that the British could not ignore.

At the same time, the government in London was running out of options in its effort to find a way to deal with its staggering war debt. Landlords and merchants in England itself were objecting strenuously to increases in what they already considered excessively high taxes. The necessity of stationing significant numbers of British troops on the Indian border after 1763 was adding even more to the cost of defending the American settlements. And the halfhearted response of the colonial assemblies to the war effort had suggested that in its search for revenue, England could not rely on any cooperation from the colonial governments. Only a system of taxation administered by London, the leaders of the empire believed, could effectively meet England's needs.

BRITAIN'S STAGGERING WAR DEBT

At this crucial moment in Anglo-American relations, with the imperial system in desperate need of redefinition, George III became king in 1760 on the death of his grandfather. He brought two particularly unfortunate qualities to the office. First, he was determined, unlike his two predecessors, to be an active and responsible monarch. In part because of pressure from his ambitious mother, he removed from power the long-standing and stable coalition of Whigs, who had (under Pitt and others) governed the empire for much of the century and whom the new king mistrusted. In their place, he created a new coalition of his own through patronage and bribes and gained an uneasy control of Parliament. The new ministries that emerged as a result of these changes were unstable, each lasting in office only about two years.

Second, the king had serious intellectual and psychological limitations that compounded his political difficulties. He suffered, apparently, from a rare disease that produced intermittent bouts of insanity. (Indeed, in the last years of his long reign he was, according to most accounts, deranged, confined to the palace and unable to perform any official functions.) Yet, even when George III was lucid and rational, which in the 1760s and 1770s was most of the time, he was painfully immature (he was only twenty-two when he ascended the throne) and insecure–striving constantly to prove his fitness for his position but time and again finding himself ill equipped to handle the challenges he seized for himself. The king's personality, therefore, contributed to both the instability and the intransigence of the British government during these critical years.

GEORGE III'S SHORTCOMINGS

GEORGE III George III was twenty-two years old when he ascended the throne in 1760, and for many years almost all portraits of him were highly formal, with the king dressed in elaborate ceremonial robes. This less formal painting dates from much later in his reign, after he had begun to suffer from the mental disorders that eventually consumed him. After 1810, he was blind and permanently deranged, barred from all official business by the Regency Act of 1811. His son (later King George IV) served as regent in those years until he became king after his father's death in 1820

The Granger Collection, New York

More immediately responsible for the problems that soon emerged with the colonies, however, was George Grenville, whom the king made prime minister in 1763. Grenville did not share his brother-in-law William Pitt's sympathy with the American point of view. He agreed instead with the prevailing opinion within Britain that the colonists had been too long indulged and that they should be compelled to obey the laws and to pay a part of the cost of defending and administering the empire. He promptly began trying to impose a new system of control upon what had been a loose collection of colonial possessions in America.

THE BRITISH AND THE NATIVE AMERICAN NATIONS

The western problem was the most urgent. With the departure of the French, settlers and traders from the English colonies moved immediately into the upper Ohio Valley. The Native Americans of the region objected to this intrusion, and an alliance of nations, under the Ottawa chieftain Pontiac, struck back. To prevent an escalation of the fighting that

Discussion and Activities

Analyzing Change Have students read the section "George III's Shortcomings." Ask them to identify and discuss examples of how George III's ascension to the throne changed the relationship between England and its American colonies. **PCE**

might threaten western trade, the British government issued a ruling–the Proclamation of 1763–forbidding settlers to advance beyond a line drawn along the Appalachian Mountains.

The Proclamation of 1763 was appealing to the British for several reasons. It would allow London, rather than the provincial governments and their land-hungry constituents, to control the westward movement of the white population. Hence, westward expansion would proceed in an orderly manner, and conflicts with the Native Americans, which were both militarily costly and dangerous to trade, might be limited. Slower western settlement would also slow the population exodus from the coastal colonies, where England's most important markets and investments were. And it would reserve opportunities for land speculation and fur trading for English rather than colonial entrepreneurs.

PROCLAMATION OF 1763

Although Native Americans were not enthusiastic about the Proclamation, which required them to cede still more land to the white settlers, many groups supported the agreement as the best bargain available to them. The Cherokee, in particular, worked actively to hasten the drawing of the boundary, hoping to end white encroachments. Relations between the western nations and the British improved in some areas after the Proclamation, partly as a result of the work of the formally appointed "Indian superintendents" installed by the British. John Stuart was in charge of Native American affairs in the southern colonies, and Sir William Johnson in the northern ones. Both lived among the Native Americans and were sympathetic to the needs of the community; Johnson married a Mohawk woman, Mary Brant, who was later to play an important role in the American Revolution.

In the end, however, the Proclamation of 1763 failed to meet even the modest expectations of the Native Americans. It had some effect in limiting colonial land speculation in the West and in controlling the fur trade, but on the crucial point of the line of settlement it was ineffective. White settlers continued to swarm across the boundary and to claim lands farther and farther into the Ohio Valley. The British authorities tried repeatedly to establish limits to the expansion but continually failed to prevent the white colonists from pushing the line of settlement still farther west.

WHITE ENCROACHMENT

THE COLONIAL RESPONSE

The Grenville ministry soon moved to increase its authority in the colonies in more direct ways. Regular British troops, London announced, would now be stationed permanently in America; and under the Mutiny Act of 1765 the colonists were required to assist in provisioning and maintaining the army. Ships of the British navy were assigned to patrol American waters and search for smugglers. The customs service was reorganized and enlarged. Royal officials were ordered to take up their colonial posts in person instead of sending substitutes. Colonial manufacturing was to be restricted so that it would not compete with the rapidly expanding industry of Great Britain.

The Sugar Act of 1764, designed in part to eliminate the illegal sugar trade between the continental colonies and the French and Spanish West Indies, strengthened enforcement of the duty on sugar (while lowering the duty on molasses, further damaging the market for sugar grown in the colonies). It also established new vice-admiralty courts in America to try accused smugglers–thus depriving them of the benefit of sympathetic local juries. The Currency Act of 1764 required the colonial assemblies to stop issuing paper money (a widespread practice during the war) and to retire on schedule all the paper money already in circulation. Most momentous of all, the Stamp Act of 1765 imposed a tax on most printed documents in the colonies: newspapers, almanacs, pamphlets, deeds, wills, licenses.

SUGAR, CURRENCY, AND STAMP ACTS

The new imperial program was an effort to reapply to the colonies the old principles of mercantilism. And in some ways, it proved highly effective. British officials were soon collecting more than ten times as much annual revenue from America as before 1763. But the new policies created many more problems than they solved.

The colonists may have resented the new imperial regulations, but at first they found it difficult to resist them effectively. Americans continued to harbor as many grievances against one another as against the authorities in London. Often, the conflicts centered around tensions between the established societies of the Atlantic coast and the "backcountry" farther west, whose residents often felt isolated from, and underrepresented in, the colonial governments. These western settlers sometimes felt resentful because they lived closer to Native American communities than the societies of the East. In 1763, for example, a band of people from western Pennsylvania known as the "Paxton Boys" descended on Philadelphia with demands for relief from colonial (not British) taxes and for money to help them defend themselves against Native Americans; the colonial government averted bloodshed only by making concessions to them.

PAXTON BOYS

In 1771, a small-scale civil war broke out as a result of the so-called Regulator movement in North Carolina. The Regulators were farmers of the Carolina upcountry who organized in opposition to the high taxes that local sheriffs (appointed by the colonial governor) collected. The western counties were badly underrepresented in the colonial assembly, and the Regulators failed to win redress of their grievances there. Finally, they armed themselves and began resisting tax collections by force. To suppress the revolt, Governor William Tryon raised an army of militiamen, mostly from the eastern counties, who defeated a band of 2,000 Regulators in the Battle of Alamance. Nine on each side were killed, and many others were wounded. Afterward, six Regulators were hanged for treason.

REGULATOR MOVEMENT

The bloodshed was exceptional, but bitter conflicts within the colonies were not. After 1763, however, the new policies of the British government began to create common grievances among virtually all colonists that to some degree counterbalanced these internal divisions.

Reasoning Processes

Causation Have students read the sections "Proclamation of 1763" and "White Encroachment." Ask them to create a two-column chart identifying motives for the Proclamation of 1763 and the effects of the Proclamation. Ask students to evaluate and discuss whether the Proclamation achieved its desired effects and whether colonial reaction to it should have been anticipated by the British government. **PCE**

Historical Thinking Skills

Sourcing and Situation Have students read the section "Sugar, Currency, and Stamp Acts." Ask them to write a sentence or two identifying the purpose of these new acts. This could be done as an exit ticket. **PCE**

Reasoning Processes

Comparing After students have read the sections "Paxton Boys" and "Regulator Movement," ask them to create a Venn diagram to compare the two movements. Then have students evaluate whether they think the differences or similarities were more important and why. This could be used as the basis for a class or small group discussion. **PCE** **SOC**

Indeed, there was something in the Grenville program to antagonize everyone. Northern merchants believed they would suffer from restraints on commerce, closing opportunities for manufacturing, and increased taxes. Settlers in the northern backcountry resented the closing of the West to land speculation and fur trading. Southern planters, in debt to English merchants, feared having to pay additional taxes and losing their ability to ease their debts by speculating in western land. Professionals–ministers, lawyers, professors, and others–depended on merchants and planters for their livelihood and thus shared their concerns about the effects of English law. Small farmers, the largest group in the colonies, believed they would suffer from increased taxes and from the abolition of paper money, which had enabled them to pay their loans. Workers in towns opposed the restraints on manufacturing.

NORTH AMERICA IN 1763 The victory of the English over the French in the Seven Years' War (or, as it was known in America, the French and Indian War) reshaped the map of colonial North America. Britain gained a vast new territory, formerly controlled by France—Canada, and a large area west of the Mississippi River—thus more than doubling the size of the British Empire in America. French possessions in the New World dwindled to a few islands in the Caribbean. Spain continued to control a substantial empire in the North American interior. The red line along the western borders of the English colonies represents the line of settlement established by Britain in 1763. White settlers were not permitted to move beyond that line.

Why did the British wish to restrict settlement of the western lands?

Answers

North America in 1763

The British wished to restrict westward settlement, mainly to minimize conflict with Native American groups in the region.

The new restrictions came, moreover, at the beginning of an economic depression. The British government, by pouring money into the colonies to finance the fighting, had stimulated a wartime boom. When the flow of funds stopped after the peace in 1763, an economic bust followed. The imperial policies would, many colonists feared, doom them to permanent economic stagnation and a declining standard of living.

POSTWAR DEPRESSION

In reality, most Americans soon found ways to live with (or circumvent) the new British policies. The American economy was not, in fact, being destroyed. But economic anxieties were rising in the colonies nevertheless, and they created a growing sense of unease.

Whatever the economic consequences of the British government's programs, the political consequences were–in the eyes of the colonists–far worse. Perhaps nowhere else in the late-eighteenth-century world did so large a proportion of the people take an active interest in public affairs. That was partly because Anglo-Americans were deeply attached to broad powers of self-government; and the colonists were determined to protect those powers. The keys to self-government, they believed, were the provincial assemblies; and the key to the power of the provincial assemblies was their long-established right to give or withhold appropriations for the colonial governments, a right the British were now challenging. Home rule, therefore, was not something new and different that the colonists were striving to attain, but something old and familiar that they desired to keep. The movement to resist the new imperial policies, a movement for which many would ultimately fight and die, was at the same time democratic and conservative. It was a movement to conserve liberties Americans believed they already possessed.

POLITICAL CONSEQUENCES OF THE GRENVILLE PROGRAM

STIRRINGS OF REVOLT

By the mid-1760s, a hardening of positions had begun in both England and America that would bring the colonies into increasing conflict with the mother country. The victorious war for empire had given the colonists a heightened sense of their own importance and a renewed commitment to protecting their political autonomy. But it had also given the British a strengthened belief in the need to tighten administration of the empire and use the colonies as a source of revenue. The result was a series of events that, more rapidly than anyone had imagined, shattered the British Empire in America.

PREPARING TO MEET THE PAXTON BOYS The "Paxton Boys" were residents of western Pennsylvania who were declared outlaws by the assembly in Philadelphia after they launched an unauthorized attack on neighboring Conestoga Indians. Instead of surrendering, they armed themselves and marched on Philadelphia. This engraving satirizes the haphazard military preparations in the city for the expected invasion. An accompanying poem, expressing the contempt some colonists felt toward the urbanized, pacifist Quakers of Philadelphia, commented: "To kill the Paxtonians, they then did Advance, With Guns on their Shoulders, but how did they Prance." Benjamin Franklin finally persuaded the Paxton rebels not to attack in return for greater representation in the legislature.

Historical Thinking Skills

Analyzing Cause and Effect Have students read the sections "Postwar Depression" and "Political Consequences of the Grenville Program." Ask them to create a two-column chart listing the economic and political effects of Grenville's colonial policies. Then have students write a thesis statement that makes a historically defensible claim about whether Grenville's policies had a greater economic or political effect. **PCE** **WXT**

Discussion and Activities

Analyzing Visuals Have students examine the illustration "Preparing to Meet the Paxton Boys." Ask them to identify details from the illustration and write a short paragraph evaluating the point of view of the artist. *(The artist appears critical of efforts to defend Philadelphia. The heading refers to the defense as a "farce," cannons are pointed in various directions, and different groups of soldiers appear to be led by different officers without any apparent overall direction.)* **PCE**

Reasoning Processes

Change Over Time Have students read the section "Effects of the Stamp Act." Ask them to think about how the Stamp Act was different from earlier British colonial laws. Then have students pair up and share their thoughts with a partner. **WXT** **PCE**

The Stamp Act Crisis

Even if he had tried, Prime Minister Grenville could not have devised a better method for antagonizing and unifying the colonies than the Stamp Act of 1765.

Effects of the Stamp Act

The Sugar Act of a year earlier had affected few people other than the New England merchants. But the new tax fell on all Americans, and it evoked particular opposition from some of the most powerful members of the population. Merchants and lawyers were obliged to buy stamps for ships' papers and legal documents. Tavern owners, often the political leaders of their neighborhoods, were required to buy stamps for their licenses. Printers–the most influential group in distributing information and ideas in colonial society–had to buy stamps for their newspapers and other publications.

The actual economic burdens of the Stamp Act were relatively light; the stamps were not expensive. What made the law offensive to the colonists was the precedent it seemed to set. In the past, Americans had rationalized the taxes and duties on colonial trade as measures to regulate commerce, not raise money. Some Americans had even managed to persuade themselves that the Sugar Act, which was in fact designed primarily to raise money, was not fundamentally different from the traditional imperial duties. The Stamp Act, however, they could interpret in only one way: it was a direct attempt by England to raise revenue in the colonies without the consent of the colonial assemblies. If this new tax passed without resistance, the door would be open for more burdensome taxation in the future.

Few colonists believed that they could do anything more than grumble and buy the stamps–until the Virginia House of Burgesses sounded what one colonist called a "trumpet of sedition" that aroused Americans to action almost everywhere. The "trumpet" was the collective voice of a group of young Virginia aristocrats. They hoped, among other things, to challenge the power of tidewater planters who (in alliance with the royal governor) dominated Virginia politics. Foremost among the malcontents was Patrick Henry, who had already achieved fame for his fiery oratory and his occasional defiance of British authority. Henry made a dramatic speech to the House of Burgesses in May 1765, concluding with a vague prediction that if present policies were not revised, George III, like earlier tyrants, might lose his head. There were shocked cries of "Treason!" and, according to one witness, an immediate apology from Henry (although many years later he was quoted as having made the defiant reply: "If this be treason, make the most of it").

Henry introduced a set of resolutions declaring that Americans possessed the same rights as the English, especially

Virginia Resolves

the right to be taxed only by their own representatives; that Virginians should pay no taxes except those voted by the Virginia assembly; and that anyone advocating the right of Parliament to tax Virginians should be deemed an enemy of the colony. The House of Burgesses defeated the most extreme

THE ALTERNATIVES OF WILLIAM BURG In the aftermath of the Boston Tea Party and in response to the Coercive Acts Great Britain enacted to punish the colonists, the First Continental Congress called on Americans to boycott British goods until the acts were repealed. In this drawing, a prosperous Virginia merchant is seen signing a pledge to honor the nonimportation agreement—not surprising, given the alternative, visible in the background of the picture: tar and feathers hanging from a post labeled "A Cure for the Refractory."

of Henry's resolutions. All of them, however, were printed and circulated as the "Virginia Resolves" (creating an impression in other colonies that the people of Virginia were more militant than they actually were).

In Massachusetts at about the same time, James Otis persuaded his fellow members of the colonial assembly to call an intercolonial congress for action against the new tax. In October 1765, the Stamp Act Congress met in New York with delegates from nine colonies and decided to petition the king and the two houses of Parliament. Their petition conceded that Americans owed to Parliament "all due subordination," but it denied that the colonies could rightfully be taxed except through their own provincial assemblies.

Meanwhile, in several colonial cities, crowds began taking the law into their own hands. During the summer of 1765,

Sons of Liberty

serious riots broke out up and down the coast, the largest of them in Boston. Men belonging to the newly organized Sons of Liberty terrorized stamp agents and burned the stamps. The agents, themselves Americans, hastily resigned; and the sale of stamps in the continental colonies ceased. In Boston, a crowd also attacked such pro-British "aristocrats" as the lieu-

Historical Thinking Skills

Contextualization Have students read the section "Virginia Resolves." Ask them to explain why Patrick Henry's threat that George III might lose his head may have caused such a strong reaction from some Virginia legislators. *(They likely would have thought of the execution of Charles I during the English Civil War and inferred that Henry was advocating such an uprising.)* **PCE**

tenant governor, Thomas Hutchinson (who had privately opposed passage of the Stamp Act but who, as an officer of the crown, felt obliged to support it once it became law). The protesters pillaged Hutchinson's elegant house and virtually destroyed it.

The Stamp Act crisis was a dangerous moment in the relationship between the colonies and the British government. But the crisis subsided, largely because England backed down. The authorities in London changed their attitude not because of the colonists' defiance but because of economic pressure. Even before the Stamp Act, many New Englanders had stopped buying English goods to protest the Sugar Act of 1764. Now the colonial boycott spread, and the Sons of Liberty intimidated colonists who were reluctant to participate in it. The merchants of England, feeling the loss of much of their colonial market, begged Parliament to repeal the Stamp Act; and stories of unemployment, poverty, and discontent arose from English seaports and manufacturing towns.

The Marquis of Rockingham, who succeeded Grenville as prime minister in July 1765, tried to appease both the English merchants and the American colonists, and he finally convinced the king to kill the Stamp Act. On March 18, 1766, Parliament repealed it. Rockingham's opponents were strong and vociferous, and they insisted that unless England compelled the colonists to obey the Stamp Act, they would soon cease to obey any laws of Parliament. So, on the same day, to satisfy such critics, Parliament passed the Declaratory Act, asserting Parliament's authority over the colonies "in all cases whatsoever." In their rejoicing over the repeal of the Stamp Act, most Americans paid little attention to this sweeping declaration of power.

PARLIAMENT RETREATS

INTERNAL REBELLIONS

The conflicts with Britain were not the only uprisings emerging in the turbulent years of the 1760s. In addition to the Stamp Act crisis and other challenges to London, there were internal rebellions that had their roots in the class system in New York and New England. In the Hudson Valley in New York, great estates had grown up, whose owners had rented their land to small farmers. The revolutionary fervor of the time led many of these tenants to demand ownership of the land they worked. To emphasize their determination, they stopped paying rents. The challenge to landownership soon failed. But other challenges to landownership continued in other colonies. In Vermont, which still was governed by New York, insurgent farmers challenged landowners (many of them the same owners whom tenants had challenged on the Hudson) by taking up arms and demanding ownership of the land they worked. Ethan Allen (later a hero of the Revolutionary War and himself a land speculator) took up the cause of the Green Mountain farmers and accused the landowners of trying to "enslave a free people." Allen eventually succeeded in making Vermont into a separate state, which broke up some of the large estates.

Library of Congress

"THE TORY'S DAY OF JUDGMENT" A mob of American Patriots hoists a Loyalist neighbor up a flagpole in this woodcut, which is obviously sympathetic to the victim. The crowd is shown as fat, rowdy, and drunken. Public humiliations of Tories were not infrequent during the war. More common, however, was seizure of their property.

THE TOWNSHEND PROGRAM

The reaction in England to the Rockingham government's policy of appeasement was less enthusiastic than it was in America. English landlords, a powerful political force, angrily protested that the government had "sacrificed the landed gentlemen to the interests of traders and colonists." They feared that backing down from taxing the colonies would lead the government to increase taxes on them. The king finally bowed to their pressure and dismissed the Rockingham ministry. To replace it, he called upon the aging but still powerful William Pitt to form a government. Pitt had been a strong critic of the Stamp Act and had a reputation in America as a friend of the colonists. Once in office, however, Pitt (now Lord Chatham) was so hobbled by gout and at times so incapacitated by mental illness that the actual leadership of his administration fell to the chancellor of the exchequer, Charles Townshend–a bril-

Discussion and Activities

Making Connections After students have read the section "Sons of Liberty," ask them to discuss in small groups how the actions of groups like the Sons of Liberty were similar to or different from contemporary protests, such as demonstrations relating to police-officer involved shootings or violations of mask mandates during the COVID-19 pandemic. **PCE** **SOC**

Historical Thinking Skills

Sourcing and Situation Have students examine the image "The Tory's Day of Judgment." Ask them to identify details from the illustration that might reveal the artist's purpose, point of view, or intended audience. *(Purpose: to reveal the lawlessness of the Patriots by showing them administering mob justice. Point of View: pro-Tory, supporting the British government by showing Patriots as unrestrained by law. Audience: likely other Tories, or those undecided about whether to support the British.)* **PCE**

Reasoning Processes

Comparing After students read the section "The Townshend Program," ask them to create a bisected Venn diagram (a Venn diagram with a horizontal line drawn through the middle) comparing the policies surrounding the colonies of Charles Townshend to those of George Grenville. Use the space above the line for economic policies and the space below the line for political policies. Ask students to evaluate whether the economic or political policies had more impact in the colonies. PCE WXT

liant, flamboyant, and at times reckless politician known to his contemporaries variously as "the Weathercock" and "Champagne Charlie."

Among Townshend's first challenges was dealing with the continuing American grievances against Parliament, now most notably the Mutiny (or Quartering) Act of 1765, which required the colonists to provide quarters and supplies for the British troops in America. The British considered this a reasonable requirement. The troops were stationed in North America to protect the colonists from Native American or French attack and to defend the frontiers; lodging the troops in coastal cities was simply a way to reduce the costs to England of supplying them. To the colonists, however, the law was another assault on their liberties.

MUTINY ACT

They did not so much object to quartering the troops or providing them with supplies; they had been doing that voluntarily ever since the last years of the French and Indian War. They resented that these contributions were now mandatory, and they considered it another form of taxation without consent. The Massachusetts Assembly refused to vote the mandated supplies to the troops. The New York Assembly soon did likewise, posing an even greater challenge to imperial authority, since the army headquarters were in New York City.

To enforce the law and to try again to raise revenues in the colonies, Townshend steered two inflammatory measures through Parliament in 1767. The first disbanded the New York Assembly until the colonists agreed to obey the Mutiny Act. (By singling out New York, Townshend thought he would avoid Grenville's mistake of arousing all the colonies at once.) The second levied new taxes (known as the Townshend Duties) on various goods imported to the colonies from England—lead, paint, paper, and tea. The colonists could not logically object to taxation of this kind, Townshend reasoned, because it met standards they themselves had accepted. Benjamin Franklin, as a colonial agent in London trying to prevent the passage of the Stamp Act, had long ago argued for the distinction between "internal" and "external" taxes and had denounced the stamp duties as internal taxation. Townshend himself had considered the distinction laughable; but he was nevertheless imposing duties on what he believed were clearly external transactions.

INTERNAL AND EXTERNAL TAXES

Yet Townshend's efforts to satisfy colonial grievances were to no avail. He might call them external taxes, but they were no more acceptable to colonial merchants than the Stamp Act. Their purpose, Americans believed, was the same as that of the Stamp Act: to raise revenue from the colonists without their consent. And the suspension of the New York Assembly, far from isolating New York, aroused the resentment of all the colonies. They considered this assault on the rights of one provincial government a precedent for the annihilation of the rights of all of them.

The Massachusetts Assembly took the lead in opposing the new measures by circulating a letter to all the colonial governments urging them to stand up against every tax, external or internal, imposed by Parliament. At first, the circular evoked little response in some of the legislatures (and ran into strong opposition in Pennsylvania's). Then Lord Hillsborough, secretary of state for the colonies, issued a circular letter of his own from London in which he warned that assemblies endorsing the Massachusetts letter would be dissolved. Massachusetts defiantly reaffirmed its support for the circular. (The vote in the Assembly was 92 to 17, and for a time "ninety-two" became a patriotic rallying cry throughout British America.) The other colonies, including Pennsylvania, promptly rallied to the support of Massachusetts.

In addition to his other unpopular measures, Townshend tried to strengthen enforcement of commercial regulations in the colonies by, among other things, establishing a new board of customs commissioners in America. Townshend hoped the new board would stop the rampant corruption in the colonial customs houses, and to some extent his hopes were fulfilled. The new commissioners ended smuggling in Boston, their headquarters, although smugglers continued to carry on a busy trade in other colonial seaports.

The Boston merchants—accustomed to loose enforcement of the Navigation Acts and doubly aggrieved now that the new commission was diverting the lucrative smuggling trade—were indignant and took the lead in organizing another boycott. In 1768, the merchants of Philadelphia and New York joined them in a nonimportation agreement, and later some southern merchants and planters also agreed to cooperate. Colonists boycotted British goods subject to the Townshend Duties; and throughout the colonies, American homespun and other domestic products became fashionable overnight, while English luxuries fell from favor.

COLONIAL BOYCOTTS

Late in 1767, Charles Townshend suddenly died—before the consequences of his ill-conceived program had become fully apparent. The question of dealing with colonial resistance to the Townshend Duties fell, therefore, to the new prime minister, Lord North. Hoping to break the nonimportation agreement and divide the colonists, Lord North secured the repeal of all the Townshend Duties except the tax on tea in March 1770.

THE BOSTON MASSACRE

The withdrawal of the Townshend Duties never had a chance to pacify colonial opinion. Before news of the repeal reached America, an event in Massachusetts raised colonial resentment to a new level of intensity. The colonists' harassment of the new customs commissioners in Boston had grown so intense that the British government had placed four regiments of regular troops inside the city. The presence of the "redcoats" was a constant affront to the colonists' sense of their independence and a constant reminder of what they considered British oppression. In addition, British soldiers, poorly paid and poorly treated by the army, wanted jobs in their off-duty hours; and they competed with local workers in an already tight market. Clashes between them were frequent.

COMPETITION FOR SCARCE EMPLOYMENT

Discussion and Activities

Analyzing Points of View Have students read the section "Mutiny Act." Ask them to write a short newspaper article or journal entry evaluating the act from the point of view of either a colonial administrator or a colonist required to house soldiers. Have students share their perspective with a student who chose the opposite role. SOC PCE

On the night of March 5, 1770, a few days after a particularly intense skirmish between workers at a ship-rigging factory and British soldiers who were trying to find work there, a crowd of dockworkers, "liberty boys," and others began pelting the sentries at the customs house with rocks and snowballs. Hastily, Captain Thomas Preston of the British regiment lined up several of his men in front of the building to protect it. There was some scuffling; one of the soldiers was knocked down; and in the midst of it all, apparently, several British soldiers fired into the crowd, killing five people (among them a sailor of Native American and African descent, Crispus Attucks).

This murky incident, almost certainly the result of panic and confusion, was quickly transformed by local resistance leaders into the "Boston Massacre"—a graphic symbol of British oppression and brutality. The victims became popular martyrs; the event became the subject of many lurid (and inaccurate) accounts. A famous engraving by Paul Revere, widely reproduced and circulated, falsely portrayed the "massacre" as a carefully organized, calculated assault on a peaceful crowd. A jury of Massachusetts colonists found two British soldiers guilty of manslaughter and acquitted six others. Colonial pamphlets and newspapers, however, convinced many Americans that all of the soldiers were guilty of official murder. Year after year, resistance leaders marked the anniversary of the massacre with demonstrations and speeches.

The leading figure in fomenting public outrage over the Boston Massacre was Samuel Adams, the most effective radical in the colonies. Adams (a distant cousin of John Adams, second

Library of Congress

THE BOSTON MASSACRE (1770), BY PAUL REVERE This is one of many sensationalized engravings, by Revere and others, of the conflict between British troops and Boston laborers that became important propaganda documents for the Patriot cause in the 1770s. Among the victims of the massacre listed by Revere was Crispus Attucks, probably the first black man to die in the struggle for American independence.

Discussion and Activities

Making Connections After students read the section "Competition for Scarce Employment," ask them to think about how the presence of British troops in Boston caused tension with the inhabitants of that city. Have students pair up and share how those tensions might be similar to tensions relating to immigration today. **WXT**

Discussion and Activities

Analyzing Visuals Have students examine the image "The Boston Massacre (1770), by Paul Revere." Ask them to list specific details from the image and discuss as a class or in small groups which details are pro-British or anti-British. *(Students will likely conclude that all details are ant-British; the heading calls the event a massacre, the unarmed Boston residents are being fired upon by well-organized British soldiers without provocation, and a British officer is clearly seen giving the order to fire.)* Conclude with a discussion about the how the impact that propaganda such as this poster might lead to greater tension in Boston. **PCE**

Historical Thinking Skills

Historical Developments and Argumentation Have students read the first two paragraphs in the section "The Philosophy of Revolt." Based on the reading and their prior knowledge, ask students to work in small groups to create a list of factors that lend support to the idea of revolution in America. *(Possible responses: Scottish immigrants suspicious of the expansion of British authority; Puritan ideal of equality of church members; Enlightenment ideas of sovereignty.)* Have groups discuss which of these factors would be most potent in supporting the idea of revolution in America, and what evidence would support those conclusions. **PCE** **WOR** **SOC**

president of the United States) was born in 1722 and was thus somewhat older than other leaders of colonial protest. As a member of an earlier generation with strong ties to New England's Puritan past, he was particularly inclined to view public events in stern moral terms. A failure in business, he became an unflagging voice expressing outrage at British oppression. England, he argued, had become a morass of sin and corruption; only in America did public virtue survive. He spoke frequently at Boston town meetings; and as one unpopular English policy followed another–the Townshend Duties, the placement of customs commissioners in Boston, the stationing of British troops in the city (with its violent results)–his message attracted increasing support. In 1772, he proposed the creation of a "committee of correspondence" in Boston to publicize the grievances against England throughout the colony. He became its first head. Other colonies followed Massachusetts's lead, and a loose network of political organizations grew up that kept the spirit of dissent alive through the 1770s.

SAMUEL ADAMS

"THE CRUEL FATE OF THE LOYALISTS" This British cartoon, published near the end of the American Revolution, shows three Native Americans, representing American revolutionaries, murdering six Loyalists: four by hanging, one by scalping, and one—appealing to Fate—about to be killed. By using Native Americans to represent Anglo-American soldiers, the British were trying to equate the presumed savagery of Native Americans with the behavior of the revolutionaries.

The Library of Congress (LC-USZ62-1540)

THE PHILOSOPHY OF REVOLT

A superficial calm settled on the colonies for approximately three years after the Boston Massacre. But the crises of the 1760s had helped arouse enduring ideological challenges to England and had produced powerful instruments for publicizing colonial grievances. Gradually a political outlook gained a following in America that would ultimately serve to justify revolt.

The ideas that would support the Revolution emerged from many sources. Some were drawn from religious (particularly Puritan) sources or from the political experiences of the colonies. Others came from abroad. Most important, perhaps, were the "radical" ideas of those in Great Britain who stood in opposition to their government. Some were Scots, who considered the English state tyrannical. Others were embittered "country Whigs," who felt excluded from power and considered the existing political system corrupt and oppressive. Drawing from some of the great philosophical minds of earlier generations–most notably John Locke–these English dissidents framed a powerful argument against their government.

Central to this emerging ideology was a new concept of what government should be. Because humans were inherently corrupt and selfish, government was necessary to protect individuals from the evil in one another. But because any government was run by corruptible people, the people needed safeguards against its possible abuses of power. Most people in both England and America had long considered the English constitution the best system ever devised to meet these necessities. By distributing power among the three elements of society–the monarchy, the aristocracy, and the common people–the English political system ensured that no individual or group could exercise authority unchecked by another. Yet, by the mid-seventeenth century, dissidents in both England and America had become convinced that the constitution was in danger. A single center of power–the king and his ministers–was becoming so powerful that it could not be effectively checked. The system, the dissidents believed, was becoming a corrupt and dangerous tyranny.

ENGLAND'S BALANCED CONSTITUTION

Such arguments found little sympathy in most of England. The English constitution was not a written document or a fixed set of unchangeable rules. It was a general sense of the "way things are done," and most people in England were willing to accept changes in it. Americans, by contrast, drew from their experience with colonial charters, in which the shape and powers of government were permanently inscribed on paper. They resisted the idea of a flexible, changing set of basic principles.

One basic principle, Americans believed, was the right of people to be taxed only with their own consent–a belief that gradually took shape in the widely repeated slogan "No taxation without representation." This clamor about "representation" made little sense to the English. According to English constitutional theory, members of Parliament did not represent individuals or particular geographic areas. Instead, each member represented the interests of the whole nation and indeed the whole empire, no matter where the member came from. The many boroughs of England that had no representative in Parliament, the whole of Ireland, and the colonies thousands of miles away–all were thus represented in the Parliament at London, even though they elected no representatives of their own. This was the theory of "virtual" representation. But Americans, drawing from their experiences with their town meetings and their colonial assemblies, believed in "actual" representation: every community was entitled to its own representative, elected by the people of that community and directly responsible to them. Since the colonists had none of their own representatives in Parliament, it followed that they were not represented there. Instead, Americans believed that the colonial assemblies played the same role within the colo-

Discussion and Activities

Analyzing Visuals Have students examine the image "The Cruel Fate of the Loyalists." Ask them why the artist might have chosen to represent Patriots as Native Americans. *(Possible response: Using a stereotype of Native Americans as uncivilized savages infers that the Patriots themselves were unprincipled savages.)* Ask how a pro-Patriot cartoon might have portrayed the same scene. *(Possible responses: Loyalists might be shown undergoing a trial by jury with legal representation. Loyalists might be shown massacring Patriots for looting or vandalizing their homes.)* Then have students draw cartoons that express either a pro-Patriot or anti-Patriot theme. **PCE** **SOC**

nies that Parliament did within England. The British Empire, the Americans began to argue, was a sort of federation of commonwealths, each with its own legislative body, all tied together by common loyalty to the king.

Such ideas illustrated a fundamental difference of opinion between England and America over the nature of sovereignty—over the question of where ultimate power lay. By arguing that Parliament had the right to legislate for England and for the empire as a whole, but that only the provincial assemblies could legislate for the individual colonies, Americans were in effect arguing for a division of sovereignty. Parliament would be sovereign in some matters; the assemblies would be sovereign in others. To the British, such an argument was absurd. In any system of government there must be a single, ultimate authority. And since the empire was, in their view, a single, undivided unit, there could be only one authority within it: the English government of king and Parliament.

VIRTUAL VERSUS ACTUAL REPRESENTATION

THE TEA EXCITEMENT

The relatively calm first years of the 1770s disguised a growing sense of resentment at the increasingly heavy-handed British enforcement of the Navigation Acts. The customs commissioners, who remained in the colonies despite the repeal of the Townshend Duties, were mostly clumsy, intrusive, and arrogant officials. They harassed colonial merchants and seamen constantly with petty restrictions, and they also enriched themselves through graft and illegal seizures of merchandise.

Colonists also kept revolutionary sentiment alive through writing and talking. Dissenting leaflets, pamphlets, and books circulated widely through the colonies. In towns and cities, men gathered in churches, schools, town squares, and above all in taverns to discuss politics and express their growing disenchantment with English policy. The rise of revolutionary ideology was not simply a result of the ideas of intellectuals. It was also a product of a social process by which ordinary people heard, discussed, and absorbed new ideas.

REVOLUTIONARY DISCOURSE

The popular anger lying just beneath the surface was also visible in occasional acts of rebellion. At one point, colonists seized a British revenue ship on the lower Delaware River. And in 1772, angry residents of Rhode Island boarded the British schooner *Gaspée*, set it afire, and sank it in Narragansett Bay. The British response to the *Gaspée* affair further inflamed American opinion. Instead of putting the accused attackers on trial in colonial courts, the British sent a special commission to America with power to send the defendants back to England for trial.

What finally revived the revolutionary fervor of the 1760s, however, was a new act of Parliament—one that the English government had expected to be relatively uncontroversial. It involved the business of selling tea. In 1773, Britain's East India Company (which had an official monopoly on trade with the Far East) was on the verge of bankruptcy and sitting on large stocks of tea that it could not sell in England. In an effort to save the company, the government passed the Tea Act of 1773, which gave the company the right to export its merchandise directly to the colonies without paying any of the navigation taxes that were imposed on the colonial merchants, who had traditionally served as the middlemen in such transactions. With these privileges, the East India Company could undersell American merchants and monopolize the colonial tea trade.

The Tea Act angered many colonists for several reasons. First, it enraged influential colonial merchants, who feared

Monday Morning December 27, 1773.

THE TEA SHIP being arrived, every Inhabitant, who wishes to preserve the Liberty of America, is desired to meet at the STATE-HOUSE, This Morning, precisely at TEN o'Clock, to advise what is best to be done on this alarming Crisis.

To the PUBLIC.

THE Senfe of the City relative to the Landing the India Company's Tea, being fignified to Captain Lockyer, by the Committee, neverthelefs, it is the Defire of a Number of the Citizens, that at his Departure from hence, he fhould fee, with his own Eyes, their Deteftation of the Meafures purfued by the Miniftry and the India Company, to enflave this Country. This will be declared by the Convention of the People at his Departure from this City; which will be on next Saturday Morning, about nine o'Clock, when no Doubt, every Friend to this Country will attend. The Bells will give the Notice about an Hour before he embarks from Murray's Wharf.

By Order of the COMMITTEE.

NEW YORK, APRIL 21ft, 1774.

THE BOSTON TEA PARTY The artist Ramberg produced this wash drawing of the Boston Tea Party in 1773. A handbill in a Philadelphia newspaper ten days later and another distributed in New York the following April illustrate how quickly the spirit of resistance spread to other colonies

Reasoning Process

Comparing Have students read the section "Virtual Versus Actual Representation." Ask them to create a T-chart to compare the attributes of each system. Then have students pair up, with one student per pair creating an argument in support of one of the two positions. Ask students to create a short dialogue/debate that could be acted out in front of the class. **PCE** **WOR** **WXT**

Historical Thinking Skills

Sourcing and Situation Have students examine the New York hand bill about "The Boston Tea Party." Ask them to compile a list of words or phrases that seem designed to evoke an emotional response (sometimes referred to as "trigger words," e.g., *destination, enslave*). Ask students to write a brief explanation of what purpose the author may have had in using those words. **PCE**

Discussion and Activities

Have students read the sections "The Tea Act" and "Boston Tea Party." Ask students to create a two-column chart listing reasons why the British imposed the Tea Act on one side and why the Patriots carried out the Boston Tea Party on the other side. Use the lists as the basis for a discussion about the motives for the Tea Act and how it led to unintended consequences. **WXT** **PCE**

being replaced and bankrupted by a powerful monopoly. The East India Company's decision to grant franchises to certain American merchants for the sale of its tea created further resentments among those excluded from this lucrative trade. More important, however, the Tea Act revived American passions about the issue of taxation without representation. The law provided no new tax on tea. But it exempted the East India Company from having to pay the normal customs duties. That put colonial merchants at a grave competitive disadvantage. British Prime Minister Lord North assumed that most colonists would welcome the new law because it would reduce the price of tea to consumers by removing the middlemen. But resistance leaders in America argued that it was another insidious example of the results of an unconstitutional tax. Many colonists responded by boycotting tea.

THE TEA ACT

The boycott was an important event in the history of colonial resistance. Unlike earlier protests, most of which had involved small numbers of people, the boycott mobilized large segments of the population. It also helped link the colonies in a common experience of mass popular protest. Particularly important to the movement were the activities of colonial women, who were among the principal consumers of tea and now became leaders of the effort to boycott it.

Women had played a significant role in resistance activities from the beginning. Several women (most prominently Mercy Otis Warren) had been important in writing the dissident literature—in Warren's case, satirical plays—that did much to fan colonial resentments in the 1760s. Women had participated actively in anti-British riots and crowd activities in the 1760s; they had formed an informal organization—the Daughters of Liberty—that occasionally mocked their male counterparts as insufficiently militant. Now, as the sentiment for a boycott grew, some women mobilized as never before, determined (as the Daughters of Liberty had written) "that rather than Freedom, we'll part with our Tea."

In the last weeks of 1773, with strong popular support, leaders in various colonies made plans to prevent the East India Company from landing its cargoes in colonial ports. In Philadelphia and New York City, determined colonists kept the tea from leaving the company's ships. In Charles Town, they stored it in a public warehouse. In Boston, after failing to turn back the three ships in the harbor, local Patriots staged a spectacular drama. On the evening of December 16, 1773, three companies of fifty men each, masquerading as Mohawks, passed through a tremendous crowd of spectators (which served to protect them from official interference), went aboard the three ships, broke open the tea chests, and heaved them into the harbor. As the electrifying news of the Boston "tea party" spread, other seaports followed the example and staged similar acts of resistance.

BOSTON TEA PARTY

When the Bostonians refused to pay for the property they had destroyed, George III and Lord North decided on a policy of coercion, to be applied only against Massachusetts—the chief center of resistance. In four acts of 1774, Parliament closed the port of Boston, drastically reduced colonial self-government, permitted royal officers to be tried in other colonies or in England when accused of crimes, and provided for the quartering of troops in the colonists' barns and empty houses.

PAYING THE EXCISEMAN This eighteenth-century satirical drawing by a British artist depicts Bostonians forcing tea down the throat of a customs official, whom they have tarred and feathered. In the background, colonists are dumping tea into the harbor (presumably a representation of the 1773 Boston Tea Party); and on the tree at right is a symbol of the Stamp Act, which the colonists had defied eight years earlier.

Parliament followed these Coercive Acts—or, as they were more widely known in America, Intolerable Acts—with the Quebec Act, which was separate from them in origin and quite different in purpose. Its object was to provide a civil government for the French-speaking Roman Catholic inhabitants of Canada and the Illinois country. The law extended the boundaries of Quebec to include the French communities between the Ohio and Mississippi Rivers. It also granted political rights to Roman Catholics and recognized the legality of the Roman Catholic Church within the enlarged province. In many ways it was a tolerant and long-overdue piece of legislation. But in the inflamed atmosphere of the time, many people in the thirteen English-speaking colonies considered it a threat. They were already alarmed by rumors that the Church of England was scheming to appoint a bishop for America who would impose Anglican authority on all the various sects. Since the line between the Church of England and the Church of Rome had always seemed to many Americans dangerously thin, the passage of the Quebec Act convinced some of them that a plot

COERCIVE ACTS

Discussion and Activities

Analyzing Visuals Have students view the image "Paying the Exciseman." The caption indicates that this is a satirical drawing. Ask students to define satire, then identify the details in the painting that indicate that it is satire. *(The colonists aren't actually paying the tea tax; they are instead forcing tea down the throat of the tax agent. The agent has also been tarred and feathered, there is a threatening noose hanging from the tree which is named the "Liberty Tree," and protesters are dumping tea from an English ship into the harbor.)* **PCE** **WXT**

CONSIDER THE SOURCE

TEA PARTIES

THE BOSTON Tea Party of 1773 was a revolt against "taxation without representation." The poem "Tea, Destroyed by Indians" celebrates the action of the Boston Tea Party, expresses the colonists' resentments and complaints against the distant London government, and calls upon Boston patriots to continue to resist British actions.

The twenty-first-century Tea Party movement became prominent in 2009. Although not an official political party, members tend to endorse Republican candidates. The modern Tea Party movement has borrowed its name from the Boston event that took place over 200 years ago, and has picked up some (although not all) of the ideas of the 1773 Boston Tea Party: hostility to distant authority (London then, Washington now) and resentment of taxes (imposed by Britain then, and by Washington now). Although taxation in our time does not really take place "without representation," today's Tea Partiers certainly feel that contemporary taxation is as illegitimate as the Bostonians felt it was in 1773.

BOSTON TEA PARTY—1773

TEA, DESTROYED BY INDIANS

Poem honoring the Boston Tea Party, Dec. 1773

CHORUS:

Bostonian's SONS keep up your Courage good,
Or Dye, like Martyrs, in fair Free-born Blood.

YE GLORIOUS SONS OF FREEDOM, brave and bold,
That has flood forth–fair LIBERTY to hold;
Though you were INDIANS, come from distant shores,
Like MEN you acted–not like savage Moors.

CHORUS

Our LIBERTY, and LIFE is now invaded,
And FREEDOM's brightest Charms are darkly shaded;
But, we will STAND–and think it noble mirth,
To DART the man that dare oppress the Earth.

CHORUS

How grand the Scene!–(No Tyrant shall oppose)
The TEA is sunk in spite of all our foes.
A NOBLE SIGHT–to see th' accursed TEA
Mingled with MUD–and ever for to be;
For KING and PRINCE shall know that we are FREE.

CHORUS

Must we be still– and live on Blood-bought Ground,
And not oppose the Tyrants cursed found?
We Scorn the thought–our views are well refin'd
We Scorn those slavish shackles of the Mind,
"We've Souls that were not made to be confin'd."

CHORUS

Could our Fore-fathers rise from their cold Graves,
And view their Land, with all their Children SLAVES;
What would they say! how would their Spirits rend,
And, Thunder-strucken, to their Graves descend.

CHORUS

Let us with hearts of steel now stand the task,
Throw off all darksome ways, nor wear a Mask.
Oh! may our noble Zeal support our frame,
And brand all Tyrants with eternal SHAME.

CHORUS

Bostonian's SONS keep up your Courage good,
And sink all Tyrants in their GUILTY BLOOD.

Source: www.masshist.org

AP Exam Tip

One way to demonstrate complexity in AP essay writing is to explain how claims or evidence support, modify, or refute an argument. The simplest way for students to do this is to demonstrate the relative importance of multiple causes or effects, different degrees of similarity or difference, or different degrees of continuity or change over time.

Historical Thinking Skills

Claims and Evidence in Sources Have students practice the AP Exam tip by asking them to construct a thesis statement that makes a historically defensible claim while distinguishing between multiple factors. Students may incorporate a formula into their theses, such as "X, however A and B, therefore Y," where X represents a concession, A and B represent the strongest arguments in support of the thesis, and Y represents the position being taken.

Historical Thinking Skills

Historical Sources and Argumentation Have students read the poem "Tea, Destroyed by Indians." Ask them to identify "virtue words," words that are used to create a positive emotional response. Ask students to discuss what type of response the author was likely trying to achieve. **NAT** **PCE**

AP Exam Practice

Short Answer Provide students with the following short-answer questions and allow 15 minutes for completion. Ask for volunteers to share their responses and discuss as a class.

Answer A, B, and C.

A) Briefly explain ONE important similarity between the British colonies in the Chesapeake region and in New England from 1607 to 1754. *(Possible responses: mostly agricultural economies; initial desire for cooperation between Native Americans and colonists; eventual wars between colonists and Native Americans due to land and cultural conflicts; indentured servitude and slavery for labor; dependence on trade from and to Britain; motivations for immigration.)*

B) Briefly explain ONE important difference between the British colonies in the Chesapeake region and in New England from 1607 to 1754. *(Possible responses: greater reliance on slavery in the Chesapeake; greater disparity in wealth between classes in the Chesapeake, mixed economy [e.g., fishing, lumber, tar, rope, small farming, etc.] in New England and reliance on agriculture and cash crops [e.g., tobacco, indigo, etc.] in the Chesapeake; large versus small farms in the regions; higher concentration of population density in New England.)*

C) Briefly explain ONE factor that accounts for the difference that you indicated in B. *(Possible responses: New England was founded more for religious reasons than the Chesapeake was; settlement in New England was more family oriented than in the Chesapeake, which was primarily young single males; more ethnic diversity in the Chesapeake; healthier climate and more stable living conditions in New England; New England town meetings versus Chesapeake landed gentry [e.g., House of Burgesses]; Powhatan Wars/Bacon's Rebellion versus Pequot Wars/King Phillip's War; greater reliance on slavery in the Chesapeake due to labor intensive agriculture demands; greater disparity in wealth in the Chesapeake due to unequal land distribution; different economies due to rocky soil in New England and nutrient rich soil in the Chesapeake.)*

TEA PARTY MOVEMENT—2010

Although the Tea Party movement has no centralized leadership, one organization that claims to be the "official" home of the American Tea Party movement is TeaParty.org. A description and set of core beliefs provided by this organization appear below.

TeaParty.org Description and Core Beliefs

What Is the Tea Party?

The Tea Party is a grassroots movement that calls awareness to any issue that challenges the security, sovereignty, or domestic tranquility of our beloved nation, the United States of America.

From our founding, the Tea Party is the voice of the true owners of the United States, WE THE PEOPLE.

Many claim to be the founders of this movement–however, it was the brave souls of the men and women in 1773, known today as the Boston Tea Party, who dared defy the greatest military might on earth.

We are the beneficiaries of their courage. By joining the Tea Party, you are taking a stand for our nation. You will be upholding the grand principles set forth in the U.S. Constitution and Bill of Rights.

Non-negotiable core beliefs

Illegal Aliens Are Here Illegally.
Pro-Domestic Employment Is Indispensable.
Stronger Military Is Essential.
Special Interests Eliminated.
Gun Ownership Is Sacred.
Government Must Be Downsized.
National Budget Must Be Balanced.
Deficit Spending Will End.
Bail-Out and Stimulus Plans Are Illegal.
Reduce Personal Income Taxes A Must.
Reduce Business Income Taxes Is Mandatory.
Political Offices Available To Average Citizens.
Intrusive Government Stopped.
English As Core Language Is Required.
Traditional Family Values Are Encouraged.
Common Sense Constitutional.
Conservative Self-Governance.

Source: Tea Party/1773 Tea Party

ANALYZING SOURCES

Questions assume cumulative content knowledge from this chapter and previous chapters.

1. The poem reflects the influence of which philosophical ideas?
   (A) religious conservatism
   (B) ideals of religious toleration
   (C) Enlightenment
   (D) British parliamentary system

2. Which political question in common is being alluded to by both the poem and the document?
   (A) degree of authority of centralized power
   (B) legitimacy of Parliamentary power
   (C) the extent of private property rights
   (D) commercial regulation

3. The poem and document best share which of the following regarding the audience being addressed?
   (A) grassroots movement
   (B) intellectual elites
   (C) women
   (D) politicians

Answers

Consider the Source

1. C; **2.** A; **3.** A

TAVERNS IN REVOLUTIONARY MASSACHUSETTS

In colonial Massachusetts, as in many other American colonies in the 1760s and 1770s, taverns (or "public houses," or "pubs," as they came to be known) were crucial to the development of popular resistance to British rule. The Puritan culture of New England created some resistance to taverns, and there were continuing efforts by reformers to regulate or close them to reduce the problems caused by "public drunkenness," "lewd behavior," and anarchy. But as the commercial life of the colonies expanded, and as increasing numbers of people began living in towns and cities, taverns became a central institution in American social life—and eventually in its political life as well.

Taverns were appealing, of course, because they provided alcoholic drinks in a culture where the craving for alcohol—and the extent of drunkenness—was very high. But taverns had other attractions as well. There were few other places where people could meet and talk openly in public, and to many colonists the life of the tavern came to seem the most democratic experience available to them. Gradually, many began to see the attacks on the public houses as efforts to increase the power of existing elites and suppress the freedoms of ordinary people. The tavern was a mostly male institution, just as politics was considered a mostly male concern. And so the fusion of male camaraderie and political discourse emerged naturally out of the tavern culture.

As the revolutionary crisis deepened, taverns and pubs became the central meeting places for discussions of the ideas that fueled resistance to British polices. Educated and uneducated men alike joined in animated discussions of events. Those who could not read—and there were many—could learn about the contents of revolutionary pamphlets from listening to tavern discussions. They could join in the discussion of the new republican ideas emerging in the Americas by participating in tavern celebrations of, for example, the anniversaries of resistance to the Stamp Act. Those anniversaries inspired elaborate toasts in public houses throughout the colonies. Such toasts were the equivalents of political speeches, and illiterate men could learn much from them about the political concepts that were circulating through the colonies.

THE SCALES OF JUSTICE This sign for a Hartford tavern promises hospitality (from "the charming Patroness") and "entertainment" as well as food and drink.

TAVERNS AND POLITICS The Green Dragon Tavern is where protestors planned the Boston Tea Party.

Taverns were important sources of information in an age before any wide distribution of newspapers. Tavernkeepers were often trusted informants and confidants to the Sons of Liberty and other activists, and they were fountains of information about the political and social turmoil of the time. Taverns were also the settings for political events. In 1770, for example, a report circulated through the taverns of Danvers, Massachusetts, about a local man who was continuing to sell tea despite the colonial boycott. The Sons of Liberty brought the seller to the Bell Tavern and persuaded him to sign a confession and apology before a crowd of defiant men.

Almost all politicians found it necessary to visit taverns in colonial Massachusetts if they wanted any real contact with the public. Samuel Adams spent considerable time in the public houses of Boston, where he sought to encourage resistance to British rule while taking care to drink moderately so as not to erode his stature as a leader. His cousin John Adams was somewhat more skeptical of taverns, more sensitive to the vices they encouraged. But he, too, recognized their political value. In taverns, he once said, "bastards, and legislatores are frequently begotten."

HISTORICAL THINKING SKILLS

1. **Evaluating Historical Significance** Describe why taverns were so important in educating colonists about the relationship with Britain.
2. **Determining Context** Explain the ways that women would have been able to express their dissatisfaction with the political and economic conditions in the colonies.
3. **Making Connections** Identify similar gathering places today that serve the same purpose as taverns did in colonial America.

Discussion and Activities

Making Connections Have students read the feature "Taverns in Revolutionary Massachusetts." Ask them to discuss how taverns provided opportunities for making connections in eighteenth-century New England towns. Ask students where or how citizens can make those connections today. *(Social media, libraries, coffee shops, etc.)* How are the connections made in these venues today different from those made in eighteenth-century taverns? (Today a person with an Internet connection can have conversations with like-minded people across the world. In the eighteenth century, taverns filled that role.) **SOC**

Answers

Historical Thinking Skills

1. Taverns served as de facto town hall meetings for all different classes in New England. These informal gatherings were the perfect place for political conversations.
2. Women were usually barred from visiting taverns, but they were often still able to participate in these informal debates. Some women modeled the reading clubs, popular in Europe, where political conversation often was the main topic of discourse. As the American Revolution came closer and closer, women ultimately used the domain that they had the most control over, the household, for political debate. Women were instrumental in protesting British injustice in the form of boycotts and the homespun movements.
3. Today, the Internet and social media platforms perform functions similar to what taverns served: they provide a place to discuss politics, join groups of people with like-minded ideas, and gain access to information quickly and easily. Unfortunately, the Internet and these social media platforms have also made the spread of disinformation quicker and easier, thus making it challenging to decipher between what is real and what is false.

Historical Thinking Skills

Evaluating Evidence Have students read the section "First Continental Congress." Ask them to list the five decisions made by the First Continental Congress and rank them in order of importance. Ask volunteers to share their lists and explain their reasoning. **PCE** **WXT**

was afoot in London to subject Americans to the tyranny of the pope. Those interested in western lands, moreover, believed that the act would hinder westward expansion.

CONSEQUENCES

The Coercive Acts, far from isolating Massachusetts, made it a martyr to residents of other colonies and sparked new resistance up and down the coast. Colonial legislatures passed a series of resolves supporting Massachusetts. Women's groups throughout the colonies mobilized to extend the boycotts of British goods and to create substitutes for the tea, textiles, and other commodities they were shunning.

COOPERATION AND WAR

Revolutions do not simply happen. They need organizers and leaders. Beginning in 1765, colonial leaders developed a variety of organizations for converting popular discontent into direct action–organizations that in time formed the basis for an independent government.

New Sources of Authority

The passage of authority from the royal government to the colonists themselves began on the local level, where the tradition of autonomy was already strong. In colony after colony, local institutions responded to the resistance movement by simply seizing authority on their own. At times, entirely new, extralegal bodies emerged semispontaneously and began to perform some of the functions of government. In Massachusetts in 1768, for example, Samuel Adams called a convention of delegates from the towns of the colony to sit in place of the General Court, which the governor had dissolved. The Sons of Liberty, which Adams had helped organize in Massachusetts and which sprang up elsewhere as well, became another source of power. Its members at times formed disciplined bands of vigilantes who made certain that all colonists respected the boycotts and other forms of popular resistance. And in most colonies, committees of prominent citizens began meeting to perform additional political functions.

FIRST CONTINENTAL CONGRESS

The most effective of these new groups were the committees of correspondence, which Adams had inaugurated in Massachusetts in 1772. Virginia later established the first intercolonial committees of correspondence, which made possible continuous cooperation among the colonies. Virginia also took the greatest step of all toward united action in 1774 when, after the royal governor dissolved the assembly, a special session met in the Raleigh Tavern at Williamsburg, declared that the Intolerable Acts menaced the liberties of every colony, and issued a call for a Continental Congress. Variously elected by the assemblies and by extralegal meetings, delegates from all the thirteen colonies except Georgia were present when, in September 1774, the First Continental Congress convened in Carpenter's Hall in Philadelphia. They made five major decisions. First, in a very close vote, they rejected a plan (proposed by Joseph Galloway of Pennsylvania) for a colonial union under British authority (much like the earlier Albany Plan). Second, they endorsed a statement of grievances, whose tortured language reflected the conflicts among the delegates between moderates and extremists. The statement seemed to concede Parliament's right to regulate colonial trade and addressed the king as "Most Gracious Sovereign"; but it also included a more extreme demand for the repeal of all the oppressive legislation passed since 1763. Third, they approved a series of resolutions, recommending, among other things, that the colonists make military preparations for defense against possible attack by the British troops in Boston. Fourth, they agreed to nonimportation, nonexportation, and nonconsumption as means of stopping all trade with Great Britain, and they formed a "Continental Association" to enforce the agreements. And fifth, when the delegates adjourned, they agreed to meet again the next spring, thus indicating that they considered the Continental Congress a continuing organization.

Through their representatives in Philadelphia the colonies had, in effect, reaffirmed their autonomous status within the empire and declared something close to economic war to maintain that position. The more optimistic of the Americans hoped that this economic warfare alone would win a quick and bloodless victory, but the more pessimistic had their doubts. "I expect no redress, but, on the contrary, increased resentment and dou-

RECRUITING PATRIOTS This Revolutionary War recruiting poster attracted recruits by appealing to their patriotism (asking them to defend "the liberties and independence of the United States"), their vanity (by showing the "handsome clothing" and impressive bearing of soldiers), and their greed (by offering them "a bounty of twelve dollars" and "sixty dollars a year").

Library of Congress

Discussion and Activities

Historical Evidence and Argumentation Have students examine the recruiting poster "Recruiting Patriots." Ask students what techniques are used in the poster to encourage enlistment. Discuss as a class how effective these techniques might have been and why. Ask them what other appeals recruiters might have made to bolster enlistment. **SOC** **PCE** **WXT**

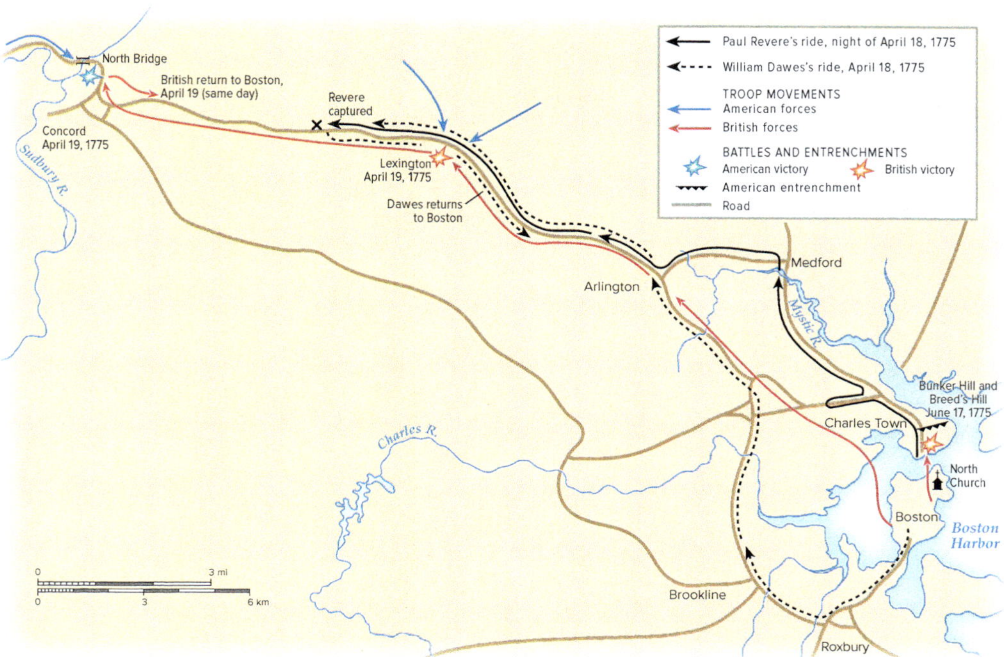

THE BATTLES OF LEXINGTON AND CONCORD, 1775 This map shows the fabled series of events that led to the first battle of the American Revolution. On the night of April 18, 1775, Paul Revere and William Dawes rode out from Boston to warn the outlying towns of the approach of British troops. Revere was captured just west of Lexington, but Dawes escaped and returned to Boston. The next morning, British forces moved out of Boston toward Lexington, where they met armed American minutemen on the Lexington common and exchanged fire. The British dispersed the Americans in Lexington. But they next moved on to Concord, where they encountered more armed minutemen, clashed again, and were driven back toward Boston. All along their line of march, they were harassed by riflemen.

What impact did the Battles of Lexington and Concord (and the later Battle of Bunker Hill, also shown on this map) have on colonial sentiment toward the British?

ble vengeance," John Adams wrote to Patrick Henry; "we must fight." And Henry replied, "By God, I am of your opinion."

During the winter, the Parliament in London debated proposals for conciliating the colonists. Lord Chatham (William Pitt), the former prime minister, urged the withdrawal of troops from America. Edmund Burke called for the repeal of the Coercive Acts. But their efforts were in vain. Lord North finally won approval early in 1775 for a series of measures known as the Conciliatory Propositions, but they were far less conciliatory than the approaches Burke or Chatham had urged. Parliament now proposed that the colonies, instead of being taxed directly by Parliament, would tax themselves at Parliament's demand. With this offer, Lord North hoped to divide the American moderates, who he believed represented the views of the majority, from the extremist minority. But his offer was too little and too late. It did not reach America until after the first shots of war had been fired.

The Conciliatory Propositions

LEXINGTON AND CONCORD

For months, the farmers and townspeople of Massachusetts had been gathering arms and ammunition and training as "minutemen," preparing to fight on a minute's notice. The Continental Congress had approved preparations for a defensive war, and the citizen-soldiers awaited an aggressive move by the British regulars in Boston.

In Boston, General Thomas Gage, commanding the British garrison, knew of the military preparations in the countryside but considered his army too small to do anything until reinforcements arrived. He resisted the advice of less cautious officers, who assured him that the Americans would never dare actually to fight, that they would back down quickly before any show of British force. Major John Pitcairn, for example, insisted that a single "small action," such as the burning of a few towns, would "set everything to rights."

General Thomas Gage

Reasoning Processes

Continuity and Change After students read the section "New Sources of Authority," ask them to create a time line listing events that represented claims of authority from 1763–1774. *(Virginia Resolves, Sons of Liberty, Stamp Act Congress, Committees of Correspondence, First Continental Congress)* Discuss as a class how these events represented a change over time in how colonists viewed sources of colonial authority. **PCE**

Answers

The Battles of Lexington and Concord, 1775

With the outbreak of violence, more colonists began to see military action more as a means to secure independence than just as a way to preserve their rights as Englishmen.

Historical Thinking Skills

Analyzing Issues After students read the section "General Thomas Gage," ask them to create a T-chart to compile reasons why General Gage should or should not have sent his forces into Lexington and Concord. Have students write a short letter to General Gage from the point of view of one of General Gage's aides arguing either for or against the mission. **PCE**

The Retreat
From Concord to Lexington of the Army of Wild Irish Asses Defeated by the Brave American Militia
Deacon Mr Loerings Mr Mulikens Mr Bonds Houses and Barn all Plunder'd and Burnt on April 19th

THE BRITISH RETREAT FROM CONCORD, 1775 This American cartoon satirizes the retreat of British forces from Concord after the battle there on April 19, 1775. Patriot forces are lined up on the left, and the retreating British forces (portrayed with dog heads, perhaps because many of the soldiers were "wild" Irish) straggle off at right—some fleeing in panic, others gloating over the booty they have plundered from the burning homes above. In its crude and exaggerated way, the cartoon depicts the success of Patriot forces at the Old North Bridge in Concord in repulsing a British contingent under the command of Lord Percy. As the redcoats retreated to Lexington and then to Boston, they continued to encounter fire from colonial forces, not arrayed in battle lines as shown here, but hidden along the road. One British soldier described the nightmarish withdrawal: "We were fired on from Houses and behind Trees . . . the Country was . . . full of Hills, Woods, stone Walls . . . which the Rebels did not fail to take advantage of."

General Gage still hesitated when he received orders from England to arrest the rebel leaders Sam Adams and John Hancock, known to be in the vicinity of Lexington. But when Gage heard that the minutemen had stored a large supply of gunpowder in Concord (eighteen miles from Boston), he finally decided to act. On the night of April 18, 1775, he sent a detachment of about 1,000 soldiers out from Boston on the road to Lexington and Concord. He intended to surprise the colonials and seize the illegal supplies without bloodshed.

But Patriots in Boston were watching the British movements closely, and during the night two horsemen, William Dawes and Paul Revere, rode out to warn the villages and farms. When the British troops arrived in Lexington the next day, several dozen minutemen awaited them on the town common. Shots were fired and minutemen fell; eight of them were killed and ten more wounded. Advancing to Concord, the British discovered that the Americans had hastily removed most of the powder supply, but the British burned what was left of it. All along the road from Concord back to Boston, farmers hiding behind trees, rocks, and stone fences harassed the British with continual gunfire. By the end of the day, the British had lost almost three times as many men as the Americans.

The first shots—the "shots heard round the world," as Americans later called them—had been fired. But who had fired them? According to one of the minutemen at Lexington, Major Pitcairn had shouted to the colonists on his arrival, "Disperse, ye rebels!" When the Americans ignored the command, he had given the order to fire. British officers and soldiers told a different story. They claimed that the minutemen had fired first, that only after seeing the flash of American guns had the British begun to shoot. Whatever the truth, the rebels succeeded in circulating their account well ahead of the British version, adorning it with lurid tales of British atrocities. The effect was to rally to the rebel cause thousands of colonists, north and south, who previously had had little enthusiasm for war. Jeremy Lister, a minuteman in Lexington, wrote later: "We got all over the bay and landed on the opposite shore betwixt twelve and one O'Clock and was on our March by one, which was at first through some swamps and slips of the Sea till we got into the Road leading to Lexington soon after which the Country people begun to fire their alarm guns light their Beacons, to raise the Country. . . . To the best of my recollection about 4 oClock in the morning being the 19th of April the 5 front Compys. was ordered to Load which we did."

Discussion and Activities

Analyzing Visuals Have students examine the image "The British Retreat From Concord, 1775." Ask them to identify details that indicate either successes or failures of General Gage's mission to Lexington and Concord. *(Failures: Redcoats are retreating; they are portrayed as animals; some have become disorderly. Successes: town in background is in flames.)* Ask students what indication the image gives that not all colonists were committed to the cause of independence. *(The Patriot flag on the left-hand side is still the British flag, just with the motto "Liberty" printed on it, which is ambivalent.)* **SOC** **PCE**

THE REVOLUTION BEGINS

It was not immediately clear to the British, and even to many Americans, that the skirmishes at Lexington and Concord were the first battles of a war. Many saw them as simply another example of the tensions that had been afflicting Anglo-American relations for years. But whether they recognized it at the time or not, the British and the Americans had taken a decisive step. The War for Independence had begun.

CHAPTER 4 REVIEW

CONNECTING THEMES

Chapter Four began by analyzing the causes of the French and Indian War in North America. The clash between France and Britain was part of a global world war known in Europe as the Seven Years' War. The British colonies were not isolated or sheltered from the conflict; on the contrary, they were instrumental in its outcome. The British victory exiled the French and removed a major European competitor in North America. But at the same time, the war empowered the colonists, and a distinct American identity began to emerge.

The war also burdened the British with a large war debt, forcing them to end their policy of political and economic neglect and turn to the colonies for economic assistance. The colonists met the resulting British taxes with violent and hostile resistance, which led to direct political and economic confrontation with Parliament. Great Britain demanded that the colonies pay their fair share to support costly military protections; in response, the colonists demanded "No taxation without representation" and articulated important political principles drawn from Enlightenment thinkers. These protests culminated in armed conflict at Lexington and Concord, which marked the beginning of the American Revolution.

You should consider the following questions as you review the themes for this chapter:

- How did the escalating conflict between Great Britain and the colonists lead to a redefining of an American identity?
- How did disagreements over trade and taxation lead to increased conflict between the colonists and Great Britain?
- What were the causes and effects of the political power struggle between the colonies and Great Britain?
- How did the conflict over taxation and representation compound problems between the colonists and Great Britain?
- What role did philosophical principles play in the revolt of the British colonies?

KEY TERMS

Admiralty Courts 119
Albany Plan 110
Benjamin Franklin 109
Boston Massacre 124
Boston Tea Party 128
Charles Townshend 123
Coercive Acts (Intolerable Acts) 128
Committees of Correspondence 132
Creoles 111
Currency Act 119
Daughters of Liberty 128
First Continental Congress 132
George Grenville 118
Imperial Authority 110
Impressment 113
Iroquois Confederacy 111
John Adams 133
Lord North 124
Mercy Otis Warren 128
Mutiny Act 116
Patrick Henry 122
Paxton Boys 119
Pontiac's Rebellion 118
Proclamation of 1763 119
Quebec Act 128
Samuel Adams 125
Seven Years' War (French and Indian War) 110
Sons of Liberty 122
Stamp Act 122
Stamp Act Congress 122
Sugar Act 119
Tea Act 128
Townshend Duties 124
Virginia Resolves 122
William Pitt 113

Discussion and Activities

Analyzing Points of View Have students read the section "Lexington and Concord." Ask them to think about the issues, decisions, and actions on both sides that led to these battles. Discuss as a class what either side may have been able to do to reconcile differences without a military conflict. Have students then write a brief paragraph containing an argument about whether the American Revolution was inevitable. **PCE**

Key Terms

Students should be familiar with the key terms and be able to define them in the context of British efforts to restore and maintain economic and political control of its North American colonies, along with growing American resistance to those efforts. Encourage students to use these terms in performing review exercises and exam practice for this chapter.

Go Online Chapter 4 Content Review

Assessing Student Understanding Use the online assessment to assess student understanding of concepts and topics within the chapter. You can assign the ready-made Chapter 4 Content Review or create your own from available questions. This easy-to-use tool helps you design assessments that meet the needs of different types of learners.

CHAPTER 4
THE EMPIRE IN TRANSITION

Answers

Multiple Choice

1. B; **2.** C; **3.** A

Short Answer

4A) The point of view is that of a British supporter, someone who is opposed to the American colonists' ways of handling the different taxes being imposed upon them.

4B) The painting depicts Bostonians forcing tea down the throat of a customs official, whom they have tarred and feathered. By 1773, the British Parliament had passed a number of measures to attempt to raise revenue in the colonies to help pay for the massive war debt incurred during the French and Indian War. The British believed that these were fair taxes and that they were only asking the colonists to pay their fair share. The colonists, on the other hand, believed these taxes were unfair and violated the terms of their agreement.

4C) Following the dumping of British tea in Boston Harbor, known as the Boston Tea Party, the British government cracked down on the colonists in Boston. They implemented a series of measures known as the Intolerable Acts. These were punitive measures designed to punish the city of Boston for its unruly behavior. These acts were extreme, but they also had a galvanizing effect within the colonies.

5A) Before and after the French and Indian War, the colonies had to contend with the presence of Native Americans. The further expansion of the eastern boundary between the two groups continued to be a source of great tension. Even though the Proclamation Line was declared in 1763 to help with this conflict, the American colonists resented this policy and largely ignored it.

5B) Following the French and Indian War, the French presence largely disappeared, thus eliminating Britain's greatest European foe in North America.

5C) The confidence that the American colonists gained from the victory in the war served as a source of self-assurance to stand up to the British at the start of the American Revolution.

AP EXAM PRACTICE

Questions assume cumulative content knowledge from this chapter and the previous chapter.

MULTIPLE CHOICE

Use the following excerpt and your knowledge of U.S. history to answer questions 1-3.

"[81] Q. Did the Americans ever dispute the controlling power of Parliament to regulate commerce?
A. No.
[82] Q. Can anything less than a military force carry the Stamp Act into execution?
A. I do not see how a military force can be applied to that purpose.
[83] Q. Why may it not?
A. Suppose a military force is sent into America, and they find nobody in arms; what are they then to do? They cannot force a man to take stamps who chooses to do without them. They will not find a rebellion; they may indeed make one.
[84] Q. If the act is not repealed, what do you think will be the consequences?
A. A total loss of the respect and affection the people of America bear to this country and of all the commerce that depends on that respect and affection.
[85] Q. How can the commerce be affected?
A. You will find, that if the act is not repealed, they will take very little of your manufactures in a short time.
[86] Q. Is it in their power to do without them?
A. I think they may very well do without them.
[87] Q. Is it their interest not to take them?
A. The goods they take from Britain are either necessaries, mere conveniences, or superfluities. The first, as cloth, &c. with a little industry they can make at home; the second they can do without, till they are able to provide them among themselves; and the last, which are much the greatest part, they will strike off immediately. They are mere articles of fashion, purchased and consumed, because of the fashion in a respected country, but will now be detested and rejected. The people have already struck off, by general agreement, the use of all goods fashionable in mournings, and many thousand pounds worth are sent back as unsaleable."

–Examination of Benjamin Franklin before the Committee of the Whole of the House of Commons, 1766

1. Why did the British Parliament begin to levy taxes, such as the Stamp Act, on the American colonies?
   - (A) The British wished to shift more population groups to North America.
   - (B) The British needed to raise funds and increase control amid intensifying colonial rivalry.
   - (C) The British wished to ally with the French for continued warfare against the Native American nations.
   - (D) The British were preparing the American colonists for their political independence.

2. What American reaction to the Stamp Act was Franklin correct in anticipating?
   - (A) the Americans' division over how to protest
   - (B) the Americans' acceptance of increased taxation
   - (C) the Americans' boycott of British stamps
   - (D) the Americans' desire to pass similar taxes in their own assemblies

3. Franklin discusses which protest strategy that involved significant participation by Patriot women?
   - (A) boycotts of British goods
   - (B) destruction of British property
   - (C) stockpiling of weaponry
   - (D) formation of communication networks

SHORT ANSWER

Use your knowledge of U.S. history to answer questions 4 and 5.

4. Use the image on page 128 to answer A, B, and C.
   - (A) Briefly describe ONE point of view about the colonists as depicted in the image.
   - (B) Briefly explain ONE specific historical cause that led to the event depicted in the image.
   - (C) Briefly explain ONE specific historical effect that resulted from the event depicted in the image.

5. Answer A, B, and C.
   - (A) Briefly describe ONE specific historical similarity between the colonies before and after the French and Indian War.
   - (B) Briefly describe ONE specific historical difference between the colonies before and after the French and Indian War.
   - (C) Explain ONE specific historical effect which resulted from the French and Indian War.

LONG ESSAY

Develop a thoughtful and thorough historical argument that addresses the statement below. Begin your essay with a thesis statement, and support it with specific historical evidence and examples.

6. Evaluate the extent of changes in the American colonies in the beginning stages of the American Revolution from 1700 to 1775.

Answers

Long Essay

6. Possible thesis: Most of the colonists, even as late as 1775, considered themselves part of the British Empire. However, following the French and Indian War, the economic relationship between the British and the American colonies underwent a serious transformation. Additionally, the confidence that the Americans gained from that event gave rise to a new independence movement. Therefore, despite some continuities, there were many more changes that took place in the American colonies from 1700 to 1775. Continuities: The American colonists still considered themselves part of the British Empire, even though they had largely been operating independently in both political and economic actions. Changes: While the colonists had largely acted independently, following the war the British policy of neglect had to end, and the colonists were asked to help pay their fair share of the defense of the colonies. Passage of the Stamp Act, Tea Act, and the Townshend Acts all served to cause debate within the colonies about their status and role within the Empire. Following the French and Indian War, some colonists began to question their role within the British Empire, and some now considered themselves independent.

5 THE AMERICAN REVOLUTION

SURRENDER OF CORNWALLIS On October 19, 1781, Lord Charles Cornwallis surrendered to George Washington at Yorktown. This painting by James S. Baillie depicts the event that ended the hostilities between Britain and the United States.

CONNECTING CONCEPTS

Chapter Five begins by looking at the American Revolution and its immediate aftermath. The colonists were reluctant revolutionaries who were bitterly divided over independence. Thomas Paine's *Common Sense*, written to convince the ordinary citizen, articulated a powerful argument in support of separation from Britain. Once the colonists committed, they needed to mobilize, which was no easy task. The biggest challenges the colonists faced were raising and organizing armies, providing them with supplies and equipment, and financing the war.

The war had three phases. The first phase took place primarily in New England, where the strongest opposition to the British existed. The second phase took place in the Mid-Atlantic region. The third and final phase took place in the South, where the British enjoyed the most colonial support. Regardless of region, the American Revolution affected all aspects of the colonies and had a significant impact on different groups of people, including women and African Americans.

After the surrender of the British, the newly formed states faced many challenges. The first was establishing a functional national government. The Articles of Confederation served relatively well during the war, but its weaknesses became apparent after hostilities ended. The debate over independence and the battle over ratification of a new federal constitution were the first significant political clashes in American politics. Other domestic challenges emerged as the westward migration, encouraged by state and national governments, increased problems with Native Americans. At the same time, economic issues drove political disputes. But the new nation also confronted serious foreign policy challenges.

Pacing Guide

Chapter 5 explores key concepts from Period 3: 1754–1800 of the AP U.S. History Curriculum Framework. The suggested instruction time for Chapter 5 is 6 days.

Key Concepts

3.2.I The ideals that inspired the revolutionary cause reflected new beliefs about politics, religion, and society that had been developing over the course of the 18th century.

3.2.II After declaring independence, American political leaders created new constitutions and declarations of rights that articulated the role of the state and federal governments while protecting individual liberties and limiting both centralized power and excessive popular influence.

3.2.III New forms of national culture and political institutions developed in the United States alongside continued regional variations and differences over economic, political, social, and foreign policy issues.

Discussion and Activities

Analyzing Visuals Ask students to examine the image "Surrender of Cornwallis." Ask them to identify which elements from the image indicate who won and who lost. *(A British officer is surrendering his sword to General Washington; American flags are flying over the scene; a British cannon is pointing at the ground uselessly.)* Have students write a short newspaper article or journal entry from the point of view of a witness to the scene. **PCE**

Historical Thinking Skills

Analyzing Perspectives Have students read the section "The Olive Branch Petition." Ask them how the Olive Branch Petition and the Declaration of the Causes and Necessity of Taking Up Arms showed division among colonial leaders. Have students create two web diagrams identifying motives linked to each of these documents. **PCE** **NAT**

As you read, you should:

- Identify how Native Americans continuously adjusted their alliances with European powers during the eighteenth century.
- Describe how the American colonies overcame significant obstacles to defeat Great Britain in the American Revolution.
- Analyze how ideas from the Enlightenment and the belief in republican ideas of self-government led to a transformation of political thought in the United States.
- Understand how westward expansion led to continued conflict with Native Americans and foreign countries.
- Evaluate the strengths and weaknesses of the Articles of Confederation and the reasons why the country moved to ratify a new constitution.

THE STATES UNITED

Although many Americans had been anticipating a military conflict with Britain for months, even years, the actual beginning of hostilities in 1775 found the colonies generally unprepared for the enormous challenges awaiting them. America was an unformed nation, with a population less than a third as large as the 9 million of Great Britain, and with vastly inferior economic and military resources. It faced the task of mobilizing for war against the world's greatest armed power at the same time Americans were deeply divided about what they were fighting for.

DEFINING AMERICAN WAR AIMS

Three weeks after the Battles of Lexington and Concord, the Second Continental Congress met in the State House in Philadelphia, with delegates from every colony except Georgia, which sent no representative until the following autumn. The members agreed to support the war, but they disagreed, at times profoundly, about its purpose.

At one pole was a group led by the Adams cousins (John and Samuel), Richard Henry Lee of Virginia, and others, who favored complete independence from Great Britain. At the other pole was a group led by such moderates as John Dickinson of Pennsylvania, who hoped for modest reforms in the imperial relationship that would permit an early reconciliation with Great Britain. Most of the delegates tried to find some middle ground between these positions. They demonstrated their uncertainty in two very different declarations, which they adopted in quick succession. They approved one last, conciliatory appeal to the king, the "Olive Branch Petition," which the British government rejected. Then, on July 6, 1775, they adopted an antagonistic "Declaration of the Causes and Necessity of Taking Up Arms." It proclaimed that the British government had left the American people with only two alternatives: "unconditional submission to the tyranny of irritated ministers or resistance by force."

OLIVE BRANCH PETITION

The attitude of much of the public mirrored that of the Congress. At first, most Americans believed they were fighting not for independence but for a redress of grievances within the British Empire. During the first year of fighting, however, many of them began to change their minds, for several reasons. First, the costs of the war–human and financial–were so high that the original war aims began to seem too modest to justify them. Second, what lingering affection American Patriots retained for England greatly diminished when the British began trying to recruit Native Americans, enslaved Africans, and foreign mercenaries (the hated Hessians) against them. Third, and most important, colonists came to believe that the British government was forcing them toward independence by rejecting the Olive Branch Petition and instead enacting a "Prohibitory Act." It closed the colonies to all overseas trade and made no concessions to American demands except an offer to pardon repentant rebels. The British enforced the Prohibitory Act with a naval blockade of colonial ports.

But the growing support for independence remained to a large degree unspoken until January 1776, when an impassioned pamphlet appeared that galvanized many Americans. It was called, simply, *Common Sense*. Its author, unmentioned on the title page, was thirty-eight-year-old Thomas Paine, who had emigrated from England to America fifteen months before. He barely survived the transatlantic voyage to America. For much of his life he lived in poverty, and he was ostracized because he openly ridiculed Christianity. But his pamphlets influenced the developing ideals of the United States. A failure in various trades, Paine now proved a brilliant success as a Revolutionary propagandist. His *Common Sense* helped

COMMON SENSE

Go Online AP Exam Preparation

AP Exam Practice Use the online assessment to help prepare students for the AP Exam. You can assign the ready-made AP-style short-answer questions, document-based questions, and multiple-choice questions assessing concepts, themes, and skills from Period 3 and AP style long-essay questions organized in sets of three questions from various time periods. You can also create your own tests from available questions. This easy-to-use tool helps you design assessments that meet the needs of different types of learners.

THOMAS PAINE Paine emigrated to America in 1774 and quickly became involved in the revolutionary circles in Philadelphia. Early in 1776, he published an anonymous pamphlet titled *Common Sense*, which called for an end to British rule in America. He served in the American army during the Revolution in New Jersey, while also writing additional tracts promoting independence. In later years, he joined the French Revolution and published *The Rights of Man* in 1791–1792.

© Corbis

change the American outlook toward the war. Paine wanted to turn the anger of Americans away from the specific parliamentary measures they were resisting and toward what he considered the root of the problem—the English constitution itself. It was not enough, he argued, for Americans to continue blaming their problems on particular ministers, or even on Parliament. It was the king, and the system that permitted him to rule, that was to blame. It was, he argued, simple common sense for Americans to break completely with a government that could produce so corrupt a monarch as George III, a government that could inflict such brutality on its own people, a government that could drag Americans into wars in which America had no interest. The island kingdom of England was no more fit to rule the American continent, Paine claimed, than a satellite was fit to rule the sun.

THE DECISION FOR INDEPENDENCE

Common Sense sold more than 100,000 copies in its first few months. To many of its readers it was a revelation. Although sentiment for independence remained far from unanimous, support for the idea grew rapidly in the first months of 1776.

At the same time, the Continental Congress was moving slowly and tentatively toward a final break with England. It declared American ports open to the ships of all nations except Great Britain's. It entered into communication with foreign powers. It recommended to the various colonies that they establish new governments independent of the British Empire, as most already were doing. Congress also appointed a committee to draft a formal declaration of independence. On July 2, 1776, it adopted a resolution: "That these United Colonies are, and, of right, ought to be, free and independent states; that they are absolved from all allegiance to the British crown, and that all political connexion between them and the state of Great Britain is, and ought to be, totally dissolved." Two days later, on July 4, Congress approved the Declaration of Independence, which provided the formal justifications for the actions the delegates had in fact taken two days earlier.

THE DECLARATION OF INDEPENDENCE

Thomas Jefferson, a thirty-three-year-old delegate from Virginia, wrote most of the Declaration, with help from Benjamin Franklin and John Adams. As Adams later observed, Jefferson said little in the document that was new. Its power lay in the eloquence with which it expressed beliefs already widespread in America. In particular, it repeated ideas that had been voiced throughout the colonies in the preceding months in the form of at least ninety local "declarations of independence"—declarations drafted up and down the coast by town meetings, artisan and militia organizations, county officials, grand juries, Sons of Liberty, and colonial assemblies. Jefferson borrowed heavily from these texts, both for the ideas he expressed and, to some extent, for the precise language he used.

The document was in two parts. In the first, the Declaration restated the familiar contract theory of John Locke: that governments were formed to protect the rights of life, liberty, and property; Jefferson gave the theory a more idealistic tone by replacing "property" with "the pursuit of happiness." In the second part, the Declaration listed the alleged crimes of the king, who, with the backing of Parliament, had violated his "contract" with the colonists and thus had forfeited all claim to their loyalty.

The Declaration's ringing endorsement of the idea that "all men are created equal"—a phrase borrowed from an earlier document by Jefferson's fellow Virginian George Mason—later helped inspire movements of liberation and reform of many kinds in the United States and abroad, among them the French Revolution's own Declaration of the Rights of Man. More immediately, the Declaration—and its bold claim that the American colonies were now a sovereign nation, "The United States of America"—led to increased foreign aid for the struggling rebels and prepared the way for France's intervention on their side. The Declaration also encouraged American Patriots, as those opposing the British called themselves, to fight on and to reject the idea of a peace that stopped short of winning independence. At the same time, it created deep divisions within American society.

Discussion and Activities

Assessing Credibility After students have read the section "Common Sense," ask them to discuss as a class or in small groups why colonists would have listened to Thomas Paine's arguments. Was there anything in his background that made people pay attention? *(Paine's background wasn't notable, but his arguments crystallized the ways in which many colonists were already thinking.)* **PCE**

Historical Thinking Skills

Explaining Significance Have students read the section "The Decision for Independence." Ask them to create a chart connecting the important ideas contained in the Declaration of Independence. Have students identify what they believe are the most important ideas, and ask them to share their thoughts in a class discussion. **PCE** **SOC** **WOR**

Discussion and Activities

Explaining Significance Have students read the section "Responses to Independence." Ask them to write a brief paragraph explaining why it was important that colonies began to call themselves "states" after the Declaration of Independence. Ask them to include an explanation of how that change was manifested in the Articles of Confederation. **PCE**

RESPONSES TO INDEPENDENCE

At the news of the Declaration of Independence, crowds in Philadelphia, Boston, and other places gathered to cheer, fire guns and cannons, and ring church bells. But there were many in America who did not rejoice. Some had disapproved of the war from the beginning. Others had been willing to support it only so long as its aims did not conflict with their basic loyalty to the king. Such people were a minority, but a substantial one. They called themselves Loyalists; supporters of independence called them Tories.

In the aftermath of the Declaration of Independence, the colonies began to call themselves "states"–a reflection of their belief that each province was now in some respects a separate and sovereign entity. Even before the Declaration, colonies were beginning to operate independently of royal authority.

DIVIDED AMERICANS

The Parliament in London had suspended representative government in America. That suspension did not end colonial self-government. It increased it, since the colonial assemblies continued to meet, now independent of imperial law. After the Declaration of 1776, the former colonies marked their independence by writing formal constitutions for themselves. By 1781, most of the new states had produced such constitutions, which established republican governments. Some of these constitutions survived for many decades without significant change.

At the national level, however, the process of forming a government was more halting and less successful. For a time, Americans were uncertain whether they even wanted a real national government; the Continental Congress had not been much more than a coordinating mechanism, and virtually everyone considered the individual colonies (now states) the real centers of authority. Yet fighting a war required a certain amount of central direction. Americans began almost immediately to do something they would continue to do for more than two centuries: balance the commitment to state and local autonomy against the need for some centralized authority.

In November 1777, Congress adopted the Articles of Confederation (which were not finally ratified until 1781). They did little more than confirm the weak, decentralized system already in operation. The Continental Congress would

ARTICLES OF CONFEDERATION

survive as the chief coordinating agency of the war effort. Its powers over the individual states would be very limited. Indeed, the Articles did not make it entirely clear that the Congress was to be a real government. As a result, the new nation had to fight a war for its own survival with a weak and uncertain central government, never sure of its own legitimacy.

MOBILIZING FOR WAR

The new governments of the states and the nation faced a series of overwhelming challenges: raising and organizing armies, providing them with supplies and equipment, and finding a way to pay for it all. Without access to the British markets on which the colonies had come to depend, finding necessary supplies was exceptionally difficult.

America had many gunsmiths, but they could not come close to meeting the wartime demand for guns and ammunition, let alone the demand for heavy arms. Although Congress created a government arsenal at Springfield, Massachusetts, in 1777, the Americans managed to manufacture only a small fraction of the equipment they needed. Instead, they relied heavily on weapons and matériel they were able to capture from the British. But they got most of their war supplies from European nations, mainly from France.

Financing the war proved in many ways the most nettlesome problem. Congress had no authority to levy taxes directly on the people; it had to requisition funds from the state governments. But hard money was scarce in America, and the states were little better equipped to raise it than Congress was. None of them contributed more than a small part of their expected share. Congress tried to raise money by selling long-term bonds, but few Americans could afford them and those who could generally preferred to invest in more-profitable ventures, such as privateering. In the end, the government had no choice but to issue paper money. Continental currency came from the printing presses in large and repeated batches. The states printed sizable amounts of paper currency of their own.

The result, predictably, was inflation. Prices rose to fantastic heights, and the value of paper money plummeted. Many

FINANCING THE WAR

American farmers and merchants began to prefer doing business with the British, who could pay for goods in gold or silver coin. (That was one reason why George Washington's troops suffered from severe food shortages at Valley Forge in the winter of 1777–1778; many Philadelphia merchants would not sell to them.) Congress tried and failed repeatedly to stem the inflationary spiral. In the end, the new American government was able to finance the war effort only by borrowing heavily from other nations.

After the first great surge of patriotism faded in 1775, few Americans volunteered for military service. As a result, the states had to resort to persuasion and force: to paying bounties to attract new recruits and to drafting them. Even when it was possible to recruit substantial numbers of militiamen, they

GENERAL GEORGE WASHINGTON

remained under the control of their respective states. Congress quickly recognized the disadvantages of this decentralized system and tried, with some success, to correct it. In the spring of 1775, it created a Continental army with a single commander in chief. George Washington, the forty-three-year-old Virginia planter-aristocrat who had commanded colonial forces during the French and Indian War, and–despite his defeat at the battle at Fort Necessity in 1754–possessed more experience than any other American-born officer available. He had also been an early advocate of independence. Above all, he was admired, respected, and trusted by nearly all Patriots. He was the unanimous choice of the delegates, and he took command in June 1775.

Reasoning Processes

Causation Have students read the section "Financing the War." Ask them to discuss in small groups how the colonies paid for their war effort and why it was so difficult for the national government to raise money. Have students write a summary statement making a claim about what the most significant cause of financial difficulty was. **PCE**

Reasoning Processes

Comparing Have students read the feature "The American Revolution." Ask them to create a T-chart listing attributes of the more conservative and more radical interpretations of the Revolution. Ask students to evaluate the differences and identify which differences they think are most important. **PCE** **SOC**

THE AMERICAN REVOLUTION

The long-standing debate over the origins of the American Revolution has tended to reflect two broad schools of interpretation. One sees the Revolution largely as a political and intellectual event and argues that the revolt against Britain was part of a defense of ideals and principles. The other views the Revolution as a social and economic phenomenon and contends that material interests were at its heart.

The Revolutionary generation itself portrayed the conflict as a struggle over ideals, and their interpretation prevailed through most of the nineteenth century. But in the early twentieth century, historians influenced by the reform currents of the progressive era (1873–1920) began to identify social and economic forces that they believed had contributed to the rebellion. In a 1909 study of New York, Carl Becker wrote that two questions had shaped the Revolution: "The first was the question of home rule; the second was the question . . . of who should rule at home." Not only were the colonists fighting the British, they were also engaged in a kind of civil war, a contest for power between radicals and conservatives that led to the "democratization of American politics and society."

Other "progressive" historians elaborated on Becker's thesis. In *The American Revolution Considered as a Social Movement* (1926), J. Franklin Jameson argued that "many economic desires, many social aspirations, were set free by the political struggle, many aspects of society profoundly altered by the forces thus let loose." In a 1917 book, Arthur M. Schlesinger maintained that colonial merchants, motivated by their own interest in escaping the restrictive policies of British mercantilism, aroused American resistance in the 1760s and 1770s.

Beginning in the 1950s, a new generation of scholars began to re-emphasize the role of ideology and to de-emphasize the role of economic interests. Robert E. Brown (in 1955) and Edmund S. Morgan (in 1956) both argued that most eighteenth-century white Americans shared basic political principles and that the social and economic conflicts the progressives had identified were not severe. The rhetoric of the Revolution, they suggested, was not propaganda but, rather, a real reflection of the colonists' ideas. Bernard Bailyn, in *The Ideological Origins of the American Revolution* (1967), demonstrated the complex roots of the ideas behind the Revolution and argued that this carefully constructed political stance was not a disguise for economic interests but a genuine ideology, rooted in deeply held convictions about rights and power.

By the late 1960s, however, a group of younger historians were challenging the ideological interpretation again by illuminating social and economic tensions within colonial society that they claimed helped shape the Revolutionary struggle. Jesse Lemisch and Dirk Hoerder pointed to the actions of mobs in colonial cities as evidence of popular resentment of both American and British elites. Joseph Ernst reemphasized the significance of economic pressures on colonial merchants and tradesmen. Gary Nash, in *The Urban Crucible* (1979), emphasized the role of growing economic distress in colonial cities in creating a climate in which Revolutionary sentiment could flourish.

Some newer social interpretations of the Revolution attempt to break free of the old debate pitting ideas against interests. The two things are not in competition with but, rather, reinforce each other, more-recent scholars argue. "Everyone has economic interests," Gary Nash has written, "and everyone . . . has an ideology." Only by exploring the relationships between the two can historians hope fully to understand either. Also, as Linda Kerber has written, newer interpretations have "reinvigorated the Progressive focus on social conflict between classes and extended it to include the experience not only of rich and poor but of a wide variety of interest groups, marginal communities, and social outsiders." That extension of focus to previously little-studied groups includes work by Mary Beth Norton on women, Silvia Frey on enslaved people, and Colin Calloway on Native Americans.

The Farmer and his Son's return from a visit to the CAMP.

FATHER and I went down to camp,
Along with Captain Gooding,
And there we see the men and boys
As thick as hasty pudding.
Yankey doodle keep it up, yankey doodle dandy,
Mind the music and the step,
And with the girls be handy.

And there we see a thousand men,
As rich as 'squire David,
And what they wasted every day,
I wish it had been saved.
Yankey doodle, &c.

And there we see a swamping gun,
Large as a log of maple,
Upon a deuced little cart,
A load for father's cattle.
Yankey doodle, &c.

And every time they shoot it off,
It takes a horn of powder,
And makes a noise like father's gun,
Only a nation louder.
Yankey doodle, &c.

And captain Davis had a gun,

And there was captain Washington,
And gentlefolks about him,
He will not ride without them.
Yankey doodle, &c.

Lock'd up in mother's chamber.
Yankey doodle, &c.

Gordon Wood, in *The Radicalism of the American Revolution* (1992) and *Empire of Liberty* (2009), helped revive a once-popular interpretation of the Revolution that had fallen out of fashion: that it was a genuinely radical event, which led to the breakdown of such long-standing patterns of society as deference, patriarchy, and traditional gender relations. Class conflict and radical goals may not have caused the Revolution; but the Revolution had a profound, even radical, ideological impact on society nevertheless.

HISTORICAL THINKING SKILLS

Questions assume cumulative content knowledge from this chapter and previous chapters.

1. **Identifying Historical Developments** Identify two broad schools of historical interpretation concerning the origins of the American Revolution.
2. **Explaining Historical Developments** Describe how twentieth century scholarship modified or altered the interpretation of the American Revolution.
3. **Developing Arguments** Analyze the school of thought you find more convincing. Be sure to provide evidence to support your point of view.

Answers

Debating the Past

1. One school sees the Revolution mainly as a political and intellectual movement and argues that the revolt against the British was largely part of a defense of ideals and principles. The other school sees the Revolution mainly as a social and economic movement, and argues that the revolt against the British was largely a defense of the colonies' material interests.
2. The Revolutionary generation viewed the Revolution in terms of a struggle over rights and ideals, but people in the twentieth century, heavily influenced by progressive ideas, began to identify the social and economic forces they believed had contributed to the Revolution.
3. Student answers will vary. One way of arguing could be to point to the concern over taxes as lending support for the economic interpretation. On the other hand, students could point to the concerns over rights (e.g., "no taxation without representation") as supporting the ideological interpretation.

Historical Thinking Skills

Predicting After students have read the section "Mobilizing for War," ask them to list the traits of George Washington that led to him being named commander of the Continental Army. Ask students to identify which trait(s) they think will be most important for General Washington's potential success. At the end of the chapter, have students return to this list to see if their thoughts have changed. **SOC** **PCE**

Congress had chosen well. Throughout the war, Washington never flagged, despite difficulties and discouragements that would have daunted a lesser man. There were serious problems of morale among soldiers who consistently received short rations and low pay. Open mutinies broke out in 1781 among the Pennsylvania and New Jersey troops. The Continental Congress always seemed too little interested in supplying him with manpower and equipment and too much interested in interfering with his conduct of military operations.

FOREIGN ASSISTANCE

Washington had some shortcomings as a military commander. But he was, in the end, a great war leader. With the aid of foreign military experts such as the Marquis de Lafayette from France and Baron von Steuben from Prussia, he succeeded in building and holding together an army of fewer than 10,000 men that, along with state militias, ultimately prevailed against the greatest military power in the world. Even more important in a new nation still unsure of either its purposes or its structure, with a central government both weak and divided, Washington provided the army—and the people—with a symbol of stability around which they could rally. He may not have been the most brilliant of the country's early leaders, but in the crucial years of the war, at least, he was the most successful in holding the new nation together.

THE WAR FOR INDEPENDENCE

On the surface, at least, all the advantages in the military struggle between America and Great Britain appeared to lie with the British. They possessed the greatest navy and the best-equipped army in the world. They had access to the resources of an empire. They had a coherent structure of command. The Americans, by contrast, were struggling to create a new army and a new government at the same time that they were trying to fight a war.

VOTING FOR INDEPENDENCE The Continental Congress actually voted in favor of independence from Great Britain on July 2, 1776. July 4, the date Americans now celebrate as Independence Day, is when the Congress formally ratified the Declaration of Independence. This painting by Edgar Pine-Savage re-creates the scene in Philadelphia as delegates from the various colonies made their momentous decision.

Discussion and Activities

Analyzing Visuals Have students examine the image "Voting for Independence." Ask them to write down the details they can discern about members of the Second Continental Congress. Then discuss as a class how this image would differ from a portrait of current members of Congress. *(They are all well dressed, most are wearing wigs, they all appear affluent, they are all male, and they are all white. A contemporary portrait would show much more greater diversity in race, ethnicity, gender, and to some extent wealth.)* **SOC** **PCE**

Yet the United States had advantages that were not at first apparent. Americans were fighting on their own ground, while the English were far from home (and from their own resources). The American Patriots were, on the whole, deeply committed to the conflict; the British people only halfheartedly supported the war. As Thomas Paine said at the time, "They cannot defeat an idea with an army." Beginning in 1777, moreover, the Americans had the benefit of substantial aid from abroad, when the American war became part of a larger world contest in which Great Britain faced the strongest powers of Europe—most notably France—in a struggle for imperial supremacy.

AMERICAN ADVANTAGES

The American victory was not, however, simply the result of these advantages—nor even of the remarkable spirit and resourcefulness of the people and the army. It was a result, too, of a series of egregious blunders and miscalculations by the British in the early stages of the fighting, when England could (and probably should) have won. And it was, finally, a result of the transformation of the war—which proceeded in three different phases—into a new kind of conflict that the British military, for all its strength, could not win.

THE FIRST PHASE: NEW ENGLAND

For the first year of the fighting, the British remained uncertain about whether or not they were actually engaged in a war. Many English authorities continued to believe that British forces were simply attempting to quell pockets of rebellion in the contentious area around Boston. Gradually, however, colonial forces took the offensive and made almost the entire territory of the American colonies a battleground.

After the British withdrawal from Concord and Lexington in April 1775, American forces besieged the army of General Thomas Gage in Boston. The Patriots suffered severe casualties in the Battle of Bunker Hill (actually fought on Breed's Hill) on June 17, 1775, and were ultimately driven from their position there. But they inflicted much greater losses on the enemy than the enemy inflicted on them. Indeed, the British suffered their heaviest casualties of the entire war at Bunker Hill. After the battle, the Patriots continued to tighten the siege.

BUNKER HILL

By the first months of 1776, the British had concluded that Boston was not the best place from which to wage war. Not only was it in the center of the most fervently anti-British

REVOLUTIONARY SOLDIERS Jean Baptiste de Verger, a nineteen-year-old French officer serving in America during the Revolution, kept a journal of his experiences illustrated with watercolors. Here he portrays four American soldiers carrying different kinds of arms: an African American infantryman with a light rifle, a musketman, a rifleman, and an artilleryman.

Reasoning Processes

Comparing After students have read the section "The War for Independence," ask them to create a Venn diagram comparing British and American advantages at the outset of the Revolutionary War. Have students add to their diagrams as they learn more throughout the chapter. **PCE**

Discussion and Activities

Analyzing Visuals Have students examine the image "Revolutionary Soldiers." Ask them to identify details in the painting that demonstrate diversity. *(There is one African American soldier in the group. The rifleman appears to be wearing frontier-style clothing with a tomahawk tucked into his belt and may have been a militiaman rather than a soldier in the regular army.)* Have students discuss in small groups how representative this image might have been of the whole army. **SOC** **PCE**

Historical Thinking Skills

Argumentation After students have read the section "The First Phase: New England," ask them to think about why the Battle of Bunker Hill could be celebrated as a victory even though the Patriots suffered heavy casualties and had to abandon their position. Have students pair up and share their thoughts with their partners. Ask for volunteers to share with the class. **NAT** **PCE** **WOR**

region of the colonies, it was also tactically indefensible–a narrow neck of land, easily isolated and besieged. By late winter, in fact, Patriot forces had surrounded the city and occupied strategic positions on the heights. On March 17, 1776 (a date still celebrated in Boston as Evacuation Day), the British departed Boston for Halifax in Nova Scotia with hundreds of Loyalist refugees. Less than a year after the firing of the first shots, the Massachusetts colonists had driven the British–temporarily–from American soil.

Elsewhere, the war proceeded fitfully and inconclusively. To the south, at Moore's Creek Bridge in North Carolina, a band of Patriots crushed an uprising of Loyalists on February 27, 1776, and in the process discouraged a British plan to invade the southern states. The British had expected substantial aid from local Tories in the South; they realized now that such aid might not be as effective as they had hoped. To the north, Americans launched an invasion of Canada–hoping to remove the British threat and win the Canadians to their cause. Benedict Arnold, the commander of a small American force, threatened Quebec in late 1775 and early 1776 after a winter march of incredible hardship. Richard Montgomery, coming to his assistance, combined his forces with Arnold's and took command of both. Montgomery died in the assault on the city; and although a wounded Arnold kept up the siege for a time, the Quebec campaign ended in frustration. Congress sent a civilian commission to Canada, headed by the seventy-year-old Benjamin Franklin. But Franklin also failed to win the allegiance of the northern colonists. Canada did not become part of the new nation.

INVASION OF CANADA

The British evacuation of Boston in 1776 was not, therefore, so much a victory for the Americans as a reflection of changing English assumptions about the war. By the spring of 1776, it had become clear to the British that England must be prepared to fight a much larger and longer conflict. The departure of the British, therefore, signaled the beginning of a new phase in the war.

THE SECOND PHASE: THE MID-ATLANTIC REGION

The next phase of the war, which lasted from 1776 until early 1778, was when the British were in the best position to win. Indeed, had it not been for a series of blunders and misfortunes, they probably would have crushed the rebellion then. During this period the struggle became, for the most part, a traditional, conventional war. And in that, the Americans were woefully overmatched.

The British regrouped quickly after their retreat from Boston. During the summer of 1776, in the weeks immediately following the Declaration of Independence, the waters around New York City grew crowded with the most formidable military force Great Britain had ever sent abroad. Hundreds of man-of-war vessels and troopships and 32,000 disciplined soldiers arrived, under the command of the affable William Howe. Howe felt no particular hostility toward the Americans. He hoped to awe them into submission rather than fight them, and he believed that most of them, if given a chance, would show their loyalty to the king. In a meeting with commissioners from Congress, he offered them a choice between submission with royal pardon and a battle against overwhelming odds.

To oppose Howe's impressive array, Washington could muster only about 19,000 poorly armed and lightly trained soldiers, even after combining the Continental army with state militias; he had no navy at all. Even so, the Americans quickly rejected Howe's offer and chose to continue the war–a decision that led inevitably to a succession of rapid defeats. The British pushed the defenders off Long Island, compelled them to abandon Manhattan, and then drove them in slow retreat over the plains of New Jersey, across the Delaware River, and into Pennsylvania.

BRITISH TAKE NEW YORK

For eighteenth-century Europeans, warfare was a seasonal activity. Fighting generally stopped in cold weather. The British settled down for the winter at various points in New Jersey, leaving an outpost of Hessians (German mercenaries) at Trenton on the Delaware River. But Washington did not sit still. On Christmas night 1776, he boldly recrossed the icy river, surprised and scattered the Hessians, and occupied the town. Then he advanced to Princeton and drove a British force from their base in the college there. But Washington was unable to hold either Princeton or Trenton, and he finally took refuge for the rest of the winter in the hills around Morristown, New Jersey.

For their campaigns of 1777, the British devised a strategy to cut the United States in two. Howe would move north from New York City up the Hudson to Albany, while another British force would come south from Canada to meet him. One of the younger British officers, the dashing John Burgoyne, secured command of this northern force and planned a two-pronged attack along both the Mohawk and the upper Hudson approaches to Albany.

BRITAIN'S STRATEGY

But after setting this plan in motion, Howe himself abandoned it. He decided instead to launch an assault on the rebel capital Philadelphia–an assault that would, he hoped, discourage the Patriots, rally the Loyalists, and bring the war to a speedy conclusion. He removed the bulk of his forces from New York by sea, landed at the head of the Chesapeake Bay, brushed Washington aside at the Battle of Brandywine Creek on September 11, and proceeded north to Philadelphia, which he was able to occupy with little resistance. Meanwhile, Washington, after an unsuccessful October 4 attack at Germantown (just outside Philadelphia), went into winter quarters at Valley Forge. The Continental Congress, now dislodged from its capital, reassembled at York, Pennsylvania.

Howe's move to Philadelphia left Burgoyne to carry out the campaign in the north alone. Burgoyne sent Colonel Barry St. Leger up the St. Lawrence River toward Lake Ontario and the headwaters of the Mohawk, while Burgoyne himself advanced directly down the upper Hudson Valley. He got off to a flying start. He seized Fort Ticonderoga easily and with it an enor-

Discussion and Activities

Evaluating Have students read the section "British Take New York." Ask them to evaluate General Howe's strategy in New York. Discuss as a class whether his approach seemed reasonable and whether the Congress ought to have seriously considered accepting Howe's offer. Have students make a list of pros and cons for accepting Howe's offer. **PCE** **NAT**

THE BATTLE OF GERMANTOWN The Battle of Germantown, a campaign intended by Washington to liberate Philadelphia from British occupation, took place on October 4, 1777. In this painting by Alonzo Chappel (1828–1887), Battle of Germantown, Attack on Judge Chew's House (1860), Washington's much larger force cannot defeat the 120 British infantrymen who barricaded themselves in the summer home of Loyalist Benjamin Chew. Twelve thousand American troops were forced to retreat into nearby Montgomery County.

mous store of powder and supplies; this caused such dismay in Congress that the delegates removed General Philip Schuyler from command of American forces in the north and replaced him with Horatio Gates.

By the time Gates took command, Burgoyne had already experienced two staggering defeats. In one of them–at Oriskany, New York, on August 6–a Patriot band of German farmers led by Nicholas Herkimer held off a force of Native Americans and Tories commanded by St. Leger. That gave Benedict Arnold time to go to the relief of Fort Stanwix and close off the Mohawk Valley to St. Leger's advance.

In the other battle–at Bennington, Vermont, on August 16–New England militiamen under the Bunker Hill veteran John Stark severely mauled a British detachment that Burgoyne had sent out to seek supplies. Short of materials, with all help cut off, Burgoyne fought several costly engagements and then withdrew to Saratoga, where Gates surrounded him. On October 17, 1777, Burgoyne ordered what was left of his army, nearly 5,000 men, to surrender to the Americans.

PATRIOT VICTORY AT SARATOGA

To the Patriots and peoples watching from around the world, the New York campaign was a remarkable victory. The British surrender at Saratoga became a major turning point in the war–above all, perhaps, because it led directly to an alliance between the United States and France.

BRITISH BLUNDERS

The British failure to win the war during this period, a period in which they had overwhelming advantages, was in large part a result of their own mistakes. And in assessing them, the role of William Howe looms large. He abandoned his own most important strategic initiative–the northern campaign–leaving Burgoyne to fight alone. And even in Pennsylvania,

Reasoning Processes

Causation After students have read the sections "Britain's Strategy" and "Patriot Victory at Saratoga," ask them to create a two-column chart with columns labeled "Patriot Successes" and "British Failures." Have students complete the chart with examples of American actions that led to the Patriot victory at Saratoga and British actions that led to their defeat. Ask students to evaluate which they think was more responsible for the Patriot victory. In other words, did the Americans win the battle, or did the British lose it? **PCE**

Discussion and Activities

Analyzing Visuals Have students examine the image "The Battle of Germantown." Ask them to consider how the artist has used light, shadow, and smoke to focus the viewer's attention. Discuss as a class or in small groups what the artist wanted the viewer to focus on, and why. *(Smoke shrouds the house, hiding the defenders. Light focusses on the solitary figure of General Washington on horseback in the center of the painting as he appears to consider his options. An artillery unit to Washington's right is also spotlighted as the Patriots attempt to dislodge the defenders. There is considerable movement in the lower-left and on the right-hand side of the painting, but the soldiers are largely in the shadows, so it is difficult to tell what they are actually doing.)* **SOC** **PCE**

Historical Thinking Skills

Evaluating Evidence Have students read the section "British Blunders." The section notes that some critics in England claimed that General Howe did not really want to win the war. Ask students to create a list of evidence from the section and their prior knowledge that would either support or refute the claim. Ask them to discuss which position they think the evidence better supports. **PCE**

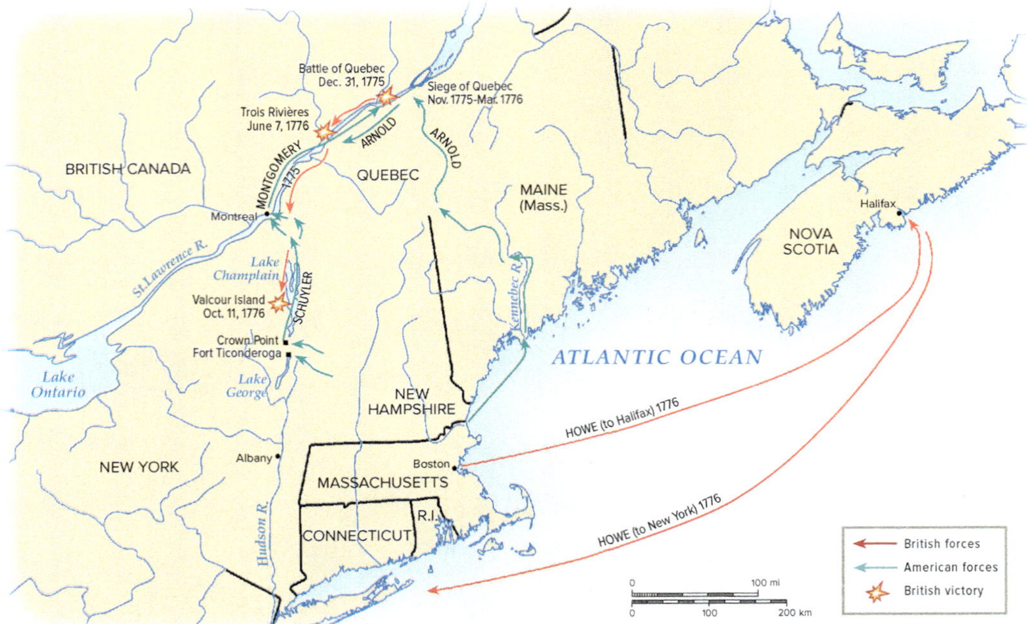

THE REVOLUTION IN THE NORTH, 1775–1776 After initial battles in and around Boston, the British forces left Massachusetts and (after a brief stay in Halifax, Canada) moved south to New York. In the meantime, American forces moved north in an effort to capture British strongholds in Montreal and Quebec, with little success.

Why would the British have considered New York a better base than Boston?

where he chose to engage the enemy, he refrained from moving in for a final attack on the weakened Continental army, even though he had several opportunities. Instead, he repeatedly allowed Washington to retreat and regroup; and he permitted the American army to spend a long winter unmolested in Valley Forge, where—weak and hungry—they might have been easy prey for a British attack. Some British critics believed that Howe did not want to win the war, that he was secretly in sympathy with the American cause. His family had close ties to the colonies, and he was linked politically to those forces within the British government that opposed the war. Others pointed to personal weaknesses: Howe's apparent alcoholism, his romantic attachment (he spent the winter of 1777–1778 in Philadelphia with his mistress when many of his advisers were urging him to move elsewhere). But the most important problem, it seems clear, was his failure to understand the nature of the war that he was fighting—or even to understand that it was truly a war.

The Iroquois and the British

The campaign in upstate New York was not just a British defeat. It was also a setback for the ambitious efforts of several Iroquois leaders, who had hoped to involve Native American forces in the English military effort, believing that a British victory would help stem white movement onto tribal lands. The Iroquois Confederacy had declared itself neutral in the war in 1776, but not all its members were content to remain passive in the northern campaign. Among those who worked to expand the Native American role in the war were a Mohawk brother and sister, Joseph Brant and Mary Brant. Both were people of stature within the Mohawk nation: Joseph was a celebrated warrior; Mary was a charismatic woman and the widow of Sir William Johnson, the British superintendent of Indians, who had achieved wide popularity among Native American groups. The Brants persuaded the Mohawk to contribute to the British cause and attracted the support of the Seneca and Cayuga as well. They played an important role in Burgoyne's unsuccessful campaigns in the north.

But the alliance was also a sign of the growing divisions within the Iroquois Confederacy. Only three of the six nations of the Confederacy supported the British. The Oneida and the Tuscarora backed the Americans; the Onondaga split into several factions. The three-century-old Confederacy, weakened by the aftermath of the French and Indian War, continued to unravel.

DIVISIONS IN THE IROQUOIS CONFEDERACY

Answers

The Revolution in the North, 1775–1776

New York has a better harbor than Boston; there were more Loyalists in New York than in Boston; New York was the focal point of early British efforts to divide the colonies.

THE BATTLE OF BUNKER HILL, 1775 British troops face Patriot forces outside Boston on June 17, 1775, in the first great battle of the American Revolution. The British ultimately drove the Americans from their positions on Breed's Hill and Bunker Hill, but only after suffering enormous casualties. General Gage, the British commander, reported to his superiors in London after the battle: "These people show a spirit and conduct against us they never showed against the French." This anonymous painting reveals the array of British troops and naval support and also shows the bombardment and burning of Charles Town from artillery in Boston.

The alliance had other unhappy consequences for the Iroquois. A year after Oriskany, Native American allies joined British troops in a series of raids on outlying white settlements in upstate New York. Months later, Patriot forces under the command of General John Sullivan harshly retaliated, wreaking such destruction on Iroquois communities that large groups of Iroquois fled north into Canada to seek refuge. Many never returned.

Securing Aid from Abroad

The failure of the British to crush the Continental army in the mid-Atlantic states, combined with the stunning American victory at Saratoga, was a turning point in the war. It transformed the conflict and ushered it into a new and final phase.

Central to this transformation of the war was American success in winning support from abroad–indirectly from several European nations and directly from France. Even before the Declaration of Independence, Congress dispatched representatives to the capitals of Europe to negotiate commercial treaties with the governments there; if America was to leave the British Empire, it would need to cultivate new trading partners. Such treaties would, of course, require European governments to recognize the United States as an independent nation. John Adams called the early American representatives abroad "militia diplomats." Unlike the diplomatic regulars of Europe, they had little experience with the formal art and etiquette of Old World diplomacy. Since transatlantic communication was slow and uncertain (it took from one to three months for a message to cross the Atlantic), they had to interpret the instructions of Congress very freely and make crucial decisions entirely on their own.

Militia Diplomats

The most promising potential ally for the United States was France. King Louis XVI, who had come to the throne in 1774, and his astute foreign minister, the Count de Vergennes, were eager to see Britain lose a crucial part of its empire. Through a series of secret bargains, facilitated by the creation of a fictional trading firm and the use of secret agents on both sides (among them the famed French dramatist Caron de Beaumarchais), France began supplying the Americans large quantities of much-needed supplies. But the French government remained reluctant to provide the United States with what it most wanted: diplomatic recognition.

Reasoning Processes

Continuity and Change After students have read the section "The Iroquois and the British," ask them to identify how participation in the American Revolution caused changes within the Iroquois Confederacy. Have students write a short paragraph predicting how those changes might impact the Iroquois after the American Revolution. *(Possible responses: Most importantly, the Iroquois will be treated as enemies by the Americans. The Confederacy will continue to weaken.)*

Historical Thinking Skills

Analyzing Point of View Have students examine the image "The Battle of Bunker Hill, 1775." Ask the class to brainstorm a list of details they notice in the painting. Ask which details add to their knowledge or understanding of the Battle of Bunker Hill. *(Possible responses: The painting emphasizes the role of the Royal Navy; the painting highlights the destruction of property in addition to the large number of casualties.)*

Reasoning Processes

Causation After students have read the section "Securing Aid From Abroad," discuss as a class why the French aided the Americans. *(France was a traditional rival of England; France began to believe that the Americans might win after the Battle of Saratoga.)* Have students write a short summary statement explaining why French support was so important for Patriot success. **WOR** **PCE**

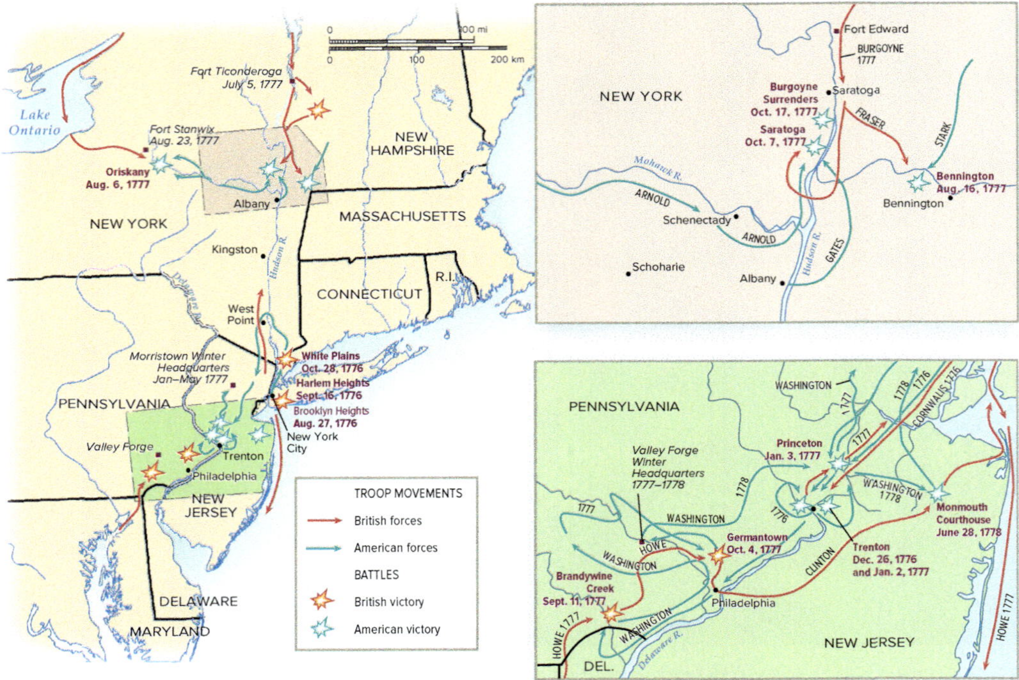

THE REVOLUTION IN THE MIDDLE COLONIES, 1776–1778 These maps illustrate the major campaigns of the Revolution in the middle colonies—New York, New Jersey, and Pennsylvania—between 1776 and 1778. The large map on the left shows the two prongs of the British strategy: first, a movement of British forces south from Canada into the Hudson Valley; and second, a movement of other British forces, under General William Howe, out from New York and south into New Jersey and Pennsylvania. The strategy was designed to trap the American army between the two British movements. The two smaller maps on the right show detailed pictures of some of the major battles. The upper one reveals the surprising American victory at Saratoga. The lower one shows a series of inconclusive battles between New York and Philadelphia in 1777 and 1778.

What movements of Howe helped thwart that plan?

Finally, Benjamin Franklin himself went to France to represent the United States. A natural diplomat, Franklin became a popular hero among the French–aristocrats and common people alike. His popularity there greatly helped the American cause. Of even greater help was the news of the American victory at Saratoga, which arrived in London on December 2, 1777, and in Paris two days later. On February 6, 1778–in part to forestall a British peace offensive that Vergennes feared might persuade the Americans to abandon the war–France formally recognized the United States as a sovereign nation and laid the groundwork for greatly expanded assistance to the American war effort.

France's intervention made the war an international conflict. In the course of the next two years, France, Spain, and the Netherlands all drifted into another general war with Great Britain in Europe, and all contributed both directly and indirectly to the ultimate American victory. But France was America's truly indispensable ally. Not only did it furnish the new nation with most of its money and munitions; it also provided a navy and an expeditionary force that proved invaluable in the decisive phase of the Revolutionary conflict.

PIVOTAL FRENCH AID

THE FINAL PHASE: THE SOUTH

The last phase of the military struggle in America was very different from either of the first two. The British government had never been fully united behind the war; after the defeat at Saratoga and the intervention of the French, it imposed new limits on its commitment to the conflict. Instead of a full-scale military struggle against the American army, therefore, the British decided to try to enlist the support of those elements of the American population–a majority, they continued to believe–who were still loyal to the Crown; in other words,

Answers

The Revolution in the Middle Colonies, 1776–1778

Howe's decision not to leave Philadelphia undermined the British plan to separate New England from the rest of the colonies along the Hudson River.

they would work to undermine the Revolution from within. Since the British believed Loyalist sentiment was strongest in the southern colonies (despite their earlier failure to enlist Loyalist support in North Carolina), the main focus of their effort shifted there; and so it was in the South, for the most part, that the final stages of the war occurred.

The new British strategy was a dismal failure. British forces spent three years (from 1778 to 1781) moving through the South, fighting small battles and large, and attempting to neutralize the territory through which they traveled. All such efforts ended in frustration. The British badly overestimated the extent of Loyalist sentiment. There were many Tories in Georgia and the Carolinas, some of them disgruntled members of the Regulator movement. But there were also many more Patriots than the British had believed. In Virginia, support for independence was as fervent as in Massachusetts. And even in the lower South, Loyalists often refused to aid the British because they feared reprisals from the Patriots around them. The British also harmed their own cause by encouraging southern enslaved people to desert their slaveholders in return for promises of emancipation. Many enslaved people (perhaps 5 percent of the total) took advantage of this offer, despite the great difficulty of doing so. But white Southerners were aghast; and even many who might otherwise have been inclined to support the Crown

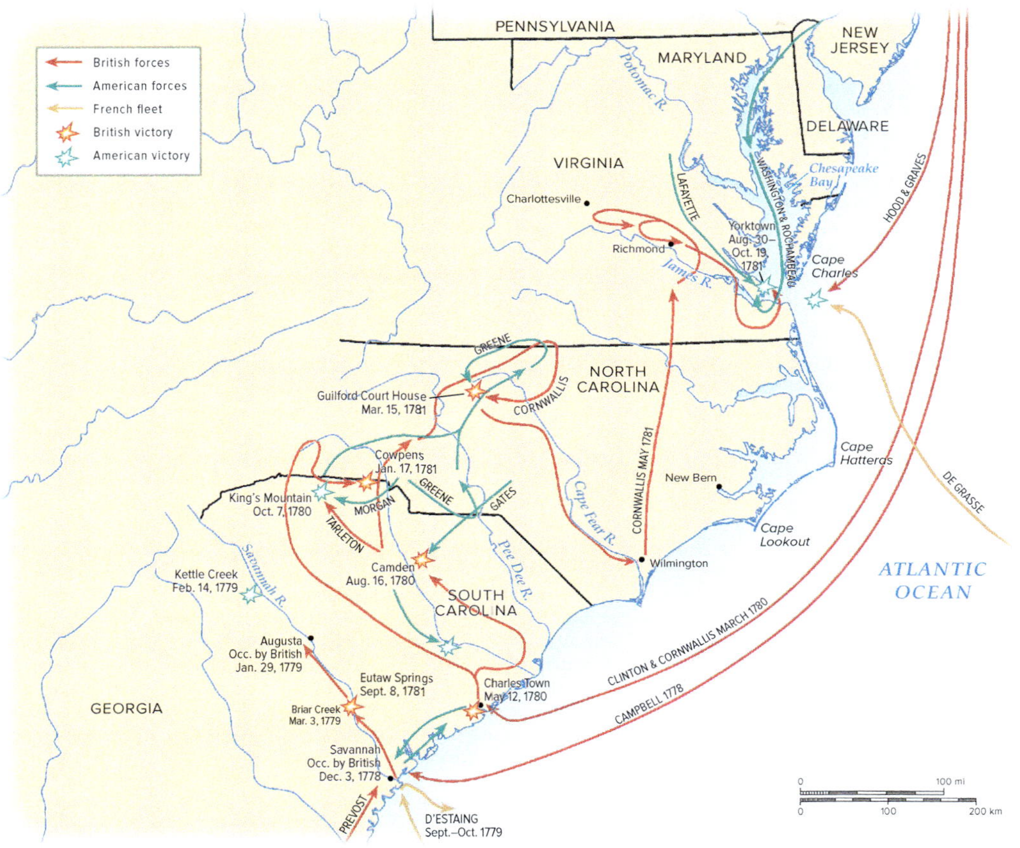

THE REVOLUTION IN THE SOUTH, 1778–1781 The final phase of the American Revolution occurred largely in the South, which the British thought would be a more receptive region for their troops. This map reveals the many, scattered military efforts of the British and the Americans in those years, none of them conclusive. It also shows the final chapter of the Revolution around the Chesapeake Bay and the James River.

What errors led the British to their surrender at Yorktown?

Reasoning Processes

Comparing After students have read the section "The Final Phase: The South," ask them to create a Venn diagram comparing British objectives in the South to British objectives in the Mid-Atlantic Region. Ask students to evaluate whether the campaigns were more similar or different. **PCE**

Answers

The Revolution in the South, 1778–1781

Cornwallis withdrew onto the Yorktown peninsula and was then cut off from support from the sea by a French squadron under Admiral DeGrasse.

Reasoning Processes

Causation After students have read the section "The Final Phase: The South," ask them to list and rank the importance of the effects of the failed British southern campaign. Have students use their lists to write thesis statements using the "X, however A and B, therefore Y" formula described in Chapter 4 to make a claim about the most important causes or effects of the British failure. **PCE**

now joined the Patriot side, which posed no such threat to slavery. The British also faced severe logistical problems in the South. Patriot forces could move at will throughout the region, living off the resources of the countryside, blending in with the civilian population and leaving the British unable to distinguish friend from foe. The British, by contrast, suffered all the disadvantages of an army in hostile territory.

It was this phase of the conflict that made the war truly "revolutionary"–not only because it introduced a new kind of combat, but also because it had the effect of mobilizing and politicizing large groups of the population who had previously remained aloof from the struggle. With the war expanding into previously isolated communities, with many civilians forced to involve themselves whether they liked it or not, the political climate of the United States grew more heated than ever. And support for independence, far from being crushed as the British had hoped, greatly increased.

That was the context in which the important military encounters of the last years of the war occurred. In the North, where significant numbers of British troops remained, the fighting settled into a relatively quiet stalemate. Sir Henry Clinton replaced the hapless William Howe in 1778 and moved what had been Howe's army from Philadelphia back to New York City. There the British troops stayed for more than a year, with Washington using his army to keep watch around them. The American forces in New York did so little fighting in this period that Washington sent some troops west to fight Native Americans who had been attacking white settlers. In that same winter, George Rogers Clark, under orders from the state of Virginia–not from either Washington or Congress–led a daring expedition over the mountains and captured settlements in the Illinois country from the British and their Native American allies.

Revolutionary Consequences of the Southern Campaign

During this period of relative calm, General Benedict Arnold shocked the American forces–and Washington in particular–by becoming a traitor. Arnold had been one of the early heroes of the war, but now, convinced that the American cause was hopeless, he conspired with British agents to betray the Patriot stronghold at West Point on the Hudson River. The scheme unraveled before Arnold could complete it, and he fled to the safety of the British camp, where he spent the rest of the war.

In the meantime, decisive fighting was in progress in the South. The British did have some significant military successes during this period. On December 29, 1778, they captured Savannah, on the coast of Georgia; and on May 12, 1780, they took the port of Charles Town, South Carolina. They also inspired some Loyalists to take up arms and advance with them into the interior. But although the British were able to win conventional battles, they were constantly harassed as they moved through the countryside by Patriot guerrillas led by such resourceful fighters as Thomas Sumter, Andrew Pickens, and Francis Marion, the "Swamp Fox."

Moving inland to Camden, South Carolina, Lord Cornwallis (Clinton's choice as British commander in the South) met and crushed a Patriot force under Horatio Gates on August 16, 1780. Congress recalled Gates, and Washington gave the southern command to Nathanael Greene, a Quaker and a former blacksmith from Rhode Island and probably the ablest of all the American generals of the time next to Washington.

Nathanael Greene

Even before Greene joined the southern army, the tide of battle began to turn against Cornwallis. At King's Mountain (near the North Carolina-South Carolina border) on October 7, 1780, a band of Patriot riflemen from the backwoods killed, wounded, or captured an entire force of 1,100 New York and South Carolina Tories that Cornwallis was using as auxiliaries. Once Greene arrived, he confused and exasperated Cornwallis further by dividing the American forces into small, fast-moving contingents and refraining from a showdown in open battle. One of the contingents inflicted what Cornwallis admitted was "a very unexpected and severe blow" at Cowpens on January 17, 1781. Finally, after receiving reinforcements, Greene combined all his forces and maneuvered to meet the British on ground of his own choosing, at Guilford Court House, North Carolina. After a hard-fought battle there on March 15, 1781, Greene withdrew from the field; but Cornwallis had lost so many men that he decided at last to abandon the Carolina campaign.

Cornwallis withdrew to the port town of Wilmington, North Carolina, to receive supplies being sent to him by sea; later he moved north to launch raids in the interior of Virginia. But Clinton, concerned for the army's safety, ordered him to take up a position on the peninsula between the York and James Rivers and wait for ships to carry his troops to New York City or Charles Town. So Cornwallis retreated to Yorktown and began to build fortifications there.

George Washington–along with Count Jean Baptiste de Rochambeau, commander of the French expeditionary force in America, and Admiral François Joseph Paul de Grasse, commander of the French fleet in American waters–set out to trap Cornwallis at Yorktown. Washington and Rochambeau marched a French-American army from New York City to join other French forces under Lafayette in Virginia, while de Grasse sailed with additional troops for Chesapeake Bay and the York River. These joint operations, perfectly timed and executed, caught Cornwallis between land and sea. After a few shows of resistance, he capitulated on October 17, 1781 (four years to the day after the surrender of Burgoyne at Saratoga). Two days later, as a military band played the old tune "The World Turn'd Upside Down," Cornwallis, claiming to be ill, sent a deputy who formally surrendered the British army of more than 7,000 men.

Yorktown

Except for a few skirmishes, the fighting was now over; but the United States had not yet won the war. British forces continued to hold the seaports of Savannah, Charles Town, Wilmington, and New York City. Before long, a British fleet met and defeated Admiral de Grasse's fleet in the West Indies, ending Washington's hopes for further French naval assistance. For more than a year, although there was no significant further combat between British and American forces, it remained possible that the war might resume and the struggle for independence might still be lost.

Discussion and Activities

Evaluating Have students read the section "Yorktown." Ask them to write a short summary about why Cornwallis withdrew to Yorktown, and how that proved to be ironic. *(Cornwallis went to Yorktown in order to be resupplied by sea. That was ironic because once at Yorktown, Cornwallis was cut off from resupply by a French squadron commanded by Admiral de Grasse.)* **PCE** **WOR**

THE BRITISH ON THE HUDSON, 1776 In one of the largest troop movements of the Revolution, English commanders sent 13,000 British and Hessian troops up the Hudson River to drive George Washington and his Patriot army from strongholds in the palisades above the river. The British took nearly 3,000 prisoners when the Patriots surrendered on November 16, 1776. Thomas Davies painted this watercolor of the British landing at the time.

Winning the Peace

Cornwallis's defeat provoked outcries in England against continuing the war. Lord North resigned as prime minister; Lord Shelburne emerged from the political wreckage to succeed him; and British emissaries appeared in France to talk informally with the American diplomats in Paris. The three American principals were Benjamin Franklin, John Adams, and John Jay.

The Americans were under instructions to cooperate fully with France in their negotiations with England. But Vergennes insisted that France could not agree to any settlement of the war with England until its ally Spain had achieved its principal war aim: winning back Gibraltar from the British. There was no real prospect of that happening soon, and the Americans began to fear that the alliance with France might keep them at war indefinitely. As a result, Franklin, Jay, and Adams began proceeding on their own, without informing Vergennes, and signed a preliminary treaty with Great Britain on November 30, 1782. Franklin, in the meantime, skillfully pacified Vergennes and avoided an immediate rift in the French-American alliance.

The British and Americans reached a final settlement—the Treaty of Paris—on September 3, 1783, when both Spain and France agreed to end hostilities. It was, on the whole, remarkably favorable to the United States in granting a clear-cut recognition of its independence and a generous, though ambiguous, cession of territory—from the southern boundary of Canada to the northern boundary of Florida and from the Atlantic to the Mississippi. With good reason, Americans celebrated in the fall of 1783 as the last of the British occupation forces embarked from New York and General Washington, at the head of his troops, rode triumphantly into the city.

TREATY OF PARIS

WAR AND SOCIETY

Historians have long debated whether the American Revolution was a social as well as a political revolution. Some have argued that the colonists were struggling not only over the question of home rule, but also over "who should rule at home." Others claim that domestic social and economic concerns had little to

Reasoning Processes

Comparing Have students read the section "Winning the Peace," and then review the Peace of Paris that ended the Seven Years' War. Ask students to create a Venn diagram comparing the terms of the Peace of Paris (1763) with the terms of the Treaty of Paris (1783). Ask them to write a short paragraph explaining at least one important reason for the differences between the two treaties. **PCE** **WOR**

Discussion and Activities

Analyzing Visuals Have students examine the image "The British on the Hudson, 1776." Ask them to discuss in small groups details from the painting that demonstrate advantages held by the British or the Americans. *(The British control the river and have large numbers of soldiers and artillery. The Americans have high ground along the riverbank that would favor defense.)* **PCE** **GEO**

Historical Thinking Skills

Analyzing Point of View Have students read the section "The Loyalists' Plight." Ask them to create a list of effects the end of the Revolutionary War had on Loyalists. Have students use that list to write a short letter or journal entry in which they describe from the point of view of a Loyalist how their lives have changed. **SOC** **PCE**

do with the conflict. Whatever the motivations of Americans, however, there can be little doubt that the War for Independence had important effects on the nature of American society.

LOYALISTS AND MINORITIES

The losers in the American Revolution included not only the British but also American Loyalists. There is no way to be sure how many Americans remained loyal to England during the Revolution, but it is clear that there were many–at least a fifth (and some historians estimate as much as a third) of the white population. Their motivations were varied. Some were officeholders in the imperial government, who stood to lose their positions as a result of the Revolution. Others were merchants engaged in trade closely tied to the imperial system. (Most merchants, however, supported the Revolution.) Still others were people who lived in relative isolation and had not been exposed to the wave of discontent that had turned so many Americans against Britain. There were cultural and ethnic minorities who feared that an independent America would not offer them sufficient protection. There were settled, cautious people who feared social instability. And there were those who, expecting the British to win the war, were simply currying favor with the anticipated victors.

What happened to these men and women during the war was a turbulent and at times tragic story. Hounded by Patriots in their communities, harassed by legislative and judicial actions, the position of many Loyalists became intolerable. Up to 100,000 fled the country. Those who could afford to moved to England, where many lived in difficult and lonely exile. Thomas Hutchinson, who was a wealthy businessman, historian, and loyalist of the king, served in the Massachusetts government for many years as lieutenant governor and from 1758 to 1774 as governor. He was a polarizing figure; and as the Revolution began, his Boston mansion was ransacked during protests against the Stamp Acts. After being replaced as governor in May 1774 by General Thomas Gage, Hutchinson left Boston and moved first to Canada and then to England.

THE LOYALISTS' PLIGHT

Loyalists of modest means moved to Canada, establishing the first English-speaking community in the province of Quebec. Some returned to America after the war and, as the earlier passions and resentments faded, managed to reenter the life of the nation. Others remained abroad for the rest of their lives.

Most Loyalists were people of average means, but a substantial minority consisted of men and women of wealth. They left behind large estates and vacated important positions of social and economic leadership. Even some who remained in the country saw their property confiscated and their positions forfeited. The result was new opportunities for Patriots to acquire land and influence, a situation that produced significant social changes in many communities.

It would be an exaggeration, however, to claim that the departure of the Loyalists was responsible for anything approaching a social revolution or that the Revolution created a general assault on the wealthy and powerful in America. When the war ended, those who had been wealthy at its beginning were, for the most part, still wealthy at the end. Most of those who had wielded social and political influence continued to wield it.

The war had a significant effect on other minorities as well, and on certain religious groups in particular. No sect suffered more than the Anglicans, many of whom were Loyalists. In Virginia and Maryland, where the colonial governments had recognized Anglicanism as the official religion and had imposed a tax for its maintenance, the new Revolutionary regimes disestablished the Anglican Church and eliminated the subsidy. By the time the fighting ended, many Anglican parishes no longer had clergymen, for there were few ministers to take the place of those who had died or who had left the country as Loyalist refugees. Anglicanism survived in America, but the losses during the Revolution permanently weakened it. The Revolution also weakened the Quakers in Pennsylvania and elsewhere. They incurred widespread unpopularity because of their pacifism, which destroyed much of the social and political prestige they had once enjoyed.

WEAKENING OF THE ANGLICAN CHURCH

While the war was weakening the Anglicans and the Quakers, it was strengthening the position of the Roman Catholic Church. On the advice of Charles Carroll of Carrollton, a Maryland statesman and Catholic lay leader, most American Catholics supported the Patriot cause during the war. The French alliance brought Catholic troops and chaplains to the country, and the gratitude with which most Americans greeted them did much to erode old and bitter hostilities toward Catholics. The Catholic Church did not greatly increase its numbers as a result of the Revolution, but it did gain considerable strength as an institution. Not long after the end of the war, the Vatican provided the United States with its own Catholic hierarchy. (Until then, Catholic bishops in Europe had controlled the American church.) Father John Carroll (also of Maryland) was named head of Catholic missions in America in 1784 and, in 1789, the first American bishop. In 1808 he became archbishop of Baltimore.

STRENGTHENING OF THE CATHOLIC CHURCH

THE WAR AND SLAVERY

For the largest of America's minorities–the African American population–the war had limited, but nevertheless profound, significance. For some, it meant freedom, because many enslaved people took advantage of the British presence in the South in the final years of the war to escape. The British enabled many of them to leave the country–not so much as any principled commitment to emancipation, but more as a way of disrupting the American war effort. In South Carolina, for example, nearly a third of all enslaved people defected during the war. Africans had constituted over 60 percent of

Historical Thinking Skills

Contextualizing Ask students to read the section "Weakening of the Anglican Church." Ask them to think about why many Anglicans would have been Loyalists. Then have students share their thoughts with a partner. Ask for volunteers to share with the class. *(The Anglican Church, also known as the Church of England, was nominally headed by the king. Religious loyalty would have correlated highly with political loyalty.)* **SOC** **NAT**

AMERICA IN THE WORLD

THE AGE OF REVOLUTIONS

The American Revolution was a result of specific tensions and conflicts between Britain and its North American colonies. But it was also a part, and a cause, of what historians have come to call an "age of revolutions" that spread through much of the Western world in the late eighteenth and early nineteenth centuries.

The modern idea of revolution—the overturning of old systems and regimes and the creation of new ones—was largely a product of the ideas of the Enlightenment. Among those ideas was the notion of popular sovereignty, articulated by the English philosopher John Locke and others. Locke argued that political authority did not derive from the divine right of kings or the inherited authority of aristocracies but, rather, from the consent of the governed. A related Enlightenment idea was the concept of individual freedom, which challenged the traditional belief that governments had the right to prescribe the way people act, speak, and even think. Champions of individual freedom in the eighteenth century—among them the French philosopher Voltaire—advocated religious toleration and freedom of thought and expression. The Swiss-French Enlightenment theorist Jean-Jacques Rousseau helped spread the idea of political and legal equality for all people—the end of special privileges for aristocrats and elites, the right of all citizens to participate in the formation of policies and laws.

The American Revolution was the first and in many ways the most influential of the Enlightenment-derived uprisings against established orders. It served as an inspiration to people in other lands who were trying to find a way to oppose unpopular regimes. In 1789, a little over a decade after the beginning of the American Revolution, revolution began in France. The monarchy was abolished (and the king and queen publicly executed in 1793), the authority of the Catholic Church was challenged and greatly weakened, and at the peak of revolutionary chaos during the Jacobin period (1793–1794), more than 40,000 suspected enemies of the revolution were executed and hundreds of thousands of others imprisoned. The most radical phase of the revolution came to an end in 1799, when Napoleon Bonaparte, a young general, seized power and began to build a new French empire. But France's *ancien régime* of king and aristocracy never wholly revived.

The American and French Revolutions helped inspire uprisings in many other parts of the Atlantic world. In 1791, a major slave uprising began in Haiti and soon attracted more than 100,000 rebels. They defeated both the white settlers of the island and the French colonial armies sent to quell their rebellion. Under the leadership of General Toussaint L'Ouverture, they began to agitate for independence, which they obtained on January 1, 1804, a few months after Toussaint's death.

Revolution spread next into the Spanish and Portuguese colonies in the Americas, particularly among the so-called Creoles, people of European ancestry born in the Americas. In the late eighteenth century, they began to resist the authority of colonial officials sent from Spain and Portugal and to demand a greater say in governing their own lands. Napoleon's invasion of Spain and Portugal in 1807 weakened the ability of the European regimes to sustain authority over their American colonies. In the years that followed, revolutions swept through much of Latin America. Mexico became an independent nation in 1821, and provinces of Central America that had once been part of Mexico (Guatemala, El Salvador, Honduras, Nicaragua, and Costa Rica) established their independence three years later. Simón Bolívar, modeling his efforts on those of George Washington, led a great revolutionary movement that won independence for Brazil in 1822 and also helped lead revolutionary campaigns in Venezuela, Ecuador, and Peru—all of which won their independence in the 1820s. Across the Atlantic, Greek patriots—drawing from the examples of other revolutionary nations—launched a movement to win their independence from the Ottoman Empire, which finally succeeded in 1830.

The age of revolutions left many new, independent nations in its wake. It did not, however, succeed in establishing the ideals of popular sovereignty, individual freedom, and political equality in all the nations it affected. Slavery survived in the United States and in many areas of Latin America. New forms of aristocracy and even monarchy emerged in France, Mexico, Brazil, and elsewhere. Women—many of whom had hoped the revolutionary age would win new rights for them—made few legal or political gains in this era. But the ideals that the revolutionary era introduced to the Western world continued to shape the histories of nations throughout the nineteenth century and beyond.

STORMING THE BASTILLE This painting portrays the storming of the great Parisian fortress and prison, the Bastille, on July 14, 1789. The Bastille was a despised symbol of royal tyranny to many of the French, because of the arbitrarily arrested and imprisoned people who were sent there. The July assault was designed to release the prisoners, but in fact the revolutionaries found only seven people in the vast fortress. Even so, the capture of the Bastille—which marked one of the first moments in which ordinary Frenchmen joined the Revolution—became one of the great moments in modern French history. The anniversary of the event, "Bastille Day," remains the French national holiday.

HISTORICAL THINKING SKILLS

1. **Determining Context** Describe the Enlightenment influences that helped bring about the American Revolution.
2. **Explaining Significance** Explain how other nations were significantly influenced by the American Revolution.
3. **Identifying Historical Developments** Analyze the ways the goals and ideals of the American Revolution, as articulated by the Founding Fathers, fell short.

AP Exam Practice

Long Essay Some historians have argued that the British victory over the French in North America inevitably led to the American Revolution a few years later. Support, modify, or refute this contention using specific evidence. *(Thesis and evidence: Students should evaluate the relative importance of causes such as British colonial policy, the end of salutary neglect, the impact of British debt, divisions over treatment of colonial militias, etc. Better responses will place students' arguments in the larger context of issues leading to the French and Indian War.)*

Answers

America in the World

1. The English philosopher John Locke argued that political power does not come from the divine right of kings; instead, it comes from the consent of the governed. The French philosopher Voltaire argued for religious freedom and freedom of thought. The Swiss-French philosopher Jean-Jacques Rousseau argued for political and legal equality for all people.
2. The main example was the French Revolution. The French drew heavily on the ideals of the American Patriots to articulate similar arguments in support of their revolution. In some instances, the same revolutionaries (e.g., Thomas Paine) took part in both the American and French Revolutions. Students may also discuss Haiti and various countries of Latin America.
3. The ideals of the American Revolution were not fully carried out as the words from the Declaration of Independence, "All men are created equal," were narrowly understood in terms of only white wealthy males. The Revolution did not succeed in carrying out a broad movement of rights and opportunities, political sovereignty, individual freedom, and political equality.

Historical Thinking Skills

Evaluating Evidence After students have read the section "The War and Slavery," ask them to create a T-chart listing ways that American independence either improved life for African Americans or made it harder. Have students evaluate which factors seem more prevalent. **PCE** **SOC**

the population in 1770; by 1790, that figure had declined to about 44 percent.

For other African Americans, the Revolution meant an increased exposure to the concept, although seldom to the reality, of liberty. Most African Americans could not read, but few could avoid the new and exciting ideas circulating through the towns and cities and even at times on the plantations. The results included incidents in several communities in which African Americans engaged in open resistance to white control. In Charles Town, South Carolina, for example, Thomas Jeremiah, a free African American, was executed in 1775 after Patriot leaders accused him of conspiring to smuggle British guns to enslaved people in South Carolina. The Revolution also produced eloquent works by African American writers (mostly in the North) to communicate their ideals to the wider community. "Liberty is a jewel which was handed Down to man from the cabinet of heaven," wrote Lemuel Haynes, an African American Patriot, in 1776. "Even an African has Equally good a right to his Liberty in common with Englishmen. . . . Shall a man's Couler Be the Decisive Criterion wherby to Judg of his natural right?"

AFRICAN AMERICAN DESIRE FOR FREEDOM

That was one reason why in South Carolina and Georgia–where enslaved people constituted half or more of the population–there was great ambivalence about the Revolution. Slaveholders opposed British efforts to emancipate enslaved people, but they also feared that the Revolution itself would foment slave rebellions. The same fears helped prevent English colonists in the Caribbean islands (who were far more greatly outnumbered by enslaved Africans) from joining with the continental Americans in the revolt against Britain. In much of the North, the combination of Revolutionary sentiment and evangelical Christian fervor helped spread antislavery sentiments widely through society. But in the South, white support for slavery survived. Southern churches rejected the antislavery ideas of the North and worked instead to develop a rationale for slavery–in part by reinforcing ideas about white superiority, in part by encouraging slaveholders to make slavery more humane.

As in so many other periods of American history, the Revolution exposed the continuing tension between the nation's commitment to liberty and its commitment to slavery. To people in our time, and even to some people in Revolutionary times, it seems obvious that liberty and slavery are incompatible. But to many white Americans in the eighteenth century, especially in the South, that did not seem obvious. Many white Southerners believed, in fact, that enslaving Africans–whom they considered inferior and unfit for citizenship–was the best way to ensure liberty for white people. They feared the impact of free African Americans living alongside white Americans. They also feared that without enslaved laborers, it would be necessary to recruit a servile white workforce in the South, and that the resulting inequalities would jeopardize the survival of liberty. One of the ironies of the American Revolution, therefore, was that white Americans were fighting both to secure freedom for themselves and to preserve slavery for others.

TENSION BETWEEN LIBERTY AND SLAVERY

NATIVE AMERICANS AND THE REVOLUTION

Most Native Americans viewed the American Revolution with considerable uncertainty. The American Patriots tried to persuade them to remain neutral in the conflict, which they described as a "family quarrel" between the colonists and Britain that had nothing to do with Native American nations.

But in fact a great deal was at stake for Native Americans in the American Revolution. During the colonial period, the British government struggled for many years to restrain the growth of white migration into the Native American lands west of the Appalachian Mountains. Such efforts were mostly unsuccessful. The white colonists, the royal governor of Virginia wrote, "do not conceive that the government has any right to forbid taking possession of a vast tract of country." But the British believed that the government did have a right to protect the lands of Native Americans–not because of benevolence, but because of their desire to avoid further conflict, especially on land that had been promised to Native Americans.

Once the Revolutionary War began, the role of Native Americans became of critical significance to both sides of the conflict. For the American Patriots, among the goals of battle for independence was their right to expand into the western lands, at the expense of Native Americans. Some of the most eminent figures in the new nation were themselves land speculators in the west, among them George Washington, and many such men had long complained about the Proclamation of 1763, which had forbidden white movement into tribal lands. Other colonial grievances against the British included the recruitment of Indians to join the Royal Army. In fact, both sides tried to recruit Indians to help them.

In the western Carolinas and Virginia, a Cherokee faction led by Dragging Canoe attacked outlying white settlements in the summer of 1776. Patriot militias responded with overwhelming force, ravaging Cherokee lands and forcing Dragging Canoe and many of his followers to flee west across the Tennessee River. Those Cherokees who remained behind agreed to a new treaty by which they gave up still more land. Not all Native American military efforts were so unsuccessful. Some Iroquois, despite the setbacks at Oriskany, continued to wage war against white Americans in the West and caused widespread destruction in large agricultural areas of New York and Pennsylvania–areas whose crops were of crucial importance to the Patriot cause. And although the retaliating United States armies inflicted heavy losses on Native Americans forces, the attacks continued throughout the war.

In the end, however, the Revolution generally weakened the position of Native Americans in several ways. The Patriot victory increased the demand for western lands; many white Americans associated restrictions on settlement with British oppression and expected the new nation to remove the obstacles. At the same time, white attitudes toward Native

Discussion and Activities

Analyzing Point of View After students have read the section "The War and Slavery," ask them to consider what incentives were offered to enslaved African Americans by the Patriots or the British. Have students write a short paragraph explaining the risks and rewards for enslaved people in choosing to support one side or the other. **SOC** **PCE**

Americans, seldom friendly in the best of times, took a turn for the worse. Many white Americans deeply resented the assistance the Mohawk and other Native American nations had given the British and insisted on treating them as conquered people. Others adopted a paternalistic view of Native Americans that was only slightly less dangerous to them. Thomas Jefferson, for example, came to view the Native Americans as "noble savages" uncivilized in their present state but redeemable if they were willing to adapt to the norms of white society.

TAKING SIDES

Among the Native American nations, the Revolution both revealed and increased the deep divisions that made it difficult for them to form a common front to resist the growing power of whites. In 1774, for example, the Shawnee Indians in western Virginia had attempted to lead an uprising against white settlers moving into the lands that would later become Kentucky. They attracted virtually no allies and (in a conflict known as Lord Dunmore's War) were defeated by the colonial militia and forced to cede more land to white settlers. And the Iroquois, whose power had been eroding since the end of the French and Indian War, were similarly unable to act in unison in the Revolution.

GROWING DIVISIONS

JOSEPH BRANT, CHIEF OF THE MOHAWKS George Romney painted this portrait, *Joseph Brant, Chief of the Mohawks*, 1742–1807, to depict the Mohawk leader who led four of the six Iroquois nations against the American forces in support of the British. He achieved a formidable reputation after participating in the Battle of Oriskany and a raid against the fortified village of Cherry Valley, New York.

Bands of Native Americans continued to launch raids against white settlers on the frontier. White militias, often using such raids as pretexts, continued to attack Native Americans who stood in the way of expansion. Perhaps the most vicious massacre of the era occurred in 1782, after the British surrender, when white militias slaughtered a peaceful band of Delaware Indians at Gnadenhuetten in Ohio. They claimed to be retaliating for the killing of a white family several days before, but few white settlers believed this band of Delaware (who were both Christian converts and pacifists) had played any role in the earlier attack. The white soldiers killed ninety-six people, including many women and children. Such massacres did not become the norm, but they did reveal how little the Revolution had done to settle the basic conflict between the two peoples.

The triumph of the American Patriots in the Revolution contributed to the ultimate defeat of the Native American nations. To white Americans, independence meant, among other things, their right to move aggressively into the western lands, despite the opposition of Native Americans. To the Native Americans, American independence was "the greatest blow that could have been dealt us," one tribal leader warned.

WOMEN'S RIGHTS AND WOMEN'S ROLES

The long Revolutionary War, which touched the lives of people in almost every region, naturally had a significant effect on American women. The departure of so many men to fight in the Patriot armies left wives, mothers, sisters, and daughters in charge of farms and businesses. Other women whose husbands or fathers went off to war did not have even a farm or shop to fall back on. Many cities and towns developed significant populations of impoverished women, who on occasion led popular protests against price increases. On a few occasions, hungry women rioted and looted for food. Elsewhere (in New Jersey and on Staten Island), women launched attacks on occupying British troops, whom they were required to house and feed at considerable expense.

Not all women, however, stayed behind when the men went off to war. Sometimes by choice, but more often out of economic necessity or because they had been driven from their homes by the enemy (and by the smallpox and dysentery the British army carried with it), women flocked in increasing numbers to the camps of the Patriot armies to join their male relatives. George Washington looked askance at these female "camp followers," convinced that they were disruptive and distracting (even though his own wife, Martha, spent the winter of 1778–1779 with him at Valley Forge). Other officers were even more hostile, voicing complaints that reflected a high level of anxiety over this seeming violation of traditional gender roles (and also, perhaps, over the generally lower-class backgrounds of the camp women). One described them in decidedly hostile terms: "their hair falling, their brows beady with the heat, their belongings slung over one shoulder, chat-

WOMEN OF THE ARMY

Reasoning Processes

Change Over Time After students have read the section "Native Americans and the Revolution," ask them to create a two-column chart to identify reasons for Native American leaders to support the Patriots or the British. At the bottom of each list, have students identify important effects of choosing the losing side. **SOC** **PCE**

Discussion and Activities

Analyzing Visuals Have students examine the image "Joseph Brant, Chief of the Mohawks." Ask them to identify details in the portrait of Joseph Brant. Ask students to discuss how this image reinforces or undermines stereotypes of Native Americans. *(Reinforces: Brant is wearing a feathered headdress and native-style sash. Undermines: Brant is wearing a European style shirt and silver pauldron. He is depicted as calm and reasonable, not as a murderous savage as Native Americans were often portrayed in art by white people.)* **SOC**

Historical Thinking Skills

Analyzing Change After students have read the section "Women of the Army," ask them to brainstorm traditional and non-traditional roles women filled during the Revolutionary War. Have students write a journal entry from the point of view of a woman who took on a non-traditional role, explaining how her life had changed. **SOC**

tering and yelling in sluttish shrills as they went." In fact, however, the women were of significant value to the new army. It had not yet developed an adequate system of supply and auxiliary services, and it profited greatly from the presence of women, who increased army morale and performed such necessary tasks as cooking, laundry, and nursing.

But female activity did not always remain restricted to "women's" tasks. In the rough environment of the camps, traditional gender distinctions proved difficult to maintain. Considerable numbers of women became involved, at least intermittently, in combat—including the legendary Molly Pitcher (so named because she carried pitchers of water to soldiers on the battlefield). She watched her husband fall during one encounter and immediately took his place at a field gun. A few women even disguised themselves as men so as to be able to fight.

After the war, of course, the soldiers and the female camp followers returned home. The experience of combat had little visible impact on how society (or on how women themselves) defined female roles in peacetime. The Revolution did, however, call certain assumptions about women into question in other ways. The emphasis on liberty and the "rights of man" led some women to begin to question their position in society as well. "By the way," Abigail Adams wrote to her husband, John Adams, in 1776, "in the new code of laws which I suppose it will be necessary for you to make, I desire you would remember the ladies and be more generous and favorable to them than your ancestors."

Adams was calling for a very modest expansion of women's rights. She wanted new protections against abusive and tyrannical men. A few women, however, went further. Judith Sargent Murray, one of the leading essayists of the late eighteenth century, wrote in 1779 that women's minds were as good as men's and that girls as well as boys therefore deserved access to education.

Some political leaders—among them Benjamin Franklin and Benjamin Rush—also voiced support for the education of women and for other feminist reforms. Yale students in the 1780s debated the question "Whether women ought to be admitted into the magistracy and government of empires and republics." And there was for a time wide discussion of the future role of women in a new republic that had broken with so many other traditions already. But few concrete reforms became either law or common social practice.

CALLS FOR WOMEN'S RIGHTS

In colonial society, under the doctrines of English common law, an unmarried woman had some legal rights (to own property, to enter contracts, and others), but a married woman had virtually no rights. She could own no property and earn no independent wages; everything she owned and everything she earned belonged to her husband. She had no legal authority

THE BRITISH INFANTRY The world's greatest military power raised its armies in almost haphazard fashion. Command of a British regiment was a favor to well-positioned gentlemen, who received a cash reward for every man they enlisted. With that incentive, they were hardly picky, and the foot soldiers of the British army were mostly men who could be persuaded (or tricked) into enlisting through a combination of liquor and cash. Even so, the rough-and-ready quality of the British infantry made them good soldiers on the whole. This drawing portrays a British encampment during the American Revolution. As with the colonial armies, the British troops attracted women, seen at left, some of whom served as "camp followers," doing chores to help the soldiers. The soldiers themselves wore highly ornamental uniforms that were in many ways very impractical. To keep himself properly groomed and attired could take a soldier up to three hours a day.

Discussion and Activities

Contrasting Have students examine the image "The British Infantry." Using the image and their prior knowledge, ask students to create a T-chart contrasting the experiences and attributes of British officers with those of British enlisted men. **SOC**

over her children; the father was, in the eyes of the law, the autocrat of the family. Because a married woman had no property rights, she could not engage in any legal transactions (buying or selling, suing or being sued, writing wills). She could not vote. Nor could she obtain a divorce in most states; that, too, was a right reserved mostly for men, although in much of the South men could not obtain divorces either. These restrictions were what Abigail Adams (who herself enjoyed a successful marriage) was describing when she appealed to her husband not to put "such unlimited power into the hands of the Husbands."

The Revolution did little to change any of these legal customs. In some states, it did become easier for women to obtain divorces. And in New Jersey, women obtained the right to vote (although that right was repealed in 1807). Otherwise, there were few advances and some setbacks—including widows' loss of the right to regain their dowries from their husbands' estates. That change left many widows without any means of support and was one of the reasons for the increased agitation for female education: such women needed a way to support themselves.

The Revolution, in other words, far from challenging the patriarchal structure of American society, actually confirmed and strengthened it. Few American women challenged the belief that they occupied a special sphere distinct from that of men. Most accepted that their place remained in the family. Nevertheless, the Revolutionary experience did contribute to a subtle but important alteration of women's roles. In the past, they had often been little better than servants in their husbands' homes. But the Revolution encouraged people of both genders to reevaluate the contribution of women to the family and the society.

One reason for this was a reevaluation of American life during and after the Revolutionary struggle. As the republic searched for a cultural identity for itself, it began to place additional value on the role of women as mothers. The new nation was, many Americans liked to believe, producing a new kind of citizen, steeped in the principles of liberty. Mothers had a particularly important task, therefore, in instructing their children in the virtues the republican citizenry was expected now to possess. Wives were still far from equal partners in marriage, but their ideas, interests, and domestic roles received increased respect from many men.

A STRENGTHENED PATRIARCHAL STRUCTURE

THE WAR ECONOMY

Inevitably, the Revolution produced important changes in the structure of the American economy. After more than a century of dependence on the British imperial system, American trade suddenly found itself on its own. No longer did it have the protection of the great British navy; on the contrary, English ships now attempted to drive American vessels from the seas. No longer did American merchants have access to the markets of the empire; those markets were now hostile ports—including, of course, the most important source of American trade: England itself.

Yet, while the Revolution disrupted traditional economic patterns, in the long run it strengthened the American economy. Well before the war was over, American ships had learned to evade the British navy with light, fast, easily maneuverable vessels. Indeed, the Yankees began to prey on British commerce with hundreds of privateers. For many shipowners, pri-

BANNER OF THE SOCIETY OF PEWTERERS Members of the American Society of Pewterers carried this patriotic banner when they marched in a New York City parade in July 1788. Its inscription celebrates the adoption of the new federal Constitution and predicts a future of prosperity and freedom in "Columbia's Land." The banner also suggests the growing importance of American manufacturing, which had received an important boost during the Revolution when British imports became unavailable.

Reasoning Processes

Continuity and Change After students read the section "A Strengthened Patriarchal Structure," ask them to create a two-column chart with the headings "Before" and "After" and rows labelled "social," "political," and "economic." Have students fill in the chart using information from the section. Use these charts as the basis for a class discussion about the extent of change for women as a result of the Revolutionary War. **PCE** **WXT** **SOC**

Discussion and Activities

Analyzing Visuals Have students examine the image "Banner of the Society of Pewterers." Ask students to identify details from the image. *(American flag, coat of arms, motto, and image depicting their work.)* Have students discuss as a class what the purpose of the image might have been. *(Advertising to create demand; demonstrating pride in their profession; demonstrating loyalty.)* **WXT** **SOC**

Reasoning Processes

Continuity and Change After students have read the section "The War Economy," ask them to brainstorm elements of the American economy at the end of the Revolutionary War. Have students discuss as a class those items that demonstrate a change from the pre-war economy. **WXT**

vateering proved to be more profitable than ordinary peacetime trade. More important in the long run, the end of imperial restrictions on American shipping opened up enormous new areas of trade to the nation. Enterprising merchants in New England and elsewhere began to develop new commerce in the Caribbean and in South America. By the mid-1780s, American merchants were developing an important new pattern of trade with Asia; and by the end of that decade, Yankee ships were regularly sailing from the eastern seaboard around Cape Horn to the Pacific coast of North America, there exchanging manufactured goods for hides and furs, and then proceeding across the Pacific to barter for goods in China. There was also a substantial increase in trade among the American states.

When English imports to America were cut off–first by the prewar boycott, then by the war itself–there were desperate efforts throughout the states to stimulate domestic manufacturing of certain necessities. No great industrial expansion resulted, but there were several signs of the economic growth that was to come in the next century. Americans began to make their own cloth–"homespun," which became both patriotic and fashionable–to replace now-unobtainable British fabrics. It would be some time before a large domestic textile industry would emerge, but the nation was never again to rely exclusively on foreign sources for its cloth. There was, of course, pressure to build factories for the manufacture of guns and ammunition. And there was a growing general awareness that America need not forever be dependent on other nations for manufactured goods.

NEW PATTERNS OF TRADE

The war stopped well short of revolutionizing the American economy; not until the nineteenth century would that begin to occur. But it did serve to release a wide range of entrepreneurial energies that, despite the temporary dislocations, encouraged growth and diversification.

THE CREATION OF STATE GOVERNMENTS

At the same time that Americans were struggling to win their independence on the battlefield, they were also struggling to create new institutions of government to replace the British system they had repudiated. That struggle continued for more than fifteen years, but its most important phase occurred during the war itself, at the state level.

THE ASSUMPTIONS OF REPUBLICANISM

If Americans agreed on nothing else when they began to build new governments for themselves, they agreed that those governments would be republican. To them, that meant a political system in which all power came from the people, rather than from some supreme authority (such as a king). The success of such a government depended on the nature of its citizenry. If the population consisted of sturdy, independent property owners imbued with civic virtue, then the republic could survive. If it consisted of a few powerful aristocrats and a great mass of dependent workers, then it would be in danger. From the beginning, therefore, the ideal of the small freeholder (the independent landowner) was basic to American political ideology.

IMPORTANCE OF CIVIC VIRTUE

Another crucial part of that ideology was the concept of equality. The Declaration of Independence had given voice to that idea in its most ringing phrase: "All men are created equal." It was a belief that stood in direct contrast to the old European assumption of an inherited aristocracy. The innate talents and energies of individuals, not their positions at birth, would determine their roles in society. Some people would inevitably be wealthier and more powerful than others. But all people would have to earn their success. There would be no equality of condition, but there would be equality of opportunity.

In reality, of course, the United States was never a nation in which all citizens were independent property holders. From the beginning, there was a sizable dependent labor force. White laborers enjoyed some of the privileges of citizenship. Free African American workers were allowed virtually none. American women remained both politically and economically subordinate. Native Americans were systematically exploited and displaced. Nor was there ever full equality of opportunity. American society was more open and more fluid than the societies of most European nations, but the condition of a person's birth was almost always a crucial determinant of success.

PERSISTENT INEQUALITY

Nevertheless, in embracing the assumptions of republicanism, Americans were adopting a powerful, even revolutionary, ideology, and their experiment in statecraft became a model for many other countries. It made the United States for a time the most admired and studied nation on earth.

THE FIRST STATE CONSTITUTIONS

The first and perhaps most basic decision about the character of government was that the constitutions were to be written down, because Americans believed the vagueness of England's unwritten constitution had produced corruption. The second decision was that the power of the executive, which Americans believed had grown too great in England, must be limited. Pennsylvania eliminated the executive altogether. Most other states inserted provisions that limited the power of governors to make appointments and veto legislation. Most states also prevented governors from dismissing the legislature. Most important, every state forbade the governor or any other executive officer from holding a seat in the legislature, thus ensuring that, unlike in England, the executive and legislative branches of government would remain wholly separate.

WRITTEN CONSTITUTIONS AND STRONG LEGISLATURES

Discussion and Activities

Making Connections Have students read the section "The Assumptions of Republicanism." Ask them to define what early Americans meant by the term "republican." Have students discuss in small groups how the meaning of the term has changed over time into the twenty-first century. **PCE** **NAT**

But the new constitutions did not embrace direct popular rule. In Georgia and Pennsylvania, the legislature consisted of one popularly elected house. But in every other state, there was an upper and a lower chamber, and in most cases, the upper chamber was designed to represent the "higher orders" of society. There were property requirements for voters–some modest, some substantial–in all states.

REVISING STATE GOVERNMENTS

By the late 1770s, many Americans were growing concerned about the apparent divisiveness and instability of their new state governments. Most states were having trouble accomplishing anything. Many believed the problem was one of too much democracy. As a result, most of the states began to revise their constitutions to limit popular power. Massachusetts, which waited until 1780 to ratify its first constitution, was the first to act on the new concerns.

Two changes in particular differentiated the Massachusetts and later constitutions from the earlier ones. The first was a change in the process of constitution writing itself. Most of the first documents had been written by state legislatures and thus could easily be amended (or violated) by them. Massachusetts and, later, other states sought a way to protect the constitutions from ordinary politics and created the constitutional convention: a special assembly of the people that would meet only for the purpose of writing the constitution and that would never (except under extraordinary circumstances) meet again.

The second change was a significant strengthening of the executive, a reaction to what many Americans believed was the instability of the original state governments that had weak governors. The 1780 Massachusetts constitution made the governor one of the strongest in any state. He was to be elected directly by the people; he was to have a fixed salary (in other words, he would not be dependent on the goodwill of the legislature each year for his wages); he would have significant appointment powers and a veto over legislation. Other states followed. Those with weak or nonexistent upper houses strengthened or created them. Most increased the powers of the governor. Pennsylvania, which had no executive at first, now produced a strong one. By the late 1780s, almost every state had either revised its constitution or drawn up a new one in an effort to produce stability in government.

SHIFT TO STRONG EXECUTIVES

TOLERATION AND SLAVERY

The states moved far in the direction of complete religious freedom. Most Americans continued to believe that religion should play some role in government, but they did not wish to give special powers to any particular denomination. The privileges that churches had once enjoyed were now largely stripped away. In 1786, Virginia enacted the Statute of Religious Liberty, written by Thomas Jefferson, which called for the complete separation of church and state.

STATUTE OF RELIGIOUS LIBERTY

A FREE BLACK MAN John Singleton Copley, the great American portraitist of the Revolutionary age, painted this picture of a young African American in 1777–1778. He was probably a worker on New England fishing boats who appeared in another Copley painting (Watson and the Shark). It is one of a small number of portrayals of the free African American in the North in this era, and one of even a smaller number that portrays them realistically and seriously.

More difficult to resolve was the question of slavery. In areas where slavery was already weak–in New England, where there had never been many enslaved people, and in Pennsylvania, where the Quakers opposed slavery–it was abolished relatively early. Even in the South, there were some pressures to amend or even eliminate the institution; every state but South Carolina and Georgia prohibited further importation of enslaved people from abroad, and South Carolina banned the slave trade during the war. Virginia passed a law encouraging manumission (the freeing of enslaved people).

Nevertheless, slavery survived in all the southern and border states. There were several reasons: racist assumptions among white people about the inferiority of African Americans; the enormous economic investments many white Southerners had in enslaved people; and the inability of even such men as Washington and Jefferson, who had moral misgivings about slavery, to envision any alternative to it. If slavery were abolished, what would happen to the enslaved people in America? Few white Americans believed African Americans could be integrated into American society as equals. In maintaining

Discussion and Activities

Analyzing Cause and Effect After students have read the section "The First State Constitutions," ask them to think about how and why states placed most power in the hands of the legislature. Then have students share their thoughts with a partner and compare. Ask for volunteers to share with the whole class. *(Having just overthrown what they considered to be an oppressive monarchy, they wanted to ensure that there would not be a strong executive. Most states limited the power of the governor, and all states produced written constitutions to protect against arbitrary exercise of power.)* **PCE**

Reasoning Processes

Continuity and Change Have students read the section "Revising State Governments." Ask them to make a list of changes that states, starting with Massachusetts, made to limit the powers of their legislatures. Ask students to write a short paragraph considering whether it is possible to have "too much democracy." Ask students if they can think of recent examples that might be considered by some to be "too much democracy." **PCE**

Discussion and Activities

Making Connections After students have read the section "Toleration and Slavery," ask them to divide into small groups. Ask the groups to consider the analogy offered by Thomas Jefferson, that the issue of slavery was like holding "a wolf by the ears." Have groups discuss whether there are issues today that raise similar challenges. **SOC** **WXT** **PCE**

slavery, Jefferson once remarked, Americans were holding a "wolf by the ears." However unappealing it was to hold on to it, letting go would be even worse.

THE SEARCH FOR A NATIONAL GOVERNMENT

Americans were much quicker to agree on state institutions than they were on the structure of their national government. At first, most believed that the central government should remain a relatively weak and unimportant force and that each state would be virtually a sovereign nation. It was in response to such ideas that the Articles of Confederation emerged.

The Confederation

The Articles of Confederation, which the Continental Congress had adopted in 1777, provided for a national government much like the one already in place. Congress wrote for ratification of the Articles: "Permit us, then, earnestly to recommend these articles to the immediate and dispassionate attention of the legislatures of the respective states. Let them be candidly reviewed under a sense of the difficulty of combining in one system the various sentiments and interests of a continent divided into so many sovereign and independent communities, under a conviction of the absolute necessity of uniting all our councils and all our strengths, to maintain and defend our common liberties."

Under the Articles, Congress remained the central–indeed the only–institution of national authority. Its powers expanded to give it authority to conduct wars and foreign relations and to appropriate, borrow, and issue money. But it did not have power to regulate trade, draft troops, or levy taxes directly on the people. For troops and taxes, it had to make formal requests to the state legislatures, which could–and often did–refuse them. There was no separate executive; the "president of the United States" was merely the presiding officer at the sessions of Congress. Each state had a single vote in Congress, and at least nine of the states had to approve the admission of a new state. All thirteen state legislatures had to approve any amendment of the Articles.

Limited Power of the National Government

THE CONFLICT OVER WESTERN LANDS The American victory in the Revolution transformed the colonies into "states" within a new nation whose central government claimed at least some sovereignty over the individual units. An early conflict between national and state power took place over the state claims to western lands—claims established during the colonial period. This map shows the extensive western lands claimed by most of the original thirteen colonies to land in the West, and it illustrates the shifting nature of those claims over time—as colonies and then states transferred land to one another. The new national government gradually persuaded the states to give it control of the western lands, and in 1784 and 1785 it issued ordinances governing the process of settling those lands.

Why did the national government consider it important for the states to give up their claim to these territories?

Answers

The Conflict Over Western Lands

The division between states that had claimed western lands and those that had not was increasing. The national government also saw the land as a potential source of revenue.

During the process of ratifying the Articles of Confederation (which required approval by all thirteen states), broad disagreements over the plan became evident. The small states had insisted on equal state representation, but the larger states wanted representation to be based on population. The smaller states prevailed on that issue. More important, the states claiming western lands wished to keep them, but the rest of the states demanded that all such territory be turned over to the national government. New York and Virginia had to give up their western claims before the Articles were finally approved. They went into effect in 1781.

The Confederation, which existed from 1781 until 1789, was not a complete failure, but it was far from a success. It lacked adequate powers to deal with interstate issues or to enforce its will on the states, and it had little stature in the eyes of the world.

Diplomatic Failures

Postwar Disputes with Britain and Spain

Evidence of the low esteem in which the rest of the world held the Confederation was its difficulty in persuading Great Britain (and to a lesser extent Spain) to live up to the terms of the peace treaty of 1783.

The British had promised to evacuate American territory, but British forces continued to occupy a string of frontier posts along the Great Lakes within the United States. Nor did the British honor their agreement to make restitution to slaveholders whose enslaved people the British army had confiscated. There were also disputes over the boundaries of the new nation. Americans wanted full access to British markets; England, however, placed sharp restrictions on that access.

THE TREATY OF GREENVILLE ON AUGUST 3, 1795 This painting, from the American School of painting, depicts the Treaty of Greenville ending the Northeast Indian War in the Ohio Country. In exchange for $20,000 worth of various goods such as blankets, utensils, and domesticated animals, the United States acquired large parts of Ohio, tracts of what would soon become Chicago, and the Fort Detroit area.

Reasoning Processes

Comparison After students have read the section "The Confederation," ask them to create a T-chart comparing the powers granted to the national government to the powers denied the national government under the Articles of Confederation. Then ask students to reflect on the powers assumed by state governments they read about earlier in the chapter. Have students write a brief paragraph explaining what level of government, state or national, would have had more impact on the daily lives of Americans at this time. **PCE**

Discussion and Activities

Analyzing Visuals Have students examine the image "The Treaty of Greenville on August 3, 1795." Ask them to imagine that they are eyewitnesses to the scene as portrayed. As a class, discuss whether students think the negotiations were peaceful or fair, and what elements from the painting support their conclusions. **PCE** **SOC** **NAT**

Reasoning Processes

Comparing Have students read the section "The Ordinances of 1784 and 1785." Ask them to create a Venn diagram comparing the terms of the two land ordinances. **PCE** **MIG**

In 1784, Congress sent John Adams as minister to London to resolve these differences, but Adams made no headway with the English, who were never sure whether he represented a single nation or thirteen different ones. Throughout the 1780s, the British government refused even to send a diplomatic minister to the American capital.

THE CONFEDERATION AND THE NORTHWEST

The Confederation's most important accomplishment was its resolution of controversies over the western lands. When the Revolution began, only a few thousand whites lived west of the Appalachian mountains; but by 1790 their numbers had increased to 120,000. The Confederation had to find a way to include these new settlements in the political structure of the nation. The landed states began to yield their western claims to the national government in 1781, and by 1784 the Confederation controlled enough land to permit Congress to begin making policy for the western lands.

THE ORDINANCES OF 1784 AND 1785

The Ordinance of 1784, based on a proposal by Thomas Jefferson, divided the western territory into ten self-governing districts, each of which could petition Congress for statehood when its population equaled the number of free inhabitants of the smallest existing state. The provision reflected the desire of the Revolutionary generation to avoid creating second-class citizens in subordinate territories. Then, in the Ordinance of 1785, Congress created a system for surveying and selling the western lands. The territory north of the Ohio River was to be surveyed and marked off into neat rectangular townships, each divided into thirty-six identical sections. In every township, four sections were to be set aside for the United States; the revenue from the sale of one of the other sections was to support creation of a public school. Sections were to be sold at auction for no less than one dollar an acre.

THE GRID

Among the many important results of the Ordinance of 1785 was the establishment of an enduring pattern of dividing up land for human use. Many such systems have emerged throughout history. Some have relied on natural boundaries (rivers, mountains, and other topographical features). Some have reflected informal claims of landlords over vast but vaguely defined territories. Some have rested on random allocations of acres, to be determined by individual landholders. But many Enlightenment thinkers began in the eighteenth century to imagine more precise, even mathematical, forms of land distribution, which required both careful surveying and a clear method for defining boundaries. The result was the method applied in 1785 in the Northwest Territory, which came to be known as "the grid"—the division of land into carefully measured and evenly divided squares or rectangles. This pattern of land distribution eventually became the norm for much of the land west of the

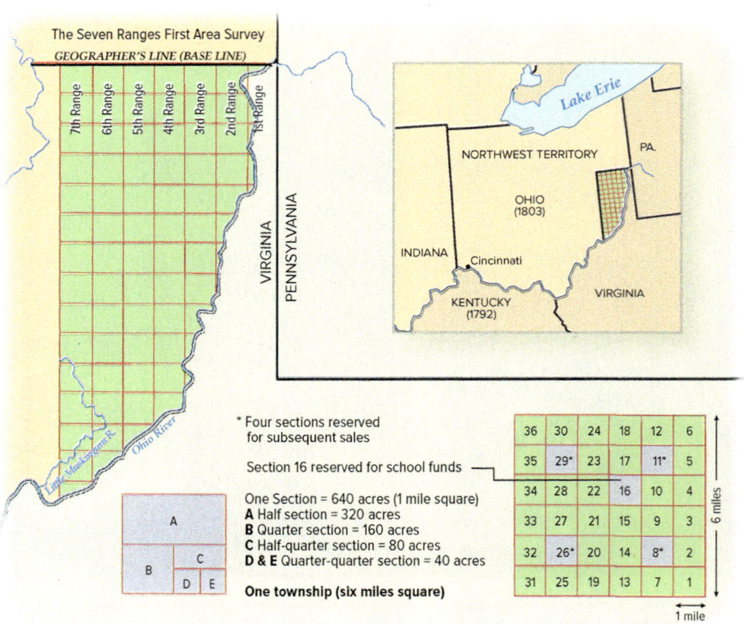

LAND SURVEY: ORDINANCE OF 1785 In the Ordinance of 1785, the Congress established a new system for surveying and selling western lands. These maps illustrate the way in which the lands were divided in an area of Ohio. Note the highly geometrical grid pattern that the ordinance imposed on these lands. Each of the squares in the map on the left was subdivided into 36 sections, as illustrated in the map at the lower right.

Why was this grid pattern so appealing to the planners of the western lands?

Answers

Land Survey: Ordinance of 1785

The grid was orderly, easy to subdivide, and easy to describe in legal documents.

Appalachians. It also became a model for the organization of many towns and cities, which distributed land in geometrical patterns within rectangular grids defined by streets. Although older land-distribution systems survive within the United States, the grid has become the most common form by which Americans impose human ownership and use on the landscape.

NORTHWEST ORDINANCE

The original ordinances were highly favorable to land speculators and less so to ordinary settlers, many of whom could not afford the price of the land. Congress compounded the problem by selling much of the best land to the Ohio and Scioto land companies before making it available to anyone else. Criticism of these policies led to the passage in 1787 of another law governing western settlement–legislation that became known as the "Northwest Ordinance." The 1787 Ordinance abandoned the ten districts established in 1784 and created a single Northwest Territory out of the lands north of the Ohio; the territory could eventually be divided into between three and five territories. It also specified a population of 60,000 as a minimum for statehood, guaranteed freedom of religion and the right to trial by jury to residents of the Northwest, and prohibited slavery throughout the territory.

The western lands south of the Ohio River received less attention from Congress, and development was more chaotic there. The region that became Kentucky and Tennessee developed rapidly in the late 1770s, and in the 1780s speculators and settlers began setting up governments and asking for recognition as states. The Confederation was never able to successfully resolve the conflicting claims in that region.

NATIVE AMERICANS AND THE WESTERN LANDS

On paper at least, the western land policies of the Confederation created a system that brought order and stability to the process of white settlement in the Northwest. But in reality, order and stability came slowly and at great cost, because much of the land the Confederation was neatly subdividing and offering for sale consisted of territory claimed by the Native Americans of the region. Congress tried to resolve that problem in 1784, 1785, and 1786 by persuading Iroquois, Choctaw, Chickasaw, and Cherokee leaders to sign treaties ceding substantial western lands in the North and South to the United States. But those agreements proved ineffective. In 1786, the leadership of the Iroquois Confederacy repudiated the treaty it had signed two years earlier and threatened to attack white settlements in the disputed lands. Other Native American nations had never accepted the treaties affecting them and continued to resist white movement into their lands.

BATTLE OF FALLEN TIMBERS

Violence between white settlers and Native Americans on the Northwest frontier reached a crescendo in the early 1790s. In 1790 and again in 1791 a group of Miami and Shawnee, led by the famed Miami warrior Little Turtle, defeated United States forces in two major battles near what is now the western border of Ohio; in the second of those battles, on November 4, 1791, 630 white Americans died in fighting at the Wabash River (the greatest military victory Native Americans had ever or would ever again achieve in their battles with white Americans). Efforts to negotiate a settlement failed because of the Miami's insistence that no treaty was possible unless it forbade white settlement west of the Ohio River. Negotiations did not resume until after General Anthony Wayne led 4,000 soldiers into the Ohio Valley in 1794 and defeated the Native American in the Battle of Fallen Timbers.

A year later, the Miami signed the Treaty of Greenville, ceding substantial new lands to the United States (which was now operating under the Constitution of 1789) in exchange for a formal acknowledgment of their claim to the territory they had managed to retain. In doing so, the United States was affirming that Native American lands could be ceded only by the Native American nations. That hard-won assurance, however, proved a frail protection against the pressure of white expansion westward in later years.

LITTLE TURTLE Little Turtle led the Miami confederacy in its wars with the United States in what is now Ohio and Indiana in the early 1790s. For a time he seemed almost invincible, but in 1794 Little Turtle was defeated in the Battle of Fallen Timbers. In this sketch (a rough copy of a painting attributed to Gilbert Stuart), Little Turtle wears a medal bearing the likeness of George Washington, awarded him by the United States after the signing of the Treaty of Greenville.

Historical Thinking Skills

Analyzing Change Have students read the section "Northwest Ordinance." Ask them to make a list of provisions found in the ordinance. Have students circle or highlight those provisions that marked a significant change from previous land ordinances, and ask them to write a short paragraph explaining what they think was the most important change and why. **PCE** **MIG**

Discussion and Activities

Historical Developments and Argumentation Have students read the section "Native Americans and the Western Lands." Ask them to write a thesis statement that makes a historically defensible claim in response to the prompt, "What were the main causes of conflict between the United States and Native Americans following the Revolutionary War?" **PCE** **MIG** **SOC**

Reasoning Processes

Causation Have students read the section "Postwar Depression." Ask them to identify the causes of the national government's debt, and to recall why the Congress had been given limited powers under the Articles of Confederation. Ask students to consider whether this was a foreseeable problem, and if so, what could have been done to prevent it. **PCE**

DEBTS, TAXES, AND DANIEL SHAYS

POSTWAR DEPRESSION

The postwar depression, which lasted from 1784 to 1787, increased the perennial American problem of an inadequate money supply, a problem that weighed particularly heavily on debtors. In dealing with this problem, Congress most clearly demonstrated its weakness.

The Confederation itself had an enormous outstanding debt that it had accumulated at home and abroad during the Revolutionary War. It had few means with which to pay it, having no power to tax. It could only make requisitions of the states, and it received only about one-sixth of the money it requisitioned. The fragile new nation was faced with the grim prospect of defaulting on its obligations.

POLITICAL DISPUTES OVER ECONOMIC ISSUES

This alarming possibility brought to the fore a group of leaders who would play a crucial role in the shaping of the republic for several decades. Committed nationalists, they sought ways to increase the powers of the central government and to meet its financial obligations. Robert Morris, the head of the Confederation's treasury; Alexander Hamilton, his young protégé; James Madison of Virginia; and others called for a "continental impost"—a 5 percent duty on imported goods to be levied by Congress and used to fund the debt. Many Americans, however, feared that the impost plan would concentrate too much financial power in the hands of Morris and his allies in Philadelphia. Congress failed to approve the impost in 1781 and again in 1783. Angry and discouraged, the nationalists largely withdrew from any active involvement in the Confederation.

The states had war debts, too, and they generally relied on increased taxation to pay them. But poor farmers, already burdened by debt and now burdened again by new taxes, considered such policies unfair, even tyrannical. They demanded that the state governments issue paper currency to increase the money supply and make it easier for them to meet their obligations. Resentment was especially high among farmers in New England, who felt that the states were squeezing them to enrich already wealthy bondholders in Boston and other towns.

SHAYS'S REBELLION

Throughout the late 1780s, therefore, mobs of distressed farmers rioted periodically in various parts of New England. Dissidents in the Connecticut Valley and the Berkshire Hills of Massachusetts, many of them Revolutionary veterans, rallied behind Daniel Shays, a former captain in the Continental army. Shays issued a set of demands that included paper money, tax relief, a moratorium on debts, the relocation of the state capital from Boston to the interior, and the abolition of imprisonment for debt. During the summer of 1786, the Shaysites concentrated on preventing the collection of debts, private or public, and used force to keep courts from sitting and sheriffs from selling confiscated property. In Boston, members of the legislature, including Samuel Adams, denounced Shays and his men as rebels and traitors. When winter came, the rebels advanced on Springfield, hoping to seize weapons from the arsenal there. An army of state militiamen, financed by a loan from wealthy merchants, set out from Boston to confront them. In January 1787, this army met Shays's band and dispersed his ragged troops.

As a military enterprise, Shays's Rebellion was a failure, although it produced some concessions to the aggrieved farmers. Shays and his lieutenants, at first sentenced to death, were later pardoned, and Massachusetts offered the protesters some tax relief and a postponement of debt payments. The rebellion had more important consequences for the future of the United States, however, for it added urgency to a movement already gathering support throughout the new nation—the movement to produce a new, national constitution.

DANIEL SHAYS AND JOB SHATTUCK Shays and Shattuck were the principal leaders of the 1786 uprising by poor farmers in Massachusetts demanding relief from their indebtedness. Shattuck led an insurrection in the east, which collapsed when he was captured on November 30. Shays organized the rebellion in the west, which continued until the state militia dispersed the rebels in late February 1787. The following year, state authorities pardoned Shays; even before that, the legislature responded to the rebellion by providing some relief to the impoverished farmers. These drawings are part of a hostile account of the rebellion published in 1787 in a Boston almanac.

Historical Thinking Skills

Contextualization Have students read the section "Shays's Rebellion." Ask them to list the issues that inspired the rebellion. In small groups, have students discuss how those issues demonstrated a social division in Massachusetts. *(The rebellion was largely comprised of farmers protesting policies implemented by wealthy merchants, traders, and financiers who made up the bulk of the Massachusetts Assembly. Those farmers were angry because many of the policies that made their economic situation more difficult benefited the wealthy assemblymen who made them.)* **PCE** **SOC**

CHAPTER 5 REVIEW

CONNECTING THEMES

Chapter Five explored the political, economic, and social consequences of the American Revolution. Before the Revolution, Americans viewed the increased attention from Great Britain as a violation of political and economic agreements. What resulted was a shift in political relations, as the colonists declared their independence from Great Britain and announced a new role for their nation in the world. But as Americans soon learned, this emerging nation would have to prove its merit if it was to gain the respect of European powers. International relations were not, however, the most pressing issues that the new country had to confront. The Revolution had transformed American society and fueled westward migration, which led to new challenges for the country.

Independence also altered the political structure of the United States at the state and national levels. The Articles of Confederation, which had guided the colonies during the conflict, now seemed inadequate for the growing needs of the young nation. The first big political battle centered on a new proposed constitution. The debate would lead to the emergence and evolution of the first two distinct political parties in the United States,. These parties would dominate political life in the new nation for years to come.

You should consider the following questions as you review the themes for this chapter:

- How did economic, political, and social factors create regional identities in the United States?
- What factors influenced western migration, and what were the consequences of that migration?
- How did the American Revolution and its aftermath alter relationships between the United States and foreign countries?
- How did Enlightenment ideas manifest themselves during and after the American Revolution?
- What role did the belief in republican principles of self-government play during and after the American Revolution?

KEY TERMS

Abigail Adams 156
American Patriots 139
Articles of Confederation 140
Battle of Fallen Timbers 163
Benedict Arnold 144
***Common Sense* 138**
Daniel Shays 164
Declaration of Independence 139
George Washington 140
Hessians 144
Jean Jacques Rousseau 153
John Burgoyne 144
John Locke 139
Loyalists (Tories) 140
Molly Pitcher 156
Nathanael Greene 150
Northwest Ordinance 163
Olive Branch Petition 138
Ordinances of 1784 and 1785 162
Prohibitory Act 138
Republicanism 158
Saratoga 145
Second Continental Congress 138
Thomas Jefferson 139
Thomas Paine 138
Valley Forge 140
Yorktown 150

Discussion and Activities

Comparing and Contrasting Divide the class into groups to review and research the impact of the American Revolution on women, Native Americans, and African Americans. Each group should investigate political, economic, and social changes that occurred as the result of the war. Then bring the class together to discuss ways in which the war affected the groups similarly or differently.

Key Terms

Students should be familiar with the key terms and be able to define them in the context of the challenges Americans faced in organizing to fight a war of independence and the war's impacts on women, minorities, and relations with other countries. Encourage students to use these terms in performing review exercises and exam practice for this chapter.

Go Online Chapter 5 Content Review

Assessing Student Understanding Use the online assessment to assess student understanding of concepts and topics within the chapter. You can assign the ready-made Chapter 5 Content Review or create your own from available questions. This easy-to-use tool helps you design assessments that meet the needs of different types of learners.

Answers

Multiple Choice

1. C; **2.** B; **3.** A

Short Answer

4A) Possible answer: The image depicts a variety of different types of soldiers carrying different types of arms. The idea is that the American Revolution was carried out by a number of different people, with different means and abilities, using a variety of different resources.

4B) Possible answer: The Stamp Act, which was the first act by the British Parliament to put a revenue tax on the colonists, was met with strong opposition. This set the stage for future protests by the American colonists. They viewed the Stamp Act as a serious violation of their rights. Many believed the British had the right to regulate and control trade, but that revenue bills must be placed by local representative bodies, such as colonial legislatures.

4C) Possible answer: The most significant effect that resulted from the American Revolution was the independence that the colonies gained from the mother country. Despite all the tactical and military advantages of the British, Americans managed to gain their independence.

5A) The Loyalists supported the British government during the American Revolution, whereas the Patriots opposed the British government.

5B) Possible answer: Both the Patriots and the Loyalists were composed of wealthy members of American colonial society. Wealthy Loyalists tended to come from older money, while the wealthy Patriots tended to come from newer money, often acquired from smuggling and other illegal activities.

5C) Possible answer: Once the American Revolution was over and the Americans had defeated the British, Loyalists found themselves in a precarious situation. During the Revolution they had property confiscated, which was to be returned according to the terms of the Paris Peace Treaty, but most of them were not able to reclaim their property. Many of the Loyalists left the mainland, traveling down south to Louisiana, or traveled back to Europe, especially Britain.

AP EXAM PRACTICE

Questions assume cumulative content knowledge from this chapter and previous chapters.

MULTIPLE CHOICE

Use the image on page 147 and your knowledge of U.S. history to answer questions 1-3.

1. Early military actions like the Battle of Bunker Hill centered in New England because
   (A) New England had a long tradition of sympathy with the French.
   (B) New England's Loyalist population threatened to overwhelm the Patriots.
   (C) New England's economic activity caused significant conflict with the British.
   (D) New England's Patriots sought early alliances with Native American nations.

2. As evidenced in the image, the British had a significant advantage in
   (A) popular support.
   (B) military weaponry and supplies.
   (C) military leadership.
   (D) geographical location.

3. Ultimately the American military victory was secured by
   (A) foreign aid from the French.
   (B) alliances with Native American nations.
   (C) the American dedication to ending slavery.
   (D) the significant participation of women in the military.

SHORT ANSWER

Use your knowledge of U.S. history to answer questions 4 and 5.

4. Use the image on page 143 to answer A, B, and C.
   (A) Briefly describe ONE point of view about the colonists as depicted in the image *Revolutionary Soldiers*.
   (B) Briefly explain ONE specific historical cause which led to the American Revolution.
   (C) Briefly explain ONE specific historical effect that resulted from the American Revolution.

5. Answer A, B, and C.
   (A) Briefly describe ONE specific historical difference between the Patriots and the Loyalists during the American Revolution.
   (B) Briefly describe ONE specific historical similarity between the Patriots and the Loyalists during the American Revolution.
   (C) Explain ONE specific historical effect of the American Revolution that directly impacted either the Patriots or the Loyalists.

LONG ESSAY

Develop a thoughtful and thorough historical argument that addresses the statement below. Begin your essay with a thesis statement, and support it with specific historical evidence and examples.

6. Evaluate the relative importance of the immediate effects of the American Revolution.

Answers

Long Essay

6. Possible thesis: Loyalists faced extreme hardships both during and after the American Revolution, as extreme violations of their property and rights were continually violated. Similarly, women were forced to take on new domestic roles but continued to be denied their most basic freedoms. African Americans suffered the most from the failed ideals of the American Revolution. They continued to be enslaved for years following the conflict. Historical evidence: Loyalists had their property confiscated during the conflict. Many were forced to flee the country both during and following the fighting. Women participated in various ways during the Revolution, from direct fighting to secondary roles. After the war, many began calling for the same political rights as their male counterparts but for the most part were denied these rights. A third affected group was African Americans. Enslaved people were promised their freedom if they fought in the war, but they were also threatened with continued servitude if they took up arms against the different sides as well. The ideals of the American Revolution were most elusive for this group of people. The words "All men are created equal" rang hollow as they continued to be enslaved long after the revolutionary fervor had died out.

6 THE CONSTITUTION AND THE NEW REPUBLIC

THE AMERICAN STAR
Frederick Kemmelmeyer painted this tribute to George Washington sometime in the 1790s. It was one of many efforts by artists and others to create an iconography for the new republic.

CONNECTING CONCEPTS

Chapter Six begins by exploring the first major political debate in the newly formed country: ratification of a new U.S. Constitution. The Federalists supported ratification and the creation of a stronger federal government. The Antifederalists accepted the need for modification of the Articles of Confederation but opposed the wide-scale changes proposed by the Constitutional Convention. These unofficial parties represented a major shift in the political atmosphere within the young nation. Following a hard-fought intellectual battle, ratification of the new U.S. Constitution resulted in a major victory for those Founding Fathers who envisioned a stronger national government.

More debates ensued as the country fought over its long-term political future. Alexander Hamilton and the Federalists endorsed a strong national government that dominated the states. Thomas Jefferson and the Democratic-Republicans favored a weak national government that was subservient to the states. The parties that formed around these two polarizing figures often had differing views on major issues facing the nation. Domestic challenges included westward expansion and growing conflicts with Native Americans. Foreign challenges included winning the respect and support of European powers, notably Great Britain. The bitter disputes of the 1790s led into the election of 1800, where the young nation faced its first great political test—the peaceful transfer of power between the two parties.

Pacing Guide

Chapter 6 explores key concepts from Period 3: 1754–1800 of the AP U.S. History Curriculum Framework. The suggested instruction time for Chapter 6 is 5 days.

Key Concepts

3.3.I In the decades after American independence, interactions among different groups resulted in competition for resources, shifting alliances, and cultural blending.

3.3.II The continued presence of European powers in North America challenged the United States to find ways to safeguard its borders, maintain neutral trading rights, and promote its economic interests.

Discussion and Activities

Analyzing Visuals Have students examine the image "The American Star." Ask them to construct a list of elements in the image that symbolically represent the United States. Have students then discuss why there was an effort to create an iconography for the new country. *(List: Portrait of George Washington, numerous national flags, shields with stars and stripes, and the eagle with arrows and olive branches in its talons. Iconography was important in helping to create a sense of national unity and identification with the new nation.)*

Historical Thinking Skills

Contextualizing Have students read the section "A Weak Central Government." Ask them to write a thesis statement that makes a historically defensible claim about why the Founders might have intentionally created a weak central government. *(The American Revolution had largely been about overthrowing what was felt to be an overly controlling central government, so the Founders naturally did not want to create a strong central government to replace it.)* **PCE**

As you read, you should:

- Evaluate how Native Americans continuously adjusted their alliances with European powers during the eighteenth century.
- Analyze how the presence of European powers on the borders of the United States forced the new nation to safeguard its territory and defend its commercial interests diplomatically and militarily.
- Consider how the ideas of the Enlightenment and the belief in republican ideas of self-government led to a transformation of political thought in the United States with the ratification of the Constitution.
- Analyze how dissatisfaction with the Articles of Confederation led to the writing of the Constitution and the creation of a stronger central government.
- Describe how the fundamentals of the newly ratified Constitution, which were based on the ideas of federalism, divided power between the states and the national government.

FRAMING A NEW GOVERNMENT

So unpopular and ineffectual had the Confederation Congress become by the mid-1780s that it began to lead an almost waiflike existence. In 1783, its members timidly withdrew from Philadelphia to escape from the clamor of army veterans demanding back pay. They took refuge for a while in Princeton, New Jersey, then moved to Annapolis, and in 1785 settled in New York. Through all of this, the delegates were often conspicuous largely by their absence. Only with great difficulty did Congress secure a quorum to ratify the treaty with Great Britain ending the Revolutionary War. Eighteen members, representing only eight states, voted on the Confederation's most important piece of legislation, the Northwest Ordinance. In the meantime, a major public debate was beginning over the future of the Confederation.

A WEAK CENTRAL GOVERNMENT

ADVOCATES OF CENTRALIZATION

Weak and unpopular though the Confederation was, it had for a time satisfied a great many–probably a majority–of the people. They believed they had fought the Revolutionary War to avert the danger of what they considered remote and tyrannical authority; now they wanted to keep political power centered in the states, where they could carefully and closely control it.

But during the 1780s, some of the wealthiest and most powerful groups in the country began to clamor for a more genuinely national government capable of dealing with the nation's problems–particularly the economic problems that most directly afflicted them. Some military men, many of them members of the exclusive and hereditary Society of the Cincinnati (formed by Revolutionary army officers in 1783), were disgruntled at the refusal of Congress to fund their pensions. They began aspiring to influence and invigorate the national government; some even envisioned a form of military dictatorship and flirted briefly (in 1783, in the so-called Newburgh Conspiracy) with a direct challenge to Congress, until George Washington intervened and blocked the potential rebellion.

SUPPORTERS OF A STRONG NATIONAL GOVERNMENT

American manufacturers–the artisans and "mechanics" of the nation's cities and towns–wanted to replace the various state tariffs with a uniformly high national duty. Merchants and shippers wanted to replace the thirteen different (and largely ineffective) state commercial policies with a single, national one. Land speculators wanted the "Indian menace" finally removed from their western tracts. People who were owed money wanted to stop the states from issuing paper money, which would lower the value of what they received in payment. Investors in Confederation securities wanted the government to fund the debt and thus enhance the value of their securities. Large property owners looked for protection from the threat of mobs, a threat that seemed particularly menacing in light of such episodes as Shays's Rebellion. This fear of disorder and violence expressed a tension between the resolute defense of individual rights, which was a core principle of the Revolution and found reflection in the Bill of Rights, and the public concern for safety and security, which the occasional chaos of the Confederation period had reinforced. Frequent conflicts between liberty and order became, and remain, a central feature of American democracy.

168 • CHAPTER 6

Go Online AP Exam Preparation

AP Exam Practice Use the online assessment to help prepare students for the AP Exam. You can assign the ready-made AP-style short-answer questions, document-based questions, and multiple-choice questions assessing concepts, themes, and skills from Period 3 and AP-style long-essay questions organized in sets of three questions from various time periods. You can also create your own tests from available questions. This easy-to-use tool helps you design assessments that meet the needs of different types of learners.

GEORGE WASHINGTON AT MOUNT VERNON Washington was in his first term as president in 1790 when an anonymous folk artist painted this view of his home at Mount Vernon, Virginia. Washington appears in uniform, along with members of his family, on the lawn. After he retired from office in 1797, Washington returned happily to his plantation and spent the two years before his death in 1799 "amusing myself in agricultural and rural pursuits." He also played host to an endless stream of visitors from throughout the country and Europe.

Courtesy, National Gallery of Art, Washington

By 1786, these diverse demands had grown so powerful that the issue was no longer whether the Confederation should be changed but how drastic the changes should be. Even the defenders of the existing system reluctantly came to agree that the government needed strengthening at its weakest point—its lack of power to tax.

ALEXANDER HAMILTON

The most resourceful of the reformers was Alexander Hamilton, political genius, New York lawyer, onetime military aide to General Washington, and illegitimate son of a Scottish merchant in the West Indies. From the beginning, Hamilton had been unhappy with the Articles of Confederation and the weak central government they had created. He now called for a national convention to overhaul the entire document. He found an important ally in James Madison of Virginia, who persuaded the Virginia legislature to convene an interstate conference on commercial questions. Only five states sent delegates to the meeting, held in Annapolis, Maryland, in 1786; but the delegates approved a proposal drafted by Hamilton (who was representing New York) recommending that Congress call a convention of special delegates from all the states to gather in Philadelphia the next year and consider ways to "render the constitution of the Federal government adequate to the exigencies of the union."

At that moment, in 1786, there seemed little possibility that the Philadelphia convention would attract any more interest than the meeting at Annapolis had attracted. Only by winning the support of George Washington, the centralizers believed, could they hope to prevail. But Washington at first showed little interest in joining the cause. Then, early in 1787, the news of Shays's Rebellion spread throughout the nation. Thomas Jefferson, then the American minister in Paris, was not alarmed. "I hold," he confided in a letter to James Madison, "that a little rebellion, now and then, is a good thing, and as necessary in the political world as storms in the physical." But Washington took the news less calmly. In May, he left his home at Mount Vernon in Virginia for the Constitutional Convention in Philadelphia. His support gave the meeting immediate credibility.

A Divided Convention

THE FOUNDING FATHERS

Fifty-five men, representing all the states except Rhode Island, attended one or more sessions of the convention that sat in the Philadelphia State House from May to September 1787. These "Founding Fathers," as they would later become known, were relatively young; their average age was forty-four, and only one delegate (Benjamin Franklin, then eighty-one) was of advanced age. They were well educated by the standards of their time. Most represented the great

Reasoning Processes

Causation After students have read the section "Advocates of Centralization," ask them to create a T-chart listing economic concerns of wealthy Americans under the Articles of Confederation in one column and proposals of Alexander Hamilton in the other. Have students draw a line connecting concerns with proposed solutions. **WXT** **SOC**

Discussion and Activities

Analyzing Visuals Have students examine the image "George Washington at Mount Vernon." Ask them to consider and discuss what they *do not* see in the image that would be important to life on the estate. *(For example, there are no enslaved people depicted in the image.)* **WXT** **SOC**

Historical Thinking Skills

Analyzing Points of View Have students read the section "The Virginia Plan." Ask them to create a concept map (a graphic organizer that uses a web to connect details to a main idea) linking the main features of the Virginia Plan. Lead a discussion over which states would support or oppose each provision, and why. **PCE**

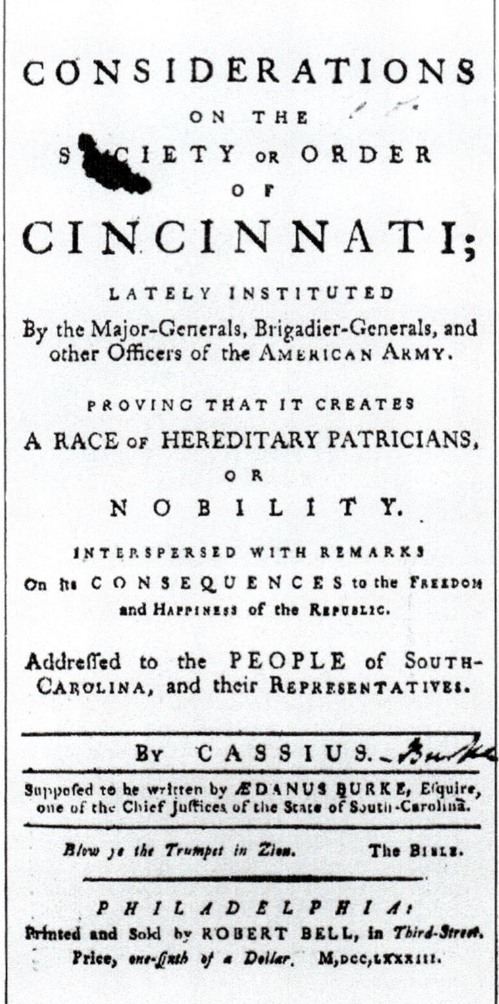

CONSIDERATIONS
ON THE
S[illegible]IETY OR ORDER
OF
CINCINNATI;
LATELY INSTITUTED
By the Major-Generals, Brigadier-Generals, and other Officers of the AMERICAN ARMY.
PROVING THAT IT CREATES
A RACE OF HEREDITARY PATRICIANS,
OR
NOBILITY.
INTERSPERSED WITH REMARKS
On its CONSEQUENCES to the FREEDOM and HAPPINESS of the REPUBLIC.
Addreſſed to the PEOPLE of SOUTH-CAROLINA, and their REPRESENTATIVES.

BY CASSIUS.

Suppoſed to be written by ÆDANUS BURKE, Eſquire, one of the Chief Juſtices of the State of South-Carolina.

Blow ye the Trumpet in Zion. The BIBLE.

PHILADELPHIA:
Printed and Sold by ROBERT BELL, in *Third-Street.*
Price, *one-ſixth of a Dollar.* M,DCC,LXXXIII.

A BROADSIDE AGAINST "NOBILITY" This 1783 pamphlet was one of many expressions of the broad democratic sentiment that the Revolution unleashed in American society. The Society of the Cincinnati was an organization created shortly after the Revolution by men who had served as high-ranking officers in the Patriot army. To many Americans, however, the society—membership in which was to be hereditary—looked suspiciously like the inherited aristocracies of England. This pamphlet, printed in Philadelphia but intended for South Carolinians, warns of the dangers the society supposedly posed to the "Freedom and Happiness of the Republic."

propertied interests of the country, and many feared what one of them called the "turbulence and follies" of democracy. Yet all were also products of the American Revolution and retained the Revolutionary suspicion of concentrated power.

The convention unanimously chose Washington to preside over its sessions and then closed its business to the public and the press. The members then ruled that each state delegation would have a single vote. Major decisions would not require unanimity, as they did in Congress, but only a simple majority. Virginia, the most populous state, sent the best-prepared delegation to Philadelphia. James Madison (thirty-six years old) was its intellectual leader. He had devised a detailed plan for a new "national" government, and the Virginians used it to control the agenda from the moment the convention began.

THE VIRGINIA PLAN

Edmund Randolph of Virginia began the discussion by proposing that "a national government ought to be established, consisting of a supreme Legislative, Executive, and Judiciary." Despite its vagueness, it was a drastic proposal. It called for the creation of a government very different from the existing Confederation, which, among other things, had no executive branch. But so committed were the delegates to fundamental reform that they approved this resolution after only perfunctory debate. Then Randolph introduced the details of Madison's plan. The Virginia Plan (as it came to be known) called for a new national legislature consisting of two houses. In the lower house, the states would be represented in proportion to their population; thus the largest state (Virginia) would have about ten times as many representatives as the smallest (Delaware). Members of the upper house were to be elected by the lower house under no rigid system of representation; thus some of the smaller states might at times have no members in the upper house.

The proposal aroused immediate opposition among delegates from Delaware, New Jersey, and other small states. Some responded by arguing that Congress had called the convention "for the sole and express purpose of revising the Articles of Confederation" and had no authority to do more than that. Eventually, however, William Paterson of New Jersey submitted a substantive alternative to the Virginia Plan, a proposal for a "federal" as opposed to a "national" government. The New Jersey Plan would preserve the existing one-house legislature, in which each state had equal representation, but it gave Congress expanded powers to tax and to regulate commerce. The delegates voted to table Paterson's proposal, but not without taking note of the substantial support for it among small-state representatives.

The Virginia Plan remained the basis for discussion. But its supporters realized they would have to make concessions to the small states if the convention was ever to reach a general agreement. They soon conceded an important point by agreeing to permit the members of the upper house to be elected by the state legislatures rather than by the lower house of the national legislature. Thus each state would always have at least one member in the upper house.

But many questions remained. Would the states be equally represented in the upper house, or would the large states have more members than the small ones? Would enslaved people

Historical Thinking Skills

Contextualization Have students examine the image "A Broadside Against 'Nobility.'" Ask them to think about why many Americans would oppose the formation of a hereditary elite class. Have students share their thoughts with a partner, then ask for volunteers to share with the class. **SOC**

THE CONSTITUTIONAL CONVENTION This painting, *Scene at the Signing of the Constitution of the United States*, is a 1940 work by Howard Chandler Christy depicting the signing of the U.S. Constitution at Independence Hall in Philadelphia on September 17, 1787.

(who could not vote) be counted as part of the population in determining the size of a state's representation in Congress, or were they to be considered simple property? Delegates from states with large and apparently permanent enslaved populations—especially those from South Carolina—wanted to have it both ways. They argued that enslaved people should be considered persons in determining representation. But they wanted enslaved people to be considered property if the new government were to levy taxes on each state on the basis of population. Representatives from states where slavery had disappeared or was expected soon to disappear argued that enslaved people should be included in calculating taxation but not representation. No one argued seriously for giving enslaved people citizenship or the right to vote.

SMALL STATES VERSUS LARGE STATES

COMPROMISE

The delegates bickered for weeks. By the end of June, as both temperature and tempers rose to uncomfortable heights, the convention seemed in danger of collapsing. Benjamin Franklin, who remained a calm voice of conciliation through the summer, warned that if they failed, the delegates would "become a reproach and by-word down to future ages. And what is worse, mankind may hereafter, from this unfortunate instance, despair of establishing governments by human wisdom, and leave it to chance, war and conquest." Partly because of Franklin's soothing presence, the delegates refused to give up.

THE GREAT COMPROMISE

Finally, on July 2, the convention agreed to create a "grand committee," with a single delegate from each state (and with Franklin as chairman), to resolve the disagreements. The committee produced a proposal that became the basis of the "Great Compromise." Its most important achievement was resolving the difficult problem of representation. The proposal called for a legislature in which the states would be represented in the lower house on the basis of population. Each enslaved person would count as three-fifths of a free person in determining the basis for both representation and direct taxation. (The three-fifths formula was based on the false assumption that a enslaved person was three-fifths as productive as a free worker and thus contributed only three-fifths as much wealth to the state.) The committee proposed that in the upper house, the states should be represented equally with two members apiece. The proposal broke the deadlock. On July 16, 1787, the convention voted to accept the compromise.

Discussion and Activities

Analyzing Issues Have students read the section "Small States Versus Large States." Ask them to write a short statement explaining the conflict between slave states and non-slave states over taxation and representation. **SOC** **WXT** **PCE**

Discussion and Activities

Analyzing Visuals Have students examine the image "The Constitutional Convention." Ask them to consider why the painting may have been composed the way that it is. You might mention that in 1940, much of the world was consumed in a war (World War II) that the United States was not yet officially a part of. *(In a time of uncertainty, the artist portrayed the signers of the Constitution essentially united with no internal conflict, gathered under patriotic symbols like the flags and drum.)* **WOR** **NAT**

AP Exam Practice

Short Answer

Answer A, B, and C.

A) Briefly explain ONE way in which the Constitution represented a conservative defense of existing economic elites. *(Beard argued that the Constitution was principally designed to create a stable government that would create conditions conducive to the promotion of business and industry.)*

B) Briefly explain ONE way in which the Constitution represented a radical effort to preserve the political ideals of the Revolution. *(Fiske argued that adoption of the Constitution restored order necessary to implement Revolutionary ideals.)*

C) Briefly explain ONE way in which interpretations of the Constitution have changed over time. *(Answers will vary.)*

THE MEANING OF THE CONSTITUTION

The constitution has inspired debate from the moment it was drafted. Some people argue that the Constitution is a flexible document intended to evolve in response to society's evolution. Others argue that it has a fixed meaning, rooted in the "original intent" of the framers, and that to move beyond that is to deny its value.

Historians, too, disagree about why the Constitution was written and what it meant. To some scholars, the creation of the federal system was an effort to preserve the ideals of the Revolution and to create a strong national government capable of exercising real authority. To others, the Constitution was an effort to protect the economic interests of existing elites, even at the cost of betraying the principles of the Revolution. To still others, the Constitution was designed to protect individual freedom and to limit the power of the federal government.

The first influential exponent of the heroic view of the Constitution as the culmination of the Revolution was John Fiske. In *The Critical Period of American History* (1888), Fiske described the many problems that beset the nation under the Articles of Confederation: economic difficulties, the weakness and ineptitude of the new national government, threats from abroad, interstate jealousies, and widespread lawlessness. Only the timely adoption of the Constitution, Fiske claimed, saved the young republic from disaster.

In *An Economic Interpretation of the Constitution of the United States* (1913), Charles A. Beard challenged Fiske's view. According to Beard, the 1780s had been a "critical period" primarily for conservative businessmen who feared that the decentralized political structure of the republic imperiled their financial position. Such men, he claimed, wanted a government able to promote industry and trade, protect private property, and make good the public debt—much of which was owed to them. The Constitution was, Beard claimed, "an economic document drawn with superb skill by men whose property interests were immediately at stake" and who won its ratification over the opposition of a majority of the people.

A series of powerful challenges to Beard's thesis emerged in the 1950s, as many scholars began to argue that the Constitution was not an effort to preserve property but, rather, an enlightened effort to ensure stability and order. Examining the debate between the Federalists and the Antifederalists, Forrest McDonald, in *We the People* (1958), concluded that there was no consistent relationship between wealth and property and support for the Constitution. Instead, opinion on the new system was far more likely to reflect local and regional interests. The cumulative effect of these challenges greatly weakened Beard's argument; few historians any longer accepted his thesis without reservation.

In the 1960s, a new group of scholars began to revive an economic interpretation of the Constitution—one that differed from Beard's in important ways but that nevertheless emphasized social and economic factors as motives for supporting the federal system. Jackson Turner Main argued, in *The Antifederalists* (1961), that supporters of the Constitution were "cosmopolitan commercialists," eager to advance the economic development of the nation; the Antifederalists, by contrast, were "agrarian localists," fearful of centralization. Gordon Wood, in *The Creation of the American Republic* (1969), suggested that the debate over the state constitutions in the 1770s and 1780s reflected profound social divisions and that those same divisions helped shape the argument over the federal Constitution. The Federalists, Wood suggested, were largely traditional aristocrats deeply concerned over the instability of life under the Articles of Confederation and particularly alarmed by the decline in popular deference toward social elites. The creation of the Constitution, Wood argued, was part of a larger search to create a legitimate political leadership based on the existing social hierarchy.

Historians have continued to examine the question of "intent." Did the framers intend a strong, centralized political system; or did they intend to create a decentralized system with a heavy emphasis on individual rights? The answer, according to Jack Rakove in *Original Meanings* (1996) and *Revolutionaries* (2010), is both—and many other things as well. The Constitution, Rakove argues, was the result of a long and vigorous debate through which the views of many different groups found their way into the document. James Madison, a strong nationalist, believed that only a powerful central government could preserve stability in a large nation. Alexander Hamilton also saw the Constitution as a way to protect order and property and to defend the nation against the dangers of too much liberty. But if Madison and Hamilton feared too much liberty, they also feared too little. And that made them receptive to the vigorous demands of the "Antifederalists" for protections of individual rights, which culminated in the Bill of Rights. The Constitution is not, Rakove argues, "infinitely malleable." But neither does it have a fixed meaning that can be a reliable guide to how we interpret it today.

HISTORICAL THINKING SKILLS

Questions assume cumulative content knowledge from this chapter and previous chapters.

1. **Identifying Historical Developments** Identify three broad schools of historical interpretation concerning the ratification of the U.S. Constitution.
2. **Determining Context** Describe how one piece of historical evidence from the time period could be used to support each of the three broad schools of historical interpretation concerning the ratification of the U.S. Constitution.
3. **Developing Arguments** Analyze which school of thought you find most convincing. Be sure to use evidence to support your reasoning.

National Archives and Records Administration

Answers

Debating the Past

1. First, the heroic view of the Constitution, promoted by John Fiske, focused on the problems of the Articles of Confederation and argued that ratification of the Constitution saved the new republic from disaster. Second, the economic view of the Constitution, promoted by Charles A. Beard, focused on the fact that many of the Founders who were present at the Constitutional Convention, as well as members of many of the state ratification conventions, were wealthy elites within American society, and that their main goal of ratification was to ensure the status quo. Third, the social view of the Constitution, promoted by Forrest McDonald, focused on the fact that the ratification debates reflected social divisions within American society.
2. The heroic view: weaknesses in the government created by the Articles of Confederation, like the inability to collect taxes or regulate trade, showed a major weakness in the first constitution. The economic view: most of the Founding Fathers were white wealthy elites within American society, and they formed the core of constituents who initiated and ratified the new U.S. Constitution. The social view: it wasn't wealth that separated the Founders who supported the ratification from those who opposed it; instead, the divisions were based on geographical, local, or regional interests. Most Federalists came from cities, whereas most Antifederalists came from rural areas.
3. Student responses will vary.

Over the next few weeks, the convention agreed to another important compromise on the explosive issue of slavery. The representatives of the southern states feared that the power to regulate trade might interfere with their agrarian economy, which relied heavily on sales abroad, and with slavery. In response, the convention agreed that the new legislature would not be permitted to tax exports; Congress would also be forbidden to impose a duty of more than $10 a head on imported enslaved people, and it would have no authority to stop the slave trade for twenty years. To those delegates who viewed the continued existence of slavery as an affront to the principles of the new nation, this was a large and difficult concession. They agreed to it because they feared that without it the Constitution would fail.

The convention chose to ignore differences of opinion it was unable to resolve, leaving important questions alive that would surface again in later years. The Constitution provided no definition of citizenship. Most important was the absence of a list of individual rights, which would restrain the powers of the national government in the way that bills of rights restrained the state governments. Madison opposed the idea, arguing that specifying rights that were reserved to the people would, in effect, limit those rights. Other delegates, however, feared that without such protections the national government might abuse its new authority.

THE CONSTITUTION OF 1787

Many people contributed to the creation of the American Constitution, but the single most important of them was James Madison—the most creative political thinker of his generation. Perhaps Madison's most important achievement was in helping resolve two important philosophical questions that had served as obstacles to the creation of an effective national government: the question of sovereignty and the question of limiting power.

JAMES MADISON

The question of sovereignty had been one of the chief sources of friction between the colonies and Great Britain, and it continued to trouble Americans as they attempted to create their own government. How could both the national government and the state governments exercise sovereignty at the same time? Where did ultimate sovereignty lie? The answer, Madison and his contemporaries decided, was that all power, at all levels of government, flowed ultimately from the people. Thus neither the federal government nor the state governments were truly sovereign. All of them derived their authority from below. The opening phrase of the Constitution (devised by Gouverneur Morris) was "We the people of the United States"—an expression of the belief that the new government derived its power not from the states but from its citizens.

THE QUESTION OF SOVEREIGNTY

Resolving the problem of sovereignty made possible one of the distinctive features of the Constitution—its distribution of powers between the national and state governments. It was, Madison wrote at the time, "in strictness, neither a national nor a federal Constitution, but a composition of both." The Constitution and the government it created were to be the "supreme law" of the land; no state would have the authority to defy it. The federal government was to have broad powers, including the power to tax, to regulate commerce, to control the currency, and to pass such laws as would be "necessary and proper" for carrying out its other responsibilities. Gone was the stipulation of the Articles that "each State shall retain every power, jurisdiction, and right not expressly delegated to the United States in Congress assembled." On the other hand, the Constitution accepted the existence of separate states and left important powers in their hands.

In addition to solving the question of sovereignty, the Constitution produced a solution to a problem troubling to Americans: the problem of concentrated authority. Nothing so frightened the leaders of the new nation as the prospect of creating a tyrannical government. That fear had been one of the chief obstacles to the creation of a national government. Drawing from the ideas of the French philosopher Baron de Montesquieu, most Americans had long believed that the best way to avoid tyranny was to keep government close to the people. A republic, they thought, must remain confined to a small area. A large nation would breed corruption and despotism because the rulers would be so distant from most of the people that there would be no way to control them. In the first years of the new American nation, these assumptions had led to the belief that the individual states must remain sovereign and that a strong national government would be dangerous.

Madison, however, helped break the grip of these assumptions by arguing that a large republic would be less, not more, likely to produce tyranny, because it would contain so many different factions that no single group would ever be able to dominate it. (In this, he drew from—among other sources—the Scottish philosopher David Hume.) This idea of many centers of power "checking each other" and preventing any single, despotic authority made possible the idea of a large republic and also helped shape the internal structure of the federal government. The Constitution's most distinctive feature was its "separation of powers" within the government, its creation of "checks and balances" among the legislative, executive, and judicial branches. The array of forces within the government would constantly compete with (and often frustrate) one another. Congress would have two chambers, the Senate and the House of Representatives, each with members elected in a different way and for different terms, and each checking the other, since both would have to agree before any law could be passed. The president would have the power to veto acts of Congress. The federal courts would have protection from both the executive and the legislature because judges and justices, once appointed by the president and confirmed by the Senate, would serve for life.

SEPARATION OF POWERS

The "federal" structure of the government, which divided power between the states and the nation, and the system of "checks and balances," which divided power among various

Historical Thinking Skills

Explaining Significance After students have read the section "Compromise," ask them to brainstorm issues resolved by compromise and issues left unresolved. Discuss as a class or in small groups which unresolved issue seems most important. **PCE** **SOC**

Discussion and Activities

Explaining Historical Concepts Have students read the section "The Question of Sovereignty." Ask them to create a 3-column chart identifying rights and powers belonging to the people, state governments, and the national government under the Constitution. **PCE**

Discussion and Activities

Argumentation After students have read the section “Separation of Powers,” ask them to create a concept map with three nodes labelled “Executive,” “Legislative,” and “Judicial.” Have them draw arrows in both directions between each set of branches, and ask them to list examples on the arrows describing ways that each branch limits and is limited by the others. **PCE**

elements within the national government, were designed to protect the United States from the kind of despotism Americans believed had emerged in England. But they were also designed to protect the nation from another kind of despotism, perhaps equally menacing: the tyranny of the people. Fear of the "mob," of an "excess of democracy," was at least as important to the framers of the Constitution as fear of a single tyrant. Shays's Rebellion had been only one example, they believed, of what could happen if a nation did not defend itself against the unchecked exercise of popular will. Thus, in the new government, only the members of the House of Representatives would be elected directly by the people. Senators, the president, and federal judges would be insulated in varying degrees from the public.

On September 17, 1787, thirty-nine delegates signed the Constitution, doubtless sharing the feelings that Benjamin Franklin expressed at the end: "Thus I consent, Sir, to this Constitution, because I expect no better, and because I am not sure it is not the best."

The Limits of the Constitution

The Constitution of 1789 was a document that established a democratic republic for white people, mostly white men. Native Americans and African Americans, the two largest population groups sharing the lands of the United States with Anglo-Americans, enjoyed virtually none of the rights and privileges provided to the white population. Native Americans had at least the semblance of a legal status within the nation, through treaties that assured them lands that would be theirs forever. But most of these treaties did not survive for long, and Native Americans found themselves driven farther and farther west with little of the protection that the government had promised them.

Among the white leaders of the United States, there were eminent figures who believed Native Americans could join the republic as citizens. Jefferson was among them, believing that Native Americans could be taught the ways of "civilization." Jefferson, and other Americans with good intentions, sought to teach Native Americans to live as white Americans did. Efforts to teach them Anglo farming methods were based on sedentary farms that relied on men doing the farming and women caring for the home. Native Americans had no interest in such ways and preferred to retain their traditional cultures. Their repudiation of white civilization contributed to the erosion of support among white Americans. Native Americans were not granted citizenship of the United States until the 1920s.

Far more removed from the guarantees of the Constitution were enslaved people, who were given virtually none of the rights and protections that the new government provided to white people. They were, one southern official noted, not "constituent members of our society." The French-Canadian writer Hector St. John de Crèvecoeur, who after the Revolution settled in the United States, wrote a famous book, *Letters from an American Farmer*, in 1782. In it, he posed what became a famous question: "What then is the American, this new man?" Crèvecoeur answered his own question by noting that "individuals of all nations" would become "melted" into a common citizenry. But he too saw no room for African Americans in the community of the "new man." Indeed, among the first laws passed by the new United States under the Constitution was the Naturalization Act of 1790, which helped legalize the stream of immigrants coming into the country and allowed them to become citizens. But it defined citizenry as a status available only to white people. Even free African Americans were barred from citizenship.

Jefferson, who had briefly tried without result to give Native Americans a legal status within the new nation, had no such aspirations for African Americans. He was an uneasy defender of slavery, worrying about excluding "a whole race of men" from the natural rights that Jefferson himself had done so much to promote. But he could never accept the idea that black men and black women could attain the level of knowledge and intelligence of white people. Jefferson's long romantic relationship with an enslaved woman, Sally Hemmings, did nothing to change his mind. Hemmings was an enslaved woman on

FEDERALIST #1 *The Federalist Papers*, gathered here in a book distributed to the people of New York, began as essays, letters, and articles published in newspapers throughout America during the debate over the Constitution. Its authors—James Madison, Alexander Hamilton, and John Jay—were defenders of the new Constitution and wrote these essays to explain its value and importance. They remain today one of the most important American contributions to political theory.

Historical Thinking Skills

Argumentation Have students read the section “The Limits of the Constitution.” Ask them to consider the quote from Crèvecoeur, “What then is the American, this new man?” Have students write a short letter to Crèvecoeur answering his question. **SOC** **WXT** **NAT**

Jefferson's plantation in Virginia. Jefferson lived with her after the death of his wife and fathered several of her children. But his intimate relationship with the Hemmings family did not ultimately change his postion on slavery. Unlike George Washington, who stipulated that the enslaved people on his estate be freed after his death, Jefferson (deeply in debt) required his heirs to sell his enslaved people after he died (after liberating the Hemmings family). Not until the end of the Civil War were black men and black women eligible to live as citizens in the United States, and even then with only partial rights until a century later.

FEDERALISTS AND ANTIFEDERALISTS

The delegates at Philadelphia had greatly exceeded their instructions from Congress and the states. Instead of making simple revisions to the Articles of Confederation, they had produced a plan for a completely different form of government. They feared, therefore, that the Constitution might never be ratified under the rules of the Articles of Confederation, which required unanimous approval by the state legislatures. So the convention changed the rules. The Constitution specified that the new government would come into existence among the ratifying states when any nine of the thirteen had ratified it. The delegates recommended to Congress that special state conventions, not state legislatures, consider the document. They were required to vote "yes" or "no" on the document. They could make no changes until after the Constitution was ratified by the required number of states, at which point the Constitution's amendment process could be used (as it was for the Bill of Rights).

The old Confederation Congress, now overshadowed by the events in Philadelphia, passively accepted the Constitutional Convention's work and submitted it to the states for approval. All the state legislatures except Rhode Island's elected delegates to ratifying conventions, most of which began meeting by early 1788. Even before the ratifying conventions convened, however, a great national debate on the new Constitution had begun–in the state legislatures, in mass meetings, in the columns of newspapers, and in ordinary conversations. Occasionally, passions rose to the point that opposing factions came to blows. In at least one place–Albany, New York–such clashes resulted in injuries and death.

Supporters of the Constitution had a number of advantages. They were better organized than their opponents, and they had the support of the two most eminent men in America, Franklin and Washington. And they seized an appealing label for themselves: "Federalists"–the term that opponents of centralization had once used to describe themselves–thus implying that they were less committed to a "nationalist" government than in fact they were. The Federalists also had the support of the ablest political philosophers of their time: Alexander Hamilton, James Madison, and John Jay. Those three men, under the joint pseudonym "Publius," wrote a series of essays–widely published in newspapers throughout the nation–explaining the meaning and virtues of the Constitution. They did so in an effort to counter the powerful arguments that those opposed to the Constitution–those who became known as the Antifederalists–were making. Without a powerful defense of the new Constitution, they feared, the Antifederalists might succeed in several crucial states, most notably in New York. The essays were later issued as a book, and they are known today as *The Federalist Papers*. They are among the most important American contributions to political theory.

THE FEDERALIST PAPERS

The Federalists called their critics "Antifederalists," implying that their rivals had nothing to offer except opposition and chaos. But the Antifederalists had serious and intelligent arguments of their own. They presented themselves as the defenders of the true principles of the Revolution. The Constitution, they believed, would betray those principles by establishing a strong, potentially tyrannical, center of power in the new national government. The "federal" government, they claimed, would increase taxes, obliterate the states, wield dictatorial powers, favor the "well born" over the common people, and put an end to individual liberty. But their biggest complaint was that the Constitution lacked a bill of rights, a concern that revealed one of the most important sources of their opposition: a basic mistrust of human nature and of the capacity of human beings to wield power. The Antifederalists argued that any government that centralized authority would inevitably produce despotism. Their demand for a bill of rights was a product of this belief: no government could be trusted to protect the liberties of its citizens; only by enumerating the natural rights of the people could there be any assurance that those rights would be preserved.

THE ANTIFEDERALISTS

At its heart, then, the debate between the Federalists and the Antifederalists was a battle between two fears. The Federalists were afraid, above all, of disorder, anarchy, chaos; they feared the unchecked power of the masses, and they sought in the Constitution to create a government that would function at some distance from popular passions. The Antifederalists were not anarchists; they too recognized the need for an effective government. But they were much more concerned about the dangers of concentrated power than about the dangers of popular will. They opposed the Constitution for some of the same reasons the Federalists supported it: because it placed obstacles between the people and the exercise of power.

DEBATING THE CONSTITUTION

Despite the Antifederalist efforts, ratification proceeded quickly (although not without occasional difficulty) during the winter of 1787–1788. The Delaware convention was the first to act, when it ratified the Constitution unanimously. The New Jersey and Georgia conventions did the same. In the larger states of Pennsylvania and Massachusetts, the Antifederalists put up a determined struggle but lost in the final vote. New Hampshire ratified the document in June 1788–the ninth state to do so. It was now theoretically possible for the Constitution to go into effect.

Reasoning Processes

Continuity and Change Have students read the section "The Federalist Papers." Ask them to consider whether the Constitution represented a legitimate transfer of power from the Articles. Discuss reasons why or why not. **PCE**

Discussion and Activities

Speculating Have students read the section "The Antifederalists." Ask them to consider why the Antifederalists wanted a Bill of Rights. Have students work with a partner or in small groups to draft a list of rights they think would be important for the new nation. **PCE** **NAT**

Discussion and Activities

Making Connections Have students read the section "The Bill of Rights." Ask them to look up the ten amendments of the Bill of Rights. Have students discuss in small groups which of the amendments they believe is the most important, then ask each student to choose one amendment to rewrite as a tweet of 140 characters or less. Ask for volunteers to share with the class. **PCE** **NAT**

A new government could not hope to flourish, however, without the participation of Virginia and New York, the two most populous states, whose conventions remained closely divided. By the end of June, first Virginia and then New York had consented to the Constitution by narrow margins. The New York convention yielded to expediency–even some of the most staunchly Antifederalist delegates feared that the state's commercial interests would suffer if, once the other states gathered under the "New Roof," New York were to remain outside. Massachusetts, Virginia, and New York all ratified, on the assumption that a bill of rights would be added to the Constitution. The North Carolina convention adjourned without taking action, waiting to see what happened to the amendments. Rhode Island, whose leaders had opposed the Constitution almost from the start, did not even call a convention to consider ratification.

COMPLETING THE STRUCTURE

The first elections under the Constitution took place in the early months of 1789. Almost all the newly elected congressmen and senators had favored ratification, and many had served as delegates to the Philadelphia convention. There was never any real doubt about who would be the first president. George Washington had presided at the Constitutional Convention, and many delegates who had favored ratification did so only because they expected him to preside over the new government as well. Washington received the votes of all the presidential electors. John Adams, a leading Federalist, became vice president. After a journey from Mount Vernon marked by elaborate celebrations along the way, Washington was inaugurated in New York–the national capital for the time being–on April 30, 1789.

The first Congress served in many ways almost as a continuation of the Constitutional Convention, because its principal responsibility was filling in the various gaps in the Constitution.

THE BILL OF RIGHTS

Its most important task was drafting a bill of rights. By early 1789, even Madison had come to agree that some sort of bill of rights was essential to legitimize the new government in the eyes of its opponents. Congress approved twelve amendments on September 25, 1789; ten of them were ratified by the states by the end of 1791. What we know as the Bill of Rights is these first ten amendments to the Constitution. Nine of them placed limitations on Congress by forbidding it to infringe on certain basic rights: freedom of religion, speech, and the press; immunity from arbitrary arrest; trial by jury; and others. The Tenth Amendment reserved to the states all powers except those specifically withheld from them or delegated to the federal government.

On the subject of the federal courts, the Constitution said only: "The judicial power of the United States shall be vested in one Supreme Court, and in such inferior courts as the Congress may from time to time ordain and establish." It was left to Congress to determine the number of Supreme Court judges to be appointed and the kinds of lower courts to be organized. In the Judiciary Act of 1789, Congress provided for a Supreme Court of six members, with a chief justice and five associate justices; thirteen district courts with one judge apiece; and three circuit courts of appeal, each to consist of one of the district judges sitting with two of the Supreme Court justices. In the same act, Congress gave the Supreme Court the power to make the final decision in cases involving the constitutionality of state laws.

The Constitution referred indirectly to executive departments but did not specify what or how many there should be. The first Congress created three such departments–state, treasury, and war–and also established the offices of the attorney general and the postmaster general. To the office of secretary of the treasury, Washington appointed Alexander Hamilton of New York, who at age thirty-two was an acknowledged expert in public finance. For secretary of war he chose a Massachusetts Federalist, General Henry Knox. As attorney general he named Edmund Randolph of Virginia, sponsor of the plan on which the Constitution had been based. As secretary of state he chose another Virginian, Thomas Jefferson, who had recently served as minister to France.

THE CABINET

FEDERALISTS AND REPUBLICANS

The resolution of these initial issues, however, did not resolve the deep disagreements about the nature of the new government. On the contrary, for the first twelve years under the Constitution, American politics was characterized by a level of acrimony seldom matched in any period since. The framers of the Constitution had dealt with many disagreements not by solving them but by papering them over with a series of vague compromises; as a result, the conflicts survived to plague the new government.

At the heart of the controversies of the 1790s was the same basic difference in philosophy that had been at the heart of the debate over the Constitution. On one side stood a powerful group that believed America required a strong, national government: that the country's mission was to become a genuine nation-state, with centralized authority, a complex commercial economy, and a proud standing in world affairs. On the other side stood another group–a minority at first, but one that gained strength during the decade–that envisioned a far weaker central government. American society should not, this group believed, aspire to be highly commercial or urban. It should remain predominantly rural and agrarian, and it should have a central government of modest size and powers that would leave most power in the hands of the states and the people. The centralizers became known as the Federalists and gravitated to the leadership of Alexander Hamilton. Their opponents took the name Republicans and gathered under the leadership of James Madison and Thomas Jefferson.

COMPETING VISIONS

Reasoning Processes

Causation Have students read the section "The Cabinet." Ask them to think about why the Constitution was relatively vague about the structure of the court system. Have students write a statement identifying at least one reason for that vagueness and at least one effect of it. *(The colonies had never really had an independent judiciary. Congress defined the structure of the courts through legislation.)* **PCE**

Historical Thinking Skills

Analyzing Issues Have students read the section "Assuming the Debt." Ask them to create a T-chart listing reasons for assuming state debts and for the creation of a national bank. Have students circle reasons that would appeal to Federalists and strike through reasons that would upset Antifederalists. (Some examples may end up both circled and crossed out.) WXT PCE NAT

ALEXANDER HAMILTON As President George Washington's secretary of the Treasury, Alexander Hamilton exerted enormous influence in both domestic and foreign affairs. Hamilton favored the establishment of an enlightened ruling class to govern the new nation. His plans for the new federal government to assume existing public debt and to establish a national bank were part of his vision of a powerful nation with a vigorous and independent commercial economy, a robust industrial sector, and a dynamic role in world economic affairs.

HAMILTON AND THE FEDERALISTS

For twelve years, control of the new government remained firmly in the hands of the Federalists. That was in part because George Washington had always envisioned a strong national government and as president had quietly supported those who were attempting to create one. His enormous prestige throughout the nation was one of the Federalists' greatest assets. But Washington also believed that the presidency should remain above political controversies, and so he avoided any personal involvement in the deliberations of Congress. As a result, the dominant figure in his administration became his talented secretary of the treasury, Alexander Hamilton, who exerted more influence on domestic and foreign policy than anyone else both during his term of office and, to an almost equal extent, after his resignation in 1794.

Of all the national leaders of his time, Hamilton was one of the most aristocratic in personal tastes and political philosophy–ironically, perhaps, since his own origins as an illegitimate child in the Caribbean had been so humble. Far from embracing the republican ideals of the virtue of the people, he believed that a stable and effective government required an enlightened ruling class. Thus the new government needed the support of the wealthy and powerful; and to get that support, it needed to give those elites a stake in its success. Hamilton proposed, therefore, that the new government take responsibility for the existing public debt. Many of the miscellaneous, uncertain, depreciated certificates of indebtedness that the old Congress had issued during and after the Revolution were now in the hands of wealthy speculators; the government should call them in and exchange them for uniform, interest-bearing bonds, payable at definite dates. (This policy was known as "funding" the debt.) He also recommended that the federal government "assume" (or take over) the debts the states had accumulated during the Revolution; this assumption policy would encourage state as well as federal bondholders to look to the central government for eventual payment. Hamilton did not, in other words, envision paying off and thus eliminating the debt. He wanted instead to create a large and permanent national debt, with new bonds being issued as old ones were paid off. The result, he believed, would be that creditors–the wealthy classes most likely to lend money to the government–would have a permanent stake in seeing the government survive.

ASSUMING THE DEBT

Hamilton also wanted to create a national bank. At the time, there were only a few banks in the country, located principally in Boston, Philadelphia, and New York City. A new, national bank would help fill the void that the absence of a well-developed banking system had created. It would provide loans and currency to businesses. It would give the government a safe place to deposit federal funds. It would help collect taxes and disburse the government's expenditures. The bank would be chartered by the federal government, would have a monopoly of the government's own banking business, and would be controlled by directors, of whom one-fifth would be appointed by the government. It would provide a stable center to the nation's small and feeble banking system.

The funding and assumption of debts would require new sources of revenue, since the government would now have to pay interest on the loans it was accepting. Up to now, most government revenues had come from the sale of public lands in the West. Hamilton proposed two new kinds of taxes. One was an excise to be paid by distillers of alcoholic liquors, a tax that would fall most heavily on the whiskey distillers of the backcountry, especially in Pennsylvania, Virginia, and North Carolina–small farmers who converted part of their corn and rye crop into whiskey. The other was a tariff on imports, which not only would raise revenue but also would protect American manufacturing from foreign competition. In his famous "Report on Manufactures" of 1791, Hamilton laid out a grand scheme for stimulating the growth of industry in the United States and wrote

HAMILTON'S REPORT ON MANUFACTURING

Discussion and Activities

Analyzing Visuals Have students examine the image "Alexander Hamilton." Ask them to write a brief summary of how the image reinforces or contradicts what they know of Hamilton. *(Hamilton was born poor in the West Indies, but is shown wearing fine clothing. He was also young for a person of great influence.)* PCE SOC

Historical Thinking Skills

Analyzing Point of View After students have read the section "Hamilton's Report on Manufacturing," ask them to write a letter to Hamilton from the point of view of either a small farmer or a prosperous merchant explaining why they support or oppose Hamilton's tax proposals. **WXT** **PCE**

glowingly of the advantages to the nation of a healthy manufacturing base.

The Federalists, in short, offered more than a vision of how to stabilize the new government. They offered a vision of the sort of nation America should become—a nation with a wealthy, enlightened ruling class, a vigorous, independent commercial economy, and a thriving industrial sector; a nation able to play a prominent role in world economic affairs.

Enacting the Federalist Program

Few members of Congress objected to Hamilton's plan for funding the national debt, but many did oppose his proposal to accept the debt "at par," that is, at face value. The old certificates had been issued to merchants and farmers in payment for war supplies during the Revolution, or to officers and soldiers of the Revolutionary army in payment for their services. But many of these original holders had sold their bonds during the hard times of the 1780s to speculators, who had bought them at a fraction of their face value. Many members of Congress believed that if the federal government was to assume responsibility for these bonds, some of them should be returned to the original purchasers. James Madison, now a representative from Virginia, proposed dividing the federally funded bonds between the original purchasers and the speculators. But Hamilton's allies insisted that such a plan was impractical and that the honor of the government required that it pay the bondholders themselves, not the original lenders who had sold their bonds of their own accord. Congress finally passed the funding bill Hamilton wanted.

Debating Hamilton's Program

Hamilton's proposal that the federal government assume the state debts encountered greater difficulty. His opponents argued that if the federal government took over the state debts, the people of states with few debts would have to pay taxes to service the larger debts of other states. Hamilton and his supporters struck a bargain with the Virginians to win passage of the bill.

The deal involved the location of the national capital. The capital had moved from New York City back to Philadelphia in 1790. But the Virginians wanted a new capital near them in the South. Hamilton met with Thomas Jefferson and agreed over dinner to provide northern support for placing the capital in the South in exchange for Virginia's votes for the assumption bill. The bargain called for the construction of a new capital city on the banks of the Potomac River, which divided Virginia and Maryland, on land to be selected by Washington himself. The government would move there by the beginning of the new century.

Location of the Capital

Hamilton argued that creation of a national bank was compatible with the intent of the Constitution, even though the document did not explicitly authorize it. But Madison, Jefferson, Randolph, and others argued that Congress should exercise no powers that the Constitution had not clearly assigned it. Nevertheless, both the House and the Senate finally agreed to Hamilton's bill. Washington displayed some uncertainty about its legality at first, but he finally signed it. The Bank of the United States began operations in 1791, under a charter that granted it the right to continue for twenty years.

Bank of the United States

Once enacted, Hamilton's program had many of the effects he had intended and won the support of influential segments of the population. It quickly restored public credit; the bonds of the United States were soon selling at home and abroad at prices even above their face value. Speculators (among them many members of Congress) reaped large profits as a result. Manufacturers profited from the tariffs, and merchants in the seaports benefited from the new banking system.

Small farmers, who formed the vast majority of the population, complained that they had to bear a disproportionate tax burden. Not only did they have to pay property taxes to their state governments, but they bore the brunt of the excise tax on distilleries that Hamilton had initiated. They also opposed a 1792 tariff, also promoted by Hamilton. Many Americans came to believe that the Federalist program served the interests not of the people but of small, wealthy elites. Partly as a result, an organized political opposition arose.

The Republican Opposition

The Constitution had made no reference to political parties, and the omission was not an oversight. Most of the framers—George Washington in particular—believed that organized parties were dangerous and should be avoided. Disagreement on particular issues was inevitable, but most of the founders believed that such disagreements need not and should not lead to the formation of permanent factions. "The public good is disregarded in the conflicts of rival parties," Madison wrote in *The Federalist Papers*, Number 10, perhaps the most influential of all the essays, "and . . . measures are too often decided, not according to the rules of justice and the rights of the minor party, but by the superior force of an interested and overbearing majority."

Yet, within just a few years after ratification of the Constitution, Madison and others became convinced that Hamilton and his followers had become just such an "interested and overbearing majority." The Hamiltonians, Madison and others agreed, had worked to establish a national network of influence that embodied all the worst features of a party. The Federalists had used their control over appointments and the awarding of government franchises to reward their supporters and win additional allies. They had encouraged the formation of local associations—largely aristocratic in nature—to strengthen their standing in local communities. They were doing many of the same things, their opponents believed, that the corrupt British governments of the early eighteenth century had done.

Establishment of the Federalist Party

Because the Federalists appeared to be creating a menacing and tyrannical structure of power, their opponents believed

Discussion and Activities

Historical Evidence and Argumentation Have students read the section "Enacting the Federalist Program." Ask them to write a short essay identifying the setting, the characters, and the problems that had to be resolved during the debate over Hamilton's financial plan. Have students conclude with a statement of the outcome. **PCE** **WXT** **NAT**

THE JEFFERSONIAN IDYLL American artists in the early nineteenth century were drawn to tranquil rural scenes, symbolic of the Jeffersonian vision of a nation of small, independent farmers. By 1822, when Francis Alexander painted this pastoral landscape of "Ralph Wheelock's Farm," the simple agrarian republic it depicts was already being transformed by rapid economic growth.

Courtesy, National Gallery of Art, Washington

that there was no alternative but to organize a vigorous opposition. The result was the emergence of an alternative political organization, which called itself the Republican Party. (This first "Republican" Party is not an ancestor of the modern Republican Party, which was born in the 1850s.) By the late 1790s, the Republicans were going to even greater lengths than the Federalists to create an apparatus of partisan influence. In every state they formed committees, societies, and caucuses. Republican groups corresponded with one another across state lines. They banded together to influence state and local elections. And they justified their actions by claiming that they and they alone represented the true interests of the nation—that they were fighting to defend the people against a corrupt conspiracy by the Federalists. Just as Hamilton believed that the network of supporters he was creating represented the only legitimate interest group in the nation, so the Republicans believed that their party organization represented the best interests of the people. Neither side was willing to admit that it was acting as a party; neither would concede the right of the other to exist. This institutionalized factionalism is known to scholars as the "first party system."

FORMATION OF THE REPUBLICAN PARTY

From the beginning, the preeminent figures among the Republicans were Thomas Jefferson and James Madison. Indeed, the two men were such intimate collaborators with such similar political philosophies that it is sometimes difficult to distinguish the contributions of one from those of the other. But Jefferson, the more charismatic personality of the two, gradually emerged as the most prominent spokesman for the Republicans. Jefferson considered himself a farmer. (He was, in fact, a substantial planter; but he had spent little time in recent years at his estate in Virginia.) He believed in an agrarian republic, most of whose citizens would be sturdy, independent farmer-citizens tilling their own soil.

Jefferson did not scorn commercial activity; he assumed farmers would market their crops in the national and even international markets. Nor did he oppose industry; he believed the United States should develop some manufacturing capacity. But he was suspicious of large cities, feared urban mobs as "sores upon the body politic," and opposed the development of an advanced industrial economy because it would, he feared, increase the number of propertyless workers packed in cities. In short, Jefferson envisioned a decentralized society, dominated by small property owners engaged largely in agrarian activities.

The difference between the Federalist and Republican social philosophies was visible in, among other things, reactions to the French Revolution. As that revolution grew increasingly radical in the 1790s, with its attacks on organized religion, the overthrow of the monarchy, and eventually the execution of the king and queen, the Federalists expressed horror. But the Republicans generally applauded the democratic, antiaristocratic spirit they believed the French Revolution embodied. Some even imitated the French radicals (the Jacobins) by cutting their hair short, wearing pantaloons, and addressing one another as "Citizen" and "Citizeness."

DIFFERENCES OVER THE FRENCH REVOLUTION

Reasoning Processes

Comparison Have students read the section "The Formation of the Republican Party." Ask them to create a Venn diagram comparing the Federalist and Republican parties. PCE NAT SOC

Discussion and Activities

Analyzing Images Have students examine the image "The Jefferson Idyll." Ask them to look up the definition of "idyll." Ask students to write a brief summary of what the image means, including details from the painting that support its title. *(The painting shows farmers working together in productive fields. Jefferson believed that working the land imbued citizens with patriotic character. Noticeably absent are depictions of any enslaved persons.)* NAT

Historical Thinking Skills

Analyzing Points of View Have students read the section "Securing the Frontier." Ask them to write a journal entry from the point of view of a Pennsylvania farmer explaining their resistance to the Whiskey Excise. **SOC** **WXT** **PCE**

Although both parties had supporters in all parts of the country and among all classes, there were regional and economic differences. The Federalists were most numerous in the commercial centers of the Northeast and in such southern seaports as Charleston; the Republicans were most numerous in the rural areas of the South and the West.

As the 1792 presidential election–the nation's second–approached, both Jefferson and Hamilton urged Washington to run for another term. The president reluctantly agreed. But while most Americans considered Washington above the partisan battle, he was actually much more in sympathy with the Federalists than with the Republicans. And during his presidency, Hamilton remained the dominant figure in government.

ESTABLISHING NATIONAL SOVEREIGNTY

The Federalists consolidated their position–and for a time attracted wide public support for the new national government–by dealing effectively with two problems the old Confederation had been unable fully to resolve. They helped stabilize the nation's western lands, and they strengthened America's international position.

SECURING THE FRONTIER

Despite the Northwest Ordinance, the Confederation Congress had largely failed to tie the outlying western areas of the country firmly to the government. Continued population growth had increased the flow of white settlers westward and fueled political, social, and ethnic tensions. Farmers in western Massachusetts had risen in revolt; settlers in Vermont, Kentucky, and Tennessee had toyed with the idea of separating from the Union. The new government under the Constitution inherited these problems.

In 1794, farmers in western Pennsylvania raised a major challenge to federal authority when they refused to pay a whiskey excise tax and began terrorizing the tax collectors (much as colonists had done at the time of the Stamp Act). But the federal government did not leave settlement of the so-called Whiskey Rebellion to Pennsylvania, as the Confederation Congress had left Shays's Rebellion to Massachusetts. At Hamilton's urging, Washington called out the militias of three states, raised an army of nearly 15,000 (a larger force than he had commanded against the British during most of the Revolution), and personally led the troops into Pennsylvania. As the militiamen approached Pittsburgh, the center of the resistance, the rebellion quickly collapsed.

WHISKEY REBELLION

The federal government won the allegiance of the whiskey rebels by intimidating them. It won the loyalties of other frontier people by accepting their territories as new states in the Union. The last of the original thirteen colonies joined the Union once the Bill of Rights had been appended to the Constitution–North Carolina in 1789 and Rhode Island in 1790. Then Vermont, which had had its own state government since the Revolution, became the fourteenth state in 1791 after New York and New Hampshire finally agreed to give up their claims to it. Next came Kentucky, in 1792, when Virginia gave up its claim to that region. After North Carolina finally ceded its western lands to the Union, Tennessee became first a territory and, in 1796, a state.

NATIVE AMERICANS AND THE NEW NATION

The new government faced a greater challenge, also inherited from the Confederation, in the more distant areas of the Northwest and the Southwest, where Native Americans (occasionally in alliance with the British and Spanish) fought to retain tribal lands that the U.S. government claimed for itself. The ordinances of 1784–1787 had produced a series of border conflicts with Native American nations resisting white settlement in what they considered their lands. Although the United States eventually defeated virtually every Native American challenge (if often at great cost), it was clear that the larger question of who was to control the lands of the West–the United States or the Native American nations–remained unanswered.

These clashes revealed another issue the Constitution had done little to resolve: the place of the Native American nations within the new federal structure. The Constitution barely mentioned Native Americans. Article I excluded "Indians not taxed" from being counted in the population totals that determined the number of seats states would receive in the House of Representatives; and it gave Congress the power to "regulate Commerce with foreign Nations, and among the several States, and with the Indian tribes." Article VI bound the new government to respect treaties negotiated by the Confederation, most of which had been with the tribes. But none of this did much to clarify the precise legal standing of Native Americans or Native American nations within the United States.

NATIVE AMERICANS AND THE CONSTITUTION

On the one hand, the Constitution seemed to recognize the existence of the Native American nations as legal entities. On the other hand, it made clear that they were not "foreign Nations" (in the same sense that European countries were); nor were their members citizens of the United States. The nations received no direct representation in the new government. Above all, the Constitution did not address the major issue that would govern relations between white settlers and Native Americans: land. Native American nations existed within the boundaries of the United States, yet they claimed (and the white government at times agreed) that they had some measure of sovereignty within their own lands. But neither the Constitution nor common law offered any clear guide to the rights of a "nation within a nation" or to the precise nature of tribal sovereignty, which ultimately depended on control of land. To assert its dominance over the western territory of Native Americans, Congress passed the Indian Trade and

Reasoning Processes

Continuity and Change Have students read the section "Securing the Frontier." Ask them to think about how the "frontier" changed from 1607 to 1794. Have students discuss the shifting of the frontier and reasons for the shift. *(Population growth led to westward movement. Defeat of the French in 1763 and British in 1783 had opened more land to settlement.)* **MIG** **PCE** **NAT** **WOR**

Intercourse Act of 1790. This act established boundaries for Native American lands and regulated commerce between settlers and Native Americans. Thus the relationship between the Native American nations and the United States continued to be determined by a series of treaties, agreements, and judicial decisions in a process that has continued for more than 200 years.

MAINTAINING NEUTRALITY

Not until 1791—eight years after the end of the Revolution—did Great Britain send a minister to the United States, and then only because Madison and the Republicans were threatening to place special trade restrictions on British ships. That was one of many symbols of the difficulty the new government had in establishing its legitimacy in the eyes of the British. Another crisis in Anglo-American relations emerged in 1793 when the new French government, created by the Revolution of 1789, went to war with Great Britain and its allies. Both the president and Congress took steps to establish American neutrality in that conflict. But the neutrality quickly encountered severe tests.

CITIZEN GENET

The first challenge to American neutrality came from revolutionary France and its first diplomatic representative to America, the brash and youthful Edmond Genet. Instead of landing at Philadelphia and presenting himself immediately to the president, Genet disembarked at Charleston. There he made plans to use American ports to outfit French warships, encouraged American shipowners to serve as French privateers, and commissioned the aging George Rogers Clark to lead a military expedition against Spanish lands to the south. (Spain was at the time an ally of Great Britain and an enemy of France.) In all of this, Genet was brazenly ignoring Washington's policies and flagrantly violating the Neutrality Act. His conduct infuriated Washington (who provided "Citizen Genet," as he was known, with an icy reception in Philadelphia) and the Federalists; it also embarrassed all but the most ardent admirers of the French Revolution among the Republicans. Washington eventually demanded that the French government recall him, but by then Genet's party was out of power in France. (The president granted him political asylum in the United States, and he settled with his American wife on a Long Island farm.) The neutrality policy had survived its first serious test.

A second and even greater challenge came from Great Britain. Early in 1794, the Royal Navy began seizing hundreds of American ships engaged in trade in the French West Indies, outraging public opinion in the United States. Anti-British feeling rose still higher at the report that the governor general of Canada had delivered a warlike speech to Native Americans on the northwestern frontier encouraging them to challenge U.S. dominance there. Hamilton was deeply concerned. War would mean an end to imports from England, and most of the revenue for maintaining his financial system came from duties on those imports.

JAY'S TREATY AND PINCKNEY'S TREATY

This was, Hamilton believed, no time for ordinary diplomacy. He did not trust the State Department to reach a settlement with Britain. Jefferson had resigned as secretary of state in 1793 to devote more time to his political activities, but his successor, Edmund Randolph, was even more ardently pro-French than Jefferson had been. So Hamilton persuaded Washington to name a special commissioner to England: John Jay, chief justice of the United States Supreme Court and a staunch New York Federalist. Jay was instructed to secure compensation for the recent British assaults on American shipping, to demand withdrawal of British forces from the frontier posts, and to negotiate a new commercial treaty.

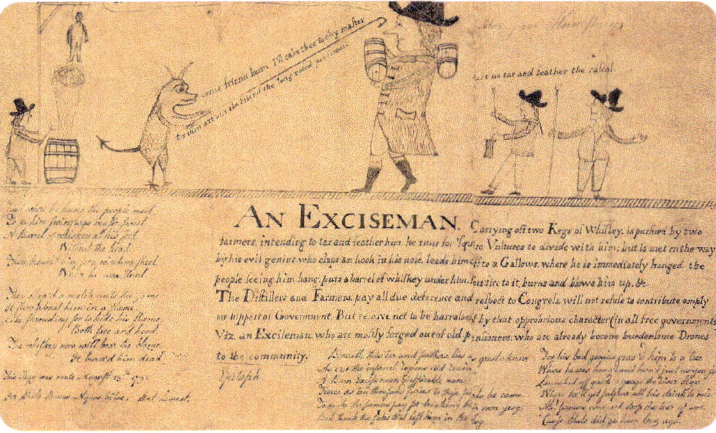

A COMMENT ON THE WHISKEY REBELLION Although Thomas Jefferson and other Republicans claimed to welcome occasional popular uprisings, the Federalists were horrified by such insurgencies as Shays's Rebellion in Massachusetts and, later, the Whiskey Rebellion in Pennsylvania. This Federalist cartoon portrays the rebels as demons who pursue and eventually hang an unfortunate "exciseman" (tax collector), who has confiscated two kegs of rum.

Discussion and Activities

Making Generalizations After students have read the section "Native Americans and the New Nation," ask them to create a list of Constitutional provisions regarding Native Americans. Have students label those provisions as economic, political, legal, or cultural. Discuss how early American leaders thought about Native Americans as evidenced by how Native Americans were treated in the Constitution. *(The Constitution did not clearly define Native Americans legally. Tax-paying Native Americans could be counted for political representation. Congress had the right to regulate trade with Native American nations.)* **PCE** **WOR** **WXT**

Historical Thinking Skills

Analyzing Significance After students have read the section "Maintaining Neutrality," ask them to create a T-chart listing reasons to remain neutral or fight Britain and/or France. Use the chart as the basis for a discussion about what the United States should have done in response to European provocations. **WOR** **PCE**

Reasoning Processes

Comparing Have students read the sections "Jays' Treaty" and "Pinckney's Treaty." Ask them to create a Venn diagram comparing the treaties. Discuss with the class how the treaties reflected America's place in the world and whether they left the United States in a weaker or stronger position relative to France, Spain, and Britain. **WOR** **PCE** **NAT**

The long and complex treaty Jay negotiated in 1794 failed to achieve these goals. But it was not without merit. It settled the conflict with Britain and helped prevent what had seemed likely to become a war between the two nations. It established undisputed American sovereignty over the entire Northwest. And it produced a reasonably satisfactory commercial relationship with Britain, whose trade was important to the United States. Nevertheless, when the terms became public in America, there were bitter public denunciations of it for having failed to extract enough promises from the British. Jay was burned in effigy in various parts of the country. Opponents of the treaty–nearly all the Republicans and even some Federalists, encouraged by agents of France–went to extraordinary lengths to defeat it in the Senate. The American minister to France, James Monroe, and even the secretary of state, Edmund Randolph, joined the desperate attempt to prevent ratification. But in the end the Senate ratified what was by then known as Jay's Treaty.

JAY'S TREATY

Among other things, the treaty made possible a settlement of America's conflict with the Spanish, because it raised fears in Spain that the British and the Americans might now join together to challenge Spanish possessions in North America. When Thomas Pinckney arrived in Spain as a special negotiator, he had no difficulty in gaining nearly everything the United States had sought from the Spaniards for more than a decade. Under Pinckney's Treaty (signed in 1795), Spain recognized the right of Americans to navigate the Mississippi to its mouth and to deposit goods at New Orleans for reloading on oceangoing ships; agreed to fix the northern boundary of Florida where Americans always had insisted it should be, along the 31st parallel; and required Spanish authorities to prevent the Native Americans in Florida from launching raids across the border.

PINCKNEY'S TREATY

MOUNT VERNON George and Martha Washington lavished enormous attention on their home at Mount Vernon, importing materials and workmen from Europe to create a house that they hoped would rival some of the elegant country homes of England. Like many wealthy planters and merchants of their time, they strove to bring refinement and gentility to their lives.

© Paul G. Rocheleau

THE DOWNFALL OF THE FEDERALISTS

The Federalists' impressive triumphs did not ensure their continued dominance in the national government. On the contrary, success seemed to produce problems of its own–problems that led to their downfall.

Since almost all Americans in the 1790s agreed that there was no place in a stable republic for an organized opposition, the emergence of the Republicans as powerful contenders for popular favor seemed to the Federalists a grave threat to national stability. Beginning in the late 1790s, when international perils confronted the government as well, the Federalists could not resist the temptation to move forcefully against the opposition. Facing what they believed was a stark choice between respecting individual liberties and preserving stability, the Federalists chose stability. The result was political disaster. After 1796, the Federalists never won another election. The popular respect for the institutions of the federal government, which they had worked so hard to produce among the people, survived. But the Federalists themselves gradually vanished as an effective political force.

THE ELECTION OF 1796

Despite strong pressure from his many admirers to run for a third term as president, George Washington insisted on retiring from office in 1797. In his Farewell Address to the American people (actually a long letter, composed in part by Hamilton and published in a Philadelphia newsletter), he reacted sharply to the Republicans. His reference to the "insidious wiles of foreign influence" was not just an abstract warning against international entanglements; it was also a specific denunciation of those Republicans who had been conspiring with the French to frustrate the Federalist diplomatic program.

WASHINGTON'S FAREWELL ADDRESS

With Washington out of the running, no obstacle remained to an open expression of the partisan rivalries that had been building over the previous eight years. Jefferson was the uncontested candidate of the Republicans in 1796. The

Discussion and Activities

Analyzing Images Have students examine the image "Mount Vernon." Ask them to consider how the Washington residence either did or did not reflect a new American sense of identity. *(Mount Vernon indicates by its European influences, materials, and craftsmen that George Washington still felt a strong identification with Europe after American independence.)* **NAT**

JOHN ADAMS John Adams's illustrious career as Revolutionary leader, diplomat, and president marked the beginning of four generations of public distinction among members of his family. His son, John Quincy Adams, served as secretary of state and president. His grandson, Charles Francis Adams, was one of the great diplomats of the Civil War era. His great-grandson, Henry Adams, was one of America's most distinguished historians and writers.

Courtesy National Gallery of Art, Washington, D.C.

Federalists faced a more difficult choice. Hamilton, the personification of Federalism, had created too many enemies to be a credible candidate. So Vice President John Adams, who had been directly associated with none of the unpopular Federalist measures, became his party's nominee for president.

The Federalists were still clearly the dominant party, and there was little doubt of their ability to win a majority of the presidential electors. But without Washington to mediate, they fell victim to fierce factional rivalries that almost led to their undoing. Hamilton and many other Federalists (especially in the South) were not reconciled to Adams's candidacy and favored his running mate, Thomas Pinckney, instead. And when, as expected, the Federalists elected a majority of the presidential electors, some of these Pinckney supporters declined to vote for Adams; he managed to defeat Jefferson by only three electoral votes. Because a still-larger number of Adams's supporters declined to vote for Pinckney, Jefferson finished second in the balloting and became vice president. (Until the Twelfth Amendment was adopted in 1804, the Constitution provided for the candidate receiving the second highest number of electoral votes to become vice president—hence the awkward result of men from different parties serving in the nation's two highest elected offices.)

Adams thus assumed the presidency under unhappy circumstances. He presided over a divided party, which faced a strong and resourceful Republican opposition committed to its extinction. Adams was not even the dominant figure in his own party; Hamilton remained the most influential Federalist, and Adams was never able to challenge him effectively. The new president was one of the country's most accomplished and talented diplomats, but he had few skills as a politician. Austere, rigid, aloof, he had little talent at conciliating differences, soliciting support, or inspiring enthusiasm. He was a man of enormous, indeed intimidating, rectitude, and he seemed to assume that his own virtue and the correctness of his positions would be enough to sustain him.

DIVIDED FEDERALISTS

THE QUASI WAR WITH FRANCE

American relations with Great Britain and Spain improved as a result of Jay's and Pinckney's Treaties. But the nation's relations with revolutionary France quickly deteriorated. French vessels captured American ships on the high seas and at times imprisoned the crews. When the South Carolina Federalist Charles Cotesworth Pinckney, brother of Thomas Pinckney, arrived in France, the government refused to receive him as the official representative of the United States.

Some of President Adams's advisers favored war, most notably Secretary of State Thomas Pickering, a stern New Englander who detested France. But Hamilton recommended conciliation, and Adams agreed. In an effort to stabilize relations, Adams appointed a bipartisan commission—consisting of Charles Cotesworth Pinckney, the recently rejected minister; John Marshall, a Virginia Federalist, later chief justice of the Supreme Court; and Elbridge Gerry, a Massachusetts Republican but a friend of the president—to negotiate with France. When the Americans arrived in Paris in 1797, three agents of the French foreign minister, Prince Talleyrand, demanded a loan for France and a bribe for French officials before any negotiations could begin. Pinckney responded: "No! No! Not a sixpence!"

When Adams heard of the incident, he sent a message to Congress denouncing the French insults and urging preparations for war. He then turned the report of the American commissioners over to Congress, after deleting the names of the three French agents and designating them only as "Messrs. X, Y, and Z." When the report was published, it created widespread popular outrage at France's actions and strong support for the Federalists' response. For nearly two years after the "XYZ Affair," as it became known, the United States found itself engaged in an undeclared war with France.

THE XYZ AFFAIR

Adams persuaded Congress to cut off all trade with France and to authorize American vessels to capture French armed ships on the high seas. In 1798, Congress created a Department of the Navy and appropriated money for the construction of new warships. The navy soon won a number of duels with

THE QUASI WAR

Historical Thinking Skills

Contrasting Have students read the section "Divided Federalists." Ask them to create a T-chart listing the positions of the Adams and Hamilton factions within the Federalist Party. Have students identify the main differences, and discuss as a class or in small groups why the Federalists remained a single party despite those differences. **PCE**

Discussion and Activities

Argumentation Have students read the section "The X, Y, Z Affair." Ask them to assume the role of an advisor to President Adams and write a short paragraph recommending a course of action to the president. **WOR** **NAT**

Reasoning Processes

Causation Have students read the section "Alien and Sedition Acts." Ask them to discuss in pairs or small groups the causes and effects of the acts and how the acts had unintended consequences for the Federalists. **PCE**

French vessels and captured eighty-five ships, including armed merchantmen. The United States also began cooperating closely with the British and became an ally of Britain in the war with France.

In the end, France chose to conciliate the United States before the conflict grew. Adams sent another commission to Paris in 1800, and the new French government (headed now by "first consul" Napoleon Bonaparte) agreed to a treaty with the United States that canceled the old agreement of 1778 and established new commercial arrangements. As a result, the "quasi war" came to a reasonably peaceful end.

REPRESSION AND PROTEST

The conflict with France helped the Federalists increase their majorities in Congress in 1798. Armed with this new strength, they began to consider ways to silence the Republican opposition. The result was some of the most controversial legislation in American history: the Alien and Sedition Acts.

ALIEN AND SEDITION ACTS

The Alien Act placed new obstacles in the way of foreigners who wished to become American citizens, and it strengthened the president's hand in dealing with aliens. The Sedition Act allowed the government to prosecute those who engaged in "sedition" against the government. In theory, only libelous or treasonous activities were subject to prosecution; but since such activities were open to widely varying definitions, the law made it possible for the federal government to stifle almost any opposition. The Republicans interpreted the new laws as part of a Federalist campaign to destroy them and fought back.

President Adams signed the new laws but was cautious in implementing them. He did not deport any aliens, and he prevented the government from launching a major crusade against the Republicans. But the legislation had a significant repressive effect nevertheless. The Alien Act helped discourage immigration and encouraged some foreigners already in the country to leave. And the administration made use of the Sedition Act to arrest and convict ten men, most of them Republican newspaper editors whose only crime had been to criticize the Federalists in government.

Republican leaders pinned their hopes for a reversal of the Alien and Sedition Acts on the state legislatures. (The Supreme Court had not yet established its sole right to nullify congressional legislation, and there were many Republican leaders who believed that the states had that power too.) The Republicans laid out a theory for state action in two sets of resolutions in 1798–1799, one written (anonymously) by Jefferson and adopted by the Kentucky legislature and the other drafted by Madison and approved by the Virginia legislature. The Virginia and Kentucky Resolutions, as they were known, used the ideas of John Locke to argue that the federal government had been formed by a "compact" or contract among the states and possessed only certain delegated powers.

VIRGINIA AND KENTUCKY RESOLUTIONS

THE XYZ AFFAIR The sensational "XYZ Affair" of 1798 is the subject of this American political cartoon. The five-headed figure in the center represents the Directory of the French government; he is demanding "money, money, money" from the three diplomats at left who were in Paris representing the United States. The monster at the top right is operating a guillotine—a symbol of the violence and terror of the later stages of the French Revolution.

Discussion and Activities

Analyzing Images Have students examine the image "The X, Y, Z Affair." Ask them to consider how the symbols used in the cartoon suggest the point of view of its author. *(Portraying representatives of the French government as a multi-headed monster, and showing the excesses of the Reign of Terror, suggest that the author was opposed to any settlement with France.)* **WOR**

Whenever the federal government exercised any undelegated powers, its acts were "unauthoritative, void, and of no force." If the parties to the contract, the states, decided that the central government had exceeded those powers, the Kentucky Resolution claimed, they had the right to "nullify" the appropriate laws. (Such claims emerged again in the South in the decades before the Civil War.)

The Republicans did not win wide support for nullification; only Virginia and Kentucky declared the congressional statutes void. The Republicans did, however, succeed in elevating their dispute with the Federalists to the level of a national crisis. By the late 1790s, the entire nation was deeply and bitterly divided politically. State legislatures at times resembled battlegrounds. Even the United States Congress was plagued with violent disagreements. In one celebrated incident in the chamber of the House of Representatives, Matthew Lyon, a Republican from Vermont, responded to an insult from Roger Griswold, a Federalist from Connecticut, by spitting in Griswold's face. Griswold attacked Lyon with his cane. Lyon fought back with a pair of fire tongs, and the two men ended up wrestling on the floor.

The "Revolution" of 1800

These bitter controversies shaped the 1800 presidential election. Adams and Jefferson were again the opposing candidates.

THE ELECTION OF 1800

But the campaign of 1800 was very different from the one preceding it. Indeed, it may have been the ugliest in American history. Adams and Jefferson themselves displayed reasonable dignity, but their supporters showed no such restraint. The Federalists accused Jefferson of being a dangerous radical and his followers of being wild men who, if they came to power, would bring on a reign of terror comparable to that of the French Revolution. The Republicans portrayed Adams as a tyrant conspiring to become king, and they accused the Federalists of plotting to subvert human liberty and impose slavery on the people. There was considerable personal invective as well. For example, it was during this campaign that the story of Jefferson's romantic involvement with an enslaved woman on his plantation was first widely aired. (Recent DNA evidence has proven that the story was true.)

The election was close, and the crucial contest was in New York. There, Aaron Burr had mobilized an organization of Revolutionary War veterans, the Tammany Society, to serve as a Republican political machine. And through Tammany's efforts, the Republicans carried the city by a large majority and, with it, the state. Jefferson was, apparently, elected.

But an unexpected complication soon jeopardized the Republican victory. The Constitution called for each elector to "vote by ballot for two persons." The normal practice was for an elector to cast one vote for his party's presidential candidate and another for the vice presidential candidate. To avoid a tie between Jefferson and Aaron Burr (the Republican vice presidential candidate), the Republicans had intended for one elector to refrain from voting for Burr. But the plan went awry. When the votes were counted, Jefferson and Burr each had 73. No candidate had a majority. According to the Constitution, the House of Representatives had to choose between the two leading candidates when no one had a majority; in this case, that meant deciding between Jefferson and Burr. Each state delegation would cast a single vote.

The new Congress, elected in 1800 with a Republican majority, was not to convene until after the inauguration of the president, so it was the Federalist Congress that had to

The Library of Congress (LC-DIG-ppmsca-31832)

CONGRESSIONAL BRAWLERS This cartoon lampoons a celebrated fight on the floor of the House of Representatives in 1798 between Matthew Lyon, a Republican from Vermont, and Roger Griswold, a Federalist from Connecticut. The conflict began when Griswold insulted Lyon by attacking his military record in the Revolutionary War. Lyon replied by spitting in Griswold's face. Two weeks later, Griswold attacked Lyon with his cane, and Lyon seized a pair of fire tongs and fought back. That later scene is depicted (and ridiculed) here. Other members of Congress are portrayed as enjoying the spectacle. On the wall is a picture titled "Royal Sport," showing animals fighting.

Historical Thinking Skills

Speculating After students have read the section "Virginia and Kentucky Resolutions," ask them to consider how the United States might have been different if the resolutions had gained broader support, and why they think that the resolutions failed to gain wider support. Ask students to summarize their thoughts in a short paragraph. *(Unity would have been harder to maintain, having just emerged from the Revolutionary War, Shays's Rebellion, and the debate over ratification of the Constitution, many Americans were likely reluctant to weaken the central government significantly.)* **NAT** **PCE**

Discussion and Activities

Making Connections Ask students to read the first paragraph of the section "The Election of 1800." Ask them to brainstorm ideas about how the presidential election of 1800 was similar to or different from recent presidential elections. **PCE**

Historical Thinking Skills

Predicting Have students read the section "The Judiciary Act of 1801." Ask them to predict how the Federalists could use control of the courts to prevent Republican domination of the government. *(The courts, in particular the Supreme Court, could use their powers to block implementation of Republican legislation.)* **PCE**

decide the question. Some Federalists hoped to use the situation to salvage the election for their party; others wanted to strike a bargain with Burr and elect him. But after a long deadlock, several leading Federalists, most prominent among them Alexander Hamilton, concluded that Burr (whom many suspected of having engineered the deadlock in the first place) was too unreliable to trust with the presidency. On the thirty-sixth ballot, Jefferson was elected.

After the election of 1800, the only branch of the federal government left in Federalist hands was the judiciary. The Adams administration spent its last months in office taking steps to make the party's hold on the courts secure. By the Judiciary Act of 1801, passed by the lame duck Congress, the Federalists reduced the number of Supreme Court justiceships by one but greatly increased the number of federal judgeships as a whole. Adams quickly appointed Federalists to the newly created positions. Indeed, there were charges that he stayed up until midnight on his last day in office to finish signing the new judges' commissions. These officeholders became known as the "midnight appointments."

THE JUDICIARY ACT OF 1801

Even so, the Republicans viewed their victory, incorrectly, as almost complete. The nation, they believed, had been saved from tyranny. A new era could now begin, one in which the true principles on which America had been founded would once again govern the land. The exuberance with which the victors viewed the future–and the importance they attributed to the Federalists' defeat–was evident in the phrase Jefferson later used to describe his election: the "Revolution of 1800." It remained to be seen how revolutionary it would really be.

AMERICAN IDENTITY AND THE ARTS

The dissolution of political and economic dependence leading up to and culminating with the American Revolution resulted in a cultural bond that united the colonies in a unique way. The eighteenth-century American states were very different from the seventeenth-century British colonies. The diversity and isolationism among the regions in 1650 changed significantly by 1750, and the country evolved into a complex set of national cultural identities. While regional variations continued, particularly between the North and South, a new national culture also began to emerge, in which Americans could see themselves as a culturally united people with a shared historical past. Americans sought ways of representing this past, and the idea of a unique American identity increasingly found expression in architecture, art, and literature.

ARCHITECTURE, ART, AND LITERATURE

The Founding Fathers were explicit about their belief in the importance of their inheritance from the classical world. Not only would they often pen writings with names which were an homage to classical writers, but they modeled Greek and Roman architectural styles. The Federal style of neoclassical architecture, emulated by Thomas Jefferson in the construction of the University of Virginia, flourished during the time period as a reflection of Greek and Roman ideals. Architects Charles Bulfinch and Benjamin Latrobe also drew on neoclassical ideals and architectural styles to create future government buildings.

ARCHITECTURE

American artists often faced great challenges. With no art schools in America, artists had to travel to Europe to study or to teach themselves, which was more common. Artists also needed patrons to be successful, and most Americans did not have the means to support the arts. The lack of interest in the arts by the Church, particularly by Puritans, limited large-scale purchases. But American artists like Benjamin West would eventually find success. Largely self-taught, he spent his entire artistic career in England and is known for his historical scenes, including *The Death of General Wolfe*. This painting aptly displays the Greek and Roman ideas of civic virtue and the sacrifice of the individual for the good of the community. West's art also focused on the competing intellectual and religious forces of Puritanism and the Enlightenment–religion versus science. But instead of seeing the two forces as being at odds with each other, West saw how they could achieve positive results when they complemented each other instead.

ART

Other artists, such as John Singleton Copley, sought to capture the American ideal. He focused much of his work on portraits, including a depiction of Paul Revere as a silversmith. The imagery of Revere as a common man, despite his prosperity, was a nod to the working people who supported the American Revolution. Painter Gilbert Stuart chose to symbolize a different aspect of the American Revolution. His life-size *Lansdowne Portrait of George Washington* in a civilian suit served as a powerful reminder that America was a country founded on political democracy, not military power.

Like visual artists of the time, writers were developing a unique American perspective. The Philadelphia author Charles Brockden Brown was one of the first important writers to develop a unique American voice. Brown's novels were among the first to situate tales inside an American geographic area and explore the Gothic dangers that influenced later American writers. Brown's first published novel, *Wieland*, explored the inherent tensions between the religious tradition of the Puritans, represented by the First Great Awakening, and those of the Enlightenment. Much like the political arguments during the founding era, Brown's literary voice looked to the classical past for both intellectual and moral guidance. This didactic element of his literature, along with the specific American elements, helped propel the idea that the founding of America represented something universal and unique, which helped create the early elements of an American identity.

LITERATURE

Discussion and Activities

Evaluating Evidence Have students read the section "Architecture, Art, and Literature." Ask them to construct a three-column chart listing achievements in each area. Have them use the chart to discuss in which area they believe Americans had the greatest impact. **SOC** **NAT**

CHAPTER 6 REVIEW

CONNECTING THEMES

Chapter Six explored the political, economic, and social consequences of the American Revolution. The country was deeply divided over the war but even more so over the issues that would confront it in the years that followed. This division led to the development of the first formal political parties in the country. The Federalists and the Democratic-Republicans had divergent views on how powerful the national government should be, along with differences on a variety of issues facing the new nation. The American Revolution had also spurred increased westward migration that ultimately led to new confrontations with Native Americans and challenges in foreign relations.

At the same time, a national culture and identity developed on the heels of the revolution, despite the persistence of regional differences. Washington's Farewell Address acknowledged the divisions and urged citizens to view themselves as a cohesive group. He also warned the nation of two major dangers: domestic political factions and entangling foreign alliances. This advice drove much of the economic and political debate for the next generation and beyond—even to present day.

You should consider the following questions as you review the themes for this chapter:

- What were the factors that encouraged western migration, and what were the consequences of that migration?
- How did political parties in the United States develop, and in what ways did their beliefs differ?
- How did American trade policy, policies of neutrality, and westward expansion lead to conflict with a variety of European countries?
- How did Enlightenment ideas and the belief in republican principles of self-government manifest themselves during and after the writing of the Constitution?
- How did the social and political consequences of the American Revolution lead to new forms of national culture and influence national identity?

KEY TERMS

Alexander Hamilton 169
Alien and Sedition Acts 184
Antifederalists 175
Bill of Rights 176
Checks and Balances 173
Citizen Genet Affair 181
Federalists 175
Federal structure (federalism) 173
French Revolution 179
Great Compromise 171
Hamilton's Financial Plan 177
James Madison 169
Jay's Treaty 181
John Adams 183
Judiciary Act of 1801 186
Neutrality Act 181
New Jersey Plan 170
Pinckney's Treaty 181
Quasi War 183
Republicans 176
Revolution of 1800 186
Separation of Powers 173
Sovereignty 173
The Federalist Papers 175
Virginia And Kentucky Resolutions 184
Virginia Plan 170
Washington's Farewell Address 182
Weaknesses in the Articles of Confederation 172
Whiskey Rebellion 180
XYZ Affair 183

Discussion and Activities

Comparing and Contrasting Have students review the section "Connecting Themes." Ask students to make a Venn diagram comparing and contrasting the Federalist and Democratic Republican political parties. Discuss as a class how the differences between those political parties are similar to or different from current political parties. **PCE** **SOC** **NAT**

Key Terms

Students should be familiar with the key terms and be able to define them in the context of the political, economic, and social effects of the Revolutionary War. Encourage students to use these terms in performing review exercises and exam practice for this chapter.

Go Online Chapter 6 Content Review

Assessing Student Understanding Use the online assessment to assess student understanding of concepts and topics within the chapter. You can assign the ready-made Chapter 6 Content Review or create your own from available questions. This easy-to-use tool helps you design assessments that meet the needs of different types of learners.

Answers

Multiple Choice

1. C; **2.** A; **3.** A

Short Answer

4A) One point of view about ratification is that the Founding Fathers were heroic figures. George Washington is standing with a very confident and proud posture. The windows are open and the figures are all represented in grand style, which was typical of the Neoclassical period, used to promote classical images of contemporary figures.

4B) The government established under the Articles of Confederation was weak and limited. It had no power to collect taxes, nor did it have the power to regulate trade.

4C) The government established under the new U.S. Constitution was much stronger than the one created under the Articles of Confederation. However, there were still questions and issues that were still unresolved (e.g., Did the new Constitution authorize the creation of a national bank?).

5A) Many of the Federalists supported the creation of a strong central executive office, whereas the Antifederalists were leery of the executive branch and believed that the office the Federalists were creating was going to take the place of a monarch in the new country.

5B) Both the Federalists and the Antifederalists wanted to replace the Articles of Confederation. Both groups agreed that the government under the Articles was too weak and was unable to handle many of the challenges of the new country.

5C) The vigorous debate between the Federalists and Antifederalists led to the passage of the first ten amendments to the U.S. Constitution, which are collectively known as the Bill of Rights.

AP EXAM PRACTICE

Questions assume cumulative content knowledge from this chapter and previous chapters.

MULTIPLE CHOICE

Use the image on page 167 and your knowledge of U.S. history to answer questions 1-3.

1. George Washington was a revered figure in the early Republic after first gaining fame during the Revolutionary War as
   (A) the president of the Continental Congress.
   (B) the governor of Virginia.
   (C) the general of the Continental Army.
   (D) the chief diplomat in Europe.

2. Images like Kemmelmeyer's painting demonstrate the attempts during the early Republic to create
   (A) a new national identity.
   (B) political party unity.
   (C) unity among geographical regions.
   (D) opposition to slavery.

3. One key challenge that Washington faced in his second term was
   (A) the escalating war between England and France.
   (B) the failure to build a national financial plan.
   (C) the lack of a written Constitution.
   (D) the inability to attract talented political leaders into public service.

SHORT ANSWER

Use your knowledge of U.S. history to answer questions 4 and 5.

4. Use the image on page 171 to answer A, B, and C.
   (A) Briefly describe ONE point of view about the ratification of the Constitution as depicted in the painting.
   (B) Briefly explain ONE specific historical cause that led to the calling of ratification conventions.
   (C) Briefly explain ONE specific historical effect that resulted from the calling of ratification conventions.

5. Answer A, B, and C.
   (A) Briefly describe ONE specific historical difference between the Federalists and the Antifederalists during the ratification debates.
   (B) Briefly describe ONE specific historical similarity between the Federalists and the Antifederalists during the ratification debates.
   (C) Explain ONE specific historical effect of the ratification of the U.S. Constitution.

LONG ESSAY

Develop a thoughtful and thorough historical argument that addresses the statement below. Begin your essay with a thesis statement, and support it with specific historical evidence and examples.

6. Evaluate the extent of changes in American politics from 1776 to 1800.

Answers

Long Essay

6. Possible thesis: The ratification of the Constitution and the peaceful transition of power between political parties were significant political changes in the country. However, the country continued to be politically divided over several issues, including war with Britain, ratification of the Constitution, and federalism. Therefore, despite some changes, there were also many political continuities from 1776 to 1800. Specific historical evidence: The country was divided over political issues. Beginning in 1776, there was division over whether the country should declare independence from the British. The Patriots and Loyalists were divided over this political question. In 1787 the new country was divided between Federalists or Antifederalists. Although not an exact alignment, this division evolved into new permanent political parties. This division within the political sphere continued under Washington's first term of office as Hamiltonians and Jeffersonians were divided over many political issues. Changes: The first political change occurred in 1787 when a group of individuals met in Philadelphia in support of adopting a new Constitution. The Articles of Confederation were sufficient during the American Revolution, but they were not adequate to handle this new political power that resulted from the American Revolution. A second change occurred in 1800, when the peaceful transfer of political power occurred as outgoing Federalist president Adams yielded to the incoming Democratic-Republican president Jefferson. This was a cause of great concern because in Europe the transition of political parties was often not peaceful and usually resulted in warfare.

UNIT 3 AP EXAM PRACTICE

AP EXAM PRACTICE

As you answer the questions, consider how the historical developments, processes, and individuals in Unit 3 connect to those in previous units.

MULTIPLE CHOICE

Use the image on page 110 and your knowledge of U.S. history to answer questions 1-3.

1. Franklin's appeal for unity was initially necessary in 1754 as the colonies were threatened by
   (A) British actions to subdue Patriot leaders.
   (B) French aggression toward British colonies.
   (C) Native American alliances with the British.
   (D) Spanish alliances with the British.

2. The argument made by the image remained important during the American Revolution as
   (A) Franklin sought French aid against the British.
   (B) Patriots sought the support of enslaved Americans.
   (C) many colonists remained loyal to the British crown.
   (D) a significant number of colonists fled to Canada to avoid the war.

3. Why was intercolonial unity challenged after the Revolution?
   (A) The British aggressively sought to overthrow the new American government.
   (B) Southern colonies objected to the Constitution's ban on slavery.
   (C) Americans objected to the imposition of high tariffs under the Articles of Confederation.
   (D) Revolutionary rhetoric highlighted inequities in American life.

Use the image on page 125 and your knowledge of U.S. history to answer questions 4 and 5.

4. Images like the one depicting the Boston Massacre were effective in impacting colonial public opinion because
   (A) they accurately represented events in distant locations.
   (B) the colonists were almost universally united behind the Patriot cause.
   (C) the colonies had a highly developed print culture and were unified by newspapers and pamphlets.
   (D) the colonists had a long tradition of tolerating violence by British soldiers.

5. Revere's image reinforces the important role played by which group in support of the Patriot cause?
   (A) yeoman farmers
   (B) French aristocrats
   (C) urban artisans
   (D) enslaved laborers

Use the excerpt and your knowledge of U.S. history to answer questions 6-8.

". . . and by the way in the new Code of Laws which I suppose it will be necessary for you to make I desire you would Remember the Ladies, and be more generous and favourable to them than your ancestors. Do not put such unlimited power into the hands of the Husbands. Remember all Men would be tyrants if they could. If perticuliar care and attention is not paid to the Laidies we are determined to foment a Rebelion, and will not hold ourselves bound by any Laws in which we have no voice, or Representation."

–Letter from Abigail Adams to John Adams, March 31, 1776

6. Abigail Adams's appeal to her husband was deeply rooted in the Patriot argument for
   (A) representation based on the consent of the governed.
   (B) the elimination of traditional gender norms.
   (C) the importance of foreign alliances.
   (D) the goal of expanding colonial territory.

7. Women's support of the Patriot cause found direction into the concept of Republican Motherhood, which encouraged women to
   (A) reeducate the children of Loyalists after the Revolution.
   (B) advocate for the overhaul of public education systems.
   (C) establish community child-care centers to enable women to take paid employment.
   (D) raise their children to embrace republican values and civic virtue.

UNIT 3
AP Exam Practice

Discussion and Activities

Analyzing Cause and Effect Direct students' attention to the Questions to Consider posed at the beginning of Unit 3:

- What were the major causes that led to the independence movement in the North American colonies?
- What were the major factors that led to the ratification of the U.S. Constitution?
- What were the major domestic and foreign challenges the newly independent country faced?

Discuss these questions as a class to review important concepts from the unit. To close the discussion, **ask:** How was the new United States similar to or different from the original vision of the English settlers?

Answers

Multiple Choice

1. B; **2.** C; **3.** D; **4.** C; **5.** C; **6.** A; **7.** D; **8.** B; **9.** A; **10.** D

Answers

Short Answer

11A) The point of view of the artist was one of support for the Patriot cause.

11B) Students may indicate that colonists were angry over what they perceived as unfair taxes or were upset over the occupation by British troops.

11C) The massacre increased support for the Patriots by colonists who were already frustrated with British rule and swayed others to support the cause. It further strained the relationship between the colonies and Great Britain.

8. President John Adams faced significant conflict at home over which issue?
   (A) the emergence of an abolitionist movement
   (B) accelerating conflict with the French
   (C) the importance of alliances with Native American nations
   (D) the imposition of a high protective tariff

Use the Land Survey graphic on page 162 and your knowledge of U.S. history to answer questions 9 and 10.

9. The Land Ordinance of 1785 eased one post-war source of conflict in creating
   (A) an orderly structure to facilitate westward expansion.
   (B) a framework for the abolition of slavery in the east.
   (C) a system for expanding the land holdings of the original states.
   (D) a plan for allowing the shared administration of French lands.

10. Population movement following the Revolution facilitated
    (A) the near total disintegration of existing gender norms.
    (B) increasing integrations of Native Americans into American citizenship.
    (C) rapid expansion of existing railroad lines.
    (D) the development of new regional variations of American culture.

SHORT ANSWER

Use the image on page 125 and your knowledge of U.S. history to answer question 11.

11. Answer A, B, and C.
    (A) Briefly describe the artist's point of view about American colonists in 1770 as depicted in the image *The Boston Massacre.*
    (B) Briefly explain ONE specific historical cause which led to the event depicted in the image *The Boston Massacre.*
    (C) Briefly explain ONE specific effect which resulted from the event depicted in the image *The Boston Massacre.*

LONG ESSAY

Develop a thoughtful and thorough historical argument that addresses the statement below. Begin your essay with a thesis statement, and support it with specific historical evidence and examples.

12. Evaluate the extent of continuities involved in developing a unique American culture from 1754 to 1800.

Answers

Long Essay

12. Possible thesis: The colonies continued to exist for different economic reasons, and the regions continue to reflect those differences. The North and the South developed as distinct entities. However, by the end of the eighteenth century, the changes in the colonies outweighed the continuities. The population growth forced more interaction with each other; this exposed them to commonalities with each other. As population growth pushed the colonies together, they also came to view themselves as a single unit with shared values and a common historical past. Continuities: The colonies founded during the early part of the seventeenth century were established for different reasons, by different types of individuals, and survived using different means. The North primarily relied on trade, fishing, shipbuilding, and subsistence farming, while the South relied on large-scale agriculture, along with trade and subsistence farming. Slavery existed primarily in the South. Changes: In the colonies, changes were also taking place. The reasons for immigration now centered mostly around economic opportunities, and what had started as religious communities grew during the eighteenth century to become prosperous commercial cities. The need for the British to offset the expensive costs of war forced them to turn to the colonies for economic revenue, which resulted in violent protests and led to the beginning of an independent movement within the American colonies.

Pacing Guide

Unit 4 explores key concepts from Period 4: 1800–1848 of the AP U.S. History Curriculum Framework. It is recommended that 10–17% of the total instruction time for the entire course be spent on Period 4.

Key Concepts

4.1 The United States began to develop a modern democracy and celebrated a new national culture, while Americans sought to define the nation's democratic ideals and change their society and institutions to match them.

4.2 Innovations in technology, agriculture, and commerce powerfully accelerated the American economy, precipitating profound changes to U.S. society and to national and regional identities.

4.3 The U.S. interest in increasing foreign trade and expanding its national borders shaped the nation's foreign policy and spurred government and private initiatives.

UNIT 4: 1800–1848

THEMATIC LEARNING OBJECTIVES

- Analyze the reasons for the push to expand democracy in the United States beginning in the 1820s.
- Compare and contrast the First and Second Party Systems that emerged in the United States during the first half of the nineteenth century.
- Assess the causes and effects of industrialization and the factory system during the first half of the nineteenth century.
- Evaluate the success of the reform movements that emerged in the United States during the first half of the nineteenth century.
- Analyze how economic development influenced trade, migration, and settlement patterns during the first half of the nineteenth century.
- Describe the causes of distinct regional differences in the United States during the first half of the nineteenth century.
- Explain the significance of the First American Renaissance.

QUESTIONS TO CONSIDER

- What were the major reasons for the emergence of official political parties in the United States during the first half of the nineteenth century?
- What were the major foreign policy challenges faced by the United States during the first half of the nineteenth century?
- What were the major factors that caused differences to grow among the different geographic regions in the United States during the first half of the nineteenth century?

HISTORICAL DEVELOPMENTS: 1800–1848

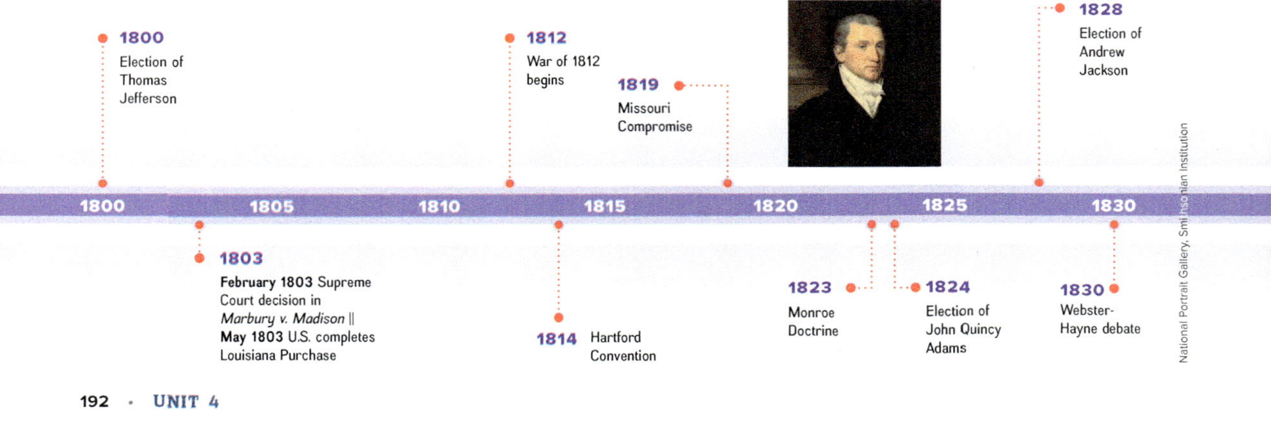

Discussion and Activities

Predicting Have students examine the timeline "Historical Developments: 1800–1848." Ask: Based on the timeline and what you already know, which events on the timeline seem to indicate growing national unity, and which events seem to indicate growing national division? *(Unity: Missouri Compromise, Compromise Tariff; division: Webster-Hayne Debate, Turner Rebellion, Garrison Calls for Disunion.)*

MAKING CONNECTIONS

Unit Four focuses on the development of the two-party political system that formed in the United States during the first half of the nineteenth century. The unit also examines the rise of the First Industrial Revolution and the resultant Market Revolution, the emergence of a number of reform movements spawned by the Second Great Awakening, and the continued rift dividing the country along geographic lines over the institution of slavery.

In the election of 1800, the United States witnessed the peaceful transition of power between political parties—something virtually unheard of in Europe. The First Party System arose out of competing visions for the country, beginning with the debate over whether the country ought to declare independence at the outset of the American Revolution and continuing through deliberation over ratification of the Constitution in 1787. During George Washington's second term, two competing ideologies emerged, championed by the supporters of Alexander Hamilton and Thomas Jefferson. The main center of dispute was how to interpret the newly adopted and ratified Constitution. Hamiltonians viewed the document as a loose set of principles with broad powers granted to the federal government. By contrast, Jeffersonians viewed the document as a strict set of principles, with limited powers granted to the federal government. These philosophical and ideological debates spilled over into practical measures, including legalization of a national bank, neutrality during the French Revolution, and federal protective tariffs.

Political challenges were not the only factors shaping the new nation. The country was also going through a number of economic transformations. Americans were slowly moving out of rural areas and migrating into urban pockets. The steady stream of European immigration, mostly from Ireland and Germany, led to huge jumps in population in urban centers and continued westward expansion. These immigrants came in pursuit of economic opportunities spurred by the beginnings of the First Industrial Revolution that was beginning to transform the economic, social, physical, and cultural landscapes of the United States.

As the nation developed, the divide between the different geographic regions grew larger. The North cultivated industry, the West relied on agriculture, and the South continued to depend on cash crops. But these economic activities also bound the distinct regions together. The Northern economy relied heavily on Southern cotton, and both regions depended on foodstuffs from the western territories. The institution of slavery was concentrated in the South, where it shaped the culture and fueled a growing sectionalism that eventually led to the Civil War in the 1860s. But slavery also played a major role in the North, where the banking industry funded slaveholders, insurance companies issued policies on enslaved people to slaveholders, and textile mills depended on Southern cotton. In addition, Northern shipping companies transported millions of bales of cotton across the Atlantic to English textile mills, thus making American slavery an international issue as well as a national one.

Americans not only wanted to assert their political independence from Britain but also their cultural independence following the American Revolution. In the first half of the nineteenth century, Americans sought to differentiate themselves from Europe in literature, art, and music. Writers sought to create an American identity by exploring the dark side of human nature and the existential quest to find meaning in the world. At the same time, artists of the Hudson River School joined the European celebration of Romanticism, which helped inspire Transcendentalism, the first unique American intellectual movement. Leading figures like Ralph Waldo Emerson and Henry David Thoreau urged Americans to "transcend" the limits imposed by logic and the senses.

Despite intense racism and prejudice, both free and enslaved African Americans created a unique culture through religion, music, art, and language, which made their harsh living conditions more tolerable. The abolitionist movement, though riven with internal divisions, grew more influential in American society. This movement, along with economic panics that left the South largely untouched, accelerated the trend in regionalism. The rise of the belief of many Southerners that "Cotton was King!" provided a false sense of security and superiority that further contributed to future conflict.

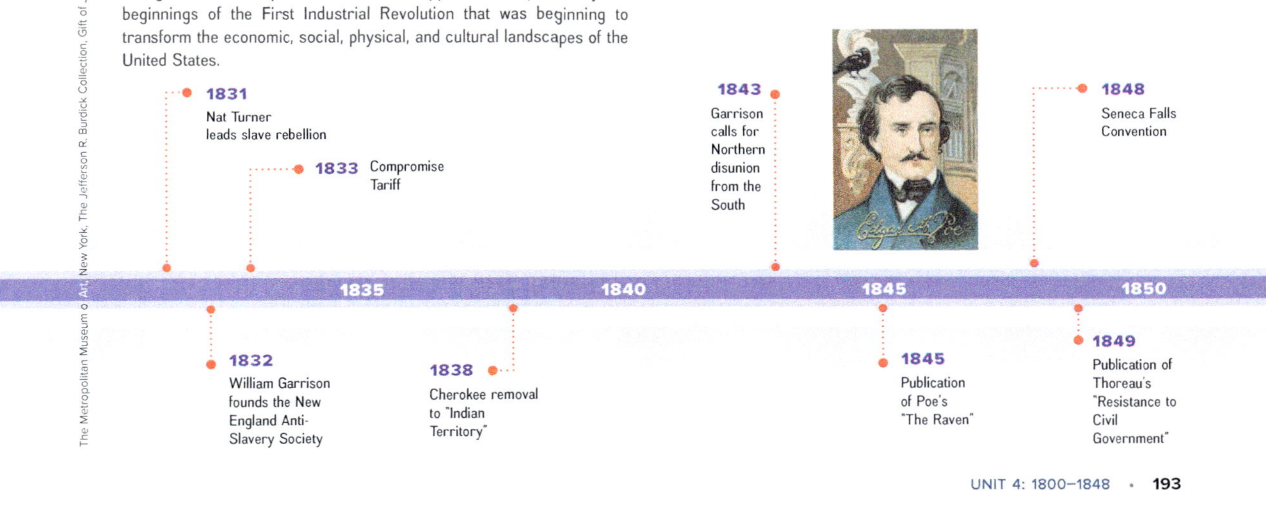

The Metropolitan Museum of Art, New York, The Jefferson R. Burdick Collection, Gift of Jefferson R. Burdick

Historical Thinking Skills

Developments and Processes Have students read the section "Making Connections." Ask them to create a T-chart with the headings "Unity" and "Division." Have students list examples of each from the section. Then ask students to identify which examples are political, economic, geographic, and cultural. **Ask:** Which seem to be more prevalent?

Go Online Additional Resources

Adaptive Learning with SmartBook A proven adaptive learning program, SmartBook offers an interactive environment that helps students learn faster, study more efficiently, and retain more knowledge.

Assign this resource to differentiate instruction for students and report on year-long progression.

Pacing Guide

Chapter 7 explores key concepts from Period 4: 1800–1848 of the AP U.S. History Curriculum Framework. The suggested instruction time for Chapter 7 is 3 days.

Key Concepts

4.1.I The nation's transition to a more participatory democracy was achieved by expanding suffrage from a system based on property ownership to one based on voting by all adult white men, and it was accompanied by the growth of political parties.

4.1.II While Americans embraced a new national culture, various groups developed distinctive cultures of their own.

7 THE JEFFERSONIAN ERA

THE BURNING OF WASHINGTON
This dramatic engraving somewhat exaggerates the extent of the blazes in Washington when the British occupied the city in August 1814. But the invaders did set fire to the Capitol, the White House, and other public buildings in retaliation for the American burning and looting of the Canadian capital at York.

CONNECTING CONCEPTS

Chapter Seven begins by exploring how educational opportunities gradually expanded in the early nineteenth century, though primarily for affluent white men and some women. Medical schools placed a greater emphasis on the scientific method and narrowed opportunities for midwives. In the arts, cultural nationalism flourished as Noah Webster produced his American dictionary and Washington Irving published popular fables about the new nation. In religion, a wave of revivalism known as the Second Great Awakening swept the country. It promoted the idea that a pious individual could affect their own destiny and earn God's grace through active faith and good works. Women flocked to the movement in large numbers in part because of their changing roles in society.

The United States also took the first tentative steps toward industrialization and urbanization. Immigrants often imported technologies from Europe, but Massachusetts-born Eli Whitney revolutionized cotton production with the cotton gin and weapons production with the innovative use of interchangeable parts. Transportation developments like the steamboat and turnpike made it easier to transport raw materials to factories and finished goods to markets. Growing cities like Philadelphia and New York were becoming major centers of commerce and learning.

As president, Thomas Jefferson oversaw the construction of the new capital city, abolished internal taxes, and reduced the armed forces. He also confronted the Barbary pirates, doubled the size of the new nation by negotiating the Louisiana Purchase with France, and authorized the Lewis and Clark expedition. Jefferson could not, however, prevent Chief Justice John Marshall from enhancing the power of the Supreme Court by establishing the principle of judicial review in the case of *Marbury v. Madison*. Then renewed conflict with Great Britain on the high seas and with Native Americans in North America led to the controversial and ambiguous War of 1812. During the conflict, British troops burned down Washington, and New England threatened to secede in the name of states' rights at the Hartford Convention. But Francis Scott Key's composition of "The Star-Spangled Banner" and Andrew Jackson's victory in the Battle of New Orleans stimulated a postwar rise in American nationalism.

Discussion and Activities

Analyzing Visuals Have students examine the image "The Burning of Washington." Ask them to list details from the image. Have students then discuss whose point of view the image presents based on the details they describe. *(Likely a British point of view as British flags can be seen, but not American. Also the destruction portrayed seems to support celebration of a British success.)* **WOR**

As you read, you should:

- Analyze the continuing debate over the power of the national government versus states' rights.
- Compare and contrast the economic, political, and social systems of the North, the South, and the West.
- Describe the causes and effects of the Second Great Awakening.
- Identify the major causes of the War of 1812.
- Evaluate the advances in technology that gave rise to the First Industrial Revolution.
- Analyze the effects of the First Industrial Revolution.
- Identify the ways that new transportation allowed for greater access to natural resources, markets, and western lands.
- Describe the ways that the United States dominated the North American continent by military, diplomatic, and demographic means.

THE RISE OF CULTURAL NATIONALISM

In many respects, American cultural life in the early nineteenth century seemed to reflect the Republican vision of the nation's future. Opportunities for education increased; the nation's literary and artistic life began to free itself from European influences; and American religion began to confront and adjust to the spread of Enlightenment rationalism. In other respects, however, the new culture was posing a serious challenge to Republican ideals.

Patterns of Education

Importance of a Virtuous Citizenry

Central to the Republican vision of America was the concept of a virtuous and enlightened citizenry. Jefferson himself called emphatically for a national "crusade against ignorance." Republicans believed, therefore, in the establishment of a nationwide system of public schools to create the educated electorate they believed a republic required. All white male citizens (the nation's prospective voters) should, they argued, receive free education.

Some states endorsed the principle of public education for all in the early years of the republic, but none actually created a working system of free schools. A Massachusetts law of 1789 reaffirmed the colonial laws by which each town was obligated to support a school, but there was little enforcement. In Virginia, the state legislature ignored Jefferson's call for universal elementary education and for advanced education for the gifted. As late as 1815, not a single state had a comprehensive public school system.

Private Schooling

Instead, schooling became primarily the responsibility of private institutions, most of which were open only to those who could afford to pay for them. In the South and in the mid-Atlantic states, religious groups ran most of the schools. In New England and elsewhere, private academies were usually secular, many of them modeled on schools founded by the Phillips family at Andover, Massachusetts, in 1778, and at Exeter, New Hampshire, three years later. By 1815, there were thirty such private secondary schools in Massachusetts, thirty-seven in New York, and several dozen more scattered throughout the country. Many were frankly

A SEMINARY FOR WOMEN Educational opportunities for women were scarce in the early nineteenth century, but by the 1820s a number of seminaries were created for young ladies, mostly affluent students. The watercolor on silk is by an unknown artist and portrays two women studying geography.

Discussion and Activities

Making Connections Have students read the section "Importance of a Virtuous Citizenry." Ask them to consider why states promoted public schools. Then have students write a short paragraph explaining how those motives are similar or different from current rationales for public education. **SOC**

Go Online AP Exam Preparation

AP Exam Practice Use the online assessment to help prepare students for the AP Exam. You can assign the ready-made AP-style short answer questions, document-based questions, and multiple-choice questions assessing concepts, themes, and skills from Period 4 and AP-style long-essay questions organized in sets of 3 questions from various time periods. You can also create your own tests from available questions. This easy-to-use tool helps you design assessments that meet the needs of different types of learners.

Reasoning Processes

Comparing After students have read the section "Patterns of Education," ask them to construct a Venn diagram comparing educational opportunities for women and Native Americans. **SOC**

aristocratic in outlook, training their students to become members of the nation's elite. There were a few schools open to the poor offering education that was clearly inferior to that provided at exclusive schools.

Private secondary schools such as those in New England, and even many public schools, accepted only male students. Yet the early nineteenth century did see some important advances in female education.

In the eighteenth century, women received very little education of any kind, and the female illiteracy rate at the time of the Revolution was very high—at least 50 percent. At the same time, however, Americans had begun to place a new value on the contribution of the "republican mother" to the training of the new generation. That raised an important question: If mothers remained ignorant, how could they raise their children to be enlightened? Beginning as early as the 1770s and accelerating thereafter, such concerns led to the creation of a network of female academies throughout the nation (usually for the daughters of affluent families). In 1789, Massachusetts required that its public schools serve females as well as males. Other states, although not all, soon followed.

NEW EDUCATIONAL OPPORTUNITIES FOR WOMEN

Most white men, at least, assumed that female education should serve only to make women better wives and mothers. Women therefore had no need for advanced or professional training; there was no reason for colleges and universities to make space for female students. Some women, however, aspired to more. In 1784, Judith Sargent Murray published an essay defending women's rights to education, a defense set in terms very different from those used by most men. Men and women were equal in intellect and potential, Murray argued. Women, therefore, should have precisely the same educational opportunities as men. Moreover, they should have opportunities to earn their own living, to establish a role for themselves in society apart from their husbands and families. Murray's ideas became an inspiration to later generations of women, but during most of her own lifetime (1751–1820) they attracted little support.

Reformers who believed in the power of education to reform and redeem ignorant and "backward" people spurred a growing interest in Native American education. Because Jefferson and his followers liked to think of Native Americans as "noble savages" (uncivilized but, unlike their view of African Americans, not necessarily innately inferior), they hoped that schooling in white culture would tame and "uplift" Native Americans. Although white governments did little to promote Native American education, missionaries and mission schools proliferated among the tribes.

NATIVE AMERICAN EDUCATION

Almost no white people in the early nineteenth century believed that there was a need to educate African Americans, almost all of whom were still enslaved. In a few northern states, some free black children attended segregated schools. In the South, slaveholders generally tried to prevent enslaved people from learning to read or write, fearful that knowledge would make them unhappy with their condition. Some African Americans managed to acquire some education despite these obstacles, by teaching themselves and their own children. But the numbers of literate enslaved people remained very small.

Higher education was much less widely available than education at lower levels, despite Republican hopes for a wide dispersion of advanced knowledge. (Jefferson founded the University of Virginia to promote that ideal.) The number of colleges and universities in America grew from nine at the start of the Revolution to twenty-two by 1800 and continued to increase thereafter. None of the new schools, however, was truly public. Even those established by state legislatures (in Georgia, North Carolina, Vermont, Ohio, and South Carolina, for example) relied on private contributions and on tuition fees. Scarcely more than one white man in a thousand (and no women, African Americans, or Native Americans) had access to college education, and those few who did attend universities were almost without exception members of prosperous, propertied families.

HIGHER EDUCATION

The education that the colleges provided was exceedingly limited—narrow training in the classics and a few other areas and intensive work in theology. Indeed, the clergy was the only profession for which college training was generally a prerequisite. A few institutions attempted to provide their students advanced education in other fields. The College of William and Mary in Virginia, the University of Pennsylvania, and Columbia College in New York all created law schools before 1800, but most lawyers continued to train for their profession simply by apprenticing themselves to practicing attorneys.

MEDICINE AND SCIENCE

The University of Pennsylvania created the first American medical school in the eighteenth century. In the early nineteenth century, however, most doctors studied medicine by working with an established practitioner. Some American physicians believed in applying new scientific methods to medicine and struggled against age-old prejudices and superstitions. Efforts to teach anatomy, for example, encountered strong public hostility because of the dissection of cadavers that the study required. Municipal authorities had no understanding of medical science and almost no idea of what to do in the face of the severe epidemics that so often swept their populations; only slowly did they respond to the warnings of, among others, Benjamin Rush, a pioneering Philadelphia physician, that lack of adequate sanitation programs was to blame for disease.

Individual patients often had more to fear from their doctors than from their illnesses. Even the leading advocates of scientific medicine often embraced useless and dangerous treatments. Benjamin Rush, for example, was an advocate of the new and supposedly scientific techniques of bleeding and purging, and many of his patients died. George Washington's death in 1799 was probably less a result of the minor throat

BENJAMIN RUSH

Discussion and Activities

Making Connections Have students read the section "Higher Education." Ask them to list reasons why students today consider going to college and then ask them to compare these reasons with students in the late eighteenth century. **SOC**

THE PENNSYLVANIA HOSPITAL The ideas of the Enlightenment spread through American culture in the eighteenth and nineteenth centuries and strengthened the belief that every individual was a divine being and could be redeemed from even the most miserable condition. Hospitals and asylums—such as this institution in Pennsylvania—began to emerge to provide settings for the redemption of the poor, the ill, and the deviant.

infection that had afflicted him than of his physicians' efforts to cure him by bleeding and purging.

The medical profession also used its newfound commitment to the "scientific" method to justify expanding its own role to kinds of care that had traditionally been outside its domain. Most childbirths, for example, had been attended by female midwives. In the early nineteenth century, physicians began to handle deliveries themselves and to demand restrictions on the role of midwives. Among the results of that change was a narrowing of opportunities for women (midwifery was an important female occupation) and a restriction of access to childbirth care for poor mothers (who could have afforded midwives, but who could not pay the higher physicians' fees).

DECLINE OF MIDWIFERY

Education and professional training in the early republic–in medicine and in many other fields–thus fell far short of the Jeffersonian vision. Indeed, efforts to promote education and increase professionalism often had the effect of strengthening existing elites rather than eroding them.

CULTURAL ASPIRATIONS IN THE NEW NATION

Many Americans in the Jeffersonian era may have repudiated the Federalist belief in political and economic centralization, but most embraced another form of nationalism with great fervor. Having won political independence from Europe, they aspired now to a form of cultural independence. In the process, they dreamed of an American literary and artistic life that would rival the greatest achievements of Europe. As a popular "Poem on the Rising Glory of America" had predicted as early as 1772, Americans believed that their "happy land" was destined to become the "seat of empire" and the "final stage" of civilization, with "glorious works of high invention and of wond'rous art." The United States, another eighteenth-century writer had proclaimed, would serve as "the last and greatest theatre for the improvement of mankind."

ESTABLISHMENT OF A NATIONAL CULTURE

Such nationalism found expression, among other places, in early American schoolbooks. The Massachusetts geographer Jedidiah Morse, author of *Geography Made Easy* (1784), said the country must have its own textbooks to prevent the aristocratic ideas of England from infecting the people. The Connecticut schoolmaster and lawyer Noah Webster argued similarly that American students should be educated as patriots, their minds filled with nationalistic, American thoughts.

To encourage a distinctive American culture and help unify the new nation, Webster insisted on a simplified and Americanized system of spelling–"honor" instead of "honour," for example. His *American Spelling Book*, first published in 1783 and commonly known as the "blue-backed speller," eventually sold over 100 million copies, to become the best-selling book (except for the Bible) in the history of American publishing. In addition, his school dictionary, issued in 1806, was republished in many editions and was eventually enlarged to become (in 1828) *An American Dictionary of the English Language*. His speller and his dictionary established a national standard of words and usages.

NOAH WEBSTER

Those Americans who aspired to create a more elevated national literary life faced a number of obstacles. There was a large potential audience for a national literature–a substantial reading public, created in part by the wide circulation of newspapers and political pamphlets during the Revolution.

Discussion and Activities

Analyzing Issues After students have read the section "Medicine and Science," ask them use a dictionary or the Internet to define the term "rent-seeking." Have students discuss how late eighteenth-century physicians were employing the tactic of rent-seeking. Ask how this practice affected their patients and what examples of this practice they can think of today. **WRX**

Reasoning Processes

Causation Have students read the section "Establishment of a National Culture." Ask them to think about how schoolbooks were used to promote a national culture. Have students share with a partner whether promoting nationalism is an appropriate task for textbooks. **SOC**

Reasoning Processes

Causation After students have read the section "Cultural Aspirations in the New Nation," ask them to consider whether new types of American literature were more a cause of American nationalism or an effect of it. Have students write a thesis statement that takes a position on that issue. **SOC**

But there were few opportunities for would-be American authors to get their work before the public. Printers preferred to publish popular works by English writers (for which they had to pay no royalties); magazine publishers filled their pages largely with items clipped from British periodicals. Only those American writers willing to pay the cost and bear the risk of publishing their own works could compete for public attention.

Even so, a growing number of American authors struggled to create a strong native literature so that, as the poet Joel Barlow wrote, "true ideas of glory may be implanted in the minds of men here, to take the place of the false and destructive ones that have degraded the species in other countries." Barlow himself, one of a group of Connecticut writers known as the "Hartford Wits," published an epic poem, *The Columbiad,* in 1807, in an effort to convey the special character of American civilization. The acclaim it received helped to encourage other native writers.

Among the most ambitious was the Philadelphian Charles Brockden Brown. Like many Americans, he was attracted to the relatively new literary form of the novel, which had become popular in England in the late eighteenth century and had been successfully imported to America. But Brown sought to do more than simply imitate the English forms; he tried to use his novels to give voice to distinctively American themes, to convey the "soaring passions and intellectual energy" of the new nation. His obsession with originality led him to produce a body of work characterized by a fascination with horror and deviant behavior. Perhaps as a result, his novels failed to develop a large popular following.

Much more successful was Washington Irving, a resident of New York State who won wide acclaim for his satirical histories of early American life and his powerful fables of society in the New World. His popular folktales, recounting the adventures of such American rustics as Ichabod Crane and Rip Van Winkle, made him the widely acknowledged leader of American literary life in his era and one of the few writers of that time whose works would continue to be read by later generations.

WASHINGTON IRVING

Perhaps the most influential works by American authors in the early republic were not poems, novels, or stories, but works of history that glorified the nation's past. Mercy Otis Warren, who had been an influential playwright and agitator during the 1770s, continued her literary efforts with a three-volume *History of the Revolution,* published in 1805 and emphasizing the heroism of the American struggle. Mason Weems, an Anglican clergyman, published a eulogistic *Life of Washington* in 1806, which became one of the best-selling books of the era. Weems had little interest in historical accuracy. He portrayed the aristocratic former president as a homespun man possessing simple republican virtues. (He also invented, among other things, the famous story of Washington and the cherry tree.) History, like literature, was serving as a vehicle for instilling a sense of nationalism in the American people.

RELIGIOUS SKEPTICISM

The American Revolution weakened traditional forms of religious practice by detaching churches from government and by elevating ideas of individual liberty and reason. By the 1790s, only a small proportion of white Americans (perhaps as few as 10 percent) were members of formal churches, and ministers were complaining often about the "decay of vital piety." Religious traditionalists were particularly alarmed about the emergence of new, "rational" theologies that reflected modern, scientific attitudes and de-emphasized the role of God in the world.

Some Americans, including Jefferson and Franklin, embraced "deism," which had originated among Enlightenment philosophers in France. Deists accepted the existence of God, but considered God a remote being who, after having created the universe, had withdrawn from direct involvement with the human race and its sins. Books and articles attacking religious "superstitions" attracted wide readerships and provoked much discussion, among them Thomas Paine's *The Age of Reason,* published in parts between 1794 and 1796. Paine once declared that Christianity was the "strangest religion ever set up," for "it committed a murder upon Jesus in order to redeem mankind from the sin of eating an apple."

DEISM

Religious skepticism also produced the philosophies of "universalism" and "unitarianism," which emerged at first as dissenting views within the New England Congregational Church. Disciples of these new ideas rejected the Calvinist belief in predestination, arguing that salvation was available to all. They rejected, too, the idea of the Trinity. Jesus was only a great religious teacher, they claimed, not the Son of God. So wide was the gulf between these dissenters and the Congregationalist establishment that it finally became a permanent schism. James Murray (who later married Judith Sargent Murray) founded the Universalist Church as a separate denomination in Gloucester, Massachusetts, in 1779; the Unitarian Church was established in Boston three years later.

Some Americans believed that the spread of rationalism marked the end of traditional, evangelistic religion in the new nation. But quite the contrary was true. In fact, most Americans continued to hold strong religious beliefs. What had declined was their commitment to organized churches and denominations, which many considered too formal and traditional for their own zealous religious faith. Deism, Universalism, Unitarianism, and other "rational" religions seemed more powerful than they actually were because for a time traditional evangelicals were confused and disorganized. But beginning in 1801, traditional religion staged a dramatic comeback in the form of a wave of revivalism known as the Second Great Awakening.

THE SECOND GREAT AWAKENING

The origins of the Second Great Awakening lay in the efforts of conservative theologians of the 1790s to fight the spread of religious rationalism, and to encourage church establishments to revitalize their organizations.

Reasoning Processes

Continuity and Change Have students read the section "Religious Skepticism." Ask them to create a Venn diagram comparing characteristics of American religion at the beginning of the nineteenth century with the characteristics of American religion in the early years of colonization. Ask students whether they think there are more similarities or differences. **SOC**

Leaders of several different denominations participated in the evangelizing efforts that drove the revival. Presbyterians tried to arouse the faithful on the western fringe of white settlement, and conservatives in the church denounced New Light dissenters (people who had altered their religious views to make them more compatible with the world of scientific rationalism). Methodism, which John Wesley had founded in England, spread to America in the 1770s and became a formal denomination in 1784 under the leadership of Francis Asbury. Authoritarian and hierarchical in structure, the Methodist Church sent itinerant preachers throughout the nation to win recruits; it soon became the fastest-growing denomination in America. Almost as successful were the Baptists, who were themselves relatively new to America; they found an especially fervent following in the South.

By 1800, the revivalist energies of all these denominations were combining to create the greatest surge of evangelical fervor since the first Great Awakening sixty years before. Beginning among Presbyterians in several eastern colleges (most notably at Yale, under the leadership of President Timothy Dwight), the new awakening soon spread rapidly throughout the country, reaching its greatest heights in the western regions. In only a few years, a large proportion of the American people were mobilized by the movement, and membership in those churches embracing the revival—most prominently the Methodists, the Baptists, and the Presbyterians—was mushrooming. At Cane Ridge, Kentucky, in the summer of 1801, a group of evangelical ministers presided over the nation's first "camp meeting"—an extraordinary revival that lasted several days and impressed all who saw it with its size (some estimated that 25,000 people attended) and its fervor. Such events became common in subsequent years, as the Methodists in particular came to rely on them as a way to "harvest" new members. The Methodist circuit-riding preacher Peter Cartwright won national fame as he traveled from region to region exhorting his listeners to embrace the church. Even Cartwright, however, was often unprepared for the results of his efforts—a religious frenzy that at times produced convulsions, fits, rolling in the dirt, and twitching "holy jerks."

CANE RIDGE

The message of the Second Great Awakening was not entirely consistent, but its basic thrust was clear: individuals must readmit God and Christ into their daily lives, must embrace a fervent, active piety, and must reject the skeptical rationalism that threatened traditional beliefs. Even so, the wave of revivalism did not serve to restore the religious ideas of the past. Few of the revivalist denominations any longer accepted the idea of predestination; and the belief that a person could affect his or her own destiny added intensity to the individual's search for salvation. The Awakening, in short, combined a more active piety with a belief in God as an active force in the world whose grace could be attained through faith and good works.

The Second Great Awakening also accelerated the growth of different sects and denominations. It helped create a broad popular acceptance of the idea that men and women could belong to different Protestant churches and still be committed to essentially the same Christian faith. Finally, the new evangelicalism—by spreading religious fervor into every area of the nation—provided a vehicle for establishing a sense of order and social stability in communities still searching for an identity.

MESSAGE OF THE SECOND GREAT AWAKENING

One of the most striking features of the Second Great Awakening was the preponderance of women (particularly young women) within it. One reason for this was that women were more numerous in certain regions than men. Adventurous young men often struck out on their own and moved west; women, for the most part, had no such options. Their marriage prospects thus diminished and their futures plagued with uncertainty, some women discovered in religion a foundation on which to build their lives. But even where there was no shortage of men, women flocked to the revivals in enormous numbers, which suggests that they were responding to their changing economic roles as well. The movement of industrial work out of the home (where women had often contributed to the family economy through spinning and weaving) and into the factory—a process making rapid strides in the early nineteenth century—deprived older women, in particular, of one of their most important social roles. Religious enthusiasm helped compensate for the losses and adjustments these transitions produced; it also provided access to a new range of activities associated with the churches—charitable societies ministering to orphans and the poor, missionary organizations, and others—in which women came to play important roles.

Although revivalism was most widespread within white society, it penetrated other cultures as well. In some areas of the country, revivals were open to people of all races, and many African Americans not only attended but eagerly embraced the new religious fervor as well. Out of these revivals, in fact, emerged a substantial group of black preachers, who became important figures within the enslaved community. Some of them translated the apparently egalitarian religious message of the Second Great Awakening—that salvation was available to all—into a similarly egalitarian message for African Americans in the present world. Out of black revival meetings in Virginia arose an elaborate plan in 1800 (devised by Gabriel Prosser, the brother of an African American preacher) for a rebellion and attack on Richmond. The plan was discovered and the rebellion forestalled by white Virginians, but revivalism continued to stir racial unrest in the South.

AFRICAN AMERICANS AND THE REVIVALS

The spirit of revivalism was also particularly strong in these years among Native Americans, although very different from revivalism in white or black society. It drew heavily from earlier tribal experiences. In the 1760s, the Delaware prophet Neolin had sparked a widespread revival in the Old Northwest with a message combining Christian and Native American imagery and bringing to Native American religion a vision of a personal God, intimately involved in the affairs of man. Neolin had also called for Native Americans to rise up in defense of

Discussion and Activities

Evaluating Evidence After students have read the section "Message of the Second Great Awakening," ask them to create a T-chart comparing the religious and social/economic impacts of the Second Great Awakening. Ask students to write a brief summary explaining whether the revival was more about religion or something else. **SOC** **WRX**

Discussion and Activities

Analyzing Cause and Effect Have students read the section "African Americans and the Revivals." Have them discuss how the idea of religious equality contributed to appeals for other types of equality. **SOC**

Reasoning Processes

Comparing Have students review the characteristics of a megachurch. Ask them to create a Venn diagram comparing churches of the Second Great Awakening with modern megachurches. **SOC**

CONSIDER THE SOURCE

RELIGIOUS REVIVALS

Camp (or revival) meetings were popular among some evangelical Christians in America as early as 1800. By the 1820s, there were approximately 1,000 meetings a year, most of them in the South and West. Estimated attendance at some of the larger meetings was as large as 25,000 people.

Today, there are many "megachurches" throughout the United States. Although opinions vary on what constitutes a "megachurch," the Hartford Institute on Religious Research lists these characteristics: (1) 2,000 or more persons in attendance at weekly worship; (2) a charismatic, authoritative senior minister; (3) a very active seven-day-a-week congregational community; (4) a multitude of social and outreach ministries; and (5) a complex differentiated organizational structure. By this definition, there are more than 1,200 megachurches in the United States, most of them located in Sunbelt states, especially California, Texas, Georgia, and Florida.

The two images that follow, the first a lithograph dated 1837 and the second a photograph of a modern megachurch, suggest both comparisons and contrasts between the two religious movements.

CAMP MEETINGS—1837

METHODIST CAMP MEETING, 1837.

Historical Thinking Skills

Analyzing Point of View After reading the section "Religious Revivals" and examining the image "Methodist Camp Meeting—1837," ask students to write a short paragraph describing the experience of a tent revival from the point of view of a first-time participant. **SOC**

MEGACHURCHES—2010

LAKEWOOD CHURCH IN HOUSTON, TEXAS Pastor Joel Osteen preaches each week to some 25,000 people in attendance and thousands more on television.

ANALYZING SOURCES

Questions assume cumulative content knowledge from this chapter and previous chapters.

1. The illustration of the camp meeting best suggests which of the following regarding a feature of the Second Great Awakening?
   - (A) Most participants were not fervent supporters.
   - (B) Large numbers of women were a part of the movement.
   - (C) Men's leadership roles were limited.
   - (D) Attendees of camps in the wilderness faced attacks by Native Americans.
2. What central belief of the Second Great Awakening is best supported by the illustration?
   - (A) that organized religious practice should be highly ritualistic and formal
   - (B) that prayer was the only means to personal salvation
   - (C) that salvation was predestined to a select few
   - (D) the role of personal action in achieving salvation
3. The illustration and photograph best offer a link concerning which aspect of American democratic ideals?
   - (A) a belief in the power of the individual vs. power stemming from hereditary privilege
   - (B) a belief that people have a responsibility to their communities
   - (C) a belief that Americans should serve as a role model for the world
   - (D) a belief that old European customs should not be a part of American democracy.

AP Exam Tip

When responding to document-based questions, students are required to explain the significance of a source's point of view, purpose, historical situation, and/or audience. Point of view often involves the ideology, opinions, or experiences of the artist or author.

Historical Thinking Skills

Analyzing Point of View To practice the skill, have students examine the image "Camp Meeting—1837." Ask them to identify details in the image that suggest whether the artist was sympathetic toward or was opposed to the Second Great Awakening. *(The artist seems sympathetic. The proceedings are portrayed as orderly; participants are well-behaved and well-dressed.)* **SOC**

Answers

Consider the Source

1. B; **2.** D; **3.** B

Reasoning Processes

Causation After students have read the section "Native Americans and the Second Great Awakening," ask them to create a T-chart listing the causes and effects of the revival. In small groups, have students discuss what they think are the most important causes and effects. **SOC** **WRX** **PCE** **NAT**

their lands and had denounced the growth of trade and other relationships with white civilization. His vehement statements had helped stimulate the Native American military efforts of 1763 and beyond.

NATIVE AMERICANS AND THE SECOND GREAT AWAKENING

The dislocations and military defeats Native Americans suffered in the aftermath of the American Revolution created a sense of crisis among many of the eastern Native American nations in particular; as a result, the 1790s and early 1800s became another era of religious fervor and prophecy. Presbyterian and Baptist missionaries were active among the southern nations and sparked a great wave of conversions. The most important revivalism came from the efforts of another great prophet: Handsome Lake, a Seneca whose seemingly miraculous "rebirth" after years of alcoholism helped give him a special stature within his tribe. Handsome Lake, like Neolin before him, called for a revival of traditional Native American ways. (He claimed to have met Jesus, who instructed him to "tell your people they will become lost when they follow the ways of the white man.") Handsome Lake's message spread through the scattered Iroquois communities and inspired many Native Americans to give up whiskey, gambling, and other destructive customs derived from white society.

But the revival did not, in fact, lead to a true restoration of traditional Iroquois culture. Instead, Handsome Lake encouraged Christian missionaries to become active within Native American communities, and he urged Iroquois men to abandon their roles as hunters (partly because so much of their hunting land had been seized by white men) and become sedentary farmers instead. Iroquois women, who had traditionally done the farming, were to move into more-domestic roles. When some women resisted the change, Handsome Lake denounced them as witches. He demanded confessions from them and killed some of those who refused.

FREETHINKERS

The Second Great Awakening also had important effects on those Americans who did not accept its teachings. The rational "freethinkers," whose skeptical philosophies had helped produce the revivals, were in many ways victims of the new religious fervor. They did not disappear after 1800, but their influence rapidly declined, and for many years they remained a small and defensive minority within American Christianity. Instead, the dominant religious characteristic of the new nation became a fervent evangelicalism, which would survive into the mid-nineteenth century and beyond.

STIRRINGS OF INDUSTRIALISM

Despite the hopes of Jefferson and his followers that the United States would remain a simple agrarian republic, the nation took its first, tentative steps in these years toward its transformation into an urban, industrial society.

TECHNOLOGY IN AMERICA

Americans imported some of these technological advances from England. The British government attempted to protect the nation's manufacturing preeminence by preventing the export of textile machinery or the emigration of skilled mechanics. Despite such efforts, immigrants arrived in the United States with advanced knowledge of English technology, eager to introduce the new machines to America. Samuel Slater, for example, used the knowledge he had acquired before leaving England to build a spinning mill for the Quaker merchant Moses Brown in Pawtucket, Rhode Island, in 1790. It was the first modern factory in America.

America in the early nineteenth century also produced several important inventors of its own. Among them was Oliver Evans of Delaware, who devised a number of ingenious new machines: an automated flour mill, a card-making machine, and others. He made several important improvements in the steam engine, and in 1795 he published America's first textbook of mechanical engineering: *The Young Mill-Wright's and Miller's Guide*. His own flour mill, which began operations in 1787, required only two men to operate: one of them emptying a bag of wheat into the machinery, another putting the lid on the barrels of flour and rolling them away.

Even more influential for the future of the nation were the inventions of the Massachusetts-born, Yale-educated Eli Whitney, who revolutionized both cotton production and weapons manufacturing. The growth of the textile industry in England had created an enormous demand for cotton, a demand that planters in the American South were finding impossible to meet. Their greatest obstacle was separating the seeds from cotton fiber—a difficult and time-consuming process that was essential before cotton could be sold. Long-staple, or Sea Island, cotton, with its smooth black seeds and

THE COTTON GIN Eli Whitney's cotton gin revolutionized the cotton economy of the South by making the processing of short-staple cotton simple and economical. With the device, a single operator could clean as much cotton in a few hours as a group of workers had once needed a whole day to do.

Discussion and Activities

Analyzing Perspectives After students have read the section "Native Americans and the Second Great Awakening," ask them to think about the messages of Neolin and Handsome Lake. Have them share with a partner which Native American leader they would have followed, and why. **SOC** **MIG**

long fibers, was easy to clean, but it grew successfully only along the Atlantic coast or on the offshore islands of Georgia and South Carolina. There was not nearly enough of it to satisfy the demand. Short-staple cotton, by contrast, could grow inland through vast areas of the South. But its sticky green seeds were extremely difficult to remove. A skilled worker could clean no more than a few pounds a day by hand. Then, in 1793, Whitney, who was working at the time as a tutor on the Georgia plantation of General Nathanael Greene's widow, invented a machine that performed the arduous task quickly and efficiently. It was dubbed the cotton gin ("gin" was an abbreviation for "engine"), and it transformed the life of the South.

ELI WHITNEY'S COTTON GIN

Mechanically, the gin was very simple. A toothed roller caught the fibers of the cotton boll and pulled them between the wires of a grating. The grating caught the seeds while a revolving brush removed the lint from the roller's teeth. With the device, a single operator could clean as much cotton in a few hours as a group of workers had once needed a whole day to do. The results were profound. Soon cotton growing spread into the upland South and beyond, and within a decade total crop production increased eightfold. African American slavery, which with the decline of tobacco production some had considered a dwindling institution, regained its importance, expanded, and became more firmly fixed upon the South.

The cotton gin not only changed the economy of the South, it also helped transform the North. The large supply of domestically produced fiber was a strong incentive to entrepreneurs in New England and elsewhere to develop an American textile industry. Few northern states could hope to thrive on the basis of agriculture alone; by learning to turn cotton into yarn and thread, plantation owners could become industrially prosperous instead. The manufacturing preeminence of the North, which emerged with the development of the textile industry in the 1820s and 1830s, helped drive a wedge between the nation's two most populous regions—one becoming increasingly industrial, the other more firmly bound to agriculture.

THE COTTON GIN'S IMPACT ON THE NORTH

Whitney also made a major contribution to the development of modern warfare and in the process made a contribution to other industrial techniques. During the two years of undeclared war with France (1798 and 1799), Americans were deeply troubled by their lack of sufficient armaments for the expected hostilities. Production of muskets—each carefully handcrafted by a skilled gunsmith—was discouragingly slow. Whitney devised a machine to make each part of a gun according to an exact pattern. Tasks could thus be divided among several workers, and one laborer could quickly assemble a weapon out of parts made by several others. Before long, manufacturers of sewing machines, clocks, and many other complicated products were using the same system.

The new technological advances were relatively isolated phenomena during the early years of the nineteenth century. Not until at least the 1840s did the nation begin to develop a true manufacturing economy. But the inventions of this period were crucial in making the eventual transformation possible.

TRANSPORTATION INNOVATIONS

One of the prerequisites for industrialization is an efficient system for transporting raw materials to factories and finished goods to markets. The United States had no such system in the early years of the republic. But work was under way that would ultimately remove the transportation obstacle.

There were several ways to solve the problem of the small American market. One was to look for customers overseas, and American merchants continued their efforts to do that. Among the first acts of the new Congress when it met in 1789 were two tariff bills giving preference to American ships in American ports, helping to stimulate an expansion of domestic shipping. More important—indeed the principal reason for the growth of American trade in this period—was the outbreak of war in Europe in the 1790s, allowing Yankee merchant vessels to take over most of the carrying trade between Europe and the Western Hemisphere. As early as 1793, the young republic had a merchant marine and a foreign trade larger than those of any country except England. In proportion to its population, the United States had more ships and international commerce than any other country. Between 1789 and 1810, the total tonnage of American vessels engaged in overseas traffic rose from less than 125,000 to nearly 1 million. American ships had carried only 30 percent of the country's exports in 1789; they were carrying over 90 percent in 1810. The figures for American ships carrying imports increased even more dramatically, from 17.5 percent to 90 percent in the same period.

RAPID GROWTH OF AMERICAN SHIPPING

Another solution to the problem of limited markets was to develop new markets at home, by improving transportation between the states and into the interior of the continent. In river transportation, a new era began with the development of the steamboat. A number of inventors began experimenting with steam-powered craft in the late eighteenth century; John Fitch exhibited a forty-five-foot vessel with paddles operated by steam to some of the delegates at the Constitutional Convention in 1787. But the real breakthrough was Oliver Evans's development of a high-pressure engine, lighter and more efficient than James Watt's, which made steam more feasible for powering boats (and, eventually, locomotives) as well as mill machinery.

The inventor Robert Fulton and the promoter Robert R. Livingston were principally responsible for perfecting the steamboat and bringing it to the attention of the nation. Their *Clermont*, equipped with paddle wheels and an English-built engine, sailed up the Hudson in the summer of 1807, demonstrating the practicability of steam navigation (even though it took the ship thirty hours to go 150 miles). In 1811, a partner of Livingston's, Nicholas J. Roosevelt (a remote

ROBERT FULTON'S STEAMBOAT

Reasoning Processes

Causation After students have read the section "Technology in America," ask them to create a list of the effects of the cotton gin. Have them rank the effects in order of importance and write a thesis statement with a claim about what the most important effects of the cotton gin were. **WRX**

Discussion and Activities

Analyzing Causes Have students read the section "Rapid Growth of American Shipping." Ask them to consider the causes of the growth of the shipping industry. Have students discuss with a partner or in small groups why war in Europe was instrumental to that growth. **WOR** **WRX**

Discussion and Activities

Historical Developments and Argumentation Have students read the section "The Turnpike Era." Ask them to consider why governments took over the construction of roads in many areas. Have students discuss recent areas where similar transitions have taken place. *(Possible responses: space exploration moving from governments to private companies; government taking a leading role in vaccine development.)*  WRX

PAWTUCKET BRIDGE AND FALLS One reason for the growth of the textile industry in New England in the early nineteenth century was that there were many sources of water power in the region to run the machinery in the factories. That was certainly the case with Slater's Mill, one of the first American textile factories. It was located in Pawtucket, Rhode Island, alongside a powerful waterfall, demonstrating the critical importance of water power to early American industry.

ancestor of Theodore Roosevelt), introduced the steamboat to the West by sending the *New Orleans* from Pittsburgh down the Ohio and Mississippi. The next year, this vessel began a profitable career of service between New Orleans and Natchez.

THE TURNPIKE ERA

Meanwhile, what was to become known as the "turnpike era" had begun. In 1792, a corporation constructed a toll road running the sixty miles from Philadelphia to Lancaster, Pennsylvania, with a hard-packed surface of crushed rock. This venture proved so successful that several other companies laid out similar turnpikes (so named from the kind of tollgate frequently used) from other cities to neighboring towns. Since the turnpikes had to produce profits for the companies that built them, construction costs had to be low enough and the prospective traffic heavy enough to ensure an early and ample return. As a result, these roads, radiating from eastern cities, ran comparatively short distances and through densely settled areas. No private operators were willing to build similar highways over the mountains and into the less populated interior. State governments and the federal government eventually had to finance them.

THE RISING CITIES

Despite all the changes and all the advances, America in the early nineteenth century remained an overwhelmingly rural and agrarian nation. Only 3 percent of the non-Indian population lived in towns of more than 8,000 at the time of the second census, in 1800. Ten percent lived west of the Appalachian Mountains, far from what urban centers there were. Much of the country remained a wilderness. Even the nation's largest cities could not begin to compare, either in size or in cultural sophistication, with such European capitals as London and Paris.

Yet here too there were signs of change. The leading American cities might not yet have become world capitals, but they were large and complex enough to rival the important secondary cities of Europe. Philadelphia, with 70,000 residents, and New York, with 60,000, were becoming major centers of commerce and learning. The cities were also developing a distinctively urban culture. So too were the next-largest cities of the new nation: Baltimore (26,000 in 1800), Boston (24,000), and Charleston (20,000).

Discussion and Activities

Analyzing Point of View After students have read the section "Robert Fulton's Steamboat," ask them to write a letter or journal article from the point of view of an eyewitness describing the *Clermont* steaming up the Hudson River. WRX

CHAPTER 7
THE JEFFERSONIAN ERA

Reasoning Processes

Comparing Have students read the section "Urban Life." Ask them to create a bisected Venn diagram comparing life for urban and rural dwellers, with economic factors above the line and social factors below the line. **SOC** **WRX** **NAT**

AMERICAN STAGE WAGGON This image of a stagecoach, by J. Stoner, shows how roads were beginning to link the disparate regions of early-nineteenth-century America.

People living in towns and cities lived differently than the vast majority of Americans who continued to work as farmers. Among other things, urban life produced affluence, and affluent people sought amenities that would not have entered the imaginings of any but the wealthiest farmers. They sought increasing elegance and refinement in their homes, their grounds, and their dress. They also looked for diversions–music, theater, dancing, and, for many people, one of the most popular entertainments of all, horse racing.

URBAN LIFE

Much remained to be done before this small and still half-formed nation would become a complex modern society. It was still possible in the early nineteenth century to believe that those changes might not ever occur. But forces were already at work that, in time, would lastingly transform the United States.

JEFFERSON THE PRESIDENT

Privately, Thomas Jefferson may well have considered his victory over John Adams in 1800 to be what he later termed it: a revolution "as real . . . as that of 1776." Publicly, however, he was restrained and conciliatory as he assumed office, attempting to minimize the differences between the two parties and to calm the passions that the bitter campaign had aroused. "We are all republicans, we are all federalists," he said in his inaugural address. And during his eight years in office, he did much to prove those words correct. There was no complete repudiation of Federalist policies, no true "revolution." Indeed, at times Jefferson seemed to outdo the Federalists at their own work–most notably in overseeing a remarkable expansion of the territory of the United States.

Reasoning Processes

Evaluating After students have read the section "The Rising Cities," ask them to think about what the largest American cities had in common. Have students compare their thoughts with a partner. *(All were ports and had economies that were highly dependent upon trade.)* **MIG** **WRX**

AP Exam Practice

Short Answer Provide students with the following short-answer questions and allow 15 minutes for completion. Ask for volunteers to share their responses and discuss as a class.

Answer A, B, and C.

A) Briefly explain one important similarity between the nineteenth-century industrial revolutions in Great Britain and the United States. *(Both began with the textile industry.)*

B) Briefly explain one important difference between the nineteenth-century industrial revolutions in Great Britain and the United States. *(America utilized considerable immigrant labor and imported technology.)*

C) Briefly explain one important reason for the difference cited in B. *(The industrial revolution started earlier in Great Britain, allowing Americans the opportunity to utilize knowledge and skills brought by British immigrants.)*

THE GLOBAL INDUSTRIAL REVOLUTION

The tentative stirrings of industrial activity in the United States in the early nineteenth century were part of a vast movement that over the course of the century transformed much of the globe. Historians differ over precisely when the industrial revolution began, but it is clear that by the end of the eighteenth century it was well under way in many parts of the world. By the beginning of the twentieth century, industrialization had transformed the societies of Britain, most of continental Europe, Japan, and the United States.

For Americans, the industrial revolution was largely a result of the rapid changes in Great Britain, the nation with which they had the closest relations. Britain was the first nation to develop significant industrial capacity. The factory system took root in England in the late eighteenth century, revolutionizing the manufacture of cotton thread and cloth. One invention followed another in quick succession. Improvements in weaving drove improvements in spinning, and these changes created a demand for new devices for carding (combing and straightening the fibers for the spinner). Water, wind, and animal power continued to be important in the textile industry; but more important was the emergence of steam power—which proliferated after the appearance of James Watt's advanced steam engine (patented in 1769). England's textile industry quickly became the most profitable in the world, and it helped encourage comparable advances in other fields of manufacturing as well. Despite the efforts of the British government to prevent the export of English industrial technology, knowledge of the new machines reached other nations quickly, usually through the emigration of people who had learned the technology in British factories.

America benefited the most from English technology, because it received more immigrants from Great Britain than from any other country. But English technology spread quickly to the nations of continental Europe as well. In Japan, the sudden intrusion of American and European traders helped cause the so-called Meiji reforms of the 1880s and 1890s, which launched a period of rapid industrialization there.

Industrialization changed not just the world's economies, but also its societies. First in England, and then in Europe, America, and Japan, social systems underwent wrenching changes. Hundreds of thousands, and eventually millions, of men and women moved from rural areas into cities to work in factories, where they experienced both the benefits and the costs of industrialization. Many of those who moved from farm to factory experienced some improvement in nutrition and other material circumstances, even in their health. But there were psychological costs to being suddenly uprooted from one way of life and thrust into another, fundamentally different one. Little in most workers' prior experience had prepared them for the nature of industrial labor. The routinized, rigidly scheduled work of the urban factory contrasted sharply with the varying, seasonal work pattern of the rural economy. Industrial workers experienced, too, a fundamental change in their relationship with their employers. Unlike rural landlords and local aristocrats, factory owners and managers—the new class of industrial capitalists, many of them accumulating unprecedented wealth—were usually remote and inaccessible. They dealt with their workers impersonally, and the result was a growing schism between the two classes—each lacking access to or understanding of the other. Working men and women throughout the globe began thinking of themselves as a distinct class, with common goals and interests. Their efforts simultaneously to adjust to their new way of life and to resist its most damaging aspects sometimes created great social turbulence. Battles between workers and employers became a characteristic feature of industrial life throughout the world.

THE ENGLISH CANAL AGE **Industrialization in England contributed, as it did in America, to the building of new transportation facilities to serve the growing commercial markets of the new economy. Among the most popular such facilities were canals, among them the Regent's Canal in London, pictured here in the 1820s.**

Life in industrial nations changed at every level. Populations in industrial countries grew rapidly, and people began to live longer. At the same time, industrial cities began to produce great increases in pollution, crime, and—until modern sanitation systems emerged—infectious disease. Around the industrial world, middle classes expanded and came to dominate the economy (although not always the culture or the politics) of their nations.

Not since the agricultural revolution thousands of years earlier, when many humans had turned from hunting to farming for sustenance, had there been an economic change of a magnitude comparable to that of the industrial revolution. Centuries of traditions, social patterns, and cultural and religious assumptions were challenged and often shattered. The social and economic consequences of industrialism were complex and profound, and they continue today to shape the nature of global society.

HISTORICAL THINKING SKILLS

1. **Explaining Historical Developments** What was the first significant industry impacted by the industrial revolution?
2. **Explaining Significance** How did the British industrial revolution impact the United States?
3. **Making Connections** What were the effects of the British industrial revolution on its population?

Answers

America in the World: The Global Industrial Revolution

1. The first industry significantly impacted by the industrial revolution was the cotton industry. Improvements in weaving drove improvements in spinning, and these changes created a demand for combing and straightening the fibers for the spinner.
2. America had more immigrants from Britain than any other country in the world. Despite the fact that Britain tried to control the information about its industrial revolution, emigration of people who had learned the technology brought it to other places around the world, including the United States.
3. Hundreds of thousands moved from rural to urban centers. Most experienced improvement in nutrition. Many suffered from psychological conditions brought on from industry work. Battles between workers and owners became common-place.

THE FEDERAL CITY AND THE "PEOPLE'S PRESIDENT"

The New Capital City

The newly founded national capital was the city of Washington. The French architect Pierre L'Enfant had designed the capital on a grand scale, with broad avenues radiating out from the uncompleted Capitol building, set on one of the area's highest hills. Washington was, many Americans believed, to become the Paris of the United States.

In reality, however, throughout Jefferson's presidency—and indeed through most of the nineteenth century—Washington remained little more than a provincial village. Although the population increased steadily from the 3,200 counted in the 1800 census, it never rivaled that of New York, Philadelphia, or the other major cities of the nation. The city remained a raw, inhospitable community with few public buildings of any consequence. Members of Congress viewed Washington not as a home but as a place to visit briefly during sessions of the legislature and leave as quickly as possible. Most lived in a cluster of simple boardinghouses in the vicinity of the Capitol. It was not unusual for a member of Congress to resign his seat in the midst of a session to return home if he had an opportunity to accept the more prestigious post of member of his state legislature.

Jefferson set out as president to act in a spirit of democratic simplicity in keeping with the frontierlike character of the unfinished federal city. He was a wealthy and aristocratic planter by background, with more than 100 enslaved people, and a man of rare cultivation and sophistication; but he conveyed to the public an image of plain, almost crude disdain for pretension. He walked like an ordinary citizen to and from his inauguration at the Capitol. In the presidential mansion, which had not yet acquired the name "White House," he disregarded the courtly etiquette of his predecessors (in part, no doubt, because as a widower he had no First Lady to take charge of social affairs). At state dinners, he let his guests scramble pell-mell for places at the table. He did not always bother to dress up, once prompting the fastidious British ambassador to complain of being received by the president in coat and pantaloons that were "indicative of utter slovenliness and indifference to appearances."

NORTH AMERICA IN 1800 This map illustrates how substantially the non-Indian settlement of British North America (much of it by 1800 the United States) had expanded since 1700. Note the new areas of settlement since the 1700s: west of the original thirteen colonies—including, in Kentucky, an area that reaches almost to the Mississippi River. Significant settlements are also now visible along the Gulf Coast, especially in the territory around New Orleans. Scattered non-Indian settlements are visible in the Southwest and along the coast of California, as well as in southern Canada (where the settlements were largely forts).

How does this map help explain the spread of settlement south from Pittsburgh into western Virginia and Kentucky?

Discussion and Activities

Analyzing Change Have students read the section "The New Capital City." Ask them to discuss why Washington, D.C., was slow to grow. *(The new capital suffered from an uncomfortable climate and did not have the amenities of larger cities, and serving in the national government was sometimes perceived as less prestigious than serving in state governments.)* **NAT** **MIG** **PCE**

Answers

North America in 1800

Settlement follows the Ohio River from Pittsburgh to northern Virginia and Kentucky.

Historical Thinking Skills

Contextualization Have students read the section "Limiting the Federal Government." Ask them to consider why Jefferson and others might have feared having a large standing army. *(The Revolution had been fought against what was thought to be an oppressive British government. Jefferson feared that a large standing army might result in similar oppression.)* **PCE** **NAT**

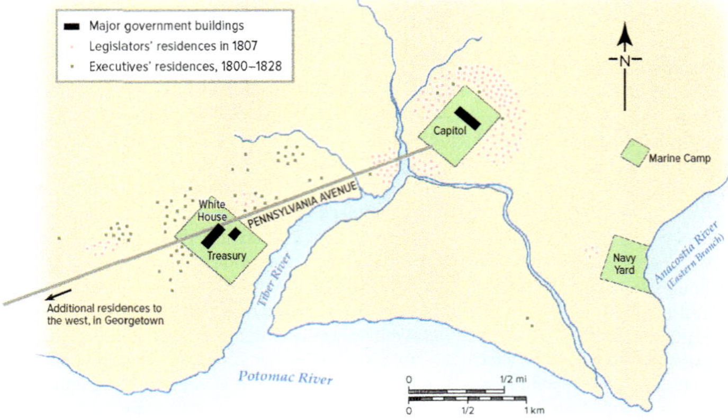

WASHINGTON, D.C., IN THE EARLY NINETEENTH CENTURY The nation's capital moved from New York City to Washington, D.C., in 1800, into a new city designed on a grand scale by the French planner Pierre L'Enfant. But in the early eighteenth century, it remained little more than a village on a marshy tract of land, with hot, humid summers. This map shows the location of the principal government buildings in the early republic, and also the sites of the homes of members of the executive and legislative branches. Note how the homes of executive officials mostly clustered around the White House and the Treasury, while those of legislators mainly clustered around the Capitol.

How did the geography of the city help shape the relationship between the executive and legislative branches?

Yet Jefferson managed nevertheless to impress most of those who knew him. He was a brilliant conversationalist, a gifted writer, and one of the nation's most intelligent and creative men, with perhaps a wider range of interests and accomplishments than any public figure in American history. In addition to politics and diplomacy, he was an active architect, educator, inventor, scientific farmer, and philosopher-scientist.

Jefferson was, above all, a shrewd and practical politician. On the one hand, he went to great lengths to eliminate the aura of majesty surrounding the presidency that he believed his predecessors had created. At the same time, however, Jefferson worked hard to exert influence as the leader of his party, giving direction to Republicans in Congress by quiet and sometimes even devious means. Although the Republicans had objected strenuously to the efforts of their Federalist predecessors to build a network of influence through patronage, Jefferson, too, used his powers of appointment as an effective political weapon. By the end of his first term about half the government jobs, and by the end of his second term practically all of them, were in the hands of loyal Republicans.

JEFFERSON THE POLITICIAN

When Jefferson ran for reelection in 1804, he won overwhelmingly. The Federalist presidential nominee, Charles C. Pinckney, could not even carry most of the party's New England strongholds. Jefferson won 162 electoral votes to Pinckney's 14, and the Republican majorities in both houses of Congress increased.

DOLLARS AND SHIPS

Under Washington and Adams, the Republicans believed, the government had been needlessly extravagant. Yearly federal expenditures had almost tripled between 1793 and 1800. Hamilton had, as he had intended, increased the public debt and created an extensive system of internal taxation, including the hated whiskey excise tax.

The Jefferson administration moved deliberately to reverse the trend. In 1802, it persuaded Congress to abolish all internal taxes, leaving customs duties and the sale of western lands as the only sources of revenue for the government. Meanwhile, Secretary of the Treasury Albert Gallatin drastically reduced government spending, cutting the already small staffs of the executive departments to minuscule levels. Although Jefferson was unable to retire the entire national debt, as he had hoped, he did cut it almost in half (from $83 million to $45 million) during his presidency.

LIMITING THE FEDERAL GOVERNMENT

Jefferson also scaled down the armed forces. He reduced the army of 4,000 men to 2,500. He cut the navy from twenty-five ships to seven and reduced the number of officers and sailors accordingly. Anything but the smallest of standing armies, he argued, might menace civil liberties and civilian control of government. And a large navy, he feared, might promote overseas commerce, which Jefferson believed should remain secondary to agriculture. Yet Jefferson was not a pacifist. At the same time that he was reducing the size of the army and navy, he was helping to establish the United States Military Academy at West Point, founded in 1802. And when trouble began brewing overseas, he began again to build up the fleet.

Such trouble appeared first in the Mediterranean, off the coast of northern Africa. For years the Barbary states of North Africa–Morocco, Algiers, Tunis, and Tripoli (now part of Libya)–had been demanding protection money from all nations whose ships sailed the Mediterranean. Even Great Britain gave regular contributions to the Barbary pirates. During the 1780s and 1790s the United States agreed to treaties providing for annual tribute to the Barbary states, but Jefferson was reluctant to continue this policy of appeasement. "Tribute or war is the usual alternative of these Barbary pirates," he said. "Why not build a navy and decide on war?"

CHALLENGING THE BARBARY PIRATES

Answers

Washington, D.C., in the Early Nineteenth Century

The rivers and marshes kept development from spreading out, and the main thoroughfare, Pennsylvania Avenue, linked the Capitol and the White House

In 1801, the pasha (leader) of Tripoli forced Jefferson's hand. Unsatisfied by the American response to his extortionate demands, he ordered the flagpole of the American consulate chopped down—a symbolic declaration of war. Jefferson responded cautiously, building up the American fleet in the region over the next several years. Finally, in 1805, the United States reached an agreement with the pasha that ended American payments of tribute to Tripoli but required the United States to pay a substantial (and humiliating) ransom of $60,000 for the release of American prisoners seized by Barbary pirates.

Conflict with the Courts

Having won control of the executive and legislative branches of government, the Republicans looked with suspicion on the judiciary, which remained largely in the hands of Federalist judges. Soon after Jefferson's first inauguration, his followers in Congress launched an attack on this last preserve of the opposition. Their first step was the repeal of the Judiciary Act of 1801, thus eliminating the judgeships to which Adams had made his "midnight appointments."

The debate over the courts led to one of the most important judicial decisions in the history of the nation. Federalists had long maintained that the Supreme Court had the authority to nullify acts of Congress (although the Constitution said nothing specifically to support the claim), and the Court itself had actually exercised the power of judicial review in 1796 when it upheld the validity of a law passed by the legislature. But the Court's authority in this area would not be secure, it was clear, until it actually declared a congressional act unconstitutional.

JUDICIAL REVIEW

In 1803, in the case of *Marbury v. Madison*, it did so. William Marbury, one of Adams's "midnight appointments," had been named a justice of the peace in the District of Columbia. But his commission, although signed and sealed, had not been delivered to him before Adams left office. Once Jefferson became president, the new secretary of state, James Madison, was responsible for transmitting appointments. He had refused to hand over the commission to Marbury. Marbury appealed to the Supreme Court for an order directing Madison to perform his official duty. In its historic ruling, the Court found that Marbury had a right to his commission but that the Court had no authority to order Madison to deliver it. On the surface, therefore, the decision was a victory for the administration. But of much greater importance than the relatively insignificant matter of Marbury's commission was the Court's reasoning in the decision.

MARBURY V. MADISON

The original Judiciary Act of 1789 had given the Court the power to compel executive officials to act in such matters as the delivery of commissions, and it was on that basis that Marbury had filed his suit. But the Court ruled that Congress had exceeded its authority in creating that statute: that the Constitution had defined the powers of the judiciary and that the legislature had no right to expand them. The relevant section of the 1789 act was therefore void. In seeming to deny its own authority, the Court was in fact radically enlarging it. The justices had repudiated a relatively minor power (the power to force the delivery of a commission) by asserting a vastly greater one (the power to nullify an act of Congress).

The chief justice of the United States at the time of the ruling was John Marshall, one of the towering figures in the history of American law. A leading Federalist and prominent Virginia lawyer, he had served John Adams as secretary of state. (It had been Marshall, ironically, who had neglected to deliver Marbury's commission in the closing hours of the administration.) In 1801, just before leaving office, Adams had appointed him chief justice, and almost immediately Marshall established himself as the dominant figure on the Court, shaping all its most important rulings—including, of course, *Marbury v. Madison*. Through a succession of Republican administrations, he established the judiciary as a branch of government coequal with the executive and the legislature—a position that the founders of the republic had never clearly indicated it should occupy.

JOHN MARSHALL

Jefferson recognized the threat that an assertive judiciary could pose to his policies. Even while the *Marbury* case was still pending, he was preparing for a renewed assault on this last Federalist stronghold. He urged Congress to impeach obstructive judges, and Congress attempted to oblige him. The Republicans successfully removed from office a district judge, John Pickering of New Hampshire (on the perhaps specious grounds that he was insane and thus unfit for office). They later targeted a justice of the Supreme Court itself: Justice Samuel Chase, a highly partisan Federalist. Chase had certainly been injudicious; he had, for example, delivered stridently partisan speeches from the bench. But he had committed no crime. Some Republicans argued, however, that impeachment was not merely a criminal proceeding. Congress could properly impeach a judge for political reasons—for obstructing the other branches of the government and disregarding the will of the people.

IMPEACHMENT OF SAMUEL CHASE

At Jefferson's urging, the House impeached Chase and sent him to trial before the Senate early in 1805. But Republican leaders were unable to get the necessary two-thirds vote for conviction in the Senate. Chase's acquittal helped establish that impeachment would not become a routine political weapon, that something more than partisan disagreement should have to underlie the process, a precedent that Congress only occasionally violated in future years. Marshall remained secure in his position as chief justice. And the judiciary survived as a powerful force within the government—more often than not ruling on behalf of the centralizing, expansionary policies that the Republicans had hoped to reverse.

Historical Thinking Skills

Argumentation After students have read the section "Challenging the Barbary Pirates," ask them to write a short letter to President Jefferson recommending whether or not to strengthen the navy. Ask them to support their positions with an argument supported by at least one specific piece of evidence. **WOR** **PCE**

Discussion and Activities

Explaining Significance Have students read the section "Conflict with the Courts." Ask them to discuss in small groups how the concept of judicial review is important to the functioning of checks and balances. *(Without judicial review, the courts would have no way to limit the powers of the executive and legislative branches by declaring their actions unconstitutional.)* **PCE**

Discussion and Activities

Analyzing Images Have students examine the image "Oakland House and Race Course." Ask them to list details from the image. Then have students discuss what inferences they could make from the painting about horse racing in the early nineteenth century. *(The large plantation house suggests horse racing was a sport for the wealthy. The formal dress and elaborate carriages of the spectators suggest this as well.)* **SOC** **PCE** **WRX**

PATTERNS OF POPULAR CULTURE

HORSE RACING IN EARLY AMERICA

Informal horse racing began in North America almost as soon as Europeans settled the English colonies. Formal racing followed quickly. The first race track in North America—New Market (named for a popular race course in England)—was established in 1665 near the site of present-day Garden City, on Long Island in New York. Tracks quickly developed wide appeal, and soon horse racing had spread up and down the Atlantic coast. By the time of the American Revolution, it had become popular in almost every colony and was moving as well into the newly settled areas of the Southwest. Andrew Jackson was a founder of the first racing track in Nashville, Tennessee, in the early nineteenth century. Kentucky—whose native bluegrass was early recognized as ideal for grazing horses—had eight tracks by 1800.

Like almost everything else in the life of early America, the world of horse racing was bounded by lines of class and race. For many years, it was considered the exclusive preserve of "gentlemen," so much so that in 1674 a court in Virginia fined James Bullocke, a tailor, for proposing a race, "it being contrary to Law for a Labourer to make a race, being a sport only for Gentlemen." But while white aristocrats retained control of racing, they were not the only people who participated in it. Southern aristocrats often trained enslaved young men and boys as jockeys for their horses, just as northern horse owners employed the services of free African Americans as riders. In the North and the South, African Americans eventually emerged as some of the most talented and experienced trainers of racing horses. And despite social and legal pressures, free African Americans and poor whites often staged their own informal races.

Racing also began early to reflect the growing sectional rivalry between the North and the South. In 1824, the Union Race Course on Long Island established an astounding $24,000 purse for a race between two famous thoroughbreds: American Eclipse (from the North) and Sir Henry (from the South). American Eclipse won two of the three heats, but a southern racehorse prevailed in another such celebrated contest in 1836. These intersectional races, which drew enormous crowds and created tremendous publicity, continued into the 1850s, until the North-South rivalry began to take a deadly form.

OAKLAND HOUSE AND RACE COURSE This 1840 painting by Robert Brammer and August A. Von Smith portrays men and women flocking to an early race course in Louisville, Kentucky, which provided entertainment to affluent white Southerners.

THE ECLIPSE-HENRY MATCH RACE "Match races" between famous horses were a popular feature of early-nineteenth-century horse racing. This famous 1823 race on Long Island, New York, pitted prize-winning horses from the North and the South against one another. American Eclipse, the northern entry, won.

Horse racing remained popular after the Civil War, but two developments changed its character considerably. One was the successful effort to drive African Americans out of the sport. At least until the 1890s, black jockeys and trainers remained central to racing. At the first Kentucky Derby, in 1875, fourteen of the fifteen horses had African American riders. One black man, Isaac Murphy, won a remarkable 44 percent of all races in which he rode, including three Kentucky Derbys. Gradually, however, the same social dynamics that enforced racial segregation in so many other areas of American life penetrated racing as well. By the beginning of the twentieth century, white jockeys and organized jockey clubs had driven almost all black riders and many black trainers out of the sport.

The second change was the introduction of formalized betting to the sport. In the late nineteenth century, race tracks began creating betting systems to lure customers to the races. At the same time that the breeding of racehorses was moving into the hands of enormously wealthy families, the audience for racing was becoming increasingly working class and lower middle class. The people who now came to tracks were mostly white men, and some white women, lured to the races not by a love of horses—which were coming to play a less central role in their everyday lives—but by the usually futile hope of quick and easy riches through gambling.

HISTORICAL THINKING SKILLS

1. **Explaining** What were the origins of horse racing in the early United States?
2. **Explaining Historical Context** How did horse racing reflect larger social issues in early America?
3. **Explaining Historical Developments** What were the two major ways that horse racing changed following the Civil War?

Answers

Patterns of Popular Culture

1. The first horse track in America was established in 1665 and was a carryover from European popular culture.
2. Like everything else in early America, horse racing was defined by race and class. It was considered the exclusive domain of "gentlemen." White aristocrats maintained control over the sport, but both in the North and the South, African Americans were used as riders. Racing also reflected the growing sectional rivalry of the larger culture, as horses from each section were selected to represent the regional section and race against the other, creating an atmosphere of regional competition.
3. Following the civil war, African Americans were driven out of the sport. The same social dynamics that enforced racial segregation in other areas of American life were reflected in racing. The other significant change following the Civil War was the introduction of formal betting.

DOUBLING THE NATIONAL DOMAIN

In the same year that Jefferson became president of the United States, Napoleon Bonaparte made himself ruler of France with the title of first consul. In the year that Jefferson was reelected, Napoleon named himself emperor. The two men had little in common. Yet for a time they were of great help to each other in international politics–until Napoleon's ambitions moved from Europe to America and created conflict and estrangement.

JEFFERSON AND NAPOLEON

Having failed in a grandiose plan to seize India from the British Empire, Napoleon turned his imperial ambitions in a new direction: he began to dream of restoring French power in the New World. The territory east of the Mississippi, which France had ceded to Great Britain in 1763, was now mostly part of the United States and lost to France forever. But Napoleon wanted to regain the lands west of the Mississippi, which now belonged to Spain, over which Napoleon now exercised strong influence. Under the secret Treaty of San Ildefonso of 1800 between the French and the Spanish, France regained title to Louisiana, which included almost the whole of the Mississippi Valley to the west of the river, plus New Orleans near its mouth. The Louisiana Territory would, Napoleon hoped, become the heart of a great French empire in America.

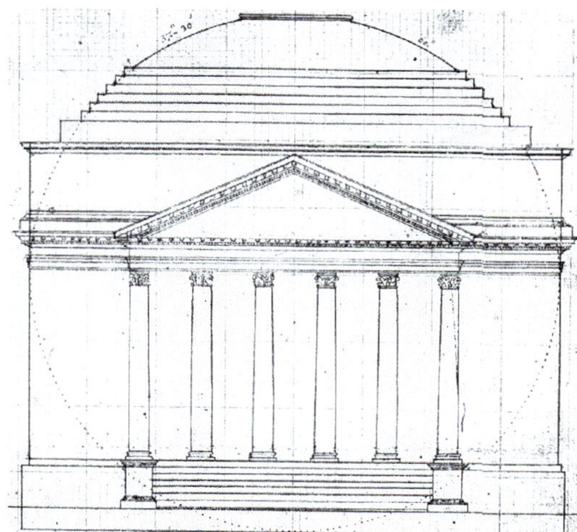

JEFFERSON THE ARCHITECT Among his many accomplishments, Thomas Jefferson was a gifted architect. This rotunda is the centerpiece of the central campus of the University of Virginia, which Jefferson designed near the end of his life. Earlier, he designed his own home near Charlottesville, Monticello; and his proposal for a president's mansion in Washington, D.C., placed second in a blind competition.

THOMAS JEFFERSON This 1805 portrait by the noted American painter Rembrandt Peale shows Jefferson at the beginning of his second term as president. It also conveys (through the simplicity of dress and the slightly unkempt hair) the image of democratic simplicity that Jefferson liked to project.

Also part of Napoleon's empire in the New World were the sugar-rich and strategically valuable West Indian islands that still belonged to France–Guadeloupe, Martinique, and above all Santo Domingo. But unrest among the Caribbean enslaved people posed a threat to Napoleon's hopes for the islands. Enslaved Africans in Santo Domingo (inspired by the French Revolution) revolted and created a republic of their own, under the remarkable black leader Toussaint L'Ouverture. Taking advantage of a truce in his war with England, Napoleon sent an army to the West Indies. It temporarily crushed the insurrection and restored French authority; but the incident was an early sign of the problems Napoleon would have in realizing his ambitions in America.

TOUSSAINT L'OUVERTURE

Jefferson was unaware at first of Napoleon's imperial ambitions in America, and for a time he pursued a foreign policy that reflected his well-known admiration for France. He appointed as American minister to Paris the ardently pro-French Robert R. Livingston. He worked to secure ratification of the Franco-American settlement of 1800 and began observing the terms of the treaty even before it was ratified. The Adams administration had joined with the British in recognizing and supporting the rebel regime of Toussaint L'Ouverture in Santo Domingo; Jefferson assured the French minister in Washington that the American people, especially those of the slaveholding states, did not approve of the black revolutionary, who they thought was setting a bad example for their enslaved

Historical Thinking Skills

Contextualization Have students read the first paragraph under the heading "Jefferson and Napoleon." Ask students to think about why Napoleon wanted the Mississippi Valley territory. Have students share their thoughts with a partner. *(The area had been a lucrative source of the fur trade prior to the French and Indian War, and Napoleon wanted the area as part of a reconstituted New World empire.)* **WOR**

Discussion and Activities

Making Connections Have students examine the image "Thomas Jefferson." Ask them to think about reasons that Jefferson may have wanted to be portrayed this way. *(He may have wanted to project an image of himself as a simple farmer to advance his agrarian ideal and to show the impact of being a widower.)* Ask students to discuss whether current politicians attempt to portray themselves this way and why. **PCE** **SOC**

Historical Thinking Skills

Analyzing Points of View After students have read the section "Napoleon's Offer," ask them to create a list of factors that led to growing tension between France and the United States. Have them rank the list in order of importance, then write a letter to President Jefferson from the point of view of an advisor to the president encouraging him to take a specific course of action. **WOR** **PCE**

people. He even implied that the United States might join with France in putting down the rebellion (although nothing ever came of the suggestion). Jefferson began to reconsider his position toward France, however, when he heard rumors of the secret transfer of Louisiana.

Jefferson was even more alarmed when, in the fall of 1802, he learned that the Spanish intendant at New Orleans (who still governed the city, since the French had not yet taken formal possession of the region) had announced a disturbing new regulation. American ships sailing the Mississippi River had for many years been accustomed to depositing their cargoes in New Orleans for transfer to oceangoing vessels. The intendant now forbade the practice—even though Spain had guaranteed Americans that right in the Pinckney Treaty of 1795—thus effectively closing the lower Mississippi to American shippers.

Westerners demanded that the federal government do something to reopen the river. The president faced a dilemma. If he yielded to the frontier clamor and tried to change the policy by force, he would run the risk of a major war with France. If he ignored the westerners' demands, he might lose political support. But Jefferson saw another solution. He instructed Robert Livingston, the American ambassador in Paris, to negotiate the purchase of New Orleans. Livingston, on his own authority, proposed that the French sell the United States the vast western part of Louisiana as well.

Napoleon's Offer

In the meantime, Jefferson persuaded Congress to appropriate funds for an expansion of the army and the construction of a river fleet, and he deliberately gave the impression that American forces might soon descend on New Orleans and that the United States might form an alliance with Great Britain if the problems with France were not resolved. Perhaps that was why Napoleon suddenly decided to accept Livingston's proposal and offer the United States the entire Louisiana Territory.

Napoleon had good reasons for the decision. His plans for an American empire had already gone seriously awry. That was partly because a yellow fever epidemic had wiped out much of the French army in the New World. But it was also because the expeditionary force Napoleon sent to take possession of Louisiana had been frozen into a Dutch harbor through the winter of 1802–1803. By the time the harbor thawed in the spring of 1803, Napoleon was preparing for a renewed war in Europe. He would not, he realized, have the resources now to secure an American empire.

WEST POINT Creating a professional military was an important task for the leaders of the early republic. Without an army, they realized, it would be difficult for the United States to win respect in the world. The establishment in 1802 of the United States Military Academy at West Point (whose parade ground is pictured here) was, therefore, an important event in the early history of the republic.

Historical Thinking Skills

Contextualization Have students examine the image "West Point." Ask them to think about and discuss what was going on in the world that led many to conclude that the American military needed to be professionalized. *(The French Revolution and wars in Europe; growing conflict with France over territories in the Americas; revolution in Haiti; conflict with the Barbary Coast pirates.)* **WOR** **PCE**

THE LOUISIANA PURCHASE

Faced with Napoleon's startling proposal, Livingston and James Monroe, whom Jefferson had sent to Paris to assist in the negotiations, had to decide first whether they should even consider making a treaty for the purchase of the entire Louisiana Territory, since they had not been authorized by their government to do so. But fearful that Napoleon might withdraw the offer, they decided to proceed without further instructions from home. After some haggling over the price, Livingston and Monroe signed the agreement on April 30, 1803.

By the terms of the treaty, the United States was to pay a total of 80 million francs ($15 million) to the French government. The United States was also to grant certain exclusive commercial privileges to France in the port of New Orleans and was to incorporate the residents of Louisiana into the Union with the same rights and privileges as other citizens. The boundaries of the purchase were not clearly defined; the treaty simply specified that Louisiana would occupy the "same extent" as it had when France and Spain had owned it.

In Washington, the president was both pleased and embarrassed when he received the treaty. He was pleased with the terms of the bargain but uncertain whether the United States had authority to accept it, since he had always insisted that the federal government could rightfully exercise only those powers explicitly assigned to it. Nowhere did the Constitution say anything about the acquisition of new territory. But Jefferson's advisers persuaded him that his treaty-making power under the Constitution would justify the purchase of Louisiana. The president finally agreed, trusting, as he said,

EXPLORING THE LOUISIANA PURCHASE, 1804–1807 When Jefferson purchased the Louisiana Territory from France in 1803, he doubled the size of the nation. But few Americans knew what they had bought. The Lewis and Clark expedition set out in 1804 to investigate the new territories, and this map shows their route, along with that of another inveterate explorer, Zebulon Pike. Note the vast distances the two parties covered (including, in both cases, a great deal of land outside the Louisiana Purchase). Note, too, how much of this enormous territory lay outside the orbit of even these ambitious explorations.

How did the American public react to the addition of these new territories?

Discussion and Activities

Analyzing Images Have students examine the image "Exploring the Louisiana Purchase, 1804–1807." Ask them to identify important rivers in the territory shown on the map. Ask students to write a short paragraph explaining the importance of these rivers to exploration. *(The Lewis and Clark expedition depended heavily on navigation of the Missouri and Columbia Rivers to travel through the territory they explored. The Pike expedition followed the Arkansas River. Rivers were vital thoroughfares in the absence of roads.)* **MIG**

Answers

Exploring the Louisiana Purchase, 1804–1807

The public was generally supportive of the acquisition of these territories, as it represented opportunity for expansion and land ownership for many and the growth of the country promoted a sense of nationalism. Many, however, were concerned about the possible future expansion of slavery into these territories. **PCE** **SOC** **WXT** **MIG** **NAT**

Discussion and Activities

Analyzing Issues Have students read the section "Jefferson's Quandary." Ask students to create a T-chart listing reasons for Jefferson to support the Louisiana Purchase and reasons to oppose it. *(Support: opportunity to add economically important land and control on navigation on the Mississippi River. Opposition: possibly unconstitutional use of executive authority.)* Then have students indicate which option they would recommend to Jefferson. **WOR** **PCE**

"that the good sense of our country will correct the evil of loose construction when it shall produce ill effects." The Republican Congress promptly approved the treaty and appropriated money to implement its provisions. Finally, late in 1803, the French assumed formal control of Louisiana from Spain just long enough to turn the territory over to General James Wilkinson, the commissioner of the United States.

JEFFERSON'S QUANDARY

The government organized the Louisiana Territory much as it had organized the Northwest Territory, with the assumption that its various territories would eventually become states. The first of these was admitted to the Union as the state of Louisiana in 1812.

Lewis and Clark Explore the West

Meanwhile, several ambitious explorations were revealing the geography of the far-flung new territory to white Americans, few of whom had ever ventured much beyond the Mississippi River. In 1803, even before Napoleon's offer to sell Louisiana, Jefferson helped plan an expedition that was to cross the continent to the Pacific Ocean, gather geographic facts, and investigate prospects for trade with the Native Americans. He named as its leader his private secretary and Virginia neighbor, the thirty-three-year-old Meriwether Lewis, a veteran of Indian wars skilled in the ways of the wilderness. Lewis chose as a colleague the twenty-nine-year-old William Clark, who—like George Rogers Clark, his older brother—was an experienced frontiersman and Indian fighter. In the spring of 1804, Lewis and Clark, with a company of four dozen men, started up the Missouri River from St. Louis. With a Shoshone woman, Sacajawea, as their guide, they eventually crossed the Rocky Mountains, descended the Snake and Columbia Rivers, and in the late autumn of 1805 camped on the Pacific coast. In September 1806, they were back in St. Louis with elaborate records of the geography and the Native American civilizations they had observed along the way, and a lengthy diary recounting their experiences.

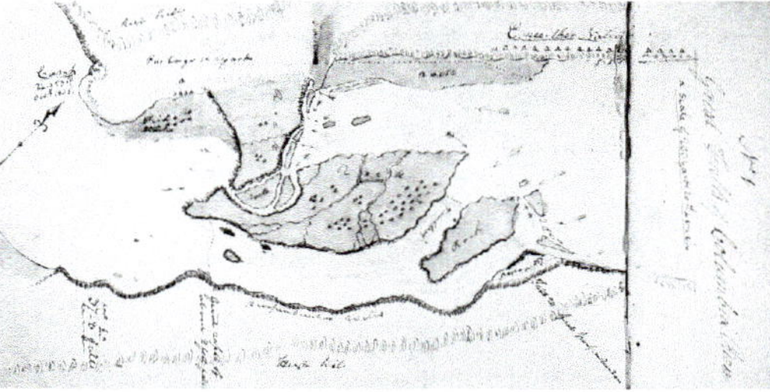

THE EXPLORATIONS OF LEWIS AND CLARK This map was drawn by William Clark while on his famous journey with Meriwether Lewis through the territory the United States had acquired in the Louisiana Purchase—and beyond. It shows the portages around the "Great Falls" of the Columbia River.

While Lewis and Clark were still on their journey, Jefferson dispatched other explorers to other parts of the Louisiana Territory. Lieutenant Zebulon Montgomery Pike, twenty-six years old, led an expedition in the fall of 1805 from St. Louis into the upper Mississippi Valley. In the summer of 1806, he set out again up the valley of the Arkansas River and into what later became Colorado, where he encountered (but failed in his attempt to climb) the peak that now bears his name. His account of his western travels created an enduring (and inaccurate) impression among many Americans in the East that the land between the Missouri River and the Rockies was an uninhabitable, uncultivable desert.

ZEBULON PIKE

The Burr Conspiracy

Jefferson's triumphant reelection in 1804 suggested that most of the nation approved the new territorial acquisition. But some New England Federalists raged against it. They realized that the more the West grew and the more new states joined the Union, the less power the Federalists and their region would retain. In Massachusetts, a group of the most extreme Federalists, known as the "Essex Junto," concluded that the only recourse for New England was to secede from the Union and form a separate "Northern Confederacy." If this confederacy was to have any hope for lasting success, the Federalists believed, it would have to include New York and New Jersey as well. But the leading Federalist in New York, Alexander Hamilton, refused to support the secessionist scheme. "Dismemberment of our empire," he wrote, "will be a clear sacrifice of great positive advantages without any counterbalancing good, administering no relief to our real disease, which is democracy."

ESSEX JUNTO

Federalists in New York then turned to Hamilton's greatest political rival: Vice President Aaron Burr. He was a politician without prospects in his own party. Jefferson had never forgiven him for the 1800 election deadlock. Burr accepted a Federalist proposal that he become their candidate for governor of New York in 1804, and there were rumors (unsupported by any evidence) that he had also agreed to support the Federalist plans for secession. Hamilton accused Burr of plotting treason and made numerous private remarks, widely reported in the press, about Burr's "despicable" character. When Burr lost the New York election, he blamed his defeat on Hamilton's malevolence. "These things must have an end," Burr wrote. He challenged Hamilton to a duel.

HAMILTON AND BURR

Dueling had by then already fallen into some disrepute in America, but many people still considered it a legitimate institution for settling matters of "honor." Hamilton feared that refusing Burr's challenge would brand him a coward. And so, on a July morning in 1804, the two men met at Weehawken, New Jersey. Hamilton was mortally wounded; he died the next day.

The resourceful and charismatic Burr was now a political outcast who had to flee New York to avoid an indictment for murder. But he found new outlets for his ambitions in the

Reasoning Processes

Comparing Have students read the section "Lewis and Clark Explore the West." Ask them to construct a Venn diagram comparing the Lewis and Clark expedition with that of Zebulon Pike. Have students then write a short statement about the most important similarity and difference between the two expeditions. **MIG**

West. Even before the duel, he had begun corresponding with prominent white settlers in the Southwest, especially with General James Wilkinson, now governor of the Louisiana Territory. Burr and Wilkinson hoped to lead an expedition that would capture Mexico from the Spanish. "Mexico glitters in all our eyes," Burr wrote; "the word is all we wait for." But there were also rumors that they wanted to separate the Southwest from the United States and create a western empire that Burr would rule. There is little evidence to support them.

Whether the rumors were true or not, many of Burr's opponents–including, ultimately, Jefferson himself–chose to believe them. When Burr led a group of armed followers down the Ohio River by boat in 1806, disturbing reports flowed into Washington. The most alarming was from Wilkinson. He had suddenly turned against Burr and now informed the president that treason was afoot and that an attack on New Orleans was imminent. Jefferson ordered Burr and his men arrested as traitors. Burr was brought to Richmond for trial. Determined to win a conviction, Jefferson carefully managed the government's case from Washington. But Chief Justice Marshall, presiding over the trial on circuit duty, limited the evidence the government could present and defined the charge in such a way that the jury had little choice but to acquit Burr.

The Burr "conspiracy" was in part the story of a single man's soaring ambitions and flamboyant personality. But it was also a symbol of the larger perils still facing the new nation. With a central government that remained deliberately weak, with vast tracts of land only nominally controlled by the United States, with ambitious political leaders willing, if necessary, to circumvent normal channels in their search for power, the legitimacy of the federal government, and indeed the existence of the United States as a stable and united nation, remained to be fully established.

EXPANSION AND WAR

Two very different conflicts were taking shape in the later years of Thomas Jefferson's presidency that would, together, draw the United States into a difficult and frustrating war. One was the continuing tension in Europe, which in 1803 escalated

THE NAPOLEONIC WARS

NEW ORLEANS IN 1803 Because of its location near the mouth of the Mississippi River, New Orleans was the principal port of western North America in the early nineteenth century. Through it, western farmers shipped their produce to markets in the East and Europe. This 1803 painting celebrates the American acquisition of the city from France as part of the Louisiana Purchase.

Reasoning Processes

Continuity and Change After students have read the section "The Burr Conspiracy," ask them to write a short paragraph explaining how the Essex Junto and the Burr Conspiracy were either continuations of earlier conflicts between Federalists and Republicans or changes from earlier conflicts. *(Earlier conflicts centered around questions of how much authority the federal government should have concerning banks, debt, whether to promote manufacturing, etc. The Essex Junto focused on the Federalist fear of growing federal power, including change from earlier conflicts where Republicans had opposed expansion of federal power. The Burr Conspiracy seemed more based on personality conflicts between Burr, Hamilton, and Jefferson.)* **PCE**

Discussion and Activities

Analyzing Details Have students examine the image "New Orleans in 1803." Ask them to brainstorm details about the painting. Discuss as a class what these details indicate about New Orleans in 1803. *(It is located on the river and appears to be a busy port. There is a row of large buildings and substantial houses indicating a wealthy class. The dike along the river starting at the bottom left indicates that much of the city was below water level. The symbolic eagle with the banner at the top indicates that the city was now under U.S. control.)* **WOR** **PCE** **SOC** **GEO**

Historical Thinking Skills

Claims and Evidence in Sources Have students read the document "Resisting the Impressment of Sailors." Ask them to evaluate what argument Madison was making in the letter. *(Madison was arguing that Britain was acting as an aggressor, violating the neutral rights of the United States and its sailors.)* **WOR**

once again into a full-scale conflict (the Napoleonic Wars). As the fighting escalated, both the British and the French took steps to prevent the United States from trading with (and thus assisting) the other.

The other conflict was in North America, a result of the ceaseless westward expansion of white settlement, which was now stretching to the Mississippi River and beyond, colliding again with Native American populations committed to protecting their lands and their trade from intruders. In both the North and the South, the threatened tribes mobilized to resist white encroachments. They began as well to forge connections with British forces in Canada and Spanish forces in Florida. The Native American conflict on land therefore became intertwined with the European conflict on the seas and ultimately helped cause the War of 1812, an unpopular conflict with ambiguous results.

Conflict on the Seas

The early nineteenth century saw a dramatic expansion of American shipping in the Atlantic. Britain retained significant naval superiority, but the British merchant marine was preoccupied with commerce in Europe and Asia and devoted little energy to trade with America. Thus the United States stepped effectively into the void and developed one of the most important merchant marines in the world, which soon controlled a large proportion of the trade between Europe and the West Indies.

In 1805, at the Battle of Trafalgar, a British fleet virtually destroyed what was left of the French navy. Because France could no longer challenge the British at sea, Napoleon now chose to pressure England through economic rather than naval means. He announced the creation of what he called the "Continental System." It was designed to close the European continent to British trade. The British government replied to Napoleon's decrees by establishing—through a series of "orders in council"—a blockade of the European coast. It required that any goods being shipped to Napoleon's Europe be carried either in British vessels or in neutral vessels stopping at British ports—precisely what Napoleon's policies forbade.

American ships were caught between Napoleon's decrees and Britain's orders in council. If they sailed directly for the European continent, they risked being captured by the British navy; if they sailed by way of a British port, they risked seizure by the French. Both of the warring powers were violating America's rights as a neutral nation. But most Americans considered the British, with their greater sea power, the worse offender. British ships pounced on Yankee merchantmen all over the ocean. Particularly infuriating to Americans, British vessels stopped United States ships on the high seas and seized sailors off the decks, making them victims of "impressment."

America's Predicament

Impressment

The British navy—with its floggings, low pay, and terrible shipboard conditions—was known as a "floating hell" to its sailors. Few volunteered. Most had to be "impressed" (forced) into the service. At every opportunity they deserted. By 1807, many of these deserters had joined the American merchant marine or the American navy. To check this loss of vital manpower, the British claimed the right to stop and search American merchant ships (although at first not naval vessels) and reimpress deserters. They did not claim the right to take native-born Americans, but they did claim the right to seize naturalized Americans born on British soil. In practice, the British navy often made no such distinctions, impressing British deserters and native-born Americans alike into service.

In the summer of 1807, the British went to more provocative extremes in an incident involving a vessel of the American

IMPORTANT
AND
LUMINOUS COMMUNICATION
ON THE
SUBJECT OF THE
IMPRESSMENT OF AMERICAN AND FOREIGN
SEAMEN
AND OTHER PERSONS.

IT has become manifest to every attentive observer, that the early and continued aggressions of Great Britain on our persons, our property, and our rights, imperiously demand a firm stand—an effectual, though calm system of measures of arrestation. For this purpose, it is our duty to make ourselves completely masters of the great truths and arguments by which our rights have been elucidated, supported and maintained.

On the 17th of January, 1806, the President of the United States communicated to Congress an extract from a dispatch of James Madison Esq. our secretary of state, to James Monroe Esq. our minister in London, which contains many facts highly important, and observations and arguments perfectly satisfactory and conclusive against "*impressments* of seamen and passengers, whether Foreign or American, on board of our vessels." The republication of that document at this crisis will at once display some of the reasons on which the government has probably declined to sanction the recent draught of a treaty with Great Britain, and will elucidate the ground on which the question of *the impressment of persons*, both native and alien, has been rested by our administration.

Extract of a letter from the Secretary of State to James Monroe Esq. dated 5th January, 1804.

We consider a neutral flag, on the high seas, as a safeguard to those sailing under it. Great Britain, on the contrary, asserts a right to search for, and seize her own subjects ; and un-

RESISTING THE IMPRESSMENT OF SAILORS On January 5, 1804, Secretary of State James Madison wrote this public letter to James Monroe on the unlawful impressment of American sailors by the British Royal Navy. The practice of boarding US ships and taking away sailors deemed by the British to be deserters from their navy came to a climax with the Chesapeake-Leopard Incident.

Discussion and Activities

Analyzing Issues Have students read the section "Conflict on the Seas." Ask them to write a short summary of the dilemma created for President Jefferson by the war between France and Britain. **WOR**

navy. Sailing from Norfolk, with several alleged deserters from the British navy among the crew, the American naval frigate *Chesapeake* encountered the British ship *Leopard*. When the American commander, James Barron, refused to allow the British to search the *Chesapeake*, the *Leopard* opened fire. Barron had no choice but to surrender, and a boarding party from the *Leopard* dragged four men off the American frigate.

CHESAPEAKE-LEOPARD INCIDENT

When news of the *Chesapeake-Leopard* incident reached the United States, there was great popular clamor for revenge. If Congress had been in session, it might have declared war. But Jefferson and Madison tried to maintain the peace. Jefferson expelled all British warships from American waters to lessen the likelihood of future incidents. Then he sent instructions to his minister in England, James Monroe, to demand that the British government renounce impressment. The British government disavowed the action of the officer responsible for the *Chesapeake-Leopard* incident and recalled him; it offered compensation for those killed and wounded in the incident; and it promised to return three of the captured sailors (one of the original four had been hanged). But the British refused to renounce impressment.

"PEACEABLE COERCION"

In an effort to prevent future incidents that might bring the nation again to the brink of war, Congress enacted a drastic measure known as "the Embargo." It became one of the most controversial political issues of its time. The Embargo prohibited American ships from leaving the United States for any foreign port anywhere in the world. The law was widely evaded, but it was effective enough to create a serious depression through most of the nation. Hardest hit were the merchants and shipowners of the Northeast, most of them Federalists.

THE EMBARGO

STRUGGLING WITH THE EMBARGO This cartoon lampoons the U.S. Embargo against Britain in 1807, a decision that created much economic hardship for many people. The word "Ograbme" (a common nickname for a snapping turtle) is "embargo" spelled backward. It shows a struggling merchant wrestling with the results of the Embargo. It was an effort to prevent the United States from being drawn into the wars between Britain and France. But the Embargo, which continued until 1812, not only hurt the American economy but also helped draw the nation into the War of 1812.

Historical Thinking Skills

Argumentation After students have read the section "Impressment," ask them to create a poster designed to recruit sailors into the British Navy. Have them include at least one argument or incentive designed to appeal to a potential recruit. **SOC** **WXT**

Discussion and Activities

Analyzing Images Have students examine the image "Struggling with the Embargo." Ask them to identify elements in the cartoon that are designed to promote opposition to the embargo. *(The embargo, in the form of a turtle, is shown biting the angered merchant. The ship off the coast flies a British flag, suggesting that Britain benefitted from the embargo. On the shore, a group of men are loading small boats, suggesting a smuggling operation.)* **WOR** **PCE** **WXT**

Reasoning Processes

Continuity and Change After students have read the section "Non-Intercourse Act," ask them to create a timeline showing legislation and events relevant to the embargo. *(Impressment; Chesapeake-Leopard affair; Embargo Act; Non-Intercourse Act; Macon's Bill No 2.)* Have them identify which of those events represented a continuity, or a change over time. **WOR** **PCE** **WXT**

The election of 1808 came in the midst of the Embargo-(1807) induced depression. James Madison, Jefferson's secretary of state and political ally, won the presidency. But the Embargo was clearly a growing political liability, and Jefferson decided to back down. A few days before leaving office, he approved a bill ending his experiment with what he called "peaceable coercion."

To replace the Embargo, Congress passed the Non-Intercourse Act just before Madison took office. The new law reopened trade with all nations but Great Britain and France. A year later, in 1810, Congress allowed the Non-Intercourse Act to expire and replaced it with Macon's Bill No. 2, which conditionally reopened free commercial relations with Britain and France. Napoleon announced that France would no longer interfere with American shipping, and Madison announced that an embargo against Great Britain alone would automatically go into effect early in 1811 unless Britain renounced its restrictions on American shipping. The British government repealed its blockade of Europe. But the repeal came too late to prevent war.

NON-INTERCOURSE ACT

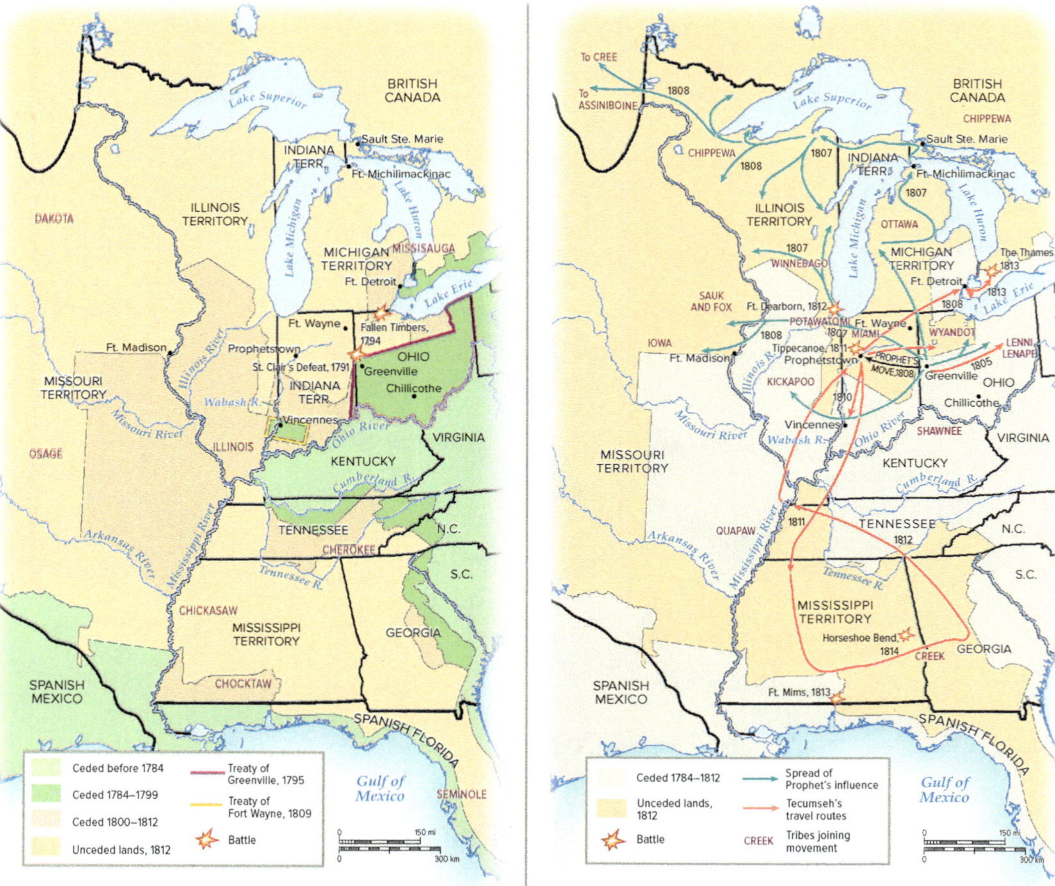

THE NATIVE AMERICAN RESPONSE TO WHITE ENCROACHMENT With land cessions and white western migration placing increased pressure on Native American cultures after 1790, news of the Prophet's revival fell on eager ears. It spread especially quickly northward along the shores of Lake Michigan and westward along Lake Superior and the interior of Wisconsin. Following the Battle of Tippecanoe, Tecumseh eclipsed the Prophet as the major leader of Native American resistance, but his trips south to forge political alliance met with less success.

Discussion and Activities

Historical Evidence and Argumentation Have students examine the map "The Native American Response to White Encroachment." Ask them to identify evidence from the map that might explain the location of major battles. *(Battles of Fallen Timbers; Ft. Wayne; defeat of St. Clair; Tippecanoe.)* **PCE** **MIG**

THE "INDIAN PROBLEM" AND THE BRITISH

The 1807 war crisis following the *Chesapeake-Leopard* incident revived the conflict between Native Americans and white Americans. Two important (and very different) leaders emerged to oppose one another in the conflict: William Henry Harrison and Tecumseh.

WILLIAM HENRY HARRISON

The Virginia-born Harrison, already a veteran of Native American conflicts, at age twenty-six, became a congressional delegate from the Northwest Territory in 1799. He was a committed advocate of growth and development in the western lands, and he was largely responsible for the passage in 1800 of the so-called Harrison Land Law, which enabled white settlers to acquire farms from the public domain on much easier terms than before.

In 1801, Jefferson appointed Harrison governor of the Indiana Territory to administer the president's proposed solution to the "Indian problem." Jefferson offered the Native Americans a choice: they could convert themselves into settled farmers and assimilate–become a part of white society; or they could migrate to the west of the Mississippi. In either case, they would have to give up their claims to tribal lands in the Northwest.

JEFFERSON'S OFFER

Jefferson considered the assimilation policy a benign alternative to continuing conflict between Native Americans and white settlers, a conflict he assumed the Native Americans were destined to lose. But to Native American nations, the new policy seemed far from benign, especially given the bludgeonlike efficiency with which Harrison set out to implement it. He played Native American nations against one another and used threats, bribes, trickery, and whatever other tactics he felt would help him conclude treaties. In the first decade of the nineteenth century, the number of white settlers east of the Appalachians had grown to more than 500,000–a population far larger than that of the Native Americans. It was becoming almost inevitable, as a result, that the Native Americans would face ever-growing pressure to move out of the way of the rapidly growing white settlements.

By 1807, the United States had extracted from reluctant tribal leaders treaty rights to eastern Michigan, southern Indiana, and most of Illinois. Meanwhile, in the Southwest, white Americans were taking millions of acres from other Native American groups in Georgia, Tennessee, and Mississippi. The Native Americans wanted to resist, but the separate groups were helpless by themselves against the power of the United States. They might have accepted their fate passively but for the emergence of two new factors.

One factor was the policy of the British authorities in Canada. After the *Chesapeake-Leopard* incident and the surge of anti-British feeling throughout the United States, the British colonial authorities began to expect an American invasion of Canada and took measures for their own defense. Among those measures were efforts to renew friendship with the Native Americans and provide them with increased supplies.

TECUMSEH AND THE PROPHET

The second, and more important, factor intensifying the border conflict was the rise of two remarkable Native American leaders, who together helped create an age of religious fervor and prophecy. One was Tenskwatawa, a charismatic religious leader and orator known as "the Prophet." He had experienced a mystical awakening in the process of recovering from alcoholism. Having freed himself from what he considered the evil

THE PROPHET'S MESSAGE

TECUMSEH Tecumseh's efforts to unite the groups of the Mississippi Valley against further white encroachments on their lands led him ultimately into an alliance with the British after the Battle of Tippecanoe in 1811. In the War of 1812, he was commissioned a brigadier general by the British and fought against the United States in the Battle of the Thames.

Discussion and Activities

Analyzing Points of View Have students read the section "The Indian Problem and the British." Ask them to write a short paragraph comparing Jefferson's offer of assimilation from the point of view of the president and from the point of view of the Native American groups. **SOC** **PCE** **MIG**

Reasoning Processes

Causation After students have read the section "The Indian Problem and the British," ask them to create a list of factors that caused increased tension between the United States and Native Americans in the early nineteenth century. Have students rank their list in order of importance, and then write a thesis that makes a claim about the most important causes of that tension. **MIG** **PCE**

Reasoning Processes

Comparison After students have read the section "The Prophet's Message," ask them to create a Venn diagram comparing the leaders Tenskwatawa and Tecumseh. Have students evaluate whether they were more similar or different, and discuss as a class which was a more effective leader and why. **PCE** **SOC**

effects of white culture, he began to speak to his people of the superior virtues of Native American civilization and the sinfulness and corruption of the white world. In the process, he inspired a religious revival that spread through numerous tribes and helped unite them. Like Neolin before him, and like his contemporary to the east, Handsome Lake, Tenskwatawa demonstrated the power of religious leaders to mobilize Native Americans behind political and military objectives. The Prophet's headquarters at the confluence of Tippecanoe Creek and the Wabash River (known as Prophetstown) became a sacred place for people of many tribes and attracted thousands of Native Americans from throughout the Midwest. Out of their common religious experiences, they began to consider joint political and military efforts as well. Tenskwatawa advocated for a Native American society entirely separate from that of white Americans and a culture rooted in tribal tradition. The effort to trade with the Anglos and to borrow from their culture would, he argued, lead to the death of Native American ways.

Tecumseh–the chief of the Shawnees called by his tribe "the Shooting Star"–was in many ways even more militant than his brother. "Where today are the Pequot?" he thundered. "Where are . . . the other powerful tribes of our people? They have vanished before the avarice and oppression of the white man." And he warned of Shawnee extermination if they did not take action against the white Americans moving into their lands.

Tecumseh understood, as few other Native American leaders had, that only through united action could the tribes hope to resist the advance of white civilization. Beginning in 1809, after groups in Indiana had ceded vast lands to the United States, he set out to unite all the Native Americans of the Mississippi Valley, north and south. Together, he promised, they would halt white expansion, recover the whole Northwest, and make the Ohio River the boundary between the United States and the Indian country. He maintained that Harrison and others, by negotiating treaties with individual groups, had obtained no real title to land. The land belonged to all Native Americans; none of them could rightfully cede any of it without the consent of the others.

In 1811, Tecumseh left Prophetstown and traveled down the Mississippi to visit the Native American nations of the South, hoping to persuade them to join the alliance. During his absence, Harrison camped near Prophetstown with 1,000 soldiers. On November 7, 1811, he provoked a battle. The white

JAMES AND DOLLEY MADISON James Madison may have been the most brilliant of the early leaders of the republic, but he was also one of the most serious and humorless, as this grim portrait suggests. His wife (born Dolley Payne in North Carolina and raised a Quaker in Virginia) was twenty-six when she married the forty-three-year-old Madison in 1794. Her charm and social grace made her one of her husband's greatest political assets. She acted as hostess for Thomas Jefferson, a widower, while her husband was secretary of state. And she presided over a lively social life during her eight years in the White House as First Lady.

Discussion and Activities

Analyzing Images Have students examine the images "James and Dolley Madison." Ask them to create a T-chart listing details from each of the portraits. Have students consider how the portraits are similar and different and what might account for the differences. *(Dolley was much younger. She was not a government leader and could be portrayed more casually.)* **SOC**

forces suffered losses as heavy as those of the Native Americans, but Harrison drove off the Native Americans and burned the town. The Battle of Tippecanoe (named for the creek near the fighting) disillusioned many of the Prophet's followers, who had believed that his magic would protect them. Tecumseh returned to find the confederacy in disarray. But there were still many warriors eager for combat, and by the spring of 1812 they were raiding white settlements and terrifying white settlers.

BATTLE OF TIPPECANOE

The bloodshed along the western borders was largely a result of the Native Americans own initiative, but Britain's agents in Canada had encouraged and helped supply the uprising. To Harrison and most white residents of the regions, there seemed only one way to make the West safe for Americans: drive the British out of Canada and annex that province to the United States.

FLORIDA AND WAR FEVER

While white "frontiersmen" in the North demanded the conquest of Canada, those in the South wanted the United States to acquire Spanish Florida, a territory that included the present state of Florida and the southern areas of what are now Alabama, Mississippi, and Louisiana. The territory was a continuing threat to white Southerners. Enslaved people escaped across the Florida border; Native Americans launched frequent raids north into white settlements from Florida. But white Southerners also coveted Florida because through it ran rivers that could provide residents of the Southwest with access to valuable ports on the Gulf of Mexico.

In 1810, American settlers in West Florida (an area that is part of Mississippi and Louisiana today) seized the Spanish fort at Baton Rouge and asked the federal government to annex the captured territory to the United States. President Madison happily agreed and then began planning to get the rest of Florida, too. The desire for Florida became yet another motivation for war with Britain. Spain was Britain's ally, and a war with Britain might provide a pretext for taking Spanish territory.

By 1812, war fever was growing on both the northern and southern borders of the United States. In the congressional elections of 1810, voters from these regions elected a large number of representatives of both parties eager for war with Britain. They became known as the "war hawks." Some of them were ardent nationalists fired by passion for territorial expansion—among them two men who would play a great role in national politics for much of the next four decades: Henry Clay of Kentucky and John C. Calhoun of South Carolina. Others were men impassioned in their defense of Republican values. Together, they formed a powerful coalition in favor of war.

WAR HAWKS

Clay became Speaker of the House in 1811, and he filled committees with those who shared his eagerness for war. He appointed Calhoun to the crucial Committee on Foreign Affairs, and both men began agitating for the conquest of Canada. Madison still hoped for peace. But he shared the concerns of other Republicans about the dangers to American trade, and he was losing control of Congress. On June 18, 1812, he gave in to the pressure and approved a declaration of war against Britain.

THE WAR OF 1812

Preoccupied with their struggle against Napoleon in Europe, the British were not eager for a conflict with the United States. Even after the Americans declared war, Britain largely ignored them for a time. But in the fall of 1812, Napoleon launched a catastrophic campaign against Russia that left his army in disarray and his power in Europe diminished. By late 1813, with the French Empire on its way to final defeat, Britain was able to turn its military attention to America.

BATTLES WITH THE TRIBES

Americans entered the War of 1812 with great enthusiasm, but events on the battlefield soon cooled their ardor. In the summer of 1812, American forces invaded Canada through Detroit. They soon had to retreat back to Detroit and in August surrendered the fort there. Other invasion efforts also failed. In the meantime, Fort Dearborn (Chicago) fell before a Native American attack.

Things went only slightly better for the United States on the seas. At first, American frigates won some spectacular victories over British warships, and American privateers destroyed or captured many British merchant ships, occasionally braving the coastal waters of the British Isles themselves and burning vessels within sight of the shore. But by 1813, the British navy—now less preoccupied with Napoleon—was counterattacking effectively, driving the American frigates to cover and imposing a blockade on the United States.

EARLY DEFEATS

The United States did, however, achieve significant early military successes on the Great Lakes. First, the Americans took command of Lake Ontario, which permitted them to raid and burn York (now Toronto), the capital of Canada. American forces then seized control of Lake Erie, mainly through the work of the youthful Oliver Hazard Perry, who engaged and dispersed a British fleet at Put-in-Bay on September 10, 1813. This made possible another invasion of Canada by way of Detroit, which Americans could now reach easily by water. William Henry Harrison, the American commander in the West, pushed up the Thames River into upper Canada and, on October 5, 1813, won a victory notable for the death of Tecumseh, who was serving as a brigadier general in the British army. The Battle of the Thames weakened and disheartened the Native Americans of the Northwest and greatly diminished their ability to defend their claims to the region.

PUT-IN-BAY

In the meantime, another white military leader was striking an even harder blow at the tribes of the Southwest. The

Discussion and Activities

Analyzing Issues After students have read the section "Battle of Tippecanoe," ask them to evaluate Tecumseh's claim that individual tribes could not cede land that belonged to all Native Americans. Discuss how persuasive this claim was then and how persuasive it would be now. **PCE** **MIG**

Reasoning Processes

Causation Have students read the section "Florida and War Fever." Ask them to brainstorm a list of factors that led to a declaration of war against Great Britain. *(Impressment; seizure of ships; supplying Native Americans; desire for territorial expansion.)* Have students write a thesis statement that makes a claim about the most important causes for the War of 1812. Ask students to share their thesis statements with a partner and give feedback to each other. **WOR** **PCE** **WXT** **GEO** **MIG** **NAT**

Discussion and Activities

Analyzing Cause and Effect After students have read the section "Battles with the Tribes," ask them to write a short paragraph explaining the effects the battles of the War of 1812 had on Native Americans. **PCE** **MIG**

Creeks, whom Tecumseh had aroused on a visit to the South and whom the Spanish had supplied with weapons, had been attacking white settlers near the Florida border. Andrew Jackson, a wealthy Tennessee planter and a general in the state militia, temporarily abandoned plans for an invasion of Florida and set off in pursuit of them. On March 27, 1814, in the Battle of Horseshoe Bend, Jackson's men took terrible revenge on the Native Americans–slaughtering women and children along with warriors–and broke the resistance of the Creek. The Creek agreed to cede most of its lands to the United States and retreated westward, farther into the interior. The battle also won Jackson a commission as a major general in the United States Army. In that capacity he led his men farther south into Florida and, on November 7, 1814, seized the Spanish fort at Pensacola.

Battles with the British

The victories over the Native Americans were not enough for the United States to win the war. After the surrender of Napoleon in 1814, England prepared to invade the United States. A British

THE BRITISH INVASION

THE WAR OF 1812 This map illustrates the military maneuvers of the British and the Americans during the War of 1812. It shows all the theaters of the war, from New Orleans to southern Canada, the extended land and water battle along the Canadian border and in the Great Lakes, and the fighting around Washington and Baltimore. Note how in all these theaters there are about the same number of British and American victories.

What finally brought this inconclusive war to an end?

Answers

The War of 1812

Both sides gave up several of their original demands and agreed to return to the status quo. **WOR** armada sailed up the Patuxent River from Chesapeake Bay and landed an army that marched a short distance overland to Bladensburg, on the outskirts of Washington, where it dispersed a poorly trained force of American militiamen. On August 24, 1814, the British troops entered Washington and set fire to several public buildings, including the White House, in retaliation for the earlier American burning of the Canadian capital at York. This was the low point of American fortunes in the war.

Leaving Washington in partial ruins, the British army proceeded up the bay toward Baltimore. But Baltimore harbor, guarded by Fort McHenry, was prepared. To block the approaching fleet, the American garrison had sunk several ships to clog the entry to the harbor, thus forcing the British to bombard the fort from a distance.

Through the night of September 13, Francis Scott Key, a Washington lawyer who was on board one of the British ships trying to secure the release of an American prisoner, watched the bombardment. The next morning, "by the dawn's early light," he could see the flag on the fort still flying; he recorded his pride in the moment by scribbling a poem—"The Star-Spangled Banner"—on the back of an envelope. The British withdrew from Baltimore, and Key's words were soon set to the tune of an old English drinking song. In 1931, "The Star-Spangled Banner" became the official national anthem.

Meanwhile, American forces repelled another British invasion in northern New York at the Battle of Plattsburgh, on September 11, 1814, which turned back a much larger British naval and land force and secured the northern border of the United States. In the South, a formidable array of battle-hardened British veterans, fresh from the campaign against the French in Spain, landed below New Orleans and prepared to advance north up the Mississippi. Awaiting the British was Andrew Jackson with a motley collection of Tennesseans, Kentuckians, Creoles, African Americans, pirates, and regular army troops behind earthen fortifications. On January 8, 1815, the British advanced, but their exposed forces were no match for Jackson's well-protected men. After the Americans had repulsed several waves of attackers, the British finally retreated, leaving behind 700 dead (including their commander, Sir Edward Pakenham), 1,400 wounded, and 500 prisoners. Jackson's losses were 8 killed and 13 wounded. Only later did news reach North America that the United States and Britain had signed a peace treaty several weeks before the Battle of New Orleans.

BATTLE OF NEW ORLEANS

THE REVOLT OF NEW ENGLAND

With a few notable exceptions, such as the Battles of Put-in-Bay and New Orleans, the military operations of the United States between 1812 and 1815 consisted of a series of humiliating failures. As a result, the American government faced increasing popular opposition as the contest dragged on. In New England, opposition both to the war and to the Republican government that was waging it was so extreme that some Federalists celebrated British victories. In Congress, in the meantime, the Republicans had persistent trouble with the Federalist opposition, led by a young congressman from New Hampshire, Daniel Webster, who missed no opportunity to embarrass the administration.

By now the Federalists were a minority in the country as a whole, but they were still the majority party in New England. Some of them began to dream again of creating a separate nation in that region, which they could dominate and in which they could escape what they saw as the tyranny of slaveholders and backwoodsmen. Talk of secession revived and reached a climax in the winter of 1814–1815.

On December 15, 1814, delegates from the New England states met in Hartford, Connecticut, to discuss their grievances.

Discussion and Activities

Analyzing Points of View After students have read the section "The British Invasion," ask them to search the Internet for the songs "The War of 1812," performed by the Canadian comedy troupe Three Dead Trolls in a Baggie, and "The Battle of New Orleans," by Johnny Horton. Ask students to find examples from the lyrics that demonstrate each song's point of view about the war. **PCE** **SOC** **NAT** **WOR**

THE BOMBARDMENT OF FORT MCHENRY The British bombardment of Fort McHenry in Baltimore harbor in September 1814 was of modest importance to the outcome of the War of 1812. It is remembered as the occasion for Francis Scott Key to write his poem "The Star-Spangled Banner," which recorded his sentiments at seeing an American flag still flying over the fort "by the dawn's early light."

The Library of Congress

Reasoning Processes

Argumentation Have students read the section "The Battle of New Orleans." Ask them to identify important results of the battle. Have students then make an argument about whether the timing of the battle was important. **NAT** **WOR**

Discussion and Activities

Analyzing Issues After students have read the section "The Hartford Convention," ask them to list the demands made by the representatives at the Convention. If necessary, have students look up a definition of treason, and then discuss whether the demands of the Hartford Convention constituted treason. **PCE**

Those who favored secession at the Hartford Convention were outnumbered by a comparatively moderate majority. But while the convention's report only hinted at secession, it reasserted the right of nullification and proposed seven amendments to the Constitution (presumably as the condition of New England's remaining in the Union)—amendments designed to protect New England from the growing influence of the South and the West.

HARTFORD CONVENTION

Because the war was going badly and the government was becoming desperate, the New Englanders assumed that the Republicans would have to agree to their demands. Soon after the convention adjourned, however, the news of Jackson's smashing victory at New Orleans reached the cities of the Northeast. A day or two later, reports arrived from abroad of a negotiated peace. In the euphoria of this apparent triumph, the Hartford Convention and the Federalists came to seem futile, irrelevant, even treasonable. The failure of the secession effort was a virtual death blow to the Federalist Party.

THE PEACE SETTLEMENT

Peace talks between the United States and Britain had begun even before fighting in the War of 1812 began. John Quincy Adams, Henry Clay, and Albert Gallatin led the American delegation.

In the negotiations, the Americans gave up their demand for a British renunciation of impressment and for the cession of Canada to the United States. The British abandoned their call for the creation of a Native American buffer state in the Northwest. The negotiators referred other disputes to arbitration. Hastily drawn up, a treaty was signed on Christmas Eve 1814. It was named the Treaty of Ghent after the Dutch city in which it was signed.

TREATY OF GHENT

Other settlements followed the Treaty of Ghent and contributed to a long-term improvement in Anglo-American relations. A commercial treaty in 1815 gave Americans the right to trade freely with England and much of the British Empire. The Rush-Bagot agreement of 1817 provided for mutual disarmament on the Great Lakes; eventually (although not until 1872) the Canadian-American boundary became the longest "unguarded frontier" in the world.

RUSH-BAGOT AGREEMENT

For the other parties to the War of 1812, the Native American nations east of the Mississippi, the Treaty of Ghent was of no lasting value. It required the United States to restore the Native American lands seized by white Americans in the fighting to the Native American nations, but those provisions were never enforced. Ultimately, the war was another disastrous blow to the capacity of Native Americans to resist white expansion. Tecumseh, their most important leader, was dead. The British, their most important allies, were gone from the Northwest. The alliance that Tecumseh and the Prophet had forged was in disarray. And the end of the war spurred a great new drive by white settlers deeper into the West, into land the Native Americans were less than ever able to defend.

ATTACKING THE FEDERALISTS A Republican cartoonist derided the secession efforts of New England Federalists at the Hartford Convention in this cartoon. It portrays timid men representing Massachusetts, Connecticut, and Rhode Island preparing to leap into the arms of George III.

The Library of Congress

Reasoning Processes

Comparing Have students read the section "The Peace Settlement." Ask them to create a T-chart identifying terms in the Treaty of Ghent that favored either the United States or Great Britain. Then have students evaluate which side, if any, appeared to have negotiated more favorable terms. **WOR**

CHAPTER 7 REVIEW

CONNECTING THEMES

Chapter Seven first explored the rise of cultural nationalism in the United States in the early nineteenth century. The Republican vision of America rested on the concept of a virtuous and enlightened citizenry. As a consequence, educational opportunities expanded for some citizens. American writers and artists also began to distance themselves from European influences, and American religion moved away from Enlightenment rationalism. But at the same time, the new culture was posing serious challenges to Republican ideals.

Jefferson and his supporters hoped that the United States would remain a simple agrarian republic. But during these years, the country began a slow and tentative transition into an urban and industrial society as cities grew and technology spread. As president, Jefferson never completely repudiated Federalist policies, and he doubled the size of the United States through the Louisiana Purchase from France.

Westward expansion, however, led to increased conflict with Native Americans. Serious tensions with Great Britain also erupted after the resumption of the Napoleonic Wars in Europe in 1803. Conflict on the seas and the frontier led to a second war with Great Britain in 1812. The clash revealed regional divisions and had an ambiguous outcome, but it also reinforced a growing sense of American nationalism.

You should consider the following questions as you review the themes for this chapter:

- How did the rise of the First Industrial Revolution and the development of a national market impact the economic, political, and social aspects of American life?
- What were the causes and effects of western migration?
- What were the causes and effects of the first American party system?
- How did American trade, neutrality, and western expansion lead to conflict with a variety of European countries?
- What was the impact of territorial acquisition on migration, political power, and foreign relations in the United States?
- How did Enlightenment ideas and the belief in the perfectibility of humanity influence the development of American culture and society?

KEY TERMS

Aaron Burr 214
American shipping 203
camp meetings 200
Cane Ridge 199
Deism 198
Eli Whitney 203
Embargo Act 217
Handsome Lake 202
Hartford Convention 223
impressment 216
Industrialism 202
John Marshall 209
judicial review 209
Judith Sargent Murray 186
Louisiana Purchase 213
Marbury vs. Madison 209
Mercy Otis Warren 198
Neolin 199
New Light dissenters 199
Noah Webster 197
Robert Fulton 203
Samuel Slater 202
Second Great Awakening 198
Tecumseh 219
The Embargo 217
The Prophet (Tenskwatawa) 219
Toussaint L'Ouverture 211
War Hawks 221
War of 1812 221
Washington Irving 198
William Henry Harrison 219

Discussion and Activities

Analyzing After students have read Chapter 7, discuss as a class whether the War of 1812 constituted a "second war for independence," as some observers have claimed. Ask them to explain the reasons for their responses. **WOR** **NAT**

Key Terms

Students should be familiar with the key terms and be able to define them in the context of religious movements, the growth of industry, and westward expansion. Encourage students to use these terms in performing review exercises and exam practice for this chapter.

Go Online Chapter 7 Content Review

Assessing Student Understanding Use the online assessment to assess student understanding of concepts and topics within the chapter. You can assign the ready-made Chapter 7 Content Review or create your own from available questions. This easy-to-use tool helps you design assessments that meet the needs of different types of learners.

CHAPTER 7
THE JEFFERSONIAN ERA

Answers

Multiple Choice

1. C; **2.** D; **3.** A

Short Answer

4A) One point of view from the image is that of a struggling merchant negatively impacted by the embargo. The caption in the cartoon says "ograbme," which is *embargo* spelled backward.

4B) Jefferson was reacting to the European policy, particularly from France and England, of impressing sailors from U.S. ships and capturing commerce. Jefferson reasoned that if the United States refused to trade with those countries, it would significantly hurt their economy as the United States was a major trading partner with both.

4C) Jefferson's embargo had devastating effects on the American economy. American merchants relied on trade with Britain and France for survival, but because the embargo forbid any commerce with either country, many businesses were effectively shut down completely. The embargo backfired on Jefferson.

5A) Both movements were reactions to the perceived secularization of the American society. There was great concern over the general lack of interest in religion within the colonies and the states, and the Great Awakenings attempted to counter that sentiment.

5B) The Second Great Awakening accelerated the growth of different sects and denominations within American religious while the First Great Awakening focused on the renewal of religious devotion largely within Protestantism.

5C) One of the most significant effects of the Second Great Awakening was the influence that women had upon the movement. Women were more numerous in certain regions than men, and many women found in religion a foundation on which to build their lives. This is also related to the fact that following the Second Great Awakening, many women got involved with reform movements.

AP EXAM PRACTICE

Questions assume cumulative content knowledge from this chapter and previous chapters.

MULTIPLE CHOICE

Use the image on page 195 and your knowledge of U.S. history to answer questions 1-3.

1. Based on the image, American beliefs in the Revolutionary Era and the early Republic were largely influenced by
   (A) the First Great Awakening.
   (B) the Second Great Awakening.
   (C) the Enlightenment.
   (D) European Romanticism.

2. After the Revolution, many sought increased educational opportunities for American women so that they could
   (A) expand their economic opportunities.
   (B) expand their access to voting rights in the new Republic.
   (C) prepare for political office to represent their communities.
   (D) raise their children to be good future citizens.

3. Increased educational opportunities were part of a larger movement to create
   (A) an independent American culture.
   (B) a new society based on gender equality.
   (C) a political system that ensured racial equity.
   (D) artistic forms that celebrated the nation's English colonial heritage.

SHORT ANSWER

Use your knowledge of U.S. history to answer questions 4-5.

4. Use the image on page 217 to answer A, B, and C.
   (A) Briefly describe ONE point of view about the U.S. embargo as depicted in the image.
   (B) Briefly explain ONE specific historical cause that led to the embargo in 1807.
   (C) Briefly explain ONE specific historical effect that resulted from the embargo in 1807.

5. Answer A, B, and C
   (A) Briefly describe ONE specific historical similarity between the First and Second Great Awakenings.
   (B) Briefly describe ONE specific historical difference between the First and Second Great Awakenings.
   (C) Briefly explain ONE specific historical effect of the Second Great Awakening.

LONG ESSAY

Develop a thoughtful and thorough historical argument that evaluates the statement below. Begin your essay with a thesis statement, and support it with specific historical evidence and examples.

6. Evaluate the relative importance of the issues and events that led to the War of 1812 between the British and the United States.

Answers

Long Essay

6. Possible thesis: There was a small segment of the U.S. population who were advocating war with Britain because they wanted to continue westward expansion northward into Canada. However, a much stronger cause was the trade war between the U.S. and Britain. Further, Britain refused to abide by the agreements of the peace treaty following the American Revolution, causing considerable havoc on the western frontier for settlers. Therefore, further expansion was a cause of the War of 1812, but the actions of the British were much stronger causes for the war. Specific historical evidence: There was a serious trade war going on between the United States and Europe (particularly Britain and France, who also happened to be at war with each other). The British were also engaged in impressment of United States vessels into the Royal Navy. The British refused to abandon the western forts, which was a direct violation of the peace treaty that ended the American Revolution. The British military was aiding the American Indians out west on the frontier. There was a segment of the United States population that advocated annexing parts of Canada. Finally, there was a segment of the United States population that was advocating for war with Britain as a way to uphold national honor from a number of British insults.

8 VARIETIES OF AMERICAN NATIONALISM

CELEBRATING THE NATION
Celebrations of Independence Day, like this one in New York City, became major festive events throughout the United States in the early nineteenth century, a sign of rising American nationalism.

CONNECTING CONCEPTS

Chapter Eight begins by exploring the rise in American nationalism following the War of 1812. Nationalism took various forms, including the growth of economic unification spurred by the American System, the reduction of political tensions during the Era of Good Feelings, and westward territorial expansion.

American nationalism also coincided with a surge in American regionalism. The acquisition of new lands, like the Louisiana Territory, led to more debates about the status of slavery. The tension between the different regions grew and hardened. Political solutions, like the Missouri Compromise, provided temporary respite, but sectionalism continued to compete with nationalism, which also affected foreign policy after the War of 1812. Through the Monroe Doctrine, the United States asserted its primacy in the Western Hemisphere.

Chief Justice John Marshall, a prominent Federalist, also dominated the Supreme Court during this era. The major decisions of the Marshall Court defined the proper balance of federalism in the United States at the time. The court's rulings reinforced the constitutional principle of federalism and the supremacy of the Constitution, paving the way for an increased federal role in economic growth.

As you read, you should:

- Analyze the way the Supreme Court, under Chief Justice Marshall, asserted federal power over the states.
- Describe the different parts of Henry Clay's American System.
- Identify the ways that the new transportation system aided the movement of goods and people as well as allowing for greater access to natural resources, markets, and western lands.
- Evaluate the ways that the United States sought to dominate the North American continent and also sought to extend its influence into Latin America with the Monroe Doctrine.
- Analyze how the geographic growth of the United States led to controversy over the expansion of slavery into new territories and increased conflict with Native Americans.

Pacing Guide

Chapter 8 explores key concepts from Period 4: 1800–1848 of the AP U.S. History Curriculum Framework. The suggested instruction time for Chapter 8 is 2 days.

Key Concepts

4.1.I The nation's transition to a more participatory democracy was achieved by expanding suffrage from a system based on property ownership to one based on voting by all adult white men, and it was accompanied by the growth of political parties.

4.2.I New transportation systems and technologies dramatically expanded manufacturing and agricultural production.

4.3.I Struggling to create an independent global presence, the United States sought to claim territory throughout the North American continent and promote foreign trade.

Discussion and Activities

Analyzing Images Have students examine the image "Celebrating the Nation." Ask them to identify details that demonstrate a sense of nationalism. *(Celebration of Independence Day; numerous American flags; soldiers marching in a parade.)* Discuss with the class how early nineteenth-century Americans celebrated Independence Day and ask them to compare with current celebrations. **NAT**

Historical Thinking Skills

Analyzing Cause and Effect Have students read the section "Banking, Currency, and Protection." Ask them to create a t-chart listing opportunities and challenges for the American economy following the War of 1812. Have students circle the items that were addressed by the federal government after the war.

WXT **PCE** **WOR**

BUILDING A NATIONAL MARKET

The end of the War of 1812 allowed the United States to resume the economic growth and territorial expansion that had characterized the first decade of the nineteenth century. A vigorous postwar boom led to a disastrous bust in 1819. Brief though it was, the collapse was evidence that the United States continued to lack some of the basic institutions necessary to sustain long-term growth. In the years to follow, there were strenuous efforts to introduce stability to the expanding economy.

BANKING, CURRENCY, AND PROTECTION

The War of 1812 may have stimulated the growth of manufacturing by cutting off imports, but it also produced chaos in shipping and banking, and it exposed dramatically the inadequacy of the existing transportation and financial systems. The aftermath of the war, therefore, saw the emergence of a series of political issues connected with national economic development.

POSTWAR ISSUES

The wartime experience underlined the need for another national bank. After the expiration of the first Bank of the United States's charter in 1811, a large number of state banks had begun operations. They issued vast quantities of bank notes but did not always retain enough reserves of gold or silver to redeem the notes on demand. The notes passed from hand to hand more or less as money, but their actual value depended on the reputation of the bank that issued them. Thus there was a wide variety of notes, of widely differing value, in circulation at the same time. The result was a confusion that made honest business difficult and counterfeiting easy.

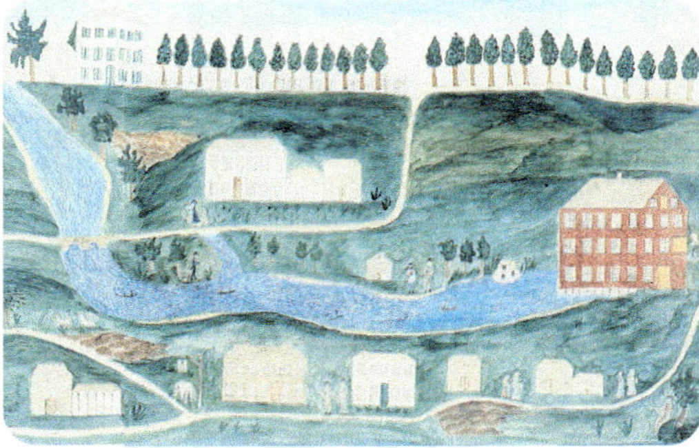

AN EARLY MILL IN NEW ENGLAND This early folk painting of about 1814 shows the small town of East Chelmsford, Massachusetts—still primarily agrarian, with its rural houses, open fields, and grazing livestock, but with a small textile mill already operating along the stream, at right. A little more than a decade later, the town had been transformed into a major manufacturing center and renamed for the family that owned the mills: Lowell.

Congress dealt with the currency problem by chartering a second Bank of the United States in 1816. It was essentially the same institution Hamilton had founded in 1791 except that it had more capital than its predecessor. The national bank could not forbid state banks to issue currency, but its size and power enabled it to dominate the state banks. It could compel them to issue only sound notes or risk being forced out of business.

SECOND BANK OF THE UNITED STATES

Congress also acted to promote the already burgeoning manufacturing sector of the nation's economy. Manufactured goods had been so scarce during the conflict that, even with comparatively unskilled labor and inexperienced management, new factories could start operations virtually assured of quick profits.

The American textile industry experienced a particularly dramatic growth. Between 1807 and 1815, the total number of cotton spindles increased more than fifteenfold, from 8,000 to 130,000. Until 1814, the textile factories—most of them in New England—produced only yarn and thread; families operating hand-looms at home did the actual weaving of cloth. Then the Boston merchant Francis Cabot Lowell, after examining textile machinery in England, developed a power loom that was better than its English counterpart. In 1813, Lowell organized the Boston Manufacturing Company and, at Waltham, Massachusetts, founded the first mill in America to carry on spinning and weaving under a single roof. Lowell's company was an important step in revolutionizing American manufacturing and in shaping the character of the early industrial workforce.

GROWTH OF THE TEXTILE INDUSTRY

But the end of the war suddenly dimmed the prospects for American industry. British ships—determined to recapture their lost markets—swarmed into American ports and unloaded cargoes of manufactured goods, many priced below cost. As one English leader explained to Parliament, it was "well worth while to incur a loss upon the first exportation, in order, by the glut, to stifle in the cradle those rising manufactures in the United States." The "infant industries" cried out for protection against these tactics, arguing that they needed time to grow strong enough to withstand the foreign competition.

In 1816, protectionists in Congress won passage of a tariff law that effectively limited competition from abroad on a wide range of items, the most important of which was cotton cloth. There were objections from agricultural interests, who would have to pay higher prices for manufactured goods as a result. But the nationalist dream of creating an important American industrial economy prevailed.

A PROTECTIVE TARIFF

TRANSPORTATION

The nation's most pressing economic need in the aftermath of the war was for a better transportation system. Without one, manufacturers would not have access to the raw materials

Port of the Town of Chelmsford, By Miss Warren. Abby Aldrich Rockefeller Folk Art Museum, Colonial Williamsburg Foundation, Williamsburg, VA

Go Online AP Exam Preparation

AP Exam Practice Use the online assessment to help prepare students for the AP Exam. You can assign the ready-made AP-style short answer questions, document-based questions, and multiple-choice questions assessing concepts, themes, and skills from Period 4 and AP style long-essay questions organized in sets of 3 questions from various time periods. You can also create your own tests from available questions. This easy-to-use tool helps you design assessments that meet the needs of different types of learners.

they needed or to domestic markets. So an old debate resumed: Should the federal government help to finance roads and other "internal improvements"?

The idea of using government funds to finance road building was not new. When Ohio entered the Union in 1803, the federal government agreed that part of the proceeds from the government's sale of public lands should finance road construction. In 1807, Jefferson's secretary of the treasury, Albert Gallatin, proposed that revenues from the Ohio land sales should help finance a National Road from the Potomac River to the Ohio River. Both Congress and the president approved. After many delays, construction of the National Road finally began in 1811 at Cumberland, Maryland, on the Potomac; and by 1818, this highway—with a crushed stone surface and massive stone bridges—ran as far as Wheeling, Virginia, on the Ohio River. Meanwhile, the state of Pennsylvania gave $100,000 to a private company to extend the Lancaster pike westward to Pittsburgh. Over both of these roads a heavy traffic soon moved: stagecoaches, Conestoga wagons, private carriages, and other vehicles, as well as droves of cattle. Despite high tolls, the roads made transportation costs across the mountains lower than ever before. Manufactures, particularly textiles, moved from the Atlantic seaboard to the Ohio Valley in unprecedented quantities.

GOVERNMENT-FUNDED ROADS

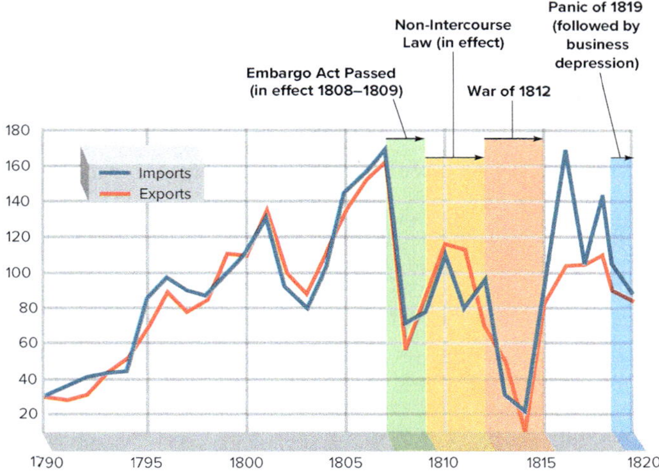

AMERICAN IMPORTS AND EXPORTS, 1790–1820 This chart shows the pattern of goods imported to and exported from the United States—the level of foreign trade, and the balance between goods bought and goods sold. Americans were heavily dependent on Britain and Europe for "finished" or "manufactured" goods in these years; and as you can see, imports grew as rapidly as, and often even more rapidly than, exports. Note how the nation's disputes with European powers depressed both exports and imports from about 1808 to 1814.

How does this chart help explain Congress's passage of a protective tariff law in 1816?

At the same time, on the rivers and the Great Lakes, steam-powered shipping was expanding rapidly. The development of steamboat lines was already well under way before the War of 1812, thanks to the technological advances introduced by Robert Fulton and others. The war had retarded expansion for a time, but by 1816, river steamers were beginning to journey up and down the Mississippi to the Ohio River, and up the Ohio as far as Pittsburgh. Within a few years, steamboats were carrying far more cargo on the Mississippi than all the earlier forms of river transport—flatboats, barges, and others—combined. They stimulated the agricultural economy of the West and the South, by providing much readier access to markets at greatly reduced cost. And they enabled eastern manufacturers to send their finished goods west.

STEAMBOATS

Despite the progress with steamboats and turnpikes, there remained serious gaps in the nation's transportation network, as the War of 1812 had shown. Once the British blockade cut off Atlantic shipping, the coastal roads became choked by the unaccustomed volume of north-south traffic. Long lines of wagons waited for a chance to use the ferries that were still the only means of crossing most rivers. Oxcarts, pressed into emergency service, took six or seven weeks to go from Philadelphia to Charleston. In some areas there were serious shortages of goods that normally traveled by sea, and prices rose to new heights. Rice cost three times as much in New York as in Charleston, flour three times as much in Boston as in Richmond—all because of the difficulty of transportation. There were military consequences, too. On the northern and western frontiers, the absence of good roads had frustrated American campaigns.

In 1815, with this wartime experience in mind, President Madison called the attention of Congress to the "great importance of establishing throughout our country the roads and canals which can be best executed under the national authority," and suggested that a constitutional amendment would resolve any doubts about Congress's authority to provide for their construction. Representative John C. Calhoun promptly introduced a bill that would have used the funds owed the government by the Bank of the United States to finance internal improvements. "Let us, then, bind the republic together with a perfect system of roads and canals," Calhoun urged. "Let us conquer space."

Congress passed Calhoun's internal improvements bill, but President Madison, on his last day in office (March 3, 1817), vetoed it. He supported the purpose of the bill, he explained, but he still believed that Congress lacked authority to fund the improvements without a constitutional amendment. It remained for state governments and private enterprise to undertake the tremendous task of building the transportation network necessary for the growing American economy.

VETOING INTERNAL IMPROVEMENTS

Reasoning Processes

Comparison After students have read the sections "Government-Funded Roads" and "Steamboats," ask them to create a Venn diagram comparing overland travel and travel using waterways. Have them draw a conclusion about which form of travel would be better for most merchants and travelers.

WXT MIG PCE GEO

Answers

American Imports and Exports, 1790–1820.

The rapid rise in imports following the War of 1812 threatened to undermine new American manufacturers.

WXT WOR PCE

CHAPTER 8
Varieties of American Nationalism

Reasoning Processes

Causation Have students read the section "Reasons for Westward Expansion." Ask them to create a list of reason for westward settlement. Have students rank the reasons from most to least important, then write a thesis statement making a claim about the most important reasons for westward expansion. **MIG** **GEO** **WXT**

EXPANDING WESTWARD

One reason for the growing interest in internal improvements was the sudden and dramatic surge in westward expansion in the years following the War of 1812. "Old America seems to be breaking up and moving westward," wrote an English observer at the time. By the time of the census of 1820, white settlers had pushed well beyond the Mississippi River, and the population of the western regions was increasing more rapidly than that of the nation as a whole. Almost one of every four white Americans lived west of the Appalachians in 1820; ten years before, only one in seven had resided there.

The Great Migrations

The westward movement of the white American population was one of the most important developments of the nineteenth century. It had a profound effect on the nation's economy, bringing vast new regions into the emerging capitalist system. It had great political ramifications, which ultimately became a major factor in the coming of the Civil War. And like earlier movements west, it thrust peoples of different cultures and traditions into intimate (and often disastrous) association with one another.

Reasons for Westward Expansion

There were several important reasons for this expansion. The pressures driving white Americans out of the East came in part from the continued growth of the nation's population—both through natural increase and through immigration. Between 1800 and 1820, the population nearly doubled—from 5.3 million to 9.6 million. The growth of cities absorbed some of that increase, but most Americans were still farmers. The agricultural lands of the East were by now largely occupied, and some of them were exhausted. In the South, the spread of the plantation system, and of an enslaved labor force, limited opportunities for new settlers.

At the same time, the West itself was becoming increasingly attractive to white settlers. The War of 1812 had helped diminish (although it did not wholly eliminate) one of the traditional deterrents to western expansion: Native American opposition. And in the aftermath of the war, the federal government continued its policy of pushing the remaining groups

STEAMBOATS ON THE HUDSON Inventor Robert Fulton developed an engine that could propel a boat from Manhattan to Albany, a distance of about 150 miles, in thirty two hours. His steam-powered vessels, first built in 1807, were the first large and reliable enough to be commercially valuable.

Photo © Tarker/The Bridgeman Art Library

Discussion and Activities

Analyzing Images Have students examine the image "Steamboats on the Hudson." Ask them to look for details that demonstrate how new and unproven steam technology was. *(The ship still had sails, an indication that Fulton wanted to have a backup source of power in case the steam engine failed.)* **WXT**

farther and farther west. A series of treaties in 1815 wrested more land from Native Americans. In the meantime, the government was erecting a chain of stockaded forts along the Great Lakes and the Mississippi to protect the frontier. It also created a "factor" system, by which government factors (or agents) supplied the Native Americans with goods at cost. This not only worked to drive Canadian traders out of the region; it also helped create a situation of dependency on the factors that made Native Americans easier to control.

THE FACTOR SYSTEM

Now that fertile lands were secure for white settlement, migrants from throughout the East flocked to the Old Northwest (now called the Midwest). The Ohio and Monongahela Rivers were the main routes westward, until the completion of the Erie Canal in 1825. Once on the Ohio, the migrants floated downstream on flatboats bearing all their possessions, then left the river (often at Cincinnati, which was becoming one of the region's–and the nation's–principal cities) and pressed on overland with wagons, handcarts, packhorses, cattle, and hogs.

THE PLANTATION SYSTEM IN THE SOUTHWEST

In the Southwest, the new agricultural economy emerged along different lines. The principal attraction was cotton. The cotton lands in the uplands of the Old South had lost much of their fertility through overplanting and erosion. But the market for cotton continued to grow, so there was no lack of ambitious farmers seeking fresh soil in a climate suitable for the crop. In the Southwest, there were vast tracts of land appropriate for growing cotton. They included what would become known as the Black Belt of central Alabama and Mississippi, a large region with a dark, productive soil of rotted limestone.

The growth of Southern settlement spread cotton, plantations, and slavery. The first arrivals in an uncultivated region were usually small farmers who made rough clearings in the forest. But wealthier planters soon followed. They bought up cleared or partially cleared land, and the original settlers moved farther west and started over again.

COTTON AND THE EXPANSION OF SLAVERY

The large planters made the westward journey in a style quite different from that of the first pioneers. Over the alternately dusty and muddy roads came great caravans consisting of herds of livestock, wagonloads of household goods, long lines of enslaved people, and–at the rear–the planter's family riding in carriages. Success in the wilderness was by no means ensured, even for the wealthiest settlers. But many planters soon expanded small clearings into vast cotton fields. They replaced the cabins of the early pioneers with sumptuous log dwellings and ultimately with imposing mansions that symbolized the emergence of a newly wealthy class. In later years, these western planters would assume the airs of a long-standing aristocracy. But by the time of the Civil War, few planter

FORT SNELLING This is an 1838 sketch of Fort Snelling (at the juncture of the Minnesota and Mississippi Rivers), containing instructions for reaching it from St. Louis. It was one of a string of fortifications built along the western edge of European settlement along the Great Lakes and the upper Mississippi in the first three decades of the nineteenth century. The forts were designed to protect the new white communities from hostile Native Americans. Fort Snelling stands today in Minnesota as a "living history" site.

"Fort Snelling from the East." Smithsonian Institution Archives, Record Unit 7290, Carl Andreas Geyer Journal, 1838, Negative # SA-861.

families in the Southwest had been there for more than one or two generations.

The rapid growth of the Northwest and Southwest resulted in the admission of four new states to the Union in the immediate aftermath of the War of 1812: Indiana in 1816, Mississippi in 1817, Illinois in 1818, and Alabama in 1819.

TRADE AND TRAPPING IN THE FAR WEST

Not many Anglo-Americans had much knowledge of or interest in the far western areas of the continent. But a significant trade nevertheless developed between these far western regions and the United States beginning early in the nineteenth century and growing steadily for decades.

Mexico, which controlled Texas, California, and much of the rest of the Southwest, won its independence from Spain in 1821. Almost immediately, it opened its northern territories to trade with the United States. American traders poured into the region–overland into Texas and New Mexico, by sea into California. Merchants from the United States quickly displaced both Native American and Mexican traders who had previ-

Discussion and Activities

Analyzing Issues Have students read the section "The Factor System." Ask them to think about how the system described could both help and hurt Native Americans at the same time. *(Factors provided goods at low cost, but by driving competitors out of the market, made Indians dependent on the factors going forward.)* Have students share their thoughts with a partner. **PCE** **WXT** **MIG**

Reasoning Processed

Continuity and Change Have students read the section "The Plantation System in the Southwest." Ask them to write a short paragraph about how westward expansion in the nineteenth century was different for westward expansion in the seventeenth century.

Discussion and Activities

Understanding Change After students have read the section "Astor's American Fur Company," ask them to discuss how fur trappers and traders contributed to westward expansion. *(Trappers and traders continually moved west seeking more opportunities. As they did so, they sometimes established small permanent settlements around trading posts.)* **MIG** **WXT** **GEO**

ously dominated trade. A steady traffic of commercial wagon trains was moving back and forth along the Santa Fe Trail between Missouri and New Mexico.

Fur traders created a wholly new commerce with the West. Before the War of 1812, John Jacob Astor's American Fur Company had established Astoria as a trading post at the mouth of the Columbia River in Oregon. But when the war came, Astor sold his suddenly imperiled interests to the Northwestern Fur Company, a British concern operating out of Canada. After the war, Astor centered his operations in the Great Lakes area and eventually extended them westward to the Rockies. Other companies carried on operations up the Missouri and its tributaries and into the Rocky Mountains.

ASTOR'S AMERICAN FUR COMPANY

At first, fur traders did most of their business by purchasing pelts from the Native Americans. But increasingly, white trappers entered the region and began to hunt beaver on their own. Substantial numbers of Anglo-Americans and French Canadians moved deep into the Great Lakes region and beyond to join the Iroquois and other Native Americans in pursuit of furs.

As the trappers, or "mountain men," moved west from the Great Lakes region, they began to establish themselves in what is now Utah and in parts of New Mexico. In 1822, Andrew Henry and William Ashley founded the Rocky Mountain Fur Company and recruited white trappers to move permanently into the Rockies in search of furs, which were becoming increasingly scarce farther east. Henry and Ashley dispatched supplies annually to their trappers in exchange for furs and skins. The arrival of the supply train became the occasion for a gathering of scores of mountain men, some of whom lived much of the year in considerable isolation.

But however isolated their daily lives, these mountain men were closely bound up with the expanding market economy of the United States. Some were employees of the Rocky Mountain Fur Company (or some other, similar enterprise), earning a salary in return for providing a steady supply of furs. Others were nominally independent but relied on the companies for credit; they were almost always in debt and hence economically bound to the companies. Some trapped entirely on their own and simply sold their furs for cash, but they too depended on merchants from the East for their livelihoods. And it was to those merchants that the bulk of the profits from the trade flowed.

THE FUR TRADE AND THE MARKET ECONOMY

Many trappers and mountain men lived peacefully and successfully with the Native Americans and Mexicans whose lands they shared. Perhaps two-thirds of the white trappers married women of Native American or Spanish backgrounds while living in the West. But relations between white trappers and Native Americans were not always friendly or peaceful. Jedediah

RENDEZVOUS, 1837 The annual gathering of fur trappers and traders was a major event in the lives of the lonely men who made their livelihoods gathering furs. It was also a meeting of representatives of the many cultures that mingled in the Far West, among them Anglo-Americans, French Canadians, and those of Spanish origins.

Discussion and Activities

Analyzing Images Have students examine the image "Rendezvous, 1837." Ask them to list details from the painting and circle any examples that show evidence of westward expansion. Use the lists as the basis for a discussion about what, if anything, in the painting, heralds a change in westward expansion. *(The scene is dominated by evidence of Native American activity. However, there are a small number of non-Natives riding through the middle of the scene, apparently present to trade for furs. This may foretell a growing American presence in the future.)* **MIG** **WXT**

S. Smith, a trapper who became an Ashley partner, led a series of forays deep into Mexican territory that ended in disastrous battles with the Mojaves and other tribes. Four years after an 1827 expedition to Oregon in which sixteen members of his party of twenty had died, Smith set out for New Mexico and was killed by Comanches, who took the weapons he was carrying and sold them to Mexican settlers.

Eastern Images of the West

Americans in the East were only dimly aware of the world the trappers were entering and helping to reshape. Smith and others became the source of dramatic (and often exaggerated) popular stories. But few trappers themselves wrote of their lives.

More important in increasing eastern awareness of the West were explorers, many of them dispatched by the U.S. government with instructions to chart the territories they visited. In 1819 and 1820, Stephen H. Long led nineteen soldiers on a journey up the Platte and South Platte Rivers through what is now Nebraska and eastern Colorado, and then returned eastward along the Arkansas River through what is now Kansas. He wrote an influential report on his trip, including an assessment of the region's potential for future settlement and development that echoed the dismissive conclusions of Zebulon Pike fifteen years before. On the published map of his expedition, he labeled the Great Plains the "Great American Desert."

STEPHEN LONG'S EXPEDITION

THE "ERA OF GOOD FEELINGS"

The expansion of the economy, the growth of white settlement and trade in the West, the creation of new states—all reflected the rising spirit of nationalism that was permeating the United States in the years following the War of 1812. That spirit found reflection for a time in the character of national politics.

The End of the First Party System

Ever since 1800, the presidency seemed to have been the special possession of Virginians. After two terms in office, Jefferson chose his secretary of state, James Madison of Virginia, to succeed him, and after two more terms, Madison secured the presidential nomination for his secretary of state, James Monroe, also of Virginia. Many in the North were expressing impatience with the so-called Virginia Dynasty, but the Republicans had no difficulty electing their candidate in the listless campaign of 1816. Monroe received 183 ballots in the electoral college; his Federalist opponent, Rufus King of New York, received only 34—from Massachusetts, Connecticut, and Delaware.

THE VIRGINIA DYNASTY

Monroe was sixty-one years old when he became president. In the course of his long career, he had served as a soldier in the Revolution, as a diplomat, and most recently as a cabinet officer. He entered office under what seemed to be remarkably favorable circumstances. With the decline of the Federalists, his party faced no serious opposition. With the conclusion of the War of 1812, the nation faced no important international threats. American politicians had dreamed since the first days of the republic of a time in which partisan divisions and factional disputes might come to an end. In the prosperous postwar years, Monroe attempted to use his office to realize that dream.

He made that clear, above all, in the selection of his cabinet. For secretary of state, he chose the New Englander and former Federalist John Quincy Adams. Jefferson, Madison, and Monroe had all served as secretary of state before becoming president;

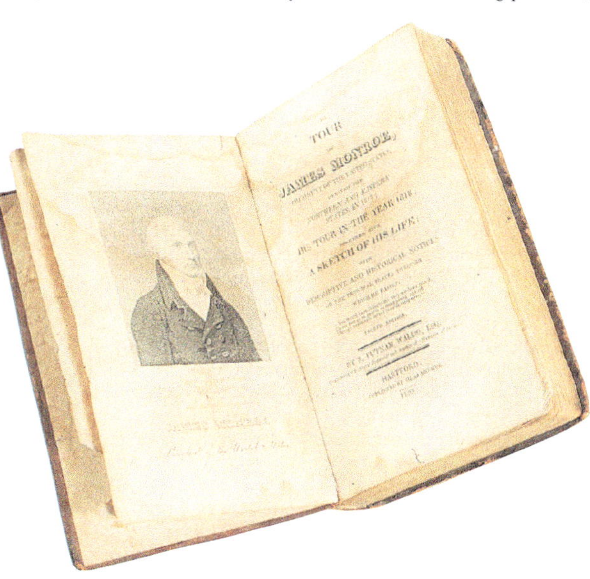

THE TRIUMPHANT TOUR OF JAMES MONROE After James Monroe's enormously successful tour of the northern and eastern states in 1818, midway through his first term as president, there was widespread self-congratulation through much of the United States for the apparent political unity that had gripped the nation. Only a few years earlier, the Northeast had been the bastion of Federalist Party opposition to the Republican governments of the early nineteenth century. At one point, some Federalist leaders had even proposed secession from the United States. But now a Virginia Republican president had been greeted as a hero in the former Federalist strongholds. This book, published in 1820 (when Monroe ran virtually unopposed for reelection), is an account of the president's triumphant tour and a short account of his life—an early version of the now-familiar campaign biography.

Reasoning Processes

Comparison Have students read the section "Stephen Long's Expedition." Ask them to create a 3-circle Venn diagram comparing Long's Expedition with the Lewis and Clark and Pike expeditions students learned about previously. Ask students to identify whether the expeditions were more similar or more different. MIG PCE NAT

Discussion and Activities

Making Connections Have students read the section "The Virginia Dynasty." Ask them to create a t-chart comparing the qualifications of James Monroe to be president with the qualifications of a recent presidential candidate with whom they may be familiar. Ask them to discuss as a class how the qualifications Americans look for in a president have changed or stayed the same. PCE SOC NAT

Discussion and Activities

Analyzing Change After students have read the section "Monroe's Goodwill Tour," ask them to write a short paragraph summarizing how the nation changed during Monroe's term, and evaluating the claim that the country had entered an "Era of Good Feelings." PCE SOC MIG

Adams, therefore, immediately became the heir apparent, suggesting that the "Virginia Dynasty" would soon come to an end. Speaker of the House Henry Clay declined an offer to be secretary of war, so Monroe named John C. Calhoun instead. In his other appointments, too, Monroe took pains to include both Northerners and Southerners, Easterners and Westerners, Federalists and Republicans.

MONROE'S GOODWILL TOUR

Soon after his inauguration, Monroe did what no president since Washington had done: he made a goodwill tour through the country. In New England, so recently the scene of rabid Federalist discontent, he was greeted everywhere with enthusiastic demonstrations. The *Columbian Centinel*, a Federalist newspaper in Boston, commenting on the "Presidential Jubilee" in that city, observed that an "era of good feelings" had arrived. And on the surface, at least, the years of Monroe's presidency did appear to be an "era of good feelings." In 1820, Monroe was reelected without opposition. For all practical purposes, the Federalist Party had now ceased to exist.

JOHN QUINCY ADAMS AND FLORIDA

Like his father, the second president, John Quincy Adams had spent much of his life in diplomatic service. Even before becoming secretary of state, he had become one of the great diplomats in American history. He was also a committed nationalist, and he considered his most important task to be the promotion of American expansion.

Adams's first challenge as secretary of state was Florida. The United States had already annexed West Florida, but that claim remained in dispute. Most Americans believed the nation should gain possession of the entire peninsula. In 1817, Adams began negotiations with the Spanish minister, Luis de Onís, in hopes of resolving the dispute and gaining the entire territory for the United States.

THE SEMINOLE WAR

In the meantime, events were taking their own course in Florida. Andrew Jackson, now in command of American troops along the Florida frontier, had orders from Secretary of War Calhoun to "adopt the necessary measures" to stop continuing raids on American territory by Seminole Indians south of the Florida border. Jackson used those orders as an excuse to invade Florida, seize the Spanish forts at St. Marks and Pensacola, and order the hanging of two British subjects on the charge of supplying and inciting Native Americans. The operation became known as the Seminole War.

Instead of condemning Jackson's raid, Adams urged the government to assume responsibility for it. The United States, he told the Spanish, had the right under international law to defend itself against threats from across its borders. Since Spain was unwilling or unable to curb those threats, America had simply done what was necessary. Jackson's raid demonstrated to the Spanish that the United States could easily take Florida by force. Adams implied that the nation might consider doing so.

SEMINOLE DANCE This 1838 drawing by a U.S. military officer portrays a dance by Seminole Indians near Fort Butler in Florida. It was made in the midst of the prolonged Second Seminole War, which ended in 1842 with the removal of most of the tribe from Florida to reservations west of the Mississippi

ADAMS-ONÍS TREATY

Onís realized, therefore, that he had little choice but to come to terms with the Americans. Under the provisions of the Adams-Onís Treaty of 1819, Spain ceded all of Florida to the United States and gave up as well its claim to territory north of the 42nd parallel in the Pacific Northwest. In return, the American government gave up its claims to Texas.

THE PANIC OF 1819

But the Monroe administration had little time to revel in its diplomatic successes, for the nation was falling victim to a serious economic crisis: the Panic of 1819. It followed a period of high foreign demand for American farm goods and thus of exceptionally high prices for American farmers (all as a result of the disruption of European agriculture caused by the Napoleonic Wars). The rising prices for farm goods had stimulated a land boom in the western United States. Fueled by speculative investments, land prices soared.

BOOM AND BUST

The availability of easy credit to settlers and speculators–from the government (under the land acts of 1800 and 1804), from state banks and wildcat banks, even for a time from the rechartered Bank of the United States–fueled the land boom. Beginning in 1819, however, new management at the national bank began tighten-

Discussion and Activities

Analyzing Issues Have students read the section "John Quincy Adams and Florida." Ask them to think about whether the Adams-Onís Treaty was the result of force or diplomacy. Have them share their thoughts with a partner. WOR PCE NAT ing credit, calling in loans, and foreclosing mortgages. This precipitated a series of failures by state banks. The result was a financial panic, which many Americans, particularly those in the West, blamed on the national bank. Six years of depression followed and began a process that would eventually make the Bank's existence one of the nation's most burning political issues.

SECTIONALISM AND NATIONALISM

For a brief but alarming moment in 1819–1820, the increasing differences between the North and the South threatened the unity of the United States—until the Missouri Compromise temporarily averted a sectional crisis.

The Missouri Compromise

When Missouri applied for admission to the Union as a state in 1819, slavery was already well established there. Even so, Representative James Tallmadge Jr. of New York proposed an amendment to the Missouri statehood bill that would prohibit the further introduction of enslaved people into Missouri and provide for the gradual emancipation of those already there. The Tallmadge Amendment provoked a controversy that raged for the next two years.

TALLMADGE AMENDMENT

Since the beginning of the republic, partly by chance and partly by design, new states had come into the Union more or less in pairs, one from the North, another from the South. In 1819, there were eleven free states and eleven slave states; the admission of Missouri as a free state would upset that balance and increase the political power of the North over the South. Hence the controversy over slavery and freedom in Missouri.

Complicating the Missouri question was the application of Maine (previously the northern part of Massachusetts) for admission as a new (and free) state. Speaker of the House Henry Clay informed northern members that if they blocked Missouri from entering the Union as a slave state, Southerners would block the admission of Maine. But Maine ultimately offered a way out of the impasse, as the Senate agreed to combine the Maine and Missouri proposals into a single bill. Maine would be admitted as a free state, Missouri as a slave state. Then Senator Jesse B. Thomas of Illinois proposed an amendment prohibiting slavery in the rest of the Louisiana Purchase territory north of the southern boundary of Missouri (the 36°30′ parallel). Congress adopted the Thomas Amendment.

MISSOURI COMPROMISE

Nationalists in both North and South hailed this settlement—which became known as the Missouri Compromise—as a happy resolution of a danger to the Union. But the debate over the bill had revealed a strong undercurrent of sectionalism that was competing with—although at the moment failing to derail—the powerful tides of nationalism.

Marshall and the Court

John Marshall served as chief justice of the United States from 1801 to 1835, and he dominated the Court more fully than anyone else before or since. More than anyone but the framers themselves, he molded the development of the Constitution: strengthening the judicial branch at the expense of the executive and legislative branches, increasing the power of the federal government at the expense of the states, and advancing the interests of the propertied and commercial classes.

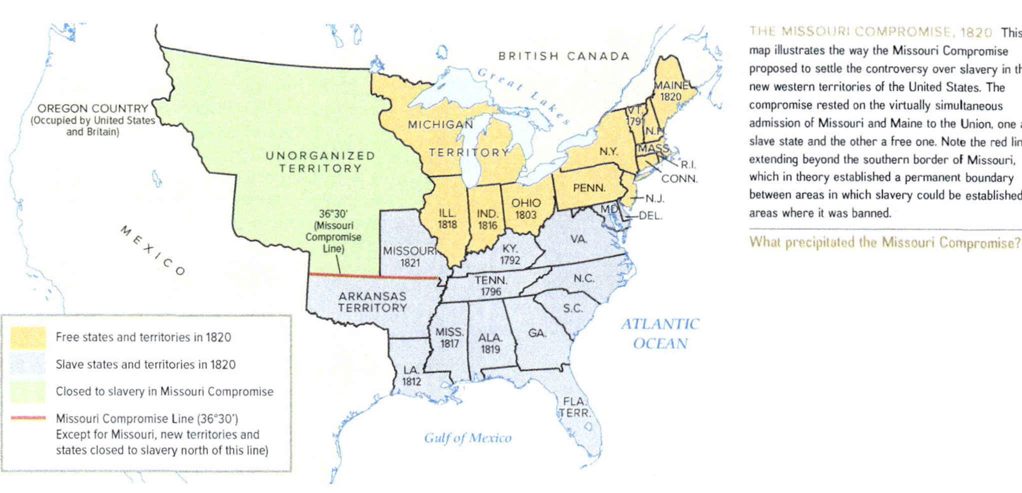

THE MISSOURI COMPROMISE, 1820 This map illustrates the way the Missouri Compromise proposed to settle the controversy over slavery in the new western territories of the United States. The compromise rested on the virtually simultaneous admission of Missouri and Maine to the Union, one a slave state and the other a free one. Note the red line extending beyond the southern border of Missouri, which in theory established a permanent boundary between areas in which slavery could be established and areas where it was banned.

What precipitated the Missouri Compromise?

Discussion and Activities

Speculating Have students read the section "The Missouri Compromise." Ask them to list the territorial provisions of the compromise. Then have students discuss in small groups whether the compromise represented a real solution to the problems of slavery, and, if not, what further problems might emerge. **PCE** **MIG** **NAT**

Answers

The Missouri Compromise, 1820.

The Missouri Compromise was precipitated by the debate over the admission of new states to the Union that might disrupt the balance between free and slave states in the U.S. Senate.

Discussion and Activities

Historical Significance and Argumentation After students have read the section "Marshall and the Court," ask them to construct a chart to record the issues at stake, the decision of the court, and effects of the decision for the Supreme Court cases *Fletcher v. Peck, Dartmouth College v. Woodward, Cohens v. Virginia, McCulloch v. Maryland,* and *Gibbons v. Ogden.* Then have students discuss which general principle(s) the Court reinforced in those decisions *(federal supremacy)*, and which decision they think was the most important and why. **PCE** **WXT** **NAT**

Committed to promoting commerce, the Marshall Court staunchly defended the inviolability of contracts. In *Fletcher v. Peck* (1810), which arose out of a series of notorious land frauds in Georgia, Marshall held that a land grant was a valid contract and could not be repealed even if corruption was involved.

Dartmouth College v. Woodward (1819) further expanded the meaning of the contract clause of the Constitution. Having gained control of the New Hampshire state government, Republicans tried to revise Dartmouth College's charter (granted by King George III in 1769) to convert the private college into a state university. Daniel Webster, a Dartmouth graduate and brilliant orator, argued the college's case. The Dartmouth charter, he insisted, was a contract, protected by the same doctrine that the Court had already upheld in *Fletcher v. Peck.* Then, according to legend, he brought some of the justices to tears with an irrelevant passage that concluded: "It is, sir, . . . a small college. And yet there are those who love it." The Court ruled for Dartmouth. The decision placed important restrictions on the ability of state governments to control corporations.

DARTMOUTH COLLEGE V. WOODWARD

In overturning the act of the legislature and the decisions of the New Hampshire courts, the justices also implicitly claimed for themselves the right to override the decisions of state courts. But advocates of states' rights, especially in the South, continued to challenge the Supreme Court's right to do so. In *Cohens v. Virginia* (1821), Marshall explicitly affirmed the constitutionality of federal review of state court decisions. The states had given up part of their sovereignty in ratifying the Constitution, he explained, and their courts must submit to federal jurisdiction; otherwise, the federal government would be powerless "at the feet of every state in the Union."

Meanwhile, in *McCulloch v. Maryland* (1819), Marshall confirmed the "implied powers" of Congress by upholding the constitutionality of the Bank of the United States. The Bank had become so unpopular in the South and the West that several of the states tried to drive branches out of business by outright prohibition or by confiscatory taxes. This case presented two constitutional questions: Could Congress charter a bank? And if so, could individual states ban it or tax it? Daniel Webster, one of the Bank's attorneys, argued that establishing such an institution came within the "necessary and proper" clause of the Constitution and that the power to tax involved a "power to destroy." If the states could tax the Bank at all, Webster said, they could "tax it to death." Marshall adopted Webster's words in deciding for the Bank.

CONFIRMING IMPLIED POWERS

In the case of *Gibbons v. Ogden* (1824), the Court strengthened Congress's power to regulate interstate commerce. The state of New York had indirectly granted Aaron Ogden the business of carrying passengers across the river between New York and New Jersey. But Thomas Gibbons, with a license granted under an act of Congress, began competing with Ogden for the ferry traffic. Ogden brought suit against him and won in the New York courts. Gibbons appealed to the Supreme Court. The most important question facing the justices was whether Congress's power to give Gibbons a license to operate his ferry superseded the state of New York's power to grant Ogden a monopoly. Marshall claimed that the power of Congress to regulate interstate commerce (which, he said, included navigation) was "complete in itself" and might be "exercised to its utmost extent." Ogden's state-granted monopoly, therefore, was void.

The decisions of the Marshall Court established the primacy of the federal government over the states in regulating the economy and opened the way for an increased federal role in promoting economic growth. They protected corporations and other private economic institutions from local government interference. They were, in short, highly nationalistic decisions, designed to promote the growth of a strong, unified, and economically developed United States.

ESTABLISHING FEDERAL PRIMACY

JOHN MARSHALL The imposing figure in this image is John Marshall, the most important chief justice of the Supreme Court in American history. A former secretary of state, Marshall served as chief justice from 1801 until his death in 1835 at the age of eighty. Such was the power of his intellect and personality that he dominated his fellow justices throughout that period, regardless of their previous party affiliations or legal ideologies. Marshall established the independence of the Court, gave it a reputation for nonpartisan integrity, and established its powers, which were only vaguely defined by the Constitution.

THE COURT AND NATIVE AMERICANS

The nationalist inclinations of the Marshall Court were visible as well in a series of decisions concerning the legal status of Native American nations within the United States. But these decisions did not simply affirm the supremacy of the United

Discussion and Activities

Analyzing Continuity Have students examine the image "John Marshall." Ask students to discuss as a class how John Marshall kept alive the ideology of the Federalist Party long after the party itself had faded away. *(After his appointment as Chief Justice by John Adams in 1801, Marshall used his position to reinforce and expand the authority of the court system, and to promote a strong central government, which was a core element of Federalist Party, for the next 35 years.)* **PCE**

States; they also carved out a distinctive position for Native Americans within the constitutional structure.

The first of the crucial decisions was in the case of *Johnson v. McIntosh* (1823). Leaders of the Illinois and Pinakeshaw nations had sold parcels of their land to a group of white settlers (including Johnson) but later signed a treaty with the federal government ceding territory that included those same parcels to the United States. The government proceeded to grant homestead rights to new white settlers (among them McIntosh) on the land claimed by Johnson. The Court was asked to decide which claim had precedence. Marshall's ruling, not surprisingly, favored the United States. But in explaining it, he offered a preliminary definition of the place of Native Americans within the nation. The tribes had a basic right to their tribal lands, he said, that preceded all other American law. Individual American citizens could not buy or take land from the tribes; only the federal government—the supreme authority—could do that.

Even more important was the Court's 1832 decision in *Worcester v. Georgia*, in which the Court invalidated Georgia laws that attempted to regulate access by U.S. citizens to Cherokee country. Only the federal government could do that, Marshall claimed, thus taking another important step in con-

WORCESTER V. GEORGIA

solidating federal authority over the states (and over the tribes). In doing so, he further defined the nature of the Native American nations. The tribes, he explained, were sovereign entities in much the same way Georgia was a sovereign entity— "distinct political communities, having territorial boundaries within which their authority is exclusive." In defending the power of the federal government, he was also affirming, indeed expanding, the rights of the Native American nations to remain free from the authority of state governments.

The Marshall decisions, therefore, did what the Constitution itself had not done: they defined a place for Native American nations within the American political system. The nations had basic property rights. They were sovereign entities not subject to the authority of state governments. But the federal government, like a "guardian" governing its "ward," had ultimate authority over tribal affairs—even if that authority was, according to the Court, limited by the government's obligation to protect the welfare of Native Americans. These provisions were seldom enough to defend Native Americans from the steady westward march of white civilization, but they formed the basis of what few legal protections they had.

THE LATIN AMERICAN REVOLUTION AND THE MONROE DOCTRINE

Americans looking southward in the years following the War of 1812 beheld a gigantic spectacle: the Spanish Empire in its

REVOLUTION IN LATIN AMERICA

death throes, a whole continent in revolt, new nations in the making. Already the United States had developed a profitable trade with Latin America and was rivaling Great Britain as the principal trading nation there. Many Americans believed the success of the anti-Spanish revolutions would further strengthen America's position in the region.

In 1815, the United States proclaimed neutrality in the wars between Spain and its rebellious colonies, implying a partial recognition of the rebels' status as nations. Moreover, the United States sold ships and supplies to the revolutionaries, a clear indication that it was not genuinely neutral but was trying to help the insurgents. In 1822, President Monroe established diplomatic relations with five new nations—La Plata (later Argentina), Chile, Peru, Colombia, and Mexico—making the United States the first country to recognize them.

In 1823, Monroe announced a policy that would ultimately be known (beginning some thirty years later) as the "Monroe

THE MONROE DOCTRINE

Doctrine," even though it was primarily the work of John Quincy Adams. "The American continents," Monroe declared, ". . . are henceforth not to be considered as subjects for future colonization by any European powers." The United States would consider any foreign challenge to the sovereignty of existing American nations an unfriendly act. At the same time, he proclaimed, "Our policy in regard to Europe . . . is not to interfere in the internal concern of any of its powers."

The Monroe Doctrine emerged directly out of America's

AMERICAN FEARS

relations with Europe in the 1820s. Many Americans feared that Spain's European

CHEROKEE LEADER SEQUOYAH Sequoyah (who also used the name George Guess) was a mixed-blood Cherokee who translated his tribe's language into writing through an elaborate syllabary (equivalent to an alphabet) of his own invention, pictured here. He opposed Native American assimilation into white society and saw the preservation of the Cherokee language as a way to protect the culture of his tribe. He moved to Arkansas in the 1820s and became a chief of the western Cherokee tribes.

Reasoning Processes

Continuity and Change After students have read the section "The Court and Native Americans." Ask them to discuss as a class how the Supreme Courts' decisions concerning Indian tribes changed the relationship between the tribes, the states, and the federal government. **PCE** **NAT**

Discussion and Activities

Historical Evidence and Argumentation After students have read the section "The Monroe Doctrine." Ask them to construct a t-chart listing American foreign policy actions that seem neutral or not neutral. Ask students to evaluate which seems more prevalent, then ask them to write a thesis statement making a claim about whether American foreign policy in the early nineteenth century was neutral. **WOR**

Reasoning Processes

Causation After students have read the section "The Latin American Revolution and the Monroe Doctrine," ask them to brainstorm reasons why the United States would want to limit the participation of European powers in the Americas. *(Support the ideals of Latin American independence movements, fear re-establishment of European colonial empires, foresaw competition with European powers for territory.)* **WOR** **MIG** **WXT**

allies (notably France) would assist Spain in an effort to retake its lost empire. Even more troubling to Adams (and many other Americans) was the fear that Great Britain had designs on Cuba. Adams wanted to keep Cuba in Spanish hands until it fell (as he believed it ultimately would) to the Americans.

The Monroe Doctrine had few immediate effects, but it was important as an expression of the growing spirit of nationalism in the United States in the 1820s. And it established the idea of the United States as the dominant power in the Western Hemisphere.

THE REVIVAL OF OPPOSITION

After 1816, the Federalist Party offered no presidential candidate and soon ceased to exist as a national political force. The

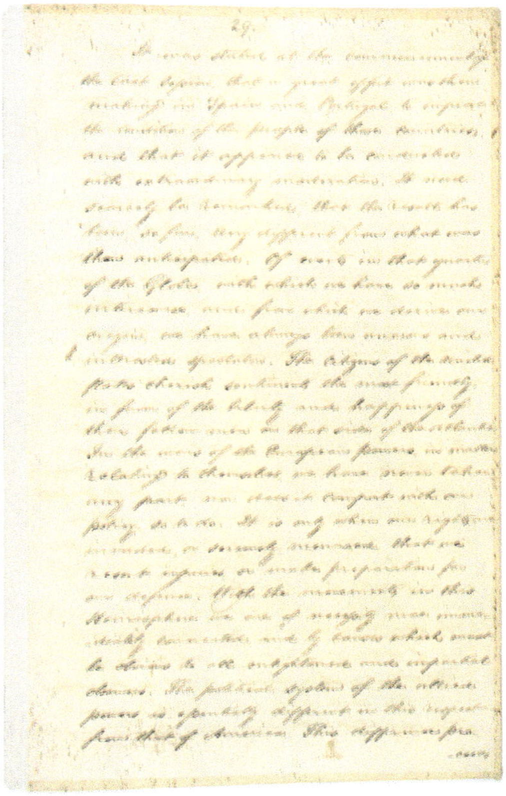

THE MONROE DOCTRINE On December 2, 1823, President James Monroe delivered his seventh annual message to Congress. In it, he outlined an important part of his foreign policy that subsequently became known as the "Monroe Doctrine." Monroe declared that henceforth any attempt by a European power to colonize any part of the "American continents" would be viewed as an "unfriendly act" toward the United States.

Republican Party (which considered itself not a party but an organization representing the whole of the population) was the only organized force in national politics.

By the late 1820s, however, partisan divisions were emerging once again. In some respects, the division mirrored the schism that had produced the first party system in the 1790s.

NEW POLITICAL DIVISIONS

The Republicans had in many ways come to resemble the early Federalist regimes in their promotion of economic growth and centralization. And the opposition, like the opposition in the 1790s, objected to the federal government's expanding role in the economy. There was, however, a crucial difference. At the beginning of the century, the opponents of centralization had also often been opponents of economic growth. Now, in the 1820s, the controversy involved not whether but how the nation should continue to expand.

THE "CORRUPT BARGAIN"

Until 1820, when the Federalist Party effectively ceased operations and James Monroe ran for reelection unopposed, presidential candidates were nominated by caucuses of the two parties in Congress. But in the presidential election of 1824, "King Caucus" was overthrown. The Republican caucus nominated William H. Crawford of Georgia, the secretary of the treasury and the favorite of the extreme states' rights faction of the party. But other candidates received nominations from state legislatures and won endorsements from irregular mass meetings throughout the country.

END OF THE CAUCUS SYSTEM

One of them was Secretary of State John Quincy Adams, who held the office that was the traditional stepping-stone to the presidency. But as he himself ruefully understood, he was a man of cold and forbidding manners, with little popular appeal. Another contender was Henry Clay, the Speaker of the House. He had a devoted personal following and a definite and coherent program: the "American System," which proposed creating a great home market for factory and farm producers by raising the protective tariff, strengthening the national bank, and financing internal improvements. Andrew Jackson, the fourth major candidate, had no significant political record—even though he had served briefly as a representative in Congress and was now a new member of the U.S. Senate. But he was a military hero and had the help of shrewd political allies from his home state of Tennessee.

Jackson received more popular and electoral votes than any other candidate, but not a majority. He had 99 electoral votes to Adams's 84, Crawford's 41, and Clay's 37. The Twelfth Amendment to the Constitution (passed in the aftermath of the contested 1800 election) required the House of Representatives to choose among the three candidates with the largest numbers of electoral votes. Crawford was by then seriously ill and not a plausible candidate. Clay was out of the running, but he was in a strong position to influence the result. Jackson was Clay's most formidable political rival in the West,

ELECTION OF 1824

Reasoning Processes

Comparison Have students read the section "New Political Divisions." Ask them to create a 3-circle Venn diagram comparing the Federalists, the Republicans, and opponents to the Republicans that emerged in the 1820s. Ask: What do the new opponents of the Republicans have in common with the Federalists, and how are they different? **PCE** **NAT**

so Clay supported Adams, in part because, alone among the candidates, Adams was an ardent nationalist and a likely supporter of the American System. With Clay's endorsement, Adams won election in the House.

The Jacksonians believed their large popular and electoral pluralities entitled their candidate to the presidency, and they were enraged when he lost. But they grew angrier still when Adams named Clay his secretary of state. The State Department was the well-established route to the presidency, and Adams thus appeared to be naming Clay as his own successor. The outrage the Jacksonians expressed at what they called a "corrupt bargain" haunted Adams throughout his presidency.

THE SECOND PRESIDENT ADAMS

Throughout Adams's term in the White House, the political bitterness arising from the "corrupt bargain" charges thoroughly frustrated his policies. Adams proposed an ambitiously nationalist program reminiscent of Clay's American System. But Jacksonians in Congress blocked most of it.

JOHN QUINCY ADAMS This photograph of the former president was taken shortly before his death in 1848 at the age of eighty—almost twenty years after he had left the White House—when he was serving as a congressman from Massachusetts. During his years as president, he was—as he had been throughout his life—an intensely disciplined and hardworking man. He rose at four in the morning and made a long entry in his diary for the previous day. He wrote so much that his right hand at times became paralyzed with writer's cramp, so he taught himself to write with his left hand as well.

Adams also experienced diplomatic frustrations. He appointed delegates to an international conference that the Venezuelan liberator, Simón Bolívar, had called in Panama in 1826. But Haiti was one of the participating nations, and Southerners in Congress opposed the idea of white Americans mingling with the black delegates. Congress delayed approving the Panama mission so long that the American delegation did not arrive until after the conference was over.

Adams also lost a contest with the state of Georgia, which wished to remove the remaining Creek and Cherokee Indians from the state to gain additional soil for cotton planters. The U.S. government, in a 1791 treaty, had guaranteed that land to the Creeks; but in 1825, white Georgians had extracted a new treaty from William McIntosh, the leader of one faction in the Creek nation and a longtime advocate of Native American cooperation with the United States. Adams believed the new treaty had no legal force, since McIntosh clearly did not represent the wishes of the Native Americans; and he refused to enforce the treaty, setting up a direct conflict between the president and the state. The governor of Georgia defied the president and proceeded with plans for the removal of Native Americans. Adams found no way to stop him.

Even more damaging to the administration was its support for a new tariff on imported goods in 1828. This measure originated with the demands of Massachusetts and Rhode Island woolen manufacturers, who complained that the British were dumping textiles on the American market at artificially low prices. But to win support from middle and western states, the administration had to accept duties on other items. In the process, it antagonized the original New England supporters of the bill; the benefits of protecting their manufactured goods from foreign competition now had to be weighed against the prospects of having to pay more for raw materials. Adams signed the bill, earning the animosity of Southerners who cursed it as the "tariff of abominations."

TARIFF OF ABOMINATIONS

JACKSON TRIUMPHANT

By the time of the 1828 presidential election, a new two-party system had begun to emerge out of the divisions among the Republicans. On one side stood the supporters of John Quincy Adams, who called themselves the National Republicans and who supported the economic nationalism of the preceding years. Opposing them were the followers of Andrew Jackson, who took the name Democratic Republicans and who called for an assault on privilege and a widening of opportunity. Adams attracted the support of most of the remaining Federalists; Jackson appealed to a broad coalition that opposed the "economic aristocracy."

But issues seemed to count for little in the end, as the campaign degenerated into a war of personal invective. The Jacksonians charged that Adams as president had been guilty of gross waste and extravagance and had used public

Reasoning Processes

Causation After students have read the section "The Corrupt Bargain," ask them to write a short paragraph explaining how the election of 1824 led to the creation of a new political party. **PCE** **NAT**

Discussion and Activities

Historical Evidence and Argumentation Have students read the section "The Second President Adams." Ask them to create a t-chart listing "successes" and "failures" of the John Quincy Adams' administration. Have students evaluate and discuss whether Adams was an effective president. **PCE** **NAT**

Reasoning Processes

Comparison After students have read the section "Jackson Triumphant," ask students to create a Venn diagram comparing Andrew Jackson and John Quincy Adams. Have students discuss which differences most likely contributed to Jackson's victory in the 1828 election. **PCE** **NAT** **SOC**

funds to buy gambling devices (a chess set and a billiard table) for the White House. Adams's supporters hurled even worse accusations at Jackson. They called him a murderer and distributed a "coffin handbill," which listed, within coffin-shaped outlines, the names of militiamen whom Jackson was said to have shot in cold blood during the War of 1812. (The men had been deserters who were legally executed after sentence by a court-martial.) And they called his wife a bigamist. Jackson had married his beloved Rachel at a time when the pair incorrectly believed her first husband had divorced her. (When Jackson's wife first read of the accusations against her shortly after the election, she collapsed and, a few weeks later, died; not without reason, Jackson blamed his opponents for her death.)

JACKSON TRIUMPHANT

Jackson's victory was decisive, but sectional. He won 56 percent of the popular vote and an electoral majority of 178 votes to 83. Adams swept virtually all of New England and showed significant strength in the mid-Atlantic region. Nevertheless, the Jacksonians considered their victory as complete and as important as Jefferson's in 1800. Once again, the forces of privilege had been driven from Washington. Once again, a champion of democracy would occupy the White House and restore liberty to the people and to the economy. America had entered, some Jacksonians claimed, a new era of democracy, the "age of the common man."

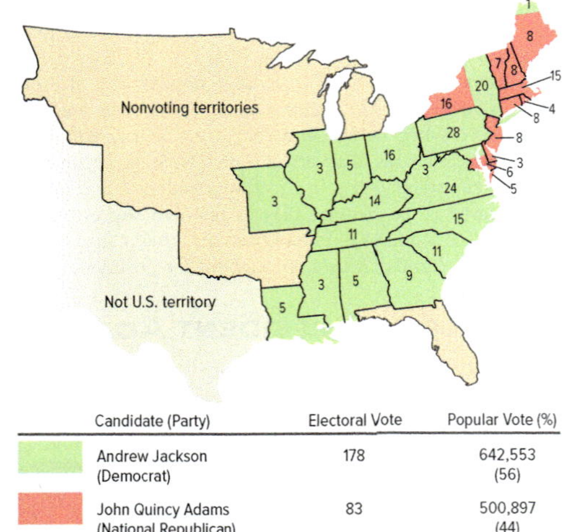

Candidate (Party)	Electoral Vote	Popular Vote (%)
Andrew Jackson (Democrat)	178	642,553 (56)
John Quincy Adams (National Republican)	83	500,897 (44)

THE ELECTION OF 1828 As this map shows, Andrew Jackson's victory over John Quincy Adams was one of the most decisive in American history for a challenger facing an incumbent president.

What accounts for this decisive repudiation of President Adams?

Answers

The Election of 1828.

Adams was viewed as a member of the elite, while Jackson appealed to the "common man" who was increasingly being given the right to vote in many states.

CHAPTER 8 REVIEW

CONNECTING THEMES

Chapter Eight covered the continuing growth of American nationalism during the first half of the nineteenth century. The chapter also examined the issues surrounding the exploration of the western territories, including more conflicts with Native Americans and the further expansion of slavery.

Slavery continued to drive the national economy, from cotton planters in the South to the textile manufacturers in the North. At the same time, it deeply divided the country along regional lines. Political parties also began to form around the issue of slavery, which would lead to the beginning of the Civil War. Particularly important was the creation of the Missouri Compromise, a short-term political solution to the growing issue over the legality and constitutionality of slavery.

Foreign policy and international affairs also underwent great changes as the United States focused on territorial acquisition and the resolution of outstanding problems with Great Britain. In addition, the Monroe Doctrine reduced European influence in Latin America and dominated American relations with other countries for decades to come.

You should consider the following questions as you review the themes for this chapter:

- How did the rise of the First Industrial Revolution and the development of a national market affect the economic, political, and social aspects of American life?
- What were the causes and effects of western expansion?
- What were the causes that led to the destruction of the first party system, and how were those issues tied to distinct regional differences in the United States?
- What were the major attempts by the United States to resolve lingering issues with foreign countries and to extend its influence into Latin America?
- How did American nationalism conflict with American regionalism?

KEY TERMS

Adams-Onis Treaty 234
American System 238
Francis Cabot Lowell 228
Gibbons v. Ogden 236
Henry Clay 234
John Quincy Adams 234
McCulloch v. Maryland 236
Missouri Compromise 235
Monroe Doctrine 237
Sectionalism 235
Seminole War 234
Sequoyah 237
Stephen H. Long 233
Tallmadge Amendment 235
Transportation improvements 229
Worcester v. Georgia 237

Discussion and Activities

Making Connections After students have read Chapter 8, ask them to create a T-chart with the headings "nationalism" and "regionalism." Have them list factors that contributed to both, then discuss as a class which grew stronger during the period 1800–1828. **NAT** **MIG** **SOC** **WXT** **WOR**

Key Terms

Students should be familiar with the key terms and be able to define them in the context of a growing national economy, continuing westward expansion and increasing sectional tensions. Encourage students to use these terms in performing review exercises and exam practice for this chapter.

 **Go Online Chapter 8 Content Review**

Assessing Student Understanding Use the online assessment to assess student understanding of concepts and topics within the chapter. You can assign the ready-made Chapter 8 Content Review or create your own from available questions. This easy-to-use tool helps you design assessments that meet the needs of different types of learners.

Answers

Multiple Choice

1. A; **2.** B; **3.** C

Short Answer

4A) Answer: In 1804 the Lewis and Clark expedition began to survey the territory acquired by the Louisiana Purchase. This land was largely unorganized and raised questions about the status of slavery within this large territory.

4B) Answer: Slavery continued to grow and expand in the young nation. The entire nation was reliant on slave labor, from Southern cotton farmers to textile manufacturers in the North. The Constitution protected the institution, but there were no laws regulating the legal status of slavery in the western territories. The Missouri Compromise was designed to be a compromise between the slave states and the free state, as it admitted a 1-for-1 ratio with Missouri and Maine. The 1-for-1 ratio allowed the country to remain evenly divided in representation of free and slave states in Congress.

4C) Answer: The Missouri Compromise temporarily solved the question of slavery, but this was only a quick fix. It settled the question of slavery within the Louisiana Territory, but it did not solve the larger issue about further western expansion.

5A) Answer: Both before and after the Era of Good Feelings, the country was marred by political parties that were strongly opposed to each other. Before the Era, the two major political parties were the Federalists and the Democratic-Republicans, after the Era the two major political parties were the Whigs and the Democrats.

5B) Answer: Before the Era, the country was stuck doing things the same way they had been done for centuries. Economically, there really was very little progress that had taken place. Following the Era, there was a massive technological revolution that fundamentally transformed the country in many ways.

5C) Answer: Despite the fact that the Era was very short lived, it did show Americans that there was political common ground. The period would often serve as an example to future times of the potential for compromise. The Missouri Compromise was often invoked in times when it seemed like compromise was at a standstill.

AP EXAM PRACTICE

Questions assume cumulative content knowledge from this chapter and previous chapters.

MULTIPLE CHOICE

Use the excerpt below and your knowledge of U.S. history to answer questions 1-3.

"If any one proposition could command the universal assent of mankind, we might expect it would be this – that the government of the Union, though limited in its powers, is supreme within its sphere of action. This would seem to result, necessarily, from its nature. It is the government of all; its powers are delegated by all; it represents all, and acts for all. Though any one state may be willing to control its operations, no state is willing to allow others to control them. The nation, on those subjects on which it can act, must necessarily bind its component parts. But this question is not left to mere reason: the people have, in express terms, decided it, by saying, *"this constitution, and the laws of the United States, *406 which shall be made in pursuance thereof," "shall be the supreme law of the land," and by requiring that the members of the state legislatures, and the officers of the executive and judicial departments of the states, shall take the oath of fidelity to it. The government of the United States, then, though limited in its powers, is supreme; and its laws, when made in pursuance of the constitution, form the supreme law of the land, "anything in the constitution or laws of any state to the contrary notwithstanding."

–John Marshall, majority opinion, *McCullogh* v *Maryland*, 1819

1. In *McCullogh* v *Maryland*, the Marshall Court upheld the constitutionality of the Bank of the United States through the
   (A) powers implied in the Constitution.
   (B) judicial review of executive actions.
   (C) supremacy of states over the federal government.
   (D) separation of powers between the branches of government.

2. The Marshall Court decisions laid the groundwork for an economic system that experienced
   (A) cycles of foreign interference and competition.
   (B) strong growth and the protection of the federal government.
   (C) varied outcomes dependent on the support of state governments.
   (D) continuing challenges in expansion.

3. Marshall Court decisions regarding Native Americans in cases such as *Johnson* v *McIntosh* and *Worcester* v *Georgia* established that
   (A) reservation land was to be solely under control of Native American nations.
   (B) Native Americans had the right to full American citizenship.
   (C) Native American nations had a distinctive, protected place in the political system.
   (D) Native American nations should be under the political control of state governments.

SHORT ANSWER

Use your knowledge of U.S. history to answer questions 4 and 5.

4. Use the map on page 235 to answer A, B, and C.
   (A) Briefly describe ONE historical situation related to the event depicted in the map.
   (B) Briefly explain ONE specific historical cause that led to the passage of the Missouri Compromise.
   (C) Briefly explain ONE specific historical effect that resulted from the passage of the Missouri Compromise.

5. Answer A, B, and C.
   (A) Briefly describe ONE specific historical similarity between the periods in American history before and after the Era of Good Feelings.
   (B) Briefly describe ONE specific historical difference between the periods in American history before and after the Era of Good Feelings.
   (C) Briefly explain ONE specific historical effect of the Era of Good Feelings.

LONG ESSAY

Develop a thoughtful and thorough historical argument that addresses the statement. Begin your essay with a thesis statement, and support it with specific historical evidence and examples.

6. Evaluate the relative importance of the causes that led to the rise in American nationalism following the War of 1812.

Answers

Long Essay

6. Thesis: The attempts to establish an American identity continued following the War of 1812. The consecutive military victories over the British brought forth a strong sense of American pride. However, it was the Era of Good Feelings and its reduction of political discourse that drew the country closest together, even though it was short lived. Further, the economic prosperity brought on by the rise of the First Industrial Revolution also gave Americans a sense of pride and economic security. Therefore, political and economic successes were the main driving forces for the rise of an American nationalism following the War of 1812. Specific Historical Evidence: America's second victory over the British was a source of great pride for Americans. The political divisions that had dominated the country's politics had died down, at least for a time during the Era of Good Feelings. Attempts to forge a national culture, with art, music, and literature, pushed artists to continue to search for a unique American identity. Washington Irving's international popularity catapulted other American writers onto the international stage. The First Industrial Revolution produced an enormous amount of economic prosperity, leading to other technological innovation. Henry Clay's American System sought to unite the country physically, with the national bank and internal improvements. Noah Webster tried to create a unified American language with the publication of his American dictionary. Finally, the judicial decisions of the Marshall Court, finally putting a legal endorsement for the superiority of the federal government over the states, also contributed to the rise and feeling of American nationalism.

9 JACKSONIAN AMERICA

GENERAL ANDREW JACKSON LEADING HIS TROOPS AT THE BATTLE OF NEW ORLEANS This scene of the battle of New Orleans during the War of 1812 shows Jackson on a white horse, leading his troops. His decisive victory in the battle cemented his reputation and led many people to call for him to run for president.

John Parrot/Stocktrek Images/Getty Images

CONNECTING CONCEPTS

Chapter Nine begins by exploring the emergence of the Second Party System during the Jacksonian Era. This phenomenon saw the rise of democracy and a push to expand the right to vote for white males. This development sought to legitimize the idea of party as a popular democratic institution during the first half of the nineteenth century in the United States.

The two parties that came to power in the Second Party System were the Democrats and the Whigs. Many of the social, political, and economic movements during this period fostered both the growing power of the federal government and an increasing sense of regional sectionalism. A strong challenge to federalism came during the Nullification Crisis, when South Carolina challenged the legitimacy and constitutionality of a federal tax. Henry Clay's role in this crisis and his American System of internal improvements also exemplified the growing division.

During the Antebellum period, sectional debates over the power of the federal government versus states' rights became more intense. The polarizing figure of Andrew Jackson and the controversy over the National Bank only added to the intensity of these disputes.

As you read, you should:

- Identity the causes which gave rise to the Second Party System in American politics.
- Analyze the strengths and weaknesses of democracy as it existed during the Jacksonian Era.
- Describe the various issues over the debate of federalism within the United States in the first half of the nineteenth century.
- Analyze how Henry Clay's American System furthered the divide between nationalism and sectionalism.
- Evaluate the causes and effects of continued western expansion in the first half of the nineteenth century.
- Analyze the causes that contributed to the divide between different geographic regions, furthering sectional controversy.

Pacing Guide

Chapter 9 explores key concepts from Period 4: 1800–1848 of the AP U.S. History Curriculum Framework. The suggested instruction time for Chapter 9 is 3 days.

Key Concepts

4.1.I The nation's transition to a more participatory democracy was achieved by expanding suffrage from a system based on property ownership to one based on voting by all adult white men, and it was accompanied by the growth of political parties.

4.3.I Struggling to create an independent global presence, the United States sought to claim territory throughout the North American continent and promote foreign trade.

4.3.II The United States's acquisition of lands in the West gave rise to contests over the extension of slavery into new territories.

Discussion and Activities

Analyzing Images Have students examine the image "General Andrew Jackson Leading His Troops at the Battle of New Orleans." Ask them to identify details from the painting and write a short summary describing the scene and how Jackson is presented in relation to the rest of his troops. *(Jackson is shown riding a big white horse and towering above his troops, with an American flag flying over his head. He appears in charge of the entire scene as the battle rages in the background.)* **PCE** **SOC** **NAT**

Reasoning Processes

Comparison Have students read the section "The Emergence of Andrew Jackson." Ask them to create a Venn diagram comparing Jackson to a previous president. **PCE** **SOC**

THE RISE OF MASS POLITICS

On March 4, 1829, an unprecedented throng–thousands of Americans from all regions of the country, including farmers, laborers, and others of modest social rank–crowded before the Capitol in Washington, D.C., to witness the inauguration of Andrew Jackson. After the ceremonies, the boisterous crowd poured down Pennsylvania Avenue, following their hero to the White House. There, at a public reception open to all, they filled the state rooms to overflowing, trampling one another, soiling the carpets, ruining elegantly upholstered sofas and chairs in their eagerness to shake the new president's hand. "It was a proud day for the people," wrote Amos Kendall, one of Jackson's closest political associates. "General Jackson is their own President." To other observers, however, the scene was less appealing. Justice of the Supreme Court Joseph Story, a friend and colleague of John Marshall, looked on the inaugural levee, as it was called, and remarked with disgust: "The reign of King 'Mob' seems triumphant."

JACKSON'S INAUGURATION

THE EMERGENCE OF ANDREW JACKSON

Jackson, one of the most powerful presidents of the nineteenth century, was born in 1767 to modest parents. They had moved from Ireland two years before Andrew was born in a small village in the Carolinas. At the age of thirteen, he was captured by the British during the American Revolution. When Jackson refused to clean the boots of a British officer, the officer cut Jackson with a sword, leaving him with scars and an enduring hatred of the British. As he became older, Jackson received only sporadic education and worked in various shops and on farms. As a young man, he studied law and was admitted to the bar.

Most of Jackson's early legal work involved disputed land-claims of which he soon tired. He was elected as a delegate to the Tennessee constitutional convention in 1796 and, later that same year, became a U.S. congressman. In 1797, he went on to become a U.S. senator but resigned within a year. In 1798, he was appointed a judge of the Tennessee Supreme Court, a position he held until 1804.

Gradually, Jackson prospered as planter and merchant. He also bought enslaved people to help his growing plantation. In 1804, he acquired an elegant home, the Hermitage, a large plantation in Davidson County, near Nashville. In time, he had one of the largest plantations in the state with up to 300 enslaved people.

Jackson joined the Tennessee militia in 1801 and in the next year was elected major general. He fought Native Americans in Alabama and Georgia. In the War of 1812, he fought against Britain. When the British threatened New Orleans, Jackson took command. In the Battle of New Orleans, his soldiers won a decisive victory over the British that ensured New Orleans would be part of the United States. He developed the reputation for being as "tough as old hickory" and thus earned the nickname "Old Hickory." Jackson left the war with many people calling for him to run for president of the United States.

EXPANDING DEMOCRACY

What some have called the "age of Jackson" did not much advance the cause of economic equality. The distribution of wealth and property in America was little different at the end of the Jacksonian era than it had been at the start. But it did mark a transformation of American politics that widely extended to new groups the right to vote.

Until the 1820s, relatively few Americans had been permitted to vote. Most states restricted the franchise to white males who were property owners or taxpayers or both, effectively barring an enormous number of the less affluent from the voting rolls. But beginning even before Jackson's election, the rules governing voting began to expand. Changes came first in Ohio and other new states of the West, which, on joining the Union, adopted constitutions that guaranteed all adult white males the right to vote and gave all voters the right to hold public office. Older states, concerned about the loss of their population to the West and thinking that extending the franchise might encourage some residents to stay, began to grant similar political rights to their citizens, dropping or reducing their property ownership or taxpaying requirements. Eventually, every state democratized its electorate to some degree, although some much later and less fully than others.

BROADENING THE FRANCHISE

ANDREW JACKSON This stern portrait suggests something of the fierce determination that characterized Andrew Jackson's military and political careers. Shattered by the death of his wife a few weeks after his election as president—a death he blamed (not without reason) on the attacks his political opponents had leveled at her—he entered office with a steely determination to live by his own principles and give no quarter to his adversaries.

Go Online AP Exam Preparation

AP Exam Practice Use the online assessment to help prepare students for the AP Exam. You can assign the ready-made AP-style short-answer questions, document-based questions, and multiple-choice questions assessing concepts, themes, and skills from Period 4 and AP-style long-essay questions organized in sets of 3 questions from various time periods. You can also create your own tests from available questions. This easy-to-use tool helps you design assessments that meet the needs of different types of learners.

Change provoked resistance, and at times the democratic trend fell short of the aims of the radical reformers, as when Massachusetts held its constitutional convention in 1820. Reform-minded delegates complained that in the Massachusetts government the rich were better represented than the poor, both because of restrictions on voting and officeholding and because of a peculiar system by which members of the state senate represented property rather than simply people. But Daniel Webster, one of the conservative delegates, opposed democratic changes on the grounds that "power naturally and necessarily follows property" and that "property as such should have its weight and influence in political arrangement." Webster and the rest of the conservatives could not prevent the reform of the rules for representation in the state senate; nor could they prevent elimination of the property requirement for voting. But, to the dismay of the radicals, the new constitution required that every voter be a taxpayer and that the governor be the owner of considerable real estate.

More often, however, the forces of democratization prevailed in the states. In the New York convention of 1821, for example, conservatives led by James Kent insisted that a taxpaying requirement for suffrage was not enough and that, at least in the election of state senators, the property qualification should survive. But reformers, citing the Declaration of Independence, maintained that life, liberty, and the pursuit of happiness, not property, were the main concerns of society and government. The property qualification was abolished.

The wave of state reforms was generally peaceful, but in Rhode Island democratization efforts created considerable instability. The Rhode Island constitution (still basically the old colonial charter) barred more than half the adult males of the state from voting. The conservative legislature, chosen by this restricted electorate, consistently blocked all efforts at reform. In 1840, the lawyer and activist Thomas W. Dorr and a group of his followers formed a "People's Party," held a convention, drafted a new constitution, and submitted it to a popular vote. It was overwhelmingly approved. The existing legislature, however, refused to accept the Dorr document and submitted a new constitution of its own to the voters. It was narrowly defeated. The Dorrites, in the meantime, had begun to set up a new government, under their own constitution, with Dorr as governor; and so, in 1842, two governments were claiming legitimacy in Rhode Island. The old state government proclaimed that Dorr and his followers were rebels and began to imprison them. Meanwhile, the Dorrites made a brief and ineffectual effort to capture the state arsenal. The Dorr Rebellion, as it was known, quickly failed. Dorr himself surrendered and was briefly imprisoned. But the episode helped pressure the old guard to draft a new constitution, which greatly expanded the suffrage.

THE DORR REBELLION

Year	Percentage
1824	26.9
1828	57.6
1832	55.4
1836	57.8
1840	80.2
1844	78.9
1848	72.7
1852	69.6
1856	78.9
1860	81.2

PARTICIPATION IN PRESIDENTIAL ELECTIONS, 1824–1860 This chart reveals the remarkable increase in popular participation in presidential elections in the years after 1824. Participation almost doubled between 1824 and 1828, and it increased substantially again beginning in 1840 and continuing through and beyond the Civil War.

What accounts for this dramatic expansion of the electorate? Who remained outside the voting population in these years?

Encyclopaedia Britannica/© UIG/The Bridgeman Art Library

THE DORR REBELLION The democratic sentiments that swept much of the nation in the 1830s and 1840s led to, among many other events, the Dorr Rebellion (as its opponents termed it) in Rhode Island. Thomas Dorr was one of many Rhode Islanders who denounced the state's constitution, which limited voting rights to a small group of property owners known as "freeholders."

Historical Thinking Skills

Contextualization After students have read the section "Broadening the Franchise," ask them to think about how westward expansion influenced suffrage. *(New western states tended not to include property ownership requirements or tax-paying restrictions on voting in their new constitutions. Existing states began to remove those restrictions in order to avoid losing more of their populations to the West.)* Have students share their thoughts with a partner. Ask for volunteers to share their thoughts with the class. **MIG** **PCE** **SOC**

Answers

Participation in Presidential Elections, 1824–1860

Many states were loosening property requirements; however, most still did not allow minorities or women to vote.

Historical Thinking Skills

Argumentation After students have read the section "Democratic Reforms," ask them to list examples of voting reforms and then rank those examples in order of importance. Ask students to write a thesis statement making a claim about the most important effects of voting reforms in the early nineteenth century. **PCE** **SOC**

The democratization process was far from complete. In much of the South, election laws continued to favor the planters and politicians of the older counties and to limit the influence of newly settled western areas. Enslaved people of course, were disenfranchised by definition; they were not considered citizens and were believed to have no legal or political rights. Free African American men could vote nowhere in the South and hardly anywhere in the North. Pennsylvania, in fact, amended its state constitution in 1838 to strip African Americans of the right to vote they had previously enjoyed. In no state could women vote. Nowhere was the ballot secret, and often voters had to cast a spoken vote rather than a written one, which meant that political bosses could, and often did, bribe and intimidate them.

DEMOCRATIC REFORMS

Despite the persisting limitations, however, the number of voters increased far more rapidly than did the population as a whole. Indeed, one of the most striking political trends of the early nineteenth century was the change in the method of choosing presidential electors and the dramatic increase in popular participation in the process. In 1800, the legislature had chosen the presidential electors in ten of the states, and the people in only six. By 1828, electors were chosen by popular vote in every state but South Carolina. In the presidential election of 1824, less than 27 percent of adult white males had voted. In the election of 1828, the figure rose to 58 percent, and in 1840 to 80 percent.

TOCQUEVILLE AND *DEMOCRACY IN AMERICA*

The rapid growth of the electorate—and the emergence of political parties—were among the most striking events of the early nineteenth century. As the right to vote spread widely in these years, it came to be the mark of freedom and democracy. One of the most important commentaries on this extraordinary moment in American life was a book by a French aristocrat, Alexis de Tocqueville. He spent two years in the United States in the 1830s watching the dramatic political changes in the age of Andrew Jackson. The French government had requested him to make a study of American prisons, which were thought to be more humane and effective institutions than prisons in Europe. But Tocqueville quickly went far beyond the study of prisons and wrote a classic study of American life, titled *Democracy in America*. Tocqueville examined not just the politics of the United States, but also the daily lives of many groups of Americans and their cultures, their associations, and their visions of democracy. In France in the early decades of the nineteenth century, the fruits of democracy were largely restricted to landowners and aristocrats. But Tocqueville recognized that traditional aristocracies were rapidly fading in America and that new elites could rise and fall no matter what their backgrounds.

Tocqueville also realized that the rising democracy of America had many limits. Democracy was a powerful, visible force in the lives of most white men. Few women could vote, although some shared the democratic ethos through their families. For many other Americans, democracy was a distant hope. Tocqueville wrote of the limits of equality and democracy:

> . . . he first who attracts the eye, the first in enlightenment, in power and in happiness, is the white man, the European, man par excellence; below him appear the Negro and the Indian. These two unfortunate races have neither birth, nor face, nor language, nor mores in common; only their misfortunes look alike. Both occupy an equally inferior position in the country that they inhabit; both experience the effects of tyranny; and if their miseries are different, they can accuse the same author for them.

Tocqueville's book helped spread the idea of American democracy into France and other European nations. Only later did it become widely read and studied in the United States as a remarkable portrait of the emerging democracy of the United States.

ALEXIS DE TOCQUEVILLE Renowned French printmaker and lithographer Honoré Daumier created this caricature of Alexis de Tocqueville in 1849. Tocqueville, also a Frenchman, traveled throughout the United States for two years in the 1830s witnessing the extraordinary growth of the U.S. electorate. In his famous book *Democracy in America*, he examined and analyzed the political, cultural, and social life of the United States. His work strongly influenced how many in France and the rest of Europe would understand the young country's experience of its emerging democracy.

Discussion and Activities

Historical Sources and Argumentation Have students read the section "Tocqueville and *Democracy in America*." Ask them to create a T-chart listing examples from Tocqueville's work that indicate that the United States either was or was not democratic. Then have students evaluate which seems truer of the United States at the time of Tocqueville's writing. **PCE** **SOC** **NAT**

The Legitimization of Party

The high level of voter participation was only partly the result of an expanded electorate. It was also the result of a growing interest in politics and a strengthening of party organization and, perhaps equally important, party loyalty. Although party competition was part of American politics almost from the beginning of the republic, acceptance of the idea of party was not. For more than thirty years, most Americans who had opinions about the nature of government considered parties evils to be avoided and thought the nation should seek a broad consensus in which permanent factional lines would not exist. But in the 1820s and 1830s, those assumptions gave way to a new view: that permanent, institutionalized parties were a desirable part of the political process, that indeed they were essential to democracy.

The elevation of the idea of party occurred first at the state level, most prominently in New York State. There Martin Van Buren led a dissident political faction (known as the "Bucktails" or the "Albany Regency"). In the years after the War of 1812, this group began to challenge the established political leadership–led by the aristocratic governor De Witt Clinton–that had dominated the state for years. Factional rivalries were not new, of course. But the nature of Van Buren's challenge was. Refuting the traditional view of a political party as undemocratic, they argued that only an institutionalized party, based in the populace at large, could ensure genuine democracy. The alternative was the sort of closed elite that Clinton had created. In the new kind of party the Bucktails proposed, ideological commitments would be less important than loyalty to the party itself. Preservation of the party as an institution–through the use of favors, rewards, and patronage–would be the principal goal of the leadership. Above all, for a party to survive, it must have a permanent opposition. Competing parties would give each political faction a sense of purpose; they would force politicians to remain continually attuned to the will of the people; and they would check and balance each other in much the same way that the different branches of government checked and balanced one another.

By the late 1820s, this new idea of party was spreading beyond New York. The election of Jackson in 1828, the result of a popular movement that seemed to stand apart from the usual political elites, seemed further to legitimize the idea of party as a popular, democratic institution. "Parties of some sort must exist," said a New York newspaper. "'Tis in the nature and genius of our government." Finally, in the 1830s, a fully formed two-party system began to operate at the national level, with each party committed to its own existence as an institution and willing to accept the legitimacy of its opposition. The anti-Jackson forces began to call themselves Whigs. Jackson's followers called themselves Democrats (no longer Democratic Republicans), thus giving a permanent name to what is now the nation's oldest political party.

The Second Party System

"President of the Common Man"

Unlike Thomas Jefferson, Jackson was no democratic philosopher. The Democratic Party, much less than Jefferson's Republicans, embraced no clear or uniform ideological position. But Jackson himself did embrace a distinct, if simple, theory of democracy. It should offer "equal protection and equal benefits" to all its white male citizens and favor no region or class over another. In practice, that meant an assault on what Jackson and his associates considered the citadels of the eastern aristocracy and an effort to extend opportunities to the rising classes of the West and the South. It also meant a firm commitment to the continuing subjugation of African Americans and Native Americans (and, although for different reasons, women), for the Jacksonians believed that only by keeping these "dangerous" elements from the body politic could the white-male democracy they valued be preserved.

Jackson's first targets were the entrenched officeholders in the federal government, many of whom had been in place for a generation or more. Official duties, he believed, could be made "so plain and simple that men of intelligence may readily qualify themselves for their performance." Offices belonged to the people, he argued, not to the entrenched officeholders. Or, as one of his henchmen, William L. Marcy of New York, cynically put it, "To the victors belong the spoils."

In the end, Jackson removed a total of no more than one-fifth of the federal officeholders during his eight years in office, many of them less for partisan reasons than because they had misused government funds or engaged in other corruption. Proportionally, Jackson dismissed no more job-holders than Jefferson had dismissed during his presidency. But by embracing the philosophy of the "spoils system," a system already well entrenched in a number of state governments, the Jackson administration helped make the right of elected officials to appoint their own followers to public office an established feature of American politics.

The Spoils System

Jackson's supporters also worked to transform the process by which presidential candidates won their party's nomination. They had long resented the congressional caucus, a process they believed favored entrenched elites. Jackson himself had avoided the caucus process in 1828. In 1832, the president's followers staged a national party convention to renominate him for the presidency–one year after the Anti-Masons became the first party to hold such a meeting. In later generations, some Americans would see the party convention as a source of corruption and political exclusivity. But those who created it in the 1830s considered it a great triumph for democracy. Through the convention, they believed, power would arise directly from the people, not from aristocratic political institutions such as the caucus.

Discussion and Activities

Making Connections After students have read the section "The Second Party System," ask them to think about and discuss how the party system that emerged in the 1820s is similar to or different from political parties today. **PCE** **SOC** **NAT**

Historical Thinking Skills

Analyzing Points of View After students have read the section "The Spoils System," ask them to think about how presidential appointments either changed or stayed the same during the Jackson administration. Have students write a letter to President Jackson from the point of view of a Jackson supporter seeking an appointment to office. **PCE** **SOC** **NAT**

Discussion and Activities

Analyzing Images Ask students to examine the portrait of President Jackson. Have them discuss as a class which interpretation(s) of Jackson's portrait is most consistent with their own perceptions of Jackson, and why. **PCE** **SOC**

DEBATING THE PAST

THE "AGE OF JACKSON"

To many Americans in the 1820s and 1830s, Andrew Jackson was a champion of democracy, a symbol of a spirit of anti-elitism and egalitarianism that was sweeping American life. In the twentieth and twenty-first centuries, however, historians have disagreed sharply not only in their assessments of Jackson himself, but also in their portrayal of American society in his era.

The "progressive" historians of the early twentieth century tended to see the politics of Jackson and his supporters as a forerunner of their own generation's battles against economic privilege and political corruption. Frederick Jackson Turner encouraged scholars to see Jacksonianism as the product of the democratic West: a protest by the people of the frontier against the conservative aristocracy of the East, which they believed restricted their own freedom and opportunity. Jackson represented those who wanted to make government responsive to the will of the people rather than to the power of special interests. The culmination of this progressive interpretation of Jacksonianism was the publication in 1945 of Arthur M. Schlesinger Jr.'s *The Age of Jackson.* Less interested in the regional basis of Jacksonianism than Turner's disciples had been, Schlesinger argued that Jacksonian democracy was an effort "to control the power of the capitalist groups, mainly Eastern, for the benefit of non-capitalist groups, farmers and laboring men, East, West, and South." He portrayed Jacksonianism as an early version of modern reform efforts to "restrain the power of the business community."

Richard Hofstadter, in an influential essay in his 1948 book *The American Political Tradition,* sharply disagreed. Jackson, he argued, was the spokesman of rising entrepreneurs—aspiring businessmen who saw the road to opportunity blocked by the monopolistic power of eastern aristocrats. The Jacksonian leaders were less sympathetic to the aspirations of those below them than they were to the destruction of obstacles to their own success. Bray Hammond, writing in 1957, argued similarly that the Jacksonian cause was "one of enterpriser against capitalist." Other historians saw Jacksonianism less as a democratic reform movement than as a nostalgic effort to restore a lost (and largely imagined) past. In *The Jacksonian Persuasion* (1957), Marvin Meyer argued that Jackson and his followers looked with misgivings on the new industrial society emerging around them and yearned instead for a restoration of the agrarian, republican virtues of an earlier time.

In the 1960s, historians examining the Jacksonian era began looking less at Jackson himself and more at the nature of American society in the early nineteenth century. Lee Benson's *The Concept of Jacksonian Democracy* (1961) used quantitative methods to demonstrate the role of religion and ethnicity in determining political divisions in the 1830s. Edward Pessen's *Jacksonian America* (1969) portrayed the Jacksonian era as an increasingly stratified society. This inclination to look more closely at society than at formal "Jacksonianism" continued into the late twentieth and early twenty-first centuries. Sean Wilentz, in *Chants Democratic* (1984) and in *The Rise of American Democracy* (2005), examined the rise in the 1820s of powerful movements among ordinary citizens, who were attracted less to Jackson than to the notion of popular democracy.

Gradually, this attention to Jacksonian-era society has led to reassessments of Jackson himself and the nature of his regime. In *Fathers and Children: Andrew Jackson and the Subjugation of the American Indian* (1975), Michael Rogin portrays Jackson as a leader of a new American revolution, not against British tyranny but against those who challenged the ability of white men to control the continent. Alexander Saxton, in *The Rise and Fall of the White Republic* (1990), makes the related point that "Jacksonian democracy" was explicitly a white man's democracy that rested on the subjugation of women, enslaved people and Native Americans. But the portrayal of Jackson as a champion of the common man has not vanished from scholarly life. The leading Jackson biographer of the postwar era, Robert V. Remini, has noted the flaws in Jackson's concept of democracy; but within the context of his time, Remini claims, Jackson was a genuine "man of the people."

The Library of Congress (3g06446u)

HISTORICAL THINKING SKILLS

Questions assume cumulative content knowledge from this chapter and previous chapters.

1. **Identifying Historical Developments** Identify three historical interpretations concerning the "Age of Jackson."
2. **Determining Context** Describe how one piece of historical evidence from the time period could be used to support each of the historical interpretations concerning the "Age of Jackson."
3. **Developing Arguments** Analyze which historical interpretation you find most convincing, and explain your reasoning.

Answers

Debating the Past

1. Progressive scholars like Turner encouraged scholars to see Jacksonianism as the product of the democratic West. This view culminated in the publication of Schlesinger Jr.'s *The Age of Jackson*, where he argued that Jacksonian democracy was an effort to control the power of the capitalist groups, mainly Eastern, for the benefit of non-capitalist groups. Hofstadter disagreed with this progressive interpretation. He argued that Jackson was the spokesman of rising entrepreneurs. But in the early twenty-first century, Wilentz examined the rise in the 1820s of powerful movements among ordinary citizens, who were attracted less to Jackson than to the notion of popular democracy.
2. Evidence of progressive interpretation points to the growing influence of the West on American politics, as Western territories grew in influence and power and more states were carved up from this region. The Populist interpretation, as presented by Hofstadter, points to the growing middle class, brought about by increased opportunities from the First Industrial Revolution and the Market Revolution. The social interpretation, as presented by Wilentz, points to the loosening of political requirements for the franchise, which in turn increased the political power of more and more white males.
3. The interpretation put forth by Alexander Saxton, in his book *The Rise and Fall of the White Republic* (1990), emphasized that Jacksonian democracy and the increased power of the white male middle class also rested on the subjugation of women, enslaved people, and Native Americans.

The "spoils" system and the political convention did serve to limit the power of two entrenched elites–permanent officeholders and the exclusive party caucus. Yet neither really transferred power to the people. Appointments to office almost always went to prominent political allies of the president and his associates. Delegates to national conventions were less often common men than members of local party organizations. Political opportunity within the party was expanding, but much less so than Jacksonian rhetoric suggested.

LIMITED NATURE OF DEMOCRATIC REFORM

"OUR FEDERAL UNION"

Jackson's commitment to extending power beyond entrenched elites led him to want to reduce the functions of the federal government. The concentration of power in Washington, he believed, restricted opportunity to people with political connections. But Jackson also believed in forceful presidential leadership and was strongly committed to the preservation of the Union. Thus, at the same time that Jackson was promoting an economic program to reduce the power of the national government, he was asserting the supremacy of the Union in the face of a potent challenge. For no sooner had he entered office than his own vice president–John C. Calhoun–began to champion a controversial (and, in Jackson's view, dangerous) constitutional theory: nullification.

CALHOUN AND NULLIFICATION

Calhoun was forty-six years old in 1828, with a distinguished past and an apparently promising future. But the smoldering issue of the tariff created a dilemma for him. Once he had been an outspoken protectionist and had strongly supported the tariff of 1816. But by the late 1820s, many South Carolinians had come to believe that the "tariff of abominations" was responsible for the stagnation of the state's economy–even though the stagnation was largely a result of the exhaustion of South Carolina's farmland, which could no longer compete effectively with the newly opened fertile lands of the Southwest. Some exasperated Carolinians were ready to consider a drastic remedy–secession.

Calhoun's future political hopes rested on how he met this challenge in his home state. He did so by developing a theory that he believed offered a moderate alternative to secession: the theory of nullification. Drawing from the ideas of Madison and Jefferson and their Virginia and Kentucky Resolutions of 1798–1799 and citing the Tenth Amendment to the Constitution, Calhoun argued that since the federal government was a creation of the states, the states–not the courts or Congress–were the final arbiters of the constitutionality of federal laws. If a state concluded that Congress had passed an unconstitutional law, then it could hold a special convention and declare the federal law null and void within the state. The nullification doctrine–and the idea of using it to nullify the 1828 tariff–quickly attracted broad support in South Carolina. But it did nothing to help Calhoun's standing within the new administration, in part because he had a powerful rival in Martin Van Buren.

CALHOUN'S THEORY OF NULLIFICATION

JOHN C. CALHOUN This photograph, by Mathew Brady, captured Calhoun toward the end of his life, when he was torn between his real commitment to the ideals of the Union and his equally fervent commitment to the interests of the South. The younger generation of southern leaders, who would dominate the politics of the region in the 1850s, were less idealistic and more purely sectional in their views.

THE RISE OF VAN BUREN

Van Buren was about the same age as Calhoun and equally ambitious. He had won election to the governorship of New York in 1828 and then resigned in 1829 when Jackson appointed him secretary of state. Alone among the figures in the Jackson administration, Van Buren soon established himself as a member both of the official cabinet and of the president's unofficial circle of political allies, known as the "Kitchen Cabinet" (which included such Democratic newspaper editors as Isaac Hill of New Hampshire and Amos Kendall and Francis P. Blair of Kentucky). Van Buren's influence with the president was unmatched and grew stronger still as a result of a quarrel over etiquette that drove a wedge between the president and Calhoun.

MARTIN VAN BUREN'S GROWING INFLUENCE

Reasoning Processes

Continuity and Change After students have read the section "Limited Nature of Democratic Reform," ask them to write a thesis statement that makes a claim about whether there was more continuity or change in presidential politics in the period from 1800 to 1832. **PCE** **NAT**

Historical Thinking Skills

Historical Reasoning and Argumentation Have students read the section "Calhoun and Nullification." Ask them to look up the Tenth Amendment in the appendix of their books or online. Have students discuss in small groups how the Tenth Amendment might be used to support Calhoun's position on nullification. *(The Tenth Amendment reserves to states powers not delegated to the federal government. Calhoun interpreted that to give states the power to overturn federal laws.)* **PCE**

Discussion and Activities

Analyzing Cause and Effect After students have read the section "Martin Van Buren's Growing Influence," ask them to create a T-chart listing political and social factors accounting for Van Buren's growing influence and then write a summary arguing which factor was more responsible for his rise. **PCE** **SOC**

Peggy O'Neale was the attractive daughter of a Washington tavernkeeper with whom both Andrew Jackson and his friend John H. Eaton had taken lodgings while serving as senators from Tennessee. O'Neale was married, but rumors circulated in Washington in the mid-1820s that she and the unmarried Senator Eaton were having an affair. O'Neale's husband died in 1828, and she and Eaton were soon married. A few weeks later, Jackson named Eaton secretary of war and thus made the new Mrs. Eaton a cabinet wife. The rest of the administration wives, led by Mrs. Calhoun, refused to receive her socially. Jackson (remembering the effects of public slander directed against his own late wife) was furious and demanded that the members of the cabinet accept her into their social world. Calhoun, under pressure from his wife, refused. Van Buren, a widower, befriended the Eatons and thus ingratiated himself with Jackson. By 1831, partly as a result of the Peggy Eaton affair, Jackson had chosen Van Buren to succeed him in the White House, apparently ending Calhoun's dreams of the presidency.

THE WEBSTER-HAYNE DEBATE

In January 1830, as the controversy over nullification grew more intense, a great debate occurred in the U.S. Senate over another sectional controversy. In the midst of a routine debate over federal policy toward western lands, a senator from Connecticut suggested that all land sales and surveys in the west be temporarily discontinued so as to slow the growth of slavery. Robert Y. Hayne, a young senator from South Carolina, responded, charging that slowing down the growth of the West was a way for the East to retain its political and economic power. Although he had no real interest in western lands, he hoped his stance would attract support from westerners in Congress for South Carolina's drive to lower the tariff. Both the South and the West, he argued, were victims of the tyranny of the Northeast. He hinted that the two regions might combine to defend themselves against that tyranny.

Daniel Webster, now a senator from Massachusetts and a nationalistic Whig, attacked Hayne the next day, and through him Calhoun, for what he considered their challenge to the integrity of the Union. He was, in fact, challenging Hayne to a debate not on public lands and the tariff but on the issue of states' rights versus national power. Hayne, coached by Calhoun, responded with a defense of the theory of nullification. Webster then spent two full afternoons delivering what became known as his "Second Reply to Hayne," a speech that northerners quoted and revered for years to come. He concluded with the ringing appeal "Liberty and Union, now and forever, one and inseparable!"

STATES' RIGHTS VERSUS NATIONAL POWER

Both sides now waited to hear what President Jackson thought of the argument. The answer became clear at the annual Democratic Party banquet in honor of Thomas Jefferson. After dinner, guests delivered a series of toasts. The president arrived with a written text in which he had underscored certain words: "Our Federal Union—It must be preserved." While he spoke, he looked directly at Calhoun. The diminutive Van Buren, who stood on his chair to see better, thought he saw Calhoun's hand shake and a trickle of wine run down his glass as he responded to the president's toast with his own: "The Union, next to our liberty most dear." The two most important figures in government had drawn sharp lines between themselves.

MARTIN VAN BUREN As leader of the so-called Albany Regency in New York in the 1820s, Van Buren helped create one of the first modern party organizations in the United States. Later, as Andrew Jackson's secretary of state and (after 1832) vice president, he helped bring party politics to the national level. In 1840, when he ran for reelection to the presidency, he lost to William Henry Harrison, whose Whig Party made effective use of many of the techniques of mass politics that Van Buren himself had pioneered.

THE NULLIFICATION CRISIS

In 1832, finally, the controversy over nullification produced a crisis. A congressional tariff bill was passed that offered South Carolinians no relief from the 1828 "tariff of abominations." Almost immediately, the legislature summoned a state convention, which voted to nullify the tariffs of 1828 and 1832 and to forbid the collection of duties within the state. At the same time, South Carolina elected Hayne to serve as governor and Calhoun (who resigned as vice president) to replace Hayne as senator.

Discussion and Activities

Contextualization and Argumentation Have students read the section "The Webster-Hayne Debate." Ask them to think about the competing toasts offered by Jackson and Calhoun at the Democratic Party banquet. Have students pair up, with each partner taking one side of the conflict. Ask them to paraphrase the toasts as tweets of 140 characters or less. Ask for volunteers to share their tweets with the class. **PCE** **NAT**

DANIEL WEBSTER The great Civil War photographer Mathew Brady took this portrait of Daniel Webster shortly before Webster's death in 1852. It conveys something of Webster's intensity of purpose—an intensity that was perhaps most famously visible in his dramatic 1830 debate with South Carolina senator Robert Y. Hayne. In his response to Hayne, he spoke words that became a rallying cry in the North: "Liberty and Union, now and forever, one and inseparable." During his long political career, Webster was one of the giants of American politics, a man of much greater stature than many of the presidents who were his contemporaries.

Jackson insisted that nullification was treason and that those implementing it were traitors. He strengthened the federal forts in South Carolina and ordered a warship and several revenue ships to Charleston. When Congress convened early in 1833, Jackson proposed a force bill authorizing the president to use the military to see that acts of Congress were obeyed. Violence seemed a real possibility.

Calhoun faced a predicament as he took his place in the Senate. Not a single state had come to South Carolina's support. Even South Carolina itself was divided and could not hope to prevail in a showdown with the federal government. But the timely intervention of Henry Clay, newly elected to the Senate, averted a crisis. Clay devised a compromise by which the tariff would be lowered gradually so that, by 1842, it would reach approximately the same level as in 1816. The compromise and the force bill were passed on the same day, March 1, 1833. Jackson signed them both. In South Carolina, the convention reassembled and repealed its nullification of the tariffs. Calhoun and his followers claimed a victory for nullification, which had, they insisted, forced the revision of the tariff. But the episode made clear that no state could defy the federal government alone.

COMPROMISE

THE REMOVAL OF NATIVE AMERICANS

There had never been any doubt about Andrew Jackson's attitude toward the Native Americans that continued to live in the eastern states and territories of the United States. He wanted them to move west, beyond the Mississippi, out of the way of expanding white settlement. Jackson's antipathy toward the Native Americans had a special intensity because of his own earlier experiences leading military campaigns against groups along the southern border. But in most respects, his views were little different from those of most other white Americans.

WHITE ATTITUDES TOWARD NATIVE AMERICANS

In the eighteenth century, many white Americans had considered the Native Americans "noble savages," peoples without real civilization but with an inherent dignity that made civilization possible among them. By the first decades of the nineteenth century, this vaguely paternalistic attitude (the attitude of Thomas Jefferson, among others) was giving way to a more hostile one, particularly among the white settlers in the western states and territories whom Jackson came to represent. Such settlers were coming to view Native Americans simply as "savages," not only uncivilized but uncivilizable. White Americans, they believed, should not be expected to live in close proximity to Native Americans.

CHANGING ATTITUDES

White westerners favored removal as well because they feared that continued contact between the expanding white settlements and the Native Americans would produce endless conflict and violence. Most of all, however, they favored removal because of their own insatiable desire for territory. The Native American nations possessed valuable land in the path of expanding white settlement. White Americans wanted it.

THE BLACK HAWK WAR

In the Old Northwest, the long process of expelling the Woodland Indians culminated in a last battle in 1831–1832, between white settlers in Illinois and an alliance of Sauk (or Sac) and Fox Indians under the fabled and now aged warrior Black Hawk. An earlier treaty had ceded tribal lands in Illinois to the United States; but Black Hawk and his followers refused to recognize the legality of the agreement, which a rival tribal faction had signed. Hungry and resentful, a thousand of them crossed the river and reoccupied vacant lands in Illinois. White settlers in the region feared that the resettlement was the beginning of a substantial invasion, and they assembled the Illinois state militia and federal troops to repel the "invaders."

Reasoning Processes

Comparison After students have read the section "The Nullification Crisis," ask them to recall the earlier compromise brokered by Henry Clay, the Missouri Compromise. Have students create a Venn diagram comparing the Missouri Compromise to the compromise that ended the Nullification Crisis. Ask them to evaluate what the most important similarities and differences were. **PCE** **SOC** **WXT**

Historical Thinking Skills

Argumentation Have students read the section "White Attitudes Toward Native Americans." Ask them to write a thesis statement making a claim about the most important changes in white attitudes toward Native Americans from 1754 to 1840. **PCE** **MIG** **SOC**

Discussion and Activities

Understanding Multiple Perspectives After students have read the section "Sauk and Fox Indians Defeated," hold a class discussion about why Andrew Jackson may have wanted to meet Black Hawk and why the tour of Black Hawk and Whirling Thunder through the East may have changed the attitudes of many white Americans toward Native Americans. **SOC** **PCE** **NAT**

NEW YORK HARBOR This aquatint, by W. J. Bennett (after the painting by John William Hill) shows Manhattan viewed from Brooklyn Heights around 1836. By this time, overseas traders had increasingly directed their business to New York, leaving much less opportunity for other cities, especially those in the South.

The Black Hawk War, as it became known, was notable chiefly for the viciousness of the white military efforts. White leaders in western Illinois vowed to exterminate the "bandit collection of Indians" and attacked them even when Black Hawk attempted to surrender. The Sauks and Foxes, defeated and starving, retreated across the Mississippi into Iowa. White troops (and some bands of Sioux whom they encouraged to join the chase) pursued them as they fled and slaughtered most of them. United States troops captured Black Hawk himself and sent him on a tour of the East, where Andrew Jackson was one of many curious white Americans who arranged to meet him. (Abraham Lincoln served as a captain of the militia, but saw no action, in the Black Hawk War; Jefferson Davis was a lieutenant in the regular army.)

SAUK AND FOX INDIANS DEFEATED

BLACK HAWK AND WHIRLING THUNDER After his defeat by white settlers in Illinois in 1832, the famed Sauk warrior Black Hawk and his son Whirling Thunder were captured and sent on a tour of the East by Andrew Jackson, displayed to the public as trophies of war. They showed such dignity through the ordeal that much of the white public quickly began to sympathize with them. This portrait, by John Wesley Jarvis, was painted on the tour's final stop, in New York City. Black Hawk wears the European-style suit, while Whirling Thunder wears native costume to emphasize his commitment to his tribal roots. Soon thereafter, Black Hawk returned to his tribe, wrote a celebrated autobiography, and died in 1838.

NATIVE AMERICAN NATIONS OF THE SOUTH

More troubling to the government in the 1830s were the Native American nations remaining in the South. In western Georgia, Alabama, Mississippi, and Florida lived what were referred to at the time as the "Five Civilized Tribes"–the Cherokee, Creek, Seminole, Chickasaw, and Choctaw–most

Reasoning Processes

Continuity and Change Have students examine the image "New York Harbor." Ask them to identify details that show how New York had changed or stayed the same over the preceding century. *(New York was still a leading port and trade center, as evidenced by the numerous ships in the harbor and warehouses around it. New technology is evident in the form of steamships that helped New York consolidate trade after completion of the Erie Canal.)* **WXT** **WOR**

of whom had established settled agricultural societies with successful economies. The Cherokees in Georgia had formed a particularly stable and sophisticated culture, with their own written language and a formal constitution (adopted in 1827) that created an independent Cherokee Nation. They were more closely tied to their lands than many of the nomadic groups to the north.

Even some white Americans argued that the Cherokees, unlike other groups, should be allowed to retain their eastern lands, since they had become such a "civilized" society and had, under pressure from missionaries and government agents, given up many of their traditional ways. Cherokee men had once been chiefly hunters and had left farming mainly to women. By now the men had given up most of their hunting and (like most white men) took over the farming themselves; Cherokee women, also like their white counterparts, restricted themselves largely to domestic tasks.

The federal government worked steadily to negotiate treaties with the southern Native American nations that would remove them to the West and open their lands for white settlement. But the negotiating process did not proceed fast enough to satisfy the region's white settlers. The state of Georgia's independent effort to dislodge the Creeks, over the objection of President Adams, was one example of this impatience. That same impatience became evident early in Jackson's administration, when the legislatures in Georgia, Alabama, and Mississippi began passing laws to regulate the Native Americans remaining in their states. They received assistance in these efforts from Congress, which in 1830 passed the Removal Act (with Jackson's approval) to appropriate money to finance federal negotiations with the southern groups aimed at relocating them to the West. The president quickly dispatched federal officials to negotiate nearly a hundred new treaties with the remaining groups. Thus the southern Native American nations faced a combination of pressures from both the state and federal governments. Most groups were too weak to resist, and they ceded their lands in return for token payments. Some, however, balked.

REMOVAL ACT

In Georgia, the Cherokees tried to stop the white encroachments (which were actively encouraged by Jackson) by appealing to the Supreme Court. The Court's decisions in *Cherokee Nation v. Georgia* and *Worcester v. Georgia* in 1831 and 1832 seemed at least partially to vindicate the tribe. But Jackson's longtime hostility toward Native Americans left him

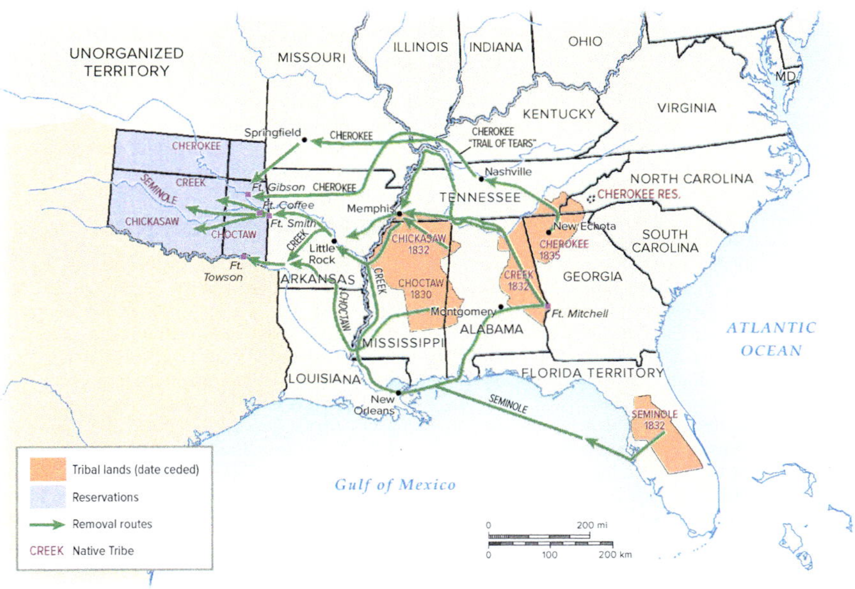

THE EXPULSION OF THE NATIVE AMERICAN NATIONS, 1830–1835 Andrew Jackson was famous well before he became president for his military exploits against Native Americans. Once in the White House, he ensured that few Native Americans would remain in the southern states of the nation, now that white settlement was increasing there. The result was a series of dramatic "removals" of Native Americans out of their traditional lands and into new territories west of the Mississippi—mostly in Oklahoma. Note the very long distance many of these tribes had to travel.

Why was the route of the Cherokees, shown in the upper portion of the map, known as the "Trail of Tears"?

Discussion and Activities

Analyzing Cause and Effect After students have read the section "Agrarian Nations of the South," discuss as a class in what ways the Five Civilized Tribes had attempted to avoid conflict with Americans and why those efforts eventually failed. **PCE** **SOC** **NAT** **MIG**

Answers

The Expulsion of the Native Americans, 1830–1835

It was known as the "Trail of Tears" due to the intense suffering and numerous deaths endured by the Cherokee Native Americans who were forced onto new lands in the West along its route.

Discussion and Activities

Historical Reasoning and Argumentation After students have read the section "Cherokee Resistance," ask them to discuss in pairs or small groups what else members of the Five Civilized Tribes could have done to preserve their land or to appeal for support from the white community. SOC PCE MIG

with little sympathy for the Cherokees and little patience with the Court. He was eager to retain the support of white Southerners and Westerners in the increasingly bitter partisan battles in which his administration was becoming engaged. When the chief justice announced the decision in *Worcester v. Georgia*, Jackson reportedly responded with contempt. "John Marshall has made his decision," he was reported to have said. "Now let him enforce it." The decision was not enforced.

CHEROKEE RESISTANCE

In 1835, the federal government extracted a treaty from a minority faction of the Cherokees, none of them a chosen representative of the Cherokee Nation. The treaty ceded the tribe's land to Georgia in return for $5 million and a reservation west of the Mississippi. The great majority of the 17,000 Cherokees did not recognize the treaty as legitimate and refused to leave their homes. But Jackson would not be thwarted. He sent an army of 7,000 under General Winfield Scott to round them up and drive them westward at bayonet point.

TRAILS OF TEARS

CHEROKEE REMOVAL

About 1,000 Cherokees fled across the state line to North Carolina, where the federal government eventually provided a small reservation for them in the Smoky Mountains, which survives today. But most of the rest made the long, forced trek to "Indian Territory" (which later became Oklahoma) beginning in the winter of 1838. Along the way, a Kentuckian observed: "Even aged females, apparently nearly ready to drop in the grave, were travelling with heavy burdens attached to their backs, sometimes on frozen ground and sometimes on muddy streets, with no covering for their feet."

INDIAN REMOVAL

Thousands, perhaps an eighth or more of the emigrés, perished before or soon after reaching their unwanted destination. In the harsh new reservations in which they were now forced to live, the survivors never forgot the hard journey. They called their route "The Trail Where They Cried," the Trail of Tears. Jackson claimed that the "remnant of that ill-fated race" was now "beyond the reach of injury or oppression," apparently trying to convince himself or others that he had supported removal as a way to protect Native Americans.

The Cherokees were not alone in experiencing the hardships of the Trail of Tears. Between 1830 and 1838, virtually all Native American nations were expelled from the Southern states and forced to relocate in the new Indian Territory, which Congress had officially created by the Indian Intercourse Act of 1834. The Choctaws of Mississippi and western Alabama were the first to make the trek, beginning in 1830. The army moved out the Creeks of eastern Alabama and western Georgia in 1836. The Chickasaws in northern Mississippi began the long march westward a year later, and the Cherokees, finally, a year after that. The government thought the Indian Territory was safely distant from existing white settlements and consisted of land that most settlers considered undesirable. It had the additional advantage, the government believed, of being on the eastern edge of what earlier white explorers had christened the "Great American Desert," land unfit for habitation. It seemed unlikely that white settlers would ever seek to settle along the western borders of the Indian Territory; and thus the prospect of settlers surrounding the reservation and producing further conflict seemed remote.

THE SEMINOLE WAR

Only the Seminoles in Florida managed to resist the pressures to relocate, and even their success was limited. Like other groups, the Seminoles had agreed under pressure to a settlement (the 1832–1833 treaties of Payne's Landing), by which they ceded their lands to the government and agreed to move to Indian Territory within three years. Most did move west, but a substantial minority, under the leadership of the chieftain Osceola, refused to leave and staged an uprising beginning in 1835 to defend their lands. (Joining the Seminoles in their struggle was a group of runaway enslaved people who had been living with the group.) The Seminole War dragged on for years. Jackson sent troops to Florida, but the Seminoles with their African American associates were masters of guerrilla warfare in the jungly Everglades. Even after Osceola had been treacherously captured by white troops while under a flag of truce and had died in prison; even after white troops had engaged in a systematic campaign of extermination against the resisting Indians and their black allies; even after 1,500 white soldiers had died and the federal government had spent $20 million on the struggle—even then, followers of Osceola remained in Florida. Finally, in 1842, the government abandoned the war. By then, many of the Seminoles had been either killed or forced westward. But the relocation of the Seminoles, unlike the relocation of most of the other groups, was never complete.

THE MEANING OF REMOVAL

By the end of the 1830s, almost all the important Native American societies east of the Mississippi had been removed to the West. The Native American nations had ceded over 100 million acres of eastern land to the federal government; they had received in return about $68 million and 32 million acres in the far less hospitable lands west of the Mississippi between the Missouri and Red Rivers. There they lived, organized by nation into a series of carefully defined reservations, in a territory surrounded by a string of United States forts to keep them in (and to keep most white Americans out), in a region whose climate and topography bore little relation to anything they had known before. Eventually, even this forlorn enclave would face serious incursions from white Americans.

What were the alternatives to the removal of the eastern Native Americans? There was probably never any realistic possibility that the government could stop white expansion westward. White people had already been penetrating the West for nearly two centuries, and such penetrations were certain to continue. But did that expansion really require removal?

Historical Thinking Skills

Argumentation Have students read the section "Trails of Tears." Ask them to write a letter to the editor of a newspaper along the route advocating for changes in the government's Native American policy. PCE SOC MIG NAT

There were, in theory at least, several alternatives to the brutal removal policy. There were many examples in the West of white settlers and Native Americans living side by side and creating a shared (if not necessarily equal) world. In the pueblos of New Mexico, in the fur trading posts of the Pacific Northwest, in parts of Texas and California, settlers from Mexico, Canada, and the United States had created societies in which Native Americans and whites were in intimate contact with each other. Even during the famous Lewis and Clark expedition, white explorers had lived with western Native Americans and had intimate relationships with Native American women. Sometimes these close contacts between white settlers and Native Americans were beneficial to both sides, even reasonably equal. Sometimes they were cruel and exploitive. But the early multiracial societies of the West did not separate white settlers and Native Americans. They demonstrated ways in which the two cultures could interact, each shaping the other.

ALTERNATIVES TO REMOVAL

By the mid-nineteenth century, however, white Americans had adopted a different model as they contemplated westward expansion. Much as the early British settlers along the Atlantic coast had established "plantations," from which Native Americans were, in theory, to be excluded, so the westward-moving white settlers of later years came to imagine the territories they were entering as virgin land, with no preexisting civilization. Native Americans, they believed, could not be partners—either equal or subordinate—in the creation of new societies in the West. They were obstacles, to be removed and, as far as possible, isolated. Native Americans, Andrew Jackson once said, had "neither the intelligence, the industry, the moral habits, nor the desire of improvement" to be fit partners in the project of extending white civilization westward. By dismissing Native American cultures in that way, white Americans justified to themselves a series of harsh policies that they believed (incorrectly) would make the West theirs alone.

ACTS
OF THE
STATE OF GEORGIA

AN ACT

To ratify and confirm certain articles of agreement and cession entered into on the 24th day of April 1802, between the Commissioners of the State of Georgia on the one part, and the Commissioners of the United States on the other part.

WHEREAS the Commissioners of the State of Georgia, to wit: James Jackson, Abraham Baldwin, and John Milledge, duly authorized and appointed by, and on the part and behalf of the said State of Georgia; and the Commissioners of the United States, James Madison, Albert Gallatin, and Levi Lincoln, duly authorized and appointed by, and on the part and behalf of the said United States, to make an amicable settlement of limits, between the two Sovereignties, after a due examination of their respective powers, did, on the 24th day of April last, enter into a deed of articles, and mutual cession, in the words following, to wit:

ARTICLES of agreement and cession, entered into on the twenty-fourth day of April, one thousand eight hundred and two, between the Commissioners appointed on the part of the United States, by virtue of an act entitled, "An act for an amicable settlement of limits

THE REMOVAL OF NATIVE AMERICANS FROM GEORGIA On April 24, 1831, Georgia issued an agreement to document the forced removal of Native Americans from the state. This policy forced thousands of Native Americans from their traditional tribal lands to new "reservations" west of the Mississippi River. The Cherokees were among the first groups forced to move. The conditions of this forced displacement were harsh and many people died, prompting survivors to call the route they had traveled the "Trail of Tears."

JACKSON AND THE BANK WAR

Jackson was quite willing to use federal power against rebellious states and Native American nations. On economic issues, however, he was consistently opposed to concentrating power either in the federal government or in powerful and, in his view, aristocratic institutions associated with it. An early example of his skeptical view of federal power was his 1830 veto of a congressional measure providing a subsidy to the proposed Maysville Road in Kentucky. The bill was unconstitutional, Jackson argued, because the road in question lay entirely within Kentucky and was not, therefore, a part of "interstate commerce." But the bill was also unwise, he believed, because it committed the government to what Jackson considered extravagant expenditures.

JACKSON'S OPPOSITION TO CONCENTRATED POWER

Jackson's opposition to federal power and aristocratic privilege lay behind the most celebrated episode of his presidency: the war against the Bank of the United States.

BIDDLE'S INSTITUTION

The Bank of the United States in the 1830s was a mighty institution, and it is not surprising that it would attract Jackson's wrath. Its stately headquarters in Philadelphia seemed to symbolize its haughty image of itself. It had branches in twenty-nine other cities, making it the most powerful and far-flung financial institution in the nation. By law, the Bank was the only place that the federal government could deposit its own funds; the government, in turn, owned one-fifth of the Bank's

NICHOLAS BIDDLE

Discussion and Activities

Historical Developments and Argumentation After students have read the section "The Meaning of Removal," ask them to consider why none of the alternatives to removal were implemented. Have students share their thoughts with a partner. **MIG** **WXT** **SOC** **PCE** **NAT**

Discussion and Activities

Analyzing Issues After students have read the section "The Meaning of Removal," ask them to write a short paragraph summarizing how Georgia was able to remove the Cherokee even though the Supreme Court had sided with the Native Americans in *Worcester v. Georgia. (This was mainly due to President Jackson's refusal to support the Court's decision, but also due to Congressional indifference and the desire of white Georgians to occupy the economically lucrative land.)* **PCE** **SOC** **WXT**

Reasoning Processes

Comparing After students have read the section "Biddle's Institution," ask them to construct a 3-circle Venn diagram comparing the positions of Biddle, "soft money" advocates, and "hard money" advocates. Have them evaluate whether there were any common ideas that could have led to compromise. **PCE** **WXT**

stock. The Bank did a tremendous business in general banking. It provided credit to growing enterprises; it issued bank notes, which served as a dependable medium of exchange throughout the country; and it exercised a restraining effect on the less well-managed state banks. Nicholas Biddle, who served as president of the Bank from 1823 on, had done much to put the institution on a sound and prosperous basis. Nevertheless, Andrew Jackson was determined to destroy it.

Opposition to the Bank came from two very different groups: the "soft-money" faction and the "hard-money" faction. Advocates of soft money–people who wanted more currency in circulation and believed that issuing bank notes unsupported by gold and silver was the best way to circulate more currency–consisted largely of state bankers and their allies. They objected to the Bank of the United States because it restrained the state banks from issuing notes freely. The hard-money people believed that gold and silver were the only basis for money. They condemned all banks that issued bank notes, including the Bank of the United States. The soft-money advocates were believers in rapid economic growth and speculation; the hard-money forces embraced older ideas of "public virtue" and looked with suspicion on expansion and speculation.

HARD AND SOFT MONEY

Jackson supported the hard-money position. Many years before, he had been involved in some grandiose land and commercial speculations based on paper credit. His business had failed in the Panic of 1797, and he had fallen deeply into debt. After that, he was suspicious of all banks and all paper currency. But as president he was also sensitive to the complaints of his many soft-money supporters in the West and the South. He made it clear that he would not favor renewing the charter of the Bank of the United States, which was due to expire in 1836.

A Philadelphia aristocrat unaccustomed to politics, Biddle nevertheless began granting financial favors to influential men who he thought might help him preserve the Bank. In particular, he turned to Daniel Webster and cultivated a close personal friendship with him. He named Webster the Bank's legal counsel and director of its Boston branch; Webster was also a frequent, heavy borrower from the Bank. He helped Biddle win the support of other important figures, among them Henry Clay.

Clay, Webster, and other advisers persuaded Biddle to apply to Congress in 1832 for a bill to renew the Bank's charter. That was four years ahead of the date the original charter was scheduled to expire. But forcing a vote now would allow the Bank to become a major issue in the 1832 national elections. Congress passed the recharter bill; Jackson, predictably, vetoed it; and the Bank's supporters in Congress failed to override the veto. Just as Clay had hoped, the 1832 campaign now centered on the future of the Bank.

JACKSON'S VETO

Clay ran for president that year as the unanimous choice of the National Republicans, who held a nominating convention in Baltimore late in 1831. But the Bank War failed to provide him with the winning issue for which he had hoped. Jackson, with Van Buren as his running mate, overwhelmingly defeated Clay (and several minor party candidates) with 55 percent of the popular vote and 219 electoral votes (more than four times as many as Clay received). These results were a defeat not only for Clay, but also for Biddle.

Candidate (Party)	Electoral Vote	Popular Vote (%)
Andrew Jackson (Democrat)	219	687,502 (55)
Henry Clay (National Republican)	49	530,189 (42)
William Wirt (Anti-Mason)	7	33,108 (3)
John Floyd (Independent Democrat)	11	
Not voted	2	

THE ELECTION OF 1832 Jackson's reelection victory in 1832 was almost as decisive as his earlier victory in 1828.

What changes are visible in party loyalties since the previous election?

THE "MONSTER" DESTROYED

Jackson was now more determined than ever to destroy the "monster" Bank as quickly as possible. He could not legally abolish the institution before the expiration of its charter. Instead, he tried to weaken it. He decided to remove the government's deposits from the Bank. His secretary of the treasury believed that such an action would destabilize the financial system and refused to give the order. Jackson fired him and appointed a new one. When the new secretary similarly balked, Jackson fired him too and named a third, more compliant secretary: Attorney General Roger B. Taney, his close friend and loyal ally. Taney began placing the government's deposits not in the Bank of the United States, as it had in the past, but in a number of state banks (which Jackson's enemies called "pet banks").

REMOVAL OF GOVERNMENT DEPOSITS

Answers

The Election of 1832

National Republicans lost support in the Northeast, though they did win Clay's home state of Kentucky. Also, third-party candidates won in Vermont and South Carolina.

Nicholas Biddle, whom Jacksonians derisively called "Czar Nicholas," did not give in without a fight. "This worthy President," he wrote sarcastically, "thinks that because he has scalped Indians and imprisoned Judges, he is to have his way with the Bank. He is mistaken." When the administration began to transfer funds directly from the Bank of the United States to the pet banks (as opposed to the initial practice of simply depositing new funds in those banks), Biddle called in loans and raised interest rates, explaining that without the government deposits the Bank's resources were stretched too thin. He realized his actions were likely to cause financial distress. He hoped a short recession would persuade Congress to recharter the Bank. "Nothing but the evidence of suffering," he told a colleague, would "produce any effect in Congress." By now, the struggle had become not just a conflict over policy and principle, but also a bitter personal battle between two proud men—both of them acting recklessly in an effort to humiliate and defeat the other.

As financial conditions worsened in the winter of 1833–1834, supporters of the Bank blamed Jackson's policies for the recession. They organized meetings around the country and sent petitions to Washington urging a rechartering of the Bank. But the Jacksonians blamed the recession on Biddle and refused to budge. When distressed citizens appealed to the president for help, he dismissively answered, "Go to Biddle."

Finally, Biddle contracted credit too far even for his own allies in the business community, who began to fear that in his effort to save his own bank he was threatening their interests. Some of them did "go to Biddle." A group of New York and Boston merchants protested. To appease the business community, Biddle at last reversed himself and began to grant credit in abundance and on reasonable terms. His vacillating and unpopular tactics ended his chances of winning a recharter of the Bank.

Jackson Victorious

Jackson had won a considerable political victory. But when the Bank of the United States died in 1836, the country lost a valuable, albeit flawed, financial institution and was left with a fragmented and chronically unstable banking system that would plague the economy for more than a century.

The Taney Court

In the aftermath of the Bank War, Jackson moved against the most powerful institution of economic nationalism of all: the Supreme Court. In 1835, when John Marshall died, the president appointed as the new chief justice his trusted ally Roger B. Taney. Taney did not bring a sharp break in constitutional interpretation, but he gradually helped modify Marshall's vigorous nationalism.

Charles River Bridge v. Warren Bridge

Perhaps the clearest indication of the new judicial mood was the celebrated case of *Charles River Bridge v. Warren Bridge* of 1837. The case involved a dispute between two Massachusetts companies over the right to build a bridge across the Charles River between Boston and Cambridge. One company had a long-standing charter from the state to operate a toll bridge and claimed that this charter guaranteed it a monopoly of the bridge traffic. Another company had applied to the legislature for authorization to construct a second, competing bridge that would—since it would be toll free—greatly reduce the value of the first company's charter.

The first company contended that in granting the second charter the legislature was engaging in a breach of contract and noted that the Marshall Court, in the *Dartmouth College* case and other decisions, had ruled that states had no right to abrogate contracts. But now Taney, speaking for the Democratic majority on the Court, supported the right of Massachusetts to award the second charter. The object of government, Taney maintained, was to promote the general happiness, an object that took precedence over the rights of contract and property. A state, therefore, had the right to amend or abrogate a contract if such action was necessary to advance the well-being of the community. Such an abrogation was clearly necessary in the case of the Charles River Bridge, he argued, because the original bridge company, by exercising a monopoly, was benefiting from unjustifiable privilege. (It did not help the first company that its members were largely Boston aristocrats closely associated with Harvard College; the challenging company, by contrast, consisted largely of newer, aspiring entrepreneurs—the sort of people with whom Jackson and his allies instinctively identified.) The decision reflected one of the cornerstones of the Jacksonian ideal: that the key to democracy was an expansion of economic opportunity, which would not occur if older corporations could maintain monopolies and choke off competition from newer companies.

The Changing Face of American Politics

Birth of the Whig Party

Jackson's forceful—some people claimed tyrannical—tactics in crushing first the nullification movement and then the Bank of the United States helped galvanize a growing opposition coalition that by the mid-1830s was ready to assert itself in national politics. Denouncing the president as "King Andrew I," they began to refer to themselves as Whigs, after the party in England that had traditionally worked to limit the power of the king. With the emergence of the Whigs, the nation once again had two competing political parties. What scholars now call the "Second Party System" began what turned out to be its relatively brief life.

Democrats and Whigs

The two parties were different from one another in their philosophies, in their constituencies, and in the character of their leaders. But they became increasingly alike in the way they approached the process of electing their followers to office.

Discussion and Activities

Historical Evidence and Argumentation After students have read the section "The Monster Destroyed," ask them to go online or use a dictionary to define the term "Pyrrhic victory." Have them discuss as a class or in small groups whether Jackson's defeat of the Bank of the United States was a "Pyrrhic victory." PCE WXT NAT

Reasoning Processes

Comparing Have students read the section "The Taney Court." Ask them to create a T-chart listing positions and decisions of the Supreme Court under Roger B. Taney and John Marshall. Ask students to evaluate how the decisions were similar or different. PCE

Reasoning Processes

Comparing After students have read the sections "Democrats' Emphasis on Opportunity" and "Whigs' Call for Economic Union," ask them to create a Janus figure comparing the economic ideology of the parties. (A Janus figure is a graphic organizer in the shape of a human figure divided vertically down the middle.) Then have them take a position about whether these policies were more similar or different. **PCE** **SOC** **WXT**

"THE DOWNFALL OF MOTHER BANK" This 1832 cartoon celebrates Andrew Jackson's destruction of the Bank of the United States. The president is shown here driving away the Bank's corrupt supporters by ordering the withdrawal of government deposits.

Democrats in the 1830s envisioned a future of steadily expanding economic and political opportunities for white males. The role of government should be limited, they believed, but it should include efforts to remove obstacles to opportunity and to avoid creating new ones. That meant defending the Union, which Jacksonians believed was essential to the dynamic economic growth they favored. It also meant attacking centers of corrupt privilege. As Jackson himself said in his farewell address, the society of America should be one in which "the planter, the farmer, the mechanic, and the laborer, all know that their success depends on their own industry and economy," in which artificial privilege would stifle no one's opportunity. Among the most radical members of the party–the so-called Locofocos, mainly workingmen and small businessmen and professionals in the Northeast–sentiment was strong for a vigorous, perhaps even violent assault on monopoly and privilege far in advance of anything Jackson himself ever contemplated.

DEMOCRATS' EMPHASIS ON OPPORTUNITY

The political philosophy that became known as Whiggery was very different. It favored expanding the power of the federal government, encouraging industrial and commercial development, and knitting the country together into a consolidated economic system. Whigs embraced material progress enthusiastically; but unlike the Democrats, they were cautious about westward expansion, fearful that rapid territorial growth would produce instability. Their vision of America was of a nation embracing the industrial future and rising to world greatness as a commercial and manufacturing power. Thus, while Democrats were inclined to oppose legislation establishing banks, corporations, and other modernizing institutions, Whigs generally favored such measures.

WHIGS' CALL FOR ECONOMIC UNION

The Whigs were strongest among the more substantial merchants and manufacturers of the Northeast; the wealthier planters of the South (those who favored commercial development and the strengthening of ties with the North); and the ambitious farmers and rising commercial class of the West–usually migrants from the Northeast–who advocated internal improvements, expanding trade, and rapid economic progress. The Democrats drew more support from smaller merchants and the workingmen of the Northeast; from southern planters suspicious of industrial growth; and from westerners–usually with southern roots–who favored a predominantly agrarian economy and opposed the development of powerful economic institutions in their region. Whigs tended to be wealthier than

Discussion and Activities

Analyzing Images Have students examine the image "The Downfall of Mother Bank." Ask them to list details that demonstrate how the image supports a pro-Jackson point of view. *(Jackson is the dominant figure; at least one of the Bank's supporters is portrayed as a demon; the other supporters are shown as small and cowering.)* **PCE** **WXT**

Democrats, to have more aristocratic backgrounds, and to be more commercially ambitious.

But Whig and Democratic politicians alike were more interested in winning elections than in maintaining philosophical purity. And both parties made frequent adjustments in their public postures to attract the largest possible number of voters. In New York, for example, the Whigs worked to develop

ANTI-MASONS

a popular following by making a connection to a movement known as Anti-Masonry. The Anti-Mason movement had emerged in the 1820s in response to widespread resentment against the secret, exclusive, and hence supposedly undemocratic, Society of Freemasons. Such resentments greatly increased in 1826 when a former Mason, William Morgan, mysteriously disappeared (and was assumed to have been murdered) from his home in Batavia, New York, shortly before he was scheduled to publish a book exposing the supposed secrets of Freemasonry. Whigs seized on the Anti-Mason frenzy to launch harsh attacks on Jackson and Van Buren (both Freemasons), implying that the Democrats were part of the antidemocratic conspiracy. In the process, the Whigs presented themselves as opponents of aristocracy and exclusivity. They were attacking the Democrats with the Democrats' own issues.

Religious and ethnic divisions also played an important role in determining the constituencies of the two parties. Irish and German Catholics, among the largest of the recent immigrant groups, tended to support the Democrats, who appeared to

CULTURAL ISSUES

share their own vague aversion to commercial development and entrepreneurial progress and who seemed to respect family- and community-centered values and habits. Evangelical Protestants gravitated toward the Whigs because they associated the party with constant development and improvement, goals their own faith embraced. These and other ethnic, religious, and cultural tensions were often more influential in determining party alignments than any concrete political or economic proposals.

The Whig Party was more successful at defining its positions and attracting a constituency than it was in uniting behind a national leader. No single person was ever able to command the loyalties of the party in the way Andrew Jackson did the Democrats. Instead, Whigs tended to divide their loyalties among three figures, each of whom was so substantial a figure that together they became known as the "Great Triumvirate": Henry Clay, Daniel Webster, and John Calhoun.

Clay won support from many of those who favored his program for internal improvements and economic development,

CLAY'S AMERICAN SYSTEM

what he called the "American System"; but his image as a devious operator and his identification with the West proved to be serious liabilities. He ran for president three times and never won. Daniel Webster, the greatest orator of his era, won broad support with his passionate speeches in defense of the Constitution and the Union; but his close connection with the Bank of the United States and the protective tariff, his reliance on rich men for financial support, and his excessive and often embarrassing fondness for brandy prevented him from developing enough of a national constituency to win him the office he so desperately wanted. John C. Calhoun, the third member of the Great Triumvirate, never considered himself a true Whig, and his identification with the nullification controversy in effect disqualified him from national leadership in any case. But he had tremendous strength in the South, supported a national bank, and shared with Clay and Webster a strong animosity toward Andrew Jackson.

The problems that emerged from this divided leadership became particularly clear in 1836. The Democrats were united

ELECTION OF 1836

behind Andrew Jackson's personal choice for president, Martin Van Buren. The Whigs could not agree on a single candidate. Instead, they ran several candidates, hoping to profit from the regional strength of each. Webster represented the party in New England; Hugh Lawson White of Tennessee ran in the South; and the military veteran and hero of the War of 1812, William Henry Harrison, from Ohio, was the candidate in the

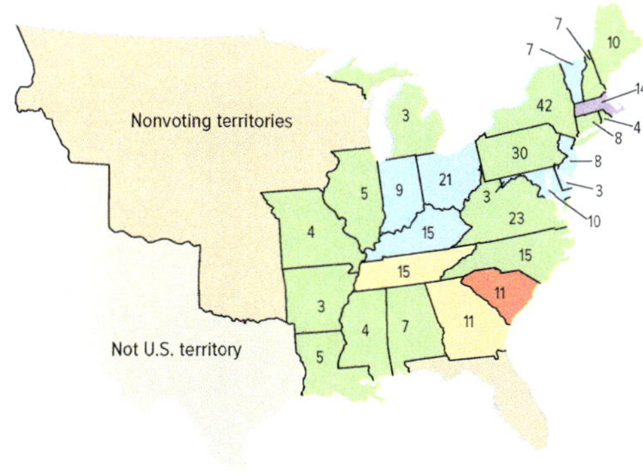

Candidate (Party)	Electoral Vote	Popular Vote (%)
Martin Van Buren (Democrat)	170	765,483 (50.9)
W. H. Harrison (Whig)	73	550,816 (36.6)
Hugh L. White (Whig)	26	146,107 (9.7)
Daniel Webster (Whig)	14	41,201 (2.7)
W. P. Magnum (Independent)	11	—

THE ELECTION OF 1836 Martin Van Buren, who had served as vice president and secretary of state for Andrew Jackson, was the Democratic candidate for president in 1836. His connection to the revered Jackson helped him easily defeat his Whig opponent, William Henry Harrison. Four years later, the same two men contested the presidency, but that time it was Harrison who won.

Historical Thinking Skills

Argumentation After students have read the section "Cultural Issues," ask them to write a thesis statement making a claim about whether political or social issues were more important in determining voters identifying as Whigs or Democrats. Have students share their thoughts with a partner and give feedback. **WXT** **SOC** **PCE**

Historical Thinking Skills

Argumentation Have students read the section "Clay's American System." Ask them to create a campaign poster making an argument for either Clay, Webster, or Calhoun to be the Whig presidential candidate. **SOC** **PCE**

Discussion and Activities

Speculating After students have read the section "Election of 1836," ask them to write a short paragraph from the point of view of the chairperson of the Whig Party describing a strategy to defeat Van Buren. **PCE**

middle states and the West. Party leaders hoped the three candidates together might draw enough votes from Van Buren to prevent his getting a majority and throw the election to the House of Representatives, where the Whigs might be able to elect one of their own leaders. In the end, however, Van Buren won easily, with 170 electoral votes to 124 for all his opponents combined.

VAN BUREN AND THE PANIC OF 1837

Andrew Jackson retired from public life in 1837, beloved by most Americans. Martin Van Buren was very different from his predecessor and far less fortunate. He was never able to match Jackson's personal popularity, and his administration encountered economic difficulties that devastated the Democrats and helped the Whigs.

Van Buren's success in the 1836 election was a result in part of a nationwide economic boom that was reaching its height in that year. Canal and railroad builders were at a peak of activity. Prices were rising, money was plentiful, and credit was easy as banks increased their loans and notes with little regard to their reserves of cash. The land business, in particular, was booming. Between 1835 and 1837, the government sold nearly 40 million acres of public land, nearly three-fourths of it to speculators, who purchased large tracts in hopes of reselling them at a profit. These land sales, along with revenues the government received from the tariff of 1833, created a series of substantial federal budget surpluses and made possible a steady reduction of the national debt (something Jackson had always advocated). From 1835 to 1837, the government for the first and only time in its history was out of debt, with a substantial surplus in the Treasury.

Congress and the administration now faced the question of what to do with the Treasury surplus. Reducing the tariff was not an option, since no one wanted to raise that thorny issue again. Instead, support grew for returning the federal surplus to the states. In 1836, Congress passed a "distribution" act requiring the federal government to pay its surplus funds to the states each year in four quarterly installments as interest-free, unsecured loans. No one expected the "loans" to be repaid. The states spent the money quickly, mainly to encourage construction of highways, railroads, and canals. The distribution of the surplus thus gave further stimulus to the economic boom.

DISTRIBUTION ACT

Congress did nothing to check the speculative fever, with which many congressmen themselves were badly infected. Webster, for one, was buying up thousands of acres in the West. But Jackson, always suspicious of paper currency, was

"THE TIMES," 1837 This savage caricature of the economic troubles besetting the United States in 1837 illustrates, among other things, popular resentment of the hard-money orthodoxies of the time. A sign on the Custom House reads: "All bonds must be paid in Specie." Next door, the bank announces: "No specie payments made here." Women and children are shown begging in the street, while unemployed workers stand shoeless in front of signs advertising loans and "grand schemes."

Discussion and Activities

Analyzing Images Have students examine the image "'The Times,' 1837." Ask them to identify details that demonstrate the severity of the Panic of 1837. *(A burning balloon labelled "safety plan" is falling from the sky; the busiest stores are the liquor store and pawnshop; the unemployed workers are wearing ragged clothing; the apparent widow and her child are begging on the street.)* **WXT**

unhappy that the government was selling good land and receiving in return various state bank notes worth no more than the credit of the issuing bank.

In 1836, not long before leaving office, he issued a presidential order, the "specie circular." It provided that in payment for public lands the government would accept only gold or silver coins or currency securely backed by gold or silver. Jackson was right to fear the speculative fever but wrong in thinking the specie circular would cure it. On the contrary, it produced a financial panic that began in the first months of Van Buren's presidency. Hundreds of banks and businesses failed. Unemployment grew. Bread riots broke out in some of the larger cities. Prices fell, especially the price of land. Many railroad and canal projects failed. Several of the debt-burdened state governments ceased to pay interest on their bonds, and a few repudiated their debts, at least temporarily. It was the worst depression in American history to that point, and it lasted for five years. It was a political catastrophe for Van Buren and the Democrats.

PANIC OF 1837

Both parties bore some responsibility for the panic. But the depression was only partly a result of American policies. England and western Europe were facing panics of their own, which caused European (and especially English) investors to withdraw funds from America, putting an added strain on American banks. A succession of crop failures on American farms reduced the purchasing power of farmers and required increased imports of food, which sent more money out of the country. But whatever its actual causes, the Panic of 1837 occurred during a Democratic administration, and the Democrats paid the political price for it. The Van Buren administration, which strongly opposed government intervention in the economy, did little to fight the depression. Some of the steps it took–borrowing money to pay government debts and accepting only specie for payment of taxes–may have made things worse. Van Buren did succeed in establishing a ten-hour workday on all federal projects, by presidential order, but he had only a few legislative achievements.

The most important and controversial of them was the creation of a new financial system to replace the Bank of the United States. Under Van Buren's plan, known as the "independent treasury" or "subtreasury" system, the government would place its funds in an independent treasury at Washington and in subtreasuries in other cities. No private banks would have the government's money or name to use as a basis for speculation; the government and the banks would be "divorced."

INDEPENDENT TREASURY

Van Buren called a special session of Congress in 1837 to consider the proposal, which failed in the House. In 1840, the last year of Van Buren's presidency, the administration finally succeeded in driving the measure through both houses of Congress.

THE LOG CABIN CAMPAIGN

As the campaign of 1840 approached, the Whigs realized that they would have to settle on one candidate for president this time if they were to have any hope of winning. As a result, they held their first national nominating convention in Harrisburg, Pennsylvania, in December 1839. Passing over the controversial Henry Clay, who had expected the nomination, the convention chose William Henry Harrison and, for vice president, John Tyler of Virginia. Harrison was a descendant of the Virginia aristocracy but had spent his adult life in the Northwest. He was a renowned soldier, famous from conflicts with Native American nations, and a popular national figure. The Democrats nominated Van Buren. But because they were not much more united than the Whigs, they failed to nominate a vice presidential candidate, leaving the choice of that office to the electors.

The 1840 campaign was the first in which the new popular "penny press" carried news of the candidates to a large audience of workers and tradespeople. It also illustrated how fully the concept of party competition, the subordination of ideology to immediate political needs, had established itself in America. The Whigs represented the affluent elements of the population, and they favored government policies that would aid business. But they presented themselves in 1840 as the party of the common people. So, of course, did the Democrats. Both parties used the

NEW TECHNIQUES OF POLITICAL CAMPAIGNING

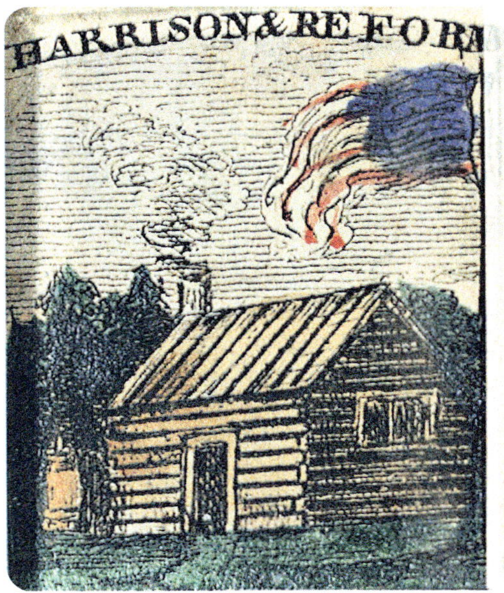

HARRISON AND REFORM This hand-colored engraving was made for a brass brooch during the 1840 presidential campaign and served the same purposes that modern campaign buttons do. It conveys Harrison's presumably humble beginnings in a log cabin. In reality, Harrison was a wealthy, aristocratic man; but the unpopularity of the aristocratic airs of his opponent, President Martin Van Buren, persuaded the Whig Party that it would be good political strategy to portray Harrison as a humble "man of the people."

Reasoning Processes

Identifying Cause and Effect Have students read the section "Panic of 1837." Ask them to create a T-chart identifying causes and effects of the recession. Have students write a thesis statement making a claim about the most important effects of the Panic of 1837. Ask for volunteers to share and give feedback. **WXT**

Discussion and Activities

Analyzing Issues Have students read the section "Independent Treasury." Ask them to discuss in pairs or small groups how an independent treasury could help prevent future economic crises. *(It could help by taking government funds out of state banks, which would make it more difficult for those state banks to finance speculators.)* **WXT**

Discussion and Activities

Making Connections After students have read the section "The Log Cabin Campaign," ask them to create a Venn diagram comparing the Harrison campaign for president in 1840 and a recent presidential campaign. **PCE** **SOC**

same techniques of mass voter appeal, the same evocation of simple, rustic values. What mattered now was not the philosophical purity of the party but its ability to win votes. The Whig campaign was particularly effective in portraying William Henry Harrison, a wealthy member of the frontier elite with a considerable estate, as a simple man of the people who loved log cabins and hard cider. They accused Van Buren of being an aloof aristocrat who used cologne, drank champagne, and ate from gold plates. The Democrats had no defense against the combination of these campaign techniques and the effects of the depression. Harrison won the election with 234 electoral votes to 60 for Van Buren and with a popular vote majority of 53 percent.

THE FRUSTRATION OF THE WHIGS

Despite their decisive victory, the Whigs found their four years in power frustrating and divisive. In large part, that was because their popular new president, "Old Tippecanoe," William Henry Harrison, died of pneumonia one month after taking office. Vice President Tyler succeeded him. Control of the administration thus fell to a man with whom the Whig party leadership had weak ties. Harrison had generally deferred to Henry Clay and Daniel Webster, whom he named secretary of state. Under Tyler, things quickly changed.

Tyler was a former Democrat who had left the party in reaction to what he considered Jackson's excessively egalitarian program and imperious methods. But there were still signs of his Democratic past in his approach to public policy. The president did agree to bills abolishing Van Buren's independent treasury system and raising tariff rates. But he refused to support Clay's attempt to recharter a Bank of the United States. And he vetoed several internal improvement bills that Clay and other congressional Whigs sponsored. Finally, a conference of congressional Whigs read Tyler out of the party. Every cabinet member but Webster resigned; five former Democrats took their places. When Webster, too, left the cabinet, Tyler appointed Calhoun, who had rejoined the Democratic Party, to replace him.

WHIGS BREAK WITH TYLER

A new political alignment was emerging. Tyler and a small band of conservative southern Whigs were preparing to rejoin the Democrats. Joining the "common man's party" of Jackson and Van Buren was a faction with decidedly aristocratic political ideas, who thought that government had an obligation to protect and even expand the institution of slavery, and who believed in states' rights with almost fanatical devotion.

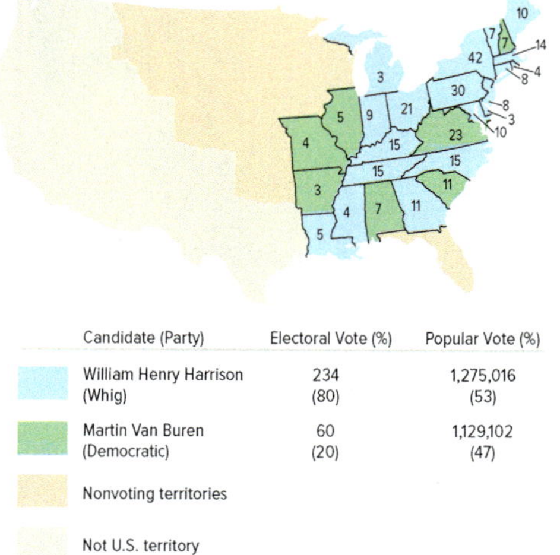

Candidate (Party) | Electoral Vote (%) | Popular Vote (%)
William Henry Harrison (Whig) | 234 (80) | 1,275,016 (53)
Martin Van Buren (Democratic) | 60 (20) | 1,129,102 (47)
Nonvoting territories
Not U.S. territory

THE ELECTION OF 1840 President Martin Van Buren was defeated in 1840 despite his close relationship to the popular former president, Andrew Jackson. Van Buren, unlike Jackson, was president during a sharp economic recession. And even though his opponent, William Henry Harrison, was a wealthy frontier aristocrat, the Whig Party effectively portrayed him as a humble man of the people, a contrast to what they claimed was Van Buren's extravagance and elitism.

WHIG DIPLOMACY

In the midst of these domestic controversies, a series of incidents in the late 1830s brought Great Britain and the United States once again to the brink of war. Residents of the eastern provinces of Canada launched a rebellion against the British colonial government in 1837, and some of the rebels chartered an American steamship, the *Caroline*, to ship supplies across the Niagara River to them from New York. British authorities in Canada seized the *Caroline* and burned it, killing one American in the process. The British government refused either to disavow the attack or to provide compensation for it, and resentment in the United States ran high. But the British soon had reasons for anger as well. Authorities in New York, attempting to exploit the *Caroline* affair, arrested a Canadian named Alexander McLeod and charged him with the murder of the American who had died in the incident. The British government, expressing majestic rage, insisted that McLeod could not be accused of murder because he had acted under official orders. The foreign secretary, the bellicose Lord Palmerston, demanded McLeod's release and threatened that his execution would bring "immediate and frightful" war.

THE *CAROLINE* AFFAIR

Webster as secretary of state did not think McLeod was worth a war, but he was powerless to release him. The prisoner was under New York jurisdiction and had to be tried in the state courts, a peculiarity of American jurisprudence that the British did not seem to understand. A New York jury did what Webster could not: it defused the crisis by acquitting McLeod.

Historical Thinking Skills

Argumentation Have students read the section "The Frustration of the Whigs." Ask them to create a T-chart listing successes and failures of the Tyler administration. Have them conclude with an argument about whether the Tyler administration experienced more successes or failures. **PCE**

Reasoning Processes

Identifying Cause and Effect After students have read the section "Whig Diplomacy," ask them to create a T-chart listing causes and effects of the Aroostook War. Ask students to discuss whether the causes they identified seemed to justify another war with Great Britain. **WOR**

A BEAUTIFUL GOBLET OF WHITE-HOUSE CHAMPAGNE
AN UGLY MUG OF LOG-CABIN HARD CIDER

AN ATTACK ON VAN BUREN This "pull card," made during the 1840 presidential campaign, which Van Buren lost to William Henry Harrison, satirizes the president as an aristocratic dandy. The card displays Van Buren grinning while he drinks champagne in the White House. Pulling a tab on the card changes his champagne glass to a mug of hard cider (with Harrison's initials on it) and changes his expression from delight to revulsion.

At the same time, tensions flared over the boundary between Canada and Maine, which had been in dispute since the Treaty of 1783. In 1838, groups of Americans and Canadians, mostly lumberjacks, began moving into the Aroostook River region in the disputed area, precipitating a violent brawl between the two groups that became known as the "Aroostook War."

Aroostook War

Several years later, there were yet more Anglo-American problems. In 1841, an American ship, the *Creole*, sailed from Virginia for New Orleans with more than 100 enslaved people aboard. En route the enslaved people mutinied, took possession of the ship, and took it to the Bahamas. British officials there declared the enslaved people free, and the English government refused to overrule them. Many Americans, especially Southerners, were furious.

At this critical juncture, a new government eager to reduce the tensions with the United States came to power in Great Britain. In the spring of 1842, it sent Lord Ashburton, an admirer of America, to negotiate an agreement on the Maine boundary and other matters. The result of his negotiations with Secretary of State Webster and representatives from Maine and Massachusetts was the Webster-Ashburton Treaty of 1842. Its terms established a firm northern boundary between the United States and Canada along the Maine-New Brunswick border that survives to this day; the new border gave the United States a bit more than half of the previously disputed territory. Other, smaller provisions placated Maine and Massachusetts and protected critical trade routes in both the northern United States and southern Canada. In a separate exchange of notes, Ashburton eased the memory of the *Caroline* and *Creole* affairs by expressing regret and promising no future "officious interference" with American ships.

Webster-Ashburton Treaty

Discussion and Activities

Analyzing Images Have students examine the image "An Attack on Van Buren." Ask students to consider the significance of the drink changing from champagne to hard cider. *(The champagne symbolized extravagance and identified Van Buren as a member of the elite, while the hard cider symbolized the common man and the campaign of Harrison, who defeated Van Buren in the 1840 election.)* **PCE** **SOC**

AP Exam Tip

One way that students can develop a point-of-view analysis in responding to document-based questions is to analyze motives for a source. Identifying a motive can help students understand why the author of a source wrote what he or she did.

Historical Thinking Skills

Sourcing and Situation To practice the AP Exam Tip, have students read the feature "The Penny Press." **Ask:** What motives did the penny press have to sensationalize stories? *(This was to attract attention and sell more papers. Higher circulation meant being able to charge higher rates for advertising.)* **WXT**

PATTERNS OF POPULAR CULTURE

THE PENNY PRESS

On September 3, 1833, a small newspaper appeared in New York City for the first time: the *New York Sun*, published by a young former apprentice from Massachusetts named Benjamin Day. Four pages long, it contained mostly trivial local news, with particular emphasis on sex, crime, and violence. It sold for a penny, launching a new age in the history of American journalism, the age of the "penny press."

Before the advent of the penny press, newspapers in America were far too expensive for most ordinary citizens to buy. But several important changes in the business of journalism and the character of American society paved the way for Benjamin Day and others to challenge the established press. New technologies—the steam-powered cylinder printing press, new machines for making paper, railroads and canals for distributing issues to a larger market—made it possible to publish newspapers inexpensively and to sell them widely. A rising popular literacy rate, a result in part of the spread of public education, created a bigger reading public.

The penny press was also a response to the changing culture of the 1820s and 1830s. The spread of an urban, market economy contributed to the growth of the penny press by drawing a large population of workers, artisans, and clerks into large cities, where they became an important market for the new papers. The spirit of democracy—symbolized by the popularity of Andrew Jackson and the rising numbers of white male voters across the country—helped create an appetite for journalism that spoke to and for "the people." Hence Benjamin Day's slogan for his new paper: "It Shines for ALL." The *Sun* and papers like it were committed to feeding the appetites of the people of modest means, who constituted most of their readership. "Human interest stories" helped solidify their hold on the working public. Condescending stories about poor black men and women—ridiculing their subjects' illiteracy and their accents—were also popular among these papers' virtually all-white readership.

Within six months of its first issue, the *Sun* had the largest circulation in New York—8,000 readers, more than twice the number of its nearest competitors. James Gordon Bennett's *New York Herald*, which began publication in 1835, soon surpassed the *Sun* in popularity with its lively combination of sensationalism and local gossip and with its aggressive pursuit of national and international stories. The *Herald* pioneered a "letters to the editor" column, was the first paper to have regular reviews of books and the arts, and launched the first daily sports section. By 1860, its circulation of more than 77,000 was the largest of any daily newspaper in the world.

THE SUN.

THE NEW YORK *SUN* This 1834 front page of *The Sun*, which had begun publication a year earlier, contains advertisements, human interest stories, a description of a slave auction in Charleston, S.C., and homespun advice: "Life is short. The poor pittance of several years is not worth being a villain for."

THE LEXINGTON BLOWS! This image in the *New York Sun* was one of the first examples of large and (in this case at least) lurid illustration in the daily press. This dramatic picture depicts an event that took place on the Long Island Sound in 1840.

Not all the new penny papers were as sensationalist as the *Sun* and the *Herald*. Both the *Philadelphia Public Ledger* and the *Baltimore Sun*, founded in 1836 and 1837 respectively, strove to provide serious coverage of the news. The *Baltimore Sun* even developed a Washington bureau, the first of the penny papers to do so. The *New York Tribune*, founded in 1841 by Horace Greeley, prided itself on serious reporting and commentary, all of it tinged with a conspicuous sympathy for socialism and for the aspirations of working people. As serious as the *Tribune*, but more sober and self-consciously "objective" in its reportage, was the *New York Times*, which Henry Raymond founded in 1851. "We do not mean to write as if we were in a passion—unless that shall really be the case," the *Times* huffily proclaimed in its first issue, in an obvious reference to Greeley and his impassioned reportage; "and we shall make it a point to get into a passion as rarely as possible."

The newspapers of the penny press initiated the process of turning journalism into a profession. They were the first to pay their reporters and the first to rely heavily on advertisements, often devoting up to half their space to paid advertising. They tended to be sensationalist and opinionated, but they were often also aggressive in uncovering serious and important news—in police stations, courts, jails, streets, and private homes as well as in city halls, state capitals, Washington, D.C., and the world.

HISTORICAL THINKING SKILLS

1. **Determining Context** How were the penny press newspapers a product of the Jacksonian era?
2. **Comparing and Contrasting** What were some of the characteristics of the early penny press newspapers? How did they differ from each other?
3. **Making Connections** How are the penny press newspapers related to the more modern newspapers of our day?

264 · CHAPTER 9

Answers

Patterns of Popular Culture

1. The first paper sold for a penny, thus making it affordable for a much larger audience. New technology also made newspapers and the printing industry more affordable and accesible to a larger audience. A rising literacy rate among the populous, one of the highest in the world at the time, created a larger reading public. The changing culture of the 1820s and 1830s brought more individuals to the cities, where they became an important market for the newspapers.
2. Many of the first papers contained stories on sex, crime, and violence. Several other newspapers focused on "human interest stories," which helped solidify their hold on the working public. Many of the papers also reinforced the societal prejudices that were imposed upon many individuals of the time. One paper included "letters to the editor," something new at the time, and also contained reviews of books and the arts and the launch of the daily sports section.
3. Many of these newspapers created the profession of journalism. Many were the first to pay their reporters and to pay for stories, and they were also the first to rely on paid advertising. They tended to sensationalize stories, and they were often aggressive in uncovering serious and important news.

During the Tyler administration, the United States established its first diplomatic relations with China. In 1842, Britain forced China to open certain ports to foreign trade. Eager to share the new privileges, American mercantile interests persuaded Tyler and Congress to send a commissioner–Caleb Cushing–to China to negotiate a treaty giving the United States some part in the China trade. In the Treaty of Wang Hya, concluded in 1844, Cushing secured most-favored-nation provisions giving Americans the same privileges as the English. He also won for Americans the right of "extraterritoriality"–the right of Americans accused of crimes in China to be tried by American, not Chinese, officials. In the next ten years, American trade with China steadily increased.

TREATY OF WANG HYA

In their diplomatic efforts, at least, the Whigs were able to secure some important successes. But by the end of the Tyler administration, the party could look back on few other victories. In the election of 1844, the Whigs lost the White House. They were to win only one more national election in their history.

CHAPTER 9 REVIEW

CONNECTING THEMES

Chapter Nine explored how non-elite white men became more important political actors in the early part of the nineteenth century. The rise of the Second Party System and the growing movement of mass politics fundamentally altered the political and social structures of the country. The political franchise continued to expand, although women and people of color remained largely excluded. As the Second Party System replaced the First Party System, politics and power continued to fuel much of the social, political, and economic insecurity that continued throughout the antebellum era. Debate continued over the delicate balance between federalism and states' rights.

The country also tried to find the proper political, economic, and social balance between federalism and regionalism. Westward migration led to growing conflicts with Native Americans, resulting in the forced removal of the Cherokee people via the Trail of Tears. Political and regional differences further divided the evolving nation.

You should consider the following questions as you review the themes for this chapter:

- How did increased sectional tension lead to threats to American nationalism?
- What led to the rise of the Second Party System?
- What were the push and pull factors that led to Americans' westward migration?
- What were the major consequences of western migration?
- How did the theory of nullification threaten the central nature of the Union?

KEY TERMS

Andrew Jackson 244
Anti-Masonry 259
Aroostook War 263
Bank War 255
***Caroline* Affair** 262
Daniel Webster 251
Democrats 247
Dorr Rebellion 245
hard money 256
Indian Territory 254
John C. Calhoun 249
John Tyler 261
Martin Van Buren 249
Nicholas Biddle 255
nullification 249
Panic of 1837 260
Removal Act 253
Roger B. Taney 256
Seminole War 254
specie circular 261
Spoils System 247
Trail of Tears 254
Webster-Ashburton Treaty 263
Webster-Hayne debate 250
Whigs 257
William Henry Harrison 261

Discussion and Activities

Evaluating Have students read the section "Treaty of Wang Hya." Ask them to create a T-chart listing concessions granted to China and received from China. Ask students to evaluate whether China or the United States, or neither, gained an advantage in the treaty. WOR WXT

Key Terms

Students should be familiar with the key terms and be able to define them in the context of the emergence of a new system of political parties, relations with Native Americans, economic crises, and new styles of political participation. Encourage students to use these terms in performing review exercises and exam practice for this chapter.

Go Online Chapter 9 Content Review

Assessing Student Understanding Use the online assessment to assess student understanding of concepts and topics within the chapter. You can assign the ready-made Chapter 9 Content Review or create your own from available questions. This easy-to-use tool helps you design assessments that meet the needs of different types of learners.

Answers

Multiple Choice

1. B; **2.** C; **3.** A

Short Answer

4A) Possible answer: One point of view was that the War of 1812 and Andrew Jackson represented the changing American political democracy. The idea of the common man having a prominent role in the nation altered political participation.

4B) Possible answer: As the population continued to grow in the United States coupled with the rise of a middle class as a result of the First Industrial Revolution, Americans increasingly pushed for a democratic revolution, hoping to a nation that was more inclusive and that reflected the ideals of the American Revolution ("all men are created equal").

4C) Possible answer: As the franchise of voting began to grow, those who were excluded (e.g., women and African Americans) began to voice their opposition to the exclusive institution. Debates continued about just how inclusive the franchise ought to grow to be.

5A) Possible answer: The Nullification Crisis was an example of sectional tensions that threatened American nationalism. South Carolina objected to a federal tax, which they believed hurt Southern interests. Lawmakers passed a resolution nullifying the tax in the state, but Jackson objected to the proposal of nullification, claiming that the states did not have the authority to nullify federal law.

5B) Possible answer: The Bank War was another example of sectional tensions that threatened American nationalism. The Bank of the United States was up for re-chartering, but Jackson and other westerners did not believe the bank was in the best interest of the entire country. They objected to the ethical and constitutional nature of the bank. They rejected Marshall's decision and believed that the bank was an overreach of national power.

5C) Possible answer: Jackson's refusal to recognize and acknowledge the right of South Carolina to nullify a federal law is one example. Congress passed the Force Bill in 1833, which allowed the national government, specifically the president, to use force to enforce federal law.

AP EXAM PRACTICE

Questions assume cumulative content knowledge from this chapter and the previous chapter.

MULTIPLE CHOICE

Use the chart on page 245 and your knowledge of U.S. history to answer questions 1-3.

1. The first big expansion of voter participation reflected in the chart may be related to
   (A) the conflict over the National Bank.
   (B) the "Corrupt Bargain" between John Quincy Adams and Henry Clay.
   (C) the backlash from Clay's American System.
   (D) the increasing embrace of differing social and economic classes.

2. The nation's expanding democracy, as reflected by the voter participation indicated in the chart, continued to be limited by
   (A) the inability of poor white men to vote due to property qualifications.
   (B) the refusal of the United States to support economic expansion.
   (C) the continuing exclusion of all women and men of color from voting.
   (D) President Jackson's insistence that the role of government is to protect the elites.

3. The increasing embrace of democratization was reflected in
   (A) the Spoils System, which increased access to political appointments.
   (B) the end of Indian Removal in response to the opposition of a majority of Americans.
   (C) the spread of women's suffrage to multiple states in the Northeast.
   (D) the widespread acceptance of the Abolitionist movement throughout the North and portions of the South.

SHORT ANSWER

Use your knowledge of U.S. history to answer questions 4 and 5.

4. Use the image on page 243 to answer A, B, and C.
   (A) Briefly describe ONE historical point of view about the nature of democracy in the image.
   (B) Explain ONE specific historical cause which led to the increase in democratic participation in America from 1800 to 1840.
   (C) Explain ONE specific historical effect that resulted from the increase in democratic participation in the United States from 1800 to 1840.

5. Answer A, B, and C.
   (A) Briefly describe ONE specific historical example of sectional tensions in the early nineteenth century that threatened American nationalism.
   (B) Briefly describe a SECOND specific historical example of sectional tensions in the early nineteenth century that threated American nationalism.
   (C) Briefly explain ONE specific example of federal government action that enforced its powers over that of the states in the early nineteenth century.

LONG ESSAY

Develop a thoughtful and thorough historical argument that addresses the statement. Begin your essay with a thesis statement, and support it with specific historical evidence and examples.

6. Evaluate the extent of similarities between the Democrats and the Whigs in American politics during the era of the Second Party System from 1824 to 1840.

Answers

Long Essay

6. Possible thesis: Both parties were united in their belief that winning party elections was more important than articulating a uniform political philosophy. However, the two parties were much more different than they were alike in a number of ways. The Democrats had a long history within the American political process, and their roots stretched back to the Antifederalists. The Whigs were a reactionary political party that rose primarily in opposition to Jackson and did not last beyond the 1830s. The Democrats' base was primarily the middle and working classes and farmers, mostly from the South and West. The Whigs were made up of a hodgepodge of different individuals from different regions of the country but were primarily concentrated in the Northeast, wealthier planters from the South, and the ambitious and rising commercial class of the West. Democrats believed in limiting the role of the government and had a growing concern about monopolies and privilege. Whigs believed in expanding the power of the federal government, encouraging industrial development, and consolidating the economic system. The Democrats tended to be able to unite around a single political figure for president, whereas the Whigs tended to be divided, as evidenced by the 1836 election.

10 AMERICA'S ECONOMIC REVOLUTION

THE LOWELL MILLS For many years, Lowell, Massachusetts, had been a small farming village known as East Chelmsford. By the 1840s, when Fitzhugh Lane painted *The Middlesex Company Woolen Mills*, the town had become one of the most famous manufacturing centers in America and a magnet for visitors from around the world. Lane's painting shows female workers, who dominated the labor force in Lowell, entering the factory.

CONNECTING CONCEPTS

Chapter 10 begins by examining the demographic shifts that occurred in the United States during the first half of the nineteenth century. The population increased throughout the century through both reproduction and European immigration. The arrival of immigrants from northern and western Europe, especially Germany and Ireland, led to rising nativist sentiments and major changes in the composition of the American workforce.

The factory system slowly began to replace the artisan tradition, despite efforts by newly established national craft unions. While some unions won small though temporary victories, the industrial capitalists maintained their control of political, social, and economic power. Despite a growing disparity between rich and poor, a new middle-class emerged during the period. Although urban growth accelerated, the United States remained primarily a rural country that relied on agriculture for its main economic activity.

Technological innovations also contributed to many of the changes taking place within American society. Railroads and canals made transportation more efficient, which fostered other economic gains and growing social links between the Northeast and Northwest. These links, however, also led to further isolation for the South, both politically and economically.

Pacing Guide

Chapter 10 explores key concepts from Period 4: 1800–1848 of the AP U.S. History Curriculum Framework. The suggested instruction time for Chapter 10 is 3 days.

Key Concepts

4.2.I New transportation systems and technologies dramatically expanded manufacturing and agricultural production.

4.2.II The changes caused by the market revolution had significant effects on U.S. society, workers' lives, and gender and family relations.

4.2.III Economic development shaped settlement and trade patterns, helping to unify the nation while also encouraging the growth of different regions.

Discussion and Activities

Analyzing Visuals Have students examine the painting "The Lowell Mills." Ask them to identify details that show the development of manufacturing since the eighteenth century, and then discuss as a class what the most significant changes were. *(Manufacturing facilities had grown larger as more workers and machines were concentrated in smaller spaces. Many workers were now women. Factories such as the Lowell Mills used steam power, as evidenced by the smoke coming from a factory chimney.)* **SOC** **WXT**

CHAPTER 10
AMERICA'S ECONOMIC REVOLUTION

Discussion and Activities

Making Connections Have students read the section "Reasons for Population Increase." Ask them to create a chart listing reasons for the dramatic population increase. Have students circle those items that may still contribute to population growth today. **SOC** **MIG** **NAT**

As you read, you should:

- Describe how industrialization increased sectional differences, which led to varied expectations on the role of government in the economy.
- Analyze how the growth in advanced technology and industrialization impacted different social and economic classes in the United States.
- Evaluate how improvements in technology tied different parts of the country together and led to further western migration.
- Identify the causes and effects of the growth of the factory system in the United States.
- Analyze the causes and effects of population growth in the United States.

THE CHANGING AMERICAN POPULATION

The American industrial revolution was a result of many factors. Before it could occur, the United States needed a population large enough both to grow its own food and to provide a surplus workforce for an industrial economy. It needed a transportation and communications system capable of sustaining commerce over a large geographic area. It needed the technology to permit manufacturing on a large scale. And it needed systems of business organization capable of managing large industrial enterprises. By 1860, the northern regions of the nation had acquired at least the beginnings of all those things.

THE AMERICAN POPULATION, 1820–1840

Three trends characterized the American population between 1820 and 1840, all of them contributing in various ways to economic growth. The population was increasing rapidly; much of it was moving from the countryside into the industrializing cities of the Northeast and Northwest; and much of it was migrating westward.

The American population had stood at only 4 million in 1790. By 1820, it had reached 10 million; by 1830, nearly 13 million; and by 1840, 17 million. The United States was growing much more rapidly in population than Britain or Europe. One reason for this substantial population growth was improvements in public health. The number and ferocity of epidemics (such as the great cholera plague of 1832)—which had periodically decimated urban and even rural populations in America—slowly declined, as did the nation's mortality rate. The population increase was also a result of a high birth rate. In 1840, white women bore an average of 6.14 children each, a decline from the very high rates of the eighteenth century but still substantial enough to produce rapid population increases, particularly since a larger proportion of children could expect to grow to adulthood than had been the case a generation or two earlier.

REASONS FOR POPULATION INCREASE

Immigration, choked off by wars in Europe and economic crises in America, contributed little to the American population in the first three decades of the nineteenth century but rapidly revived beginning in the 1830s. Of the total 1830 population of nearly 13 million, the foreign-born numbered fewer than 500,000. But the number of immigrants climbed by 60,000 in 1832 and nearly 80,000 in 1837. Reduced transportation costs and increasing economic opportunities helped stimulate the immigration boom, as did deteriorating economic conditions in some areas of Europe. The migrations introduced new groups to the United States. In particular, the number of immigrants arriving from the southern counties of Ireland began to grow, marking the beginning of a tremendous influx of Irish Catholics that would continue through the three decades before the Civil War.

Much of this new European immigration flowed into the rapidly growing cities of the Northeast. But urban growth was a result of substantial internal migration as well. As the agricultural regions of New England and other areas grew less profitable, more and more people picked up stakes and moved—some to more promising agricultural regions in the West, but many to eastern cities. In 1790, one person in thirty had lived in a city (defined as a community of 8,000 or more); in 1820, one in twenty; and in 1840, one in twelve.

The rise of New York City was particularly dramatic. By 1810, it was the largest city in the United States. That was partly a result of its superior natural harbor. It was also a result of the Erie Canal (completed in 1825), which gave the city unrivaled access to the interior, and of liberal state laws that made the city attractive for both foreign and domestic commerce.

Go Online AP Exam Preparation

AP Exam Practice Use the online assessment to help prepare students for the AP Exam. You can assign the ready-made AP-style short-answer questions, document-based questions, and multiple-choice questions assessing concepts, themes, and skills from Period 4 and AP-style long-essay questions organized in sets of 3 questions from various time periods. You can also create your own tests from available questions. This easy-to-use tool helps you design assessments that meet the needs of different types of learners.

POPULATION GROWTH, 1620–1860 From its tiny beginnings in the seventeenth century, the American population grew rapidly and dramatically so that by 1860—with more than 31 million people—the United States was one of the most populous countries in the world.

How did this growing population contribute to the nation's economic transformation?

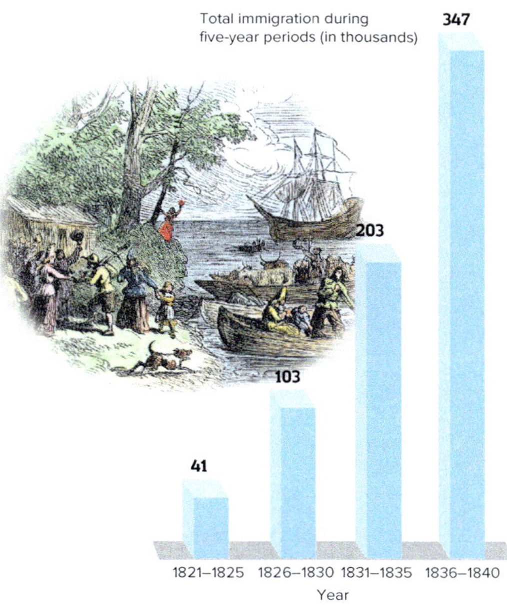

IMMIGRATION, 1821–1840 Among the sources of the nation's growing population in the nineteenth century was rapidly increasing immigration. This graph shows how rapidly immigration to the United States increased in the 1820s and 1830s. The 347,000 immigrants in the second half of the 1830s were almost nine times the number in the first half of the 1820s.

Where did most of these new immigrants settle?

IMMIGRATION AND URBAN GROWTH, 1840–1860

The growth of cities accelerated even more dramatically between 1840 and 1860. The population of New York, for example, rose from 312,000 to 805,000. (New York's population would have numbered 1.2 million in 1860 if Brooklyn, which was then a separate municipality, had been included in the total.) Philadelphia's population grew over the same twenty-year period from 220,000 to 565,000; Boston's from 93,000 to 177,000. By 1860, 26 percent of the population of the free states was living in towns (places of 2,500 people or more) or cities (8,000 people or more), up from 14 percent in 1840. That percentage was even higher for the industrializing states of the Northeast. (In the South, by contrast, the increase of urban residents was only from 6 percent in 1840 to 10 percent in 1860.)

RAPID URBANIZATION

The booming agricultural economy of the western regions of the nation produced significant urban growth as well. Between 1820 and 1840, communities that had once been small western villages or trading posts became major cities: St. Louis, Pittsburgh, Cincinnati, Louisville. All of them benefited from strategic positions on the Mississippi River or one of its major tributaries. All of them became centers of the growing carrying trade that connected the farmers of the Midwest with New Orleans and, through it, the cities of the Northeast. After 1830, however, substantial shipping began from the Mississippi River to the Great Lakes, creating major new urban centers that gradually superseded the river ports. Among them were Buffalo, Detroit, Milwaukee, Cleveland, and–most important–Chicago.

The enlarged urban population was in part a reflection of the growth of the national population as a whole, which rose by more than a third–from 23 million to over 31 million–in the decade of the 1850s alone. By 1860, the American population was larger than Britain's and quickly approaching that of France and Germany. Urban growth was also a result of the increasing flow of people into cities from the farms of the Northeast. Immigration from abroad continued to increase as well. Between 1840 and 1850, more than 1.5 million Europeans moved to America, three times the number of arrivals in the 1830s. Still greater numbers arrived in the 1850s–over 2.5 million. Almost half the residents of New York City in the 1850s were recent immigrants. In St. Louis, Chicago, and Milwaukee, the

SURGING IMMIGRATION

Historical Thinking Skills

Analyzing Points of View Have students read the section "Rapid Urbanization." Ask them to write a letter or journal entry from the point of view of a new arrival to a major city describing how their life has changed. **SOC** **WXT**

Answers

Population Growth, 1620–1860

Population growth created a huge new workforce to support growing industrialization.

Immigration, 1821–1840

Most new immigrants settled in the eastern seaboard cities they arrived in.

Historical Thinking Skills

Claims and Evidence in Sources Have students examine the map "American Population Density, 1820." Ask them to list evidence that explains the patterns of settlement, and then use the lists as the basis for a whole class or small group discussion. *(Population was densest in eastern seaboard ports, then spread out along the Atlantic Coast and moved westward along the rivers.)* **MIG** **WXT**

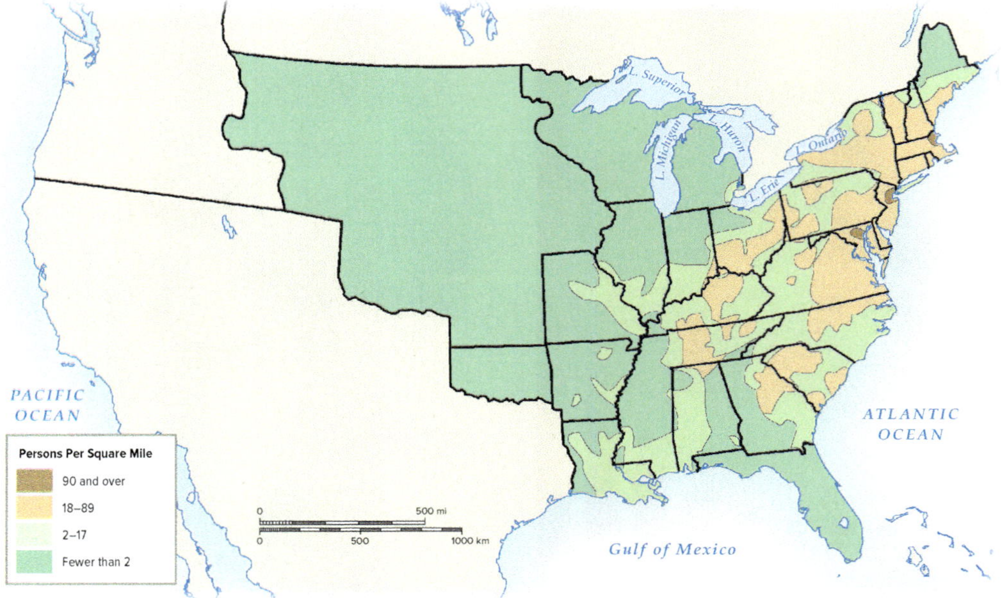

AMERICAN POPULATION DENSITY, 1820 The population of the United States in 1820 was still overwhelmingly rural and agrarian and was still concentrated largely in the original thirteen states, although settlement was growing in the Ohio River valley to the west. Note how few areas of the country were populated really densely: a small area in northeastern Massachusetts, the area around New York City, and the area in Maryland adjoining Baltimore.

What accounts for the density in these areas?

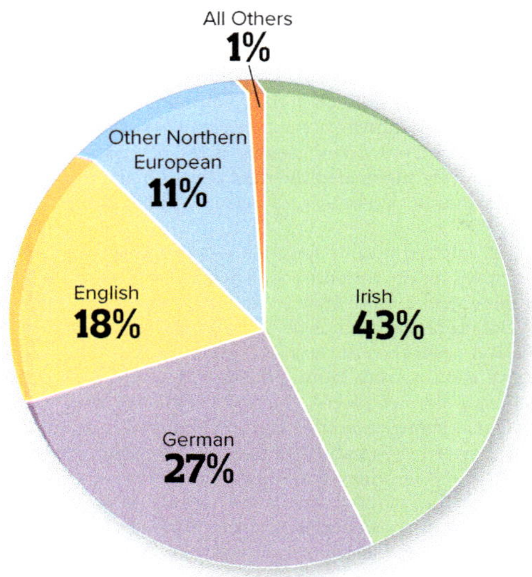

SOURCES OF IMMIGRATION, 1820–1840 The chart illustrates the nationalities of the large numbers of immigrants to the U.S. between 1820 and 1840. Note the very large number of Irish immigrants.

Why were Irish immigrants among the most likely groups to become part of the industrial workforce?

Answers

American Population Density, 1820

The densest settlement occurred around the major port cities on the East Coast.

Sources of Immigration, 1820–1840

They were unlikely to become farmers because they had little to access to land. The alternative was to work in manufacturing.

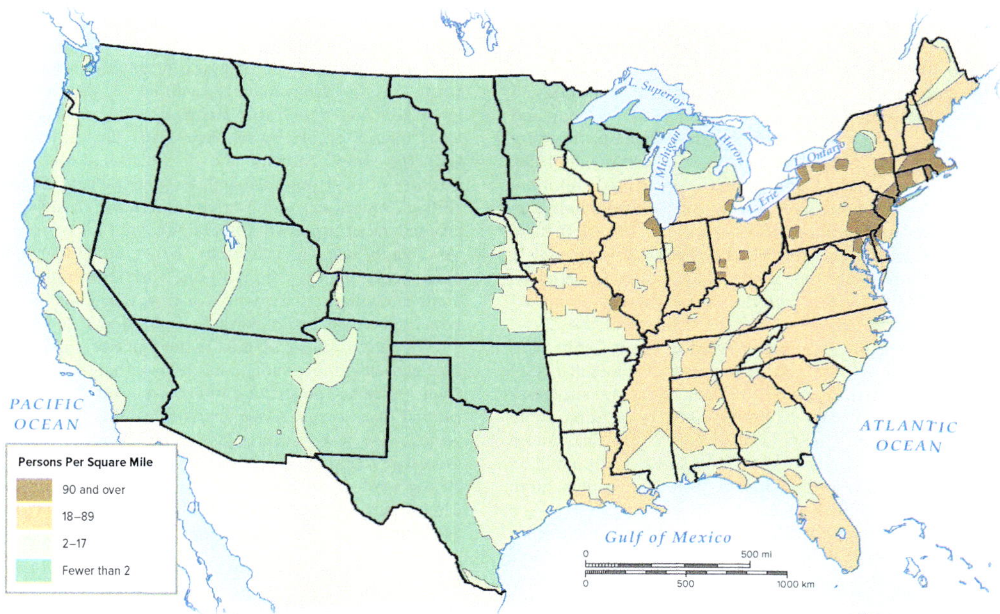

AMERICAN POPULATION DENSITY, 1860 By 1860, the population of the United States had spread much more evenly across the entire country. Communities that had once been small trading posts emerged as major cities. Among them were St. Louis, Pittsburgh, Cincinnati, and Louisville. In the meantime, the Erie Canal had opened up a large and prosperous market area for New York City. Note the larger and more numerous areas of dense population, including many in the Midwest.

What accounts for the growing population density in some areas of the South?

BROADWAY IN 1836 This image of the area of New York City's Broadway in what is now lower Manhattan suggests the way in which New York was becoming an increasingly important center of trade and commerce—and a densely urban place—in the 1830s.

Discussion and Activities

Analyzing Visuals Have students examine the image "Broadway in 1836." Ask them as a class to identify details from the image that indicate growing urbanization. Then ask students to discuss as a class or in small groups how they think the city of New York might change in the future. *(Multi-story buildings indicate growing population density; the gridded street network allows for systematic growth; a considerable amount of business activity and pedestrian traffic is shown.)* **MIG** **SOC** **WXT**

Answers

American Population Density, 1860

Increasing use of slavery in the cotton growing regions (the Black Belt) of the South led to increased population density. **MIG** **WXT** **SOC**

Reasoning Processes

Comparing Have students read the section "German and Irish Immigrants." Ask them to construct a Venn diagram comparing the two groups. **SOC** **WXT** **MIG**

foreign-born outnumbered those of native birth. Few immigrants settled in the South. Only 500,000 lived in the slave states in 1860, and a third of these were concentrated in Missouri, mostly in St. Louis.

The newcomers came from many different countries and regions: England, France, Italy, Scandinavia, Poland, and Holland. But the overwhelming majority came from Ireland and Germany. In 1850, Irish immigrants constituted approximately 45 percent and German immigrants over 20 percent of the foreign-born in America. By 1860, there were more than 1.5 million Irish-born and approximately 1 million German-born people in the United States. In Germany, the economic dislocations of the industrial revolution had caused widespread poverty, and the collapse of the liberal revolution there in 1848 also persuaded many Germans to emigrate. In Ireland, the oppressiveness and unpopularity of English rule drove many people out. But even more important was the greatest disaster in Ireland's history: a catastrophic failure of the potato crop (and other food crops) that caused the devastating "potato famine" of 1845–1849. Nearly a million people died of starvation and disease. Well over a million more emigrated to the United States.

GERMAN AND IRISH IMMIGRANTS

The great majority of Irish immigrants settled in the eastern cities, where they swelled the ranks of unskilled labor. Most German immigrants moved on to the Northwest, where they became farmers or went into business in the western towns. One reason for the difference was wealth: German immigrants generally arrived with at least some money; Irish immigrants had practically none. Another important reason was gender. Most German immigrants were members of family groups or were single men, for whom movement to the agricultural frontier was both possible and attractive. Many Irish immigrants were young, single women, for whom movement west was much less plausible. They were more likely to stay in the eastern cities, where factory and domestic work was available.

THE RISE OF NATIVISM

Some native-born Americans welcomed the new immigration, which provided a large supply of cheap labor that they believed would help keep wage rates low. Land speculators and others with investments in the sparsely populated West hoped that immigrants would move into the region and help expand the population, and thus the market for land and goods, there. Political leaders in western states and territories wanted the immigrants to swell their population, which would increase the political influence of the region. Wisconsin, for example, permitted foreign-born residents to become voters as soon as they had declared their intention of seeking citizenship and had resided in the state for a year; other western states soon followed its lead. In eastern cities, too, urban political organizations eagerly courted immigrant voters, hoping to enhance their own political strength.

Other Americans, however, viewed the growing foreign-born population with alarm. Their fears led to the rise of what is known as "nativism," a defense of native-born people and a hostility to the foreign-born, usually combined with a desire to stop or slow immigration. The emerging nativism took many forms. Some of it was a result of simple racism. Many nativists (conveniently overlooking their own immigrant heritage) argued that the new immigrants were inherently inferior to older-stock Americans. Some viewed them with the same contempt and prejudice—and the same low estimate of their potential abilities—with which they viewed African Americans and Native Americans. Many nativists avoided racist arguments but argued nevertheless that the newcomers were socially unfit to live alongside people of older stock, that they did not bring with them sufficient standards of civilization. Evidence for that, they claimed, was the wretched urban and sometimes rural slums in which they lived. (Many nativists seemed to assume that such wretchedness was something immigrants chose, rather than the result of their extreme poverty.) Others—especially workers—complained that because foreigners were willing to work for low wages, they were stealing jobs from the native labor force. Protestants, observing the success of Irish Catholics in establishing footholds in urban politics, warned that the Catholic Church and the pope were gaining a foothold in American government. Whig politicians were outraged because so many

IMMIGRATION, 1841–1860 Immigration continued to increase in the forty years before the Civil War. This chart illustrates the much higher levels of growth than in the previous forty years. The low point in this era was the first half of the 1840s, in which 430,000 new immigrants entered the United States. That was significantly higher than the largest number of the previous twenty years. In the early 1850s, the number of immigrants grew to nearly 2 million.

What events in Europe contributed to this increase in immigration?

Answers

Immigration, 1841–1860

Much of the immigration was caused by famine in Ireland and political upheaval in central Europe.

CONSIDER THE SOURCE

NATIVISM AND ANTI-IMMIGRATION SENTIMENT

ANTI-IMMIGRATION SENTIMENT AND NATIVISM HAVE LONG BEEN PRESENT IN THE NATION, as indicated by the first two items below: an 1852 broadside announcing publication of The *American Patriot*, a nativist newspaper, and a cartoon from 1850. The broadside issues a dire warning: "Already the enemies of our dearest institutions, like the foreign spies in the Trojan horse of old, are within our gates. They are disgorging themselves upon us, at the rate of Hundreds of Thousands Every Year! They aim at nothing short of conquest and supremacy over us."

Fast-forward to April 2010 when Arizona Senate Bill 1070 was signed into law by Governor Jan Brewer. Provisions of the law include the right of law enforcement agents to ask for a person's immigration documents during routine stops and a mandate that any illegal immigrant convicted of a crime or misdemeanor be turned over to federal immigration agents. Critics claim that the law is a product of nativism and anti-immigration sentiment directed specifically at those of Hispanic origin, which will result in persecution of both legal and undocumented immigrants. See the excerpt on p. 261.

ANTI-IMMIGRATION SENTIMENT—1850/1852

AP Exam Practice

Short Answer Provide students with the following short-answer questions and allow 15 minutes for completion. Students may use their Venn diagrams from the previous page to answer A and B. Ask for volunteers to share their responses and discuss as a class.

Answer A, B, and C.

A) Briefly explain ONE similarity between Irish and German immigrants from 1820 to 1860. *(Both groups were seeking better economic opportunities and political liberty in America.)*

B) Briefly explain ONE difference between Irish and German immigrants from 1820 to 1860. *(German immigrants generally had better financial resources when they arrived. German immigrants were more likely to arrive in family groups, whereas most Irish immigrants were single men.)*

C) Briefly explain how the difference cited in B led to different experiences for Irish and German immigrants. *(Irish immigrants were more likely to stay in the port cities they arrived in due to lack of resources to move farther, and many of them worked in industry. Many German immigrants moved farther west and were more likely to establish farms.)*

Discussion and Activities

Making Connections Have students examine the image "American Patriot." Ask them to discuss as a class what "patriot" meant in the context of the advertisement and how that is similar to or different from what that term means to them today. **SOC** **PCE** **NAT**

Discussion and Activities

Making Connections Have students examine the cartoon "Irish and Germans Steal the Ballot Box." Ask them to discuss in small groups how the concern about election integrity in the mid-nineteenth century was similar to or different from concerns surrounding recent elections. **PCE** **SOC**

"IRISH AND GERMANS STEAL THE BALLOT BOX."

ARIZONA SENATE BILL 1070—2010

Notwithstanding any other law, a law enforcement agency may securely transport an alien who is unlawfully present in the United States and who is in the agency's custody to a federal facility in this state or to any other point of transfer into federal custody that is outside the jurisdiction of the law enforcement agency.

E. A law enforcement officer, without a warrant, may arrest a person if the officer has probable cause to believe that the person has committed any public offense that makes the person removable from the United States.

F. Except as provided in federal law, officials or agencies of this state and counties, cities, towns and other political subdivisions of this state may not be prohibited or in any way be restricted from sending, receiving or maintaining information relating to the immigration status of any individual or exchanging that information with any other federal, state or local governmental entity for the following official purposes:

1. Determining eligibility for any public benefit, service or license provided by any federal, state, local or other political subdivision of this state.
2. Verifying any claim of residence or domicile if determination of residence or domicile is required under the laws of this state or a judicial order issued pursuant to a civil or criminal proceeding in this state.
3. Confirming the identity of any person who is detained.
4. If the person is an alien, determining whether the person is in compliance with the federal registration laws prescribed by Title II, Chapter 7 of the Federal Immigration and Nationality Act.

Source: State of Arizona Senate Bill 1070, 2010.

ANALYZING SOURCES

Questions assume cumulative content knowledge from this chapter and previous chapters.

1. Both the broadside and cartoon from the 1850s and the excerpt of the 2010 Arizona law—particularly section E—demonstrate what commonality in the anti-immigrant attitudes from both time periods?

(A) Anti-immigrant attitudes in both time periods were solely based on economic issues.

(B) Anti-immigrant attitudes in both time periods carried a strong nativist component.

(C) Anti-immigrant attitudes in both time periods revolved around voting rights.

(D) Anti-immigrant attitudes in both time periods stemmed from religious differences.

2. Both the broadside and cartoon from the 1850s and the excerpt from the Arizona law most strongly illustrate which bias in their view of the immigrants they are targeting?

(A) The immigrants are gentle folk, but are paupers.

(B) The immigrants bring new economic opportunities.

(C) The immigrants take away economic opportunities from American citizens.

(D) The immigrants are criminal or deceptive.

Answers

Consider the Source

1. A; **2.** B

of the newcomers voted Democratic. Others complained that the immigrants corrupted politics by selling their votes. Many older-stock Americans of both parties feared that immigrants would bring new, radical ideas into national life.

Out of these tensions and prejudices emerged a number of new secret societies created to combat what nativists had come to call the "alien menace." Most of them originated in the Northeast. Some later spread to the West and even to the South. The first of these, the Native American Association, began agitating against immigration in 1837. In 1845, nativists held a convention in Philadelphia and formed the Native American Party (unaware that the term they used to describe themselves would one day become a common label for American Indians). Many of the nativist groups combined in 1850 to form the Supreme Order of the Star-Spangled Banner. It endorsed a list of demands that included banning Catholics or the foreign-born from holding public office, more-restrictive naturalization laws, and literacy tests for voting. The order adopted a strict code of secrecy, which included the secret password, used in lodges across the country, "I know nothing." Ultimately, members of the movement became known as the "Know-Nothings."

NATIVE AMERICAN PARTY

Gradually, the Know-Nothings turned their attention to party politics, and after the election of 1852 they created a new political organization that they called the American Party. In the East, the new organization scored an immediate and astonishing success in the elections of 1854: the Know-Nothings cast a large vote in Pennsylvania and New York and won control of the state government in Massachusetts.

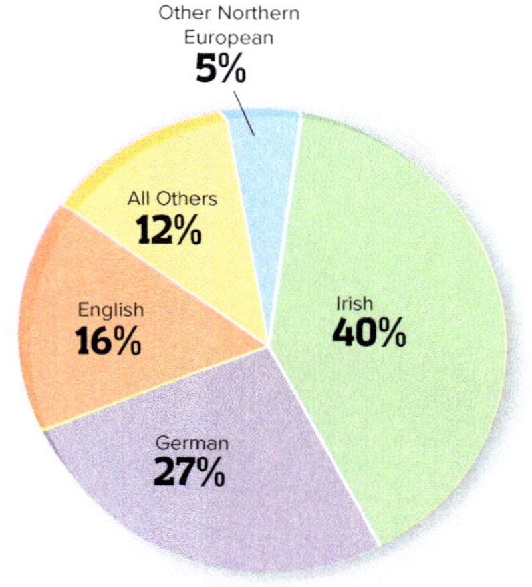

SOURCES OF IMMIGRATION, 1840–1860 Although the extent of immigration increased dramatically in the two decades after 1840, the sources of it remained remarkably stable. Note how closely the distribution of immigrant groups portrayed in this pie chart parallels that in the similar chart for the 1820–1840 period.

What were some of the differences between what German and Irish immigrants did once they arrived in America?

THE LAMENT OF THE IRISH EMIGRANT This poem, written by Helen Selina Blackwood and set to music by William R. Dempster captures the painful time in Ireland during the potato famine from the mid 1840s to the early 1850s. During this period an estimated 1 million people died of starvation and another million emigrated, many to the United States. The protagonist of the poem sings of his grief from having lost his wife and his promise to remember her in the new land.

THE KNOW-NOTHINGS

Elsewhere, the progress of the Know-Nothings was modest. Western members of the party, because of the presence of many German voters in the area, found it expedient not to oppose naturalized Protestants. After 1854, the strength of the Know-Nothings declined.

TRANSPORTATION, COMMUNICATIONS, AND TECHNOLOGY

Just as the industrial revolution needed a growing population, it also required an efficient system of transportation and communications. Such a system was essential in creating regional,

Historical Thinking Skills

Historical Developments and Argumentation After students have read the section "The Rise of Nativism," ask them to create a chart of reasons why many Americans opposed immigration in the mid-nineteenth century. Have students organize their charts around political, economic, and social factors. Ask them to evaluate their lists and then write a thesis statement making a claim about whether political, economic, or social factors were the most important causes of nativism. MIG NAT SOC WXT PCE

Sources of Immigration, 1840–1860

Most Irish immigrants remained in their cities of arrival, while most German immigrants moved farther west.

Historical Thinking Skills

Claims and Evidence in Sources Have students examine the image "Know-Nothing Soap." Ask them to discuss with a partner what evidence they see that shows the advertisement might be supporting a nativist argument. *(Soap cleanses, and the inference is that foreigners and other outsiders, such as the Native Americans pictured, are dirty.)* **MIG** **SOC**

national, and ultimately international markets. Progress in this area required not just significant investment, but also important advances in technological knowledge.

THE CANAL AGE

From 1790 until the 1820s, the so-called turnpike era, Americans had relied largely on roads for internal transportation. But in a country as large as the United States was becoming, roads alone (and the mostly horse-drawn vehicles that used them) were not adequate for the nation's expanding needs. And so, in the 1820s and 1830s, Americans began to turn to other means of transportation as well.

The larger rivers, especially the Mississippi and the Ohio, had been important transportation routes for years, but most of the traffic on them consisted of flat barges–little more than rafts–that floated downstream laden with cargo and were broken up at the end of their journeys because they could not navigate back upstream. To return north, shippers had to send goods by land or by agonizingly slow upstream vessels that sometimes took up to four months to travel the length of the Mississippi.

STEAMBOATS

These rivers became vastly more important by the 1820s, as steamboats grew in number and improved in design. The new riverboats carried the corn and wheat of northwestern farmers and the cotton and tobacco of southwestern planters to New Orleans in a fraction of the time of the old barges. From New Orleans, oceangoing ships

KNOW-NOTHING SOAP This illustrated advertising label for soap manufactured in Boston alludes to the Know Nothing or nativist movement. The Native Americans depicted in the foreground and the teepees and camp in the background symbolize the movement's prejudice against foreigners.

THE ERIE CANAL This lithograph suggests something of the enormous engineering challenges faced by the builders of the Erie Canal. This picture shows a deep cutting at Lockport, New York. The canal was completed in 1825 and connected New York to the Great Lakes via the Hudson River.

Discussion and Activities

Analyzing Visuals Ask students to examine the image "The Erie Canal." Ask them to write a short journal entry from the point of view of a traveler on an Erie Canal boat describing their experience. **GEO** **MIG**

took the cargoes on to eastern ports. Steamboats also developed a significant passenger traffic, and companies built increasingly lavish vessels to compete for this lucrative trade.

But neither the farmers of the West nor the merchants of the East were wholly satisfied with this pattern of trade. Farmers would pay less to transport their goods (and eastern consumers would pay less to consume them) if they could ship them directly eastward to market, rather than by the roundabout river-sea route; and northeastern merchants, too, could sell larger quantities of their manufactured goods if they could transport their merchandise more directly and economically to the West. New highways across the mountains provided a partial solution to the problem. But the costs of hauling goods overland, although lower than before, were still too high for anything except the most compact and valuable merchandise. The thoughts of some merchants and entrepreneurs began, therefore, to turn to an alternative: canals.

A team of four horses could haul one and a half tons of goods eighteen miles a day on the turnpikes. But the same four horses, walking along the "towpaths" next to canals while yoked to barges, could draw a boatload of a hundred tons twenty-four miles a day. By the 1820s, the economic advantages of canals had generated a booming interest in expanding the water routes to the West. Canal building was too expensive for private enterprise, and the job of digging canals fell largely to the states. The ambitious state governments of the Northeast took the lead in constructing them. New York was the first to act. It had the natural advantage of a good land route between the Hudson River and Lake Erie through the only real break in the Appalachian chain. But the engineering tasks were still imposing. The distance was more than 350 miles, several times the length of any of the existing canals in America. The route was interrupted by high ridges and a wilderness of woods. After a long public debate over whether the scheme was practical, canal advocates prevailed when De Witt Clinton, a late but ardent convert to the cause, became governor in 1817. Digging began on July 4, 1817.

Economic Advantages of Canals

The building of the Erie Canal was the greatest construction project the United States had ever undertaken. The canal itself was simple: a ditch forty feet wide and four feet deep, with towpaths along the banks. But hundreds of difficult cuts and fills, some of them enormous, were required to enable the canal to pass through hills and over valleys; stone aqueducts were

The Erie Canal

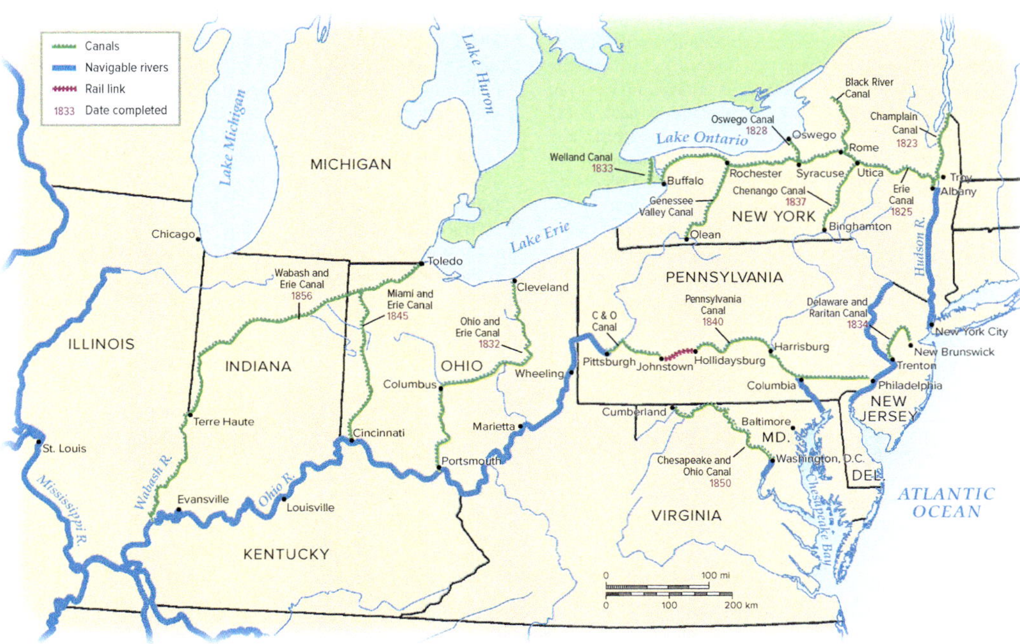

CANALS IN THE NORTHEAST, 1823–1860 The great success of the Erie Canal, which opened in 1825, inspired decades of energetic canal building in many areas of the United States, as this map illustrates. But none of the new canals had anything like the impact of the original Erie Canal, and thus none of New York City's competitors—among them Baltimore, Philadelphia, and Boston—were able to displace it as the nation's leading commercial center.

What form of transportation ultimately displaced the canals?

Reasoning Processes

Comparing and Contrasting After students have read the section "Economic Advantages of Canals," ask them to construct a chart identifying costs and benefits of turnpikes and canals. Use the chart as the basis for a class discussion about which mode of transportation better met the needs of mid-nineteenth century America. **WXT** **GEO** **MIG**

Answers

Canals in the Northeast, 1823–1860

Railroads ultimately displaced canals.

Reasoning Processes

Comparing After students have read the section "The Erie Canal," ask them to create a Venn diagram comparing the Erie Canal to other canal operations. Have students evaluate why the Erie Canal was more successful financially. *(It connected New York to a vast hinterland; New York City had a great natural harbor to receive imports and ship out exports; it was the first to be completed.)* **WXT** **MIG** **GEO**

necessary to carry it across streams; and eighty-eight locks, of heavy masonry with great wooden gates, were needed to permit ascents and descents. The Erie Canal was not just an engineering triumph, but an immediate financial success as well. It opened in October 1825, amid elaborate ceremonies and celebrations, and traffic was soon so heavy that within about seven years tolls had repaid the entire cost of construction. By providing a route to the Great Lakes, the canal gave New York City direct access to Chicago and the growing markets of the West. New York City could now compete with (and increasingly replace) New Orleans as a destination for agricultural goods (particularly wheat) and other products of the West, and as a source for manufactured goods to be sold in the region.

The system of water transportation–and the primacy of New York City–extended farther when the states of Ohio and Indiana, inspired by the success of the Erie Canal, provided water connections between Lake Erie and the Ohio River. These canals helped connect them by an inland water route all the way to New York, although it was still necessary to transfer cargoes several times between canal, lake, and river craft. One of the immediate results of these new transportation routes was increased white settlement in the Northwest, because canals made it easier for migrants to make the westward journey and to ship their goods back to eastern markets.

Rival cities along the Atlantic seaboard took alarm at the prospect of New York's acquiring so vast a hinterland. But they had limited success in catching up. Boston, its way to the Hudson River blocked by the Berkshire Mountains, did not even try to connect itself to the West by canal; its hinterland would remain confined largely to New England. Philadelphia and Baltimore had the still more formidable Allegheny Mountains to contend with. They made a serious effort at canal building, nevertheless, but with discouraging results. Pennsylvania's effort ended in an expensive failure. Maryland constructed part of the Chesapeake and Ohio Canal beginning in 1828, but completed only the stretch between Washington, D.C., and Cumberland, Maryland, and thus never crossed the mountains. In the South, Richmond and Charleston also aspired to build water routes to the Ohio Valley, but never completed them.

In the end, canals did not provide a satisfactory route to the West for any of New York's rivals. Some cities, however, saw their opportunity in a different and newer means of transportation. Even before the canal age had reached its height, the era of the railroad was already beginning.

THE EARLY RAILROADS

Eventually, railroads became the primary transportation system for the United States, and they remained so until the construction of the interstate highway system in the mid-twentieth century.

Railroads emerged from a combination of technological and entrepreneurial innovations. The technological breakthroughs included the invention of tracks, the creation of steam-powered locomotives, and the development of railroad cars that could serve as public carriers of passengers and freight. By 1804, both English and American inventors had experimented with steam engines for propelling land vehicles. In 1820, John Stevens ran a locomotive and cars around a circular track on his New Jersey estate. And in 1825, the Stockton and Darlington Railroad in England opened a short length of track and became the first line to carry general traffic.

TECHNOLOGICAL BASIS OF THE RAILROAD

American entrepreneurs, especially in those northeastern cities that sought better communication with the West, quickly grew interested in the English experiment. The first company to begin actual operations was the Baltimore and Ohio, which opened a thirteen-mile stretch of track in 1830. In New York, the Mohawk and Hudson began running trains along the sixteen miles between Schenectady and Albany in 1831. By 1836, more than a thousand miles of track had been laid in eleven states.

But there was not yet a true railroad system. Even the longest of the lines was comparatively short in the 1830s, and most of them served simply to connect water routes, not to link one railroad to another. Even when two lines did connect, the tracks often differed in gauge (width), so that cars from one line often could not fit onto the tracks of another.

RACING ON THE RAILROAD Peter Cooper, who in later years was best known as a philanthropist and as the founder of the Cooper Union in New York City, was also a successful iron manufacturer. Cooper designed and built the first steam-powered locomotive in America in 1830 for the Baltimore and Ohio Railroad. On August 28 of that year, he raced his locomotive (the Tom Thumb) against a horse-drawn railroad car. This sketch depicts the moment when Cooper's engine overtook the horsecar.

Discussion and Activities

Explaining Significance Have students examine the image "Racing on the Railroad." Ask them to write a short newspaper article from the point of view of a local reporter who witnessed the race. Have students consider what sights and sounds the reporter may have witnessed, and then write a description of the significance of the event. **WXT** **MIG** **NAT**

Schedules were erratic, and wrecks were frequent. But railroads made some important advances in the 1830s and 1840s. The introduction of heavier iron rails improved the roadbeds. Steam locomotives became more flexible and powerful. Redesigned passenger cars became stabler, more comfortable, and larger.

Competition between Railroads and Canals

Railroads and canals were soon competing bitterly. For a time, the Chesapeake and Ohio Canal Company blocked the advance of the Baltimore and Ohio Railroad through the narrow gorge of the upper Potomac, which it controlled; and the state of New York prohibited railroads from hauling freight in competition with the Erie Canal and its branches. But railroads had so many advantages that when they were able to compete freely with other forms of transportation they almost always prevailed.

The Triumph of the Rails

After 1840, railroads gradually supplanted canals and all other modes of transport. In 1840, there were 2,818 miles of railroad tracks in the United States; by 1850, there were 9,021. An unparalleled burst of railroad construction followed in the 1850s, tripling the amount of trackage in just ten years. The most comprehensive and efficient system was in the Northeast, which had twice as much trackage per square mile as the Northwest and four times as much as the South. But the expansion of the rails left no region untouched. Railroads were even reaching west of the Mississippi, which was spanned at several points by great iron bridges. One line ran from Hannibal to St. Joseph on the Missouri River, and another was under construction between St. Louis and Kansas City.

Consolidation

An important change in railroad development was the trend toward the consolidation of short lines into longer lines (known as "trunk lines"). By 1853, four major railroad trunk lines had crossed the Appalachian Mountains to connect the Northeast with the Northwest. The New York Central and the New York and Erie gave New York City access to the Lake Erie ports. The Pennsylvania railroad linked Philadelphia and Pittsburgh, and the Baltimore and Ohio connected Baltimore with the Ohio River at Wheeling. From the terminals of these lines, other railroads into the interior touched the Mississippi River at eight points. Chicago became the rail center of the West, served by fifteen lines and more than a hundred daily trains. The appearance of the great trunk lines tended to divert traffic from the main water routes–the Erie Canal and the Mississippi River. By lessening the dependence of the West on the Mississippi, the railroads helped weaken further the connection between the Northwest and the South.

Capital to finance the railroad boom came from many sources. Private American investors provided part of the necessary funding, and railroad companies borrowed large sums from abroad. But local governments–states, counties, cities, towns–also often contributed capital, because they were eager to have railroads serve them. The railroads obtained substantial additional assistance from the federal government in the form of public land grants. In 1850, Senator Stephen A. Douglas of Illinois and other railroad-minded politicians persuaded Congress to grant federal lands to aid the Illinois Central, which was building from Chicago toward the Gulf of Mexico. Other states and their railroad promoters demanded the same privileges, and by 1860, Congress had allotted over 30 million acres to eleven states to assist railroad construction.

Innovations in Communications and Journalism

Critical to the railroads was an important innovation in communications: the magnetic telegraph. Telegraph lines extended along the tracks, connecting one station with another and aiding the scheduling and routing of trains. But the telegraph also permitted instant communication between distant cities, tying the nation together as never before. At the same time, it helped reinforce the schism between the North and the South. Like railroads, telegraph lines were far more extensive in the North than in the South, and they helped similarly to link the North to the Northwest (and thus to separate the Northwest further from the South).

The Telegraph

The telegraph burst into American life in 1844, when Samuel F. B. Morse, after several years of experimentation, succeeded in transmitting from Baltimore to Washington, D.C., the news of James K. Polk's nomination for the presidency. The relatively low cost of constructing wire systems made the Morse telegraph system seem the ideal answer to the problems of long-distance communication. By 1860, more than 50,000 miles of wire connected most parts of the country; and a year later, the Pacific telegraph, with 3,595 miles of wire, opened between New York City and San Francisco. By then, nearly all the independent lines had joined in one organization, the Western Union Telegraph Company.

The Associated Press

New forms of journalism also drew communities into a common communications system. In 1846, Richard Hoe invented the steam cylinder rotary press, making it possible to print newspapers rapidly and cheaply. The development of the telegraph, together with the introduction of the rotary press, made possible much speedier collection and distribution of news than ever before. In 1846, newspaper publishers from around the nation formed the Associated Press to promote cooperative news gathering by wire; no longer did they have to depend on the cumbersome exchange of newspapers for out-of-town reports.

Major metropolitan newspapers began to appear in the larger cities of the Northeast. In New York alone, there were Horace Greeley's *Tribune*, James Gordon Bennett's *Herald*, Henry J. Raymond's *Times*, and others. All gave serious attention to national and even international events and had substantial circulations beyond the city.

In the long run, journalism would become an important unifying factor in American life. In the 1840s and 1850s, however, the rise of the new journalism helped to feed sectional discord. Most of the major magazines and newspapers were in

Discussion and Activities

Making Generalizations Have students read the section "The Triumph of the Rails." Ask them to discuss in pairs or small groups why state and local governments would work so hard to bring railroads to their jurisdictions. *(Railroads brought trade, jobs, and migrants.)* WXT 

Discussion and Activities

Drawing Conclusions Have students read the section "The Telegraph." Ask them to create a T-chart listing ways in which the railroads and the telegraph promoted unity or division. Have students conclude whether unity or division was more prevalent. NAT WXT

Discussion and Activities

Drawing Conclusions Have students examine the map "Railroad Growth, 1850–1860." Ask them to think about the implications for regionalism of the North and South operating on almost entirely different railroad gauges. Have them share their thoughts with a partner. Ask for volunteers to share with the class. *(Different gauges made it harder for trade across regional boundaries. Goods would have to be unloaded from one train and then loaded onto a new train to continue the journey. Less economic integration led to less social and political integration.)* **WXT** **NAT**

RAILROAD GROWTH, 1850–1860 These two maps illustrate the dramatic growth in the extent of American railroads in the 1850s. Note the particularly extensive increase in mileage in the upper Midwest (known at the time as the Northwest). Note too the relatively smaller increase in railroad mileage in the South. Railroads forged a close economic relationship between the upper Midwest and the Northeast, and weakened the Midwest's relationship to the South.

How did the growth of railroads in the North contribute to the South's growing sense of insecurity within the Union?

280 · CHAPTER 10

Answers

Railroad Growth, 1850–1860

The South was not able to integrate its economy fully with the North due to limited transportation.

THE TELEGRAPH The telegraph provided rapid communication across the country—and eventually across oceans—for the first time. Samuel F. B. Morse was one of a number of nineteenth-century inventors who helped create the telegraph, but Morse was the most commercially successful of the rivals, he nce his greater reputation than others who helped create it.

The Library of Congress [LCUSZC4-5040]

the North, reinforcing the South's sense of subjugation.

FUELING SECTIONAL DISCORD

Southern newspapers tended to have smaller budgets and reported largely local news. Few had any impact outside their immediate communities. The combined circulation of the *Tribune* and the *Herald* exceeded that of all the daily newspapers published in the South put together.

COMMERCE AND INDUSTRY

By the middle years of the nineteenth century, the United States had developed the beginnings of a modern capitalist

IMPACT OF THE MARKET ECONOMY

economy and an advanced industrial capacity. This emerging economy created enormous wealth and changed the face of all areas of the nation. But it did not, of course, affect everyone equally. Some classes and regions benefited from the economic development far more than others.

THE EXPANSION OF BUSINESS, 1820–1840

American business grew rapidly in the 1820s and 1830s, partly because of population growth and the transportation revolution, but also because of the daring, imagination, and ruthlessness of a new generation of entrepreneurs whose enormous wealth allowed for lifestyles of "conspicuous consumption."

One important change came in the retail distribution of goods. In the larger cities, stores specializing in groceries, dry goods, hardware, and other lines appeared, although residents of smaller towns and villages still depended on general stores (stores that did not specialize). In these less populous areas, many people did much of their business by barter.

The organization of business was also changing. Individuals or limited partnerships continued to operate most businesses, and the dominating figures were still the great merchant capitalists, who generally had sole ownership of their enterprises. In some larger businesses, however, the individual merchant capitalist was giving way to the corporation. Corporations

ADVANTAGES OF THE CORPORATION

began to develop particularly rapidly in the 1830s, when some legal obstacles to their formation were removed. Previously, a corporation could obtain a charter only by a special act of the state legislature–a cumbersome process that stifled corporate growth. By the 1830s, however, states were beginning to pass general incorporation laws, under which a group could secure a charter merely by paying a fee.

The new laws also permitted a system of limited liability, which meant that individual stockholders risked losing only the value of their own investment if a corporation should fail, and that they were not liable (as they had been in the past) for the corporation's larger losses. The rise of these new corporations made possible the accumulation of much greater amounts of capital and hence made possible much larger manufacturing and business enterprises.

Investment alone, however, still provided too little capital to meet the demands of the most ambitious businesses. Such

INADEQUATE CREDIT

businesses relied heavily on credit, and their borrowing often created dangerous instability. Credit mechanisms remained very crude in the early nineteenth century. The government alone could issue official currency, but the official currency consisted only of gold and silver (or paper certificates backed literally by gold and silver), and there was thus too little of it to support the growing demand for credit. Under pressure from corporate promoters, many banks issued large quantities of bank notes–unofficial currency that circulated in much the same way that government currency did but was of much less stable value. But the notes had value only to the degree that the bank could sustain public confidence in their value; and some banks issued so many notes that their own reserves could not cover them. As a result, bank failures were frequent, and bank deposits were often insecure. The difficulty of obtaining credit for business investment remained, therefore, an impediment to economic growth.

Discussion and Activities

Understanding Change Have students read the section "Advantages of the Corporation." Ask them to discuss in small groups how the principle of limited liability benefited corporations. *(The principle of limited liability protected individual investors from being held responsible for a corporation's losses or liabilities. In other words, all the investor had at stake was the amount of the original investment. This protection made investment in corporations much more attractive.)* **WXT**

Reasoning Processes

Comparing and Contrasting Have students read the section "Inadequate Credit." Ask them to create a T-chart listing advantages and disadvantages of a specie-backed monetary system. Have them make an argument about which was greater, the advantages or the disadvantages. *(Advantages: stable; predictable; reliable; universally accepted. Disadvantages: difficulty in increasing the money supply when the economy was growing, as this would require additional supplies of gold or silver. Students' arguments will vary.)* **WXT** **PCE**

Discussion and Activities

Causation and Argumentation Have students read the section "The Emergence of the Factory." Ask them to discuss as a class reasons why manufacturing was so heavily concentrated in the Northeast. *(Expansion of existing manufacturing; access to raw materials and labor; easy access to export through ports.)* **WXT** **NAT**

THE EMERGENCE OF THE FACTORY

The most profound economic development in mid-nineteenth-century America was the rise of the factory. Before the War of 1812, most of what manufacturing there was in the United States took place within private households or in small, individually operated workshops. Men and women built or made products by hand, or with simple machines such as hand-operated looms. Gradually, however, improved technology and increasing demand produced a fundamental change. It came first in the New England textile industry. There, entrepreneurs were beginning to make use of new and larger machines driven by water power that allowed them to bring textile operations together under a single roof. This factory system, as it came to be known, spread rapidly in the 1820s and began to make serious inroads into the old home-based system of spinning thread and weaving cloth.

Factories also penetrated the shoe industry, concentrated in eastern Massachusetts. Shoes were still largely handmade, but manufacturers were beginning to employ workers who specialized in one or another of the various tasks involved in production. Some factories began producing large numbers of identical shoes in ungraded sizes and without distinction as to rights and lefts. By the 1830s, factory production was spreading from textiles and shoes into other industries and from New England to other areas of the Northeast.

TRANSFORMATION OF THE SHOE INDUSTRY

Between 1840 and 1860, American industry experienced even more dramatic growth as the factory system spread rapidly. In 1840, the total value of manufactured goods produced in the United States stood at $483 million; ten years later the figure had climbed to over $1 billion; and in 1860 it reached close to $2 billion. For the first time, the value of manufactured goods was approximately equal to that of agricultural products.

Of the approximately 140,000 manufacturing establishments in the country in 1860, 74,000 were located in the Northeast. The Northeast plants were so large that the region produced more than two-thirds of the nation's manufactured goods. Of the 1,311,000 workers in manufacturing in the United States, about 938,000 were employed in the mills and factories of New England and the mid-Atlantic states.

THE INDUSTRIAL NORTHEAST

ADVANCES IN TECHNOLOGY

Even the most highly developed industries were still immature by later standards. American cotton manufacturers, for example, produced goods of coarse grade; fine items continued to come from England. But machine technology advanced more rapidly in the United States in the mid-nineteenth century than in any other country in the world. The American economy was growing so rapidly that the rewards of technological innovation were very great. Change was so rapid, in fact, that some manufacturers built their new machinery out of wood; by the time the wood wore out, they reasoned, improved

CARGO IN CHICAGO This engraving of cargo ships docked in the Chicago River illustrates the rapid growth of the city in the 1850s as it was becoming the great trading center of the central part of the United States.

Historical Thinking Skills

Claims and Evidence in Sources Have students examine the image "Cargo in Chicago." Ask them to list details that demonstrate what type of trade Chicago mainly participated in. *(The image shows grain elevators that stored grain from the Midwest prior to shipment eastward through the Great Lakes and Erie Canal to New York and beyond.)* **WXT**

technology would have made the machine obsolete. By the beginning of the 1830s, American technology had become so advanced–particularly in textile manufacturing–that industrialists in Britain and Europe were beginning to travel to the United States to learn new techniques, instead of the other way around.

The manufacturing of machine tools–the tools used to make machinery parts–was an important contribution to manufacturing. The government supported much of the research and development of machine tools, often in connection with supplying the military. For example, a government armory in Springfield, Massachusetts, developed two important tools–the turret lathe (used for cutting screws and other metal parts) and the universal milling machine (which replaced the hand chiseling of complicated parts and dies)–early in the nineteenth century. The precision grinding machine (which became critical to, among other things, the construction of sewing machines) was designed in the 1850s to help the United States Army produce standardized rifle parts. The federal armories such as those at Springfield and Harpers Ferry, Virginia, became the breeding ground for many technological discoveries, and a magnet for craftsmen and factory owners looking for ideas that could be useful to them. By the 1840s, the machine tools used in the factories of the Northeast were already better than those in most European factories.

Interchangeable Parts

Interchangeable parts, which Eli Whitney and Simeon North had tried to introduce into gun factories, now found their way into many industries. Eventually, interchangeability would revolutionize watch and clock making, the manufacturing of locomotives and steam engines, and the making of many farm tools. It would also help make possible such newer devices as bicycles, sewing machines, typewriters, cash registers, and eventually the automobile.

Industrialization was also profiting from the introduction of new sources of energy. Coal was replacing wood and water power as fuel for many factories. The production of coal, most of it mined around Pittsburgh in western Pennsylvania, leaped from 50,000 tons in 1820 to 14 million tons in 1860. The new power source made it possible to locate mills away from running streams and thus permitted industry to expand still more widely.

Technological Innovations

The great technological advances in American industry owed much to American inventors, as the patent records of the time make clear. In 1830, the number of inventions patented was 544; by 1850, the figure had risen to 993; and in 1860, it stood at 4,778. In 1839, Charles Goodyear, a New England hardware merchant, discovered a method of vulcanizing rubber (treating it to give it greater strength and elasticity); by 1860, his process had found over 500 uses and had helped create a major American rubber industry. In 1846, Elias Howe of Massachusetts constructed a sewing machine; Isaac Singer made improvements on it, and the Howe-Singer machine was soon being used in the manufacture of ready-to-wear clothing.

For all the technological innovations that characterized the early factory system, most American industry remained dependent on the most traditional source of power: water. In the 1820s and 1830s, water power remained the most important source of power for manufacturing. The first important factory towns in New England–Lawrence, Lowell, and others–emerged where they did because of the natural waterfalls that could be channeled to provide power for the mills built along their banks. This sometimes required factories to close for periods in the winter when rivers were frozen. That was one reason factory owners began to look for alternative forms of energy that could be used throughout the year, which led them by the late 1830s to rely more and more on steam and other transportable forms of energy that could be fueled by wood, coal, or (later) petroleum.

MEN AND WOMEN AT WORK

However sophisticated industrial firms became technologically and administratively, manufacturers still relied above all on a supply of labor. In the 1820s and 1830s, factory labor came primarily from the native-born population. After 1840, the growing immigrant population became the most important new source of workers.

Recruiting a Native Workforce

Recruiting a labor force was not an easy task in the early years of the factory system. Ninety percent of Americans in the 1820s still lived and worked on farms, and many urban residents were skilled artisans–independent crafts workers who owned and managed their own shops as small businessmen; they were not likely to flock to factory jobs. The available unskilled workers were not numerous enough to form a reservoir from which the new industries could draw.

Transformation of American Agriculture

The beginnings of an industrial labor supply came instead from the transformation of American agriculture in the nineteenth century. The opening of vast, fertile new farmlands in the Midwest, the improvement of transportation systems, the development of new farm machinery–all combined to increase food production dramatically. New farming methods were also less labor-intensive than the old ones; the number of workers required to produce large crops in the West was much smaller than the number required to produce smaller crops in the less fertile Northeast. No longer did each region have to feed itself entirely from its own farms; it could import food from other regions. As as result, farmers and their families began to abandon some of the relatively unprofitable farming areas of the East. In the Northeast, especially in New England, where poor land had always placed harsh limits on farm productivity, rural people began leaving the land to work in the factories.

Two systems of recruitment emerged to bring this new labor supply to the expanding textile mills. One, common in

Discussion and Activities

Speculating Have students read the section "Interchangeable Parts." Ask them to write a short paragraph explaining why they think federal armories became early centers for innovation. *(Government contracts for weapons provided a steady stream of money for projects and created an incentive for manufacturers to innovate in order to win these contracts.)* **WXT** **PCE**

Discussion and Activities

Explaining Significance After students have read the section "Advances in Technology," ask them to list important technological advances and then rank them by order of importance. Discuss as a class to try to develop a consensus on which advance was most important and why. **WXT**

Reasoning Processes

Change Over Time Have students examine the image "Women at Work." Ask them to create a Venn diagram comparing working women in factories such as the one depicted with working women in the eighteenth century. **WXT**

WOMEN AT WORK This wood engraving from an American newspaper of 1859 shows women working in a skirt factory. Aside from the overcrowding of the factory, none of the usual primitive and unsafe conditions characteristic of many work environments of the time are shown.

the mid-Atlantic states (especially in such major manufacturing centers as New York City and Philadelphia), brought whole families from the farm to the mill. Parents tended looms alongside their children, some of whom were no more than four or five years old. The second system, common in Massachusetts, enlisted young women, mostly farmers' daughters in their late teens and early twenties. It was known as the Lowell or Waltham System, after the factory towns in which it first emerged. Many of these women worked for several years in the factories, saved their wages, and returned home to marry and raise children. Others married men they met in the factories or in town and remained part of the industrial world, but often stopped working in the mills to take up domestic roles instead.

Labor conditions in these early years of the factory system were significantly better than those in English industry, better too than they would ultimately become in much of the United States. The employment of young children created undeniable hardships. But the misery was not as great as in European factories, since working children in America usually remained under the supervision of their parents. In England, by contrast, asylum authorities often hired out orphans to factory owners who showed little concern for their welfare and kept them in something close to slavery.

Even more different from the European labor pattern was the "Lowell System," which relied heavily, indeed almost exclusively, on young unmarried women. In England and other areas of industrial Europe, the conditions of work for women were often horrifyingly bad. A British parliamentary investigation revealed, for example, that women workers in the coal mines endured unimaginably wretched conditions. Some had to crawl on their hands and knees, naked and filthy, through cramped, narrow tunnels, pulling heavy coal carts behind them. It was little wonder that English visitors to America considered the Lowell mills a female paradise by contrast. The Lowell workers lived in clean boardinghouses and dormitories, which the factory owners maintained for them. They were well fed and carefully supervised. Because many New Englanders considered the employment of women to be vaguely immoral, the factory owners placed great emphasis on maintaining a proper environment for their employees, enforcing strict curfews and requiring regular church attendance. Employers quickly dismissed women suspected of immoral conduct. Wages for the Lowell workers were generous by the standards of the time. The women even found time to write and publish a monthly magazine, the *Lowell Offering*.

THE LOWELL SYSTEM

Yet even these relatively well-treated workers often found the transition from farm life to factory work difficult, even traumatic. Uprooted from everything familiar, forced to live among strangers in a regimented environment, many women suffered from severe loneliness and disorientation. Still more had difficulty adjusting to the nature of factory work—the repetition of fixed tasks hour after hour, day after day. That the women had to labor from sunrise to sunset was not in itself a new experience; many of them had worked similarly long days on the farm. But that they now had to spend those days performing tedious, unvarying chores, and that their schedules did not change from week to week or season to season, made the adjustment to factory work especially painful. But however uncomfortable women may have found factory work, they had few other options. They were barred from such manual labor as construction or from work as sailors or on the docks. Most of society considered it unthinkable

WOMEN WORKERS

Discussion and Activities

Analyzing Points on View Have students read the section "The Lowell System." Ask them to write a short journal entry from the point of view of a young woman working at the Lowell Mills describing a typical work day. **WXT**

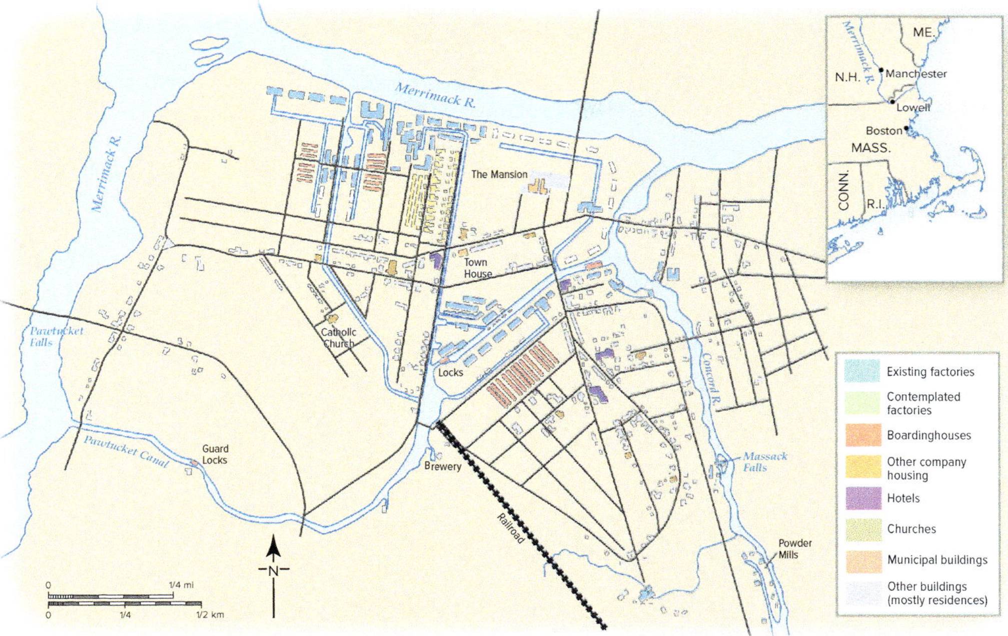

LOWELL, MASSACHUSETTS, 1832 Lowell was one of the leading manufacturing centers of New England in the 1830s, and one of the largest textile centers in America. Lowell relied heavily on women workers. Company owners—in deference to popular uneasiness about women working outside the home—created a paternalistic system of boardinghouses for them, where they could be carefully supervised. This map shows the clusters of boardinghouses adjacent to groups of factories. Note how concentrated the manufacturing center of the town was, and how the transportation system (rail and water) served the factories. Note also the many churches, which women workers were usually required to attend.

What happened to this labor system in the 1840s and 1850s?

for women to travel the country alone, as many men did, in search of opportunities. Work in the mills was in many cases the only alternative to returning to farms that could no longer support them.

The paternalistic factory system of Lowell did not, in any case, survive for long. In the competitive textile market as it developed in the 1830s and 1840s–a market prey to the booms and busts that afflicted the American economy as a whole–manufacturers found it difficult to maintain the high living standards and the attractive working conditions with which they had begun. Wages declined; the hours of work lengthened; the conditions of the boardinghouses deteriorated as the buildings decayed and overcrowding increased.

DECLINE OF THE LOWELL SYSTEM

In 1834, mill workers in Lowell organized a union–the Factory Girls Association–which staged a strike to protest a 25 percent wage cut. Two years later, the association struck again–against a rent increase in the boardinghouses. Both strikes failed, and a recession in 1837 virtually destroyed the organization. Eight years later the Lowell women, led by the militant Sarah Bagley, created the Female Labor Reform Association and began demanding a ten-hour day (some women worked twelve-hour shifts) and for improvements in conditions in the mills. The new association not only made demands of management; it also turned to state government and asked for legislative investigation of conditions in the mills. By then, however, the character of the factory workforce was changing again. The young women who had worked in the mills were gradually moving into other occupations–teaching or domestic service–or they got married. And textile manufacturers were turning to a less contentious labor supply: immigrants.

THE IMMIGRANT WORKFORCE

The rapidly increasing supply of immigrant workers after 1840 was a boon to manufacturers and other entrepreneurs. At last they had access to a source of labor that was both large and inexpensive. These new workers, because of their vast numbers and unfamiliarity with their new country, had less leverage than the women they at times displaced. As a result, they often encountered far worse working conditions. Construction

Discussion and Activities

Historical Evidence and Argumentation Have students read the section "Decline of the Lowell System." Ask them to list and rank the reasons for the decline of the Lowell Mills. Discuss whether these reasons were inevitable or could have been avoided, and if they could have been avoided, how so? WXT 

Answers

Lowell, Massachusetts, 1832

Managers increasingly hired cheaper immigrant laborers to replace more costly American workers.

AP Exam Tip

When responding to document-based questions, students will be asked to analyze sourcing and situations of primary and secondary sources. One way to do that is to place a document in its historical context.

Historical Thinking Skills

Analyzing Sources To practice the exam tip, have students read the source "Handbook to Lowell: Factory Rules." Ask them to discuss what was going on at Lowell by 1848 that may have influenced the rules. *(Recent immigrants had largely replaced local young women in the workforce. These new workers might have been considered less trustworthy, leading to an emphasis on reducing theft and tamping down behaviors that were considered immoral.)* **WXT** **SOC**

CONSIDER THE SOURCE

RULES FOR EMPLOYEES

STRICT RULES GOVERNED THE WORKING LIFE OF THE YOUNG WOMEN who worked in the textile mills in Lowell, Massachusetts, in the first half of the nineteenth century. Equally strict rules regulated their time away from work (what little leisure time they enjoyed) in the company-supervised boardinghouses in which they lived. The excerpts from the *Handbook to Lowell* from 1848 that follow suggest the tight supervision under which the Lowell mill girls worked and lived.

Many companies today publish employee handbooks that provide information about employee responsibilities, including working hours and days, and expectations of employee performance. They may also outline employee benefits, such as compensation, vacation policies, and medical benefits. Some companies issue formal rules of conduct and ethics by which their employees must abide. The example from the Simpson Manufacturing Company, which makes building products, provides an interesting comparison to the Lowell guidelines.

HANDBOOK TO LOWELL—1848

Handbook to Lowell

Factory Rules

REGULATIONS TO BE OBSERVED by all persons employed in the factories of the Hamilton Manufacturing Company. The overseers are to be always in their rooms at the starting of the mill, and not absent unnecessarily during working hours. They are to see that all those employed in their rooms are in their places in due season, and keep a correct account of their time and work. They may grant leave of absence to those employed under them, when they have spare hands to supply their places and not otherwise, except in cases of absolute necessity.

All persons in the employ of the Hamilton Manufacturing Company are to observe the regulations of the room where they are employed. They are not to be absent from their work without the consent of the overseer, except in cases of sickness, and then they are to send him word of the cause of their absence. They are to board in one of the houses of the company and give information at the counting room, where they board, when they begin, or, whenever they change their boarding place; and are to observe the regulations of their boarding-house.

Those intending to leave the employment of the company are to give at least two weeks' notice thereof to their overseer.

All persons entering into the employment of the company are considered as engaged for twelve months, and those who leave sooner, or do not comply with all these regulations, will not be entitled to a regular discharge.

The company will not employ anyone who is habitually absent from public worship on the Sabbath, or known to be guilty of immorality.

A physician will attend once in every month at the counting-room, to vaccinate all who may need it, free of expense.

Anyone who shall take from the mills or the yard, any yarn, cloth or other article belonging to the company will be considered guilty of stealing and be liable to prosecution.

Payment will be made monthly, including board and wages. The accounts will be made up to the last Saturday but one in every month, and paid in the course of the following week.

These regulations are considered part of the contract, with which all persons entering into the employment of the Hamilton Manufacturing Company, engage to comply.

Discussion and Activities

Making Connections Have students read the source "Handbook to Lowell: Factory Rules." Ask them to paraphrase the rules presented and discuss as a class how they compare to current workplace rules with which they are familiar. **WXT**

Boarding House Rules

REGULATIONS FOR THE BOARDING-HOUSES of the Hamilton Manufacturing Company. The tenants of the boarding-houses are not to board, or permit any part of their houses to be occupied by any person, except those in the employ of the company, without special permission.

They will be considered answerable for any improper conduct in their houses, and are not to permit their boarders to have company at unseasonable hours.

The doors must be closed at ten o'clock in the evening, and no person admitted after that time, without some reasonable excuse.

The keepers of the boarding-houses must give an account of the number, names and employment of their boarders, when required, and report the names of such as are guilty of any improper conduct, or are not in the regular habit of attending public worship.

The buildings, and yards about them, must be kept clean and in good order; and if they are injured, otherwise than from ordinary use, all necessary repairs will be made, and charged to the occupant.

The sidewalks, also, in front of the houses, must be kept clean, and free from snow, which must be removed from them immediately after it has ceased falling; if neglected, it will be removed by the company at the expense of the tenant.

It is desirable that the families of those who live in the houses, as well as the boarders, who have not had the kine pox, should be vaccinated, which will be done at the expense of the company, for such as wish it.

Some suitable chamber in the house must be reserved, and appropriated for the use of the sick, so that others may not be under the necessity of sleeping in the same room.

JOHN AVERY, Agent.

Source: The Handbook to Lowell (1848)

SIMPSON MANUFACTURING CODE OF CONDUCT—2011

Simpson Manufacturing: Code of Business Conduct and Ethics

November 1, 2011

At Simpson Manufacturing Co., Inc. and its subsidiaries (Company), we expect that all of our employees, officers and directors will treat each other, our customers, and our suppliers with goodwill, trust, and respect. As a Company, we value honesty, high ethical standards and compliance with laws, rules and regulations

The following provides guidance on the application of these principles:

Compliance with laws, rules and regulations

. . .

Accounting Requirements: Follow the accepted rules and controls required by the U.S. Securities and Exchange Commission (SEC), Financial Accounting Standards Board (FASB), and New York Stock Exchange (NYSE). For additional information on these rules and controls, contact the Company's Chief Financial Officer.

Equal Employment Opportunity (EEO) and Discrimination Laws: It continues to be the practice of the Company to employ positive business and personnel practices designed to ensure the full realization of equal employment opportunity. Further, we expect all employees to accomplish their work in a businesslike manner with a concern for the well-being of their co-workers. Harassment of any employee by any other employee is prohibited, regardless of their working relationship. Any employee who experiences harassment should bring it to the attention of his/her supervisor or branch manager. If the employee is not satisfied that the matter has been appropriately addressed, the employee should feel free to contact the President of Simpson Strong-Tie or the President of Simpson Manufacturing.

Securities Laws: All employees of the Company are prohibited from transacting in the Company's securities, for themselves, family members, friends or any other person, while in the possession of material, nonpublic (inside) information concerning the Company. In addition employees must not give inside information to anyone. Inside information is information that the Company has not

AP Exam Practice

Short Answer Provide students with the following short-answer questions and allow 15 minutes for completion. Ask for volunteers to share their responses and discuss as a class.

Answer A, B, and C.

A) Briefly explain ONE important reason for the development of the Lowell Mills. *(Investors saw an opportunity for profit; technological advances made larger-scale industrialization possible.)*

B) Briefly explain ONE important effect of the development of the Lowell Mills. *(See possible answers under question C.)*

C) Briefly explain a SECOND important effect of the development of the Lowell Mills. *(Manufacturing output increased, making more goods available at lower prices; workers were increasingly forced into routine and unskilled jobs; workers often faced long hours, low wages, and unsafe working conditions.)*

Discussion and Activities

Analyzing Points of View Have students read the "Boarding House Rules" from Lowell, 1848. Ask them to write a short journal entry or letter home from the point of view of one of the residents. **WXT** **SOC**

AP Exam Tip

When responding to document-based questions, students will be asked to analyze sourcing and situation of primary and secondary sources. One way to do that is to explain a document's purpose.

Historical Thinking Skills

Sourcing and Situation To practice the exam tip, ask student to write a short paragraph explaining the purpose of the Simpson Manufacturing Code of Business Conduct and Ethics of 2011.

made public about any Company activities, such as earnings estimates, the commencement or outcome of litigation, mergers and acquisitions, or any other information that could affect the Company's fortunes and therefore the price of the stock. For more detailed information, please refer to Insider Trading-Policies and Procedures, available from the Company's Chief Financial Officer.

Antitrust Laws: We do not discuss our prices with our competitors. We do not enter into illegal agreements or engage in illegal practices in restraint of trade. For additional information on antitrust laws, contact the President of Simpson Strong-Tie or the President of Simpson Manufacturing.

Anti Corruption Laws: Our officers, directors, employees and agents are expected to comply with all U.S. and foreign laws while conducting business outside the United States, including, but not limited to, the United States Foreign Corrupt Practices Act ("FCPA").

Health and safety
The Company seeks to provide a clean, safe and healthy place to work. All employees are expected to observe all safety rules and practices and to follow instructions concerning safe work practices.

Record keeping and reporting of information
All records and reported information must be accurate, complete, honest and timely.

Conflicts of interest
Every employee, officer and director, is expected to make decisions in the best interest of the Company and not for personal gain. A conflict of interest can arise when an employee, officer or director takes action or has a personal interest that may make it difficult to perform his or her work for the Company objectively and effectively. This may include outside business interests, outside employment, outside investments and business relationships with friends or relatives that could cause a conflict of interest. Employees, officers and directors should report potential conflicts of interest and are prohibited from taking for themselves personally opportunities that are discovered or may be available through the use of the Company's property, information or position. Employees are prohibited from accepting meals, entertainment, travel, gratuities, merchandise or promotional material that could influence objectivity in making business decisions. Employees are generally prohibited from accepting any such item worth more than $50. Certain business events may require an employee's participation in excess of this amount. These must be approved by their supervisor.

Fair dealing
Employees, officers and directors should endeavor to deal fairly with the Company's customers and suppliers and each other. No one should take unfair advantage of anyone else through manipulation or misrepresentation of material facts.

Quality
Products that meet our quality standards are essential to our success. Everyone in the Company is responsible for product quality and must be committed to ensuring the effectiveness of the Quality Management System. For more information on the Company's Quality Principles, please see your supervisor.

Protection and proper use of Company assets
All employees, officers and directors should protect the Company's assets and ensure their efficient use.

Confidentiality
Employees, officers and directors should maintain the confidentiality of information entrusted to them by the Company, its customers, and its vendors and suppliers, except when disclosure is authorized or legally mandated. Confidential information includes all non-public information.

Encouraging the reporting of any illegal or unethical behavior
Many areas of the law, such as securities and antitrust, are very complicated. The Company encourages employees to talk to supervisors, managers or other appropriate personnel when in doubt about the best course of action in a particular situation. Additionally, employees should report violations of laws, rules, regulations or the Code of Business Conduct and Ethics to the President of the Company or the subsidiary or an ombudsman appointed for this purpose. There will be no retaliation against anyone who presents this type of information in good faith.

Waiver of the Code of Business Conduct and Ethics
There will be no waivers to the Code of Business Conduct and Ethics.

Reasoning Processes

Comparing and Contrasting After students have read the Simpson Manufacturing Code of Business Conduct and Ethics, ask them to create a Venn diagram comparing those rules with the rules of the Lowell Mills. Have students write a short summary of how the codes are similar and different. **WXT** **SOC**

ANALYZING SOURCES

Questions assume cumulative content knowledge from this chapter and previous chapters.

1. The difference in the nature of the content from the Lowell handbook from that of the Simpson guidelines best indicates which of the following regarding attitudes toward the workers in the textile mills of Lowell?
   (A) The textile workers were given greater personal freedom during the workday.
   (B) The textile workers were treated in a much more paternalistic manner.
   (C) The textile workers were looked upon with suspicion and distrust.
   (D) Professionalism was not expected of the textile workers.

2. What do the differences in the issues disccused in each of the documents best suggest about big business in the 19th century versus that in the 21st century?
   (A) Businesses in the 19th century contended with fewer government regulations.
   (B) Businesses in the 19th century had greater expectations for worker conduct.
   (C) Businesses in the 19th century faced more government regulations.
   (D) Issues surrounding ethics were of greater concern to businesses in the 19th century.

3. Which of the following best describes a commonality between the two documents?
   (A) The purpose of both documents is to recruit employees.
   (B) The purpose of both documents is, ultimately, to protect the company.
   (C) The purpose of both documents is to ensure the well-being of its employees.
   (D) The purpose of both documents is to, ultimately, ensure employee morality.

4. Based on the documents, which statement best describes the differences in employment between the 19th and 21st centuries?
   (A) Workers had more rights and privileges in the 19th century.
   (B) Workers have more rights and privileges in the 21st century.
   (C) Workers had fewer rights in the 19th century but were provided greater benefits.
   (D) Workers in the 21st century have fewer rights but are provided greater benefits.

Discussion and Activities

Making Connections After students have read the sections listing the rules for employers and employees under the Simpson Manufacturing Code of Business Conduct and Ethics, ask them to discuss as a class what else may have changed in the relationship between employers and employees in addition to the rules presented in the feature.

Answers

Consider the Source

1. B; **2.** A; **3.** B; **4.** B

Reasoning Processes

Continuity and Change After students have read the section "The Immigrant Workforce," ask them to discuss in small groups how workplaces had changed from previous eras by the 1840s. Have them address whether these changes generally benefted workers or management. **WXT** **SOC**

FOUR WOMEN WEAVERS This tintype shows four young women employed in the textile factories of Lowell, Massachusetts. Neatly dressed in matching uniforms, they conveyed the image the factory managers wanted the public to absorb: that women could work in the mills and still be protected from the rough-and-tumble world of industrialization.

gangs, made up increasingly of Irish immigrants, performed the heavy, unskilled work on turnpikes, canals, and railroads under often intolerable conditions. Because most of these workers had no marketable skills and because of native prejudice against them, they received wages so low (and so intermittently, since the work was seasonal and uncertain) that they generally did not earn enough to support their families in even minimal comfort. Many of them lived in flimsy shanties, in grim conditions that endangered the health of their families (and reinforced native prejudices toward the "shanty Irish").

ECONOMIC ADVANTAGES OF IMMIGRANT LABOR

The arrival of Irish workers accelerated the deterioration of working conditions in New England. There was far less social pressure on owners to provide a decent environment for Irish workers than there had been for native women. Employers began paying piece rates (wages tied to how much a worker produced) rather than a daily wage and employed other devices to speed up production and use the labor force more profitably and efficiently. By the mid-1840s, the town of Lowell—once a model for foreign visitors of enlightened industrial development—had become a squalid slum. Similarly miserable working-class neighborhoods were emerging in other northeastern cities.

HARSH WORK CONDITIONS

Conditions were still not as bad as in most factory towns in England and Europe, but in almost all industrial areas, factories themselves were becoming large, noisy, unsanitary, and often dangerous places to work. The average workday was extending to twelve, often fourteen hours. Wages were declining, so that even skilled male workers could hope to earn only from $4 to $10 per week, while unskilled laborers were likely to earn only about $1 to $6 per week. Women and children, whatever their skills, also earned less than most men.

THE FACTORY SYSTEM AND THE ARTISAN TRADITION

It was not only the mill workers who suffered from the transition to the modern factory system. It was also the skilled artisans whose trades the factories were displacing. The artisan tradition was as much a part of the older, republican vision of America as the tradition of sturdy, independent, yeoman farmers. Independent craftsmen considered themselves embodiments of the American ideal; they clung to a vision of economic life that was in some ways very different from what the new capitalist class was promoting. Skilled artisans valued their independence; they also valued the stability and relative equality within their economic world.

DE-SKILLING

The factory system threatened that world with obsolescence. Some artisans made successful transitions into small-scale industry. But others found themselves unable to compete with the new factory-made goods that sold for a fraction of the artisans' prices. In the face of this competition from industrial capitalists, craftsmen began early in the nineteenth century to form organizations—workingmen's political parties and the first American labor unions—to protect their endangered positions and to resist the new economic order. As early as the 1790s, printers and cordwainers (makers of high-quality boots and shoes) took the lead. Members of other skilled trades—carpenters, joiners, masons, plasterers, hatters, and shipbuilders—felt similarly vulnerable.

NATIONAL TRADE UNIONS

In such cities as Philadelphia, Baltimore, Boston, and New York, the skilled workers of each craft formed societies for mutual aid. During the 1820s and 1830s, the craft societies began to combine on a citywide basis and set up central organizations known as trade unions. With the widening of markets, the

Discussion and Activities

Analyzing Points of View Have students read the section "De-skilling." Ask them to write a journal entry or letter from the point of view of a skilled laborer who has just been displaced by a factory. **WXT** **SOC**

economies of cities were interconnected, so workers soon realized there were advantages in joining forces. They established national unions or federations of local ones. In 1834, delegates from six cities founded the National Trades' Union; and in 1836, the printers and the cordwainers set up their own national craft unions.

This early craft union movement fared poorly. Labor leaders struggled against the handicap of hostile laws and hostile courts. The common law, as interpreted by the courts in the industrial states, viewed a combination among workers as an illegal conspiracy. The Panic of 1837, a dramatic financial collapse that produced a severe recession, weakened the movement further.

Fighting for Control

Workers at all levels of the emerging industrial economy attempted to improve their lots. They tried, with little success, to persuade state legislatures to pass laws setting a maximum workday. Two states–New Hampshire in 1847 and Pennsylvania in 1848–passed ten-hour laws, limiting the workday unless the workers agreed to an "express contract" calling for more time on the job. Such measures were virtually without impact, however, because employers could simply require prospective employees to sign the "express contract" as a condition of hiring. Three states–Massachusetts, New Hampshire, and Pennsylvania–passed laws regulating child labor. But again, the results were minimal. The laws simply limited the workday to ten hours for children unless their parents agreed to something longer; employers had little difficulty persuading parents to consent to additional hours.

Commonwealth v. Hunt

Perhaps the greatest legal victory of industrial workers came in Massachusetts in 1842, when the supreme court of the state, in *Commonwealth v. Hunt*, declared that unions were lawful organizations and that the strike was a lawful weapon. Other state courts gradually accepted the principles of the Massachusetts decision. On the whole, however, the union movement of the 1840s and 1850s remained generally ineffective. Some workers were reluctant to think of themselves as members of a permanent laboring force and resisted joining unions. But even those unions that did manage to recruit significant numbers of industrial workers were usually not large enough or strong enough to stage strikes, and even less frequently strong enough to win them.

Artisans and skilled workers, despite their setbacks in the 1830s, had somewhat greater success than did factory workers. But their unions often had more in common with preindustrial guilds than with modern labor organizations. In most cases, their primary purpose was to protect the favored position of their members in the labor force by restricting admission to the skilled trades. The organizing effort that had floundered in the 1830s revived impressively in the 1850s. Among the new organizations skilled workers created were the National Typographical Union, founded in 1852, the Stone Cutters in 1853, the Hat Finishers in 1854, and the Molders and the Machinists, both in 1859.

Female Protective Unions

Virtually all the early craft unions excluded women, even though female workers were numerous in almost every industry and craft. As a result, women began establishing their own protective unions by the 1850s, often with the support of middle-class female reformers. Like the male craft unions, the female protective unions had little power in dealing with employers. They did, however, serve an important role as mutual-aid societies for women workers.

America's Divided Working Class

Despite these persistent efforts at organization and protest, the American working class in the 1840s and 1850s was notable for its relatively modest power. In England, workers were becoming a powerful, united, and often violent economic and political force. They were creating widespread social turmoil and helping to transform the nation's political structure. In America, nothing of the sort happened. Many factors combined to inhibit the growth of effective labor resistance. Among the most important was the flood of immigrant laborers into the country. The newcomers were usually willing to work for lower wages than native workers. Because they were so numerous, manufacturers had little difficulty replacing disgruntled or striking workers with eager immigrants. Ethnic divisions and tensions–both between natives and immigrants and among the various immigrant groups themselves–often led workers to channel their resentments into internal bickering rather than into their shared grievances against employers. There was, too, the sheer strength of the industrial capitalists, who had not only economic but also political and social power and could usually triumph over even the most militant challenges.

"Free Labor"

Despite the many obstacles and challenges that faced northern workers in the first half of the nineteenth century, nothing was more important than the idea of personal freedom. Most workers had hard lives, but they were proud of their personal freedoms and considered themselves what some people called the "sovereign individual"–people who could, at least in theory, make choices and change their lives.

Modern notions of freedom are much more robust than those of the early nineteenth century, when only a few men (and no women) were able to vote; when workers were sometimes bound to their employers for years; when husbands subjugated their wives and when, of course, millions of African Americans were living with almost no freedom. But even in the early years of American history, the belief in the freedom of the individual was strong. In the North in particular, personal liberty was growing exponentially for more and more Americans. By the mid-nineteenth century, most white Americans identified themselves as free individuals, no matter what their occupations or means.

Discussion and Activities

Analyzing Issues After students have read the section "National Trade Unions," ask them to create a T-chart listing advantages and disadvantages for workers joining a union. Have them write a short statement making a recommendation to a mid-nineteenth century worker on whether or not to join a union. **WXT**

Discussion and Activities

Historical Reasoning and Argumentation Have students read the section "Fighting for Control." Ask them to create a poster advocating for membership in a union. Ask for volunteers to share their posters, and discuss as a class what the most powerful inducements for joining and for not joining unions would have been. **WXT** **SOC**

Discussion and Activities

Making Connections After students have read the section "'Free Labor,'" ask them to discuss in small groups what freedom meant to mid-nineteenth century workers compared to what it means for workers today. **WXT** **SOC** **NAT**

Some of the great philosophers of nineteenth-century America argued that the "independency of the individual" required free people to escape from the market economy and find freedom in solitude and the wonders of nature–as Henry David Thoreau tried to do in his famous retreat to live alone in a cabin on Walden Pond in Concord, Massachusetts. But for most Americans, the opportunities for solitude and communion with nature were slim. For most northern workers, freedom meant the absence of slavery. It meant that they could leave jobs they did not want, move to new areas of the country, and seek opportunities to change their lives. Their material circumstances were sometimes far worse than those of many enslaved people in the South. Still, they believed that their lives were better than those who lacked freedom. And when the great debate over slavery began in the 1840s and 1850s, northern laborers–however bad their own lots–abhorred slavery, both because it was the antithesis of freedom and because they feared that slavery threatened the jobs of free laborers.

Not only were enslaved people denied the freedom that most Americans valued. The more than 200,000 free African American men and women living in the North (and a few in the South) remained ineligible to vote and were not considered legal citizens. Many of the free African Americans in the North were people who had been skilled crafts workers as enslaved people and who bought or were given their freedom. But their lots were in many ways worse than when they were working in the South. In the Northern cities to which many free African Americans moved, there were many white craftsmen already who saw black workers as rivals. Most free African Americans worked in menial jobs and as domestic servants.

PATTERNS OF INDUSTRIAL SOCIETY

The industrial revolution made the United States–and particularly its more economically developed regions–dramatically wealthier almost every year. It was also making society more unequal, and it transformed social relationships and everyday life at almost every level–from the workplace to the family.

THE RICH AND THE POOR

The commercial and industrial growth of the United States greatly elevated the average income of the American people. But this increasing wealth was being distributed highly unequally. Substantial groups of the population shared hardly at all in the economic growth: enslaved people, Native Americans, landless farmers, and many of the unskilled workers on the fringes of the manufacturing system. But even among the rest of the population, disparities of income were marked. Wealth had always been unequally distributed in the United States, to be sure. Even in the era of the Revolution, according to some estimates, 45 percent of the wealth was concentrated in the hands of about 10 percent of the population. But by the mid-nineteenth century, that concentration had become far more pronounced. In Boston in 1845, for example, 4 percent of the citizens are estimated to have owned more than 65 percent of the wealth; in Philadelphia in 1860, 1 percent of the population possessed more than half the wealth. Among the American people overall in 1860, according to scholarly estimates, 5 percent of the families possessed more than 50 percent of the wealth.

INCREASING INEQUALITY IN WEALTH

There had been wealthy classes in America almost from the beginning of European settlement. But the extent and character of wealth were changing in response to the commercial revolution of the mid-nineteenth century. Merchants and industrialists were accumulating enormous fortunes; and because there was now a significant number of rich people living in cities, a distinctive culture of wealth began to emerge. In large cities, people of great wealth gathered together in neighborhoods of great opulence. They founded clubs and developed elaborate social rituals. They looked increasingly for ways to display their wealth–in the great mansions they built, the showy carriages in which they rode, the lavish household goods they accumulated, the clothes they wore, the elegant social establishments they patronized. New York City, which had more wealthy families than anywhere else, developed a particularly elaborate high society.

POVERTY IN NEW YORK CITY This wood engraving from 1869 shows "squatters" and their dilapidated shanties. This group of extremely poor people lived on hilly land near New York City's new Central Park, an urban retreat designed for the city's wealthier classes. Compare the circumstances of these homeless people with those of the aristocrats shown in the Central Park image.

Discussion and Activities

Analyzing Visuals Have students examine the image "Poverty in New York City." Ask them to identify details from the image that indicate poverty. Have them compare the image to the previous image of Broadway in 1836 and create a Venn diagram comparing the images. **WXT** **SOC**

CENTRAL PARK To affluent New Yorkers, the construction of the city's great Central Park was important because it provided them with an elegant setting for their daily carriage rides—an activity ostensibly designed to expose the riders to fresh air but that was really an occasion for them to display their finery to their neighbors.

New Yorkers in 1857 were trying to make the city as important as London and Paris. To achieve this goal, they decided to build a great park that would impart elegance to the city and draw New Yorkers to the upper part of the city where new real estate was available. Two great landscape architects–Frederick Law Olmsted and Calvert Vaux–developed a vast part of Manhattan, displacing people from their houses in the process. The result was one of the largest parks in America. Olmsted called Central Park a place of "great importance as the first real park in this country." Designed with hills, lakes, paths, bridges, and elegant buildings, it began as a place for wealthy New Yorkers, but very soon became important to almost everyone in the city.

CENTRAL PARK

There was also a significant population of genuinely destitute people emerging in the growing urban centers of the nation. These were people who were not merely poor, in the sense of having to struggle to sustain themselves–most Americans were poor in that sense. They were almost entirely without resources, often homeless, dependent on charity or crime or both for survival.

THE URBAN POOR

Some of these "paupers," as contemporaries called them, were recent immigrants who had failed to find work or to adjust to life in the New World. Some were widows and orphans, stripped of the family structures that allowed most working-class Americans to survive. Some were people suffering from alcoholism or mental illness, unable to work. Others were victims of native prejudice–barred from all but the most menial employment because of race or ethnicity. Irish immigrants were particular victims of such prejudice.

Among the worst off were free African Americans. African American communities in antebellum northern cities were small by later standards, but most major urban areas had significant black populations. Some of these African Americans were descendants of families that had lived in the North for generations. Others were former enslaved people who had escaped from the South or been released by slaveholders or had bought their freedom; some former enslaved people, once free, then worked to buy the freedom of relatives left behind. In material terms, at least, life was not always much better for them in the North than it had been in slavery. Most had access only to very menial jobs, which usually paid too little to allow workers to support their families or educate their children; in bad times, many had access to no jobs at all. In most parts of the North, African Americans could not vote, could not attend public schools, indeed could not use any of the public

AFRICAN AMERICAN POVERTY

Discussion and Activities

Analyzing Issues Have students examine the image "Central Park." Ask them to think about where the people who used to live in the area that became Central Park ended up. Discuss with the class how the creation of this park represents class division. *(Those displaced to make room for the park may have ended up in shanty towns like the one shown on the previous page. There is a stark contrast between the poor who were displaced to make room for the park and the wealthy who used it as a venue to display their wealth. The neighborhoods surrounding the park also became some of the most valuable land in New York.)* **SOC**

Historical Thinking Skills

Argumentation After students have read the section "The Urban Poor," ask them to make a list of different groups of urban poor. Have them rank the list in order of sympathy poor people likely would have received from the rest of society and explain their rankings. *(Widows and orphans would have likely been viewed most sympathetically, since their poverty would not have been seen as their own fault. Recent immigrants and those with mental illness or addictions would have been viewed less sympathetically, as many in society would have viewed their situations as their own fault.)* **SOC** **WXT** **NAT**

Reasoning Processes

Comparing Have students read the section "Social Mobility." Ask them to create a T-chart comparing the importance of social mobility and geographic mobility in terms of reducing worker discontent. Have students write a thesis statement making a claim about which was the greater cause of reducing worker discontent. **WXT** **SOC** **MIG**

services available to white residents. Still, most African Americans preferred life in the North, however arduous, to life in the South because it permitted them at least some level of freedom.

SOCIAL MOBILITY

One might expect the contrasts between conspicuous wealth and conspicuous poverty in antebellum America to have encouraged more class conflict than actually occurred. But a number of factors operated to limit resentments. For one thing, however much the relative economic position of American workers may have been declining, the absolute living standard of most laborers was improving. Life, in material terms at least, was usually better for factory workers than it had been on the farms or in the European societies from which they had migrated. They ate better, they were often better clothed and housed, and they had greater access to consumer goods.

There was also a significant amount of mobility within the working class, which helped to limit discontent. Opportunities for social mobility, for working one's way up the economic ladder, were relatively modest. A few workers did manage to move from poverty to riches by dint of work, ingenuity, and luck—a very small number, but enough to support the dreams of those who watched them. And a much larger number of workers managed to move at least one notch up the ladder—for example, becoming in the course of a lifetime a skilled, rather than an unskilled, laborer. Such people could envision their children and grandchildren moving up even further.

SOCIAL MOBILITY

More common than social mobility was geographic mobility, which was even more extensive in the United States than in Europe, where it was considerable. America had a huge expanse of uncultivated land in the West, much of it open for settlement for the first time in the 1840s and 1850s. Some workers saved money, bought land, and moved west to farm it. The historian Frederick Jackson Turner later referred to the availability of western lands as a "safety valve" for discontent, a basic explanation for the relative lack of social conflict in the antebellum United States. But few urban workers, and even fewer poor ones, could afford to make such a move or had the expertise to know how to work land even if they could. Much more common was the movement of laborers from one industrial town to another. Restless, questing, sometimes hopeful, sometimes despairing, these frequently moving people were often the victims of layoffs, looking for better opportunities elsewhere. Their searches may seldom have led to a marked improvement in their circumstances, but the rootlessness of this large segment of the workforce—one of the most distressed segments—made effective organization and protest difficult.

There was, finally, another "safety valve" for working-class discontent: politics. Economic opportunity may not have greatly expanded in the nineteenth century, but opportunities to participate in politics did. And to many white, male working people, access to the ballot seemed to offer a way to help guide their society and to feel like a significant part of their communities.

MIDDLE-CLASS LIFE

For all the visibility of the very rich and the very poor in antebellum society, the fastest-growing group in America was the middle class. The expansion of the middle class was in part a result of the growth of the industrial economy and the increasing commercial life that accompanied it. Economic development opened many more opportunities for people to own or work in businesses, to own shops, to engage in trade, to enter professions, and to administer organizations. In earlier times, when ownership of land had been the only real basis of wealth, society had been divided between people with little or no land (people Europeans generally called peasants) and a landed gentry (which in Europe usually meant an inherited aristocracy). Once commerce and industry became a source of wealth, these rigid distinctions broke down, and many people who did not own land could become prosperous by providing valuable services to the new economy or by owning capital other than land.

RAPIDLY EXPANDING MIDDLE CLASS

Middle-class life in the years before the Civil War rapidly established itself as the most influential cultural form of urban America. Middle-class families lived in solid and often substantial homes, which, like the wealthy, they tended to own. Workers and artisans were increasingly becoming renters—a relatively new phenomenon in American cities that spread widely in the early nineteenth century.

Middle-class women tended to remain in the home and care for the children and the household, although increasingly they were also able to hire servants—usually young, unmarried immigrant women who put in long hours of arduous work for very little money. One of the aspirations of middle-class women in an age when doing the family's laundry could take an entire day was to escape from some of the drudgery of housework.

New household inventions altered, and greatly improved, the character of life in middle-class homes. Perhaps the most important was the invention of the cast-iron stove, which began to replace fireplaces as the principal vehicle for cooking and also as an important source of heat. These wood- or coal-burning devices were hot, clumsy, and dirty by the standards of the twenty-first century; but compared to the inconvenience and danger of cooking on an open hearth, they seemed a great luxury. Stoves gave cooks more control over the preparation of food and allowed them to cook several things at once.

NEW HOUSEHOLD INVENTIONS

Middle-class diets were changing rapidly in the antebellum years, and not just because of the wider range of cooking the stove made possible. The expansion and diversification of American agriculture, and the ability of farmers to ship goods to urban markets by rail from distant regions, greatly

Discussion and Activities

Analyzing Change Have students read the section "Rapidly Expanding Middle Class." Ask them to think about and discuss as a class ways the expansion of the middle class changed the role and status of women and ways that the role and status of women stayed the same. **SOC** **PCE**

increased the variety of food available in cities. Fruits and vegetables were difficult to ship over long distances in an age with little refrigeration, but families had access to a greater variety of meats, grains, and dairy products than they had had in the past. A few households acquired iceboxes in the years before the Civil War, and the sight of wagons delivering large chunks of ice to wealthy and middle-class homes began to become a familiar part of urban life. Iceboxes allowed their owners to keep fresh meat and dairy products for as long as several days without spoilage. Most families, however, did not yet have any kind of refrigeration. Preserving food for them meant curing meat with salt and preserving fruits in sugar. Diets were generally much heavier and starchier than they are today, and middle-class people tended to be considerably stouter than would be fashionable in the twenty-first century.

Middle-class homes came to differentiate themselves from those of workers and artisans in other ways as well. They were more elaborately decorated and furnished, with household goods made available for the first time through factory production. Houses that had once had bare walls and floors now had carpeting, wallpaper, and curtains. The spare, simple styles of eighteenth-century homes gave way to the much more elaborate, even baroque household styles of the early Victorian era–styles increasingly characterized by crowded, even cluttered rooms, dark colors, lush fabrics, and heavy furniture and draperies. Middle-class homes also became larger. It became less common for children to share beds and less common for all family members to sleep in the same room. Parlors and dining rooms separate from the kitchen–once a luxury reserved largely for the wealthy–became the norm for the middle class as well. Some urban middle-class homes had indoor plumbing and indoor toilets by the 1850s–a significant advance over the outdoor wells and privies that had been virtually universal only a few years earlier (and that remained common among working-class people).

GROWING CLASS DISTINCTIONS

THE CHANGING FAMILY

The new industrializing society of the northern regions of the United States produced profound changes in the nature and function of the family. At the heart of the transformation was the movement of families from farms to urban areas, where jobs, not land, were the most valued commodities. The patriarchal system of the countryside, whereby fathers controlled their children's futures by controlling the distribution of land to them, could not survive the move to a city or town. Sons and daughters were much more likely to leave the family in search of work than they had been in the rural world.

Another important change was the shift of income-earning work out of the home and into the shop, mill, or factory. In the early decades of the nineteenth century (and for many years before that), the family had been the principal unit of economic activity. Family farms, family shops, and family industries were the norm throughout most of the United States. Men, women, and children worked together, sharing tasks and jointly earning the income that sustained the family. But as farming spread to the fertile lands of the Northwest and as the size and profitability of farms expanded, agricultural work became more commercialized. Farm owners in need of labor began to rely less on their families (which often were not large enough to satisfy the demand) and more on hired male workers. These farmhands performed many of the tasks that on smaller farms had once been the jobs of the women and children of the family. As a result, farm women tended to work increasingly at domestic tasks–cooking, sewing, gardening, and dairying–a development that spared them from some heavy labor but that also removed them from the principal income-producing activities of the farm.

DECLINING ECONOMIC ROLE OF THE FAMILY

In the industrial economy of the rapidly growing cities, there was an even more significant decline in the traditional economic function of the family. The urban household became less important as a center of production. Instead, most income earners left home each day to work elsewhere. A sharp distinction began to emerge between the public world of the workplace–the world of commerce and industry–and the private world of the family. The world of the family was now more often dominated not by production, but by housekeeping, child rearing, and other primarily domestic concerns. It was also a world dominated by women.

Accompanying (and perhaps in part caused by) the changing economic function of the family was a decline in the birth rate. In 1800, the average American woman could be expected to give birth to approximately seven children during her childbearing years. By 1860, the average woman bore five children. The birth rate fell most quickly in urban areas and among middle-class women. Mid-nineteenth-century Americans had access to some birth-control devices, which undoubtedly contributed in part to the change. There was also a significant rise in abortions, which remained legal in some states until after the Civil War and which, according to some estimates, may have terminated as many as 20 percent of all pregnancies in the 1850s. But the most important cause of the declining birth rate was changes in sexual behavior–including increased abstinence.

FALLING BIRTH RATES

WOMEN AND THE "CULT OF DOMESTICITY"

The emerging distinction between the public and private worlds, between the workplace and the home, led to increasingly sharp distinctions between the social roles of men and women. Those distinctions affected not only factory workers and farmers, but members of the growing middle class as well. There had, of course, always been important differences between the male and female spheres in American society.

Discussion and Activities

Analyzing Change After students have read the section "Growing Class Distinctions," ask them to create a list of changes many middle-class families experienced in their standards of living at this time. Ask them to discuss in pairs or small groups which of those changes would have been the most important or would have most impacted daily life.

Reasoning Processes

Identifying Cause and Effect Have students read the section "The Changing Family." Ask them to create a chart identifying social and economic causes and effects of the changes to families. Ask them to evaluate what they think were the most important causes and effects. WXT SOC

Historical Thinking Skills

Argumentation After students have read the section "Female Education," ask them to create an advertisement designed to attract both male and female students to Oberlin College. Have students incorporate images and words designed to overcome societal resistance to female education. **SOC** **PCE**

PASTORAL AMERICA, 1848 This painting by the American artist Edward Hicks suggests the degree to which Americans continued to admire the "Peaceable Kingdom" (the name of another, more famous Hicks work) of the agrarian world. Hicks titled this work *An Indian Summer View of the Farm w. Stock of James C. Cornell of Northampton Bucks County Pennsylvania. That Took the Premium in the Agricultural Society, October the 12, 1848.* It portrays the diversified farming of a prosperous Pennsylvania family, shown here in the foreground with their cattle, sheep, and workhorses. In the background stretches a field ready for plowing and another ready for harvesting.

Courtesy National Gallery of Art, Washington

Women had long been denied many legal and political rights enjoyed by men; within the family, the husband and father had traditionally ruled, and the wife and mother had generally bowed to his demands and desires. It had long been practically impossible for most women to obtain divorces, although divorces initiated by men were often easier to arrange. (Men were also far more likely than women to win custody of children in case of a divorce.) In most states, husbands retained almost absolute authority over both the property and persons of their wives. Wife beating was illegal in only a few areas, and the law did not acknowledge that rape could occur within marriage. Women traditionally had very little access to the worlds of business or politics. Indeed, in most communities custom dictated that women never speak in public before audiences that included men.

FEMALE EDUCATION

Most women also had much less access to education than men, a situation that survived into the mid-nineteenth century. Although they were encouraged to attend school at the elementary level, they were strongly discouraged—and in most cases effectively barred—from pursuing higher education. Oberlin in Ohio became the first college in America to accept female students; it permitted four to enroll in 1837, despite criticism that coeducation was a rash experiment approximating free love. Oberlin authorities were confident that "the mutual influence of the sexes upon each other is decidedly happy in the cultivation of both mind & manners." But few other institutions shared their views. Coeducation remained extraordinarily rare until long after the Civil War; and only a very few women's colleges—such as Mount Holyoke, founded in Massachusetts by Mary Lyon in 1837—emerged.

NEW ROLES FOR WOMEN

No longer income producers, middle-class women became guardians of the "domestic virtues." Their role as mothers, entrusted with the nurturing of the young, seemed more central to the family than it had in the past. And their role as wives—as companions and helpers to their husbands—grew more important as well. Middle-class women also became more important as consumers. They learned to place a high value on keeping a clean, comfortable, and well-appointed home, on entertaining, and on dressing elegantly and stylishly.

Discussion and Activities

Analyzing Visuals Have students examine the image "Pastoral America, 1848." Ask them to identify the point of view of the artist regarding the importance of agriculture, and discuss as a class how this represents either a continuity or change from earlier ideas about the importance of agriculture. *(The image clearly echoes the Jeffersonian ideal of an agrarian-based economy.)* **WXT** **NAT**

CONSIDER THE SOURCE

FAMILY TIME

HOW A FAMILY SPENDS TIME TOGETHER has been a favorite subject of artists for centuries. Studying where families gather, how they celebrate, and how they interact and communicate when relaxing or playing is a powerful way to gather information about conventional roles of mothers, fathers, extended family members, children, and sometimes servants.

The two images following are separated by 172 years yet strive to tell a similar story about family life. The first image, of a parlor in antebellum Philadelphia, appeared in *Godey's Lady's Book* in May 1842. Focused on the lives of better-off white women, *Godey's Lady's Book* featured advice columns on fashion, manners, home decoration, and child rearing. The second, by photographer Eric Audras, is set in present-day America. Audras, who chronicles the joys and struggles of modern families, has a keen eye for catching what fascinates parents and children today.

Much is communicated in the small details of each composition: the style of dress, the type of activities being pursued, and the spatial organization of family members. When such details are collectively analyzed, they tell us about the evolution of family life in America.

FAMILY TIME—1842

FAMILY DEVOTION-MORNING

AP Exam Tip

When responding to document-based questions, students will be asked to analyze the sourcing and situation of primary and secondary sources. One way to do that is to evaluate the purpose of a document.

Historical Thinking Skills

Sourcing and Situation Have students practice the exam tip by examining the image "Family Devotion–Morning," and then writing a short paragraph explaining the purpose of the image. *(*Godey's Lady's Book *was a publication intended to provide helpful advice to middle-class women about how to fulfill their roles as wives and mothers. The purpose of the image is likely to reinforce traditional ideas about men being the leaders of the household.)* **SOC**

Discussion and Activities

Analyzing Visuals Have students examine the image "Family Devotion–Morning." Ask them to discuss in small groups details that reveal the social hierarchy portrayed in the image. *(The male leads the devotion while his wife and child face him from across the table. Two other adult females, possibly sisters of the husband or wife or servants, sit in the corner in apparently submissive positions.)* **SOC**

Reasoning Processes

Continuity and Change After students have examined the images "Family Devotion–Morning" and "Family Time–2013," ask them to create a Venn diagram comparing the images. Ask students to discuss what they see as the greatest changes, as well the greatest continuities. **SOC**

FAMILY TIME—2013

ANALYZING SOURCES

Questions assume cumulative content knowledge from this chapter and previous chapters.

1. What does the illustration from *Godey's Lady's Book* most suggest about the value of reading as a leisure activity—at least for middle class families—in the first half of the 19th century?
   (A) Reading was one among a great variety of leisure activities highly valued.
   (B) Reading was not highly valued, as only the father is reading in the illustration.
   (C) Reading was given high importance, as the father, who is central in the illustration, is prominently shown reading to an attentive family.
   (D) Books were mostly used as decorative items to display social status.

2. What does the difference in the ways that the pursuit of leisure activity is shown and the spatial organization of the family members in both images most suggest about family life in the first half of the 19th century, compared to family life of today?
   (A) Family life in the early half of the 19th century was less patriarchal.
   (B) Family life in the early half of the 19th century was more patriarchal.
   (C) Children had greater independence within the family, in the early half of the 19th century.
   (D) Family life in the early half of the 19th century was matriarchal.

3. What does the difference in the activities of the parents in both images best suggest about middle-class, domestic gender roles in the first half of the 19th century, compared to middle-class, domestic gender roles of today?
   (A) The gender roles within domestic life were much more distinct in the 19th century.
   (B) In the 19th century, both genders shared equally in the domestic roles.
   (C) The distinction between domestic gender roles was less sharp in the 19th century.
   (D) There was less formality in gender roles in the 19th century.

4. What does the illustration from *Godey's Lady Book* most suggest about the ideal of women in the 19th century?
   (A) Expectations of women to direct the social life within the family became more prominent.
   (B) Women were increasingly expected to display independence.
   (C) The role of women as nurturers became more prominent.
   (D) The role of women as nurturers became less important.

Answers

Consider the Source

1. C; **2.** B; **3.** A; **4.** C

NATHAN HAWLEY AND FAMILY Nathan Hawley, seated at center in this 1801 painting, was typical of many early-nineteenth-century fathers in having a very large family. Nine members are visible here. Hawley at the time was the warden of the Albany County jail in New York, and the painting was by William Wilkie, one of the inmates there. The painting suggests that Hawley was a man of modest but not great means. His family is fashionably dressed, and there are paintings on the walls—signs of style and affluence. But the house is very simply furnished, without drapes for the windows, with a simple painted floor cloth in the front room, and a bare floor in the back.

WOMEN'S SEPARATE SPHERE

Occupying their own "separate sphere," some women began to develop a distinctive female culture. Friendships among women became increasingly intense; women began to form their own social networks (and, ultimately, to form female clubs and associations that were of great importance to the advancement of various reforms). A distinctive feminine literature began to emerge to meet the demands of middle-class women. There were women's magazines, of which the most prominent was *Godey's Lady's Book*, edited after 1837 by Sarah Hale. The magazine scrupulously avoided dealing with public controversies or political issues and focused instead on fashions, shopping and homemaking advice, and other purely domestic concerns. Politics and religion were inappropriate for the magazine, Hale explained in 1841, because "other subjects are more important for our sex and more proper for our sphere."

By the standards of a later era, the increasing isolation of women from the public world seems to be a form of oppression and discrimination. And it is true that few men considered women fit for business, politics, or the professions. On the other hand, most middle-class men—and many middle-class women as well—considered the new female sphere a vehicle for expressing special qualities that made women in some ways superior to men. Women were to be the custodians of morality and benevolence, just as the home—shaped by the influence of women—was to be a refuge from the harsh, competitive world of the marketplace. It was women's responsibility to provide religious and moral instruction to their children and to counterbalance the acquisitive, secular impulses of their husbands.

BENEFITS AND COSTS

Thus the "cult of domesticity," as some scholars have called it, brought both benefits and costs to middle-class women. It allowed them to live lives of greater material comfort than in the past, and it placed a higher value on their "female virtues" and on their roles as wife and mother. At the same time, it left women increasingly detached from the public world, with few outlets for their other interests and energies.

The costs of that detachment were particularly clear among unmarried women of the middle class. By the 1840s, the ideology of domesticity had grown so powerful that few genteel women would any longer consider working (as many had in the past) in shops or mills, and few employers would consider hiring them. But unmarried women nevertheless required some income-producing activity. They had few

Discussion and Activities

Evaluating Evidence After students have read the section "Women's Separate Sphere," ask them to create a T-chart listing responsibilities and privileges of middle-class women in this system of a separate sphere. Discuss as a class whether students believe women were better or worse off in this system.

Discussion and Activities

Analyzing Perspectives Have students examine the image "Nathan Hawley and Family." Ask them to identify details that give insight to family life in the situation depicted. Have students write a short journal entry from the point of view of any member of the family describing family life. Ask for volunteers to share perspectives of various family members.

SOC

Reasoning Processes

Comparing After students have read the section "Working Class Women," ask them to create a Venn diagram comparing the lives of middle- and lower-class women under the system of separate spheres. SOC

choices. Some could become teachers or nurses, professions that seemed to call for the same female qualities that made women important within the home; and both of those professions began in the 1840s and 1850s to attract significant numbers of women, although not until the Civil War did females begin to dominate them. Otherwise, unmarried females were largely dependent on the generosity of relatives or hired as governesses for children or companions for widows and other women.

Middle-class people gradually came to consider work by women outside the household to be unseemly, something characteristic of the lower classes—as indeed it was. But working-class women could not afford to stay home and cultivate the "domestic virtues." They had to produce income for their families. They continued to work in factories and mills, but under conditions far worse than those that the original, more "respectable" women workers had once enjoyed. They also frequently found employment in middle-class homes. Domestic service became one of the most frequent sources of female employment. In other words, now that production had moved outside the household, women who needed to earn money had to move outside their own households to do so.

WORKING-CLASS WOMEN

LEISURE ACTIVITIES

Leisure time was scarce for all but the wealthiest Americans in the mid-nineteenth century. Most people worked long hours. Saturday was a normal working day. Vacations—paid or unpaid—were rare. For most people, Sunday was the only respite from work and was generally reserved for religion and rest. Almost no commercial establishments did any business on Sunday, and even within the home many families frowned upon playing games or engaging in other kinds of entertainment on the Sabbath. For working-class and middle-class people, therefore, holidays took on a special importance. That was one reason for the strikingly elaborate Fourth of July celebrations throughout the country. The celebrations were not just expressions of patriotism. They were also a way of enjoying one of the few holidays from work available to virtually all Americans.

In rural America, where most people still lived, the erratic pattern of farmwork gave many people some relief from the relentless work schedules of city residents. For urban people, however, leisure was something to be seized in what few free moments they had. Men gravitated to taverns for drinking, talking, and game-playing. Women gathered in one another's homes for conversation or card games or to share work on such household tasks as sewing. For educated people, whose numbers were rapidly expanding, reading became one of the principal leisure activities. Newspapers and magazines proliferated rapidly, and books—novels, histories, autobiographies, biographies, travelogues, and others—became staples of affluent homes. Women were particularly avid readers, and women writers created a new genre of fiction specifically for females—the "sentimental novel," which often offered idealized visions of women's lives and romances.

There was also a vigorous culture of public leisure, even if many families had to struggle to find time or means to participate in it. In larger cities, theaters were becoming increasingly popular; and while some of them catered to particular social groups, others attracted audiences that crossed class lines. Wealthy people, middle-class people, workers and their families: all could sometimes be found watching a performance of Shakespeare or a melodrama based on a popular novel or an American myth. Minstrel shows—in which white actors mimicked (and ridiculed) African American culture—became increasingly popular. Public sporting events—boxing, horse racing, cockfighting (already becoming controversial), and others—often attracted considerable crowds. Baseball—not yet organized into professional leagues—was beginning to attract large crowds when played in city parks or fields on the edges of towns. A particularly exciting event in many communities was the arrival of the circus—a traveling entertainment with roots in the Middle Ages that continued to entertain, delight, and bamboozle children and adults alike.

MINSTREL SHOWS

Popular tastes in public spectacle tended toward the bizarre and the fantastic. Most men and women lived in a constricted world of familiar things. Relatively few people traveled; and in the absence of film, radio, television, or even much photography, they hungered for visions of unusual phenomena that contrasted with their normal experiences. People going to the theater or the circus or the museum wanted to see things that amazed and even frightened them. Perhaps the most celebrated provider of such experiences was the famous and unscrupulous showman P. T. Barnum, who opened the American Museum in New York City in 1842—not a showcase for art or nature, but a great freak show populated by midgets (the most famous named Tom Thumb), Siamese twins, magicians, and ventriloquists. Barnum was a genius in publicizing his ventures with garish posters and elaborate newspaper announcements. Only later, in the 1870s, did he launch the famous circus for which he is still best remembered. But he was always a pioneer in exploiting public tastes for the wild and exotic.

P. T. BARNUM

One of the ways Barnum tried to draw visitors to his museum was by engaging lecturers. He did so because he understood that the lecture was one of the most popular forms of entertainment in nineteenth-century America. Men and women flocked in enormous numbers to lyceums, churches, schools, and auditoriums to hear lecturers explain the latest advances in science, to describe their visits to exotic places, to provide vivid historical narratives, or to rail against the evils of alcohol or slavery. Messages of social uplift and reform attracted rapt audiences, particularly among women eager for guidance as they adjusted to the often jarring changes in the character of family life in the industrializing world.

Discussion and Activities

Making Connections Have students read the section "Leisure Activities." Ask them to discuss as a class how students today celebrate holidays like Independence Day and attend various entertainment events and how and why these celebrations are so different compared to those of the mid-nineteenth century. SOC NAT

P. T. BARNUM AND TOM THUMB P. T. Barnum, circus producer, next to a table on which stands Charles Stratton, a little person who came to be known as General Tom Thumb. Hoping to capitalize on the popular fascination with the bizarre and the fantastic, Barnum hired Stratton at the age of five to tour the country with his circus. Stratton sang, danced, and impersonated famous people such as Napoleon Bonaparte.

THE AGRICULTURAL NORTH

Even in the rapidly urbanizing and industrializing Northeast, and more so in what nineteenth-century Americans called the Northwest (and what Americans today call the Midwest), most people remained tied to the agricultural world. But agriculture, like industry and commerce, was becoming increasingly a part of the new capitalist economy, linked to the national and international market. Where agriculture could not compete in this new commercial world, it declined. Where it could compete, it simultaneously flourished and changed.

RISE OF COMMERCIAL AGRICULTURE

NORTHEASTERN AGRICULTURE

The story of agriculture in the Northeast after 1840 is one of decline and transformation. The reason for the decline was simple: the farmers of the section could no longer compete with the new and richer soil of the Northwest. Centers of production were gradually shifting westward for many of the farm goods that had in the past been most important to northeastern agriculture: wheat, corn, grapes, cattle, sheep, and hogs.

Some eastern farmers responded to these changes by moving west themselves and establishing new farms. Still others moved to mill towns and became laborers. Some farmers, however, remained on the land and managed to hold their own. As the eastern urban centers increased in population, many farmers turned to the task of supplying food to nearby cities; they raised vegetables (truck farming) or fruit and sold it in local towns. New York, for example, led all other states in apple production.

TRUCK FARMING IN THE NORTHEAST

The rise of cities also stimulated the rise of profitable dairy farming. Approximately half the dairy products of the country were produced in the East; most of the rest came from the West, where Ohio was the leading dairy state. Partly because of the expansion of the dairy industry, the Northeast led other sections in the production of hay. New York was the leading hay state in the nation; Pennsylvania and New England grew large crops as well. The Northeast also exceeded other areas in producing potatoes.

But while agriculture in the region remained an important part of the economy, it was steadily becoming less important than the industrial growth of the Northeast itself. As a result, the rural population in many parts of the Northeast continued to decline.

THE OLD NORTHWEST

There was some industry in the states of the Northwest, more than in the South; and in the two decades before the Civil War, the region experienced steady industrial growth. By 1860, it had 36,785 manufacturing establishments employing 209,909 workers. There was a flourishing industrial and commercial area along the shore of Lake Erie, with Cleveland at its center. Another manufacturing region was in the Ohio River valley; the meatpacking city of Cincinnati was its nucleus. Farther west, the rising city of Chicago, destined to become the great metropolis of the region, was emerging as the national center of the agricultural machinery and meatpacking industries.

INDUSTRIALIZATION IN THE OLD NORTHWEST

Most of the major industrial activities of the West either served agriculture (as in the case of farm machinery) or relied on agricultural products (as in flour milling, meatpacking, whiskey distilling, and the making of leather goods). As this suggests, industry was much less important in the Northwest than farming.

Discussion and Activities

Analyzing Cause and Effect After students have read the section "Northeastern Agriculture," ask them to think about why truck farmers in this region would mainly grow fruits and vegetables to sell in nearby towns. Have students share their thoughts with a partner. Ask for volunteers to share with the class. *(Northeastern farmers grew perishable crops with short shelf lives to transport to local cities, since competitors from farther away could not ship perishables long distances without their products spoiling. Northeastern farmers could not compete with grain producers from the Midwest, whose crops were relatively non-perishable.)* **WXT** **GEO**

Discussion and Activities

Analyzing Perspectives Have students examine the image "P.T. Barnum and Tom Thumb." Ask them to write a short paragraph making an argument about whether Barnum was exploiting his "freak show" performers or offering them opportunities. **SOC** **WXT**

Historical Thinking Skills

Comparison and Argumentation After students have read the section "Agricultural Specialization," ask them to create a T-chart comparing the impacts of industry and agriculture in the Northwest. Have students write a summary statement containing an argument about which was more important to the region. **WXT** **GEO**

Some areas of the Northwest were not yet dominated by white settlers. Native Americans remained the most numerous inhabitants of much of the upper third of the Great Lakes states until after the Civil War. In those areas, hunting and fishing, along with some sedentary agriculture, remained the principal economic activities of both white settlers and Native Americans. But Native Americans did not become integrated into the new commercialized economy that was emerging elsewhere in the Northwest.

For the white (and occasionally black) settlers who populated the lands farther south, the Northwest was primarily an agricultural region. Its rich and plentiful lands made farming a lucrative and expanding activity there, in contrast to the declining agrarian Northeast. Thus the typical citizen of the Northwest was not an industrial worker or poor, marginal farmer, but the owner of a reasonably prosperous family farm. The average size of western farms was 200 acres, the majority owned by the people who worked them.

Rising farm prices around the world provided a strong incentive for these western farmers to engage in commercial agriculture. That usually meant concentrating on a single crop for market (corn, wheat, cattle, sheep, hogs, and others). In the early years of white settlement in the Northwest, farm prices rose because of the debilitation of European agriculture in the aftermath of the Napoleonic Wars and the growing urban population (and hence the growing demand for food) of industrializing areas of Europe. The Northwest, with good water routes on the Mississippi for getting its crops to oceangoing vessels, profited from this international trade.

AGRICULTURAL SPECIALIZATION

But industrialization, in both the United States and Europe, provided the greatest boost to agriculture. With the growth of factories and cities in the Northeast, the domestic market for farm goods increased dramatically. The growing national and worldwide demand for farm products resulted in steadily rising farm prices. For most farmers, the 1840s and early 1850s were years of increasing prosperity.

To meet the increasing demand for its farm products, residents of the Northwest worked strenuously, and often frantically, to increase their productive capacities. Many tried to take advantage of the large areas of still-uncultivated land and to enlarge the area of white settlement during the 1840s. By 1850, the growing western population was moving into the prairie regions both east and west of the Mississippi: into areas of Indiana, Michigan, Illinois, Missouri, Iowa, and Minnesota. Residents cleared forest lands or made use of fields Native Americans had cleared many years earlier. And they began to develop a timber industry to make use of the forests that remained. Wheat was the staple crop of the region, but other crops–corn, potatoes, and oats–and livestock were also important.

The Northwest increased production not only by expanding the area of settlement, but also by adopting new agricultural technologies that greatly reduced the labor necessary for producing a crop and slowed the exhaustion of the region's rich soil. Farmers began to cultivate new varieties of seed, notably Mediterranean wheat, which was hardier than the native type; and they imported better breeds of animals, such as hogs and sheep from England and Spain, to take the place of native stock. Most important were improved tools and farm machines, which American inventors and manufacturers produced in rapidly increasing numbers. During the 1840s, more-efficient grain drills, harrows, mowers, and hay rakes came into wide use. The cast-iron plow, an earlier innovation, remained popular because its parts could be replaced when broken. An even better tool appeared in 1847, when John Deere established at Moline, Illinois, a factory to manufacture steel plows, which were more durable than those made of iron.

NEW AGRICULTURAL TECHNOLOGIES

CYRUS MCCORMICK'S AUTOMATIC REAPER Cyrus McCormick invented an automatic reaper in 1831 and had it patented in 1834. The machine, drawn by a horse, cut wheat, corn, or other crops and left it lying in swaths in the field where farmworkers would gather it up and store it in stacks. The reaper allowed one worker to harvest as much wheat in a day as five could harvest using earlier methods.

Two new machines heralded a coming revolution in grain production. The most important was the automatic reaper, the invention of Cyrus H. McCormick of Virginia. The reaper enabled one worker to harvest as much wheat (or any other small grain) in a day as five could harvest using older methods. McCormick, who had patented his device in 1834, established a factory at Chicago, in the heart of the grain belt, in 1847. By 1860, more than 100,000 reapers were in use on western farms. Almost as important to the grain grower was the thresher–a machine that separated the grain from the wheat stalks. Threshers appeared in large numbers after 1840. Before that, farmers generally flailed grain by hand (seven bushels a day was a good average for a farm) or used farm animals to tread it (twenty bushels a day on the average). A threshing machine, such as those manufactured by the Jerome I. Case factory in Racine, Wisconsin, could thresh twenty-five bushels or more in an hour.

MCCORMICK REAPER

The Northwest considered itself the most democratic section of the country. But its democracy was based on a defense of economic freedom and the rights of property–a white, middle-class vision of democracy that was becoming common

Reasoning Processes

Continuity and Change After students have read the section "New Agricultural Technologies," ask them to discuss in pairs or small groups the ways the introduction of new crops was similar to or different from the Columbian Exchange discussed in Unit 1. **WXT**

in many other parts of the country as well. Abraham Lincoln, an Illinois Whig, voiced the economic opinions of many of the people of his section. "I take it that it is best for all to leave each man free to acquire property as fast as he can," said Lincoln. "Some will get wealthy. I don't believe in a law to prevent a man from getting rich; it would do more harm than good. . . . When one starts poor, as most do in the race of life, free society is such that he knows he can better his condition; he knows that there is no fixed condition of labor for his whole life."

RURAL LIFE

Rural life for people farming the land was very different from life in towns and cities. It also varied greatly from one farming region to another. In the more densely populated farm areas east of the Appalachians and in the easternmost areas of the Northwest, farmers were usually part of vibrant communities and made extensive use of the institutions of those communities–the churches, schools, stores, and taverns. As white settlement moved farther west, farmers became isolated and had to struggle to find any occasions for contact with people outside their own families.

IMPORTANCE OF RELIGION IN RURAL COMMUNITIES

Religion drew farm communities together perhaps more than any other force, particularly since so many farm areas were populated by people of common ethnic (and therefore religious) backgrounds. Town or village churches were popular meeting places, for both services and social events–most of them dominated by women. Even in areas with no organized churches, farm families–and, again, women in particular–gathered in one another's homes for prayer meetings, Bible readings, and other religious activities. Weddings, baptisms, and funerals also brought communities together in celebration or mourning.

But religion was only one of many reasons for interaction. Farm people joined together frequently to share tasks that a single family would have difficulty performing on its own; festive barn raisings were among the most frequent. Women prepared large suppers while the men worked on the barn and the children played. Large numbers of families also gathered together at harvest time to help bring in crops, husk corn, or thresh wheat. Women came together to share domestic tasks as well, holding "bees" in which groups of women joined together to make quilts, baked goods, preserves, and other products.

But despite the many social gatherings farm families managed to create, they lived in a world with much less contact with popular culture and public social life than people who lived in towns and cities. Rural people, often even more than urban ones, treasured their links to the outside world–letters from relatives and friends in distant places, newspapers and magazines from cities they had never seen, catalogs advertising merchandise that their local stores never had. Yet many also valued their separation from urban culture and cherished the relative autonomy that farm life gave them. One reason many rural Americans looked back nostalgically on country life once they moved to the city was that they sensed that in the urban world they did not have as much control over the patterns of their daily lives as they had once known.

Discussion and Activities

Contextualization and Argumentation After students have read the section "McCormick Reaper," ask them to create advertisements for the McCormick Reaper, keeping in mind the target audience and the advantages the reaper would offer to that market. **WXT**

Discussion and Activities

Understanding Multiple Perspectives Have students read the section "Rural Life." Ask them to write a short letter from the point of view of a farm family member writing to a relative living in an Eastern city describing their experience of a barn raising. **SOC**

Discussion and Activities

Evaluating Evidence After finishing the chapter, have students work in small groups to brainstorm and research the key economic, social, and political changes that impacted family life and gender roles during this era. Have each group create a 3-column chart listing those factors. Then, bring the class together to discuss which factors they believe were most important in causing the changes in family life and gender roles. 

Key Terms

Students should be familiar with the key terms and be able to define them in the context of economic and social changes precipitated by ongoing immigration, industrialization, and westward expansion. Encourage students to use these terms in performing review exercises and exam practice for this chapter.

CHAPTER 10 REVIEW

CONNECTING THEMES

Chapter 10 examined the causes and effects of rapid population growth in the United States during the first half of the nineteenth century. European immigration brought major changes to the labor force and American society, including growing nativism and diverging regional identities.

Technological innovations, both in agriculture and transportation, complemented the rise of the factory system and revolutionized American society in many ways. The nation experienced increased urbanization and wealth inequality, which led to greater leisure time for some. Family and gender roles underwent significant social changes that most significantly affected working and middle-class women. Finally, the development of a national market contributed to the growing sectionalism and regional divisions between the North, South, and West.

You should consider the following questions as you review the themes for this chapter:

- How did European migration in the first half of the nineteenth century impact notions of an American identity?
- How did technological innovations affect the labor force, class distinctions, and social mobility?
- What were the causes and effects of rapid population growth in the United States?
- How did movement toward a national market economy and the factory system lead to political divisions and increased sectional tensions?
- How did the natural environment influence the development of regional political and economic identities?
- What were the changes in the roles of women during the first half of the nineteenth century?

KEY TERMS

agricultural specialization 302
Canal Age 276
Commonwealth vs. Hunt 291
corporations 281
"Cult of Domesticity" 295
early skilled worker unions 290
Erie Canal 277
factory system 282
Free Labor 291
Godey's Lady's Book 299
immigrant labor 290
interchangeable parts 283
Know-Nothings 275
Lowell System 284
machine tools 283
middle class 294
nativism 272
Old Northwest 301
P. T. Barnum 299
Samuel F. B. Morse 279
Sarah Bagley 285
social mobility 294
steamboats 276
steel plow 302
truck farming 301
women's "separate sphere" 299

304 · CHAPTER 10

Go Online Chapter 10 Content Review

Assessing Student Understanding Use the online assessment to assess student understanding of concepts and topics within the chapter. You can assign the ready-made Chapter 10 Content Review or create your own from available questions. This easy-to-use tool helps you design assessments that meet the needs of different types of learners.

AP EXAM PRACTICE

Questions assume cumulative content knowledge from this chapter and previous chapters.

MULTIPLE CHOICE

Use the image advertising the *American Patriot* on page 273 and your knowledge of U.S. history to answer questions 1-3.

1. The immigrants arriving in the 1840s and 1850s largely came from
   (A) Italy and Russia.
   (B) England and Scotland.
   (C) Ireland and Germany.
   (D) France and Austria.

2. Concerns like those reflected in the image partly centered around the fear that
   (A) immigrants settling in cities would be competition for employment.
   (B) immigrants were generally well-educated and could dominate elections.
   (C) immigrants would favor politically radical beliefs and candidates.
   (D) immigrants would settle in agricultural areas and refuse to integrate in urban centers.

3. Those who shared concerns with the creators of the image ultimately reflected their nativism politically by
   (A) supporting the passage of restrictive immigration legislation.
   (B) passing a law that established English as the official language of the United States.
   (C) forming a political party commonly known as the "Know-Nothing Party."
   (D) forming institutions to speed up the cultural integration of immigrants.

SHORT ANSWER

Use your knowledge of U.S. history to answer questions 4 and 5.

4. Use the image on page 274 to answer A, B, and C.
   (A) Briefly describe ONE historical point of view about European immigration in the image.
   (B) Briefly explain ONE specific historical cause of European immigration to the United States during the first half of the nineteenth century.
   (C) Briefly explain ONE specific historical effect of European immigration to the United States during the first half of the nineteenth century.

5. Answer A, B, and C.
   (A) Briefly describe ONE specific historical similarity about Americans before and after the emergence of the factory system.
   (B) Briefly describe ONE specific historical difference about Americans before and after the emergence of the factory system.
   (C) Briefly explain ONE specific historical effect that resulted from the emergence of the factory system.

LONG ESSAY

Develop a thoughtful and thorough historical argument that addresses the statement. Begin your essay with a thesis statement, and support it with specific historical evidence and examples.

6. Evaluate the relative importance of the effects of the technological revoltuion on the United States in the first half of the nineteenth century.

Answers

Multiple Choice

1. C; **2.** A; **3.** C

Short Answer

4A) Possible answer: One point of view of European immigration is that of a nativist. Nativists viewed the foreign-born population with alarm, believing that immigrants were inherently inferior. In this particular image, the artist is reinforcing a specific stereotype about the Irish and Germans–that they are heavy drinkers. The image is also implying that these immigrants are also diluting the vote by "stealing" the ballot box.

4B) Possible answer: During the 1840s and 1850s, Ireland was hit with the Potato Famine, which decimated the population, especially in southern Ireland. The economic opportunities in the United States drew many Irish and other Europeans to the new country.

4C) Possible answer: Increased population growth due to European immigration caused the rise of nativist sentiment and the rise of nativist political parties like the Know-Nothing Party. The party became a powerful albeit short-lived force, especially in the North, where in 1854 they gained control of the Massachusetts state government. However, the party, because of its narrow focus, lost steam after 1854.

5A) Possible answer: Americans, both before and after the emergence of the factory system, were overwhelmingly still rural and farmers.

5B) Possible answer: Following the emergence of the factory system, Americans saw the rise in two new and distinct social and economic classes: the middle class and the working class.

5C) Possible answer: The rise of the factory system served as both push and pull factors for European immigration during the first half of the nineteenth century. Many Europeans faced mounting hardships back in their home countries (e.g., famine and political upheavals), and the United States offered up many opportunities for these individuals looking for a fresh start.

Answers

Long Essay

6. Possible thesis: The technological revolution affected the growth of population, as immigrants sought new economic opportunities in America. But more importantly, the country began to notice a shift in the geography of the population as more people were moving to urban settings because of these opportunities. Finally, the technology allowed faster and easier migration to the West, continuing the influx of western settlers. Historical evidence: The U.S. population grew significantly during this area, spurred by increased immigration due to economic hardships in Europe and economic opportunities in the United States. Population growth also affected urban growth in the country. While much slower in the South, there was still a general trend of urban growth throughout the entire country. Despite this, the country still remained largely agricultural. The growth of industry also contributed to a shift in the workplace, as families moved out of the home to the factory system. Labor also becomes more unskilled, as the apprentice system began to die out. The growth in transportation opened up opportunities for continued western migration. Canals, roads, bridges, and railroads all provided faster and more convenient opportunities to move out west. This, of course, also had political ramifications, as new territories became states, thus shifting the political dynamics in Congress.

Pacing Guide

Chapter 11 explores key concepts from Period 4: 1800–1848 of the AP U.S. History Curriculum Framework. The suggested instruction time for Chapter 11 is 3 days.

Key Concepts

4.2.I New transportation systems and technologies dramatically expanded manufacturing and agricultural production.

4.2.II The changes caused by the market revolution had significant effects on U.S. society, workers' lives, and gender and family relations.

4.2.III Economic development shaped settlement and trade patterns, helping to unify the nation while also encouraging the growth of different regions.

11 COTTON, SLAVERY, AND THE OLD SOUTH

THE OLD PLANTATION This painting, by an unidentified folk artist of the early nineteenth century, suggests the importance of music in plantation slavery life in America. The banjo, which the musician with the hat is playing, was originally an African instrument.

CONNECTING CONCEPTS

Chapter 11 begins by examining the complex nature of Southern society and the impact that cotton production had on its development. The large-scale agricultural economy of the South ensured that the institution of slavery would remain a vital part of the social fabric of the region. Slavery led to great wealth for a small number of plantation farmers, but it also created a regional society heavily dependent on cotton production. This complicated relationship created a structured hierarchy, with clearly defined gender and class roles for both Southern whites and African Americans.

The nature of slavery, the development of slave culture, and resistance to slavery were integral to the development of Southern society. The institution of slavery itself varied greatly from place to place, and variations developed as the region split between an Upper South and a Lower (or Deep) South. In addition, urban and rural African Americans also had different experiences that contributed to the great diversity of African American culture.

As you read, you should:

- Analyze how the South remained politically, culturally, and ideologically different from other regions of the United States, despite certain economic ties between the South and the North.
- Identify how both free and enslaved African Americans developed a distinct society and created networks of support for each other.
- Evaluate the ways many Southerners defended the institution of slavery.

Discussion and Activities

Analyzing Visuals Have students examine the image "The Old Plantation." Ask them to create a KWL chart listing what they know, what they want to know, and what they learned about the lives of enslaved people. Have students add to their charts throughout the chapter. **SOC** **WXT** **PCE**

- Analyze the similarities and differences in labor systems in the North and the South.
- Assess the ways that slavery was both a regional and national issue.
- Identify the different ways that enslaved African Americans developed various means of resistance to the institution of slavery.
- Analyze the ways that the cotton economy and slavery shaped the political, economic, and social development of the South.

THE COTTON ECONOMY

The most important economic development in the mid-nineteenth-century South was the shift of economic power from the "upper South" (the original southern states along the Atlantic coast) to the "lower South" (the expanding agricultural regions in the new states of the Southwest). That shift reflected above all the growing dominance of cotton in the Southern economy.

The Rise of King Cotton

Much of the upper South continued in the nineteenth century to rely, as it always had, on the cultivation of tobacco. But the market for that crop was notoriously unstable. Tobacco prices were subject to frequent depressions, including a prolonged one that began in the 1820s and extended into the 1850s. Tobacco also rapidly exhausted the land on which it grew; it was difficult for most growers to remain in business in the same place for very long. By the 1830s, therefore, many farmers in the old tobacco-growing regions of Virginia, Maryland, and North Carolina were shifting to other crops–notably wheat–while the center of tobacco cultivation was moving westward, into the Piedmont area.

DECLINE OF THE TOBACCO ECONOMY

The southern regions of the coastal South–South Carolina, Georgia, and parts of Florida–continued to rely on the cultivation of rice, a more stable and lucrative crop than tobacco. Rice, however, demanded substantial irrigation and needed an exceptionally long growing season (nine months), so cultivation of that staple remained restricted to a relatively small area. Sugar growers along the Gulf Coast, similarly, enjoyed a reasonably profitable market for their crop. But sugar cultivation required intensive (and debilitating) labor and a long growing time. Only relatively wealthy planters could afford to engage in it, and they faced major competition from the great sugar plantations of the Caribbean. Sugar cultivation, therefore, did not spread much beyond a small area in southern Louisiana and eastern Texas. Long-staple (Sea Island) cotton was another lucrative crop, but like rice and sugar, it could grow only in a limited area–the coastal regions of the Southeast.

The decline of the tobacco economy in the upper South, and the limits of the sugar, rice, and long-staple cotton economies farther south, might have forced the region to shift its attention in the nineteenth century to other nonagricultural pursuits, had it not been for the growing importance of a new product that soon overshadowed all else: short-staple cotton. This was a hardier and coarser strain of cotton that could grow successfully in a variety of climates and in a variety of soils. It was harder to process than the long-staple variety; its seeds were more difficult to remove from the fiber. But the 1793 invention of the cotton gin had largely solved that problem.

SHORT-STAPLE COTTON

Demand for cotton was growing rapidly. The growth of the textile industry in Britain in the 1820s and 1830s, and in New England in the 1840s and 1850s, created an enormous new demand for the crop. As a result, ambitious men and women rapidly moved into previously uncultivated lands–many of them newly open to planter settlement after the relocation of the tribes in the 1820s and 1830s–to establish new cotton-growing regions.

Beginning in the 1820s, therefore, cotton production spread rapidly. From the western areas of South Carolina and Georgia, production moved steadily westward–first into Alabama and Mississippi, then into northern Louisiana, Texas, and Arkansas. By the 1850s, cotton had become the linchpin of the Southern economy. In 1820, the South had produced about 500,000 bales of cotton. By 1850 it was producing nearly 3 million bales a year, and by 1860 nearly 5 million. There were periodic fluctuations in cotton prices, resulting generally from overproduction; periods of boom frequently gave

SPREAD OF COTTON PRODUCTION

Reasoning Processes

Comparing After students have read the section "Short-Staple Cotton," ask them to create a chart listing the advantages and disadvantages of cultivating tobacco, rice, sugar, and cotton. Have students write a short summary explaining why cotton cultivation became more prevalent than other crops in the South. **GEO** **WXT**

Go Online AP Exam Preparation

AP Exam Practice Use the online assessment to help prepare students for the AP Exam. You can assign the ready-made AP-style short-answer questions, document-based questions, and multiple-choice questions assessing concepts, themes, and skills from Period 4 and AP-style long-essay questions organized in sets of 3 questions from various time periods. You can also create your own tests from available questions. This easy-to-use tool helps you design assessments that meet the needs of different types of learners.

Discussion and Activities

Speculating After students have read the section "Spread of Cotton Production," ask them to list reasons for the dominance of cotton over other crops in the South. Discuss as a class the potential implications of being overly dependent on a single crop. *(Failure of the crop due to pests or crop disease could lead to economic disaster; could potentially be replaced by supplies from competitors overseas.)* **WXT**

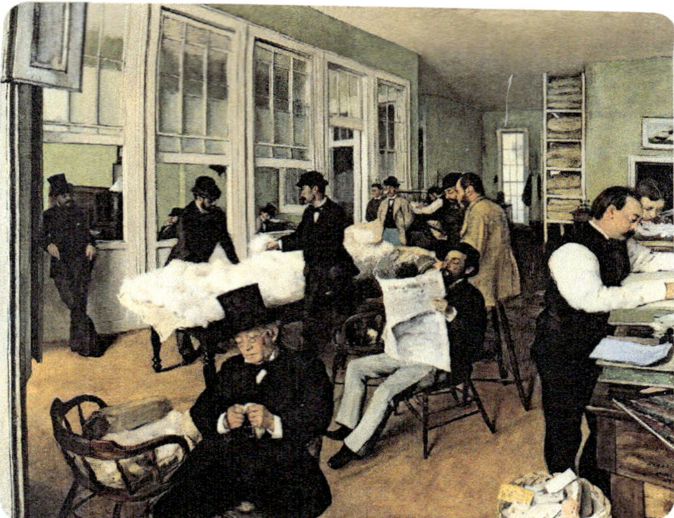

THE NEW ORLEANS COTTON EXCHANGE Edgar Degas, the French impressionist, painted this scene of cotton traders examining samples in the New Orleans cotton exchange in 1873. By this time the cotton trade was producing less impressive profits than those that had made it the driving force of the booming Southern economy of the 1850s. Degas's mother came from a Creole family of cotton brokers in New Orleans, and two of the artist's brothers (depicted here reading a newspaper and leaning against a window) joined the business in America.

way to abrupt busts. But the cotton economy continued to grow, even if in fits and starts. By the time of the Civil War, cotton constituted nearly two-thirds of the total export trade of the United States and was bringing in nearly $200 million a year. The annual value of the rice crop, in contrast, was $2 million. It was little wonder that southern politicians now proclaimed: "Cotton is king!"

Cotton production dominated the more recently settled areas of what came to be known as the "lower South" (or, in a later era, the "Deep South"). Many people began to call this region the "Cotton Kingdom." Settlement of the area resembled in some ways the rush of gold seekers to a new strike. The prospect of tremendous profits from growing cotton drew white settlers to the lower South by the thousands. Some were wealthy planters from the older states who transferred their assets and enslaved people to a cotton plantation. Most were small slaveholders or slaveless farmers who hoped to move into the planter class.

A similar shift, if an involuntary one, occurred in the enslaved population. Between 1820 and 1860, the number of enslaved people in Alabama leaped from 41,000 to 435,000, and in Mississippi from 32,000 to 436,000. In the same period, the increase in Virginia was only from 425,000 to 490,000. Between 1840 and 1860, according to some estimates, 410,000 enslaved people moved from the upper South to the cotton states—either accompanying slaveholders who were themselves migrating to the Southwest or (more often) sold to planters already there. Indeed, the sale of enslaved people to the Southwest became an important economic activity in the upper South and helped the troubled planters of that region compensate for the declining value of their crops.

EXPANSION OF SLAVERY

SOUTHERN TRADE AND INDUSTRY

In the face of this booming agricultural expansion, other forms of economic activity developed slowly in the South. The business classes of the region—the manufacturers and merchants—were not unimportant. There was growing activity in flour milling and in textile and iron manufacturing, particularly in the upper South. The Tredegar Iron Works in Richmond, for example, compared favorably with the best iron mills in the Northeast. But industry remained an insignificant force in comparison with the agricultural economy. The total value of Southern textile manufactures in 1860 was $4.5 million—a threefold increase over the value of those goods twenty years before, but only about 2 percent of the value of the raw cotton exported that year.

WEAK MANUFACTURING SECTOR

To the degree that the South developed a nonfarm commercial sector, it was largely to serve the needs of the plantation economy. Particularly important were the brokers, or "factors," who marketed the planters' crops. These merchants tended to live in such towns as New Orleans, Charleston, Mobile, and Savannah, where they worked to find buyers for cotton and other crops and where they purchased goods for the planters they served. The South had only a very rudimentary financial system, and the factors often also served the planters as bankers, providing them with credit. Planters frequently accumulated substantial debts, particularly during periods when cotton prices were in decline; and the Southern merchant-bankers thus became figures of considerable influence and importance in the region. There were also substantial groups of professional people in the South—lawyers, editors,

Discussion and Activities

Analyzing Change Have students read the section "Expansion of Slavery." Ask them to write a short paragraph explaining why slavery was growing so much faster in the deep South than elsewhere. *(Expansion of cotton planting in the deep South; rich farmland leading planters to relocate from the upper South.)* **MIG** **WXT** **GEO**

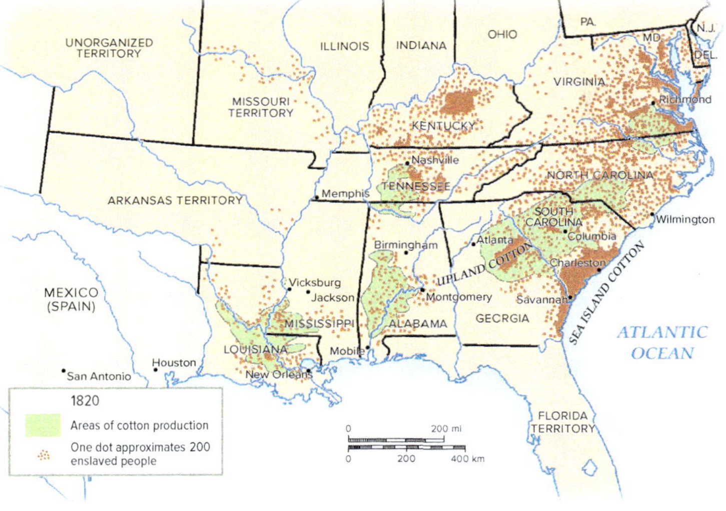

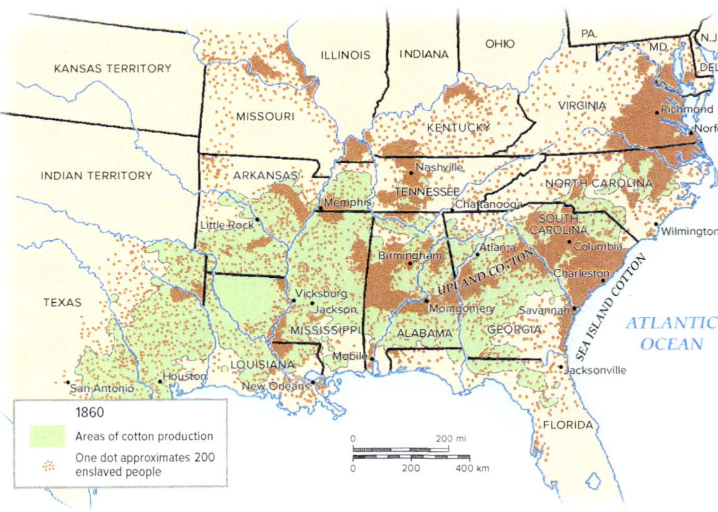

SLAVERY AND COTTON IN THE SOUTH, 1820 AND 1860 These two maps show the remarkable spread of cotton cultivation in the South in the decades before the Civil War. Both maps show the areas of cotton cultivation (the green-colored areas) as well as areas with large populations of enslaved people (the brown-dotted areas). Note how in the top map, which represents 1820, cotton production is concentrated largely in the East, with a few areas scattered among Alabama, Mississippi, Louisiana, and Tennessee. Slavery is most concentrated along the Georgia and South Carolina coast, areas in which long-staple cotton was grown, with only a few other areas of highly dense enslaved populations. By 1860, the South had changed dramatically. Cotton production had spread throughout the lower South, from Texas to northern Florida, and slavery had moved with it. Slavery was also much denser in the tobacco-growing regions of Virginia and North Carolina, which had also grown.

How did this economic shift affect the white South's commitment to slavery?

doctors, and others. In most parts of the region, however, they too were closely tied to and dependent on the plantation economy. However important manufacturers, merchants, and professionals might have been to Southern society, they were relatively unimportant in comparison with the manufacturers, merchants, and professionals of the North, on whom Southerners were coming more and more (and increasingly unhappily) to depend.

The primitive character of the region's banking system matched a lack of development in other basic services and structures necessary for industrial development. Perhaps most notable was the South's inadequate transportation system. In the North in the antebellum period, enormous sums were invested in roads, canals, and above all railroads to knit the region together into

INADEQUATE REGIONAL TRANSPORTATION SYSTEM

Reasoning Processed

Comparing After students have read the section "Weak Manufacturing Sector," ask them to discuss in pairs or small groups why the Southern economy remained so much less diverse than the Northern economy, particularly with regards to the limited development of industry. **WXT** **NAT**

Answers

Slavery and Cotton in the South, 1820 and 1860

As the South become more financially dependent on cotton, white southerners of all classes became more supportive of the system of slavery used to produce cotton.

Reasoning Processes

Comparing After students have read the section "Inadequate Regional Transportation System," ask them to create a Venn diagram comparing transportation in the North and the South. Have students discuss as a class how the disparities increased regional division. **NAT** **WXT**

an integrated market. In the South there were no such investments. Canals were almost nonexistent; most roads were crude and unsuitable for heavy transport; and railroads, although they expanded substantially in the 1840s and 1850s, failed to tie the region together effectively. Such towns as Charleston, Atlanta, Savannah, and Norfolk had direct connections with Memphis, and thus with the Northwest; and Richmond was connected, via the Virginia Central, with the Memphis and Charleston Railroad. In addition, several independent lines furnished a continuous connection between the Ohio River and New Orleans. Most of the South, however, remained unconnected to the national railroad system. Most lines in the region were short and local. The principal means of transportation was water. Planters generally shipped their crops to market along rivers or by sea; most manufacturing was in or near port towns.

Perceptive Southerners recognized the economic subordination of their region to the North. "From the rattle with which the nurse tickles the ear of the child born in the South to the shroud that covers the cold form of the dead, everything comes to us from the North" the Arkansas journalist Albert Pike lamented. Perhaps the most prominent advocate of Southern economic independence was James B. D. De Bow, a resident of New Orleans. He published a magazine advocating Southern commercial and agricultural expansion, *De Bow's Review*, which survived from its founding in 1846 until 1880.

DE BOW'S REVIEW

De Bow made his journal into a tireless advocate of Southern economic independence from the North, warning constantly of the dangers of the "colonial" relationship between the sections. One writer noted in the pages of his magazine: "I think it would be safe to estimate the amount which is lost to us annually by our vassalage to the North at $100,000,000. Great God!" Yet *De Bow's Review* was itself evidence of the dependency of the South on the North. It was printed in New York, because no New Orleans printer had facilities adequate for the task; it was filled with advertisements from Northern manufacturing firms; and its circulation was always modest in comparison with those of Northern publications. In Charleston, for

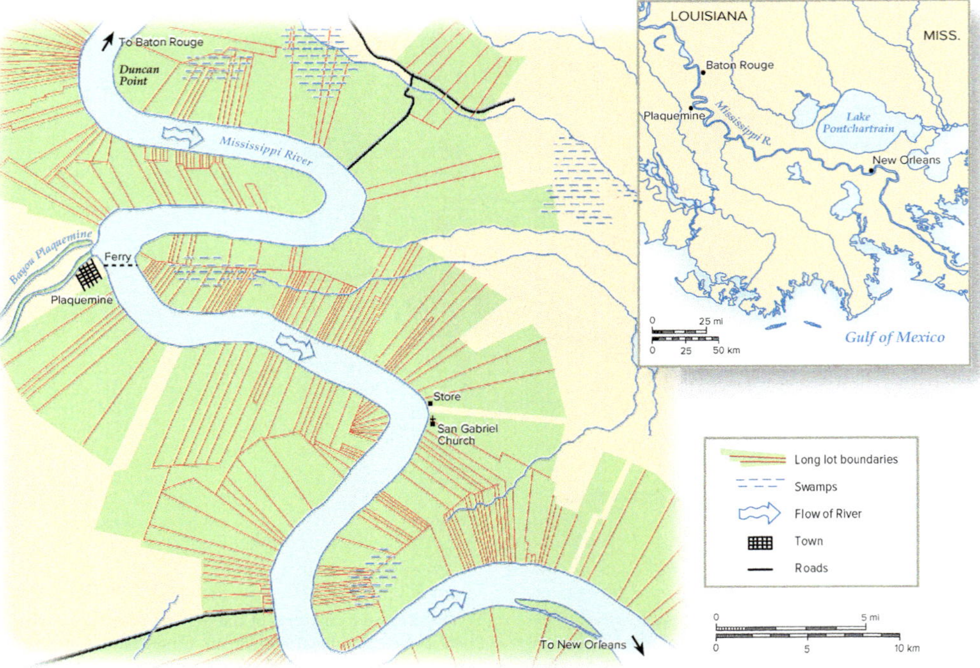

PLANTATIONS IN LOUISIANA, 1858 This map provides a detailed view of plantation lands along a stretch of the Mississippi River between New Orleans and Baton Rouge, Louisiana. Note the long, narrow shapes of these landholdings—known as "long lots." This system was designed to give as many planters as possible frontage on the river, which they needed to transport their crops to market and to receive goods in return. The river also deposited rich soil on the lands near its banks, which made cultivation of crops easier. Note how towns, stores, and churches all are near the riverbank, so planters and others living on plantations nearby could reach them easily by boat.

How is this landscape different from that of the newly opened federal lands in the West?

Answers

Plantations in Louisiana, 1858

Louisiana was a landscape dominated by the presence of water; the West was a landscape dominated by a lack of water.

example, it sold an average of 173 copies per issue; *Harper's Magazine* of New York, in contrast, regularly sold 1,500 copies to South Carolinians.

SOURCES OF SOUTHERN DIFFERENCE

Despite this growing concern about the region's "colonial dependency," the South made few serious efforts to build an economy that might challenge its dependency. An important question about antebellum Southern history, therefore, is why the region did so little to develop a larger industrial and commercial economy of its own. Why did it remain so different from the North?

Part of the reason was the great profitability of the South's agricultural system, particularly of cotton production. In the Northeast, many people had turned to manufacturing as the agricultural economy of the region declined. In the South, the agricultural economy was booming, and ambitious people eager to profit from the emerging capitalist economy had little incentive to look beyond it. Another reason was that wealthy Southerners had so much capital invested in their land and, particularly, enslaved people, they had little left for other investments. Some historians have suggested that the climate–with its long, hot, steamy summers–was less suitable for industrial development than the climate of the North. Still others have claimed that Southern work habits (perhaps a reflection of the debilitating effects of the climate) impeded industrialization; some white Southerners appeared–at least to many Northern observers–not to work very hard, to lack the strong work ethic that fueled Northern economic development.

REASONS FOR COLONIAL DEPENDENCY

But the Southern failure to create a flourishing commercial or industrial economy was also in part the result of a set of values distinctive to the South that discouraged the growth of cities and industry. Many white Southerners liked to think of themselves as representatives of a special way of life based on traditional values of chivalry, leisure, and elegance. White Southerners were, they argued, "cavaliers"–people happily free from the base, acquisitive instincts of the "yankees" to their north. Southern white people were, they believed, more concerned with a refined and gracious way of life than with rapid growth and development. Appealing as the "cavalier" image was to white Southerners, however, it conformed to the reality of Southern society in very limited ways.

THE CAVALIER IMAGE

WHITE SOCIETY IN THE SOUTH

Only a small minority of white Southerners were slaveholders. In 1850, when the total white population of the South was over 6 million, the number of slaveholders was 347,525. In 1860, when the white population was just above 8 million, the number of slaveholders had risen to 383,637. These figures are somewhat misleading, since each slaveholder was normally the head of a family averaging five members. But even with all members of slaveholding families included in the figures, those with enslaved people still amounted to perhaps no more than one-quarter of the white population. And of the minority of white slaveholders, only a small proportion had substantial numbers of enslaved people.

THE PLANTER CLASS

How, then, did the South come to be seen–both by the outside world and by many Southerners themselves–as a society dominated by great plantations and wealthy landowning planters? In large part, it was because the planter aristocracy–the cotton magnates, the sugar, rice, and tobacco nabobs, the slaveholders with at least 40 or 50 enslaved people and 800 or more acres–exercised power and influence far in excess of their numbers. They stood at the apex of society, determining the political, economic, and even social life of their region. Enriched by vast annual incomes, dwelling in palatial homes, surrounded by broad acres and many enslaved laborers, they became a class to which all other Southerners deferred. The wealthiest planters also maintained homes in towns or cities and spent several months of the year there, engaged in a glittering social life. Others traveled widely, especially to Europe, as an antidote to the isolation of plantation life. And many used their plantations to host opulent social events.

PLANTER ARISTOCRACY

White Southerners liked to compare their planter class to the old upper classes of England and Europe: true aristocracies, long entrenched. In fact, however, the Southern upper class was in most cases not at all similar to the landed aristocracies of the Old World. In some areas of the upper South–the Tidewater region of Virginia, for example–some of the great aristocrats were indeed people whose families had occupied positions of wealth and power for generations. In most of the South, however, a long-standing landed aristocracy, although central to the "cavalier" image, was largely a myth. Even the most important planters in the cotton-growing areas of the South were, typically, new to their wealth and power. As late as the 1850s, many of the great landowners in the lower South were still first-generation settlers, who had arrived with only modest resources, struggled for years to clear land and develop a plantation in what was at first a rugged wilderness, and only recently had started to live in the comfort and luxury for which they became famous. Large areas of the "Old South" (as Americans later called the South of the pre-Civil War era) had been settled and cultivated for less than two decades at the time of the Civil War.

Nor was the world of the planter nearly as leisured and genteel as the "cavalier" myth would suggest. Growing staple crops was a business that was in its own way just as competitive and just as risky as the industrial enterprises of the North. Planters had to supervise their operations carefully if they hoped to make a profit. They were, in many respects, just as much competitive capitalists as the industrialists of the North whose lifestyles they claimed to hold in contempt. Even many

PLANTATION MANAGEMENT

Reasoning Processes

Comparing and Contrasting Have students read the section "Sources of Southern Difference." Ask them to create a T-chart listing social and economic differences between the North and the South. Have students discuss in small groups which was type of difference was greater. **NAT** **SOC** **WXT**

Discussion and Activities

Assessing Credibility Have students read the section "Planter Aristocracy." As a class, discuss how the attempts by Southern planters to portray themselves as a landed aristocracy similar to Old World elites were accurate, exaggerated, or false. **SOC** **PCE**

Discussion and Activities

Analyzing Perspectives After students have read the section "Aristocratic Values," ask them to discuss in pairs or small groups ways that Southern planters tried to promote the image of themselves as landed aristocrats. Have students consider whether these portrayals showed strength or weakness. **SOC**

affluent planters lived modestly, their wealth so heavily invested in land and enslaved people that there was little left for personal comfort. And white planters, even some substantial ones, tended to move frequently as new and presumably more-productive areas opened up to cultivation.

Indeed, it may have been the very newness and precariousness of the plantation way of life, and the differences between the reality of that life and the image of it, that made many Southern planters determined to portray themselves as genteel aristocrats. Having struggled so hard to reach and maintain their positions, they were all the more determined to defend them. Perhaps that was why the defense of slavery and of the South's "rights" was stronger in the new, booming regions of the lower South and weaker in the more established and less flourishing areas of the Tidewater.

ARISTOCRATIC VALUES

Wealthy white Southerners sustained their image of themselves as aristocrats in many ways. They avoided such "coarse" occupations as trade and commerce; those who did not become planters often gravitated toward the military, a "suitable" career for men raised in a culture in which medieval knights (as portrayed in the novels of Walter Scott) were a powerful and popular image. The aristocratic ideal also found reflection in the definition of a special role for Southern white women.

"HONOR"

Above all, perhaps, white males adopted an elaborate code of chivalry, which obligated them to defend their "honor," often through dueling—which survived in the South long after it had largely vanished in the North. Southern white males placed enormous stock in conventional forms of courtesy and respect in their dealings with one another—perhaps to distance themselves from the cruelty and disrespect that were so fundamental to the slave system they controlled. Violations of such forms often brought what seemed to outsiders a disproportionately heated and even violent response.

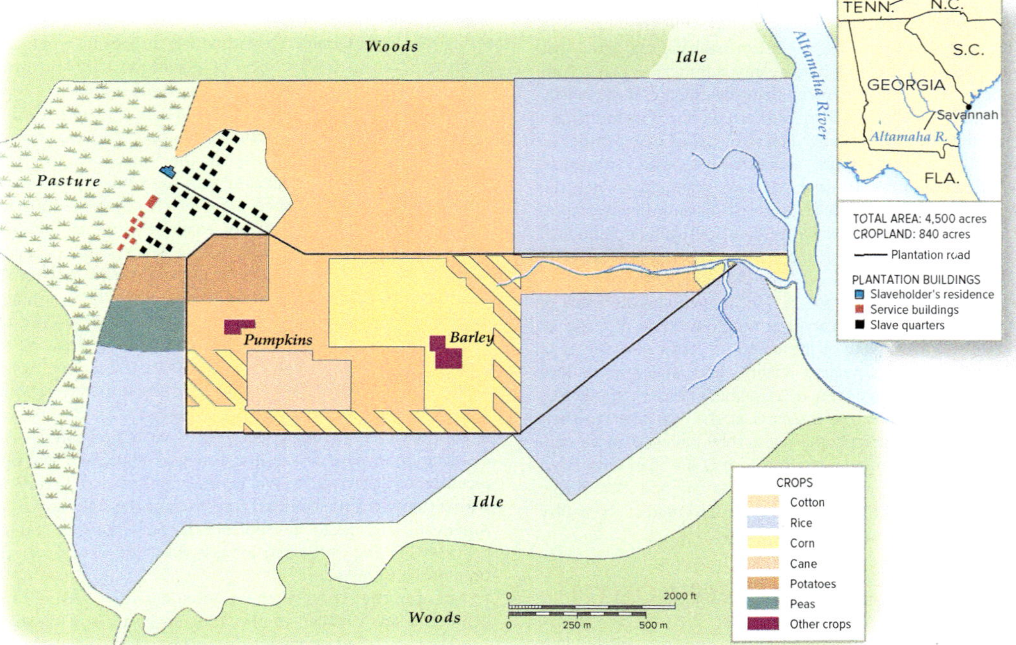

A GEORGIA PLANTATION This map of the Hopeton Plantation in Georgia shows both how much plantations were connected to the national and world markets, and how much they tried to be self-sufficient. Note the large areas of land devoted to growing cotton, rice, and sugarcane, all of them crops for the market. Note also the many crops grown for the local market or for consumption by residents of the plantation—potatoes, vegetables, corn, and others. The top left of the map shows the distribution of living quarters, with slaves' quarters grouped together very near the slaveholder's residence.

Why would a plantation in this part of the South be so much more diversified in the market crops it raised than the cotton plantations in the Mississippi Delta? Why would planters want enslaved people living nearby? Why might enslaved people be unhappy about being so close to slaveholders?

Answers

A Georgia Plantation

Georgia plantations may have been less well-connected to other markets, necessitating greater self-sufficiency. Slaveholders may have wanted quarters for enslaved people close by in order to keep watch over their activities, while enslaved people most likely resented being so closely watched.

The idea of honor in the South was only partly connected to the idea of ethical behavior and bravery. It was also tied to the importance among white males of the public appearance of dignity and authority–of saving face in the presence of others. Anything that seemed to challenge the dignity, social station, or "manhood" of a white Southern male might be the occasion for a challenge to duel, or at least for a stern public rebuke. When the South Carolina congressman Preston Brooks strode into the chamber of the United States Senate and savagely beat Senator Charles Sumner of Massachusetts with a cane to retaliate for what he considered an insult to a relative, he was acting wholly in accord with the idea of Southern honor. In the North, he was reviled as a savage. In the South, he became a popular hero. But Brooks was only the most public example of a code of behavior that many white Southern men followed. Avenging insults was a social necessity in many parts of Southern society, and avenging insults to white Southern women was perhaps the most important obligation of a white Southern "gentleman."

CULT OF HONOR

THE "SOUTHERN LADY"

In some respects, affluent white women in the South occupied roles very similar to those of middle-class white women in the North. Their lives generally centered in the home, where they served as companions to and hostesses for their husbands and as nurturing mothers for their children. Even less frequently than in the North did "genteel" Southern white women engage in public activities or find income-producing employment.

But the life of the "Southern lady" was also in many ways very different from that of her Northern counterpart. For one thing, the cult of honor in the region meant in theory that Southern white men gave particular importance to the "defense" of women. In practice, this generally meant that white men were even more dominant and white women even more subordinate in Southern culture than they were in the North. George Fitzhugh, one of the South's most important social theorists, wrote in the 1850s: "Women, like children, have but one right, and that is the

SUBORDINATE STATUS OF WOMEN

© Louisiana State Museum, USA/Bridgeman Images

THE OLIVIER PLANTATION In this watercolor on paper, Adrien Persac (1823–1873) places the main house of this sugar plantation on the left with additional dwellings towards the right, on the east bank of the Bayou Teche, an important waterway in Louisiana. Also on the right, he depicts the sugar house and a floating pontoon bridge. The artist represents the self-consciously elegant life of the planter and his family.

Discussion and Activities

Making Connections After students have read the section "Honor," discuss as a class what "honor" meant to Southern planters and how that perception is similar to or different from what students consider "honor" to mean today. Have students write a short paragraph describing what "honor" means to them. **SOC**

Discussion and Activities

Analyzing Points of View Have students examine the image "The Olivier Plantation." Ask them to identify details from the painting that support the efforts of Southern planters to portray themselves as landed aristocrats. *(The elegant manor house and grounds; the formal dress of the residents; the apparent leisure that the residents enjoy.)* Have students write a journal entry from the point of view of one of the residents portrayed in the painting describing the scene. **SOC**

Reasoning Processes

Comparing After students have read the section "The Subordinate Status of Women," ask them to create a T-chart listing similarities and differences between Northern and Southern women of the middle and upper classes. Have them identify and discuss in small groups what they believe are the most important similarities and differences. SOC PCE

right to protection. The right to protection involves the obligation to obey."

More important in determining the role of Southern white women, however, were the social and economic realities in which they lived. The vast majority of females in the region lived on farms, isolated from people outside their own families, with virtually no access to the "public world" and thus few opportunities to look beyond their roles as wives and mothers. Because the family was the principal economic unit on most farms, the dominance of husbands and fathers over wives and children was even greater than in those Northern families in which income-producing activities had moved out of the home and into the factory or office. For many white women, living on farms of modest size meant a fuller engagement in the economic life of the family than was becoming typical for middle-class women in the North. These women engaged in spinning, weaving, and other production; they participated in agricultural tasks; they helped supervise the enslaved workforce. On some of the larger plantations, however, even these limited roles were sometimes considered unsuitable for white women; and the "plantation mistress" became, in some cases, more an ornament for her husband than an active part of the economy or the society.

Southern white women also had less access to education than their Northern counterparts. Nearly a quarter of all white women over twenty were completely illiterate; relatively few women had more than a rudimentary exposure to schooling. Even wealthy planters were not interested in extensive schooling for their daughters. The few female "academies" in the South trained women primarily to be suitable wives.

OTHER BURDENS

Southern white women had other special burdens as well. The Southern white birth rate remained nearly 20 percent higher than that of the nation as a whole, and infant mortality in the region remained higher than elsewhere; nearly half the children born in the South in 1860 died before they reached five years of age. The slave-labor system had a mixed impact on white women. It helped spare many of them from certain kinds of arduous labor, but it also threatened their relationships with their husbands. Male slaveholders had frequent sexual relationships with the enslaved women on their plantations; the children of those unions became part of the plantation labor force and served as a constant reminder to white women of their husbands' infidelity. Black women (and men) were obviously the most important victims of such practices. But white women suffered too.

CLEAR STARCHING IN LOUISIANA This 1837 etching by Auguste Hervieu offers a strikingly unromanticized view of plantation women in the South. The white woman, soberly dressed, speaks harshly to two black household servants, presumably criticizing the way they are doing the laundry. The enslaved people cower, carefully hiding whatever resentment they might feel behind a submissive pose. Nothing in this picture suggests anything like the kind of ease and luxury often associated with plantation life in popular mythology at the time and since.

The Life and Adventures of Jonathan Jefferson Whitlaw, by Frances Trollope, 1836

A few Southern white women rebelled against their roles and against the prevailing assumptions of their region. Some became outspoken abolitionists and joined Northerners in the crusade to abolish slavery. Some agitated for other reforms within the South itself. Most white women, however, found few outlets for whatever discontent they may have felt with their lives. Instead, they generally convinced themselves of the benefits of their position and—even more fervently than Southern white men—defended the special virtues of the Southern way of life. Upper-class white women in the South were particularly energetic in defending the class lines that separated them from poorer whites Southerners.

THE PLAIN FOLK

The typical white Southerner was not a great planter and slaveholder, but a modest yeoman farmer. Some of these "plain folk," as they have become known, owned a few enslaved people, with whom they worked and lived far more closely than did the larger planters. Most (in fact, three-quarters of all white families) owned no enslaved people. Some plain folk, most of whom owned their own land, devoted themselves largely to subsistence farming; others grew cotton or other crops for the market, but usually could not produce enough to allow them to expand their operations or even get out of debt. During the 1850s, the number of nonslaveholding landowners increased much faster than the number of slaveholding landowners. While there were occasional examples of poor farmers moving into the ranks of the planter class, such cases were rare. Most yeomen knew that they had little prospect of substantially bettering their lot.

LIMITED EDUCATIONAL OPPORTUNITIES

One reason was the Southern educational system, which provided poor whites with few opportunities to learn and thus limited their chances of advancement. For the sons of wealthy planters, the region provided ample opportunities to gain an education. In 1860 there were 260 Southern colleges and universities, public and private, with 25,000 students enrolled in them, or more than half the total number of students in the United States. But universities were within the reach of only the upper class. The elementary and secondary schools of the South were not only fewer but also inferior to those of the Northeast (although not much worse than the crude schools of the Northwest), and a higher proportion of white Southerners were illiterate than in other parts of the country.

Discussion and Activities

Analyzing Visuals Have students examine the image "Clear Starching in Louisiana." Ask them to think about and share with a partner what the role of the white man in the background might have been. *(The well-dressed man is likely the owner of the plantation. The white woman might have felt compelled to chastise the enslaved people to show her husband that she was in control.)* SOC

That a majority of the South's white population consisted of modest farmers largely excluded from the dominant plantation society raises another important question about the antebellum South. Why did the plain folk have so little power in the public world of the Old South? Why did they not oppose the aristocratic social system in which they shared so little? Why did they not resent the system of slavery, from which they generally did not benefit?

Some white Southerners that were not slaveholders did oppose the planter elite, but for the most part in limited ways and in a relatively few, isolated areas. These were Southern highlanders, the "hill people," who lived in the Appalachian ranges east of the Mississippi, in the Ozarks to the west of the river, and in other "hill country" or "backcountry" areas cut off from the commercial world of the plantation system. Of all white Southerners, they were the most isolated from the mainstream of the region's life. They practiced a simple form of subsistence agriculture, held practically no enslaved people, and had a proud sense of seclusion. They were, in most respects, unconnected to the new commercial economy that dominated the great cotton-planting region of the South. They produced almost no surplus for the market, had little access to money, and often bartered for the goods they could not grow themselves.

HILL PEOPLE

To such men and women, slavery was unattractive for many of the same reasons it was unappealing to workers and small farmers in the North: because it threatened their sense of their own independence. Hill country farmers lived in a society defined by individual personal freedom and unusual isolation from modern notions of property. They also held to older political ideals, which for many included the ideal of fervent loyalty to the nation.

Such white Southerners frequently expressed animosity toward the planter aristocracy of the other regions of the South. The mountain region was the only part of the South to defy the trend toward sectional conformity, and the only part to resist the movement toward secession when it finally developed. Even during the Civil War, many hill country Southerners refused to support the Confederacy; some even fought for the Union.

Far greater in number, however, were the nonslaveholding white Southerners who lived in the midst of the plantation system. Many, perhaps most of them, accepted that system because they were tied to it in important ways. Small farmers depended on the local plantation aristocracy for many things: access to cotton gins, markets for their modest crops and their livestock, credit or other financial assistance. In many areas, there were also extensive kinship networks linking lower- and upper-class white Southerners. The poorest resident of a county might be a cousin of the richest aristocrat. Together, these mutual ties helped mute what might otherwise have been pronounced class tensions.

CLOSE RELATIONS WITH THE PLANTATION ARISTOCRACY

Small farmers felt tied to the plantation society in other ways as well. For white men, at least, the South was an unusually democratic society, in that participation in politics—both through voting and through attending campaign meetings and barbecues—was even more widespread than in the North, where participation was also high. Just as political participation gave workers in the North a sense of connection to the social order, so it did for farmers in the South—although officeholders in the South, even more than in the North, were almost always members of the region's elites. In the 1850s, moreover, the boom in the cotton economy allowed many small farmers to improve their economic fortunes. Some bought more land, became slaveholders, and moved into at least the fringes of plantation society. Others simply felt more secure in their positions as independent yeomen and hence more likely to embrace the fierce regional loyalty that was spreading throughout the white South in these years.

Small farmers, even more than great planters, were also committed to a traditional, male-dominated family structure. Their household-centered economies required the participation of all family members and, they believed, a stable system of gender relations to ensure order and stability. Men were the unquestioned head of the household; women and children, who were both family and workforce, were firmly under his control. As the Northern attack on slavery increased in the 1840s and 1850s, it was easy for such farmers to believe—and easy for ministers, politicians, and other propagandists for slavery to persuade them—that an assault on one hierarchical system (slavery) would open the way to an assault on another such system (patriarchy).

COMMITMENT TO PATERNALISM

There were other white Southerners, however, who did not share in the plantation economy in even limited ways and yet continued to accept its premises. These were the members of a particularly degraded class—numbering perhaps a half million in 1850—known to other classes variously and demeaningly as "crackers," "sand hillers," or "poor white trash" (a phrase used as a chapter title in Harriet Beecher Stowe's *Uncle Tom's Cabin*). Occupying the infertile lands of the pine barrens, the red hills, and the swamps, they lived in miserable cabins amid genuine destitution. Many owned no land (or owned land on which nothing could be grown) and supported themselves by foraging or hunting. Others worked as common laborers for their neighbors, although the slave system limited their opportunities. Their degradation resulted partly from dietary deficiencies and disease. Some resorted at times to eating clay (hence the tendency of affluent white Southerners to refer to them disparagingly as "clay eaters"); and they suffered from pellagra, hookworm, and malaria. Planters and small farmers alike held them in contempt. They formed a true underclass. In some material respects, their plight was worse than that of the enslaved African Americans (who themselves often looked down on the poor white Southerners).

Yet, even among these Southerners—the true outcasts of white society in the region—there was no real opposition to the plantation system or slavery. In part, undoubtedly, this was because these men and women were so benumbed by

LIMITED CLASS CONFLICT

Reasoning Processes

Comparing After students have read the section "Hill People," ask them to create a Venn diagram comparing the planter elite with the "plain folk." Have students discuss as a class what they believe to be the most important differences between these two groups and the reasons for those differences. **SOC** **WXT** **PCE**

Discussion and Activities

Analyzing Cause and Effect After students have read the section "Commitment to Paternalism," ask them to write a short paragraph explaining why they think poor Southerners largely supported a social and economic system that benefited the planter class much more than themselves. **SOC** **PCE**

Discussion and Activities

Analyzing Issues After students have read the section "Limited Class Conflict," ask them to work in small groups to create a flow chart demonstrating the socio-economic hierarchy of the South.

poverty that they had little strength to protest. But their relative passivity resulted also from perhaps the single greatest unifying factor among the Southern white population, the one force that was most responsible for reducing tensions among the various classes: their perception of race. However poor and miserable these white Southerners were, they could still consider themselves members of a ruling race; they could still look down on the black population of the region and feel a bond with fellow white Southerners born of a determination to maintain their racial supremacy. As Frederick Law Olmsted, a Northerner who visited the South and chronicled Southern society in the 1850s, wrote: "From childhood, the one thing in their condition which has made life valuable to the mass of whites has been that the niggers are yet their inferiors."

SLAVERY: THE "PECULIAR INSTITUTION"

White Southerners often referred to slavery as the "peculiar institution." By that they meant not that the institution was odd, but that it was distinctive, special. The description was apt, for American slavery was indeed distinctive. The South in the mid-nineteenth century was the only area in the Western world—except for Brazil, Cuba, and Puerto Rico—where slavery still existed. Slavery, more than any other single factor, isolated the South from the rest of American society. And as that isolation increased, so did the commitment of Southerners to defend the institution.

Within the South itself, the institution of slavery had paradoxical results. On the one hand, it isolated black people from white people, drawing a sharp and inviolable racial line dividing one group of Southerners from another. As a result, African Americans under slavery began to develop a society and culture of their own, one unrelated to the white civilization around them. On the other hand, slavery created a unique bond between enslaved people and slaveholders in the South. The two groups may have maintained separate spheres, but each sphere was deeply influenced by, indeed dependent on, the other.

VARIETIES OF SLAVERY

LEGAL BASIS OF SLAVERY

Slavery was an institution established and regulated in detail by law. The slave codes of the Southern states forbade enslaved people to hold property, to leave the slaveholders premises without permission, to be out after dark, to congregate with other enslaved people except at church, to carry firearms, or to strike a white person, even in self-defense. The codes of some states prohibited whites from teaching enslaved people to read or write and denied enslaved people the right to testify in court against white people. The laws contained no provisions to legalize slave marriages or divorces. If a slaveholder killed an enslaved person while punishing him, the act was generally not considered a crime. Enslaved people however, faced the death penalty for killing or even resisting a white person and for inciting revolt. The codes also contained extraordinarily rigid provisions for defining a person's race. Anyone with even a trace of African ancestry was defined as a black person. And anyone even rumored to possess any such trace was presumed to be African American unless he or she could prove otherwise—which was, of course, almost impossible to do.

REALITY OF SLAVERY

These and dozens of other restrictions might seem to suggest that enslaved people lived under a uniformly harsh and dismal regime. Had the laws been rigidly enforced, that might have been the case. In fact, however, enforcement was spotty and uneven. Some enslaved people did acquire property, did learn to read and write, and did assemble with other enslaved people, in spite of laws to the contrary. Although the major slave offenses generally fell under the jurisdiction of the courts (and thus of the slave codes), slaveholders handled most transgressions and inflicted widely varying punishments. In other words, despite the rigid provisions of law, there was in reality considerable variety within the slave system. Some enslaved people lived in almost prisonlike conditions, rigidly and harshly controlled by their slaveholders. Many (probably most) others enjoyed some flexibility and (at least in comparison to the regimen prescribed by law) a significant degree of autonomy.

Most slaveholders held very few enslaved people, and their experience with (and image of) slavery was a reflection of the special nature of slavery on the small farm. White farmers with fewer enslaved people generally supervised their workers directly and often worked closely alongside them. On such farms, enslaved people and slaveholders developed a form of intimacy unknown on larger plantations. The paternal relationship between such slaveholders and enslaved people could, like relationships between fathers and children, be warm and affectionate. It could also be tyrannical and cruel. In either case, it was a relationship based on the relative powerlessness of enslaved people.

Although the majority of slaveholders were small farmers, the majority of enslaved people lived on plantations of medium or large size, with sizable enslaved workforces. Substantial planters often hired overseers and even assistant overseers to represent them. "Head drivers," trusted and responsible enslaved people often assisted by several subdrivers, acted under the overseer as foremen.

TASK AND GANG SYSTEMS

Larger planters generally used one of two methods of assigning labor. One was the task system (most common in rice culture), under which enslaved people were assigned a particular task in the morning, for example, hoeing one acre; after completing the job, they were free for the rest of the day. The other, far more common, was the gang system (employed on the cotton, sugar, and tobacco plantations), under which enslaved people were simply divided into groups, each of them directed by a driver, and compelled to work for as many hours as the overseer considered a reasonable workday.

Discussion and Activities

Historical Developments and Argumentation After students have read the section "Reality of Slavery," discuss as a class how and why the actual experiences of enslaved people sometimes varied from the legal restrictions imposed upon enslaved people. SOC WXT PCE

LIFE UNDER SLAVERY

Enslaved people generally received at least enough necessities to enable them to live and work. Slaveholders usually furnished them with an adequate, if mostly coarse, diet, consisting mainly of cornmeal, salt pork, molasses, and on special occasions fresh meat or poultry. Many enslaved people cultivated gardens for their own use. They received cheap clothing and shoes. They lived in crude cabins, called slave quarters, usually clustered in a complex near the slaveholder's house. The planter's wife or a doctor retained by the slaveholder provided some medical care; but enslaved women themselves—as "healers" and midwives, or simply as mothers—were the more important source.

Enslaved people worked hard, beginning with light tasks as children. Their workdays were longest at harvest time.

SPECIAL POSITION OF WOMEN

Enslaved women worked particularly hard. They generally labored in the fields with the men, and they assumed as well the crucial chores traditionally reserved for women—cooking, cleaning, and child rearing. Because enslaved families were often divided, with husbands and fathers frequently living on neighboring plantations (or, at times, sold to plantation owners far away), enslaved women often found themselves acting in effect as single parents. Within the family, therefore, enslaved women had special burdens but also a special authority.

Enslaved people were, as a group, much less healthy than white Southerners. After 1808, when the international slave

HIGH MORTALITY RATES

trade became illegal in America, the proportion of African Americans to the white population steadily declined. In 1820, there was one African American to every four white American; in 1840, one to every five. The slower increase of the black population was a result of its comparatively high death rate. Enslaved mothers had large families, but the enforced poverty in which virtually all African Americans lived ensured that fewer of their children would survive to adulthood than the children of white parents. Even those who did survive typically died at a younger age than the average white person.

Even so, according to some scholars, the actual material conditions of slavery may have been better than those of some Northern factory workers and better than those of both peasants and industrial workers in much of nineteenth-century

WAVING FROM THE SHORE This image, from the mid-1800s, depicts enslaved people picking cotton along a riverbank. They are waving to men sitting on bales as they ride the barge on route to the market.

Reasoning Processes

Causation Have students read the section "Special Position of Women." Ask them to think about why enslaved women may have exercised more authority than enslaved men. Have students share their thoughts with a partner, and ask for volunteers to share with the class. **SOC**

Discussion and Activities

Analyzing Visuals Have students examine the image "Waving from the Shore." Ask them to identify details that may reinforce stereotypes of enslaved African Americans. *(Enslaved people are depicted as easily distracted and possibly lazy, with several figures laying on the ground or on the hay bales, and possibly joyful, evidenced by the celebratory atmosphere among those on the shore and the banjo player on the barge.)* Have students discuss in pairs or small groups what the artist's purpose might have been. **SOC**

CHAPTER 11

Cotton, Slavery, and the Old South

Historical Thinking Skills

Sourcing and Situation Have students examine the image "Nursing the Slaveholder's Child." Ask them to discuss in pairs or small groups who would have had the portrait taken and what the purpose would have been. *(The portrait almost certainly would have been arranged by the slaveholder. The purpose likely would have been to perpetuate the idea that enslaved people were well treated and accepted almost as family members.)* **SOC** **PCE**

Europe. The conditions of enslaved people in America were certainly less severe than those of enslaved people in the Caribbean and South America where the crops required more arduous labor. Sugar production in the Caribbean islands, in particular, involved extraordinarily backbreaking work and a high risk of fatal tropical diseases. Caribbean and South American planters continued to use the African slave trade well into the nineteenth century to replenish their labor supply, so they had less incentive than American planters (who no longer had access to that trade) to protect their existing laborers. Growing cotton, the principal activity for most enslaved people in the United States, was much less debilitating than growing sugar; and planters had strong economic incentives to maintain a healthy enslaved population. One result of this was that America became the only country where an enslaved population actually increased through natural reproduction (although it grew much more slowly than the white population).

Most slaveholders did make some effort to preserve the health–and thus the usefulness–of enslaved people. One example was the frequent practice of protecting enslaved children from hard work until early adolescence. Slaveholders believed that doing so would make young enslaved people more loyal and would also ensure better health as adults. Another example was the use of hired labor, when available, for the most unhealthy or dangerous tasks. A traveler in Louisiana noted, for example, that Irishmen were employed to clear malarial swamps and to handle cotton bales at the bottom of chutes extending from the river bluff down to a boat landing. If an Irish worker died of disease or in an accident, a slaveholder could hire another for a dollar a day or less. But a slaveholder would lose an investment of perhaps $1,000 or more if an enslaved field laborer died. Still, cruel slaveholders might forget their pocketbooks in the heat of anger. Enslaved laborers were often left to the discipline of overseers, who had less of an economic stake in their well-being; overseers were paid in proportion to the amount of work they could get out of the enslaved people they supervised.

Enslaved household laborers had a somewhat easier life–physically at least–than did enslaved field laborers. On a small plantation, the same enslaved person might do both field work and housework. But on a large estate, there would generally be a separate enslaved people as: nursemaids, housemaids, cooks, butlers, coachmen. These enslaved people lived close to the slaveholder and his family, eating the leftovers from the family table and in some cases even sleeping in the "big house." Between the slaveholders and enslaved people of such households affectionate, almost familial relationships might sometimes develop. More often, however, enslaved people laboring within households resented their isolation from other enslaved people and the lack of privacy that came with living in such close proximity to the slaveholder's family. Among other things, that proximity meant that their transgressions were more visible than those of field hands, and so they received punishments more often than did other enslaved people. When emancipation came

Enslaved Household Laborers

NURSING THE SLAVEHOLDER'S CHILD This photograph shows an enslaved woman caring for a white child. The image was taken in Arkansas in 1855. Black women typically cared for white children on plantations, sometimes with great affection and sometimes—as this photograph may suggest—dutifully and without enthusiasm.

The Library of Congress (LC-USZC4-5251)

after the Civil War, it was often the enslaved people laboring in households who were the first to leave the plantations of their former slaveholders.

Enslaved women laboring in households were especially vulnerable to sexual abuse by their slaveholders and white overseers, who sometimes pressured them into supposedly consensual sexual relationships and sometimes raped them. In addition to unwanted sexual attention from white men, enslaved women often received vindictive treatment from white women. The wives of plantation owners naturally resented the sexual liaisons between their husbands and enslaved women. Punishing their husbands was not usually possible, so they often punished enslaved women instead–with arbitrary beatings, increased workloads, and various forms of psychological torment.

Sexual Abuse

Slavery in the Cities

The conditions of slavery in the cities differed significantly from those in the countryside. On relatively isolated plantations, enslaved people had little contact with free African Americans and lower class white people, and slaveholders maintained direct and effective control; a deep and seemingly unbridgeable chasm yawned between slavery and freedom. In the city, however, a slaveholder often could not supervise enslaved people closely and at the same time use them profitably. Even if they slept at night in carefully watched backyard

Discussion and Activities

Historical Reasoning and Argumentation After students have read the section "Life Under Slavery," ask them to work in small groups to create a chart demonstrating the hierarchy on a Southern cotton plantation. Have them include the planter and his family, field hands, and household servants, taking into account gender differences. **SOC**

THE CHARACTER OF SLAVERY

No issue in American history has produced a richer literature or a more spirited debate than the nature of American slavery. The debate began even before the Civil War, when abolitionists strove to expose slavery to the world as a brutal, dehumanizing institution, while Southern defenders of slavery tried to depict it as a benevolent, paternalistic system. But by the late nineteenth century, as historian David Blight noted in *Race and Reunion* (2002), with white Americans eager for sectional conciliation, both Northern and Southern chroniclers of slavery began to accept a romanticized and unthreatening picture of the Old South and its "peculiar institution."

The first major scholarly examination of slavery was Ulrich B. Phillips's *American Negro Slavery* (1918), which portrayed slavery as an essentially benign institution in which kindly slaveholders looked after submissive, childlike, and generally contented African Americans. Phillips's apologia for slavery remained the authoritative work on the subject for nearly thirty years.

Challenges to Phillips began to emerge in the 1940s, as concern about racial injustice increasingly engaged the attention of white Americans. In 1941, Melville J. Herskovits challenged Phillips's contention that black Americans retained little of their African cultural inheritance. In 1943, Herbert Aptheker published a chronicle of slave revolts as a way of refuting Phillips's claim that enslaved people were submissive and content.

A somewhat different challenge to Phillips emerged in the 1950s from historians who emphasized the brutality of the institution. Kenneth Stampp's *The Peculiar Institution* (1956) and Stanley Elkins's *Slavery* (1959) described a labor system that did serious physical and psychological damage to its victims. Stampp, and especially Elkins, portrayed slavery as something like a prison, in which men and women had no space in which to develop their own social and cultural lives.

In the 1970s, new scholarship on slavery focused on the success of enslaved people in building a culture of their own despite their enslavement. John Blassingame in 1973 argued that "the most remarkable aspect of the whole process of enslavement is the extent to which the American-born enslaved people were able to retain their ancestors' culture." Herbert Gutman, in *The Black Family in Slavery and Freedom* (1976), challenged the prevailing belief that slavery had weakened and even destroyed the African American family. On the contrary, he argued, the black family survived slavery with impressive strength. Eugene Genovese's *Roll, Jordan, Roll* (1974) and other works revealed how African Americans manipulated the paternalist assumptions at the heart of slavery to build a large cultural space of their own within the system where they could develop their own family life, social traditions, and religious patterns. That same year, Robert Fogel and Stanley Engerman published their controversial *Time on the Cross*, a highly quantitative study that supported some of the claims of Gutman and Genovese about black achievement, but that went much further in portraying slavery as a successful and reasonably humane (if ultimately immoral) system. Enslaved laborers, they argued, were better treated and lived in greater comfort than most Northern industrial workers of the same era.

Other scholarship on slavery has focused on the role of women within it. Elizabeth Fox-Genovese's *Within the Plantation Household* (1988) examined the lives of both white and black women on the plantation. Rejecting the claims of some feminist historians that black and white women shared a common female identity born of their shared subordination to men, she portrayed enslaved women as defined by their dual roles as members of the plantation workforce and anchors of the black family.

Recent works by Walter Johnson and Ira Berlin mark at least a partial return to the "damage" thesis. In *Soul by Soul* (2000), a study of the New Orleans slave market, Johnson contends that for white people, procuring enslaved people was a way of fulfilling the middle-class fantasy of success and independence, but for enslaved people the trade was destructive and dehumanizing. Ira Berlin's *Many Thousands Gone* (2000), *Generation of Captivity* (2003), and *The Making of African America* (2010) similarly emphasize the dehumanizing character of the slave market and argue that slavery was less a social system than a commodification of human beings.

HISTORICAL THINKING SKILLS

Questions assume cumulative content knowledge from this chapter and previous chapters.

1. **Identifying Historical Developments** Identify three broad schools of historical interpretation concerning the nature and character of slavery.
2. **Determining Context** Describe how one piece of historical evidence from the time period could be used to support each of the three broad schools of historical interpretation concerning the nature and character of slavery.
3. **Developing Arguments** Analyze which school of thought you find most convincing, and explain your reasoning.

Discussion and Activities

Analyzing Visuals Have students examine the image accompanying the feature "Debating the Past." Ask them to list details in the image that demonstrate the authority of the slaveholder. *(The slaveholder is mounted on horseback, towering over the enslaved people. He is dressed in fine clothing, in contrast to the ragged clothing of the enslaved people. The distant manor house demonstrates the size of the slaveholder's estate.)* Have students discuss in small groups what the purpose of the image might have been.

WXT **SOC** **PCE**

Answers

Debating the Past

1. Phillips's interpretation portrayed slavery as an essentially benign institution in which kindly masters looked after submissive, childlike African Americans. The interpretations of Stampp and Elkins challenged the paternalistic interpretation of Southern slaveholders, focusing on slavery's brutality. Fogel and Engerman compared the Southern institution of slavery with the situation of Northern industrial workers and found that enslaved workers were sometimes treated better and lived in greater comfort than many Northern workers.
2. First, enslaved people in the Upper South generally lived on relatively smaller plantations, and many worked alongside their slaveholders. They often lived in the main house. Second, pictures coming out of this time period showing African Americans with scars and other injuries reinforces the fact that enslaved people were often subjected to extreme punishment to ensure compliance with work. Third, recent research has shown that enslaved people who lived on large plantations in the Lower South often lived in communities where there was opportunity to socialize with others, despite brutal working conditions.
3. Student responses will vary.

Reasoning Processes

Comparing and Contrasting After students have read the section "Autonomy of Urban Enslaved People," ask them to create a Janus figure using symbols and words to compare and contrast the lives of urban enslaved people with those of enslaved people working on plantations. **SOC** **WXT**

barracks, enslaved people moved about during the day alone, performing errands of various kinds. Thus urban enslaved people gained numerous opportunities to mingle with free African Americans and white people. In the cities, the line between slavery and freedom became increasingly indistinct.

AUTONOMY OF URBAN ENSLAVED PEOPLE

There was a considerable market in the South for common laborers, particularly since, unlike in the North, there were few European immigrants to perform menial chores. Even the poorest white people tended to prefer working on farms to doing ordinary labor, and so slaveholders often hired out enslaved people for such tasks. Enslaved people on contract worked in mining and lumbering (often far from cities); but others worked on the docks and on construction sites, drove wagons, and performed other unskilled jobs in cities and towns. Enslaved women and children worked in the region's few textile mills. Particularly skilled workers such as blacksmiths or carpenters were also often hired out.

Many white Southerners considered slavery to be incompatible with city life, and as Southern cities grew the number of enslaved people in them declined, relatively if not absolutely. Fearing conspiracies and insurrections, many urban slaveholders sold off enslaved men to rural slaveholders. The remaining enslaved women outnumbered enslaved men. The same cities also had more white men than women—a situation that helped account for the birth of many mulattoes, as they were referred to at the time. Even while slavery in the cities was declining, the forced segregation of urban blacks, both free and enslaved, from white society increased. Segregation was a means of social control intended to make up for the loosening of the discipline of slavery in urban areas.

FREE AFRICAN AMERICANS

There were about 250,000 free African Americans in the slaveholding states by the start of the Civil War, more than half of them in Virginia and Maryland. In some cases, they were formerly enslaved people who had somehow earned money with which they managed to buy their own and their families' freedom, usually by developing a skill they could market independently of slaveholders. It was usually urban enslaved people, with their greater freedom of movement and activity, who could take that route. One example was Elizabeth Keckley, an enslaved woman who bought freedom for herself and her son with proceeds from sewing. She later became a seamstress, personal servant, and companion to Mary Todd Lincoln in the White House. But few slaveholders had any incentive, or inclination, to give up their enslaved people, so this route was open to relatively few people.

TIGHTENED RESTRICTIONS

Some enslaved people were sometimes set free by a slaveholder who had moral qualms about slavery, or by a slaveholder's will after his death—for example, the more than 400 enslaved people held by John Randolph of Roanoke, freed in 1833. From the 1830s on, however, state laws governing slavery became more rigid. That was in part a response to the fears Nat Turner's revolt created among white Southerners: free African Americans, removed from close supervision by white people, might generate more violence and rebellion than enslaved people. It was also in part because the community of free African Americans in Southern cities was becoming larger and, to white people, more threatening—a dangerous example to enslaved people. The rise of abolitionist agitation in the North—and the fear that it would inspire enslaved people to rebel—also persuaded Southern whites to tighten their system. The new laws made it more and more difficult, and in some cases practically impossible, for slaveholders to set free (or "manumit") enslaved people; all Southern states forbade free African Americans from entering. Arkansas even forced the freed African Americans living there to leave.

A few free African Americans (generally those on the northern fringes of the slaveholding regions) attained wealth and prominence. Some were slaveholders themselves, usually relatives whom they had bought in order to ensure their ultimate emancipation. In a few cities—New Orleans, Natchez, Charleston—free black communities managed to flourish relatively unmolested by white people and with some economic stability. Most free African Americans, however, lived in abject poverty, under conditions worse than those of African Americans in the North. Law or custom closed many occupations to them, forbade them to assemble without white supervision, and placed numerous other restraints on them. They were only quasi-free, but they had all the burdens of freedom: the necessity to support themselves, to find housing, to pay taxes. Yet, great as were the hardships of freedom, these African Americans preferred them to slavery.

THE SLAVE TRADE

SLAVE MARKETS

The transfer of enslaved people from one part of the South to another was one of the most important and terrible consequences of slavery. Sometimes enslaved people moved to the new cotton lands in the company of their original slaveholders, who were migrating themselves. But more often, the transfer occurred through the efforts of professional slave traders. For shorter journeys enslaved people traveled on foot, trudging in coffles of hundreds along dusty highways. For transfers over longer distances, the traders conveyed enslaved people via river or ocean steamers. Central slave markets included Natchez, New Orleans, Charleston, and Mobile. In the 1840s and 1850s, healthy young field hands could fetch between $500 and $1,700, depending on the fluctuations in the market.

The domestic slave trade, essential to the growth and prosperity of the system, was one of its most horrible aspects. The trade dehumanized all who were involved in it. It separated children from their parents and parents from each other. Even families who had long been together might be broken up by new slaveholders in the division of the estate after a slaveholder's death. Planters might deplore the trade, but they eased their consciences by holding traders in contempt.

Discussion and Activities

Analyzing Point of View Have students read the section "Free African Americans." Ask them to write a short paragraph describing both the opportunities and challenges free African Americans faced. **SOC** **WXT** **PCE**

THE BUSINESS OF SLAVERY The offices of slave dealers were familiar sights on the streets of pre–Civil War Southern cities and towns. They provide testimony to the way in which slavery was not just a social system, but a business, deeply woven into the fabric of Southern economic life.

The Foreign Slave Trade

The foreign slave trade was usually badly conducted, resulting in many people dying along the way. Although federal law had prohibited the importation of enslaved people from 1808 on, some continued to be smuggled into the United States as late as the 1850s when the supply of enslaved people had become inadequate. At the annual Southern commercial conventions, planters began to discuss the legal reopening of the trade. "If it is right to buy slaves in Virginia and carry them to New Orleans," William L. Yancey of Alabama asked his fellow delegates in 1858, "why is it not right to buy them in Cuba, Brazil, or Africa?" The convention that year voted to repeal all the laws against importation of enslaved people, but the government never acted on its proposal.

The continued smuggling was not without resistance from the enslaved people themselves. In 1839, a group of fifty-three enslaved people in Cuba took charge of the ship *Amistad* that was transporting them to another part of Cuba. Their goal was to sail back to their homeland in Africa. The enslaved people had no experience with sailing, and they tried to compel the crew to steer them across the Atlantic. Instead, the ship sailed up the Atlantic coast until it was captured by a ship of the United States Revenue Service. Many Americans, including President Van Buren, thought the enslaved people should be returned to Cuba. But at the request of a group of abolitionists, former president John Quincy Adams went before the Supreme Court to argue that they should be freed. Adams argued that the foreign slave trade was illegal and thus the *Amistad* rebels could not be returned to slavery. The Court accepted his argument in 1841, and most of the former enslaved people were returned to Africa, with funding from American abolitionists.

Two years later, in 1841, another group of enslaved people revolted on board a ship and took control of it–this time an American vessel bound from Norfolk, Virginia, to New Orleans–

REVOLT ON THE *AMISTAD* Joseph Cinquez led the revolt of enslaved Africans on the Spanish vessel *Amistad* en route to Cuba in June 1839. Once exonerated of charges of murder and piracy, he was reported to have said, "Brothers, we have done that which we purposed, our hands are now clean for we have Striven to regain the precious heritage we received from our fathers. . . . I am resolved it is better to die than to be a white man's slave."

Discussion and Activities

Historical Developments and Argumentation Have students read the section "The Foreign Slave Trade." Ask them to go online to http://tracesofthetrade.org/synopsis to read a synopsis of the film "Traces of the Trade: Tales from the Deep North." As a class, discuss how the slave trade was able to continue after 1808. **PCE** **WXT** **SOC**

Discussion and Activities

Analyzing Visuals Have students examine the image "Revolt on the *Amistad*." Ask them to write a short paragraph describing the details of the scene. *(Onboard the* Amistad, *African Americans rally around their leader. They have apparently already taken over the ship, though there is no sign of violence or struggle between them and the officers and crew of the ship, who appear more curious than anything else.)* **SOC** **PCE**

Discussion and Activities

Comparison and Argumentation Have students have read the beginning of the section "Slave Resistance." In pairs, have them create charts listing what they believe the advantages and disadvantages might have been to each of the two types of response methods to slavery discussed in the section.

and steered it (and its 135 enslaved people) to the British Bahamas, where slavery was illegal and the enslaved people were given sanctuary. Such shipboard revolts were rare, but they were symbols of the continued efforts by Africans to resist slavery.

SLAVE RESISTANCE

Few issues have sparked as much debate among historians as the effects of slavery on African Americans themselves. Slaveholders, and many white Americans after emancipation, liked to argue that enslaved people were generally content, "happy with their lot." That may have been true in some cases. But it is clear that the vast majority of Southern African Americans were not content being enslaved and, that they yearned for freedom even though most realized there was little they could do to secure it. Evidence for that conclusion can be found, if nowhere else, from the reaction of enslaved people when emancipation finally came. Virtually all reacted to freedom with joy and celebration; few chose to remain in the service of slaveholders (although most African Americans remained for many years subservient to white people in one way or another).

Rather than contented acceptance, the dominant response of African Americans to slavery was a complex one: a combination of adaptation and resistance. At the extremes, slavery could produce two very different reactions, each serving as the basis for a powerful stereotype in white society. One extreme was what became known as the "Sambo"—the shuffling, grinning, head-scratching, deferential enslaved person who acted out the role that he recognized the white world expected of him. More often than not, the "Sambo" pattern of behavior was a charade, a façade assumed in the presence of white people. The other extreme was the slave rebel—the African American who could not bring himself or herself to either acceptance or accommodation but remained forever rebellious. Actual slave revolts were extremely rare, but the knowledge that they were possible struck terror into the hearts of white Southerners everywhere. In 1800, Gabriel Prosser gathered 1,000 enslaved people in preparation for a revolt outside Richmond; but two Africans gave the plot away, and the Virginia militia stymied the uprising before it could begin. Prosser and thirty-five others were executed. In 1822, the Charleston free black Denmark Vesey and his followers—rumored to total 9,000—made preparations for revolt; but again word leaked out, and suppression and retribution followed. In 1831, Nat Turner, a slave preacher, led a band of African Americans who armed themselves with guns and axes and, on a summer night, went

PROSSER AND TURNER REBELLIONS

HARRIET TUBMAN WITH ESCAPED ENSLAVED PEOPLE Harriet Tubman (c. 1820–1913) was born into slavery in Maryland. In 1849, when her slaveholder died, she escaped to Philadelphia to avoid being sold out of state. Over the next ten years, she assisted first members of her own family and then up to 300 other enslaved people to escape from Maryland to freedom. During the Civil War, she served alternately as a nurse and as a spy for Union forces in South Carolina. She is shown here, on the left, with some of the enslaved people she had helped to free.

Reasoning Processes

Comparing Have students examine the image "Harriet Tubman With Escaped Enslaved People." As a class, discuss how Harriet Tubman's acts of resistance to slavery were similar to or different from other acts of resistance.

THE ROLE OF MUSIC

For African Americans living as enslaved people on Southern plantations, there was little leisure time—and little opportunity for the kinds of cultural activities that were beginning to appeal to other groups of Americans. But enslaved people managed nevertheless to create a culture of their own. And among its most distinctive and pervasive features was music.

Indeed, to white observers at least, nothing was more striking about the life of enslaved people than the role music played within it. African Americans sang frequently, sometimes alone, more often in groups. They sang while they worked together in the fields, as they shucked corn, slaughtered hogs, or repaired fences. They sang whenever they had social gatherings—on Sundays or on the rare other holidays from work. They sang when they gathered for chores in the evenings. They sang during their religious services. And they sang with a passion, at times even an ecstasy, that was completely unfamiliar to white Americans—and sometimes troubling to them.

Their songs were rarely written down and often seemed entirely spontaneous; but much of the music was really derived from African and Caribbean traditions passed on through generations and from snatches of other songs the performers had heard before and from which they improvised variations. In its emotionalism, its pulsing rhythms, and its lack of conventional formal structure, it resembled nothing its white listeners had ever heard before.

Enslaved people sang whether or not there were any musical instruments to accompany them, but they often created instruments for themselves out of whatever materials were at hand. "Us take pieces of sheep's rib or cow's jaw or a piece of iron, with an old kettle or a hollow gourd and some horsehair to make the drum," one former enslaved person recalled years later. "They'd take the buffalo horn and scrape it out to make the flute." When they could, they would build banjos, an instrument that had originated in Africa. Slaveholders sometimes gave them violins and guitars. When the setting permitted it, African Americans danced to their music—dances very different from and much more spontaneous than the formal steps that nineteenth-century white people generally learned. They also used music to accompany one of their other important cultural traditions: storytelling. Black music on the plantations took a number of forms. The most common was religious songs, the precursors of modern gospel music, which expressed—in terms that slaveholders, who usually did not listen to the words very carefully, found acceptable—a faith in their eventual freedom and salvation and often spoke of Africans as a chosen people waiting for redemption. At other times, the songs would express a bitterness toward white slaveholders. The great black abolitionist Frederick Douglass remembered one:

We raise de wheat,
Dey gib us de corn;
We bake de bread,
Dey gib us de crust;
We sif the meal,
Dey gib us de huss;
We peel de meat,
Dey gib us de skin;
And dat's de way
Dey take us in;
We skim de pot,
Dey gib us de liquor,
And say dat's good enough for nigger.
Your butter and the fat;
Poor nigger, you can't ever get that.

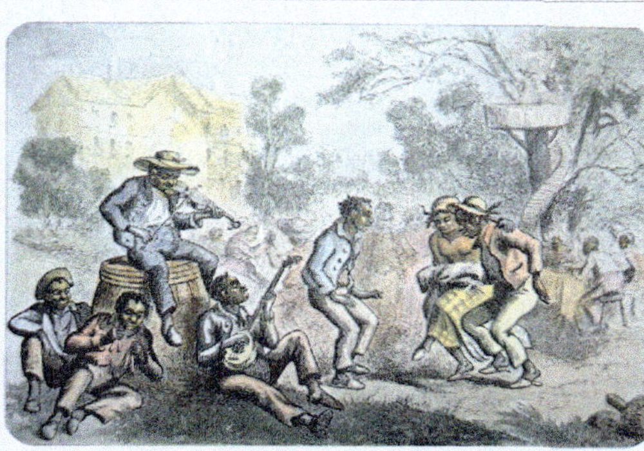

SLAVE MUSIC This folk painting illustrates the importance of music to enslaved people (and at times to slaveholders). The banjo in the hands of the man in the center was an instrument that originated in Africa.

To African Americans, music was a treasured avenue of escape from the hardships of slavery. It was also a vehicle through which they could express anger, resentment, and hope. Slaveholders generally tolerated African American music—and even valued it, both because they often enjoyed listening to it and because the more intelligent understood that without this means of emotional and spiritual release, active resistance to slavery might be more frequent.

The powerful music that emerged from slavery helped shape the lives of African Americans on the plantations. It also helped lay the foundations for music that almost all Americans later embraced: gospel, blues, jazz, rhythm and blues, rock, and rap.

HISTORICAL THINKING SKILLS

1. **Drawing Conclusions** Does the prominent place of music in slave culture support the thesis that slavery was essentially a benign institution? Why or why not?
2. **Explaining Historical Developments** What were some of the different functions that music played in African American slave culture and society?
3. **Identifying Historical Developments** What more recent musical forms continue to shape a distinct African American culture?

Discussion and Activities

Making Connections Ask students to read the song lyrics included in the feature. Have them work in small groups to create a list of definitions of slang terms used in the lyrics, and then rewrite the song in the form of a tweet or social media post.

Answers

Patterns of Popular Culture

1. Possible response: The prominence of slave music does not support this thesis. In fact, the opposite could be argued—that slave music was one of the few tools available to enslaved people to cope with and sometimes fight back against the brutality of slavery.
2. Music served different functions for African Americans then much like it does for everyone today. Music was often a form of entertainment, it was used in religious ceremonies, and it was also used to vent frustration. It also served an educational purpose, especially as the Civil War drew closer. African Americans often used music as a way to resist slavery and provide information about ways of escape.
3. Music is always a representation of culture, regardless of the group or time period one might study. Later music within the African American community included genres like gospel, blues, jazz, rhythm and blues, rock, and rap. All of these also served, and continue to serve, the purpose of entertainment, instruction, and venting frustration.

Reasoning Processes

Evaluating After students have read the section "Prosser and Turner Rebellions," ask them to create a Venn diagram comparing these two resistance movements. Then, discuss as a class which one was more important or effective, and why. **SOC** **PCE**

from house to house in Southampton County, Virginia. They killed sixty white men, women, and children before being overpowered by state and federal troops. More than a hundred African Americans were executed in the aftermath. Nat Turner's was the only large-scale slave insurrection in the nineteenth-century South, but fear of slave conspiracies and renewed violence pervaded the section as long as slavery lasted.

For the most part, however, resistance to slavery took less drastic forms such as running away. A small number of enslaved people managed to escape to the North or to Canada, especially after sympathetic whites began organizing the so-called underground railroad to assist them in flight. But the odds against a successful escape, particularly from the Deep South, were almost impossibly high. The hazards of distance and the lack of geographical knowledge were serious obstacles for enslaved people seeking freedom. So were the white "slave patrols," which stopped African Americans on sight throughout the South demanding to see travel permits. Without such a permit, enslaved people were presumed to be runaways and were taken captive. Slave patrols often employed bloodhounds to track African Americans who attempted to escape through the woods. Despite all the obstacles to success, however, African Americans continued to run away from their slaveholders in large numbers. Some did so repeatedly, undeterred by the whippings and other penalties inflicted on them when captured.

But perhaps the most important method of resistance was simply a pattern of everyday behavior by which enslaved people defied slaveholders. That white people so often considered African Americans to be lazy and shiftless suggests one means of resistance: refusal to work hard.

SLAVE RESISTANCE

Some enslaved people stole from their slaveholders or from neighboring white people. Some performed isolated acts of sabotage: losing or breaking tools (Southern planters gradually began to buy unusually heavy hoes because so many of the lighter ones got broken) or performing tasks improperly. Many enslaved people resisted by building into their normal patterns of behavior subtle methods of rebellion.

THE CULTURE OF SLAVERY

Resistance was only part of the response of enslaved people to slavery. Another was an elaborate process of adaptation. The process did not imply contentment with bondage. It represented a recognition that there was no realistic alternative. One of the ways enslaved people adapted was by developing their own, separate culture, one that enabled them to sustain a sense of racial pride and unity.

LANGUAGE AND MUSIC

In many areas, enslaved people retained a language of their own, sometimes incorporating African speech patterns into English. Having arrived in America speaking many different African languages, the first generations of enslaved people had as much difficulty communicating with one another as they did with white people. To overcome these barriers, they learned a simple, common language (known to linguists as "pidgin"). It retained some African words, but it drew primarily, if selectively, from English. And while slave language grew more sophisticated as enslaved Africans spent more time in America—and as new generations grew up never having known African tongues—some features of this early pidgin survived in black speech for many generations.

PIDGIN

Music was especially important in slave society. In some ways, it was as important to African Americans as language. Most important were voices and song. Enslaved field workers often used songs to pass the time in the fields; since they sang them in the presence of white people, they usually attached relatively innocuous words to them. But African Americans also created emotionally rich and politically challenging music in the relative privacy of their religious services. It was there that the tradition of the spiritual emerged in the early nineteenth century.

IMPORTANCE OF SPIRITUALS

AFRICAN AMERICAN RELIGION

A separate slave religion was not supposed to exist. Almost all African Americans were Christians by the early nineteenth century. Some had converted voluntarily, and some were coerced by their slaveholders and by the Protestant missionaries who evangelized among them. Slaveholders expected enslaved people to worship under the supervision of white ministers. Indeed, autonomous black churches were banned by law; and many enslaved people became members of the same denominations as the slaveholders—usually Baptist or Methodist. In the 1840s and 1850s, as slavery expanded in the South, missionary efforts increased. Vast numbers of African Americans became members of Protestant churches in those years.

Nevertheless, African Americans throughout the South developed their own version of Christianity, at times incorporating into it such practices as voodoo or other polytheistic religious traditions of Africa. Or they simply bent religion to the special circumstances of bondage. Natural leaders emerging within the slave community rose to the rank of preacher.

African American religion was often more emotional than that of its white counterparts and reflected the influence of African customs and practices. Slave prayer meetings routinely involved fervent chanting, spontaneous exclamations from the congregation, and ecstatic conversion experiences. Black religion was also more joyful and affirming than that of many white denominations. And above all, African American religion emphasized the dream of freedom and deliverance. In their prayers and songs and sermons, black Christians talked and sang of the day when the Lord would "call us home," "deliver us to freedom," "take us to the Promised Land." And while slaveholders generally chose to interpret such language merely as the expression of hopes for life after death, many African

SLAVE RELIGION

Discussion and Activities

Historical Reasoning and Argumentation Have students read the section "Language and Music." Ask them to write a short paragraph explaining how new dialects and music enabled enslaved people to form new communities despite all the challenges they faced. **SOC**

Americans themselves used the images of Christian salvation to express their own dream of freedom in the present world. Christian images, and biblical injunctions, were central to Gabriel Prosser, Denmark Vesey, Nat Turner, and others who planned or engaged in open resistance to slavery.

In cities and towns in the South, some African Americans had their own churches, where free African Americans occasionally worshiped alongside enslaved people. In the countryside, however, enslaved people usually attended the same churches as slaveholders–sometimes a chapel on the plantation itself, sometimes a church serving a larger farm community. Seating in such churches was usually segregated. Enslaved people sat in the rear or in balconies. They held their own services later, often in secret, usually at night.

THE SLAVE FAMILY

The slave family was the other crucial institution of black culture in the South. Like religion, it suffered from certain legal restrictions–most notably the lack of legal marriage. Nevertheless, what we now call the "nuclear family" consistently emerged as the dominant kinship model among African Americans.

Such families did not always operate according to white customs. Black women generally began bearing children at younger ages than most white women, often as early as age fourteen or fifteen. Slave communities did not condemn premarital pregnancy in the way white society did, and African American couples would often begin living together before marrying. It was customary, however, for couples to marry–in a ceremony involving formal vows–soon after conceiving a child. Often, marriages occurred between enslaved people living on neighboring plantations. Husbands and wives sometimes visited each other with the permission of slaveholders, but often such visits had to be in secret, at night. Family ties were no less strong than those of white families, and many slave marriages lasted throughout the course of long lifetimes.

SLAVE MARRIAGES

When marriages did not survive, it was often because of circumstances over which enslaved people had no control. Up to a third of all families were broken apart by the slave trade; an average enslaved person might expect during a lifetime to see ten or more relatives sold. And that accounted for some of the other distinctive characteristics of the black family, which adapted itself to the cruel realities of its own uncertain future. Extended kinship networks–which grew to include not only spouses and their children, but also aunts, uncles, grandparents, even distant cousins–were strong and important and often helped compensate for the breakup of nuclear families. An enslaved person forced suddenly to move to a new area, far from his or her family, might create fictional kinship ties and become "adopted" by a family in the new community. Even so, the impulse to maintain contact with a spouse and children remained strong long after the breakup of a family. One of the most frequent causes of flight from the plantation was an enslaved persons desire to find a husband, wife, or child who had been sent elsewhere.

IMPORTANCE OF KINSHIP NETWORKS

It was not only by breaking up families through sale that slaveholders intruded on black family life. Enslaved women, usually powerless to resist the sexual advances of slaveholders, often bore the children of white men–children whom slaveholders almost never recognized as their own and who were consigned to slavery from birth.

In addition to establishing social and cultural institutions of their own, enslaved people adapted themselves to slavery by forming complex relationships with slaveholders. However much enslaved people resented their lack of freedom, they often found it difficult to maintain an entirely hostile attitude toward slaveholders. Not only were they dependent on slaveholders for the material means of existence–food, clothing, and shelter; they also often derived a sense of security and protection. There was, in short, a paternal relationship between enslaved person and slaveholder–sometimes harsh, sometimes kindly, but almost invariably important. Paternalism, in fact, became (even if not always consciously) a vital instrument of white control. By creating a sense of mutual dependence, white slaveholders helped reduce resistance to an institution that, in essence, served only the interests of the ruling race.

PATERNAL NATURE OF SLAVERY

Historical Thinking Skills

Argumentation After students have read the section "African American Religion," ask them to discuss in pairs or small groups how religious expression by African Americans could be viewed as both conforming to and defying the expectations of white society. *(While some African Americans did become members of the same churches as white slaveholders, others incorporated non-Christian elements into their religious practices or maintained a façade of orthodox Christianity while attaching subversive meanings to it.)* **SOC** **PCE**

Discussion and Activities

Analyzing Continuity Have students read the section "The Slave Family." As a class, discuss how communities of enslaved African Americans were able to maintain a sense of family despite all the challenges and restrictions they faced. **SOC** **PCE**

Discussion and Activities

Understanding Change Have the class divide into four groups to research how the lives of white men, white women, African American men, and African American women in the South changed as a result of the South's growing economic reliance on cotton. Then, have a representative from each group share their group's conclusions with the class. **SOC** **WXT** **PCE** **NAT**

Key Terms

Students should be familiar with the key terms and be able to define them in the context of how increased Southern reliance on the cultivation of cotton and the use of the labor of enslaved African Americans redefined the economy and culture of the South. Encourage students to use these terms in performing review exercises and exam practice for this chapter.

CHAPTER 11 REVIEW

CONNECTING THEMES

Chapter 11 examined the importance of both cotton production and the institution of slavery in forming a distinct Southern regional identity. The South also developed a rigid class system. Most white people were poor farmers who lived in rural areas, but a small group of wealthy planters dominated the region's economy, politics, and society.

African Americans, both free and enslaved, experienced a variety of conditions in the South. The region's political and economic structure deeply affected their lives. Adaptation and resistance to slavery, along with racism aimed at both urban and rural African Americans, influenced the development of a unique culture, which to this day has greatly affected American culture as a whole.

You should consider the following questions as you review the themes for this chapter:

- What were the factors that led to the creation of a distinct regional identity for white Southerners and the characteristics that set that society apart from that of other regions?
- How did the nature of the Southern economy impact the development of Southern society?
- How did the labor system in the South compare and contrast with the labor system in the North?
- How did the development of "King Cotton" and the institution of slavery lead to a distinct regional political system in the South?
- In what ways did the natural environment impact the development of the South's political and economic identities?
- How were gender roles similar and different within both white and slave societies in the South?

KEY TERMS

cult of honor 313
De Bow's Review 310
Denmark Vesey 322
Gabriel Prosser 322
gang system 316
Nat Turner 320
paternalism 315
pidgin 324
"Sambo" 322
Slave Codes 316
spirituals 324
task system 303

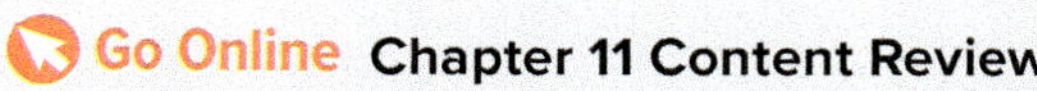

Go Online Chapter 11 Content Review

Assessing Student Understanding Use the online assessment to assess student understanding of concepts and topics within the chapter. You can assign the ready-made Chapter 11 Content Review or create your own from available questions. This easy-to-use tool helps you design assessments that meet the needs of different types of learners.

AP EXAM PRACTICE

Questions assume cumulative content knowledge from this chapter and previous chapters.

MULTIPLE CHOICE

Use the maps on page 309 and your knowledge of U.S. history to answer questions 1-3.

1. Which of the following most significantly led to the trends shown by the maps?
   (A) the development of technology that streamlined the processing of cotton
   (B) prohibition of international slave trade, leading to a decrease in reliance on enslaved laborers
   (C) significant investment by Southern states in a canal network to improve the transport of cotton
   (D) abolition of slavery by multiple states in the South, leading to a search for alternate labor sources

2. What national policy enabled the trend shown by the maps?
   (A) the arrival of Irish and German immigrants, who served as agricultural workers
   (B) the development of a separate spheres ideology to open up agricultural work to women
   (C) the removal of Native Americans, which allowed expansion across the Southeast
   (D) the spread of the Second Great Awakening and the formation of new religious groups

3. Which of the following most accurately reflects the economic relationship that developed between U.S. regions by 1860?
   (A) a strong national banking system that supported agricultural interests of both the North and the South
   (B) the North supplying the labor force to build Southern canals and railroads
   (C) the South supplying the majority of food products for Northern factory workers
   (D) the South supplying the cotton for Northern textile factories

SHORT ANSWER

Use your knowledge of U.S. history to answer questions 4 and 5.

4. Use the image on page 306 to answer A, B, and C.
   (A) Briefly describe ONE historical perspective about slavery in the image.
   (B) Briefly explain ONE specific historical difference within slave communities as they existed in the United States.
   (C) Briefly explain ONE specific historical similarity within slave communities as they existed in the United States.

5. Answer A, B, and C.
   (A) Briefly describe ONE specific historical similarity between the North and the South in antebellum America.
   (B) Briefly describe ONE specific historical difference between the North and South in antebellum America.
   (C) Briefly explain ONE specific effect that resulted from a difference between the North and the South in antebellum America.

LONG ESSAY

Develop a thoughtful and thorough historical argument that addresses the statement. Begin your essay with a thesis statement, and support it with specific historical evidence and examples.

6. Evaluate the relative importance of the effects of the institution of slavery in the South from 1800 to 1850.

Answers

Multiple Choice

1. A; **2.** C; **3.** D

Short Answer

4A) Possible answer: This painting was very controversial because it presented slave life in a relatively positive light. The couple in the middle of the painting is getting married, and the ceremony is part of the African American tradition of the bride and groom jumping over a stick to signify the ending of the ceremony.

4B) Possible answer: The life of African Americans differed depending on where one lived. Life in the Upper South differed greatly from life in the Deep (or Lower) South. Life in the city also differed from life on the plantations. Enslaved people living on the plantations often had little contact with free African Americans or lower-class whites.

4C) Possible answer: Enslaved people, whether they lived in cities or in urban centers, were still considered property. They had little to no legal rights.

5A) Possible answer: Both the North and the South relied heavily on the institution of slavery to fuel their economies. The South relied more directly, by using slave labor to work in the cotton fields. The North relied more indirectly, as Southern cotton was used in much of the Northern textile mills. This was also true in other industries. Northern bankers provided slaveholders with loans to purchase more enslaved people, Northern insurance companies insured enslaved people, and Northern shipping provided transportation overseas to European textile manufacturing.

5B) Possible answer: As the country overall progressed and evolved, the South continued to remain largely an agricultural economy. The North, on the other hand, relied more on a variety of different industries to fuel its economy.

5C) Possible answer: As the two geographic regions continued to diverge economically, this spilled over into political issues. Federal taxes were viewed as protecting Northern industry at the expense of Southern agriculture. The resulting feelings of neglect and resentment helped fuel the fire of the Civil War during the 1860s.

Answers

Long Essay

6. Possible thesis: Slavery affected all parts of the South. It created a dependent economy, and that dependence ended up being a huge liability once the Civil War began. Slavery created a wedge between the North and the South. The most significant effect of slavery was on African Americans. They were forced to live a life completely opposed to the principles that America claimed it was founded on. Despite this, African Americans were resilient and developed a unique culture. Historical evidence: The tobacco economy was in decline in the South, but the boom of the textile industry in both England and the North, along with the development of the cotton gin, created a huge demand for slave labor to cultivate cotton. But this Southern cotton agriculture, while it brought great wealth to a small number of plantation farmers, also hamstringed the Southern economy by making it dependent on one crop. This weakened the Southern economy as a whole. As the country developed and evolved, two regions developed in the South: the Upper South and the Lower South. Enslaved people were "sold down the river" as the Upper South's economy slowly moved away from the need for large-scale slave labor. However, this meant that slavery grew exponentially in the Lower South.

Pacing Guide

Chapter 12 explores key concepts from Period 4: 1800–1848 of the AP U.S. History Curriculum Framework. The suggested instruction time for Chapter 12 is 3 days.

Key Concepts

4.1.II While Americans embraced a new national culture, various groups developed distinctive cultures of their own.

4.1.III Increasing numbers of Americans, many inspired by new religious and intellectual movements, worked primarily outside of government institutions to advance their ideals.

12 ANTEBELLUM CULTURE AND REFORM

GIRLS' EVENING SCHOOL (C. 1840), ANONYMOUS Schooling for women, which expanded significantly in the mid-nineteenth century, included training in domestic arts (as indicated by the sewing table at right), as well as in reading, writing, and other basic skills.

CONNECTING CONCEPTS

Chapter 12 begins by exploring how Romanticism inspired the artistic and literary movements sometimes known as the First American Renaissance. This movement rejected much of the ideas of the Enlightenment and its emphasis on the individual's ability to reason to the point of discovering absolute truth through scientific understanding and exploration. American intellectuals in the early nineteenth century worked to establish an artistic world that was both independent of Europe and that expressed the unique virtues of the nation.

Reform movements stimulated by growing urbanization and the Second Great Awakening were also important developments. Often these movements promoted responses to major issues of the time, such as temperance, women's rights, abolitionism, education, and prison reform. The abolitionist movement, although initially small and fragmented, gathered strength and influence as the nation veered toward conflict. Many reformers also believed in the perfectibility of the individual and society, an idea known as utopianism. From this idea, various communitarian experiments emerged, although most were short lived.

Discussion and Activities

Comparing and Contrasting Have students examine the image "Girls' Evening School." Discuss as a class how the scene depicted is similar to or different from the school they currently attend. **SOC**

CHAPTER 12
ANTEBELLUM CULTURE AND REFORM

As you read, you should:

- Analyze the causes and effects of the American Renaissance, especially with regard to art and literature.
- Evaluate the causes and effects of the Second Great Awakening.
- Describe the ways that African Americans participated in the abolitionist movement.
- Identify ways that the women's rights movement challenged traditional beliefs about gender roles.
- Describe how the South remained politically, culturally, and ideologically distinct from other geographic regions of the country.
- Assess the ways that abolitionists, despite being a small minority in the North, intensified sectional conflict.

THE ROMANTIC IMPULSE

"In the four quarters of the globe," wrote the English wit Sydney Smith in 1820, "who reads an American book? or goes to an American play? or looks at an American picture or statue?" The answer, he assumed, was obvious: no one. American intellectuals were fully aware of the low regard in which Europeans held their artistic and intellectual life. In the middle decades of the nineteenth century, they continued to work for both an elevation and a liberation of their nation's culture–for the creation of an American artistic world independent of Europe, one that would express their nation's special virtues.

NATIONAL CULTURAL ASPIRATIONS

At the same time, however, some of the nation's cultural leaders were beginning to strive for another kind of liberation, one that would eventually overshadow their self-conscious nationalism. That impulse–which was, ironically, largely an import from Europe–was the spirit of romanticism. In literature, philosophy, art, even in politics and economics, American intellectuals were committing themselves to the liberation of the human spirit.

NATIONALISM AND ROMANTICISM IN AMERICAN PAINTING

When Sydney Smith asked in 1820 who looked at an American painting, he was expressing the belief among European artists that they–and they alone–stood at the center of the world of art. But in the United States, many people were looking at American paintings in the antebellum era–and they were doing so not because the paintings introduced them to the great traditions of Europe, but because they believed Americans were creating important new artistic traditions.

The most important and popular American paintings of the first half of the nineteenth century set out to evoke the wonder of the nation's landscape. Unlike their European counterparts, American painters did not favor gentle scenes of carefully cultivated countrysides. They sought instead to capture the undiluted power of nature by portraying some of the nation's wildest and most spectacular areas–to evoke what many nineteenth-century people called the "sublime," the feeling of awe and wonderment and even fear of the grandeur of nature. The first great school of American painters emerged in New York. Frederic Church, Thomas Cole, Thomas Doughty, and Asher Durand–known, along with others, as the Hudson River School–painted the spectacular vistas of the rugged and still largely unsettled Hudson Valley. Like Emerson and Thoreau, whom many of the painters read and admired, they considered nature–more than civilization–the best source of wisdom and spiritual fulfillment. In portraying the Hudson Valley, they seemed to announce that in America, unlike in Europe, "wild nature" still existed; and that America, therefore, was a nation of greater promise than the played-out lands of the Old World. Yet there was also a sense of nostalgia in many of the Hudson River paintings, an effort to preserve and cherish a kind of nature that many Americans feared was fast disappearing.

HUDSON RIVER SCHOOL

In later years, some of the Hudson River painters traveled farther west, in search of more profound spiritual experiences. They found an even more rugged and spectacular natural world. Their enormous canvases of great natural wonders–the Yosemite Valley, Yellowstone, the Rocky Mountains–touched a passionate chord among the American public. Some of the most famous of their paintings–particularly the works of Albert Bierstadt and Thomas Moran–traveled around the country attracting enormous crowds.

Discussion and Activities

Explaining Historical Concepts Have students read the section "National Cultural Aspirations." Ask them to create a KWL chart listing what they know about nineteenth century American art and Romanticism, what they want to know, and later, what they learned. Have students add to their charts as they read the chapter. **SOC** **ARC**

Go Online AP Exam Preparation

AP Exam Practice Use the online assessment to help prepare students for the AP Exam. You can assign the ready-made AP-style short-answer questions, document-based questions, and multiple-choice questions assessing concepts, themes, and skills from Period 4 and AP style long-essay questions organized in sets of 3 questions from various time periods. You can also create your own tests from available questions. This easy-to-use tool helps you design assessments that meet the needs of different types of learners.

Discussion and Activities

Making Generalizations After students have read the section "Literature and the Quest for Liberation," have them create 5-column charts listing the main characteristics of the works of Scott, Cooper, Whitman, Melville, and Poe. As a class, discuss how these different types of literature worked together to begin to create a new American identity. **SOC**

LITERATURE AND THE QUEST FOR LIBERATION

American readers in the first decades of the nineteenth century were relatively indifferent to the work of their nation's own writers. The most popular novelist in America in these years was the British writer Sir Walter Scott, whose swashbuckling historical novels set in eighteenth-century England and Scotland won him an impassioned readership in both Britain and America. When Americans read books written in their own country, many were likely to turn to the large number of "sentimental novels," written mostly by and for women.

But even during the heyday of Scott in the 1820s, the effort to create a distinctively American literature—which Washington Irving and others had advanced in the first decades of the century—made considerable progress with the emergence of the first great American novelist: James Fenimore Cooper. The author of more than thirty novels in the space of three decades, Cooper was known to his contemporaries as a master of adventure and suspense. What most distinguished his work, however, was its evocation of the American wilderness. Cooper had grown up in central New York, at a time when the edge of white settlement was not far away; and he retained throughout his life a fascination with man's relationship to nature and with the challenges (and dangers) of America's expansion westward. His most important novels were known as the "Leatherstocking Tales." Among them were *The Last of the Mohicans* (1826) and *The Deerslayer* (1841), which explored the American frontiersman's experience with Native Americans, pioneers, violence, and the law.

COOPER AND THE AMERICAN WILDERNESS

Cooper's novels were a continuation of the early-nineteenth-century effort to produce a truly American literature. But they also served as a link to the concerns of later intellectuals. For in the "Leatherstocking Tales" could be seen not only a celebration of the American spirit and landscape but also an evocation, through the central character of Natty Bumppo, of the ideal of the independent individual with a natural inner goodness. There was also evidence of another impulse that would motivate American reform: the fear of disorder. Many of Cooper's less savory characters illustrated the vicious, grasping nature of some of the nation's western settlers and suggested a need for social discipline even in the wilderness.

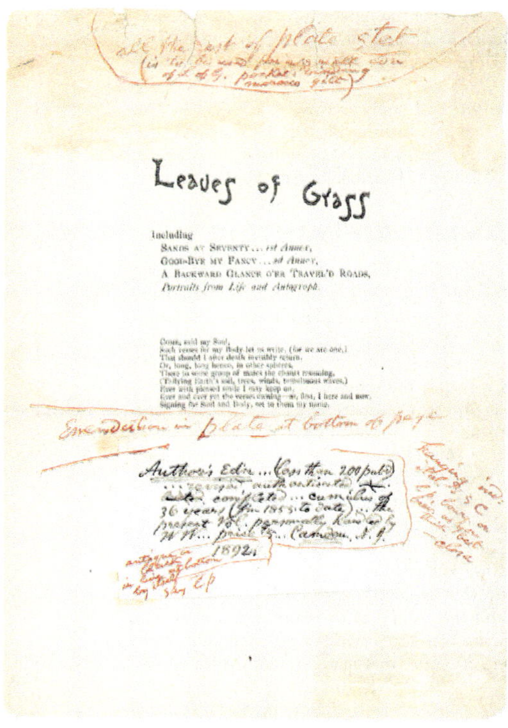

TITLE PAGE FOR WHITMAN'S *LEAVES OF GRASS* For more than thirty years after the publication of the original *Leaves of Grass* in 1855, Walt Whitman constantly revised and expanded the collection of poems and issued numerous subsequent editions. This sample title page, with notations by Whitman indicating changes and additions he wanted made, is for the final such edition, published in 1892, the year of Whitman's death. In a statement Whitman wrote to announce publication, he said that "the book *Leaves of Grass,* which he has been working on at great intervals and partially issued for the past thirty-five or forty years, is now completed. . . . Faulty as it is, he decides it is by far his special and entire self-chosen poetic utterance."

The Library of Congress

Walt Whitman, the self-proclaimed poet of American democracy, became one of the most important writers of his time. He was born in 1819, on Long Island, to Quaker parents—the second of nine children. As he grew older, he worked as an apprentice in newspapers. At age sixteen, he moved to New York City, where he worked as a printer and later taught at several schools. After his teaching attempts, Whitman went to Huntington, New York, to found his own newspaper, the *Long Islander,* and served as its publisher, editor, pressman, and distributor and even provided home delivery. But he began to write poetry when he could and eventually left his newspaper. In 1855, he hired a printer and published a first volume of work: *Leaves of Grass.* His poems were an unrestrained celebration of democracy, of the liberation of the individual, and of the pleasures of the flesh as well as of the spirit. They also expressed Whitman's personal yearning for emotional and physical release and personal fulfillment—a yearning perhaps rooted in part in his own experience as a homosexual living in a society profoundly intolerant of unconventional sexuality. In his large body of poems, Whitman not only helped liberate verse from traditional, restrictive conventions but also helped express the soaring spirit of individualism that characterized his age.

HERMAN MELVILLE

The new literary concern with the unleashing of human emotions did not always produce such optimistic works, as the work of Herman Melville suggests. Born in New York in 1819, Melville ran away to sea as a youth and spent years sailing the world before returning home to become the greatest

Reasoning Processes

Comparing and Contrasting After students have read the section "Cooper and the American Wilderness," ask them to create a Venn diagram comparing the novels of James Fenimore Cooper with European literature, such as the works of Sir Walter Scott. Ask students to discuss in small groups whether they were more similar or different. **ARC** **SOC**

American novelist of his era. The most important of his novels was *Moby Dick*, published in 1851. His portrayal of Ahab, the powerful, driven captain of a whaling vessel, was a story of courage and of the strength of individual will; but it was also a tragedy of pride and revenge. Ahab's maniacal search for Moby Dick, a great white whale that had maimed him, suggested how the search for personal fulfillment and triumph could not only liberate but destroy as well. The result of Ahab's great quest was his own annihilation, reflecting Melville's conviction that the human spirit was a troubled, often self-destructive force.

Even more bleak were the works of one of the few Southern writers of the time to embrace the search for the essence of the human spirit: Edgar Allan Poe. In the course of his short and unhappy life (he died in 1849 at the age of forty), Poe produced stories and poems that were primarily sad and macabre. His first book, *Tamerlane and Other Poems* (1827), received little recognition. But later works, including his most famous poem, "The Raven" (1845), established him as a major, if controversial, literary figure. Poe evoked images of individuals rising above the narrow confines of intellect and exploring the deeper world of the spirit and the emotions. Yet that world, he seemed to say, contained much pain and horror. Other American writers were contemptuous of Poe's work and his message, but he was ultimately to have a profound effect on European poets such as Baudelaire.

Literature in the Antebellum South

Poe, however, was something of an exception in the world of Southern literature. Like the North, the South experienced a literary flowering in the mid-nineteenth century, and produced writers and artists who were concerned with defining the nature of American society and the American nation. But white Southerners produced very different images of what that society was and should be.

Southern Romanticism

Southern novelists of the 1830s (among them Beverly Tucker, William Alexander Caruthers, and John Pendleton Kennedy), some of them writers of great talent, many of them residents of Richmond, produced historical romances or romantic eulogies of the plantation system of the upper South. In the 1840s, the Southern literary capital moved to Charleston, home of the most distinguished of the region's men of letters: William Gilmore Simms. For a time, Simms's work expressed a broad nationalism that transcended his regional background; but by the 1840s he too had become a strong defender of Southern institutions–especially slavery–against the encroachments of the North. There was, he believed, a unique quality to Southern life that it was the duty of intellectuals to defend.

One group of Southern writers, however, produced works that were more broadly American and less committed to a glorification of the peculiarities of Southern life. These were writers from the fringes of plantation society, who depicted the world of the backwoods rural areas. Augustus B. Longstreet, Joseph G. Baldwin, Johnson J. Hooper, and others focused not on aristocratic "cavaliers," but on ordinary people and poor white characters. Instead of romanticizing their subjects, they were deliberately and sometimes painfully realistic. And they seasoned their sketches with a robust, vulgar humor that was new to American literature. These Southern realists established a tradition of American regional humor that was ultimately to find its most powerful voice in Mark Twain.

The Transcendentalists

One of the outstanding expressions of the romantic impulse in America came from a group of New England writers and philosophers known as the transcendentalists. Borrowing heavily from German philosophers such as Kant, Hegel, and Schelling, and from the English writers Coleridge and Carlyle, the transcendentalists embraced a theory of the individual that rested on a distinction (first suggested by Kant) between what they called "reason" and "understanding"–words they used in ways that seem unfamiliar, even strange, to modern ears. Reason, as they defined it, had little to do with rationality. It was, rather, the individual's innate capacity to grasp beauty and truth through giving full expression to the instincts and emotions; and as such, it was the highest human faculty. Understanding, the transcendentalists argued, was the use of intellect in the narrow, artificial ways imposed by society; it involved the repression of instinct and the victory of externally imposed learning. Every person's goal, therefore, should be liberation from the confines of "understanding" and the cultivation of "reason." Each individual should strive to "transcend" the limits of the intellect and allow the emotions, the "soul," to create an "original relation to the Universe."

Ralph Waldo Emerson

Transcendentalist philosophy emerged first among a small group of intellectuals centered in Concord, Massachusetts. Their leader and most eloquent voice was Ralph Waldo Emerson. A Unitarian minister in his youth, Emerson left the church in 1832 to devote himself entirely to writing and teaching the elements of transcendentalism. He was a dazzling figure to his contemporaries–a lecturer whose public appearances drew rapturous crowds; a conversationalist who drew intellectuals to his Concord home almost daily. He was the most important intellectual of his age.

Emerson produced a significant body of poetry, but he was most renowned for his essays and lectures. In "Nature" (1836), one of his best-known essays, Emerson wrote that in the quest for self-fulfillment, individuals should work for a communion with the natural world: "in the woods, we return to reason and faith. . . . Standing on the bare ground–my head bathed by the blithe air, and uplifted into infinite space–all mean egotism vanishes. . . . I am part and particle of God." In other essays, he was even more explicit. "Nothing is at last sacred," he wrote in "Self-Reliance" (1841), perhaps his most famous essay, "but the integrity of your own mind." The quest for self-reliance, he explained, was really a search for communion with the unity of the universe, the wholeness of God, the great spiritual force

Historical Thinking Skills

Argumentation After students have read the section "Herman Melville," ask them to write a short paragraph explaining why *Moby Dick* is considered to be one of the greatest American novels. **ARC**

Reasoning Processes

Comparing and Contrasting Have students read the section "Literature in the Antebellum South." Ask them to create a T-chart listing features of Northern and Southern Romanticism. Ask them to discuss in small groups whether these two genres are more similar or different and to consider reasons for the differences. *(Differences are largely related to growing economic regionalism and sectional tension over the issue of slavery.)* **ARC** **SOC** **WXT**

Discussion and Activities

Analyzing Issues After students have read the section "The Transcendentalists," ask them to write a short paragraph explaining how transcendentalism could produce both Emerson's nationalism and Thoreau's civil disobedience. *(Emerson's nationalism was based on individual independence from European systems of thought, and Thoreau's civil disobedience was also based on individual independence from the arbitrary rule of law.)* **ARC** **SOC**

that he described as the "Oversoul." Each person's innate capacity to become, through his or her private efforts, a part of this essence was perhaps the classic expression of the romantic belief in the "divinity" of the individual.

Emerson was also a committed nationalist, an ardent proponent of American cultural independence. In a famous 1837 lecture, "The American Scholar," he boasted that "our day of dependence, our long apprenticeship to the learning of other lands, draws to a close." His belief that truth and beauty could be derived as much from instinct as from learning suggested that Americans, lacking the rich cultural heritage of European nations, could still aspire to artistic and literary greatness. Artistic and intellectual achievement need not rely on tradition and history; it could come from the instinctive creative genius of individuals. "Let the single man plant himself indomitably on his instincts and there abide," Emerson once said, "and the huge world will come round to him."

Almost as influential as Emerson was another leading Concord transcendentalist, Henry David Thoreau. Thoreau went even further than his friend Emerson in repudiating the repressive forces of society, which produced, he said, "lives of quiet desperation." Individuals should work for self-realization by resisting pressures to conform to society's expectations and responding instead to their own instincts. Thoreau's own effort to free himself–immortalized in his most famous book, *Walden* (1854)–led him to build a small cabin in the Concord woods on the edge of Walden Pond, where he lived alone for two years as simply as he could. "I went to the woods," he explained, "because I wished to live deliberately, to front only the essential facts of life, and see if I could not learn what it had to teach, and not, when I came to die, discover that I had not lived." Living simply, Thoreau believed, was a desirable alternative to the rapidly modernizing world around him–a world, he believed, that the disruptive and intrusive railroad unhappily symbolized.

Thoreau's rejection of what he considered the artificial constraints of society extended as well to his relationship with government. In 1846, he went to jail (briefly) rather than agree to pay a poll tax. He would not, he insisted, give financial support to a government that permitted the existence of slavery. In his 1849 essay "Resistance to Civil Government," Thoreau explained his refusal by claiming that the individual's personal morality had the first claim on his or her actions, that a government which required violation of that morality had no legitimate authority. The proper response was "civil disobedience," or "passive resistance"–a public refusal to obey unjust laws.

THOREAU AND CIVIL DISOBEDIENCE

THE DEFENSE OF NATURE

The transcendentalists, and others, feared the impact of the new capitalist enthusiasms on the integrity of the natural world. "The mountains and cataracts, which were to have made poets and painters," wrote the essayist Oliver Wendell Holmes, "have been mined for anthracite and dammed for water power."

Nature was not just a setting for economic activity, as many farmers, miners, and others believed; and it was not simply a body of data to be catalogued and studied, as many scientists thought. It was the source of human inspiration–the vehicle through which individuals could best realize the truth within their own souls. Genuine spirituality, they argued, came not from formal religion but through communion with the natural world. "In wildness is the preservation of the world." Thoreau once wrote. Humans separated from nature, he believed, would lose a substantial part of their humanity.

In making such claims, the transcendentalists were among the first Americans to anticipate the environmental movement of the twentieth century. They had no scientific basis for their defense of the wilderness, no knowledge of modern ecology, little sense of the twentieth-century notion of the interconnectedness of species. But they did believe in, and articulate, an essential unity between humanity and nature–a spiritual unity, they believed, without which civilization would be impoverished. They looked at nature, they said, "with new eyes," and with those eyes they saw that "behind nature, throughout nature, spirit is present."

VISIONS OF UTOPIA

Although transcendentalism was above all an individualistic philosophy, it helped spawn the most famous of all nineteenth-century experiments in communal living: Brook Farm, which the Boston transcendentalist George Ripley established as an experimental community in West Roxbury, Massachusetts, in 1841. There, according to Ripley, individuals would gather to create a new form of social organization. All residents would share equally in the labor of the community so that all could share too in the leisure, because leisure was the first necessity for cultivation of the self. (Ripley was one of the first Americans to attribute positive connotations to the idea of leisure; most of his contemporaries equated it with laziness and sloth.) Participation in manual labor served another purpose as well: it helped individuals bridge the gap between the world of the intellect and learning, and the world of instinct and nature. The obvious tension between the ideal of individual freedom and the demands of a communal society took their toll on Brook Farm. Many residents became disenchanted and left; when a fire destroyed the central building of the community in 1847, the experiment dissolved.

BROOK FARM

Among the original residents of Brook Farm was the writer Nathaniel Hawthorne, who expressed his disillusionment with the experiment and, to some extent, with transcendentalism in a series of notable novels. In *The Blithedale Romance* (1852), he wrote scathingly of Brook Farm itself, portraying the disastrous consequences of the experiment on the individuals who had submitted to it.

The failure of Brook Farm did not, however, prevent the formation of other experimental communities. Some borrowed, as Ripley had done, from the ideas of the French philosopher Charles Fourier, whose ideas of socialist communities organized as cooperative "phalanxes" received wide attention

Discussion and Activities

Making Connections Have students read the section "The Defense of Nature." Ask them to discuss in pairs or small groups how the transcendentalists' defense of nature was similar to or different from contemporary debates over protection of the environment versus resource utilization. **ARC** **WXT**

in America. Others drew from the ideas of the Scottish industrialist and philanthropist Robert Owen. Owen himself founded an experimental community in Indiana in 1825, which he named New Harmony. It was to be a "Village of Cooperation," in which every resident worked and lived in total equality. The community was an economic failure, but the vision that had inspired it continued to enchant Americans. Dozens of other "Owenite" experiments began in other locations in the following years.

NEW HARMONY

Redefining Gender Roles

One of the principal concerns of many of the new utopian communities (and of the new social philosophies on which they rested) was the relationship between men and women. Transcendentalism and other movements of this period fostered expressions of a kind of feminism that would not gain a secure foothold in American society until the late twentieth century.

One of those most responsible for raising issues of gender was Margaret Fuller. A leading transcendentalist and a close associate of Emerson, she suggested the important relationship between the discovery of the "self" that was so central to antebellum reform and the questioning of gender roles: "Many women are considering within themselves what they need and what they have not," she wrote in a famous feminist work, *Woman in the Nineteenth Century* (1844). "I would have Woman lay aside all thought, such as she habitually cherishes, of being taught and led by men." Fuller herself, before her premature death in a shipwreck in 1850, lived a life far different from the domestic ideal of her time. She had intimate relationships with many men; became a great admirer of European socialists and a great champion of the Italian revolution of 1848, which she witnessed during travels there; and established herself as an intellectual leader whose power came in part from her perspective as a woman.

MARGARET FULLER As a leading transcendentalist, Fuller argued for the important relationship between the discovery of the "self" and the questioning of the prevailing gender roles of her era. In her famous feminist work, *Women in the Nineteenth Century*, Fuller wrote, "Many women are considering within themselves what they need and what they have not." She encouraged her readers, especially women, to set aside conventional thinking about the role of women in society: "I would have Woman lay aside all thought, such as she habitually cherishes, of being taught and led by men." Fuller provided a strong voice in the redefinition of gender roles in the nineteenth century.

A redefinition of gender roles was crucial to one of the most enduring utopian colonies of the nineteenth century: the Oneida Community, established in 1848 in upstate New York by John Humphrey Noyes. The Oneida "Perfectionists," as residents of the community called themselves, rejected traditional notions of family and marriage. All residents, Noyes declared, were "married" to all other residents; there were no permanent conjugal ties. But Oneida was not, as its horrified critics often claimed, an experiment in "free love." It was a place where the community carefully monitored sexual behavior; where women were to be protected from unwanted childbearing; in which children were raised communally, often seeing little of their own parents. The Oneidans took special pride in what they considered the liberation of their women from the demands of male "lust" and from the traditional bonds of family.

REDEFINED GENDER ROLES AT THE ONEIDA COMMUNITY

The Shakers, even more than the Oneidans, made a redefinition of traditional sexuality and gender roles central to their society. Founded by "Mother" Ann Lee in the 1770s, the society of the Shakers survived throughout the nineteenth century and into the twentieth. (A tiny remnant survives today.) But the Shakers attracted a particularly large following in the antebellum period and established more than twenty communities throughout the Northeast and Northwest in the 1840s. They derived their name from a unique religious ritual, a sort of ecstatic dance, in which members of a congregation would "shake" themselves free of sin while performing a loud chant.

The most distinctive feature of Shakerism, however, was its commitment to complete celibacy—which meant, of course, that no one could be born to Shakerism; all Shakers had to choose the faith voluntarily. Shaker communities attracted about 6,000 members in the 1840s, more women than men; and members lived in conditions in which contact between men and women was very limited. Shakers openly endorsed the idea of sexual equality; they even embraced the idea of a God who was not clearly male or female. Within the Shaker society as a whole, it was women who exercised the most power. Mother Ann Lee was succeeded as leader of the movement by Mother Lucy Wright. Shakerism, one observer wrote in the 1840s, was a refuge from the "perversions of marriage" and "the gross abuses which drag it down."

THE SHAKERS

The Shakers were not, however, motivated only by a desire to escape the burdens of traditional gender roles. They were trying as well to create a society separated and protected from

Historical Thinking Skills

Argumentation After students have read the section "Visions of Utopia," ask them to discuss in pairs or small groups why communities such as Brook Farm and New Harmony typically did not last more than a few years. SOC WXT

Discussion and Activities

Analyzing Points of View Have students read the section "Redefined Gender Roles at the Oneida Community." Ask them to write a short letter or journal entry from the point of view of either a supporter or critic of Margaret Fuller. Have students consider how Fuller's writings and actions challenged traditional gender roles. SOC

Reasoning Processes

Continuity and Change After students have read the section "Redefining Gender Roles," discuss as a class how successful various groups were in challenging traditional gender roles. Ask them to identify important ways that gender roles changed or stayed the same. **ARC** **SOC**

the chaos and disorder that they believed had come to characterize American life as a whole. Less interested in personal freedom than in social discipline, they were like some other dissenting religious sects and utopian communities of their time. Another example was the Amana Community, founded by German immigrants in 1843, whose members settled in Iowa in 1855 and attempted to realize Christian ideals by creating an ordered, socialist society.

THE MORMONS

Among the most important efforts to create a new and more ordered society within the old was that of the Church of Jesus Christ of Latter-Day Saints—the Mormons. Mormonism began in upstate New York as a result of the efforts of Joseph Smith, a young, energetic, but economically unsuccessful man, who had spent most of his twenty-four years moving restlessly through New England and the Northeast. Then, in 1830, he published a remarkable document—the Book of Mormon, named for the ancient prophet who he claimed had written it. It was, Smith said, a translation of a set of golden tablets he had found in the hills of New York, revealed to him by an angel of God. The Book of Mormon told the story of an ancient and successful civilization in America, peopled by one of the lost tribes of Israel who had found their way to the New World centuries before Columbus. Its members waited patiently for the appearance of the Messiah, and they were rewarded when Jesus came to America after his resurrection. Subsequent generations, however, strayed from the path of righteousness that Jesus had laid out for them. Ultimately, their civilization collapsed, and God punished the sinful by making their skin dark. These darkened people, Smith believed, were the descendants of the American Indians, although the modern groups had no memory of their origins. But while the ancient Hebrew kingdom in America had ultimately vanished, Smith believed, its history as a righteous society could serve as a model for a new holy community in the United States.

JOSEPH SMITH

In 1831, gathering a small group of believers around him, Smith began searching for a sanctuary for his new community of "saints," an effort that would continue unhappily for more than twenty years. Time and again, the Mormons attempted to establish their "New Jerusalem." Time and again, they met with persecution from surrounding communities suspicious of their radical religious doctrines—which included polygamy (the right of men to take several wives), a rigid form of social organization, and, particularly damaging to their image, an intense secrecy, which gave rise to wild rumors among their critics of conspiracy and depravity.

Driven from their original settlements in Independence, Missouri, and Kirtland, Ohio, the Mormons moved on to the new town of Nauvoo, Illinois, which by the early 1840s had become an imposing and economically successful community. In 1844, however, Joseph Smith was arrested, charged with treason (for allegedly conspiring against the government to win foreign support for a new Mormon colony in the Southwest), and imprisoned in Carthage, Illinois. There an angry mob attacked the jail, forced Smith from his cell, and shot and killed him. The Mormons now abandoned Nauvoo and, under the leadership of Smith's successor, Brigham Young, traveled across the desert—a society of 12,000 people, in one of the largest single group migrations in American history—and established a new community in Utah, the present Salt Lake City. There, at last, the Mormons were able to create a lasting settlement.

ESTABLISHMENT OF SALT LAKE CITY

Like other experiments in social organization of the era, Mormonism reflected a belief in human perfectibility. God had once been a man, the church taught, and thus every man or woman could aspire to become—as Joseph Smith had become—a saint. But unlike other new communities, such as the Oneidans, the Mormons did not embrace the doctrine of individual liberty. Instead, they created a highly organized, centrally directed, almost militarized social structure, a refuge against the disorder and uncertainty of the secular world. They placed particular emphasis on the structure of the family. Mormon religious rituals even included a process by which men and women went through baptism ceremonies in the name of deceased ancestors; as a result, they believed, they would be reunited with those ancestors in heaven. The intense Mormon interest in genealogy, which continues today, is a reflection of this belief in the possibility of reuniting present generations with those of the past.

The original Mormons were, for the most part, men and women who felt displaced in their rapidly changing society—people left behind or troubled by the material growth and social progress of their era. In the new religion, they found genuine faith. In the society Mormonism created, they found security and order.

REMAKING SOCIETY

The simultaneous efforts to liberate the individual and impose order on a changing world also helped create a wide range of new movements to remake society—movements in which, to a striking degree, women formed the real rank and file and often the leadership as well. By the 1830s, such movements had taken the form of organized reform societies. "In no country in the world," Tocqueville had observed, "has the principle of association been more successfully used, or more unsparingly applied to a multitude of different objects, than in America."

The new organizations did indeed work on behalf of a wide range of issues: temperance; education; peace; the care of the poor, the handicapped, and the mentally ill; the treatment of criminals; the rights of women; and many more. Few eras in American history have witnessed as wide a range of reform efforts as emerged in the mid-nineteenth century. And few eras have exposed more clearly the simultaneous attraction of Americans to the ideas of personal liberty and social order.

NEW REFORM MOVEMENTS

Reasoning Processes

Comparing Have students read the section "The Mormons." Ask them to create a Venn diagram comparing the Mormons at this time to existing Christian denominations, such as Baptists, Methodists, or Presbyterians. Have students write a summary explaining why Mormons faced greater discrimination than other groups. **SOC**

CHAPTER 12
ANTEBELLUM CULTURE AND REFORM

MORMONS HEADING WEST This lithograph, by William Henry Jackson (1843–1942), shows Mormon handcart pioneers heading west to Utah in 1850.

REVIVALISM, MORALITY, AND ORDER

The philosophy of reform arose from several distinct sources. One was the optimistic vision of those who, like the transcendentalists, rejected Calvinist doctrines and preached the divinity of the individual. These included not only Emerson, Thoreau, and their followers, but also a much larger group of Americans who embraced the doctrines of Unitarianism and Universalism and absorbed European romanticism.

A second, and in many respects more important, source was Protestant revivalism–the movement that had begun with the Second Great Awakening early in the century and had, by the 1820s, evolved into a powerful force for social reform. Although the New Light revivalists were theologically far removed from the transcendentalists and Unitarians, they had come to share the optimistic belief that every individual was capable of salvation. According to Charles Grandison Finney, an evangelistic Presbyterian minister who became the most influential revival leader of the 1820s and 1830s, traditional Calvinist doctrines of predestination and individual human helplessness were both obsolete and destructive. Each person, he preached, contained within himself or herself the capacity to experience spiritual rebirth and achieve salvation. A revival of faith need not depend on a miracle from God; it could be created by individual effort.

Finney enjoyed particular success in upstate New York, where he helped launch a series of passionate revivals in towns along the Erie Canal–a region so prone to religious awakenings that it was known as the "burned-over district." It was no coincidence that the new revivalism should prove so powerful there, for this region of New York was experiencing–largely as a result of the construction of the canal–a major economic transformation. And with that transformation had come changes in the social fabric so profound that many men and women felt baffled and disoriented. (It was in roughly this same area of New York that Joseph Smith first organized the Mormon church.)

REVIVALISM IN THE BURNED-OVER DISTRICT

In Rochester, New York, the site of his greatest success, Finney staged a series of emotionally wrenching religious

Discussion and Activities

Analyzing Visuals Have students examine the image "Mormons Heading West." Ask them to identify and discuss as a class details from the painting that reveal the challenges of the Mormon Trek. *(Rugged terrain; harsh climate; lack of draft animals to pull wagons or carts.)* Then have students discuss what they can infer about the Mormons based on their willingness to endure such hardships. **GEO** **SOC**

Reasoning Processes

Causation Have students read the section "Revivalism in the Burned-Over District." Ask them to list and rank reasons for the beginnings of a religious revival in western New York. *(Rejection of traditional doctrine; belief in individual salvation; leadership of ministers like Charles Finney.)* Then have students write a thesis statement making a claim about the most important reasons for the revival. **ARC** **SOC**

Historical Thinking Skills

Argumentation Have students read the section "Finney's Doctrine of Personal Regeneration." Ask them to discuss in pairs or small groups why Finney's message resonated with western New Yorkers. Have students consider whether the responses of New Yorkers were more motivated by religious beliefs or social concerns. **SOC** **ARC**

meetings that aroused a large segment of the community. He had particular success in mobilizing women, on whom he tended to concentrate his efforts–both because women found the liberating message of revivalism particularly appealing and because, Finney discovered, they provided him with access to their male relatives. Gradually, he developed a large following among the prosperous citizens of the region. They were enjoying the economic benefits of the new commercial growth, but they were also uneasy about some of the social changes accompanying it (among them the introduction into their community of a new, undisciplined pool of transient laborers). For them, revivalism became not only a means of personal salvation but also a mandate for the reform (and control) of their society. Finney's revivalism became a call for a crusade against personal immorality. "The church," he maintained, "must take right ground on the subject of Temperance, the Moral Reform, and all the subjects of practical morality which come up for decision from time to time."

FINNEY'S DOCTRINE OF PERSONAL REGENERATION

CHARLES GRANDISON FINNEY Evangelistic Presbyterian minister Charles Grandison Finney became the most influential revival leader of the 1820s and 1830s. He argued that each person contained within herself or himself the capacity to experience spiritual rebirth and achieve salvation. Finney's views on revivalist faith contrasted with earlier Calvinist doctrines of predestination and individual human helplessness.

THE TEMPERANCE CRUSADE

Evangelical Protestantism added major strength to one of the most influential reform movements of the era: the crusade against drunkenness. No social vice, argued some reformers (including many of Finney's converts in cities such as Rochester), was more responsible for crime, disorder, and poverty than the excessive use of alcohol. Women, who were particularly active in the temperance movement, claimed that alcoholism placed a special burden on wives: men spent money on alcohol that their families needed for basic necessities, and drunken husbands often abused their wives and children.

In fact, alcoholism was an even more serious problem in antebellum America than it has been in the twentieth and twenty-first centuries. The supply of alcohol was growing rapidly, particularly in the West; farmers there grew more grain than they could sell in the still-limited markets in this prerailroad era, so they distilled much of it into whiskey. But in the East, too, commercial distilleries and private stills were widespread. The appetite for alcohol was growing along with the supply: in isolated western areas, where drinking provided a social pastime in small towns and helped ease the loneliness and isolation on farms; in pubs and saloons in eastern cities, where drinking was the principal leisure activity for many workers. The average male in the 1830s drank nearly three times as much alcohol as the average person does today. And as that figure suggests, many people drank habitually and excessively, with bitter consequences for themselves and others. Among the many supporters of the temperance movement were people who saw it as a way to overcome their own problems with alcoholism.

Although advocates of temperance had been active since the late eighteenth century, the new reformers gave the movement an energy and influence it had never previously known. In 1826, the American Society for the Promotion of Temperance emerged as a coordinating agency among various groups; it attempted to use many of the techniques of revivalism in preaching abstinence. Then, in 1840, six reformed alcoholics in Baltimore organized the Washington Temperance Society and began to draw large crowds–in which workers (many of them attempting to overcome their own alcoholism) were heavily represented–to hear their impassioned and intriguing confessions of past sins. By then, temperance advocates had grown dramatically in numbers; more than a million people had signed a formal pledge to forgo hard liquor.

AMERICAN SOCIETY FOR THE PROMOTION OF TEMPERANCE

As the movement gained in strength, it also became divided in purpose. Some temperance advocates now urged that abstinence include not only liquor but beer and wine as well. Not everyone agreed. Some began to demand state legislation to restrict the sale and consumption of alcohol (Maine passed such a law in 1851); others insisted that temperance must rely on the conscience of the individual. Whatever their disagreements, by promoting abstinence reformers were attempting to

Reasoning Processes

Causation Have students read the section "American Society for the Promotion of Temperance." Ask them to list the causes for the emergence of the temperance movement, identify which causes were economic, social, or religious, and identify which of those categories seems most influential. **SOC**

promote the moral self-improvement of individuals. They were also trying to impose discipline on society.

The search for social discipline was particularly clear in the battle over prohibition laws, which pitted established Protestants against new Catholic immigrants, to many of whom drinking was an important social ritual and an integral part of the life of their communities. The arrival of the immigrants was profoundly disturbing to established residents of many communities, and the restriction of alcohol seemed to them a way to curb the disorder they believed the new population was creating.

CULTURAL DIVISIONS OVER ALCOHOL

HEALTH FADS AND PHRENOLOGY

For some Americans, the search for individual and social perfection led to an interest in new theories of health and knowledge. Threats to public health were critical to the sense of insecurity that underlay many reform movements, especially after the terrible cholera epidemics of the 1830s and 1840s. Cholera is a severe bacterial infection of the intestines, usually a result of consuming contaminated food or water. In the nineteenth century, long before the discovery of antibiotics, less than half of those who contracted the disease survived. Thousands of people died of cholera during its occasional outbreaks, and in certain cities—New Orleans in 1833 and St. Louis in 1849—the effects were truly catastrophic. Nearly a quarter of the population of New Orleans died in the 1833 epidemic. Many municipalities, pressured by reformers, established city health boards to try to find solutions to the problems of epidemics. But the medical profession of the time, unaware of the nature of bacterial infections, had no answers; and the boards therefore found little to do.

Instead, many Americans turned to nonscientific theories for improving health. Affluent men and, especially, women flocked to health spas for the celebrated "water cure," which purported to improve health through immersing people in hot or cold baths or wrapping them in wet sheets. Although the water cure delivered few of the benefits its promoters promised, it did have some therapeutic value; some forms of hydrotherapy are still in use today. Other people adopted new dietary theories. Sylvester Graham, a Connecticut-born Presbyterian minister and committed reformer, won many followers with his prescriptions for eating fruits, vegetables, and bread made from coarsely ground flour—a prescription not unlike some dietary theories today—instead of meat. (The "Graham cracker" is made from a kind of flour named for him.) Graham accompanied his dietary prescriptions with moral warnings about the evils of excess and luxury.

Perhaps strangest of all to modern sensibilities was the widespread belief in the new "science" of phrenology, which appeared first in Germany and became popular in the United

THE DRUNKARD'S PROGRESS This 1846 lithograph by Nathaniel Currier shows what temperance advocates argued was the inevitable consequence of alcohol consumption. Beginning with an apparently innocent "glass with a friend," the young man rises step by step to the summit of drunken revelry, then declines to desperation and suicide while his abandoned wife and child grieve.

Historical Thinking Skills

Argumentation After students have read the section "The Temperance Crusade," ask them to create a poster encouraging people to make a temperance pledge to forgo hard liquor. **SOC** **ARC**

Discussion and Activities

Analyzing Visuals Have students examine the image "The Drunkard's Progress." Ask them to brainstorm in small groups to identify details that are intended to discourage drinking. *(Drinking is portrayed as an activity that may seem harmless in the beginning but leads to the death of the individual and widowhood and orphanhood for the drinker's family. Many specific examples may be cited.)* Have students assess whether materials like this would have been effective at reducing alcohol consumption. **SOC**

Discussion and Activities

Speculating After students have read the section "Health Fads and Phrenology," discuss as a class why people were so willing to embrace treatments that had no scientific basis. *(In the nineteenth century, much less was known about the causes of disease. People tried treatments that seem outrageous to us today, rather than do nothing then.)* SOC

States beginning in the 1830s through the efforts of Orson and Lorenzo Fowler, publishers of the *Phrenology Almanac*. Phrenologists argued that the shape of an individual's skull was an important indicator of his or her character and intelligence. They made elaborate measurements of bumps and indentations to calculate the size (and, they claimed, the strength) of different parts of the brain, each of which, they argued, controlled a specific kind of intelligence or behavior. For a time, phrenology seemed to many Americans an important vehicle for improving society. It provided a way of measuring an individual's fitness for various positions in life and seemed to promise an end to the arbitrary process by which people matched their talents to occupations and responsibilities. The theory is now universally believed to have no scientific value.

PHRENOLOGY

Medical Science

In an age of rapid technological and scientific advances, the science of medicine sometimes seemed to lag behind. In part, that was because of the greater difficulty of experimentation in medicine, which required human subjects as compared to other areas of science and technology that relied on inanimate objects. In part, it was because of the character of the medical profession, which—in the absence of any significant regulation—attracted many poorly educated people and many quacks, in addition to trained physicians. Efforts to regulate the profession were opposed in the 1830s and 1840s by those who considered the licensing of physicians to be a form of undemocratic monopoly. The prestige of the profession, therefore, remained low, and it was for many people a career of last resort.

The biggest problem facing American medicine, however, was the absence of basic knowledge about disease. The great medical achievement of the eighteenth century—the development of a vaccination against smallpox by the English Physician Edward Jenner—came from no broad theory of infection, but from a brilliant adaptation of folk practices among country people. The development of anesthetics came not from medical doctors at first, but from a New England dentist, William Morton, who was looking for ways to help his patients endure the extraction of teeth. Beginning in 1844, Morton began experimenting with using sulphuric ether. John Warren, a Boston surgeon, soon began using ether to sedate surgical patients. Even these advances met with stiff resistance from traditional physicians, some of whom continued to believe that all medical knowledge derived from timeless truths and ancient scholars and who mistrusted innovation and experimentation. Others rejected scientific advances because of unorthodox, and untested "medical" techniques popularized by entrepreneurs, many of them charlatans.

In the absence of any broad acceptance of scientific methods and experimental practice in medicine, it was very difficult for even the most talented doctors to succeed in treating disease. Even so, halting progress toward the discovery of the germ theory did occur in antebellum America. In 1843, the Boston essayist, poet, and physician Oliver Wendell Holmes published his findings from a study of large numbers of cases of "puerperal fever" (septicemia in children) and concluded that the disease could be transmitted from one person to another. This discovery of contagion met with a storm of criticism, but was later vindicated by the clinical success of the Hungarian physician Ignaz Semmelweis, who noticed that the infection seemed to be spread by medical students who had been working with corpses. Once he began requiring students to wash their hands and disinfect their instruments, the infections virtually disappeared.

DISCOVERY OF CONTAGION

Reforming Education

One of the outstanding reform movements of the mid-nineteenth century was the effort to produce a system of universal public education. As of 1830, no state yet had such a system, although some states—such as Massachusetts—had supported a limited version for many years. In the 1830s, however, interest in public education grew rapidly. It was a reflection of the new belief in the innate capacity of every person and of society's obligation to tap that capacity; but it was a reflection, too, of the desire to expose students to stable social values as a way to resist instability.

The greatest educational reformer was Horace Mann, the first secretary of the Massachusetts Board of Education, which was established in 1837. To Mann and his followers, education

"SPOUT BATH AT WARM SPRINGS" Among the many fads and theories about human health to gain currency in the 1830s and 1840s, one of the most popular was the idea that bathing in warm, sulphurous water was restorative. Visitors to "warm springs" all over the United States and Europe "took the baths," drank the foul-smelling water, and sometimes stayed for weeks as part of a combination vacation and "cure." This 1837 drawing is by Sophie Dupont, a visitor to a popular spa. She wrote to a friend that the water, "notwithstanding its odour of half spoiled eggs and its warmth, is not very nauseous to the taste."

Discussion and Activities

Explaining Significance Have students read the section "Medical Science." Ask them to list and rank in order of importance nineteenth century advancements in medical science. Then have students write a thesis statement that makes a claim about what the most important advances were. SOC WXT

Discussion and Activities

Making Connections Have students read the section "Rapid Growth of Public Education." Ask them to create a Venn diagram comparing the purposes and forms of public education in the nineteenth century and today. Discuss as a class what students believe are the greatest similarities and differences. **SOC**

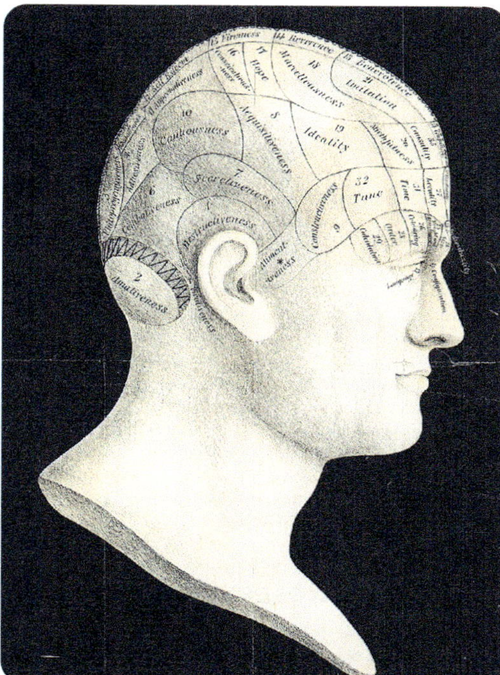

PHRENOLOGY This lithograph illustrates some of the ideas of the popular "science" of phrenology in the 1830s. Drawing from the concepts of the German writer Johann Gaspar Spurzheim, American phrenologists promoted the belief that a person's character and talents could be understood by the formation of his or her skull; that the brain was, in fact, a cluster of autonomous organs, each controlling some aspect of human thought or behavior. In this diagram, the areas of the brain that supposedly control "identity," "acquisitiveness," "secretiveness," "marvelousness," and "hope" are clearly identified. The theory has no scientific basis.

The Library of Congress

was the only way to "counterwork this tendency to the domination of capital and the servility of labor." The only way to protect democracy, Mann believed, was to create an educated electorate. He reorganized the Massachusetts school system, lengthened the academic year (to six months), doubled teachers' salaries (although he did nothing to eliminate the large disparities between the salaries of male and female teachers), enriched the curriculum, and introduced new methods of professional training for teachers.

Rapid Growth of Public Education

Other states experienced similar expansion and development. They built new schools, created teachers' colleges, and offered large new groups of children access to education. Henry Barnard helped produce a educational system in Connecticut and Rhode Island. Pennsylvania passed a law in 1835 appropriating state funds for the support of universal education. Governor William Seward of New York extended public support of schools throughout the state in the early 1840s. By the 1850s, the principle of tax-supported elementary schools had been accepted in all the states; and all were making at least a start toward putting the principle into practice.

Yet the quality of the new education continued to vary widely. In some places–Massachusetts, for example, where Mann established the first American state-supported teachers' college in 1839 and where the first professional association of teachers was created in 1845–educators were usually capable men and women, often highly trained, and with an emerging sense of themselves as career professionals. In other areas, however, teachers were often barely literate, and limited funding for education restricted opportunities severely. In the newly settled regions of the West, where the white population was highly dispersed, many children had no access to schools. In the South, the entire black population was barred from formal education (although approximately 10 percent of enslaved people achieved literacy anyway), and only about a third of all white children of school age actually enrolled in schools in 1860. In the North the percentage was 72 percent, but even there, many students attended classes only briefly and casually.

The interest in education was visible too in the growing movement to educate American Indians in the antebellum period. Some reformers held racist assumptions about the unredeemability of nonwhite peoples; but even many who accepted that idea about African Americans continued to believe that Native Americans could be "civilized" if only they could be taught the ways of the white world. Efforts to educate Native Americans and encourage them to assimilate were particularly prominent in such areas of the Far West as Oregon. Substantial numbers of white Americans were beginning to settle there in the 1840s. Nevertheless, the great majority of Native Americans remained outside the reach of educational reform, either by choice or by circumstance or both.

Achievements of Educational Reform

Despite limitations and inequities, the achievements of the school reformers were impressive by any standard. By the beginning of the Civil War, the United States had one of the highest literacy rates of any nation: 94 percent of the population of the North and 83 percent of the white population of the South (58 percent of the total Southern population).

The conflicting impulses underlying the movement for school reform were visible in some of the different educational institutions that emerged. In New England, for example, the transcendentalist Bronson Alcott established a controversial experimental school in Concord that reflected his strong belief in the importance of complete self-realization. He urged children to learn from their own inner wisdom, not from the imposition of values by the larger society. Children were to teach themselves, rather than rely on teachers.

The Benevolent Empire

A similar emphasis on the potential of the individual sparked the creation of new institutions to help the handicapped, institutions that formed part of a great network of charitable activities known as the Benevolent Empire. Among

Reasoning Processes

Causation Have students read the section "Achievements of Educational Reform." Ask them to list and discuss the effects of the public education reform movement. Have students consider what they believe to be the most important effects. **SOC**

Discussion and Activities

Contrasting After students have read the section "The Benevolent Empire," ask them to discuss in pairs or small groups how the motives behind educational reform may have been contradictory. *(Some reforms were motivated by a desire to help individuals reach their full potential, while others were motivated by a desire to strengthen social order.)* **SOC**

them was the Perkins School for the Blind in Boston, the first such school in America. Nothing better exemplified the romantic impulse of the era than the belief of those who founded Perkins that even society's supposedly least-favored members—the blind and otherwise handicapped—could be helped to discover inner strength and wisdom.

More typical of educational reform, however, were efforts to use schools to impose a set of social values on children—the values that reformers believed were appropriate for their new, industrializing society. These values included thrift, order, discipline, punctuality, and respect for authority. Horace Mann, for example, spoke frequently of the role of public schools in extending democracy and expanding individual opportunity. But he spoke, too, of their role in creating social order. "The unrestrained passions of men are not only homicidal, but suicidal," he said, suggesting a philosophy very different from that of Alcott and other transcendentalists, who emphasized instinct and emotion. "Train up a child in the way he should go, and when he is old he will not depart from it."

REHABILITATION

Similar impulses helped create another powerful movement of reform: the creation of "asylums" (as they now were called) for criminals and for the mentally ill. On the one hand, in advocating prison and hospital reform, Americans were reacting to one of society's most glaring ills. Criminals of all kinds, debtors unable to pay their debts, the mentally ill, even senile paupers—all were crowded together indiscriminately into prisons and jails, which in some cases were holes in the ground; one jail in Connecticut was an abandoned mine shaft. Beginning in the 1820s, numerous states replaced these antiquated facilities with new "penitentiaries" and mental institutions designed to provide a proper environment for inmates. New York built the first penitentiary at Auburn in 1821. In Massachusetts, the social reformer Dorothea Dix began a national movement for new methods of treating the mentally ill. Imprisonment of debtors and paupers gradually disappeared, as did such traditional practices as legal public hangings.

THE ASYLUM MOVEMENT

But the creation of "asylums" for social deviants was not simply an effort to curb the abuses of the old system. It was also an attempt to reform and rehabilitate the inmates. New forms of rigid prison discipline were designed to rid criminals of the "laxness" that had presumably led them astray. Solitary confinement and the imposition of silence on work crews (both adopted in Pennsylvania and New York in the 1820s) were meant to give prisoners opportunities to meditate on their wrongdoings (hence the term "penitentiary": a place for individuals to cultivate penitence). Some reformers argued that the discipline of the asylum could serve as a model for other potentially disordered environments—for example, factories and schools. But penitentiaries and mental hospitals often fell victim to overcrowding, and the original reform ideal gradually faded. Many prisons ultimately degenerated into little more than warehouses for criminals, with scant emphasis on rehabilitation, which was far from the original, optimistic vision.

PRISON REFORM

The "asylum" movement was not, however, restricted to criminals and people otherwise considered "unfit." The idea that a properly structured institution could prevent moral failure or rescue individuals from failure and despair helped spawn the creation of new orphanages designed as educational institutions. Such institutions, reformers believed, would provide an environment in which children who might otherwise be drawn into criminality could be trained to become useful citizens. Similar institutions emerged to provide homes for "friendless" women—women without families or homes, but otherwise "respectable," for whom the institutions might provide an opportunity to build a new life. (Such homes were in part an effort to prevent such women from turning to prostitution.) There were also new facilities for the poor: almshouses and workhouses, which created closely supervised environments for those who had failed to work their way up in society. Such an environment, reformers believed, would train them to live more productive lives.

THE INDIAN RESERVATION

Some of these same beliefs underlay the emergence in the 1840s and 1850s of a new "reform" approach to the problems of Native Americans: the idea of the reservation. For several decades, the dominant thrust of U.S. policy toward the Native Americans in areas of white settlement had been relocation. The principal motive behind relocation had always been a simple one: getting Native American nations out of the way of white civilization. But among some white Americans there had also been another, if secondary, intent: to move the Native Americans to a place where they would be protected from white settlers and allowed to develop to a point where assimilation might be possible. Even Andrew Jackson, whose animus toward Native Americans was legendary, once described the removals as part of the nation's "moral duty . . . to protect and if possible to preserve and perpetuate the scattered remnants of the Indian race."

It was a small step from the idea of relocation to the idea of the reservation: the idea of creating an enclosed region in which Native Americans would live in isolation from white society. The reservations served white economic purposes above all—moving Native Americans out of good lands that white settlers wanted. But they were also supposed to serve a reform purpose. Just as prisons, asylums, and orphanages would provide society with an opportunity to train and uplift misfits and unfortunates within white society, so the reservations might provide a way to undertake what one official called "the great work of regenerating the Indian race." Native Americans on reservations, reformers argued, would learn the ways of civilization in a protected setting.

Discussion and Activities

Making Connections Have students read the section "Rehabilitation." Ask them to create a chart listing the motives and methods of the asylum and prison reform movements. Have students indicate which of those motives or methods are still valid today. **SOC** **ARC**

PERKINS SCHOOL FOR THE BLIND The Perkins School in Boston was the first school for the blind in the United States and was committed to the idea that the blind could be connected effectively to the world through the development of new skills, such as reading through the relatively new technique of embossed writing systems. This woodcut shows Perkins's main building in the mid-1850s, by which time the school was already over twenty years old. It continues to educate the blind today.

Discussion and Activities

Analyzing Visuals Have students examine the image "Perkins School for the Blind." Ask them to write a short letter or journal entry from the point of view of a visually impaired student arriving at the institution. Have students address the hopes and fears those students may have experienced. **SOC** **ARC**

THE EMERGENCE OF FEMINISM

The reform ferment of the antebellum period had a particular meaning for American women. They played central roles in a wide range of reform movements and a particularly important role in the movements on behalf of temperance and the abolition of slavery. In the process, they expressed their awareness of the problems that women themselves faced in a male-dominated society. The result was the creation of the first important American feminist movement, one that laid the groundwork for more than a century of agitation for women's rights.

Women in the 1830s and 1840s faced not only all the traditional restrictions imposed on members of their sex by society, but also a new set of barriers that had emerged from the doctrine of "separate spheres" and the transformation of the family. Many women who began to involve themselves in reform movements in the 1820s and 1830s came to look on such restrictions with rising resentment. Some began to defy them. Sarah and Angelina Grimké, sisters born in South Carolina who had become active and outspoken abolitionists, ignored attacks by men who claimed that their activities were inappropriate for their sex. "Men and women were CREATED EQUAL," they argued. "They are both moral and accountable beings, and whatever is right for man to do, is right for women to do." Other reformers—Catharine Beecher, Harriet Beecher Stowe (her sister), Lucretia Mott, Elizabeth Cady Stanton, and Dorothea Dix—also chafing at the restrictions placed on them by men, similarly pressed at the boundaries of "acceptable" female behavior.

REFORM MOVEMENTS AND THE RISE OF FEMINISM

Finally, in 1840, the patience of several women snapped. A group of American female delegates arrived at a world antislavery convention in London, only to be turned away by the men who controlled the proceedings. Angered at the rejection, several of the delegates—notably Lucretia Mott and Elizabeth Cady Stanton—became convinced that their first duty as reformers should now be to elevate the status of women. Over the next several years, Mott, Stanton, Susan B. Anthony, and others began drawing pointed parallels between the plight of women and the plight of enslaved people; and in 1848, they organized a convention in Seneca Falls, New York, to discuss the question of women's rights. Out of the meeting emerged a "Declaration of Sentiments" (patterned on the 1776 Declaration of Independence), which stated that "all men and women are created equal," that women no less than men have certain inalienable rights. Their most prominent demand was for the right to vote, thus launching a movement for woman suffrage that would continue until 1920. But the document was in many ways more important for its rejection of the whole notion that men and women should be assigned separate "spheres" in society.

SENECA FALLS CONVENTION

It should not be surprising, perhaps, that many of the women involved in these feminist efforts were Quakers. Quakerism had long embraced the ideal of sexual equality and had tolerated, indeed encouraged, the emergence of women as preachers and community leaders. Women taught to expect the absence of gender-based restrictions in their own communities naturally resented the restrictions they encountered when they moved outside them. Quakers had also been among the leaders of the antislavery movement, and Quaker women

Reasoning Processes

Continuity and Change Have students read the section "Reform Movements and the Rise of Feminism." Discuss as a class how the feminist movement was either a continuation of other reform movements, a departure from them, or both. *(Many feminists were inspired by unequal treatment while participating in other movements. Some were motivated by new resentment of traditional gender norms, such as those enforced by the system of separate spheres.)* **SOC** **ARC**

AP Exam Tip

When writing responses to document-based questions, students will be asked to analyze the sourcing and situation of primary and secondary sources. One way to do that is to place a document in its historical context.

Historical Thinking Skills

Sourcing and Situation Have students practice the exam tip by writing a short paragraph explaining the context of the "Declaration of Sentiments." *(The feminist movement was part of the broader Antebellum reform movement inspired by a desire to improve society. Many women became feminist reformers due to their own experiences of discrimination while participating in other reform movements.)* **SOC** **ARC**

CONSIDER THE SOURCE

THE RISE OF FEMINISM

IN THE 1840S, a group of women who had started out as abolitionists began to advocate for the rights of women. "All men and women are created equal," they declared. They argued that women should have the same opportunities as men and should no longer be restricted to the domestic sphere. This effort reached its peak at the 1848 convention in Seneca Falls, New York, where a Declaration of Sentiments was proclaimed.

Just as the women's rights movement of the nineteenth century grew out of the abolitionist movement, so the feminist movement of the twentieth century built upon the civil rights movement. The modern feminist movement often marks its beginning with the publication of Betty Friedan's *The Feminine Mystique* in 1963 and the formation of the National Organization for Women (NOW) in 1966. Despite the more than one hundred years separating the two documents that follow, the basic sentiments of the Seneca Falls Declaration bear many similarities to the ideas that have shaped feminist thinking of the twentieth and twenty-first centuries.

SENECA FALLS—1848

The Declaration of Sentiments, Seneca Falls Convention, 1848

When, in the course of human events, it becomes necessary for one portion of the family of man to assume among the people of the earth a position different from that which they have hitherto occupied, but one to which the laws of nature and of nature's God entitle them, a decent respect to the opinions of mankind requires that they should declare the causes that impel them to such a course.

We hold these truths to be self-evident: that all men and women are created equal; that they are endowed by their Creator with certain inalienable rights; that among these are life, liberty, and the pursuit of happiness; that to secure these rights governments are instituted, deriving their just powers from the consent of the governed. Whenever any form of government becomes destructive of these ends, it is the right of those who suffer from it to refuse allegiance to it, and to insist upon the institution of a new government, laying its foundation on such principles, and organizing its powers in such form, as to them shall seem most likely to effect their safety and happiness. . . . Such has been the patient sufferance of the women under this government, and such is now the necessity which constrains them to demand the equal station to which they are entitled. The history of mankind is a history of repeated injuries and usurpations on the part of man toward woman, having in direct object the establishment of an absolute tyranny over her. . . .

Now, in view of this entire disfranchisement of one-half the people of this country, . . . because women do feel themselves aggrieved, oppressed, and fraudulently deprived of their most sacred rights, we insist that they have immediate admission to all the rights and privileges which belong to them as citizens of the United States.

From Elizabeth Cady Stanton, *A History of Woman Suffrage*, vol. 1 (Rochester, NY: Fowler and Wells, 1889), pp. 70–71.

Historical Thinking Skills

Contextualization Have students read the document "The Declaration of Sentiments." Ask them to consider the inspiration for the wording of the document, and have them discuss in small groups why organizers of the convention may have chosen this wording. *(The wording parallels the beginning of the Declaration of Independence.)* **ARC** **SOC**

NATIONAL ORGANIZATION FOR WOMEN (NOW)—1966

THE NATIONAL ORGANIZATION FOR WOMEN'S 1966 STATEMENT OF PURPOSE

We, men and women who hereby constitute ourselves as the National Organization for Women, believe that the time has come for a new movement toward true equality for all women in America, and toward a fully equal partnership of the sexes, as part of the worldwide revolution of human rights now taking place within and beyond our national borders.

The purpose of NOW is to take action to bring women into full participation in the mainstream of American society now, exercising all the privileges and responsibilities thereof in truly equal partnership with men.

We believe the time has come to . . . confront, with concrete action, the conditions that now prevent women from enjoying the equality of opportunity and freedom of choice which is their right, as individual Americans, and as human beings.

NOW is dedicated to the proposition that women, first and foremost, are human beings, who, like all other people in our society, must have the chance to develop their fullest human potential. We believe that women can achieve such equality only by accepting to the full the challenges and responsibilities they share with all other people in our society, as part of the decision-making mainstream of American political, economic and social life.

. . .

WE BELIEVE that the power of American law, and the protection guaranteed by the U.S. Constitution to the civil rights of all individuals, must be effectively applied and enforced to isolate and remove patterns of sex discrimination, to ensure equality of opportunity in employment and education, and equality of civil and political rights and responsibilities on behalf of women, as well as for Negroes and other deprived groups.

. . .

WE BELIEVE THAT women will do most to create a new image of women by acting now, and by speaking out in behalf of their own equality, freedom, and human dignity–not in pleas for special privilege, nor in enmity toward men, who are also victims of the current, half-equality between the sexes–but in an active, self-respecting partnership with men. By so doing, women will develop confidence in their own ability to determine actively, in partnership with men, the conditions of their life, their choices, their future and their society.

This Statement of Purpose was written by Betty Friedan, author of The Feminine Mystique.

Source: National Organization for Women Statement of Purpose (1966).

ANALYZING SOURCES

Questions assume cumulative content knowledge from this chapter and previous chapters.

1. Which best describes what both documents are responding to, regarding social ideals of womanhood?
   (A) the ideal that women are the keepers of American democratic principles
   (B) the ideal of the woman's "separate sphere"
   (C) the romantic ideal of the "Southern lady"
   (D) the ideal that women were highly sensitive creatures, occupying solely the realm of emotions.

2. Which of the following best describes the similarity in sentiments between the two documents?
   (A) Both documents assert that women need to unite to overthrow a tyrannical government.
   (B) Both documents assert the right of women to vote.
   (C) Both documents assert the right of women to the American democratic ideals of liberty and equal opportunity.
   (D) Both documents assert the rights of other disenfranchised groups.

3. Both documents were most strongly influenced by which of the following?
   (A) 19th century Romanticism
   (B) the Enlightenment
   (C) federalist notions of a strong union
   (D) the religious skepticism of the late 18th century

AP Exam Practice

Short Answer Provide students with the following short-answer questions and allow 15 minutes for completion. Ask for volunteers to share their responses and discuss as a class.

Answer A, B, and C.

A) Briefly explain ONE important similarity between the feminist movement and another Antebellum reform movement from 1800–1848. *(The reform movements were motivated by a desire to improve society. Many of the reform leaders were women.)*

B) Briefly explain ONE important difference between the feminist movement and another Antebellum reform movement from 1800–1848. *(The feminist movement had much less male participation. The feminist movement was less successful during this time period at achieving its goals than the asylum, prison reform, and education reform movements were.)*

C) Briefly explain ONE reason for the difference cited in B. *(Many men and some women continued to believe that women should not play significant roles in politics, society, or the economy.)*

Answers

Consider the Source

1. B; **2.** C; **3.** B

Discussion and Activities

Analyzing Cause and Effect Have students read the section "Limited Progress for Women." Discuss as a class reasons why feminists in the nineteenth century failed to accomplish all their goals and how some women succeeded individually despite various barriers. Have students consider whether barriers to gender equality still exist, and if so, to what extent they are similar to those facing nineteenth-century women. **SOC** **ARC**

7

FREDERICK DOUGLASS, AMY POST, CATHARINE STEBBINS, and ELIZABETH C. STANTON, and was unanimously adopted, as follows:

DECLARATION OF SENTIMENTS.

When, in the course of human events, it becomes necessary for one portion of the family of man to assume among the people of the earth a position different from that which they have hitherto occupied, but one to which the laws of nature and of nature's God entitle them, a decent respect to the opinions of mankind requires that they should declare the causes that impel them to such a course.

THE "DECLARATION OF SENTIMENTS" Frederick Douglass joined female abolitionists in signing the famous "Declaration of Sentiments" that emerged out of the Women's Rights Convention at Seneca Falls, New York, in 1848—one of the founding documents of American feminism.

played a leading role within those efforts. Of the women who drafted the Declaration of Sentiments, all but Elizabeth Cady Stanton were Quakers.

Progress toward feminist goals was limited in the antebellum years, but individual women did manage to break the social barriers to advancement. Elizabeth Blackwell, born in England, gained acceptance and fame as a physician. Her sister-in-law Antoinette Brown Blackwell became the first ordained woman minister in the United States; and another sister-in-law, Lucy Stone, took the revolutionary step of retaining her maiden name after marriage (as did the abolitionist Angelina Grimké). Stone became a successful and influential lecturer on women's rights. Emma Willard, founder of the Troy Female Seminary in 1821, and Catharine Beecher, who founded the Hartford Female Seminary in 1823, worked on behalf of women's education. Some women expressed their feminist sentiments even in their choice of costume—by wearing a distinctive style of dress (introduced in the 1850s) that combined a short skirt with full-length pantalettes—an outfit that allowed freedom of movement without loss of modesty. Introduced by the famous actress Fanny Kemble, it came to be called the "bloomer" costume, after one of its advocates, Amelia Bloomer. (It provoked so much controversy that feminists finally abandoned it, convinced that the furor was drawing attention away from their more important demands.)

LIMITED PROGRESS FOR WOMEN

There was an irony in this rise of interest in the rights of women. Feminists benefited greatly from their association with other reform movements, most notably abolitionism; but they also suffered from them. For the demands of women were usually assigned—even by some women themselves—a secondary position to what many considered the far greater issue of the rights of enslaved people.

THE CRUSADE AGAINST SLAVERY

The antislavery movement was not new to the mid-nineteenth century. There had been efforts even before the Revolution to limit, and even eliminate, the institution. Those efforts had helped remove slavery from most of the North by the end of the eighteenth century and had led to the legal prohibition of the international slave trade in 1808. There were powerful antislavery movements in Europe that cried out forcefully against human bondage, perhaps most notably from Britain, where the great antislavery leader, William Wilberforce, had led the effort to abolish the slave trade, and later slavery itself, from the British Empire. But American anti-slavery sentiment remained relatively muted in the first decades after independence. Not until 1830 did it begin to gather the force that would ultimately enable it to overshadow virtually all other efforts at social reform.

EARLY OPPOSITION TO SLAVERY

In the early years of the nineteenth century, those who opposed slavery were, for the most part, a calm and genteel lot, expressing moral disapproval but engaging in few overt activities. To the extent that there was an organized antislavery movement, it centered on the concept of colonization—the effort to encourage the resettlement of African Americans in Africa or the Caribbean. In 1817, a group of prominent white Virginians organized the American Colonization Society (ACS), which worked carefully to challenge slavery without challenging property rights or Southern sensibilities. The ACS proposed a gradual manumission (or freeing) of enslaved people, with slaveholders receiving compensation through funds raised by private charity or appropriated by state legislatures. The Society would then transport liberated enslaved people out of the country and help them to establish a new society of their own elsewhere.

AMERICAN COLONIZATION SOCIETY

The ACS was not without impact. It received some funding from private donors, some from Congress, some from the legislatures of Virginia and Maryland. And it arranged the shipment of several groups of African Americans out of the country, some of them to the west coast of Africa, where in 1830 they established the nation of Liberia (which became an independent republic in 1846—its capital, Monrovia, was named for the American president who had presided over the initial settlement).

But the ACS was in the end a negligible force. Neither private nor public funding was nearly enough to carry out the vast projects its supporters envisioned. In the space of a decade, they managed to "colonize" fewer enslaved people than were born in the United States in a month. No amount of funding, in fact, would have been enough; there were far too many black men and women in America in the nineteenth

FAILURE OF COLONIZATION

Discussion and Activities

Analyzing Issues Have students read the section "American Colonization Society." Ask them to think about why the American Colonization Society would want to end slavery but then remove formerly enslaved people from the country. *(Although ACS members believed slavery was harmful to society and the economy, they did not believe that African Americans were equal to white Americans, and they did not want to live among formerly enslaved people.)* Have students share their thoughts with a partner, and then ask for volunteers to share their thoughts with the class. **SOC** **ARC**

century to be transported to Africa by any conceivable program. And in any case, the ACS met resistance from African Americans themselves, many of whom were now three or more generations removed from Africa and had no wish to move to a land of which they knew almost nothing. (The Massachusetts free black Paul Cuffe had met similar resistance from members of his own race in the early 1800s when he proposed a colonization scheme of his own.)

By 1830, in other words, the early antislavery movement was rapidly losing strength. Colonization was proving not to be a viable method of attacking the institution, particularly since the cotton boom in the Deep South was increasing the commitment of planters to their "peculiar" labor system. Those opposed to slavery had reached what appeared to be a dead end.

Garrison and Abolitionism

At this crucial juncture, with the antislavery movement seemingly on the verge of collapse, a new figure emerged to transform it into a dramatically different phenomenon. He was William Lloyd Garrison. Born in Massachusetts in 1805, Garrison was an assistant in the 1820s to the New Jersey Quaker Benjamin Lundy, who published the leading antislavery newspaper of the time—the *Genius of Universal Emancipation*—in Baltimore. Garrison shared Lundy's abhorrence of slavery, but he soon grew impatient with his employer's moderate tone and mild proposals for reform. In 1831, therefore, he returned to Boston to found his own weekly newspaper, the *Liberator*.

Garrison and the *Liberator*

Garrison's simple philosophy was genuinely revolutionary. Opponents of slavery, he said, should view the institution from the point of view of the black man, not the white slaveholder. They should not, as earlier reformers had done, talk about the evil influence of slavery on white society; instead, they should talk about the damage the system did to Africans. And they should, therefore, reject "gradualism" and demand the immediate, unconditional, universal abolition of slavery. Garrison spoke with particular scorn about the advocates of colonization. They were not emancipationists, he argued; on the contrary, their real aim was to strengthen slavery by ridding the country of those African Americans who were already free. The true aim of foes of slavery, he insisted, must be to extend to African Americans all the rights of American citizenship. As startling as the drastic nature of his proposals was the relentless, uncompromising tone with which he promoted them. "I am aware," he wrote in the first issue of the *Liberator*, "that many object to the severity of my language; but is there not cause for severity? I will be as harsh as truth, and as uncompromising as justice. . . . I am in earnest—I will not equivocate—I will not excuse—I will not retreat a single inch—AND I WILL BE HEARD."

Garrison soon attracted a large group of followers throughout the North, enough to enable him to found the New England Anti-Slavery Society in 1832 and a year later, after a convention in Philadelphia, the American Anti-Slavery Society. Membership in the new organizations mushroomed. By 1835, there were more than 400 chapters of the societies; by 1838, there were 1,350 chapters, with more than 250,000 members. Antislavery sentiment was developing a strength and assertiveness greater than at any other point in the nation's past history.

American Anti-Slavery Society

Black Abolitionists

Abolitionism had a particular appeal to the free African Americans of the North, who in 1850 numbered about 250,000, mostly concentrated in cities. They lived in conditions of poverty and oppression often worse than those of their enslaved counterparts in the South. An English traveler who had visited both sections of the country wrote in 1854 that he was "utterly at a loss to imagine the source of that prejudice which subsists against [African Americans] in the Northern states, a prejudice unknown in the South, where the relations between the Africans and the European [white American] are so much more intimate." This confirmed an earlier observation by the French observer Alexis de Tocqueville that "the prejudice which repels the Negroes seems to increase in proportion as they are emancipated." Northern African Americans were often victimized by mob violence; they had virtually no access to education; they could vote in only a few states; and they were barred from all but the most menial of occupations. Most worked either as domestic servants or as sailors in the American merchant marine, and their wages were such that they lived in squalor. Some were kidnapped by white men and forced back into slavery.

For all their problems, however, Northern African Americans were aware of, and fiercely proud of, their freedom. And they remained acutely sensitive to the plight of those members of their race who remained in bondage, aware that their own position in society would remain precarious as long as slavery existed. Many in the 1830s came to support Garrison, to subscribe to his newspaper, and to sell subscriptions to it in their own communities. Indeed, the majority of the *Liberator*'s early subscribers were free African Americans.

Commitment to Abolition

There were also important African American leaders who expressed the aspirations of their race. One of the most militant was David Walker, a free African American from Boston, who in 1829 published a harsh pamphlet: *Walker's Appeal . . . to the Colored Citizens*. In it he declared: "America is more our country than it is the whites'—we have enriched it with our blood and tears." He warned: "The whites want slaves, and want us for their slaves, but some of them will curse the day they ever saw us." Slaves should, he declared, cut their masters' throats, should "kill, or be killed!"

Most African American critics of slavery, however, were less violent in their rhetoric. Sojourner Truth, a freed black woman, spent several years involved in a strange religious cult in upstate New York. She emerged as a powerful and eloquent spokeswoman for the abolition of slavery.

Discussion and Activities

Analyzing Change Have students read the section "Garrison and the *Liberator*." Discuss as a class how Garrison's approach to abolitionism was a departure from the approaches of earlier abolitionists. **SOC** **ARC**

Reasoning Processes

Comparing After students have read the section "Commitment to Abolition," ask them to create a Venn diagram comparing Garrison's *Liberator* with Walker's *Appeal to the Colored Citizens*. Have them discuss with a partner the greatest similarities and differences and which approach they think would be more successful. **ARC** **SOC**

Historical Thinking Skills

Sourcing and Situation After students have read the section "Black Abolitionists," discuss as a class how black abolitionist leaders may have used different approaches to appeal to different audiences. **SOC**

FUGITIVE SLAVE LAW CONVENTION
Abolitionists gathered in Cazenovia, New York, in August 1850 to consider how to respond to the law recently passed by Congress requiring Northern states to return fugitive enslaved people to their owners. Frederick Douglass is seated just to the left of the table in this photograph of some of the participants. The gathering was unusual among abolitionist gatherings in including substantial numbers of African Americans.

From the Collection of the Madison County Historical Society, Oneida, New York

FREDERICK DOUGLASS

The greatest African American abolitionist of all—and one of the most electrifying orators of his time, black or white—was Frederick Douglass. Born into slavery in Maryland, Douglass escaped to Massachusetts in 1838, became an outspoken leader of antislavery sentiment, and spent two years lecturing in England, where members of that country's vigorous antislavery movement lionized him. On his return to the United States in 1847, Douglass purchased his freedom from his Maryland slaveholder and founded an antislavery newspaper, the *North Star*, in Rochester, New York. He achieved wide renown as well for his autobiography, *Narrative of the Life of Frederick Douglass* (1845), in which he presented a damning picture of slavery. Douglass demanded for African Americans not only freedom but full social and economic equality as well. "What, to the American slave, is your 4th of July?" Douglass harshly asked in an Independence Day speech in Rochester, New York, in 1852. "I answer: a day that reveals to him, more than all other days in the year, the gross injustice and cruelty to which he is the constant victim. . . . There is not a nation on earth guilty of practices, more shocking and bloody, than are the people of these United States at this very hour."

Black abolitionists had been active for years before Douglass emerged as a leader of their cause; they had held their first national convention in 1830. But with Douglass's leadership, they became a more influential force; and they began, too, to forge alliances with white antislavery leaders such as Garrison.

ANTI-ABOLITIONISM

Abolitionism was a powerful force, but it provoked a powerful opposition as well. Almost all white Southerners, of course, looked on the movement with fear and contempt. But so too did many white Northerners. Indeed, even in the North, abolitionists were never more than a small, dissenting minority.

To its critics, the abolitionist crusade was a dangerous and frightening threat to the existing social system. Some white Americans correctly warned that it would produce a terrible war between the sections. Others feared, also correctly, that it might lead to a great influx of free African American into the North. The strident, outspoken abolition movement seemed to many white Northerners a sign of the disorienting social changes their society was experiencing—yet another threat to stability and order. To other Northerners, mostly men of business, abolition was a threat to lucrative trade with the South.

VIOLENT REPRISALS

The result was an escalating wave of violence directed against abolitionists in the 1830s. When Prudence Crandall attempted to admit several African American girls to her private school in Connecticut, local citizens had her arrested, threw filth into her well, and forced her to close down the school. A mob in Philadelphia attacked the abolitionist headquarters, the "Temple of Liberty," in 1834, burned it to the ground, and began a bloody race riot. Another mob seized Garrison on the streets of Boston in 1835 and threatened to hang him. Authorities saved him from death only by locking him in jail. Elijah Lovejoy, the editor of an abolitionist newspaper in Alton,

Discussion and Activities

Analyzing Perspectives Have students examine the image "Fugitive Slave Law Convention." Ask them to list details from the image that describe the tone of the gathering. *(African American and white participants are seated together; formal attire; formal postures; outdoor setting.)* Have students write a short paragraph explaining the effect(s) this photo may have had on different groups who viewed it in 1850. **SOC** **ARC**

Illinois, was a repeated victim of mob violence. Three times, angry white mobs invaded his offices and smashed his presses. Three times, Lovejoy installed new machines and began publishing again. When a mob attacked his office a fourth time, late in 1837, he tried to defend his press. The attackers set fire to the building and, as Lovejoy fled, shot and killed him.

That so many men and women continued to embrace abolitionism in the face of such vicious opposition from within their own communities suggests much about the nature of the movement. Abolitionists were not people who made their political commitments lightly or casually. They were strong-willed, passionate crusaders, displaying enormous courage and moral strength, and displaying, too, at times a level of fervor that many of their contemporaries found disturbing. Abolitionists were widely denounced, even by some who shared their aversion to slavery, as wild-eyed fanatics bent on social revolution. The anti-abolitionist mobs, in other words, were only the most violent expression of a sentiment that many other white Americans shared.

WILLIAM LLOYD GARRISON Garrison was the first member of the antislavery movement to call publicly for "immediate and complete emancipation" of enslaved people. That was in 1831, and for the next three decades he remained a stern and uncompromising enemy of slavery. After the Civil War, however, Garrison displayed little interest in the plight of the African Americans he had tried to emancipate. Instead, he turned to women's suffrage, Native American rights, and the prohibition of alcohol.

Abolitionism Divided

By the mid-1830s, the abolitionist crusade had become impossible to ignore. It had also begun to experience serious internal strains and divisions. One reason was the violence of the anti-abolitionists, which persuaded some members of the movement that a more moderate approach was necessary. Another reason was the growing radicalism of William Lloyd Garrison, who shocked even many of his own allies (including Frederick Douglass) by attacking not only slavery but the government itself. The Constitution, he said, was "a covenant with death and an agreement with hell." The nation's churches, he claimed, were bulwarks of slavery. In 1840, finally, Garrison precipitated a formal division within the American Anti-Slavery Society by insisting that women, who had always been central to the organization's work, be permitted to participate in the movement on terms of full equality. He continued after 1840 to arouse controversy with new, more-radical stands: an extreme pacifism that rejected even defensive wars; opposition to all forms of coercion—not just slavery but prisons and asylums as well; and finally, in 1843, a call for Northern disunion from the South. The nation could, Garrison suggested, purge itself of the sin of slavery by expelling the slave states from the Union.

MODERATES VERSUS EXTREMISTS

From 1840 on, therefore, abolitionism moved in many channels and spoke with many different voices. The Garrisonians remained influential, with their uncompromising moral stance. Others operated in moderate ways, arguing that abolition could be accomplished only as the result of a long, patient, peaceful struggle—"immediate abolition gradually accomplished," as they called it. At first, such moderates depended on "moral suasion." They would appeal to the conscience of the slaveholders and convince them that their institution was sinful. When that produced no results, they turned to political action, seeking to induce the Northern states and the federal government to aid the cause wherever possible. They joined the Garrisonians in helping runaway enslaved people find refuge in the North or in Canada through the so-called underground railroad (although their efforts were never as highly organized as the term suggests). They helped fund the legal battle over the Spanish slave vessel *Amistad*.

Later, after the Supreme Court (in *Prigg v. Pennsylvania*, 1842) ruled that states need not aid in enforcing the 1793 law requiring the return of fugitives to slaveholders, abolitionists secured the passage of "personal liberty laws" in several Northern states. These laws forbade state officials to assist in the capture and return of runaways. Above all, the antislavery societies petitioned Congress to abolish slavery in places where the federal government had jurisdiction—in the territories and in the District of Columbia—and to prohibit the interstate slave trade. But political abolitionism had severe limits. Few members of the movement believed that Congress could constitutionally interfere with a "domestic" institution such as slavery within the individual states themselves.

The abolitionists never formed a political party. Antislavery sentiment underlay the formation in 1840 of the Liberty Party,

Reasoning Processes

Comparing After students have read the section "Anti-Abolitionism," ask them to create a T-chart listing reactions to abolitionism in the North and the South. Have students discuss in small groups which reactions they think were more surprising. **SOC** **ARC**

Reasoning Processes

Comparing Have students read the section "Moderates Versus Extremists." Ask them to create a Venn diagram comparing the two groups. Have students discuss whether there was common ground the groups could have found to advance the cause of abolitionism together. **SOC** **ARC**

Discussion and Activities

Comparing and Contrasting Have students examine the image "Anti-Slave Message." Then have them use the Internet to find the image "Am I Not a Woman and a Sister." Discuss as a class the similarities and differences between the two images and how effective the imagery and phrases would have been in promoting the abolitionist cause. **SOC** **ARC**

AMERICA IN THE WORLD

The Abolition of Slavery

The Thirteenth Amendment to the Constitution, ratified in 1865, following the Civil War, abolished slavery in the United States. But the effort to abolish slavery did not begin or end in North America. Emancipation in the United States was part of a worldwide antislavery movement that had begun in the late eighteenth century and continued through the end of the nineteenth.

The movement to end slavery reflected the ideals of the Enlightenment, which inspired new concepts of individual freedom and political equality. As Enlightenment ideas spread throughout the Western world in the seventeenth and eighteenth centuries, introducing human rights and individual liberty to the concept of civilization, people on both sides of the Atlantic began to ask whether slavery was compatible with these new ideas. Some Enlightenment thinkers, including some of the founders of the American republic, believed that freedom was appropriate for white people, but not for people of color. But others came to believe that all human beings had an equal claim to liberty, and their views became the basis for an escalating series of antislavery movements.

Opponents of slavery first targeted the slave trade—the vast commerce in human beings that had grown up in the seventeenth and eighteenth centuries and had come to involve large parts of Europe, Africa, the Caribbean, and North and South America. In the aftermath of the revolutions in America, France, and Haiti in the late eighteenth and early nineteenth centuries, the attack on the slave trade gained momentum. The English reformer William Wilberforce spent years attacking Britain's connection with the slave trade, arguing against it on moral and religious grounds. After the Haitian revolution, he argued as well that the continuation of slavery would create more slave revolts. In 1807, he persuaded Parliament to pass a law ending the slave trade within the entire British Empire. The British example—combined with political, economic, and military pressure from London—persuaded many other nations to make the international slave trade illegal: the United States in 1808, France in 1814, Holland in 1817, and Spain in 1845. Trading in enslaved people continued within countries and colonies where slavery remained legal (including the United States), and some illegal slave trading continued throughout the Atlantic world. But the sale of enslaved people steadily declined after 1807. The last known shipment of enslaved people across the Atlantic—from Africa to Cuba—occurred in 1867.

Ending the slave trade was a great deal easier than ending slavery itself. But pressure to abolish slavery grew steadily throughout the nineteenth century, with Wilberforce once more helping lead the international outcry against the institution. In Haiti, the slave revolts that began in 1791 eventually abolished not only slavery but also French rule. In some parts of South America, slavery came to an end with the overthrow of Spanish rule in the 1820s. Simón Bolívar, the great leader of Latin American independence, considered abolishing slavery an important part of his mission. He freed enslaved people who joined his armies, and he insisted on prohibitions of slavery in several of the constitutions he helped frame. In 1833, the British Parliament passed a law abolishing slavery throughout the British Empire and compensated slaveholders for freeing enslaved people. France abolished slavery in its empire in 1848. In the Caribbean, Spain followed Britain in slowly eliminating slavery from its colonies. Puerto Rico abolished slavery in 1873 and Cuba became the last colony in the Caribbean to end slavery, in 1886, in the face of increasing slave resistance and the declining profitability of slave-based plantations. Brazil was the last nation in the Americas to end the system, in 1888. The Brazilian military began to turn against slavery after the valiant participation of slaves in Brazil's war with Paraguay in the late 1860s; eventually, educated Brazilian civilians began to oppose the system too, arguing that it obstructed economic and social progress.

ANTI-SLAVE MESSAGE **This sampler conveys a potent anti-slave message, "Thou God Seest Me." Originally from the Bible (Genesis 16:13), this quote expresses the sentiment that the enslaved man should be seen as a man rather than chattel.**

In the United States, the power of world opinion—and the example of Wilberforce's movement in England—became an important spur to the abolitionist movement as it gained strength in the 1820s and 1830s. American abolitionism, in turn, helped reinforce the movements abroad. Frederick Douglass, the former enslaved man turned abolitionist, became a major figure in the international antislavery movement and was a much-admired and much-sought-after speaker in England and Europe in the 1840s and 1850s. No other nation paid as terrible a price for abolishing slavery as did the United States during its Civil War, but American emancipation was nevertheless a part of a worldwide movement toward ending legalized human bondage.

HISTORICAL THINKING SKILLS

1. **Explaining Historical Developments** Why did opponents of slavery focus first on ending the slave trade, rather than abolishing slavery itself? Why was ending the slave trade easier than ending slavery?
2. **Analyzing Perspectives** How do William Wilberforce's arguments against slavery compare with those of the abolitionists in the United States?
3. **Developing Arguments** How could a nation that declared "all men are created equal" justify slavery?

Answers

America in the World

1. Both were complex issues at the time. One major question was how to compensate slaveholders. The other question concerned safety and security in the South. Some formerly enslaved people did not have employable skills, nor could they read or write. Without the proper skills and training for many people, abolition created a situation where a large number of people had nothing to do.
2. For the most part, the arguments of U.S. abolitionists were similar to those of Wilberforce. Some, like Thomas Paine, argued about the immorality of slavery. Paine did not believe the institution could coexist in a country that called itself Christian. Others, however, also relied on economic and political arguments, as well as philosophical ones.
3. Slavery was an established labor system in the Americas even before the arrival of Europeans, as many Native American groups used enslaved people for labor. Slavery varied from place to place, but the system was established and heavily rooted into the economic fabric of American society. Most Americans, even those that enslaved people, believed that the institution was going to go away eventually, but most were skeptical about how that was going to work in practice.

which chose the Kentucky antislavery leader James G. Birney as its presidential candidate. But this party, and its successors, never campaigned for outright abolition (an illustration of the important fact that "antislavery" and "abolitionism" were not always the same thing). They stood instead for "free soil," for keeping slavery out of the territories. Some free-soilers were concerned about the welfare of African Americans; others cared nothing about the enslaved people but simply wanted to keep the West a country for white Americans. Garrison dismissed free-soilism as "white-manism." But the free-soil position would ultimately do what abolitionism never could accomplish: attract the support of large numbers, even a majority, of the white population of the North.

The frustrations of political abolitionism drove some critics of slavery to embrace more drastic measures. A few began to advocate violence; a group of prominent abolitionists in New England, for example, funneled money and arms to John Brown to enable bloody uprisings in Kansas and Virginia. Others attempted to arouse widespread public anger through propaganda. Abolitionist descriptions of slavery–for example, Theodore Dwight Weld and Angelina Grimké's *American Slavery as It Is: Testimony of a Thousand Witnesses* (1839)–presented what the authors claimed were careful, factual pictures of slavery, but what were in fact highly polemical, often wildly distorted images.

Harriet Beecher Stowe

The most powerful document of abolitionist propaganda, however, was a work of fiction: Harriet Beecher Stowe's *Uncle Tom's Cabin*. It appeared first, in 1851–1852, as a serial in an antislavery weekly. Then, in 1852, it was published as a book. It rocked the nation, selling more than 300,000 copies within a year of publication, and was later issued again and again to become one of the most remarkable best-sellers in American history.

Stowe's novel emerged not just out of abolitionist politics, but also out of a popular tradition of sentimental novels written by, and largely for, women. Stowe combined the emotional conventions of the sentimental novel with the political ideas of the abolition movement, and to sensational effect. Her novel, by embedding the antislavery message within a familiar and popular literary form, succeeded in bringing the message of abolitionism to an enormous new audience–not only those who read the book but also those who watched dramatizations of its story by countless theater companies throughout the nation. The novel's emotional portrayal of good, kindly enslaved people victimized by a cruel system; of the loyal, trusting Uncle Tom; of the vicious overseer Simon Legree (described as a New Englander so as to prevent the book from seeming to be an attack on white Southerners); of the escape of the beautiful Eliza; of the heartrending death of Little Eva–all became a part of American popular legend. Reviled throughout the South, Stowe became a hero to many in the North. And in both regions, her novel helped to inflame sectional tensions to a new level of passion. Few books in American history have had so great an impact on the course of public events.

Abolitionism's Enduring Influence

Even divided, therefore, abolitionism remained a powerful influence on the life of the nation. Only a relatively small number of people before the Civil War ever accepted the abolitionist position that slavery must be entirely eliminated in a single stroke. But the crusade that Garrison had launched, and that thousands of committed men and women kept alive for three decades, was a constant, visible reminder of how deeply the institution of slavery was dividing America.

Discussion and Activities

Analyzing Cause and Effect Have students read the section "Harriet Beecher Stowe." Ask them to write a short paragraph explaining why *Uncle Tom's Cabin* had such a great impact on abolitionism. **SOC** **ARC**

Reasoning Processes

Comparing Have students read the section "Abolitionism's Enduring Influence." Ask them to construct a Janus figure (a human outline figure divided down the middle) illustrating symbols and ideas that represent an abolitionist on one side and an anti-abolitionist on the other. **SOC** **ARC**

Discussion and Activities

Making Connections Have students read the feature "Sentimental Novels." As a class, discuss how these novels are similar to or different from literary genres that are popular now. **SOC**

SENTIMENTAL NOVELS

"America is now wholly given over to a damned mob of scribbling women," Nathaniel Hawthorne complained in 1855, "and I should have no chance of success while the public taste is occupied with their trash." Hawthorne, one of the leading novelists of his time, was complaining about the most popular form of fiction in mid-nineteenth-century America—not his own dark and serious works, but the "sentimental novel," a genre of literature written and read mostly by middle-class women.

In an age when affluent women occupied primarily domestic roles, and in which finding a favorable marriage was the most important thing many women could do to secure or improve their lots in life, the sentimental novel gave voice to both female hopes and female anxieties. The plots of sentimental novels were usually filled with character-improving problems and domestic trials, but most of them ended with the heroine securely and happily married. They were phenomenally successful, many of them selling more than 100,000 copies each—far more than almost any other books of the time.

Sentimental heroines were almost always beautiful and endowed with specifically female qualities—"all the virtues," one novelist wrote, "that are founded in the sensibility of the heart: Pity, the attribute of angels, and friendship, the balm of life, delight to dwell in the female breast." Women were highly sensitive creatures, the sentimental writers believed, incapable of disguising their feelings, and subject to fainting, mysterious illnesses, trances, and, of course, tears—things rarely expected of men. But they were also capable of a kind of nurturing love and natural sincerity that was hard to find in the predominantly male public world. In Susan Warner's *The Wide, Wide World* (1850), for example, the heroine, a young girl named Ellen Montgomery, finds herself suddenly thrust into the "wide, wide world" of male competition after her father loses his fortune. She is unable to adapt to this world, but she is saved in the end when she is taken in by wealthy relatives, who will undoubtedly prepare her for a successful marriage. They restore to her the security and comfort to which she had been born and without which she seemed unable to thrive.

Sentimental novels accepted uncritically the popular assumptions about women's special needs and desires, and they offered stirring tales of how women satisfied them. But sentimental novels were not limited to romanticized images of female fulfillment through protection and marriage. They hinted as well at the increasing role of women in reform movements. Many such books portrayed women dealing with social and moral problems—and using their highly developed female sensibilities to help other women escape from their troubles. Women were particularly suitable for such reform work, the writers implied, because they were specially gifted at helping and nurturing others.

The most famous sentimental novelist of the nineteenth century was Harriet Beecher Stowe. Most of her books—*The Minister's Wooing, My Wife and I, We and Our Neighbors,* and others—portrayed the travails and ultimate triumphs of women as they became wives, mothers, and hostesses. But Stowe was and remains best known for her 1852 antislavery novel, *Uncle Tom's Cabin,* one of the most influential books ever published in America. As a story about slavery, and about an aging black man—Uncle Tom—who is unfailingly submissive to his white slaveholders, it is in many ways very different from her other novels. But *Uncle Tom's Cabin* is a sentimental novel, too. Stowe's critique of slavery is based on her belief in the importance of domestic values and family security. Slavery's violation of those values, and its denial of that security, is what made it so abhorrent to her. The simple, decent Uncle Tom faces many of the same dilemmas that the female heroines of other sentimental novels encounter in their struggles to find security and tranquillity in their lives.

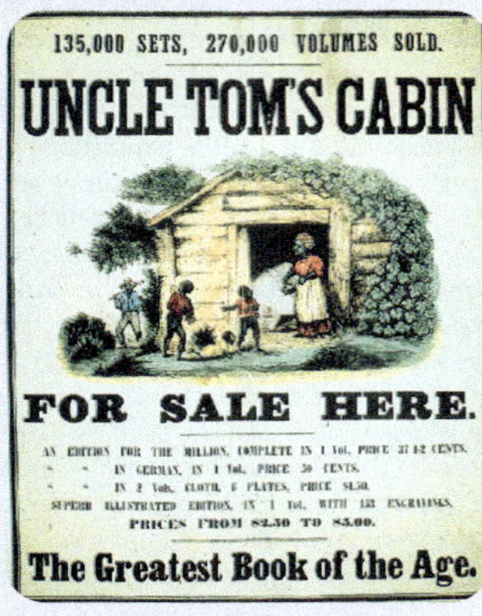

UNCLE TOM'S CABIN Uncle Tom's Cabin did much to inflame public opinion in both the North and the South in the last years before the Civil War. When Abraham Lincoln was introduced to Stowe once in the White House, he reportedly said to her: "So you are the little lady that has brought this great war." At the time, however, Stowe was equally well known as one of the most successful American writers of sentimental novels.

Another way in which women were emerging from their domestic sphere was in becoming consumers of the expanding products of America's industrializing economy. The female characters in sentimental novels searched not just for love, security, and social justice; they also searched for luxury and for the pleasure of buying some favored item. Susan Warner illustrated this aspect of the culture of the sentimental novel—and the desires of the women who read them—in *The Wide, Wide World,* in her description of the young Ellen Montgomery in an elegant bookstore, buying a Bible: "Such beautiful Bibles she had never seen; she pored in ecstasy over their varieties of type and binding, and was very evidently in love with them all."

HISTORICAL THINKING SKILLS

1. **Comparing** How did the lives of the heroines of sentimental novels compare with the lives of real women of the nineteenth century?
2. **Evaluating** Did sentimental novels reinforce prevailing attitudes toward women or broaden the perception of women's "proper role"?
3. **Making Connections** *Uncle Tom's Cabin* is probably one of the best known works of American fiction from this time period. Why was this novel so much more powerful than other sentimental novels?

Answers

Patterns of Popular Culture

1. In the mid-nineteenth century, the main goal of most American women was to find a favorable marriage and secure a good home. These novels reinforced these issues and almost always portrayed a positive, happy outcome. For real women, these goals were not always attainable. Also, some women had other goals that were not necessarily acceptable in society at the time.
2. Most of these novels reinforced the traditional roles of women, but some did portray women as grappling with various moral and social issues in society.
3. This novel touched on an issue that was ripping the country apart—slavery. The story tugged at the heartstrings of many readers because it portrayed the brutality of slavery and the effect it had on families. The book was not only popular in the United States but in Europe as well. The book also elicited a number of responses from Southerners, many of whom claimed that the book was written by someone who had never experienced slavery first hand.

CHAPTER 12 REVIEW

CONNECTING THEMES

Chapter 12 explored the impact of art and literature on American culture and society during a prolific period of creativity. The First American Renaissance, the Second Great Awakening, and other factors also led to a growing number of reform movements. Two in particular – abolitionism and women's rights – would have major and long-lasting effects on the nation.

The philosophical and literary movement known generally as Romanticism stressed the importance of the individual. But many reformers also developed a faith in utopianism, which emphasized the possibility of creating ideal communities. As the nation experienced different influences at different times and in different places, society became less cohesive, helping to set the stage for the advent of the Civil War.

You should consider the following questions as you review the themes for this chapter:

- What were the factors that led to the creation of distinct identities for reform movements and utopian ventures?
- What did reform movements accomplish during this period?
- How did utopian ideals encourage western settlement?
- How did women and African Americans attempt to influence the political culture of the United States during the time period?
- How successful were the political efforts of African Americans and women in this time period?
- What was the continuing impact of the natural environment on the development of regional political and economic identities?
- How did science and technology influence American culture during the antebellum period?
- What were the causes and effects of the rise of art and literature during the Romantic period in American history?

KEY TERMS

abolitionists 344
American Colonization Society 344
Amistad 347
anti-abolitionism 346
Charles Grandison Finney 335
David Walker 345
Edgar Allan Poe 331
Elizabeth Cady Stanton 341
feminism 341
Frederick Douglass 346
Fugitive Slave Law 346
Harriet Beecher Stowe 349
Henry David Thoreau 332
Herman Melville 330
Horace Mann 338
Hudson River School 329
Indian reservation 340
James Fenimore Cooper 330
Joseph Smith 334
Lucretia Mott 341
Margaret Fuller 333
Nathaniel Hawthorne 332
Protestant revivalism 335
public education 338
Ralph Waldo Emerson 331
Sarah and Angelica Grimke 341
Seneca Falls Convention 341
Shakers 333
Susan B. Anthony 341
Temperance Crusade 334
Transcendentalism 331
utopian societies 333
Walt Whitman 330
William Lloyd Garrison 345

Discussion and Activities

Argumentation Divide the class into groups and assign each group a topic from the following list: Romanticism, Transcendentalism, asylum and prison reform, education reform, feminism, and abolitionism. Have each group review what they have learned and construct a short argument about why that movement was the most important of those assigned. They could frame their argument around a poster, a short speech, or a short essay. **SOC** **ARC**

Key Terms

Students should be familiar with the key terms and be able to define them in the context of literary, artistic, and social reform movements that emerged in the United States in the nineteenth century. Encourage students to use these terms in performing review exercises and exam practice for this chapter.

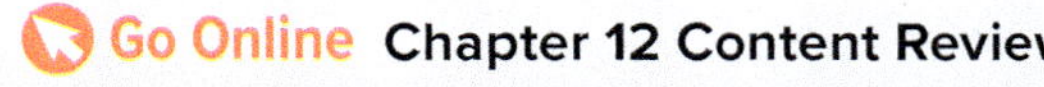

Go Online Chapter 12 Content Review

Assessing Student Understanding Use the online assessment to assess student understanding of concepts and topics within the chapter. You can assign the ready-made Chapter 12 Content Review or create your own from available questions. This easy-to-use tool helps you design assessments that meet the needs of different types of learners.

CHAPTER 12

Antebellum Culture and Reform

Answers

Multiple Choice

1. A; **2.** C; **3.** C

Short Answer

4A) Possible answer: The point of view is that of a reformer who supports the temperance movement. The image shows the "progress" that individuals go through once they begin drinking alcohol—an activity that begins innocently but can lead to death.

4B) Possible answer: Drinking became a problem for some individuals during the first half of the nineteenth century. Evangelical Protestants and others argued that drinking affected individuals adversely in many ways, leading to crime, disorder, and poverty.

4C) Possible answer: Organization against drinking solidified into the creation of several temperance groups, with one of the more prominent being the American Society for the Promotion of Temperance. Organizations like this spurred opposition to drinking to grow to include millions of people.

5A) Possible answer: Both groups looked to nature as a guiding principle, but they differed in how to read nature. For the Dark Romantics, nature was something to be feared because of the danger that it potentially posed. For Transcendentalists, nature was something to be embraced for its beauty and as a way to understand their relationship to the world.

5B) Possible answer: Both groups believed in the ability of the individual to construct their own reality. For Transcendentalists, that reality meant breaking away from the constraints of society to pursue higher levels of understanding. For the Dark Romantics, that reality was one devoid of universal meaning.

5C) Possible answer: Both groups were reacting to the philosophy of the Enlightenment and its emphasis upon reason as a guide to truth. For both the Dark Romantics and the Transcendentalists, truth was not something that could be obtained only from reason. They emphasized the importance of intuition as a better guide to higher understanding.

AP EXAM PRACTICE

Questions assume cumulative content knowledge from this chapter and previous chapters.

MULTIPLE CHOICE

Use the image on page 337 and your knowledge of U.S. history to answer questions 1-3.

1. What belief held by many reform movements of the Second Great Awakening is reflected in the image?
   - (A) the importance of a "virtuous citizenry"
   - (B) the focus on individuals as distinct from greater society
   - (C) the belief in predestination
   - (D) the idea of women as belonging in a separate sphere
2. Which of the following most influenced the adherents of the Second Great Awakening to improve society?
   - (A) influences from European Romanticism
   - (B) popular desire for a new, uniquely American culture
   - (C) concern over social changes accelerated by industrialization and immigration
   - (D) increasing acceptance of new Enlightenment ideals
3. Which demographic group emerged as leaders for the first time within multiple reform movements during the Second Great Awakening?
   - (A) middle-class men
   - (B) religious leaders
   - (C) working-class men
   - (D) middle-class women

SHORT ANSWER

Use your knowledge of U.S. history to answer questions 4 and 5.

4. Use the image on page 337 to answer A, B, and C.
   - (A) Briefly describe ONE historical point of view about drinking in the image.
   - (B) Briefly explain ONE specific historical cause that led to the reform movements during the first half of the nineteenth century.
   - (C) Briefly explain ONE specific historical effect that resulted from the reform movements during the first half of the nineteenth century.
5. Answer A, B, and C.
   - (A) Briefly describe ONE specific historical difference between the Dark Romantics, such as Poe, and the Transcendentalists, such as Thoreau.
   - (B) Briefly describe ONE specific historical similarity between the Dark Romantics and the Transcendentalists.
   - (C) Explain ONE specific cause that led to the rise of either of these literary movements.

LONG ESSAY

Develop a thoughtful and thorough historical argument that addresses the statement. Begin your essay with a thesis statement, and support it with specific historical evidence and examples.

6. Evaluate the extent that individualism led to the rise of a women's rights movement from 1800 to 1850.

Answers

Long Essay

6. Possible thesis: The guiding principle of individualism played an important role in leading to a women's rights movement in the first half of the nineteenth century. This philosophy was rooted deep in the American psyche from the founding of the nation. However, the notion of equality and the social and political consequences of that concept would play greater roles within the women's rights movement between 1800 and 1850. The philosophy of individualism is grounded in the Lockean social contract theory, which drove much of the American Revolution. It is also inherently woven within the fabric of the Romantic Movement, which dominated American art and literature in the first half of the nineteenth century. However, this ideal, while embraced by many important figures and movements between 1800 and 1850, was also limited in its scope. For the most part, it only included white males. Women were also generally left out of any social or political conversations, as their social roles were embodied by the concepts of "Republican Motherhood" and the "Cult of Domesticity." America's general lack of official hierarchy also led to the importance of the concept of individualism within the American psyche. The Constitution abolishes social titles, thus reinforcing the belief that all are equal (at least on paper, if not in reality). This fact also contributed to the rise of the women's movement.

AP EXAM PRACTICE

As you answer the questions, consider how the historical developments, processes, and individuals in Unit 4 connect to those in previous units.

MULTIPLE CHOICE

Use the image on page 202 and your knowledge of U.S. history to answer questions 1 and 2.

1. Eli Whitney's cotton gin was instrumental in what significant shift?
   - (A) the movement from exclusively cotton cultivation to a diversified economy
   - (B) the inclusion of textile mills into southern cities
   - (C) the shift from tobacco cultivation to cotton cultivation
   - (D) the movement of cotton cultivation to the western territories

2. The cotton gin affected the larger American economy by
   - (A) placing the South and North in direct economic competition as both grew significant cotton crops.
   - (B) slowing the movement westward as Americans instead took jobs in textile mills.
   - (C) preventing the development of transportation networks as focus increased on agriculture.
   - (D) connecting the South and North as Northern mills processed Southern cotton.

Use the image on page 274 and your knowledge of U.S. history to answer questions 3–5.

3. The image reflects the concern that
   - (A) Americans of Irish and German descent would use their economic dominance to gain political control.
   - (B) recently arrived Irish and German immigrants would unfairly seize elections.
   - (C) the lack of overall political interest would allow Irish and German immigrants to win elections uncontested.
   - (D) Irish and German immigrants would not show interest in participating in American elections.

4. Nativists largely objected to Irish and German immigrants because many of the immigrants
   - (A) held politically radical ideals.
   - (B) dominated the economic system.
   - (C) were religiously Roman Catholic.
   - (D) refused to assimilate into American society.

5. The rise of a political party in response to feelings such as those reflected in the image served to disrupt
   - (A) the Era of Good Feelings.
   - (B) the formation of the Republican Party.
   - (C) one-party rule by the Democratic Party.
   - (D) the Second Party System.

Use the image on page 321 and your knowledge of U.S. history to answer questions 6 and 7.

6. Images such as "The Business of Slavery" are evidence of
   - (A) the significant economic integration of the system of slavery into American culture.
   - (B) the separation of the system of slavery from the rest of the economy.
   - (C) the solely agricultural nature of slavery in the United States.
   - (D) the dispersed presence of enslaved workers throughout the United States.

7. Throughout early years of the United States, how did the institution of slavery change?
   - (A) The institution of slavery became increasingly uniform in all regions as the nation united economically.
   - (B) As the institution of slavery began to contract wage laborers, they eventually replaced enslaved people.
   - (C) As the institution of slavery began to contract Southerners, slavery was increasingly seen as being in conflict with Revolutionary ideals of freedom.
   - (D) The institution of slavery continued to expand as Americans moved westward.

Discussion and Activities

Analyzing Cause and Effect Direct students' attention to the Questions to Consider posed at the beginning of Unit 4:

- What were the major reasons for the emergence of official political parties in the United States during the first half of the nineteenth century?
- What were the major foreign policy challenges faced by the United States during the first half of the nineteenth century?
- What were the major factors that caused differences to grow among the different geographic regions in the United States during the first half of the nineteenth century?

Discuss these questions as a class to review important concepts from the unit. To close the discussion, **ask:** Do the various reform movements of the first half of the nineteenth century show increasing unity or division in the United States?

Answers

Multiple Choice

1. C; **2.** D; **3.** B; **4.** C; **5.** D; **6.** A; **7.** D; **8.** A; **9.** C; **10.** B

Answers

Short Answer

11A) Possible answer: In the image, two women are sitting around studying geography. This image presents the view that women are just as capable as men of higher intellectual pursuits. Despite the limited opportunities for women, by the 1820s, a number of seminaries had been created for young women.

11B) Possible answer: In 1776, Abigail Adams called for a democratic revolution of women if the Founding Fathers did not include them in the political discourse at the start of the American Revolution. This call to action was one step in the gradual call for more women's rights.

11C) Possible answer: In 1848, a group of women met at Seneca Falls, New York, for the first official women's rights convention. The document that emerged from this event mimicked the wording of the Declaration of Independence, calling for the political equality of women in the United States. Despite its failure to achieve any real or lasting change, this event did serve as a model for later movements.

Use the excerpt from "Declaration of Sentiments" on page 342 and your knowledge of U.S. history to answer questions 8–10.

8. The excerpt from the "Declaration of Sentiments" indicates that advocates for women's rights
   (A) sought to include women in the freedoms and rights secured in the Revolution.
   (B) were focused on economic rights and financial independence for women.
   (C) wanted to create a new place for women in American society.
   (D) felt that women should have equal educational opportunities as men.

9. The women's movement arose to counter the increasing cultural belief in
   (A) the value of women in the industrial workplace.
   (B) the need to move away from the ideals of the Revolution.
   (C) the importance of separate spheres for men and women.
   (D) the need to permanently entrench Republican Motherhood.

10. Many of the activists who supported the Declaration of Sentiments
    (A) were members of the working class.
    (B) were active in many reform movements.
    (C) kept undivided focus on women's suffrage.
    (D) were overwhelmingly male.

SHORT ANSWER

Use the image *A Seminary for Women* on page 195 and your knowledge of U.S. history to answer question 11.

11. Answer A, B, and C.
    (A) Briefly describe ONE point of view about women in the first half of the nineteenth century as depicted in the image.
    (B) Briefly explain ONE specific historical cause for the rise of a woman's rights movement in the first half of the nineteenth century.
    (C) Briefly explain ONE specific historical effect that resulted from the rise of a woman's rights movement in the first half of the nineteenth century.

LONG ESSAY

Develop a thoughtful and thorough historical argument that addresses the statement. Begin your essay with a thesis statement, and support it with specific historical evidence and examples.

12. Evaluate the extent of continuities in the lives of African Americans in the United States from 1800 to 1850.

Answers

Long Essay

12. Possible thesis: In 1800, African Americans had very little political and legal rights, and most were enslaved on the plantations in the South; much of this had not changed by 1850. Slave labor was still protected in the United States, despite the fact that by 1850 some individual states had begun outlawing the institution within their own borders. Despite the fact that slavery continued to be protected and recognized by federal law in the first half of the nineteenth century, there were a number of significant changes taking place. Several federal laws were enacted prohibiting the expansion of slavery into designated territories. In 1800, virtually no states had outlawed the institution of slavery, but by 1850, virtually every state in the North had abolished the institution. Enslaved people also began to assert their independence, as a number of slave revolts took place across the South during the early 1800s. Unfortunately, none of these was very successful and often resulted in beefed-up slave laws. African Americans found continuity in the rich culture they developed, particularly in the South, and especially in the areas of religion, language, and music.

Pacing Guide

Unit 5 explores key concepts from Period 5: 1844–1877 of the AP U.S. History Curriculum Framework. It is recommended that 10–17% of the total instruction time for the entire course be spent on Period 5.

Key Concepts

5.1 The United States became more connected with the world, pursued an expansionist foreign policy in the Western Hemisphere, and emerged as the destination for many migrants from other countries.

5.2 Intensified by expansion and deepening regional divisions, debates over slavery and other economic, cultural, and political issues led the nation into civil war.

5.3 The Union victory in the Civil War and the contested reconstruction of the South settled the issues of slavery and secession, but left unresolved many questions about the power of the federal government and citizenship rights.

UNIT 5: 1844–1877

CHAPTER 13: THE IMPENDING CRISIS

CHAPTER 14: THE CIVIL WAR

CHAPTER 15: RECONSTRUCTION AND THE NEW SOUTH

THEMATIC LEARNING OBJECTIVES

- Analyze the causes and effects of the ideology known as Manifest Destiny.
- Compare and contrast the compromises that led to the Civil War.
- Explain the impact of major elections on the regional divide between the North and the South.
- Assess the advantages and disadvantages of the North and the South at the start of the Civil War.
- Describe the different phases of the Civil War.
- Analyze the policies of the Lincoln administration during the Civil War.
- Evaluate the impact of Reconstruction on both the North and the South.

QUESTIONS TO CONSIDER

- What were the major causes of the Civil War?
- How were the North and the South politically, socially, and economically similar and different before and after the Civil War?
- What were the major effects of the Civil War?

HISTORICAL DEVELOPMENTS: 1844–1877

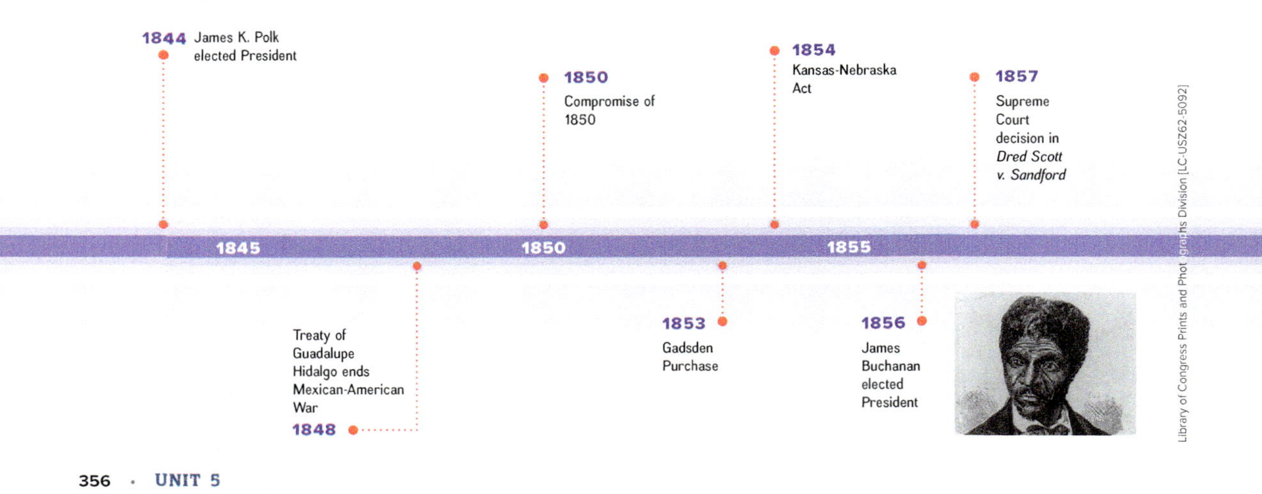

Library of Congress Prints and Photographs Division [LC-USZ62-5092]

Discussion and Activities

Comparison and Argumentation Have students examine the time line "Historical Developments: 1844–1877." **Ask:** Based on the time line and what you already know, which events on the time line seem to indicate growing national unity, and which events seem to indicate growing national division? *(Unity: End of the Mexican-American War; Compromise of 1850. Division: Civil War begins.)*

MAKING CONNECTIONS

Unit Five focuses on further U.S. expansion west, the causes and conduct of the Civil War, the impact of the conflict on Northern and Southern societies, and the immediate and lasting effects of Reconstruction on the United States.

White Americans often justified the wave of expansion in the 1840s with the ideology of Manifest Destiny, which contended that the United States was destined by God and history to gain territory and extend liberty across the continent. This expansion led to many conflicts, including a major war with Mexico and many clashes with Native Americans. The Mexican War resulted in a vast territorial acquisition for the United States and a new array of divisive issues. Most critical was whether to allow slavery in these new territories. Eventually, Congress enacted the Compromise of 1850, which was not the product of widespread agreement and failed to satisfy either the pro- or anti-slavery forces. The Fugitive Slave Act and the Kansas-Nebraska Act that followed the compromise only deepened the sectional divide. Finally, the Supreme Court enraged the anti-slavery movement in the North with the *Dred Scott* decision, while John Brown's raid at Harpers Ferry alarmed the South.

The election of Abraham Lincoln in 1860 led South Carolina to issue the first Declaration of Secession. Other Southern states quickly followed. The Civil War was now at hand. The North held advantages based on population, industry, and transportation, while the South had the advantage of fighting a defensive war in familiar territory. Following one of the bloodiest and most costly wars in American history, the two sides signed a peace treaty in 1865.

The grieving country now faced the task of rebuilding the Union. President Lincoln proposed a relatively swift and lenient policy of Reconstruction, but Radical Republicans in Congress wanted a harsher policy. White Southerners increasingly objected to the governments imposed on them during Reconstruction. Passage of the Civil War amendments to the Constitution further angered white Southerners. For African Americans and poor whites, Reconstruction increased access to public education. But sharecropping and the crop-lien system, which could trap farmers in a cycle of debt, overshadowed limited gains in land and income redistribution.

Southern states pushed to reverse the effects of the war and Reconstruction. Secret societies like the Ku Klux Klan used violence and intimidation to disenfranchise and repress African Americans. White Southerners passed Black Codes and Jim Crow laws to institutionalize the system of segregation that touched nearly every aspect of Southern life. These laws eliminated most of the social, economic, and political gains made by African Americans in the late 1800s.

In the aftermath of Civil War and Reconstruction, the North continued to absorb millions of European immigrants and focus on the growth of industry and commerce. The South attempted to rebuild with a new emphasis on factories and railroads. Agriculture, however, still dominated the region, which remained underdeveloped as white politicians prioritized racial segregation over economic modernization. As the United States began to look outward, serious internal divisions and challenges remained.

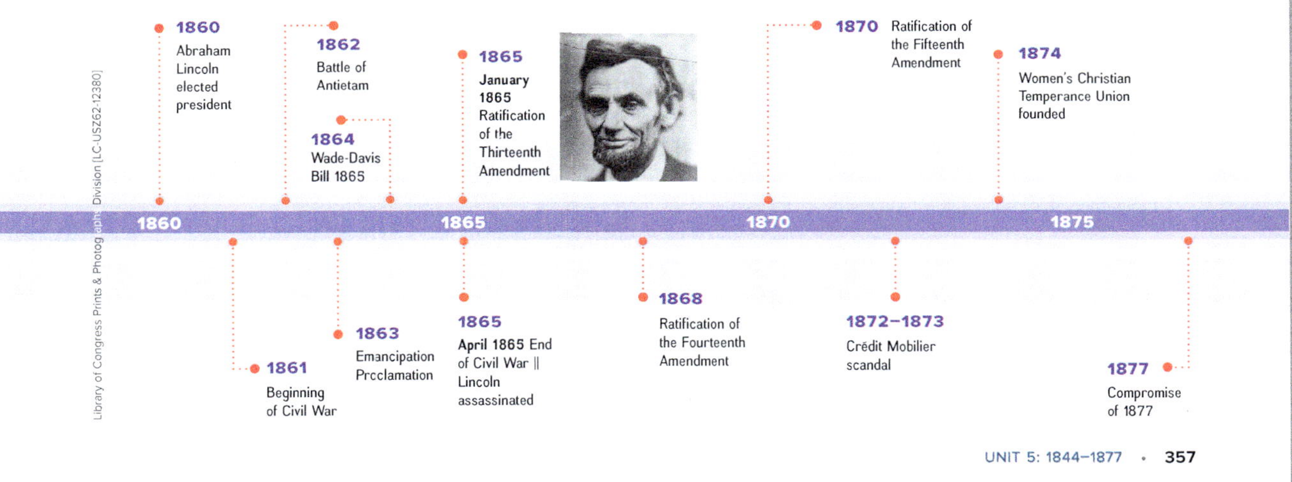

Library of Congress Prints & Photographs Division [LC-USZ62-12380]

Historical Thinking Skills

Historical Reasoning and Argumentation Have students read the section "Making Connections." Ask them to create a T-chart with the headings "Unity" and "Division." Have students list examples of each from the section. Then ask students to identify which examples are political, economic, geographic, or cultural. **Ask:** Which type of example seems most significant?

Go Online Additional Resources

Adaptive Learning with SmartBook A proven adaptive learning program, SmartBook offers an interactive environment that helps students learn faster, study more efficiently, and retain more knowledge.

Assign this resource to differentiate instruction for students and report on year-long progression.

Pacing Guide

Chapter 13 explores key concepts from Period 5: 1844–1877 of the AP U.S. History Curriculum Framework. The suggested instruction time for Chapter 13 is 5 days.

Key Concepts

5.1.I Popular enthusiasm for U.S. expansion, bolstered by economic and security interests, resulted in the acquisition of new territories, substantial migration westward, and new overseas initiatives.

5.1.II In the 1840s and 1850s, Americans continued to debate questions about rights and citizenship for various groups of U.S. inhabitants.

13 THE IMPENDING CRISIS

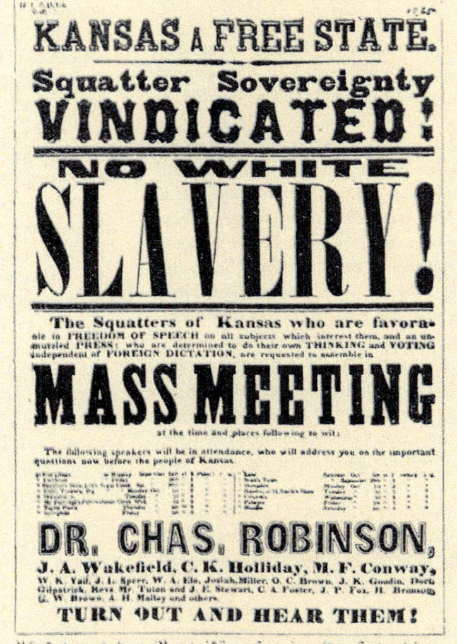

"BLEEDING KANSAS"
The battle over the fate of slavery in Kansas was one of the most turbulent events of the 1850s. This 1855 poster invites antislavery forces to a meeting to protest the actions of the "bogus" pro-slavery territorial legislature, which had passed laws that, among other things, made it illegal to speak or write against slavery. "Squatter sovereignty" was another term for "popular sovereignty," the doctrine that gave residents of a prospective state the power to decide the fate of slavery there.

CONNECTING CONCEPTS

Chapter Thirteen begins by explaining the ideology known as Manifest Destiny. Many Americans viewed the continuing westward expansion and the acquisition of territory outside of North America as destined by God and history. Some people further justified U.S. expansion through arguments about the superiority of white Americans. The Mexican War, the Oregon dispute, and the Kansas crisis also led to competing ideologies. In the South, white politicians like John Calhoun now contended that slavery was a "positive good," not a "necessary evil." In the North and the West, a "free-soil" ideology emerged which emphasized that slavery posed a threat to democracy and opportunity for white Americans.

Westward expansion led to military and diplomatic crises during the 1850s. The sectional divide between the North and the South grew larger. When the U.S. Supreme Court endorsed the constitutional and legal status of slavery in *Dred Scott v. Sandford*, most northern states and abolitionists refused to accept the decision. The controversy not only focused on the status of slavery and the fate of millions of African Americans, but also concerned the balance of power between the slave and free states in Congress. Once again, Henry Clay tried to broker a sectional compromise.

Clay proposed a comprehensive, and he believed, permanent solution to the sectional crisis, but it was defeated in Congress following months of debate. A younger group of leaders emerged in the Senate and put forth a series of separate measures, passed individually, that created the Compromise of 1850. The act was not the result of widespread agreement among members of Congress and only briefly relieved sectional conflict. Tensions soon increased and the sectional crisis escalated with John Brown's raid at Harpers Ferry and the election of Abraham Lincoln in 1860.

Discussion and Activities

Evaluating Evidence Have students examine the image "Bleeding Kansas." Ask them to create a KWL chart identifying what they know, what they want to know, and later what they have learned about the conflict over slavery prior to the Civil War. Have students add to their charts as they read through the chapter. **PCE** **SOC** **ARC** **NAT** **WXT**

CHAPTER 13
THE IMPENDING CRISIS

As you read, you should:

- Analyze the reasons why territorial acquisition increased sectional tensions.
- Describe the ways that slavery highlighted cultural differences between the North and the South.
- Identify the historical arguments for and against the institution of slavery.
- Describe the attempts at compromise during the 1850s.
- Evaluate the cause and effects of a Third Party system in the antebellum United States.
- Analyze the causes which ultimately led to the secession movement following Lincoln's election in 1860.

Historical Thinking Skills

Contextualization Have students read the introductory section "Looking Westward." Ask them to recall and discuss as a class previous events in westward expansion. *(Louisiana Purchase; Adams-Onís Treaty; Black Hawk War; King Philip's War; Anglo-Powhatan War)* **MIG** **WOR**

LOOKING WESTWARD

The United States acquired more than a million square miles of new territory in the 1840s–the greatest wave of expansion since the Louisiana Purchase nearly forty years before. By the end of the decade, the nation possessed all the territory of the present-day United States except Alaska, Hawaii, and a few relatively small areas acquired later through border adjustments. Many factors accounted for this great new wave of expansion, the most important of which were the hopes and ambitions of the many thousands of white Americans who moved into or invested in these new territories. Advocates of expansion justified their goals with a carefully articulated set of ideas–an ideology known as "Manifest Destiny," which became one of the factors driving white Americans to look to the West.

MANIFEST DESTINY

Manifest Destiny reflected both the burgeoning pride that characterized American nationalism in the mid-nineteenth century and the idealistic vision of social perfection that fueled so much of the reform energy of the time. It rested on the idea that America was destined–by God and by history–to expand its boundaries over a vast area, an area that included, but was not necessarily restricted to, the continent of North America. American expansion was not selfish, its advocates insisted; it was an altruistic attempt to extend American liberty to new realms. John L. O'Sullivan, the influential Democratic editor who gave the movement its name, wrote in 1845 that the American claim to new territory

> is by the right of our manifest destiny to overspread and to possess the whole of the continent which Providence has given us for the development of the great experiment of liberty and federative self government entrusted to us.

Manifest Destiny represented more than pride in the nation's political system. Running throughout many of the arguments for expansion was an explicitly racial justification. Throughout the 1840s, many Americans defended the idea of westward expansion by citing the superiority of the "American race"–white people of northern European origins. The "nonwhite" peoples of the territories could not be absorbed into the republican system. The Native Americans, Mexican populations, and others in the western regions were racially unfit to be part of an "American" community, Manifest Destiny advocates insisted. Westward expansion was, therefore, a movement to spread both a political system and a racially defined society. O'Sullivan called "racial purity" (or "whiteness") the "key" to the triumph of the nation.

RACIAL JUSTIFICATION

By the 1840s, the idea of Manifest Destiny had spread throughout the nation, publicized by the new "penny press" (inexpensive newspapers aimed at a mass audience) and fanned by the rhetoric of nationalist politicians. Advocates of Manifest Destiny disagreed, however, about how far and by what means the nation should expand. Some had relatively limited territorial goals; others envisioned a vast new "empire of liberty" that would include Canada, Mexico, Caribbean and Pacific islands, and ultimately, a few dreamed, much of the rest of the world. Some believed America should use force to achieve its expansionist goals, while others felt that the nation should expand peacefully or not at all.

Not everyone embraced the idea of Manifest Destiny. Henry Clay and other prominent politicians feared, correctly as it turned out, that territorial expansion would reopen the painful controversy over slavery and threaten the stability of the Union. But their voices were barely audible over the clamor of enthusiasm for expansion in the 1840s, which began with the issues of Texas and Oregon.

OPPOSITION TO FURTHER EXPANSION

Go Online AP Exam Preparation

AP Exam Practice Use the online assessment to help prepare students for the AP Exam. You can assign the ready-made AP-style short-answer questions, document-based questions, and multiple-choice questions assessing concepts, themes, and skills from Period 5 and AP-style long-essay questions organized in sets of 3 questions from various time periods. You can also create your own tests from available questions. This easy-to-use tool helps you design assessments that meet the needs of different types of learners.

Historical Thinking Skills

Argumentation After students have read the section "Manifest Destiny," discuss as a class arguments in favor of and against Manifest Destiny and what general philosophy the idea was based upon. *(Manifest Destiny was based on the belief, stated or implied, that white Americans were more entitled to western lands than other groups and would make more productive use of it.)* **MIG** **NAT** **WXT** **SOC**

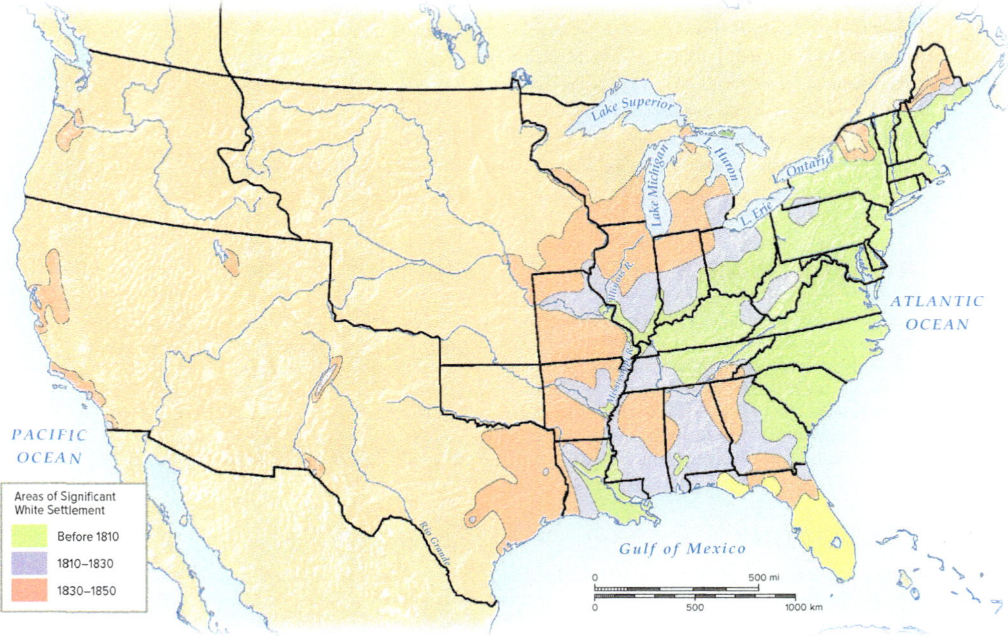

EXPANDING SETTLEMENT, 1810–1850 This map shows the dramatic expansion of the territorial boundaries of the United States in the decades after the Louisiana Purchase. By 1850, the nation had reached its present boundaries (with the exception of Alaska and Hawaii, which it acquired later). Much of this acquisition occurred in the 1840s. It also shows the spread of white settlement within the territories and states.

What events contributed to the annexation of new land to the United States in those years?

THE LONE STAR FLAG Almost from the moment Texas won its independence from Mexico in 1836, it sought admission to the United States as a state. Controversies over the status of slavery in the territories prevented its admission until 1845, and so for nine years it was an independent republic. The tattered banner pictured here was one of the republic's original flags.

AMERICANS IN TEXAS

The United States had once claimed Texas–which until the 1830s was part of the Republic of Mexico–as a part of the Louisiana Purchase, but it had renounced the claim in 1819. Twice thereafter the United States had offered to buy Texas, only to meet with indignant Mexican refusals.

But in the early 1820s, the Mexican government launched an ill-advised experiment that would eventually cause it to lose its great northern province: it encouraged American emigration to Texas. The Mexican government hoped to strengthen the economy of the territory and increase their own tax revenues. They also liked the idea of American settlers sitting between Mexican settlement and the large and sometimes militant Native American groups to the north. They convinced themselves, too, that settlers in Texas would serve as an effective buffer against United States expansion into the region; the Americans, they thought, would soon become loyal to the Mexican government. An 1824 colonization law designed to attract American settlers promised the newcomers cheap land and a four-year exemption from taxes.

Answers

Expanding Settlement, 1810–1850

Louisiana Purchase; Adams-Onís Treaty; Black Hawk War; King Philip's War; Anglo-Powhatan War

Thousands of Americans, attracted by the rich soil in Texas, took advantage of Mexico's welcome. Since much of the available land was suitable for growing cotton, the great majority of the immigrants were Southerners, many of whom brought enslaved people with them. By 1830, there were about 7,000 Americans living in Texas, more than twice the number of Mexican residents there.

Most of the settlers came to Texas through the efforts of American intermediaries, who received sizable land grants from Mexico in return for promising to bring settlers into the region. The most successful of them was Stephen F. Austin, a young immigrant from Missouri who had established the first legal American settlement in Texas in 1822. Austin and other intermediaries were effective in recruiting American immigrants to Texas, but they also created centers of power in the region that competed with the Mexican government. In 1826, one of these American intermediaries led a revolt to establish Texas as an independent nation (which he proposed calling Fredonia). The Mexican government quickly crushed the revolt and, four years later, passed new laws barring any further American immigration into the region. They were too late. Americans kept flowing into the territory, and in 1833 Mexico dropped the futile immigration ban. By 1835 more than 30,000 Americans, white and black, had settled in Texas.

STEPHEN AUSTIN

TENSIONS BETWEEN THE UNITED STATES AND MEXICO

Friction between the American settlers and the Mexican government continued to grow. It arose from the continuing ties of the immigrants to the United States, and it arose, too, from their desire to legalize slavery, which the Mexican government had made illegal in Texas in 1830. But the Americans were divided over how to address their unhappiness with Mexican rule. Austin and his followers wanted to reach a peaceful settlement that would give Texas more autonomy within the Mexican republic. Other Americans wanted to fight for independence.

In the mid-1830s, instability in Mexico drove General Antonio Lopez de Santa Anna to seize power as a dictator and impose a new, more autocratic regime on the nation and its territories. A new law increased the powers of the national government of Mexico at the expense of the state governments, a measure that Texans from the United States assumed Santa Anna was aiming specifically at them. The Mexican government even imprisoned Stephen Austin in Mexico City for a time, claiming that he was encouraging revolts among his fellow American settlers in Texas. Sporadic fighting between Americans and Mexicans in Texas began in 1835 and escalated as the Mexican government sent more troops into the territory. In 1836, the American settlers defiantly proclaimed their independence from Mexico.

Santa Anna led a large army into Texas, where the American settlers were having difficulties organizing an effective defense of their new "nation." Several different factions claimed to be the legitimate government of Texas, and the rebels could not even agree on who their commanders were. Mexican forces annihilated an American garrison at the Alamo mission in San Antonio after a famous, if futile, defense by a group of Texas patriots, a group that included, among others, the renowned frontiersman and former Tennessee congressman Davy Crockett. Another garrison, at Goliad, suffered substantially the same fate when the Mexican army executed most of the force after it had surrendered. By March 1836, the rebellion appeared to have collapsed. Americans were fleeing east toward Louisiana to escape Santa Anna's army.

But General Sam Houston managed to keep a small force together. And on April 23, 1836, at the Battle of San Jacinto (near the present-day city of Houston), he defeated the Mexican army and took Santa Anna prisoner. During the surrender, American troops killed many of the Mexican soldiers in retribution for the executions at Goliad. Santa Anna, under pressure from his captors, signed a treaty giving Texas independence. The Mexican government repudiated the treaty, and Mexican troops briefly occupied San Antonio in 1842 but were unable to win Texas back.

SAN JACINTO

A number of Mexican residents of Texas (known as "Tejanos") had fought with the Americans in the revolution. But soon after Texas won its independence, their positions grew difficult. The Americans did not trust the Mexican residents, fearing that they were agents of the Mexican government, and in effect drove many of them out of the new republic. Most of those who stayed had to settle for a politically and economically subordinate status within the fledgling nation.

Above all, American Texans hoped for annexation by the United States. One of the first acts of the new president of Texas, Sam Houston, was to send a delegation to Washington with an offer to join the Union. There were supporters of expansion in the United States who welcomed these overtures; indeed, expansionists in the United States had been supporting and encouraging the revolt against Mexico for years. But there was also opposition. Many American Northerners opposed acquiring a large new slave territory, and others opposed increasing the Southern votes in Congress and in the electoral college. Unfortunately for the Texans, one of the opponents was President Jackson, who feared annexation might cause a dangerous sectional controversy and even a war with Mexico. He therefore did not support annexation and even delayed recognizing the new republic until 1837. Presidents Martin Van Buren and William Henry Harrison also refrained from pressing the issue during their terms of office.

OPPOSITION TO ANNEXATION

Spurned by the United States, Texas cast out on its own. Its leaders sought money and support from Europe. Some of them dreamed of creating a vast southwestern nation, stretching to the Pacific, that would rival the United States–a dream that appealed to European nations eager to counter the growing power of America. England and France quickly recognized and concluded trade treaties with Texas. In response, President Tyler persuaded Texas to apply for statehood again in 1844.

Reasoning Processes

Comparing After students have read the section "Americans in Texas," ask them to discuss reasons the Mexican government offered land to American settlers and why American settlers moved to Mexico. Ask students to make an argument about which side gained more from the deal. **MIG** **WXT**

Historical Thinking Skills

Identifying Cause and Effect Have students read the section "San Jacinto." Ask them to create a list of causes of the fighting between the Mexican government and American settlers in Texas. Have students rank their lists in order of importance, and then write a thesis statement that makes a claim about the most important causes of the war. **MIG** **PCE** **NAT**

Discussion and Activities

Analyzing Issues After students have read the section "Tensions Between the United States and Mexico," ask them to write a short paragraph explaining why the United States did not annex Texas in 1836. *(Abolitionists feared the expansion of slavery into the new territory; President Jackson did not want to precipitate war with Mexico.)* **SOC** **PCE** **MIG** **WOR**

AUSTIN, TEXAS, 1840 Four years after Texas declared its independence from Mexico, the new republic's capital, Austin, was still a small village, most of whose buildings were rustic cabins, as this hand-colored lithograph from the time suggests. The imposing house atop the hill at right was a notable exception. It was the residence of President Mirabeau Lamar.

But when Secretary of State Calhoun presented an annexation treaty to Congress as if its only purpose were to extend slavery, Northern senators rebelled and defeated it. Rejection of the treaty only spurred advocates of Manifest Destiny to greater efforts toward their goal. The Texas question quickly became the central issue in the election of 1844.

OREGON

Control of what was known as Oregon Country, in the Pacific Northwest, was another major political issue in the 1840s. Its half-million square miles included the present states of Oregon, Washington, and Idaho, parts of Montana and Wyoming, and half of British Columbia. Both Britain and the United States claimed sovereignty in the region–the British on the basis of explorations in the 1790s by George Vancouver, a naval officer; the Americans on the basis of simultaneous claims by Robert Gray, a fur trader. Unable to resolve their conflicting claims diplomatically, they agreed in an 1818 treaty to allow citizens of each country equal access to the territory. This arrangement, known as "joint occupation," continued for twenty years.

DISPUTED CLAIMS

In fact, by the time of the treaty neither Britain nor the United States had established much of a presence in Oregon Country. White settlement in the region consisted largely of American and Canadian fur traders; and the most significant white settlements were the fur trading post established by John Jacob Astor's company at Astoria and other posts built by the British Hudson's Bay Company north of the Columbia River–where residents combined fur trading with farming and recruited Native American labor to compensate for their small numbers.

But American interest in Oregon grew substantially in the 1820s and 1830s. Missionaries considered the territory an attractive target for evangelical efforts, especially after the strange appearance of four Nez Percé and Flathead Indians in St. Louis in 1831. White Americans never discovered what had brought the Native Americans (who spoke no English) from Oregon to Missouri, and all four died before they could find out. But some missionaries considered the visit a divinely inspired invitation to extend their efforts westward. They were also motivated by a desire to counter the Catholic missionaries from Canada, whose presence in Oregon, many settlers believed, threatened American hopes for annexation. The missionaries had little success with the tribes they attempted to convert, and some–embittered by Native American resistance to their efforts–began encouraging white emigration to the region, arguing that by repudiating Christianity the Native Americans had abdicated their right to the land. "When a people refuse or neglect to fill the designs of Providence, they ought not to complain of the results," said the missionary Marcus Whitman, who, with his wife, Narcissa, had established an important, if largely unsuccessful, mission among the Cayuse Indians east of the Cascade Mountains.

Significant numbers of white Americans began emigrating to Oregon in the early 1840s, and they soon substantially outnumbered the British settlers there. They also devastated much of the Native American population, in part through a measles epidemic that spread through the Cayuse. The Cayuse blamed the Whitman mission for the plague, and in 1847 they attacked it and killed thirteen white settlers, including Marcus and Narcissa. But such resistance did little to stem the white immigration. By the mid-1840s, American settlements had spread up and down the Pacific coast; and the new settlers (along with advocates of Manifest Destiny in the East) were urging the U.S. government to take possession of the disputed Oregon Country.

CONFLICT BETWEEN SETTLERS AND NATIVE AMERICANS

WESTWARD MIGRATION

The migrations into Texas and Oregon were part of a larger movement that took hundreds of thousands of white and black Americans into the far western regions of the continent

Discussion and Activities

Analyzing Cause and Effect Have students read the section "Oregon." Ask them to create a T-chart listing causes and effects of American settlement in Oregon. *(Causes: desire to proselytize to Native Americans; farmers wanting to claim the fertile river valleys; fur trappers and traders looking for pelts. Effects: epidemic disease among Native Americans; conflict with Native Americans and the British.)* **MIG** **PCE** **SOC**

between 1840 and 1860. Southerners flocked mainly to Texas. But the largest number of migrants came from the Old Northwest–white men and women, and a few African Americans, who undertook arduous journeys in search of new opportunities. Most traveled in family groups, until the early 1850s, when the great California gold rush attracted many single men. Most were relatively prosperous young people. Poor people could not afford the expensive trip, and those who wished to migrate usually had to do so by joining established families or groups as laborers–men as farm or ranch hands, women as domestic servants, teachers, or, in some cases, prostitutes. The character of the migrations varied according to the destination of the migrants. Groups headed for areas where mining or lumbering was the principal economic activity consisted mostly of men. Those heading for farming regions traveled mainly as families.

All the migrants were in search of a new life, but they harbored many different visions of what a new life would bring. Some–particularly after the discovery of gold in California in 1848–hoped for quick riches. Others planned to take advantage of the vast public lands the federal government was selling at modest prices to acquire property for farming or speculation. Still others hoped to establish themselves as merchants and serve the new white communities developing in the West. Some (among them the Mormons) were on religious missions or were attempting to escape the epidemic diseases plaguing many cities in the East. But the vast majority of migrants were looking for economic opportunities. They formed a vanguard for the expanding capitalist economy of the United States.

Life on the Trail

Most migrants–about 300,000 between 1840 and 1860–traveled west along the great overland trails. They generally gathered in one of several major depots in Iowa and Missouri (Independence, St. Joseph, or Council Bluffs), joined a wagon train led by hired guides, and set off with their belongings piled in covered wagons, livestock trailing behind. The major route west was the 2,000-mile Oregon Trail, which stretched from Independence across the Great Plains and through the South Pass of the Rocky Mountains. From there, migrants moved north into Oregon or south (along the California Trail) to the northern California coast. Other migrations moved along the Santa Fe Trail, southwest from Independence into New Mexico.

Oregon Trail

However they traveled, overland migrants faced considerable hardships–although the death rate for travelers was only slightly higher than the rate for the American population as a whole. The mountain and desert terrain in the later portions of the trip were particularly difficult. Most journeys lasted five or six months (from May to November), and there was always pressure to get through the Rockies before the snows began, not always an easy task given the very slow pace of most wagon trains (about fifteen miles a day). And although some migrants were moving west at least in part to escape the epidemic diseases of eastern cities, they were not immune from plagues. Thousands of people died on the trail of cholera during the great epidemic of the early 1850s.

WESTWARD HO! *Westward the Course of Empire Takes Its Way*, painted by Emanuel Gottlieb Leutze (1816–1868) in 1861, is a pictorial representation of Manifest Destiny. It symbolizes the belief held by many during the mid-1800s that the United States was destined by divine plan and authority for western exploration and expansion. This mural is displayed in the House of Representatives in the United States Capitol building.

Reasoning Processes

Causation After students have read the section "Westward Migration," ask them to create a list of motives drawing settlers to the West in the 1840s and 1850s. Have them rank their lists in order of importance and write a thesis statement that makes a claim about the most important causes of westward migration in the mid-nineteenth century. **MIG** **SOC** **WXT** **ARC**

Reasoning Processes

Comparing Have students read the section "Oregon Trail." Ask them to go online and search for an online version of the classic video game "Oregon Trail." Have students play through the game and then write a short summary of the challenges faced in the game compared with the challenges faced by actual travelers. **MIG**

Discussion and Activities

Analyzing Visuals Have students examine the map "Western Trails in 1860." Ask them to identify and discuss what geographic challenges settlers had to overcome on their journeys westward. *(Mountains; deserts; rivers.)* Have students discuss why settlers would have been willing to take the risks involved in moving west. **MIG** **WXT** **SOC**

In the years before the Civil War, fewer than 400 migrants (about one-tenth of 1 percent) died in conflicts with the tribes. In fact, Native Americans were usually more helpful than dangerous to the white migrants. They often served as guides through difficult terrain or aided travelers in crossing streams or herding livestock. They maintained an extensive trade with the white travelers in horses, clothing, and fresh food. But stories of the occasional conflicts between migrants and Native Americans on the trail created widespread fear among white travelers, even though more Native Americans than white people (and relatively few of either) died in those conflicts.

LIFE ON THE TRAIL

Life on the trail was obviously very different from life on a farm or in a town. But the society of the trail re-created many of the patterns of conventional American society. Families divided tasks along gender lines: the men driving and, when necessary, repairing the wagons or hunting game; the women cooking, washing clothes, and caring for children. Almost everyone, male or female, walked the great majority of the time, to lighten the load for the horses drawing the wagons; and so the women, many of whose chores came at the end of the day, generally worked much harder than the men, who usually rested when the caravan halted.

WESTERN TRAILS IN 1860 As settlers began the long process of exploring and establishing farms and businesses in the West, major new trails began to facilitate travel and trade between the region and the more thickly settled areas to the east. Note how many of the trails led to California and how few of them led into any of the far northern regions of United States territory. Note too the important towns and cities that grew up along these trails.

What forms of transportation later performed the functions that these trails performed prior to the Civil War?

Answers

Western Trails in 1860

Railroads would take the place of the overland trails.

Discussion and Activities

Analyzing Visuals Have students examine the image "Crossing the Sierras." Ask them to write a short letter or journal entry from the point of view of a traveler describing their experiences crossing the mountains. **MIG**

CROSSING THE SIERRAS A wagon train struggles across the rugged trails over the Sierra Nevada, as migrants travel in California. The image is a black-and-white photograph that was colored by paint. Only a few years later, the same trip could be achieved much easier because of the transcontinental railroad.

Despite the traditional image of westward migrants as rugged individualists, most travelers found the journey a highly collective experience. That was partly because many expeditions consisted of groups of friends, neighbors, or relatives who had decided to pull up stakes and move west together. And it was partly because of the intensity of the experience: many weeks of difficult travel with no other human contacts except, occasionally, with Native Americans. Indeed, one of the most frequent causes of disaster for travelers was the breakdown of the necessarily communal character of the migratory companies. It was a rare expedition in which there were not some internal conflicts before the trip was over.

THE OREGON BOUNDARY, 1846 One of the last major boundary disputes between the United States and Great Britain involved the territory known as Oregon—the large region on the Pacific coast north of California (which in 1846 was still part of Mexico). For years, America and Britain had overlapping claims on the territory. The British claimed land as far south as the present state of Oregon, while the Americans claimed land extending well into what is now Canada. Tensions over the Oregon border at times rose to the point that many Americans were demanding war, some using the slogan "54–40 or fight," referring to the latitude of the northernmost point of the American claim.

How did President James K. Polk DEFUSE the crisis?

EXPANSION AND WAR

The growing number of white Americans in the lands west of the Mississippi put great pressure on the government in Washington to annex Texas, Oregon, and other territory. In the 1840s, these expansionist pressures helped push the United States into a war that–however dubious its origins–became a triumph for the advocates of Manifest Destiny.

The Democrats and Expansion

In preparing for the presidential election of 1844, the two leading candidates–Henry Clay and former president Martin Van Buren–both tried to avoid taking a stand on the controversial issue of the annexation of Texas. Sentiment for expansion was mild within the Whig Party, and Clay had no difficulty securing the nomination despite his noncommittal position. But many Southern Democrats supported annexation, and the party passed over Van Buren to nominate a strong supporter of annexation, the previously unheralded James K. Polk.

JAMES K. POLK

Polk was not as obscure as his Whig critics claimed. He had represented Tennessee in the House of Representatives for fourteen years, four of them as Speaker, and had subsequently served as governor. But by 1844, he had been out of public office–and for the most part out of the public mind–for three years. What made his victory possible was his support for the position, expressed in the Democratic platform, "that the re-occupation of Oregon and the re-annexation of Texas at the earliest practicable period are great American measures." By combining the Oregon and Texas questions, the Democrats hoped to appeal to both Northern and Southern expansionists. Polk carried the election by 170 electoral votes to 105, although his popular majority was less than 40,000.

Answers

The Oregon Boundary, 1846

Polk negotiated a compromise with Great Britain to divide the territory at the 49th parallel.

Reasoning Processes

Comparing After students have read the section "The Democrats and Expansion," ask them to write a short paragraph comparing the settlement of the boundary disputes over Texas and Oregon. *(Texas was admitted as a state by joint resolution of Congress, while the Oregon boundary dispute was settled by a treaty with Great Britain.)* **WOR** **MIG**

Polk entered office with a clear set of goals and with plans for attaining them. John Tyler accomplished the first of Polk's goals for him. Interpreting the election returns as a mandate for the annexation of Texas, the outgoing president won congressional approval for it in February 1845. That December, Texas became a state.

Polk himself resolved the Oregon question. The British minister in Washington brusquely rejected a compromise Polk offered that would establish the United States-Canadian border at the 49th parallel; he did not even refer the proposal to London. Incensed, Polk again asserted the American claim to all of Oregon. There was loose talk of war on both sides of the Atlantic–talk that in the United States often took the form of the bellicose slogan "54-40 or fight!" (a reference to where the Americans hoped to draw the northern boundary of their part of Oregon). But neither country really wanted war. Finally, the British government accepted Polk's original proposal. On June 15, 1846, the Senate approved a treaty that fixed the boundary at the 49th parallel, where it remains today.

COMPROMISE OVER OREGON

THE SOUTHWEST AND CALIFORNIA

One of the reasons the Senate and the president had agreed so readily to the British offer to settle the Oregon question was that new tensions were emerging in the Southwest–tensions that ultimately led to a war with Mexico. As soon as the United States admitted Texas to statehood in 1845, the Mexican government broke diplomatic relations with Washington. Mexican-American relations grew still worse when a dispute developed over the boundary between Texas and Mexico. Texans claimed the Rio Grande as their western and southern border, a claim that would have added much of what is now New Mexico to Texas. Mexico, although still not conceding the loss of Texas, argued nevertheless that the border had always been the Nueces River, to the north of the Rio Grande. Polk accepted the Texas claim, and in the summer of 1845 he sent a small army under General Zachary Taylor to Texas to protect it against a possible Mexican invasion.

Part of the area in dispute was New Mexico, whose Spanish and Native American residents lived in a multiracial society that by the 1840s had endured for nearly a century and a half. In the 1820s, the Mexican government had invited American traders into the region (just as it invited American settlers into Texas), hoping to speed development of the province. And New Mexico, like Texas, began to become more American than Mexican. A flourishing commerce soon developed between Santa Fe and Independence, Missouri.

Americans were also increasing their interest in an even more distant province of Mexico: California. In this vast region lived members of several western Native American groups and perhaps 7,000 Mexicans, mostly descendants of Spanish colonists. Gradually, however, white Americans began to arrive: first maritime traders and captains of Pacific whaling ships, who stopped to barter goods or buy supplies; then merchants, who established stores, imported merchandise, and developed a profitable trade with the Mexicans and Native Americans; and finally pioneering farmers, who entered California from the east, by land, and settled in the Sacramento Valley. Some of these new settlers began to dream of bringing California into the United States.

AMERICAN INTERESTS IN CALIFORNIA

President Polk soon came to share their dream and committed himself to acquiring both New Mexico and California for the United States. At the same time that he dispatched troops to Texas, he sent secret instructions to the commander of the Pacific naval squadron to seize the California ports if Mexico declared war. Representatives of the president quietly informed Americans in California that the United States would respond sympathetically to a revolt against Mexican authority there.

THE MEXICAN WAR

Having appeared to prepare for war, Polk turned to diplomacy and dispatched a special minister, John Slidell, to try to buy off Mexican leaders. But Mexican leaders rejected Slidell's offer to purchase the disputed territories. On January 13, 1846, as soon as he heard the news, Polk ordered Taylor's army in Texas to move across the Nueces River, where it had been stationed, to the Rio Grande. For months, Mexican troops refused to fight. But finally, according to disputed American

FAILURE OF THE SLIDELL MISSION

SACRAMENTO IN THE 1850S The busy river port of Sacramento served the growing agricultural and mining economies of north central California in the 1850s—years in which the new state began the dramatic population growth that a century later would make it the nation's largest.

The Library of Congress (LC-USZC4-2853)

Reasoning Processes

Comparing and Contrasting Have students read the section "The Southwest and California." Ask them to create a three-circle Venn diagram comparing American interests in Texas, New Mexico, and California. Have them discuss as a class how these interests led to increased tension between the United States and Mexico. **WOR** **MIG** **WXT**

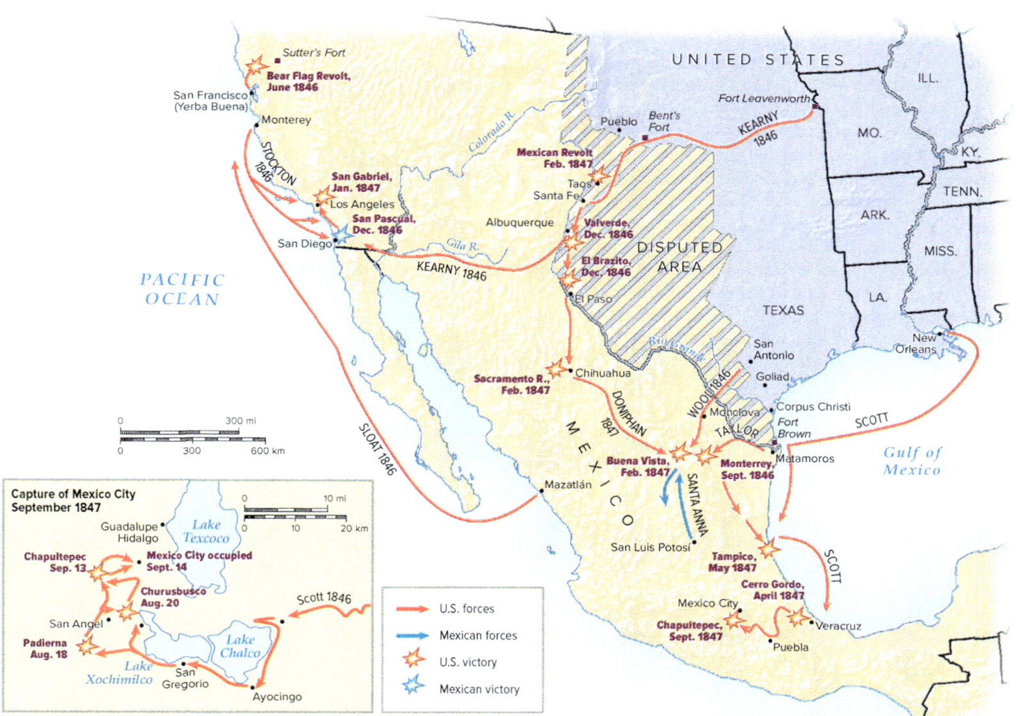

THE MEXICAN WAR, 1846–1848 Shortly after the settlement of the Oregon border dispute with Britain, the United States entered a war with Mexico over another contested border. This map shows the movement of Mexican and American troops during the fighting, which extended from the area around Santa Fe south to Mexico City and west to the coast of California. Note the American use of its naval forces to facilitate a successful assault on Mexico City, and other attacks on the coast of California. Note, too, how unsuccessful the Mexican forces were in their battles with the United States. Mexico won only one battle—a minor one at San Pasqual near San Diego—in the war.

How did President Polk deal with the popular clamor for the United States to annex much of present-day Mexico?

accounts, some Mexican troops crossed the Rio Grande and attacked a unit of American soldiers. Polk now told Congress: "War exists by the act of Mexico herself." On May 13, 1846, Congress declared war by votes of 40 to 2 in the Senate and 174 to 14 in the House.

The war had many opponents in the United States. Whig critics charged from the beginning (and not without justification) that Polk had deliberately maneuvered the country into the conflict and had staged the border incident that had precipitated the declaration. Many other critics argued that the hostilities with Mexico were draining resources and attention away from the more important issue of the Pacific Northwest. Even when the United States finally reached its agreement with Britain on the Oregon question, opponents claimed that Polk had settled for less than he should have because he was preoccupied with Mexico. Opposition intensified as the war continued and as the public became aware of the casualties and expense.

OPPOSITION TO THE WAR

To others, the war was a moral crime. Ulysses Grant, then an officer in the Mexican War, called it "one of the most unjust ever waged." Abraham Lincoln criticized the war on the grounds that it gave the president too much power. "Allow the President to invade a neighboring country whenever he shall deem it necessary . . . ," he said, "and you allow him to make war at pleasure." Pacifists were particularly dismayed. Henry David Thoreau was so horrified by the war that he refused to pay taxes (which he said financed the conflict) and spent time in jail.

American forces did well against the Mexican troops, but victory did not come as quickly as Polk had hoped. The president ordered Taylor to cross the Rio Grande, seize parts of northeastern Mexico, beginning with the city of Monterrey, and then march on to Mexico City itself. Taylor captured

Discussion and Activities

Analyzing Cause and Effect After students have read the section "Opposition to the War," ask them to list and discuss as a class the arguments for and against going to war with Mexico and whether they think President Polk was justified in asking Congress to declare war. **WOR** **MIG** **NAT**

Answers

The Mexican War, 1846–1848

President Polk sent troops into disputed territory and asked Congress for a declaration of war when those troops were allegedly fired upon.

Discussion and Activities

Evaluating Evidence After students have read the section "Bear Flag Revolution," have them write a short paragraph describing the American strategy in the war against Mexico. *(A small force was sent to secure California, while a two-pronged invasion from across the Rio Grande and from Veracruz on the Gulf Coast led to the capture of Mexico City.)* **WOR**

Monterrey in September 1846, but he let the Mexican garrison evacuate without pursuit. Polk now began to fear that Taylor lacked the tactical skill for the planned advance against Mexico City. He also feared that, if successful, Taylor would become a powerful political rival (as, in fact, he did).

In the meantime, Polk ordered other offensives against New Mexico and California. In the summer of 1846, a small army under Colonel Stephen W. Kearny captured Santa Fe with no opposition. Then Kearny proceeded to California, where he joined a conflict already in progress that was being staged jointly by American settlers, a well-armed exploring party led by John C. Frémont, and the United States Navy: the so-called Bear Flag Revolution. Kearny brought the disparate American forces together under his command, and by the autumn of 1846 he had completed the conquest of California.

BEAR FLAG REVOLUTION

The United States now controlled the two territories for which it had gone to war. But Mexico still refused to concede defeat. At this point, Polk and General Winfield Scott, the commanding general of the army and its finest soldier, launched a bold new campaign. Scott assembled an army at Tampico, which the navy transported down the Mexican coast to Veracruz. With an army that never numbered more than 14,000, Scott advanced 260 miles along the Mexican National Highway toward Mexico City, kept American casualties low, and never lost a battle before finally seizing the Mexican capital. A new Mexican government took power and announced its willingness to negotiate a peace treaty.

President Polk was now unclear about his objectives. He continued to encourage those who demanded that the United States annex much of Mexico itself. At the same time, concerned about the approaching presidential election, he was growing anxious to finish the war quickly. Polk had sent a special presidential envoy, Nicholas Trist, to negotiate a settlement. On February 2, 1848, Trist reached agreement with the new Mexican government on the Treaty of Guadalupe Hidalgo, by which Mexico agreed to cede California

TREATY OF GUADALUPE HIDALGO

THE BATTLE OF MONTERREY The Battle of Monterrey in 1846 was one of the most important conflicts of the Mexican War. Troops under the command of General Zachary Taylor defeated the Mexican forces, but not without significant American casualties. The surrender of the Mexican army on September 26 was a result of the Americans surrounding the Mexican soldiers. It was an important step in the American victory in the Mexican War.

Discussion and Activities

Analyzing Visuals Have students examine the image "The Battle of Monterrey." Have them list and discuss in pairs or small groups details that reveal the nature of the fighting in the Mexican War. *(Soldiers were fighting at close quarters, even hand-to-hand, using rifles, bayonets, swords, cannons, and possibly even their bare hands.)* **WOR**

and New Mexico to the United States and acknowledge the Rio Grande as the boundary of Texas. In return, the United States promised to assume any financial claims its new citizens had against Mexico and to pay the Mexican government $15 million. Trist had obtained most of Polk's original demands, but he had not satisfied the new, more expansive dreams of acquiring additional territory in Mexico itself. Polk angrily claimed that Trist had violated his instructions, but he soon realized that he had no choice but to accept the treaty to silence a bitter battle growing between ardent expansionists demanding the annexation of "All Mexico!" and antislavery leaders charging that the expansionists were conspiring to extend slavery to new realms. The president submitted the Trist treaty to the Senate, which approved it by a vote of 38 to 14. The war was over, and America had gained a vast new territory. But it had also acquired a new set of troubling and divisive issues.

THE SECTIONAL DEBATE

James Polk tried to be a president whose policies transcended sectional divisions. But conciliating the sections was becoming an almost impossible task. Polk gradually earned the enmity of Northerners and Westerners alike, who believed his policies (particularly his enthusiasm for territorial expansion in the Southwest) favored the South at their expense.

SLAVERY AND THE TERRITORIES

In August 1846, while the Mexican War was still in progress, Polk asked Congress to appropriate $2 million for purchasing peace with Mexico. Representative David Wilmot of Pennsylvania, an antislavery Democrat, introduced an amendment to the appropriation bill prohibiting slavery in any territory acquired from Mexico. The so-called Wilmot Proviso passed the House but failed in the Senate. It would be called up, debated, and voted on repeatedly for years. Southern militants, in the meantime, contended that all Americans had equal rights in the new territories, including the right to move their "property" (enslaved people) there.

As the sectional debate intensified, President Polk supported a proposal to extend the Missouri Compromise line through the new territories to the Pacific coast, banning slavery north of the line and permitting it south of the line.

SOUTHWESTERN EXPANSION, 1845–1853 The annexation of much of what is now Texas in 1845, the much larger territorial gains won in the Mexican War in 1848, and the purchase of additional land from Mexico in 1853 completed the present continental border of the United States.

What great event shortly after the Mexican War contributed to a rapid settlement of California by migrants from the eastern United States?

Discussion and Activities

Analyzing Issues After students have read the section "Treaty of Guadalupe Hidalgo," ask them to create a list of the concessions made by each side in the conflict. Have students discuss as a class which provision in the treaty was most predictable, which was most surprising, and which benefited the United States the most. **WOR** **WXT** **PCE**

Answers

Southwestern Expansion, 1845–1853

The event was the discovery of gold near Sacramento.

Reasoning Processes

Causation After students have read the section "Slavery and the Territories," ask them to create a T-chart listing examples of how the end of the Mexican War either strengthened unity or created division within the United States. Have students evaluate which result they think had the most impact. **NAT** **ARC** **PCE**

Other politicians supported a plan, originally known as "squatter sovereignty" and later by the more dignified phrase "popular sovereignty," which would allow the people of each territory (acting through their legislature) to decide the status of slavery there. The debate over these various proposals dragged on for many months, and the issue remained unresolved when Polk left office in 1849.

COMPETING PLANS

The presidential campaign of 1848 dampened the controversy for a time as both Democrats and Whigs tried to avoid the slavery question. When Polk, in poor health, declined to run again, the Democrats nominated Lewis Cass of Michigan, a dull, aging party regular. The Whigs nominated General Zachary Taylor of Louisiana, hero of the Mexican War but a man with no political experience. Opponents of slavery found the choice of candidates unsatisfying, and out of their discontent emerged the new Free-Soil Party, which drew from the existing Liberty Party and the antislavery wings of the Whig and Democratic Parties and which endorsed the Wilmot Proviso. Its candidate was former president Martin Van Buren.

Taylor won a narrow victory. But while Van Buren failed to carry a single state, he polled an impressive 291,000 votes (10 percent of the total), and the Free-Soilers elected ten members to Congress. The emergence of the Free-Soil Party as an important political force, like the emergence of the Know-Nothing and Liberty Parties before it, signaled the inability of the existing parties to contain the political passions slavery was creating.

FREE-SOIL PARTY

THE CALIFORNIA GOLD RUSH

By the time Taylor took office, the pressure to resolve the question of slavery in the far western territories had become more urgent as a result of dramatic events in California. In January 1848, James Marshall, a carpenter working on one of rancher John Sutter's sawmills, found traces of gold in the foothills of the Sierra Nevada. Sutter tried to suppress the news, fearing a gold rush would destroy his own substantial empire in the region. But by May, word of the discovery had reached San Francisco; by late summer, it had reached the east coast of the United States and much of the rest of the world. Almost immediately, hundreds of thousands of people from around the world began flocking to California in a frantic search for gold. California's non-Indian population increased nearly twentyfold in four years: from 14,000 in 1848 to over 220,000 in 1852.

The atmosphere in California at the peak of the gold rush was one of crazed excitement and greed. For a short time, San Francisco was almost completely depopulated as residents raced to the mountains to search for gold; the city's principal newspaper (which had been criticizing the gold mania) had to stop publication because it could no longer find either staff or readers. "Nothing but the introduction of insane asylums can effect a cure," one visitor remarked of the gold mania.

Most pre-gold-rush migrants to the Far West had prepared carefully before making the journey. But the gold-rush migrants (known as "Forty-niners") threw caution to the winds. They abandoned farms, jobs, homes, families; they piled onto ships and flooded the overland trails–many carrying only what they could pack on their backs. The overwhelming majority of the Forty-niners (perhaps 95 percent) were men, and the society they created on their arrival in California was unusually volatile because of the absence of women, children, and families.

FORTY-NINERS

The gold rush also attracted some of the first Chinese migrants to the western United States. News of the discoveries created great excitement in China, particularly in impoverished areas, where letters from Chinese immigrants already in California and reports from Americans visiting in China spread the word. It was, of course, extremely difficult for a poor Chinese peasant to get to America; but many young, adventurous people (mostly men) decided to go anyway–believing that they could quickly become rich and then return to China. Emigration brokers loaned many migrants money for passage to California, which the migrants would pay off out of their earnings there. The migration was almost entirely voluntary (unlike the forced movement of kidnapped Chinese men to such places as Peru and Cuba at about the same time). The Chinese migrants in California were, therefore, free laborers and merchants, looking for gold or, more often, hoping to profit from other economic opportunities the gold boom was creating.

The gold rush created a serious labor shortage in California, as many male workers left their jobs and flocked to the gold fields. This shortage created opportunities for many people who needed work (including Chinese immigrants). It also led to an overt exploitation of Native Americans that resembled slavery in all but name. White vigilantes, who called themselves "Indian hunters," were already hunting down and killing thousands of Native Americans before the gold rush (contributing to the process by which the Native American population of California declined from 150,000 to 30,000 between the 1850s and 1870). Now a new state law permitted the arrest of "loitering" or orphaned Native Americans and their assignment to a term of "indentured" labor.

NATIVE AMERICAN SLAVERY

The gold rush was of critical importance to the growth of California, but not for the reasons most of the migrants hoped. There was substantial gold in the hills of the Sierra Nevada, and many people got rich from it. But only a tiny fraction of the Forty-niners ever found gold, or even managed to stake a claim to land on which they could look for gold. Some disappointed migrants returned home after a while. But many stayed in California and swelled both the agricultural and urban populations of the territory. By 1856, for example, San Francisco–whose population had been 1,000 before the gold rush (and at one point declined to about 100 as people left for the mines)–was the home of over 50,000 people. By the early 1850s, California's population, which had always been diverse, had become even more so. The gold rush had attracted not just white Americans, but also people from Europe, China, South America, Mexico, and free African Americans, and enslaved people who accompanied Southern migrants.

Discussion and Activities

Analyzing Change Have students read the section "Forty-Niners." Discuss as a class how the California gold rush changed the patterns of migration to the West. **MIG**

LOOKING FOR GOLD Finding gold in California was not, for the most part, a task for lone prospectors. More common were teams of people who, together, built elaborate mining technologies. As this 1852 photograph shows, the mining teams were often interracial. The white miners on the left stand conspicuously apart from the Chinese workers on the right, but both groups were essential parts of the enterprise.

Conflicts over gold intersected with racial and ethnic tensions to make the territory an unusually turbulent place. As a result, pressure grew to create a stable and effective government. The gold rush, therefore, became another factor putting pressure on the United States to resolve the status not only of California, but of all territories—and of slavery within them—as well.

RISING SECTIONAL TENSIONS

Zachary Taylor believed statehood could become the solution to the issue of slavery in the territories. As long as the new lands remained territories, the federal government was responsible for deciding the fate of slavery within them. But once they became states, he thought, their own governments would be able to settle the slavery question. At Taylor's urging, California quickly adopted a constitution that prohibited slavery, and in December 1849 Taylor asked Congress to admit California as a free state. New Mexico, he added, should also be granted statehood as soon as it was ready and should, like California, be permitted to decide for itself what it wanted to do about slavery.

Congress balked, in part because of several other controversies concerning slavery that were complicating the debate. One was the effort of antislavery forces to abolish slavery in the District of Columbia, a movement bitterly resisted by Southerners. Another was the emergence of personal liberty laws in Northern states, which barred courts and police officers from helping to return runaway enslaved people to slaveholders. In response, Southerners demanded a stringent law that would require Northern states to return fugitive enslaved peo-

Discussion and Activities

Historical Evidence and Argumentation After students have read the section "Native American Slavery," ask them to create a list of the effects of the California Gold Rush. Have students rank their lists in order of importance and then write a thesis statement that makes a claim about the most important effects of the California Gold Rush. **MIG** **WXT** **SOC**

Discussion and Activities

Analyzing Visuals Have students examine the image "Looking for Gold." Ask them to list and discuss the tools the prospectors are using to find gold. *(Shovel; pan; water sluice.)* As a class, discuss what conclusions students can draw regarding the importance of geography to these prospectors. *(A source of flowing water was necessary for this operation in order to wash lighter sediments away while hopefully leaving the heavier gold nuggets behind.)* **MIG** **WXT** **GEO**

Reasoning Processes

Comparing After students have read the section "Rising Sectional Tensions," ask them to review the arguments for nullification during the Nullification Crisis and in the Virginia and Kentucky Resolutions. **Ask:** How were the Northern personal liberty laws similar to or different from these examples? *(They were similar in that in all cases, states were arguing they had the authority to block enforcement of federal laws within their borders.)* **PCE**

ple to slaveholders. But the biggest obstacle to the president's program was the white South's fear that two new free states would be added to the Northern majority. The number of free and slave states was equal in 1849—fifteen each. But the admission of California would upset the balance; and New Mexico, Oregon, and Utah might upset it further, leaving the South in a minority in the Senate, as it already was in the House.

SECTIONAL CONFLICT OVER SLAVERY IN THE TERRITORIES

Tempers were now rising to dangerous levels. Even many otherwise moderate Southern leaders were beginning to talk about secession from the Union. In the North, every state legislature but one adopted a resolution demanding the prohibition of slavery in the territories.

THE COMPROMISE OF 1850

CLAY'S PROPOSED SOLUTION

Faced with this mounting crisis, moderates and unionists spent the winter of 1849–1850 trying to frame a great compromise. The aging Henry Clay, who was spearheading the effort, believed that no compromise could last unless it settled all the issues in dispute between the sections. As a result, he took several measures that had been proposed separately, combined them into a single piece of legislation, and presented it to the Senate on January 29, 1850. Among the bill's provisions were the admission of California as a free state; the formation of territorial governments in the rest of the lands acquired from Mexico, without restrictions on slavery; the abolition of the slave trade, but not slavery itself, in the District of Columbia; and a new, more effective fugitive slave law. These resolutions launched a debate that raged for seven months—both in Congress and throughout the nation. The debate occurred in two phases, the differences between which revealed much about how American politics was changing in the 1850s.

In the first phase of the debate, the dominant voices in Congress were those of old men—national leaders who still remembered Jefferson, Adams, and other founders—who argued for or against the compromise on the basis of broad ideals. Clay himself, seventy-three years old in 1850, appealed to shared national sentiments of nationalism. Early in March, another of the older leaders—John C. Calhoun, sixty-eight years old and so ill that he had to sit grimly in his seat while a colleague read his speech for him—joined the debate. He insisted that the North grant the South equal rights in the territories, that it agree to observe the laws concerning fugitive enslaved people, that it cease attacking slavery, and that it amend the Constitution to create dual presidents, one from the North and one from the South, each with a veto. Calhoun was making radical demands that had no chance of passage. But like Clay, he was offering what he considered a comprehensive, permanent solution to the sectional problem that would, he believed, save the Union. After Calhoun came the third of the elder statesmen, sixty-eight-year-old Daniel Webster, one of the great orators of his time. Still nourishing presidential ambitions, he delivered an eloquent address in the Senate, trying to rally Northern moderates to support Clay's compromise.

But in July, after six months of this impassioned, nationalistic debate, Congress defeated the Clay proposal. And with that, the controversy moved into its second phase, in which a very different cast of characters predominated. Clay, ill and tired, left Washington to spend the summer resting in the mountains. Calhoun had died even before the vote in July. And Webster accepted a new appointment as secretary of state, thus removing himself from the Senate and from the debate.

NEW LEADERSHIP

In place of these leaders, a new, younger group now emerged. One spokesman was William H. Seward of New York, forty-nine years old, a wily political operator who staunchly opposed the proposed compromise. The ideals of union were to him less important than the issue of eliminating slavery. Another was Jefferson Davis of Mississippi, forty-two years old, a representative of the new, cotton South. To him, the slavery issue was less one of principles and ideals than one of economic self-interest. Most important of all, there was Stephen A. Douglas, a thirty-seven-year-old Democratic senator from Illinois. A westerner from a rapidly growing state, he was an open spokesman for the economic needs of his section—especially for the construction of railroads. His was a career devoted not to any broad national goals but to sectional gain and personal self-promotion.

The new leaders of the Senate were able, as the old leaders had not been, to produce a compromise. One spur to the compromise was the disappearance of the most powerful obstacle to it: the president. Zachary Taylor had been adamant that only after California and possibly New Mexico were admitted as states could other measures be discussed. But on July 9, 1850, Taylor suddenly died—the victim of a violent stomach disorder. He was succeeded by Millard Fillmore of New York—a dull, handsome, dignified man who understood the political importance of flexibility. He supported the compromise and used his powers of persuasion to swing Northern Whigs into line.

TEMPORARY COMPROMISE

The new leaders also benefited from their own pragmatic tactics. Douglas's first step, after the departure of Clay, was to break up the "omnibus bill" that Clay had envisioned as a great, comprehensive solution to the sectional crisis and to introduce instead a series of separate measures to be voted on one by one. Thus representatives of different sections could support those elements of the compromise they liked and oppose those they did not. Douglas also gained support with complicated backroom deals linking the compromise to such nonideological matters as the sale of government bonds and the construction of railroads. As a result of his efforts, by mid-September Congress had enacted and the president had signed all the components of the compromise.

The Compromise of 1850, unlike the Missouri Compromise thirty years before, was not a product of widespread agreement on common national ideals. It was, rather, a victory of bargaining and self-interest. Still, members of Congress hailed the measure as a triumph of statesmanship; and Millard Fillmore, signing it, called it a just settlement of the sectional problem, "in its character final and irrevocable."

Discussion and Activities

Evaluating Evidence Have students read the section "The Compromise of 1850." Ask them to create a T-chart listing the provisions that would have been favorable to the North or to the South. Have students discuss which side seems to have gained more (or given up less) in the compromise. **PCE** **ARC**

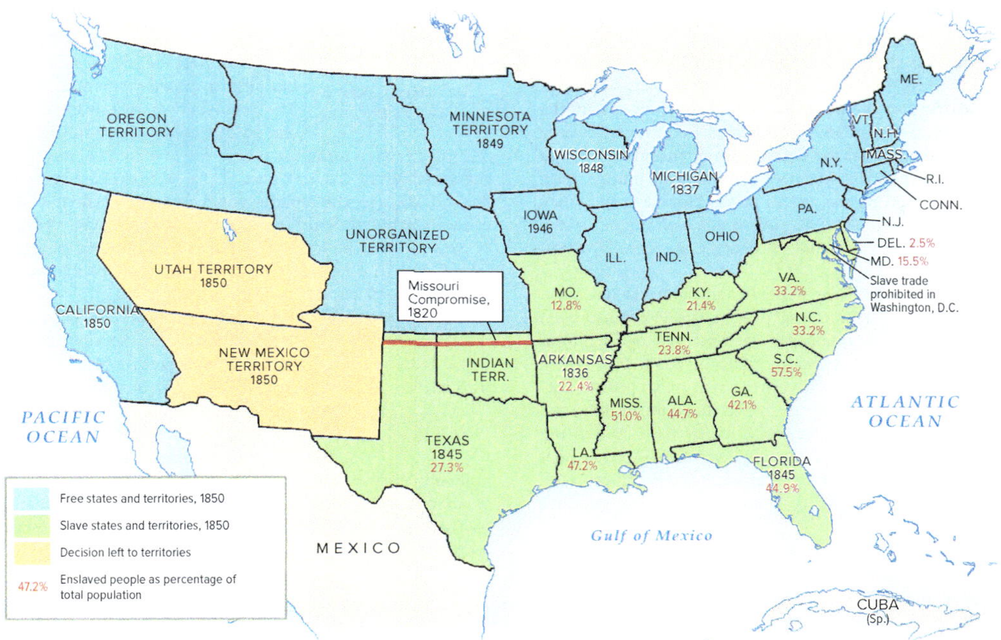

SLAVE AND FREE TERRITORIES UNDER THE COMPROMISE OF 1850 The acquisition of vast new western lands raised the question of the status of slavery in new territories organized for statehood by the United States. Tension between the North and the South on this question led in 1850 to a great compromise, forged in Congress, to settle this dispute. The compromise allowed California to join the Union as a free state and introduced the concept of "popular sovereignty" for other new territories.

How well did the Compromise of 1850 work?

THE CRISES OF THE 1850S

For a few years after the Compromise of 1850, the sectional conflict seemed briefly to have succeeded amid booming prosperity and growth. But the tensions between North and South remained, and the crisis continued to smolder until–in 1854–it once more burst into the open.

THE UNEASY TRUCE

Both major parties endorsed the Compromise of 1850 in 1852, and both nominated presidential candidates unidentified with sectional passions. The Democrats chose the obscure New Hampshire politician Franklin Pierce, and the Whigs the military hero General Winfield Scott, a man of unknown political views. But the sectional question was a divisive influence in the election anyway, and the Whigs were the principal victims. They suffered the massive defection of antislavery members angered by the party's evasiveness on the issue. Many of them flocked to the Free-Soil Party, whose antislavery presidential candidate, John P. Hale, repudiated the Compromise of 1850. The divisions among the Whigs helped produce a victory for the Democrats in 1852.

Franklin Pierce, a charming, amiable man of no particular distinction, attempted to maintain party–and national–harmony by avoiding divisive issues, particularly by avoiding the issue of slavery. But it was an unachievable goal. Northern opposition to the Fugitive Slave Act intensified quickly after 1850, when Southerners began appearing in Northern states to pursue people they claimed were fugitives. Mobs formed in some Northern cities to prevent enforcement of the law, and several Northern states also passed their own laws barring the deportation of fugitive enslaved people. White Southerners watched with growing anger and alarm as the one element of the Compromise of 1850 that they had considered a victory seemed to become meaningless as a result of Northern defiance.

OPPOSITION TO THE FUGITIVE SLAVE ACT

Discussion and Activities

Historical Evidence and Argumentation
Have students read the section "The Uneasy Truce." Have them discuss in small groups what issues almost immediately put the Compromise of 1850 under strain, and what, if anything, political leaders could have done differently to reduce tensions. **PCE**

Answers

Slave and Free Territories Under the Compromise of 1850

The compromise only temporarily postponed sectional conflict over the issue of slavery.

Discussion and Activities

Analyzing Issues Have students read the section "Young America." Ask them to write a short paragraph explaining how the conflict over slavery kept the United States from expanding its territory and from promoting democracy abroad. **WOR** **PCE**

"YOUNG AMERICA"

One of the ways Franklin Pierce hoped to dampen sectional controversy was through his support of a movement in the Democratic Party known as "Young America." Its adherents saw the expansion of American democracy throughout the world as a way to divert attention from the controversies over slavery. The great liberal and nationalist revolutions of 1848 in Europe stirred them to dream of a republican Europe with governments based on the model of the United States. They dreamed as well of expanding American commerce in the Pacific and acquiring new territories in the Western Hemisphere.

But efforts to extend the nation's domain could not avoid becoming entangled with the sectional crisis. Pierce had been pursuing unsuccessful diplomatic attempts to buy Cuba from Spain (efforts begun in 1848 by Polk). In 1854, however, a group of his envoys sent him a private document from Ostend, Belgium, making the case for seizing Cuba by force. When the Ostend Manifesto, as it became known, was leaked to the public, it enraged many antislavery Northerners, who charged the administration with conspiring to bring a new slave state into the Union.

OSTEND MANIFESTO

The South, for its part, opposed all efforts to acquire new territory that would not support a slave system. The kingdom of Hawaii agreed to join the United States in 1854, but the treaty died in the Senate because it contained a clause prohibiting slavery in the islands. A powerful movement to annex Canada to the United States–a movement that had the support of many Canadians eager for access to American markets–similarly foundered, at least in part because of slavery.

SLAVERY, RAILROADS, AND THE WEST

What fully revived the sectional crisis was the same issue that had produced it in the first place: slavery in the territories. By the mid-1850s, the line of substantial white settlement had moved beyond the boundaries of Missouri, Iowa, and what became Minnesota into a great expanse of plains, which many white Americans had once believed was unfit for cultivation. Now it was becoming apparent that large sections of this region were, in fact, suitable for farming and ranching. In the states of the Old Northwest, therefore, prospective settlers urged the government to open the area to them, provide territorial governments, and–despite the solemn assurance the United States had earlier given the Native Americans of the sanctity of their reservations–dislodge the tribes located there to make room for white settlers. There was relatively little opposition from any segment of white society to this proposed violation of Native Americans rights. But the interest in further settlement raised two divisive issues that gradually became entwined with each other: railroads and slavery.

As the nation expanded westward, the problem of communication between the older states and the areas west of the Mississippi River became more and more critical. As a result, broad support began to emerge for building a transcontinental railroad. The problem was where to place it–and in particular, where to locate the railroad's eastern terminus, where the line could connect with the existing rail network east of the Mississippi. Northerners favored Chicago, the rapidly growing capital of the free states of the Northwest. Southerners supported St. Louis, Memphis, or New Orleans–all located in slave states. The transcontinental railroad, in other words, had become part of the struggle between the North and the South.

TRANSCONTINENTAL RAILROAD AND SLAVERY

Pierce's secretary of war, Jefferson Davis of Mississippi, removed one obstacle to a southern route. Surveys indicated that a railroad with a southern terminus would have to pass through an area in Mexican territory. But in 1853 Davis sent James Gadsden, a Southern railroad builder, to Mexico, where he persuaded the Mexican government to accept $10 million in exchange for a strip of land that today comprises part of Arizona and New Mexico and that would have facilitated a southern route for the transcontinental railroad. The so-called Gadsden Purchase only accentuated the sectional rivalry.

GADSDEN PURCHASE

THE KANSAS-NEBRASKA CONTROVERSY

As a senator from Illinois, a resident of Chicago, and the acknowledged leader of northwestern Democrats, Stephen A. Douglas naturally wanted the transcontinental railroad for his own city and section. He also realized the strength of the principal argument against the northern route west of the Mississippi: that it would run mostly through country with a substantial Native American population. As a result, he introduced a bill in January 1854 to organize (and thus open to white settlement) a huge new territory, known as Nebraska, west of Iowa and Missouri.

Douglas knew the South would oppose his bill because it would prepare the way for a new free state; the proposed territory was in the area of the Louisiana Purchase north of the Missouri Compromise line (36°30′) and hence closed to slavery. In an effort to make the measure acceptable to Southerners, Douglas inserted a provision that the status of slavery in the territory would be determined by the territorial legislature–that is, according to "popular sovereignty." In theory, the region could choose to open itself to slavery (although few believed it actually would). When Southern Democrats demanded more, Douglas agreed to an additional clause explicitly repealing the Missouri Compromise. He also agreed to divide the area into two new territories–Nebraska and Kansas–instead of one. The new, second territory (Kansas) was more likely to become a slave state. In its final form the measure was

KANSAS-NEBRASKA ACT

Historical Thinking Skills

Argumentation Have students read the section "Slavery, Railroads, and the West." Ask them to discuss in pairs or small groups how the issue of slavery became a barrier to railroad construction in the West. *(Northerners and Southerners wanted railroads that connected to their own region and not to the other.)* **PCE**

known as the Kansas-Nebraska Act. President Pierce supported the bill, and after a strenuous debate, it became law in May 1854 with the unanimous support of the South and the partial support of Northern Democrats.

Perhaps no piece of legislation in American history produced so many immediate, sweeping, and ominous consequences. It divided and destroyed the Whig Party, which nearly disappeared by 1856. It divided the Northern Democrats (many of whom were appalled at the repeal of the Missouri Compromise, which they considered an almost sacred part of the fabric of the Union) and drove many of them from the party. Most important, it spurred the creation of a new party that was frankly sectional in composition and creed. People in both major parties who opposed Douglas's bill began to call themselves Anti-Nebraska Democrats and Anti-Nebraska Whigs. In 1854, they formed a new organization and named it the Republican Party. It instantly became a major force in American politics. In the elections of that year, the Republicans won enough seats in Congress to permit them, in combination with allies among the Know-Nothings, to organize the House of Representatives.

BIRTH OF THE REPUBLICAN PARTY

"BLEEDING KANSAS"

Events in Kansas in the next two years increased the political turmoil in the North. White settlers from both the North and the South began moving into the territory almost immediately after the passage of the Kansas-Nebraska Act. In the spring of 1855, elections were held for a territorial legislature. There were only about 1,500 legal voters in Kansas by then, but thousands of Missourians, some traveling in armed bands into Kansas, swelled the vote to over 6,000. The result was that pro-slavery forces elected a majority to the legislature, which immediately legalized slavery. Outraged free-staters elected their own delegates to a constitutional convention, which met at Topeka and adopted a constitution excluding slavery. They then chose their own governor and legislature and petitioned Congress for statehood. President Pierce denounced them as traitors and threw the full support of the federal government behind the pro-slavery territorial legislature. A few months later a pro-slavery federal marshal assembled a large posse, consisting mostly of Missourians, to arrest the free-state leaders, who had set up their headquarters in Lawrence. The posse sacked the town, burned the "governor's" house, and destroyed several printing presses. Retribution came quickly.

Among the most fervent abolitionists in Kansas was John Brown, a fiercely committed foe of slavery who considered himself an instrument of God's will to destroy slavery. He had moved to Kansas with his sons so that they could fight to make it a free state. After the events in Lawrence, he gathered six followers (including four of his sons) and in one night murdered five pro-slavery settlers, leaving their mutilated bodies to discourage other supporters of slavery from entering Kansas. This bloody episode, known as the Potawatomie Massacre, led to more civil strife in Kansas–irregular, guerrilla warfare conducted by armed bands, some of them more interested in land claims or loot than in ideologies. Northerners and Southerners alike came to believe that the events in Kansas illustrated (and were caused by) the aggressive designs of the other section. "Bleeding Kansas" became a symbol of the sectional controversy.

POTAWATOMIE MASSACRE

Another symbol soon appeared, in the United States Senate. In May 1856, Charles Sumner of Massachusetts–a militant and passionate opponent of slavery–rose to give a speech titled "The Crime Against Kansas." In it, he gave particular attention to Senator Andrew P. Butler of South Carolina, an outspoken defender of slavery. The South Carolinian was, Sumner claimed, the "Don Quixote" of slavery, having "chosen a mistress . . .

"BLEEDING KANSAS" During the bitter battles over slavery in 1856, the slave state of Missouri tried to prevent antislavery emigrants from passing through their territory en route to Kansas. Free-staters responded by organizing a large emigration through Iowa, circumventing Missouri. Those who entered Kansas by that route tended to arrive armed, some of them with large cannons—among them the one pictured here, which free-staters brought with them to Topeka that year.

Discussion and Activities

Explaining Significance After students have read the section "The Kansas-Nebraska Controversy," have them create a list of the consequences of the Kansas-Nebraska Act. Discuss as a class why the repeal of the Missouri Compromise was so controversial. **PCE** **ARC**

Discussion and Activities

Analyzing Point of View After students have read the section "Potawatomie Massacre," ask them to write a journal entry from the point of view of a resident of either Lawrence or Potawatomie Creek describing the attack on their settlement. **PCE** **ARC**

Discussion and Activities

Historical Developments and Argumentation After students have read the section "Preston Brooks and Charles Sumner," ask them to discuss in small groups the causes and effects of the beating of Senator Sumner and how the incident demonstrated increasing tensions between the North and the South. **PCE** **ARC**

who, though ugly to others, is always lovely to him, though polluted in the sight of the world, is chaste in his sight . . . the harlot slavery."

The pointedly sexual references and the viciousness of the speech enraged Butler's nephew, Preston Brooks, a member of the House of Representatives from South Carolina. Several days after the speech, Brooks approached Sumner at his desk in the Senate chamber during a recess, raised a heavy cane, and began beating him repeatedly on the head and shoulders. Sumner, trapped in his chair, rose in agony with such strength that he tore the desk from the bolts holding it to the floor. Then he collapsed, bleeding and unconscious. So severe were his injuries that he was unable to return to the Senate for four years. Throughout the North, he became a hero–a martyr to the barbarism of the South. In the South, Preston Brooks became a hero, too. Censured by the House, he resigned his seat, returned to South Carolina, and stood successfully for reelection.

PRESTON BROOKS AND CHARLES SUMNER

THE FREE-SOIL IDEOLOGY

What had happened to produce such deep hostility between the two sections? In part, the tensions were reflections of the two sections' differing economic and territorial interests. But they were also reflections of a hardening of ideas in both North and South. As the nation expanded and political power grew more dispersed, each section became concerned with ensuring that its vision of America's future would be the dominant one.

In the North, assumptions about the proper structure of society came to center on the belief in "free soil" and "free labor." Although abolitionists generated some support for their argument that slavery was a moral evil and must be eliminated, most white Northerners came to believe that the existence of slavery was dangerous not because of what it did to African Americans but because of what it threatened to do to white people. At the heart of American democracy, they argued, was the right of all citizens to own property, to control their own labor, and to have access to opportunities for advancement.

"FREE-SOIL" IDEOLOGY

According to this Northern vision, the South was the antithesis of democracy–a closed, static society, in which slavery preserved an entrenched aristocracy and in which common white people had no opportunity to improve themselves. While the North was growing and prospering, the South was stagnating, rejecting the values of individualism and progress. The South was, Northern free-laborites further maintained, engaged in a conspiracy to extend slavery throughout the nation and thus to destroy the openness of Northern capitalism and replace it with the closed, aristocratic system of the South. The only solution to this "slave power conspiracy" was to fight the spread of slavery and extend the nation's democratic, free-labor ideals to all sections of the country.

"SLAVE POWER CONSPIRACY"

This ideology, which lay at the heart of the new Republican Party, also strengthened the commitment of Republicans to the Union. Since the idea of continued growth and progress was central to the free-labor vision, the prospect of dismemberment of the nation–a diminution of America's size and economic power–was unthinkable.

THE PRO-SLAVERY ARGUMENT

In the South, in the meantime, a very different ideology–entirely incompatible with the free-labor ideology–was emerging among white Southerners on the issue of slavery. It was a result of many things: the Nat Turner uprising in 1831, which terrified Southern whites and made them more determined than ever to make slavery secure; the expansion of the cotton economy into the Deep South, which made slavery unprecedentedly lucrative; and the growth of the Garrisonian abolitionist movement, with its strident attacks on Southern society. The popularity of Harriet Beecher Stowe's *Uncle Tom's*

ANTI-ABOLITIONIST VIOLENCE This 1838 woodcut depicts the anti-abolitionist riot in Alton, Illinois, in which Elijah P. Lovejoy, publisher of an abolitionist newspaper, was slain on November 7, 1837. The death of Lovejoy aroused the antislavery movement throughout the United States.

The Library of Congress

Historical Thinking Skills

Argumentation Have students read the section "The Free-Soil Ideology." Ask them to create a campaign poster promoting Free-Soil Party candidates using symbols and slogans appropriate to the ideology of the party. **PCE** **ARC** **SOC** **WXT**

Cabin was perhaps the most glaring evidence of the success of those attacks, but other abolitionist writings had been antagonizing white Southerners for years.

In response to these pressures, a number of white Southerners produced a new intellectual defense of slavery. Professor Thomas R. Dew of the College of William and Mary helped begin that effort in 1832. Twenty years later, supporters of slavery summarized their views in an anthology titled *The Pro-Slavery Argument*. John C. Calhoun stated the essence of the case in 1837: Southerners should stop apologizing for slavery as a necessary evil and defend it as "a good—a positive good." It was good for the enslaved people, white Southerners argued, because they enjoyed better conditions than industrial workers in the North. Slavery was good for Southern society as a whole because it was the only way the two races could live together in peace. It was good for the entire country because the Southern economy, based on slavery, was the key to the prosperity of the nation.

THE PRO-SLAVERY ARGUMENT

Above all, Southern apologists argued, slavery was good because it served as the basis for the Southern way of life—a way of life superior to any other in the United States, perhaps in the world. White Southerners looking at the North saw a spirit of greed, debauchery, and instability. "The masses of the North are venal, corrupt, covetous, mean and selfish," wrote one Southerner. Others wrote with horror of the factory system and the crowded, pestilential cities filled with unruly immigrants. The South, by contrast, was a stable, orderly society, operating at a slow and human pace. It was free from the feuds between capital and labor plaguing the North. It protected the welfare of its workers. And it allowed the aristocracy to enjoy a refined and accomplished cultural life. It was, in short, an ideal social order in which all elements of the population were secure and content.

The defense of slavery rested, too, on increasingly elaborate arguments about the biological inferiority of African Americans, who were, many white Southerners claimed, inherently unfit to take care of themselves, let alone exercise the rights of citizenship. And just as abolitionist arguments drew strength from Protestant theology in the North, the pro-slavery defense mobilized the Protestant clergy in the South to give the institution a religious and biblical justification.

BUCHANAN AND DEPRESSION

In this unpromising climate, the presidential campaign of 1856 began. Democratic Party leaders wanted a candidate who, unlike President Pierce, was not closely associated with the explosive question of "Bleeding Kansas." They chose James Buchanan of Pennsylvania, a reliable Democratic stalwart who as minister to England had been safely out of the country during the recent controversies. The Republicans, participating in their first presidential contest, denounced the Kansas-Nebraska Act and the expansion of slavery but also endorsed a Whiggish program of internal improvements, thus combining the idealism of antislavery with the economic aspirations of the North. As eager as the Democrats to present a safe candidate, the Republicans nominated John C. Frémont, who had made a national reputation as an explorer of the Far West and who had no political record. The Native American, or Know-Nothing, Party was beginning to break apart, but it nominated former president Millard Fillmore, who also received the endorsement of a small remnant of the Whig Party.

ELECTION OF 1856

After a heated, even frenzied campaign, Buchanan won a narrow victory over Frémont and Fillmore. A slight shift of votes in Pennsylvania and Illinois would have elected the Republican candidate. Particularly significant was that Frémont had attracted virtually no votes in the South while outpolling all other candidates in the North. At the time of his inauguration, Buchanan was, at age sixty-five, the oldest president, except for William Henry Harrison, ever to have taken office. Whether because of age and physical infirmities or because of a fundamental weakness of character, he was a painfully timid and indecisive president at a critical moment in history.

In the year Buchanan took office, a financial panic struck the country, followed by a depression that lasted several years. In the North, the depression strengthened the Republican Party because distressed manufacturers, workers, and farmers came to believe that the hard times were the result of the unsound policies of Southern-controlled Democratic administrations. They expressed their frustrations by moving into an alliance with antislavery elements and thus into the Republican Party.

THE *DRED SCOTT* DECISION

On March 6, 1857, the Supreme Court of the United States projected itself into the sectional controversy with one of the most controversial and notorious decisions in its history—its ruling in the case of *Dred Scott v. Sandford*, handed down two days after Buchanan was inaugurated. Dred Scott was an enslaved man in Missouri, once owned by an army surgeon who had taken Scott with him into Illinois and Wisconsin, where slavery was forbidden. In 1846, after the surgeon died, Scott sued his slaveholder's widow for freedom on the grounds that his residence in free territory had liberated him from slavery. The claim was well grounded in Missouri law, and in 1850 the circuit court in which Scott filed the suit declared him free. By now, John Sanford, the brother of the surgeon's widow, was claiming ownership of Scott, and he appealed the circuit court ruling to the state supreme court, which reversed the earlier decision. When Scott appealed to the federal courts, Sanford's attorneys claimed that Scott had no standing to sue because he was not a citizen, but private property.

The Supreme Court (which misspelled Sanford's name in its decision) was so divided that it was unable to issue a single ruling on the case. The thrust of the various rulings, however, was a stunning defeat for the antislavery movement. Chief Justice Roger Taney, who wrote one of the majority opinions, declared that Scott could not bring a suit in the federal courts because he was not a citizen. African

TANEY'S SWEEPING OPINION

Discussion and Activities

Distinguishing Fact From Opinion After students have read the section "The Pro-Slavery Argument," ask them to write a short paragraph summarizing the main points of the pro-slavery argument. Have students address in what ways Southern apologists for slavery argued the slavery was a "positive good," and then write a paragraph of rebuttal to this argument. SOC WXT PCE

Discussion and Activities

Analyzing Issues Have students read the section "Buchanan and Depression." Discuss as a class why Buchanan was able to win the election of 1856. *(Buchanan, the Democratic candidate, was the only candidate who received significant votes from all parts of the country. Fillmore, representing the remaining Whigs and the Know-Nothings, had weak support everywhere and only managed to win one state. Fremont, the candidate of the new Republican Party, terrified Southerners due to their fear that Republicans might act to limit slavery.)* PCE

Historical Thinking Skills

Argumentation After students have read the section "The *Dred Scott* Decision," ask them to consider the fact that some legal scholars have described the decision as the worst in the history of the Supreme Court. Have students write a thesis that supports, refutes, or modifies that claim. **PCE**

Americans had no claim to citizenship, Taney argued, and virtually no rights under the Constitution. Enslaved people were property, and the Fifth Amendment prohibited Congress from taking property without "due process of law." Consequently, Taney concluded, Congress possessed no authority to pass a law depriving persons of their slave property in the territories. The Missouri Compromise, therefore, had always been unconstitutional.

The ruling did nothing to challenge the right of an individual state to prohibit slavery within its borders, but the statement that the federal government was powerless to act on the issue was drastic and startling. Few judicial opinions have ever created as much controversy. White Southerners were elated: the highest tribunal in the land had sanctioned some of the most extreme Southern arguments. In the North, the decision produced widespread fury and dismay. The decision, the *New York Tribune* wrote, "is entitled to just so much moral weight as would be the judgment of a majority of those congregated in any Washington bar-room." Republicans threatened that when they won control of the national government, they would reverse the decision–by "packing" the Court with new members.

DEADLOCK OVER KANSAS

President Buchanan timidly endorsed the *Dred Scott* decision. At the same time, he tried to resolve the controversy over Kansas by supporting its admission to the Union as a slave state. In response, the pro-slavery territorial legislature called an election for delegates to a constitutional convention. The free-state residents refused to participate, claiming that the legislature had discriminated against them in drawing district lines. As a result, the pro-slavery forces won control of the convention, which met in 1857 at Lecompton, framed a constitution legalizing slavery, and refused to give voters a chance to reject it. When an election for a new territorial legislature was called, the antislavery groups turned out to vote and won a majority. The new legislature promptly submitted the Lecompton constitution to the voters, who rejected it by more than 10,000 votes.

Both sides had resorted to fraud and violence, but it was clear nevertheless that a majority of the people of Kansas opposed slavery. Buchanan, however, pressured Congress to admit Kansas under the Lecompton constitution. Stephen A. Douglas and other western Democrats refused to support the president's proposal, which died in the House of Representatives. Finally, in April 1858, Congress approved a compromise: The Lecompton constitution would be submitted to the voters of Kansas again. If it was approved, Kansas would be admitted to the Union; if it was rejected, statehood would be postponed. Again, Kansas voters decisively rejected the Lecompton constitution. Not until the closing months of Buchanan's administration in early 1861, after several Southern states had already withdrawn from the Union, did Kansas enter the Union–as a free state.

LECOMPTON CONSTITUTION REJECTED

THE EMERGENCE OF LINCOLN

Given the gravity of the sectional crisis, the congressional elections of 1858 took on a special importance. Of particular note was the United States Senate election in Illinois, which pitted Stephen A. Douglas, the most prominent Northern Democrat, against Abraham Lincoln, who was largely unknown outside Illinois but who quickly emerged as one of the most skillful politicians in the Republican Party.

Lincoln was a successful lawyer who had long been involved in state politics. He had served several terms in the Illinois legislature and one undistinguished term in Congress. He was not a national figure like Douglas, so he tried to increase his visibility by engaging Douglas in a series of debates. The Lincoln-Douglas debates attracted enormous crowds and received wide attention in newspapers across the country. By the time the debates ended, Lincoln's increasingly eloquent and passionate attacks on slavery had made him nationally prominent.

LINCOLN-DOUGLAS DEBATES

At the heart of the debates was a basic difference on the issue of slavery. Douglas appeared to have no moral position on the issue. "One of the reserved rights of the states," he said, "was the right to regulate the relations between master and servant, on the slavery question." But Douglas went further, endorsing what was still the dominant sentiment among white people (both North and South) of his time: "I am opposed to negro citizenship in any and every form. I believe this government was made on the white basis. I believe it was made by white men for the benefit of white men and their posterity forever." Lincoln's opposition to slavery was different. If the nation could accept that African Americans were not entitled to basic human rights, he argued, then it could accept that other groups–immigrant laborers, for example–could be deprived of rights, too. And if slavery were to extend into the western territories, he claimed, opportunities for poor white laborers to better their lots in life would be lost. The nation's future, he argued (reflecting the central idea of the Republican Party), rested on the spread of free labor.

Lincoln believed slavery was morally wrong, but he was not an abolitionist. That was in part because he could not envision an easy alternative to slavery in the areas where it already existed. He shared the prevailing view among white Northerners that African Americans were not prepared (and perhaps never would be) to live on equal terms with white people. But even while Lincoln accepted the inferiority of black people, he continued to believe that they were entitled to basic rights. "I have no purpose to introduce political and social equality between the white and the black races. . . . But I hold that . . . there is no reason in the world why the negro is not entitled to all the natural rights enumerated in the Declaration of Independence, the right to life, liberty, and the pursuit of happiness. I hold that he is as much entitled to these as the white man." Lincoln and his party wanted to "arrest the further spread" of slavery–that is, prevent its expansion into the

LINCOLN'S POSITION

Discussion and Activities

Evaluating Evidence Have students read the section "Deadlock Over Kansas." Discuss as a class how the debate over Kansas statehood demonstrated growing division surrounding the issue of slavery. **PCE**

THE HARPERS FERRY ARSENAL John Brown's famous raid on Harpers Ferry in 1859 centered on this arsenal, from which he and his followers tried, in vain, to foment slave rebellion throughout the South.

National Park Service, Harper's Ferry, U.S. Department of the Interior/National Archives and Records Administration

territories; but they would not directly challenge it where it already existed and would instead trust that the institution would gradually die there of its own accord.

Douglas's position satisfied his followers sufficiently to win him reelection to the Senate in 1858, but it aroused little enthusiasm and did nothing to enhance his national political ambitions. Lincoln, by contrast, lost the election but emerged with a growing following both in and beyond the state. And outside Illinois, the elections went heavily against the Democrats, who lost ground in almost every Northern state. The Democratic Party retained control of the Senate but lost its majority in the House, with the result that the congressional sessions of 1858 and 1859 were bitterly deadlocked.

JOHN BROWN'S RAID

The battles in Congress, however, were overshadowed by a spectacular event that enraged and horrified the entire South and greatly hastened the rush toward disunion. In the fall of 1859, John Brown, the antislavery zealot whose bloody actions in Kansas had inflamed the crisis there, staged an even more dramatic episode, this time in the South itself. With private encouragement and financial aid from some prominent eastern abolitionists, he made elaborate plans to seize a mountain fortress in Virginia from which, he believed, he could foment a slave insurrection in the South. On October 16, he and a group of eighteen followers attacked and seized control of a U.S. arsenal in Harpers Ferry, Virginia. But the slave uprising Brown hoped to inspire did not occur, and he quickly found himself besieged by citizens, local militia companies, and, before long, U.S. troops under the command of Robert E. Lee. After ten of his men were killed, Brown surrendered. He was promptly tried in a Virginia court for treason against the state, found guilty, and sentenced to death. He and six of his followers were hanged.

JOHN BROWN'S RAID

No other single event did more than the Harpers Ferry raid to convince white Southerners that they could not live safely in the Union. John Brown's raid, many Southerners believed (incorrectly) had the support of the Republican Party, and it suggested to them that the North was now committed to producing a slave insurrection.

THE ELECTION OF LINCOLN

The presidential election of 1860 had the most momentous consequences of any in American history. It was also among the most complex.

The Democratic Party was torn apart by a battle between Southerners, who demanded a strong endorsement of slavery, and Westerners, who supported the idea of popular sovereignty. The party convention met in April in Charleston, South Carolina. When the convention endorsed popular sovereignty, delegates from eight states in the lower South walked out. The remaining delegates could not agree on a presidential candidate and finally adjourned after agreeing to meet again in Baltimore

DIVIDED DEMOCRATS

Discussion and Activities

Historical Reasoning and Argumentation After students have read the section "The Emergence of Lincoln," ask them to go online and search the C-SPAN website for its reenactment of the Lincoln-Douglas debates, in particular Douglas's exposition of the "Freeport Doctrine." (https://www.c-span.org/video/?c4185844/user-clip-freeport-doctrine) **Ask:** How did Douglas try to answer Lincoln's charge that popular sovereignty (as authorized by the Kansas-Nebraska Act) had been nullified by the Supreme Court's decision in *Dred Scott v. Sandford*? *(Douglas implied that the Supreme Court decision didn't matter, as the people would use the laws and the enforcement of laws in the territories to keep slavery out if they were opposed to it.)* **PCE**

Discussion and Activities

Identifying Bias Have students read the section "John Brown's Raid." Ask them to discuss in small groups how the raid was interpreted differently by those in the North and the South and how the different interpretations indicated growing sectional division. **ARC** **PCE**

Historical Thinking Skills

Argumentation After students have read the section "The Election of Lincoln," divide them into groups of four. In their groups, have one student write a short campaign speech for each of the four leading candidates and then deliver their speeches to the other members of their groups. **PCE**

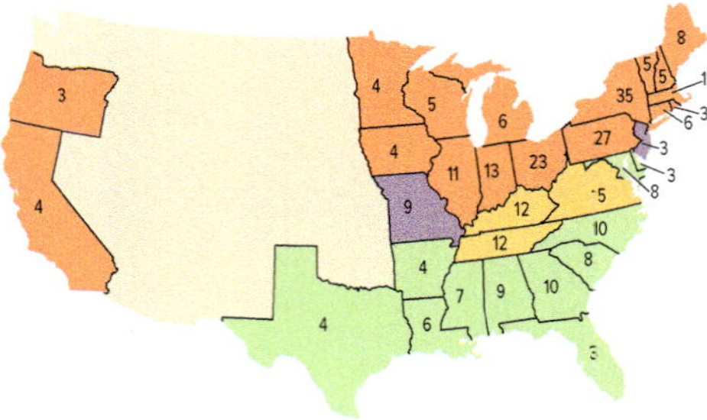

	Candidate (Party)	Electoral Vote	Popular Vote (%)
	Abraham Lincoln (Republican)	180	1,865,593 (39.9)
	J. C. Breckinridge (Southern Democratic)	72	848,356 (18.1)
	John Bell (Constitutional Union)	39	592,906 (12.6)
	Stephen A. Douglas (Northern Democratic)	12	1,382,713 (29.4)
	Nonvoting territories		

81.2% of electorate voting

THE ELECTION OF 1860 The stark sectional divisions that helped produce the Civil War were clearly visible in the results of the 1860 presidential election. Abraham Lincoln, the antislavery Republican candidate, won almost all of the free states. Stephen Douglas, a Northern Democrat with no strong position on the issue of slavery, won only one border and one free state, and John Bell, a supporter of both slavery and union, won three border states. John Breckinridge, a strong pro-slavery Southern Democrat, carried the entire Deep South. Lincoln won less than 40 percent of the popular vote but, because of the four-way division in the race, managed to win a clear majority of the electoral vote.

What impact did the election of Lincoln have on the sectional crisis?

in June. The decimated convention at Baltimore nominated Stephen Douglas for president. In the meantime, disenchanted Southern Democrats met in Richmond and nominated John C. Breckinridge of Kentucky. Later, a group of conservative ex-Whigs met in Baltimore to form the Constitutional Union Party, with John Bell of Tennessee as their presidential candidate. They endorsed the Union and remained silent on slavery.

The Republican leaders, in the meantime, were trying to broaden their appeal so as to attract every major interest group in the North. They warned that the South was blocking the North's economic aspirations. The platform endorsed such traditional Whig measures as a high tariff, internal improvements, a homestead bill, and a Pacific railroad to be built with federal financial assistance. It supported the right of each state to decide the status of slavery within its borders. But it also insisted that neither Congress nor territorial legislatures could legalize slavery in the territories. The Republican convention chose Abraham Lincoln as the party's presidential nominee. Lincoln was appealing because of his growing reputation for eloquence, because of his firm but moderate position on slavery, and because his relative obscurity ensured that he would have none of the drawbacks of other, more prominent (and therefore more controversial) Republicans. He was a representative of the West, a considerable asset in a race against Douglas.

In the November election, Lincoln won the presidency with a majority of the electoral votes but only about two-fifths of the fragmented popular vote. The Republicans, moreover, failed to win a majority in Congress. Even so, the election of Lincoln became the final signal to many white Southerners that their position in the Union was hopeless. And within a few weeks of Lincoln's victory, the process of disunion began—a process that would quickly lead to a prolonged and bloody war between two groups of Americans, each heir to more than a century of struggling toward nationhood, each now convinced that it shared no common ground with the other.

DISUNION

Answers

The Election of 1860

After Lincoln's election, several Southern states, convinced that Lincoln intended to abolish slavery, began secession proceedings.

CHAPTER 13 REVIEW

CONNECTING THEMES

Chapter Thirteen explored the ideology behind Manifest Destiny and the impact that territorial acquisition had on the intensifying sectional divide between the North and the South during the antebellum period in the United States. The expansionist government policies, specifically the presidential agenda of James K. Polk, entangled the issue of slavery into debates over territorial acquisition.

The Compromise of 1850 and the Fugitive Slave Act were among a series of events that would eventually lead to the Civil War. The Kansas-Nebraska Act and the concept of "popular sovereignty" were part of efforts to find a solution to the problem of territorial expansion and slavery. But the legislation could not bridge the divisions. Ultimately, it led to the demise of the Second Party System and the emergence of the Third American Party System.

A number of issues continued to polarize the sectional divide: increasing emotionalism over slavery, the growing abolitionist movement, the Free-Soil movement within the North, and the apologist defense of slavery in the South. At the heart of the conflict was the issue of slavery. Both regions wanted their political, economic, social, and cultural vision of America to dominate the future. Among the final events leading to the impending crisis were the Dred Scott decision, John Brown's raid at Harpers Ferry, and the election of Lincoln in 1860.

You should consider the following questions as you review the themes for this chapter:

- What were the major historical arguments both for and against the institution of slavery?
- How did regional differences affect the political environment during the antebellum period?
- How did territorial acquisition intensify sectional conflict?
- What were the ways that the arguments over slavery intensified and worsened the sectional crisis?

KEY TERMS

Abraham Lincoln 378
Compromise of 1850 372
***Dred Scott* decision** 377
Election of 1860 379
Fugitive Slave Act 373
gold rush 370
Free-Soil ideology 376
Free-Soil Party 370
Gadsden Purchase 374
General Antonio Lopez de Santa Anna 361
Harpers Ferry 379
Henry Clay 372
James K. Polk 365
John Brown 375
John C. Calhoun 372
Kansas-Nebraska Act 374
Manifest Destiny 359
Mexican War 366
Oregon border dispute 362
Oregon Trail 363
popular sovereignty 370
Republican Party 375
Sam Houston 361
Stephen A. Douglas 372
Stephen F. Austin 361
Tejanos 361
Texas annexation 361
The Alamo 361
Transcontinental Railroad 374
Treaty of Guadalupe-Hidalgo 368
Wilmot Proviso 369
Winfield Scott 373
"Young America" 374
Zachary Taylor 366

Discussion and Activities

Contextualization and Argumentation Ask students to review the compromises that attempted to resolve divisions over slavery (The Wilmot Proviso; the Compromise of 1850; the Kansas-Nebraska Act). As a class, discuss why each of those compromises failed and what political leaders might have done differently, if anything, to resolve the conflict short of going to war. Have students write a summary of what they think the best approach to avoiding war might have been. **PCE** **ARC** **SOC** **WXT**

Key Terms

Students should be familiar with the key terms and be able to define them in the context of the growing sectional tension over slavery and the failure of attempted compromises. Encourage students to use these terms in performing review exercises and exam practice for this chapter.

Go Online Chapter 13 Content Review

Assessing Student Understanding Use the online assessment to assess student understanding of concepts and topics within the chapter. You can assign the ready-made Chapter 13 Content Review or create your own from available questions. This easy-to-use tool helps you design assessments that meet the needs of different types of learners.

Answers

Multiple Choice

1. B; **2.** D; **3.** D

Short Answer

4A) Possible answer: The point of view in the image is that of someone who supports and believes in the philosophy of Manifest Destiny, the idea that western expansion was sanctioned by a divine plan. The image is a bit different from other depictions of this philosophy as this one shows some examples of struggle.

4B) Possible answer: Expansion of slavery was one of the drivers for western expansion and Manifest Destiny. As soil exhaustion depleted needed minerals, farmers sought out new land to cultivate.

4C) Possible answer: As western expansion continued, new territories lobbied for statehood. This led to debates about the expansion of slavery and the political power that slave states had in Congress. New territory from the Mexican War was a focal point for disagreement.

5A) Possible answer: Both proposals attempted to deal with the constitutional and legal issues over the spread of slavery into the Mexican cession territory. The first, proposed by Free-Soil proponents, supported the idea to ban all slavery from all territory acquired in the Mexican War. The second, brokered by Henry Clay, proposed a compromise between the North and the South.

5B) Possible answer: The Wilmot Proviso proposed to ban all slavery from the Mexican cession territory but ultimately failed in the Senate. The Compromise of 1850 proposed a balance between the North and the South and ultimately passed in both the House and the Senate.

5C) Possible answer: The Compromise of 1850 caused anger and frustration in both the North and the South. It gave each something they wanted, but it also gave up too much, according to both sides. The North was angry over the beefed-up Fugitive Slave Law, and the South was angry about limiting the spread of slavery.

AP EXAM PRACTICE

Questions assume cumulative content knowledge from this chapter and previous chapters.

MULTIPLE CHOICE

Use the map on page 380 and your knowledge of U.S. history to answer questions 1-3.

1. What divisive issue continually led to conflict throughout the decades preceding the election of 1860?
   (A) the regulation of protective tariffs
   (B) the expansion of slavery into new territories and states
   (C) the question of expansion into Cuba
   (D) the working conditions in the expanding textile industry

2. The pattern demonstrated on the map reflects which reality?
   (A) The North and the South voted in uniform regional blocks.
   (B) Lincoln won a majority of votes cast in the election.
   (C) The Democratic Party remained unified through the election.
   (D) Lincoln failed to win any slave states.

3. What was the most immediate impact of the election shown on the map?
   (A) The Missouri Compromise was repealed.
   (B) The Dred Scott decision was reversed.
   (C) Kansas was admitted to the Union as a free state.
   (D) The Southern states began to secede.

SHORT ANSWER

Use your knowledge of U.S. history to answer questions 4 and 5.

4. Use the image on page 363 to answer A, B, and C.
   (A) Briefly describe ONE historical point of view about western migration illustrated by the image *Westward the Course of Empire Takes Its Way*.
   (B) Briefly explain ONE specific historical cause of Manifest Destiny during the first half of the nineteenth century.
   (C) Briefly explain ONE specific historical effect that resulted from Manifest Destiny during the first half of the nineteenth century.

5. Answer A, B, and C.
   (A) Briefly describe ONE specific historical similarity between the Wilmot Proviso and the Compromise of 1850.
   (B) Briefly describe ONE specific historical difference between the Wilmot Proviso and the Compromise of 1850.
   (C) Briefly explain ONE specific historical effect of the Compromise of 1850.

LONG ESSAY

Develop a thoughtful and thorough historical argument that addresses the statement. Begin your essay with a thesis statement, and support it with specific historical evidence and examples.

6. Evaluate the relative importance of causes that led to the crises of the 1850s in the United States.

Answers

Long Essay

6. Possible thesis: During this time, there were significant cultural and social differences between the North and South as the two continued to grow further apart. The issue over slavery was the most significant of these differences, along with other political divisions. Specific historical evidence: First, the debate over the expansion of slavery was an overwhelming cause that led the country to severe sectional tensions. The U.S. Supreme Court, finally, weighed in on the issue over the constitutional and legal status of the institution. But many Northern states began passing personal liberty laws, nullifying federal laws that protected slavery. Second, concerns grew over not just the institution of slavery but the political power that slave states held over free states. Both the Missouri Compromise and the Compromise of 1850 attempted to deal with these issues. Third, there were growing differences that were developing between the industrial North and the agricultural South, and western expansion and the alignment between the North and the West further alienated Southerners. Finally, there were cultural differences between the two regions. These differences had always existed, but they became more prominent as the country moved closer to civil war.

14 THE CIVIL WAR

UNION SOLDIERS AT REST
The Civil War was one of the bloodiest conflicts in American history. But there were many times at which the armies were not in battle. This photograph of Union soldiers was taken at a large supply base in northern Virginia in 1862—one of many sites in which soldiers spent long, idle periods.

The Library of Congress

CONNECTING CONCEPTS

Chapter Fourteen begins by examining the causes and beginning of the Civil War. It concludes by analyzing the impact of the conflict on Northern and Southern society. After the secession crisis and the firing on Fort Sumter, the North had huge advantages in terms of population, industry, and transportation systems, but the South had the advantage of fighting a defensive war on familiar terrain with the nearly full support of its white population.

In the North, the Civil War stimulated economic growth and prosperity. Republicans used their control of Congress to pass higher tariffs, the National Bank Acts, and the Morrill Land Grant Act. President Lincoln, however, faced strong opposition from Peace Democrats and often resorted to extralegal measures to silence political critics. Conscription was also unpopular with workers, who objected to wealthy people avoiding military service by hiring substitutes. On both sides, many protested that it was a "rich man's war, and a poor man's fight."

In the South, the Civil War devastated the economy, which rested on the production and export of cotton. The Confederacy also faced funding problems, manpower shortages, supply shortfalls, and ideological battles over states' rights versus the power of centralized government. In the end, President Davis was unsuccessful at meeting these difficult challenges, although only a few close calls on the battlefield prevented the South from gaining political independence and international recognition.

Both the North and the South were initially reluctant to mobilize black soldiers. But after Lincoln issued the Emancipation Proclamation in 1862 and made the elimination of slavery a central goal of the war, African Americans enlisted in the Union Army in large numbers. The Proclamation had little impact at first, but it ultimately led to passage of the Thirteenth Amendment, which abolished the institution of slavery, although parts of it survived in different forms for decades to come.

Pacing Guide

Chapter 14 explores key concepts from Period 5: 1844–1877 of the AP U.S. History Curriculum Framework. The suggested instruction time for Chapter 14 is 6 days.

Key Concepts

5.2.I Ideological and economic differences over slavery produced an array of diverging responses from Americans in the North and the South.

5.2.II Debates over slavery came to dominate political discussion in the 1850s, culminating in the bitter election of 1860 and the secession of Southern states.

Discussion and Activities

Speculating Have students examine the photo "Union Soldiers at Rest." Ask them to write a short journal entry from the point of view of one of the soldiers pictured describing his thoughts, hopes, and fears during this break from fighting. **SOC**

Discussion and Activities

Analyzing Cause and Effect Have students read the section "The Withdrawal of the South." Ask them to create a T-chart listing causes and effects of the initial secession of Southern states. Have students discuss which, if any, of the causes might still have been resolved by compromise at this point. **PCE** **ARC**

By choice or necessity, women had to assume new and unfamiliar roles during the Civil War. Although traditional gender roles remained largely in place, women took over positions vacated by men in the workplace. They also entered the field of nursing and dominated it by the end of the war. Some women, like Elizabeth Cady Stanton, saw the war as an opportunity to gain support for their goals of abolitionism and voting rights for women. Ultimately, the Civil War had lasting social, political, and economic effects for the United States and its people.

As you read, you should:

- Identify the ways in which the abolition of slavery led to the reshaping of cultural identities and concepts of citizenship.
- Analyze how the Civil War generated new social, political, and economic opportunities for many Americans.
- Evaluate the reasons for the repeated attempts at compromise and why they failed to prevent the Civil War.
- Describe the advantages and disadvantages of both the North and the South during the Civil War.
- Explain the ways the Emancipation Proclamation and the Thirteenth Amendment offered new opportunities for African Americans.

THE SECESSION CRISIS

"SOUTHERN NATIONALISM"

Almost as soon as the news of Abraham Lincoln's election reached the South, the militant leaders of the region—the champions of the new concept of "Southern nationalism," men known both to their contemporaries and to history as the "fire-eaters"—began to demand an end to the Union.

The Withdrawal of the South

South Carolina, long the hotbed of Southern separatism, seceded first. It called a special convention, which voted unanimously on December 20, 1860, to withdraw the state from the Union. Horace Greeley of the *New York Tribune* wrote three days before secession, "We fully realize that the dilemma of the incoming administration will be a critical one. It must endeavor to uphold and enforce laws, as well against rebellious slaveholders as fugitives."

ESTABLISHMENT OF THE CONFEDERACY

By the time Lincoln took office, six other states from the lower South—Mississippi (January 9, 1861), Florida (January 10), Alabama (January 11), Georgia (January 19), Louisiana (January 26), and Texas (February 1)—had seceded. In February 1861, representatives of the seven seceded states met at Montgomery, Alabama, and announced the formation of a new nation: the Confederate States of America. The response from the North was confused and indecisive. President James Buchanan told Congress in December 1860 that no state had the right to secede from the Union but suggested that the federal government had no authority to stop a state if it did.

The seceding states immediately seized the federal property—forts, arsenals, government offices—within their boundaries. Robert Toombs, a Confederate cabinet member and general, said, "Our property has been stolen, our people murdered; felons and assassins have found sanctuary in the arms of the party which elected Mr. Lincoln. The Executive power, the last bulwark of the Constitution to defend us against these enemies of the Constitution, has been swept away, and we now stand without a shield, with bare bosoms presented to our enemies." At first they did not have sufficient military power to seize two fortified offshore military installations: Fort Sumter, on an island in the harbor of Charleston, South Carolina, garrisoned by a small force under Major Robert Anderson; and Fort Pickens, in the harbor of Pensacola, Florida. South Carolina sent commissioners to Washington to ask for the surrender of Sumter; but Buchanan, timid though he was, refused to yield it. Indeed, in January 1861 he ordered an unarmed merchant ship to proceed to Fort Sumter with additional troops and supplies. Confederate guns on shore fired at the vessel—the first shots between North and South—and turned it back. Still, neither section was yet ready to concede that war had begun. And in Washington, efforts began once more to forge a compromise.

The Failure of Compromise

CRITTENDEN COMPROMISE

Gradually, compromise forces gathered behind a proposal first submitted by Senator John J. Crittenden of Kentucky and known as the Crittenden Compromise. It called for several constitutional amendments, which would guarantee the permanent existence of slavery in the slave states and would satisfy Southern demands on such issues as fugitive enslaved people and slavery in

Go Online AP Exam Preparation

AP Exam Practice Use the online assessment to help prepare students for the AP Exam. You can assign the ready-made AP-style short-answer questions, document-based questions, and multiple-choice questions assessing concepts, themes, and skills from Period 5 and AP style long-essay questions organized in sets of 3 questions from various time periods. You can also create your own tests from available questions. This easy-to-use tool helps you design assessments that meet the needs of different types of learners.

the District of Columbia. But the heart of Crittenden's plan was a proposal to reestablish the Missouri Compromise line in all present and future territory of the United States: Slavery would be prohibited north of the line and permitted south of it. The remaining Southerners in the Senate seemed willing to accept the plan, but the Republicans were not. The compromise would have required the Republicans to abandon their most fundamental position: that slavery not be allowed to expand.

And so nothing had been resolved when Abraham Lincoln arrived in Washington for his inauguration–sneaking into the city in disguise on a night train to avoid assassination as he passed through the slave state of Maryland. In his inaugural address, which dealt directly with the secession crisis, Lincoln laid down several basic principles. Since the Union was older than the Constitution, no state could leave it. Acts of force or violence to support secession were insurrectionary. And the government would "hold, occupy, and possess" federal property in the seceded states–a clear reference to Fort Sumter.

Fort Sumter

Conditions at Fort Sumter were deteriorating quickly. Union forces were running short of supplies; unless they received fresh provisions, the fort would have to be evacuated. Lincoln believed that if he surrendered Sumter, his commitment to maintaining the Union would no longer be credible. So he sent a relief expedition to the fort, carefully informing the South Carolina authorities that there would be no attempt to send troops or munitions unless the supply ships met with resistance.

The new Confederate government now faced a dilemma. Permitting the expedition to land would seem to be a tame submission to federal authority. Firing on the ships or the fort would seem (to the North at least) to be aggression. But Confederate leaders finally decided that to appear cowardly would be worse than to appear belligerent, and they ordered General P. G. T. Beauregard, commander of Confederate forces at Charleston, to take the island, by force if necessary. When Anderson refused to surrender the fort, the Confederates bombarded it for two days, April 12–13, 1861. On April 14, Anderson surrendered. The Civil War had begun.

The War Begins

As the Southern states began to secede, Abraham Lincoln spoke of American liberty: "It was not the mere matter of the separation of the Colonies from the motherland; but that sentiment in the Declaration of Independence which gave liberty, not alone to the people of this country, but, I hope, to the world, for all future time. It was that which gave promise that in due time the weight would be lifted from the shoulders of all men. This is a sentiment embodied in the Declaration of Independence. Now, my friends, can this country be saved upon that basis? If it can, I will consider myself one of the happiest men in the world, if I can help to save it. If it cannot be saved, upon that principle, it will be truly awful."

Almost immediately, Lincoln began mobilizing the North for war. And equally promptly, four more slave states seceded from the Union and joined the Confederacy: Virginia (April 17, 1861), Arkansas (May 6), North Carolina (May 20), and Tennessee (June 8). The four remaining slave states–Maryland, Delaware, Kentucky, and Missouri–cast their lot with the Union (under heavy political and even military pressure from Washington).

Was there anything that Lincoln (or those before him) could have done to settle the sectional conflict peaceably? That question has preoccupied historians for more than a century without resolution. There were, of course, actions that might have prevented a war: if, for example, Northern leaders had decided to let the South withdraw in peace. The real question, however, is not what hypothetical situations might have

FORT SUMTER DURING THE BOMBARDMENT This graphic drawing shows the interior of Fort Sumter during its bombardment by Confederate forces in April 1861. Union forces faced the dual problem of heavy Confederate artillery and cannon fire, and dwindling supplies—since the Confederates had blockaded the Charleston harbor to prevent the North from resupplying the fort.

Reasoning Processes

Comparing After students have read the section "The Failure of Compromise," ask them to create a chart comparing the Crittenden Compromise with earlier compromises about the issue of slavery, such as the Missouri Compromise, the Compromise of 1850, and the Kansas-Nebraska Act. Have students evaluate why these attempts at compromise all failed to prevent war. **PCE** **ARC** **SOC**

Discussion and Activities

Analyzing Visuals Have students examine the image "Fort Sumter During the Bombardment." Ask them to identify details in the image that demonstrate the artist's point of view. *(The apparent calm of the Union soldiers during the barrage and the amount of damage done to the fort by the Confederate bombardment seem to indicate a pro-Union point of view.)* **PCE** **ARC**

Historical Thinking Skills

Argumentation After students have read the section "Fort Sumter," discuss as a class the dilemma facing Southern leaders concerning Fort Sumter. Have students talk about what course of action they would have recommended. **PCE** **ARC**

reversed the trend toward war but whether the preponderance of forces in the nation were acting to hold the nation together or to drive it apart. And by 1861, it seems clear that in both the North and the South, sectional antagonisms–whether justified or not–had risen to such a point that the existing terms of union had become untenable.

People in both regions had come to believe that two distinct and incompatible civilizations had developed in the United States and that those civilizations were incapable of living together in peace. Ralph Waldo Emerson, speaking for much of the North, said at the time: "I do not see how a barbarous community and a civilized community can constitute one state." And a slaveholder, expressing the sentiments of much of the South, said shortly after the election of Lincoln: "These [Northern] people hate us, annoy us, and would have us assassinated by our slaves if they dared. They are a different people from us, whether better or worse, and there is no love between us. Why then continue together?"

That the North and the South had come to believe these things helped lead to secession and war. Whether these things were actually true–whether the North and the South were really as different and incompatible as they thought–is another question, one that the preparations for and conduct of the war help to answer.

THE OPPOSING SIDES

As the war began, only one thing was clear: all the important material advantages lay with the North. Its population was more than twice as large as that of the South (and nearly four times as large as the nonslave population of the South), so

UNION ADVANTAGES

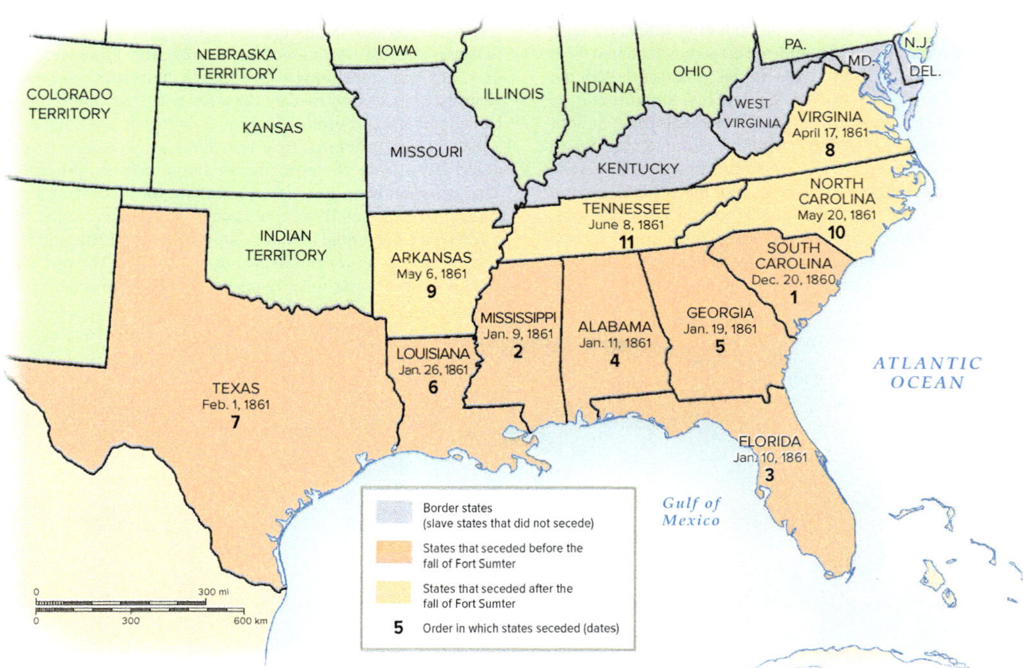

THE PROCESS OF SECESSION The election of Lincoln, the candidate of the antislavery Republican Party, to the presidency had the immediate result of inspiring many of the states in the Deep South to secede from the Union, beginning with South Carolina only a little more than a month after the November election. Other states nearer the northern border of the slaveholding region remained in the Union for a time, but the U.S. attempt to resupply Fort Sumter (and the bombardment of the fort by the new Confederate army) mobilized the upper South to secede as well. Only enormous pressure from the federal government kept the slaveholding states of Maryland, Delaware, Kentucky, and Missouri in the Union.

What accounted for the creation of the state of West Virginia in 1861?

Answers

The Process of Secession

Some of the western counties of Virginia that had less economic dependence upon slavery seceded from the state.

the Union had a much greater manpower reserve for both its armies and its workforce. The North had an advanced industrial system and was able by 1862 to manufacture almost all its own war materials. The South had almost no industry at all and, despite impressive efforts to increase its manufacturing capacity, had to rely on imports from Europe throughout the war.

In addition, the North had a much better transportation system than did the South and, in particular, more and better railroads: twice as much trackage as the Confederacy and a much better integrated system of lines. During the war, moreover, the already inferior Confederate railroad system steadily deteriorated and by the beginning of 1864 had almost collapsed.

But in the beginning the North's material advantages were not as decisive as they appear in retrospect. The South was, for the most part, fighting a defensive war on its own land and thus had the advantage of local support and familiarity with the territory. The Northern armies, on the other hand, were fighting mostly within the South, with long lines of communications, amid hostile local populations, and with access only to the South's own inadequate transportation system. The commitment of the white population of the South to the war was, with limited exceptions, clear and firm. In the North, opinion about the war was divided and support for it remained shaky until near the end. A major Southern victory at any one of several crucial moments might have proved decisive by breaking the North's will to continue the struggle. Finally, many Southerners believed that the dependence of the English and French textile industries on American cotton would require those nations to intervene on the side of the Confederacy.

SOUTHERN ADVANTAGES

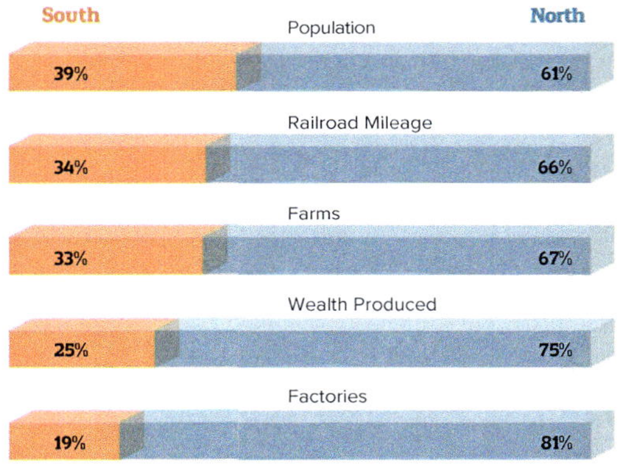

UNION AND CONFEDERATE RESOURCES Virtually all the material advantages—population, manufacturing, railroads, wealth, even agriculture—lay with the North during the Civil War, as this chart shows.

What advantages did the South have in the conflict?

THE MOBILIZATION OF THE NORTH

In the North, the war produced considerable discord, frustration, and suffering. But it also produced prosperity and economic growth by giving a major stimulus to both industry and agriculture.

ECONOMIC MEASURES

With Southern forces now gone from Congress, the Republican Party could exercise virtually unchallenged authority. During the war, it enacted an aggressively nationalistic program to promote economic development, particularly in the West. The Homestead Act of 1862 permitted any citizen or prospective citizen to claim 160 acres of public land and to purchase it for a small fee after living on it for five years. The Morrill Land Grant Act of the same year transferred substantial public acreage to the state governments, which were to sell the land and use the proceeds to finance public education. This act led to the creation of many new state colleges and universities, the so-called land-grant institutions. Congress also passed a series of tariff bills that by the end of the war had raised duties to the highest level in the nation's history—a great boon to domestic industries eager for protection from foreign competition.

REPUBLICAN ECONOMIC POLICY

Congress also moved to complete the dream of a transcontinental railroad. It created two new federally chartered corporations: the Union Pacific Railroad Company, which was to build westward from Omaha, and the Central Pacific, which was to build eastward from California, settling the prewar conflict over the location of the line. The two projects were to meet in the middle and complete the link. The government provided free public lands and generous loans to the companies.

The National Bank Acts of 1863–1864 created a new national banking system. Existing or newly formed banks could join the system if they had enough capital and were willing to invest one-third of it in government securities. In return, they could issue U.S. Treasury notes as currency. The new system eliminated much of the chaos and uncertainty in the nation's currency and created a uniform system of national bank notes.

NATIONAL BANK ACTS

More difficult than promoting economic growth was financing the war. The government tried to do so in three ways: by levying taxes, issuing paper currency, and borrowing. Congress levied new taxes on almost all goods and services; and in 1861 the government levied an income tax for the first time, with rates that eventually rose to 10 percent on incomes above $5,000. But taxation raised only a small proportion of the funds necessary for financing the war, and strong popular resistance prevented the government from raising the rates. At least equally controversial was the printing of paper currency, or "greenbacks." The new currency was backed not by gold or silver, but simply by the good faith and credit of the government

FINANCING THE WAR

Reasoning Processes

Comparing After students have read the section "The Opposing Sides," have them create a chart listing Union and Confederate advantages and disadvantages. Have students rank those advantages and disadvantages in order of importance and write a short paragraph explaining the balance of forces at the outset of the Civil War. **PCE** **ARC** **WXT**

Answers

Union and Confederate Resources

The main Southern advantage was that they were fighting a defensive war and did not have to invade the North to win. Southerners were also generally more committed to their cause than those in the North at the start of the war.

Historical Thinking Skills

Contextualization After students have read the section "Economic Measures," ask them to discuss in small groups how the Union Congress was able to pass measures like the Homestead Act and the Pacific Railway Act. *(Southern congressmen had consistently blocked the Homestead Act out of fear that westward expansion would lead to the creation of new free states. Congress had never been able to agree on funding a transcontinental railroad out of disagreement over its route. With almost all Southern congressmen now gone, the remaining Congress, dominated by Republicans, was able to pass these measures.)* **PCE** **ARC** **WXT** **MIG**

WAR BY RAILROAD Union soldiers pose beside a mortar mounted on a railroad car in July 1864, during the siege of Petersburg, Virginia. Railroads played a critical role in the Civil War, and the superiority of the North's rail system was an important factor in its victory. It was appropriate, perhaps, that the battle for Petersburg, the last great struggle of the war, was over control of critical railroad lines.

National Archives and Records Administration

(much like today's currency). The value of the greenbacks fluctuated according to the fortunes of the Northern armies. Early in 1864, with the war effort bogged down, a greenback dollar was worth only 39 percent of a gold dollar. Even at the close of the war, it was worth only 67 percent of a gold dollar. Because of the difficulty of making purchases with this uncertain currency, the government used greenbacks sparingly. The Treasury issued only $450 million worth of paper currency–a small proportion of the cost of the war but enough to produce significant inflation.

By far the largest source of financing for the war was loans from the American people. In previous wars, the government had sold bonds only to banks and to a few wealthy investors. Now, however, the Treasury persuaded ordinary citizens to buy over $400 million worth of bonds–the first example of mass financing of a war in American history. Still, bond purchases by individuals constituted only a small part of the government's borrowing, which in the end totaled $2.6 billion. Most of the loans to finance the war came from banks and large financial interests.

Raising the Union Armies

Over 2 million men served in the Union armed forces during the course of the Civil War. But at the beginning of 1861, the regular army of the United States consisted of only 16,000 troops, many of them stationed in the West to protect white settlers from Native Americans. So the Union, like the

Discussion and Activities

Analyzing Visuals Have students view the image "War by Railroad." Ask them to identify and list examples of how Northern advantages in industry and transportation impacted the war effort. *(The advantage in railroad miles gave the Union greater ability to transport soldiers and supplies quickly and efficiently. Advantages in industry allowed the Union to produce greater volumes of weapons and ammunition for the war effort.)* **ARC** **WXT**

Confederacy, had to raise its army mostly from scratch. Lincoln called for an increase of 23,000 in the regular army, but the bulk of the fighting, he knew, would have to be done by volunteers in state militias. When Congress convened in July 1861, it authorized enlisting 500,000 volunteers for three-year terms (as opposed to the customary three-month terms). This voluntary system of recruitment produced adequate forces only briefly. After the first flush of enthusiasm for the war, enlistments declined. By March 1863, Congress was forced to pass a national draft law. Virtually all young adult males were eligible to be drafted; but a man could escape service by hiring someone to go in his place or by paying the government a fee of $300. Only about 46,000 men were ever actually conscripted, but the draft greatly increased voluntary enlistments.

DRAFT RIOTS

To a people accustomed to a remote and inactive national government, conscription was strange and threatening. Opposition to the law was widespread, particularly among laborers, immigrants, and Democrats opposed to the war (known as "Peace Democrats" or "Copperheads" by their opponents). Occasionally, opposition to the draft erupted into violence. Demonstrators against the draft rioted in New York City for four days in July 1863, after the first names were selected for conscription. It was among the most violent urban uprisings in American history. More than 100 people died. Irish workers were at the center of the violence. They were angry because black strikebreakers had been used against them in a recent longshoremen's strike; and they blamed African Americans generally for the war, which they thought was being fought for the benefit of enslaved people who would soon be competing with white workers for jobs. The rioters lynched a number of African Americans, burned down homes and businesses (mostly those of freemen), and even destroyed an orphanage for African American children. Only the arrival of federal troops subdued the rioters.

WARTIME POLITICS

When Abraham Lincoln arrived in Washington early in 1861, many politicians—noting his lack of national experience and his folksy, unpretentious manner—considered him a minor politician from the prairies, a man whom the real leaders of his party would easily control. But the new president moved quickly to establish his own authority. He assembled a cabinet representing every faction of the Republican Party and every segment of Northern opinion—men of exceptional prestige and influence and in some cases arrogance, several of whom believed that they, not Lincoln, should be president. Lincoln moved boldly as well to use the war powers of the presidency, ignoring what he considered inconvenient parts of the Constitution because, he said, it would be foolish to lose the whole by being afraid to disregard a part. He sent troops into battle without asking Congress for a declaration of war. (Lincoln insisted on calling the conflict a domestic insurrection, which required no formal declaration of war; to ask for a declaration would, he believed, constitute implicit recognition of the Confederacy as an independent nation.) He increased the size of the regular army without receiving legislative authority to do so. He unilaterally proclaimed a naval blockade of the South.

WARTIME REPRESSION

Lincoln's greatest political problem was the widespread popular opposition to the war, mobilized by factions in the Democratic Party. The Peace Democrats feared that the agricultural Northwest was losing influence to the industrial East and that Republican nationalism was eroding states' rights. Lincoln used extraordinary methods to suppress them. He ordered military arrests of civilian dissenters and suspended the right of habeas corpus (the right of a person to be released by a judge or court from unlawful detention, as in the case of insufficient evidence). At first, Lincoln used these methods only in

SENDING THE BOYS OFF TO WAR In this painting, *The Departure of the Seventh Regiment to the War,* by Thomas Nast, New York's Seventh Regiment parades down Broadway in April 1861, to the cheers of exuberant, patriotic throngs, shortly before departing to fight in what most people then assumed would be a brief war. Thomas Nast is better known for his famous political cartoons of the 1870s.

Discussion and Activities

Analyzing Change After students have read the section "Raising the Union Armies," have them discuss in pairs or small groups why, after an initial wave of enlistments, the Union had to pass a draft law. *(After an initial wave of nationalistic fervor led to large numbers of enlistments, the harsh realities of the war began to sink in, and enlistments diminished.)* **SOC** **PCE**

Discussion and Activities

Analyzing Visuals Have students examine the image "Sending the Boys Off to War." Ask them to list details that illustrate the initial wave of nationalism after the war began. Have students write a short letter or journal entry from the point of view of either one of the soldiers or a member of the crowd, describing the emotions and sensations being experienced. **PCE** **NAT** **ARC**

Discussion and Activities

Historical Developments and Argumentation After students have read the section “Wartime Repression,” ask them to list and discuss as a class measures taken by President Lincoln to maintain order in the North. Have them discuss whether such actions were necessary as part of the war effort or justified by the Constitution. **PCE**

THE NEW YORK CITY DRAFT RIOT, 1863 Opposition to the Civil War draft was widespread in the North and in July 1863 produced a violent four-day uprising in New York City in which as many as 100 people died. The riot began on July 13 with a march by 4,000 men, mostly poor Irish laborers, who were protesting the provisions by which some wealthy people could be exempted from conscription. "Rich man's war, poor man's fight," the demonstrators cried (just as some critics of the war chanted at times in the South). Many New Yorkers also feared that the war would drive black workers north to compete for their jobs. The demonstration turned violent when officials began drawing names for the draft. The crowd burned the draft building and then split into factions. Some rioters attacked symbols of wealth such as exclusive shops and mansions. Others terrorized black neighborhoods and lynched some residents. This contemporary engraving depicts one such lynching. Only by transferring five regiments to the city from Gettysburg (less than two weeks after the great battle there) was the government able to restore order.

sensitive areas such as the border states; but in 1862, he proclaimed that all persons who discouraged enlistments or engaged in disloyal practices were subject to martial law. In all, more than 13,000 persons were arrested and imprisoned for varying periods. The most prominent Copperhead in the country–Ohio Congressman Clement L. Vallandigham–was seized by military authorities and exiled to the Confederacy after he made a speech claiming that the purpose of the war was to free African Americans and enslave white people. Lincoln defied all efforts to curb his authority to suppress opposition, even those of the Supreme Court. When Chief Justice Taney issued a writ (*Ex parte Merryman*) requiring him to release an imprisoned Maryland secessionist leader, Lincoln simply ignored it. (After the war, in 1866, the Supreme Court ruled in *Ex parte Milligan* that military trials in areas where the civil courts existed were unconstitutional.)

Repression was not the only tool the North used to strengthen support for the war. In addition to arresting "disloyal" Northerners, Lincoln's administration used new tools of persuasion to build popular opinion in favor of the war. In addition to pro-war pamphlets, posters, speeches, and songs, the war mobilized a significant corps of photographers–organized by the renowned Mathew Brady, one of the first important photographers in American history–to take pictures of the war. The photographs that resulted from this effort–new to warfare–were among the grimmest ever made to that point, many of them displaying the vast numbers of dead on the Civil War battlefields. For some Americans, the images of death contributed to a revulsion from the war. But for most Northerners, they gave evidence of the level of sacrifice that had been made for the preservation of the Union and thus spurred the nation on to victory. (Southerners used similar propaganda in the Confederacy, although less effectively.)

The presidential election of 1864 occurred, therefore, in the midst of considerable political dissension. The Republicans had suffered heavy losses in the congressional elections of 1862, and in response leaders of the party tried to create a broad coalition of all the groups that supported the war. They called the new organization the Union Party, but in reality it was little more than the Republican Party and a small faction of War Democrats. The Union Party nominated Lincoln for another term as president and Andrew Johnson of Tennessee, a War Democrat who had opposed his state's decision to secede, for the vice presidency.

The Democrats nominated George B. McClellan, a celebrated former Union general who had been relieved of his command by Lincoln. The party adopted a platform denouncing the war and calling for a truce. McClellan repudiated that demand, but the Democrats were clearly the peace party in the campaign, trying to profit from growing war weariness and from the Union's discouraging military position in the summer of 1864.

1864 ELECTION

At this crucial moment, however, several Northern military victories, particularly the capture of Atlanta, Georgia, early in September, rejuvenated Northern morale and boosted Republican prospects. Lincoln won reelection comfortably, with 212 electoral votes to McClellan's 21; the president carried every state except Kentucky, New Jersey, and Delaware. But Lincoln's lead in the popular vote was a modest 10 percent. Had Union victories not occurred when they did, and had Lincoln not made special arrangements to allow Union troops to vote, McClellan might have won.

THE POLITICS OF EMANCIPATION

Despite their surface unity in 1864 and their general agreement on most economic matters, the Republicans disagreed sharply on the issue of slavery. Radicals–led in Congress by such men as Representative Thaddeus Stevens of Pennsylvania and Senators Charles Sumner of Massachusetts and Benjamin Wade of Ohio–wanted to use the war to abolish slavery immediately and completely. Conservatives favored a slower, more gradual, and, they believed, less disruptive process for ending slavery. In the beginning, at least, they had the support of the president.

Despite Lincoln's cautious view of emancipation, momentum began to gather behind it early in the war. In 1861, Congress passed the Confiscation Act, which declared that all

Discussion and Activities

Analyzing Issues Have students read the section “1864 Election.” Ask them to create a campaign poster promoting either Lincoln or McClellan. Ask for volunteers to share their posters with the class when finished. **PCE**

DEBATING THE PAST

THE CAUSES OF THE CIVIL WAR

In his second inaugural address in March 1865, Abraham Lincoln looked back at the beginning of the Civil War four years earlier. "All knew," he said, that slavery "was somehow the cause of the war." Few historians doubt the basic truth of Lincoln's statement, but they have disagreed sharply about whether slavery was the only, or even the principal, cause of the war.

This debate began even before the war itself and continued to dominate the politics and culture of the next half century, as David Blight demonstrated in *Race and Reunion: The Civil War in American Memory* (2001). In 1858, Senator William H. Seward of New York took note of two competing explanations of the sectional tensions that were then inflaming the nation. On one side, he claimed, stood those who believed the sectional hostility to be "accidental, unnecessary, the work of interested or fanatical agitators." Opposing them stood those (like Seward himself) who believed there to be "an irrepressible conflict between opposing and enduring forces."

The "irrepressible conflict" argument dominated historical discussion of the war from the 1860s to the 1920s. Because the North and the South had reached positions on the issue of slavery that were both irreconcilable and seemingly unalterable, some historians claimed, the conflict had become "inevitable." James Rhodes, in his seven-volume *History of the United States from the Compromise of 1850 . . .* (1893–1900), placed greatest emphasis on the moral conflict over slavery, but he suggested as well that the struggle also reflected fundamental differences between the Northern and Southern economic systems. Charles and Mary Beard, in *The Rise of American Civilization* (2 vols., 1927), also viewed the war as an irrepressible economic, rather than moral, conflict. Ultimately, however, most of those who believed the Civil War to have been "irrepressible" returned to an emphasis on social and cultural factors. Allan Nevins, in *The Ordeal of the Union* (8 vols., 1947–1971), argued that the "problem of slavery" lay at the root of the cultural differences between the North and the South, but that the "fundamental assumptions, tastes, and cultural aims" of the two regions were diverging in other ways as well.

More-recent proponents of the "irrepressible conflict" argument have taken different views of the Northern and Southern positions on the conflict but have been equally insistent on the role of culture and ideology in creating them. Eric Foner, in *Free Soil, Free Labor, Free Men* (1970) and other writings, emphasized the importance of the "free-labor ideology" to Northern opponents of slavery. Most Northerners (including Abraham Lincoln), Foner claimed, opposed slavery largely because they feared it might spread to the North and threaten the position of free white laborers. Eugene Genovese, writing of Southern slaveholders in *The Political Economy of Slavery* (1965), argued that just as Northerners were becoming convinced of a Southern threat to their economic system, so Southerners believed that the North had aggressive and hostile designs on the Southern way of life. Like Foner, therefore, Genovese saw cultural differences as the source of an all but inevitable conflict.

Other historians have argued that the Civil War might have been avoided, that the differences between North and South were not so fundamental as to have necessitated war. The idea of the war as avoidable gained wide recognition among historians in the 1920s and 1930s, when a group known as the "revisionists" began to offer new accounts of the origins of the conflict. One of the leading revisionists was James G. Randall, who saw in the social and economic systems of the North and the South no differences so fundamental as to require a war. Avery Craven, another leading revisionist, argued similarly in *The Coming of the Civil War* (1942) that slave laborers were not much worse off than Northern industrial workers, that the institution was already on the road to "ultimate extinction," and that war could therefore have been averted had skillful and responsible leaders worked to produce compromise.

More-recent students of the Civil War have emphasized the role of political agitation and ethnocultural conflicts in the coming of the war. Michael Holt, in *The Political Crisis of the 1850s* (1978), emphasized the role of political parties and especially the collapse of the Second Party System, rather than the irreconcilable differences between sections, in explaining the conflict, although he avoided placing blame on any one group. Along with Paul Kleppner, Joel Silbey, and William Gienapp, Holt was one of the creators of an "ethnocultural" interpretation of the war. These scholars argue that the Civil War began in large part because the party system—the most effective instrument for containing and mediating sectional differences—collapsed in the 1850s and produced a new Republican Party that aggravated, rather than calmed, the divisions in the nation. William Gienapp, in *The Origins of the Republican Party, 1852–1856* (1987), argued that the disintegration of the party system in the early 1850s was less a result of the debate over slavery in the territories than of such ethnocultural issues as temperance and nativism. Gienapp and the other ethnoculturalists would not entirely dispute Lincoln's claim that slavery was "somehow the cause of the war." But they do challenge the arguments of Eric Foner and others that the "free labor ideal" of the North—and the challenge slavery, and its possible expansion into the territories, posed to that ideal—was the principal reason for the conflict. Slavery became important, they suggest, less because of irreconcilable differences of attitude than because of the collapse of parties and other structures that might have contained the conflict.

ON TO LIBERTY This painting by Theodore Kaufmann shows a group of fugitive enslaved people escaping from the South in the late years of the Civil War. Thousands of former enslaved people crossed the Union lines, where they were given their freedom. Many of them joined the Union army.

HISTORICAL THINKING SKILLS

Questions assume cumulative content knowledge from this chapter and previous chapters.

1. **Identifying Historical Developments** Identify three broad schools of historical interpretation concerning the causes of the Civil War.
2. **Determining Context** Describe how one piece of historical evidence from the time period could be used to support each of the three broad schools of historical interpretation concerning the causes of the Civil War.
3. **Developing Arguments** Analyze which school of thought you find more convincing, and explain why by using evidence to support your reasoning.

Historical Thinking Skills

Sourcing and Situation Have students examine the image "On to Liberty." As a class, discuss which interpretation of the causes of the Civil War this painting most closely represents. *(This image would probably most closely align with the "irrepressible conflict" school of thought that saw the clash over free and enslaved labor at the heart of the conflict. Arguments could be made in support of other interpretations as well.)* **SOC** **WXT**

Answers

Debating the Past

1. Civil War scholarship began early, even before the start of the war. In 1858, William H. Seward delivered a speech that has come to be known as the "Irrepressible Conflict" speech. In it, Seward argued that the war was an irrepressible conflict between opposing forces. Charles and Mary Beard gave one of the earliest economic arguments for the major cause of the war, a theory that has found strong support in recent scholarship. Michael Holt and others emphasized the roles of political parties in the war.
2. Arguments for the irrepressible conflict theory can be traced back to the 1820s, when Jefferson warned about slavery's impact with his famous analogy of holding a wolf by the ears. Economically, the North and the South were conceived differently from the outset. The Southern states relied heavily on large-scale agriculture, requiring massive amounts of labor that drove their support of slavery; the industrial North did not face this issue. Finally, while the political parties for years found ways to compromise with each other over the institution of slavery, these compromises eventually broke down.
3. Student answers will vary but may cite Beard's argument in support of economic reasons, Nevins in support of cultural reasons, or Gienapp in support of political causes.

Discussion and Activities

Analyzing Points of View After students have read the section "The Politics of Emancipation," ask them to consider the opportunities and risks for President Lincoln in issuing the Emancipation Proclamation. Have students write a short letter to Lincoln from the point of view of one of his Cabinet members advising him what to do. **PCE** **ARC**

enslaved people used for "insurrectionary" purposes (that is, in support of the Confederate military effort) would be considered freed. Subsequent laws in the spring of 1862 abolished slavery in Washington, D.C., and in the western territories, and compensated slaveholders. In July 1862, the Radicals pushed through Congress the second Confiscation Act, which again declared free the enslaved people of persons aiding and supporting the insurrection (whether or not the enslaved people themselves were doing so) and which also authorized the president to employ African Americans, including freedmen, as soldiers. As the war progressed, much of the North seemed slowly to accept emancipation as a central war aim; nothing less would justify the enormous sacrifices of the struggle, many Northerners believed. As a result, the Radicals increased their influence within the Republican Party—a development that did not go unnoticed by the president, who decided to seize the leadership of the rising antislavery sentiment himself.

CONFISCATION ACTS

On September 22, 1862, after the Union victory at the Battle of Antietam, the president announced his intention to use his war powers to issue an executive order freeing all enslaved people in the Confederacy. And on January 1, 1863, he formally signed the Emancipation Proclamation, which declared forever free enslaved people in all areas of the Confederacy except those already under Union control: Tennessee, western Virginia, and southern Louisiana. The proclamation did not apply to the border slave states, which had never seceded from the Union and therefore were not subject to the president's war powers. On the day of Emancipation, Ralph Waldo Emerson wrote a "Boston Hymn":

EMANCIPATION PROCLAMATION

> Today unbind the captive
> So only are ye unbound;
> Lift up a people from the dust,
> Trump of their rescue sound . . .
>
> Pay ransom to the owner,
> And fill the bag to the brim,
> Who is the owner? The slave is owner,
> And ever was. Pay him.
>
> **Source**: English Poetry III: From Tennyson to Whitman. Vol. XLII. The Harvard Classics, edited by Charles W. Eliot (New York: P. F. Collier & Son, 1909-1914).

The immediate effect of the proclamation was limited, since it applied only to enslaved people still under Confederate control. But the document was of great importance nevertheless, because it clearly and irrevocably established that the war was being fought not only to preserve the Union but also to eliminate slavery. Eventually, as federal armies occupied much of the South, the proclamation became a practical reality and led directly to the freeing of thousands of enslaved people. Even in areas not directly affected by the proclamation, the antislavery impulse gained strength.

The U.S. government's tentative measures against slavery were not, at first, a major factor in the liberation of enslaved people. Instead, the war helped African Americans to liberate themselves, and they did so in increasing numbers as the war progressed. Many enslaved people were taken from their plantations and put to work building defenses and other chores. Once transported to the front, many of them found ways to escape across Northern lines, where they were treated as "contraband"—goods seized from people who had no right to them. They could not be returned to their slaveholders. By 1862, the Union army often penetrated deep into the Confederacy. Almost everywhere they went, escaped enslaved people, often whole families, flocked to join them by the thousands. Some of them joined the Union army, others simply stayed with the troops until they could find their way to free states. When the Union captured New Orleans and much of southern Louisiana, enslaved people refused to work for their former slaveholders, even though the Union occupiers had not made any provisions for liberating African Americans.

By the end of the war, slavery had been abolished in two Union slave states—Maryland and Missouri—and in three Confederate states occupied by Union forces—Tennessee, Arkansas, and Louisiana. The final step came in 1865, when Congress approved and the necessary states ratified the Thirteenth Amendment, abolishing slavery as an institution in all parts of the United States. After more than two centuries, legalized slavery finally ceased to exist in the United States.

AFRICAN AMERICANS AND THE UNION CAUSE

About 186,000 emancipated African Americans served as soldiers, sailors, and laborers for the Union forces, joining a significant number of free African Americans from the North. The services of African Americans to the Union military were significant in many ways, not least because of the substantial obstacles many black men had to surmount in order to enlist.

In the first months of the war, African Americans were largely excluded from the military. A few black regiments eventually took shape in some of the Union-occupied areas of the Confederacy, mainly because they were a ready source of manpower in these defeated regions. But once Lincoln issued the Emancipation Proclamation, African American enlistment increased rapidly and the Union military began actively to recruit African American soldiers and sailors in both the North and, where possible, the South.

AFRICAN AMERICAN ENLISTMENT

Some of these men were organized into fighting units. The best known was probably the Fifty-fourth Massachusetts Infantry, which (like most black regiments) had a white commander: Robert Gould Shaw, a member of an aristocratic Boston family. Shaw and more than half his regiment died during a battle near Charleston, South Carolina, in the summer of 1863.

Most African American soldiers, however, were assigned menial tasks behind the lines, such as digging trenches and transporting water. Even though fewer African American

Historical Thinking Skills

Argumentation Have students read the section "African American Enlistment." Ask them to go online and search for images of the Robert Gould Shaw and Massachusetts 54th Regiment Memorial. Discuss as a class whether the monument is a fitting tribute to African American soldiers in the Civil War. **SOC** **ARC** **PCE**

Reasoning Processes

Comparing After students have read the section "Mistreatment of Black Soldiers," ask them to create a Venn diagram comparing the experiences of African American and white soldiers during the Civil War. Have students write a short paragraph accounting for the differences. **SOC** **ARC** **WXT**

AFRICAN AMERICAN TROOPS Although most of the black soldiers who enlisted in the Union army during the Civil War performed noncombat jobs behind the lines, there were also black combat regiments—members of one of which are pictured here—who fought with great success and valor in critical battles.

The Library of Congress

soldiers than white soldiers died in combat, the black mortality rate was higher than the rate for white soldiers because so many died of disease from working long, arduous hours in unsanitary conditions. Conditions for African American and white soldiers were unequal in other ways as well. African American soldiers were paid a third less than were white soldiers (until Congress changed the law in mid-1864). But however dangerous, onerous, or menial the tasks African American soldiers were given, most of them felt enormous pride in their service–pride they retained throughout their lives and often through the lives of their descendants. Many moved from the army into politics and other forms of leadership (in both the North and, after the war, the Reconstruction South).

MISTREATMENT OF BLACK SOLDIERS

African American soldiers captured by the Confederates were, unlike white prisoners, not returned to the North in exchange for Southern soldiers being returned to the South. They were sent back to their slaveholders (if they were fugitive enslaved men) or often executed. In 1864, Confederate soldiers killed more than 260 African Americans after capturing them in Tennessee.

THE WAR AND ECONOMIC DEVELOPMENT

The Civil War did not, as some historians used to claim, transform the North from an agrarian to an industrial society. Industrialization was already far advanced when the war began, and in some areas, the war retarded growth–by cutting manufacturers off from their Southern markets and sources of raw material, and by diverting labor and resources to military purposes.

On the whole, however, the war sped the economic development of the North. That was in part a result of the political dominance of the Republican Party and its promotion of nationalistic economic legislation. But it was also because the war itself required the expansion of certain sectors of the economy. Coal production increased by nearly 20 percent during the war. Railroad facilities improved–mainly through the adoption of a standard gauge (track width) on new lines. The loss of farm labor to the military forced many farmers to increase the mechanization of agriculture.

The war was a difficult experience for many American workers. For industrial workers, there was a substantial loss of purchasing power, as prices in the North rose by more than 70 percent during the war, while wages rose only about 40 percent. That was partly because liberalized immigration laws permitted a flood of new workers into the labor market and helped keep wages low. It was also because the increasing mechanization of production eliminated the jobs of many skilled workers. One result of these changes was a substantial increase in union membership in many industries and the creation of several national unions, for coal miners, railroad engineers, and others–organizations bitterly opposed and rigorously suppressed by employers.

HARD TIMES FOR WORKERS

Historical Thinking Skills

Argumentation Have students read the section "Hard Times for Workers." Ask them to list and rank in order of importance the economic changes that impacted workers and their families in the Union. *(Increased mechanization; high inflation; rise in labor union membership.)* Then have students write a thesis statement that makes a claim about the most important economic impact of the Civil War. **WXT**

AP Exam Tip

When answering document-based questions, students will be asked to analyze the sourcing and situation of primary and secondary sources. One way to do this is to analyze the author's purpose.

Historical Thinking Skills

Sourcing and Situation Have students practice the tip by reading the Gettysburg Address and then think about and share with a partner why President Lincoln chose the words and setting he did to deliver this speech. *(The speech recalls the Revolutionary War and compares the Civil War to it. By using the dedication of a battlefield cemetery as his backdrop, he may have been appealing to his audience to continue the fight so that the deaths of the soldiers buried there would not be wasted.)*

CONSIDER THE SOURCE

WARTIME ORATORY

The causes of wars are rather different from their *meanings*. Presidents often use wartime speeches to shape public understanding of those meanings–to articulate their visions of what wars are really about. They tend to emphasize broad principles and cherished ideals rather than more-narrow economic concerns or even national security arguments.

More than four months after the pivotal battle at Gettysburg, President Abraham Lincoln traveled there to dedicate a military cemetery. A crowd of 15,000 listened first to the famed orator Edward Everett's two-hour account of the battle. Then came Lincoln. His speech was much shorter–just over two minutes. The President touched briefly on American history before turning to the Civil War and what it meant. The Gettysburg Address is reproduced here in its entirety (the "1863" document).

Almost a hundred and fifty years later, President George W. Bush also appealed to the past in explaining the conflict of his time, the war on terrorism of the early twenty-first century. The occasion was Bush's second inaugural address, delivered in January 2005 after his victory over the Democratic nominee, John Kerry. His speech came in the middle of the ongoing wars in Iraq and Afghanistan that had been prompted by the terrorist attacks of September 11, 2001. Though the context couldn't have been more different, Bush devoted part of his address to themes similar to Lincoln's so many years before. That excerpt is included here as the "2005" document.

LINCOLN—1863

THE GETTYSBURG ADDRESS, NOVEMBER 19, 1863

Four score and seven years ago our fathers brought forth on this continent, a new nation, conceived in Liberty, and dedicated to the proposition that all men are created equal.

Now we are engaged in a great civil war, testing whether that nation, or any nation so conceived and so dedicated, can long endure. We are met on a great battle-field of that war. We have come to dedicate a portion of that field, as a final resting place for those who here gave their lives that that nation might live. It is altogether fitting and proper that we should do this.

But, in a larger sense, we can not dedicate–we can not consecrate–we can not hallow–this ground. The brave men, living and dead, who struggled here, have consecrated it, far above our poor power to add or detract. The world will little note, nor long remember what we say here, but it can never forget what they did here. It is for us the living, rather, to be dedicated here to the unfinished work which they who fought here have thus far so nobly advanced. It is rather for us to be here dedicated to the great task remaining before us–that from these honored dead we take increased devotion to that cause for which they gave the last full measure of devotion–that we here highly resolve that these dead shall not have died in vain–that this nation, under God, shall have a new birth of freedom–and that government of the people, by the people, for the people, shall not perish from the earth.

Source: abrahamlincolnonline.org

Discussion and Activities

Making Connections Have students reread the Gettysburg Address. Discuss as a class whether any of the words or phrases Lincoln used are familiar to them and in what context they may have heard them.

BUSH—2005

George W. Bush's Second Inaugural Address, January 20, 2005

We are led, by events and common sense, to one conclusion: The survival of liberty in our land increasingly depends on the success of liberty in other lands. The best hope for peace in our world is the expansion of freedom in all the world.

America's vital interests and our deepest beliefs are now one. From the day of our Founding, we have proclaimed that every man and woman on this earth has rights, and dignity, and matchless value, because they bear the image of the Maker of Heaven and earth. Across the generations we have proclaimed the imperative of self-government, because no one is fit to be a master, and no one deserves to be a slave. Advancing these ideals is the mission that created our Nation. It is the honorable achievement of our fathers. Now it is the urgent requirement of our nation's security, and the calling of our time.

So it is the policy of the United States to seek and support the growth of democratic movements and institutions in every nation and culture, with the ultimate goal of ending tyranny in our world.

This is not primarily the task of arms, though we will defend ourselves and our friends by force of arms when necessary. Freedom, by its nature, must be chosen, and defended by citizens, and sustained by the rule of law and the protection of minorities. And when the soul of a nation finally speaks, the institutions that arise may reflect customs and traditions very different from our own. America will not impose our own style of government on the unwilling. Our goal instead is to help others find their own voice, attain their own freedom, and make their own way.

Source: http://georgewbush-whitehouse.archives.gov

ANALYZING SOURCES

Questions assume cumulative content knowledge from this chapter and previous chapters.

1. Which of the following groups might most applaud Lincoln's message regarding the meaning for fighting the war?
   (A) those who supported the formation of political parties in the early years of the nation
   (B) those in the early 1800s who opposed a strong, national bank
   (C) Those who, at the time of the American Revolution, supported the formation of America as a confederation of states
   (D) those who at the time of the Constitutional Convention wished to build a stronger central government

2. Which of the following best describes the common vision expressed in both documents regarding the respective war's meaning?
   (A) ending tyranny in the world
   (B) spread of American democracy through all the nations
   (C) fulfillment of the American democratic ideal of individual freedom of opportunity and choice
   (D) the need for America to adopt a policy of imperialism

3. How does Bush's speech reflect his articulation about the larger meaning for the war on terrorism?
   (A) By stating that America will not impose its political and social systems on a country, but will, instead, help that country determine its own freedom.
   (B) By stating that it will overthrow tyranny in the world and establish American-style democracy throughout the world.
   (C) By stating that the security of America depends on the security of all nations.
   (D) By stating that America is a blessed country.

Reasoning Processes

Comparing After students have read George Bush's Second Inaugural Address, ask them to create a Venn diagram comparing this speech with Lincoln's Gettysburg Address. Have students write an explanation for the differences they identify.

Answers

Consider the Source

1. D; **2.** C; **3.** A

Reasoning Processes

Continuity and Change Have students read the section "Women, Nursing, and the War." Ask them to create a T-chart listing ways in which women's roles either changed or stayed the same as a result of participating in the Civil War. Have them write a short summary explaining whether there was more change or continuity in women's roles. **SOC** **WXT**

WOMEN, NURSING, AND THE WAR

Responding not only to the needs of employers for additional labor, but to their own, often desperate, need for money, women found themselves, by either choice or necessity, thrust into new and often unfamiliar roles during the war. They took over positions vacated by men and worked as teachers, retail salesclerks, office workers, and mill and factory hands.

Above all, women entered nursing, a field previously dominated by men. The U.S. Sanitary Commission, an organization of civilian volunteers led by social reformer Dorothea Dix, mobilized large numbers of female nurses to serve in field hospitals. By the end of the war, women were the dominant force in nursing; by 1900, nursing had become an almost entirely female profession. Female nurses not only cared for patients but also performed other tasks considered appropriate for women: cooking, cleaning, and laundering.

U.S. SANITARY COMMISSION

Female nurses encountered considerable resistance from male doctors, many of whom considered women too weak for medical work and who, in any case, thought it inappropriate that women were taking care of men who were strangers to them. The Sanitary Commission tried to counter such arguments by attributing to nursing many of the domestic ideals that American society attributed to women's work in the home: women as nurses would play the same maternal, nurturing, instructive role they played as wives and mothers. "The right of woman to her sphere, which includes housekeeping, cooking, and nursing, has never been disputed," one Sanitary Commission official insisted. But not all women who worked for the commission were content with a purely maternal role; some challenged the dominance of men in the organization and even stood up against doctors whom they considered incompetent, increasing the resentment felt toward them by many men. In the end, though, the work of female nurses was so indispensable to the military that the complaints of male doctors were irrelevant.

TRADITIONAL GENDER ROLES REINFORCED

Nurses, and many other women, found the war a liberating experience, in which (as one Sanitary Commission nurse later wrote) the American woman "had developed potencies and possibilities of which she had been unaware and which surprised her, as it did those who witnessed her marvelous achievement." Some women, especially those who had been committed to feminist causes earlier, came to see the war as an opportunity to win support for their own goals. Elizabeth Cady Stanton and Susan B. Anthony, who together founded the National Woman's Loyal League in 1863, worked simultaneously for the abolition of slavery and the awarding of suffrage to women. Clara Barton, who was active during the war in collecting and distributing medical supplies and who later became an important figure in the nursing profession (and a founder of the American Red Cross), said in 1888: "At the war's end, woman was at least fifty years in advance of the normal position which continued peace would have assigned her." That may have been an exaggeration; but it captured the degree to which many women looked back on the war as a crucial moment in the redefinition of female roles and in the awakening of a sense of independence and new possibilities.

Whatever nursing may have done for the status of women, it had an enormous impact on the medical profession and on the treatment of wounded soldiers during the war. The U.S. Sanitary Commission not only organized women to serve at the front; it also funneled medicine and supplies to badly overtaxed field hospitals. The commission also (as its name suggests) helped spread ideas about the importance of sanitary conditions in hospitals and clinics and probably contributed to the relative decline of death by disease in the Civil War. Nevertheless, twice as many soldiers died of diseases—malaria, dysentery, typhoid, gangrene, and others—as died in combat during the war. Even minor injuries could lead to fatal infections.

NURSING AND MEDICINE

THE U.S. SANITARY COMMISSION Mathew Brady took this photograph of female nurses and Union soldiers standing before an infirmary at Brandy Station, Virginia, near Petersburg, in 1864. The infirmary was run by the U.S. Sanitary Commission, the government-supported nursing corps that became important to the medical care of wounded soldiers during the Civil War.

National Archives and Records Administration

Discussion and Activities

Analyzing Visuals Have students examine the image "The U.S. Sanitary Commission," and ask them to list details from the photo. **Ask:** How is the image similar to or different from what they might have expected?

THE MOBILIZATION OF THE SOUTH

Many Southerners boasted loudly of the differences between their new nation and the nation they had left. The differences were real. But there were also important similarities between the Union and the Confederacy, which became clear as the two sides mobilized for war: similarities in their political systems, in the methods they used for financing the war and conscripting troops, and in the way they fought.

THE CONFEDERATE GOVERNMENT

The Confederate constitution was largely identical to the Constitution of the United States, but with several significant exceptions: it explicitly acknowledged the sovereignty of the individual states (although not the right of secession), and it specifically sanctioned slavery and made its abolition (even by one of the states) practically impossible.

The constitutional convention at Montgomery named a provisional president and vice president: Jefferson Davis of Mississippi and Alexander H. Stephens of Georgia, who were later chosen by the general electorate, without opposition, for six-year terms. Davis had been a moderate secessionist before the war; Stephens had argued against secession. The Confederate government, like the Union government, was dominated throughout the war by moderate leaders. Also like the Union's, it was dominated less by the old aristocracy of the East than by the newer aristocrats of the West, of whom Davis was the most prominent example.

DAVIS'S LEADERSHIP

Davis was, in the end, an unsuccessful president. He was a reasonably able administrator and the dominating figure in his government, encountering little interference from the generally tame members of his unstable cabinet and serving as his own secretary of war. But he rarely provided genuinely national leadership. One shrewd Confederate official wrote: "All the revolutionary vigor is with the enemy. . . . With us timidity-hair splitting."

SOUTHERN DIVISIONS

There were no formal political parties in the Confederacy, but its congressional and popular politics were rife with dissension nevertheless. Some white Southerners (and of course most African Americans who were aware of the course of events) opposed secession and war. Many white people in poorer "backcountry" and "upcountry" regions, where slavery was limited, refused to recognize the new Confederate government or to serve in the Southern army; some worked or even fought for the Union. Most white Southerners supported the war; but as in the North, many were openly critical of the government and the military, particularly as the tide of battle turned against the South and the Confederate economy decayed.

MONEY AND MANPOWER

Financing the Confederate war effort was a monumental and ultimately impossible task. It involved creating a national revenue system in a society unaccustomed to significant tax burdens. It depended on a small and unstable banking system that had little capital to lend. Because most wealth in the South was invested in enslaved people and land, liquid assets were scarce; and the Confederacy's only gold–seized from U.S. mints located in the South–was worth only about $1 million.

FUNDING PROBLEMS

The Confederate congress tried at first not to tax the people directly but to requisition funds from the individual states. Most of the states, however, were also unwilling to tax their citizens and paid their shares, when they paid them at all, with bonds or notes of dubious worth. In 1863, the congress enacted an income tax–which planters could pay "in kind" (as a percentage of their produce). But taxation never provided the Confederacy with much revenue; it produced only about 1 percent of the government's total income. Borrowing was not much more successful. The Confederate government issued bonds in such vast amounts that the

CONFEDERATE VOLUNTEERS Young Southern soldiers posed for this photograph in 1861, shortly before the First Battle of Bull Run. The Civil War was the first major military conflict in the age of photography, and it launched the careers of many of America's early photographers.

Discussion and Activities

Analyzing Issues Have students read the section "Davis's Leadership." Ask them to write a short paragraph describing Davis's challenges. *(The Confederacy was founded on the principle of states' rights, and states were reluctant to give up power to the central government.)* **PCE** **ARC**

Discussion and Activities

Analyzing Perspectives Have students read the section "Southern Division." Have them discuss in pairs or small groups how socio-economic status correlated with support for secession. *(In general, poorer whites who lived in areas where slavery was limited showed less support for secession.)* **SOC**

Historical Thinking Skills

Argumentation After students have read the section "Money and Manpower," ask them to create a recruiting poster designed to encourage Southern men to either enlist or resist enlisting in the Confederate army. After they are finished, ask the class to discuss how the messages would have had to change over time. **SOC** **WXT** **PCE**

public lost faith in them and stopped buying them. Efforts to borrow money in Europe using cotton as collateral fared no better.

As a result, the Confederacy had to pay for the war through the least stable, most destructive form of financing: paper currency, which it began issuing in 1861. By 1864, the Confederacy had issued the staggering total of $1.5 billion in paper money, more than twice what the Union had produced. And unlike the Union, the Confederacy did not establish a uniform currency system; the national government, states, cities, and private banks all issued their own notes, producing widespread chaos and confusion. The result was a disastrous inflation, far worse than anything the North experienced. Prices in the North rose 80 percent in the course of the war; in the South they rose 9,000 percent, with devastating effects on the South's morale.

Like the United States, the Confederacy first raised a military by calling for volunteers. And as in the North, by the end of 1861 voluntary enlistments were declining. In April 1862, therefore, the congress enacted a Conscription Act, which subjected all white males between the ages of eighteen and thirty-five to military service for three years. As in the North, a draftee could avoid service if he furnished a substitute. But since the price of substitutes was high, the provision aroused such opposition from poorer white Southerners that it was repealed in 1863. Even more controversial was the exemption from the draft of one white man on each plantation with twenty or more enslaved people, a provision that caused smaller farmers to make the same complaint some Northerners made: "It's a rich man's war but a poor man's fight." Many more white Southerners were exempted from military service than were Northerners.

RAISING THE CONFEDERATE ARMY

Even so, conscription worked for a time. At the end of 1862, about 500,000 men were in the Confederate military. (A total of approximately 900,000 served in the course of the entire war.) That number did not include the many enslaved men and enslaved women recruited by the military to perform such services as cooking, laundry, and manual labor, hence freeing additional white manpower for fighting. After 1862, however, conscription began producing fewer men–in part because the Union had by then begun to seize large areas of the Confederacy and thus had cut off much of the population from conscription or recruitment.

Early in 1864, the government faced a critical manpower shortage. In a desperate move, the Confederate congress began trying to draft men as young as seventeen and as old as fifty. But in a nation suffering from intense war weariness, where many had concluded that defeat was inevitable, nothing could attract or retain an adequate army any longer. In 1864–1865 there were 100,000 desertions. In a frantic final attempt to raise men, the Confederate congress authorized the conscription of 300,000 enslaved men, but the war ended before the government could attempt this incongruous experiment.

MANPOWER SHORTAGE

STATES' RIGHTS VERSUS CENTRALIZATION

The greatest sources of division in the South, however, were differences of opinion over the doctrine of states' rights. States' rights had become such a cult among many white Southerners that they resisted all efforts to exert national authority, even those necessary to win the war. They restricted Davis's ability to impose martial law and suspend habeas corpus. They obstructed conscription. Recalcitrant governors such as Joseph Brown of Georgia and Zebulon M. Vance of North Carolina tried at times to keep their own troops apart from the Confederate forces and insisted on hoarding surplus supplies for their own states' militias.

Even so, the Confederate government did make substantial strides in centralizing power in the South. By the end of the war, the Confederate bureaucracy was larger than its counterpart in Washington. The central government experimented, successfully for a time, with a "food draft"–which permitted soldiers to feed themselves by seizing crops from farms in their path. The government impressed enslaved people, often over the objections of slaveholders, to work as laborers on military projects. The Confederacy seized control of the railroads and shipping; it imposed regulations on industry; it limited corporate profits. States' rights sentiment was a significant handicap, but the South nevertheless took important steps in the direction of centralization–becoming in the process increasingly like the region whose institutions it was fighting to escape.

CENTRALIZATION

ECONOMIC AND SOCIAL EFFECTS OF THE WAR

The war had a devastating effect on the economy of the South. It cut off Southern planters and producers from the markets in the North on which they had depended; it made the sale of cotton overseas much more difficult; it robbed farms and industries that did not have large enslaved populations of a male workforce, leaving some of them unable to function effectively. While in the North production of all goods, agricultural and industrial, increased somewhat during the war, in the South production declined by more than a third.

Most of all, perhaps, the fighting itself wreaked havoc on the Southern economy. Almost all the major battles of the war occurred within the Confederacy; both armies spent most of their time on Southern soil. As a result of the savage fighting, the South's already inadequate railroad system was nearly destroyed; much of its most valuable farmland and many of its most successful plantations were ruined by Union troops (especially in the last year of the war).

Once the Northern naval blockade became effective in 1862, the South experienced massive shortages of almost everything. The region was overwhelmingly agricultural, but since it had concentrated so single-mindedly on producing cotton and other export crops, it did not grow enough food to meet its

Historical Thinking Skills

Contextualization Have students read the section "States' Rights Versus Centralization." Discuss as a class how the challenges facing the Confederate government were similar to or different from the challenges faced by Congress under the Articles of Confederation during the American Revolution. *(Neither had much power to collect taxes, raise an army, or even coordinate military participation by the states.)* **PCE**

own needs. And despite the efforts of women and enslaved laborers to keep farms functioning, the departure of white male workers seriously diminished the region's ability to keep up what food production there had been. Large numbers of doctors were conscripted to serve the needs of the military, leaving many communities without any medical care. Blacksmiths, carpenters, and other craftsmen were similarly in short supply.

ECONOMIC WOES

As the war continued, the shortages, the inflation, and the suffering created increasing instability in Southern society. There were major food riots, some led by women, in Georgia, North Carolina, and Alabama in 1863, as well as a large demonstration in Richmond that quickly turned violent. Resistance to conscription, food impressment, and taxation increased throughout the Confederacy, as did hoarding and black-market commerce.

Despite the economic woes of the South, the war transformed Confederate society in many of the same ways that it was changing the society of the Union. The changes were particularly significant for Southern women. Because so many men left the farms and plantations to fight, the task of keeping families together and maintaining agricultural production fell increasingly to women. Slaveholders' wives often became responsible for managing large enslaved workforces; the wives of modest farmers learned to plow fields and harvest crops. Substantial numbers of females worked as schoolteachers or in government agencies in Richmond. Even larger numbers chose nursing, both in hospitals and in temporary facilities set up to care for wounded soldiers.

NEW ROLES FOR WOMEN

The long-range results of the war for Southern women are more difficult to measure but equally profound. The experience of the 1860s forced many women to question the prevailing Southern assumption that females were unsuited for certain activities, that they were not fit to participate actively in the public sphere. A more concrete legacy was the decimation of the male population and the creation of a major gender imbalance in the region. After the war, there were many thousands more women in the South than there were men. In Georgia, for example, women outnumbered men by 36,000 in 1870; in North Carolina by 25,000. The result, of course, was a large number of unmarried or widowed women who, both during and after the war, had to find employment—thus, by necessity rather than choice, expanding the number of acceptable roles for women in Southern society.

Even before emancipation, the war had far-reaching effects on the lives of enslaved people. Confederate leaders, who were more terrified of slave revolts during the war than they had been in peacetime, enforced slave codes and other regulations with particular severity. Even so, many enslaved people—especially those near the front—found ways to escape their slaveholders and cross behind Union lines in search of freedom. Those who had no realistic avenue for escape seemed, to slaveholders at least, to be particularly resistant to authority during the war. That was in part because on many plantations, the slaveholders and overseers for whom they were accustomed to working were away at war; they found it easier to resist the authority of the women and boys left behind to manage the farms.

ATLANTA AFTER THE BURNING General Sherman captured Atlanta on September 2, 1864, evacuated most of the population, and set fire to the city. This photograph shows the extent of the devastation. The destruction of Atlanta was the beginning of Sherman's famous "March to the Sea." It also signaled the beginning of a new kind of warfare, waged not just against opposing armies but also against the economies and even the populations of the enemy.

Discussion and Activities

Evaluating Evidence After students have read the section "Economic and Social Effects of the War," ask them to construct a T-chart listing economic and social effects of the Civil War in the South. Have students evaluate whether economic or social effects made a greater impact on Southern society. **WXT** **SOC** **PCE** **ARC**

Discussion and Activities

Analyzing Points of View Have students examine the image "Atlanta After the Burning." Ask them to write a short journal entry from the point of view of an evacuated resident of Atlanta returning to the city after its destruction. Have students address whether scenes like this would harden their resolve to continue fighting or cause them to seek peace to end the destruction. **SOC** **PCE** **ARC**

Reasoning Processes

Comparing After students have read the section "Robert E. Lee," have them create a Venn diagram comparing the leadership styles of Abraham Lincoln and Jefferson Davis. Ask students to discuss in small groups what may have accounted for the differences. **PCE**

STRATEGY AND DIPLOMACY

Militarily, the initiative in the Civil War lay mainly with the North, since it needed to destroy the Confederacy, while the South needed only to avoid defeat. Diplomatically, however, the initiative lay with the South. It needed to enlist the recognition and support of foreign governments; the Union wanted to preserve the status quo prior to the war.

THE COMMANDERS

LINCOLN'S LEADERSHIP

The most important Union military commander was Abraham Lincoln, whose previous military experience consisted only of brief service in his state militia during the Black Hawk War. Lincoln was a successful commander in chief because he realized that numbers and resources were on his side, and because he took advantage of the North's material advantages. He realized, too, that the proper objective of his armies was the destruction of the Confederate armies, not the occupation of Southern territory. It was important that Lincoln had a good grasp of strategy, because many of his generals did not. The problem of finding adequate commanders for the troops in the field plagued him throughout the first three years of the war.

From 1861 to 1864, Lincoln tried time and again to find a chief of staff capable of orchestrating the Union war effort. He turned first to General Winfield Scott, the aging hero of the Mexican War. But Scott was unprepared for the magnitude of the new conflict and retired on November 1, 1861. Lincoln replaced him with the young George B. McClellan, commander of the Union armies in the East, the Army of the Potomac; but the proud, arrogant McClellan had a wholly inadequate grasp of strategy and returned to the field in March 1862. For most of the rest of the year, Lincoln had no chief of staff. And when he finally appointed General Henry W. Halleck to the post, he found him an ineffectual strategist who left all substantive decision making to the president. Not until March 1864 did Lincoln finally find a general he trusted to command the war effort: Ulysses S. Grant, who shared Lincoln's belief in making enemy armies and resources, not enemy territory, the target of military efforts. Lincoln gave Grant a relatively free hand, but the general always submitted at least the broad outlines of his plans to the president for advance approval.

Lincoln's (and later Grant's) handling of the war effort faced constant scrutiny from the Committee on the Conduct of the War, a joint investigative committee of the two houses of Congress and the most powerful voice the legislative branch has ever had in formulating war policies. Established in December 1861 and chaired by Senator Benjamin F. Wade of Ohio, it complained constantly of the insufficient ruthlessness of Northern generals, which Radicals on the committee attributed (largely inaccurately) to a secret sympathy among the officers for slavery. The committee's efforts often seriously interfered with the conduct of the war.

Southern command arrangements centered on President Davis, who, unlike Lincoln, was a trained professional soldier.

ULYSSES S. GRANT One observer said of Grant (seen here posing for a photograph during the Wilderness campaign of 1864): "He habitually wears an expression as if he had determined to drive his head through a brick wall, and was about to do it." It was an apt metaphor for Grant's military philosophy, which relied on constant, unrelenting assault. One result was that Grant was willing to fight when other Northern generals held back. Another was that Grant presided over some of the worst carnage of the Civil War.

ROBERT E. LEE

Nevertheless, he failed to create an effective command system. Early in 1862, Davis named General Robert E. Lee as his principal military adviser. But in fact, Davis had no intention of sharing control of strategy with anyone. After a few months, Lee left Richmond to command forces in the field, and for the next two years Davis planned strategy alone. In February 1864, he named General Braxton Bragg as a military adviser; but Bragg never provided much more than technical advice. Not until February 1865 did the Confederate Congress create the formal position of general in chief. Davis named Lee to the post but made clear that he expected to continue to make all basic decisions. In any case, the war ended before this last command structure had time to take shape.

At lower levels of command, men of markedly similar backgrounds controlled the war in both the North and the South. Many of the professional officers on both sides were graduates of the U.S. Military Academy at West Point and the U.S. Naval Academy at Annapolis, and thus had been trained in similar

Discussion and Activities

Comparison and Argumentation Have students examine the image "Ulysses S. Grant" and read the section "Lincoln's Leadership." Have them discuss in small groups the challenges Lincoln had in securing effective military leadership and what distinguished Grant from his predecessors. **PCE**

ROBERT E. LEE Lee, who was a moderate by the standards of Southern politics in the 1850s, opposed secession and was ambivalent about slavery. But he could not bring himself to break with his region, and he left the U.S. Army to lead Confederate forces beginning in 1861. He was (and remains) the most revered of all the white Southern leaders of the Civil War. For decades after his surrender at Appomattox, Lee was a symbol to white Southerners of the "Lost Cause."

ways. Many were closely acquainted, even friendly, with their counterparts on the other side. And all were imbued with the classic, eighteenth-century models of warfare that the service academies still taught. The most successful officers were those who, like Grant and William Tecumseh Sherman, were able to see beyond their academic training and envision a new kind of warfare in which destruction of resources was as important as battlefield tactics.

Amateur officers played an important role in both armies as commanders of volunteer regiments. In both North and South, such men were usually economic or social leaders in their communities who appointed themselves officers and rounded up troops to lead. This system was responsible for recruiting considerable numbers of men into the armies of the two nations. Only occasionally, however, did it produce officers of real ability.

The Role of Sea Power

The Union had an overwhelming advantage in naval power, and it gave its navy two important roles in the war. One was enforcing a blockade of the Southern coast, which the president ordered on April 19, 1861. The other was assisting the Union armies in field operations.

The blockade of the South was never fully effective, but it had a major impact on the Confederacy nevertheless. The U.S. Navy could generally keep oceangoing ships out of Confederate ports. For a time, small blockade runners continued to slip through. But gradually, federal forces tightened the blockade by seizing the ports themselves. The last important port in Confederate hands–Wilmington, North Carolina–fell to the Union early in 1865.

THE UNION BLOCKADE

The Confederates made bold attempts to break the blockade with new weapons. Foremost among them was an ironclad warship, constructed by plating with iron a former U.S. frigate, the *Merrimac*, which the Yankees had scuttled in Norfolk harbor when Virginia seceded. On March 8, 1862, the refitted *Merrimac*, renamed the *Virginia*, left Norfolk to attack a blockading squadron of wooden ships at nearby Hampton Roads. It destroyed two of the ships and scattered the rest. But the Union government had already built ironclads of its own. And one of them, the *Monitor*, arrived off the coast of Virginia only a few hours after the *Virginia's* dramatic foray. The next day, it met the *Virginia* in the first battle between ironclad ships. Neither vessel was able to sink the other, but the *Monitor* put an end to the *Virginia's* raids and preserved the blockade. The Confederacy experimented as well with other naval innovations, such as small torpedo boats and hand-powered submarines. But despite occasional small successes with these new weapons, the South never managed to overcome the Union's naval advantages.

IRONCLADS

As a supporter of land operations, the Union navy was particularly important in the western theater of war–the vast region between the Appalachian Mountains and the Mississippi River–where the major rivers were navigable by large vessels. The navy transported supplies and troops and joined in attacking Confederate strong points. With no significant navy of its own, the South could defend only with fixed land fortifications, which proved no match for the mobile land-and-water forces of the Union.

Europe and the Disunited States

Judah P. Benjamin, the Confederate secretary of state for most of the war, was a clever and intelligent man, but he confined most of his energy to routine administrative tasks. William Seward, his counterpart in Washington, gradually became one of the great American secretaries of state. He had invaluable assistance from Charles Francis Adams, the American minister to London, who had inherited the considerable diplomatic talents of his father, John Quincy Adams, and his grandfather, John Adams.

At the beginning of the war, the ruling classes of England and France, the two nations whose support was most crucial to both sides, were generally sympathetic to the Confederacy,

Discussion and Activities

Comparing and Contrasting After students have read the section "Robert E. Lee," ask them to create a T-chart listing similarities and differences between Union and Confederate army officers. Have students evaluate whether the similarities or differences were greater and what might account for the similarities. *(Many officers from both armies had served together before the war, and many had attended the same military academies.)* **SOC** **ARC**

Historical Thinking Skills

Argumentation Have students read the section "The Role of Sea Power." Discuss as a class why Union naval supremacy was important in determining the outcome of the Civil War. *(The Union Navy was increasingly able to blockade Southern ports, denying the Confederacy imported supplies and the ability to earn revenue from exports. The Union Navy also supported field operations, particularly in the West.)* **PCE**

Historical Thinking Skills

Historical Reasoning and Argumentation After students have read the section "Europe and the Disunited States," have them create a chart listing reasons Britain and France considered supporting the Confederacy, along with reasons why they ultimately did not. Have students write a letter from the point of view of either Confederate Secretary of State Judah P. Benjamin or Union Secretary of State William Seward to the Foreign Minister of France or Great Britain expressing an argument about why those countries should either enter the Civil War or remain neutral. **PCE** **WOR**

for several reasons. The two nations imported much Southern cotton for their textile industries; they were eager to weaken the United States, an increasingly powerful commercial rival; and some British and French citizens admired the supposedly aristocratic social order of the South, which they believed resembled the hierarchical structures of their own societies. But France was unwilling to take sides in the conflict unless England did so first. And in England, the government was reluctant to act because there was powerful popular support for the Union. Important English liberals such as John Bright and Richard Cobden considered the war a struggle between free and slave labor and urged their followers to support the Union cause. The politically conscious but largely unenfranchised workers in Britain expressed their sympathy for the North frequently and unmistakably—in mass meetings, in resolutions, and through their champions in Parliament. After Lincoln issued the Emancipation Proclamation, these groups worked particularly avidly for the Union.

Southern leaders hoped to counter the strength of the British antislavery forces by arguing that access to Southern cotton was vital to the English and French textile industries. But this "King Cotton diplomacy," on which the Confederacy had staked so many of its hopes, failed. English manufacturers had a surplus of both raw cotton and finished goods on hand in 1861 and could withstand a temporary loss of access to American cotton. Later, as the supply of American cotton began to diminish, both England and France managed to keep some of their mills open by importing cotton from Egypt, India, and other sources. Equally important, English workers, the people most seriously threatened by the cotton shortage, did not clamor to have the blockade broken. Even most of the 500,000 English textile workers thrown out of jobs as a result of mill closings continued to support the North. In the end, therefore, no European nation offered diplomatic recognition to the Confederacy or intervened in the war. No nation wanted to antagonize the United States unless the Confederacy seemed likely to win, and the South never came close enough to victory to convince its potential allies to support it.

KING COTTON DIPLOMACY

Even so, there was considerable tension, and on occasion near hostilities, between the United States and Britain, beginning in the first days of the war. Great Britain declared itself neutral as soon as the fighting began, followed by France and other nations. The Union government was furious: neutrality implied that the two sides to the conflict had equal stature. Leaders in Washington were insisting that the conflict was simply a domestic insurrection, not a war between two legitimate governments.

A more serious crisis, the so-called Trent affair, began in late 1861. Two Confederate diplomats, James M. Mason and John Slidell, had slipped through the then-ineffective Union blockade to Havana, Cuba, where they boarded an English steamer, the *Trent*, for England. Waiting in Cuban waters was the American frigate *San Jacinto*, commanded by the impetuous Charles Wilkes. Acting without authorization, Wilkes stopped the British vessel, arrested the diplomats, and carried them in triumph to Boston. The British government demanded the release of the prisoners, reparations, and an apology. Lincoln and Seward, aware that Wilkes had violated maritime law and unwilling to risk war with England, stalled the negotiations until American public opinion had cooled off, then released the diplomats with an indirect apology. A second diplomatic crisis lasted for years. Unable to construct large vessels itself, the Confederacy bought six ships, known as commerce destroyers, from British shipyards. The best known of them were the *Alabama*, the *Florida*, and the *Shenandoah*. The United States protested that this sale of military equipment to a belligerent violated the laws of neutrality, and the protests became the basis, after the war, of damage claims by the United States against Great Britain.

TRENT AFFAIR

THE AMERICAN WEST AND THE WAR

Except for Texas, which joined the Confederacy, all the western states and territories remained officially loyal to the Union—but not without controversy and conflict. Southerners and Southern sympathizers were active throughout the West. And, in some places, there was actual combat between Unionists and secessionists.

There was particularly vicious fighting in Kansas and Missouri, the scene of so much bitterness before the war. The same pro-slavery and free-state forces who had fought one another in the 1850s continued to do so, with even more deadly results. William C. Quantrill, an Ohio native who had spent much of his youth in the West, became a captain in the Confederate army after he organized a band of guerrilla fighters (mostly teenage boys) with which he terrorized areas around the Kansas-Missouri border. Quantrill and his band were an exceptionally murderous group, notorious for killing almost everyone in their path. Their most infamous act was a siege of Lawrence, Kansas, during which they slaughtered 150 civilians, adults and children alike. Union troops killed Quantrill shortly after the end of the war. Union sympathizers in Kansas, organized in bands known as the Jayhawkers, were only marginally less savage, as they moved across western Missouri exacting reprisals for the actions of Quantrill and other Confederate guerrillas. One Jayhawk unit was jointly commanded by the son of John Brown and the brother of Susan B. Anthony, men who brought the fervor of abolitionists to their work. Even without a major battle, the border areas of Kansas and Missouri were among the bloodiest and most terrorized places in the United States during the Civil War.

GUERRILLA WAR IN THE WEST

Not long after the war began, Confederate agents tried to negotiate alliances with the Five Civilized Tribes living in Indian Territory (later Oklahoma), in hopes of recruiting their support against Union forces in the West. The Native Americans themselves were divided. Some wanted to support the South, both because they resented the way the U.S. government had treated them and because some tribal leaders were themselves slaveholders. But other Native Americans supported the North out of a general hostility to slavery (in both the South and their own nation).

Historical Thinking Skills

Contextualization Have students read the section "Guerilla War in the West." Ask them to consider and discuss as a class what they already know about Kansas that would help to explain the intense violence there during the Civil War. *(After the Kansas-Nebraska Act was passed, there was intense conflict over whether Kansas would become a free or slave state. This conflict included several fraudulent elections, the Potawatomie Massacre perpetrated by John Brown, and fighting between pro- and anti-slavery forces that led to Kansas being described as "Bleeding Kansas.")* **PCE** **ARC**

PATTERNS OF POPULAR CULTURE

BASEBALL AND THE CIVIL WAR

Long before the great urban stadiums, long before the lights and the cameras and the multimillion-dollar salaries, long before the Little Leagues and the high school and college teams, baseball was the most popular game in America. And during the Civil War, it was a treasured pastime for soldiers, and for thousands of men (and some women) behind the lines, in both North and South.

The legend that baseball was invented by Abner Doubleday, who probably never even saw the game, came from Albert G. Spalding, a patriotic sporting-goods manufacturer eager to prove that the game had purely American origins and to dispel the notion that it came from England. In fact, baseball was derived from a variety of earlier games, especially the English pastimes of cricket and rounders. American baseball took its own distinctive form beginning in the 1840s, when Alexander Cartwright, a shipping clerk, formed the New York Knickerbockers, laid out a diamond-shaped field with four bases, and declared that batters with three strikes were out and that teams with three outs were retired.

Alexander Cartwright moved west in search of gold in 1849, ultimately grew rich, and settled finally in Hawaii (where he brought the game to Americans in the Pacific). But the game did not languish in his absence. Henry Chadwick, an English-born journalist, spent much of the 1850s popularizing the game (and regularizing its rules). By 1860, baseball was being played by college students and Irish workers, by urban elites and provincial farmers, by people of all classes and ethnic groups from New England to Louisiana. It was also attracting the attention of women. Students at Vassar College formed "ladies" teams in the 1860s, and in Philadelphia, free black men formed the first of what would become a great network of African American baseball teams, the Pythians. From the beginning, they were barred from playing against most white teams.

When young men marched off to war in 1861, some took their bats and balls with them. Almost from the start of the fighting, soldiers in both armies took advantage of idle moments to lay out baseball diamonds and organize games. There were games in prison camps; games on the White House lawn (where Union soldiers were sometimes billeted); and games on battlefields that were sometimes interrupted by gunfire and cannonfire. "It is astonishing how indifferent a person can become to danger," a soldier wrote home to Ohio in 1862. "The report of musketry is heard but a very little distance from us, . . . yet over there on the other side of the road is most of our company, playing Bat Ball." After a skirmish in Texas, another Union soldier lamented that, in addition to casualties, his company had lost "the only baseball in Alexandria, Texas." Far from discouraging baseball, military commanders—and the United States Sanitary Commission, the Union army's medical arm—actively encouraged the game during the war. It would, they believed, help keep up the soldiers' morale.

Away from the battlefield, baseball continued to flourish. In New York City, games between local teams drew crowds of ten or twenty thousand. The National Association of Baseball Players (founded in 1859) had recruited ninety-one clubs in ten Northern states by 1865; a North Western Association of Baseball Players, organized in Chicago in 1865, indicated that the game was becoming well established in the West as well. In Brooklyn, William Cammeyer drained a skating pond on his property, built a board fence around it, and created the first enclosed baseball field in America—the Union Grounds. He charged 10 cents admission. The professionalization of the game was under way.

BATS BEHIND BARS Baseball was a popular recreation for troops on both sides of the Civil War. This image depicts Union prisoners playing the game while incarcerated in a prison camp at Salisbury, North Carolina, in about 1863.

Despite the commercialization and spectacle that became associated with baseball in the years after the Civil War, the game remained for many Americans what it was to millions of young men fighting in the most savage war in the nation's history—an American passion that at times, even if briefly, erased the barriers dividing groups from one another. "Officers and men forget, for a time, the differences in rank," a Massachusetts private wrote in 1863, "and indulge in the invigorating sport with a schoolboy's ardor."

HISTORICAL THINKING SKILLS

1. **Determining Context** How could a competitive game of baseball erase "the barriers dividing groups from one another"?
2. **Identifying Historical Concepts** How and why did baseball take on a unique American identity?
3. **Making Connections** Baseball during the Civil War crossed the lines of cultural differences between the North and the South. Does baseball today, professional or amateur, continue to cross lines of cultural differences? Explain your reasoning.

AP Exam Tip

When answering document-based questions, students will be asked to analyze the sourcing and situation of primary and secondary sources. One way to do that is to analyze an artist's intended audience.

Historical Thinking Skills

Sourcing and Situation Have students practice the tip by examining the image "Bats Behind Bars" and discussing in small groups what the intended audience for this painting might have been. *(The likely intended audience was Northern critics of conditions in Confederate prisoner-of-war camps, as it demonstrates supposed humane treatment of prisoners.)* **PCE** **ARC** **SOC**

Answers

Patterns of Popular Culture

1. The game provides a sense of shared values, connecting the players no matter where they are from, with common rules and expectations.
2. Baseball had its origins in English cricket and rounders, but American baseball took on its own unique form in the 1840s when Alexander Cartwright made his presence known in the field and defined some of the early rules of the game. Baseball, as a reflection of culture, became important for Americans as they continued to find ways to define themselves, separated from their European past.
3. Possible response: Today, all professional sports have become about big money, in terms of contracts for athletes and profits for owners. All of this comes at the expense of the consumer. Ticket prices for professional events have skyrocketed over the past few decades. One game for a single family could result in hundreds of dollars spent. But the reality is that baseball, as America's game, also symbolizes the United States. Fans at the games represent a cross-section of the country; wealthy and poor, different ethnicities, different political ideologies, etc., are represented at all sporting events, including baseball.

Discussion and Activities

Making Connections Have students read the section "High Casualties." Ask them to go online to look up the number of American casualties during recent military interventions in Iraq and Afghanistan. Discuss as a class what the reaction of contemporary Americans would have been if casualties in those conflicts had been as proportionally high as those in the Civil War. **PCE** **SOC**

One result of these divisions was a civil war within Indian Territory. Another was that Native American regiments fought for both the Union and the Confederacy during the war. But the tribes themselves never formally allied themselves with either side.

THE COURSE OF BATTLE

In the absence of direct intervention by the European powers, the two contestants in America were left to resolve the conflict between themselves. They did so in four long years of bloody combat that produced more carnage than any war in American history, before or since. More than 618,000 Americans died in the Civil War, far more than the 115,000 who perished in World War I or the 318,000 who died in World War II—more, indeed, than died in all other American wars combined prior to Vietnam. There were nearly 2,000 deaths for every 100,000 of population during the Civil War. In World War I, the comparable figure was 109 deaths; in World War II, 241 deaths. Massive death, and along with it massive grief, shadowed both North and South during and after the war.

HIGH CASUALTIES

Despite the gruesome cost, the Civil War has become the most romanticized and the most intently studied of all American wars. In part, that is because the conflict produced—in addition to terrible fatalities—a series of military campaigns of classic strategic interest and a series of military leaders who displayed unusual brilliance and daring.

THE TECHNOLOGY OF BATTLE

Much of what happened on the battlefield in the Civil War was a result of new technologies that transformed the nature of combat. The Civil War has often been called the first "modern" war and the first "total" war. The great conflict between the North and the South was unlike any war fought before it, and it suggested what warfare would be like in the future.

The most obvious change in the character of warfare in the 1860s was the nature of the armaments that both sides used in battle. Among the most important was the introduction of repeating weapons. Samuel Colt had patented a repeating pistol (the revolver) in 1835, but more important for military purposes was the repeating rifle, introduced in 1860 by Oliver Winchester. Also important were greatly improved cannons and artillery, a result of advances in iron and steel technology of the previous decades.

REPEATING WEAPONS

These devastating advances in the effectiveness of arms and artillery changed the way soldiers in the field fought. It was now impossibly deadly to fight battles as they had been fought for centuries, with lines of infantry soldiers standing erect in the field firing volleys at their opponents until one side withdrew. Fighting in that way now produced almost inconceivable slaughter, and soldiers quickly learned that the proper position for combat was staying low to the ground and behind cover. For the first time in the history of organized warfare infantry did not fight in formation, and the battlefield became a more chaotic place. Gradually, the deadliness of the new weapons encouraged armies on both sides to spend a great deal of time building elaborate fortifications and trenches to protect themselves from enemy fire. The sieges of Vicksburg and Petersburg, the defense of Richmond, and many other sieges led to the construction of vast fortifications around cities and attacking armies. (They were the predecessors to the great network of trenches that became so central a part of World War I.)

Other weapons technologies were less central to the fighting of the war, but important nevertheless. There was sporadic use of the relatively new technology of hot-air balloons, employed intermittently to provide a view of enemy formations in the field. (During one battle, a Union balloonist took a telegraph line aloft with him in his balloon and tapped out messages about troop movements to the commanders below.) Ironclad ships such as the *Merrimac* (or *Virginia*) and the *Monitor*, torpedoes, and submarine technology all suggested the dramatic changes that would soon overtake naval warfare, although none played a major role in the Civil War.

Critical to the conduct of the war, however, were two other relatively new technologies: the railroad and the telegraph. The railroad was particularly important in a war in which millions of soldiers were being mobilized and transferred to the front, and in which a single field army could number as many as 250,000 men. Transporting such enormous numbers of soldiers, and the supplies necessary to sustain them, would have been almost impossible without railroads. But they also limited mobility. Railroad lines and stations are, of course, in fixed positions. Commanders, therefore, were forced to organize their campaigns around the location of the railroads whether the location was optimal or not.

IMPORTANCE OF THE RAILROAD

The impact of the telegraph on the war was limited both by the scarcity of qualified telegraph operators and by the difficulty of bringing telegraph wires into the fields where battles were being fought. The situation improved somewhat after the new U.S. Military Telegraph Corps, headed by Thomas Scott and Andrew Carnegie, trained and employed over 1,200 operators. Gradually, too, both the Union and Confederate armies learned to string telegraph wires along the routes of their troops so that field commanders were able to stay in close touch with one another during battles. Both the North and the South sent spies behind enemy lines who tried to tap the telegraph lines of their opponents and send important information back about troop movements and formations.

THE TELEGRAPH

THE OPENING CLASHES, 1861

The Union and the Confederacy fought their first major battle of the war in northern Virginia. A Union army of over 30,000 men under the command of General Irvin McDowell was stationed just outside Washington. About thirty miles away, at

Reasoning Processes

Comparing Have students read the section "The Technology of Battle." Ask them to create a Venn diagram comparing new weapons of the Civil War with the technologies used to fight previous wars. Have students discuss why the new technologies led to much higher casualty numbers. **PCE** **WXT**

THE CONSOLIDATION OF NATIONS

The American Civil War was an event largely rooted in conditions particular to the United States. But it was also a part of a worldwide movement in the nineteenth century to create large, consolidated nations. A commitment to preserving the Union—to consolidating, rather than dismantling, the nation—was one of the principal motives for the North's commitment to fighting a war against the seceding states. Similar efforts at expansion, consolidation, and unification were occurring in many other nations around the same time.

The consolidation of nation-states was, of course, not new to the nineteenth century. The revolutions in America and France in the late eighteenth century—and the subsequent strengthening of the French concept of nationhood under Napoleon in the early nineteenth century—inspired new nationalist enthusiasms in other parts of Europe. Nationalist sentiment also grew among peoples who shared language, culture, ethnicity, and tradition and who came to believe that a consolidated nation was the best vehicle for strengthening their common bonds.

In 1848, a wave of nationalist revolutions erupted in Italy, France, and Austria, challenging the imperial powers that many Europeans believed were subjugating national cultures. Those revolutions failed, but they helped lay the groundwork for the two most important national consolidations of nineteenth-century Europe.

One of these consolidations occurred in Germany, which was divided into numerous small, independent states in the early nineteenth century but where popular sentiment for German unification had been growing for decades. It was spurred in part by new histories of the German Volk (people) and by newly constructed images of German traditions, visible in such literature as the Grimms' fairy tales—an effort to record and popularize German folk traditions and make them the basis of a shared sense of a common past. In 1862, King Wilhelm I of Prussia—the leader of one of the most powerful of the scattered German states—appointed an aristocratic landowner, Otto von Bismarck, as his prime minister. Bismarck exploited the growing nationalism throughout the various German states and helped develop a strong popular base for unification. He did so in part by launching Prussian wars against Denmark, Austria, and France—wars Prussia easily won, inspiring pride in German power that extended well beyond Prussia. The Franco-Prussian War of 1870 was particularly important, because Prussia fought it to take possession of the French provinces of Alsace and Lorraine—provinces the Prussians claimed were part of the German "national community" because its people, although legally French citizens, were ethnically and linguistically German. In 1871, capitalizing on the widespread nationalist sentiment the war had created throughout the German-speaking states, Bismarck persuaded the German king to proclaim himself emperor (or Kaiser) of a new empire that united all German peoples except those in Austria and Switzerland.

The second great European movement for national unification occurred in Italy, which had long been divided into small kingdoms, city-states, and regions controlled by the Vatican. Beginning in the early nineteenth century, Italian nationalists formed what became known as the "Young Italy" movement, under the leadership of Giuseppe Mazzini. The movement demanded an end to foreign control in Italy and the unification of the Italian people into a single nation. Peoples with common language, culture, and tradition, Mazzini believed, should be free to unite and govern themselves. More important than this growing popular nationalism as a cause of Italian unification were the efforts of powerful and ambitious leaders. The most powerful Italian state in the mid-nineteenth century was the kingdom of the Piedmont and Sardinia, in the northwestern part of the peninsula. Its king, Victor Emmanuel II, appointed his own version of Bismarck—Camillo di Cavour—as prime minister in 1852. Cavour joined forces with nationalists in other areas of Italy to drive the Spanish and the Austrians out of Italian territory. Having first won independence for northern Italy, Cavour joined forces with the Southern nationalist leader Giuseppe Garibaldi, who helped win independence in the south and then agreed to a unification of the entire Italian nation under Victor Emmanuel II in 1860.

THE UNIFICATION OF ITALY **This engraving shows the Battle of Volturno, which was really a series of skirmishes that took place in September and October 1860. The main battle, between Garibaldi's volunteers and the troops of the Kingdom of the Two Sicilies, occurred on October 1. Although the immediate aftermath of the battle left Garibaldi's forces exhausted, they did go on to successfully unify Italy under King Victor Emmanuel II.**

Other nations in these years were also trying to create, preserve, and strengthen nation-states. Some failed to do so—Russia, for example, despite the reform efforts of several tsars, never managed to create a stable nation-state from among its broad and diverse peoples. But others succeeded—Meiji Japan, for example, instituted a series of reforms in the 1880s and 1890s that created a powerful new Japanese nation-state.

In fighting and winning the Civil War, the nationalists of the Northern parts of the United States not only preserved the unity of their nation. They also became part of a movement toward the consolidation of national cultures and national territories that extended through many areas of the globe.

HISTORICAL THINKING SKILLS

1. **Comparing and Contrasting** How were the problems Bismarck faced similar to and different from those faced by Lincoln?
2. **Drawing Conclusions** Which man—Mazzini, Cavour, or Garibaldi—in the struggle to achieve the unification of Italy most closely parallels Lincoln and the fight to preserve the Union?
3. **Developing Arguments** Does Mazzini's argument—that peoples with common language, culture, and tradition should be free to unite and govern themselves—apply to the North's attempt to preserve the Union, or does it better fit the South's attempt to secede and form a separate nation?

Reasoning Processes

Comparing Have students read the feature, and then ask them to construct a 3-circle Venn diagram comparing the American Civil War, German Unification, and Italian Unification. Ask students to discuss in pairs or small groups how nationalism played similar or different roles in the three events. **WOR** **PCE**

Answers

America in the World

1. Bismarck launched wars in an effort to generate German pride. Lincoln tried to avoid a civil war; he argued that his intention (and that of the Republican Party) was not to end the institution of slavery. Both used language in speeches that roused nationalistic sentiment. Both Bismarck and Lincoln used the rhetoric of nationalism to garner support for their cause.
2. Lincoln shared commonalities with all three Italian leaders, but the figure he had the most in common with was Mazzini. Both used the language of shared ideals to try and unite the different parts of the country. For Lincoln, however, this came in the context of social, political, and economic values. Lincoln believed that the North and the South shared too many bonds to effectively separate. He also believed that the Southern states had no legal or constitutional right to separate from the rest of the Union.
3. Both the North and the South made similar arguments. Neither focused exclusively on culture, though. Both sides presented deep and complicated arguments arguing that differences and similarities of social, political, and economic issues must be factored into any decision with regard to secession. The South tended to rely more on cultural arguments than the North.

Discussion and Activities

Analyzing Change After students have read the section "The Opening Clashes, 1861," ask them to write a short paragraph explaining how the First Battle of Bull Run changed the nature of the war. *(The battle dispelled the illusion that the war would be short, leading to changes in how both sides approached the conflict. The Confederate victory may have led to some overconfidence on their part.)* **PCE**

the town of Manassas, was a slightly smaller Confederate army under General P. G. T. Beauregard. If the Northern army could destroy the Southern one, Union leaders believed, the war might end at once. In mid-July, McDowell marched his inexperienced troops toward Manassas. Beauregard moved his troops behind Bull Run, a small stream north of Manassas, and called for reinforcements, which reached him the day before the battle. The two armies were now approximately the same size.

On July 21, in the First Battle of Bull Run, or First Battle of Manassas, McDowell almost succeeded in dispersing the Confederate forces. But the Southerners stopped a last strong Union assault and then began a savage counterattack. The Union troops, exhausted after hours of hot, hard fighting, suddenly panicked. They broke ranks and retreated chaotically. McDowell was unable to reorganize them, and he had to order a retreat to Washington–a disorderly withdrawal complicated by the presence along the route of many civilians who had ridden down from the capital, picnic baskets in hand, to watch the battle from nearby hills. The Confederates, as disorganized by victory as the Union forces were by defeat, and short of supplies and transportation, did not pursue. The battle was a severe blow to Union morale and to President Lincoln's confidence in his officers. It also dispelled the illusion that the war would be a brief one.

FIRST BATTLE OF BULL RUN

Elsewhere in 1861, Union forces were achieving some small but significant victories. In Missouri, rebel forces gathered behind Governor Claiborne Jackson and other state officials who wanted to secede from the Union. Nathaniel Lyon, who commanded a small regular army force in St. Louis, moved his troops into southern Missouri to face the secessionists. On August 10, at the Battle of Wilson's Creek, Lyon was defeated and killed–but not before he had seriously weakened the striking power of the Confederates. Union forces were subsequently able to hold most of the state.

WILSON'S CREEK

Meanwhile, a Union force under George B. McClellan moved east from Ohio into western Virginia. By the end of 1861, it had "liberated" the anti-secession mountain people of the region. They created their own state government loyal to the Union and were admitted to the Union as West Virginia in 1863. The occupation of western Virginia was of limited military value, since the mountains cut the area off from the rest of Virginia. It was, however, an important symbolic victory for the North.

THE WESTERN THEATER

After the First Battle of Bull Run, military operations in the East settled into a long and frustrating stalemate. The first decisive operations in 1862 occurred in the West. Union forces were trying to seize control of the southern Mississippi River, which would divide the Confederacy and give the North easy transportation into the heart of the South. Northern soldiers advanced on the river from both the north and south, moving downriver from Kentucky and upriver from the Gulf of Mexico toward New Orleans.

In April, a Union squadron of ironclads and wooden vessels commanded by David G. Farragut gathered in the Gulf of Mexico, then smashed past weak Confederate forts near the mouth of the Mississippi, and from there sailed up to New Orleans, which was defenseless because the Confederate high command had expected the attack to come from the north. The city surrendered on April 25–the first major Union victory and an important turning point in the war. From then on, the mouth of the Mississippi was closed to Confederate trade; and the South's largest city and most important banking center was in Union hands.

NEW ORLEANS CAPTURED

Farther north in the western theater, Confederate troops under the command of Albert Sidney Johnston were stretched out in a long defensive line centered at two forts in Tennessee, Fort Henry and Fort Donelson, on the Tennessee and Cumberland Rivers, respectively. But the forts were well behind the main Southern flanks, a fatal weakness that Union commanders recognized and exploited. Early in 1862, Ulysses S. Grant attacked Fort Henry, whose defenders, awed by the ironclad riverboats accompanying the Union army, surrendered with almost no resistance on February 6. Grant then moved both his naval and ground forces to Fort Donelson, where the Confederates put up a stronger fight but finally, on February 16, had to surrender. By cracking the Confederate center, Grant had gained control of river communications and forced Confederate forces out of Kentucky and half of Tennessee.

With about 40,000 men, Grant now advanced south along the Tennessee River to seize control of railroad lines vital to the Confederacy. From Pittsburg Landing, he marched to nearby Shiloh, Tennessee, where a force almost equal to his own, commanded by Albert Sidney Johnston and P. G. T. Beauregard, caught him by surprise. The result was the Battle of Shiloh, April 6–7. In the first day's fighting (during which Johnston was killed), the Southerners drove Grant back to the river. But the next day, reinforced by 25,000 fresh troops, Grant recovered the lost ground and forced Beauregard to withdraw. After the narrow Union victory at Shiloh, Northern forces occupied Corinth, Mississippi, the hub of several important railroads, and established control of the Mississippi River as far south as Memphis.

SHILOH

Braxton Bragg, who succeeded Johnston as commander of the Confederate army in the West, gathered his forces at Chattanooga, in eastern Tennessee, which the Confederacy still controlled. He hoped to win back the rest of the state and then move north into Kentucky. But first he had to face a Union army (commanded by Don Carlos Buell and later William S. Rosecrans), whose assignment was to capture Chattanooga. The two armies maneuvered for advantage inconclusively in northern Tennessee and southern Kentucky for several months until they finally met, December 31–January 2, in the Battle of Murfreesboro, or Stone's River. Bragg was forced to withdraw to the south, his campaign a failure. By the end of 1862, Union forces had made considerable progress in the West. But the major conflict remained in the East, where they were having much less success.

Historical Thinking Skills

Argumentation Have students read the section "The Western Theater." Discuss as a class why conflict in the West was so important to the success of Union efforts to control the rivers and railroads. **PCE**

The Virginia Front, 1862

Union operations were being directed in 1862 by George B. McClellan, commander of the Army of the Potomac and the most controversial general of the war. McClellan was a superb trainer of men, but he often appeared reluctant to commit his troops to battle. Opportunities for important engagements came and went, and McClellan seemed never to take advantage of them—claiming always that his preparations were not yet complete or that the moment was not right. During the winter of 1861–1862, McClellan concentrated on training his army of 150,000 men near Washington. Finally, he designed a spring campaign whose purpose was to capture the Confederate capital at Richmond. But instead of heading overland directly toward Richmond, McClellan chose a complicated, round-about route that he thought would circumvent the Confederate defenses. The navy would carry his troops down the Potomac to a peninsula east of Richmond, between the York and James Rivers. The army would approach the city from there. It became known as the Peninsular campaign.

George McClellan

McClellan began the campaign with only part of his army. Approximately 100,000 men accompanied him down the Potomac. Another 30,000—under General Irvin McDowell—

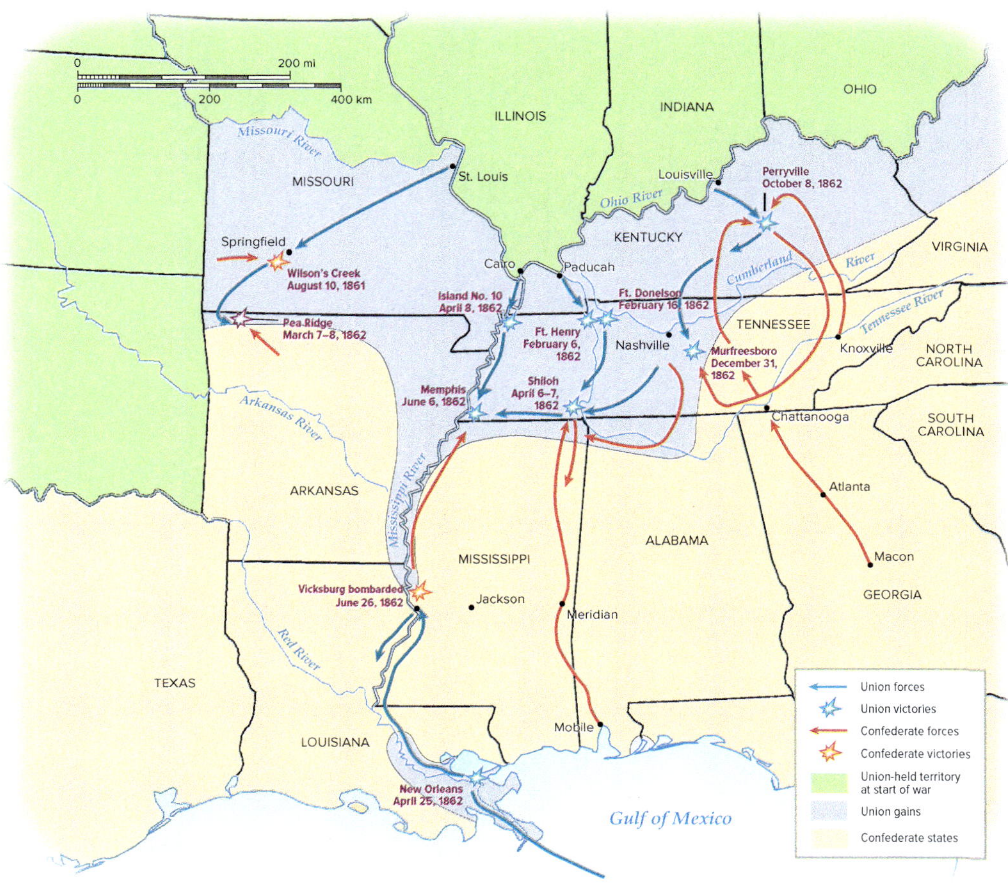

THE WAR IN THE WEST, 1861–1863 While the Union armies in Virginia were meeting with repeated frustrations, the Union armies in the West were scoring notable successes in the first two years of the war. This map shows a series of Union drives in the western Confederacy. Admiral David Farragut's ironclads led to the capture of New Orleans—a critical Confederate port—in April 1862, while forces farther north under the command of Ulysses S. Grant drove the Confederate army out of Kentucky and western Tennessee. These battles culminated in the Union victory at Shiloh, which led to Union control of the upper Mississippi River.

Why was control of the Mississippi so important to both sides?

Discussion and Activities

Analyzing Evidence Have students examine the map "The War in the West, 1861–1863." Have them discuss in pairs or small groups why Kentucky and Missouri remaining in the Union was so important to the Union cause. *(It allowed free navigation of the Ohio River all the way to the Mississippi River.)* **GEO**

Answers

The War in the West, 1861–1863

Control of the Mississippi was essential to control of trade throughout the Confederacy and to maintaining the integrity of Confederate territory by maintaining contact with Texas, Arkansas, and Louisiana.

Reasoning Processes

Comparing Have students examine the maps "The Virginia Theater, 1861–1863." Ask them to create a Venn diagram comparing the Virginia Theater to the Western Theater. *(Similarities: In both theaters, Union commanders tried to utilize rivers for transportation. Differences: The area involved in the Virginia Theater was much smaller, and the battles were more compressed.)* **GEO**

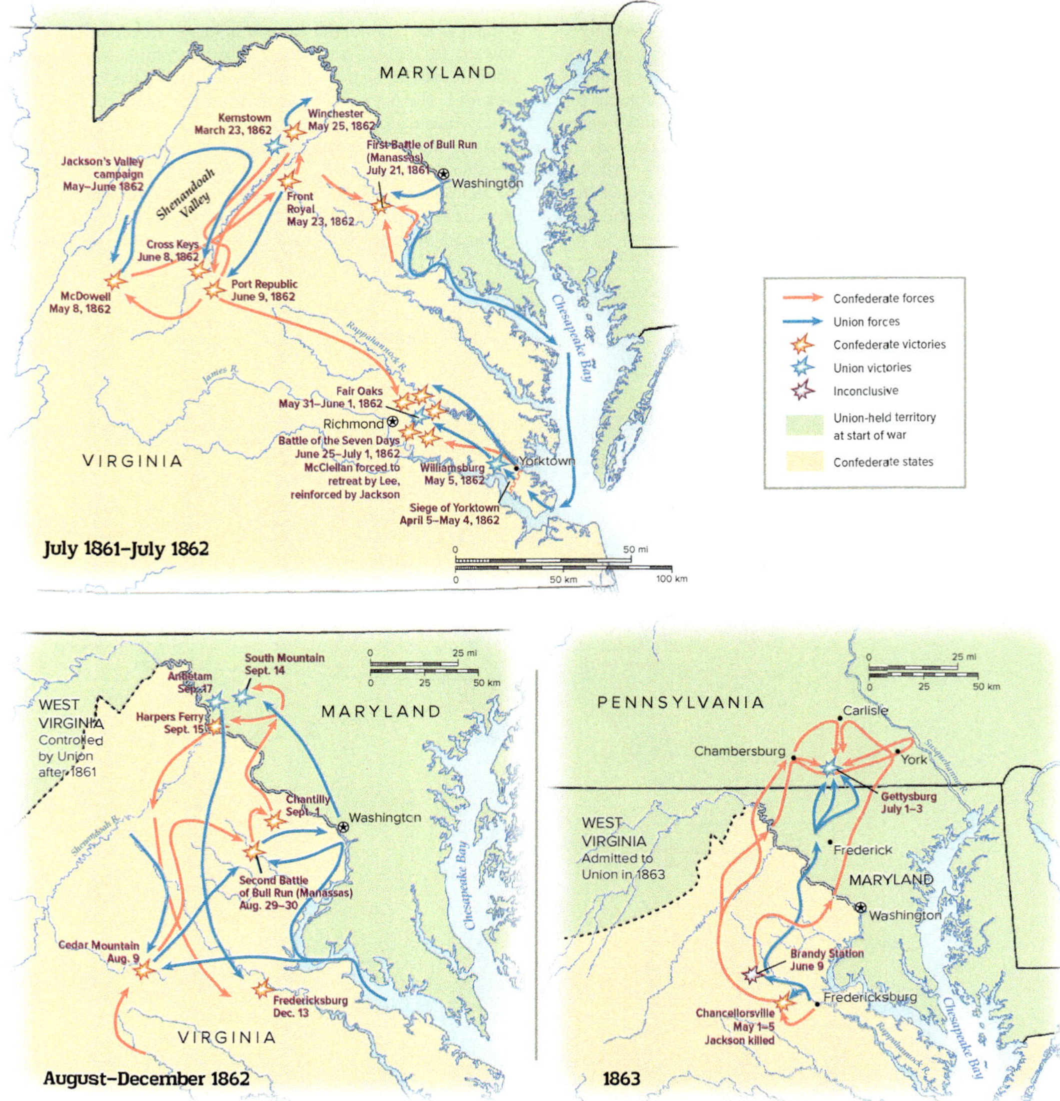

THE VIRGINIA THEATER, 1861–1863 Much of the fighting during the first two years of the Civil War took place in what became known as the Virginia theater—although the campaigns in this region eventually extended north into Maryland and Pennsylvania. The Union hoped for a quick victory over the newly created Confederate army. But as these maps show, the Southern forces consistently thwarted such hopes. The map at top left shows the battles of 1861 and the first half of 1862, almost all of them won by the Confederates. The map at lower left shows the last months of 1862, during which the Southerners again defeated the Union in most of their engagements—although Northern forces drove the Confederates back from Maryland in September. The map on the right shows the troop movements that led to the climactic battle of Gettysburg in 1863.

Why were the Union forces unable to profit more from their material advantages during these first years of the war?

Answers

The Virginia Theater, 1861–1863

The main cause of the Union's inability to capitalize on its material advantages was inconsistent military leadership.

remained behind to protect Washington. McClellan insisted that Washington was safe as long as he was threatening Richmond, and finally persuaded Lincoln to promise to send him the additional men. But before the president could do so, a Confederate army under Thomas J. ("Stonewall") Jackson changed his plans. Jackson staged a rapid march north through the Shenandoah Valley, as if he were planning to cross the Potomac and attack Washington. Alarmed, Lincoln dispatched McDowell's corps to head off Jackson. In the brilliant Valley campaign of May 4–June 9, 1862, Jackson defeated two separate Union forces and slipped away before McDowell could catch him.

SEVEN PINES

Meanwhile, Confederate troops under Joseph E. Johnston were attacking McClellan's advancing army outside Richmond. But in the two-day Battle of Fair Oaks, or Seven Pines (May 31–June 1), they could not repel the Union forces. Johnston, badly wounded, was replaced by Robert E. Lee, who then recalled Stonewall Jackson from the Shenandoah Valley. With a combined force of 85,000 to face McClellan's 100,000, Lee launched a new offensive, known as the Battle of the Seven Days (June 25–July 1). Lee wanted to cut McClellan off from his base on the York River and then destroy the isolated Union army. But McClellan fought his way across the peninsula and set up a new base on the James. There, with naval support, the Army of the Potomac was safe.

McClellan was now only twenty-five miles from Richmond, with a secure line of water communications, and thus in a good position to renew the campaign. Time and again, however, he found reasons for delay. Instead of replacing McClellan with a more aggressive commander, Lincoln finally ordered the army to move to northern Virginia and join a smaller force under John Pope. The president hoped to begin a new offensive against Richmond on the direct overland route that he himself had always preferred.

As the Army of the Potomac left the peninsula by water, Lee moved north with the Army of Northern Virginia to strike Pope before McClellan could join him. Pope was as rash as McClellan was cautious, and he attacked the approaching Confederates without waiting for the arrival of all of McClellan's troops. In the ensuing Second Battle of Bull Run, or Second Battle of Manassas (August 29–30), Lee threw back the assault and routed Pope's army, which fled to Washington. With hopes for an overland campaign against Richmond now in disarray, Lincoln removed Pope from command and put McClellan in charge of all the Union forces in the region.

Lee soon went on the offensive again, heading north through western Maryland, and McClellan moved out to meet him. McClellan had the good luck to get a copy of Lee's orders,

ANTIETAM

which revealed that a part of the Confederate army, under Stonewall Jackson, had separated from the rest to attack Harpers Ferry. But instead of attacking quickly before the Confederates could recombine, McClellan delayed and gave Lee time to pull most of his forces together behind Antietam Creek, near the town of Sharpsburg. There, on September 17, in the bloodiest single-day engagement of the war, McClellan's 87,000-man army repeatedly attacked Lee's force of 50,000, with enormous casualties on both sides. Six thousand soldiers died, and 17,000 sustained injuries. Late in the day, just as the Confederate line seemed ready to break, the last of Jackson's troops arrived from Harpers Ferry to reinforce it. McClellan might have broken through with one more assault. Instead, he allowed Lee to retreat into Virginia. Technically, Antietam was a Union victory, but in reality, it was an opportunity squandered. In November, Lincoln finally removed McClellan from command for good.

McClellan's replacement, Ambrose E. Burnside, was a short-lived mediocrity. He tried to move toward Richmond by crossing the Rappahannock at Fredericksburg, the strongest defensive point on the river. There, on December 13, he launched a series of attacks against Lee, all of them bloody, all of them hopeless. After losing a large part of his army, Burnside withdrew to the north bank of the Rappahannock. He was relieved at his own request.

THE PROGRESS OF THE WAR

Why did the Union—with its much larger population and its much better transportation and technology than the Confederacy—make so little progress in the first two years of the war? Had there been a decisive and dramatic victory by either side early in the war—for example, a major victory by the Union at the First Battle of Bull Run—the conflict might have ended quickly by destroying the Confederacy's morale. But no such decisive victory occurred in the first two years of the war.

Many Northerners blamed the military stalemate on timid or incompetent Union generals, and there was some truth to that view. But the more important reason for the drawn-out conflict was that it was not a traditional war of tactics and military strategy. It was, even if the leaders of both sides were not yet fully aware of it, a war of attrition. Winning or losing battles here and there would not determine the outcome of the war. What would bring the war to a conclusion was the steady destruction of the resources that were necessary for victory. More than two bloody years of fighting was still to

THE FIRST CONNECTICUT ARTILLERY Mathew Brady's photograph shows the First Connecticut Artillery at Fort Richardson, Virginia.

Discussion and Activities

Historical Evidence and Argumentation After students have read the section "The Virginia Front, 1862," ask them to create a chart listing Union commanders and their strengths and weaknesses. Have students discuss in pairs or small groups how fighting in the Virginia front may have gone differently with more effective Union military leadership. **PCE**

Discussion and Activities

Analyzing Visuals Have students examine the image "The First Connecticut Artillery." Ask them to list and discuss in pairs or small groups details that show how fighting changed during the Civil War compared with past wars. *(There were extensive fortifications in response to new repeating weapons, as well as large numbers of weapons produced by Northern industry.)* **WXT**

Discussion and Activities

Explaining Significance After students have read the section, "The Progress of the War," ask them to write a short paragraph evaluating the impact of a war of attrition on the civilian population of the South. **PCE** **WXT**

come. But those last years were a testimony to the slow, steady deterioration of the Confederacy's ability to maintain the war and to the consistent growth of the resources that allowed the Union armies to grow steadily stronger.

With the federal blockade growing tighter and tighter, the Confederacy found it difficult to secure food. On April 2, 1863, a Confederate soldier received a letter from Richmond from a friend. "Something very sad has just happened in Richmond," she said, "something that makes me ashamed of all my . . . hats, bonnets, gowns, stationery, books, magazines, dainty food." She saw hundreds of young women and men looking for food. "The crowd now rapidly increased and numbered, I am sure, more than a thousand women and children. It grew and grew until it reached the dignity of a mob–a bread riot. . . . While I write women and children are still standing in the streets, demanding food."

1863: Year of Decision

At the beginning of 1863, General Joseph Hooker was in command of the still formidable Army of the Potomac, whose 120,000 troops remained north of the Rappahannock, opposite Fredericksburg. But despite his reputation as a fighter (his popular nickname was "Fighting Joe"), Hooker showed little resolve as he launched his own campaign in the spring. Taking part of his army, Hooker crossed the river above Fredericksburg and moved toward the town and Lee's army. But at the last minute, he apparently lost his nerve and drew back to a defensive position in a desolate area of brush and scrub trees known as "the Wilderness." Lee had only half as many men as Hooker did, but he boldly divided his forces for a dual assault on the Union army. In the Battle of Chancellorsville, May 1–5, Stonewall Jackson attacked the Union right and Lee himself charged the front. Hooker barely managed to escape with his army. Lee had defeated the Union objectives, but he had not destroyed the Union army. And his ablest officer, Jackson, was wounded during the battle and subsequently died of pneumonia.

BATTLE OF CHANCELLORSVILLE

While the Union forces were suffering repeated frustrations in the East, they were continuing to achieve important victories in the West. In the spring of 1863, Ulysses S. Grant was driving at Vicksburg, Mississippi, one of the Confederacy's two remaining strongholds on the southern Mississippi River. Vicksburg was well protected, surrounded by rough country on the north and low, marshy ground on the west, and with good artillery coverage of the river itself. But in May, Grant boldly moved men and supplies–overland and by water–to an area south of the city, where the terrain was better. He then attacked Vicksburg from the rear. Six weeks later, on July 4, Vicksburg–whose residents were by then literally starving as a result of a prolonged siege–surrendered. At almost the same time, the other Confederate strong point on the river, Port Hudson, Louisiana, also surrendered–to a Union force that had moved north from New Orleans. The Union had achieved one of its basic military aims: control of the whole length of the Mississippi. The Confederacy was split in two, with Louisiana, Arkansas, and Texas cut off from the other seceded states. The victories on the Mississippi were among the great turning points of the war.

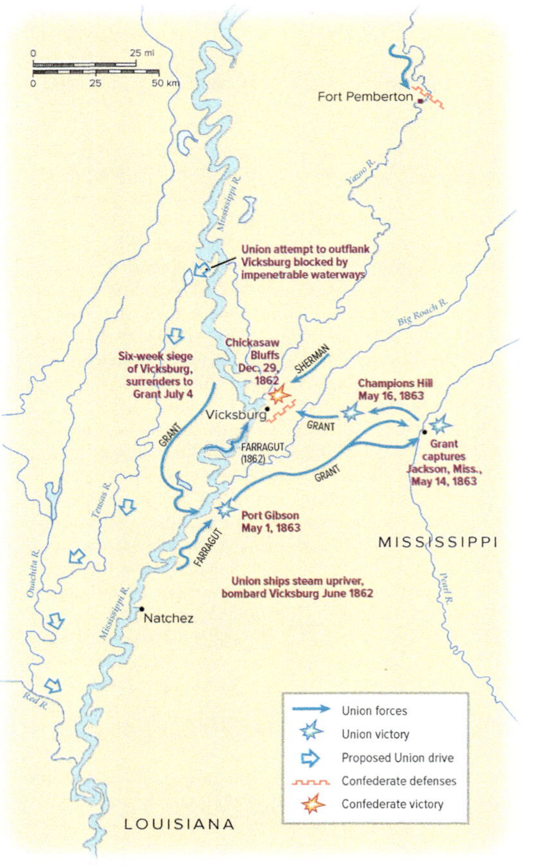

VICKSBURG

THE SIEGE OF VICKSBURG, MAY–JULY 1863 In the spring of 1863, Grant began a campaign to win control of the final piece of the Mississippi River still controlled by the Confederacy. To do that required capturing the Southern stronghold at Vicksburg—a well-defended city sitting above the river. Vicksburg's main defenses were in the North, so Grant boldly moved men and supplies around the city and attacked it from the south. Eventually, he cut off the city's access to the outside world, and after a six-week siege, its residents finally surrendered.

What impact did the combined victories at Vicksburg and Gettysburg have on Northern commitment to the war?

During the siege of Vicksburg, Lee proposed an invasion of Pennsylvania, which would, he argued, divert Union troops north and remove the pressure on the lower Mississippi.

Answers

The Siege of Vicksburg, May–July 1863

The dual victories, announced to the public on July 4, gave a tremendous boost to Northern morale.

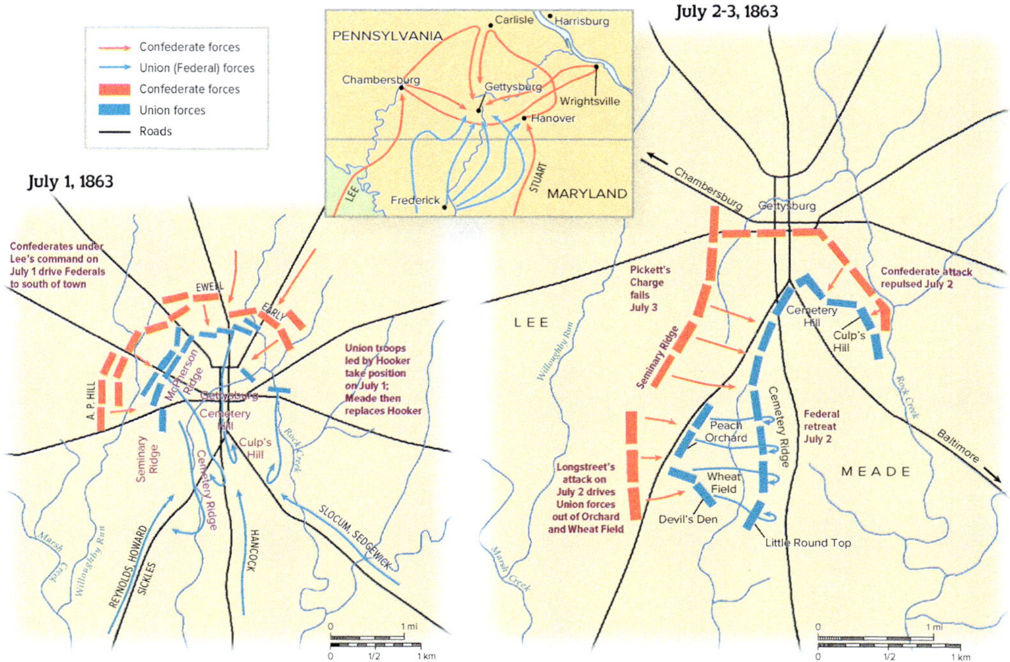

GETTYSBURG, JULY 1–3, 1863 Gettysburg was the most important single battle of the Civil War. The map on the left shows the distribution of Union and Confederate forces at the beginning of the battle, July 1, after Lee had driven the Northern forces south of town. The map on the right reveals the pattern of the attacks on July 2 and 3. Note, in particular, Pickett's bold and costly charge, whose failure on July 3 was the turning point in the battle and, some chroniclers have argued, the war.

Why did Robert E. Lee believe that an invasion of Pennsylvania would advance the Confederate cause?

Further, he argued, if he could win a major victory on Northern soil, England and France might come to the Confederacy's aid. The war-weary North might even quit the war before Vicksburg fell.

In June 1863, Lee moved up the Shenandoah Valley into Maryland and then entered Pennsylvania. The Union Army of the Potomac, commanded first by Hooker and then by George C. Meade, also moved north, parallel with the Confederates' movement, staying between Lee and Washington. The two armies finally encountered each other at the small town of Gettysburg, Pennsylvania. There, on July 1–3, 1863, they fought the most celebrated battle of the war.

Meade's army established a strong, well-protected position on the hills south of the town. The confident and combative

GETTYSBURG

Lee attacked, even though his army was outnumbered 75,000 to 90,000. His first assault on the Union forces on Cemetery Ridge failed. A day later he ordered a second, larger effort. In what is remembered as Pickett's Charge, a force of 15,000 Confederate soldiers advanced for almost a mile across open country while being swept by Union fire. Only about 5,000 made it up the ridge, and this remnant finally had to surrender or retreat. By now Lee had lost nearly a third of his army. On July 4, the same day as the surrender of Vicksburg, he withdrew from Gettysburg—another major turning point in the war. Never again were the weakened Confederate forces able to threaten Northern territory seriously.

Before the end of 1863, there was a third important turning point, this one in Tennessee. After occupying Chattanooga on September 9, Union forces under William Rosecrans began an unwise pursuit of Bragg's retreating Confederate forces. Bragg was waiting for them just across the Georgia line, with reinforcements from Lee's army. The two armies engaged in the Battle of Chickamauga (September 19–20), one of the few battles in which the Confederates enjoyed a numerical superiority (70,000 to 56,000). Union forces could not break the Confederate lines and retreated back to Chattanooga.

Bragg now began a siege of Chattanooga itself, seizing the heights nearby and cutting off fresh supplies to the

Historical Thinking Skills

Argumentation After students have read the section "Gettysburg," ask them to write a thesis statement that supports, refutes, or modifies the claim that Gettysburg was the most important battle of the Civil War. **PCE**

Answers

Gettysburg, July 1–3 1863

Lee believed that a victory in the North would strengthen the Northern peace movement and create pressure on the Union government to negotiate a settlement.

Discussion and Activities

Comparing After students have read the section "The Battle of Chattanooga," discuss as a class how this battle was similar to or different from previous Union campaigns. **PCE**

Union forces. Grant came to the rescue. In the Battle of Chattanooga (November 23–25), the reinforced Union army drove the Confederates back into Georgia. Northern troops then occupied most of eastern Tennessee. Union forces had now achieved a second important objective: control of the Tennessee River. Four of the eleven Confederate states were now effectively cut off from the Southern nation. No longer could the Confederacy hope to win independence through a decisive military victory. They could hope to win only by holding on and exhausting the Northern will to fight.

BATTLE OF CHATTANOOGA

THE LAST STAGE, 1864–1865

By the beginning of 1864, Ulysses S. Grant had become general in chief of all the Union armies. At long last, President Lincoln had found a commander whom he could rely on to pursue the war doggedly and tenaciously. Grant was not a subtle strategic or tactical general; he believed in using the North's overwhelming advantage in troops and material resources to overwhelm the South. He was not afraid to absorb massive casualties as long as he was inflicting similar casualties on his opponents.

Grant planned two great offensives for 1864. In Virginia, the Army of the Potomac (technically under Meade's command, but really now under Grant's) would advance toward Richmond and force Lee into a decisive battle. In Georgia, the western army, under William Tecumseh Sherman, would advance east toward Atlanta and destroy the remaining Confederate force farther south, which was now under the command of Joseph E. Johnston. The northern campaign began when the Army of the Potomac, 115,000 strong, plunged into the rough, wooded Wilderness area of northwestern Virginia in pursuit of Lee's 75,000-man army. After avoiding an engagement for several weeks, Lee turned Grant back in the Battle of the Wilderness (May 5–7). But Grant was undeterred. Without stopping to rest or reorganize, he resumed his march toward Richmond. He met Lee again in the bloody, five-day Battle of Spotsylvania Court

GRANT'S STRATEGY

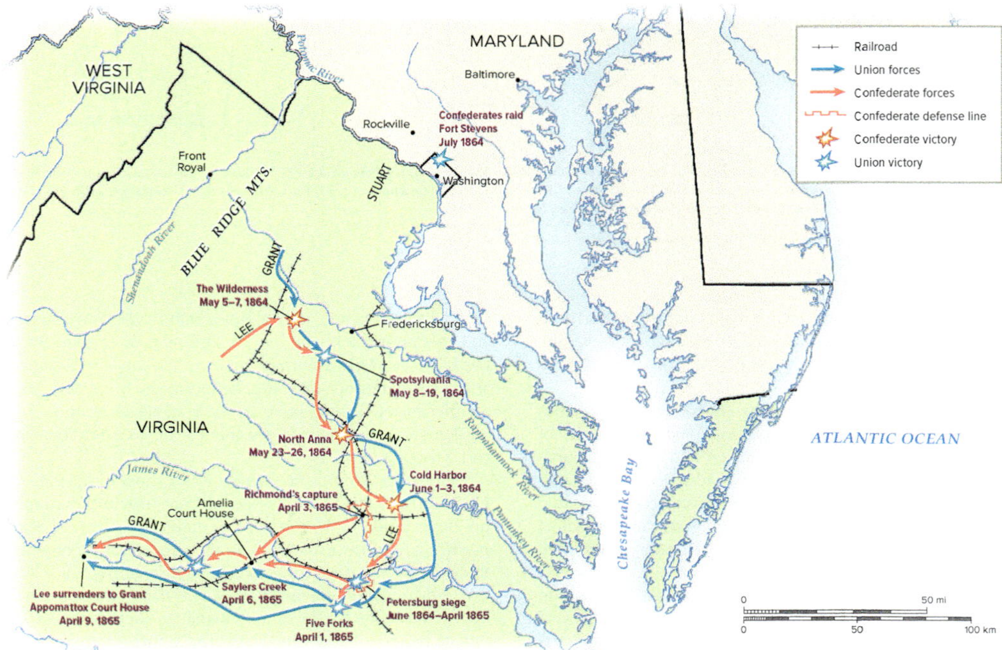

VIRGINIA CAMPAIGNS, 1864–1865 From the Confederate defeat and retreat from Gettysburg until the end of the war, most of the eastern fighting took place in Virginia. By now, Ulysses S. Grant was commander of all Union forces and had taken over the Army of the Potomac. Although Confederate forces won a number of important battles during the Virginia campaign, the Union army grew steadily stronger and the Southern forces steadily weaker. Grant believed that the Union strategy should reflect the North's greatest advantage: its superiority in men and equipment.

What effect did this decision have on the level of casualties?

Answers

Virginia Campaigns, 1864–1865

Grant's decision led to a series of frontal attacks utilizing the Union's advantages in manpower and equipment, but this led to high casualties.

MOBILE BAY, 1864 This image by Currier and Ives portrays a famous naval battle at the entrance to Mobile Bay between a Union sloop-of-war, the USS Richmond, part of a fleet commanded by Admiral David Farragut, and a Confederate ironclad, the CSS Tennessee. Although Confederate mines were scattered across the entrance to the harbor, Farragut ordered his ships into battle with the memorable command "Damn the torpedoes! Full speed ahead!" The Union forces defeated the Confederate flotilla and three weeks later captured the forts defending the harbor—thus removing from Confederate control the last port on the Gulf Coast available to the blockade runners who were attempting to supply the South's war needs.

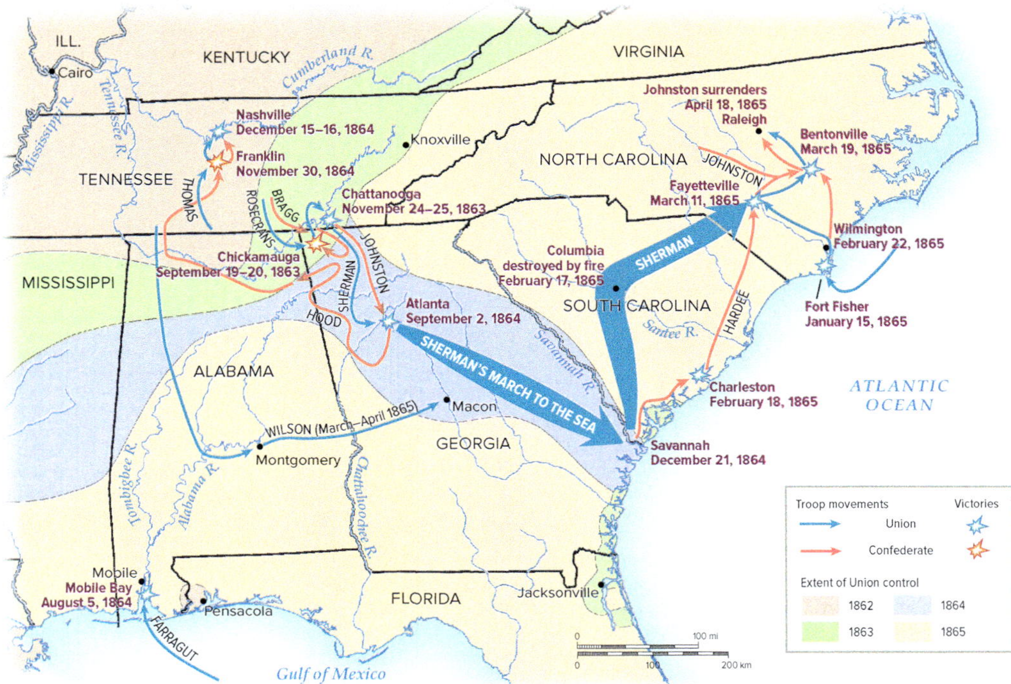

SHERMAN'S MARCH TO THE SEA, 1864–1865 While Grant was wearing Lee down in Virginia, General William Tecumseh Sherman was moving east across Georgia. After a series of battles in Tennessee and northwest Georgia, Sherman captured Atlanta and then marched unimpeded to Savannah, on the Georgia coast—deliberately devastating the towns and plantations through which his troops marched. Note that after capturing Savannah by Christmas 1864, Sherman began moving north through the Carolinas. A few days after Lee surrendered to Grant at Appomattox, Confederate forces farther south surrendered to Sherman.

What did Sherman believe his devastating March to the Sea would accomplish?

Discussion and Activities

Evaluating Evidence Have students examine the image "Mobile Bay, 1864." Have them discuss in pairs or small groups how the image demonstrates advances in naval technology and Union naval superiority. *(Ironclads, built by Union industry, helped to blockade Southern ports. Most of the navy had remained loyal to the Union at the outbreak of the war.)* **WXT** **PCE** **ARC**

Answers

Sherman's March to the Sea, 1864–1865

Sherman believed his march would deprive the South of the resources they needed to fight and undermine their will to continue.

Historical Thinking Skills

Argumentation Have students read the section "Capture of Atlanta." Have them discuss in pairs or small groups what political consequences this Union victory had. *(This victory silenced much anti-war talk in the North and united the Republican Party behind Lincoln, contributing to Lincoln's reelection in 1864.)* **PCE**

House, in which 12,000 Union troops and a large but unknown number of Confederates died or were wounded. Despite the enormous losses, Grant kept moving. But victory continued to elude him.

Lee kept his army between Grant and the Confederate capital and on June 1–3 repulsed the Union forces again, just northeast of Richmond, at Cold Harbor. The month-long Wilderness campaign had cost Grant 55,000 men (killed, wounded, and captured) to Lee's 31,000. And Richmond still had not fallen.

Grant now changed his strategy. He moved his army east of Richmond, bypassing the capital altogether, and headed south toward the railroad center at Petersburg. If he could seize Petersburg, he could cut off the capital's communications with the rest of the Confederacy. But Petersburg had strong defenses; and once Lee came to the city's relief, the assault became a prolonged siege, which lasted nine months.

CAPTURE OF ATLANTA

In Georgia, meanwhile, Sherman was facing less ferocious resistance. With 90,000 men, he confronted Confederate forces of 60,000 under Johnston, who was unwilling to risk a direct engagement. As Sherman advanced, Johnston tried to delay him by maneuvering. The two armies fought only one real battle—at Kennesaw Mountain, northwest of Atlanta, on June 27—where Johnston scored an impressive victory. Even so, he was unable to stop the Union advance toward Atlanta. President Davis replaced Johnston with the combative John B. Hood, who twice daringly attacked Sherman's army but accomplished nothing except seriously weakening his own forces. Sherman took Atlanta on September 2. News of the victory electrified the North and helped unite the previously divided Republican Party behind President Lincoln.

A young Union drummer boy, William Bircher, left an account of the burning of Atlanta. "At night we destroyed the city by fire," he wrote. "A grand and awful spectacle it presented to the beholder. . . . The heaven was one expanse of lurid fire; the air was filled with flying, burning cinders. Buildings, covering two hundred acres, were in ruins or in flames; every instant there was the sharp detonation of the smothered booming sound of exploding shells and powder concealed in the buildings, and then the sparks and flames would shoot up into the black and red roof. . . . I heard the real fine band of the Thirty-third Massachusetts playing, 'John Brown's soul goes marching on.'"

Hood now tried unsuccessfully to draw Sherman out of Atlanta by moving back up through Tennessee and threatening an invasion of the North. Sherman did not take the bait. But he did send Union troops to reinforce Nashville. In the Battle of Nashville, on December 15–16, 1864, Northern forces practically destroyed what was left of Hood's army.

MARCH TO THE SEA

Meanwhile, Sherman had left Atlanta to begin his soon-to-be-famous March to the Sea. Living off the land, destroying supplies it could not use, his army cut a sixty-mile-wide swath of desolation across Georgia. "War is all hell," Sherman had once said. By that he meant not that war is a terrible thing to be avoided, but that it should be made as horrible and costly as possible for the opponent. He sought not only to deprive the Confederate army of war materials and railroad communications but also to break the will of the Southern people, by burning towns and plantations along his route. By December 20, he had reached Savannah, which surrendered two days later. Sherman offered it to President Lincoln as a Christmas gift. Early in 1865, having left Savannah largely undamaged, Sherman continued his destructive march northward through South Carolina. He was virtually unopposed until he was well inside North Carolina, where a small force under Johnston could do no more than cause a brief delay.

In April 1865, Grant's Army of the Potomac—still engaged in the prolonged siege at Petersburg—finally captured a vital railroad junction southwest of the town. Without rail access to the South, cut off from other Confederate forces, Lee could no

A LETTER FROM THE FRONT Charles Wellington Reed, a nineteen-year-old Union soldier who was also a talented artist, sent illustrated letters to the members of his family throughout the war. In this 1863 letter to his mother, he portrays the Ninth Massachusetts Battery leaving Centreville, Virginia, on its way to Gettysburg. Two weeks later, Reed fought in the famous battle and eventually received the Congressional Medal of Honor for his bravery there. "Such a shrieking, hissing, seathing I never dreamed was imaginable," he wrote of the fighting at the time.

Discussion and Activities

Analyzing Issues Have students read the section "March to the Sea." Ask them to write a letter to President Lincoln either praising or condemning this action. **PCE**

longer hope to defend Richmond. With the remnant of his army, now about 25,000 men, Lee began moving west in the forlorn hope of finding a way around the Union forces so that he could head south and link up with Johnston in North Carolina. But the Union army pursued him and blocked his escape route. Finally recognizing that further bloodshed was futile, Lee arranged to meet Grant at a private home in the small town of Appomattox Court House, Virginia. There, on April 9, he surrendered what was left of his forces. Nine days later, near Durham, North Carolina, Johnston surrendered to Sherman.

Appomattox Court House

In military terms, at least, the long war was now effectively over, even though Jefferson Davis refused to accept defeat. He fled south from Richmond and was finally captured in Georgia. A few Southern diehards continued to fight, but even their resistance collapsed before long. Well before the last shot was fired, the difficult process of reuniting the shattered nation had begun.

The war ensured the permanence of the Union, but many other issues remained far from settled. What would happen to the freedmen (the term used for enslaved people who were now liberated)? Could the South and the North reconcile? Would the massive industrial growth in the North during the Civil War spread to the South, or would the South remain an agrarian region with much less wealth than in the North? The end of the war was the beginning of more than a generation of struggle to determine the legacy of the Civil War.

The North's victory was not just a military one. The war strengthened the North's economy, giving a spur to industry and railroad development. It greatly weakened the South's economy, by destroying millions of dollars of property and depleting the region's young male population. Southerners had gone to war in part because of their fears of growing Northern dominance. The war itself, ironically, confirmed and strengthened that dominance. There was no doubt by 1865 that the future of the United States lay in the growth of industry and commerce, which would occur for many years primarily outside the South.

Impact of the North's Victory

But most of all, the Civil War was a victory for the millions of enslaved people, over whose plight the conflict had largely begun in the first place. The war produced Abraham Lincoln's epochal Emancipation Proclamation and, later, the Thirteenth Amendment to the Constitution, which abolished slavery. It also encouraged hundreds of thousands of enslaved people to free themselves, to desert their slaveholders and seek refuge behind Union lines–at times to fight in the Union armies. The future of the freed African Americans was not to be without challenges and hardships, but 3.5 million people who had once lived in bondage emerged from the war as free men and women.

Discussion and Activities

Analyzing Points of View After students have read the section "Appomattox Court House," ask them to write a short journal entry from the point of view of a Union or Confederate soldier who witnessed Lee's surrender. **PCE**

Discussion and Activities

Analyzing Significance Have students read the section "Impact of the North's Victory." Ask them to create a list of effects of the Union victory and rank them in order of importance. Have students write a thesis statement that makes a claim about the most important effects of the Civil War. **PCE** **NAT** **ARC** **WXT** **SOC**

Discussion and Activities

Analyzing Issues Divide students into three groups to research the political, economic, and social effects of the Civil War. Ask each group to review the chapter and go online to find supporting information about their assigned topic. Then form groups of three, including one student from each of the original three groups, to share what they learned about their topics. **PCE** **ARC** **NAT** **SOC** **WXT**

Key Terms

Students should be familiar with the key terms and be able to define them in the context of the causes of the Civil War, the failure of pre-war attempts at compromise, and the political, economic, and social effects of the war. Encourage students to use these terms in performing review exercises and exam practice for this chapter.

CHAPTER 14 REVIEW

CONNECTING THEMES

Chapter Fourteen explored the causes of the Civil War and the failure of compromise. The war had a major and lasting impact on the social, political, and economic institutions of both the North and the South. Each side had significant, though different, advantages. But neither accurately predicted the length or toll of the war, which was the most devastating in U.S. history.

The Emancipation Proclamation led the North to recruit black soldiers and hindered the efforts of the South to gain recognition from Britain. The Proclamation also established a second overriding war aim beyond reunion and led to the ratification in 1865 of the Thirteenth Amendment, which abolished the institution of slavery. Yet African Americans would continue to face great challenges in both the South and the North for many years to come, and several of those challenges exist to this day.

The roles and responsibilities of women changed during and after the war as more entered the field of nursing and the workforce, often out of necessity. The decimation of the male population in the South further expanded the number of acceptable roles for Southern women after the war. Women in both the North and the South found more independence and sought opportunities to win support for other goals such as suffrage.

The Civil War accelerated industrial growth and railroad development in the North. The belief in the South that "King Cotton" was vital to the European textile industries proved unfounded. With no access to Northern or international markets, the Southern economy suffered greatly during the war. The South also experienced widespread physical destruction and an immense cost in human life, which devastated the region for decades. Ultimately, the growth of industry and commerce was concentrated in the North after the Civil War.

You should consider the following questions as you review the themes for this chapter:

- How did the idea of American identity, particularly for African Americans, change during and after the Civil War?
- What role did the differences in regional economic systems play in the causes and outcomes of the Civil War?
- How did the Civil War affect the social, political, and economic institutions of both the North and the South?
- In what ways did the Civil War alter existing labor systems?
- How was the population of the United States affected by the Civil War and by nineteenth century immigration?
- What political changes were brought about by the Northern victory in the Civil War?
- How was Southern infrastructure affected by the Civil War?
- How did the Civil War alter perceptions of government and democratic ideals?

KEY TERMS

Abraham Lincoln 385
Antietam 409
Appomattox Court House 415
Bull Run 406
Clara Barton 396
Emancipation Proclamation 392
Fort Sumter 385
George B. McClellan 407
Gettysburg 411
Gettysburg Address 394
greenbacks 387
Homestead Act 387
Jefferson Davis 397
March to the Sea 414
Morrill Land Grant Act 387
Robert E. Lee 400
Shiloh 406
Thomas "Stonewall" Jackson 409
Ulysses S. Grant 412
U.S. Sanitary Commission 396
William Tecumseh Sherman 412

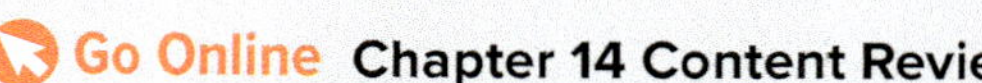

Assessing Student Understanding Use the online assessment to assess student understanding of concepts and topics within the chapter. You can assign the ready-made Chapter 14 Content Review or create your own from available questions. This easy-to-use tool helps you design assessments that meet the needs of different types of learners.

AP EXAM PRACTICE

Questions assume cumulative content knowledge from this chapter and previous chapters.

MULTIPLE CHOICE

Use the excerpt from the Gettysburg Address on page 394 and your knowledge of U.S. history to answer questions 1-3.

1. What foundational document does Lincoln reference in the introductory sentence?
   (A) the Olive Branch Petition
   (B) the Declaration of Independence
   (C) the Constitution
   (D) the Bill of Rights
2. Earlier in 1863, the "New Birth of Freedom" that Lincoln referenced was supported by
   (A) the treaty between the Confederacy and Great Britain.
   (B) the ratification of the Thirteenth Amendment.
   (C) the issuance of the Emancipation Proclamation.
   (D) the declaration of the draft.
3. What was a unique feature of the Battle of Gettysburg?
   (A) It was fought completely on the water.
   (B) It was the first battle in which African American troops saw front line combat.
   (C) It convinced several European nations to aid the Confederacy.
   (D) It was the last time the Confederates threatened Northern territory.

SHORT ANSWER

Use your knowledge of U.S. history to answer questions 4 and 5.

4. Use the image of the draft riot on page 390 to answer A, B, and C.
   (A) Describe ONE historical context illustrated by the image.
   (B) Briefly explain ONE specific historical cause that led to the New York draft riots during the Civil War.
   (C) Briefly explain ONE specific historical effect that resulted from the New York draft riots during the Civil War.
5. Answer A, B, and C.
   (A) Briefly describe ONE specific historical difference between the border and seceding states in the South at the beginning of the Civil War.
   (B) Briefly describe ONE specific historical similarity between border and seceding states in the South at the start of the Civil War.
   (C) Briefly explain ONE specific historical effect that resulted from the border states remaining in the Union during the Civil War.

LONG ESSAY

Develop a thoughtful and thorough historical argument that addresses the statement. Begin your essay with a thesis statement, and support it with specific historical evidence and examples.

6. Evaluate the extent of similarities between the North and the South at the beginning of the Civil War.

Answers

Multiple Choice

1. B; **2.** C; **3.** D

Short Answer

4A) Possible response: The notion that all Northerners were strong abolitionists and all Southerners supported slavery is too simplistic. As the image depicts, not all Northerners supported the war effort. The New York race riots showed the complexity of the issues of the Civil War. Northerners, particularly Irish laborers, believed that the war drove African Americans north, causing competition for jobs.

4B) Possible response: One similarity between the North and the South during the war was the belief held by many that it was a "rich man's war and a poor man's fight." Both the North and the South had provisions in place that exempted wealthy individuals from having to enlist. This caused resentment on the part of the poor toward the rich in both regions, leading to outbreaks of violence like the New York draft riots.

4C) Possible response: The need for manpower forced the Union, despite opposition by some of its leaders, to institute a draft and allow African Americans the ability to enlist in the military. The policy of allowing wealthy individuals the opportunity to pay for a substitute for draft selection caused great animosity between the rich and poor during the Civil War.

5A) Possible response: The border states opted to stay within the Union, although some were forced and compelled through military force to do so. The seceding states did so by choice.

5B) Possible response: States in the Upper South, representing the border states, had constitutional and legal protections for the institution of slavery, as did the seceding states.

5C) Tensions remained high in the border states, as some were forced to remain in the Union through military force. Kentucky was viewed as an essential resource for the food that it could provide the Union army, as well as the fact that it also housed a cannon factory.

Answers

Long Essay

6. Possible thesis: The North had serious economic, military, and tactical advantages over the South at the start of the Civil War. These advantages gave the North confidence, leading them to believe the war would be over quickly. However, there were more similarities than differences between the two regions. Both sides believed their causes were just, and both sides also believed that loyalty from their respective populations would provide the resources necessary to end the war quickly and decisively. Similarities: Both the North and the South believed they were waging a war for the survival of their respective cultures. Both believed they would win the war fairly quickly, and both believed they had God on their side. Both sides believed they had the loyalty and support from their respective populations in a way that would give them military superiority. Differences: The North's advantages included a greater population, railroads, and factories. The South's advantages included skilled fighters, strong leadership, and the fact that they only had to defend their territory, not invade new territory. Southerners also believed that Europe would intervene on their behalf, as many European textile factories relied heavily upon Southern cotton.

Pacing Guide

Chapter 15 explores key concepts from Period 5: 1844–1877 of the AP U.S. History Curriculum Framework. The suggested instruction time for Chapter 15 is 6 days.

Key Concepts

5.3.I The North's greater manpower and industrial resources, the leadership of Abraham Lincoln and others, and the decision to emancipate slaves eventually led to the Union military victory over the Confederacy in the devastating Civil War.

5.3.II Reconstruction and the Civil War ended slavery, altered relationships between the states and the federal government, and led to debates over new definitions of citizenship, particularly regarding the rights of African Americans, women, and other minorities.

15 RECONSTRUCTION AND THE NEW SOUTH

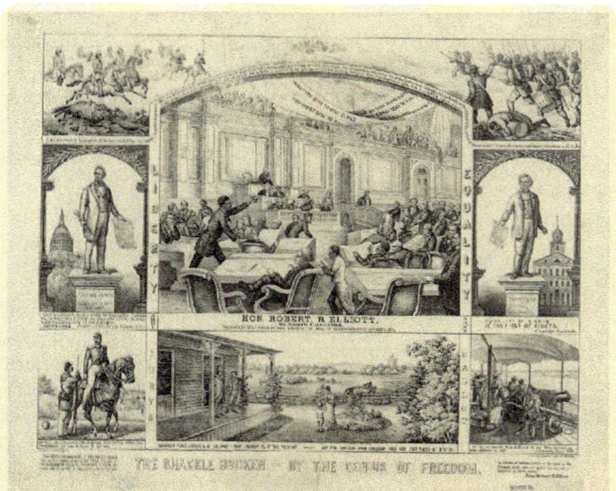

THE GENIUS OF FREEDOM
This 1874 lithograph portrays a series of important moments in the history of African Americans in the South during Reconstruction—among them the participation of African American soldiers in the Civil War, a speech by an African American representative in the North Carolina legislature, and the movement of formerly enslaved African Americans into a system of free labor. It also portrays some of the white leaders (among them Lincoln and Charles Sumner) who had promoted the cause of the freedmen.

CONNECTING CONCEPTS

Chapter Fifteen begins by examining the impact of the Civil War and the tremendous challenge of rebuilding the Union. The terms that would allow Southern states to rejoin the Union had significant implications for both Republicans and Democrats. Reconstruction would also alter the relationship and balance of power between the three branches of the federal government.

President Lincoln and Congress had differing ideas about Reconstruction. Lincoln proposed a swift and lenient plan that he believed would result in rapid reunification. Radical Republicans, however, wanted to punish the South for imposing a devastating war on the nation. After the assassination of Lincoln, President Johnson implemented a plan for "Restoration" that the Radicals in Congress rejected. They then tried to remove Johnson via impeachment and instituted Radical Reconstruction, which divided the South into military regions overseen by federal troops. It ended after the election of 1876 and the Compromise of 1877 placed President Hayes in the White House.

Southern states resisted Reconstruction from the start. Through violence and intimidation of African Americans by secret societies like the Ku Klux Klan, Southern whites retained or regained a majority of the electorate. Southern legislatures also passed Black Codes and Jim Crow laws, which perpetrated a system of segregation and eliminated most of the modest and hard-won social, economic, and political gains made by African Americans in the late 1800s. In *Plessy* v. *Ferguson*, the Supreme Court upheld the widespread practice of racial segregation reinforced by Jim Crow laws.

Reasoning Processes

Continuity and Change Have students examine the image "The Genius of Freedom." Ask them to list and discuss details that provide evidence of change over time. *(Union leaders, not Confederate ones, are portrayed. African Americans are portrayed in the role of legislators, as well as in the roles of voting and serving on juries.)* **SOC**

As you read, you should:

- Analyze how the abolition of slavery led to a reshaping of cultural identities and new concepts of citizenship.
- Identify how the Civil War created a stronger sense of nationalism.
- Evaluate how Jim Crow laws, segregation, and rulings by the U.S. Supreme Court stripped the rights granted to African Americans by the Thirteenth, Fourteenth, and Fifteenth Amendments to the Constitution.
- Analyze the effects of Reconstruction on social and economic patterns in the South.
- Explain how Reconstruction affected the balance of power between the legislative and executive branches.
- Identify the Constitutional changes brought about by the Civil War and Reconstruction for women and African Americas.

THE PROBLEMS OF PEACEMAKING

In 1865, as it became clear that the war was almost over, no one in Washington had yet formed a plan for what would happen to the defeated South. Lincoln could not negotiate a treaty with the Confederate government; he continued to insist that the Confederate government had no legal right to exist. Yet neither could he simply readmit the Southern states into the Union as if nothing had happened.

THE AFTERMATH OF WAR AND EMANCIPATION

The Civil War was a catastrophe for the South with no parallel in America's experience as a nation. Towns had been gutted, plantations burned, fields neglected, bridges and railroads destroyed. Many white Southerners, stripped of their enslaved laborers through emancipation and stripped of the capital they had invested in now-worthless Confederate bonds and currency, had almost no personal property. Many families had to rebuild their fortunes without the help of adult males, massive numbers of whom had died in the war. Some white Southerners faced starvation and homelessness.

THE DEVASTATED SOUTH

The more than 258,000 Confederate soldiers who had died in the war constituted over 20 percent of the adult white male population of the region; thousands more returned home wounded or sick. Almost all surviving white Southerners had lost people close to them in the fighting. A cult of ritualized mourning developed throughout the region in the late 1860s, particularly among white women–many of whom wore mourning clothes (and jewelry) for two years or longer. At the same time, white Southerners began to romanticize the "Lost Cause" and its leaders, and to look back nostalgically at the South as it had existed before the terrible disruptions of war. Such Confederate heroes as Robert E. Lee, Stonewall Jackson, and (later) Jefferson Davis were treated with extraordinary reverence, almost as religious figures. Communities throughout the South built elaborate monuments in town squares to commemorate their war dead. The tremendous sense of loss that pervaded the white South reinforced the determination of many white people to protect what remained of their now-vanished world.

MYTH OF THE "LOST CAUSE"

If conditions were bad for many white Southerners, they were worse for most black Southerners–the 4 million men and women emerging from bondage. Some of them had also seen service during the war–as servants to Confederate officers or as teamsters and laborers for the Southern armies. Nearly 200,000 had fought for the Union, and 38,000 had died. Others had worked as spies or scouts for Union forces in the South. Many more had flocked to the Union lines to escape slavery. Even before Emancipation, thousands of enslaved people in many parts of the South had taken advantage of wartime disruptions to leave slaveholders and move off in search of freedom. As soon as the war ended, hundreds of thousands more former enslaved people–young and old, healthy and sick–left their plantations. Some went in search of family members who had been sold by their former slaveholders. But many others had nowhere to go. Some trudged to the nearest town or city, roamed the countryside camping at night on the bare ground, or gathered around Union occupation forces, hoping for assistance. Virtually none owned any land or property. Most had no possessions except the clothes they wore.

In 1865, in short, Southern society was in vast disarray. Men and women, regardless of race, faced a future of great uncertainty. Yet all Southerners faced this future with some very clear aspirations. For both African Americans and white people, Reconstruction became a struggle to define the meaning of freedom. But the former enslaved people and the defeated white people had very different conceptions of what freedom meant.

Historical Thinking Skills

Contextualization Have students read the section "The Devastated South." Ask them to consider and discuss why the South suffered so much more damage as a result of the Civil War than the North did. *(Because of Southern and Northern strategy, almost of all the actual fighting took place in the South. Late in the conflict, the Union adopted a strategy of total war, which led to great devastation—for example, during Sherman's March to the Sea. The Union Navy successfully blockaded Southern ports, denying access to supplies.)* **PCE**

Go Online AP Exam Preparation

AP Exam Practice Use the online assessment to help prepare students for the AP Exam. You can assign the ready-made AP-style short-answer questions, document-based questions, and multiple-choice questions assessing concepts, themes, and skills from Period 5 and AP-style long-essay questions organized in sets of 3 questions from various time periods. You can also create your own tests from available questions. This easy-to-use tool helps you design assessments that meet the needs of different types of learners.

Reasoning Processes

Comparing After students have read the section "Myth of the 'Lost Cause'," ask them to create a Venn diagram comparing the toll of the Civil War on African American and white Southerners. Have students discuss upon which group they believe the costs weighed more heavily. **PCE** **WXT** **SOC**

RICHMOND, 1865 By the time Union forces captured Richmond in early 1865, the Confederate capital had been under siege for months and much of the city lay in ruins, as this photograph reveals. On April 4, President Lincoln, accompanied by his son Tad, visited Richmond. As he walked through the streets of the shattered city, hundreds of former enslaved people emerged from the rubble to watch him pass. "No triumphal march of a conqueror could have equalled in moral sublimity the humble manner in which he entered Richmond," a black soldier serving with the Union army wrote. "It was a great deliverer among the delivered. No wonder tears came to his eyes."

The Library of Congress

Competing Notions of Freedom

For African Americans, freedom meant above all an end to slavery and to all the injustices and humiliation they associated with it. But it also meant the acquisition of rights and protections that would allow them to live as free men and women in the same way white people did. "If I cannot do like a white man," one African American man told his former slaveholder, "I am not free."

African Americans differed with one another on how to achieve that freedom. Some demanded a redistribution of economic resources, especially land, because, as a convention of Alabama freedmen put it in a formal resolution, "The property which they hold was nearly all earned by the sweat of our brows." Others asked simply for legal equality, confident that given the same opportunities as white citizens they could advance successfully in American society. But whatever their particular demands, virtually all former enslaved people were united in their desire for independence from white control. Freed from slavery, African Americans throughout the South began almost immediately to create autonomous communities. They pulled out of white-controlled churches and established their own. They created fraternal, benevolent, and mutual-aid societies. When they could, they began their own schools.

For most white Southerners, freedom meant something very different. It meant the ability to control their own destinies without interference from the North or the federal government. And in the immediate aftermath of the war, they attempted to exercise this version of freedom by trying to restore their society to its antebellum form. Slavery had been abolished in the former Confederacy by the Emancipation Proclamation, and everywhere else (as of December 1865) by the Thirteenth Amendment. But many white planters continued a kind of slavery in an altered form by keeping black workers legally tied to the plantations. When many white Southerners fought for what they considered freedom, they were fighting above all to preserve local and regional autonomy and white supremacy.

The federal government kept troops in the South after the war to preserve order and protect the freedmen. In March 1865, Congress established the Freedmen's Bureau, an agency of the army directed by General Oliver O. Howard. The Freedmen's Bureau distributed food to millions of for-

THE FREEDMEN'S BUREAU

Discussion and Activities

Analyzing Points of View Have students examine the image "Richmond, 1865." Ask them to consider and discuss the reaction the publication of this image would have created in both the North and the South. As a class, discuss how these different reactions might have affected efforts to heal divisions between the regions. **PCE** **ARC**

Historical Thinking Skills

Argumentation After students have read the section "Competing Notions of Freedom," ask them to write a short paragraph explaining how the ideas of freedom differed for African American and white Southerners, and what compromise, if any, could be found to reconcile the differences. SOC PCE ARC

A MONUMENT TO THE "LOST CAUSE" This monument in the town square of Monroe, Georgia, was typical of many such memorials erected all across the South after the Civil War. They served both to commemorate the Confederate dead and to remind white Southerners of what was by the 1870s already widely known and romanticized as the "Lost Cause."

A FREEDMEN'S BUREAU SCHOOL African American students and teachers stand outside a school for former enslaved people, one of many run by the Freedmen's Bureau throughout the defeated Confederacy in the first years after the war.

mer enslaved people. It established schools staffed by missionaries and teachers who had been sent to the South by Freedmen's Aid Societies and other private and church groups in the North. It made modest efforts to settle African Americans on lands of their own. (The bureau also offered considerable assistance to poor white people, many of whom were similarly destitute and homeless after the war.) But the Freedmen's Bureau was not a permanent solution. It had authority to operate for only one year; and in any case it was far too small to deal effectively with the enormous problems facing Southern society. By the time the war ended, other proposals for reconstructing the defeated South were emerging.

ISSUES OF RECONSTRUCTION

Reconstruction was determined not just by social realities or ideals. It was also determined by partisan politics. The terms by which the Southern states rejoined the Union had important implications for both major political parties. The Republican victories in 1860 and 1864 had been a result in large part of the division of the Democratic Party and, later, the removal of the South from the electorate. Readmitting the South, leaders of both parties believed, would reunite the Democrats and weaken the Republicans. In addition, the Republican Party had taken advantage of the South's absence from Congress to pass a program of nationalistic economic legislation–railroad subsidies, protective tariffs, banking and currency reforms, and other measures to benefit Northern business leaders and industrialists. Should the Democratic Party regain power with heavy Southern support, these programs would be in jeopardy. Complicating these practical questions were emotional concerns. Many Northerners believed the South should be punished in some way for the suffering and sacrifice its rebellion had caused. Many Northerners believed, too, that the South should be transformed, made over in the North's urbanized image–its supposedly backward, feudal, undemocratic society civilized and modernized.

Even among the Republicans in Congress, there was considerable disagreement about the proper approach to Reconstruction–disagreement that reflected the same factional divisions that had created disputes over emancipation during the war. Conservatives insisted that the South accept the abolition of slavery, but proposed few other conditions for the readmission of the seceded states. The Radicals, led by Representative Thaddeus Stevens of Pennsylvania and Senator Charles Sumner of Massachusetts, urged that the civil and military leaders of the Confederacy be punished, that large numbers of white Southerners be disenfranchised, that the legal rights of former enslaved people be protected, and that the property of wealthy white Southerners who had aided the Confederacy be confiscated and distributed among the freedmen. Some Radicals favored granting suffrage to the former enslaved people. Others hesitated, since few Northern states permitted African Americans to vote. Between the Radicals and the Conservatives stood a faction of uncommitted Republicans, the Moderates, who rejected the punitive goals of the Radicals but supported extracting at least some concessions from the South on African American rights.

CONSERVATIVE AND RADICAL REPUBLICANS

Historical Thinking Skills

Argumentation Have students read the section "Issues of Reconstruction." Ask students to list the issues and then rank them in order of importance. Discuss as a class which issues students believe were the most difficult to resolve. PCE SOC

Reasoning Processes

Comparing After students read the section "Plans for Reconstruction," have them create a T-chart listing the provisions of each plan and identifying which parts of each plan were similar or different. As a class, discuss which plan seems more practical and which seems to be the most effective. **SOC** **NAT**

PLANS FOR RECONSTRUCTION

President Lincoln's sympathies lay with the Moderates and Conservatives of his party. He believed that a lenient Reconstruction policy would encourage Southern unionists and other former Whigs to join the Republican Party and would thus prevent the readmission of the South from strengthening the Democrats. More immediately, the Southern unionists could become the nucleus of new, loyal state governments in the South. Lincoln was not uninterested in the fate of the freedmen, but he was willing to defer questions about their future for the sake of rapid reunification.

LINCOLN'S 10% PLAN

Lincoln's Reconstruction plan, which he announced in December 1863, offered a general amnesty to white Southerners–other than high officials of the Confederacy–who would pledge loyalty to the government and accept the elimination of slavery. Whenever 10 percent of the number of voters in 1860 took the oath in any state, those loyal voters could set up a state government. Lincoln also hoped to extend suffrage to African Americans who were educated, owned property, and had served in the Union army. Three Southern states–Louisiana, Arkansas, and Tennessee, all under Union occupation–reestablished loyal governments under the Lincoln formula in 1864.

WADE-DAVIS BILL

The Radical Republicans were astonished at the mildness of Lincoln's program. They persuaded Congress to deny seats to representatives from the three "reconstructed" states and refused to count the electoral vote of those states in the election of 1864. But for the moment, the Radicals were uncertain about what form their own Reconstruction plan should take. Their first effort to resolve that question was the Wade-Davis Bill, passed by Congress in July 1864. It authorized the president to appoint a provisional governor for each conquered state. When a majority (not Lincoln's 10 percent) of the white males of the state pledged their allegiance to the Union, the governor could summon a state constitutional convention, whose delegates were to be elected by those who would swear (through the so-called Ironclad Oath) that they had never borne arms against the United States–another departure from Lincoln's plan. The new state constitutions would have to abolish slavery, disenfranchise Confederate civil and military leaders, and repudiate debts accumulated by the state governments during the war. After a state had met these conditions, Congress would readmit it to the Union. Like the president's proposal, the Wade-Davis Bill left up to the states the question of political rights for African Americans. Congress passed the bill a few days before it adjourned in 1864, and Lincoln disposed of it with a pocket veto. His action enraged the Radical leaders, and the pragmatic Lincoln became convinced he would have to accept at least some of the Radical demands. He began to move toward a new approach to Reconstruction.

THE DEATH OF LINCOLN

What plan Lincoln might have produced no one can say. On the night of April 14, 1865, the president and his wife attended a play at Ford's Theater in Washington. As they sat in the presidential box, John Wilkes Booth, a member of a distinguished family of actors and a zealous advocate of the Southern cause, entered the box from the rear and shot Lincoln in the head. The president was carried unconscious to a house across the street, where early the next morning, surrounded by family, friends, and political associates (among them a tearful Charles Sumner), he died.

The circumstances of Lincoln's death earned him immediate martyrdom. It also produced something close to hysteria throughout the North. There were accusations that Booth had acted as part of a great conspiracy–accusations that contained some truth. Booth did indeed have associates, one of whom stabbed and wounded Secretary of State Seward the night of the assassination, another of whom abandoned at the last moment a plan to murder Vice President Johnson. Booth himself escaped on horseback into the Virginia countryside, where, on April 26, he was cornered by Union troops and shot to death in a blazing barn. A military tribunal convicted eight other people of participating in the conspiracy (at least two of them on the basis of virtually no evidence). Four were hanged.

ABRAHAM LINCOLN This haunting photograph of Abraham Lincoln, showing clearly the weariness and aging that four years as a war president had created, was taken in Washington only four days before his assassination in 1865.

Discussion and Activities

Analyzing Issues Have students read the section "Wade-Davis Bill." Ask them to discuss in pairs or small groups why the provisions of the bill would have been difficult for Southern states to implement. *(The bill required over 50% of Southern males to swear allegiance to the Union, and the electors of the constitutional conventions would have to swear they had never borne arms against the United States. These requirements would have been difficult to meet if those affected were truthful.)* **PCE**

To many Northerners, however, the murder of the president seemed evidence of an even greater conspiracy—one masterminded and directed by the unrepentant leaders of the defeated South. Militant Republicans exploited such suspicions relentlessly for months, ensuring that Lincoln's death would help doom his plans for a relatively easy peace.

JOHNSON AND "RESTORATION"

Leadership of the Moderates and Conservatives fell to Lincoln's successor, Andrew Johnson, who was not well suited, by either circumstance or personality, for the task. A Democrat until he had joined the Union ticket with Lincoln in 1864, he became a Republican president at a moment when partisan passions were growing. Johnson himself was an intemperate and tactless man, filled with resentments and insecurities. He was also openly hostile to the freed African Americans and unwilling to support any plans that guaranteed them civil equality or enfranchisement. He once declared, "White men alone must manage the South."

ANDREW JOHNSON'S PERSONALITY

Johnson revealed his plan for Reconstruction—or "Restoration," as he preferred to call it—soon after he took office, and he implemented it during the summer of 1865, when Congress was in recess. Like Lincoln, he offered amnesty to those Southerners who would take an oath of allegiance. (High-ranking Confederate officials and any white Southerner with land worth $20,000 or more would have to apply to the president for individual pardons. Johnson, a self-made man, apparently liked the thought of the great planter aristocrats humbling themselves before him.) In most other respects, however, his plan resembled that of the Wade-Davis Bill. For each state, the president appointed a provisional governor, who was to invite qualified voters to elect delegates to a constitutional convention. Johnson did not specify how many qualified voters were necessary, but he implied that he would require a majority (as had the Wade-Davis Bill). In order to win readmission to Congress, a state had to revoke its ordinance of secession, abolish slavery, ratify the Thirteenth Amendment, and repudiate the Confederate and state war debts. The final procedure before restoration was for a state to elect a state government and send representatives to Congress.

Whereas Johnson helped white Southerners to return to their land, he did little in support of former enslaved people. Although freedmen had been given their liberty, holding on to it proved difficult. Many freedmen who returned to work for white planters found themselves almost enslaved people again. Johnson offered no help. "Are not our rights as a free people and good citizens of the United States to be considered?" asked a petition against the president. It was a long time before freedmen truly found liberty.

By the end of 1865, all the seceded states had formed new governments—some under Lincoln's plan, some under Johnson's—and were prepared to rejoin the Union as soon as Congress recognized them. But Radical Republicans vowed not to recognize the Johnson governments, just as they had previously refused to recognize the Lincoln regimes; for by now, Northern opinion had hardened and become more hostile toward the South than it had been a year earlier when Congress passed the Wade-Davis Bill. Many Northerners were disturbed by the apparent reluctance of some delegates to the Southern conventions to abolish slavery, and by the refusal of all the conventions to grant suffrage to any African Americans. They were astounded that states claiming to be "loyal" should elect prominent leaders of the recent Confederacy as state officials and representatives to Congress. Particularly hard to accept was Georgia's choice of Alexander H. Stephens, former Confederate vice president, as a United States senator.

NORTHERN ATTITUDES HARDEN

RADICAL RECONSTRUCTION

Reconstruction under Johnson's plan—often known as "presidential Reconstruction"—continued only until Congress reconvened in December 1865. At that point, Congress refused to seat the representatives of the "restored" states and created a new Joint Committee on Reconstruction to frame a Reconstruction policy of its own. The period of "congressional," or "Radical," Reconstruction had begun.

THE BLACK CODES

Meanwhile, events in the South were driving Northern opinion in more-radical directions. Throughout the South in 1865 and early 1866, state legislatures were enacting sets of laws known as the "Black Codes," designed to give white people substantial control over freed African Americans. The codes authorized local officials to apprehend unemployed African Americans, fine them for vagrancy, and hire them out to private employers to satisfy the fine. Some of the codes forbade African Americans to own or lease farms or to take any jobs other than as plantation workers or domestic servants.

Congress first responded to the Black Codes by passing an act extending the life of the Freedmen's Bureau and widening its powers so that it could nullify work agreements forced on freedmen under the Black Codes. Then, in April 1866, Congress passed the first Civil Rights Act, which declared African Americans to be citizens of the United States and gave the federal government power to intervene in state affairs to protect the rights of citizens. Johnson vetoed both bills, but Congress overrode him on each of them.

JOHNSON'S VETOES

THE FOURTEENTH AMENDMENT

In April 1866, the Joint Committee on Reconstruction proposed a new amendment to the Constitution, which Congress approved in early summer and sent to the states for ratification. Eventually, it became one of the most important provisions in the Constitution.

Discussion and Activities

Analyzing Points of View After students have read the section "The Death of Lincoln," ask them to write a journal entry from the point of view of a Northerner or Southerner capturing their thoughts and emotions upon hearing about the assassination of President Lincoln.

Reasoning Processes

Comparing Have students read the section "Johnson and 'Restoration'." Ask them to create a Venn diagram comparing Johnson's and Lincoln's plans for Reconstruction. Have students identify in what ways these plans were similar or different and write a short explanation for the similarities or differences. **PCE** **NAT**

Discussion and Activities

Making Connections After students have read the section "The Fourteenth Amendment," ask them to create a list of the provisions of this amendment. Have students discuss which of those provisions would have been most important at the time and which seem most important now. **SOC** **PCE** **NAT**

The Fourteenth Amendment offered the first constitutional definition of American citizenship: everyone born in the United States, and everyone naturalized, was automatically a citizen and entitled to all the "privileges and immunities" guaranteed by the Constitution, including equal protection of the laws by both the state and national governments. There could be no other requirements (for example, being a white person) for citizenship. The amendment also imposed penalties–reduction of representation in Congress and in the electoral college–on states that denied suffrage to any adult male inhabitants. (The wording reflected the prevailing view in Congress and elsewhere that the franchise was properly restricted to men.) Finally, it prohibited former members of Congress or other former federal officials who had aided the Confederacy from holding any state or federal office unless two-thirds of Congress voted to pardon them.

CITIZENSHIP FOR AFRICAN AMERICANS

Congressional Radicals offered to readmit to the Union any state whose legislature ratified the Fourteenth Amendment. Only Tennessee did so. All the other former Confederate states, along with Delaware and Kentucky, refused, leaving the amendment temporarily without the necessary approval of three-fourths of the states.

FOURTEENTH AMENDMENT Among its provisions, the Fourteenth Amendment provided the first constitutional definition of U.S. citizenship. Everyone born in the United States, and everyone naturalized, was automatically a citizen and entitled to all the "privileges and immunities" guaranteed by the Constitution, including equal protection of the laws by both the state and national governments. This amendment also imposed penalties on states that did not extend the right to vote to all male citizens, including African American men. African American women, like all women, had to wait until 1920 and the ratification of the Nineteenth Amendment before legally entitled to vote.

But by now, the Radicals were growing more confident and determined. Bloody race riots in New Orleans and other Southern cities–riots in which African Americans were the principal victims–were among the events that strengthened their hand. In the 1866 congressional elections, Johnson actively campaigned for Conservative candidates, but he did his own cause more harm than good with his intemperate speeches. The voters returned an overwhelming majority of Republicans, most of them Radicals, to Congress. In the Senate, there were now 42 Republicans to 11 Democrats; in the House, 143 Republicans to 49 Democrats. (The South remained largely unrepresented in both chambers.) Congressional Republicans were now strong enough to enact a plan of their own even over the president's objections.

THE CONGRESSIONAL PLAN

The Radicals passed three Reconstruction bills early in 1867 and overrode Johnson's vetoes of all of them. These bills finally established, nearly two years after the end of the war, a coherent plan for Reconstruction.

THREE RECONSTRUCTION BILLS

Under the congressional plan, Tennessee, which had ratified the Fourteenth Amendment, was promptly readmitted. But Congress rejected the Lincoln-Johnson governments of the other ten Confederate states and, instead, combined those states into five military districts. A military commander governed each district and had orders to register qualified voters (defined as all adult black males and those white males who had not participated in the rebellion). Once registered, voters would elect conventions to prepare new state constitutions, which had to include provisions for black suffrage. Once voters ratified the new constitutions, they could elect state governments. Congress had to approve a state's constitution, and the state legislature had to ratify the Fourteenth Amendment. Once that happened, and once enough states ratified the amendment to make it part of the Constitution, then the former Confederate states could be restored to the Union.

By 1868, seven of the ten former Confederate states (Arkansas, North Carolina, South Carolina, Louisiana, Alabama, Georgia, and Florida) had fulfilled these conditions (including ratification of the Fourteenth Amendment, which now became part of the Constitution). They were readmitted to the Union. Conservative white voters held up the return of Virginia and Texas until 1869 and Mississippi until 1870. By then, Congress had added one more requirement for readmission–ratification of another constitutional amendment, the Fifteenth, which forbade the states and the federal government to deny suffrage to any citizen on account of "race, color, or previous condition of servitude."

FIFTEENTH AMENDMENT

To stop the president from interfering with their plans, the congressional Radicals passed two remarkable laws of dubious

Discussion and Activities

Analyzing Issues After students have read the section "Fifteenth Amendment," ask them to think about whether this amendment was necessary and to share their thoughts with a partner. **PCE**

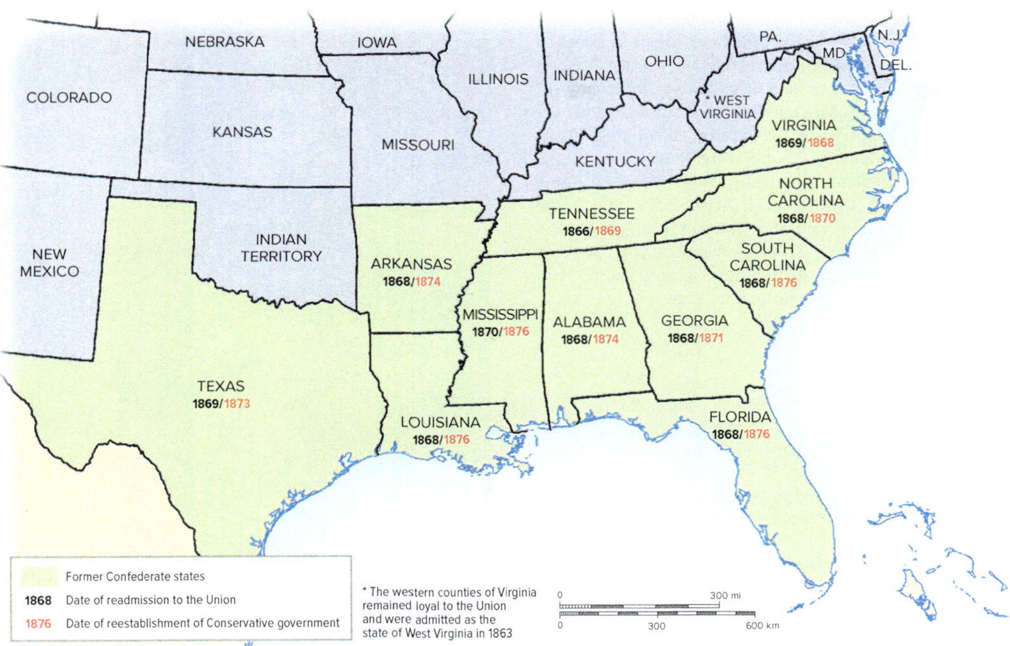

RECONSTRUCTION, 1866–1877 This map shows the former Confederate states and provides the date when each was readmitted to the Union as well as a subsequent date when each state managed to return political power to traditional white, conservative elites—a process white Southerners liked to call "redemption."

What had to happen for a state to be readmitted to the Union? What had to happen before a state could experience "redemption"?

constitutionality in 1867. One, the Tenure of Office Act, forbade the president to remove civil officials, including members of his own cabinet, without the consent of the Senate. The principal purpose of the law was to protect the job of Secretary of War Edwin M. Stanton, who was cooperating with the Radicals. The other law, the Command of the Army Act, prohibited the president from issuing military orders except through the commanding general of the army (General Grant), who could not be relieved or assigned elsewhere without the consent of the Senate.

The congressional Radicals also took action to stop the Supreme Court from interfering with their plans. In 1866, the Court had declared in the case of *Ex parte Milligan* that military tribunals were unconstitutional in places where civil courts were functioning, a decision that seemed to threaten the system of military government the Radicals were planning for the South. Radicals in Congress immediately proposed several bills that would require two-thirds of the justices to support any decision overruling a law of Congress, would deny the Court jurisdiction in Reconstruction cases, would reduce its membership to three, and would even abolish it. The justices apparently took notice. Over the next two years, the Court refused to accept jurisdiction in any cases involving Reconstruction (and the congressional bills concerning the Court never passed).

The Impeachment of the President

President Johnson had long since ceased to be a serious obstacle to the passage of Radical legislation, but he was still the official charged with administering the Reconstruction programs. As such, the Radicals believed, he remained a serious impediment to their plans. Early in 1867, they began looking for a way to impeach him and remove him from office. Republicans found grounds for impeachment, they believed, when Johnson dismissed Secretary of War Stanton despite Congress's refusal to agree, thus deliberately violating the Tenure of Office Act in hopes of testing the law before the courts. Elated Radicals in the House quickly impeached the president and sent the case to the Senate for trial. By that time, the

TENURE OF OFFICE ACT

Discussion and Activities

Historical Reasoning and Argumentation After students have read the section "The Congressional Plan," have them form small groups to create their own plans for Reconstruction. Their plans should address what rights formerly enslaved people should have and how they would be protected, and how states should be readmitted the Union. Ask for a representative from each group to share details of their group's plan with the class. PCE NAT ARC SOC WXT

Answers

Reconstruction, 1866–1877

For a state to be readmitted, it had to adopt a constitution that incorporated the Thirteenth, Fourteenth, and Fifteenth Amendments. For a state to experience "redemption," it had to restore state autonomy.

CHAPTER 15

Reconstruction and the New South

Historical Thinking Skills

Contextualization After students have read the section "The Impeachment of the President," ask them to discuss as a class who would have become president if Johnson had been removed from office. *(At the time, there was no Constitutional provision for the vice president to fill a presidential vacancy, so next in the line of succession would have been the Speaker of the House, a Radical Republican.)* **PCE**

Radicals were determined to impeach President Johnson. "Who does not know," said Benjamin Butler, an opponent of Johnson, "that from the hour [Johnson] began these, his usurpations of power, he everywhere denounced Congress, the legality and constitutionality of its action, and defied its legitimate power."

The trial before the Senate lasted throughout April and May 1868. The Radicals put heavy pressure on all the Republican senators, but the Moderates (who were losing faith in the Radical program) vacillated. On the first three charges to come to a vote, seven Republicans joined the Democrats and independents to support acquittal. The vote was 35 to 19, one short of the constitutionally required two-thirds majority. After that, the Radicals dropped the impeachment effort.

JOHNSON ACQUITTED

THE SOUTH IN RECONSTRUCTION

When white Southerners spoke bitterly in later years of the effects of Reconstruction, they referred most frequently to the governments Congress helped impose on them–governments they claimed were both incompetent and corrupt, that saddled the region with enormous debts, and that trampled on the rights of citizens. When black Southerners and their defenders condemned Reconstruction, in contrast, they spoke of the failure of the national and state governments to go far enough to guarantee freedmen even the most elemental rights of citizenship–a failure that resulted in a harsh new system of economic subordination.

The Reconstruction Governments

In the ten states of the South that were reorganized under the congressional plan, approximately one-fourth of the white males were at first excluded from voting or holding office. That produced black majorities among voters in South Carolina, Mississippi, and Louisiana (states where African Americans were also a majority of the population), and in Alabama and Florida (where they were not). But the government soon lifted most suffrage restrictions so that nearly all white males could vote. After that, Republicans maintained control only with the support of many white Southerners.

Critics called these Southern white Republicans "scalawags." Many were former Whigs who had never felt comfortable in the Democratic Party–some of them wealthy (or once wealthy) planters or businessmen interested in the economic development of the region. Others were farmers who lived in remote areas where there had been little or no slavery and who hoped the Republican program of internal improvements would help end their economic isolation. Despite their diverse social positions, scalawags shared a belief that the Republican Party would serve their economic interests better than the Democrats.

"SCALAWAGS"

THE "STRONG" GOVERNMENT 1869–1877.

THE BURDENED SOUTH This Reconstruction-era cartoon expresses the South's sense of its oppression at the hands of Northern Republicans. President Grant (whose hat bears Abraham Lincoln's initials) rides in comfort in a giant carpetbag, guarded by bayonet-wielding soldiers, as the South staggers under the burden in chains. More evidence of destruction and military occupation is visible in the background.

White men from the North also served as Republican leaders in the South. Critics of Reconstruction referred to them pejoratively as "carpetbaggers," which conveyed an image of penniless adventurers who arrived with all their possessions in a carpetbag (a common kind of cheap suitcase covered with carpeting material). In fact, most of the so-called carpetbaggers were well-educated people of middle-class origin, many of them doctors, lawyers, and teachers. Most were veterans of the Union army who looked on the South as a new frontier, more promising than the West. They had settled there at war's end as hopeful planters or as business and professional people.

"CARPETBAGGERS"

But the most numerous Republicans in the South were the black freedmen, most of whom had no previous experience in politics and who tried, therefore, to build institutions through which they could learn to exercise their power. In several states, African American voters held their own conventions to chart their future course. One such "colored convention," as white Southerners called them, assembled in Alabama in 1867 and announced: "We claim exactly the same rights, privileges and immunities as are enjoyed by white men–we ask nothing more and will be content with nothing else." The black churches that freedmen created after emancipation also helped

FREEDMEN

Reasoning Processes

Comparison After students have read the section "'Carpetbaggers'," ask them to create a Venn diagram comparing "Carpetbaggers" and "Scalawags." Have them discuss in small groups which faction was more disliked in the South and why. **SOC** **PCE**

Discussion and Activities

Historical Evidence and Argumentation After students have read the section "The Reconstruction Governments," ask them to create a T-chart listing successes and failures of the new state governments. Discuss as a class whether successes or failures were more prevalent, and reasons for the failures. **PCE** **SOC** **NAT** **ARC**

NEW ORLEANS RIOT On July 30, 1866, a violent conflict took place outside the Mechanics Institute in New Orleans. White men attacked African Americans parading outside the building where a reconvened Louisiana Constitutional Convention was being held. The state's Radical Republicans had called for the Convention because they were angered by the legislature's enactment of the Black Codes that restricted the rights of African Americans to travel and work. An estimated thirty-eight people were killed and forty-six wounded, most of them African American.

give unity and political self-confidence to former enslaved people. African Americans played a significant role in the politics of the Reconstruction South. They served as delegates to the constitutional conventions. They held public offices of practically every kind. Between 1869 and 1901, twenty African Americans served in the U.S. House of Representatives, two in the Senate (Hiram Revels of Mississippi and Blanche K. Bruce of Mississippi). African Americans served, too, in state legislatures and in various other state offices. White Southerners complained loudly (both at the time and for generations to come) about "Negro rule" during Reconstruction, but no such thing ever actually existed in any of the states. No black man was ever elected governor of a Southern state (although Lieutenant Governor P. B. S. Pinchback briefly performed gubernatorial duties in Louisiana). African Americans never controlled any of the state legislatures, although they held a majority in the lower house in South Carolina for a short time. In the South as a whole, the percentage of black officeholders was always far lower than the percentage of African Americans in the population.

The record of the Reconstruction governments is mixed. Critics at the time and since denounced them for corruption and financial extravagance, and there is some truth to both charges. Officeholders in many states enriched themselves through graft and other illicit activities. State budgets expanded to hitherto unknown totals, and state debts soared to previously undreamed-of heights. In South Carolina, for example, the public debt increased from $7 million to $29 million in eight years.

But the corruption in the South, real as it was, was hardly unique to the Reconstruction governments. Corruption was at least as rampant in the Northern states. And in both North and South, it was a result of the same thing: a rapid economic expansion of government services (and revenues) that put new strains on (and new temptations before) elected officials everywhere. The end of Reconstruction did not end corruption in Southern state governments. In many states, in fact, corruption increased.

And the state expenditures of the Reconstruction years were huge only in comparison with the meager budgets of the antebellum era. They represented an effort to provide the South with urgently needed services that antebellum governments had never offered: public education, public works programs, relief for the poor, and other costly new commitments. There were, to be sure, graft and extravagance in Reconstruction governments; there were also positive and permanent accomplishments.

EDUCATION

Perhaps the most important of those accomplishments was a dramatic improvement in the education of African Americans and white Southerners with scant learning. In the first years of Reconstruction, much of the impetus for educational reform in the South came from outside groups—from the Freedmen's Bureau, from Northern private philanthropic organizations, from many Northern women, black and white, who traveled to the South to teach in freedmen's schools—and from black Southerners themselves. Over the opposition of many white Southerners, who feared that education would give African Americans "false notions of equality," these reformers established a large network of schools for former enslaved people—4,000 schools by 1870, staffed by 9,000 teachers (half of them African American), teaching 200,000 students (about 12 percent of the total school-age population of the freedmen). In the 1870s, Reconstruction governments also began to build a comprehensive public school system in the South. By 1876, more than half of all white children and about 40 percent of all black children were attending schools in the South. Several black "academies," offering more advanced education, also began operating. Gradually, these academies grew into an important network of black colleges and universities, which included such distinguished schools as Fisk and Atlanta Universities and Morehouse College.

Already, however, Southern education was becoming divided into two separate systems based on race. Early efforts to integrate the schools of the region were a dismal failure. The Freedmen's Bureau schools, for example, were open to students of all races, but almost no white students attended them. New Orleans set up an integrated school system under the Reconstruction government; again, white students almost universally stayed away. The one federal effort to mandate school integration—the Civil Rights Act of 1875—had its provisions for educational desegregation removed before it was passed. As soon as the Republican governments of Reconstruction were replaced, the new Southern Democratic regimes quickly abandoned all efforts to promote integration.

SEGREGATED SCHOOLS

Reasoning Processes

Comparing Have students read the section "Education." Ask them to discuss in pairs or small groups how education changed or remained the same during Reconstruction. **SOC** **PCE**

Historical Thinking Skills

Argumentation Have students read the section "Failure of Land Redistribution." Ask them to write a short paragraph explaining why efforts at distributing land to formerly enslaved people largely failed. Have students draw a conclusion about the most important reason for this failure. **SOC** **PCE** **WXT**

LANDOWNERSHIP AND TENANCY

The most ambitious goal of the Freedmen's Bureau, and of some Radical Republicans in Congress, was to make Reconstruction the vehicle for a fundamental reform of landownership in the South. The effort failed. In the last years of the war and the first years of Reconstruction, the Freedmen's Bureau did oversee the redistribution of substantial amounts of land to freedmen in a few areas—notably the Sea Islands of South Carolina and Georgia, and areas of Mississippi that had once belonged to the family of Jefferson Davis. By June 1865, the bureau had settled nearly 10,000 black families on their own land—most of it drawn from abandoned plantations—arousing dreams among former enslaved people throughout the South of "forty acres and a mule." By the end of that year, however, the experiment was already collapsing. Southern plantation owners were returning and demanding the restoration of their property, and President Johnson was supporting their demands. Despite the resistance of the Freedmen's Bureau, the government eventually returned most of the confiscated land to the original white owners.

FAILURE OF LAND REDISTRIBUTION

Very few Northern Republicans believed that the federal government had the right to confiscate property. Even so, distribution of landownership in the South changed considerably in the postwar years. Among white Southerners, there was a significant decline in landownership, from 80 percent before the war to 67 percent by the end of Reconstruction. Some white Southerners lost their land because of unpaid debt or increased taxes; some left the marginal lands they had owned to move to more-fertile areas, where they rented.

During the same period, the number of African Americans who owned land rose from virtually none to more than 20 percent. Many black landowners acquired their property through hard work or luck or both. But some relied unwisely on assistance from white-dominated financial or philanthropic institutions. One of them was the Freedman's Bank, established in 1865 in an effort to promote landownership among African Americans. They persuaded thousands of freedmen to deposit their modest savings in the bank, but then invested heavily in

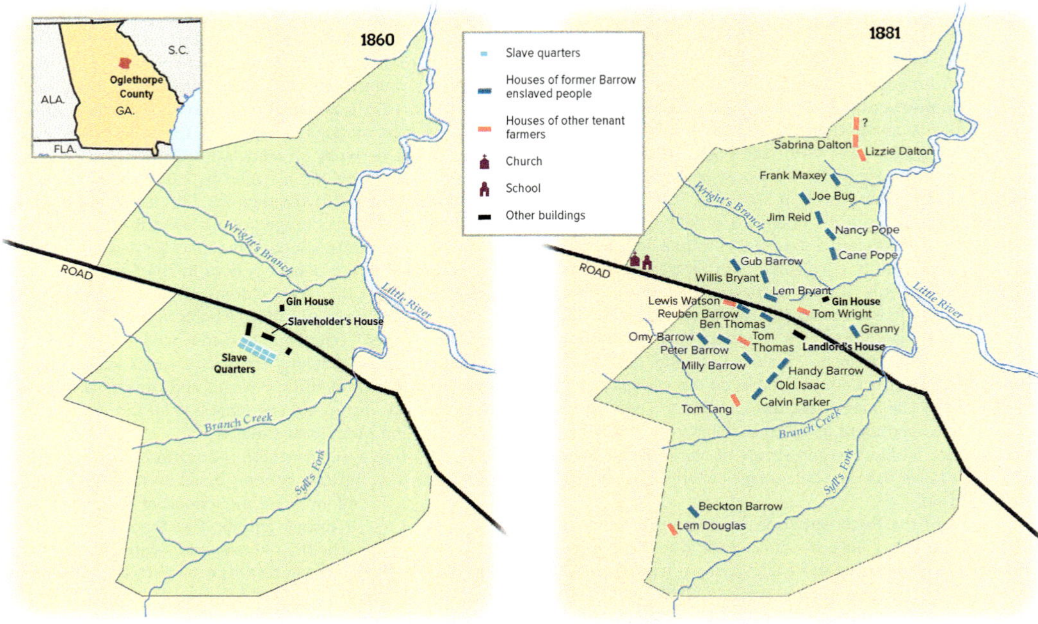

THE SOUTHERN PLANTATION BEFORE AND AFTER EMANCIPATION This map shows the distribution of lands and dwellings on the Barrow Plantation in Oglethorpe County, Georgia, before and after the emancipation of enslaved people at the close of the Civil War. The map on the left shows the plantation in 1861, as the war began. Like the Hopeton Plantation, the Barrow Plantation was highly centralized before the war, with all enslaved people living together in a complex of dwellings near the slaveholder's house. Twenty years later, as the map on the right shows, the same landscape was very differently divided. Housing was now widely dispersed, as African Americans became tenants or sharecroppers and began working their own small pieces of land and living independently. Churches had sprung up away from the landowner's house as well.

Why did former enslaved people move so quickly to relocate their homes and churches away from slaveholders?

Answers

The Southern Plantation Before and After Emancipation

They wanted to assert their independence, even if they were unable to leave the plantation.

unsuccessful enterprises. It was ill prepared, therefore, for the national depression of the 1870s and it failed in 1874.

SHARECROPPING

Still, most African Americans, and a growing minority of white Southerners, did not own their own land during Reconstruction; and some who acquired land in the 1860s had lost it by the 1890s. These people worked for others in one form or another. Many African American agricultural laborers–perhaps 25 percent of the total–simply worked for wages. Most, however, became tenants of white landowners–working their own plots of land and paying their landlords either a fixed rent or a share of their crop.

The new system was a repudiation of African Americans of the gang-labor system of the antebellum plantation, in which enslaved people had lived and worked together under the direction of a slaveholder. As tenants and sharecroppers, African Americans enjoyed at least a physical independence from their landlords and had the sense of working their own land, even if in most cases they could never hope to buy it. But tenantry also benefited landlords in some ways, relieving them of any responsibility for the physical well-being of their workers.

The Crop-Lien System

In some respects, the postwar years were a period of remarkable economic progress for African Americans. If the material benefits they had received under slavery are calculated as income, then prewar African Americans had earned about a 22 percent share of the profits of the plantation system. By the end of Reconstruction, they were earning 56 percent. Measured another way, the per capita income of black Southerners rose 46 percent between 1857 and 1879, while the per capita income of white Southerners declined 35 percent. This represented one of the most significant redistributions of income in American history.

But these figures are somewhat misleading. While the African American share of profits was increasing, the total profits of Southern agriculture were declining–a result of the dislocations of the war and a reduction in the world market for cotton. In addition, while African Americans were earning a greater return on each hour of labor than they had under slavery, they were working fewer hours. Women and children were less likely to labor in the fields than in the past. Adult men tended to work shorter days. In all, the black labor force worked about one-third fewer hours during Reconstruction than enslaved people had been compelled to work under slavery–a reduction that brought the working schedule of African Americans roughly into line with that of white farm laborers. Nor did the income redistribution of the postwar years lift many African Americans out of poverty. Black per capita income rose from about one-quarter of white per capita income to about one-half in the first few years after the war. And after this initial increase, it rose hardly at all.

For African Americans and poor white Southerners alike, whatever gains there might have been as a result of land and income redistribution were often overshadowed by the ravages of the crop-lien system. Few of the traditional institutions of credit in the South–the "factors" and banks–returned after the war. In their stead emerged a new system of credit, centered in large part on local country stores, some of them owned by planters, others by independent merchants. African Americans and Southern whites, landowners and tenants–all depended on these stores for such necessities as food, clothing, seed, and farm implements. And since farmers did not have the same steady cash flow as other workers, customers usually had to rely on credit from these merchants in order to purchase what they needed. Most local stores had no competition (and went to great lengt hs to ensure that things stayed that way). As a result, they were able to set interest rates as high as 50 or 60 percent. Farmers had to give the merchants a lien (or claim) on their crops as collateral for the loans (thus the term "crop-lien system"). Farmers who suffered a few bad years in a row, as often happened, could become trapped in a cycle of debt from which they could never escape.

NEW SYSTEM OF CREDIT

SHARECROPPERS, 1879 This painting, by Winslow Homer (1836–1910), depicts sharecroppers picking cotton. In sharecropping, a landowner permits tenants to use the land in exchange for a share of the crops produced.

Reasoning Processes

Continuity and Change After students have read the section "Sharecropping," ask them to create a Venn diagram comparing sharecropping to conditions experienced by enslaved people prior to the end of the Civil War. Ask them to identify ways in which sharecroppers were or were not better off compared to the previous system. **SOC** **PCE** **WXT**

Reasoning Processes

Continuity and Change Have students examine the image "Sharecroppers, 1879." Ask them to identify and discuss details from the image that indicate how much life had changed for formerly enslaved people following emancipation. **SOC** **WXT** **PCE**

Historical Thinking Skills

Argumentation After students have read the section "The Crop-Lien System," ask them to create a list of the effects of the transition to sharecropping and the crop-lien system. Have students write a thesis statement that makes a claim about the most important economic changes in the South following the Civil War. **PCE** **WXT** **SOC**

WASH DAY ON THE PLANTATION One of the most common occupations of women recently emancipated from slavery was taking in laundry from white families who no longer had enslaved people as household servants. This photograph of a group of African American women illustrates how arduous a task laundry was.

The Library of Congress

This burdensome credit system had a number of effects on the region, almost all of them unhealthy. One effect was that some African Americans who had acquired land during the early years of Reconstruction gradually lost it as they fell into debt. So, to a lesser extent, did white small landowners. Another effect was that Southern farmers became almost wholly dependent on cash crops–and most of all on cotton–because only such marketable commodities seemed to offer any possibility of escape from debt. Thus Southern agriculture, never sufficiently diversified even in the best of times, became more one-dimensional than ever. The relentless planting of cotton, moreover, was contributing to an exhaustion of the soil. The crop-lien system, in other words, was not only helping to impoverish small farmers; it was also contributing to a general decline in the Southern agricultural economy.

THE AFRICAN AMERICAN FAMILY IN FREEDOM

One of the most striking features of the African American response to Reconstruction was the effort to build or rebuild family structures and to protect them from the interference they had experienced under slavery. A major reason for the rapid departure of so many emancipated enslaved people from plantations was the desire to find lost relatives and reunite families. Thousands of African Americans wandered through the South–often over vast distances–looking for husbands, wives, children, or other relatives from whom they had been separated. In the few black newspapers that circulated in the South, there were many advertisements by people searching for information about their relatives. Former enslaved people rushed to have marriages, previously without legal standing,

Discussion and Activities

Analyzing Visuals Have students examine the image "Wash Day on the Plantation." Ask them to list details from the photograph and discuss as a class what it reveals about work and family life for formerly enslaved people. **SOC** **WXT**

sanctified by church and law. Black families resisted living in the former slave quarters and moved instead to small cabins scattered widely across the countryside, where they could enjoy at least some privacy. Within the black family, the definition of male and female roles quickly came to resemble that within white families. Many women and children ceased working in the fields. Such work, they believed, was a badge of slavery. Instead, many women restricted themselves largely to domestic tasks—cooking, cleaning, gardening, sewing, raising children, attending to the needs of their husbands. Some black husbands refused to allow their wives to work as servants in white homes. "When I married my wife I married her to wait on me," one freedman told a former slaveholder who was attempting to hire his wife as a servant. "She got all she can do right here for me and the children."

CHANGING GENDER ROLES

Still, middle-class notions of domesticity were often difficult to sustain in the impoverished circumstances of most former enslaved people. Economic necessity required many black women to engage in income-producing activities, including activities that they and their husbands resisted: working as domestic servants, taking in laundry, or helping in the field. By the end of Reconstruction, half of all black women over the age of sixteen were working for wages. And unlike white working women, most black female income-earners were married.

THE GRANT ADMINISTRATION

Exhausted by the political turmoil of the Johnson administration, American voters in 1868 yearned for a strong, stable figure to guide them through the troubled years of Reconstruction. They turned trustingly to General Ulysses S. Grant, the hero of the war and, by 1868, a revered national idol.

THE SOLDIER PRESIDENT

U.S. GRANT

Grant could have had the nomination of either party in 1868. But believing that Republican Reconstruction policies were more popular in the North, he accepted the Republican nomination. The Democrats nominated former governor Horatio Seymour of New York. The campaign was a bitter one, and Grant's triumph was surprisingly narrow. Without the 500,000 new black Republican voters in the South, he would have had a minority of the popular vote.

Grant entered the White House with no political experience, and his performance was clumsy and ineffectual from the start. Except for Hamilton Fish, whom Grant appointed secretary of state and who served for eight years with great distinction, most members of the cabinet were ill equipped for their tasks. Grant relied chiefly, and increasingly, on established party leaders—the group most ardently devoted to patronage. His administration used the spoils system even more blatantly than most of its predecessors, embittering reform-minded members of his party. Grant also alienated the many Northerners who were growing disillusioned with Radical Reconstruction policies, which the president continued to support. Some Republicans suspected, correctly, that there was also corruption in the Grant administration itself.

LIBERAL REPUBLICANS

By the end of Grant's first term, therefore, members of a substantial faction of the party—who referred to themselves as Liberal Republicans—had come to oppose what they called "Grantism." In 1872, hoping to prevent Grant's reelection, they bolted the party and nominated their own presidential candidate: Horace Greeley, veteran editor and publisher of the *New York Tribune*. The Democrats, somewhat reluctantly, named Greeley their candidate as well, hoping that the alliance with the Liberals would enable them to defeat Grant. But the effort was in vain. Grant won a substantial victory, polling 286 electoral votes to Greeley's 66, and nearly 56 percent of the popular total.

THE GRANT SCANDALS

CRÉDIT MOBILIER

During the 1872 campaign, the first of a series of political scandals came to light that would plague Grant and the Republicans for years. It involved the Crédit Mobilier construction company, which had helped build the Union Pacific Railroad. The heads of Crédit Mobilier had used their positions as Union Pacific stockholders to steer large fraudulent contracts to their construction company, thus bilking the Union Pacific (and the federal government, which provided large subsidies to the railroad) of millions. To prevent investigations, the directors had given Crédit Mobilier stock to key members of Congress. In 1872, Congress launched an investigation, which revealed that some highly placed Republicans—including Schuyler Colfax, now Grant's vice president—had accepted some of the stock.

CREDIT MOBILIER This political cartoon by Thomas Nast, called "The Cherubs of Crédit Mobilier," depicts the censure by the House of Representatives of Congressmen James Brooks of New York and Oakes Ames of Massachusetts for their involvement in the Crédit Mobilier scandal, one of several scandals to stain the Grant administration.

Discussion and Activities

Analyzing Change After students have read the section "The African American Family in Freedom," ask them to discuss in small groups changes in African American families due to emancipation. Have them consider in what ways formerly enslaved people were still not completely free. *(Due to poverty, many formerly enslaved people, particularly women, had to work in occupations that they did not want to work in.)* **SOC** **WXT** **PCE**

Discussion and Activities

Speculating Have students read the section "The Soldier President." Ask them to create a T-chart listing ways that Grant was similar to or different from previous presidents. Have students discuss in small groups how those similarities and differences may have enhanced or undermined Grant's effectiveness as president. *(Being a political novice with no previous experience undermined his prestige with Congress. His loyalty to incompetent or corrupt subordinates undermined his reputation, though his military record made him popular with the public in the North, at least at the beginning of his administration.)* **PCE**

Reasoning Processes

Comparing Have students read the section "The Greenback Question." Ask them to list the causes of the Panic of 1873 and discuss how this economic crash was similar to or different from earlier economic crashes. *(All crashes were at least partly caused by over-speculation and questions about the integrity of the money supply.)* **PCE** **WXT**

One dreary episode followed another in Grant's second term. Benjamin H. Bristow, Grant's third Treasury secretary, discovered that some of his officials and a group of distillers operating as a "whiskey ring" were cheating the government out of taxes by filing false reports. Then a House investigation revealed that William W. Belknap, secretary of war, had accepted bribes to retain an Indian-post trader in office (the so-called Indian ring). Other, lesser scandals added to the growing impression that "Grantism" had brought rampant corruption to government.

The Greenback Question

Compounding Grant's, and the nation's, problems was a financial crisis, known as the Panic of 1873. It began with the failure of a

PANIC OF 1873

leading investment banking firm, Jay Cooke and Company, which had invested too heavily in postwar railroad building. There had been panics before—in 1819, 1837, and 1857—but this was worse than any earlier economic crisis. The depression it produced lasted four years.

Debtors now pressured the government to redeem federal war bonds with greenbacks, paper currency of the sort printed during the Civil War, which would increase the amount of money in circulation. But Grant and most Republicans wanted a "sound" currency—based solidly on gold reserves—which would favor the interests of banks and other creditors. Approximately $356 million in paper currency issued during the Civil War was still in circulation. In 1873, the Treasury issued more in response to the panic. But in 1875, Republican leaders in Congress, in an effort to crush the greenback movement for good, passed the Specie Resumption Act. It provided that after January 1, 1879, the greenback dollars, whose value constantly fluctuated, would be redeemed by the government and replaced with new certificates, firmly pegged to the price of gold. The law satisfied creditors, who had worried that debts would be repaid in paper currency of uncertain value. But "resumption" made things more difficult for debtors, because the gold-based money supply could not easily expand.

In 1875, the "greenbackers," as the inflationists were called, formed their own political organization: the National Greenback Party. It was active in the next three presidential

NATIONAL GREENBACK PARTY

elections, but it failed to gain widespread support. It did, however, keep the money issue alive. The question of the proper composition of the currency was to remain one of the most controversial and enduring issues in late-nineteenth-century American politics.

Republican Diplomacy

The Johnson and Grant administrations achieved their greatest successes in foreign affairs. The accomplishments were the work not of the presidents themselves, who displayed little aptitude for diplomacy, but of two outstanding secretaries of state: William H. Seward, who had served Lincoln and who remained in office until 1869; and Hamilton Fish, who served throughout the two terms of the Grant administration.

An ardent expansionist, Seward acted with as much daring as the demands of Reconstruction politics and the Republican

"SEWARD'S FOLLY"

hatred of President Johnson would permit. Seward accepted a Russian offer to sell Alaska to the United States for $7.2 million, despite criticism from many Americans who considered Alaska a frozen wasteland and derided it as "Seward's Folly." In 1867, Seward also engineered the American annexation of the tiny Midway Islands, west of Hawaii.

Hamilton Fish's first major challenge was resolving the long-standing controversy with England over the American claims that the British government had violated neutrality laws during the Civil War by permitting English shipyards to

ALABAMA CLAIMS

build ships (among them the *Alabama*) for the Confederacy. American demands that England pay for the damage these vessels had caused became known as the "*Alabama* claims." In 1871, after a number of failed efforts, Fish forged an agreement, the Treaty of Washington, which provided for international arbitration and in which Britain expressed regret for the "escape" of the *Alabama* from England.

The Abandonment of Reconstruction

As the North grew increasingly preoccupied with its own political and economic problems, interest in Reconstruction began to wane. The Grant administration continued to protect Republican governments in the South, but less because of any interest in ensuring the position of freedmen than because of a desire to prevent the reemergence of a strong Democratic Party in the region. But even the presence of federal troops was not enough to prevent white Southerners from overturning the Reconstruction regimes. By the time Grant left office, Democrats had taken back (or, as white Southerners called it, "redeemed") the governments of seven of the eleven former Confederate states. For three other states—South Carolina, Louisiana, and Florida—the end of Reconstruction had to wait for the withdrawal of the last federal troops in 1876, a withdrawal that was the result of a long process of political bargaining and compromise at the national level. (One former Confederate state, Tennessee, had never been part of the Reconstruction process because it had ratified the Fourteenth Amendment and rejoined the Union in 1866.)

The Southern States "Redeemed"

In the states where white people constituted a majority—the states of the upper South—overthrowing Republican control was relatively simple. By 1872, all but a handful of white Southerners had regained suffrage. Now a clear majority of the electorate, they needed only to organize and vote for their candidates.

Discussion and Activities

Making Connections Have students read the section "Republican Diplomacy." Ask them to discuss as a class what they know about Alaska today that would contradict the criticism that Secretary of State Seward's negotiation to purchase Alaska from Russia was a "folly." *(Discovery of gold and later large reserves of oil have made Alaska economically valuable.)* **PCE** **WOR**

In other states, where African Americans were a majority or the black and white populations were almost equal, white people used intimidation and violence to undermine the Reconstruction regimes. Secret societies–the Ku Klux Klan, the Knights of the White Camellia, and others–used terrorism to frighten or physically bar African Americans from voting or otherwise exercising citizenship. Paramilitary organizations–the Red Shirts and White Leagues–armed themselves to "police" elections and worked to force all white males to join the Democratic Party and to exclude all African Americans from meaningful political activity.

The Ku Klux Klan was the largest and most effective of these organizations. Formed in 1866 and led by former Confederate general Nathan Bedford Forrest, it gradually absorbed many of the smaller terrorist organizations in the South. Its leaders devised rituals, costumes, secret languages, and other airs of mystery to create a bond among its members and make the organization seem even more terrifying to those it was attempting to intimidate. The Klan's "midnight rides"–bands of men clad in white sheets and masks, their horses covered with white robes and with hooves muffled–created terror in black communities throughout the South.

KU KLUX KLAN

Many white Southerners considered the Klan and the other secret societies and paramilitary groups proud, patriotic societies. Together such groups served, in effect, as a military force (even if a decentralized and poorly organized one) continuing the battle against Northern rule. They worked in particular to advance the interests of those with the most to gain from a restoration of white supremacy–above all the planter class and the Southern Democratic Party. Even stronger than the Klan in discouraging black political power, however, was the simple weapon of economic pressure: some planters refused to rent land to black Republicans; storekeepers refused to extend them credit; employers refused to give them work.

THE KU KLUX KLAN ACTS

The Republican Congress tried for a time to turn back this new wave of white repression. In 1870 and 1871, it passed two Enforcement Acts, also known as the Ku Klux Klan Acts, which were in many ways the most radical measures of the era. The Enforcement Acts prohibited the states from discriminating against voters on the basis of race and gave the federal government power to supersede the state courts and prosecute violations of the law. It was the first time the federal government had ever claimed the power to prosecute crimes by individuals under federal law. Federal district attorneys were now empowered to take action against conspiracies to deny African Americans such rights as voting, holding office, and serving on juries. The new laws also authorized the president to use the military to protect civil rights and to suspend the right of habeas corpus when violations of the rights seemed particularly egregious. In October 1871, President Grant used this provision of the law when he declared a "state of lawlessness" in nine counties in South Carolina and sent in federal troops to occupy the area. Hundreds of suspected Klan members were arrested; some were held for long periods without trial; some were eventually convicted under the law and sent to jail.

ENFORCEMENT ACTS

The Enforcement Acts were seldom used as severely as they were in South Carolina, but they were effective in the effort by African Americans and white Northerners to weaken the Klan. By 1872, Klan violence against African Americans was in decline throughout the region.

DECLINE OF THE KLAN

WANING NORTHERN COMMITMENT

The Ku Klux Klan Acts marked the peak of Republican commitment to enforce the new rights Reconstruction was extending to black citizens. But that commitment did not last for long. Black Southerners were gradually losing the support of many of their former backers in the North. As early as 1870, after the adoption of the Fifteenth Amendment, some Northern reformers convinced themselves that their long campaign on behalf of black people was now over–that with the vote, African Americans ought to be able to take care of themselves. Over the next several years, former Radical leaders such as Charles Sumner and Horace Greeley now began calling themselves Liberals, cooperating with Democrats and, at times, outdoing even the Democrats in denouncing what they viewed as black and carpetbag misgovernment. Within the South itself, many white Republicans joined the Liberals and eventually moved into the Democratic Party.

The Panic of 1873 further undermined support for Reconstruction. The economic crisis spurred Northern industrialists and their allies to find an explanation for the poverty and instability around them. They found it in a new idea known as "Social Darwinism", a harsh theory that argued that individuals who failed did so because of their own weakness and "unfitness." Those influenced by Social Darwinism came to view the large number of unemployed vagrants in the North–and poor African Americans in the South–as irredeemable misfits. Social Darwinism also encouraged a broad critique of government intervention in social and economic life, which further weakened commitment to the Reconstruction program. Support for land redistribution, never great, and willingness to spend money from the depleted federal treasury to aid the freedmen, waned quickly after 1873. State and local governments also found themselves short of funds, and rushed to cut back on social services–which in the South meant the end of almost all services to the former enslaved people.

IMPACT OF SOCIAL DARWINISM

In the congressional elections of 1874, the Democrats won control of the House of Representatives for the first time since 1861. Grant took note of the changing temper of the North and made use of military force to prop up the Republican regimes that were still standing in the South. By the end of 1876, only three Southern states were left in the hands of the Republicans–South Carolina, Louisiana, and Florida. In state

Discussion and Activities

Analyzing Cause and Effect After students have read the section "The Southern States 'Redeemed'," ask them to write a short paragraph explaining how most Southern states overthrew Republican control. **PCE** **SOC**

Historical Thinking Skills

Argumentation Have students read the section "The Ku Klux Klan Acts." Ask them to discuss in small groups whether the Enforcement Acts were an appropriate response to Klan violence. Have students consider what should have been done differently or in addition to these acts. **PCE** **SOC**

Reasoning Processes

Causation After students have read the section "Waning Northern Commitment," ask them to list the reasons for decreasing levels of support in the North for continuing Reconstruction policies. Have students rank their lists in order of importance and write a thesis statement that makes a claim about the most important causes of this waning support.
PCE

elections that year, Democrats (after using terrorist tactics) claimed victory in all three. But the Republicans challenged the results and claimed victory as well, and they were able to remain in office because of the presence of federal troops. Without federal troops, it was now clear, the last of the Republican regimes would quickly fall.

THE COMPROMISE OF 1877

Grant had hoped to run for another term in 1876. But most Republican leaders were shaken by recent Democrat success, afraid of the scandals with which Grant was associated, and concerned about the president's declining health. Instead, they sought a candidate not associated with the problems of the Grant years, one who might entice Liberals and unite the party again. They settled on Rutherford B. Hayes of Ohio, a former Union army officer, governor, and congressman, champion of civil service reform. The Democrats united behind Samuel J. Tilden, the reform governor of New York who had been instrumental in challenging the corrupt Tweed Ring of New York City's Tammany Hall.

HAYES VERSUS TILDEN

Although the campaign was a bitter one, there were few differences of principle between the candidates, both of whom were conservatives committed to moderate reform. The November election produced an apparent Democratic victory. Tilden carried the South and several large Northern states, and his popular margin over Hayes was nearly 300,000 votes. But disputed returns from Louisiana, South Carolina, Florida, and Oregon, whose total electoral vote was 20, threw the election in doubt. Tilden had undisputed claim to 184 electoral votes, only one short of a majority. But Hayes could still win if he managed to receive all 20 disputed votes.

The Constitution had established no method to determine the validity of disputed returns. It was clear that the decision lay with Congress, but it was not clear with which house or through what method. (The Senate was Republican, the House, Democratic.) Members of each party naturally supported a solution that would yield them the victory.

Finally, late in January 1877, Congress tried to break the deadlock by creating a special electoral commission to judge the disputed votes. The commission would be composed of five senators, five representatives, and five justices of the Supreme Court. The congressional delegation would consist of five Republicans and five Democrats. The Court delegation would include two Republicans, two Democrats, and an independent. But the independent seat ultimately went to a justice whose real sympathies were with the Republicans. The commission voted along straight party lines, 8 to 7, awarding every disputed vote to Hayes. Congress accepted their verdict on March 2. Two days later, Hayes was inaugurated.

SPECIAL ELECTORAL COMMISSION

Behind the resolution of the deadlock, however, lay a series of elaborate compromises among leaders of both parties. When a Democratic filibuster threatened to derail the commission's report, Republican Senate leaders met secretly with Southern Democratic leaders to work out terms by which the Democrats would allow the election of Hayes. According to traditional accounts, Republicans and Southern Democrats met at Washington's Wormley Hotel. In return for a Republican pledge that Hayes would withdraw the last federal troops from the South, thus permitting the overthrow of the last Republican governments there, the Southerners agreed to abandon the filibuster.

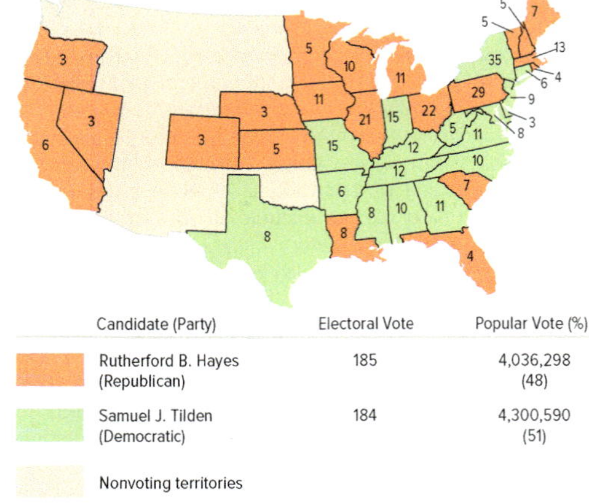

	Candidate (Party)	Electoral Vote	Popular Vote (%)
(orange)	Rutherford B. Hayes (Republican)	185	4,036,298 (48)
(green)	Samuel J. Tilden (Democratic)	184	4,300,590 (51)
(cream)	Nonvoting territories		

81.8% of electorate voting

THE ELECTION OF 1876 The election of 1876 was one of the most controversial in American history. As in the elections of 1824, 1888, and 2000, the winner of the popular vote—Samuel J. Tilden—was not the winner of the electoral college, which he lost by one vote. The final decision as to who would be president was not made until the day before the official inauguration in March.

How did the Republicans turn this apparent defeat into a victory?

Actually, the story behind the "Compromise of 1877" is more complex. Hayes was already on record favoring withdrawal of the troops, so Republicans needed to offer more than that if they hoped for Democratic support. The real agreement, the one that won over the Southern Democrats, was reached well before the Wormley meeting. As the price of their cooperation, the Southern Democrats (among them some former Whigs) exacted several pledges from the Republicans in addition to withdrawal of the troops: the appointment of at least one Southerner to the Hayes cabinet, control of federal patronage in their areas, generous internal improvements, and federal aid for the Texas and Pacific Railroad. Many powerful Southern Democrats supported industrializing their region. They believed Republican programs of federal support for business would aid the South more than the states' rights policies of the Democrats.

COMPROMISE OF 1877

In his inaugural address, Hayes announced that the South's most pressing need was the restoration of "wise, honest, and

Answers

The Election of 1876

The Republicans negotiated a deal with Democrats, making concessions in exchange for Democrats dropping challenges to Hayes's election.

DEBATING THE PAST

RECONSTRUCTION

Debate over the nature of Reconstruction has created so much controversy over the decades that one scholar, writing in 1959, described the issue as a "dark and bloody ground." For many years, a relatively uniform and highly critical view of Reconstruction prevailed among historians. William A. Dunning offered the principal scholarly expression of this view in *Reconstruction, Political and Economic* (1907), the first major historical interpretation of Reconstruction. Dunning portrayed Reconstruction as a corrupt outrage perpetrated on the prostrate South by a vicious and vindictive group of Northern Republican Radicals. Unscrupulous carpetbaggers flooded the South to profit from the misery of the defeated region. Ignorant, illiterate African Americans were thrust into positions of power for which they were entirely unfit. The Reconstruction experiment survived only because of the determination of the Republican Party to keep itself in power. Some later writers, notably Howard K. Beale, added an economic motive—to protect Northern business interests.

Dunning's interpretation shaped the views of several generations of historians and helped shape popular depictions of Reconstruction such as those expressed in the 1915 film *The Birth of a Nation* and then the 1936 book and 1939 movie *Gone with the Wind*.

The great African American scholar W. E. B. Du Bois was among the first to challenge the Dunning view. In *Black Reconstruction* (1935), Du Bois argued that Reconstruction politics in the Southern states had been an effort on the part of the masses, black and white, to create a more democratic society. The misdeeds of the Reconstruction governments, he claimed, had been greatly exaggerated, and their achievements overlooked. In the 1940s, the historians C. Vann Woodward, David Herbert Donald, Thomas B. Alexander, and others began to reexamine the Reconstruction governments in the South and to suggest that their records were not nearly as inaccurate and incomplete as most historians had previously assumed.

By the early 1960s, a new view of Reconstruction was emerging. The revisionist approach was summarized by John Hope Franklin in *Reconstruction after the Civil War* (1961) and Kenneth Stampp in *The Era of Reconstruction* (1965), who claimed that the postwar Republicans had been engaged in a genuine, if flawed, effort to solve the problem of race in the South by providing much-needed protection to the freedmen. The Reconstruction governments, for all their faults, had been bold experiments in interracial politics. The congressional Radicals were not saints, but they had displayed a genuine concern for the rights of enslaved people. Andrew Johnson was not a martyred defender of the Constitution, but an inept, racist politician who resisted reasonable compromise and brought the government to a crisis. African Americans had played only a small part in Reconstruction governments and had generally acquitted themselves well. The Reconstruction regimes had, in fact, brought important progress to the South, establishing the region's first public school system and other important social changes. Corruption in the South had been no worse than corruption in the North at that time. What was tragic about Reconstruction, the revisionist view claimed, was not what it did to white Southerners but, rather, what it did not do for black Southerners. By stopping short of the reforms necessary to ensure African Americans genuine equality, Reconstruction had consigned them to more than a century of injustice and discrimination.

In later years, scholars began to question the revisionist view in an attempt to draw attention to the achievements of Reconstruction. Eric Foner, in *Nothing but Freedom* (1983) and *Reconstruction: America's Unfinished Revolution* (1988), emphasized how far former enslaved people moved toward freedom and independencein a short time and how large a role African Americans played in shaping Reconstruction. During Reconstruction, African Americans won a certain amount of legal and political power in the South; even though they held that power only

THE FREEDMEN'S BUREAU For four years after the Civil War, the Freedmen's Bureau served newly freed African Americans, helping them to get housing, food, education, and other services. This image shows African American men and women waiting for rations, most of them old and sick.

temporarily, they used it to strengthen their economic and social positions and to win a position of limited but genuine independence. Though they failed to achieve equality, they won a measure of individual and community autonomy that they used as building blocks of the freedom that emancipation alone had not guaranteed. Leon Litwack argued similarly in *Been in the Storm So Long* (1979) that former enslaved people used the relative latitude they enjoyed under Reconstruction to build a certain independence for themselves within Southern society. They strengthened their churches; they reunited their families; by refusing to work in the "gang-labor" system of the plantations, they forced the creation of a new labor system in which they had more control over their own lives. Writing from the perspective of women's history, Amy Dru Stanley and Jacqueline Jones have both argued that the freed African Americans displayed considerable independence in constructing their households on their own terms and asserting their control over family life, reproduction, and work. According to Jones in *Labor of Love, Labor of Sorrow* (1985), women in particular sought the opportunity "to labor on behalf of their own families and kin within the protected spheres of household and community."

Some historians have begun to argue that Reconstruction was not restricted to the South alone. Heather Richardson, in *West from Appomattox* (2007) and *The Death of Reconstruction* (2001), shows how the entire nation changed during the Civil War and Reconstruction—with the South, perhaps, changing least of all. The age of Reconstruction was also the age of western expansion and industrialization.

HISTORICAL THINKING SKILLS

Questions assume cumulative content knowledge from this chapter and previous chapters.

1. **Identifying Historical Developments** Identify three broad schools of historical interpretation concerning Reconstruction.
2. **Determining Context** Describe how one piece of historical evidence, from the time period, could be used to support each of the three broad schools of historical interpretation concerning Reconstruction.
3. **Developing Arguments** Analyze which school of thought you find more convincing and explain why using historical evidence to support your argument.

Discussion and Activities

Evaluating Evidence Have students examine the image "The Freedmen's Bureau." Ask them to think about which historical interpretation(s) of Reconstruction described in the feature would be supported by the image. Have students share their thoughts with a partner. *(The image would support any interpretation other than Dunning's as it shows an apparently successful implementation of a Reconstruction program.)* **PCE**

Answers

Debating the Past

1. The African American historian and sociologist W. E. B. Du Bois argued, in his book *Black Reconstruction* (1935), that Reconstruction was largely an attempt to create a more democratic society. During the 1960s, a new take on Reconstruction took hold in much of the scholarship, led by Kenneth Stampp in his book *The Era of Reconstruction* (1965), which argued that Reconstruction was largely an attempt to provide protection for freedmen. During the 1980s, Eric Foner, in his books *Nothing But Freedom* (1983) and *Reconstruction: America's Unfinished Revolution* (1987), emphasized how far formerly enslaved people had moved toward freedom and independence.
2. The passage of the 13th, 14th, and 15th Amendments supported the Du Bois interpretation as the country moved to protect the rights of all people. The establishment of the Freedmen's Bureau supports Stampp's interpretation as the agency attempted to provide education and other rights to freedmen in the South. Following the Civil War amendments, a record number of African Americans were elected to public offices; this political achievement supports Foner's belief that Reconstruction sought to protect freedom and independence for newly freed African Americans.
3. Recent scholarship, published by Heather Richardson in her books *West from Appomattox* (2007) and *The Death of Reconstruction* (2001), argues that the same racism and elitism that existed in the South simply moved out West following Reconstruction.

Discussion and Activities

Analyzing Issues After students have read the section "The Compromise of 1877," ask them to create a T-chart listing provisions of the compromise that benefited Democrats or Republicans. Have students discuss in pairs or small groups which group they believe gained more from the deal. **PCE**

peaceful local self-government"—a signal that he planned to withdraw federal troops and let white Democrats take over the state governments. That statement, and Hayes's subsequent actions, supported the widespread charges that he was paying off the South for acquiescing in his election and strengthened those who referred to him as "his Fraudulency." Hayes tried to counter such charges by projecting an image of stern public (and private) rectitude. But the election had already created such bitterness that even Hayes's promise to serve only one term could not mollify his critics.

The president and his party had hoped to build up a "new Republican" organization in the South drawn from Whiggish conservative white groups and committed to some modest acceptance of African American rights. But all such efforts failed. Although many white Southern leaders sympathized with Republican economic policies, popular resentment of Reconstruction and its attack on white supremacy was so deep that supporting the party was politically impossible. At the same time, the withdrawal of federal troops signaled that the national government was giving up its attempts to control Southern politics and to improve the lot of African Americans in Southern society.

REPUBLICAN FAILURE IN THE SOUTH

THE LEGACIES OF RECONSTRUCTION

Reconstruction made some important contributions to the efforts of former enslaved people to achieve dignity and equality in American life. And it was not as disastrous an experience for white Southerners as most of them believed at the time. But Reconstruction was in the end largely a failure, for in those years the United States abandoned its first serious effort to resolve the nation's oldest and deepest social problem—the problem of race. Moreover, the experience so disappointed, disillusioned, and embittered white Americans that it would be nearly a century before they would try again in any serious way.

Why did this great assault on racial injustice not achieve more? In part, it was because of the weaknesses and errors of the people who directed it. But in greater part, it was because attempts to produce solutions ran up against conservative obstacles so deeply embedded in the nation's life that they could not be dislodged. Veneration of the Constitution sharply limited the willingness of national leaders to infringe on the rights of states and individuals. A profound respect for private property and free enterprise prevented any real assault on economic privilege in the South. Above all, perhaps, a pervasive belief among many of even the most liberal white people that African Americans were inherently inferior served as an obstacle to equality. Given the context within which Americans of the 1860s and 1870s were working, what is surprising is not that Reconstruction did so little, but that it did as much as it did.

IDEOLOGICAL LIMITS

Considering the odds confronting them, therefore, African Americans had reason for pride in the gains they made during Reconstruction. And future generations had reason for gratitude for two great charters of freedom—the Fourteenth and Fifteenth Amendments to the Constitution—which, although largely ignored at the time, would one day serve as the basis for a "Second Reconstruction" that would renew the drive to bring freedom and equality to all Americans.

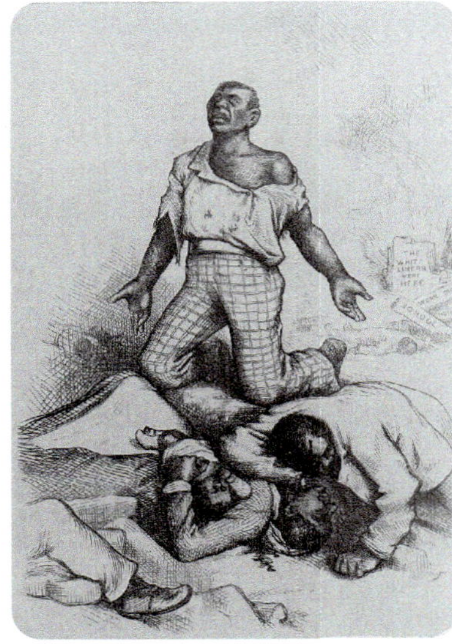

"IS *THIS* A REPUBLICAN FORM OF GOVERNMENT?" The New York artist and cartoonist Thomas Nast marked the end of Reconstruction in 1876 with this biting cartoon in Harper's Weekly, expressing his dismay at what he considered the nation's betrayal of former enslaved people, who still had not received adequate guarantees of their rights. The caption of the cartoon continued: "Is this protecting life, liberty, or property? Is this equal protection of the laws?"

THE NEW SOUTH

The agreement between Southern Democrats and Northern Republicans that helped settle the disputed election of 1876 was supposed to be the first step toward developing a stable, permanent Republican Party in the South. In that respect, at least, it failed. In the years following the end of Reconstruction, white Southerners established the Democratic Party as the only viable political organization for the region's white voters. Even so, the South did change in the years after Reconstruction in some of the ways the framers of the Compromise of 1877 had hoped.

THE "REDEEMERS"

By the end of 1877—after the last withdrawal of federal troops—every Southern state government had been "redeemed" by

Discussion and Activities

Explaining Significance Have students read the section "The Legacies of Reconstruction." Ask them to create a list of the impacts of Reconstruction and rank items in their lists in order of importance. Have students write a thesis statement that makes a claim about the most import consequence of Reconstruction. Ask for volunteers to share and give feedback as a class. **PCE** **WXT** **SOC** **NAT** **ARC**

white Democrats. Many white Southerners rejoiced at the restoration of what they liked to call "home rule." But in reality, political power in the region was soon more restricted than at any time since the Civil War. Once again, the South fell under the control of a powerful, conservative oligarchy, whose members were known variously as the "Redeemers" (to themselves and their supporters) or the "Bourbons" (a term for aristocrats used by some of their critics).

BOURBON RULE

In a few places, this post-Reconstruction ruling class was much the same as the ruling class of the antebellum period. In Alabama, for example, the old planter elite–despite challenges from new merchant and industrial forces–retained much of its former power and continued largely to dominate the state for decades. In most areas, however, the Redeemers constituted a genuinely new ruling class. They were merchants, industrialists, railroad developers, and financiers. Some of them were former planters, some of them Northern immigrants who had become absorbed into the region's life, some of them ambitious, upwardly mobile white Southerners from the region's lower social tiers. They combined a commitment to "home rule" and social conservatism with a commitment to economic development.

The various Bourbon governments of the New South behaved similarly to one another. Conservatives had complained that the Reconstruction governments fostered widespread corruption, but the Redeemer regimes were even more awash in waste and fraud. (In this, they were little different from governments in every region of the country.) At the same time, virtually all the new Democratic regimes lowered taxes, reduced spending, and drastically diminished state services–including many of the most important accomplishments of Reconstruction. In one state after another, for example, state support for public school systems was reduced or eliminated. "Schools are not a necessity," an economy-conscious governor of Virginia commented.

By the late 1870s, significant dissenting groups were challenging the Bourbons: protesting the cuts in services and denouncing the commitment of the Redeemer governments to paying off the prewar and Reconstruction debts in full, at the original (usually high) rates of interest. In Virginia, for example, a vigorous "Readjuster" movement emerged, demanding that the state revise its debt payment procedures so as to make more money available for state services. In 1879, the Readjusters won control of the legislature, and in the next few years they captured the governorship and a U.S. Senate seat. Other states produced similar movements, some of them adding demands as well for greenbacks, debt relief, and other economic reforms. (A few such independent movements included significant numbers of African Americans in their ranks, but all consisted primarily of lower-income white people.) By the mid-1880s, however, conservative Southerners–largely by exploiting racial prejudice–had destroyed most of the dissenting movements.

THE READJUSTER CHALLENGE

INDUSTRIALIZATION AND THE "NEW SOUTH"

Some white Southern leaders in the post-Reconstruction era hoped to see their region become the home of a vigorous industrial economy. The South had lost the war, such leaders argued, because its economy had been unable to compete with the modernized manufacturing capacity of the North. Now the region must "out-Yankee the Yankees" and build a "New South." Henry Grady, editor of the *Atlanta Constitution*, and other prominent spokesmen for a New South seldom challenged white supremacy, but they did advocate other important changes in Southern values. Above all, they promoted the virtues of thrift, industry, and progress–qualities that prewar Southerners had often denounced in Northern society. "We have sown towns and cities in the place of theories," Grady boasted to a New England audience in the 1880s, "and put business above politics. . . . We have fallen in love with work." But even the most fervent advocates of the New South creed were generally unwilling to break entirely with the Southern past. That was evident in, among other things, the popular literature of the region. At the same time that white Southern writers were extolling the virtues of industrialization in newspaper editorials and speeches, they were painting nostalgic portraits of the Old South in their literature. Few Southerners advocated a literal return to the old ways, but most white Southerners eagerly embraced romantic talk of the "Lost Cause." And they responded warmly to the local-color fiction of such writers as Joel Chandler Harris, whose folktales–the most famous being *Uncle Remus* (1880)–portrayed the slave society of the antebellum years as a harmonious world marked by engaging dialect and close emotional bonds between the races. The writer Thomas Nelson Page similarly extolled the old Virginia aristocracy. The growing popularity of minstrel shows also reflected the romanticization of the Old South. The white leaders of the New South, in short, faced their future with one foot still in the past.

HENRY GRADY

Even so, Southern industry expanded dramatically in the years after Reconstruction and became a more important part of the region's economy than ever before. Most visible was the growth in textile manufacturing, which increased ninefold in the last twenty years of the century. In the past, Southern planters had usually shipped their cotton out of the region to manufacturers in the North or in Europe. Now textile factories appeared in the South itself–many of them drawn to the South from New England by the abundance of water power, the ready supply of cheap labor, the low taxes, and the accommodating conservative governments. The tobacco-processing industry, similarly, established an important foothold in the region, largely through the work of James B. Duke of North Carolina, whose American Tobacco Company established for a time a virtual monopoly over the processing of raw tobacco into marketable materials. In the lower South, particularly in Birmingham, Alabama, the iron (and, later, steel) industry grew rapidly. By 1890, the Southern iron and steel industry represented nearly a fifth of the nation's total capacity.

Reasoning Processes

Comparing After students have read the section "The 'Redeemers'," ask them to create a Venn diagram comparing the Redeemer (or Bourbon) governments that emerged in the 1870s with the pre-war governments in the South. Ask students to discuss as a class what accounts for the similarities and differences. **PCE** **ARC** **SOC**

Reasoning Processes

Continuity and Change Have students read the section "Henry Grady." Ask them to discuss as a class how successful Grady and other "New South" leaders were in bringing economic and social change to the South. Have students consider why some changes proved harder to make than others. **ARC** **SOC** **WXT**

Discussion and Activities

Analyzing Points of View After students have read the section "Industrialization and the New South," ask them to write a short letter or journal entry from the point of view of a worker in a Southern mill town explaining their hopes and frustrations. **WXT** **SOC**

Railroad development increased substantially in the post-Reconstruction years–at a rate far greater than that of the nation at large. Between 1880 and 1890, trackage in the South more than doubled. And the South took a major step toward integrating its transportation system with that of the rest of the country when, in 1886, it changed the gauge (distance between the two rails) of its trackage to correspond with the standards of the North. Yet Southern industry developed within strict limits, and its effects on the region were never even remotely comparable to the effects of industrialization on the North. The Southern share of national manufacturing doubled in the last twenty years of the century, to 10 percent of the total. But that percentage was the same the South had claimed in 1860; the region, in other words, had done no more than regain what it had lost during the war and its aftermath. The region's per capita income increased 21 percent in the same period. But at the end of the century, average income in the South was only 40 percent of that in the North; in 1860 it had been more than 60 percent. And even in those areas where development had been most rapid–textiles, iron, railroads–much of the capital had come from the North. In effect, the South was developing a colonial economy.

RAILROAD DEVELOPMENT

The growth of industry in the South required the region to recruit a substantial industrial workforce for the first time. From the beginning, a high percentage of the factory workers (and an especially high percentage of textile workers) were women. Heavy male casualties in the Civil War had helped create a large population of unmarried women who were in dire need of employment. Factories also hired entire families, many of whom were moving into towns from failed farms. Workdays were long (often twelve hours a day) and wages were far below the northern equivalent; indeed, one of the greatest attractions of the South to industrialists was that employers were able to pay workers there as little as one-half what northern workers received.

Life in most mill towns was rigidly controlled by the owners and managers of the factories, who rigorously suppressed attempts at protest or union organization. Company stores sold goods to workers at inflated prices and issued credit at exorbitant rates (much like country stores in agrarian areas), and mill owners ensured that no competitors were able to establish themselves in the community. At the same time, however, the conditions of the mill town helped create a strong sense of community and solidarity among workers (even if they seldom translated such feelings into militancy).

Some industries, textiles for example, offered virtually no opportunities to African American workers. Others–including tobacco, iron, and lumber–did provide some employment for African Americans, usually the most menial and lowest-paid positions. Some mill towns, therefore, were places where black and white culture came into close contact. That proximity contributed less to the growth of racial harmony than to the determination of white leaders to take additional measures to protect white supremacy.

At times, industrialization proceeded on the basis of no wage-paying employment. Through the "convict-lease" system, Southern states leased gangs of convicted criminals to private interests as a cheap labor supply. The system exposed the convicts to brutal and at times fatal mistreatment. It paid them nothing (the leasing fees went to the states, not the workers). And it denied employment in railroad construction and other projects to the free labor force.

"CONVICT-LEASE" SYSTEM

TENANTS AND SHARECROPPERS

Despite significant growth in Southern industry, the region remained primarily agrarian. The most important economic reality in the post-Reconstruction South, therefore, was the impoverished state of agriculture. The 1870s and 1880s saw an acceleration of the trends that had begun in the immediate postwar years: the imposition of systems of tenantry and debt peonage on much of the region; the reliance on a few cash crops rather than on a diversified agricultural system; and increasing absentee ownership of valuable farmlands (many of them purchased by merchants and industrialists who paid little attention to whether the land was being properly used). During Reconstruction, perhaps a third or more of the farmers in the South were tenants; by 1900, the figure had increased to 70 percent. That was in large part the result of the crop-lien system, the system by which farmers borrowed money against their future crops and often fell deeper and deeper into debt.

Tenantry took several forms. Farmers who owned tools, equipment, and farm animals–or who had the money to buy them–usually paid an annual cash rent for their land. But many farmers (including most black farmers) had no money or equipment. Landlords would supply them with land, a crude house, a few tools, seed, and sometimes a mule. In return, farmers would promise the landlord a large share of the annual crop–hence the term "sharecropping." After paying their landlords and their local merchants (who were often the same people), sharecroppers seldom had anything left to sell on their own.

AFRICAN AMERICANS AND THE NEW SOUTH

The "New South creed" was not the property of white Southerners alone. Many African Americans were attracted to the vision of progress and self-improvement as well. Some African Americans succeeded in elevating themselves into a distinct middle class–most of them economically inferior to the white middle class, but nevertheless significant. These were former enslaved people (and, as the decades passed, their offspring) who managed to acquire property, build small businesses, or enter professions. A few African Americans accumulated substantial fortunes by establishing banks and insurance companies to serve the black community. One of those was Maggie Lena, a black woman who became the first female bank president in the United States when she founded

BLACK MIDDLE CLASS

Discussion and Activities

Analyzing Issues Have students read the section "The Convict-Lease System." Ask them to review the text of the Thirteenth Amendment, then discuss in small groups how the convict-lease system could be, or IF it could be, justified constitutionally. *(It could be argued that persons convicted of crimes have surrendered rights that allow the states to use their labor without compensation.)* **PCE**

Discussion and Activities

Analyzing Visuals Have students examine the image "Minstrelsy at High Tide." Ask them to identify and discuss in small groups details from the image that demonstrate social division. *(White and Black performers of the same troupe are posed on opposite sides of the illustration. The highlighted leaders of the troupe are both white.)* **SOC**

PATTERNS OF POPULAR CULTURE

THE MINSTREL SHOW

The minstrel show was one of the most popular forms of entertainment in America in the second half of the nineteenth century. It was also a testament to the high awareness of race (and the high level of racism) in American society both before and after the Civil War. Minstrel performers were mostly white men, usually disguised as black men. But African American performers also formed their own minstrel shows and transformed them into vehicles for training black entertainers and developing new forms of music and dance.

Before and during the Civil War, when minstrel shows consisted almost entirely of white performers, performers blackened their faces with cork and presented grotesque stereotypes of the slave culture of the American South. Among the most popular of the stumbling, ridiculously ignorant characters invented for these shows were such figures as "Zip Coon" and "Jim Crow" (whose name later resurfaced as a label for late-nineteenth-century segregation laws). A typical minstrel show presented a group of seventeen or more men seated in a semicircle facing the audience. The man in the center ran the show, played the straight man for the jokes of others, and led the music—lively dances and sentimental ballads played on banjos, castanets, and other instruments and sung by soloists or the entire group.

After the Civil War, white minstrels began to expand their repertoire. Drawing from the famous and successful freak shows of P. T. Barnum and other entertainment entrepreneurs, some began to include Siamese twins, bearded ladies, and even a supposedly 8-foot 2-inch "Chinese giant" in their shows. They also incorporated sex, both by including women in some shows and, even more popularly, by recruiting female impersonators. One of the most successful minstrel performers of the 1870s was Francis Leon, who delighted crowds with his female portrayal of a flamboyant "prima donna."

One reason white minstrels began to move in these new directions was that they were now facing competition from black performers, who could provide more-authentic versions of black music, dance, and humor. They usually brought more talent to the task than white performers. The Georgia Minstrels, organized in 1865, was one of the first all-black minstrel troupes, and it had great success in attracting white audiences in the Northeast for several years. By the 1870s,

MINSTRELSY AT HIGH TIDE The Primrose & West minstrel troupe—a lavish and expensive entertainment that drew large crowds in the 1800s—was one of many companies to offer this brand of entertainment to eager audiences all over the country. Although minstrelsy began with white musicians performing in blackface, the popularity of real African American minstrels encouraged the impresarios of the troupe to include groups of white and black performers alike.

AG FIELD MINSTRELS This famous minstrel group stands in front of a huge promotional poster sometime in the late 1890s.

touring African American minstrel groups were numerous. The black minstrels used many of the conventions of the white shows. There were dances, music, comic routines, and sentimental recitations. Some black performers even chalked their faces to make themselves look as dark as the white blackface performers with whom they were competing. Black minstrels sometimes denounced slavery (at least indirectly) and did not often speak demeaningly of the capacities of their race. But they could not entirely escape caricaturing African American life as they struggled to meet the expectations of their white audiences.

The black minstrel shows had few openly political aims. They did help develop some important forms of African American entertainment and transform them into a part of the national culture. Black minstrels introduced new forms of dance, derived from the informal traditions of slavery and black community life. They showed the "buck and wing," the "stop time," and the "Virginia essence," which established the foundations for the tap and jazz dancing of the early twentieth century. They also improvised musically and began experimenting with forms that over time contributed to the growth of ragtime, jazz, and rhythm and blues.

Eventually, black minstrelsy—like its white counterpart—evolved into other forms of theater, including the beginnings of serious black drama. At Ambrose Park in Brooklyn in the 1890s, for example, the celebrated black comedian Sam Lucas (a veteran of the minstrel circuit) starred in the play *Darkest America*, which one black newspaper later described as a "delineation of Negro life, carrying the race through all their historical phases from the plantation, into reconstruction days and finally painting our people as they are today, cultured and accomplished in the social graces, [holding] the mirror faithfully up to nature."

But interest in the minstrel show did not die altogether. In 1927, Hollywood released *The Jazz Singer*, the first feature film with sound. It was about the career of a white minstrel performer, and its star was one of the most popular singers of the twentieth century: Al Jolson, whose career had begun on the blackface minstrel circuit years before.

HISTORICAL THINKING SKILLS

1. **Explaining Historical Context** How did minstrel shows performed by white minstrels reinforce prevailing attitudes toward African Americans?
2. **Determining Context** Minstrel shows performed by black minstrels often conformed to existing stereotypes of African Americans. Why?
3. **Making Connections** Can you think of any popular entertainments today that carry remnants of the minstrel shows of the nineteenth century?

Answers

Patterns of Popular Culture

1. The shows often caricatured stereotypes of African Americans. Two characters that became popular in these minstrel shows were "Zip Coon" and "Jim Crow."
2. White audiences often went to see these shows for the way they portrayed African Americans. The shows reinforced racist stereotypes, thereby justifying discrimination within American society.
3. Music videos that portray African Americans predominately as gang members reinforce many stereotypes about young Black men. The 1992 comedy film "White Men Can't Jump" played on the stereotype that white people are less athletic than people of color.

Discussion and Activities

Analyzing Issues After students have read the section "African Americans and the New South," ask them to write a short paragraph summarizing Booker T. Washington's vision for African American self-improvement. Discuss as a class how Washington's proposals both challenged and reassured white Southerners. **PCE** **SOC** **WXT**

FAMILY PORTRAIT This photograph of an African American family of four generations was taken in the late nineteenth century. Every member of this family was born on the plantation of J. J. Smith of Beaufort, South Carolina. The youngest members, while certainly touched by slavery, were not born into that institution.

the St. Luke Penny Savings Bank in Richmond in 1903. Most middle-class African Americans experienced more-modest gains by becoming doctors, lawyers, nurses, or teachers serving African American communities.

A cardinal tenet of this rising group of African Americans was that education was vital to the future of their race. With the support of Northern missionary societies and, to a far lesser extent, a few Southern state governments, they expanded the network of black colleges and institutes that had taken root during Reconstruction into an important educational system.

BOOKER T. WASHINGTON

The chief spokesman for this commitment to education, and for a time the major spokesman for African Americans in the South (and beyond), was Booker T. Washington, founder and president of the Tuskegee Institute in Alabama. Born into slavery, Washington had worked his way out of poverty after acquiring an education (at Virginia's famous Hampton Institute). He urged other African Americans to follow the same road to self-improvement.

Washington's message was both cautious and hopeful. African Americans should attend school, learn skills, and establish a solid footing in agriculture and the trades. Industrial, not classical, education should be their goal. They should, moreover, refine their speech, improve their dress, and adopt habits of thrift and personal cleanliness; they should, in short, adopt the standards of the white middle class. Only thus, he claimed, could they win the respect of the white population, the prerequisite for any larger social gains. African Americans should forgo agitating for political rights, he said, and concentrate on self-improvement and preparation for equality. In a famous speech in Georgia in 1895, Washington outlined a philosophy of race relations that became widely known as the Atlanta Compromise.

THE ATLANTA COMPROMISE

"The wisest among my race understand," he said, "that the agitation of questions of social equality is the extremest folly." Rather, African Americans should engage in "severe and constant struggle" for economic gains; for, as he explained, "no race that has anything to contribute to the markets of the world is long in any degree ostracized." If African Americans were ever to win the rights and privileges of citizenship, they must first show that they were "prepared for the exercise of these privileges." Washington offered a powerful challenge to those white people who wanted to discourage African Americans from acquiring an education or winning any economic gains. He helped awaken the interest of a new generation to the possibilities for self-advancement through self-improvement. But his message was also an implicit promise that African Americans would not overtly challenge the system of segregation that white people were then in the process of erecting.

THE BIRTH OF JIM CROW

Few white Southerners had ever accepted the idea of racial equality. That former enslaved people acquired any legal and political rights at all after emancipation was in large part the result of federal support. That support all but vanished after 1877. Federal troops withdrew. Congress lost interest. And the Supreme Court effectively stripped the Fourteenth and Fifteenth Amendments of much of their significance. In the so-called civil rights cases of 1883, the Court ruled that the Fourteenth Amendment prohibited state governments from discriminating against people because of race but did not restrict private organizations or individuals from doing so. Thus railroads, hotels, theaters, and workplaces could legally practice segregation.

PLESSY V. FERGUSON

Eventually, the Court also validated state legislation that institutionalized the separation of the races. In *Plessy v. Ferguson* (1896), a case involving a Louisiana law that required separate seating arrangements for the races on railroads, the Court held that separate accommodations did not deprive African Americans of equal rights if the accommodations were equal, a decision that survived for years as part of the legal basis for segregated schools. In *Cumming v. County Board of Education* (1899), the Court ruled that laws establishing separate schools for white students were valid even if there were no comparable schools for African Americans.

Before these decisions, white Southerners were working to strengthen white supremacy and to separate the races to the greatest extent possible. One illustration of this movement from subordination to segregation was black voting rights. In

Discussion and Activities

Historical Developments and Argumentation After students have read the section "*Plessy v. Ferguson*," ask them to discuss in small groups how the courts weakened protections extended to African Americans through the Thirteenth, Fourteenth, and Fifteenth Amendments. **PCE**

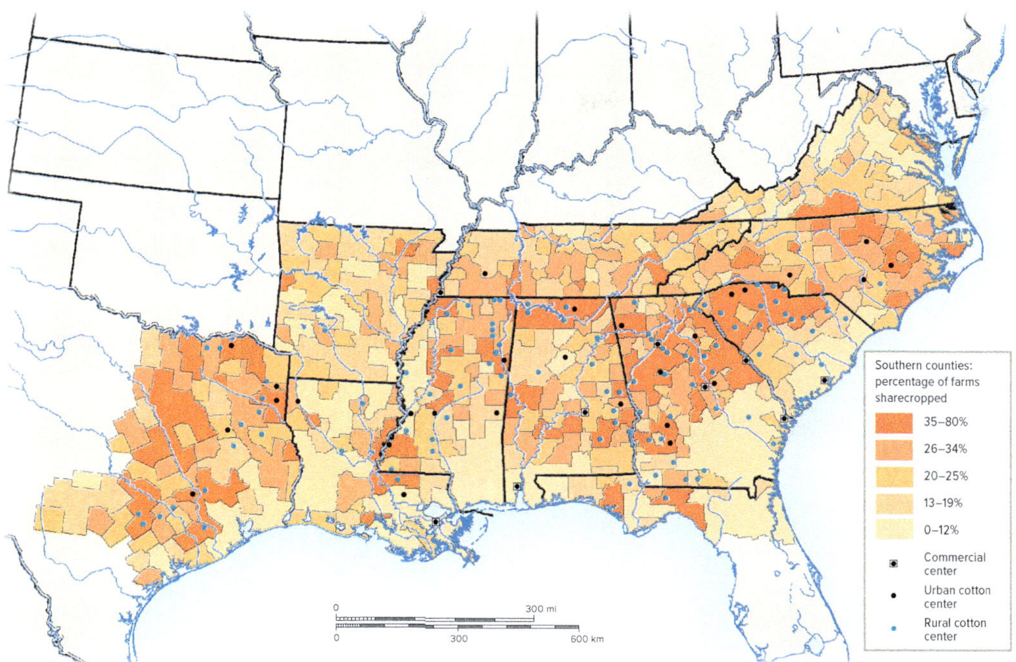

THE CROP-LIEN SYSTEM IN 1880 In the years after the Civil War, more and more Southern farmers—white and black—became tenants or sharecroppers on land owned by others. This map shows the percentage of farms that were within the so-called crop-lien system, the system by which people worked their lands for someone else, who had a claim (or "lien") on a part of the farmers' crops. Note the high density of sharecropping and tenant farming in the most fertile areas of the Deep South, the same areas where slaveholding had been most dominant before the Civil War.

How did the crop-lien system contribute to the shift in Southern agriculture toward one-crop farming?

some states, disenfranchisement had begun almost as soon as Reconstruction ended. But in other areas, black voting continued for some time after Reconstruction–largely because white conservatives believed they could control the black electorate and use it to beat back the attempts of poor white farmers to take control of the Democratic Party. In the 1890s, however, franchise restrictions became much more rigid. During those years, some small white farmers began to demand complete black disenfranchisement–both because of racial prejudice and because they objected to the black vote being used against them by the conservative planters (known as "Bourbons"). At the same time, many members of the conservative elite began to fear that poor white Southerners might unite politically with poor African Americans to challenge them. They too began to support further franchise restrictions.

In devising laws to disenfranchise black males, the Southern states had to find ways to evade the Fifteenth Amendment, which prohibited states from denying anyone the right to vote because of race. Two devices emerged before 1900 to accomplish this goal. One was the poll tax or some form of property qualification; few African Americans were prosperous enough to meet such requirements. Another was the "literacy" or "understanding" test, which required voters to demonstrate an ability to read and interpret the Constitution. Even those African Americans who could read had trouble passing the difficult test white officials gave them. Such restrictions were often applied unequally. Literacy tests for white people, for example, were sometimes much easier than those for African Americans. Even so, the laws affected poor white voters as well as African Americans. By the late 1890s, the black vote had decreased by 62 percent, the white vote by 26 percent. One result was that some states passed so-called grandfather laws, permitting men who could not meet the literacy and property qualifications to be enfranchised if their ancestors had voted before Reconstruction began, thus barring the descendants of enslaved people from the polls while allowing poor white men access to them. In many areas, however, ruling elites were quite content to see poor white men, a potential source of opposition to their power, barred from voting.

RESTRICTING THE FRANCHISE

The Supreme Court proved as compliant in ruling on the disenfranchising laws as it was in dealing with the civil rights

Discussion and Activities

Analyzing Continuity Have students examine the map "The Crop-Lien System in 1880." Ask them to discuss in small groups details from the map that show continuities with previous maps of economic activity. *(The areas with the heaviest concentration of sharecropping and the crop-lien system run across the so-called "black belt," where rich soil had supported the heaviest production of cotton and the most intensive use of slavery.)* **GEO** **WXT** **SOC**

Answers

The Crop-Lien System in 1880

The crop-lien system created pressure on farmers to grow cash crops to earn income with which to pay off debt.

Discussion and Activities

Analyzing Visuals Have students examine the image "Tuskegee Institute, 1881." Ask them to create a list of details from the image and then write a short paragraph describing the scene from the point of view of someone who did not know that this was the Tuskegee Institute. *(Simple buildings; lack of windows in most cases; resemble farm sheds and barns; workers building; rustic, almost wilderness setting. It would be easy to conclude that this was a homesteader's farm.)* **SOC** **WXT**

TUSKEGEE INSTITUTE, 1881 From these modest beginnings, Booker T. Washington's Tuskegee Institute in Alabama became the preeminent academy offering technical and industrial training to black men. It deliberately de-emphasized the traditional liberal arts curricula of most colleges. Washington considered such training an unnecessary frill and encouraged his students to work on developing practical skills.

cases. The Court eventually voided the grandfather laws, but it validated the literacy test (in the 1898 case of *Williams v. Mississippi*) and displayed a general willingness to let the Southern states define their own suffrage standards as long as evasions of the Fifteenth Amendment were not too glaring.

Laws restricting the franchise and segregating schools were only part of a network of state statutes—known as the Jim Crow laws—that by the first years of the twentieth century had institutionalized an elaborate system of segregation reaching into almost every area of Southern life. African Americans and white people could not ride in the same railroad cars, sit in the same waiting rooms, use the same washrooms, eat in the same restaurants, or sit in the same theaters. African Americans had no access to many public parks, beaches, and picnic areas; they could not be patients in many hospitals. Much of the new legal structure did no more than confirm what had already been widespread social practice in the South since well before the end of Reconstruction. But the Jim Crow laws also stripped African Americans of many of the modest social, economic, and political gains they had made in the more fluid atmosphere of the late nineteenth century. The laws served, too, as a means for white Southerners to retain control of social relations between the races in the newly growing cities and towns of the South, where traditional patterns of deference and subjugation were more difficult to preserve than in the countryside. What had been maintained by custom in the rural South was to be maintained by law in the urbanizing South.

WHITE CONTROL PERPETUATED

More than legal efforts were involved in this process. The 1890s witnessed a dramatic increase in white violence against African Americans, which, along with the Jim Crow laws, served to inhibit black agitation for equal rights. The worst such violence—lynching of African Americans by white mobs, either because the victims were accused of crimes or because they had seemed somehow to violate their expected station—reached appalling levels. In the nation as a whole in the 1890s, there was an average of 187 lynchings each year, more than 80 percent of them in the South. The vast majority of victims were black. One African American woman, Lucy McMillan, said, "John Hunter's wife

LYNCHINGS

Discussion and Activities

Analyzing Issues Have students read the section "White Control Perpetuated." Ask them to list and discuss as a class how Jim Crow laws denied rights to African Americans. **PCE** **SOC** **WXT**

Discussion and Activities

Analyzing Points of View After students have read the section "Lynchings," ask them to write a short journal entry from the point of view of a witness to one of these events.

A LYNCH MOB, 1893 A large, almost festive crowd gathers to watch the lynching of a black man accused of the murder of a three-year-old white girl. Lynchings remained frequent in the South until as late as the 1930s, but they reached their peak in the 1890s and the first years of the twentieth century. Lynchings such as this one—published well in advance and attracting whole families who traveled great distances to see them—were infrequent. Most lynchings were the work of smaller groups, operating with less visibility.

The Library of Congress

came to my house on Saturday morning, and told they were going to whip me. I was afraid of them. There was so much talk of Ku-Klux drowning people, and killing them."

The most celebrated lynchings occurred in cities and towns, where large, well-organized mobs–occasionally with the tacit cooperation of local authorities–seized black prisoners from the jails and hanged them in great public rituals. Such public lynchings were often planned well in advance and elaborately organized. They attracted large audiences from surrounding regions. Entire families traveled many miles to witness the spectacles. But such great public lynchings were relatively rare. Much more frequent, and more dangerous to African Americans because less visible or predictable, were lynchings performed by small vigilante mobs, often composed of friends or relatives of the victim (or supposed victim) of a crime. Those involved in lynchings often saw their actions as a legitimate form of law enforcement; and indeed, some victims of lynchings had in fact committed crimes. But lynchings were also a means by which white people controlled the black population through terror and intimidation. Thus, some lynch mobs killed African Americans whose only "crime" had been presumptuousness. Others chose as victims outsiders in the community, whose presence threatened to disturb the normal pattern of race relations. Black men who had made any sexual advances toward white women (or who white men thought had done so) were particularly vulnerable to lynchings; the fear of black sexuality, and the unspoken fear among many men that white women might be attracted to that sexuality, was always an important part of the belief system that supported segregation. Whatever the reasons or circumstances, the victims of lynch mobs were denied the protection of the laws and the opportunity to prove their innocence.

The rise of lynchings shocked the conscience of many white Americans in a way that other forms of racial injustice did not. Almost from the start there was a substantial anti-lynching movement. In 1892 Ida B. Wells, a committed black journalist, launched what became an international anti-lynching movement with a series of impassioned articles after the lynching of three of her friends in Memphis, Tennessee, her home. The movement gradually gathered strength in the first years of the twentieth century, attracting substantial support from white people (particularly white women) in both the North and the

Discussion and Activities

Evaluating Evidence Have students examine the image "A Lynch Mob, 1893." Ask them to discuss as a class whether such a gathering could likely take place without the knowledge of, and likely at least tacit support of, local officials.
PCE **SOC**

AP Exam Practice

Short Answer Provide students with the following short-answer questions and allow 15 minutes for completion. Ask for volunteers to share their responses and discuss as a class.

Answer A, B, and C.

A) Briefly explain ONE important similarity between the Shaw and King monuments. *(Possible answer: They both commemorate important African American achievements.)*

B) Briefly explain ONE important difference between the Shaw and King monuments. *(Possible answer: The Shaw monument focuses on the white officer; the King monument focuses on Dr. King individually. The Shaw monument is in Boston, while the King monument is in Washington, D.C.)*

C) Briefly explain ONE historical reason for the difference cited in B. *(Possible answer: Attitudes about race and racism changed in the more than 100 years between the creation of the monuments.)*

CONSIDER THE SOURCE

REMEMBERING BLACK HISTORY

How we remember the past can tell us a great deal about our values and priorities as a nation. When these memories take official form, as in a public monument erected in a culturally significant setting, they offer a view into how Americans understood history in a particular time. What is revealed, however, is rarely a popular consensus about what individuals or events were worthy of being celebrated. Rather, the final construction and placement of any public monument typically reflects a series of tough debates between people with different views of the meaning of the past.

The two monuments pictured on the following page are among the most famous in American history in general and African American history in particular. The first is a bronze relief by Augustus Saint-Gaudens commemorating the Fifty-Fourth Massachusetts Volunteer Infantry Regiment, the first military unit composed of black soldiers raised in the North during the Civil War. At full fighting strength, with over 1000 African American men led by an all-white officer corps, the 54th became a national symbol of African American freedom. Leading the assault on July 18, 1863, against the Confederate stronghold, Fort Wagner, on Morris Island, South Carolina, it sustained heavy losses, including that of its commanding officer, Colonel Robert Shaw. Despite failing to take the fort, the black troops fought passionately and with discipline, thereby silencing critics who doubted the very ability of African Americans to stand strong in battle.

Saint-Gaudens unveiled his memorial in May 1897. Eleven feet high and 14 feet long, it depicts the 54th marching through Boston in the first leg of its journey to the battlefront. Leading the unit is Colonel Shaw, on horseback. It still sits in its original locale, at the edge of the Boston Common in the shadow of the Massachusetts State House.

The second monument is a white granite statue by Lie Yixin, a sculptor from the People's Republic of China, honoring the life of civil rights pioneer, Martin Luther King, Jr. King, a Baptist minister born in Atlanta, Georgia, who led the fight to end segregation in the South in the 1950s and 1960s. He spearheaded the drive to pass the Civil Rights Act of 1964 and the Voting Rights Act of 1965. He was assassinated in 1968.

The King statue is actually part of a larger, four-acre park dedicated to his life that sits in the southwest corner of the National Mall in Washington, D.C. The 30-foot high statue has a clear view of the Lincoln Memorial and the Jefferson Memorial and is accompanied by a 450-foot long inscription wall that bears quotes from King's most famous speeches. The King Memorial is the first dedicated to a black American on the National Mall.

Discussion and Activities

Analyzing Points of View

Have students read the feature "Remembering Black History," and then ask them to write a journal entry from the point of view of an American citizen present at the dedication of either of the monuments. **SOC** **PCE** **NAT**

MEMORIALIZING BLACK HISTORY IN 1897 Memorial to Robert Gould Shaw and the Fifty-Fourth Regiment.

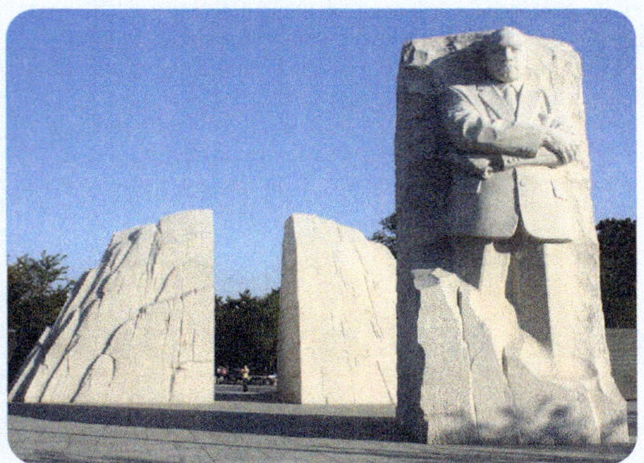

MEMORIALIZING BLACK HISTORY IN 2011 The Martin Luther King, Jr. National Memorial.

ANALYZING SOURCES

Questions assume cumulative content knowledge from this chapter and previous chapters.

1. Which statement best describes what the monument from 1897 suggests about general societal attitudes towards African Americans at the turn of the 20th century in America?
   - (A) Efforts of African Americans to achieve social equality came to be deeply appreciated by American society in general.
   - (B) The inordinate prominence of the white officer suggests that American society still did not fully appreciate African Americans as equals.
   - (C) The dominance of the number of African Americans suggests that turn-of-the-century America experienced a boom in African American population.
   - (D) The placement of the African American soldiers in the background suggests that around the turn of the 20th century, American society developed great interest in viewing American history from an African American lens.

2. How does the memorial honoring Martin Luther King, Jr., differ from the monument from 1897?
   - (A) The Martin Luther King, Jr., monument suggests that African Americans have achieved social equality, due to the use of white granite.
   - (B) The Martin Luther King, Jr., monument reflects less societal appreciation for African American achievement.
   - (C) The Martin Luther King, Jr., monument reflects a greater appreciation by American society for African American achievement—in this case, that of Martin Luther King, Jr.
   - (D) The Martin Luther King, Jr., monument suggests more than the monument from 1897 that more progress needs to be made towards racial equality.

3. In what way might the establishment of the monument from 1897 be viewed as a significant event in black history?
   - (A) by offering the public a glimpse of the perspective of African Americans during the war
   - (B) by the mere fact of the public memorializing of the role of African Americans in the Civil War
   - (C) by revealing through public art the plight of African Americans
   - (D) by reinforcing to the public the dominance of white society

Discussion and Activities

Historical Significance and Argumentation Have students examine the monuments shown in the feature. Ask them to work in small groups to consider the features of the existing monuments, and then to design a monument they believe would be appropriate to recognize the actions and achievements of African Americans, either collectively or individually, during Reconstruction. SOC PCE

Answers

Consider the Source

1. B; **2.** C; **3.** B

Discussion and Activities

Analyzing Issues Divide the class into three groups and assign each group to review and research the successes and failures of Reconstruction in one of these categories: political, economic, and social. Then have students form groups of three, including one student from each of the original three groups, to share their conclusions. **PCE** **NAT** **ARC** **SOC** **WXT**

Key Terms

Students should be familiar with the key terms and be able to define them in the context of disputes over and the successes and failures of Reconstruction politically, economically, and socially. Encourage students to use these terms in performing review exercises and exam practice for this chapter.

South. Its goal was a federal anti-lynching law, which would allow the national government to do what state and local governments in the South were generally unwilling to do: punish those responsible for lynchings.

But the substantial white opposition to lynchings stood as an exception to the general white support for suppression of African Americans. Indeed, just as in the antebellum period, **WHITE UNITY** the shared commitment to white supremacy helped dilute class animosities between poorer white Southerners and the Bourbon oligarchies. Economic issues tended to play a secondary role to race in Southern politics, distracting people from the glaring social inequalities that afflicted all races. The commitment to white supremacy, in short, was a burden for poor Southern whites as well as for African Americans.

CHAPTER 15 REVIEW

CONNECTING THEMES

Chapter Fifteen examined the disputes over Reconstruction between the North and the South, Democrats and Republicans, Radicals and Conservatives, and the various branches of government. Competing notions of freedom between African Americans and white Americans also made Reconstruction controversial from the start.

Reconstruction ultimately had varying degrees of success economically, politically, and socially. African Americans made modest and temporary gains at first. But white Southerners soon passed legislation to promote segregation and disenfranchisement as white Northerners lost interest. Oppressive economic practices in the South such as sharecropping and the crop-lien system also limited economic opportunities for African Americans. In the end, Reconstruction was largely a failure despite passage of the Fourteenth and Fifteenth Amendments, which aided the modern civil rights movement.

In the 1880s, Southern leaders like Henry Grady promoted the idea of a "New South" based on industry and commerce. But the South remained economically underdeveloped despite the growth of factories and railroads. Agriculture was dominant and many farmers were tenants or sharecroppers. Some African Americans managed to climb into the middle class, but Southern whites used public lynchings and Jim Crow to maintain political and economic control while white Northerners lost interest and shifted their attention to other issues.

You should consider the following questions as you review the themes for this chapter:

- How were American concepts of identity changed during and after the Civil War and Reconstruction, particularly for African Americans?
- How did the Civil War and Reconstruction affect the economies of both the North and the South, including existing labor systems?
- How did the Civil War and Reconstruction affect migration and immigration in the second half of the nineteenth century?
- What were the political changes brought about as a result of the Civil War and Reconstruction?
- What was the impact of the Civil War and Reconstruction on the infrastructure of the South?
- How were the beliefs of Northerners and Southerners affected by the Civil War and Reconstruction?

KEY TERMS

Andrew Johnson 423
Atlanta Compromise 440
Black Codes 423
Blanche Bruce 427
Booker T. Washington 440
Carpetbaggers 426
Charles Sumner 433
Compromise of 1877 434
crop-lien system 438
Enforcement Acts 433
Fifteenth Amendment 424
Fourteenth Amendment 423
Freedmen's Bureau 420
Hamilton Fish 431
Hiram Revels 427
Ida B. Wells 443
Jim Crow laws 442
Ku Klux Klan 433
New South 436
Panic of 1873 432
Plessy vs. Ferguson 440
Radical Republicans 421
Redeemers 436
Reconstruction bills 424
Scalawags 426
segregated schools 440
sharecropping 438
Thaddeus Stevens 421
Thirteenth Amendment 423
Wade-Davis Bill 423
William Seward 432

Go Online **Chapter 15 Content Review**

Assessing Student Understanding Use the online assessment to assess student understanding of concepts and topics within the chapter. You can assign the ready-made Chapter 15 Content Review or create your own from available questions. This easy-to-use tool helps you design assessments that meet the needs of different types of learners.

AP EXAM PRACTICE

Questions assume cumulative content knowledge from this chapter and the previous chapter.

MULTIPLE CHOICE

Use the excerpt below and your knowledge of U.S. history to answer questions 1-3.

"All persons born or naturalized in the United States, and subject to the jurisdiction thereof, are citizens of the United States and of the state wherein they reside. No state shall make or enforce any law which shall abridge the privileges or immunities of citizens of the United States; nor shall any state deprive any person of life, liberty, or property, without due process of law; nor deny to any person within its jurisdiction the equal protection of the laws."

–14th Amendment to the U.S. Constitution, Section 1

1. The 14th Amendment confirmed the concept of
   - (A) women's equality under the law.
   - (B) natural born citizenship.
   - (C) the rights of all immigrants to naturalization.
   - (D) the legality of the death penalty.
2. The 14th Amendment was necessary due to the
   - (A) creation of the Freedmen's Bureau.
   - (B) Emancipation Proclamation.
   - (C) the passage of Black Codes
   - (D) Enforcement Acts
3. Which of the following most directly attacked the main concept of the 14th Amendment during the time period?
   - (A) passage of Jim Crow laws
   - (B) ratification of the 15th Amendment
   - (C) industrialization of the Southern economy
   - (D) integration of new immigrants into Southern society

SHORT ANSWER

Use your knowledge of U.S. history to answer questions 4 and 5.

4. Use the image on page 426 to answer A, B, and C.
   - (A) Describe ONE point of view about Reconstruction illustrated by the image.
   - (B) Briefly explain ONE specific historical cause which led to military Reconstruction.
   - (C) Briefly explain ONE specific historical effect which resulted from military Reconstruction.
5. Answer A, B, and C.
   - (A) Briefly describe ONE specific historical similarity Southern African American faced before and after the Civil War.
   - (B) Briefly describe ONE specific historical difference Southern African Americans faced before and after the Civil War.
   - (C) Briefly explain ONE major effect of Reconstruction on African Americans in both the North and the South.

LONG ESSAY

Develop a thoughtful and thorough historical argument that addresses the statement. Begin your essay with a thesis statement, and support it with specific historical evidence and examples.

6. Evaluate the relative importance of effects of the Civil War and Reconstruction from 1876 to 1900 in the United States.

Answers

Multiple Choice

1. B; **2.** C; **3.** A

Short Answer

4A) The point of view in the image is that of a Southerner. President Grant, who wears the initials of Lincoln in his hat, rides on the back of the "Solid South" under a Carpetbag regime with bayonet rule. The state of the economy and society within the South is shown as terribly oppressed and burdened by the Northern policies of Reconstruction.

4B) Because the states of the Deep South seceded from the Union at the start of the Civil War, many of them refused to accept the terms of the peace agreement. The North was forced to implement military rule, ensuring safety and complicity with the terms, most importantly the Civil War amendments.

4C) Many Southerners resented the continued occupation of the South after the war was over; this led to much of the South viewing the terms of the agreement as unacceptable. Many states rushed to reinstate the Redeemer governments and implement the oppressive Jim Crow laws of segregation.

5A) The African American community continued to face de facto and de jure discrimination within American society. Before the Civil War they faced Black Codes in the South, which severely limited their freedom. After the Civil War, they faced Jim Crow laws, which sought to continue to limit their freedoms.

5B) Before the Civil War, most African Americans lived under legal slavery, protected by the Constitution and the U.S. Supreme Court. Following the Civil War, with the passage of the 13th Amendment, slavery was now officially and legally abolished in the United States.

5C) The African American community in both the North and the South faced extreme resentment from many other Americans, who accused them of being the cause of the Civil War. They faced extreme de jure discrimination in the form of Jim Crow laws, and they also faced de facto discrimination throughout the North and the South long after Reconstruction.

Answers

Long Essay

6. Possible thesis: The Democratic Party was forced to become no more than a regional party following the war and Reconstruction. However, the effects the war and Reconstruction had on the African American community was complicated. There were freedoms gained; however, these freedoms faced extensive opposition from Southern proponents. The Southern economy also suffered at this time. Their continued reliance on a single cash-crop economy kept them hampered socially, politically, and economically. Specific historical evidence: First, the effect that these two events had on the lives of African Americans was profound. It abolished slavery, but Southerners responded with de facto laws that were harsh and discriminatory. The institution of slavery was gone, but sharecropping and the crop-lien system were also repressive. With passage of the Civil War amendments, African Americans supposedly had the same protections under the law as every other American, but the South passed Jim Crow laws that forced a whole new discriminatory system on African Americans. Second, because Southerners relied on a single-crop, their economy was largely unable to adjust to the changing demands of the world economy. Additionally, while the South was lobbying for needed economic changes, some cities did industrialize; however, the South largely stayed agricultural, with a heavy reliance on cotton.

Discussion and Activities

Analyzing Cause and Effect Direct students' attention to the Questions to Consider posed at the beginning of Unit 5:

- What were the major causes of the Civil War?
- How were the North and the South politically, socially, and economically similar and different before and after the Civil War?
- What were the major effects of the Civil War?

Discuss these questions as a class to review important concepts from the unit. To close the discussion, **ask:** How did the Civil War and Reconstruction alter the identity of the United States? **NAT** **ARC** **SOC** **WXT**

UNIT 5 AP EXAM PRACTICE

AP EXAM PRACTICE

As you answer the questions, consider how the historical developments, processes, and individuals in Unit 5 connect to those in previous units.

MULTIPLE CHOICE

Use the map on page 367 and your knowledge of U.S. history to answer questions 1-3.

1. The conflict illustrated by the map reflected continuing tensions from
   (A) the Texan Revolution and American annexation of Texas.
   (B) disputes in the Northwest Territory.
   (C) the Mormon trek into Utah.
   (D) disputes surrounding the California Gold Rush.

2. The conflict illustrated by the map was part of the larger movement known as
   (A) the Second Great Awakening.
   (B) the Cult of Domesticity.
   (C) Manifest Destiny.
   (D) popular sovereignty.

3. In the aftermath of the conflict illustrated by the map, political tensions flared over the status of
   (A) taxation in the new territory.
   (B) slavery in the new territory.
   (C) immigration in the new territory.
   (D) Senate representation for the new territory.

Use the chart on page 387 and your knowledge of U.S. history to answer questions 4 and 5.

4. The advantages of the Union as shown in the chart were balanced by which advantage held by the Confederacy?
   (A) significant numbers of African Americans willing to fight for the Confederacy
   (B) the support of foreign powers
   (C) the ability to fight a largely defensive war
   (D) a large immigrant population moving into Southern regions

5. What group of Americans enlisted in large numbers and proved to be crucial to the Union's victory?
   (A) Native Americans
   (B) Midwesterners
   (C) naturalized citizens
   (D) African Americans

Use the photograph on page 409 and your knowledge of U.S. history to answer questions 6 and 7.

6. What development transformed the nature of combat in the Civil War?
   (A) the shots fired at Fort Sumter
   (B) advances made to the railroad in the South
   (C) new technologies used in armaments and artillery
   (D) enlistment of Native Americans and African Americans in the Union Army

7. What trend contributed to the Union victory in the Civil War?
   (A) England provided naval support and personnel to aid the Union.
   (B) The Union was able to enlist Canadian soldiers in large numbers.
   (C) The Confederacy failed to gain the support of European powers.
   (D) The infrastructure in Southern states did not support military demands.

Answers

Multiple Choice

1. A; **2.** C; **3.** B; **4.** C; **5.** D; **6.** C; **7.** C; **8.** B; **9.** B; **10.** A

Use the image on page 421 to answer questions 8–10.

8. Which Amendment most directly made the scene in the "Freedmen's Bureau School" image possible?
   (A) 12th Amendment
   (B) 13th Amendment
   (C) 14th Amendment
   (D) 15th Amendment

9. Institutions such as the "Freedmen's Bureau School" could be best described as
   (A) an attempt to recreate previous social structures.
   (B) a limited attempt to provide educational opportunities to African Americans.
   (C) dedicated to immediate legal and economic equality.
   (D) focused on access to higher education.

10. Opponents of schools for African Americans were successful in instituting
   (A) the economic system of sharecropping.
   (B) laws that nullified the Black Codes.
   (C) expanded access to voting.
   (D) a political system that enabled racially mixed political leadership.

SHORT ANSWER

Use the image on page 436 and your knowledge of U.S. history to answer question 11.

11. Answer A, B, and C.
   (A) Describe ONE point of view about Reconstruction as depicted in the image.
   (B) Briefly explain ONE specific historical cause of the Compromise of 1877.
   (C) Briefly explain ONE specific historical effect of the Compromise of 1877.

LONG ESSAY

Develop a thoughtful and thorough historical argument that addresses the statement below. Begin your essay with a thesis statement. and support it with specific historical evidence and examples.

12. Evaluate the extent of continuities involved in developing a unique American culture from 1754 to 1800.

Answers

Short Answer

11A) Possible answer: The point of view of the image is that of an abolitionist, someone who sympathized with the plight of African Americans. The image focuses on the failure of Reconstruction to solve any of the issues facing African Americans. They still faced economic hardships, racial discrimination, and violence.

11B) Possible answer: The Election of 1876 continued to show the flaws in the electoral system established by the Founding Fathers. Because elections required a majority and not just a plurality of Electoral College votes, in 1876, three states challenged the results of their popular vote, which would be problematic for the electoral vote. Florida, South Carolina, and Louisiana would send back multiple, conflicting results. The Constitution did not provide a solution to this electoral dilemma. A commission was established that gave the Electoral College votes to Hayes, but the Democrats protested. To solve the problem, the Compromise of 1877 ended Reconstruction when Democrats promised to accept the results of the commission if Republicans left the South and ended Reconstruction.

11C) Possible answer: The Compromise effectively ended Reconstruction, and because oversight of the South was now nonexistent, Southerners simply reverted back to the pre-Civil War days as Redeemer governments instituted Jim Crow policies. The Compromise showed a serious flaw in the argument of Republicans as defenders of African Americans as Republicans abandoned all hope of protection to guarantee victory in the election of 1876.

Answers

Long Essay

12. Possible thesis: There were efforts to revitalize the Southern economy following the Civil War with some cities becoming important national industrial sites. However, the economy remained largely agricultural, continuing to rely on farming cotton. Further, the racism and discrimination faced by African Americans continued following the Civil War in the form of Jim Crow laws. Therefore, despite some small changes, the South remained largely like it was before the Civil War. Continuities: The South had always relied heavily on large numbers of agricultural workers. Early on they used indentured servants, but eventually they turned to enslaved African Americans. Following the Civil War, the South began using other systems that turned out to be almost as repressive: sharecropping and the crop-lien system. Before the passage of the Civil War amendments, discrimination had taken the form of Black Codes. These continued in different forms, including Jim Crow laws, with much of the same results following the Civil War. Changes: In addition to the switch from slavery to sharecropping and the crop-lien system as a new economic model, other changes occurred. Following the Civil War, "New South" proponents tried to push for economic reform, and attempts were made to industrialize the South. In some areas, these attempts were successful, but overwhelmingly, the South remained an agriculture-based economy.

Pacing Guide

Unit 6 explores key concepts from Period 6: 1865–1898 of the AP U.S. History Curriculum Framework. It is recommended that 10–17% of the total instruction time for the entire course be spent on Period 6.

Key Concepts

6.1 Technological advances, large-scale production methods, and the opening of new markets encouraged the rise of industrial capitalism in the United States

6.2 The migrations that accompanied industrialization transformed both urban and rural areas of the United States and caused dramatic social and cultural change.

6.3 The Gilded Age produced new cultural and intellectual movements, public reform efforts, and political debates over economic and social policies.

UNIT 6: 1865–1898

CHAPTER 16:
THE CONQUEST OF THE FAR WEST

CHAPTER 17:
INDUSTRIAL SUPREMACY

CHAPTER 18:
THE AGE OF THE CITY

CHAPTER 19:
GILDED AGE POLITICS

THEMATIC LEARNING OBJECTIVES

- Analyze the reasons for the continued western expansion and migration in the United States during the last half of the nineteenth century.
- Explain the consequences of western expansion and white settlement on the Native American population.
- Explain the significance of the Second Industrial Revolution.
- Assess the rise of and changes to big business during the Gilded Age.
- Describe the causes and effects of the rise of agricultural and urban labor movements in the United States during the last half of the nineteenth century.
- Analyze the reasons for and the consequences of the rise of urbanization in the United States during the Gilded Age.
- Evaluate the significance of the following elections: 1876, 1884, 1892, 1896, and 1900.

QUESTIONS TO CONSIDER

- What were the major causes and effects of western migration during the Gilded Age?
- What were the reasons for and consequences of the rise of the Second Industrial Revolution in the United States?
- What were the reasons for and effects of the rise of agricultural labor movements during the Gilded Age?

HISTORICAL DEVELOPMENTS: 1865–1898

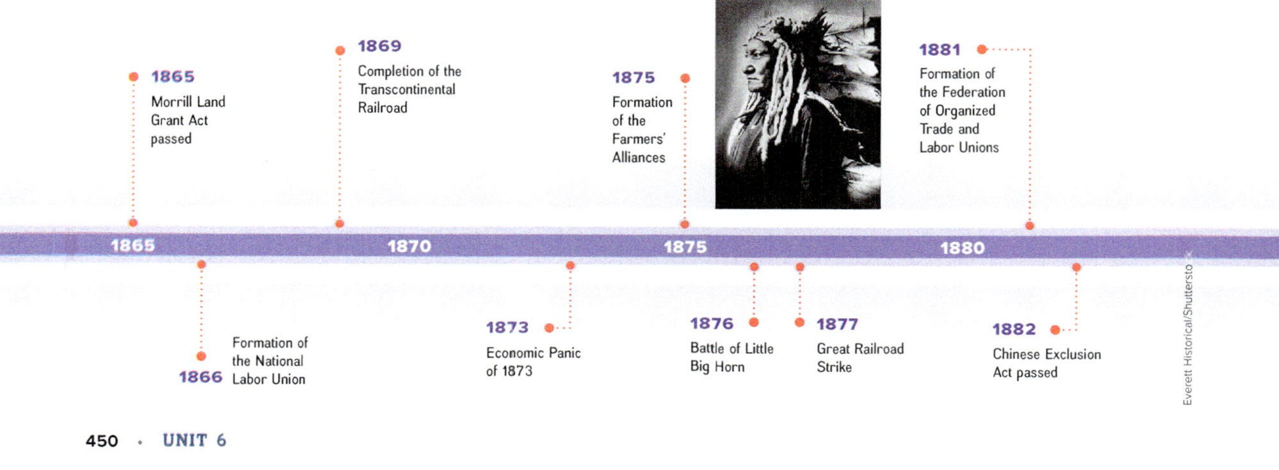

Discussion and Activities

Evaluating Have students examine the time line "Historical Developments: 1865–1898." **Ask:** Based on the time line and what you already know, which events on the time line appear to deal with social, economic, or political issues? *(Social: Farmers' Alliance; Economic: National Labor Union, Interstate Commerce Act, Panic of 1873, Great Railroad Strike, Federation of Organized Trade and Labor Unions, Panic of 1893; Political: Chinese Exclusion Act, Populist Party, Coxey's Army.)* Which category seems to be most prevalent? **PCE** **WXT** **SOC**

MAKING CONNECTIONS

Unit Six focuses on the latter decades of the nineteenth century. The period is often called the Gilded Age—a reference to the novel that Mark Twain co-authored in 1873. The era featured great political, social, economic, and cultural changes as the country struggled to rebuild following the Civil War of the 1860s.

The United States continued to expand westward, and the region grew in economic and political importance. A number of factors drew white settlers to the West. The Homestead Act provided free land. The railroads, which grew exponentially after the Civil War with the financial support of the federal government, provided transportation for people and products. However, the influx of white settlers led to many conflicts with Native American nations and existing Hispanic communities of the region. The United States government also forced Native Americans to assimilate into American culture and caused great harm to Native American identity.

The West was not the only region experiencing tremendous change. Technological advancements, the factory system, and a labor force that was greatly expanding through increasing migration and immigration drove the growth of American industry. Large corporations exerted great influence on the government at all levels and relied on the federal government for protection and support. Big business increased productivity and efficiency. Workers saw some improvement in their standard of living, but their lives remained difficult, insecure, and dangerous. Attempts by labor leaders to form unions in an effort to improve pay, hours, and working conditions were largely unsuccessful.

Industrial growth helped spur rapid urbanization. Cities provided opportunities for immigrants and rural migrants, both culturally and economically. Yet the rise in immigration also provoked a nativist response in some Americans and these sentiments would influence politics and legislation. Urbanization brought with it a new wave of problems including overcrowding, dangerous living conditions, and the spread of disease. Crime escalated and poverty was widespread in cities. Artists and writers depicted the negative aspects of urbanization and industrialization in the new Realist and Naturalist cultural movements.

During the Gilded Age, the electorate divided evenly between Democrats and Republicans. Voter turnout was high and voter loyalty was fierce, driven by religion, race, and region as well as cultural factors. The federal government played a relatively minor role in national affairs, but the political, economic, and social crisis of the 1890s led to the emergence of the People's Party, which attracted widespread support from small farmers who felt powerless and insecure. After the election of 1896, the Populists faded into history, but the issues they raised continued to affect American politics in the twentieth century.

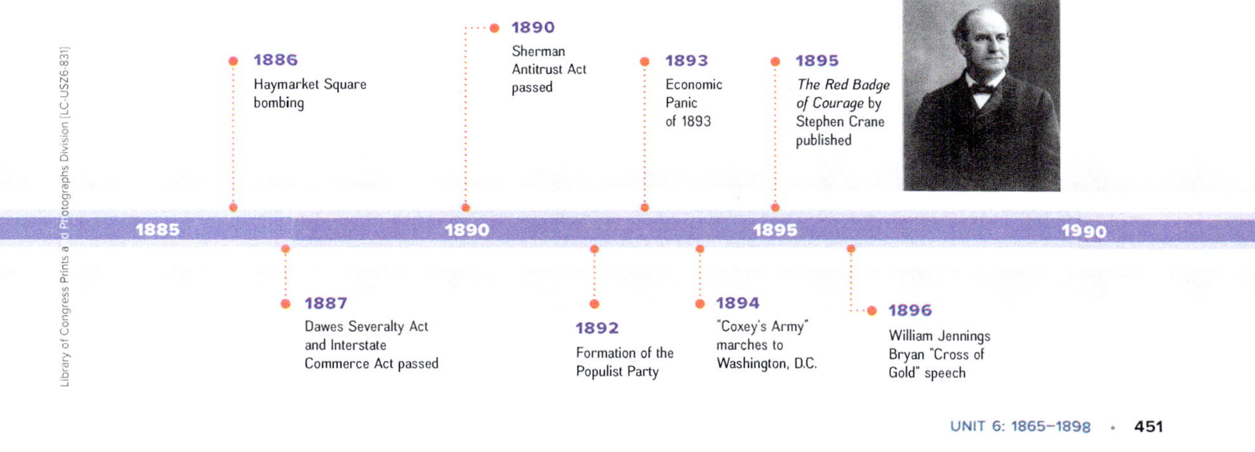

Library of Congress Prints and Photographs Division [LC-USZ6-831]

Historical Thinking Skills

Contextualization Have students read the section "Making Connections." Ask them to discuss as a class the state of the nation as of 1865. *(The nation was concerned with westward expansion, sectional division over tariffs and slavery, differing economic developments of the North and South, and most importantly, the Civil War and the beginning of Reconstruction.)* **PCE** **NAT** **ARC** **WXT** **SOC** **MIG**

Go Online Additional Resources

Adaptive Learning with SmartBook A proven adaptive learning program, SmartBook offers an interactive environment that helps students learn faster, study more efficiently, and retain more knowledge.

Assign this resource to differentiate instruction for students and report on year-long progression.

Pacing Guide

Chapter 16 explores key concepts from Period 6: 1865–1898 of the AP U.S. History Curriculum Framework. The suggested instruction time for Chapter 16 is 5 days.

Key Concepts

6.1.I Large-scale industrial production—accompanied by massive technological change, expanding international communication networks, and pro-growth government policies—generated rapid economic development and business consolidation.

6.1.II A variety of perspectives on the economy and labor developed during a time of financial panics and downturns.

6.1.III New systems of production and transportation enabled consolidation within agriculture, which, along with periods of instability, spurred a variety of responses from farmers.

16 THE CONQUEST OF THE FAR WEST

AMERICAN PROGRESS, 1872
The Brooklyn artist John Gast painted this tribute to westward expansion—an image of hardy pioneers marching toward the frontier, protected by the goddess of progress. It was designed for travel guides to encourage tourists and migrants to travel to the West.

The Library of Congress (LC-USZC4-668)

CONNECTING CONCEPTS

Chapter Sixteen begins by describing the many peoples of the Far West. The largest group consisted of Native Americans. Some were displaced members of Eastern nations like the Cherokee and Creek. But most were Native Americans who had always lived in the West. The diversity of these peoples and their reliance on the buffalo made it difficult for them to effectively resist the white settlers who poured into the West. Eventually, the federal government dispersed Native Americans onto isolated reservations and then tried to eradicate their traditional cultures through the Dawes Act. Much of the Far West was previously part of the Spanish Empire, and, later, the Mexican Republic. In the 1840s, many Mexican people became residents of the territory. Spanish-speaking communities throughout the Southwest shared the concern of Native American groups – that they might lose their land and culture to white settlers, who often arrived by railroad.

The transcontinental railroad transformed the West socially, politically, and economically. Chinese immigrants, many of whom had arrived during the Gold Rush of 1849, comprised 90 percent of the railroad workforce. While welcomed at first, they soon became the targets of racism and discrimination. California passed laws to limit Chinese immigrants from participating in mining and farming. Then Congress in 1882 issued the Chinese Exclusion Act, which barred immigration to the United States.

Federal and state governments subsidized the development of railroads through land grants. Railroad companies actively promoted western settlement, offering low rates for white settlers to increase the value of their land holdings. The romance

Discussion and Activities

Analyzing Visuals Have students examine the image "*American Progress*, 1872." Ask them to identify and discuss in small groups archetypes used in the painting and what message they believe the artist was trying to convey by using them. *(The sky is lighter in the East and darker and stormier in the West. Native Americans and wild animals are fleeing from the arrival of white settlers, shown in waves of miners and farmers, and the progression from covered wagons to stagecoaches to steam locomotives is clear. The figure of "Progress" is carrying a book, implying knowledge, and is stringing telegraph wire across the plains. In the background, bridges have been built over what appears to be the Mississippi River, and steamboats populate its waters.* **PCE** **NAT** **MIG** **WXT** **SOC**

of the Far West – the landscapes, the Cowboy Culture, and the idea of the frontier as a land of opportunity – also led to increased agricultural settlement. At first farmers had some success, thanks in part to innovations like barbed wire. But drought, overproduction, and debt led farmers in the West to complain bitterly about railroads, banks, and manufacturers in the East, who always seemed to keep the prices of agricultural commodities low and manufactured goods high. Small farmers would continue to face challenges in a commercial world of international markets and powerful corporations.

As you read, you should:

- Analyze how territorial acquisitions in the West opened new markets, led to claims of white racial superiority, and increased ideological conflict.
- Identify the ways that increased western settlement led to the transformation of the environment.
- Evaluate how westward expansion led to conflicts over American identity, citizenship, and the protection of individual rights.
- Describe how the federal government encouraged western settlement through subsidizing transportation systems and offering federal lands to settlers at low prices.
- Analyze how western migration led to political and popular conflicts.
- Assess how the rise of corporate agriculture led individual farmers to organize in order to remedy their grievances.
- Analyze how completion of the transcontinental railroad threatened Native American culture and identity.

THE SOCIETIES OF THE FAR WEST

The Far West (or what many nineteenth-century Americans called the "Great West")–the region beyond the Mississippi River into which millions of Anglo-Americans moved in the years after the Civil War–was in fact many lands. It contained some of the most arid territory in the United States, and some of the wettest and lushest. It contained the flattest plains and the highest mountains. It contained vast treeless prairies and deserts and great forests. And it contained many peoples.

THE WESTERN TRIBES

The largest and most important western population group before the great Anglo-American migration was the Native American nations. Some were members of eastern nations–Cherokee, Creek, and others–who had been forcibly resettled west of the Mississippi to "Indian Territory" (later Oklahoma) and elsewhere before the Civil War. But most were members of nations that had always lived in the West.

The western groups had developed several forms of civilization. More than 300,000 Native Americans (among them the Serrano, Chumash, Pomo, Maidu, Yurok, and Chinook) had lived on the Pacific coast before the arrival of Spanish settlers. Disease and dislocation decimated Native American populations, but in the mid-nineteenth century 150,000 remained–some living within the Hispanic society the Spanish and Mexican settlers had created, many still living within their own tribal communities. The Pueblos of the Southwest had long lived largely as farmers and had established permanent settlements there even before the Spanish settlers arrived in the seventeenth century. The Pueblos grew corn; they built towns and cities of adobe houses; they practiced elaborate forms of irrigation; and they participated in trade and commerce. In the eighteenth and nineteenth centuries, their intimate relationship with Spanish settlers (later Mexican people) produced, in effect, an alliance against the Apaches, Navajos, and Comanches of the region.

The complex interaction between the Pueblos and the Spanish settlers produced an elaborate caste system in the Southwest. At the top were the Spanish or Mexican peoples, who owned the largest estates and controlled the trading centers at Santa Fe and elsewhere. The Pueblos, subordinate but stilllargely free, were below them. Apaches, Navajos, and others–some captured in war and enslaved for a fixed time, others men and women who had voluntarily left their own tribal communities–were at the bottom. They were known as *genizaros*, Native Americans without tribes, and they had become in many ways part of Spanish society. This caste system reflected how the Spanish Empire in America was preoccupied with racial ancestry; almost every group in the Southwest–not just Spanish and Native Americans, but several categories of mulattoes and mestizos (people of mixed race) as well–had a clear place in an elaborate social hierarchy.

CASTE SYSTEM

Discussion and Activities

Analyzing Change Have students read the section "The Societies of the Far West." Ask them to think about and share with a partner how the idea of "the West" changed over time in American history. *(At the time of Independence, the West was anything west of the original 13 states—for example, Kentucky, Tennessee, and the Northwest Territory. As the center of population shifted westward, so did the idea of what constituted "the West.")* **MIG** **GEO**

Go Online AP Exam Preparation

AP Exam Practice Use the online assessment to help prepare students for the AP Exam. You can assign the ready-made AP-style short-answer questions, document-based questions, and multiple-choice questions assessing concepts, themes, and skills from Period 6 and AP-style long-essay questions organized in sets of 3 questions from various time periods. You can also create your own tests from available questions. This easy-to-use tool helps you design assessments that meet the needs of different types of learners.

Reasoning Processes

Comparing After students have read the section "Plains Indians," ask them to create a T-chart identifying roles and activities usually assigned to men or women in the Plains Indian groups. Have students discuss how these roles and activities were similar to or different from those in white society at the time. **SOC** **WXT**

PLAINS INDIANS

The most widespread Native American presence in the West was the Plains Indians, a diverse group of Native American nations and language groups. Some groups formed alliances with one another; others were in constant conflict. Some lived sedentary lives as farmers; others were highly nomadic hunters. Despite their differences, however, the Plains Indians shared some traits. Their cultures were based on close and extended family networks and on an intimate relationship with nature. Tribes (which sometimes numbered several thousand) were generally subdivided into "bands" of up to 500 men and women. Each band had its own governing council, but the community had a decision-making process in which most members participated. Within each band, tasks were divided by gender. Women's roles were largely domestic and artistic: raising children, cooking, gathering roots and berries, preparing hides, and creating many of the impressive artworks of tribal culture. They also tended fields and gardens in those places where bands remained settled long enough to raise crops. Men worked as hunters and traders and supervised the religious and military life of the band. Most of the Plains Indians practiced a religion centered on a belief in the spiritual power of the natural world—of plants and animals and the rhythms of the days and the seasons.

Many of the Plains Indians—including some of the most powerful groups in the Sioux Nation—subsisted largely through hunting buffalo. Riding small but powerful horses, descendants of Spanish stock, the tribes moved through the grasslands following the herds. Permanent settlements were rare. When a band halted, it constructed tepees as temporary dwellings; when it departed, it left the landscape almost completely undisturbed, a reflection of the deep reverence for nature that was central to Native American culture and religion.

ECONOMIC IMPORTANCE OF THE BUFFALO

The buffalo, or bison, provided the economic basis for the Plains Indians' way of life. Its flesh was their principal source of food, and its skin supplied materials for clothing, shoes, tepees, blankets, robes, and utensils. "Buffalo chips"—dried manure—provided fuel; buffalo bones became knives and arrow tips; buffalo tendons formed the strings of bows.

The Plains Indians were proud and aggressive warriors, scooled in warfare from their frequent (and usually brief) skirmishes with rival groups. The male members of each group were, in effect, a warrior class. They competed with one another to develop reputations for fierceness and bravery as both hunters and soldiers. By the early nineteenth century, the Sioux had become the most powerful nation in the Missouri River valley and had begun expanding west and south until they dominated much of the plains.

The Plains warriors proved to be the most formidable foes white settlers encountered. But the nations also suffered from several serious weaknesses that in the end made it impossible for them to prevail. One weakness was the inability of the various groups (and often even of the bands within groups) to unite against white aggression. They were seldom able to draw together a coalition large enough to counter white power. They were also frequently distracted from their battles with white settlers by conflicts among the nations themselves. At times, warriors faced white forces who were being assisted by guides and even fighters from other, usually rival, groups.

NATIVE AMERICAN WEAKNESSES

Even so, some nations were able to overcome their divisions and unite effectively for a time. By the mid-nineteenth century, for example, the Sioux, Arapaho, and Cheyenne had forged a powerful alliance that dominated the northern plains. But there remained other important

BUFFALO CHASE The painter George Catlin captured this scene of Plains Indians in the 1830s hunting among the great herds of buffalo, which provided the food and materials on which many nations relied.

Discussion and Activities

Making Connections Have students read the section "Economic Importance of the Buffalo." Ask them to think about the groceries their families consume in a week and to write a sample grocery list. Have students then mark which items would have been replaced by buffalo for late nineteenth-century Plains Indians. **WXT** **GEO**

ecological and economic weaknesses of the western nations in their contest with white society. Native Americans were tragically vulnerable to eastern infectious diseases. Smallpox epidemics, for example, decimated the Pawnees in Nebraska in the 1840s and many of the California nations in the early 1850s. And the nations were, of course, at a considerable disadvantage in any long-term battle with an economically and industrially advanced people. They were, in the end, outmanned and outgunned.

Hispanic New Mexico

For centuries, much of the Far West had been part of, first, the Spanish Empire and, later, the Mexican Republic. Although the lands the United States acquired in the 1840s did not include any of Mexico's most populous regions, considerable numbers of Mexican people did live in them and suddenly became residents of American territory. Most of them stayed.

Spanish-speaking communities were scattered throughout the Southwest, from Texas to California. All of them were transformed in varying degrees by the arrival of Anglo-American migrants and, equally important, by the expansion of the American capitalist economy into the region. For some Spanish-speaking westerners, the changes created opportunities for greater wealth. But for most it meant an end to the communal societies and economies they had built over many generations.

In New Mexico, the centers of Spanish-speaking society were the farming and trading communities the Spanish had established in the seventeenth century. Descendants of the original Spanish settlers (and more recent migrants from Mexico) lived alongside the Pueblo Indians and some American traders and engaged primarily in cattle and sheep ranching. There was a small aristocracy of great landowners, whose estates radiated out from the major trading center at Santa Fe. And there was a large population of Spanish (later Mexican) peasants, who worked on the great estates, farmed small plots of their own, or otherwise scraped out a subsistence. There were also large groups of Native American laborers, some enslaved or indentured.

When the United States acquired title to New Mexico in the aftermath of the Mexican War, General Stephen Kearny–who had commanded the American troops in the region during the conflict–tried to establish a territorial government that excluded the established Mexican ruling class (the landed aristocrats from around Santa Fe and the most influential priests). He drew most of the officials from among the approximately 1,000 Anglo-Americans in the region, ignoring the more than 50,000 Hispanics. There were widespread fears among Hispanic people and Native Americans alike that the new American rulers of the region would confiscate their lands and otherwise threaten their societies. In 1847, Taos Indians rebelled; they killed the new governor and other Anglo-American officials before being subdued by U.S. Army forces. New Mexico remained under military rule for three years, until the United States finally organized a territorial government there in 1850.

TAOS INDIAN REBELLION

By the 1870s, the government of New Mexico was dominated by one of the most notorious of the many "territorial rings" that sprang up in the West in the years before statehood. These were circles of local Anglo businesspeople and ambitious politicians with access to federal money who worked together to make the territorial government mutually profitable. In Santa Fe, the ring used its influence to gain control of over 2 million acres of land, much of which had long been in the possession of the original Mexican residents of the territory. The old Hispanic elite in New Mexico had lost much of its political and economic authority.

Even without its former power and despite the expansion of Anglo-American settlement, Hispanic society in New Mexico survived and grew. The U.S. Army finally did what the Hispanic residents had been unable to accomplish for 200 years: it broke the power of the Navajo, Apache, and other nations that had so often harassed the residents of New Mexico and had prevented them from expanding their society and commerce. The defeat of the Native American nations led to substantial Hispanic migration into other areas of the Southwest and as far north as Colorado. Most of the expansion involved peasants and small tradespeople who were looking for land or new opportunities for commerce.

Hispanic societies survived in the Southwest in part because they were so far from the centers of English-speaking society that Anglo-American migrants (and the railroads that carried them) were slow to get there. But Mexican Americans in the region also fought at times to preserve control of their societies.

HISPANIC RESISTANCE

HISPANIC WEST This color lithograph, *Tejano Ranchers, 1877*, is by James Walker (1818–1889). Walker, a painter known for depicting military subjects, here shows the lively activities on a Tejano ranch in Texas.

Historical Thinking Skills

Argumentation After students have read the section "Native American Weaknesses," ask them to list and rank in order of importance the factors that caused Plains Indians to succumb to the aggressions of white settlers. Have students write a thesis statement that makes a claim about the most important causes of the defeat of the Plains Indians. PCE SOC

Discussion and Activities

Analyzing Change Have students read the section "Taos Indian Rebellion." Ask them to write a short paragraph explaining how the exercise of power changed in New Mexico in the aftermath of the Mexican War. PCE ARC SOC

Reasoning Processes

Comparing After students have read the section "Hispanic Resistance," ask them to create a Venn diagram comparing the lives of Hispanics and Native Americans in New Mexico under American rule. Have students conclude whether their new lives were more similar to or different from their previous ones. **PCE** **WXT** **SOC**

In the late 1880s, for example, Mexican peasants in an area of what is now Nevada successfully fended off the encroachment of English-speaking cattle ranchers.

But by then, such successes were already the exception. The Anglo-American presence in the Southwest grew rapidly once the railroads established lines into the region in the 1880s and early 1890s. With the railroads came extensive new ranching, farming, and mining. The expansion of economic activity in the region attracted a new wave of Mexican immigrants—perhaps as many as 100,000 by 1900—who moved across the border (which was unregulated until World War I) in search of work. But the new immigrants, unlike the earlier Hispanic residents of the Southwest, were coming to a society in which they were from the beginning subordinate to Anglo-Americans. The English-speaking proprietors of the new enterprises restricted most Mexican immigrants to the lowest-paying and least stable jobs.

HISPANIC CALIFORNIA AND TEXAS

In California, Spanish settlement began in the eighteenth century with a string of Christian missions along the Pacific coast. The missionaries and the soldiers who accompanied them gathered most of the coastal Native Americans into their communities, some forcibly and some by persuasion. The Native Americans were targets of the evangelizing efforts of the missionaries, who baptized more than 50,000 of them. But they were also a labor force for the flourishing and largely self-sufficient economies the missionaries created; Spanish settlers forced most of these laborers into a state of servitude little different from slavery. The missions had enormous herds of cattle, horses, sheep, and goats, most of them tended by Native American workers; they had brickmakers, blacksmiths, weavers, and farmers, most of them Native Americans as well. Few of the profits of the mission economy flowed to the workers.

In the 1830s, after the new Mexican government had begun reducing the power of the church, the mission society largely collapsed, despite strenuous resistance from the missionaries themselves. In its place emerged a secular Mexican aristocracy, which controlled a chain of large estates (some of them former missions) in the fertile lands west of the Sierra Nevada. For them, the arrival of Anglo-Americans before and after the Civil War was disastrous. So vast were the numbers of English-speaking immigrants that the *californios* (as the Hispanic residents of the state were known) had little power to resist the onslaught. In the central and northern parts of the state, where the Anglo population growth was greatest, the *californios* experienced a series of defeats. English-speaking prospectors organized to exclude them, sometimes violently, from the mines during the gold rush. Many *californios* also lost their lands—either through corrupt business deals or through outright seizure (sometimes with the help of the courts and often through simple occupation by squatters). Years of litigation by the displaced Hispanics had very little effect on the changing distribution of landownership.

DECLINE OF MISSION SOCIETY

In the southern areas of California, where there were at first fewer migrants than in other parts of the state, some Mexican landowners managed to hang on for a time. The booming Anglo communities in the north of the state created a large market for the cattle that southern *rancheros* were raising. But a combination of reckless expansion, growing indebtedness, and a severe drought in the 1860s devastated the Mexican ranching culture. By the 1880s, the Hispanic aristocracy in California had largely ceased to exist. Increasingly, Mexican immigrants and Mexican Americans became part of the lower end of the state's working class, clustered in barrios in Los Angeles or elsewhere, or becoming migrant farmworkers. Even small landowners who managed to hang on to their farms found themselves unable to raise livestock, as the once-communal grazing lands fell under the control of powerful Anglo ranchers. The absence of herding destroyed many family economies and, by forcing farmers into migrant work, displaced much of the peasantry.

A similar pattern of dispossession occurred in Texas, where many Mexican landowners lost their land after the territory joined the United States. This occurred as a result of fraud, coercion, and the inability of even the most substantial Mexican ranchers to compete with the enormous emerging Anglo-American ranching kingdoms. In 1859, resentments erupted in an armed challenge to American power: a raid on a jail in Brownsville, led by the rancher Juan Cortina, who freed all the Mexican prisoners inside. But such resistance had little long-term effect. Cortina continued to harass Anglo communities in Texas until 1875, but the Mexican government finally captured and imprisoned him. As in California, Mexican residents in southern Texas (who constituted nearly three-quarters of the population there) became an increasingly impoverished working class relegated largely to unskilled farm or industrial labor.

DECLINING STATUS OF HISPANICS

On the whole, the great Anglo-American migration was less catastrophic for the Hispanic population of the West than it was for Native Americans. Indeed, for some Hispanic residents, it created new opportunities for wealth and station. For the most part, however, the late nineteenth century saw the destruction of Mexican Americans' authority in a region they had long considered their own; and it saw the movement of large numbers of Hispanic people—both longtime residents of the West and more recent immigrants—into an impoverished working class serving the expanding capitalist economy of the United States.

THE CHINESE MIGRATION

At the same time that ambitious or impoverished Europeans were crossing the Atlantic in search of opportunities in the New World, many Chinese people crossed the Pacific in hopes of better lives than they could expect in their own poverty-stricken land. Not all came to the United States. Many Chinese people immigrated to Hawaii, Australia, South and Central America, South Africa, and even the Caribbean—some as "coolies" (indentured servants whose condition was close to slavery).

Discussion and Activities

Analyzing Points of View Have students read the section "Hispanic California and Texas." Ask them to write a short letter or journal entry from the point of view of a Hispanic landowner protesting the seizure of his land. **PCE** **WXT** **SOC**

A few Chinese people had come to California even before the gold rush, but after 1848 the flow increased dramatically. By 1880, more than 200,000 Chinese immigrants had settled in the United States, mostly in California, where they constituted nearly a tenth of the population. Almost all came as free laborers. For a time, white Americans welcomed Chinese immigrants as a conscientious, hardworking people. In 1852, the governor of California called them "one of the most worthy classes of our newly adopted citizens" and called for more Chinese immigration to swell the territory's inadequate labor force. Very quickly, however, white opinion turned hostile–in part because Chinese immigrants were so industrious and successful that some white Americans began considering them rivals, even threats. The experience of Chinese immigrants in the West became, therefore, a struggle to advance economically in the face of racism and discrimination.

RACISM

In the early 1850s, large numbers of Chinese immigrants worked in the gold mines, and for a time some of them enjoyed considerable success. But opportunities for Chinese immigrants to prosper in the mines were fleeting. In 1852, the California legislature began trying to exclude the Chinese immigrants from gold mining by enacting a "foreign miners" tax (which also helped exclude Mexican miners).

A series of other laws in the 1850s were designed to discourage Chinese emigration to the territory. Gradually, the effect of the discriminatory laws, the hostility of white miners, and the declining profitability of the surface mines drove most Chinese immigrants out of prospecting. Those who remained in the mountains became primarily hired workers in the mines built by corporations with financing from the East. These newer mines–which extended much deeper into the mountains than individual prospectors or small, self-financed groups had been able to go–replaced the early, smaller operations.

Universal History Archive/© UIG/The Bridgeman Art Library

THE TRANSCONTINENTAL RAILROAD This complicated trestle under construction by the Union Pacific was one of many large spans necessary for the completion of the transcontinental railroad. It gives some indication of the enormous engineering challenges the railroad builders had to overcome.

Discussion and Activities

Analyzing Change Have students read the section "Racism." Ask them to write a short paragraph explaining how and why attitudes toward Chinese immigrants changed during the decades after the start of the California Gold Rush. *(As more immigrants came to California, Chinese laborers were increasingly seen as a threat to white workers, and various measures were enacted to limit their opportunities.)* **MIG** **PCE** **SOC** **WXT**

Discussion and Activities

Analyzing Visuals Have students examine the image "The Transcontinental Railroad." Ask them to identify and discuss in pairs or small groups details from the photo that indicate the nature of the work that was done. *(Workers had to clear rubble, secure pilings to the rocks at the bottom and along the sides of the ravine, and build the intricate framework of the trestle, all in rugged, inhospitable terrain.)* **WXT**

Historical Thinking Skills

Argumentation Have students read the section "Building the Transcontinental Railroad." Ask them to create a poster advertising for workers to work on the Central Pacific Railroad. Have students consider what to include and what to exclude in order to entice workers to commit to the job. **WXT**

As mining declined as a source of wealth and jobs for Chinese immigrants, railroad employment grew. Beginning in 1865, more than 12,000 Chinese immigrants found work building the transcontinental railroad. In fact, Chinese workers formed 90 percent of the labor force of the Central Pacific and were mainly responsible for construction of the western part of the new road. The company preferred them to white workers because they had no experience of labor organization. They worked hard, made few demands, and accepted low wages. Many railroad workers were recruited in China by agents for the Central Pacific. Once employed, they were organized into work gangs under Chinese supervisors.

BUILDING THE TRANSCONTINENTAL RAILROAD

Work on the Central Pacific was arduous and often dangerous. As the railroad moved through the mountains, the company made few concessions to the difficult conditions and provided its workers with little protection from the elements. Work continued through the winter, and many Chinese laborers tunneled into snowbanks at night to create warm sleeping areas for themselves. The tunnels frequently collapsed, suffocating those inside; but the company allowed nothing to disrupt construction.

Chinese laborers, however, were not always as docile as their employers imagined them to be. In the spring of 1866, 5,000 Chinese railroad workers went on strike, demanding higher wages and a shorter workday. The company isolated them, surrounded them with strikebreakers, and starved them. The strike failed, and most of the workers returned to their jobs.

In 1869 the transcontinental railroad was completed. Thousands of Chinese immigrants were now out of work. Some hired themselves out on the vast new drainage and irrigation projects in the agricultural valleys of central California. Some became common agricultural laborers, picking fruit for low wages. Some became tenant farmers, often on marginal lands that white owners saw no profit in working themselves. Some managed to acquire land of their own and establish themselves as modestly successful truck farmers.

Increasingly, however, Chinese immigrants flocked to cities. By 1900, nearly half the Chinese population of California lived in urban areas. By far the largest single Chinese community was in San Francisco. Much of community life there, and in other "Chinatowns" throughout the West, revolved around powerful organizations—usually formed by people from a single clan or community in China—that functioned as something like benevolent societies to address common social and financial issues and filled many of the roles that political machines often served in immigrant communities in eastern cities. They were often led by prominent merchants. (In San Francisco, the leading merchants—known as the "Six Companies"—often worked together to advance their interests in the city and state.) These organizations became, in effect, employment brokers, unions, arbitrators of disputes, defenders of the community against outside persecution, and dispensers of social services. They also organized the elaborate festivals and celebrations that were such a conspicuous and important part of life in Chinatowns.

ESTABLISHMENT OF "CHINATOWNS"

Other Chinese organizations were secret societies, known as "tongs." Some of the tongs were violent criminal organizations, involved in the opium trade and prostitution. Few people outside the Chinese communities were aware of their existence, except when rival tongs engaged in violent conflict (or "tong wars"), as occurred frequently in San Francisco in the 1880s.

Life was hard for most urban Chinese immigrants, in San Francisco and elsewhere. Chinese immigrants usually occupied the lower rungs of the employment ladder, working as common laborers, servants, and unskilled factory hands. Some established their own small businesses, especially laundries. They moved into this business not because of experience—there were few commercial laundries in China—but because they were excluded from so many other areas of employment. Laundries could be started with very little capital and required only limited command of English. By the 1890s, Chinese immigrants constituted over two-thirds of all the laundry workers in California, many of them in shops they themselves owned and ran.

The relatively small number of Chinese women fared even worse. During the earliest Chinese migrations to California, virtually all the women who made the journey did so because they had been sold into prostitution. As late as 1880, nearly half the Chinese women in California were prostitutes. Both Anglo and Chinese reformers tried to stamp out the prostitution in Chinatowns in the 1890s, but more effective than their efforts was the growing number of Chinese women in America. Once the sex ratio became more balanced, Chinese men were more likely to seek companionship in families.

ANTI-CHINESE SENTIMENTS

As Chinese communities grew larger and more conspicuous in western cities, anti-Chinese sentiment among white residents became increasingly strong. Anti-coolie clubs emerged in the 1860s and 1870s. They sought a ban on employing Chinese immigrants and organized boycotts of products made with Chinese labor. Some of these clubs attacked Chinese workers in the streets and were suspected of setting fire to factories in which Chinese immigrants worked. Such activities reflected the resentment of many white workers toward Chinese laborers for accepting low wages and thus undercutting union members.

ANTI-COOLIE CLUBS

As the political value of attacking Chinese immigrants grew in California, the Democratic Party took up the call. So did the Workingmen's Party of California—created in 1878 by Denis Kearney, an Irish immigrant—which gained significant political power in the state largely on the basis of its hostility to Chinese immigrants. By the mid-1880s, anti-Chinese agitation and violence had spread up and down the Pacific coast and into other areas of the West.

But anti-Chinese sentiment did not rest on economic grounds alone. It rested on cultural and racial arguments as well. For example, the reformer Henry George, a critic of capitalism and a champion of the rights of labor, described Chinese

Discussion and Activities

Analyzing Points of View Have students read the section "Establishment of Chinatowns." Ask them to write a short letter or journal entry from the point of view of a Chinese worker in an American city in the late nineteenth century. **WXT** **SOC**

A CHINESE FAMILY IN SAN FRANCISCO Like many other Americans, Chinese families liked to pose for photograph portraits in the late nineteenth century. And like many other immigrants, they often sent such pictures back to relatives in China. This portrait of Chun Duck Chin and his seven-year-old son, Chun Jan Yut, was taken in a studio in San Francisco in the 1870s. Both father and son appear to have dressed up for the occasion, in traditional Chinese garb, and the studio—which likely took many such portraits of Chinese families—provided a formal Chinese backdrop. The son is holding what appears to be a chicken, perhaps to impress relatives in China with the family's prosperity.

National Archives and Records Administration

immigrants as products of a civilization that had failed to progress, that remained mired in barbarism and savagery. They were, therefore, "unassimilable" and should be excluded.

In 1882, Congress responded to the political pressure and the growing violence by passing the Chinese Exclusion Act, which banned Chinese emigration to the United States for ten years and barred Chinese immigrants already in the country from becoming naturalized citizens. Support for the act came from representatives from all regions of the country. It reflected the growing fear of unemployment and labor unrest throughout the nation and the belief that excluding "an industrial army of Asiatic laborers" would protect "American" workers and help reduce class conflict. Congress renewed the law for another ten years in 1892 and made it permanent in 1902. It had a dramatic effect on the Chinese population, which declined by more than 40 percent in the forty years after its passage.

CHINESE EXCLUSION ACT

Chinese immigrants in America did not accept the new laws quietly. They were shocked by the anti-Chinese rhetoric. The Chinese workers considered themselves descendants of a great and enlightened civilization. They also believed that they had proven themselves to be industrious and law-abiding citizens. The Six Companies in San Francisco organized strenuous letter-writing campaigns and filed suit in federal court. Their efforts had little effect.

CHINESE RESISTANCE

MIGRATION FROM THE EAST

The great wave of new settlers in the West after the Civil War came on the heels of important earlier migrations. California and Oregon were both already states of the Union by 1860. There were large and growing Anglo-American and African American communities in Texas, which had entered the Union as a state in 1845 and had been part of the Confederacy during the war. And from Texas and elsewhere, traders, farmers, and ranchers had begun to establish Anglo-American outposts in parts of New Mexico, Arizona, and other areas of the Southwest.

But the scale of the postwar migration dwarfed everything that had preceded it. In previous decades, the settlers had come in thousands. Now they came in millions, spreading throughout the vast western territories–into empty and inhabited lands alike. Most of the new settlers were from the established Anglo-American societies of the eastern United States, but substantial numbers–more than 2 million between 1870 and 1900–were foreign-born immigrants from Europe: Scandinavians, Germans, Irish, Russians, Czechs, and others. Settlers were attracted by gold and silver deposits, by the shortgrass pastures for cattle and sheep, and ultimately by the sod of the plains and the meadowlands of the mountains, which they discovered were suitable for farming or ranching. Settlement was also encouraged by the completion of the transcontinental railroad in 1869 and the construction of the many subsidiary lines that spread out from it.

The land policies of the federal government also encouraged settlement. The Homestead Act of 1862 permitted settlers to buy plots of 160 acres for a small fee if they occupied the land they purchased for five years and improved it. The Homestead Act was intended as a progressive measure. It would give a free farm to any American who needed one. It would be a form of government relief to people who otherwise might have no prospects. And it would help create new markets and new outposts of commercial agriculture for the nation's growing economy.

HOMESTEAD ACT

But the Homestead Act rested on a number of misperceptions. The framers of the law had assumed that mere possession of land would be enough to sustain a farm family. They had not recognized the effects of the increasing mechanization of agriculture and the rising costs of running a farm. Moreover, they had made many of their calculations on the basis of eastern agricultural experiences that were inappropriate for the region west of the Mississippi. A unit of 160 acres

Historical Thinking Skills

Argumentation After students have read the section "Chinese Exclusion Act," ask them to create a T-chart listing economic and social reasons for the passage of the act. Have them discuss in small groups which factors seem more important. PCE WXT SOC

Discussion and Activities

Making Connections Have students examine the image "A Chinese Family in San Francisco." Ask them to think about and share with a partner what item(s) they would include in a family portrait today to demonstrate wealth. SOC

Discussion and Activities

Analyzing Issues After students have read the section "Migration from the East," ask them to create a T-chart listing opportunities and challenges facing homesteaders. Have students discuss as a class what the most important factors determining the success or failure of homesteads were. **GEO** **MIG** **WXT**

SODBUSTERS As farmers moved onto the Great Plains in Nebraska and other states on the agrarian frontier, their first task was to cut through the sod that covered the land to get to soil in which they could plant crops. The sod itself was so thick and solid that some settlers (including the Summers family of West Custer County, Nebraska, pictured here in 1888) used it to build their houses. The removal of the sod made cultivation of the plains possible; it also removed the soil's protective covering and contributed to the great dust storms that plagued the region in times of drought.

was too small for the grazing and grain farming of much of the Great Plains. Although more than 400,000 homesteaders stayed on Homestead Act claims long enough to gain title to their land, a much larger number abandoned the region before the end of the required five years, unable to cope with the bleak life on the windswept plains and the economic realities that were making it difficult for families without considerable resources to thrive.

Not for the last time, beleaguered westerners looked to the federal government for solutions to their problems. In response to their demands, Congress increased the homestead allotments. The Timber Culture Act (1873) permitted homesteaders to receive grants of 160 additional acres if they planted 40 acres of trees on them. The Desert Land Act (1877) provided that claimants could buy 640 acres at $1.25 an acre provided they irrigated part of their holdings within three years. The Timber and Stone Act (1878), which presumably applied to nonarable land, authorized sales at $2.50 an acre. These laws ultimately made it possible for individuals to acquire as much as 1,280 acres of land at little cost. Some enterprising settlers got much more. Fraud ran rampant in the administration of the acts. Lumber, mining, and cattle companies, by employing "dummy" registrants and using other illegal devices, seized millions of acres of the public domain.

GOVERNMENT ASSISTANCE

Political organization followed on the heels of settlement. After the admission of Kansas as a state in 1861, the remaining territories of Washington, New Mexico, Utah, and Nebraska were divided into smaller units that would presumably be easier to organize. By the close of the 1860s, territorial governments were in operation in the new provinces of Nevada, Colorado, Dakota, Arizona, Idaho, Montana, and Wyoming. Statehood soon followed. Nevada became a state in 1864, Nebraska in 1867, and Colorado in 1876. In 1889, North and South Dakota, Montana, and Washington won admission; Wyoming and Idaho entered the next year. Congress denied Utah statehood until its Mormon leaders convinced the government in 1896 that polygamy (the practice of a man having more than one wife at a time) had been abandoned. At the turn of the century, only three territories remained outside the Union. Arizona and New Mexico were excluded because their scanty white populations remained minorities in the territories, because their politics were predominantly Democratic in a Republican era, and because they were unwilling to accept admission as a single state. Oklahoma (formerly Indian Territory) was opened to white settlement and granted territorial status in 1889–1890.

THE CHANGING WESTERN ECONOMY

Among the many effects of the new wave of Anglo-American settlement in the Far West was a transformation of the region's economy. The new American settlers tied the West firmly to the growing industrial economy of the East (and of much of the rest of the world). Mining, cutting and selling timber,

Discussion and Activities

Evaluating Evidence Have students examine the image "Sodbusters." Ask them to identify and discuss details that demonstrate how settlers adapted to the environment. *(Sod was used for structures in the absence of many trees to use for lumber. Lumber that was brought from the East was reserved for window and door frames and probably roof trusses to hold the weight of the sod-covered roof.)* **GEO**

ranching, commercial farming, and many other economic activities relied on the East for markets and for capital. Some of the most powerful economic institutions in the West were great eastern corporations that controlled mines, ranches, and farms.

LABOR IN THE WEST

As commercial activity increased, many farmers, ranchers, and miners found it necessary to recruit a paid labor force—not an easy task for those far away from major population centers and unable or unwilling to hire Native American workers. The labor shortage of the region led to higher wages for workers than were typical in most areas of the East. But working conditions were often arduous, and job security was almost nonexistent. Once a railroad was built, a crop harvested, a herd sent to market, a mine played out, hundreds and even thousands of workers could find themselves suddenly unemployed. Competition from Chinese immigrants, whom employers could usually hire for considerably lower wages than they had to pay whites, also forced some Anglo-Americans out of work. Communities of the jobless gathered in the region's few cities, in mining camps, and elsewhere; other unemployed people moved restlessly from place to place in search of work.

Those who owned no land were highly mobile, mostly male, and seldom married. Indeed, the West had the highest percentage of single adults (10 percent) of any region in the country—one reason why single women found working in dance halls and as prostitutes among the most readily available forms of employment.

LIMITED SOCIAL MOBILITY

Despite the enormous geographic mobility in western society, actual social mobility was limited. Many Americans thought of the West as a land of limitless opportunity, but, as in the rest of the country, advancement was easiest and most rapid for those who were economically advantaged to begin with. Studies of western communities suggest that social mobility in most of them was no greater than it was in the East. And the distribution of wealth in the region was little different from that in the older states as well.

RACIALLY STRATIFIED WORKING CLASS

Even more than in many parts of the East, the western working class was highly multiracial. English-speaking white laborers worked alongside African Americans and immigrants from southern and eastern Europe, as they did in the East. Even more, they worked with immigrants from China, the Philippines, and Mexico as well as Native Americans. But the workforce was highly stratified along racial lines. In almost every area of the western economy, white workers (whatever their ethnicity) occupied the upper tiers of employment: management and skilled labor. The lower tiers—people who did unskilled and often arduous work in the mines, on the railroads, or in agriculture—consisted overwhelmingly of nonwhites.

Reinforcing this dual labor system was a set of racial assumptions developed and sustained largely by white employers. Chinese, Mexican, and Filipino immigrants, they argued, were genetically or culturally suited to manual labor. Because they were smaller than many Anglo-Americans, those who promoted these racist stereotypes argued, they could work better in deep mines than white laborers. Because they were accustomed to heat, they could withstand arduous work in the fields. Because they were unambitious and unconcerned about material comfort, they would accept low wages and live in conditions that white people would not tolerate. These racial myths served the interests of employers above all, but white workers tended to embrace them too. That was in part because the myths supported a system that reserved whatever mobility there was largely for white people. An Irish common laborer might hope in the course of a lifetime to move several rungs up the occupational ladder. A Chinese or Mexican worker in the same job had no realistic prospects of doing the same.

THE ARRIVAL OF THE MINERS

One of the great economic boons in the Far West after the gold rush was a result of the mineral-rich region of mountains and plateaus, where settlers hoped to make quick fortunes by finding precious metals. The life span of this mining boom was relatively brief. It began in earnest around 1860 and flourished until the 1890s. Then it abruptly declined.

LIFE CYCLE OF A MINING BOOM

News of a gold or silver strike in an area usually began with a stampede reminiscent of the California gold rush of 1849. Individual prospectors would exploit the first shallow deposits of ore largely by hand, with pan and placer mining. After these surface deposits dwindled, corporations moved in to engage in lode or quartz mining, which dug deeper beneath the surface. Then, as those deposits dwindled, commercial mining either disappeared or continued on a restricted basis, and ranchers and farmers moved in and established a more permanent economy.

The first great mineral strikes since the California gold rush occurred just before the Civil War. In 1858, gold was discovered in the Pike's Peak district of what would soon be the territory of Colorado; the following year, 50,000 prospectors stormed in from California, the Mississippi Valley, and the East. Denver and other mining camps blossomed into "cities" overnight. Almost as rapidly as it had developed, the boom ended. After the mining frenzy died down, corporations, notably the Guggenheim interests, revived some of the profits of the gold boom, and the discovery of silver near Leadville supplied a new source of mineral wealth.

COMSTOCK LODE

While the Colorado rush of 1859 was still in progress, news of another strike drew miners to Nevada. Gold had been found in the Washoe district, but the most valuable ore in the great Comstock Lode (first discovered in 1858 by Henry Comstock) and other veins was silver. The first prospectors to reach the Washoe fields came from California; and from the beginning, Californians dominated the settlement and development of Nevada. In a remote desert without railroad transportation, the territory produced no supplies of its own, and everything—from food and machinery to

Reasoning Processes

Comparing Have students read the section "Labor in the West." Ask them to create a Venn diagram comparing challenges facing laborers in the East and the West. Have students discuss why so many laborers migrated westward despite the challenges that awaited them. **GEO** **WXT** **PCE** **SOC**

Discussion and Activities

Analyzing Points of View Have students read the section "Life Cycle of a Mining Boom." Ask them to write a short journal entry or letter from the point of view of a prospector who has just learned of the discovery of gold or silver nearby. Have students consider the hopes, fears, and daily experiences of the prospectors. **WXT** **SOC**

Historical Thinking Skills

Argumentation After students have read the section "Comstock Lode," ask them to discuss in small groups why mining copper, lead, zinc, and quartz often was better for local economies than gold and silver mining. *(Gold and silver deposits often led to swift growth but generally played out more quickly, leaving behind ghost towns.)* **GEO** **MIG** **WXT**

COLORADO BOOMTOWN The Colorado silver boom began in 1879, bringing many people into the newly admitted state in search of opportunity. By the 1890s, with dwindling silver deposits, many recently wealthy communities went bust.

whiskey—had to be shipped from California to Virginia City, Carson City, and other gold rush settlements and towns. When the first placer (or surface) deposits ran out, California and eastern capitalists bought the claims of the pioneer prospectors and began to use the more difficult process of quartz mining, which enabled them to retrieve silver from deeper veins. For a few years these outside owners reaped tremendous profits; from 1860 to 1880, the Nevada lodes yielded bullion worth $306 million. After that, the mines quickly played out.

The next important mineral discoveries came in 1874, when gold was found in the Black Hills of southwestern Dakota Territory. Prospectors swarmed into the area until surface resources faded and corporations took over. One enormous company, the Homestake, came to dominate the fields.

In the long run, other, less glamorous natural resources proved more important to the development of the West than gold and silver. The great Anaconda copper mine launched by William Clark in 1881 marked the beginning of an industry that would remain important to Montana for many decades. In other areas, mining operations had significant success with lead, tin, quartz, and zinc.

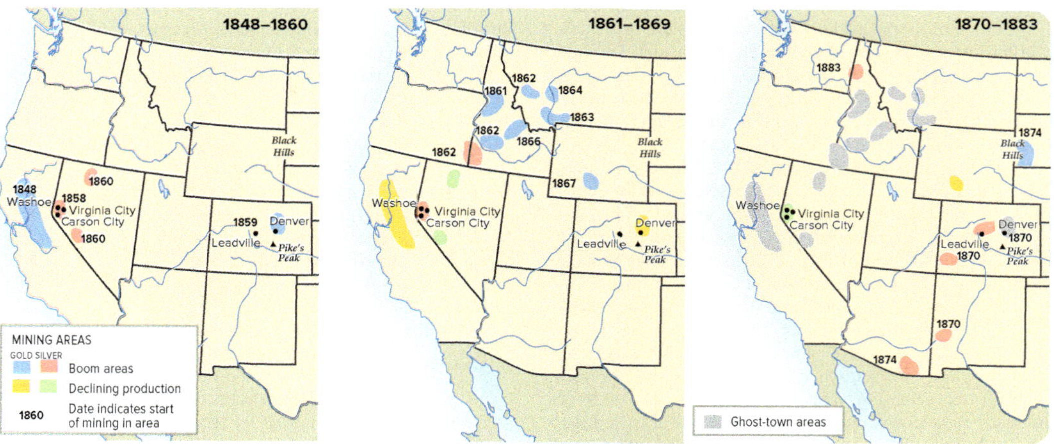

MINING TOWNS, 1848–1883 These three maps illustrate the rapid movement from boom to bust in the western mining industry in the mid-nineteenth century. Note how quickly the "boom" areas of gold and silver mining turn into places of "declining production," often in less than a decade. Note, too, how mining for both metals moved from California and Nevada in the 1860s to areas farther east and north in the 1870s and beyond. The map also shows the areas in which "ghost towns"—mining communities abandoned by their residents once production ceased—proliferated.

What impact did mining have on the population of the West?

Answers

Mining Towns, 1848–1883

In most cases, mining towns caused temporary surges in local population as prospectors and others arrived to create boom towns. However, these towns often faded away after local mines played out.

The conditions of mine life in the boom period–the presence of precious minerals, the vagueness of claim boundaries, the cargoes of gold being shipped out–attracted outlaws and "bad men," operating as individuals or gangs. When the situation became intolerable in a community, those members interested in order began enforcing their own laws through vigilante committees, an unofficial system of social control used earlier in California. Vigilantes were unconstrained by the legal system. Some vigilantes continued to operate as private "law" enforcers after the creation of regular governments.

Men greatly outnumbered women in the mining towns, and younger men in particular had difficulty finding female companions of comparable age. Those women who did gravitate to the new communities often came with their husbands, and their activities were generally (although not always) confined to the same kinds of domestic tasks that eastern women performed. Single women, or women whose husbands were earning no money, did choose (or find it necessary) to work for wages at times, as cooks, laundresses, and tavernkeepers. And in the sexually imbalanced mining communities, there was always a ready market for prostitutes.

GENDER IMBALANCE

The thousands of people who flocked to the mining towns in search of quick wealth and who failed to find it often remained as wage laborers in corporate mines after the boom period. Working conditions were almost uniformly terrible. The corporate mines were deep and extremely hot, with temperatures often exceeding 100 degrees Fahrenheit. Some workers died of heatstroke (or of pneumonia, a result of experiencing sudden changes of temperature when emerging from the mines). Poor ventilation meant large accumulations of poisonous carbon dioxide, which caused dizziness, nausea, and headaches. Lethal dusts stayed in the stagnant air to be inhaled over and over by the miners, many of whom developed silicosis (a disabling disease of the lungs) as a result. There were frequent explosions, cave-ins, and fires, and there were many accidents with the heavy machinery the workers used to bore into the earth. In the 1870s, before technological advances eliminated some of the dangers, one worker in every thirty was disabled in the mines, and one in every eighty was killed. That rate fell later in the nineteenth century, but mining remained one of the most dangerous and arduous working environments in the United States.

The Cattle Kingdom

Another important element of the changing economy of the Far West was cattle ranching. The open range–the vast grasslands of the public domain–provided a huge area on the Great Plains where cattle raisers could graze their herds free of charge and unrestricted by the boundaries of private farms.

The western cattle industry was Mexican and Texan by ancestry. Long before citizens of the United States invaded the Southwest, Mexican ranchers had developed the techniques and equipment that the cattlemen and cowboys of the Great Plains later employed: branding (a device known in all frontier areas where stock was common), roundups, roping, and the gear of the herders–their lariats, saddles, leather chaps, and spurs. Americans in Texas adopted these methods and carried them to the northernmost ranges of the cattle kingdom. Texas also had the largest herds of cattle in the country; the animals were descended from imported Spanish stock–wiry, hardy longhorns–and allowed to run wild or semiwild. From Texas, too, came small, muscular broncos or mustangs well suited to the requirements of cattle country.

MEXICAN ORIGINS

At the end of the Civil War, an estimated 5 million cattle roamed the Texas ranges. Early in 1866, some Texas cattle ranchers began driving their combined herds, as many as 260,000 cattle, north to Sedalia, Missouri, on the Missouri Pacific Railroad. Traveling over rough country and beset by outlaws, Native Americans, and property-conscious farmers, the caravan suffered heavy losses. Only a fraction of the animals

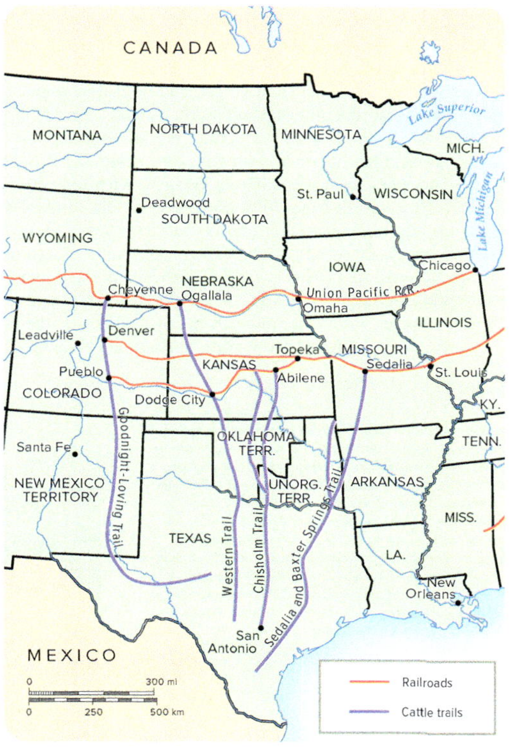

THE CATTLE KINGDOM, C. 1866–1887 Cattle ranching and cattle drives are among the most romanticized features of the nineteenth-century West. But they were also hardheaded businesses, made possible by the growing eastern market for beef and the availability of inexpensive transportation to take cattle to urban markets.

What brought an end to the open range?

Historical Thinking Skills

Argumentation Have students read the section "The Arrival of the Miners." Ask them to create a T-chart listing challenges and opportunities facing miners in the late nineteenth century. Ask students to discuss as a class why miners continued to move west despite the challenges. MIG WXT

Answers

The Cattle Kingdom, c. 1866–1887

Farming and the arrival of the railroads led to the end of the open range.

Discussion and Activities

Analyzing Change After students have read the section "Chisholm Trail," ask them to write a short paragraph explaining why the cattle trails shifted west through the 1860s and 1870s. *(The routes had to shift to avoid agricultural development and to meet the extending railheads.)* **WXT** **GEO**

arrived in Sedalia. But the drive proved that cattle could be driven to distant markets and pastured along the trail, and that they would even gain weight during the journey. This earliest of the "long drives," in other words, established the first, tentative link between the isolated cattle breeders of south and west Texas and the booming urban markets of the East. The drive laid the groundwork for the explosion of the "cattle kingdom."

CHISHOLM TRAIL

Market facilities grew up at Abilene, Kansas, on the Kansas Pacific Railroad, and for years the town reigned as the railhead of the cattle kingdom. Between 1867 and 1871, cattlemen drove nearly 1.5 million head up the Chisholm Trail to Abilene—a town that, when filled with rampaging cowboys at the end of a drive, rivaled the mining towns in rowdiness. But by the mid-1870s, agricultural development in western Kansas was eating away at the open range land at the same time that the supply of animals was increasing. Cattlemen therefore had to develop other trails and other market outlets farther west: Dodge City and Wichita in Kansas, Ogallala and Sidney in Nebraska, Cheyenne and Laramie in Wyoming, Miles City and Glendive in Montana.

A long drive was a spectacular sight, and not surprisingly, it became the most romanticized and mythologized aspect of life in the West. It began with the spring, or calf, roundup. The cattlemen rounded up stock from the open range, herds containing the stock of many different owners, with only their brands to distinguish them from one another. The combined herds, usually numbering from 2,000 to 5,000 head, moved out. Cowboys representing each of the major ranchers accompanied them. Most of the cowboys in the early years were veterans of the Confederate army. The next-largest group consisted of African Americans—more than half a million of them. They were more numerous than white Northerners or Mexican cowboys and other foreigners. They were usually assigned such jobs as wrangler (herdsman) or cook.

Every cattleman had to have a permanent base from which to operate, and so the ranch emerged. A ranch consisted of the employer's dwelling, quarters for employees, and a tract of grazing land. In the early years of the cattle kingdom, most ranches were small, since so much of the grazing occurred in the vast, open areas that cattlemen shared. But as farmers and sheep breeders began to compete for the open plains, ranches became larger and more clearly defined; cattlemen gradually had to learn to raise their stock on their own fenced land.

Farmers ("nesters") from the East threw fences around their claims, blocking trails and breaking up the open range. A series of "range wars"—between sheepmen and cattlemen, between ranchers and farmers—erupted out of the tensions between these competing groups, resulting in significant loss of life and extensive property damage.

Accounts of the lofty profits to be made in the cattle business—it was said that an investment of $5,000 would return $45,000 in four years—tempted eastern, English, and Scottish capital to the plains. Increasingly, the structure of the cattle economy became corporate; in one year, twenty corporations with a combined capital of $12 million were chartered in Wyoming. The inevitable result of this frenzied, speculative expansion was that the ranges, already diminished by the railroads and the farmers, became overstocked. There was not enough grass to support the crowding herds or sustain the long drives. Finally nature intervened. Two severe winters, in 1885–1886 and 1886–1887, with a searing summer between them, stung and scorched the plains. Hundreds of thousands of cattle died, streams and grass dried up, princely ranches and costly investments disappeared in a season.

The open-range industry never recovered; the long drive disappeared for good. Railroads displaced the trail as the route to

COWBOYS ON A "LONG DRIVE" The "long drive" not only provided cattle for the eastern market, it also created communities of men who spent much of their lives on the trail, working for ranchers tending cattle. These cowboys were mostly young, unmarried men, including many African Americans. Most of them later settled down with families, but many agreed with the former cowboy Charles Goodknight, who wrote years later, "All in all, my years on the trail were the happiest I ever lived. There were many hardships and dangers . . . but when all went well, there was no other life so pleasant. Most of the time we were solitary adventurers in a great land, . . . and we were free and full of the zest of darers." This photograph, dating from the 1890s, depicts cowboys herding cattle at the end of a long drive in the stockyards at Kansas City, Missouri.

Discussion and Activities

Analyzing Visuals Have students examine the image "Cowboys on a 'Long Drive'." Ask them to identify and discuss in small groups details from the photo that help explain elements of the long drive. *(The cowboy in the foreground is helping to herd the cattle; the cattle pictured are longhorns that had been rounded up in Texas; some of the cattle [on the right of the photo] bear markings that identified which ranch the cattle belonged to.)* **WXT**

market for livestock. But the established cattle ranches—with fenced-in grazing land and stocks of hay for winter feed—survived, grew, and prospered, eventually producing more beef than ever.

Although the cattle industry was overwhelmingly male in its early years, there were always a few women involved in ranching and driving. As ranching became more sedentary, the presence of women greatly increased. By 1890, more than 250,000 women owned ranches or farms in the western states (many of them as proxies for their husbands or fathers, but some in their own right). Indeed, the region provided women with many opportunities that were closed to them in the East—including the opportunity to participate in politics. Wyoming was the first state in the Union to guarantee woman suffrage; and throughout the West, women established themselves as an important political presence (and occasionally as significant officeholders).

Women won the vote earlier in the West than they did in the rest of the nation, although for different reasons in different places. In Utah, the Mormons granted women suffrage in an effort to stave off criticism of their practice of polygamy. In some places, women won suffrage before statehood to swell the electorate to the number required by Congress. In others, women won the vote by persuading men that they would help bring a "moral" voice into the politics of the region and strengthen the sense of community in the West. Most men (and many women) believed that women were more "generous and virtuous" than men. They might bring these special qualities to the raw societies of the region. (Many of the same arguments were ultimately used to justify suffrage in the East as well.)

POLITICAL GAINS FOR WOMEN

THE ROMANCE OF THE WEST

The supposedly unsettled West had always occupied a special place in the Anglo-American imagination, beginning in the seventeenth century when the first white settlers along the Atlantic coast began to look to the interior. They were searching for new opportunities or for refuge from the civilized world. The vast regions of this "last frontier" had a particularly strong romantic appeal to many people.

THE WESTERN LANDSCAPE

The allure of the West was obvious. The Great Plains, the Rocky Mountains, the basin and plateau region beyond the Rockies, the Sierra Nevada, and the Cascade Range—all constituted a landscape of brilliant diversity and spectacular grandeur, different from anything white Americans had encountered before. It was little wonder that newcomers looked on the West with reverence and wonder. Painters of the "Rocky Mountain School"—of whom the best known were Albert Bierstadt and Thomas Moran—celebrated the new West in grandiose canvases, some of which were taken on tours around eastern and midwestern states and attracted enormous crowds, eager for a vision of the Great West. Such paintings emphasized the ruggedness and dramatic variety of the region, and reflected the same awe toward the land that earlier regional painters had displayed toward the Hudson River valley and other areas.

"ROCKY MOUNTAIN SCHOOL"

The interest in paintings of the West helped inspire a growing wave of tourism. Increasingly in the 1880s and 1890s, as railroads extended farther into the region and as the Indian wars subsided, resort hotels began to spring up near some of the most spectacular landscapes in the region; and easterners began to come for visits of several weeks or more, combining residence in a comfortable hotel with hikes and excursions into the "wilderness."

THE COWBOY CULTURE

Even more appealing than the landscape was the rugged, free-spirited lifestyle that many Americans associated with the West—a lifestyle that supposedly stood in sharp contrast to the increasingly stable and ordered world of the East. Many nineteenth-century Americans came to romanticize, especially, the figure of the cowboy and transformed him remarkably quickly from the low-paid worker he actually was into a powerful and enduring figure of myth.

MYTH OF THE COWBOY

Admiring Americans seldom thought about the many dismal aspects of the cowboy's life: the tedium, the loneliness, the physical discomforts, the low pay, the few opportunities for advancement. Instead, in popular western novels such as Owen Wister's *The Virginian* (1902), they romanticized his freedom from traditional social constraints, his affinity with nature, even his supposed propensity for violence. Wister's character was a semi-educated man whose natural decency, courage, and compassion made him a powerful symbol of the supposed virtues of the frontier. But *The Virginian* was only the most famous example of a type of literature that soon swept throughout the United States: novels and stories about the West, and about the lives of cowboys in particular, that appeared in boys' magazines, pulp novels, theater, and even serious literature. The enormous popularity of traveling Wild West shows spread the cult of the cowboy still further.

The cowboy had become perhaps the most widely admired popular hero in America, and a powerful and enduring symbol of the important American ideal of the "natural man." That symbol has survived into the twenty-first century—in popular literature, in song, in film, and on television.

THE IDEA OF THE FRONTIER

Yet it was not simply the character of the new West that made it so important to the nation's imagination. It was also that many Americans considered it the last frontier. Since the earliest moments of European settlement in America, the image of uncharted territory to the west had always comforted

Reasoning Processes

Causation After students have read the section "The Cattle Kingdom," ask them to discuss as a class the causes and effects of the cattle industry in the West. WXT SOC

Discussion and Activities

Comparing Have students have read the section "The Cowboy Culture." Ask them to create a Janus figure (an outline of a human figure with two faces with a vertical line drawn down the middle) comparing the realities of cowboy life with the myth of the cowboy. WXT SOC

Discussion and Activities

Analyzing Points of View After students have read the feature "The Wild West Show," ask them to write a short letter or journal entry from the point of view of an Easterner who had just attended a show. Have students consider how the audience member might have been influenced to think about cowboys, Native Americans, and the West in general. **GEO** **SOC**

PATTERNS OF POPULAR CULTURE

THE WILD WEST SHOW

For many Americans, the "Old West" has always been a place of myth—a source of romantic and exciting stories. One reason the romantic depiction of the Old West persisted was the astonishing popularity of the "Wild West show" in the late nineteenth and early twentieth centuries. This colorful entertainment may have had little connection with the reality of western life, but it gave its audiences an image of the West as a place of adventure and romance that has lasted for generations. The Wild West show emerged out of a number of earlier entertainment traditions. The great showman P. T. Barnum had begun popularizing the "Wild West" as early as the 1840s when he staged a "Grand Buffalo Hunt" for spectators in New York, and such shows continued into the 1870s. At about the same time, western cowboys began staging versions of the modern rodeo when their cattle drives passed near substantial towns. But the first real Wild West show opened in Omaha, Nebraska, in 1883. Its organizer was William F. Cody, better known as "Buffalo Bill."

Cody had ridden for the Pony Express, fought in the Civil War, and been a supplier of buffalo meat to workers on the transcontinental railroad (hence his celebrated nickname). But his real fame was a result of his work as a scout for the U.S. Cavalry during the Indian wars of the 1870s and as a guide for hunting parties of notable Easterners.

Cody's Wild West shows included mock Native American attacks (by real Native Americans) on stagecoaches and wagon trains; portrayals of the Pony Express; and shooting, riding, and roping exhibitions. The grand finale—"A Grand Hunt on the Plains"—featured buffalo, elk, deer, mountain sheep, longhorn cattle, and wild horses. Cody's shows inspired dozens of imitators. Always, at the center of every show—whether Cody's or one of his imitators—was the effort to evoke the mythic romance of the Old West.

Buffalo Bill was always the star performer in his own productions. But the show had other celebrities, too. Annie Oakley became wildly popular for her shooting acts, during which she would throw into the air small cards with her picture on them, shoot a hole through their middle, and toss them into the audience as souvenirs.

Native Americans were important parts of the Wild West shows, and hundreds of them participated—showing off their martial skills and exotic costumes and customs. The great Sioux leader Sitting Bull toured with the show for four months in 1885, during which he discussed Native American affairs with President Cleveland, who was a member of one of Sitting Bull's audiences. The famous Chiricahua Apache warrior Geronimo, who had fought against the United States until 1886, spent a season touring with one of Buffalo Bill's competitors—having previously been paraded around the country as a prisoner by the U.S. Army.

An immediate success, Buffalo Bill's Wild West show traveled across the nation and throughout Europe. More than 41,000 people saw it on one day in Chicago in 1884. In 1886, it played for six months on Staten Island in New York, where General William T. Sherman, Mark Twain, P. T. Barnum, Thomas A. Edison, and the widow of General Custer all saw and praised it. Members of the royal family attended the show in England, and it drew large crowds as well in France, Germany, and Italy.

The Wild West shows died out not long after World War I, but many of their features survived in circuses and rodeos, and later in films, radio and television shows, and theme parks. Their popularity was evidence of the nostalgia with which late-nineteenth-century Americans looked at their own imagined past, and their eagerness to remember a "Wild West" that had never really been what they liked to believe. Buffalo Bill and his imitators confirmed the popular image of the West as a place of romance and glamour and helped keep that image alive for later generations.

ANNIE OAKLEY Annie Oakley had been a vaudeville and circus entertainer for years before joining Buffalo Bill's Wild West show in 1885. She was under five feet tall and weighed less than a hundred pounds, but her exploits with pistols, rifles, and horses earned her a reputation as a woman of unusual strength and skill.

PROMOTING THE WEST, C. 1895 Buffalo Bill's Wild West show was popular all over the United States and, indeed, through much of the world. He was so familiar a figure that many of his posters contained only his picture with the words "He is Coming." This more conventional poster announces a visit of the show to Brooklyn.

HISTORICAL THINKING SKILLS

1. **Comparing and Contrasting** Compare and contrast the portrayal of the West in Wild West shows to the real West.
2. **Explaining Historical Context** Why do you think Native Americans participated in the Wild West shows? How did their participation affect white audiences' perception of Native Americans?
3. **Identifying Historical Developments** Why has the romantic image of the Wild West remained so long-lived in American popular culture?

Answers

Patterns of Popular Culture

1. Possible answer: The Wild West shows of the nineteenth century would portray what life was like out West, but with a much romanticized flare. The shows had little connection to reality, as life out West was tough and dangerous. Instead, the shows focused on the adventure and romance that could be a part of the Western experience.
2. Possible answer: Participating in the shows was probably better than other alternatives, including fighting with the settlers. They probably paid Native Americans money to perform, and the use of real Native Americans added reality to the shows.
3. Possible answer: The West was a popular concept, and the lure of western expansion had been a part of the American psyche from the beginning of colonization. Americans were always on the move, both out of necessity and because of a search for adventure. The American experiment was, at least partly, based on the desire for adventure. In the early twentieth century, however, the shows died out, but with the advent of radio and television, Americans could still get their taste of the western experience through these media outlets.

and inspired those who dreamed of starting life anew. Now, with the last of that unsettled land being slowly absorbed into the nation's civilization, that image exercised a stronger pull than ever.

ROMANTIC IMAGE OF THE WEST

Mark Twain, one of the great American writers of the nineteenth century, gave voice to this romantic vision of the frontier in a series of brilliant novels and memoirs. In some of his writings–notably *Roughing It* (1872)–he wrote of the Far West and of his own experience as a newspaper reporter in Nevada during the mining boom. His greatest works, however, were novels that dealt with life on an earlier frontier: the Mississippi Valley of Twain's boyhood. In *The Adventures of Tom Sawyer* (1876) and *The Adventures of Huckleberry Finn* (1885), he produced characters who repudiated the constraints of organized society and attempted to escape into a natural world. For Huck Finn, the vehicle of escape was a small raft on the Mississippi, but the yearning for freedom reflected a larger vision of the West as the last refuge from the constraints of civilization.

The painter and sculptor Frederic Remington also captured the romance of the West and its image as an alternative to the settled civilization of the East. He portrayed the cowboy as a natural aristocrat, much like Wister's Virginian, living in a natural world in which all the normal supporting structures of "civilization" were missing. The romantic quality of his work made Remington one of the most beloved and successful artists of the nineteenth century.

FREDERIC REMINGTON

Theodore Roosevelt, who was, like both Wister and Remington, a man born and raised in the East, traveled to the Dakota Badlands in the mid-1880s to help himself recover from the sudden death of his young wife. He had long romanticized the West as a place of physical regeneration–a place where a man could gain strength through rugged activity (just as Roosevelt, a sickly, asthmatic boy, had hardened himself through adherence to the idea of a strenuous life). His long sojourn into the Badlands in the 1880s cemented his love of the region, which continued to the end of his life. And like Wister and Remington, he made his own fascination with the West a part of the nation's popular culture. In the 1890s, he published a four-volume history, *The Winning of the West*, with a romanticized account of the spread of white civilization into the frontier. These and other books on the West enhanced his own reputation. They also contributed to the public's fascination with the "frontier."

FREDERICK JACKSON TURNER

Perhaps the clearest and most influential statements of the romantic vision of the frontier came from the historian Frederick Jackson Turner, of the University of Wisconsin. In 1893, the thirty-three-year-old Turner delivered a memorable paper to a meeting of the American Historical Association in Chicago titled "The Significance of the Frontier in American History," in which he argued that the end of the "frontier" also marked the end of one of the most important democratizing forces in American life.

TURNER'S FRONTIER THESIS

In fact, Turner's assessments were both inaccurate and premature. The West had never been a "frontier" in the sense he meant the term: an empty, uncivilized land awaiting settlement. White migrants who moved into the region had joined (or displaced) already-established societies and cultures. At the same time, considerable unoccupied land remained in the West for many years to come. But Turner did express a growing and generally accurate sense that much of the best farming and grazing land was now taken, that in the future it would be more difficult for individuals to acquire valuable land for little or nothing.

THE LOSS OF UTOPIA

In accepting the idea of the "passing of the frontier," many Americans were acknowledging the end of one of their most cherished myths. As long as it had been possible for them to

Courtesy Beinecke Rare Book and Manuscript Library, Yale University

TWILIGHT ENCAMPMENT The western photographer Walter McClintock took this dramatic photograph of a Blackfoot Indian camp in the 1890s. By the time this picture was taken, the Native American nations were already dwindling, and artists, photographers, and ethnographers were flocking to the West to record aspects of Indian civilization that they feared would soon disappear.

Discussion and Activities

Historical Developments and Argumentation After students have read the section "The Idea of the Frontier," ask them to create a T-chart listing ways that the West was portrayed in art and literature. Have students discuss in small groups how art and literature romanticized the West. **GEO** **ARC**

Historical Thinking Skills

Argumentation Have students read the section "Frederick Jackson Turner." Ask them to discuss as a class what Jackson got right and wrong about the West. Have students consider what might have been a more accurate description. **GEO** **WXT** **SOC** **MIG**

Discussion and Activities

Making Connections After students have read the feature "The 'Frontier' and the West," ask them to discuss in small groups what they think the frontier(s) of today and the near future might be. *(Exploration of outer space; new developments in science and technology.)* Have students consider whether the idea of a "frontier" is still important as part of the story of America. **GEO** **WXT** **SOC**

DEBATING THE PAST

The "Frontier" and the West

The American West, the Native American population, and the people of European descent who settled there have been central to the national imagination and to American historical scholarship.

Through most of the nineteenth century, the history of the West reflected the romantic and optimistic view of the region as a place of adventure and opportunity where brave and enterprising people endured great hardships to begin building a new civilization. The emergence of western history as an important field of scholarship can be traced to Frederick Jackson Turner's "The Significance of the Frontier in American History," a paper he delivered at a meeting of the American Historical Association in 1893.

Turner stated his thesis simply. The settlement of the West by white people—"the existence of an area of free land, its continuous recession, and the advance of American settlement westward"—was the central story of American history. The process of westward expansion transformed a desolate and savage land into a modern civilization. It also continually renewed American ideas of democracy and individualism. It shaped not just the West but the nation as a whole. The Turner thesis shaped American history for a generation, and it shaped western American history for even longer. In the first half of the twentieth century, virtually everyone who wrote about the West echoed at least part of Turner's argument. Ray Allen Billington's *Westward Expansion* (1949), a skillful revision of Turner's thesis, kept the idea of what Billington called the "westward course of empire" (the movement of Europeans into an unsettled land) at the center of scholarship. In *The Great Plains* (1931) and *The Great Frontier* (1952), Walter Prescott Webb similarly emphasized the bravery and ingenuity of white settlers in the Southwest.

Serious efforts to displace Turner's thesis as the explanation of western American history did not begin in earnest until after World War II. In *Virgin Land* (1950), Henry Nash Smith examined many of the same heroic images of the West that Turner and his disciples. He treated those images less as descriptions of reality than as myths. Earl Pomeroy challenged Turner's notion of the West as a place of individualism, innovation, and democratic renewal, claiming that "conservatism, inheritance, and continuity bulked at least as large."

FRONTIER TOWN GROWS UP This picture of present-day San Francisco conveys a very different view of a city that, at about the time just before the gold rush (about 1848), had only 1,000 people. Today, the city has left behind many overt traces of its earlier status as a frontier community. The city now has nearly a million citizens with diverse backgrounds living within the Bay Area of nearly 8.5 million people.

The western historians of the late 1970s launched an even more emphatic attack on the Turner thesis and the idea of the "frontier." New western historians such as Richard White, Patricia Nelson Limerick, William Cronon, Donald Worster, Peggy Pascoe, and many others challenged the Turnerians on a number of points.

Turner saw the nineteenth-century West as "free land" awaiting the expansion of Anglo-American settlement and American democracy. Pioneers settled the region by conquering the "obstacles" that stood in the way of civilization. The new western historians rejected the concept of a "frontier" and emphasized, instead, the elaborate and highly developed civilizations that already existed in the region. White, English-speaking Americans, they argued, did not so much settle the West as conquer it, though their conquest was never complete. Anglo-Americans in the West continued to share the region not only with the Native American and Hispanic peoples who preceded them there, but also with African Americans, Asians, Latino Americans, and others who flowed into the West at the same time they did.

The Turnerian West was a place of heroism, triumph, and, above all, progress, dominated by the feats of brave white men. More-recent historians describe the West as a less triumphant (and less masculine) place in which bravery and success coexist with oppression, greed, and failure; in which decaying ghost towns, bleak Native American reservations, impoverished barrios, and ecologically devastated landscapes are as characteristic of western development as great ranches, rich farms, and prosperous cities; and in which women are as important as men in shaping the societies that emerged. This aspect of the "new western history" has attracted particular criticism from those attached to traditional accounts. The novelist Larry McMurtry, for example, has denounced the newer scholarship as "Failure Studies." He has insisted that in rejecting the romantic image westerners had of themselves, the revisionists omit an important part of the western experience.

To Turner and his disciples, the nineteenth-century West was a place where rugged individualism flourished and replenished American democracy. The newer western scholars contend that western individualism is a self-serving myth. Western "pioneers," they argue, were never self-sufficient but depended on government-subsidized railroads for access to markets, federal troops for protection from Native Americans, and (later) government-funded dams and canals for irrigating their fields and sustaining their towns.

While Turner defined the West as a process—a process of settlement that came to an end with the "closing of the frontier" in the late nineteenth century—more-recent historians see the West as a region whose distinctive history did not end in 1890 but continues into our own time.

HISTORICAL THINKING SKILLS

Questions assume cumulative content knowledge from this chapter and previous chapters.

1. **Identifying Historical Developments** Identify three broad schools of historical interpretation concerning the West.
2. **Determining Context** Describe how one piece of historical evidence, from the time period, could be used to support each of the three broad schools of historical interpretation concerning the West.
3. **Developing Arguments** Analyze which school of thought you find more convincing and why.

Answers

Debating the Past

1. Possible answer: First, Western scholarship really began with Frederick Jackson Turner with his paper, "The Significance of the Frontier in American History," delivered in 1893. Turner's argument is that America had always been a land of western migration. Second, Turner's Thesis was picked up by a new wave of historians. Ray Allen Billington and Walter Prescott Webb argued that the West was a built on bravery and ingenuity. Third, following WWII, western scholarship began to take a different turn. Beginning with Henry Nash Smith, *Virgin Land* (1950), an attempt to demythologize the western image rooted in the Turner Thesis began to take hold.
2. Possible answer: Turner's Thesis does have some aspects of truth in it. Western expansion began immediately once the first colonists settled in Jamestown. The West provided new land, new opportunity, and a chance to make something of oneself. But the post-WWII scholarship also correctly points to the ugly side of the West. Native Americans were displaced almost immediately as the government forced them off their land. Women often found the western experience very difficult. As men left the home, women were forced to take on all the roles within the house and family, and loneliness and depression were a common experience for women on the frontier.
3. Student responses will vary.

consider the West an empty, open land, it was possible to believe that there were constantly revitalizing opportunities in American life. Now there was a vague and ominous sense of opportunities foreclosed, of individuals losing their ability to control their own destinies. The psychological loss was all the greater because of what historian Henry Nash Smith would later call, in *Virgin Land* (1950), the "myth of the garden": the once widely shared belief that the West had the potential to be a virtual Garden of Eden, where a person could begin life anew and where the ideals of democracy could be restored.

PSYCHOLOGICAL LOSS

THE DISPERSAL OF NATIVE AMERICANS

Having imagined the West as a "virgin land" awaiting civilization by white people, many Americans tried to force the region to match their image of it. That meant, above all, ensuring that Native American nations tribes would not remain obstacles to the spread of white society.

WHITE TRIBAL POLICIES

The traditional policy of the federal government was to regard the tribes simultaneously as independent nations and as wards of the president, and to negotiate treaties with them that were solemnly ratified by the Senate. This limited concept of Native American sovereignty had been responsible for the government's attempt before 1860 to erect a permanent frontier between white settlers and Native Americans, to reserve the region west of the bend of the Missouri River as permanent Indian country. However, treaties or agreements with Native Americans seldom survived the pressure of white settlers eager for access to Native American lands. The history of relations between the United States and the Native Americans was, therefore, one of nearly endless broken promises.

By the early 1850s, the idea of establishing one great enclave in which many Native American nations could live gave way, in the face of white demands for access to lands in Indian Territory, to a new reservations policy, known as "concentration." In 1851, each nation was assigned its own defined reservation, confirmed by separate treaties—treaties often illegitimately negotiated with unauthorized representatives, known sarcastically as "treaty chiefs," chosen by white people. The new arrangement had many benefits for white settlers and few for Native Americans. It divided the nations from one another and made them easier to control. It allowed the government to force Native Americans into scattered locations and to take over the most desirable lands for white settlement. But it did not survive as the basis of Indian policy for long.

"CONCENTRATION" POLICY

In 1867, in the aftermath of a series of bloody conflicts, Congress established an Indian Peace Commission, composed of soldiers and civilians, to recommend a new and presumably permanent Indian policy. The commission recommended replacing the "concentration" policy with a plan to move all the Plains Indians into two large reservations—one in Indian Territory (Oklahoma), the other in the Dakotas. At a series of meetings with the nations, government agents cajoled, bribed, and tricked representatives of the Arapaho, Cheyenne, Sioux, and other nations into agreeing to treaties establishing the new reservations.

This solution worked little better than previous ones. White management of Native American matters was entrusted to the Bureau of Indian Affairs, a branch of the Department of the Interior responsible for distributing land, making payments, and supervising the shipment of supplies. Its record was appalling. The bureau's agents in the West, products of political patronage, were often men of extraordinary incompetence and dishonesty. But even the most honest and diligent agents were generally ill prepared for their jobs, had no understanding of tribal ways, and had little chance of success.

POORLY ADMINISTERED RESERVATIONS

CHIEF GARFIELD Edward Curtis, one of the most accomplished photographers of tribal life in the early twentieth century, made this portrait of a Jicarilla Apache chief in 1904. By then, the Jicarilla were living in a reservation in northern New Mexico, and white officials had assigned all members of the tribe Spanish or English names. The man depicted here, the head chief, had chosen the name Garfield himself.

Discussion and Activities

Analyzing Issues After students have read the section "The Loss of Utopia," ask them to discuss as a class how the idea of the West as a Utopia could exist simultaneously with the struggles of miners and sod-busting farmers and the experiences of Hispanics, Native Americans, and Chinese living in the West. *(The romantic view was reinforced by art, literature, and entertainment in Eastern audiences who had never experienced any of the hardships personally.)* **SOC** **WXT**

Reasoning Processes

Continuity and Change Have students read the section "'Concentration Policy'." Ask them to write a short paragraph explaining how the policy was a continuation of or change from earlier policies concerning Native Americans. *(Similar: Treaties were still negotiated with Native American groups; groups were removed to reservations; treaties were broken when white settlers decided to infringe upon Native American lands. Different: Groups were now to be removed to only a couple of large reservations, rather than scattered small reservations.)* **MIG** **PCE**

Discussion and Activities

Analyzing Points of View After students have read the section "White Tribal Policies," ask them to write a short letter or journal entry from the point of view of a railroad passenger who has witnessed a professional buffalo hunt. Have students consider why a traveler may have either supported or condemned such activity. **WXT** **GEO**

Worsening the fate of Native Americans was the white Anglos' relentless slaughtering of the buffalo herds that supported their way of life. Even in the 1850s, white settlers had been killing buffalo at a rapid rate to provide food and supplies for the large bands of migrants traveling to the gold rush in California. After the Civil War, the white demand for buffalo hides became a national phenomenon–partly for economic reasons and partly as a fad. (Everyone east of the Missouri seemed to want a buffalo robe from the romantic West, and there was a strong demand for buffalo leather, which was used to make machine belts in eastern factories.) Gangs of professional hunters swarmed over the plains to shoot the huge animals. Railroad companies hired riflemen (such as Buffalo Bill Cody) and arranged shooting expeditions to kill large numbers of buffalo, hoping to thin the herds, which were obstructions to railroad traffic. Some Native American nations (notably the Blackfeet) also began killing large numbers of buffalo to sell in the booming new market.

It was not just the hunting that threatened the buffalo. The ecological changes accompanying white settlement–the reduction, and in some areas virtual disappearance, of the open plains–also decimated the buffalo population. The southern herd was virtually exterminated by 1875, and within a few years the smaller northern herd had met the same fate. In 1865, there had been at least 15 million buffalo; a decade later, fewer than a thousand of the great beasts survived. The army and the agents of the Bureau of Indian Affairs condoned and even encouraged the killing. By destroying the buffalo herds, whites were destroying the Native Americans' source of food and supplies and their ability to resist the white advance. They were also contributing to a climate in which Native American warriors felt the need to fight to preserve their way of life.

DECIMATION OF THE BUFFALO

THE INDIAN WARS

There was almost incessant fighting between white settlers and Native Americans from the 1850s to the 1880s, as Native Americans struggled against the growing threats to their civilization. Native American warriors, usually traveling in raiding parties of thirty to forty men, attacked wagon trains, stagecoaches, and isolated ranches, often in retaliation for earlier attacks. As the U.S. Army became more deeply involved in the fighting, Native Americans began to focus more of their attacks on white soldiers.

INDIAN RESISTANCE

At times, this small-scale fighting escalated into something close to a war. During the Civil War, the eastern Sioux in Minnesota, cramped on an inadequate reservation and exploited by corrupt white agents, suddenly rebelled against the restrictions imposed on them by the government's policies. Led by Little Crow, they killed more than 700 white people before being subdued by a force of regulars and militiamen. Thirty-eight Native Americans were hanged, and the Sioux were exiled to the Dakotas.

At the same time, fighting flared up in eastern Colorado, where the Arapaho and Cheyenne were coming into conflict with white miners settling in the region. Bands of Native Americans attacked stagecoach lines and settlements in an effort to regain lost territory. In response, white settlers called up a large territorial militia. The governor urged all friendly Native Americans to congregate at army posts for protection before the army began its campaign. One Arapaho and Cheyenne band under Chief Black Kettle, apparently in response to the invitation, camped near Fort Lyon on Sand Creek in November 1864. Some members of the party were warriors, but Black Kettle believed he was under official protection and exhibited no hostile intention. Nevertheless, Colonel J. M. Chivington, apparently encouraged by the army commander of the district, led a volunteer militia force–largely consisting of unemployed miners, many of whom were apparently drunk–to the unsuspecting camp and massacred 133 people, 105 of them women and children. Black Kettle escaped the Sand Creek massacre. Four years later, in 1868, he and his Cheyennes, some of whom were now at war with white settlers and troops, were caught on the Washita

SAND CREEK MASSACRE

HELD UP BY BUFFALO Once among the most numerous creatures in North America, the buffalo almost became extinct as a result of indiscriminate slaughter by white settlers and travelers, who often fired at herds from moving trains simply for the sport of it.

Discussion and Activities

Analyzing Cause and Effect Have students examine the image "Held Up by Buffalo." Ask them to identify details from the image and discuss in small groups how the arrival of railroads impacted Native Americans. *(Railroad companies hunted buffalo to feed work crews, and railroads brought sport hunters who decimated the buffalo populations many Native American groups were dependent upon. Railroads also brought increasing numbers of settlers who desired land, thus putting pressure on existing Native American populations.)* **MIG** **WXT** **GEO**

River, near the Texas border, by Colonel George A. Custer. White troops killed the chief and slaughtered his people.

At the end of the Civil War, white troops stepped up their wars against the western Native Americans on several fronts. The most serious and sustained conflict was in Montana, where the army was attempting to build a road to connect Fort Laramie, Wyoming, to the new mining centers. The western Sioux resented this intrusion into the heart of their buffalo range. Led by one of their great chiefs, Red Cloud, they so harried the soldiers and the construction party—among other things, burning the forts that were supposed to guard the route—that the road could not be used.

It was not only the U.S. Army that threatened Native Americans. It was also unofficial violence by white vigilantes

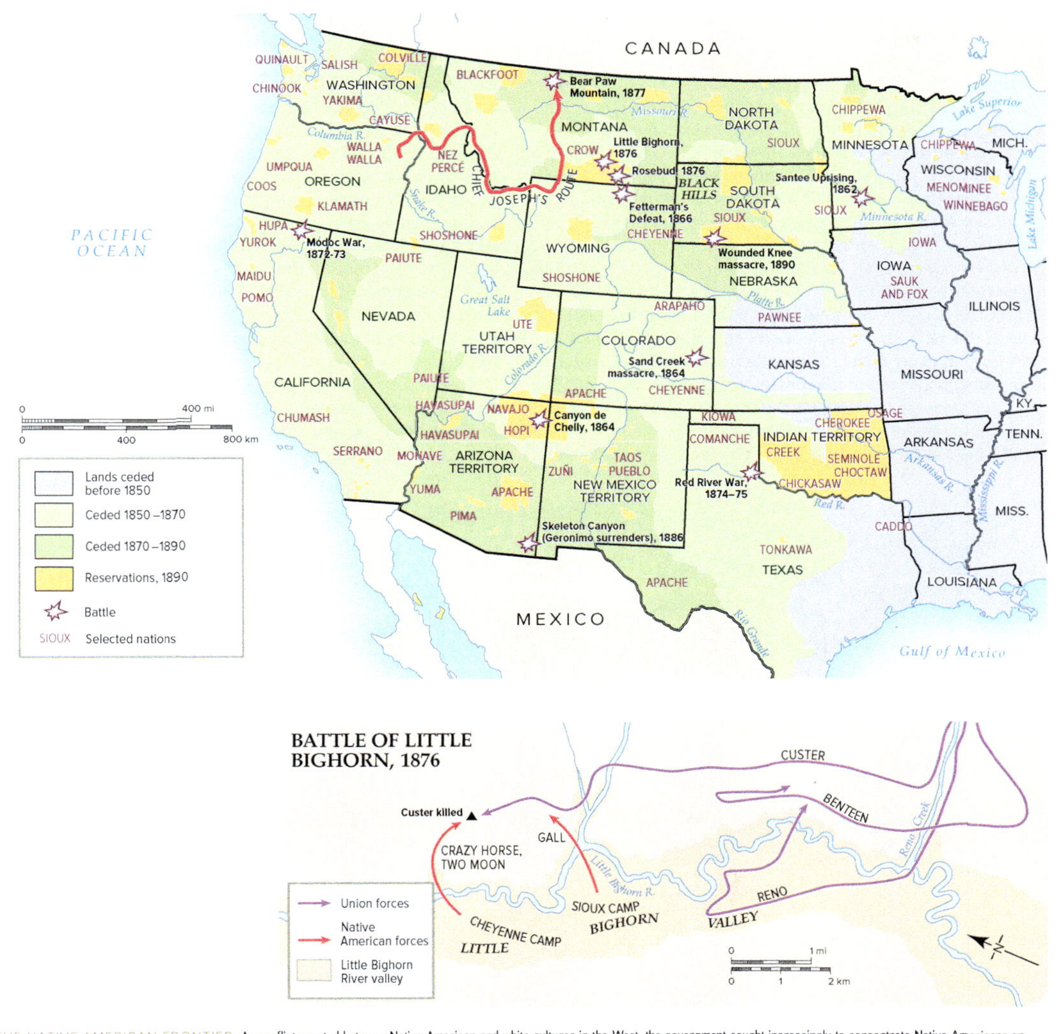

THE NATIVE AMERICAN FRONTIER As conflict erupted between Native American and white cultures in the West, the government sought increasingly to concentrate Native Americans on reservations. Resistance to the reservation concept helped unite the Sioux and Cheyenne, traditionally enemies, in the Dakotas during the 1870s. Along the Little Bighorn River, the impetuous Custer underestimated the strength of his Native American opponents and attacked before the supporting troops of Reno and Benteen were in a position to aid him.

What did the defeat of Custer's army do for the Sioux?

Discussion and Activities

Speculating After students have read the section "Sand Creek Massacre," ask them to discuss as a class whether the clashes between whites and Native Americans were avoidable, and what could have been done to prevent them. *(Better treatment and conditions on reservations; greater respect for Native American territorial claims; less reliance on untrained militias.)* **PCE**

Answers

The Native American Frontier

The Sioux victory at Little Bighorn provided only a temporary reprieve in the struggle to preserve their independence.

Historical Thinking Skills

Argumentation After students have read the section "Little Bighorn," ask them to list reasons why Native American groups were not able to follow up on the victory at Little Bighorn. Have students rank their lists in order of importance and write a thesis statement that makes a claim about the most important reasons Native Americans lost the Indian wars. **PCE** **GEO** **SOC**

who engaged in what became known as "Indian hunting." In California, in particular, tracking down and killing Native Americans became for some white men a kind of sport. Some who did not engage in killing offered rewards (or bounties) to those who did; these bounty hunters brought back scalps and skulls as proof of their deeds. Sometimes the killing was in response to raids on white communities. But often it was in service to a more basic and terrible purpose. Considerable numbers of white people were committed to the goal of literal "elimination" of Native Americans, a goal that rested on the belief in the inhumanity of Native Americans and the impossibility of white society's coexisting with them. In Oregon in 1853, for example, white people who had hanged a seven-year-old Native American boy explained themselves by saying simply "nits breed lice." In California, civilians killed close to 5,000 Native Americans between 1850 and 1880—one of many factors (disease and poverty being the more important) that reduced the Native American population of the state from 150,000 before the Civil War to 30,000 in 1870.

"Indian Hunting"

The treaties negotiated in 1867 brought a temporary lull to many of the conflicts. But new forces soon shattered the peace again. In the early 1870s, more waves of white settlers, mostly miners, began to penetrate some of the lands in Dakota Territory supposedly guaranteed to the Native American nations in 1867.

Native American resistance flared anew, this time with even greater strength. In the northern plains, the Sioux rose up in 1875 and left their reservation. When white officials ordered them to return, bands of warriors gathered in Montana and united under two great leaders: Crazy Horse and Sitting Bull.

Three army columns set out to round them up and force them back onto the reservation. With the expedition, as colonel of the famous Seventh Cavalry, was the colorful and controversial George A. Custer, a golden-haired, romantic glory seeker. At the Battle of the Little Bighorn in southern Montana in 1876—the most famous conflict between white troops and Native Americans—the warriors surprised Custer and 264 members of his regiment, surrounded them, and killed every man. Custer was accused of rashness, but he encountered something that no white man would likely have predicted. The chiefs had gathered as many as 2,500 warriors, one of the largest Native American armies ever assembled at one time in the United States.

Little Bighorn

But the Native Americans did not have the political organization or the supplies to keep their troops united. Soon the warriors drifted off in bands to elude pursuit or search for food, and the army eventually forced them back to the Dakota reservations. The power of the Sioux was soon broken. The proud leaders, Crazy Horse and Sitting Bull, accepted defeat and the monotony of life on reservations. Both were later killed by reservation police after being tricked or taunted into a last pathetic show of resistance.

One of the most dramatic episodes in Native American history occurred in Idaho in 1877. The Nez Percé were a small and relatively peaceful tribe, some of whose members had managed to live unmolested in Oregon into the 1870s without

THE BATTLE OF THE LITTLE BIGHORN This 1898 watercolor by one of the Native American participants portrays the aftermath of the Battle of the Little Bighorn, June 25–26, 1876, in which an army unit under the command of General George Armstrong Custer was surrounded and wiped out by Sioux and Cheyenne warriors. This grisly painting shows Native Americans on horseback riding over the corpses of Custer and his men. Custer can be seen lying at left center, dressed in yellow buckskin with his hat beside him. The four standing men at center are Sitting Bull, Rain-in-the-Face, Crazy Horse, and Kicking Bear (the artist). At lower right, Native American women begin preparations for a ceremony to honor the returning warriors.

Discussion and Activities

Analyzing Visuals Have students examine the image "The Battle of the Little Bighorn." Ask them to identify and discuss in small groups details that indicate that the battle was a Native American victory. Have students also discuss details that indicate costs of the victory for Native Americans. *(No soldiers survived; Sioux leaders were surrounded by the enemy dead; the Sioux village at the lower right is intact. Costs include the bodies of numerous Native American casualties on the battlefield.)* **SOC** **ARC**

ever signing a treaty with the United States. But under pressure from white settlers, the government forced them to move into a reservation that another branch of the Nez Percé had accepted by treaty in the 1850s. With no realistic prospect of resisting, the Nez Percé began the journey to the reservation; but on the way, several younger Native Americans, drunk and angry, killed four white settlers.

The leader of the Nez Percé, Chief Joseph, urged his followers to flee from the American troops. They scattered in several directions and became part of a remarkable chase. Joseph moved with 200 men and 350 women, children, and elders in an effort to reach Canada and take refuge with the Sioux there. Pursued by four columns of American soldiers, the Nez Percé group covered 1,321 miles in seventy-five days, repelling or evading the army time and again. They were finally caught just short of the Canadian boundary. Some escaped and slipped across the border; but Joseph and most of his followers, weary and discouraged, finally gave up. "Hear me, my chiefs," Joseph said after meeting with the American general Nelson Miles. "I am tired. My heart is sick and sad. From where the sun now stands, I will fight no more forever." He surrendered to Miles in exchange for a promise that his band could return to the Nez Percé reservation in Idaho. But the government refused to honor Miles's promise, and the Nez Percé were moved from one place to another for several years; in the process, many of them died of disease and malnutrition (although Joseph himself lived until 1908).

CHIEF JOSEPH

The last Native Americans to maintain organized resistance against white forces were the Chiricahua Apaches, who fought intermittently from the 1860s to the late 1880s. The two ablest chiefs were Mangas Colorados and Cochise. Mangas was murdered during the Civil War by white soldiers who tricked him into surrendering, and in 1872 Cochise agreed to peace in exchange for a reservation that included some of the Apaches traditional land. But Cochise died in 1874, and his successor, Geronimo–unwilling to bow to white pressures to assimilate–fought on for more than a decade establishing bases in the mountains of Arizona and Mexico and leading warriors in intermittent raids against white outposts. With each raid, however, the number of warring Apaches dwindled, as some warriors died and others drifted away to the reservation. By 1886, Geronimo's plight was hopeless. His band consisted of only about thirty people, including women and children, while his white pursuers numbered perhaps ten thousand. Geronimo recognized the odds and surrendered, an event that marked the end of formal warfare between Native Americans and white people. The Apache wars were the most violent of all the conflicts, perhaps because the Native Americans were now the most desperate. But it was white people who committed the most flagrant and vicious atrocities. In 1871, for example, a mob of white miners invaded an Apache camp, slaughtered more than a hundred Native Americans, and captured children, whom they enslaved and sold to rival Native American groups. On other occasions, white troops murdered Native Americans who responded to invitations to peace conferences, once killing them with poisoned food.

Nor did the atrocities end with the conclusion of the Apache wars. Another tragic encounter occurred in 1890 as a result of a religious revival among the Sioux–a revival that itself symbolized the catastrophic effects of the white assaults on Native American civilization. The Sioux were by now aware that their culture and their glories were irrevocably fading; some were also near starvation because corrupt government agents had reduced their food rations. As other groups had done in trying times in the past, many of these Native Americans turned to a prophet who led them into a religious revival.

This time the prophet was Wovoka, a Paiute who inspired a spiritual awakening that began in Nevada and spread quickly to the plains. The new revival emphasized the coming of a messiah, but its most conspicuous feature was a mass, emotional "Ghost Dance," which inspired ecstatic visions. Among these

"GHOST DANCE"

WOUNDED KNEE This grim photograph shows Big Foot, chief of the Lakota Sioux, lying dead in the snow near Wounded Knee in South Dakota. He was one of many victims of an 1890 massacre of more than 300 members of the Sioux nation, killed by U.S. Army soldiers after the Sioux had surrendered their weapons. Whether the massacre was planned and deliberate, or whether it was a result of confusion and fear, remains in dispute.

Discussion and Activities

Speculating After students have read the section "Chief Joseph," ask them to discuss in small groups why they think the U.S. government did not simply allow the Nez Perce to enter Canada. *(Most likely they wanted to prevent the Nez Perce from setting a precedent that would lead other Native American groups to challenge the government's authority.)* **PCE**

Historical Thinking Skills

Sourcing and Situation Have students examine the image "Wounded Knee." Ask them to write a short paragraph explaining the photographer's possible purpose in taking the photo. *(It could be intended to encourage sympathy for the plight of Native Americans by showing their brutal treatment. On the other hand, it could be intended as a warning to other Native American groups to respect the authority of the U.S. government and military.)* **PCE** **SOC**

Historical Thinking Skills

Argumentation After students have read the section "Wounded Knee," ask them to discuss as a class what they would have recommended Native American leaders should have done in the face of repeated aggressions by white settlers, the U.S. Army, and Native American agents. What options did Native American leaders have? **PCE** **SOC**

visions were images of a retreat of white people from the plains and a restoration of the great buffalo herds. White agents on the Sioux reservation watched the dances in bewilderment and fear; some believed they might be the preliminary to hostilities.

On December 29, 1890, the Seventh Cavalry (which had once been Custer's regiment) tried to round up a group of about 350 cold and starving Sioux at Wounded Knee, South Dakota. Fighting broke out in which about 40 white soldiers and more than 300 of the Native Americans, including women and children, died. What precipitated the conflict is a matter of dispute. But the battle soon turned into a one-sided massacre, as the white soldiers turned their revolving cannons on the Native Americans and mowed them down in the snow.

WOUNDED KNEE

THE DAWES ACT

Even before the Ghost Dance and the Wounded Knee tragedy, the federal government had moved to destroy forever the tribal structure that had always been the cornerstone of Native American culture. Reversing its policy of nearly fifty years of creating reservations in which the Native American nations would be isolated from white society, Congress abolished the practice by which nations owned reservation lands communally. Some supporters of the new policy believed they were acting for the good of Native Americans, whom they considered a "vanishing race" in need of rescue by white society. But whatever the motives, the policy was designed to force Native Americans to become landowners and farmers, to abandon their collective society and culture and become part of white civilization.

The Dawes Severalty Act of 1887 (usually known simply as the Dawes Act) provided for the gradual elimination of tribal ownership of land and the allotment of tracts to individual owners: 160 acres to the head of a family, 80 acres to a single adult or orphan, 40 acres to each dependent child. Adult owners were given United States citizenship, but unlike other citizens, they could not gain full title to their property for twenty-five years (supposedly to prevent them from selling the land to speculators). The act applied to most of the western tribes. The Pueblo, who continued to occupy lands long ago guaranteed them, were excluded from its provisions. In applying the Dawes Act, the Bureau of Indian Affairs relentlessly promoted the idea of assimilation that lay behind it. Not only did they try to move Native American families onto their own plots of land; they also took some Native American children away from their families and sent them to boarding schools run by white people, where they believed the young people could be educated to abandon tribal ways. The bureau also moved to stop Native American religious rituals and encouraged the spread of Christianity and the creation of Christian churches on the reservations.

ASSIMILATION

Few Native Americans were prepared for this wrenching change from their traditional collective society to capitalist individualism. In any case, white administration of the program was so corrupt and inept that ultimately the government simply abandoned it. Much of the reservation land, therefore, was never distributed to individual owners. Congress attempted to speed the transition with the Burke Act of 1906, but Native Americans continued to resist forced assimilation.

Neither then nor later did legislation provide a satisfactory solution to the plight of the Native Americans, largely because there was no entirely happy solution to be had. The interests of the Native Americans were not compatible with those of the expanding white civilization. White Americans successfully settled the West only at the expense of the region's indigenous peoples.

THE RISE AND DECLINE OF THE WESTERN FARMER

The arrival of the miners, the empire building of the cattle ranchers, the dispersal of the Native American nations—all served as a prelude to the decisive phase of white settlement of the Far West. Even before the Civil War, farmers had begun moving into the plains region, challenging the dominance of the ranchers and Native Americans and occasionally coming into conflict with both. By the 1870s, what was once a trickle had become a deluge. Farmers poured into the plains and beyond, enclosed land that had once been hunting territory for Native Americans and grazing territory for cattle, and established a new agricultural region.

For a time in the late 1870s and early 1880s, the new western farmers flourished, enjoying the fruits of an agricultural economic boom comparable in many ways to the booms that eastern industry periodically enjoyed. Beginning in the mid-1880s, however, the boom turned to bust. American agriculture—not only in the new West but in the older Midwest and the South as well—was producing more than it ever had, too much for the market to absorb. For that and other reasons, prices for agricultural goods declined. Both economically and psychologically, the agricultural economy began a long, steady decline.

FARMING ON THE PLAINS

Many factors combined to produce this surge of western settlement, but the most important was the railroads. Before the Civil War, the Great Plains had been accessible only through a difficult journey by wagon. But beginning in the 1860s, a great new network of railroad lines developed, spearheaded by the transcontinental routes Congress had authorized and subsidized in 1862. They made huge new areas of settlement accessible.

The completion of the transcontinental line was a dramatic and monumental achievement. The two lines joined at Promontory Point in northern Utah in the spring of 1869.

Discussion and Activities

Analyzing Issues Have students read the section "The Dawes Act." Ask them to create a T-chart listing provisions of the Act and the assimilation policy and consequences of each provision. Have students discuss in small groups what they think the most significant impacts were and why. **PCE** **SOC** **ARC**

But while this first transcontinental line captured the public imagination, the construction of subsidiary lines in the following years proved of greater importance to the West. State governments encouraged railroad development by offering financial aid, favorable loans, and more than 50 million acres of land (on top of the 130 million acres the federal government had already provided). Although operated by private corporations, the railroads were essentially public projects.

KEY ROLE OF THE RAILROAD

It was not only by making access to the Great Plains easier that the railroads helped spur agricultural settlement there. The railroad companies themselves actively promoted settlement, both to provide themselves with customers for their services and to increase the value of their vast landholdings. In addition, the companies set rates so low for settlers that almost anyone could afford the trip west. And they sold much of their land at very low prices and provided liberal credit to prospective settlers.

Contributing further to the great surge of white agricultural expansion was a temporary change in the climate of the Great Plains. For several years in succession, beginning in the 1870s, rainfall in the plains states was well above average. White Americans now rejected the old idea that the region was the Great American Desert. Some even claimed that cultivation of the plains itself actually encouraged rainfall.

Even under the most favorable conditions, farming on the plains presented special problems. First was the challenge of fencing. Farmers had to enclose their land, if for no other reason than to protect it from the herds of the open-range cattlemen. But traditional wood or stone fences were too expensive and were ineffective as barriers to cattle. In 1873, however, two Illinois farmers, Joseph H. Glidden and I. L. Ellwood, solved

BARBED WIRE

this problem by developing and marketing barbed wire, which became standard equipment on the plains and revolutionized fencing practices all over the country.

The second problem was water. Much of the land west of the Mississippi was considerably more arid than the lands to the east. Some of it was literally desert. As a result, the growth of the West depended heavily on irrigation–providing water from sources other than rainfall. Water was diverted from rivers and streams and into farmlands throughout the West–in California and in the Southwest more than anywhere else. In other areas, farmers drilled wells or found other methods of

The Library of Congress (LC-USZ62-55422)

CARLISLE INDIAN SCHOOL Government authorities and private philanthropists tried in many ways to encourage Native Americans to assimilate into mainstream white American society after the end of the Indian wars of the late nineteenth century. The Carlisle Indian Industrial School, founded by Captain Richard Henry Pratt in 1879, was the first federally funded Native American off-reservation boarding school. Educators there believed that Native Americans were the equals of people from European backgrounds. The curriculum was designed to help Native Americans gain the skills necessary to advance in mainstream American society.

Discussion and Activities

Evaluating Evidence After students have read the section "Barbed Wire," ask them to discuss in small groups the impact that technology had on farming in the West. **WXT**

Discussion and Activities

Analyzing Points of View Have students examine the image "Carlisle Indian School." Ask them to write a short letter or journal entry from the point of view of one of the students pictured in the photo. Have students consider the thoughts, emotions, and experiences the students were undergoing in this boarding school. **SOC** **ARC**

Historical Thinking Skills

Argumentation After students have read the section "Farming on the Plains," ask them to list and rank in order of importance the challenges facing farmers on the Great Plains. *(Competition with ranchers; challenges in getting crops to market; dependence upon the railroad; lack of consistent rainfall.)* Have students write a thesis statement that makes a claim about the most difficult challenge facing farmers on the Plains. **WXT** **GEO**

channeling water onto their lands. The search for water–and the resulting battles over control of water (between different landowners and even between different states)–became a central and enduring characteristic of western life.

In the plains states, the problems of water created an epic disaster. After 1887, a series of dry seasons began, and lands that had been fertile now returned to semidesert. Some farmers dealt with the problem by using deep wells pumped by steel windmills, by turning to what was called dryland farming (a system of tillage designed to conserve moisture in the soil by covering it with a dust blanket), or by planting drought-resistant crops. In many areas of the plains, however, only large-scale irrigation could save the endangered farms. But irrigation projects of the necessary magnitude required government assistance, and neither the state nor federal governments were prepared to fund the projects.

DROUGHT

Most of the people who moved into the region had previously been farmers in the Midwest, the East, or Europe. In the booming years of the early 1880s, with land values rising, the new farmers had no problem obtaining extensive and easy credit and had every reason to believe they would soon be able to retire their debts. But the arid years of the late 1880s–during which crop prices were falling while production was becoming more expensive–changed that prospect. Tens of thousands of farmers could not pay their debts and were forced to abandon their farms. There was, in effect, a reverse migration: white settlers moved back east, sometimes turning once-flourishing communities into desolate ghost towns. Those who remained continued to suffer from falling prices (for example, wheat, which had sold for $1.60 a bushel at the end of the Civil War, dropped to 49 cents in the 1890s) and persistent indebtedness.

HARD TIMES FOR FARMERS

COMMERCIAL AGRICULTURE

American farming by the late nineteenth century no longer bore much relation to the comforting image many Americans continued to cherish. The sturdy, independent farmer of popular myth was being replaced by the commercial farmer–attempting to do in the agricultural economy what industrialists were doing in the manufacturing economy.

Commercial farmers were not self-sufficient and made no effort to become so. They specialized in cash crops, which they sold in national or world markets. They did not make their own household supplies or grow their own food but bought them instead at town or village stores. This kind of farming, when it was successful, raised the farmers' living standards. But it also made them dependent on bankers and interest rates, railroads and freight rates, national and European markets, world supply and demand. And unlike the capitalists of the industrial order, they could not regulate their production or influence the prices of what they sold.

Between 1865 and 1900, agriculture became an international business. Farm output increased dramatically, not only in the United States but also in Brazil, Argentina, Canada, Australia, New Zealand, Russia, and elsewhere. At the same time, modern forms of communication and transportation–the telephone, telegraph, steam navigation, railroads–were creating new markets around the world for agricultural goods. American commercial farmers, constantly opening new lands, produced much more than the domestic market could absorb; they relied on the world market to absorb their surplus, but in that market they faced major competition. Cotton farmers depended on export sales for 70 percent of their annual income, wheat farmers for 30 to 40 percent; but the volatility of the international market put them at great risk.

Beginning in the 1880s, worldwide overproduction led to a drop in prices for most agricultural goods and hence to great economic distress for many of the more than 6 million American farm families. By the 1890s, 27 percent of the farms in the country were mortgaged; by 1910, 33 percent. In 1880, 25 percent of all farms had been operated by tenants; by 1910, the proportion had grown to 37 percent. Commercial farming made some people fabulously wealthy. But the farm economy as a whole was suffering a significant decline relative to the rest of the nation.

CONSEQUENCES OF OVERPRODUCTION

THE FARMERS' GRIEVANCES

American farmers were painfully aware that something was wrong. But few yet understood the implications of national and world overproduction. Instead, they concentrated their attention and anger on immediate, comprehensible–and no less real–problems: inequitable freight rates, high interest charges, and an inadequate currency.

The farmers' first and most burning grievance was against the railroads. In many cases, the railroads charged higher freight rates for farm goods than for other goods, and higher rates in the South and West than in the Northeast. Railroads also controlled elevator and warehouse facilities in buying centers and charged arbitrary storage rates.

Farmers also resented the institutions controlling credit–banks, loan companies, insurance corporations. Since sources of credit in the West and South were few, farmers had to take loans on whatever terms they could get, often at interest rates ranging from 10 to 25 percent. Many farmers had to pay these loans back in years when prices were dropping and currency was becoming scarce. Increasing the volume of currency eventually became an important agrarian demand.

A third grievance concerned prices–both the prices farmers received for their products and the prices they paid for goods. Farmers sold their products in a competitive world market over which they had no control and of which they had no advanced knowledge. A farmer could plant a large crop at a moment when prices were high and find that by harvesttime the price had declined, sometimes substantially. Farmers' fortunes rose and fell in response to unpredictable forces. But many farmers became convinced (often with valid reason) that "middlemen"–speculators, bankers, regional and local agents–

Discussion and Activities

Evaluating Evidence Have students read the section "Commercial Agriculture." Ask them to create a T-chart listing opportunities and risks for commercial farmers. Have students discuss in small groups whether they think the potential rewards outweighed the risks. **WXT** **GEO** **WOR**

were combining to fix prices so as to benefit themselves at the growers' expense. Many farmers also came to believe (again, not entirely without reason) that manufacturers in the East were conspiring to keep the prices of farm goods low and the prices of industrial goods high. Although farmers sold their crops in a competitive world market, they bought manufactured goods in a domestic market protected by tariffs and dominated by trusts and corporations.

THE AGRARIAN MALAISE

ISOLATION

These economic difficulties produced a series of social and cultural resentments. Farm families in some parts of the country–particularly in the prairie and plains regions, where large farms were scattered over vast areas–were virtually cut off from the outside world and human companionship. During the long winter months and spells of bad weather, the loneliness and boredom could become nearly unbearable. Many farmers lacked access to adequate education for their children, to proper medical facilities, to recreational or cultural activities, to virtually anything that might give them a sense of being members of a community. Older farmers felt the sting of watching their children leave the farm for the city. They felt the humiliation of being ridiculed as "hayseeds" by the new urban culture that was coming to dominate American life.

The result of this sense of isolation and obsolescence was a growing malaise among many farmers, a discontent that would help create a great national political movement in the 1890s. It found reflection, too, in the literature that emerged from rural America. Late nineteenth century writers often romanticized the rugged life of the cowboy and the western miner. For the farmer, however, the image was often different. Hamlin Garland, for example, reflected the growing disillusionment in a series of novels and short stories. In the past, Garland wrote in the introduction to his novel *Jason Edwards* (1891), the agrarian frontier had seemed to be "the Golden West, the land of wealth and freedom and happiness. All of the associations called up by the spoken word, the West, were fabulous, mythic, hopeful." Now, however, the bright promise had faded. The trials of rural life were crushing the human spirit. "So this is the reality of the dream!" a character in *Jason Edwards* exclaims. "A shanty on a barren plain, hot and lone as a desert. My God!" Once, sturdy yeoman farmers had viewed themselves as the backbone of American life. Now they were becoming painfully aware that their position was declining in relation to the rising urban-industrial society to the east.

Historical Thinking Skills

Argumentation After students have read the section "The Farmers' Grievances," ask them to create a poster protesting the actions of either the railroads or the banks and proposing a solution to the issue. **WXT**

Reasoning Processes

Comparing Have students read the section "The Agrarian Malaise." Ask them to create a Venn diagram comparing the portrayal of farmers and cowboys in popular culture. Have students discuss in pairs or small groups the reasons for the differences. **ARC** **SOC** **WXT**

Discussion and Activities

Analyzing Change Have students divide into three groups to review and research the impact of mining, cattle ranching, and farming on the social and economic development of the West and the consequences of that development for existing populations of Hispanics and Native Americans. Have a representative of each group split into groups of three to discuss which activity had the greatest impact on western development and the greatest consequences for Hispanics and Native Americans already living in the West. **MIG** **WXT** **PCE** **SOC** **ARC**

Key Terms

Students should be familiar with the key terms and be able to define them in the context of westward expansion due to mining, cattle raising, and farming, and the impact of that settlement on existing populations, in particular Native Americans. Encourage students to use these terms in performing review exercises and exam practice for this chapter.

CHAPTER 16 REVIEW

CONNECTING THEMES

Chapter Sixteen examined the rising economic and political importance of the Far West along with the social and cultural changes brought by white settlement. The white settlement of the Far West had tremendous consequences for vast populations of Native Americans and existing Mexican communities. As white settlers arrived in large numbers via the transcontinental railroad, so too did conflict with other peoples.

New technologies had a significant impact on the social, political, and economic development of the West. The mining, cattle, timber, and agriculture of the region each played a vital role in the development of the nation. The West also helped create and reshape the notion of a unique American identity through renewed ideas of individualism, democracy, opportunity, and adventure. These ideas continued to influence portrayals of the region for years to come.

You should consider the following questions as you review the themes for this chapter:

- How did American concepts of national identity change as a result of westward expansion?
- How did changes in technology and transportation affect the settlement of the Far West?
- What were the causes and effects of western population growth?
- How did the ethnic makeup of the Far West change and what were the consequences of those changes?
- How did the growth of the Far West influence politics in the United States?
- What impact did the environment have on western settlement and how did settlement, in turn, affect the environment of the region?
- How did settlement of the Far West influence the cultural values and artistic expression in the United States?

KEY TERMS

buffalo, economic importance 454
buffalo, destruction 470
Californios 456
Chief Joseph 473
Chinatowns 458
Chinese Exclusion Act 459
Chisholm Trail 464
Commercial agriculture 476
"concentration" policy 469
coolies 456
cowboy 465
Dawes Severalty Act 474
Frederick Jackson Turner 467
Frederic Remington 467
genizaros 453
George A. Custer 471
Geronimo 473
Ghost Dance Movement 474
Homestead Act 459
Little Bighorn 472
long drive 464
Mark Twain 467
mestizos 453
mining 461
missions, decline 456
mulatto 453
"passing of the frontier" 467
Plains Indians 454
Rocky Mountain School 465
Sand Creek Massacre 470
Taos Indian rebellion 455
Transcontinental Railroad 458
Turner thesis 467
Western tribes 453
Wounded Knee 474

Go Online **Chapter 16 Content Review**

Assessing Student Understanding Use the online assessment to assess student understanding of concepts and topics within the chapter. You can assign the ready-made Chapter 16 Content Review or create your own from available questions. This easy-to-use tool helps you design assessments that meet the needs of different types of learners.

AP EXAM PRACTICE

Questions assume cumulative content knowledge from this chapter and previous chapters.

MULTIPLE CHOICE

Use the map on page 471 and your knowledge of U.S. history to answer questions 1-3.

1. Native American nations in the Great Plains had their lives most directly impacted by what trend?
   (A) imposition of Jim Crow laws
   (B) construction of the transcontinental railroad
   (C) consolidation of major corporations
   (D) influx of large immigrant populations

2. The land taken from Native Americans, as illustrated in the map, was used extensively for all of the following economic activities except
   (A) cattle ranching.
   (B) farming.
   (C) mining.
   (D) factories.

3. Conflicts resulting from the trends shown on the map resulted in
   (A) more restrictive immigration legislation.
   (B) legislation extending citizenship rights to Native Americans.
   (C) attempts to change Native American cultural patterns through boarding schools and legislation.
   (D) the expansion of Native American representation in state legislatures.

SHORT ANSWER

Use your knowledge of U.S. history to answer questions 4 and 5.

4. Use the image on page 452 to answer A, B, and C.
   (A) Describe ONE point of view about the West as depicted in the image *American Progress*.
   (B) Briefly explain ONE specific historical cause which led to western expansion during the second half of the nineteenth century.
   (C) Briefly explain ONE specific historical effect which resulted from western expansion during the second half of the nineteenth century.

5. Answer A, B, and C.
   (A) Briefly describe ONE specific historical similarity between western migration before and after the Civil War.
   (B) Briefly describe ONE specific historical difference between western migration before and after the Civil War
   (C) Briefly explain ONE specific historical effect that western expansion had on Native Americans in the region.

LONG ESSAY

Develop a thoughtful and thorough historical argument that addresses the statement. Begin your essay with a thesis statement, and support it with specific historical evidence and examples.

6. Evaluate the relative importance of the effects of western migration in the latter half of the nineteenth century.

Answers

Multiple Choice

1. B; **2.** D; **3.** C

Short Answer

4A) Possible answer: One point of view about the West in the image is that of a proponent of western expansion. The image depicts an idealized vision of the West and western expansion. The image emphasizes the technology relevant to western expansion, and the white settlers are being led and protected by the goddess of progress.

4B) Possible answer: The desire for new land for farming was one of the most significant causes leading to western expansion.

4C) Possible answer: One effect of western expansion was that of the transportation revolution. In the image, one can see various examples of transportation being utilized to make western travel easier and more convenient. As settlers continued out west, newer transportation methods were developed to make that travel quicker and safer.

5A) Possible answer: Both before and after the Civil War, Americans found themselves needing fresh land for agriculture. As the population continued to grow, more immigrants pushed farther and farther west, if they had the means to do so.

5B) Possible answer: Transportation was the biggest difference between western migration before and after the Civil War. Before the war, movement was slow and methodical, and often settlers only had access to horses and carriages. After the war, however, because of the expansion of rail lines, more settlers had access to the railroad. This made travel much quicker and safer.

5C) Possible answer: Native Americans were probably the biggest victims of western expansion. From the start of the colonization venture with Jamestown in 1607, English settlers pushed Native Americans off their lands. From informal wars to the Indian Removal Act to forced settlement on reservations, actions by settlers dislocated Native Americans, forcing them to defend their homes, which caused many wars throughout the nineteenth century.

Answers

Long Essay

6. Possible thesis: The West was promoted as a place of great adventure and wealth. However, displacement and discrimination continued against Native Americans and the Chinese. Further, technology had to keep pace with western expansion. New forms of technology made western expansion safer and faster and helped farmers get produce to markets. Therefore, while there was some wealth available to some, continued discrimination and advances in technology were the most important effects of western expansion. Specific historical evidence: First, settlers continued to push Native Americans off their lands through various forced policies. They also began a program of forced assimilation (e.g., through the establishment of tribal schools) or forced cultural destruction (e.g., through the Dawes Act). Second, Chinese immigrants also became the targets of racism. For the first time in American history, restricted immigration of a targeted ethnic group became law with the Chinese Exclusion Act. Third, technology had to keep pace with western migration; vast improvements in transportation encouraged more expansion. Fourth, a new myth emerged about the West. Settlers were encouraged to migrate with offers of free land and promised adventure and wealth. The cowboy image emerged and was promoted through popular culture. Finally, agriculture took on a characteristic in and of itself as it broke with other labor movements from the North, where the focus was primarily on industry.

Pacing Guide

Chapter 17 explores key concepts from Period 6: 1865–1898 of the AP U.S. History Curriculum Framework. The suggested instruction time for Chapter 17 is 5 days.

Key Concepts

6.1.I Large-scale industrial production—accompanied by massive technological change, expanding international communication networks, and pro-growth government policies—generated rapid economic development and business consolidation.

6.1.II A variety of perspectives on the economy and labor developed during a time of financial panics and downturns.

17 INDUSTRIAL SUPREMACY

CELEBRATING A CITY AND A NATION The new industrial economy made possible many great feats that only decades before would have been unthinkable. Here is the world's first Ferris wheel, which was unveiled in 1893 at the World's Columbian Exposition in Chicago. The fair, designed in large part by Daniel Burnham and Frederick Law Olmsted, celebrated the 400th anniversary of Columbus's arrival in the New World in 1492. The grand scale and technological innovation on display at the fair not only announced a renewed city that had been severely damaged by fire, it also heralded the growing sense of American exceptionalism.

CONNECTING CONCEPTS

Chapter Seventeen begins by exploring the many sources of industrial growth. New technologies like the Bessemer process revolutionized iron and steel production. The development of gasoline fueled the rise of the airplane and automobile. Corporations funded large-scale research and development. The science of production – pioneered by Frederick Winslow Taylor – increased industrial efficiency and railroad expansion drove economic gains. The emergence of the modern limited-liability corporation, holding companies, and industrial integration led to corporate consolidation. The most celebrated – and controversial – corporate empire of the era was Standard Oil, created by John D. Rockefeller.

Big business increased productivity and efficiency but had critics. Many farmers and workers felt the new corporate power centers threatened the older idea of a society where wealth and authority were widely distributed. The middle class pointed to the warping of the capitalist system and political corruption at every level. Writers like Edward Bellamy offered alternative visions of the social order. In response, business leaders argued that modern corporations increased individual opportunity

Discussion and Activities

Analyzing Visuals Have students examine the image "Celebrating a City and a Nation." Ask them to identify and discuss as a class details from the image that suggest what would attract visitors to this exposition and what the city of Chicago hoped to gain by hosting it. *(The image suggests excitement and opportunities for entertainment. The Ferris wheel, electric lighting in the fairgrounds, and the all-new buildings suggest novelty. Chicago hoped to attract tourists and business investors to bring wealth to the city.)* **NAT** **WXT** **SOC**

and reflected the theory of Social Darwinism, where only the fittest survived and succeeded in the marketplace. Successful individuals like Andrew Carnegie also promoted the "gospel of wealth," which asserted that the wealthy had a responsibility to use their riches to advance society.

While many workers experienced a rise in their standard of living during the Gilded Age, they also worked in dangerous conditions with little job security and no control over the conditions of their labor. The hiring of unskilled women and young children grew as they could be paid substantially lower wages than men. Labor leaders attempted to fight back and form unions but with little success. The failure of the railroad strike of 1877, the nation's first national labor conflict, weakened efforts to organize workers, who failed to make significant gains during the era. Tensions between racial and ethnic groups divided laborers. Some immigrant workers, intending to remain in America for only a short time, were also reluctant to organize. Ultimately, corporations had the advantages of wealth and power along with the authority of local, state, and federal governments to protect their interests.

As you read, you should:

- Analyze how large-scale production and technological innovation led to urbanization, mass migration, and significant social changes during the Gilded Age.
- Describe how the increasing efficiency of industry made America a worldwide economic force.
- Assess the ways Social Darwinism was used to justify the great disparity in wealth and power during the Gilded Age, including the "conspicuous consumption" of the wealthy.
- Describe how the industrial workforce expanded through internal and international migration.
- Evaluate how workers organized labor unions to fight corporate power for better working conditions and wages.
- Analyze how industrialization led to greater opportunities for immigrants, women, and minorities.
- Evaluate why critics of the excesses of the capitalistic system emerged.
- Explain the alternatives offered by critics of the capitalistic system.

SOURCES OF INDUSTRIAL GROWTH

Many factors contributed to the growth of American industry: abundant raw materials; a large and growing labor supply; a surge in technological innovation; the emergence of a talented, ambitious, and often ruthless group of entrepreneurs; a federal government eager to assist the growth of business; and a great and expanding domestic market for the products of manufacturing.

INDUSTRIAL TECHNOLOGIES

Perhaps the most important technological development in a nation whose economy rested so heavily on railroads and urban construction was the revolutionizing of iron and steel production in the late nineteenth century. Iron production had developed slowly in the United States through most of the nineteenth century; steel production had developed hardly at all by the end of the Civil War. In the 1870s and 1880s, however, iron production soared as railroads added 40,000 new miles of track, and steel production made great strides toward what would soon be its dominance in the metals industry.

The story of the rise of steel is, like so many other stories of economic development, a story of technological discovery. An Englishman, Henry Bessemer, and an American, William Kelly, had developed, almost simultaneously, a process for converting iron into the much more durable and versatile steel. (The process, which took Bessemer's name, consisted of blowing air through molten iron to burn out the impurities.) The Bessemer process also relied on the discovery by the British metallurgist Robert Mushet that ingredients could be added to the iron during conversion to transform it into steel. In 1868, the New Jersey ironmaster Abram S. Hewitt introduced from Europe another method of making steel–the open-hearth process, which ultimately largely supplanted the Bessemer process. These techniques made possible the production of steel in great quantities and large dimensions, for use in the manufacture of locomotives, steel rails, and girders for the construction of tall buildings.

NEW STEEL PRODUCTION TECHNIQUES

Discussion and Activities

Explaining Significance Have students read the section "New Steel Production Techniques." Ask them to discuss in small groups why the production of large quantities of inexpensive steel would be important for economic growth. *(Steel would be used as a building block for railroads and locomotives, new buildings and factories, and many other important commodities.)* **WXT** **NAT**

Go Online AP Exam Preparation

AP Exam Practice Use the online assessment to help prepare students for the AP Exam. You can assign the ready-made AP-style short-answer questions, document-based questions, and multiple-choice questions assessing concepts, themes, and skills from Period 6 and AP-style long-essay questions organized in sets of 3 questions from various time periods. You can also create your own tests from available questions. This easy-to-use tool helps you design assessments that meet the needs of different types of learners.

Reasoning Processes

Causation Have students read the section "Pittsburgh." Ask them to discuss in pairs or small groups why the steel industry first emerged around Pittsburgh and what pattern(s) they can discern in the spread of the steel industry. **WXT** **GEO**

The steel industry emerged first in western Pennsylvania and eastern Ohio. That was partly because iron ore could be found there in abundance and because there was already a flourishing iron industry in the region. It was also because the new forms of steel production created a demand for new kinds of fuel–particularly a demand for the anthracite (or hard) coal that was plentiful in Pennsylvania. Later, new techniques made it possible to use bituminous (soft) coal (easily mined in western Pennsylvania), which could then be converted to coke to fuel steel furnaces. As a result, Pittsburgh quickly became the center of the steel world. But the industry was growing so fast that new sources of ore were soon necessary. The upper peninsula of Michigan, the Mesabi Range in Minnesota, and the area around Birmingham, Alabama, became important ore-producing centers by the end of the century, and new centers of steel production grew up near them in Cleveland, Detroit, Chicago, and Birmingham, among others.

PITTSBURGH

Until the Civil War, iron and steel furnaces were mostly made of stone and usually built against the side of a hill to reduce construction demands. In the 1870s and after, however, furnaces were redesigned as cylindrical iron shells lined with brick. These massive new furnaces were 75 feet tall and higher and could produce more than 500 tons of steel a week.

As the steel industry spread, new transportation systems emerged to serve it. The steel production in the Great Lakes region was possible only because of the availability of steam freighters that could carry ore on the lakes, which contributed to development of new and more powerful steam engines. Shippers also used new steam engines to speed the unloading of ore, a task that previously had been performed, slowly and laboriously, by men and horses.

A close relationship grew up between the emerging steel companies and the railroads. Steel manufacturers provided rails and parts for railroad cars. The Pennsylvania Railroad, for example, literally created the Pennsylvania Steel Company, provided it with substantial initial capital, and ensured it a market for its products with an immediate contract for steel rails.

The steel industry's need for lubrication for its machines helped create another important new industry in the late nineteenth century–oil. (Not until later did oil become important primarily for its potential as a fuel.) The existence of petroleum reserves in western Pennsylvania had been common knowledge for some time. In the 1850s,

RISE OF THE PETROLEUM INDUSTRY

PIONEER OIL RUN, 1865 The American oil industry emerged first in western Pennsylvania, where speculators built makeshift facilities almost overnight. An oil field on the other side of the hill depicted here had been producing 600 barrels a day, and the wells quickly spilled over the hill and down the slope shown in this photograph.

The Library of Congress

Discussion and Activities

Analyzing Points of View Have students examine the image "Pioneer Oil Run, 1865." Ask them to write a short paragraph from the point of view of a nearby resident describing the spread of the oil fields. Would they be more filled with fascination or dread? **WXT**

Pennsylvania businessman George Bissell showed that the substance could be burned in lamps and that it could also yield such products as paraffin, naphtha, and lubricating oil. Bissell raised money to begin drilling; and in 1859, Edwin L. Drake, one of Bissell's employees, established the first oil well, near Titusville, Pennsylvania, which was soon producing 500 barrels of oil a month. Demand for petroleum grew quickly, and promoters soon developed other fields in Pennsylvania, Ohio, and West Virginia.

THE AIRPLANE AND THE AUTOMOBILE

Two technologies were critical to the development of the automobile. One was the creation of gasoline (or petrol). It was the result of an extraction process developed in the late nineteenth century in the United States by which lubricating oil and fuel oil were separated from crude oil. In the 1870s, designers in France, Germany, and Austria–inspired by the success of railroad engines–had begun to develop an "internal combustion engine," which used the expanding power of burning gas to drive pistons. A German, Nicolaus August Otto, created a gas-powered engine in the mid-1860s, a precursor to automobile engines. But he did not develop a way to untether it from gas lines to be used portably in machines. One of Otto's former employees, Gottfried Daimler, later perfected an engine that could be used in automobiles (including the famous early car that took Daimler's name).

HENRY FORD

The American automobile industry developed rapidly in the aftermath of these breakthroughs. Charles and Frank Duryea built the first gasoline-driven motor vehicle in America in 1893. Three years later, Henry Ford produced the first of the famous cars that would eventually bear his name. By 1910, the industry had become a major force in the economy and the automobile was beginning to reshape American social and cultural life, as well as the nation's landscape. In 1895, there were only four automobiles on the American highways. By 1917, there were nearly 5 million.

The search for a means of human flight was as old as civilization, and had been almost entirely futile until the late nineteenth century, when engineers, scientists, and tinkerers in both the United States and Europe began to experiment with a wide range of aeronautic devices. Balloonists began to

John T. Daniels (photographer), Orville Wright (American aviator, 1871–1948), Wilbur Wright (American aviator, 1867–1912)/Wright Brothers Negatives, Library of Congress, LC-DIG-ppprs-00626

THE FLIGHT OF THE WRIGHT BROTHERS Orville and Wilbur Wright became great celebrities after their famous flight at Kitty Hawk, North Carolina in 1903. They made few original contributions to the development of aviation technology, but their flight (with Wilbur piloting) helped publicize the "flying machine" that would soon revolutionize travel.

Historical Thinking Skills

Contextualization After students have read the section "Rise of the Petroleum Industry," ask them to discuss in small groups how the petroleum industry got started and what consumers had used previously for light and lubrication. *(Primarily whale oil.)* **WXT**

Discussion and Activities

Making Connections Have students examine the image "The Flight of the Wright Brothers." Ask them to create a Venn diagram comparing the Wright Flyer to a modern commercial airliner.

Historical Thinking Skills

Argumentation After students have read the section "The Airplane and the Automobile," ask them to create a poster advertising one of Henry Ford's new automobiles for sale. Have students consider what advantages the auto might provide to consumers. **WXT**

consider ways to turn dirigibles into useful vehicles of transportation. Others experimented with kites and gliders to see if they could somehow be used to propel humans through the air.

Among those testing gliders were two brothers in Ohio, Wilbur and Orville Wright, who owned a bicycle shop in which they began to construct a glider that could be propelled through the air by an internal combustion engine (the same kind of engine that was propelling automobiles). In 1903, four years after they began their experiments, Orville made a celebrated test flight near Kitty Hawk, North Carolina, in which an airplane took off by itself and traveled 120 feet in 12 seconds under its own power before settling back to earth. By the fall of 1904, the Wright brothers had improved the plane to the point where they were able to fly over 23 miles, and in the following year they began to take a few passengers with them on their flights.

Although the first working airplane was built in the United States, aviation technology was slow to gain a foothold in America. Most of the early progress in airplane design occurred in France, where there was substantial government funding for research and development. The U.S. government created the National Advisory Committee on Aeronautics in 1915, twelve years after the Wright brothers' flight, and American airplanes became a significant presence in Europe during World War I. But the prospects for commercial flight seemed dim until the 1920s, when Charles Lindbergh's famous solo flight from New York to Paris electrified the nation and the world and helped make aviation a national obsession.

RESEARCH AND DEVELOPMENT

The rapid development of new industrial technologies encouraged business leaders to sponsor their own research to allow them to keep up with the rapid changes in industry. General Electric, fearful of technological competition, created one of the first corporate laboratories in 1900. By 1913, Bell Telephone, Du Pont, General Electric, Eastman Kodak, and about fifty other companies were budgeting hundreds of thousands of dollars each year for research by their own engineers and scientists. The emergence of corporate research and development laboratories coincided with a decline in government support for research. That helped corporations to attract skilled researchers who had once worked for government agencies. It also decentralized the sources of research funding and ensured that inquiry would move in many different directions, not just along paths determined by the government.

CORPORATE RESEARCH AND DEVELOPMENT

A rift began to emerge between scientists and engineers. Engineers—both inside and out of universities—became increasingly tied up with the research and development agendas of corporations and worked hard to be of practical use to the new economy. Many scientists scorned this "commercialization" of knowledge and preferred to stick to basic research that had no immediate practical applications. Even so, American scientists were more closely connected to practical challenges than were their European counterparts, and some joined engineers in corporate research and development laboratories, which over time began to sponsor not just practical but also basic research.

TRANSFORMATION OF HIGHER EDUCATION

American universities in the late nineteenth and early twentieth centuries developed a growing connection between university-based research and the needs of the industrial economy. University faculty and laboratories began to receive funding from corporations for research, and a partnership began to develop between the academic world and the commercial world that continued into the twenty-first century. No comparable partnership emerged in European universities in these years, and some scholars have argued that America's more rapid development in the twentieth century is in part a product of the market's success in harnessing knowledge—from the academic world and elsewhere—more effectively than the nation's competitors abroad.

THE SCIENCE OF PRODUCTION

By the beginning of the twentieth century, many industrialists were turning to new principles of "scientific management." Those principles were often known as "Taylorism," after their leading theoretician, Frederick Winslow Taylor. Taylor's ideas were controversial during his lifetime and have remained controversial since.

Taylor urged employers to reorganize the production process by subdividing tasks. This would speed up production; it would also make workers more interchangeable and thus diminish a manager's dependence on any particular employee. And it would reduce

"TAYLORISM"

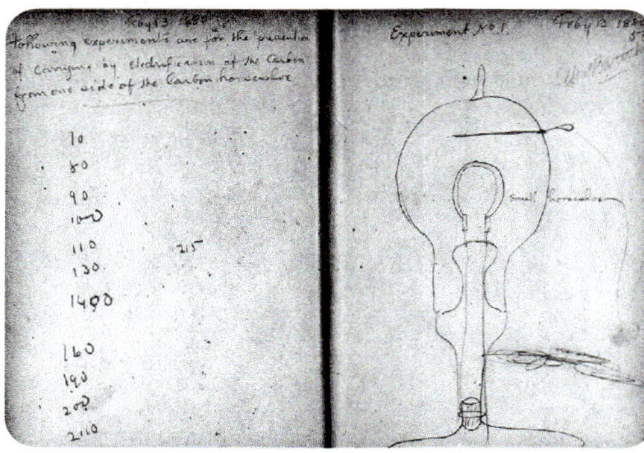

EDISON'S NOTEBOOK This page from one of Thomas Edison's notebooks shows sketches of and notes on some of his early experiments on an incandescent lamp—what we know as an electric lightbulb. Edison was not only the most celebrated inventor of his day but also, by the early twentieth century, one of the greatest popular heroes in American life in a time when scientific and technological progress was considered the defining feature of the age.

Fotosearch/Getty Images

Discussion and Activities

Historical Reasoning and Argumentation Have students read the section "Research and Development." As a class, discuss whether basic research (gaining knowledge for its own sake) or applied research (seeking knowledge to solve specific problems) is more important, and why. **WXT**

INDUSTRIAL PRODUCTION This postcard conveys the assembly line at the Caterpillar manufacturing company. The factory shown here was enormous, occupying 151 acres, 53.8 of which were enclosed building areas. The men are assembling diesel engines. The company has been well known for building tractors, engines, and road machinery.

Rykoff Collection/Corbis Historical/Getty Images

the need for highly trained skilled workers. If properly managed by trained experts, Taylor claimed, workers using modern machines could perform simple tasks at much greater speed, significantly increasing productive efficiency. Taylor and his many admirers argued that scientific management was a way to make human labor compatible with the demands of the machine age. Scientific management was also a way to increase the employer's control of the workplace and to make working people less independent.

MOVING ASSEMBLY LINE

The most important change in production technology in the industrial era was the emergence of mass production and, above all, the moving assembly line, which Henry Ford introduced in his automobile plants in 1914. This revolutionary technique cut the time for assembling a chassis from 12½ hours to 1½ hours. It enabled Ford to raise the wages and reduce the hours of his workers while cutting the base price of his Model T from $950 in 1914 to $290 in 1929. Ford's assembly line became a model for many other industries.

RAILROAD EXPANSION

Despite important advances in many other forms of technology and communication, the principal agent of industrial progress in the late nineteenth century remained the railroad. Railroads were the nation's principal form of transportation. They helped determine the path by which agricultural and industrial economies developed. When railroad lines ran through sparsely populated regions, new farms and other economic activity quickly sprang up along the routes. When they reached forests, lumberers came quickly in their wake and began cutting down timber to send back to towns and cities for sale. When railroads moved through the great plains of the West, they brought buffalo hunters who nearly exterminated the great herds of bison and, later, helped transport cattle into the region and carry meat back into the cities. Because Chicago was the principal railroad hub of the central United States, it also became the place where railroads brought livestock, making the city the slaughterhouse of the nation.

Railroads even altered concepts of time. Until the 1880s, there was no standard method of keeping time from one community to another. In most places, the position of the sun determined the time, which meant that clocks were set differently even between nearby towns. This created great difficulties for railroads, which were trying to set schedules for the entire nation. On November 18, 1883, the railroad companies, working together, agreed to create four time zones across the continent, each an hour apart from its closest neighbor. Although not until 1918 did the federal government make these time zones standard for all purposes, the action by the railroads very quickly solidified the idea of "standard time" through most of the United States.

RAPID EXPANSION OF THE RAILROAD

Every decade in the late nineteenth century, total railroad trackage increased dramatically: from 30,000 miles in 1860 to 52,000 miles in 1870, to 93,000 in 1880, to 163,000 in 1890, and to 193,000 by 1900. Subsidies from federal, state, and local governments—as well as investments from abroad—were vital to these vast undertakings, which required far more capital than private entrepreneurs in America could raise by themselves. Equally important was the emergence of great railroad combinations that brought most of the nation's rails under the control of a very few men. Many railroad combinations continued to be dominated by individuals. The achievements (and excesses) of these tycoons—Cornelius Vanderbilt, James J. Hill, Collis P. Huntington, and others—became symbols to much of the nation of great economic power concentrated in individual hands. But railroad development was less significant for the individual barons it

Discussion and Activities

Making Connections After students have read the section "The Science of Production," ask them to identify a simple task that they do regularly and to write a short paragraph breaking that task down to its simplest steps and estimating the amount of time the task should take. Have students take their paragraphs home and time themselves as they attempt to complete the task described. Ask students to then share with the class how accurate their time predictions were. **WXT**

Discussion and Activities

Analyzing Points of View Have students examine the image "Industrial Production." Ask them to write a short journal entry from the point of view of a worker on the assembly line shown. Have students describe the type of work being done, the working conditions, and their job satisfaction. **WXT**

Reasoning Processes

Causation and Argumentation After students have read the section "Railroad Expansion," ask them to create a T-chart listing causes and effects of railroad expansion in the late nineteenth century. Using their charts, have students discuss in pairs or small groups what the most important causes and effects were. **WXT** **SOC** **NAT**

RAILROADS, 1870–1890 This map illustrates the rapid expansion of railroads in the late nineteenth century. In 1870, there was already a dense network of rail lines in the Northeast and Midwest, illustrated here by the green lines. The red lines show the further expansion of rail coverage between 1870 and 1890, much of it in the South and the areas west of the Mississippi River.

Why were railroads so essential to the nation's economic growth in these years?

created than for its contribution to the growth of a new institution: the modern corporation.

THE CORPORATION

There had been various forms of corporations in America since colonial times, but the modern corporation emerged as a major force only after the Civil War, when railroad magnates and other industrialists realized that no single person or group of limited partners, no matter how wealthy, could finance their great ventures.

LIMITED LIABILITY

Under the laws of incorporation passed in many states in the 1830s and 1840s, business organizations could raise money by selling stock to members of the public; after the Civil War, one industry after another began doing so. At the same time, affluent Americans began to consider the purchase of stock a good investment even if they were not involved in the business whose stock they were purchasing. What made the practice appealing was that investors had only "limited liability"—that is, they risked only the amount of their investments; they were not liable for any debts the corporation might accumulate beyond that. The ability to sell stock to a broad public made it possible for entrepreneurs to gather vast sums of capital and undertake great projects.

ANDREW CARNEGIE

The Pennsylvania Railroad and others were among the first to adopt the new corporate form of organization. But it quickly spread beyond the railroad industry. In steel, the central figure was Andrew Carnegie, a Scottish immigrant who had worked his way up from modest beginnings and in 1873 opened his own steelworks in Pittsburgh. Soon he dominated the industry. His methods were much like those of other industrial titans. He cut costs and prices by striking deals with the railroads and then bought out rivals who could not compete with him. With his associate Henry Clay Frick, he bought up coal mines and leased part of the Mesabi iron-ore range in Minnesota, operated a fleet of ore ships on the Great Lakes, and acquired railroads. Ultimately, Carnegie controlled the processing of his steel from mine to market. He financed his undertakings not only out of his own profits but out of the sale of stock as well. Then, in 1901, he sold out for $450 million to the banker J. Pierpont Morgan, who merged the Carnegie interests with others to create the giant United States Steel Corporation—a $1.4 billion enterprise that controlled almost two-thirds of the nation's steel production.

There were similar developments in other industries. Gustavus Swift developed a relatively small Chicago meatpacking

Answers

Railroads, 1870–1890

Railroads facilitated the quick, inexpensive movement of raw materials and finished products over long distances.

ANDREW CARNEGIE Carnegie was one of a relatively small number of great industrialists of the late nineteenth century who genuinely rose "from rags to riches." Born in Scotland, he came to the United States in 1848, at the age of thirteen, and soon found work as a messenger in a Pittsburgh telegraph office. His skill in learning to transcribe telegraphic messages (he became one of the first telegraphers in the country able to take messages by sound) brought him to the attention of a Pennsylvania Railroad official, and before he was twenty, he had begun his ascent to the highest ranks of industry. After the Civil War, he shifted his attention to the growing iron industry; in 1873 he invested all his assets in the development of the first American steel mills. Two decades later Carnegie was one of the wealthiest men in the world. In 1901 he abruptly resigned from his businesses and spent the remaining years of his life as a philanthropist. By the time of his death in 1919, he had given away more than $350 million, which by some measures would be worth well over a hundred billion dollars in 2014.

company into a great national corporation, in part because of profits he earned selling to the military in the Civil War. Isaac Singer patented a sewing machine in 1851 and created I. M. Singer and Company, one of the first modern manufacturing corporations.

Many of the corporate organizations developed a new approach to management. Large, national business enterprises needed more-systematic administrative structures than the limited, local ventures of the past. As a result, corporate leaders introduced a set of managerial techniques–the genesis of modern business administration–that relied on the division of responsibilities, a carefully designed hierarchy of control, modern cost-accounting procedures, and above all, a new breed of business executive: the "middle manager," who formed a layer of command between workers and owners. Beginning in the railroad corporations, these new management techniques moved quickly into virtually every area of large-scale industry. Efficient administrative capabilities helped make possible another major feature of the modern corporation: consolidation.

New Managerial Techniques

Consolidating Corporate America

Businessmen created large, consolidated organizations primarily through two methods. One was "horizontal integration"–the

JOHN D. ROCKEFELLER Rockefeller's Standard Oil Company became perhaps the largest and most powerful monopoly in America in the late nineteenth century, and Rockefeller became one of the nation's wealthiest and most controversial men. Some historians consider Rockefeller to have been the richest person in history with a personal fortune at the time of his death of up to over a half-trillion dollars adjusted for the late 2000s.

Discussion and Activities

Making Generalizations After students have read the section "The Corporation," ask them to create a T-chart listing the methods that Carnegie and Swift used to dominate their industries. Have students look for similarities in the lists to identify tactics that might generally contribute to business success. **WXT**

Discussion and Activities

Analyzing Visuals Have students examine the portraits of Andrew Carnegie and John D. Rockefeller. Ask them to identify differences in the two portraits and explain what those differences might suggest. *(The portrait of Carnegie is candid, unposed, and taken outdoors. The portrait of Rockefeller is indoors, with Rockefeller dressed somewhat more formally. It is likely that Rockefeller was trying to put forth an impression of a successful businessman with this portrait.)* **SOC**

Reasoning Processes

Comparing After students have read the section "Consclidating Corporate America," ask them to create a Venn diagram comparing horizontal and vertical integration. Have students discuss what advantages each system would have created. **WXT**

combining of a number of firms engaged in the same enterprise into a single corporation. The consolidation of many different railroad lines into one company was an example. Another method, which became popular in the 1890s, was "vertical integration"–the taking over of all the different businesses on which a company relied for its primary function (as in the case of Carnegie Steel).

HORIZONTAL AND VERTICAL INTEGRATION

The most celebrated corporate empire of the late nineteenth century was John D. Rockefeller's Standard Oil, a great combination created through both horizontal and vertical integration. Shortly after the Civil War, Rockefeller launched a refining company in Cleveland and immediately began trying to eliminate his competition. Allying himself with other wealthy capitalists, he proceeded methodically to buy out competing refineries. In 1870, he formed the Standard Oil Company of Ohio; within a few years it had acquired twenty of the twenty-five refineries in Cleveland, as well as plants in Pittsburgh, Philadelphia, New York City, and Baltimore. So far, Rockefeller had expanded only horizontally. But soon he began expanding vertically as well. He built his own barrel factories, terminal warehouses, and pipelines. Standard Oil owned its own freight cars and developed its own marketing organization. By the 1880s, Rockefeller had established such dominance within the petroleum industry that to much of the nation he served as the leading symbol of monopoly. He controlled access to 90 percent of the refined oil in the United States.

ROCKEFELLER'S STANDARD OIL

Rockefeller and other industrialists saw consolidation as a way to cope with what they believed was the greatest curse of the modern economy: "cutthroat competition." Most businessmen claimed to believe in free enterprise and a competitive marketplace, but in fact they feared the existence of too many competing firms, convinced that substantial competition could spell instability and ruin for all. A successful enterprise, many capitalists believed (but did not say publicly), was one that could eliminate or absorb its competitors.

As the movement toward combination accelerated, new vehicles emerged to facilitate it. The railroads began making so-called pool arrangements–informal agreements among various companies to stabilize rates and divide markets (arrangements known as cartels that would later become illegal). But the pools did not work very well. If even a few firms in an industry were unwilling to cooperate (as was almost always the case), the pool arrangements collapsed.

THE TRUST AND THE HOLDING COMPANY

The failure of the pools led to new techniques of consolidation, resting less on cooperation than on centralized control. At first, the most successful such technique was the creation of the "trust"–pioneered by Standard Oil in the early 1880s and perfected by the banker J. P. Morgan. Over time, "trust" became a term for any great economic combination. But the trust was in fact a particular kind of organization. Under a trust agreement, stockholders in individual corporations transferred their stocks to a small group of trustees in exchange for shares in the trust itself. Owners of trust certificates often had no direct control over the decisions of the trustees; they simply received a share of the profits of the combination. The trustees themselves, on the other hand, might literally own only a few companies but could exercise effective control over many.

THE TRUST AGREEMENT

In 1889, the State of New Jersey helped produce a third form of consolidation by changing its laws of incorporation to permit companies to buy up other companies. Other states soon followed. That made the trust unnecessary and permitted actual corporate mergers. Rockefeller, for example, quickly relocated Standard Oil to New Jersey and created there what became known as a "holding company"–a central corporate body that would buy up the stock of various members of the Standard Oil trust and establish direct, formal ownership of the corporations in the trust.

J. PIERPONT MORGAN This arresting portrait captures something of the intimidating power of J. Pierpont Morgan, the most powerful financier in America for decades until his death in 1913.

Discussion and Activities

Contrasting Have students read the section "The Trust Agreement." Ask them to discuss in small groups how the original trust was different from other forms of economic organization. *(Stockholders in corporations owned shares of a specific company, while stockholders in trusts owned shares in a "trust" that owned multiple other companies, all managed by the same trustees.)* **WXT**

By the end of the nineteenth century, as a result of corporate consolidation, 1 percent of the corporations in America were able to control more than 33 percent of the manufacturing. A system of economic organization was emerging that lodged enormous power in the hands of a very few men: the great bankers of New York such as J. P. Morgan, industrial titans such as Rockefeller (who gained control of a major bank), and others.

RAPID CORPORATE CONSOLIDATION

Whether or not this relentless concentration of economic power was the only way or the best way to promote industrial expansion became a major source of debate in America. But it is clear that, whatever else they may have done, the industrial giants of the era were responsible for substantial economic growth. They were integrating operations, cutting costs, creating a great industrial infrastructure, stimulating new markets, creating jobs for a vast new pool of unskilled workers, and opening the way to large-scale mass production. They were also creating the basis for some of the greatest public controversies of their era.

CAPITALISM AND ITS CRITICS

The rise of big business produced many critics. Farmers and workers saw in the growth of the new corporate power centers a threat to notions of a republican society in which wealth and authority were widely distributed. Middle-class critics pointed to the corruption that the new industrial titans seemed to produce in their own enterprises and in local, state, and national politics. The growing criticisms challenged the captains of industry to defend the new corporate economy, to convince the public (and themselves) that it was compatible with the ideology of individualism and equal opportunity that had long been central to the American self-image.

THE "SELF-MADE MAN"

The most common rationale for modern capitalism rested squarely on the older ideology of individualism. The new industrial economy, its defenders argued, was not reducing opportunities for individual advancement, but expanding them. It was providing every individual with a chance to succeed and attain great wealth.

There was an element of truth in such claims, but only a small one. Before the Civil War there had been few millionaires in America; by 1892 there were more than 4,000. Some were in fact what almost all millionaires claimed to be: "self-made men." Andrew Carnegie had worked as a bobbin boy in a Pittsburgh cotton mill; John D. Rockefeller had begun as a clerk in a Cleveland commission house; E. H. Harriman, a great railroad tycoon, had begun as a broker's office boy. But most of the new business tycoons had begun their careers from positions of wealth and privilege.

MYTH OF THE SELF-MADE MAN

Nor was their rise to power and prominence always a result simply of hard work and ingenuity, as they liked to claim. It was also a result of ruthlessness, arrogance, and, at times, rampant corruption. The railroad magnate Cornelius Vanderbilt expressed the attitude of many corporate tycoons with his belligerent question: "What do I care about the law? H'aint I got the power?" So did his son William, with his oft-quoted statement: "The public be damned." Industrialists made large financial contributions to politicians, political parties, and government officials in exchange for assistance and support. And more often than not, politicians responded as they hoped. Cynics said that

"MODERN COLOSSUS OF (RAIL) ROADS" Cornelius Vanderbilt, known as the "Commodore," accumulated one of America's great fortunes by consolidating several large railroad companies under his control in the 1860s. His name became a synonym not only for enormous wealth, but also (in the eyes of many Americans) for excessive corporate power—as suggested in this cartoon, showing him standing astride his empire and manipulating its parts.

The Library of Congress (LC-DIG-ds-05068)

Discussion and Activities

Analyzing Issues After students have read the section "Rapid Corporate Consolidation," ask them to write a short paragraph explaining the benefits and costs of corporate consolidation. Have students use their paragraphs to discuss as a class who most enjoyed the benefits and who most bore the costs. **WXT** **SOC**

Historical Thinking Skills

Sourcing and Situation Have students examine the image "Modern Colossus of (Rail) Roads." Ask them to go online to research the Colossus of Rhodes, one of the seven wonders of the ancient world. Have students discuss in small groups the appropriateness of the historical comparison and what purpose the cartoonist had in publishing this cartoon. **WXT** **SOC**

AP Exam Practice

Short Answer Provide students with the following short-answer questions and allow 15 minutes for completion. Ask for volunteers to share their responses and discuss as a class.

Answer A, B, and C.

A) Briefly explain one important innovation in business organization in the late nineteenth century. *(Responses could include any of the answers listed in B.)*

B) Briefly explain a second important innovation in business organization in the late nineteenth century. *(Horizontal and vertical integration; pools; trusts.)*

C) Briefly explain one important consequence of new types of business organization in the late nineteenth century. *(Rise of a class of extremely wealthy businessmen such as Carnegie, Rockefeller, and Morgan; concentration of wealth in the hands of a relative few; lack of concern for working conditions of laborers.)*

CONSIDER THE SOURCE

PHILANTHROPY

The word *philanthropy* originally meant love of humanity or goodwill toward fellow humans, but over time the term has come to mean large-scale giving by wealthy individuals. Steel magnate Andrew Carnegie accumulated a huge fortune in industry but devoted the last two decades of his life to philanthropy, establishing more than 2,500 libraries in the United States, endowing universities, and building Carnegie Hall in New York City and the Peace Palace in The Hague. In 1911, he established the Carnegie Corporation of New York "to promote the advancement and diffusion of knowledge and understanding." Carnegie articulated his philosophy of the obligation of the wealthy to use their fortunes to improve the world in the essay "Wealth," published in *North American Review* in 1889 and excerpted in the first source document below.

Investor and philanthropist Warren Buffett is the chairman and chief executive officer of Berkshire Hathaway, a conglomerate holding company whose assets include GEICO, The Pampered Chef, Fruit of the Loom, See's Candies, and Benjamin Moore & Co., among many others. Known as the "Sage of Omaha," Buffett was born in Omaha, Nebraska, in 1930 and still resides in the house he bought there in 1957 for $31,500. He made his first stock purchase at age 11 when he bought shares of Cities Service Preferred. Today Buffett is one of the world's richest men, with an estimated net worth of $45 billion in 2010. In 2006, Buffett announced that he intended to give away most of his fortune during his lifetime, rather than having the funds distributed after his death. The majority of Buffett's wealth will go to the Bill and Melinda Gates Foundation, the charitable foundation established by his close friend, bridge partner, and fellow philanthropist Bill Gates.

ANDREW CARNEGIE—1889

WEALTH

Andrew Carnegie

This, then, is held to be the duty of the man of wealth: first, to set an example of modest, unostentatious living, shunning display or extravagance; to provide moderately for the legitimate wants of those dependent upon him; and after doing so to consider all surplus revenues which come to him simply as trust funds which he is called upon to administer, and strictly bound as a matter of duty to administer in the manner which, in his judgment, is best calculated to produce the most beneficial results for the community—the man of wealth thus becoming the mere agent and trustee for his poorer brethren, bringing to their service his superior wisdom, experience, and ability to administer, doing for them better than they would or could do for themselves. . . .

In bestowing charity, the main consideration should be to help those who will help themselves; to provide part of the means by which those who desire to improve may do so; to give those who desire to rise the aids by which they may rise; to assist, but rarely or never to do all. Neither the individual nor the race is improved by almsgiving. Those worthy of assistance, except in rare cases, seldom require assistance. The really valuable men of the race never do, except in cases of accident or sudden change. Everyone has, of course, cases of individuals brought to his own knowledge where temporary assistance can do genuine good, and these he will not overlook. But the amount which can be wisely given by the individual for individuals is necessarily limited by his lack of knowledge of the circumstances connected with each. He is the only true reformer who is as careful and as anxious not to aid the unworthy as he is

Reasoning Processes

Comparing After students have read the section "Philanthropy," ask them to create a Venn diagram comparing Carnegie and Buffett. Ask students to discuss in small groups whether these two entrepreneurs share any similarities that might help to understand why both became major philanthropists. **SOC**

to aid the worthy, and, perhaps, even more so, for in almsgiving more injury is probably done by rewarding vice than by relieving virtue. . . .

Thus is the problem of rich and poor to be solved. The laws of accumulation will be left free; the laws of distribution free. Individualism will continue, but the millionaire will be but a trustee for the poor; entrusted for a season with a great part of the increased wealth of the community, but administering it for the community far better than it could or would have done for itself. The best minds will thus have reached a stage in the development of the race in which it is clearly seen that there is no mode of disposing of surplus wealth creditable to thoughtful and earnest men into whose hands it flows save by using it year by year for the general good.

This day already dawns. But a little while, and although, without incurring the pity of their fellows, men may die sharers in great business enterprises from which their capital cannot be or has not been withdrawn, and is left chiefly at death for public uses, yet the man who dies leaving behind him millions of available wealth, which was his to administer during life, will pass away "unwept, unhonored, and unsung," no matter to what uses he leaves the dross which he cannot take with him. Of such as these the public verdict will then be: "The man who dies thus rich dies disgraced."

Such, in my opinion, is the true gospel concerning wealth, obedience to which is destined some day to solve the problem of the rich and the poor, and to bring "Peace on earth, among men goodwill."

Source: *North American Review* (June 1889). Reprinted in *The Annals of America*, vol. 11, 1884-1894 (Chicago: Encyclopaedia Britannica, 1968), 222-226.

WARREN BUFFETT—2010

My Philanthropic Pledge

Warren Buffett

In 2006, I made a commitment to gradually give all of my Berkshire Hathaway stock to philanthropic foundations. I couldn't be happier with that decision.

Now, Bill and Melinda Gates and I are asking hundreds of rich Americans to pledge at least 50% of their wealth to charity. So I think it is fitting that I reiterate my intentions and explain the thinking that lies behind them.

First, my pledge: More than 99% of my wealth will go to philanthropy during my lifetime or at death. Measured by dollars, this commitment is large. In a comparative sense, though, many individuals give more to others every day.

Millions of people who regularly contribute to churches, schools, and other organizations thereby relinquish the use of funds that would otherwise benefit their own families. The dollars these people drop into a collection plate or give to United Way mean forgone movies, dinners out, or other personal pleasures. In contrast, my family and I will give up nothing we need or want by fulfilling this 99% pledge.

Moreover, this pledge does not leave me contributing the most precious asset, which is time. Many people, including—I'm proud to say—my three children, give extensively of their own time and talents to help others. Gifts of this kind often prove far more valuable than money. A struggling child, befriended and nurtured by a caring mentor, receives a gift whose value far exceeds what can be bestowed by a check. My sister, Doris, extends significant person-to-person help daily. I've done little of this.

What I can do, however, is to take a pile of Berkshire Hathaway stock certificates—"claim checks" that when converted to cash can command far-ranging resources—and commit them to benefit others who, through the luck of the draw, have received the short straws in life. To date about 20% of my shares have been distributed (including shares given me by my late wife, Susan Buffett). I will continue to annually distribute about 4% of the shares I retain. At the latest, the proceeds from all of my Berkshire shares will be expended for philanthropic purposes by 10 years after my estate is settled. Nothing will go to endowments; I want the money spent on current needs.

AP Exam Tip

One way that students can identify the purpose of a document is to consider the motives the author may have had in creating the document.

Historical Thinking Skills

Sourcing and Situation Have students practice the tip by discussing in pairs or small groups what Carnegie's motive(s) might have been in writing the article "Wealth." *(He may have had a sincere desire to do good with the wealth he had amassed and hoped that other wealthy businessmen would follow his example.)*

Discussion and Activities

Evaluating Evidence After students have read the document "Wealth," ask them to list words and phrases that help to identify Carnegie's main argument. *("help those who will help themselves"; "Those worthy of assistance, except in rare cases, seldom require assistance"; "The really valuable men of the race never do, . . .:; "He is the only true reformer who is as careful and as anxious not to aid the unworthy as he is to aid the worthy . . .")*

Discussion and Activities

Evaluating Evidence After students have read the document "My Philanthropic Pledge," ask them to list words and phrases that help to identify Buffett's main argument. *("commit them to benefit others who, through the luck of the draw, have received the short straws in life"; Nothing will go to endowments; I want the money spent on current needs"; "My wealth has come from a combination of living in America, some lucky genes, and compound interest"; "I've worked in an economy that rewards someone who saves the lives of others on a battlefield with a medal, rewards a great teacher with thank-you notes from parents, but rewards those who can detect the mispricing of securities with sums reaching into the billions.")* Have students discuss as a class how Carnegie's and Buffett's philanthropic philosophies are similar or different. **WXT** **SOC**

This pledge will leave my lifestyle untouched and that of my children as well. They have already received significant sums for their personal use and will receive more in the future. They live comfortable and productive lives. And I will continue to live in a manner that gives me everything I could possibly want in life.

Some material things make my life more enjoyable; many, however, would not. I like having an expensive private plane, but owning a half-dozen homes would be a burden. Too often, a vast collection of possessions ends up possessing its owner. The asset I most value, aside from health, is interesting, diverse, and long-standing friends.

My wealth has come from a combination of living in America, some lucky genes, and compound interest. Both my children and I won what I call the ovarian lottery. (For starters, the odds against my 1930 birth taking place in the U.S. were at least 30 to 1. My being male and white also removed huge obstacles that a majority of Americans then faced.)

My luck was accentuated by my living in a market system that sometimes produces distorted results, though overall it serves our country well. I've worked in an economy that rewards someone who saves the lives of others on a battlefield with a medal, rewards a great teacher with thank-you notes from parents, but rewards those who can detect the mispricing of securities with sums reaching into the billions. In short, fate's distribution of long straws is wildly capricious.

The reaction of my family and me to our extraordinary good fortune is not guilt, but rather gratitude. Were we to use more than 1% of my claim checks on ourselves, neither our happiness nor our well-being would be enhanced. In contrast, the remaining 99% can have a huge effect on the health and welfare of others. That reality sets an obvious course for me and my family: Keep all we can conceivably need and distribute the rest to society, for its needs. My pledge starts us down that course.

Warren Buffett

ANALYZING SOURCES

Questions assume cumulative content knowledge from this chapter and previous chapters.

1. How does Carnegie's text best reflect ideas from the times in which Carnegie lived?
   - (A) Carnegie's text reflects humility, as American society at the turn of the 20th century believed that wealthy men should display modesty.
   - (B) Carnegie's text reflects the influence of Social Darwinism by asserting the natural superiority of the wealthy person.
   - (C) Carnegie's text reveals the wealthy industrialist's contempt for politics, which was a prevalent attitude in turn-of-the-20th century America.
   - (D) Carnegie's text reflects the view at the turn of the 20th century that government should play a role in shaping the economy to meet the needs of the rich and poor.

2. Which best describes Buffett's view of his own fortune versus Carnegie's view of his own fortune?
   - (A) success by way of hard work and thrift vs. success through being blessed
   - (B) achievement through help from the government vs. achievement strictly through individual ability
   - (C) luck of circumstance vs. deserved success through talent
   - (D) earnest action and devotion of time vs. pluck and wise decision-making

3. Which best describes commonalities shared by Carnegie and Buffett, as conveyed in their respective texts?
   - (A) to live moderately and provide their wealth for the advancement of society
   - (B) to set up large endowments for their families and use what is left for the advancement of society
   - (C) commit to living a life of poverty, so that all of their fortune can be given to address societal problems
   - (D) to live modestly and save their money for distribution in the future, upon their deaths

Answers

Consider the Source

1. B; **2.** C; **3.** A

Standard Oil did everything to the Ohio legislature except refine it. A member of the Pennsylvania legislature once reportedly said: "Mr. Speaker, I move we adjourn unless the Pennsylvania Railroad has more business for us to transact."

The average industrialist of the late nineteenth century was not, however, a Rockefeller or a Vanderbilt. For every successful millionaire, there were dozens of aspiring businessmen whose efforts failed. Some industries fell under the monopolistic control of a single firm or a small group of large firms. But most industries remained fragmented, with many small companies struggling to carve out a stable position for themselves in an uncertain, highly competitive environment. The annals of business did indeed include real stories of individuals rising from rags to riches. They also included stories of people moving from riches back to rags.

SURVIVAL OF THE FITTEST

Most tycoons liked to claim that they had attained their wealth and power through hard work, acquisitiveness, and thrift—the traditional virtues of Protestant America. Those who succeeded, they argued, deserved their success. "God gave me my money," explained John D. Rockefeller, expressing the assumption that riches were a reward for worthiness. Those who failed, they said, had earned their failure—through their own laziness, stupidity, or carelessness. "Let us remember," said a prominent Protestant minister, "that there is not a poor person in the United States who was not made poor by his own shortcomings."

Such assumptions helped strengthen a popular social theory of the late nineteenth century: Social Darwinism, the application of Charles Darwin's laws of evolution and natural selection among species to human society. Just as only the fittest survived in the process of evolution, Social Darwinists claimed, so in human society only the fittest individuals survived and flourished in the marketplace.

SOCIAL DARWINISM

The English philosopher Herbert Spencer was the first and most important proponent of this theory. Society, he argued, benefited from the elimination of the unfit and the survival of the strong and talented. Spencer's books were popular in America in the 1870s and 1880s. And his teachings found prominent supporters among American intellectuals, most notably William Graham Sumner of Yale University who promoted similar ideas in lectures, articles, and a famous 1906 book, *Folkways*. Sumner did not agree with everything Spencer wrote, but he did share Spencer's belief that individuals must have absolute freedom to struggle, to compete, to succeed, or to fail. Many industrialists seized on the theories of Spencer and Sumner to justify their own power. "The growth of a large business is merely the survival of the fittest," Rockefeller proclaimed. "This is not an evil tendency in business. It is merely the working out of the law of nature and a law of God."

Social Darwinism appealed to businessmen because it seemed to legitimize their success and confirm their virtues. It also appealed to them because it placed their activities within the context of traditional American ideas of freedom and individualism. Above all, it appealed to them because it justified their tactics. Social Darwinists insisted that all attempts by labor to raise wages by forming unions and all endeavors by government to regulate economic activities would fail, because economic life was controlled by a natural law, the law of competition. And Social Darwinism coincided with another "law" that seemed to justify business practices and business dominance: the law of supply and demand as defined by Adam Smith and the classical economists. The economic system, they argued, was like a great and delicate machine functioning by the "invisible hand" of market forces.

JUSTIFYING THE STATUS QUO

But Social Darwinism and the ideas of classical economics did not have much to do with the realities of the corporate economy. At the same time that businessmen were celebrating the virtues of competition and the free market, they were actively seeking to protect themselves from competition and to replace the natural workings of the marketplace with control by great combinations. Rockefeller's great Standard Oil monopoly was the clearest example of the effort to free an enterprise from competition. Many other businessmen made similar attempts on a smaller scale. Vicious competitive battle—something Spencer and Sumner celebrated and called a source of healthy progress—was in fact the very thing that American businessmen most feared and tried to eliminate.

THE GOSPEL OF WEALTH

Some businessmen attempted to temper the harsh philosophy of Social Darwinism with a more gentle, if in some ways equally self-serving, idea: the "gospel of wealth." People of great wealth, advocates of this idea argued, had not only great power but great responsibilities as well. It was their duty to use their riches to advance social progress. Andrew Carnegie elaborated on the creed in his 1901 book, *The Gospel of Wealth*, in which he wrote that the wealthy should consider all revenues in excess of their own needs as "trust funds" to be used for the good of the community; the person of wealth, he said, was "the mere trustee and agent for his poorer brethren." Carnegie was only one of many great industrialists who devoted large parts of their fortunes to philanthropic works—much of it to libraries and schools, institutions he believed would help the poor to help themselves.

The notion of private wealth as a public blessing existed alongside another popular concept: the notion of great wealth as something available to all. Russell H. Conwell, a Baptist minister, became the most prominent spokesman for the idea by delivering one lecture, "Acres of Diamonds," reportedly more than 6,000 times between 1880 and 1900. Conwell told a series of stories, which he claimed were true, of individuals who had found opportunities for extraordinary wealth in their own backyards. (One such story involved a modest farmer who discovered a vast diamond mine in his own fields in the course

RUSSELL CONWELL

Discussion and Activities

Assessing Credibility After students have read the section "The 'Self-Made Man'," ask them to discuss in small groups why they believe millionaires in the late nineteenth century promoted the idea of the "self-made" man. *(It would justify their wealth as earned; it suggested that anyone could get ahead with skill and hard work.)* **SOC**

Discussion and Activities

Assessing Credibility Have students read the section "Survival of the Fittest." Ask them to write a short paragraph explaining how capitalists both promoted and undermined capitalism. *(Many capitalists extolled the virtues of competition, but some actively strove to protect themselves from it.)* **WXT** **PCE**

Discussion and Activities

Analyzing Visuals Have students examine the image "Risen from the Ranks." Ask them to identify and discuss in pairs or small groups details from the image that reinforce Alger's message. *(The title suggests upward mobility; the cover illustration shows a newsboy working hard.)* **SOC** **WXT**

PATTERNS OF POPULAR CULTURE

THE NOVELS OF HORATIO ALGER

A young boy, perhaps an orphan, makes his perilous way through life on the rough streets of the city by selling newspapers or peddling matches. One day, his energy and determination catch the eye of a wealthy man, who gives him a chance to improve himself. Through honesty, charm, hard work, and aggressiveness, the boy rises in the world to become a successful man.

That, in a nutshell, is the story that Horatio Alger presented to his readers in novel after novel—more than 100 of them in all—for over forty years. During Alger's lifetime, Americans bought many million copies of his novels. After his death in 1899, his books (and others written in his name) continued to sell at an astonishing rate.

Alger was born in 1832 into a middle-class New England family, attended Harvard, and spent a short time as a Unitarian minister. He never experienced the hardships he later chronicled. In the mid-1850s, he turned to writing stories and books. His most famous novel, *Ragged Dick*, was published in 1868; but there were many others almost identical to it: *Tom, the Bootblack; Sink or Swim; Jed, the Poorhouse Boy; Phil, the Fiddler; Andy Grant's Pluck.* Most of his books were aimed at young people, and almost all of them were fables of a young man's rise "from rags to riches." The purpose of his writing, he claimed, was twofold. He wanted to "exert a salutary influence upon the class of whom [I] was writing, by setting before them inspiring examples of what energy, ambition, and an honest purpose may achieve." He also wanted to show his largely middle-class readers "the life and experiences of the friendless and vagrant children to be found in all our cities."

Most Americans of the late nineteenth and early twentieth centuries were attracted to Alger because his stories helped reinforce one of the most cherished of their national myths: that with willpower and hard work, anyone could become a "self-made man." That belief was all the more important in the late nineteenth century, when the rise of large-scale corporate industrialization was making it increasingly difficult for individuals to control their own fates.

Alger placed great emphasis on the moral qualities of his heroes; their success was a reward for their virtue. But many of his readers ignored the moral message and clung simply to the image of sudden and dramatic success. After the author's death, his publishers responded to that yearning by abridging many of Alger's works to eliminate the parts of his stories where the heroes do good deeds. Instead, they focused solely on the success of Alger's heroes in rising in the world.

Alger had very mixed feelings about the new industrial order he described. His books were meant to reveal not just the opportunities for advancement it sometimes created, but also its cruelty. To Alger, the modern age did not guarantee success through hard work alone; there had to be some providential assistance as well. That was one reason that in almost all his books, his heroes triumphed not just because of their own virtues or efforts, but because of some amazing stroke of luck as well. Over time Alger's admirers came to ignore his own misgivings about industrialism and to portray his books purely as celebrations of (and justifications for) laissez-faire capitalism and the accumulation of wealth.

Today, though his books are largely forgotten, the name Horatio Alger lives on, representing the idea of individual advancement through (in a phrase Alger coined) "pluck and luck." An example of the transformation of Alger into a symbol of individual achievement is the Horatio Alger Award, established in 1947 by the American Schools and Colleges Association to honor "living individuals who by their own efforts had pulled themselves up by their bootstraps in the American tradition." Among its recipients have been Presidents Dwight D. Eisenhower and Ronald Reagan, evangelist Billy Graham, and U.S. Supreme Court Justice Clarence Thomas.

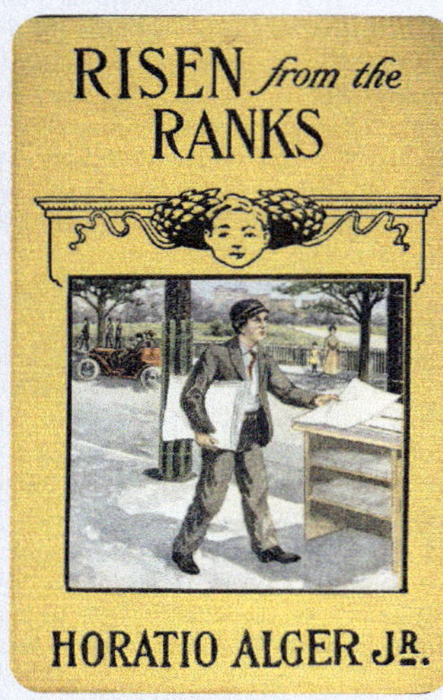

RISEN FROM THE RANKS Alger's novels were even more popular after his death in 1899 than they had been in his lifetime. This is a reprint of the cover of one of his many "rags-to-riches" books. *Risen from the Ranks* is about the rise of a young boy, Harry Walton, who rises from newsboy to newspaper editor.

HISTORICAL THINKING SKILLS

1. **Drawing Conclusions** How do Alger's novels both defend industrial capitalism and criticize it?
2. **Explaining Historical Context** According to the essay, Alger placed great emphasis on the moral qualities of his heroes, but his publishers later eliminated that aspect of the novels. Why?
3. **Making Connections** Do Alger's themes – "rags to riches," success as a reward for virtue, "pluck to luck" – live on in contemporary popular culture? If so, cite some examples where you find these themes portrayed.

Answers

Patterns of Popular Culture

1. Possible answer: Alger's stories both defend and criticize capitalism because the protagonists are always rewarded for their hard work, but their success also involves luck. Hard work is not the only formula at work in Alger's stories, as the young boys (usually) have to have a bit of good luck as well. Usually, they are recognized and aided by some rich person, often a long-lost relative.
2. Possible answer: Alger died in 1899, during the Gilded Age. In the first part of the twentieth century, Social Darwinism was very much on the American mind. Watching out for oneself was what was emphasized; thus, the publishers tended to focus on this part of the Alger "myth" instead of the other side of it.
3. Possible answer: Certainly, professional athletes in some way represent the "rags to riches" myth, as many of them rise from poor or middle-class backgrounds to making millions of dollars.

of working his land.) "I say to you," he told his rapt audiences, "that you have 'acres of diamonds' beneath you right here . . . that the men and women sitting here have within their reach opportunities to get largely wealthy. . . . I say that you ought to get rich, and that it is your duty to get rich." Most of the millionaires in the country, Conwell claimed (inaccurately), had begun on the lowest rung of the economic ladder and had worked their way to success. Every industrious individual had the chance to do likewise.

HORATIO ALGER

Horatio Alger was the most famous promoter of the success story. Alger was originally a minister in a small town in Massachusetts but was driven from his pulpit as a result of a sexual scandal. He moved to New York, where he wrote his celebrated novels about poor boys who rise "from rags to riches"–more than 100 in all, which together sold more than 20 million copies. He became something of a folk hero in American culture. Few of his many fans were aware of his homosexuality. Like most other gay men of his era, he kept his private life carefully hidden, fearful that publicity would destroy his reputation and his career.

ALTERNATIVE VISIONS

Alongside the celebrations of competition, the justifications for great wealth, and the legitimization of the existing order stood a group of alternative philosophies, challenging the corporate ethos and at times capitalism itself.

LESTER FRANK WARD

One such philosophy emerged in the work of the sociologist Lester Frank Ward. Ward was a Darwinist, but he rejected the application of Darwinian laws to human society. In *Dynamic Sociology* (1883) and other books, he argued that civilization was governed not by natural selection but by human intelligence, which was capable of shaping society as it wished. Unlike Sumner, who believed that state intervention to remodel the environment was futile, Ward thought that an active government engaged in positive planning was society's best hope. The people, through their government, could intervene in the economy and adjust it to serve their needs.

Other Americans skeptical of the laissez-faire ideas of the Social Darwinists adopted drastic approaches to reform. Some dissenters joined the Socialist Labor Party, founded in the 1870s and led for many years by Daniel De Leon, an immigrant from the West Indies. De Leon attracted a modest following in the industrial cities, but the party failed to become a major political force. It never polled more than 82,000 votes. A dissident faction of his party, eager to forge ties with organized labor, broke away and in 1901 formed the more enduring American Socialist Party.

HENRY GEORGE

Other radicals gained a wider following. One of the most influential was Henry George of California. His angrily eloquent *Progress and Poverty*, published in 1879, became one of the best-selling nonfiction works in American publishing history. George tried to explain why poverty existed amid the wealth created by modern industry. "This association of poverty with progress is the great enigma of our times," he wrote. "So long as all the increased wealth which modern progress brings goes but to build up great fortunes, to increase luxury and make sharper the contrast between the House of Have and the House of Want, progress is not real and cannot be permanent."

George blamed social problems on the ability of a few monopolists to grow wealthy as a result of rising land values. An increase in the value of land, he claimed, was a result not of any effort by the owner, but of the growth of society around the land. It was an "unearned increment," and it was rightfully the property of the community. And so George proposed a "single tax," to replace all other taxes, which would return the increment to the people. The tax, he argued, would destroy monopolies, distribute wealth more equally, and eliminate poverty. Single-tax societies sprang up in many cities. George moved east to New York; and in 1886, with the support of labor and the socialists, he narrowly missed being elected mayor.

LOOKING BACKWARD

Rivaling George in popularity was Edward Bellamy, whose utopian novel *Looking Backward*, published in 1888, sold more than 1 million copies. It described the experiences of a young Bostonian who went into a hypnotic sleep in 1887 and awoke in the year 2000 to find a new social order where want, politics, and vice were unknown. The new society had emerged from a peaceful, evolutionary process. The large trusts of the late nineteenth century had continued to grow and combine until they formed a single great trust, controlled by the government, which absorbed all the businesses of all the citizens and distributed the abundance of the industrial economy equally among all the people. Society had become a great machine, "so logical in its principles and direct and simple in its workings" that it almost ran itself. "Fraternal cooperation" had replaced competition. Class divisions had disappeared. Bellamy labeled the philosophy behind this vision "nationalism," and his work inspired the formation of more than 160 Nationalist Clubs to propagate his ideas.

THE PROBLEMS OF MONOPOLY

Relatively few Americans shared the views of those who questioned capitalism itself. But by the end of the century a growing number of people were becoming deeply concerned about a particular, glaring aspect of capitalism: the growth of monopoly (control of the market by large corporate combinations). Laborers, farmers, consumers, small manufacturers, conservative bankers and financiers, advocates of radical change–all began to assail monopoly and economic concentration.

They blamed monopoly for creating artificially high prices and for producing a highly unstable economy. In the absence of competition, they argued, monopolistic industries could charge whatever prices they wished; railroads, in particular, charged very high rates along some routes because, in the absence of competition, they knew their customers had no choice but to pay them. Artificially high prices, moreover, contributed to the economy's instability, as production consistently outpaced demand. Beginning in 1873, the economy fluctuated erratically, with severe recessions creating havoc every five or six

Historical Thinking Skills

Argumentation After students have read the section "Russell Conwell," ask them to create a poster advertising one of Conwell's lectures. Have students consider what images or slogans would attract an audience to hear his message. **SOC**

Discussion and Activities

Making Connections Have students read the section "Alternative Visions." Ask them to create a chart comparing the ideas of Lester Frank Ward, Henry George, and Edward Bellamy. Have students discuss as a class which, if any, of the ideas of these men are still influential today. **WXT** **SOC** **PCE**

Historical Thinking Skills

Sourcing and Situation After students have read the feature, ask them to think about why Alcott would have published under a pen name that was not gender-specific early in her career. Have them share their thoughts with a partner. *(It was likely easier to get published if publishers thought the author was male; readers at this time may not have found a female author writing about male characters credible.)* **SOC**

PATTERNS OF POPULAR CULTURE

THE NOVELS OF LOUISA MAY ALCOTT

If Horatio Alger's rags-to-riches tales captured the aspirations of many men of the late nineteenth century, Louisa May Alcott's enormously popular novels helped give voice to the often-unstated ambitions of many young women.

Alcott was born in 1832, the daughter of a prominent if generally impoverished reformer and educator, Bronson Alcott—a New England transcendentalist committed to abolishing slavery and advancing women's rights. Louisa May Alcott grew up wanting to write, one of the few serious vocations available to women. As a young adult, she wrote a series of popular adventure novels under the pen name A. M. Barnard, populated by conventional male heroes. While serving as a nurse in the Civil War, she contracted typhoid and recovered, but developed mercury poisoning through her treatment and suffered from it until her death in 1888. After the war, she chose a different path—writing realistic fiction and basing it on the lives and experiences of women. The publication of *Little Women* (1868, 1869) established Alcott as a major literary figure and as an enduring, if sometimes puzzling, inspiration for girls and, indeed, women of all ages.

Little Women—and its successors *Little Men* (1871) and *Jo's Boys* (1886)—were unlike the formulaic Horatio Alger stories, in which young men inevitably rose from humble circumstances to great success. And yet they both echoed and altered the message of those books. The fictional March family in the novels was in fact modeled on Alcott's own impoverished if intellectually lively childhood, and much of *Little Women* is a chronicle of poverty, suffering, and even death. But it is also the story of a young girl—Jo March, modeled to some degree on Alcott herself—who struggles to build a life for herself that is not defined by conventional women's roles and ambitions. Jo March, like Louisa May Alcott, becomes a writer. She spurns a conventional marriage (to her attractive and wealthy neighbor Laurie). Unlike Alcott, who never married, Jo does find a husband—an older man, a German professor who does not support Jo's literary ambitions.

Many readers have found this marriage troubling—and false to the message of the rest of the book. It seems to contradict Alcott's belief that women can have intellectual independence and achievement. But to Alcott, this unconventional marriage was a symbol of her own repudiation of an ordinary domestic life. "Girls write to ask who the little women marry, as if that was the only end and aim of a woman's life," Alcott wrote a friend after the publication of the first volume of the novel. "I won't marry Jo to Laurie to please any one." Jo's marriage to Professor Bhaer is in many ways a concession. "Jo should have remained a literary spinster [like Alcott herself]," she once wrote, "but so many enthusiastic ladies wrote to me clamorously demanding that she should marry Laurie, or somebody, that I didn't dare to refuse and out of perversity went and made a funny match for her."

It is tempting to see Louisa May Alcott's life—as an independent woman, a writer, and an active suffragist—as a better model to her readers than the characters in her fiction. Jo March is willful, rebellious, stubborn, ambitious, and often selfish, not the poised, romantic, submissive woman of most sentimental novels of her time. She hates housekeeping and drudgery. She yearns at times to be a boy. She resists society's expectations—through her literary aspirations, her sharp temper, and ultimately her unconventional marriage. Through those qualities, she captured the imaginations of late-nineteenth-century female readers and continues to capture the imaginations of readers today. *Little Women* has survived far longer than the Horatio Alger stories did precisely because it presents a story of growing up that, unlike Alger's, is not predictable but complicated, conflicted, and surprising.

Bettmann/Getty Images

HISTORICAL THINKING SKILLS

1. **Explaining Historical Context** Do the female characters of Alcott's novels reflect the actual status of women in the late nineteenth century?
2. **Comparing and Contrasting** In what ways are Alcott's novels similar to Alger's? How do they differ?
3. **Evaluating Historical Significance** *Little Women* has continued to be popular as a novel, and it has been made into movies and a Broadway musical. What accounts for its enduring popularity?

Answers

Patterns of Popular Culture

1. Possible answer: The main character in *Little Women,* Jo March, defies traditional stereotypes by becoming a professional writer (something very difficult for women to do during the time period), but the character also gets married. In many ways, Alcott's real life is a more liberating message to young women than those of many of her main characters.
2. Possible answer: Both reflect a sort of "rags to riches" motif; however, whereas Alger's characters follow standard societal male norms, Alcott's characters often buck up against society and the gender norms of the Gilded Age.
3. Possible answer: *Little Women* has endured, moreso than Alger's stories, because the characters and situations are much more complex, complicated, and surprising. They may be more relatable to contemporary readers, especially girls and women, than Alger's characters are.

Historical Thinking Skills

Argumentation After students have read the section "The Problems of Monopoly," ask them to list and rank in order of importance the problems caused by corporate monopolies. Have students write a thesis statement that makes a claim about the most important effect of monopolies. **WXT** **SOC** **PCE**

CHILDREN OF WEALTH Amy Elizabeth du Pont (1880–1962), the heiress of the American industrialist du Pont family, drives her younger sister, Julia, in their own pony-driven buggy. The photograph, taken by Pierre A. Gentieu, shows the children enjoying themselves while traveling with their family in France.

years, each recession worse than the previous one, until finally, in 1893, the system seemed on the verge of total collapse.

Hostility to monopoly was based on more than a concern about prices. Many Americans considered monopoly dangerous because the rise of large combinations seemed to threaten the ability of individuals to advance in the world. If a single person, or a small group, could control all economic activity in an industry, what opportunities would be left for others? To men, in particular, monopoly threatened the ideal of the wage-earning husband capable of supporting a family and prospering, because combinations seemed to reduce opportunities to succeed—to make less likely the idea of the "self-made man" memorialized in the novels of Horatio Alger. Monopoly, therefore, threatened not just competition, but certain notions of manhood as well.

Adding to the resentment of monopoly was the emergence of a new class of enormously and conspicuously wealthy people, whose lifestyles became an affront to those struggling to stay afloat. According to one estimate early in the century, 1 percent of the families in America controlled nearly 88 percent of the nation's assets. Some of the wealthy—Andrew Carnegie, for example—lived unostentatiously and donated large sums to charities. Others, however, lived in almost grotesque luxury. Like a clan of feudal barons, the Vanderbilts maintained, in addition to many country estates, seven opulent mansions on seven blocks of New York City's Fifth Avenue. Other wealthy New Yorkers lavished vast sums on parties. The most notorious, a ball on which Mrs. Bradley Martin spent $368,000, created such a furor that she and her husband fled to England to escape public abuse.

Observing their flagrant displays of wealth were the four-fifths of the American people who lived modestly and at least 10 million people who lived below the commonly accepted poverty line. The standard of living was rising for everyone, but the gap between rich and poor was increasing. To those in difficult economic circumstances, the sense of relative deprivation could be almost as frustrating and embittering as poverty itself.

INCREASING INEQUALITY

INDUSTRIAL WORKERS IN THE NEW ECONOMY

The American working class was both a beneficiary and a victim of the growth of industrial capitalism. Many workers in the late nineteenth century experienced a real rise in their standard of living. But they did so at the cost of arduous and

Discussion and Activities

Analyzing Points of View Have students examine the image "Children of Wealth." Ask them to write a short journal entry from the point of view of one of the children in the buggy or from the point of view of a working-class child who witnessed the scene. **SOC**

Reasoning Processes

Comparing Have students read the section "The Immigrant Workforce." Ask them to create a Venn diagram comparing immigrants in the 1880s and later with earlier immigrants. Have students discuss as a class the most important similarities and differences. **MIG** **SOC** **WXT**

often dangerous working conditions, diminishing control over their own work, and a growing sense of powerlessness.

THE IMMIGRANT WORKFORCE

The industrial workforce expanded dramatically in the late nineteenth century as demand for factory labor grew. There was a continuing flow of rural Americans into factory towns and cities—people disillusioned with or bankrupted by life on the farm and eager for new economic and social opportunities. And there was a great wave of immigration from Mexico, Asia, Canada, and above all Europe in the decades following the Civil War—an influx greater than that of any previous era. The 25 million immigrants who arrived in the United States between 1865 and 1915 were more than four times the number who had arrived in the fifty years before.

In the 1870s and 1880s, most of the immigrants to eastern industrial cities came from the nation's traditional sources: England, Ireland, and northern Europe. By the end of the century, however, the major sources of immigration had shifted, with large numbers of southern and eastern Europeans (Italians, Poles, Russians, Greeks, Slavs, and others) moving to America (among other nations) and into the industrial workforce. In the West, the major sources of immigration were Mexico and, until the Chinese Exclusion Act of 1882, Asia. No reliable figures are available for either group, but an estimated 1 million people from Mexico immigrated in the first three decades of the twentieth century, many of them swelling the industrial workforce of western cities.

NEW SOURCES OF IMMIGRATION

The new immigrants were coming to America in part to escape poverty and oppression in their homelands. But they were also lured to the United States by expectations of new opportunities. Sometimes such expectations were realistic, but often they were the result of false promises. Railroads tried to lure immigrants into their western landholdings by distributing misleading advertisements overseas. Industrial employers actively recruited immigrant workers under the Contract Labor Law, which—until its repeal in 1885—permitted them to pay for the passage of workers in advance and deduct the amount later from their wages. Even after the repeal of the law, employers continued to encourage the immigration of unskilled laborers, often with the assistance of foreign-born labor brokers, such as the Greek and Italian padrones, who recruited work gangs of their fellow nationals.

The arrival of these new groups introduced heightened ethnic tensions into the dynamic of the working class. Low-paid Polish, Greek, and French Canadian immigrants began to displace higher-paid British and Irish workers in the textile factories of New England. Italian, Slavic, and Polish immigrants emerged as a major source of labor for the mining industry in the East, traditionally dominated by native workers or northern European immigrants. Chinese and Mexican immigrants competed with Anglo-Americans and African Americans in mining, farmwork, and factory labor in California, Colorado, and Texas.

HEIGHTENED ETHNIC TENSIONS

APPROACHING SHORE This image of European immigrants aboard a ship approaching the American shore captures both the excitement and the tension of these newcomers to the United States.

The Library of Congress (LC-USZ62-7307)

WAGES AND WORKING CONDITIONS

The average standard of living for workers rose in the years after the Civil War, but for many laborers, the return for their labor remained very small. At the turn of the century, the average income of the American worker was $400 to $500 a year—below the $600 figure widely considered the minimum for a reasonable level of comfort. Nor did workers have much job security. All workers were vulnerable to the boom-and-bust cycle of the industrial economy, and some lost their jobs because of technological advances or because of the cyclical or seasonal nature of their work. Even those who kept their jobs could find their wages suddenly and substantially cut in hard times. Few workers, in other words, were ever far from poverty.

American laborers faced other hardships as well. For first-generation workers accustomed to the patterns of agrarian life, there was a difficult

Discussion and Activities

Analyzing Visuals Have students examine the image "Approaching Shore." Ask them to identify and discuss in small groups details that demonstrate the nature of the voyage. *(The ship is crowded; people are exposed to the elements; they are apparently sleeping on deck.)* **SOC** **MIG**

WOMEN ON THE ASSEMBLY LINE This image, from 1902, shows women at work on the lock and drill department assembly line at the National Cash Register Company in Dayton, Ohio. The photograph suggests the growing scale of factory enterprise at the turn of the twentieth century.

adjustment to the nature of modern industrial labor: the performance of routine, repetitive tasks, often requiring little skill, on a strict and monotonous schedule. To skilled artisans whose once-valued tasks were now performed by machines, the new system was impersonal and demeaning. Factory laborers worked ten- to twelve-hour days, six days a week; in the steel industry they worked twelve hours a day. Many worked in appallingly unsafe or unhealthy factories. Industrial accidents were frequent and severe. Compensation to the victims, from either their employers or the government, was often limited, until many states began passing workmen's compensation laws in the early twentieth century.

For many workers, the most disturbing aspect of factory labor in the new industrial system was their loss of control over the conditions of their labor. Even semiskilled workers and common laborers had managed to maintain some control over their labor in the relatively informal working conditions of the early and mid-nineteenth century. As the corporate form of organization spread, employers set out to make the factory more efficient (often in response to the principles of scientific management). That meant, they believed, centralizing control of the workplace in the hands of managers, ensuring that workers had no authority or control that might disrupt the flow of production. This loss of control, as much as the low wages and long hours, lay behind the substantial working-class militancy in the late nineteenth century.

LOSS OF CONTROL

WOMEN AND CHILDREN AT WORK

The decreasing need for skilled work in factories induced many employers to increase the use of unskilled women and children, whom they could hire for lower wages than adult males. By 1900, women made up 17 percent of the industrial workforce, a fourfold increase since 1870; and 20 percent of all women (well over 5 million) were wage earners. Some of these working women were single and took jobs to support themselves or their parents or siblings. Many others were married and had to work to supplement the inadequate earnings of their husbands; for many working-class families, two incomes were required to support even a minimal standard of living. Many reformers, including many females, saw women as particularly vulnerable to exploitation and injury in the rough environment of the factory. They considered it inappropriate for women to work independently. The "problem" of women in the workforce became a significant public issue. In some communities the aversion to seeing married women work was so strong—among both men and women—that families struggled on inadequate wages rather than see a wife and mother take a job.

Women industrial workers were overwhelmingly white and mostly young, 75 percent of them under twenty-five. The vast majority were immigrants or the daughters of immigrants. There were some women in all areas of industry, even in some of the most arduous jobs. Most women, however, worked in a few industries where unskilled and semiskilled machine labor (as opposed to heavy manual labor) prevailed. The textile industry remained the largest single industrial employer of women. (Domestic service remained the most common female occupation overall.) Women worked for wages as low as $6 to $8 a week, well below the minimum necessary for survival (and well below the wages paid to men working the same jobs). At the turn of the century, the average annual wage for a male

POORLY PAID WOMEN

Discussion and Activities

Analyzing Issues After students have read the section "Wages and Working Conditions," ask them to discuss as a class the challenges facing workers in the late nineteenth century and why workers were so powerless to force improvements. *(The rapidly growing population created a labor surplus, making it easy for management to replace troublesome workers; governments had not yet started to impose meaningful regulation on industry; workers came from many different parts of the world and often saw each other as competitors for jobs and therefore did not band together to force improvements.)* **PCE** **WXT**

Reasoning Processes

Comparing Have students examine the image "Women on the Assembly Line." Ask then to create a T-chart listing similarities and differences between this image and the image "Industrial Production" from earlier in the chapter. Have students discuss as a class reasons for the similarities and differences. **WXT** **SOC**

Discussion and Activities

Analyzing Points of View After students have read the section "Women and Children at Work," ask them to write a short journal entry from the point of view of a working woman or child describing their experiences in the workplace. **WXT** **SOC**

SPINDLE BOYS Young boys, some of them barefoot, clamber among the great textile machines in a Georgia cotton mill adjusting spindles. Many of them were the children of women who worked in the plants. The photograph is by Lewis Hine.

Bettmann/Corbis via Getty Images

industrial worker was $597; for a woman, it was $314. Even highly skilled women workers made about half what men doing the same job earned. Advocates of a minimum-wage law for women created a sensation when several women testified at a hearing in Chicago that low wages and desperate poverty had driven them to prostitution. (The testimony was not, however, sensational enough for the Illinois legislature, which promptly defeated the bill.)

At least 1.7 million children under sixteen years of age were employed in factories and fields in 1900, more than twice the number of thirty years before. Ten percent of all girls aged ten to fifteen, and 20 percent of all boys, held jobs. This was partly because some families so desperately needed additional wages that parents and children alike were pressed into service. It was also because in some families the reluctance to permit wives to work led parents to send their children into the workforce to avoid forcing mothers to go. This did not, however, prevent reformers from seeing children working in factories as a significant social problem. Under the pressure of outraged public opinion, thirty-eight state legislatures passed child-labor laws in the late nineteenth century; but these laws were of limited impact. Sixty percent of child workers were employed in agriculture, which was typically exempt from the laws; such children often worked twelve-hour days picking or hoeing in the fields. And even for children employed in factories, the laws merely set a minimum age of twelve years and a maximum workday of ten hours, standards that employers often ignored. In the cotton mills of the South, children working at the looms all night were kept awake by having cold water thrown in their faces. In canneries, little girls cut fruits and vegetables sixteen hours a day. Exhausted children were particularly susceptible to injury while working at dangerous machines, and they were maimed and even killed in industrial accidents at an alarming rate.

INEFFECTIVE CHILD-LABOR LAWS

As much as the appalling conditions of women and child workers troubled the national conscience, conditions for many men were at least equally dangerous. In mills and mines, and on the railroads, the American accident rate was higher than that of any industrial nation in the world. As late as 1907, an average of twelve railroad men a week died on the job. In factories, thousands of workers faced such occupational diseases as lead or phosphorus poisoning, against which few employers took precautions.

THE STRUGGLE TO UNIONIZE

Labor leaders attempted to fight back against the poor conditions in the workplace by adopting some of the same tactics their employers had used so effectively: creating large combinations, or unions. But by the end of the century their efforts had met with little success.

There had been craft unions in America, representing small groups of skilled workers, since well before the Civil War. Alone, however, individual unions could not hope to exert significant power in the new corporate economy, and in the 1860s some labor leaders began to search for ways to combine the energies of the various labor organizations. The first attempt to federate separate unions into a single national organization came in 1866, when William H. Sylvis founded the National Labor Union—a polyglot association, claiming 640,000 members, that included a variety of reform groups having lit-

NATIONAL LABOR UNION

Discussion and Activities

Analyzing Visuals Have students examine the image "Spindle Boys." Ask them to list and discuss in pairs or small groups details that demonstrate dangerous workplace conditions. *(Some boys are working barefoot on machinery; they are working around moving and unshielded spindles, belts, and pulleys.)* **WXT**

KEHOE HANGED.

Last Scenes in the Life of the King of the Molly Maguires.

I AM NOT GUILTY.

History of Kehoe's Prominent Share in the Many Murders in the Coal Region.

EVIDENCE FROM SPIES.

Little Excitement in Pottsville on the Occasion of the Execution.

[BY TELEGRAPH TO THE HERALD.]

POTTSVILLE, Pa., Dec. 18, 1878.

The people of Pottsville have become so accustomed to executions of Molly Maguires that there is no excitement attendant upon this occasion. Jack Kehoe, the terror of the coal fields, the braggart and desperado, passed a most miserable night. The guards say that he only got a few moments' sleep. He

MOLLY MCGUIRES The Molly Maguires were known for their harsh, intimidating, and at times violent tactics against the owners and managers of anthracite coal mines. This newspaper notice announces the execution of Jack Kehoe—both high constable of Mahanoy County in Pennsylvania and a member of the Molly McGuires—who was found guilty of multiple murders in this coal-producing region. He was posthumously pardoned of these crimes in 1979 suggesting that his cry "I am not guilty" was indeed true.

tle direct relationship with labor. After the Panic of 1873, the National Labor Union disintegrated and disappeared.

The National Labor Union, like most of the individual unions that joined it, excluded women workers. Male workers argued (not entirely incorrectly) that women were used to drive down their wages; and they justified their hostility by invoking the ideal of domesticity. "Woman was created to be man's companion," a National Labor Union official said, "to be the presiding deity of the home circle." Most women workers agreed that "man should be the breadwinner," as one female union organizer said. But many argued that as long as conditions made it impossible for men to support their families, women should have full and equal opportunities in the workplace.

Unions faced special difficulties during the recession years of the 1870s. Not only was there widespread unemployment; there was also widespread middle-class hostility toward the unions. When labor disputes with employers turned bitter and violent, as they occasionally did, much of the public instinctively blamed the workers (or the "radicals" and "anarchists" they believed were influencing the workers) for the trouble, rarely the employers. Particularly alarming to middle-class Americans was the emergence of the "Molly Maguires," a militant labor organization in the anthracite coal region of Pennsylvania. The Mollies operated within the Ancient Order of Hibernians, an Irish fraternal society. They attempted to intimidate the coal operators through violence and occasionally murder, and they added to the growing perception that labor activism was motivated by dangerous radicals. Much of the violence attributed to the Molly Maguires, however, was instigated or performed by informers and agents employed by the mine owners, who wanted a pretext for ruthless measures to suppress unionization.

MOLLY MAGUIRES

THE GREAT RAILROAD STRIKE

Excitement over the Molly Maguires paled beside the near hysteria that gripped the country during the railroad strike of 1877, which began when the eastern railroads announced a 10 percent wage cut and which soon expanded into something approaching a class war. Strikers disrupted rail service from Baltimore to St. Louis, destroyed equipment, and rioted in the streets of Pittsburgh and other cities. State militias were called out, and in July President Hayes ordered federal troops to suppress the disorders in West Virginia. In Baltimore, eleven demonstrators died and forty were wounded in a conflict between workers and militiamen. In Philadelphia, state militia opened fire on thousands of workers and their families who were attempting to block the railroad crossings and killed twenty people. In all, more than 100 people died before the strike finally collapsed several weeks after it had begun.

NATIONAL STRIKE

The great railroad strike was America's first major, national labor conflict, and it illustrated how disputes between workers and employers could no longer be localized in the increasingly national economy. It illustrated as well the depth of resentment among many American workers toward their employers (and toward the governments allied with them) and the lengths to which they were prepared to go to express that resentment. And finally, it was an indication of the frailty of the labor movement. The failure of the strike seriously weakened the railroad unions and damaged the reputation of labor organizations in other industries as well.

Discussion and Activities

Historical Evidence and Argumentation After students have read the section "The Great Railroad Strike," ask them to create a chart listing reasons laborers had difficulty organizing. Have students discuss in small groups what the most important reasons were. **WXT** **SOC** **PCE**

Historical Thinking Skills

Sourcing and Situation Have students examine the image "Molly McGuires." Ask them to identify and discuss with a partner details from the newspaper clipping that indicate the point of view of the author. *(Jack Kehoe, a Molly Maguire leader, is described as a "braggart," a "desperado," and as having contributed to many murders. This indicates the newspaper was anti-labor.)* **SOC** **WXT**

Reasoning Processes

Comparing and Contrasting Have students read the section "The Knights of Labor." Ask them to create a Venn diagram comparing the Knights of Labor with the National Labor Union. Have students discuss as a class the most important similarities and differences. **WXT** **SOC** **PCE**

THE KNIGHTS OF LABOR

The first genuinely national labor organization was the Noble Order of the Knights of Labor, founded in 1869 under the leadership of Uriah S. Stephens. Membership was open to all who "toiled," a definition that included all workers and most business and professional people. The only excluded groups were lawyers, bankers, liquor dealers, and professional gamblers. Unlike most labor organizations of the time, the Knights welcomed women members–not just female factory workers, but domestic servants and women who worked in their own homes. Leonora Barry, an Irish immigrant who had worked in a New York hosiery factory, ran the Woman's Bureau of the Knights. Under her effective leadership, the Knights enlisted 50,000 white and African American women members and created over a hundred all-female locals.

The Knights were loosely organized, without much central direction. Members met in local "assemblies," which took many different forms. They were loosely affiliated with a national "general assembly." Their program was similarly vague. Although they championed an eight-hour day and the abolition of child labor, the leaders were more interested in long-range reform of the economy. Leaders of the Knights hoped to replace the "wage system" with a new "cooperative system," in which workers would themselves control a large part of the economy.

DISSOLUTION OF THE KNIGHTS OF LABOR

For several years, the Knights remained a secret fraternal organization. But in the late 1870s, under the leadership of Terence V. Powderly, the order moved into the open and entered a spectacular period of expansion. By 1886, it claimed a total membership of over 700,000, including some militant elements that the moderate leadership could not always control. Local unions or assemblies associated with the Knights launched a series of strikes in the 1880s in defiance of Powderly's wishes. In 1885, striking railway workers forced the Missouri Pacific, a link in the Gould system, to restore wage cuts and recognize their union. But the victory was temporary. In the following year, a strike on another Gould railroad, the Texas and Pacific, was crushed, and the power of the unions in the Gould system was broken. Their failure helped discredit the organization. By 1890, the membership of the Knights had shrunk to 100,000. A few years later, the organization disappeared.

THE AFL

Even before the Knights began to decline, a rival organization based on a very different organizational concept appeared. In 1881, representatives of a number of existing craft unions formed the Federation of Organized Trade and Labor Unions of the United States and Canada. Five years later, it changed its name to the American Federation of Labor (AFL), and it soon became the most important and enduring labor group in the country. Rejecting the Knights' idea of one big union for everybody, the Federation was an association of autonomous craft unions and represented mainly skilled workers. It was generally hostile to organizing unskilled workers, who did not fit comfortably within the craft-based structure of existing organizations.

OPPOSITION TO FEMALE EMPLOYMENT

Toward women, the AFL adopted an apparently contradictory policy. On the one hand, the male leaders of the AFL were hostile to the idea of women entering the paid workforce. Because women were weak, they believed, employers could easily take advantage of them by paying them less than

KNIGHTS OF LABOR DELEGATES, 1886 The Knights of Labor was the first, and for many years the only, labor organization to welcome women unreservedly, as this portrait of delegates to the Knights 1886 convention indicates.

The Library of Congress (LC-USZ62-12485)

Discussion and Activities

Analyzing Visuals Have students examine the image "Knights of Labor Delegates, 1886." Ask them to write a short paragraph describing challenges faced by working women like the ones shown. **SOC** **WXT**

men. As a result, women workers drove down wages for everyone. "It is the so-called competition of the unorganized, defenseless woman worker, the girl and the wife, that often tends to reduce the wages of the father and husband," Samuel Gompers, the powerful leader of the AFL, once said. He talked often about the importance of women remaining in the home and argued (incorrectly) that "there is no necessity of the wife contributing to the support of the family by working." More than that, female labor was, the AFL newspaper wrote, "the knife of the assassin, aimed at the family circle." Gompers himself believed strongly that a test of a man's worth was his ability to support a family and that women in the workforce would undermine men's positions as heads of their families.

Although hostile to the idea of women workers, the AFL nevertheless sought equal pay for those women who did work and even hired some female organizers to encourage unionization in industries dominated by women. These positions were, in fact, less contradictory than they seem. By raising the pay of women, the AFL could make them less attractive to employers and, in effect, drive them out of the workforce.

Gompers accepted the basic premises of capitalism; his goal was simply to secure for workers a greater share of capitalism's material rewards. Gompers opposed the creation of a worker's party; he was generally hostile to any government efforts to

THE AFL'S AGENDA

protect labor or improve working conditions, convinced that what government could give it could also take away. The AFL concentrated instead on the relationship between labor and management. It supported the immediate objectives of most workers: better wages and working conditions. And while the AFL hoped to attain its goals by collective bargaining, it was ready to use strikes if necessary.

As one of its first objectives, the AFL demanded a national eight-hour day and called for a general strike if workers did not achieve the goal by May 1, 1886. On that day, strikes and demonstrations calling for a shorter workday took place all over the country, most of them staged by AFL unions but a few by radical groups.

In Chicago, a center of labor and radical strength, a strike was

HAYMARKET SQUARE

already in progress at the McCormick Harvester Company when the general strike began. City police had been harassing the strikers, and labor and radical leaders called a protest meeting at Haymarket Square. When the police ordered the crowd to disperse, someone threw a bomb that killed seven officers and injured sixty-seven other people. The police, who had killed four strikers the day before, fired into the crowd and killed four more people. Conservative, property-conscious Americans, frightened and outraged, demanded retribution, even though no one knew who had thrown the bomb. Chicago officials finally rounded up eight anarchists and charged them with murder, on the grounds that their statements had incited whoever had hurled the bomb. All eight scapegoats were found guilty after a remarkably injudicious trial. Seven were sentenced to death. One of the condemned committed suicide, four were executed, and two had their sentences commuted to life imprisonment.

To most middle-class Americans, the Haymarket bombing was an alarming symbol of social chaos and radicalism. "Anarchism" now became a code word in the public mind for terrorism and violence, even though most anarchists were relatively peaceful visionaries dreaming of a new social order. For the next thirty years, the specter of anarchism remained one of the most frightening concepts in the American middle-class imagination. It also became a constant obstacle to the goals of the AFL and other labor organizations, and it was particularly devastating to the Knights of Labor, which, as the most radical of the major labor organizations, never recovered from the post-Haymarket hysteria. However much they tried to distance themselves from radicals, unions were always vulnerable to accusations of anarchism, as the violent strikes of the 1890s occasionally illustrated.

THE HOMESTEAD STRIKE

The Amalgamated Association of Iron and Steel Workers, which was affiliated with the American Federation of Labor, was the most powerful trade union in the country. Its members were skilled workers, in great demand by employers and thus able to exercise significant power in the workplace. Employers sometimes called such workers "little shopfloor autocrats," and they resented the substantial control over working conditions these skilled laborers often had. The union had a rulebook with fifty-six pages of what workers called "legislation" limiting the power of employers. In the emerging corporate world of the late nineteenth century, such challenges to management control were beginning to seem intolerable to many employers.

By the mid-1880s, the steel industry had introduced new production methods and new patterns of organization that were streamlining the steelmaking process and, at the same time, reducing the companies' dependence on skilled labor. In the Carnegie system, the union had a foothold in only one of the corporation's three major factories—the Homestead plant

HENRY CLAY FRICK

near Pittsburgh. By 1890, Carnegie and his chief lieutenant, Henry Clay Frick, had decided that the Amalgamated "had to go," even at Homestead. Over the next two years, they repeatedly cut wages at Homestead. At first, the union acquiesced, aware that it was not strong enough to wage a successful strike.

In 1892, the company stopped even discussing its decisions with the Amalgamated, in effect denying the union's right to negotiate. Finally, when Frick announced another wage cut at Homestead and gave the union two days to accept it, the Amalgamated called for a strike. Frick abruptly shut down the plant and called in 300 guards from the Pinkerton Detective Agency to enable the company to hire nonunion workers. The hated Pinkertons were well-known strikebreakers, and their mere presence was often enough to incite workers to violence.

The Pinkertons approached the plant by river on barges on July 6, 1892. The strikers prepared for them by pouring oil on the water and setting it on fire, and they met the guards at the docks with guns and dynamite. After several hours of pitched

Historical Thinking Skills

Argumentation After students have read the section "The AFL's Agenda," ask them to create a poster either encouraging workers to join the AFL or discouraging them from doing so. WXT SOC PCE

Discussion and Activities

Evaluating Evidence Have students read the section "Haymarket Square." Ask them to discuss as a class what they think most likely actually happened there and why so many people were convicted of serious crimes on so little evidence. PCE WXT SOC

Reasoning Processes

Causation and Argumentation After students have read the section "The Homestead Strike," ask them to create a T-chart listing causes and effects of the Homestead Strike. Have students identify what they believe are the most important causes and effects. Have them discuss as a class how this strike was similar to or different from earlier strikes, such as the Great Railroad Strike and the strike at the McCormick factory in Chicago. **WXT** **PCE**

battle, during which three guards and ten strikers were killed and many others injured, the Pinkertons surrendered and were escorted roughly out of town.

But the workers' victory was temporary. The governor of Pennsylvania, at the company's request, sent the state's entire National Guard contingent, some 8,000 troops, to Homestead. Production resumed, with strikebreakers now protected by troops. Public opinion turned against the strikers when a radical made an attempt to assassinate Frick. Slowly, workers drifted back to their jobs; and finally–four months after the strike began–the Amalgamated surrendered. By 1900, every major steel plant in the Northeast had broken with the Amalgamated, which now had no power to resist. Its membership shrank from a high of 24,000 in 1891 (two-thirds of all eligible steelworkers) to fewer than 7,000 a decade later. Its decline was symbolic of the general erosion of union strength in the late nineteenth century, as factory labor became increasingly unskilled and workers thus became easier to replace. The AFL unions were often powerless in the face of these changes.

THE UNION DEFEATED

The Pullman Strike

A dispute of greater magnitude and equal bitterness, if less violence, was the Pullman strike in 1894. The Pullman Palace Car Company manufactured sleeping and parlor cars for railroads, which it built and repaired at a plant near Chicago. The company built a 600-acre town, named Pullman, and rented its trim, orderly houses to the employees. George M. Pullman, owner of the company, considered the town a model solution to the industrial problem; he referred to the workers as his "children." But many residents chafed at the regimentation and the high rents.

In the winter of 1893–1894, the Pullman Company slashed wages by about 25 percent, citing the declining revenues the depression that began in 1983 was causing. At the same time, Pullman refused to reduce rents in its model town, which were 20 to 25 percent higher than rents for comparable accommodations in surrounding areas. Workers went on strike and persuaded the militant American Railway Union, led by Eugene V. Debs, to support them by refusing to handle Pullman cars and equipment. Opposing the strikers was the General Managers' Association, a consortium of twenty-four Chicago railroads. It persuaded its member companies to discharge switchmen who refused to handle Pullman cars. Every time this happened, Debs's union instructed its members who worked for the offending companies to walk off their jobs. Within a few days thousands of railroad workers in twenty-seven states and territories were on strike, and transportation from Chicago to the Pacific coast was paralyzed.

EUGENE DEBS

Most state governors responded readily to appeals from strike-threatened businesses; but the governor of Illinois, John Peter Altgeld, was a man with demonstrated sympathies for workers and their grievances. Altgeld had criticized the trials of the Haymarket anarchists and had pardoned the convicted men who were still in prison when he took office. He refused to call out the militia to protect employers now. Bypassing Altgeld, railroad operators asked the federal government to send regular army troops to Illinois, on the pretext that the strike was preventing the movement of mail on the trains. President Grover Cleveland and Attorney General Richard Olney, a former railroad lawyer and a bitter foe of unions, complied. In July 1894, over Altgeld's objections, the president ordered 2,000 troops to the Chicago area. A federal court issued an injunction forbidding the union to continue

THE PULLMAN STRIKE These two images portray two aspects of the great Pullman strike of 1894. The photograph above shows U.S. troops, ordered to Chicago to quell the strike, camping on the lakefront. The drawing below shows freight cars and an engine destroyed by striking workers. These images were published together in *Harper's Weekly* to illustrate the ferocity of the Pullman battle.

Historical Thinking Skills

Sourcing and Situation Have students examine the image "The Pullman Strike." Ask them to identify and discuss in small groups details from the images that may help identify the purpose and point of view of *Harper's Weekly* in publishing these images. *(One image is a close-up scene of destruction caused by strikers; the orderly line of soldiers with their organized camp juxtaposed against the unorganized mass of strikers suggests that the magazine was sympathetic to the government's position.)* **PCE** **WXT** **SOC**

the strike. When Debs and his associates defied it, they were arrested and imprisoned. With federal troops protecting the hiring of new workers and with the union leaders in a federal jail, the strike quickly collapsed.

SOURCES OF LABOR WEAKNESS

The last decades of the nineteenth century were years in which labor, despite its organizing efforts, made few real gains and suffered many important losses. In a rapidly expanding industrial economy, wages for workers rose hardly at all, and not nearly enough to keep up with the rising cost of living. Labor leaders won a few legislative victories: the abolition by Congress in 1885 of the Contract Labor Law; the establishment by Congress in 1868 of an eight-hour day on public works projects and in 1892 of an eight-hour day for government employees; state laws governing hours of labor and safety standards; and gradually some guaranteed compensation for workers injured on the job. But many of these laws were not enforced, and neither strikes nor protests seemed to have much effect. The end of the century found most workers with less political power and considerably less control of the workplace than they had had forty years before.

Workers failed to make greater gains for many reasons. The principal labor organizations represented only a small percentage of the industrial workforce. Four percent of all workers (fewer than 1 million) belonged to unions in 1900. The AFL, the most important, excluded unskilled workers, who were emerging as the core of the industrial workforce, and along with them most women, African Americans, and recent immigrants. Women responded to this exclusion in 1903 by forming their own organization, the Women's Trade Union League (WTUL). But after several frustrating years of attempting to unionize women, the WTUL turned the bulk of its attention to securing protective legislation for women workers, not general organization and mobilization of labor. Other divisions within the workforce contributed further to union weakness. Tensions between different ethnic and racial groups kept laborers divided.

Another source of labor weakness was the shifting nature of the workforce. Many immigrant workers came to America intending to remain only briefly, to earn some money and return home. The assumption that they had no long-range future in the country (even though it was often a mistaken one) eroded their willingness to organize. Other workers–natives and immigrants alike–were in constant motion, moving from one job to another, one town to another, seldom in one place long enough to establish institutional ties or exert real power. A study of Newburyport, Massachusetts, over a thirty-year period shows that 90 percent of the workers there vanished from the town records in those years, many of them because they moved elsewhere. Even workers who stayed put often did not remain in the same job for long.

SHIFTING NATURE OF THE WORKFORCE

Some real social mobility did exist. Workers might move from unskilled to semiskilled or skilled jobs during their lifetimes; their children might become foremen or managers. The gains were small, but they were enough to inspire considerable (and often unrealistic) hopes and to persuade some workers that they were not part of a permanent working class.

Above all, workers made few gains in the late nineteenth century because of the strength of the forces arrayed against them. They faced corporate organizations of vast wealth and power, which were generally determined to crush any efforts by workers to challenge their prerogatives–not just through brute force, but also through infiltration of unions, espionage within working-class communities, and sabotage of organizational efforts. And as the Homestead and Pullman strikes suggest, the corporations usually had the support of local, state, and federal authorities, who were willing to send in troops to "preserve order" and crush labor uprisings on demand.

CORPORATE STRENGTH

Despite the creation of new labor unions, despite a wave of strikes and protests that in the 1880s and 1890s reached startling proportions, workers in the late nineteenth century failed to create successful organizations or to protect their interests in the way the large corporations managed to do. In the battle for power within the emerging industrial economy, almost all the advantages seemed to lie with capital.

Discussion and Activities

Analyzing Points of View After students have read the section "The Pullman Strike," ask them to write a short letter to President Cleveland from the point of view of a striking Pullman Company employee or an officer in the company advising the president what course of action he should take. PCE WXT

Historical Thinking Skills

Argumentation Have students read the section "Sources of Labor Weakness." Ask them to list and rank in order of importance the causes of labor's failures. Have students write a thesis statement that makes a claim about the most important reasons labor unions failed to achieve their goals in the late nineteenth century. WXT SOC PCE

Discussion and Activities

Evaluating Have students review the chapter and discuss as a class how to evaluate industrial leaders like Andrew Carnegie, Cornelius Vanderbilt, John D. Rockefeller, J.P. Morgan, and others. **Ask:** Were these industrial leaders "Robber Barons" or "Captains of Industry"? Have students consider late nineteenth-century income distribution, justifications for wealth, treatment of worker with a focus on women, children, and minorities, the growth of the middle class, and rising standards of living. Have them write a short paragraph outlining their views on these themes. **PCE** **NAT** **WXT** **SOC**

Key Terms

Students should be familiar with the key terms and be able to define them in the context of the rapid growth of American industry and the increasing tension between industrial leaders and their workers over wages and working conditions during this time period. Encourage students to use these terms in performing review exercises and exam practice for this chapter.

CHAPTER 17 REVIEW

CONNECTING THEMES

Chapter Seventeen focused on the reasons for industrial growth, the development of the corporation, and how businesses consolidated into monopolies and trusts. The chapter also explored the impact of industrialization and the growth of big business on all aspects of American society.

Many factors led to the growth of American industry. As corporations took advantage of the abundant supply of raw materials and a continually increasing labor supply, they also utilized technology to increase efficiencies and production. These in turn contributed to inequalities in wealth distribution and dangerous working conditions for laborers. While defenders of industry used the theory of Social Darwinism and the "gospel of wealth" to legitimize corporate success and frame it within traditional American ideals of freedom and individualism, other ideas emerged to challenge corporate principles and sometimes capitalism itself. Yet large corporations, supported by government at all levels, remained powerful. Labor leaders had limited success in fighting big business despite the formation of unions and repeated strikes and protests. As the United States moved into the twentieth century, large corporations would maintain their dominant position in the emerging industrial economy.

You should consider the following questions as you review the themes for this chapter:

- What were the ways that migration led to changes in American identity for immigrants, working class people, and first-time urban residents?
- How did changes in technology and the organizational structure of business affect the economic and social development of the United States?
- What were the major sources of urban population growth during the Gilded Age?
- Why did a relationship develop between the federal government and big business during the Gilded Age?
- What was the impact of urbanization and industrialization on the American environment?
- What were the major abuses in capitalism that led to an outcry for social and philosophical change?

KEY TERMS

Go Online **Chapter 17 Content Review**

Assessing Student Understanding Use the online assessment to assess student understanding of concepts and topics within the chapter. You can assign the ready-made Chapter 17 Content Review or create your own from available questions. This easy-to-use tool helps you design assessments that meet the needs of different types of learners.

AP EXAM PRACTICE

Questions assume cumulative content knowledge from this chapter and the previous chapter.

MULTIPLE CHOICE

Use the photograph on page 499 and your knowledge of U.S. history to answer questions 1-3.

1. The workers in the photograph experienced which of the following situations that were common in factories during the Gilded Age?
   (A) independence from the monotonous, repetitive, and unskilled labor such as farm work
   (B) loss of control over their work conditions
   (C) racially integrated workplaces
   (D) support for unionization among industrial leaders

2. The photograph reflects the increased hiring of women that was largely due to
   (A) laws that restricted child labor.
   (B) increased interest in women's educational opportunities.
   (C) lack of skilled workers to fill a boom in factory jobs.
   (D) changes in factory technology and management structure that decreased the demand for skilled labor.

3. Women working in factories during the Gilded Age, such as those in the photograph, were typically
   (A) widowed without other means of financial support.
   (B) young, white, and from immigrant families.
   (C) single, as laws restricted the paid labor of married women.
   (D) immigrants from northern and western European countries.

SHORT ANSWER

Use your knowledge of U.S. history to answer questions 4 and 5.

4. Use the image on page 489 to answer A, B, and C.
   (A) Describe ONE specific point of view about business owners during the Gilded Age.
   (B) Briefly explain ONE specific historical cause that led to the rise of monopolies during the Gilded Age.
   (C) Briefly explain ONE specific historical effect that resulted from the rise of monopolies during the Gilded Age.

5. Answer A, B, and C.
   (A) Briefly explain the historical context which gave rise to the labor movement during the Gilded Age.
   (B) Briefly describe ONE specific historical difference between the Knights of Labor and the American Federation of Labor.
   (C) Briefly describe ONE specific historical similarity between the Knights of Labor and the American Federation of Labor.

LONG ESSAY

Develop a thoughtful and thorough historical argument that addresses the statement. Begin your essay with a thesis statement, and support it with specific historical evidence and examples.

6. Evaluate the relative importance of causes that spurred the growth of industry in the United States during the Gilded Age.

Answers

Long Essay

6. Possible thesis: Many Gilded Age industries were protected by the government, and some were encouraged with subsidies and other government programs. However, the Second Industrial Revolution was a revolution of the machine. Further, millions of immigrants fueled the growth of industry and business during the Gilded Age. Therefore, it was the machine and the labor sources that fueled the Second Industrial Revolution. Specific historical evidence: The rise of industrial technology was one of the important causes that gave rise to the Second Industrial Revolution. This revolution distinguished itself from the First Industrial Revolution in that it was a revolution of the machine. The efficiency of the workplace was another important factor along with the continued increase in immigration from Europe. Much like the first half of the century, the population increase continued rapidly in the second half of the century. Immigrants poured in by the millions, thus providing the economy with a steady supply of workers. Another important factor in the rise of industry was the protections and subsidies that business owners received from the government. American society also sought to encourage and support these monopolists by using philosophical ideas like Social Darwinism and the Gospel of Wealth; these ideas encouraged monopolists to further consolidate their holdings. Vertical and horizontal integration also allowed the monopolists to build up and consolidate their holdings in ways that provided security and protection, thus allowing them to accumulate even more wealth and power as they cornered markets.

Answers

Multiple Choice

1. B; **2.** D; **3.** B

Short Answer

4A) Possible answer: Many of the large business owners were viewed as "robber barons," a derogatory term used to describe them and their business practices during the second half of the nineteenth century.

4B) Possible answer: Railroads were among the first large businesses to develop in the United States. The owners of these businesses, of which there were only a handful, controlled all the rail lines in the country, wielded enormous power, and controlled a tremendous amount of wealth. Other businesses mostly failed to secure the same kinds of wealth and control that the railroads did, but once a business controlled a market, it led to tremendous wealth and power.

4C) Possible answer: The concentration of wealth during the Gilded Age led to the rise of monopolies. Owners of monopolies, who controlled the market, wielded tremendous power and wealth. Because these owners often cut corners on wages and working conditions, this led to the rise of the labor movement. A number of labor organizations rose in response to these abuses and the concentrations of wealth.

5A) Possible answer: Monopolies sought to maximize profits and thus paid workers as low a wage as possible. Many workers also toiled in extremely dangerous working conditions. Workers during the Gilded Age had very few rights and almost no way of defending themselves against the monopolists and owners of businesses. These business leaders often had the support of the government and were protected against any attempts to rectify poor working conditions.

5B) Possible answer: The Knights of Labor was a broad organization made up of virtually anyone who "toiled." The American Federation of Labor was much narrower in its inclusivity; it only included "skilled" workers.

5C) Possible answer: Both groups lobbied on behalf of female workers, albeit begrudgingly on the part of the AFL.

Pacing Guide

Chapter 18 explores key concepts from Period 6: 1865–1898 of the AP U.S. History Curriculum Framework. The suggested instruction time for Chapter 18 is 5 days.

Key Concepts

6.2.I International and internal migration increased urban populations and fostered the growth of a new urban culture.

6.3.I New cultural and intellectual movements both buttressed and challenged the social order of the Gilded Age.

6.3.II Dramatic social changes in the period inspired political debates over citizenship, corruption, and the proper relationship between business and government.

18 THE AGE OF THE CITY

SNOW IN NEW YORK, 1902 Robert Henri Cozad (1865–1929) was one of a number of painters who, in the early twentieth century, created what became known as the "Ashcan" school of painting. These artists painted scenes of the urban underworld—tenements, saloons, boxing rings.

CONNECTING CONCEPTS

Chapter Eighteen begins by examining the emergence of urbanization in the United States during the Gilded Age. The rise of cities was due primarily to migration, not natural population growth. Railroads made it easier for young men and, especially, women from rural communities to pursue economic advancement. African Americans, however, found limited opportunities. Ocean liners enabled immigrants, especially from southern and eastern Europe, to travel to cities like Chicago and New York, where the foreign-born population often exceeded 80 percent. Ethnic communities reinforced cultural values and collective identity, but also fed a new wave of nativism. Politicians and organizations like the American Protective Association sought to create barriers to entry for immigrants.

The urban landscape was a study in contrasts. The wealthy lived in palatial homes while the middle class settled into new suburbs linked by streetcars. The poor crowded into squalid tenements with inadequate sanitation and polluted air. Disease and fires were common. Congestion and crime were the norm. The "city beautiful" movement led to the creation of urban parks, public spaces, and great buildings – museums, galleries, and theaters. But suffering was widespread and assistance was limited. Political machines like Tammany Hall in New York extended help to the urban poor in return for votes.

Urban life facilitated the rise of a new, middle-class culture. Chain stores, mail-order catalogs, and department stores changed how Americans shopped and ate. Women found new opportunities as consumers and workers, especially in retail. Leisure

Discussion and Activities

Analyzing Visuals Have students examine the image "Snow in New York, 1902." Ask them to list details from the painting. Have students think about what it would be like to be present on the street portrayed and share their thoughts with a partner. **SOC** **WXT**

time grew and mass communications affected how Americans lived. Spectator sports like college football and professional baseball became popular, in part due to newspaper and magazine coverage. Working men and women flocked to ethnic theater, vaudeville shows, boxing matches, and motion pictures. The middle class gravitated toward art and literature that offered realistic depictions of urban life, which spurred reform efforts.

As you read, you should:

- Describe how urban centers grew both in size and number during the Gilded Age.
- Evaluate how the increasing efficiency of American industry made it a worldwide economic force.
- Analyze how Darwinism contributed to the divide between the culture of the city and more provincial culture.
- Evaluate how improvements in urban transportation led to class, racial, and ethnic segregation in urban housing patterns.
- Explain how immigrants faced social prejudice and were conflicted between Americanizing and maintaining their cultural identity.
- Examine how political machines provided services for the poor in exchange for political support.
- Analyze the criticisms of the capitalistic system that arose during the Gilded Age along with the alternatives critics proposed.

THE URBANIZATION OF AMERICA

The great migration from the countryside to the city was not unique to the United States. It was occurring simultaneously throughout much of the Western world in response to industrialization and the factory system. America, a society with little experience of great cities, found urbanization both jarring and alluring.

THE LURE OF THE CITY

RAPID URBAN GROWTH

"We cannot all live in cities," the journalist Horace Greeley wrote shortly after the Civil War, "yet nearly all seem determined to do so." The urban population of America increased sevenfold in the half century after the Civil War. And in 1920, the census revealed that for the first time, a majority of the American people lived in "urban" areas–communities of 2,500 people or more. New York City and its environs grew from 1 million in 1860 to over 3 million in 1900. Chicago had 100,000 residents in 1860 and more than a million in 1900. Cities were experiencing similar growth in all areas of the country.

Natural increase accounted for only a small part of the urban growth. In fact, urban families experienced a high rate of infant mortality, a declining fertility rate, and a high death rate from disease. Without immigration, cities would have grown slowly, if at all. The city attracted people from the countryside because it offered conveniences, entertainments, and cultural experiences unavailable in rural communities. Cities gave women the opportunity to act in ways that in smaller communities would have been seen to violate "propriety." They gave gay men and lesbian women space in which to build a culture (even if still a mostly hidden one) and experiment sexually at least partly insulated from the hostile gaze of others. But most of all, cities attracted people because they offered more and better-paying jobs than were available in rural America or in the foreign economies many immigrants were fleeing.

People moved to cities, too, because new forms of transportation made it easier for them to get there. Railroads made simple, quick, and inexpensive what once was a daunting journey from parts of the American countryside to nearby cities. The development of large, steam-powered ocean liners created a highly competitive shipping industry, allowing Europeans and Asians to cross the oceans to America much more cheaply and quickly than they had in the past.

MIGRATIONS

GEOGRAPHIC MOBILITY

As a result of urbanization, the late nineteenth century became an age of unprecedented geographic mobility, as Americans left the declining agricultural regions of the East at a dramatic rate. Some who left were moving to the newly developing farmlands of the West. But many were moving to the cities of the East and the Midwest.

Reasoning Processes

Causation Have students read the section "The Lure of the City." Ask them to create a list of the causes of rapid urban growth, then rank the causes in order of importance. Have students write a thesis statement that makes a claim about the most important causes of urbanization in the late nineteenth century. *(High birth rates; immigration; internal migration.)* **SOC** **MIG**

Go Online AP Exam Preparation

AP Exam Practice Use the online assessment to help prepare students for the AP Exam. You can assign the ready-made AP-style short-answer questions, document-based questions, and multiple-choice questions assessing concepts, themes, and skills from Period 6 and AP-style long-essay questions organized in sets of 3 questions from various time periods. You can also create your own tests from available questions. This easy-to-use tool helps you design assessments that meet the needs of different types of learners.

Reasoning Processes

Comparing After students have read the section "Geographic Mobility," ask them to create a T-chart listing reasons why women and African Americans started moving to cities. Have students identify which reasons are similar and different between the two groups. **SOC** **WXT** **PCE** **MIG**

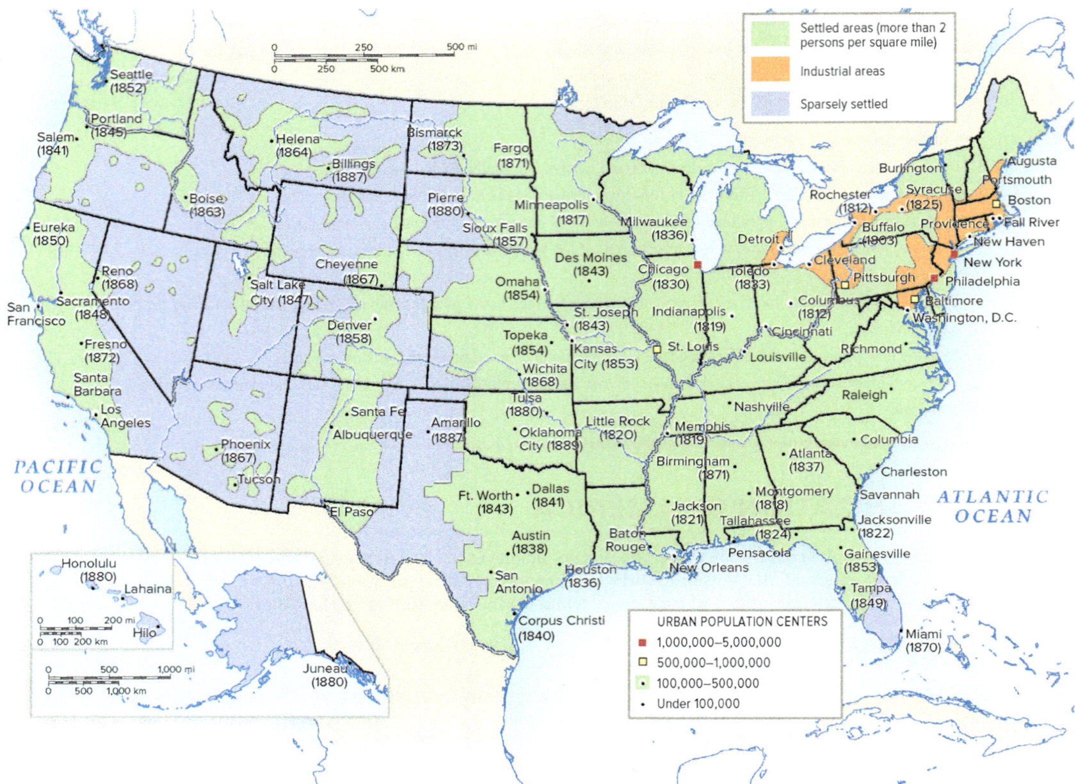

THE UNITED STATES IN 1900 This map helps illustrate the enormous increase in the nation's urban population in the nineteenth century. The map of America in 1800, in Chapter 7, reveals a nation with very few significant cities and with a population clustered largely along the eastern seaboard. By 1900, a much larger area of the United States had consistent areas of settlement, and many more of those areas consisted of towns and cities—including three cities (Chicago, New York, and Philadelphia) with populations of over a million and a considerable number of other cities with 100,000 or more people. Also striking, however, is the amount of land in the West with very light settlement or no settlement.

Do climate and geography help explain the variable patterns of settlement?

Among those leaving rural America for industrial cities in the late nineteenth century were young rural women, for whom opportunities in the farm economy were limited. As farms grew larger, more commercial, and more mechanized, they became increasingly male preserves; and since much of the workforce on many farms consisted of unskilled and often transient workers, there were fewer family units than before. Farm women had once been essential for making clothes and other household goods, but those goods were now available in stores or through catalogs. Hundreds of thousands of women moved to the cities, therefore, in search of work and community.

Southern African Americans were also beginning what would be a nearly century-long exodus from the countryside into the cities. Their withdrawal was a testament to the poverty, debt, violence, and oppression African Americans encountered in the late-nineteenth-century rural South. The opportunities they found in cities were limited. Factory jobs for African Americans were rare, and professional opportunities almost nonexistent. Urban African Americans tended to work as cooks, janitors, domestic servants, and in other low-paying service occupations. Because many such jobs were considered women's work, black women often outnumbered black men in the cities.

By the end of the nineteenth century, there were substantial African American communities (10,000 people or more) in over thirty cities–many of them in the South, but some (New York City, Chicago, Washington, D.C., Baltimore) in the North

AFRICAN AMERICAN COMMUNITIES

Answers

The United States in 1900

Early cities were clustered along ports on the eastern seaboard. Development tended to spread along rivers and railroads. The arid regions of the West remained the most sparsely populated. **MIG** **GEO**

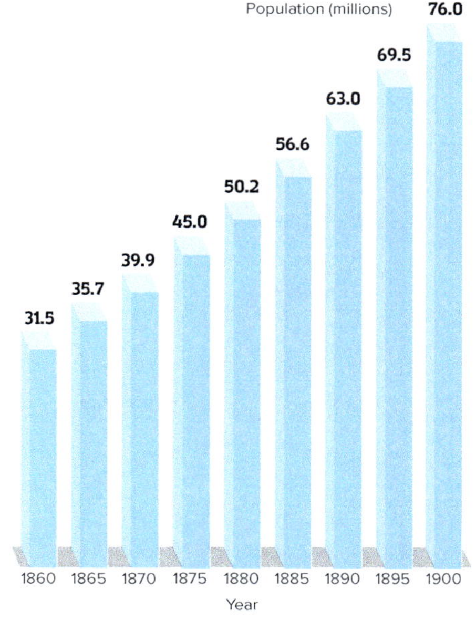

POPULATION GROWTH, 1860–1900 This chart illustrates the rapid increase in the nation's population in the last forty years of the nineteenth century. As you can see, the American population more than doubled in those years.

What were the principal factors behind this substantial population growth?

or in border states. Much more substantial African American migration would come during World War I and after; but the black communities established in the late nineteenth century paved the way for the great population movements of the future.

The most important source of urban population growth in the late nineteenth century, however, was the arrival of great numbers of new immigrants from abroad: 10 million between 1860 and 1890, 18 million more in the three decades after that. Some came from Canada, Mexico, Latin America, and–particularly on the West Coast–China and Japan. But by far the greatest number came from Europe. After 1880, the flow of new arrivals began for the first time to include large numbers of people from southern and eastern Europe: Italians, Greeks, Slavs, Slovaks, Russian Jews, Armenians, and others. By the 1890s, more than half of all immigrants came from these new regions, as opposed to less than 2 percent in the 1860s.

In earlier stages of immigration, most new immigrants from Europe (with the exception of Irish immigrants) were at least modestly prosperous and educated. German and Scandinavian immigrants in particular had headed west on their arrival, either to farm or to work as businessmen, merchants, professionals, or skilled laborers in midwestern cities such as St. Louis, Cincinnati, and Milwaukee. Most of the new immigrants of the late nineteenth century, however, lacked the capital to buy farmland and lacked the education to establish themselves in professions. So, like the poor Irish immigrants before the Civil War, they settled overwhelmingly in industrial cities, where most of them took unskilled jobs.

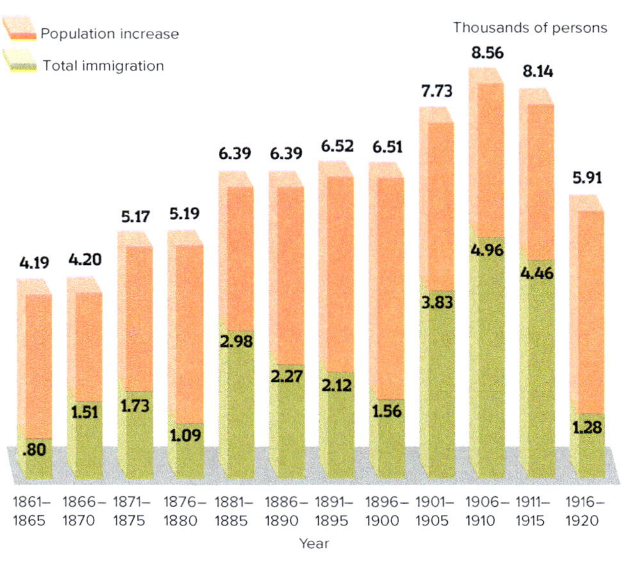

IMMIGRATION'S CONTRIBUTION TO POPULATION GROWTH, 1860–1920 Immigration, mostly from Europe, was responsible for about 20 percent of the nation's population growth in the late nineteenth and early twentieth centuries.

What factors drew so many immigrants to the United States in these years?

Discussion and Activities

Analyzing Change Have students examine the graph "Immigration's Contribution to Population Growth, 1860–1920. With a partner, have them identify the three years on the graph that show the greatest population growth and discuss the reasons for this. **MIG** **GEO**

Answers

Population Growth, 1860–1900

The main causes of population growth were high birth rates, immigration, and internal migration.

Immigration's Contribution to Population Growth, 1860–1920

The most important factors drawing immigrants to the United State were the desire for greater economic opportunity and greater freedom from political and religious oppression.

Historical Thinking Skills

Analyzing Evidence Have students examine the image "Ready Made Farms in Western Canada." Ask students to discuss in small groups what the railroad would gain by promoting settlement in the Canadian West. *(They would have more passengers as people moved west along the railroad route; there would be a greater demand for goods by the growing population that would be transported by the railroad; the railroad likely owned the land along the route to sell to the new settlers.)* **MIG** **WXT**

AMERICA IN THE WORLD

GLOBAL MIGRATIONS

The large waves of immigration that transformed American society in the late nineteenth and early twentieth centuries were not unique to the United States. They were part of a worldwide movement of peoples that affected every continent. These epic migrations were the product of two related forces: population growth and industrialization.

The population of Europe grew faster in the second half of the nineteenth century than it had ever grown before—almost doubling between 1850 and the beginning of World War I. The population growth was a result of growing economies able to support more people and productive agriculture that helped end debilitating famines. But the rapid growth nevertheless strained the resources of many parts of Europe and affected, in particular, rural people, who were now too numerous to live off the available land. Many decided to move to other parts of the world, where land was more plentiful or jobs were more available.

At the same time, industrialization drew millions of people from rural areas into cities—sometimes cities in their own countries, but often industrial cities in other, more economically advanced nations. From 1800 to the start of World War I, 50 million Europeans migrated to new lands overseas—people from almost all areas of Europe, but, in the later years of the century (when migration reached its peak), mostly from poor rural areas in southern and eastern Europe. Italy, Russia, and Poland were among the biggest sources of late-nineteenth-century migrants. Almost two-thirds of these immigrants came to the United States. But nearly 20 million Europeans migrated to other lands, to Canada, Australia, New Zealand, South Africa, Argentina, and other parts of South America. Many of these migrants moved to vast areas of open land in these countries and established themselves as farmers. Many others settled in the industrial cities that were growing up in all these regions.

It was not only Europeans who were transplanting themselves in these years. Vast numbers of migrants—usually poor, desperate people—left Asia, Africa, and the Pacific islands in search of better lives. Most of them could not afford the journey abroad on their own. They moved instead as indentured servants, agreeing to a term of servitude in their new land in exchange for food, shelter, and transportation. Recruiters of indentured servants fanned out across China, Japan, areas of Africa and the Pacific islands, and, above all, India. French and British recruiters brought hundreds of thousands of Indian migrants to work in plantations in their own Asian and African colonies. Chinese laborers were recruited to work on plantations in Cuba and Hawaii; mines in Malaya, Peru, South Africa, and Australia; and railroad projects in Canada, Peru, and the United States. African indentured servants moved in large numbers to the Caribbean, and Pacific islanders tended to move to other islands or to Australia.

The migration of European peoples to new lands was largely voluntary. Most migrants moved to the United States, where indentured servitude was illegal. Non-European migration brought relatively small numbers of people to the United States, but together, these various forms of migration produced one of the greatest population movements in the history of the world and transformed not just the United States, but much of the globe as well.

Private Collection/© Peter Newark American Pictures/Bridgeman Images

HISTORICAL THINKING SKILLS

1. **Making Connections** What were the factors that led to the increase in population in the United States during the Gilded Age?
2. **Explaining Historical Context** Why did some European countries encourage immigration to the United States?
3. **Identifying Historical Developments** Why were there more Europeans than non-Europeans immigrating to the United States during the Gilded Age?

Answers

America in the World

1. Possible answer: The availability of land in the United States and the Second Industrialization Revolution both provided opportunities that many individuals did not have back in their home countries.
2. Possible answer: Population growth was not just a phenomenon in the United States; it was happening all around the world. In Europe especially, the population grew more rapidly in the second half of the nineteenth century than it had previously. This caused an enormous strain on European resources, and it limited the amount of land available to rural individuals, so America offered opportunities that were not readily available in Europe.
3. Possible answer: Non-European individuals were generally poorer than their European counterparts. Many non-Europeans had to agree to indentured contracts for a specified amount of time in order to have their transportation costs covered. In the United States, indentured servitude was illegal at this time; therefore, fewer non-Europeans came to the United States during the Gilded Age.

THE ETHNIC CITY

By 1890, the population of some major urban areas consisted of a majority of foreign-born immigrants and their children: 87 percent of the population of Chicago, 80 percent in New York City, 84 percent in Milwaukee and Detroit. (London, the largest industrial city in Europe, by contrast, had a population that was 94 percent native.) New York had more Irish people than Dublin and more German people than Hamburg. Chicago eventually had more Polish people than Warsaw.

THE DIVERSE AMERICAN CITY

Equally striking was the diversity of the new immigrant populations. In other countries experiencing heavy immigration in this period, most of the new arrivals were coming from one or two sources: Argentina, for example, was experiencing great migrations too, but almost everyone was coming from Italy and Spain. In the United States, however, no single national group dominated. In the last four decades of the nineteenth century, substantial groups arrived from Italy, Germany, Scandinavia, Austria, Hungary, Russia, Great Britain, Ireland, Poland, Greece, Canada, Japan, China, Holland, Mexico, and many other nations. In some towns, a dozen different ethnic groups found themselves living in close proximity.

Most of the new immigrants were rural people, and their adjustment to city life was often painful. To help ease the transition, many national groups formed close-knit ethnic communities within the cities: Italian, Polish, Jewish, Slavic, Chinese, French-Canadian, Mexican, and other neighborhoods (often called "immigrant ghettos") that attempted to re-create in the New World many of the features of the Old.

BENEFITS OF ETHNIC COMMUNITIES

Some ethnic neighborhoods consisted of people who had migrated to America from the same province, town, or village. Even when the population was more diverse, however, the immigrant neighborhoods offered newcomers much that was familiar. They could find newspapers and theaters in their native languages, stores selling their native foods, churches or synagogues, and fraternal organizations that provided links with their national pasts. Many immigrants also maintained close ties with their native countries. They stayed in touch with relatives who had remained behind. Some (perhaps as many as a third in the early years) returned to Europe or Asia or Mexico after a short time; others helped bring the rest of their families to America.

The cultural cohesiveness of the ethnic communities clearly eased the pain of separation from the immigrants' native lands. What role it played in helping immigrants become absorbed into the economic life of America is a more difficult question to answer. It is clear that some ethnic groups (Jewish and German immigrant groups in particular) advanced economically more rapidly than others (for example, Irish immigrants). One explanation is that, by huddling together in ethnic neighborhoods, immigrant groups tended to reinforce the cultural values of their previous societies. When those values were particularly well suited to economic advancement in an industrial society—as was, for example, the high value Jewish immigrants placed on education—ethnic identification may have helped members of a group to improve their lots. When other values predominated—maintaining community solidarity, sustaining family ties, preserving order—progress could be less rapid.

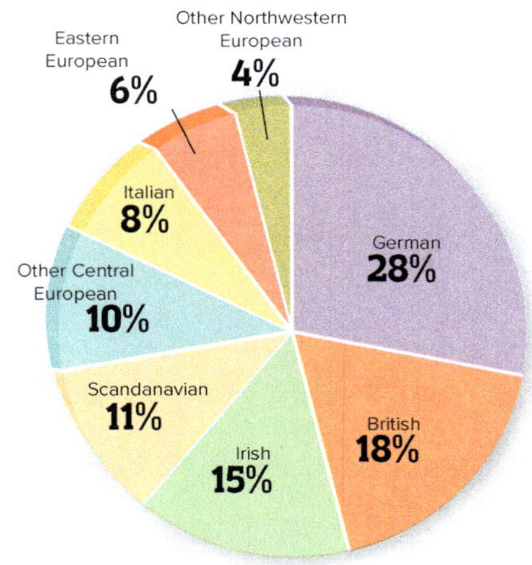

SOURCES OF IMMIGRATION FROM EUROPE, 1860–1900 This pie chart shows the sources of European immigration in the late nineteenth century. The largest number of immigrants continued to come from traditional sources (Britain, Ireland, Germany, Scandinavia), but the beginnings of what in the early twentieth century would become a major influx of immigrants from new sources—southern and eastern Europe in particular—are already visible here. Immigration from other sources—Mexico, South and Central America, and Asia—was also significant during this period.

Why would these newer sources of European and other kinds of immigration create controversy among older-stock Americans?

ASSIMILATION

Despite the substantial differences among the various immigrant communities, virtually all groups of the foreign-born had certain things in common. Most immigrants, of course, shared the experience of living in cities (and of adapting from a rural past to an urban present). Most were young; the majority of newcomers were between fifteen and forty-five years old. And in virtually all communities of foreign-born immigrants, the strength of ethnic ties had to compete against another powerful force: the desire for assimilation.

AMERICANIZATION

Many of the new arrivals from abroad had come to America with romantic visions of the New World. And however disillusioning they might find their first contact with the United States, they usually retained the dream of becoming true "Americans." Some first-generation immigrants even worked hard to rid themselves of all vestiges of their old cultures, to become more thoroughly Americanized. Second-generation

Discussion and Activities

Making Connections Have students read the section "The Ethnic City." Ask the class whether any of them have been to a modern ethnic community in an American city (for example a "Chinatown" or "Little Italy"), and discuss as a class how strong the ethnic identities expressed today are compared to those of the late nineteenth century. **MIG** **SOC** **WXT**

Answers

Sources of Immigration from Europe, 1860–1900

These newer immigrants encountered a stronger resistance because they were no longer mostly from western and northern Europe as earlier immigrants largely had been, and they were generally poorer and less literate than earlier European immigrants had been. Many of them were also Catholic or Jewish, two groups that faced discrimination in America at this time.

Historical Thinking Skills

Argumentation After students have read the section "Assimilation," ask them to write a short paragraph explaining whether they would encourage new immigrants to assimilate into American culture or work to maintain their traditional culture. **MIG** **SOC**

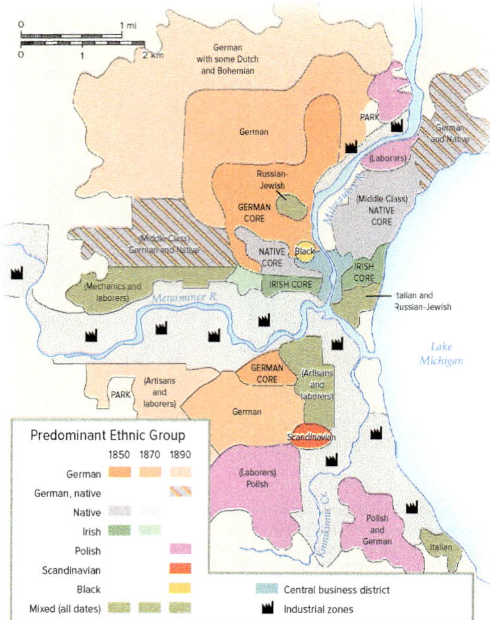

ETHNIC AND CLASS SEGREGATION IN MILWAUKEE, 1850–1890 This map illustrates the complex pattern of settlement in Milwaukee, a pattern that was in many ways typical of many industrial cities, in the late nineteenth century. Two related phenomena—industrialization and massive immigration from abroad—shaped the landscape of the city in these years. By 1890, first- and second-generation immigrants made up 84 percent of the city's population. Note the complicated distribution of ethnic groups in distinctive neighborhoods throughout the city, and note too the way in which middle-class people (especially "native-born" middle-class people, which included many people of German descent whose families had been in the United States for generations) isolated themselves from the areas in which the working class lived.

What were some of the advantages and disadvantages of this ethnic clustering to the immigrants who lived in these communities?

immigrants were even more likely to attempt to break with the old ways, to try to assimilate completely into what they considered the real American culture. Some even looked with contempt on parents and grandparents who continued to preserve traditional ethnic habits and values.

The urge to assimilate put a particular strain on relations between men and women in immigrant communities. Many of the foreign-born came from cultures in which women were more subordinate to men, and more fully lodged within the family, than most women in the United States. In some immigrant cultures, parents expected to arrange their children's marriages and to control almost every moment of their daughters' lives until marriage. But out of either choice or economic necessity, many immigrant women (and even more of the American-born daughters of immigrants) began working outside the home and developing friendships, interests, and attachments outside the family. The result was not the collapse of the family-centered cultures of immigrant communities; those cultures proved remarkably durable. But there were adjustments to the new and more fluid life of the American city, and often considerable tension in the process.

CHANGING GENDER ROLES

Assimilation was not entirely a matter of choice. Native-born Americans encouraged it, both deliberately and inadvertently, in countless ways. Public schools taught children in English, and employers often insisted that workers speak English on the job. Although there were merchants in immigrant communities who sold ethnically distinctive foods and clothing, most stores by necessity sold mainly American products, forcing immigrants to adapt their diets, wardrobes, and lifestyles to American norms. Church leaders were often native-born Americans or assimilated immigrants who encouraged their parishioners to adopt American ways. Some even reformed their theology and liturgy to make it more compatible with the norms of the new country. Reform Judaism, imported from Germany to the United States in the mid-nineteenth century, was an effort by American Jewish leaders (as it had been among German leaders) to make their faith less "foreign" to the dominant culture of a largely Christian nation.

EXCLUSION

The arrival of so many new immigrants, and the way many of them clung to old ways and created culturally distinctive communities, provoked fear and resentment among some native-born Americans, just as earlier arrivals had done. Some people reacted against the immigrants out of generalized fears and prejudices, seeing in their "foreignness" the source of all the disorder and corruption of the urban world. "These people," a Chicago newspaper wrote shortly after the Haymarket bombing, referring to striking immigrant workers, "are not American, but the very scum and offal of Europe . . . Europe's human and inhuman rubbish." Native-born Americans on the West Coast had a similar cultural aversion to Mexican, Chinese, and Japanese immigrants. Other native laborers were often incensed by the willingness of the immigrants to accept lower wages and to take over the jobs of strikers.

NATIVISM

The rising nativism provoked political responses. In 1887, Henry Bowers, a self-educated lawyer obsessed with a hatred of Catholics and foreigners, founded the American Protective Association, a group committed to stopping the immigrant tide. By 1894, membership in the organization had reportedly reached 500,000, with chapters throughout the Northeast and Midwest. That same year a more genteel organization, the Immigration Restriction League, was founded in Boston by five Harvard alumni. It was dedicated to the

IMMIGRATION RESTRICTION LEAGUE

Answers

Ethnic and Class Segregation in Milwaukee, 1850–1890

Advantages: Surrounded by familiar languages and culture; supported by earlier arrivals from their home countries; access to goods they were accustomed to. Disadvantages: Cut off from the larger society and economy; less likely to learn English and therefore had a harder time assimilating into workplaces and American culture.

Historical Thinking Skills

Argumentation After students have read the section "Immigration Restriction League," ask them to list and rank in order of importance the reasons why many Americans wanted to restrict immigration. *(Fear of foreign cultures and religions; fear of competition for jobs.)* Have students write a thesis statement that makes a claim about what they think the most important reason for the rise of Nativism was. **MIG** **SOC** **WXT** **PCE**

PUSHCART VENDOR Many immigrants to American cities aspired to be merchants. But many people with such aspirations could not afford to rent or buy a shop. So they set up business instead in pushcarts, which they parked along sidewalks and from which they sold a variety of wares. This pushcart was photographed with its owner on the Lower East Side of Manhattan around the end of the nineteenth century.

belief that immigrants should be screened, through literacy tests and other standards designed to separate the desirable from the undesirable. The league avoided the crude conspiracy theories and the rabid xenophobia of the American Protective Association. Its sophisticated nativism made it possible for many educated, middle-class people to support the restrictionist cause.

Even before the rise of these new organizations, politicians were struggling to find answers to the "immigration question." In 1882 Congress had responded to strong anti-Asian sentiment in California and elsewhere and restricted Chinese immigration, even though Chinese people made up only 1.2 percent of the population of the West Coast. In the same year, Congress denied entry to "undesirables"—convicts, paupers, the mentally incompetent—and placed a tax of 50 cents on each person admitted. Later legislation of the 1890s enlarged the list of those barred from immigrating and increased the tax.

PRO-IMMIGRATION This political cartoon from 1880, by Joseph Keppler, expresses the view that people from all over the world should be welcomed into the ever-expanding United States. While opposition to immigration from the restrictionist camp was great, immigrants were seen by many employers as a large and cheap labor supply necessary to support a rapidly growing economy.

Discussion and Activities

Analyzing Points of View Have students examine the image "Pushcart Vendor." Ask them to write a short journal entry from the point of view of the pushcart vendor or a member of his family briefly describing daily life. **SOC** **WXT**

Discussion and Activities

Making Connections through Argumentation Have students read the section "Frederick Law Olmsted and Calvert Vaux." Ask them to design a park for the community in which they live that would provide a change of pace from daily life. **SOC**

These laws kept out only a small number of aliens, however, and more-ambitious restriction proposals made little progress. Congress passed a literacy requirement for immigrants in 1897, but President Grover Cleveland vetoed it. The restrictions had limited success because many native-born Americans, far from fearing immigration, welcomed it and exerted strong political pressure against the restrictionists. Immigration was providing a rapidly growing economy with a cheap and plentiful labor supply; many employers argued that America's industrial (and indeed agricultural) development would be impossible without it.

ADVANTAGES OF CHEAP LABOR

CENTRAL PARK BAND CONCERT By the late nineteenth century, New York City's Central Park was already considered one of the great urban landscapes of the world. To New Yorkers, it was an irresistible escape from the crowded, noisy life of the rest of the city. But the park itself sometimes became enormously crowded as well, as this well-dressed audience at a band concert makes clear.

THE URBAN LANDSCAPE

The city was a place of remarkable contrasts. It had homes of almost unimaginable size and grandeur, and hovels of indescribable squalor. It had conveniences unknown to earlier generations, and problems that seemed beyond society's capacity to solve. Both the attractions and the problems were a result of the stunning pace at which cities were growing. The expansion of the urban population helped spur important new technological and industrial developments. But the rapid growth also produced misgovernment, poverty, congestion, filth, epidemics, and great fires. Planning and building simply could not match the pace of growth.

THE CREATION OF PUBLIC SPACE

In the eighteenth and early nineteenth centuries, cities had generally grown up haphazardly, with little central planning. By the mid-nineteenth century, however, reformers, planners, architects, and others began to call for a more ordered vision of the city. The result was the self-conscious creation of public spaces and public services.

Among the most important innovations of the mid-nineteenth century were great urban parks, which reflected the desire of a growing number of urban leaders to provide an antidote to the congestion of the city landscape. The most successful American promoters of this notion of the park as refuge were the landscape designers Frederick Law Olmsted and Calvert Vaux, who teamed up in the late 1850s to design New York City's Central Park. They deliberately created a public space that would look as little like the city as possible. Instead of the ordered, formal spaces common in some European cities, they created a space that seemed to be entirely natural—even though almost all of Central Park was carefully designed and constructed. Central Park was from the start one of the most popular and admired public spaces in the world, and as a result Olmsted and Vaux were recruited to design great parks and public spaces in other cities: Brooklyn, Boston, Philadelphia, Chicago, and Washington, D.C.

FREDERICK LAW OLMSTED AND CALVERT VAUX

At the same time that cities were creating great parks, they were also creating great public buildings: libraries, art galleries, natural history museums, theaters, concert halls, and opera houses. New York City's Metropolitan Museum of Art was only the largest and best known of many great museums taking shape in the late nineteenth century; others were created in such cities as Boston, Chicago, Philadelphia, and Washington, D.C. In one city after another, new and lavish public libraries appeared as if to confirm the city's role as a center of learning and knowledge.

Wealthy residents of cities were the principal force behind the creation of the great public buildings and at times even parks. As their own material and social aspirations grew, they wanted the public life of the city to provide them with amenities to match their expectations. Becoming an important patron of a major cultural institution was an especially effective route to social distinction. But this philanthropy, whatever the motives behind it, also produced valuable assets for the city as a whole.

As the size and aspirations of the great cities increased, urban leaders launched monumental projects to remake the way their cities looked. Inspired by massive city rebuilding projects in Paris, London, Berlin, and other European cities, some American cities began to clear away older neighborhoods and streets and create grand, monumental avenues lined with new, more impressive buildings. A particularly important event in inspiring this effort to remake the city was the 1893 Columbian Exposition in Chicago, a world's fair constructed to honor the 400th anniversary of Columbus's first voyage to America. At the center of the wildly popular exposition was a

"CITY BEAUTIFUL" MOVEMENT

Discussion and Activities

Analyzing Visuals Have students examine the image "Central Park Band Concert." Ask them to list details from the photo and discuss in small groups how they think New Yorkers thought about cultural events such as the one depicted. *(Most are well dressed, suggesting that this was considered a special event; there is a considerable crowd, indicating that this was a popular event.)* **SOC**

cluster of neoclassical buildings–the "Great White City"–constructed in the fashionable "beaux-arts" style of the time, arranged symmetrically around a formal lagoon. It became the inspiration for what became known as the "city beautiful" movement, led by the architect of the Great White City, Daniel Burnham. The movement aimed to impose a similar order and symmetry on the disordered life of cities around the country. "Make no little plans," Burnham liked to tell city planners. His influence led to the remaking of cities all across the country–from Washington, D.C., to Chicago and San Francisco. Only rarely, however, were planners able to overcome the obstacles of private landowners and complicated urban politics. They rarely achieved more than a small portion of their dreams. There were no reconstructions of American cities to match the elaborate nineteenth-century reshaping of Paris and London.

The effort to remake the city did not just focus on redesigning the existing landscape. It occasionally led to the creation of entirely new ones. In Boston in the late 1850s, a large area of marshy tidal land was gradually filled in to create the neighborhood known as "Back Bay." The landfill project took more than forty years to complete and was one of the largest public works projects ever undertaken in America to that point. But Boston was not alone. Chicago reclaimed large areas from Lake Michigan as it expanded and at one point raised the street level for the entire city to help avoid the problems the marshy land created. In Washington, D.C., another marshy site, large areas were filled in and slated for development. In New York and other cities, the response to limited space was not so much creating new land as annexing adjacent territory. A great wave of annexations expanded the boundaries of many American cities in the 1890s and beyond.

THE BACK BAY

Housing the Well-to-Do

One of the greatest problems of this precipitous growth was finding housing for the thousands of new residents who were pouring into the cities every day. For the prosperous, however, housing was seldom a worry. The availability of cheap labor and the reduced cost of building let anyone with even a moderate income afford a house.

Many of the richest urban residents lived in palatial mansions in the heart of the city and created lavish "fashionable districts"–Fifth Avenue in New York City, Back Bay and Beacon Hill in Boston, Society Hill in Philadelphia, Lake Shore Drive in Chicago, Nob Hill in San Francisco, and many others.

The moderately well-to-do (and as time went on, increasing numbers of wealthy people as well) took advantage of the less expensive land on the edges of the city and settled in new suburbs, linked to the downtowns by trains or streetcars or improved roads. Chicago in the 1870s, for example, boasted nearly 100 residential suburbs connected with the city by railroad and offering the joys of "pure air, peacefulness, quietude, and natural scenery." Boston, too, saw the development of some of the earliest "streetcar suburbs"–Dorchester, Brookline, and others–which catered to both the wealthy and the middle class. New Yorkers of moderate means settled in new suburbs on the northern fringes of Manhattan and commuted downtown by trolley or riverboat. Real estate developers worked to create and promote suburban communities that would appeal to nostalgia for the countryside that many city dwellers felt. Affluent suburbs, in particular, were notable for lawns, trees, and houses designed to look manorial. Even modest communities strove to emphasize the opportunities suburbs provided for owning land.

GROWTH OF SUBURBS

Housing Workers and the Poor

Most urban residents, however, could not afford either to own a house in the city or to move to the suburbs. Instead, they stayed in the city centers and rented. Because demand was so high and space so scarce, they had little bargaining power in the process. Landlords tried to squeeze as many rent-paying residents as possible into the smallest available space. In Manhattan, for example, the average population density in 1894 was 143 people per acre–a higher rate than that of the most crowded cities of Europe (Paris had 127 per acre, Berlin 101) and far higher than in any other American city then or since. In some neighborhoods–the Lower East Side of New York City, for example–density was more than 700 people per acre, among the highest levels in the world.

Landlords were reluctant to invest much in immigrant housing, confident they could rent dwellings for a profit regardless of their conditions. In the cities of the South–Charleston, New Orleans, Richmond–poor African Americans lived in crumbling former slave quarters. In Boston, they moved into cheap three-story wooden houses ("triple deckers"), many of them decaying fire hazards. In Baltimore and Philadelphia, they crowded into narrow brick row houses. And in New York, as in many other cities, more than a million people lived in tenements.

The word "tenement" had originally referred simply to a multiple-family rental building, but by the late nineteenth century it was being used to describe slum dwellings only. The first tenements, built in New York City in 1850, had been hailed as a great improvement in housing for the poor. "It is built with the design of supplying the laboring people with cheap lodgings," a local newspaper commented, "and will have many advantages over the cellars and other miserable abodes which too many are forced to inhabit." But tenements themselves soon became "miserable abodes," with many windowless rooms, little or no plumbing or central heating, and often a row of privies in the basement. A New York state law of 1870 required a window in every bedroom of tenements built after that date; developers complied by adding small, sunless air shafts to their buildings. Most of all, tenements were incredibly crowded, with three, four, and, sometimes many more people crammed into each small room.

TENEMENTS

Jacob Riis, a Danish immigrant and New York newspaper reporter and photographer, shocked many middle-class Americans with his sensational (and some claimed sensationalized) descriptions and

JACOB RIIS

Historical Thinking Skills

Evaluating Evidence After students have read the section "The Creation of Public Space," ask them to list the benefits to urban dwellers of new parks and public buildings. Have students identify whether each benefit was enjoyed more by the rich or the poor in the city. **Ask:** Who benefited the most from the "City Beautiful" movement? **SOC** **PCE**

Discussion and Activities

Historical Developments and Argumentation Have students read the section "Housing the Well-to-Do." Ask them to write a short paragraph explaining why it was relatively easy for the middle and upper classes to own a home. *(Cheap labor; expansion of cities into less expensive areas; improving access to work through public transportation.)* **WXT** **MIG**

Reasoning Processes

Comparing After students have read the section "Housing Workers and the Poor," ask them to create a Venn diagram comparing housing for the poor and the well-to-do. **Ask:** What, if any, similarities were there between how the rich and poor lived? **WXT** **SOC** **PCE**

A TENEMENT LAUNDRY Immigrant families living in tenements, in New York and in many other cities, earned their livelihoods as they could. This woman, shown here with some of her children, was typical of many working-class mothers who found income-producing activities they could pursue in the home (in this case, laundry). This room, dominated by large vats and piles of other people's laundry, is also the family's home, as the crib and religious pictures make clear.

© Bettmann/Corbis

pictures of tenement life in his 1890 book, *How the Other Half Lives*. Slum dwellings, he said, were almost universally sunless, practically airless, and "poisoned" by "summer stenches." "The hall is dark and you might stumble over the children pitching pennies back there." But the solution many reformers (including Riis) favored, and that governments sometimes adopted, was to raze slum dwellings without building any new or better housing to replace them.

Urban Transportation

Urban growth posed monumental transportation challenges. Old downtown streets were often too narrow for the heavy traffic that was beginning to move over them. Most were without a hard, paved surface producing either a sea of mud or a cloud of dust. In the last decades of the nineteenth century, more and more streets were paved, usually with wooden blocks, bricks, or asphalt; but paving could not keep up with the number of new thoroughfares the expanding cities were creating. By 1890, Chicago had paved only about 600 of its more than 2,000 miles of streets.

TRANSPORTATION PROBLEMS

But it was not simply the conditions of the streets that impeded urban transportation. It was the numbers of people who needed to move every day from one part of the city to another, numbers that mandated the development of mass transportation. Streetcars drawn on tracks by horses had been introduced into some cities even before the Civil War. But the horsecars were not fast enough, so many communities developed new forms of mass transit.

In 1870, New York opened its first elevated railway, whose noisy, filthy steam-powered trains moved rapidly above the city streets on massive iron structures. New York, Chicago, San Francisco, and other cities also experimented with cable cars, towed by continuously moving underground cables. Richmond, Virginia, introduced the

MASS TRANSIT

Discussion and Activities

Analyzing Visuals Have students examine the image "A Tenement Laundry." Ask them to identify details from the photo and discuss in pairs or small groups the challenges faced by poor families having to work from home. **SOC** **WXT**

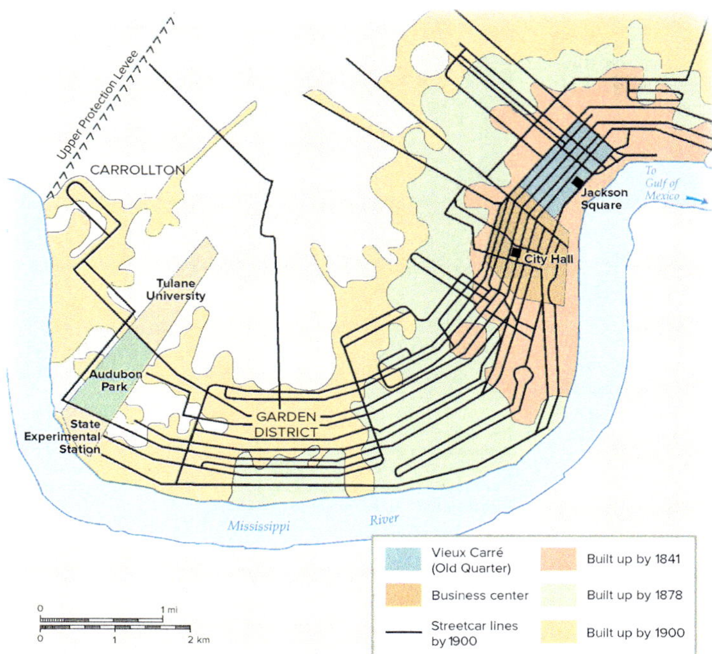

STREETCAR SUBURBS IN NINETEENTH-CENTURY NEW ORLEANS This map of streetcar lines in New Orleans reveals a pattern that repeated itself in many cities: changing residential patterns emerging in response to new forms of transportation. The map reveals the movement of population outward from the central city as streetcar lines emerged to make access to the downtown easier. Note the dramatic growth of residential suburbs in the last forty years of the nineteenth century in particular.

What other forms of mass transportation were emerging in American cities in these years?

Historical Thinking Skills

Analyzing Change Have students read the section "The 'Skyscraper'." Ask them to write a short paragraph explaining how this structure was different from earlier buildings. **Ask:** How do late nineteenth-century skyscrapers compare with modern skyscrapers? **WXT**

first electric trolley line in 1888, and by 1895 such systems were operating in 850 towns and cities. In 1897, Boston opened the first American subway when it put some of its trolley lines underground. At the same time, cities were developing new techniques of road and bridge building. One of the great technological marvels of the 1880s was the completion of the Brooklyn Bridge in New York City, a dramatic steel-cable suspension span designed by John A. Roebling.

The "Skyscraper"

Cities were growing upward as well as outward. Until the mid-nineteenth century, almost no buildings more than four or five stories high could be constructed. Construction techniques were such that it was difficult and expensive to build adequate structural supports for tall buildings. There was also a limit to the number of flights of stairs the users of buildings could be expected to climb. But by the 1850s, there had been successful experiments with machine-powered passenger elevators; and by the 1870s, new methods of construction using cast iron and steel beams made it easier to build tall buildings.

Not long after the Civil War, therefore, tall buildings began to appear in the major cities. The Equitable Building in New York City, completed in 1870 and rising seven and a half floors above the street, was one of the first in the nation to be built with an elevator. A few years later, even taller buildings of ten and twelve stories were appearing elsewhere in New York, in Chicago, and in other growing cities around the country. With each passing decade, the size and number of tall buildings increased until, by the 1890s, the term "skyscraper" became a popular description of them.

STRAINS OF URBAN LIFE

The increasing congestion of the cities and the absence of adequate public services produced many hazards. Crime, fire, disease, indigence, and pollution all placed strains on the capacities of metropolitan institutions, and both governments and private institutions were for a time poorly equipped to respond to them.

Fire and Disease

One serious problem was fires. In one major city after another, fires destroyed large downtown areas, where many buildings were still constructed of wood. Chicago and Boston suffered "great fires" in 1871. Other cities–among them Baltimore and San Francisco, where a tremendous earthquake produced a

Answers

Streetcar Suburbs in Nineteenth Century New Orleans

Other forms of mass transit were cable cars, elevated railroads, horse-drawn streetcars, and electric streetcars.

Historical Thinking Skills

Evaluating Evidence Have students read the section "Environmental Degradation." Ask them to create a T-chart listing the causes of environmental damage and the responses to that damage. Have students identify the example of each they think is most important. GEO WXT PCE

catastrophic fire in 1906—experienced similar disasters. The great fires were terrible and deadly experiences, but they also encouraged the construction of fireproof buildings and the development of professional fire departments. They also forced cities to rebuild at a time when new technological and architectural innovations were available. Some of the modern, high-rise downtowns of American cities arose out of the rubble of great fires.

DEVELOPMENT OF PROFESSIONAL FIRE DEPARTMENTS

Environmental Degradation

Modern notions of environmentalism were unknown to most Americans in the late nineteenth and early twentieth centuries. But the environmental degradation of many American cities was a visible and disturbing fact of life in those years. The frequency of great fires, the dangers of disease and plague, the extraordinary crowding of working-class neighborhoods were all examples of the environmental costs of industrialization and rapid urbanization.

Improper disposal of human and industrial waste was a common feature of almost all large cities in these years. Such practices contributed to the pollution of rivers and lakes and also, in many cases, to the compromising of the city's drinking water. This was particularly true in poor neighborhoods with primitive plumbing (and sometimes no indoor plumbing), outdoor privies that leaked into the groundwater, and overcrowded tenements. The presence of domestic animals—horses, which were the principal means of transportation until the late nineteenth century, but in poor neighborhoods also cows, pigs, and other animals—contributed as well to the environmental problems.

Air quality in many cities was poor as well. Few Americans had the severe problems that London experienced in these years with its perpetual "fogs" created by the debris from the burning of soft coal. But air pollution from factories and from stoves and furnaces in offices, homes, and other buildings was constant and at times severe. The incidence of respiratory infection and related diseases was much higher in cities than it was in nonurban areas, and it accelerated rapidly in the late nineteenth century.

AIR POLLUTION

By the early twentieth century, reformers were actively crusading to improve the environmental conditions of cities and were beginning to achieve some notable successes. By 1910, most large American cities had constructed sewage disposal systems, often at great cost, to protect the drinking water of their inhabitants and to prevent the great bacterial plagues that impure water had helped create in the past—such as the 1873 yellow fever epidemic in Memphis that killed more than 5,000 people.

Alice Hamilton, a physician who became an investigator for the U.S. Bureau of Labor, was a pioneer in the identification of pollution in the workplace. She documented ways in which improper disposal of such potentially dangerous substances as lead (she was one of the first physicians to identify lead poisoning), chemical waste, and ceramic dust was creating widespread sickness. And despite considerable resistance from many factory owners, she did bring such problems to public attention and, in some states at least, inspired legislation to require manufacturers to solve them. In 1912, the federal government created the Public Health Service, which was charged with preventing such occupational diseases as tuberculosis, anemia, and carbon dioxide poisoning, which were common in the garment industry and other trades. It attempted to create common health standards for all factories; but since the agency had few powers of enforcement, it had limited impact. It did, however, establish the protection of public health as a responsibility of the federal government and also helped bring to public attention the environmental forces that endangered health. The creation of the Occupational Health and Safety Administration in 1970, which gave government the authority to require employers to create safe and healthy workplaces, was a legacy of the Public Health Service's early work.

PUBLIC HEALTH SERVICE

THE GREAT FIRE IN CHICAGO This haunting photograph shows the intersection of State and Madison Streets, which Chicagoans liked to call "the world's busiest intersection," in the aftermath of the great fire of 1871. It destroyed much of the city's downtown. Horse-drawn streetcars are shown here traveling the ghostly, still smoke-filled streets. At left, posters advertise the new locations of displaced stores and offices—prompting the photographer to attach the optimistic title "Back in Business" to this image.

Urban Poverty

Above all, perhaps, the expansion of the cities created widespread and often desperate poverty. Despite the rapid growth of urban economies, the sheer number of new residents ensured that many people would be unable to earn enough for a decent subsistence.

Public agencies and private philanthropic organizations offered very limited relief. They were generally dominated by middle-class people, who tended to believe that too much assistance would breed dependency and that poverty was the fault of the poor themselves—a result of laziness or alcoholism

Historical Thinking Skills

Argumentation Have students examine the image "The Great Fire in Chicago." Have them discuss in pairs or small groups how the fire represented both a challenge and an opportunity for the city. Then have them write a short paragraph explaining their conclusions. WXT PCE or other kinds of irresponsibility. Most tried to restrict aid to the "deserving poor"–those who truly could not help themselves (at least according to the standards of the organizations themselves, which conducted elaborate "investigations" to separate the "deserving" from the "undeserving").

Other charitable societies–for example, the Salvation Army, which began operating in America in 1879, one year after it was founded in London–concentrated more on religious revivalism than on the relief of the homeless and hungry. Tensions often arose between native Protestant philanthropists and Catholic immigrants over religious doctrine and standards of morality.

SALVATION ARMY

Middle-class people grew particularly alarmed over the rising number of poor children in the cities, some of them orphans or runaways, living alone or in small groups scrounging for food. These "street arabs," as they were often called, attracted more attention from reformers than any other group–although that attention produced no serious solutions to their problems.

CRIME AND VIOLENCE

Poverty and crowding naturally bred crime and violence. Much of it was relatively minor, the work of pickpockets, con artists, swindlers, and petty thieves. But some was more dangerous. The American murder rate rose rapidly in the late nineteenth century (even as such rates were declining in Europe), from 25 murders for every million people in 1880 to over 100 by the end of the century–a rate slightly higher than the relatively high rates of the 1980s and 1990s. That reflected in part a very high level of violence in some nonurban areas: the American South, where rates of lynching and homicide were particularly high; and the West, where the rootlessness and instability of new communities (cow towns, mining camps, and the like) created much violence. But the cities contributed their share to the increase in crime as well. Native-born Americans liked to believe that crime was a result of the violent proclivities of immigrant groups, and they cited the rise of gangs and criminal organizations in various ethnic communities. But native-born Americans were as likely to commit crimes as immigrants.

HIGH CRIME RATES

The rising crime rates encouraged many cities to develop larger and more professional police forces. In the early nineteenth century, police forces had often been private and informal organizations; urban governments had resisted professionalized law enforcement. By the end of the century, however, professionalized public police departments were a part of the life of virtually every city and town. They worked closely with district attorneys and other public prosecutors, who were also becoming more numerous and more important in city life. Police forces themselves could also spawn corruption and brutality, particularly since jobs on them were often filled through political patronage. And complaints about police dealing differently with white and black suspects, or with rich and poor communities, were common in the late nineteenth century.

Some members of the middle class, fearful of urban insurrections, felt the need for even more substantial forms of protection. Urban national guard groups (many of them created and manned by middle-class elites) built imposing armories on the outskirts of affluent neighborhoods and stored large supplies of weapons and ammunition in preparation for uprisings that, in fact, never occurred.

THE MACHINE AND THE BOSS

Newly arrived immigrants, many of whom could not speak English, needed help in adjusting to American urban life: its laws, its customs, usually its language. Some ethnic communities created their own self-help organizations. But for many residents of the inner cities, the principal source of assistance was the political machine.

The urban machine was one of America's most distinctive political institutions. It owed its existence to the power vacuum that the chaotic growth of cities (and the very limited growth of city governments)

BOSS RULE

PUCK MAGAZINE *Puck* was the first successful humor magazine published in the United States. Issues were published from 1871 to 1918. It offered political cartoons, caricatures, and satire on the issues of the day. This cover takes on the graft and corruption of Tammany Hall.

Discussion and Activities

Contrasting After students have read the section "Urban Poverty," ask them to discuss as a class what might have been the distinction between the "deserving" and "undeserving" poor. *(The "deserving" poor would have included widows and orphans and possibly those incapable of work due to injuries or disease. The "undeserving" poor would have been most everyone else.)* **SOC** **WXT**

Discussion and Activities

Making Connections Have students read the section "Crime and Violence." Ask them to create a Venn diagram comparing the newly professionalized police forces of the late nineteenth century with the police today. **Ask:** What is the most notable similarity and the most notable difference? **SOC** **WXT** **PCE**

Historical Thinking Skills

Argumentation After students have read the section "Graft and Corruption," ask them to create a T-chart listing ways that boss rule benefited communities and ways in which it hurt communities. Have students write a thesis statement that supports, modifies, or refutes the statement, "Boss rule created more harm than benefits in late nineteenth-century American cities." **PCE** **SOC** **WXT**

had created. It was also a product of the potential voting power of large immigrant communities. Any politician who could mobilize that power stood to gain enormous influence, if not public office. And so there emerged a group of urban "bosses," themselves often of foreign birth or parentage. Many were Irish, because they spoke English and because some had acquired previous political experience from the long Irish struggle against the English at home. Almost all were men (in most states women could not yet vote). The principal function of the political boss was simple: to win votes for his organization. That meant winning the loyalty of his constituents. To do so, a boss might provide potential voters with occasional relief–baskets of groceries, bags of coal. He might step in to save those arrested for petty crimes from jail. He rewarded many of his followers with patronage: with jobs in city government or in such city agencies as the police (which the machine's elected officials often controlled); with jobs building or operating the new transit systems; and with opportunities to rise in the political organization itself.

Machines were also vehicles for making money. Politicians enriched themselves and their allies through various forms of graft and corruption. Some of it might be fairly open–what George Washington Plunkitt of New York City's Tammany Hall called "honest graft." For example, a politician might discover in advance where a new road or streetcar line was to be built, buy an interest in the land near it, and profit when the city had to buy the land from him or when property values rose as a result of the construction. But there was also covert graft: kickbacks from contractors in exchange for contracts to build streets, sewers, public buildings, and other projects; the sale of franchises for the operation of such public utilities as street railways, waterworks, and electric light and power systems. The most famously corrupt city boss was William M. Tweed, boss of New York City's Tammany Hall in the 1860s and 1870s, whose excesses finally landed him in jail in 1872.

GRAFT AND CORRUPTION

Middle-class critics saw the corrupt machines as blights on the cities and obstacles to progress. In fact, political organizations were often responsible not just for corruption, but also for modernizing city infrastructures, for expanding the role of government, and for creating stability in a political and social climate that otherwise would have lacked a center. The motives of the bosses may have been largely venal, but their achievements were sometimes greater than those of the scrupulous reformers who challenged them.

Several factors made boss rule possible. One was the power of immigrant voters, who were less concerned with middle-class ideas of political morality than with obtaining the services that machines provided and reformers did not. Another was the link between the political organizations and wealthy, prominent citizens who profited from their dealings with bosses. Still another was the structural weakness of city governments. The boss, by virtue of his control over his machine, formed an "invisible government" that provided an alternative to what was often the inadequacy of the regular government.

REASONS FOR BOSS RULE

The urban machine was not without competition. Reform groups frequently mobilized public outrage at the corruption of the bosses and often succeeded in driving machine politicians from office. Tammany, for example, saw its candidates for mayor and other high city offices lose almost as often as they won in the last decades of the nineteenth century. But the reform organizations typically lacked the permanence of the machine. Thus, many critics of machines began to argue for more-basic reforms: for structural changes in the nature of city government.

THE RISE OF MASS CONSUMPTION

For urban middle-class Americans, the last decades of the nineteenth century were a time of dramatic advances. The growth of the middle class partly stemmed from the need of industries and corporations for a wide range of employees, including managers and clerical workers. An expanding labor market also offered new opportunities for women in the workforce and growing access to education improved prospects for many employees, all of which contributed to the rise of a distinctive middle class. During those years, a middle-class culture began to exert a powerful influence over American life. Much of the rest of American society–the majority of the population, which was neither urban nor middle class–advanced less rapidly or not at all; but almost no one was unaffected by the rise of a new urban, consumer culture.

MIDDLE-CLASS CULTURE

PATTERNS OF INCOME AND CONSUMPTION

American industry could not have grown as it did without the expansion of markets. The growth of demand occurred at almost all levels of society, a result not just of the new techniques of production and mass distribution that were making consumer goods less expensive, but also of rising incomes.

Incomes in the industrial era were rising for almost everyone, although at highly uneven rates. The most conspicuous result of the new economy was the creation of vast fortunes. But more important for society as a whole were the growth and increasing prosperity of the middle class. The salaries of clerks, accountants, middle managers, and other "white-collar" workers rose on average by a third between 1890 and 1910–and in some parts of the middle class, salaries rose by much more. Doctors, lawyers, and other professionals, for example, experienced a particularly dramatic increase in the prestige and profitability of their professions.

RISING INCOME

Working-class incomes rose too in those years, although from a much lower base and considerably more slowly. Iron- and steelworkers, despite the setbacks their unions suffered, saw their hourly wages increase by a third between 1890 and 1910; but industries with large female, African American, or Mexican workforces–shoes, textiles, paper, laundries, many

Discussion and Activities

Historical Developments and Argumentation Have students read the section "Middle-Class Culture." Ask them to discuss in pairs or small groups what they believe the most important contributors to the expansion of the middle class might have been. *(Creation of new management positions; increasing access to education; greater opportunities for some women.)* **WXT** **SOC**

areas of commercial agriculture—saw very small increases, as did almost all industries in the South.

Also important to the new mass market were the development of affordable products and the creation of new merchandising techniques, which made many consumer goods available to a broad market for the first time. A good example of such changes was the emergence of ready-made clothing. In the early nineteenth century, most Americans had made their own clothing—usually from cloth they bought from merchants, at times from fabrics they spun and wove themselves. Affluent people contracted with private tailors to make their clothes. But the invention of the sewing machine and the spur that the Civil War (and its demand for uniforms) gave to the manufacture of clothing created an enormous industry devoted to producing ready-made garments. By the end of the century, almost all Americans bought their clothing from stores.

NEW MERCHANDISING TECHNIQUES

Partly as a result, much larger numbers of people became concerned with personal style. Interest in women's fashion, for example, had once been a luxury reserved for the affluent. Now middle-class and even working-class women could strive to develop a distinctive style of dress. New homes, even modest ones, now included clothes closets. Even people in remote rural areas could develop stylish wardrobes by ordering from the new mail-order houses.

Another example of the rise of the mass market was the way Americans bought and prepared food. The development and mass production of tin cans in the 1880s created a large new industry devoted to packaging and selling canned food and (as a result of the techniques Gail Borden, an inventor and politician, developed in the 1850s) condensed milk. Refrigerated railroad cars made it possible for perishables—meats, vegetables, dairy products, and other foodstuffs—to travel long distances without spoiling. The development of artificially frozen ice made it possible for many more households to afford iceboxes. Among other things, the changes meant improved diets and better health; life expectancy rose six years in the first two decades of the twentieth century.

DEPARTMENT STORES Department stores often created "events" to help promote sales of their many wares. Here, Strawbridge and Clothier department store creates quite a stir on Market Street in Philadelphia in 1907.

© Corbis

CHAIN STORES AND MAIL-ORDER HOUSES

Changes in marketing also altered the way Americans bought goods. Small local stores faced competition from new "chain stores." The Great Atlantic & Pacific Tea Company (A & P) began creating a national network of grocery stores as early as the 1850s and expanded it rapidly after the Civil War.

CHAIN STORES

F. W. Woolworth opened his first "Five and Ten Cent Store" in Utica, New York, in 1879 and went on to build a national chain of dry goods stores. Chain stores were able to sell manufactured goods at lower prices than the local, independent stores because the chains had so much more volume. From the beginning, the chains faced opposition from the established merchants they threatened to displace, and from others who feared that they would jeopardize the character of their communities. (Similar controversies have continued into the twenty-first century over the spread of large chains such as Wal-Mart and Barnes & Noble.) But most customers, however loyal they might feel to a local merchant, found it difficult to resist the greater variety and lower prices the chains provided them.

Chain stores were slow to reach remote, rural areas, which remained dependent on poorly stocked and often very expensive country stores. But rural people gradually gained access to the new consumer world through the great mail-order houses. In 1872, Montgomery Ward—a Chicago-based traveling salesman—distributed a catalog of consumer goods in association with the farmers' organization, the Grange. By the 1880s, he was offering thousands of items at low prices to farmers throughout the Midwest and beyond. He soon faced stiff competition from Sears Roebuck, first established by Richard Sears in Chicago in 1887. Together, the bulky catalogs from Ward and Sears changed the lives of many isolated people—introducing them to (and explaining for them) new trends of fashion and home decor as well as making available new tools, machinery, and technologies for the home.

SOCIAL CONSEQUENCES OF MAIL-ORDER CATALOGS

DEPARTMENT STORES

In larger cities, the emergence of great department stores (which had appeared earlier in Europe) helped transform buying habits and turn shopping into an alluring and glamorous activity. Marshall Field in Chicago created one of the

IMPACT OF THE DEPARTMENT STORE

Historical Thinking Skills

Argumentation After students have read the section "Patterns of Income and Consumption," ask them to create a poster advertising ready-made clothing or prepared food. Have them highlight in their posters the benefits of these consumer product. *(e.g., convenience; saving time)* **WXT** **SOC**

Discussion and Activities

Comparing and Contrasting Have students read the section "Chain Stores and Mail-Order Houses." Ask them to compare these retail outlets with the shopping experiences they have available to them today. Have students discuss as a class the greatest similarities and differences. **SOC** **WXT**

Discussion and Activities

Making Connections After students have read the section "Department Stores," ask them to go online to find a definition of "economies of scale." Have students discuss as a class how retailers today attempt to take advantage of the same principle. **WXT**

first American department stores, and others soon followed: Macy's in New York City, Abraham and Straus in Brooklyn, Jordan Marsh and Filene's in Boston, Wanamaker's in Philadelphia.

Department stores transformed the concept of shopping in several ways. First, they brought together under one roof an enormous array of products that had previously been sold in separate shops. Second, they sought to create an atmosphere of wonder and excitement, to make shopping a glamorous activity. Department stores were elaborately decorated to suggest great luxury and elegance. They included restaurants and tearooms and comfortable lounges, to suggest that shopping could be a social event as well as a practical necessity. They hired well-dressed salesclerks, mostly women, to provide attentive service to their mostly female customers. Third, department stores—like mail-order houses—took advantage of economies of scale to sell merchandise at lower prices than many of the individual shops with which they competed.

Women as Consumers

The rise of mass consumption had particularly dramatic effects on American women. Women's clothing styles changed much more rapidly and dramatically than men's, which encouraged frequent purchases. Women generally bought and prepared food for their families, so the availability of new food products changed not only the way everyone ate, but also the way women shopped and cooked.

The consumer economy produced new employment opportunities for women as salesclerks in department stores and as waitresses in the rapidly proliferating restaurants. And it spawned the creation of a new movement in which women were to play a vital role: the consumer protection movement. The National Consumers League, formed in the 1890s under the leadership of Florence Kelley, a prominent social reformer, attempted to mobilize the power of women as consumers to force retailers and manufacturers to improve wages and working conditions for women workers. By defining themselves as consumers, many middle-class women were able to find a stance from which they could become active participants in public life. Indeed, the mobilization of women behind consumer causes—and eventually many other causes—was one of the most important political developments of the late nineteenth century.

National Consumers League

Leisure in the Consumer Society

Closely related to the growth of consumption was an increasing interest in leisure, in part because time away from work was expanding rapidly for many people. Members of the urban middle and professional classes had increasingly large blocks of time in which they were not at work—evenings, weekends, even vacations (previously almost unknown among salaried workers). Working hours in many factories declined, from an average of nearly seventy hours a week in 1860 to under sixty in 1900. Industrial workers might still be on the job six days a week, but many of them had more time off in the evenings. Even farmers found that the mechanization of agriculture gave them more free time. The lives of many Americans were becoming compartmentalized, with clear distinctions between work and leisure.

Redefining Leisure

The growth of free time produced a redefinition of the idea of "leisure." In earlier eras, relatively few Americans had considered leisure a valuable thing. On the contrary, many equated it with laziness or sloth. "Rest," as in the relative inactivity many Americans considered appropriate for the Sabbath, was valued because it offered time for spiritual reflection and prepared people for work. But leisure—time spent amusing oneself in nonproductive pursuits—was not only unavailable to most Americans, but faintly scorned as well.

New Conceptions of Leisure

But with the rapid expansion of the economy and the increasing number of hours workers had away from work, it became possible to imagine leisure time as a normal part of the lives of many people. Industrial workers, in pursuit of shorter hours, adopted the slogan "Eight hours for work, eight hours for rest, and eight hours for what we will." Others were equally adamant in claiming that leisure time was both a right and an important contribution to an individual's emotional and even spiritual health.

The economist Simon Patten was one of the first intellectuals to articulate this new view of leisure, which he tied closely to the rising interest in consumption. Patten, in *The Theory of Prosperity* (1902), *The New Basis of Civilization* (1910), and other works, challenged the centuries-old assumption that the normal condition of civilization was a scarcity of goods. "We are now in the transition stage," he wrote, "from this pain economy [the economy of scarcity] to a pleasure economy." The principal goal of such an economy, he claimed, "should be an abundance of goods and the pursuit of pleasure."

Simon Patten

As Americans became more accustomed to leisure as a normal part of their lives, they began to look for new experiences with which to entertain themselves. Entertainment usually meant "going out," spending leisure time in public places where there would be not only entertainment, but also other people. Thousands of working-class New Yorkers flocked to the amusement park at Coney Island, for example, not just for the rides and shows, but for the excitement of the crowds as well. So did the thousands who spent evenings in dance halls, vaudeville houses, and concert halls. Affluent New Yorkers enjoyed afternoons in Central Park, where a principal attraction was seeing other people (and being seen by them). Moviegoers were attracted not just by the movies themselves, but also by the energy of the audiences at the lavish "movie palaces" that

Public Leisure

Discussion and Activities

Analyzing Points of View Have students read the section "Women as Consumers." Ask them to write a short journal entry from the point of view of a wife or mother describing how the rise of mass consumption impacted her role as manager of the household. **SOC** **WXT**

began to appear in cities in the early twentieth century, just as sports fans were drawn by the crowds as well as by the games.

Mass entertainment did not always bridge differences of class, race, or gender. Saloons and most sporting events tended to be male preserves. Shopping (itself becoming a valued leisure-time activity) and going to tearooms and luncheonettes were more characteristic of female leisure. Theaters, pubs, and clubs were often specific to particular ethnic communities or particular work groups. There were, in fact, relatively few places where people of widely diverse backgrounds gathered together.

When the classes did meet in public spaces–as they did, for example, in city parks–there was often conflict over what constituted appropriate public behavior. Elites in New York City, for example, tried to prohibit anything but quiet, "genteel" activities in Central Park, while working-class people wanted to use the public spaces for sports and entertainments. But even divided by class, ethnicity, and gender, leisure and popular entertainment did help sustain a vigorous public culture.

SPECTATOR SPORTS

The search for forms of public leisure hastened the rise of organized spectator sports, especially baseball, which by the end of the century was well on its way to becoming the national pastime. A game much like baseball, known as "rounders" and derived from cricket, had enjoyed limited popularity in Great Britain in the early nineteenth century. Versions of the game began to appear in America in the early 1830s, well before Abner Doubleday supposedly "invented" baseball. (Doubleday, in fact, had little to do with the creation of baseball and actually cared little for sports. Alexander Cartwright, a member of a New York City baseball club in the 1840s, defined many of the rules and features of the game as we know it today.)

By the end of the Civil War, interest in baseball had grown rapidly. More than 200 amateur or semiprofessional teams or clubs existed, many of which joined a national association and agreed on standard rules. The first salaried team, the Cincinnati Red Stockings, was formed in 1869. Other cities soon fielded professional teams, and in 1876, at the urging of Albert Spalding, they banded together in the National League. A rival league, the American Association, soon appeared. It eventually collapsed, but in 1901 the American League emerged to replace it. In 1903, the first modern World Series was played, in which the American League Boston Red Sox beat the National League Pittsburgh Pirates. By then, baseball had become an important business and a great national preoccupation (at least among men), attracting paying crowds in the thousands.

MAJOR LEAGUE BASEBALL

The second most popular game, football, appealed at first to an elite segment of the male population, in part because it originated in colleges and universities. The first intercollegiate football game in America occurred between Princeton and Rutgers in 1869, and soon the game became entrenched as part of collegiate life. Early intercollegiate football bore only an indirect relation to the modern game; it was more similar to what is now known as rugby. By the late 1870s, however, the game was becoming standardized and was taking on the outlines of its modern form.

As college football grew in popularity, it spread to other sections of the country, notably to the midwestern state universities, which were destined soon to replace the eastern schools as the great powers of the game. It also began to exhibit the taints of professionalism that have marked it ever

GROWTH OF COLLEGE FOOTBALL

THE AMERICAN NATIONAL GAME Long before the modern major leagues began, local baseball clubs were active throughout much of the United States, establishing the game as the "national pastime." This print of a "grand match for the championship" depicts an 1866 game at Elysian Fields, a popular park just across the river from New York City in Hoboken, New Jersey.

Discussion and Activities

Analyzing Issues After students have read the section "Redefining Leisure," ask them to valid a T-chart that lists ways that leisure activities like sports, parks, and concerts either brought people together or divided them. Have students write a short paragraph summarizing which conclusion seems most valid. **SOC**

Discussion and Activities

Comparing and Contrasting Have students examine the image "The American National Game." Ask them to list details from the image and discuss in small groups how the nineteenth-century version of baseball is similar to and different from modern baseball. *(Similar: layout of the field; positioning of players; the wearing of uniforms. The game continues to revolve around pitching and hitting. Different: modern professional baseball is played in large stadiums with seating for fans, fences, and concession stands.)* **SOC**

AP Exam Tip

The AP Exam requires students to analyze the sourcing and situation of primary and secondary sources. One way students can accomplish that is by explaining the intended audience of a document.

Historical Thinking Skills

Sourcing and Situation Have students practice the tip by examining the image "Postcard from Luna Park" and writing a short paragraph explaining who the target audience was for the postcard. *(Primarily residents of the area who might be persuaded to go to Coney Island for entertainment.)*

PATTERNS OF POPULAR CULTURE

CONEY ISLAND

People who lived in the crowded cities of early-twentieth-century America yearned at times for ways to escape the noise, smells, heat, and stress of the urban world. Wealthy families could travel to resorts or country houses. But most city dwellers could not afford to venture far, and for them ambitious entrepreneurs tried to provide dazzling escapes close to home. The most celebrated such escape was Coney Island in Brooklyn, New York—which became for a time the most famous and popular urban resort in America.

With its broad oceanfront beach, Coney Island, located in Brooklyn, had been an attractive destination for visitors since the early nineteenth century. In the 1870s and 1880s, investors built railroad lines from the city to the beach and began to create spectacular amusements to induce New Yorkers to visit. But the real success of Coney Island began in the 1890s, when the amusements and spectacles reached a new level. Sea Lion Park, which opened in 1895, showcased trained sea lions and exotic water rides. Steeplechase Park opened two years later, attracting visitors with a mechanical steeplechase ride in which visitors could pretend to be jockeys, and stunt rooms with moving floors and powerful blasts of compressed air.

By then, Coney Island was a popular site for real horse racing, boxing matches, and other sports. It was also attracting gambling casinos, saloons, and brothels. From the beginning, among affluent middle-class people at least, Coney Island had a reputation as a rough and unsavory place. But to the working-class immigrants and lower-middle-class people, it was a place of wonder, excitement, and escape.

The greatest Coney Island attraction, Luna Park, opened in 1903. It provided not just rides and stunts, but lavish reproductions of exotic places and spectacular adventures: Japanese gardens, Venetian canals with gondoliers, a Chinese theater, a simulated trip to the moon, and reenactments of such disasters as burning buildings, earthquakes, and even the volcanic eruption that destroyed Pompeii. A year later, a competing company opened Dreamland, which tried to outdo even Luna Park with a 375-foot tower, a three-ring circus, chariot races, and a Lilliputian village inspired by *Gulliver's Travels*. (A fire destroyed Dreamland in 1911.)

The popularity of Coney Island in these years was phenomenal. Thousands of people flocked to the large resort hotels that lined the beaches. Many thousands

POSTCARD FROM LUNA PARK Visitors to Coney Island sent postcards to friends and relatives by the millions, and those cards were among the most effective promotional devices for the amusement parks. This one shows the brightly lit entrance to Luna Park, Coney Island's most popular attraction for many years.

THE ELEPHANT HOTEL One of the early attractions of Coney Island as it became a popular resort was this hotel, built inside a large wooden elephant. This picture, taken in 1890, shows Coney Island at a point when development was still relatively modest.

more made day trips out from the city by train and (after 1920) subway. In 1904, the average daily attendance at Luna Park alone was 90,000 people. On weekends, the Coney Island post office handled over 250,000 postcards, through which visitors helped spread the reputation of the resort across the nation.

Coney Island's popularity reflected a number of powerful impulses among urban Americans at the turn of the century. It provided visitors with an escape from the heat and crowding of the vast metropolis around it. It gave people who had few opportunities for travel a simulated glimpse of exotic places and events that they would never be able to experience in reality. For immigrants, many of whom lived in insular ethnic communities, Coney Island provided a way of experiencing American mass culture on an equal footing with people of backgrounds different from their own. Almost everyone who found Coney Island appealing did so in part because it provided an escape from the genteel standards of behavior that governed so much of American life at the time. In the amusement parks of Coney Island, people delighted in finding themselves in situations that in any other setting would have seemed embarrassing or improper: women's skirts blown above their heads with hot air; people pummeled with water and rubber paddles by clowns; hints of sexual freedom as strangers were forced to come into physical contact with one another on rides and amusements and as men and women revealed themselves to each other wearing bathing suits on the beach.

Discussion and Activities

Evaluating Have students examine the image "The Elephant Hotel." Ask them to write a short letter to a friend from the point of view of a customer of the hotel describing the experience of staying in this novel structure. Have students consider what the outer shape of the structure might mean for the shape and size of the guest rooms and accessibility from the ground level. **SOC**

LUNA PARK Luna Park opened in 1903 and immediately began attracting crowds eager to experience a variety of rides and visit reproductions of exotic locations.

Coney Island remained popular throughout the first half of the twentieth century, and it continues to attract visitors today (although in much smaller numbers). But its heyday was in the years before World War I, when the exotic sights and thrilling adventures it offered had almost no counterparts elsewhere in American culture. When radio, movies, and eventually television began to offer their own kind of mass escapism, Coney Island gradually ceased to be the dazzling, unmatchable marvel it had seemed to earlier generations.

HISTORICAL THINKING SKILLS

1. **Determining Context** How did Coney Island reflect the new culture of mass consumption?
2. **Explaining Historical Context** What new ideas about leisure help account for the popularity of Coney Island in the early twentieth century?
3. **Making Connections** What forms of popular culture today continue the Coney Island tradition of offering escapism, adventure, and excitement to a mass audience?

since. Some schools used "ringers," tramp athletes who were not even registered as students. In an effort to eliminate such abuses, Amos Alonzo Stagg, athletic director and coach at the University of Chicago, led in forming the Western Conference, or Big Ten, in 1896, which established rules governing eligibility.

Football also became known for a high level of violence on the field; eighteen college students died of football-related injuries and over a hundred were seriously hurt in 1905. The carnage prompted a White House conference on organized sports convened by President Theodore Roosevelt. As a result of its deliberations, a new intercollegiate association (which in 1910 became known as the National College Athletic Association, the NCAA) revised the rules and the required equipment of the game in an effort to make it more honest and safer.

Other popular spectator sports were emerging at about the same time. Basketball was invented in 1891 at Springfield, Massachusetts, by Dr. James A. Naismith, a Canadian working as athletic director for a local college. Boxing, which had long been a disreputable activity concentrated primarily among the urban working classes, had become by the 1880s a more popular and in some places more reputable sport, particularly after the adoption of the Marquis of Queensberry rules (by which fighters wore padded gloves and fought in three-minute rounds). The first modern boxing hero, John L. Sullivan, became heavyweight champion of the world in 1882. Even so, boxing remained illegal in some states until after World War I. Horse racing, popular since colonial times, became increasingly commercialized with the construction of large tracks and the establishment of large-purse races such as the Kentucky Derby.

GAMBLING AND SPORTS

Even in their infancy, spectator sports were closely associated with gambling. There was elaborate betting—some of it organized by underground gambling syndicates—on baseball and football almost from the start. One of the most famous incidents in the history of baseball was the alleged "throwing" of the 1919 World Series by the Chicago White Sox because of gambling (an incident that became known as the "Black Sox Scandal"). That event resulted in the banning of some of the game's most notable figures from the sport for life and the establishment of the office of commissioner of baseball to "clean up" the game. Boxing was troubled throughout its history by the influence of gambling and the frequent efforts of managers to "fix" fights in the interests of bettors. Horse racing as it became commercialized was openly organized around betting, with the race tracks themselves establishing odds and taking bets.

The rise of spectator sports and gambling was largely a response to the desire of men to create a distinctively male culture in cities. But not all sports were the province of men. A number of sports were emerging in which women became important participants. Golf and tennis seldom attracted crowds in the late nineteenth century, but both experienced a rapid increase in participation among relatively wealthy men and women. Bicycling and croquet also enjoyed widespread popularity in the 1890s among women as well as men. Women's colleges were beginning to introduce their students to strenuous sports as well—track, crew, swimming, and

AP Exam Practice

Short Answer Provide students with the following short-answer questions and allow 15 minutes for completion. Ask for volunteers to share their responses and discuss as a class.

Answer A, B, and C.

A) Briefly explain ONE new form of entertainment that became popular in the late nineteenth century. *(Baseball, football, amusement parks, etc.)*

B) Briefly explain ONE existing form of entertainment at the time that remained popular into the late nineteenth century. *(Horse racing, theater, music halls, etc.)*

C) Briefly explain ONE reason for the rise of new forms of entertainment. *(Increasing amount of leisure time for many; rising incomes for many.)*

Answers

Patterns of Popular Culture

1. Possible answer: It provided an avenue of escape, where everyone could find something to do. It provided people with a space to escape the noise, smells, heat, and stress of the city. Rides, games, shows, etc., provided the urban city resident a place to go and have fun for a day.
2. Possible answer: Industrialization provided more leisure time for city dwellers, and places like Coney Island provided the escapism that many of these individuals desired with the free time they now had. Wealthy individuals could escape the city, but middle-class and working-class people (as well as the poor) could also go to Coney Island during their leisure time.
3. Possible answer: Places like Six Flags, Sea World, Disney Land, etc., provide the same opportunities for escapism for contemporary Americans as Coney Island provided in the first half of the twentieth century.

Reasoning Processes

Comparing After students have read the section "Gambling and Sports," ask them to create a T-chart listing sports that were commonly participated in by men and women. Have students discuss in pairs or small groups how the lists are similar or different. **Ask:** What do you think accounts for the differences? **SOC**

(beginning in the late 1890s) basketball—challenging the once prevalent notion that vigorous exercise was dangerous to women.

MUSIC AND THEATER

Many ethnic communities maintained their own theaters, in which immigrants listened to the music of their homelands and heard comedians making light of their experiences in the New World. Italian theaters often drew on the traditions of Italian opera to create sentimental musical events. The Yiddish theater built on the experiences of American Jewish people—and was the training ground for a remarkable group of musicians and playwrights who later went on to play a major role in mainstream, English-speaking theater.

ETHNIC THEATER

Urban theaters also introduced one of the most distinctively American entertainment forms: the musical comedy, which evolved gradually from the comic operettas of European theater. George M. Cohan, an Irish vaudeville entertainer, became the first great creator of musical comedies in the early twentieth century; in the process of creating his many shows, he wrote a series of patriotic songs—"Yankee Doodle Dandy," "Over There," and "You're a Grand Old Flag"—that remained popular many decades later. Irving Berlin, a veteran of the Yiddish theater, wrote more than 1,000 songs for the musical theater during his long career, including such popular favorites as "Alexander's Ragtime Band" and "God Bless America."

Vaudeville, a form of theater adapted from French models, was the most popular urban entertainment in the first decades of the twentieth century. Even saloons and small community theaters could afford to offer their customers vaudeville, which consisted of a variety of acts (musicians, comedians, magicians, jugglers, and others) and was, at least in the beginning, inexpensive to produce. As the economic potential of vaudeville grew, some promoters—most prominently Florenz Ziegfeld of New York—staged much more elaborate spectacles. Vaudeville was also one of the few entertainment media open to African American performers. They brought to it elements of the minstrel shows they had earlier developed for African American audiences in the late nineteenth century.

VAUDEVILLE

THE MOVIES

The most important form of mass entertainment (until the invention of radio and television) was the movies. Thomas Edison and others had created the technology of the motion picture in the 1880s. Not long after, short films became available to individual viewers through "peep shows" in pool halls, penny arcades, and amusement parks. Soon larger projectors made it possible to project the images onto big screens, which permitted substantial audiences to see films in theaters.

By 1900, Americans were becoming attracted in large numbers to these early movies—usually plotless films of trains or waterfalls or other spectacles designed mainly to show off the technology. D. W. Griffith carried the motion picture into a new era with his silent epics—*The Birth of a Nation* (1915), *Intolerance* (1916), and others—which introduced serious plots and elaborate productions to filmmaking. Some of these films—most notably *The Birth of a Nation*, with its celebration of the

THE BIRTH OF A NATION

THE FLORADORA SEXTET The Floradora Sextet was a popular vocal group of the late nineteenth and early twentieth centuries and became fixtures on the vaudeville and burlesque stages of many cities and resorts. They are shown here in an elaborately costumed production number at the famous Weber and Fields Music Hall in New York City, which opened in 1896.

Bettmann/Getty Images

Historical Thinking Skills

Contextualization Have students read the section "Music and Theater." Ask them to create a poster advertising a musical comedy or vaudeville show. **SOC** **ARC**

Ku Klux Klan and its demeaning portraits of African Americans—also contained notoriously racist messages, an indication, among other things, that the audiences for these early films were overwhelmingly white. Nevertheless, motion pictures were the first truly mass entertainment medium, reaching all areas of the country and almost all groups in the population.

A NICKELODEON Before the rise of the great movie palaces, urban families flocked to "nickelodeons," small theaters that charged five cents for admission and showed many different films each day, including serials—dramas that drew audiences back into theaters day after day with new episodes of a running story.

Working-Class Leisure

Leisure had a particular importance to working-class men and women—in part because it was a relatively new part of their lives and in part because it stood in such sharp contrast to the grueling environments in which many industrial workers labored. More than most other groups in society, workers spent their leisure time on the streets—walking alone or in groups, watching street entertainers, meeting friends, talking and joking. For people with time but little money, the life of the street was an appealing source of camaraderie and energy.

Another important setting for the leisure time of working-class men was the neighborhood saloon, which became a place where a worker could be sure of encountering a regular circle of friends. Saloons were often ethnically specific, in part because they served particular neighborhoods dominated by particular national groups. They also became political centers. Saloonkeepers were especially important figures in urban political machines, largely because they had regular contact with so many men in a neighborhood. When the Anti-Saloon League and other temperance organizations attacked the saloon, one of the reasons they cited was that eliminating saloons would weaken political machines. Opponents also noted correctly that saloons were sometimes places of crime, violence, and prostitution—an entryway into the dark underworld of urban life.

Importance of the Saloon

Boxing was a particularly popular sport among working-class men. Many workers could not afford to attend the great public boxing matches pairing such popular heroes as John L. Sullivan and "Gentleman Jim" Corbett. But there were less glittering boxing matches in small rings and even in saloons—bare-knuckled fights organized by ethnic clubs and other groups that gave men an opportunity to demonstrate their strength and courage, something that the working world did not always provide them.

The Fourth of July

The Fourth of July played a large role in the lives of many working-class Americans. That was in part because in an age of six-day (and sometimes seven-day) workweeks and before regular vacations, it was for many decades one of the few full days of leisure—other than the Sabbath, during which activities were often restricted by law—that many workers had. Fourth of July celebrations were one of the highlights of the year in many ethnic, working-class communities. In Worcester, Massachusetts, for example, the Ancient Order of Hibernians (an Irish organization) sponsored boisterous picnics for the Irish working class of the city. Competing with them were Irish temperance organizations, which offered more sober and "respectable" entertainments to those relatively few workers who wished to avoid the heavy drinking at the Hibernian affairs. Other ethnic groups organized their own Fourth of July events—picnics, games, parades—making the day a celebration not just of the nation's independence, but of the cultures of immigrant communities. The city's affluent middle class, in the meantime, tended to stay away, remaining indoors or organizing family picnics at resort areas outside the city.

Importance of the Fourth of July

Mass Communications

Urban industrial society created a vast market for new methods of transmitting news and information. Between 1870 and 1910, the circulation of daily newspapers increased nearly ninefold (from under 3 million to more than 24 million), a rate three times as great as the rate of population increase. And while standards varied widely from one paper to another, American journalism began to develop the beginnings of a professional identity. Salaries of reporters increased; many newspapers began separating the reporting of news from the expression of opinion; and newspapers themselves became important businesses.

One striking change was the emergence of national press services, which made use of the telegraph to supply news and features to papers throughout the country and which contributed as a result to the standardization of the product. By the turn of the century, important newspaper chains had emerged as well. The most powerful was William Randolph Hearst's,

Discussion and Activities

Analyzing Issues After students have read the section "The Movies," ask them to create a T-chart listing ways that movies drew audiences together or divided them. Have students discuss in small groups whether they think that late nineteenth-century movies more greatly promoted unity or division. **SOC** **ARC**

Discussion and Activities

Making Connections Have students read the section "The Fourth of July." Ask them to write a short paragraph explaining how the late nineteenth-century celebration of the holiday is similar to or different from recent celebrations in their community. **SOC** **NAT**

Reasoning Processes

Continuity and Change After students have read the section "Mass Communications," ask them to write a short paragraph explaining how newspapers changed in the late nineteenth century. **SOC** **ARC** **WXT**

which by 1914 controlled nine newspapers and two magazines. Hearst and rival publisher Joseph Pulitzer helped popularize what became known as "yellow journalism"—a deliberately sensational, often lurid style of reporting presented in bold graphics, designed to reach a mass audience. Another major change occurred in the nature of American magazines. Beginning in the 1880s, new kinds of magazines appeared that were designed for a mass audience. One of the pioneers was Edward W. Bok, who took over the *Ladies' Home Journal* in 1899 and, by targeting a mass female audience, built its circulation to over 700,000.

EMERGENCE OF NEWSPAPER CHAINS

HIGH CULTURE IN THE AGE OF THE CITY

In addition to the important changes in popular culture that accompanied the rise of cities and industry, there were profound changes in the realm of "high culture"—in the ideas and activities of intellectuals and elites. Even the notion of a distinction between "highbrow" and "lowbrow" culture was relatively new to the industrial era. In the early nineteenth century, many cultural activities attracted people of widely varying backgrounds and targeted people of all classes. By the late nineteenth century, however, elites were developing a cultural and intellectual life quite separate from the popular amusements of the urban masses.

THE LITERATURE OF URBAN AMERICA

Some writers and artists—the local-color writers of the South, for example, and Mark Twain, in such novels as *Huckleberry Finn* and *Tom Sawyer*—responded to the new industrial civilization by evoking an older, more natural world. But others grappled directly with the modern order.

One of the strongest impulses in late-nineteenth- and early-twentieth-century American literature was the effort to re-create urban social reality. This trend toward realism found an early voice in Stephen Crane, who—although best known for his novel of the Civil War, *The Red Badge of Courage* (1895)—was the author of an earlier, powerful indictment of the plight of the working class. Crane created a sensation in 1893 when he published *Maggie: A Girl of the Streets*, a grim picture of urban poverty and slum life. Theodore Dreiser was even more influential in encouraging writers to abandon the genteel traditions of earlier times and turn to the social dislocations and injustices of the present. He did so both in *Sister Carrie* and in other, later novels (including *An American Tragedy*, published in 1925).

SOCIAL REALISM

Many of Dreiser's contemporaries followed him in chronicling the oppression of America's poor. In 1901 Frank Norris published *The Octopus*, an account of a struggle between oppressed wheat farmers and powerful railroad interests in California. The socialist writer Upton Sinclair published *The Jungle* in 1906, a novel designed to reveal the depravity of capitalism. It exposed abuses in the American meatpacking industry; and while it did not inspire the kind of socialist response for which Sinclair had hoped, it did help produce legislative action to deal with the problem. Kate Chopin, a Southern writer who explored the oppressive features of traditional marriage, encountered widespread public abuse after publication of her shocking novel *The Awakening* in 1899. It described a young wife and mother who abandons her family in search of personal fulfillment. It was formally banned in some communities. William Dean Howells, in *The Rise of Silas Lapham* (1884) and other works, described what he considered the shallowness and corruption in the search for wealth.

Other critics of American society responded to the new civilization not by attacking it but by withdrawing from it. The historian Henry Adams published a classic autobiography in 1906, *The Education of Henry Adams*, in which he portrayed himself as a man disillusioned with and unable to relate to his society, even though he continued to live in it. The novelist Henry James lived the major part of his adult life in England and Europe and produced a series of coldly realistic novels—*The American* (1877), *Portrait of a Lady* (1881), *The Ambassadors* (1903), and others—that showed his ambivalence about the character of modern, industrial civilization.

The growing popularity of literature helped spawn a remarkable network of clubs, mostly formed and populated by women, to bring readers together to talk about books. Reading clubs proliferated rapidly in cities and even small towns, among African American as well as white women. They made literature a social experience for hundreds of thousands of women and created a tradition that has continued into the twenty-first century.

ART IN THE AGE OF THE CITY

American art through most of the nineteenth century had been overshadowed by the art of Europe. Many American artists studied and even lived in Europe. But others broke from the Old World traditions and experimented with new styles. Winslow Homer was vigorously American in his paintings of New England maritime life and other native subjects. James McNeil Whistler was one of the first Western artists to appreciate the beauty of Japanese color prints and to introduce Oriental concepts into American and European art.

By the first years of the new century, some American artists were turning decisively away from the traditional academic style, a style perhaps best exemplified in America by the brilliant portraitist John Singer Sargent. Instead, many younger painters were exploring the same grim aspects of modern life that were becoming the subject of American literature. Members of the so-called Ashcan school produced work startling in its naturalism and stark in its portrayal of the social realities of the era. John Sloan portrayed the dreariness of American urban slums; George

ASHCAN SCHOOL

Historical Thinking Skills

Historical Reasoning and Argumentation Have students read the section "The Literature of Urban America." Ask them to discuss as a class ways in which literature offered a critique of late nineteenth-century American life. *(Indictment of industrial oppression; the shallowness of consumerism; rejection of traditional roles and expectations.)* Have students discuss what medium or media would most likely be used for those sorts of critiques today. **ARC** **SOC** **PCE** **WXT**

Discussion and Activities

Evaluating Evidence After students have read the section "Art in the Age of the City," ask them to go online to find examples of Ashcan School paintings. Have students choose one painting, and ask for volunteers to explain to the class how it fits the genre of modernism. **ARC**

Bellows caught the vigor and violence of his time in paintings and drawings of prize fights; Edward Hopper explored the starkness and loneliness of the modern city. The Ashcan artists were also among the first Americans to appreciate expressionism and abstraction; and they showed their interest in new forms in 1913 when they helped stage the famous and controversial Armory Show in New York City, which displayed works of the French Postimpressionists and of some American moderns.

The work of these and other artists marked the beginning in America of an artistic movement known as modernism, a movement that had counterparts in many other areas of cultural and intellectual life as well. Rejecting the heavy reliance on established forms that characterized the "genteel tradition" of the nineteenth-century art world, modernists rejected the grip of the past and embraced new subjects and new forms. Where the genteel tradition emphasized the "dignified" and "elevated" aspects of civilization (and glorified the achievements of gifted elites), modernism gloried in the ordinary, even the coarse. Where the genteel tradition placed great importance on respect for the past and the maintenance of "standards," modernism looked to the future and gloried in the new. Eventually, modernism developed strict orthodoxies of its own. But in its early stages, it seemed to promise an escape from rigid, formal traditions and an unleashing of individual creativity.

ON THE STEPS This painting is by George Luks (1867–1933), an American artist who belonged to the so-called Ashcan school. Luks and others revolted against what they considered the sterile formalism of academic painting and chose instead to portray realistic scenes of ordinary life. In 1913 they stirred the art world with a startling exhibition in New York, known as the Armory Show. In it they displayed not only their own work (which was relatively conventional in technique, even if sometimes daring in its choice of subjects), but also the work of innovative European artists, who were already beginning to explore wholly new artistic forms.

THE IMPACT OF DARWINISM

The single most profound intellectual development in the late nineteenth century was the widespread acceptance of the theory of evolution, associated most prominently with the English naturalist Charles Darwin. Darwinism argued that the human species had evolved from earlier forms of life (and most recently from simian creatures similar to apes) through a process of "natural selection." It challenged the biblical story of the Creation and almost every other tenet of traditional American religious faith. History, Darwinism suggested, was not the working out of a divine plan, as most Americans had always believed. It was a random process dominated by the fiercest or luckiest competitors.

"NATURAL SELECTION"

The theory of evolution met widespread resistance at first from educators, theologians, and even many scientists. By the end of the century, however, the evolutionists had converted most members of the urban professional and educated classes. Even many middle-class Protestant religious leaders had accepted the doctrine, making significant alterations in theology to accommodate it. Evolution had become enshrined in schools and universities; few serious scientists any longer questioned its basic validity.

Unseen by most urban Americans at the time, however, the rise of Darwinism was contributing to a deep schism between the new, cosmopolitan culture of the city—which was receptive to new ideas such as evolution—and a traditional, provincial culture located mainly (although not wholly) in rural areas—which remained wedded to fundamentalist religious beliefs and older values. Thus the late nineteenth century saw not only the rise of a liberal Protestantism in tune with new scientific discoveries but also the beginning of an organized Protestant fundamentalism, rejecting evolution, which would make its presence felt politically in the 1920s and again in the late twentieth century and beyond.

Darwinism helped spawn other new intellectual currents. There was the Social Darwinism of William Graham Sumner and others, which industrialists used so enthusiastically to justify their favored position in American life. But there were also more sophisticated philosophies, among them a doctrine that became known as "pragmatism," which seemed peculiarly a product of

"PRAGMATISM"

Discussion and Activities

Analyzing Visuals Have students examine the image "On the Steps." Ask them to write a short journal entry from the point of view of a passerby observing the scene, describing one of the people portrayed in the painting. **ARC** **SOC**

Discussion and Activities

Analyzing Significance After students have read the section "The Impact of Darwinism," ask them to create a list of the impacts of Darwin's Theory of Evolution. *(Social Darwinism; anti-evolution backlash; pragmatism; discussion of anthropology.)* Have students discuss in pairs or small groups which impact they believe was the most important, and why. **ARC** **SOC**

DEMPSEY AND FIRPO The artist George Bellows began painting fight scenes in the first years of the twentieth century, when boxing appealed primarily to working-class urban communities. By 1924, when he painted this view of the Dempsey-Firpo fight, prizefighting had become one of the most popular sports in America.

America's changing material civilization. William James, a Harvard psychologist (and brother of the novelist Henry James), was the most prominent publicist of the new theory, although earlier intellectuals such as Charles S. Peirce and later ones such as John Dewey were also important to its development and dissemination. According to the pragmatists, modern society should rely for guidance not on inherited ideals and moral principles but on the test of scientific inquiry. No idea or institution (not even religious faith) was valid, they claimed, unless it worked and unless it stood the test of experience. "The ultimate test for us of what a truth means," James wrote, "is the conduct it dictates or inspires."

A similar concern for scientific inquiry was intruding into the social sciences and challenging traditional orthodoxies. Economists such as Richard T. Ely and Simon Patten argued for a more active and pragmatic use of scientific discipline. Sociologists such as Edward A. Ross and Lester Frank Ward urged applying the scientific method to the solution of social and political problems. Historians such as Frederick Jackson Turner and Charles Beard argued that economic factors more than spiritual ideals had been the governing force in historical development. John Dewey proposed a new approach to education that placed less emphasis on the rote learning of traditional knowledge and more on a flexible, democratic approach to schooling, one that enabled students to acquire knowledge that would help them deal with the realities of their society.

GROWTH OF ANTHROPOLOGY

The relativistic implications of Darwinism also promoted the growth of anthropology and encouraged some scholars to begin examining other cultures—most significantly, perhaps, the culture of Native Americans—in new ways. A few white Americans began to look at Native American society as a coherent culture with its own norms and values that were worthy of respect and preservation, even though different from those of white society. But such ideas about Native Americans found very little support outside a few corners of the intellectual world until much later in the twentieth century.

TOWARD UNIVERSAL SCHOOLING

A society that was coming to depend increasingly on specialized skills and scientific knowledge was, of course, a society with a high demand for education. The late nineteenth century, therefore, was a time of rapid expansion and reform of American schools and universities.

SPREAD OF PUBLIC EDUCATION

One example was the spread of free public primary and secondary education. In 1860, there were only 100 public high schools in the entire United States. By 1900, the number had reached 6,000, and by 1914 over 12,000. By 1900, compulsory school attendance laws were in effect in thirty-one states and territories. But education was still far from universal. Rural areas lagged far behind urban-industrial ones in funding public education. And in the South, many African Americans had no access to schools.

Educational reformers, few of whom shared the relativistic views of anthropologists, sought to provide educational opportunities for Native Americans as well, in an effort to "civilize" them and help them adapt to white society. In the 1870s, reformers recruited small groups of Native Americans to attend Hampton Institute, a primarily black college. In 1879, Richard Henry Pratt, a former army officer, organized the Carlisle Indian Industrial School in Pennsylvania. Carlisle emphasized the kind of practical "industrial" education that Booker T. Washington had urged at his school at Tuskegee. Equally important, it Native Americans from their nations and tried to force them to assimilate to white norms. The purpose, Pratt said, was to "kill the Indian and save the man." Carlisle inspired other, similar schools in the West. Ultimately, the reform efforts failed, both because of Native American resistance and because of inadequate funding, incompetent administration, and poor teaching.

"LAND-GRANT" INSTITUTIONS

Colleges and universities were also proliferating rapidly in the late nineteenth century. They benefited particularly from the Morrill Land Grant Act of the Civil War era, by which the federal government had donated land to states for the establishment of colleges. After 1865, states in the South and West took particular advantage of the law. In all, sixty-nine "land-grant" institutions were established in the last decades of the century—among them the state university systems of California, Illinois, Minnesota, and Wisconsin.

Reasoning Processes

Continuity and Change Have students read the section "Spread of Public Education." Ask them to create a Venn diagram comparing primary and secondary schools of the late nineteenth century with those of today. Have students discuss as a class how schools have changed over time and how they have remained the same. **SOC** **ARC**

WILLIAM GRAHAM SUMNER William Graham Sumner was an influential scholar who was appointed the first professor of sociology at Yale. A dynamic writer and teacher, he is best known for his promotion of "Social Darwinism"—a now-discredited theory that used the theory of evolution to explain differences among peoples.

Other universities benefited from millions of dollars contributed by business and financial tycoons. Rockefeller, Carnegie, and others gave generously to such schools as the University of Chicago, Columbia, Harvard, Northwestern, Princeton, Syracuse, and Yale. Other philanthropists founded new universities or reorganized and renamed older ones to perpetuate their family names–Vanderbilt, Johns Hopkins, Cornell, Duke, Tulane, and Stanford.

Education for Women

The post-Civil War era saw, too, an important expansion of educational opportunities for women, although such opportunities continued to lag far behind those available to men and were almost always denied to black women.

Most public high schools accepted women readily, but opportunities for higher education were few. At the end of the Civil War, only three American colleges were coeducational. In the years after the war, some of the land-grant colleges and universities in the Midwest and such private universities as Cornell and Wesleyan began to admit women along with men. But coeducation provided fewer opportunities than the creation of a network of women's colleges. Mount Holyoke, which had begun its life in 1836 as a "seminary" for women, became a full-fledged college in the 1880s. At about the same time, new female institutions were emerging: Vassar, Wellesley, Smith, Bryn Mawr, Wells, and Goucher. A few of the larger private universities created separate colleges for women on their campuses (Barnard at Columbia and Radcliffe at Harvard, for example). Proponents of women's colleges saw the institutions as places where female students would not be treated as "second-class citizens" by predominantly male student bodies and faculties.

WOMEN'S COLLEGES

The female college was part of an important phenomenon in the history of modern American women: the emergence of a distinctive women's community. Most faculty members and many administrators were women (often unmarried). And the life of the college produced a spirit of sorority and commitment among educated women that had important effects in later years, as women became the leaders of many reform activities. Most female college graduates eventually married, but many married at a later age than their non-college-educated counterparts and in some cases continued to pursue careers after marriage and motherhood. A significant minority, perhaps over 25 percent, did not marry, but devoted themselves exclusively to careers. A leader at Bryn Mawr remarked, "Our failures marry." That was surely rhetorical excess. The growth of female higher education clearly became for some women a liberating experience, persuading them that they had roles to perform in society in addition to those of wives and mothers.

Discussion and Activities

Making Connections After students have read the section "'Land-Grant' Institutions," ask them to go online and search for land-grant schools in their home state. Have students research what the focus of these institutions was originally. *(Agriculture; engineering; teacher education; etc.)* **ARC** **SOC**

Reasoning Processes

Causation Have students read the section "Education for Women." Ask them to create a T-chart identifying the causes and effects of the development of women's colleges. Have students discuss in small groups what they believe the most important effects were. **SOC** **ARC** **WXT**

Discussion and Activities

Comparison and Argumentation Divide the class into four groups to review and research each of the following topics relating to the effects of urbanization: the rise of mass consumption, the rise of leisure activities, the effects of machine politics and boss rule, and developments in art and literature. Have each group prepare a short report to deliver to the class that briefly describes their assigned development and evaluates whether it was the most significant of the four. SOC WXT NAT ARC MIG

Key Terms

Students should be familiar with the key terms and be able to define them in the context of the causes of urbanization and the effects of it, both positive and negative. Encourage students to use these terms in performing review exercises and exam practice for this chapter.

CHAPTER 18 REVIEW

CONNECTING THEMES

Chapter Eighteen focused on the reasons for urban growth and the effects of a rapidly growing urban population. The city offered a variety of opportunities for rural migrants along with foreign immigrants. Mass immigration from southern and eastern Europe provoked a nativist response among some Americans, but others welcomed the new arrivals as a source of labor. The wave of immigration also affected urban growth, spurring the rise of ethnic communities as immigrants sought ways to maintain connections to their values and culture.

Improvements in transportation such as the streetcar affected patterns of urban settlement and growth. Cities also had to confront many challenges such as poverty, crime, fire, disease, and pollution. Municipal governments sought ways to handle these new issues, with limited success. Urban machines often assisted the poor in return for political support.

Urbanization was not without positive effects. The middle class benefited from the increase in leisure time and a growing mass market that allowed for many conveniences and advancements, such as the consumption of packaged foods. Art and literature began to emphasize "social realism," which promoted calls to improve urban conditions, particularly for immigrants and the poor.

You should consider the following questions as you review the themes for this chapter:

- How did migration lead to changes in American identity for immigrants, working class people, and first-time urban residents?
- What were the sources and migration patterns that drove urban population growth?
- What were the reasons America moved to a mass consumption society?
- What were the effects of increased leisure time on the population?
- What were the causes and effects of urban population growth during the Gilded Age?
- What were the positive and negative effects of machine politics and boss rule on urban residents?
- How did urbanization and industrialization impact the American environment?

KEY TERMS

Alice Hamilton 520
Armory Show 531
Ashcan School 530
assimilation 413
boss rule 522
"city beautiful" movement 517
Darwinism 531
department stores 523
D.W. Griffith 528
Edward Hopper 531
Henry James 530
Jacob Riis 517
Kate Chopin 530
mass transit 518
modernism 531
movies 528
National Consumers League 524
newspaper chains 530
social realism 530
Stephen Crane 530
Tammany Hall 522
tenements 517
Theodore Dreiser 530
Upton Sinclair 530
William James 532
William M. Tweed 522
women's colleges 533
yellow journalism 530
Yiddish theater 528

Go Online Chapter 18 Content Review

Assessing Student Understanding Use the online assessment to assess student understanding of concepts and topics within the chapter. You can assign the ready-made Chapter 18 Content Review or create your own from available questions. This easy-to-use tool helps you design assessments that meet the needs of different types of learners.

AP EXAM PRACTICE

Questions assume cumulative content knowledge from this chapter and previous chapters.

MULTIPLE CHOICE

Use the graph, "Immigration's Contribution to Population Growth," on page 511 and your knowledge of U.S. history to answer questions 1–3.

1. What was a direct impact of the immigration shown in the graph on urban centers in America during the Gilded Age?
   (A) dramatic slowing of migration of native-born Americans from rural areas to urban centers
   (B) greater independence for immigrant women
   (C) growth of distinct, ethnic neighborhoods
   (D) city governments expanding subsidized housing for new arrivals

2. What trend developed in reaction to the immigration changes depicted in the graph?
   (A) decreasing availability of employment for newly arriving immigrants
   (B) growth of settlement in suburban areas
   (C) movement by African Americans out of Northern cities into the South
   (D) rise in nativist sentiment and organizations

3. Some Americans welcomed the trends depicted in the graph as they allowed for
   (A) significant cultural diversity to encounter in urban populations.
   (B) a plentiful supply of cheap labor.
   (C) a sharp increase in housing demand.
   (D) an increase in religious diversity among Americans.

SHORT ANSWER

Use your knowledge of U.S. history to answer questions 4 and 5.

4. Use the political cartoon on page 515 to answer A, B, and C.
   (A) Describe ONE point of view about immigration in the Gilded Age as depicted in the political cartoon.
   (B) Briefly explain ONE specific historical cause of the population increase during the Gilded Age.
   (C) Briefly explain ONE specific historical effect of the population increase during the Gilded Age.

5. Answer A, B, and C.
   (A) Briefly describe ONE specific similarity between the artistic movements of Realism during the Gilded Age and Romanticism of the antebellum period.
   (B) Briefly describe ONE specific difference between the artistic movements of Realism during the Gilded Age and Romanticism of the antebellum period.
   (C) Briefly explain ONE specific historical effect which resulted from the literary output during the Gilded Age.

LONG ESSAY

Develop a thoughtful and thorough historical argument that addresses the statement. Begin your essay with a thesis statement, and support it with specific historical evidence and examples.

6. Evaluate the relative importance of causes that led to urbanization in the United States from 1870 to 1900.

Answers

Multiple Choice

1. C; **2.** D; **3.** B

Short Answer

4A) Possible answer: The point of view about immigration in the image is that of someone who welcomed the new immigrants. This was possibly a business owner who viewed immigrants as a cheap source of labor. Uncle Sam is opening his arms welcoming the immigrants, and signs to the right and left of him underscore the positive benefits of the United States.

4B) Possible answer: Two things that attracted immigrants to the United States: first, the availability of land, which was not readily available back in Europe, and second, industrialization provided employment opportunities for individuals settling in the cities.

4C) Possible answer: As with any period in history where there is a population increase due to immigration, there was push back, with an increase of nativist sentiment. In the United States, this took the form of the Immigration Restriction League, a group that was committed to stopping the immigrant tide.

5A) Possible answer: Both Romanticism and Realism were responding to the geographic dynamic popular during their respective time periods. Romanticism was responding to western expansion, portraying the beauty of nature and issuing warnings to humanity, and Realism was responding to the urban environment that was dominating geographic centralization.

5B) Possible answer: Romanticism tended to be more positive, with its portrayals of human nature as well as its belief in the beauty of nature. Realism, on the other hand, focused on negative aspects of American life, usually portraying the brutal and dangerous nature of urban living.

5C) Possible answer: Social Realism, a popular literary movement, led to a number of important developments. It brought attention to the plight of the urban worker, resulting in more legislation protecting women, children, and all urban workers. It also gave rise to a new social movement known as the Social Gospel movement.

Long Essay

6. Possible thesis: Urbanization was a product of the industrialization of the American economy. The population wave from Europe, along with natural population gains in the United States, saw the growth of cities. Additionally, many of these immigrants remained in the cities, taking advantage of the economic opportunities for poor and working-class individuals. Specific historical evidence: First, the advent of the Second Industrial Revolution and the mechanization of America were important factors leading to the rise of cities during the second half of the nineteenth century. As the United States became an industrial power, the population of cities exploded due to an abundance of job opportunities. Second, these job opportunities led some individuals and families to move from rural to urban settings. Third, because of continuing immigration from Europe, most individuals seeking opportunities in the United States were poor and did not have the means to move farther west upon arrival. The cities provided much needed economic opportunities as business leaders looked to these immigrants as a valuable source of cheap labor. Finally, cities in the Midwest of the United States also grew as mid-points for western agriculture; many of these became middle grounds for trade between the West and the East.

Pacing Guide

Chapter 19 explores key concepts from Period 6: 1865–1898 of the AP U.S. History Curriculum Framework.
The suggested instruction time for Chapter 19 is 3 days.

Key Concepts

6.3.I New cultural and intellectual movements both buttressed and challenged the social order of the Gilded Age.

6.3.II Dramatic social changes in the period inspired political debates over citizenship, corruption, and the proper relationship between business and government.

19 GILDED AGE POLITICS

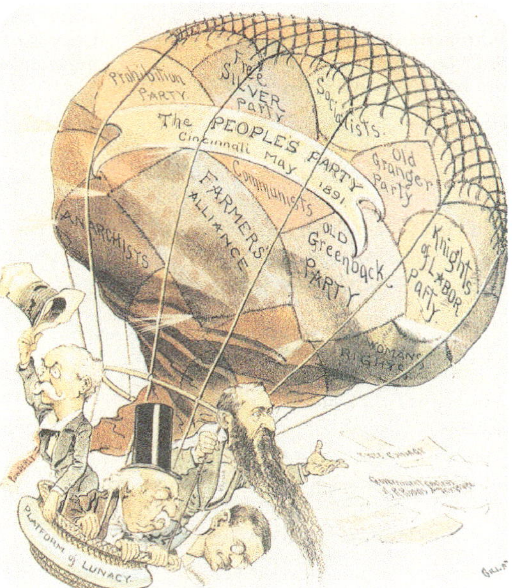

"A PARTY OF PATCHES," *JUDGE* MAGAZINE, JUNE 6, 1891 This political cartoon suggests the contempt and fear with which many easterners, in particular, viewed the emergence of the People's Party in 1891.

CONNECTING CONCEPTS

Chapter Nineteen examines the politics of the Gilded Age, beginning with a focus on the high turnout, voter loyalty, and electoral stability of the party system, which featured an almost equal balance of Republicans and Democrats. The federal government had few responsibilities aside from issuing land grants to railroads and granting annual pensions to retired Civil War veterans and their widows. Presidents and parties spent an inordinate amount of time on political appointments for supporters, which led to demands for patronage reform. Other important issues emerged, such as antitrust legislation, railroad regulation, and tariff revision, which inflamed public opinion.

High tariffs were among the major grievances of American farmers, who suffered from economic decline and cultural isolation in the 1870s and 1880s. In response, they formed organizations like the Grange and the Farmers' Alliances, which created cooperatives and welcomed women as members. Then the People's, or Populist, Party emerged in 1892. It appealed primarily to small, single-crop farmers who felt culturally marginal, politically ignored, and economically vulnerable in the new world of commercial agriculture. The Populist platform called for government loans to farmers, the abolition of the national bank, the direct election of U.S. senators (rather than appointment by state legislatures), railroad regulation, and a currency system based on gold and silver, also known as bimetallism.

The early 1890s featured a severe depression that was precipitated by the Panic of 1893, labor unrest, social violence, and a political crisis when both major parties failed to act. The Republicans in 1896 nominated for president Ohio Governor William McKinley, a staunch conservative who supported high tariffs and the gold standard. In a huge surprise, the Democrats nominated Nebraska Congressman William Jennings Bryan after he electrified the convention with his "Cross of Gold"

Discussion and Activities

Analyzing Visuals Have students examine the image *"A Party of Patches."* Ask them to think about what the creator of the cartoon was trying to communicate by portraying the Populist Party in this way. *(The patchwork implies that the party may have drawn its ideas from many different sources, and that it will not hang together as well as a party with more homogenous membership and ideas.)* Have students share their ideas with a partner, and then ask for volunteers to share their thoughts with the class. **PCE** **SOC**

speech, which endorsed bimetallism. The Populist Party then followed suit, choosing "fusion" with the Democrats. It proved a mistake. In the end, the Republicans won and the Populists dissolved. Nevertheless, their demands remained part of American politics and Bryan pioneered modern campaigning by traveling across the country and appealing directly to voters.

As you read, you should:

- Describe the major issues which separated the Democrats and the Republicans during the Gilded Age.
- Identify the causes and effects of the rise of an agricultural labor movement during the Gilded Age in the United States.
- Analyze the different organizations which arose to represent the agricultural movement in the United States.
- Evaluate the rise of the People's Party and explain its effects.
- Describe the different ways that government intervention helped or harmed agricultural interests in the United States during the Gilded Age.
- Identify the causes and consequences of the Panic of 1893.
- Analyze the importance of the Election of 1896

THE POLITICS OF EQUILIBRIUM

The most striking feature of late-nineteenth-century politics was the remarkable stability of the party system. From the end of Reconstruction until the late 1890s, the electorate was divided almost precisely evenly between the Republicans and the Democrats. Sixteen states were solidly and consistently Republican, and fourteen states (most in the South) were solidly and consistently Democratic. Only five states (most importantly New York and Ohio) were usually in doubt, and their voters generally decided the results of national elections. The Republican Party captured the presidency in all but two of the elections of the era, but in the five presidential elections beginning in 1876, the average popular-vote margin separating the Democratic and Republican candidates was 1.5 percent. The congressional balance was similarly stable, with the Republicans generally controlling the Senate and the Democrats generally controlling the House.

Electoral Stability

As striking as the balance between the parties was the intensity of public loyalty to them. In most of the country, Americans viewed their party affiliations with a passion and enthusiasm that is difficult for later generations to understand. Voter turnout in presidential elections between 1860 and 1900 averaged over 78 percent of all eligible voters (as compared with only about 50 percent in most recent elections). Even in nonpresidential years, from 60 to 80 percent of the voters turned out to cast ballots for congressional and local candidates. Large groups of potential voters were disenfranchised in these years: women in most states; almost all African Americans and many poor white people in the South. But for adult white males, there were few franchise restrictions.

High Turnout

What explains this extraordinary loyalty to the two political parties? It was not, certainly, that the parties took distinct positions on important public issues. They did so rarely. Party loyalties reflected other factors. Region was perhaps the most important. To white Southerners, loyalty to the Democratic Party was a matter of unquestioned faith. It was the vehicle by which they had triumphed over Reconstruction and preserved white supremacy. To many white and black Northerners, Republican loyalties were equally intense. To them, the party of Lincoln remained a bulwark against slavery and treason.

Religious and ethnic differences also shaped party loyalties. The Democratic Party attracted most of the Catholic voters, recent immigrants, and poorer workers–groups that often overlapped. The Republican Party appealed to northern Protestants, citizens of old stock, and much of the middle class–groups that also had considerable overlap. Among the few substantive issues on which the parties took clearly different stands were matters connected with immigrants. Republicans tended to support measures restricting immigration and to favor temperance legislation, which many of them believed would help discipline immigrant communities. Catholics and immigrants viewed such proposals as assaults on them and their cultures and opposed them; the Democratic Party followed their lead.

Cultural Basis of Party Identification

Party identification, then, was usually more a reflection of cultural inclinations than a calculation of economic interest. Individuals might affiliate with a party because their parents had done so, or because it was the party of their region, their church, or their ethnic group.

Discussion and Activities

Making Connections Have students read the section "Electoral Stability." Ask them to use the index to locate the results of recent presidential elections. Have students discuss in small groups whether they see evidence that the electoral stability of the late nineteenth century still exists today. **PCE**

Go Online AP Exam Preparation

AP Exam Practice Use the online assessment to help prepare students for the AP Exam. You can assign the ready-made AP-style short-answer questions, document-based questions, and multiple-choice questions assessing concepts, themes, and skills from Period 6 and AP-style long-essay questions organized in sets of 3 questions from various time periods. You can also create your own tests from available questions. This easy-to-use tool helps you design assessments that meet the needs of different types of learners.

Discussion and Activities

Making Connections Have students read the section "The National Government." Ask them to create a Venn diagram comparing the powers of the national government in the late nineteenth century with those of today. **PCE**

THE NATIONAL GOVERNMENT

One reason the two parties managed to avoid substantive issues was that the federal government (and, to some degree, state and local governments as well) did relatively little. The government in Washington was responsible for delivering the mail, maintaining a military, conducting foreign policy, and collecting tariffs and taxes. It had few other responsibilities and few institutions with which it could have undertaken additional responsibilities even if it had chosen to do so.

There were significant exceptions. The federal government had been supporting the economic development of the nation for decades. In the late nineteenth century, that mostly meant giving tremendous subsidies to railroads, usually in the form of grants of federal land, to encourage them to extend their lines deeper into the nation. And as President Cleveland's intervention in the Pullman strike suggests, the government was also not averse to using its military and police power to protect capitalists from challenges from their workers.

In addition, the federal government administered a system of annual pensions for Union Civil War veterans who had retired from work and for their widows. At its peak, this pension system was making payments to a majority of white and African American male citizens of the North and to many women as well. Some reformers hoped to make the system permanent and universal. But their efforts failed, in part because the Civil War pension system was awash in party patronage and corruption. Other reformers–believers in "good government"–saw elimination of the pension system as a way to fight graft, corruption, and party rule. When the Civil War generation died out, the pension system died with it.

CIVIL WAR PENSION SYSTEM

In most other respects, however, the United States in the late nineteenth century was a society without a modern, national government. The most powerful institutions were the two political parties (and the bosses and machines that dominated them) and the federal courts.

PRESIDENT CHESTER A. ARTHUR Although originally a Stalwart and a follower of Roscoe Conkling, upon becoming president on the assassination of James A. Garfield, Chester A. Arthur attempted to reform the spoils system. The Pendleton Act, passed by Congress in 1883, required that some civil service jobs be filled by competitive examinations rather than patronage.

PRESIDENTS AND PATRONAGE

The power of party bosses had an important effect on the power of the presidency. The office had great symbolic importance, but its occupants were unable to do very much except distribute government appointments. A new president and his tiny staff had to make almost 100,000 appointments (most of them in the post office, the only really large government agency); and even in that function, presidents had limited latitude, since they had to avoid offending the various factions within their own parties.

Sometimes that proved impossible, as the presidency of Rutherford B. Hayes (1877–1881) demonstrated. By the end of his term, two groups–the Stalwarts, led by Roscoe Conkling of New York, and the Half-Breeds, captained by James G. Blaine of Maine–were competing for control of the Republican Party. Rhetorically, the Stalwarts favored traditional, professional machine politics, while the Half-Breeds favored reform. In fact, both groups were mainly interested in a larger share of the patronage pie. Hayes tried to satisfy both and ended up satisfying neither.

STALWARTS AND HALF-BREEDS

The battle over patronage overshadowed all else during Hayes's unhappy presidency. His one important substantive initiative–an effort to create a civil service system–attracted no support from either party. And his early announcement that he would not seek reelection only weakened him further. (His popularity in Washington was not enhanced by the decision of his wife, a temperance advocate widely known as "Lemonade Lucy," to ban alcoholic beverages from the White House.) Hayes's presidency was a study in frustration.

The Republicans managed to retain the presidency in 1880 in part because they agreed on a ticket that included a Stalwart and a Half-Breed. They nominated James A. Garfield, a veteran congressman from Ohio and a Half-Breed, for president and Chester A. Arthur of New York, a Stalwart, for vice president. The Democrats nominated General Winfield Scott Hancock, a

Historical Thinking Skills

Contextualization Have students read the section "Stalwarts and Half-Breeds." Ask them to review the election of 1876 and the circumstances of Hayes's election as president. Have students discuss in pairs or small groups how the circumstances of Hayes's election might have contributed to his challenges as president. **PCE**

minor Civil War commander with no national following. Benefiting from the end of the recession of 1879, Garfield won a decisive electoral victory, although his popular-vote margin was very thin. The Republicans also captured both houses of Congress.

Garfield began his presidency by trying to defy the Stalwarts in his appointments and by showing support for civil service reform. He soon found himself embroiled in an ugly public quarrel with Conkling and the Stalwarts. It was never resolved. On July 2, 1881, only four months after his inauguration, Garfield was shot twice while standing in the Washington railroad station by an apparently deranged gunman (and unsuccessful office seeker) who shouted, "I am a Stalwart and Arthur is president now!" Garfield lingered for nearly three months but finally died, a victim as much of inept medical treatment as of the wounds themselves.

GARFIELD ASSASSINATED

Chester A. Arthur, who succeeded Garfield, had spent a political lifetime as a devoted, skilled, and open spoilsman and a close ally of Roscoe Conkling. But on becoming president, he tried—like Hayes and Garfield before him—to follow an independent course and even to promote reform, aware that the Garfield assassination had discredited the traditional spoils system. To the dismay of the Stalwarts, Arthur kept most of Garfield's appointees in office and supported civil service reform. In 1883, Congress passed the first national civil service measure, the Pendleton Act, which required that some federal jobs be filled by competitive written examinations rather than by patronage. Relatively few offices fell under civil service at first, but its reach extended steadily.

PENDLETON ACT

Cleveland, Harrison, and the Tariff

In the unsavory election of 1884, the Republican candidate for president was Senator James G. Blaine of Maine—known to his admirers as the "Plumed Knight" but to many others as a symbol of seamy party politics. A group of disgruntled "liberal Republicans," known by their critics as the "mugwumps," announced they would bolt the party and support an honest Democrat. Rising to the bait, the Democrats nominated Grover Cleveland, the reform governor of New York. He differed from Blaine on no substantive issues but had acquired a reputation as an enemy of corruption.

In a campaign filled with personal invective, what may have decided the election was the last-minute introduction of a religious controversy. Shortly before the election, a delegation of Protestant ministers called on Blaine in New York City; their spokesman, Dr. Samuel Burchard, referred to the Democrats as the party of "rum, Romanism, and rebellion." Blaine was slow to repudiate Burchard's indiscretion, and Democrats quickly spread the news that Blaine had tolerated a slander on the Catholic Church. Cleveland's narrow victory was probably a result of an unusually heavy Catholic vote for the Democrats in New York. Cleveland won 219 electoral votes to Blaine's 182; his popular margin was only 23,000.

ELECTION OF 1884

Grover Cleveland was respected, if not often liked, for his stern and righteous opposition to politicians, grafters, pressure groups, and Tammany Hall. He had become famous as the "veto governor," as an official who was not afraid to say no. He was the embodiment of an era in which few Americans believed the federal government could, or should, do very much. Cleveland had always doubted the wisdom of protective tariffs. The existing high rates, he believed, were responsible for the annual surplus in federal revenues, which was tempting Congress to pass "reckless" and "extravagant" legislation, which he frequently vetoed. In December 1887, therefore, he asked Congress to reduce the tariff rates. Democrats in the House approved a tariff reduction, but Senate Republicans defiantly passed a bill of their own actually raising the rates. The resulting deadlock made the tariff an issue in the election of 1888.

The Democrats renominated Cleveland and supported tariff reductions. The Republicans settled on former senator Benjamin Harrison of Indiana, who was obscure but respectable (the grandson of President William Henry Harrison); he endorsed high tariffs. The campaign was the first since the Civil War to involve a clear question of economic difference between the parties. It was also one of the most corrupt (and closest) elections in American history. Harrison won an electoral majority of 233 to 168, but Cleveland's popular vote exceeded Harrison's by 100,000.

New Public Issues

Benjamin Harrison's record as president was little more substantial than that of his grandfather, who had died a month after taking office. Harrison had few visible convictions, and he made no effort to influence Congress. And yet during Harrison's passive administration, public opinion was beginning to force the government to confront some of the pressing social and economic issues of the day. Most notably, sentiment was rising in favor of legislation to curb the power of trusts.

By the mid-1880s, fifteen western and southern states had adopted laws prohibiting combinations that restrained competition. But corporations found it easy to escape limitations by incorporating in states, such as New Jersey and Delaware, that offered them special privileges. If antitrust legislation was to be effective, its supporters believed, it would have to come from the national government. Responding to growing popular demands, both houses of Congress passed the Sherman Antitrust Act in July 1890, almost without dissent. Most members of Congress saw the act as a symbolic measure, one that would help deflect public criticism but was not likely to have any real effect on corporate power. For over a decade after its passage, the Sherman Act—indifferently enforced and steadily weakened by the courts—had almost no impact. As of 1901, the Justice Department had

SHERMAN ANTITRUST ACT

Discussion and Activities

Comparing and Contrasting After students have read the section "Presidents and Patronage," ask them to create a Janus person (an outline of a human figure with a face pointing both directions and divided in half by a vertical line) comparing the characteristics of the Stalwart and Half-Breed factions. PCE SOC

Historical Thinking Skills

Argumentation Have students read the section "Cleveland, Harrison, and the Tariff." Ask them to write a short campaign speech advocating for either Cleveland or Harrison in the election of 1888. Ask for volunteers to deliver their speeches, and hold an informal mock election. PCE WXT

Historical Thinking Skills

Argumentation After students have read the section "Sherman Antitrust Act," ask them to write a letter to a Congressperson from the point of view of an industrial worker advocating for antitrust regulation. **PCE** **WXT**

LABOR AND MONOPOLY This 1883 cartoon appeared in Puck, a magazine popular for its satirical treatment of American politics. It expresses a common sentiment of the Populists and many others: that ordinary men and women (portrayed here by the pathetic figure of "labor" and by the grim members of the audience) were almost hopelessly overmatched by the power of corporate monopolies. The knight's shield, labeled "corruption of the legislature," and his spear, labeled "subsidized press," make clear that—in the view of the cartoonist at least—corporations had many allies in their effort to oppress workers.

instituted many antitrust suits against labor unions, but only fourteen against business combinations; there had been few convictions.

McKinley Tariff

The Republicans were more interested, however, in the issue they believed had won them the 1888 election: the tariff. Representative William McKinley of Ohio and Senator Nelson W. Aldrich of Rhode Island drafted the highest protective measure ever proposed to Congress. Known as the McKinley Tariff, it became law in October 1890. But Republican leaders apparently misinterpreted public sentiment. The party suffered a stunning reversal in the 1890 congressional election. The Republicans' substantial Senate majority was slashed to 8; in the House, the party retained only 88 of the 323 seats. McKinley himself was among those who went down in defeat. Nor were the Republicans able to recover in the course of the next two years. In the presidential election of 1892, Benjamin Harrison once again supported protection; Grover Cleveland, renominated by the Democrats, once again opposed it. A new third party, the People's Party, with James B. Weaver as its candidate, advocated substantial economic reform. Cleveland won 277 electoral votes to Harrison's 145 and had a popular margin of 380,000. Weaver ran far behind. For the first time since 1878, the Democrats won a majority of both houses of Congress.

The policies of Cleveland's second term were much like those of his first—devoted to minimal government and hostile to active efforts to deal with social or economic problems. Again, he supported a tariff reduction, which the House approved but the Senate weakened. Cleveland denounced the result but allowed it to become law as the Wilson-Gorman Tariff. It included only very modest reductions.

But public pressure was growing in the 1880s for other reforms, among them regulation of the railroads. Farm organizations in the Midwest (most notably the Grangers) had persuaded several state legislatures to pass regulatory legislation in the early 1870s. In *Munn v. Illinois*, the Supreme Court agreed in 1876 that the states had authority to regulate intrastate commerce (as opposed to interstate commerce) in industries that affected the "common good." But in 1886, the Supreme Court—in *Wabash, St. Louis, and Pacific Railway Co. v. Illinois*, known as the *Wabash* case—ruled one of the Granger Laws in Illinois unconstitutional. According to the Court, the law was an attempt to control interstate commerce and thus infringed on the exclusive power of Congress. Later, the federal courts limited the powers of the states to regulate commerce

Historical Thinking Skills

Sourcing and Situation Have students examine the image "Labor and Monopoly." Ask them to identify details that help determine the artist's purpose or point of view. *(The one-sided armaments of the combatants; the differences in the audiences supporting each contestant; the size difference between the combatants.)* **Ask:** What is the significance of the locomotive carrying the figure of "Monopoly?" *(Railroads were frequently criticized as monopolies that took advantage of customers, particularly farmers.)* **PCE** **SOC** **WXT**

SHACKLED BY THE TARIFF This 1894 cartoon by the political satirist Louis Dalrymple portrays an unhappy Uncle Sam bound hand and foot by the McKinley Tariff and by what tariff opponents considered a closely related evil—monopoly. Members of the Senate are portrayed as tools of the various industries and special interests protected by the tariff. The caption, "A Senate for Revenue Only," is a parody of the antitariff rallying cry, "A tariff for revenue only," meaning that duties should be designed only to raise money for the government, not to stop imports of particular goods to protect domestic industries. A particularly provocative element of the cartoon is the image of two African American legislators promoting another controversial issue: "free silver."

even within their own boundaries. President Grover Cleveland, acting under the Sherman Antitrust Act, blocked the American Sugar Refining Company in 1892 from gaining control of the E.C. Knight Company and creating a nearly total monopoly of the sugar refining industry. But in *United States v. E. C. Knight Co.*, the Supreme Court decided in 1895 that the Commerce Clause only applied to commerce, not manufacturing, although the high court reconsidered a few years later in *Swift & Co v. United States* and ruled that Congress could regulate manufacturing when it affected interstate commerce.

Effective railroad regulation, it was now clear, could come only from the federal government. Congress responded to public pressure in 1887 with the Interstate Commerce Act, which banned discrimination in rates between long and short hauls, required that railroads publish their rate schedules and file them

INTERSTATE COMMERCE ACT

THE STATE, WAR, AND NAVY BUILDING This sprawling Victorian office building was one of the largest in Washington, D.C., when it was constructed shortly after the Civil War. It housed the State, War, and Navy Departments until not long before World War II. It suggests both the degree to which the federal government was growing in the late nineteenth century and, more importantly, the degree to which it remained a tiny entity compared to what it would later become. This building, which stands directly next door to the White House, today houses a part (but only a part) of the president's staff.

Discussion and Activities

Making Connections After students have read the section "McKinley Tariff," have them discuss as a class how important an issue tariff policy would be in contemporary elections and what issues would generate the most attention. **PCE**

Discussion and Activities

Analyzing Visuals Have students examine the image "The State, War, and Navy Building." Ask them to identify details from the image. **Ask:** How did this building demonstrate the nature and role of the federal government in the late nineteenth century? *(As large as it is, it housed three major executive departments responsible for foreign policy and national defense. This is an indication that the federal government was still quite small relative to the size of the country that it governed. These departments were arguably the most prestigious, and yet most Americans would not have interacted with them on a regular basis unless they were in the military.)* **PCE** **NAT**

Historical Thinking Skills

Analyzing Cause and Effect After students have read the section "Interstate Commerce Act," ask them to create a chart that lists the purpose, terms, and effects of the Sherman Antitrust Act, the McKinley Tariff, and the Interstate Commerce Act. Have students discuss in pairs or small groups how well each act achieved its goals. **Ask:** How effective was the federal government at regulating the economy in the late nineteenth century? **PCE** **WXT**

with the government, and declared that all interstate rail rates must be "reasonable and just"–although the act did not define what that meant. A five-person agency, the Interstate Commerce Commission (ICC), was to administer the act. But it had to rely on the courts to enforce its rulings. For almost twenty years after its passage, the Interstate Commerce Act–which was, like the Sherman Act, haphazardly enforced and narrowly interpreted by the courts–had little practical effect.

THE AGRARIAN REVOLT

No group watched the performance of the federal government in the 1880s with more dismay than American farmers. Suffering from a long economic decline, afflicted with a painful sense of obsolescence, rural Americans were keenly aware of the problems of the modern economy and particularly eager for government assistance in dealing with them. The result of their frustrations was the emergence of one of the most powerful movements of political protest in American history: what became known as Populism.

THE GRANGERS

According to popular myth, American farmers were the most individualistic of citizens. In reality, however, farmers had been making efforts to organize for many decades. The first major farm organization appeared in the 1860s: the Grange.

"THE GRANGE AWAKENING THE SLEEPERS" This 1873 cartoon illustrates the way the Grange embraced many of the same concerns that the Farmers' Alliances and their People's Party later expressed. A farmer is attempting to arouse passive citizens (lying in place of the "sleepers," or cross ties on railroad tracks), who are about to be crushed by a train. The cars bear the names of the costs of the railroads' domination of the agrarian economy.

A POPULIST GATHERING Populism was a response to real economic and political grievances. But like most political movements of its time, it was also important as a cultural experience. For farmers in sparsely settled regions in particular, it provided an antidote to isolation and loneliness. This gathering of Populist farmers in Dickinson County, Kansas, shows how the political purposes of the movement were tightly bound up with its social purposes.

Discussion and Activities

Evaluating Evidence Have students examine the image "The Grange Awakens the Sleepers." Discuss as a class the implication of the description of the figures replacing the railroad ties as being asleep. *(The implication is that they are unaware of the danger that they are in, or that they can't do anything about it.)* **PCE**

Discussion and Activities

Analyzing Points of View After students have read the section "Economic Grievances," ask them to write a short journal entry from the point of view of a Granger explaining how big business and government hurt farmers economically, and how the Grange attempted to solve those issues. **PCE** **WXT**

The Grange had its origins shortly after the Civil War in a tour through the South by a minor Agriculture Department official, Oliver H. Kelley. Kelley was appalled by what he considered the isolation and drabness of rural life. In 1867 he left the government and, with other department employees, founded the National Grange of the Patrons of Husbandry, to which he devoted years of labor as secretary and from which emerged a network of local organizations. At first, the Grangers defined their purposes modestly. They attempted to bring farmers together to learn new scientific agricultural techniques—to keep farming "in step with the music of the age." The Grangers also hoped to create a feeling of community, to relieve the loneliness of rural life.

ORIGINS

The Grangers grew slowly for a time. But when the depression of 1873 caused a major decline in farm prices, membership rapidly increased. By 1875, the Grange claimed more than 800,000 members and 20,000 local lodges; it had chapters in almost every state but was strongest in the great staple-producing regions of the South and the Midwest.

As membership grew, the lodges in the Midwest began to focus less on the social benefits of organization and more on the economic possibilities. They attempted to organize marketing cooperatives to allow farmers to circumvent the hated "middlemen" (people who managed the sale of farmers' crops, taking a large cut of the profits for themselves) And they urged cooperative political action to curb monopolistic practices by railroads and warehouses.

ECONOMIC GRIEVANCES

The Grangers set up cooperative stores, creameries, elevators, warehouses, insurance companies, and factories that produced machines, stoves, and other items. More than 400 enterprises were in operation at the height of the movement, and some of them forged lucrative relationships with existing businesses. One corporation emerged specifically to meet the needs of the Grangers: the first mail-order business, Montgomery Ward and Company, founded in 1872, which helped farmers escape from overpriced local stores. Eventually, however, most of the Grange enterprises failed, both because of the inexperience of their operators and because of the opposition of the middlemen they were challenging.

The Grangers also worked to elect state legislators pledged to their program. Usually they operated through the existing parties, although occasionally they ran candidates under such independent party labels as "Antimonopoly" and "Reform." At their peak, they managed to gain control of the legislatures in most of the midwestern states. Their purpose was to subject the railroads to government controls. The Granger laws of the early 1870s imposed strict regulations on railroad rates and practices.

POLITICAL PROGRAM

But the new regulations were soon destroyed by the courts. That defeat, combined with the political inexperience of many Grange leaders and, above all, the temporary return of agricultural prosperity in the late 1870s, produced a dramatic decline in the power of the association. Some of the Granger cooperatives survived as effective economic vehicles for many years, but the movement as a whole dwindled rapidly. By 1880, its membership had shrunk to 100,000.

THE FARMERS' ALLIANCES

The successor to the Grange as the leading vehicle of agrarian protest began to emerge even before the Granger movement had faded. As early as 1875, farmers in parts of the South (most notably in Texas) were banding together in so-called Farmers' Alliances. By 1880, the Southern Alliance had more than 4 million members; and a comparable Northwestern Alliance was taking root in the plains states and the Midwest and developing ties with its southern counterpart.

Like the Granges, the Alliances were principally concerned with local problems. They formed cooperatives and other marketing mechanisms. They established stores, banks, processing plants, and other facilities for their members—to free them from the hated "furnishing merchants" who kept so many farmers in debt. Some Alliance leaders, however, also saw the movement as an effort to build a society in which economic competition might give way to cooperation. They argued for a sense of mutual, neighborly responsibility that would enable farmers to resist oppressive outside forces. Alliance lecturers

MARY E. LEASE The fiery Populist orator Mary E. Lease was a fixture on the Alliance lecture circuit in the 1890s. She made some 160 speeches in 1890 alone. Her critics called her the "Kansas Pythoness," but she was popular among populist farmers with her denunciations of banks, railroads, and "middlemen," and her famous advice to "raise less corn and more hell."

Discussion and Activities

Analyzing Issues Have students read the section "Political Program." Ask them to discuss as a class why the Grangers' efforts at political reform largely failed at the national level. *(The Grange had by far its biggest support in the agricultural Midwest and West and virtually no support along the populous East Coast. Although they won many seats in state legislatures, they rarely had an opportunity to appoint judges, and many of their initiatives were undermined in court.)* **PCE**

Reasoning Processes

Comparing Have students read the section "Mary Lease." Ask them to create a Venn diagram comparing the Grange with the Farmers' Alliances. Have students discuss in small groups which they think was more effective and why. **PCE** **WXT** **SOC**

BEARING THE CROSS OF GOLD The cartoonist Grant Hamilton created this image of William Jennings Bryan shortly after he made his famous "Cross of Gold" speech at the Democratic National Convention, which led to his nomination for president. The cartoon highlights two of the most powerful images in Bryan's speech—a "crown of thorns" and a "cross of gold," both biblical references and both designed to represent the oppression that the gold standard imposed on working people.

traveled throughout rural areas attacking the concentration of power in great corporations and financial institutions and promoting cooperation as an alternative economic system.

From the beginning, women were full voting members in most local Alliances. Many held offices and served as lecturers.

MARY LEASE

A few, most notably Mary E. Lease, went on to become fiery Populist orators. (Lease was famous for urging farmers to "raise less corn and more hell.") Others emphasized issues of particular concern to women, especially temperance. Like their urban counterparts, agrarian women argued that sobriety was a key to stability in rural society. Alliances (and the Populist Party they eventually created) advocated extending the vote to women in many areas of the country.

Although the Alliances quickly became far more widespread than the Granges had ever been, they suffered from similar problems. Their cooperatives did not always work well, partly because the market forces operating against them were sometimes too strong to be overcome, partly because the cooperatives themselves were often mismanaged. These economic frustrations helped push the movement into a new phase at the end of the 1880s: the creation of a national political organization.

In 1889, the Southern and Northwestern Alliances, despite continuing differences between them, agreed to a loose merger. The next year the Alliances held a national convention at Ocala, Florida, and issued the so-called Ocala Demands, which were, in effect, a party platform. In the 1890 off-year elections, candidates supported by the Alliances won partial or complete control of the legislatures in twelve states. They also won six governorships, three seats in the U.S. Senate, and approximately fifty in the U.S. House of Representatives. Many of the successful Alliance candidates were Democrats who had benefited—often passively—from Alliance endorsements. But dissident farmers drew enough encouragement from the results to contemplate further political action, including forming a party of their own.

Discussion and Activities

Evaluating Evidence Have students examine the cartoon "Bearing the Cross of Gold." Ask them to identify details in the cartoon that illustrate whether or not the cartoonist was sympathetic to Bryan. *(The cross and crown of thorns are labeled as if they are props; the cross rests on, and may be damaging, an open Bible; Bryan's foot is standing on the Bible as well. The papers in the pouches appear to be pages torn from a Bible for political use. The flag waved by the Bryan supporter in the background says "anarchy.")* **PCE** **WXT**

Sentiment for a third party was strongest among the members of the Northwestern Alliance. But several southern leaders supported the idea as well—among them Tom Watson of Georgia, the only southern congressman elected in 1890 openly to identify with the Alliance, and Leonidas L. Polk of North Carolina, perhaps the ablest mind in the movement. Alliance leaders discussed plans for a third party at meetings in Cincinnati in May 1891 and St. Louis in February 1892. Then, in July 1892, 1,300 exultant delegates poured into Omaha, Nebraska, to proclaim the creation of the new party, approve an official set of principles, and nominate candidates for the presidency and vice presidency. The new organization's official name was the People's Party, but its members were more commonly known as Populists.

Birth of the People's Party

The election of 1892 (which restored Grover Cleveland to the presidency) demonstrated the potential power of the new movement. The Populist presidential candidate was James B. Weaver of Iowa, a former Greenbacker who received the nomination after the death of Leonidas Polk, the early favorite. Weaver polled more than 1 million votes, 8.5 percent of the total, and carried six mountain and plains states for 22 electoral votes. Nearly 1,500 Populist candidates won election to seats in state legislatures. The party elected three governors, five senators, and ten congressmen. It could also claim the support of many Republicans and Democrats in Congress who had been elected by appealing to populist sentiment.

The Populist Constituency

The Populists dreamed of creating a broad political coalition. But populism always appealed principally to farmers, particularly to small farmers with little long-range economic security—people whose operations were minimally mechanized, if at all, who relied on one crop, and who had access only to limited credit. In the Midwest, the Populists were usually family farmers struggling to hold on to their land (or to get it back). In the South, there were many modest landowners too, but in addition there were significant numbers of sharecroppers and tenant farmers. Whatever their differences, however, most Populists had at least one thing in common: they were engaged in a type of farming that was becoming less viable in the face of new, mechanized, diversified, and consolidated commercial agriculture.

Populists tended to be not only economically but also culturally marginal. The movement appealed above all to geographically isolated farmers who felt cut off from the mainstream of national life and resented their isolation. Populism gave such people an outlet for their grievances; it also provided them with a social experience, a sense of belonging to a community that they had previously lacked.

The Populists were also notable for the groups they failed to attract. There were energetic efforts to include labor within the coalition. Representatives of the Knights of Labor attended early organizational meetings; the new party added a labor plank to its platform—calling for shorter hours for workers and restrictions on immigration, and denouncing the use of private detective agencies as strikebreakers in labor disputes. On the whole, however, Populism never attracted significant labor support, in part because the economic interests of labor and the interests of farmers were often at odds.

One exception was the Rocky Mountain states, where the Populists did have some significant success in attracting miners to their cause. They did so partly because local Populist leaders endorsed a demand for "free silver," the idea of permitting silver to become, along with gold, the basis of the currency so as to expand the money supply. In Colorado, Idaho, Nevada, and other areas of the Far West, silver mining was an important activity, and the People's Party enjoyed substantial, if temporary, success there.

"Free Silver"

In the South, white Populists struggled with the question of whether to accept African Americans into the party. Their numbers and poverty made black farmers possibly valuable allies. There was an important black component to the movement—a network of "Colored Alliances" that by 1890 had more than one and a quarter million members. But most white Populists were willing to accept the assistance of African Americans only as long as it was clear that white Populists would remain indisputably in control. When southern conservatives began to attack the Populists for undermining white supremacy, the interracial character of the movement quickly faded.

"Colored Alliances"

Most of the Populist leaders were members of the rural middle class: professional people, editors and lawyers, or longtime politicians and agitators. Many active Populists were women. Some Populist leaders were somber, serious theoreticians; others were semihysterical rabble-rousers. In the South, in particular, Populism produced the first generation of what was to become a distinctive and enduring political breed—the "southern demagogue." Tom Watson in Georgia, Jeff Davis in Arkansas, and others attracted widespread popular support by arousing the resentment of poor Southerners against the entrenched planter aristocracy.

Populist Ideas

The reform program of the Populists was spelled out first in the Ocala Demands of 1890 and then, even more clearly, in the Omaha platform of 1892. It proposed a system of "subtreasuries," which would replace and strengthen the cooperatives of Grangers and Alliances that had been experimenting for years. The government would establish a network of warehouses, where farmers could deposit their crops. Using those crops as collateral, growers could then borrow money from the government at low rates of interest and wait for the price of their goods to go up before selling them. In addition, the Populists called for the abolition of national banks, the end of absentee ownership of land, the direct election of U.S. senators (which would weaken the power of conservative state legislatures), and other devices to improve the ability of the people to influence the political process. They called as well for regulation

Populist Platform

Historical Thinking Skills

Argumentation Have students read the section "Birth of the People's Party." Ask them to create a campaign poster promoting or opposing the candidacy of James Weaver for president. **PCE** **WXT** **ARC** **SOC**

Discussion and Activities

Analyzing Issues Have students read the section "The Populist Constituency." Ask them to discuss as a class whether the Populist Party should have made a concerted effort to enlist the support of the Colored Farmers' Alliances. **Ask:** What would have been the costs and benefits to the Populist Party of embracing the Colored Farmers' Alliances? **SOC** **PCE** **WXT** **ARC**

Reasoning Processes

Comparing Have students examine the images "Chautauqua Assembly" and "Bryan at Chautauqua." Ask them to create a Venn diagram comparing Chautauqua to the tent meetings of the Second Great Awakening. **SOC** **ARC**

PATTERNS OF POPULAR CULTURE

THE CHAUTAUQUAS

Education and oratory were part of American life in the nineteenth century. Starting in 1826, lyceums were among the first public organizations to provide adults with both. Participants met in libraries, vacant schools, and elsewhere. Organizers estimated that 13,000 people attended public lectures. An even-larger movement to provide instructional lectures and speeches arose during the 1880s and 1890s from the Populist movement. Men and women flocked by the hundreds or even thousands to hear speeches and discussions provided by itinerant speakers.

The most famous of these lectures were the Chautauquas, founded in the summer of 1874 by two enterprising men from the Chautauqua Lakes area in western New York State. Within a few years, the Chautauqua Assembly had expanded to include lectures on literary, scientific, theological, and practical subjects and was attracting ever-larger audiences for one- or two-week "schools." In 1883, the New York State legislature granted the Assemblies a charter and gave them the name "The Chautauqua University."

So successful (and profitable) were the Chautauqua Assemblies that scores of towns and villages began establishing lecture series of their own—"Little Chautauquas"—throughout the Midwest. At the peak of this movement, a Chicago promoter organized traveling programs to tour rural areas across the United States—visiting more than 8,000 different communities within a single year.

From 1904 through the mid-1920s, these "traveling Chautauquas" attracted enormous crowds and generated great excitement almost everywhere they went. On the day of a Chautauqua lecture, roads were sometimes clogged for miles in every direction with buggies and, later, automobiles transporting farm families dressed in their best clothes, carrying picnic baskets, straining excitedly to see the tents, posters, and crowds.

Chautauqua speakers were drawn from many walks of life, but they included some of the greatest figures of the age: William Jennings Bryan, William McKinley, Theodore Roosevelt, Booker T. Washington, Eugene V. Debs, and many others. The Chautauquas themselves also made some speakers rich and famous. The Philadelphia minister Russell Conwell, for example, made a great name (and a great fortune) with his famous "Acres of Diamonds" lectures, which he delivered thousands of times over the course of several decades, preaching a simple and attractive message: "Get rich . . . for money is power and power ought to be in the hands of good people." Conwell's sermon was characteristic of one kind of popular Chautauqua event—lectures that stressed self-improvement. Other such lectures stressed religion and health. The Chautauqua circuit was one of the best ways for a speaker to reach large numbers of people, which is one reason why so many progressive leaders and feminist reformers eagerly joined in. It was, for a time, one of the most powerful forms of communication in the nation.

The traveling Chautauquas declined during the 1920s and almost vanished in the 1930s—victims of radio, movies, and the automobile; the spread of public education to rural areas; and the reckless overexpansion of ambitious organizers. But the original Chautauqua Assembly in upstate New York survived, although in much-diminished form. It exists today as a resort that continues to offer lectures and other educational events to a large and dedicated clientele.

CHAUTAUQUA ASSEMBLY This Chautauqua meeting occurred in Clarinda, Iowa. It was one of hundreds of such meetings during the 1880s and 1890s that met the need of thousands of people across the country for knowledge and learning.

BRYAN AT CHAUTAUQUA William Jennings Bryan, the most famous orator of the early twentieth century, was a fixture at Chautauqua meetings, not only at the original Chautauqua in New York but also at the traveling and tented Chautauquas that spread across the country. Here he is shown speaking in Madison, Wisconsin.

HISTORICAL THINKING SKILLS

1. **Explaining Historical Context** Why would farmers have found the Chautauquas so appealing during a time when they faced so many economic problems?
2. **Drawing Conclusions** Why would so many prominent public figures have participated in the Chautauquas?
3. **Making Connections** Can you think of any parallels today to the Chautauqua movement of the early twentieth century?

Answers

Patterns of Popular Culture

1. Possible answer: Many of the ideas and philosophies of the Chautauquas would have been supportive of the needs of farmers facing economic challenges.
2. Possible answer: The Chautauquas, with their lectures and ideas, were very popular at this time with people across a wide range of backgrounds, occupations, and concerns. The participation of public figures would have brought these figures exposure to many different people and possibly the support of the people who supported the Chautauquas.
3. Student responses will vary.

and (after 1892) government ownership of railroads, telephones, and telegraphs. And they demanded a system of government-operated postal savings banks, a graduated income tax, and the inflation of the currency. Eventually, the party as a whole embraced the demand of its western members for the remonetization of silver.

Some Populists were openly anti-Semitic, pointing to Jewish people as leaders of the obscure financial forces attempting to enslave them. Others were anti-intellectual, anti-eastern, and anti-urban. A few of the leading Populists gave an impression of personal failure, brilliant instability, and brooding communion with mystic forces. Ignatius Donnelly, for example, wrote one book locating the lost isle of Atlantis, another claiming that Bacon had written Shakespeare's plays, and still another–*Caesar's Column* (1891)–presenting a deranged vision of bloody revolution and the creation of a populist utopia. Tom Watson, once a champion of interracial harmony, ended his career baiting African Americans and Jewish people.

Yet the occasional bigotry of some Populists should not dominate the image of Populism as a whole, which was a serious effort to find solutions to real problems. Populists emphatically rejected the laissez-faire orthodoxies of their time, including the idea that the rights of ownership are absolute. They raised one of the most overt and powerful challenges of the era to the direction in which American industrial capitalism was moving.

POPULISM'S IDEOLOGICAL CHALLENGE

THE CRISIS OF THE 1890s

The agrarian protest was only one of many indications of the national political crisis emerging in the 1890s. There was a severe depression, widespread labor unrest and violence, and the continuing failure of either major party to respond to the growing distress. The rigid conservatism of Grover Cleveland, who took office for the second time just at the moment the economy collapsed, meant that the federal government did little to alleviate the crisis. Out of this growing sense of urgency came some of the most heated political battles in American history, culminating in the dramatic campaign of 1896, on which, many Americans came to believe, the future of the nation was hanging.

THE PANIC OF 1893

The Panic of 1893 precipitated the most severe depression the nation had yet experienced. It began in March 1893, when the Philadelphia and Reading Railroad, unable to meet payments on loans, declared bankruptcy. Two months later, the National Cordage Company failed as well. Together, the two corporate failures triggered a collapse of the stock market. And since many of the major New York banks were heavy investors in the stock market, a wave of bank failures soon began. That caused a contraction of credit, which meant that many of the new, aggressive, and loan-dependent businesses soon went bankrupt.

There were other, longer-range causes of the financial collapse. Depressed prices in agriculture since 1887 had weakened the purchasing power of farmers, the largest group in the population. Depression conditions in Europe caused a loss of American markets abroad and a withdrawal by foreign investors of gold invested in the United States. Railroads and other major industries had expanded too rapidly, well beyond market demand. The depression reflected the degree to which the American economy was now interconnected, the degree to which failures in one area affected all other areas. And the depression showed how dependent the economy was on the health of the railroads, which remained the nation's most powerful corporate and financial institutions. When the railroads suffered, as they did beginning in 1893, everything suffered.

OVEREXPANSION AND WEAK DEMAND

Once the panic began, its effects spread with startling speed. Within six months, more than 8,000 businesses, 156 railroads, and 400 banks failed. Already low agricultural prices tumbled further. Up to 1 million workers, 20 percent of the labor force, lost their jobs–the highest level of unemployment in American history to that point. The depression was unprecedented not only in its severity but also in its persistence. Although there was some improvement beginning in 1895, prosperity did not fully return until 1901.

The suffering the depression caused naturally produced social unrest, especially among the enormous numbers of unemployed workers. In 1894, Jacob S. Coxey, an Ohio businessman and Populist, began advocating a massive public works program to create jobs for the unemployed and an inflation of the currency. When it became clear that his proposals were making no progress in Congress, Coxey announced that he would "send a petition to Washington with boots on"–a march of the unemployed to the capital to present their demands to the government. "Coxey's Army," as it was known, numbered only about 500 when it reached Washington, D.C., after having marched on foot from Masillon, Ohio. Armed police barred them from the Capitol and arrested Coxey. He and his followers were herded into camps because their presence supposedly endangered public health. Congress took no action on their demands.

"COXEY'S ARMY"

To many middle-class Americans, the labor turmoil of the time–the Homestead and Pullman strikes, for example–was a sign of a dangerous instability, even perhaps a revolution. Labor radicalism–some of it real, more of it imagined by t he frightened middle class–heightened the general sense of crisis among the public.

THE SILVER QUESTION

The financial panic weakened the government's monetary system. President Cleveland believed that the instability of the currency was the primary cause of the depression. The "money question," therefore, became the basis for some of the most dramatic political conflicts of the era.

At the heart of the complicated debate was the question of what would form the basis of the dollar. Today, the value of

Discussion and Activities

Analyzing Issues After students have read the section "Populist Ideas," ask them to discuss in pairs or small groups whether the proposals of the Omaha Platform would have solved the problems facing farmers and laborers in the late nineteenth century. Have them write a short paragraph outlining their thoughts and ideas. **PCE** **WXT**

Historical Thinking Skills

Argumentation Have students read the section "The Panic of 1893." Ask them to list and rank in order of importance the causes of the Panic of 1893. Have students write a thesis statement that makes a claim about the most important cause(s) of the panic. **WXT** **PCE**

Discussion and Activities

Analyzing Issues After students have read the section "Crime of '73," ask them to discuss as a class why the Populists focused on silver coinage as a primary issue. *(Coining silver would increase the money supply, which would make it easier for farmers to make debt payments and lead to rising prices for agricultural commodities. The money supply had not been able to grow due to shortages of gold, while the economy did grow, resulting in an economic condition known as deflation.)* **PCE** **WXT**

the dollar rests on little more than public confidence in the government. But in the nineteenth century, many people believed that currency was worthless if there was not something concrete behind it—precious metal (specie), which holders of paper money could collect if they presented their currency to a bank or to the Treasury.

During most of its existence as a nation, the United States had recognized two metals—gold and silver—as a basis for the dollar, a situation known as "bimetallism." In the 1870s, however, that had changed. The official ratio of the value of silver to the value of gold for purposes of creating currency (the "mint ratio") was 16 to 1: sixteen ounces of silver equaled one ounce of gold. But the actual commercial value of silver (the "market ratio") was much higher than that. Owners of silver could get more by selling it for manufacture into jewelry and other objects than they could by taking it to the mint for conversion to coins. So they stopped taking it to the mint, and the mint stopped coining silver.

In 1873, Congress passed a law that seemed simply to recognize the existing situation by officially discontinuing silver coinage. Few people objected at the time. But in the course of the 1870s, the market value of silver fell well below the official mint ratio of 16 to 1. (Sixteen ounces of silver, in other words, were now worth less, not more, than one ounce of gold.) Silver became attractive for coinage again. In discontinuing silver coinage, Congress had eliminated a potential method of expanding the currency (and had eliminated a potential market for silver miners). Before long, many Americans concluded that a conspiracy of big bankers had been responsible for the "demonetization" of silver and referred to the law as the "Crime of '73."

"Crime of '73"

Two groups of Americans were especially determined to undo the "Crime of '73." One consisted of the silver-mine owners, now understandably eager to have the government take their surplus silver and pay them much more than the market price. The other group consisted of discontented farmers, who wanted an increase in the quantity of money—an inflation of the currency—as a means of raising the prices of farm products and easing payment of the farmers' debts. The inflationists demanded that the government return at once to "free silver"—that is, to the "free and unlimited coinage of silver" at the old ratio of 16 to 1. But by the time the depression began in 1893, Congress had made no more than a token response to their demands.

At the same time, the nation's gold reserves were steadily dropping. President Cleveland believed that the chief cause of the weakening gold reserves was the Sherman Silver Purchase Act of 1890 (a sop to silver miners), which had required the government to purchase (but not to coin) silver and to pay for it in gold. Early in his second administration, therefore, a special session responded to Cleveland's request and repealed the Sherman Act—although only after a bitter and divisive battle that helped create a permanent split in the Democratic Party. The president's gold policy had aligned the southern and western Democrats in a solid alliance against him and his eastern followers.

TAKING ARMS AGAINST THE POPULISTS Kansas was a Populist stronghold in the 1890s, but the new party faced powerful challenges. In 1893, state Republicans disputed an election that the Populists believed had given them control of the legislature. When the Populists occupied the statehouse, Republicans armed themselves, drove out the Populists, and seized control of the state government. Republican members of the legislature pose here with their weapons in a photograph perhaps intended as a warning to any Populists inclined to challenge them.

Discussion and Activities

Analyzing Points of View Have students examine the image "Taking Arms Against the Populists." Ask them to write a short letter or journal entry from the point of view of an eyewitness to the event depicted. The eyewitness could be either a Republican or a Populist. Ask for volunteers to share their writing with the class. **PCE**

Discussion and Activities

Making Connections Have students read the section "Symbolic Importance of the Currency Question." Ask them to discuss in small groups any issues they can think of today that are the focus of more attention than the actual issue seems to be worth.

COXEY'S ARMY Jacob S. Coxey leads his "army" of unemployed men through the town of Allegheny, Pennsylvania, in 1894, en route to Washington, D.C., where he hoped to pressure Congress to approve his plans for a massive public works program to put people back to work.

Symbolic Importance of the Currency Question

By now, both sides had invested the currency question with great symbolic and emotional importance. Indeed, the issue aroused passions rarely seen in American politics, culminating in the tumultuous presidential election of 1896. Supporters of the gold standard considered its survival essential to the honor and stability of the nation. Supporters of free silver considered the gold standard an instrument of tyranny. "Free silver" became to them a symbol of liberation. Silver would be a "people's money," as opposed to gold, the money of oppression and exploitation. It would eliminate the indebtedness of farmers and of whole regions of the country. A graphic illustration of the popularity of the silver issue was the enormous success of William H. Harvey's *Coin's Financial School*, published in 1894, which became one of the great best-sellers of its age. The fictional Professor Coin ran an imaginary school specializing in finance, and the book consisted of his lectures and his dialogues with his students. The professor's brilliant discourses left even his most vehement opponents dazzled as he persuaded his listeners, with simple logic, of the almost miraculous restorative qualities of free silver: "It means the reopening of closed factories, the relighting of fires in darkened furnaces; it means hope instead of despair; comfort in place of suffering; life instead of death."

"A CROSS OF GOLD"

Most Populists did not pay much attention to the silver issue at first. But as the party developed strength, the money question became more important to its leaders. The Populists desperately needed funds to finance their campaigns. Silver-mine

Discussion and Activities

Analyzing Visuals Have students examine the image "Coxey's Army." Ask them to identify and discuss as a class details from the image that support or undermine what they learned about this event earlier in the chapter. *(It is clearly a popular movement, with many supporters. Though most participants were unemployed, they appear dressed in suits and hats for the most part. The marchers appear orderly.)* **PCE** **WXT**

AP Exam Practice

Short Answer Provide students with the following short-answer questions and allow 15 minutes for completion. Ask for volunteers to share their responses and discuss as a class.

Answer A, B, and C.

A) Briefly explain ONE important cause of the development of the Populist Party. *(Agricultural depression; political failures of the Grange and Farmers' Alliance.)*

B) Briefly explain ONE important success of the Populist Party. *(Populists won majorities in several state legislatures, and elected several governors and congressmen.)*

C) Briefly explain ONE important failure of the Populist Party. *(Nothing in the Populist platform was adopted until after the party had largely disappeared.)*

DEBATING THE PAST

POPULISM

The scholarly debates over Populism have tended to reflect a larger debate among historians on populist politics. Some historians viewed the Populists with suspicion and hostility. Others have viewed Populism approvingly. To them, the Populists have appeared as essentially admirable, democratic activists.

This latter view shaped the first, and for many years the only, general history of Populism: John D. Hicks's *The Populist Revolt* (1931). Hicks described Populists as people reacting rationally and progressively to economic misfortune. They were proposing reforms that would limit the power of the new financial titans and restore a measure of control to the farmers. Populism was, he wrote, "the last phase of a long and perhaps a losing struggle—the struggle to save agricultural America from the devouring jaws of industrial America." A losing struggle, perhaps, but not a vain one; for many of the reforms the Populists advocated, Hicks implied, became the basis of later progressive legislation.

An alternative to this generally approving view of Populism appeared in the early 1950s when some scholars, recalling the European fascism of World War II and wary about contemporary communism, took a more hostile view of mass popular politics. A leading proponent of this harsh new view was Richard Hofstadter. In *The Age of Reform* (1955), Hofstadter conceded that Populism embraced some progressive ideas and advocated some sensible reforms, but he concentrated primarily on exposing both the "soft" and the "dark" sides of the movement. Populism was "soft," Hofstadter claimed, because it rested on a nostalgic and unrealistic myth, because it romanticized the nation's agrarian past and refused to confront the realities of modern life. It was "dark," he argued, because it was permeated with bigotry and ignorance. Populists, he claimed, revealed anti-Semitic tendencies, and they displayed animosity toward intellectuals, easterners, and urbanites as well.

Challenges to Hofstadter's thesis arose almost immediately. Norman Pollack argued in a 1962 study, *The Populist Response to Industrial America*, that the agrarian revolt had rested not on nostalgic, romantic concepts but, rather, on a sophisticated, farsighted, and even radical vision of reform—one that recognized the realities of an industrial economy, but that sought to make that economy more equitable and democratic by challenging many of the premises of capitalism. Walter T. K. Nugent, in *Tolerant Populists* (1963), argued that the Populists in Kansas were far from bigoted, that they not only tolerated but welcomed Jews and other minorities into their party, and that they offered a practical, sensible program. Lawrence Goodwyn, in *Democratic Promise* (1976), argued similarly that the Populists advocated an intelligent, and above all a democratic, alternative to the inequities of modern capitalism.

Historians were debating not only the question of what Populism meant. They were also arguing over who the Populists were. Hicks, Hofstadter, and Goodwyn disagreed on many things, but they shared a general view of the Populists as victims of economic distress—usually one-crop farmers in marginal agricultural regions victimized by drought and debt. Other scholars, however, suggested that the problem of identifying the Populists is more complex. Sheldon Hackney, in *Populism to Progressivism in Alabama* (1969), argued that the Populists were not only economically troubled but also socially rootless, "only tenuously connected to society by economic function, by personal relationships, by stable community membership, by political participation, or by psychological identification with the South's distinctive myths." Peter Argersinger, Stanley Parsons, James Turner, and others have similarly suggested that Populists were characterized by a form of social and even geographic isolation. Steven Hahn's 1983 study, *The Roots of Southern Populism*, identified poor white farmers in the "upcountry" as the core of Populist activity in Georgia; and Hahn argued that

Populists were reacting not simply to the psychic distress of being "left behind," but also to a real economic threat to their way of life—to the encroachments of a new commercial order of which they had never been a part.

Another debate concerns the legacy of Populism. In *Roots of Reform* (1999), Elizabeth Sanders contends that Populism did not die as a movement after the 1896 election. On the contrary, she argues, the Populists succeeded in dominating much of the Democratic Party in the following decades and turning it into a vehicle for advancing the interests of farmers and the broader reform causes for which Populists had fought. Michael Kazin, in *The Populist Persuasion* (1994), argues that a Populist tradition has survived throughout much of American history, influencing movements as disparate as those led by Huey Long in the 1930s, the New Left and George Wallace in the 1960s, Ross Perot in the 1990s, and the Tea Party movement in the aftermath of the 2008 economic collapse. Other historians, however, maintain that the term *populism* has been used (and misused) so widely as to have become virtually meaningless, that it really applies only to the agrarian insurgents of the 1890s.

HISTORICAL THINKING SKILLS

Questions assume cumulative content knowledge from this chapter and previous chapters.

1. **Identifying Historical Developments** Identify three broad schools of historical interpretation concerning Populism.
2. **Evaluating Evidence** Describe how one piece of historical evidence from the time period could be used to support each of the three broad schools of historical interpretation concerning Populism.
3. **Developing Arguments** Analyze the school of thought you find more convincing. Explain why you feel this way and be sure to use evidence to support your argument.

The Library of Congress (LC-USZC4-1473)

Answers

Debating the Past

1. Possible answer: The first systematic and historical interpretation of the Populists came in the 1930s when John D. Hicks, in his book *The Populist Revolt* (1931), argued that the movement was a reaction to the industrialization of America. A second wave came in the 1950s, when Richard Hofstadter, in his classic survey "The Age of Reform (1955)," argued that the Populists represented some things that were good but also some things that were not so good. A new wave of scholarship rose in the 1990s, led by Elizabeth Sanders in her book *Roots of Reform* (1999), in which she argues that Populism never really died and that it still alive and well today.
2. Possible answer: The initial stirrings of Populism came from farmers protesting the railroads. Much of the rail lines during the second half of the nineteenth century were controlled by only a handfull of individuals. Also, the first part of the 21st century has shown a tremendous amount of interest in and examples of contemporary populism. The Tea Party movement in 2008, along with the 2016 election of Donald Trump to the presidency, both point to the continued presence of Populist movements, although these had very different goals from the original Populists.
3. Student responses will vary.

owners were willing to provide assistance but insisted on an elevation of the currency plank. The Populists also needed to form alliances with other political groups. The "money question" seemed a way to win the support of many people not engaged in farming but nevertheless starved for currency.

The Emergence of Bryan

As the election of 1896 approached, Republicans, watching the failure of the Democrats to deal effectively with the depression, were confident of success. Party leaders, led by the Ohio boss Marcus A. Hanna, settled on Governor William McKinley of Ohio, who had as a member of Congress authored the 1890 tariff act, as the party's presidential candidate. The Republican platform opposed the free coinage of silver except by agreement with the leading commercial nations (which everyone realized was unlikely). Thirty-four delegates from the mountain and plains states walked out of the convention in protest and joined the Democratic Party.

William McKinley

The Democratic National Convention of 1896 was the scene of unusual drama. Southern and Western delegates, eager to neutralize the challenge of the People's Party, were determined to seize control of the party from conservative easterners and incorporate some Populist demands—among them free silver—into the Democratic platform. They wanted as well to nominate a pro-silver presidential candidate.

Defenders of the gold standard seemed to dominate the debate, until the final speech. Then William Jennings Bryan, a handsome, thirty-six-year-old congressman from Nebraska already well known as an effective orator, mounted the podium to address the convention. His great voice echoed through the hall as he defended "free silver" in what became one of the most famous political speeches in American history. The closing passage sent his audience into something close to a frenzy: "Having behind us the producing masses of this nation and the world, supported by the commercial interests, the laboring interests and the toilers everywhere, we will answer their demand for a gold standard by saying to them: 'You shall not press down upon the brow of labor this crown of thorns; you shall not crucify mankind upon a cross of gold.'" It became known as the "Cross of Gold" speech.

"Cross of Gold" Speech

In the aftermath of Bryan's powerful speech, the convention voted to adopt a pro-silver platform. And the following day, Bryan (as he had eagerly and not entirely secretly hoped) was nominated for president on the fifth ballot. He was, and remains, the youngest person ever nominated for president by a major party. Republican and conservative Democrats attacked Bryan as a dangerous demagogue. But his many admirers hailed him as the Great Commoner. He was a potent symbol of rural, Protestant, middle-class America.

The choice of Bryan and the nature of the Democratic platform created a quandary for the Populists. They had expected both major parties to adopt conservative programs and nominate conservative candidates, leaving the Populists to represent the growing forces of protest. But now the Democrats had stolen much of their thunder. The Populists faced the choice of naming their own candidate and splitting the protest vote or endorsing Bryan and losing their identity as a party. By now, the Populists had embraced the free-silver cause, but most Populists still believed that other issues were more important. Many argued that "fusion" with the Democrats—who had endorsed free silver but ignored most of the other Populist demands—would destroy their party. But the majority concluded that there was no viable alternative. Amid considerable acrimony, the convention voted to support Bryan.

"Fusion"

The Conservative Victory

The campaign of 1896 produced desperation among conservatives. The business and financial community, frightened beyond reason at the prospect of a Bryan victory, contributed lavishly to the Republican campaign, which may have spent as much as $7 million, as compared to the Democrats' $300,000. From his home at Canton, Ohio, McKinley hewed to the tradition by which candidates for president did not actively campaign for the office. He conducted a dignified "front-porch" campaign by receiving pilgrimages of the Republican faithful, organized and paid for by Hanna.

Bryan showed no such restraint. He became the first presidential candidate in American history to stump every section of the country systematically, to appear in villages and hamlets, indeed the first to say frankly to the voters that he wanted to be president. He traveled 18,000 miles and addressed an estimated 5 million people. But Bryan may have done himself more harm than good. By violating a long-standing tradition of presidential candidates' remaining aloof from their own campaigns (the tradition by which they "stood" for office rather than "running" for it), Bryan helped establish the modern form of presidential politics. But he also antagonized many voters, who considered his campaign undignified.

Birth of Modern Campaigning

On election day, McKinley polled 271 electoral votes to Bryan's 176 and received 51.1 percent of the popular vote to Bryan's 47.7. Bryan carried the areas of the South and West where miners or struggling staple farmers predominated. The Democratic program, like that of the Populists, had been too narrow to win a national election.

For the Populists and their allies, the election results were a disaster. They had gambled everything on their "fusion" with the Democratic Party and lost. Within months of the election, the People's Party began to dissolve. Never again would American farmers unite so militantly to demand economic reform.

End of the People's Party

McKinley and Recovery

The administration of William McKinley, which began in the aftermath of turmoil, saw a return to relative calm. One reason was the exhaustion of dissent. By 1897, when McKinley took

Historical Thinking Skills

Argumentation Have students read the section "The Emergence of Bryan." Ask them to write a short letter to a leader of the Populist Party advising whether or not the Populists should join with the Democrats for the 1896 presidential election. **PCE** **WXT** **SOC**

Discussion and Activities

Making Connections Have students read the section "The Conservative Victory." Ask them to discuss as a class how the presidential campaign discussed here was similar to or different from recent presidential campaigns. **PCE** **SOC** **ARC**

Discussion and Activities

Speculating Have students read the section "Currency Act." Ask them to go online to research when the United States officially went off of the gold standard for good. Have students discuss in small groups why they think the gold standard lasted so long. *(Tradition; the stability of a metallic standard; international agreements.)* **WXT** **PCE**

BRYAN WHISTLE-STOPPING By long-established tradition, candidates for the presidency did not actively campaign after receiving their party's nomination. Nineteenth-century Americans considered public "stumping" to be undignified and inappropriate for a future president. But in 1896, William Jennings Bryan—a young candidate little known outside his own region, a man without broad support even among the leaders of his own party—decided that he had no choice but to go directly to the public for support. He traveled widely and incessantly in the months before the election, appearing before hundreds of crowds and hundreds of thousands of people.

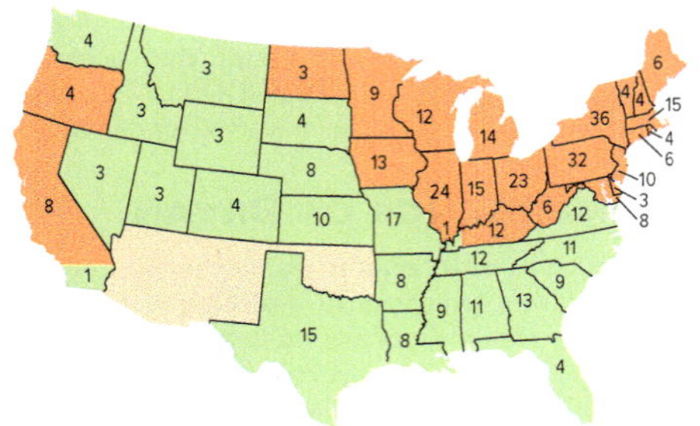

Candidate (Party)	Electoral Vote	Popular Vote (%)
William McKinley (Republican)	271	7,104,779 (51.1)
William Jennings Bryan (Democratic)	176	6,502,925 (47.7)

ELECTION OF 1896 The results of the presidential election of 1896 are, as this map shows, striking for the regional differentiation they reveal. William McKinley won the election by a comfortable but not enormous margin, but his victory was not broad-based. He carried all the states of the Northeast and the industrial Midwest, along with California and Oregon, but virtually nothing else. Bryan carried the entire South and almost all of the agrarian West.

What campaign issues in 1896 help account for the regional character of the results?

office, the labor unrest that had so frightened many middle-class Americans and so excited working-class people had subsided. With the simultaneous decline of agrarian protest, the greatest destabilizing forces in the nation's politics were—temporarily at least—in retreat. Another reason was the shrewd character of the McKinley administration itself, committed as it was to reassuring stability. Most important, however, was the gradual easing of the economic crisis, a development that undercut many of those who were agitating for change.

McKinley and his allies committed themselves fully to only one issue, one on which they knew virtually all Republicans agreed: the need for higher tariff rates. Within weeks of his inauguration, the administration won approval of the Dingley Tariff, raising duties to the highest point in American history. The administration dealt more gingerly with the explosive silver question (an issue that McKinley himself had never considered very important in any case). McKinley sent a commission to Europe to explore the possibility of a silver agreement with Great Britain and France. As he and everyone else anticipated, the effort produced no agreement. The Republicans then enacted the Currency, or Gold Standard, Act of 1900, which confirmed the nation's commitment to the gold standard by assigning a specific gold value to the dollar and requiring all currency issued by the United States to hew to that value.

CURRENCY ACT

And so the "battle of the standards" ended in victory for the forces of conservatism. Economic developments at the time seemed to vindicate the Republicans. Prosperity began to return in 1898. Foreign crop failures sent farm prices surging upward, and American business entered another cycle of expansion. Prosperity and the gold standard, it seemed, were closely allied.

But while the free-silver movement had failed, it had raised an important question for the American economy. In the quarter-century before 1900, the countries of the Western world had experienced a spectacular growth in productive facilities and population. Yet the supply of money had not kept pace with economic progress, because the supply was tied to gold and the amount of gold had remained practically constant. Had it not been for a dramatic increase in the gold supply in the late 1890s (a result of new techniques for extracting gold from low-content ores and the discovery of huge new gold deposits in Alaska, South Africa, and Australia), Populist predictions of

The Library of Congress (LC-USZC2-6259)

Answers

Election of 1896

Farmers and Populists, concentrated in the Midwest and South, supported the Democratic candidate Bryan because he advocated for "free silver." That issue never gained much traction among Eastern laborers and was actively opposed by business leaders, who largely voted Republican.

financial disaster might in fact have proved correct. In 1898, two and a half times as much gold was produced as in 1890, and the currency supply was soon inflated far beyond anything Bryan and the free-silver forces had anticipated.

By then, however, Bryan—like many other Americans—was becoming engaged with another major issue: a growing United States presence in world affairs and the possibility of America becoming an imperialist nation.

CHAPTER 19 REVIEW

CONNECTING THEMES

Chapter Nineteen explored the politics of equilibrium during the Gilded Age, when the Democrats and Republicans were evenly divided. The electoral system featured high turnouts and voter loyalty based on religion, region, race, and culture. Demands for political and economic reform led to passage of the Pendleton Civil Service Act, the Sherman Antitrust Act, and the Interstate Commerce Act, although the impact of these laws was limited or uneven.

The economic, political, and social crisis of the 1890s led to widespread protests by industrial workers and small farmers, who were economically insecure and politically marginal. The emergence of the People's Party in 1892 represented a major agrarian challenge to the Democrats and Republicans. But in the election of 1896, the Populists chose to endorse the Democratic presidential nominee, William Jennings Bryan. When he lost to Republican William McKinley, the People's Party disappeared. Nevertheless, the issues it raised would continue to influence the reform agenda of the twentieth century.

You should consider the following questions as you review the themes for this chapter:

- What were the reasons for the stability of the party system in the late-nineteenth century?
- What were the similarities and differences between the two major parties during the Gilded Age?
- How did the Granger movement and the Farmers' Alliances reflect the regional concerns?
- What were the reasons for the third party movement and how did they tie to major party platform issues of the Populist movement?
- How did the Panic of 1893 effect the social, political, and economic institutions in the United States?
- What were the major issues of the monetary debate between the silver and gold standard?
- What was significant about the Election of 1896?

KEY TERMS

Discussion and Activities

Comparison and Argumentation
After students have finished reading Chapter 19, have them discuss as a class how successful the farmer's revolt of the late nineteenth century was, taking into consideration new legislation like the Sherman Antitrust Act, the Sherman Silver Purchase Act, the Interstate Commerce Act, and the Granger laws, as well as the advocacy for an eight-hour work day, the federal subtreasury plan, regulation of railroads, etc. It may be helpful to assign these topics to small groups to review, research, and present prior to the class discussion. **PCE** **WXT** **SOC** **ARC**

Key Terms

Students should be familiar with the key terms and be able to define them in the context of the political equilibrium of the period, taking into consideration the major issues of tariff and monetary policy and the emergence of farmers' organizations and the Populist Party that pressed for political and economic reform. Encourage students to use these terms in performing review exercises and exam practice for this chapter.

Go Online Chapter 19 Content Review

Assessing Student Understanding Use the online assessment to assess student understanding of concepts and topics within the chapter. You can assign the ready-made Chapter 19 Content Review or create your own from available questions. This easy-to-use tool helps you design assessments that meet the needs of different types of learners.

Answers

Multiple Choice

1. C; **2.** A; **3.** C

Short Answer

4A) Possible answer: The point of view in the image is that of someone who is sympathetic to the plight of workers. The "monopoly" is fitted out with heavy armor, riding on the back of a horse represented as a railroad car, versus the little guy of "labor," who only has a small hammer to battle the long spear of the monopolist.

4B) Possible answer: The Sherman Antitrust Act was the first piece of federal legislation that attempted to try and rein in the monopolies. The legislation was largely ineffective, because it lacked any enforcement power and was misinterpreted by the U.S. Supreme Court and targeted labor unions.

4C) Possible answer: In 1886, the U.S. Supreme Court ruled in the *Wabash* case that an Illinois Granger Law, which regulated the price of railroad rates, was unconstitutional because the law violated the commerce clause of the U.S. Constitution. Because railroad lines crossed state boundaries, the state of Illinois had no authority to regulate the rates.

5A) Possible answer: Both groups responded to specific concerns that they had against the monopolist. Both groups believed that the government was supporting these individuals over the interests of labor.

5B) Possible answer: Industrial labor movements focused their energy on the cities and the industrial workforce. Agricultural labor movements instead focused their energy on rural America and farmers. The Populist movement had no support outside parts of the South and the West.

5C) Possible answer: After initial unsuccessful state-level attempts to regulate big business, the federal government stepped in and began passing legislation which would deal with the issues raised by both the industrial and agricultural labor movements.

AP EXAM PRACTICE

Questions assume cumulative content knowledge from this chapter and previous chapters.

MULTIPLE CHOICE

Use the image on page 544 and your knowledge of U.S. history to answer questions 1-3.

1. William Jennings Bryan argued in his famous "Cross of Gold" speech for what Populist position?
   (A) government regulation of all major industries
   (B) significant restriction of immigration
   (C) monetary policy based on a silver standard
   (D) popular election of Senators

2. The Populists gained political support as
   (A) farmers increasingly became politically organized through the Grange and Farmers' Alliances.
   (B) urban factory workers joined forces with farmers to battle the increasing power of industrialists.
   (C) they welcomed new immigrants and African Americans into their ranks.
   (D) they spread their membership into the growing ranks of middle management in consolidating industries.

3. What economic trends accelerated political discord in the 1890s?
   (A) The increasing wealth of farmers distanced them from average Americans.
   (B) The boom in factory workers' wages created economic tensions with farmers.
   (C) The Panic of 1893 precipitated a depression that led to widespread economic hardship.
   (D) Significant immigration brought economic tension as immigrants filled all the higher paying jobs.

SHORT ANSWER

Use your knowledge of U.S. history to answer questions 4 and 5.

4. Use the image on page 540 to answer A, B, and C.
   (A) Describe ONE point of view about the nature of capitalism during the Gilded Age in the United States.
   (B) Briefly explain ONE specific historical action by government that attempted to control the monopolies during the Gilded Age.
   (C) Briefly explain ONE specific historical action by government that supported the monopolies during the Gilded Age.

5. Answer A, B, and C.
   (A) Briefly describe ONE specific historical similarity between the industrial labor movement and the agricultural labor movement during the Gilded Age.
   (B) Briefly describe ONE specific historical difference between the industrial labor movements and the agricultural labor movements during the Gilded Age.
   (C) Briefly explain ONE specific historical effect that resulted from the agricultural labor movements during the Gilded Age.

LONG ESSAY

Develop a thoughtful and thorough historical argument that addresses the statement. Begin your essay with a thesis statement, and support it with specific historical evidence and examples.

6. Evaluate the relative importance of the causes of the agricultural labor movement during the Gilded Age in the United States.

554 · CHAPTER 19

Answers

Long Essay

6. Possible thesis: Monetary policy was a source of great concern for the agricultural labor movement. However, regulation of big business, especially that of the railroads, as well as agricultural opposition to tariffs, were more important causes which gave rise to an agricultural labor movement during the Gilded Age. Specific historical evidence: Railroads impacted every other economic venture in the United States. Railroads had control over farmers and industry in the South and West. Since only a handful of individuals controlled most of the rail lines in America, these individuals controlled a tremendous amount of power over the agricultural industry. Farmers voiced protests against what they believed to be unfair practices of regulating prices and controlling rates. The Populists supported government control of certain industries, like transportation and communications industries. Because industrial labor had organizations that lobbied on their behalf, farmers also believed that they needed some organized support against industry. Monetary issues were also a main concern for agricultural labor movements during the second half of the nineteenth century. Since farmers were often in debt to banks for loans for land and other things, they generally supported an inflationary monetary policy. Bankers, on the other hand, supported a deflationary monetary policy. The silver and gold issue, reaching its height with Bryan's "Cross of Gold" speech, highlighted the differences between agricultural interests and those of big business and banking.

UNIT 6 AP EXAM PRACTICE

AP EXAM PRACTICE

As you answer the questions, consider how the historical developments, processes, and individuals in Unit 6 connect to those in previous units.

MULTIPLE CHOICE

Use the excerpt and your knowledge of U.S. history to answer questions 1-3.

"Since the days when the fleet of Columbus sailed into the waters of the New World, America has been another name for opportunity, and the people of the United States have taken their tone from the incessant expansion which has not only been open but has even been forced upon them... Movement has been its dominant fact... each frontier did indeed furnish a new field of opportunity, a gate of escape from the bondage of the past; and freshness, and confidence, and scorn of older society, impatience of its restraints and its ideas, and indifference to its lessons, have accompanied the frontier."

–Frederick Jackson Turner, "The Significance of the Frontier in American History," 1893

1. Which best describes the American democratic tradition that Turner argues the frontier enabled?
   (A) freedom of religion
   (B) orderly settlement of society
   (C) desirability of utopian societies
   (D) ideal of equal opportunity

2. Which of the following most closely reflects Turner's perspective?
   (A) mercantilism
   (B) Manifest Destiny
   (C) Calvinist predestination
   (D) abolitionism

3. Turner's thesis does not account for what related historical conflicts?
   (A) disagreements over immigration policy
   (B) racial disparities in legal structures after the Civil War
   (C) legal battles over the denial of women's suffrage
   (D) conflicts over land between Native Americans and white settlers

Use the political cartoon on page 489 and your knowledge of U.S. history to answer question 4-6.

4. What would supporters of the cartoonist's perspective have argued?
   (A) industrialists had too much control over the economy
   (B) industrialists are important moral leaders in America
   (C) industrialists should be subject to more stringent government oversight
   (D) industrialists should pay a higher tax rate

5. Industrialists were able to amass such significant fortunes through
   (A) new means of transportation.
   (B) new approaches to factory organization designed to increase workers' job satisfaction.
   (C) new forms of corporate consolidation and managerial techniques.
   (D) new philanthropy designed to encourage racial justice.

6. Individuals such as those pictured in the cartoon justified their massive fortunes through the ideology of
   (A) Republican motherhood.
   (B) Manifest Destiny.
   (C) Social Darwinism.
   (D) the Social Gospel.

Discussion and Activities

Analyzing Cause and Effect Direct students' attention to the Questions to Consider posed at the beginning of Unit 6:

- What were the major causes and effects of western migration during the Gilded Age?
- What were the reasons for and consequences of the rise of the Second Industrial Revolution in the United States?
- What were the reasons for and effects of the rise of the agricultural labor movements during the Gilded Age?

Discuss these questions as a class to review important concepts from the unit. To close the discussion, **ask:** How appropriate is the label "Gilded Age?" What, if any, significant advances were made in the United States culturally, socially, and economically during the time period? **WXT** **SOC** **ARC**

Answers

Multiple Choice

1. D; **2.** B; **3.** D; **4.** A; **5.** C; **6.** C; **7.** D; **8.** C; **9.** A; **10.** C

Answers

Short Answer

11A) Possible answer: The point of view about the Populists in the image is one critical of the party. The balloon is made up of a "hodge-podge" of different movements, some of them not having much to do with each other. Many of them were considered minor movements, without any uniform direction, which is indicated by the puffs of air coming from the balloon (that also indicates that the movement is losing momentum).

11B) Possible answer: Farmers had begun uniting under different organizations during the Gilded Age, but initially they were little more than random organizations with essentially no power or authority. The Populist Party united the different groups and inserted themselves as a political player in local, state, and national politics. The party gave farmers a united voice in American politics.

11C) Possible answer: During the elections of 1892 and 1896, the Populists played a significant role as they battled with Democrats, especially for votes. However, the party soon died out as the United States became a majority urban society.

Use the map on page 510 and your knowledge of U.S. history to answer questions 7 and 8.

7. What population trend is illustrated by the map?
   (A) Large numbers of African Americans were moving from the South to Northern cities.
   (B) Most immigrants settled in the Great Plains rather than urban areas.
   (C) Great numbers of older Americans moved to cities to escape the challenges of rural life.
   (D) Significant numbers of young rural women and African Americans migrated to cities.

8. Which best describes the cause for the settlement patterns illustrated by the map?
   (A) availability of new farmlands in the Great Plains and West
   (B) industrialization and mechanization of farming techniques
   (C) the large number of immigrants arriving in the United States
   (D) the sharp increase of cotton and tobacco production

Use the political cartoon on page 536 and your knowledge of U.S. history to answer questions 9 and 10.

9. The groups represented in the image all struggled with which reality of Gilded Age politics?
   (A) The American political system was plagued with patronage politics and significant corruption.
   (B) Elected officials wielded significant power and used it to protect the working class.
   (C) The Presidency was too powerful and blocked all Congressional attempts at reform.
   (D) Government programs focused solely on westward expansion and virtually ignored industrial leaders.

10. Repeated attempts to unite the groups represented in the image found the most political success in which party or movement?
   (A) the Republican Party
   (B) the Farmers' Alliances
   (C) the Populist Party
   (D) the Grange

SHORT ANSWER

Use the image on page 536 and your knowledge of U.S. history to answer question 11.

11. Answer A, B, and C.
   (A) Describe ONE point of view about Populists presented in the image, "A Party of Patches."
   (B) Explain ONE specific historical cause that led to the formation of the Populist Party in 1892.
   (C) Explain ONE specific historical effect of the formation of the Populist Party in 1892.

LONG ESSAY

Develop a thoughtful and thorough historical argument that addresses the statement below. Begin your essay with a thesis statement, and support it with specific historical evidence and examples.

12. Evaluate the extent of continuities within the American party system from 1860 to 1900.

556 · UNIT 6

Answers

Long Essay

12. Possible thesis: Despite a short stint of supporting civil rights during and immediately following the Civil War, the Republican Party became the party of money and wealth. Both parties' ideologies remained similar to those of when they were founded, and the two-party system remained the major dynamic in American politics during the Gilded Age. Continuities: America during the Gilded Age remained largely a two-party system. The Democrats and the Republicans would remain the major and national parties for the rest of America's political life, up to present. The ideological and geographic focus of these parties remained the same throughout the duration of the Gilded Age; Democrats represented largely agricultural and Southern interests, while Republicans represented largely industrial and Northern interests. Changes: The short life of the Republicans as the party dedicated to civil rights would change within a decade. This party, which had emerged as the party of Lincoln, opposed the expansion of slavery and eventually championed the Thirteenth, Fourteenth, and Fifteenth Amendments, but it abandoned many of these principles following the Compromise of 1877. They became the party of big business and monopolies, turning a blind eye to the violations of those amendments in the reconstituted South. Third parties emerged, but many of these, with the possible exception of the Populists, were simply specific-interest parties with little value or lasting importance.

Pacing Guide

Unit 7 explores key concepts from Period 7: 1890–1945 of the AP U.S. History Curriculum Framework. It is recommended that 10–17% of the total instruction time for the entire course be spent on Period 7.

Key Concepts

7.1 Growth expanded opportunity, while economic instability led to new efforts to reform U.S. society and its economic system.

7.2 Innovations in communications and technology contributed to the growth of mass culture, while significant changes occurred in internal and international migration patterns.

7.3 Participation in a series of global conflicts propelled the United States into a position of international power while renewing domestic debates over the nation's proper role in the world.

UNIT 7: 1890–1945

THEMATIC LEARNING OBJECTIVES

- Analyze the causes and effects of the new imperialism, including the Spanish-American War.
- Explain the reasons for and the impact of the rise of the Progressive movement in the United States.
- Analyze the continuities and changes in America's foreign policy during the first half of the twentieth century.
- Assess the home front mobilization efforts by the United States in preparation for both world wars.
- Evaluate the reasons for and consequences of the changes in migration patterns during both world wars.
- Identify the efforts that Roosevelt took to counter the effects of the Great Depression during the 1930s.
- Describe the cultural controversies that drove social, political, and economic changes in the United States during the first half of the twentieth century.

QUESTIONS TO CONSIDER

- What were the continuities and changes within American foreign policy during the first half of the twentieth century?
- What were the reasons for and effects of the rise of a Progressive movement in the first decade of the twentieth century?
- What major issues propelled the cultural wars during the first half of the twentieth century in the United States?

HISTORICAL DEVELOPMENTS: 1890–1945

1898
Spanish-American War begins
1904
"Roosevelt Corollary" to the Monroe Doctrine
1909
National Association for the Advancement of Colored People established
1915
German submarine sinks British passenger liner Lusitania
1919
League of Nations formed
1895
1900
1905
1910
1915
1900
Boxer Rebellion begins in China
Niagara Movement organized by W.E.B. Du Bois 1905
1906
The Jungle by Upton Sinclair published
1914
Federal Trade Commission Act and Clayton Antitrust Act passed
1917
United States enters World War I

Discussion and Activities

Evaluating Evidence Have students examine the time line "Historical Developments: 1890–1945." **Ask:** Based on the time line and what you already know, which events on the time line appear to deal with social, economic, diplomatic, or political issues? *(Social: NAACP formed,* The Great Gatsby *published, Zoot Suit riots; Economic: FTC formed, stock market crash, SEC formed; Diplomatic: "Roosevelt Corollary," League of Nations, Kellogg-Briand Pact; Political: FTC formed, Nineteenth Amendment, Emergency Quota Act, Korematsu decision*). Which category seems to be most prevalent? **PCE** **WXT** **SOC**

MAKING CONNECTIONS

Unit Seven focuses on the period from 1890 to 1945. Prior to the outbreak of war with Spain in 1898, the United States had traditionally pursued a policy of isolationism. But by the 1890s America was on the verge of becoming a world power, thanks in part to industrial development. Growing European imperialism, however, caused some American leaders to fear that the United States lacked access to raw materials and markets. Victory over Spain in the Spanish-American War provided territorial expansion, which American imperialists desired and celebrated, but now the nation had to deal with the challenging political and economic consequences of these acquisitions.

The urbanization and industrialization of America led to a political movement known as Progressivism. These reformers adopted a different approach to the relationship between government and business. Presidents like Theodore Roosevelt and Woodrow Wilson attempted to monitor, regulate, and legislate the behavior of large corporations. Authors and journalists known as "muckrakers" also exposed political and economic corruption, which led to federal laws such as the Pure Food and Drug Act and the Meat Inspection Act.

Overseas, Roosevelt adopted a more interventionist foreign policy, while his successor William Howard Taft advocated economic pressure known as "Dollar Diplomacy." Wilson initially tried to promote pro-democracy policies – sometimes known as "Moral Diplomacy"—but soon had the United States embroiled in the Mexican Revolution as war erupted in Europe in 1914. Three years later, America entered the Great War and became a major player on the world stage.

During the 1920s, a series of Republican presidents — Warren Harding, Calvin Coolidge, and Herbert Hoover — sought a return to "Normalcy." Progressivism faded as coordination between government and business again became commonplace. New technologies and growing consumerism fueled the economic growth of the "Roaring Twenties."

At the same time, the nation experienced a clash of cultures between more traditional rural Americans and more modern urban Americans over religion, immigration, and Prohibition. A new, secular view of womanhood inspired some women to continue to press for reforms. The "New Negro" also emerged, in part due to the Great Migration of African Americans from the rural South to the industrial North during and after World War I. Racial tensions often exploded in violence, but the art, music, and literature of the Harlem Renaissance was extraordinary.

During the 1930s, the country experienced an economic crisis known as the Great Depression, which eroded the popularity of Hoover. The election of Franklin Roosevelt in 1932 led to the "New Deal," which dramatically expanded the role of the federal government in relation to the day-to-day lives of Americans. But the New Deal failed to end the Great Depression, which continued until America went to war again in 1941 after the Japanese attack on Pearl Harbor. World War II transformed the United States into an economic and military superpower. But it also placed the nation on a collision course with the Soviet Union, the other superpower to emerge from the conflict. The Cold War would dominate world affairs for the next half century.

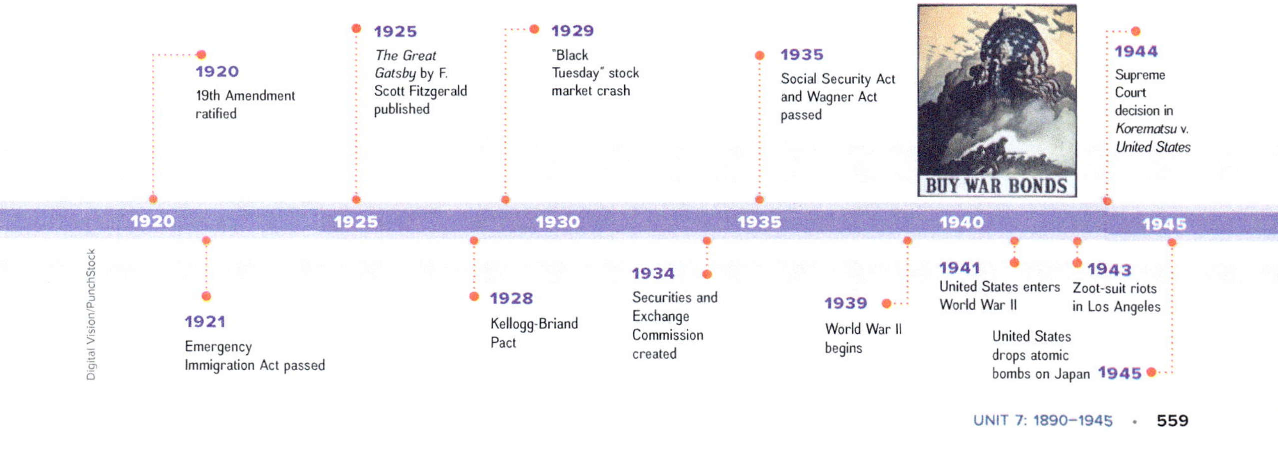
1920
19th Amendment ratified
1921
Emergency Immigration Act passed
1925
The Great Gatsby by F. Scott Fitzgerald published
1928
Kellogg-Briand Pact
1929
"Black Tuesday" stock market crash
1934
Securities and Exchange Commission created
1935
Social Security Act and Wagner Act passed
1939
World War II begins
BUY WAR BONDS
1941
United States enters World War II
1943
Zoot-suit riots in Los Angeles
1944
Supreme Court decision in *Korematsu v. United States*
1945
United States drops atomic bombs on Japan
1920
1925
1930
1935
1940
1945

Digital Vision/PunchStock

Historical Thinking Skills

Contextualization Have students read the section "Making Connections." Discuss as a class the state of the nation and important developments. *(Discussion topics include: Gilded Age, Second Industrial Revolution, urbanization, machine politics, and farmers' revolt.)*

PCE **NAT** **ARC** **WXT** **SOC** **MIG**

Go Online Additional Resources

Adaptive Learning with SmartBook A proven adaptive learning program, SmartBook offers an interactive environment that helps students learn faster, study more efficiently, and retain more knowledge.

Assign this resource to differentiate instruction for students and report on year-long progression.

Pacing Guide

Chapter 20 explores key concepts from Period 7: 1890–1945 of the AP U.S. History Curriculum Framework. The suggested instruction time for Chapter 20 is 2 days.

Key Concepts

7.3.I In the late 19th century and early 20th century, new U.S. territorial ambitions and acquisitions in the Western Hemisphere and the Pacific accompanied heightened public debates over America's role in the world.

20 IMPERIALISM

"REMEMBER THE *MAINE*!"
President McKinley sent the battleship USS *Maine* to Cuba. When the vessel exploded, an enraged nation blamed Spain. "Remember the *Maine*!" became the battle cry for war.

Everett Historical/Shutterstock

CONNECTING CONCEPTS

Chapter Twenty focuses on the reasons for and consequences of American emergence onto the world stage as both an economic and military power three decades after the Civil War. The Panic of 1893 caused businesses to look overseas for foreign markets and natural resources. Some imperialists used Social Darwinism to capitalize on the fear that European powers were gaining in the race for global dominance. Others contended that America had the duty and obligation to spread democracy and civilization to other countries. A new sense of Manifest Destiny led the United States to intervene in Venezuela in defense of the Monroe Doctrine, acquire Samoa, and support a revolution in Hawaii staged by American planters.

War with Spain in 1898 gave the United States an overseas empire. President McKinley was reluctant to declare war, but the American press blamed Spain for the brutal mistreatment of Cuban revolutionaries and the accidental explosion of the battleship *Maine* in Havana harbor. Although the war spotlighted racial tensions and glaring deficiencies in the U.S. military, which subsequently modernized, the fighting was brief and led to the capture of Cuba, control of the Philippines, and the annexation of Puerto Rico. The Treaty of Paris ended the conflict with Spain, but sparked an intense debate over the acquisition of the Philippines. Anti-imperialists feared an influx of Asian immigrants and job competition with American workers. But imperialists successfully argued that the precedent set with Native Americans — annexing land without absorbing people as citizens — justified ratification of the treaty.

The new American empire was small by European standards and three of the new dependencies — Hawaii, Alaska (acquired from Russia in 1867), and Puerto Rico posed few problems. But annexation of the Philippines resulted in a brutal, though little-remembered, war from 1898 to 1902 between American soldiers and Filipino revolutionaries led by Emilio Aguinaldo. The eventual victory over the revolutionaries increased American interest in Asia, especially China, where Japan and European powers had established spheres of influence. To gain equal access to markets in China, the United States issued the "Open Door notes," participated in the suppression of the Boxer Rebellion, and began to take its place on the world stage.

560 · CHAPTER 20

Discussion and Activities

Analyzing Images Have students examine the image "Remember the *Maine*!" Ask them to identify and discuss in small groups details from the image that would inspire support for a war against Spain. *(American flag being knocked into the water; sailors being blown into the sky and water; destruction of an American battleship engaged in a peaceful mission.)* **WOR** **PCE**

As you read, you should:

- Analyze the efforts of the United States to expand its presence in world affairs to gain greater influence, open new markets, and gain access to new sources of raw materials.
- Evaluate the economic, social, and political arguments the United States used to justify its new imperialism.
- Identify how the United States acquired new territories and expanded its military and economic presence in the world.
- Analyze the major causes that led the United States to declare war on Spain in 1898.
- Explain the debate between imperialists and anti-imperialists that divided the country in the late nineteenth century.

STIRRINGS OF IMPERIALISM

For over two decades after the Civil War, the United States expanded hardly at all. By the 1890s, however, some Americans were ready—indeed, eager—to resume the course of Manifest Destiny that had inspired their ancestors to wrest an empire from Mexico in the expansionist 1840s.

IMPERIALISM AT HIGH TIDE: 1900

The United States became a formal imperial power in 1898, when it acquired colonies in the aftermath of the Spanish American War. But the U.S. was a decided latecomer to imperialism. During the nineteenth century, European nations dramatically expanded the reach of their empires, moving in particular into Africa and Asia. Although the British remained the world's largest imperial power by a significant margin, vast areas of the globe came under the control of other European colonizers, as this map shows.

How did the United States and the European imperial nations justify their acquisition of empire?

Answers

Imperialism at High Tide: 1900

They claimed the need for new markets and sources of raw materials for manufactured goods, the need to control strategic locations, and the superiority of people of European descent.

Go Online AP Exam Preparation

AP Exam Practice Use the online assessment to help prepare students for the AP Exam. You can assign the ready-made AP-style short-answer questions, document-based questions, and multiple-choice questions assessing concepts, themes, and skills from Period 7 and AP-style long-essay questions organized in sets of 3 questions from various time periods. You can also create your own tests from available questions. This easy-to-use tool helps you design assessments that meet the needs of different types of learners.

Historical Thinking Skills

Argumentation Have students read the section "Increasing Importance of Trade." Ask them to write a short paragraph explaining how the Turner Thesis created pressure for the United States to expand overseas. *(The closing of the frontier represented the end of new discovery, and eventually, the depletion of natural resources. New sources of raw materials might be secured overseas.)* **WXT** **WOR**

THE NEW MANIFEST DESTINY

Several developments helped shift American attention to lands across the seas. The experience of subjugating the Native American nations had established a precedent for exerting colonial control over dependent peoples. The concept of the "closing of the frontier," widely heralded by Frederick Jackson Turner and many others in the 1890s, produced fears that natural resources would soon dwindle and that alternative sources must be found abroad. The depression of the 1890s encouraged some businessmen to look overseas for new markets. The bitter social protests of the time–the Populist movement, the free-silver crusade, the bloody labor disputes–led some politicians to urge a more aggressive foreign policy as an outlet for frustrations that would otherwise destabilize domestic life.

INCREASING IMPORTANCE OF TRADE

Foreign trade became increasingly important to the American economy in the late nineteenth century. The nation's exports had totaled about $392 million in 1870; by 1890, the figure was $857 million; and by 1900, $1.4 billion. Many Americans began to consider the possibility of acquiring colonies that might expand such markets further.

Americans were well aware of the imperialist fever that was raging through Europe and leading the major powers to partition most of Africa among themselves and to turn eager eyes on the Far East and the feeble Chinese Empire. Some Americans feared that their nation would soon be left out, that no territory would remain to be acquired. Senator Henry Cabot Lodge of Massachusetts, a leading imperialist, warned that the United States "must not fall out of the line of march." The same distortion of Darwinism that industrialists and others had long been applying to domestic economic affairs in the form of Social Darwinism was now applied to world affairs. Many writers and public figures contended that nations or "races," like biological species, struggled constantly for existence and that only the fittest could survive. For strong nations to dominate weak ones was, therefore, in accordance with the laws of nature.

The popular writer John Fiske predicted in an 1885 article in *Harper's Magazine* that the English-speaking peoples would eventually control every land that was not already the seat of an

Historical Thinking Skills

Contextualization Have students examine the map "Imperialism at High Tide: 1900." Ask them to think about why there is so little European involvement in the Western Hemisphere compared to the Eastern Hemisphere, then share their thoughts with a partner. *(This had much to do with the Monroe Doctrine and Latin American independence movements in the early nineteenth century.)* **WOR** **PCE**

"established civilization." The experience of white Americans in subjugating the indigenous population of their own continent, Fiske argued, was "destined to go on" in other parts of the world.

John W. Burgess, founder of Columbia University's School of Political Science, gave a stamp of scholarly approval to imperialism. In his 1890 study: *Political Science and Comparative Law*, he flatly stated that the Anglo-Saxon and Teutonic nations possessed the highest political talents. It was their duty, therefore, to uplift less fortunate peoples, even to force superior institutions on them if necessary. "There is," he wrote, "no human right to the status of barbarism."

INTELLECTUAL JUSTIFICATIONS FOR IMPERIALISM

The ablest and most effective apostle of imperialism was Alfred Thayer Mahan, a captain and later admiral in the U.S. Navy. Mahan's thesis, presented in *The Influence of Sea Power upon History* (1890) and other works, was simple: countries with sea power were the great nations of history; the greatness of the United States, bounded by two oceans, would rest on its naval strength. The prerequisites for sea power were a productive domestic economy, foreign commerce, a strong merchant marine, a navy to defend trade routes–and colonies, which would provide raw materials and markets and could serve as naval bases. Mahan advocated that the United States construct a canal across the isthmus of Central America to join the oceans, acquire defensive bases on both sides of the canal in the Caribbean and the Pacific, and take possession of Hawaii and other Pacific islands.

ALFRED THAYER MAHAN

Mahan feared the United States did not have a large enough navy to play the great role he envisioned. But during the 1870s and 1880s, the government launched a shipbuilding program that by 1898 had moved the United States to fifth place among the world's naval powers, and by 1900 to third.

HEMISPHERIC HEGEMONY

James G. Blaine, who served as secretary of state in two Republican administrations in the 1880s, led early efforts to

HAWAIIAN SUGARCANE PLANTATION The sugarcane plantations of nineteenth-century Hawaii (like the sugar plantations of Barbados in the seventeenth and eighteenth centuries) required a vast labor force that the island's indigenous population could not provide. The mostly American owners of the plantations imported more than 300,000 Asian workers from China, Japan, and Korea to work in the fields between 1850 and 1920. The work was arduous, as the words of a song by Japanese sugar workers suggests: "Hawaii, Hawaii, But when I came what I saw was Hell. The boss was Satan, The lunas [overseers] his helpers."

Reasoning Processes

Comparing and Contrasting After students have read the section "The New Manifest Destiny," ask them to create a Venn diagram comparing the new Manifest Destiny with that of the mid-nineteenth century. Have students evaluate what they believe to be the most important similarity and difference. **PCE** **WOR** **WXT** **SOC** **MIG**

Discussion and Activities

Analyzing Images Have students examine the image "Hawaiian Sugar Plantation." Ask them to write a short newspaper article or investigative report describing the working and living conditions of plantation workers. **SOC** **WXT**

Discussion and Activities

Comparing and Contrasting Have students read the feature "Imperialism." Ask them to discuss in small groups how the motivation of the United States in seeking colonies was different from or similar to those of European nations. **WOR**

AMERICA IN THE WORLD

IMPERIALISM

Empires were not, of course, new to the nineteenth century, when the United States acquired its first overseas colonies. They have existed since the early moments of recorded history—in ancient Greece, Rome, China, and many other parts of the world. But in the mid- and late nineteenth century, the construction of empires took on a new and different form from those of earlier eras, and the word "imperialism" emerged for the first time to describe it. European powers now created colonies not by sending large numbers of migrants to settle and populate new lands but, instead, by creating military, political, and business structures that allowed them to dominate and profit from the existing populations. This new imperialism changed the character of the imperial nations themselves, enriching them greatly and producing new classes of people whose lives were shaped by the demands of imperial business and administration. It changed the character of colonized societies even more, by drawing them into the vast nexus of global industrial capitalism and by introducing European customs, institutions, and technologies to the subject peoples.

Champions of the new imperialism argued that the acquisition of colonies was essential for the health, even the survival, of their own industrializing nations. Colonies were sources of raw materials vital to industrial production, they were markets for manufactured goods, and they could be suppliers of cheap labor. Defenders of the idea of empire argued as well that imperialism was good for the colonized people too. Many saw colonization as an opportunity to export Christianity to "heathen" lands, while secular apologists argued that imperialism helped bring colonized people into the modern world. The British poet Rudyard Kipling was perhaps the most famous spokesman for empire. In his celebrated poem "The White Man's Burden," he spoke of the duty of the colonizers to lift up primitive peoples, to "fill full the mouth of famine and bid the sickness cease."

The greatest imperial power of the nineteenth century, indeed one of the greatest imperial powers in all of human history, was Great Britain. By 1800, despite its recent loss of the colonies that became the United States, it already possessed vast territory in North America, the Caribbean, and the Pacific—most notably Canada and Australia. But in the second half of the nineteenth century, Britain greatly expanded its empire. Its most important acquisition was India. In 1857, when native Indians revolted against British authority, British forces brutally crushed the rebellion and established formal colonial control over the land. British officials, backed by substantial military power, now governed India through a large civil service staffed mostly by people from England and Scotland, but with some Indians serving in minor or symbolic positions. The British invested heavily in railroads, telegraphs, canals, harbors, and agricultural improvements to enhance the economic opportunities available to them. They created schools for Indian children in an effort to draw them into British culture and make them supporters of the imperial system.

Britain also extended its empire into Africa and other parts of Asia. Cecil Rhodes expanded a small existing British colony at Cape Town into a substantial colony that included what is now South Africa. In 1895, he added new territories to the north, which he named Rhodesia (today, Zimbabwe and Zambia). Other imperialists spread British authority into Kenya, Uganda, Nigeria, and much of Egypt. With the acquisition of Singapore, Hong Kong, Burma, and Malaya, Britain extended its empire into east Asia.

Other European states, watching the vast expansion of the British Empire, quickly jumped into the race for colonies. France created colonies in Indochina (Vietnam and Laos), Algeria, west Africa, and Madagascar. Belgium moved into the Congo in west Africa. Germany established colonies in the Cameroons, Tanganyika, and other parts of Africa, and in the Pacific islands north of Australia. Dutch, Italian, Portuguese, Spanish, Russian, and Japanese imperialists created colonies in Africa, Asia, and the Pacific—driven both by their own commercial interests and by the frenzied competition that had developed among rival imperial powers. In 1898, the United States was drawn into the imperial race as an unanticipated result of the Spanish-American War. But Americans also sought colonies, although only a few, as a result of the efforts of pro-imperialists (among them Theodore Roosevelt), who believed that in the modern industrial-imperial world a nation without colonies would have difficulty remaining, or becoming, a true great power.

THE BRITISH RAJ The Drum Corps of the Royal Fusiliers in India poses here for a formal portrait, taken in 1877. Although the drummers are British, an Indian associate is included at top left. This blending of the dominant British with subordinate Indians was characteristic of the administration of the British Empire in India—a government known as the "raj," from the Indian word for "rule."

Time & Life Pictures/Getty Images

HISTORICAL THINKING SKILLS

1. **Evaluating Evidence** What motivated the European nations' drive for empire in the late nineteenth century and how did they justify their efforts?
2. **Drawing Conclusions** Why was Great Britain so successful in acquiring its vast empire?
3. **Comparing** How do the imperial efforts and ambitions of the United States at the end of the nineteenth century compare with those of the European powers that were also acquiring empires at this time?

Answers

America in the World

1. European countries argued that in order for their survival, they must engage in imperialistic efforts. They could get raw materials from the colonies, the colonies provided a market for finished goods, and the colonists served as sources of cheap labor.
2. Despite losing the colonies that would eventually become the United States, the British Empire still retained a tremendous number of colonies, including India. They had one of the most powerful militaries in the world and were able to crush rebellions in their colonies.
3. At this time, the United States wanted to achieve the same level of success that various European powers had in their imperial efforts. Pro-imperialists, in the U.S. and elsewhere, believed that nations without colonies would have difficulty maintaining their position in the world and have little economic success.

expand American influence into Latin America, where, he believed, the United States must look for markets for its surplus goods. In October 1889, Blaine helped organize the first Pan-American Congress, which attracted delegates from nineteen nations. The delegates agreed to create the Pan-American Union, a weak international organization located in Washington, D.C., that served as a clearinghouse of information to the member nations. But they rejected Blaine's more substantive proposals: for an inter-American customs union and arbitration procedures for hemispheric disputes.

The Cleveland administration took a similarly active interest in Latin America. In 1895, it supported Venezuela in a dispute with Great Britain. When the British ignored American demands that the matter be submitted to arbitration, Secretary of State Richard Olney charged that Britain was violating the Monroe Doctrine. Cleveland then created a special commission to settle the dispute: if Britain resisted the commission's decision, he insisted, the United States should be willing to go to war to enforce it. As war talk raged throughout the country, the British government prudently agreed to arbitration.

VENEZUELAN DISPUTE

HAWAII AND SAMOA

The islands of Hawaii in the mid-Pacific had been an important way station for American ships in the China trade since the early nineteenth century. By the 1880s, officers of the expanding American navy were looking covetously at Pearl Harbor on the island of Oahu as a possible permanent base for U.S. ships. Pressure for an increased American presence in Hawaii was emerging from another source as well: the growing number of Americans who had settled on the islands and who had gradually come to dominate their economic and political life.

In doing so, the Americans had been wresting authority away from the leaders of an ancient civilization. Settled by Polynesian people beginning in about 1500 BCE, Hawaii had developed an agricultural and fishing society in which different islands (and different communities on the same islands), each with its own chieftain, lived more or less self-sufficiently. When the first Americans arrived in Hawaii in the 1790s on merchant ships from New England, there were perhaps a half-million people living there. Battles among rival communities were frequent, as ambitious chieftains tried to consolidate power over their neighbors. In 1810, after a series of such battles, King Kamehameha I established his dominance, welcomed American traders, and helped them develop a thriving trade between Hawaii and China, from which the Hawaiians profited along with the merchants. But Americans soon wanted more than trade. Missionaries began settling there in the early nineteenth century; and in the 1830s, William Hooper, a Boston trader, became the first of many Americans to buy land and establish a sugar plantation on the islands.

SELF-SUFFICIENT SOCIETIES

The arrival of these merchants, missionaries, and planters was devastating to traditional Hawaiian society. The newcomers inadvertently brought infectious diseases to which the Hawaiians, like the Native Americans before them, were tragically vulnerable. By the mid-nineteenth century, more than half the indigenous population had died. By 1900, disease had more than halved the population again. But the Americans brought other incursions as well. Missionaries worked to undermine native religion. Other white settlers introduced liquor, firearms, and a commercial economy, all of which eroded the traditional character of Hawaiian society. By the 1840s, American planters had spread throughout the islands; and an American settler, G. P. Judd, had become prime minister of Hawaii under King Kamehameha III, who had agreed to establish a constitutional monarchy. Judd governed Hawaii for over a decade.

In 1887, the United States negotiated a treaty with Hawaii that permitted it to open a naval base at Pearl Harbor. By then, growing sugar for export to America had become the basis of the Hawaiian economy—as a result of an 1875 agreement allowing Hawaiian sugar to enter the United States duty-free. The American-dominated sugar plantation system not only displaced native Hawaiians from their lands but also sought to build a workforce with Asian immigrants, whom the Americans considered more reliable and more docile than the Hawaiians.. Indeed, finding adequate labor and keeping it under control were the principal concerns of many planters. Some planters deliberately sought to create a mixed-race workforce using workers from China, Japan, the Philippines, and Portugal along with indigenous Hawaiians as a way to keep the workers divided and unlikely to challenge them.

Indigenous Hawaiians did not accept their subordination without protest. In 1891, they elevated a powerful nationalist to the throne: Queen Liliuokalani, who set out to challenge the growing American control of the islands. But she remained in power only two years. By 1890, the United States had eliminated the privileged position of Hawaiian sugar in international trade. The result was devastating to the economy of the islands, and American planters concluded that the only way for them to recover was to become part of the United States (and hence exempt from its tariffs). In 1893, they staged a revolution and called on the United States for protection. After the American minister ordered marines from a warship in Honolulu harbor to go ashore to aid the rebels, the queen yielded her authority.

QUEEN LILIUOKALANI

A provisional government, dominated by Americans (who constituted less than 5 percent of the population of the islands), immediately sent a delegation to Washington to negotiate a treaty of annexation. But debate continued until 1898, when the Republicans returned to power and approved the agreement.

Three thousand miles south of Hawaii, the Samoan islands had also long served as a way station for American ships in the Pacific trade. As American commerce with Asia increased, business groups in the United States and the American navy began urging the government to annex the Samoan harbor at Pago Pago. In 1878, the Hayes administration extracted a treaty from Samoan leaders for an American naval station there.

But Great Britain and Germany were also interested in the islands, and they too secured treaty rights from Samoan leaders.

Reasoning Processes

Continuity and Change After students have read the section "Hemispheric Hegemony," ask them to write a thesis statement that makes a claim about whether American foreign policy in Latin America at the end of the nineteenth century represented more of a continuity of or change from previous American foreign policy in the region. **WOR**

Discussion and Activities

Analyzing Cause and Effect After students have read the section "Queen Liliuokalani," ask them to create a T-chart listing positive and negative effects of the arrival of Americans in Hawaii. Have students discuss in pairs or small groups whether the positive or negative effects were greater. **WOR** **PCE** **WXT** **SOC**

AP Exam Tip

The AP Exam requires students to identify and explain a source's point of view, purpose, historical situation, and/or audience. One way students can identify the point of view of a source is to evaluate its motives or biases.

Historical Thinking Skills

Sourcing and Situation Have students practice the tip by examining the image "The Yellow Press and the Wreck of the *Maine*" and identifying words or images that seem intended to produce a particular response from readers. *(The false dichotomy of whether the explosion was caused by a bomb or torpedo; the captain's assertion that the explosion was caused by an enemy; the reporting of rumors; the predisposition of experts to state a conclusion before examining evidence; the graphic image showing the destruction of the ship and bodies being blown skyward.)* **WOR** **PCE**

PATTERNS OF POPULAR CULTURE

YELLOW JOURNALISM

Joseph Pulitzer was a successful newspaper publisher in St. Louis, Missouri, when he traveled to New York City in 1883 to buy a struggling paper, the *New York World.* "There is room in this great and growing city," he wrote in one of his first editorials, "for a journal that is not only cheap, but bright, not only bright but large, not only large but truly democratic . . . that will serve and battle for the people with earnest sincerity." Within a year, the *World's* daily circulation had soared from 10,000 to over 60,000. By 1886, it had reached 250,000 and was making enormous profits.

The success of Pulitzer's *World* marked the birth of what came to be known as "yellow journalism," a phrase that reportedly derived from a character in one of the *World's* comic strips: "the Yellow Kid." Color printing in newspapers was relatively new, and yellow was the most difficult color to print; so in the beginning, the term "yellow journalism" was a comment on the new technological possibilities that Pulitzer was so eagerly embracing. Eventually, however, it came to refer to a sensationalist style of reporting and writing that spread quickly through urban America and changed the character of newspapers forever.

Sensationalism was not new to journalism in the late nineteenth century, of course. Political scandal sheets had been publishing lurid stories since before the American Revolution. But the yellow journalism of the 1880s and 1890s took the search for a mass audience to new levels. The *World* created one of the first Sunday editions, with lavishly colored special sections, comics, and illustrated features. It expanded coverage of sports, fashion, literature, and theater. It pioneered large, glaring, overheated headlines that captured the eyes of people who were passing newsstands. It published exposés of political corruption. It made considerable efforts to bring drama and energy to its coverage of crime. It tried to involve readers directly in its stories (as when a *World* campaign helped raise $300,000 to build a base for the Statue of Liberty, with much of the money coming in donations of five or ten cents from working-class readers). And it introduced a self-consciously populist style of writing that appealed to working-class readers. "The American people want something terse, forcible, picturesque, striking," Pulitzer said. His reporters wrote short, forceful sentences. They did not shy away from expressing sympathy or outrage. And they were not always constrained by the truth.

Pulitzer very quickly produced imitators, the most important of them the California publisher William Randolph Hearst, who in 1895 bought the *New York Journal,* cut its price to one cent (Pulitzer quickly followed suit), copied many of the *World's* techniques, and within a year raised its circulation to 400,000. Hearst soon made the *Journal* the largest-circulation paper in the country—selling more than a million copies a day. Pulitzer, whose own circulation was not far behind, accused him of "pandering to the worst tastes of the prurient and the horror-loving" and "dealing in bogus news." But the *World* wasted no time before imitating the *Journal.* The competition between these two great "yellow" journals soon drove both to new levels of sensationalism. Their success drove newspapers in other cities around the nation to copy their techniques.

The civil war in Cuba in the 1890s gave both papers their best opportunities yet for combining sensational reporting with shameless appeals to patriotism and moral outrage. They avidly published exaggerated reports of Spanish atrocities toward the Cuban rebels, fanning popular anger toward Spain. When the

863,956 The World. 863,956

MAINE EXPLOSION CAUSED BY BOMB OR TORPEDO?

Capt. Sigsbee and Consul-General Lee Are in Doubt--The World Has Sent a Special Tug, With Submarine Divers, to Havana to Find Out--Lee Asks for an Immediate Court of Inquiry--Capt. Sigsbee's Suspicions.

CAPT. SIGSBEE, IN A SUPPRESSED DESPATCH TO THE STATE DEPARTMENT, SAYS THE ACCIDENT WAS MADE POSSIBLE BY AN ENEMY.

Dr. E. C. Pendleton, Just Arrived from Havana, Says He Overheard Talk There of a Plot to Blow Up the Ship--Capt. Zalinski, the Dynamite Expert, and Other Experts Report to The World that the Wreck Was Not Accidental--Washington Officials Ready for Vigorous Action if Spanish Responsibility Can Be Shown--Divers to Be Sent Down to Make Careful Examinations.

THE YELLOW PRESS AND THE WRECK OF THE *MAINE* No evidence was ever found tying the Spanish to the explosion in Havana harbor that destroyed the American battleship *Maine* in February 1898. Indeed, most evidence indicated that the blast came from inside the ship, a fact that suggests an accident rather than sabotage. Nevertheless, the newspapers of Joseph Pulitzer and William Randolph Hearst ran sensational stories about the incident that were designed to arouse public sentiment in support of a war against the Spanish. This front page from Pulitzer's *New York World* is an example of the lurid coverage the event received. Circulation figures at the top right of the page indicate, too, how successful the coverage was in selling newspapers.

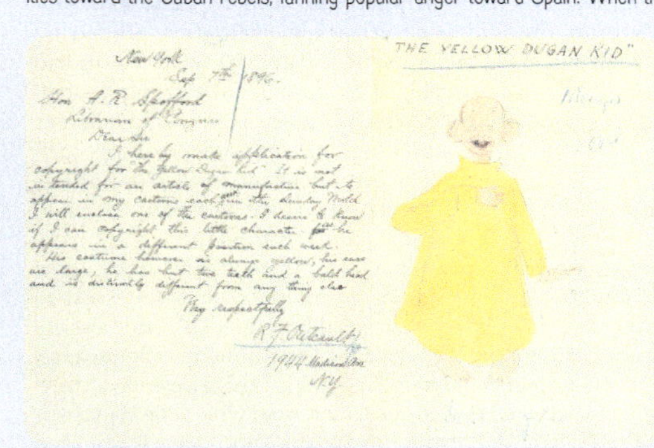
New York
Sep 7th 1896.
Hon A. R. Spofford
Librarian of Congress
Dear Sir
I hereby make application for copyright for "the Yellow Dugan Kid". It is not intended for an article of manufacture but to appear in my cartoons each [illegible] the Sunday World. I will enclose one of the cartoons. I desire to know if I can copyright this little character for he appears in a different position each week.
His costume however is always yellow, his ears are large, he has but two teeth and a bald head and is distinctly different from any thing else.
Very respectfully
R. F. Outcault
1944 Madison Ave
N.Y.

"THE YELLOW DUGAN KID" *Hogan's Alley,* one of the most popular cartoons of the late nineteenth and early twentieth centuries, debuted in the *New York World* in 1895. Perhaps its best-known character was Mickey Dugan, the goofy-looking creation of cartoonist Richard Outcault, known as "the Yellow Kid," whose nickname very likely was the source of the term "yellow journalism." *Hogan's Alley* was the forerunner of modern serial cartoons—not least because it was one of the first newspaper features to make elaborate use of color. (The drawing above accompanied Outcault's letter requesting copyright registration for the character of what he called "the yellow Dugan kid.")

566 · CHAPTER 20

Discussion and Activities

Making Connections Have students study the image "The Yellow Press and the Wreck of the *Maine*." Ask them to create a sensational headline concerning a current event that is intended to lead readers to a particular position regarding that event. **SOC** **PCE**

American battleship *Maine* mysteriously exploded in Havana harbor in 1898, both papers (without any evidence) immediately blamed Spanish authorities. The *Journal* offered a $50,000 reward for information leading to the conviction of those responsible for the explosion, and it crowded all other stories off its front page ("There is no other news," Hearst told his editors) to make room for such screaming headlines as THE WHOLE COUNTRY THRILLS WITH WAR FEVER and HAVANA POPULACE INSULTS THE MEMORY OF THE *MAINE* VICTIMS. In the three days following the *Maine* explosion, the *Journal* sold more than 3 million copies, a new world's record for newspaper circulation.

In the aftermath of the *Maine* episode, the more conservative press launched a spirited attack on yellow journalism. That was partly in response to Hearst's boast that the conflict in Cuba was "the *Journal's* war." He sent a cable to one of his reporters in Cuba saying: "You furnish the pictures, and I'll furnish the war." Growing numbers of critics tried to discourage yellow journalism, which "respectable" editors both deplored and feared. Some schools, libraries, and clubs began to banish the papers from their premises. But the techniques the "yellow" press pioneered in the 1890s helped map the way for a tradition of colorful, popular journalism—later embodied in "tabloids," some elements of which eventually found their way into television news—that has endured into the present day.

HISTORICAL THINKING SKILLS

1. **Determining Context** Did Pulitzer's *World*, Hearst's *Journal*, and their imitators report the news or manufacture it?
2. **Drawing Conclusions** How did the "yellow" press influence the public's perception of the Spanish-American War?
3. **Making Connections** How does television news continue the tradition of "yellow" journalism? In what other mass media do you see the style and techniques pioneered by the "yellow" press?

For the next ten years the three powers jockeyed for dominance in Samoa, occasionally coming dangerously close to war. Finally, the three nations agreed to share power over Samoa. The three-way arrangement failed to halt the rivalries of its members; and in 1899, the United States and Germany divided the islands between them, compensating Britain with territories elsewhere in the Pacific. The United States retained the harbor at Pago Pago.

ACQUISITION OF SAMOA

WAR WITH SPAIN

Imperial ambitions had thus begun to stir within the United States well before the late 1890s. But a war with Spain in 1898 turned those stirrings into overt expansionism. The war transformed America's relationship to the rest of the world and left the nation with a far-flung overseas empire.

CONTROVERSY OVER CUBA

The Spanish-American War was a result of events in Cuba, which along with Puerto Rico now represented all that remained of Spain's once extensive American empire. Cuban rebels had been resisting Spanish rule since at least 1868. Many Americans had sympathized with the Cuban rebels during that long struggle, but the United States had not intervened.

In 1895, the Cuban rebels launched a new rebellion. This revolution produced a ferocity on both sides that horrified many Americans. The Cuban rebels deliberately devastated the island to force the Spaniards to leave. Spanish forces, commanded by General Valeriano Weyler, confined civilians in some areas to hastily prepared concentration camps, where they died by the thousands, victims of disease and malnutrition. The American press took to calling the general "Butcher Weyler." The Spaniards had used some of these same savage methods during earlier struggles in Cuba without shocking American sensibilities. But the revolt of 1895 was reported more fully and sensationally by the American press, which helped create the impression that the Spaniards were committing all the atrocities, when in fact there was considerable brutality on both sides.

CUBAN REVOLT

The conflict in Cuba came at a particularly opportune moment for the publishers of some American newspapers, Joseph Pulitzer with his *New York World* and William Randolph Hearst with his *New York Journal*. In the 1890s, Hearst and Pulitzer were engaged in a ruthless circulation war, and they both sent batteries of reporters and illustrators to the island with orders to provide accounts of Spanish atrocities. A growing population of Cuban émigrés in the United States–centered in Florida, New York City, Philadelphia, and Trenton, New Jersey–gave extensive support to the Cuban Revolutionary Party (whose headquarters were in New York City) and helped publicize the Cuban cause as effectively as those of the yellow journalists in generating American support for the revolution.

Discussion and Activities

Making Connections After students have read the feature "Yellow Journalism," ask them to discuss in small groups to what extent media today sensationalizes stories to boost readership or viewership and to give examples. **SOC**

Answers

Patterns of Popular Culture

1. They were responsible for doing both. There were stories that they reported on that were grounded in truth; however, they often embellished stories to generate more interest from the reading public and to be more competitive with other papers.
2. When the "yellow" press reported on the *Maine* explosion, despite evidence that the explosion came from the inside the ship, they reported the story differently to drum up support for the war against Spain.
3. Student answers will vary. Possible answers include: The current political environment is taking a cue from the "yellow" journalism of the late nineteenth century. Many of the major television stations are more interested in pushing their political ideology (e.g., CNN pushing a progressive liberal agenda and FOX pushing a right-wing conservative agenda) at the expense of neutral and unbiased reporting.

Reasoning Processes

Causation After students have read the section "Controversy over Cuba," ask them to list and rank in order of importance the reasons the United States declared war on Spain. Have students write a thesis statement that makes a claim about the most important cause(s) of the Spanish-American War. **WOR** **PCE** **WXT** **SOC**

CUBA
SPANISH MISRULE
ANARCHY
THE DUTY OF THE HOUR:—TO SAVE HER NOT ONLY FROM SPAIN BUT FROM A WORSE FATE.

"THE DUTY OF THE HOUR" This 1892 lithograph was no doubt inspired by the saying "Out of the frying pan and into the fire." A despairing Cuba, struggling to escape from the frying pan of Spanish misrule, contemplates an even more dangerous alternative: "anarchy" (or home rule). Cartoonist Louis Dalrymple here suggests that the only real solution to Cuba's problems is control by the United States, whose "duty" to Cuba is "To Save Her Not Only from Spain but from a Worse Fate."

The mounting storm of indignation against Spain did not persuade President Cleveland to support intervention. But when McKinley became president in 1897, he formally protested Spain's "uncivilized and inhuman" conduct, causing the Spanish government (fearful of American intervention) to recall Weyler, modify the concentration policy, and grant the island a qualified autonomy.

But whatever chances there were for a peaceful settlement vanished as a result of two dramatic incidents in February 1898. The first occurred when a Cuban agent stole a private letter written by Dupuy de Lôme, the Spanish minister in Washington, and turned it over to the American press. The letter described McKinley as a weak man and "a bidder for the admiration of the crowd." This was no more than many Americans, including some Republicans, were saying about their president. (Theodore Roosevelt described McKinley as having "no more backbone than a chocolate eclair.") But coming from a foreigner, it created intense popular anger. Dupuy de Lôme promptly resigned.

THE *MAINE*

While excitement over the de Lôme letter was still high, the American battleship *Maine* blew up in Havana harbor with a loss of more than 260 people. The ship had been ordered to Cuba in January to protect American lives and property. Many Americans assumed that the Spanish had sunk the ship, particularly when a naval court of inquiry hastily and inaccurately reported that an external explosion by a submarine mine had caused the disaster. (Later evidence suggested that the disaster was actually the result of an accidental explosion inside one of the engine rooms.) War hysteria swept the country, and Congress unanimously appropriated $50 million for military preparations. "Remember the *Maine*!" became a national chant for revenge.

McKinley still hoped to avoid a conflict. But others in his administration (including Assistant Secretary of the Navy Theodore Roosevelt) were clamoring for war. In March 1898, the president asked Spain to agree to an armistice, negotiations for a permanent peace, and an end to the concentration camps. Spain agreed to stop the fighting and eliminate the concentration camps but refused to negotiate with the rebels and reserved the right to resume hostilities at its discretion. That satisfied neither public opinion nor the Congress; and a few days later the United States declared war on Spain.

"A Splendid Little War"

Secretary of State John Hay called the Spanish-American conflict "a splendid little war," an opinion that most Americans—except many of the enlisted men who fought in it—seemed to

Historical Thinking Skills

Sourcing and Situation Have students examine the image "The Duty of the Hour." Ask them to identify and discuss in small groups the details that illustrate the purpose of the cartoon. *(The skillet labeled "Spanish Misrule," the island with "Anarchy" superimposed, and the caption all seek to call for the United States to go to war due to Spanish incompetence and/or brutality.)* **WOR** **PCE**

share. Declared in April, it was over in August, in part because Cuban rebels had already greatly weakened the Spanish resistance, which made the American intervention in many respects little more than a "mopping-up" exercise. Only 460 Americans were killed in battle or died of wounds, although some 5,200 others perished of disease: malaria, dysentery, and typhoid, among others. Casualties among Cuban insurgents, who continued to bear the brunt of the fighting, were much higher.

SUPPLY AND MOBILIZATION PROBLEMS

And yet the American war effort was not without difficulties. United States soldiers faced serious supply problems: a shortage of modern rifles and ammunition, uniforms too heavy for the warm Caribbean weather, inadequate medical services, and skimpy, almost indigestible food. The regular army numbered only 28,000 troops and officers, most of whom had experience in quelling Native American outbreaks but none in larger-scale warfare. As in the Civil War, the United States had to rely heavily on National Guard units, organized by local communities and commanded for the most part by local leaders without military experience.

There were racial conflicts. A significant proportion of the American invasion force consisted of black soldiers. Some were volunteer troops put together by African American communities (although some governors refused to allow the formation of such units). Others were members of the four black regiments in the regular army, who had been stationed on the frontier to defend white settlements against Native Americans and were now transferred east to fight in Cuba. As the black soldiers traveled through the South toward the training camps, they chafed at the rigid segregation to which they were subjected and occasionally resisted the restrictions openly. African American soldiers in Georgia deliberately made use of a "whites only" park; in Florida, they beat a soda-fountain operator for refusing to serve them; in Tampa, white provocations and black retaliation led to a nightlong riot that left thirty people wounded.

Racial tensions continued in Cuba, where African Americans played crucial roles in some of the important battles of the war (including the famous charge at San Juan Hill) and won many medals. Nearly half the Cuban insurgents fighting with the Americans were of African descent, and unlike their American counterparts they were fully integrated into the rebel army. (Indeed, one of the leading insurgent generals, Antonio Maceo, was a black man.) The sight of black Cuban soldiers fighting alongside white soldiers as equals gave African Americans a stronger sense of the injustice of their own position.

SEIZING THE PHILIPPINES

By an accident of history, the assistant secretary of the navy during the Cuban revolution was Theodore Roosevelt, an ardent Anglophile eager to see the United States join the British and other nations as imperial powers. Roosevelt was, in fact, a relatively minor figure in the Navy Department, but he was determined to expand his power. British friends had persuaded him that the war in Cuba gave the United States a rare opportunity to expand the American empire. Roosevelt responded by sending the navy's Pacific fleet to the Philippines, with orders to attack as soon as American declared war. On May 1, 1898, Commodore George Dewey led the fleet into Manila Harbor, quickly destroyed the aging Spanish fleet, and forced the Spanish government to surrender with hardly a shot fired. He became the first American hero of the war.

In the rejoicing over Dewey's victory, few Americans paused to note that the character of the war was changing. What had begun as a war to free Cuba was becoming a war to strip Spain of its colonies. The United States was now confronted with the question of what to do with the Spanish possessions it was suddenly acquiring.

THE BATTLE FOR CUBA

The war in Cuba continued after the capture of the Philippines. At first, the American commanders planned a long period of training before actually sending troops into combat. But when a Spanish fleet under Admiral Pascual Cervera slipped past the American navy into Santiago harbor on the southern coast of Cuba, plans changed quickly. The American Atlantic fleet quickly bottled Cervera up in the harbor. And the U.S. Army's commanding general, Nelson A. Miles, hastily altered his strategy and left Tampa in June with a force of 17,000 to attack Santiago. Both the departure from Florida and the landing in Cuba were scenes of fantastic incompetence. It took five days for this relatively small army to go ashore, even with the enemy offering no opposition.

General William R. Shafter, the American commander, moved toward Santiago, which he planned to surround and capture. On the way he met and defeated Spanish forces at Las Guasimos and, a week later, in two simultaneous battles, El Caney and San Juan Hill. At the center of the fighting (and on the front pages of the newspapers) during many of these engagements was a cavalry unit known as the Rough Riders. Nominally commanded by General Leonard Wood, its real leader was Colonel Theodore Roosevelt, who had resigned from the Navy Department to get into the war and who had struggled to ensure that his regiment made it to the front before the fighting ended. His passion to join the war undoubtedly reflected the decision of his beloved father, Theodore Roosevelt Sr., not to fight in the Civil War, a source of private shame within his family that his son sought to erase.

THE ROUGH RIDERS

Roosevelt rapidly emerged as a hero of the conflict. His fame rested in large part on his role in leading a bold, if perhaps reckless, charge up Kettle Hill (a charge that was a minor part of the larger battle for the adjacent San Juan Hill) directly into the face of Spanish guns. Roosevelt himself emerged unscathed, but nearly a hundred of his soldiers were killed or wounded. He remembered the battle as "the great day of my life."

Discussion and Activities

Analyzing Continuity and Change
After students have read the section *"A Splendid Little War,"* ask them to create a T-chart listing successes and challenges experienced by the U.S. military in Cuba. Have students discuss in small groups whether these represented continuities or changes from previous American military engagements. **WOR** **PCE** **SOC**

Discussion and Activities

Analyzing Change Have students read the section "Seizing the Philippines." Ask them to discuss with a partner how the seizure of the Philippines marked a change in American goals for the Spanish-American War. **WOR** **PCE**

AP Exam Tip

The AP Exam requires students to identify and explain a source's point of view, purpose, historical situation, and/or audience. One way students can identify the point of view of a source is to evaluate its motives or biases.

Historical Thinking Skills

Sourcing and Situation Have students practice the tip by examining the images in the *Maine* memorial. Ask them to identify details of the memorial that explain who the intended audience of the memorial was. *(The location in Arlington National Cemetery suggests an intended audience of veterans and their families. The mast of the ship might attract the attention of naval veterans.)*

CONSIDER THE SOURCE

MEMORIALIZING NATIONAL HISTORY

Public monuments are constructed for a variety of reasons: to remember tragedy, to commemorate sacrifice, to celebrate specific persons or groups, and to honor acts of courage, heroism, and endurance. The structures differ in purpose, theme, and meaning, but all serve to satisfy our need to reflect upon the meaning of events, groups, or people memorialized.

The explosion of the battleship *Maine* in Havana Harbor in February 1898 resulted in the deaths of 266 men and served to propel the United States into war with Spain. Twelve years after the conclusion of the short-lived war, work began on a monument to memorialize the *Maine* and commemorate the men who died in the explosion. Dedicated on February 15, 1915, the monument, located in Arlington National Cemetery and pictured in the first two images below, includes the main mast from the *Maine*. The names of those killed in the disaster are inscribed around the base of the monument, which represents the turret of a battleship.

A memorial commemorating those killed in the terrorist attacks of September 11, 2001, in New York City, Pennsylvania, and at the Pentagon, as well as those killed in the February 1993 bombing of the World Trade Center in New York, opened at the site of the attack on September 12, 2011. A museum dedicated to the events around the destruction of the World Trade Towers opened in May of 2014. The memorial consists of two pools, each approximately one acre in size, set within the footprints of the Twin Towers of the World Trade Center. The names of every person killed have been inscribed around the edges of the pools. Four hundred oak trees have been planted to add to the site a sense of quiet solemnity and reminder of enduring life.

THE MAINE—1898/1915

(l) The Library of Congress (381569pu); (r) The Library of Congress (381579pu)

Discussion and Activities

Explaining Significance Have students read the section "Memorializing National History." Ask them to create a poster of their own monument for the victims of the *Maine* disaster that take into account what is now known of the causes. **SOC**

THE VICTIMS OF TERRORISM—2014

(l) © Drew Angerer/Getty Images; (r) © Atlantide Phototravel/Corbis Documentary/Getty Images

ANALYZING SOURCES

Questions assume cumulative content knowledge from this chapter and previous chapters.

1. Based on the images and the information provided, what is a common feature shared by both memorials?
   - (A) Each image is highly representational, or realistic, in artistic style.
   - (B) Each image is located at the place in which the event happened.
   - (C) Each image references the main structural object(s) that suffered destruction in the respective event.
   - (D) Each image focuses on a physical part of the main structural object(s) that suffered destruction in the respective event.

2. Each memorial includes inscriptions of the names of those killed in the event. What do the respective decisions for the locale of the memorial most suggest about differences between each event?
   - (A) The location of the *Maine* memorial suggests that military lives were lost, while the locale of the September 11 memorial suggests that civilian lives were lost.
   - (B) The location of the *Maine* memorial suggests that the event was a national matter, while the location of the September 11 memorial suggests that the event was not.
   - (C) The differences in the kind of locale selected for each respective memorial suggest that the September 11 memorial was more controversial.
   - (D) The differences in the kind of locale selected for each respective memorial suggest that the *Maine* event was more controversial.

3. Consider what you have learned about the national response to and the consequences of the destruction of the *Maine*. What does the construction of these particular memorials most suggest about why a nation might choose to memorialize certain events over other events?
   - (A) A nation will memorialize events that only celebrate its victories overseas.
   - (B) A nation will only memorialize events that celebrate heroes.
   - (C) A nation most typically will memorialize events that individual citizens petition for.
   - (D) A nation is more likely to memorialize events that unite a nation and propel it to major national political action.

AP Exam Practice

Short Answer Provide students with the following short-answer questions and allow 15 minutes for completion. Ask for volunteers to share their responses and discuss as a class.

Answer A, B, and C.

A) Briefly explain ONE important cause of the Spanish-American War. *(Reports of Spanish atrocities; the desire to access Cuban sugar, the destruction of the* Maine, *the de Lôme letter.)*

B) Briefly explain a second important cause of the Spanish-American War. *(Students may list any of the answers from question A.)*

C) Briefly explain ONE important effect of the Spanish-American War. *(The United States was seen as an emerging military power; the acquisition of colonies in the Philippines and Pacific Ocean, control of Cuba.)*

Answers

Consider the Source

1. A; **2.** A; **3.** D

Discussion and Activities

Historical Evidence and Argumentation
After students have read the section "The Battle for Cuba," ask them to create a T-chart listing land and naval battles in the fight for Cuba. Ask students to discuss in small groups which battle was most important to American success in the war. **WOR**

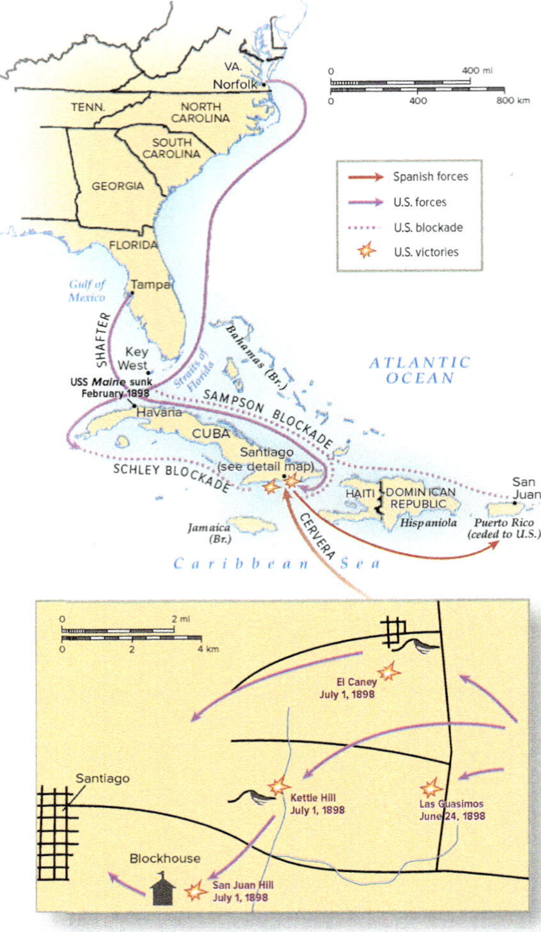

THE SPANISH-AMERICAN WAR IN CUBA, 1898 The military conflict between the United States and Spain in Cuba was a brief affair. The Cuban rebels and an American naval blockade had already brought the Spanish to the brink of defeat. The arrival of American troops was simply the final blow. In the space of about a week, U.S. troops won four decisive battles in the area around Santiago in southeast Cuba—one of them (the Battle of Kettle Hill) the scene of Theodore Roosevelt's famous charge up the adjacent San Juan Hill. This map shows the extent of the American naval blockade, the path of American troops from Florida to Cuba, and the location of the actual fighting.

What were the implications of the war in Cuba for Puerto Rico?

Although Shafter was now in position to assault Santiago, his army was so weakened by sickness that he feared he might have to abandon his position, particularly once the commander of the American naval force blockading Santiago refused to enter the harbor because of mines. But unknown to the Americans, the Spanish government had by now decided that Santiago was lost and had ordered Cervera to evacuate. On July 3, Cervera tried to escape from the harbor. The waiting American squadron destroyed his entire fleet. On July 16, the commander of Spanish ground forces in Santiago surrendered. At about the same time, an American army landed in Puerto Rico and occupied it against virtually no opposition. On August 12, an armistice ended the war.

Under the terms of the armistice, Spain recognized the independence of Cuba. It ceded Puerto Rico (now occupied by American troops) and the Pacific island of Guam to the United States. And it accepted continued American occupation of Manila pending the final disposition of the Philippines.

Puerto Rico and the United States

Annexation of Puerto Rico

The annexation of Puerto Rico produced relatively little controversy in the United States. The island of Puerto Rico had been a part of the Spanish Empire since Ponce de León arrived there in 1508, and it had contained Spanish settlements since the founding of San Juan in 1521. The indigenous people of the island, the Arawaks, had mostly disappeared as a result of infectious diseases, Spanish brutality, and poverty. Puerto Rican society developed, therefore, with a Spanish ruling class and a large African workforce for the coffee and sugar plantations that came to dominate its economy.

As Puerto Rican society became increasingly distinctive, resistance to Spanish rule began to emerge, just as it had in Cuba. Uprisings occurred intermittently beginning in the 1820s; the most important of them—the so-called Lares Rebellion—was, like the others, effectively crushed by Spanish forces in 1868. But the growing resistance did prompt some reforms: the abolition of slavery in 1873, representation in the Spanish parliament, and other changes. Demands for independence continued to grow, and in 1898, in response to political pressure organized by the popular politician Luis Muñoz Rivera, Spain granted the island a degree of independence. But before the changes had any chance to take effect, control of Puerto Rico shifted to the United States. American military forces occupied the island during the war. They remained in control until 1900, when the Foraker Act ended military rule and established a formal colonial government: an American governor and a two-chamber legislature (the members of the upper chamber appointed by the United States, the members of the lower elected by the Puerto Rican people). The United States could amend or veto any legislation the Puerto Rican legislators passed. Agitation for independence

Answers

The Spanish-American War in Cuba: 1898

Puerto Rice came under American control as a result of the Spanish-American War. **WOR**

AFRICAN AMERICAN CAVALRY Substantial numbers of African Americans fought in the U.S. Army during the Spanish-American War. Although confined to all-black units, they engaged in combat alongside white units and fought bravely and effectively. This photograph shows a troop of African American cavalry in formation in Cuba.

continued, and in 1917, under pressure to clarify the relationship between Puerto Rico and America, Congress passed the Jones Act, which declared Puerto Rico to be United States territory and made all people of Puerto Rico American citizens.

The Puerto Rican sugar industry flourished as it took advantage of the American market that was now open to it without tariffs. As in Hawaii, Americans began establishing large sugar plantations on the island and hired indigenous people to work them; many of the planters did not even live in Puerto Rico. The growing emphasis on sugar as a cash crop, and the transformation of many Puerto Rican farmers into paid laborers, led to a reduction in the growing of food for the island. The Puerto Rican people became increasingly dependent on imported food and hence increasingly a part of the international commercial economy. When international sugar prices were high, Puerto Rico did well. When they dropped, the island's economy sagged, pushing the many plantation workers—already poor—into destitution. Unhappy with the instability, the poverty among indigenous people, and the American threat to Latino culture, many Puerto Rican people continued to agitate for independence. Others, however, began to envision closer relations with the United States, even statehood.

SUGAR ECONOMY

THE DEBATE OVER THE PHILIPPINES

Although the annexation of Puerto Rico produced relatively little controversy, the annexation of the Philippines created a long and impassioned debate. Controlling a nearby Caribbean island fit reasonably comfortably into the United States's sense of itself as the dominant power in the Western Hemisphere. Controlling a large and densely populated territory thousands of miles away seemed different and, to many Americans, more ominous.

McKinley claimed to be reluctant to support annexation. But, according to his own accounts, he came to believe there were no acceptable alternatives. Emerging from what he described as an "agonizing night of prayer," he claimed divine guidance for his decision to annex the islands. Returning them to Spain would be "cowardly and dishonorable," he claimed. Turning them over to another imperialist power (France, Germany, or Britain) would be "bad business and discreditable." Granting the islands independence would be irresponsible; the Filipino people were "unfit for self government." The only solution was "to take them all and to educate the Filipinos, and uplift and Christianize them, and by God's grace do the very best we could by them."

THE PHILIPPINES QUESTION

THE ROUGH RIDERS Theodore Roosevelt resigned as assistant secretary of the navy to lead a volunteer regiment in the Spanish-American War. They were known as the Rough Riders, and their bold charge during the battle of San Juan Hill made Roosevelt a national hero. Roosevelt is shown here (at center with glasses) posing with the other members of the regiment.

Reasoning Processes

Comparing After students have read the section "Puerto Rico and the United States," ask them to create a Venn diagram comparing Puerto Rico to Cuba prior to and during the Spanish-American War. Have students discuss in small groups whether they seem more similar or different, and why. **WOR** **SOC** **WXT**

Reasoning Processes

Comparing and Contrasting Have students examine the images "African American Cavalry" and "The Rough Riders." Ask them to identify and discuss as a class how the two images are similar and different. *(Similarities: American soldiers; located in Cuba; both cavalry units. Differences: One unit is all African American, while the other is all white; the Rough Riders are pictured without horses; and the Rough Riders received far more attention in the media.)* Have students explain reasons for the similarities and differences. **PCE** **SOC** **WXT**

Discussion and Activities

Historical Significance and Argumentation After students have read the section "Anti-Imperialist League," ask them to list and rank in order of importance the reasons for opposition to imperialism. Ask them to identify which reasons are mainly political, economic, or social. Then have students evaluate which category seemed most important. **SOC** **WOR** **WXT**

The Treaty of Paris, signed in December 1898, brought a formal end to the war. It confirmed the terms of the armistice concerning Cuba, Puerto Rico, and Guam. American negotiators startled the Spanish by demanding that they cede the Philippines to the United States, something the original armistice had not included. Spain objected briefly, but an American offer of $20 million for the islands softened their resistance. They accepted all the American terms.

In the U.S. Senate, however, resistance was fierce. During debate over ratification of the treaty, a powerful anti-imperialist movement arose around the country to oppose acquisition of the Philippines. The anti-imperialists included some of the nation's wealthiest and most powerful figures: Andrew Carnegie, Mark Twain, Samuel Gompers, Senator John Sherman, and others. Their motives were various. Some believed simply that imperialism was immoral, a repudiation of America's commitment to human freedom. Some feared "polluting" the American population by introducing "inferior" Asian races into it. Industrial workers feared being undercut by a flood of cheap laborers from the new colonies. Conservatives worried about the large standing army and entangling foreign alliances that they believed imperialism would require and that they feared would threaten American liberties. Sugar growers and others feared unwelcome competition from the new territories. The Anti-Imperialist League, established late in 1898 by upper-class Bostonians, New Yorkers, and others to fight against annexation, attracted a widespread following in the Northeast and waged a vigorous campaign against ratification of the Paris treaty.

ANTI-IMPERIALIST LEAGUE

Favoring ratification was an equally varied group. There were the exuberant imperialists such as Theodore Roosevelt, who saw the acquisition of empire as a way to reinvigorate the nation and keep alive what they considered the healthy, restorative influence of the war. Some businessmen saw opportunities to dominate the Asian trade. And most Republicans saw partisan advantages in acquiring valuable new territories through a war fought and won by a Republican administration. Perhaps the strongest argument in favor of annexation, however, was that the United States already possessed the islands.

When anti-imperialists warned of the danger of acquiring territories with large populations who might have to become citizens, the imperialists had a ready answer: the nation's long-standing policies toward Native Americans—treating them as dependents rather than as citizens—had created a precedent for annexing land without absorbing people. Supporters of annexation argued that the "uncivilized" Filipino people "would occupy the same status precisely as our Indians. . . . They are, in fact, 'Indians'—and the Fourteenth Amendment does not make citizens of Indians." Likewise, the U.S. Supreme Court, in a 1901 decision now known as the Insular Cases, ruled that constitutional protection of rights does not automatically extend to all places under American control. The inhabitants of unincorporated territories like Puerto Rico, Guam, and the Philippines, even if they are U.S. citizens, may lack some constitutional rights. The court established the principle that the Constitution fully applied only to incorporated territories, or those territories on the path to statehood, such as Alaska and Hawaii.

The fate of the treaty remained in doubt for weeks, until it received the unexpected support of William Jennings Bryan, a fervent anti-imperialist. He backed ratification not because he approved of annexation but because he hoped to move the issue out of the Senate and make it the subject of a national referendum in 1900, when he expected to be the Democratic presidential candidate again. Bryan persuaded a number of anti-imperialist Democrats to support the treaty so as to set up the 1900 debate. The Senate ratified it finally on February 6, 1899.

But Bryan miscalculated. If the election of 1900 was in fact a referendum on the Philippines, as Bryan expected, it proved beyond doubt that the nation had decided in favor of imperialism. Once again Bryan ran against McKinley; and once again McKinley won—even more decisively than in 1896. It was not only the issue of the colonies, however, that ensured McKinley's victory. The Republicans were the beneficiaries of growing prosperity—and also of the colorful personality of their vice presidential candidate, Theodore Roosevelt, the hero of San Juan Hill.

ELECTION OF 1900

THE REPUBLIC AS EMPIRE

The new American empire was small by the standards of the great imperial powers of Europe. But it embroiled the United States in the politics of both Europe and the Far East in ways the nation had always tried to avoid in the past. It also drew Americans into a brutal war in the Philippines.

GOVERNING THE COLONIES

Three of the American dependencies—Hawaii, Alaska (acquired from Russia in 1867), and Puerto Rico—presented relatively few problems. They received territorial status (and their residents American citizenship) relatively quickly: Hawaii in 1900, Alaska in 1912, and Puerto Rico in 1917. The U.S. Navy took control of the Pacific islands of Guam and Tutuila. Some of the smallest, least populated Pacific islands now under American control the United States simply left alone. Cuba was a thornier problem. American military forces, commanded by General Leonard Wood, remained there until 1902 to prepare the island for independence. They built roads, schools, and hospitals, reorganized the legal, financial, and administrative systems, and introduced medical and sanitation reforms. But the United States also laid the basis for years of American economic domination of the island.

When Cuba drew up a constitution that made no reference to the United States, Congress responded by passing the Platt Amendment in 1901 and pressured Cuba into incorporating its terms into its constitution. The Platt Amendment barred Cuba from making treaties with other nations (thus, in effect, giving the United States control of Cuban foreign policy); it gave the

PLATT AMENDMENT

Historical Thinking Skills

Argumentation After students have read the section "The Philippines Question," ask them to list and rank in order of importance the reasons for annexing the Philippines. Have students write a thesis statement that makes a claim about the most important cause(s) of the annexation of the Philippines. **WOR** **SOC** **WXT**

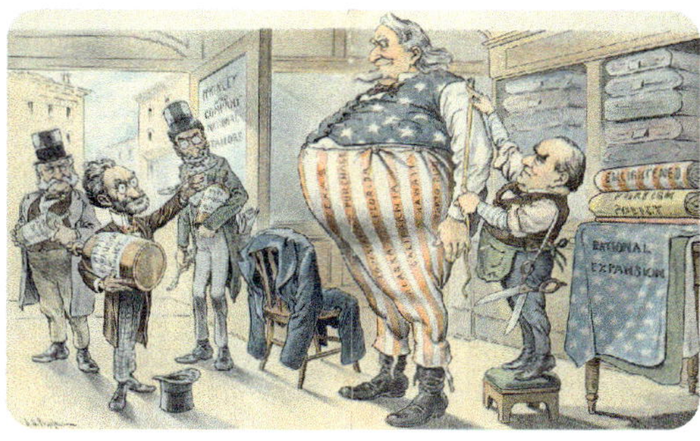

"MEASURING UNCLE SAM FOR A NEW SUIT," BY J. S. PUGHE, IN *PUCK MAGAZINE*, 1900 President William McKinley is favorably depicted here as a tailor, measuring his client for a suit large enough to accommodate the new possessions the United States obtained in the aftermath of the Spanish-American War. This detail from a larger cartoon tries to link this expansion with earlier, less controversial ones such as the Louisiana Purchase.

The Library of Congress (LC-DIG-ppmsca-25453)

United States the right to intervene in Cuba to preserve independence, life, and property; and it required Cuba to permit American naval stations on its territory. The amendment left Cuba with only nominal political independence.

American investments, which quickly took over the island's economy, made the new nation an American economic appendage as well. Americans poured into Cuba, buying up plantations, factories, railroads, and refineries. Absentee American ownership of many of the island's most important resources was the source of resentment and agitation for decades. Resistance to "Yankee imperialism" produced intermittent revolts against the Cuban government–revolts that at times prompted U.S. military intervention. American troops occupied the island from 1906 to 1909 after one such rebellion; they returned again in 1912, to suppress a revolt by black plantation workers. As in Puerto Rico and Hawaii, sugar production–spurred by access to the American market–increasingly dominated the island's economy and subjected it to the same cycle of booms and busts that so plagued other sugar-producing appendages of the United States economy.

American Economic Dominance

THE PHILIPPINE WAR

Americans did not like to think of themselves as imperial rulers in the European mold. Yet, like other imperial powers, the United States soon discovered–as it had discovered at home in its relations with Native Americans–that subjugating another people required more than ideals; it also required strength and brutality. That, at least, was the lesson of the American experience in the Philippines, where American forces soon became engaged in a long and bloody war with insurgent forces fighting for independence.

The conflict in the Philippines is the least remembered of all American wars. It was also one of the longest, lasting from 1898 to 1902, and one of the most vicious. It involved 200,000 American troops and resulted in 4,300 American deaths, nearly ten times the number who had died in combat in the Spanish-American War. The number of Filipino people killed in the conflict has long been a matter of dispute, but it seems likely that at least 50,000 (and perhaps many more) died. The American occupiers faced brutal guerrilla tactics in the Philippines, very similar to those the Spanish occupiers had faced prior to 1898 in Cuba. And they soon found themselves drawn into the same pattern of brutality that had outraged so many Americans when Weyler had used them in the Caribbean.

The Filipino people had been rebelling against Spanish rule even before 1898. And as soon as they realized American occupiers had come to stay, they rebelled against them as well. Ably led by Emilio Aguinaldo, who claimed to head the legitimate government of the nation, Filipino rebels harried the American army of occupation from island to island for more than three years. At first, American commanders believed the rebels had only a small popular following. But by early 1900, General Arthur MacArthur, an American commander in the islands (and father of General Douglas MacArthur), was writing: "I have been reluctantly compelled to believe that the Filipino masses are loyal to Aguinaldo and the government which he heads."

Emilio Aguinaldo

To MacArthur and others, that realization was not a reason to moderate American tactics or conciliate the rebels. It was a reason to adopt much more severe measures. Gradually, the American military effort became more systematically vicious and brutal. Captured Filipino guerrillas were treated not as prisoners of war, but as murderers. Many were summarily executed. On some islands, entire communities were evacuated–the residents forced into concentration camps while American troops destroyed their villages, farms, crops, and livestock. A spirit of savagery grew among some American soldiers, who came to view the Filipino people as almost subhuman and at times seemed to take pleasure in killing arbitrarily. One American commander ordered his troops "to kill and burn, the more you kill and burn the better it will please me. . . . Shoot everyone over the age of 10." Over fifteen Filipino people were killed for every one wounded; in the American Civil War–the bloodiest conflict in U.S. history to that point–one person had died for every five wounded.

By 1902, reports of the brutality and of the American casualties had soured the American public on the war. But by then, the rebellion had largely exhausted itself and the occupiers had established control over most of the islands. The key to their victory was the March 1901 capture of Aguinaldo, who later signed a document urging his followers to stop fighting and declaring his own allegiance to the United States. (Aguinaldo then retired from public life and lived quietly until 1964.) Fighting continued in some places for another year, and the war revived intermittently until as late as 1906; but American possession of the Philippines was now secure. In the summer of 1901, the military transferred authority over

Growing Economic Dependence

Discussion and Activities

Analyzing Issues After students have read the section "Governing the Colonies," ask them to create a T-chart listing costs and benefits to the United States of annexing territories after the Spanish-American War. Have students identify each example as being primarily economic, social, or diplomatic. **WOR** **PCE** **WXT** **SOC**

Discussion and Activities

Analyzing Visuals Have students examine the image "Measuring Uncle Sam for a New Suit." Ask them to identify and discuss in small groups details that demonstrate support for the annexation of the Philippines. **WOR** **WXT** **SOC**

Discussion and Activities

Historical Evidence and Argumentation
After students have read the section "The Philippine War," ask them to discuss as a class whether the costs of fighting the Philippine Insurrection was worth the benefits to the United States. Have students consider the economic and strategic value to the United States of controlling the Philippines, as well as the economic, social, and political costs. **WOR** **SOC** **WXT**

FILIPINO PRISONERS American troops guard captured Filipino guerrillas in Manila. The suppression of the Filipino insurrection was a much longer and costlier military undertaking than the Spanish-American War, by which the United States first gained possession of the islands. By mid-1900 there were 70,000 American troops in the Philippines, under the command of General Arthur MacArthur (whose son Douglas won fame in the Philippines during World War II).

the islands to William Howard Taft, who became their first civilian governor. Taft announced that the American mission in the Philippines was to prepare the islands for independence, and he gave the Filipino people broad local autonomy. The American government also built roads, schools, bridges, and sewers; instituted major administrative and financial reforms; and established a public health system. The Philippine economy–dominated by fishing, agriculture, timber, and mining–also became increasingly linked to the economy of the United States. American investors did not make many investments in the Philippines, and few American people moved there. But trade with the United States grew to the point that the islands were almost completely dependent on American markets.

In the meantime, a succession of American governors gradually increased Filipino political autonomy. On July 4, 1946, the islands gained their independence.

THE OPEN DOOR

The acquisition of the Philippines greatly increased the already strong American interest in Asia. Americans were particularly concerned about the future of China, with which the United States had an important trade and which was now so enfeebled that it provided a tempting target for exploitation by stronger countries. By 1900, England, France, Germany, Russia, and Japan were beginning to carve up China among themselves. They pressured the Chinese government for "concessions," which gave them effective control over various regions, most along the coast of China. In some cases, they simply seized Chinese territory and claimed it as their own. Many Americans feared that the process would soon cut them out of the China trade altogether.

Eager for a way to advance American interests in China without risking war, McKinley issued a statement in September 1898 saying the United States wanted access to China, but no special advantages there. "Asking only the open door for ourselves, we are ready to accord the open door to others." The next year, Secretary of State John Hay translated those words into policy when he addressed identical messages–which became known as the "Open Door notes"–to England, Germany, Russia, France, Japan, and Italy. He asked them to approve three principles: each nation with a sphere of influence in China was to respect the rights and privileges of other nations in its sphere; Chinese officials were to continue to collect tariff duties in all spheres (the existing tariff favored the United States); and nations were not to discriminate against other nations in levying port dues and railroad rates within their

HAY'S "OPEN DOOR NOTES"

Discussion and Activities

Analyzing Points of View Have students examine the image "Filipino Prisoners." Ask them to write a short letter or journal entry from the point of view of one of the prisoners or guards pictured explaining their experiences, hopes, fears, and motivations. **WOR** **WXT** **SOC** **PCE**

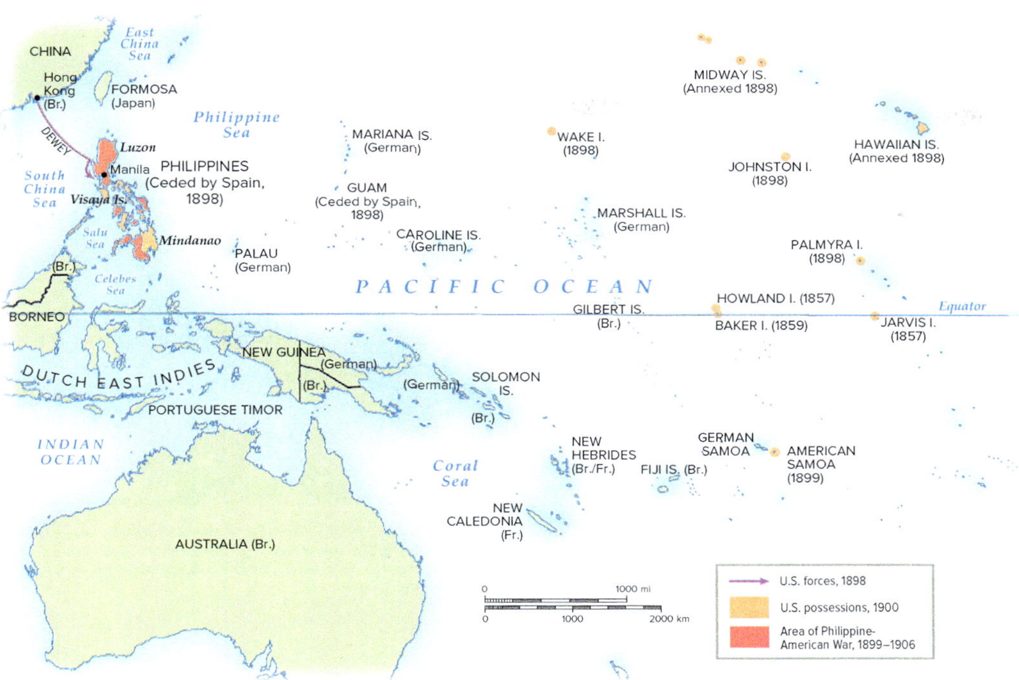

THE AMERICAN SOUTH PACIFIC EMPIRE, 1900 Except for Puerto Rico, all of the colonial acquisitions of the United States in the wake of the Spanish-American War occurred in the Pacific. The new attraction of imperialism persuaded the United States to annex Hawaii in 1898. The war itself gave America control of the Philippines, Guam, and other, smaller Spanish possessions in the Pacific. When added to the small, scattered islands that the United States had acquired as naval bases earlier in the nineteenth century, these new possessions gave the nation a far-flung Pacific empire, even if one whose total territory and population remained small by the standards of the other great empires of the age.

What was the reaction in the United States to the acquisition of this new empire?

own spheres. Together, these principles would allow the United States to trade freely with China without fear of interference and without having to become militarily involved in the region. They would also retain the illusion of Chinese sovereignty and thus prevent formal colonial dismemberment of China, which might also create obstacles to American trade.

Europe and Japan received the Open Door proposals coolly. Russia openly rejected them; the other powers claimed to accept them in principle but to be unable to act unless all the other powers agreed. But Hay refused to consider this a rebuff. He boldly announced that all the powers had accepted the principles of the Open Door in "final and definitive" form and that the United States expected them to observe those principles.

No sooner had the diplomatic maneuvering over the Open Door ended than the Boxers, a secret Chinese martial-arts society with highly nationalist convictions and a somewhat mystical vision of their invulnerability to bullets, launched a revolt against foreigners in China. The Boxer Rebellion spread widely across eastern China, attacking Westerners wherever they could find them—including many Christian missionaries. But the climax of the revolt was a siege of the entire Western foreign diplomatic corps, which took refuge in the British embassy in Beijing. The imperial powers (including the United States) sent an international expeditionary force into China to rescue the diplomats. In August 1900, it fought its way into Peking and broke the siege.

The Boxer Rebellion became an important event for the role of the United States in China. McKinley and Hay had agreed to American participation in quelling the Boxer Rebellion so as to secure a voice in the settlement of the uprising and to prevent the partition of China by the European powers. Hay now won support for his Open Door approach from England and Germany and induced the other participating powers to accept compensation from China for the damages the Boxer Rebellion had caused. Chinese territorial integrity survived at least in name, and the United States retained access to its lucrative trade.

BOXER REBELLION

Reasoning Processes

Continuity and Change After students have read the section "The Open Door," ask them to discuss in small groups how the Open Door policy represented both continuity and change in American foreign policy. *(Continuity: desire for increased American participation in Asia following annexation of the Philippines, similar to the Perry Expedition opening Japan to American trade in the 1850s. Change: United States gained control over large territories outside of its own borders for the first time in Puerto Rico, the Philippines, the Mariana Islands, and Hawaii.)* **WOR**

Answers

The American South Pacific Empire, 1900

The reaction was mixed. Some welcomed the economic opportunities afforded by the acquisition of new territories, as well as the strategic advantages it gave. Others protested the treatment of those living in the new territories or opposed expansion of moral grounds.

Historical Thinking Skills

Argumentation Have students read the section "A Modern Military System." Ask them to create a recruiting poster encouraging enlistment in the enlarged and modernized military described in the section. Have students keep in mind the failures the military experienced in the Spanish-American War that might have made potential recruits hesitate. **PCE** **WXT** **SOC**

A Modern Military System

The war with Spain had revealed glaring deficiencies in the American military system. The army had exhibited the greatest weaknesses, but the entire military organization had demonstrated problems of supply, training, and coordination. Had the United States been fighting a more powerful foe, disaster might have resulted. After the war, McKinley appointed Elihu Root, an able corporate lawyer in New York, as secretary of war to supervise a major overhaul of the armed forces. (Root was one of the first of several generations of attorney-statesmen who moved easily between public and private roles and constituted much of what has often been called the American "foreign policy establishment.")

Between 1900 and 1903, the Root reforms enlarged the regular army from 25,000 to a maximum of 100,000. They established federal army standards for the National Guard, ensuring that never again would the nation fight a war with volunteer regiments trained and equipped differently than those in the regular army. They sparked the creation of a system of officer training schools, including the Army Staff College (later the Command and General Staff School) at Fort Leavenworth, Kansas, and the Army War College in Washington. And in 1903, a general staff (named the Joint Chiefs of Staff) was established to act as military advisers to the secretary of war. It was this last reform that Root considered most important: the creation of a central planning agency modeled on the example of European general staffs. The Joint Chiefs were charged with many functions. They were to "supervise" and "coordinate" the entire army establishment and to establish an office that would plan for possible wars. An Army and Navy Board was to foster interservice cooperation. As a result of the new reforms, the United States entered the twentieth century with something resembling a modern military system.

ROOT'S MILITARY REFORMS

THE BOXER REBELLION, 1900 This photograph shows imprisoned Boxers in Beijing. Days earlier, they had been involved in the siege of the compound in which Western diplomats lived. An expeditionary force of numerous European powers in China, and of the United States, had broken the siege and captured the Boxers.

Discussion and Activities

Analyzing Visuals Have students examine the image "The Boxer Rebellion, 1900." Ask them to identify details and discuss in small groups evidence that would help to explain why the United States participated in putting down this movement. *(There was considerable anti-Chinese discrimination in the United States, as evidenced by the Chinese Exclusion Act and discrimination against Chinese immigrants in America.)* **WOR** **PCE**

CHAPTER 20 REVIEW

CONNECTING THEMES

Chapter Twenty focused on the causes and ramifications of the expansion pursued by the United States. Imperialists defended expansion by citing the need for foreign markets and access to natural resources. They also used Social Darwinism to justify competing with European powers like Britain, France, and Germany. Anti-imperialists reminded Americans of traditional isolationist principles and stoked the fears of workers about competition for jobs. Imperialists emphasized that the nation's policies toward Native Americans set a precedent for the peoples, who were treated as dependents rather than citizens.

The Spanish-American War helped lead to a new American overseas empire and immersed the United States in the politics of Europe and Asia. Governing new acquisitions proved more difficult than expected in some cases, with a long and brutal war in the Philippines generating large-scale public disapproval by the end of the conflict. American expansionism would affect the social, political, and economic structures within the United States and its new territories into the twentieth century.

You should consider the following questions as you review the themes for this chapter:

- How was the new imperialism similar to and different from the Manifest Destiny of the first half of the nineteenth century?
- What were the economic, social, and political motivations for the new imperialism?
- What were the major factors that led the United States to declare war against Spain in 1898?
- What were the most significant effects of the Spanish-American War?
- How did the new imperialism of the late nineteenth century change America's status in the world?
- What were the debates over imperialism, and what justifications did each side use to defend their position?

KEY TERMS

Alfred Thayer Mahan 563
Anti-Imperialist League 574
Boxer Rebellion 577
Cuban Revolt 567
Emilio Aguinaldo 575
Hawaii 565
imperialism 561
Insular Cases 574
The *Maine* 568
"Open Door" notes 576
Philippines 573
Platt Amendment 574
Puerto Rico 572
Rough Riders 569
Rudyard Kipling 564
Spanish-American War 567
"The White Man's Burden" 564
Venezuelan dispute 565
William Jennings Bryan 574
William McKinley 568
William Randolph Hearst 567
yellow journalism 566

Discussion and Activities

Analyzing Cause and Effect Divide the class in half. Have one group evaluate the causes and effects of American intervention in Latin America and the other group evaluate the causes and effects of American intervention in Asia. When finished, ask members of each group to pair up with a student from the other group to exchange information. **WOR PCE WXT SOC NAT MIG**

Key Terms

Students should be familiar with the key terms and be able to define them in the context of the causes and effects of American expansionism beginning at the end of the nineteenth century. Encourage students to use these terms in performing review exercises and exam practice for this chapter.

Go Online Chapter 20 Content Review

Assessing Student Understanding Use the online assessment to assess student understanding of concepts and topics within the chapter. You can assign the ready-made Chapter 20 Content Review or create your own from available questions. This easy-to-use tool helps you design assessments that meet the needs of different types of learners.

Answers

Multiple Choice

1. A; **2.** B; **3.** D

Short Answer

4A) Possible answer: The point of view in the image is that of an imperialist. The image depicts the Cuban people as being subjected to misrule by the Spanish, leading to anarchy within the country itself. The caption at the bottom concludes that the United States has a moral responsibility to intervene on behalf of the Cuban people.

4B) Possible answer: The protection of Cubans as Cubans had attempted several revolutions in trying to overthrow Spanish rule. The latest one occurred in 1895, which saw the Spanish brutally crush the rebellion.

4C) Possible answer: The United States had vested business interests in Cuba. U.S. businesses had tons of land on which to grow sugar within Cuba, and there were concerns over this with the Spanish cracking down on growing dissent.

5A) Possible answer: Both concepts and movements were about the United States expanding its sphere of influence, and both movements were driven by economic needs of the country during their respective times.

5B) Possible answer: Manifest Destiny involved expansion across the continent, but imperialism was expansion across the globe. Expansion during Manifest Destiny, was primarily about western expansion for land and later for resources and minerals. Expansion during the second half of the nineteenth century as an imperialistic venture was about raw materials, cheap labor, and places for markets.

5C) Possible answer: The United States was looking to assert itself as a world power, tantamount to that of the Europeans, and the U.S. gained power on the world stage.

AP EXAM PRACTICE

Questions assume cumulative content knowledge from this chapter and previous chapters.

MULTIPLE CHOICE

Use the image on page 575 and your knowledge of U.S. history to answer questions 1-3.

1. The political cartoon reflects the attempts to
   - (A) position newly acquired lands as a continuation of previous American foreign policy.
   - (B) build opposition to the expansion of American economic interests overseas.
   - (C) integrate new immigrants into American culture.
   - (D) criticize President McKinley for the expansion of American land holdings.

2. The first major challenge to the expanding American empire was
   - (A) the continuation of land wars with Native American nations within the continental boundaries
   - (B) the resistance of the Filipino people to American control after the Spanish-American War.
   - (C) the diplomatic challenges of acquiring the land needed for construction of the Panama Canal.
   - (D) the outbreak of military conflict with the British over disputed territory in Hawaii.

3. United States policy regarding China was different than its interactions in other regions because
   - (A) it resulted in military conflict with several European nations.
   - (B) it fostered a closer bond with the Chinese government.
   - (C) it prevented the negotiation of a trade alliance.
   - (D) it sought shared access with other powerful nations.

SHORT ANSWER

Use your knowledge of U.S. history to answer questions 4 and 5.

4. Use the image on page 568 to answer A, B, and C.
   - (A) Describe ONE point of view about America's role in Cuba in 1892.
   - (B) Briefly explain ONE specific historical argument Americans gave for intervening in Cuba.
   - (C) Briefly explain a SECOND specific historical argument Americans gave for intervening in Cuba.

5. Answer A, B, and C.
   - (A) Briefly describe ONE specific historical similarity between Manifest Destiny and imperialism.
   - (B) Briefly describe ONE specific historical difference between Manifest Destiny and imperialism.
   - (C) Briefly explain ONE specific historical effect that resulted from American imperialism during the second half of the nineteenth century.

LONG ESSAY

Develop a thoughtful and thorough historical argument that addresses the statement below. Begin your essay with a thesis statement, and support it with specific historical evidence and examples.

6. Evaluate the relative importance of causes that led to the United States becoming an imperialist power during the second half of the nineteenth century.

Answers

Long Essay

6. Possible thesis: There were intellectual arguments made in support of the United States's turn toward imperialism. However, the economic demands of the Second Industrial Revolution forced the country to look outside its traditional borders for support and growth. Further, the United States was interested in taking its place among the European powers, which required it to engage in diplomatic issues around the world. Therefore, despite arguments in support of imperialism, the economic and diplomatic causes were more important. Specific historical evidence: First, the advent of the Second Industrial Revolution brought about significant changes within the United States. The country now needed raw materials, cheap labor, and places to sell their finished goods to, and this led the country to look outside its traditional borders. Second, the United States was interested in imposing hemispheric hegemony within the Americas. This would prove costly and challenging, as Spain still controlled parts of the Americas, especially Cuba, where the United States had vested business interests.

21 THE PROGRESSIVES

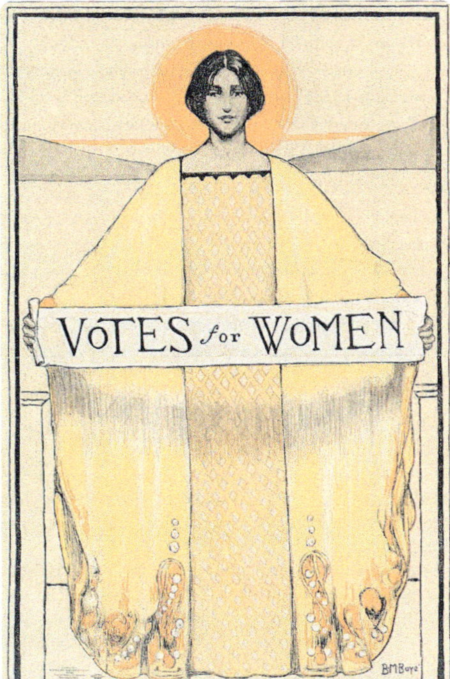

"VOTES FOR WOMEN," BY B. M. BOYE This striking poster was the prize-winning entry in a 1911 contest sponsored by the College Equal Suffrage League of Northern California.

CONNECTING CONCEPTS

Chapter Twenty-One begins by examining the vision of Progressives, who believed in the idea of societal progress but not if left solely to the "natural laws" of the marketplace or Social Darwinism. The reformers had different motivations — some had an abiding faith in knowledge and expertise while others had a religious comment to social justice. They also had different objectives — "muckraking" journalists like Ida Tarbell and Lincoln Steffens wanted to expose corruption while urban activists like Jane Addams created settlement houses to assist new immigrants. Middle-class, college-educated women played a key role in the Progressive movement, which dovetailed with the fight for woman suffrage and passage of the Nineteenth Amendment.

Progressives were highly critical of existing political institutions and parties. Middle-class reformers on the East Coast dominated the public image of the Progressive Movement, but western activists, working-class whites, and African Americans also contributed to the cause in critical ways. Soon after W.E.B. Du Bois and others formed the NAACP in 1905, it began to win important legal victories. Some Progressives advocated for social reform and moral issues like temperance because alcohol abuse contributed to domestic violence, political corruption, and industrial inefficiency. Female activists often led the charge — the Women's Christian Temperance Union had almost a quarter-million members by 1911. Eight years later, the states

Pacing Guide

Chapter 21 explores key concepts from Period 7: 1890–1945 of the AP U.S. History Curriculum Framework. The suggested instruction time for Chapter 21 is 3 days.

Key Concepts

7.1.I The United States continued its transition from a rural, agricultural economy to an urban, industrial economy led by large companies.

7.1.II In the Progressive Era of the early 20th century, Progressives responded to political corruption, economic instability, and social concerns by calling for greater government action and other political and social measures.

Discussion and Activities

Analyzing Visuals Have students examine the image "Votes for Women." Ask them to identify and discuss in small groups details from the image that promote the idea of women's suffrage. *(The motto is displayed by the figure in the image; the woman in the image has the sun behind her head, suggesting a halo; the robe the woman is wearing resembles a representation of angel's wings.)* **PCE** **SOC**

Discussion and Activities

Explaining Historical Concepts Have students read the section "Varieties of Progressivism." Ask them to create a chart listing the main ideas of Progressivism. Have students add to the chart as they learn more about the Progressive movement throughout the chapter.

ratified the Eighteenth Amendment. But other Progressives concentrated on social order. Believing that efforts at assimilation had failed or were inadequate, they supported immigration restriction as eugenicist beliefs reinforced a nativist tide.

Theodore Roosevelt helped modernize the presidency and became an idol to Progressives because he used the power of government to regulate corporate behavior, mediate labor disputes, promote environmental conservation, and inspect unsafe food and drugs. But William Howard Taft, Roosevelt's handpicked successor in 1908, disappointed Progressives when he sided with Republican conservatives. In 1912 they rejected a return by Roosevelt, who promised a "New Nationalism," and nominated Taft for a second term. But voters elected Woodrow Wilson, who championed a "New Freedom." As president, he backed Progressive efforts to curb child labor and limit corporate power, but he also condoned the racial resegregation of the federal government and refused to support woman suffrage.

As you read, you should:

- Describe the different ways that Progressives sought to curb the power of big business within American society.
- Analyze the concept of the "new woman" within the Progressive movement.
- Identify the ways that Progressives pressured government to take a more active role in democratizing the political system and enacting social welfare legislation.
- Explain the ways that Progressives sought to continue and build upon the reform tradition within the United States.
- Analyze the differences in Progressive philosophy from the three Progressive presidents: Roosevelt, Taft, and Wilson.

THE PROGRESSIVE IMPULSE

Progressivism was, first, an optimistic vision. Progressives believed, as their name implies, in the idea of progress. They believed that society was capable of improvement and that continued growth and advancement were a large part of the nation's destiny.

But progressives believed, too, that growth and progress could not continue to occur recklessly, as they had in the late nineteenth century. The "natural laws" of the marketplace, and the doctrines of laissez faire and Social Darwinism that celebrated those laws, were not sufficient. Direct, purposeful human intervention in social and economic affairs was, they argued, essential to ordering and bettering society.

VARIETIES OF PROGRESSIVISM

Progressives did not always agree on the form their intervention should take, and the result was a variety of reform impulses that sometimes seemed to have little in common. One powerful impulse was the spirit of "anti-monopoly," the fear of concentrated power and the urge to limit and disperse authority and wealth. This vaguely populist impulse appealed not only to many workers and farmers but to some middle-class Americans as well. And it encouraged government to regulate or break up trusts at both the state and national level.

"ANTIMONOPOLY"

Another progressive impulse was a belief in the importance of social cohesion: the belief that individuals are part of a great web of social relationships, that each person's welfare is dependent on the welfare of society as a whole. That assumption produced a concern about the "victims" of industrialization and other people who had difficult lives.

Still another impulse was a deep faith in knowledge—in the possibilities of applying to society the principles of natural and social sciences. Many reformers believed that knowledge was more important than anything else as a vehicle for making society more equitable and humane. Most progressives believed, too, that a modernized government could—and must—play an important role in the process of improving and stabilizing society. Modern life was too complex to be left in the hands of party bosses, untrained amateurs, and antiquated institutions.

FAITH IN KNOWLEDGE

THE MUCKRAKERS

Among the first people to articulate the new spirit of reform were crusading journalists who began to direct public attention toward social, economic, and political injustices. They became known as the "muckrakers," after

Go Online AP Exam Preparation

AP Exam Practice Use the online assessment to help prepare students for the AP Exam. You can assign the ready-made AP-style short-answer questions, document-based questions, and multiple-choice questions assessing concepts, themes, and skills from Period 7 and AP-style long-essay questions organized in sets of 3 questions from various time periods. You can also create your own tests from available questions. This easy-to-use tool helps you design assessments that meet the needs of different types of learners.

Theodore Roosevelt accused one of them of raking up muck through his writings. They were committed to exposing scandal, corruption, and injustice to public view.

At first, their major targets were the trusts and particularly the railroads, which the muckrakers considered powerful and deeply corrupt. Exposés of the great corporate organizations began to appear as early as the 1860s, when Charles Francis Adams Jr. and others uncovered corruption among the railroad barons. One of the most notable muckrakers was the journalist Ida Tarbell's enormous study of the Standard Oil trust (published first in magazines and then as a two-volume book in 1904). By the turn of the century, many muckrakers were turning their attention to government, particularly to the urban political machines. The most influential, perhaps, was Lincoln Steffens, a reporter for *McClure's* magazine and the author of a famous book based on his articles, *The Shame of the Cities* (1904). His portraits of "machine government" and "boss rule"; his exposure of "boodlers" in cities as diverse as St. Louis, Minneapolis, Cleveland, Cincinnati, Chicago, Philadelphia, and New York; his tone of studied moral outrage—all helped arouse sentiment for urban political reform. The alternative to leaving government in the hands of corrupt party leaders, the muckrakers argued, was for the people themselves to take a greater interest in public life.

IDA TARBELL AND LINCOLN STEFFENS

The muckrakers reached the peak of their influence in the first decade of the twentieth century. By presenting social problems to the public with indignation and moral fervor, they helped inspire other Americans to take action.

THE SOCIAL GOSPEL

The growing outrage at social and economic injustice helped produce many reformers committed to the pursuit of what came to be known as "social justice." (Social justice is a term widely used around the world to describe a kind of justice that goes beyond the individual, seeking justice for society as a whole. Advocates of social justice are likely to believe in an egalitarian society and support for poor and oppressed people.) That impulse helped create the rise of what became known as the "Social Gospel." By the early twentieth century, it had become a powerful movement within American Protestantism (and, to a lesser extent, within American Catholicism and Judaism). It was chiefly concerned with redeeming the nation's cities.

The Salvation Army, which began in England but soon spread to the United States, was one example of the fusion of religion with reform. A Christian social welfare organization with a vaguely military structure, by 1900 it had recruited 3,000 "officers" and 20,000 "privates" and was offering both material aid and spiritual service to the urban poor. In addition, many ministers, priests, and rabbis left traditional parish work to serve in the troubled cities. Charles Sheldon's *In His Steps* (1898), the story of a young minister who abandoned a comfortable post to work among the needy, sold more than 15 million copies. It was one of the most successful novels of the era.

Walter Rauschenbusch, a Protestant theologian from Rochester, New York, published a series of influential discourses on the possibilities for human salvation through Christian reform. To him, the message of Darwinism was not the survival of the fittest. He believed, rather, that all individuals should work to ensure a humanitarian evolution of the social fabric. Some American Catholics seized on the 1893 publication of Pope Leo XIII's encyclical *Rerum Novarum* (New Things) as justification for their own crusade for social justice. Catholic liberals such as Father John A. Ryan took to heart the pope's warning that "a small number of very rich men have been able to lay upon the masses of the poor a yoke little better than slavery itself." For decades, he worked to expand the scope of Catholic social welfare organizations.

FATHER JOHN RYAN

THE SETTLEMENT HOUSE MOVEMENT

An element of much progressive thought was the belief in the influence of the environment on individual development. Social Darwinists such as William Graham Sumner had argued that people's fortunes reflected their inherent "fitness" for survival. Progressive theorists disagreed. Ignorance, poverty, even criminality, they argued, were not the result of inherent genetic failings or of the workings of providence; they were, rather, the effects of an unhealthy environment. To elevate the distressed, therefore, required an improvement of the conditions in which they lived.

Nothing produced more distress, many urban reformers believed, than crowded immigrant neighborhoods, which publicists such as Jacob Riis were exposing through vivid photographs and lurid descriptions. One response to the problems of such communities, borrowed from England, was the settlement house. The most famous, and one of the first, was Hull House, which opened in 1889 in Chicago as a result of the efforts of the social worker Jane Addams. It became a model for more than 400 similar institutions throughout the nation. Staffed by members of the educated middle class, settlement houses sought to help immigrant families adapt to the language and customs of their new country. Settlement houses avoided the condescension and moral disapproval of earlier philanthropic efforts. But they generally embraced a belief that middle-class Americans had a responsibility to impart their own values to immigrants and to teach them how to create middle-class lifestyles.

JANE ADDAMS AND HULL HOUSE

Young college women (mostly unmarried) were important participants in the settlement house movement. Working in a settlement house, which was a protected site that served mostly women, was consistent with the widespread assumption that women needed to be sheltered from difficult environments. The clean and well-tended buildings that settlement houses created were not only a model for immigrant women, but an appropriate site for elite women as well.

Discussion and Activities

Making Connections After students have read the section "The Muckrakers," ask them to discuss in pairs or small groups what, if any, group or institution fills the role today played by muckrakers at the beginning of the twentieth century. **SOC**

Reasoning Processes

Continuity and Change Have students read the section "The Social Gospel." Ask them to discuss as a class how the Social Gospel represents a continuation or change over time in the role of the church in society. *(Some elements of the Social Gospel could be viewed as a continuation of the impulse to perfect society in the Second Great Awakening, but with less emphasis on personal conversion to achieve salvation.)* **SOC**

Discussion and Activities

Analyzing Points of View After students have read the section "The Settlement House Movement," ask them to write a journal entry from the point of view of an immigrant describing the services they received from a settlement house and how it impacted their lives. **SOC**

"THE BOSSES OF THE SENATE" (1889), BY JOSEPH KEPPLER Keppler was a popular political cartoonist of the late nineteenth century who shared the growing concern about the power of the trusts—portrayed here as bloated, almost reptilian figures standing menacingly over the members of the U.S. Senate, to whose chamber the "people's entrance" is "closed."

The settlement houses helped create another important element of progressive reform: the profession of social work. Workers at Hull House, for example, maintained a close relationship with the University of Chicago's pioneering work in the field of sociology. A growing number of programs for the professional training of social workers began to appear in the nation's leading universities, partly in response to the activities of the settlements.

The Allure of Expertise

As the emergence of the social work profession suggests, progressives involved in humanitarian efforts placed a high value on knowledge and expertise. Even nonscientific problems, they believed, could be analyzed and solved scientifically. Many reformers came to believe that only enlightened experts and well-designed bureaucracies could create the stability and order America needed.

Some reformers even spoke of the creation of a new civilization, in which the expertise of scientists and engineers could be brought to bear on the problems of the economy and society. The social scientist Thorstein Veblen, for example, proposed a new economic system in which power would reside in the hands of highly trained engineers. Only they, he argued, could fully understand the "machine process" by which modern society must be governed.

The Professions

The late nineteenth century saw a dramatic expansion in the number of Americans engaged in administrative and professional tasks. Industries needed managers, technicians, and accountants as well as workers. Cities required commercial, medical, legal, and educational services. New technology required scientists and engineers, who, in turn, required institutions and instructors to train them. By the turn of the century, those performing these services had come to constitute a distinct social group–what some historians have called a new middle class.

The new middle class placed a high value on education and individual accomplishment. By the early twentieth century, its millions of members were building organizations and

Discussion and Activities

Analyzing Visuals Have students examine the image "The Bosses of the Senate." Ask them to identify and discuss in small groups images in the cartoon that reinforce the cartoon's message. *(The trusts are represented as money bags towering over the senators; various signs on the wall indicate that the business of the senate is to promote the business interests of the trusts.)* **PCE**

establishing standards to secure their position in society. The idea of professionalism had been a frail one in America even as late as 1880. When every patent-medicine salesman could claim to be a doctor, when every frustrated politician could set up shop as a lawyer, when anyone who could read and write could pose as a teacher, a professional label by itself carried little weight. There were, of course, skilled and responsible doctors, lawyers, teachers, and others; but they had no way of controlling or distinguishing themselves clearly from the amateurs, charlatans, and incompetents who presumed to practice their trades. As the demand for professional services increased, so did the pressures for reform.

Among the first to respond was the medical profession. In 1901, doctors who considered themselves trained professionals reorganized the American Medical Association into a national professional society. By 1920, nearly two-thirds of all American doctors were members. The AMA quickly called for strict, scientific standards for admission to the practice of medicine, with doctors themselves serving as protectors of the standards. State governments responded by passing new laws requiring the licensing of all physicians. By 1900, medical education at a few medical schools—notably Johns Hopkins in Baltimore (founded in 1893)—compared favorably with that in the leading institutions of Europe. Doctors such as William H. Welch at Hopkins revolutionized the teaching of medicine by moving students out of the classrooms and into laboratories and clinics.

AMERICAN MEDICAL ASSOCIATION

There was similar movement in other professions. By 1916, lawyers in all forty-eight states had established professional bar associations. The nation's law schools accordingly expanded greatly. Businessmen supported the creation of schools of business administration and created their own national organizations: the National Association of Manufacturers in 1895 and the United States Chamber of Commerce in 1912. Even farmers, long the symbol of the romantic spirit of individualism, responded to the new order by forming, through the National Farm Bureau Federation, a network of agricultural organizations designed to spread scientific farming methods.

NATIONAL ASSOCIATION OF MANUFACTURERS

While removing the untrained and incompetent, the admission requirements also protected those already in the professions from excessive competition and lent prestige and status to their trades. Some professionals used their entrance requirements to exclude African Americans, women, immigrants, and other "undesirables" from their ranks. Others used them simply to keep the numbers down, to ensure that demand would remain high.

The Library of Congress (LC-DIG-npcc-33267)

THE INFANT WELFARE SOCIETY, CHICAGO The Infant Welfare Society was one of many "helping" organizations in Chicago and other large cities—many of them closely tied to the settlement houses—that strove to help immigrants adapt to American life and create safe and healthy living conditions. Here, a volunteer helps an immigrant mother learn to bathe her baby.

WOMEN AND THE PROFESSIONS

Both by custom and by active barriers of law and prejudice, American women found themselves excluded from most of the emerging professions. But a substantial number of middle-class women—particularly those emerging from the new women's colleges and coeducational state universities—entered professional careers nevertheless.

A few women managed to establish themselves as physicians, lawyers, engineers, scientists, and corporate managers in the early 1900s. Several leading medical schools admitted women, and in 1900 about 5 percent of all American physicians were female (a proportion that remained unchanged until the 1960s). Most, however, turned by necessity to those "helping" professions that society considered vaguely domestic and thus suitable for women: settlement houses, social work, and most important, teaching. Indeed, in the late nineteenth century, more than two-thirds of all grammar school teachers were women, and perhaps 90 percent of all professional women were teachers. For educated black women, in particular, the existence of segregated schools in the South created a substantial market for African American teachers.

FEMALE-DOMINATED PROFESSIONS

Women also dominated other professional activities. Nursing had become primarily a women's field during and after the Civil War. By the early twentieth century, it was adopting professional standards. And many women entered academia—often receiving advanced degrees at such

Discussion and Activities

Analyzing Issues After students have read the section "The Professions," ask them to create a T-chart listing the benefits and costs to society of the formation of various professional organizations. Have students discuss as a class whether the overall benefits or costs were greater, and if that still holds true today. **SOC** **WXT**

Discussion and Activities

Evaluating Evidence Have students examine the image "The Infant Welfare Society, Chicago." Ask them to discuss in small groups what the purpose or intent may have been behind publication of this photo. *(The photo was likely intended to contradict negative stereotypes about immigrants being unsanitary and unhealthy, and to attract monetary support and volunteers for the settlement house.)* **SOC**

Historical Thinking Skills

Sourcing and Situation Have students examine the image "Woman's Holy War." Ask them to identify and discuss in small groups details from the image that support the purpose of the poster. *(The women in the poster are shown wearing armor and wielding weapons that bring to mind a medieval crusade tying into the caption of the poster.)* **SOC**

DEBATING THE PAST

PROGRESSIVISM

Until the early 1950s, most historians generally agreed on the central characteristics of progressivism. It was just what progressives themselves said it was: a movement by the "people" to curb the power of the "special interests."

George Mowry challenged this traditional view in *The California Progressives* (1951). He described the reform movement in California not as a people's protest, but, rather, as an effort by a small and privileged group of business and professional men to limit the power of large new corporations and labor unions. Richard Hofstadter expanded on this idea in *The Age of Reform* (1955), describing progressives throughout the country as people suffering from "status anxiety"—old, formerly influential, upper-middle-class families seeking to restore their fading prestige by challenging the powerful new institutions that had begun to displace them.

The Mowry-Hofstadter thesis provoked new challenges and new interpretations of the meaning of progressivism. Gabriel Kolko, in *The Triumph of Conservatism* (1963), rejected the Mowry-Hofstadter idea that progressivism represented the efforts of a displaced elite. Progressivism, he argued, was an effort to regulate business undertaken, not by the "people" or "displaced elites," but by corporate leaders, who saw in government supervision a way to protect themselves from competition. Martin Sklar's *The Corporate Reconstruction of American Capitalism* (1988) is a more sophisticated version of a similar argument.

A more moderate challenge to the "psychological" interpretation of progressivism came from historians embracing a new "organizational" view of history. In *The Search for Order, 1877–1920* (1967), Robert Wiebe presented progressivism as a response to dislocations in American life brought on by rapid changes in the economy. Economic power had moved to large, national organizations, while social and political life remained centered primarily in local communities. The result was widespread disorder and unrest. Progressivism, Wiebe argued, was the effort of a "new middle class"—a class tied to the emerging national economy—to stabilize and enhance their position in society by creating national institutions suitable for the new national economy.

Some historians continued to argue that progressivism was a movement of the people against the special interests. J. Joseph Huthmacher argued in 1962 that much of the force behind progressivism came from members of the working class, especially immigrants, who pressed for such reforms as workmen's compensation and wage and hour laws. John Buenker, in *Urban Liberalism and Progressive Reform* (1973), claimed that political machines and urban "bosses" were important sources of reform energy and helped create twentieth-century liberalism.

Other historians writing in the 1970s and 1980s attempted to link reform to some of the broad processes of political change that had created the public battles of the era. Richard L. McCormick's *From Realignment to Reform* (1981), a study of political change in New York State, argued that the crucial change in this era was the decline of the political parties and the rise of interest groups working for particular social and economic goals.

Many historians see progressivism as rooted in gender and have focused on the role of women (and the vast network of voluntary associations they created) in shaping and promoting progressive reform. Historians Kathryn Sklar, Linda Gordon, Ruth Rosen, and Elaine Tyler May, among others, argued that some progressive battles were part of an effort by women to protect their interests within the domestic sphere in the face of jarring challenges from the new industrial world. This protective urge drew women reformers to such issues as temperance, divorce, prostitution, and the regulation of female and child labor. Other women worked to expand their own roles in the public world. Progressivism cannot be understood, historians of women contend, without understanding the role of women and the importance of issues involving the family and the private world within it.

WOMAN'S HOLY WAR.
Grand Charge on the Enemy's Works

Other historians have sought to place progressivism in a broader context. Daniel Rodgers's *Atlantic Crossings* (1998) is a study of how European reforms influenced American progressives. Both Michael McGerr, in *A Fierce Discontent* (2003), and Alan Dawley, in *Changing the World* (2003), have characterized progressivism as a fundamentally moral undertaking. McGerr viewed it as an effort by the middle class to create order and stability, whereas Dawley saw it as an effort by groups on the left to attack social injustice.

Given the range of disagreement over the nature of the progressive movement, it is hardly surprising that some historians have despaired of finding any coherent definition for the term. Peter Filene, for one, suggested in 1970 that the concept of progressivism as a "movement" had outlived its usefulness. But Daniel Rodgers, in an important 1982 article, "In Search of Progressivism," disagreed. The very diversity of progressivism, he argued, accounted both for its enormous impact on its time and for its capacity to reveal to us today the "noise and tumult" of an age of rapid social change.

HISTORICAL THINKING SKILLS

Questions assume cumulative content knowledge from this chapter and previous chapters.

1. **Identifying Historical Developments** Identify three broad schools of historical interpretation regarding Progressivism.
2. **Evaluating Evidence** Describe how historical evidence, from the time period, could be used to support each of the three broad schools of historical interpretation regarding Progressivism.
3. **Developing Arguments** Analyze which school of thought you find more convincing and explain why using evidence from the text to support your argument.

Answers

Debating the Past

1. Richard Hofstadter argued that progressivism was fundamentally about people suffering from "status anxiety." It was mainly made up of formally influential upper middle-class families who were seeking to restore their prestige by challenging the powerful new institutions that had begun to displace them. Huthmacher argued that progressivism was largely a movement of the working class, especially immigrants, who pressed for such reforms. Others have seen Progressivism primarily as a movement by women to protect their interests within the domestic sphere in the face of challenges from the new industrial world.
2. Progressives built upon the small gains of the Populist movement by aggressively going after corporations and using the tools of the federal government to regulate and break up monopolies. Progressives not only pushed to control and regulate business but also advocated for broader laws protecting workers and the population in general.
3. Student answers will vary. Daniel Rodgers, in his 1982 article "In Search of Progressivism," argues that progressivisms' enduring legacy is the fact that it involved a wide diversity of interests and individuals.

predominantly male institutions as the University of Chicago, MIT, or Columbia, and finding professional opportunities in the new and expanding women's colleges.

WOMEN AND REFORM

The prominence of women in reform movements is one of the most striking features of progressivism. In most states during the early twentieth century, women could not vote. They almost never held public office. They had footholds in only a few (and usually primarily female dominated) professions and lived in a culture in which most people, male and female, believed that women were not suited for the public world. What, then, explains the prominent role so many women played in the reform activities of the time period?

THE "NEW WOMAN"

SOCIOECONOMIC ORIGINS OF THE NEW WOMAN

The phenomenon of the "new woman," widely remarked upon at the time, was a product of social and economic changes that affected the private world as much as the public one, even if such changes affected mostly middle-class people. By the end of the nineteenth century, almost all income-producing activity had moved out of the home and into the factory or the office. At the same time, children were beginning school at earlier ages and spending more time there. For many wives and mothers who did not work for wages, the home was no longer an all-consuming place. Technological innovations such as running water, electricity, and eventually household appliances made housework less onerous (even if higher standards of cleanliness counterbalanced many of these gains).

Declining family size also changed the lives of many women. Middle-class white women in the late nineteenth century had fewer children than their mothers and grandmothers had borne. They also lived longer. Many women thus now spent fewer years with young children in the home and lived more years after their children were grown.

Some educated women shunned marriage, believing that only by remaining single could they play the roles they envisioned in the public world. Single women were among the most prominent female reformers of the time: Jane Addams and Lillian Wald in the settlement house movement, Frances Willard in the temperance movement, Anna Howard Shaw in the suffrage movement, and many others. Some of these women lived alone. Others lived with other women, often in long-term relationships—some of them quietly romantic—that were known at the time as "Boston marriages." The divorce rate also rose rapidly in the late nineteenth century, from one divorce for every twenty-one marriages in 1880 to one in nine by 1916; women initiated the majority of them.

"BOSTON MARRIAGES"

THE CLUBWOMEN

Among the most visible signs of the increasing public roles of women in the late nineteenth and early twentieth centuries were the women's clubs, which proliferated rapidly beginning in the 1880s and 1890s and became the vanguard of many important reforms.

The women's clubs began largely as cultural organizations to provide middle- and upper-class women with an outlet for their intellectual energies. In 1892, when women formed the General Federation of Women's Clubs to coordinate the activities of local organizations, there were more than 100,000 members in nearly 500 clubs. By 1917, there were over 1 million.

GFWC

By the early twentieth century, the clubs were becoming less concerned with cultural activities and more concerned with contributing to social betterment. Because many club members were from wealthy families, some organizations had substantial funds at their disposal to make their influence felt. And ironically, because women could not vote, the clubs had a nonpartisan image that made them difficult for politicians to dismiss.

Black women occasionally joined clubs dominated by white women. But most such clubs excluded African Americans, and so black women formed clubs of their own. Some of them affiliated with the General Federation, but most became part of the independent National Association of Colored Women. Some black clubs also took positions on issues of particular concern to African Americans, such as lynching and aspects of segregation.

The women's club movement seldom raised overt challenges to prevailing assumptions about the proper role of women in society. Few clubwomen were willing to accept the arguments of such committed feminists as Charlotte Perkins Gilman, who in her 1898 book, *Women and Economics*, argued that the traditional definition of gender roles was exploitive and obsolete. Instead, the club movement allowed women to define a space for themselves in the public world without openly challenging the existing, male-dominated order.

A PUBLIC SPACE FOR WOMEN

Much of what the clubs did was uncontroversial: planting trees; supporting schools, libraries, and settlement houses; building hospitals and parks. But clubwomen were also an important force in winning passage of state (and ultimately federal) laws that regulated the conditions of woman and child labor, established government inspection of workplaces, regulated the food and drug industries, reformed policies toward Native Americans, applied new standards to urban housing, and, perhaps most notably, outlawed the manufacture and sale of alcohol. They were instrumental in pressuring state legislatures in most states to provide "mother's pensions" to widowed or abandoned mothers with small children—a system that ultimately became absorbed into the Social Security system. In 1912, they pressured Congress into establishing the Children's Bureau in the Labor Department, an agency directed to develop policies to protect children.

Reasoning Processes

Continuity and Change After students have read the section "Women and the Professions," ask them to think about and share with a partner whether the numbers and roles of women in the professions by the beginning of the twentieth century represented a continuity or change over time in ideas about gender roles. *(Although the increased number of female doctors and lawyers suggests a change, the concentration of women in helping professions, such as teaching and nursing, represents a continuity from the ideas of separate spheres.)* **SOC**

Discussion and Activities

Analyzing Change Have students read the section "The 'New Woman.'" Ask them to discuss as a class how the "New Woman" of the early twentieth century differed from previous generations of American women. **SOC**

Discussion and Activities

Evaluating Evidence After students have read the section "The Clubwomen," ask them to create a chart listing economic, social, and political accomplishments of women's clubs. Have students evaluate in which area the clubs had their greatest impact. **SOC** **WXT** **PCE**

THE COLORED WOMEN'S LEAGUE OF WASHINGTON, D.C. The women's club movement spread widely through American life and produced a number of organizations through which African American women gathered to improve social and political conditions. The Colored Women's League of Washington, D.C., members of which appear in this 1894 photograph, was founded in 1892 by Sara Fleetwood, a registered nurse who was the wife of Christian Fleetwood, one of the first African American soldiers to receive the Congressional Medal of Honor for his heroism in the Civil War. The league she founded was committed to "racial uplift," and it consisted mostly of teachers, who created nurseries for the infants of women who worked and evening schools for adults. Members of the League are shown here gathered on the steps of Frederick Douglass's home on Capitol Hill. Sara Fleetwood is in the second row on the far right.

Library of Congress, Rare Book and Special Collections Division, Daniel A.P. Murray Pamphlets Collection

WOMEN'S TRADE UNION LEAGUE

In many of these efforts, the clubwomen formed alliances with other women's groups, such as the Women's Trade Union League (WTUL), founded in 1903 by female union members and upper-class reformers. It was committed to persuading women to join unions. In addition to working on behalf of protective legislation for women, WTUL members held public meetings on behalf of female workers, raised money to support strikes, marched on picket lines, and bailed striking women out of jail.

WOMAN SUFFRAGE

Perhaps the largest single reform movement of the progressive era, indeed one of the largest in American history, was the fight for woman suffrage.

It is sometimes difficult for today's Americans to understand why the suffrage issue could have become the source of such enormous controversy. But at the time, suffrage seemed to many of its critics a very radical demand, in part because of the rationale some of its early supporters used to advance it. Throughout the late nineteenth century, many suffrage advocates presented their views in terms of "natural rights," arguing that women deserved the same rights as men—including, first and foremost, the right to vote. Elizabeth Cady Stanton, for example, wrote in 1892 of woman as "the arbiter of her own destiny . . . if we are to consider her as a citizen, as a member of a great nation, she must have the same rights as all other members." This was an argument that boldly challenged the views of the many men and women who believed that society required a distinctive female "sphere" in which women would serve first and foremost as wives and mothers. And so a powerful antisuffrage movement emerged, dominated by men but with the active support of many women. Opponents railed against the threat suffrage posed to the "natural order" of civilization. Antisuffragists, many of them women, associated suffrage with

RADICAL CHALLENGE OF WOMEN'S SUFFRAGE

Discussion and Activities

Analyzing Visuals Have students examine the image "The Colored Women's League of Washington, D.C." Ask them to identify and discuss in small groups details that demonstrate characteristics of the members. *(Most are women, though there a few men also pictured. A few women pictured appear to be dressed as servants, but most are dressed in middle-class clothing.)* **SOC**

SHIRTWAIST WORKERS ON STRIKE The Women's Trade Union League was notable for bringing educated, middle-class women together with workers in efforts to improve factory and labor conditions. These picketing women are workers in the "Ladies Tailors" garment factory in New York.

divorce (not without some reason, since many suffrage advocates also supported making it easier for women to obtain a divorce). They linked suffrage with promiscuity, immorality, and neglect of children.

In the first years of the twentieth century, the suffrage movement began to overcome this opposition and win some substantial victories, in part because suffragists were becoming better organized and more politically sophisticated than their opponents. Under the leadership of Anna Howard Shaw, a Boston social worker, and Carrie Chapman Catt, a journalist from Iowa, membership in the National American Woman Suffrage Association (NAWSA) grew from about 13,000 in 1893 to over 2 million in 1917. The movement gained strength because many of its most prominent leaders began to justify suffrage in "safer," less threatening ways. Suffrage, some supporters began to argue, would not challenge the "separate sphere" in which women resided. It was, they claimed, precisely because women occupied a distinct sphere—because as mothers and wives and homemakers they had special experiences and special sensitivities to bring to public life—that woman suffrage could make such an important contribution to politics.

NAWSA

In particular, many suffragists argued that enfranchising women would help the temperance movement, by giving its largest group of supporters a political voice. Some suffrage advocates claimed that once women had the vote, war would become a thing of the past, since women would—by their calming, maternal influence—help curb the belligerence of men. That was one reason why World War I gave a final, decisive push to the movement for suffrage.

Suffrage also attracted support for other, less optimistic reasons. Many middle-class people found persuasive the argument that if African Americans, immigrants, and other "base" groups had access to the franchise, then it was a matter not only of justice but of common sense to allow educated, "well-born" women to vote.

CONSERVATIVE ARGUMENTS FOR SUFFRAGE

The principal triumphs of the suffrage movement began in 1910, when Washington became the first state in fourteen years to extend suffrage to women. California followed a year later, and four other western states in 1912. In 1913, Illinois became the first state east of the Mississippi to embrace woman suffrage. And in 1917 and 1918, New York and Michigan—two of the most populous states in the Union—gave women the vote. By 1919, thirty-nine states had granted women the right to vote in at least some elections; fifteen had allowed them full participation. In 1920, finally, suffragists won ratification of the Nineteenth Amendment, which guaranteed political rights to women throughout the nation.

NINETEENTH AMENDMENT

To some feminists, however, the victory seemed less than complete. Alice Paul, head of the militant National Woman's Party (founded in 1916), never accepted the relatively conservative "separate sphere" justification for suffrage. She argued that the Nineteenth Amendment alone would not be sufficient to protect women's rights. Women needed more: a constitutional amendment that would provide clear, legal protection for their rights and would prohibit all discrimination on the basis of sex. But Alice Paul's argument found limited favor even among many of the most important leaders of the recently triumphant suffrage crusade.

Historical Thinking Skills

Argumentation After students have read the section "Woman Suffrage," ask them to create a T-chart listing arguments for and against the right of women to vote. Have students discuss in small groups which, if any, of the arguments against women voting still exist in the minds of some people. **SOC** **PCE**

Discussion and Activities

Analyzing Points of View Have students examine the image "Shirtwaist Workers on Strike." Ask them to write a short journal article from the point of view of either a supporter or opponent of the women shown on strike. **SOC** **PCE** **WXT**

Historical Thinking Skills

Contextualization After students have read the section "Early Attacks," ask them to discuss in pairs or small groups why they think the secret ballot was such a powerful reform and what problems it resolved. *(Previously, poll watchers could see how individuals were voting, leading to the potential and common practice of intimidating voters—for example, voters of color in the post-Reconstruction South or workers in Eastern cities.)* **PCE**

SUFFRAGE PAGEANT, 1913 On March 3, 1913—the day before Woodrow Wilson's inauguration as president—more than 5,000 supporters of woman suffrage staged a parade in Washington, D.C., that overshadowed Wilson's own arrival there. Crowds estimated at over half a million watched the parade, not all of them admirers of the woman suffrage movement, and some of the onlookers attacked the marchers. The police did nothing to stop the attacks. This photograph depicts a suffragist, Florence Noyes, costumed as Liberty, posing in front of the U.S. Treasury Building, part of a pageant accompanying the parade. Woman suffrage was one of the most important and impassioned reform movements of the progressive era.

THE ASSAULT ON THE PARTIES

Sooner or later, most progressive goals required the involvement of government. Only government, reformers agreed, could effectively counter the many powerful private interests that threatened the nation. But American government at the dawn of the new century was, progressives believed, poorly adapted to perform their ambitious tasks. At every level, political institutions were outmoded, inefficient, and corrupt. Before progressives could reform society effectively, they would have to reform government itself. Many reformers believed the first step must be an assault on the dominant role the political parties played in the life of the state.

EARLY ATTACKS

Attacks on party dominance had been frequent in the late nineteenth century. Greenbackism and Populism, for example, had been efforts to break the hammerlock with which the Republicans and Democrats controlled public life. The Independent Republicans (or mugwumps) had also attempted to challenge the grip of partisanship.

These early assaults enjoyed some success. In the 1880s and 1890s, for example, most states adopted the secret ballot. Prior to that, the political parties themselves had printed ballots (or "tickets"), with the names of the party's candidates, and no others. They distributed the tickets to their supporters, who then simply went to the polls to deposit them in the ballot box. The old system had made it possible for bosses to monitor the voting behavior of their constituents; it had also made it difficult for voters to "split" their tickets–to vote for candidates of different parties for different offices. The new secret ballot–printed by the government and distributed at the polls to be filled out and deposited in secret–helped chip away at the power of the parties over voters.

MUNICIPAL REFORM

Many progressives, such as Lincoln Steffens, believed the impact of party rule was most damaging in the cities. Municipal government therefore became one of the first targets of those working for political reform.

The muckrakers struck a responsive chord among a powerful group of urban, middle-class progressives. For several decades after the Civil War, "respectable" citizens of the nation's large cities had avoided participation in municipal government. Viewing politics as a debased and demeaning activity, they shrank from contact with the "vulgar" elements who were coming to dominate public life. By the end of the century, however, a new generation of activists–some of them members of old aristocratic families, others a part of the new middle class–were taking a growing interest in government.

MIDDLE-CLASS PROGRESSIVES

These activists faced a formidable array of opponents. In addition to challenging the powerful city bosses and their entrenched political organizations, they were attacking a large group of special interests: saloon owners, brothel keepers, and, perhaps most significantly, those businessmen who had established lucrative relationships with the urban political machines and who viewed reform as a threat to their profits. Finally, there was the great constituency of urban working people, many of them recent immigrants, to whom the machines were a source of needed jobs and services. Gradually, however, the reformers gained in political strength.

Historical Thinking Skills

Sourcing and Situation Have students examine the image "Suffrage Pageant, 1913." As a class, identify and discuss the symbolism captured in the photo that was intended to promote woman suffrage. *(Most of the women are dressed in white, evoking purity. The central character is cloaked in what may be an American flag, and she is wearing Roman-style armor and carrying a staff with an eagle, suggesting the ideal of civic virtue.)* **SOC** **PCE**

Historical Thinking Skills

Argumentation After students have read the section "Municipal Reform," ask them to create a list of obstacles municipal reformers faced and rank them in order of importance. Have students write a thesis statement that makes a claim about the most important barrier to municipal reform. **PCE**

NEW FORMS OF GOVERNANCE

One of the first major successes came in Galveston, Texas, where the old city government proved unable to deal with the effects of a destructive tidal wave in 1900. Capitalizing on public dismay, reformers, many of them local businessmen, won approval of a new city charter. The mayor and council were replaced by an elected, nonpartisan commission. In 1907, Des Moines, Iowa, adopted its own version of the commission plan, and other cities followed.

COMMISSION PLAN

Another approach to municipal reform was the city-manager plan, by which elected officials hired an outside expert—often a professionally trained business manager or engineer—to take charge of the city government. The city manager would presumably remain untainted by the corrupting influence of politics. By the end of the progressive era in the early 1920s, almost 400 cities were operating under commissions, and another 45 employed city managers.

CITY-MANAGER PLAN

TOM JOHNSON As sentiment for municipal reform grew in intensity in the late nineteenth century, it became possible for progressive mayors committed to ending "boss rule" to win election over machine candidates in some of America's largest cities. One of the most prominent was Tom Johnson, the reform mayor of Cleveland. Johnson made a fortune in the steel and streetcar business and then entered politics, partly as a result of reading Henry George's Poverty and Progress. He became mayor in 1901 and in his four terms waged strenuous battles against party bosses and corporate interests. He won many fights, but he lost what he considered his most important one: the struggle for municipal ownership of public utilities.

In most urban areas, the enemies of partnership had to settle for less absolute victories. Some cities made the election of mayors nonpartisan (so that the parties could not choose the candidates) or moved them to years when no presidential or congressional races were in progress (to reduce the influence of the large turnouts that party organizations produced). Reformers tried to make city councilors run at large, to limit the influence of ward leaders and district bosses. They tried to strengthen the power of the mayor at the expense of the city council, on the assumption that reformers were more likely to succeed in getting a sympathetic mayor elected than they were to win control of the entire council.

Some of the most successful reformers emerged from conventional political structures that progressives came to control. Tom Johnson, the celebrated reform mayor of Cleveland, waged a long war against the powerful streetcar interests in his city, fighting to lower streetcar fares to 3 cents, and ultimately to impose municipal ownership on certain basic utilities. After Johnson's defeat and death, his talented aide Newton D. Baker won election as mayor and helped maintain Cleveland's reputation as the best-governed city in America. Hazen Pingree of Detroit, Samuel "Golden Rule" Jones of Toledo, and other mayors effectively challenged local party bosses to bring the spirit of reform into city government.

TOM JOHNSON

STATEHOUSE PROGRESSIVISM

The assault on boss rule in the cities did not, however, always produce results. Consequently, many progressives turned to state government as an agent for reform. They looked with particular scorn on state legislatures, whose ill-paid, undistinguished members, they believed, were generally incompetent, often corrupt, and totally controlled by party bosses. Reformers began looking for ways to circumvent the boss-controlled legislatures by increasing the power of the electorate.

Two of the most important changes were innovations first proposed by Populists in the 1890s: the initiative and the referendum. The initiative allowed reformers to circumvent state legislatures by submitting new legislation directly to the voters in general elections. The referendum provided a method by which actions of the legislature could be returned to the electorate for approval. By 1918, more than twenty states had enacted one or both of these reforms.

INITIATIVE AND REFERENDUM

Similarly, the direct primary and the recall were efforts to limit the power of party and improve the quality of elected officials. The primary election was an attempt to take the selection of candidates away from the bosses and give it to the people. (In the South, it was also an effort to limit black voting—since primary voting, many white Southerners believed, would be easier to control than general elections.) The recall gave voters the right to remove a public official from office at a special election, which could be called after a sufficient number of citizens had signed a petition.

DIRECT PRIMARY AND RECALL

Reasoning Processes

Comparing Have students read the section "New Forms of Governance." Ask them to create a Venn diagram comparing the Commission Plan and the City-Manager Plan. Have students discuss as a class what they believe are the most important similarities and differences and how effective each system would have been at controlling municipal corruption. **PCE**

Discussion and Activities

Analyzing Issues After students have read the feature "Social Democracy," ask them to discuss as a class whether they think that American reformers were more influenced by ideas from other parts of the world or whether foreign reformers were more influenced by American ideas. **WOR** **PCE** **SOC** **WXT**

AMERICA IN THE WORLD

SOCIAL DEMOCRACY

Enormous energy, enthusiasm, and organization drove the reform efforts in America in the late nineteenth and early twentieth centuries, much of it a result of social crises and political movements in the United States. But the "age of reform," as some scholars have called it, was not just an American phenomenon. It was part of a wave of social experimentation that was occurring through much of the industrial world.

Several industrializing nations—the United States, Britain, Germany, and France—adopted the term "progressivism" for their efforts, but the term that most broadly defined the new reform energies was "social democracy." Social democrats in many countries shared a belief in the betterment of society, not through religion or inherited ideology, but through the accumulation of knowledge. They favored improving the social condition of all people through economic reforms and government programs of social protection. And they believed that these changes could come through peaceful political change, rather than through radicalism or revolution. Political parties committed to these goals emerged in several countries: the Labour Party in Britain, Social Democratic parties in various European nations, and the short-lived Progressive Party in the United States. Intellectuals, academics, and government officials across the world shared the knowledge they were accumulating and observed social programs. An important moment in the growth of social democracy were the many Paris expositions of 1889 and 1900. Their symbol was the famous Eiffel Tower, and their meaning for many progressives was the possibilities of progress through industrial innovation. Not only tourists, but progressive experts as well, visited the Paris expositions; and they held meetings while they were there to share their visions of the future.

At the turn of the century, American reformers visited Germany, France, Britain, Belgium, and the Netherlands, observing the reforms in progress there, while European reformers visited the United States. Reformers from both the United States and Europe were also fascinated by the advanced social experiments in Australia and, especially, New Zealand—which the American reformer Henry Demarest Lloyd once called "the political brain of the modern world." New Zealand's dramatic experiments in factory regulation, woman suffrage, old-age pensions, progressive taxation, and labor arbitration gradually found counterparts in many other nations. William Allen White, a progressive journalist from Kansas, said of this time: "We were parts of one another, in the United States and Europe. Something was welding us into one social and economic whole with local political variations . . . [all] fighting a common cause."

Social democracy—or, as it was sometimes called in the United States and elsewhere, social justice or the Social Gospel—was responsible for many public programs. Germany began a system of social insurance for its citizens in the 1880s while undertaking a massive study of society that produced more than 140 volumes of "social investigation" of almost every aspect of the nation's life. French reformers pressed in the 1890s for factory regulation, assistance to the elderly, and progressive taxation. Britain pioneered the settlement houses in working-class areas of London—a movement that soon spread to the United States as well—and, like the United States, witnessed growing challenges to the power of monopolies at both the local and national level.

In many countries, social democrats felt pressure from the rising worldwide labor movement and from the rise of socialist parties in many industrial countries. Strikes, sometimes violent, were common in France, Germany, Britain, and the United States in the late nineteenth century. The more militant workers became, the more unions grew. Social democrats did not always welcome the rise of militant labor movements, but they took them seriously and tried to use them to support their own reform efforts.

The politics of social democracy represented a great shift in the character of public life all over the industrial world. Instead of battles over the privileges of aristocrats or the power of monarchs, reformers now focused on the social problems of ordinary people and attempted to improve their lot. "The politics of the future are social politics," the British reformer Joseph Chamberlain said in the 1880s, referring to efforts to deal with the problems of ordinary citizens. That belief was fueling progressive efforts across the world in the years that Americans have come to call the "progressive era."

HISTORICAL THINKING SKILLS

1. **Explaining Historical Concepts** What is social democracy? How does it differ from socialism?
2. **Making Connections** What progressive era reforms in American social and political life can be seen in other nations as well?
3. **Analyzing Change** Social democratic political parties continue to exist in many countries throughout the world. Why was the Progressive Party in the United States so short-lived?

Answers

America in the World

1. Social democracy believed in the betterment of society not through religion or inherited ideology but through the accumulation of knowledge. Two major differences between social democracy and socialism were the belief in capitalism and the belief that change within society ought to be peaceful and within the legal and political structures of society.
2. Several other countries had just as strong Progressive movements as did the United States, including the rise of the Labour Party in Britain and other social democratic parties across Europe. The American social reformer Henry Demarest Lloyd looked to New Zealand as the "political brain of the modern world."
3. The movement seems to come and go within the scope of American politics. It had largely died out by the 1920s because of pushback on the part of business leaders and American presidents during the era and because the 1920s represented an economic boom to a large section of the country.

By 1915, every state in the nation had instituted primary elections for at least some offices. The recall encountered more strenuous opposition, but a few states (such as California) adopted it as well.

Other reform measures attempted to clean up the legislatures themselves. Between 1903 and 1908, twelve states passed laws restricting lobbying by business interests in state legislatures. In those same years, twenty-two states banned campaign contributions by corporations, and twenty-four states forbade public officials to accept free passes from railroads. Many states also struggled successfully to create systems of workmen's compensation for workers injured on the job. And starting in 1911, reformers successfully created pensions for widows with dependent children.

Reform efforts proved most effective in states that elevated vigorous and committed politicians to positions of leadership. In New York, Governor Charles Evans Hughes exploited progressive sentiment to create a commission to regulate public utilities. In California, Governor Hiram Johnson limited the political power of the Southern Pacific Railroad. In New Jersey, Woodrow Wilson, the Princeton University president elected governor in 1910, used executive leadership to win reforms designed to end New Jersey's widely denounced position as the "mother of trusts."

ROBERT LA FOLLETTE

The most celebrated state-level reformer was Robert M. La Follette of Wisconsin. Elected governor in 1900, he helped turn his state into what reformers across the nation described as a "laboratory of progressivism." Under his leadership the Wisconsin progressives won approval of direct primaries, initiatives, and referendums. They regulated railroads and utilities. They passed laws to regulate the workplace and provide compensation for laborers injured on the job. They instituted graduated taxes on inherited fortunes, and they nearly doubled state levies on railroads and other corporate interests. La Follette used his personal magnetism to widen public awareness of progressive goals. Reform was the responsibility not simply of politicians, he argued, but of newspapers, citizens' groups, educational institutions, and business and professional organizations as well.

PARTIES AND INTEREST GROUPS

DECLINE OF PARTY INFLUENCE

The reformers did not, of course, eliminate parties from American political life. But they did contribute to a decline in party influence. Evidence of their impact came from, among other things, the decline in voter turnout. In the late nineteenth century, up to 81 percent of eligible voters routinely turned out for national elections because of the strength of party loyalty. In the early twentieth century, while turnout remained high by today's standards, the figure declined markedly as parties grew weaker. In the presidential election of 1900, 73 percent of the electorate voted. By 1912, that figure had declined to about 59 percent. Never again did voter turnout reach as high as 70 percent.

ROBERT LA FOLLETTE CAMPAIGNING IN WISCONSIN After three terms as governor of Wisconsin, La Follette began a long career in the U.S. Senate in 1906, during which he worked uncompromisingly for advanced progressive reforms—so uncompromisingly, in fact, that he was often almost completely isolated. He titled a chapter of his autobiography "Alone in the Senate." La Follette had a greater impact on his own state, whose politics he and his sons dominated for nearly forty years and where he was able to win passage of many reforms that the federal government resisted.

Why did voter turnout decline in these years? The secret ballot was one reason. Party bosses had less ability to get voters to the polls. Illiterate voters had trouble reading the new ballots. Party bosses lost much of their authority and were unable to mobilize voters as successfully as they had in the past. But perhaps the most important reason for the decline of party rule (and voter turnout) was that other power centers were beginning to replace them. They have become known as "interest groups." Beginning late in the nineteenth century and accelerating rapidly in the twentieth, new organizations emerged outside the party system: professional organizations, trade associations representing businesses and industries, labor organizations, farm lobbies, and many others. Social workers, the settlement house movement, women's clubs, and others learned to operate as interest groups to advance their demands.

SOURCES OF PROGRESSIVE REFORM

Middle-class reformers, most of them from the East, dominated the public image and much of the substance of progressivism in the late nineteenth and early twentieth centuries. But they were not alone in seeking to improve social conditions. Working-class Americans, African Americans, Westerners, and even party bosses also played crucial roles in advancing some of the important reforms of the era.

Discussion and Activities

Analyzing Issues After students have read the section "Statehouse Progressivism," ask them to discuss in small groups how the direct primary could be used to both expand and restrict suffrage. *(Individual voters had more influence over the selection of candidates, but party control of primaries could lead to disenfranchisement of minority voters.)* **PCE** **SOC**

Discussion and Activities

Analyzing Change Have students read the section "Parties and Interest Groups." Ask them to write a short paragraph explaining how voting reform led to a decline in voter turnout. **PCE**

Discussion and Activities

Analyzing Issues Have students read the section "Labor, the Machine, and Reform." Ask them to discuss in small groups how the Triangle Shirtwaist Factory fire led the Tammany Hall political machine to advocate for Progressive reforms. **PCE** **WXT** **SOC**

LABOR, THE MACHINE, AND REFORM

Although the American Federation of Labor, and its leader Samuel Gompers, remained largely aloof from many of the reform efforts of the time (reflecting Gompers's firm belief that workers should not rely on government to improve their lot), some unions played important roles in reform battles. Between 1911 and 1913, thanks to political pressure from labor groups such as the newly formed Union Labor Party, California passed a child-labor law, a workmen's compensation law, and a limitation on working hours for women. Union pressures contributed to the passage of similar laws in many other states as well.

One result of the assault on the parties was a change in the party organizations themselves, which attempted to adapt to the new realities so as to preserve their influence. They sometimes allowed their machines to become vehicles of social reform. One example was New York City's Tammany Hall, the nation's oldest and most notorious city machine. Its astute leader, Charles Francis Murphy, began in the early years of the century to fuse the techniques of boss rule with some of the concerns of social reformers. Tammany began to use its political power on behalf of legislation to improve working conditions, protect child laborers, and eliminate the worst abuses of the industrial economy.

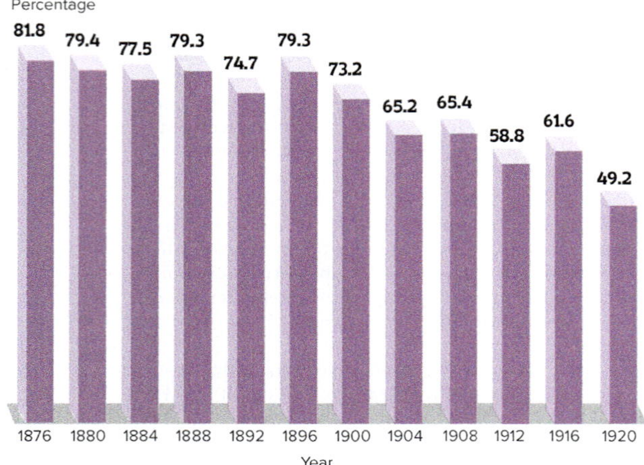

VOTER PARTICIPATION IN PRESIDENTIAL ELECTIONS, 1876–1920 One of the striking developments of early-twentieth-century politics was the significant decline in popular participation in politics. This chart shows the steady downward progression of voter turnout in presidential elections from 1876 to 1920. Turnout remained high by modern standards (except for the aberrant election of 1920, in which turnout dropped sharply because women had recently received the vote but had not yet begun to participate in elections in large numbers). But from an average rate of participation of about 79 percent in the last quarter of the nineteenth century, turnout dropped to an average of about 65 percent between 1900 and 1916.

What were some of the reasons for this decline?

TRIANGLE SHIRTWAIST FIRE

In 1911, a terrible fire swept through the factory of the Triangle Shirtwaist Company in New York City; 146 workers, most of them women, died. Many of them had been trapped inside the burning building because management had locked the emergency exits to prevent malingering. For the next three years, a state commission studied not only the background of the fire but also the general condition of the industrial workplace. It was responding to intense public pressure from women's groups and New York City labor unions—and to quiet pressure from Tammany Hall. By 1914, the commission had issued a series of reports calling for major reforms in the conditions of modern labor. The report itself was a classic progressive document, based on the testimony of experts, filled with statistics and technical data.

Yet, when its recommendations reached the New York legislature, its most effective supporters were not middle-class progressives but two Tammany Democrats from working-class backgrounds: Senator Robert F. Wagner and Assemblyman Alfred E. Smith. With the support of Murphy and the backing of other Tammany legislators, they steered through a series of pioneering labor laws that imposed strict regulations on factory owners and established effective mechanisms for enforcement.

WESTERN PROGRESSIVES

The American West produced some of the most notable progressive leaders of the time: Hiram Johnson of California, George Norris of Nebraska, William Borah of Idaho, and others—almost all of whom spent at least some of their political careers in the U.S. Senate. For western states, the most important target of reform energies was not state or local governments, which had relatively little power, but the federal government, which exercised a kind of authority in the West that it had never possessed in the East. That was in part because some of the most important issues to the future of the West required action above the state level. Disputes over water, for example, almost always involved rivers and streams that crossed state lines. The question of which states had the rights to the waters of the Colorado River created a political battle that no state government could resolve; the federal government had to arbitrate.

More significant, perhaps, the federal government exercised enormous power over the lands and resources of the western states and provided substantial subsidies to the region in the form of land grants and support for railroad and water projects. Huge areas of the West remained (and still remain) public lands, controlled by Washington—a far greater proportion than in any states east of the Mississippi. Much of the growth of the West was (and continues to be) a result of federally funded dams and water projects.

Answers

Voter Participation in Presidential Elections, 1876–1920

Political parties lost control over voting due to the secret ballot, and interest groups challenged the power of political parties.

AFRICAN AMERICANS AND REFORM

One social question that received little attention from white progressives was race. But among African Americans themselves, the progressive era produced some significant challenges to existing racial norms.

African Americans faced greater obstacles than any other group in challenging their own oppressed status and seeking reform. Thus it was not surprising, perhaps, that so many embraced the message of Booker T. Washington in the late nineteenth century, to "put down your bucket where you are," to work for immediate self-improvement rather than long-range social change. Not all African Americans, however, were content with this approach. And by the turn of the century a powerful challenge was emerging—a challenge to the philosophy of Washington but, more important, to the entire structure of race relations. The chief spokesman for this new approach was W. E. B. Du Bois.

W. E. B. Du Bois

Du Bois, unlike Washington, had never known slavery. Born in Massachusetts, educated at Fisk University in Nashville and at Harvard, he grew to maturity with a more expansive view than Washington of the goals of his race and the responsibilities of white society to eliminate prejudice and injustice. In *The Souls of Black Folk* (1903), he launched an open attack on the philosophy of Washington, accusing him of encouraging white efforts to impose segregation and of limiting the aspirations of his race. "Is it possible and probable," he asked, "that nine millions of men can make effective progress in economic lines if they are deprived of political rights, made a servile caste, and allowed only the most meager chance for developing their exceptional men? If history and reason give any distinct answer to these questions, it is an emphatic No."

Rather than content themselves with education at the trade and agricultural schools, Du Bois advocated, talented African Americans should accept nothing less than a full university education. They should aspire to the professions. They should,

VICTIMS OF THE TRIANGLE FIRE, 1911 In this bleak photograph, victims of the fire in the factory of the Triangle Shirtwaist Company are laid out on the sidewalk near the building, as police and passersby look up at the scene of the blaze. The tragedy of the Triangle Fire galvanized New York legislators into passing laws to protect women workers.

Reasoning Processes

Comparing After students have read the section "Western Progressives," ask them to create a Venn diagram comparing progressivism in the East and the West. Have students evaluate in which region Progressives were more successful at achieving their agenda and why. PCE WXT SOC

Historical Thinking Skills

Argumentation Have students examine the image "Victims of the Triangle Fire, 1911." Ask them to write a short editorial responding to the disaster and commenting on working conditions in the factory, as well as the governmental response. PCE WXT

Discussion and Activities

Analyzing Change After students have read the section "African Americans and Reform," ask them to discuss as a class how the philosophy of W.E.B. Du Bois was different from that of Booker T. Washington. **PCE** **WXT** **SOC**

above all, fight for their civil rights, not simply wait for them to be granted as a reward for patient striving. In 1905, Du Bois and a group of his supporters met at Niagara Falls—on the Canadian side of the border because no hotel on the American side of the Falls would have them—and launched what became known as the Niagara Movement. Four years later, after a race riot in Springfield, Illinois, they joined with white progressives sympathetic to their cause to form the National Association for the Advancement of Colored People (NAACP). White men held most of the offices at first, but Du Bois, its director of publicity and research, was the guiding spirit. In the ensuing years, the new organization led the drive for equal rights, using as its principal weapon lawsuits in the federal courts.

NAACP FOUNDED

Within less than a decade, the NAACP had begun to win some important victories. In *Guinn v. United States* (1915), the Supreme Court supported its position that the grandfather clause in an Oklahoma law was unconstitutional. (The statute denied the vote to any citizen whose ancestors had not been enfranchised in 1860.) In *Buchanan v. Worley* (1917), the Court struck down a Louisville, Kentucky, law requiring residential segregation. The NAACP established itself, particularly after Booker T. Washington's death in 1915, as one of the nation's leading black organizations, a position it would maintain for many years.

THE YOUNG W. E. B. DU BOIS This formal photograph of W. E. B. Du Bois was taken in 1899, when he was thirty-one years old and a professor at Atlanta University. He had just published The Philadelphia Negro, a classic sociological study of an urban community, which startled many readers with its description of the complex class system among African Americans in the city.

Among the many issues that engaged the NAACP and other African American organizations was the phenomenon of lynching in the South. Du Bois was an outspoken critic of lynching and an advocate of a federal law making it illegal (since state courts in the South routinely refused to prosecute lynchers). But the most determined opponents of lynching were Southern women. They included white women such as Jessie Daniel Ames. The most effective crusader was a black woman, Ida Wells Barnett, who worked both on her own (at great personal risk) and with such organizations as the National Association of Colored Women and the Women's Convention of the National Baptist Church to try to discredit lynching and challenge segregation.

CRUSADE FOR SOCIAL ORDER AND REFORM

Reformers directed many of their energies at the political process. But they also crusaded on behalf of what they considered moral issues. There were campaigns to eliminate alcohol from national life, to curb prostitution, to limit divorce, and to restrict immigration. Proponents of each of those reforms believed that success would help regenerate society as a whole.

THE TEMPERANCE CRUSADE

Many progressives considered the elimination of alcohol from American life a necessary step in restoring order to society. Scarce wages vanished as workers spent hours in the saloons. Drunkenness spawned violence, and occasionally murder, within urban families. Working-class wives and mothers hoped through temperance to reform male behavior and thus improve women's lives. Employers, too, regarded alcohol as an impediment to industrial efficiency; workers often missed time on the job because of drunkenness or came to the factory intoxicated. Critics of economic privilege denounced the liquor industry as one of the nation's most sinister trusts. And political reformers, who (correctly) looked on the saloon as one of the central institutions of the urban machine, saw an attack on drinking as part of an attack on the bosses. Out of such sentiments emerged the temperance movement.

Temperance had been a major reform movement before the Civil War, mobilizing large numbers of people in a crusade with strong evangelical overtones. In 1873, the movement developed new strength. Temperance advocates formed the Women's Christian

WCTU

Historical Thinking Skills

Argumentation After students have read the section "African Americans and Reform," ask them to create a poster condemning lynching. Have students consider what arguments or images would have been effective in conveying their message to an early twentieth-century audience. **SOC** **PCE**

Temperance Union (WCTU), led after 1879 by Frances Willard. By 1911, it had 245,000 members and had become the single largest women's organization in American history to that point. In 1893, the Anti-Saloon League joined the temperance movement and, along with the WCTU, began to press for a specific legislative solution: the legal abolition of saloons. Gradually, that demand grew to include the complete prohibition of the sale and manufacture of alcoholic beverages.

Despite substantial opposition from immigrant and working-class voters, pressure for prohibition grew steadily through the first decades of the new century. By 1916, nineteen states had passed prohibition laws. But since the consumption of alcohol was actually increasing in many unregulated areas, temperance advocates were beginning to advocate a national prohibition law. America's entry into World War I, and the moral fervor it unleashed, provided the last push to the advocates of prohibition. In 1917, with the support of rural fundamentalists who opposed alcohol on moral and religious grounds, progressive advocates of prohibition steered through Congress a constitutional amendment embodying their demands. Two years later, after ratification by every state in the nation except Connecticut and Rhode Island (bastions of Catholic immigrants), the Eighteenth Amendment became law, to take effect in January 1920.

EIGHTEENTH AMENDMENT

IMMIGRATION RESTRICTION

Virtually all reformers agreed that the growing immigrant population had created social problems, but there was wide disagreement on how best to respond. Some progressives believed that the proper approach was to help the new residents adapt to American society. Others argued that efforts at assimilation had failed and that the only solution was to limit the flow of new arrivals.

In the first decades of the century, pressure grew to close the nation's gates. New scholarly theories, appealing to the progressive respect for expertise, argued that the introduction of immigrants into American society was polluting the nation's racial stock. Among the theories created to support this argument was eugenics, the science of altering the reproductive processes of plants and animals to produce new hybrids or breeds. In the early twentieth century, there was an effort, funded by the Carnegie Foundation, to turn eugenics into a method of altering human reproduction as well. But the eugenics movement when applied to humans was not an effort to "breed" new people, an effort for which no scientific tools existed. It was, rather, an effort to grade races and ethnic groups according to their genetic qualities. Eugenicists advocated the forced sterilization of people with intellectual

EUGENICS AND NATIVISM

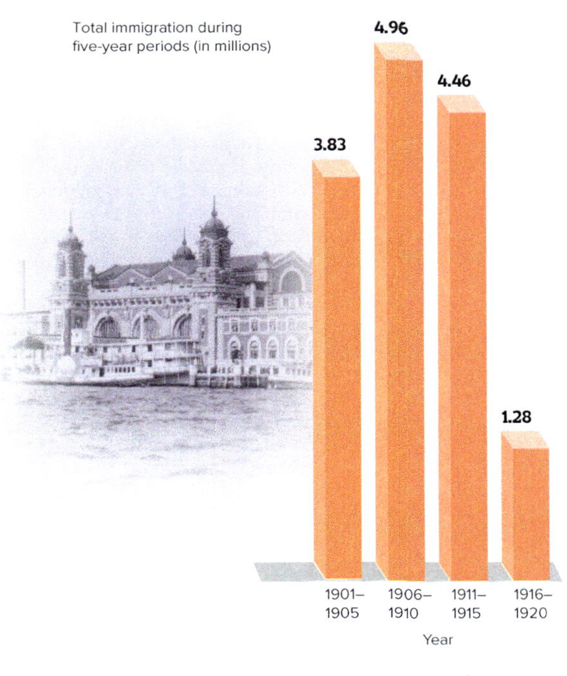

The Library of Congress (3a38144u)

TOTAL IMMIGRATION, 1900–1920 Emigration to the United States reached the highest level in the nation's history to that point in the first fifteen years of the twentieth century. In the nineteenth century, there was no five-year period when as many as 3 million immigrants arrived in America. In the first fifteen years of the twentieth century, more than 3 million newcomers arrived in every five-year period—and in one of them, as this chart reveals, the number reached almost 5 million.

Why did the flow of immigrants drop so sharply in the period 1916–1920?

Reasoning Processes

Continuity and Change After students have read the section "The Temperance Crusade," ask them to create a T-chart comparing the temperance movements of the early nineteenth and early twentieth centuries. Have students form small groups and discuss the important similarities and differences. **SOC**

Answers

Total Immigration, 1900–1920

Immigration dropped largely due to World War I.

Reasoning Processes

Continuity and Change After students have read the section "Immigration Restriction," ask them to create a Venn diagram comparing the Nativist movement of the mid-nineteenth century with the movement to restrict immigration in the early twentieth century. Have students discuss as a class important continuities and changes over time. **PCE** **SOC**

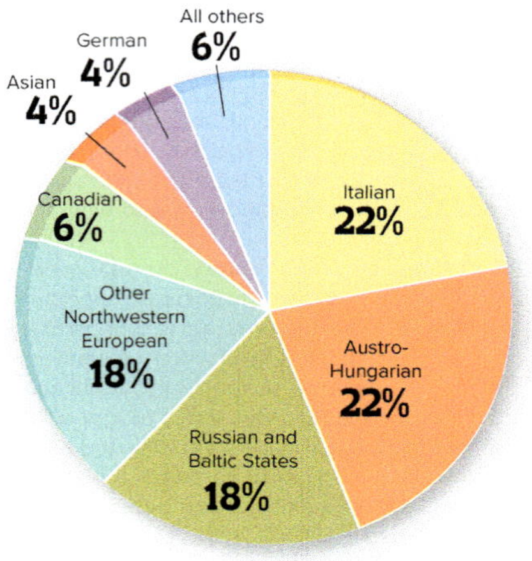

SOURCES OF IMMIGRATION, 1900–1920 At least as striking as the increase in immigration in the early twentieth century was the change in its sources. In the nineteenth century, the vast majority of immigrants to the United States had come from northern and western Europe (especially Britain, Ireland, Germany, and Scandinavia). Now, as this chart shows, the major sources were southern and eastern Europe, with over 60 percent coming from Italy, Russia, and the eastern European regions of the Austro-Hungarian Empire.

What impact did these changing sources have on attitudes toward immigration in the United States?

disabilities, criminals, and others. But they also spread the belief that human inequalities were hereditary and that immigration was contributing to the multiplication of the unfit. Skillful publicists such as Madison Grant, whose *The Passing of the Great Race* (1916) established him as the nation's most effective nativist, warned of the dangers of racial "mongrelization" and of the importance of protecting the purity of Anglo-Saxon and other Nordic stock from pollution by immigrants from eastern Europe, Latin America, and Asia.

A special federal commission of "experts," chaired by Senator William P. Dillingham of Vermont, issued a study filled with statistics and scholarly testimony. It argued that the newer immigrant groups–largely southern and eastern Europeans–had proven themselves less assimilable than earlier immigrants. Immigration, the report implied, should be restricted by nationality. Many people who rejected these racial arguments nevertheless supported limiting immigration as a way to solve such urban problems as overcrowding, unemployment, strained social services, and social unrest.

The combination of these concerns gradually won for the nativists the support of some of the nation's leading progressives, among them former president Theodore Roosevelt. Powerful opponents–employers who saw immigration as a source of cheap labor, immigrants themselves, and their political representatives–managed to block the restriction movement for a time. But by the beginning of World War I (which effectively blocked immigration temporarily), the nativist tide was gaining strength.

CHALLENGING THE CAPITALIST ORDER

If there was one issue that overshadowed, and helped to shape, all others in the minds of reformers, it was the character of the dramatically growing modern industrial economy. Most of the problems that concerned progressives could be traced back, directly or indirectly, to the growing power and influence–and also, reformers believed, corruption–of corporate America. So it is not surprising that prominent among progressive concerns was reshaping or reforming the behavior of the capitalist world.

THE DREAM OF SOCIALISM

At no time in the history of the United States to that point, and seldom after, did radical critiques of the capitalist system attract more support than in the period 1900–1914. Although never a force to rival or even seriously threaten the two major parties, the Socialist Party of America grew during these years into a force of considerable strength. In the election of 1900, it had attracted the support of fewer than 100,000 voters; in 1912, its durable leader and perennial presidential candidate, Eugene V. Debs, received nearly 1 million ballots. Strongest in urban immigrant communities, particularly among Germans and Jews, it also attracted the loyalties of a substantial number of Protestant farmers in the South and Midwest. Socialists won election to over 1,000 state and local offices. And they had the support at times of such intellectuals as Lincoln Steffens, the crusader against municipal corruption, and Walter Lippmann, the brilliant young journalist and social critic. Florence Kelley, Frances Willard, and other women reformers were attracted to socialism, too, in part because of its support for pacifism and labor organizing.

EUGENE DEBS

Virtually all socialists agreed on the need for basic structural changes in the economy, but they differed widely on the extent of those changes and the tactics necessary to achieve them. Some socialists endorsed the radical goals of European Marxists; others envisioned a moderate reform that would allow small-scale private enterprise to survive but would nationalize major industries. Some believed in working for reform through electoral politics; others favored militant direct action. Among the militants was the radical labor union the Industrial Workers of the World (IWW), known to opponents as the "Wobblies" (a nickname of unknown origin). Under the leadership of William ("Big Bill") Haywood, the IWW advocated a single union for all workers and abolition of the "wage slave" system; it rejected political action in favor of strikes–especially the general strike.

"WOBBLIES"

Answers

Sources of Immigration, 1900–1920

"New" immigrants coming increasingly from Southern and Eastern Europe were more likely to be Catholic or Jewish than previous immigrants. They were also generally poorer and less educated. They seemed extremely different from established Americans, and therefore seemed to pose a greater threat to American society.

Reasoning Processes

Comparing and Contrasting After students have read the section "The Dream of Socialism," ask them to create a Venn diagram comparing the IWW to the earlier AFL. Have students discuss as a class how they were similar and different. (*Both included unskilled laborers and used the strike. The AFL focused on "bread and butter issues," while the IWW advocated for wider social and economic reforms. The IWW seemed more open to the use of violence.*) PCE WXT

MAY DAY, 1908 The American Socialist Party staged this vast rally in New York City's Union Square to celebrate May Day in 1908. The Second Socialist International had designated May Day as the official holiday for radical labor in 1899.

The Wobblies were widely believed to have been responsible for the dynamiting of railroad lines and power stations and other acts of terror in the first years of the twentieth century.

The IWW was one of the few labor organizations of the time to champion the cause of unskilled workers and had particular strength in the West–where a large group of migratory laborers (miners, timbermen, and others) found it very difficult to organize or sustain conventional unions. In 1917, a strike by IWW timber workers in Washington and Idaho shut down production in the industry. That brought down upon the union the wrath of the federal government, which had just begun mobilizing for war and needed timber for war production. Federal authorities imprisoned the leaders of the union, and state governments between 1917 and 1919 passed a series of laws that outlawed the IWW. The organization survived for a time but never fully recovered.

Moderate socialists who advocated peaceful change through political struggle dominated the Socialist Party. They emphasized a gradual education of the public to the need for change and patient efforts within the system to enact it. But World War I dramatically weakened the socialists. They had refused to support the war effort, and a growing wave of antiradicalism subjected them to enormous harassment and persecution.

SOCIALISM'S DEMISE

DECENTRALIZATION AND REGULATION

Most progressives retained a faith in the possibilities of reform within a capitalist system. Rather than nationalize basic industries, many reformers hoped to restore the economy to a "more human" scale. Few envisioned a return to a society of small, local enterprises; some consolidation, they recognized, was inevitable. They did, however, argue that the federal government should work to break up the largest combinations and enforce a balance between the need for bigness and the need for competition.

This viewpoint came to be identified particularly closely with Louis D. Brandeis, a brilliant lawyer and later justice of the Supreme Court, who wrote widely (most notably in his 1913 book, *Other People's Money*) about the "curse of bigness."

Discussion and Activities

Analyzing Points of View Have students examine the image "May Day, 1908." Ask them to write a short letter or journal article about the march from the point of view of an observer who was either pro- or anti-labor. WXT PCE

Discussion and Activities

Analyzing Issues After students have read the section "Decentralization and Regulation," ask them to discuss as a class whether big corporations were inherently good or bad for the economy and consumers. Have students consider how much government regulation is necessary to protect the interests of consumers. **PCE** **WXT** **SOC**

LOUIS BRANDEIS Brandeis graduated from Harvard Law School in 1877 with the best academic record of any student in the school's previous or subsequent history. His success in his Boston law practice was such that by the early twentieth century he was able to spend much of his time in unpaid work for public causes. His investigations of monopoly power soon made him a major figure in the emerging progressive movement. Woodrow Wilson nominated him for the U.S. Supreme Court in January 1916. He was one of the few nominees in the Court's history never to have held prior public office, and he was the first Jew ever to have been nominated. The appointment aroused five months of bitter controversy in the Senate before Brandeis was finally confirmed. For the next twenty years, he was one of the Court's most powerful members—all the while lobbying behind the scenes on behalf of the many political causes (preeminent among them Zionism, the founding of a Jewish state) to which he remained committed.

© Bettmann/Getty Images

THE PROBLEM OF CORPORATE CENTRALIZATION

Brandeis and his supporters opposed bigness in part because they considered it inefficient. But their opposition had a moral basis as well. Bigness was a threat not just to efficiency but to freedom as well. It limited the ability of individuals to control their own destinies. It encouraged abuses of power. Government must, Brandeis insisted, regulate competition in such a way as to ensure that large combinations did not emerge.

"GOOD TRUSTS" AND "BAD TRUSTS"

Other progressives were less enthusiastic about the virtues of competition. More important to them was efficiency, which they believed economic concentration encouraged. What government should do, they argued, was not to fight "bigness," but to guard against abuses of power by large institutions. It should distinguish between "good trusts" and "bad trusts," encouraging the good while disciplining the bad. Since economic consolidation was destined to remain a permanent feature of American society, continuing oversight by a strong, modernized government was essential. One of the most influential spokesmen for this emerging "nationalist" position was Herbert Croly, whose 1909 book, *The Promise of American Life*, became an influential progressive document.

Increasingly, the attention of nationalists such as Croly focused on some form of coordination of the industrial economy. Society must act, Walter Lippmann wrote in a notable 1914 book, *Drift and Mastery*, "to introduce plan where there has been clash, and purpose into the jungles of disordered growth." To some nationalists, that meant businesses themselves learning new ways of cooperation and self-regulation. To others, the solution was for government to play a more active role in regulating and planning economic life. One of those who came to endorse that position (although not fully until after 1910) was Theodore Roosevelt, who once said: "We should enter upon a course of supervision, control, and regulation of those great corporations." Roosevelt became for a time the most powerful symbol of the reform impulse at the national level.

THEODORE ROOSEVELT AND THE MODERN PRESIDENCY

"Presidents in general are not lovable," the famous writer and columnist Walter Lippmann, who had known many, said near the end of his life. "They've had to do too much to get where they are. But there was one President who was lovable–Teddy Roosevelt–and I loved him."

Lippmann was not alone. To a generation of progressive reformers, Theodore Roosevelt was more than an admired public figure; he was an idol. No president before, and few since, had attracted such attention and devotion. Yet, for all his popularity among reformers, Roosevelt was in many respects decidedly conservative. He earned his extraordinary popularity less because of the extent of the reforms he championed than because he brought to his office a broad conception of its powers and invested the presidency with something of its modern status as the center of national political life.

THE ACCIDENTAL PRESIDENT

When President William McKinley suddenly died in September 1901, the victim of an assassination, Roosevelt (who had been elected vice president less than a year before) was only forty-two years old, the youngest man ever to assume the presidency. "I told William McKinley that it was a mistake to nominate that wild man at Philadelphia," party boss Mark Hanna was reported to have exclaimed. "Now look, that damned cowboy is President of the United States!"

Discussion and Activities

Analyzing Perspectives Have students examine the image "Louis Brandeis" and its caption. Ask them to write a letter to a senator recommending either Brandeis's confirmation as a Supreme Court justice or his denial. **PCE**

Discussion and Activities

Evaluating Evidence After students have read the section "The Accidental President," ask them to write a short paragraph evaluating how well qualified Theodore Roosevelt was to become president in 1901. **PCE**

Roosevelt's reputation as a wild man was a result less of the substance of his early political career than of its style. As a young member of the New York legislature, he had displayed an energy seldom seen in that lethargic body. As a rancher in the Dakota Badlands (where he retired briefly after the sudden death of his first wife), he had helped capture outlaws. As New York City police commissioner, he had been a flamboyant battler against crime and vice. As assistant secretary of the navy, he had been a bold proponent of American expansion. As commander of the Rough Riders, he had led a heroic, if militarily useless, charge in the battle of San Juan Hill in Cuba during the Spanish-American War.

ROOSEVELT'S BACKGROUND

But Roosevelt as president rarely rebelled against the leaders of his party. He became, rather, a champion of cautious, moderate change. Reform, he believed, was a vehicle less for remaking American society than for protecting it against radical challenges.

Government, Capital, and Labor

Roosevelt allied himself with those progressives who urged regulation (but not destruction) of the trusts. At the heart of Roosevelt's policy was his desire to win for government the power to investigate the activities of corporations and publicize the results. The new Department of Commerce and Labor, established in 1903 (later to be divided into two separate departments), was to assist in this task through its investigatory arm, the Bureau of Corporations.

ROOSEVELT'S VISION OF FEDERAL POWER

Although Roosevelt was not a trustbuster at heart, he made a few highly publicized efforts to break up combinations. In 1902, he ordered the Justice Department to invoke the Sherman Antitrust Act against a great new railroad monopoly in the Northwest, the Northern Securities Company, a $400 million enterprise pieced together by J. P. Morgan and others. To Morgan, accustomed to a warm, supportive relationship with Republican administrations, the action was baffling. He told the president, "If we have done anything wrong, send your man to my man and they can fix it up." Roosevelt proceeded with the case nonetheless, and in 1904 the Supreme Court ruled that the Northern Securities Company must be dissolved. Although he filed more than forty additional antitrust suits during the remainder of his presidency, Roosevelt had no serious commitment to reverse the prevailing trend toward economic concentration.

NORTHERN SECURITIES COMPANY

A similar commitment to establishing the government as an impartial regulatory mechanism shaped Roosevelt's policy toward labor. In the past, federal intervention in industrial disputes had almost always meant action on behalf of employers. Roosevelt was willing to consider labor's position as well. When a bitter 1902 strike by the United Mine Workers endangered coal supplies for the coming winter, Roosevelt asked

PRESIDENT THEODORE ROOSEVELT To a generation of progressive reformers, Theodore Roosevelt was an idol. No president before, and few since, had attracted such attention and devotion from the American people.

both the operators and the miners to accept impartial federal arbitration. When the mine owners balked, Roosevelt threatened to send federal troops to seize the mines. The operators finally relented. Arbitrators awarded the strikers a 10 percent wage increase and a nine-hour day, although no recognition of their union—less than they had wanted but more than they would likely have won without Roosevelt's intervention. Roosevelt viewed himself as no more the champion of labor than as a champion of management. On several occasions, he ordered federal troops to intervene in strikes on behalf of employers.

The "Square Deal"

During Roosevelt's first years as president, he was principally concerned with winning reelection, which required that he not antagonize the conservative Republican Old Guard. By skillfully dispensing patronage to conservatives and progressives alike, and by winning the support of Northern businessmen while making adroit gestures to reformers, Roosevelt had neutralized his opposition within the party by early 1904. He won its presidential nomination with ease. And in the general election, where he faced a dull conservative Democrat, Alton B. Parker, he captured over 57 percent of the popular vote and lost no states outside the South.

Discussion and Activities

Historical Evidence and Argumentation Have students read the section "Government, Capital, and Labor." Ask them to discuss in small groups whether Roosevelt's interventions in the economy more greatly benefited workers or management. **PCE** **WXT**

Discussion and Activities

Analyzing Change Have students read the section "Dedicated to Conserving America." Ask them to discuss as a class how Muir's arguments about setting aside land to protect it from development represented a continuation or change from previous land policies. *(Previous land policies, such as the Northwest Ordinance, Louisiana Purchase, Mexican Cession, etc., had largely been about making land available for economic development.)* **PCE**

CONSIDER THE SOURCE

DEDICATED TO CONSERVING AMERICA

A Leader in America's Conservation Movement, naturalist John Muir (1838-1914) was born in Scotland and grew up in Wisconsin. He went to California in 1868 and spent several years in the American West exploring the land and studying the trees, forests, and glaciers of the area before settling permanently in California in 1880. He campaigned for the establishment of Yosemite National Park, a goal achieved in 1890. Through his friendship with President Theodore Roosevelt, he persuaded the president to greatly increase the amount of protected public land. As a dedicated conservationist, Muir wrote articles attempting to rouse the public to the need to protect public lands. In addition to the public lands he helped protect and preserve, Muir created another lasting legacy–the Sierra Club, an organization that he co-founded and that is still thriving today.

The two source documents below are thus both connected to John Muir. The first is an excerpt from his book *Our National Parks*. The second is a reprinting of the Sierra Club's current stated purposes and goals.

OUR NATIONAL PARKS—1901

FROM CHAPTER 1, "THE WILD PARKS AND FOREST RESERVATIONS OF THE WEST," BY JOHN MUIR

The tendency nowadays to wander in wildernesses is delightful to see. Thousands of tired, nerve-shaken, over-civilized people are beginning to find out that going to the mountains is going home; that wildness is a necessity; and that mountain parks and reservations are useful not only as fountains of timber and irrigating rivers, but as fountains of life. Awakening from the stupefying effects of the vice of over-industry and the deadly apathy of luxury, they are trying as best they can to mix and enrich their own little ongoings with those of Nature, and to get rid of rust and disease. Briskly venturing and roaming, some are washing off sins and cobweb cares of the devil's spinning in all-day storms on mountains; sauntering in rosiny pinewoods or in gentian meadows, brushing through chaparral, bending down and parting sweet, flowery sprays; tracing rivers to their sources, getting in touch with the nerves of Mother Earth; jumping from rock to rock, feeling the life of them, learning the songs of them, panting in whole-souled exercise, and rejoicing in deep, long-drawn breaths of pure wildness. This is fine and natural and full of promise. So also is the growing interest in the care and preservation of forests and wild places in general, and in the half wild parks and gardens of towns. . . .

When, like a merchant taking a list of his goods, we take stock of our wildness, we are glad to see how much of even the most destructible kind is still unspoiled. Looking at our continent as scenery when it was all wild, lying between beautiful seas, the starry sky above it, the starry rocks beneath it, to compare its sides, the East and the West, would be like comparing the sides of a rainbow. But it is no longer equally beautiful. . . . [T]he continent's outer beauty is fast passing away, especially the plant part of it, the most destructible and most universally charming of all.

Only thirty years ago, the great Central Valley of California, five hundred miles long and fifty miles wide, was one bed of golden and purple flowers. Now it is ploughed and pastured out of existence, gone forever,–scarce a memory of it left in fence corners and along the bluffs of the streams. . . . The same fate, sooner or later, is awaiting them all, unless awakening public opinion comes forward to stop it. . . .

The Grand Cañon Reserve of Arizona, of nearly two million acres, or the most interesting part of it, as well as the Rainier region, should be made into a national park, on account of their supreme grandeur and beauty. . . . No matter how far you have wandered hitherto, or how many famous gorges and valleys you have seen, this one,

Discussion and Activities

Making Connections Have students go online to research information about current national parks. Ask them to select one of interest and create a short summary of the history and features of that park to share with the class.

the Grand Cañon of the Colorado, will seem as novel to you, as unearthly in the color and grandeur and quantity of its architecture, as if you had found it after death, on some other star; so incomparably lovely and grand and supreme is it above all the other cañons in our fire-moulded, earthquake-shaken, rain-washed, wave-washed, river and glacier sculptured world. . . .

Source: Library of Congress, Materials from the General Collection and Rare Book and Special Collections Division of the Library of Congress.

SIERRA CLUB—2006

Sierra Club Purposes and Goals

The purposes of the Sierra Club are to explore, enjoy, and protect the wild places of the earth; to practice and promote the responsible use of the earth's ecosystems and resources; to educate and enlist humanity to protect and restore the quality of the natural and human environment; and to use all lawful means to carry out these objectives.

Ideal Goals for Environment and Society

- To sustain natural life-support systems, avoid impairing them, and avoid irreversible damage to them.
- To facilitate species survival; to maintain genetic diversity; to avoid hastened extinction of species; to protect prime natural habitat.
- To establish and protect natural reserves, including representative natural areas, wilderness areas in each biome, displays of natural phenomena, and habitats for rare and endangered species.
- To control human population growth and impacts; to limit human population numbers and habitat needs within Earth's carrying capacity; to avoid needless human consumption of resources; to plan and control land use, with environmental impact assessment and safeguards, and rehabilitation of damaged sites.
- To learn more about the facts, interrelationships, and principles of the Earth's ecosystems, and the place and impact of humans in them; to understand the consequences of human activities within the biosphere.
- To develop responsible and appropriate technology matched to end-uses; to introduce sophisticated technology gradually after careful assessment and with precautionary monitoring.
- To control pollution of the biosphere; to minimize waste residuals with special care of hazardous materials; to use the best available control technology at sources; and to recycle wastes.
- To manage resources soundly; to avoid waste with long-term plans; to sustain the yield of living resources and maintain their productivity and breeding stocks; to prolong availability of nonliving resources such as fossil fuels, minerals, and water.
- To impart a sense of social responsibility among consumers, developers, and public authorities concerning environmental protection; to regulate threats to public health; to avoid private degradation of public resources; to minimize impacts on innocent parties and future generations.

As the Sierra Club prepares for its second century, we offer to America and the world our vision of humanity living in harmony with nature. We dedicate ourselves to achieving this vision as we reaffirm our passionate commitment to explore, enjoy, and protect the Earth.

(*From the Current Articles of Incorporation & Bylaws*, June 20, 1981, updated July 13, 2006. Excerpted from, Sierra Club Goals Pamphlet, 1985-1989. Reproduced from sierraclub.org with permission of the Sierra Club.)

Discussion and Activities

Evaluating Evidence After students have read the document "Our National Parks–1901," ask them to identify and discuss in small groups words and phrases from the excerpt that help the author achieve his purpose. *(Many of the words and phrases the author uses involve various descriptions of natural beauty juxtaposed with the negative impacts upon people of industrialization.)* **PCE** **GEO**

Reasoning Processes

Comparing and Contrasting After students have read the document "Sierra Club–2006," ask them to create a Venn diagram comparing the Sierra Club document to the Muir excerpt. Have students discuss in small groups how the goals and language are similar and different.

Discussion and Activities

Argumentation After students have read the feature "Consider the Source," ask them to select a natural feature and write a short speech or create a poster arguing that feature either needs protection or no longer needs protection from development. **PCE** **GEO**

ANALYZING SOURCES

Questions assume cumulative content knowledge from this chapter and previous chapters.

1. Which of the following groups would most agree with the excerpt from *Our National Parks*?
   - (A) Southern romantic aristocrats
   - (B) Western settlers in the 19th century
   - (C) those who championed ideas of self-reliance and self-realization in the mid-19th century
   - (D) Protestant evangelists

2. Which best describes how Muir's argument in *Our National Parks* reflects the economic and social history of the time?
   - (A) Muir is responding to a sense of societal disorder due to developments of his time, such as rapid industrialization.
   - (B) Muir is responding to a sense of political injustice, due to the relationship between government and big business at the time.
   - (C) Muir is responding to the social critiques of the power of monopolies to do as they please.
   - (D) Muir is responding to the demands of farmers to increase arable lands through irrigation projects.

3. Which progressive value does the Sierra Club's statement of purposes and goals best reflect?
   - (A) a strong belief in the ideal of spiritual self-improvement
   - (B) a strong belief in the role of government in regulating use of environmental resources
   - (C) a strong belief in the role of purposeful human action in bettering a society
   - (D) a strong belief in social justice

Answers

Consider the Source

1. C; **2.** A; **3.** C

Discussion and Activities

Explaining Significance After students have read the section "The 'Square Deal'," ask them to think about which element they believe was the most important of this deal and why, and share with a partner. **PCE** **GEO** **WXT**

BOYS IN THE MINES These young boys, covered in grime and no more than twelve years old, pose for the noted photographer Lewis Hine outside the coal mine in Pennsylvania where they separated coal from slate in coal breakers. The rugged conditions endured by mine workers were one cause of the great strike of 1902, in which Theodore Roosevelt intervened.

The Library of Congress

During the 1904 campaign, Roosevelt boasted that he had worked in the anthracite coal strike to provide everyone with a "square deal." One of his first targets after the election was the powerful railroad industry. The Interstate Commerce Act of 1887, establishing the Interstate Commerce Commission (ICC), had been an early effort to regulate the industry; but over the years, the courts had sharply limited its influence. Roosevelt asked Congress for legislation to increase the government's power to oversee railroad rates. The Hepburn Railroad Regulation Act of 1906 sought to restore some regulatory authority to the government, although the bill was so cautious that it satisfied few progressives.

HEPBURN ACT

Roosevelt also pressured Congress to enact the Pure Food and Drug Act, which restricted the sale of dangerous or ineffective medicines. When Upton Sinclair's powerful novel *The Jungle* appeared in 1906, featuring appalling descriptions of conditions in the meatpacking industry, Roosevelt pushed for passage of the Meat Inspection Act, which helped eliminate many diseases once transmitted in impure meat. Starting in 1907, he proposed, but mostly failed to achieve, even more stringent reforms: an eight-hour workday, broader compensation for victims of industrial accidents, inheritance and income taxes, regulation of the stock market, and others. He also started openly to criticize conservatives in Congress and the judiciary who were obstructing these programs. The result was a widening gulf between the president and the conservative wing of his party.

PURE FOOD AND DRUG ACT

ROOSEVELT AND CONSERVATION

Roosevelt's aggressive policies on behalf of conservation contributed to that gulf. Using executive powers, he restricted private development on millions of acres of undeveloped government land–most of it in the West–by adding them to the previously modest national forest system. When conservatives in Congress restricted his authority over public lands in 1907, Roosevelt and his chief forester, Gifford Pinchot, seized all the forests and many of the water power sites still in the public domain before the bill became law.

Roosevelt was the first president to take an active interest in the new and struggling American conservation movement. In the early twentieth century, the idea of preserving the natural world for ecological reasons was not well established. Instead, many people who considered themselves "conservationists"–such as Pinchot, the first director of the National Forest Service (which he helped to create)–promoted policies to protect land for carefully managed development.

The Old Guard eagerly supported another important aspect of Roosevelt's natural resource policy: public reclamation and irrigation projects. In 1902, the president backed the National Reclamation Act, better known as the Newlands Act (named for its sponsor, Nevada senator Francis Newlands). The Newlands Act provided federal funds for the construction of dams, reservoirs, and canals in the West–projects that would open new lands for cultivation and (years later) provide cheap electric power.

FEDERAL AID TO THE WEST

ROOSEVELT AND PRESERVATION

Despite his sympathy with Pinchot's vision of conservation, Roosevelt also shared some of the concerns of the naturalists–those within the conservation movement committed to protecting the natural beauty of the land and the health of its wildlife from human intrusion. Early in his presidency, Roosevelt even spent four days camping in the Sierras with

Discussion and Activities

Making Connections Have students read the section "Roosevelt and Conservation." Ask them to consider and discuss in small groups whether the construction of dams, reservoirs, and canals would be considered "conservation" today. **PCE** **GEO**

Discussion and Activities

Historical Evidence and Argumentation After students have read the section "Roosevelt and Preservation," ask them to create a T-chart listing Roosevelt's actions that could be considered conservation and preservation. Have students discuss as a class which category they think better describes Roosevelt. **PCE** **GEO**

John Muir, the nation's leading preservationist and the founder of the Sierra Club.

Roosevelt added significantly to the still-young National Park System, whose purpose was to protect public land from any exploitation or development. Congress had created the first national park–Yellowstone, in Wyoming, in 1872–and had authorized others in the 1890s: Yosemite and Sequoia in California, and Mount Rainier in Washington State. Roosevelt added land to several existing parks and also created new ones: Crater Lake in Oregon, Mesa Verde in Utah, Platt in Oklahoma, and Wind Cave in South Dakota.

THE HETCH HETCHY CONTROVERSY

The contending views of the early conservation movement came to a head beginning in 1906 in a sensational controversy over the Hetch Hetchy Valley in Yosemite National Park. Hetch Hetchy (a name derived from a local Native American term meaning "grassy meadows") was a spectacular, high-walled valley popular with naturalists. But many residents of San Francisco, worried about finding enough water to serve their growing population, saw Hetch Hetchy as an ideal place for a dam, which would create a large reservoir for the city–a plan that Muir and other naturalists furiously opposed.

In 1906, San Francisco suffered a devastating earthquake and fire. Widespread sympathy for the city strengthened the case for the dam; and Theodore Roosevelt–who had initially expressed some sympathy for Muir's position–turned the decision over to Gifford Pinchot. Pinchot had no interest in Muir's aesthetic and spiritual arguments. He approved construction of the dam.

For over a decade, a battle raged between naturalists and the advocates of the dam, a battle that consumed the energies of John Muir for the rest of his life and that eventually, many

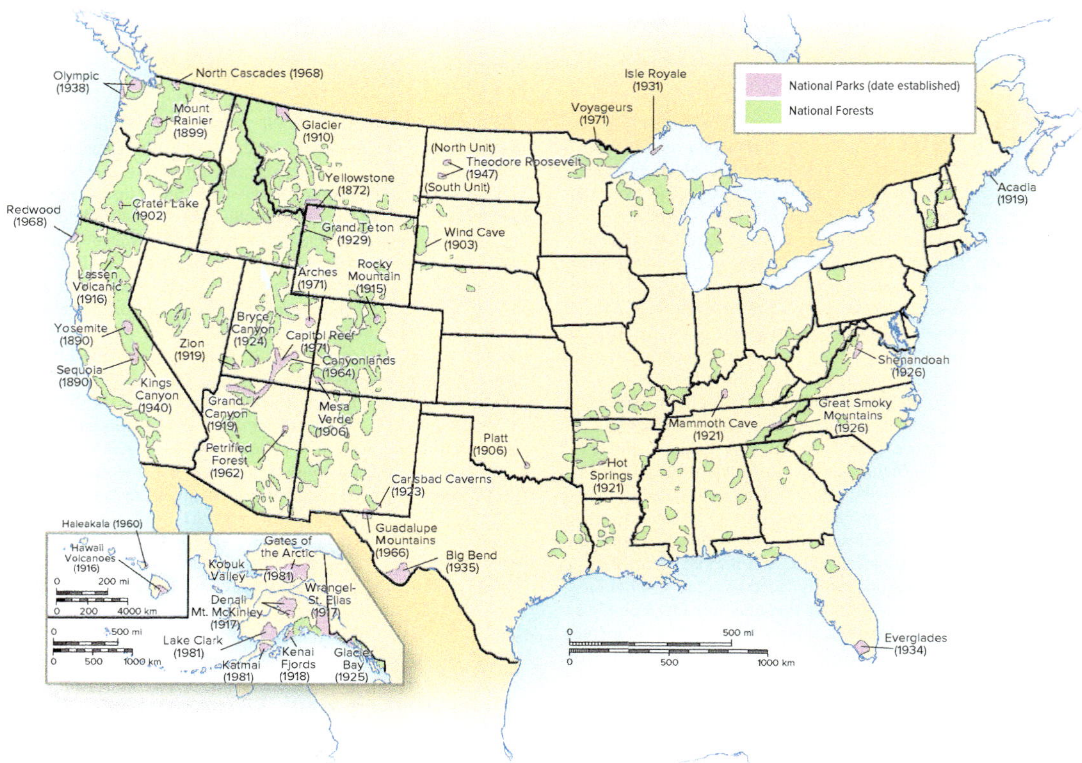

ESTABLISHMENT OF NATIONAL PARKS AND FORESTS This map illustrates the steady growth throughout the late nineteenth and early twentieth centuries of the systems of national parks and national forests in the United States. Although Theodore Roosevelt is widely and correctly remembered as a great champion of national parks and forests, the greatest expansions of these systems occurred after his presidency. Note, for example, how many new areas were added in the 1920s.

What is the difference between national parks and national forests?

Answers

Establishment of National Parks and Forests

National parks are protected from almost all development, while National forests allow some activities, such as mining, logging, and drilling.

people believed, led to his death. "Dam Hetch Hetchy!" Muir once said. "As well dam for water-tanks the people's cathedrals and churches, for no holier temple has ever been consecrated by the heart of man." To Pinchot, there was no question that the needs of the city were more important than the claims of preservation. Muir helped place a referendum question on the ballot in 1908, certain that the residents of the city would oppose the project "as soon as light is cast upon it." Instead, San Franciscans approved the dam by a huge margin. Although there were many more delays in succeeding years, construction of the dam finally began after World War I.

COMPETING CONSERVATIONIST VISIONS

This setback for the naturalists was not, however, a total defeat. The fight against Hetch Hetchy helped mobilize a new coalition of people committed to preservation, not "rational use," of wilderness.

THE PANIC OF 1907

Despite the flurry of reforms Roosevelt was able to enact, the government still had relatively little control over the industrial economy. That became clear in 1907, when a serious panic and recession began.

Conservatives blamed Roosevelt's "mad" economic policies for the disaster. And while the president naturally (and correctly) disagreed, he nevertheless acted quickly to reassure business leaders that he would not interfere with their recovery efforts. J. P. Morgan, in a spectacular display of his financial power, helped construct a pool of the assets of several important New York banks to prop up shaky financial institutions. The key to the arrangement, Morgan told the president, was the purchase by U.S. Steel of the shares of the Tennessee Coal and Iron Company, currently held by a threatened New York bank. He would, he insisted, need assurances that the purchase would not prompt antitrust action. Roosevelt tacitly agreed, and the Morgan plan proceeded. Whether or not as a result, the panic soon subsided.

TENNESSEE COAL AND IRON COMPANY

Roosevelt loved being president. As his years in office produced increasing political successes, as his public popularity continued to rise, more and more observers began to assume that he would run for reelection in 1908, despite the long-standing tradition of presidents serving no more than two terms. But the Panic of 1907, combined with Roosevelt's growing "radicalism" during his second term, so alienated conservatives in his own party that he might have had difficulty winning the Republican nomination. In 1904, moreover, he had made a public promise to step down four years later. And so in 1909, Roosevelt, fifty years old, retired from public life—briefly.

THE TROUBLED SUCCESSION

William Howard Taft, who assumed the presidency in 1909, had been Theodore Roosevelt's most trusted lieutenant and his hand-picked successor; progressive reformers believed him to be one of their own. But Taft had also been a restrained and moderate jurist, a man with a punctilious regard for legal process; conservatives

ROOSEVELT AND MUIR IN YOSEMITE John Muir, founder and leader of the Sierra Club, considered Theodore Roosevelt a friend and ally—a relationship cemented by a four-day camping trip the two men took together in Yosemite National Park in 1903. Roosevelt was indeed a friend to the national park and national forest systems and added considerable acreage to both. Among other things, he expanded Yosemite (at Muir's request). But unlike Muir, Roosevelt was also committed to economic development. As a result, he was not always a reliable ally of the most committed preservationists.

Discussion and Activities

Making Connections After students have read the section "The Hetch Hetchy Controversy," ask them to discuss as a class more recent examples of conflicts over preservation or development of natural resources. *(Drilling for oil in Alaska; oil pipelines; mining for coal in Appalachia and the West; and many others.)* GEO PCE

Discussion and Activities

Evaluating Evidence Have students read the section "The Panic of 1907." Ask them to write a short paragraph explaining whether Roosevelt's handling of the crisis supported or undermined his image as a "trustbuster." PCE WXT

Historical Thinking Skills

Argumentation Have students read the section "Taft and the Progressives." Ask them to write a short letter to President Taft advising him on how to handle the Ballinger-Pinchot controversy. **PCE**

expected him to abandon Roosevelt's aggressive use of presidential powers. By seeming acceptable to almost everyone, Taft easily won election to the White House in 1908. He received his party's nomination virtually uncontested. His victory in the general election in November–over William Jennings Bryan, running for the Democrats for the third time–was a foregone conclusion.

Four years later, however, Taft would leave office the most decisively defeated president of the twentieth century, his party deeply divided and the government in the hands of a Democratic administration for the first time in twenty years.

Taft and the Progressives

Taft's first problem arose in the opening months of the new administration, when he called Congress into special session to lower protective tariff rates, an old progressive demand. But the president made no effort to overcome the opposition of the congressional Old Guard, arguing that to do so would violate the constitutional doctrine of separation of powers. The result was the feeble Payne-Aldrich Tariff, which reduced tariff rates scarcely at all and in some areas raised them. Progressives resented the president's passivity.

PAYNE-ALDRICH TARIFF

Taft may not have been a champion of reform, but neither was he a consistent opponent of change. In 1912, he supported and signed legislation to create a federal Children's Bureau to investigate "all matters pertaining to the welfare of children and child life." Julia Lathrop, the first chief of the bureau, was a veteran of Hull House and a close associate of Jane Addams. She helped make the Children's Bureau a force for progressive change not just in federal policy, but also in state and local governments.

But a sensational controversy broke out late in 1909 that helped put an end to Taft's popularity with reformers. Many progressives had been unhappy when Taft replaced Roosevelt's secretary of the interior, James R. Garfield, an aggressive conservationist, with Richard A. Ballinger, a conservative corporate lawyer. Suspicion of Ballinger grew when he attempted to invalidate Roosevelt's removal of nearly 1 million acres of forests and mineral reserves from private development.

In the midst of this mounting concern, Louis Glavis, an Interior Department investigator, charged Ballinger with having once connived to turn over valuable public coal lands in Alaska to a private syndicate for personal profit. Glavis took the evidence to Gifford Pinchot, still head of the Forest Service and a critic of Ballinger's policies. Pinchot took the charges to the president. Taft investigated them and decided they were groundless. But Pinchot was not satisfied, particularly after Taft fired Glavis for his part in the episode. He leaked the story to the press and asked Congress to investigate the scandal. The president discharged him for insubordination. The congressional committee appointed to study the controversy, dominated by Old Guard Republicans, exonerated Ballinger. But progressives throughout the country supported Pinchot. The controversy aroused as much public passion as any dispute of its time; and when it was over, Taft had alienated the supporters of Roosevelt completely and, it seemed, irrevocably.

BALLINGER-PINCHOT DISPUTE

WILLIAM HOWARD TAFT Taft could be a jovial companion in small groups, but his public image was of a dull, stolid man who stood in sharp and unfortunate contrast to his dynamic predecessor, Theodore Roosevelt. Taft also suffered public ridicule for his enormous size. He weighed as much as 350 pounds at times, and wide publicity accompanied his installation of an oversized bathtub in the White House.

The Return of Roosevelt

During most of these controversies, Theodore Roosevelt was far away: on a long hunting safari in Africa and an extended tour of Europe. To the American public, however, Roosevelt remained a formidable presence thanks to intensive newspaper coverage of his every move abroad. His return to New York in the spring of 1910 was a major public event. Roosevelt insisted that he had no plans to reenter politics, but within a month he announced that he would embark on a national speaking tour before the end of the summer. Furious with Taft, he was becoming convinced that he alone was capable of reuniting the Republican Party.

Discussion and Activities

Analyzing Visuals Have students examine the image "William Howard Taft" and compare it to the image "Roosevelt and Muir in Yosemite" in the previous section. Have students list differences in the style and setting of the photos and discuss in small groups possible reasons for the differences.

The real signal of Roosevelt's decision to assume leadership of Republican reformers came in a speech he gave on September 1, 1910, in Osawatomie, Kansas. In it he outlined a set of principles, which he labeled the "New Nationalism," that made clear he had moved a considerable way from the cautious conservatism of the first years of his presidency. He argued that social justice was possible only through the vigorous efforts of a strong federal government whose executive acted as the "steward of the public welfare." Those who thought primarily of property rights and personal profit "must now give way to the advocate of human welfare." He supported graduated income and inheritance taxes, workers' compensation for industrial accidents, regulation of the labor of women and children, tariff revision, and firmer regulation of corporations.

"New Nationalism"

Spreading Insurgency

The congressional elections of 1910 provided further evidence of how far the progressive revolt had spread. In primary elections, conservative Republicans suffered defeat after defeat while almost all the progressive incumbents were reelected. In the general election, the Democrats, who were now offering progressive candidates of their own, won control of the House of Representatives for the first time in sixteen years and gained strength in the Senate. But Roosevelt still denied any presidential ambitions and claimed that his real purpose was to pressure Taft to return to progressive policies. Two events, however, changed his mind. The first, on October 27, 1911, was the announcement by the administration of a suit against U.S. Steel, which charged, among other things, that the 1907 acquisition of the Tennessee Coal and Iron Company had been illegal. Roosevelt had approved that acquisition in the midst of the 1907 panic, and he was enraged by the implication that he had acted improperly.

Roosevelt was still reluctant to become a candidate for president because Senator Robert La Follette, the great Wisconsin progressive, had been working since 1911 to secure the presidential nomination for himself. But La Follette's candidacy stumbled in February 1912 when, exhausted, and distraught over the illness of a daughter, he appeared to suffer a nervous breakdown during a speech in Philadelphia. Roosevelt announced his candidacy on February 22.

Roosevelt versus Taft

La Follette retained some die-hard support. But for all practical purposes, the campaign for the Republican nomination had now become a battle between Roosevelt and Taft. Roosevelt scored overwhelming victories in all thirteen presidential primaries. Taft, however, remained the choice of most party leaders, who controlled the nominating process.

The battle for the nomination at the Chicago convention revolved around an unusually large number of contested delegates: 254 in all. Roosevelt needed fewer than half the disputed seats to clinch the nomination. But the Republican National Committee, controlled by the Old Guard, awarded all but 19 of them to Taft. At a rally the night before the convention opened, Roosevelt addressed 5,000 cheering supporters. "We stand at Armageddon," he told the roaring crowd, "and we battle for the Lord." The next day, he led his supporters out of the convention, and out of the party. The convention then quietly nominated Taft on the first ballot.

Roosevelt called his supporters back to Chicago in August for another convention, this one to launch the new Progressive Party and nominate himself as its presidential candidate. Roosevelt approached the battle feeling, as he put it, "fit as a bull moose" (thus giving his new party an enduring nickname).

The Progressive Party

ROOSEVELT AT OSAWATOMIE
Roosevelt's famous speech at Osawatomie, Kansas, in 1910 was the most radical of his career and openly marked his break with the Taft administration and the Republican leadership. "The essence of any struggle for liberty," he told his largely conservative audience, "has always been, and must always be to take from some one man or class of men the right to enjoy power, or wealth, or position or immunity, which has not been earned by service to his or their fellows."

Discussion and Activities

Assessing Credibility After students have read the section "The Return of Roosevelt," ask them to discuss in small groups whether they agree with Roosevelt's assertion that he reentered public life only to unify the Republican Party. **PCE**

Historical Thinking Skills

Argumentation Have students read the section "Spreading Insurgency." Ask them to write a short letter to Roosevelt encouraging him to either run for president or withdraw from the campaign. **PCE**

Discussion and Activities

Analyzing Perspectives After students have read the section "Roosevelt Versus Taft," ask them to discuss as a class why Republican Party leaders chose Taft as their candidate even though Roosevelt had won all the primaries. PCE

The "Bull Moose" party was notable for its strong commitment to a wide range of progressive causes that had grown in popularity over the previous two decades. The party advocated additional regulation of industry and trusts, sweeping reforms of many areas of government, compensation by the government for workers injured on the job, pensions for the elderly and for widows with children, and (alone among the major parties) woman suffrage. The delegates left the party's convention filled with hope and excitement.

Roosevelt himself, however, entered the fall campaign aware that his cause was almost hopeless, partly because many of the insurgents who had supported him during the primaries refused to follow him out of the Republican Party. His pessimism was also a result of the man the Democrats had nominated for president.

WOODROW WILSON AND THE NEW FREEDOM

The 1912 presidential contest was not simply one between conservatives and reformers. It was also one between two brands of progressivism. And it matched the two most important national leaders of the early twentieth century in unequal contest.

WOODROW WILSON

Reform sentiment had been gaining strength within the Democratic as well as the Republican Party in the first years of the century. At the 1912 Democratic National Convention in Baltimore in June, Champ Clark, the conservative Speaker of the House, was unable to assemble the two-thirds majority necessary for nomination because of progressive opposition. Finally, on the forty-sixth ballot, Woodrow Wilson, the governor of New Jersey and the only genuinely progressive candidate in the race, emerged as the party's nominee.

Wilson's "New Freedom"

Wilson had risen to political prominence by an unusual path. He had been a professor of political science at Princeton until 1902, when he was named president of the university. Elected governor of New Jersey in 1910, he demonstrated a commitment to reform. During his two years in the statehouse, he earned a national reputation for winning passage of progressive legislation. As a presidential candidate in 1912, Wilson presented a progressive program that came to be called the "New Freedom." Roosevelt's New Nationalism advocated accepting economic concentration and using government to regulate and control it. But Wilson seemed to side with those who (like Louis Brandeis) believed that bigness was both unjust and inefficient, that the proper response to monopoly was not to regulate it but to destroy it.

The 1912 presidential campaign was an anticlimax. William Howard Taft, resigned to defeat, barely campaigned. Roosevelt campaigned energetically (until a gunshot wound from a would-be assassin forced him to the sidelines during the last weeks before the election), but he failed to draw any significant numbers of Democratic progressives away from Wilson. In November, Roosevelt and Taft split the Republican vote; Wilson held on to most Democrats and won. He polled only 42 percent of the vote, compared with 27 percent for Roosevelt, 23 percent for Taft, and 6 percent for the socialist Eugene V. Debs. But in the electoral college, Wilson won 435 of the 531 votes. Roosevelt had carried only six states, Taft two, Debs none.

THE SCHOLAR AS PRESIDENT

Wilson was a bold and forceful president. He exerted firm control over his cabinet, and he delegated real authority only to those whose loyalty to him was beyond question. His most powerful adviser, Colonel Edward M. House, was an intelligent and ambitious Texan who held no office and whose only claim to authority was his personal intimacy with the president.

Lowering the Tariff

In legislative matters, Wilson skillfully welded together a coalition that would support his program. Democratic majorities in both houses of Congress made his task easier. Wilson's first triumph as president was the fulfillment of an old Democratic (and progressive) goal: a substantial lowering of the protective tariff. The Underwood-Simmons Tariff provided cuts substantial enough, progressives believed, to introduce real competition into American markets and thus to help break the power of trusts. To make up for the loss of revenue under the new tariff, Congress approved a graduated income tax, which the recently adopted Sixteenth Amendment to the Constitution now permitted. This first modern income tax imposed a 1 percent tax on individuals and corporations earning more than $4,000 a year, with rates ranging up to 6 percent on annual incomes over $500,000.

Federal Reserve Act

Wilson held Congress in session through the summer to work on a major reform of the American banking system: the Federal Reserve Act, which Congress passed and the president signed on December 23, 1913. It created twelve regional banks, each to be owned and controlled by the individual banks of its district. The regional Federal Reserve banks would hold a certain percentage of the assets of their member banks in reserve; they would use those reserves to support loans to private banks at an interest (or "discount") rate that the Federal Reserve system would set; they would issue a new type of paper currency–Federal Reserve notes–that would become the nation's basic medium of trade and would be backed by the government. Most important, they would be able to shift funds quickly to troubled areas–to meet increased demands for credit or to protect imperiled banks. Supervising and regulating the entire system was a national Federal Reserve Board, whose members were appointed by the president. Nearly half the nation's banking resources were represented in the system within a year, and 80 percent by the late 1920s.

In 1914, turning to the central issue of his 1912 campaign, Wilson proposed two measures to deal with the problem of monopoly. In the process he revealed how his own approach to the issue was beginning to change. There was a proposal to

Reasoning Processes

Comparing and Contrasting Have students read the section "Woodrow Wilson." Ask them to create a Venn diagram to compare Wilson's New Freedom with Roosevelt's New Nationalism. Have students discuss as a class what they believe are the most important similarities and differences. PCE WXT SOC

WOODROW WILSON Woodrow Wilson, the 28th president of the United States, was a Virginian (the first Southerner to be elected president since before the Civil War), a professor of political science and later president of Princeton University, governor of New Jersey, and known as a brilliant progressive. His election to the presidency brought the first Democrat to the White House since 1896.

The Library of Congress (3a21763v)

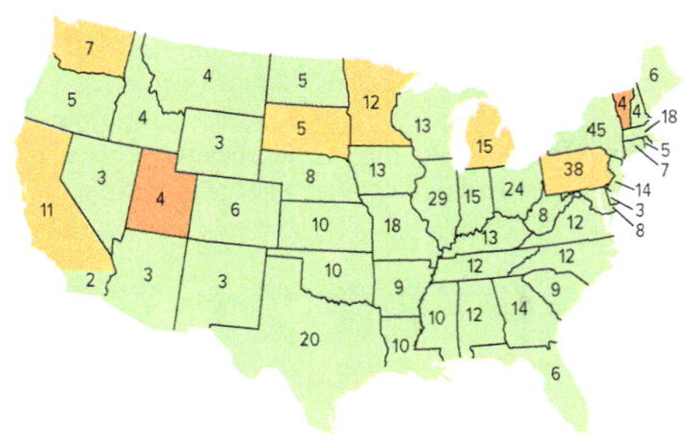

	Candidate (Party)	Electoral Vote	Popular Vote (%)
	Woodrow Wilson (Democratic)	435	6,293,454 (41.9)
	Theodore Roosevelt (Progressive/Bull Moose)	88	4,119,538 (27.4)
	William H. Taft (Republican)	8	3,484,980 (23.2)
	Eugene V. Debs (Socialist)	–	900,672 (6.0)
	Other parties (Prohibition; Socialist Labor)	–	235,025

58.8% of electorate voting

ELECTION OF 1912 The election of 1912 was one of the most unusual in American history because of the dramatic schism within the Republican Party. Two Republican presidents—William Howard Taft, the incumbent, and Theodore Roosevelt, his predecessor—ran against each other in 1912, opening the way for a victory by the Democratic candidate, Woodrow Wilson, who won with only about 42 percent of the popular vote. A fourth candidate, the socialist Eugene V. Debs, received a significant 6 percent of the vote.

What events caused the schism between Taft and Roosevelt?

create a federal agency through which the government would help business police itself–a regulatory commission of the type Roosevelt had advocated in 1912. There were also proposals to strengthen the government's ability to break up trusts–a decentralizing approach characteristic of Wilson's 1912 campaign. The two measures took shape as the Federal Trade Commission Act and the Clayton Antitrust Act. The Federal Trade Commission Act created a regulatory agency that would help businesses determine in advance whether their actions would be acceptable to the government. The agency would also have authority to launch prosecutions against "unfair trade practices," and it would have wide power to investigate corporate behavior. Wilson signed the Federal Trade Commission Bill happily. But he seemed to lose interest in the Clayton Antitrust Bill and did little to protect it from conservative assaults, which greatly weakened it. The future, he had apparently decided, lay with government supervision.

RETREAT AND ADVANCE

By the fall of 1914, Wilson believed that the program of the New Freedom was essentially complete and that agitation for reform would now subside. He refused to support the movement for national woman suffrage. Deferring to Southern Democrats, and reflecting his own Southern background, he condoned the reimposition of segregation in the agencies of the federal government (in contrast to Roosevelt, who had ordered the elimination of many such barriers). When congressional progressives attempted to enlist his support for new reform legislation, Wilson dismissed their proposals as unconstitutional or unnecessary.

The congressional elections of 1914, however, shattered the president's complacency. Democrats suffered major losses in Congress, and voters who in 1912 had supported the Progressive Party began returning to the Republicans. Wilson would not be able to rely on a divided opposition when he ran for reelection in 1916. By the end of 1915, therefore, Wilson had begun to support a second flurry of reforms. In January 1916, he appointed Louis Brandeis to the Supreme Court, making him not only the first Jew but also the most progressive justice to serve there. Later, he supported a measure to make it easier for farmers to receive credit and one creating a system of workers' compensation for federal employees.

Wilson was sponsoring measures that expanded the powers of the national government in important ways. In 1916, for example, he supported the Keating-Owen Act, the first federal law regulating child labor. The measure prohibited the shipment

CHILD-LABOR LAWS

Discussion and Activities

Explaining Significance After students have read the section "The Scholar as President," ask them to create a chart listing key elements of the Underwood-Simmons Tariff, the Federal Reserve Act, the Federal Trade Commission Act, and the Clayton Antitrust Act. Have students discuss as a class which of these they believe had the greatest impact on the economy and which represented the greatest change from previous economic policy. **PCE** **WXT**

Answers

Election of 1912

Roosevelt was upset with Taft for his handling of the Ballinger-Pinchot controversy and the antitrust suit against United States Steel.

CHAPTER 21
THE PROGRESSIVES

Discussion and Activities

Argumentation Divide the class into three groups and ask them to review and research the actions of presidents Roosevelt, Taft, and Wilson. Have each group create a brief presentation arguing that their president was the most "Progressive." **PCE** **WXT** **SOC** **GEO**

Key Terms

Students should be familiar with the key terms and be able to define them in the context of causes and effects of the Progressive movement at the state and national levels. Encourage students to use these terms in performing review exercises and exam practice for this chapter.

of goods produced by underage children across state lines, thus giving an expanded importance to the constitutional clause assigning Congress the task of regulating interstate commerce. The president similarly supported measures that used federal taxing authority as a vehicle for legislating social change. After the Court struck down Keating-Owen, a new law attempted to achieve the same goal by imposing a heavy tax on the products of child labor. (The Court later struck it down too.) And the Smith-Lever Act of 1914 demonstrated another way in which the federal government could influence local behavior; it offered matching federal grants to support agricultural extension education. Over time, these innovative uses of government overcame most of the constitutional objections and became the foundation of a long-term growth in federal power over the economy.

CHAPTER 21 REVIEW

CONNECTING THEMES

Chapter Twenty One explored the goals, successes, and limitations of the progressive movement. Crusading journalists known as muckrakers sought to expose political scandals and corporate misbehavior to the public. Middle-class women took active roles in promoting social reforms as industrialization and immigration grew. The growing demand for educated workers, driven by urbanization and technology, spurred the rise of a new middle class. While white men benefited the most from professional opportunities, white women gained more access to education and found more employment in fields like teaching and nursing. Educated black women were in high demand as teachers in the growing numbers of segregated schools in the South. The woman suffrage movement capitalized on the changes of the era and won ratification of the Nineteenth Amendment.

African Americans also pursued social change during the era despite pervasive racism, discrimination, and segregation. W.E.B. DuBois launched both the Niagara Movement and the NAACP in his drive to win equal rights. The NAACP won important victories in the Supreme Court becoming the leading civil rights organization in America.

As large corporations dominated the economic landscape, Roosevelt, Taft, and Wilson sought to regulate and control big business. Each had their own take on the proper role and balance between government and the economy. Debates raged over tariffs, trusts, and monopolies along with issues such as the preservation of wilderness areas and natural resources. By the end of the era, the federal government had assumed a larger role in managing the economy and conservationists had successfully advocated for the National Park System, although they lost many battles along the way.

You should consider the following questions as you review the themes for this chapter:

- How was class consciousness accentuated during the progressive era?
- How did the perception of traditional gender roles change during the progressive era?
- What were the causes and effects of economic hardship on both the domestic and international scene?
- Why did the attitude toward big business and the economy change during the progressive era?
- How successful was the progressive movement in making the national, state, and local government more responsible to the people?
- How did the debate between conservation and preservation shape the attitude and debate about environmentalism during the progressive era?
- How did ideas about the role of the federal government in the welfare of its citizens change during the progressive era?
- How did the reform movements of the progressive era compare with those of previous time periods?

KEY TERMS

Alice Paul 589
"Bad Trusts" 600
"Bull Moose" party 609
Elizabeth Cady Stanton 588
Eugene Debs 598
eugenics 597
Father John Ryan 583
Federal Reserve Act 610
Gifford Pinchot 606
"Good Trusts" 600
Hetch Hetchy 606
Hull House 583
Ida Tarbell 583
Interstate Commerce Act 605
IWW ("Wobblies") 598
Jane Addams 583
Lincoln Steffens 583
Louis Brandeis 599
muckrakers 582
municipal reforms 590
NAACP 596
National American Woman Suffrage Association (NAWSA) 589
New Freedom 610
Newlands Act 605
New Nationalism 609
Panic of 1907 607
professional associations 585
Prohibition 597
Pure Food and Drug Act 605
referendum 591
Robert La Follette 593
settlement houses 583
Sierra Club 603
Social Gospel 583
social work 583
Tammany Hall 594
Thorstein Veblen 584
Triangle Shirtwaist Company fire 594
W.E.B. Du Bois 595
Western progressives 594
Women's Christian Temperance Union 596
woman's club movement 587

Go Online Chapter 21 Content Review

Assessing Student Understanding Use the online assessment to assess student understanding of concepts and topics within the chapter. You can assign the ready-made Chapter 21 Content Review or create your own from available questions. This easy-to-use tool helps you design assessments that meet the needs of different types of learners.

AP EXAM PRACTICE

Questions assume cumulative content knowledge from this chapter and the previous chapter.

MULTIPLE CHOICE

Use the photograph on page 585 and your knowledge of U.S. history to answer questions 1-3.

1. The activities portrayed in the photograph most reflect the Progressive belief in
   (A) participation in municipal government.
   (B) the "natural laws" of the marketplace.
   (C) individual accomplishment and professionalism.
   (D) the influence of the environment on human development.
2. Many activists of the Progressive movement tended to be
   (A) Southern African-Americans.
   (B) middle class women.
   (C) urban economic elites.
   (D) rural farmers and ranchers.
3. Progressive reformers found the most success in their attempts to
   (A) eliminate trusts from the economic system.
   (B) establish racial equity in voting.
   (C) eliminate gender as a barrier to voting.
   (D) establish ethnically neutral immigration guidelines.

SHORT ANSWER

Use your knowledge of U.S. history to answer questions 4 and 5.

4. Use the image on page 586 to answer A, B, and C.
   (A) Describe ONE point of view about the relationship between women and the Progressive movement.
   (B) Explain ONE specific historical cause that led to women becoming active in the Progressive movement.
   (C) Explain ONE specific historical effect that resulted from women becoming active in the Progressive movement.
5. Answer A, B, and C.
   (A) Describe ONE specific historical difference between Populism and Progressivism.
   (B) Describe ONE specific historical similarity between Populism and Progressivism.
   (C) Explain ONE specific piece of historical context that explains the shift from Populism to Progressivism.

LONG ESSAY

Develop a thoughtful and thorough historical argument that addresses the statement. Begin your essay with a thesis statement, and support it with specific historical evidence and examples.

6. Evaluate the relative importance of causes that gave rise to the Progressive movement within the United States from 1900 to 1920.

Answers

Multiple Choice

1. D; **2.** B; **3.** C

Short Answer

4A) Possible answer: In the political cartoon "Woman's Holy War," the central figure is wielding a battle ax and the background shows other women waging war for reforms. The image is from the point of view of a reformer, showing the important role that women played within the Progressive and reform movements.

4B) Possible answer: Women were empowered following the Second Great Awakening. The Gilded Age had been an age of the white male monopolist and a time for women that reinforced the traditional image. With the advent of Progressivism, women felt empowered to take an active role within American society.

4C) Possible answer: Women were essential within the Progressive movement; Jane Addams' Hull House movement was a significant contribution on the part of women reformers.

5A) Possible answer: Populists were primarily agrarian and represented the West and farmer's interests, while Progressives were primarily urban and represented industrial worker's interests.

5B) Possible answer: Both groups rose in response to the rise of monopolies in the Gilded Age. Both groups saw the monopolists as symbolic of unchecked capitalism and economic greed at its peak, which needed to be checked by middle-class and working-class individuals.

5C) Possible answer: An important piece of historical context explaining the shift from Populism to Progressivism was the rise of urbanization and industrialization in the first few decades in the history of the United States. By 1920 more Americans lived in cities than lived in rural communities, and this paradigm shift represented a major geographical move that had ramifications all throughout American society.

Answers

Long Essay

6. Possible thesis: Progressives built upon the small gains that were made by the Populists during the Gilded Age in America. However, with the shift in population, the Progressive movement focused on the issues of the cities. Reform movements were generally no longer concerned with agricultural reform but now focused on labor and industry. Further, Progressive women built upon the reform gains during the Second Great Awakening to further advance the causes of middle-class America. Specific historical evidence: First, Progressives built upon the gains that were made by Populists decades before the twentieth century. Second, Progressives were concerned about the rise in power and wealth by the unchecked monopolists within the American economy. The monopolists' had a general lack of concern about the middle class, working class, and the poor within the United States. Third, women were active within the Progressive movement, building upon the reforms of the Second Great Awakening. Fourth, Progressives sought ways to control and reform government through advocating for the initiative, the referendum, and the recall. Fifth, presidents during the Progressive era sought more control and regulation of the U.S. economy. Finally, Progressives made the environment an important part of their agenda.

Pacing Guide

Chapter 22 explores key concepts from Period 7: 1890–1945 of the AP U.S. History Curriculum Framework. The suggested instruction time for Chapter 22 is 3 days.

Key Concepts

7.3.I In the late 19th century and early 20th century, new U.S. territorial ambitions and acquisitions in the Western Hemisphere and the Pacific accompanied heightened public debates over America's role in the world.

7.3.II World War I and its aftermath intensified ongoing debates about the nation's role in the world and how best to achieve national security and pursue American interests.

22 AMERICA AND THE GREAT WAR

THE WAR TO END ALL WARS
The horror of World War I was unprecedented in human history. More than 9 million people died between July 28, 1914, when the war started and November 11, 1918, when it came to an end. The astronomical number of casualties was due to advanced technologies of combat. Here, an American soldier is succumbing to poison gas, one of the most feared weapons of the war.

Private Collection/© Peter Newark Pictures/Bridgeman Images

CONNECTING CONCEPTS

Chapter Twenty-Two begins by examining Theodore Roosevelt's use of American power in the world, which he divided between "civilized" and "uncivilized" nations. In Asia, he protected the "Open Door"; in Latin America, he intervened through the "Roosevelt Corollary" to the Monroe Doctrine and built the Panama Canal. His successor, William Howard Taft, worked to advance the nation's economic interests in Nicaragua through "Dollar Diplomacy." Woodrow Wilson entered office determined to pursue "Moral Diplomacy," but soon embroiled the United States in the Mexican Revolution as a devastating war erupted in Europe in 1914 between two competing alliances.

At first Wilson urged neutrality. But economic and cultural ties to Britain and France made it difficult, especially when U.S. trade with and loans to the Allies led Germany to launch submarine warfare in the Atlantic. After winning reelection on a peace platform in 1916, Wilson asked Congress to declare war on Germany in 1917. The arrival in 1918 of the American Expeditionary Force (including fifty thousand black soldiers) in France eventually tipped the balance in favor of the Allies and broke the deadly stalemate of trench warfare. But new technology, including machine guns and poison gas, had already cost millions of lives.

At home the Great War had profound effects. The economy boomed and workers enjoyed important, if temporary, gains. The government found new ways to organize production and financed the war by raising taxes and selling bonds. Yet the war failed to unify American society. The Espionage and Sedition Acts restricted civil liberties and suppressed political dissent. Patriotism was compulsory. The "Great Migration" of African Americans from the rural South to the industrial North in search of political, social, and economic freedom and opportunity led to racial conflict with white residents.

Discussion and Activities

Analyzing Visuals Have students examine the image "The War to End All Wars." Ask them to identify and discuss in small groups details from the photo that shed light on conditions for American soldiers in World War I. *(Heavy woolen uniforms and leather boots would be uncomfortable in hot or wet conditions. Facing weapons such as poison gas would be terrifying. Soldiers are having to advance in the open with no cover.)* **WOR** **WXT**

Wilson planned to lead the fight for a just and lasting peace with his Fourteen Points. But at the Paris Peace Conference, he encountered opposition from Britain and France, who wanted to punish Germany. The U.S. Senate then refused to ratify the Treaty of Versailles and blocked U.S. participation in the League of Nations. The end of the war brought turmoil and reaction, not idealism or reform. A postwar recession, labor strife, and a radical mail-bombing campaign terrified middle-class white Americans, who in the aftermath of the Russian Revolution saw them as frightening omens. The Red Scare led to mass deportations and arrests – but also to a vigorous defense of civil liberties. Meanwhile, black veterans demanded racial equality despite more race riots in cities like Chicago, and Marcus Garvey attracted a wide following by insisting on racial pride and black nationalism.

As you read, you should:

- Describe the ways that changing demography led to cultural and racial conflict.
- Identify how America's involvement in World War I increased xenophobic tendencies among portions of the American population.
- Analyze the ways that World War I created a climate in which civil liberties were significantly restricted.
- Describe how labor strikes and racial tensions disrupted American society, partially enabling the Red Scare.
- Explain how World War I significantly altered migration patterns both internally and externally.
- Analyze how the United States shed its isolationistic background and became a major player on the world stage.
- Evaluate how the United States justified expansion on the basis of economic, political, and social motives.
- Analyze the reasons why the United States entered World War I.

THE "BIG STICK": AMERICA AND THE WORLD, 1901–1917

To the general public, foreign affairs remained largely remote. Walter Lippmann once wrote: "I cannot remember taking any interest whatsoever in foreign affairs until after the outbreak of the First World War." But to Theodore Roosevelt and later presidents, that made foreign affairs even more appealing. There the president could act with less regard for the Congress or the courts. There he could free himself from concerns about public opinion. Overseas, the president could exercise power unfettered and alone.

Roosevelt and "Civilization"

Theodore Roosevelt believed in the value and importance of using American power in the world (a conviction he once described by citing the proverb "Speak softly, but carry a big stick"). But he had two different standards for using that power.

Roosevelt believed that an important distinction existed between the "civilized" and "uncivilized" nations of the world. "Civilized" nations, as he defined them, were predominantly white and Anglo-Saxon or Teutonic; "uncivilized" nations were generally nonwhite, Latin, or Slavic. But racism was only partly the basis of the distinction. Equally important was economic development. He believed, therefore, that Japan, a rapidly industrializing society, had earned admission to the ranks of the civilized. A civilized society, he argued, had the right and duty to intervene in the affairs of a "backward" nation to preserve order and stability. That belief was one important reason for Roosevelt's early support of the development of American sea power. By 1906, the American navy had attained a size and strength surpassed only by that of Great Britain (although Germany was fast gaining ground).

Racial and Economic Basis of Roosevelt's Diplomacy

Protecting the "Open Door" in Asia

In 1904, the Japanese staged a surprise attack on the Russian fleet at Port Arthur in southern Manchuria, a province of China that both Russia and Japan hoped to control. Roosevelt, hoping to prevent either nation from

Historical Thinking Skills

Contextualization Have student discuss as a class how the United States became more active overseas in the last part of the nineteenth century. *(This was due to the Spanish-American War, the annexation of the Philippines, the purchase of Alaska, the mediation of the Venezuela Boundary dispute, etc.)* **WOR**

Go Online AP Exam Preparation

AP Exam Practice Use the online assessment to help prepare students for the AP Exam. You can assign the ready-made AP-style short-answer questions, document-based questions, and multiple-choice questions assessing concepts, themes, and skills from Period 7 and AP-style long-essay questions organized in sets of 3 questions from various time periods. You can also create your own tests from available questions. This easy-to-use tool helps you design assessments that meet the needs of different types of learners.

Historical Thinking Skills

Argumentation After students have read the section "Protecting the 'Open Door' in Asia," ask them to write a press release explaining why Roosevelt won the Nobel Peace Prize. **WOR** **NAT** **PCE**

"THE NEW DIPLOMACY" This 1904 drawing by the famous Puck cartoonist Louis Dalrymple conveys the new image of America as a great power that Theodore Roosevelt was attempting to project to the world. Roosevelt the world policeman deals effectively with "less civilized" peoples (Asians and Latin Americans, seen clamoring at left) by using the "big stick" and deals equally effectively with the "civilized" nations (at right) by offering arbitration.

becoming dominant there, agreed to a Japanese request to mediate an end to the conflict. Russia, faring badly in the war, had no choice but to agree. At a peace conference in Portsmouth, New Hampshire, in 1905, Roosevelt extracted from the embattled Russians a recognition of Japan's territorial gains and from the Japanese an agreement to cease the fighting and expand no further. At the same time, he negotiated a secret agreement with the Japanese to ensure that the United States could continue to trade freely in the region.

Roosevelt won the Nobel Peace Prize in 1906 for his work in ending the Russo-Japanese War. But in the years that followed, relations between the United States and Japan steadily deteriorated. Japan now emerged as the preeminent naval power in the Pacific and soon began to exclude American trade from many of the territories it controlled. To be sure the Japanese government recognized the power of the United States, he sent sixteen battleships of the new American navy (known as the "Great White Fleet" because the ships were temporarily painted white for the voyage) on an unprecedented journey around the world that included a call on Japan.

"GREAT WHITE FLEET"

THE IRON-FISTED NEIGHBOR

Roosevelt took a particular interest in events in what he (and most other Americans) considered the nation's special sphere of interest: Latin America. He established a pattern of U.S. intervention in the region that would long survive his presidency.

Early in 1902, the financially troubled government of Venezuela began to renege on debts to European bankers. Naval forces of Britain, Italy, and Germany blockaded the Venezuelan coast in response. Then German ships began to bombard a Venezuelan port amid rumors that Germany planned to establish a permanent base in the region. Roosevelt used the threat of American naval power to pressure the German navy to withdraw.

The incident helped persuade Roosevelt that European intrusions into Latin America could result not only from aggression but also from instability or irresponsibility (such as defaulting on debts) within the Latin American nations themselves. As a result, in 1904 he announced what came to be known as the "Roosevelt Corollary" to the Monroe Doctrine.

"ROOSEVELT COROLLARY"

Historical Thinking Skills

Analyzing Images Have students examine the image "The New Diplomacy." Ask them to identify and discuss in small groups details from the cartoon that would help to identify the author's point of view. *(Roosevelt, dressed as a policeman, stands astride the United States. He towers over all the other figures from Asia, the Americas, and Europe. He swings his "Big Stick" over Latin America and Asia in a manner that suggests dominance. He holds "arbitration" toward the European states. The cartoon portrays Roosevelt as both a deal-maker and an enforcer, the representative of an increasingly strong and involved American foreign policy.)* **WOR**

THE UNITED STATES AND LATIN AMERICA, 1895–1941 Except for Puerto Rico, the Virgin Islands, and the Canal Zone, the United States had no formal possessions in Latin America and the Caribbean in the late nineteenth century and the first half of the twentieth. But as this map reveals, the U.S. exercised considerable influence in these regions throughout this period—political and economic influence, augmented at times by military intervention. Note the particularly intrusive presence of the United States in the affairs of Cuba, Haiti, and the Dominican Republic—as well as the canal-related interventions in Colombia and Panama.

What were some of the most frequent reasons for U.S. intervention in Latin America?

The United States, he claimed, had the right not only to oppose European intervention in the Western Hemisphere but also to intervene in the domestic affairs of its neighbors if those neighbors proved unable to maintain order and national sovereignty on their own.

The immediate motivation for the Roosevelt Corollary, and the first opportunity for using it, was a crisis in the Dominican Republic. A revolution had toppled its corrupt and bankrupt government in 1903, but the new regime proved no better able to make good on the country's $22 million in debts to European nations. Roosevelt established, in effect, an American receivership, assuming control of Dominican customs and distributing 45 percent of the revenues to the Dominicans and the rest to foreign creditors. This arrangement lasted, in one form or another, for more than three decades.

In 1902, the United States granted political independence to Cuba, but only after the new government had agreed to the Platt Amendment to its constitution. The amendment gave the United States the right to prevent any other foreign power from intruding into the new nation. In 1906, when domestic uprisings seemed to threaten the internal stability of the island, American troops landed in Cuba, quelled the fighting, and remained there for three years.

PLATT AMENDMENT

THE PANAMA CANAL

The most celebrated accomplishment of Roosevelt's presidency was the construction of the Panama Canal, which linked the Atlantic and the Pacific. At first, Roosevelt and many advocates of a canal favored a route across Nicaragua, which would permit a sea-level canal requiring no locks. But they soon turned instead to the narrow Isthmus of Panama in Colombia, the site of an earlier, failed effort by a French company to construct a channel. Although the Panama route was not at sea level (and would thus require locks), it was shorter than the one in Nicaragua. And construction was already about 40 percent complete. When the French company lowered the price for its holdings, the United States chose Panama.

Roosevelt dispatched John Hay, his secretary of state, to negotiate an agreement with Colombian diplomats in Washington that would allow construction to begin without delay. Under heavy American pressure, the Colombian chargé d'affaires, Tomas Herrén, unwisely signed an agreement giving

Reasoning Processes

Comparison After students have read the section "The Iron-Fisted Neighbor," ask them to create a T-chart comparing U.S. intervention in the Dominican Republic and Cuba. Have students discuss in small groups reasons for any similarities or differences. WOR

Answers

The United States and Latin America, 1895–1941

The United States frequently justified intervention in Latin American countries by claiming it was doing so to restore political and economic order. WOR PCE

Discussion and Activities

Analyzing Issues After students have read the section "The Panama Canal," ask them to discuss in small groups whether they believe the American recognition of Panama was legitimate. **WOR** **PCE**

the United States perpetual rights to a six-mile-wide "canal zone" across Colombia. The outraged Colombian senate refused to ratify it. Colombia then sent a new representative to Washington with instructions to demand a higher payment from the Americans plus a share of the payment to the French.

Roosevelt was furious and began to look for ways to circumvent the Colombian government. Philippe Bunau-Varilla, chief engineer of the French canal project, was a ready ally. In November 1903, he helped organize and finance a revolution in Panama.

PANAMANIAN REVOLT

There had been many previous revolts, all of them failures, but this one had the support of the United States. Roosevelt landed troops from the USS *Nashville* in Panama to "maintain order." Their presence prevented Colombian forces from suppressing the rebellion, and three days later Roosevelt recognized Panama as an independent nation. The new Panamanian government quickly agreed to the terms the Colombian senate had rejected. Work on the canal proceeded rapidly, and it opened in 1914.

Taft and "Dollar Diplomacy"

Like his predecessor, William Howard Taft worked to advance the nation's economic interests overseas. But he showed little interest in Roosevelt's larger vision of world stability. Taft's secretary of state, the corporate attorney Philander C. Knox, worked aggressively to extend American investments into less developed regions. Critics called his policies "Dollar Diplomacy."

It was particularly visible in the Caribbean. When a revolution broke out in Nicaragua in 1909, the administration quickly

INTERVENTION IN NICARAGUA

sided with the insurgents (who had been inspired to revolt by an American mining company) and sent troops into the country to seize the customs houses. As soon as peace was restored, Knox encouraged American bankers to offer substantial loans to the new government, thus increasing Washington's financial leverage over the country. When the new pro-American government faced an insurrection less than two years later, Taft again landed troops in Nicaragua, this time to protect the existing regime. The troops remained there for more than a decade.

Diplomacy and Morality

Woodrow Wilson entered the presidency with relatively little interest or experience in international affairs. Yet he faced international challenges of a scope and gravity unmatched by those of any president before him. In many respects, he continued–and even strengthened–the Roosevelt-Taft approach to foreign policy.

OPENING THE PANAMA CANAL The great Miraflores locks of the Panama Canal open in October 1914 to admit the first ship to pass through the channel. The construction of the canal was one of the great engineering feats of the early twentieth century. But the heavy-handed political efforts of Theodore Roosevelt were at least equally important to its completion.

Reasoning Processes

Comparing and Contrasting Have students read the section "Taft and Dollar Diplomacy." Ask them to create a Venn diagram comparing Dollar Diplomacy to the Roosevelt Corollary. Have students discuss as a class the most important differences and the reasons for them. **WOR** **WXT** **PCE**

Having already seized control of the finances of the Dominican Republic in 1905, the United States established a military government there in 1916. The military occupation lasted eight years. In neighboring Haiti, Wilson landed marines in 1915 to quell a revolution, in the course of which a mob had murdered an unpopular president. American military forces remained in the country until 1934, and American officers drafted the new Haitian constitution adopted in 1918. When Wilson began to fear that the Danish West Indies might be about to fall into the hands of Germany, he bought the colony from Denmark and renamed it the Virgin Islands. Concerned about the possibility of European influence in Nicaragua, he signed a treaty with that country's government ensuring that no other nation would build a canal there and winning for the United States the right to intervene in Nicaragua to protect American interests.

But Wilson's view of America's role in the world was not entirely similar to the views of his predecessors, as became clear in his dealings with Mexico. For many years, under the friendly auspices of the corrupt dictator Porfirio Díaz, American businessmen had been establishing an enormous economic presence in Mexico. In 1910, however, Díaz had been overthrown by the popular leader Francisco Madero, who seemed hostile to American businesses in Mexico. The United States quietly encouraged a reactionary general, Victoriano Huerta, to depose Madero early in 1913, and the Taft administration, in its last weeks in office, prepared to recognize the new Huerta regime and welcome back a receptive environment for American investments in Mexico. Before it could do so, however, the new government murdered Madero, shortly before Woodrow Wilson took office in Washington. The new president instantly announced that he would never recognize Huerta's "government of butchers."

WILSON'S MORAL DIPLOMACY

At first, Wilson hoped that simply by refusing to recognize Huerta he could help topple the regime and bring to power the opposing Constitutionalists, led by Venustiano Carranza. But when Huerta, with the support of American business interests, established a full military dictatorship in October 1913, the president became more assertive. In April 1914, an officer in Huerta's army briefly arrested several American sailors from the USS *Dolphin* who had gone ashore in Tampico, on Mexico's east coast. The men were immediately released, but the American admiral—unsatisfied with the apology he received—demanded that the Huerta forces fire a twenty-one-gun salute to the American flag as a public display of penance. The Mexicans refused. Wilson used the trivial incident as a pretext for seizing the Mexican port of Veracruz.

VERACRUZ

Wilson had envisioned a bloodless action, but in a clash with Mexican troops in Veracruz, the Americans killed 126 Mexican soldiers and suffered 19 casualties of their own. Now at the brink of war, Wilson began to look for a way out. His show of force, however, had helped strengthen the position of the Carranza faction, which captured Mexico City in August and forced Huerta to flee the country. At last, it seemed, the crisis might be over.

But Wilson was not yet satisfied. He reacted angrily when Carranza refused to accept American guidelines for the creation of a new government, and he briefly considered throwing his support to still another aspirant to leadership: Carranza's erstwhile lieutenant Pancho Villa, who was now leading

PANCHO VILLA AND HIS TROOPS Pancho Villa (fourth from left in the front row) poses with some of the leaders of his army, whose members Americans came to consider bandits once they began staging raids across the U.S. border. He was a national hero in Mexico.

Reasoning Processes

Comparing After students have read the section "Wilson's Moral Diplomacy," ask them to create a three-column chart comparing the main ideas behind the Roosevelt Corollary, Dollar Diplomacy, and Moral Diplomacy. Have students discuss as a class which approach they think would best represent American interests. **WOR** **NAT**

Historical Thinking Skills

Argumentation After students have read the section "Wilson's Moral Diplomacy," ask them to write a short letter to President Wilson from the point of view of an American citizen advising him on which faction to support in the Mexican civil war. **WOR** **SOC** **PCE**

Discussion and Activities

Historical Evidence and Argumentation After students have read the section "Diplomacy and Morality," ask them to create a T-chart comparing costs and benefits of American involvement in Mexico. Have students discuss in small groups whether the benefits were worth the costs. **WOR** **PCE**

a rebel army of his own. When Villa's military position deteriorated, however, Wilson abandoned him and finally, in October 1915, granted preliminary recognition to the Carranza government. By now, however, he had created yet another crisis. Villa, angry at what he considered an American betrayal, retaliated in January 1916 by shooting sixteen American mining engineers in northern Mexico. Two months later, he led his soldiers (or "bandits," as the United States called them) across the border into Columbus, New Mexico, where they killed seventeen more Americans.

With the permission of the Carranza government, Wilson ordered General John J. Pershing to lead an American expeditionary force across the Mexican border in pursuit of Villa. The American troops never found Villa, but they did engage in two ugly skirmishes with Carranza's army, in which forty Mexican soldiers and twelve American soldiers died. Again, the United States and Mexico stood at the brink of war. But at the last minute, Wilson drew back. He quietly withdrew American troops from Mexico, and in March 1917, he at last granted formal recognition to the Carranza regime. By now, however, Wilson's attention was turning elsewhere–to the far greater international crisis engulfing the European continent and ultimately much of the world.

INTERVENTION IN MEXICO

THE ROAD TO WAR

The causes of the war in Europe–indeed the question of whether there were any significant causes at all, or whether the entire conflict was the result of a tragic series of blunders–have been the subject of continued debate for nearly a century. What is clear is that the European nations had by 1914 created an unusually precarious international system that careened into war very quickly on the basis of what most historians agree was a relatively minor series of provocations.

THE COLLAPSE OF THE EUROPEAN PEACE

The major powers of Europe were organized by 1914 in two great, competing alliances. The "Triple Entente" linked Britain, France, and Russia. The "Triple Alliance" united Germany, the Austro-Hungarian Empire, and Italy. The chief rivalry, however, was not between the two alliances, but between the great powers that dominated them: Great Britain and Germany–the former long established as the world's most powerful colonial and commercial nation, the latter ambitious to expand its own empire and become at least Britain's equal. The Anglo-German rivalry may have been the most important underlying source of the tensions that led to World War I, but it was not the immediate cause of its outbreak. The conflict emerged most directly out of a controversy involving nationalist movements within the Austro-Hungarian Empire. On June 28, 1914, Archduke Franz Ferdinand, heir to the throne of the tottering empire, was assassinated while paying a state visit to Sarajevo. Sarajevo was the capital of Bosnia, a province of Austria-Hungary that Slavic nationalists wished to annex to neighboring Serbia; the archduke's assassin was a Serbian nationalist.

COMPETING ALLIANCES

This local controversy quickly escalated through the workings of the system of alliances that the great powers had constructed. With support from Germany, Austria-Hungary launched a punitive assault on Serbia. The Serbians called on Russia to help with their defense. The Russians began mobilizing their army on July 30. Things quickly careened out of control. By August 3, Germany had declared war on both Russia and France and had invaded Belgium in preparation for a thrust across the French border. On August 4, Great Britain–ostensibly to honor its alliance with France but, more importantly, to blunt the advance of its principal rival–declared war on Germany. Russia and the Austro-Hungarian Empire formally began hostilities on August 6. Italy, although an ally of Germany in 1914, remained neutral at first and later entered the war on the side of the British and French. The Ottoman Empire (centered in Turkey) and other, smaller nations all joined the fighting later in 1914 or in 1915. Within less than a year, virtually the entire European continent and part of Asia were embroiled in a catastrophic war.

WILSON'S NEUTRALITY

Wilson called on his fellow citizens in 1914 to remain "impartial in thought as well as deed." But that was an impossible task, for several reasons. Some Americans sympathized with the German cause (German Americans because of affection for Germany, Irish Americans because of hatred of Britain). Many more (including Wilson himself) sympathized with Britain. Wilson was only one of many Americans who fervently admired England–its traditions, its culture, its political system; almost instinctively, these Americans attributed to the cause of the Allies (Britain, France, Italy, Russia) a moral quality that they denied to the Central Powers (Germany, the Austro-Hungarian Empire, and the Ottoman Empire). Lurid reports of German atrocities in Belgium and France, skillfully exaggerated by British propagandists, strengthened the hostility of many Americans toward Germany.

Economic realities also made it impossible for the United States to deal with the belligerents on equal terms. The British had imposed a naval blockade on Germany to prevent munitions and supplies from reaching the enemy. As a neutral, the United States had the right, in theory, to trade with both Britain and Germany; but for Americans to trade with Germany, they would have to defy the British blockade. A truly neutral response to the blockade would have been to stop trading with Britain as well. But while the United States could survive an interruption of its relatively modest trade with the Central Powers, it could not easily weather an embargo on its much more extensive trade with the Allies, particularly when war orders from Britain and France soared after 1914, helping to produce one of the greatest economic booms in the nation's history. So America

ECONOMIC TIES TO BRITAIN

Discussion and Activities

Speculating Have students read the section "Collapse of the European Peace." Ask them to discuss in pairs or small groups whether war would have broken out in Europe if Franz Ferdinand had not been assassinated. **WOR** **PCE** **SOC**

IT IS FAR BETTER
TO FACE THE BULLETS
THAN TO BE KILLED
AT HOME BY A BOMB
JOIN THE ARMY AT ONCE
& HELP TO STOP AN AIR RAID
GOD SAVE THE KING

BULLETS BETTER THAN BOMBS? At the beginning of World War I, Britain largely relied on a volunteer army. To attract recruits, the government used propaganda posters such as the one shown here. While this was very successful in attracting recruits, the need for soldiers was enormous, compelling Parliament to enact in January 1916 a Military Service Bill that introduced conscription. By the end of the war, more than 5 million men had joined up.

tacitly ignored the blockade of Germany and continued trading with Britain. By 1915, the United States had gradually transformed itself from a neutral power into the arsenal of the Allies.

The Germans, in the meantime, were resorting to a new and, in American eyes, barbaric tactic: submarine warfare. Unable to challenge British domination on the ocean's surface, Germany began early in 1915 to use the newly improved submarine to try to stem the flow of supplies to England. Enemy vessels, the Germans announced, would be sunk on sight. Months later, on

LUSITANIA

May 7, 1915, a German submarine sank the British passenger liner *Lusitania* without warning, causing the deaths of 1,198 people, 128 of them Americans. The ship was, it later became clear, carrying both passengers and munitions; but most Americans considered the attack what Theodore Roosevelt called it: "an act of piracy."

Wilson angrily demanded that Germany promise not to repeat such outrages and that the Central Powers affirm their commitment to neutral rights. The Germans finally agreed to Wilson's demands, but tensions between the nations continued to grow. Early in 1916, in response to an announcement that the Allies were now arming merchant ships to sink submarines, Germany proclaimed that it would fire on such vessels without warning. A few weeks later Germany attacked the unarmed French steamer *Sussex*, injuring several American passengers. Again Wilson demanded that Germany abandon its "unlawful" tactics; again the German government relented, still hoping to keep America out of the war.

Preparedness Versus Pacifism

Despite the president's increasing bellicosity in 1916, he was still far from ready to commit the United States to war. One obstacle was American domestic politics. Facing a difficult battle for reelection, Wilson could not ignore the powerful factions that continued to oppose intervention.

The question of whether America should make military and economic preparations for war provided the first issue over which pacifists and interventionists could openly debate. Wilson at first sided with the antipreparedness forces, denouncing the idea of an American military buildup as needless and provocative. As tensions between the United States and Germany grew, however, he changed his mind. In the fall of 1915, he endorsed an ambitious proposal for a large and rapid increase in the nation's armed forces. Amid expressions of outrage from pacifists in Congress and elsewhere, he worked hard to win approval of it, even embarking on a national speaking tour early in 1916 to arouse support for the proposal.

Still, the peace faction wielded considerable political strength, as became clear at the Democratic Convention in the

1916 ELECTION

summer of 1916. The convention became especially enthusiastic when the keynote speaker punctuated his list of Wilson's diplomatic achievements with the chant "What did we do? What did we do? . . . We didn't go to war! We didn't go to war!" That speech helped produce one of the most prominent slogans of Wilson's reelection campaign: "He kept us out of war." During the campaign, Wilson did nothing to discourage those who argued that the Republican candidate, the progressive New York governor Charles Evans Hughes (supported by the bellicose Theodore Roosevelt), was more likely than he to lead the nation into war. And when pro-war rhetoric became particularly heated, Wilson spoke defiantly of the nation being "too proud to fight." He ultimately won reelection by a small margin: fewer than 600,000 popular votes and only 23 electoral votes. The Democrats retained a precarious control over Congress.

A War for Democracy

The election was behind him, and tensions between the United States and Germany remained high. But Wilson still required a justification for American intervention that would unite public opinion and satisfy his own sense of morality. In the end, he created that rationale himself. The United States,

Discussion and Activities

Analyzing Issues After students have read the section "Wilson's Neutrality," ask them to discuss in pairs or small groups how the United States should have responded to German submarine warfare from 1915 to 1917. **WOR** **SOC** **NAT**

Discussion and Activities

Analyzing Issues Have students read the section "Preparedness Versus Pacifism." Ask them to create a Janus person (an outline of a human figure with a face pointing in both directions and divided in half by a vertical line) showing the statements and actions of President Wilson in advocating for neutrality yet preparing for war. **WOR** **SOC** **NAT**

Historical Thinking Skills

Argumentation After students have read the section "A War for Democracy," ask them to create a list of motives for the United States's declaration of war against Germany. Have students write a thesis statement that makes a claim about the most important cause(s) of American entrance into World War I. **WOR** **SOC** **PCE**

Wilson insisted, had no material aims in the conflict. Rather, the nation was committed to using the war as a vehicle for constructing a new world order, one based on some of the same progressive ideals that had motivated reform in America. In a speech before Congress in January 1917, he presented a plan for a postwar order in which the United States would help maintain peace through a permanent league of nations–a peace that would ensure self-determination for all nations, a "peace without victory." These were, Wilson believed, goals worth fighting for if there was sufficient provocation. Provocation came quickly.

In January, after months of inconclusive warfare in the trenches of France, the military leaders of Germany decided on one last dramatic gamble to achieve victory. They launched a series of major assaults on the enemy's lines in France. At the same time, they began unrestricted submarine warfare (against American as well as Allied ships) to cut Britain off from vital supplies. The Allied defenses would collapse, they hoped, before the United States could intervene.

ZIMMERMANN TELEGRAM

The new German policy made American entry into the war virtually inevitable. Two additional events helped clear the way. On February 25, the British gave Wilson a telegram intercepted from the German foreign minister, Arthur Zimmermann, to the government of Mexico. It proposed that in the event of war between Germany and the United States, the Mexicans should join with Germany against the Americans to regain their "lost provinces" (Texas and much of the rest of the American Southwest) when the war was over. Widely publicized by British propagandists and in the American press, the Zimmermann telegram inflamed public opinion and helped build popular sentiment for war. A few weeks later, in March 1917, a revolution in Russia toppled the reactionary czarist regime and replaced it with a new, republican government. The United States would now be spared the embarrassment of allying itself with what most Americans considered a despotic monarchy.

On the rainy evening of April 2, two weeks after German submarines had torpedoed three American ships, Wilson appeared before a joint session of Congress and asked for a declaration of war:

> It is a fearful thing to lead this great peaceful people into war, into the most terrible and disastrous of all wars, civilization itself seeming to be in the balance. But the right is more precious than peace, and we shall fight for the things which we have always carried nearest our hearts–for democracy, for the right of those who submit to authority to have a voice in their own Governments, for the rights and liberties of small nations, for a universal dominion of right by such a concert of free peoples as shall bring peace and safety to all nations and make the world itself at last free.

Even then, opposition remained. For four days, pacifists in Congress carried on a futile struggle. When the declaration of war finally passed on April 6, fifty representatives and six senators voted against it.

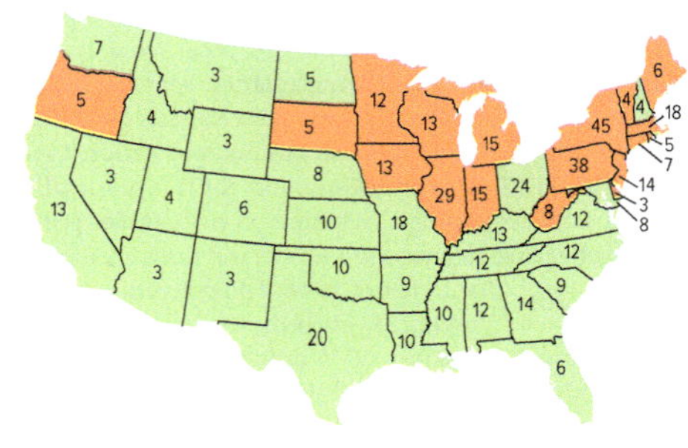

	Candidate (Party)	Electoral Vote	Popular Vote (%)
(orange)	Charles E. Hughes (Republican)	254	8,538,221 (46.2)
(green)	Woodrow Wilson (Democratic)	277	9,129,606 (49.4)
	A. L. Benson (Socialist)	—	585,113 (3.2)
	Other parties (Prohibition; Socialist Labor)	—	233,909

61.6% of electorate voting

ELECTION OF 1916 Woodrow Wilson had good reason to be concerned about his reelection prospects in 1916. He had won only about 42 percent of the vote in 1912, and the Republican Party—which had been divided four years earlier—was now reunited around the popular Charles Evans Hughes. In the end, Wilson won a narrow victory over Hughes with just under 50 percent of the vote and an even narrower margin in the electoral college. Note the striking regional character of his victory.

How did Wilson use the war in Europe to bolster his election prospects?

"WAR WITHOUT STINT"

Armies on both sides in Europe were decimated and exhausted by the time of Woodrow Wilson's declaration of war. The German offensives of early 1917 had failed to produce an end to the struggle, and French and British counteroffensives had accomplished little beyond adding to the casualties. The Allies looked to the United States for help. Wilson, who had called on the nation to wage war "without stint or limit," was ready to oblige.

ENTERING THE WAR

By the spring of 1917, Great Britain was suffering such vast losses from attacks by German submarines–one of every four ships setting sail from British ports never returned–that its ability to continue receiving vital supplies from across the Atlantic was in question. Within weeks of joining the war, a fleet of American destroyers began aiding the British navy in its assault on German submarines. Other American warships

Answers

Election of 1916

Wilson and his supporters suggested that he was more likely to keep the United States out of the war in Europe than his opponent was.

Discussion and Activities

Analyzing Significance After students have read the section "Entering the War," ask them to think about and discuss with a partner why the timing of American entrance into the war was so critical to the Allies. *(Within a few months of American entrance into the war on the Allied side, Russian withdrew.)* **WOR**

escorted merchant vessels across the Atlantic. Americans also helped sow antisubmarine mines in the North Sea. The results were dramatic. Sinkings of Allied ships had totaled nearly 900,000 tons in April 1917; by December, the figure had dropped to 350,000, and by October 1918 to 112,000. The convoys also helped the United States protect its own soldiers en route to Europe. No American troop ship was lost at sea in World War I.

Many Americans had hoped that providing naval assistance alone would be enough to turn the tide in the war, but it quickly became clear that American ground forces would also be necessary to shore up the tottering Allies. Britain and France had few remaining reserves. By early 1918, Russia had withdrawn from the war. After the Bolshevik Revolution in November 1917, the new government, led by V.I. Lenin, negotiated a hasty and costly peace with the Central Powers, thus freeing additional German troops to fight on the western front.

RUSSIAN REVOLUTION

THE AMERICAN EXPEDITIONARY FORCE

There were only about 120,000 soldiers in the army in 1917 and perhaps 80,000 more in the National Guard. Neither group had any combat experience; and except for the small number of officers who had participated in the Spanish-American War two decades before and the Mexican intervention of 1916, few commanders had any experience in battle either.

Some politicians urged a voluntary recruitment process to raise the needed additional forces. Among the advocates of this approach was Theodore Roosevelt, now old and ill, who swallowed his hatred of Wilson and called on him at the White House with an offer to raise a regiment to fight in Europe. Wilson rejected his offer. In the new age of warfare, he sensed, the old tradition of civilians becoming officers and recruiting troops (a common practice in the Civil War), seemed obsolete. The president and his secretary of war, Newton D. Baker, decided that only a national draft could provide the needed men; and despite the protests of those who agreed with House Speaker Champ Clark that "there is precious little difference between a conscript and a convict," he won passage of the Selective Service Act in mid-May. The draft brought nearly 3 million men into the army; another 2 million joined various branches of the armed services voluntarily. Together, they formed what became known as the American Expeditionary Force (AEF).

SELECTIVE SERVICE ACT

It was the first time in American history that any substantial number of soldiers and sailors had fought overseas for an

The Library of Congress (LC-DIG-npcc-00293)

THE WARTIME DRAFT The World War I draft was the first centrally organized effort by the federal government to require military service from its citizens. Although some Americans evaded the draft in 1917 and 1918 (and were reviled by others as "shirkers"), most of those drafted complied with the law.

Discussion and Activities

Analyzing Visuals Have students examine the image "The Wartime Draft." Ask them to identify and discuss in small groups details from the photo that suggest the level of popular support for the war. *(The men pictured appear calm and orderly, and there is no indication of any organized opposition to the draft.)* **WOR** **PCE** **SOC**

Discussion and Activities

Analyzing Issues After students have read the section "American Expeditionary Force," ask them to write a short paragraph describing how the armed forces simultaneously provided opportunities for minorities and women while still denying them equal treatment. **PCE** **SOC**

A WOMEN'S MOTOR CORPS Although the most important new role that women performed during World War I was probably working in factories that male workers had left, many women also enlisted in auxiliary branches of the military—among them these uniformed women who served as drivers for the U.S. Army.

The Library of Congress (LC-DIG-ggbain-26109)

extended period. The military did its best to keep up morale among men who spent most of their time living in the trenches, but it was a difficult task. The trenches were frequently shelled and even when calm were muddy, polluted, and infested with rats. But when soldiers had time away from the front, they were usually less interested in the facilities the Red Cross tried to make available for them than in exploring the bars and brothels of local towns. More than one in every ten American soldiers in Europe contracted venereal disease during World War I, which inspired elaborate official efforts to prevent infection and to treat it when it occurred.

In some respects, the AEF was the most diverse fighting force the United States had ever assembled. For the first time, women were permitted to enlist in the military—more than ten thousand in the navy and a few hundred in the marines. They were not allowed to participate in combat, but they served auxiliary roles in hospitals and offices.

AFRICAN AMERICAN SOLDIERS

Nearly 400,000 African Americans enlisted in or were drafted into the army and navy as well. (The marines would not accept them.) And while most of them performed menial tasks on military bases in the United States, more than 50,000 went to France. African American soldiers served in segregated, all-black units under white commanders; and even in Europe, most of them were assigned to noncombat duty. But some black units fought valiantly in the great offensives of 1918. Most African American soldiers learned to live with the racism they encountered—in part because they hoped their military service would ultimately improve their status. But a few responded to provocations violently. In August 1917, a group of black soldiers in Houston, Texas, subjected to continuing abuse by people in the community, used military weapons to kill seventeen white people. Thirteen African American soldiers were hanged, and another forty were sentenced to life terms in military jails.

Having assembled this first genuinely national army, the War Department permitted the American Psychological Association to study it. The psychologists gave thousands of soldiers new tests designed to measure intelligence: the "Intelligence Quotient," or "IQ," test and other newly designed aptitude tests. In fact, the tests were less effective in measuring intelligence than in measuring education; and they reflected the educational expectations of the white middle-class people who had devised them. Half the white soldiers and the vast majority of the African American soldiers taking the test scored at levels that classified them as "morons." In reality, most of them were simply people who had not had much access to education.

THE MILITARY STRUGGLE

GENERAL JOHN PERSHING

The engagement of these forces in combat was intense but brief. Not until the spring of 1918 were significant numbers of American ground troops available for battle. Eight months later, the war was over. Under the command of General John J. Pershing, who had only recently led the unsuccessful American pursuit of Pancho Villa, the American Expeditionary Force—although it retained a command structure independent of the other Allies—joined the existing Allied forces.

The experience of American troops during World War I was very different from those of other nations, which had already been fighting for nearly four years by the time the U.S. forces arrived in significant numbers. British, French, German, and other troops had by then spent years living in

Discussion and Activities

Analyzing Visuals Have students examine the image "A Women's Motor Corps." Ask them to identify and discuss in pairs or small groups details that shed light on women's participation in the armed forces. *(The women wore uniform skirts, suggesting that they would not participate in combat or heavy labor. The uniformed man in the center of the group is likely the commanding officer of the unit.)* **SOC** **NAT**

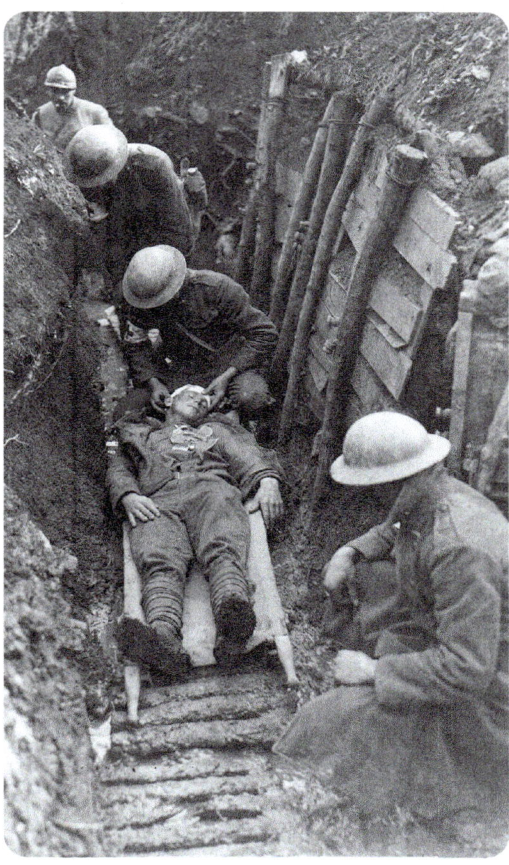

LIFE IN THE TRENCHES For most British, French, German, and ultimately American troops in France, the most debilitating part of World War I was the seeming endlessness of life in the trenches. Some young men lived in these cold, wet, muddy dugouts for months, even years, surrounded by filth, sharing their space with vermin, eating mostly rotten food. Occasional attacks to try to dislodge the enemy from its trenches usually ended in failure and became the scenes of terrible slaughters.

National Archives and Records Administration (530724)

the vast network of trenches that had been dug into the French countryside. Modern weapons made conventional, frontal battles a recipe for mass suicide. Instead, the two sides relied on heavy shelling of each other's trenches and occasional, usually inconclusive, and always murderous assaults across the "no-man's land" dividing them. Life in the trenches was almost indescribably terrible. The trenches were places of extraordinary physical stress and discomfort. They were also places of intense boredom, laced with fear. By the time the Americans arrived, morale on both sides was declining, and many soldiers had come to believe that the war would be virtually endless.

Although the American forces had trench experiences of their own, they were very brief compared to those of the European armies. Instead, the United States tipped the balance of power in the battle and made it possible for the Allies at last to break out of their entrenched positions and advance against the Germans. In early June 1918, American forces at Château-Thierry assisted the French in repelling a German offensive that had brought German forces within fifty miles of Paris. Six weeks later, after over a million American troops had flooded into France, the Americans helped turn away another assault, at Rheims, farther south. By July 18, the Allies had halted the German advance and were beginning a successful offensive of their own.

CHÂTEAU-THIERRY

On September 26, the American fighting force joined a large assault against the Germans in the Argonne Forest that lasted nearly seven weeks. By the end of October, despite terrible weather, they had helped push the Germans back toward their own border and had cut the enemy's major supply lines to the front.

MEUSE-ARGONNE OFFENSIVE

Faced with an invasion of their own country, German military leaders now began to seek an armistice—an immediate cease-fire that would, they hoped, serve as a prelude to negotiations among the belligerents. Pershing wanted to drive on into Germany itself; but other Allied leaders, after first insisting on terms that made the agreement little different from a surrender, accepted the German proposal. On November 11, 1918, the Great War shuddered to a close.

THE NEW TECHNOLOGY OF WARFARE

World War I was a proving ground for a range of military and other technologies. The trench warfare that characterized the conflict was necessary because of the enormous destructive power of newly improved machine guns and higher-powered artillery. It was no longer feasible to send troops out into an open field, or even to allow them to camp in the open. The new weaponry would slaughter them in an instant. Trenches sheltered troops while allowing limited, and usually inconclusive, fighting. But technology overtook the trenches, too, as mobile weapons—tanks and flamethrowers—proved capable of piercing entrenched positions. Most terrible of all, new chemical weapons—poisonous mustard gas, which required troops to carry gas masks at all times—made it possible to attack entrenched soldiers without direct combat.

The new forms of technological warfare required elaborate maintenance. Faster machine guns needed more ammunition. Motorized vehicles required fuel and spare parts and mechanics capable of servicing them. The logistical difficulties of supply became a major factor in planning tactics and strategy. Late in the war, when advancing toward Germany, Allied armies frequently had to stop for days at a time to wait for their equipment to catch up with them.

Discussion and Activities

Explaining Significance After students have read the section "The Military Struggle," ask them to write a short paragraph about how important the role played by the United States was in the closing stages of the fighting on the Western Front. Remind students to use evidence from the text to support their argument. **WOR**

Discussion and Activities

Analyzing Points of View Have students examine the image "Life in the Trenches." Ask them to write a short letter or journal entry from the point of view of an American soldier describing the experiences of trench warfare. If writing a letter, have students keep in mind how soldiers might want to shield loved ones from some of the harsher realities of their situation. **SOC**

Discussion and Activities

Historical Evidence and Argumentation
After students have read the section "The New Technology of Warfare," ask them to create a chart listing new weapons employed in World War I and their effects. Have students discuss in small groups which new weapons had the greatest impact on the outcome of the war. **WOR** **WXT**

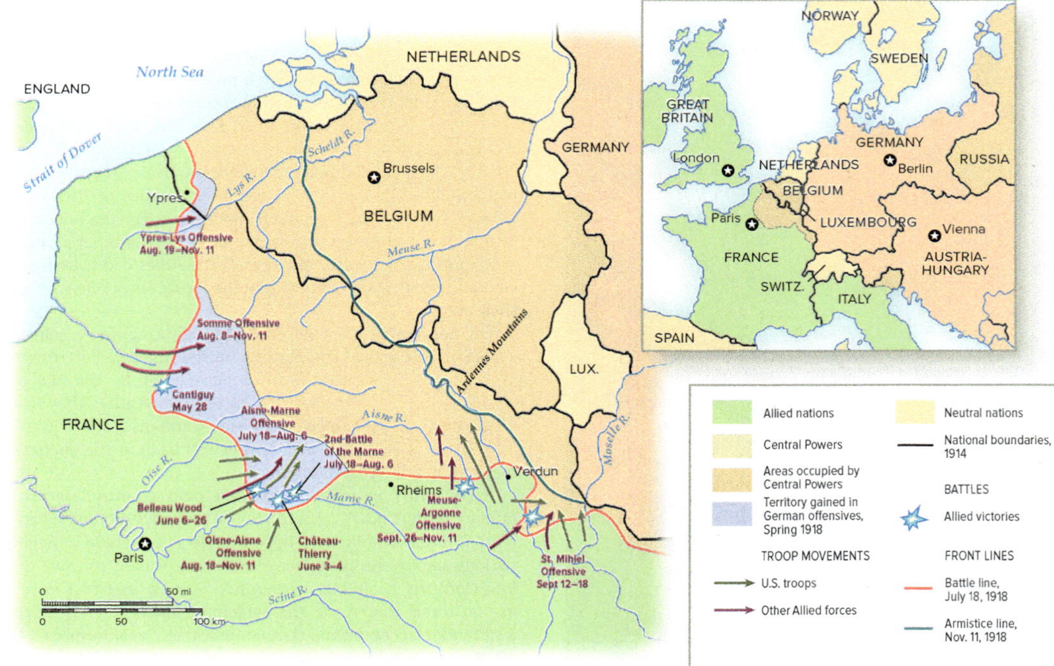

AMERICA IN WORLD WAR I: THE WESTERN FRONT, 1918 These maps show the principal battles in which the United States participated in the last year of World War I. The small map on the upper right helps locate the area of conflict within the larger European landscape. The larger map at left shows the long, snaking red line of the western front in France—stretching from the border between France and southwest Germany all the way to the northeast border between Belgium and France. Along that vast line, the two sides had been engaged in murderous, inconclusive warfare for over three years by the time the Americans arrived. Beginning in the spring and summer of 1918, bolstered by reinforcements from the United States, the Allies began to win a series of important victories that finally enabled them to begin pushing the Germans back. American troops, as this map makes clear, were decisive along the southern part of the front.

At what point did the Germans begin to consider putting an end to the war?

World War I was the first conflict in which airplanes played a significant role. The planes themselves were relatively simple and not very maneuverable; but anti-aircraft technology was not yet highly developed either, so their effectiveness was still considerable. Planes began to be constructed to serve various functions: bombers, fighters (planes that would engage in "dogfights" with other planes), and reconnaissance aircraft.

The most "modern" part of the military during World War I was the navy. New battleships emerged–of which the British *Dreadnought* was perhaps the most visible example–that made use of new technologies such as turbine propulsion, hydraulic gun controls, electric light and power, wireless telegraphy, and advanced navigational aids. Submarines, which had made a brief appearance in the American Civil War, now became significant weapons (as the German U-boat campaign in 1915 and 1916 made clear). The new submarines were driven by diesel engines, which had the advantage of being more compact than a steam engine and whose fuel was less explosive than that of a gasoline engine. The diesel engine also had a much greater range than ships powered by other fuels.

The new technologies were to a large degree responsible for the most stunning and horrible characteristic of World War I–its appalling level of casualties. A million men representing the British Empire (Britain, Canada, Australia, India, and others) died. France lost 1.7 million men; Germany, 2 million; the former Austro-Hungarian Empire, 1.5 million; Italy, 460,000; and Russia, 1.7 million. The number of Turkish dead, which was surely large, was never known. In Britain, one-third of the men born between 1892 and 1895 died in the war. Similarly terrible percentages could be calculated for other warring nations. Even greater numbers of men returned home with

HIGH CASUALTY RATES

Answers

America in World War I: The Western Front, 1918

Germany considered seeking an end to the war after the failure of their spring offensive in 1918.

injuries, some of them permanently crippling. The United States, which entered the war near its end and became engaged only in the last successful offensives, suffered very light casualties in comparison—112,000 dead, half of them victims of influenza, not battle. But the American casualties were very high in the battles in which U.S. troops were centrally involved.

THE WAR AND AMERICAN SOCIETY

The American experience in World War I was relatively brief, but it had profound effects on the government, the economy, and society. Mobilizing an industrial economy for total war required an unprecedented degree of government involvement in industry, agriculture, and other areas. It also required, many Americans believed, a strenuous effort to ensure the loyalty and commitment of the people.

ORGANIZING THE ECONOMY FOR WAR

By the time the war ended, the U.S. government had spent $32 billion for expenses directly related to the conflict. This was a staggering sum by the standards of the time. The entire federal budget had seldom exceeded $1 billion before 1915, and as recently as 1910 the nation's entire gross national product had been only $35 billion. To finance the war, the government relied on two devices. First, it launched a major drive to solicit loans from the American people by selling "Liberty Bonds" to the public. By 1920, the sale of bonds, to both individuals and institutions, accompanied by elaborate patriotic appeals, had produced $23 billion. At the same time, new taxes were bringing in an additional sum of nearly $10 billion—some from levies on the "excess profits" of corporations, much from new, steeply graduated income and inheritance taxes that ultimately rose as high as 70 percent in some brackets.

FINANCING THE WAR

An even greater challenge was organizing the economy to meet war needs. In 1916, Wilson established a Council of National Defense, composed of members of his cabinet, and a Civilian Advisory Commission, which set up local defense councils in every state and locality. Economic mobilization, according to this first plan, was to rest on a dispersal of power to local communities.

But this early administrative structure soon proved unworkable. Some members of the Council of National Defense, many of them disciples of the social engineering gospel of Thorstein Veblen and the "scientific management" principles of Frederick Winslow Taylor, urged a centralized approach. Instead of dividing the economy geographically, they proposed dividing it functionally by organizing a series of planning bodies, each to supervise a specific sector of the economy. The administrative structure that slowly emerged from such proposals was dominated by a series of "war boards," one to oversee the railroads, one to supervise fuel supplies (largely coal), another to handle food (a board that helped elevate to prominence the brilliant young engineer and business executive Herbert Hoover). The boards generally succeeded in meeting essential war needs without paralyzing the domestic economy.

At the center of the effort to rationalize the economy was the War Industries Board (WIB), an agency created in July 1917 to coordinate government purchases of military supplies. Casually organized at first, it stumbled badly until March 1918, when Wilson restructured it and placed it under the control of the Wall Street financier Bernard Baruch. From then on, the board wielded powers greater (in theory at least) than any other government agency had ever possessed. Baruch decided which factories would convert to the production of which war materials and set prices for the goods they produced. When materials were scarce, Baruch decided to whom they should go. When corporations were competing for government contracts, he chose among them. He was, it seemed, providing the centralized regulation of the economy that some progressives had long urged.

WAR INDUSTRIES BOARD

In reality, the celebrated efficiency of the WIB was something of a myth. The agency was, in fact, plagued by mismanagement and inefficiency. Its apparent success rested in large part on the sheer extent of American resources and productive capacities. Nor was the WIB in any real sense an example of state control of the economy. Baruch viewed himself as the partner of business; and within the WIB, businessmen themselves—the so-called dollar-a-year men, who took paid leave from their corporate jobs and worked for the government for a token salary—supervised the affairs of the private economy. Baruch ensured that manufacturers who coordinated their efforts with his goals would be exempt from antitrust laws. He helped major industries earn enormous profits from their efforts.

The effort to organize the economy for war produced some spectacular accomplishments: Hoover's efficient organization of domestic food supplies, William McAdoo's success in untangling the railroads, and others. In some areas, however, progress was so slow that the war was over before many of the supplies ordered for it were ready. Even so, many leaders of both government and industry emerged from the experience convinced of the advantages of a close, cooperative relationship between the public and private sectors. Some hoped to continue the wartime experiments in peacetime.

LESSONS OF THE MANAGED ECONOMY

LABOR AND THE WAR

The growing link between the public and private sectors extended, although in greatly different form, to labor. The National War Labor Board, established in April 1918 to resolve labor disputes, pressured industry to grant important concessions to workers: an eight-hour day, the maintenance of

Discussion and Activities

Speculating Have students read the section "High Casualty Rates." Ask them to graph the casualties from the leading Allied and Central Powers. Have students discuss in pairs or small groups how the different casualty figures might influence how different countries might approach peace negotiations. *(Allied countries with higher casualty numbers might demand greater concessions from the defeated enemy powers.)* **WOR**

Discussion and Activities

Historical Developments and Argumentation Have students read the section "Organizing the Economy for War." Ask them to discuss as a class how the war transformed the economy. **WXT** **NAT**

Reasoning Processes

Continuity and Change After students have read the section "Labor and the War," ask them to discuss as a class how the war impacted relations between labor and management. Have students consider which changes were the most important for labor. **WXT**

minimal living standards, equal pay for women doing equal work, recognition of the right of unions to organize and bargain collectively. In return, it insisted that workers forgo all strikes and that employers not engage in lockouts. Membership in labor unions increased by more than 1.5 million between 1917 and 1919.

The war provided workers with important, if usually temporary, gains. But it did not stop labor militancy. That was particularly clear in the West, where the Western Federation of Miners staged a series of strikes to improve the terrible conditions in the underground mines. The bloodiest of them occurred just before the war. In Ludlow, Colorado, in 1914, workers (mostly Italians, Greeks, and Slavs) walked out of coal mines owned by John D. Rockefeller. Joined by their wives and daughters, they continued the strike even after they had been evicted from company housing and had moved into hastily erected tents. The state militia was called into the town to protect the mines, but in fact (as was often the case), it actually worked to help employers defeat the strikers.

Joined by strikebreakers and others, the militia attacked the workers' tent colony; and in the battle that followed, thirty-nine people died, among them eleven children. But these events, which became known as the Ludlow Massacre, were only precursors to continued conflict in the mines that the war itself did little to discourage.

LUDLOW MASSACRE

ECONOMIC AND SOCIAL RESULTS OF THE WAR

Whatever its other effects, the war helped produce a remarkable period of economic growth in the United States–a boom that began in 1914 (when European demands for American products began to increase) and accelerated after 1917

ON THE TOWN IN HARLEM Harlem, once a suburb of Manhattan where middle-class commuters lived, became in the early twentieth century the center of African American life in New York. The Lafayette Theatre was the first New York theater to desegregate, in as early as 1912. African American theatergoers could sit in the orchestra section rather than just in the balcony as was the practice in other New York theaters.

Discussion and Activities

Analyzing Points of View Have students examine the image "On the Town in Harlem." Ask them to write a short newspaper article about the night life in Harlem based on the image. Have students consider how the experience would have been different from that in other clubs at the time. **ARC** **SOC**

WOMEN INDUSTRIAL WORKERS
In World War II, such women were often called "Rosie the Riveter." Their presence in these previously all-male work environments was no less startling to Americans during World War I. These women are shown working with acetylene torches to bevel armor plate for tanks.

(in response to demand from the United States war effort). Industrial production soared, and manufacturing activity expanded in regions that had previously had relatively little of it. The shipbuilding industry, for example, grew rapidly on the West Coast (enabled by the Panama Canal). Employment increased dramatically; and because so many white men were away at war, new opportunities for female, African American, Mexican, and Asian workers appeared. Some workers experienced a significant growth in income, but inflation cut into the wage increases and often produced a net loss in purchasing power. The agricultural economy profited from the war as well. Farm prices rose to their highest levels in decades, and agricultural production increased dramatically as a result.

One of the most important social changes of the war years was the migration of hundreds of thousands of African Americans from the rural South into northern industrial cities. It became known as the "Great Migration." Like most migrations, it was a result of both a "push" and a "pull." The push was the poverty, indebtedness, racism, and violence many black men and women experienced in the South. The pull was the prospect of factory jobs in the urban North and the opportunity to live in communities where African Americans could enjoy more freedom and autonomy. In the labor-scarce economy of the war years, northern factory owners dispatched agents to the South to recruit African American workers. Black newspapers advertised the prospects for employment in the North. And perhaps most important, those who migrated sent word back to friends and families of the opportunities they encountered—which explains the heavy concentration of migrants from a single area of the South in certain cities in the North. In Chicago, for example, the more than 70,000 new black residents came disproportionately from a few areas of Alabama and Mississippi.

"GREAT MIGRATION"

The result was a dramatic growth in black communities in northern industrial cities such as New York, Chicago, Cleveland, and Detroit. Some older, more established African American residents of these cities were unsettled by these new arrivals, with their country ways and their revivalistic religion; many people in the existing African American communities considered the newcomers coarse and feared that their presence would increase their own vulnerability to white racism. But the movement could not be stopped. New churches sprang up in black neighborhoods (many of them simple storefronts, from which self-proclaimed preachers searched for congregations). Low-paid black workers crowded into inadequate housing. As the black communities expanded, they inevitably began to rub up against white neighborhoods, with occasionally violent results. In East St. Louis, Illinois, a white mob attacked a black neighborhood on July 2, 1917, burned down many houses, and shot the residents of some of them as they fled. As many as forty African Americans died.

RACE RIOTS

For American women, black and white, the war meant new opportunities for employment. A million or more women worked in a wide range of industrial jobs that, in peacetime, were considered male preserves: steel, munitions, trucking, public transportation. Most of them had been working in other, lower-paying jobs. But whatever changes the war brought were temporary ones. As soon as the war was over, almost all of the women working in previously male industrial jobs quit or were fired; in fact, the percentage of women working for wages actually declined between 1910 and 1920. The government had created the Women in Industry Board to oversee the movement of these women into the jobs left behind by men. After the war, the board became the Women's Bureau, a permanent agency dedicated to protecting the interests of women in the workforce.

Discussion and Activities

Historical Significance and Argumentation After students have read the section "Economic and Social Results of the War," ask them to create a T-chart listing economic and social effects of World War I in the United States. Have students identify which category indicates greater change. **NAT** **ARC** **SOC** **WXT**

Reasoning Processes

Continuity and Change Have students examine the image "Women Industrial Workers." Ask them to discuss as a class how the image demonstrates continuities or changes over time in the role of women in the workplace. **WXT** **SOC**

Historical Thinking Skills

Argumentation Have students read the section "Woman's Peace Party." Ask them to discuss in small groups why they think some members of the Woman's Peace Party began to support the war effort once the United States declared war. *(Opposition to the war could be seen as unpatriotic; suffrage leaders saw support for the war as a way to gain support for the right of women to vote.)* **SOC** **PCE**

THE FUTILE SEARCH FOR SOCIAL UNITY

The idea of unity–not only in the direction of the economy but in the nation's social purpose as well–had been the dream of many progressives for decades. To them, the war seemed to offer an unmatched opportunity for America to close ranks behind a great common cause. In the process, they hoped, society could achieve a lasting sense of collective purpose. The dream of social unity helped drive many efforts–the peace movement, the labor movement, and even the government. But it also drove a period of political and social oppression and an egregious violation of civil liberties.

The Peace Movement

Government leaders, and many others, realized that public sentiment about American involvement in the war had been deeply divided before April 1917 and remained so even after the declaration of war.

The peace movement in the United States before 1917 had many constituencies: German Americans, Irish Americans, religious pacifists (Quakers, Mennonites, and others), intellectuals and groups on the left such as the Socialist Party and the Industrial Workers of the World, all of whom considered the war a meaningless battle among capitalist nations for commercial supremacy–an opinion many others, in America and Europe, later came to share. But the most active and widespread peace activism came from the women's movement. In 1915, Carrie Chapman Catt, a leader of the fight for woman suffrage, helped create the Woman's Peace Party, with a small but active membership. As the war in Europe intensified, the party's efforts to keep the United States from intervening grew.

Woman's Peace Party

Women peace activists were sharply divided once America entered the war in 1917. The National American Woman Suffrage Association, the largest women's organization, supported the war and, more than that, presented itself as a patriotic organization dedicated to advancing the war effort. Its membership grew dramatically as a result. Catt, who was among those who abandoned the peace cause, now began calling for woman suffrage as a "war measure," to ensure that women (whose work was essential to the war effort) would feel fully a part of the nation. But many other women refused to support the war even after April 1917. Among them were Jane Addams, who was widely reviled as a result, and Charlotte Perkins Gilman, a leading feminist activist.

Women peace activists shared many of the same objections to the war as did the members of the Socialist Party (to which some of them belonged). But some criticized the war on other grounds as well, arguing that as "the mother half of humanity," they had a special moral and maternal basis for their pacifism.

Maternal Opposition to War

Selling the War and Suppressing Dissent

World War I was not as popular among the American people as World War II would be, but most of the country supported the intervention once it began. In communities across the nation, there were outbursts of fervent patriotism, floods of voluntary enlistments in the military, and greatly increased displays of patriotism. Women joined their local Red Cross in an effort to contribute to the war effort. Children raised money for war bonds in their schools. Churches included prayers for the president and the troops in their services. And the war also gave a large boost to the wave of religious revivalism that had been growing for a decade before 1917; revivalism, in turn, became a source of support for the war. Billy Sunday, the leading revivalist of his time, dropped his early opposition to intervention in 1917 and became a fervent champion of the American military effort.

Nevertheless, government leaders (and many others) remained deeply concerned about the significant minorities who continued to oppose the war even after the United States entered the conflict. Many believed that a crucial prerequisite for victory

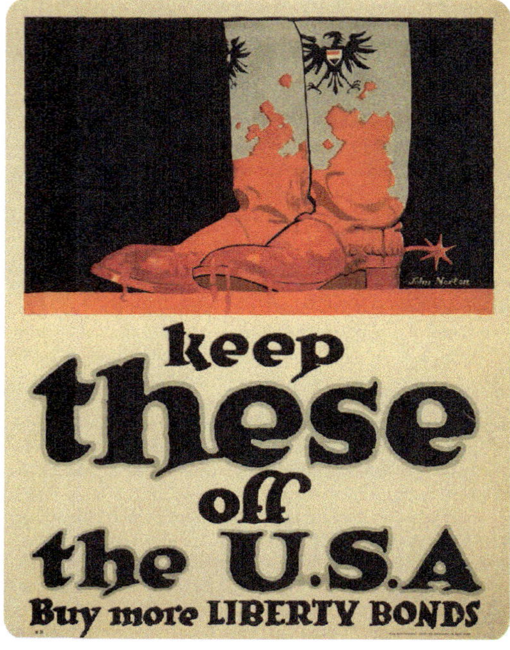

WARTIME PROPAGANDA This poster—one of many lurid images of imperial Germany used by the U.S. government to generate enthusiasm for American involvement in World War I—shows bloodstained German boots with the German eagle clearly visible. The demonization of Germany was at the heart of government efforts to portray the war to Americans.

Reasoning Processes

Comparing Have students read the section "Maternal Opposition to War." Ask them to create a Venn diagram comparing the views of women anti-war advocates with other groups, such as the Socialist Party and the Industrial Workers of the World. **WOR** **WXT** **PCE**

CONSIDER THE SOURCE

RACE, GENDER, AND MILITARY SERVICE

Much can be learned about a society's values from how it handles the raising of an army. In wartime, nations typically clarify the terms of citizenship and service–asking some people to fight, others to stay home, and appealing to the public for participation and support. The government sets the terms of service, but they must align with popular values to be successful.

During World War I, as part of the broad national effort to explain, justify, and fight the war, the government disseminated the two posters below (the "1917-1918" documents). The first poster was part of a recruiting drive for the U.S. Navy; the second was part of a campaign to sell "liberty loans," interest-bearing bonds that funded roughly two-thirds of the war's $32 billion price tag. Both images suggest that women not only served in the military and industrial sectors–they also served as *symbols*.

By the time of the war on terrorism of the early twenty-first century, the landscape of military recruitment had changed dramatically. The new war was more limited in scale than World War I, and the draft had been suspended in 1973, converting the military to an all-volunteer force. This put a high premium on recruiting and marketing–and the materials used for those purposes remained just as illuminating as ever (see the "2006-2014" documents). In 2006, the U.S. Army launched its "Army Strong" campaign to communicate the message that the army builds not only physical but also mental and emotional strengths in its recruits. The second images shows the welcoming attitude of today's army.

WORLD WAR I—1917–1918

Wartime Posters

Discussion and Activities

Making Connections Have students read the section "Race, Gender, and Military Service." Ask them to discuss in small groups how they have experienced armed forces recruiting. *(Recruiters meeting with students on high school campuses; letters and emails addressed to high school students explaining benefits of enlistment, such as job training and money for college.)*

Historical Thinking Skills

Argumentation Have students examine the WWI posters. Ask them to design a poster that encourages women to take a more active role in supporting or opposing the American war effort. **ARC** **WXT** **SOC**

AP Exam Tip

The AP Exam requires students to identify and explain a source's point of view, purpose, historical situation, and/or audience. One way students can identify the point of view of a source is to evaluate its motives or biases.

Historical Thinking Skills

Sourcing and Situation Have students practice the tip by examining each of the four posters in the feature. Ask students to discuss in small groups examples from each poster that explain what the purpose of the poster is. *(Enlistment through an appeal to masculinity; supporting the war effort financially; enlistment through training opportunities; enlistment through opportunities to advance education.)* **NAT** **SOC** **WXT**

WAR ON TERRORISM—2006–2014

Army Recruitment and Marketing

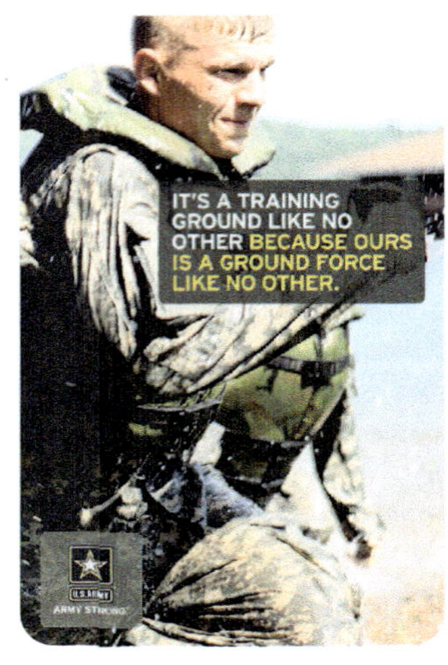

IT'S A TRAINING GROUND LIKE NO OTHER BECAUSE OURS IS A GROUND FORCE LIKE NO OTHER.
U.S. ARMY

ANALYZING SOURCES

Questions assume cumulative content knowledge from this chapter and previous chapters.

1. The World War I recruiting posters depict only white people, despite the fact that many African Americans and ethnic minorities served in World War I. What does that difference say about mainstream attitudes toward race and ethnicity during World War I?
   (A) African Americans were integrated with white society
   (B) white people were viewed as superior and the legitimate citizens of the nation
   (C) for recruitment purposes, all races were considered part of the "white" population
   (D) white people were viewed as equally desirable as recruits from minority groups
2. In comparing the way the genders are portrayed between the posters from the different time periods, which best describes the general societal understanding of gender roles in the early 20th century?
   (A) There was a general expectation that women would enlist in addition to men.
   (B) Women were viewed as equal to men.
   (C) Men played subordinate roles to women.
   (D) Women were generally expected to embody virtue.
3. What do the different styles of persuasion between the posters of the two time periods suggest about changing popular attitudes towards military enlistment from the early 20th century to the early 21st century?
   (A) a continuation of the idea of military enlistment as one of patriotic duty
   (B) a change from a romantic idea of duty to one of practical personal benefit and opportunity
   (C) a change from the idea of military enlistment as protecting the nation to one of adventure
   (D) a continuation of the ideal of practical benefit for the individual

Answers

Consider the Source

1. B; **2.** D; **3.** B

was an energetic, even coercive, effort to unite public opinion behind the military effort.

The most conspicuous government effort to rally public support was a vast propaganda campaign orchestrated by the new Committee on Public Information (CPI). It was directed by the Denver journalist George Creel, who spoke openly of the importance of achieving social unity. The CPI supervised the distribution of tons of pro-war literature (75 million pieces of printed material). War posters plastered the walls of offices, shops, theaters, schools, churches, and homes. Newspapers dutifully printed official government accounts of the reasons for the war and the prospects for quick victory. Creel encouraged reporters to exercise "self-censorship" when reporting news about the conflict.

CPI

As the war continued, the CPI's tactics became increasingly crude. Government-promoted posters and films became lurid portrayals of the savagery of the Germans, bearing such titles as *The Prussian Cur* and *The Kaiser: Beast of Berlin*, encouraging Americans to think of the German people as something close to savages.

The government soon began more coercive efforts to suppress dissent. The CPI ran full-page advertisements in popular magazines like the *Saturday Evening Post* urging citizens to notify the Justice Department when they encountered "the man who spreads the pessimistic stories . . . , cries for peace, or belittles our efforts to win the war." The Espionage Act of 1917 gave the government new tools with which to respond to such reports. It created stiff penalties for spying, sabotage, or obstruction of the war effort (crimes that were often broadly defined); and it empowered the Post Office Department to ban "seditious" material from the mails. Sedition, Postmaster General Albert Sidney Burleson said, included statements that might "impugn the motives of the government and thus encourage insubordination," anything that suggested "that the government is controlled by Wall Street or munitions manufacturers, or any other special interests." He included in that category all publications of the Socialist Party.

ESPIONAGE ACT

More repressive were two measures of 1918: the Sabotage Act of April 20 and the Sedition Act of May 16. These bills expanded the meaning of the Espionage Act to make illegal any public expression of opposition to the war; in practice, it allowed officials to prosecute anyone who criticized the president or the government.

SEDITION ACT

The most frequent targets of the new legislation (and one of the reasons for its enactment in the first place) were such anticapitalist groups (and antiwar) groups as the Socialist Party and the Industrial Workers of the World (IWW). Many Americans had favored the repression of socialists and radicals even before the war; the wartime policies now made it possible to move against them legally. Eugene V. Debs, the humane leader of the Socialist Party and an opponent of the war, was sentenced to ten years in prison in 1918. Only a pardon by President Warren G. Harding ultimately won his release in 1921. Big Bill Haywood and members of the IWW were especially energetically prosecuted. Only by fleeing to the Soviet Union did Haywood avoid long imprisonment. More than 1,500 people were arrested in 1918 for the crime of criticizing the government.

State and local governments, corporations, universities, and private citizens contributed as well to the climate of repression. Vigilante mobs sprang up to "discipline" those who dared challenge the war. A dissident Protestant clergyman in Cincinnati was pulled from his bed one night by a mob, dragged to a nearby hillside, and whipped "in the name of the women and children of Belgium." An IWW organizer in Montana was seized by a mob and hanged from a railroad bridge.

REPRESSING DISSENT

A cluster of citizens' groups emerged to mobilize "respectable" members of their communities to root out disloyalty. The American Protective League, probably the largest of such groups, enlisted the services of 250,000 people, who served as "agents"—prying into the activities and thoughts of their neighbors, opening mail, tapping telephones, and in general attempting to impose unity of opinion on their communities. It received government funds to support its work. Attorney General Thomas W. Gregory, a particularly avid supporter of repressing dissent, described the league and similar organizations approvingly as "patriotic organizations." Other vigilante organizations—the National Security League, the Boy Spies of America, the American Defense Society—performed much the same function.

There were many victims of such activities: socialists, labor activists, female pacifists. But the most frequent targets of repression were immigrants: Irish Americans because of their historic animosity toward the British, Jewish people because many had expressed opposition to the anti-Semitic policies of the Russian government, and others. "Loyalist" citizens' groups policed immigrant neighborhoods. They monitored meetings and even conversations for signs of disloyalty. Even some settlement house workers, many of whom had once championed ethnic diversity, contributed to such efforts. The director of the National Security League described the origins of the anti-immigrant sentiment, which was producing growing support for what many citizens were now calling "100 percent Americanism":

"100 PERCENT AMERICANISM"

> The melting pot has not melted. . . . There are vast communities in the nation thinking today not in terms of America, but in terms of Old World prejudices, theories, and animosities.

The greatest target of abuse was the German American community. Most German Americans supported the American war effort once it began. Still, public opinion turned bitterly hostile. A campaign to purge society of all things German quickly gathered speed, at times assuming ludicrous forms. Sauerkraut was renamed "liberty cabbage." Frankfurters became "liberty sausage." Performances of German music were frequently banned. German books were removed from the shelves of libraries. Courses in the German language were removed from school curricula; the California Board of Education called it "a language that disseminates the ideals of autocracy, brutality, and hatred." Germans were routinely fired from jobs in war

Historical Thinking Skills

Argumentation Have students read the section "CPI." Ask them to write a short speech or elevator pitch either demonizing the enemy or encouraging support of the war effort as if they were working for the Committee for Public Information. **ARC** **SOC** **NAT**

Discussion and Activities

Speculating After students have read the section "Repressing Dissent," ask them to discuss as a class whether the Espionage Act, the Sedition Act, or the work of organizations like the American Protective League would have been effective at suppressing dissent or might have stirred up more resentment. **WOR** **SOC**

Historical Thinking Skills

Argumentation Have students read the section "The Fourteen Points." Ask them to write a short letter to President Wilson from the point of view of an American citizen or soldier advising the president on what to ask for in peace negotiations. **WOR** **NAT**

industries, lest they "sabotage" important tasks. Some were fired from positions entirely unrelated to the war–for example, Karl Muck, the German-born conductor of the Boston Symphony Orchestra. Vigilante groups routinely subjected German Americans to harassment and beatings, including a lynching in southern Illinois in 1918. Relatively few Americans favored such extremes, but many came to agree with the belief of the eminent psychologist G. Stanley Hall that "there is something fundamentally wrong with the Teutonic soul."

THE SEARCH FOR A NEW WORLD ORDER

Woodrow Wilson had led the nation into war promising a more just and stable peace at its conclusion. Well before the armistice, he was preparing to lead the fight for what he considered a democratic postwar settlement.

THE FOURTEEN POINTS

On January 8, 1918, Wilson appeared before Congress to present the principles for which he claimed the nation was fighting. The war aims had fourteen distinct provisions, widely known as the Fourteen Points; but they fell into three broad categories. First, Wilson's proposals contained eight specific recommendations for adjusting postwar boundaries and for establishing new nations to replace the defunct Austro-Hungarian and Ottoman Empires. Those recommendations reflected his belief in the right of all peoples to self-determination. Second, there were five general principles to govern international conduct in the future: freedom of the seas, open covenants instead of secret treaties, reductions in armaments, free trade, and impartial mediation of colonial claims. Finally, there was a proposal for a league of nations that would help implement these new principles and territorial adjustments and resolve future controversies.

WILSON'S IDEALISTIC VISION

There were serious flaws in Wilson's proposals. He provided no formula for deciding how to implement the "national self-determination" he promised for subjugated peoples. He said little about economic rivalries and their effect on international relations, even though such economic tensions had been in large part responsible for the war. Nevertheless, Wilson's international vision quickly came to enchant not only much of his own generation (in both America and Europe), but also members of generations to come. It reflected his belief, strongly rooted in the ideas of progressivism, that the world was as capable of just and efficient government as were individual nations; that once the international community accepted certain basic principles of conduct, and once it constructed modern institutions to implement them, the human race could live in peace.

The Fourteen Points were also an answer to the new Bolshevik government in Russia. In December 1917, Lenin had issued his own statement of war aims, strikingly similar to Wilson's. Wilson's announcement, which came just three weeks later, was, among other things, a last-minute (and unsuccessful) effort to persuade the Bolshevik regime to keep Russia in the war. But Wilson also realized that Lenin was now a competitor in the effort to lead the postwar order. And he announced the Fourteen Points in part to ensure that the world looked to the United States, not Russia, for guidance.

LENIN'S CHALLENGE

EARLY OBSTACLES

Wilson was confident, as the war neared its end, that popular support would enable him to win Allied approval of his peace plan. But there were ominous signs both at home and abroad that his path might be more difficult than he expected. In Europe, leaders of the Allied forces, many resenting what they considered Wilson's tone of moral superiority, were preparing to resist him even before the armistice was signed. They had reacted unhappily when Wilson refused to make the United States their "ally" but had kept his distance as an "associate" of his European partners, keeping American military forces separate from the Allied armies they were joining.

Most of all, however, Britain and France, having suffered incalculable losses in their long years of war, and having stored up an enormous reserve of bitterness toward Germany as a result, were in no mood for a benign and generous peace. The British prime minister, David Lloyd George, insisted for a time that the German kaiser be captured and executed. He and Georges Clemenceau, president of France, remained determined to the end to gain something from the struggle to compensate them for the catastrophe they had suffered.

ALLIED INTRANSIGENCE

At the same time, Wilson was encountering problems at home. In 1918, with the war almost over, he unwisely appealed to the American voters to support his peace plans by electing Democrats to Congress in the November elections. A Republican victory, he declared, would be "interpreted on the other side of the water as a repudiation of my leadership." Days later, the Republicans captured majorities in both houses. Domestic economic troubles, more than international issues, had been the most important factor in the voting; but because of the president's ill-timed appeal, the results damaged his ability to claim broad popular support for his peace plans.

The leaders of the Republican Party, in the meantime, were developing their own reasons for opposing Wilson. Some were angry that he had tried to make the 1918 balloting a referendum on his war aims, especially since many Republicans had been supporting the Fourteen Points. Wilson further antagonized them when he refused to appoint any important Republicans to the negotiating team that would represent the United States at the peace conference in Paris. But the president considered such matters unimportant. Only one member of the American negotiating party would have any real authority: Wilson himself. And once he had produced a just and moral treaty, he believed, the weight of world and American opinion would compel his enemies to support him.

Discussion and Activities

Analyzing Perspectives Have students read the section "Early Obstacles." Ask them to discuss as a class whether President Wilson could have or should have modified his stance on the Fourteen Points to produce a satisfactory peace agreement for the United States. **WOR** **NAT**

THE PARIS PEACE CONFERENCE

Wilson arrived in Europe to a welcome such as few men in history have experienced. To the war-weary people of the Continent, he was nothing less than a savior, the man who would create a new and better world. When he entered Paris on December 13, 1918, he was greeted, some observers claimed, by the largest crowd in the history of France. The negotiations themselves, however, proved less satisfying.

The principal figures in the negotiations were the leaders of the victorious Allied nations: David Lloyd George representing Great Britain; Georges Clemenceau representing France; Vittorio Orlando, the prime minister of Italy; and Wilson, who hoped to dominate them all. From the beginning, the atmosphere of idealism Wilson had sought to create was competing with a spirit of national aggrandizement. There was, moreover, a strong sense of unease about the unstable situation in eastern Europe and the threat of communism. Russia, whose new Bolshevik government was still fighting "White" counterrevolutionaries, was unrepresented in Paris; but the radical threat it seemed to pose to Western governments was never far from the minds of any of the delegates, least of all Wilson himself.

THE BIG FOUR

Indeed, not long before he came to Paris, Wilson ordered the landing of American troops in the Soviet Union. They were there, he claimed, to help a group of 60,000 Czech soldiers trapped in Russia to escape. But the Americans soon became involved, at least indirectly, in assisting the White Russians (the anti-Bolsheviks) in their fight against the new regime. Some American troops remained in Russia as late as April 1920. Lenin's regime survived these challenges. Wilson refused to recognize the new government. Diplomatic relations between the United States and the Soviet Union were not restored until 1933.

In the tense and often vindictive atmosphere of the negotiations in Paris, Wilson was unable to win approval of many of the broad principles he had espoused: freedom of the seas, which the British refused even to discuss; free trade; "open covenants openly arrived at" (the Paris negotiations themselves were often conducted in secret). Despite his support for "impartial mediation" of colonial claims, he was forced to accept a transfer of German colonies in the Pacific to Japan; the British had promised them in exchange for Japanese assistance in the war. Wilson's pledge of "national self-determination" for all peoples suffered numerous assaults. Economic and strategic demands were constantly coming into conflict with the principle of cultural nationalism.

WILSON'S RETREAT

The treaty departed most conspicuously from Wilson's ideals on the question of reparations. As the conference began, the president opposed demanding compensation from the defeated Central Powers. The other Allied leaders, however, were insistent, and slowly Wilson gave way and accepted the principle of reparations, the specific sum to be set later by a commission. That figure, established in 1921, was $56 billion, supposedly to pay for damages to civilians and for military pensions. Continued negotiations over the next decade scaled the sum back considerably. In the end, Germany paid only $9 billion, which was still more than its crippled economy could afford. The reparations, combined with other territorial and economic penalties,

REPARATIONS

THE BIG FOUR IN PARIS Surface cordiality during the Paris Peace Conference disguised serious tensions among the so-called Big Four, the leaders of the victorious nations in World War I. As the conference progressed, the European leaders developed increasing resentment of Woodrow Wilson's high (and some of them thought sanctimonious) moral posture in the negotiations. Shown here are, from left to right, David Lloyd George of Great Britain, Vittorio Orlando of Italy, Georges Clemenceau of France, and Wilson.

The Library of Congress (LC-DIG-ggbain-29038)

Discussion and Activities

Speculating After students have read the section "Wilson's Retreat," ask them to discuss in small groups whether and how the number of casualties suffered by Great Britain and France may have factored into the negotiations. **WOR** **NAT**

Discussion and Activities

Analyzing Visuals Have students examine the image "The Big Four in Paris." Ask them to write a new caption for the photo the captures the scene, taking into consideration the arrangement and attire of the leaders in the photo and how they seem to be interacting. **WOR** **NAT**

Discussion and Activities

Historical Reasoning and Argumentation After students have read the section "The Paris Peace Conference," ask them to create a T-chart listing President Wilson's successes and failures in the negotiations at the Paris Peace Conference. Have students discuss as a class whether they think there were more successes or more failures, and why. **WOR** **NAT** **SOC** **PCE**

constituted an effort to keep Germany weak for the indefinite future. Never again, the Allied leaders believed, should the Germans be allowed to become powerful enough to threaten the peace of Europe.

Wilson did manage to win some important victories in Paris in setting boundaries and dealing with former colonies. He secured approval of a plan to place many former colonies and imperial possessions (among them Palestine) in "trusteeship" under the League of Nations–the so-called mandate system. He blocked a French proposal to break up western Germany into a group of smaller states. He helped design the creation of two new nations: Yugoslavia and Czechoslovakia, which were welded together out of, among other territories, pieces of the former Austro-Hungarian Empire. Each nation contained an uneasy collection of ethnic groups that had frequently battled one another in the past.

But Wilson's most visible triumph, and the one most important to him, was the creation of a permanent international organization to oversee world affairs and prevent future wars. On January 25, 1919, the Allies voted to accept the "covenant" of the League of Nations; and with that, Wilson believed, the peace treaty was transformed from a disappointment into a success. Whatever mistakes and inequities had emerged from the peace conference, he was convinced, could be corrected later by the League.

League of Nations

The covenant provided for an assembly of nations that would meet regularly to debate means of resolving disputes and protecting the peace. Authority to implement League decisions would rest with a nine-member executive council; the United States would be one of five permanent members of the council, along with Britain, France, Italy, and Japan. The covenant left many questions unanswered, most notably how the League would enforce its decisions. Wilson, however, was confident that once established, the new organization would find suitable answers.

The Ratification Battle

Wilson was well aware of the political obstacles awaiting him at home. Many Americans, accustomed to their nation's isolation from Europe, questioned the wisdom of this major new commitment to internationalism. Others had serious reservations about the specific features of the treaty and the covenant. After a brief trip to Washington in February 1919, during which he listened to harsh objections to the treaty from members of the Senate and others, he returned to Europe and insisted on several modifications in the covenant to satisfy his critics. The revisions ensured that the United States would not be obliged to accept a League mandate to oversee a territory and that the League would not challenge the Monroe Doctrine. But the changes were not enough to mollify his opponents, and Wilson refused to go further.

Wilson presented the Treaty of Versailles (which took its name from the palace outside Paris where the final negotiating sessions had taken place) to the Senate on July 10, 1919, asking, "Dare we reject it and break the heart of the world?" In the weeks that followed, he refused to consider even the most innocuous compromise. His deteriorating physical condition–he was suffering from hardening of the arteries and had apparently experienced something like a mild stroke (undiagnosed) in Paris–may have contributed to his intransigence.

Wilson's Intransigence

The Senate, in the meantime, was raising many objections. Some senators–the fourteen so-called irreconcilables, many of them western isolationists–opposed the agreement on principle. But other opponents, with less fervent convictions, were principally concerned with constructing a winning issue for the Republicans in 1920 and with weakening a president whom some members of the Senate had come to despise. Most notable of these was Senator Henry Cabot Lodge of Massachusetts, the powerful chairman of the Foreign Relations Committee. A man of stunning arrogance and a close friend of Theodore Roosevelt (who had died early in 1919, spouting hatred of Wilson to the end), Lodge loathed the president with genuine passion. "I never thought I could hate a man as I hate Wilson," he once admitted. He used every possible tactic to obstruct, delay, and amend the treaty. Wilson, for his part, despised Lodge as much as Lodge despised him.

Henry Cabot Lodge

Public sentiment clearly favored ratification, so at first Lodge could do little more than play for time. When the document reached his committee, he spent two weeks slowly reading aloud each word of its 300 pages; then he held six weeks of public hearings to air the complaints of every disgruntled minority (Irish Americans, for example, angry that the settlement made no provision for an independent Ireland). Gradually, Lodge's general opposition to the treaty crystallized into a series of "reservations"–amendments to the League covenant limiting American obligations to the organization.

At this point, Wilson might still have won approval if he had agreed to some relatively minor changes in the language of the treaty. But the president refused to yield. When he realized the Senate would not budge, he decided to appeal to the public.

Wilson's Ordeal

What followed was a political disaster and a personal tragedy. Wilson embarked on a grueling, cross-country speaking tour to arouse public support for the treaty. In a little more than three weeks, he traveled over 8,000 miles by train, speaking as often as four times a day, resting hardly at all. Finally, he reached the end of his strength. After speaking at Pueblo, Colorado, on September 25, he collapsed with severe headaches. Canceling the rest of his itinerary, he rushed back to Washington, D.C., where, a few days later, he suffered a major stroke. For two weeks he was close to death; for six weeks more, he was so seriously ill that he could conduct virtually no public business. His wife and his doctor formed an almost impenetrable barrier around him, shielding him from any official pressures that might impede his recovery, preventing the public from receiving any accurate information about the gravity of his condition.

Discussion and Activities

Historical Reasoning and Argumentation Have students read the section "The Ratification Battle." Ask them to discuss in pairs or small groups what Wilson could have done differently to secure ratification of the Treaty of Versailles in the Senate. **WOR** **PCE** **NAT**

Wilson ultimately recovered enough to resume a limited official schedule, but he was essentially an invalid for the remaining eighteen months of his presidency. His left side was partially paralyzed; more important, like many stroke victims, he had only partial control of his mental and emotional state. His condition only intensified what had already been his strong tendency to view public issues in moral terms and to resist any attempts at compromise. When the Senate Foreign Relations Committee finally sent the treaty to the full Senate for ratification, recommending nearly fifty amendments and reservations, Wilson refused to consider any of them. When the full Senate voted in November to accept fourteen of the reservations, Wilson gave stern directions to his Democratic allies: they must vote only for a treaty with no changes whatsoever; any other version must be defeated. On November 19, 1919, forty-two Democrats, following the president's instructions, joined with the thirteen Republican "irreconcilables" to reject the amended treaty. When the Senate voted on the original version without any reservations, thirty-eight senators, all but one Democrats, voted to approve it; fifty-five senators (some Democrats among them) voted no.

LEAGUE MEMBERSHIP REJECTED

There were sporadic efforts to revive the treaty over the next few months. But Wilson's opposition to anything but the precise settlement he had negotiated in Paris remained too formidable an obstacle. He was, moreover, becoming convinced that the 1920 national election would serve as a "solemn referendum" on the League. By now, however, public interest in the peace process had begun to fade—partly as a reaction against the tragic bitterness of the ratification fight, but more in response to a series of other crises.

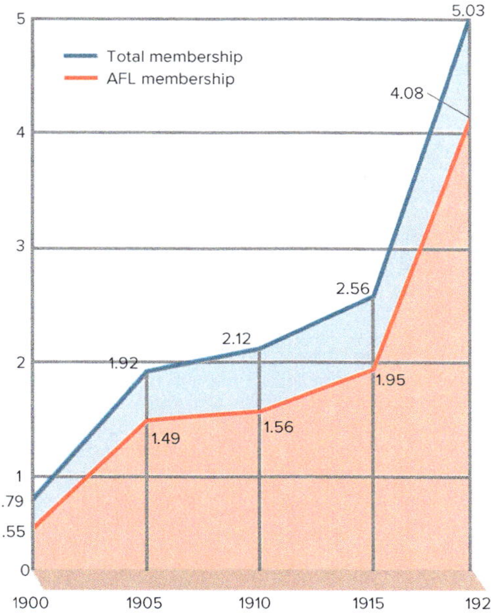

UNION MEMBERSHIP, 1900–1920 This chart illustrates the steady increase in union membership in the first part of the twentieth century—a membership dominated by unions associated with the AFL. Note the particularly sharp increase between 1915 and 1920, the years of World War I.

Why did the war years see such an expansion of union labor?

A SOCIETY IN TURMOIL

Even during the Paris Peace Conference, many Americans were less concerned about international matters than about turbulent events at home. The American economy experienced a severe postwar recession. And much of middle-class America responded to demands for change with a fearful, conservative hostility. The aftermath of war brought not the age of liberal reform that progressives had predicted, but a period of repression and reaction.

INDUSTRY AND LABOR

Citizens of Washington, D.C., on the day after the armistice, found it impossible to place long-distance telephone calls: the lines were jammed with officials of the war agencies canceling government contracts. The fighting had ended sooner than anyone had anticipated, and without warning, without planning, the nation was launched into the difficult task of economic reconversion.

At first, the wartime boom continued. But the postwar prosperity rested largely on the lingering effects of the war (government deficit spending continued for some months after the armistice) and on sudden, temporary demands (a booming market for scarce consumer goods at home and a strong market for American products in the war-ravaged nations of Europe). This brief postwar boom was accompanied, however, by raging inflation, a result in part of the rapid abandonment of wartime price controls. Through most of 1919 and 1920, prices rose at an average of more than 15 percent a year.

Finally, late in 1920, the economic bubble burst, as many of the temporary forces that had created it disappeared and as inflation began killing the market for consumer goods. Between 1920 and 1921, the gross national product (GNP) declined nearly 10 percent; 100,000 businesses went bankrupt; 453,000 farmers lost their land; nearly 5 million Americans lost their jobs. In this unpromising economic environment, leaders of organized labor set out to consolidate the advances they had made in the war, which now seemed in danger of being lost. The raging inflation of 1919 wiped out the modest wage gains workers had achieved during the war; many laborers worried about job security as hundreds of thousands of veterans returned to the workforce; arduous working conditions—such as the twelve-hour workday in the steel industry—continued to be a source of discontent. Employers aggravated the resentment by using the end of the war (and the end of government controls) to

POSTWAR RECESSION

Discussion and Activities

Speculating After students have read the section "Wilson's Ordeal," ask them to discuss in pairs or small groups whether they think that President Wilson would have been able to secure ratification of the Treaty of Versailles had his health not been compromised. NAT PCE

Answers

Union Membership, 1900–1920

Union membership increased due to efforts to maintain improvements in working conditions and wages that had been achieved during the war with the aid of the National War Labor Board. WXT PCE

Discussion and Activities

Making Generalizations After students have read the section "Industry and Labor," ask them to discuss in pairs or small groups why they think that strikes by Seattle shipyard workers, Boston police, and steelworkers all failed. **WXT** **SOC** **PCE**

rescind benefits they had been forced to give workers in 1917 and 1918—most notably recognition of unions.

The year 1919, therefore, saw an unprecedented wave of strikes—more than 3,600 in all, involving over 4 million workers. In January, a walkout by shipyard workers in Seattle, Washington, evolved into a general strike that brought the entire city almost to a standstill. The mayor requested and received the assistance of U.S. Marines to keep the city running, and eventually the strike failed. But the brief success of a general strike, something Americans associated with European radicals, made the Seattle incident reverberate loudly throughout the country.

BOSTON POLICE STRIKE

In September, there was a strike by the Boston police force, which was responding to layoffs and wage cuts by demanding recognition of its union. Seattle had remained generally calm during its strike; but with its police off the job, Boston erupted in violence and looting. Efforts by local businessmen, veterans, and college students to patrol the streets proved ineffective; and finally Governor Calvin Coolidge called in the National Guard to restore order. (His public statement that "there is no right to strike against the public safety by anybody, anywhere, any time" attracted national acclaim.) Eventually, Boston officials dismissed the entire police force and hired a new one.

STEELWORKERS' STRIKE DEFEATED

In September 1919, the greatest strike in American history began, when 350,000 steelworkers in several eastern and midwestern cities walked off the job, demanding an eight-hour workday and recognition of their union. The steel strike was long, bitter, and violent—most of the violence coming from employers, who hired armed guards to disperse picket lines and escort strikebreakers into factories. It climaxed in a riot in Gary, Indiana, in which eighteen strikers were killed. Steel executives managed to keep most plants running with nonunion labor, and public opinion was so hostile to the strikers that the AFL—having at first endorsed the strike—soon timidly repudiated it. By January, the strike had collapsed. It was a setback from which organized labor would not recover for more than a decade.

THE DEMANDS OF AFRICAN AMERICANS

The nearly 400,000 black men who had served in the armed forces during the war came home in 1919 and marched

THE BOSTON POLICE STRIKE National Guardsmen stand guard in front of a store where broken windows suggest looting has already occurred, during the Boston Police Strike of 1919.

Discussion and Activities

Analyzing Points of View Have students examine the image "The Boston Police Strike." Ask them to write a letter to the editor of a Boston newspaper from the point of view of either a supporter or critic of the Boston Police Strike. **WXT** **SOC** **PCE**

down the main streets of the industrial cities with other returning troops. And then (in New York and other cities), they marched again through the streets of black neighborhoods such as Harlem, led by jazz bands, cheered by thousands of African Americans, worshiped as heroes. The black soldiers were an inspiration to thousands of urban African Americans, a sign, they thought, that a new age had come, that the glory of black heroism in the war would make it impossible for white society ever again to treat African Americans as less than equal citizens. W. E. B. Du Bois, watching the African American soldiers returning home, conveyed his hopes for a new life for them. "We are returning from war!" he wrote, "The Crisis and tens of thousands of black men were drafted into the great struggle . . . we fought gladly and to the last drop of blood; for America and her highest ideals, we fought in far-off hope." But recalling the past he added, "This country of ours, despite all its better souls have done and dreamed, is yet a shameful land."

New Black Attitudes

In fact, that black soldiers had fought in the war had almost no impact on white attitudes. But it did have a profound effect on black attitudes: it accentuated African American bitterness—and increased black determination to fight for their rights. For soldiers, there was an expectation of some social reward for their service. For many other African Americans, the war had raised economic expectations, as they moved into industrial and other jobs vacated by white workers, jobs to which they had previously had no access. Just as black soldiers expected their military service to enhance their social status, so black factory workers regarded their move north as an escape from racial prejudice and an opportunity for economic gain.

By 1919, however, the racial climate had become savage and murderous. In the South, there was a sudden increase in lynchings: more than seventy African Americans, some of them war veterans, died at the hands of white mobs in 1919 alone. In the North, black factory workers faced widespread layoffs as white veterans displaced them from their jobs. African American veterans found no significant new opportunities for advancement. Rural black migrants to Northern cities encountered white communities unfamiliar with and generally hostile to them; and as white workers became convinced that black workers with lower wage demands were hurting them economically, animosity grew rapidly.

The wartime riots in East St. Louis and elsewhere were a prelude to a summer of much worse racial violence in 1919. In

Chicago Race Riots

Chicago, a black teenager swimming in Lake Michigan on a hot July day happened to drift toward a white beach. White beachgoers on shore allegedly stoned him unconscious; he sank and drowned. African Americans gathered in crowds and marched into white neighborhoods to retaliate; white people formed even larger crowds and roamed into black neighborhoods shooting, stabbing, and beating passersby, destroying homes and properties. For more than a week, Chicago was virtually at war. In the end, 38 people died—15 white people and 23 African Americans—and 537 were injured; over 1,000 people were left homeless. The Chicago riot was the worst but not the only racial violence during the so-called red summer of 1919; in all, 120 people died in such racial outbreaks in little more than three months.

Racial violence, and even racially motivated urban riots, was not new. The deadliest race riot in American history had

THE FIFTEENTH REGIMENT ON FIFTH AVENUE The all-black Fifteenth Army Regiment marches up Fifth Avenue in New York City in 1917, shortly after the United States entered World War I. They are en route to an army training camp in New York State before traveling to the front in Europe. Less than two years later, many of these same men marched through Harlem on their return from the war, and again down Fifth Avenue, before cheering crowds—convinced, wrongly, that their service in the war would win them important new freedoms at home.

Discussion and Activities

Historical Developments and Argumentation After students have read the section "New Black Attitudes," ask them to discuss in pairs or small groups why the service of black soldiers produced such different responses in white and African American communities. **ARC** **NAT** **SOC**

Discussion and Activities

Analyzing Perspectives Have students examine the image "The Fifteenth Regiment on Fifth Avenue." Ask them to create a newsreel script centered around the image to boost enlistment or inspire patriotism within the American public of the time. **NAT** **SOC**

Reasoning Processes

Causation After students have read the section "The Demands of African Americans," ask them to create a chart listing the economic, political, and social demands of African Americans following World War I. Have students discuss as a class which, if any, of those demands were met, and why so much violence resulted. **NAT** **SOC** **PCE**

occurred in New York during the Civil War. But the 1919 riots were different in one respect: they did not just involve white people attacking African Americans; they also involved African Americans fighting back. The NAACP signaled this change by urging African Americans not just to demand government protection, but also to retaliate, to defend themselves. The poet Claude McKay, one of the major figures of what would shortly be known as the Harlem Renaissance, wrote a poem after the Chicago riot called "If We Must Die":

> Like men we'll face the murderous cowardly pack.
> Pressed to the wall, dying, but fighting back.

MARCUS GARVEY'S BLACK NATIONALISM

At the same time, a Jamaican, Marcus Garvey, began to attract a wide American following–mostly among poor urban African Americans–with an ideology of black nationalism. Garvey encouraged African Americans to take pride in their own achievements and to develop an awareness of their African heritage–to reject assimilation into white society and develop pride in what Garvey argued was their own superior race and culture. His United Negro Improvement Association (UNIA) launched a chain of black-owned grocery stores and pressed for the creation of other black businesses. Eventually, Garvey began urging his supporters to leave America and "return" to Africa, where they could create a new society of their own. In the 1920s, the Garvey movement experienced explosive growth for a time; and the UNIA became notable for its mass rallies and parades, for the opulent uniforms of its members, and for the growth of its enterprises. It began to decline, however, after Garvey was indicted in 1923 on charges of business fraud. He was deported to Jamaica two years later. But the allure of black nationalism, which he helped make visible to millions of African Americans, survived in black culture long after Garvey himself was gone.

THE RED SCARE

To much of the white middle class at the time, the industrial warfare, the racial violence, and other forms of dissent all appeared to be frightening omens of instability and radicalism. This was in part because the Russian Revolution of November 1917 made it clear that communism was no longer simply a theory, but now an important regime.

Concerns about the communist threat grew in 1919 when the Soviet government announced the formation of the Communist International (or Comintern), whose purpose was to export revolution around the world. And in America itself, there were, in addition to the great number of imagined radicals, a modest number of real ones. The American Communist Party was formed in 1919, and there were other radical groups (many of them dominated by immigrants from Europe who had been involved in radical politics before coming to America). Some of these radicals were presumably responsible for a series of bombings in the spring of 1919 that produced great national alarm. In April, the Post Office Department, intercepted several dozen parcels addressed to leading businessmen and politicians that were triggered to explode when opened. Several of them reached their destinations, and one of them exploded, severely injuring a domestic servant of a public official in Georgia. Two months later, eight bombs exploded in eight cities within minutes of one another, suggesting a nationwide conspiracy. One of them damaged the

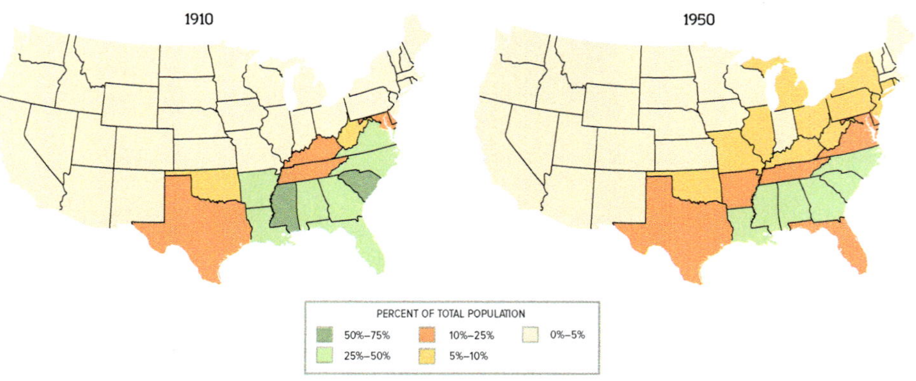

AFRICAN AMERICAN MIGRATION, 1910–1950 Two great waves of migration produced a dramatic redistribution of the African American population in the first half of the twentieth century—one around the time of World War I, the other during and after World War II. The map on the left shows the almost exclusive concentration of African Americans in the South as late as 1910. The map on the right shows both the tremendous increase of black populations in northern states by 1950 and the relative decline of black populations in parts of the South. Note in particular the changes in Mississippi and South Carolina.

Why did the wars produce such significant migration out of the South?

Answers

African American Migration, 1910–1950

Many African Americans left the South to find work in war industries in the North during both of the wars.

MARCUS GARVEY Marcus Garvey rejected the idea of African Americans assimilating into white society. Instead, he encouraged his supporters to leave America and "return" to Africa to create their own society.

facade of Attorney General A. Mitchell Palmer's home in Washington. In 1920, there was a terrible explosion in front of the Morgan bank on Wall Street, which killed thirty people (only one of them–a clerk–in the bank itself).

The bombings crystallized what was already a growing determination among many middle-class Americans (and some government officials) to fight back against radicalism–a determination steeled by the repressive atmosphere of the war years. This antiradicalism accompanied, and reinforced, the already strong commitment among old-stock Protestants to the idea of "100 percent Americanism." And it produced what became known as the Red Scare.

POPULAR ANTIRADICALISM

Antiradical newspapers and politicians now began to portray almost every form of instability or protest as a sign of a radical threat. Race riots, one newspaper claimed, were the work of "armed revolutionaries running rampant through our cities." The steel strike, the *Philadelphia Inquirer* claimed, was "penetrated with the Bolshevik idea . . . steeped in the doctrines of the class struggle and social overthrow." Nearly thirty states enacted new peacetime sedition laws imposing harsh penalties on those who promoted revolution; some 300 people went to jail as a result–many of them people whose "crime" had been nothing more than opposition to the war. There were spontaneous acts of violence against supposed radicals in some communities. A mob of off-duty soldiers in New York City ransacked the offices of a socialist newspaper and beat up its staff. Another mob, in Centralia, Washington, dragged an IWW agitator from jail and castrated him before hanging him from a bridge. Citizens in many communities removed "subversive" books from the shelves of libraries; administrators in some universities dismissed "radical" members from their faculties. Women's groups such as the National Consumers League came under attack by antiradicals because so many feminists had opposed American intervention in the fighting in Europe.

Perhaps the greatest contribution to the Red Scare came from the federal government. On New Year's Day, 1920, Attorney General A. Mitchell Palmer and his ambitious assistant, J. Edgar Hoover, orchestrated a series of raids on alleged radical centers throughout the country and arrested more than 6,000 people.

PALMER RAIDS

The Palmer Raids had been intended to uncover large caches of weapons and explosives; they discovered only three pistols. Most of those arrested were ultimately released, but about 500 who were not American citizens were summarily deported.

SACCO AND VANZETTI

The ferocity of the Red Scare soon abated, but its effects lingered well into the 1920s, most notably in the celebrated case of Sacco and Vanzetti. In May 1920, two Italian immigrants, Nicola Sacco and Bartolomeo Vanzetti, were charged with the murder of a paymaster in Braintree, Massachusetts. The evidence against them was questionable; but because both men were confessed anarchists, they faced a widespread public presumption of guilt. They were convicted in a trial of extraordinary injudiciousness, before an openly prejudiced judge, Webster Thayer, and were sentenced to death. Over the next several years, public support for Sacco and

Reasoning Processes

Causation After students have read the section "Palmer Raids," ask them to create a T-chart listing causes and effects of anti-Bolshevik fears following World War I. Have students discuss in small groups which causes and effects they believe were the most important. **NAT** **WXT** **SOC**

Discussion and Activities

Analyzing Visuals Have students examine the image "Marcus Garvey." Ask them to identify and discuss in pairs or small groups details from the photo that are consistent with Garvey's ideas of black nationalism. *(Garvey's supporters are wearing middle-class and academic dress, signifying economic and academic achievement; Garvey is being chauffeured; Garvey is wearing what appears to be a military-style uniform.)* **NAT** **SOC** **WXT** **PCE**

Historical Thinking Skills

Argumentation After students have read the section "Sacco and Vanzetti," ask them to write a letter to the governor of Massachusetts asking for either a pardon or a new trial for Sacco and Vanzetti. **PCE** **WXT** **SOC**

Vanzetti grew to formidable proportions. But all requests for a new trial or a pardon were denied. On August 23, 1927, amid widespread protests around the world, Sacco and Vanzetti, still proclaiming their innocence, died in the electric chair. Theirs was a cause that a generation of Americans never forgot.

REFUTING THE RED SCARE

An unexpected result of postwar turmoil was the emergence of a vigorous defense of civil liberties that not only discredited the Red Scare, but helped give new force of the Bill of Rights as well. The heavy-handed actions of the federal government after the war created a powerful backlash. It destroyed the career of A. Mitchell Palmer. It almost nipped in the bud the ascent of J. Edgar Hoover. It damaged the Democratic Party. And it led to an organization committed to protecting civil liberties: the National Civil Liberties Bureau, launched in 1917, which in 1920 was renamed the American Civil Liberties Union (ACLU), which remains a prominent institution today. At the same time, members of the Supreme Court–most notably Justices Oliver Wendell Holmes and Louis Brandeis–gradually moved toward a strong position of defense of unpopular speech. The clash of "fighting faiths," Holmes wrote in a dissent in 1920, was best resolved "by free trade in ideas–that the best test of truth is . . . the competition of the market." This and other dissents eventually became law as other justices committed themselves to a robust defense of speech, however unpopular.

THE PALMER RAIDS In the years following World War I, many Americans feared political radicalism, especially from the left. The United States Department of Justice, led by Attorney General A. Mitchell Palmer, conducted raids and arrested and deported more than 500 foreign citizens, including several prominent leftist leaders.

THE RETREAT FROM IDEALISM

On August 26, 1920, the Nineteenth Amendment, guaranteeing women the right to vote, became part of the Constitution. To the woman suffrage movement, this was the culmination of nearly a century of struggle. To many progressives, who had seen the inclusion of women in the electorate as a way of bolstering their political strength, it seemed to promise new support for reform. In some respects, the amendment helped fulfill that promise. Because of woman suffrage, members of Congress–concerned that women would vote as a bloc on the basis of women's issues–passed the Sheppard-Towner Maternity and Infancy Act in 1921, one of the first pieces of federal welfare legislation that provided funds for supporting the health of women and infants. Concern about the women's vote also appeared to create support for the 1922 Cable Act, which granted women the rights of U.S. citizenship independent of their husbands' status, and for the proposed (but never ratified) 1924 constitutional amendment to outlaw child labor.

In other ways, however, the Nineteenth Amendment marked less the beginning of an era of reform than an ending. Economic problems, feminist demands, labor unrest, racial tensions, and the intensity of the antiradicalism they helped create–all combined in the years immediately following the war to produce a general sense of disillusionment.

That became particularly apparent in the election of 1920. Woodrow Wilson wanted the campaign to be a referendum on the League of Nations, and the Democratic candidates, Ohio governor James M. Cox and Assistant Secretary of the Navy Franklin D. Roosevelt, tried to keep Wilson's ideals alive. The Republican presidential nominee, however, offered a different vision. He was Warren Gamaliel Harding, an obscure Ohio senator whom party leaders had chosen as their nominee confident that he would do their bidding once in office. Harding offered few ideals, only a vague promise of a return, as he later phrased it, to "normalcy." He won in a landslide. The Republican ticket received 61 percent of the popular vote and carried every state outside the South. The party made major gains in Congress as well. Woodrow Wilson, who had tried and failed to create a postwar order based on democratic ideals, stood repudiated. Early in 1921, he retired to a house on S Street in Washington, where he lived quietly until his death in 1924. In the meantime, for most Americans, a new era had begun.

RETURN TO "NORMALCY"

Reasoning Processes

Continuity and Change After students have read the section "The Retreat from Idealism," have them create a T-chart listing ways in which civil liberties were strengthened or weakened during and immediately after World War I. Have students discuss in small groups whether Americans' civil liberties protections were stronger or weaker as a result of the war. **PCE** **NAT**

CHAPTER 22 REVIEW

CONNECTING THEMES

Chapter Twenty-Two explored how the United States assumed a major role in world affairs during the first two decades of the twentieth century. The presidents during this period — Roosevelt, Taft, and Wilson — shaped American foreign policy through a series of economic, diplomatic, and military interventions, particularly in Latin America and Western Europe. By the conclusion of World War I, the United States was an important global power, even if it never joined the League of Nations as Wilson had hoped with his Fourteen Points.

The entry of the United States into World War I also had important domestic consequences. Federal laws, government agencies, and citizen groups suppressed dissent and disloyalty by targeting radicals, immigrants, and those not identified as "100 Percent American." The racism, violence, and poverty many African Americans experienced in the rural South fueled a "Great Migration" to the industrial North, where greater political freedom, personal autonomy, and economic opportunity awaited. But racial violence, driven by white racism, often erupted. As the economic boom of the war years faded, labor conflict grew. This instability raised fears of radicalism and revolution, which culminated in the Red Scare.

You should consider the following questions as you review the themes for this chapter:

- How did World War I change perceptions of American identity?
- What were the effects of World War I on the American economy?
- How did World War I impact women and minorities?
- Why did America's involvement in World War I cause conflict between the political parties, both before and after the war?
- What were the causes and effects of increasing U.S. involvement in world affairs?
- Why did racial tensions increase in the United States during and after World War I?
- How did beliefs about what constituted loyalty in American society change during and after World War I?

KEY TERMS

Allies 620
American Expeditionary Force 623
Central Powers 620
Dollar Diplomacy 618
General John J. Pershing 620
"Great Migration" 629
League of Nations 634
Ludlow Massacre 628
Lusitania 621
Marcus Garvey 640
Nicola Sacco and Bartolomeo Vanzetti 641
Nineteenth Amendment 642
Palmer Raids 641
Pancho Villa 620
Red Scare 640
Roosevelt Corollary 616
Senator Henry Cabot Lodge 636
The Fourteen Points 634
Treaty of Versailles 636
trench warfare 625
Triple Alliance 620
Triple Entente 620
United Negro Improvement Association 640
Zimmermann telegram 622

Discussion and Activities

Analyzing Issues Divide students into three groups to review and evaluate the economic, social, and political changes in the United States as a result of its increasing involvement in Latin America and its participation in World War I. Have each group make a short presentation to the rest of the class arguing why their category of change was the most important. **WOR** **SOC** **WXT** **NAT**

Key Terms

Students should be familiar with the key terms and be able to define them in the context of the political, economic, and social causes and effects of America's increasing involvement in world affairs, culminating in World War I. Encourage students to use these terms in performing review exercises and exam practice for this chapter.

Go Online Chapter 22 Content Review

Assessing Student Understanding Use the online assessment to assess student understanding of concepts and topics within the chapter. You can assign the ready-made Chapter 22 Content Review or create your own from available questions. This easy-to-use tool helps you design assessments that meet the needs of different types of learners.

CHAPTER 22

AMERICA AND THE GREAT WAR

Answers

Multiple Choice

1. C; **2.** A; **3.** B

Short Answer

4A) Possible answer: The point of view about U.S. foreign policy as depicted in the image is that of an advocate of American imperialism. The central figure, representing Roosevelt, is overwhelming others as he imposes his will on other countries. On the left, with the "inferior" nations, he uses his "Big Stick." On the right, with "equal" nations, he uses arbitration.

4B) Possible answer: Due to the rise of the Second Industrial Revolution in the United States, America was looking for other markets in which to sell its goods. . Additionally, if the United States was going to keep up with other world powers, particularly those in Europe, it would have to reassess its foreign policy.

4C) Possible answer: Despite its efforts to remain isolationist, U.S. involvement in World War I and subsequently in World War II caused the United States to realize that becoming a world power economically also meant being a world power diplomatically.

5A) Possible answer: Even though the United States began to reassess its foreign policy during World War I, both before and after the war, the nation promoted an isolationist approach.

5B) Possible answer: Before World War I, the United States generally was not a major player on the international scene. Following World War I, the United States was recognized as a leading world player.

5C) Possible answer: Following World War I and America's failure to join the League of Nations, the United States realized its role in world affairs, and became more active on the world stage.

AP EXAM PRACTICE

Questions assume cumulative content knowledge from this chapter and the previous chapter.

MULTIPLE CHOICE

Use the United States Navy poster on page 631 and your knowledge of U.S. history to answer questions 1-3.

1. The poster was created by the government during World War I to address the challenges of
   (A) growing enough food to supply the troops and Allies.
   (B) funding the war effort.
   (C) enlisting soldiers.
   (D) raising awareness of potential security threats.

2. Conflicts on the homefront during World War I largely centered around
   (A) questions of loyalty and challenges of internal migration.
   (B) allocation of scare economic resources in urban areas.
   (C) incentivization of farmers to limit crops due to overproduction.
   (D) low worker pay in war related industries.

3. Woodrow Wilson's effort to achieve lasting peace through the Treaty of Versailles largely centered around
   (A) the rebuilding of Allied nations through the payment of German reparations.
   (B) the creation of the League of Nations.
   (C) the creation of new nations such as Czechoslovakia and Yugoslavia.
   (D) the recognition of maritime neutrality rights.

SHORT ANSWER

Use your knowledge of U.S. history to answer questions 4 and 5.

4. Use the image on page 616 and your knowledge of U.S. history to answer A, B, and C.
   (A) Describe ONE point of view in the image about U.S. foreign policy at the beginning of the twentieth century.
   (B) Briefly explain ONE specific historical cause that led America to reevaluate its foreign policy.
   (C) Briefly explain ONE specific historical effect that resulted from America reevaluating its foreign policy.

5. Answer A, B, and C.
   (A) Briefly describe ONE specific historical similarity of American foreign policy before and after World War I.
   (B) Briefly describe ONE specific historical difference of American foreign policy before and after World War I.
   (C) Briefly explain ONE specific historical effect of America's involvement in World War I.

LONG ESSAY

Develop a thoughtful and thorough historical argument that addresses the statement. Begin your essay with a thesis statement, and support it with specific historical evidence and examples.

6. Evaluate the relative importance of causes that led to the ratification of the Nineteenth Amendment in the United States in 1920.

Answers

Long Essay

6. Possible thesis: From the start of the American Revolution, women were bringing attention to inequalities in the American political system. Specific historical evidence: First, there have been advocates for political equality including Abigail Adams and her famous letter warning John Adams to "remember the ladies" in political conversations. Second, the major move on the part of women to voice political dissent with the Seneca Falls Convention. There, they drafted the Declaration of Rights and Sentiments. Third, following the American Revolution, the "Republican Motherhood" movement set the stage for women to influence the politics of the day. Fourth, during the Second Great Awakening, women became leaders in reform movements and exerted a tremendous amount of influence in American society. Fifth, this reform-minded activism continued into the second half of the nineteenth century and into the twentieth century with the urban reforms of the Progressives. Sixth, Teddy Roosevelt's push to include women, despite it being based on self-interests, did contribute to legitimizing the movement. Finally, women's active engagement and involvement with World War I politics and their confrontation of Woodrow Wilson directly put their plight in the limelight and garnered national and international recognition.

23 THE "NEW ERA"

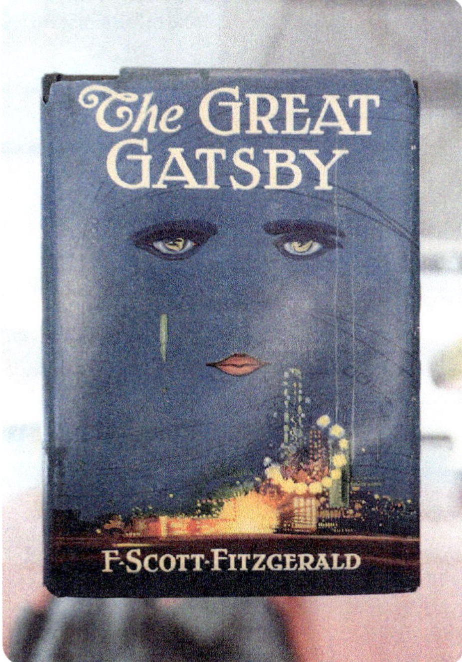

THE GREAT GATSBY
F. Scott Fitzgerald's great novel, one of the most famous of the "Lost Generation," critiques the excesses of capitalism and explores the personal sense of alienation experienced by many in the years following World War I.

CONNECTING CONCEPTS

Chapter Twenty-Three begins by examining the economic boom of the 1920s. Technology made a great industrial expansion possible. New industries like radio and aviation emerged, and new forms of corporate organization helped industries to consolidate and achieve efficiency. Yet economic growth was accompanied by economic inequality. Employers like Henry Ford offered workers "welfare capitalism" — higher wages and some benefits. But labor unions experienced hard times and half of all Americans, especially women, minorities, and farmers, lived at or below the level of "subsistence and poverty" in 1929.

Although the United States remained a diverse nation, more Americans in different regions began to lead more similar lives. Mass consumption enabled middle-class families to purchase new appliances, clothing, and cosmetics. Above all, the automobile transformed American life, offering increased mobility and enabling life in the suburbs. Mass advertising now provided more than information — it identified products with lifestyle. For college-educated women, professional opportunities remained limited. But for middle-class women, the decade offered new ideas of marriage. Younger women also challenged older ideas of respectability, although the "flapper" was as much myth as reality. The writers and intellectuals in the "Lost Generation" felt a profound sense of personal alienation from the materialist culture, and African American artists, poets, and musicians of the Harlem Renaissance drew heavily from both American and African roots.

Pacing Guide

Chapter 23 explores key concepts from Period 7: 1890–1945 of the AP U.S. History Curriculum Framework. The suggested instruction time for Chapter 23 is 2 days.

Key Concepts

7.2.I Popular culture grew in influence in U.S. society, even as debates increased over the effects of culture on public values, morals, and American national identity.

7.2.II Economic pressures, global events, and political developments caused sharp variations in the numbers, sources, and experiences of both international and internal migrants.

Discussion and Activities

Speculating Based on the chapter title, *The "New Era,"* have students create a KWL chart listing things they know and things they want to know about this time period. Ask students to add to the chart as they read the chapter. **WOR** **PCE** **SOC** **WXT** **ARC** **NAT**

Reasoning Processes

Causation Have students read the section "Sources of the Boom." Ask them to list and rank in order of importance the causes of the economic boom of the early 1920s. Have students write a thesis statement that makes a claim about the most important cause(s) of the economic boom of the 1920s. **WXT** **SOC** **WOR**

During the 1920s, urban Americans who embraced the more modern and secular culture often clashed with rural Americans who held more traditional and religious views. Prohibition soon seemed like a failure to many Americans, who witnessed widespread evasion and growing crime, but many others continued to defend the "noble experiment." Nativist sentiment led to immigration restriction and a New Klan, which claimed to defend traditional values as it targeted Catholic, Jewish, and foreign-born people. At the same time, Protestants divided into modernist and fundamentalist factions over Charles Darwin's theory of evolution.

The Republican Party dominated national politics largely because Prohibition and the Klan divided the Democratic Party, which had rural and urban factions. As president, neither Warren Harding nor Calvin Coolidge distinguished themselves. But the federal government, led by Treasury Secretary Andrew Mellon and Commerce Secretary Herbert Hoover, worked hard to ensure that business and industry operated with maximum efficiency and productivity by lowering taxes, removing regulations, and encouraging cooperation among companies. In 1928, Hoover became president when he defeated New York Governor Al Smith, a Catholic who opposed Prohibition.

As you read, you should:

- Describe how the United States, during the 1920s, moved from a rural agrarian society to an urban industrial society.
- Evaluate the revolutionary changes in communications and technology and how those changes influenced a new "mass culture."
- Analyze how the rise of an urban industrial society created new challenges and opportunities for women and African Americans.
- Describe how World War I intensified nativist sentiment and led to increasingly restrictive immigration laws.
- Analyze the reasons why the United States turned to a more isolationistic and conservative stance during the 1920s.

THE NEW ECONOMY

After the recession of 1921–1922, the United States began a period of almost uninterrupted prosperity and economic expansion. Less visible at the time, but equally significant, was the survival (and even the growth) of inequalities and imbalances.

TECHNOLOGY AND ECONOMIC GROWTH

No one could deny the remarkable, some believed miraculous, feats of the American economy in the 1920s. The nation's manufacturing output rose by more than 60 percent during the decade. Per capita income grew by a third. Inflation was negligible. A mild recession in 1923 interrupted the pattern of growth, but when it subsided early in 1924, the economy expanded with greater vigor than before.

SOURCES OF THE BOOM

The economic boom was a result of many factors. An immediate cause was the debilitation of European industry in the aftermath of World War I, which left the United States for the next ten years or so the only truly healthy industrial power in the world. More important in the long run was technology and the great industrial expansion it made possible. The automobile industry, as a result of the development of the assembly line and other innovations, now became one of the most important industries in the nation. It stimulated growth in many related industries as well. Auto manufacturers purchased the products of steel, rubber, glass, and tool companies. Auto owners bought gasoline from the oil corporations. Road construction in response to the proliferation of motor vehicles became an important industry. The increased mobility the automobile made possible increased the demand for suburban housing, fueling a boom in the construction industry.

RADIO

Other new industries benefiting from technological innovations contributed as well to the economic growth. Radio began to become a popular technology even before commercial broadcasting began in 1920. Early radio had been able to broadcast little besides pulses, which meant that radio communication could occur only through the Morse code. But with the discovery of the theory of modulation, pioneered by the Canadian scientist Reginald Fessenden, it became possible to transmit speech and music. (Modulation also eventually made possible the transmission of video signals that later helped create radar and

Go Online AP Exam Preparation

AP Exam Practice Use the online assessment to help prepare students for the AP Exam. You can assign the ready-made AP-style short-answer questions, document-based questions, and multiple-choice questions assessing concepts, themes, and skills from Period 7 and AP-style long-essay questions organized in sets of 3 questions from various time periods. You can also create your own tests from available questions. This easy-to-use tool helps you design assessments that meet the needs of different types of learners.

THE STEAMFITTER Lewis Hine was among the first American photographers to recognize his craft as an art. In this photograph from the mid-1920s, Hine made a point that many other artists were making in other media: The rise of the machine could serve human beings, but might also bend them to its own needs. The steamfitter (carefully posed by the photographer) is forced to shape his body to the contours of his machine in order to complete his task.

television.) Once commercial broadcasting began, families flocked to buy conventional radio sets, which, unlike the cheaper "shortwave" or "ham" radios, could receive high-quality signals over short and medium distances. They were powered by vacuum tubes that were much more reliable than earlier models. By 1925, there were 2 million sets in American homes, and by the end of the 1920s almost every family had one.

Commercial aviation developed slowly in the 1920s, beginning with the use of planes to deliver mail. On the whole, airplanes remained curiosities and sources of entertainment. But technological advances—the development of the radial engine and the creation of pressurized cabins—were laying the groundwork for the great increase in commercial travel in the 1930s and beyond. Trains became faster and more efficient as well with the development of the diesel-electric engine. Electronics, home appliances, plastics and synthetic fibers such as nylon (both pioneered by researchers at Du Pont), aluminum, magnesium, oil, electric power, and other industries fueled by technological advances—all grew and spurred the economic boom.

Telephones continued to proliferate. By the late 1930s, there were approximately 25 million telephones in the United States, approximately one for every six people.

The seeds of future technologies were also visible in the 1920s and 1930s. In both England and America, scientists and engineers were working to transform primitive calculating machines into devices capable of performing more complicated tasks. By the early 1930s, researchers at MIT, led by Vannevar Bush, had created an instrument capable of performing a variety of complicated tasks—the first analog computer, which became the starting point for dramatic progress over the next several decades. A few years later, Howard Aiken, with financial assistance from Harvard and MIT, built a much more complex computer with memory, capable of multiplying eleven-digit numbers in three seconds.

EARLY COMPUTERS

Genetic research had begun in Austria in the mid-nineteenth century through the work of Gregor Mendel, a Catholic monk who performed experiments on the hybridization of vegetables in the garden of his monastery. His findings attracted little attention during his lifetime, but in the early twentieth century they were discovered by several investigators and helped shape modern genetic research. Among the American pioneers was Thomas Hunt Morgan of Columbia University and later Cal Tech, whose experiments with fruit flies revealed how several genes could be transmitted together (as opposed to Mendel's belief that they could only be transferred separately). Morgan also revealed the way in which genes were arranged along the chromosome. His work helped open the path to understanding how genes could recombine—a critical discovery that led to advanced experiments in hybridization and genetics.

ECONOMIC ORGANIZATION

Large sectors of American business were accelerating their drive toward national organization and consolidation. Certain industries—notably those, such as steel, dependent on large-scale mass production—seemed naturally to move toward concentrating production in a few large firms; U.S. Steel, the nation's largest corporation, was so dominant that almost everyone used the term "Little Steel" to refer to all of its competitors combined. Other industries, such as textiles, that were less dependent on technology and less susceptible to great economies of scale, proved more resistant to consolidation, despite the efforts of many businessmen to promote it.

In those areas where industry did consolidate, new forms of corporate organization emerged to advance the trend. General Motors, by 1920 not only the largest automobile manufacturer but also the fifth-largest American corporation, was a classic example. GM's founder, William Durant, had expanded the company dramatically but had never replaced the informal, personal management style with which he began. When GM foundered in the recession of the early 1920s, leadership of the company fell to Alfred P. Sloan, who created a modern administrative system with an efficient divisional organization. The new system not only made it

MODERN ADMINISTRATIVE SYSTEMS

Discussion and Activities

Making Connections After students have read the section "Early Computers," ask them to create a Venn diagram comparing early twentieth-century computers with those of today. **WXT**

Historical Thinking Skills

Argumentation After students have read the section "Technology and Economic Growth," ask them to list and rank in order of importance the inventions described in the text. Have students discuss in small groups which invention they believe was the most important and why. **WXT**

Reasoning Processes

Comparing After students have read the section "Economic Organization," ask them to create a Venn diagram comparing industrial consolidation as in the case of General Motors with industrial consolidation as in the case of trade associations. **WXT**

easier for GM to control its many subsidiaries; it also made it simpler for it–and for the many other corporations that adopted similar administrative systems–to expand further.

Some industries less susceptible to domination by a few great corporations attempted to stabilize themselves not through consolidation but through cooperation. An important vehicle was the trade association–a national organization created by various members of an industry to encourage coordination in production and marketing techniques. Trade associations worked reasonably well in the mass-production industries that had already succeeded in limiting competition through consolidation. But in more decentralized industries, such as cotton textiles, their effectiveness was limited.

TRADE ASSOCIATIONS

The strenuous efforts by industrialists throughout the economy to find ways to curb competition through consolidation or cooperation reflected a strong fear of overproduction. Even in the booming mid-1920s, industrialists remembered how too-rapid expansion had helped produce recessions in 1893, 1907, and 1920. The great, unrealized dream of the New Era was to find a way to stabilize the economy so that such collapses would never occur again.

LABOR IN THE NEW ERA

The remarkable economic growth was accompanied by a continuing, and in some areas even increasing, maldistribution of wealth and purchasing power. More than two-thirds of the American people in 1929 lived at no better than what one major study described as the "minimum comfort level." Half of those languished at or below the level of "subsistence and poverty."

American industrial workers experienced both the successes and the failures of the 1920s as much as any other group. On the one hand, most workers saw their standard of living rise during the decade; many enjoyed greatly improved working conditions and other benefits. Some employers in the 1920s, eager to avoid disruptive labor unrest and the growth of independent trade unions, adopted paternalistic techniques that came to be known as "welfare capitalism." Henry Ford, for example, shortened the workweek, raised wages, and instituted paid vacations. U.S. Steel made conspicuous efforts to improve safety and sanitation in its factories. For the first time, some workers became eligible for pensions on retirement–nearly 3 million by 1926. (Women workers in such companies tended to receive other kinds of benefits–less often pensions, more often longer rest periods and vacations.) When labor grievances surfaced despite these efforts, workers could voice them through the so-called company unions that were emerging in many industries. These were workers' councils and shop committees, organized by the corporations themselves and thus without the independence later unions demanded.

"WELFARE CAPITALISM"

Welfare capitalism brought many workers important economic benefits, but it did not help them gain any real control over their own fates. Company unions were feeble vehicles, forbidden in most industries to raise the issues most important to workers. And welfare capitalism survived only as long as industry prospered. After 1929, with the economy in crisis, the system quickly collapsed.

Welfare capitalism affected only a relatively small number of workers in any case. Most employers were interested primarily in keeping their labor costs to a minimum. Workers as a whole, therefore, received wage increases at a rate far below increases in production and profits. Unskilled workers, in particular, saw their wages increase by only a little over 2 percent between 1920 and 1926. In the end, American workers in the 1920s remained a relatively impoverished and powerless group. Their wages rose; but the average annual income of a worker remained below $1,500 a year when $1,800 was considered necessary to maintain a minimally decent standard of living. Only by relying on the earnings of several family members could many working-class families make ends meet. And almost all such families had to live with the very real possibility of one or more members losing their jobs. Unemployment was lower in the 1920s than it had been in the previous two decades, and much lower than it would be in the 1930s. But a large proportion of the workforce (estimated at 5–7 percent at any given time) was out of work for at least some period during the decade–in part because the rapid growth of industrial technology made many jobs obsolete.

Many laborers continued to regard an effective, independent union movement as their best hope. But the New Era was a bleak time for labor organization, in part because the unions themselves were generally conservative and failed to adapt to the realities of the modern economy. The American Federation of Labor (AFL) remained committed to the concept of the craft union, in which workers were organized on the basis of particular skills. It continued to make no provision for the fastest-growing area of the workforce: unskilled, industrial workers, who had few organizations of their own. William Green, who became president of the AFL in 1924, was committed to peaceful cooperation with employers and to strident opposition to communism and socialism. He frowned on strikes.

HARD TIMES FOR ORGANIZED LABOR

WOMEN AND MINORITIES IN THE WORKFORCE

A growing proportion of the workforce consisted of women, who were concentrated in what have since become known as "pink-collar" jobs–low-paying service occupations with many of the same problems as manufacturing employment. Large numbers of women worked as secretaries, salesclerks, telephone operators, and in other, similarly underpaid jobs. Because technically such positions were not industrial jobs, the AFL and other labor organizations were generally uninterested in organizing these workers.

"PINK-COLLAR" JOBS

Similarly, the half-million African Americans who had migrated from the rural South to the cities during the Great

Historical Thinking Skills

Argumentation Have students read the section "Labor in the New Era." Ask them to discuss in small groups whether workers were better off in workplaces that implemented "welfare capitalism" than in those that did not. **WXT**

CONSIDER THE SOURCE

COMMUNICATIONS TECHNOLOGY

Scottish-Born Inventor and Scientist Alexander Graham Bell received a patent for his invention of the telephone on March 7, 1876. The Bell Telephone Company was formed in July of the following year; in the first month of the company's existence, it sold only six phones. By the end of the year, however, more than 3,000 telephones were in service in the United States. The nation's first telephone system (or exchange) was installed in Hartford, Connecticut, that same year. The first exchange linking two major cities was established in 1883 between New York City and Boston. By the turn of the century there were more than 5 million phones in the United States. As the map below shows, in 1914 telephone exchanges linked more than 70,000 places and 8 million subscribers in the United States. The telephone served as the basic communication link in the United States for over 100 years.

One of the next big revolutions in communications technology occurred in the 1970s, with the development of the Internet. The Soviet Union's launch of the satellite *Sputnik* in 1957 spurred the United States to develop computers and computer communications technology largely for defense-related purposes. The Department of

THE TELEPHONE—1914

What the Telephone Map Shows

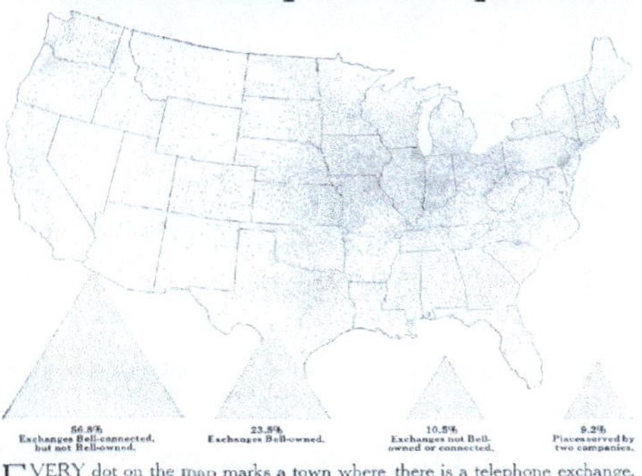

EVERY dot on the map marks a town where there is a telephone exchange, the same sized dot being used for a large city as for a small village. Some of these exchanges are owned by the Associated Bell companies and some by independent companies. Where joined together in one system they meet the needs of each community and, with their suburban lines, reach 70,000 places and over 8,000,000 subscribers.

The pyramids show that only a minority of the exchanges are Bell-owned, and that the greater majority of the exchanges are owned by independent companies and connected with the Bell System.

At comparatively few points are there two telephone companies, and there are comparatively few exchanges, chiefly rural, which do not have outside connections.

The recent agreement between the Attorney General of the United States and the Bell System will facilitate connections between all telephone subscribers regardless of who owns the exchanges.

Over 8,000 different telephone companies have already connected their exchanges to provide universal service for the whole country.

AMERICAN TELEPHONE AND TELEGRAPH COMPANY
AND ASSOCIATED COMPANIES

One Policy *One System* *Universal Service*

For our Mutual Advantage mention Popular Electricity and Modern Mechanics when writing to Advertisers.

Popular Electricity and Modern Mechanics, September, 19, 1914

Discussion and Activities

Making Connections Have students examine the image "What the Telephone Map Shows." Ask them to discuss in small groups how the image is similar to or different from current maps showing cellular network coverage. **WXT** **SOC**

Discussion and Activities

Analyzing Points of View Have students read the first paragraph of the feature. Ask them to write a short journal entry from the point of view of a new telephone customer in the early twentieth century describing how the telephone has changed their everyday life. **SOC** **WXT** **NAT**

Discussion and Activities

Making Connections After students have read the feature, ask them to create a Venn diagram comparing the impact of the telephone in the early twentieth century with the impact of the Internet in the late twentieth century. **WXT** **SOC** **NAT** **PCE**

Defense's Advanced Research Projects Agency (ARPA) formed the first computer network (ARPANET) in 1969, linking the computers of four universities–Stanford, UCLA, the University of California at Santa Barbara, and the University of Utah. By 1971, the ARPANET had expanded to twenty-three hosts at universities and government research centers throughout the United States. The Department of Defense withdrew from ARPANET in the early 1980s for security reasons. Now free to develop independently, the network–renamed the Internet–expanded rapidly, not only throughout the United States but across the globe as well.

GLOBAL COMMUNICATION NETWORKS

esenkartal/Getty Images

ANALYZING SOURCES

Questions assume cumulative content knowledge from this chapter and previous chapters.

1. What similar effect did both the telephone and Internet have on American society?
   (A) each was controlled by a dominant communications company
   (B) each greatly expanded Americans' communications ability
   (C) each was initially developed for national defense purposes
   (D) each greatly reduced the need for the American people to travel

2. Which pattern is most supported by the illustrations?
   (A) The coastal regions have or had the most access to the new respective technologies, when compared to the other regions of the U.S.
   (B) The northern Midwest region and the Northeast have or had greater access to the new technology of the time, in comparison to other regions of the U.S.
   (C) The Northwest has or had the most access to the new technology of the time, in both eras.
   (D) The Great Basin and Great Plains had the most access to both technologies.

3. Based on what you have learned about the Southern region of the U.S, which best explains the pattern of telephone exchanges in the South in 1914?
   (A) Due to the romantic cultural legacy of the South, fewer individuals in the South sought to purchase the new technology.
   (B) The South was more rural and, therefore, less densely populated between cities and villages.
   (C) The Northern cities took up most of the available capacity, leaving little for the South.
   (D) The technology was not available in the South.

650 · CHAPTER 23

Answers

Consider the Source

1. B; **2.** B; **3.** B

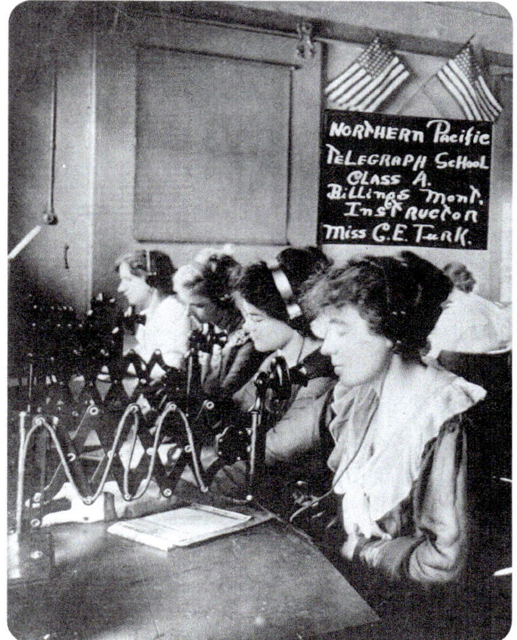

PREPARING WOMEN FOR WORK This school was established during World War I by the Northern Pacific Telegraph Company to train new women employees to be telephone operators. Both during and after the war, telephone companies were among the largest employers of women.

Migration after 1914 had few opportunities for union representation. The skilled crafts represented in the AFL often worked actively to exclude African Americans from their trades and organizations. Most African Americans worked in jobs in which the AFL took no interest–as janitors, dishwashers, garbage collectors, commercial laundry attendants, and domestics, and in other types of service jobs. This general reluctance to organize service-sector workers was in part because AFL leaders did not want women and minorities to become union members. The Brotherhood of Sleeping Car Porters, founded in 1925 and led for years by A. Philip Randolph, was a notable exception: a vigorous union, led by an African American and representing a virtually all-black workforce. Over time, Randolph won some significant gains for his members–increased wages, shorter working hours, and other benefits. He also enlisted the union in battles for civil rights for African Americans.

A. PHILIP RANDOLPH

In the West and the Southwest, the ranks of unskilled workers included considerable numbers of Asian and Hispanic people, few of them organized, most of them actively excluded from white-dominated unions. In the wake of the Chinese Exclusion Acts of the late nineteenth century, Japanese immigrants increasingly took the place of Chinese immigrants in menial jobs in California, despite the continuing hostility of the white population. They worked on railroads, construction sites, and farms, and in many other low-paying workplaces. Some Japanese immigrants managed to escape the ranks of the unskilled by forming their own small businesses or setting themselves up as truck farmers (farmers who grow small food crops for local sale). Many of the *Issei* (Japanese immigrants) and *Nisei* (their American-born children) enjoyed significant economic success–so much so that California passed laws in 1913 and 1920 to make it more difficult for them to buy land. Other Asian immigrants–most notably Filipinos–also swelled the unskilled workforce and generated considerable hostility. Anti-Filipino riots in California beginning in 1929 helped produce legislation in 1934 virtually eliminating immigration from the Philippines.

Mexican immigrants formed a major part of the unskilled workforce throughout the Southwest and California. Nearly half a million Mexican immigrants entered the United States in the 1920s, more than any other national group, increasing the total Mexican population to over a million. Most lived in California, Texas, Arizona, and New Mexico; and by 1930, most

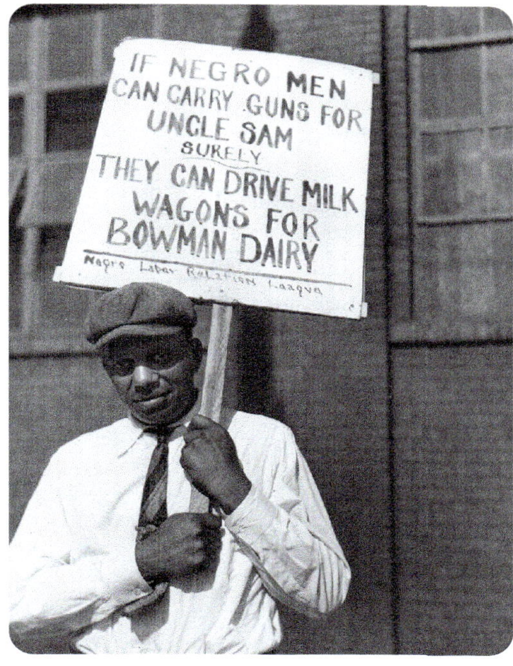

AFRICAN AMERICAN WORKER PROTESTING The frail union movement among African Americans in the 1920s, led by A. Philip Randolph and others against imposing obstacles, slowly built up a constituency within the black working class. Here, an aspiring black dairy worker draws attention to the contrast between African American patriotism in war and the discriminatory treatment African Americans faced at home.

Discussion and Activities

Historical Reasoning and Argumentation Have students read the section "A. Phillip Randolph." Ask them to think about and share with a partner the challenges facing African American workers trying to organize and reasons why Randolph may have been successful. *(Existing unions like the AFL tried to keep women and minorities out because they believed they had stronger bargaining positions without them. Randolph was successful because he focused narrowly on a service industry [railroad porters] that was dominated by African American men.)* **WXT** **SOC** **PCE**

Discussion and Activities

Analyzing Images Have students examine the images "Preparing Women for Work," and "African American Worker Protesting." Ask them to create a T-chart listing details from each photo. Have students discuss in small groups the similarities and differences between the two photos. *(Similarities: Both photos show disadvantaged workers. Women and African Americans often worked in different jobs than white men. Differences: The women are receiving training, while the black worker is unemployed.)* **WXT** **SOC**

Reasoning Processes

Comparing After students have read the section "Women and Minorities in the Workforce," ask them to create a Venn diagram comparing the challenges facing women and minorities in the workplace during the time period. **WXT** **SOC**

lived in cities. Large Mexican barrios—usually raw urban communities, often without even such basic services as plumbing and sewage—grew up in Los Angeles, El Paso, San Antonio, Denver, and many other cities and towns. Some of the residents found work locally in factories and shops; others traveled to mines or did migratory labor on farms, but returned to the cities between jobs. Mexican workers, too, faced hostility and discrimination from the Anglo population of the region; but there were few efforts actually to exclude them. Employers in the relatively underpopulated West needed this ready pool of low-paid, unskilled, and unorganized workers.

THE "AMERICAN PLAN"

Whatever the weaknesses of the unions and of unorganized, unskilled workers, the strength of the corporations was the principal reason for the absence of effective labor organization. After the turmoil of 1919, corporate leaders worked hard to spread the doctrine that unionism was somehow subversive, that a crucial element of democratic capitalism was the protection of the open shop (a shop in which no worker could be required to join a union). The crusade for the open shop, euphemistically titled the "American Plan," received the endorsement of the National Association of Manufacturers in 1920 and became a pretext for a harsh campaign of union busting across the country.

PROTECTING THE OPEN SHOP

When such tactics proved insufficient to counter union power, government assistance often made the difference. In 1921, the Supreme Court upheld a lower-court ruling that declared picketing illegal and supported the right of courts to issue injunctions against strikers. In 1922, the Justice Department intervened to quell a strike by 400,000 railroad workers. In 1924, the courts refused protection to members of the United Mine Workers Union when mine owners launched a violent campaign in western Pennsylvania to drive the union from the coal fields. As a result of these developments, union membership fell from more than 5 million in 1920 to under 3 million in 1929.

AGRICULTURAL TECHNOLOGY AND THE PLIGHT OF THE FARMER

Like industry, American agriculture in the 1920s was embracing new technologies for increasing production. The number

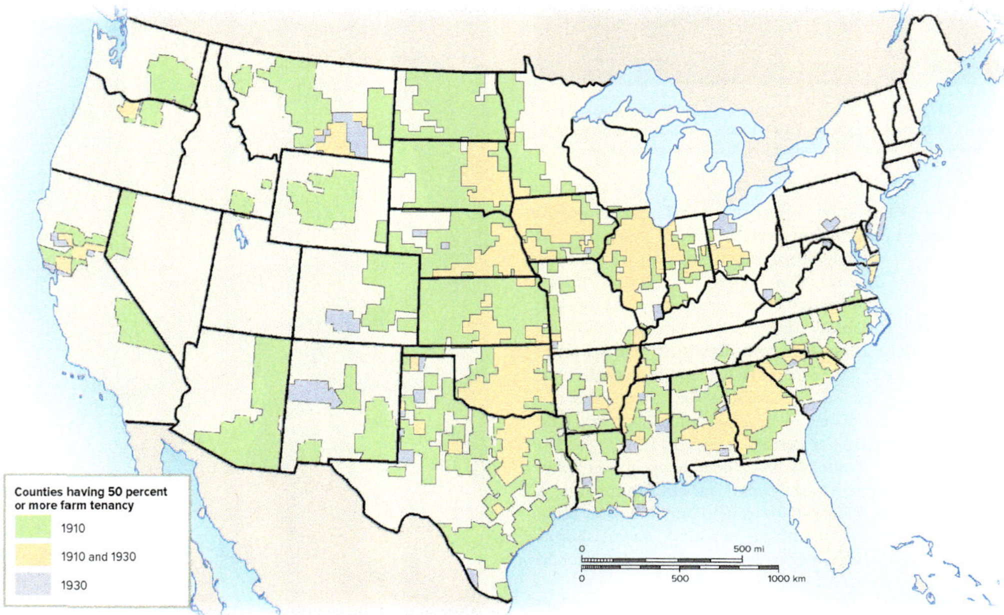

FARM TENANCY, 1910–1930 This map illustrates the significant increase in farm tenancy—that is, the number of farmers who did not own their land but worked as tenants for others—between 1910 and 1930. The dark green areas of the map show how extensive tenancy was even in 1910; over 50 percent of the land in those areas was farmed by tenants. The gold and purple parts of the map show the significant expansion of tenancy between 1910 and 1930—creating many new areas in which more than half the farmers were tenants.

How did the increasing efficiency and technological progress of agriculture in these years contribute to the growth of tenancy?

Answers

Farm Tenancy, 1910–1930

Mechanization increased farm productivity, but farmers who could not afford new equipment were increasingly forced to sell their farms.

MECHANIZED FARMING

of tractors on American farms, for example, quadrupled during the 1920s, especially after they began to be powered by internal combustion engines (like automobiles) rather than by the cumbersome steam engines of the past. They helped to open 35 million new acres to cultivation. Increasingly sophisticated combines and harvesters were proliferating, helping make it possible to produce more crops with fewer workers.

Agricultural researchers were already at work on other advances that would later transform food production in America and around the world: the invention of hybrid corn (made possible by advances in genetic research), which became available to farmers in 1921 but was not grown in great quantities until the 1930s; and the creation of chemical fertilizers and pesticides, which also began to have limited use in the 1920s but proliferated quickly in the 1930s and 1940s.

The new technologies greatly increased agricultural productivity, both in the United States and in other parts of the world. But the demand for agricultural goods was not rising as fast as production. The results were substantial surpluses, a disastrous decline in food prices, and a severe drop in farmers' income beginning early in the 1920s. More than 3 million people left agriculture in the course of the decade. Of those who remained, many lost ownership of their lands and had to rent instead from banks or other landlords.

In response, some farmers began to demand relief in the form of government price supports. One price-raising scheme

"PARITY"

in particular came to dominate agrarian demands: the idea of "parity." Parity was a complicated formula for setting an adequate price for farm goods and ensuring that farmers would earn back at least their production costs no matter how the national or world agricultural market might fluctuate. Champions of parity urged high tariffs against foreign agricultural goods and a government commitment to buy surplus domestic crops at parity and sell them abroad at whatever the market would bring.

The legislative expression of the demand for parity was the McNary-Haugen Bill, named after its two principal sponsors in

MCNARY-HAUGEN BILL

Congress and introduced repeatedly between 1924 and 1928. In 1926 and again in 1928, Congress (where farm interests enjoyed disproportionate influence) approved a bill requiring parity for grain, cotton, tobacco, and rice, but President Coolidge vetoed it both times.

THE NEW CULTURE

The increasingly urban and consumer-oriented culture of the 1920s helped many Americans in all regions live their lives and perceive their world in increasingly similar ways. That same culture exposed them to a new set of values that reflected the prosperity and complexity of the modern economy. But the new culture could not, of course, erase the continuing, and indeed increasing, diversity of the United States.

CONSUMERISM

Among the many changes industrialization produced in the United States was the creation of a mass consumer culture. By

GROWING MASS CONSUMPTION

the 1920s, America was a society in which many men and women could afford not merely the means of subsistence, but a considerable measure of additional, discretionary goods and services; a society in which people could buy items not just because of need but for pleasure as well. Middle-class families purchased such new appliances as electric refrigerators, washing machines, electric irons, and vacuum cleaners, which revolutionized housework and had a particularly dramatic impact on the lives of women. Men and women wore wristwatches and smoked cigarettes. Women purchased cosmetics and mass-produced fashions. Above all, Americans bought automobiles. By the end of the decade, there were more than 30 million cars on American roads.

The automobile affected American life in countless ways. It greatly expanded the geographic horizons of millions of

SOCIAL IMPACT OF THE AUTOMOBILE

people who in the past had seldom ventured far from their homes. Rural men and women, in particular, found in the automobile a means of escaping the isolation of farm life; now they could visit friends or drive into town quickly and at will, rather than spending hours traveling by horse or foot. City dwellers found in the automobile an escape from the congestion of urban life. Weekend drives through the countryside became a staple of urban leisure. Many families escaped the city in a permanent sense: by moving to the new suburbs that were rapidly growing up around large cities in response to the ease of access the automobile had created.

The automobile also transformed the idea of vacations. In the past, the idea of traveling for pleasure had been a luxury reserved for the wealthy. Now many middle-class and even working-class people could aspire to travel considerable distances for vacations, which were a new concept for most men and women in this era. Many businesses and industries began to include paid vacations among their employee benefits; and many employers encouraged their vacationing workers to travel, on the assumption that a change of scene would help restore their energy and vigor at work.

For young people in families affluent enough to afford a car, the automobile was often a means of a different kind of escape. It allowed them to move easily away from parents and family and to develop social lives of their own. It contributed to one of the distinctive developments of the early twentieth century: the emergence of a well-developed and relatively independent youth culture.

ADVERTISING

No group was more aware of the emergence of consumerism (or more responsible for creating it) than the advertising industry. The first advertising and public relations firms (N. W. Ayer and

Discussion and Activities

Evaluating Evidence After students have read the section "Agricultural Technology and the Plight of the Farmer," ask them to write a short letter or journal entry from the point of view of a farmer facing the decision about whether to take out a loan to purchase a new tractor, combine, or harvester. Have students consider whether the risks (being unable to repay debt) outweigh the potential rewards (increased productivity). **WXT**

Discussion and Activities

Analyzing Change Have students read the section "Consumerism." Ask them to discuss as a class how the purchase of an automobile would have changed life for an American family. **WXT** **SOC** **NAT**

Historical Thinking Skills

Argumentation After students have read the section "Advertising," ask them to create an advertisement for one of the new household appliances described earlier in the chapter (electric refrigerators, washing machines, electric irons, vacuum cleaners, etc.) using methods described in this section. **WXT** **SOC**

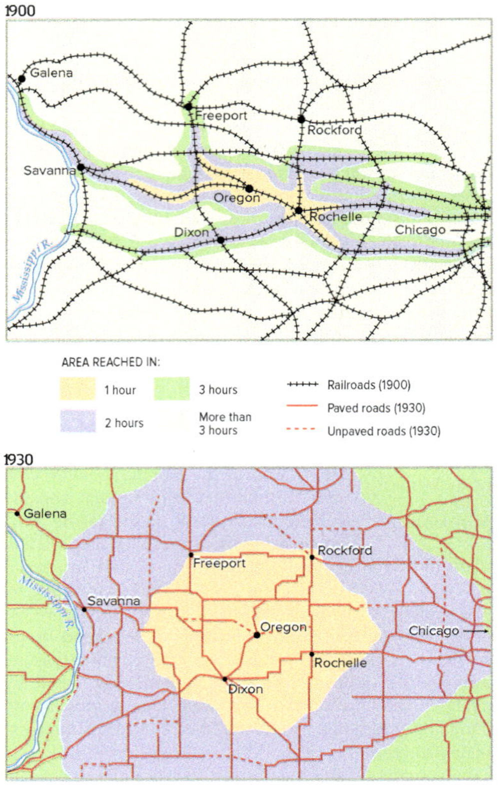

BREAKING DOWN RURAL ISOLATION: THE EXPANSION OF TRAVEL HORIZONS IN OREGON, ILLINOIS This map uses the small town of Oregon, Illinois—west of Chicago—to illustrate the way in which railroads and then automobiles reduced the isolation of rural areas in the first decades of the twentieth century. The gold and purple areas of the two maps show the territory that residents of Oregon could reach within two hours. Note how small that area was in 1900 and how much larger it was in 1930, by which time an area of over a hundred square miles had become easily accessible to the town. Note, too, the significant network of paved roads in the region by 1930, few of which had existed in 1900.

Why did automobile travel do so much more than railroads to expand the travel horizons of small towns?

J. Walter Thompson) had appeared well before World War I; but in the 1920s, partly as a result of techniques pioneered by wartime propaganda, advertising came of age. Publicists no longer simply conveyed information; they sought to identify products with a particular lifestyle, to invest them with glamour and prestige, and to persuade potential consumers that purchasing a commodity could be a personally fulfilling and enriching experience.

Advertisers also encouraged the public to absorb the values of promotion and salesmanship and to admire those who were effective "boosters" and publicists. One of the most successful books of the 1920s was *The Man Nobody Knows*, by advertising executive Bruce Barton. It portrayed Jesus Christ as not only a religious prophet but also a "super salesman," who "picked up twelve men from the bottom ranks of business and forged them into an organization that conquered the world." The parables, Barton claimed, were "the most powerful advertisements of all time." Barton's message was fully in tune with the new spirit of the consumer culture. Jesus had been a man concerned with living a full and rewarding life in this world; twentieth-century men and women should do the same. ("Life is meant to live and enjoy as you go along," Barton once wrote.) Jesus had succeeded because he knew how to make friends, to become popular, to please others; that talent was a prescription for success in the modern era as well.

THE MAN NOBODY KNOWS

The advertising industry could never have had the impact it did without the emergence of new vehicles of communication that made it possible to reach large audiences quickly and easily. Newspapers were being absorbed into national chains, and wire services were making it possible even for independent newspapers to carry nationally syndicated material.

New or expanded mass-circulation magazines also attracted broad, national audiences. *The Saturday Evening Post*, which began publication as a magazine in 1871, appealed to rural and small-town families with its homey stories and its conspicuous traditionalism; its popularity was, in some respects, evidence of a yearning for an earlier time. But other magazines responded directly to the realities of modern, urban life. The *Reader's Digest*, founded in 1921 by DeWitt and Lila Wallace, condensed stories and even books originally published in other places in an effort to make the expanding world of knowledge and information available in a brief, efficient form for people who would otherwise have no access to it. *Time* magazine, founded in 1923 by Henry Luce and Briton Hadden, set out to condense the news of the week into a brief, accessible, lively format for busy people who did not have the time or desire to read newspapers.

MASS-CIRCULATION MAGAZINES

THE MOVIES AND BROADCASTING

At the same time, movies were becoming an ever more popular and powerful form of mass communication. More than 100 million people saw films in 1930, as compared to 40 million in 1922. The addition of sound to motion pictures–beginning in 1927 with the first feature-length "talkie," *The Jazz Singer* with Al Jolson–created nationwide excitement. An embarrassing scandal in 1921 involving the popular comedian Fatty Arbuckle produced public outrage and political pressure to "clean up" Hollywood. In response, the film industry introduced "standards" to its films. Studio owners created the Motion Picture Association, a new trade association, and hired former postmaster general Will Hays to head it. More important, they gave Hays broad

HOLLYWOOD

Answers

Breaking Down Rural Isolation: The Expansion of Travel Horizons in Oregon, Illinois

Railroads connected towns and cities to one another but followed a fixed schedule and did not stop in between all towns. An automobile, on the other hand, could travel and stop anywhere along existing roads and travel whenever it was convenient for the driver. **SOC** **WXT** **ARC** **GEO** powers to review films and to ban anything likely to offend viewers (or politicians). Hays exercised his powers broadly and imposed on the film industry a safe, sanctimonious conformity for many years.

The most important communications vehicle was the only one truly new to the 1920s: radio. The first commercial radio station in America, KDKA in Pittsburgh, began broadcasting in 1920; and the first national radio network, the National Broadcasting Company, was formed in 1927. By 1923, there were more than 500 radio stations, covering every area of the country. The radio industry, too, feared government regulation and control, and thus monitored program content carefully and excluded controversial or provocative material. But radio was much less centralized than filmmaking. Individual stations had considerable autonomy, and even carefully monitored stations and networks could not control the countless hours of programming as effectively as the Hays office could control films. Radio programming, therefore, was more diverse—and at times more controversial and even subversive—than film.

MODERNIST RELIGION

The influence of the consumer culture, and its increasing emphasis on immediate, personal fulfillment, was visible even in religion. Theological modernists taught their followers to abandon some of the traditional tenets of evangelical Christianity (literal interpretation of the Bible, belief in the Trinity, attribution of human traits to the deity) and to accept

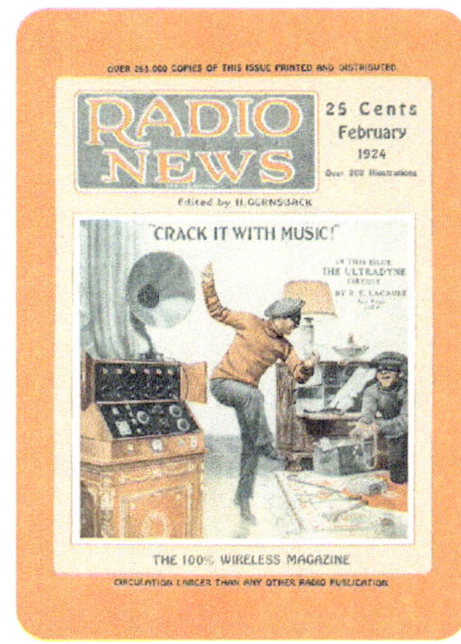

RADIO NEWS In the early 1920s, when radio was still new, many people considered it a "hobby," appropriate to people interested in technology. By the end of the decade, radio was a normal part of the everyday lives of almost everyone. *Radio News* started off in 1919 as a magazine for amateur radio enthusiasts. By the time of its last issue, in 1971, the magazine had expanded to cover all technical aspects of radio and electronics.

a faith that would help individuals to live more fulfilling lives in the present world.

The most influential spokesman for liberal Protestantism in the 1920s was Harry Emerson Fosdick, the pastor of Riverside Church in New York City. The basis of Christian religion, he claimed, was not unexamined faith, but a fully developed personality. In his 1926 book, *Abundant Religion*, he argued that Christianity would "furnish an inward spiritual dynamic for radiant and triumphant living."

HARRY EMERSON FOSDICK

Most Americans, even most middle-class Americans, stopped well short of this view of religion as a vehicle for advancing "man's abundant life" and remained faithful to traditional religious messages. But many other middle-class Americans were gradually devaluing religion, assigning it a secondary role (or at times no role) in their lives. When the sociologists Robert and Helen Merrell Lynd studied the society of Muncie, Indiana, in the mid-1920s, they were struck by how many people there claimed that they paid less attention to religion than their parents had. They no longer devoted much time to teaching their children the tenets of their faith; they seldom prayed at home or attended church on any day but Sunday. Even the Sabbath was becoming not a day of rest and religious reflection but, rather, a holiday filled with activities and entertainments.

PROFESSIONAL WOMEN

In the 1920s, college-educated women were no longer pioneers. There were now two and even three generations of graduates of women's or coeducational colleges and universities; many such women were making their presence felt in professional areas that in the past they had rarely penetrated.

Still, professional opportunities for women remained limited by prevailing assumptions (prevalent among many women as well as men) about what were suitable female occupations. Although there were notable success stories about female business executives, journalists, doctors, and lawyers, most professional women remained confined to such traditionally "feminine" fields as fashion, education, social work, and nursing, or to the lower levels of business management. Some middle-class women now combined marriage and careers, but most still had to choose between work and family. The majority of the 25 percent of married women who worked outside the home in the 1920s were working class. The "new professional woman" was a vivid and widely publicized image in the 1920s. In reality, however, most middle-class married women did not work outside the home.

LIMITED OPPORTUNITIES FOR WOMEN

CHANGING IDEAS OF MOTHERHOOD

Yet the 1920s constituted a new era for middle-class women nonetheless. In particular, the decade saw a redefinition of the idea of motherhood. Shortly after World War I, an influential group of psychologists—the "behaviorists," led by John B. Watson—

Reasoning Processes

Comparing and Contrasting After students have read the section "The Movies and Broadcasting," ask them to create a T-chart comparing the traits of radio and film. Have students discuss as a class the similarities and differences and what they feel would have been the most important difference during the time period. **WXT** **SOC** **ARC**

Reasoning Processes

Continuity and Change Have students read the section "Modernist Religion." Ask them to discuss in small groups how this movement represented a continuity or change over time from earlier religious movements in America, such as the First and Second Great Awakenings and the Social Gospel. *(Differences: less emphasis on obedience or personal responsibility to God or the Church; emphasis on this life rather than salvation.)* **SOC** **ARC**

Discussion and Activities

Analyzing Change After students have read the section "Changing Ideas of Motherhood," ask them to identify the factors that led to changes in family relationships in the early twentieth century. Have students discuss in pairs or small groups which of these they believe were most important and whether men or women were more greatly impacted. SOC ARC

began to challenge the long-held assumption that women had an instinctive capacity for motherhood. Maternal affection was not, they claimed, sufficient preparation for child rearing. Instead, mothers should rely on the advice and assistance of experts and professionals: doctors, nurses, and trained educators in nursery schools and kindergartens.

For many middle-class women, these changes helped redefine what had been an all-consuming activity. Motherhood was no less important in behaviorist theory than it had been before; if anything, it was more so. But for many women it was less emotionally fulfilling, less connected to their instinctive lives, more dependent on (and tied to) people and institutions outside the family. Many attempted to compensate by devoting new attention to their roles as wives and companions, to developing what became known as "companionate marriage." The middle-class wife shared increasingly in her husband's social life; she devoted more attention to cosmetics and clothing; she was less willing to allow children to interfere with their marriage. Most of all, many more women considered their sexual relationships with their husbands not simply as a means of procreation, as earlier generations had been taught to do, but as an important and pleasurable experience in its own right, as the culmination of romantic love.

"COMPANIONATE MARRIAGES"

Progress in the development of birth control was both a cause and a result of this change. The pioneer of the American birth-control movement was Margaret Sanger, who had become committed to the cause in part because of the influence of Emma Goldman—a Russian immigrant and political radical who had agitated for birth control before World War I. Sanger began her career promoting the diaphragm and other birth-control devices out of a concern for working-class women, believing that large families were among the major causes of poverty and distress in poor communities. By the 1920s, partly because she had limited success in persuading working-class women to accept her teachings, she was becoming more concerned with persuading middle-class women of the benefits of birth control. Women, she argued, should be free to enjoy the pleasures of sexual activity without any connection to procreation. Birth-control devices began to find a large market among middle-class women, even though some techniques remained illegal in many states (and abortion remained illegal nearly everywhere).

BIRTH CONTROL

THE "FLAPPER": IMAGE AND REALITY

The new, more secular view of womanhood had effects on women beyond the middle class as well. Some women concluded that in the "New Era" it was no longer necessary to maintain a rigid, Victorian female "respectability." Women could smoke, drink, dance, wear seductive clothes and makeup, and attend lively parties. They could strive for physical and emotional fulfillment, for release from repression and inhibition. (The wide popularity of Freudian ideas in the 1920s—often simplified and distorted for mass consumption—contributed to the growth of these attitudes.)

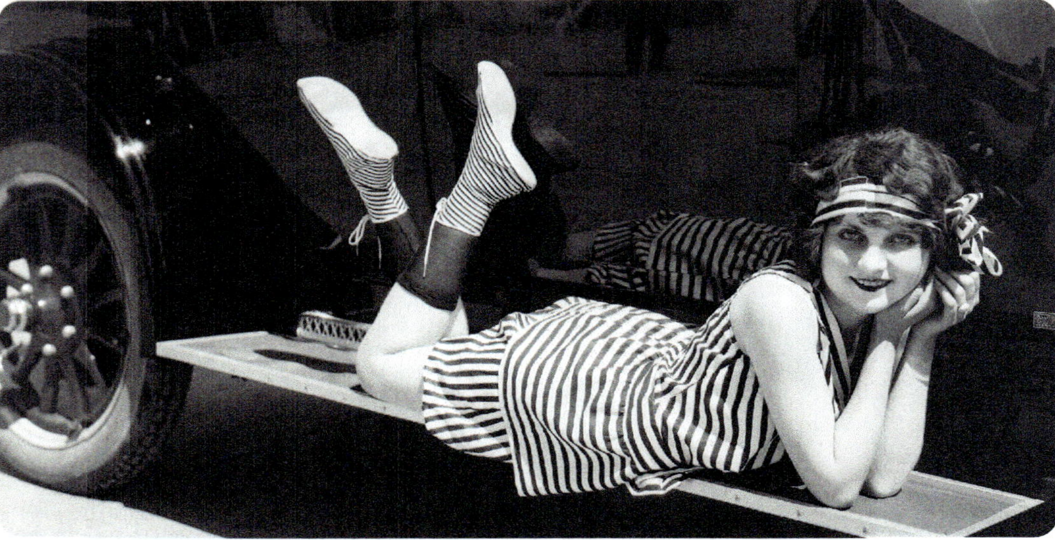

THE FLAPPER By the mid-1920s, the flapper—the young woman who challenged traditional expectations—had become not only a social type but a movement in fashion as well. Here, Catherine Dear is shown posing in the latest "beach costume," a fashion a long way from the rigid "respectability" of Victorian age women.

Bettmann/Getty Images

Discussion and Activities

Analyzing Visuals Have students examine the image "The Flapper." Ask them to identify and share with a partner details that illustrate social changes for women in the 1920s. *(The relatively revealing swimsuit suggests greater independence for young women. The automobile the model is posing on the running-board of represents independence of movement.)* ARC SOC

AMERICA IN THE WORLD

THE CINEMA

There is probably no cultural or commercial product more closely identified with the United States than motion pictures—or, as they are known in much of the world, the cinema. Although the technology of cinema emerged from the work of inventors in England and France as well as the United States, the production and distribution of films has been dominated by Americans almost from the start. The United States was the first nation to create a film "industry," and it did so at a scale vaster than that of any other country. The 700 feature films a year that Hollywood produced in the 1920s was more than ten times the number created by any other nation, and its films were dominating not only the vast American market, but much of the world's market as well. Seventy percent of the films seen in France, 80 percent of those seen in Latin America, and 95 percent of the movies viewed in Canada and Great Britain were produced in the United States in the 1920s.

As early as the 1930s, the penetration of other nations by American movies was already troubling many governments. The Soviet Union responded to the popularity of Walt Disney's Mickey Mouse cartoons by inventing a cartoon hero of its own—a porcupine, designed to entertain in a way consistent with socialist values and not the capitalist ones that the Soviets believed Hollywood conveyed. During World War II, American films were banned in occupied France (prompting some antifascist dissidents to screen such American films as Frank Capra's *Mr. Smith Goes to Washington* in protest).

American dominance was a result in part of World War I and its aftermath, which debilitated European filmmaking just as movies were vigorously growing in the United States. By the end of World War I, half the theaters of the world were in America. Two decades later, despite an extraordinary expansion of theaters in other nations, the United States continued to have over 40 percent of the world's cinemas. And while the spread of theaters through other areas of the world helped launch film industries in many other countries, it also increased the market (and the appetite) for American films and strengthened American supremacy in their production. "The sun, it now appears," *The Saturday Evening Post* commented in the mid-1920s, "never sets on the British empire and the American motion picture." Movies were then, and perhaps remain still, America's most influential cultural export. Even American popular music, which has enormous global reach, faces more significant local competition than American movies do in most parts of the world.

Despite this American dominance, however, filmmaking has flourished—and continues to flourish—in many countries around the world. India's fabled "Bollywood," for example, produces an enormous number of movies for its domestic market—almost as many as the American industry creates, even though few of them are widely exported. The global cinema has had a significant impact on American filmmaking, just as American films have influenced filmmakers abroad. The small British film industry had a strong early influence on American movies partly because of the quality and originality of British films, and partly because of the emigration of talented actors, directors, and screenwriters to the United States. The great Alfred Hitchcock, for example, made his first films in London before moving to Hollywood, where he spent the rest of his long career. After World War II, French "new wave" cinema helped spawn a new generation of highly individualistic directors in the United States. Asian cinema—especially the thriving film industry in Hong Kong, with its gritty realism—helped lead to some of the powerfully violent American films of the 1980s and beyond, as well as the genre of martial-arts films that has become popular around the world. German, Italian, Swedish, Dutch, Japanese, Australian, and Indian filmmakers also had influence on Hollywood—and over time perhaps even greater influence on the large and growing "independent film" movement in the United States.

VALENTINO The popularity of the film star Rudolph Valentino among American women was one of the most striking cultural phenomena of the 1920s. Valentino was slight and delicate, not at all like the conventional image of "manliness." But he developed an enormous following among women, in part—as this poster is obviously intended to suggest—by baring his body on screen. Valentino was Italian, which made him seem somehow strange and foreign to many older-stock Americans, and he was almost always cast in exotic roles, never as an American. His sudden death in 1926 (at the age of 31) created enormous outpourings of grief among many American women.

In recent decades, as new technologies and new styles have transformed films around the world, the American movie industry has continued to dominate global cinema. But national boundaries no longer adequately describe moviemaking in the twenty-first century. It is becoming a truly globalized enterprise in the same way that so many other commercial ventures are becoming international. "American" films today are often produced abroad, often have non-American directors and actors, and are often paid for with international financing. Hollywood still dominates worldwide filmmaking, but Hollywood itself is now an increasingly global community.

HISTORICAL THINKING SKILLS

1. **Explaining Historical Developments** Why did the American movie industry dominate global cinema during the 1920s and beyond?
2. **Analyzing Perspectives** Did American movies, as the Soviet Union claimed in the 1930s, promote capitalism?
3. **Developing Arguments** With the increasingly globalism of the movie industry, is there still an identifiable American cinema?

Discussion and Activities

Making Connections Have students examine the image "Valentino." Ask them to discuss as a class how celebrity is promoted today. SOC ARC WXT

Answers

America in the World

1. As the world was attempting to recover from the physical devastation of World War I, American infrastructure was unaffected. This gave the United States the opportunity and resources to advance in cinema.
2. The First Red Scare, which came about during World War I and especially during the 1920s, pitted the United States against the Soviet Union, despite their being allies in World War I. The ideological differences between the two nations caused a tremendous amount of suspicion and ideological warfare and the film industries of both countries reflected predominate views of its citizens.
3. Student answers will vary. With increasing globalization, there is more integration of multiple cultures in cinema industries around the world. While there is more cultural representation in American films, there remains an identifiable American cinema.

Discussion and Activities

Making Connections Have students read the section "The 'Flapper': Image and Reality." Ask them to go online and research the Equal Rights Amendment. Have students discuss as a class how the arguments on both sides were similar or different, and why they think the amendment failed in the 1920s and in the late-twentieth century. ARC SOC PCE

Such assumptions became the basis of the "flapper"–the modern woman whose liberated lifestyle found expression in dress, hairstyle, speech, and behavior. The flapper lifestyle had a particular impact on lower-middle-class and working-class single women, who were flocking to new jobs in industry and the service sector. (The young, affluent, upper-class "Bohemian" women most often associated with the flapper image were, in fact, imitating a style that emerged first among this larger working-class group.) At night, such women flocked, often alone, to clubs and dance halls in search of excitement and companionship.

Despite the image of liberation the flapper evoked in popular culture, most women remained highly dependent on men–both in the workplace, where they were usually poorly paid, and in the home–and relatively powerless when men exploited that dependence.

Pressing for Women's Rights

The realization that the "new woman" was as much myth as reality inspired some American feminists to continue their crusade for reform. The National Woman's Party, under the leadership of Alice Paul, pressed on with its campaign to make the Equal Rights Amendment, first proposed in 1923, a part of the Constitution, although it found little support in Congress (and met continued resistance from other feminist groups). Nevertheless, women's organizations and female political activities grew in many ways in the 1920s. Responding to the suffrage victory, women organized the League of Women Voters and the women's auxiliaries of both the Democratic and Republican Parties. Female-dominated consumer groups grew rapidly and increased the range and energy of their efforts.

EQUAL RIGHTS AMENDMENT

Women activists won a significant triumph in 1921, when they helped secure passage in Congress of a measure in keeping with the traditional feminist goal of securing "protective" legislation for women: the Sheppard-Towner Act. It provided federal funds to states to establish prenatal and child health-care programs. From the start, however, the bill produced controversy. Alice Paul and her supporters opposed the measure, arguing that it classified all women as mothers. Margaret Sanger's objection was that the new programs would discourage birth-control efforts. More important, the American Medical Association fought Sheppard-Towner, warning that it would introduce untrained outsiders into the health-care field. In 1929, Congress terminated the program.

SHEPPARD-TOWNER ACT

Education and Youth

The growing secularism of American culture and its expanding emphasis on training and expertise found reflection in the increasingly important role of education in the lives of American youth. First, more people were going to school in the 1920s than ever before. High-school attendance more than doubled during the decade, from 2.2 million to more than 5 million. Enrollment in colleges and universities increased threefold between 1900 and 1930, with much of that increase occurring after World War I. In 1918, there had been 600,000 college students; in 1930, there were 1.2 million, nearly 20 percent of the college-age population. Attendance was increasing as well at trade and vocational schools and in other institutions providing the specialized training that the modern economy demanded. Schools were beginning to offer instruction not only in the traditional disciplines, but also in modern technical skills: engineering, management, and economics.

The growing importance of education contributed to the emergence of a separate youth culture. The idea of adolescence as a distinct period in the life of an individual was for the most part new to the twentieth century. In some measure it was a result of the influence of Freudian psychology. But it was a result, too, of society's recognition that a more extended period of training and preparation was necessary before a young person was ready to move into the workplace. Schools and colleges provided adolescents with a setting in which they could develop their own social patterns, their own hobbies, their own interests and activities. An increasing number of students saw school as a place not just for academic training, but also for organized athletics, extracurricular activities, clubs, and fraternities and sororities–that is, as an institution that allowed them to define themselves less in terms of their families and more in terms of their peer group.

YOUTH CULTURE

The Disenchanted

The generation that lived through (and in many cases fought in) the Great War quickly came to see the conflict as a useless waste of lives lost for no purpose. For many young people in the 1920s, disenchantment with the war contributed to a growing disenchantment with the United States. The newly prosperous and consumer-driven era they encountered seemed meaningless and vulgar to many artists and intellectuals in particular. As a result, they came to view their own culture with contempt. Rather than trying to influence and reform their society, they isolated themselves from it and embarked on a restless search for personal fulfillment. The American writer Gertrude Stein once referred to the young Americans emerging from World War I as a "Lost Generation." For some writers and intellectuals, at least, it was an apt description.

At the heart of the Lost Generation's critique of modern society was a sense of personal alienation. The repudiation of Wilsonian idealism, the restoration of "business as usual," the growing emphasis on materialism and consumerism suggested that the war had been a fraud; that the suffering and the dying had been in vain. Ernest Hemingway, one of the most celebrated (and most commercially successful) of the new breed of writers, expressed the generation's contempt for the war in his novel *A Farewell to Arms* (1929). Its

LOST GENERATION'S CRITIQUE

Discussion and Activities

Making Connections Have students read the section "Education and Youth." Ask them to discuss as a class whether they think the idea of adolescence as a distinct stage of life has benefited them today or not. SOC ARC WXT

DANCE HALLS

In the booming, boisterous, consumer-oriented world of the 1920s, many Americans—especially those living in urban areas—challenged the inhibitions of traditional public culture. They looked instead for freedom, excitement, and release. Nowhere did they do so more vigorously and visibly than in the great dance halls that were proliferating in cities across the nation in these years.

The dance craze that swept urban America in the 1920s and 1930s was a result of many things. The great African American migration during World War I had helped bring new forms of jazz out of the South and into the urban North—where the phonograph and the radio popularized it. The growth of a distinctive youth culture—and the increasing tendency of men and women to socialize together in public—created an audience for uninhibited, sexually titillating entertainment. The relative prosperity of the 1920s enabled many young working-class people to afford to spend evenings out. And prohibition, by closing down most saloons and taverns, limited their other options.

Night after night, in big cities and small, young people flocked to dance halls to hear the powerful, pulsing new music; to revel in dazzling lights and ornate surroundings; to show off new clothes and hairstyles; and, of course, most of all, to dance. Like the new movie palaces that were being built at the same time, many of the dance halls provided a sense of grandiosity and glamour. Some of the larger dance halls in the big cities—Roseland and the Savoy in New York, the Trianon and the Aragon in Chicago, the Raymor in Boston, the Greystone in Detroit, the Hollywood Paladium, and many others—were truly cavernous, capable of accommodating thousands of couples at once. Over 10 percent of the men and women between the ages of 17 and 40 in New York went dancing at least once a week, and the numbers were comparable in other large cities.

What drew so many people to the dance halls? In large part, it was the music, which both its defenders and critics recognized as something very new in mainstream American culture. Dancing was "moral ruin," the *Ladies' Home Journal* primly warned in 1921, prompting "carelessness, recklessness, and laxity of moral responsibility" with its "direct appeal to the body's sensory centers." Many young dancers might have agreed with the description, if not with the moral judgment. Jazz encouraged a kind of uninhibited, even frenetic dancing—expressive, athletic, sensual—that young couples, in particular, found

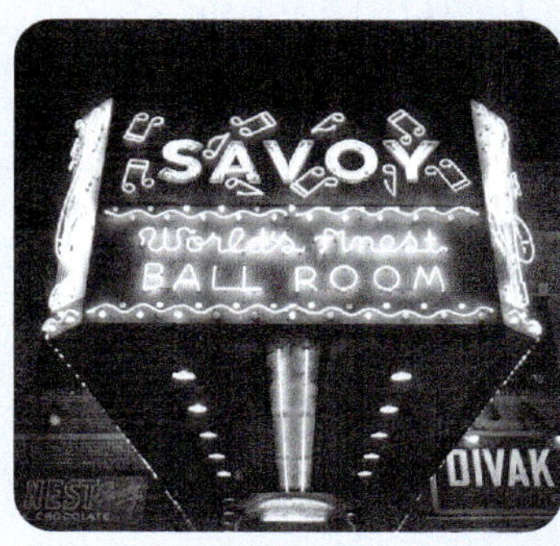

THE SAVOY The Savoy ballroom in New City's Harlem was one of the largest and most popular dance halls in America, and a regular home to many of the most noted dance bands in the 1920s and 1930s.

JITTERBUGGERS As dance halls became more popular, dancing became more exuberant—perhaps never more so than when the "jitterbug" became popular in the 1930s. This photograph shows an acrobatic pair of dancers during a huge dance event in Los Angeles designed to raise money for the Salvation Army. More than 10,000 people attended the event, and the police on hand to keep order had to call for reinforcements as the crowd became more and more frenzied and enthusiastic.

extraordinarily exciting, a welcome release from the often staid worlds of family, school, or work. Performances by some of the most famous bands and musicians of the day, Paul Whiteman, Ben Pollack, Fletcher Henderson, Bix Beiderbecke, Louis Armstrong, and Duke Ellington—already familiar to everyone through radio performances and recordings—drew enormous crowds.

Some of the less savory halls also attracted dancers for illicit reasons—as sources of bootleg liquor or as places to buy drugs. "Taxi-dance" ballrooms, which allowed men without their own partners to buy tickets to dance with "hostesses" and "instructresses," were sometimes closed by municipal authorities for "lewd" dancing and prostitution. Managers of the larger ballrooms tried to distance themselves from the unsavory image of the taxi-dance halls by imposing dress codes and making at least some efforts, usually futile, to require "decorum" among their patrons.

Dance halls were particularly popular with young men and women from working-class, immigrant communities. For them, going dancing was part of becoming American, a way to escape—even if momentarily—the insular world of the immigrant neighborhood. (Their parents saw it that way too, and often tried to stop their children from going because they feared the dance halls would pull them out of the family and the community.) Going dancing was a chance to mingle with hundreds, sometimes thousands, of strangers of diverse backgrounds, and to participate in a cultural ritual that had no counterpart in ethnic cultures.

But dance halls were not melting pots. African Americans—who flocked to ballrooms at least as eagerly as white Americans—usually gathered at clubs in black neighborhoods, where there were only occasional white patrons. White working-class people might encounter a large number of different ethnic groups in a great hall at once, but the groups did not mix very much. In

AP Exam Practice

Short Answer Provide students with the following short-answer questions and allow 15 minutes for completion. Ask for volunteers to share their responses and discuss as a class.

Answer A, B, and C.

A) Briefly describe ONE important new form of entertainment in the 1920s. *(Students may describe features of radio, movies, magazines, dance halls, etc.)*

B) Briefly describe a second important new form of entertainment in the 1920s. *(Students may describe any of the entertainment forms listed in Question A.)*

C) Briefly explain ONE important reason for the development of one of the forms of entertainment explained above. *(Increasing affluence of upper and middle classes; more discretionary income; new technologies like motion pictures with sound.)*

Discussion and Activities

Analyzing Visuals Have students examine the image "Jitterbuggers." Ask them to identify and discuss in small groups details from the image that show cultural changes in the 1920s. *(Shorter skirts worn by young women; African Americans and white participants on the dance floor together.)* **SOC** **ARC**

Reasoning Processes

Comparing After students have read the section "The Disenchanted," ask them to create a chart listing attributes of Hemingway, Mencken, Lewis, and Fitzgerald. Have students identify traits that all four have in common. **ARC**

DANCING AT THE SAVOY This photograph of the interior of the famous Savoy ballroom shows the crowds of men and women who typically flocked there to dance to the great black jazz bands of the 1920s and 1930s.

Chicago's Dreamland, for example, Italian groups congregated near the door, Polish groups gathered near the band, and Jewish people grouped together in the middle of the floor. Still, the experience of the dance hall—like the experience of the movie palace or the amusement park—drew people into the growing mass culture that was competing with and beginning to overwhelm the close-knit ethnic cultures into which many young Americans had been born.

HISTORICAL THINKING SKILLS

1. **Drawing Conclusions** Besides the music, what was the appeal of the dance hall?
2. **Explaining Historical Context** Although thousands of young people attended dance halls, why were the halls unable to break down the ethnic or racial barriers of those who flocked to them?
3. **Making Connections** Is there an equivalent today of the dance hall of the 1920s and 1930s?

WORKERS AT SCHOOL The progressive ethos of the early twentieth century inspired many groups to fight for reform. These working-class women enrolled in a labor summer school at Bryn Mawr College in the summer of 1916 to prepare to become politically active.

protagonist, an American officer fighting in Europe, decides that there is no justification for his participation in the conflict and deserts the army with a nurse with whom he has fallen in love. Hemingway suggested that the officer was to be admired for doing so.

One result of this alienation was a series of savage critiques of modern society by a wide range of writers, some of whom were known as the "debunkers." Among them was the Baltimore journalist H. L. Mencken. His magazines–first the *Smart Set* and later the *American Mercury*–ridiculed everything most middle-class Americans held dear: religion, politics, the arts, even democracy itself. Mencken could not believe, he claimed, that "civilized life was possible under a democracy," because it was a form of government that placed power in the hands of the common people, whom he ridiculed as the "booboisie." Echoing Mencken's contempt was the novelist Sinclair Lewis, the first American to win a Nobel Prize in Literature. In a series of savage novels–*Main Street* (1920), *Babbitt* (1922), *Arrowsmith* (1925), and others–he lashed out at one aspect of modern society after another: the small town, the modern city, the medical profession, popular religion. The novelist F. Scott Fitzgerald ridiculed the American obsession with material success in *The Great Gatsby* (1925). The novel's title character, Jay Gatsby, spends his life accumulating wealth and social prestige in order to win the woman he loves. The world to which he has aspired, however, turns out to be one of pretension, fraud, and cruelty, and it ultimately destroys him.

H. L. MENCKEN

REJECTING SUCCESS

Answers

Patterns of Popular Culture

1. The dance halls of the 1920s were places where freedom could be celebrated and inhibitions could be tossed aside, which was very much in keeping with the prevailing ideology of the decade.
2. The dance halls, while a source of freedom and experimentation, were still cultural products of the segregated society of the 1920s.
3. Yes, contemporary dance clubs are the equivalent of the dance halls of the 1920s. These are popular for the same reasons and often attract a similar age cohort.

THE ART OF THE HARLEM RENAISSANCE Aaron Douglas (1899–1979), one of the most significant African American artists of the 1920s, combined an interest in African and African American themes with an attraction to the modernist trends in American art during this period.

THE HARLEM RENAISSANCE

In postwar Harlem in New York City, a new generation of black artists and intellectuals created a flourishing African American culture widely described as the "Harlem Renaissance." There were nightclubs (among them the famous Cotton Club) featuring many of the great jazz musicians who would later become staples of national popular culture: Duke Ellington, Jelly Roll Morton, Fletcher Henderson, and others. There were theaters featuring ribald musical comedies and vaudeville acts. Many white New Yorkers traveled up to Harlem for the music and theater, but the audiences were largely black New Yorkers.

Harlem in the 1920s was above all a center of literature, poetry, and art that drew heavily from both American and African roots. Black artists were trying in part to demonstrate the richness of their own racial heritage (and, not incidentally, to prove to white people that their race was worthy of respect). The poet Langston Hughes captured much of the spirit of the movement in a single sentence: "I am a Negro–and beautiful." One of the leaders of the Harlem Renaissance was Alain Locke, who assembled a notable collection of black writings published in 1925 as *The New Negro*. Gradually, white publishers began to notice and take an interest in the writers Locke helped launch. Hughes, Zora Neale Hurston, Countee Cullen, Claude McKay, James Weldon Johnson, and others gradually found readerships well beyond the black community. The painter Aaron Douglas, talented chronicler of the African American experience, eventually found himself commissioned to create important murals in universities and public buildings.

AFRICAN AMERICAN PRIDE

A CONFLICT OF CULTURES

The modern, secular culture of the 1920s was not unchallenged. It grew up alongside older, more traditional cultures, with which it continually and often bitterly competed.

PROHIBITION

When the prohibition of the sale and manufacture of alcohol went into effect in January 1920, it had the support of most members of the middle class and most of those who considered themselves progressives. Within a year, however, it had become clear that the "noble experiment," as its defenders called it, was not working well. Prohibition did substantially reduce drinking, at least in some regions of the country. But it also produced conspicuous and growing violations that made the law an almost immediate source of disillusionment and controversy. The federal government hired only 1,500 agents to enforce the prohibition laws, and in many places they received little help from local police. Before long, it was almost as easy to acquire illegal alcohol in much of the country as it had once been to acquire legal alcohol. And since an enormous, lucrative industry was now barred to legitimate businessmen, organized crime figures took it over. In Chicago, Al Capone built a criminal empire based largely on illegal alcohol. He guarded it against interlopers with an army of as many as 1,000 gunmen, whose zealousness contributed to the violent deaths of more than 250 people in the city between 1920 and 1927. Other regions produced gangsters and gang wars of their own.

FAILURE OF PROHIBITION

ALCOHOL AND ORGANIZED CRIME

Many middle-class progressives who had originally supported prohibition soon soured on the experiment. But an enormous constituency of provincial, largely rural, Protestant Americans continued vehemently to defend it.

HARLEM, 1925 Well-dressed schoolchildren gather on a street in Harlem, illustrating the growing affluence of the African American elite in New York.

Discussion and Activities

Analyzing Points of View Have students read the section "The Harlem Renaissance." Ask them to write a advertisement for a social, cultural, or artistic activity taking place in Harlem at the time. **ARC** **SOC** **WXT**

Discussion and Activities

Analyzing Visuals Have students examine the image "Harlem, 1925." Ask them to identify and discuss in small groups details from the image that give an impression of life in Harlem at that time. *(Many children, suggesting a relatively young population; well-dressed children suggesting material success; school children suggesting access to education.)* **ARC** **SOC**

Reasoning Processes

Causation After students have read the section "Prohibition," ask them to list and rank in order of importance the reasons for the failure of Prohibition. Have students write a thesis statement that makes a claim about the most important effect(s) of Prohibition. **ARC** **NAT** **SOC** **WXT**

Opponents of prohibition (or "wets," as they came to be known) gained steadily in influence. Not until 1933, however, when the Great Depression added weight to their appeals, were they finally able effectively to challenge the "drys" and win repeal of the Eighteenth Amendment.

PROHIBITION, 1921 A New York City police commissioner oversees agents pouring illegal liquor into the street. This raid occurred in the early months of prohibition, when the battle against alcohol was still popular—hence the eagerness of the commissioner to appear in the photograph.

The Library of Congress (LC-USZ62-123257)

NATIVISM AND THE KLAN

Agitation for a curb on foreign emigration to the United States had begun in the nineteenth century; and like the prohibition movement, it had gathered strength in the years before the war largely because of the support of middle-class progressives. Such concerns had not been sufficient in the first years of the century to win passage of curbs on immigration; too many employers fought to keep low-paid immigrant workers flooding into the country. But in the troubled and repressive years immediately following the war, many old-stock Americans began to associate immigration with radicalism.

Sentiment on behalf of restriction grew rapidly as a result. In 1921, Congress passed an emergency immigration act, establishing a quota system by which annual immigration from any country could not exceed 3 percent of the number of persons of that nationality who had been in the United States in 1910. The new law cut immigration from 800,000 to 300,000 in any single year, but nativists remained unsatisfied and pushed for a harsher law. The National Origins Act of 1924 strengthened the exclusionist provision of the 1921 law. It banned immigration from east Asia entirely. That provision deeply angered Japanese people, who understood that they were the principal target; Chinese immigration had been illegal since 1882. The law also reduced the quota for European immigrants from 3 percent to 2 percent. The quota would be based, moreover, not on the 1910 census, but on the census of 1890, a year in which there had been many fewer southern and eastern Europeans in the country. What immigration there was, in other words, would heavily favor northwestern Europeans—people of "Nordic" or "Teutonic" stock. Five years later, a further restriction set a rigid limit of 150,000 immigrants a year. In the years that followed, immigration officials seldom permitted even half that number actually to enter the country.

NATIONAL ORIGINS ACT OF 1924

But the nativism of the 1920s extended well beyond restricting immigration. Among other things, this nativism helped instigate the rebirth of the Ku Klux Klan as a major force in American society.

The first Klan, founded during Reconstruction, had died in the 1870s. But in 1915, another group of white Southerners met on Stone Mountain near Atlanta and established a new version of the society. Nativist passions had swelled in Georgia and elsewhere in response to the case of Leo Frank, a Jewish factory manager in

THE NEW KLAN

Total immigration during five-year periods (in millions)

Year	Total immigration (millions)
1921–1925	2.64
1926–1930	1.47
1931–1935	0.22
1936–1940	0.31
1941–1945	0.17
1946–1950	0.86
1951–1955	1.09
1956–1960	1.43

TOTAL IMMIGRATION, 1920–1960 After many years of extremely high rates of immigration from Europe and elsewhere, the United States experienced several decades of much lower immigration beginning in the 1920s. Immigration-restriction legislation passed in 1921 and 1924 was one important reason for the decline.

What other factors depressed immigration in the 1930s and 1940s?

Answers

Total Immigration, 1920–1960

World War II interfered with immigration during the 1930s and 1940s.

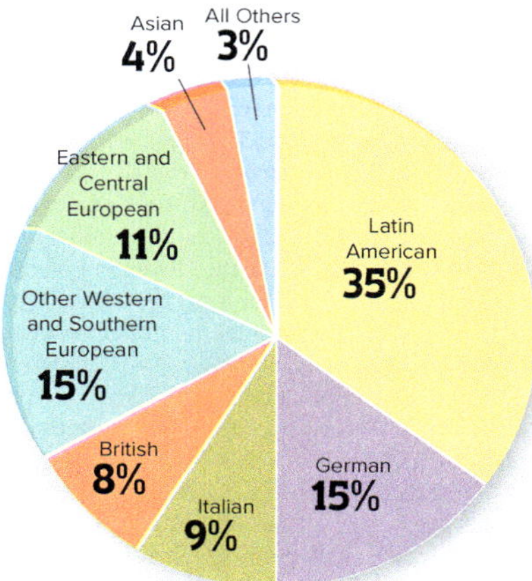

SOURCES OF IMMIGRATION, 1920–1960 This chart shows a significant change in the sources of immigration between 1920 and 1960, a direct result of the National Origins Act of 1924, which established national quotas for immigrants to the United States based on the number of such immigrants who had been in the country in 1890. Note the shift back toward northern and western Europe and away from Italy and other southern and eastern European nations (which had not been heavily represented in the immigration of the 1890s). But the most dramatic change was the huge increase in the proportion of immigrants from Latin America, a region explicitly exempted from the quota system established in 1924.

Why were Latin Americans treated differently than Europeans in immigration law in these years?

Atlanta convicted in 1914 (on very flimsy evidence) of murdering a female employee; a mob stormed Frank's jail cell and lynched him. The premiere (also in Atlanta) of D. W. Griffith's film *The Birth of a Nation*, which glorified the early Klan, also helped inspire white Southerners to form a new one. At first the new Klan, like the old, was largely concerned with intimidating African Americans, who, according to Klan leader William J. Simmons, were becoming insubordinate. And at first it remained small, obscure, and almost entirely Southern. After World War I, however, concern about African Americans became secondary to concern about Catholic, Jewish, and foreign people. At that point, membership in the Klan expanded rapidly and dramatically, not just in the small towns and rural areas of the South, but also in industrial cities in the North and Midwest. Indiana had the largest Klan membership of any state, and there were substantial Klans in Chicago, Detroit, and other Northern industrial cities. The Klan was also strong in the West, with large and active chapters in Oregon and Colorado. By 1924, there were reportedly 4 million members.

In some communities, where Klan leaders came from the most "respectable" segments of society, the organization operated much like a fraternal society, engaging in nothing more dangerous than occasional political pronouncements. Many Klan units (or "klaverns") tried to present themselves as patriots and community leaders. Some established women's and even children's auxiliaries to demonstrate their commitment to the family. Often, however, the Klan also operated as a brutal, even violent, opponent of "alien" groups and as a defender

KLAN INITIATION A Ku Klux Klan chapter in Jackson, Mississippi, holds an initiation ceremony for new members in August 1923.

Discussion and Activities

Analyzing Visuals Have students examine the image "Klan Initiation." Ask them to identify and discuss in small groups details from the image that illustrate Klan tactics. *(Nighttime rituals and costumes covering heads and bodies suggesting secrecy; the large circle symbolizing unity.)* **SOC**

Answers

Sources of Immigration, 1920–1960

Immigrants from Latin America were exempt from the National Origins Act and were often sought after as a source of low-wage labor.

Reasoning Processes

Comparing and Contrasting After students have read the section "Nativism and the Klan," ask them to create a Venn diagram comparing the "New" Klan with the original Klan that emerged during Reconstruction. Have students discuss as a class the most important similarities and differences. **ARC** **SOC**

of traditional, fundamentalist morality. Some Klansmen systematically terrorized African Americans as well as Catholic, Jewish, and foreign people and boycotted their businesses, threatened their families, and attempted to drive them out of their communities. Occasionally, they resorted to violence: public whipping, tarring and feathering, arson, and lynching.

What the Klan feared, it soon became clear, was not simply "foreign" or "racially impure" groups; it was anyone who posed a challenge to "traditional values," as the Klan defined them. Klansmen persecuted not only immigrants and African Americans, but also those white Protestants they considered guilty of irreligion, sexual promiscuity, or drunkenness. The Klan worked to enforce prohibition; it attempted to institute compulsory Bible reading in schools; it worked to punish divorce. It also provided its members, many of them people of modest means with little real power in society, with a sense of community and seeming authority. Its bizarre costumes, its elaborate rituals, its "secret" language, its burning crosses—all helped produce a sense of excitement and cohesion.

DEFENDING "TRADITIONAL VALUES"

The Klan declined quickly after 1925, when a series of internal power struggles and several sordid scandals discredited some of its most important leaders. The most damaging episode involved David Stephenson, head of the Indiana Klan, who raped a young secretary, kidnapped her, and watched her die rather than call a doctor after she swallowed poison. The Klan staggered on in some areas into the 1930s, but by World War II it was effectively dead. (The postwar Ku Klux Klan, which still survives, is modeled on but has no direct connection to the Klan of the 1920s and 1930s.)

DAVID STEPHENSON

RELIGIOUS FUNDAMENTALISM

Another bitter cultural controversy of the 1920s challenged the place of religion in contemporary society. By 1921, American Protestantism was divided into two warring camps. On one side stood the modernists: mostly urban, middle-class people who had attempted to adapt religion to the teachings of science and to the realities of their modern, secular society. On the other side stood the defenders of traditional faith: provincial, largely rural men and women, fighting to maintain the centrality of traditional religion in American life. They became known as "fundamentalists," a term derived from an influential set of pamphlets, *The Fundamentals*, published before World War I. The fundamentalists were outraged at the abandonment of traditional beliefs in the face of scientific discoveries. They insisted the Bible was to be interpreted literally. Above all, they opposed the teachings of Charles Darwin, who had openly challenged the biblical story of the Creation. Human beings had not evolved from lower orders of animals, the fundamentalists insisted; they had been created by God, as described in Genesis.

Fundamentalism was a highly evangelical movement, interested in spreading the doctrine to new groups. Fundamentalist evangelists, among them the celebrated Billy Sunday, traveled from state to state (particularly in the South and parts of the West) attracting huge crowds to their revival meetings. Protestant modernists looked on much of this activity with condescension and amusement. But by the mid-1920s, to their great alarm, evangelical fundamentalism was gaining political strength in some states with its demands for legislation to forbid the teaching of evolution in the public schools. In

BRYAN AND DARROW IN DAYTON
Clarence Darrow (left), a famous lawyer who defended Scopes, and William Jennings Bryan, an even more famous politician who supported the prosecution, pose for photographers during the 1925 Scopes trial. Both men had removed their jackets because of the intense heat, and Bryan had shocked many of his admirers by revealing that he was not wearing suspenders (as most country people did), but a belt—which in rural Tennessee was a symbol of urban culture.

Hulton Archive/Getty Images

Discussion and Activities

Analyzing Issues Have students read the section "David Stephenson." Ask them to think about and discuss with a partner why the case discussed was so damaging to the Klan. *(The Klan consistently used rhetoric about protecting the purity of the white race and protecting the virtue of white women. News of the rape and complicity in the death of a white woman at the hands of a Klan leader dramatically undercut those claims.)* **SOC**

Tennessee in March 1925, the legislature adopted a measure making it illegal for any public school teacher "to teach any theory that denies the story of the divine creation of man as taught in the Bible."

The Tennessee law attracted the attention of the fledgling American Civil Liberties Union, which had been founded in 1920 by men and women alarmed by the repressive legal and social climate of World War I and its aftermath. The ACLU offered free counsel to any Tennessee educator willing to defy the law and become the defendant in a test case. A twenty-four-year-old biology teacher in the town of Dayton, John T. Scopes, agreed to have himself arrested. And when the ACLU decided to send the famous attorney Clarence Darrow to defend Scopes, the aging William Jennings Bryan (now an important fundamentalist spokesman) announced that he would travel to Dayton to assist the prosecution. Journalists from across the country flocked to Tennessee to cover what became known as the "Monkey Trial," which opened in an almost circuslike atmosphere. Scopes had, of course, clearly violated the law; and a verdict of guilty was a foregone conclusion, especially when the judge refused to permit "expert" testimony by evolution scholars. Scopes was fined $100, and the case was ultimately dismissed in a higher court because of a technicality. Nevertheless, Darrow scored an important victory for the modernists by calling Bryan to the stand to testify as an "expert on the Bible." In the course of the cross-examination, which was broadcast by radio to much of the nation, Darrow made Bryan's stubborn defense of biblical truths appear foolish and finally tricked him into admitting the possibility that not all religious dogma was subject to only one interpretation.

SCOPES "MONKEY TRIAL"

The Scopes trial was a traumatic experience for many fundamentalists. It isolated and ultimately excluded them from many mainstream Protestant denominations. It helped put an end to much of their political activism. But it did not change their religious convictions. Even without connection to traditional denominations, fundamentalists continued to congregate in independent churches or new denominations of their own.

THE DEMOCRATS' ORDEAL

The anguish of provincial Americans attempting to defend an embattled way of life proved particularly troubling to the Democratic Party, which suffered during the 1920s as a result of tensions between its urban and rural factions. More than the Republicans, the Democrats were a diverse coalition of interest groups, linked to the party by local traditions. Among those interest groups were prohibitionists, Klansmen, and fundamentalists on one side and Catholics, urban workers, and immigrants on the other.

In 1924, the tensions between them proved devastating. At the Democratic National Convention in New York City that summer, bitter conflict broke out over the platform when the party's urban wing attempted to win approval of planks calling for the repeal of prohibition and a denunciation of the Klan. Both planks narrowly failed. More damaging to the party was a deadlock in the balloting for a presidential candidate. Urban Democrats supported Alfred E. Smith, the Irish Catholic Tammanyite who had risen to become a progressive governor of New York. Rural Democrats backed William McAdoo, Woodrow Wilson's Treasury secretary (and son-in-law), later to become a senator from California; he had skillfully positioned himself to win the support of southern and western delegates suspicious of Tammany Hall and modern urban life. The convention dragged on for 103 ballots, until finally, after both Smith and McAdoo withdrew, the party settled on a compromise: the bland corporate lawyer John W. Davis, who had served as solicitor general and ambassador to Britain under Wilson. He was easily defeated by President Calvin Coolidge.

A similar schism plagued the Democrats again in 1928, when Al Smith finally secured his party's nomination for president after a much shorter battle. Smith was not, however, able to unite his divided party—largely because of widespread anti-Catholic sentiment, especially in the South. He was the first Democrat since the Civil War not to carry the entire South. Elsewhere, although he did well in the large cities, he carried only Massachusetts and Rhode Island. Smith's opponent, and the

AL SMITH

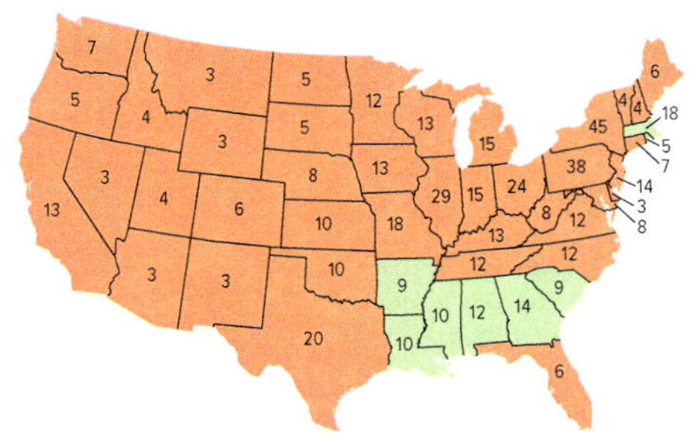

Candidate (Party)	Electoral Vote	Popular Vote (%)
Herbert Hoover (Republican)	444	21,391,381 (58.2)
Alfred E. Smith (Democratic)	87	15,016,443 (40.9)
Norman Thomas (Socialist)	—	267,835 (0.7)
Other parties (Socialist Workers, Prohibition)	—	62,890

56.9% of electorate voting

ELECTION OF 1928 The election of 1928 was, by almost any measure, highly one-sided. Herbert Hoover won over 58 percent of the vote to Alfred Smith's 41. Smith carried only Massachusetts, Rhode Island, and some traditionally Democratic states in the South.

Why did Smith do so poorly even in some of the South?

Discussion and Activities

Analyzing Issues After students have read the section "Religious Fundamentalism," ask them to discuss in small groups how the court ruling in the Scopes trial could represent both a victory and a defeat for both sides. **SOC** **ARC** **PCE**

Answers

Election of 1928

Al Smith was Catholic, and there was considerable anti-Catholic sentiment in the nation at this time.

Historical Thinking Skills

Evaluating Historical Significance After students have read the section "The Democrats' Ordeal," ask them to create a campaign poster for one of the major party candidates in the presidential elections of 1924 and 1928. You may want to assign candidates to four different groups of students. Have students consider what messages would appeal to each candidate's existing supporters and what messages might appeal to voters of the other party. **PCE** **SOC** **ARC** **WXT**

victor in the presidential election, was a man who perhaps more than any other contemporary politician seemed to personify the modern, prosperous, middle-class society of the New Era: Herbert Hoover.

REPUBLICAN GOVERNMENT

For twelve years, beginning in 1921, both the presidency and the Congress were in the hands of the Republican Party–a party in which the power of reformers had greatly dwindled since the heyday of progressivism before the war. For most of those years, the federal government enjoyed a warm and supportive relationship with the American business community. Yet the government of the New Era was more than the passive, pliant instrument that critics often described. It also attempted to serve as an active agent of economic change.

HARDING AND COOLIDGE

Nothing seemed more clearly to illustrate the unadventurous character of 1920s politics than the characters of the two men who served as president during most of the decade: Warren G. Harding and Calvin Coolidge.

Harding was elected to the presidency in 1920, having spent many years in public life doing little of note. An undistinguished senator from Ohio, he had received the Republican presidential nomination as a result of an agreement among leaders of his party, who considered him, as one noted, a "good second-rater." Harding appointed capable men to the most important cabinet offices, and he attempted to stabilize the nation's troubled foreign policy. But even as he attempted to rise to his office, he seemed baffled by his responsibilities, as if he recognized his own unfitness. "I am a man of limited talents from a small town," he reportedly told friends on one occasion. "I don't seem to grasp that I am President." Harding's intellectual limits were compounded by personal weaknesses: his penchant for gambling, illegal alcohol, and attractive women.

Teapot Dome

Harding lacked the strength to abandon the party hacks who had helped create his political success. One of them, Harry Daugherty, the Ohio party boss principally responsible for his meteoric political ascent, he appointed attorney general. Another, New Mexico senator Albert B. Fall, he made secretary of the Interior. Members of the so-called Ohio Gang filled important offices throughout the administration. Unknown to the public (and perhaps also to Harding), Daugherty, Fall, and others were engaged in fraud and corruption. The most spectacular scandal involved the rich naval oil reserves at Teapot Dome, Wyoming, and Elk Hills, California. At the urging of Fall, Harding transferred control of those reserves from the Navy Department to the Interior Department. Fall then secretly leased them to two wealthy businessmen and received in return nearly half a million dollars in "loans" to ease his private financial troubles. Fall was ultimately convicted of bribery and sentenced to a year in prison; Daugherty barely avoided a similar fate for his part in another scandal.

In the summer of 1923, only months before Senate investigations and press revelations brought the scandals to light, a tired and depressed Harding left Washington for a speaking tour in the West. In Seattle late in July, he suffered severe pain, which his doctors wrongly diagnosed as food poisoning. A few days later, in San Francisco, he suffered two major heart attacks and died.

Calvin Coolidge

In many ways, Calvin Coolidge, who succeeded Harding in the presidency, was utterly different from his predecessor. Where Harding was genial, garrulous, and debauched, Coolidge was dour, silent, even

HARDING AND FRIENDS President Warren G. Harding (center left, holding a rod) poses with companions during a fishing trip to Miami in 1921. He enjoyed these social and sporting events with wealthy friends and political cronies. Two of his companions here, Attorney General Harry Daugherty (to the left of Harding) and Interior Secretary Albert Fall (at far right) were later principal figures in the scandals that rocked the administration before and after Harding's death.

Historical Thinking Skills

Argumentation Have students read the section "Teapot Dome." Ask them to discuss in pairs or small groups how Harding should have handled the Teapot Dome scandal. **PCE**

CALVIN COOLIDGE AT LEISURE Coolidge was a silent man of simple tastes. But he was not really an outdoorsman, despite his efforts to appear so. He is shown here fishing in Simsbury, Connecticut, carefully attired in suit, tie, hat, and rubber boots.

puritanical. And while Harding was, if not perhaps personally corrupt, then at least tolerant of corruption in others, Coolidge seemed honest beyond reproach. In other ways, however, Harding and Coolidge were similar figures. Both took an essentially passive approach to their office.

Like Harding, Coolidge had risen to the presidency on the basis of few substantive accomplishments. Elected governor of Massachusetts in 1919, he had won national attention with his laconic response to the Boston police strike that year. That was enough to make him his party's vice presidential nominee in 1920. Three years later, after Harding's death, he took the oath of office from his father, a justice of the peace, by the light of a kerosene lamp.

If anything, Coolidge was even less active as president than Harding, partly as a result of his conviction that government should interfere as little as possible in the life of the nation. In 1924, he received his party's presidential nomination virtually unopposed. Running against John W. Davis, he won a comfortable victory: 54 percent of the popular vote and 382 of the 531 electoral votes. Robert La Follette, the candidate of the reincarnated Progressive Party, received 16 percent of the popular vote but carried only his home state of Wisconsin. Coolidge probably could have won renomination and reelection in 1928. Instead, in characteristically laconic fashion, he walked into a press room one day and handed each reporter a slip of paper containing a single sentence: "I do not choose to run for president in 1928."

GOVERNMENT AND BUSINESS

The story of Harding and Coolidge themselves, however, is only a part—and by no means the most important part—of the story of their administrations. However passive the New Era presidents may have been, much of the federal government was working effectively and efficiently during the 1920s to adapt public policy to the widely accepted goal of the time: helping business and industry operate with maximum efficiency and productivity. The close relationship between the private sector and the federal government that had been forged during World War I continued. Secretary of the Treasury Andrew Mellon, a wealthy steel and aluminum tycoon, devoted himself to working for substantial reductions in taxes on corporate profits, personal incomes, and inheritances. Largely because of his efforts, Congress cut them all by more than half. Mellon also worked closely with President Coolidge after 1924 on a series of measures to trim dramatically the already modest federal budget. The administration even managed to retire half the nation's World War I debt.

ANDREW MELLON

The most energetic member of the cabinet was Commerce Secretary Herbert Hoover, who considered himself, and was considered by others, a notable progressive. During his eight years in the Commerce Department, Hoover encouraged voluntary cooperation in the private sector as the best avenue to stability. But the idea of voluntarism, he believed, did not require that the government remain passive; on the contrary, public institutions, Hoover insisted, should play an active role in creating the new, cooperative order. Above all, Hoover became the champion of the concept of business "associationalism"—a concept that envisioned the creation of national organizations of businessmen in particular industries. Through these trade associations, private entrepreneurs could, Hoover believed, stabilize their industries and promote efficiency in production and marketing.

HOOVER'S "ASSOCIATIONALISM"

Many progressives derived encouragement from the election of Herbert Hoover to the presidency in 1928. Hoover easily defeated Al Smith, the Democratic candidate. And he entered office promising bold new efforts to solve the nation's remaining economic problems. But Hoover had few opportunities to prove himself. Less than a year after his inauguration, the nation plunged into the severest and most prolonged economic crisis in its history—a crisis that brought many of the optimistic assumptions of the New Era crashing down and launched the nation into a period of unprecedented social innovation and reform.

Discussion and Activities

Analyzing Visuals After students have read the section "Calvin Coolidge," ask them to examine the image "Calvin Coolidge at Leisure." Have students discuss as a class how the image either supports or refutes the popular conception of President Coolidge. **PCE**

Discussion and Activities

Evaluating Evidence Have students read the section "Government and Business." Ask them to create a T-chart listing successes and failures of the Republican administrations of the 1920s. Have students discuss whether they think the administrations were characterized more by success or failure politically, economically, socially, and diplomatically. **WOR** **PCE** **ARC** **SOC** **WXT**

Discussion and Activities

Historical Significance and Argumentation Divide the class into three groups. Assign each group to review and research political, economic, or social events, issues, or developments of the 1920s. Have each group create a short presentation or skit that explains the most important event(s) of the decade in each category. **PCE** **WXT** **SOC** **ARC**

Key Terms

Students should be familiar with the key terms and be able to define them in the context of social and cultural changes during this era, including new ideas about gender roles, new expressions of modern art and the Harlem Renaissance, and the conservative backlash against these new ideas. Encourage students to use these terms in performing review exercises and exam practice for this chapter.

CHAPTER 23 REVIEW

CONNECTING THEMES

Chapter Twenty-Three examined the 1920s, with particular focus on social and cultural change. The impact of technology, particularly communications, played a major role in creating a mass culture and consumer society. New ideas surrounding motherhood and a more secular view of womanhood inspired some feminists to press for more reform as roles for women continued to evolve. American society saw a birth of a modernist movement in art, literature, and music. Black artists, musicians, and intellectuals in particular flourished during the Harlem Renaissance.

But the changing culture and emergence of more secular views were often at odds with traditional culture. Nativism and fundamentalism gained political strength as rural Protestants sought to limit immigration, protect Prohibition, and defend the Bible against Charles Darwin's theory of evolution. In the midst of this clash of cultures, the country was also undergoing a political change. The Republican presidents of the 1920s sought a return to "normalcy" as they lowered taxes and reduced regulations on American business.

You should consider the following questions as you review the themes for this chapter:

- How did perceptions of American identity change during the 1920s?
- How did technology and communications contribute to the growth of a mass consumer society?
- What were the causes and effects of the country moving toward a more conservative political posture?
- Why did the United States, during the 1920s, reduce its role in world affairs?
- What were the reasons for and consequences of the United States challenging traditional cultural values during the 1920s?

KEY TERMS

A. Philip Randolph 651
Alain Locke 661
Al Smith 665
"American Plan" 652
automobile 653
Duke Ellington 661
H. L. Mencken 660
Harlem Renaissance 661
Herbert Hoover 667
Issei 651
Jelly Roll Morton 661
Ku Klux Klan 662
Langston Hughes 661
Lost Generation 658
Margaret Sanger 656
National Origins Act of 1924 662
Nisei 651
parity 653
Scopes "Monkey Trial" 665
Sinclair Lewis 661
Teapot Dome 666
The Jazz Singer 654
welfare capitalism 648

Go Online Chapter 23 Content Review

Assessing Student Understanding Use the online assessment to assess student understanding of concepts and topics within the chapter. You can assign the ready-made Chapter 23 Content Review or create your own from available questions. This easy-to-use tool helps you design assessments that meet the needs of different types of learners.

AP EXAM PRACTICE

Questions assume cumulative content knowledge from this chapter and the previous chapter.

MULTIPLE CHOICE

Use the maps on page 654 and your knowledge of U.S. history to answer questions 1–3.

1. Which social change in America in the first half of the twentieth century was most directly a result of the trends shown in the maps?
   (A) Railroads greatly expanded their short lines and linked into many major rail lines.
   (B) Americans had increased access to urban employment.
   (C) Americans experienced greater personal mobility.
   (D) Rural Americans were increasingly isolated from urban areas.

2. The development depicted by the maps most likely suggests that fewer Americans were able to
   (A) purchase consumer goods.
   (B) travel cross-country via railroads.
   (C) identify culturally through regional distinctions.
   (D) freely access consumer goods.

3. The trends illustrated by the maps contributed to social conflicts in the 1920s through
   (A) the influx of immigrants, primarily in rural areas.
   (B) the widening income gap in small towns.
   (C) religious fundamentalism in rural areas limiting the social changes driven by urban culture.
   (D) the encouragement of more racial cooperation in cities.

SHORT ANSWER

Use your knowledge of U.S. history to answer questions 4 and 5.

4. Use the image on page 656 to answer A, B, and C.
   (A) Describe ONE point of view of women promoted by the image during the 1920s.
   (B) Briefly explain ONE specific cause that gave rise to a counter-culture movement during the 1920s.
   (C) Briefly explain ONE specific effect that resulted from the rise of a counter-culture movement during the 1920s.

5. Answer A, B, and C.
   (A) Briefly describe ONE specific similarity in government attitudes toward business and industry before and after World War I.
   (B) Briefly describe ONE specific difference in government attitudes toward business and industry before and after World War I.
   (C) Briefly explain ONE specific effect that resulted from government attitudes toward business during the 1920s.

LONG ESSAY

Develop a thoughtful and thorough historical argument that addresses the statement. Begin your essay with a thesis statement, and support it with specific historical evidence and examples.

6. Evaluate the relative importance of effects that resulted from the counter-culture movement during the 1920s.

Answers

Multiple Choice

1. C; **2.** D; **3.** C

Short Answer

4A) Possible answer: The point of view in the image is one of a supporter of the woman's movement as it was taking shape during the 1920s. The young lady is supporting the newest fashion representing changing views of women.

4B) Possible answer: Following World War I young people were feeling a sense of independence. This sense of independence gave rise to a new counter culture.

4C) Possible answer: Push-back from conservatives took many shapes during the culture war of the 1920s. A sharp rise in Fundamentalism, with its opposition to much of the new cultural movements, contributed to new laws being passed to regulate social behavior.

5A) Possible answer: The presidents of the Progressive Era and the 1920s both believed in the importance of business to stimulate the economy. A strong economy was necessary for America to continue its rise within the world.

5B) Possible answer: Before World War I, the Progressive presidents believed that it was government's responsibility to regulate and control business for the betterment of the country. Following World War I in the 1920s, the Conservative presidents began to believe it was not the responsibility of the government to regulate business.

5C) Possible answer: The largely "hands off" attitude of the 1920s presidents continued the philosophy of the "do nothing" attitude which had guided much of governmental beliefs throughout the decade. Hoover, especially, was partly responsible for the economic crisis to come.

Answers

Long Essay

6. Possible thesis: Women and African Americans were emboldened during the 1920s as they asserted new freedom and independence in response to the counter-culture. However, America was also caught in the grips of a conservative movement that saw the rise of new racist and nativist organizations as well as attempts to stifle intellectual freedom and discourse. Specific historical evidence: Women exerted a tremendous amount of change within American society during the 1920s. Voting finally became a nationally protected right with the passage of the 19th Amendment in 1920. The Harlem Renaissance celebrated the cultural contributions of African Americans, not just in New York's Harlem but all over the country. On the other hand, as more immigrants poured into the country, there was a rise in nativism. Conservative politics returned to "normalcy" as the presidents of the 1920s embraced a "hands off" philosophy toward society and the economy, which was partly responsible for the upcoming economic crisis.

Pacing Guide

Chapter 24 explores key concepts from Period 7: 1890–1945 of the AP U.S. History Curriculum Framework. The suggested instruction time for Chapter 24 is 2 days.

Key Concepts

7.1.III During the 1930s, policymakers responded to the mass unemployment and social upheavals of the Great Depression by transforming the U.S. into a limited welfare state, redefining the goals and ideas of modern American liberalism.

7.2.II Economic pressures, global events, and political developments caused sharp variations in the numbers, sources, and experiences of both international and internal migrants.

24 THE GREAT DEPRESSION

WOMAN OF THE HIGH PLAINS "IF YOU DIE, YOU'RE DEAD—THAT'S ALL." This poignant photograph, taken by Dorothea Lange (1895–1965) in 1938, shows a plains woman, Nettie Featherston, enduring one of the great natural disasters in U.S. history: the Dust Bowl of the 1930s. Featherston, a migrant laborer's wife and mother of three, lived in the drought-ridden Texas Panhandle. Her despair could not be more evident.

CONNECTING CONCEPTS

Chapter Twenty-Four begins by examining the coming of the Great Depression. The stock market crash of October 1929 was a sign of weakness and contributed to a banking crisis. But the Great Depression had more important causes, such as the lack of diversification in the American economy, the maldistribution of wealth, declining exports, and an unstable international debt structure caused by World War I. By 1932 the American gross national product had declined 25 percent and depositors had lost more than $2.5 billion as a result of bank closings.

Mass unemployment led to mass suffering. Most Americans — especially adult men — blamed themselves for their failure. Private charities were overwhelmed as breadlines stretched for blocks. A catastrophic drought led to a "Dust Bowl" in the Great Plains, driving many farmers ("Okies") to migrate to California. African Americans, Mexican Americans, and Asian Americans faced discrimination and prejudice, suffering higher rates of unemployment and poverty than white Americans. The economic crisis strengthened the widespread belief that a woman's place was in the home — but many had to seek employment with so many men out of work and families strained to the breaking point.

The Great Depression had a mixed impact on American culture. On the one hand, it did not seriously erode the popular belief in the "success ethic" and individual responsibility. The movies and radio also offered escapist programming. On the screen were lavish musicals and historical dramas. On the air were soap operas, comedy programs, and serial dramas. On the other

Discussion and Activities

Analyzing Points of View Have students examine the image "Woman of the High Plains 'If You Die, You're Dead—That's All.'" Ask them to write a short journal entry from the point of view of the woman in the photo describing her situation and her emotions concerning it. **SOC** **GEO**

hand, writers and intellectuals criticized capitalism in books like *The Grapes of Wrath* while photographers like Dorothea Lange exposed the widespread poverty and hardship.

The Great Depression shattered the presidency of Herbert Hoover. He tried to restore public confidence with government programs and spending, but he was unwilling to commit the funds needed or offer direct assistance to desperate Americans. As his popularity plummeted, protests mounted among farmers and veterans. When the U.S. Army violently evicted a "Bonus Army" of unemployed World War I veterans in July 1932, it sealed Hoover's political fate. That fall voters overwhelmingly elected New York Governor Franklin Roosevelt, who avoided divisive cultural issues like Prohibition and vaguely promised a "new deal" for the nation.

As you read, you should:

- Analyze how the Great Depression exposed weaknesses in the American economy.
- Evaluate how the Great Depression challenged Americans' sense of identity along with ideas about the social and economic roles of the federal and state government.
- Analyze how the reaction to the Great Depression produced powerful social criticism as well as reaffirmation of traditional American values.
- Identify the reasons why many Americans migrated during the Great Depression.
- Evaluate the reasons for and consequences of the additional hardships farmers, women, and minorities experienced during the Great Depression.

THE COMING OF THE GREAT DEPRESSION

The sudden economic decline that began in 1929 came as an especially severe shock because it followed so closely a period in which the New Era seemed to be performing another series of economic miracles.

The Great Crash

In February 1928, stock prices began a steady rise that continued, with only a few temporary lapses, for a year and a half. Between May 1928 and September 1929, the average price of stocks increased over 40 percent. The stocks of the major industrials–the stocks that are used to determine the Dow Jones Industrial Average–doubled in value in that same period. Trading mushroomed from 2 or 3 million shares a day to over 5 million and, at times, to as many as 10 or 12 million. A widespread speculative fever grew steadily more intense, particularly once brokerage firms began encouraging the mania by recklessly offering easy credit.

Stock Market Boom

In the autumn of 1929, the great bull market began to fall apart. On October 21 and again on October 23, there were alarming declines in stock prices, in both cases followed by temporary recoveries (the second of them engineered by J. P. Morgan and Company and other big bankers, who conspicuously bought up stocks to restore public confidence). But on October 29, "Black Tuesday," all efforts to save the market failed. Sixteen million shares of stock were traded; the industrial index dropped 43 points; stocks in many companies became worthless. The market remained deeply depressed for more than four years.

"Black Tuesday"

Many people believed that the stock market crash was the beginning, and even the cause, of the Great Depression. But although October 1929 might have been the first visible sign of the crisis, the Depression had earlier beginnings and more important causes.

Causes of the Depression

Economists, historians, and others have argued for decades about the causes of the Great Depression without reaching any consensus. But most agree on several things. They agree, first, that what is remarkable about the crisis is not that it occurred; periodic recessions are a normal feature of capitalist economies. What is remarkable is that it was so severe and that it lasted so long. The important question, therefore, is not so much why there was a depression, but why it was such a bad one. Most observers agree, too, that a number of different

Reasoning Processes

Comparison Have students read the section "The Great Crash." Ask them to create a Venn diagram comparing the stock market crash in 1929 to previous economic crashes. *(Similarities: most crashes involved overspeculation in some commodity, such as land, tobacco, or cotton. Differences: The 1929 crash followed overspeculation in stocks, and a broader cross section of the public participated in the speculation.)* **WXT**

Go Online AP Exam Preparation

AP Exam Practice Use the online assessment to help prepare students for the AP Exam. You can assign the ready-made AP-style short-answer questions, document-based questions, and multiple-choice questions assessing concepts, themes, and skills from Period 7 and AP-style long-essay questions organized in sets of 3 questions from various time periods. You can also create your own tests from available questions. This easy-to-use tool helps you design assessments that meet the needs of different types of learners.

Discussion and Activities

Analyzing Points of View After students have examined the image "Aftermath of the Crash," ask them to write a short journal entry from the point of view of Walker Thornton in the photo explaining why he had invested everything in the stock market and how he planned to survive going forward. **SOC** **WXT**

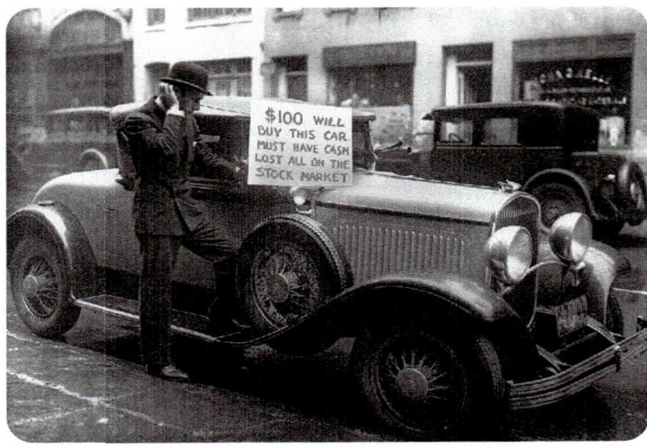

AFTERMATH OF THE CRASH Walter Thornton, shown here in October 1929 next to an expensive roadster he had bought not long before, was one of the affluent Americans who suffered substantial losses in the crash of the stock market in the fall of 1929. In popular mythology, many such people committed suicide in despair. In reality, very few people did. Much more common were efforts such as this to sell off assets to make up for the losses. Thornton was more fortunate than many victims of the Depression. Most had few assets to sell.

factors account for the severity of the crisis, even if there is considerable disagreement about which was the most important.

One of those factors was a lack of diversification in the American economy in the 1920s. Prosperity had depended excessively on a few basic industries, notably construction and automobiles. In the late 1920s, those industries began to decline. Expenditures on construction fell from $11 billion to less than $9 billion between 1926 and 1929. Automobile sales fell by more than a third in the first nine months of 1929. Newer industries were emerging to take up the slack–among them petroleum, chemicals, plastics, and others oriented toward the expanding market for consumer goods–but had not yet developed enough strength to compensate for the decline in other sectors.

LACK OF DIVERSIFICATION

A second factor was the maldistribution of purchasing power and, as a result, a weakness in consumer demand, which was too small to create an adequate market for the goods the economy was producing. Even in 1929, after nearly a decade of economic growth, more than half the families in America lived on the edge of or below the minimum subsistence level–too poor to buy the goods the industrial economy was producing.

MALDISTRIBUTION OF WEALTH

Another major problem was the credit structure of the economy. Farmers were deeply in debt–their land mortgaged, crop prices too low to allow them to pay off what they owed. Small banks, especially those tied to the agricultural economy, were in constant trouble in the 1920s as their customers defaulted on loans; many of these small banks failed. Large banks were in trouble, too. Although most

THE UNEMPLOYED, 1930 Thousands of unemployed men wait to be fed outside the Municipal Lodgers House in New York City.

Discussion and Activities

Analyzing Visuals Have students examine the image "The Unemployed, 1930." Ask them to identify and discuss in small groups details from the photo that illustrate the hardships facing the unemployed. *(Large crowds of men waiting to be fed and possibly housed at a homeless shelter; most men are dressed in hats and coats as if they were going to work on a chilly day, but there is no work for them; many men have their heads down as if they are worn out or ashamed.)* **WXT** **ARC** **SOC**

DEBATING THE PAST

CAUSES OF THE GREAT DEPRESSION

What were the causes of the Great Depression? Economists and historians have debated this question since the economic collapse began and still have not reached anything close to agreement on an answer to it. In the process, however, they have produced several very different theories about how a modern economy works.

During the Depression itself, different groups offered interpretations of the crisis that fit comfortably with their own self-interests. Some corporate leaders claimed that the Depression was the result of a lack of "business confidence," that businessmen were reluctant to invest because they feared government regulation and high taxes. The Hoover administration, unable to solve the crisis with the tools it considered acceptable, blamed international economic forces and sought, therefore, to stabilize world currencies and debt structures. New Dealers, determined to find a domestic solution to the crisis and ideologically inclined to place limits on corporate power, argued that the Depression was a crisis of "underconsumption"—that low wages and high prices had made it too difficult to buy the products of the industrial economy—and that a lack of demand had led to the economic collapse.

Scholars in the years since the Great Depression have also created interpretations that fit their views of how the economy works. One of the first important postwar interpretations came from the economists Milton Friedman and Anna Schwartz, in their *Monetary History of the United States* (1963). In a chapter titled "The Great Contraction," they argued for what has become known as the "monetary" interpretation. The Depression, they claimed, was a result of a drastic contraction of the currency (a result largely of mistaken decisions by the Federal Reserve Board, which raised interest rates when it should have lowered them). These deflationary measures, Friedman and Schwartz argue, turned an ordinary recession into the Great Depression. Friedman, in particular, advocated for many years that sound monetary policy is the best way to solve economic problems—as opposed to fiscal policies, such as taxation and spending.

A second, very different argument, known as the "spending" interpretation, is identified with, among others, the economist Peter Temin and his book *Did Monetary Forces Cause the Great Depression?* (1976). Temin's answer to his own question is "no." The cause of the crisis was not monetary contraction (although the contraction made it worse), but a drop in investment and consumer spending, which preceded the decline in the money supply and helped to cause it. Here again, there are obvious political implications. If a decline in spending was the cause of the Depression, then the proper response was an effort to stimulate demand—raising government spending, increasing purchasing power, redistributing wealth. According to this theory, the New Deal never ended the Depression because it did not spend enough. World War II did end it because it pumped so much public money into the economy. This is a liberal, Keynesian explanation, just as the "monetary hypothesis" is a conservative explanation.

In *The Great Depression* (1987), the economic historian Michael Bernstein avoids trying to explain why the economic downturn occurred and asks, instead, why it lasted so long. The reason the recession of 1929 became the Depression of the 1930s, he argues, was the timing of the collapse. The recession began as an ordinary cyclical downturn. Had it begun a few years earlier, the basic strength of the automobile and construction industries in the 1920s would have led to a reasonably speedy recovery. Had it begun a few years later, a group of newer, emerging industries would have helped produce a recovery in a reasonably short time. But the recession began in 1929, too late for the automobile and construction industries to help and too soon for emerging new industries to help, since they were still in their infancies. One of the reasons World War II was so important to the long-term recovery of the U.S. economy, Bernstein's argument suggests, was not just that it pumped money into the economy, but that much of that money contributed to developing new industries that would help sustain prosperity after the war. This is, in other words, an explanation of the Depression that seems to support some of the economic ideas that became popular in the 1970s and 1980s calling for a more direct government role in stimulating the growth of new industries. Other explanations include the rise of protectionism (increased by the ill-advised Smoot-Hawley Tariff of 1931, which stifled international trade); the weakness of the banking system; the reckless credit policies of the 1920s; and many others.

SHOP WINDOW Arthur Rothstein, one of the most significant photographers of the Great Depression, photographed this shop window in West Frankfort, Illinois, in 1939. The windows are plastered with signs pleading for customers to help them by purchasing their goods.

In the end, however, no single explanation of the Great Depression has ever seemed adequate to most scholars. The event, the economist Robert Lucas once argued, is simply "inexplicable" by any rational calculation.

HISTORICAL THINKING SKILLS

Questions assume cumulative content knowledge from this chapter and previous chapters.

1. **Explaining Historical Developments** Explain the three arguments made by groups concerning causes of the Great Depression. How were the arguments affected by the self-interests and values of each group?
2. **Evaluating Evidence** Describe how historical evidence, from the time period, could be used to support each of the three arguments concerning the causes of the Great Depression.
3. **Developing Arguments** Analyze the argument you find most convincing and explain why using evidence from the text.

Historical Thinking Skills

Argumentation Have students examine the image "Shop Window." Ask them to discuss in small groups how effective the ads in the shop window were likely to have been and why. **WXT**

Answers

Debating the Past

1. During the 1960s, Friedman and Schwartz put forth the "monetary" interpretation of the cause of the Great Depression - or it was the result of monetary contraction (or deflation). During the 1970s, Temin argued that it was a drop in investment and consumer spending. In the 1980s, Bernstein reframed the question to ask not what caused the Depression but why did it last so long? Bernstein argued that the timing was the perfect storm for a depression, as this was part of the normal economic cycle.
2. Friedman and Schwartz argued that the Federal Reserve should have lowered interest rates; instead, it raised them, creating a deflationary environment. For Temin, the drop in investment and consumer spending both preceded the decline in the money supply, leading to the Depression. Finally, Bernstein argued that the Depression came at a bad time between two major economic events, and if these had occurred earlier, the Depression could have been much shorter and less severe.
3. Student answers will vary. They may argue that Robert Lucas is correct, and the number of explanations is simply "inexplicable" by any rational calculation.

Reasoning Processes

Causation After students have read the section "Causes of the Depression," ask them to list and rank in order of importance the main causes of the Great Depression. Have students write a thesis statement that makes a claim about the most important cause(s) of the Great Depression. Ask for volunteers to share their thoughts with the class and receive feedback. **WXT**

American bankers were very conservative, some of the nation's biggest banks were investing recklessly in the stock market or making unwise loans. When the stock market crashed, many of these banks suffered losses greater than they could absorb.

A fourth factor contributing to the coming of the Depression was America's position in international trade. Late in the 1920s, European demand for American goods began to decline. That was partly because of high American tariffs, partly because European industry and agriculture were becoming more productive, and partly because some European nations (most notably Germany, under the Weimar Republic) were having financial difficulties and could not afford to buy goods from overseas. But it was also because the European economy was being destabilized by, a fifth factor contributing to the Depression, the international debt structure that had emerged in the aftermath of World War I.

DECLINING EXPORTS

When the war ended in 1918, all the European nations that had been allied with the United States owed large sums of money to American banks, sums much too large to be repaid out of their shattered economies. That was one reason the Allies had insisted (over Woodrow Wilson's objections) on reparation payments from Germany and Austria. Reparations, they believed, would provide them with a way to pay off their own debts. But Germany and Austria were themselves in economic trouble after the war; they were no more able to pay the reparations than the Allies were able to pay their debts.

UNSTABLE INTERNATIONAL DEBT STRUCTURE

The U.S. government refused to forgive or reduce the debts. Instead, American banks began making large loans to European governments, with which they paid off their earlier loans. Thus debts (and reparations) were being paid only by piling up new and greater debts. In the late 1920s, particularly after the American economy began to weaken in 1929, the European nations found it much more difficult to borrow money from the United States. At the same time, high American protective tariffs were making it difficult for them to sell their goods in American markets. Without any source of foreign exchange with which to repay their loans, they began to default. The collapse of the international credit structure was one of the reasons the Depression spread to Europe (and grew much worse in America) after 1931.

PROGRESS OF THE DEPRESSION

The stock market crash of 1929 did not so much cause the Depression, then, as help trigger a chain of events that exposed long-standing weaknesses in the American economy. During the next three years, the crisis steadily worsened.

A collapse of much of the banking system followed the stock market crash. More than 9,000 American banks either went bankrupt or closed their doors to avoid bankruptcy between 1930 and 1933. Depositors lost over $2.5 billion in deposits. Partly as a result of these banking closures, the total money supply of the nation fell by more than a third between 1930 and 1933. The declining money supply meant a decline in purchasing power, and thus deflation. Manufacturers and merchants began reducing prices, cutting back on production, and laying off workers. Some economists argue that a severe depression could have been avoided if the Federal Reserve system had acted more responsibly. But the members of the Federal Reserve Board, concerned about protecting its own solvency in a dangerous economic environment, raised interest rates in 1931, which contracted the money supply even further.

BANKING COLLAPSE

The American gross national product plummeted from more than $104 billion in 1929 to $76.4 billion in 1932–a 25 percent decline in three years. In 1929, Americans had spent $16.2 billion in capital investment; in 1933, they invested only a third of a billion. The consumer price index declined 25 percent between 1929 and 1933, the wholesale price index 32 percent. Gross farm income dropped from $12 billion to $5 billion in four years.

SEVERE CONTRACTION

THE AMERICAN PEOPLE IN HARD TIMES

Someone asked the British economist John Maynard Keynes in the 1930s whether he was aware of any historical era comparable to the Great Depression. "Yes," Keynes replied. "It was called the Dark Ages, and it lasted 400 years." The Depression did not, of course, last 400 years, but it did bring unprecedented despair to the economies of the United States and much of the Western world. And it had far-reaching effects on American society and culture.

UNEMPLOYMENT AND RELIEF

In the industrial Northeast and Midwest, cities were becoming paralyzed by unemployment. Cleveland, Ohio, in 1932 had an unemployment rate of roughly 50 percent; Akron, 60 percent; Toledo, 80 percent. Many industrial workers were accustomed to periods of unemployment, but no one was prepared for the scale and duration of the joblessness of the 1930s.

Most Americans had been taught to believe that every individual was responsible for his or her own fate, that unemployment and poverty were signs of personal failure. Many adult men, in particular, felt deeply ashamed of their joblessness; the helplessness of unemployment was a challenge to traditional notions of masculinity. Unemployed workers walked through the streets day after day looking for jobs that did not exist.

BELIEF IN PERSONAL RESPONSIBILITY

An increasing number of families were turning to state and local public relief systems, just to be able to eat. But those systems, which in the 1920s had served only a small number of indigent persons, were unequipped to handle the new

Discussion and Activities

Analyzing Evidence Have students read the section "Progress of the Depression." Ask them to write a short paragraph describing how banks failed and, using evidence from the text, indicate what possible warning signs preceded the bank failures. **SOC** **WXT**

AMERICA IN THE WORLD

THE GLOBAL DEPRESSION

The Great Depression began in the United States, but it did not end there. The collapse of the American economy—the largest in the world—sent shock waves around the globe. By 1931, the American depression had become a world depression.

The origins of the worldwide depression lay in the pattern of debts that had emerged during and after World War I, when the United States loaned billions of dollars to European nations. In 1931, large banks in New York began calling in their loans from Germany and Austria. That precipitated the failure of one of Austria's largest banks, which in turn created panic through much of central Europe. The economic collapse in Germany and Austria meant that those nations could not continue paying reparations to Britain and France (required by the Treaty of Versailles of 1919), which meant in turn that Britain and France could not continue paying off their loans to the United States.

This spreading financial crisis was accompanied by a dramatic contraction of international trade, precipitated in part by the Smoot-Hawley Tariff in the United States, which established the highest import duties in history and stifled much global commerce. Depressed agricultural prices—a result of worldwide overproduction—also contributed to the downturn. By 1932, worldwide industrial production had declined by more than a third, and world trade had plummeted by nearly two-thirds. By 1933, thirty million people in industrial nations were unemployed, five times the number four years before.

But the Depression was not confined to industrial nations. Imperialism and industrialization drew almost all regions of the world into the international industrial economy. Colonies and nations in Africa, Asia, and South America—critically dependent on exporting raw materials and agricultural goods to industrial countries—experienced a decline in demand for their products, which led to rising levels of poverty and unemployment. Some nations—among them the Soviet Union and China—remained unconnected to the global economy and suffered relatively little from the Great Depression. But in most parts of the world, the Depression caused tremendous social and economic hardship.

It also created political turmoil. Among the countries hardest hit by the Depression was Germany, where industrial production had declined by 50 percent and unemployment reached 35 percent in the early 1930s. The desperate economic conditions there contributed greatly to the rise of the Nazi Party and its leader, Adolf Hitler, who became chancellor in 1932. Japan suffered greatly as well, and as in Germany, Japan's economic troubles produced political turmoil and aided the rise of a new militaristic regime. In Italy, the fascist government of Benito Mussolini, which had first taken power in the 1920s, also saw militarization and territorial expansion as a way out of economic difficulties.

In other nations, governments sought solutions to the Depression through reform of their domestic economies. Among the most common responses to the Depression around the world was substantial government investment in public works. The United States, Britain, France, Germany, Italy, the Soviet Union, and other countries made substantial investments in roads, bridges, dams, public buildings, and other large projects. All the industrial countries of the world also experimented with some form of government-funded relief for the unemployed, often borrowing ideas from one another in the process.

Furthermore, because classical models of economic behavior seemed unable to explain, or provide solutions to, the crisis, the Depression helped create new approaches to economics. The great British economist John Maynard Keynes revolutionized economic thought in much of the world. His 1936 book, *The General Theory of Employment, Interest, and Money*, despite its bland title, created a sensation by arguing that the Depression was a result not of declining production but, rather, of inadequate consumer demand. Governments, he said, could stimulate their economies by increasing the money supply and creating investment—through a combination of lowering interest rates and public spending. Keynesianism, as Keynes's theories became known, began to have an impact in the United States in 1938, and in much of the rest of the world in subsequent years.

The Great Depression was an important turning point not only in American history, but in the history of the twentieth-century world as well. It transformed ideas of public policy and economics in many nations. It toppled old regimes and created new ones. Above all, it was a major factor—maybe the single most important factor—in the coming of World War II.

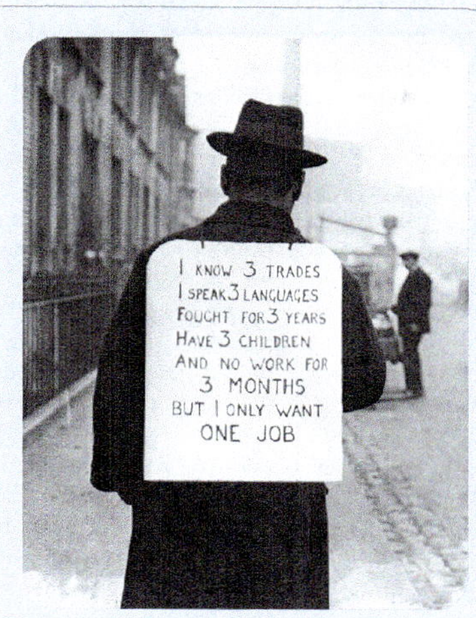

LOOKING FOR WORK IN LONDON, 1935 **An unemployed London man wears a sign that seems designed to convince passersby that he is an educated, respectable person despite his present circumstances.**

General Photographic Agency/Hulton Archive/Getty Images

HISTORICAL THINKING SKILLS

1. **Explaining Historical Developments** How did the 1919 Treaty of Versailles and the Hawley-Smoot Tariff contribute to the global depression of the 1930s?
2. **Evaluating** How did the governments of European nations respond to the depression?
3. **Making Connections** What effect did the global depression have on economic theory? Why was Keynes's economic theory so revolutionary?

AP Exam Tip

The AP Exam requires students to identify and explain a source's point of view, purpose, historical situation, and/or audience. One way students can identify the historical situation of a source is to explain other events happening at the same time that relate to the content of the document.

Historical Thinking Skills

Sourcing and Situation Have students practice the tip by examining the image "Looking for Work in London, 1935." Ask them to list and discuss events happening in England and other parts of the world at the time of the photo that help explain its significance. **WXT** **SOC**

Answers

America in the World

1. Following World War I, the pattern of debt was disrupted when a New York bank called in its loans from Germany and Austria. This caused the collapse of one of Austria's largest banks, which then caused a ripple effect all across Europe. Trade was also significantly affected by the Hawley-Smoot Tariff, which raised protection levels to their highest levels ever in the United States. Europe responded, which essentially cut off most international trade.
2. Germany saw the rise of Hitler and the Nazi Party, which promised to end the depression for Germany. Japan also suffered. Like Germany, their economic troubles resulted in political turmoil and aided the rise of a new militaristic regime. But the most common response by nations to the global depression was an investment in public works, which were designed to rebuild infrastructure and provide much needed jobs to citizens.
3. Classic economic models were not able to explain or provide a solution to the economic crisis. Keynes argued that governments could stimulate their economies by increasing the money supply and creating investment through a combination of lowering interest rates and increasing public spending.

Discussion and Activities

Analyzing Change After students have read the section "Unemployment and Relief," ask them to discuss as a class the challenges facing the long-term unemployed. *(Lack of available jobs; limited welfare programs to provide support; loss of self-esteem.)* **WXT** **SOC** **NAT**

demands. In many places, relief simply collapsed. Private charities attempted to supplement the public relief efforts, but the problem was far beyond their capabilities as well. State governments felt pressure to expand their own assistance to the unemployed; but tax revenues were declining along with everything else, and state leaders balked at placing additional strains on already tight budgets. Moreover, many public officials believed that an extensive welfare system would undermine the moral fiber of its clients.

Breadlines stretched for blocks outside Red Cross and Salvation Army kitchens. Thousands of people sifted through garbage cans for scraps of food or waited outside restaurant kitchens in hopes of receiving plate scrapings. Nearly 2 million men, most of them young (and a much smaller number of women), took to the roads, riding freight trains from city to city, living as nomads.

Farm income declined by 60 percent between 1929 and 1932. A third of all American farmers lost their land. In addition, a large area of agricultural settlement in the Great Plains of the South and West was suffering from a catastrophic natural disaster: one of the worst droughts in the history of the nation. Beginning in 1930, a large area of the nation, stretching north from Texas into the Dakotas, came to be known as the "Dust Bowl." It began to experience a steady decline in rainfall and an accompanying increase in heat. The drought continued for a decade, turning what had once been fertile farm regions into deserts. In Kansas, the soil in some places was without moisture as far as three feet below the surface. In Nebraska, Iowa, and other affected states, summer temperatures were averaging over 100 degrees. Swarms of grasshoppers were moving from region to region, devouring what meager crops farmers were able to raise, often even devouring fenceposts or clothes hanging out to dry. Great dust storms—called "black blizzards"—swept across the plains, blotting out the sun and suffocating livestock as well as people unfortunate or foolish enough to stay outside.

"DUST BOWL"

Even with these disastrous conditions, the farm economy continued through the 1930s to produce far more food than American consumers could afford to buy. Farm prices fell so low that few growers made any profit on their crops. As a result, many farmers, like many urban unemployed, left their homes in search of work. In the South, in particular, many dispossessed farmers—black and white—wandered from town to town, hoping to find jobs or handouts. Hundreds of thousands of families from the Dust Bowl (often known as "Okies," since many came from Oklahoma) traveled to California and other states, where they found conditions little better than those they had left. Many worked as agricultural migrants, traveling from farm to farm picking fruit and other crops at starvation wages.

"OKIES"

Throughout the nation, problems resulting from malnutrition and homelessness grew at an alarming rate. Hospitals pointed to a striking increase in deaths from starvation. On the outskirts of cities, families lived in makeshift shacks constructed of flattened tin cans, scraps of wood, abandoned crates, and other debris. Many homeless Americans simply kept moving—sleeping in freight cars, city parks, subways, or unused sewer ducts.

AFRICAN AMERICANS AND THE DEPRESSION

As the Depression began, over half of all African Americans still lived in the South. Most were farmers. The collapse of prices for cotton and other staple crops left some with no income. Many left the land altogether—either by choice or forced by landlords who no longer found the sharecropping system profitable. Some migrated to Southern cities. But unemployed white men in the urban South believed they had first claim to all work and began to take positions as janitors, street cleaners, and domestic servants, displacing the African Americans who formerly had occupied such jobs.

AFRICAN AMERICAN SUFFERING

As the Depression deepened, white people in many Southern cities began to demand that all African Americans be dismissed from their jobs. In Atlanta in 1930, an organization calling itself the Black Shirts organized a campaign with the slogan "No Jobs for Niggers Until Every White Man Has a Job!" In other areas, white people used intimidation and violence to drive African Americans from jobs. By 1932, over half the African Americans in the South were without employment. And what limited relief there was went almost invariably to white people first.

Unsurprisingly, therefore, many black Southerners—perhaps 400,000—left the South in the 1930s and journeyed to the cities of the North. There they generally found less blatant discrimination. But conditions were little better than in the South. In New York, and in many other cities, black unemployment was 50 percent or more. In other cities, it was higher. Two million African Americans were on some form of relief by 1932.

Traditional patterns of segregation and disenfranchisement in the South survived the Depression largely unchallenged. But a few particularly notorious examples of racism did attract national attention. The most notorious was the Scottsboro case. In March 1931, nine black teenagers were taken off a freight train in Alabama (in a small town near Scottsboro) and arrested for vagrancy and disorder. Later, two white women who had also been riding the train accused them of rape. In fact, there was overwhelming evidence, medical and otherwise, that the women had not been raped—that they may have made their accusations out of fear of being arrested themselves. Nevertheless, an all-white jury in Alabama quickly convicted all nine of the "Scottsboro boys" (as they were known to both friends and foes) and sentenced eight of them to death.

SCOTTSBORO CASE

The Supreme Court overturned the convictions in 1932, and a series of new trials began that attracted increasing national attention. The International Labor Defense, an organization associated with the Communist Party, came to the aid of the accused youths and began to publicize the case. Later, the National Association for the Advancement of Colored

Reasoning Processes

Comparing and Contrasting Have students read the section "African American Suffering." Ask them to create a T-chart comparing challenges faced by African Americans and white Americans during the Great Depression. Have students discuss as a class the ways in which the challenges were similar or different and why experiences varied. **WXT** **SOC**

MIGRANT FAMILY Dorothea Lange, one of the great photographers of the Depression era, worked in the 1930s for the photographic division of the Farm Security Administration (FSA). The FSA photographers sought to record the conditions of life in America's troubled agrarian world during the Great Depression in the hopes of stimulating reform. Lange's photograph here represents a family in transit as they, like thousands of others, moved from the Great Plains to California.

Photo by Dorothea Lange/© Time & Life Pictures/Getty Images

People (NAACP) provided assistance as well. The trials continued throughout the 1930s. Although the white Southern juries who sat on the case never acquitted any of the defendants, all of them eventually gained their freedom–four because the charges were dropped, four because of early paroles, and one because he escaped. But the last of the Scottsboro defendants did not leave prison until 1950.

The Depression was a time of important changes in the role and behavior of leading black organizations. The NAACP, for example, began to work diligently to win a position for African Americans within the emerging labor movement, supporting the formation of the Congress of Industrial Organizations and helping to break down racial barriers within labor unions. Walter White, secretary of the NAACP, once made a personal appearance at an auto plant to implore African Americans not to work as strikebreakers. Partly as a result of such efforts, more than half a million African Americans were able to join the labor movement. In the Steelworkers Union, for example, African Americans constituted about 20 percent of the membership.

NAACP's Changing Role

Mexican Americans in Depression America

Similar patterns of discrimination confronted the large and growing population of Mexican immigrants and Mexican Americans, which numbered approximately 2 million in the 1930s.

Mexican Americans filled many of the same menial jobs in the West and elsewhere that African Americans filled in other regions. Some farmed small, marginal tracts. Some became agricultural migrants, traveling from region to region harvesting fruit, lettuce, and other crops. But most lived in urban areas–in California, New Mexico, and Arizona, but also in Detroit, Chicago, New York, and other eastern industrial cities–and occupied the lower ranks of the unskilled labor force in such industries as steel, automobiles, and meatpacking.

As in the South, unemployed white Anglos in the Southwest demanded jobs held by Hispanic people. Thus Mexican unemployment rose quickly to levels far higher than those for Anglos. Some Mexican immigrants were, in effect, forced to leave the country by officials who arbitrarily removed them from relief rolls or simply rounded them up and transported them across the border. Perhaps half a million left the United States for Mexico in the first years of the Depression. Most relief programs excluded Hispanic people from their rolls or offered them benefits far below those available to white people. Latinos generally had no access to American schools. Many hospitals refused them admission.

Discrimination in the Southwest

Occasionally, there were signs of organized resistance by Mexican Americans themselves, most notably in California, where some formed a union of migrant farmworkers. But harsh repression by local growers and the public authorities allied with them prevented such organizations from having much impact. Like African American farmworkers, many Latino people began as a result to migrate to cities such as Los Angeles, where they lived in a poverty comparable to that of urban African Americans in the South and Northeast.

Asian Americans in Hard Times

For Asian Americans, too, the Depression reinforced long-standing patterns of discrimination and economic marginalization. In California, where the largest Japanese American and Chinese American populations resided, even educated Asian Americans had always found it difficult, if not impossible, to move into mainstream professions. Japanese American college graduates often found themselves working at family

Reasoning Processes

Comparing Have students read the section "Mexican Americans in Depression America." Ask them to create a Venn diagram comparing the experiences of Black and Hispanic Americans during the Great Depression. **WXT** **SOC**

Historical Thinking Skills

Sourcing and Situation Have students examine the image "Migrant Family." Ask them to discuss in small groups the historical situation of the photo. *(The family pictured had left the Great Plains, likely due to long-term drought, the Dust Bowl, and the collapse of the farm economy starting in 1929, and was seeking better opportunities they believed existed in California.)* **WXT** **SOC**

Discussion and Activities

Analyzing Points of View Have students examine the image "Dust Storm, Southwest Plains, 1937." Ask them to write a short journal entry from the point of view of a resident of the town pictured in the photo or from a nearby farm describing their thoughts and feelings at the approach of the storm. **SOC** **WXT** **GEO**

DUST STORM, SOUTHWEST PLAINS, 1937 The dust storms of the 1930s were a terrifying experience for all who lived through them. Resembling a black wall sweeping in from the western horizon, such a storm engulfed farms and towns alike, blotting out the light of the sun and covering everything with fine dirt.

BLACK MIGRANTS The Great Migration of African Americans from the rural South into the cities had begun before World War I. But in the 1930s and 1940s the movement accelerated. Northerners were not always so welcoming. Here, vans move African Americans to the federal Sojourner Truth Housing Project in Detroit under the guard of Michigan state troopers and police.

Discussion and Activities

Analyzing Issues Have students examine the image "Black Migrants." Ask them to discuss as a class how the black migration of the 1930s would have been similar to or different from African American migrations of the earlier 1900s. *(Similarities: Previously, black migrants leaving the South were seeking better economic opportunities in Northern industrial cities. These migrants were often greeted with indifference or hostility over competition for jobs. Differences: Black migrants in the 1930s were less likely to find work in the North, although they still faced hostility.)* **SOC** **WXT** **MIG**

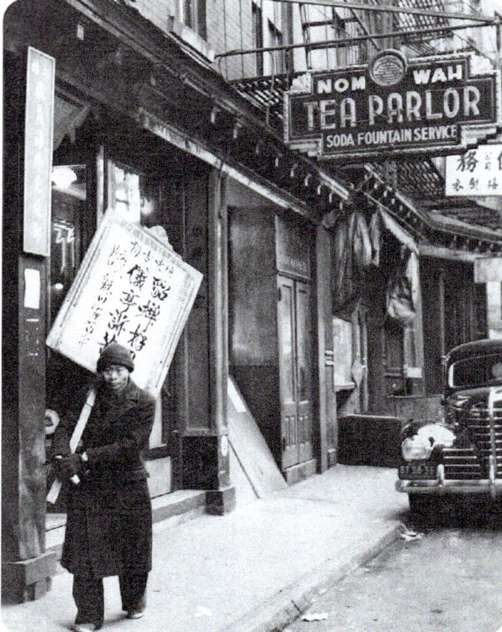

CHINATOWN, NEW YORK A Chinese man carries a "sandwich board" through the streets of New York's Chinatown bearing the latest news of the war between China and Japan, which in 1938 was already well under way. Chinese Americans had the dual challenge in the 1930s of dealing both with large-scale unemployment and with continuing news of catastrophe from China, where most still had many family members.

Fox Photos/Hulton Archive/Getty Images

fruit stands; 20 percent of all Japanese Americans in Los Angeles worked at such stands at the end of the 1930s. For those who found jobs (usually poorly paid) in the industrial or service economy, employment was precarious; like African Americans and Hispanic Americans, they often lost jobs to white Americans desperate for work that a few years earlier they would not have considered. Japanese farmworkers, like Chicano farmworkers, suffered from the increasing competition for even these low-paying jobs from white migrants from the Great Plains.

In California, younger men and women organized Japanese American Democratic Clubs in several cities, which worked for, among other things, laws protecting racial and ethnic minorities from discrimination. At the same time, some Japanese American businessmen and professionals tried to overcome obstacles by encouraging other Japanese to become more assimilated, more "American." They formed the Japanese American Citizens League in 1930 to promote their goals. By 1940, it had nearly 6,000 members.

JAPANESE AMERICAN CITIZENS LEAGUE

Chinese Americans fared no better. The overwhelming majority continued to work in Chinese-owned laundries and restaurants. Those who moved outside the Asian community could rarely find jobs above the entry level.

Women and the Workplace in the Great Depression

The economic crisis served in many ways to strengthen the widespread belief that a woman's proper place was in the home. Most men and many women believed that what work there was should go to men. Many people believed that no woman whose husband was employed should accept a job.

POPULAR DISAPPROVAL OF WOMEN'S EMPLOYMENT

But the widespread assumption that married women, at least, should not work outside the home did not stop them from doing so. Both single and married women worked in the 1930s, despite public condemnation of the practice, because they or their families needed the money. In fact, the largest new group of female workers consisted of wives and mothers. By the end of the Depression, 20 percent more women were working than had been doing so at the beginning.

INCREASED FEMALE EMPLOYMENT

The increase occurred despite considerable obstacles. Professional opportunities for women declined because unemployed men began moving into professions, such as teaching and social work, that had previously been considered women's fields. Female industrial workers were more likely to be laid off or to experience wage reductions than their male counterparts. But white women also had certain advantages in the workplace. The nonprofessional jobs that women traditionally held—as salesclerks and stenographers, and in other service positions—were less likely to disappear than the predominantly male jobs in heavy industry. Nor were many men, even unemployed men, likely to ask for such jobs.

Black women suffered massive unemployment because of a great reduction of domestic service jobs. As many as half of all black working women lost their jobs in the 1930s. Even so, at the end of the 1930s, 38 percent of black women were employed, as compared to 24 percent of white women. That was because black women—both married and unmarried—had always been more likely to work than white women, less out of preference than out of economic necessity.

For American feminists, the Depression years were, on the whole, a time of frustration. Although economic pressures pushed more women into the workforce, those same pressures helped to erode the frail support that feminists had won in the 1920s for the idea of women becoming economically and professionally independent.

Depression Families

The economic hardships of the Depression years placed great strains on American families, many of whom had become

Historical Thinking Skills

Argumentation After students have read the section "Asian Americans in Hard Times," ask them to write a letter to the editor of a newspaper encouraging Japanese Americans to either assimilate despite the discrimination they faced or to resist assimilation. **WXT** **SOC** **NAT** **MIG**

Historical Thinking Skills

Argumentation Have students read the section "Women and the Workplace in the Great Depression." Ask them to discuss in small groups how the Great Depression created both challenges and opportunities for women. *(The percentage of women working increased due to the financial needs of their families, but there was growing backlash against women working due to the belief that working women were taking jobs away from men.)* **WXT** **SOC** **ARC**

Discussion and Activities

Historical Reasoning and Argumentation Have students read the section "Depression Values." Ask them to discuss as a class why they think so many Americans blamed themselves for their circumstances during the Great Depression rather than outside forces. **WXT** **SOC** **NAT**

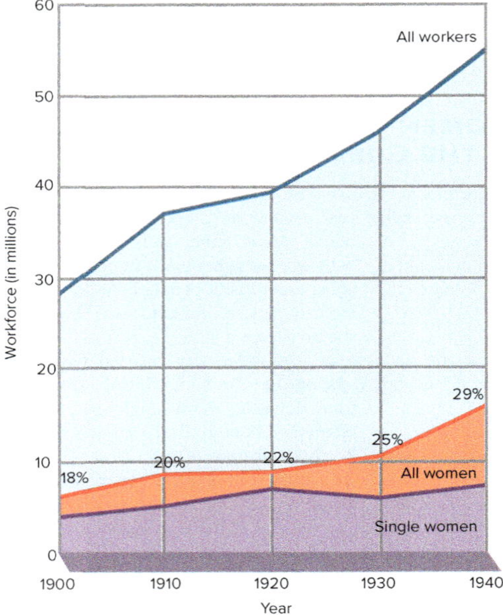

WOMEN IN THE PAID WORKFORCE, 1900–1940 The participation of women in the paid workforce increased slowly but steadily in the first forty years of the twentieth century. Note, however, the general leveling off of the participation of single women—who traditionally accounted for the vast majority of women workers—after 1920, at the same time that the total number of women in the paid workforce was rising. Many more married women began entering the paid workforce in these years, particularly in the 1930s.

Why did so many married women begin doing paid work during the Great Depression?

accustomed in the 1920s to a steadily rising standard of living but now found themselves plunged suddenly into uncertainty.

Such circumstances forced many families to retreat from the consumer patterns they had developed in the 1920s. Women often returned to sewing clothes for themselves and their families and to preserving their own food rather than buying such products in stores. Others engaged in home businesses—taking in laundry, selling baked goods, accepting boarders. Many households expanded to include distant relatives. Parents often moved in with their children and grandparents with their grandchildren, or vice versa.

RETREAT FROM CONSUMERISM

But the Depression also eroded the strength of many family units. There was a decline in the divorce rate, but largely because divorce was now too expensive for some. More common was the informal breakup of families, particularly the desertion of families by unemployed men bent on escaping the humiliation of being unable to earn a living. The marriage and birth rates declined simultaneously for the first time since the early nineteenth century.

THE DEPRESSION AND AMERICAN CULTURE

The Great Depression was a traumatic experience for millions of Americans, and it shook the confidence of many people in themselves or in their nation or both. Out of the crisis emerged some of the most probing criticisms of American society and the American economic system of the industrial age. At the same time, the Depression produced powerful confirmations of traditional values and reinforced many traditional goals. There was not one Depression culture, but many.

DEPRESSION VALUES

American social values seemed to change relatively little in response to the Depression. Instead, many people responded to hard times by redoubling their commitment to familiar ideas and goals. The sociologists Robert Lynd and Helen Merrell Lynd, who had published a celebrated study of Muncie, Indiana, *Middletown*, in 1929, returned there in the mid-1930s to see how the city had changed. They concluded in their 1937 book, *Middletown in Transition*, that in most respects "the texture of Middletown's culture has not changed. . . . Middletown is overwhelmingly living by the values by which it lived in 1925." Above all, the men and women of "Middletown"—and by implication many other Americans—remained committed to the traditional American emphasis on the individual.

In some respects, the economic crisis worked to undermine the traditional "success ethic" in America. Many people began to look to government for assistance; many blamed corporate moguls, international bankers, "economic royalists," and others for their distress. Yet the Depression did not, in the end, seriously erode the success ethic.

PERSISTENCE OF THE "SUCCESS ETHIC"

Some victims of the Depression expressed anger and struck out at the economic system. Many, however, seemed to blame themselves. Nothing so surprised foreign observers of America in the 1930s as the apparent passivity of the unemployed, many of whom were so ashamed of their joblessness that they refused to leave their homes.

SELF-BLAME

At the same time, millions of people responded eagerly to reassurances that they could, through their own efforts, restore themselves to prosperity and success. The writer and lecturer Dale Carnegie's self-help manual *How to Win Friends and Influence People* (1936) was one of the best-selling books of the decade. Carnegie's message was not only that personal initiative was the route to success; it was also that the best way for people to get ahead was to fit in and make other people feel important.

Answers

Women in the Paid Workforce, 1900–1940

More married women entered the workforce during the Great Depression due to the unemployment or underemployment of their husbands and to meet the financial needs of their families. **WXT** **SOC**

ARTISTS AND INTELLECTUALS IN THE GREAT DEPRESSION

Just as many progressives had become alarmed when, early in the twentieth century, they "discovered" the existence of widespread poverty in the cities, so many Americans were shocked during the 1930s at their discovery of debilitating rural poverty. Among those who were most effective in conveying the dimensions of this poverty was a group of documentary photographers, many of them employed by the federal Farm Security Administration in the late 1930s, who traveled through the South recording the nature of agricultural life. Roy Stryker, Walker Evans, Arthur Rothstein, Ben Shahn, Margaret Bourke-White, Dorothea Lange, and others produced memorable studies of farm families and their surroundings, studies often designed to reveal the savage impact of a hostile environment on its victims.

"DISCOVERY" OF RURAL POVERTY

Many writers, similarly, turned away from the personal concerns of the 1920s and devoted themselves to exposés of social injustice. Erskine Caldwell's *Tobacco Road* (1932), which later became a long-running Broadway play, was an exposé of poverty in the rural South. Richard Wright, a major African American novelist, exposed the plight of residents of the urban ghetto in *Native Son* (1940). John Steinbeck's novels portrayed the trials of workers and migrants in California. John Dos Passos's trilogy, *U.S.A.* (1930–1936), attacked modern capitalism outright. Playwright Clifford Odets provided an explicit demonstration of the appeal of political radicalism in *Waiting for Lefty* (1935).

DEPRESSION LITERATURE

But the cultural products of the 1930s that attracted the widest popular audiences were those that diverted attention away from the Depression. And they came to Americans primarily through the two most powerful instruments of popular culture in the 1930s–radio and the movies.

RADIO

Almost every American family had a radio in the 1930s. In cities and towns, radio consoles were now as familiar a part of the furnishing of parlors and kitchens as tables and chairs. Even in remote rural areas without access to electricity, many families purchased radios and hooked them up to car batteries when they wished to listen.

Unlike in later times, radio in the 1930s was often a community experience. Young people would place radios on their front porches and invite friends over to sit, talk, or dance. In poor urban neighborhoods, many people who could not afford other kinds of social activities would gather on a street or in a backyard to listen to sporting events or concerts. Within families, the radio often drew parents and children together in the evening to listen to favorite programs.

What did Americans hear on the radio? Although radio stations occasionally carried socially and politically provocative programs, the staple of broadcasting was escapism: comedies such as *Amos 'n Andy* (with its humorous, if demeaning, picture of urban African Americans); adventures such as *Superman, Dick Tracy*, and *The Lone Ranger;* and other entertainment programs. Radio brought a new kind of comedy–

ESCAPIST PROGRAMMING

A RADIO PLAY Among the most popular entertainments of the 1930s were live readings of plays over the radio—many of them mysteries or romances written specifically for the new medium. Here, a group of actors performs a radio comedy over WNBC in New York City in the early 1930s. The actors (from left to right) are Jack Benny, George Murphy, Jean Cranford, and Reginald Gardiner.

Discussion and Activities

Identifying Bias Have students read the section "Artists and Intellectuals in the Great Depression." Ask them to discuss in small groups why rural poverty was not "discovered" by much of the rest of America until after the start of the Great Depression. **SOC** **WXT** **GEO** **NAT**

Discussion and Activities

Speculating Have students examine the image "A Radio Play" and read the "Radio" section. Ask them to write a short paragraph describing what they feel the impact of radio might have been for different groups of people during the 1930s. **SOC** **ARC** **NAT**

Discussion and Activities

Analyzing Change After students have read the section "Radio," ask them to discuss as a class how radio changed American life. *(Radio provided low-cost entertainment, gave listeners common experiences, and provided news and weather information.)* **WXT** **SOC** **NAT** **ARC**

A NIGHT AT THE OPERA The antic comedy of the Marx Brothers provided a popular and welcome escape from the rigors of the Great Depression. The Marx Brothers, shown here in a poster for one of their most famous films, effectively lampooned dilemmas that many Americans faced in their ceaseless, and usually unsuccessful, efforts to find an easy route to wealth and comfort.

previously limited to vaudeville or to ethnic theaters—to a wide audience. Jack Benny, George Burns and Gracie Allen, and other masters of elaborately timed jokes and repartee began to develop broad followings (that they would later take with them to television).

Soap operas, also later to become staples of television programming, were enormously popular on radio in the 1930s, especially with women who were alone in the house during the day. (That was one reason they became known as soap operas; soap companies—whose advertising was targeted at women—generally sponsored them.)

Almost invariably, radio programs were broadcast live; and as a result, radio spawned an enormous number of public performances. Radio comedies and dramas were often performed before audiences in theaters or studios. Band concerts were broadcast from dance halls, helping jazz and swing bands to achieve broad popularity. Classical music, too, was broadcast live from studios.

RADIO'S IMPACT

Radio provided Americans with their first direct access to important public events, and radio news and sports divisions grew rapidly to meet the demand. Some of the most dramatic moments of the 1930s were a result of radio coverage of celebrated events: the World Series, major college football games, the Academy Awards, political conventions, presidential inaugurations. When the German dirigible the *Hindenburg* crashed in flames in Lakehurst, New Jersey, in 1937 after a transatlantic voyage, it produced an enormous national reaction largely because of the live radio account by a broadcaster overcome with emotion who cried out, as he watched the terrible crash, "Oh the humanity! Oh the humanity!" The actor/director Orson Welles created another memorable event in 1938 when he broadcast "War of the Worlds," which created panic among millions of people who believed for a while that the fictional events it described were real.

Radio was important for the way it drew the nation together by creating the possibility of shared experiences and common access to culture and information. It was also significant for the way it helped reshape the social life of the nation, for the way it encouraged many families and individuals to center their lives more around the home than they had in the past.

MOVIES IN THE NEW ERA

CONTINUING POPULARITY OF MOVIES

Moviegoing would seem particularly vulnerable to hard times. Families struggling to pay the rent or buy food could easily decide to forgo an evening at the movies. In the first years of the Depression, movie attendance did drop significantly. By the mid-1930s, however, most Americans had resumed their moviegoing habits—in part because movies were a less expensive entertainment option than many other possibilities, and in part because the movies themselves (all of them now with sound, and by the end of the decade many of them in color) were becoming more appealing.

In many ways, movies were as safely conventional in the 1930s as they had been in the late 1920s. Hollywood continued to exercise tight control over its products in the 1930s through its resilient censor Will Hays, who ensured that most movies carried no sensational or controversial messages. The studio system—through which a few large movie companies exercised iron control over actors, writers, and directors, and through which a few great moguls, such as Louis B. Mayer or Jack Warner, could single-handedly decide the fate of most projects—also worked to ensure that Hollywood films avoided controversy.

But neither the censor nor the studio system could (or wished to) prevent films from exploring social questions altogether. A few films, such as King Vidor's *Our Daily Bread* (1932) and John Ford's adaptation of John Steinbeck's novel *The Grapes of Wrath* (1940), did explore political themes. The director Frank Capra provided a muted social message in several of his comedies—*Mr. Deeds Goes to Town* (1936), *Mr. Smith Goes to Washington* (1939), and *Meet John Doe* (1941)—which celebrated the virtues of the small town and the decency of the common people in contrast to the selfish, corrupt values of the city and the urban rich. Gangster movies such as *Little Caesar* (1930) and *The Public Enemy* (1931) portrayed a dark, gritty, violent world with which few Americans were familiar, but their desperate stories were popular nevertheless with those engaged in their own difficult struggles.

More often, however, the commercial films of the 1930s were deliberately and explicitly escapist: lavish musicals such

Discussion and Activities

Analyzing Visuals Have students examine the image "A Night at the Opera." Ask them to identify and discuss in small groups details from the poster designed to increase public interest in the movie being advertised. *(Funny caricatures of the actors; promises of hilarity, making "a night at the opera," normally a formal cultural activity, into a comedy. All of these details are designed to promote the idea that attending the movie would make one laugh and take one's mind off of the difficulties of the Depression.)* **SOC** **ARC**

THE FILMS OF FRANK CAPRA

Frank Capra is probably best remembered today for his last successful film, *It's a Wonderful Life* (1946), widely replayed every year at Christmas. In it, George Bailey, a kind and compassionate small-town savings-and-loan operator (played by Jimmy Stewart), is almost destroyed by a wealthy, greedy, and malicious banker. In despair and contemplating suicide, Bailey receives a visit from an angel who shows him what life in his community, Bedford Falls, would have been like had George never been born. After a few hours of wandering through a coarse, corrupt, degraded version of the town he knew, Bailey comes to understand the value of his own life. He returns to the real Bedford Falls to find that his family, friends, and neighbors have rallied together to rescue him from his financial difficulties and affirm his value to them, and theirs to him.

By the time *It's a Wonderful Life* appeared, Frank Capra had been the most famous and successful director in Hollywood for more than a decade. His films during those years had almost all been great commercial and critical successes. Capra's popularity was a result in part of his tremendous talent as a director. But it was also a result of his ideas. Most of his films expressed a vision of society, and of politics, that resonated clearly with the concerns of millions of Americans as they struggled through the years of the Great Depression.

Capra was born in 1897 in a small village in Sicily and moved with his family to America six years later. After working his way through college, he found a job in the still-young movie industry in California and eventually became a director of feature films. His greatbreakthrough came in 1934 with *It Happened One Night*, a now-classic comedy that won five major Academy Awards, including best picture and best director. Over the next seven years, he built on that success by making a series of more-pointed films through which he established himself as a powerful voice of a comfortably populist vision of democracy and American life.

Capra made no secret of his romantic image of the small town and the common man, his distaste for cities, his contempt for opportunistic politicians, and his condemnation of what he considered the amoral (and often immoral) capitalist marketplace. In *Mr. Deeds Goes to Town* (1936), a simple man from a small town inherits a large fortune, moves to the city, and—not liking the greed and dishonesty he finds there—gives the money away and moves back home. In *Mr. Smith Goes to Washington* (1939), a decent man from a western state is elected to the U.S. Senate, refuses to join in the self-interested politics of Washington, and dramatically exposes the corruption and selfishness of his colleagues. (The rugged western actor Gary Cooper portrayed Mr. Deeds, and Jimmy Stewart played Mr. Smith.) In *Meet John Doe* (1941), released on the brink of American entry into World War II, an ordinary man—played again by Gary Cooper—is manipulated by a fascist cartel to dupe the public on their behalf. He comes to his senses just in time and, by threatening suicide, rallies ordinary people to turn against the malign plans of the fascists. He then disappears into the night.

MR. DEEDS GOES TO TOWN Gary Cooper, playing the newly wealthy Longfellow Deeds, leaves the friendly, virtuous small town of Mandrake Falls en route to New York to receive the fortune he has inherited. Capra's evocation of the warmth and generosity of Mandrake Falls was part of his effort to contrast the decent America of ordinary people with the grasping and corrupt America of the wealthy and the city.

THE GREATEST OF ALL CAPRA HITS...
FRANK CAPRA'S
MR. SMITH GOES TO WASHINGTON
JEAN ARTHUR ★ JAMES STEWART

PROMOTING CAPRA Capra was unusual among directors of the 1930s in having a distinct following of his own. Most films attempted to attract audiences by highlighting their stars. Capra films highlighted Capra himself.

Capra was entirely conscious of the romantic populism that he brought to his films. He was intensely patriotic, and he believed fervently that America stood for individual opportunity and was defined by the decency of ordinary people. He did not like the term "masses" and found it "insulting, degrading." He saw the people, rather, as a "collection of free individuals . . . each an island of human dignity."

When America entered World War II, Capra collaborated with the government (and the Walt Disney studios) to make a series of films designed to explain to new soldiers what the war was about—a series known as *Why We Fight*. They contrasted the individualistic democracy of the American small town with the dark collectivism of the Nazis and Fascists. Capra poured into them all his skills as a filmmaker and all his romantic, patriotic images. *It's a Wonderful Life*, released a year after the war ended, continued his evocation of the decency of ordinary people.

Historical Thinking Skills

Sourcing and Situation Have students examine the image *Mr. Deeds Goes to Town*. Ask students to consider in pairs or small groups the point of view of the director by discussing how Frank Capra's background may have influenced the type of films he directed. **NAT** **MIG** **WXT** **SOC** **ARC**

Historical Thinking Skills

Sourcing and Situation Have students examine the image "Promoting Capra." Ask them to write a short paragraph evaluating the purpose of the poster promoting a film by highlighting the director instead of the actors. *(Frank Capra had directed several popular films by this time, and by promoting the fact that he had directed the film in the poster, the studio hoped to attract audiences of viewers who had enjoyed the previous films.)* **WXT** **ARC**

Discussion and Activities

Historical Evidence and Argumentation
After students have read the section "Movies in the New Era," ask them to create a chart capturing reasons for motion picture attendance and reasons for the types of movies being produced. Have students discuss in small groups whether moviegoers would have wanted to see films different from the ones being produced by the studios. **WXT** **SOC** **ARC**

FRANK CAPRA **Frank Capra was one of the most famous and successful Hollywood movie directors of the 1930s and 1940s. His films evoked a romantic populism and patriotism during a time of great stress and deprivation.**

In the decades that followed, Capra ceased to be an important force in American cinema. The sentimental populism and comic optimism that had been so appealing to audiences during the hard years of the Depression and the war gave way to a harder, more realistic style of filmmaking in the 1950s and 1960s; and Capra—a romantic to the end—was never fully able to adjust. But in a time of crisis, Capra had helped his audiences find solace in his romantic vision of the American past, and in the warmth and goodness of small towns and the decency of ordinary people.

HISTORICAL THINKING SKILLS

1. **Explaining Historical Context** Why were Capra's films so popular with people suffering through the economic crisis of the Great Depression?
2. **Evaluating Historical Significance** What social messages do Capra's films convey and what vision of American life did they present?
3. **Making Connections** If Capra's style was considered dated after World War II, why has his film *It's a Wonderful Life* continued to be so popular?

as *Gold Diggers of 1933* (whose theme song was "We're in the Money"), "screwball" comedies such as Capra's *It Happened One Night*, or the many films of the Marx Brothers–films designed to divert audiences from their troubles and, often, indulge their fantasies about quick and easy wealth.

The 1930s saw the beginning of Walt Disney's long reign as the champion of animation and children's entertainment. After producing cartoon shorts for theaters in the late 1920s–many of them starring the newly created character of Mickey Mouse, who made his debut in the 1928 cartoon *Steamboat Willie*–Disney began to produce feature-length animated films, starting in 1937 with *Snow White*. Other enormously popular films of the 1930s were adaptations of popular novels: *The Wizard of Oz* and *Gone with the Wind*, both released in 1939.

WALT DISNEY

POPULAR LITERATURE AND JOURNALISM

The social and political strains of the Great Depression found voice much more successfully in print than they did on the airwaves or the screen. Much literature and journalism in the 1930s dealt directly or indirectly with the tremendous disillusionment, and the increasing radicalism, of the era.

Not all literature, of course, was challenging or controversial. The most popular books and magazines of the time were as escapist and romantic as the most popular radio shows and movies. Two of the best-selling novels of the decade were romantic sagas set in earlier eras: Margaret Mitchell's *Gone with the Wind* (1936) and Hervey Allen's *Anthony Adverse* (1933). Leading magazines focused more on fashions, stunts, scenery, and the arts than on the social conditions of the nation. The enormously popular new photographic journal *Life*, which began publication in 1936 and quickly became one of the most successful magazines in American history, had one of the largest readerships of any publication in the United States. It devoted some attention to politics and to the economic conditions of the Depression, more, in fact, than did many of its competitors. But it was best known for stunning photographs of sporting and theater events, natural landscapes, and impressive public projects. Its first cover was a striking photograph by Margaret Bourke-White of a New Deal hydroelectric project. One of its most popular features was "*Life* Goes to a Party," which took the chatty social columns of daily newspapers and turned them into glossy photographic glimpses of Americans having fun.

LIFE MAGAZINE

Other Depression writing, however, was frankly and openly challenging to the dominant values of American popular culture. In the first years of the Depression, some of the most significant literature offered corrosive portraits of the harshness and emptiness of American life: Nathanael West's *Miss Lonelyhearts* (1933), the story of an advice columnist overwhelmed by the sadness he encounters in the lives of those who consult him; Jack Conroy's *The Disinherited* (1933), a harsh portrait of the lives of coal miners; and James T. Farrell's *Studs Lonigan* (1932), a portrait of a lost, hardened working-class youth.

Answers

Patterns of Popular Culture

1. Capra's films offered a positive message. They gave people hope that there was still good in society and that individuals who work hard will make it through desperate times.
2. His messages included the power of the people to make significant change, belief in the fundamental goodness of individuals, and the power of populism.
3. The film, still shown multiple times during the December holidays, has a timeless message about redemption and the positive force that family and friends can be in times of desperation.

The Popular Front and the Left

In the later 1930s, much of the political literature was a result of the rise of the Popular Front, a broad coalition of "antifascist" groups on the left, of which the most important was the American Communist Party. The party had long been a harsh and unrelenting critic of American capitalism and the government it claimed was controlled by it. But in 1935, under instructions from the Soviet Union, the party softened its attitude toward Franklin Roosevelt (whom Stalin considered a potential ally in the coming battle against Hitler) and formed loose alliances with many other "progressive" groups. The party began to praise the New Deal. It even supported John L. Lewis, a powerful (and strongly anticommunist) labor leader. The party adopted the slogan "Communism is twentieth-century Americanism." In its heyday, the Popular Front did much to enhance the reputation and influence of the Communist Party, whose formal membership grew to perhaps 100,000 in the mid-1930s, the highest it had ever been or would be again. But it also helped mobilize writers, artists, and intellectuals—many of them unconnected with (and many of them uninterested in) the Communist Party—behind a pattern of social criticism.

For some intellectuals, the Popular Front offered an escape from the lonely and difficult stance of detachment and alienation they had embraced in the 1920s. The Spanish Civil War was important to many American intellectuals, especially those on the left. It helped give meaning and purpose to individual lives. The war in Spain pitted the fascists of Francisco Franco (who was receiving support from Hitler and Mussolini) against the existing republican government. It attracted a substantial group of young Americans—more than 3,000—who formed the Abraham Lincoln Brigade (directed and in part created by the American Communist Party) and traveled to Spain to join the fight against the fascists. About a third of its members died in combat. Ernest Hemingway, who spent time as a correspondent in Spain during the conflict, wrote in his novel *For Whom the Bell Tolls* (1940) of how the war provided those Americans who fought in it with "a part in something which you could believe in wholly and completely and in which you felt an absolute brotherhood with others who were engaged in it."

Spanish Civil War

The Communist Party was active as well in organizing the unemployed in the early 1930s and staged a hunger march in Washington, D.C., in 1931. Party members were among the most effective union organizers in some industries. And the party was among the few political organizations that took a firm stand in favor of racial justice; its active defense of the Scottsboro defendants was but one example of its efforts to ally itself with the aspirations of African Americans.

The American Communist Party was not, however, the open, patriotic organization it tried to appear. It was always under the close and rigid supervision of the Soviet Union. Its leaders took their orders from the Comintern in Moscow. Most members obediently followed the "party line" (although there were many areas in which Communists were active for which there was no party line, areas in which members acted independently). The subordination of the party leadership to the Soviet Union was most clearly demonstrated in 1939, when Stalin signed a nonaggression pact with Nazi Germany. Moscow then sent orders to the American Communist Party to abandon the Popular Front and return to its old stance of harsh criticism of American liberals; and Communist Party leaders in the United States immediately obeyed—although thousands of disillusioned members left the party as a result.

The Socialist Party of America, under the leadership of Norman Thomas, also cited the economic crisis as evidence of the failure of capitalism and sought vigorously to win public support for its own political program. Among other things, it attempted to mobilize support among the rural poor. The Southern Tenant Farmers' Union (STFU), supported by the party and organized by a young socialist, H. L. Mitchell, attempted to create a biracial coalition of sharecroppers, tenant farmers, and others to demand economic reform. Neither the STFU nor the party itself, however, made any real progress toward establishing socialism as a major force in American politics. By 1936, membership in the Socialist Party had fallen below 20,000.

Southern Tenant Farmers' Union

Antiradicalism was a powerful force in the 1930s, just as it had been during and after World War I and would be again in the 1940s and 1950s. Hostility toward the Communist Party, in particular, was intense at many levels of government. Congressional committees chaired by Hamilton Fish of New York and Martin Dies of Texas investigated communist influence wherever they could find it (or imagine it). State and local governments harried and sometimes imprisoned communist organizers. White Southerners tried to drive communist organizers out of the countryside, just as growers in California and elsewhere tried (unsuccessfully) to keep communists from organizing Mexican American and other workers.

Even so, only a few times before in American history (and in few since) did being part of the left seem so respectable and even conventional among workers, intellectuals, and others. Thus the 1930s witnessed a significant, if temporary, widening of the ideological range of mainstream art and politics. The New Deal sponsored artistic work through the Works Projects Administration that was frankly challenging to the capitalist norms of the 1920s. The filmmaker Pare Lorentz, with funding from New Deal agencies, made a series of powerful and polemical documentaries—*The Plow That Broke the Plains* (1936), *The River* (1937)—that combined a celebration of New Deal programs with a harsh critique of the exploitation of people and the environment that industrial capitalism had produced.

The Left's Newfound Respectability

Perhaps the most successful chronicler of social conditions in the 1930s was the novelist John Steinbeck, particularly in his celebrated novel *The Grapes of Wrath*, published in 1939.

Historical Thinking Skills

Argumentation Have students read the section "Spanish Civil War." Ask them to create a poster designed to attract attendance to a Popular Front rally. Have students consider how the appeal might be presented in a way to minimize traditional American suspicion of communism and socialism. **PCE** **WXT** **SOC**

Discussion and Activities

Understanding Multiple Perspectives After students have read the section "The Left's Newfound Respectability," ask them to discuss as a class arguments in favor of and in opposition to the rise of support for socialism and communism in the 1930s. **PCE** **WXT** **SOC** **NAT**

Historical Thinking Skills

Argumentation After students have read the section "The Popular Front and the Left," ask them to list and rank in order of importance the reasons for the rise in popularity of socialism and communism in the 1930s. Have students write a thesis statement that makes a claim about the most important cause(s) of the rise of radicalism in the 1930s. **SOC** **WXT** **ARC** **NAT**

MIGRANT FAMILY This photograph by the great Depression photographer Dorothea Lange portrays a family of migrants leaving Texas in search of work in California. It suggests the plight of hundreds of thousands of families who fled the regions affected by drought in the 1930s—a devastation that became known as the Dust Bowl.

THE GRAPES OF WRATH

In telling the story of the Joad family, migrants from the Dust Bowl to California who encounter an unending string of calamities and failures, he offered not only a harsh portrait of the exploitive features of agrarian life in the West, but also a tribute to the endurance of his main characters—and to the spirit of community they represent.

THE UNHAPPY PRESIDENCY OF HERBERT HOOVER

Herbert Hoover began his presidency in March 1929 believing, like most Americans, that the nation faced a bright and prosperous future. For the first six months of his Republican administration, he attempted to expand the policies he had advocated during his eight years as secretary of commerce, policies that would, he believed, complete a stable system of cooperative individualism and sustain a successful economy. The economic crisis that began before the year was out forced the president to deal with a new set of problems, but for most of the rest of his term, he continued to rely on the principles that had always governed his public life.

THE HOOVER PROGRAM

Hoover's first response to the Depression was to attempt to restore public confidence in the economy. "The fundamental business of this country, that is, production and distribution of commodities," Hoover said in 1930, "is on a sound and prosperous basis." He then summoned leaders of business, labor, and agriculture to the White House and urged them to adopt a program of voluntary cooperation for recovery. He implored businessmen not to cut production or lay off workers; he talked labor leaders into forgoing demands for higher wages or better hours. But by mid-1931, economic conditions had deteriorated so much that the modest structure of voluntary cooperation he had erected collapsed.

FAILURE OF VOLUNTARISM

Hoover also attempted to use government spending as a tool for fighting the Depression. The president proposed to Congress an increase of $423 million—a significant sum by the

Discussion and Activities

Analyzing Images Have students examine the image "Migrant Family." Ask them to identify and discuss in small groups details that illustrate conditions for poor families struggling during the Great Depression. *(Old, dirty car; children crowded into the back of the car; the family's possessions strapped to the back of the car.)* **SOC** **WXT** **MIG**

standards of the time—in federal public works programs, and he exhorted state and local governments to fund public construction. But the spending was not nearly enough in the face of such devastating problems. And when economic conditions worsened, he became less willing to increase spending, worrying instead about creating large government deficits. In 1932, at the depth of the Depression, he proposed a tax increase to help the government avoid a deficit.

Even before the stock market crash, Hoover had begun to construct a program to assist the already troubled agricultural economy. In April 1929, he proposed the Agricultural Marketing Act, which established the first major government program to help farmers maintain prices. A federally sponsored Farm Board would make loans to national marketing cooperatives or establish corporations to buy surpluses and thus raise prices. At the same time, Hoover attempted to protect American farmers from international competition by raising agricultural tariffs. The Tariff Act of 1930 (also known as the Smoot-Hawley Tariff and the Hawley-Smoot Tariff) increased protection on seventy-five farm products. But neither the Agricultural Marketing Act nor the Hawley-Smoot Tariff ultimately helped American farmers significantly. The tariff, on the contrary, harmed the agricultural economy by stifling exports of food.

AGRICULTURAL MARKETING ACT

By the spring of 1931, Herbert Hoover's political position had deteriorated considerably. In the 1930 congressional elections, Democrats won control of the House and made substantial inroads in the Senate by promising increased government assistance to the economy. Many Americans held the president personally to blame for the crisis and began calling the shantytowns that unemployed people established on the outskirts of cities "Hoovervilles." Democrats urged the president to support more-vigorous programs of relief and public spending. Hoover continued to believe his policies were working.

HOOVER'S DECLINING POPULARITY

The international financial panic of the spring of 1931 destroyed the illusion that the economic crisis was coming to an end. Throughout the 1920s, European nations had depended on loans from American banks to allow them to make payments on their debts. After 1929, when they could no longer get such loans, the financial fabric of several European nations began to unravel. In May 1931, one of the largest banks in Austria collapsed. Over the next several months, panic gripped the financial institutions of neighboring countries. The American economy rapidly declined to new lows.

By the time Congress convened in December 1931, conditions had grown so desperate that Hoover supported a series of measures designed to keep endangered banks afloat and protect homeowners from foreclosure on their mortgages. More important was a bill passed in January 1932 establishing the Reconstruction Finance Corporation (RFC), a government agency whose purpose was to provide federal loans to troubled banks, railroads, and other businesses. It even made funds available to local governments to support public works projects and assist relief efforts. Unlike some earlier Hoover programs, it operated on a large scale. In 1932, the RFC had a budget of $1.5 billion for public works alone.

RECONSTRUCTION FINANCE CORPORATION

HOOVER THE PATRICIAN Although Herbert Hoover grew up in a family of modest means in a small town in Iowa, his critics in the 1930s delighted in portraying him as an aloof aristocrat, fond of fancy dinners and elegant surroundings. As this formal portrait shows, Hoover gave his critics many opportunities to strengthen that image.

Nevertheless, the new agency failed to deal directly or forcefully enough with the real problems of the economy to produce any significant recovery. The RFC lent funds only to financial institutions with sufficient collateral; much of its money went to large banks and corporations. At Hoover's insistence, it helped finance only those public works projects that promised ultimately to pay for themselves (toll bridges, public housing, and others). Above all, the RFC did not have enough money to make any real impact on the Depression, and it did not even spend all the money it had. Of the $300 million available to support local relief efforts, the RFC lent out only $30 million in 1932. Of the $1.5 billion public works budget, it released only about 20 percent.

POPULAR PROTEST

For the first several years of the Depression, most Americans were either too stunned or too confused to raise any effective protest. By the middle of 1932, however, dissident voices began to be heard.

Discussion and Activities

Evaluating After students have read the section "The Hoover Program," ask them to create a three-column chart listing the most important programs proposed by Hoover to address the Depression, what they were intended to accomplish, and how effective they were. Have students discuss in small groups what other measures the Hoover Administration might have taken to address the Great Depression. **PCE** **WXT** **NAT**

Discussion and Activities

Analyzing Visuals Have students examine the image "Hoover the Patrician." Ask them to discuss as a class how the photo of Hoover would have been interpreted by Americans struggling during the Depression, and how they might have advised President Hoover to present himself. **PCE** **SOC**

Discussion and Activities

Analyzing Points of View After students have read the section "Popular Protest," ask them to write a short journal entry from the point of view of a bystander who witnessed the arrival of the Bonus Army in Washington, D.C., and its subsequent removal by the U.S. Army. **SOC** **PCE**

HOOVERVILLES Herbert Hoover remained a symbol of despair for many Americans enduring the stresses of the Great Depression. This shanty town in Seattle and many others throughout the country were called by critics of the president "Hoovervilles."

World History Archive/Alamy Stock Photo

In the summer of 1932, a group of unhappy farm owners gathered in Des Moines, Iowa, to establish a new organization: the Farmers' Holiday Association, which endorsed the withholding of farm products from the market–in effect a farmers' strike. The strike began in August in western Iowa, spread briefly to a few neighboring areas, and succeeded in blockading several markets, but in the end it dissolved in failure.

FARMERS' HOLIDAY ASSOCIATION

A more celebrated protest movement emerged from American veterans. In 1924, Congress had approved the payment of a $1,000 bonus to all those who had served in World War I, the money to be paid beginning in 1945. By 1932, however, many veterans were demanding that the bonus be paid immediately. Hoover, concerned about balancing the budget, rejected their appeal. In June, more than 20,000 veterans, members of the self-proclaimed Bonus Expeditionary Force, or "Bonus Army," marched into Washington, built crude camps around the city, and promised to stay until Congress approved legislation to pay the bonus. Some of the veterans departed in July, after Congress voted down their proposal. Many, however, remained where they were.

Their continued presence in Washington disturbed President Hoover. Finally, in mid-July, he ordered police to clear the marchers out of several abandoned federal buildings in which they had been staying. A few marchers threw rocks at the police, and someone opened fire; two veterans fell dead. Hoover considered the incident evidence of growing violence and radicalism, and he ordered the U.S. Army to assist the police in clearing out the buildings.

General Douglas MacArthur, the army chief of staff, carried out the mission himself (with the assistance of his aide, Dwight D. Eisenhower) and greatly exceeded the president's orders. He led the Third Cavalry (under the command of George S. Patton), two infantry regiments, a machine-gun detachment, and six tanks down Pennsylvania Avenue in pursuit of the Bonus Army. The veterans fled in terror. MacArthur followed them across the Anacostia River, where he ordered the soldiers to burn their tent city to the ground. More than 100 marchers were injured.

DEMISE OF THE BONUS ARMY

The incident served as perhaps the final blow to Hoover's already-battered political standing. Hoover's own reserved personality reinforced the public image of him as aloof and unsympathetic to distressed people. The Great Engineer, the personification of the optimistic days of the 1920s, had become a symbol of the nation's failure to deal effectively with its startling reversal of fortune.

THE ELECTION OF 1932

As the 1932 presidential election approached, few people doubted the outcome. The Republican Party dutifully renominated Herbert Hoover for a second term of office, but the gloomy atmosphere of the convention made it clear that few delegates believed he could win. The Democrats, in the meantime, gathered jubilantly in Chicago to nominate the governor of New York, Franklin Delano Roosevelt.

FDR NOMINATED

Roosevelt had been a well-known figure in the party for many years already. A Hudson Valley aristocrat, a distant cousin of Theodore Roosevelt (a connection strengthened by his marriage in 1904 to the president's niece, Eleanor), and a handsome, charming young man, he progressed rapidly: from a seat in the New York State legislature to a position as assistant secretary of the navy during World War I to his party's vice presidential nomination in 1920 on the ill-fated ticket with James M. Cox. Less than a year later, he was stricken with

Discussion and Activities

Analyzing Visuals Have students examine the image "Hoovervilles." Ask them to identify and discuss in small groups details from the photo that demonstrate what life was like in one of these encampments. *(Small shanties built out of found materials; no apparent utilities; haphazard arrangement; no evidence of vehicular traffic.)* **WXT** **SOC** **MIG**

CLEARING OUT THE BONUS MARCHERS In July 1932, President Hoover ordered the Washington, D.C., police to evict the Bonus marchers from some of the public buildings and land they had been occupying. The result was a series of pitched battles (one of them visible here), in which both veterans and police sustained injuries. Such skirmishes persuaded Hoover to call out the U.S. Army to finish the eviction.

polio. Although he never regained use of his legs (and eventually could appear to walk only by using crutches and braces), he built up sufficient physical strength to return to politics in 1928. When Al Smith received the Democratic nomination for president that year, Roosevelt was elected to succeed him as governor of New York. In 1930, he easily won reelection.

Roosevelt worked no miracles in New York, but he did initiate enough positive programs of government assistance to be able to present himself as a more energetic and imaginative leader than Hoover. In national politics, he avoided such divisive cultural issues as religion and prohibition and emphasized the economic grievances that most Democrats shared. He was able as a result to assemble a broad coalition within the party and win his party's nomination. In a dramatic break with tradition, he flew to Chicago to address the convention in person and accept the nomination. In the course of his acceptance speech, Roosevelt aroused the delegates with his ringing promise: "I pledge you, I pledge myself, to a new deal for the American people," giving his future program a name that would long endure. Neither then nor in the subsequent campaign did Roosevelt give much indication of what that program would be. But Herbert Hoover's unpopularity virtually ensured Roosevelt's election.

1932 ELECTION

In November, to the surprise of no one, Roosevelt won by a landslide. He received 57.4 percent of the popular vote to Hoover's 39.7. In the electoral college, the result was even more overwhelming. Hoover carried Delaware, Pennsylvania, Connecticut, Vermont, New Hampshire, and Maine. Roosevelt won everything else. Democrats won majorities in both houses of Congress. It was a broad and convincing mandate.

THE "INTERREGNUM"

The period between the election and the inauguration (which in the early 1930s lasted more than four months) was a season of growing economic crisis. Presidents-elect traditionally do not involve themselves directly in government. But in a series of brittle exchanges with Roosevelt in the months following the election, Hoover tried to exact from the president-elect a pledge to maintain policies of economic orthodoxy. Roosevelt genially refused.

BANKING CRISIS

In February, only a month before the inauguration, a new crisis developed when the collapse of the American banking system suddenly and rapidly accelerated. Public confidence in

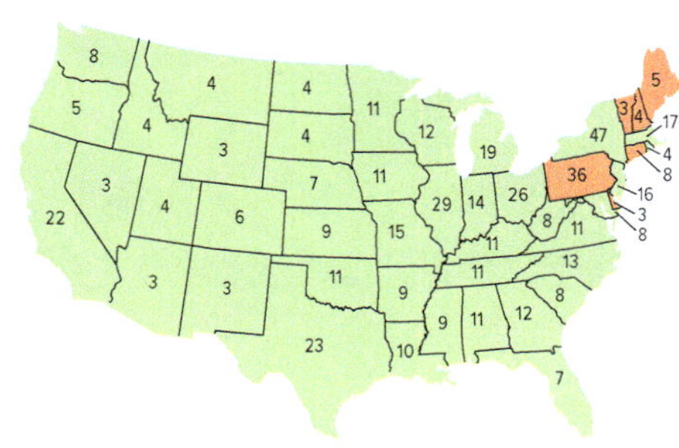

	Candidate (Party)	Electoral Vote	Popular Vote (%)
(green)	Franklin D. Roosevelt (Democratic)	472	22,821,857 (57.4)
(orange)	Herbert Hoover (Republican)	59	15,761,841 (39.7)
	Norman Thomas (Socialist)	—	881,951 (2.2)
	Other candidates (Communist, Prohibition, Socialist Labor, Liberty)	—	271,355

56.9% of electorate voting

ELECTION OF 1932 Like the election of 1928, the election of 1932 was exceptionally one-sided. But this time, the landslide favored the Democratic candidate, Franklin Roosevelt, who overwhelmed Herbert Hoover in all regions of the country except New England. Roosevelt obviously benefited primarily from popular disillusionment with Hoover's response to the Great Depression.

But what characteristics of Roosevelt himself contributed to his victory?

Historical Thinking Skills

Argumentation After students have read the section "The Election of 1932," ask them to create a campaign poster advocating for the election of either Hoover or Roosevelt as president. **PCE** **SOC** **NAT** **WXT**

Answers

Election of 1932

Roosevelt gave voters hope for a fresh start and promises of vigorous government intervention to end the Depression. He communicated a sense of caring for the well-being of the people.

Historical Thinking Skills

Argumentation After students have read the section "The 'Interregnum,'" ask them to write a letter to President-elect Roosevelt advising him on the first actions he should take as president considering the challenges facing the country. **PCE** **WXT** **SOC**

the banks was ebbing; depositors were withdrawing their money in panic; and one bank after another was closing its doors and declaring bankruptcy. Hoover again asked Roosevelt to give prompt public assurances that there would be no tinkering with the currency, no heavy borrowing, no unbalancing of the budget. Roosevelt again refused.

March 4, 1933, was, therefore, a day of both economic crisis and considerable personal bitterness. On that morning, Herbert Hoover, convinced that the United States was headed for disaster, rode glumly down Pennsylvania Avenue with a beaming, buoyant Franklin Roosevelt, who would shortly be sworn in as the thirty-second president of the United States.

THE CHANGING OF THE GUARD Herbert Hoover and Franklin D. Roosevelt travel together to the Capitol for Roosevelt's inauguration. The ride appeared uncomfortable for the outgoing president. Hoover seems glum and uncommunicative whereas Roosevelt seems ready to take on his new responsibilities.

Reasoning Processes

Comparing Have students examine the image "The Changing of the Guard." Ask them to discuss in pairs or small groups details from the photo that illustrate the differing personalities and circumstances of the two men.

CHAPTER 24 REVIEW

CONNECTING THEMES

Chapter Twenty-Four examined the causes and effects of the Great Depression. The Depression had both short-term and long-term consequences for American economic, social, and political institutions. Hundreds of thousands of farmers in the Great Plains fled the "Dust Bowl" and migrated to California hoping to find work. Local governments and white workers often used violence, intimidation, and deportation to displace African Americans, Mexican Americans, and Asian Americans from their jobs and keep them out of the workforce.

Some radical writers and photographers exposed the extreme poverty and social injustices of the period. But most Hollywood movies and radio shows defended the capitalist system, reinforced traditional values, and offered escapist entertainment from the economic realities of the Great Depression. Mass unemployment overwhelmed private charities and led to a public rethinking of the government's responsibility to address the issue. But most Americans continued to embrace the "success ethic" and blame themselves for their struggles during the crisis.

You should consider the following questions as you review the themes for this chapter:

- How did the Great Depression affect American identity and values?
- How were minorities affected by the Great Depression?
- Why did technological advances and foreign trade policies help lead to the Great Depression?
- How was the election of 1932 a significant turning point in American history?
- What affect did the Great Depression have on migration patterns in the United States?
- How did the Great Depression affect the evolution of literature and other forms of culture in the United States during the 1930s?

KEY TERMS

Agricultural Marketing Act 687
"Black Tuesday" 671
Bonus Army 688
Clifford Odets 681
Dust Bowl 676
Erskine Caldwell 681
Frank Capra 682
Hindenburg 682
Hoovervilles 687
John Dos Passos 681
John Steinbeck 681
Life Magazine 684
"Okies" 676
Orson Welles 682
Popular Front 685
Reconstruction Finance Corporation 687
Richard Wright 681
Scottsboro case 676
soap operas 682
Tariff Act of 1930 687

Discussion and Activities

Explaining Effects Divide the class into three groups and have them review and research the political, economic, and social effects of the Great Depression. Assign a topic to each group, and have each group prepare a short presentation or skit to share their results with the class. **PCE** **WXT** **SOC** **ARC** **NAT** **MIG** **GEO**

Key Terms

Students should be familiar with the key terms and be able to define them in the context of the causes of the Great Depression and its political, economic, and social effects. Encourage students to use these terms in performing review exercises and exam practice for this chapter.

Go Online Chapter 24 Content Review

Assessing Student Understanding Use the online assessment to assess student understanding of concepts and topics within the chapter. You can assign the ready-made Chapter 24 Content Review or create your own from available questions. This easy-to-use tool helps you design assessments that meet the needs of different types of learners.

Answers

Multiple Choice

1. D; **2.** B; **3.** A

Short Answer

4A) Possible response: The photo depicts a group of radio performers in the middle of a live reading of a play over the radio. The radio emerged during the 1920s as a popular piece of communication technology. It was used extensively during the Depression for many different purposes.

4B) Possible response: Radios provided a form of escape, which became very important during the Depression of the 1930s.

4C) Possible response: Radios provided direct access to important information, from news to weather to sports. The radio fundamentally drew the nation together; it generated a sense of unity and universality.

5A) Possible response: Major pieces of literature of both the 1920s and the 1930s reflected the major social, political, and economic conditions of the times. *The Great Gatsby,* published in 1925, presented the glamour and glitz of the Jazz Age and the Roaring Twenties. *The Grapes of Wrath,* published in 1939, represented the hardships faced by farmers during the Great Depression. Both novels are considered classics of their time and possibly representative of the Great American Novel.

5B) Possible response: *The Great Gatsby* focused on the lives of the rich and wealthy (and those who wanted to be), whereas *The Grapes of Wrath* focused on the lives of poor farmers. These two iconic novels represented the extreme social, political, and economic differences between two classes and two eras.

5C) Possible response: Literature, like the radio, provided opportunities for escapism. But more importantly, it reflected the fears and concerns of the country as a whole. It also mixed modernism and realism.

AP EXAM PRACTICE

Questions assume cumulative content knowledge from this chapter and previous chapters.

MULTIPLE CHOICE

Use the photograph on page 677 and your knowledge of U.S. history to answer questions 1-3.

1. How did many Americans respond to the conditions created in agrarian communities by the Great Depression?
   (A) They migrated overseas in search of stable employment.
   (B) They advocated for high protective tariffs.
   (C) They remained on farms and continued to over-cultivate the land.
   (D) They migrated to western states such as California to work as migrant laborers.

2. Photographers such as Dorothea Lange presented the conditions some Americans faced in order to
   (A) help the subjects of the photograph find employment.
   (B) stimulate reforms in hopes of gaining support for struggling rural families.
   (C) generate work in the midst of the economic downturn.
   (D) document the era for their personal memoirs.

3. Hardships such as those faced by the family in the photograph challenged Americans' traditional cultural belief that
   (A) hard work would lead to personal prosperity.
   (B) the government should protect Americans from economic ruin.
   (C) all Americans deserved equal opportunities regardless of ethnic or racial background.
   (D) local communities should provide for members in their times of need.

SHORT ANSWER

Use your knowledge of U.S. history to answer questions 4 and 5.

4. Use the photograph on page 681 to answer A, B, and C.
   (A) Describe ONE important historical context of the photograph.
   (B) Explain ONE specific effect that radio had on American society during the 1930s.
   (C) Explain a SECOND specific effect that radio had on American society during the 1930s

5. Answer A, B, and C.
   (A) Briefly describe ONE specific historical similarity between literature of the 1920s and literature of the 1930s.
   (B) Briefly describe ONE specific historical difference between literature of the 1920s and literature of the 1930s.
   (C) Briefly explain ONE specific historical effect literature had on American society during the 1930s.

LONG ESSAY

Develop a thoughtful and thorough historical argument that addresses the statement. Begin your essay with a thesis statement, and support it with specific historical evidence and examples.

6. Evaluate the extent of continuities Americans faced in the post-World War I and pre-World War II society, from 1920 to 1940.

Answers

Long Essay

6. Possible thesis: Even though the United States faced great changes between the wars, some continuities endured. During the inter-war period, Americans shared a common sense of value, shaped largely by radio and other popular cultural activities. However, economic conditions radically changed from the 1920s to the 1930s. For African Americans and women, this period represented both a time of excitement and a time of concern. African Americans faced racism, segregation, and discrimination while also creating a flourishing artistic and intellectual culture. While women were making some great strides, social and cultural expectations had changed very little. Both of these groups continued to work for change to make their lives better. For the nation overall, the radio tended to play a significant impact on the social, political, and economic conditions of the country. It united the country and provided individuals with important information.

25 THE NEW DEAL

TVA JOBS ARE WAR JOBS
The Tennessee Valley Authority, a federally owned corporation, sought to revitalize a region devastated by depression and other catastrophes. By the time of World War II, much of the work of the TVA centered on producing hydroelectric power with which to build war materiel.

CONNECTING CONCEPTS

Chapter Twenty-Five begins by examining Franklin Roosevelt's efforts to restore American confidence and end the Great Depression. He declared a "bank holiday," supported the repeal of Prohibition, and communicated his optimism directly to families through "fireside chats" on radio. Roosevelt also tried, with limited success, to revive the agricultural and industrial sectors. Regulation of the banking system and stock market followed. Finally, the New Deal began to offer direct assistance in the form of grants and jobs to desperate Americans.

Yet the Great Depression continued and critics of the New Deal emerged. On the right, conservatives contended that Roosevelt was anti-capitalist. On the left, radicals asserted that the New Deal was too supportive of the free market. Populists like Father Charles Coughlin and Huey Long offered an assortment of criticisms. In response, Roosevelt launched a "Second New Deal," which featured the Social Security Act and the Works Progress Administration. The government also encouraged the rapid growth of industrial unions, which used frequent strikes to win better wages from the auto and steel industries.

Roosevelt easily won reelection in 1936. But the recession of 1937 and his controversial plan to add justices to the Supreme Court, which had struck down several of his programs, damaged his popularity and stalled his agenda, although he continued to promote economic development in the West and South. The New Deal also remained sympathetic to the aspirations of African Americans, Native Americans, and American women, but often settled for symbolic actions. Ultimately, the New Deal

Pacing Guide

Chapter 25 explores key concepts from Period 7: 1890–1945 of the AP U.S. History Curriculum Framework. The suggested instruction time for Chapter 25 is 3 days.

Key Concepts

7.1.III During the 1930s, policymakers responded to the mass unemployment and social upheavals of the Great Depression by transforming the U.S. into a limited welfare state, redefining the goals and ideas of modern American liberalism.

Discussion and Activities

Evaluating Evidence Have students examine the image "TVA Jobs are War Jobs." Ask them to identify and discuss in small groups the implications of the poster's slogan. *(If the TVA is vital to the war effort, its workers are as well. TVA workers would be encouraged to think of their labor as contributing to the security of the country, not just providing an income for themselves, and therefore the workers should be willing to make sacrifices for the good of the country.)*
PCE **WXT**

Historical Thinking Skills

Developments and Processes Have students read the section "Roosevelt's Personality." Ask them to discuss as a class how Roosevelt was able to reassure the nation that economic relief was coming even before any legislation was passed. **PCE** **SOC** **NAT**

failed to end the Great Depression, but transformed American politics by remaking the Democratic Party, creating the welfare state, and raising public expectations of the federal government.

As you read, you should:

- Analyze how the Great Depression led to calls to increase the regulatory powers of the federal government.
- Describe how national reformers responded to the Great Depression by transforming the United States into a limited welfare state.
- Evaluate how New Deal programs that focused on promoting relief for those in need, recovery of the American economy, and reform of the economic system to prevent future depressions of such severity, met or fell short of their goals.
- Identify ways conservatives and the U.S. Supreme Court worked to limit the New Deal, while other dissident political movements pushed for further measures.
- Describe how the New Deal failed to end the Great Depression, but how it led to political realignment that strengthened the Democratic Party.
- Analyze the increase in the power of trade unions during the time period.

LAUNCHING THE NEW DEAL

Roosevelt's first task upon taking office was to alleviate the panic that was threatening the financial system. He did so in part by force of personality and in part by constructing very rapidly an ambitious and diverse program of legislation.

RESTORING CONFIDENCE

Much of Roosevelt's success was a result of his ebullient personality. In his inaugural address, he assured the American people that "the only thing we have to fear is fear itself," and promised to take drastic, even warlike, action against the emergency. He projected an infectious optimism that helped alleviate the growing despair. He was the first president to make regular use of the radio, and his friendly "fireside chats," during which he explained his programs and plans to the people, helped build public confidence in the administration. Roosevelt held frequent informal press conferences and won the respect and friendship of most reporters. Their regard for him was such that by unwritten agreement, no journalist ever photographed the president getting into or out of his car or sitting in his wheelchair. Much of the American public remained unaware throughout the Roosevelt years that the president's legs were completely paralyzed.

ROOSEVELT'S PERSONALITY

But Roosevelt could not rely on image alone. On March 6, 1933, two days after taking office, he issued a proclamation closing all American banks for four days until Congress could meet in special session to consider banking-reform legislation. So great was the panic about bank failures that the "bank holiday," as the president euphemistically described it, created a general sense of relief. Three days later, Roosevelt sent to Congress the Emergency Banking Act, a generally conservative bill (much of it drafted by Hoover administration holdovers) designed primarily to protect the larger banks from being dragged down by the weakness of smaller ones. The bill provided for Treasury Department inspection of all banks before they would be allowed to reopen, for federal assistance to some troubled institutions, and for a thorough reorganization of those in the greatest difficulty. A confused and frightened Congress passed the bill within four hours of its introduction. "I can assure you," Roosevelt told the public on March 12, in his first fireside chat, "that it is safer to keep your money in a reopened bank than under the mattress." Whatever else the new law accomplished, it helped dispel the panic. Three-quarters of the banks in the Federal Reserve system reopened within the next three days, and $1 billion in hoarded currency and gold flowed back into them within a month. The immediate banking crisis was over.

"BANK HOLIDAY"

On the morning after passage of the Emergency Banking Act, Roosevelt sent to Congress another measure–the Economy Act–designed to convince fiscally conservative Americans (especially the business community) that the federal government was in safe, responsible hands. The act proposed to balance the federal budget by cutting the salaries of government employees and reducing pensions to veterans by as much as 15 percent. Otherwise, the president warned, the nation faced a $1 billion budget deficit. Like the banking bill, this one passed Congress almost instantly–despite heated protests from some congressional progressives.

Go Online AP Exam Preparation

AP Exam Practice Use the online assessment to help prepare students for the AP Exam. You can assign the ready-made AP-style short-answer questions, document-based questions, and multiple-choice questions assessing concepts, themes, and skills from Period 7 and AP-style long-essay questions organized in sets of 3 questions from various time periods. You can also create your own tests from available questions. This easy-to-use tool helps you design assessments that meet the needs of different types of learners.

THE "RADIO PRESIDENT" Franklin D. Roosevelt was the first American president to master the use of radio. Beginning in his first days in office, he regularly bypassed the newspapers and communicated directly with the people through his famous "fireside chats." He is shown here speaking in 1938, urging communities to continue to provide work relief for the unemployed.

© Bettmann/Getty Images

Roosevelt also moved in his first days in office to put to rest one of the divisive issues of the 1920s. He supported and then signed a bill to legalize the manufacture and sale of beer with a 3.2 percent alcohol content—an interim measure pending the repeal of prohibition, for which a constitutional amendment (the Twenty-First) was already in process. The amendment was ratified later in 1933.

PROHIBITION REPEALED

AGRICULTURAL ADJUSTMENT

These initial actions were largely stopgaps, to buy time for comprehensive programs. The first of them was the Agricultural Adjustment Act, which Congress passed in May 1933. Its most important feature was its provision for reducing crop production to end agricultural surpluses and halt the downward spiral of farm prices.

Under the provisions of the act, producers of seven basic commodities (wheat, cotton, corn, hogs, rice, tobacco, and dairy products) would decide on production limits for their crops. The government, through the Agricultural Adjustment Administration (AAA), would then tell individual farmers how much they should produce and would pay them subsidies for leaving some of their land idle. A tax on food processing (for example, the milling of wheat) would provide the funds for the new payments. Farm prices would be subsidized up to the point of parity.

AAA

The AAA helped bring about a rise in prices for farm commodities in the years after 1933. Gross farm income increased by half in the first three years of the New Deal, and the agricultural economy emerged from the 1930s much more stable and prosperous than it had been in many years. The AAA did, however, favor larger farmers over smaller ones, particularly since local administration of its programs often fell into the hands of the most powerful producers in a community. By distributing payments to landowners, not those who worked the land, the government did little to discourage planters who were reducing their acreage from evicting tenants and sharecroppers and firing field hands.

In January 1936, the Supreme Court struck down the crucial provisions of the Agricultural Adjustment Act, arguing that the government had no constitutional authority to require farmers to limit production. But within a few weeks the administration had secured passage of new legislation (the Soil Conservation and Domestic Allotment Act), which permitted the government to pay farmers to reduce production so as to "conserve soil," prevent erosion, and accomplish other secondary goals. The Court did not interfere with the new laws.

The administration launched several efforts to assist poor farmers as well. The Resettlement Administration, established in 1935, and its successor, the Farm Security Administration, created in 1937, provided loans to help farmers cultivating submarginal soil to relocate to better lands. But the programs never moved more than a few thousand farmers. More effective was the Rural Electrification Administration, created in 1935, which worked to make electric power available for the first time to thousands of farmers through utility cooperatives.

"RURAL ELECTRIFICATION"

INDUSTRIAL RECOVERY

Ever since 1931, leaders of the U.S. Chamber of Commerce and many others had been urging the government to adopt an anti-deflation scheme that would permit trade associations to cooperate in stabilizing prices within their industries. Existing antitrust laws clearly forbade such practices, and Herbert Hoover had refused to endorse suspension of the laws. The Roosevelt administration was more receptive. In exchange for relaxing antitrust provisions, however, New Dealers insisted on other provisions. Business leaders would have to make important concessions to labor—recognize the workers' right to bargain collectively through unions—to ensure that the incomes of workers would rise along with prices. And to help create jobs and increase consumer buying power, the administration added a major program of public works spending. The result of these and many other impulses was the National Industrial Recovery Act, which Congress passed in June 1933.

At first, the new industrial recovery program appeared to work well. At its center was a new federal agency, the National Recovery Administration (NRA), under the direction of the flamboyant and energetic Hugh S. Johnson. Johnson called on every business establishment in the nation to accept a temporary "blanket code": a minimum wage of between 30 and 40 cents an hour, a maximum workweek of thirty-five to forty hours, and the abolition of child labor. Adherence to the code, he claimed, would raise consumer purchasing power and increase employment. At the same time, Johnson negotiated another, more specific set of

NRA

Discussion and Activities

Historical Reasoning and Argumentation After students have read the section "Restoring Confidence," ask them to think about and discuss with a partner whether the Emergency Banking Act of Roosevelt's radio address was influential in ending the banking crisis. **WXT** **PCE**

Historical Thinking Skills

Argumentation Have students read the section "Agricultural Adjustment." Ask them to create a poster designed to persuade farmers that they would be better off producing less food. **WXT** **PCE**

AP Exam Tip

The AP Exam requires students to identify and explain a source's point of view, purpose, historical situation, and/or audience. One way students can identify the purpose of a source is to explain how the author of the source would benefit from creating the source.

Historical Thinking Skills

Sourcing and Situation Have students practice the tip by reading the first paragraph of the First Fireside Chat. Ask them to discuss in small groups what President Roosevelt would gain by briefly explaining what banks did with customer's money. *(Roosevelt would hope that bank customers would be reassured that banks were acting appropriately and that they would understand that a bank run was counterproductive since banks did not keep all deposits in the bank.)* **PCE** **WXT**

CONSIDER THE SOURCE

BANKING CRISES

When Franklin Delano Roosevelt took Office as President in 1933, the U.S. banking system was close to collapse. As depositors, panicked by the worsening Depression, withdrew their savings from the banks, bank after bank was forced to close. To prevent a complete collapse of the banking system, FDR first declared a "bank holiday," calling for the closing of all banks, and then called Congress into special session to pass banking-reform legislation, the Emergency Banking Act. In his first fireside chat on March 12, 1933–excerpted in the first source document below–the president sought to explain to the public the actions he and Congress had undertaken and to reassure his listeners that their money would be safe in banks.

Some seventy-five years after the Great Depression of the 1930s, the nation once again experienced a serious financial crisis in the Great Recession of 2007-2010. Once again, Congress passed banking-reform legislation calling for closer regulation of banks and providing greater protections for consumers. In his address of July 21, 2010, President Barack Obama outlined the provisions of the new legislation and sought to reassure the public. Excerpts from this address comprise the second source in this feature.

THE GREAT DEPRESSION—1933

Franklin Delano Roosevelt: "The Banking Crisis (First Fireside Chat)"

First of all, let me state the simple fact that when you deposit money in a bank, the bank does not put the money into a safe deposit vault. It invests your money in many different forms of credit in bonds, in commercial paper, in mortgages and in many other kinds of loans. In other words, the bank puts your money to work to keep the wheels of industry and of agriculture turning around. . . .

What, then, happened during the last few days of February and the first few days of March? Because of undermined confidence on the part of the public, there was a general rush by a large portion of our population to turn bank deposits into currency or gold, a rush so great that the soundest banks couldn't get enough currency to meet the demand. . . . By the afternoon of March third, a week ago last Friday, scarcely a bank in the country was open to do business. Proclamations closing them, in whole or in part, had been issued by the Governors in almost all the states. It was then that I issued the proclamation providing for the national bank holiday, and this was the first step in the Government's reconstruction of our financial and economic fabric.

The second step, last Thursday, was the legislation promptly and patriotically passed by the Congress confirming my proclamation and broadening my powers so that it became possible in view of the requirement of time to extend the holiday and lift the ban of that holiday gradually in the days to come. This law also gave authority to develop a program of rehabilitation of our banking facilities. . . .

The new law allows the twelve Federal Reserve Banks to issue additional currency on good assets and thus the banks that reopen will be able to meet every legitimate call. . . . It is necessary that the reopening of banks be extended over a period [of several days] in order to permit the banks to make applications for the necessary loans, to obtain currency needed to meet their requirements, and to enable the Government to make common sense checkups. . . .

We have had a bad banking situation. Some of our bankers had shown themselves either incompetent or dishonest in their handling of the people's funds. They had used the money entrusted to them in speculations and unwise loans. This was, of course, not true in the vast majority of our banks, but it was true in enough of them to shock the people of the United States, for a time, into a sense of insecurity and to put them into a frame of mind where they did not differentiate, but seemed to assume

Historical Thinking Skills

Contextualization Have students read the section "Banking Crises." Ask them to review the causes of the Great Depression and discuss as a class why the banking system was close to collapse by 1933. *(The collapse of the Dawes Plan; numerous runs on banks; lack of deposit insurance.)* **WXT**

that the acts of a comparative few had tainted them all. And so it became the Government's job to straighten out this situation and do it as quickly as possible. And that job is being performed. . . .

[T]here is an element in the readjustment of our financial system more important than currency, more important than gold, and that is the confidence of the people themselves. Confidence and courage are the essentials of success in carrying out our plan. You people must have faith; you must not be stampeded by rumors or guesses. Let us unite in banishing fear. We have provided the machinery to restore our financial system, and it is up to you to support and make it work.

Source: whitehouse.c-span.org

THE GREAT RECESSION OF 2007–2010

Barack Obama: Signing of Dodd-Frank Wall Street Reform and Consumer Protection Act

Over the past two years, we have faced the worst recession since the Great Depression. Eight million people lost their jobs. Tens of millions saw the value of their homes and retirement savings plummet. Countless businesses have been unable to get the loans they need and many have been forced to shut their doors. And although the economy is growing again, too many people are still feeling the pain of the downturn.

Now, while a number of factors led to such a severe recession, the primary cause was a breakdown in our financial system. It was a crisis born of a failure of responsibility from certain corners of Wall Street to the halls of power in Washington. For years, our financial sector was governed by antiquated and poorly enforced rules that allowed some to game the system and take risks that endangered the entire economy.

Unscrupulous lenders locked consumers into complex loans with hidden costs. Firms like AIG placed massive, risky bets with borrowed money. And while the rules left abuse and excess unchecked, they also left taxpayers on the hook if a big bank or financial institution ever failed.

Now, let's put this in perspective. The fact is, the financial industry is central to our nation's ability to grow, to prosper, to compete and to innovate. There are a lot of banks that understand and fulfill this vital role, and there are a whole lot of bankers who want to do right–and do right–by their customers. This reform will help foster innovation, not hamper it. It is designed to make sure that everybody follows the same set of rules, so that firms compete on price and quality, not on tricks and not on traps. . . .

[R]eform will also rein in the abuse and excess that nearly brought down our financial system. It will finally bring transparency to the kinds of complex and risky transactions that helped trigger the financial crisis. Shareholders will also have a greater say on the pay of CEOs and other executives, so they can reward success instead of failure.

And finally, because of this law, the American people will never again be asked to foot the bill for Wall Street's mistakes. There will be no more tax-funded bailouts–period. If a large financial institution should ever fail, this reform gives us the ability to wind it down without end angering the broader economy. And there will be new rules to make clear that no firm is somehow protected because it is "too big to fail." . . .

The fact is every American–from Main Street to Wall Street–has a stake in our financial system. Wall Street banks and firms invest the capital that makes it possible for start-ups to sell new products. They provide loans to businesses to expand and to hire. They back mortgages for families purchasing a new home. That's why we'll all stand to gain from these reforms. We all win when investors around the world have confidence in our markets. We all win when shareholders have more power and more information. We all win when consumers are protected against abuse. And we all win when folks are rewarded based on how well they perform, not how well they evade accountability.

Source: www.whitehouse.gov

AP Exam Practice

Short Answer Provide students with the following short-answer questions and allow 15–20 minutes for completion. Ask for volunteers to share their responses and discuss as a class.

Answer A, B, and C.

A) Briefly explain ONE important cause of the banking crisis of the early 1930s. *(Students may explain any of the following: the collapse of the Dawes Plan; the stock market crash; runs on banks; lack of deposit insurance.)*

B) Briefly explain ONE important response to the banking crisis of the 1930s by the Hoover Administration. *(Students should explain the Hawley-Smoot Tariff.)*

C) Briefly explain ONE important response to the banking crisis of the 1930s by the Roosevelt Administration. *(Students should describe the Emergency Banking Act, Roosevelt's First Fireside Chat, and the "bank holiday.")*

Reasoning Processes

Comparing and Contrasting Have students read both document excerpts. Ask them to create a Venn diagram comparing the tone, wording, and main ideas of the speeches. Have students discuss in small groups what they believe are the most important similarities and differences. **PCE** **WXT**

Discussion and Activities

Historical Sources and Argumentation After students have read the "Banking Crises" feature, ask them to discuss in small groups which president's approach to economic crisis was more effective. Ask: Which speech would you have found more reassuring if you had been a nervous bank customer? **PCE** **WXT** **SOC**

ANALYZING SOURCES

Questions assume cumulative content knowledge from this chapter and previous chapters.

1. Based on the excerpts, which major cause did both crises share?
   - (A) banks refused to lend money to individuals
   - (B) the public withdrew their savings from banks
   - (C) irresponsible speculation by banks
   - (D) no public understanding of how the financial system worked

2. A comparison of the documents provides the most evidence of which difference in the lead-up to the Great Recession versus the Great Depression?
   - (A) no panic on the part of the public vs. great panic on the part of the public
   - (B) failure of the government to enforce banking regulations vs. very little to no government regulation of banks
   - (C) strict of government enforcement of banking and finance regulations vs. no government enforcement
   - (D) too many government regulations to keep track of vs. no government regulations

3. What governmental banking policies changed as a result of the Great Depression and also led to President Obama stating, "(lender policies) left taxpayers on the hook if a big bank or financial institution ever failed?"
   - (A) more regulations placed on bank loaning policies
   - (B) more disclosures required by government regulators to ensure truth in bank assets
   - (C) a government program insured bank savings accounts
   - (D) a government regulation required all bank loans be backed by government funds

Answers

Consider the Source

1. C; **2.** B; **3.** D

SALUTING THE BLUE EAGLE Several thousand San Francisco schoolchildren assembled on a baseball field in 1933 to form the symbol of the National Recovery Administration: an eagle clutching a cogwheel (to symbolize industry) and a thunderbolt (to symbolize energy). This display is evidence of the widespread (if brief) popular enthusiasm the NRA produced. NRA administrators drew from their memories of World War I Liberty Loan drives and tried to establish the Blue Eagle as a symbol of patriotic commitment to recovery.

Reasoning Processes

Comparing and Contrasting
After students have read the section "Industrial Recovery," ask them to create a Venn diagram comparing the National Recovery Administration and the Agricultural Adjustment Administration. Have students discuss in small groups the most important similarities and differences. **PCE** **WXT**

codes with leaders of the nation's major industries. These industrial codes set floors below which no company would lower prices or wages in its search for a competitive advantage. He quickly won agreements from almost every major industry in the country.

From the beginning, however, the NRA encountered serious difficulties. The codes themselves were hastily and often poorly written. Administering them was beyond the capacities of federal officials with no prior experience in running so vast a program. Large producers consistently dominated the code-writing process and ensured that the new regulations would work to their advantage and to the disadvantage of smaller firms. And the codes at times did more than simply set floors under prices; they actively and artificially raised them—sometimes to levels higher than the market could sustain.

Other NRA goals did not progress as quickly as the efforts to raise prices. Section 7(a) of the National Industrial Recovery Act promised workers the right to form unions and engage in collective bargaining and encouraged many workers to join unions for the first time. But Section 7(a) contained no enforcement mechanisms. Hence recognition of unions by employers (and thus the significant wage increases the unions were committed to winning) did not follow. The Public Works Administration (PWA), established in 1933 to administer the National Industrial Recovery Act's spending programs, only gradually allowed the $3.3 billion in public works funds to trickle out. Not until 1938 was the PWA budget pumping an appreciable amount of money into the economy.

SECTION 7(A)

Perhaps the clearest evidence of the NRA's failure was that industrial production actually declined in the months after the agency's establishment—from an index of 101 in July 1933 to 71 in November—despite the rise in prices that the codes had helped to create. By the spring of 1934, the NRA was besieged by criticism, and businessmen were ignoring many of its provisions. That fall, Roosevelt pressured Johnson to resign and established a new board of directors to oversee the NRA. Then, the Supreme Court intervened.

In 1935, a case came before the Court involving alleged NRA code violations by the Schechter brothers, who operated a wholesale poultry business confined to Brooklyn, New York. The Court ruled unanimously that the Schechters were not engaged in interstate commerce (and thus not subject to federal regulation) and, further, that Congress had unconstitutionally delegated legislative power to the president to draft the NRA codes. The justices struck down the legislation establishing the agency. Roosevelt denounced the justices for their "horse-and-buggy" interpretation of the interstate commerce clause. He was rightly concerned, for the reasoning in the Schechter case threatened many other New Deal programs as well. But the Court's destruction of the NRA itself gave the New Deal a convenient excuse for ending a failed experiment.

REGIONAL PLANNING

The AAA and the NRA largely reflected the beliefs of New Dealers who favored economic planning but wanted private interests (farmers or business leaders) to dominate the planning process. Other reformers believed that the government itself should be the chief planning agent in the economy. Their most conspicuous success, and one of the most celebrated accomplishments of the New Deal, was an unprecedented experiment in regional planning: the Tennessee Valley Authority (TVA).

The TVA had its roots in a political controversy of the 1920s. Progressive reformers had agitated for years for public development of the nation's water resources as a source of cheap electric

TVA

Discussion and Activities

Analyzing Visuals Have students examine the image "Saluting the Blue Eagle." Ask them to identify and discuss in small groups details from the image that indicate the public's response to the NRA and the New Deal generally. *(The symbol was prominently displayed in many businesses. A large number of children were gathered for this display, indicating support of the program from those who organized it. However, the school children in the photo would not have been directly affected by the program. A gathering of adults who worked under the NRA's direction would have been more convincing.)* **PCE** **WXT** **SOC**

Discussion and Activities

Historical Evidence and Argumentation
After students have read the section "Regional Planning," ask them to create a T-chart listing costs and benefits of the Tennessee Valley Authority. Have students discuss as a class whether the benefits outweighed the costs. **PCE** **WXT** **SOC** **GEO**

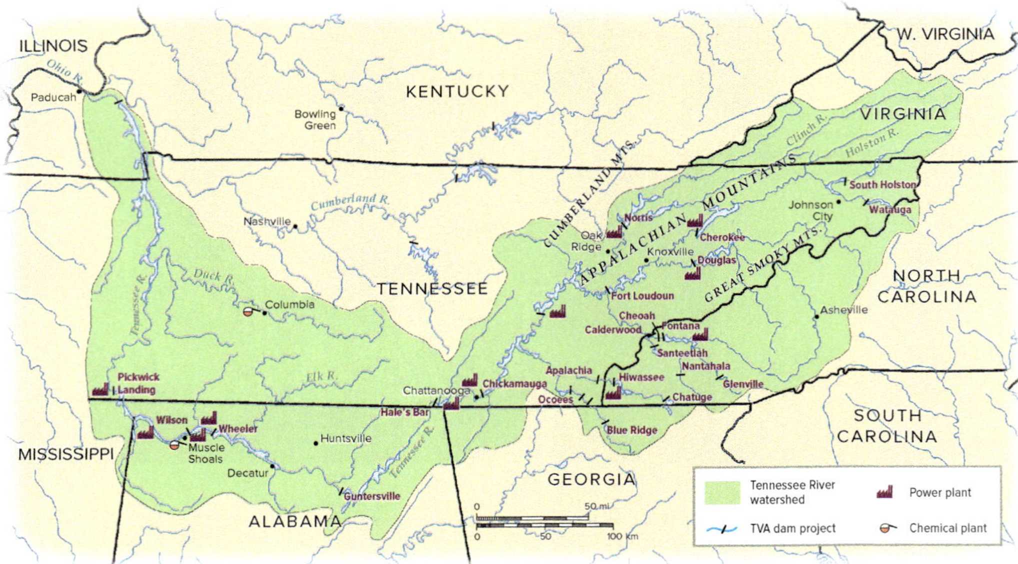

THE TENNESSEE VALLEY AUTHORITY The Tennessee Valley Authority was one of the largest experiments in government-funded public works and regional planning in American history to that point. The federal government had helped fund many projects in its history—canals, turnpikes, railroads, bridges, dams, and others. But never before had it undertaken a project of such great scope, and never before had it maintained such close control and ownership over the public works it helped create. This map illustrates the broad reach of the TVA within the Tennessee Valley region, which spanned seven states. TVA dams throughout the region helped control floods and also provided a source for hydroelectric power, which the government sold to consumers. Note the dam near Muscle Shoals, Alabama, in the bottom left of the map. It was begun during World War I, and efforts to revive it in the 1920s helped create the momentum that produced the TVA.

Why were progressives so eager to see the government enter the business of hydroelectric power in the 1920s?

power. In particular, they had urged completion of a great dam at Muscle Shoals on the Tennessee River in Alabama—a dam begun during World War I and left unfinished when the war ended. But opposition from the utility companies had been too powerful to overcome.

In 1932, however, one of the great utility empires—that of the electricity magnate Samuel Insull—collapsed spectacularly, amid widely publicized exposés of corruption. Hostility to the utilities soon grew so intense that the companies were no longer able to block the public power movement. The result in May 1933 was the Tennessee Valley Authority. The TVA was authorized to complete the dam at Muscle Shoals and build others in the region, and to generate and sell electricity from them to the public at reasonable rates. It was also intended to be an agent for a comprehensive redevelopment of the entire region: for stopping the disastrous flooding that had plagued the Tennessee Valley for centuries, for encouraging the development of local industries, for supervising a substantial program of reforestation, and for helping farmers improve productivity.

The TVA revitalized the region in numerous ways. It improved water transportation, virtually eliminated flooding in the region, and provided electricity to thousands who had never before had it. Throughout much of the country, largely because of the "yardstick" provided by the TVA's cheap production of electricity, private power rates declined. Even so, the Tennessee Valley remained a generally impoverished region despite the TVA's efforts. And like many other New Deal programs, the TVA made no serious effort to challenge local customs and racial prejudices.

CURRENCY, BANKS, AND THE STOCK MARKET

Roosevelt soon came to consider the gold standard a major obstacle to the restoration of adequate prices. On April 18, 1933, he made the shift off the gold standard official with an executive order. By itself, the repudiation of the gold standard meant relatively little. But both before and after the April decision, the administration experimented in various ways with manipulating the value of the dollar—by making substantial purchases of gold and silver and later by establishing a new, fixed standard for the dollar (reducing its gold content substantially from the 1932 amount). The resort to government-managed currency—that is, to a dollar whose value could be

Answers

The Tennessee Valley Authority

Progressives saw government operation of the Tennessee Valley Authority as a way to bring electricity to poorer, rural parts of the South that were not well served by private utility companies.

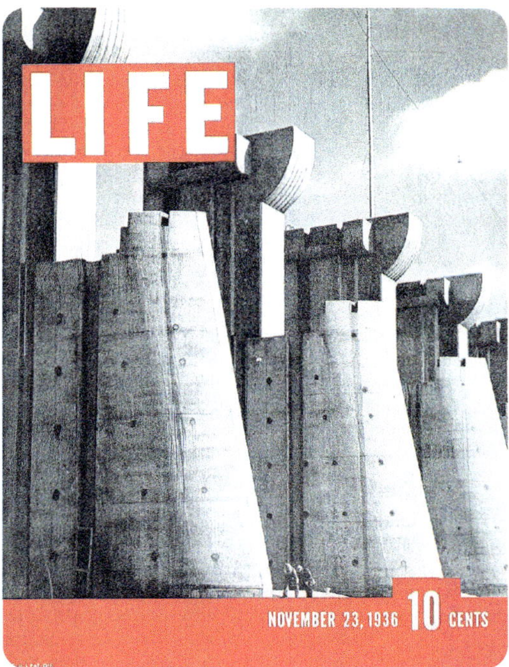

PUBLIC WORKS Among the most visible products of the New Deal was a vast network of public works in almost all areas of the country, but concentrated particularly in the South and the West. The great dams that the government built in the Tennessee Valley and elsewhere were particularly effective at capturing the public imagination. This dramatic photograph by Margaret Bourke-White appeared on the cover of the first issue of Life in 1936, which very quickly became the most popular and successful magazine in America. It shows the Fort Peck Dam on the Missouri River.

raised or lowered by government policy according to economic circumstances—created an important precedent for future federal policies and permanently altered the relationship between the public and private sectors. It did not, however, have any immediate impact on the depressed American economy.

GLASS-STEAGALL ACT

Through other legislation, the early New Deal increased federal authority over previously unregulated or weakly regulated areas of the economy. The Glass-Steagall Act of June 1933 gave the government authority to curb irresponsible speculation by banks. It also established a wall between commercial banking and investment banking. Equally important, it established the Federal Deposit Insurance Corporation, which guaranteed all bank deposits up to $2,500. Finally, in 1935, Congress passed a major banking act that transferred much of the authority once wielded by the regional Federal Reserve banks to the Federal Reserve Board in Washington.

SEC

To protect investors in the stock market, Congress passed the so-called Truth in Securities Act of 1933, requiring corporations issuing new securities to provide full and accurate information about them to the public. Another act of June 1934 established the Securities and Exchange Commission (SEC) to police the stock market. Among other things, the establishment of the SEC was an indication of how far the financial establishment had fallen in public estimation. The criminal trials of a number of once-respected Wall Street figures for grand larceny and fraud eroded the public stature of the financial community still further.

The Growth of Federal Relief

Among Roosevelt's first acts in office was the establishment of the Federal Emergency Relief Administration (FERA), which provided cash grants to states to prop up bankrupt relief agencies. To administer the program, he chose the director of the New York State relief agency, Harry Hopkins, who disbursed the FERA grants widely and rapidly. But both Hopkins and Roosevelt had misgivings about establishing a government "dole."

CWA

They felt more comfortable with another form of government assistance: work relief. Thus, when it became clear that the FERA grants were not enough, the administration established a second program: the Civil Works Administration (CWA). Between November 1933 and April 1934, it put more than 4 million people to work on temporary projects. Some of the projects were of lasting value, such as the construction of roads, schools, and parks; others were little more than make-work. To Hopkins, however, the important thing was pumping money into an economy badly in need of it and providing assistance to people with nowhere else to turn.

CCC

Roosevelt's favorite relief project was the Civilian Conservation Corps (CCC). Established in the first weeks of the new administration, the CCC was designed to provide employment to the millions of young men who could find no jobs in the cities. The CCC created camps in national parks and forests and in other rural and wilderness settings. There young men (women were largely excluded from the program) worked in a semimilitary environment on such projects as planting trees, building reservoirs, developing parks, and improving agricultural irrigation. CCC camps were segregated by race. The vast majority of them were restricted to white men, but a few were available to African Americans, Mexican Americans, and Native Americans.

Mortgage relief was a pressing need for millions of farm owners and homeowners. The Farm Credit Administration, which within two years refinanced one-fifth of all farm mortgages in the United States, was one response to that problem. The Frazier-Lemke Farm Bankruptcy Act of 1933 was another. It enabled some farmers to regain their land even after foreclosure on their mortgages. Despite such efforts, however, 25 percent of all American farm owners had lost their land by 1934. Homeowners were similarly troubled, and in June 1933

Historical Thinking Skills

Argumentation After students have read the section "Currency, Banks, and the Stock Market," ask them to discuss in pairs or small groups what they think the Roosevelt Administration's most important economic regulation was. **PCE** **WXT**

Discussion and Activities

Analyzing Visuals Have students examine the image "Public Works." Ask them to write a short paragraph explaining how the photo communicates the power of the federal government and the effectiveness of the New Deal. *(The photo shows a massive, castle-like structure that required large amounts of money and manpower to build. The dam created a reservoir that could be used for irrigation and that generated electricity that would help people in the area have access to the electric power grid.)* **PCE** **WXT** **SOC** **NAT**

Reasoning Processes

Comparing After students have read the section "The Growth of Federal Relief," ask them to create a chart comparing the provisions of the CWA, CCC, and FHA. Have students discuss as a class which programs would have affected the most people and/or would have had the greatest impact on the economy. **PCE** **WXT** **SOC**

the administration established the Home Owners Loan Corporation, which by 1936 had refinanced the mortgages of more than 1 million householders. A year later, Congress established the Federal Housing Administration to insure mortgages for new construction and home repairs.

THE NEW DEAL IN TRANSITION

Seldom has an American president enjoyed such remarkable popularity as Franklin Roosevelt did during his first two years in office. But with no end to the Depression yet in sight, the New Deal gradually found itself the target of fierce public criticism. In the spring of 1935, partly in response to these growing attacks, Roosevelt launched an ambitious new program of legislation that has often been called the "Second New Deal."

CRITICS OF THE NEW DEAL

Some of the most strident attacks on the New Deal came from critics on the right. Roosevelt had tried for a time to conciliate conservatives and business leaders. By the end of 1934, however, it was clear that the American right in general, and much of the corporate world in particular, had become irreconcilably hostile to the New Deal. In August 1934, a group of the most fervent (and wealthiest) Roosevelt opponents, led by members of the Du Pont family, reshaped the American Liberty League (formed initially to oppose prohibition of liquor), to arouse public opposition to the New Deal's "dictatorial" policies and its supposed attacks on free enterprise. But the new organization was never able to expand its constituency much beyond the Northern industrialists who had founded it.

AMERICAN LIBERTY LEAGUE

Roosevelt's critics on the far left also managed to produce alarm among some supporters of the administration, but like the conservatives, they proved to have only limited strength. The Communist Party, the Socialist Party, and other radical and semiradical organizations were at times harshly critical of the New Deal. But they, too, failed to attract genuine mass support.

More menacing to the New Deal than either the far right or the far left was a group of dissident political movements that defied easy ideological classification. Some gained substantial public support within particular states and regions. And three men succeeded in mobilizing genuinely national followings. Dr. Francis E. Townsend, an elderly California physician, rose from obscurity to lead a movement of more than 5 million members with his plan for federal pensions for the elderly. According to the Townsend Plan, all Americans over the age of sixty would receive monthly government pensions of $200, provided they retired (thus freeing jobs for younger, unemployed Americans) and spent the money in full each month (which would pump needed funds into the economy). By 1935, the Townsend Plan had attracted the support of many older men and women. And while the plan itself was defeated in Congress in 1935, the public sentiment behind it helped build support for the Social Security system, which Congress did approve in 1935.

TOWNSEND PLAN

Father Charles E. Coughlin, a Catholic priest in the Detroit suburb of Royal Oak, Michigan, achieved even greater renown through his weekly sermons, launched in 1926 and broadcast nationally over the radio. In later years, Coughlin became notorious for his sympathy for fascism and his outspoken anti-Semitism. But until at least 1937, he was known primarily as an advocate for changing the banking and currency systems. He proposed a series of monetary reforms–remonetization of silver, issuing of greenbacks, and nationalization of the banking system–that he insisted would restore prosperity and ensure economic justice. At first a warm supporter of Franklin Roosevelt, by late 1934 Coughlin had become disheartened by what he claimed was the president's failure to deal harshly enough with the "money powers." In the spring of 1935, he established his own political organization, the National Union for Social Justice. He was widely believed to have one of the largest regular radio audiences of anyone in America.

More alarming to the administration was the growing national popularity of Senator Huey P. Long of Louisiana. Long had risen to power in his home state through his strident attacks on the banks, oil companies, and utilities and on the conservative political oligarchy allied with them. Elected governor in 1928, he launched an assault on his opponents so thorough and forceful that they were soon left with virtually no political power. Many critics in Louisiana claimed that Long had, in effect, become a dictator. But he also maintained the overwhelming support of the

HUEY LONG

THE NEW DEAL Of the many resources at Roosevelt's disposal was the impression of his sunny personality during dark times. It conveyed to many a sense of hope and optimism. In this political cartoon from about 1934, Roosevelt is seen steering the ship of state towards economic recovery. His detractors are shown grumbling under the cloud of depression.

Historical Thinking Skills

Analyzing Perspectives Have students examine the image "The New Deal." Ask them to discuss in small groups the point of view of the cartoon's author. *(The cartoon's creator appears to have been a supporter of the New Deal. The cartoon shows an upright Roosevelt (no wheelchair) easily steering the economy toward the clear skies and rainbow of recovery, while the detractors, dressed as wealthy businessmen, continue to be soaked by the receding storm cloud labeled "Depression.")* **PCE** **WXT**

Louisiana electorate, in part because of his flamboyant personality and in part because of his solid record of conventional progressive accomplishments: building roads, schools, and hospitals; revising the tax codes; distributing free textbooks; lowering utility rates. Barred by law from succeeding himself as governor, he ran in 1930 for a seat in the U.S. Senate and won easily.

Long, like Coughlin, supported Franklin Roosevelt in 1932. But within six months of Roosevelt's inauguration, he had broken with the president. As an alternative to the New Deal, he advocated a drastic program of wealth redistribution, a program he ultimately named the Share-Our-Wealth Plan. The government, he claimed, could end the Depression easily by using the tax system to confiscate the surplus riches of the wealthiest men and women in America and distribute these surpluses to the rest of the population. That would, he claimed, allow the government to guarantee every family a minimum "homestead" of $5,000 and an annual wage of $2,500. In 1934, Long established his own national organization: the Share-Our-Wealth Society, which soon attracted a large following through much of the nation. A poll by the Democratic National Committee in the spring of 1935 disclosed that Long might attract more than 10 percent of the vote if he ran as a third-party candidate, possibly enough to tip a close election to the Republicans.

SHARE-OUR-WEALTH SOCIETY

HUEY LONG Few public speakers could arouse a crowd more effectively than Huey Long of Louisiana, known to many as "the Kingfish" (a nickname borrowed from the popular radio show *Amos 'n Andy*). It was Long's effective use of radio, however, that contributed most directly to his spreading national popularity in the early 1930s.

THE "SECOND NEW DEAL"

Roosevelt launched the so-called Second New Deal in the spring of 1935 in response both to the growing political pressures and to the continuing economic crisis. The new proposals represented, if not a new direction, at least a shift in the emphasis of New Deal policy. Perhaps the most conspicuous change was in the administration's attitude toward big business. Symbolically at least, the president was now willing to attack corporate interests openly. In March, for example, he proposed to Congress an act designed to break up the great utility holding companies, and he spoke harshly of monopolistic control of their industry. The Holding Company Act of 1935 was the result, although furious lobbying by the utilities led to amendments that sharply limited its effects.

Equally alarming to affluent Americans was a series of tax reforms proposed by the president in 1935, a program conservatives quickly labeled a "soak-the-rich" scheme. Apparently designed to undercut the appeal of Huey Long's Share-Our-Wealth Plan, the Roosevelt proposals called for establishing the highest and most progressive peacetime tax rates in history–although the actual impact of these rates was limited.

The Supreme Court decision in 1935 to strike down the National Industrial Recovery Act also invalidated Section 7(a) of the act, which had guaranteed workers the right to organize and bargain collectively. A group of progressives in Congress led by Senator Robert F. Wagner of New York introduced what became the National Labor Relations Act of 1935. The new law, popularly known as the Wagner Act, provided workers with a crucial enforcement mechanism missing from the 1933 law: the National Labor Relations Board (NLRB), which would have power to compel employers to recognize and bargain with legitimate unions. The president was not entirely happy with the bill, but he signed it anyway. That was in large part because American workers themselves had by 1935 become so important and vigorous a force that Roosevelt realized his own political future would depend in part on responding to their demands.

NATIONAL LABOR RELATIONS BOARD

LABOR MILITANCY

The emergence of a powerful trade union movement in the 1930s was one of the most important social and political developments of the decade. It occurred partly in response to government efforts to enhance the power of unions, but it was also a result of the increased pressure from American workers and their leaders.

The growing labor militancy first became obvious in 1934, when recently organized workers (many of them inspired by the collective bargaining provisions of the National Industrial Recovery Act) demonstrated a new assertiveness. It was soon clear, however, that without stronger legal protection, most organizing drives would end in frustration. Once the Wagner Act became law, the search for more-effective forms of organization rapidly gained strength in labor ranks.

Reasoning Processes

Comparison After students have read the section "Critics of the New Deal," ask them to create a Venn diagram comparing the ideas of Francis Townsend and Huey Long. Have students discuss as a class which ideas the general public would have found more appealing and which might have posed a greater challenge to Roosevelt's New Deal. **PCE** **WXT** **SOC** **NAT**

Discussion and Activities

Speculating Have students read the section "The 'Second New Deal.'" Ask them to discuss as a class why Roosevelt might have thought a "second" New Deal was needed. *(The economy continued to struggle; important programs from the first New Deal had been ruled unconstitutional; several important challengers were proposing competing ideas.)* **PCE** **WXT** **SOC**

Reasoning Processes

Causation After students have read the section "Labor Militancy," ask them to create a T-chart identifying important causes and effects of rising union activity. Have students discuss in small groups how the union activity of the 1930s was similar to or different from earlier union activity. **PCE** **WXT** **SOC**

The American Federation of Labor (AFL) remained committed to the idea of the craft union: organizing workers on the basis of their skills. But that concept had little to offer unskilled laborers, who now constituted the bulk of the industrial workforce. During the 1930s, therefore, a newer concept of labor organization challenged the craft union ideal: industrial unionism. Advocates of this approach argued that all workers in a particular industry should be organized in a single union, regardless of what functions the workers performed: all autoworkers should be in a single automobile union; all steelworkers should be in a single steel union. United in this way, workers would greatly increase their power.

INDUSTRIAL UNIONISM

Leaders of the AFL craft unions for the most part opposed the new concept. But industrial unionism found a number of important advocates, most prominent among them John L. Lewis, the talented, flamboyant, and eloquent leader of the United Mine Workers. At first, Lewis and his allies attempted to work within the AFL, but friction between the new industrial organizations Lewis was promoting and the older craft unions grew rapidly. At the 1935 AFL convention, Lewis became embroiled in a series of angry confrontations (and one celebrated fistfight) with craft union leaders before finally walking out. A few weeks later, he created the Committee on Industrial Organization. When the AFL expelled the new committee and all the industrial unions it represented, Lewis renamed the committee the Congress of Industrial Organizations (CIO), established it in 1936 as an organization directly rivaling the AFL, and became its first president.

CIO

The CIO expanded the constituency of the labor movement. It was more receptive to women and to African Americans than the AFL had been, in part because women and African Americans were more likely to be relegated to unskilled jobs and in part because CIO organizing drives targeted previously unorganized industries (textiles, laundries, tobacco factories, and others) where women and minorities constituted much of the workforce. The CIO was also a more militant organization than the AFL. By the time of the 1936 schism, it was already engaged in major organizing battles in the automobile and steel industries.

ORGANIZING BATTLES

Out of several competing auto unions, the United Auto Workers (UAW) was gradually emerging preeminent in the early and mid-1930s. But although it was gaining recruits, it was making little progress in winning recognition from the automobile corporations. In December 1936, however, autoworkers employed a controversial and effective new technique for challenging corporate opposition: the sit-down strike. Employees in several General Motors plants in Detroit simply sat down inside the plants, refusing either to work or to leave, thus preventing the company from using strikebreakers. The tactic spread to other locations, and by February 1937 strikers had occupied seventeen GM plants. While male workers remained in the factories, female supporters–relatives, friends, and coworkers of the strikers–demonstrated on behalf of the strikers, lobbied on their behalf with state and local officials, and provided food, clothing, and other necessities to the men inside. The strikers ignored court orders and local police efforts to force them to vacate the buildings. When Michigan's governor, Frank Murphy, a liberal Democrat, refused to call up the National Guard to clear out the strikers, and when the federal government also refused to intervene on behalf of employers, General Motors relented. In February 1937, GM became the first major manufacturer to recognize the UAW; other automobile companies soon did the same. The sit-down strike proved effective for rubber workers and others as well, but it survived only briefly as a labor technique. Its apparent illegality aroused so much public opposition that labor leaders soon abandoned it.

SIT-DOWN STRIKE

In the steel industry, the battle for unionization was less easily won. In 1936, the Steel Workers' Organizing Committee (SWOC; later the United Steelworkers of America) began a major organizing drive involving thousands of workers and frequent, at times bitter, strikes. In March 1937, U.S. Steel, the giant of the industry, recognized the union rather than risk a costly strike at a time when it sensed itself on the verge of recovery from the Depression. But the smaller companies (known collectively as "Little Steel") were less accommodating. On Memorial Day 1937, a group of striking workers from Republic Steel gathered with their families for a picnic and demonstration in South Chicago. When they attempted to march peacefully (and legally) toward the steel plant, police opened fire on them. Ten demonstrators were killed; another ninety were wounded. Despite a public outcry against the "Memorial Day Massacre," the harsh tactics of Little Steel companies succeeded. The 1937 strike failed.

But the victory of Little Steel was one of the last gasps of the kind of brutal strikebreaking that had proved so effective in the past. In 1937 alone, there were 4,720 strikes–over 80 percent of them settled in favor of the unions. By the end of the year, more than 8 million workers were members of unions recognized as official bargaining units by employers (compared with 3 million in 1932). By 1941, that number had expanded to 10 million and included the workers of Little Steel, whose employers had finally recognized the SWOC.

ORGANIZED LABOR'S RAPID GROWTH

SOCIAL SECURITY

In 1935, Roosevelt gave public support to what became the Social Security Act, which Congress passed the same year. It established several distinct programs. For the elderly, there were two types of assistance. Those who were presently destitute could receive up to $15 a month in federal assistance. More important for the future, many Americans presently working were incorporated into a pension system, to which they and their employers would contribute by paying a payroll tax; it would provide them with an income on retirement. Pension payments would not begin until 1942 and even then

Reasoning Processes

Continuity and Change Have students read the section "Organizing Battles." Ask them to discuss as a class the reasons for the rapid growth of unions in the 1930s. Have students compare and contrast union tactics of the 1930s with earlier union activities. **PCE** **WXT**

Reasoning Processes

Comparing After students have read the section "Social Security," ask them to create a T-chart comparing Social Security to the Townsend Plan. Have students discuss in small groups which plan would better support retirees and which plan would be better for the overall economy. **PCE** **WXT** **SOC**

THE "MEMORIAL DAY MASSACRE" The bitterness of the labor struggles of the 1930s was nowhere more evident than in Chicago in 1937, when striking workers attempting to march on a Republic Steel plant were brutally attacked by Chicago police, who used clubs, tear gas, and guns to turn the marchers away. Ten strikers were killed and many others were injured.

would provide only $10 to $85 a month to recipients. And broad categories of workers (including domestic servants and agricultural laborers, occupations with disproportionate numbers of African Americans and women) were excluded from the program. But the act was a crucial first step in building the nation's most important social program for the elderly.

In addition, the Social Security Act created a system of unemployment insurance, which employers alone would finance and which made it possible for workers laid off from their jobs to receive temporary government assistance. It also established a limited system (later expanded) of federal aid to people with disabilities and a program of aid to dependent children.

UNEMPLOYMENT INSURANCE

The framers of the Social Security Act wanted to create a system of "insurance," not "welfare." And the largest programs (old-age pensions and unemployment insurance) were in many ways similar to private insurance programs, with contributions from participants and benefits available to all. But the act also provided considerable direct assistance based on need–to the elderly poor, to those with disabilities, to dependent children and their mothers. These groups were widely perceived to be small and genuinely unable to support themselves. But in later generations the programs for these groups would expand considerably.

NEW DIRECTIONS IN RELIEF

Social Security was designed primarily to fulfill long-range goals. But unemployed Americans had immediate needs. To help them, the Roosevelt administration established the Works Progress Administration (WPA) in 1935. Like the Civil Works Administration and earlier efforts, the WPA established a system of work relief for the unemployed. But it was much bigger than the earlier agencies, both in the size of its budget ($5 billion in its first two years) and in the energy and imagination of its operations.

WPA

Historical Thinking Skills

Sourcing and Situation Have students examine the image "The 'Memorial Day Massacre.'" Ask them to discuss in small groups the historical situation of the photo. *(Following a successful strike against "Big Steel," steelworkers struck against "Little Steel." The strike was crushed by police and strikebreakers, but this ultimately led to increasing public support for the steelworkers.)* **PCE** **WXT** **SOC**

Discussion and Activities

Comparing and Contrasting After students have read the section "New Directions in Relief," ask them to discuss in pairs or small groups how women and men were treated differently by most New Deal programs and what the rationale for the differing treatment was. Have students consider whether they are aware of similar discrepancies in government programs today. **PCE** **WXT** **SOC**

Under the direction of Harry Hopkins, the WPA was responsible for building or renovating 110,000 public buildings (schools, post offices, government office buildings) and for constructing almost 600 airports, more than 500,000 miles of roads, and over 100,000 bridges. In the process, the WPA kept an average of 2.1 million workers employed and pumped needed money into the economy.

The WPA displayed flexibility and imagination in offering assistance to those whose occupations did not fit into any traditional category of relief. The Federal Writers' Project of the WPA, for example, gave unemployed writers a chance to do their work and receive a government salary. The Federal Arts Project, similarly, helped painters, sculptors, and others to continue their careers. The Federal Music Project and the Federal Theater Project oversaw the production of concerts and plays, creating work for unemployed musicians, actors, and directors. Other relief agencies emerged alongside the WPA. The National Youth Administration (NYA) provided work and scholarship assistance to high-school and college-age men and women. The Emergency Housing Division of the Public Works Administration began federal sponsorship of public housing.

SOCIAL SECURITY POSTER, 1935 Within months of the passage of the Social Security Act of 1935, the new Social Security Board began publicizing the benefits the new system offered to working Americans—the most dramatic of which was a monthly pension to retired Americans who had paid into the system.

Men and women alike were in distress in the 1930s (as in all difficult times). But the new welfare system dealt with members of the two sexes in very different ways. For men, the government concentrated mainly on work relief–on such programs as the CCC, the CWA, and the WPA, all of which were overwhelmingly male, and–through the Social Security Act–pensions and unemployment insurance, both structured initially to assist mostly men. The principal government aid to women was not work relief but cash assistance–most notably through the Aid to Dependent Children program of Social Security, which was designed largely to assist single mothers. This disparity in treatment reflected a widespread assumption that men constituted the bulk of the paid workforce and that women needed to be treated within the context of the family. In fact, millions of women were already employed by the 1930s.

THE 1936 "REFERENDUM"

ALF LANDON

For a time in 1935 there had seemed reason to question the president's prospects for reelection. But by the middle of 1936–with the economy visibly reviving–there could be little doubt that he would win a second term. The Republican Party nominated the moderate governor of Kansas, Alf M. Landon, who waged a weak campaign. Roosevelt's dissident challengers now appeared powerless. One reason was the violent death of their most effective leader, Huey Long, who was assassinated in Louisiana in September 1935. Another reason was the ill-fated alliance among Father Coughlin, Dr. Townsend, and Gerald L. K. Smith (an intemperate henchman of Huey Long), who joined forces that summer to establish a new political movement–the Union Party, which nominated an undistinguished North Dakota congressman, William Lemke, for president.

The result was the greatest landslide in American history to that point. Roosevelt polled just under 61 percent of the vote to Landon's 36 percent and carried every state except Maine and Vermont. The Democrats increased their already large majorities in both houses of Congress. The Union Party received fewer than 900,000 votes.

ELECTORAL REALIGNMENT

The election results demonstrated the party realignment that the New Deal had produced. The Democrats now controlled a broad coalition of Western and Southern farmers, the urban working classes, the poor and unemployed, and the black communities of Northern cities, as well as traditional progressives and committed new liberals–a coalition that constituted a substantial majority of the electorate. It would be decades before the Republican Party could again create a lasting majority coalition of its own.

Historical Thinking Skills

Argumentation Have students examine the image "Social Security Poster, 1935." Ask them to create an advertisement intended to persuade young workers to support the Social Security program. **PCE** **WXT** **SOC** **NAT**

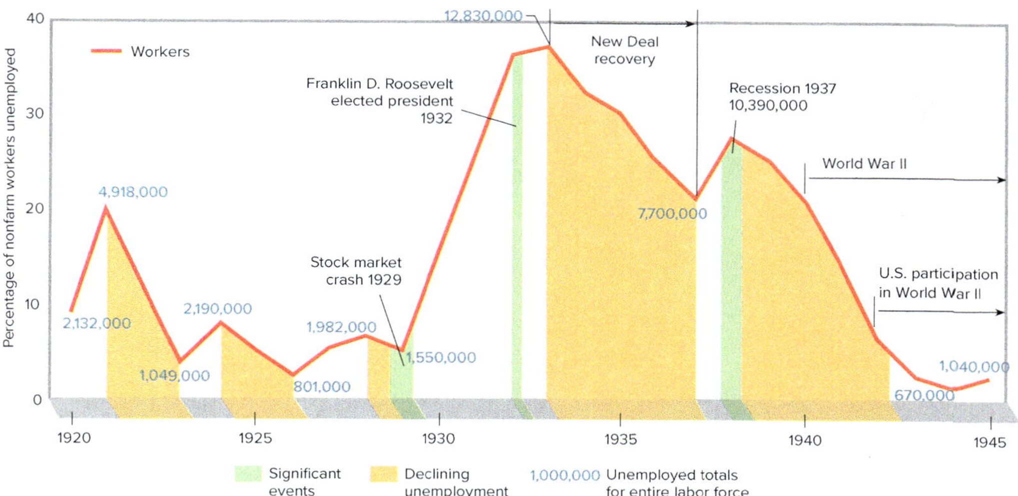

UNEMPLOYMENT, 1920–1945 This chart shows the shifting patterns of unemployment from 1920 to the end of World War II. As it reveals, nonfarm unemployment was very high in the early 1920s, in the last year of the postwar recession, but remained relatively low from 1923 to 1929. The beginning of the Great Depression sent unemployment soaring—to a peak of nearly 13 million people in early 1933—an unemployment rate of 25 percent. The New Deal helped create a partial recovery from the Depression over the next four years, but unemployment remained very high throughout the 1930s, and spiked sharply higher again during the recession of 1937–1938, before falling rapidly after war began in Europe.

Why was the war so much more successful than the New Deal in ending unemployment?

WPA WORKERS ON THE JOB The Works Progress Administration funded an enormous variety of work projects to provide jobs for the unemployed. But most WPA employees worked on construction sites of one kind or another.

Historical Thinking

Argumentation After students have read the section "The 1936 'Referendum,'" ask them to create a campaign poster for either Roosevelt or Landon encouraging Americans to vote for them. **PCE** **WXT** **SOC** **NAT**

Answers

Unemployment, 1920–1945

World War II created huge demand for labor in the armed forces as well as industry. It also created huge demand for industrial production to supply the military.

Historical Thinking Skills

Argumentation Have students read the section "The Court Fight." Ask them to write a short letter to President Roosevelt from the point of view of an ordinary American advising the president on how to respond to the Supreme Court's decisions striking down the AAA and the NRA. **PCE** **WXT**

WPA MURAL ART The Federal Arts Project of the Works Progress Administration commissioned an impressive series of public murals from the artists it employed. Many of these murals adorned post offices, libraries, and other public buildings constructed by the WPA. Shown here is a portion of a mural of workers at the Rincon Center, San Francisco. This mural is unusual in showing African American and Asian workers. Most WPA iconography portrayed workers as white men only.

Historic Collection/Alamy Stock Photo

THE NEW DEAL IN DISARRAY

Roosevelt emerged from the 1936 election at the zenith of his popularity. Within months, however, the New Deal was mired in serious new difficulties–a result of continuing opposition, the president's own political errors, and major economic setbacks.

THE COURT FIGHT

The 1936 mandate, Franklin Roosevelt believed, made it possible for him to do something about the problem of the Supreme Court. No program of reform, he had become convinced, could long survive the conservative justices, who had already struck down the NRA and the AAA and threatened to invalidate even more legislation.

COURT PACKING

In February 1937, Roosevelt sent a surprise message to Capitol Hill proposing a general overhaul of the federal court system; included among the many provisions was one to add up to six new justices to the Supreme Court, with a new justice added for every sitting justice over the age of seventy. The courts were "overworked," he claimed, and needed additional manpower and fresh ideas to enable them to cope with their increasing burdens. But Roosevelt's real purpose was to give himself the opportunity to appoint new, liberal justices and change the ideological balance of the Court.

Conservatives were outraged at the "Court-packing plan," and even many Roosevelt supporters were disturbed by what they considered evidence of the president's hunger for power. Still, Roosevelt might well have persuaded Congress to approve at least a compromise measure had not the Supreme Court itself intervened. Of the nine justices, three reliably supported the New Deal, and four reliably opposed it. Of the remaining two, Chief Justice Charles Evans Hughes often sided with the progressives and Associate Justice Owen J. Roberts usually voted with the conservatives. On March 29, 1937, Roberts, Hughes, and the three progressive justices voted together to uphold a state minimum-wage law–in the case of *West Coast Hotel v. Parrish*–thus appearing to reverse a 5-to-4 decision of the previous year invalidating a similar law. Two weeks later, again by a 5-to-4 margin, the Court upheld the Wagner Act, and in May it validated the Social Security Act. Whether or not for that reason, the Court's newly moderate position made the Court-packing bill seem unnecessary. Congress ultimately defeated it.

On one level, the affair was a significant victory for Franklin Roosevelt. The Court was no longer an obstacle to New Deal reforms, particularly after the older justices began to retire, to be replaced by Roosevelt appointees. But the Court-packing episode did lasting political damage to the administration. From 1937 on, Southern Democrats and other conservatives voted against Roosevelt's measures much more often than they had in the past.

RETRENCHMENT AND RECESSION

By the summer of 1937, the gross national product, which had dropped from $82 billion in 1929 to $40 billion in 1932, had risen back to nearly $72 billion. Other economic indices showed similar advances. Roosevelt seized on these improvements as an excuse to try to balance the federal budget, convinced by Treasury Secretary Henry Morgenthau and many economists that the real danger now was no longer depression but inflation. Between January and August 1937, he cut the WPA in half, laying off 1.5 million relief workers. A few weeks later, the fragile boom collapsed. Other cuts in spending followed. The index of industrial production dropped from 117 in August 1937 to 76 in May 1938. Four million additional workers lost their jobs. Economic conditions were soon almost as bad as they had been in the bleak days of 1932–1933.

Historical Thinking Skills

Sourcing and Situation Have students view the image "WPA Mural Art." Ask them to discuss in small groups what the purpose of the painting would have been. *(The Federal Artists Project, part of the WPA, was designed to create jobs for unemployed artists while at the same time beautifying public buildings and spaces.)* **PCE** **WXT**

PATTERNS OF POPULAR CULTURE

THE GOLDEN AGE OF COMIC BOOKS

In the troubled years of the Great Depression and World War II, many Americans sought release from their anxieties in fantasy. Movies, plays, books, radio shows, and other diversions drew people out of their own lives and into a safer or more glamorous or more exciting world. Beginning in 1938, one of the most popular forms of escape for many young Americans became the comic book.

In February 1935, Malcolm Wheeler-Nicholson founded the first comics magazine—what we now know as the "comic book"—titled *New Fun*. *New Fun* was not successful, but Wheeler founded a new company, Detective Comics, and began in 1937 to design a new magazine called *Action Comics*. Wheeler ran out of money before he could publish anything, but the company continued without him. In 1938, the first issue of *Action Comics* appeared with a startling and controversial cover—a powerful man in a skintight suit lifting a car over his head. His name was Superman, and he became the most popular cartoon character of all time.

Within a year, Superman had a comic book named after him, which was selling over 1.2 million copies each issue. By 1940, there was a popular Superman radio show introduced by a breathless announcer crying, "It's a bird! It's a plane! It's . . . Superman!" Soon other publishers began developing new "superheroes" (a term invented by the creators of Superman) to capitalize on this growing new popular appetite. In 1939, a second great comic book publisher appeared—Marvel Comics. By the early 1940s, Superman had been joined by other superheroes: the Human Torch, the Sub-Mariner, Batman, the Flash, and Wonder Woman, a character created in part to signal the importance of women to the war effort.

It is not hard to imagine why superheroes would be so appealing to Americans—particularly to the teenage boys who were the largest single purchasers of comic books—in the 1930s and 1940s. Superman and other superheroes were idealized versions of the ideal boy—smart, good, "the perfect Boy Scout," as one fan put it. But they were also all-powerful, capable of righting wrong and preventing catastrophe. At a time when catastrophe was an ever-present possibility in the world, superheroes were a comforting escape from fear.

Many of the early comic book writers were young Jewish men, conscious of their outsider status in an American culture not yet wholly open to them. Almost all the characters they created had alter egos, identities they used while living within the normal world. Superman was Clark Kent, a "mild-mannered reporter." Batman was Bruce Wayne, a wealthy heir. The superhero characters were outsiders themselves—but outsiders endowed with special powers and abilities unavailable to ordinary people.

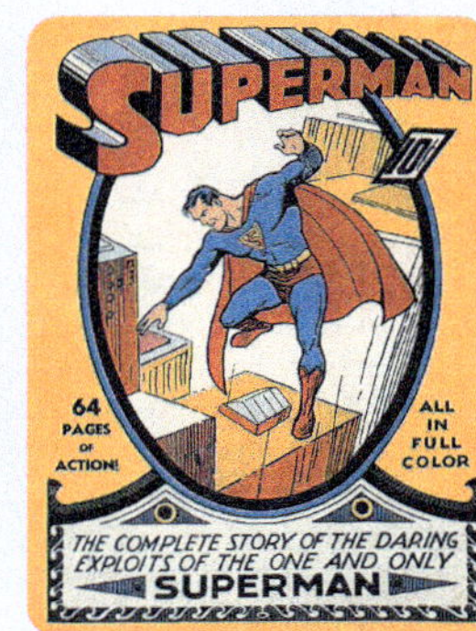

SUPERMAN The most popular action figure in the history of comic books was Superman, whose superhuman powers were particularly appealing fantasies to Americans suffering through the Depression and, later, World War II.

(t) © Warner Bros./Photofest, (b) © Hulton Archive/Getty Images

SUPERMAN TODAY Superman continues to appeal to the fantasies of Americans, as shown by this poster of the movie *Superman Returns* from 2006. Another film, *Man of Steel*, was released in 2013. And yet another is in the works for 2015 or 2016.

Even before America entered World War II, the comic superheroes were battling the Axis powers. Marvel's the Human Torch and the Sub-Mariner joined forces against the German navy. Superman fought spies and saboteurs at home. Captain America, a new character created in March 1941, was a frail young man rejected by the army who, after being given a secret serum by a military doctor, became extraordinarily powerful. The cover of the first issue of *Captain America* showed the title character punching Hitler in his headquarters in Germany.

The end of the war was also the end of this first "golden age" of American comic books. Many superhero magazines ceased publication as peacetime reduced the popular appetite for fantasy. In their place emerged new comic books, which emphasized romance and even mild sexuality.

In the late 1940s and early 1950s, comic books began to come under attack from educators, psychiatrists, journalists, and even the federal government. Congress took no legal action against comic book publishers or writers, but the comic book industry itself created a trade association, which produced a "Comics Code" to prevent indecency in the industry.

Comic books experienced an unexpected revival in the late 1950s and 1960s. Old superheroes—Captain America, the Human Torch, and others—reappeared. New ones—Spiderman, Iron Man, the Silver Surfer—joined them. Superman, who had never disappeared, enjoyed newfound popularity and became the hero for a time of a popular television show. But these new or revised heroes were not entirely like those of the 1930s and 1940s. They reflected the realities of an increasingly complex and complicated world, which their characters—like their mostly young readers—were struggling to understand.

HISTORICAL THINKING SKILLS

1. **Drawing Conclusions** What could comic books offer readers suffering through the crisis of the Great Depression?
2. **Explaining Historical Developments** How and why have comic book superheroes changed over time?
3. **Making Connections** What might account for the upsurge in comic books' popularity in the late 1950s and 1960s?

Discussion and Activities

Making Connections Have students examine the images "Superman," and "Superman Today." Ask them to discuss as a class why the Superman character in particular would have captured the public's imagination in the 1930s, and why this character still resonates with many today. **SOC** **ARC** **NAT**

Answers

Consider the Source

1. Elements of popular culture (e.g., comic books, radio, television, movies, Cony Island, etc.) often served to distract people from day-to-day hardships. Comic books offered an escape into a fantasy world where an idealized hero fights against evil and always averts catastrophic events.
2. Comic books superheroes began to represent an increasing complex culture and world.
3. The contentious political environment of the first half of the twenty-first century, along with questions and fear that many Americans held, called out for various means of escape from reality.

Reasoning Processes

Causation After students have read the section "Retrenchment and Recession," ask them to create a T-chart listing causes and effects of the "Roosevelt recession." Have students discuss in small groups what they believe to have been the most important effect(s). **PCE** **WXT** **SOC**

Federal Budget and Surplus/Deficit, 1920–1940

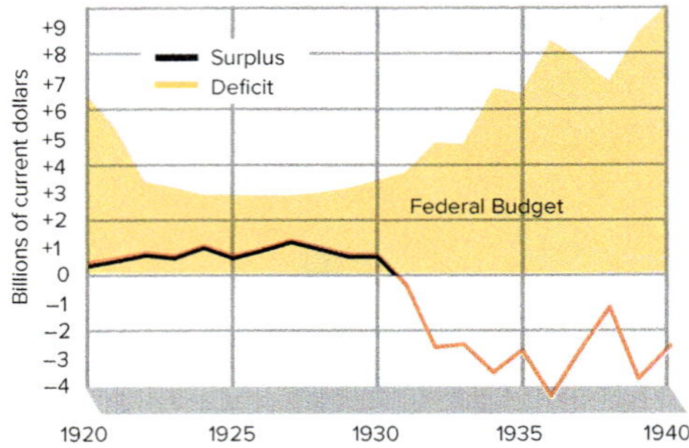

Gross National Product, 1920–1940

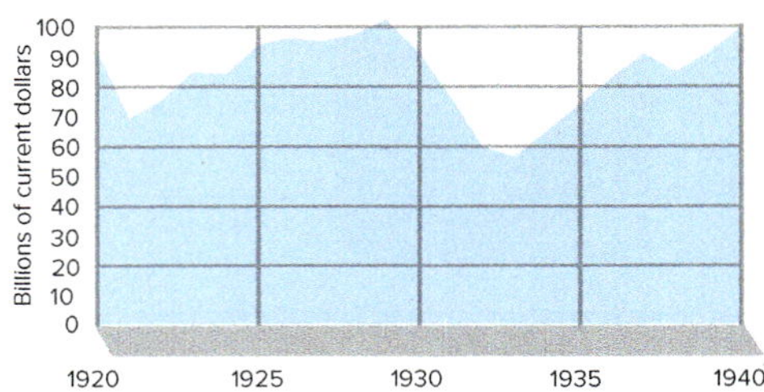

Budget and Surplus/Deficit as Percentage of GNP, 1920–1940

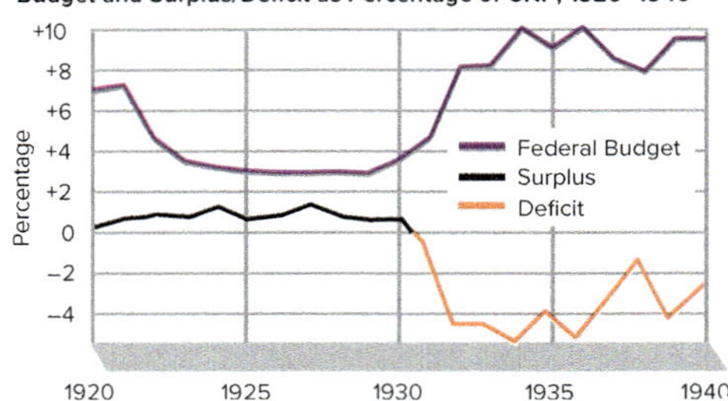

FEDERAL BUDGET SURPLUS/DEFICIT AND GNP, 1920–1940 Among its many other effects, the Great Depression produced dramatic changes in the fiscal condition of the federal government. In the first of these three charts, note the sharp decline in federal spending in the early 1920s (as the nation demobilized from World War I) and the appearance of significant budget surpluses. Note, too, the dramatic increase in government spending (and the appearance of significant deficits) once the Depression began and, particularly, once Franklin Roosevelt became president. The second chart illustrates the varying fortunes of the nation's economy by showing the rise and fall of gross national product—the total of goods and services produced by the economy. The GNP fell sharply in the first years of the Depression, but by the end of the 1930s was nearing its 1929 levels again. The final chart gives some perspective on these figures by illustrating the relationship between federal spending (and federal surpluses and deficits) and the total size of the economy. At its peak in these years, federal spending was never more than about 9 percent of the GNP and the deficit never more than about 5 percent. In recent decades, the federal budget has often exceeded 20 percent of the GNP. Deficits—much higher in absolute numbers than those of the 1930s—were rarely higher as a percentage of the GNP than those of the 1930s until the first decade of the twenty-first century.

Why did government deficits increase so sharply during the Great Depression?

The recession of 1937, known to the president's critics as the "Roosevelt recession," was a result of many factors. But to many observers at the time (including, apparently, the president himself), it seemed to be a direct result of the administration's unwise decision to reduce spending. And so in April 1938, the president asked Congress for an emergency appropriation of $5 billion for public works and relief programs, and government funds soon began pouring into the economy once again. Within a few months, another tentative recovery seemed to be under way, and the advocates of spending pointed to it as proof of the validity of their approach.

ROOSEVELT RECESSION

At about the same time, at the urging of a group of younger, anti-monopolist liberals in the administration, Roosevelt sent a stinging message to Congress, vehemently denouncing what he called an "unjustifiable concentration of economic power" and asking for the creation of a commission to consider major reforms in the antitrust laws. In response, Congress established the Temporary National Economic Committee (TNEC), whose members included representatives of both houses of Congress and officials from several executive agencies. Also that spring, Roosevelt appointed a new head of the antitrust division of the Justice Department: Thurman Arnold, a Yale Law School professor who soon proved to be the most vigorous director ever to serve in that office.

Later in 1938, the administration successfully supported one of its most ambitious pieces of labor legislation, the Fair Labor Standards Act, which for the first time established a national minimum wage and a forty-hour workweek, and which also placed strict limits on child labor. Like Social Security, the act at first excluded from its provisions the great majority of women and minority workers.

Despite these achievements, however, by the end of 1938 the New Deal had essentially come to an end. Congressional opposition now made it difficult for the president to enact any major new programs. But more important, perhaps, the threat of world crisis hung heavy in the political atmosphere, and Roosevelt was gradually growing more concerned with persuading a reluctant nation to prepare for war than with pursuing new avenues of reform.

END OF THE NEW DEAL

LIMITS AND LEGACIES OF THE NEW DEAL

In the 1930s, Roosevelt's principal critics were conservatives, who accused him of abandoning the Constitution and establishing a menacing, even tyrannical, state. In later years, the New Deal's most visible critics attacked it from the left, pointing to the major problems it left unsolved and the important groups it failed to represent. And beginning in the early twenty-first century, conservative attacks on the New Deal would emerge again. A full understanding of the New Deal requires coming to terms with the sources of both critiques, by examining both its achievements and its limits.

Answers

Federal Budget Surplus/Deficit and GNP, 1920–1940

Deficits increased sharply mainly due to large increases in spending to support New Deal programs.

THE IDEA OF THE "BROKER STATE"

In 1933, many New Dealers dreamed of using their new popularity and authority to remake American capitalism—to produce new forms of cooperation and control that would create a genuinely harmonious, ordered economic world. By 1939, it was clear that what they had created was in fact something quite different. But rather than bemoan the gap between their original intentions and their ultimate achievements, New Deal liberals, both in 1939 and in later years, chose to accept what they had produced and to celebrate it—to use it as a model for future reform efforts.

ESTABLISHMENT OF THE "BROKER STATE"

What they had created was something that in later years would become known as the "broker state." Instead of forging all elements of society into a single, harmonious unit, as some reformers had once hoped to do, the real achievement of the New Deal was to elevate and strengthen new interest groups so as to allow them to compete more effectively in the national marketplace. The New Deal made the federal government a mediator in that continuous competition—a force that could intervene when necessary to help some groups and limit the power of others. In 1933, there had been only one great interest group (albeit a varied and divided one) with genuine power in the national economy: the corporate world. By the end of the 1930s, American business found itself competing for influence with an increasingly powerful labor movement, an organized agricultural economy, and aroused consumers. In later years, the "broker state" idea would expand to embrace other groups as well: racial, ethnic, and religious minorities; women; and many others. Thus, one of the enduring legacies of the New Deal was to make the federal government a protector of interest groups and a supervisor of the competition among them, rather than an instrument attempting to create a universal harmony of interests.

What determines which interest groups receive government assistance in a "broker state"? The experience of the New Deal suggests that such assistance goes largely to those groups able to exercise enough political or economic power to demand it. Thus in the 1930s, farmers—after decades of organization and agitation—and workers—as the result of militant action and mass mobilization—won from the government new and important protections. Other groups, less well organized, perhaps, but politically important because so numerous and visible, won limited assistance as well: imperiled homeowners, the unemployed, the elderly.

By the same token, the interest-group democracy that the New Deal came to represent offered much less to those groups either too weak to demand assistance or not visible enough to arouse widespread public support. And yet those same groups were often the ones most in need of help from their government. One of the important limits of the New Deal, therefore, was its very modest record on behalf of several important social groups.

AFRICAN AMERICANS AND THE NEW DEAL

One group the New Deal did relatively little to assist was African Americans. The administration was not hostile to the aspirations of African Americans. On the contrary, the New Deal was probably more sympathetic to them than any previous

George Rinhart/Corbis/Getty Images

ELEANOR ROOSEVELT First Lady Eleanor Roosevelt was among the first women to play an important role in politics and government. She oversaw Franklin Roosevelt's political campaigns before he became president as well as developed an important career of her own working on social programs in New York. When she moved to the White House, she served her husband by traveling widely (something that Franklin Roosevelt, whose legs were paralyzed by polio, could not often do), and she took on issues that her husband chose not to embrace. An example is this photograph of Eleanor Roosevelt riding in a car to a Washington, D.C., jail to inspect the facility, which had a reputation for being overcrowded and obsolete.

Discussion and Activities

Making Connections Have students read the section "The Idea of the 'Broker State.'" Ask them to discuss as a class whether a "broker state" still exists, and if so, which groups participate in it. PCE WXT SOC NAT

Discussion and Activities

Analyzing Points of View Have students examine the image "Eleanor Roosevelt." Ask them to write a short letter to Eleanor Roosevelt from the point of view of an ordinary American expressing their opinions about the First Lady and her activities during the Roosevelt administration. PCE SOC

Discussion and Activities

Making Connections After students have read "The New Deal" feature, ask them to contact older relatives or other people who may have lived through the New Deal era. Have students prepare short presentations to the class highlighting the experiences of these people during the New Deal. **SOC**

DEBATING THE PAST

THE NEW DEAL

For many years, debate among historians over the nature of the New Deal mirrored the debate among Americans in the 1930s over the achievements of the Roosevelt administration. Historians struggled, just as contemporaries had done, to decide whether the New Deal was a good thing or a bad thing.

By far the dominant view of the New Deal among scholars has been an approving, liberal interpretation, and the first important voice of that view was Arthur M. Schlesinger Jr., who argued in the three volumes of *The Age of Roosevelt* (1957–1960) that the New Deal marked a continuation of the long struggle between public power and private interests. Roosevelt had moved that struggle to a new level, challenging the unrestrained power of the business community and offering far more protection for workers, farmers, consumers, and others than they had enjoyed in the past.

The first systematic "revisionist" interpretation of the New Deal came in 1963, in William Leuchtenburg's *Franklin D. Roosevelt and the New Deal*. Leuchtenburg was a sympathetic critic, arguing that most of the limitations of the New Deal were a result of the restrictions imposed on Roosevelt by the political and ideological realities of his time—that the New Deal probably could not have done much more than it did. Nevertheless, Leuchtenburg could not agree with others who called the New Deal a revolution in social policy. He was able to muster only enough enthusiasm to call it a "halfway revolution," one that enhanced the positions of some previously disadvantaged groups (notably farmers and factory workers) but did little or nothing for many others (including African Americans, sharecroppers, and the urban poor). Ellis Hawley augmented these moderate criticisms of the Roosevelt record in *The New Deal and the Problem of Monopoly* (1966). In examining 1930s economic policies, Hawley argued that New Deal efforts were in many cases designed to enhance the position of private entrepreneurs—even, at times, at the expense of some of the liberal reform goals that administration officials espoused.

Much harsher criticisms of the New Deal emerged in the 1960s and later. Barton Bernstein in a 1968 essay concluded that the Roosevelt administration may have saved capitalism, but it failed to help—and in many ways actually harmed—groups most in need of assistance. Ronald Radosh, Thomas Ferguson, and, more recently, Colin Gordon took such arguments further. They cited the close ties between the New Deal and internationalist financiers and industrialists; the liberalism of the 1930s was a product of their shared interest in protecting capitalists and stabilizing capitalism.

Most scholars in the 1980s and 1990s, however, seemed largely to have accepted the revised liberal view: that the New Deal was a significant (and, most agreed, valuable) chapter in the history of reform, but one that worked within rigid, occasionally crippling limits. Much of the recent work on the New Deal has focused on the constraints within which it was operating. The sociologist Theda Skocpol (along with other scholars) has emphasized the issue of "state capacity" as an important New Deal constraint; ambitious reform ideas often foundered, she argued, because no government bureaucracy had sufficient strength and expertise to shape or administer them. James T. Patterson, Barry Karl, Mark Leff, and others have emphasized the political constraints the New Deal encountered. Both in Congress and among the public, conservative inhibitions about government remained strong.

Frank Freidel, Ellis Hawley, Herbert Stein, and many others point as well to the ideological constraints affecting Franklin Roosevelt and his supporters. Alan Brinkley, in *The End of Reform* (1995), described an ideological shift in New Deal liberalism that shifted from the initial regulatory view of government to one that envisioned relatively little direct governmental interference in the corporate world and centered instead on Keynesian welfare state programs. David Kennedy, in *Freedom from Fear* (1999), argued by contrast that the aggressive anticapitalism of early New Deal liberalism actually hampered the search for recovery. Only when Roosevelt embraced measures that unleashed the power of the market did prosperity begin to return.

FDR IN ALBANY **Before he became president, Franklin Roosevelt served as governor of New York, where he developed a reputation of being an activist working to confront the Great Depression. In this 1930 photograph, he is sitting at his desk in the state capitol. Two years later, he would be elected president.**

The phrase "New Deal liberalism" has come in the postwar era to seem synonymous with modern ideas of aggressive federal management of the economy, elaborate welfare systems, a powerful bureaucracy, and large-scale government spending. Many historians of the New Deal, however, would argue that the modern idea of "New Deal liberalism" bears only a limited relationship to the ideas that New Dealers themselves embraced. The liberal accomplishments of the 1930s can be understood only in the context of their own time; later liberal efforts drew from that legacy but also altered it to fit the needs and assumptions of very different eras.

HISTORICAL THINKING SKILLS

Questions assume cumulative content knowledge from this chapter and previous chapters.

1. **Identifying Historical Developments** Identify three broad schools of historical interpretation of the New Deal.
2. **Determining Context** Describe how one piece of historical evidence, from the time period, could be used to support each of the three broad schools of historical interpretation concerning the New Deal.
3. **Developing Arguments** Analyze which historical interpretation you find most convincing and explain why using evidence from the text to support your argument.

Answers

Consider the Source

1. Arthur M. Schlesinger, Jr., argued for the success of the programs of the New Deal in ending the Great Depression. Later historians like Bernstein and Leuchtenburg were more critical of the New Deal. The New Deal is now viewed in a more complex light as the lasting effects on the role of government, on capitalism, and on various groups in American society are widely debated.
2. One argument is that the New Deal should be seen as an extension of the Progressive movement, which sought to regulate and control industry in favor of workers. Some may argue the New Deal did very little in way of ending the Great Depression, as unemployment continued to be very high and, in fact, some individuals were actually harmed by the New Deal.
3. Student responses will vary based on their argument. They may argue that the New Deal was somewhat successful or that its benefits varied widely.

government of the twentieth century. Eleanor Roosevelt spoke throughout the 1930s on behalf of racial justice and put continuing pressure on her husband and others in the federal government to ease discrimination against African Americans. She was also partially responsible for what was, symbolically at least, one of the most important events of the decade for African Americans. When the renowned African American concert singer Marian Anderson was refused permission in the spring of 1939 to give a concert in the auditorium of the Daughters of the American Revolution (Washington's only major concert hall), Eleanor Roosevelt resigned from the organization and then (along with Interior Secretary Harold Ickes, another champion of racial equality) helped secure government permission for her to sing on the steps of the Lincoln Memorial. Anderson's Easter Sunday concert attracted 75,000 people and became, in effect, one of the first modern civil rights demonstrations.

The president himself appointed a number of black officials to significant second-level positions in his administration. Roosevelt appointees such as Robert Weaver, William Hastie, and Mary McLeod Bethune created an informal network of officeholders who consulted frequently with one another and who became known as the "Black Cabinet." Eleanor Roosevelt, Harold Ickes, and Harry Hopkins all made efforts to ensure that New Deal relief programs did not exclude African Americans; and by 1935, perhaps a quarter of all African Americans were receiving some form of government assistance. One result was a historic change in black electoral behavior. As late as 1932, most African Americans were voting Republican, as they had since the Civil War. By 1936, more than 90 percent of them were voting Democratic–the beginnings of a political alliance that would endure for decades.

"BLACK CABINET"

African Americans supported Franklin Roosevelt because they knew he was not their enemy. But they had few illusions that the New Deal represented a major turning point in American race relations. For example, the president was never willing to risk losing the backing of Southern Democrats by supporting legislation to make lynching a federal crime. Nor would he endorse efforts in Congress to ban the poll tax, one of the most potent tools by which white Southerners kept African Americans from voting.

New Deal relief agencies did not challenge, and indeed reinforced, existing patterns of discrimination. The Civilian Conservation Corps established separate black camps. The NRA codes tolerated paying African Americans less than white workers doing the same jobs. African Americans were largely excluded from employment in the TVA. The Federal Housing Administration refused to provide mortgages to African Americans moving into white neighborhoods, and the first public housing projects financed by the federal government were racially segregated. The WPA routinely relegated black, Hispanic, and Asian workers to the least-skilled and lowest-paying jobs, or excluded them altogether; when funding ebbed, nonwhites, like women, were among the first to be dismissed.

EXISTING DISCRIMINATION REINFORCED

The New Deal was not hostile to African Americans, and it did much to help them advance. But it refused to make the issue of race a significant part of its agenda.

THE NEW DEAL AND THE "INDIAN PROBLEM"

In many respects, government policies toward the Native American nations in the 1930s were simply a continuation of the long-established effort to encourage Native Americans to assimilate into the larger society and culture.

But the principal elements of federal policy in the New Deal years worked to advance a very different goal, largely because of the efforts of the extraordinary commissioner of Indian affairs in those years, John Collier. Collier was a former social worker who had become committed to the cause of the Native Americans after exposure to tribal cultures in New Mexico in the 1920s. More important, he was greatly influenced by the work of twentieth-century anthropologists who promoted the idea of cultural relativism, which challenged the three-centuries-old assumption among white Americans that Native Americans were "savages" and that white society was inherently superior and more "civilized."

JOHN COLLIER

Collier promoted legislation that would, he hoped, reverse the pressures on Native Americans to assimilate and would allow them the right to live in traditional Native American ways. Not all Native American leaders agreed with Collier; indeed, his belief in the importance of preserving Native American culture would not find its broadest support among the Native American nations until the 1960s. Nevertheless, Collier effectively promoted legislation–which became the Indian Reorganization Act of 1934–that restored to the nations the right to own land collectively. (It reversed the allotment policy adopted in 1887, which encouraged the breaking up of tribal lands into individually owned plots–a policy that had led to the loss of over 90 million acres of tribal land to white speculators and others.) In the thirteen years after passage of the 1934 bill, tribal land increased by nearly 4 million acres, and Native American agricultural income increased from under $2 million in 1934 to over $49 million in 1947.

INDIAN REORGANIZATION ACT

Even with the redistribution of lands under the 1934 act, however, Native Americans continued to possess, for the most part, only territory white Americans did not want–much of it arid, some of it desert. And as a group, they continued to constitute the poorest segment of the population. The efforts of the 1930s did not solve what some white people called the "Indian problem." They did, however, provide Native Americans with some tools for rebuilding the viability of their nations.

WOMEN AND THE NEW DEAL

As with African Americans, the New Deal was not hostile to feminist aspirations, but neither did it do a great deal to advance them. That was largely because such aspirations did not have sufficiently widespread support (even among women)

Discussion and Activities

Analyzing Points of View After students have read the section "African Americans and the New Deal," ask them to write a newspaper review describing the experience of watching Marian Anderson sing "My Country, 'Tis of Thee" from the steps of the Lincoln Memorial. **SOC** **NAT**

Reasoning Processes

Comparing Have students read the section "The New Deal and the 'Indian Problem.'" Ask them to create a Venn diagram comparing the experiences of African Americans and Native Americans during the New Deal. **PCE** **WXT** **SOC** **NAT**

Reasoning Processes

Continuity and Change After students have read the section "Women and the New Deal," ask them to discuss as a class how the New Deal expanded opportunities for women, yet at the same time reinforced traditional gender roles. **PCE** **SOC**

to make it politically advantageous for the administration to back them.

There were, to be sure, important symbolic gestures on behalf of women. Roosevelt appointed the first female cabinet member in the nation's history, Secretary of Labor Frances Perkins. He also named more than 100 other women to positions at lower levels of the federal bureaucracy. They created an active female network within the government and cooperated with one another in advancing causes of interest to women. Such appointments were in part a response to pressure from Eleanor Roosevelt, who was a committed advocate of women's rights and a champion of humanitarian causes. Molly Dewson, head of the Women's Division of the Democratic National Committee, was also influential in securing federal appointments for women as well as in increasing their role within the Democratic Party. Several women received appointments to the federal judiciary. And one, Hattie Caraway of Arkansas, became in 1934 the first woman elected to a full term in the U.S. Senate. (She was running to succeed her husband, who had died in office.)

SYMBOLIC GAINS FOR WOMEN

But New Deal support for women operated within limits, partly because New Deal women themselves had limited views of what their aims should be. Frances Perkins and many others in the administration emerged out of the feminist tradition of the progressive era, which emphasized not so much gender equality as special protections for women. Perkins and other women reformers were instrumental in creating support for, and shaping the character of, the Social Security Act of 1935. But they built into that bill their own notion of women's special place in a male-dominated economy. The principal provision of the bill specifically designed for women—the Aid to Dependent Children program—was modeled on the state-level mothers' pensions that generations of progressive women had worked to pass earlier in the century.

The New Deal generally supported the prevailing belief that in hard times women should withdraw from the workplace to open up more jobs for men. New Deal relief agencies offered relatively little employment for women. The NRA sanctioned wage practices that discriminated against women. The Social Security program at first excluded domestic servants, waitresses, and other predominantly female occupations.

PREVAILING GENDER NORMS BUTTRESSED

THE NEW DEAL IN THE WEST AND THE SOUTH

Two regions of the United States that did receive special attention from the New Deal were the West and the South, both of which benefited disproportionately from New Deal relief and public works programs. The West received more federal funds per capita through New Deal relief programs than any other region, and parts of the South were not far behind.

HARLEM, THE "NEGRO CAPITAL OF AMERICA" Photographer Jack Manning took this picture, *Street Portrait 5 Young Boys*, as part of Aaron Siskind's project called the "Harlem Document," which portrayed life in what *Look* magazine called "the Negro capital of America." This photo was taken in 1938 or 1939.

Most Westerners were eager for the assistance New Deal agencies provided, but their political leaders were not always as supportive. In Colorado, for example, the state legislature refused to provide the required matching funds for FERA relief in 1933. When, in response, Harry Hopkins cut Colorado off from the program, unemployed people rioted in Denver and looted food stores. Only then did the legislature reverse course and provide funding.

In the South, locally administered New Deal relief programs did not challenge prevailing racial norms. In the West, too, New Deal programs accepted existing racial and ethnic prejudices. In several states, relief agencies paid different groups at different rates: white Anglos received the most generous aid; African Americans, Native Americans, and Mexican Americans received lower levels of support. In the CCC camps in New Mexico, Hispanic and white workers were sometimes in the same camps, but there were frequent tensions and occasional conflicts between them. But the main reason for the New Deal's impact on the West was that conditions in the region made the government's programs especially important. Federal agricultural programs had an enormous impact on the West because farming remained so much more central to the economy of the region than it did in much of the East. The largest New Deal public works programs—the great dams and power stations—were mainly in the West, both because the best locations for

FAILURE TO CHALLENGE JIM CROW

Discussion and Activities

Analyzing Points of View Have students examine the image "Harlem, the 'Negro Capital of America.'" Ask them to write a short paragraph exploring the purpose and point of view of the photographer taking the photo. **SOC** **NAT** **WXT** **ARC**

such facilities were there and because the West had the most need for new sources of water and power. The Grand Coulee Dam on the Columbia River was the largest public works project in American history to that point. It provided cheap electric power for much of the Northwest and, along with the construction of smaller dams and water projects nearby, created a basis for economic development in the region.

Without this enormous public investment by the federal government, much of the economic development that transformed the West after World War II would have been much more difficult, if not impossible, to achieve. But the region paid a price for the government's beneficence: for generations after the Great Depression, the federal government maintained a much greater and more visible bureaucratic presence in the West than in any other region.

NEW DEAL'S LEGACY IN THE WEST

The New Deal located fewer great infrastructure projects in the South than it did in the West—although the largest of them, the TVA, was an entirely Southern venture. But many of the economic development efforts the Roosevelt administration undertook were of disproportionate benefit to the South, largely because the South was the least economically developed region of the nation in the 1930s. One example was rural electrification, which had a large impact on many agrarian areas of the nation but a particular impact on the South, where vast parts of the countryside remained without access to power lines until the Rural Electrification Administration provided them.

The New Deal also directed national attention toward the economic condition of the South in a way that no previous administration had done. Many Americans outside the South had long believed the South to be "backward," but they tended to attribute that backwardness to racism, segregation, and prejudice. In a 1938 economic report sponsored by the federal government, a group of social scientists and others called the South "the nation's number one economic problem." Although the report made some reference to the South's racial customs, it spoke mostly about its lack of sufficiently developed economic institutions and facilities.

THE NEW DEAL AND THE NATIONAL ECONOMY

The most frequent criticisms of the New Deal involve its failure genuinely to revive or reform the American economy. New Dealers never fully embraced government spending as a vehicle for recovery, and their efforts along other lines never succeeded in ending the Depression. The economic boom sparked by World War II, not the New Deal, finally ended the crisis. Nor did the New Deal substantially alter the distribution of power within American capitalism; and it had only a small impact on the distribution of wealth among the American people.

FAILURE TO ACHIEVE RECOVERY

Nevertheless, the New Deal did have important and lasting effects on both the behavior and the structure of the American economy. It helped elevate new groups—workers, farmers, and others—to positions from which they could at times effectively challenge the power of the corporations. It contributed to the economic development of the West and, to a lesser degree, the South. It increased the regulatory functions of the federal government in ways that helped stabilize previously troubled areas of the economy: the stock market, the banking system, and many others. (Many of these regulations were weakened or repealed beginning in the 1970s and beyond.) And the administration helped establish the basis for new forms of federal fiscal policy, which in the postwar years would give the government tools for promoting and regulating economic growth.

The New Deal also created the basis of the federal welfare state, through its many relief programs and above all through the Social Security system. The conservative inhibitions New Dealers brought to this task ensured that the welfare system would be limited in its impact (at least in comparison with those of other industrial nations), would reinforce some traditional patterns of gender and racial discrimination, and would be expensive and cumbersome to

FEDERAL WELFARE STATE ESTABLISHED

MAJOR LEGISLATION OF THE NEW DEAL

Year	Legislation	Year	Legislation
1933	Emergency Banking Act	1935	Works Progress Administration
	Economy Act		National Youth Administration
	Civilian Conservation Corps		Social Security Act
	Agricultural Adjustment Act		National Labor Relations Act
	Tennessee Valley Authority		Public Utilities Holding Company Act
	National Industrial Recovery Act		Resettlement Administration
	Banking Act		Rural Electrification Administration
	Federal Emergency Relief Act		Revenue Act ("wealth tax")
	Home Owners Refinancing Act	1936	Soil Conservation and Domestic Allotment Act
	Civil Works Administration	1937	Farm Security Administration
	Federal Securities Act		National Housing Act
1934	National Housing Act	1938	Second Agricultural Adjustment Act
	Securities and Exchange Act		Fair Labor Standards Act
	Home Owners Loan Act	1939	Executive Reorganization Act

Reasoning Processes

Comparison After students have read the section "The New Deal in the West and the South," ask them to discuss as a class how and why the New Deal provided additional benefits to the West and the South and why the New Deal failed to challenge racial discrimination. **PCE** **WXT** **SOC**

Discussion and Activities

Making Generalizations Have students examine the chart "Major Legislation of the New Deal." Ask them to identify which programs were intended to provide immediate relief for workers, which were temporary programs intended to stimulate the recovery of consumer demand, and which were intended to be permanent reforms designed to prevent a recurrence of the Great Depression. **WXT** **PCE**

Discussion and Activities

Evaluating Divide the class into three groups. Ask students to refer to the chart they made dividing New Deal Legislation into relief, recovery, and reform programs. Assign one category to each group, and have the groups identify what they believe to be the most important examples in each category. Have each group present to the rest of the class what those programs were intended to achieve, how successful they were, and how they ended (unless they are still in existence). **PCE** **WXT** **SOC** **ARC** **NAT**

Key Terms

Students should be familiar with the key terms and be able to define them in the context of the Roosevelt Administration's efforts to address the challenges of the Great Depression and the mixed effectiveness of New Deal programs. Encourage students to use these terms in performing review exercises and exam practice for this chapter.

administer. But for all its limits, the new system marked a historic break with the federal government's traditional reluctance to offer public assistance to its neediest citizens.

THE NEW DEAL AND AMERICAN POLITICS

Perhaps the most dramatic effect of the New Deal was on the structure and behavior of American government and on the character of American politics. Franklin Roosevelt helped enhance the power of the federal government. By the end of the 1930s, state and local governments were clearly of secondary importance to the government in Washington. Roosevelt also established the presidency as the preeminent center of authority within the federal government.

NEW EXPECTATIONS OF GOVERNMENT

Finally, the New Deal had a profound impact on how the American people defined themselves politically. It took a weak, divided Democratic Party, which had been a minority force in American politics for many decades, and turned it into a mighty coalition that would dominate national party competition for more than thirty years. It turned the attention of many voters away from some of the cultural issues that had preoccupied them in the 1920s and awakened in them an interest in economic matters of direct importance to their lives. And it created among the American people greatly increased expectations of government—expectations that the New Deal did not always fulfill but that survived to become the basis of new liberal crusades in the postwar era.

CHAPTER 25 REVIEW

CONNECTING THEMES

Chapter Twenty-Five explored the specific acts and consequences of the New Deal's attempts to end the Great Depression. Roosevelt tried to use radio broadcasts and his ebullient personality to restore confidence in the American economy. The First and Second New Deals had varying degrees of success economically, socially, and politically. But they failed to end the Great Depression. This led to criticism from the left for not doing enough and from the right for giving the government too much power and interfering too much with the capitalist system.

First Lady Eleanor Roosevelt spoke often about racial justice and pushed, along with black officeholders, to ensure that African Americans had access to New Deal programs. The Roosevelt administration was also sympathetic to the plight of working people, poor farmers, labor unions, Native Americans, and women. While the New Deal often settled for symbolic actions and left significant barriers to equal opportunity in place, it won the allegiance of many members of these groups, which led to a political realignment that would transform American politics in the decades to come.

You should consider the following questions as you review the themes for this chapter:

- How did the works projects of the New Deal impact the American economy and the self-image of unemployed workers?
- What were the causes and effects of the political realignment of the political parties during the Great Depression?
- What was the impact of climate changes on the economy, and how did New Deal programs influence environmental reclamation?
- How did the New Deal change the philosophical mindset of the American people toward the role of the federal government in the economy?

KEY TERMS

Agricultural Adjustment Act (AAA) 695
"bank holiday" 694
broker state 711
Charles E. Coughlin 702
Congress of Industrial Organizations (CIO) 704
Court-packing plan 708
Eleanor Roosevelt 713
Federal Writers' Project 706
Frances Perkins 714
Francis E. Townsend 702
Glass-Steagall Act 701
Harry Hopkins 701
Huey Long 702
John Collier 713
John L. Lewis 704
Marian Anderson 713
National Recovery Administration (NRA) 695
Schechter brothers case 699
Second New Deal 703
Securities and Exchange Commission (SEC) 701
sit-down strike 704
Social Security Act 704
Tennessee Valley Authority (TVA) 699

Go Online Chapter 25 Content Review

Assessing Student Understanding Use the online assessment to assess student understanding of concepts and topics within the chapter. You can assign the ready-made Chapter 25 Content Review or create your own from available questions. This easy-to-use tool helps you design assessments that meet the needs of different types of learners.

AP EXAM PRACTICE

Questions assume cumulative content knowledge from this chapter and previous chapters.

MULTIPLE CHOICE

Use the excerpt from Roosevelt's first fireside chat on page 696 and your knowledge of U.S. history to answer questions 1–3.

1. In the excerpt, Roosevelt is communicating with Americans in order to
   (A) convince them that they need to withdraw their savings from banks.
   (B) restore their confidence in the financial system after years of despair.
   (C) inform them that they need to make different decisions when planting crops.
   (D) persuade them to shop at merchants who support New Deal programs.

2. Roosevelt's New Deal programs sought to do all of the following except
   (A) promote restoration of traditional laissez-faire economic beliefs.
   (B) promote relief from the immediate challenges of the Great Depression.
   (C) promote recovery for the overall American economy.
   (D) promote reform to prevent a future downturn of such severity.

3. The New Deal was not embraced by
   (A) the Executive Branch.
   (B) the Legislative Branch.
   (C) the Judicial Branch.
   (D) state governments.

SHORT ANSWER

Use your knowledge of U.S. history to answer questions 4 and 5.

4. Use the image on page 702 to answer A, B, and C.
   (A) Describe ONE point of view about Roosevelt as depicted in the image.
   (B) Explain ONE specific historical example of why Roosevelt's New Deal program was challenged by individuals or a group on the left.
   (C) Explain ONE specific historical example of why Roosevelt's New Deal program was challenged by individuals or a group on the right.

5. Answer A, B, and C.
   (A) Describe ONE specific historical similarity between American society before and after the implementation of the New Deal.
   (B) Describe ONE specific historical difference between American society before and after the implementation of New Deal.
   (C) Explain ONE specific historical context that gave rise to New Deal.

LONG ESSAY

Develop a thoughtful and thorough historical argument that addresses the statement. Begin your essay with a thesis statement, and support it with specific historical evidence and examples.

6. Evaluate the relative importance of causes that led to the New Deal during the Great Depression in the United States.

Answers

Long Essay

6. Possible thesis: The actions of Hoover led the country to seek new leadership. However, the historical progress that had been moving toward regulation, as well as the effects that the Great Depression was having on the country, led the nation to elect FDR specifically as a move to action in dealing with the greatest economic catastrophe in the nation's history. Specific historical evidence: First, the country had been going through a shift in thinking and beginning to embrace the belief that government needed to take a more active role in curtailing the abuses of big business. Second, the Great Depression was the factor driving FDR to reimagine the relationship between individuals and the government. Third, unemployment was at a record high and the country needed action.

Answers

Multiple Choice

1. B; **2.** A; **3.** C

Short Answer

4A) Possible answer: The point of view in the image is that of a supporter of FDR and the New Deal program. The American people are looking toward recovery, and FDR is steering the ship toward a brighter future.

4B) Possible answer: Huey Long and his Share-Our-Wealth Plan argued that FDR did not go far enough in helping individuals suffering from the effects of the Great Depression.

4C) Possible answer: The American Liberty League argued that FDR and the New Deal were an assault on the very heart of capitalism and that the regulatory nature of the program was tantamount to an all-out war on the economic institutions of the country.

5A) Possible answer: American unemployment was at an all-time high during the early stages of the Great Depression, but even after significant programs to get the unemployment rate under control, the New Deal programs did very little to move the national unemployment rate.

5B) Possible answer: Before the New Deal programs, Americans had a very limited sense of the relationship between citizens and their government. Following the implementation of many New Deal programs like Social Security, however, the fundamental relationship between the individual and government was altered.

5C) Possible answer: FDR ran in 1932 on the idea that he would get the country out of the Great Depression. He was largely vague on specifics, but his positive attitude was a welcomed change from that of the previous administration. This set the stage for a shift in the role of government.

CHAPTER 26
The Global Crisis, 1921–1941

Pacing Guide

Chapter 26 explores key concepts from Period 7: 1890–1945 of the AP U.S. History Curriculum Framework. The suggested instruction time for Chapter 26 is 2 days.

Key Concepts

7.2.II Economic pressures, global events, and political developments caused sharp variations in the numbers, sources, and experiences of both international and internal migrants.

7.3.II World War I and its aftermath intensified ongoing debates about the nation's role in the world and how best to achieve national security and pursue American interests.

26 THE GLOBAL CRISIS, 1921–1941

"DEFENDING MADRID"
The Spanish Civil War, in which the forces led by Francisco Franco overturned the existing republican government, was an early signal to many Americans of the dangers of fascism and the threat to democracy. Although the United States government remained aloof from the conflict, several thousand Americans volunteered to fight on behalf of the republican forces. This 1938 Spanish war poster contains the words "Defending Madrid Is Defending Catalonia," an effort by the government in Madrid to enlist the support of the surrounding regions to defend the capital against Franco forces.

CONNECTING CONCEPTS

Chapter Twenty-Six examines the changes in U.S. foreign policy from the 1920s through the Japanese attack on Pearl Harbor and American entry into World War II. In the decade after World War I, the United States was not isolationist. To promote peace, it hosted a naval arms reduction conference and signed a multinational treaty to outlaw war. To promote prosperity and protect the overseas interests of U.S. corporations, it arranged for private investments and loans to European and Latin American nations. But by 1929 the international system of voluntary cooperation had collapsed due to U.S. tariff barriers, the financial crisis, foreign debts, and Japanese aggression in Manchuria.

Franklin Roosevelt had to confront a global economic crisis and a rising fascist threat from Germany and Italy. He worked to repair relations with the Soviet Union and Latin America. But a resurgence of isolationism — highlighted by the Neutrality Acts imposed by Congress — limited his options in Europe and Asia. The Great Depression was the focus of most Americans, who reacted negatively when Roosevelt tried to condemn Japanese aggression in China in 1937. Meanwhile, British and

Discussion and Activities

Analyzing Visuals Have students examine the image "Defending Madrid." Have them discuss in small groups details the artist used in the poster to convey a sense of fear. *(Faceless soldiers advancing with bayonets mounted; stark colors; battlefield imagery in the foreground.)*

French efforts to appease Hitler at the Munich Conference failed, leading to the German invasion of Poland in 1939 and the start of World War II in Europe.

Roosevelt and a majority of Americans favored the Allies. But it was unclear how best to help them, and a powerful anti-interventionist lobby — the America First Committee — opposed measures that might lead to U.S. participation in another European war. Roosevelt was able to send lend-lease military aid directly to Britain only after France fell and he won a third term in 1940. The following year, Hitler invaded the Soviet Union and made an alliance with Japan, which launched a surprise attack on the Pacific fleet at Pearl Harbor in December 1941. Overnight, the bitter debate between isolationists and interventionists ended as the attack unified the American people in their commitment to victory.

As you read, you should:

- Describe the causes that led to the United States adopting a more isolationistic stance.
- Identify the major events, from 1920 to 1941, that led the United States to rethink its role in global affairs.
- Analyze the reasons the United States pursued a foreign policy of independent internationalism during the 1920s, choosing when and where to become involved.
- Evaluate why the American people generally opposed U.S. involvement in global disputes until the attack on Pearl Harbor in 1941.

THE DIPLOMACY OF THE NEW ERA

Critics of American foreign policy in the 1920s often used a single word to describe the cause of their disenchantment: isolationism. Having rejected the Wilsonian vision of a new world order, they claimed, the nation had turned its back on the rest of the globe and repudiated its international responsibilities. This was a myth as, in fact, the United States played a more active role in world affairs in the 1920s than it had at almost any previous time in its history–even if not the role the Wilsonians had prescribed.

REPLACING THE LEAGUE

It was clear when the Harding administration took office in 1921 that American membership in the League of Nations was no longer a realistic possibility. As if finally to bury the issue, Secretary of State Charles Evans Hughes secured legislation from Congress in 1921 declaring the war with Germany at an end, and then proceeded to negotiate separate peace treaties with the former Central Powers. Through these treaties, American policymakers believed, the United States would receive all the advantages of the Versailles Treaty with none of the burdensome responsibilities. But Hughes was also committed to finding something to replace the League as a guarantor of world peace and stability. He embarked, therefore, on a series of efforts to build safeguards against future wars–but safeguards that would not hamper American freedom of action in the world.

WASHINGTON CONFERENCE OF 1921

The most important such effort was the Washington Conference of 1921–an attempt to prevent what was threatening to become a costly and destabilizing naval armaments race between the United States, Britain, and Japan. In his opening speech, Hughes startled the delegates by proposing a plan for dramatic reductions in the fleets of all three nations and a ten-year moratorium on the construction of large warships. He called for the scrapping of nearly 2 million tons of existing shipping. Far more surprising than the proposal was the fact that the conference ultimately agreed to accept most of its terms, something that Hughes apparently had not anticipated. The Five-Power Pact of February 1922 established both limits for total naval tonnage and a ratio of armaments among the signatories. For every 5 tons of American and British warships, Japan would maintain 3 and France and Italy 1.75 each. (Although the treaty seemed to confirm the military inferiority of Japan, in fact it sanctioned Japanese dominance in East Asia. The United States and Britain had to spread their fleets across the globe; Japan was concerned only with the Pacific.) The Washington Conference also produced two other, related treaties: the Nine-Power Pact, pledging a continuation of the Open Door policy in China, and the Four-Power Pact, by which the United States, Britain, France, and Japan promised to respect one another's Pacific territories and cooperate to prevent aggression.

Historical Thinking Skills

Contextualization Have students read the section "The Diplomacy of the New Era." Ask them to discuss as a class examples of American interventionism between 1898–1920. *(Spanish American War; annexation of Hawaii; Teller Amendment; interventions in Latin America.)* **WOR** **PCE**

Go Online AP Exam Preparation

AP Exam Practice Use the online assessment to help prepare students for the AP Exam. You can assign the ready-made AP-style short-answer questions, document-based questions, and multiple-choice questions assessing concepts, themes, and skills from Period 7 and AP-style long-essay questions organized in sets of 3 questions from various time periods. You can also create your own tests from available questions. This easy-to-use tool helps you design assessments that meet the needs of different types of learners.

Discussion and Activities

Speculating After students have read the section "Replacing the League," ask them to create a T-chart listing key elements of the Washington Naval Conference and the Kellogg-Briand Pact. Have students discuss in small groups which treaty was more likely to result in permanent change. **WOR** **PCE**

The Washington Conference began the New Era effort to protect the peace (and the international economic interests of the United States) without accepting active international duties. The Kellogg-Briand Pact of 1928 concluded it. When the French foreign minister, Aristide Briand, asked the United States in 1927 to join an alliance against Germany, Secretary of State Frank Kellogg (who had replaced Hughes in 1925) instead proposed a multilateral treaty outlawing war as an instrument of national policy. Fourteen nations signed the agreement in Paris on August 27, 1928, amid great solemnity and wide international acclaim. Forty-eight other nations later joined the pact. It contained no instruments of enforcement but rested, as Kellogg put it, on the "moral force" of world opinion.

KELLOGG-BRIAND PACT

DEBTS AND DIPLOMACY

The first responsibility of diplomacy, Hughes, Kellogg, and others agreed, was to ensure that American overseas trade faced no obstacles to expansion and would remain free of interference. Preventing a dangerous armaments race and reducing the possibility of war were steps to that end. So were new financial arrangements that emerged at the same time.

The United States was most concerned about Europe, on whose economic health American prosperity in large part depended. Not only were the major European industrial powers suffering from the devastation World War I had produced; they were also staggering under a heavy burden of debt. The Allied forces were struggling to repay $11 billion in loans they had contracted with the United States during and shortly after the war, loans that the Republican administrations were unwilling to reduce or forgive. "They hired the money, didn't they?" Calvin Coolidge once replied when asked if he favored offering Europe relief from their debts. At the same time, an even more debilitated Germany was attempting to pay the reparations levied against it by the Allies. With the financial structure of Europe on the brink of collapse, the United States stepped in with a solution.

In 1924 Charles G. Dawes, an American banker and diplomat, negotiated an agreement under which American banks would provide enormous loans to the Germans, enabling them to meet their reparations payments; in return, Britain and France would agree to reduce the amount of those payments. Dawes won the Nobel Peace Prize for his efforts, but in fact the Dawes Plan did little to solve the problems it addressed. It led to a troubling circular pattern in international finance. America would lend money to Germany, which would use that money to pay reparations to France and England, which would in turn use those funds (as well as large loans they themselves were receiving from American banks) to repay war debts to the United States. The flow was able to continue only by virtue of the enormous debts Germany and the other European nations were accumulating to American banks and corporations.

CIRCULAR LOANS

U.S. PRODUCTION METHODS IN THE SOVIET UNION This photograph, from about 1930, shows American turbines used in a Soviet power station built by Americans as part of the first Five Year Plan of Soviet economic growth. Soviet planners were so impressed with American methods of mass production, they called the system of large-scale factory production "Fordism," after American automobile manufacturer Henry Ford.

Those banks and corporations were doing more than providing loans. They were becoming a daily presence in the economic life of Europe. American automobile manufacturers were opening European factories, capturing a large share of the overseas market. Other American industries in the 1920s were establishing subsidiaries worth more than $10 billion throughout the Continent, taking advantage of the devastation of European industry and the inability of domestic corporations to recover. Some groups within the U.S. government warned that the reckless expansion of overseas loans and investments, many in enterprises of dubious value, threatened disaster; that the United States was becoming too dependent on unstable European economies.

The high tariff barriers that the Republican Congress had erected (through the Fordney-McCumber Act of 1922) were creating additional problems, such skeptics warned. European nations, unable to export their goods to the United States, were finding it difficult to earn the money necessary to repay their loans. Such warnings fell for the most part on deaf ears.

The U.S. government felt even fewer reservations about assisting American economic expansion in Latin America. During the 1920s, American military forces maintained a presence in numerous countries in the region. United States investments in Latin America more than doubled between 1924 and 1929; American corporations built roads and other facilities in many areas—partly, they argued, to weaken the appeal of revolutionary forces in the region, but at least equally to increase their own access to Latin America's rich natural resources. United States banks were offering large loans to Latin American governments, just as they were in Europe; and just as in Europe, the Latin Americans were having great difficulty earning the money to repay them in the face of the formidable U.S. tariff barrier. By the end of the

ECONOMIC EXPANSION IN LATIN AMERICA

Discussion and Activities

Explaining Historical Developments Have students read the section "Circular Loans." Ask them to discuss in pairs or small groups the apparent risks and rewards of the system of finance established by the Dawes Plan. *(Rewards: Germany and the Allies able to make debt and reparations payments. Risks: International economy dependent upon loans from American banks.)* **WOR** **WXT**

1920s, resentment of "Yankee imperialism" was growing rapidly. The economic troubles after 1929 would only accentuate such problems.

HOOVER AND THE WORLD CRISIS

After the relatively placid international climate of the 1920s, the diplomatic challenges facing the Hoover administration must have seemed ominous and bewildering. The world financial crisis that began in 1929 and greatly intensified after 1931 was not only creating economic distress; it was also producing a dangerous nationalism that threatened the weak international agreements established during the previous decade. Above all, the Depression was toppling some existing political leaders and replacing them with powerful, belligerent governments bent on expansion as a solution to their economic problems. Hoover was confronted, therefore, with the beginning of a process that would ultimately lead to war.

In Latin America, Hoover worked studiously to repair some of the damage created by earlier American policies. He made a ten-week goodwill tour through the region before his inauguration. Once in office, he tried to abstain from intervening in the internal affairs of neighboring nations and moved to withdraw American troops from Haiti. When economic distress led to the collapse of one Latin American regime after another, Hoover announced a new policy: the United States would grant diplomatic recognition to any sitting government in the region without questioning the means it had used to obtain power. He even repudiated the Roosevelt corollary to the Monroe Doctrine by refusing to permit U.S. intervention when several Latin American countries defaulted on debt obligations to the United States in October 1931.

In Europe, the administration enjoyed few successes in its efforts to promote economic stability. When Hoover's proposed moratorium on debts in 1931 failed to attract broad support or produce financial stability, many economists and political leaders appealed to the president to cancel all war debts to the United States. Like his predecessors, Hoover refused; and several European nations promptly went into default, severely damaging an already tense international climate.

The ineffectiveness of diplomacy in Europe was particularly troubling in view of some of the new governments coming to power on the Continent. Benito Mussolini's Fascist Party had been in control of Italy since the early 1920s; by the 1930s, the regime was growing increasingly nationalistic and militaristic, and Fascist leaders were loudly threatening an active campaign of imperial expansion. More ominous was the growing power of the National Socialist (or Nazi) Party in Germany. By the late 1920s, the Weimar Republic, the nation's government since the end of World War I, had lost virtually all popular support, discredited by, among other things, a ruinous inflation. Adolf Hitler, the stridently nationalistic leader of the Nazis, was rapidly growing in popular favor. Although he lost a 1932 election for chancellor, Hitler would sweep into power less than a year later. His belief in the racial superiority of the Aryan (German) people, his commitment to providing *Lebensraum* (living space) for his "master race," his pathological anti-Semitism, and his passionate militarism—all posed a great threat to European, and world, peace.

More immediately alarming to the Hoover administration was a major crisis in Asia—another early step toward World War II. Japan, reeling from an economic depression of their own, were concerned about the

MANCHURIA

© Popperfoto/Getty Images

HITLER AND MUSSOLINI The German and Italian dictators (shown here reviewing Nazi troops in the mid-1930s) acted publicly as if they were equals. Privately, Hitler treated Mussolini with contempt, and Mussolini complained constantly of being a junior partner in the relationship.

Reasoning Processes

Comparison After students have read the section "Debts and Diplomacy," ask them to create a Venn diagram comparing American involvement in the economies of Europe and Latin America. Have students discuss as a class the potential advantages and disadvantages of American involvement in each region. **WOR** **PCE** **WXT**

Discussion and Activities

Analyzing Visuals Have students examine the image "Hitler and Mussolini." Ask them to identify and discuss in small groups details from the photo that are intended to reinforce the two dictators' projection of power. *(Military uniforms; reviewing troops to project command of the military; the use of banners and flags creating a pageant of power.)*

Reasoning Processes

Comparison After students have read the section "Hoover and the World Crisis," ask them to create a chart comparing the diplomacy of the Hoover Administration in Latin America, Europe, and Asia. Have students discuss as a class in which region diplomacy was most and least effective and why. **WOR** **PCE**

increasing strength of the Soviet Union and of Premier Chiang Kai-shek's nationalist China. In particular, they were alarmed at Chiang's insistence on expanding his government's power in Manchuria, which remained officially a part of China but over which Japan had maintained effective economic control since 1905. When the moderate government of Japan failed to take forceful steps to counter Chiang's ambitions, Japan's military leaders staged what was, in effect, a coup in the autumn of 1931—seizing control of foreign policy from the weakened liberals. Weeks later, they launched a major invasion of northern Manchuria.

The American government had few options. For a while, Secretary of State Henry Stimson (who had served as secretary of war under Taft) continued to hope that Japanese moderates would regain control of the Tokyo government and halt the invasion. The militarists, however, remained in command; and by the beginning of 1932, the conquest of Manchuria was complete. Stimson issued stern (but ineffectual) warnings to Japan and tried to use moral suasion to end the crisis. But Hoover forbade him to cooperate with the League of Nations in imposing economic sanctions against Japan. Stimson's only real tool in dealing with the Manchurian invasion was a refusal to grant diplomatic recognition to the new Japanese territories. Japan was unconcerned and early in 1932 expanded its aggression farther into China, attacking the city of Shanghai and killing thousands of civilians.

By the time Hoover left office early in 1933, it was clear that the international system the United States had attempted to create in the 1920s—a system based on voluntary cooperation among nations and on an American refusal to commit to the interests of other countries—had collapsed. The United States faced a choice. It could adopt a more energetic form of internationalism and enter into firmer and more meaningful associations with other nations. Or it could resort to nationalism and rely on its own devices for dealing with its own (and the world's) problems. For the next six years, it experimented with elements of both approaches.

FAILURE OF AMERICA'S INTERWAR DIPLOMACY

ISOLATIONISM AND INTERNATIONALISM

The administration of Franklin Roosevelt faced a dual challenge as it entered office in 1933: it had to deal with the worst economic crisis in the nation's history, and it had to deal with

THE BOMBING OF CHUNGKING, 1940 Chungking (now Chongqing) was the capital of China under the nationalist government of Chiang Kai-shek during World War II. It was also the site of some of the most savage fighting of the Sino-Japanese War. This photograph shows buildings in Chungking burning after Japanese bombing in 1940.

Discussion and Activities

Analyzing Visuals Have students examine the image "The Bombing of Chungking, 1940." Ask them to discuss in pairs or small groups evidence from the photo that suggests how warfare had changed since World War I. *(Nations now had access to bombers that could severely damage distant cities.)*

the effects of a decaying international structure. The two problems were not unrelated. It was the worldwide Depression itself that was producing much of the political chaos throughout the globe.

Through most of the 1930s, however, the United States was unwilling to make more than faint gestures toward restoring stability to the world. Like many other peoples suffering economic hardship, most Americans were turning inward. Yet the realities of world affairs were not to allow the nation to remain isolated for very long–as Franklin Roosevelt soon realized.

Depression Diplomacy

Perhaps Roosevelt's sharpest break with the policies of his predecessor was on the question of American economic relations with Europe. Hoover had argued that only by resolving the question of war debts and reinforcing the gold standard could the American economy hope to recover. He had therefore agreed that the United States would participate in the World Economic Conference, to be held in London in June 1933, to try to resolve these issues. By the time the conference assembled, however, Roosevelt was president. He had already decided to allow the gold value of the dollar to fall to enable American goods to compete in world markets. Shortly after the conference convened, Roosevelt released a famous "bombshell" message repudiating the orthodox views of most of the delegates and rejecting any agreement on currency stabilization. The conference quickly dissolved without reaching agreement, and not until 1936 did the administration finally agree to new negotiations to stabilize Western currencies.

FDR's "Bombshell"

At the same time, Roosevelt abandoned the commitments of the Hoover administration to settle the issue of war debts through international agreement. In effect, he simply let the issue die. In April 1934, he signed a bill to forbid American banks to make loans to any nation in default on its debts. The result was to stop the old, circular system; within months, war-debt payments from every nation except Finland stopped for good.

Although the new administration had no interest in international currency stabilization or settlement of war debts, it did have an active interest in improving America's position in world trade. Roosevelt approved the Reciprocal Trade Agreement Act of 1934, authorizing the administration to negotiate treaties lowering tariffs by as much as 50 percent in return for reciprocal reductions by other nations. By 1939, Secretary of State Cordell Hull, a devoted free trader, had negotiated new treaties with twenty-one countries. The result was an increase in American exports of nearly 40 percent. But most of the agreements admitted only products not competitive with American industry and agriculture, so imports into the United States continued to lag. Thus other nations were not obtaining the American currency needed to buy American products or pay off debts to American banks.

Reciprocal Trade Agreement Act

America and the Soviet Union

America's hopes of expanding its foreign trade helped produce efforts by the Roosevelt administration to improve relations with the Soviet Union. The United States and Russia had viewed each other with mistrust and even hostility since the Bolshevik Revolution of 1917, and the American government still had not officially recognized the Soviet regime by 1933. But powerful voices within the United States were urging a change in policy because the Soviet Union appeared to be a possible source of trade. The Russians, too, were eager for a new relationship. They were hoping in particular for American cooperation in containing the power of Japan, which Soviet leaders feared as a threat to Russia from the southeast. In November 1933, therefore, Soviet foreign minister Maxim Litvinov reached an agreement with President Roosevelt in Washington: the Soviets would cease their propaganda efforts in the United States and protect American citizens in Russia; in return, the United States would recognize the Soviet regime.

Despite this promising beginning, however, relations with the Soviet Union soon soured once again. American trade failed to establish much of a foothold in Russia; and the Soviets received no reassurance from the United States that it was interested in stopping Japanese expansion in Asia. By the end of 1934, as a result of these disappointed hopes on both sides, the Soviet Union and the United States were once again viewing each other with considerable mistrust.

The Good Neighbor Policy

Somewhat more successful were American efforts to enhance both diplomatic and economic relations with Latin America through what became known as the "Good Neighbor Policy." Latin America was one of the most important targets of the new policy of trade reciprocity. During the 1930s, the United States succeeded in increasing both exports to and imports from the other nations of the Western Hemisphere by over 100 percent. Closely tied to these new economic relationships was a new U.S. attitude toward intervention in Latin America. The Hoover administration had unofficially abandoned the earlier U.S. practice of using military force to compel Latin American governments to repay debts, respect foreign investments, or otherwise behave "responsibly." The Roosevelt administration went further. At the Inter-American Conference in Montevideo in December 1933, Secretary of State Hull signed a formal convention declaring: "No state has the right to intervene in the internal or external affairs of another." Roosevelt respected that pledge throughout his years in office. The Good Neighbor Policy did not mean, however, that the United States had abandoned its influence in Latin America. Instead of military force, Americans now tried to use economic influence. The new reliance on economic pressures eased tensions between the United States and its neighbors considerably. It did nothing to stem the growing U.S. domination of the Latin American economies.

Inter-American Conference

Discussion and Activities

Historical Developments and Argumentation Have students read the section "Depression Diplomacy." Ask them to discuss in small groups how effective the Reciprocal Trade Agreements were in stimulating the economies of the United States and its Latin American trade partners. *(They initially increased U.S. exports, but limits on imports from Latin America threatened the ability of Latin American nations to continue to buy American goods.)* **WOR** **WXT**

Discussion and Activities

Analyzing Points of View Have students read the section "America and the Soviet Union." Ask them to write a letter to President Roosevelt from the point of view of either a business owner or an industrial laborer advising the president on whether to officially recognize the Soviet Union. **WOR** **SOC**

Discussion and Activities

Speculating After students have read "The Sino-Japanese War" feature, ask them to discuss as a class what measures, if any, the United States could have enacted in an effort to end the war. **Ask:** Was there any way that war between China and Japan have been avoided? **WOR** **WXT**

AMERICA IN THE WORLD

THE SINO-JAPANESE WAR, 1931–1941

Long before Pearl Harbor, well before war broke out in Europe in 1939, the first shots of what would become World War II had been fired in the Pacific in a conflict between Japan and China.

Japan emerged from World War I as a great world power, with a proud and powerful military and growing global trade. But the Great Depression created severe economic problems for Japan (in part because of stiff new American tariffs on silk imports). As in other parts of the world, the crisis strengthened the political influence of highly nationalistic and militaristic leaders. Japanese militarists dreamed of a new empire in the Pacific that would give Japan access to fuel, raw materials, and markets for its industries, as well as land for its agricultural needs and its rapidly increasing population. Such an empire, they argued, would free Asia from exploitation by Europe and America and would create a "new world order based on moral principles."

During World War I, Japan had seized territory and economic concessions in China and had created a particularly strong presence in the northern Chinese region of Manchuria. There, in September 1931, a group of militant young army officers seized on a railway explosion to justify a military campaign through which they conquered the entire province. Both the United States government and the League of Nations demanded that Japan evacuate Manchuria. Japan ignored them and, for the next six years, consolidated their control over their new territory.

On July 7, 1937, Japan began a wider war when it attacked Chinese troops at the Marco Polo Bridge outside Beijing. Over the next few weeks, Japanese forces overran a large part of southern China, including most of the port cities, killing many Chinese soldiers and civilians in the process. Particularly notorious was the annihilation of many thousands of civilians in the city of Nanjing (the number has long been in dispute, but estimates range from 80,000 to more than 300,000) by Japanese forces in an event that became known in China and the West as the Nanjing Massacre. The Chinese government fled to the mountains. As in 1931, the United States and the League of Nations protested in vain.

The China that Japan had invaded was a nation in turmoil. It was engaged in a civil war between the so-called Kuomintang, a nationalist party led by Chiang Kai-shek, and the Chinese Communist Party, led by Mao Zedong; and this internal struggle weakened China's capacity to resist invasion. But beginning in 1937, the two Chinese rivals agreed to an uneasy truce and began fighting Japan together, with some success—bogging the Japanese military down in a seemingly endless war and imposing hardships on the Japanese people at home. The Japanese government and the military, however, remained determined to continue the war against China, whatever the sacrifices.

One result of the costs of the war for Japan was its growing dependence on the United States for steel and oil to meet civilian and military needs. In July 1941, in an effort to pressure Japan to stop their expansion, the Roosevelt administration made it impossible for Japan to continue buying American oil. Japan now faced a choice between ending its war in China and finding other sources of fuel to keep its war effort (and its civilian economy) going. It chose to extend the war beyond China in a search for oil. The best available sources were in the Dutch East Indies; but the only way to secure that European colony, the Japanese government believed, would be to neutralize the United States in Asia. Visionary military planners in Japan began advocating a daring move to immobilize the Americans in the Pacific before expanding the war elsewhere—with an attack on the U.S. naval base at Pearl Harbor. The first blow of World War II in America, therefore, was the culmination of more than a decade of efforts by Japan to conquer China.

ENTERING MANCHURIA, 1931 Japanese troops pour into Mukden (now Shenyang), the capital of the Chinese province of Manchuria, in 1931—following a staged incident that allowed Japan to claim that its troops had been attacked. The so-called Mukden Incident marked the beginning of the long Sino-Japanese War.

Keystone/Getty Images

HISTORICAL THINKING SKILLS

1. **Explaining Historical Developments** What were the goals of the Japanese militarists in the 1930s that led to the attacks on China?
2. **Evaluating Evidence** Why was China unable to stop Japanese aggression in the 1930s?
3. **Making Connections** What role did the United States play in the Sino-Japanese War?

724 · CHAPTER 26

Answers

America in the World

1. Japan emerged from World War I as a world empire, with goals of independence and freedom from European and American influence. To accomplish this goal, Japan began, during World War I, to seize territory in China and to demand economic concessions.
2. China was involved in a civil war between nationalists and communists. This internal war weakened China's ability to resist invasion and made the country vulnerable to external threats.
3. The United States, along with the League of Nations, protested the start of the Japanese invasion of China. In an effort to halt further aggressions, the United States put a blockade on Japan's ability to purchase American oil. This move forced the hand of Japan, and they felt their only option was to obtain fuel sources from the Dutch East Indies.

THE RISE OF ISOLATIONISM

The first years of the Roosevelt administration marked not only the death of Hoover's hopes for international economic agreements, but the end of any hopes for world peace through treaties and disarmament as well.

The arms control conference in Geneva had been meeting, without result, since 1932; and in May 1933, Roosevelt attempted to spur it to action by submitting a new American proposal for arms reductions. Negotiations stalled and then broke down; and only a few months later, first Hitler and then Mussolini withdrew from the talks. Two years later, Japan withdrew from the London Naval Conference, which was attempting to draw up an agreement to continue the limitations on naval armaments negotiated at the Washington Conference of 1921.

Faced with a choice between more-active efforts to stabilize the world and more-energetic attempts to isolate the nation from it, most Americans unhesitatingly chose the latter. Support for isolationism emerged from many quarters. Old Wilsonian internationalists had grown disillusioned with the League of Nations and its inability to stop Japanese aggression in Asia. Other Americans were listening to the argument (popular among populist-minded politicians in the Midwest and West) that powerful business interests—Wall Street, munitions makers, and others—had tricked the United States into participating in World War I. An investigation by a Senate committee chaired by Senator Gerald Nye of North Dakota revealed exorbitant profiteering and blatant tax evasion by many corporations during the war, and it suggested (on the basis of little evidence) that bankers had pressured Wilson to intervene in the war so as to protect their loans abroad. Roosevelt himself shared some of the suspicions voiced by the isolationists and claimed to be impressed by the findings of the Nye investigation. Nevertheless, he continued to hope for at least a modest American role in maintaining world peace. In 1935, he asked the Senate to ratify a treaty to make the United States a member of the World Court—a treaty that would have expanded America's symbolic commitment to internationalism without increasing its actual responsibilities in any important way. Nevertheless, isolationist opposition (spurred by unrelenting hostility from the Hearst newspapers and a passionate broadcast by Father Charles Coughlin on the eve of the Senate vote) resulted in the defeat of the treaty. It was a devastating political blow to the president, and he did not soon again attempt to challenge the isolationist tide.

SOURCES OF ISOLATIONISM

That tide seemed to grow stronger in the following months. Through the summer of 1935, it became clear that Mussolini's Italy was preparing to invade Ethiopia in an effort to expand its colonial holdings in Africa. Fearing that a general European war would result, American legislators began to design legal safeguards to prevent the United States from being dragged into the conflict. The result was the Neutrality Act of 1935.

The 1935 act, and the Neutrality Acts of 1936 and 1937 that followed, was designed to prevent a recurrence of the events that many Americans now believed had pressured the United States into World War I. The 1935 law established a mandatory arms embargo against both victim and aggressor in any military conflict and empowered the president to warn American citizens that they might travel on the ships of warring nations only at their own risk. Thus, isolationists believed, the "protection of neutral rights" could not again become an excuse for American intervention in war. The 1936 Neutrality Act renewed these provisions. And in 1937, with world conditions growing even more precarious, Congress passed a new Neutrality Act that established the so-called cash-and-carry policy, by which belligerents could purchase only nonmilitary goods from the United States and had to pay cash and carry the goods away on their own vessels.

NEUTRALITY ACTS

The American stance of militant neutrality gained support in October 1935 when Mussolini finally launched his long-anticipated attack on Ethiopia. When the League of Nations protested, Italy simply resigned from the organization, completed its conquest of Ethiopia, and formed an alliance (the "Axis") with Nazi Germany. Most Americans responded to the news with renewed determination to isolate themselves from European instability. Two-thirds of those responding to public opinion polls at the time opposed any American action to deter aggression. Isolationist sentiment showed its strength once again in 1936–1937 in response to the civil war in Spain. The Falangists, a group much like the Italian fascists, revolted in July 1936 against the existing republican government. Hitler and Mussolini supported General Francisco Franco, who became the leader of the Falangists in 1937, both vocally and with weapons and supplies. Some individual Americans traveled to Spain to assist the republican cause; but the U.S. government joined with Britain and France in an agreement to offer no assistance to either side—although all three governments were sympathetic to the republicans.

ETHIOPIA

Particularly disturbing was the deteriorating situation in Asia. Japan's aggressive designs against China had been clear since the invasion of Manchuria in 1931. In the summer of 1937, Tokyo launched an even broader assault, attacking China's five northern provinces. The United States, Roosevelt believed, could not allow the Japanese aggression to go unremarked or unpunished. In a speech in Chicago in October 1937, therefore, the president warned forcefully of the dangers that Japanese aggression posed to world peace. Aggressors, he proclaimed, should be "quarantined" by the international community to prevent the contagion of war from spreading. The president was deliberately vague about what such a "quarantine" would mean. Nevertheless, public response to the speech was disturbingly hostile. As a result, Roosevelt drew back.

"QUARANTINE" SPEECH

Discussion and Activities

Analyzing Cause and Effect Have students read the section "Sources of Isolationism." Ask them to list the sources of isolationism and then identify which were economic, political or diplomatic, and social. Have students discuss in small groups which type of motive seemed the strongest. **WOR** **WXT** **SOC**

Reasoning Processes

Continuity and Change Have students read the section "Neutrality Acts." Ask them to discuss as a class how neutral the acts seemed to be and whether they became more or less neutral over time. **WOR** **WXT**

Historical Thinking Skills

Argumentation After students have read the section "The Rise of Isolationism," ask them to write a letter to President Roosevelt from the point of view of an ordinary American citizen advising the president on whether to pursue a policy of intervention or isolation. **WOR**

THE SPANISH CIVIL WAR Many Americans took up arms to help the republican forces fight against Franco and his army. The novelist Ernest Hemingway joined them in Spain as a reporter (and supporter of the republicans), and he spent much of his time talking with both American and Spanish troops. His novel *For Whom the Bell Tolls* was inspired by his experience in the civil war.

Only months later, another episode provided renewed evidence of how formidable the obstacles to Roosevelt's efforts remained. On December 12, 1937, Japanese aviators bombed and sank the U.S. gunboat *Panay* as it sailed the Yangtze River in China. The attack was almost undoubtedly deliberate. It occurred in broad daylight, with clear visibility. A large American flag had been painted conspicuously on the *Panay's* deck. Even so, isolationists seized eagerly on protestations that the bombing had been an accident and pressured the administration to accept Japan's apologies.

The Failure of Munich

Hitler's determination to expand German power became fully visible in 1936, when he moved the revived German army into the Rhineland, violating the Versailles treaty and rearming an area that France had, in effect, controlled since World War I. In March 1938, German forces marched into Austria, and Hitler proclaimed a union (or *Anschluss*) between Austria, his native land, and Germany, his adopted one–thus fulfilling his long-time dream of uniting the German-speaking peoples in one great nation. Neither in America nor in most of Europe was there much more than a murmur of opposition. The Austrian invasion, however, soon created another crisis, because Hitler had by now occupied territory surrounding three sides of western Czechoslovakia, a region he dreamed of annexing to provide Germany with the *Lebensraum* (living space) he believed it needed. In September 1938, he demanded that Czechoslovakia cede to him part of that region, the Sudetenland, an area on the Austro-German border in which many ethnic Germans lived. Czechoslovakia, which possessed substantial military power of its own, was prepared to fight rather than submit. But it realized it could not hope for success without help from other European nations. It received none. Most Western nations were appalled at the prospect of another war and were willing to pay almost any price to settle the crisis peacefully. Anxiety ran almost as high in the United States as it did in Europe during and after the crisis, and helped produce such strange expressions of fear as the hysterical response to the famous "War of the Worlds" radio broadcast in October.

On September 29, Hitler met with the leaders of France and Great Britain at Munich in an effort to resolve the crisis. The French and British agreed to accept the German demands for Czechoslovakia in return for Hitler's promise to expand no farther. "This is the last territorial claim I have to make in Europe," the führer solemnly declared. And Prime Minister Neville Chamberlain returned to England to a hero's welcome, assuring his people that the agreement ensured "peace in our time." Among those who had cabled him with encouragement at Munich was Franklin Roosevelt.

MUNICH CONFERENCE

The Munich accords were the most prominent element of a policy that came to be known as "appeasement" and that came to be identified (not altogether fairly) almost exclusively with Chamberlain. Whoever was to blame, however, it became clear almost immediately that the policy was a failure. In March 1939, Hitler occupied the remaining areas of Czechoslovakia,

FAILURE OF "APPEASEMENT"

Historical Thinking Skills

Argumentation Have students examine the image "The Spanish Civil War." Ask them to discuss in small groups whether the United States should have intervened in the Spanish Civil. Have each group explain their reasoning to the rest of the class. **WOR**

violating the Munich agreement unashamedly. And in April, he began issuing threats against Poland. At that point, both Britain and France gave assurances to the Polish government that they would come to its assistance in case of an invasion; they even flirted, too late, with the Stalinist regime in Russia, attempting to draw it into a mutual defense agreement. Stalin, however, had already decided that he could expect no protection from the West; after all, he had not even been invited to attend the Munich Conference. Accordingly, he signed a nonaggression pact with Hitler in August 1939, freeing the Germans for the moment from the danger of a two-front war. For a few months, Hitler had been trying to frighten the Poles into submitting to German demands. When that failed, he staged an incident on the Polish border to allow him to claim that Germany had been attacked; and on September 1, 1939, he launched a full-scale invasion of Poland. Britain and France, true to their pledges, declared war on Germany two days later. World War II in Europe had begun.

THE OCCUPATION OF POLAND, 1939 A German motorized detachment enters a Polish town that has already been battered by heavy bombing from the German air force (the *Luftwaffe*). The German invasion of Poland, which began on September 1, 1939, sparked the formal beginning of World War II.

FROM NEUTRALITY TO INTERVENTION

"This nation will remain a neutral nation," the president declared shortly after the hostilities began in Europe, "but I cannot ask that every American remain neutral in thought as well." It was a statement that stood in stark and deliberate contrast to Woodrow Wilson's 1914 plea that the nation remain neutral in both deed and thought; and it was clear from the start that among those whose opinions were decidedly unneutral in 1939 was the president himself.

NEUTRALITY TESTED

There was never any question that both the president and the majority of the American people favored Britain, France, and the other Allied nations in the conflict. The question was how much the United States was prepared to do to assist them. At the very least, Roosevelt believed, the United States should make armaments available to the Allied armies to help them counter the highly productive German munitions industry.

CASH-AND-CARRY

In September 1939, he asked Congress for a revision of the Neutrality Acts. The original measures had forbidden the sale of American weapons to any nation engaged in war; Roosevelt wanted the arms embargo lifted. Powerful isolationist opposition forced him to accept a weaker revision than he would have liked; as passed by Congress, the 1939 measure maintained the prohibition on American ships entering war zones. It did, however, permit belligerents to purchase arms on the same cash-and-carry basis that the earlier Neutrality Acts had established for the sale of nonmilitary materials.

After the German armies had quickly subdued Poland, the war in Europe settled into a long, quiet lull that lasted through the winter and spring—a "phony war," many people called it. The only real fighting during this period occurred not between the Allies and the Axis, but between Russia and its neighbors. Taking advantage of the situation in the West, the Soviet Union overran and annexed the small Baltic republics of Latvia, Estonia, and Lithuania and then, in late November, invaded Finland. Most Americans were outraged, but neither Congress nor the president was willing to do more than impose an ineffective "moral embargo" on the shipment of armaments to Russia. By March 1940, the Soviet advance was complete.

Whatever illusions anyone may have had about the reality of the war in western Europe were shattered in the spring of 1940 when Germany launched an invasion to the west—first attacking Denmark and Norway, sweeping next across the Netherlands and Belgium, and driving finally deep into the heart of France. Allied efforts proved futile against the Nazi blitzkrieg.

FALL OF FRANCE

Discussion and Activities

Analyzing Effects After students have read the section "The Failure of Munich," ask them to write a brief paragraph explaining why the appeasement policy failed. **WOR**

Discussion and Activities

Analyzing Change Have students examine the image "The Occupation of Poland, 1939." Ask them to identify and discuss in small groups details from the photo that demonstrate how warfare had changed since World War I. *(Increased mobility with the use of motor vehicles; destruction of fortifications from the air and by artillery.)*

AP Exam Tip

The document-based question and long essay question on the AP Exam require students to create an argument that describes a broader historical context relevant to the prompt. Encourage students to think about what was happening in the United States and around the world in the months and years prior to historical events.

Historical Thinking Skills

Contextualization Have students practice the tip by writing a paragraph that describes social, economic, and diplomatic events that preceded and contributed to the hysteria that resulted from the "War of the Worlds" broadcast. **WOR** **WXT** **SOC**

PATTERNS OF POPULAR CULTURE

ORSON WELLES AND THE "WAR OF THE WORLDS"

On the evening of October 30, 1938, about 6 million Americans were listening to the weekly radio program *The Mercury Theatre on the Air,* produced by the actor/filmmaker Orson Welles and broadcast over the CBS network. A few minutes into the show, an announcer interrupted some dance music with a terrifying report:

> At least forty people, including six state troopers, lie dead in a field east of Grover's Mill [New Jersey], their bodies burned and distorted beyond recognition. . . . Good heavens, something's wriggling out of the shadow like a gray snake! Now it's another one and another. . . . It's large as a bear and it glistens like black leather. But that face . . . it's indescribable! I can hardly force myself to keep looking at it.

The panicky announcer was describing the beginning of an alien invasion of earth and the appearance of Martians armed with "death rays," determined to destroy the planet. Later in the evening, an announcer claiming to be broadcasting from Times Square reported the destruction of New York City before falling dead at the microphone.

The dramatic "news bulletins" were part of a radio play by Howard Koch, loosely adapted from H. G. Wells's 1898 novel, *The War of the Worlds.* Announcers reminded the audience repeatedly throughout the broadcast that they were listening to a play, but many people either did not hear or did not notice the disclaimers. By the end of the hour, according to some estimates, as many as a million Americans were flying into panics, convinced that the end of the world was imminent.

Thousands of listeners in New York and New Jersey fled their homes and tried to drive along clogged highways into the hills or the countryside. In Newark, people ran from their buildings with wet towels wrapped around their faces or wearing gas masks—as if defending themselves against the chemical warfare that many remembered from the trenches in World War I. In cities across the country, people flocked into churches to pray; called police and hospitals for help; flooded the switchboards of newspapers, magazines, and radio stations desperate for information. "I never hugged my radio so closely as I did last night," one woman later explained. "I held a crucifix in my hand and prayed while looking out of my open window for falling meteors." The *New York Times* described it the next day as "a wave of mass hysteria." For weeks thereafter, Orson Welles and other producers of the show were the focus of a barrage of criticism for what many Americans believed had been a deliberate effort to create public fear. For years, sociologists and other scholars studied the episode for clues about mass behavior.

THE MERCURY THEATRE ON THE AIR **Orson Welles, the founder and director of The Mercury Theatre on the Air, directs a corps of actors during a rehearsal for one of the show's radio plays.**

WELLES ON THE AIR **Welles is shown here during the broadcast of the "War of the Worlds" in 1938. Although announcers told listeners throughout the broadcast that it was fiction, Welles came under intense criticism in following days for the panic it caused among many listeners.**

Welles and his colleagues claimed to be surprised by the reaction their show created. The broadcast proved more effective than they had expected because it touched on anxieties that ran deep in American life at the time. The show aired only a few weeks after the war fever that had preceded the Munich pact among Germany, Britain, and France; Americans already jittery about the possibility of war proved easy prey to fears of another kind of invasion. The show also tapped longer-standing anxieties about the fragility of life that afflicted many Americans during the long depression of the 1930s, and it seemed to frighten working-class people—those most vulnerable to unexpected catastrophes—in particular.

Most of all, however, the "War of the Worlds" unintentionally exploited the enormous power that radio had come to exercise in American life, and the great trust many people had developed in what they heard over the air. For many people, the broadcasts they received over the radio had become their principal, even their only, source of information about the outside world. When the actors from *The Mercury Theatre* began to use the familiar phrases and cadences of radio news announcers, it was easy for members of their audience to assume that they were hearing the truth.

Welles concluded the broadcast by describing the play as "the Mercury Theater's own radio version of dressing up in a sheet and jumping out of a bush and saying Boo! . . . So good-bye everybody, and remember, please, for

Discussion and Activities

Speculating Have students examine the image "Welles on the Air." Ask them to think about and share with a partner whether the same story in written or motion picture form would have produced the same response. **SOC** **ARC**

CHAPTER 26

Patterns of Popular Culture

DAILY NEWS FINAL

NEW YORK'S PICTURE NEWSPAPER

FAKE RADIO 'WAR' STIRS TERROR THROUGH U.S.

MASS HYSTERIA A *New York Daily News* headline the morning after the famous "War of the Worlds" broadcast of *The Mercury Theatre on the Air* reports on the panic the radio show caused the night before. Thousands of listeners throughout the nation panicked as they listened to a broadcast based on H. G. Wells's fantasy *The War of the Worlds*. Many believed that an interplanetary conflict had started with invading Martians spreading wide death and destruction in New Jersey and New York.

the next day or so, the terrible lesson you learned tonight. The grinning, glowing, globular invader of your living room is an inhabitant of the pumpkin patch, and if your doorbell rings and there's no one there, that was no Martian . . . it's Halloween." But the real lesson of the "War of the Worlds" was the lesson of the enormous, and at times frightening, power of the medium of broadcasting.

From *War of the Worlds* by Howard Koch. Copyright © 1938 Howard Koch.

HISTORICAL THINKING SKILLS

1. **Explaining Historical Developments** Why did Welles's "War of the Worlds" broadcast create so much panic and hysteria?
2. **Explaining Historical Context** What responsibility did Welles and his producers bear for the hysteria that followed the program? Could they have done more to prevent that hysteria and reassure their audience? If so, should they have done more?
3. **Making Connections** Do the media today hold as much power and influence as radio did in the 1930s? Would an audience today be as likely to react with panic and hysteria to a broadcast similar to that of the "War of the Worlds"?

One western European stronghold after another fell into German hands. On June 10, Mussolini brought Italy into the war, invading France from the south as Hitler was attacking from the north. On June 22, finally, France fell to the German onslaught. Nazi troops marched into Paris; a new collaborationist regime assembled in Vichy; and in all Europe, only the shattered remnants of the British army, rescued from the beaches of Dunkirk by a flotilla of military and civilian vessels assembled miraculously quickly, remained to oppose the Axis forces.

Roosevelt had already begun to increase American aid to the Allies. He also began preparations to resist a possible Nazi invasion of the United States. On May 16, he asked Congress for an additional $1 billion for defense (much of it for the construction of an enormous new fleet of warplanes) and received it quickly. With France weakening a few weeks later, he proclaimed that the United States would "extend to the opponents of force the material resources of this nation." And on May 15, Winston Churchill, the new British prime minister, sent Roosevelt the first of many long lists of requests for ships, armaments, and other assistance without which, he insisted, England could not long survive. Many Americans (including the U.S. ambassador to London, Joseph P. Kennedy) argued that the British plight was already hopeless, that any aid to the English was a wasted effort. The president, however, made the politically dangerous decision to make war materials available to Churchill. He even circumvented the cash-and-carry provisions of the Neutrality Act by trading fifty American destroyers (most of them left over from World War I) to England in return for the right to build American bases on British territory in the Western Hemisphere; and he returned to the factories a number of new airplanes purchased by the American government so that the British could buy them instead.

Roosevelt was able to take such steps in part because of a major shift in American public opinion. Before the invasion of France, most Americans had believed that a German victory in the war would not be a threat to the United States. By July, with France defeated and Britain threatened, more than 66 percent of the American public (according to opinion polls) believed that Germany posed a direct threat to the United States. Congress was aware of the change and was becoming more willing to permit expanded American assistance to the Allies. It was also becoming more concerned about the need for internal preparations for war, and in September it approved the Burke-Wadsworth Act, inaugurating the first peacetime military draft in American history.

SHIFTING PUBLIC OPINION

But while the forces of isolation may have weakened, they were far from dead. A spirited and at times vicious debate began in the spring of 1940 between those activists who advocated expanded American involvement in the war (who were termed, often inaccurately, "interventionists") and those who continued to insist on neutrality. The celebrated journalist William Allen White served as chairman of a new Committee to Defend America by Aiding the Allies whose members lobbied actively for increased American assistance to the Allies but opposed actual intervention. Other activists went so far as

Discussion and Activities

Analyzing Cause and Effect After students have read the section "Fall of France," ask them to discuss in small groups how the fall of France contributed to shifting American foreign policy and public opinion concerning the war in Europe. *(Foreign policy shifted to more directly supporting Great Britain in its efforts to resist German expansion. Public opinion shifted more in favor of intervention in Europe.)* **WOR** **SOC** **PCE**

Answers

Patterns of Popular Culture

1. The United States, at the time of the broadcast in 1938, was paranoid and fearful of another world war and largely trusted the information broadcast on the radio.
2. Student responses will vary. Some may say that by continually reminding the audience that the broadcast was fiction, the producers really did not bear any responsibility for the mistaken judgment on the part of their listeners. Others may respond that the show should never have been produced in the first place.
3. Student responses will vary, but they should mention that both national news channels and social media greatly influence public perception today. Students may use examples such as when the news media reports on a product shortage, often the immediate effect is that the public rushes out to buy and stockpile the item based on the information given by the media.

Reasoning Processes

Comparing and Contrasting After students have read the section "Neutrality Tested," ask them to create a Venn diagram comparing the Committee to Defend America by Aiding the Allies and the America First Committee. Have students discuss in small groups the most important similarities and differences between the two groups. **WOR** **PCE** **SOC**

THE BLITZ, LONDON The German *Luftwaffe* terrorized London and other British cities in 1940–1941 and again late in the war by bombing civilian areas indiscriminately in an effort to break the spirit of the English people. The effort failed, and the fortitude of the British in the face of the attack did much to arouse support for their cause in the United States. St. Paul's Cathedral, largely undamaged throughout the raids, looms in the background of this photograph, as other buildings crumble under the force of German bombs.

Shawshots/Alamy Stock Photo

to urge an immediate declaration of war (a position that as yet had little public support) and in April 1941 created an organization of their own, the Fight for Freedom Committee.

Opposing them was a powerful new lobby called the America First Committee, which attracted some of America's most prominent leaders. Its chairman was General Robert E. Wood, until recently the president of Sears Roebuck; and its membership included Charles Lindbergh, General Hugh Johnson, Senator Gerald Nye, and Senator Burton Wheeler. It won the editorial support of the Hearst chain and other influential newspapers, and it had at least the indirect support of a large proportion of the Republican Party. (It also, inevitably, attracted a fringe of Nazi sympathizers and anti-Semites.) The debate between the two sides was loud and bitter. Through the summer and fall of 1940, moreover, it was complicated by a presidential campaign.

AMERICA FIRST COMMITTEE

The Third-Term Campaign

For many months, the politics of 1940 revolved around the question of Franklin Roosevelt's intentions. Would he break with tradition and run for an unprecedented third term? The president never publicly revealed his own wishes. But by refusing to withdraw from the contest, he made it impossible for any rival Democrat to establish a foothold within the party. Just before the Democratic National Convention in July, he let it be known that he would accept a "draft" from his party. The Democrats quickly renominated him and even reluctantly swallowed his choice for vice president: Agriculture Secretary Henry A. Wallace, a man too liberal for the taste of many party leaders.

With Roosevelt effectively straddling the center of the defense debate, favoring neither the extreme isolationists nor the extreme interventionists, the Republicans had few obvious alternatives. Succumbing to a remarkable popular movement (carefully orchestrated by, among others, *Time* and *Life* magazines), they nominated a dynamic and attractive but politically inexperienced businessman, Wendell Willkie.

WENDELL WILLKIE

Willkie took positions little different from Roosevelt's: he would keep the country out of war but would extend generous assistance to the Allies. An appealing figure and a vigorous campaigner, he managed to evoke more public enthusiasm than any Republican candidate in decades. In the end, however, he was no match for Franklin Roosevelt. The election was closer than it had been in either 1932 or 1936, but Roosevelt nevertheless won decisively. He received 55 percent of the popular vote to Willkie's 45 percent, and won 449 electoral votes to Willkie's 82.

Neutrality Abandoned

In the last weeks of 1940, with the election behind him, Roosevelt began to make subtle but profound changes in the American role in the war. More than aiding Britain, he was moving the United States closer to entering the war.

In December 1940, Great Britain was virtually bankrupt. No longer could the British meet the cash-and-carry requirements imposed by the Neutrality Acts; yet England's needs, Churchill insisted, were greater than ever. The president, therefore, suggested a method that would "eliminate the dollar sign" from all arms transactions. The new system was labeled "lend-lease." It would allow the government not only to sell but also to lend or lease armaments to any nation deemed "vital to the defense of the United States." In other words, America could funnel weapons to England on the basis of no more than Britain's promise to return or pay for them when the war was over. Isolationists attacked the measure bitterly, arguing (correctly) that it was simply a device to tie the United States more closely to the Allies; but Congress enacted the bill by wide margins.

LEND-LEASE

With lend-lease established, Roosevelt soon faced another serious problem: ensuring that the American supplies would actually reach Great Britain. Shipping lanes in the Atlantic had become extremely dangerous; German submarines destroyed as much as a half-million tons of shipping each month. The British navy was losing ships more rapidly than it could replace them and was finding it difficult to transport materials across the Atlantic from America. Secretary of War Henry Stimson (who had been Hoover's secretary of state and who returned to the cabinet at Roosevelt's request in 1940) argued that the

Discussion and Activities

Analyzing Issues Have students read the section "Third Term Campaign." Ask them to discuss in pairs or small groups how President Roosevelt justified violating the two-term tradition for presidents and how Americans responded to his campaign. **PCE** **SOC** **WXT**

United States should itself convoy vessels to England; but Roosevelt decided to rely instead on the concept of "hemispheric defense," by which the United States navy would defend transport ships only in the western Atlantic—which he argued was a neutral zone and the responsibility of the American nations. By July 1941, American ships were patrolling the ocean as far east as Iceland, escorting convoys of merchant ships, and radioing information to British vessels about the location of Nazi submarines.

At first, Germany did little to challenge these obviously hostile American actions. By the fall of 1941, however, events in Europe changed its position. German forces had invaded the Soviet Union in June of that year, shattering the 1939 Nazi-Soviet pact. The Germans drove quickly and forcefully deep into Russian territory. When the Soviets did not surrender, as many military observers had predicted they would, Roosevelt persuaded Congress to extend lend-lease privileges to them—the first step toward creating a new relationship with Stalin that would ultimately lead to a formal Soviet-American alliance. Now American industry was providing crucial assistance to Hitler's foes on two fronts, and the navy was playing a more active role than ever in protecting the flow of goods to Europe.

GERMANY INVADES THE USSR

In September, Nazi submarines began a concerted campaign against American vessels. Early that month, a German U-boat fired on the American destroyer *Greer* (which was radioing the U-boat's position to the British at the time). Roosevelt responded by ordering American ships to fire on German submarines "on sight." In October, Nazi submarines hit two American destroyers and sank one of them, the *Reuben James*, killing many American sailors. Enraged members of Congress now voted approval of a measure allowing the United States to arm its merchant vessels and to sail all the way into belligerent ports. The United States had, in effect, launched a naval war against Germany.

At the same time, a series of meetings, some private and one public, were tying the United States and Great Britain more closely together. In April 1941, senior military officers of the two nations met in secret and agreed on the joint strategy they would follow if the United States entered the war. In August, Roosevelt met with Churchill aboard a British vessel anchored off the coast of Newfoundland. The president made no military commitments, but he did join the prime minister in releasing a document that became known as the Atlantic Charter, in which the two nations set out "certain common principles" on which to base "a better future for the world." It was, in only vaguely disguised form, a statement of war aims that called openly for, among other things, "the final destruction of the Nazi tyranny."

ATLANTIC CHARTER

By the fall of 1941, it seemed only a matter of time before the United States became an official belligerent. Roosevelt remained convinced that public opinion would support a declaration of war only in the event of an actual enemy attack. But an attack seemed certain to come, if not in the Atlantic, then in the Pacific.

THE ROAD TO PEARL HARBOR

Japan took advantage of the crisis that had preoccupied the Soviet Union and the two most powerful colonial powers in Asia, Britain and France, to extend its empire in the Pacific. In September 1940, Japan signed the Tripartite Pact, a loose defensive alliance with Germany and Italy that seemed to extend the Axis into Asia. (In reality, the European Axis powers never developed a strong relationship with Japan, and the wars in Europe and the Pacific were largely separate conflicts.)

TRIPARTITE PACT

Roosevelt had already displayed his animosity toward Japanese policies by harshly denouncing their assault on China and by terminating a long-standing American commercial treaty with the Tokyo government. Still the Japanese drive continued. In July 1941, imperial troops moved into Indochina and seized the capital of Vietnam, a colony of France. The United States, having broken the Japanese codes, knew that Japan's next target would be the Dutch East Indies; and when Tokyo failed to respond to Roosevelt's stern warnings, the president froze all Japanese assets in the United States and established a complete trade embargo, severely limiting Japan's ability to purchase essential supplies (including oil). American public opinion, shaped by strong anti-Japanese prejudices developed over several decades, generally supported these hostile actions.

Tokyo now faced a choice. Either it would have to repair relations with the United States to restore the flow of supplies, or it would have to find those supplies elsewhere, most notably by seizing British and Dutch possessions in the Pacific. At first the Japanese prime minister, Prince Konoye, seemed willing to compromise. In October, however, militants in Tokyo forced Konoye out of office and replaced him with the leader of the war party, General Hideki Tojo. With Japan's need for new sources of fuel becoming desperate, there now seemed little alternative to war.

For several weeks, the Tojo government kept up a pretense of wanting to continue negotiations. On November 20, 1941, Tokyo proposed a modus vivendi highly favorable to itself and sent its diplomats in Washington to the State Department to discuss it. But Tokyo had already decided that it would not yield on the question of China, and Washington had made clear that it would accept nothing less than a reversal of that policy. Secretary of State Cordell Hull rejected the Japanese overtures out of hand; on November 27, he told Secretary of War Henry Stimson, "I have washed my hands of the Japanese situation, and it is now in the hands of you and [Secretary of the Navy Frank] Knox, the Army and Navy." He was not merely speculating. American intelligence had already decoded Japanese messages, which made clear that war was imminent, that after November 29 an attack would be only a matter of days.

TOKYO'S DECISION FOR WAR

But Washington did not know where the attack would take place. Most officials were convinced that Japan would move first not against American territory but against British or

Discussion and Activities

Historical Reasoning and Argumentation After students have read the section "Neutrality Abandoned," ask them to discuss as a class exactly how neutral actions like lend-lease and attacking German submarines were, and why the United States did not declare war in early- to mid-1940. **WOR** **PCE**

Discussion and Activities

Speculating Have students read the section "Tripartite Pact." Ask them to think about and share with a partner whether there was any way for the United States to avoid war after freezing Japanese assets and enacting an embargo against Japan. **WOR**

Discussion and Activities

Analyzing Points of View Have students examine the image "Pearl Harbor, December 7, 1941." Ask them to write a journal entry from the point of view of a high school senior about to turn 18 years old describing their reactions to images like this photo. **SOC**

DEBATING THE PAST

The Question of Pearl Harbor

The phrase "Remember Pearl Harbor!" became a rallying cry during World War II—reminding Americans of the surprise Japanese attack on the American naval base in Hawaii and arousing the nation to exact revenge. But within a few years of the end of hostilities, some Americans began to challenge the official version of the attack on December 7, 1941, and their charges sparked a debate that has never fully subsided. Was the Japanese attack on Pearl Harbor unprovoked, and did it come without warning? Or was it part of a deliberate plan by the Roosevelt administration to make the Japanese attack to force a reluctant United States into the war? Most controversial of all, did the administration know of the attack in advance? Did Roosevelt deliberately refrain from warning the commanders in Hawaii so that the air raid's effect on the American public would be more profound?

Among the first to challenge the official version of Pearl Harbor was the historian Charles A. Beard, who maintained in *President Roosevelt and the Coming of the War* (1948) that the United States had deliberately forced Japan into a position whereby they had no choice but to attack. By cutting off Japan's access to the raw materials it needed for its military adventure in China, by stubbornly refusing to compromise, the United States ensured that Japan would strike out into the southwest Pacific to take the needed supplies by force—even at the risk of war with the United States. The administration, which had some time before cracked the Japanese code, must have known weeks in advance of Japan's plan to attack—although Beard did not claim that officials knew the attack would come at Pearl Harbor. Beard supported his argument by citing Secretary of War Henry Stimson's comment in his diary: "The question was how we should maneuver them into the position of firing the first shot." This view has reappeared more recently in Thomas Fleming, *The New Dealers' War* (2001), which also argues that Roosevelt deliberately (and duplicitously) maneuvered the United States into war with Japan.

Basil Rauch, in *Roosevelt from Munich to Pearl Harbor* (1950), challenged Beard's thesis. Rauch argued that the administration did not know in advance of the planned attack on Pearl Harbor. It did, however, expect an attack somewhere; and it made subtle efforts to "maneuver" Japan into firing the first shot in the conflict. Richard N. Current, in *Secretary Stimson: A Study in Statecraft* (1954), offered an even stronger challenge to Beard. Stimson did indeed anticipate an attack, Current argued, but not an attack on American territory; rather, he anticipated an assault on British or Dutch possessions in the Pacific. The problem confronting the administration was how to find a way to make a Japanese attack on British or Dutch territory appear to be an attack on America. Only thus, Stimson believed, could Congress be persuaded to approve a declaration of war.

Roberta Wohlstetter, in *Pearl Harbor: Warning and Decision* (1962), the most thorough scholarly study to appear to that point, undertook to answer the question of whether the Roosevelt administration knew of the attack in advance. She concluded that the United States had ample warning of Japan's intentions and should have realized that the Pearl Harbor raid was imminent. But government officials failed to interpret the evidence correctly, largely because their preconceptions about Japanese intentions were at odds with the evidence they confronted. Admiral Edwin T. Layton, who had been a staff officer at Pearl Harbor in 1941, also blamed political and bureaucratic failures for the absence of advance warning of the attack. In a 1985 memoir, *And I Was There*, he argued that the Japanese attack was a result not only of "audacious planning and skillful execution" by Japan, but also of "a dramatic breakdown in our intelligence process . . . related directly to feuding among high-level naval officers in Washington."

PEARL HARBOR, DECEMBER 7, 1941 **At least seven 18-inch aerial torpedoes and two bombs struck the battleship USS *West Virginia* on that fateful morning. Repair workers discovered 66 bodies of *West Virginia* crewmembers. After it was restored to fighting condition, the ship reentered the war and participated in the Battles of Iwo Jima and Okinawa.**

The most thorough study of Pearl Harbor to date is Gordon W. Prange's *At Dawn We Slept* (1981). Like Wohlstetter, Prange concluded that the Roosevelt administration was guilty of a series of disastrous blunders in interpreting Japanese strategy; the American government had possession of enough information to predict the attack, but failed to do so. But Prange dismissed the arguments of the "revisionists" (Beard and his successors) that the president had deliberately maneuvered the nation into the war by permitting Japan to attack. Instead, he emphasized the enormous daring and great skill with which Japan orchestrated an ambitious operation that few Americans believed possible.

The revisionist claims have not been laid to rest. John Toland revived the charges of a Roosevelt betrayal in 1982, in *Infamy: Pearl Harbor and Its Aftermath*, claiming to have discovered new evidence (the testimony of an unidentified seaman) that proves the navy knew at least five days in advance that Japanese aircraft carriers were heading toward Hawaii. From that, Toland concluded that Roosevelt must have known that an attack was forthcoming and that he allowed it to occur in the belief that a surprise attack would arouse popular support for entering the war. But like the many other writers who have made the same argument, Toland was unable to produce any direct evidence of Roosevelt's knowledge of the planned attack.

HISTORICAL THINKING SKILLS

Questions assume cumulative content knowledge from this chapter and previous chapters.

1. **Identifying Historical Developments** Identify three broad schools of historical interpretation of the attack on Pearl Harbor.
2. **Determining Context** Describe how one piece of historical evidence, from the time period, could be used to support each of the three broad schools of historical interpretation concerning the attack on Pearl Harbor.
3. **Developing Arguments** Analyze which school of thought you find most convincing and explain why using evidence from the text to support your argument.

Answers

Debating the Past

1. Beard argued that the United States provoked the Japanese into attacking with its aggressiveness regarding Japan's involvement in China. Wohlstetter argued that the United States failed to interpret the intelligence correctly. Prange argued that the Roosevelt administration was guilty of possessing enough information to predict the attack and underestimated the effectiveness of Japanese forces.
2. The U.S. blockade on Japan's ability to procure more fuel did force the hand of the Japanese. There are also documented testimonies from individuals who have claimed that the United States had knowledge of the Japanese attack on the United States. There is disagreement, however, as to where this attack would take place, which questions the culpability of the Roosevelt administration's failure to act to prevent the attack on Pearl Harbor.
3. Student responses will vary but must use specific evidence in support of their argument.

Dutch possessions to the south. American intelligence took note of a Japanese naval task force that began sailing east from the Kuril Islands in the general direction of Hawaii on November 25, and radioed a routine warning to the U.S. naval facility at Pearl Harbor, near Honolulu. But officials were paying more attention to a large Japanese convoy moving southward through the China Sea. A combination of confusion and miscalculation led the government to overlook indications that Japan intended a direct attack on American forces—partly because Hawaii was so far from Japan that few officials believed such an attack possible.

At 7:55 a.m. on Sunday, December 7, 1941, a wave of Japanese bombers—taking off from aircraft carriers hundreds of miles away—attacked the United States naval base at Pearl Harbor. A second wave came an hour later. Military commanders in Hawaii had taken no precautions against such an attack and had allowed ships to remain bunched up defenselessly in the harbor and airplanes to remain parked in rows on airstrips. The consequences of the raid were disastrous for America. Within two hours, the United States lost 8 battleships, 3 cruisers, 4 other vessels, 188 airplanes, and several vital shore installations. More than 2,000 soldiers and sailors died, and another 1,000 were injured. The Japanese forces suffered only light losses.

PEARL HARBOR

American forces were now greatly diminished in the Pacific (although by a fortunate accident, none of the American aircraft carriers—the heart of the Pacific fleet—had been at Pearl Harbor on December 7). Nevertheless, the raid on Pearl Harbor did virtually overnight what more than two years of effort by Roosevelt and others had been unable to do: it unified the American people in a fervent commitment to war. On December 8, the president traveled to Capitol Hill, where he grimly addressed a joint session of Congress: "Yesterday, December 7, 1941—a date which will live in infamy—the United States of America was suddenly and deliberately attacked by the naval and air forces of the Empire of Japan." Within four hours, the Senate unanimously and the House 388 to 1 (the lone dissenter being Jeannette Rankin of Montana, who had voted against war in 1917 as well) approved a declaration of war against Japan. Three days later, Germany and Italy, Japan's European allies, declared war on the United States; and on the same day, December 11, Congress reciprocated without a dissenting vote. For the second time in twenty-five years, the United States was engaged in a world war.

HIDEKI TOJO Tojo was a general of the Imperial Japanese Army and, for most of World War II, the prime minister of Japan. He was directly responsible for the attack on Pearl Harbor, although planning for it had begun before he took office. After the war, Tojo was arrested, convicted of war crimes, and hanged.

Historical Thinking Skills

Argumentation After students have read the section "Tokyo's Decision for War," ask them to discuss in small groups what actions they think the U.S. government and military should have taken in the days prior to December 7, 1941. **WOR** **PCE** **WXT**

Reasoning Processes

Comparison Have students read the section "Pearl Harbor." Ask them to create a chart listing American conflicts with Japan in Asia and American conflicts with Germany in Europe. Have students rank the importance of these conflicts and then discuss in small groups whether the United States should have prioritized the conflict with Germany or with Japan. **WOR** **PCE** **WXT**

Discussion and Activities

Causation Divide the class in half and have each half review and research either causes for American isolationism or causes for American interventionism in the years prior to the attack on Pearl Harbor. Have each group prepare at least three arguments about the causes they've researched to present to the class. You may have students from each group alternate their presentations. **WOR** **WXT** **PCE** **SOC** **NAT**

Key Terms

Students should be familiar with the key terms and be able to define them in the context of the arguments for isolationism and interventionism in the years leading up to the attack on Pearl Harbor. Encourage students to use these terms in performing review exercises and exam practice for this chapter.

CHAPTER 26 REVIEW

CONNECTING THEMES

Chapter Twenty Six explored the involvement of the United States in world affairs between World War I and World War II. During the 1920s, the U.S. was active in international affairs, but as the threat of fascism rose in the 1930s many Americans retreated into a policy of isolationism.

The Depression spurred Roosevelt to pursue expansion of trade by improving relationships with the Soviet Union and Latin America. The "Good Neighbor Policy" endorsed the use of economic pressure rather than military force to win influence in Latin America. But U.S. domination of Latin American economies increased even as tensions diminished.

As Germany, Japan, and Italy began to threaten world stability, the United States maintained a position of neutrality as powerful isolationists dominated Congress. But Roosevelt was able to send aid directly to Britain after France fell to Hitler in 1940 and he won a third term as president. Then the Japanese attack on Pearl Harbor united the American public in support of the war in the Pacific. World War II eventually reshaped the role and identify of the United States in the global community.

You should consider the following questions as you review the themes for this chapter:

- How did World War I affect the views of Americans in the 1920s and 1930s?
- How did public opinion influence U.S. involvement in world affairs?
- What actions of the federal government altered public opinion on foreign affairs?
- How did American foreign policy change in the decades following World War I?
- In what ways did the debate in the United States over isolationism versus internationalism change between 1920 and 1941?

KEY TERMS

Adolf Hitler 721
appeasement 726
Atlantic Charter 731
Benito Mussolini 721
Cordell Hull 723
Dawes Plan 720
Good Neighbor Policy 723
Henry Stimson 730
Hideki Tojo 731
Kellogg-Briand Pact 720
Lend-lease 730
Neutrality Acts 720
Pearl Harbor 733
Washington Conference of 1921 719

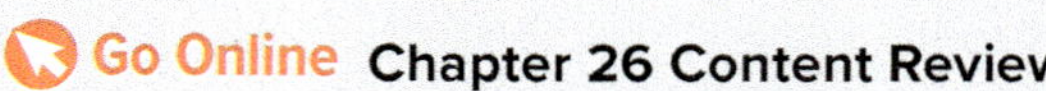

Go Online **Chapter 26 Content Review**

Assessing Student Understanding Use the online assessment to assess student understanding of concepts and topics within the chapter. You can assign the ready-made Chapter 26 Content Review or create your own from available questions. This easy-to-use tool helps you design assessments that meet the needs of different types of learners.

AP EXAM PRACTICE

Questions assume cumulative content knowledge from this chapter and previous chapters.

MULTIPLE CHOICE

Use the photograph on page 721 and your knowledge of U.S. history to answer questions 1-3.

1. One commonality between the European dictators in the photograph was their embrace of
   (A) international peacekeeping organizations.
   (B) fascist government systems.
   (C) strong alliances with African nations.
   (D) Communist ideals.
2. In response to the increasing tensions, the United States
   (A) issued a series of demands threatening military action.
   (B) aligned with the Germans and Italians.
   (C) continued to seek solutions through the League of Nations.
   (D) passed a series of Neutrality Acts.
3. When the European war began in 1939, the American public can most accurately be described as
   (A) divided over the most appropriate path forward.
   (B) unified in its support of the Allied powers.
   (C) fully supportive of the Axis powers.
   (D) anxious to enter the war as soon as possible.

SHORT ANSWER

Use your knowledge of U.S. history to answer questions 4 and 5.

4. Use the image on page 718 to answer A, B, and C.
   (A) Briefly describe ONE specific point of view about the threat of fascism during the first half of the twentieth century.
   (B) Briefly explain ONE specific historical cause of isolationism during the first half of the twentieth century.
   (C) Briefly explain ONE specific historical effect of isolationism during the first half of the twentieth century
5. Answer A, B, and C.
   (A) Briefly describe ONE specific similarity in the foreign policy of the United States before World War I and before World War II.
   (B) Briefly describe ONE specific difference in the foreign policy of the United States before World War I and before World War II.
   (C) Briefly explain ONE specific effect of the foreign policy of the United States before World War II.

LONG ESSAY

Develop a thoughtful and thorough historical argument that addresses the statement. Begin your essay with a thesis statement, and support it with specific historical evidence and examples.

6. Evaluate the relative importance of causes that led to the United States involvement in World War II.

Answers

Multiple Choice

1. B; **2.** D; **3.** A

Short Answer

4A) Possible answer: The point of view in the image is that of someone who is trying to enlist support and help in an effort to fend off Franco's forces and fight fascism during the Spanish Civil War.

4B) Possible answer: Many in the United States were concerned about becoming involved in another world war following World War I. Isolationists saw the potential financial and human costs of another war, and they were not interested in using U.S. resources for what they viewed as a largely European war.

4C) Possible answer: The failure of the United States to join the League of Nations and take a more active role in foreign affairs in part allowed the rise of fascist governments.

5A) Possible answer: With a few exceptions, the United States's attitude toward foreign policy issues was one of isolationism before both wars.

5B) Possible answer: Before World War I, the United States remained true to its isolationist policy. Before World War II, the situation slowly began to change as the United States gradually began to grow into a world power.

5C) Possible answer: The United States's failure to get involved in world affairs resulted in an atmosphere that allowed the rise of fascist governments and people who were willing to follow anyone who offered economic remedies.

Answers

Long Essay

6. Possible thesis: The direct attack on Pearl Harbor and Hitler's direct attack on European democracies and U.S. allies were the most important causes that led the United States to abandon its isolationist foreign policy and enter into a second world war. Specific historical evidence: First, the attack on Pearl Harbor and the declaration of war on the United States by Japan and Germany. Second, Germany's growing threat to Europe and the democracies across the globe posed an indirect threat to the United States. Third, the U.S. government was slowly realizing the extent of its influence on global foreign affairs.

Pacing Guide

Chapter 27 explores key concepts from Period 7: 1898–1945 of the AP U.S. History Curriculum Framework. The suggested instruction time for Chapter 27 is 3 days.

Key Concepts

7.3.III U.S. participation in World War II transformed American society, while the victory of the United States and its allies over the Axis powers vaulted the U.S. into a position of global, political, and military leadership.

27 AMERICA IN A WORLD AT WAR

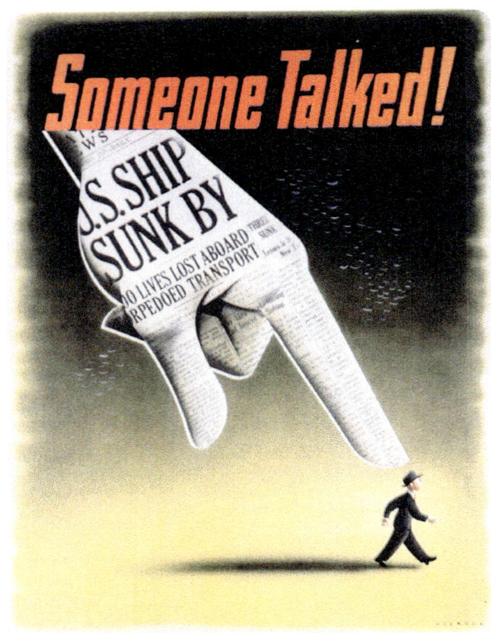

"SOMEONE TALKED"
This World War II poster, created by the graphic artist Henry Koerner, was one of many stern reminders to Americans from the government of the dangers of disclosing military secrets. In particular, wartime leaders were worried about soldiers and their families talking loosely about troop and ship locations (hence the title of another such poster: "Loose Lips Sink Ships").

CONNECTING CONCEPTS

Chapter Twenty-Seven begins by examining how the United States fought World War II on two fronts. In the Pacific, America first had to contain the Japanese advance until victory at Midway turned the tide of battle. In Europe, the United States had to coordinate with Great Britain and the Soviet Union, which achieved a major victory at Stalingrad. As news of the Holocaust reached the Allies, President Roosevelt resisted public pressure to take direct action and insisted that the best way to halt the atrocities was to defeat Germany as quickly as possible.

At home the war ended the Great Depression. Federal spending on military production and new technologies rose sharply, especially in the West, and workers and unions made gains. Labor shortages also led to new opportunities for African Americans and Mexican Americans, although discrimination and segregation remained rampant. Despite limited child care, many women entered the service sector or joined the industrial workforce, where they were known as "Rosie the Riveter." Unlike in World War I, German Americans faced little ethnic or cultural animosity. But in response to pressure from the military, Roosevelt authorized the mass internment of Japanese Americans in remote prisons which the government misleadingly described as "relocation centers."

Discussion and Activities

Analyzing Visuals Have students examine the image "'Someone Talked'." Ask them to discuss as a class what the implication of the poster is and the effectiveness of its message. *(The implication is that someone talking led to the sinking of the ship mentioned in the headline.)* **WOR** **SOC**

By mid-1943, the Allies had halted the Axis advance in Europe and the Pacific. The invasion and liberation of France came in 1944. The following year, the Allies forced Germany to surrender after Hitler committed suicide. But Japan continued to fight despite bombing raids on Tokyo and substantial casualties at Okinawa. As moderate Japanese leaders struggled for power, the United States made the controversial decision to drop atomic weapons on the cities of Hiroshima and Nagasaki. At last Japan surrendered and the most catastrophic war in history ended. The United States emerged in a position of unprecedented power, influence, and prestige — but a new conflict with the Soviet Union already loomed on the horizon.

As you read, you should:

- Describe how World War II led to greater internal migration in the United States.
- Analyze the ways that World War II contributed to ending the Great Depression.
- Identify the ways World War II led to increased opportunities for those who were traditionally underemployed.
- Describe how the development of new technology influenced the outcome of the war and affected America's role in world affairs.
- Evaluate the ways that World War II transformed the role of the United States in world affairs to that of a dominant world power.

WAR ON TWO FRONTS

Whatever political disagreements and social tensions that may have existed among the American people during World War II, there was striking unity of opinion about the conflict itself–"a unity," as one member of Congress proclaimed shortly after Pearl Harbor, "never before witnessed in this country." America's unity and confidence were severely tested in the first, troubled months of 1942. Despite the impressive display of patriotism and the dramatic flurry of activity across the United States, the war was going very badly. Britain appeared ready to collapse. The Soviet Union was staggering. One after another, Allied strongholds in the Pacific were falling to the forces of Japan. The first task facing the United States, therefore, was less to achieve victory than to stave off defeat.

CONTAINING JAPAN

Ten hours after the strike at Pearl Harbor, Japanese airplanes attacked the American airfields at Manila in the Philippines, destroying much of America's remaining air power in the Pacific. Three days later Guam, an American possession, fell to Japan; then Wake Island and the British colony Hong Kong. The great British fortress of Singapore surrendered in February 1942, the Dutch East Indies in March, Burma in April. In the Philippines, exhausted Filipino and American troops gave up their defense of the islands on May 6.

American strategists planned two broad offensives to turn the tide against Japan. One, under the command of General Douglas MacArthur, would move north from Australia, through New Guinea, and eventually back to the Philippines. The other, under Admiral Chester Nimitz, would move west from Hawaii toward major Japanese island outposts in the central Pacific. Ultimately, the two offensives would come together to invade Japan itself.

MIDWAY

The Allies achieved their first important victory in the Battle of Coral Sea, just northwest of Australia, on May 7-8, 1942, when American forces turned back the previously unstoppable Japanese fleet. A month later, there was an even more important turning point northwest of Hawaii. An enormous battle raged for four days, June 3-6, 1942, near the small American outpost at Midway Island, at the end of which the United States, despite great losses, was clearly victorious. The American navy destroyed four Japanese aircraft carriers while losing only one, and regained control of the central Pacific for the United States.

GUADALCANAL

The Americans took the offensive for the first time several months later in the southern Solomon Islands, to the east of New Guinea. In August 1942, American forces assaulted three of the islands: Gavutu, Tulagi, and Guadalcanal. A ferocious struggle (with, before it was over, terrible savagery) developed at Guadalcanal and continued for six months, inflicting heavy losses on both sides. In the end, however, the Japanese troops were forced to abandon the island–and with it their last chance of launching an effective offensive to the south.

Thus, in both the southern and central Pacific, the initiative had shifted to the United States by mid-1943. The Japanese advance had come to a stop. With aid from Australians and New Zealanders, the Americans now began

Historical Thinking Skills

Contextualization Have students read the section "War on Two Fronts." Ask them to discuss as a class the ways in which the United States demonstrated both unity and division between the end of World War I and the bombing of Pearl Harbor. **WOR** **WXT** **SOC** **ARC** **NAT**

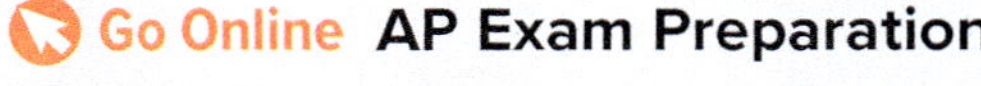

Go Online AP Exam Preparation

AP Exam Practice Use the online assessment to help prepare students for the AP Exam. You can assign the ready-made AP-style short-answer questions, document-based questions, and multiple-choice questions assessing concepts, themes, and skills from Period 7 and AP-style long-essay questions organized in sets of 3 questions from various time periods. You can also create your own tests from available questions. This easy-to-use tool helps you design assessments that meet the needs of different types of learners.

Discussion and Activities

Analyzing Issues After students have read the section "Containing Japan," ask them to go online to research code breaking in World War II. Then have them write a short paragraph explaining how code breaking played a key role in the Battle of Midway. *(Cryptography gave Allied planners advance knowledge of Japan's advance on Midway and allowed for the advantageous positioning of the American fleet.)* **WOR**

the slow, arduous process of moving toward the Philippines and toward Japan itself.

HOLDING OFF THE GERMANS

In the European war, the United States had less control over military operations. It was fighting in cooperation with Britain and with the exiled "Free French" forces in the west; and it was trying also to conciliate its new ally, the Soviet Union, which was fighting Hitler in the east. The army chief of staff, General George C. Marshall, supported a plan for a major Allied invasion of France across the English Channel in the spring of 1943. But the American plan faced challenges from the Allies. The Soviet Union, which was absorbing (as it would throughout the war) the brunt of the German effort, wanted the Allied invasion to proceed at the earliest possible moment. The British, on the other hand, wanted first to launch a series of Allied offensives around the edges of the Nazi empire—in northern Africa and southern Europe—before undertaking the major invasion of France.

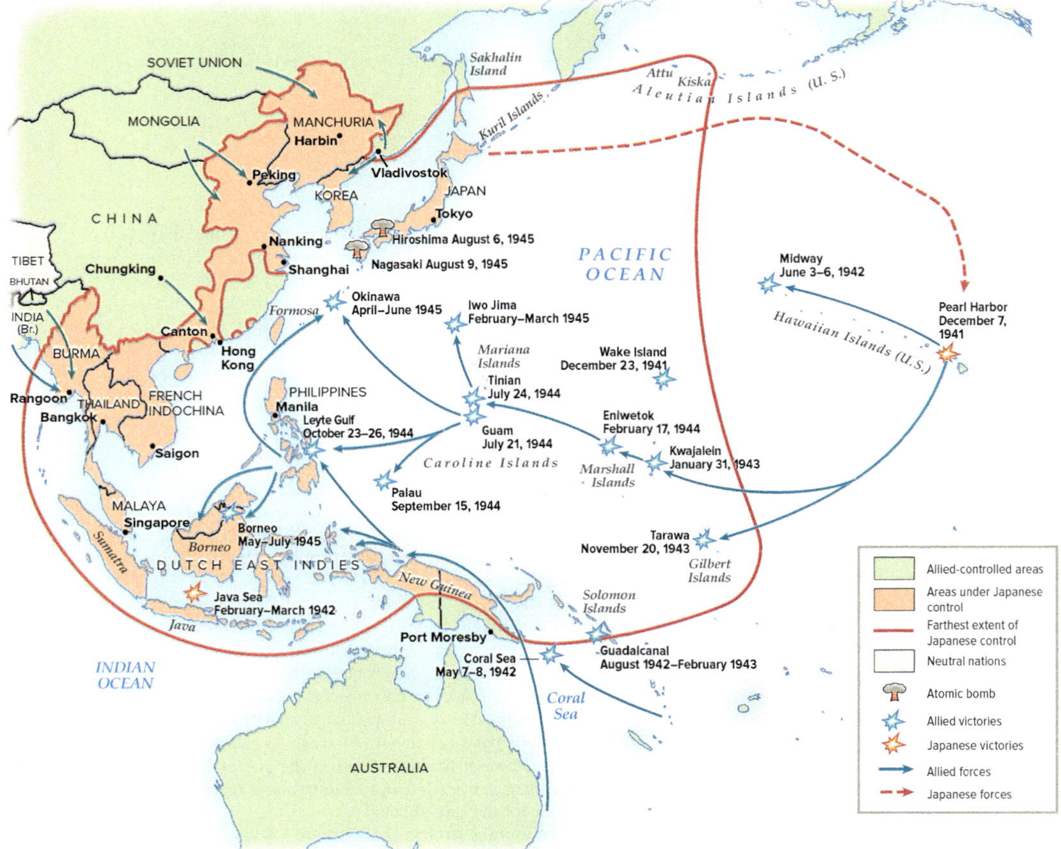

WORLD WAR II IN THE PACIFIC This map illustrates the changing fortunes of the two combatants in the Pacific phase of World War II. The long red line stretching from Burma to Manchuria represents the eastern boundary of the vast areas of the Pacific that had fallen under Japanese control by the summer of 1942. The blue lines illustrate the advance of American forces back into the Pacific beginning in May 1942 and accelerating in 1943 and after, which drove the Japanese forces back. The American advance was a result of two separate offensives—one in the central Pacific, under the command of Chester Nimitz, which moved west from Hawaii; the other, under the command of Douglas MacArthur, which moved north from Australia. By the summer of 1945, American forces were approaching the Japanese mainland and were bombing Tokyo. The dropping of two American atomic bombs, on Hiroshima and Nagasaki, finally brought the war to an end.

Why did the Soviet Union enter the Pacific war in August 1945, as shown in the upper left corner of the map?

Answers

World War II in the Pacific

The Soviet Union hoped to regain territory it had lost during the Russo-Japanese War.

Roosevelt realized that to support the British plan would antagonize the Soviets and might delay the important cross-channel invasion. But he also knew that the invasion of Europe would take a long time to prepare, and he was reluctant to wait so long before getting American forces into combat. And so, over the objections of some of his most important advisers, he decided to support the British plan. At the end of October 1942, the British opened a counteroffensive against Nazi forces in North Africa under General Erwin Rommel, who was threatening the Suez Canal at El Alamein, and forced the Germans to retreat from Egypt. On November 8, Anglo-American forces landed at Oran and Algiers in Algeria and at Casablanca in Morocco–areas under the Nazi-controlled French government at Vichy–and began moving east toward Rommel.

The Germans threw the full weight of their forces in Africa against the inexperienced Americans and inflicted a serious defeat on them at the Kasserine Pass in Tunisia. General George S. Patton, however, regrouped the American troops and began an effective counteroffensive. With the help of Allied air and naval power and of British forces attacking from the east under General Bernard Montgomery (the hero of El Alamein), the American offensive finally drove the last Germans from Africa in May 1943. The North Africa campaign had tied up a large proportion of the Allied resources and contributed to the postponement of the planned May 1943 cross-channel invasion of France. That produced angry complaints from the Soviet Union. By now, however, the threat of a Soviet collapse seemed much diminished, for during the winter of 1942–

STALINGRAD

1943 the Red Army had successfully held off a major German assault at Stalingrad in southern Russia. Hitler had committed such enormous forces to the battle, and had suffered such appalling losses, that he could not continue his eastern offensive.

The Soviet victory had come at a horrible cost. The German siege of Stalingrad had decimated the civilian population of the city and devastated the surrounding countryside. Indeed, throughout the war, the Soviet Union absorbed losses far greater than any other warring nation (up to 20 million casualties)–a fact that continued to haunt the Russian memory and affect Soviet policy generations later. But the Soviet success in beating back the German offensive persuaded Roosevelt to agree, in a January 1943 meeting with Churchill in Casablanca, to an Allied invasion of Sicily. General Marshall opposed the plan, arguing that it would further delay the vital invasion of France. But Churchill prevailed with the argument that the operation in Sicily might knock Italy out of the war and tie up German divisions that might otherwise be stationed in France. On the night of July 9, 1943, American and British armies landed in southeast Sicily; thirty-eight days later they had conquered the island and were moving onto the Italian mainland. In the face of these setbacks, Mussolini's government collapsed and the deposed dictator fled north to Germany. Mussolini's successor, Pietro Badoglio, quickly committed Italy to the Allies, but Germany moved eight divisions into the country and established a powerful defensive line south of Rome. The Allied offensive on the Italian peninsula, which began on September 3, 1943, soon bogged down, especially after a serious setback at Monte Cassino that winter. Not until May 1944 did the Allies resume their northward advance. On June 4, 1944, they captured Rome.

AUSCHWITZ, DECEMBER 1944 This photograph, taken near the end of World War II, shows a group of imprisoned children behind a barbed wire fence in one of the most notorious Nazi concentration camps. By the time this picture was taken, the Nazis had been driven out of Auschwitz and were under the control of Allied soldiers.

Discussion and Activities

Historical Developments and Argumentation After students have read the section "Stalingrad," ask them to discuss in small groups how the North African campaign and the Battle of Stalingrad marked a turning point in the war in Europe. *(German forces would now be on the defensive; resources were freed up for a large-scale Allied invasion in western Europe.)* **WOR** **PCE**

Discussion and Activities

Analyzing Points of View Have students examine the image "Auschwitz, December 1944." Ask them to write a journal entry from the point of view of a soldier involved in the liberation of a camp like the one in the photo that describes his reactions to the scene.

Historical Thinking Skills

Argumentation After students have read the section "Holding Off the Germans," ask them to write a letter from President Roosevelt to Joseph Stalin explaining the need to delay a cross-channel invasion. **WOR**

The invasion of Italy contributed to the Allied war effort in several important ways. But it postponed the invasion of France by as much as a year, deeply embittering the Soviet Union, many of whose leaders believed that the United States and Britain were deliberately delaying the cross-channel invasion in order to allow the Russians to absorb the brunt of the fighting. The postponement also gave the Soviets time to begin moving toward the countries of eastern Europe.

Dispute over the Second Front

America and the Holocaust

In dealing with the global crisis, the leaders of the American government were confronted with one of history's great horrors: the Nazi campaign to exterminate the Jewish people of Europe—the Holocaust. As early as 1942, high officials in Washington had incontrovertible evidence that Hitler's forces were rounding up Jewish people and others (including non-Jewish Poles, gypsies, homosexuals, and communists) from all over Europe, transporting them to concentration camps in eastern Germany and Poland, and systematically murdering them, often in factory-like gas chambers. (The death toll would ultimately reach 6 million Jewish people and approximately 4 million others.) News of the atrocities was reaching the public as well, and public pressure began to build for an Allied effort to end the killing or at least to rescue some of the Jewish survivors.

The American government consistently resisted almost all such entreaties. Although Allied bombers were flying missions within a few miles of the most notorious death camp at Auschwitz in Poland, pleas that the planes try to destroy the crematoria at the camp were rejected as militarily unfeasible. So were similar requests that the Allies try to destroy railroad lines leading to the camps.

The United States also resisted entreaties that it admit large numbers of the Jewish refugees attempting to escape Europe—a pattern established well before Pearl Harbor. One ship, the German passenger liner *St. Louis*, had arrived off Miami in 1939 (after having already been turned away from Havana, Cuba) carrying nearly 1,000 escaped German Jewish people, only to be refused entry and forced to return to Europe. Both before

WORLD WAR II IN NORTH AFRICA AND ITALY: THE ALLIED COUNTEROFFENSIVE, 1942–1943 The United States and Great Britain understood from the beginning that an invasion of France across the English Channel would eventually be necessary for a victory in the European war. In the meantime, however, they began a campaign against Axis forces in North Africa, and in the spring of 1943 they began an invasion across the Mediterranean into Italy. This map shows the points along the coast of North Africa where Allied forces landed in 1942—with American forces moving east from Morocco and Algeria, and British forces moving west from Egypt. The two armies met in Tunisia and moved into Italy from there.

Why were America and Britain reluctant to launch the cross-channel invasion in 1942 or 1943?

Answers

World War II in North Africa and Italy: The Allied Counteroffensive, 1942–1943

The western Allies hoped to knock Italy out of the war before launching a cross-channel invasion.

and during the war, the State Department did not even use up the number of visas permitted by law; almost 90 percent of the quota remained untouched. This disgraceful record was not a result of inadvertence. There was a deliberate effort by officials in the State Department–spearheaded by Assistant Secretary Breckinridge Long, a genteel anti-Semite–to prevent Jewish people from entering the United States in large numbers. One opportunity after another to assist imperiled Jewish people was either ignored or rejected.

OFFICIAL ANTI-SEMITISM

After 1941, there was probably little American leaders could have done, other than defeat Germany, to save most of Hitler's victims. But more forceful action by the United States (and Britain, which was even less amenable than America to Jewish requests for assistance) might well have saved some lives. Policymakers at the time justified their inaction by arguing that most of the proposed actions–bombing the railroads and the death camps, for example–would have had little effect. They insisted that the most effective thing they could do for the victims of the Holocaust was to concentrate their attention solely on the larger goal of winning the war.

THE AMERICAN PEOPLE IN WARTIME

"War is no longer simply a battle between armed forces in the field," an American government report of 1939 concluded. "It is a struggle in which each side strives to bring to bear against the enemy the coordinated power of every individual and of every material resource at its command. The conflict extends from the soldier in the front line to the citizen in the remotest hamlet in the rear." The United States had experienced wars before. But not since the Civil War had the nation undergone so consuming a military experience as World War II. American armed forces engaged in combat around the globe for nearly four years. American society, in the meantime, underwent changes that reached into virtually every corner of the nation.

PROSPERITY

World War II had its most profound impact on American domestic life by at last ending the Great Depression. By the middle of 1941, the economic problems of the 1930s–unemployment, deflation, industrial sluggishness–had virtually vanished before the great wave of wartime industrial expansion.

WAR-INDUCED ECONOMIC RECOVERY

The most important agent of the new prosperity was federal spending, which after 1939 was pumping more money into the economy each year than all the New Deal relief agencies combined had done. In 1939, the federal budget had been $9 billion, the highest level it had ever reached in peacetime; by 1945, it had risen to $100 billion. Largely as a result, the gross national product soared: from $91 billion in 1939 to $166 billion in 1945. Personal incomes in some areas grew by as much as 100 percent or more. The demands of wartime production created a shortage of consumer goods, so many wage earners diverted much of their new affluence into savings, which would help keep the economic boom alive in the postwar years.

Bettmann/Getty Images

THE *ST. LOUIS* The fate of the German liner *St. Louis* has become a powerful symbol of the indifference of the United States and other nations to the fate of European Jewish people during the Holocaust, even though its forlorn journey preceded both the beginning of World War II and the beginning of systematic extermination of Jewish people by the Nazi regime. The *St. Louis* carried a group of over 900 Jewish people fleeing from Germany in 1939, carrying exit visas of dubious legality cynically sold to them by members of Hitler's Gestapo. It became a ship without a port as it sailed from country to country—Mexico, Paraguay, Argentina, Costa Rica, and Cuba—where its passengers were refused entry time and again. Most of the passengers were hoping for a haven in the United States, but the U.S. State Department refused to allow the ship even to dock as it sailed up the American eastern seaboard. Eventually, the *St. Louis* returned to Europe and distributed its passengers among Britain, France, Holland, and Belgium (where this photograph was taken showing refugees smiling and waving as they prepare to disembark in Antwerp in June 1939). Less than a year later, all those nations except Britain fell under Nazi control.

Historical Thinking Skills

Argumentation After students have read the section "America and the Holocaust," ask them to discuss as a class what they think the policy of the United States should have been concerning the Holocaust. **WOR** **NAT** **SOC** **PCE**

Discussion and Activities

Analyzing Points of View Have students examine the image "The *St. Louis*." Ask them to write a letter to the editor from the point of view of an American business owner or laborer advising whether to grant asylum to the passengers on the *St. Louis*. **WOR** **PCE** **SOC** **NAT**

AP Exam Tip

Document-based questions on the AP Exam require students to explain the point of view, purpose, historical situation, or audience of a document. One way to accomplish this is by explaining inferences that are made in the document.

Historical Thinking Skills

Sourcing and Situation Have students practice the tip by examining the cartoon "What Have You Done Today to Save the Country from Them?" and asking them to explain inferences made by the cartoonist. *(The cartoonist depends upon the reader to understand that the characters portrayed are Hitler and Tojo.)* **WOR**

CONSIDER THE SOURCE

THE FACE OF THE ENEMY

Political cartoonists use a variety of techniques to present their message, including caricature, symbolism, exaggeration, irony, and juxtaposition. Their work both reflects and draws public attention to contemporary issues, and often captures the emotional response to an issue better than the written word. Theodore Geisel, better known as Dr. Seuss, drew some 400 cartoons for *PM*, a left-wing daily newspaper, during World War II in which he lambasted the wartime enemies of the United States. One of these cartoons ("What have YOU done today to help save your country from them?") is reproduced below. The second image from World War II, depicting Japanese prime minister Hideki Tojo, was drawn by Arthur Szyk and appeared on the cover of *Collier's* magazine in December 1942.

Political cartoons were also used during earlier conflicts. The image on page 711 was drawn during the War of 1812 to celebrate American naval victories and portrays American President James Madison giving Britain's King George III a bloody nose.

WORLD WAR II—1942

"WHAT HAVE YOU DONE TODAY TO HELP SAVE YOUR COUNTRY FROM THEM?"

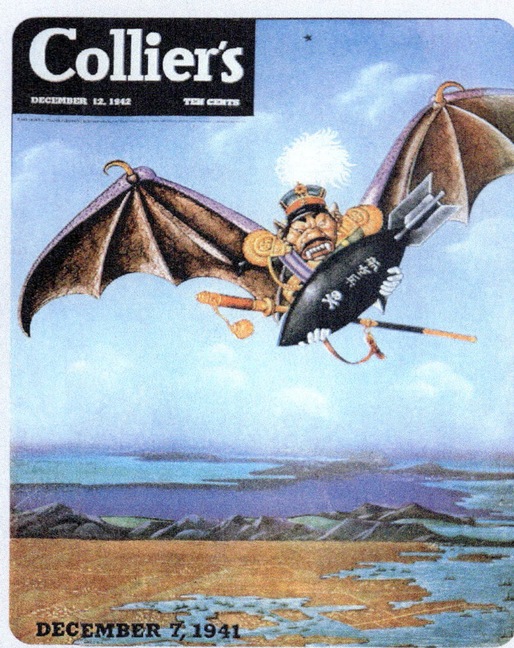

ARTHUR SZYK, *COLLIER'S* COVER, DECEMBER 12, 1942

Historical Thinking Skills

Sourcing and Situation Have students examine the *Collier's* cover. Ask them to identify and discuss in small groups details from the illustration that reveal the artist's purpose. *(Portraying the Japanese character as a bat with exaggerated features is designed to dehumanize the enemy to make it easier to justify fighting them.)* **WOR** **ARC**

WAR OF 1812—1812

A BOXING MATCH, OR ANOTHER BLOODY NOSE FOR JOHN BULL, WILLIAM CHARLES, 1813

ANALYZING SOURCES

Questions assume cumulative content knowledge from this chapter and previous chapters.

1. The first World War II cartoon's perspective most suggests which attitude towards the two individuals and their respective countries in 1942?
   (A) one was viewed as self-important and the other, inferior
   (B) one was viewed as humble, and the other, silly
   (C) one was viewed as superior, and the other, imperial
   (D) both were viewed as imperious

2. What can most likely be deduced from the fact that the Szyk cartoon was the cover page for a popular magazine almost exactly one year after the event?
   (A) The Japanese people were determined to achieve their goals.
   (B) The event was a turning point in American history.
   (C) The event did not have a great impact on America.
   (D) The event was more about Japanese aggression than about America's response.

3. What do the Seuss and the Charles cartoons share in their suggestion about American identity in the face of the two different crises at different time periods?
   (A) Americans react recklessly to such crises.
   (B) Americans are inexperienced against such crises.
   (C) Americans are steadfast against aggression.
   (D) Americans are singularly united and do not experience differences of opinion within their society during such crises.

Reasoning Processes

Comparing Have students examine the cartoon "A Boxing Match, or Another Bloody Nose for John Bull." Ask them to create a Venn diagram comparing this cartoon with the images on the previous page. **WOR** **SOC** **ARC**

Answers

Consider the Source

1. A; **2.** B; **3.** C

Discussion and Activities

Analyzing Change Have students read the section "The War and the West." Ask them to discuss in small groups how the war effort transformed the West. **WXT** **SOC**

THE WAR AND THE WEST

The impact of government spending was perhaps most dramatic in the West, which had long relied on federal largesse more than other regions. The West Coast, naturally, became the launching point for most of the naval war against Japan; and the government created large manufacturing facilities in California and elsewhere to serve the needs of its military. Altogether, the government made almost $40 billion worth of capital investments (factories, military and transportation facilities, highways, power plants) in the West during the war, more than in any other region. Ten percent of all the money the federal government spent between 1940 and 1945 went to California. Other western states also shared disproportionately in war contracts and government-funded capital investments.

By the end of the war, the economy of the Pacific Coast and, to a lesser extent, other areas of the West had been transformed. The Pacific Coast had become the center of the growing American aircraft industry. New yards in southern California, Washington State, and elsewhere made the West a center of the shipbuilding industry. Los Angeles, formerly a medium-sized city notable chiefly for its film industry, now became a major industrial center as well.

Once a lightly industrialized region, parts of the West were now among the most important manufacturing areas in the country. Once a region without adequate facilities to support substantial economic growth, the West now stood poised to become the fastest-growing region in the nation after the war.

LABOR AND THE WAR

Instead of the prolonged and debilitating unemployment that had been the most troubling feature of the Depression economy, the war created a serious labor shortage. The armed forces took more than 15 million men and women out of the civilian workforce at the same time that the demand for labor was rising rapidly. Nevertheless, the civilian workforce increased by almost 20 percent during the war. The 7 million people who had previously been unemployed accounted for some of the increase; the employment of many people previously considered inappropriate for the workforce–the very young, the elderly, and, most important, several million women–accounted for the rest.

UNION GAINS

The war gave an enormous boost to union membership, which rose from about 10.5 million members in 1941 to more than 13 million in 1945. But it also created important new restrictions on the ability of unions to fight for their members' demands. The government was principally interested in preventing inflation and in keeping production moving without disruption. It managed to win important concessions from union leaders on both scores. One was the so-called Little Steel formula, which set a 15 percent limit on wartime wage increases. Another was the "no-strike" pledge, by which unions agreed not to stop production in wartime. In return, the government provided labor with a "maintenance-of-membership" agreement, which insisted that the thousands of new workers pouring into unionized defense plants would be automatically enrolled in the unions. The agreement ensured the continued health of the union organizations, but in return workers had to give up the right to demand major economic gains during the war.

Many rank-and-file union members, and some local union leaders, resented the restrictions imposed on them by the government and the labor movement hierarchy. Despite the no-strike pledge, there were nearly 15,000 work stoppages during the war, mostly wildcat strikes (strikes unauthorized by the union leadership). When the United Mine Workers defied the government by striking in May 1943, Congress reacted by passing, over Roosevelt's veto, the Smith-Connally Act (or the War Labor Disputes Act), which required unions to wait thirty days before striking and empowered the president to seize a struck war plant. In the meantime, public animosity toward labor rose rapidly, and many states passed laws to limit union power.

STABILIZING THE BOOM

OFFICE OF PRICE ADMINISTRATION

The fear of deflation, the central concern of the 1930s, gave way during the war to a fear of inflation, particularly after prices rose 25 percent in the two years before the attack on Pearl Harbor. In October 1942, Congress grudgingly responded to the president's request and passed the Anti-Inflation Act, which gave the administration authority to freeze agricultural prices, wages, salaries, and rents throughout the country. Enforcement of these provisions was the task of the Office of Price Administration (OPA), led first by Leon Henderson and then by Chester Bowles. In part because of its success, inflation was a much less serious problem during World War II than it had been during World War I.

Even so, the OPA was never popular. There was widespread resentment of its controls over wages and prices. And there was only grudging acquiescence in its complicated system of rationing scarce consumer goods: coffee, sugar, meat, butter, canned goods, shoes, tires, gasoline, and fuel oil. Black-marketing and overcharging grew to proportions far beyond OPA policing capacity.

From 1941 to 1945, the federal government spent a total of $321 billion–twice as much as it had spent in the entire 150 years of its existence to that point, and ten times as much as the cost of World War I. The national debt rose from $49 billion in 1941 to $259 billion in 1945. The government borrowed about half the revenues it needed by selling $100 billion worth of bonds–some sold to ordinary citizens, but most to financial institutions. Much of the rest it raised by radically increasing income taxes through the Revenue Act of 1942, which established a 94 percent rate for the highest brackets and, for the first time, imposed taxes on the lowest-income families as well. To simplify collection, Congress enacted a withholding system of payroll deductions in 1943.

Discussion and Activities

Analyzing Issues Have students read the section "Labor and the War." Ask them to write a short paragraph explaining how the war effort both helped and hindered union activities. **WXT** **PCE**

MOBILIZING PRODUCTION

The search for an effective mechanism to mobilize the economy for war began as early as 1939 and continued for nearly four years. One failed agency after another attempted to bring order to the mobilization effort. Finally, in January 1942, the president responded to widespread criticism by creating the War Production Board (WPB), under the direction of former Sears Roebuck executive Donald Nelson. In theory, the WPB was to be a "superagency," with broad powers over the economy. In fact, it never had as much authority as its World War I equivalent, the War Industries Board. And the genial Donald Nelson never displayed the administrative or political strength of his 1918 counterpart, Bernard Baruch.

WAR PRODUCTION BOARD

The WPB was never able to win control over military purchases; the army and navy often circumvented the board entirely in negotiating contracts with producers. It was never able to satisfy the complaints of small business, which charged (correctly) that most contracts were going to large corporations. Gradually, the president transferred much of the WPB's authority to a new office located within the White House: the Office of War Mobilization, directed by former Supreme Court justice and South Carolina senator James F. Byrnes. But the OWM was only slightly more successful than the WPB.

Despite the administrative problems, the war economy managed to meet almost all the nation's critical war needs. Enormous new factory complexes sprang up in the space of a few months, many of them funded by the federal government's Defense Plants Corporation. An entire new industry producing synthetic rubber emerged, to make up for the loss of access to natural rubber in the Pacific. By the beginning of 1944, American factories were, in fact, producing more of most goods than the government needed. Their output was twice that of all the Axis countries combined. There were even complaints late in the war from some officials that military production was becoming excessive, that a limited resumption of civilian production should begin before the fighting ended. The military staunchly and successfully opposed almost all such demands.

WARTIME SCIENCE AND TECHNOLOGY

More than any previous American war, World War II was a watershed for technological and scientific innovation. That was partly because the American government poured substantial funds into research and development beginning in 1940. In that year the government created the National Defense Research Committee, headed by the MIT scientist Vannevar Bush, who had been a pioneer in the early development of the computer. By the end of the war, the new agency had spent more than $100 million on research, more than four times the amount spent by the government on military research and development in the previous forty years.

NATIONAL DEFENSE RESEARCH COMMITTEE

In the first years of the war, all the technological advantages seemed to lie with Germany and Japan. Germany had made great advances in tanks and other mechanized armor in the 1930s, particularly during the Spanish Civil War, when it had helped arm Franco's fascist forces. It used its armor effectively during its blitzkrieg in Europe in 1940 and again in North Africa in 1942. German submarine technology was significantly advanced compared to British and American capabilities in 1940, and German U-boats were, for a time, devastatingly effective in disrupting Allied shipping. Japan had developed extraordinary capacity in its naval-air technology. Its highly sophisticated fighter planes, launched from distant aircraft carriers, conducted the successful raid on Pearl Harbor in December 1941.

But Britain and America had advantages of their own, which quickly helped redress these imbalances. American techniques of mass production—the great automotive assembly lines in particular—were converted efficiently to military production in 1941 and 1942 and soon began producing airplanes, ships, tanks, and other armaments in much greater numbers than the Germany and Japan could produce. Allied scientists and engineers moved quickly as well to improve Anglo-American aviation and naval technology, particularly to improve the performance of submarines and tanks. By late 1942, Allied weaponry was at least as advanced as that of the enemy.

In addition, each technological innovation by the enemy produced a corresponding innovation to limit the damage of the new techniques. American and British physicists made rapid advances in improving radar and sonar technology—taking advantage of advances in radio technology in the 1920s and beyond—which helped Allied naval forces decimate German U-boats in 1943 and effectively end their effectiveness in the naval war. Particularly important was the creation in 1940 of "centimetric radar," which used narrow beams of short wavelength that made radar more efficient and effective than ever before—as the British navy discovered in April 1941 when the instruments on one of its ships detected a surfaced submarine ten miles away at night and, on another occasion, spotted a periscope at three-quarters of a mile range. With earlier technologies, the sub and periscope would have been undetectable. This new radar could also be effectively miniaturized, which was critical to its use on airplanes and submarines in particular. It required only a small rotating aerial, and it used newly advanced cavity magnetron valves of great power. These innovations put the Allies far in advance of Germany and Japan in radar and sonar technology. The Allies also learned early how to detect and disable German naval mines; and when the Germans tried to counter this progress by introducing an "acoustic" mine, which detonated when a ship came near it, not necessarily just on contact, the Allies developed acoustical countermeasures of their own, which transmitted sounds through the water to detonate mines before ships came near them.

RADAR AND SONAR

Anglo-American antiaircraft technology—both on land and on sea—also improved, although never to the point where it

Historical Thinking Skills

Argumentation After students have read the section "Stabilizing the Boom," ask them to create a poster either encouraging or discouraging price controls. **WXT** **PCE**

Discussion and Activities

Evaluating Evidence Have students read the section "Mobilizing Production." Ask them to discuss in small groups the successes and failures of the War Production Board and the Office of War Management. *(Successes: Production either met or exceeded goals. Failures: Big businesses favored over smaller businesses; never gained control of military purchasing.)* **WXT** **PCE**

Reasoning Processes

Comparing After students have read the section "Radar and Sonar," ask them to create a Venn diagram comparing the two systems. Have students discuss in pairs or small groups which they believe had a greater impact on the war effort. **PCE** **WOR** **WXT**

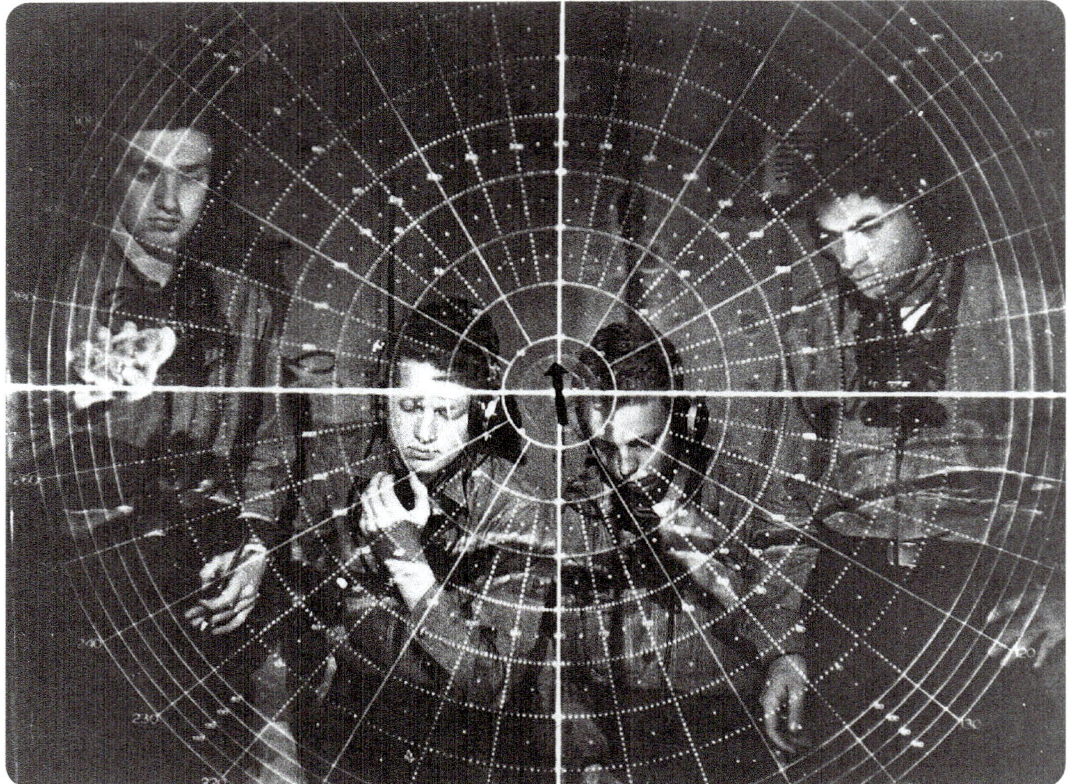

RADAR SCOPE, 1944 Navy technicians are shown here demonstrating the new radar scopes that revolutionized the tracking of ships and planes during World War II.

could stop bombing raids. Germany made substantial advances in the development of rocket technology in the early years of the war, and it managed to launch some rocket-propelled bombs (the V1s and V2s) across the English Channel, aimed at London. The psychological effects of the rockets on the British people were considerable. But the Germans were never able to create a production technology capable of building enough such rockets to make a real difference in the balance of military power.

Beginning in 1942, British and American forces seized the advantage in the air war by producing new and powerful four-engine bombers in great numbers—among them the British Lancaster B1 and the American Boeing B17F, capable of flying a bomb load of 6,000 pounds for 1,300 miles, and capable of reaching 37,500 feet. Because they were able to fly higher and longer than the German equivalents, they were able to conduct extensive bombing missions over Germany (and later Japan) with much less danger of being shot down. But the success of the bombers rested heavily as well on new electronic devices capable of guiding their bombs to their targets. The Gee navigation system, which was also valuable to the navy, used electronic pulses to help pilots plot their exact location—something that in the past only a highly skilled navigator could do, and then only in good weather. In March 1942, eighty Allied bombers fitted with Gee systems staged a devastatingly effective bombing raid on German industrial and military installations in the Ruhr Valley. Studies showed that the Gee system doubled the accuracy rate of night bombing raids. Also effective was the Oboe system, a radio device that sent a sonic message to airplanes to tell them when they were within twenty yards of their targets, first introduced in December 1942.

The area in which the Allies had perhaps the greatest advantages in technology and knowledge was the gathering of intelligence, much of it through Britain's top-secret Ultra project. Some of the advantages the

ULTRA

National Archives and Records Administration

Discussion and Activities

Analyzing Visuals Have students examine the image "Radar Scope, 1944." Ask them to discuss in small groups details from the photo that illustrate features of the American war effort. *(Technology was increasingly important, and there were still clearly defined gender roles. Women were not allowed in combat but were confined to support roles, such as the radar plotters shown in the photo.)* **SOC** **WOR** **PCE**

Allies enjoyed came from successful efforts to capture or steal German and Japanese intelligence devices. More important, however, were the efforts of cryptologists to puzzle out the enemy's systems, and advances in computer technology that helped the Allies decipher coded messages sent by Japan and Germany. Much of Germany's coded communication made use of the so-called Enigma machine, which was effective because it constantly changed the coding systems it used.

In the first months of the war, Polish intelligence had developed an electro-mechanical computer, which it called the "Bombe," that could decipher some Enigma messages. After the fall of Poland, British scientists, led by the brilliant computer pioneer Alan Turing, took the Bombe, which was too slow to keep up with the increasingly frequent changes of coding the Germans were using, and greatly improved it. On April 15, 1940, the new, improved, high-speed Bombe broke the coding of a series of German messages within hours (not days, as had previously been the case). A few weeks later, it began decrypting German messages at the rate of 1,000 a day, providing the British (and later the Americans) with a constant flow of information about enemy operations that continued–unknown to the Germans–until the end of the war.

Later in the war, British scientists working for the intelligence services built the first real programmable, digital computer–the Colossus II, which became operational less than a week before the beginning of the Normandy invasion. It was able to decipher an enormous number of intercepted German messages almost instantly.

The United States also had some important intelligence breakthroughs, including, in 1941, a dramatic success by the American Magic operation (the counterpart to the British Ultra) in breaking a Japanese coding system not unlike the German Enigma, a mechanical device known to the Allies as Purple. The result was that Americans had access to intercepted information that, if properly interpreted, could have alerted them to the Japanese raid on Pearl Harbor in December 1941. But because such a raid had seemed entirely inconceivable to most American officials prior to its occurrence, those who received the information failed to understand or disseminate it in time.

MAGIC

AFRICAN AMERICANS AND THE WAR

During World War I, many African Americans had eagerly seized the chance to serve in the armed forces, believing that their patriotic efforts would win them an enhanced position in postwar society. They had been cruelly disappointed. As World War II approached, African Americans were again determined to use the conflict to improve their position in society–this time, however, not by currying favor but by making demands.

In the summer of 1941, A. Philip Randolph, president of the predominantly black Brotherhood of Sleeping Car Porters, began to insist that the government require companies receiving defense contracts to integrate their workforces. To mobilize support for the demand, Randolph planned a massive march on Washington, which would, he promised, bring more than 100,000 demonstrators to the capital. Roosevelt was afraid of both the possibility of violence and the certainty of political embarrassment. He finally persuaded Randolph to cancel the march in return for a promise to establish a Fair Employment Practices Commission (FEPC) to investigate discrimination in war industries. The FEPC's enforcement powers, and thus its effectiveness, were limited, but its creation was a rare symbolic victory for African Americans making demands of the government.

FEPC

The demand for labor in war plants greatly increased the migration of African Americans from the rural areas of the South into industrial cities–a migration that continued for more than a decade after the war and brought many more African Americans into Northern cities than the Great Migration of 1914–1919 had done. The migration bettered the economic condition of many African Americans, but it also created urban tensions. On a hot June day in Detroit in 1943, a series of altercations between African Americans and white people at a city park led to two days of racial violence in which thirty-four people died, twenty-five of them African Americans.

Despite such tensions, the leading black organizations redoubled their efforts during the war to challenge the system of segregation. The Congress of Racial Equality (CORE), organized in 1942, mobilized mass popular resistance to discrimination in a way that the older, more conservative organizations had never done. Randolph, Bayard Rustin, James Farmer, and other, younger black leaders helped organize sit-ins and demonstrations in segregated theaters and restaurants. In 1944, CORE won a much-publicized victory by forcing a Washington, D.C., restaurant to agree to serve African Americans. CORE's defiant spirit would survive into the 1950s and help produce the civil rights movement.

CORE

Pressure for change was also growing within the military. At first, the armed forces maintained their traditional practice of limiting African Americans to the most menial assignments, keeping them in segregated training camps and units, and barring them entirely from the Marine Corps and the Army Air Forces. Gradually, however, military leaders were forced to make adjustments–in part because of public and political pressures, but also because they recognized that these forms of segregation were wasting manpower. By the end of the war, the number of black servicemen had increased sevenfold, to 700,000; some training camps were being at least partially integrated; African Americans were beginning to serve on ships with white sailors; and more black units were being sent into combat than at the beginning of the war. But tensions remained. In some of the partially integrated army bases–Fort Dix, New Jersey, for example–riots occasionally broke out when African Americans protested having to serve in segregated divisions. Substantial discrimination survived in all the services until well after the war. But within the military, as within the society at large, the traditional pattern of race relations was slowly eroding.

Discussion and Activities

Evaluating Evidence After students have read the section "Wartime Science and Technology," ask them to create a chart of all the inventions described, their purpose, and their impact. Have students discuss as a class which they think was the most important in advancing the war effort, and why. **WOR** **WXT**

Discussion and Activities

Historical Evidence and Argumentation Have students read the section "African Americans and the War." Ask them to discuss as a class challenges and opportunities that World War II presented to African Americans. **WXT** **SOC** **NAT** **PCE**

Discussion and Activities

Analyzing Points of View Have students read the section "Native Americans and the War." Have students work in groups to discuss the impact of the war on Native Americans and the challenges faced by Native Americans in the armed forces. Have groups share with the class and discuss if the treatment of Native Americans changed after the war and if their contributions were recognized. **PCE** **SOC** **NAT**

NATIVE AMERICANS AND THE WAR

Approximately 25,000 Native Americans performed military service during World War II. Many of them served in combat (among them Ira Hayes, one of the men who memorably raised the American flag at Iwo Jima). Others worked as "code-talkers," working in military communications and speaking their own languages (which enemy forces would be unlikely to understand) over the radio and the telephones.

"CODE-TALKERS"

The war had important effects, too, on those Native Americans who remained civilians. Little war work reached the Native American nations, and government subsidies dwindled. Many talented young people left the reservations, some to serve in the military, others (more than 70,000) to work in war plants. This brought many Native Americans into close contact with white society for the first time and awakened in some of them a taste for the material benefits of life in capitalist America that they would retain after the war. Some never returned to the reservations, but chose to remain in the non-Indian world and assimilate to its ways. Others found that after the war, employment opportunities that had been available to them during the fighting became unavailable once again, drawing them back to the reservations.

The wartime emphasis on national unity undermined support for the revitalization of tribal autonomy that the Indian Reorganization Act of 1934 had launched. New pressures emerged to eliminate the reservation system and require the nations to assimilate into white society–pressures so severe that John Collier, the director of the Bureau of Indian Affairs who had done so much to promote the reinvigoration of the reservations, resigned in 1945.

MEXICAN AMERICAN WAR WORKERS

Large numbers of Mexican workers entered the United States during the war in response to labor shortages on the Pacific Coast, in the Southwest, and eventually in almost all areas of the nation. The American and Mexican governments agreed in 1942 to a program by which *braceros* (contract laborers) would be admitted to the United States for a limited time to work at specific jobs, and American employers in some parts of the Southwest began actively recruiting Mexican American workers.

During the Depression, many Mexican American farmworkers had been deported to make room for unemployed white workers. The wartime labor shortage caused farm owners to begin hiring Mexican Americans again. More important, however, Mexican Americans were able for the first time to find significant numbers of factory jobs. They formed the second-largest group of migrants (after African Americans) to American cities in the 1940s. Over 300,000 of them served in the United States military.

EMPLOYMENT GAINS FOR MEXICAN AMERICANS

The sudden expansion of Mexican American neighborhoods created tensions and occasionally conflict in some

VICTORY GARDENS During both World War I and II, private and public lands were cultivated by non-combattant civilians, often children, to reduce the pressure on the public food supply. In addition to help solving practical needs of food production, these gardens served to boost the morale of citizens across the country as they supported the war effort. Here, gardeners work a plot of land in Saint Gabriel's Park, in New York City, with the Chrysler Building looming in the background.

ClassicStock/Alamy Stock Photo

American cities. Some white residents of Los Angeles became alarmed at the activities of Mexican American teenagers, many of whom were joining street gangs *(pachucos)*. The *pachucos* were particularly distinctive because of their members' style of dress, which whites considered outrageous. They wore "zoot suits"–long, loose jackets with padded shoulders, baggy pants tied at the ankles–long watch chains, broad-brimmed hats, and greased, ducktail hairstyles. (It was a style borrowed in part from fashions in Harlem.)

In June 1943, animosity toward the zoot-suiters produced a four-day riot in Los Angeles, during which white sailors stationed at a base in Long Beach invaded Mexican American communities and attacked zoot-suiters (in response to alleged attacks). The city police did little to restrain the sailors, who grabbed Mexican American teenagers, tore off and burned their clothes, cut off their ducktails, and beat them. But when Mexican Americans tried to fight back, the police moved in and arrested them. In the aftermath of the "zoot-suit riots," Los Angeles passed a law prohibiting the wearing of zoot suits.

ZOOT-SUIT RIOTS

WOMEN AND CHILDREN AT WAR

The war drew increasing numbers of women into roles from which, by either custom or law, they had been largely barred. The number of women in the workforce increased by nearly 60 percent, and women accounted for a third of paid workers in 1945 (as opposed to a quarter in 1940). These wage-earning women were more likely to be married and older than most women who had entered the workforce in the past.

DRAMATIC INCREASE IN FEMALE EMPLOYMENT

Reasoning Processes

Comparing and Contrasting After students have read the section "Mexican American War Workers," ask them to discuss as a class how the experiences of African Americans, Native Americans, and Mexican Americans were similar and different during World War II. **PCE** **WXT** **SOC** **NAT**

Many women entered the industrial workforce to replace male workers serving in the military. But while economic and military necessity eroded some of the popular objections to women in the workplace, obstacles remained. Many factory owners continued to categorize jobs by gender. (Female work, like male work, was also categorized by race: black women were usually assigned more menial tasks, and paid at a lower rate, than their white counterparts.) Employers also made substantial investments in automated assembly lines to reduce the need for heavy labor.

Special recruiting materials for women made domestic analogies. Cutting airplane wings was compared to making a dress pattern, mixing chemicals to making a cake. Still, women did make important inroads in industrial employment during the war. Women had been working in industry for over a century, but some began now to take on heavy industrial jobs that had long been considered "men's work." The famous wartime image of "Rosie the Riveter" symbolized the new importance of the female industrial workforce. Women workers joined unions in substantial numbers, and they helped erode at least some of the prejudice, including the prejudice against working mothers, that had previously kept many of them from paid employment.

"ROSIE THE RIVETER"

Most women workers during the war were employed not in factories but in service-sector jobs. Above all, they worked for the government, whose bureaucratic needs expanded dramatically alongside its military and industrial needs. Washington, D.C., in particular, was flooded with young female clerks, secretaries, and typists—known as "government girls"—most of whom lived in cramped quarters in boardinghouses, private homes, and government dormitories and worked long hours in the war agencies. Public and private clerical employment for women expanded in other urban areas as well, creating high concentrations of young women in places largely depleted of young men. Even within the military, which enlisted substantial numbers of women as WACs (army) and WAVEs (navy), most female work was clerical.

The new opportunities produced new problems. Many women whose husbands were in the military had to combine working with caring for their children. The scarcity of child-care facilities or other community services meant that some women had no choice but to leave young children—often known as "latchkey children" or "eight-hour orphans"—at home alone (or sometimes locked in cars in factory parking lots) while they worked.

LIMITED CHILD CARE

Perhaps in part because of the family dislocations the war produced, juvenile crime rose markedly in the war years. Young boys were arrested at rapidly increasing rates for car theft and burglary, vandalism, and vagrancy. The arrest rate for prostitutes, many of whom were teenage girls, rose too, as did the incidence of sexually transmitted disease. For many children, however, the distinctive experience of the war years was not crime but work. More than a third of all teenagers between the ages of fourteen and eighteen were employed late in the war, causing some reduction in high-school enrollments.

The return of prosperity during the war helped increase the rate and lower the age of marriage after the Depression decline, but many of these young marriages were unable to survive the pressures of wartime separation. The divorce rate rose rapidly. The rise in the birth rate that accompanied the increase in marriages was the first sign of what would become the great postwar "baby boom."

BEGINNING OF THE "BABY BOOM"

WOMEN AT WAR Many American women enlisted in the army and navy women's corps during World War II, but an equally important contribution of women to the war effort was their work in factories and offices—often in jobs that would have been considered inappropriate for them in peacetime but that they were now encouraged to assume because of the absence of so many men.

Discussion and Activities

Speculating After students have read the section "Women and Children at War," ask them to create a T-chart listing opportunities and challenges for women entering the workforce during the war. Have students discuss as a class which was greater and how lasting the changes were likely to be after the war ended. **WXT** **SOC**

Discussion and Activities

Analyzing Visuals Have students examine the image "Women at War." Ask them to identify the types of work displayed in the poster, and then have them discuss in small groups how representative those jobs would have been in the actual workforce. *(Only one woman in the poster is shown doing clerical work, when in reality a majority of women worked in those types of jobs.)* **WXT** **SOC**

Discussion and Activities

Making Connections Ask students to think about how many, if any, periodicals their families subscribe to. Have them discuss as a class why their experience with periodicals is likely different from families in the 1940s.

PATTERNS OF POPULAR CULTURE

LIFE: THE GREAT MAGAZINE

The birth of a great era of photographs in the twentieth century created many new magazines. One of the finest was *Life,* first published in 1936 by Henry Luce. It soon became the most popular magazine in America. Luce himself wrote a minor classic of journalism for his new magazine:

> To see life; to see the world; to eyewitness great events; to watch the faces of the poor and the gestures of the proud; to see strange things—machines, armies, multitudes, shadows in the jungle and on the moon; to see man's work. . . . Thus to see, and to be shown, is now the will and new expectancy of half of mankind.

Luce and his partner, Briton Hadden, began a remarkable empire when they started *Time* magazine in 1923. But Hadden died suddenly in 1929, and Luce took charge. He began a successful business magazine—*Fortune.* But it was *Life* that made Luce famous and wealthy. The Cowles family of Iowa followed Luce with *Look,* which was also successful. But for most Americans, *Life* was the most important magazine.

Life, which began just three years before World War II presented many stories on the coming conflict. Building for the war was growing fast by 1942. Detroit and other cities turned their automobile production into the manufacture of planes, armored vehicles, jeeps, and other war matériel. *Life* reporters warned that "the morale situation is perhaps worst in the U.S. . . . For Detroit can either blow up Hitler or it can blow up the U.S."

Life sent a large pool of photographers and graphic artists across the Atlantic to cover the war. The magazine turned the conflict into a great visual story and became renowned for its striking imagery.

Life's remarkable popularity continued throughout the war. It's first issue after the Japanese attack on Pearl Harbor featured the word "WAR" set in large black type on its first page. Photographers were not allowed to use many of the pictures they took of the tremendous damage until 1943, because editors feared that people at home would be shocked if they saw military personnel who were injured or killed. But, eventually, Americans saw what the war really was through images that included flag-draped coffins. At the end of the war, on VJ Day, the great photographer Alfred Eisenstadt captured a moment of peace and joy when he took the famous picture of a sailor embracing a young woman in Times Square.

THE STORY OF WAR *Life* reporters and photographers told the story of the war to everyone, including these soldiers, shown reading the magazine that they will in turn appear in.

HENRY LUCE

After the war, although there were still serious essays on politics and foreign affairs, *Life* began another effort—to show America as a prosperous and happy nation. The magazine began to show "Modern Living," along with "football games, automobile trips, family trips, and all the pleasant trivia of the American way of life." *Life* was eager to show the great bounty of American life. "How can one feel thankful for too much," one reporter wrote.

Through most of the 1950s, *Life* remained an enormously prosperous venture. But toward the end of that decade, *Life* started to decline, as many magazines began to lose their impact with the growing popularity of television. Advertisers who would have bought ad space in magazines began buying television advertisements. Magazines, including *Life,* lost a vital source of their revenue. In December 1972, *Life* published its last issue. But the great *Life* photographs remain a remarkable archive of events around the world during a large part of the twentieth century.

HISTORICAL THINKING SKILLS

1. **Explaining Historical Context** In what ways did *Life* magazine influence the way news stories were reported during the 1930s, 40s, and 50s?
2. **Evaluating** What were the messages the magazine wanted to convey about the war to its readers?
3. **Making Connections** How does the motive of making a profit influence how the news is reported?

Answers

Patterns of Popular Culture

1. *Life,* along with other magazines, focused on photography to tell their stories.
2. *Life* captured images of soldiers and the dangerous and heroic aspects of their efforts in defeating the enemy but largely avoided images of injuries and death.
3. Magazines, like any business, must make money to stay in business. As television became more affordable, the influence that magazines had slowly diminished.

WARTIME LIFE AND CULTURE

The war created considerable anxiety in American life. Families worried about loved ones at the front and struggled to adjust to the absence of husbands, fathers, brothers, sons–and to the new mobility of women, which also drew family members away from home. Businesses and communities struggled to compensate for shortages of goods and the absence of men.

But the abundance of the war years also created a striking buoyancy in American life that the conflict itself only partially subdued. Suddenly, people had money to spend again and–despite the many shortages of consumer goods–at least some things to spend it on. Audiences equal to about half the population attended movies each week, often to watch heroic war films. Magazines, particularly pictorial ones such as *Life*, reached the peak of their popularity, satisfying the seemingly insatiable hunger of readers for pictures of and stories about the war. Radio ownership and listening also increased, for the same reason.

ECONOMIC GOOD TIMES

Resort hotels, casinos, and race tracks were jammed with customers. Dance halls were packed with young people drawn to the seductive music of swing bands; soldiers and sailors home on leave, or awaiting shipment overseas, were especially attracted to the dances and the big band.

Advertisers, and at times even the government, exhorted Americans to support the war effort to ensure a future of material comfort and consumer choice for themselves and their children. "Your people are giving their lives in useless sacrifice," *The Saturday Evening Post* wrote in a mock letter to the leaders of wartime Japan. "Ours are fighting for a glorious future of mass employment, mass production and mass distribution and ownership." Even troops at the front seemed at times to justify their efforts with reference to the comforts of home more than to the character of the enemy or the ideals America claimed to be defending. "They are fighting for home," the writer John Hersey once wrote from Guadalcanal (with at least a trace of dismay), because "Home is where the good things are–the generosity, the good pay, the comforts, the democracy, the pie."

FIGHTING FOR FUTURE PROSPERITY

For men at the front, the image of home was a powerful antidote to the rigors of wartime. They dreamed of music, food, movies, material comforts. Many also dreamed of women–wives and girlfriends, but also movie stars and others who became the source of one of the most popular icons of the front: the pinup.

For the servicemen who remained in America during the war, and for soldiers and sailors in cities far from home in particular, the company of friendly, "wholesome" women was, the military believed, critical to maintaining morale. USOs recruited thousands of young women to serve as hostesses in their clubs–women who were expected to dress nicely, dance well, and chat happily with lonely men. Other women joined "dance brigades" and traveled by bus to military bases for social evenings with servicemen. They, too, were expected to be pretty, to dress attractively (and conservatively), and to interact comfortably with men they had never met before and would likely never see again. The USO forbade women to have dates with soldiers after parties in the clubs, and the members of the "dance brigades" were expected to have no contact with servicemen except during the dances. Clearly, such regulations were sometimes violated. But while the military took elaborate measures to root out homosexual men and women from their ranks (unceremoniously dismissing many of them with undesirable discharges), it quietly tolerated "healthy heterosexuality."

USO

THE INTERNMENT OF JAPANESE AMERICANS

World War I had produced widespread hatred, vindictiveness, and hysteria in America, as well as widespread and flagrant violations of civil liberties. World War II did not produce a comparable era of repression. The government barred from the mails a few papers it considered seditious, among them Father Coughlin's anti-Semitic and pro-fascist *Social Justice*, but there was no general censorship of dissident publications. The most ambitious effort to punish domestic fascists, a sedition trial of twenty-eight people, ended in a mistrial, and the defendants went free. Unlike during World War I, the government generally left socialists and communists (most of whom strongly supported the war effort) alone–although the Roosevelt administration summarily and secretly executed a number of German spies who had entered the country.

Nor was there much of the ethnic or cultural animosity that had shaped the social climate of the United States during World War I. The "zoot-suit" riots in Los Angeles and occasional racial conflicts in American cities and on military bases made clear that traditional racial and ethnic hostilities had not disappeared. So did wartime restrictions imposed on some Italians–including provisions forbidding many of them to travel and imprisoning several hundred. The great opera singer Ezio Pinza was classified as an "enemy alien." But on the whole, the war worked more to blur ethnic distinctions than to heighten them. Americans continued to eat sauerkraut without calling it by the World War I name "liberty cabbage." They displayed relatively little hostility toward German or Italian Americans. Instead, they seemed to share the view of their government's propaganda: that the enemy was less the German and Italian people than the vicious political systems to which they had succumbed. In popular culture, and in everyday interactions, ethnicity seemed less a source of menacing difference–as it often had in the past–and more evidence of healthy diversity. The participation and frequent heroism of American soldiers of many ethnic backgrounds encouraged this change.

ETHNIC DISTINCTIONS BLURRED

But there was a glaring exception to the general rule of tolerance: the treatment of the small, politically powerless group of Japanese Americans. From the beginning, Americans adopted a different attitude toward their Asian enemy than they did toward their European foes. Both government and

Discussion and Activities

Evaluating Perspectives Have students read the section "Wartime Life and Culture." Ask them to write a short paragraph in which they attempt to reconcile the apparent wartime abundance promoted by businesses and the entertainment industry with the sacrifices being asked of military personnel fighting overseas. **ARC** **WXT** **SOC** **NAT**

Discussion and Activities

Analyzing Issues Have students read the section "Ethnic Distinctions Blurred." Ask them to discuss in small groups why they think there was less overt hostility toward those of German descent than there had been during World War I. **SOC** **NAT**

Reasoning Processes

Comparison After students have read the section "'Relocation Centers'," ask them to discuss as a class why Japanese Americans were treated so differently than German and Italian Americans during World War II. **SOC** **NAT**

private propaganda encouraged Americans to believe that Japanese people were devious and cruel. The infamous attack on Pearl Harbor seemed to many Americans to confirm that assessment.

ANTI-JAPANESE PREJUDICE

This racial animosity soon extended to Americans of Japanese descent. There were not many Japanese Americans in the continental United States–only about 127,000, most of them concentrated in a few areas in California. About a third of them were unnaturalized, first-generation immigrants (Issei); two-thirds were naturalized or native-born citizens of the United States (Nisei). Japanese Americans, like Chinese Americans, had long been the target of ethnic and racial animosity; and unlike members of European ethnic groups, who had encountered similar resentment, Asian Americans seemed unable to dispel prejudice against them no matter how assimilated they became. Many white Americans continued to consider Asian Americans (even native-born citizens) so "foreign" that they could never become "real" Americans. Partly as a result, much of the Japanese American population in the West continued to live in close-knit, to some degree even insular, communities, which reinforced the belief that they were alien and potentially menacing.

The attack on Pearl Harbor inflamed these long-standing suspicions and turned them into active animosity. Wild stories circulated about how the Japanese Americans in Hawaii had helped sabotage Pearl Harbor and how Japanese Americans in California were conspiring to aid an enemy landing on the Pacific coast. There was no evidence to support any of these charges; but according to Earl Warren, then attorney general of California, the apparent passivity of the Japanese Americans was itself evidence of the danger they posed. Because they did nothing to allow officials to gauge their intentions, Warren claimed, it was all the more important to take precautions against conspiracies.

Although there was some public pressure in California to remove the Japanese "threat," popular sentiment was generally more tolerant of the Nisei and Issei (and more willing to make distinctions between them and the Japanese people in Japan) than was official sentiment. The real impetus for taking action came from the government. Secretary of the Navy Frank Knox, for example, said shortly after Pearl Harbor that "the most effective fifth column [a term for internal sabotage] work of the entire war was done in Hawaii." That statement–clearly referring to the large Japanese population there–later proved to be entirely false. General John L. DeWitt, the senior military commander on the West Coast, claimed to have "no confidence in [Japanese American] loyalty whatsoever." When asked about the distinction between unnaturalized Japanese immigrants and American citizens, he said, "A Jap is a Jap. It makes no difference whether he is an American citizen or not."

"RELOCATION CENTERS"

In February 1942, in response to such pressure (and over the objections of the attorney general and J. Edgar Hoover, the director of the FBI), President Roosevelt authorized the army to "intern" the Japanese Americans. He created the War Relocation Authority (WRA) to oversee the project. More than 100,000 people (Issei and Nisei alike) were rounded up, told to dispose of their property however they could (which often meant simply abandoning it), and taken to what the government euphemistically termed "relocation centers" in the "interior." In fact, they were facilities little different from prisons, many of them located in the western mountains and the desert. Conditions in the internment camps were not brutal, but they were harsh and uncomfortable. Government officials talked of them as places where Japanese Americans could be socialized and "Americanized." But the internment camps were more a target of white economic aspirations than of missionary work. The governor of Utah, where many of the internees were located, wanted the federal government to turn over thousands of Japanese Americans to serve as forced laborers. Washington did not comply, but the WRA did hire out many inmates as agricultural laborers.

The internment never produced significant popular opposition. For the most part, once Japanese Americans were in the camps, other Americans (including their former neighbors on the West Coast) largely forgot about them–except to make strenuous efforts to acquire the property they had abandoned. Even so, beginning in 1943 conditions slowly improved. Some young Japanese Americans left the camps to attend colleges and universities (mostly in the East–the WRA continued to be wary of letting Japanese Americans return to the Pacific Coast). Others were permitted to move to cities to take factory and service jobs (although, again, not on the West Coast). Some young men joined and others were drafted into the American military; a Nisei army unit fought with distinction in Europe.

MANZANAR RELOCATION CENTER During World War II, more than 100,000 Japanese Americans were interned by the government in "relocation centers" such as the one shown here. Many of these U.S. citizens were forced to give up their property and to work for little or no money. Here, sequestered citizens wait for lunch.

Discussion and Activities

Analyzing Points of View Have students examine the image "Manzanar Relocation Center." Ask them to write a short paragraph about the experience of Japanese Americans during the internment process. **SOC** **NAT**

In 1944, the Supreme Court ruled in *Korematsu v. U.S.* that military necessity made the forced relocation constitutionally permissible. In another case the same year, it barred the internment of "loyal" citizens, but General DeWitt contended in his "Final Report" that it was impossible to determine who fit that category. Nevertheless, by the end of 1944, most of the internees had been released; and in early 1945, they were finally permitted to return to the West Coast–where they faced continuing harassment and persecution, and where many found their property and businesses irretrievably lost. In 1988, after years of agitation by survivors of the camps and their descendants, Congress voted to award them reparations. But the compensation was limited, and by then many of the former internees had died.

KOREMATSU V. U.S.

CHINESE AMERICANS AND THE WAR

Just as America's conflict with Japan undermined the position of Japanese Americans, the American alliance with China during World War II significantly enhanced both the legal and social status of Chinese Americans. In 1943, partly to improve relations with the government of China, Congress finally repealed the Chinese Exclusion Act, which had barred almost all Chinese immigration since 1882. The new quota for Chinese immigrants was minuscule (105 a year), but a substantial number of Chinese women managed to gain entry into the country through other provisions covering war brides and fiancées. Over 4,000 Chinese women entered the United States in the first three years after the war. Permanent residents of the United States who were of Chinese descent were finally permitted to become citizens.

CHINESE EXCLUSION ACTS REPEALED

Racial animosity toward Chinese Americans did not disappear, but it did decline–in part because government propaganda and popular culture began presenting positive images of Chinese people (partly to contrast them with Japanese people); in part because Chinese Americans (like African Americans and other previously marginal groups) began taking jobs in war plants and other booming areas suffering from labor shortages and hence moving out of the isolated world of the Chinatowns. A higher proportion of Chinese Americans (22 percent of all adult males) were drafted than of any other national group, and the entire Chinese community in most cities worked hard and conspicuously for the war effort.

THE RETREAT FROM REFORM

Late in 1943, Franklin Roosevelt publicly suggested that "Dr. New Deal," as he called it, had served its purpose and should now give way to "Dr. Win-the-War." The statement reflected the president's own genuine shift in concern: that victory was now more important than reform. But it also reflected the political reality that had emerged during the first two years of war. Liberals in government were finding themselves unable to enact new programs. They were even finding it difficult to protect existing ones from conservative assault.

Within the administration itself, many liberals found themselves displaced by the new managers of the wartime agencies, who came overwhelmingly from large corporations and conservative Wall Street law firms. But the greatest assault on New Deal reforms came from conservatives in Congress, who seized on the war as an excuse to do what many of them had wanted to do in peacetime: dismantle many of the achievements of the New Deal. They were assisted by the end of mass unemployment, which decreased the need for such relief programs as the Civilian Conservation Corps and the Works Progress Administration (both of which were abolished by Congress). They were assisted, too, by their own increasing numbers. In the congressional elections of 1942, Republicans gained 47 seats in the House and 10 in the Senate. Roosevelt continued to talk at times about his commitment to social progress and liberal reform, in part to bolster the flagging spirits of his traditional supporters. But increasingly, the president quietly accepted the defeat or erosion of New Deal measures in order to win support for his war policies and peace plans. He also accepted the changes because he realized that his chances for reelection in 1944 depended on his ability to identify himself less with domestic issues than with world peace.

DISMANTLING THE NEW DEAL

Republicans approached the 1944 election determined to exploit what they believed was resentment of wartime regimentation and privation and unhappiness with Democratic reform. They nominated as their candidate the young and vigorous governor of New York, Thomas E. Dewey. Roosevelt was unopposed within his party, but Democratic leaders pressured him to abandon the controversial Vice President Henry Wallace, an outspoken liberal and hero of the CIO. Roosevelt, tired and frail, seemed to take little interest in the matter and passively acquiesced in the selection of Senator Harry S. Truman of Missouri, a man he barely knew. Truman was not a prominent figure in the party, but he had won acclaim as chairman of the Senate War Investigating Committee (known as the Truman Committee), which had compiled an impressive record of uncovering waste and corruption in wartime production.

The conduct of the war was not an issue in the campaign. Instead, the election revolved around domestic economic issues and, indirectly, the president's health. The president was in fact gravely ill, suffering from, among other things, arteriosclerosis. But the campaign seemed momentarily to revive him. He made several strenuous public appearances late in October, which dispelled popular doubts about his health and ensured his reelection. Roosevelt captured 53.5 percent of the popular vote to Dewey's 46 percent, and won 432 electoral votes to Dewey's 99. Democrats lost 1 seat in the Senate, gained 20 in the House, and maintained control of both.

1944 ELECTION

Reasoning Processes

Comparing Have students read the section "Chinese Americans and the War." Ask them to create a Venn diagram comparing the treatment of Japanese Americans and Chinese Americans during the war. Have students discuss in small groups why the treatment of the groups may have been different. **SOC** **NAT**

Reasoning Processes

Causation Have students read the section "Dismantling the New Deal." Ask them to discuss as a class why even some Democrats moved away from previous New Deal policies during Roosevelt's third term. *(War mobilization removed the need for relief programs; Roosevelt himself transitioned to war leadership; Roosevelt moved away from some reform policies to bolster support for his war aims.)* **PCE** **WXT**

Historical Thinking Skills

Argumentation After students have read the section "1944 Election," ask them to create a campaign poster for either Roosevelt or Dewey emphasizing one of main arguments advanced by his campaign. **PCE** **WXT** **SOC**

WORLD WAR II IN EUROPE: THE ALLIED COUNTEROFFENSIVE, 1943–1945 This map illustrates the climactic movements in the war in Europe—the two great offensives against Germany that began in 1943 and culminated in 1945. From the east, the armies of the Soviet Union, having halted the Germans at Stalingrad and Moscow, swept across eastern Europe toward Germany. From the west and the south, American, British, and other Allied forces moved toward Germany through Italy and—after the Normandy invasion in June 1944—through France. The two offensives met in Berlin in May 1945.

What problems did the position of the Allied forces at the end of the war help to produce?

THE DEFEAT OF THE AXIS

By the middle of 1943, America and its allies had succeeded in stopping the Axis advance in both Europe and the Pacific. In the next two years, the Allies themselves seized the offensive and launched a series of powerful drives that rapidly led the way to victory.

THE LIBERATION OF FRANCE

By early 1944, American and British bombers were attacking German industrial installations and other targets almost around the clock, drastically cutting production and impeding transportation. Especially devastating was the massive bombing of

STRATEGIC BOMBING

Answers

World War II in Europe: The Allied Counteroffensive, 1943–1945

At the end of the war, the Allies occupied different parts of Germany, leading to conflicts over how post-war Germany should be administered.

such German cities as Leipzig, Dresden, and Berlin—attacks that often made few distinctions between industrial sites and residential ones. A February 1945 incendiary raid on Dresden created a great firestorm that destroyed three-fourths of the previously undamaged city and killed approximately 135,000 people, almost all civilians.

Military leaders claimed that the bombing destroyed industrial facilities, demoralized the population, and cleared the way for the great Allied invasion of France planned for the late spring. The air battles over Germany considerably weakened the *Luftwaffe* (the German air force) and made it a less formidable obstacle to the Allied invasion. Preparations for the invasion were also assisted by the breaking of the Enigma code.

An enormous invasion force had been gathering in England for two years: almost 3 million troops, and perhaps the greatest array of naval vessels and armaments ever assembled in one place. On the morning of June 6, 1944, D-Day, General Dwight D. Eisenhower, the Supreme Commander of the Allied forces, sent this vast armada into action. The landing came not at the narrowest part of the English Channel, where the Germans had expected and prepared for it, but along sixty miles of the Cotentin Peninsula on the coast of Normandy. While airplanes and battleships offshore bombarded the Nazi defenses, 4,000 vessels landed troops and supplies on the beaches. (Three divisions of paratroopers had been dropped behind the German lines the night before, amid scenes of great confusion, to seize critical roads and bridges for the push inland.) Fighting was intense along the beach, but the superior manpower and equipment of the Allied forces gradually prevailed. Within a week, the German forces had been dislodged from virtually the entire Normandy coast.

D-DAY

For the next month, further progress remained slow. But in late July in the Battle of Saint-Lô, General Omar Bradley's First Army smashed through the German lines. General George S. Patton's Third Army, spearheaded by heavy tank attacks, then moved through the hole Bradley had created and began a drive into the heart of France. On August 25, Free French forces arrived in Paris and liberated the city from four years of German occupation. And by mid-September, the Allied armies had driven the Germans almost entirely out of France and Belgium.

The great Allied drive came to a halt, however, at the Rhine River in the face of a firm line of German defenses and a period of cold weather, rain, and floods. In mid-December, German forces struck in desperation along fifty miles of front in the Ardennes Forest. In the Battle of the Bulge (named for a large bulge that appeared in the American lines as the Germans pressed forward), they drove fifty-five miles toward Antwerp before

BATTLE OF THE BULGE

THE NORMANDY INVASION This photograph, taken from a landing craft, shows American troops wading ashore and onto the Normandy beaches, where one of the decisive battles of World War II was taking shape. The invasion was launched despite threatening weather and rough seas.

Historical Thinking Skills

Argumentation After students have read the section "D-Day," organize the class into two groups and discuss whether the aerial bombardment of Germany was warranted. Have each half of the class prepare a defense of one side of the argument to present to the other side. **WOR**

Discussion and Activities

Analyzing Points of View Have students examine the image "The Normandy Invasion." Ask them to write a journal entry from the point of view of a soldier participating in the landing describing his thoughts, actions, and emotions of that day. **WOR** **SOC**

Discussion and Activities

Historical Evidence and Argumentation After students have read the section "The Liberation of France," ask them to identify and discuss in small groups the events that led to the Allied victory over Germany. Have students attempt to form a consensus over what the most important factors were in the Allied victory. **WOR** **WXT**

they were finally stopped at Bastogne. The battle ended serious German resistance in the west.

While the Allies were fighting their way through France, Soviet forces were sweeping westward into central Europe and the Balkans. In late January 1945, the Russians launched a great offensive toward the Oder River inside Germany. In early spring, they were ready to launch a final assault against Berlin. By then, Omar Bradley's First Army was pushing into Germany from the west. Early in March, his forces captured the city of Cologne, on the west bank of the Rhine. The next day, in a remarkable stroke of good fortune, he discovered and seized an undamaged bridge over the river at Remagen; Allied troops were soon pouring across the Rhine. In the following weeks the British field marshal Bernard Montgomery, commander of Allied ground operations on D-Day and after, pushed into northern Germany with a million troops, while Bradley's army, sweeping through central Germany, completed the encirclement of 300,000 German soldiers in the Ruhr.

The German resistance was now broken on both fronts. American forces were moving eastward faster than they had anticipated and could have beaten the Russians to Berlin and Prague. Instead, the American and British high commands decided to halt the advance along the Elbe River in central Germany to await the Russians. That decision enabled the Soviets to occupy eastern Germany and Czechoslovakia.

On April 30, with Soviet forces on the outskirts of Berlin, Adolf Hitler killed himself in his bunker in the capital. And on May 8, 1945, the remaining German forces surrendered unconditionally. V-E (Victory in Europe) Day prompted great celebrations in western Europe and in the United States, tempered by the knowledge of the continuing war against Japan.

GERMANY DEFEATED

THE PACIFIC OFFENSIVE

In February 1944, American naval forces under Admiral Chester Nimitz won a series of victories in the Marshall Islands and cracked the outer perimeter of the Japanese Empire. Within a month, the navy had destroyed other vital Japanese bastions. American submarines, in the meantime, were decimating Japanese shipping and crippling the nation's domestic economy. By the summer of 1944, the already skimpy food rations for the Japanese people had been reduced by nearly a quarter; there was also a critical gasoline shortage.

America's principal ally in Asia was China, and the United States hoped that the Chinese forces would help defeat Japan.

Anthony Camerano/AP Photo

COMING HOME Euphoric American soldiers arrive in New York Harbor back aboard the *Queen Elizabeth* after the end of the war in Europe in 1945.

Discussion and Activities

Analyzing Points of View Have students examine the image "Coming Home." Ask them to write a journal entry from the point of view of a soldier arriving on the ship in the photo describing his thoughts, actions, and emotions of that day. **WOR** **SOC**

To assist them, the army sent General Joseph W. Stilwell to help provide critical supplies to China by a land route through India and across the Himalayas. It was a brutal task. The Japanese blocked them at several points, and Stilwell had to rely for a time on airlifts of supplies over the mountains. But finally in the fall of 1944, Stilwell's forces succeeded in constructing a road and pipelines across the mountains into China—a route that came to be known by several names: the Burma Road, the Ledo Road, and at times the Stilwell Road.

Japanese forces consistently threatened the Burma Road. More dangerously, Japan was also threatening the wartime capital of China in Chungking. Chiang Kai-shek, the Chinese premier, was reluctant to use his troops against Japanese forces and seemed more concerned with attacking Chinese communists, who were also fighting Japan. This helped create a famous feud between Stilwell and Chiang. Stilwell began to call Chiang—not entirely privately—the "peanut." The dispute continued for many months until Stilwell finally left China. Stilwell's successors had little more success in prodding Chiang to confront the Japanese forces.

The decisive battles of the Pacific war occurred not in China but at sea. In mid-June 1944, an enormous American armada struck the heavily fortified Mariana Islands and, after some of the bloodiest operations of the war, captured Tinian, Guam, and Saipan, 1,350 miles from Tokyo. In September, American forces landed on the western Carolines. And on October 20, General MacArthur's troops landed on Leyte Island in the Philippines. As the American forces pushed closer to Japan itself, Japanese forces used their entire fleet against the Allied invaders in three major encounters—which together constituted the decisive Battle of Leyte Gulf, the largest naval engagement in history. American forces held off the onslaught and sank four Japanese carriers, all but destroying Japan's capacity to continue a serious naval war.

BATTLE OF LEYTE GULF

Nevertheless, the Japanese forces seemed only to increase their resistance. In February 1945, American marines seized the tiny volcanic island of Iwo Jima, only 750 miles from Tokyo, but only after the costliest single battle in the history of the Marine Corps. The marines suffered over 25,000 casualties, and the Japanese forces suffered even greater losses.

The battle for Okinawa, an island only 370 miles south of Japan, was further evidence of the strength of the Japanese resistance in those last desperate months. Week after week, Japan sent kamikaze (suicide) planes against American and British ships, sacrificing 3,500 of them while inflicting great damage. Japanese troops on shore launched desperate nighttime attacks on the American lines. The United States and its allies suffered nearly 50,000 casualties before finally capturing Okinawa in late June 1945. More than 100,000 Japanese people died in the siege.

OKINAWA

The same kind of bitter fighting seemed to await the Americans in Japan itself. But there were also signs early in 1945 that such an invasion might not be necessary. The

© Bettmann/Getty Images

OKINAWA The invasion of Okinawa, an island near Japan, was one of the last major battles of World War II. In this photograph, taken June 18, 1945, a bullet-scarred monument provides shelter to members of the 7th Infantry of the U.S. Tenth Army as they look ahead at Japanese action. Over 11,000 Americans (and more than 80,000 Japanese forces) died in the rugged battle for the island, which consumed nearly three months. It ended three days after this photograph was taken. Two months later—after the bombing of Hiroshima and Nagasaki—Japan surrendered.

Discussion and Activities

Historical Reasoning and Argumentation After students have read the section "Battle of Leyte Gulf," ask them to discuss in small groups why the decisive actions in the Pacific theater occurred at sea rather than on land. *(The Pacific theater was spread over the vast Pacific Ocean. Control of the seas meant the ability to deny supplies and reinforcements to the enemy.)* **WOR** **GEO**

Discussion and Activities

Argumentation Have students read the section "Okinawa." Ask them to write a persuasive argument about how the president should proceed regarding Japan to end the war in the Pacific. **WOR** **PCE** **SOC**

Discussion and Activities

Historical Evidence and Argumentation After students have read the section "The Pacific Offensive," ask them to identify and discuss in small groups the events that led to American victory over Japan. Have students attempt to form a consensus over what the most important factor was in the victory. **WOR** **WXT**

Japanese forces had almost no ships or planes left with which to fight. In July 1945, for example, American warships stood off the shore of Japan and shelled industrial targets (many already in ruins from aerial bombings) with impunity. A brutal firebombing of Tokyo in March, in which American bombers dropped napalm on the city, created a massive firestorm in which at least 83,000 and perhaps as many as 100,000, mostly civilians, died. It further weakened Japan's will to resist. Moderate Japanese leaders, who had long since decided that the war was lost, were struggling for power within the government and were looking for ways to bring the war to an end. After the invasion of Okinawa, Emperor Hirohito appointed a new premier and gave him instructions to sue for peace; but the new leader could not persuade military leaders to give up the fight. The premier did try, along with the emperor, to obtain mediation through the Soviet Union. The Russians, however, showed little interest in playing the role of arbitrator.

Whether the moderates could ultimately have prevailed is a question about which historians and others continue to disagree. In any case, the question eventually became moot. In mid-July, American scientists conducted a successful test of a new atomic bomb, which led to a major event in world history, significant only in part because it ended World War II.

THE MANHATTAN PROJECT

Reports had reached the United States in 1939 that Nazi scientists had taken the first step toward the creation of an atomic bomb. The United States and Britain immediately began a race to develop the weapon before the Germans did.

The search for the new weapon emerged from theories developed by atomic physicists, beginning early in the century, and particularly from some of the founding ideas of modern science developed by Albert Einstein. Einstein's famous theory of relativity had revealed the relationships between mass and energy. More precisely, he had argued that, in theory at least, matter could be converted into a tremendous force of energy. It was Einstein, by then living in the United States, who warned Franklin Roosevelt that the Germans were developing atomic weapons and that the United States must begin trying to do the same. The effort to build atomic weapons centered on the use of uranium, whose atomic structure made possible the creation of a nuclear chain reaction. A nuclear chain reaction occurs when the atomic nuclei in radioactive matter are split (a process known as nuclear fission) by neutrons. Each fission creates new neutrons that produce fissions in additional atoms at an ever-increasing and self-sustaining pace.

ENRICO FERMI

The construction of atomic weapons had become feasible by the 1940s because of the discovery of the radioactivity of uranium in the 1930s by Enrico Fermi in Italy. In 1939, the great Danish physicist Niels Bohr sent news of German experiments in radioactivity to the United States. In 1940, scientists at Columbia University began chain-reaction experiments with uranium and produced persuasive evidence of the feasibility of using uranium as fuel for a weapon. The Columbia experiments stalled in 1941, and the work moved to UC Berkeley and the University of Chicago, where Enrico Fermi (who had emigrated to the United States in 1938) achieved the first controlled fission chain reaction in December 1942.

By then, the army had taken control of the research and appointed General Leslie Groves to reorganize the project–which soon became known as the Manhattan Project (because it was devised in the Manhattan Engineer District Office of the Army Corps of Engineers). Over the next three years, the U.S. government secretly poured nearly $2 billion into the Manhattan Project–a massive scientific and technological effort conducted at hidden laboratories in Oak Ridge, Tennessee; Los Alamos, New Mexico; Hanford, Washington; and other sites. Scientists in Oak Ridge, who were charged with finding a way to create a nuclear chain reaction that could be feasibly replicated within the confined space of a bomb, began experimenting with plutonium–a derivative of uranium first discovered by scientists at UC Berkeley. Plutonium proved capable of providing a practical fuel for the weapon. Scientists in Los Alamos, under the direction of J. Robert Oppenheimer, were charged with the construction of the actual atomic bomb.

THE TRINITY BOMB

Despite many unforeseen problems, the scientists pushed ahead much faster than anyone had predicted. Even so, the war in Europe ended before they were ready to test the first weapon. Just before dawn on July 16, 1945, in the desert near Alamogordo, New Mexico, the scientists gathered to witness the first atomic explosion in history: the detonation of a plutonium-fueled bomb that its creators had named Trinity. The explosion–a blinding flash of light, probably brighter than any ever seen on earth, followed by a huge, billowing mushroom cloud–created a vast crater in the barren desert.

ATOMIC WARFARE

News of the explosion reached President Harry S. Truman (who had taken office in April on the death of Roosevelt) in Potsdam, Germany, where he was attending a conference of Allied leaders. He issued an ultimatum to Japan (signed jointly by the British) demanding that they surrender by August 3 or face complete devastation. The Japanese premier wanted to accept the Allied demand, but he still could not persuade the military leaders to agree. There was a hint from Tokyo that the government might agree to surrender, in return for a promise that the Japan could retain its emperor. The American government, firmly committed to the idea of "unconditional surrender," dismissed those proposals. They were convinced (perhaps correctly) that the moderates who were making the peace overtures did not have the power to deliver them. When the deadline passed with no surrender, Truman ordered the air force to use the new atomic weapons against Japan.

Controversy has raged for decades over whether Truman's decision to use the bomb was justified and what his motives were. Some people have argued that the atomic attack was

Discussion and Activities

Evaluating Evidence Have students read the section "The Manhattan Project." Ask them to create a T-chart listing examples of the scientific and military value of the Manhattan Project. Have students draw a conclusion about which category was more significant. **WOR** **WXT**

THE EMPEROR SURVEYS THE RUINS In the aftermath of the American firebombing of Tokyo, which caused as much damage and death as the atomic bomb attacks on Hiroshima and Nagasaki, and just before the formal Japanese surrender in September 1945, Emperor Hirohito—previously visible to most Japanese people only in formal portraits—walked through the ruins of the city and allowed himself to be photographed. This photograph is widely considered the first picture of the emperor to reveal any expression on his face. It was taken by Carl Mydans, a photographer for *Life* magazine.

Discussion and Activities

Evaluating Evidence Have students read the section "Debating the Bomb's Use." Ask them to create a T-chart listing arguments in favor of and opposing the use of the atomic bomb on Japan. Have students identify what they believe to be the most persuasive argument for and against. **WOR** **WXT**

DEBATING THE BOMB'S USE

unnecessary, that had the United States agreed to the retention of the emperor (which it ultimately did agree to, in any case), or waited only a few more weeks, the Japanese government would have surrendered. Others argue that nothing less than the atomic bombs could have persuaded the hard-line military leaders of Japan to surrender without a costly American invasion. Some critics of the decision, including some of the scientists involved in the Manhattan Project, have argued that whatever the Japanese intentions, the United States, as a matter of morality, should not have used the terrible new weapon. One horrified physicist wrote the president shortly before the attack: "This thing must not be permitted to exist on this earth. We must not be the most hated and feared people in the world."

The nation's military and political leaders, however, showed little concern about such matters. Truman, who had not even known of the existence of the Manhattan Project until he became president, was apparently making what he believed to be a simple military decision. A weapon was available that would end the war quickly; he could see no reason not to use it.

Still more controversy has existed over whether there were other motives at work behind Truman's decision. With the Soviet Union poised to enter the war in the Pacific, did the United States want to end the conflict quickly to forestall an expanded communist presence in Asia? Did Truman use the bomb to intimidate Stalin, with whom he was engaged in difficult negotiations, so that the Soviet leader would accept American demands? Little direct evidence is available to support (or definitively refute) either of these accusations.

HIROSHIMA

On August 6, 1945, an American B-29, the *Enola Gay*, dropped an atomic weapon on the Japanese industrial center at Hiroshima. With a single bomb, the United States completely incinerated a four-square-mile area at the center of the previously undamaged city. More than 80,000 civilians died, according to later American estimates. Many more survived to suffer the crippling effects of radioactive fallout or to pass those effects on to their children in the form of birth defects.

NAGASAKI

The Japanese government, stunned by the attack, was at first unable to agree on a response. Two days later, on August 8, the Soviet Union declared war on Japan. And the following day, the United States sent another American plane to drop another atomic weapon–this time on the city of Nagasaki–causing more than 100,000 deaths in another unfortunate community. Finally, the emperor intervened to break the stalemate in the cabinet, and on August 14 the government announced that it was ready to give up. On September 2, 1945, on board the American battleship *Missouri*, anchored in Tokyo Bay, Japanese officials signed the articles of surrender.

The most catastrophic war in the history of mankind had come to an end, and the United States had emerged not only victorious but in a position of unprecedented power, influence, and prestige as well. It was a victory, however, that few could greet with unambiguous joy. Fourteen million combatants had died in the struggle. As many as 40 million civilians may have died–mostly from bombings, from disease and starvation, from genocidal campaigns of extermination. The United

Discussion and Activities

Historical Significance and Argumentation After students have read the section "Nagasaki," ask them to discuss as a class whether the benefits of using atomic bombs against Japan was worth the cost. **WOR** **WXT** **PCE**

Discussion and Activities

Analyzing Points of View Have students examine the image "Nagasaki Survivors." Ask them to write a short paragraph describing what they think the experience of the people pictured in the photo was probably like on the day the photo was taken, and to speculate about what their lives were like immediately after the bombing. **SOC**

DEBATING THE PAST

THE DECISION TO DROP THE ATOMIC BOMB

In the fall of 1994, the Air and Space Museum of the Smithsonian Institution in Washington, D.C., installed in its main hall the fuselage of the *Enola Gay*, the airplane that dropped the first atomic bomb ever used in warfare. It was used in 1945 on the Japanese city of Hiroshima. Originally, the airplane was to have been accompanied by an exhibit that would include discussions of the many popular and academic controversies over whether the United States should have used the bomb. But a powerful group of critics demanded that the exhibit should reflect only the "official" explanation of the decision. In the end, the museum decided to mount no exhibit at all. The *Enola Gay* hangs in the Smithsonian today without any explanation for the millions of tourists who see it each year.

The furor that surrounded the *Enola Gay* exhibit reflects the passions that the bombing of Hiroshima and Nagasaki continue to arouse among people around the world. It also reflects the continuing debate since 1945 among historians about how to explain and evaluate President Truman's decision to use the atomic bomb in the war against Japan.

Truman himself, both at the time and in his 1955 memoir, insisted that the decision was a simple and straightforward one. The alternative to using atomic weapons, he claimed, was an invasion of mainland Japan that might have cost as many as a million American lives. Given that choice, he said, the decision was easy. "I regarded the bomb as a military weapon and never had any doubt that it should be used." Truman's explanation of his decision has been supported by the accounts of many of his contemporaries: Secretary of War Henry Stimson, Winston Churchill, and several of Truman's senior military advisers. It has also received considerable support from historians. Herbert Feis argued in *The Atomic Bomb and the End of World War II* (1966) that Truman had made his decision on purely military grounds—to ensure a speedy American victory. David McCullough, author of the popular biography Truman, published in 1992, also accepted Truman's own account of his actions largely uncritically, as did Alonzo L. Hamby in *Man of the People* (1995), an important scholarly study of Truman. "One consideration weighed most heavily on Truman," Hamby concluded. "The longer the war lasted, the more Americans killed." Robert J. Donovan, author of an extensive history of the Truman presidency, *Conflict and Crisis* (1977), reached the same conclusion: "The simple reason Truman made the decision to drop the bomb was to end the war quickly and save lives."

Other scholars have strongly disagreed. As early as 1948, a British physicist, P. M. S. Blackett, wrote in *Fear, War, and the Bomb* that the destruction of Hiroshima and Nagasaki was "not so much the last military act of the second World War as the first major operation of the cold diplomatic war with Russia."

An important critic of Truman's decision is the historian Gar Alperovitz, the author of two influential books on the subject: *Atomic Diplomacy: Hiroshima and Potsdam* (1965) and *The Decision to Use the Atomic Bomb and the Architecture of an American Myth* (1995). Alperovitz dismissed the argument that the bomb was used to shorten the war and save lives. Japan was likely to have surrendered soon even if the bomb had not been used, he claimed. Instead, he argued, the United States used the bomb less to influence Japan than to intimidate the Soviet Union. Truman made his decision to bomb Hiroshima following a discouraging meeting with Stalin at Potsdam. He was heavily influenced, therefore, by his belief that America needed a new way to force Stalin to change his behavior, "to make Russia more manageable in Europe."

Martin J. Sherwin, in *A World Destroyed* (1975), argued similarly that the danger Stalin posed to the peace made American policymakers aware that the effective use of atomic weapons could help strengthen the American hand in the nation's critical relationship with the Soviet Union.

NAGASAKI SURVIVORS **A Japanese woman and child look grimly at a photographer as they hold pieces of bread in the aftermath of the dropping of the second American atomic bomb—this one on Nagasaki.**

John W. Dower's *War Without Mercy* (1986) contributed, by implication at least, to another controversial explanation of the American decision: racism. Throughout World War II, many Americans looked upon the Japanese people as members of an almost bestial race, almost a subhuman species. And while Dower himself stops short of saying so, other historians have suggested that this racialized image of the Japanese people contributed to American willingness to drop atomic bombs on Japanese cities. Even many of Truman's harshest critics, however, note that it is, as Alperovitz has written, "all but impossible to find specific evidence that racism was an important factor in the decision to attack Hiroshima and Nagasaki."

The debate over the decision to drop the atomic bomb is an unusually emotional one, and it has inspired bitter professional and personal attacks on advocates of almost every position. It illustrates clearly how history has often been, and remains, a powerful force in the way societies define their politics, their values, and their character.

HISTORICAL THINKING SKILLS

Questions assume cumulative content knowledge from this chapter and previous chapters.

1. **Identifying Historical Developments** Identify the broad schools of historical interpretation regarding dropping the atomic bomb.
2. **Determining Context** Describe how one piece of historical evidence, from the time period, could be used to support each of the broad schools of historical interpretation concerning the decision to drop the atomic bomb.
3. **Developing Arguments** Analyze which school of thought you find most convincing and explain why using evidence from the text to support your argument.

Answers

Debating the Past

1. Debates over the decision to drop the bomb fell into two general camps. First there were those who supported the decision as a war-ending strategy that saved American lives and prevented the necessity of a ground invasion of Japan. Others maintain it showed the Soviet Union the power of the U.S. and gave America the advantage in the Cold War that followed. Dower argued that Americans saw the Japanese people as inferior which made dropping the atomic bomb easier.
2. First, the Japanese had shown no proclivity to surrender. Secondly, Truman was influenced by Soviet positioning, following a concerning meeting with Stalin at Potsdam. Finally, the famous political cartoons of the era show a concerted racial bias against Japanese people.
3. Student responses will vary. They may mention that the fact that Japanese soldiers were willing to die and sacrifice their lives for the emperor or that the United States had a responsibility to end the war without more American lives lost.

States had suffered only light casualties in comparison with many other nations, but the cost had still been high: 322,000 dead, another 800,000 injured. And despite the sacrifices, the world continued to face an uncertain future, menaced by the threat of nuclear warfare and by the emerging antagonism between the world's two strongest nations–the United States and the Soviet Union–that would darken the peace for many decades to come.

CHAPTER 27 REVIEW

CONNECTING THEMES

Chapter Twenty-Seven focused on the conduct of World War II and the impact of the war on every aspect of American society. The war ended the Great Depression and created an industrial boom, which raised incomes and created opportunities for African Americans, Mexican Americans, and American women. But discrimination and prejudice remained prevalent, even in the military where difficult questions about racial segregation arose.

The United States began World War II as a second-tier military power but emerged as a superpower. This important shift for the United States set the stage for a bitter rivalry with the other great superpower to arise from the war, the Soviet Union. The Cold War would pose major challenges to America's political, cultural, educational, and social institutions during the next half-century.

You should consider the following questions as you review the themes for this chapter:

- How did World War II reshape American identity?
- How did World War II alter the makeup and organization of the labor force in the United States?
- What changes to internal and external migration patterns in the United States were instigated by World War II?
- How did World War II change the political landscape of the United States?
- What were the causes and effects of the United States becoming a dominant world power?
- How did the development of atomic energy impact physical and human geography?
- Why did World War II lead to debates over traditional American values?

KEY TERMS

atomic bomb 758
A. Philip Randolph 747
Battle of the Bulge 755
braceros 748
Colossus II 747
Congress of Racial Equality (CORE) 747
D-Day 755
Dwight D. Eisenhower 755
Enola Gay 759
Enrico Fermi 758
Guadalcanal 737
Harry S. Truman 753
Hiroshima 759
Holocaust 740
Korematsu v. U.S. 753
Luftwaffe 755
Manhattan Project 758
Midway 737
Nisei unit 752
Office of Price Administration (OPA) 744
Okinawa 757
"relocation centers" 752
"Rosie the Riveter" 749
sonar 745
Vichy 739
zoot suits 748

Discussion and Activities

Evaluating Evidence Organize the class into three groups. Assign one of the following to each group: the impact of the war on the U.S. military, the impact of the war on the U.S. economy, or the impact of the war on American society. Have each group prepare a short presentation to share with the rest of the class. **WOR** **WXT** **SOC** **ARC** **NAT**

Key Terms

Students should be familiar with the key terms and be able to define them in the context of American military participation during World War II and the impact of the war on the American economy and society. Encourage students to use these terms in performing review exercises and exam practice for this chapter.

Go Online Chapter 27 Content Review

Assessing Student Understanding Use the online assessment to assess student understanding of concepts and topics within the chapter. You can assign the ready-made Chapter 27 Content Review or create your own from available questions. This easy-to-use tool helps you design assessments that meet the needs of different types of learners.

Answers

Multiple Choice

1. C; **2.** D; **3.** A

Short Answer

4A) Possible answer: Millions of men enlisted in the military following the bombing of Pearl Harbor, leaving huge holes in the workforce. This hole was filled by millions of women.

4B) Possible answer: In the United States during the interwar period of the 1920s and 1930s, the lives of women went through a radical transformation. Women gained the right to vote through the 19th Amendment, and views about the roles of women in the home and workforce changed.

4C) Possible answer: Once servicemen returned from the war, the same women who had helped with the war effort were forced out of the workforce to ensure the returning veterans had jobs. Some women resented the treatment as they had discovered they enjoyed the new freedom they experienced during the war years.

5A) Possible answer: Women and African Americans contributed greatly to the success of the Allied war effort. Women enlisted in the women's corps, and African Americans also enlisted but in segregated units.

5B) Possible answer: Women were welcomed into the workforce. As millions of men enlisted, millions of women took their place, performing tasks that would have been considered off limits to them otherwise. African Americans, on the other hand, were forced to continue to live and work within a racially segregated world.

5C) Possible answer: Despite the contributions of African Americans during World War II, they still faced discrimination and segregation at home and in the armed forces, leading more people to question these practices and actively work against them.

AP EXAM PRACTICE

Questions assume cumulative content knowledge from this chapter and previous chapters.

MULTIPLE CHOICE

Use the poster on page 749 and your knowledge of U.S. history to answer questions 1-3.

1. In what way does the poster provide evidence that World War II ended the Great Depression in the United States?
   (A) Women were finally allowed to work and thus expanded the economy.
   (B) The government funded the war through expanded taxation.
   (C) The demands of the wartime economy created an abundance of jobs.
   (D) The United States's refusal to enter the war allowed trade to continue.

2. What does the poster most indicate about the role of women in the war effort?
   (A) Women were focused on traditional roles on the home front.
   (B) Women were able to fill traditionally male jobs in the military.
   (C) Women occupied leadership positions in government agencies and elected offices.
   (D) Women filled important jobs in heavy industry to build war materials.

3. Workforce demands at the start of the war were complicated by
   (A) racial tensions caused by discrimination against African Americans.
   (B) women's refusal to seek employment to support the war effort.
   (C) employers' rejection of job applicants from rural communities.
   (D) the government's refusal to cooperate with the private sector to meet wartime demand.

SHORT ANSWER

Use your knowledge of U.S. history to answer questions 4 and 5.

4. Use the image on page 749 to answer A, B, and C.
   (A) Briefly describe ONE specific historical context of the image "Women at War."
   (B) Briefly explain ONE specific cause, during the period 1920 to 1940, that led to the development depicted in the image "Women at War."
   (C) Briefly explain ONE specific effect, from the period of the 1940s and 50s, that resulted from the development depicted in the image "Women at War."

5. Answer A, B, and C.
   (A) Describe ONE specific similarity in the experience of women and African Americans during the 1940s.
   (B) Describe ONE specific difference in the experience of women and African Americans during the 1940s.
   (C) Explain ONE specific historical effect that resulted from the experience of African Americans during World War II.

LONG ESSAY

Develop a thoughtful and thorough historical argument that addresses the statement. Begin your essay with a thesis statement, and support it with specific historical evidence and examples.

6. Evaluate the extent that World War II contributed to the end of the Great Depression in the United States.

Answers

Long Essay

6. Possible thesis: American businesses were supplying U.S. allies and the military in ways that continued postwar, effectively ending the Great Depression. This, more than the New Deal, led to the United States pulling itself out of the global economic depression. Specific historical evidence: World War II led to a tremendous economic boom within the United States. European countries scrambled to buy military weapons and equipment. The federal government, in order to supply forces with equipment and weapons, also purchased millions of supplies from U.S. businesses. The war did not damage industry and infrastructure in the United States as it did in Europe, allowing the U.S. to continue to supply Europe as it rebuilt.

UNIT 7 AP EXAM PRACTICE

AP EXAM PRACTICE

As you answer the questions, consider how the historical developments, processes, and individuals in Unit 7 connect to those in previous units.

MULTIPLE CHOICE

Use the image on page 616 and your knowledge of U.S. history to answer questions 1-3.

1. The foreign policy approach embraced by Theodore Roosevelt, as portrayed in the political cartoon, can be best described as
   (A) concerned with establishing America as a power among "civilized" nations.
   (B) focused primarily on American economic interests.
   (C) centered on the spread of democracy.
   (D) focused on removing American military forces from entanglements in Asia.

2. Roosevelt's approach to foreign policy was best illustrated by his decision to
   (A) send American troops to Cuba after the sinking of the USS *Maine*.
   (B) issue the Roosevelt Corollary which fundamentally altered U.S. relationships in Latin America.
   (C) end the military conflict with the Filipino people and recognize their independence.
   (D) protect Columbian control over Panama amidst French efforts to build the Panama Canal.

3. President Taft's foreign policy approach centered around the concept that
   (A) the U.S. should advance human rights and democracy around the world.
   (B) America should avoid possession of permanent territories and protectorates.
   (C) all actions should benefit the American economy.
   (D) demonstrations of American military strength facilitated treaty efforts.

Use the image on page 628 and your knowledge of U.S. history to answer questions 4-6.

4. Which significant social change in early 20th century American is most clearly represented in the photograph?
   (A) the sharp rise in ethnic tensions among communities in the urban North
   (B) the "Great Migration" of African Americans from the rural South to the industrial North
   (C) the desegregation policies in the South
   (D) the dramatic surge in American cultural production modeled after European styles

5. The rise of communities like those represented in the photograph best demonstrate
   (A) public enthusiasm for embracing a vision of self-determination and peace in the aftermath of World War I.
   (B) increased job opportunities following World War I.
   (C) greater personal freedom following World War I.
   (D) poor economic conditions due to economic strains of World War I.

6. The growth of the communities like those represented in the photograph created conditions for
   (A) racial and ethnic integration.
   (B) expanded tenement settlements.
   (C) a wave of public recognitions of women's rights.
   (D) an explosion of African American cultural achievement.

Discussion and Activities

Continuity and Change Direct students' attention to the Questions to Consider posed at the beginning of Unit 7:

- What were the continuities and changes within American foreign policy during the first half of the twentieth century?
- What were the reasons for and effects of the rise of a Progressive movement in the first decade of the twentieth century?
- What major issues propelled the cultural wars during the first half of the twentieth century in the United States?

Discuss these questions as a class to review important concepts from the unit. To close the discussion, **ask:** What was the most important development in the United States from 1890–1945?

Answers

Multiple Choice

1. A; **2.** B; **3.** C; **4.** B; **5.** B; **6.** D; **7.** B; **8.** B; **9.** C; **10.** B

Answers

Short Answer

11A) Possible answer: The WPA created murals between 1935 and 1943. At the start of World War II, everyone had a part to play in the mobilization of the home front. The mural shows both black and white men engaged in welding, which was used to help build the military machine of the United States.

11B) Possible answer: African Americans continued to face segregation and discrimination during the first half of the twentieth century in the United States. The *Plessy* decision ensured that a segregated society would be the norm and constitutionally protected throughout the entire country.

11C) Possible answer: Beginning in the twentieth century, many African Americans participated in the Great Migration, where they left the South for economic opportunities in the North. Unfortunately, they still faced extreme discrimination and racism in the North. The emergence of the "Harlem Renaissance" saw a new sense of pride and opportunity for many African Americans.

Use the chart on page 707 and your knowledge of U.S. history to answer questions 7 and 8.

7. Which New Deal programs most directly impacted the trend illustrated by the chart in the period between 1933 and 1936?
   (A) establishment of old age pensions through the Social Security Act
   (B) establishment of work relief programs such as the Civilian Conservation Corps
   (C) establishment of a more stable banking system through the Emergency Banking Act
   (D) establishment of programs for more effective agriculture through the Agricultural Adjustment Act

8. What American approach to World War II most likely accounts for the trends illustrated by the chart?
   (A) The United States prioritized sending overwhelming numbers of military personnel to all battlefront locations.
   (B) The United States prioritized helping its Allies through significant industrial production as the Arsenal of Democracy.
   (C) The United States successfully avoided joining in military conflicts in Asia, concentrating troops in Europe.
   (D) The United States limited industrial production.

Use the image on page 730 and your knowledge of U.S. history to answer questions 9 and 10.

9. German actions, like those in the photograph, significantly impacted the U.S. foreign policy debates concerning
   (A) increasing imports from belligerent nations.
   (B) continued implementation of Manifest Destiny.
   (C) isolationism vs. intervention.
   (D) imperialism vs. anti-imperialism.

10. Which of the following best describes a characteristic of America's war effort in World War II?
    (A) The creation of patriotic campaigns that focused on the destitution of the Great Depression.
    (B) A commitment by Americans to advance democratic ideals abroad.
    (C) A commitment by Americans to remain neutral in judgment about the motivations of various belligerent nations.
    (D) The conviction of Americans that early assistance to British allies had been foolish.

SHORT ANSWER

Use the image on page 708 and your knowledge of U.S. history to answer question 11.

11. Answer A, B, and C
    (A) Describe ONE specific historical context of the WPA mural.
    (B) Explain ONE specific historical continuity that African Americans faced during the first half of the twentieth century.
    (C) Explain ONE specific historical change that African Americans faced during the first half of the twentieth century.

ESSAY

Develop a thoughtful and thorough historical argument that addresses the statement. Begin your essay with a thesis statement, and support it with specific historical evidence and examples.

12. Evaluate the extent of continuities in U.S. foreign policy from 1890 to 1950.

Answers

Long Essay

12. Possible thesis: America tried at times to maintain the tradition established by Washington with the Farewell Address yet became involved in conflicts based largely on expansionist ideals along with world wars. Specific historical evidence: In 1898 the United States declared war on Spain, and America took its seat at the imperialistic table with many European countries. Roosevelt, Taft, and Wilson all viewed the country from a diplomatic standpoint, but each had their own vision as to what that specific diplomacy should look like. It was Wilson's vision, with the League of Nations, which would have radically shifted the international relationship of the U.S. to the rest of the world, but Congress pushed back. The economic woes of the Great Depression led to many changes across Europe and Asia that would eventually bring America into another world war.

Pacing Guide

Unit 8 explores key concepts from Period 8: 1945–1980 of the AP U.S. History Curriculum Framework. It is recommended that 10–17% of the total instruction time for the entire course be spent on Period 8.

Key Concepts

8.1 The United States responded to an uncertain and unstable postwar world by asserting and working to maintain a position of global leadership, with far-reaching domestic and international consequences.

8.2 New movements for civil rights and liberal efforts to expand the role of government generated a range of political and cultural responses.

8.3 Postwar economic and demographic changes had far-reaching consequences for American society, politics, and culture.

UNIT 8: 1945–1980

THEMATIC LEARNING OBJECTIVES

- Analyze the major causes and effects of the Cold War from 1945 to 1980.
- Explain the significance of the rise of a modern civil rights movement during the second half of the twentieth century.
- Evaluate the reasons for and consequences of the Korean and Vietnam Wars.
- Assess the significance of the rise of the "New Left" and the counterculture movement in the United States following World War II.
- Identify continuities and changes in the role of government in the economy during the second half of the twentieth century.

QUESTIONS TO CONSIDER

- What were the major causes and effects of the Cold War following World War II?
- What were the major continuities and changes during the modern civil rights movement in the second half of the twentieth century?
- What were the major causes and effects of the counterculture movement in the United States following World War II?

HISTORICAL DEVELOPMENTS: 1945–1980

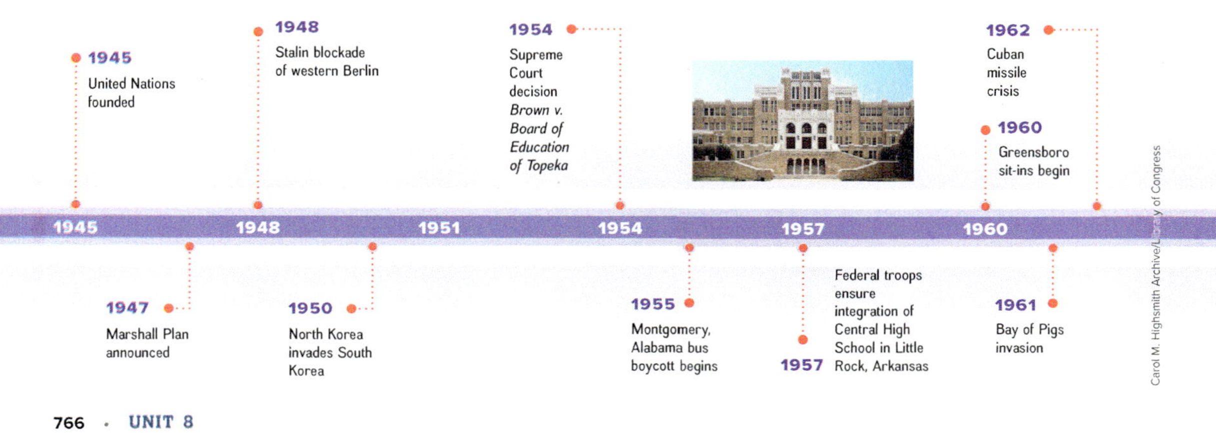

1945 United Nations founded
1948 Stalin blockade of western Berlin
1954 Supreme Court decision Brown v. Board of Education of Topeka
1962 Cuban missile crisis
1960 Greensboro sit-ins begin
1945
1948
1951
1954
1957
1960
1947 Marshall Plan announced
1950 North Korea invades South Korea
1955 Montgomery, Alabama bus boycott begins
1957 Federal troops ensure integration of Central High School in Little Rock, Arkansas
1961 Bay of Pigs invasion
Carol M. Highsmith Archive/Library of Congress

Discussion and Activities

Evaluating Evidence Have students examine the time line "Historical Developments: 1945–1980." **Ask:** Based on the time line and what you already know, which events on the time line appear to deal with social, economic, diplomatic, or political issues? *(Social: Supreme Court decision Brown v. Board of Education of Topeka, Montgomery, Alabama, bus boycott, Greensboro sit-ins begin, NOW founded, Stonewall "Riots,"; Diplomatic: United Nations founded, SALT I Treaty; Political: Voting Rights Act, Roe v. Wade; Economic: March on Washington).* Which category seems to be most prevalent? **PCE** **WXT** **SOC**

MAKING CONNECTIONS

Unit Eight focuses on the period from 1945 to 1980. After World War II, the relationship between the United States and the Soviet Union deteriorated and the rivalry known as the Cold War developed. To stop the spread of communism, the United States pursued a foreign policy of containment, which drove U.S. intervention in military conflicts around the world, including in South Korea and Vietnam.

American society underwent great changes following World War II. The post-war baby boom, increased housing demand, and government spending helped create a thriving economy by the 1950s. Many Americans had more disposable income than ever before, which altered the social and physical landscape of the United States. America became a country dominated by the suburb, as families flooded to the outskirts of major cities. Two technological innovations, the television and the automobile, helped drive the demographic shift. The automobile provided Americans the ability to travel greater distances and to live outside the cities where they worked. The television, with its ever increasing homogenization of American society and culture, extolled the suburb as an ideal utopia. But while the suburb offered solace to many white Americans, it excluded African Americans. Racial minorities, rural Americans, and most elderly also failed to share fully in the new prosperity of the postwar era.

Decades of efforts by African Americans to end school segregation contributed to the Supreme Court decision in *Brown v. Board of Education of Topeka* that overturned the precedent of "separate but equal." The modern civil rights movement gained strength through the 1960s with large scale protests. Other minorities, inspired by the modern civil rights movement, also advocated for equal rights and opportunities. Native American and Latino American movements struggled with cohesion, but brought increased political and economic power. The women's movement, energized by the new feminism, significantly changed women's role in society as they made progress in business and politics.

The various civil rights movements along with the "New Left" and counterculture challenged the traditional norms of American society. To some conservative Americans, this came at the cost of stability and order within society. Opposition to the Vietnam War also contributed to a greater distrust of the military and the federal government. Richard Nixon capitalized on the domestic disorder and growing opposition to the Vietnam War to win the presidency in 1968. Relations with China and the Soviet Union improved under Nixon and the Cold War waned, but the Watergate crisis resulted in his resignation in the middle of his second term in office. The Watergate crisis also left the American public more divided and more distrustful of the government than ever.

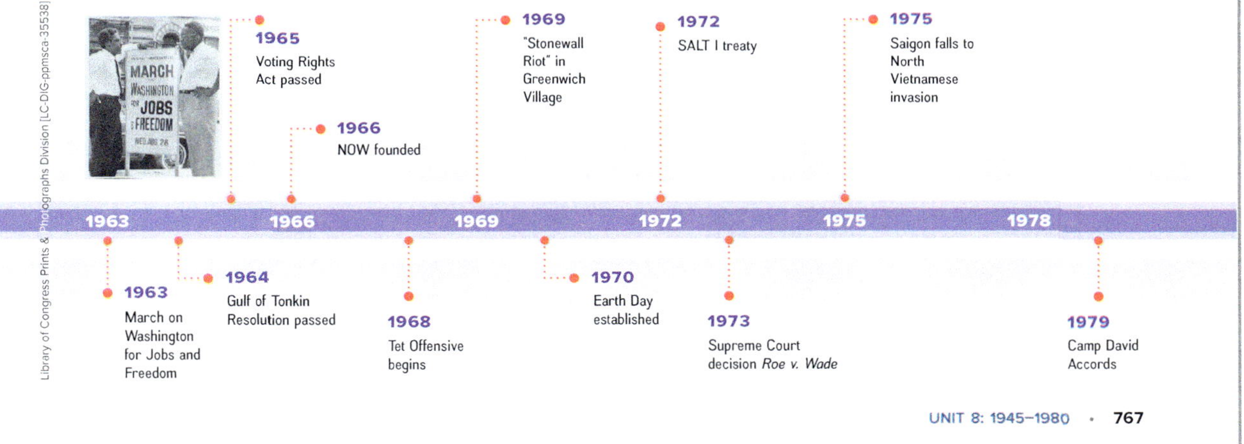

MARCH
WASHINGTON
JOBS
FREEDOM
1965
Voting Rights Act passed
1966
NOW founded
1969
"Stonewall Riot" in Greenwich Village
1972
SALT I treaty
1975
Saigon falls to North Vietnamese invasion
1963
1966
1969
1972
1975
1978
1963
March on Washington for Jobs and Freedom
1964
Gulf of Tonkin Resolution passed
1968
Tet Offensive begins
1970
Earth Day established
1973
Supreme Court decision *Roe v. Wade*
1979
Camp David Accords

Library of Congress Prints & Photographs Division [LC-DIG-ppmsca-35538]

Historical Thinking Skills

Contextualization Have students read the section "Making Connections." Discuss as a class the state of the nation as of 1945. *(end of World War II; demobilization of the armed forces; division and rebuilding of Europe; tension with the Soviet Union)* **PCE** **NAT** **ARC** **WXT** **SOC** **WOR**

Go Online Additional Resources

Adaptive Learning with SmartBook A proven adaptive learning program, SmartBook offers an interactive environment that helps students learn faster, study more efficiently, and retain more knowledge.

Assign this resource to differentiate instruction for students and report on year-long progression.

Pacing Guide

Chapter 28 explores key concepts from Period 8: 1945–1980 of the AP U.S. History Curriculum Framework. The suggested instruction time for Chapter 28 is 4 days.

Key Concepts

8.1.I U.S. policymakers engaged in a cold war with the authoritarian Soviet Union, seeking to limit the growth of Communist military power and ideological influence, create a free-market global economy, and build an international security system.

8.1.II Cold War policies led to public debates over the power of the federal government and acceptable means for pursuing international and domestic goals while protecting civil liberties.

28 THE EARLY COLD WAR

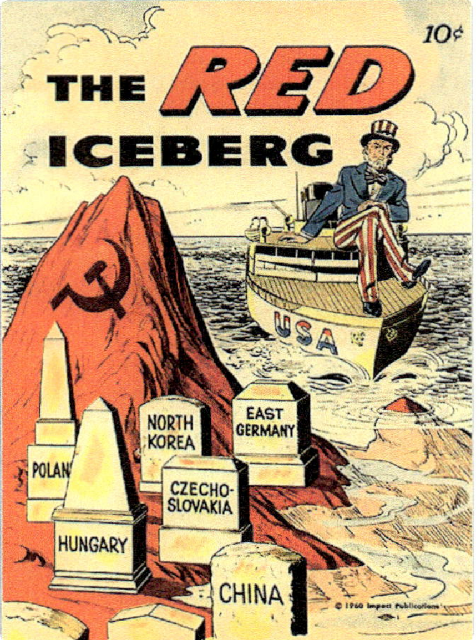

THE RED ICEBERG This magazine cover suggests how much attention was directed to the threat of communism. The illustration depicts the Soviet Union as the red iceberg that sank, or influenced, communism in Poland, Hungary, North Korea, Czechoslovakia, East Germany, and China. The United States is shown heading toward the tip of an iceberg to indicate the threat communism posed.

CONNECTING CONCEPTS

Chapter Twenty-Eight begins by examining the controversial origins of the Cold War, which at heart reflected a fundamental difference in the ways the great powers envisioned the aftermath of World War II. The United States saw a world in which nations abandoned their traditional beliefs in military alliances and pursued peace through international organizations like the United Nations. The Soviet Union foresaw a future where great powers would continue to dominate areas of strategic interest. The two nations had a common interest in defeating Germany during the war, but serious strains in the alliance became apparent at the Yalta and Potsdam conferences.

After the surrender of Japan, the United States developed a policy known as containment, which sought to prevent the further expansion of Soviet influence. The Truman Doctrine offered military aid to nations facing communist aggression; the Marshall Plan offered economic assistance to Western Europe, which formed the North Atlantic Treaty Organization after the Berlin Blockade. Some conservatives opposed containment, but the National Security Act of 1947 created the Central Intelligence Agency while reshaping other military and diplomatic institutions. The invasion of South Korea by North Korea in 1950 seemed to confirm that communism was on the march, although the United States was able to halt the advance despite limited mobilization and the direct intervention of Chinese forces.

Dwight Eisenhower kept the United States at peace after the Korean War, but efforts to improve relations with the Soviet Union collapsed during the U-2 Incident. The threat of nuclear war with the Soviet Union heightened anxiety in the United States and around the world throughout the 1950s.

Discussion and Activities

Analyzing Visuals Have students examine the image "The Red Iceberg." Ask them to discuss in small groups the implications of the iceberg used in the cartoon. *(The implication is that the danger is far greater than it appears on the surface. The challenges represented in the cartoon are only the beginning of the challenges for the United States.)* **WOR** **PCE** **SOC**

As you read, you should:

- Evaluate the attempts by the United States to limit the extension of the Soviet Union's military and ideological expansion through a policy of military and economic containment.
- Analyze the foreign policy stance of the United Sates following World War II.
- Explain how decolonization of European colonies led to deteriorating relations between the United States and developing nations.
- Analyze the causes and effects of America's entry into the Korean War.
- Describe the effects of the threat of nuclear war following World War II.

ORIGINS OF THE COLD WAR

Few issues in twentieth-century American history have aroused more debate than the question of the origins of the Cold War. Some historians have claimed that Soviet duplicity and expansionism created the international tensions, while others have proposed that American provocations and imperial ambitions were at least equally to blame. Most historians agree, however, that wherever the preponderance of blame may lie, both the United States and the Soviet Union contributed to the atmosphere of hostility and suspicion that quickly clouded the peace.

Sources of Soviet-American Tension

At the heart of the rivalry between the United States and the Soviet Union in the 1940s was a fundamental difference in the ways the great powers envisioned the postwar world. One vision, first openly outlined in the Atlantic Charter in 1941, was of a world in which nations abandoned their traditional beliefs in military alliances and spheres of influence and governed their relations with one another through democratic processes, with an international organization serving as the arbiter of disputes and the protector of every nation's right of self-determination. That vision–inspired in part by Woodrow Wilson–appealed to many Americans, including Franklin Roosevelt.

America's Postwar Vision

The other vision was that of the Soviet Union and to some extent, it gradually became clear, of Great Britain. Both Stalin and Churchill had signed the Atlantic Charter. But Britain had always been uneasy about the implications of the self-determination ideal for its own enormous empire. And the Soviet Union was determined to create a secure sphere for itself in Central and Eastern Europe as protection against possible future aggression from the West. Both Churchill and Stalin, therefore, tended to envision a postwar structure in which the great powers would control areas of strategic interest to them, in which something vaguely similar to the traditional European balance of power would reemerge. Gradually, the differences between these two positions would turn the peacemaking process into a form of warfare.

Spheres of Influence

Wartime Diplomacy

Serious strains had already begun to develop in the alliance with the Soviet Union in January 1943, when Roosevelt and Churchill met in Casablanca, Morocco, to discuss Allied strategy. (Stalin had declined Roosevelt's invitation to attend.) The two leaders could not accept Stalin's most important demand–the immediate opening of a second front in western Europe. But they tried to reassure Stalin by announcing that they would accept nothing less than the unconditional surrender of the Axis powers, thus indicating that they would not negotiate a separate peace with Hitler and leave the Soviets to fight on alone.

In November 1943, Roosevelt and Churchill traveled to Teheran, Iran, for their first meeting with Stalin. By now, however, Roosevelt's most effective bargaining tool–Stalin's need for American assistance in his struggle against Germany–had been largely removed. The German advance against Russia had been halted; Soviet forces were now launching their own westward offensive. Nevertheless, the Teheran Conference seemed in most respects a success. Roosevelt and Stalin established a cordial personal relationship. Stalin agreed to an American request that the Soviet Union enter the war in the Pacific soon after the end of hostilities in Europe. Roosevelt, in turn, promised that an Anglo-American second front would be established within six months.

On other matters, however, the origins of future disagreements were already visible. Most important was the question of the future of Poland. Roosevelt and Churchill were willing to agree to a movement of the Soviet

Discussion and Activities

Historical Developments and Argumentation Have students read the section "Sources of Soviet-American Tension." Ask them to discuss in small groups how the post-war vision of the United States differed from that of its wartime allies. Have students evaluate whether the differences were primarily based on economic or political considerations. WOR PCE WXT

Go Online AP Exam Preparation

AP Exam Practice Use the online assessment to help prepare students for the AP Exam. You can assign the ready-made AP-style short-answer questions, document-based questions, and multiple-choice questions assessing concepts, themes, and skills from Period 8 and AP style long-essay questions organized in sets of 3 questions from various time periods. You can also create your own tests from available questions. This easy-to-use tool helps you design assessments that meet the needs of different types of learners.

Discussion and Activities

Analyzing Issues After students have read the section "Wartime Diplomacy," ask them to create a T-chart listing areas of agreement and disagreement between the United States and the Soviet Union at the Casablanca and Teheran conferences. **WOR** **PCE**

YALTA Churchill, Roosevelt, and Stalin (known during the war as the "Big Three") meet at Yalta in the Crimea in February 1945 to try to agree on the outlines of the peace that they knew was soon to come. Instead, they settled on a series of vague compromises that ultimately left all parties feeling betrayed.

Bettmann/Getty Images

border westward, allowing Stalin to annex some historically Polish territory. But on the nature of the postwar government in the rest of Poland, there were sharp differences. Roosevelt and Churchill supported the claims of the Polish government-in-exile that had been functioning in London since 1940; Stalin wished to install another pro-communist exiled government that had spent the war in Lublin, in the Soviet Union. The three leaders avoided a bitter conclusion to the Teheran Conference only by leaving the issue unresolved.

DISPUTE OVER POLAND

YALTA

More than a year later, in February 1945, Roosevelt joined Churchill and Stalin for a peace conference in the Soviet city of Yalta–a resort on the Black Sea that was once a summer palace for the tsars. On a number of issues, the "Big Three," as Roosevelt, Churchill, and Stalin were known, reached agreements. In return for Stalin's renewed promise to enter the Pacific war, Roosevelt agreed that the Soviet Union should receive some of the territory in the Pacific that Russia had lost in the 1904 Russo-Japanese War.

The negotiators also agreed to a plan for a new international organization, a plan that had been hammered out the previous summer at a conference in Washington, D.C., at the Dumbarton Oaks estate. The new United Nations would contain a General Assembly, in which every member would be represented, and a Security Council, with permanent representatives of the five major powers (the United States, Britain, France, the Soviet Union, and China), each of which would have veto power. The Security Council would also have temporary delegates from several other nations. These agreements became the basis of the United Nations charter, drafted at a conference of fifty nations beginning April 25, 1945, in San Francisco. The U.S. Senate ratified the charter in July by a vote of 80 to 2 (in striking contrast to the slow and painful defeat it had administered to the charter of the League of Nations twenty-five years before).

UNITED NATIONS

On other issues, however, the Yalta Conference produced no real accord. Basic disagreement remained about the postwar Polish government. Stalin, whose armies now occupied Poland, had already installed a government composed of the pro-communist "Lublin" Poles. Roosevelt and Churchill insisted that the pro-Western "London" Poles must be allowed a place in the Warsaw regime. Roosevelt envisioned a government based on free, democratic elections–which both he and Stalin recognized the pro-Western forces would win. Stalin agreed only to a vague compromise by which an unspecified number of pro-Western Poles would be granted a place in the government. He reluctantly consented to hold "free and unfettered elections" in Poland on an unspecified future date. They did not take place for almost fifty years.

Nor was there agreement about the future of Germany. Roosevelt seemed to want a reconstructed and reunited Germany. Stalin wanted to impose heavy reparations on Germany and to ensure a permanent dismemberment of the nation. The final agreement was, like the Polish accord, vague and unstable. The

DISAGREEMENTS OVER GERMANY

Reasoning Processes

Continuity and Change Have students read the section "United Nations." Discuss as a class why the United Nations charter was ratified easily, while the Treaty of Versailles that established the League of Nations was never ratified by the Senate. *(The United States assumed a new leadership role in world affairs after WWII in contrast to its retreat back to isolationism after WWI. Many in the United States believed that the nation had a responsibility imposed by its status as an economic and military superpower.)* **WOR** **PCE** **WXT**

decision on reparations would be referred to a future commission. The United States, Great Britain, France, and the Soviet Union would each control its own "zone of occupation" in Germany—the zones to be determined by the position of troops at the end of the war. Berlin, the German capital, was already well inside the Soviet zone, but because of its symbolic importance it would be divided into four sectors, one for each nation to occupy. At an unspecified date, Germany would be reunited; but there was no agreement on how the reunification would occur. As for the rest of Europe, the conference produced a murky accord on the establishment of governments "broadly representative of all democratic elements" and "responsible to the will of the people."

The Yalta accords, in other words, were less a settlement of postwar issues than a set of loose principles that sidestepped the most difficult questions. Roosevelt, Churchill, and Stalin returned home from the conference each apparently convinced that he had signed an important agreement. But the Soviet interpretation of the accords differed so sharply from the Anglo-American interpretation that the illusion endured only briefly. In the weeks following the Yalta Conference, Roosevelt watched with growing alarm as the Soviet Union moved systematically to establish pro-communist governments in one Central or Eastern European nation after another and as Stalin refused to make the changes in Poland that the president believed he had promised.

But Roosevelt did not abandon hope. Still believing the differences could be settled, he left Washington early in the spring for a vacation at his retreat in Warm Springs, Georgia. There, on April 12, 1945, he suffered a sudden, massive stroke and died.

THE COLLAPSE OF THE PEACE

Harry S. Truman, who succeeded Roosevelt in the presidency, had little familiarity with international issues. And he did not share Roosevelt's apparent faith in the flexibility of the Soviet Union. Roosevelt had hoped that Stalin was a reasonable man with whom an ultimate accord might be reached. Truman, in contrast, sided with those in the government (and there were many) who considered the Soviet Union fundamentally untrustworthy and who viewed Stalin with suspicion and even loathing.

THE FAILURE OF POTSDAM

TRUMAN'S "GET TOUGH" POLICY

Truman had been in office only a few days before he decided to, as he put it, "get tough" with the Soviet Union. Truman met on April 23 with Soviet foreign minister Molotov and sharply chastised him for violations of the Yalta accords. In fact, Truman had only limited leverage by which to compel the Soviet Union to carry out its agreements. Truman insisted that the United States should be able to get "85 percent" of what it wanted, but he was ultimately forced to settle for much less.

Truman conceded first on Poland. When Stalin made a few minor concessions to the pro-Western exiles, Truman recognized the Warsaw government, hoping that noncommunist forces might gradually expand their influence there. Until the 1980s, they did not. Other questions remained, above all the question of Germany. To settle them, Truman met in July at Potsdam, in Russian-occupied Germany, with Churchill (who, after elections in Britain in the midst of the talks, was replaced as prime minister by Clement Attlee) and Stalin. Truman reluctantly accepted the adjustments of the Polish-German border that Stalin had long demanded; he refused, however, to permit the Russians to claim any reparations from the American, French, and British zones of Germany. This stance effectively confirmed that Germany would remain divided, with the western zones united into one nation, friendly to the United States, and the Russian zone surviving as another nation, with a Soviet-dominated, communist government.

THE CHINA PROBLEM

CHIANG KAI-SHEK

Central to American hopes for an open, peaceful world "policed" by the great powers was a strong, independent China. But even before the war ended, the American government was aware that those hopes faced a major, perhaps insurmountable, obstacle: the Chinese government of Chiang Kai-shek. Chiang was generally friendly to the United States, but his government was corrupt and incompetent with feeble popular support, and Chiang was unable or unwilling to face the problems that were threatening to engulf him. Since 1927, the nationalist government he headed had been engaged in a prolonged and bitter rivalry with the communist armies of Mao Zedong. So successful had the communist challenge grown that Mao was in control of one-fourth of the population by 1945.

Some Americans urged the government to find a "third force" to support as an alternative to either Chiang or Mao. A few argued that the United States should try to reach some accommodation with Mao. Truman, however, decided reluctantly that he had no choice but to continue supporting Chiang. For the next several years, as the long struggle between the nationalists and the communists erupted into a full-scale civil war, the United States continued to send money and weapons to Chiang. Eventually, Truman sent General George Marshall, former army chief of staff and future secretary of state, to study the Chinese problem and recommend a policy for the United States. Many American friends in China—known generally as the China Lobby—pressured Marshall to expand the American military presence as a way to combat the continuing expansion of communist control. Marshall came to believe that nothing short of an all-out war with China would be necessary to defeat the communists, and he was unwilling to recommend that the president should accept such a war. That decision was the source of many embittered attacks on Marshall, Truman, and many others for decades to come.

Discussion and Activities

Analyzing Cause and Effect After students have read the section "Yalta," ask them to identify the important agreements reached at the Yalta Conference. Discuss as a class how and why those agreements disintegrated. **WOR** **PCE** **WXT**

Discussion and Activities

Analyzing Points of View Have students read the section "The Failure of Potsdam." Ask them to write a letter to President Truman from the point of view of an American citizen advising the president on his negotiating strategy with Stalin. **WOR**

Discussion and Activities

Speculating After students have read the feature "Origins of the Cold War," ask them to discuss in small groups how different the Cold War might have been if the United States had not used the atomic bomb during World War II. **WOR** **PCE** **WXT**

DEBATING THE PAST

ORIGINS OF THE COLD WAR

The Cold War may be over, but the debate over its origins is not.

For more than a decade after the end of World War II, few historians in the United States challenged the official American interpretation of the beginnings of the Cold War. Most students of the conflict agreed that relations with the Soviet Union broke down because Stalin violated the Yalta accords and because he was spreading communism throughout the world.

Not long after the war, as communism was spreading in Europe, George F. Kennan wrote an important telegraph arguing that the Soviet Union needed to be "contained," that while the United States should not invade communist nations it should work to stop their growing influence. Over time, he suggested, containment would weaken the Soviet Union.

In debates from the 1950s on, scholars began to offer different, more critical views about the Cold War. William Appleman Williams, writing in *The Tragedy of American Diplomacy* (1959), disagreed with the containment theory. The Cold War, he said, was simply the most recent version of a consistent American effort in the twentieth century to maintain an "open door" for American trade in world markets. According to Williams, the confrontation with the Soviet Union was less a response to Russian aggressive designs than an expression of the American belief in the necessity of capitalist expansion.

Later revisionists modified Williams's claims, but most accepted his basic outlook. The United States had been primarily to blame for the Cold War, many scholars asserted. Claims were made that the Soviet Union was too weak and exhausted at the end of World War II to pose a serious threat to America; that the United States used its nuclear monopoly to threaten and intimidate Stalin; that Harry Truman recklessly abandoned the conciliatory tone taken by Franklin Roosevelt (who died in 1945), taking instead a provocative hard line against the Russians. The Soviet response, these scholars asserted, reflected a legitimate fear of capitalist encirclement. Walter LaFeber, in *America, Russia, and the Cold War, 1945–1966* (1967 and later editions), maintained that America's supposedly idealistic internationalism at the close of the war was in reality an effort to ensure a world shaped in the American image that would guarantee its influence, especially regarding trade.

Ultimately, the revisionist interpretation began to produce a reaction of its own, a "post revisionist" view of the conflict. Some manifestations of this reaction consisted of little more than a reaffirmation of the traditional view of the Cold War, but the dominant works of post revisionist scholarship attempted to strike a balance between the two camps, to identify areas of blame and misperception on both sides of the conflict. Thomas G. Paterson, in *Soviet-American Confrontation* (1973), viewed Russian hostility and American efforts to dominate the postwar world as equally responsible for the Cold War. John Lewis Gaddis, in *The United States and the Origins of the Cold War, 1941–1947* (1972) and other works, similarly maintained that "neither side can bear sole responsibility for the onset of the Cold War." American policymakers, he argued, had only limited options because of the pressures of domestic politics. And Stalin was immobilized by his obsessive concern with maintaining his own power and ensuring absolute security for the Soviet Union. But if neither side was entirely to blame, Gaddis concluded, the Soviets must be held more accountable for the problems, for Stalin was in a much better position to compromise, given his broader power within his own government, than the politically hamstrung Truman. Melvyn Leffler's *Preponderance of Power* (1991) argued similarly that American policymakers genuinely believed in the existence of a Soviet threat and were determined to remain consistently stronger than the Soviets in response.

National Archives and Records Administration [NWDNS-342-AF-78460AC]

A more complex view of the Cold War has emerged out of the post revisionist literature. The Cold War, historians now suggest, was not so much the fault of one side or the other as it was the natural, perhaps inevitable, result of tensions between the world's two most powerful nations—nations that had been suspicious of, if not hostile toward, one another for nearly a century. "The United States and the Soviet Union were doomed to be antagonists," Ernest May wrote in 1984. "There probably was never any real possibility that the post-1945 relationship could be anything but hostility verging on conflict."

Since the fall of the Soviet Union in 1991, scholars have had access to Russian archives that have enriched—though not fundamentally changed—the way historians view the Cold War. John Lewis Gaddis, in *We Now Know: Rethinking Cold War History* (1998) and *The Cold War: A History* (2005), argues that the strong anticommunist positions of Margaret Thatcher, Ronald Reagan, and Pope John Paul II had a larger impact on the weakening of the Soviet Union than was previously understood. In *The Global Cold War* (2005), Arne Westad, also making use of the released archives, roots the origins of the dangerous instability in the so-called Third World in the frequent interventions of both the Soviet Union and the United States in the Cold War era. And John Lewis Gaddis, in *The Cold War: A History*, looks back on the Cold War that he chronicled for several decades in the midst of the Cold War. He argues that, despite all the anxieties it raised and all the violence it helped to create, the containment policy that shaped American foreign policy beginning in the mid-1940s was ultimately a significant success.

HISTORICAL THINKING SKILLS

Questions assume cumulative content knowledge from this chapter and previous chapters.

1. **Identifying Historical Developments** Identify three historical debates about the origins of the Cold War.
2. **Evaluating Evidence** Describe how historical evidence could be used to support each of the three broad schools of historical interpretation concerning the origins of the Cold War.
3. **Developing Arguments** Using historical evidence to develop your argument, analyze the school of thought you find most convincing.

772 · CHAPTER 28

Answers

Debating the Past

1. Possible answer: Kennan argued that the U.S. should work to "contain" communism. Williams argued that the Cold War was the result of a consistent effort by the U.S. to maintain an "open door" trade policy. Gaddis argued that the Cold War was a combination of U.S. efforts to dominate the post-World War II world and the Soviets' desire to strengthen its position in the world.
2. Possible answer: The Marshall Plan and the Truman Doctrine were both part of containment strategies. The global interventions of both the United States and the Soviet Union illustrate the drive for dominance and the purported desire to eliminate roadblocks to trade.
3. Possible answer: Student responses will vary. They may mention that containment was the ideology that drove much of U.S. foreign policy. Students may also support their argument with examples of U.S. military engagement or diplomatic efforts that were designed to promote democratic and capitalistic structures.

Instead, the American government was beginning to consider an alternative to China as the strong, pro-Western force in Asia: a revived Japan. Abandoning the strict occupation policies of the first years after the war (when General Douglas MacArthur had governed the nation), the United States lifted restrictions on industrial development and encouraged rapid economic growth in Japan. The vision of an open, united world was giving way in Asia, as it was in Europe, to an acceptance of a divided world with a strong, pro-American sphere of influence.

RESTORING JAPAN

THE CONTAINMENT DOCTRINE

By the end of 1945, any realistic hope of a postwar world constructed according to the Atlantic Charter ideals that Roosevelt and Churchill had agreed upon was in shambles. Instead, a new American policy, known as containment, was slowly emerging. Rather than attempting to create a unified, "open" world, the United States and its allies would work to "contain" the threat of further Soviet expansion.

The new doctrine emerged in part as a response to events in Europe in 1946. In Turkey, Stalin was trying to win control over the vital sea lanes to the Mediterranean. In Greece, communist forces were threatening the pro-Western government. The British had announced they could no longer provide assistance. Faced with these challenges, Truman decided to enunciate a firm new policy. In doing so, he drew from the ideas of the influential American diplomat George F. Kennan, who had warned not long after the war that the only appropriate diplomatic approach to dealing with the Soviet Union was "a long-term, patient but firm and vigilant containment of Russian expansive tendencies." On March 12, 1947, Truman appeared before Congress and used Kennan's warnings as the basis of what became known as the Truman Doctrine. "I believe," he argued, "that it must be the policy of the United States to support free peoples who are resisting attempted subjugation by armed minorities or by outside pressures." In the same speech he requested $400 million–part of it to bolster the armed forces of Greece and Turkey, another part to provide economic assistance to Greece. Congress quickly approved the measure.

TRUMAN DOCTRINE

The American commitment ultimately helped ease Soviet pressure on Turkey and helped the Greek government defeat the communist insurgents. More important, it established a basis for American foreign policy that would survive for more than forty years.

THE MARSHALL PLAN

An integral part of the containment policy was a proposal to aid in the economic reconstruction of Western Europe. There were many motives: humanitarian concern for the European people; a fear that Europe would remain an economic drain on the United States if it could not quickly rebuild and begin to feed itself; a desire for a strong European market for American goods. But above all, American policymakers believed that unless something could be done to strengthen the shaky pro-American governments in Western Europe, those governments might fall under the control of rapidly growing domestic communist parties.

REBUILDING EUROPE

In June 1947, therefore, Secretary of State George C. Marshall announced a plan to provide economic assistance to all European nations (including the Soviet Union) that would join in drafting a program for recovery. Although Russia and its Eastern satellites quickly and predictably rejected the plan, sixteen Western European nations eagerly participated. Whatever domestic opposition to the plan there was in the United States largely vanished after a sudden coup in Czechoslovakia in February 1948 that established a Soviet-dominated communist government there. In April, Congress approved the creation of the Economic Cooperation Administration, the agency that would administer the Marshall Plan, as it became known. Over the next three years, the Marshall Plan channeled over $12 billion of American aid into Europe, helping to spark a substantial economic revival. By the end of 1950, European industrial production had risen 64 percent, communist strength in the member nations had declined, and opportunities for American trade had revived.

SALUTING THE MARSHALL PLAN In another age, a chimney spouting smoke would evoke environmental damage. But in the aftermath of World War II, the rebuilding of Europe's industrial capacity was a great achievement—helped by (and celebrated by) the United States and the Marshall Plan.

Historical Thinking Skills

Argumentation After students have read the section "The China Problem," ask them to write a letter to the editor arguing for a specific policy to pursue with respect to China. WOR PCE WXT

Reasoning Processes

Continuity and Change Have students read the section "The Containment Doctrine." Discuss as a class how the Truman Doctrine represented a continuity or change from previous American foreign policy. *(Continuity: anti-communism dating back to refusal to recognize the Soviet Union until 1933. Change: long-term, open-ended commitment to use U.S. military and economic power in foreign countries departed from previous isolationism.)* WOR

Discussion and Activities

Making Connections Have students read the section "Mobilization at Home." Discuss as a class how the expanded powers of the government described in the text are similar to or different from governmental powers implemented to deal with current issues, such as terrorism. **WOR** **PCE**

Mobilization at Home

That the United States had accepted a continuing commitment to the containment policy became clear in 1947 and 1948 through a series of measures designed to maintain American military power at near wartime levels. In 1948, at President Truman's request, Congress approved a new military draft and revived the Selective Service System. In the meantime, the United States, having failed to reach agreement with the Soviet Union on international control of nuclear weapons, redoubled its own efforts in atomic research, elevating nuclear weaponry to a central place in its military arsenal. The Atomic Energy Commission, established in 1946, became the supervisory body charged with overseeing all nuclear research, both civilian and military. And in 1950, the Truman administration approved the development of the new hydrogen bomb, a nuclear weapon far more powerful than the bombs the United States had used in 1945.

NATIONAL SECURITY ACT OF 1947

The National Security Act of 1947 reshaped the nation's major military and diplomatic institutions. It created a new Department of Defense to oversee all branches of the armed services, combining functions previously performed separately by the War and Navy Departments. A National Security Council (NSC), operating out of the White House, would oversee foreign and military policy. A Central Intelligence Agency (CIA) would replace the wartime Office of Strategic Services and would be responsible for collecting information through both open and covert methods; as the Cold War continued, the CIA would also engage secretly in political and military operations. The National Security Act, in other words, gave the president expanded powers with which to pursue the nation's international goals.

The Road to NATO

At about the same time, the United States was moving to strengthen the military capabilities of Western Europe. Convinced that a reconstructed Germany was essential to the hopes of the West, Truman reached an agreement with England and France to merge the three western zones of occupation into a new West German republic (which would include the former American, British, and French sectors of Berlin, even though that city lay well within the East German zone). Stalin responded quickly. On June 24, 1948, he imposed a tight blockade around the western sectors of Berlin. If Germany was to be officially divided, he was implying, then the country's western government would have to abandon its outpost in the heart of the Soviet-controlled eastern zone. Truman refused to do so. Unwilling to risk war through a military challenge to the blockade, he ordered a massive airlift to supply the city with food, fuel, and other needed goods. The airlift continued for more than ten months, transporting nearly 2.5 million tons of material, keeping a city of 2 million people alive, and transforming West Berlin into a symbol of the West's resolve to resist communist expansion. In the spring of 1949, Stalin lifted the now-ineffective blockade. And in October, the division of Germany into two nations–the Federal Republic in the west and the Democratic Republic in the east–became official.

4 PREPARING THE HOUSE

Guard against Fire

The H-bomb's heat could not set fire to the brick or stone of a house but, striking through unprotected windows, it could set fire to the contents.

Stop the heat from entering the house

Whitewash your windows; those at the top of the building matter most. The whitewash will greatly reduce the fire risk by reflecting away much of the heat, which would have passed by the time the slower moving blast wave arrived. The blast might shatter the glass, but keeping out the heat-flash for those few seconds would prevent countless fires.

Reduce the risk of fires

Dispose of any inflammable material lying around in attics and upper storeys. Here the heat could strike most easily, but fire would be hardest to put out.

Clear away newspapers and magazines.

Get rid of boxes, firewood and inflammable rubbish from around the outside of the building.

14

Prepare to put out fires

Fires can be put out quite easily if tackled at once, while they are still small. If left, they spread rapidly and soon get out of control. Water is still the most effective way of dealing with fire.

Keep buckets of water on each floor

A stirrup pump or garden syringe would be very useful. If you have one, test it and make sure that it works. Keep it close to your fall-out room.

Guard against Flying Glass

Draw curtains and keep blinds lowered and closed. This will help to prevent injury from splinters of flying glass if the windows were shattered by the blast.

Other things to do

You will see later in this booklet (page 22) that after an attack you and your family might have to be moved away from where you had taken shelter. Pack necessities and any small valuables against this possibility. You would also need a change of clothing, and eating and drinking utensils; a blanket or travelling rug should be taken if possible. Pack your belongings in suitcases, travel bags or haversacks or, if you prefer, and know how to do this, in securely strapped blanket packs. Remember that you may be out in any weather and that your belongings may need protection from the rain.

KEEP YOUR LUGGAGE DOWN TO A WEIGHT YOU AND YOUR FAMILY CAN CARRY

If you have a car, make sure that the petrol tank is kept full, and that the car is ready for a journey at any time.

15

SURVIVING NUCLEAR WAR Preoccupation with the possibility of a nuclear war reached a fever pitch in the first years of the atomic era. These rules describe actions for civilians to take following an atomic attack.

Discussion and Activities

Analyzing Points of View Have students examine the diagram "Surviving Nuclear War." Ask them to write a short journal entry from the point of view of any member of an American family describing their reaction to reading the pamphlet shown. **SOC** **WXT**

DIVIDED EUROPE AFTER WORLD WAR II This map shows the sharp division that emerged in Europe after World War II between the area under the control of the Soviet Union and the area allied with the United States. In the east, Soviet control or influence extended into all the nations shaded brown—including the eastern half of Germany. In the west and south, the green-shaded nations were allied with the United States as members of the North Atlantic Treaty Organization (NATO). The countries shaded gold were aligned with neither of the two superpowers. The small map in the upper right shows the division of Berlin among the various occupying powers at the end of the war. Eventually, the American, British, and French sectors were combined to create West Berlin, a city governed by West Germany but entirely surrounded by communist East Germany.

How did the West prevent East Germany from absorbing West Berlin?

NATO

The crisis in Berlin accelerated the consolidation of what was already in effect an alliance among the United States and the countries of Western Europe. On April 4, 1949, twelve nations signed an agreement establishing the North Atlantic Treaty Organization (NATO) and declaring that an armed attack against one member would be considered an attack against all. The NATO countries would, moreover, maintain a standing military force in Europe to defend against what many policymakers believed was the threat of a Soviet invasion. The formation of NATO eventually spurred the Soviet Union to create an alliance of its own with the communist governments in Eastern Europe–an alliance formalized in 1955 by the Warsaw Pact.

REEVALUATING COLD WAR POLICY

A series of events in 1949 propelled the Cold War in new directions. An announcement in September that the Soviet Union had successfully exploded its first atomic weapon, years earlier than predicted, shocked and frightened many Americans. So did the collapse of Chiang Kai-shek's nationalist government in China, which occurred with startling speed in the last months

Discussion and Activities

Historical Developments and Argumentation After students have read the section "Road to NATO." Ask students to work in pairs to discuss why Berlin became the focal point of the Cold War in Europe. Ask for volunteers to share the main points of their discussion with the class. **WOR** **PCE** **WXT**

Answers

Divided Europe After WWII

The Western powers supplied West Berlin by air to prevent it from falling under Soviet control.

Discussion and Activities

Analyzing Points of View After students have read the section "Reevaluating Cold War Policy," ask them to write a short journal entry from the point of view of an American high school student describing their reaction upon hearing the news of the Soviet Union's detonation of an atomic bomb. **WOR** **SOC**

of 1949. Chiang fled with his political allies and the remnants of his army to the offshore island of Formosa (Taiwan), and the entire Chinese mainland came under the control of a communist government that many Americans believed to be an extension of the Soviet Union. The United States refused to recognize the new communist regime and, instead, devoted increased attention to the revitalization of Japan as a buffer against Asian communism, ending the American occupation in 1952.

In this atmosphere of escalating crisis, Truman called for a thorough review of American foreign policy. The result was a National Security Council report, issued in 1950 and commonly known as NSC-68, which outlined a shift in the American position. The first statements of the containment doctrine–the writings of George Kennan, the Truman Doctrine speech–had made at least some distinctions between areas of vital interest to the United States and areas of less importance to the nation's foreign policy and called on America to share the burden of containment with its allies. But the April 1950 document argued that the United States could no longer rely on other nations to take the initiative in resisting communism. It must itself establish firm and active leadership of the noncommunist world. And it must move to stop communist expansion virtually anywhere it occurred, regardless of the intrinsic strategic or economic value of the lands in question. Among other things, the report called for a major expansion of American military power, with a defense budget almost four times the previously projected figure.

NSC-68

PROCLAIMING THE VICTORY OF THE REVOLUTION Chairman Mao Zedong, standing on the rostrum of the Tiananmen Square Gate in Beijing, speaks by radio to the Chinese people on October 1, 1949, to proclaim the founding of the People's Republic of China. This was shortly after the communist victory in the nation's civil war and the departure of Chiang Kai-shek and his followers to the island of Taiwan.

© AP Images

THE CONSERVATIVE OPPOSITION TO CONTAINMENT

The containment doctrine for dealing with the Cold War attracted broad bipartisan support. But not everyone believed that containment was the right approach to take. Some Americans on the left believed that containment was unnecessarily belligerent and that the United States could have made peace with the Russians. But greater opposition to containment came from conservative Americans who believed that it was too weak a response to communism and saw containment as a kind of appeasement.

Among the conservatives who disdained containment was an anticommunist organization known as the John Birch Society. Its leader was Robert Welch, a man so fearful of communism that he believed some of the most important leaders of American government were trying to undermine the United States by collaborating with the Soviets. Welch presented his opposition in *The Blue Book of the John Birch Society*, in which he argued that much of the American government was riddled with treason. "For years," he wrote, "we have been taken steadily down the road to Communism by steps supposedly designed . . . as ways of *fighting* communism." But instead, he argued, it was communist Americans themselves who were undermining the nation. "Both the U.S. and Soviet governments are controlled by the same furtive conspiratorial cabal of internationalists, greedy bankers, and corrupt politicians," Welch wrote. "If left unexposed, the traitors inside the U.S. government would betray the country's sovereignty to the United Nations for a collectivist New World Order, managed by a 'one-world government.'" Among the sources of treason, Welch claimed, were the United Nations and other international institutions. Many Americans considered the John Birch Society an extremist organization, but the belief that communism was the greatest danger facing the United States was widely supported by many people.

The opposition to containment reached some of the highest levels of the government. John Foster Dulles, who would become secretary of state in the Eisenhower administration, wrote the foreign policy plank of the Republican platform in 1952. "We charge that the leaders of the Administration in power lost the peace so dearly earned by World War II," Dulles stated. "They abandoned friendly nations such as Latvia, Lithuania, Estonia, Poland, and Czechoslovakia." Containment, opponents such as Dulles argued, was a policy of weakness that had allowed the communists to take over much of the world. Many of those who argued against containment called for what was known as "rollback": instead of containing com-

Discussion and Activities

Analyzing Change Have students examine the image "Proclaiming the Victory of the Revolution." Ask them to discuss in small groups how the fall of Chiang Kai-Shek's government changed American foreign policy in Asia. *(Japan became the focal point of America's Asian foreign policy, and efforts would begin to contain Chinese communism.)* **WOR**

munism, the United States should be pushing back the borders of communism, despite the possibility of another war. President Eisenhower, however, did not share Dulles's belief in rollback, and the government abided by the containment strategy throughout the 1950s and beyond.

THE KOREAN WAR

On June 24, 1950, the armies of communist North Korea swept across their southern border and invaded the pro-Western half of the Korean peninsula to the south. Within days, they had occupied much of South Korea, including Seoul, its capital. Almost immediately, the United States committed itself to defeating the North Korean offensive. It was the nation's first military engagement of the Cold War.

THE DIVIDED PENINSULA

Before the end of World War II, both the United States and the Soviet Union had sent troops into Korea in an effort to weaken Japanese occupation. Once the war was over and the Japanese expelled, the United States and the Soviet Union each supported different governments–the Soviets supporting a communist regime in the North and the United States supporting a pro-Western government in the South. Instead, they had divided the nation, supposedly temporarily, along the 38th parallel. The Russians departed in 1949, leaving behind a communist government in the north with a strong, Soviet-equipped army. The Americans left a few months later, handing control to the pro-Western government of Syngman Rhee, who was anticommunist but only nominally democratic. He had a relatively small military, which he used primarily to suppress internal opposition.

SYNGMAN RHEE

The relative weakness of the south offered a strong incentive to nationalists in the North Korean government who wanted to reunite the country. The temptation to invade grew stronger when the American government implied that it did not consider South Korea within its own "defense perimeter." The role of the Soviet Union in North Korea's calculations prior to the 1950 invasion remains unclear; there is reason to believe that the North Korean government acted without Stalin's prior approval. But the Soviets supported the offensive once it began.

The Truman administration responded quickly to the invasion. On June 27, 1950, the president appealed to the United Nations to intervene. The Soviet Union was boycotting the Security Council at the time (to protest the council's refusal to recognize the new communist government of China) and thus was unable to exercise its veto power. As a result, American delegates were able to win UN agreement to a resolution calling for international assistance to the Rhee government. On June 30, the United States ordered its own ground forces into Korea, and Truman appointed General Douglas MacArthur to command the overwhelmingly American UN operations there.

The intervention in Korea was the first expression of the newly expansive American foreign policy outlined in NSC-68. But the administration quickly went beyond NSC-68 and decided that the war would be an effort not simply at containment but also at "liberation." After a surprise American invasion at Inchon in September had routed the North Korean forces from the south and sent them fleeing back across the 38th parallel, Truman gave MacArthur permission to pursue the communists into their own territory. His aim, as an American-sponsored UN resolution proclaimed in October, was to create "a unified, independent and democratic Korea."

"LIBERATION"

FROM INVASION TO STALEMATE

For several weeks, MacArthur's invasion of North Korea proceeded smoothly. On October 19, the capital, Pyongyang, fell to the UN forces. Victory seemed near–until the new communist government of China, alarmed by the movement of American forces toward its border, intervened. By November 4, eight divisions of the Chinese army had entered the war. The UN offensive stalled and then collapsed. Through December 1950, outnumbered American forces fought a bitter, losing battle against the Chinese divisions, retreating at almost every juncture. Within weeks, communist forces had pushed the Americans back below the 38th parallel once again and had captured the South Korean capital of Seoul a second time. By mid-January 1951 the rout had ceased; and by March the UN armies had managed to regain much of the territory they had recently lost, taking back Seoul and pushing the communists north of the 38th parallel once more. But with that, the war degenerated into a protracted stalemate.

From the start, Truman was determined to avoid a direct conflict with China, which he feared might lead to a new world war. Once China entered the war, he began seeking a negotiated solution to the struggle, and for the next two years he insisted that there be no wider war. But he faced a formidable opponent in General MacArthur, who resisted any limits on his military discretion. The United States was fighting the Chinese army, he argued. It should therefore attack China itself, if not through an actual invasion, then at least by bombing communist forces massing north of the Chinese border. In March 1951, MacArthur indicated his unhappiness in a public letter to House Republican leader Joseph W. Martin that concluded: "There is no substitute for victory." His position had wide popular support.

The Martin letter came after nine months during which MacArthur had opposed Truman's decisions. More than once, the president had warned the general to keep his objections to himself. The release of the Martin letter, therefore, struck the president as intolerable insubordination. On April 11, 1951, he relieved MacArthur of his command.

TRUMAN-MACARTHUR CONTROVERSY

There was a storm of public outrage. Sixty-nine percent of the American people supported MacArthur, a Gallup poll

Discussion and Activities

Evaluating Evidence Have students read the section "The Conservative Opposition to Containment." Ask them to list the reasons for many Americans' opposition to communism and to evaluate which they believe was the most compelling. **WOR** **PCE**

Discussion and Activities

Speculating Have students read the section "The Divided Peninsula." Discuss as a class how the United States might have acted differently with respect to Korea to prevent war. **WOR**

Historical Thinking Skills

Argumentation After students have read the section "From Invasion to Stalemate," ask them to consider and discuss in pairs or small groups the costs and benefits of UN forces advancing north of the 38th parallel. Have students consider what other courses of action, if any, might have led to a better outcome for the United States. **WOR** **PCE**

DISARRAY IN KOREA This disturbing picture by the noted *Life* magazine photographer Carl Mydans conveys something of the air of catastrophe that surrounded the rout of Americans from North Korea by the Chinese army in 1951. Having approached the Chinese border, the Americans confronted a massive invasion of Korea by Chinese troops, who soon pushed them back below the border between the North and the South and well beyond. Shown here are U.S. Marines following a vehicle carrying corpses after a battle with Chinese and North Korean troops. They had been trapped by the enemy in North Korea and had fought their way forty miles south before being rescued.

Photo by Carl Mydans/© Time & Life Pictures/Getty Images

reported. When the general returned to the United States later in 1951, he was greeted with wild enthusiasm. His televised farewell appearance before a joint session of Congress—which he concluded by saying, "Old soldiers never die, they just fade away"—attracted an audience of millions. Public criticism of Truman abated somewhat when a number of prominent military figures, including General Omar Bradley, publicly supported the president's decision. But substantial hostility toward Truman remained. In the meantime, the Korean stalemate continued. Negotiations between the opposing forces began at Panmunjom in July 1951, but the talks—and the war—dragged on until 1953.

LIMITED MOBILIZATION

Just as the war in Korea produced only a limited American military commitment abroad, so it created only a limited economic mobilization at home. Still, the government did try to control the wartime economy in several important ways.

First, Truman set up the Office of Defense Mobilization to fight inflation by holding down prices and discouraging high union wage demands. When these cautious regulatory efforts failed, the president took more-drastic action. When railroad workers walked off the job in 1951, Truman ordered the government to seize control of the railroads. That helped keep the trains running, but it had no effect on union demands. Workers ultimately got most of what they had demanded. In 1952, during a nationwide steel strike, Truman seized the steel mills, citing his powers as commander in chief. But in a 6-to-3 decision, the Supreme Court ruled that the president had exceeded his authority, and Truman was forced to relent.

WARTIME ECONOMIC REGULATION

The Korean War gave a significant boost to economic growth by pumping new government funds into the economy at a point when many people believed a recession was about to begin. But as the long stalemate continued, leaving 140,000 Americans dead or wounded, frustration turned to anger. Many began to believe that something must be deeply wrong—

Discussion and Activities

Analyzing Perspectives Have students examine the image "Disarray in Korea." Ask them to write a short letter home from the point of view of one of the soldiers in the photo. Have students consider what they would include or omit from their experiences for the sake of the recipients of the letter. **WOR** **SOC** **ARC** **GEO**

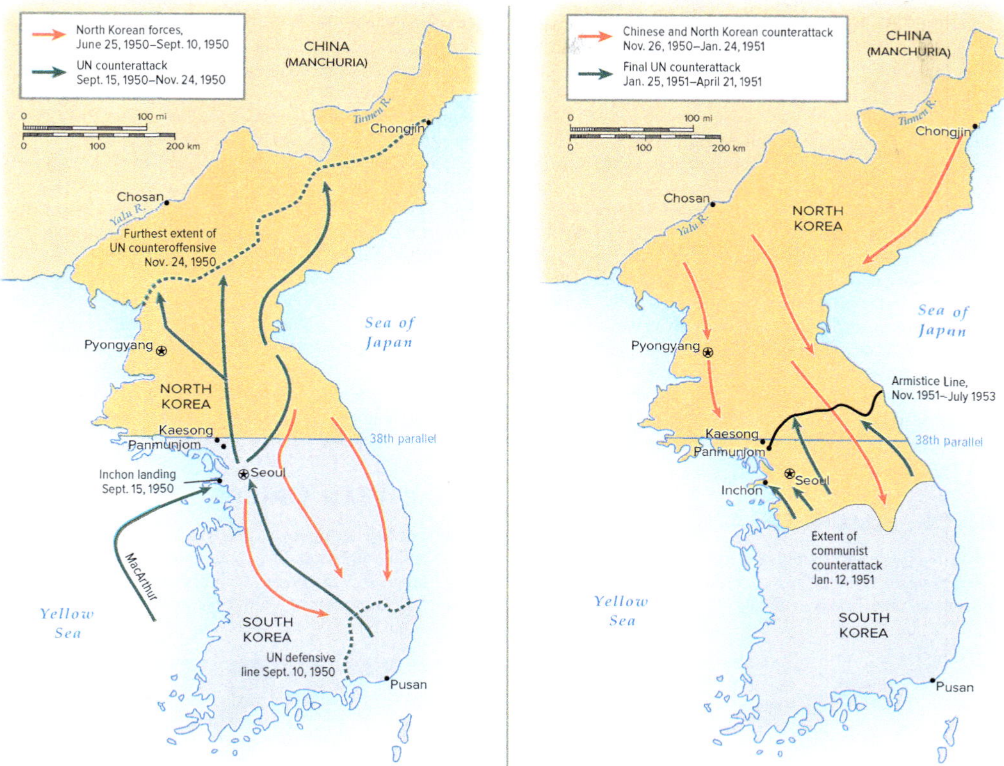

THE KOREAN WAR, 1950–1953 These two maps illustrate the changing fortunes of UN forces (which were mostly American) during the 1950–1953 Korean War. The map at the left shows the extent of the North Korean invasion of the South in 1950; communist forces for a time controlled all of Korea except a small area around Pusan in the southeast. On September 15, 1950, UN troops under Douglas MacArthur landed in force at Inchon and soon drove North Korean forces back across the border. MacArthur then pursued the North Korean forces well into their own territory. The map at right shows the very different circumstances once China entered the war in November 1950. Chinese forces drove the UN army back below the 38th parallel and, briefly, deep into South Korea, below Seoul. The UN troops fought back to the prewar border between North and South Korea late in 1951, but the war then bogged down into a stalemate that continued for a year and a half.

What impact did the Korean War have on American politics in the early 1950s?

not only in Korea but within the United States as well. Such fears contributed to the rise of the second major campaign of the century against domestic communism.

EISENHOWER, DULLES, AND THE COLD WAR

The threat of nuclear war with the Soviet Union created a sense of high anxiety in international relations in the 1950s. But the nuclear threat had another effect as well. With the potential devastation of an atomic war so enormous, both superpowers began to edge away from direct confrontations. The attention of both the United States and the Soviet Union began to turn to the rapidly escalating instability in the poor and developing nations of the Third World.

Dulles and "Massive Retaliation"

Eisenhower's secretary of state, and (except for the president himself) the dominant figure in the nation's foreign policy in the 1950s, was John Foster Dulles, an aristocratic corporate lawyer with a stern moral revulsion to communism. He entered office denouncing the containment policies of the Truman years as excessively passive, arguing that the United States

Reasoning Processes

Comparing After students have read the section "Limited Mobilization," ask them to create a Venn diagram comparing resources committed by the United States to the Korean War and to World War II. Have students discuss in small groups reasons for the differences. **WOR** **PCE** **WXT** **NAT** **GEO**

Answers

The Korean War: 1950–1953

The Korean War generated a wave of anti-communism in domestic politics.

Reasoning Processes

Comparing After students have read the section "Dulles and 'Massive Retaliation,'" ask them to create a Venn diagram comparing Truman's containment policy with Dulles's "Massive Retaliation." **WOR** **PCE** **NAT**

should pursue an active program of "liberation," which would lead to a "rollback" of communist expansion. Once in power, however, he had to defer to the more moderate views of the president himself.

The most prominent of Dulles's innovations was the policy of "massive retaliation," which Dulles announced early in 1954. The United States would, he explained, respond to communist threats to its allies not by using conventional forces in local conflicts (a policy that had led to so much frustration in Korea) but by relying on "the deterrent of massive retaliatory power" (by which he meant nuclear weapons). In part, the new doctrines reflected Dulles's inclination for tense confrontations, an approach he once defined as "brinksmanship"–pushing the Soviet Union to the brink of war in order to exact concessions. But the real force behind the massive-retaliation policy was economics. With pressure growing both in and out of government for a reduction in American military expenditures, an increasing reliance on atomic weapons seemed to promise, as some advocates put it, "more bang for the buck."

ECONOMIC BENEFITS OF "MASSIVE RETALIATION"

FRANCE, AMERICA, AND VIETNAM

What had been the most troubling foreign policy concern of the Truman years–the war in Korea–plagued the Eisenhower administration only briefly. On July 27, 1953, negotiators at Panmunjom finally signed an agreement ending the hostilities. Each antagonist was to withdraw its troops a mile and a half from the existing battle line, which ran roughly along the 38th parallel, the prewar border between North and South Korea. A conference in Geneva was to consider means by which to reunite the nation peacefully–although in fact the 1954 meeting produced no agreement and left the cease-fire line as the apparently permanent border between the two countries.

Almost simultaneously, however, the United States was being drawn into a long, bitter struggle in Southeast Asia. Vietnam, a colony of France, was facing strong opposition from nationalists, led by Ho Chi Minh, a communist.

When French troops became surrounded in a disastrous siege in North Vietnam, only American intervention, it was clear, could prevent the total collapse of the French military effort. Yet despite the urgings of Secretary of State Dulles, Vice President Nixon, and others, Eisenhower refused to permit direct American military intervention in Vietnam, claiming that neither Congress nor America's other allies would support such action.

DIEN BIEN PHU

COLD WAR CRISES

American foreign policy in the 1950s rested on a reasonably consistent foundation: the containment policy, as revised by the Truman and Eisenhower administrations. But the nation's leaders spent much of their time reacting to both real and

EISENHOWER AND DULLES Although President Eisenhower was a somewhat colorless television personality, his was the first administration to make extensive use of the new medium to promote its policies and dramatize its actions. The president's press conferences were frequently televised, and on several occasions Secretary of State John Foster Dulles reported to the president in front of the cameras. Dulles is shown here in the Oval Office on May 17, 1955, reporting after his return from Europe, where he had signed the treaty restoring sovereignty to Austria.

Discussion and Activities

Speculating Have students read the section "France, America, and Vietnam." Discuss as a class why the United States might have been more willing to intervene in Vietnam on behalf of France if it hadn't recently negotiated a cease-fire in Korea. **WOR** **PCE** **WXT**

THE STATE OF ISRAEL The prime minister of Israel, David Ben-Gurion (in suit and open collar shirt), watches the departure of the last British troops from Palestine shortly after the United Nations approved (and the United States recognized) in 1948 the existence of a new Jewish state in part of the region.

© Bettmann/Getty Images

imagined crises in far-flung areas of the world. Among the Cold War challenges the Eisenhower administration confronted were a series of crises in the Middle East, a region in which the United States had been little involved until after World War II.

On May 14, 1948, after years of Zionist efforts and a dramatic decision by the new United Nations, Israel proclaimed its independence. President Truman recognized the new Jewish homeland the next day. But the creation of Israel, while it resolved some conflicts, created others. Palestinian Arabs, unwilling to accept being displaced from what they considered their own country, joined with Israel's Arab neighbors and fought determinedly against the new state in 1948—the first of several Arab-Israeli wars.

RECOGNIZING ISRAEL

Committed as the American government was to Israel, it was also concerned about the stability and friendliness of the Arab regimes in the oil-rich Middle East, in which American petroleum companies had major investments. Thus the United States reacted with alarm as it watched Mohammad Mossadegh, the nationalist prime minister of Iran, begin to resist the presence of Western corporations in his nation in the early 1950s. In 1953, the American CIA joined forces with conservative Iranian military leaders to engineer a coup that drove Mossadegh from office. To replace him, the CIA helped elevate the young shah of Iran, Mohammad Reza Pahlevi, from his position as token constitutional monarch to that of virtually absolute ruler. The shah remained closely tied to the United States for the next twenty-five years.

American policy was less effective in dealing with the nationalist government of Egypt, under the leadership of General Gamal Abdel Nasser, which began to develop a trade relationship with the Soviet Union in the early 1950s. In 1956, to punish Nasser for his friendliness toward the communists, Dulles withdrew American offers to assist in building the great Aswan Dam across the Nile. A week later, Nasser retaliated by seizing control of the Suez Canal from the British, saying that he would use the income from it to build the dam himself.

SUEZ CRISIS

On October 29, 1956, Israeli forces attacked Egypt. The next day the British and French landed troops in the Suez to drive the Egyptians from the canal. Dulles and Eisenhower feared that the Suez crisis would drive the Arab states toward the Soviet Union and precipitate a new world war. By refusing to support the invasion, and by joining in a United Nations denunciation of it, the United States helped pressure the French and British to withdraw and helped persuade Israel to agree to a truce with Egypt.

Cold War concerns affected American relations in Latin America as well. In 1954, the Eisenhower administration ordered the CIA to help topple the new, leftist government of Jacobo Arbenz Guzmán in Guatemala, a regime that Dulles (responding to the entreaties of the United Fruit Company, a major investor in Guatemala fearful of Arbenz) argued was potentially communist.

No nation in the region had been more closely tied to America than Cuba. Its leader, Fulgencio Batista, had ruled as a military dictator since 1952, when with American assistance he had toppled a more moderate government. Cuba's relatively prosperous economy had become a virtual fiefdom of American corporations, which controlled almost all the island's natural resources and had cornered over half the vital sugar crop. American organized-crime syndicates controlled much of Havana's lucrative hotel and nightlife business. In 1957, a popular movement of resistance to the Batista regime began to gather strength

FIDEL CASTRO

Historical Thinking Skills

Argumentation After students have read the section "Suez Crisis," discuss as a class why the United States supported the creation of the state of Israel but sided with Egypt during the Suez Crisis. *(The United States supported the creation of Israel largely due to sympathy to the cause of creating a Jewish homeland following the Holocaust. The United States supported Egypt in the Suez Crisis to attempt to persuade Egypt to align with the United States rather than the Soviet Union.)* **WOR** **PCE** **WXT**

Discussion and Activities

Analyzing Visuals Have students examine the image "The State of Israel." Discuss as a class evidence from the photo that speaks to the state of Israel at its inception. *(There was already an army and an elected government with a national symbol and flag.)* **WOR** **PCE**

Discussion and Activities

Historical Evidence and Argumentation After students have read the section "Cold War Crises," ask them to create a chart listing reasons for American involvement in Israel, Egypt, Iran, Guatemala, and Cuba. Have students identify motives for each intervention and discuss as a class whether American involvement was primarily politically or economically motivated. **WOR** **PCE** **WXT** **GEO**

under the leadership of Fidel Castro. On January 1, 1959, with Batista having fled to exile in Spain, Castro marched into Havana and established a new government.

Castro soon began implementing radical policies of land reform and expropriating foreign-owned businesses and resources. Cuban-American relations deteriorated rapidly as a result. When Castro began accepting assistance from the Soviet Union in 1960, the United States cut back the "quota" by which Cuba could export sugar to America at a favored price. Early in 1961, as one of its last acts, the Eisenhower administration severed diplomatic relations with Castro. Isolated by the United States, Castro soon cemented an alliance with the Soviet Union.

Europe and the Soviet Union

Although the problems of the Third World were moving slowly toward the center of American foreign policy, the direct relationship with the Soviet Union and the effort to resist communist expansion in Europe remained the principal concerns of the Eisenhower administration. In 1955, Eisenhower and other NATO leaders met with the Soviet premier, Nikolai Bulganin, at a cordial summit conference in Geneva. But when a subsequent conference of foreign ministers met to try to resolve specific issues, they could find no basis for agreement. Relations between the Soviet Union and the West soured further in 1956 in response to the Hungarian Revolution. Hungarian dissidents had launched a popular uprising in November to demand democratic reforms. Before the month was out, Soviet tanks and troops entered Budapest to crush the uprising and restore an orthodox, pro-Soviet regime. The Eisenhower administration refused to intervene.

HUNGARIAN REVOLUTION OF 1956

The U-2 Crisis

In November 1958, Nikita Khrushchev, who had succeeded Bulganin as Soviet premier and Communist Party chief earlier that year, renewed the demands of his predecessors that the NATO powers abandon West Berlin. When the United States and its allies predictably refused, Khrushchev suggested that

THE CUBAN REVOLUTION Fidel Castro is shown here in the Cuban jungle in 1957 with a small group of his staff and their revolutionary forces. Kneeling in the foreground is Castro's brother Raoul. Two years later, Castro's forces toppled the existing government and elevated Fidel to the nation's leadership, where he remained for almost fifty years.

Discussion and Activities

Analyzing Issues After students have read the section "Europe and the Soviet Union," ask them to discuss in pairs or small groups how the "massive retaliation" policy affected the American response to events in Hungary. *(Massive retaliation would have likely meant a nuclear strike against the Soviet Union. Most American leaders were unwilling to use nuclear weapons in the defense of Hungary.)* **WOR** **PCE** **GEO**

he and Eisenhower discuss the issue personally, both in visits to each other's countries and at a summit meeting in Paris in 1960. The United States agreed. Khrushchev's 1959 visit to America produced a cool but mostly polite public response. Plans proceeded for the summit conference and for Eisenhower's visit to Moscow shortly thereafter. Only days before the scheduled beginning of the Paris meeting, however, the Soviet Union announced that it had shot down an American U-2, a high-altitude spy plane, over Russian territory. Its pilot, Francis Gary Powers, was in captivity. Khrushchev lashed out angrily at the American incursion into Soviet air space, breaking up the Paris summit almost before it could begin and withdrawing his invitation to Eisenhower to visit the Soviet Union.

After eight years in office, Eisenhower had failed to eliminate, and in some respects had actually increased, the tensions between the United States and the Soviet Union. Yet Eisenhower had brought to the Cold War his own sense of the limits of American power. He had resisted military intervention in Vietnam. And he had placed a measure of restraint on those who urged the creation of an enormous American military establishment. In his Farewell Address in January 1961, he warned of the "unwarranted influence" of a vast "military-industrial complex." His caution, in both domestic and international affairs, stood in marked contrast to the attitudes of his successors, who argued that the United States must act more boldly and aggressively on behalf of its goals at home and abroad.

EISENHOWER'S RESTRAINT

CHAPTER 28 REVIEW

CONNECTING THEMES

Chapter Twenty-Eight examined the development of the Cold War and the international tensions following World War II. The United States and the Soviet Union emerged from World War II as superpowers with vastly different worldviews. The United States envisioned greater reliance on international organizations to maintain peace, whereas the Soviet Union anticipated that powerful nations would dominate the world stage.

The United States moved to a policy of containment after World War II to prevent the Soviet Union from extending its influence. Integral to the policy of containment were the Marshall Plan and the Truman Doctrine, both designed to stop the spread of communism. Critics of containment felt the policy was not a strong enough response to the threat of communism. The invasion of South Korea by communist North Korean forces drew the United States into its first military engagement of the Cold War. As the Cold War continued, U.S. leaders reacted to crises around the world, including Southeast Asia and the Middle East. At the same time, domestic issues grew and occupied the attention of many Americans.

You should consider the following questions as you review the themes for this chapter:

- How did the Cold War affect foreign trade and the American economy?
- How did the Cold War alter the international relationships of the United States?
- What were the major foreign policy challenges for the United States following World War II?
- Why did the United States adopt the policy of containment and how did the policy lead to further involvement in conflicts?

KEY TERMS

Atlantic Charter 769
brinksmanship 780
containment 773
Dien Bien Phu 780
Douglas MacArthur 777
Fidel Castro 781
George F. Kennan 773
John Foster Dulles 779
Korean War 777
Mao Zedong 771
Marshall Plan 773
massive retaliation 779
National Security Act 774
North Atlantic Treaty Organization (NATO) 775
NSC-68 776
Syngman Rhee 777
Truman Doctrine 773
United Nations 770
Warsaw Pact 775
Yalta Conference 770

Discussion and Activities

Evaluating Evidence After students have read the section "The U-2 Crisis," ask them to discuss as a class whether the United States moved closer to war or peace in the years following World War II. WOR PCE WXT NAT GEO

Key Terms

Students should be familiar with the key terms and be able to define them in the context of the implementation of the foreign policies of containment and massive retaliation in Europe, Asia, and Latin America. Encourage students to use these terms in performing review exercises and exam practice for this chapter.

Go Online Chapter 28 Content Review

Assessing Student Understanding Use the online assessment to assess student understanding of concepts and topics within the chapter. You can assign the ready-made Chapter 28 Content Review or create your own from available questions. This easy-to-use tool helps you design assessments that meet the needs of different types of learners.

CHAPTER 28
THE EARLY COLD WAR

Answers

Multiple Choice

1. B; **2.** D; **3.** A

Short Answer

4A) Possible answer: Following World War II, Europe was devastated physically and economically. In order to prevent the Soviets from providing aid, the U.S. intervened through the Truman Doctrine and the Marshall Plan.

4B) Possible answer: Following World War I, the U.S. Senate refused to join the League of Nations; after World War II, the U.S. joined and took a leadership role in the United Nations.

4C) Possible answer: The Truman Doctrine and the Marshall Plan aided in the rebuilding of Europe and helped those countries maintain independence from the Soviet Union, which was also trying to extend its sphere of influence.

5A) Possible answer: The failure of the United States to enter the League of Nations following World War I led to instability within Europe. The need for stability was one cause in the creation of NATO.

5B) Possible answer: The creation of NATO by the Western countries led to the creation of the Warsaw Pact, an organization of Eastern European countries.

5C) Possible answer: Division of the world between democratic capitalist nations and communist countries helped fuel the Cold War.

AP EXAM PRACTICE

Questions assume cumulative content knowledge from this chapter and previous chapters.

MULTIPLE CHOICE

Use the map on page 775 and your knowledge of U.S. history to answer questions 1-3.

1. The political division of countries as shown on the map was most directly a result of
   (A) The Soviet Union's drive to create fair trade zones to allow for the expansion of capitalism.
   (B) The American policy of containment to stop the expansion of communism.
   (C) The American commitment to maintaining the same military presence in Europe as during World War II.
   (D) The desire by both the United States and the Soviet Union to avoid all forms of conflict.

2. Which best explains the reason for America's economic approach to its allies in the years immediately following World War II?
   (A) The United States wanted to prevent an economic power from developing in Asia.
   (B) The United States wanted to prevent any disputes from arising between any allied nations.
   (C) The United States wanted to pursue an international organization that would enforce the right to economic self-determination for all nations.
   (D) The United States wanted allied nations to have strong economies in order to resist communism.

3. Which best describes how American foreign policy toward the Cold War shifted during the 1950s?
   (A) U.S. policy became more aggressive as it asserted the right to actively intervene anywhere communism threatened an allied nation.
   (B) U.S. policy shifted to focus on European allies and allowed communism to spread throughout Asia without attempting to challenge its spread.
   (C) U.S. policy shifted to focus on the Americas as it ignored communist aggression against countries outside the Western Hemisphere.
   (D) U.S. policy became less aggressive as it no longer directly assisted allied nations who faced communist aggression.

SHORT ANSWER

Use your knowledge of U.S. history to answer questions 4-5.

4. Use the Marshall Plan image on page 773 to answer A, B, and C.
   (A) Briefly describe the historical developments that led to the events promoted by the image.
   (B) Briefly explain ONE specific foreign policy change in the United States between 1945 to 1965.
   (C) Briefly explain ONE specific foreign policy continuity in the United States between 1945 to 1965.

5. Answer A, B, and C.
   (A) Briefly describe ONE specific cause that led to the creation of NATO.
   (B) Briefly describe ONE specific effect of the creation of NATO.
   (C) Briefly explain a SECOND specific effect of the creation of NATO.

LONG ESSAY

Develop a thoughtful and thorough historical argument that answers the question. Begin your essay with a thesis statement, and support it with specific historical evidence and examples.

6. Evaluate the relative importance of causes that led to the Cold War between the United States and the Soviet Union following World War II.

Answers

Long Essay

6. Possible Thesis: The desire of nations following World War II to increase their sphere of influence, the fear of falling behind technologically, and the policy of containment were all factors in the rise of a Cold War. Specific historical evidence: The Truman Doctrine and the Marshall Plan to aid Europe put the U.S. and Soviet Union at odds. The policy of containment led to military interventions by the U.S. around the world. The race for technological advancements, especially those with atomic and hydrogen weapons, drove anxieties surrounding nuclear war and increased competition between the U.S. and the Soviet Union.

29 POST-WAR AMERICA

AMERICAN TV The arrival of television into American homes signaled a rapid, pervasive, and profound change in American life. TV viewing affected how Americans experienced entertainment and received their news. Television advertising helped create an enormous market for American products. Newspapers, radios, and the movies all lost some of their impact on American culture with the arrival of television.

CONNECTING CONCEPTS

Chapter Twenty-Nine begins by examining the labor unrest and price inflation the United States faced immediately after World War II, although the GI Bill enabled many veterans to pursue higher education and join the middle class. Harry Truman won a surprising victory in the 1948 election, but public and congressional conservatism blocked his liberal program known as the "Fair Deal." In the 1950s, government spending, suburban expansion, and corporate consolidation fueled economic growth, especially in the West. New technologies like computers and television promoted prosperity, while scientists raised life expectancy with pesticides, antibiotics, and a vaccine for polio.

The middle class expanded in the 1950s, and a consumer culture developed based on credit cards, new appliances, automobile ownership, travel, and the growth of suburbs. Television and suburbanization reinforced traditional gender and societal roles, but a youth culture that was critical of materialism and conformity emerged around the poets and writers of the Beat Generation. The birth of rock 'n' roll, which had black roots in rhythm and blues, also provided a backbeat of rebellion from white musicians like Elvis Presley.

Fears of communist subversion led to a second Red Scare headlined by Wisconsin Senator Joseph McCarthy. The sensational investigation of Alger Hiss and the Rosenberg case also convinced many Americans that communist spies or sympathizers were widespread. The fever of anti-communism would not break until the Army-McCarthy Hearings of 1954 when millions of Americans watched the senator make groundless accusations on national television.

Although white middle-class Americans dominated popular culture, tens of millions of other people lived on the margins of society. Tenant farmers and migrant workers struggled to survive as rural America continued to shrink. The expanding

Pacing Guide

Chapter 29 explores key concepts from Period 8: 1945–1980 of the AP U.S. History Curriculum Framework. The suggested instruction time for Chapter 29 is 4 days.

Key Concepts

8.3.I Rapid economic and social changes in American society fostered a sense of optimism in the postwar years.

8.3.II New demographic and social developments, along with anxieties over the Cold War, changed U.S. culture and led to significant political and moral debates that sharply divided the nation.

Discussion and Activities

Making Connections Have students examine the image "American TV." Discuss as a class how the scene might be different today. *(Large, flat-screen TV, more casual clothing.)* **WXT** **SOC** **ARC**

Historical Thinking Skills

Argumentation Have students read the section "GI Bill." Ask them to create a list of the benefits afforded to veterans. Have students discuss in small groups which of the benefits would be most useful for returning servicemen and women, and why. PCE WXT SOC ARC

suburbs excluded non-whites and poor inner-city neighborhoods filled with African Americans and other minorities. Yet Dwight Eisenhower, a war hero and moderate Republican, was among the most popular and politically successful presidents of the postwar era. He was pro-business and favored limited government, although he expanded social security and signed the Federal Highway Act, the largest public works project in American history.

As you read, you should:

- Describe the economic and social challenges faced by the United States during the post-World War II era.
- Evaluate the emergence of an "affluent society" despite the continuing poverty in many areas of the United States.
- Explain how government spending, the consolidation of industry, and a dramatically increased birth rate resulted in an economic boom in the United States following World War II.
- Describe how the second Red Scare led to renewed debate over the limiting of personal liberty versus the federal government's attempts to ensure national security.
- Analyze how migration patterns underwent significant changes following World War II.

SOCIETY AND POLITICS AFTER THE WAR

The crises overseas were not the only frustrations the American people encountered after the war. The nation also faced serious economic difficulties in adapting to peacetime. The resulting instability contributed to an increasingly heated political climate.

THE PROBLEMS OF RECONVERSION

The bombs that destroyed Hiroshima and Nagasaki ended the war months earlier than almost anyone had predicted and propelled the nation precipitously into a process of reconversion.

There had been many predictions that peace would bring a return of Depression unemployment, as war production ceased and returning soldiers flooded the labor market. But there was no general economic collapse in 1946–for several reasons. Government spending did drop sharply and abruptly, with around $35 billion dollars worth of war contracts canceled within weeks of the Japanese surrender. But increased consumer demand soon compensated. Consumer goods had been generally unavailable during the war, so many workers had saved a substantial portion of their wages and were now ready to spend. A $6 billion tax cut pumped additional money into general circulation. The Servicemen's Readjustment Act of 1944, better known as the GI Bill of Rights, provided economic and educational assistance to veterans, increasing spending even further.

GI BILL

This flood of consumer demand ensured that there would be no new depression, but it contributed to more than two years of serious inflation, during which prices rose at rates of 14 to 15 percent annually. In the summer of 1946, President Truman vetoed an extension of the authority of the wartime Office of Price Administration, thus eliminating price controls. (He was opposed not to the controls, but to congressional amendments that had weakened the OPA.) Inflation soared to 25 percent before he relented a month later and signed a bill little different from the one he had rejected.

Compounding the economic difficulties was a sharp rise in labor unrest, driven in part by the impact of inflation. By the end of 1945, there had already been major strikes in the automobile, electrical, and steel industries. In April 1946, John L. Lewis led the United Mine Workers on strike, shutting down the coal fields for forty days. Fears grew rapidly that without vital coal supplies, the entire economy might grind to a halt. Truman finally forced the miners to return to work by ordering government seizure of the mines. But in the process, he pressured mine owners to grant the union most of its demands, which he had earlier denounced as inflationary. Almost simultaneously, the nation's railroads suffered a total shutdown–the first in the nation's history–as two major unions walked out on strike. By threatening to use the army to run the trains, Truman pressured the workers back to work after only a few days.

POSTWAR LABOR UNREST

Reconversion was particularly difficult for the millions of women and minorities who had entered the workforce during the war. With veterans returning home and looking for jobs in the industrial economy, employers tended to push minority workers and women laborers out of the plants to make room for white males. Some of the war workers, particularly women, left the workforce voluntarily, out of a desire to return to their former

Go Online AP Exam Preparation

AP Exam Practice Use the online assessment to help prepare students for the AP Exam. You can assign the ready-made AP-style short-answer questions, document-based questions, and multiple-choice questions assessing concepts, themes, and skills from Period 8 and AP-style long-essay questions organized in sets of 3 questions from various time periods. You can also create your own tests from available questions. This easy-to-use tool helps you design assessments that meet the needs of different types of learners.

THE GI BILL The Servicemen's Readjustment Act of 1944, better known as the GI Bill, provided a wide range of benefits to all honorably discharged service personnel who served during the war. Benefits included low-cost mortgages, low-interest loans to start a business, cash payments of tuition and living expenses to attend university, high school or vocational education, as well as one year of unemployment compensation. By 1956, roughly 2.2 million veterans had used the GI Bill education benefits to attend colleges or universities. An additional 5.6 million veterans used these benefits for some kind of training program.

domestic lives. But as many as 80 percent of women workers, and virtually all black, Hispanic, and Asian workers, wanted to continue working. The postwar inflation, the pressure to meet the rising expectations of a high-consumption society, the growing divorce rate, which left many women responsible for their own economic well-being—all combined to create among women a high demand for paid employment. As they found themselves excluded from industrial jobs, therefore, women workers moved increasingly into other areas of the economy (above all, the service sector).

THE FAIR DEAL REJECTED

Days after the Japanese surrender, Truman submitted to Congress a twenty-one-point domestic program outlining what he later termed the "Fair Deal." It called for expansion of Social Security benefits, the raising of the legal minimum wage from 40 to 65 cents an hour, a program to ensure full employment through aggressive use of federal spending and investment, a permanent Fair Employment Practices Act, public housing and slum clearance, long-range environmental and public works planning, and government promotion of scientific research. Weeks later he added other proposals: federal aid to funding for the St. Lawrence Seaway, nationalization of atomic energy, and, perhaps most important, national health insurance—a dream of welfare-state liberals for decades, but one deferred in 1935 when the Social Security Act was written. The president was declaring an end to the wartime moratorium on liberal reform. He was also symbolizing, as he later wrote, "my assumption of the office of President in my own right."

TRUMAN'S "FAIR DEAL"

But many of the Fair Deal programs fell victim to the same public and congressional conservatism that had crippled the last years of the New Deal. Indeed, that conservatism seemed to be intensifying, as the November 1946 congressional elections suggested. Using the simple but devastating slogan "Had Enough?," the Republican Party won control of both houses of Congress.

The new Republican Congress quickly moved to reduce government spending and chip away at New Deal reforms. The president bowed to what he claimed was the popular mandate to lift most remaining wage and price controls, and Congress moved further to deregulate the economy. Inflation rapidly increased. When a public outcry arose over the soaring prices for meat, Senator Robert Taft, perhaps the most influential Republican conservative in Congress, advised consumers to "eat less," and added, "We have got to break with the corrupting idea that we can legislate prosperity, legislate equality, legislate opportunity." True to the spirit of Taft's words, the Republican Congress refused to appropriate funds to aid education, increase Social Security, or support reclamation and power projects in the West. It defeated a proposal to raise the minimum wage. It passed tax measures that cut rates dramatically for high-income families and moderately for those with lower incomes. Only vetoes by the president finally forced a more progressive bill.

The most notable action of the new Congress was its assault on the Wagner Act of 1935. Conservatives had always resented the new powers the legislation had granted unions; and in light of the labor difficulties during and after the war, such resentments intensified sharply. The result was the Labor-Management Relations Act of 1947, better known as the Taft-Hartley Act. It made illegal the so-called closed shop (a workplace in which no one can be hired without first being a member of a union). And although it continued to permit the creation of so-called union shops (in which workers must join a union after being hired), it permitted states to pass "right-to-work" laws prohibiting even that. Repealing this provision, the controversial Section 14(b), would remain a goal of the labor movement for decades. Outraged workers and union leaders denounced the measure as a "slave labor bill." Truman vetoed it, but both the House and the Senate easily overruled him the same day.

TAFT-HARTLEY ACT

The Taft-Hartley Act did not destroy the labor movement, as many union leaders had predicted. But it did damage weaker unions in relatively lightly organized industries such as chemicals and textiles; and it made more difficult the organizing of workers who had never been union members, especially women, minorities, and most workers in the South.

THE ELECTION OF 1948

Truman and his advisers believed the American public was not ready to abandon the achievements of the New Deal, despite the 1946 election results. As they planned strategy for the 1948 campaign, therefore, they placed their hopes in an appeal to enduring Democratic loyalties. Throughout 1948, Truman

Historical Thinking Skills

Analyzing Point of View After students have read the section "The Problems of Reconversion," ask them to create a poster from the point of view of a coal miner or railroad worker supporting or opposing a strike in the industry. **WXT** **SOC** **PCE**

Discussion and Activities

Historical Reasoning and Argumentation Have students read the section "The Fair Deal Rejected." Ask them to discuss in pairs or small groups whether Truman's Fair Deal would have passed if President Truman and the Democratic Party had followed a different strategy. **PCE** **WXT** **SOC** **NAT**

CHAPTER 29
POST-WAR AMERICA

Reasoning Processes

Comparing After students have read the section "Democratic Defections," ask them to create a 3-circle Venn diagram identifying similarities and differences in the Democratic Party, the Dixiecrat Party, and the Progressive Party. Have students discuss in small groups whether there were enough similarities to give the Democratic Party a chance at victory in the 1948 Presidential election. **PCE** **WXT** **SOC** **ARC**

ELECTION NIGHT, 1948 Throughout the 1948 campaign, Harry Truman was considered a very unlikely victor for a new term as president. But the combination of an energetic campaign by Truman, a lack of enthusiasm for his opponent, Thomas Dewey, and the lingering loyalty to the New Deal led to a surprise victory. *The Chicago Daily Tribune*, a strongly Republican paper, was so certain of Dewey's victory that it published this headline, which hit the newsstands just after it became clear that Truman won. This picture is one of the most famous political photographs of the twentieth century.

proposed one reform measure after another. Although Congress ignored or defeated them all, the president was building campaign issues for the fall.

DEMOCRATIC DEFECTIONS

There remained, however, the problems of Truman's personal unpopularity–the belief among much of the electorate that he and his administration were weak and inept–and the deep divisions within the Democratic Party. At the Democratic National Convention that summer, two factions abandoned the party: Southern conservatives reacted angrily to Truman's proposed civil rights bill (the first major one of the century) and to the approval at the convention of a civil rights plank in the platform (engineered by Hubert Humphrey, the mayor of Minneapolis). These two factions formed the States' Rights (or "Dixiecrat") Party, with Governor Strom Thurmond of South Carolina as its presidential nominee. At the same time, the Democratic Party's left wing formed a new Progressive Party, with Henry A. Wallace as its candidate. Wallace supporters objected to what they considered the slow and ineffective domestic policies of the Truman administration, but they resented even more the president's confrontational stance toward the Soviet Union.

In addition, many Democratic liberals unwilling to leave the party attempted to dump the president in 1948. The Americans for Democratic Action (ADA), a coalition of liberals, tried to entice Dwight D. Eisenhower, the popular war hero, to contest the nomination. Only after Eisenhower had refused did liberals bow to the inevitable and concede the nomination to Truman. The Republicans, in the meantime, had once again nominated Governor Thomas E. Dewey of New York, whose substantial reelection victory in 1946 had made him one of the nation's leading political figures. Austere, dignified, and competent, he seemed to offer an unbeatable alternative to the president. Polls showed Dewey with an apparently insurmountable lead in September, so much so that some opinion analysts stopped taking surveys. Dewey conducted a subdued, statesmanlike campaign and tried to avoid antagonizing anyone. But Truman, seemingly alone, believed he could win. As the campaign gathered momentum, Truman became more and more aggressive, turning the fire away from himself and toward Dewey and the "do-nothing, good-for-nothing" Republican Congress, which was, he told the voters, responsible for fueling inflation and abandoning workers and the middle class. To dramatize his point, he called Congress into a special session in July to give it a chance, he said, to enact the liberal measures the Republicans had recently written into their platform. Congress met for two weeks and, predictably, did almost nothing.

TRUMAN'S SURPRISING VICTORY

The president traveled nearly 32,000 miles and made 356 speeches, delivering blunt, extemporaneous attacks. He had told Senator Alben Barkley of Kentucky, his running mate, "I'm going to fight hard. I'm going to give them hell." He called for repeal of the Taft-Hartley Act, increased price supports for farmers, and strong civil rights protection for blacks. (He was the first president to campaign in Harlem.) He sought, in short, to re-create much of Franklin Roosevelt's New Deal coalition. To the surprise of virtually everyone, he succeeded. On election night, Truman won a narrow but deci-

Discussion and Activities

Analyzing Visuals Have students examine the image "Election Night, 1948." Ask them to identify and discuss in small groups details from the photo that identify the winner of the 1948 presidential election. *(Although the headline indicates that he lost, Truman's broad smile indicates he was happy with the outcome and was victorious. The Chicago Tribune was published by Truman's political adversary Robert McCormick, which made the irony even more satisfying for Truman.)* **PCE**

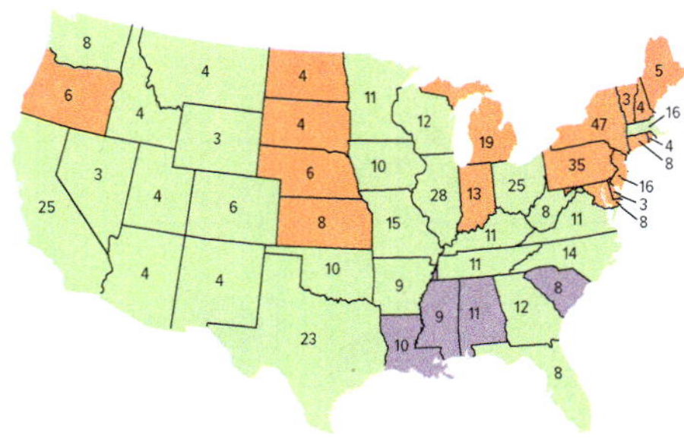

Candidate (Party)	Electoral Vote	Popular Vote (%)
Harry S. Truman (Democratic)	303	24,105,695 (49.5)
Thomas E. Dewey (Republican)	189	21,969,170 (45.1)
Strom Thurmond (States' Rights)	39	1,169,021 (2.4)
Henry A. Wallace (Progressive)	–	1,156,103 (2.4)
Other Candidates (Prohibition; Socialist Labor, Socialist, Socialist Workers)	–	272,713

53% of electorate voting

ELECTION OF 1948 Despite the widespread expectation that the Republican candidate, Thomas Dewey, would easily defeat Truman in 1948, the president in fact won a substantial reelection victory that year. This map shows the broad geographic reach of Truman's victory. Dewey swept most of the Northeast, but Truman dominated almost everywhere else. Strom Thurmond, the States' Rights candidate, carried four states in the South.

What had prompted Thurmond to desert the Democratic Party and run for president on his own?

sive victory: 49.5 percent of the popular vote to Dewey's 45.1 percent (with the two splinter parties dividing the small remainder between them), and an electoral vote margin of 303 to 189. Democrats, in the meantime, regained both houses of Congress by substantial margins.

THE FAIR DEAL REVIVED

Despite the Democratic victories, the Eighty-First Congress was little more hospitable to Truman's Fair Deal reform than its Republican predecessor. Truman did win some important victories. Congress raised the legal minimum wage from 40 cents to 75 cents an hour. It approved an important expansion of the Social Security system, increasing benefits by 75 percent and extending them to 10 million additional people. And it passed the National Housing Act of 1949, which provided for the construction of 810,000 units of low-income housing, accompanied by long-term rent subsidies. (Inadequate funding plagued the program for years, and it reached its initial goal only in 1972.)

But on other issues—among them national health insurance and aid to education—Truman made no progress. Nor was he able to persuade Congress to accept the civil rights legislation he proposed in 1949, which would have made lynching a federal crime, provided federal protection of black voting rights, abolished the poll tax, and established a new Fair Employment Practices Commission to curb discrimination in hiring (to replace the wartime commission Roosevelt had established in 1941). Southern Democrats filibustered to kill the bill.

TRUMAN STYMIED

Truman did proceed on his own to battle several forms of racial discrimination. He ordered an end to discrimination in the hiring of government employees. He began to dismantle segregation within the armed forces. And he allowed the Justice Department to become actively involved in court battles against discriminatory statutes. In the meantime, the Supreme Court signaled its own growing awareness of the issue by ruling, in *Shelley v. Kraemer* (1948), that the courts could not be used to enforce private "covenants" meant to bar African Americans from residential neighborhoods.

THE NUCLEAR AGE

Looming over the political, economic, and diplomatic struggles of the postwar years was the image of the great and terrible mushroom clouds that had risen over Alamogordo, Hiroshima, and Nagasaki. Americans greeted these terrible new instruments of destruction with fear and awe, but also with expectation. Postwar culture, therefore, was torn in many ways. There was the dark image of the nuclear war that many Americans feared would be a result of the rivalry with the Soviet Union. But there was also the bright image of a dazzling technological future that atomic power might help to produce.

CONFLICTING VIEWS OF NUCLEAR POWER

The fear of nuclear weapons was not hard to find in popular culture, even if it was often disguised in other ways. The late 1940s and early 1950s were the heyday of the *film noir*, a kind of filmmaking that had originated in France and had been named for the dark lighting characteristic of the genre. American *film noir* movies portrayed the loneliness of individuals in an impersonal world—a staple of American culture for many decades—but also suggested the menacing character of the age, the looming possibility of vast destruction. Sometimes, films and television programs addressed nuclear fear explicitly—for example, the celebrated television show of the 1950s and early 1960s *The Twilight Zone*, which frequently featured dramatic portrayals of the aftermath of nuclear war; or postwar comic books, which depicted powerful superheroes saving the world from destruction.

Such images resonated with the public because awareness of nuclear weapons was increasingly built into their daily lives. Schools and office buildings had regular air raid drills, to prepare people for the possibility of nuclear attack. Radio stations regularly tested the emergency broadcast systems. Fallout

Discussion and Activities

Evaluating Evidence Have students read the section "The Fair Deal Revived." Ask students to create a T-chart listing the successes and failures of Truman's legislative agenda following his reelection in 1948. Have students discuss in small groups which successes and failures were the most significant. **PCE** **WXT** **SOC** **ARC**

Answers

Election of 1948

Thurmond chose to run a separate campaign for the presidency after President Truman issued an executive order integrating the armed forces.

Discussion and Activities

Making Connections After students have read the section "The Nuclear Age," ask them to discuss as a class what, if any, issues today generate anxiety the way the nuclear power and weapons scare did in the 1950s and 1960s. *(Terrorism, pollution, and climate change are a few possibilities.)* **ARC** **NAT** **WXT** **SOC**

shelters sprang up in public buildings and private homes, stocked with water and canned goods. America was a nation filled with anxiety.

And yet at the same time, the United States was also an exuberant nation, dazzled by its own prosperity and excited by the technological innovations that were transforming the world. Among those innovations was nuclear power–which offered the possibility that the same scientific knowledge that could destroy the world might also lead it into a dazzling future. A Gallup poll late in 1948 revealed that approximately two-thirds of those who had an opinion on the subject believed that, "in the long run," atomic energy would "do more good than harm." Nuclear power plants began to spring up in many areas of the country, welcomed as the source of cheap and unlimited electricity, their potential dangers scarcely even discussed by those who celebrated the creation of atomic power.

PROMISE OF CHEAP NUCLEAR POWER

"THE ECONOMIC MIRACLE"

Among the most striking features of American society in the 1950s and early 1960s was a booming economic growth that made even the heady 1920s seem pale by comparison. It was a better-balanced and more widely distributed prosperity than that of thirty years earlier, but it was not as universal as some Americans liked to believe.

SOURCES OF ECONOMIC GROWTH

Between 1945 and 1960, the gross national product grew by 250 percent, from $200 billion to over $500 billion. Unemployment, which during the Depression had averaged between 15 and 25 percent, remained throughout the 1950s and early 1960s at about 5 percent or lower. Inflation, in the meantime, hovered around 3 percent a year or less.

The causes of this growth and stability were varied. Government spending, which had ended the Depression in the 1940s, continued to stimulate growth through public funding of schools, housing, veterans' benefits, welfare, the $100 billion interstate highway program, which began in 1956, and above all, military spending. Economic growth was at its peak (averaging 4.7 percent a year) during the first half of the 1950s, when military spending was highest because of the Korean War. In the late 1950s, with spending on armaments in decline, the annual rate of growth declined by more than half, to 2.25 percent.

GOVERNMENT SPENDING

The national birth rate reversed a long pattern of decline with the so-called baby boom, which had begun during the war and peaked in 1957. The nation's population rose almost 20 percent in the decade, from 150 million in 1950 to 179 million in 1960. The baby boom contributed to increased consumer demand and expanding economic growth.

The rapid expansion of suburbs–the suburban population grew 47 percent in the 1950s, more than twice as fast as the population as a whole–helped stimulate growth in several important sectors of the economy. The number of privately owned cars (essential for most suburban living) more than doubled in a decade, sparking a great boom in the automobile industry. Demand for new homes helped sustain a vigorous housing industry. The construction of roads and highways stimulated the economy as well.

SUBURBAN GROWTH

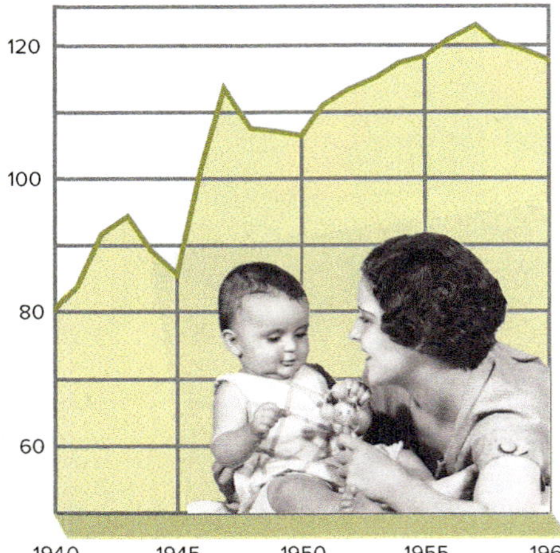

THE AMERICAN BIRTH RATE, 1940–1960 This chart shows how the American birth rate grew rapidly during and after World War II (after a long period of decline in the 1930s) to produce what became known as the "baby boom." At the peak of the baby boom, during the 1950s, the nation's population grew by 20 percent.

What impact did the baby boom have on the nation's economy?

Because of this unprecedented growth, the economy grew nearly ten times as fast as the population in the thirty years after the war. And while that growth was far from equally distributed, it affected most of society. The average American in 1960 had over 20 percent more purchasing power than in 1945, and more than twice as much as during the prosperous 1920s. By 1960, per capita income was over $1,800, $500 more than it had been in 1945. The American people had achieved the highest standard of living of any society in the history of the world.

THE RISE OF THE MODERN WEST

No region of the country profited more from economic growth than the American West. Its population expanded dramatically; its cities boomed; its industrial economy flourished. Before World War II, most of the West had been, economically at least, an appendage of the great industrial economy of the East. The West provided the East with raw materials and agricultural goods. By the 1960s, however, some parts of the West had become among the most important (and populous)

Answers

The American Birthrate: 1940–1960

Rapid population growth spurred increased demand for housing and many other consumer goods.

industrial and cultural centers of the nation in their own right. As during World War II, much of the growth of the West was a result of federal spending and investment—on the dams, power stations, highways, and other infrastructure projects that made economic development possible; and on the military contracts that continued to flow disproportionately to factories in California and Texas, many of them built with government funds during the war. But other factors played a role as well. The enormous increase in automobile use after World War II—a result, among other things, of suburbanization and improved highway systems—gave a large stimulus to the petroleum industry and contributed to the rapid growth of oil fields in Texas and Colorado, and also to the metropolitan centers serving them: Houston, Dallas, and Denver. State governments in the West invested heavily in their universities. The University of Texas and University of California systems, in particular, became among the nation's largest and best; as centers of research, they helped attract technology-intensive industries to the region.

FAVORABLE CLIMATE

Climate also contributed to economic growth. California, Nevada, and Arizona, in particular, attracted many migrants from the East because of their warm, dry climates. The growth of Los Angeles after World War II was a particularly remarkable phenomenon. More than 10 percent of all new businesses in the United States between 1945 and 1950 began in Los Angeles. Its population rose by over 50 percent between 1940 and 1960.

THE NEW ECONOMICS

The discovery of the power of the American economic system was a major cause of the confident tone of much American political life in the 1950s. During the Depression, politicians, intellectuals, and others had often questioned the viability of capitalism. In the 1950s, such doubt vanished. Two features in particular made the postwar economy a source of national confidence.

KEYNESIAN ECONOMICS

First was the belief that Keynesian economics made it possible for government to regulate and stabilize the economy without intruding directly into the private sector. The British economist John Maynard Keynes had argued as early as the 1920s that by varying the flow of government spending and taxation (fiscal policy) and managing the supply of currency (monetary policy), the government could stimulate the economy to cure recession and dampen growth to prevent inflation. The experience of the last years of the Depression and the first years of the war had seemed to confirm this argument. By the mid-1950s, Keynesian theory was rapidly becoming a fundamental article of faith—not only among professional economists but also among much of the public.

The "new economics," as its supporters came to call it, finally won official acceptance in 1963, when John Kennedy proposed a tax cut to stimulate economic growth. Although it took Kennedy's death and the political skills of Lyndon Johnson to win passage of the measure in 1964, the result seemed to confirm all that the Keynesians had predicted: an increase in private demand, which stimulated economic growth and reduced unemployment.

ENDING POVERTY THROUGH ECONOMIC GROWTH

As the economy continued to expand far beyond what anyone had predicted only a few years before, many Americans assumed that such growth was now without bounds. By the mid-1950s, reformers concerned about poverty were arguing that the solution lay not in redistribution but in economic growth. The affluent would not have to sacrifice in order to eliminate poverty; the nation would simply have to produce more abundance, thus raising the quality of life of even the poorest citizens to a level of comfort and decency.

CAPITAL AND LABOR

CORPORATE CONSOLIDATION

Over 4,000 corporate mergers took place in the 1950s; and more than ever before, a relatively small number of large-scale organizations controlled an enormous proportion of the nation's economic activity. This was particularly true in industries benefiting from government defense spending. As during World War II, the federal government tended to award military contracts to a few large corporations. In 1959, for example, half of all defense contracts went to only twenty firms. By the end of the decade, half the net corporate income in the nation was going to only slightly more than 500 firms, or one-tenth of 1 percent of the total number of corporations.

A similar consolidation was occurring in the agricultural economy. As increasing mechanization reduced the need for farm labor, the agricultural workforce declined by more than half in the two decades after the war. Mechanization also endangered one of the most cherished American institutions: the family farm. By the 1960s, relatively few individuals could any longer afford to buy and equip a modern farm, and much of the nation's most productive land had been purchased by financial institutions and corporations.

Corporations enjoying booming growth were reluctant to allow strikes to interfere with their operations. As a result, business leaders made important concessions to unions. As early as 1948, Walter Reuther, president of the United Automobile Workers, obtained a contract from General Motors that included a built-in "escalator clause"—an automatic cost-of-living increase pegged to the consumer price index. In 1955, Reuther received a guarantee from Ford Motor Company of continuing wages to auto workers even during layoffs. By the mid-1950s, factory wages in all industries had risen substantially.

THE "POSTWAR CONTRACT"

By the early 1950s, large labor unions had developed a new kind of relationship with employers, a relationship sometimes known as the "postwar contract." Workers in steel, automobiles, and other large unionized industries were receiving generous increases in wages and benefits; in return, the unions tacitly

Historical Thinking Skills

Argumentation After students have read the section "The Rise of the Modern West," ask them to list the factors that led to the rapid economic development of the West during and after World War II. Have students write a thesis statement that makes a claim about the most important cause of the economic development of the West. **WXT** **GEO**

Discussion and Activities

Speculating Have students read the section "The New Economics." Ask them to discuss as a class why the anticipated uninterrupted economic growth did not occur following the tax cut of 1964. *(Economic growth was unevenly distributed. Factors leading to economic growth or contraction were not as well understood or predictable as many argued.)* **WXT** **PCE**

Discussion and Activities

Analyzing Visuals Have students examine the image "Route 66." Ask them to identify and discuss in small groups details from the image that would help to explain its appeal in 1960s society. *(The lure of wide-open spaces; the freedom of the road; the bonding of the two leads through their shared adventures.)* **SOC** **ARC** **NAT** **GEO** **WXT**

PATTERNS OF POPULAR CULTURE

ON THE ROAD

People have traveled across the Americas for thousands of years, often with considerable difficulty. Indians had to make paths over rough terrain. Immigrants from England, Scotland, Mexico, and many other places began to move from town to town often on log roads. Later, they used stones and pebbles to create new byways. Wagons and carriages often rode on bumpy or muddy surfaces. Of course, many years later more-efficient, comfortable roads were built across the American continent, a development that changed American life dramatically.

In the mid-twentieth century, automobiles traveled more slowly than they do today. But cars allowed travelers to discover interesting places and meet new people as they moved from town to town. Jack Kerouac, in his famous book *On the Road* (1957), was one of the first to capture in writing the new spirit of automobile travel. "It was drizzling and mysterious at the beginning of our journey," Kerouac wrote as he got his battered car ready. "I could see that it was all going to be one big saga of the mist. . . . We were all delighted, when we all realized we were leaving confusion and nonsense behind and performing our one and noble function of the time, *move.* And we moved!"

In the 1950s, Route 66 was one of the first highways to cross most of the United States, from the West Coast to Chicago. But Route 66 became more than a road; it became a popular symbol of a country on the move. Travelers could drive along the famous highway while listening to the hit song "(Get Your Kicks On) Route 66" on the radio. A television series called *Route 66* depicted characters becoming involved in all sorts of drama as they traveled the storied route.

People traveling long distances, perhaps even across the continent, needed restaurants, motels, and shops, a development that encouraged the creation of fast-food chains, many of which began with drive-in restaurants where customers could be served and eat in their cars. The first drive-in restaurant, Royce Hailey's Pig Stand, opened in Dallas in 1921, followed later in the decade by the White Tower. Ray Kroc's McDonald's opened its first outlets in Des Plaines, Illinois, and southern California in 1955. Five years later, there were 228 outlets. In time, with thousands of restaurants, McDonald's became the most recognizable symbol of food in the world. Large supermarket chains—catering to customers with automobiles—replaced smaller, family-owned markets in town centers. Large centers and shopping malls moved the center of retailing out of cities and into separate, sprawling complexes surrounded by large parking lots.

Eventually, with President Eisenhower's encouragement, the Federal Aid Highway Act of 1956 provided money to build the interstate highway system. This network of highways made it possible for people to travel long distances quickly and efficiently.

ROUTE 66 The television show *Route 66*, starring George Maharis and Martin Milner, conveyed in popular culture the optimistic energy of a driving nation.

JACK KEROUAC Beat author Jack Kerouac's *On the Road* captured in literature the energy of a country on the move. The book's emphasis on jazz, beat poetry, and drugs, however, made it a notorious expression of the prevailing counterculture.

HISTORICAL THINKING SKILLS

1. **Explaining Historical Context** How did television programs like *Route 66* of the mid-1950s reflect much older American myths about the American West?
2. **Making Connections** In what ways, other than those described in the feature, did the interstate highway system help the American economy?
3. **Drawing Conclusions** What military advantages did the highway system provide?

(l) John Cohen/Hulton Archive/Getty Images, (r) CBS/Photofest

792 · CHAPTER 29

Answers

Patterns of Popular Culture

1. Possible answer: There had always been a fascination with expansion, and this trend continued as technology made it possible to travel farther and more quickly. Television shows like *Route 66* captured the imagination of Americans.
2. Possible answer: Interstates drove the rise of other industries, including restaurants, motels, and shops. Especially important was the creation of fast-food chains and the further development of suburbia.
3. Possible answer: The creation of highways allowed for faster mobilization of the military in case of an emergency.

agreed to refrain from raising other issues—issues involving control of the workplace and a voice for workers in the planning of production. Strikes became far less frequent.

The economic successes of the 1950s helped pave the way for a reunification of the labor movement. In December 1955,

AFL-CIO

the American Federation of Labor and the Congress of Industrial Organizations ended their twenty-year rivalry and merged to create the AFL-CIO, under the leadership of George Meany. Relations between the leaders of the former AFL and the former CIO were not always comfortable. CIO leaders believed (correctly) that the AFL hierarchy was dominating the relationship. AFL leaders were suspicious of what they considered the radical past of the CIO leadership. Even so, the union of the two great labor movements of the 1930s survived and gradually tensions subsided.

Success bred corruption in some union bureaucracies. In 1957, the powerful Teamsters Union became the subject of a congressional investigation, and its president, David Beck, was charged with misappropriation of union funds. Beck ultimately stepped down to be replaced by Jimmy Hoffa, whom government investigators pursued for nearly a decade before finally winning a conviction against him (for tax evasion) in 1967. The United Mine Workers, the union that had spearheaded the industrial movement in the 1930s, similarly became tainted by suspicions of corruption and by violence. John L. Lewis's last years as head of the union were plagued with scandals and dissent within the organization. His successor, Tony Boyle, was ultimately convicted of complicity in the 1969 murder of the leader of a dissident faction within the union.

While the labor movement enjoyed significant success in winning better wages and benefits for workers already organized in strong unions, the majority of laborers who were as yet

LIMITED GAINS FOR UNORGANIZED WORKERS

unorganized made fewer advances. Total union membership remained relatively stable throughout the 1950s, at about 16 million; and while this was in part a result of a shift in the workforce from blue-collar to white-collar jobs, it was also a result of new obstacles to organization. The 1947 Taft-Hartley Act and the state "right-to-work" laws that it created made it more difficult to form (or even sustain) many unions. The CIO launched a major organizing drive in the South shortly after World War II, targeting the poorly paid workers in textile mills in particular. But "Operation Dixie," as it was called, was a failure—as were most other organizing drives for at least thirty years after World War II.

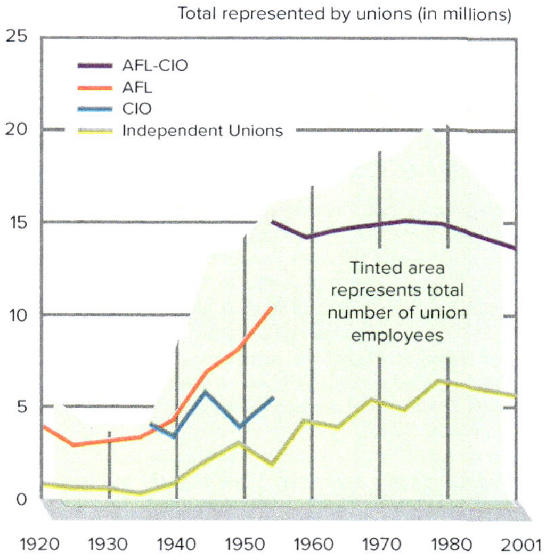

Total represented by unions (in millions)

AFL-CIO
AFL
CIO
Independent Unions

Tinted area represents total number of union employees

25 20 15 10 5 0

1920 1930 1940 1950 1960 1970 1980 2001

WORKERS REPRESENTED BY UNIONS, 1920–2001 This chart shows the number of workers represented by unions over an eighty-year period. Note the dramatic rise in the unionized workforce during the 1930s and 1940s, the slower but still-significant rise in the 1960s and 1970s, and the steady decline that began in the 1980s. The chart, in fact, understates the decline of unionized labor in the postwar era, since it shows union membership in absolute numbers and not as a percentage of the rapidly growing workforce.

Why did unions cease recruiting new members successfully in the 1970s, and why did they begin losing members in the 1980s?

THE EXPLOSION OF SCIENCE AND TECHNOLOGY

In 1961, *Time* magazine selected as its "man of the year" not a specific person but "the American Scientist." The choice was an indication of the widespread fascination with which Americans viewed science and technology. But it was also a sign of the remarkable, and remarkably rapid, scientific and technological advances in many areas during the postwar years.

MEDICAL BREAKTHROUGHS

A particularly important advance in medical science was the development of new antibacterial drugs capable of fighting infections that in the past had been all but untreatable.

The development of antibiotics had its origins in the discoveries of Louis Pasteur and Jules-François Joubert. Working

ANTIBIOTICS

in France in the 1870s, they produced the first conclusive evidence that virulent bacterial infections could be defeated by other, more ordinary bacteria. Using their discoveries, the English physician Joseph Lister revealed the value of antiseptic solutions in preventing infection during surgery.

But the practical use of antibacterial agents to combat disease did not begin until many decades later. In the 1930s, scientists in Germany, France, and England demonstrated the power of so-called sulfa drugs—drugs derived from an antibacterial agent known as sulfanilamide—which could be used effectively to treat streptococcal blood infections. New sulfa drugs were soon being developed at an astonishing rate, and were steadily improved, with dramatic results in treating what had once been a major cause of death.

Reasoning Processes

Comparing After students have read the section "Capital and Labor," ask them to create a T-chart listing gains and losses for workers during the 1950s. Have students evaluate whether they believe workers were better off at the beginning or end of the decade. **PCE** **WXT** **SOC**

Answers

Workers Represented by Unions: 1920–2001

Unions lost membership due to corruption scandals among union leaders and legislation like the Taft-Hartley Act.

Discussion and Activities

Evaluating Evidence After students have read the section "Medical Breakthroughs," ask them to discuss as a class which scientific advance they believe had the greatest impact on the United States at the time. **WXT** **SOC** **NAT**

In 1928, in the meantime, Alexander Fleming, an English medical researcher, accidentally discovered the antibacterial properties of an organism that he named penicillin. There was little progress in using penicillin to treat human illness, however, until a group of researchers at Oxford University, directed by Howard Florey and Ernest Chain, learned how to produce stable, potent penicillin in sizable enough quantities to make it a practical weapon against bacterial disease. The first human trials of the new drug, in 1941, were dramatically successful, but progress toward the mass availability of penicillin was stalled in England because of World War II. American laboratories took the next crucial steps in developing methods for the mass production and commercial distribution of penicillin, which became widely available to doctors and hospitals around the world by 1948. Since then, a wide range of new antibiotics of highly specific character have been developed so that bacterial infections are now among the most successfully treated of all human illnesses.

PENICILLIN

There was also dramatic progress in immunization. The first great triumph was the development of the smallpox vaccine by the English researcher Edward Jenner in the late eighteenth century. A vaccine effective against typhoid was developed by an English bacteriologist, Almorth Wright, in 1897, and was in wide use by World War I. Vaccination against tetanus became widespread in many countries just before and during World War II. Medical scientists also developed a vaccine, BCG, against another major killer, tuberculosis, in the 1920s; but controversy over its safety stalled its adoption, especially in the United States, for many years. It was not widely used in the United States until after World War II, when it largely eliminated tuberculosis.

Viruses are much more difficult to prevent and treat than bacterial infections, and progress toward vaccines against viral infections–except for smallpox–was relatively slow. Not until the 1930s, when scientists discovered how to grow viruses in laboratories in tissue cultures, could researchers study them with any real effectiveness. Gradually, they discovered how to produce forms of a virus incapable of causing a disease but capable of triggering antibodies in vaccinated people that would protect them from contracting the disease. An effective vaccine against yellow fever was developed in the late 1930s, and one against some forms of influenza–one of the great killers of the first half of the twentieth century–appeared in 1945.

A particularly dramatic postwar triumph was the development of a vaccine against polio. In 1954, the American scientist Jonas Salk introduced an effective vaccine against the virus that had killed and crippled thousands of children and adults (among them Franklin Roosevelt). It was provided free to the public by the federal government beginning in 1955. After 1960, an oral vaccine developed by Albert Sabin–usually administered in a sugar cube–made widespread vaccination even easier. By the early 1960s, these vaccines had virtually eliminated polio from American life and much of the rest of the world.

SALK VACCINE

As a result of these and many other medical advances, both infant mortality and the death rate among young children declined significantly in the first twenty-five years after the war (although not by as much as in Western Europe). Average life expectancy in that same period rose by five years, to seventy-one.

PESTICIDES

At the same time that medical researchers were finding cures and vaccines against infectious diseases, other scientists were developing new kinds of chemical pesticides, which they hoped would protect crops from destruction by insects and protect humans from such insect-carried diseases as typhus and malaria. The most famous of the new pesticides was dichlorodiphenyltrichloroethane, generally known as DDT, a compound discovered in 1939 by a Swiss chemist named Paul Muller. He had found that although DDT seemed harmless to human beings and other mammals, it was extremely toxic to insects. American scientists learned of Muller's discovery in 1942, just as the army was grappling with the insect-borne tropical diseases–especially malaria and typhus–that threatened American soldiers overseas during World War II.

DDT

Under these circumstances, DDT seemed a godsend. It was first used on a large scale in Italy in 1943–1944 during a typhus outbreak, which it quickly helped end. Soon it was being sprayed in mosquito-infested areas of Pacific islands where American troops were fighting the Japanese. No soldiers suffered any apparent ill effects from the sprayings, and the incidence of malaria dropped precipitously. DDT quickly gained a reputation as a miraculous tool for controlling insects, and it undoubtedly saved thousands of lives. Only later did scientists recognize that DDT had long-term toxic effects on animals and humans.

POSTWAR ELECTRONIC RESEARCH

The 1940s and 1950s saw dramatic new developments in electronic technology. Researchers in the 1940s produced the first commercially viable televisions and created a technology that made it possible to broadcast programming over large areas. Later, in the late 1950s, scientists at RCA's David Sarnoff Laboratories in New Jersey developed the technology for color television, which first became widely available in the early 1960s.

INVENTION OF TELEVISION

In 1948 Bell Labs, the research arm of AT&T, produced the first transistor, a small solid-state device capable of amplifying electrical signals, which was much smaller and more efficient than the cumbersome vacuum tubes that had powered most electronic equipment in the past. Transistors made possible the miniaturization of many devices (radios, televisions, audio equipment, hearing aids) and were also important in aviation, weaponry, and satellites. They contributed as well to another major breakthrough in electronics: the development of integrated circuitry in the late 1950s.

Integrated circuits combined a number of once-separate electronic elements (transistors, resistors, diodes, and others) and embedded them into a single, microscopically small device. They made it possible to create increasingly complex

Historical Thinking Skills

Argumentation Have students read the section "Pesticides." Ask them to create a poster advocating for more or less use of chemical pesticides based on what was known in the 1960s. **WXT** **SOC** **PCE**

THE SALK VACCINE Dr. Jonas Salk, a medical researcher at the University of Pittsburgh, developed in the mid-1950s the first vaccine that proved effective in preventing polio. In its aftermath, scenes similar to this one—a mass inoculation of families in a municipal stadium in Evansville, Indiana—repeated themselves all over the country. A few years later, Dr. Albert Sabin of the University of Cincinnati created a vaccine that could be administered more easily, through sugar cubes.

electronic devices requiring complicated circuitry that would have been impractical to produce through other means. Most of all, integrated circuits helped advance the development of the computer.

POSTWAR COMPUTER TECHNOLOGY

Prior to the 1950s, computers had been constructed mainly to perform complicated mathematical tasks, such as those required to break military codes. In the 1950s, they began to perform commercial functions for the first time, as data-processing devices used by businesses and other organizations.

UNIVAC

The first significant computer of the 1950s was the Universal Automatic Computer (or UNIVAC), which was developed initially for the U.S. Bureau of the Census by the Remington Rand Company. It was the first computer able to handle both alphabetical and numerical information easily. It used tape storage and could perform calculations and other functions much faster than its predecessor, the ENIAC, developed in 1946 by the same researchers at the University of Pennsylvania who were responsible for the UNIVAC. Searching for a larger market than the census for their very expensive new device, Remington Rand arranged to use a UNIVAC to predict the results of the 1952 election for CBS television news. It would, they believed, produce valuable publicity for the machine. Analyzing early voting results, the UNIVAC accurately predicted an enormous landslide victory for Eisenhower over Stevenson. Few Americans had ever heard of a computer before that night, and the UNIVAC's television debut became, therefore, a critical breakthrough in public awareness of computer technology.

Remington Rand had limited success in marketing the UNIVAC, but in the mid-1950s the International Business Machines Company (IBM) introduced its first major data-processing computers and began to find a wide market for them among businesses in the United States and abroad. These early successes, combined with the enormous amount of money IBM invested in research and development, made the company the worldwide leader in computers for many years.

THE DAWN OF THE COMPUTER AGE This massive computer, powered by tubes, was part of the first generation of mainframes developed after World War II. They served mostly government agencies and large corporations. By the 1990s, a small desktop computer could perform all the functions of this huge computer at much greater speed.

BOMBS, ROCKETS, AND MISSILES

THE HYDROGEN BOMB

In 1952, the United States successfully detonated the first hydrogen bomb. (The Soviet Union tested its first H-bomb a year later.) Unlike the plutonium and uranium bombs developed during World War II, the hydrogen bomb derives its power not from fission (the splitting of atoms) but from fusion (the joining of lighter atomic elements with heavier ones). It is capable of producing explosions of vastly greater power than the earlier, fission bombs.

The development of the hydrogen bomb gave considerable impetus to a stalled scientific

Discussion and Activities

Historical Evidence and Argumentation Have students read the section "Postwar Computer Technology." Ask them to discuss in small groups why new computer technology was slow to catch on at this time. *(Large, expensive machines were only able to do limited calculations.)* Discuss as a class if there are any areas of technology where this is true today. **WXT**

Discussion and Activities

Making Connections Have students examine the image "The Dawn of the Computer Age." Ask them to write a short paragraph explaining how the scene depicted might appear different today. **WXT**

Reasoning Processes

Causation After students have read the section "Bombs, Rockets, and Missiles," ask them to discuss as a class why the development of new weapons technologies was such a high priority for the United States. *(The United States was looking for an edge in its Cold War competition with the Soviet Union.)* **WXT** **WOR**

project in both the United States and the Soviet Union–the effort to develop unmanned rockets and missiles capable of carrying the new weapons, which were not suitable for delivery by airplanes, to their targets. Both nations began to put tremendous resources into their development. The United States, in particular, benefited from the emigration to America of some of the German scientists who had helped develop rocketry for Germany during World War II.

In the United States, early missile research was conducted almost entirely by the Air Force. There were significant early successes in developing rockets capable of traveling several hundred miles. But American and Soviet leaders were both struggling to build longer-range missiles that could cross oceans and continents–intercontinental ballistic missiles, or ICBMs, capable of traveling through space to distant targets. American scientists experimented in the 1950s with first the Atlas and then the Titan ICBM. There were some early successes, but there were also many setbacks, particularly because of the difficulty of massing sufficient, stable fuel to provide the tremendous power needed to launch missiles beyond the atmosphere. By 1958, scientists had created a solid fuel to replace the volatile liquid fuels of the early missiles; and they had also produced miniaturized guidance systems capable of ensuring that missiles could travel to reasonably precise destinations. Within a few years, a new generation of missile, known as the Minuteman, with a range of several thousand miles, became the basis of the American atomic weapons arsenal. American scientists also developed a nuclear missile capable of being carried and fired by submarines–the Polaris, which could launch from below the surface of the ocean by compressed air. A Polaris was first successfully fired from underwater in 1960.

LAUNCHING A SATELLITE, 1961 Four years after the successful Russian launching of the satellite *Sputnik* in 1957 threw Americans into something close to a panic, a Thor-Able Star rocket takes off from Cape Canaveral, Florida, carrying an American satellite. The satellite contained a nuclear generator capable of providing it with extended continuous power for its radio transmitters.

THE SPACE PROGRAM

The origins of the American space program can be traced most directly to a dramatic event in 1957, when the Soviet Union announced that it had launched an earth-orbiting satellite–*Sputnik*–into outer space. The United States had yet to perform any similar feats, and the American government (and much of American society) reacted to the announcement with alarm, as if the Soviet achievement was also a massive American failure. Federal policy began encouraging (and funding) strenuous efforts to improve scientific education in the schools, to create more research laboratories, and, above all, to speed the development of America's own exploration of outer space. The United States launched its first satellite, *Explorer I*, in January 1958.

THE SHOCK OF *SPUTNIK*

The centerpiece of space exploration, however, soon became the manned space program, established in 1958 through the creation of a new agency, the National Aeronautics and Space Administration (NASA), and through the selection of the first American space pilots, or "astronauts." They quickly became among the nation's most revered heroes. NASA's initial effort, the Mercury Project, was designed to launch manned vehicles into space to orbit the earth. On May 5, 1961, Alan Shepard became the first American launched into space. But his short, suborbital flight came several months after a Soviet "cosmonaut," Yuri Gagarin, had made a flight in which he had orbited the earth. On February 2, 1962, John Glenn (later a U.S. senator) became the first American to orbit the globe. NASA later introduced the Gemini program, whose spacecraft could carry two astronauts at once.

Mercury and Gemini were followed by the Apollo program, whose purpose was to land men on the moon. It had some catastrophic setbacks, most notably a fire in January 1967 that killed three astronauts. But on July 20, 1969, Neil Armstrong, Edwin Aldrin, and Michael Collins successfully traveled in a space capsule into orbit around the moon. Armstrong and Aldrin then detached a smaller craft from the capsule, landed

THE APOLLO PROGRAM

Discussion and Activities

Analyzing Points of View Have students read the section "The Shock of *Sputnik*." Ask them to write a short paragraph explaining why the news of the Soviet Union's launch of the *Sputnik* satellite caused such alarm in the United States. *(The implication was that if the Soviet Union could launch a satellite into orbit, they could also launch a nuclear warhead at the United States.)* **WOR** **NAT** **WXT**

APOLLO 11 Edwin ("Buzz") Aldrin is photographed by his fellow astronaut Neil Armstrong in August 1969, when they became the first humans to set foot on the surface of the moon. They traveled into orbit around the moon in the spaceship *Apollo 11* and then traveled from the spaceship to the moon in a "lunar module," which they then used to return to the ship for the journey home.

NASA

on the surface of the moon, and became the first humans to walk on a body other than earth. Six more lunar missions followed, the last in 1972. Not long after that, however, the government began to cut the funding for missions, and popular enthusiasm for the program began to wane.

The future of the manned space program did not lie primarily in efforts to reach distant planets, as originally envisioned. Instead, the program became a more modest effort to make travel in near space easier and more practical through the development of the "space shuttle," an airplane-like device launched by a missile but capable of both navigating in space and landing on earth much like a conventional aircraft. The first space shuttle was successfully launched in 1982. The explosion of one shuttle, *Challenger*, in January 1986 shortly after takeoff, killing all seven astronauts, stalled the program for two years. Missions resumed in the late 1980s, driven in part by commercial purposes. The space shuttle launched and repaired communications satellites, and inserted the Hubble Space Telescope into orbit in 1990 (and later repaired its flawed lens). But problems continued to plague the program into the early twenty-first century.

The space program, like the military development of missiles, gave a tremendous boost to the American aeronautics industry and was responsible for the development of many technologies that proved valuable in other areas.

PEOPLE OF PLENTY

Among the most striking social developments of the postwar era was the rapid expansion of a middle-class lifestyle and outlook. The new prosperity of social groups that had previously lived on the margins; the growing availability of consumer products at affordable prices and the rising public fascination with such products; and the massive population movement from the cities to the suburbs—all helped make the American middle class a larger, more powerful, more homogeneous, and more dominant force than ever before.

THE CONSUMER CULTURE

At the center of middle-class culture in the 1950s, as it had been for many decades before, was a growing absorption with consumer goods. That was a result of increased prosperity, of the increasing variety and availability of products, and of advertisers' adeptness in creating a demand for those products. It was also a result of the growth of consumer credit, which increased by 800 percent between 1945 and 1957 through the development of credit cards, revolving charge accounts, and easy-payment plans. Prosperity fueled the automobile industry, and Detroit responded to the boom with ever-flashier styling and accessories. Consumers also responded eagerly to the development of such new products as dishwashers, garbage disposals, televisions, hi-fis, and stereos. To a large degree, the prosperity of the 1950s and 1960s was consumer driven (as opposed to investment driven).

Because consumer goods were so often marketed (and advertised) nationally, the 1950s were notable for the rapid spread of great national consumer crazes. For example, children, adolescents, and even some adults became entranced in the late 1950s with the hula hoop—a large plastic ring kept spinning around the waist. The popularity of the Walt Disney-produced children's television show *The Mickey Mouse Club* created a national demand for related products such as Mickey Mouse watches and hats. It also helped produce the stunning success of Disneyland, an amusement park near Los Angeles that re-created many of the characters and events of Disney entertainment programs.

CONSUMER CRAZES

Discussion and Activities

Evaluating Evidence After students have read the section "The Space Program," ask them to create a T-chart comparing the costs and benefits of the space program. Have students discuss in small groups to what extent, if any, the benefits outweighed the costs. WXT NAT PCE WOR

Discussion and Activities

Analyzing Points of View Have students examine the image "Apollo 11." Ask them to write a journal entry from the point of view of an American high school student describing his or her reaction to the moon landing. NAT

Discussion and Activities

Making Connections After students have read the section "The Consumer Culture," discuss as a class "consumer crazes" students have witnessed in their lifetimes. Ask students to explain how their examples are similar to or different from those described in the text. **WXT**

THE DAVY CROCKETT CRAZE In the 1950s Walt Disney introduced a television show about American folk hero Davy Crockett. This boy wears to school his hero's famous "coon-skin" (that is, raccoon skin) cap and Davy Crockett T-shirt as he reads about Crockett. In addition to merchandising products associated with Crockett, Disney believed that it was time for Americans "to get acquainted, or renew acquaintance with, the robust, cheerful, energetic and representative folk heroes" from the American past.

THE LANDSCAPE AND THE AUTOMOBILE

The success of Disneyland depended largely on the ease of highway access from the dense urban areas around it, as well as the vast parking lots that surrounded the park. It was, in short, a symbol of the overwhelming influence of automobiles on American life and on the American landscape in the postwar era. Between 1950 and 1980, the nation's population increased by 50 percent, but the numbers of automobiles owned by Americans increased by 400 percent.

The Federal Highway Act of 1956, which appropriated $25 billion for highway construction, was one of the most important alterations of the national landscape in modern history. Great ribbons of concrete–40,000 miles of them–spread across the nation, spanning rivers and valleys, traversing every state, and providing links to every major city (and between cities and their suburbs). These highways dramatically reduced the time necessary to travel from one place to another. They also made trucking a more economical way than railroads to transport goods to markets. They made travel by automobile, truck, and bus as fast as or faster than travel by trains, resulting in the long, steady decline of railroads.

INTERSTATE HIGHWAYS

Highways also encouraged the movement of economic activities–manufacturing in particular–out of cities and into suburban and rural areas where land was cheaper. The decline of many traditional downtowns soon followed, as many workers moved outside the urban core. There was rapid growth of what eventually became known as "edge cities" and other new centers of industry and commerce outside traditional city centers.

The proliferation of automobiles and the spread of highways also made it easier for families to move into homes that were far away from where they worked. This enabled many people to live in larger houses with larger lots than they could have afforded previously. Garages began to be built onto houses in great numbers after World War II, and such suburban amenities as swing sets, barbecues, and private swimming pools became more common as backyards became more the focus of family life. The shift of travel from train to automobile helped launch a tremendous proliferation of motels–26,000 by 1948, 60,000 by 1960, well over 100,000 by 1970. The first Holiday Inn (starting what would soon become the largest motel chain in America) opened along a highway connecting Memphis and Nashville, Tennessee, in 1952. Drive-in theaters–a distinctively American phenomenon that had begun to appear in the 1930s–spread rapidly after the war. There were 4,000 drive-ins by 1958.

THE SUBURBAN NATION

By 1960, a third of the nation's population was living in suburbs. Suburbanization was partly a result of important innovations in home-building, which made single-family houses affordable to millions of people. The most famous of the postwar suburban developers, William Levitt, used new mass-production techniques to construct a large housing development on Long Island, near New York City. This first "Levittown" (there would later be others in New Jersey and Pennsylvania) consisted of several thousand two-bedroom Cape Cod–style houses, with identical interiors and only slightly varied facades, each perched on its own concrete slab (to eliminate excavation costs), facing curving, treeless streets. Levittown houses, and other, similarly low-priced homes, sold for under $10,000, and they helped meet an enormous and growing demand for housing. Young couples–often newly married and the husband a war veteran, eager to start a family, assisted by low-cost, government-subsidized mortgages provided by the GI Bill–rushed to purchase the inexpensive homes.

"LEVITTOWN"

Why did so many Americans want to move to the suburbs? One reason was the enormous importance postwar Americans

Reasoning Processes

Causation Have students read the section "The Landscape and the Automobile." Ask them to create a T-chart listing causes and effects of the development of highways. Have students classify effects as being economic, social, or political and evaluate which type of effect was most prevalent. **WXT** **SOC** **NAT** **PCE**

INTERSTATES The interstate highway system changed the physical landscape of the United States. Its great, sprawling ribbons of concrete—such as this photograph that shows the Hollywood Freeway, Harbor Freeway, and Arroyo Seco Freeway intersecting on multiple levels—sliced through cities, towns, and rural areas. But its biggest impact was in facilitating the movement of urban populations out of cities and into increasingly distant suburbs.

placed on family life after five years of disruptive war. Suburbs provided families with larger homes than they could find (or afford) in the cities. Many people were attracted by the idea of living in a community populated largely by people of similar age and background and found it easier to form friendships and social circles there than in the city. Women in particular often valued the presence of other nonworking mothers living nearby to share the tasks of child raising. Another factor motivating white Americans to move to the suburbs was race. There were some African American suburbs, but most suburbs were restricted to white Americans—both because relatively few black Americans could afford to live in them and because formal and informal barriers kept out even prosperous African Americans. In an era when the black population of most cities was rapidly growing, many white families moved to the suburbs to escape the integration of urban neighborhoods and schools.

Suburban neighborhoods had many things in common with one another. But they were not uniform. Levittowns and inexpensive developments like them ultimately became the homes of mainly lower-middle-class people one step removed from the inner city. Other, more affluent suburbs became enclaves of wealthy families. In virtually every city, a clear hierarchy emerged of upper-class suburban neighborhoods and more modest ones, just as such gradations had emerged years earlier among urban neighborhoods.

The Suburban Family

For professional men (many of whom worked in cities, at some distance from their homes), suburban life generally meant a rigid division between their working and personal worlds. For many middle-class, married women, it meant increased isolation from the workplace. The enormous cultural emphasis on family life in the 1950s strengthened popular prejudices against women entering the professions, or occupying any paid job at all. Many middle-class husbands considered it demeaning for their wives to be employed. And many women shied away from the workplace when they could afford to stay at home full-time with their children.

"PREVAILING GENDER ROLES REINFORCED"

One of the most influential books in postwar American life was a famous guide to child rearing: Dr. Benjamin Spock's *Baby and Child Care*, first published in 1946 and reissued (and revised) repeatedly for decades thereafter. Dr. Spock's approach to raising babies was child-centered, as opposed to parent-centered. The purpose of motherhood, he taught, was to help children learn and grow and realize their potential. All other considerations, including the mother's own physical and emotional requirements, should be subordinated to the needs of the child. Dr. Spock at first envisioned only a very modest role for fathers in the process of child rearing, although he changed his views on this (and on many other issues) over time.

DR. BENJAMIN SPOCK

Women who could afford not to work faced pressures to remain in the home and concentrate on raising their children. But as expectations of material comfort rose, many middle-class families needed a second income to maintain the standard of living they desired. As a result, the number of married women working outside the home actually increased in the postwar years—even as the social pressure for them to stay out of the workplace grew. By 1960, nearly a third of all married women were part of the paid workforce.

The Birth of Television

Television, the most powerful medium of mass communication in the second half of the twentieth century, was central to the culture of the postwar era. Experiments in broadcasting pictures (along with sound) had begun as early as the 1920s, but commercial television began only shortly after World War II. Its growth was phenomenally rapid. In 1946, there were only 17,000 sets in the country; by 1957, there were 40 million television sets in use—almost as many sets as there were families. More people had television sets, according to one report, than had refrigerators.

The television industry emerged directly out of the radio industry, and all three major networks—the National Broadcasting Company, the Columbia Broadcasting System, and the American Broadcasting Company—had started as radio companies. Like radio, the television business was driven by advertising. The need to attract advertisers determined most programming decisions; and in the early days of television, sponsors often played a direct, powerful, and continuing role in determining the content of the programs they chose to sponsor. Many early television shows bore the names of the

Historical Thinking Skills

Argumentation After students have read the section "The Suburban Nation," ask them to create an advertisement for Levittown or a similar suburban development. Have students consider what features of suburban living would have been most appealing for American families following World War II. WXT SOC NAT GEO

Discussion and Activities

Making Connections Have students read the section "The Suburban Family." Ask them to discuss in small groups how American families have changed or stayed the same since 1950. SOC GEO WXT

Discussion and Activities

Making Connections After students have read the section "The Birth of Television," ask them to create a Venn diagram comparing how viewers experienced television in the 1950s compared to the present day. SOC

OZZIE AND HARRIET In addition to depicting American life as predominantly white, middle class, and suburban, television in the 1950s and 1960s often portrayed Americans as optimistic and upwardly mobile. Here the Nelson family, characters from the show *The Adventures of Ozzie and Harriet*, enjoys time together in their backyard pool.

corporations that were paying for them: the GE Television Theater, the Chrysler Playhouse, the Camel News Caravan, and others. Some daytime serials were actually written and produced by Procter & Gamble and other companies.

The impact of television on American life was rapid, pervasive, and profound. By the late 1950s, television news had replaced newspapers, magazines, and radios as the nation's most important vehicle of information. Television advertising helped create a vast market for new fashions and products. Televised athletic events gradually made professional and college sports one of the most important sources of entertainment (and one of the biggest businesses) in America. Television entertainment programming–almost all of it controlled by the three national networks and their corporate sponsors–replaced movies and radio as the principal source of diversion for American families.

SOCIAL CONSEQUENCES OF TELEVISION

Much of the programming of the 1950s and early 1960s created a common image of American life–an image that was predominantly white, middle-class, and suburban, and that was epitomized by such popular situation comedies as *Ozzie and Harriet* and *Leave It to Beaver*. Programming also reinforced the concept of gender roles that most men (and many women) unthinkingly embraced. Most situation comedies, in particular, showed families in which, as the title of one of the most popular put it, *Father Knows Best*, and in which most women were mothers and housewives striving to serve their children and please their husbands.

TELEVISION'S HOMOGENIZING MESSAGE

But television also conveyed other images: gritty, urban, working-class families in Jackie Gleason's *The Honeymooners;* the childless show-business family of the early *I Love Lucy;* unmarried professional women in *Our Miss Brooks* and *My Little Margie;* hapless African Americans in *Amos 'n Andy*. Television not only sought to create an idealized image of a homogeneous suburban America. It also sought to convey experiences at odds with that image–but to convey them in warm, unthreatening terms.

Yet television also, inadvertently, created conditions that could accentuate social conflict. Even those unable to share in the affluence of the era could, through television news and other venues, acquire a vivid picture of how the rest of their society lived. And at the same time that television was reinforcing the homogeneity of the white middle class, it was also contributing to the sense of alienation and powerlessness among groups excluded from the world it portrayed.

TRAVEL, OUTDOOR RECREATION, AND ENVIRONMENTALISM

The idea of a paid vacation for American workers, and the association of that idea with travel, entered American culture beginning in the 1920s. But it was not until the postwar years that vacation travel became truly widespread among middle-income Americans. The construction of the interstate highway system contributed dramatically to the growth of travel. So did the increasing affluence of workers, which made it possible for them to buy cars.

Nowhere was this surge in travel and recreation more visible than in America's national parks, which experienced the beginnings of what became a permanent surge in attendance

Discussion and Activities

Evaluating Evidence Have students examine the image "Ozzie and Harriet." Discuss as a class the ways in which television shows like the one pictured reinforced gender and family roles. *(The reinforcement of stereotypes with the father and children relaxing in the pool while the mother serves them refreshments. Women had the responsibility of maintaining the home and for child-centered parenting.)* WXT SOC

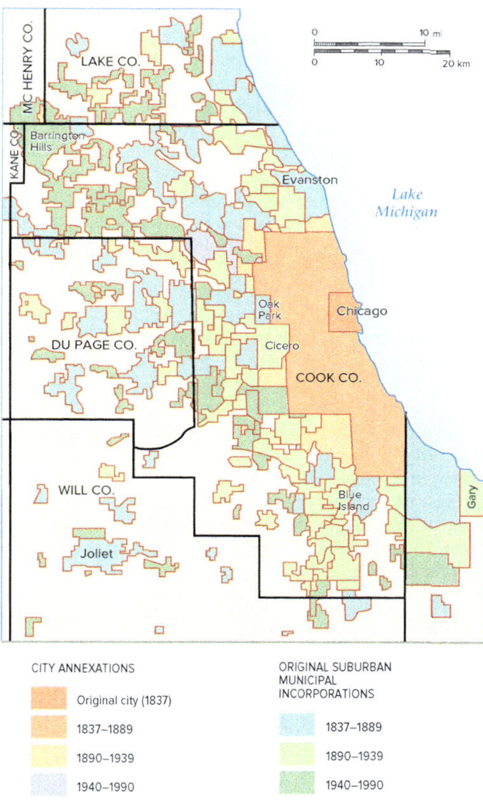

CHICAGO'S ANNEXATIONS AND THE SUBURBAN NOOSE This map uses Chicago as an example of two important processes in the growth of American cities—municipal consolidation and suburbanization. In 1837, Chicago consisted of a small area on the shore of Lake Michigan (represented by the small dark orange area on the right center of the map. Over the next fifty years, Chicago annexed an enormous amount of additional land around its original borders, followed by a few smaller annexations in the twentieth century. At the same time, however, many of the areas around Chicago were separating themselves from the city by incorporating as independent communities—suburbs—with a particular wave of such incorporations in the first decades of the twentieth century, continuing into the 1990s. A map of New York, and of many other cities, would reveal a similar pattern.

What were the consequences for the city of its legal and financial separation from so many suburban communities?

in the 1950s. People who traveled to national parks did so for many reasons–some to hike and camp; some to fish and hunt (activities that themselves grew dramatically in the 1950s and helped create a large number of clubs); some simply to look in awe at the landscape. Many visitors to national parks came in search less of conventional recreation than of wilderness. The importance of that search became clear in the early 1950s in the first of many battles over development of wilderness areas: the fight to preserve Echo Park.

ECHO PARK

Echo Park is a spectacular valley in the Dinosaur National Monument, on the border between Utah and Colorado, near the southern border of Wyoming. In the early 1950s, the federal government's Bureau of Reclamation–created early in the century to encourage irrigation, develop electric power, and increase water supplies–proposed building a dam across the Green River, which runs through Echo Valley, so as to create a lake for recreation and a source of hydroelectric power. The American environmental movement had been relatively quiet since its searing defeat early in the century in its effort to stop a similar dam in the Hetch Hetchy Valley at Yosemite National Park. But the Echo Park proposal helped rouse it from its slumber.

In 1950, Bernard DeVoto–a well-known writer and a great champion of the American West–published an essay in *The Saturday Evening Post* titled "Shall We Let Them Ruin Our National Parks?" It had a sensational impact, arousing opposition to the Echo Valley dam from many areas of the country. The Sierra Club, relatively quiet in previous decades, moved into action; the controversy helped elevate a new and aggressive leader, David Brower, who eventually transformed the club into the nation's leading environmental organization. By the mid-1950s, a large coalition of environmentalists, naturalists, and wilderness vacationers had been mobilized in opposition to the dam, and in 1956 Congress–bowing to the public pressure–blocked the project and preserved Echo Park in its natural state. The controversy was a major victory for those who wished to preserve the sanctity of the national parks, and it was an important impetus to the dawning environmental consciousness that would become so important in later decades.

SIERRA CLUB REBORN

ORGANIZED SOCIETY AND ITS DETRACTORS

White-collar workers came to outnumber blue-collar laborers for the first time in the 1950s, and an increasing proportion of them worked in corporate settings with rigid hierarchical structures. Industrial workers also confronted large bureaucracies, both in the workplace and in their own unions. Consumers discovered the frustrations of bureaucracy in dealing with the large national companies from whom they bought goods and services. More and more Americans were becoming convinced that the key to a successful future lay in acquiring the specialized training and skills necessary for work in large organizations.

The American educational system responded to the demands of this increasingly organized society by experimenting with changes in curriculum and philosophy. Elementary and secondary schools gave increased attention to the teaching of science, mathematics, and foreign languages (particularly after the launching of the Soviet Union's *Sputnik*)–all of which educators considered important for the development of skilled, specialized professionals. Universities in the meantime were expanding their curricula

GROWTH OF SPECIALIZED EDUCATION

Discussion and Activities

Analyzing Issues After students have read the section "Travel, Outdoor Recreation, and Environmentalism," ask them to write a short paragraph explaining how the Echo Park controversy demonstrated the tension between advocates of development and supporters of conservation. **WXT** **GEO**

Answers

Chicago's Annexations and the Suburban Noose

While cities expanded rapidly through annexation, they often found themselves hemmed in by the suburban areas that formed around them.

Reasoning Processes

Comparing After students have read the section "Organized Society and Its Detractors," ask them to discuss in pairs or small groups the similarities and differences between secondary education in the 1950s and today. **WXT** **ARC**

to provide more opportunities for students to develop specialized skills. The idea of the "multiversity"–a phrase first coined by the chancellor of the University of California at Berkeley to describe his institution's diversity–represented a commitment to making higher education a training ground for specialists in a wide variety of fields.

The debilitating impact of bureaucratic life on the individual slowly became a central theme of popular and scholarly debate. William H. Whyte Jr. produced one of the most widely discussed books of the decade: *The Organization Man* (1956), which attempted to describe the special mentality of the worker in a large, bureaucratic setting. Self-reliance, Whyte claimed, was losing place to the ability to "get along" and "work as a team" as the most valued trait in the modern character. Sociologist David Riesman had made similar observations in *The Lonely Crowd* (1950), in which he argued that the traditional "inner-directed" man, who judged himself on the basis of his own values and the esteem of his family, was giving way to a new "other-directed" man, more concerned with winning the approval of the larger organization or community.

Novelists, too, expressed misgivings in their work about the impersonality of modern society. Saul Bellow produced a series of novels–*The Adventures of Augie March* (1953), *Seize the Day* (1956), *Herzog* (1964), and many others–that chronicled the difficulties American Jewish men had in finding fulfillment in modern urban America. J. D. Salinger wrote in *The Catcher in the Rye* (1951) of a prep-school student, Holden Caulfield, who was unable to find any area of society–school, family, friends, city–in which he could feel secure or committed.

The Beats and the Restless Culture of Youth

The most caustic critics of bureaucracy, and of middle-class society in general, were a group of young poets, writers, and artists generally known as the "beats" (or, derisively, as "beatniks").

THE BEAT GENERATION'S CRITIQUES

They wrote harsh critiques of what they considered the sterility and conformity of American life, the meaninglessness of American politics, and the banality of popular culture. Allen Ginsberg's dark, bitter poem "Howl" (1955) decried the "Robot apartments! invincible suburbs! skeleton treasuries! blind capitals! demonic industries!" of modern life. Jack Kerouac produced the bible of much of the Beat Generation in his novel *On the Road* (1957)–an account of a cross-country automobile trip that depicted the rootless, iconoclastic lifestyle of Kerouac and his friends.

The beats were the most visible evidence of a widespread restlessness among young Americans in the 1950s. In part, that restlessness was a result of prosperity itself–of a growing sense among young people of limitless possibilities, and of the declining power of such traditional values as thrift, discipline, and self-restraint. Young middle-class Americans were growing up in a culture that encouraged them to expect rich and fulfilling lives; but they were living in a world in which almost all of them experienced obstacles to that fulfillment.

Tremendous public attention was directed at the phenomenon of "juvenile delinquency," and in both politics and popular culture there were dire warnings about the growing criminality of American youth. The 1955 film *Blackboard Jungle*, for example, was a frightening depiction of crime and violence in city schools. Scholarly studies, presidential commissions, and journalistic exposés all contributed to the sense of alarm about the spread of delinquency–although in fact youth crime did not dramatically increase in the 1950s.

The culture of alienation that the beats so vividly represented had counterparts even in ordinary middle-class behavior: teenage rebelliousness toward parents, youthful fascination with fast cars and motorcycles, and the increasing visibility of teenage sex, assisted by the greater availability of birth-control devices. The popularity of James Dean, in such movies as *Rebel Without a Cause* (1955), *East of Eden* (1955), and *Giant* (1956), conveyed a powerful image of youth culture in the 1950s. Both in the roles he played (moody, alienated teenagers and young men with a streak of self-destructive violence) and in the way he lived his own life (he died in 1955, at the age of 24,

ELVIS Elvis Presley is almost certainly the most famous and influential rock musician of the twentieth century. Born in Mississippi and influenced by the African American of the South, he became a singer in the mid-1950s and continued to be extraordinarily popular until his death in 1977. This photograph shows him very early in his career.

Discussion and Activities

Analyzing Points of View Have students examine the image "Elvis." Ask them to write a short journal entry from the point of view of either an American teenager or the parent of a teenager explaining their reaction to rock 'n' roll artists like Elvis Presley. **SOC** **ARC**

LUCY AND DESI

The most popular show in the history of television began as an effort by a young comedian to strengthen her troubled marriage. In 1950, Lucille Ball was performing in a popular weekly CBS radio comedy, *My Favorite Husband*, in which she portrayed a slightly zany housewife who tangled frequently with her banker husband, played by Richard Denning. The network proposed to transfer the show from radio to television. Lucy said she would do so only if she could replace Denning with her real-life husband of ten years, Desi Arnaz—a Cuban-born bandleader whose almost constant traveling was putting a strain on their marriage. Network officials tried in vain to talk her out of the idea. Arnaz had no acting experience, they told her. Lucy herself recognized another reason for their reluctance: the radicalism of portraying an ethnically mixed marriage on the air. But she held her ground.

On Monday, October 15, 1951, the first episode of *I Love Lucy* was broadcast over CBS. Desi Arnaz played Ricky Ricardo, a Cuban bandleader and singer who spoke, at times, with a comically exaggerated Latin accent. Lucille Ball was Lucy Ricardo, his stage-struck and slightly dizzy wife. Performing with them were William Frawley and Vivian Vance, who played their neighbors and close friends, Fred and Ethel Mertz. In the premiere episode, "The Girls Want to Go to a Nightclub," Ricky and Fred want to go to a boxing match on the night of Fred and Ethel's anniversary, while the wives are arranging an evening at a nightclub.

The opening episode contained many of the elements that characterized the show throughout its long run and ensured its extraordinary success: the remarkable chemistry among the four principal actors, the unexpected comedic talent of Desi Arnaz, and most of all the brilliance of Lucille Ball. She was a master of physical comedy, and many of her funniest moments involved scenes of absurdly incongruous situations (Lucy working an assembly line, Lucy stomping grapes in Italy). Her characteristic yowl of frustration became one of the most familiar sounds in American culture. She was a beautiful woman, but she never hesitated to make herself look ridiculous. "She was everywoman," her longtime writer Jess Oppenheim once wrote; "her little expressions and inflections stimulated the shock of recognition in the audience."

But it was not just the great talents of its cast that made *I Love Lucy* such a phenomenon. It was the skill of its writers in evoking some of the most common experiences and desires of television viewers in the 1950s. Lucy, in particular, mined the frustrations of domestic life for all they were worth, constantly engaging in zany and hilarious schemes to break into show business or somehow expand her world. The husbands wanted calm and conventional domestic lives—and time to themselves for conspicuously male activities: boxing, fishing, baseball. In the first seasons, the fictional couples lived as neighbors, without children, in a Manhattan apartment building. Later, Lucy had a child and they all moved to the suburbs. (The show used Lucy's real-life pregnancy on the air; and on January 19, 1953—only hours after Lucille Ball gave birth to her realson and second child—CBS aired a previously filmed episode of the fictional Lucy giving birth to a fictional son, "Little Ricky" Ricardo.)

VITAMEATAVEGAMIN One of the most popular episodes of *I Love Lucy* portrays Lucy at a trade show promoting a new health product called "Vitameatavegamin." In the course of the show, she herself drinks a great deal of the concoction, which has a high alcohol content and leaves her hilariously drunk.

PROMOTING THE SHOW The marriage of Lucille Ball and Desi Arnaz, which paralleled the television marriage of Lucy and Ricky Ricardo, was one of the most effective promotional devices for *I Love Lucy*. Here, Lucy and Desi pose for a promotional still—one of many they made for advertisements, magazine covers, and posters until their marriage (and the show) dissolved in 1960.

LUCY AT HOME Although Lucy and Desi at first portrayed a childless, ethnically mixed couple living in a Manhattan apartment, many of the comic situations in the early years of the show were purely domestic. Here, Lucy, wearing an apron, deals with one of her many household predicaments with the extraordinary physical comedy that was part of her great success. Desi, watching skeptically, was a talented straight man to Lucy's zaniness.

Lucille Ball remained a major television star for nearly twenty years after *I Love Lucy* (and its successor, *The Lucille Ball–Desi Arnaz Comedy Hour*) left the air in 1960. Desi Arnaz, whom Lucy divorced in 1960, remained for a time one of Hollywood's most powerful and successful studio executives as the head of Desilu Productions. And nearly sixty-five years after the first episode of *I Love Lucy* aired, the series remains extraordinarily popular all over the world—shown so frequently in reruns that in some American cities it is sometimes possible to see six Lucy episodes in a single evening. "People identified with the Ricardos," Lucille Ball once said, "because we had the same problems they had. We just took ordinary situations and exaggerated them."

HISTORICAL THINKING SKILLS

1. **Explaining Historical Developments** In what ways did *I Love Lucy* reflect American society and family life of the 1950s?
2. **Making Connections** How have television situation comedies since *I Love Lucy* copied the formula for success established by that program? Do you see elements of the *I Love Lucy* pattern in today's situation comedies?
3. **Explaining Significance** Why do you think *I Love Lucy* has continued to be so popular, both in the United States and throughout the world?

AP Exam Tip

The Advanced Placement Exam will require students to explain the purpose, point of view, historical situation, and/or audience of a document or image. One way students can demonstrate this is to explain a motive for the creation of a document or image.

Historical Thinking Skills

Sourcing and Situation Have students practice the tip by writing a short paragraph explaining the motive(s) behind one of the images included in the feature "Lucy and Desi." *(A possible response is to increase the audience by reinforcing gender roles or by showcasing the real-life relationship between the stars of the show.)* **ARC** 

Answers

Patterns of Popular Culture

1. Possible answer: The show depicted a married couple that had the same issues and problems as many Americans. As Lucille Ball stated, "We just took ordinary situations and exaggerated them." The show also explored the shared anxieties of the post-World War II American society and culture.
2. Possible answer: Like *I Love* Lucy, many situational comedies today portray the challenges faced by ordinary people. Likewise, shows today also take on societal issues and anxieties.
3. Possible answers: The characters were believable, the episodes had a wide range of emotional appeal, and the themes and stories they explored were universal.

Discussion and Activities

Making Connections After students have read the section "The Beats and the Restless Culture of Youth," ask them to create a Venn diagram comparing the youth culture of the 1950s with that of today. Have students discuss as a class the similarities and differences between the time periods. **ARC** **SOC** **WXT**

in a car accident), Dean became an icon of the unfocused rebelliousness of American youth in his time.

ROCK 'N' ROLL

One of the most powerful cultural forces for American youth was the enormous popularity of rock 'n' roll–and of the greatest early rock star, Elvis Presley. Presley became a symbol of a youthful determination to push at the borders of the conventional and acceptable. His sultry good looks; his self-conscious effort to dress in the vaguely rebellious style of urban gangs (motorcycle jackets and slicked-back hair); and most of all, the open sexuality of his music and his public performances made him wildly popular among young Americans in the 1950s. His first great hit, "Heartbreak Hotel," established him as a national phenomenon in 1956, and he remained a powerful figure in American popular culture until–and indeed beyond–his death in 1977.

ELVIS PRESLEY

Presley's music, like that of most early white rock musicians, drew heavily from black rhythm and blues traditions, which appealed to some white youths in the early 1950s because of their pulsing, sensual rhythms and their hard-edged lyrics. Sam Phillips, a local record promoter who had recorded some of the important black rhythm and blues musicians of his time (among them B. B. King), reportedly said in the early 1950s: "If I could find a white man with a Negro sound, I could make a billion dollars." Soon after that, he found Presley. But there were others as well. Among them were Buddy Holly and Bill Haley (whose 1955 song "Rock Around the Clock"–used in the film *Blackboard Jungle*–served to announce the arrival of rock 'n' roll to millions of young people), who were closely connected to African American musical traditions. Rock drew from other sources too: from country western music (another strong influence on Presley), from gospel music, even from jazz. But its most important influence was its roots in rhythm and blues.

ROCK 'N' ROLL'S BLACK ROOTS

The rise of such white rock musicians as Presley was a result in part of the limited willingness of white audiences to accept black musicians. But the 1950s did see a growth in the popularity of African American bands and singers among both black and white audiences. Chuck Berry, Little Richard, B. B. King, Chubby Checker, the Temptations, and others–many of them recorded by the African American producer Berry Gordy, the founder and president of Motown Records in Detroit–never rivaled Presley in their popularity among white youths. But they did develop a significant multiracial audience of their own.

The rapid rise and enormous popularity of rock owed a great deal to innovations in radio and television programming. By the 1950s, radio stations no longer felt obliged to present mostly live programming. Instead, many radio stations devoted themselves to playing recorded music. Early in the 1950s, a new breed of radio announcers, known now as "disc jockeys," began to create programming aimed specifically at young fans of rock music; and when those programs became wildly successful, other stations followed suit. *American Bandstand*, a televised showcase for rock 'n' roll hits that began in 1957, featured a live audience dancing to mostly recorded music. The show helped spread the popularity of rock–and made its host, Dick Clark, one of the best-known figures in America among young Americans.

Radio and television were important to the recording industry, of course, because they encouraged the sale of records. Also important were jukeboxes, which played individual songs on 45s (records with one song on each side) and proliferated in soda fountains, diners, bars, and other places where young people were likely to congregate. Sales of records increased threefold–from $182 million to $521 million–between 1954 and 1960. So eager were record promoters to get their songs on the air that some routinely made secret payments to station owners and disc jockeys to encourage them to showcase their artists. These payments, which became known as "payola," produced a briefly sensational series of scandals when they were exposed in the late 1950s and early 1960s.

"PAYOLA" SCANDALS

THE "OTHER AMERICA"

It was relatively easy for white, middle-class Americans in the 1950s to believe that the world they knew–a world of economic growth, personal affluence, and cultural homogeneity–was the world all Americans experienced; that the values and assumptions they shared were ones that most other Americans shared too. But such assumptions were false. Even within the middle class, there was considerable restiveness–among women, intellectuals, young people, and others who found the middle-class consumer culture somehow unsatisfying, even stultifying. More importantly, large groups of Americans remained outside the circle of abundance and shared in neither the affluence of the middle class nor its values.

ON THE MARGINS OF THE AFFLUENT SOCIETY

In 1962, the socialist writer Michael Harrington created a sensation by publishing a book called *The Other America*, in which he chronicled the continuing existence of poverty in America. The conditions he described were not new. Only the attention he was bringing to them was.

THE OTHER AMERICA

The great economic expansion of the postwar years reduced poverty significantly but did not eliminate it. In 1960, at any given moment, more than a fifth of all American families (over 30 million people) continued to live below what the government defined as the poverty line (down from a third of all families fifteen years before). Many millions more lived just above the official poverty line, but with incomes that gave them little comfort and no security.

Most of the poor experienced poverty intermittently and temporarily. Eighty percent of those classified as poor at any particular moment were likely to have moved into poverty

Historical Thinking Skills

Identifying Cause and Effect Have students read the section "Rock 'n' Roll." Ask them to discuss in small groups the causes and effects of the rise in popularity of rock 'n' roll music. **ARC** **SOC** **WXT**

recently and might move out of it again as soon as they found a job—an indication of how unstable employment could be at the lower levels of the job market. But approximately 20 percent of the poor were people for whom poverty was a continuous, debilitating reality, from which there was no easy escape. That included approximately half the nation's elderly and a large proportion of African Americans and Hispanics. Native Americans constituted the single poorest group in the country, a result of government policies that undermined the economies of the reservations and drove many Indians into cities, where some lived in a poverty worse than that they had left. These were the people Harrington had written about in *The Other America*, people who suffered from what he called "a system designed to be impervious to hope."

PERSISTENT POVERTY

This "hard-core" poverty rebuked the assumptions of those who argued that economic growth would eventually lead everyone into prosperity; that, as many claimed, "a rising tide lifts all boats." It was a poverty that the growing prosperity of the postwar era seemed to affect hardly at all.

RURAL POVERTY

Among those on the margins of the affluent society were many rural Americans. In 1948, farmers had received 8.9 percent of the national income; in 1956, they received only 4.1 percent. In part, this decline reflected the steadily shrinking farm population; in 1956 alone, nearly 10 percent of the rural population moved into or was absorbed by cities. But it also reflected declining farm prices. Because of enormous surpluses in basic staples, prices fell 33 percent in those years, even though national income as a whole rose 50 percent at the same time. Even most farmers who managed to survive experienced substantial losses of income at the same time that the prices of many consumer goods rose.

DECLINING AGRICULTURAL PRICES

Not all farmers were poor. Some substantial landowners weathered, and even managed to profit from, the changes in American agriculture. Others moved from considerable to only modest affluence. But the agrarian economy did produce substantial numbers of genuinely impoverished people. Black sharecroppers and tenant farmers continued to live at or below subsistence level throughout the rural South—in part because of the mechanization of cotton picking beginning in 1944, in part because of the development of synthetic fibers that reduced demand for cotton. (Two-thirds of the cotton acreage of the South went out of production between 1930 and 1960.) Migrant farmworkers, a group concentrated especially in the West and Southwest and containing many Mexican American and Asian American workers, lived in similarly dire circumstances. In rural areas without much commercial agriculture—such as the Appalachian region in the East, where the decline of the coal economy reduced the one significant source of support for the region—whole communities lived in desperate poverty, increasingly cut off from the market economy. All these groups were vulnerable to malnutrition and even starvation.

THE INNER CITIES

As white families moved from cities to suburbs in vast numbers, many inner-city neighborhoods became vast repositories for the poor, "ghettos" from which there was no easy escape. The growth of these neighborhoods owed much to a vast migration of African Americans out of the countryside and into industrial cities. More than 3 million black men and women moved from the South to northern cities between 1940 and 1960. Chicago, Detroit, Cleveland, New York, and other eastern and midwestern industrial cities experienced a great expansion of their black populations—both in absolute numbers and, even more, as a percentage of the whole, since so many white people were leaving these cities at the same time.

BLACK URBAN MIGRATION

Similar migrations from Mexico and Puerto Rico expanded poor Hispanic neighborhoods at the same time. Between 1940 and 1960, nearly a million Puerto Ricans moved into American cities (the largest group to New York). Mexican workers crossed the border in Texas and California and swelled the already substantial Latino communities of such cities as San Antonio, Houston, San Diego, and Los Angeles (which by 1960 had the largest Mexican American population of any city, approximately 500,000 people).

Why so many inner-city communities, populated largely by racial and ethnic minorities, remained so poor in the midst of growing affluence has been the subject of considerable debate. Some critics have argued that the new migrants were victims, in part, of their own pasts, that the work habits, values, and family structures they brought with them from their rural homes were poorly adapted to the needs of the modern industrial city. Others have argued that the inner city itself—its crippling poverty, its crime, its violence, its apparent hopelessness—created a "culture of poverty" that made it difficult for individuals to advance.

Many others argue that a combination of declining blue-collar jobs, inadequate support for minority-dominated public schools, and barriers to advancement rooted in racism—not the culture and values of the poor themselves—was the source of inner-city poverty. It is indisputable that inner cities were filling up with poor minority residents at the same time that the unskilled industrial jobs they were seeking were diminishing. Employers were relocating factories and mills from old industrial cities to new locations in suburbs, smaller cities, and even abroad—places where the cost of labor was lower. Even in the factories that remained, automation was reducing the number of unskilled jobs. The economic opportunities that had helped earlier immigrant groups to rise up from poverty were unavailable to most of the postwar migrants. Nor can there be any doubt that historic patterns of racial discrimination in hiring, education, and housing doomed many members of these communities to continuing, and in some cases increasing, poverty.

For many years, the principal policy response to the poverty of inner cities was "urban renewal": the effort to tear down buildings in the poorest and most degraded areas. In the

Historical Thinking Skills

Drawing Conclusions After students have read the section "On the Margins of the Affluent Society," discuss as a class why poverty persisted despite the economic growth of the 1950s. *(Unequal opportunities for women and minorities; waning influence of unions; discriminatory government policies.)* **WXT** **PCE** **SOC**

Historical Thinking Skills

Identifying Cause and Effect Have students read the section "Rural Poverty." Ask them to create a T-chart listing causes and effects of rural poverty. Have students work in small groups to classify the causes and effects they identified as economic, social, or political. **WXT** **PCE** **SOC**

Reasoning Processes

Comparing After students have read the section "The Inner Cities," ask them to create a Venn diagram comparing conditions in the inner cities and the suburbs they read about earlier in the chapter. Have students discuss the reasons for the similarities and differences. WXT SOC PCE GEO ARC

AFRICAN AMERICAN MIGRATION, 1950–1980 Although there had been a substantial migration of African Americans out of the South and into northern industrial cities around the time of World War I and again during World War II, that process accelerated in the thirty years after 1950. By 1980, fewer southern states had black populations that accounted for 25 percent or more of their total population than in 1950. In the rest of the country, the number of states whose black populations exceeded 5 and 10 percent (the states shaded orange and purple) greatly increased.

What were some of the factors that produced the African American migration in this period?

"URBAN RENEWAL"

twenty years after World War II, urban renewal projects destroyed over 400,000 buildings, among them the homes of nearly 1.5 million people. In some cases, urban renewal provided new public housing for poor city residents. Some of it was considerably better than the housing they left; some of it was poorly designed and constructed, and deteriorated rapidly into dismal and dangerous slums.

THE CRUSADE AGAINST SUBVERSION

The cultural homogeneity white, middle-class Americans imagined was also threatened by a growing fear of internal communist subversion that by the early 1950s had reached the point of near hysteria.

DALTON TRUMBO Screenwriter Dalton Trumbo was a member of the "Hollywood Ten." He refused to testify before the House Un-American Activities Committee in its investigation of communist influences in Hollywood. As a result, Trumbo was blacklisted and could not find work. While blacklisted, Trumbo won two Academy Awards; one was given to a "front" writer who pretended to be the author of the script and the other was awarded to "Robert Rich," Trumbo's pseudonym.

Answers

African American Migration: 1950–1980

This migration was primarily motivated by a search for work in the face of changes in industry and agriculture.

Communism was not an imagined enemy in the 1950s. It had tangible shape, in Joseph Stalin and the Soviet Union. In addition, America had encountered setbacks in its battle against communism: the Korean stalemate, the "loss" of China, the Soviet development of an atomic bomb. Searching for someone to blame, many people were attracted to the idea of a communist conspiracy within American borders. But there were other factors as well, rooted in American domestic politics.

SOURCES OF THE RED SCARE

HUAC and Alger Hiss

Much of the anticommunist furor emerged out of the Republican Party's search for an issue with which to attack the Democrats, and out of the Democrats' efforts to stifle that issue. Beginning in 1947 (with Republicans temporarily in control of Congress), the House Un-American Activities Committee (HUAC) held widely publicized investigations to prove that, under Democratic rule, the government had tolerated (if not actually encouraged) communist subversion. The committee turned first to the movie industry, arguing that communists had infiltrated Hollywood. Writers and producers, some of them former communists, were called to testify; and when several of them ("the Hollywood Ten") refused to answer questions about their own political beliefs and those of their colleagues, they were jailed for contempt. Some writers were barred from employment in the movie industry when Hollywood, attempting to protect its public image, adopted a blacklist of those of "suspicious loyalty."

More alarming to much of the public was HUAC's investigation into charges of disloyalty leveled against a former high-ranking member of the State Department: Alger Hiss. In 1948, Whittaker Chambers, a self-avowed former communist agent who had turned vehemently against the party and become an editor at *Time* magazine, told the committee that Hiss had passed classified State Department documents through him to the Soviet Union in 1937 and 1938. When Hiss sued him for slander, Chambers produced microfilms of the documents (called the "pumpkin papers," because Chambers had kept them hidden in a pumpkin in his garden). Hiss could not be tried for espionage because of the statute of limitations (a law that protects individuals from prosecution for most crimes after seven years have passed). But largely because of the relentless efforts of Richard M. Nixon, a freshman Republican congressman from California and a member of HUAC, Hiss was convicted of perjury and served several years in prison. The Hiss case not only discredited a prominent young diplomat; it also cast suspicion on a generation of liberal Democrats and made it possible for many Americans to believe that communists had actually infiltrated the government.

ALGER HISS

The Federal Loyalty Program and the Rosenberg Case

Partly to protect itself against Republican attacks, partly to encourage support for the president's foreign policy initiatives, the Truman administration in 1947 initiated a widely publicized program to review the loyalty of federal employees. In August 1950, the president authorized sensitive agencies to fire people deemed "bad security risks." By 1951, more than 2,000 government employees had resigned under pressure and 212 had been dismissed.

The employee loyalty program established a widely cited list of supposedly subversive organizations. The director of the Federal Bureau of Investigation (FBI), J. Edgar Hoover, investigated and harassed alleged radicals. In 1950, Congress passed the McCarran Internal Security Act, requiring all communist organizations to register with the government. Truman vetoed the bill. Congress easily overrode his veto.

THE MCCARRAN INTERNAL SECURITY ACT

The successful Soviet detonation of a nuclear weapon in 1949 convinced many people that there had been a conspiracy to pass American atomic secrets to the Russians. In 1950, Klaus Fuchs, a young British scientist, seemed to confirm those fears when he testified that he had delivered to the Russians details of the manufacture of the bomb. The case ultimately settled on an obscure New York couple, Julius and Ethel Rosenberg, members of the Communist Party, whom the federal government claimed had been the masterminds of the conspiracy. The case against them rested in large part on testimony by Ethel's brother, David Greenglass, a machinist who had worked on the Manhattan Project. Greenglass admitted to channeling secret information to the Soviet Union through other agents (including Fuchs). His sister and brother-in-law had, he claimed, planned and orchestrated the espionage. The Rosenbergs were convicted and, on April 5, 1951, sentenced to death. After two years of appeals and protests by sympathizers, they died in the electric chair on June 19, 1953.

All these factors—the HUAC investigations, the Hiss trial, the loyalty investigations, the McCarran Act, the Rosenberg case—helped to intensify public fear of communist subversion. By the early 1950s, the fear seemed to have gripped much of the country. State and local governments, the judiciary, schools and universities, labor unions—all sought to purge themselves of real or imagined subversives. A pervasive fear settled on the country—not only the fear of communist infiltration but also the fear of being suspected of communist subversion. It was a climate that made possible the rise of an extraordinary public figure, whose behavior at any other time might have been dismissed as preposterous.

ANTICOMMUNIST HYSTERIA

McCarthyism

Joseph McCarthy was a relatively undistinguished first-term Republican senator from Wisconsin when, in February 1950, he suddenly burst into national prominence. In the midst of a speech in Wheeling, West Virginia, he raised a sheet of paper and claimed to "hold in my hand" a list of 205 known communists currently working in the U.S. State Department. No person of comparable stature had ever made so bold a charge against the federal government; and in the weeks to come, as

Historical Thinking Skills

Contextualization Have students read the section "HUAC and Alger Hiss." Discuss as a class how the Hollywood Ten and Alger Hiss cases might have been influenced by Cold War tensions between the United States and Soviet Union. *(Fear of the spread of communism and the nuclear arms race caused many Americans to question the loyalty of others.)* **WOR** **PCE** **SOC**

Historical Thinking Skills

Evaluating Evidence Have students read the section "The Federal Loyalty Program and the Rosenberg Case." Then, ask students to write a letter to President Truman recommending either enforcement of the Rosenberg sentence or a pardon based on their interpretation of the evidence. **PCE**

Reasoning Processes

Causation After students have read the section "McCarthyism," ask them to discuss the reasons for McCarthy's popularity and whether or not President Eisenhower should have publicly spoken out against him. PCE SOC

McCarthy repeated and expanded his accusations, he emerged as the nation's most prominent leader of the crusade against domestic subversion.

Within weeks of his charges against the State Department, McCarthy was leveling accusations at other agencies. After 1952, with the Republicans in control of the Senate and McCarthy the chairman of a special subcommittee, he conducted highly publicized investigations of subversion in many areas of the government. His ambitious assistants, Roy Cohn and David Schine, sauntered arrogantly through federal offices and American embassies overseas looking for evidence of communist influence. One hapless government official after another appeared before McCarthy's subcommittee, where the senator belligerently and often cruelly badgered witnesses and destroyed public careers. McCarthy never produced solid evidence of actual communist subversion. But a growing constituency adored him nevertheless for his coarse, "fearless" assaults on a government establishment that many Americans considered arrogant, elitist, even traitorous. Republicans, in particular, rallied to his claims that the Democrats had been responsible for "twenty years of treason," that only a change of parties could rid the country of subversion. McCarthy, in short, provided his followers with an issue into which they could channel a wide range of resentments: fear of communism, animosity toward the country's "eastern establishment," and frustrated partisan ambitions.

McCarthyism's Appeal

For a time, McCarthy intimidated all but a few people from opposing him. Even the highly popular Dwight D. Eisenhower, running for president in 1952, did not speak out against him, although he disliked McCarthy's tactics and was outraged at McCarthy's attacks on General George Marshall.

The Republican Revival

Public frustration over the stalemate in Korea and popular fears of internal subversion combined to make 1952 a bad year for the Democratic Party. Truman, whose popularity had greatly diminished, wisely decided not to run again. The party united instead behind Governor Adlai E. Stevenson of Illinois, whose dignity, wit, and eloquence made him a beloved figure to many liberals and intellectuals. But Republicans charged that Stevenson lacked the strength or the will to combat communism sufficiently. McCarthy described him as "soft" and took delight in deliberately confusing him with Alger Hiss.

Stevenson's greatest problem, however, was the Republican candidate opposing him. Rejecting the efforts of conservatives to nominate Robert Taft or Douglas MacArthur, the Republicans turned to a man who had no previous identification with the party: General Dwight D. Eisenhower, military hero, commander of NATO, president of Columbia University in New York. Eisenhower won nomination on the first ballot. He chose as his running mate the young California senator who had gained national prominence through his crusade against Alger Hiss: Richard M. Nixon. Eisenhower and Nixon were a powerful combination in the autumn campaign. While Eisenhower attracted support through his geniality and his statesmanlike pledges to settle the Korean conflict (at one point dramatically promising to "go to Korea" himself), Nixon effectively exploited the issue of communist subversion. After surviving early accusations of financial improprieties (which he effectively neutralized in a famous television address, the "Checkers speech"), Nixon went on to launch harsh attacks on Democratic "cowardice," "appeasement," and "treason."

Dwight Eisenhower

Eisenhower won by both a popular and electoral landslide: 55 percent of the popular vote to Stevenson's 44 percent, 442 electoral votes to Stevenson's 89. Republicans gained control of both houses of Congress for only the second time in two decades. The election of 1952 ended twenty years of Democratic government. And while it might not have seemed so at the time, it also signaled the end of some of the worst turbulence of the postwar era.

Eisenhower Republicanism

Dwight D. Eisenhower was one of the least experienced politicians to serve in the White House in the twentieth century. He was also among the most popular and politically successful presidents of the postwar era. At home, he pursued essentially moderate policies, avoiding most new initiatives but accepting the work of earlier reformers. Abroad, he continued and even intensified American commitments to oppose communism but brought to some of those commitments a measure of restraint that his successors did not always match.

"What Was Good for . . . General Motors"

The first Republican administration in twenty years staffed itself with men drawn from the same quarter as those who had staffed Republican administrations in the 1920s: the business community. But by the 1950s, many business leaders had acquired a social and political outlook very different from that of their predecessors. Above all, many had reconciled themselves to at least the broad outlines of the Keynesian welfare state the New Deal had launched. Indeed, some corporate leaders had come to see it as something that actually benefited them—by helping maintain social order, by increasing mass purchasing power, and by stabilizing labor relations.

Business Leaders' New Outlook

To his cabinet, Eisenhower appointed wealthy corporate lawyers and business executives who were not apologetic about their backgrounds. Charles Wilson, president of General Motors, assured senators considering his nomination for secretary of defense that he foresaw no conflict of interest because he was certain that "what was good for our country was good for General Motors, and vice versa."

Eisenhower's consistent inclination was to limit federal activities and encourage private enterprise. He supported the private rather than public development of natural resources.

Historical Thinking Skills

Argumentation Have students read the section "The Republican Revival." Ask them to create a campaign poster supporting either Eisenhower or McCarthy in the 1952 presidential election. PCE

DEBATING THE PAST

"MCCARTHYISM"

When the American Civil Liberties Union warned in the early 1950s, at the peak of the anticommunist fervor that is now known as "McCarthyism," that "the threat to civil liberties today is the most serious in the history of our country," it was expressing a view with which many Americans wholeheartedly agreed. But while many Americans accept that there were unusually powerful challenges to freedom of speech and association in the late 1940s and early 1950s, there is wide disagreement about the causes and meaning of those challenges.

The simplest argument—and one that continues to attract scholarly support—is that the postwar Red Scare expressed real and legitimate concerns about communist subversion in the United States. William O'Neill, in *A Better World* (1982), and Richard Gid Powers, in *Not Without Honor* (1995), have both argued that anticommunism was a serious, intelligent, and patriotic movement, despite its excesses. The American Communist Party, according to this view, was an agent of Stalin and the Soviet Union within the United States, actively engaged in espionage and subversion. The effort to root communists out of public life was both understandable and justifiable—and the hysteria it sometimes produced was an unhappy but predictable by-product of an essentially rational and justifiable effort. "Anticommunism," Powers wrote, "expressed the essential American determination to stand against attacks on human freedom and foster the growth of democracy throughout the world. . . . To superimpose on this rich history the cartoon features of Joe McCarthy is to reject history for the easy comforts of moralism."

Most interpretations, however, have been much less charitable. In the 1950s, in the midst of the Red Scare, an influential group of historians and social scientists began to portray the anticommunist fervor of their time as an expression of social maladjustment—an argument perhaps most closely associated with Richard Hofstadter's essay "The Paranoid Style in American Politics." There was, they argued, no logical connection between the modest power of actual communists in the United States and the anticommunist hysteria. The fear of communism, they maintained, was rooted in social and cultural anxieties that had only an indirect connection with the political world. Extreme anticommunism, they claimed, was something close to a pathology; it expressed fear of and alienation from the modern world. A person afflicted with the "paranoid style," Hofstadter wrote:

> believes himself to be living in a world in which he is spied upon, plotted against, betrayed, and very likely destined for total ruin. He feels that his liberties have been arbitrarily and outrageously invaded. He is opposed to almost everything that has happened in American politics in the past twenty years.

Other scholars, writing not long after the decline of McCarthyism, rejected the sociocultural argument but shared the belief that the crusade against subversion was a distortion of normal public life. They saw the anticommunist crusade as an example of party politics run amok. Richard Freeland, in *The Truman Doctrine and the Origins of McCarthyism* (1971), argued that the Democrats began the effort to purge the government of radicals to protect themselves from attacks by the Republicans. Nelson Polsby, Robert Griffith, and others have noted how Republicans seized on the issue of communism in government in the late 1940s to reverse their nearly twenty-year exclusion from power. With each party trying to outdo the other in its effort to demonstrate its anticommunist credentials, it was hardly surprising that the crusade reached extraordinarily intense proportions.

Still other historians have emphasized the role of powerful government officials and agencies with a strong commitment to anticommunism—most notably J. Edgar Hoover and the FBI. Athan Theoharis and Kenneth O'Reilly introduced the idea of an anticommunist bureaucracy in work published in the 1970s and 1980s. Ellen Schrecker, in *Many Are the Crimes* (1998), argues that the Red Scare was, at its heart, directed largely against the left and that it was orchestrated by an interlocking cluster of official agencies with a deep commitment to the project.

Several scholars, finally, have presented an argument that does not so much challenge other interpretations as complement them. Anticommunist zealots were not alone to blame for the excesses of McCarthyism, they argue. It was also the fault of liberals—in politics, in academia, and perhaps above all in the media—who were so intimidated by the political climate, or so imprisoned within the conventions of their professions, that they found themselves unable to respond effectively to the distortions and excesses they recognized around them.

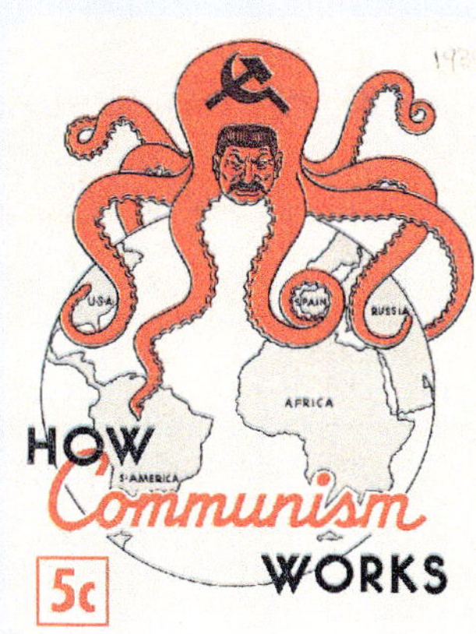

Rare Book and Special Collections Division, The Library of Congress

HISTORICAL THINKING SKILLS

Questions assume cumulative content knowledge from this chapter and previous chapters.

1. **Identifying Historical Concepts** Identify five different historical arguments discussed regarding McCarthyism.
2. **Evaluating Evidence** Describe how historical evidence could be used to support three of the historical arguments concerning McCarthyism.
3. **Developing Arguments** Analyze the school of thought you find most convincing making sure to use evidence from the text to support your argument.

Discussion and Activities

Analyzing Visuals Have students examine the image "How Communism Works." Ask them to discuss with a partner the symbolism associated with the octopus in the image. *(The octopus symbolizes an effort to control everything within its grasp. It was previously used to criticize the control of trusts.)* **WXT** **WOR** **PCE**

Answers

Debating the Past

1. Possible answer: O'Neill and Powers argued that the Red Scare represented a legitimate threat to the United States. Hofstadter argued that the real fear of communism in the United States was linked more to social and cultural anxieties. Freeland, Polsby, and Griffith blamed Democrats and Republicans for McCarthyism stating it was propagated for a political advantage. Schrecker argued it was the right directing attacks against the left. Theoharis and O'Reilly argued that government agencies like the FBI promoted a "anticommunism bureaucracy" that supported McCarthyism.
2. Possible answer: The conviction of Julius and Ethel Rosenberg clearly demonstrated that the communist threat to America was a real and legitimate phenomenon. The establishment of HUAC and its attacks on different aspects of American society clearly showed that the Red Scare was a movement controlled and run by political parties.
3. Possible answer: The existence of legitimate threats to American society were real, although over-exaggerated by members on both sides of the political spectrum in order to establish political hegemony.

Reasoning Processes

Comparing After students have read the section "What Was Good for . . . General Motors," ask them to create a Venn diagram comparing the economic policies of the Eisenhower administration with those of the Truman administration. PCE WXT

To the chagrin of farmers, he lowered federal support for farm prices. He also removed the last limited wage and price controls maintained by the Truman administration. He opposed the creation of new social service programs such as national health insurance. He strove constantly to reduce federal expenditures (even during the recession of 1958) and balance the budget. He ended 1960, his last full year in office, with a $1 billion budget surplus.

THE SURVIVAL OF THE WELFARE STATE

The president took few new initiatives in domestic policy, but he resisted pressure from the right wing of his party to dismantle those welfare policies of the New Deal that had survived the conservative assaults of the war years and after. He agreed to extend the Social Security system to an additional 10 million people and unemployment compensation to an additional 4 million, and he agreed to increase the legal minimum hourly wage from 75 cents to $1. Perhaps the most significant legislative accomplishment of the Eisenhower administration was the Federal Highway Act of 1956, which authorized $25 billion for a ten-year project that built over 40,000 miles of interstate highways–the largest public works project in American history. The program was to be funded through a highway "trust fund," whose revenues would come from new taxes on the purchase of fuel, automobiles, trucks, and tires.

FEDERAL HIGHWAY ACT OF 1956

In 1956, Eisenhower ran for a second term, even though he had suffered a serious heart attack the previous year. With Adlai Stevenson opposing him once again, he won by another, even greater landslide, receiving nearly 57 percent of the popular vote and 457 electoral votes to Stevenson's 73. Democrats retained control of both houses of Congress, which they had won back in 1954. And in 1958–during a serious recession–they increased that control by substantial margins.

THE DECLINE OF MCCARTHYISM

The Eisenhower administration did little in its first years in office to discourage the anticommunist furor that had gripped the nation. By 1954, however, the crusade against subversion was beginning to produce significant popular opposition–an indication that the anticommunist passion of several years earlier was beginning to abate. The clearest signal of that change was the political demise of Senator Joseph McCarthy.

During the first year of the Eisenhower administration, McCarthy continued to operate with impunity. But in January 1954 he overreached when he attacked Secretary of the Army Robert Stevens and the armed services in general. At that point, the administration and influential members of Congress organized a special investigation of the charges, which became known as the Army-McCarthy hearings. They were among the first congressional hearings to be nationally televised. The result was devastating to McCarthy. Watching McCarthy in action–bullying witnesses, hurling groundless (and often cruel) accusations, evading issues–much of the public began to see him as a villain, and even a buffoon. In December 1954, the Senate voted 67 to 22 to condemn him for "conduct unbecoming a senator." Three years later, with little public support left, he died–a victim, apparently, of complications arising from alcoholism.

ARMY-MCCARTHY HEARINGS

THE "HIGHWAY BILL" President Dwight Eisenhower signs the Federal Highway Act of 1956 into law from the Oval Office at the White House. This initiative authorized $25 billion to build more than 40,000 miles of interstate highway.

Discussion and Activities

Making Connections Have students read the section "Federal Highway Act of 1956." Ask them to discuss in small groups ways in which the interstate highway system impacts them today. SOC GEO WXT ARC NAT

CHAPTER 29 REVIEW

CONNECTING THEMES

Chapter Twenty-Nine explored the social and economic changes to American society following World War II. Truman continued much of the philosophical approach of the "New Deal" with his "Fair Deal," but conservatives blocked much of his agenda. The economy initially struggled to adapt to peacetime production. Government spending, the post-war baby and housing boom, technological advancements, and infrastructure spending spurred economic growth. This growth brought advantages and prosperity to segments of the population, but poverty continued to be a reality for minorities, the elderly, and many rural Americans. Television, movies, and suburbanization reinforced traditional gender roles in American society. The mass consumerism of plentiful manufactured goods helped grow the economy but drew criticism from the poets and writers of the Beat Generation.

The rise of a second Red Scare created political tension within the country. General fears of communist subversion contributed to Republican dominance in the 1952 election. Eisenhower easily won the presidency, and Republicans gained control of both houses of Congress. Eisenhower largely embraced moderate domestic policies but strengthened American commitments to oppose communism. Domestic and foreign tensions continued to rise during Eisenhower's second term and accelerated as the nation moved into the 1960s.

You should consider the following questions as you review the themes for this chapter:

- How did technology and automation change the economy and impact American society?
- What were the major causes for and the effects of the rise of a second Red Scare in the United States during the Cold War?
- What changes in migration were brought about by increased affluence, white flight, and the post-war baby boom in the United States?
- What influenced gender and societal roles in the 1950s?
- What impact did the Cold War have on the economy and consumer culture during the 1950s?

KEY TERMS

Alger Hiss 807
Allen Ginsberg 802
"Beats" 802
Echo Park 801
Elvis Presley 804
Fair Deal 787
House Un-American Committee (HUAC) 807
J. D. Salinger 802
Jack Kerouac 802
Jonas Salk 794
Joseph McCarthy 807
Julius and Ethel Rosenberg 807
Levittown 798
McCarthyism 807
Michael Harrington 804
Saul Bellow 802
Sputnik 796
Taft-Hartley Act 787
Thomas E. Dewey 788
UNIVAC 795
Whittaker Chambers 807
William H. Whyte Jr. 802
William Levitt 798

Discussion and Activities

Drawing Conclusions After students have read the section "The Decline of McCarthyism," ask them to discuss as a class how television demonstrated its influence in politics during this era. **SOC**

Key Terms

Students should be familiar with the key terms and be able to define them in the context of the economic, political, and social developments of the Truman and Eisenhower administrations. Encourage students to use these terms in performing review exercises and exam practice for this chapter.

 Go Online **Chapter 29 Content Review**

Assessing Student Understanding Use the online assessment to assess student understanding of concepts and topics within the chapter. You can assign the ready-made Chapter 29 Content Review or create your own from available questions. This easy-to-use tool helps you design assessments that meet the needs of different types of learners.

Answers

Multiple Choice

1. B; **2.** A; **3.** D

Short Answer

4A) Possible answer: Following World War II there were fears that the country would return to the economic depression of pre-World War II. The consumer culture that drove the economy following the war brought a level of unprecedented prosperity to many Americans.

4B) Possible answer: Both radio and television served as key factors related to consumerism during this time period. Both were consumer items that drove the economy and provided a cultural connection. They linked the country in a meaningful way and set societal and cultural expectations.

4C) Possible answer: The consumerism of the 1920s, which contributed to the subsequent depression of the 1930s, never really materialized following World War II. The post-war economy thrived and led to enormous economic growth in American society.

5A) Possible answer: Both the 1920s and the 1950s saw the emergence of a counterculture. During the 1920s, the Harlem Renaissance and the rise of the "New Negro" movement rebelled against previously held racial stereotypes. Similarly, the 1950s saw the emergence of its own counterculture, beginning with the Beats.

5B) Possible answer: Following World War I, the United States had a more isolationist attitude as it withdrew from global affairs. Following World War II, the United States embraced its leadership position by joining and taking the lead in major international initiatives.

5C) Possible answer: The United States embraced its global leadership position. The U.S. joined the United Nations and helped form NATO. The division between capitalist and communist countries helped fuel the Cold War.

AP EXAM PRACTICE

Questions assume cumulative content knowledge from this chapter and previous chapters.

MULTIPLE CHOICE

Use the photograph on page 799 and your knowledge of U.S. history to answer questions 1-3.

1. In what way did the construction of government public works projects such as the ones in the photograph alter the United States?
   (A) More Americans moved to rural areas as farming held increasing appeal to Americans in the postwar decades.
   (B) Economic activities shifted from urban to suburban and rural areas, negatively impacting downtown areas.
   (C) Downtown urban areas grew as increased transportation led to the building of new urban manufacturing centers.
   (D) America remained largely rural as cars became financially inaccessible.
2. The movement facilitated by interstate highways allowed for
   (A) the development of demographically homogeneous suburban areas.
   (B) the explosive growth of diverse rural populations.
   (C) the contraction of suburban populations as Americans preferred the ease of urban living.
   (D) the increase in urban populations as people moved closer to factories.
3. The construction of interstate highways encouraged the expansion of
   (A) childcare.
   (B) radio and television industries.
   (C) railroads and high speed trains.
   (D) motels and travel related industries.

SHORT ANSWER

Use your knowledge of U.S. history to answer questions 4 and 5.

4. Use the image on page 785 to answer A, B, and C.
   (A) Briefly describe the historical situation which gave rise to the event depicted in the image.
   (B) Briefly explain ONE specific historical continuity with regard to consumerism in American society from 1920 to 1960.
   (C) Briefly explain ONE specific historical change with regard to consumerism in American society from 1920 to 1960.
5. Answer A, B, and C.
   (A) Briefly describe ONE specific historical similarity between the 1920s and the 1950s.
   (B) Briefly describe ONE specific historical difference between the 1920s and the 1950s.
   (C) Briefly explain ONE specific historical effect which resulted from the difference identified in 5B.

LONG ESSAY

Develop a thoughtful and thorough historical argument that answers the question. Begin your essay with a thesis statement, and support it with specific historical evidence and examples.

6. Evaluate the relative importance of causes that led to the rise of youth culture and the Beats in post-World War II American society.

Answers

Long Essay

6. Possible thesis: The baby boom increased the number of teenagers who were feeling the existential alienation of earlier generations which, along with the rise of political conservatism, helped fueled the fire of a counterculture. Specific historical evidence: Television promoted consumer items and fueled the consumer society. The counterculture challenged consumer culture and the idea of the nuclear family. The Beats represented a continued existential alienation that was started by the "Lost Generation" of earlier decades. Art, literature, rock music, radio, and television shows reflected the changing culture.

30 THE QUEST FOR EQUALITY

SELMA MARCH In March 1965, Martin Luther King, Jr. and civil rights activists led a 54 mile march from Selma to Montgomery, Alabama to raise awareness of the struggles faced by African American voters and the need for a Voting Rights Act. The march garnered support across the United States as shown in the photograph of 15,000 marchers in Harlem, New York carrying a banner reading, "We march with Selma!"

CONNECTING CONCEPTS

Chapter Thirty begins by examining the emergence of the modern civil rights movement in the 1950s. Important causes were the legacy of World War II, the growth of an urban black middle class, and the Cold War, which made racial injustice an international embarrassment to the United States. The movement was sparked by the Montgomery Bus Boycott, which first brought Dr. Martin Luther King, Jr. to national prominence, and the Brown decision, which banned racial segregation in public education. But "massive resistance" by Southern whites culminated in a clash at Little Rock High School in 1957 between federal authority and states' rights.

The battle for racial equality expanded in the 1960s. The "Freedom Rides" sponsored by SNCC and the Birmingham demonstrations convinced John Kennedy to introduce a civil rights bill in Congress. The March on Washington in 1963 added to the pressure on Congress, and the assassination of Kennedy increased public support for both the Civil Rights Act of 1964 and the Voting Rights Act of 1965. The new president, Lyndon Johnson, signed both measures into law, but had to contend with urban violence as well as new issues like Black Power and de facto segregation in northern cities. New leaders like Malcolm X also signaled different directions and deepening divisions within the movement.

The civil rights movement inspired other minorities and American women to demand equal rights and opportunities. Native Americans formed the American Indian Movement and occupied Wounded Knee in 1973 as a protest against political persecution. Latino Americans challenged cultural and economic barriers, while Cesar Chavez battled on behalf of itinerant farm workers. LBGT+ Americans fought to win social acceptance and political rights — the "Stonewall Uprising" of 1969 helped make the gay liberation movement a significant public force. Finally, young feminists in the 1960s and 1970s, though sharply divided on important issues and unable to secure an Equal Rights Amendment, changed American society and transformed personal relations between many women and men.

Pacing Guide

Chapter 30 explores key concepts from Period 8: 1945–1980 of the AP U.S. History Curriculum Framework. The suggested instruction time for Chapter 30 is 4 days.

Key Concepts

8.2.I Seeking to fulfill Reconstruction-era promises, civil rights activists and political leaders achieved some legal and political successes in ending segregation, although progress toward racial equality was slow.

8.2.II Responding to social conditions and the African American civil rights movement, a variety of movements emerged that focused on issues of identity, social justice, and the environment.

8.2.III Liberalism influenced postwar politics and court decisions, but it came under increasing attack from the left as well as from a resurgent conservative movement.

Discussion and Activities

Evaluating Evidence Have students examine the image "Selma March." Discuss as a class the details from the image that illustrate tactics of the civil rights movement. *(mass gathering, peaceful marchers, demands clearly stated)* **SOC** **PCE**

Discussion and Activities

Analyzing Points of View Have students examine the image "Little Rock, Arkansas." In pairs or small groups, ask them to discuss what thoughts and feelings they think may have been experienced by the student depicted in the photo. **SOC**

As you read, you should:

- Describe the causes and effects of the Brown v. Board of Education Supreme Court decision on the civil rights movement.
- Evaluate the ways that the early civil rights movement sought to expand within American society.
- Analyze the different approaches to the civil rights movement by leaders within the African American community.
- Identify the goals and actions of various civil rights movements of the late 1960s and 1970s.
- Describe the causes and effects of the rise of the contemporary women's liberation movement.

THE RISE OF THE CIVIL RIGHTS MOVEMENT

After decades of skirmishes, an open battle began in the 1950s against racial segregation and discrimination. Although white Americans played an important role in the civil rights movement, pressure from African Americans themselves was the crucial element in raising the issue of race to prominence.

THE *BROWN* DECISION AND "MASSIVE RESISTANCE"

BROWN V. BOARD OF EDUCATION

On May 17, 1954, the Supreme Court announced its decision in the case of *Brown v. Board of Education of Topeka*. In considering the legal segregation of a Kansas public school system, the Court rejected its own 1896 *Plessy v. Ferguson* decision, which had ruled that communities could provide African Americans with separate facilities as long as the facilities were equal to those of white Americans.

The *Brown* decision was the culmination of many decades of effort by black opponents of segregation, and particularly by a group of talented NAACP lawyers, many of them trained at Howard University in Washington, D.C., by the great legal educator Charles Houston. Thurgood Marshall, William Hastie, James Nabrit, and others spent years filing legal challenges to segregation in one state after another, nibbling at the edges of the system, and accumulating precedents to support their assault on the "separate but equal" doctrine itself. The same lawyers filed the suits against the school boards of Topeka, Kansas, and several other cities that became the basis for the *Brown* decision.

"SEPARATE BUT EQUAL" DOCTRINE OVERTURNED

The Topeka suit involved the case of an African American girl who had to travel several miles to a segregated public school every day even though she lived virtually next door to a white elementary school. When the case arrived before the Supreme Court, the justices examined it not simply in terms of legal precedent but in terms of history, sociology, and psychology. They concluded that school segregation inflicted unacceptable damage on those it affected, regardless of the relative quality of the separate schools. Chief Justice Earl Warren explained the unanimous opinion of his colleagues: "We conclude

LITTLE ROCK, ARKANSAS African American student Elizabeth Eckford passes by jeering whites on her way to Little Rock Central High School, newly integrated by federal court order. The black students later admitted that they had been terrified during the first difficult weeks of integration. But in public, most of them acted with calm and dignity.

Go Online AP Exam Preparation

AP Exam Practice Use the online assessment to help prepare students for the AP Exam. You can assign the ready-made AP-style short-answer questions, document-based questions, and multiple-choice questions assessing concepts, themes, and skills from Period 8 and AP-style long-essay questions organized in sets of 3 questions from various time periods. You can also create your own tests from available questions. This easy-to-use tool helps you design assessments that meet the needs of different types of learners.

that in the field of public education the doctrine of 'separate but equal' has no place. Separate educational facilities are inherently unequal." The following year, the Court issued another decision (known as "*Brown* II") to provide rules for implementing the 1954 order. It ruled that communities must work to desegregate their schools "with all deliberate speed," but it set no timetable and left specific decisions up to lower courts.

"MASSIVE RESISTANCE"

In some communities–for example, Washington, D.C.–compliance came relatively quickly and quietly. More often, however, strong local opposition (what came to be known in the South as "massive resistance") produced long delays and bitter conflicts. Some school districts ignored the ruling altogether. Others attempted to circumvent it with purely token efforts to integrate. More than 100 southern members of Congress signed a "manifesto" in 1956 denouncing the *Brown* decision and urging their constituents to defy it. Southern governors, mayors, local school boards, and nongovernmental pressure groups (including hundreds of "White Citizens' Councils") all worked to obstruct desegregation. Many school districts enacted "pupil placement laws" allowing school officials to place students in schools according to their scholastic abilities and social behavior. Such laws were transparent devices for maintaining segregation; but in 1958, the Supreme Court (in *Shuttlesworth v. Birmingham Board of Education*) refused to declare them unconstitutional.

By the fall of 1957, only 684 of 3,000 affected school districts in the South had even begun to desegregate their schools. Many white parents simply withdrew their children from the public schools and enrolled them in all-white "segregation academies"; some state and local governments diverted money from newly integrated public schools and used it to fund the new, all-white academies. The *Brown* decision, far from ending segregation, had launched a prolonged battle between federal authority and state and local governments, and between those who believed in racial equality and those who did not.

LITTLE ROCK

The Eisenhower administration was not eager to commit itself to that battle. The president himself had greeted the *Brown* decision with skepticism (and once said it had set back progress on race relations "at least fifteen years"). But in September 1957, he faced a case of direct state defiance of federal authority and felt compelled to act. Federal courts had ordered the desegregation of Central High School in Little Rock, Arkansas. An angry white mob tried to prevent implementation of the order by blockading the entrances to the school, and Governor Orval Faubus refused to do anything to stop the obstruction. President Eisenhower responded by federalizing the Arkansas National Guard and sending troops to Little Rock to restore order and ensure that the court orders would be obeyed. Only then did Central High School admit its first black students.

THE EXPANDING MOVEMENT

The *Brown* decision helped spark a growing number of popular challenges to segregation in the South. On December 1, 1955, Rosa Parks, an African American woman, was arrested in Montgomery, Alabama, when she refused to give up her seat on a Montgomery bus to a white passenger. Parks, an active civil rights leader in the community, had apparently decided spontaneously to resist the order to move. Her feet were tired, she later explained. But black leaders in Montgomery had been waiting for such an incident, which they wanted to use to challenge the segregation of the buses. The arrest of this admired woman produced outrage in the city's African American community and helped local leaders organize a successful boycott of the bus system to demand an end to segregated seating.

MONTGOMERY BUS BOYCOTT

The bus boycott owed much of its success to the prior existence of well-organized black citizens' groups. A black women's political caucus had, in fact, been developing plans for a boycott of the segregated buses for some time. They seized on Rosa Parks as a symbol of the movement. Once launched, the boycott was almost completely effective. Black workers who needed to commute to their jobs (of whom the largest group consisted of female domestic servants) formed car pools to ride back and forth to work, or simply walked, at times over long distances. The boycott put economic pressure not only on the bus company (a private concern) but on many Montgomery merchants as well. The bus boycotters found it difficult to get to downtown stores and tended to shop instead in their own neighborhoods. Still, the boycott might well have failed had it not been for a Supreme Court decision late in 1956, inspired in part by the protest, that declared segregation in public transportation to be illegal. The buses in Montgomery abandoned their discriminatory seating policies, and the boycott came to a close.

An important result of the Montgomery boycott was the rise to prominence of a new figure in the movement for civil rights. The man chosen to head the boycott movement was a local Baptist pastor, Martin Luther King Jr., the son of a prominent Atlanta minister, a powerful orator, and a gifted leader. At first King was reluctant to lead the movement. But once he accepted the role, he became consumed by it.

MARTIN LUTHER KING'S STRATEGY

King's approach to black protest was based on the doctrine of nonviolence–that is, of passive resistance even in the face of direct attack. He drew from the teachings of Mahatma Gandhi, the Indian nationalist leader; from Henry David Thoreau and his doctrine of civil disobedience; and from Christian doctrine. And he produced an approach to racial struggle that captured the moral high ground for his supporters. He urged African Americans to engage in peaceful demonstrations; to allow themselves to be arrested, even beaten, if necessary; and to respond to hate with love. For the next thirteen years–as leader of the Southern Christian Leadership Conference, an interracial group he founded shortly after the bus boycott–he was the most influential and most widely admired black leader in the country. The popular movement he came to represent soon spread throughout the South and throughout the country.

Reasoning Processes

Identifying Cause and Effect After students have read the section "The *Brown* decision and 'Massive Resistance,'" ask them to create a T-chart listing causes and effects of the *Brown v. Board of Education of Topeka* decision. **PCE** **SOC**

Historical Thinking Skills

Evaluating Have students read the section "Montgomery Bus Boycott." Discuss as a class the factors that led to the success of the Montgomery bus boycott. **PCE** **SOC** **WXT**

Discussion and Activities

Analyzing Points of View After students have read the section "The Expanding Movement," ask them to work in small groups to identify how the actions of civil rights activists led to the "Second Reconstruction." Ask groups to share the main points of their group discussion with the class. PCE WXT SOC

Pressure from the courts, from northern liberals, and from African Americans themselves also speeded the pace of racial change in other areas. One important color line had been breached as early as 1947, when the Brooklyn Dodgers signed Jackie Robinson as the first African American to play Major League baseball. By the mid-1950s, African Americans had established themselves as a powerful force in almost all professional sports. Within the government, President Eisenhower completed the integration of the armed forces, attempted to desegregate the federal workforce, and in 1957 signed a civil rights act (passed, without active support from the White House, by a Democratic Congress) providing federal protection for African Americans who wished to register to vote. It was a weak bill, with few mechanisms for enforcement, but it was the first civil rights bill of any kind to win passage since the end of Reconstruction, and it served as a signal that the executive and legislative branches were beginning to join the judiciary in the federal commitment to the "Second Reconstruction."

Causes of the Civil Rights Movement

Why did a civil rights movement begin to emerge at this particular moment? The injustices it challenged and the goals it promoted were hardly new; in theory, African Americans could have launched the same movement fifty or a hundred years earlier, or decades later. Why did they do so in the 1950s and 1960s?

Several factors contributed to the rise of African American protest in these years. The legacy of World War II was one of the most important. Millions of black men and women had served in the military or worked in war plants during the war and had derived from the experience a broader view of the world, and of their place in it.

Legacy of World War II

Another factor was the growth of an urban black middle class, which had been developing for decades but which began to flourish after the war. Much of the impetus for the civil rights movement came from the leaders of urban black communities–ministers, educators, professionals–and much of it came as well from students at black colleges and universities, which had expanded significantly in the previous decades. Men and women with education and a stake in society were often more aware of the obstacles to their advancement than poorer and more oppressed people, to whom the possibility of advancement may have seemed too remote even to consider. And urban African Americans had considerably more freedom to associate with one another and to develop independent institutions than did rural African Americans, who were often under the very direct supervision of white landowners.

Urban Black Middle Class

Television and other forms of popular culture were another factor in the rising consciousness of racism among African Americans. More than any previous generation, postwar African Americans had constant, vivid reminders of how the white majority lived–of the world from which they were effectively excluded. Television also conveyed the activities of demonstrators to a national audience, ensuring that activism in one community would inspire similar protests in others. In addition to the forces that were inspiring African Americans to mobilize, other forces were at work mobilizing many white Americans to support the movement once it began. One was the Cold War, which made racial injustice an embarrassment to Americans trying to present their nation as a model to the world. Another was the political mobilization of northern African Americans, who were now a substantial voting bloc within the Democratic Party; politicians from northern industrial states could not ignore their views. Labor unions with substantial black memberships also played an important part in supporting (and funding) the civil rights movement.

THE BATTLE FOR RACIAL JUSTICE

The nation's most important domestic initiative in the 1960s was the effort to provide justice and equality to African Americans. It was the most difficult commitment, the one that produced the severest strains on American society. It was also the most urgent. Black Americans were themselves ensuring that the nation would have to deal with the problem of race.

Expanding Protests

John Kennedy had long been sympathetic to the cause of racial justice, but he was hardly a committed crusader. His intervention during the 1960 campaign to help win the release of Martin Luther King Jr. from a Georgia prison won him a large plurality of the black vote. But like many presidents before him, he feared alienating southern Democratic voters and members of Congress. His administration set out to contain the racial problem by expanding enforcement of existing laws and supporting litigation to overturn existing segregation statutes, hoping to make modest progress without creating politically damaging divisions.

But the pressure for more fundamental change could not be contained. In February 1960, black college students in Greensboro, North Carolina, staged a sit-in at a segregated Woolworth's lunch counter; and in the following weeks, similar demonstrations spread throughout much of the South, forcing many merchants to integrate their facilities. In the fall of 1960, some of those who had participated in the sit-ins formed the Student Nonviolent Coordinating Committee (SNCC), which worked to keep the spirit of resistance alive.

SNCC

In 1961, an interracial group of students, working with the Congress of Racial Equality (CORE), began what they called "freedom rides" (reviving a tactic CORE had tried, without much success, in the 1940s). Traveling by bus throughout the South, the freedom riders tried to force the desegregation of bus stations. In some places, they met with such savage violence at the hands of enraged whites that the president finally

"Freedom Rides"

Historical Thinking Skills

Drawing Conclusions After students have read the section "Causes of the Civil Rights Movement," ask them to create a T-chart listing causes and effects of the Civil Rights Movement. Have students write a thesis statement making a claim about what they believe to be the most important cause(s) or effect(s). PCE WXT SOC

BIRMINGHAM, 1963 In one of the scenes that horrified many Americans watching on television, police in Birmingham, Alabama, turn fire hoses full force on civil rights demonstrators, knocking many of them to the ground.

Bill Hudson/AP Images

dispatched federal marshals to help keep the peace. Kennedy also ordered the integration of all bus and train stations. In the meantime, SNCC workers began fanning out through black communities and even into remote rural areas to encourage African Americans to challenge the obstacles to voting that the Jim Crow laws had created. The Southern Christian Leadership Conference (SCLC) also created citizen-education and other programs—many of them organized by Ella Baker, one of the most successful grassroots leaders of the movement—to mobilize black workers, farmers, housewives, and others to challenge segregation, disenfranchisement, and discrimination.

Continuing judicial efforts to enforce the integration of public education increased the pressure on national leaders to respond to the civil rights movement. In October 1962, a federal court ordered the University of Mississippi to enroll its first black student, James Meredith; Governor Ross Barnett, a strident segregationist, refused to enforce the order. When angry whites in Oxford, Mississippi, began rioting to protest the court decree, President Kennedy sent federal troops to the city to restore order and protect Meredith's right to attend the university.

BIRMINGHAM

Events in Alabama in 1963 helped bring the growing movement to something of a climax. In April, Martin Luther King Jr. helped launch a series of nonviolent demonstrations in Birmingham, Alabama, a city perhaps unsurpassed in its commitment to segregation. Police Commissioner Eugene "Bull" Connor supervised a brutal effort to break up the peaceful marches, arresting hundreds of demonstrators and using attack dogs, tear gas, electric cattle prods, and fire hoses—at times even against small children—as much of the nation watched televised reports in horror. Two months later, Governor George Wallace—who had won election in 1962 pledging staunch resistance to integration—pledged to stand in the doorway of a building at the University of Alabama to prevent the court-ordered enrollment of several black students. Only after the arrival of federal marshals and a visit from Attorney General Robert Kennedy did Wallace give way. His stand won him wide popularity among whites throughout the nation who were growing uncomfortable with the pace of integration. That same night, NAACP official Medgar Evers was murdered in Mississippi.

A National Commitment

The events in Alabama and Mississippi were a warning to the president that he could no longer contain or avoid the issue of race. In an important television address the night of the University of Alabama confrontation and the murder of Evers, President Kennedy spoke eloquently of the "moral issue" facing the nation. "If an American," he asked, "because his skin is dark, . . . cannot enjoy the full and free life which all of us want, then who among us would be content to have the color of his skin changed and stand in his place? Who among us would then be content with the counsels of patience and delay?" Days later, he introduced a series of new legislative proposals prohibiting segregation in "public accommodations" (stores, restaurants, theaters, hotels), barring discrimination in employment, and increasing the power of the government to file suits on behalf of school integration.

MARCH ON WASHINGTON

To generate support for the legislation, and to dramatize the power of the growing movement, more than 200,000 demonstrators marched down the Mall in Washington, D.C., in August 1963 and gathered before the Lincoln Memorial for the greatest civil rights demonstration in the nation's history. President Kennedy, who had at first opposed the idea of the march, in the end gave it his open support after receiving pledges from organizers that speakers would not criticize the administration. Martin Luther King Jr., in one of the greatest speeches of his distinguished oratorical career, roused the crowd with a litany of images prefaced again and again by the phrase "I have a dream." The march was the high-water mark of the peaceful, interracial civil rights movement.

The assassination of President Kennedy three months later gave new impetus to the battle for civil rights legislation. The ambitious measure that Kennedy had proposed in June 1963 had stalled in the Senate after having passed through the House of Representatives with relative ease. Early in 1964, after Johnson applied both public and private pressure, supporters of the measure finally mustered the two-thirds majority necessary to close debate and end a filibuster by southern senators; and the Senate passed the most comprehensive civil rights bill in the nation's history.

Reasoning Processes

Comparison After students have read the section "Expanding Protests," ask them to create a Venn diagram comparing the tactics and ideology of the SNCC with that of Dr. King's Southern Christian Leadership Conference. PCE SOC WXT

Discussion and Activities

Speculating Have students read the section "A National Commitment." Ask them to discuss in small groups whether they believe the Civil Rights Act of 1964 would have passed if President Kennedy had not introduced the legislation and later been assassinated. PCE

Historical Thinking Skills

Contextualization Have students read the section "The Battle for Voting Rights." Discuss as a class why attaining voting rights was such a struggle in light of the 15th Amendment that had guaranteed African American males the right to vote. PCE SOC WXT

THE BATTLE FOR VOTING RIGHTS

Having won a significant victory in one area, the civil rights movement shifted its focus to another: voting rights. During the summer of 1964, thousands of civil rights workers, black and white, northern and southern, spread out through the South, but primarily in Mississippi, to work on behalf of black voter registration and participation. The campaign was known as "freedom summer," and it produced a violent response from some southern whites. Three of the first freedom workers to arrive in the South–two whites, Andrew Goodman and Michael Schwerner, and one African American, James Chaney–were brutally murdered by Ku Klux Klan members with the support of local police in Neshoba County, Mississippi.

"FREEDOM SUMMER"

The "freedom summer" also produced the Mississippi Freedom Democratic Party (MFDP), an integrated alternative to the regular state party organization. Under the leadership of Fannie Lou Hamer and others, the MFDP challenged the regular party's right to its seats at the Democratic National Convention that summer. President Johnson, eager to avoid antagonizing anyone (even southern white Democrats who seemed likely to support his Republican opponent), enlisted King's help to broker a compromise. It permitted the MFDP to be seated as observers, with promises of party reforms later on, while the regular state party retained its official standing. Both sides grudgingly accepted the agreement. Both were embittered by it.

A year later, in March 1965, King helped organize a major demonstration in Selma, Alabama, to press the demand for the right of African Americans to register to vote. Selma sheriff Jim Clark led local police in a brutal attack on the demonstrators–which, as in Birmingham, received graphic television coverage and horrified many viewers across the nation. Two white Northerners participating in the Selma march were murdered in the course of the effort there–one, a minister, beaten to death in the streets of the town; the other, a Detroit housewife, shot as she drove along a highway at night with a black passenger in her car. The national outrage that followed the events in Alabama helped push Lyndon Johnson to propose and win passage of the Civil Rights Act of 1965, better known as the Voting Rights Act, which provided federal protection to African Americans attempting to exercise their right to vote. But important as such gains were, they failed to satisfy the rapidly rising expectations of African Americans as the focus of the movement began to move from political to economic issues.

VOTING RIGHTS ACT

MARTIN LUTHER KING JR. IN WASHINGTON, D.C. Moments after completing his memorable speech during the August 1963 March on Washington, King waves to the vast and enthusiastic crowd that has gathered in front of the Lincoln Memorial to demand "equality and jobs."

THE CHANGING MOVEMENT

For decades, the nation's African American population had been undergoing a major demographic shift; and by the 1960s, the problem of racial injustice was no longer primarily Southern and rural, as it had been earlier in the century. By 1966, 69 percent of black Americans were living in metropolitan areas and 45 percent outside the South. Although the economic condition of much of American society was improving, in the poor urban communities in which the black population was concentrated, things were getting significantly worse. Well over half of all nonwhite Americans lived in poverty at the beginning of the 1960s; black unemployment was twice that of white Americans.

By the mid-1960s, therefore, the issue of race was moving out of the South and into the rest of the nation. The battle against school desegregation had moved beyond the initial assault on de jure segregation (segregation by law) to an attack on de

DE JURE AND DE FACTO SEGREGATION

Discussion and Activities

Analyzing Points of View

Have students examine the image "Martin Luther King, Jr. in Washington, D.C." Ask them to write a journal entry from the point of view of a person who attended Dr. King's "I Have a Dream" speech during the 1963 March on Washington. PCE SOC

DEBATING THE PAST

THE CIVIL RIGHTS MOVEMENT

The early histories of the civil rights movement rest on a heroic narrative of moral purpose and personal courage by which great men and women inspired ordinary people to rise up and struggle for their rights. This narrative generally begins with the *Brown* decision of 1954 and the Montgomery bus boycott of 1955, continues through the civil rights campaigns of the early 1960s, and culminates in the Civil Rights Acts of 1964 and 1965. Central events in this narrative are the 1963 March on Washington, with Martin Luther King Jr.'s famous "I Have a Dream" speech, and King's assassination in 1968, which has often symbolized the end of the movement and the beginning of a different, more complicated period of the black freedom struggle. The key element of these narratives is the central importance to the movement of a few great leaders, most notably King himself. Among the best examples of this kind of narrative are Taylor Branch's powerful studies of the life and struggles of King, *Parting the Waters* (1988), *Pillar of Fire* (1998), and *At Canaan's Edge* (2006), as well as David Garrow's important study, *Bearing the Cross* (1986).

Few historians would deny the importance of King and other leaders to the successes of the civil rights movement. But a number of scholars have argued that the leader-centered narrative obscures the vital contributions of ordinary people in communities throughout the South, and the nation, to the struggle. John Dittmer's *Local People: The Struggle for Civil Rights in Mississippi* (1994) and Charles Payne's *I've Got the Light of Freedom* (1995) both examine the day-to-day work of the movement's rank and file in the early 1960s and argue that their collective efforts were at least as important as those of King and other leaders. Only by understanding the local origins of the movement, these and other scholars argue, can we understand its true character.

Scholars also disagree about the time frame of the movement. Rather than beginning the story in 1954 or 1955 (as in Robert Weisbrot's excellent 1991 synthesis *Freedom Bound* or William Chafe's important 1981 local study *Civilities and Civil Rights*, which examined the Greensboro sit-ins of 1961), a number of scholars have tried to move the story into both earlier periods and later ones. Robin Kelley's *Race Rebels* (1994) emphasizes the important contributions of working-class African Americans, who organized some of the earliest civil rights demonstrations—sit-ins, marches, and other efforts to challenge segregation—long before the conventional dates for the beginning of the movement. Gail O'Brien's *The Color of the Law* (1999) examines a 1946 "race riot" in Columbia, Tennessee, citing it as a signal of the early growth of African American militancy.

Other scholars have looked beyond the 1960s and beyond the South to incorporate events outside the orbit of the formal "movement" in the history of the civil rights struggle. A growing literature on northern, urban, and relatively radical activists emphasizes the challenges facing northern African Americans and the very different tactics and strategies that they often chose to pursue their goals. The enormous attention historians have given to the life and legacy of Malcolm X—among them Alex Haley's influential *Autobiography of Malcolm X* (1965) and Michael Eric Dyson's *Making Malcolm* (1996)—is one example of this, as is the increasing attention scholars have given to black radicalism in the late 1960s and beyond and to such militant groups as the Black Panthers.

Even *Brown v. Board of Education* (1954), the great landmark of the legal challenge to segregation, has been subject to reexamination. Richard Kluger's narrative history of the *Brown* decision, *Simple Justice* (1975), is a classic statement of the traditional view of *Brown* as a triumph over injustice. But critics have been less certain of the dramatic success of the ruling. James T. Patterson's *Brown v. Board of Education: A Civil Rights Milestone and Its Troubled Legacy* (2001) argues that the *Brown* decision long preceded any national consensus on the need to end segregation and that its impact was far less decisive than earlier scholars have suggested. Michael Klarman's *From Jim Crow to Civil Rights* (2004) examines the role of the Supreme Court in advancing civil rights and suggests, among other things, that the *Brown* decision may actually have retarded racial progress in the South for a time because of the enormous backlash it created. Charles Ogletree's *All Deliberate Speed* (2004) and Derrick Bell's *Silent Covenants* (2004) both argue that the Court's decision did not provide an effective enforcement mechanism for desegregation and in many other ways failed to support measures that would have made school desegregation a reality. They note as evidence for this view that American public schools are now more segregated—even if not forcibly by law—than they were at the time of the *Brown* decision.

As the literature on the African American freedom struggles of the twentieth century has grown, historians have begun to speak of civil rights *movements*, rather than a single, cohesive movement. In this way, scholars recognize that struggles of this kind take many more forms, and endure through many more periods of history, than the traditional accounts suggest.

BROWN V. BOARD OF EDUCATION This photograph, taken for an Atlanta newspaper, illustrated the long and dangerous walk that Linda Brown, one of the plaintiffs in the famous desegregation case that ultimately reached the Supreme Court, had to travel each day on her way to a segregated school in Topeka, Kansas. An all-white school was located close to her home, but to reach the black school she had to attend required a long walk and a long bus ride each day. Not only does the picture illustrate the difficulties segregation created for Linda Brown, it was also a part of a broad publicity campaign launched by the supporters of the case.

Photo by Carl Iwasaki/© Time & Life Pictures/Getty Images

HISTORICAL THINKING SKILLS

Questions assume cumulative content knowledge from this chapter and previous chapters.

1. **Explaining Historical Developments** Describe three broad schools of historical interpretation regarding the origins of the civil rights movement.
2. **Evaluating Evidence** Explain how one piece of historical evidence could be used to support each of the three broad schools of historical interpretation concerning the civil rights movement.
3. **Developing Arguments** Analyze the school of thought you find most convincing. Use evidence from the text to support your argument.

Historical Thinking Skills

Sourcing and Situation Have students examine the image "*Brown v. Board of Education.*" Ask them to discuss in small groups what they believe could have been the photographer's purpose, point of view, or intended audience for the photograph. *(Purpose: to arouse sympathy for the Brown court case. Point of view: supported expansion of civil rights for African Americans. Audience: white Southerners who were not committed segregationists)* **SOC** **WXT**

Answers

Debating the Past

1. Possible answer: Branch and Garrow cite the heroic efforts of great men and women in leading the movement and in inspiring others to rise up and seek change. Dittmer and Payne emphasize the work of ordinary men and women as the true nature of the movement. Weisbrot and Chafe argue that the movement had begun much earlier than the 1950s through efforts of ordinary African Americans.
2. Possible answer: King's leadership within the modern civil rights movement places him at the center of most major events during the period. But the mobilization of ordinary Americans promoted and encouraged change. Earlier efforts by African Americans support the idea that seeds of the modern civil rights movement occurred earlier with events such as the race riots during the 1940s.
3. Student responses will vary. They may claim that the modern civil rights movement would not have flourished were it not for the millions of Americans who rallied around the messages of leaders like King.

Discussion and Activities

Identifying Bias After students have read the section "The Changing Movement," ask them to discuss as a class how it might be more difficult to eliminate *de facto* segregation compared to *de jure* segregation. **SOC** **WXT**

facto segregation (segregation in practice, as through residential patterns), thus carrying the fight into Northern cities. Many African American leaders (and their white supporters) were demanding, similarly, that the battle against job discrimination move to a new level: employers not only should abandon negative measures to deny jobs to African Americans; they also should adopt positive measures to recruit minorities, thus compensating for past injustices. Lyndon Johnson gave his tentative support to the concept of "affirmative action" in 1965. Over the next decade, affirmative action guidelines gradually extended to all institutions doing business with or receiving funds from the federal government (including schools and universities)—and to many others as well.

A symbol of the movement's new direction, and of the problems it would cause, was a major campaign in the summer of 1966 in Chicago, in which King played a prominent role. Organizers of the Chicago campaign hoped to direct national attention to housing and employment discrimination in Northern industrial cities in much the same way similar campaigns had exposed legal racism in the South. But the Chicago campaign not only evoked vicious and at times violent opposition from white residents of that city; it also failed to arouse the national conscience in the way events in the South had.

URBAN VIOLENCE

Well before the Chicago campaign, the problem of urban poverty was thrust into national attention when violence broke out in black neighborhoods in major cities. There were a few scattered disturbances in the summer of 1964, most notably in Harlem. The first large race riot since the end of World War II occurred the following summer in the Watts section of Los Angeles. In the midst of a seemingly routine traffic arrest, a white police officer struck a protesting black bystander with his club. The incident triggered a storm of anger and a week of violence (and revealed how deeply African Americans in Los Angeles, and in other cities, resented their treatment at the hands of local police). As many as 10,000 people were estimated to have participated in the violence in Watts—attacking white motorists, burning buildings, looting stores, and sniping at policemen. Thirty-four people died during the Watts uprising, which was eventually quelled by the National Guard; twenty-eight of the dead were black. In the summer of 1966, there were forty-three additional outbreaks, the most serious of them in Chicago and Cleveland. And in the summer of 1967, there were eight major outbreaks, including the largest of them all—a racial clash in Detroit in which forty-three people (thirty-three of them black) died.

WATTS RIOT

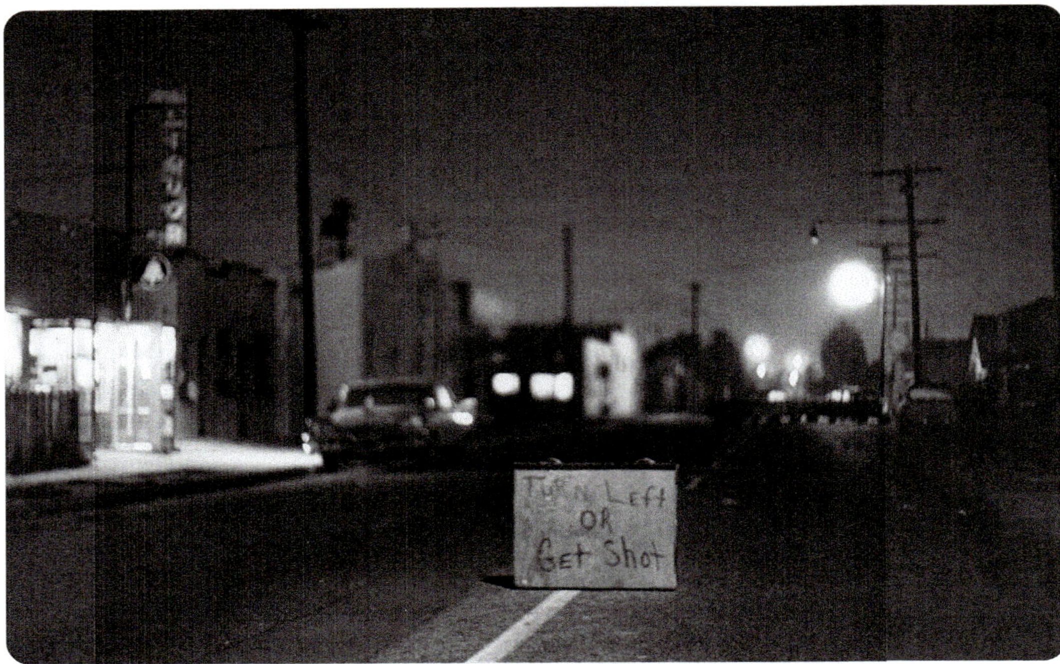

"TURN LEFT OR GET SHOT" This chilling sign, erected at an intersection in the Watts neighborhood in Los Angeles during the 1965 riot there, illustrates the escalating racial tensions that were beginning to explode in American cities in the mid-1960s.

Discussion and Activities

Analyzing Points of View Have students examine the image "Turn Left or Get Shot." Have students discuss with a partner the possible reactions to the sign that either a black resident of the neighborhood where the sign was located or a white passerby might have experienced. **SOC** **PCE**

Discussion and Activities

Historical Reasoning and Argumentation After students have read the section "Urban Violence," ask them to discuss in pairs or small groups whether it was appropriate to label the summers of 1966 and 1967 as "long, hot summers," as many in the media did at the time. SOC PCE WXT GEO

Televised reports of the violence alarmed millions of Americans and created both a new sense of urgency and a growing sense of doubt among many of those whites who had embraced the cause of racial justice only a few years before. A special Commission on Civil Disorders, created by the president in response to the disturbances, issued a celebrated report in the spring of 1968 recommending massive spending to eliminate the abysmal conditions of the ghettos. "Only a commitment to national action on an unprecedented scale," the commission concluded, "can shape a future compatible with the historic ideals of American society." To many white Americans, however, the lesson of the riots was the need for stern measures to stop violence and lawlessness.

Black Power

Disillusioned with the ideal of peaceful change in cooperation with whites, an increasing number of African Americans were turning to a new approach to the racial issue: the philosophy of "black power." Black power could mean many different things. But in all its forms, it suggested a move away from interracial cooperation and toward increased awareness of racial distinctiveness. It was part of a long nationalist tradition among African Americans that extended back into slavery and that had its most visible twentieth-century expression in the Garvey movement of the 1920s.

Shift from Integration to Racial Distinction

Perhaps the most enduring impact of the black-power ideology was a social and psychological one: instilling racial pride in African Americans, who lived in a society whose dominant culture generally portrayed African Americans as inferior to whites. It encouraged the growth of black studies in schools and universities. It helped stimulate important black literary and artistic movements. It produced a new interest among many African Americans in their African roots. It led to a rejection by some African Americans of certain cultural practices borrowed from white society: "Afro" hairstyles began to replace artificially straightened hair; some black Americans began to adopt African styles of dress and new, African names.

But black power had political manifestations as well, most notably in creating a deep schism within the civil rights movement. Traditional black organizations that had emphasized cooperation with sympathetic whites–groups such as the NAACP, the Urban League, and King's Southern Christian Leadership Conference–now faced competition from radical groups. The Student Nonviolent Coordinating Committee and the Congress of Racial Equality had both begun as relatively moderate, interracial organizations; SNCC was originally a student branch of the SCLC. By the mid-1960s, however, these and other groups were calling for radical and occasionally even violent action against the racism of white society and were openly rejecting the approaches of older, more established black leaders.

An Increasingly Divided Civil Rights Movement

Particularly alarming to many whites (and to some African Americans as well) were organizations that existed outside the mainstream civil rights movement. In Oakland, California, the Black Panther Party (founded by Huey Newton and Bobby Seale) promised to defend black rights even if that required violence. Black Panthers organized along semimilitary lines and wore weapons openly and proudly. They were, in fact, more the victims of violence from the police than they were practitioners of violence themselves. But they created an image, quite deliberately, of militant radicals willing to fight for justice, in Newton's words, "through the barrel of a gun."

Malcolm X

In Detroit, a once-obscure black nationalist group, the Nation of Islam, gained new prominence. Founded in 1931 by Elijah Poole (who converted to Islam and renamed himself Elijah Muhammad), the movement taught African Americans to take responsibility for their own lives, to live by strict codes of behavior, and

Nation of Islam

MALCOLM X Malcolm X, a leader of the militant Nation of Islam, arrives in Washington, D.C., in May 1963 to set up a headquarters for the organization there. Malcolm was hated and feared by many whites during his lifetime. After he was assassinated in 1965, he became a widely revered hero among African Americans.

Discussion and Activities

Evaluating Evidence Have students read the section "Black Power." Ask them to create a T-chart listing political and social expressions of "black power." Have students share with a partner which they think was most important. PCE SOC WXT

Reasoning Processes

Comparing After students have read the section "Malcolm X," ask them to create a Venn diagram comparing the message and tactics of Malcolm X and Martin Luther King, Jr. Have students discuss as a class which approach would have been more effective in the 1960s and why. You may ask students to recall the division between Booker T. Washington and W.E.B. Du Bois at the beginning of the 20th century and ask them to compare the differences across time periods. **PCE** **SOC** **WXT**

to reject any dependence on white Americans. The most celebrated of the Black Muslims, as whites often termed them, was Malcolm Little, a former drug addict and pimp who had spent time in prison and had rebuilt his life after joining the movement. He adopted the name Malcolm X ("X" to denote his lost African surname).

Malcolm became one of the movement's most influential spokesmen, particularly among younger African Americans as a result of his intelligence, his oratorical skills, and his harsh, uncompromising opposition to all forms of racism and oppression. He did not advocate violence, as his critics often claimed; but he insisted that black people had the right to defend themselves, violently if necessary, from those who assaulted them. Malcolm died in 1965 when black gunmen, presumably under orders from rivals within the Nation of Islam, assassinated him in New York.

But Malcolm's influence did not die with him. A book he had been working on before his death with the writer Alex Haley *(The Autobiography of Malcolm X)* attracted wide attention after its publication in 1965 and spread his reputation broadly through the nation. Years after his death, he was to many African Americans as important and revered a symbol as Martin Luther King Jr.

THE MOBILIZATION OF MINORITIES

The growth of African American protest, the New Left, and the counterculture encouraged other minorities to assert themselves and demand redress of their grievances. For Native Americans, Hispanic Americans, gay men and women, and minorities, the late 1960s and the 1970s were a time of growing self-expression and political activism.

SEEDS OF NATIVE AMERICAN MILITANCY

Few minorities had deeper or more justifiable grievances against the prevailing culture than American Indians—or Native Americans, as some began to call themselves in the 1960s. Native Americans were the least prosperous, least healthy, and least stable group in the nation. They were also one of the smallest, constituting less than 1 percent of the population. Average annual family income for Native Americans was $1,000 less than that for African Americans. The Native American unemployment rate was ten times the national rate. Joblessness was particularly high on the reservations, where nearly half of Native American populations lived. But even most Native Americans living in cities suffered from their limited education and training and could find only menial jobs. Life expectancy among Native Americans was some twenty years less than the national average. Suicides among Native American youths were a hundred times more frequent than among white youths. And while black Americans attracted the attention (for good or for ill) of many white Americans, Native Americans for many years remained largely ignored.

NATIVE AMERICAN GRIEVANCES

For much of the postwar era, particularly after the resignation of John Collier as commissioner of Indian Affairs in 1946, federal policy moved toward incorporating Native Americans into mainstream American society. (This policy was similar to failed "assimilation" efforts in the late nineteenth century.) Two laws passed in 1953 established what became known as "termination." Through termination, the federal government withdrew all official recognition of the tribes as legal entities, administratively separate from state governments, and made them subject to the same local jurisdictions as white residents. At the same time, the government encouraged Native Americans to assimilate into the larger society and worked to funnel Native Americans into cities, where, presumably, they would adapt to the white world and lose their cultural distinctiveness.

To some degree, the termination and assimilation policies achieved their objectives. The tribes grew weaker, and many Native Americans adapted to life in the cities became less able to fend off white influence. On the whole, however, the new policies were a disaster for the tribes and a failure for the reformers who had promoted them. Termination led to widespread corruption and abuse. And Native Americans fought so bitterly against it that in 1958 the Eisenhower administration barred further "terminations" without the consent of the affected tribes. In the meantime, the struggle against termination had mobilized a new generation of Indian militants and had breathed life into the principal Native American organization, the National Congress of American Indians (NCAI), created in 1944. The new militancy also benefited from the rapid increase in the Indian population, which was growing much faster than that of the rest of the nation (nearly doubling between 1950 and 1970, to a total of about 800,000).

FAILURE OF "TERMINATION"

THE NATIVE AMERICAN CIVIL RIGHTS MOVEMENT

In 1961, more than 400 members of 67 tribes gathered in Chicago to discuss ways of bringing all Native Americans together in an effort to redress common wrongs. The manifesto they issued, the Declaration of Indian Purpose, stressed the "right to choose our own way of life." One result of the movement was a gradual change in the way popular culture depicted Native American. By the 1970s, almost no films or television westerns portrayed Native Americans as brutal savages attacking peaceful white people. Native American activists even persuaded some white institutions to abandon what they considered demeaning references to them; Dartmouth College, for example, ceased referring to its athletic teams as the "Indians." In 1968, a group of young militant Native Americans established the American Indian Movement (AIM), which drew its greatest support from those Native Americans who lived in urban areas but soon established a significant presence on the reservations as well.

AIM

Historical Thinking Skills

Contextualization Have students read the section "Seeds of Native American Militancy." Ask them to discuss in small groups the reasons that Native Americans were the least prosperous, least healthy, and least stable group in the nation during this time. **PCE** **MIG** **GEO**

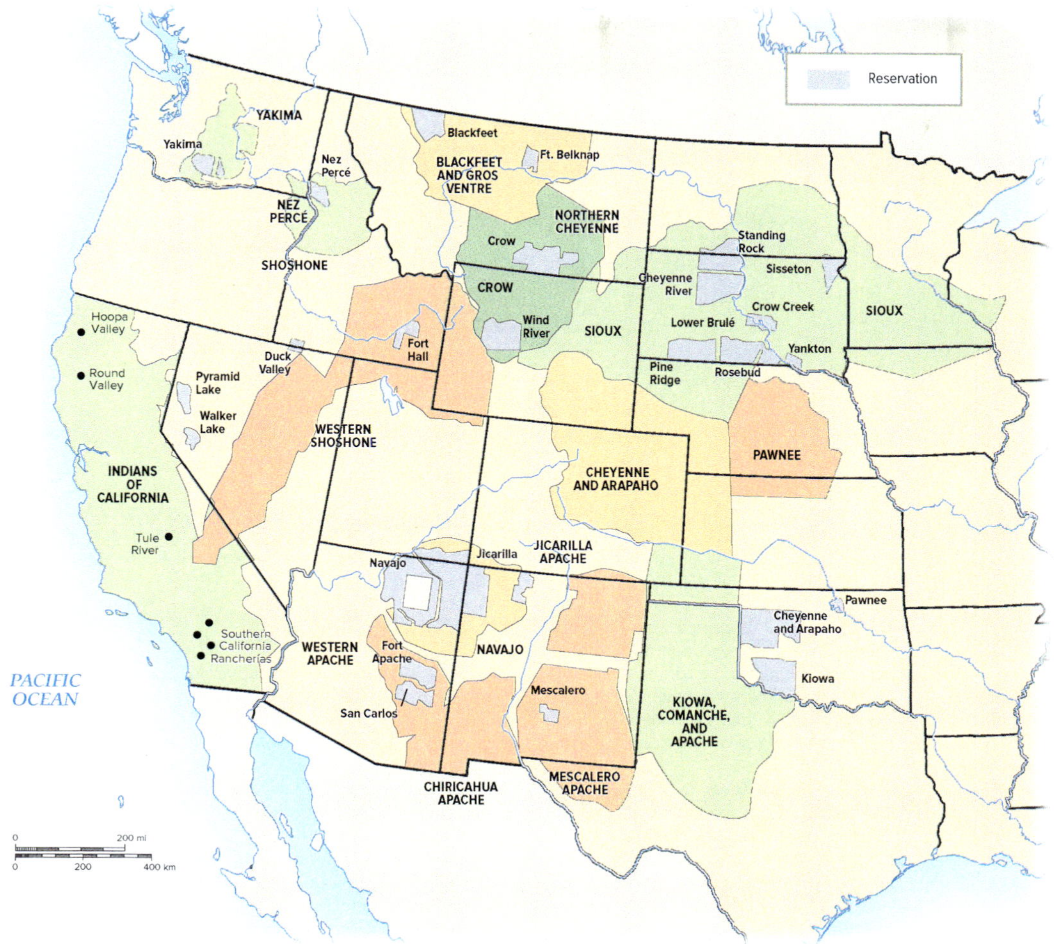

ABORIGINAL TERRITORIES AND MODERN RESERVATIONS OF WESTERN NATIVE AMERICAN NATIONS This map shows the rough distribution of the Native American population in the western United States before the establishment of reservations by the federal government in the nineteenth century. The large shaded regions in colors other than purple represent the areas in which the various groups were dominant a century and more ago. The purple shaded areas show the much smaller areas set aside for them as reservations after the Indian wars of the late nineteenth century.

What impact did life on the reservations have on the rise of Native American activism in the 1960s and 1970s?

The new activism had some immediate political results. In 1968, Congress passed the Indian Civil Rights Act, which recognized the legitimacy of tribal laws within the reservations. But leaders of AIM and other insurgent groups were not satisfied and turned increasingly to direct action. In 1968, Native American fishermen clashed with Washington State officials on the Columbia River and in Puget Sound, where Native Americans claimed that treaties gave them the exclusive right to fish. The following year, members of several tribes made a symbolic protest by occupying the abandoned federal prison on Alcatraz Island in San Francisco Bay and claiming the site "by right of discovery."

In response to the growing pressure, the Nixon administration appointed a Mohawk-Sioux to the position of commissioner of Indian Affairs in 1969; and in 1970, the president promised both increased tribal self-determination and an

Discussion and Activities

Making Connections After students have read the section "AIM," discuss as a class current examples of the ways Native Americans are depicted in popular culture—for example, on television and film or in conflicts over sports team mascots and nicknames. **SOC** **ARC**

Answers

Aboriginal Territories and Modern Reservations of Western Native American Nations

Reservations tended to be located on economically unproductive land, leading to high rates of poverty and related social issues.

Reasoning Processes

Comparing After students have read the section "The Native American Civil Rights Movement," ask them to create a Venn diagram comparing the Native American civil rights movement with the movement for African American civil rights. Have students consider the goals, tactics, and results of each movement. PCE WXT SOC NAT

THE OCCUPATION OF ALCATRAZ Alcatraz, an island in San Francisco Bay, once housed a large federal prison that by the late 1960s had been abandoned. In 1969, a group of Native American activists occupied the island and claimed it as Indian land—precipitating a long standoff with authorities.

© AP Images

increase in federal aid. But the protests continued. In November 1972, nearly a thousand demonstrators, most of them Sioux, forcibly occupied the building of the Bureau of Indian Affairs in Washington, D.C., for six days.

A more celebrated protest occurred in February 1973 at Wounded Knee, South Dakota, the site of the 1890 massacre of Sioux by federal troops. Members of AIM seized and occupied the town of Wounded Knee for two months, demanding radical changes in the administration of the reservation and insisting that the government honor its long-forgotten treaty obligations. A brief clash between the occupiers and federal forces left one Native American dead and another wounded.

OCCUPATION OF WOUNDED KNEE

More immediately effective than these militant protests were the victories that various groups were achieving in the federal courts. In *United States v. Wheeler* (1978), the Supreme Court confirmed that Native American nations had independent legal standing and could not be "terminated" by Congress. Other decisions ratified the authority to impose taxes on businesses within their reservations and to perform other sovereign functions. In 1985, the U.S. Supreme Court, in *County of Oneida v. Oneida Indian Nation*, supported Oneida claims to 100,000 acres in upstate New York that the Oneida tribe claimed by virtue of treaty rights.

The Native American civil rights movement, like other civil rights movements of the same time, fell far short of winning full justice and equality for its constituents. To some Native Americans, the principal goal was to defend tribal autonomy, to protect the right of Native Americans (and, more to the point, individual tribal groups) to remain separate and distinct. To others, the goal was equality—to win for Native Americans a place in society equal to that of other groups of Americans. Because there was no single Native Americans culture or tradition in America, the movement never united all Native Americans.

IMPORTANT LEGAL VICTORIES

For all its limits, however, the Native American civil rights movement helped win a series of new legal rights and protections that gave Native American nations a stronger position than they had enjoyed at any previous time in the twentieth century.

LATINO ACTIVISM

Far more numerous than Native Americans were Latino Americans (or Hispanic Americans), the fastest-growing minority group in the United States. They were no more a single, cohesive group than the Native Americans were. Some—including the descendants of early Spanish settlers in New Mexico—had roots as deep in American history as those of any other group. Others were men and women who had immigrated since World War II.

Large numbers of people from Puerto Rico had migrated to eastern cities, particularly New York City. South Florida's substantial Cuban population began with a wave of middle-class refugees fleeing the Castro regime in the early 1960s, followed by a second, much poorer wave of Cuban immigrants in 1980—the so-called Marielitos, named for the port from which they left Cuba. Later in the 1980s, large numbers of immigrants (both legal and illegal) began to arrive from the troubled nations of Central and South America—from Guatemala, Nicaragua, El Salvador, Peru, and others. But the most numerous and important Latino group in the United States was Mexican Americans.

During World War II, large numbers of Mexican Americans had entered the country in response to the labor shortage, and many had remained in the cities of the Southwest and the Pacific Coast. After the war, when the legal agreements that had allowed Mexican contract workers to enter the country expired, large numbers of immigrants continued to move to the United States illegally. In 1953, the government launched

Historical Thinking Skills

Sourcing and Situation Have students examine the image "The Occupation of Alcatraz." Ask them to discuss in small groups what they believe could have been the photographer's purpose, point of view, and intended audience of the photo. Ask groups to describe the historical situation of the photo and to share their discussion with the class. *(Purpose: to raise awareness of the movement for Native American rights. Point of view: sympathetic toward the movement for Native American rights. Audience: anyone who might have been unaware of the movement for Native American rights. Historical situation: part of the campaign by AIM to raise awareness of the movement for Native American rights by occupation.)* PCE SOC WXT GEO what it called Operation Wetback to deport illegal immigrants, but the effort failed to stem the flow of new arrivals. By 1960, there were substantial Mexican American neighborhoods (barrios) in American cities from El Paso to Detroit. The largest (with more than 500,000 people, according to census figures) was in Los Angeles, which had a bigger Mexican population than any other place except Mexico City.

SURGING LATINO IMMIGRATION

But the greatest expansion in the Mexican American population was yet to come. In 1960, the census reported slightly more than 3 million Latino people living in the United States (the great majority of them Mexican Americans). By 1970, that number had grown to 9 million, and by 2009 to 48 million. Since there was also an uncounted but very large number of illegal immigrants in those years, the real number was undoubtedly larger.

By the late 1960s, Mexican Americans were one of the largest population groups in the West–outnumbering African Americans–and had established communities in most other parts of the nation as well. They were also among the most urbanized groups in the population; almost 90 percent lived and worked in cities. Many of them (particularly members of the older and more assimilated families of Mexican descent) were affluent and successful. Wealthy Cuban Americans in Miami filled influential positions in the professions and local government; in the Southwest, Mexican Americans elected their own leaders to seats in Congress and to governorships.

But most newly arrived Mexican Americans and other Hispanic immigrants were less well educated than either "Anglo" or African Americans and hence less well prepared for high-paying jobs. Some of them found good industrial jobs in unionized industries, and some Mexican Americans became important labor organizers in the AFL-CIO. But many more (including most illegal immigrants) worked in low-paying service jobs, with few if any benefits and no job security.

"CHICANO" ACTIVISM

Partly because of language barriers, partly because the family-centered culture of many Latino communities discouraged effective organization, and partly because of discrimination, Mexican Americans and other Hispanic groups were slower to develop political influence than other minorities. But some did respond to the highly charged climate of the 1960s by strengthening their ethnic identification and organizing for political and economic power. Young Mexican American activists began to call themselves "Chicanos" (once a term of derision used by white Americans) as a way of emphasizing the shared culture of Spanish-speaking Americans. Some Chicanos advocated a form of nationalism not unlike the ideas of black power advocates. The Texas leaders of La Raza Unida, a Chicano political party in the Southwest, called for the creation of an autonomous Mexican American state within a state; it demonstrated significant strength at the polls in the 1970s.

One of the most visible efforts to organize Mexican Americans occurred in California, where an Arizona-born Latino farmworker, César Chávez, created an effective union of itinerant farmworkers. In 1965, his United Farm Workers (UFW), a largely Mexican American organization, launched a

CÉSAR CHÁVEZ

prolonged strike against growers to demand recognition of their union and increased wages and benefits. When employers resisted, Chávez enlisted the cooperation of college students, churches, and civil rights groups (including CORE and SNCC) and organized a nationwide boycott, first of table grapes and then of lettuce. In 1968, Chávez campaigned openly for Robert Kennedy. Two years later, he won a substantial victory when the growers of half of California's table grapes signed contracts with his union.

Latino Americans were at the center of another controversy of the 1970s and beyond: the issue of bilingualism. It was a question that aroused the opposition not only of many white Americans but of some Hispanic Americans as well. Supporters of bilingualism in education argued that non-English-speaking Americans were entitled to schooling in their own language, that otherwise they would be at a grave disadvantage in comparison with native English speakers. The U.S. Supreme Court confirmed the right of non-English-speaking students to schooling in their native language in 1974. Opponents cited not only the cost and difficulty of bilingualism but also the dangers it posed to students' ability to assimilate into the mainstream of American culture.

GAY LIBERATION

Another important liberation movement that made gains in the 1960s was the effort gay and lesbian people to win political and economic rights and, equally important, social acceptance. Gay and lesbian people had been unacknowledged realities throughout American history; not until many years after their deaths did many Americans know, for example, that revered cultural figures such as Walt Whitman and Horatio Alger were homosexuals. But by the late 1960s, the liberating impulses that had affected other groups helped mobilize gay men and lesbians to fight for their own rights.

On June 27, 1969, police officers raided the Stonewall Inn, a gay bar in New York City's Greenwich Village, and began arresting patrons simply for frequenting the place. The raid was not unusual; police had been harassing gay bars (and gay and lesbian people) for years. The accumulated resentment of this long history of assaults and humiliations caused the extraordinary response that summer night. Onlookers taunted the police, then attacked them. Someone started a blaze in the Stonewall Inn, almost trapping the policemen inside. Rioting continued throughout Greenwich Village (a center of New York's gay community) through much of the night.

"STONEWALL RIOT"

The "Stonewall Riot" helped make the gay liberation movement–a movement that had been gaining strength since at least the 1950s–a significant and highly public force. New organizations sprang up around the country. Public discussion and media coverage of homosexuality, long subject to an unofficial taboo, quickly and dramatically increased. Gay and lesbian activists had some success in challenging the long-standing assumption that their relationships were "aberrant"

Reasoning Processes

Comparing and Contrasting After students have read the section "Latino Activism," ask them to create a Venn diagram comparing the goals and methods of Native American and Latino civil rights activists. Have students discuss as a class how these movements, as well as the African American civil rights movement, were similar to or different from each other. **PCE** **WXT** **SOC** **NAT**

Historical Thinking Skills

Argumentation After students have read the section "Latino Activism," ask them to create a poster advocating for a boycott of produce in support for the United Farm Workers. **PCE** **WXT**

Historical Thinking Skills

Argumentation After students have read the section "Impact of the Gay Liberation Movement," ask them to identify and evaluate the causes of the gay liberation movement. Have students write a thesis statement that makes a claim about the most important cause of the movement. **PCE** **SOC**

KENNEDY AND CHÁVEZ César Chávez, the magnetic leader of the largely Mexican American United Farm Workers, a union that represented mostly migrant workers, staged a hunger strike in 1968 to demand that its members receive better treatment by growers. Robert F. Kennedy, just beginning his campaign for the presidency, paid him a visit in Delano, California, to show his support. Chávez, who had by then been fasting for many weeks, looks visibly weak here. Kennedy's visit helped persuade him to end the fast.

Photo by Michael Rougier/© Time & Life Pictures/Getty Images

behavior. They argued that no sexual orientation was any more "normal" than another.

Most of all, however, the gay liberation movement transformed the outlook of gay men and lesbians themselves. It helped them to "come out," to express their orientation openly and unapologetically, and to demand from society a recognition that gay relationships could be as significant and worthy of respect as heterosexual ones. Even the ravages of the AIDS epidemic, which affected the gay community more disastrously than it affected any other group, failed to halt the growth of gay liberation. In many ways, it strengthened it.

IMPACT OF THE GAY LIBERATION MOVEMENT

By the early 1990s, gay men and lesbians were achieving some of the same milestones that other oppressed minorities had attained in earlier decades. Some openly gay politicians won election to public office. Universities were establishing gay and lesbian studies programs. And laws prohibiting discrimination on the basis of sexual orientation were making slow, halting progress at the local level.

But gay liberation also produced a powerful backlash. This became especially evident in 1993, when President Bill Clinton's effort to lift the ban on gay and lesbian people serving in the military met a storm of criticism from members of Congress and from within the military itself. The backlash proved so strong that the administration retreated from its position and settled for a weak compromise ("Don't ask, don't tell") by which the military would not ask recruits about their sexual orientation, while those who enlisted in the military were expected not to reveal them.

A decade later, issues involving gay and lesbian people reached a high level of intensity again, sparked in part by the efforts of several cities and states to legalize same-sex marriage. President George W. Bush proposed a constitutional amendment to ban same-sex marriage, and the issue became a major element of Republican election campaigns. Many states put referenda on their ballots banning gay marriage, and most such referenda were decisively approved by the voters.

By 2014, the federal government, 17 states, and the District of Columbia authorized same-sex marriage. In 2013, the Supreme Court bolstered the rights of same-sex couples when it ruled, in *United States v. Windsor*, that restricting the definition of marriage to include only heterosexual couples was unconstitutional. The ruling extended on the federal level the

Discussion and Activities

Evaluating Evidence Have students examine the image "Kennedy and Chávez." Ask them to discuss in small groups the tactics demonstrated by Chávez and the United Farm Workers in the photo. *(Hunger strike designed to attract publicity and force government intervention; peaceful protest; economic pressure through boycotts.)* **PCE** **WXT**

THE QUILT In the early years of gay liberation, the movement focused mostly on ending discrimination and harassment. By the 1990s, however, with the AIDS epidemic affecting large numbers of gay men, activists shifted much of their attention to pressing for a cure and to remembering those who had died. One of the most remarkable results of that effort was the AIDS Quilt. Friends and relatives of victims of the disease made individual patches in memory of those they had lost. Then, in many different cities, thousands of quilters would join their pieces to create a vast testament to bereavement and memory. The enormity of the project was most visible in October 1996, when hundreds of thousands of pieces of the quilt were laid out on the Mall in Washington, stretching from the Washington Monument to the Capitol.

© Ron Edmunds/AP Images

same rights enjoyed by married heterosexuals to same-sex couples. The ruling left intact any state laws prohibiting same-sex marriage. Also in 2013, Congress passed the Don't Ask, Don't Tell Repeal Act, making it possible for gay people to serve openly in the military.

THE NEW FEMINISM

American women constitute a slight majority of the population. But during the 1960s and 1970s, many women began to identify with minority groups and to demand a liberation of their own. As a result, the role of women in American life changed more dramatically than that of any other group in the nation.

THE REBIRTH

Feminism had been a weak and often-embattled force in American life for more than forty years after the adoption of the woman suffrage amendment in 1920. Yet in the 1960s and 1970s, it evolved very quickly from relative obscurity to one of the most powerful social movements in American history.

THE FEMININE MYSTIQUE

The 1963 publication of Betty Friedan's *The Feminine Mystique* is often cited as an important early event of contemporary women's liberation. Friedan, a magazine journalist, had traveled around the country interviewing the women who had graduated with her from Smith College in 1942. Most of these women were living out the dream that postwar American society had created for them: they were affluent wives and mothers living in comfortable suburbs. And yet many of them were deeply frustrated and unhappy. The suburbs, Friedan claimed, had become a "comfortable concentration camp," providing the women who inhabited them with no outlets for their intelligence, talent, and education. The "feminine mystique," she wrote, was responsible for "burying millions of women alive." By chronicling their unhappiness and frustration, Friedan did not so much cause the revival of feminism as help give voice to a movement that was already stirring.

By the time *The Feminine Mystique* appeared, John Kennedy had established the President's Commission on the Status of Women; it brought national attention to sexual discrimination and helped create important networks of feminist activists who would lobby for legislative redress. Also in 1963, the Kennedy administration helped win passage of the Equal Pay Act, which barred the pervasive practice of paying women less than men for equal work. A year later, Congress incorporated into the Civil Rights Act of 1964 an amendment—Title VII—that extended to women many of the same legal protections against discrimination that were being extended to African Americans.

The events of the early 1960s helped expose a contradiction that had been developing for decades between the image of happy domesticity, what Friedan had called the "feminine mystique," and the reality of women's roles in America. The reality was that increasing numbers of women (including, by 1963, over a third of all married women) had already entered the workplace and were encountering widespread discrimination there; and that many other women were finding their domestic lives suffocating and frustrating.

NOW FOUNDED

In 1966, Friedan joined with other feminists to create the National Organization for Women (NOW), which soon became the nation's largest and most influential feminist organization. Like other movements for liberation, feminism drew much of its inspiration from the black struggle for freedom.

Discussion and Activities

Analyzing Points of View Have students examine the image "The Quilt." Ask them to write a journal entry from the point of view of an observer of the quilt in Washington, D.C., describing it physically as well as discussing its purpose and goals. SOC

Discussion and Activities

Analyzing Issues Have students read the section "*The Feminine Mystique.*" Ask them to think about and share with a partner in their own words what they believe Friedan meant by the term "feminine mystique." SOC WXT ARC

Reasoning Processes

Continuity and Change Have students read the section "Women's Liberation." Ask them to discuss in small groups how the women's movement changed from the 1960s into the 1970s and beyond. **PCE** **SOC** **WXT**

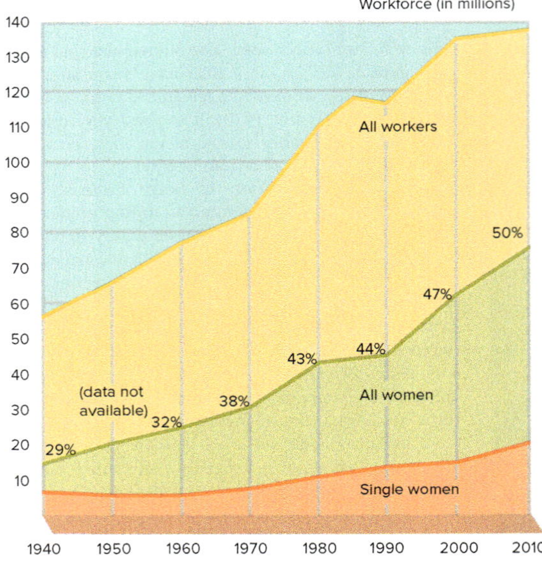

WOMEN IN THE PAID WORKFORCE, 1940–2010 The number of women working for wages steadily expanded from 1940 on, to the point that in 2010, they constituted half the total workforce.

What role did this growing participation in the paid workforce have on the rise of feminism in the 1960s and beyond?

The new organization responded to the complaints of the women Friedan's book had examined–affluent suburbanites with no outlet for their interests–by demanding greater educational opportunities for women and denouncing the domestic ideal and the traditional concept of marriage. But the heart of the movement, at least in the beginning, was directed toward the needs of women already in the workplace. NOW denounced the exclusion of women from professions, from politics, and from countless other areas of American life. It decried legal and economic discrimination, including the practice of paying women less than men for equal work (a practice the Equal Pay Act had not effectively eliminated). The organization called for "a fully equal partnership of the sexes, as part of the worldwide revolution of human rights."

WOMEN'S LIBERATION

By the late 1960s, new and more radical feminist demands were also attracting a large following. The new feminists were mostly younger, the vanguard of the baby-boom generation. Many of them drew inspiration from the New Left and the counterculture. Some were involved in the civil rights movement, others in the antiwar crusade. Many had found that even within those movements, they faced discrimination and exclusion or subordination to male leaders.

NEW DIRECTIONS IN THE WOMEN'S MOVEMENT

By the early 1970s, a significant change was visible in the tone and direction of the women's movement. New books by younger feminists expressed a harsher critique of American society than Friedan had offered. Kate Millett's *Sexual Politics* (1969) signaled the new direction by arguing that "every avenue of power within the society is entirely within male hands." The answer to women's problems, in other words, was not, as Friedan had suggested, for individual women to search for greater personal fulfillment; it was for women to band together to assault the male power structure. Shulamith Firestone's *The Dialectic of Sex* (1970) was subtitled "The Case for Feminist Revolution." By the early 1970s, large numbers of women were coming to see themselves as an exploited group organizing against oppression and developing a culture and communities of their own.

EXPANDING ACHIEVEMENTS

By the early 1970s, the public and private achievements of the women's movement were already substantial. In 1971, the government extended its affirmative action guidelines to include women–linking sexism with racism as an officially acknowledged social problem. In the meantime, women were making rapid progress in their efforts to move into the economic and political mainstream. The nation's major all-male educational institutions began to open their doors to women. (Princeton and Yale did so in 1969, and most other all-male colleges and universities soon followed.) Some women's colleges, in the meantime, began accepting male students.

Women were also becoming an important force in business and the professions. Nearly half of all married women held jobs by the mid-1970s, and almost 90 percent of all women with college degrees worked. (By 2010, women constituted half the total workforce.) The two-career family, in which both husband and wife maintained active professional lives, was becoming a widely accepted norm; many women were postponing marriage or motherhood for the sake of their careers. There were also important symbolic changes, such as the refusal of many women to adopt their husbands' names when they married and the use of the term "Ms." in place of "Mrs." or "Miss" to denote the irrelevance of a woman's marital status in the public world. In politics, women were beginning to compete effectively with men for both elected and appointive positions. By 2010, considerable numbers of women were serving in both houses of Congress (including a Speaker of the House, Nancy Pelosi), in numerous federal cabinet positions (including three secretaries of state), as governors, and in many other positions. Ronald Reagan appointed the first female Supreme Court justice, Sandra Day O'Connor, in 1981; in 1993, Bill Clinton appointed the second, Ruth Bader Ginsburg; and Barack Obama appointed two women justices, Sonia Sotomayor

POLITICAL AND ECONOMIC SUCCESS

Answers

Women in the Paid Workforce, 1940–2010

Greater participation in the workforce led to greater political, social, and economic independence for more women.

Discussion and Activities

Evaluating Evidence After students have read the section "Expanding Achievements," ask them to create a T-chart listing political and economic successes of the women's movement. Discuss as a class the areas that the movement was most successful in achieving its goals. **PCE** **SOC** **WXT**

MARCHING FOR WOMEN'S RIGHTS By the end of the 1960s, the struggle for individual rights—which the African American civil rights movement had helped push to the center of national consciousness—had inspired a broad range of movements. Perhaps the most important in the long run was the drive for women's rights, which was already formidable in the summer of 1970, when thousands of women joined this march through New York City.

and Elena Kagan in 2009 and 2010, respectively. In 1984, the Democratic Party chose Representative Geraldine Ferraro of New York as its vice presidential candidate, and in 2008, Hillary Clinton became a formidable candidate in the race for the Democratic presidential nomination. In academia, women were expanding their presence in traditional scholarly fields; they were also creating a field of their own–women's studies, which in the 1980s and early 1990s was among the fastest-growing areas of American scholarship.

In professional athletics, women were beginning to compete with men both for attention and for an equal share of prize money. By the late 1970s, the federal government was pressuring colleges and universities to provide women with athletic programs equal to those available to men.

FAILURE OF ERA

In 1972, Congress approved the Equal Rights Amendment to the Constitution, which some feminists had been promoting since the 1920s, and sent it to the states. For a while, ratification seemed almost certain. By the late 1970s, however, the momentum behind the amendment had died. The ERA was in trouble not because of indifference but because of a rising chorus of objections to it from people (including many antifeminist women) who feared it would disrupt traditional social patterns. In 1982, the amendment died when the time allotted for its ratification expired.

THE ABORTION CONTROVERSY

A vital element of American feminism since the 1920s has been women's effort to win greater control of their own sexual and reproductive lives. In its least controversial form, this impulse helped produce an increasing awareness in the 1960s and 1970s of the problems of rape, sexual abuse, and wife beating. There continued to be some controversy over the dissemination of contraceptives and birth-control information; but that issue, at least, seemed to have lost much of the explosive character it had had in the 1920s. A related issue, however, stimulated as much popular passion as any question of its time: abortion.

Abortion had once been legal in much of the United States, but by the beginning of the twentieth century it was banned by statute in most of the country and remained so into the

Discussion and Activities

Analyzing Points of View

Have students examine the image "Marching for Women's Rights." Ask them to write a journal entry from the point of view of either a participant in or an observer of the march, describing their experiences. **SOC** **PCE**

Discussion and Activities

Making Connections After students have read the section "The Abortion Controversy," ask them to research recent legislation and court decisions relating to abortion. Have students discuss as a class how various abortion laws have changed since the *Roe v. Wade* decision. **SOC** **PCE**

Key Terms

Students should be familiar with the key terms and be able to define them in the context of the post-World War II struggle for equal rights by African Americans, Native Americans, Latinos, the LGBTQ community, and women. Encourage students to use these terms in performing review exercises and exam practice for this chapter.

1960s (although many abortions continued to be performed quietly, and often dangerously, out of sight of the law). But the women's movement created strong new pressures on behalf of legalizing abortion. Several states had abandoned restrictions on abortion by the end of the 1960s. And in 1973, the Supreme Court's decision in *Roe v. Wade*, based on a relatively new theory of a constitutional "right to privacy," first recognized by the Court only a few years earlier in *Griswold v. Connecticut* (1965), invalidated all laws prohibiting abortion during the "first trimester"–the first three months of pregnancy. The decision would become the most controversial ruling of the century.

ROE V. WADE

CHAPTER 30 REVIEW

CONNECTING THEMES

Chapter Thirty explored the rise and growth of the modern civil rights movement during the second half of the twentieth century in American society. The modern civil rights movement brought tremendous change to America's political, economic, and social institutions. Decades of challenges to segregation finally met with success in the Supreme Court decision that overturned the long-standing "separate but equal" doctrine established by *Plessy v. Ferguson* at the end of the nineteenth century. More challenges to segregation and inequality arose and were met with stiff opposition from some segments within American society. White Americans often reacted with anger or violence to demonstrations and protests. As African Americans made political and social gains the civil rights movement began to focus on economic issues, including job and housing discrimination.

The modern civil rights movement also served as a catalyst for other minorities within American society to advocate for equal rights and opportunities. Native Americans organized and won new legal rights and protections. Likewise, Latino Americans organized to advocate for more political and economic power, but struggled to form a cohesive movement partly due to the variety of cultures and the language barrier. The gay rights movement challenged long-held assumptions and demanded recognition from American society. The women's movement gained strength and successfully moved women into the economic and political mainstream. The civil rights movements of the era challenged American identity and raised issues that continue to impact American society today.

You should consider the following questions as you review the themes for this chapter:

- What were the major causes and effects of the rise of the modern civil rights movement?
- What was the impact of ideas about social conformity and non-conformity and the civil rights movement on American identity and values?
- How did the modern civil rights movement change or challenge Americans' ideas about democracy, freedom, and individualism?
- How did the growing protests by minority groups change both their perception of themselves and the perception of others toward them?
- What were the major similarities and differences faced by African American and other minority groups as they all sought to achieve equal rights within American society?
- How did the new feminist movement transform gender roles in the United States during the second half of the twentieth century?

KEY TERMS

American Indian Movement (AIM) 822
Betty Friedan 827
Black Panther Party 821
Brown v. Board of Education 814
Cesar Chavez 825
Civil Rights Act of 1964 827
Congress of Racial Equality (CORE) 816
Equal Pay Act 827
Equal Rights Amendment (ERA) 829
Fannie Lou Hamer 818
Freedom Rides 816
Freedom Summer 818
Gay Liberation Movement 825
George Wallace 817
Jackie Robinson 815
James Meredith 817
La Raza Unida 825
Little Rock Central High School 815
Malcolm X 821
March on Washington 817
Martin Luther King, Jr. 814
Mississippi Freedom Democratic Party (MFDP) 818
Montgomery Bus Boycott 814
National Organization for Women (NOW) 827
Operation Wetback 825
Roe v. Wade 830
Rosa Parks 815
Southern Christian Leadership Conference (SCLC) 817
Stonewall Riot 825
Student Nonviolent Coordinating Committee (SNCC) 816
The Feminine Mystique 827
Voting Rights Act of 1965 818
Watts Riot 820
Wounded Knee 824

Go Online **Chapter 30 Content Review**

Assessing Student Understanding Use the online assessment to assess student understanding of concepts and topics within the chapter. You can assign the ready-made Chapter 30 Content Review or create your own from available questions. This easy-to-use tool helps you design assessments that meet the needs of different types of learners.

AP EXAM PRACTICE

Questions assume cumulative content knowledge from this chapter and previous chapters.

MULTIPLE CHOICE

Use the image on page 814 and your knowledge of U.S. history to answer questions 1-3.

1. Activists in the civil rights movement, such as the individual in the photograph, included
   (A) governmental leaders.
   (B) children and teenagers.
   (C) the elderly.
   (D) military personnel.
2. The students who integrated in Little Rock Central High School were supported by
   (A) the Arkansas governor, Orval Faubus.
   (B) other integrated schools in the Southern states.
   (C) the Supreme Court decision in *Brown v Board of Education*.
   (D) the recent passage of the Voting Rights Act.
3. Many activists for racial justice were met, as illustrated by the photograph, with
   (A) local resistance and threats of violence.
   (B) significant and vocal support from other community members.
   (C) the protection of local police and elected officials.
   (D) immediate and full support from all branches of the federal government.

SHORT ANSWER

Use your knowledge of U.S. history to answer questions 4 and 5.

4. Use the photograph on page 814 to answer A, B, and C.
   (A) Briefly describe ONE historical situation in the United States during the 1950s illustrated by the image.
   (B) Briefly explain how ONE specific historical event or development before 1955 led to the historical situation illustrated by the image.
   (C) Briefly explain ONE specific historical event or development that resulted from the historical situation illustrated by the image.
5. Answer A, B, and C.
   (A) Briefly describe ONE specific historical difference between the philosophy of Martin Luther King, Jr. and Malcolm X.
   (B) Briefly describe ONE specific historical similarity between the philosophy of Martin Luther King, Jr. and Malcolm X.
   (C) Briefly explain ONE specific effect that resulted from the philosophy of Martin Luther King, Jr. or Malcolm X.

LONG ESSAY

Develop a thoughtful and thorough historical argument that answers the question. Begin your essay with a thesis statement, and support it with specific historical evidence and examples.

6. Evaluate the extent of continuities in the lives of African Americans from 1940 to 1980 in American society.

Answers

Multiple Choice

1. B; **2.** C; **3.** A

Short Answer

4A) Possible answer: The changes in American society during the time period were not embraced by everyone. The image depicts the desegregation of Little Rock Central High School, where the military was called in to enforce the federal court order.

4B) Possible answer: The *Brown v. Board of Education* Supreme Court decision ruled that segregated schools were in violation of the U.S. Constitution and overturned the *Plessy* decision, which had legalized the concept of "separate but equal."

4C) Possible answer: Following the *Brown* decision, Southern states mounted a "massive resistance" movement. Many places implemented "Pupil Placement Laws" that allowed schools and officials to place students according to their academic abilities and social behavior. These placement laws allowed segregation to continue.

5A) Possible answer: Martin Luther King, Jr., supported passive, nonviolent protest, whereas Malcolm X and other more radical members supported a more confrontational approach to injustices.

5B) Possible answer: Both philosophies maintained that it was time to confront racism and advocated for immediate change within the political, economic, and social structures of American society.

5C) Possible answer: The nonviolent approach of Martin Luther King, Jr., drew sympathy from lawmakers and the general public as the violence that was used against peaceful protesters was on view for all to see as many of these events were televised. Two pieces of legislation resulted: the Civil Rights Act and the Voting Rights Act.

Answers

Long Essay

6. Possible thesis: Passage of major pieces of legislation helped further the idea that American society was undergoing significant changes, especially for African Americans. However, African Americans continued to face discrimination and racism. Therefore, there were more continuities in the lives of African Americans than there were changes during the second half of the twentieth century. Specific historical evidence: African Americans continued to face discrimination and racism following the post–World War II era in American history. The *Plessy* decision, which constitutionalized the concept of "separate but equal," was tightly entrenched in all aspects of American society. Segregation was a part of daily life for African Americans. Jim Crow–era laws continued throughout the first part of the twentieth century. While both the Civil Rights Act and the Voting Rights Act were passed, voter suppression and discrimination continued in more subtle ways.

Pacing Guide

Chapter 31 explores key concepts from Period 8: 1945–1980 of the AP U.S. History Curriculum Framework. The suggested instruction time for Chapter 31 is 4 days.

Key Concepts

8.1.I United States policymakers engaged in a cold war with the authoritarian Soviet Union, seeking to limit the growth of Communist military power and ideological influence, create a free-market global economy, and build an international security system.

8.1.II Cold War policies led to public debates over the power of the federal government and acceptable means for pursuing international and domestic goals while protecting civil liberties.

8.3.II New demographic and social developments, along with anxieties over the Cold War, changed U.S. culture and led to significant political and moral debates that sharply divided the nation.

31 THE LATER COLD WAR

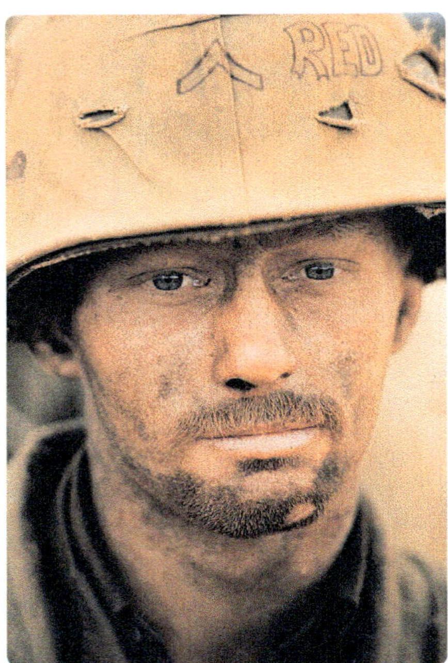

KHE SANH, VIETNAM, 1968
A beleaguered American soldier shows his exhaustion during the 76-day siege of the American marine base at Khe Sanh, which began shortly before the 1968 Tet offensive in Vietnam. American forces sustained record casualties in the fierce fighting at Khe Sanh; the Vietnamese communist forces suffered far more.

CONNECTING CONCEPTS

Chapter Thirty-One begins by examining the later Cold War during the Kennedy and Nixon administrations. John Kennedy tried to overthrow Cuban dictator Fidel Castro at the Bay of Pigs in 1961. The failed attempt led to the Cuban missile crisis of 1962, the most dangerous and dramatic moment of the Cold War when the United States and Soviet Union almost went to war.

Kennedy inherited from Eisenhower the obligation to defend South Vietnam from communist aggression after the French abandoned the struggle in 1954. At first, the United States sent military aid and advisors to oppose Ho Chi Minh and his followers. But after steady communist gains and the Gulf of Tonkin Resolution, Lyndon Johnson deployed ground troops in 1965. The war of attrition soon became a quagmire and generated increasing opposition at home. Although the Tet Offensive of 1968 was a military defeat for North Vietnam, it was a political and psychological victory. The broadcast of violent images from Vietnam across the United States convinced many Americans that victory was impossible and the war was not worth fighting.

Richard Nixon in 1968 promised voters "peace with honor" in Southeast Asia. He then scaled back the ground war – what he called "Vietnamization" – and escalated the air war against North Vietnam. But the Easter Offensive of 1972 demonstrated that the communists remained dominant and determined to prevail. The Paris Peace Accords of 1973 led the United States to withdraw from Southeast Asia, and two years later, North Vietnam conquered South Vietnam. By that time, Nixon had thawed the Cold War and improved relations with the Soviet Union and Communist China while adapting the United States to a new "multipolar" international structure.

Discussion and Activities

Analyzing Points of View Have students examine the image "Khe Sanh, Vietnam, 1968." Ask them to write a journal entry from the point of view of the soldier in the photo describing the hopes and fears he experienced upon deployment to Vietnam. **WOR** **SOC** **WXT**

As you read, you should:

- Describe the reasons for and consequences of the continued Cold War with the Soviet Union.
- Evaluate the escalation of the Vietnam War and the polarization of American society in response to the war.
- Analyze the factors which caused the year 1968 to become such a traumatic year in American history.
- Identify the reasons why the United States escalated its presence in Vietnam, despite large-scale protests within American society.
- Explain the efforts of the Nixon administration in creating a new international order.

KENNEDY AND "FLEXIBLE RESPONSE"

Those who yearned for a more active government in the late 1950s, and who accused the Eisenhower administration of allowing the nation to "drift," looked above all to the presidency for leadership. The two men who served in the White House through most of the 1960s–John Kennedy and Lyndon Johnson–seemed for a time to be the embodiment of these liberal hopes.

JOHN KENNEDY

The presidential campaign of 1960 produced two young candidates who claimed to offer the nation active leadership. The Republican nomination went almost uncontested to Vice President Richard Nixon, who promised moderate reform. The Democrats, in the meantime, emerged from a spirited primary campaign united, somewhat uneasily, behind John Fitzgerald Kennedy, an attractive and articulate senator from Massachusetts who had narrowly missed being the party's vice presidential candidate in 1956.

ELECTION OF 1960

John Kennedy was the son of the wealthy, powerful, and highly controversial Joseph P. Kennedy, former American ambassador to Britain. But while he had grown up in a world of ease and privilege, he became a spokesman for personal sacrifice and energetic progress. His appealing public image was at least as important as his political positions in attracting popular support. He overcame doubts about his youth (he turned forty-three in 1960) and religion (he was Catholic) to win with a tiny plurality of the popular vote (49.7 percent to Nixon's 49.6 percent) and only a slightly more comfortable electoral majority (303 to 219).

Kennedy had campaigned promising a set of domestic reforms more ambitious than any since the New Deal, a program he described as the "New Frontier." But his thin popular mandate and a Congress dominated by a coalition of Republicans and conservative Democrats frustrated many of his hopes. Kennedy did manage to win approval of tariff reductions his administration had negotiated, and he began to build an ambitious legislative agenda that he hoped he might eventually see enacted–including a call for a significant tax cut to promote economic growth.

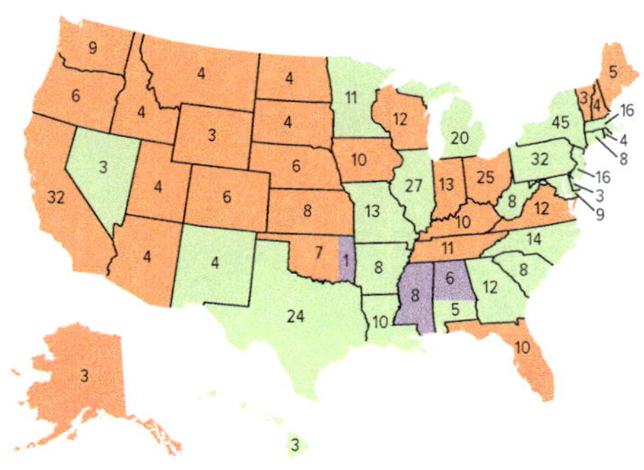

Candidate (Party)	Electoral Vote	Popular Vote (%)
John F. Kennedy (Democratic)	303	34,227,096 (49.7)
Richard M. Nixon (Republican)	219	34,108,546 (49.6)
Harry F. Byrd (Dixiecrat)	15	501,643 (0.7)
Other candidates (Prohibition; Socialist Labor; Constitution; Socialist Workers; States' Rights)	–	197,029

64% of electorate voting

THE ELECTION OF 1960 The election of 1960 was, in the popular vote at least, one of the closest in American history. John Kennedy's margin over Richard Nixon was less than one-third of 1 percent of the total national vote, but greater in the electoral college. Note the distribution of electoral strength of the two candidates. Kennedy was strong in the industrial Northeast and the largest industrial states of the Midwest, and he retained at least a portion of his party's traditional strength in the South and Southwest. But Nixon made significant inroads into the upper South, carried Florida, and swept most of the Plains and Mountain states.

What was the significance of this distribution of strength to the future of the two parties?

DIVERSIFYING FOREIGN POLICY

In international affairs as much as in domestic reform, the optimistic liberalism of the Kennedy and Johnson administrations

Answers

The Election of 1960.

Kennedy's dependence upon conservative Southern Democrats, who arguably had more in common with Republicans than with the president, undermined his social policies.

Go Online AP Exam Preparation

AP Exam Practice Use the online assessment to help prepare students for the AP Exam. You can assign the ready-made AP-style short-answer questions, document-based questions, and multiple-choice questions assessing concepts, themes, and skills from Period 8 and AP-style long-essay questions organized in sets of 3 questions from various time periods. You can also create your own tests from available questions. This easy-to-use tool helps you design assessments that meet the needs of different types of learners.

Historical Thinking Skills

Argumentation After students have read the section "John Kennedy," ask them to create a campaign poster supporting either Kennedy or Nixon. **PCE** **SOC** **GEO**

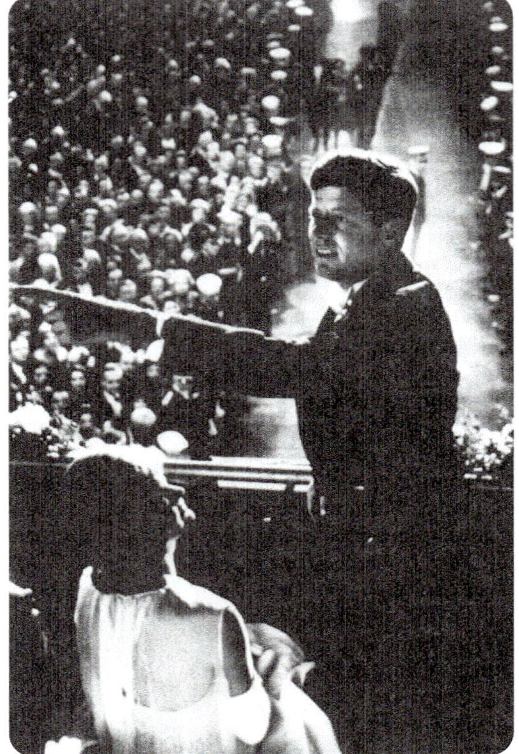

JOHN KENNEDY The new president and his wife, Jacqueline, attend one of the five balls in Washington marking Kennedy's inauguration in 1961.

dictated a more positive, more active approach to dealing with the nation's problems than in the past. And just as the new activism in domestic reform proved more difficult and divisive than liberals had imagined, so too it created frustrations and failures in foreign policy.

The Kennedy administration entered office convinced that the United States needed to be able to counter communist aggression in more-flexible ways than the atomic-weapons-oriented defense strategy of the Eisenhower years had permitted. In particular, Kennedy was unsatisfied with the nation's ability to meet communist threats in "emerging areas" of the Third World–the areas in which, Kennedy believed, the real struggle against communism would be waged in the future. He gave enthusiastic support to the expansion of the Special Forces (or "Green Berets," as they were soon known)–soldiers trained specifically to fight guerrilla conflicts and other limited wars.

"FLEXIBLE RESPONSE"

Kennedy also favored expanding American influence through peaceful means. To repair the badly deteriorating relationship with Latin America, he proposed an "Alliance for Progress": a series of projects for peaceful development and stabilization of the nations of that region. Kennedy also inaugurated the Agency for International Development (AID) to coordinate foreign aid. And he established what became one of his most popular innovations: the Peace Corps, which sent young American volunteers abroad to work in developing areas.

Among the first foreign policy ventures of the Kennedy administration was a disastrous assault on the Castro government in Cuba. The Eisenhower administration had begun the project; and by the time Kennedy took office, the CIA had been working for months to train a small army of anti-Castro Cuban exiles in Central America. On April 17, 1961, with the approval of the new president, 2,000 of the armed exiles landed at the Bay of Pigs in Cuba, expecting first American air support and then a spontaneous uprising by the Cuban people on their behalf. They received neither. At the last minute, as it became clear that things were going badly, Kennedy withdrew the air support, fearful of involving the United States too directly in the invasion. The expected uprising did not occur. Instead, well-armed Castro forces easily crushed the invaders, and within two days the entire mission had collapsed.

BAY OF PIGS

CONFRONTATIONS WITH THE SOVIET UNION

In the grim aftermath of the Bay of Pigs, Kennedy traveled to Vienna in June 1961 for his first meeting with Soviet premier Nikita Khrushchev. Their frosty exchange of views did little to reduce tensions between the two nations–nor did Khrushchev's veiled threat of war if the United States continued to support a noncommunist West Berlin in the heart of East Germany.

Khrushchev was particularly unhappy about the mass exodus of residents of East Germany to the West through the easily traversed border in the center of Berlin. But he ultimately found a method short of war to stop it. Before dawn on August 13, 1961, the East German government, complying with directives from Moscow, began constructing a wall between East and West Berlin. Guards fired on those who continued to try to escape from East to West. For nearly thirty years, the Berlin Wall served as the most potent physical symbol of the conflict between the communist and noncommunist worlds.

The rising tensions culminated the following October in the most dangerous and dramatic crisis of the Cold War. On October 14, aerial reconnaissance photos produced clear evidence that the Soviets were constructing sites in Cuba for offensive nuclear weapons. To the Soviets, placing missiles in Cuba probably seemed a reasonable–and relatively inexpensive–way to counter the presence of American missiles in Turkey (and a way to deter any future American invasion of Cuba). But to Kennedy and most other Americans, the missile sites represented an act of aggression by the Soviets toward

CUBAN MISSILE CRISIS

Reasoning Processes

Comparing and Contrasting After students have read the section "Diversifying Foreign Policy," discuss as a class how the new policy of "flexible response" was similar to or different from the Eisenhower administration's "massive retaliation" policy. **WOR** **PCE**

THE UNITED STATES IN LATIN AMERICA, 1954–1996 The Cold War greatly increased the readiness of the United States to intervene in the affairs of its Latin American neighbors. This map presents the many times and ways in which Washington ordered interventions in Central America, the Caribbean, and the northern nations of South America. During much of this period, the interventions were driven by Cold War concerns—by fears that communists might take over nations near the United States as they had taken over Cuba in the early 1960s.

What other interests motivated the United States to exert influence in Latin America, even after the end of the Cold War?

KENNEDY IN BERLIN, 1963 President John F. Kennedy looks across the Berlin Wall from a platform built to allow him to see into East Berlin. Shortly afterward he gave a powerful speech to a vast crowd of West Berliners. The speech was well received in Europe and America. But it followed another important speech in which Kennedy spoke of easing the tensions between the West and the communist world.)

the United States. Almost immediately, the president decided that the weapons could not be allowed to remain. On October 22, he ordered a naval and air blockade around Cuba, a "quarantine" against all offensive weapons. Preparations were under way for an American air attack on the missile sites when, late in the evening of October 26, Kennedy received a message from Khrushchev implying that the Soviet Union would remove the missile bases in exchange for an American pledge not to invade Cuba. Ignoring other, tougher Soviet messages, the president agreed. The crisis was over.

JOHNSON AND THE WORLD

Lyndon Johnson entered the presidency lacking John Kennedy's prior, albeit limited, experience with international affairs. He was eager, therefore, not only to continue the policies of his predecessor but also to prove quickly that he too was a strong and forceful leader.

An internal rebellion in the Dominican Republic gave him an early opportunity to do so. A 1961 assassination had toppled the repressive dictatorship of

Discussion and Activities

Analyzing Issues After students have read the section "Confrontations with the Soviet Union," ask them to discuss in small groups whether the quarantine ordered by President Kennedy constituted an act of war. **WOR**

Answers

The United States in Latin America, 1954–1996

The United States continued to fear the influence of communism in Latin America, particularly in Nicaragua and Cuba.

AP Exam Tip

The Advanced Placement Exam will require students to explain the purpose, point of view, historical situation, and/or audience of a document. One way students can demonstrate this is to explain historical events that led to the event being portrayed.

Historical Thinking Skills

Sourcing and Situation Have students practice the tip by examining the image of the wounded soldier. Ask them to discuss in small groups how American soldiers came to be in Vietnam. **WOR** **PCE**

DEBATING THE PAST

THE VIETNAM COMMITMENT

In 1965, the Department of Defense released a film intended for American soldiers about to embark for service in Vietnam and designed to explain why the United States had found it necessary to commit so many lives and resources to the defense of a small and distant land. The film was titled *Why Vietnam?*—a question many Americans have pondered and debated in the decades since. The debate has centered on two questions. One is an effort to assess the broad objectives Americans believed they were pursuing in Vietnam. The other is an effort to explain how and why policymakers made the specific decisions that led to the American commitment.

The Defense Department film offered one answer to the question of America's broad objectives: the United States was fighting in Vietnam to defend freedom and stop aggression and to prevent the spread of communism. This explanation continued to attract support well after the war ended. Political scientist Guenter Lewy contended, in *America in Vietnam* (1978), that the United States entered Vietnam to help an ally combat "foreign aggression." Historian Ernest R. May stated: "The paradox is that the Vietnam War, so often condemned by its opponents as hideously immoral, may well have been the most moral or at least the most selfless war in all of American history. For the impulse guiding it was not to defeat an enemy or to serve a national interest; it was simply not to abandon friends."

Other scholars have taken a starkly different view. They see America's intervention in Vietnam as a form of imperialism—part of a larger effort by the United States after World War II to impose a particular political and economic order on the world. "The Vietnam War," historian Gabriel Kolko wrote in *Anatomy of a War* (1985), "was for the United States the culmination of its frustrating postwar effort to merge its arms and politics to halt and reverse the emergence of states and social systems opposed to the international order Washington sought to establish." Marilyn Young, in *The Vietnam Wars, 1945–1990* (1991), argued that the United States intervened in Vietnam as part of a broad and continuing effort to organize the post–World War II world along lines compatible with American interests and ideals.

Those who looked less at the nation's broad objectives than at the internal workings of the policymaking process likewise produced competing explanations. Journalist David Halberstam's *The Best and the Brightest* (1972) argued that policymakers deluded themselves into thinking they could achieve their goals in Vietnam by ignoring, suppressing, or dismissing the information that might have suggested otherwise. The foreign policy leaders of the Kennedy and Johnson administrations were so committed to the idea of American activism and success that they refused to consider the possibility of failure; the Vietnam disaster was thus, at least in part, a result of the arrogance of the nation's leaders.

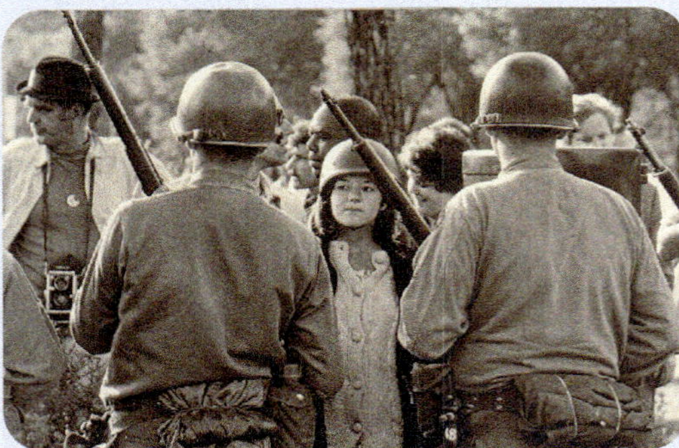

Larry Berman offered a somewhat different view in *Planning a Tragedy* (1982) and *Lyndon Johnson's War* (1989). Berman argued that Johnson committed American troops to the war in Vietnam in 1965 not because he expected to win (in fact, he never believed that a real victory was within sight), but because he feared that allowing Vietnam to fall would ruin him politically. To do otherwise, Johnson feared, would destroy his hopes for winning approval of his Great Society legislation at home.

Leslie H. Gelb and Richard K. Betts saw the roots of the involvement in the larger imperatives of the American foreign policy system. In *The Irony of Vietnam: The System Worked* (1979), they argued that intervention in Vietnam was the logical, perhaps even inevitable, result of a political and bureaucratic order shaped by the doctrine of containment. American foreign policy operated in response to a single, overriding imperative: the need to prevent the expansion of communism. Only when the national and international political situation had shifted to the point where it was possible for American policymakers to reassess the costs of the commitment (a shift that began to occur in the early 1970s) was it possible for the United States to begin disengaging.

More-recent studies have questioned the idea that intervention was inevitable or that there were no viable alternatives. David Kaiser, in *American Tragedy* (2000), argues that John Kennedy was not a hawkish supporter of escalation. Rather, his skepticism about the judgment of his military advisers had led him to believe that the United States should find a negotiated settlement to the war. His successor, Lyndon Johnson, harbored no such skepticism and sided with those who favored a military solution. The death of John Kennedy, therefore, becomes a vital event in the history of America in Vietnam. Fredrik Logevall, in *Choosing War: The Lost Chance for Peace and the Escalation of the War in Vietnam* (1999), argues that there were significant opportunities for a negotiated settlement of the war in the early 1960s, but that American leaders (including both Kennedy and Johnson) chose a military response instead—in part to protect themselves politically from charges of weakness.

Discussion and Activities

Analyzing Points of View Have students examine the images in the feature. Ask students to work in small groups to discuss the point of view and possible purpose and audience of each image. Ask for volunteers to share their discussions with the class. **PCE** **SOC**

That the debate over the Vietnam War has been so continuous over the past few decades is a reflection of the enormous role the U.S. failure there has played in shaping the way Americans have thought about politics and policy ever since. Because the "lessons of Vietnam" remain a subject of intense popular concern, the debate over the history of Vietnam is likely to continue.

HISTORICAL THINKING SKILLS

Questions assume cumulative content knowledge from this chapter and previous chapters.

1. **Identifying Historical Developments** Identify three broad schools of historical interpretation presented in the discussion of why America committed to the Vietnam War.
2. **Evaluating Evidence** Describe how historical evidence could be used to support three broad schools of historical interpretation concerning the U.S. commitment to the Vietnam War.
3. **Developing Arguments** Analyze which school of thought you find most convincing and develop your argument using evidence from the text.

INTERVENTION IN THE DOMINICAN REPUBLIC

General Rafael Trujillo, and for the next four years various factions in the country had struggled for dominance. In the spring of 1965, a conservative military regime began to collapse in the face of a revolt by a broad range of groups on behalf of the left-wing nationalist Juan Bosch. Arguing (without any evidence) that Bosch planned to establish a pro-Castro, communist regime, Johnson dispatched 30,000 American troops to quell the disorder. Only after a conservative candidate defeated Bosch in a 1966 election were the forces withdrawn.

From Johnson's first moments in office, however, his foreign policy was almost totally dominated by the bitter civil war in Vietnam and by the expanding involvement of the United States there.

THE AGONY OF VIETNAM

George Kennan, who helped devise the containment doctrine that drew America into war in Vietnam, once called the conflict "the most disastrous of all America's undertakings over the whole 200 years of its history." Yet at first, the Vietnam War seemed simply one more Third World struggle on the periphery of the Cold War, a struggle in which the United States would try to tip the balance against communism without becoming too deeply or directly engaged. No single president really "decided" to go to war in Vietnam. Rather, the American involvement there emerged from years of gradually increasing commitments that slowly and almost imperceptibly expanded.

THE FIRST INDOCHINA WAR

Vietnam had a long history both as an independent kingdom and a major power in its region, and as a subjugated province of China. In the mid-nineteenth century, Vietnam became a colony of France. And like other European possessions in Asia, it fell under the control of Japan during World War II. After the defeat of Japan, the question arose of what was to happen to Vietnam in the postwar world. There were two opposing forces attempting to answer that question, both of them appealing to the United States for help. The French wanted to reassert their colonial control over Vietnam. Challenging them was a powerful nationalist movement within Vietnam committed to creating an independent country. The nationalists were organized into a political party, the Vietminh, which had been created in 1941 and led ever since by Ho Chi Minh, a communist educated in Paris and Moscow, and a fervent Vietnamese nationalist. In the fall of 1945, after the collapse of Japan and before the Western powers had time to return, the Vietminh declared Vietnam an independent nation and set up a nationalist government under Ho Chi Minh in Hanoi.

THE VIETMINH

President Truman was under heavy pressure from both the British and the French to support France in its effort to reassert its control over Vietnam. The French argued that without

Discussion and Activities

Explaining Historical Concepts After students have read the section "Johnson and the World," ask them to discuss in small groups how intervention in the Dominican Republic reflected American Cold War fears. **WOR**

Answers

Debating the Past

1. Possible answer: Lewy argued that America entered Vietnam to help an ally combat "foreign aggression." Kolko argued that America's intervention in Vietnam was the culmination of its political and military imposition upon the larger world community. Similarly, Gelb and Betts argued that America's involvement in Vietnam was the inevitable effect of the doctrine of containment.
2. Possible answer: Going back to Wilson's "Moral Diplomacy," the country has often couched its foreign policy in terms of aid to weaker countries or allies. During the Cold War, America sought ways of asserting its influence, which can be argued was the continuation of the imperialistic foreign policy going back to the Spanish-American War.
3. Possible answer: Student responses will vary. They may say that there is some truth in all three arguments. The United States likes to phrase its foreign policy goals in terms of humanitarian aid, but at the same time, it's likely that foreign policy directives also have to have America's interests at heart, whether they be social, political, or economic.

Historical Thinking Skills

Argumentation After students have read the section "The First Indochina War," ask them to discuss with a partner whether the United States should have supported France or the Vietminh in setting up a government. Have each partner make the case for one side. **WOR**

Vietnam, their domestic economy would collapse. And since the economic revival of Western Europe was quickly becoming one of the Truman administration's top priorities, the United States did nothing to stop the French as they moved back into Vietnam in 1946 and began a struggle with the Vietminh to reestablish control over the country.

For the next four years, during what has become known as the First Indochina War, Truman and then Eisenhower supported the French military campaign against the Vietminh; by 1954, by some calculations, the United States was paying 80 percent of France's war costs. But the war went badly for the French in spite of the American support. Finally, late in 1953, Vietminh forces engaged the French in a major battle in the far northwest corner of the country, at Dien Bien Phu, an isolated and almost indefensible site. The French were surrounded, and the battle turned into a prolonged and horrible siege, with the French position steadily deteriorating. It was at this point that the Eisenhower administration decided not to intervene to save the French. The defense of Dien Bien Phu collapsed and the French government decided the time had come to get out. The First Indochina War had come to an end.

Geneva and the Two Vietnams

An international conference at Geneva, planned many months before to settle the Korean dispute and other controversies, now took up the fate of Vietnam as well. The Geneva Conference produced an agreement to end the Vietnam conflict without American participation. There would be an immediate cease-fire in the war; Vietnam would be temporarily partitioned along the 17th parallel, with the Vietminh in control of North Vietnam and a pro-Western regime in control of the South. In 1956, elections would be held to reunite the country under a single government.

GENEVA CONFERENCE

America and Diem

As soon as the Geneva accords established the partition, the French finally left Vietnam. The United States almost immediately stepped into the vacuum and became the principal benefactor of the new government in the South, led by Ngo Dinh Diem. Diem was an aristocratic Catholic from central Vietnam, an outsider in the South. But he was also a nationalist, uncontaminated by collaboration with the French. And he was, for a time, successful. With the help of the American CIA, Diem waged an effective campaign against some of the powerful religious sects and the South Vietnamese mafia, which had challenged the authority of the central government. As a result, the United States came to regard Diem as a powerful and impressive alternative to Ho Chi Minh. Lyndon Johnson once called him the "Churchill of Southeast Asia."

NGO DINH DIEM

The U.S. government supported South Vietnamese President Diem's refusal in 1956 to permit the elections called for by the Geneva accords (see above), reasoning, correctly, that Ho Chi Minh would easily win any such election. He could count on almost 100 percent of the vote in the north, with its much larger population, and at least some support in the south. In the meantime, the United States poured military and economic aid into South Vietnam. By 1956, it was the second largest recipient of American military aid in the world, after Korea.

Diem's early successes in suppressing the sects in Vietnam led him in 1959 to begin a similar campaign to eliminate the Vietminh supporters who had stayed behind in the south after the partition. He was quite successful for a time, so successful, in fact, that the North Vietnamese found it necessary to respond. Ho Chi Minh resumed his armed struggle for national unification. In 1959, the Vietminh cadres in the south created the National Liberation Front (NLF), known to many Americans as the Viet Cong–an organization closely allied with the North Vietnamese government. It was committed to overthrowing the "puppet regime" of Diem and reuniting the nation. In 1960, under orders from Hanoi, and with both material and manpower support from North Vietnam, the NLF began military operations in the South.

THE NLF

By 1961, NLF forces were very successfully destabilizing the Diem regime. They were killing more than 4,000 government officials a year (mostly village leaders) and establishing effective control over many areas of the countryside. Diem was also by now losing the support of many other groups in South Vietnam, and he was even losing support within his own military. In 1963, the Diem regime precipitated a major crisis by trying to discipline and repress the South Vietnamese Buddhists in an effort to make Catholicism the dominant religion of the country. The Buddhists began to stage enormous antigovernment demonstrations. Several Buddhist monks doused themselves with gasoline, sat cross-legged in the streets of downtown Saigon, and set themselves on fire–in view of photographers and television cameras.

The Buddhist crisis caused the U.S. government to reconsider its commitment to Diem–although not to the survival of South Vietnam. American officials pressured Diem to reform his government, but Diem made no significant concessions. In the fall of 1963, Kennedy gave his tacit approval to a plot by a group of South Vietnamese generals to topple Diem. In early November 1963, the generals staged the coup, assassinated Diem and his brother and principal adviser, Ngo Dinh Nhu (murders the United States had not wanted or expected), and established the first of a series of new governments, which were, for over three years, even less stable than the one they had overthrown. A few weeks after the coup, John Kennedy too was dead.

DIEM OVERTHROWN

From Aid to Intervention

Lyndon Johnson thus inherited what was already a substantial American commitment to the survival of an anticommunist South Vietnam. During his first two years in office, he expanded that commitment into a full-scale American war. Why he did so has long been a subject of debate.

Discussion and Activities

Historical Evidence and Argumentation Have students read the section "America and Diem." Ask them to create a T-chart listing the advantages of supporting Diem in South Vietnam. Have students consider whether the advantages outweighed the disadvantages, and if there was a better alternative. **WOR**

Many factors played a role in Johnson's decision. But the most obvious explanation is that the new president faced many pressures to expand the American involvement and very few to limit it. As the untested successor to a revered and martyred president, he felt obliged to prove his worthiness for the office by continuing the policies of his predecessor. Johnson also felt it necessary to retain in his administration many of the important figures of the Kennedy years. In doing so, he surrounded himself with a group of foreign policy advisers–Secretary of State Dean Rusk, Secretary of Defense Robert McNamara, National Security Adviser McGeorge Bundy, and others–who firmly believed that the United States had an obligation to resist communism in Vietnam. Congress raised little protest to, and indeed at one point openly endorsed, Johnson's use of executive powers to lead the nation into war.

PRESSURE FOR AMERICAN INTERVENTION

Above all, intervention in South Vietnam was fully consistent with nearly twenty years of American foreign policy. An anticommunist ally was appealing to the United States for assistance; all the assumptions of the containment doctrine, as it had come to be defined by the 1960s, seemed to require the nation to intervene. Vietnam, Johnson believed, was a test of American willingness to fight communist aggression, a test he was determined not to fail.

During his first months in office, Johnson expanded the American involvement in Vietnam only slightly, sending an additional 5,000 military advisers there and preparing to send 5,000 more. Then, early in August 1964, the president announced that American destroyers on patrol in international waters in the Gulf of Tonkin had been attacked by North Vietnamese torpedo boats. Later information raised doubts as to whether the administration reported the attacks accurately. At the time, however, virtually no one questioned Johnson's portrayal of the incident as a serious act of aggression, or his insistence that the United States must respond. By a vote of 416 to 0 in the House and 88 to 2 in the Senate, Congress hurriedly passed the Gulf of Tonkin Resolution, which authorized the president to "take all necessary measures" to protect American forces and "prevent further aggression" in Southeast Asia. The resolution became, in Johnson's view at least, an open-ended legal authorization for escalation of the conflict.

GULF OF TONKIN RESOLUTION

With the South Vietnamese leadership still in disarray, more and more of the burden of opposition to the Viet Cong fell on the United States. In February 1965, seven marines died when communist forces attacked an American military base at Pleiku. Johnson retaliated by ordering the first American bombings of the north since the 1964 Tonkin crisis in an attempt to destroy the depots and transportation lines responsible for the flow of North Vietnamese soldiers and supplies into South Vietnam. The bombing continued intermittently until 1972. A month later, in March 1965, two battalions of American marines landed at Da Nang in South Vietnam. There were now more than 100,000 American troops in Vietnam.

Four months later, the president finally admitted that the character of the war had changed. American soldiers would now, he announced, begin playing an active combat role in the conflict. By the end of the year, there were more than 180,000 American combat troops in Vietnam; in 1966, that number doubled; and by the end of 1967, over 500,000 American soldiers were there–along with a considerable number of civilian personnel working in various capacities. In the meantime, the air war intensified; ultimately the tonnage of bombs dropped on North Vietnam would exceed that in all theaters during World War II. And American casualties were mounting. In 1961,14 Americans had died in Vietnam. By the spring of 1966, more than 4,000 Americans had been killed.

MOUNTING CASUALTIES

The United States finally succeeded in 1965 in creating a reasonably stable government in the south under General Nguyen Van Thieu. But the new regime was hardly less corrupt or brutal than its predecessors, and no more able than they to establish its authority in its own countryside. The Viet Cong, not the Thieu regime, controlled the majority of South Vietnam's villages and hamlets.

THE QUAGMIRE

Central to the American war effort was a commitment to what the military called "attrition," a strategy premised on the belief that the United States could inflict so many casualties and so much damage on the enemy that eventually they would be unable and unwilling to continue the struggle. But the attrition strategy failed because the North Vietnamese proved willing to commit many more soldiers to the conflict than the United States had expected. The United States relied heavily on its bombing of the north to eliminate the communists' war-making capacity. By the end of 1967, most of the identifiable targets of any strategic importance in North Vietnam had been destroyed. But the bombing had produced none of the effects that the United States had expected. North Vietnam was not a modern, industrial society; it had few of the sorts of targets against which bombing is effective. The North Vietnamese responded to the air raids with ingenuity: They created a great network of underground tunnels, shops, and factories. They also secured increased aid from the Soviet Union and China. Infiltration of the south was unaffected; the North Vietnamese kept moving the Ho Chi Minh Trail, the routes by which North Vietnam soldiers infiltrated the South.

STRATEGY OF "ATTRITION"

Another crucial part of the American strategy was the "pacification" program, which was intended to push the Viet Cong from areas chosen by the United States and then "pacify" those regions by winning the "hearts and minds" of the people. But American forces were not adept at establishing the kind of rapport with provincial Vietnamese that the Viet Cong had created.

"HEARTS AND MINDS"

Gradually, the pacification program gave way to a heavy-handed relocation strategy, through which American troops uprooted villagers from their homes, sent them fleeing to refugee camps or into the cities (producing by 1967 more than

Reasoning Processes

Continuity and Change After students have read the section "From Aid to Intervention," ask them to discuss in small groups how the Gulf of Tonkin Resolution represented a continuation of or departure from the policy of containment. *(Continuity: There was still a commitment to resist spread of communism. Change: Previously, most containment had been pursued in Europe rather than Asia.)* **WOR**

Reasoning Processes

Comparing Have students read the section "Strategy of Attrition." Ask them to create a Venn diagram comparing the attrition strategy to military operations in World War II and Korea. **WOR** **WXT**

Discussion and Activities

Analyzing Points of View After students have read the section "The Quagmire," ask them to write a short letter to President Johnson advising him on Vietnam policy from the point of view of an American high school student in 1967. **WOR** **PCE** **WXT**

THE WAR IN VIETNAM AND INDOCHINA, 1964–1975 Much of the Vietnam War was fought in small engagements in widely scattered areas and did not conform to traditional notions of combat. But as this map shows, there were traditional battles and invasions and supply routes as well. The red arrows in the middle of the map show the general path of the Ho Chi Minh Trail, the main supply route by which North Vietnam supplied its troops and allies in the South. The blue arrow in southern South Vietnam indicates the point at which American troops invaded Cambodia in 1970.

What is there in the geography of Indochina, as presented on this map, that helps to explain the great difficulty the American military had in securing South Vietnam against communist attacks?

3 million refugees), and then destroyed the vacated villages and surrounding countryside. But the Viet Cong responded by moving to new sanctuaries elsewhere. The futility of the United States's effort was suggested by the statement of an American officer after flattening one such hamlet that it had been "necessary to destroy [the village] in order to save it."

As the war dragged on and victory remained elusive, some American officers and officials began to urge the president to expand the military efforts. The Johnson administration, however, resisted. Unwilling to abandon its commitment to South Vietnam for fear of destroying American "credibility" in the world, the government was also unwilling to expand the war too far, for fear of provoking direct intervention by the Chinese, the Soviets, or both. In the meantime, the president began to encounter additional obstacles and frustrations at home.

THE WAR AT HOME

As late as the end of 1965, few Americans, and even fewer influential ones, had protested the American involvement in Vietnam. But as the war dragged on, political support for it began to erode. A series of "teach-ins" on university campuses, beginning at the University of Michigan in 1965, sparked a national debate over the war. By the end of 1967, American

Answers

The War in Vietnam and Indochina: 1964–1975

South Vietnam shared long, rugged borders with noncombatant nations, which made it difficult for American and South Vietnamese forces to stop the flow of enemy soldiers and supplies.

PATTERNS OF POPULAR CULTURE

THE FOLK-MUSIC REVIVAL

Two impulses of the 1960s—the renewed interest among young people in the politics of the left, and the search for an "authentic" alternative to what many considered the artificial, consumerist culture of modern America—helped produce the revived popularity of folk music in that turbulent era. Although the harder, harsher, and more sensual music of rock 'n' roll was more visible and more popular in the 1960s, folk music more clearly expressed many of the political ideas and aspirations that were welling up in the youth culture of the time.

The folk-music tradition, like most American musical traditions, had many roots. It drew from some of the black musical traditions of the South, and from the white country music of Appalachia. And it drew most immediately from a style of music developed by musicians associated with the Communist Party's Popular Front in the 1930s. Woody Guthrie, Pete Seeger, the Weavers, and others whose music would become popular again in the 1960s began their careers singing in Popular Front and union rallies during the Great Depression. Their music, like the Popular Front itself, set out to seem entirely American, rooted in the nation's folk traditions.

Folk music remained alive in the 1940s and 1950s, but it had only a modest popular following. Pete Seeger and the Weavers continued to perform and to attract attention on college campuses. Harry Belafonte and the Kingston Trio recorded slick, pop versions of folk songs in an effort to bring them to mass audiences. In 1952, Folkway Records released the *Anthology of American Folk Music*, a collection of eighty-four performances recorded in the 1920s and 1930s that became an inspiration and an important source of material to many younger folk musicians. Folk-music festivals—at Berkeley, Newport, and Chicago—began to proliferate beginning in 1959. And an important community of folk musicians lived and performed together in the 1950s and early 1960s in New York City's Greenwich Village.

As the politics of the 1960s became more heated, and as young people in particular became politically aroused, it was folk music that most directly reflected their new values and concerns. Peter, Paul, and Mary—although only intermittently political—became icons to much of the New Left, beginning with their 1962 recording of "If I Had a Hammer," a song first performed at Communist Party rallies in the 1940s by Pete Seeger and the Weavers. Bob Dylan, whose own politics were never wholly clear to the public, had a large impact on the 1960s left, even inadvertently providing a name to the most radical offshoot of Students for a Democratic Society (SDS), the Weathermen, who named themselves after a line from one of his songs: "You don't need a weatherman to know which way the wind blows."* Joan Baez, whose politics were no secret to anyone, was actively engaged in the antiwar movement and was arrested several times for participating in militant protests.

But it was not just the overt political messages of folk musicians that made them so important to young Americans in the 1960s. In addition, folk was a kind of music that seemed to reflect the "authenticity" the youth culture was attempting to find. In truth, neither the musicians themselves nor the young Americans attracted to them had much real connection with the traditions they were trying to evoke. The audiences for folk music—a product of rural and working-class traditions—were overwhelmingly urban, middle-class people. But the message of folk music—that there is a "real" America rooted in values of sharing and community, hidden beneath the crass commercialism of modern culture—resonated with the yearnings of many people in the 1960s (and beyond) for an alternative to their own troubled world. When young audiences responded to Woody Guthrie's famous ballad "This Land Is Your Land," they were expressing a hope for a different America—more democratic, more honest, and more natural than the land they knew.

RALLYING AGAIN The music of Woody Guthrie and other musicians of the 1930s, 1940s and 1950s inspired a revival of popular music sympathetic to the protesting generation of the 1960s.

PETE SEEGER Pete Seeger was one of several folk musicians who provided a link between the Popular Front–labor movement folk music of the 1930s and the folk revival of the 1960s. He is shown here in concert in 1966.

COFFEEHOUSE MUSIC The Feejon Coffee House in Manhattan was popular among young writers, poets, and others in the late 1950s, in part because it was a gathering place for folk musicians, two of whom are shown here performing at right.

HISTORICAL THINKING SKILLS

1. **Drawing Conclusions** What did folk music, with roots in the musical traditions of blacks, rural folk, and working-class people, offer that made it so appealing to and popular with urban, middle-class audiences?
2. **Comparing** What similarities between the 1930s and the 1960s help explain the popularity of folk music during both decades?
3. **Making Connections** What musical style or form today continues the folk music tradition of expressing a political message and reflecting the search for "authenticity"?

AP Exam Tip

The Advanced Placement Exam will require students to explain the purpose, point of view, historical situation, and/or audience of a document or other primary source. One way students can describe a historical situation is to explain the historical events that led to the event being portrayed.

Historical Thinking Skills

Sourcing and Situation Have students practice the tip by examining the image "Coffeehouse Music." Ask them to discuss in small groups why young people in the 1960s may have become interested in performing folk music. *(Folk music had traditionally been used to express unrest or discontent of the lower classes. Young people harnessed this history in the 1960s to express support for Civil Rights and opposition to the war in Vietnam.)* **SOC** **PCE** **ARC**

Answers

Patterns of Popular Culture

1. Possible Answer: It resonated with people looking for an alternative to the troubled times they were living in by promoting community values.
2. Possible answer: The 1920s and the 1950s were both decades that saw the growth of a counterculture.
3. Possible answer: Many genres of music today reflect political messages and the search for "authenticity." Country music tends to align with conservative political ideologies, rap tends to align with urban concerns of the African American community, and alternative rock often speaks to elements critical of the status quo within society.

Reasoning Processes

Identifying Cause and Effect After students have read the section "The War at Home," ask them to create a T-chart listing causes and effects of the growing domestic opposition to the war in Vietnam. Have students discuss in small groups what they believe the most important cause(s) and effect(s) to be. **WOR** **PCE** **SOC**

SEARCH AND DESTROY U.S. troops in Vietnam, often unable to distinguish enemy forces from the civilian population, increasingly sought to destroy places they considered possible enemy sanctuaries. Here an American soldier watches the burning of a village, one of many that U.S. troops destroyed.

students opposed to the war had become a significant political force. Enormous peace marches in New York, Washington, D.C., and other cities drew broad public attention to the antiwar movement. Opposition to the war became a central issue in left-wing politics and in the culture of colleges and universities. It had penetrated popular cultures as well–most visibly in the rising popularity of folk musicians, many of whom used their songs to express opposition to the war. In the meantime, a growing number of journalists, particularly reporters who had spent time in Vietnam, helped sustain the antiwar movement with their frank revelations about the brutality and apparent futility of the war. The growing chorus of popular protest soon began to stimulate opposition to the war from within the government.

GROWING OPPOSITION TO THE WAR

Senator J. William Fulbright of Arkansas, chairman of the powerful Senate Foreign Relations Committee, turned against the war and in January 1966 began to stage highly publicized congressional hearings to air criticisms of it. Distinguished figures such as George F. Kennan and retired general James Gavin testified against the conflict, giving opposition to the war greater respectability. Other members of Congress joined Fulbright in opposing Johnson's policies–including, in 1967, Robert F. Kennedy, brother of the slain president and now a senator from New York. Even within the administration, the consensus seemed to be crumbling. Robert McNamara, who had done much to help extend the American involvement in Vietnam, quietly left the government, disillusioned, in 1968. His successor as secretary of defense, Clark Clifford, became a quiet but powerful voice within the administration on behalf of a cautious scaling down of the commitment in troops and funding.

In the meantime, the American economy was beginning to suffer. Johnson's commitment to fighting the war while continuing his Great Society reforms–his promise of "guns and butter"–proved impossible to maintain. The inflation rate, which had remained at 2 percent through most of the early 1960s, rose to 3 percent in 1967, 4 percent in 1968, and 6 percent in 1969. In August 1967, Johnson asked Congress for a tax increase–a 10 percent surcharge that was widely labeled a "war tax"–which he knew was necessary if the nation was to avoid even more ruinous inflation. In return, congressional conservatives demanded and received a $6 billion reduction in the funding for Great Society programs.

WAR-INDUCED INFLATION

Discussion and Activities

Evaluating Evidence Have students examine the image "Search and Destroy." Ask them to think about and share with a partner how details in the photo illustrate the new strategy of "attrition." *(A soldier has burned a structure in a village, denying its use to the enemy.)* **WOR**

THE TRAUMAS OF 1968

By the end of 1967, the twin crises of the war in Vietnam and the deteriorating racial situation at home–crises that fed upon and inflamed each other–had produced profound social and political tensions. In the course of 1968, those tensions seemed suddenly to burst to the surface and to threaten the nation with genuine chaos.

THE TET OFFENSIVE

On January 31, 1968, the first day of the Vietnamese New Year (Tet), communist forces launched an enormous, concerted attack on American strongholds throughout South Vietnam. A few cities fell to the communists. During their occupation of the provincial capital, Hue, the communist forces rounded up supporters of the Saigon regime and massacred them. Other cities suffered major disruptions.

Americans saw vivid reports on television of communist forces in the heart of Saigon, setting off bombs, shooting South Vietnamese officials and troops, and holding down fortified areas (including, briefly, the grounds of the American embassy). Such images shocked many Americans and proved devastating to popular support for the war. The Tet offensive also suggested to the American public something of the brutality of the struggle in Vietnam. In the midst of the fighting, television cameras recorded the sight of a captured Viet Cong soldier being led up to a South Vietnamese officer in the streets of Saigon. Without a word, the officer pulled out his pistol and shot the young man in the head, leaving him lying dead in the street. Few single events did more to galvanize support for the war in the United States.

American forces soon dislodged the Viet Cong from most of the positions they had seized, and the Tet offensive in the end cost the communists such appalling casualties that they were significantly weakened for months to come. The Tet defeats permanently depleted the ranks of the NLF and forced North Vietnamese troops to take on a much larger share of the subsequent fighting. Tet may have been a military victory for the United States, but it was a political defeat for the administration.

POLITICAL AND PSYCHOLOGICAL DEFEAT

MY LAI MASSACRE On March 16, 1968 U.S. Army soldiers killed between 347 and 504 unarmed men, women, and children in South Vietnam. Twenty-six soldiers were charged with criminal offenses. Only Lieutenant William Calley, Jr., a platoon leader, was convicted. The incident increased domestic opposition to the war when its horrific scope and the initial attempt by the army to cover it up were exposed.

Reasoning Processes

Causation Have students read the section "The Tet Offensive." Ask them to discuss as a class why the Tet Offensive had such a galvanizing effect on the American anti-war movement. *(Many Americans had believed assurances that the war was going well, but the brutality of the Tet Offensive turned public opinion about the war.)* **WOR** **PCE** **SOC**

Discussion and Activities

Analyzing Points of View Have students examine the image "My Lai Massacre." Ask them to write a journal entry from the point of view of an American seeing the evidence of the massacre for the first time. **WOR** **PCE** **SOC**

Historical Thinking Skills

Sourcing and Situation Have students examine the image "Prague Spring." Ask them to discuss in small groups the possible purpose and point of view of the photograph. *(Purpose: to publicize the uprising; to encourage support for the protesters. Point of view: possibly sympathetic to the demonstrators' cause.)*

AMERICA IN THE WORLD

1968

The year 1968 was one of the most turbulent in the postwar history of the United States. Much of what caused these upheavals was specifically American events—the growing controversy over the war in Vietnam, the assassinations of Martin Luther King Jr. and Robert Kennedy, racial unrest in the nation's cities, and student protests on campuses throughout America. But the turmoil of 1968 was not confined to the United States. There were tremendous upheavals in many parts of the world that year.

The most common form of turbulence around the world in 1968 was student unrest. A student uprising in France in May 1968 far exceeded in size and ferocity anything that occurred in the United States. It attracted the support of French workers, briefly paralyzed Paris and other cities, and contributed to the downfall of the government of Charles de Gaulle a year later. In England, Ireland, Germany, Italy, the Netherlands, Mexico, Canada, Japan, and South Korea, students and other young people also demonstrated in great numbers, sometimes violently, against governments and universities and other structures of authority. In Czechoslovakia, hundreds of thousands of citizens took to the streets in support of what became known as "Prague Spring"—a demand for greater democracy and a repudiation of many of the oppressive rules and structures imposed on the nation by its Soviet-dominated communist regimes—until Russian tanks rolled into the city to crush the uprising.

One factor that contributed to the worldwide turbulence of 1968 was simple numbers. The postwar baby boom, which occurred in many nations, had created a very large age cohort that by the late 1960s was reaching adulthood. The sheer size of the new generation produced a tripling of the number of people attending colleges and universities, and a heightened sense of the power of youth. The long period of postwar prosperity and relative peace in which this generation had grown up contributed to heightened expectations of what the world should offer them—and a greater level of impatience than previous generations had demonstrated with the obstacles that stood in the way of their hopes. A new global youth culture emerged that was in many ways at odds with the dominant culture of older generations. It valued nonconformity, personal freedom, and even rebellion.

A second force contributing to the widespread turbulence of 1968 was the power of global media. Satellite technology introduced in the early 1960s made it possible to transmit live news instantly across the world. Videotape technology and the creation of lightweight portable television cameras enabled media organizations to respond to events much more quickly and flexibly than in the past. And the audience for these televised images was by now global and enormous, particularly in industrial nations but even in the poorest areas of the world. Protests in one country were suddenly capable of inspiring protests in others. Demonstrators in Paris, for example, spoke openly of how campus protests in the United States in 1968—for example, the student uprising at Columbia University in New York City—had helped motivate French students to rise up as well. Just as American students were protesting against what they considered the antiquated paternalistic features of their universities, French students demanded an end to the rigid, autocratic character of their own academic world.

In most parts of the world, the 1968 uprisings came and went without fundamentally altering the institutions and systems they were attacking. But many changes came in the wake of these protests. Universities around the globe undertook significant reforms. Religious observance in mainstream churches and synagogues in the West declined dramatically after 1968. New concepts of personal freedom gained legitimacy, helping to inspire new social movements in the years that followed—among them the dramatic growth of feminism in many parts of the world. The events of 1968 did not produce a revolution, in the United States or in most of the rest of the world, but they did help launch a period of dramatic social, cultural, and political change that affected the peoples of many nations.

PRAGUE SPRING Czech demonstrators march through Wenceslas Square in Prague following a radio address by their reform president, Alexander Dubcek, in August 1968. By this time, the great hopes awakened by Dubcek's reforms during the "Prague Spring" of several months ago had been crushed by Soviet pressure, including the arrival of Soviet tanks in the streets of Prague. These demonstrators are demanding the "brutal truth" from their leaders about the price Czechoslovakia paid to keep Dubcek in power.

HISTORICAL THINKING SKILLS

1. **Explaining Historical Developments** What factors combined to produce the turbulence that resulted in the uprisings of 1968?
2. **Evaluating Evidence** Did the demonstrators of 1968 succeed or fail to achieve their objectives? What were the long-term effects of the 1968 uprisings?
3. **Making Connections** Has there been a year or period since 1968 in which similar worldwide protests and uprisings have occurred? If so, what events triggered these later demonstrations?

Answers

America in the World

1. Possible answer: The global baby boom helped lead to the turbulence during the global uprisings of 1968. The increasing number of youth, along with a relatively positive post-war economy, led to increased demands on what they thought society should offer them. Technology also contributed to the turbulence of 1968, as it allowed faster and more accessible media coverage.
2. Possible answer: The demonstrations of 1968 achieved a certain level of success. After them, a great deal of societal change occurred across the nation.
3. Possible answer: The Trump presidency caused a tremendous amount of societal polarization within the United States and around the world. A number of events: the Black Lives Matter movement, the #MeToo movement, and the COVID-19 pandemic were factors in the polarization of American society during this time.

In the following weeks, opposition to the war grew substantially. Leading newspapers and magazines, television commentators, and mainstream politicians began taking public stands in favor of de-escalation of the conflict. Within weeks of the Tet offensive, public opposition to the war had almost doubled. And Johnson's personal popularity rating had slid to 35 percent, the lowest of any president since Harry Truman.

THE POLITICAL CHALLENGE

Beginning in the summer of 1967, dissident Democrats (led by the activist Allard Lowenstein) tried to mobilize support behind an antiwar candidate who would challenge Lyndon Johnson in the 1968 primaries. When Robert Kennedy declined their invitation, they turned to Senator Eugene McCarthy of Minnesota. A brilliantly orchestrated campaign by Lowenstein and thousands of young volunteers in the New Hampshire primary produced a startling showing by McCarthy in March; he nearly defeated the president.

A few days later, Robert Kennedy entered the campaign, embittering many McCarthy supporters, but bringing his own substantial strength among African Americans, the poor, and workers to the antiwar cause. Polls showed the president trailing badly in the next scheduled primary, in Wisconsin. Indeed, public animosity toward the president was now so intense that Johnson did not even dare leave the White House to campaign. On March 31, Johnson went on television to announce a limited halt in the bombing of North Vietnam—his first major concession to the antiwar forces—and, more surprising, his withdrawal from the presidential contest.

ROBERT KENNEDY

Robert Kennedy quickly established himself as the champion of the Democratic primaries. In the meantime, however, Vice President Hubert Humphrey, with the support of President Johnson, entered the contest and began to attract the support of party leaders and of the many delegations that were selected not by popular primaries but by state party organizations. He soon appeared to be the front-runner in the race.

THE KING AND KENNEDY ASSASSINATIONS

In the midst of this bitter political battle, in which the war had been the dominant issue, attention suddenly turned back to the nation's bitter racial conflicts. On April 4, Martin Luther King Jr., who had traveled to Memphis, Tennessee, to lend his support to striking black sanitation workers in the city, was shot and killed while standing on the balcony of his motel. The presumed assassin, James Earl Ray, who was captured days later in London and eventually convicted, had no apparent motive. Later evidence suggested that he had been hired by others to do the killing, but he never revealed the identity of his employers.

King's tragic death produced an outpouring of grief matched in recent memory only by the reaction to the death of John Kennedy. Among African Americans, it also produced anger. In the days after the assassination, major riots broke out in more than sixty American cities. Forty-three people died; more than 3,000 suffered injuries; as many as 27,000 people were arrested.

RIOTS

For two months following the death of King, Robert Kennedy continued his campaign for the presidential nomination. Late on the night of June 6, he appeared in the ballroom of a Los Angeles hotel to acknowledge his victory in that day's California primary. As he left the ballroom after his victory statement, Sirhan Sirhan, a young Palestinian apparently enraged by pro-Israeli remarks Kennedy had recently made, emerged from a crowd and shot him in the head. Early the next morning, Kennedy died.

By the time of his death, Robert Kennedy—who earlier in his career had been widely considered a cold, ruthless agent of his more appealing brother—had emerged as a figure of enormous popular appeal. More than John Kennedy, Robert identified his hopes with the American "underclass"—with blacks, Hispanics, Native Americans, the poor. Indeed, Robert Kennedy, much more than John, shaped what some would later call the "Kennedy legacy," a set of ideas that would for a time become central to American liberalism: the fervent commitment to using government to help the powerless. The passions Kennedy aroused made his violent death a particularly shattering experience for many Americans.

THE "KENNEDY LEGACY"

The presidential campaign continued gloomily during the last weeks before the convention. Hubert Humphrey, who had seemed likely to win the nomination even before Robert Kennedy's death, now faced only minor opposition. The approaching Democratic National Convention, therefore, began to take on the appearance of an exercise in futility; and antiwar activists, despairing of winning any victories within the convention, began to plan major demonstrations outside it.

When the Democrats finally gathered in Chicago in August, even the most optimistic observers were predicting a turbulent convention. Inside the hall, delegates bitterly debated an antiwar plank in the party platform that both Kennedy and McCarthy supporters favored. Miles away, in a downtown park, thousands of antiwar protesters were staging demonstrations. On the third night of the convention, as the delegates were beginning their balloting on the now inevitable nomination of Hubert Humphrey, demonstrators and police clashed in a bloody riot in the streets of Chicago. Hundreds of protesters were injured as police attempted to disperse them with tear gas and billy clubs. Aware that the violence was being televised, the demonstrators taunted the authorities with the chant, "The whole world is watching!" And Hubert Humphrey, who had spent years dreaming of becoming his party's candidate for president, received a nomination that appeared at the time to be almost worthless.

DEMOCRATIC NATIONAL CONVENTION

THE CONSERVATIVE RESPONSE

The turbulent events of 1968 persuaded many observers that American society was in the throes of revolutionary change. In

Historical Thinking Skills

Argumentation Have students read the section "The Political Challenge." Ask them to create a campaign poster supporting McCarthy, Kennedy, or Humphrey for the Democratic presidential nomination in 1968. **PCE**

Discussion and Activities

Speculating Have students read the section "The King and Kennedy Assassinations." Discuss as a class the effects of the assassinations. Ask students to consider how things might have been different in the nation if both men had lived.
WOR **PCE** **SOC** **ARC**

Reasoning Processes

Causation Have students read the section "George Wallace." Ask them to create a T-chart listing the causes and effects of Wallace's third-party campaign. **PCE** **SOC**

CHICAGO, 1968 Demonstrators climb on a statue in a Chicago park during the 1968 Democratic National Convention, protesting both the Vietnam War and the harsh treatment they had received from Mayor Richard Daley's Chicago police.

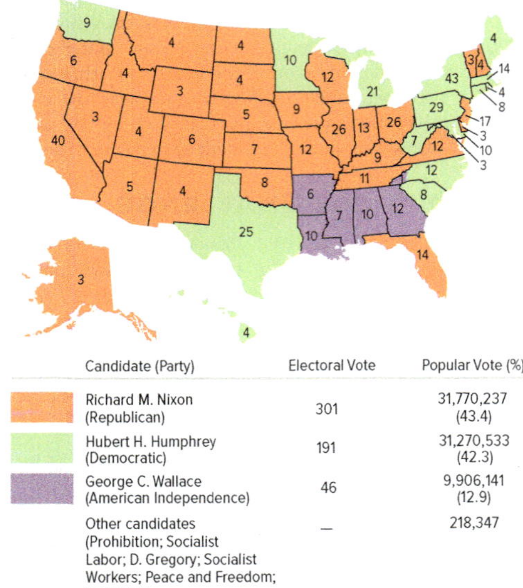

	Candidate (Party)	Electoral Vote	Popular Vote (%)
Orange	Richard M. Nixon (Republican)	301	31,770,237 (43.4)
Green	Hubert H. Humphrey (Democratic)	191	31,270,533 (42.3)
Purple	George C. Wallace (American Independence)	46	9,906,141 (12.9)
	Other candidates (Prohibition; Socialist Labor; D. Gregory; Socialist Workers; Peace and Freedom; McCarthy)	—	218,347

60.6% of electorate voting

THE ELECTION OF 1968 The 1968 presidential election, which Richard Nixon won, was almost as close as the election of 1960, which he had lost. Nixon might have won a more substantial victory had it not been for the independent candidacy of Governor George C. Wallace, who attracted many of the same conservative voters to whom Nixon appealed.

How does the distribution of Democratic and Republican strength in this election compare to that in 1960?

fact, however, the response of most Americans to the turmoil was a conservative one.

The most visible sign of the conservative backlash was the surprising success of the campaign of the segregationist Alabama governor George Wallace for the presidency. In 1964, he had run in a few Democratic presidential primaries and had done surprisingly well, even in several states outside the South. In 1968, he became a third-party candidate for president, basing his campaign on a host of conservative grievances, not all of them connected to race. He denounced the forced busing of students, the proliferation of government regulations and social programs, and the permissiveness of authorities toward race riots and antiwar demonstrations. There was never any serious chance that Wallace would win the election; but his standing in the polls at times rose to over 20 percent.

GEORGE WALLACE

A more effective effort to mobilize the "silent majority" in favor of order and stability was under way within the Republican Party. Richard Nixon, whose political career had seemed at an end after his losses in the presidential race of 1960 and a California gubernatorial campaign two years later, reemerged as the preeminent spokesman for what he called "Middle America." Nixon recognized that many Americans were tired of hearing about their obligations to the poor, tired of hearing about the sacrifices necessary to achieve racial justice, tired of judicial reforms that seemed designed to help criminals. By offering a vision of stability, law and order, government retrenchment, and "peace with honor" in Vietnam, he easily captured the Republican presidential nomination. And after the spectacle of the Democratic National Convention, he enjoyed a commanding lead in the polls as the November election approached.

That lead diminished greatly in the last weeks before the voting. Old doubts about Nixon's character continued to haunt the Republican candidate. A skillful last-minute surge by Hubert Humphrey, who managed to restore a tenuous unity to the Democratic Party, narrowed the gap further. And the Wallace campaign appeared to be hurting the Republicans more than the Democrats. In the end, however, Nixon eked out a victory almost as narrow as his defeat in 1960. He received 43.4 percent of the popular vote to Humphrey's 42.3 percent (a margin of only about 800,000 votes), and 301 electoral votes to Humphrey's 191. George Wallace, who like most third-party

Answers

The Election of 1968

Compared to 1960 Republicans made significant gains in the West and Midwest in 1968, while Democrats lost strength in these areas.

candidates faded in the last weeks of the campaign, still managed to poll 12.9 percent of the popular vote and to carry five southern states with a total of 46 electoral ballots—the best showing by a third-party candidate since the 1920s. Nixon had not won a decisive personal mandate. But the election made clear that a majority of the American electorate was more interested in restoring stability than in promoting social change.

NIXON VICTORIOUS

NIXON, KISSINGER, AND THE WAR

Richard Nixon assumed office in 1969 committed not only to restoring stability at home but also to creating a new and more stable order in the world. Central to his hopes was a resolution of the stalemate in Vietnam. Yet the new president felt no freer than his predecessor to abandon the American commitment there. He realized that the war was threatening both the nation's domestic stability and its position in the world. But he feared that a precipitous retreat would destroy American honor and "credibility." American involvement in Indochina continued for four more years, during which the war expanded in its geographic scope and its bloodiness.

VIETNAMIZATION

Despite Nixon's own passionate interest in international affairs, he brought with him into government a man who ultimately seemed to overshadow him in the conduct of diplomacy: Henry Kissinger, a Harvard professor whom the president appointed as his national security adviser. Kissinger quickly established dominance over the secretary of state, William Rogers, and the secretary of defense, Melvin Laird, who were both more experienced in public life than Kissinger was. That was in part a result of Nixon's passion for concentrating decision making in the White House. But Kissinger's keen intelligence, bureaucratic skills, and success in handling the press were at least equally important. Together, Nixon and Kissinger set out to find an acceptable solution to the stalemate in Vietnam.

HENRY KISSINGER

The new Vietnam policy moved along several fronts. One was an effort to limit domestic opposition to the war. Aware that the military draft was one of the most visible targets of dissent, the administration devised a new "lottery" system, through which only a limited group—those nineteen-year-olds with low lottery numbers—would be subject to conscription. Later, the president urged the creation of an all-volunteer army. By 1973, the Selective Service System was on its way to at least temporary extinction.

More important in stifling dissent, however, was the new policy of "Vietnamization" of the war—the training and equipping of the South Vietnamese military to take over the burden of combat from American forces. In the fall of 1969, Nixon announced reduction of American ground troops from Vietnam by 60,000, the first reduction in U.S. troop strength since the beginning of the war. The reductions continued steadily for more than three years. From a peak of more than 540,000 American troops in 1969, the number had dwindled to about 60,000 by 1972.

CONSEQUENCES OF "VIETNAMIZATION"

Vietnamization helped quiet domestic opposition to the war. But it did nothing to break the stalemate in the negotiations with the North Vietnamese in Paris. The new administration quickly decided that new military pressures would be necessary to do that.

ESCALATION

By the end of their first year in office, Nixon and Kissinger had concluded that the most effective way to tip the military balance in America's favor was to destroy the bases in Cambodia from which, the American military believed, the North Vietnamese were launching many of their attacks. Very early in his presidency, Nixon ordered the air force to begin bombing Cambodian territory to destroy the enemy sanctuaries. He kept the raids secret from Congress and the public. In the spring of 1970, possibly with U.S. encouragement and support, conservative military leaders overthrew the neutral government of Cambodia and established a new, pro-American regime under General Lon Nol. Lon Nol quickly gave his approval to American incursions into his territory; and on April 30, Nixon went on television to announce that he was ordering American troops across the border into Cambodia to "clean out" the bases that the enemy had been using for its "increased military aggression."

Almost overnight, the Cambodian invasion restored the dwindling antiwar movement to vigorous life. The first days of May saw the most widespread and vocal antiwar demonstrations since the beginning of the war. Hundreds of thousands of protesters gathered in Washington, D.C., to denounce the president's policies. Millions, perhaps, participated in other demonstrations on campuses nationwide. The mood of crisis intensified greatly on May 4, when four college students were killed and nine others injured when members of the National Guard opened fire on antiwar demonstrators at Kent State University in Ohio. Ten days later, police killed two black students at Jackson State University in Mississippi during a demonstration there.

KENT STATE

The clamor against the war quickly spread into the government and the press. Congress angrily repealed the Gulf of Tonkin Resolution in December, stripping the president of what had long served as the legal basis for the war. Nixon ignored the action. Then, in June 1971, first the *New York Times* and later other newspapers began publishing excerpts from a secret study of the war prepared by the Defense Department during the Johnson administration. What came to be known as the Pentagon Papers, leaked to the press by former Defense Department official Daniel Ellsberg, provided evidence of what many critics of the war had long believed: that the government had been dishonest, both in reporting the military progress of the war and in explaining its own motives for American involvement. The administration went to court

Discussion and Activities

Analyzing Cause and Effect
Have students read the section "Vietnamization." Organize students into small groups to discuss the reasons for and the effects of the Vietnamization policy. Have groups consider what other actions the Nixon administration could have taken, and if any of those actions would have been more effective in easing the combat burden on the United States.
WOR **PCE**

Discussion and Activities

Analyzing Points of View Have students read the section "Kent State." Ask them to write a journal entry from the point of view of a student demonstrator, a member of the Ohio National Guard, or a bystander describing the events and emotions of the encounter. **PCE** **SOC**

Discussion and Activities

Speculating After students have read the section "Escalation," ask them to discuss as a class the reasons why the military was having problems with desertion, drug use, racial violence, and violence against officers. *(The military was still mostly made up of draftees. The middle and upper classes had many means of avoiding the draft, so the army was predominantly made up of lower-income people. There was resentment about fighting a war the soldiers didn't understand, uncertainty over who the enemy was, and a cheap and abundant supply of drugs.)* **SOC** **WXT**

to suppress the documents, but the Supreme Court finally ruled that the press had the right to publish them.

Morale and discipline were rapidly deteriorating among U.S. troops in Vietnam, who had been fighting a savage and inconclusive war for more than five years. The trial and conviction in 1971 of Lieutenant William Calley, who was charged with overseeing a massacre of more than 300 unarmed South Vietnamese civilians, attracted wide public attention. Many Americans believed that the My Lai tragedy was not an isolated incident. Less publicized were other, more widespread problems among American troops in Vietnam: desertion, drug addiction, racial hostilities, refusal to obey orders, even the occasional killing of unpopular officers by enlisted men.

MY LAI MASSACRE

By 1971, nearly two-thirds of those interviewed in public opinion polls were urging American withdrawal from Vietnam, including many conservatives, who considered Nixon's policies as too timid. If the war was not designed for victory, they believed, it should not be fought.

In March 1972, the North Vietnamese mounted the biggest offensive since 1968 (the so-called Easter offensive). American and South Vietnamese forces managed to halt the North Vietnam advance, but it was clear that without American support the offensive would have succeeded. At the same time, Nixon ordered American planes to bomb targets near Hanoi, the capital of North Vietnam, and Haiphong, its principal port, and called for the mining of seven North Vietnamese harbors to stop the flow of supplies from China and the Soviet Union.

EASTER OFFENSIVE

"PEACE WITH HONOR"

As the 1972 presidential election approached, the administration stepped up its efforts to produce a breakthrough in negotiations with the North Vietnamese. In April 1972, the president dropped his longtime insistence on a removal of North Vietnamese troops from the south before any American withdrawal. Meanwhile, Henry Kissinger was meeting privately in Paris with the North Vietnamese foreign secretary, Le Duc Tho, to work out terms for a cease-fire. On October 26, only days before the presidential election, Kissinger announced that "peace is at hand." But several weeks later (after the election), negotiations broke down once again. The American and the North Vietnamese governments appeared ready to accept the Kissinger-Tho plan for a cease-fire, but the regime of General Nguyen Van Thieu balked, still insisting on a full withdrawal of North Vietnamese forces from the south. Kissinger tried to win additional concessions from the communists to meet Thieu's objections, but on December 16 talks broke off.

The next day, December 17, American B-52s began the heaviest and most destructive air raids of the entire war on Hanoi, Haiphong, and other North Vietnamese targets. Civilian casualties were high, and fifteen American B-52s were shot down by the North Vietnamese; in the entire war to that point, the United States had lost only one of the giant bombers. On December 30, Nixon terminated the "Christmas bombing." The United States and the North Vietnamese soon returned to the conference table. And on January 27, 1973, they signed an "agreement on ending the war and restoring peace in Vietnam." Nixon claimed that the Christmas bombing had forced the North Vietnamese to relent. At least equally important, however, was the enormous American pressure on Thieu to accept the cease-fire.

"CHRISTMAS BOMBING"

The terms of the Paris accords were little different from those Kissinger and Tho had accepted in principle a few months before. There would be an immediate cease-fire. The North Vietnamese would release several hundred American prisoners of war. The Thieu regime would survive for the moment—the principal North Vietnamese concession to the United States—but North Vietnamese forces already in the south would remain there. An undefined committee would work out a permanent settlement.

DEFEAT IN INDOCHINA

American forces were hardly out of Indochina before the Paris accords collapsed. During the first year after the cease-fire, the contending Vietnamese armies suffered greater battle losses than the Americans had absorbed during ten years of fighting. Finally, in March 1975, the North Vietnamese launched a full-scale offensive against the now greatly weakened forces of the south. Thieu appealed to Washington for assistance; the president (now Gerald Ford; Nixon had resigned in 1974) appealed to Congress for additional funding; Congress refused. Late in April 1975, communist forces marched into Saigon, shortly after officials of the Thieu regime and the staff of the American embassy had fled the country in humiliating disarray. Communist forces quickly occupied the capital, renamed it Ho Chi Minh City, and began the process of reuniting Vietnam under the Hanoi government. At about the same time, the Lon Nol regime in Cambodia fell to the murderous communists of Pol Pot and the Khmer Rouge—whose genocidal policies led to the deaths of more than a third of the country's people over the next several years. That was the grim end of over a decade of direct American military involvement in Vietnam. More than 1.2 million Vietnamese soldiers had died in combat, along with countless civilians throughout the region. The United States paid a heavy price as well. The war had cost the nation almost $150 billion in direct costs and much more indirectly. It had resulted in the deaths of over 55,000 young Americans and the injury of 300,000 more. And the nation had suffered a heavy blow to its confidence and self-esteem.

FALL OF SAIGON

NIXON, KISSINGER, AND THE WORLD

The continuing war in Vietnam provided a dismal backdrop to what Nixon considered his larger mission in world affairs: the construction of a new international order. The president had

Discussion and Activities

Analyzing Issues Have students read the section "Peace with Honor." Ask them to list the terms of the Paris Peace Accord. Have students analyze which of these terms favored the United States and South Vietnam and which favored North Vietnam and the Viet Cong. **WOR**

AMERICA IN THE WORLD

The End of Colonialism

On July 4, 1946, less than a year after the close of World War II, the United States voluntarily ended its five-decade-old colonial control of the Philippines, which it had acquired as part of the spoils from the 1898 Spanish-American War. Philippine independence was only a small part of a dramatic change in the political structure of the world. The close of World War II marked not only the defeat of fascism in Germany, Italy, and Japan, but also the beginning of the end of the formal system of imperialism that European powers had maintained for centuries. Like most fundamental geopolitical changes, the drive for colonial independence was turbulent and often violent.

Although its divestiture of the Philippines was relatively peaceful, the United States was not quite as ready to cede its military and economic presence in the region as it was to give up political responsibility over the islands. Philippine independence came with important caveats: the United States maintained control of its military bases there, forbade the Philippines to engage in any direct economic competition with the United States, and required the new Philippine government to revise its constitution to allow American interests free access to the nation's natural resources. In fact, many Filipinos argue that their nation only achieved full independence in 1991, after the Philippine Senate refused to ratify a treaty that would have extended the American lease on the Subic Bay Naval Base. A year later, the United States closed the base and left, marking the first time in 400 years that the Philippines (once a Spanish possession) were not home to a foreign military power.

Britain, whose imperial holdings were the vastest in the world, withdrew from most of its colonies after World War II—beginning in 1947 with India, its largest and most important colony. As often happened when colonial rule ended, suppressed conflicts in the native population quickly emerged—in the case of India, between Hindus and Muslims. The price of Indian independence was the partition of the country into India and Pakistan (and, several decades later, Bangladesh). A year later, Britain gave up its World War I mandate of Palestine, ceding the territory to the United Nations (and allowing for the creation of Israel), as well as many of its holdings in Southeast Asia. In 1982, Britain passed the Canada Act, effectively severing Canada from the United Kingdom and culminating a move toward full Canadian self-government. Finally, in 1997, Britain returned Hong Kong to the control of China, effectively bringing an end to the era of the British Empire.

The dissolution of the British Empire did not always proceed smoothly. The Suez Crisis of 1956 dealt a decisive blow to Britain's status as a major power in the Middle East. The efforts of Britain, France, and Israel to prevent Egypt from seizing the British-controlled Suez Canal, which ran through Egyptian territory, ended in a humiliating defeat. In 1982, a dispute over the tiny Falkland Islands (just off the coast of Argentina) soon erupted into war between Britain and Argentina, which claimed the islands as its own. After the deaths of 258 British and 649 Argentine soldiers, Britain maintained its control of the Falklands, although Argentina continues to assert its right to the islands.

Despite these controversies, the dissolution of the British Empire proceeded relatively smoothly compared to the experience of the French. In late 1946, Vietnamese nationalists rose up against the French colonial government that controlled the region. The French effort to return to Vietnam culminated ultimately in the French defeat at Dien Bien Phu in 1954 and their subsequent withdrawal from Indochina. France also became embroiled in—and tried to suppress by force—other violent colonial uprisings, in Madagascar, Cameroon, and most notably Algeria. The Algerian War (1954–1962) was a particularly bloody and costly conflict, involving guerrilla warfare, torture, acts of terrorism, and, eventually, the collapse of the French Fourth Republic in 1958. Algeria ultimately won its independence, but the scars created by the long and ugly war were slow to heal.

The end of the colonial system had its greatest impact on Africa. European powers had carved up almost all of sub-Saharan Africa in the nineteenth century. But in the decades after World War II, almost all the African colonies won their independence even if not always easily. African nationalism, however, was troubled for decades by political instability and, in some countries, extreme poverty. Africa is currently home to 34 of the 48 poorest and 24 of the 32 least developed countries in the world, in no small part a result of the lingering shadow cast by centuries of colonial exploitation of the continent.

The most recent epicenter of independence movements has been in the lands that used to comprise the former Soviet Union. A long and costly war in Afghanistan began in the 1970s as the Soviet Union struggled to retain control of the nation in the face of powerful local insurgencies. The war was one of the principal factors in the unraveling of the Soviet Empire that began in 1991. Many of the former Soviet republics—which considered themselves colonies of Russia—soon separated from Russia and became independent nations in their own right. Even after the dissolution of the Soviet Union, Russia continues to deal with the problems of empire. A vicious conflict with Chechnya, an Islamic area of Russia insisting on independence, has created terror and instability for years. In 2014, Russia reclaimed Crimea, which since the collapse of the Soviet Union had been a part of Ukraine. This action threatened to heighten tensions between Russia and the West to levels not seen since the Cold War.

The end of colonialism marked the end to an imperial system that was based on the assumption of European (and American) superiority over non-Western peoples. But if formal colonialism came to an end in the post–World War II era, other aspects of imperialism did not. Many former colonies still struggle with the indirect exercise of power, especially economic power, that wealthy Western nations continue to exert over much of the nonindustrialized world.

HISTORICAL THINKING SKILLS

1. **Drawing Conclusions** How did the experience of World War II contribute to the end of colonialism?
2. **Explaining Historical Developments** Why was the end of colonialism so often accompanied by violence?
3. **Making Connections** What have been the effects of colonialism—and the end of colonialism—on Africa? Why have the effects been so pronounced on that continent, more so than in other areas of the world?

Discussion and Activities

Analyzing Points of View After students have read the feature, ask them to write a journal entry from the point of view of a resident of one of the newly independent former colonies describing their hopes and fears for the future.

Answers

America in the World

1. Possible answer: Many countries began to move into a different phase as they began giving up their territorial control of areas long held as colonies.
2. Possible answer: When countries leave a territory, it often results in a power vacuum that gives way to the rise of smaller groups within the territory to vie for political and economic power.
3. Possible answer: The effects have often been costly and deadly. Western powers have stripped Africa of much of its resources, which has had a devastating effect on the continent economically and environmentally.

Reasoning Processes

Comparing Have students read the section "China and the Soviet Union." Ask them to create a Venn diagram comparing American foreign policy with that of China and the Soviet Union at this time. **WOR**

become convinced that old assumptions of a "bipolar" world—in which the United States and the Soviet Union were the only truly great powers—were now obsolete. Instead, America must adapt to the new "multipolar" international structure, in which China, Japan, and Western Europe would become major, independent forces. "It will be a safer world and a better world," he said in 1971, "if we have a strong, healthy United States, Europe, Soviet Union, China, Japan—each balancing the other, not playing one against the other, an even balance."

TOWARD A "MULTIPOLAR" WORLD

CHINA AND THE SOVIET UNION

For more than twenty years, ever since the fall of Chiang Kai-shek in 1949, the United States had treated China, the second-largest nation on earth, as if it did not exist. Instead, America recognized the regime-in-exile on the island of Taiwan as the legitimate government of mainland China. Nixon and Kissinger wanted to forge a new relationship with the Chinese communists—in part to strengthen them as a counterbalance to the Soviet Union. The Chinese communists, for their part, were eager to forestall what they feared was the possibility of a Soviet-American alliance against China and to end China's own isolation from the international arena.

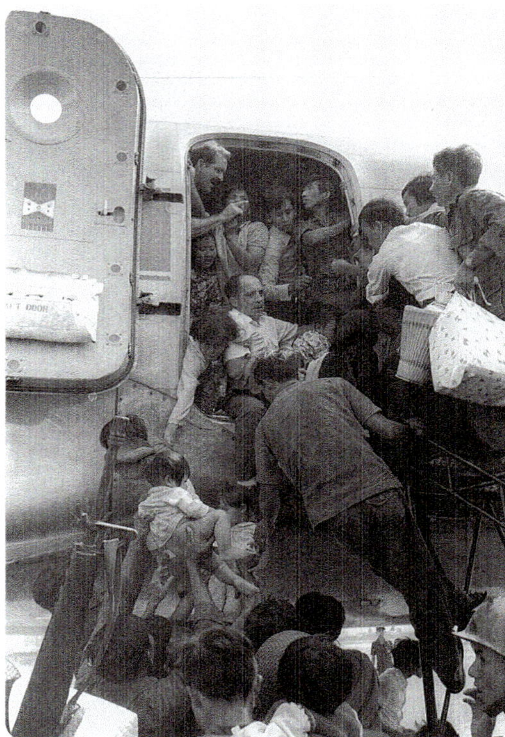

THE EVACUATION OF SAIGON A harried U.S. official struggles to keep panicking Vietnamese from boarding an already-overburdened helicopter on the roof of the American embassy in Saigon. The hurried evacuation of Americans took place only hours before the arrival of North Vietnamese troops, signaling the final defeat of South Vietnam.

© AP Images

In July 1971, Nixon sent Henry Kissinger on a secret mission to Beijing. When Kissinger returned, the president made the startling announcement that he would visit China within the next few months. That fall, with American approval, the United Nations admitted the communist government of China and expelled the representatives of the Taiwan regime. Finally, in February 1972, Nixon paid a formal visit to China, which erased much of the deep American animosity toward the Chinese communists.

NIXON'S CHINA VISIT

The initiatives in China coincided with (and probably assisted) an effort by the Nixon administration to improve relations with the Soviet Union. In 1969, American and Soviet diplomats met in Helsinki, Finland, to begin talks on limiting nuclear weapons. In 1972, they produced the first Strategic Arms Limitation Treaty (SALT I), which froze the nuclear missiles (ICBMs) of both sides at present levels.

SALT I

THE PROBLEMS OF MULTIPOLARITY

Nixon and Kissinger believed that great-power relationships could not alone ensure international stability, for the "Third World" remained the most volatile and dangerous source of international tension.

Central to the Nixon-Kissinger policy toward the Third World was the effort to maintain a stable status quo without involving the United States too deeply in local disputes. In 1969 and 1970, the president described what became known as the Nixon Doctrine, by which the United States would "participate in the defense and development of allies and friends" but would leave the "basic responsibility" for the future of those "friends" to the nations themselves.

NIXON DOCTRINE

In the Middle East, conditions grew more volatile in the aftermath of the 1967 "Six-Day War," in which Israel routed Egyptian, Syrian, and Jordanian forces, gained control of the whole of the long-divided city of Jerusalem, and occupied substantial new territories: on the west bank of the Jordan River, the Gaza Strip, the Golan Heights, and elsewhere. The war also increased the number of refugee Palestinians—Arabs who claimed the lands now controlled by Israel and who, dislodged from their homes, became a source of considerable instability in Jordan, Lebanon, and the other surrounding countries into which they now moved.

"SIX-DAY WAR"

In October 1973, on the Jewish High Holy Day of Yom Kippur, Egyptian and Syrian forces again attacked Israel. For ten days, the Israelis struggled to recover from the surprise attack; finally, they launched an effective counteroffensive against Egyptian forces in the Sinai. At that point, the United

Discussion and Activities

Analyzing Visuals Have students examine the image "The Evacuation of Saigon." Ask them to discuss in small groups how the photo depicts American intervention in Vietnam. **WOR**

NIXON IN CHINA President Richard Nixon's 1972 visit to China was an important step in normalizing relations between the US and the People's Republic of China. Here Nixon toasts the developing relationship with Prime Minister Zhou Enlai.

States intervened, placing heavy pressure on Israel to accept a cease-fire rather than press its advantage.

The imposed settlement of the Yom Kippur War demonstrated the growing dependence of the United States and its allies on Arab oil. Permitting Israel to continue its drive into Egypt might have jeopardized the ability of the United States to purchase needed petroleum from the Arab states. A brief but painful embargo by the Arab governments on the sale of oil to supporters of Israel (including America) in 1973 provided an ominous warning of the costs of losing access to the region's resources.

ARAB OIL EMBARGO

CHAPTER 31 REVIEW

CONNECTING THEMES

Chapter Thirty-One explored the events of the later Cold War along with the increased tension in American society and politics. This tension, driven by domestic and foreign policies and actions, deeply affected the American identity.

The strain on Soviet and U.S. relations continued with the failed attempt by the United States to overthrow the Cuban government. The resulting Cuban missile crisis brought the powers close to nuclear war. The United States, following the policy of containment, also found itself gradually drawn deeper into the conflict in Vietnam. After President Johnson announced the North Vietnamese had attacked U.S. destroyers, Congress passed the Gulf of Tonkin Resolution, which authorized the president to "take all necessary measures" in Southeast Asia. The United States increased forces in and attacks on North Vietnam, but the attrition strategy failed to quell the North Vietnamese. As television and newspapers depicted increasingly violent scenes, particularly from the Tet Offensive, many Americans began to doubt that victory was possible.

Opposition to the war and rising racial tensions created a volatile domestic state. The assassination of Martin Luther King, Jr. and Robert Kennedy spurred more violence. The turmoil resulted in a conservative backlash, and the election of Richard Nixon, as a majority of Americans sought a return to stability. Nixon improved relations with the Soviet Union and China and instituted what became known as the "Nixon Doctrine" to limit American involvement in disputes in developing nations. These actions would affect American foreign policy until the end of the century.

You should consider the following questions as you review the themes for this chapter:

- How did American foreign policy during the time period reduce and intensify Cold War tensions?
- What factors led the United States to enter into the Vietnam War?
- Why did the events of 1968 produce social and political tensions within the United States?
- What were the causes and effects of America's long term commitment into the Vietnam War?
- How did the presidencies of Kennedy, Johnson, and Nixon shape both domestic and foreign policy for the United States during the second half of the twentieth century?

KEY TERMS

Bay of Pigs 834
Cuban missile crisis 834
Dien Bien Phu 838
Gulf of Tonkin resolution 839
Henry Kissinger 847
Ho Chi Minh 837
Ho Chi Minh trail 840
John Kennedy 833
New Frontier 833
Ngo Dinh Diem 838
Nixon Doctrine 850
Richard Nixon 847
Robert Kennedy 845
Tet offensive 843
Viet Cong 838
Vietnamization 847

Discussion and Activities

Comparing After students have read the section "The Problems of Multipolarity," ask them to create a Venn diagram comparing the Six-Day War with the Yom Kippur War. Have students consider how both wars might impact the United States in the future, both diplomatically and economically. **WOR**

Key Terms

Students should be familiar with the key terms and be able to define them in the context of the ongoing conflicts of the Cold War in Asia and Latin America and their effects on American politics and society. Encourage students to use these terms in performing review exercises and exam practice for this chapter.

Go Online Chapter 31 Content Review

Assessing Student Understanding Use the online assessment to assess student understanding of concepts and topics within the chapter. You can assign the ready-made Chapter 31 Content Review or create your own from available questions. This easy-to-use tool helps you design assessments that meet the needs of different types of learners.

Answers

Multiple Choice

1. C; **2.** C; **3.** D

Short Answer

4A) Possible answer: Tensions between the U.S. and the Soviet Union gave rise to a Cold War. This tension led to events like the building of the Berlin Wall. The wall separated East and West Berlin and became a symbol of the Cold War.

4B) Possible answer: Kennedy had inherited a plan to overthrow Fidel Castro, who was backed by the Soviet Union. In April 1961, Kennedy authorized the invasion and 2000 armed exiles landed at the Bay of Pigs. The exiles received neither American air support nor the support by the Cuban people, and the invasion was a failure.

4C) Possible answer: In 1962, aerial photographs showed that the Soviets were constructing sites in Cuba for offensive weapons. Kennedy immediately ordered a blockade of the island. In a tense moment, a Soviet ship headed toward the blockade turned back and confrontation was avoided.

5A) Possible answer: Both were proxy wars and were fought as part of the U.S. foreign policy of containment.

5B) Possible answer: The level of public support for each war was very different with much of the American population opposing the Vietnam War in its final years.

5C) Possible answer: The U.S. withdraw in Vietnam did not result in the spread of communism throughout the region which disproved the domino theory the U.S. used as a reason for intervention during the era.

AP EXAM PRACTICE

Questions assume cumulative content knowledge from this chapter and previous chapters.

MULTIPLE CHOICE

Use the election graphic on page 846 and your knowledge of U.S. history to answer questions 1-3.

1. Opposition to the Vietnam War grew in 1968 as many Americans were shocked by televised scenes of
   - (A) the Gulf of Tonkin attack.
   - (B) U.S. forces turning on their South Vietnamese allies.
   - (C) the Tet Offensive.
   - (D) invasion of Cambodia and Laos.

2. The election of 1968, as illustrated by the graphic, was similar to Nixon's experience in 1960 in that
   - (A) the election was closely contested.
   - (B) a third party candidate failed to gain any votes.
   - (C) Nixon scored an overwhelming victory in the Electoral College.
   - (D) Nixon ran on a mixed ticket with a Democratic Vice-Presidential running mate.

3. The cultural turbulence of 1960s America was perhaps most visible in what aspect of the 1968 election?
   - (A) The victory of the Republican Richard Nixon after the string of Republican political failures in the Vietnam War.
   - (B) The candidacy of Hubert Humphrey after he defeated incumbent Lyndon Johnson in the primary elections.
   - (C) The failure of any candidate to win a majority in the Electoral College.
   - (D) The number of votes for independent candidate George Wallace.

SHORT ANSWER

Use your knowledge of U.S. history to answer questions 4 and 5.

4. Use the image on page 835 to answer A, B, and C.
   - (A) Briefly describe ONE historical development following World War II that gave rise to the event depicted in the image.
   - (B) Briefly explain ONE specific historical event during the Kennedy administration that was a result of Cold War tensions between the U.S. and the Soviet Union.
   - (C) Briefly explain a SECOND specific historical event during the Kennedy administration that was a result of Cold War tensions between the U.S. and the Soviet Union.

5. Answer A, B, and C.
   - (A) Briefly describe ONE specific historical similarity between the Korean and Vietnam Wars.
   - (B) Briefly describe ONE specific historical difference between the Korean and Vietnam Wars.
   - (C) Briefly explain ONE specific historical effect that resulted from America's involvement in the Vietnam War.

LONG ESSAY

Develop a thoughtful and thorough historical argument that answers the question. Begin your essay with a thesis statement, and support it with specific historical evidence and examples.

6. Evaluate the relative importance of the effects of the Cold War between the United States and the Soviet Union.

Answers

Long Essay

6. Possible Thesis: The cost of the Cold War put tremendous strain on the American economy and the anti-war movement divided American society in the second half of the twentieth century. Historical Evidence: The rising cost of containment and other Cold War policies had ramifications domestically as social programs were put on the back burner at the expense of foreign entanglements. Eisenhower, Kennedy, Johnson, and Nixon were all hamstrung due to the rising costs of the Cold War on the American economy. The anti-war movement and the counterculture converged with the civil rights movement to create domestic upheaval and divisions within American society. The Cold War heightened the sense of anxiety Americans had surrounding nuclear warfare and pushed domestic initiatives, like the space program, as a way to gain a technological advantage over the Soviets.

32 TURBULENT TIMES

"SOME MEN SEE
THINGS AS THEY ARE
AND SAY WHY, I
DREAM THINGS THAT
NEVER WERE AND SAY
WHY NOT"

ROBERT KENNEDY THE ICON
This photo and statement from Robert Kennedy date from 1968, the year of his presidential campaign and assassination. Almost immediately after his death, Kennedy became a symbol of a lost era—and he remains a powerful image into our own time. In 2008, the Triborough Bridge in New York City was renamed the RFK Bridge.

CONNECTING CONCEPTS

Chapter Thirty-Two begins by examining the domestic liberalism of John Kennedy and Lyndon Johnson, who declared a "war on poverty" and created important new social programs such as Medicare and Medicaid. But the anti-poverty effort and Great Society were controversial, especially with conservatives who were critical of the high costs. The youth culture of the 1960s and 1970s also alarmed conservatives. Radicals in the "New Left" protested against the Vietnam War, while the "hippies" of the counterculture rebelled against traditional values by promoting drug use, alternative lifestyles, and a "sexual revolution."

Environmentalism emerged as a powerful and enduring movement during the 1970s. The movement gained attention partly due to the new science of ecology, which stressed the interrelatedness of the natural world, and a growing awareness of the threat that pollution posed to clean air and water. Richard Nixon, a conservative, even supported the creation of the Environmental Protection Agency as he tried to dismantle many of the Great Society's social programs. Nixon also attempted to steer the Supreme Court, which issued a series of liberal rulings such as *Miranda v. Arizona* and *Baker v. Carr* in the 1960s, in a new direction with his judicial appointments.

By appealing to the "silent majority," or the conservative white middle class, Nixon won an overwhelming victory in 1972. But two years later, the Watergate Scandal led to his resignation — the first by an American president. The pardon of Nixon by the new president, Gerald Ford, contributed greatly to the election in 1976 of Jimmy Carter, who assumed office at a difficult

Pacing Guide

Chapter 32 explores key concepts from Period 8: 1945–1980 of the AP U.S. History Curriculum Framework. The suggested instruction time for Chapter 32 is 4 days.

Key Concepts

8.2.II Responding to social conditions and the African American civil rights movement, a variety of movements emerged that focused on issues of identity, social justice, and the environment.

8.2.III Liberalism influenced postwar politics and court decisions, but it came under increasing attack from the left as well as from a resurgent conservative movement.

Historical Thinking Skills

Contextualization Have students examine the image "Robert Kennedy the Icon." Ask them to discuss as a class the events and ideas that led to the creation of the memorial to Robert Kennedy. **PCE** **SOC**

Discussion and Activities

Speculating Have students read the introduction to the section "Expanding the Liberal State." Ask them to discuss in small groups why they think that Kennedy remained popular so long after his death. *(His image was frozen in time as youthful, vigorous, and glamorous. There is nostalgia for a simpler time prior to the assassination.)* **SOC** **PCE**

moment. At home, the economy struggled from high inflation, deindustrialization, and energy shortages. Abroad, the Soviet invasion of Afghanistan and the Iran Hostage Crisis made Carter seem like a weak and ineffective leader. The stage was set for the rise of the "New Right" — American conservatism.

As you read, you should:

- Describe the reasons for and the results of the liberalism of the 1960s, including the resulting conservative backlash.
- Explain how the youth culture of the 1960s and 1970s challenged traditional American values. Identify the reasons for and consequences of the rise of environmentalism in the 1960s.
- Analyze the impact of the court cases which arose during the Warren Court in an effort to try and extend equal rights to different individuals and groups.
- Identify the major foreign and domestic troubles faced by the Nixon administration during his presidency.
- Evaluate the challenges faced by Ford and Carter following Nixon's resignation.

EXPANDING THE LIBERAL STATE

More than any other president of the century (except perhaps the two Roosevelts and, later, Ronald Reagan), Kennedy made his own personality an integral part of his presidency and a central focus of national attention. Nothing illustrated that more clearly than the popular reaction to the tragedy of November 22, 1963. Kennedy had traveled to Texas with his wife and Vice President Lyndon Johnson for a series of political appearances. While the presidential motorcade rode slowly through the streets of Dallas, shots rang out. Two bullets struck the president–one in the throat, the other in the head. He was sped to a nearby hospital, where minutes after arriving he was pronounced dead. Lee Harvey Oswald, who appeared to be a confused and embittered Marxist, was arrested for the crime later that day, and then mysteriously murdered by a Dallas nightclub owner, Jack Ruby, two days later. Most Americans at the time accepted the conclusions of a federal commission, appointed by President Johnson and chaired by Chief Justice Earl Warren, which found that both Oswald and Ruby had acted alone, that there was no conspiracy. In later years, however, many Americans came to believe that the Warren Commission report had ignored evidence of a broad conspiracy behind the murders. Even after fifty years, some people still believe in the conspiracies associated with the president's assassination. And fifty years after his death, Kennedy's popularity remains high.

LYNDON JOHNSON

The Kennedy assassination was a national trauma–a defining event for almost everyone old enough to be aware of it. At the time, however, much of the nation took comfort in the personality and performance of Kennedy's successor in the White House, Lyndon Baines Johnson. Johnson was a native of the poor "hill country" of west Texas and had risen to become majority leader of the U.S. Senate by dint of extraordinary, even obsessive, effort and ambition. Having failed to win the Democratic nomination for president in 1960, he surprised many who knew him by agreeing to accept the second position on the ticket with Kennedy. The events in Dallas thrust him into the White House.

Johnson's rough-edged, even crude personality could hardly have been more different from Kennedy's. But like Kennedy, Johnson was a man who believed in the active use of power. Between 1963 and 1966, he compiled the most impressive legislative record of any president since Franklin Roosevelt. He was aided by the tidal wave of emotion that followed the death of President Kennedy, which helped win support for many New Frontier proposals. But Johnson also constructed a remarkable reform program of his own, one that he ultimately labeled the "Great Society." And he won approval of much of it through the same sort of skillful lobbying in Congress that had made him an effective majority leader.

THE "GREAT SOCIETY"

Johnson envisioned himself as a great "coalition builder." He wanted the support of everyone, and for a time he nearly got it. His first year in office was, by necessity, dominated by the campaign for reelection. There was little doubt that he would win–particularly after the Republican Party fell under the sway of its right wing and nominated the conservative Senator Barry Goldwater of Arizona. In the November 1964 election, the president received a larger plurality of the popular vote, over 61 percent, than any candidate before or since. Goldwater managed to carry only his home state of Arizona and five states in the Deep South. Record Democratic majorities

Go Online AP Exam Preparation

AP Exam Practice Use the online assessment to help prepare students for the AP Exam. You can assign the ready-made AP-style short answer questions, document-based questions, and multiple-choice questions assessing concepts, themes, and skills from Period 8 and AP style long-essay questions organized in sets of 3 questions from various time periods. You can also create your own tests from available questions. This easy-to-use tool helps you design assessments that meet the needs of different types of learners.

in both houses of Congress, many of whose members had been swept into office only because of the margin of Johnson's victory, ensured that the president would be able to fulfill many of his goals.

The Assault on Poverty

For the first time since the 1930s, the federal government took steps in the 1960s to create important new social welfare programs. The most important of these, perhaps, was Medicare: a program to provide federal aid to the elderly for medical expenses. Its enactment in 1965 came at the end of a bitter, twenty-year debate between those who believed in the concept of national health assistance and those who denounced it as "socialized medicine." But the program as it went into effect pacified many critics. For one thing, it avoided the stigma of "welfare" by making Medicare benefits available to all elderly Americans, regardless of need (just as Social Security had done with pensions). That created a large middle-class constituency for the program. The program also defused the opposition of the medical community by allowing doctors serving Medicare patients to practice privately and to charge their normal fees; Medicare simply shifted responsibility for paying those fees from the patient to the government. In 1966, Johnson steered to passage the Medicaid program, which extended federal medical assistance to welfare recipients and other indigent people of all ages.

MEDICARE AND MEDICAID

Medicare and Medicaid were early steps in a much larger assault on poverty–one that Kennedy had been planning in the last months of his life and that Johnson launched only weeks after taking office. The centerpiece of this "war on poverty," as Johnson called it, was the Office of Economic Opportunity (OEO), which created an array of new educational, employment, housing, and health-care programs. But the OEO was controversial from the start, in part because of its commitment to the idea of "Community Action."

Community Action was an effort to involve members of poor communities themselves in the planning and administration of the programs designed to help them. The Community Action programs provided jobs for many poor people and gave them valuable experience in administrative and political work. Many men and women who went on to significant careers in politics or community organizing, including many black and Hispanic politicians, as well as many Native Americans, got their start in Community Action programs. But despite its achievements, the Community Action approach proved impossible to sustain, both because of administrative failures and because the apparent excesses of a few agencies damaged the popular image of the Community Action programs and, indeed, the war on poverty as a whole.

COMMUNITY ACTION PROGRAM

ETERNAL FLAME The John F. Kennedy Eternal Flame memorializes the slain president. It is located at Kennedy's grave site in Arlington National Cemetery. The site was designed by architect John Carl Warnecke, a long-time friend of the president.

The OEO spent nearly $3 billion during its first two years of existence, and it helped reduce poverty in some areas. But it fell far short of eliminating poverty. That was in part because of the weaknesses of the programs themselves and in part because funding for them, inadequate from the beginning, dwindled as the years passed and a costly war in Southeast Asia became the nation's first priority.

Cities, Schools, and Immigration

Closely tied to the antipoverty program were federal efforts to promote the revitalization of decaying cities and to strengthen the nation's schools. The Housing Act of 1961 offered $4.9 billion in federal grants to cities for the preservation of open spaces, the development of mass-transit systems, and the subsidization of middle-income housing. In 1966, Johnson established a new cabinet agency, the Department of Housing and Urban Development (whose first secretary, Robert Weaver, was the first African American ever to serve in the cabinet). Johnson also inaugurated the Model Cities program, which offered federal subsidies for urban redevelopment pilot programs.

HOUSING AND URBAN DEVELOPMENT

Kennedy had long fought for federal aid to public education, but he had failed to overcome two important obstacles: many Americans feared that aid to education was the first step toward federal control of the schools, and Catholics insisted that federal assistance must extend to parochial as well as public schools. Johnson managed to circumvent both objections with the Elementary and Secondary Education Act of 1965 and a series of subsequent measures. The bills extended aid to both private and parochial schools and based the aid on the economic conditions of the students, not on the needs of the

Discussion and Activities

Speculating After students have read the section "Lyndon Johnson," ask them to discuss in small groups whether President Kennedy would have been able to build the same support for social programs as Johnson had he not been assassinated. **PCE**

Reasoning Processes

Comparing and Contrasting Have students read the section "The Assault on Poverty," and ask them to create a Venn diagram comparing Medicare and Medicaid. Have students consider how these programs represented continuity or change in the involvement of the federal government in providing healthcare. **PCE** **WXT** **SOC**

Discussion and Activities

Making Connections After students have read the section "Cities, Schools, and Immigration," ask them to look up the Elementary and Secondary Education Act and its successor, Every Student Succeeds Act. Have students discuss in small groups what elements of the law have changed over time, and which have stayed the same. **PCE**

THE JOHNSON TREATMENT Lyndon Johnson was legendary for his powers of persuasion—for a combination of charm and intimidation that often worked on even the most experienced politicians. He is shown here in the Oval Office meeting with his old friend Senator Richard Russell of Georgia and demonstrating one of his most powerful and unsettling techniques of persuasion: moving so close to the person with whom he was talking as to be almost touching him.

LBJ Library Photo by Yoichi Okamoto

schools themselves. Total annual federal expenditures for education and technical training rose from $5 billion to $12 billion between 1964 and 1967.

IMMIGRATION ACT OF 1965

The Johnson administration also supported the Immigration Act of 1965, one of the most important pieces of legislation of the 1960s. The law maintained a strict limit on the number of newcomers admitted to the country each year (170,000), but it eliminated the "national origins" system established in the 1920s, which gave preference to immigrants from northern Europe over those from other parts of the world. It continued to restrict immigration from some parts of Latin America, but it allowed people from all parts of Europe, Asia, and Africa to enter the United States on an equal basis. By the early 1970s, the character of American immigration had changed, with members of new national groups–and particularly large groups of Asians–entering the United States and changing the character of the American population.

LEGACIES OF THE GREAT SOCIETY

Taken together, the Great Society reforms meant a significant increase in federal spending. For a time, rising tax revenues from the growing economy nearly compensated for the new expenditures. In 1964, Johnson managed to win passage of the $11.5 billion tax cut that Kennedy had first proposed in 1962. The cut increased the federal deficit, but substantial economic growth over the next several years made up for much of the revenue initially lost. As Great Society programs began to multiply, however, and particularly as they began to compete with the escalating costs of America's military ventures, federal spending rapidly outpaced increases in revenues. In 1961, the federal government had spent $94.4 billion. By 1970, that sum had risen to $196.6 billion.

FAILURES AND ACHIEVEMENTS OF THE GREAT SOCIETY

The high costs of the Great Society programs, the deficiencies and failures of many of them, and the inability of the government to find the revenues to pay for them contributed to a growing disillusionment in later years with the idea of federal efforts to solve social problems. By the 1980s, many Americans had become convinced that the Great Society experiments had not worked and that, indeed, government programs to solve social problems could not work. But the Great Society, despite many failures, was also responsible for some significant achievements. It substantially reduced hunger in America. It made medical care available to millions of elderly and poor people who would otherwise have had great difficulty affording it. It contributed to the greatest reduction in poverty in American history. In 1959, according to the most widely accepted estimates, 21 percent of the American people lived below the official poverty line. By 1969, only 12 percent remained below that line. The improvements affected black and white Americans in about the same proportion: 56 percent of the black population had lived in poverty in 1959, while only 32 percent did so ten years later–a 42 percent reduction; 18 percent of all white Americans had been poor in 1959, but only 10 percent were poor a decade later–a 44 percent reduction. Much of that progress was a result of economic growth, but some of it was a result of Great Society programs.

THE YOUTH CULTURE

Perhaps most alarming to conservative Americans in the 1960s and 1970s was a pattern of social and cultural protest that was emerging from younger Americans, who were giving vent to two related impulses. One was the impulse, originating with

Discussion and Activities

Analyzing Points of View Have students examine the image "The Johnson Treatment." Discuss as a class how and/or why this was a useful technique for President Johnson. Ask students if they think the technique is still useful today. **PCE**

the political left, to create a great new community of "the people," which would rise up to break the power of elites and force the nation to end the war, pursue racial and economic justice, and transform its political life. The other, equally powerful, impulse was the vision of "liberation." It found expression through the efforts of particular groups—African Americans, Native Americans, Hispanic Americans, women, gays and lesbians, and others—to define and assert themselves and make demands on the larger society. It also found expression through the efforts of individuals to create a new culture that would allow them to escape from what they considered the dehumanizing pressures of what some called the modern "technocracy."

"LIBERATION"

"THE NEW LEFT"

In retrospect, it seems unsurprising that young Americans became so assertive and powerful in American culture and politics in the 1960s. The postwar baby-boom generation—the unprecedented number of people born in a few years just after World War II—was growing up. By 1970, more than half the American population was under thirty years old; more than 8 million Americans—eight times the number in 1950—were attending college. This was the largest generation of youth in American history, and it was coming to maturity in a time of unprecedented affluence, opportunity, and—for many—frustration.

One of the most visible results of the increasingly assertive youth movement was a radicalization of many American college and university students, who in the 1960s formed what became known as the New Left—a large, diverse group of men and women energized by the polarizing developments of their time. The New Left embraced the cause of African Americans and other minorities, but its own ranks consisted overwhelmingly of white people. African Americans and minorities formed political movements of their own. Some members of the New Left were the children of radical parents (members of the so-called Old Left of the 1930s and 1940s).

SOURCES OF THE NEW LEFT

The New Left drew from the writings of some of the important social critics of the 1950s—among them C. Wright Mills, a sociologist at Columbia University who wrote a series of scathing and brilliant critiques of modern bureaucracies. Relatively few members of the New Left were communists, but many were drawn to the writings of Karl Marx and of contemporary Marxist theorists. Some came to revere Third World Marxists such as Che Guevara, the South American revolutionary and guerrilla leader; Mao Zedong; and Ho Chi Minh. But the New Left drew its inspiration above all from the civil rights movement, in which many idealistic young white Americans had become involved in the early 1960s.

In 1962, a group of students, most of them from prestigious universities, gathered in Michigan to form an organization to give voice to their demands: Students for a Democratic Society (SDS). Their declaration of beliefs, the Port Huron Statement, expressed their disillusionment with the society they had inherited and their determination to build a new politics.

SDS

Some members of SDS moved into inner-city neighborhoods and tried for a time, without great success, to mobilize poor, working-class people politically. But most members of the New Left were students, and their radicalism centered in part on issues related to the modern university. A 1964 dispute at the University of California at Berkeley over the rights of students to engage in political activities on campus gained national attention. The Free Speech Movement, as it called itself, created turmoil at Berkeley as students challenged campus police, occupied administrative offices, and produced a strike in which nearly three-quarters of the Berkeley students participated. The immediate issue was the right of students to pass out literature and recruit volunteers for political causes on campus. But the protest quickly became as well an expression of a basic critique of the university and the society it seemed to represent.

FREE SPEECH MOVEMENT

CHE ERNESTO "Che" Guevara was an Argentine Marxist revolutionary who played a significant role in the Cuban Revolution. His stylized portrait remains a major symbol of countercultural rebellion the world over.

Discussion and Activities

Analyzing Issues After students have read the section "Legacies of the Great Society," ask them to create a t-chart listing the successes and failures of the Great Society and its programs. Have students discuss as a class which programs were most and least successful, and if the successes outweighed the failures. **PCE** **SOC** **WXT**

Historical Thinking Skills

Argumentation Have students read the section "Sources of the New Left." Ask them to discuss in small groups why so many young people were attracted to the New Left movement even though they were part of the most affluent, opportunity-filled society in history. Ask for volunteers to share their discussion with the class. *(Many young people were frustrated by the slow progress of the civil rights movement, the costly war in Vietnam, and believed that the American economic and political systems were fundamentally unfair.)* **PCE** **SOC** **WXT**

AP Exam Tip

The Advanced Placement Exam will require students to explain the purpose, point of view, historical situation, and/or audience of a document. One way students can demonstrate this is to explain the motives of a source in presenting information in a particular way.

Historical Thinking Skills

Sourcing and Situation Have students practice the tip by examining the image "Reporting Woodstock." Have students work in small groups to identify and discuss evidence from the photo that illustrates the *New York Daily News* biases. *(Students may identify the use of the word "hippies," and the suggestion of the headline that the lack of planning and organization left people stranded.)* **WOR** **PCE**

PATTERNS OF POPULAR CULTURE

Rock Music in the Sixties

The rock music of the late 1960s and 1970s, even more than the rock 'n' roll of the 1950s and early 1960s, emphasized release. It gave vent to impulse and instinct, to physical and emotional urges. That was one reason it was so enormously popular among young people in an age of cultural and sexual revolution. It was also why it seemed so menacing and dangerous to many conservative Americans seeking to defend traditional values and behavior.

Rock in the late 1960s seemed simultaneously subversive and liberating. That was partly because of the behavior and lifestyles of rock musicians, whose appearance and behavior were often deliberately outrageous. Rock musicians were connected at times to the drug culture of the 1960s (especially through the so-called psychedelic-rock groups inspired by experiences with the hallucinogen LSD). They had links to mystical Eastern religions (most notably the Beatles, who had spent time in India studying Transcendental Meditation and who, beginning in 1967 with their album *Sergeant Pepper's Lonely Hearts Club Band,* incorporated those themes into their music). And they often reveled in flouting social conventions, beginning with the Rolling Stones and culminating, perhaps, in the extreme and self-destructive behavior of Jimi Hendrix, Jim Morrison, and Janis Joplin, all of whom died very young of drug-related causes.

Late-sixties rock was among many expressions of the impulses that came to be known as the counterculture; and like the counterculture, it inspired widely varying reactions. To its defenders, the new rock, with its emphasis on emotional release, was a healthy rebuke to the repressive norms of mainstream culture. To them, its virtues were symbolized by the great rock festival at Woodstock, New York, in August 1969, where over 400,000 young people gathered on a remote piece of farmland for several days to hear performances by such artists as the Who, Jimi Hendrix, the Grateful Dead, Janis Joplin, Joe Cocker, the Jefferson Airplane, and many others. The festival was marred by heavy rains that produced a sea of mud and by supplies and facilities completely inadequate for the unexpectedly large crowd. Drugs were everywhere in evidence, as was a kind of open sexual freedom that a decade earlier would have seemed unthinkable to all but a few Americans. But Woodstock remained peaceful, friendly, and harmonious. There was rhapsodic talk at the time of how Woodstock represented the birth of a new youth culture, the "Woodstock nation."

Critics of the new rock, and the counterculture, were not impressed with the idea of the "Woodstock nation." To them, the essence of the counterculture was a kind of numbing hopelessness and despair, with a menacing and violent underside. To them, the appropriate symbol was not Woodstock, but another great rock concert, which more than 300,000 people attended only four months after Woodstock, at the Altamont Speedway east of San Francisco. The concert featured many of the groups that had been at Woodstock, but the Rolling Stones, who had organized the event, were the main attraction. As at Woodstock, drugs were plentiful and sexual exhibitionism was frequent. But unlike Woodstock, Altamont was far from peaceful. Instead, it became ugly, brutal, and violent, and resulted in the deaths of four people. Several of them died accidentally, one, for example, from a bad drug trip, during which he fell into a stream and drowned. But numerous people were brutally beaten by members of the Hell's Angels motorcycle gang, who had been hired by the Rolling Stones as security guards. One man was beaten and stabbed to death in front of the stage while the Stones were playing "Sympathy for the Devil."

Woodstock and Altamont, then, became symbols of two aspects of the counterculture of the late 1960s and early 1970s, and of the rock music that created its anthems. The beat poet Allen Ginsberg wrote an ecstatic poem proclaiming that at Woodstock "a new kind of man has come to his bliss / to end the cold war he has borne / against his own kind of flesh." The festival and its music, many claimed, had shown the path to an age of love and peace and justice. Altamont, however, suggested a dark underside of the rock culture, its potential for destruction and violence. "As far as I was concerned," one participant said, "Altamont was the death knell of all those things that we thought would last forever. I personally felt like the sixties had been an extravagant stage show and I had been a spectator in the audience. Altamont had rung down the curtain to no applause."*

*Allen Ginsberg's estate is affiliated with the Naropa Institute, Boulder, CO.

WITH

FRI. AUG. 15 SAT. AUG. 16 SUN. AUG. 17

ADVERTISING WOODSTOCK Even before the thousands of spectators gathered for the famous rock concert at Woodstock in 1969, organizers envisioned it as something more than a performance. It would, this poster claims, be a search for peace as well as for music.

FINAL SUNDAY NEWS 20¢

HIPPIES MIRED IN SEA OF MUD

They Don't Melt . . .

REPORTING WOODSTOCK The *New York Daily News,* whose largely working-class readership was not notably sympathetic toward the young people at Woodstock, ran this slightly derisive front-page story on the concert as heavy rains turned the concert site into a sea of mud. ["They Don't Melt," the caption said.]

Discussion and Activities

Analyzing Points of View

After students have read the feature, ask them to write a newspaper article from either the point of view of an audience member at Woodstock or a nearby resident observing the scene. Ask for volunteers to share their work with the class and discuss the different points of view presented by students in their articles. **SOC**

ALTAMONT Hell's Angels "security guards" club a spectator near the stage during the rock concert at Altamont as other concertgoers—some curious, some aghast—watch. One spectator died as a result of the beatings.

© Photofest

HISTORICAL THINKING SKILLS

1. **Analyzing Change** How does rock music of the 1960s differ from rock 'n' roll of the 1950s? What accounts for these differences?
2. **Explaining Historical Context** What two characteristics of the counterculture are represented by Woodstock and Altamont? Was there an "Altamont" nation, just as there was a "Woodstock" nation?
3. **Evaluating Historical Significance** Does popular music today challenge the prevailing culture, as rock music of the 1960s challenged the culture of that era? What lasting effects, if any, did 1960s rock have on U.S. society and culture?

The revolt at Berkeley was the first outburst of what was to be nearly a decade of campus turmoil. Students at Berkeley and elsewhere protested the impersonal character of the modern university, and they denounced the role of educational institutions in sustaining what they considered corrupt or immoral public policies. The antiwar movement greatly inflamed the challenge and expanded it to the universities; and beginning in 1968, campus demonstrations, riots, and building seizures became almost commonplace. At Columbia University in New York City, students seized several buildings, including the offices of the president, and occupied them for days until local police forcibly and violently ejected them. Harvard University had a similar, and even more violent, experience a year later.

Also in 1969, Berkeley became the scene of perhaps the most prolonged and traumatic conflict of any American college campus in the 1960s: a battle over the efforts of a few students to build a "People's Park" on a vacant lot the university planned to use to build a parking garage. This seemingly minor event precipitated weeks of impassioned and often violent conflicts between the university administration, which sought to evict the intruders from the land, and the students, many of whom supported the advocates of the park and who saw the university's efforts to close it as a symbol of the struggle between liberation and oppression.

By the end of the People's Park battle, which lasted for over a week, the Berkeley campus was completely polarized; even students who had not initially supported or even noticed the People's Park (the great majority) were, by the end, committed to its defense; 85 percent of the 15,000 students voted in a referendum to leave the park alone. Student radicals were, for the first time, winning large audiences for their extravagant rhetoric linking university administrators, the police, and the larger political and economic system, describing them all as part of one united, oppressive force.

PEOPLE'S PARK

Most campus radicals were rarely if ever violent (except at times in their rhetoric). But the popular image of student radicalism in mainstream culture was one of chaos and disorder, based in part on the disruptive actions of small groups of militants, among them the "Weathermen," a violent offshoot of SDS. The Weathermen were responsible for several cases of arson and bombing that destroyed campus buildings and claimed several lives. Not many people, not even many students, ever accepted the most radical political views that lay at the heart of the New Left. But many supported the position of SDS and other groups on particular issues and, above all, on the Vietnam War. Student activists tried to drive out training programs for military officers (ROTC) and bar military recruiters from college campuses. They attacked the laboratories and corporations that were producing weapons for the war. And between 1967 and 1969, they organized some of the largest political demonstrations in American history. The October 1967 march on the Pentagon, where demonstrators were met by a solid line of armed troops; the "spring mobilization" of April 1968, which attracted hundreds of thousands of demonstrators in cities

Reasoning Processes

Comparison After students have read the section "Free Speech Movement," ask them to create a Venn diagram comparing the Free Speech Movement with SDS. **PCE** **SOC**

Answers

Patterns of Popular Culture

1. Possible answer: The music of the 1960s reflected physical and emotional urges and was a response to the times. It defied authority in a way that was just beginning in the 1950s.
2. Possible answer: Drugs and sex were prevalent at both concerts. Woodstock was largely a peaceful concert, whereas Altamont turned violent. Only a "Woodstock nation" emerged during the period.
3. Possible answer: Student answers will vary but may include that music can have an element of challenging tradition and authority. Students may indicate that music reflects the cultural, social, political, and economic concerns of the larger society, and reflection of these concerns was part of the lasting impact of the era's music.

Historical Thinking Skills

Argumentation After students have read the section "The New Left," ask them to create a chart listing the causes and effects of opposition to the draft. Have students discuss in small groups why some men facing the draft would have refused to serve in the armed forces. PCE SOC WXT WOR

around the country; the Vietnam "moratorium" of the fall of 1969, during which millions of opponents of the war gathered in major rallies across the nation; and countless other demonstrations, large and small—all helped thrust the issue of the war into the center of American politics.

Closely related to opposition to the war was opposition to the military draft. The gradual abolition of many traditional deferments—for graduate students, teachers, husbands, fathers, and others—swelled the ranks of those faced with conscription (and thus of those likely to oppose it). Some draft-age Americans simply refused induction, accepting what occasionally were long terms in jail as a result. Others fled to Canada, Sweden, and elsewhere (where they were joined by deserters from the armed forces) to escape conscription. Not until 1977, when President Jimmy Carter issued a general pardon to draft resisters and a limited amnesty for deserters, did the Vietnam exiles begin to return to the country in substantial numbers.

THE COUNTERCULTURE

"HIPPIES"

Closely related to the New Left was a new youth culture openly scornful of the values and conventions of middle-class society. As if to display their contempt for conventional standards, young Americans flaunted long hair, shabby or flamboyant clothing, and a rebellious disdain for traditional speech and decorum. Also central to the counterculture, as it became known, were drugs: marijuana—which after 1966 became almost as common a youthful diversion as beer—and the less widespread but still substantial use of other, more potent hallucinogens, such as LSD.

There was also a new, more permissive view of sexual behavior—the beginnings of what came to be known as a "sexual revolution." To some degree, the emergence of relaxed approaches to sexuality was a result less of the counterculture than of the new accessibility of effective contraceptives, most notably the birth-control pill and, after 1973, legalized abortion. But the new sexuality also reflected the counterculture's belief that individuals should strive for release from inhibitions and give vent to their instincts and desires.

HAIGHT-ASHBURY

The counterculture challenged the structure of modern American society, attacking its banality, hollowness, artificiality, materialism, and isolation from nature. The most committed adherents of the counterculture—the hippies, who came to dominate the Haight-Ashbury neighborhood of San Francisco and other places, and the social dropouts, some of whom retreated to rural communes—rejected modern society and attempted to find refuge in a simpler, more "natural" existence.

The effects of the counterculture reached out to the larger society and helped create a new set of social norms that many young people (and some adults) chose to imitate. Long hair

BERKELEY, 1969 The People's Park controversy at the University of California at Berkeley turned the campus and the town into something close to a war zone. In this photograph, National Guardsmen with fixed bayonets stand in the way of a planned march to protest the closing of People's Park on May 30, 1969, more than two weeks after they first arrived to keep peace in Berkeley.

Discussion and Activities

Evaluating Evidence Have students examine the image "Berkeley, 1969." Ask them to identify and discuss with a partner the details from the photo that illustrate the tension on the University of California campus. *(Police in riot gear and demonstrators erecting makeshift barricades)* PCE SOC

WOODSTOCK In the summer of 1969, more than 400,000 people gathered for a rock concert on a farm near Woodstock, New York. Despite mostly terrible weather, the gathering was remarkably peaceful—sparking talk among some enthusiasts of the new youth culture about the "Woodstock nation."

and freakish clothing became the badge not only of hippies and radicals but of an entire generation as well. The use of marijuana, the freer attitudes toward sex, the iconoclastic (and sometimes obscene) language—all spread far beyond the realm of the true devotees of the counterculture.

Perhaps the most pervasive element of the new youth society was one that even the least radical members of the generation embraced: rock music. Rock 'n' roll, drawn in part from African American music, first achieved wide popularity in the 1950s, on the strength of such early performers as Buddy Holly and, above all, Elvis Presley. Early in the 1960s, its influence spread, largely as a result of the phenomenal popularity of the Beatles, the English group whose first visit to the United States in 1964 created a remarkable sensation, "Beatlemania." For a time, most rock musicians—like most popular musicians before them—concentrated largely on uncontroversial, romantic themes. By the late 1960s, however, rock had begun to reflect many of the new iconoclastic values of its time. The Beatles, for example, abandoned their once simple and seemingly innocent style for a new, experimental, even mystical approach that reflected the growing popular fascination with drugs and Eastern religions. Other groups, such as the Rolling Stones, turned even more openly to themes of anger, frustration, and rebelliousness. Rock's driving rhythms, its sensuality, its often harsh and angry tone—all made it an appropriate vehicle for expressing the themes of the social and political unrest of the late 1960s. A powerful symbol of the fusion of rock music and the counterculture was the great music festival at Woodstock, New York, in the summer of 1969.

GROWING INFLUENCE OF ROCK 'N' ROLL

THE EMERGENCE OF ENVIRONMENTALISM

Like feminism, environmentalism entered the 1960s with a long history and little public support. Also like feminism, environmentalism both profited from and transcended the turbulence of the era and emerged by the 1970s as a powerful and enduring force in American and global life.

The rise of this new movement was in part a result of the environmental degradation that had become increasingly evident in the advanced industrial society of the late twentieth century. It was a result, too, of the growth of the science of

Reasoning Processes

Causation After students have read the section "The Counterculture," ask them to list the motives for those who participated in the counterculture. Have students write a thesis statement that makes a claim about the most important cause(s) of the rise of the counterculture. **SOC**

Discussion and Activities

Analyzing Visuals Have students examine the image "Woodstock." Ask them to discuss with a partner how details from the photo either support or undermine the ideals or expressions of the counterculture. **SOC**

Discussion and Activities

Speculating Have students read the section "The New Science of Ecology." Ask them to think about and share with a partner why ten years elapsed between the publication of *Silent Spring* and the ban on DDT. *(The slow pace of legislation and opposition from the chemical industry.)* **PCE** **WXT**

ecology, which provided environmentalists with new and powerful arguments. And it was a product of some of the countercultural movements of the time: movements that rejected aspects of the modern, industrial, consumer society and called for a return to a more "natural" existence.

THE NEW SCIENCE OF ECOLOGY

Until the mid-twentieth century, most people who considered themselves environmentalists (or, to use the traditional term, conservationists) based their commitment on aesthetic or moral grounds: they wanted to preserve nature because it was too beautiful to despoil, or because it was a mark of divinity on the world. In the course of the twentieth century, however, scientists in the United States and other nations—drawing from earlier, relatively obscure scientific writings—began to create a new rationale for environmentalism. They called it "ecology."

IDEA OF AN INTERRELATED WORLD

Ecology is the science of the interrelatedness of the natural world. It rests on an assumption—as the American zoologist Stephen A. Forbes wrote as early as 1880—that "primeval nature . . . presents a settled harmony of interaction among organic groups," and that this harmony "is in strong contrast with the many serious maladjustments of plants and animals found in countries occupied by man." Such problems as air and water pollution, the destruction of forests, the extinction of species, and toxic wastes are not, ecology teaches, separate, isolated problems. All elements of the earth's environment are intimately and delicately linked. Damaging any one of those elements, therefore, risks damaging all the others.

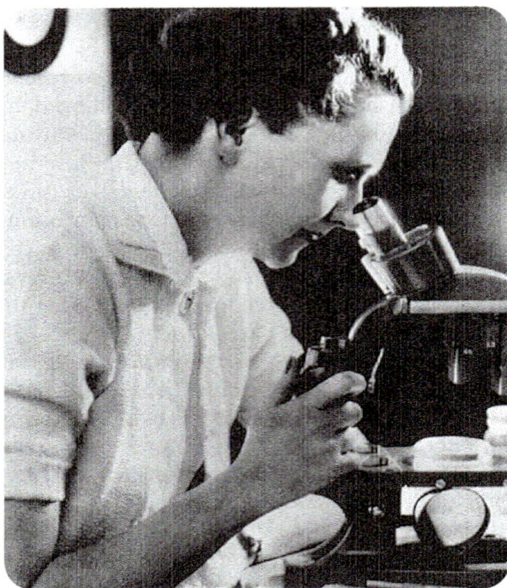

RACHEL CARSON Rachel Carson, who began her career as a marine biologist, wrote the world's best-selling book about the ocean environment in the 1950s. Carson's abiding love for the creatures of shore and surf led to her concern about the harm pesticides might do them.

A number of American scientists built on Forbes's ideas in the early twentieth century, but perhaps the greatest early-contribution to popular knowledge of ecology came not from a scientist, but from the writer and naturalist Aldo Leopold. During a career in forest management, Leopold sought to apply the new scientific findings on ecology to his interactions with the natural world. And in 1949, he published a classic of environmental literature, *The Sand County Almanac*, in which he argued that humans have a responsibility to understand and maintain the balance of nature, that they should behave in the natural world according to a code that he called the "land ethic." By then, the science of ecology was spreading widely in the scientific community. Among the findings of ecologists were such now-common ideas as the "food chain," the "ecosystem," "biodiversity," and "endangered species."

The influence of these emerging ideas of ecology could be seen especially clearly in the sensational 1962 book by Rachel Carson, *Silent Spring*. Carson was a marine biologist who had become a successful science writer. In 1957, she received a letter from a friend reporting the deaths of songbirds in her yard after the area had been sprayed with the insecticide DDT—the chemical developed in the 1930s to kill mosquitoes. Carson began investigating the impact of DDT and discovered growing signs of danger. DDT was slowly being absorbed into the food chain through water and plants, and the animals who ate and drank them. It was killing some animals (especially birds and fish) and inhibiting the ability of others to reproduce. Carson wrote eloquently about the growing danger of a "silent spring," in which birds would no longer sing and in which sickness and death would soon threaten large numbers of animals and, perhaps, people.

Silent Spring was an enormously influential book and had a direct, if delayed, influence on the decision to ban DDT in the United States in 1972. It was evidence of the growing power of environmentalism, and of the science of ecology, on public policy and national culture. But *Silent Spring* was also a very controversial book that enraged the chemical industry. Critics of Carson attempted to suppress the book and, when that effort failed, to discredit its findings.

ECOLOGY'S POSTWAR GROWTH

Between 1945 and 1960, the number of ecologists in the United States grew rapidly, and that number doubled again between 1960 and 1970. Funded by government agencies, by universities, by foundations, and eventually even by some corporations, ecological science gradually established itself as a significant field of its own. By the early twenty-first century, there were programs in and departments of ecological science in major universities throughout the United States and in many other nations.

Much more than other scientists, however, ecologists tend to fuse their commitment to research with a commitment to publicizing their work and promoting responsible public action to deal with environmental crises.

George Rinhart/Corbis/Getty Images

Discussion and Activities

Making Connections After students read the section "The New Science of Ecology," discuss as a class some of the environmental issues that are currently in the news. *(Global warming, air and water pollution, recycling, soil depletion, extreme weather events, etc.)* **PCE** **WXT** **GEO**

Environmental Advocacy

Among the most important environmental organizations of the late twentieth and early twenty-first centuries were the Wilderness Society, the Sierra Club, the National Audubon Society, the Nature Conservancy, the National Wildlife Federation, and the National Parks and Conservation Association. All of these organizations predated the rise of modern ecological science, but all of them entered the twenty-first century reenergized and committed to the new concepts of environmentalism. They found allies among other not-for-profit organizations that had no previous experience with environmentalism but now chose to join the battle—among them such groups as the American Civil Liberties Union, the League of Women Voters, the National Council of Churches, and even the AFL-CIO.

New Professional Environmental Activists

Out of these organizations emerged a new generation of professional environmental activists able to contribute to the legal and political battles of the movement. Scientists provided the necessary data. Lawyers fought battles with government agencies and in the courts. Lobbyists used traditional techniques of political persuasion with legislators and other officials—knowing that many corporations and other opponents of environmental efforts would be doing the same in opposition to their goals. Perhaps most of all, these organizations learned how to mobilize public opinion on their behalf.

Environmental Degradation

Water and Air Pollution

Perhaps the greatest force behind environmentalism was the condition of the environment itself. By the 1960s, the damage to the natural world from the dramatic economic growth of the postwar era was becoming impossible to ignore. Water pollution—which had been a problem in some areas of the country for many decades—was becoming so widespread that almost every major city was dealing with the unpleasant sight and odor, as well as the very real health risks, of polluted rivers and lakes. In Cleveland, Ohio, for example, the Cuyahoga River burst into flame from time to time beginning in the 1950s from the petroleum waste being dumped into it.

Perhaps more alarming was the growing awareness that the air itself was becoming unhealthy, that toxic fumes from factories and power plants and, most of all, automobiles were poisoning the atmosphere. Weather forecasts and official atmospheric information began to refer to "smog" levels—using a new word formed from a combination of "smoke" and "fog." In some large cities—Los Angeles and Denver among them—smog became a perpetual fact of life, rising steadily through the day, blotting out the sun, and creating respiratory difficulties for many citizens.

Environmentalists also brought to public attention some longer-term dangers of unchecked industrial development: the rapid depletion of oil and other irreplaceable fossil fuels; the destruction of lakes and forests as a result of "acid rain" (rainfall polluted by chemical contaminants); the rapid destruction of vast rain forests, in Brazil and elsewhere, which limited the earth's capacity to replenish its oxygen supply; the depletion of the ozone layer as a result of the release of chlorofluorocarbons into the atmosphere, which threatened to limit the earth's protection from dangerous ultraviolet rays from the sun; and most alarming, global warming, which if unchecked would create dramatic changes in the earth's climate and would threaten existing cities and settlements in coastal areas all over the world by causing a rise in ocean levels. Many of these claims became controversial, with skeptics arguing that environmentalists had not conclusively proven their cases. But most environmentalists—and many scientists—came to believe that the problems were real and deserving of immediate, urgent attention.

Earth Day and Beyond

On April 22, 1970, people all over the United States gathered in schools and universities, in churches and clubs, in parks and

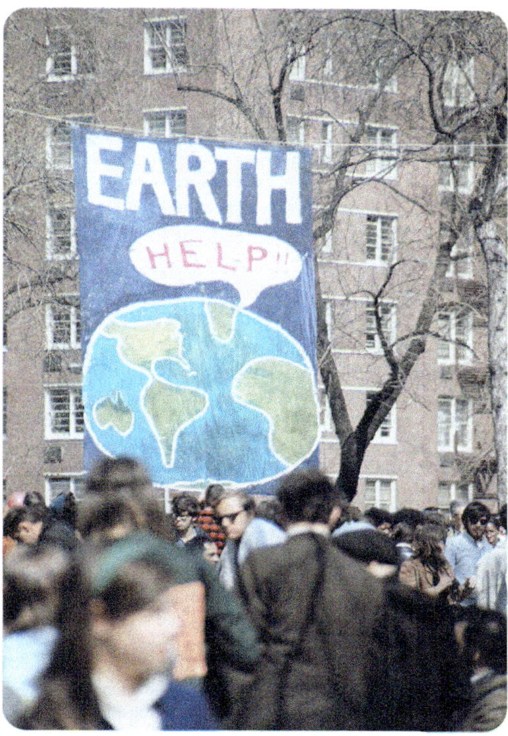

EARTH DAY, 1970 The first "Earth Day," April 22, 1970, was an important event in the development of the environmental movement. Conceived by Wisconsin senator Gaylord Nelson, Earth Day quickly gathered support in many areas of the United States and produced large demonstrations such as this one in New York City, where crowds surrounded a large banner portraying the earth crying out for help.

Reasoning Processes

Comparison Have students read the section "Environmental Advocacy." Ask them to create a Venn diagram comparing late twentieth century environmental advocacy with early twentieth century conservation and preservation activism. PCE GEO

Discussion and Activities

Evaluating Evidence Have students read the section "Environmental Degradation." Ask students to work in small groups to discuss what type of evidence described in the section they believe would have been most persuasive in convincing Americans to protect the environment at that time. GEO PCE

Discussion and Activities

Analyzing Points of View After students have read the section "Earth Day and Beyond," ask them to write a journal entry from the point of view of a participant or observer of an Earth Day demonstration describing their experiences. **PCE** **SOC**

auditoriums, for the first "Earth Day." Originally proposed by Wisconsin senator Gaylord Nelson as a series of teach-ins on college campuses, Earth Day gradually took on a much larger life. Carefully managed by people who wanted to avoid associations with the radical left, it had an unthreatening quality that appealed to many people for whom antiwar demonstrations and civil rights rallies seemed threatening. According to some estimates, over 20 million Americans participated in some part of the Earth Day observances, which may have made it the largest single demonstration in the nation's history.

THE FIRST "EARTH DAY"

The cautious, centrist character of Earth Day and related efforts to popularize environmentalism helped create a movement that had little of the divisiveness of other, more controversial causes. Gradually, environmentalism became more than simply a series of demonstrations and protests. It became part of the consciousness of the vast majority of Americans—absorbed into popular culture, built into primary and secondary education, endorsed by almost all politicians (even if many of them opposed some environmental goals).

It also became part of the fabric of public policy. In 1970, Congress passed and President Nixon signed the National Environmental Protection Act, which created a new agency—the Environmental Protection Agency—to enforce antipollution standards on businesses and consumers. The Clean Air Act, also passed in 1970, and the Clean Water Act, passed in 1972, added tools to the government's arsenal of weapons against environmental degradation.

EPA ESTABLISHED

POLITICS AND ECONOMICS UNDER NIXON

The Nixon administration described its policies as an attempt to restore balance: between the needs of the poor and the desires of the middle class, between the power of the federal government and the interests of states and local communities. In the end, however, economic and political crises—some beyond the administration's control, some of its own making—sharply limited Nixon's ability to fulfill his domestic goals.

DOMESTIC INITIATIVES

Many of Nixon's domestic policies were a response to what he believed to be the demands of his own constituency—conservative, middle-class people whom he liked to call the "silent majority" and who wanted to reduce federal "interference" in local affairs. Nixon tried, unsuccessfully, to persuade Congress to pass legislation prohibiting the use of forced busing to achieve school desegregation. He blocked the Department of Health, Education, and Welfare from cutting off federal funds from school districts that had failed to comply with court orders to integrate. At the same time, he began to reduce or dismantle many of the social programs of the Great Society and the New Frontier. In 1973, for example, he abolished the Office of Economic Opportunity, the centerpiece of the antipoverty program of the Johnson years.

DISMANTLING THE GREAT SOCIETY

Yet Nixon's domestic efforts were not entirely conservative. One of the administration's boldest efforts was an attempt to overhaul the nation's enormous welfare system. Nixon proposed replacing the existing system, which almost everyone agreed was cumbersome, expensive, and inefficient, with what he called the Family Assistance Plan (FAP). It would in effect have created a guaranteed annual income for all Americans: $1,600 in federal grants, which could be supplemented by outside earnings up to $4,000. Even many liberals applauded the proposal as an important step toward expanding federal responsibility for the poor. Nixon, however, presented the plan in conservative terms: as something that would reduce the role of government and transfer to welfare recipients themselves daily responsibility for their own lives. Although the FAP won approval in the House in 1970, concerted attacks by welfare recipients (who considered the benefits inadequate), members of the welfare bureaucracy (whose own influence stood to be sharply diminished by the bill), and conservatives (who opposed a guaranteed income on principle) helped kill it in the Senate.

FROM THE WARREN COURT TO THE NIXON COURT

Of all the liberal institutions that had aroused the enmity of the "silent majority" in the 1950s and 1960s, none had evoked more anger and bitterness than the Supreme Court. Not only had its rulings on racial matters disrupted traditional social patterns, but its staunch defense of civil liberties had, in the opinions of many Americans, contributed to the increase in crime, disorder, and moral decay. In *Engel v. Vitale* (1962), the Court ruled that prayers in public schools violated the constitutional separation of church and state, sparking outrage among religious fundamentalists and others. In *Roth v. United States* (1957), the Court had sharply limited the authority of local governments to curb pornography. In *Gideon v. Wainwright* (1963), the Court ruled that every felony defendant was entitled to a lawyer regardless of his or her ability to pay. In *Escobedo v. Illinois* (1964), it ruled that a defendant must be allowed access to a lawyer before questioning by police. In *Miranda v. Arizona* (1966), the Court confirmed the obligation of authorities to inform a criminal suspect of his or her rights. By 1968, the Warren Court had become the target of Americans of all kinds who felt the balance of power in the United States had shifted too far toward the poor and dispossessed at the expense of the middle class, and toward criminals at the expense of law-abiding citizens.

One of the most important decisions of the Warren Court in the 1960s was *Baker v. Carr* (1962), which required state legislatures to apportion electoral districts so that all citizens' votes would have equal weight. In dozens of states, systems of legislative districting had given disproportionate representation to sparsely populated

BAKER V. CARR

Discussion and Activities

Making Connections Have students read the section "Domestic Initiatives." Organize students into small groups to discuss whether Nixon would be considered a liberal, moderate, or conservative today. Ask groups to share their choice and reasoning with the class. **PCE**

rural areas, hence diminishing the voting power of urban residents. The reapportionment that the decision required greatly strengthened the voting power of African Americans, Hispanics, and other groups concentrated in cities.

Nixon was determined to use his judicial appointments to give the Court a more conservative cast. His first opportunity came almost as soon as he entered office. When Chief Justice Earl Warren resigned early in 1969, Nixon replaced him with a federal appeals court judge of conservative leanings, Warren Burger. A few months later, Associate Justice Abe Fortas resigned after allegations of financial improprieties. To replace him, Nixon named Clement F. Haynsworth, a respected federal circuit court judge from South Carolina. But Haynsworth came under fire from Senate liberals, black organizations, and labor unions for his conservative record on civil rights and for what some critics claimed was a conflict of interest in several of the cases on which he had sat. The Senate rejected him. Nixon's next choice was G. Harrold Carswell, a judge of the Florida federal appeals court of little distinction and widely considered unfit for the Supreme Court. The Senate rejected his nomination too.

Nixon was careful thereafter to choose justices of standing within the legal community to fill vacancies on the Supreme Court: Harry Blackmun, a moderate jurist from Minnesota; Lewis F. Powell Jr., a respected judge from Virginia; and William Rehnquist, a member of the Nixon Justice Department.

The new Court, however, fell short of what many conservatives had expected. Rather than retreating from its commitment to social reform, the Court in many areas became more committed. In *Swann v. Charlotte-Mecklenburg Board of Education* (1971), it ruled in favor of the use of forced busing to achieve racial balance in schools. In *Furman v. Georgia* (1972), the Court overturned existing capital punishment statutes and established strict new guidelines for such laws in the future. In *Roe v. Wade* (1973), it struck down laws forbidding abortions. In other decisions, however, the Burger Court was more moderate.

Bakke v. Board of Regents of California

Although the justices approved busing as a tool for achieving integration, they rejected, in *Milliken v. Bradley* (1974), a plan to transfer students across district lines (in this case, between Detroit and its suburbs) to achieve racial balance. While the Court upheld the principle of affirmative action in its celebrated 1978 decision *Bakke v. Board of Regents of California*, it established restrictive new guidelines for such programs in the future.

The Election of 1972

Nixon entered the presidential race in 1972 with a substantial reserve of strength. He had made significant achievements in foreign policy and in the de-escalation of the Vietnam War. His energetic reelection committee collected enormous sums of money to support the campaign. The president himself used the powers of incumbency with great effect, refraining from campaigning and concentrating on highly publicized international decisions and state visits. Agencies of the federal government dispensed funds and favors to strengthen Nixon's political standing in critical areas.

Nixon was most fortunate in 1972, however, in his opposition. The return of George Wallace to the presidential fray caused some early concern. Nixon was delighted to see Wallace run in the Democratic primaries and quietly encouraged him to do so. But he feared that Wallace would again launch a third-party campaign. The possibility of such a campaign vanished in May, when a would-be assassin shot the Alabama governor during a campaign rally in Maryland. Paralyzed from the waist down, Wallace was unable to continue campaigning.

George McGovern

The Democrats, in the meantime, were making their own contributions to the Nixon cause by nominating for president a representative of their most liberal wing: Senator George S. McGovern of South Dakota. An outspoken critic of the war, a forceful advocate of advanced liberal positions on most social and economic issues, McGovern seemed to embody many aspects of the turbulent 1960s that middle-class Americans were most eager to reject. McGovern profited greatly from party reforms (which he had helped to draft) that reduced the power of party leaders and gave increased influence to inexperienced delegates in the selection of the Democratic ticket. But those same reforms helped make the Democratic Convention of 1972 an unappealing spectacle to much of the public.

Nixon's Landslide

On election day, Nixon won reelection by one of the largest margins in history: 60.7 percent of the popular vote compared with 37.5 percent for the forlorn McGovern, and an electoral margin of 520 to 17.

The Troubled Economy

For three decades, the American economy had been the envy of the world. It had produced as much as a third of the world's industrial goods and had dominated international trade. The American dollar had been the strongest currency in the world,

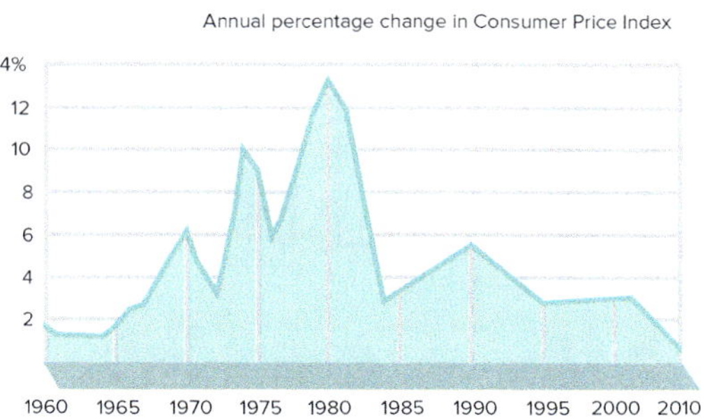

INFLATION, 1960–2010 Inflation was the biggest economic worry of most Americans in the 1970s and early 1980s, and this chart shows why. Having remained very low through the early 1960s, inflation rose slowly in the second half of the decade and then dramatically in the mid- and late 1970s, before beginning a long and steady decline in the early 1980s.

What caused the great spike in inflation in the 1970s?

Historical Thinking Skills

Argumentation Have students read the section "The Election of 1972." Ask them to create a campaign poster supporting either McGovern or Nixon in the presidential election of 1972. **PCE** **SOC** **WXT**

Answers

Inflation, 1960–2010.

Inflation in the 1970s was largely due to sharp increases in prices of imported oil.

Discussion and Activities

Analyzing Points of View Have students examine the image "Nixon Quits." Ask them to write a journal entry from the point of view of a Nixon supporter or Nixon critic describing their response to the news of Nixon's resignation. **PCE**

DEBATING THE PAST

WATERGATE

Decades after Watergate—one of the most famous political scandals in American history—historians and others continue to argue about its causes and significance. Their interpretations fall into several broad categories.

One argument emphasizes the evolution of the institution of the presidency over time and sees Watergate as the result of a much larger pattern of presidential usurpations of power that stretched back at least several decades. Arthur Schlesinger Jr. helped develop this argument in his 1973 book, *The Imperial Presidency*, which argues that ever since World War II, Americans have believed that the nation was in a state of permanent crisis, threatened from abroad by the menace of communism, threatened from within by the danger of insufficient will. The belief of a succession of presidents in the urgency of this crisis, and in their duty to take whatever measures might be necessary to combat it, led them gradually to usurp more and more power from Congress, the courts, and the public. Initially, this expansion of presidential power came in the realm of international affairs: covert and at times illegal activities overseas.

But in the postwar world, domestic politics began to seem inseparable from international politics. Gradually, presidents began to look for ways to circumvent constraints in domestic matters as well. Nixon's actions in the Watergate crisis were, in other words, a culmination of this long and steady expansion of covert presidential power. Jonathan Schell, in *The Time of Illusion* (1975), offers a variation of this argument, tying the crisis of the presidency to the pressure that nuclear weapons place on presidents to protect the nation's—and their own—"credibility." Other commentators (but few serious historical studies) go even further and argue that what happened to produce the Watergate scandals was not substantively different from the normal patterns of presidential behavior, that Nixon simply got caught where other presidents had not, and that a long-standing liberal hostility toward Nixon ensured that he would pay a higher price for his behavior than other presidents would.

A second explanation of Watergate emphasizes the difficult social and political environment of the late 1960s and early 1970s. Nixon entered office, according to this view, facing an unprecedentedly radical opposition that would stop at nothing to discredit the war and destroy his authority. He found himself, therefore, drawn into taking similarly desperate measures of his own to defend himself from these extraordinary challenges. Nixon made this argument in his own 1975 memoirs:

It was this epidemic of unprecedented domestic terrorism that prompted our efforts to discover the best means by which to deal with this new phenomenon of highly organized and highly skilled revolutionaries dedicated to the violent destruction of our democratic system.*

The historian Herbert Parmet echoes parts of this argument in *Richard Nixon and His America* (1990). Stephen Ambrose offers a more muted version of the same view in *Richard Nixon* (1989).

Most of those who have written about Watergate, however, search for the explanation not in institutional or social forces, but in the personalities of the people involved and, most notably, in the personality of Richard Nixon. Even many of those who have developed structural explanations (Schlesinger, Schell, and Ambrose, for example) return eventually to Nixon himself as the most important explanation for Watergate. Others begin there, perhaps most notably Stanley I. Kutler, in *The Wars of Watergate* (1990) and, later, *Abuse of Power* (1997), in which he presents extensive excerpts from conversations about Watergate taped in the Nixon White House. Kutler emphasizes Nixon's lifelong resort to vicious political tactics and his long-standing belief that he was a special target of unscrupulous enemies and had to "get" them before they got him. Watergate was rooted, Kutler argues, "in the personality and history of Nixon himself." A "corrosive hatred," he claims, "decisively shaped Nixon's own behavior, his career, and eventually his historical standing."

*From *RN: The Memoirs of Richard Nixon* (New York: Grosset & Dunlap, 1978). Copyright © 1978 by Richard Nixon.

NIXON QUITS Tourists outside the White House learn that Nixon will likely resign the presidency the next day: August 9, 1974.

© Bettmann/Getty Images

HISTORICAL THINKING SKILLS

Questions assume cumulative content knowledge from this chapter and previous chapters.

1. **Identifying Historical Developments** Identify three broad schools of historical interpretation regarding Watergate.
2. **Evaluating Evidence** Describe how historical evidence could be used to support each of the three broad schools of historical interpretation concerning Watergate.
3. **Developing Arguments** Analyze the school of thought you find most convincing. Be sure to support your argument using historical evidence from the text.

866 · CHAPTER 32

Answers

Debating the Past

1. Possible answer: Arthur Schlesinger, Jr. argues that presidential power had been increasing over a long period of time due to threats such as communism to the United States. Parmet and Ambrose, along with Nixon, argue that Nixon took the actions he did in order to defend himself and his reputation. Kutler suggests that Nixon had a long history of using harsh political methods to defend himself against his perceived enemies.
2. Possible answer: With the advent of the Cold War and unrest abroad as well as at home, Nixon felt it was necessary to take unprecedented action to counter these threats. Nixon's unstable personality and predilection to authoritarian tendencies led to his actions.
3. Student answers will vary, but they must cite specific historical evidence in their answer.

and the American standard of living had risen steadily from its already substantial heights. Many Americans assumed that this remarkable prosperity was the normal condition of their society. In fact, however, it rested in part on several advantages that were rapidly disappearing by the late 1960s: above all, the absence of significant foreign competition and easy access to raw materials in the Third World.

Inflation, which had been creeping upward for several years when Richard Nixon took office, soon began to soar; it would be the most disturbing economic problem of the 1970s. Its most visible cause was a significant increase in federal deficit spending that began in the 1960s, when the Johnson administration tried to fund the war in Vietnam and its ambitious social programs without raising taxes. But there were other, equally important causes. No longer did the United States have exclusive access to cheap raw materials around the globe; not only were other industrial nations now competing for increasingly scarce raw materials, but Third World suppliers of those materials were beginning to realize their value and to demand higher prices for them.

INFLATION

The greatest immediate blow to the American economy was the increasing cost of energy. More than any nation on earth, the United States based its economy on the easy availability of cheap and plentiful fossil fuels. Domestic petroleum reserves were no longer sufficient to meet this demand, and the nation was heavily dependent on imports from the Middle East and Africa.

For many years, the Organization of Petroleum Exporting Countries (OPEC) had operated as an informal bargaining unit for the sale of oil by Third World nations, but had seldom managed to exercise any real strength. But in the early 1970s, OPEC began to use its oil as both an economic tool and a political weapon. In 1973, in the midst of the Yom Kippur War, Arab members of OPEC announced that they would no longer ship petroleum to nations supporting Israel—which meant the United States and its allies in Western Europe. At about the same time, the OPEC nations agreed to raise their prices by 400 percent. These twin shocks produced momentary economic chaos in the West. The United States suffered its first fuel shortage since World War II. And although the boycott ended a few months later, the price of energy continued to skyrocket both because of OPEC's new militant policies and because of the weakening competitive position of the dollar in world markets.

OPEC

But inflation was only one of the new problems facing the U.S. economy. Another was the decline of the nation's manufacturing sector. American industry had flourished in the aftermath of World War II. By the 1970s, however, the climate for American manufacturing had changed significantly. Many of the great industrial plants were now many decades old, much less efficient than the newer plants that Japan and European industrial nations had constructed after the war. In some industries (notably steel and automobiles), management had become complacent and bureaucratic. Most important, American manufacturing now faced major competition from abroad—not only in world trade (which still constituted only a small part of the U.S. economy) but also at home. Automobiles, steel, and many other manufactured goods from Japan and Europe established major footholds in the U.S. markets. Some of America's new competitors benefited from lower labor costs than their U.S. counterparts.

Thus the 1970s marked the beginning of a long, painful process of deindustrialization, during which thousands of factories across the country closed their gates and millions of workers lost their jobs. New employment opportunities were becoming available in other, growing areas of the economy: technology, information systems, and many other "knowledge-based" industries that would ultimately drive an extraordinary (if unbalanced) economic revival in the 1980s and 1990s. But many industrial workers were poorly equipped to move into those jobs. The result was a growing pool of unemployed and underemployed workers; the virtual disappearance of industrial jobs from many inner cities, where large numbers of minorities lived; and the impoverishment of communities dependent on particular industries. Some of the nation's manufacturing sectors ultimately revived, but few regained the size and dominance they had enjoyed in the 1950s and 1960s.

DEINDUSTRIALIZATION

INEQUALITY

Inequality in income and wealth is a characteristic of every nation; but in the last four decades, that inequality has become dramatically more unequal in the United States. From the end of World War II to the middle of the 1970s, increases in incomes (and, to a lesser extent, increases in total wealth) grew at about the same rate across the range of incomes. People in the bottom 20 percent of the income scale saw their incomes increase at about the same rate that people in the top 20 percent of the income scale did. But beginning in about 1973, that pattern began to change dramatically. The top 20 percent of earners saw their incomes rise at a much higher rate than did the earners below them. The top 5 percent did even better. And the top 1 percent did far better still—earning 24 percent of total income. At the same time, people in the bottom 20 percent saw their incomes slowly decrease, while the middle-class earners saw their earnings remain relatively stagnant, with incomes rising at about the same rate as inflation.

There are many explanations for this growing inequality. The decline of industry in the United States has pushed many once-well-paid workers into much-lower-paid nonunion jobs. Income tax reductions have increased the incomes of the wealthiest Americans much more rapidly than they have increased the incomes of lower-income people. The growth of the financial sector, and the extraordinary wealth that many financiers have accumulated in recent decades, has helped concentrate income and wealth at the top in unprecedented ways. Whether this inequality is a danger to American democracy, as many people believe, or a product of economic success that has improved, or will improve, the lot of everyone, as many others believe, it is nevertheless the case that the incomes in the United States are far more unequal today than they were a generation or more ago.

Historical Thinking Skills

Argumentation After students have read the section "The Troubled Economy," ask them to make a list of the causes of American industrial struggles. Have students write a thesis statement that makes a claim about the most important cause(s) of the decline. **WOR** **WXT** **PCE**

Discussion and Activities

Making Connections Have students read the section "Inequality." Ask them to discuss as a class whether they believe that income inequality has increased or decreased since the 1970s. **WXT**

Reasoning Processes

Causation Have students read the section "The Nixon Response." Ask them to create a chart listing the causes of stagflation and the responses of the Nixon administration. Have students discuss in small groups whether they think the responses were more political or economic in nature. **PCE** **WXT**

THE NIXON RESPONSE

The Nixon administration responded to these mounting economic problems by focusing on the one thing it thought it could control: inflation. Placing conservative economists at the head of the Federal Reserve Board, he ensured sharply higher interest rates and a contraction of the money supply. But the tight money policy did little to curb inflation: the cost of living rose a cumulative 15 percent during Nixon's first two and a half years in office. Economic growth, in the meantime, declined. The United States was encountering a new and puzzling dilemma: "stagflation," a combination of rising prices and general economic stagnation.

"STAGFLATION"

In the summer of 1971, Nixon imposed a ninety-day freeze on all wages and prices at their existing levels. Then, in November, he launched what he called Phase II of his economic plan: mandatory guidelines for wage and price increases, to be administered by a federal agency. Inflation subsided temporarily, but the recession continued. Fearful that the recession would be more damaging than inflation in an election year, the administration reversed itself late in 1971: interest rates were allowed to drop sharply, and government spending grew. The new tactics helped revive the economy in the short term, but inflation rose substantially—particularly after the administration abandoned the strict Phase II controls.

In 1973, prices rose 9 percent; in 1974, after the Arab oil embargo and the OPEC price increases, they rose 12 percent—the highest rate since the relaxation of price controls shortly after World War II. The value of the dollar continued to slide, and the nation's international trade continued to decline.

THE WATERGATE CRISIS

Although economic problems greatly concerned the American people in the 1970s, another stunning development almost entirely preoccupied the nation beginning early in 1973: the fall of Richard Nixon.

THE SCANDALS

Nixon's crisis was in part a result of long-term changes in the presidency. Public expectations of the president had increased dramatically in the years since World War II; yet the constraints placed on the authority of the office had grown as well. In response, a succession of presidents had sought new methods for the exercise of power, often stretching the law, occasionally breaking it. Nixon greatly accelerated these trends. Facing a Democratic Congress hostile to his goals, he attempted to find ways to circumvent the legislature whenever possible. Saddled with a federal bureaucracy unresponsive to his wishes, he constructed a hierarchy in which virtually all executive power became concentrated in the White House. Operating within a rigid, even autocratic staff structure, the president became a solitary, at times brooding figure. Unknown to all but a few intimates, he also became mired in a pattern of illegalities and abuses of power that in late 1972 began to break through to the surface.

THE CHANGING PRESIDENCY

Early on the morning of June 17, 1972, police arrested five men who had broken into the offices of the Democratic National Committee in the Watergate office building in Washington, D.C. Two others were seized a short time later and charged with supervising the break-in. When reporters for the *Washington Post* began researching the backgrounds of the culprits, they discovered that among those involved in the burglary were former employees of the Committee for the Re-election of the President. One of them had worked in the White House. Moreover, they had been paid to execute the break-in from a secret fund of the reelection committee, a fund controlled by members of the White House staff.

THE WATERGATE BREAK-IN

Public interest in the disclosures grew slowly in the last months of 1972. Early in 1973, however, the Watergate burglars went on trial; and under relentless prodding from federal judge John J. Sirica, one of the defendants, James W. McCord, agreed to cooperate both with the grand jury and with a special Senate investigating committee. McCord's testimony opened a floodgate of confessions, and for months a parade of White House and campaign officials exposed one illegality after another. Foremost among them was a member of the inner circle of the White House, counsel to the president John Dean, who leveled allegations against Nixon himself.

Two different sets of scandals emerged from the investigations. One was a general pattern of abuses of power involving both the White House and the Nixon campaign committee, which included, but was not limited to, the Watergate break-in. The other scandal, and the one that became the major focus of public attention for nearly two years, was the way in which the administration tried to manage the investigations of the Watergate break-in and other abuses—a pattern of behavior that became known as the "cover-up." There was never any conclusive evidence that the president had planned or approved the Watergate burglary in advance. But there was evidence that he had been involved in illegal efforts to obstruct investigations and withhold information. Testimony before the Senate provided evidence of the complicity of Dean, Attorney General John Mitchell, top White House assistants H. R. Haldeman and John Ehrlichman, and others. As interest in the case grew to something approaching a national obsession, the investigation focused increasingly on a single question: in the words of Senator Howard Baker of Tennessee, "What did the President know and when did he know it?"

"COVER-UP"

Nixon accepted the departure of those members of his administration implicated in the scandals. But he continued to insist that he himself was innocent. There the matter might have rested, had it not been for the disclosure during the Senate hearings of a White House taping system that had recorded virtually every conversation in the president's office during the period in question. All the groups investigating the scandals sought access to the tapes; Nixon, pleading "executive

Discussion and Activities

Historical Reasoning and Argumentation Have students read the section "The Changing Presidency." Ask them to discuss with a partner whether Nixon's centralization of executive power was reasonable in response to rising expectations of the presidency and Democratic opposition in Congress. **PCE**

privilege," refused to release them. A special prosecutor appointed by the president to handle the Watergate cases, Harvard law professor Archibald Cox, took Nixon to court in October 1973 in an effort to force him to relinquish the recordings. Nixon fired Cox and suffered the humiliation of watching both Attorney General Elliot Richardson and his deputy resign in protest. This "Saturday night massacre" made the president's predicament infinitely worse. Not only did public pressure force him to appoint a new special prosecutor, Texas attorney Leon Jaworski, who proved just as determined as Cox to subpoena the tapes; but the episode also precipitated an investigation by the House of Representatives into the possibility of impeachment.

"SATURDAY NIGHT MASSACRE"

THE FALL OF RICHARD NIXON

Nixon's situation deteriorated further in the following months. Late in 1973, Vice President Spiro Agnew became embroiled in a scandal of his own when evidence surfaced that he had accepted bribes and kickbacks while serving as governor of Maryland and even as vice president. In return for a Justice Department agreement not to press the case, Agnew pleaded no contest to a lesser charge of income-tax evasion and resigned from the government. With the controversial Agnew no longer in line to succeed to the presidency, the prospect of removing Nixon from the White House became less worrisome to his opponents. The new vice president (the first appointed under the terms of the Twenty-Fifth Amendment, which had been adopted in 1967) was House Minority Leader Gerald Ford, an amiable and popular Michigan congressman.

In April 1974, in an effort to head off further subpoenas of the tapes, the president released transcripts of a number of relevant conversations, claiming that they proved his innocence. But even these edited tapes seemed to suggest Nixon's complicity in the cover-up. In July, the crisis reached a climax. First the Supreme Court ruled unanimously, in *United States v. Richard M. Nixon*, that the president must relinquish the tapes to Special Prosecutor Jaworski. Days later, the House Judiciary Committee voted to recommend three articles of impeachment, charging that Nixon had, first, obstructed justice in the Watergate cover-up; second, misused federal agencies to violate the rights of citizens; and third, defied the authority of Congress by refusing to deliver tapes and other materials subpoenaed by the committee.

U.S. v. RICHARD M. NIXON

NIXON'S FAREWELL Only moments before, Nixon had been in tears saying good-bye to his staff in the East Room of the White House. But as he boarded a helicopter to begin his trip home to California shortly after resigning as president, he flashed his trademark "victory" sign to the crowd on the White House lawn.

Discussion and Activities

Evaluating Evidence After students have read the section "The Scandals," ask them to discuss as a class whether President Nixon was guilty of a crime, and if so, what crime did he commit. Have students consider if Nixon could have remained in office if he had responded differently. **PCE**

Discussion and Activities

Analyzing Visuals Have students examine the image "Nixon's Farewell." Ask them to discuss in small groups if the details of the photo seem consistent with the occasion that it captures. **PCE**

Historical Thinking Skills

Argumentation After students have read the section "The Fall of Richard Nixon," ask them to discuss with a partner the evidence that led to Nixon's resignation. Have students consider what evidence was most problematic for the President, and if the evidence justified impeachment had Nixon not resigned. **PCE**

Even without additional evidence, Nixon might well have been impeached by the full House and convicted by the Senate. Early in August, however, he provided at last what many wavering members of Congress had begun to call the "smoking gun." Among the tapes that the Supreme Court compelled Nixon to relinquish were several that offered apparently incontrovertible evidence of his involvement in the Watergate cover-up. Only days after the burglary, the recordings disclosed, the president had ordered the FBI to stop investigating the break-in. Impeachment and conviction now seemed inevitable.

Nixon Resigns

For several days, Nixon brooded in the White House. Finally, on August 8, 1974, he announced his resignation–the first president in American history ever to do so. At noon the next day, while Nixon and his family were flying west to their home in California, Gerald Ford took the oath of office as president.

Many Americans expressed relief and exhilaration that, as the new president put it, "Our long national nightmare is over." But the wave of good feeling could not obscure the deeper and more lasting damage of the Watergate crisis. In a society in which distrust of leaders and institutions of authority was already widespread, the fall of Richard Nixon seemed to confirm the most cynical assumptions about the character of American public life.

POLITICS AND DIPLOMACY AFTER WATERGATE

In the aftermath of Richard Nixon's departure from office, many Americans wondered whether trust in the presidency, and in the government as a whole, could easily be restored. The administrations of the two presidents who succeeded Nixon tried to answer those questions.

THE FORD CUSTODIANSHIP

Gerald Ford inherited the presidency under unenviable circumstances. He had to try to rebuild confidence in government after the Watergate scandals and to restore economic prosperity in the midst of difficult domestic and international conditions.

Nixon Pardoned

The new president's effort to establish himself as a symbol of political integrity suffered a setback only a month after he took office, when he granted Richard Nixon "a full, free, and absolute pardon" for any crimes he may have committed during his presidency. Much of the public suspected a secret deal with the former president. The pardon caused a decline in Ford's popularity from which he never fully recovered.

The Ford administration enjoyed less success in its effort to solve the problems of the American economy. In his efforts to curb inflation, the president rejected the idea of wage and price controls and called instead for largely ineffective voluntary efforts. Ford had to deal with a serious recession in 1974 and 1975–a task made more difficult by the continuing energy crisis. In the aftermath of the Arab oil embargo of 1973, the OPEC cartel began to raise the price of oil–by 400 percent in 1974 alone, one of the principal reasons why inflation reached 11 percent in 1976.

Ford's Diplomatic Successes

Ford retained Henry Kissinger as secretary of state and continued the policies of the Nixon years. Late in 1974, Ford met with Soviet premier Leonid Brezhnev at Vladivostok in Siberia and signed an arms control accord that was to serve as the basis for SALT II, thus achieving a goal the Nixon administration had long sought. Meanwhile, in the Middle East, Henry Kissinger helped produce a new accord, by which Israel agreed to return large portions of the occupied Sinai to Egypt.

Ford's policies came under attack from both the right and the left. In the 1976 Republican primary campaign, Ford faced a powerful challenge from former California governor Ronald Reagan, leader of the party's conservative wing. He spoke for many on the right who were unhappy with any conciliation of communists. The president only barely survived the assault to win his party's nomination. The Democrats, in the meantime, were gradually uniting behind a new and, before 1976, little-known candidate: Jimmy Carter, a former governor of Georgia who organized a brilliant primary campaign by offer-

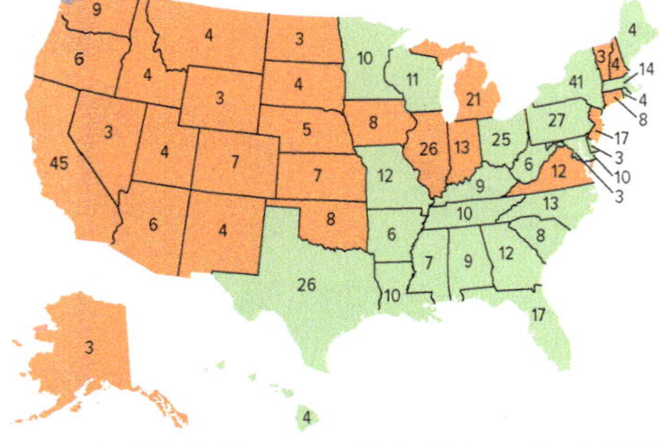

Candidate (Party)	Electoral Vote	Popular Vote (%)
Jimmy Carter (Democratic)	297	40,828,587 (50.0)
Gerald R. Ford (Republican)	240	39,147,613 (47.9)
Ronald Reagan (Independent Republican)	1	–
Other candidates (McCarthy [Ind.], Libertarian)	–	1,575,459 (2.1)

53.5% of electorate voting

THE ELECTION OF 1976 Jimmy Carter, a former governor of Georgia, swept the South in the 1976 election and carried enough of the industrial states of the Northeast and Midwest to win a narrow victory over President Gerald R. Ford. His showing indicated the importance to the Democratic Party of having a candidate capable of attracting support in the South, which was becoming increasingly Republican by the 1970s.

What drove so many southerners into the Republican Party?

Answers

The Election of 1976.

Many Southerners were attracted to Nixon's law-and-order policies, and were fearful of Democrats' efforts to expand civil rights.

ing honesty, piety, and an outsider's skepticism of the federal government. And while Carter's mammoth lead in opinion polls dwindled by election day, unhappiness with the economy and a general disenchantment with Ford enabled the Democrat to hold on for a narrow victory. Carter emerged with 50 percent of the popular vote to Ford's 47.9 percent and 297 electoral votes to Ford's 240.

THE TRIALS OF JIMMY CARTER

Like Ford, Jimmy Carter assumed the presidency at a moment when the nation faced problems of staggering complexity and difficulty.

CARTER'S LACK OF DIRECTION

Carter had campaigned for the presidency as an "outsider," representing Americans suspicious of entrenched bureaucracies and complacent public officials. He surrounded himself in the White House with a group of close-knit associates from Georgia. Carter was exceptionally intelligent, but his critics charged that he provided no overall vision or direction to his government. His ambitious legislative agenda included major reforms of the tax and welfare systems; Congress passed virtually none of it.

HIGH INTEREST RATES

Carter devoted much of his time to the problems of energy and the economy. Entering office in the midst of a recession, he moved first to reduce unemployment by raising public spending and cutting federal taxes. Unemployment declined, but inflation soared—largely because of the continuing increases in energy prices imposed on the West by OPEC. During Carter's last two years in office, oil prices rose at well over a 10 percent annual rate. Like Nixon and Ford before him, Carter responded with a combination of tight money and calls for voluntary restraint. By 1980, interest rates had risen to the highest levels in American history; at times, they exceeded 20 percent.

In the summer of 1979, instability in the Middle East produced a second major fuel shortage in the United States. OPEC announced another major price increase. Faced with increasing pressure to act (and with a dismal approval rating of 26 percent), Carter retreated to Camp David, the presidential retreat in the Maryland mountains. Ten days later, he emerged to deliver a remarkable television address. It included a series of proposals for resolving the energy crisis. But it was most notable for Carter's bleak assessment of the national condition. Speaking with unusual fervor, he complained of a "crisis of confidence" that had struck "at the very heart and soul of our national will." The address became known as the "malaise" speech (although Carter himself had never used that word), and it helped fuel charges that the president was trying to blame his inability to deal with the nation's problems on the American people.

CARTER IN THE WHITE HOUSE Jimmy Carter made a strenuous effort to bring a sense of informality to the presidency, in contrast to the "imperial" style many people had complained about during the Nixon years. He began on his inauguration day, when he and his family walked down Pennsylvania Avenue from the Capitol to the White House instead of riding in the traditional limousines. Here, Carter sits in a room in the White House preparing for a television address. He is sitting in front of a fire wearing a cardigan sweater, with his notes in his lap rather than on a desk.

HUMAN RIGHTS AND NATIONAL INTERESTS

Among Carter's most frequent campaign promises was a pledge to build a new basis for American foreign policy, one in which the defense of "human rights" would replace the pursuit of "selfish interests." Carter spoke out sharply and often about violations of human rights in many countries (including, most prominently, the Soviet Union). Beyond that general commitment, the Carter administration focused on several more traditional concerns. Carter completed negotiations begun several years earlier on a pair of treaties to turn over control of the Panama Canal to the government of Panama. After an acrimonious debate, the Senate ratified the treaties by 68 to 32, only one vote more than the necessary two-thirds majority.

Carter's greatest achievement was his success in arranging a peace treaty between Egypt and Israel. Middle East negotiations between Egyptian president Anwar Sadat and Israeli prime minister Menachem Begin had begun in 1977. When those talks stalled, Carter invited Sadat and Begin to a summit conference at Camp David in September 1978, and persuaded them to remain there for two weeks while he and others helped

Discussion and Activities

Evaluating Evidence After students have read the section "The Ford Custodianship," ask them to discuss in small groups whether President Ford should have pardoned Nixon. **PCE**

Historical Thinking Skills

Argumentation Have students read the section "The Trials of Jimmy Carter." Ask them to write a short letter to President Carter advising him on how to address the nation about instability in the Middle East and rising oil prices. **PCE** **SOC** **NAT**

Reasoning Processes

Continuity and Change Have students examine the image "Signing the Camp David Accords." Ask them to discuss in small groups how the document being signed represented continuity or change in American foreign policy. *(Continuity: The United States had supported Israel since its inception. Change: The Accord represented the first time an Arab state had recognized Israel.)* **WOR** **PCE**

SIGNING THE CAMP DAVID ACCORDS Jimmy Carter experienced many frustrations during his presidency, but his successful efforts in 1978 to negotiate a peace treaty between Israel and Egypt was his finest hour. Egyptian president Anwar Sadat and Israeli prime minister Menachem Begin join Carter here in the East Room of the White House in March 1979 to sign the accords.

mediate the disputes between them. On September 17, Carter announced agreement on a framework for an Egyptian-Israeli peace treaty. On March 26, 1979, Begin and Sadat returned together to the White House to sign a formal peace treaty—known as the Camp David accords—between their two nations.

CAMP DAVID ACCORDS

In the meantime, Carter tried to improve relations with China and the Soviet Union and to complete a new arms

WAITING FOR KHOMEINI Iranian women, dressed in traditional Islamic garb, stand in a crowd in Teheran waiting for a glimpse of the Ayatollah Khomeini, the spiritual and eventually also political leader of the Iranian Revolution.

Historical Thinking Skills

Contextualization Have students examine the image "Waiting for Khomeini." Ask them to discuss as a class the history of U.S.- Iranian relations prior to 1978. *(The U.S. supported the overthrow of Mossadegh in 1954 and the rule of the Shah in order to promote stability in the Middle East and to secure the supply of oil.)* **WOR** **PCE** **WXT**

agreement. He responded eagerly to the overtures of Deng Xiaoping, the new Chinese leader who was attempting to open his nation to the outside world. On December 15, 1978, Washington and Beijing announced the resumption of formal diplomatic relations. A few months later, Carter traveled to Vienna to meet with the aging Brezhnev to finish drafting the new SALT II arms control agreement. The treaty set limits on the number of long-range missiles, bombers, and nuclear warheads for both the United States and the USSR. Almost immediately, however, SALT II met with fierce conservative opposition in the United States.

The Year of the Hostages

Ever since the early 1950s, the United States had provided political support and military assistance to the government of the shah of Iran, hoping to make his nation a bulwark against Soviet expansion in the Middle East. By 1979, however, many Iranian people had come to resent his autocratic rule. At the same time, Islamic clergies (and much of the fiercely religious populace) opposed his efforts to modernize and Westernize a fundamentalist society. That produced a powerful revolutionary movement. In January 1979, the shah fled the country.

IRANIAN REVOLUTION

The United States made cautious efforts in the first months after the shah's abdication to establish cordial relations with the militant regimes that followed. By late 1979, however, revolutionary chaos in Iran was making any normal relations impossible. What power there was resided with a zealous religious leader, the Ayatollah Ruhollah Khomeini. In late October 1979, the deposed shah arrived in New York to be treated for cancer. Days later, on November 4, an armed group of militants invaded the American embassy in Teheran, seized the diplomats and military personnel inside, and demanded the return of the shah to Iran in exchange for their freedom. Fifty-three Americans remained hostages in the embassy for over a year.

Only weeks after the hostage seizure, on December 27, 1979, Soviet troops invaded Afghanistan, the mountainous Islamic nation lying between the USSR and Iran. The Soviet Union had in fact been a power in Afghanistan for years, and the dominant force since April 1978, when a coup had established a Marxist government there with close ties to the Kremlin. Carter called it the "gravest threat to world peace since World War II" and angrily imposed a series of economic sanctions on the Russians, canceled American participation in the 1980 summer Olympic Games in Moscow, and announced the withdrawal of SALT II from Senate consideration. The Soviet invasion of Afghanistan became a military quagmire and seriously weakened the Soviet regime.

The combination of domestic economic troubles and international crises created widespread anxiety, frustration, and anger in the United States—damaging President Carter's already low standing with the public and giving added strength to an alternative political force that had already made great strides. A diverse and powerful coalition, the "New Right," would dominate politics in the 1980s.

CARTER'S FALLING POPULARITY

Discussion and Activities

Evaluating Evidence After students have read the section "Human Rights and National Interests," ask them to make a list of the foreign policy accomplishments of the Carter Administration. Have students discuss as a class to what extent President Carter was able to accomplish his goal of a foreign policy based on the promotion of human rights. **WOR** **PCE**

Discussion and Activities

Analyzing Points of View Have students read the section "The Year of the Hostages." Ask them to write a journal entry from the point of view of one of the American hostages describing their experiences after the takeover of the U.S. embassy. **WOR** **PCE**

Discussion and Activities

Historical Developments Organize the class into two groups to review either the liberal expansion of the Kennedy and Johnson administrations or the conservative response under Nixon. Have representatives of each group present the most important social, economic, and political development of each period. You may conclude by having a class discussion to see if students can come to a consensus on the most important events covered in the chapter. **PCE** **WXT** **SOC** **NAT**

Key Terms

Students should be familiar with the key terms and be able to define them in the context of the expansion of liberalism during the Kennedy and Johnson administrations, and the conservative reaction starting with the Nixon administration Encourage students to use these terms in performing review exercises and exam practice for this chapter.

CHAPTER 32 REVIEW

CONNECTING THEMES

Chapter Thirty-Two explored the factors that led to an initial wave of liberalism in the Kennedy and Johnson administrations, along with the realized and unrealized accomplishments of the New Frontier and Great Society. The rise of a "New Left" and the counterculture significantly impacted the country's social, political, and economic direction. The counterculture movement energized the environmental movement, which challenged the nation to confront the unmistakable degradation of the environment.

The decades of the 1960s and 1970s illuminated the growing divide in American society. The decisions of the Warren Court expanded civil rights and liberties, which created intense division within the country. More conservative Americans felt these decisions increased disorder and shifted power too far to the left. Richard Nixon capitalized on these feelings to win reelection but quickly became embroiled in the Watergate crisis that led to his resignation. Upon assuming the presidency, Gerald Ford attempted to rebuild confidence in the government. But his popularity suffered when he pardoned Nixon and failed to revive the struggling economy. Democrat Jimmy Carter capitalized on these issues to win the presidency in 1976. Carter faced a multitude of issues, including a recession, soaring inflation, and an energy crisis. Public anxiety and opposition from the right only increased with the Iran Hostage Crisis and the Soviet invasion of Afghanistan in 1979. On the back of these anxieties, the coming decade would see a new force in American politics.

You should consider the following questions as you review the themes for this chapter:

- What caused the backlash against the liberal policies of the Great Society?
- How did the "New Left" and the counterculture impact American society and institutions?
- What were the short-term and long-term effects of the environmental movement on the United States?
- What was the effect of Nixon's domestic policies?
- What were the social, political, and economic challenges faced by Ford and Carter, following the resignation of Nixon?

KEY TERMS

Ayatollah Ruhollah Khomeini 873
Camp David Accords 872
Community Action Program 855
counterculture 860
George McGovern 865
Gerald Ford 869
Great Society 854
Immigration Act of 1965 856
Jimmy Carter 870
Medicaid 855
Medicare 855
New Left 857
OPEC 867
Rachel Carson 862
"silent majority" 864
Spiro Agnew 869
"stagflation" 868
Students for a Democratic Society (SDS) 857
Watergate 868
Weathermen 859

Go Online Chapter 32 Content Review

Assessing Student Understanding Use the online assessment to assess student understanding of concepts and topics within the chapter. You can assign the ready-made Chapter 32 Content Review or create your own from available questions. This easy-to-use tool helps you design assessments that meet the needs of different types of learners.

AP EXAM PRACTICE

Questions assume cumulative content knowledge from this chapter and previous chapters.

MULTIPLE CHOICE

Use the graph on page 865 and your knowledge of U.S. history to answer questions 1-3.

1. What was the most visible cause of the trend shown in the graph during the Nixon Administration?
   (A) Deflation occurred as Americans paid less for oil and the energy markets declined.
   (B) Inflation slowly impacted the economy as Americans were able to achieve independence from foreign sources of oil.
   (C) Inflation soared partly due to the increase in federal deficit spending.
   (D) Prices fell as other nations slashed their prices for increasingly scarce raw materials.
2. Overall economic changes during the time period led to
   (A) a shift from manufacturing to service and knowledge based jobs.
   (B) a shift from manufacturing in the Sun Belt to manufacturing in the Midwest and Northeast.
   (C) a shift from independent workers to union shops.
   (D) a shift from urban manufacturing to rural agriculture.
3. What foreign policy challenge contributed to the inflation trends illustrated by the chart during the Nixon administration?
   (A) Soviet invasion of Afghanistan
   (B) OPEC embargo in the midst of American support for Israel
   (C) withdrawal of American troops from Vietnam
   (D) Iran Hostage Crisis

SHORT ANSWER

Use your knowledge of U.S. history to answer questions 4 and 5.

4. Use the image on page 860 to answer A, B, and C.
   (A) Briefly describe ONE historical situation during the 1960s that gave rise to the event depicted in the photograph.
   (B) Briefly explain ONE specific historical event that gave rise to the counterculture during the 1960s.
   (C) Briefly explain ONE specific historical effect that was a result of the counterculture movement during the 1960s.
5. Answer A, B, and C.
   (A) Briefly describe ONE specific historical similarity between the counterculture movements of the 1920s and the 1960s.
   (B) Briefly describe ONE specific historical difference between the counterculture movements of the 1920s and the 1960s.
   (C) Briefly explain ONE specific historical effect which resulted from the rise of the counterculture movement of the 1960s.

LONG ESSAY

Develop a thoughtful and thorough historical argument that answers the question. Begin your essay with a thesis statement, and support it with specific historical evidence and examples.

6. Evaluate the extent of changes within American society that gave rise to a number of counterculture movements during the twentieth century.

Answers

Multiple Choice

1. C; **2.** A; **3.** B

Short Answer

4A) Possible answer: The escalation of the Vietnam War and the emergence of the modern civil rights movement both gave way to a sometimes violent counterculture that pitted the youth of America against authorities such as the police and National Guard.

4B) Possible answer: The post- World War II baby boom gave rise to the large number of youths during the 60s and 70s that largely comprised the counterculture.

4C) Possible answer: The backlash of the counterculture movement was the rise of conservative movements that would dominate American politics from the 80s forward.

5A) Possible answer: Both movements followed major world events, World War I and World War II. The counterculture movements following these events sought clarification on the essence of an American identity in the twentieth century.

5B) Possible answer: The counterculture movement of the 1920s was spurred by the economic growth following World War I and was disbanded by the Great Depression whereas the counterculture movement of the 60s was in some ways a response to the cultural components that accompanied consumerism.

5C) Possible answer: The counterculture of the 1960s created divisions within the American population which polarized partisan politics.

Answers

Long Essay

6. Possible Thesis: The anti-war movement was consistently active in American society during the twentieth century, but the Vietnam War divided people to a greater extent. Specific Historical Evidence: There was opposition to both world wars, but the counterculture was particularly focused on the Vietnam War. The media, particularly television, played a significant role in counterculture movements. The ability to broadcast images and news from the war to the American public helped fuel the counterculture.

Discussion and Activities

Making Connections Direct students' attention to the Questions to Consider posed at the beginning of Unit 8:

- What were the major causes and effects of the Cold War following World War II?
- What were the major continuities and changes during the modern civil rights movement in the second half of the twentieth century?
- What were the major causes and effects of the counterculture movement in the United States following World War II?

Discuss these questions as a class to review important concepts from the unit. To close the discussion, **ask:** What was the most important development in the United States between 1945 and 1980?

UNIT 8 AP EXAM PRACTICE

AP EXAM PRACTICE

As you answer the questions, consider how the historical developments, processes, and individuals in Unit 8 connect to those in previous units.

MULTIPLE CHOICE

Use the image on page 773 and your knowledge of U.S. history to answer questions 1 and 2.

1. As represented in the image, the Marshall Plan focused on what U.S. postwar effort?
   (A) the effort to form political alliances to counter Soviet aggression
   (B) the effort to withdraw from the European economy to focus on domestic issues
   (C) the effort to assist in rebuilding allied economies so nations could resist communist aggression
   (D) the effort to invade former allies to establish military bases in Europe

2. The Marshall Plan was an important part of the U.S. effort to
   (A) contain the spread of communism.
   (B) actively eliminate communism around the world.
   (C) assist in integrating European nations into the communist system.
   (D) encourage Allies to remain unaligned with either postwar superpower.

Use the image on page 800 and your knowledge of U.S. history to answer questions 3-5.

3. Which of the following developments in the 1950s most directly led to the lifestyle depicted in the photograph?
   (A) The widespread viewing of television and movies.
   (B) The widespread use of automobiles and the construction of interstate highways.
   (C) The growth of large suburban shopping centers.
   (D) The creation of increased consumer demand brought about through advertising.

4. What notable feature of American society in the 1950s is most reinforced in the photograph?
   (A) The desire of Americans to live in demographically homogenous neighborhoods.
   (B) The increase in the number of homes owning televisions.
   (C) The increase in women working outside the home to maintain a desired standard of living.
   (D) The idealization of traditional gender roles.

5. What postwar demographic trend most contributed to the lifestyle depicted in the photograph?
   (A) an increase in the birth rate and the centrality of children in daily life
   (B) the delay of marriage and focus on career advancement by women
   (C) the idealization of alternative and communal living arrangements
   (D) the movement of large populations into urban centers

Use the image on page 817 and your knowledge of U.S. history to answer questions 6-8.

6. Images were instrumental in gaining support for the civil rights movement as they were
   (A) published in textbooks across the country.
   (B) broadcast nationwide on television.
   (C) graphically described by national radio announcers.
   (D) largely restricted to black-owned media outlets.

7. The reaction to protests, such as the one in the image, convinced leaders of the civil rights movement of the importance of
   (A) a Supreme Court decision to order the desegregation of schools.
   (B) the passage of a national Civil Rights Act.
   (C) the passage of a constitutional amendment protecting equal employment.
   (D) the focus on state level legislation and enforcement policies.

8. Backlash against the civil rights movement could be witnessed in the support for which 1968 presidential candidate?
   (A) Hubert Humphrey
   (B) Robert Kennedy
   (C) Lyndon Johnson
   (D) George Wallace

Answers

Multiple Choice

1. C; **2.** A; **3.** B; **4.** D; **5.** A; **6.** B; **7.** B; **8.** D; **9.** A; **10.** D

Use the image on page 872 and your knowledge of U.S. history to answer questions 9-10.

9. Foreign policy achievements, such as the one in the image, represented an important settling of tensions that had been inflamed when the United States
   (A) supported Israel through ongoing Middle Eastern conflicts.
   (B) withdrew from South Vietnam in the midst of the Vietnam War.
   (C) refused to negotiate the peaceful end of the Korean conflict.
   (D) supported the French in their reassertion of colonial control in Vietnam.

10. In addition to the foreign policy turbulence of the 1970s, Americans had experienced domestic upheaval surrounding
   (A) the heavily contested Presidential election of 1972.
   (B) increasing economic division as more American workers joined unions and participated in large scale strikes.
   (C) the continued movement of the American population into Northeastern regions.
   (D) the resignation of President Richard Nixon as a result of the Watergate scandal.

SHORT ANSWER

Use the photograph on page 817 and your knowledge of U.S. history to answer question 11.

11. Answer A, B, and C.
   (A) Briefly describe a point of view illustrated by the photograph about civil rights demonstrators during the 1960s in the United States.
   (B) Briefly explain ONE specific cause that led to the event depicted in the photograph.
   (C) Briefly explain ONE specific effect that resulted from the event depicted in the photograph.

ESSAY

Develop a thoughtful and thorough historical argument that addresses the statement. Begin your essay with a thesis statement, and support it with specific historical evidence and examples.

12. Evaluate the extent of continuities in U.S. foreign policy from 1945 to 1980.

Answers

Short Answer

11A) Possible answer: One point of view illustrated by the photograph is that law enforcement in the South viewed African Americans and/or civil rights demonstrators as less than human and were willing to use violence against them.

11B) Possible answer: The increasing pressure of the judiciary and the federal government to enforce integration in Southern states encouraged civil rights activists to launch a series of nonviolent demonstrations in Birmingham.

11C) Possible answer: Many Americans were watching these scenes on television and were horrified. This helped garner more support for the civil rights movement and increased pressure on the federal government to take action.

Answers

Long Essay

12. Possible Thesis: Following the end of World War II, the U.S. and the Soviet Union were engaged in a Cold War. The policy of containment drove much of American foreign policy. Containment impacted international conflicts and increases in military spending. Specific Historical Evidence: The U.S. fought two major wars during this period based on containment: Korea and Vietnam. For these wars, containment meant military intervention. But containment also took the form of economic intervention through the implementation of policies like the Truman Doctrine and the Marshall Plan.

UNIT 9: 1980–PRESENT

Pacing Guide

Unit 9 explores key concepts from Period 9: 1980–Present of the AP U.S. History Curriculum Framework. It is recommended that 4–6% of the total instruction time for the entire course be spent on Period 9.

Key Concepts

9.1 A newly ascendant conservative movement achieved several political and policy goals during the 1980s and continued to strongly influence public discourse in the following decades.

9.2 Moving into the 21st century, the nation experienced significant technological, economic, and demographic changes.

9.3 The end of the Cold War and new challenges to U.S. leadership forced the nation to redefine its foreign policy and role in the world.

UNIT 9: 1980–PRESENT

CHAPTER 33: THE AGE OF REAGAN

CHAPTER 34: GLOBALIZATION AND POLARIZATION

THEMATIC LEARNING OBJECTIVES

- Analyze the rise of the "New Right" and its impact on the last decades of the twentieth century.
- Describe the domestic and foreign challenges faced by the U.S. administration at the end of the twentieth century and the beginning of the twenty-first century.
- Evaluate the reasons for and consequences of the "War on Terror."
- Compare and contrast the social and political climate during the Reagan and Trump administrations.
- Analyze the social, economic, and political effects of the COVID-19 pandemic on the United States.
- Identify the most significant challenges for the United States following the first two decades of the twenty-first century.

QUESTIONS TO CONSIDER

- What impact did the end of the Cold War have on U.S. domestic and foreign policies?
- What were the major causes and effects of conservative movements during the last 50 years in the United States?
- What were the most important continuities and changes in U.S. foreign policy during the "War on Terror?"

HISTORICAL DEVELOPMENTS: 1980–PRESENT

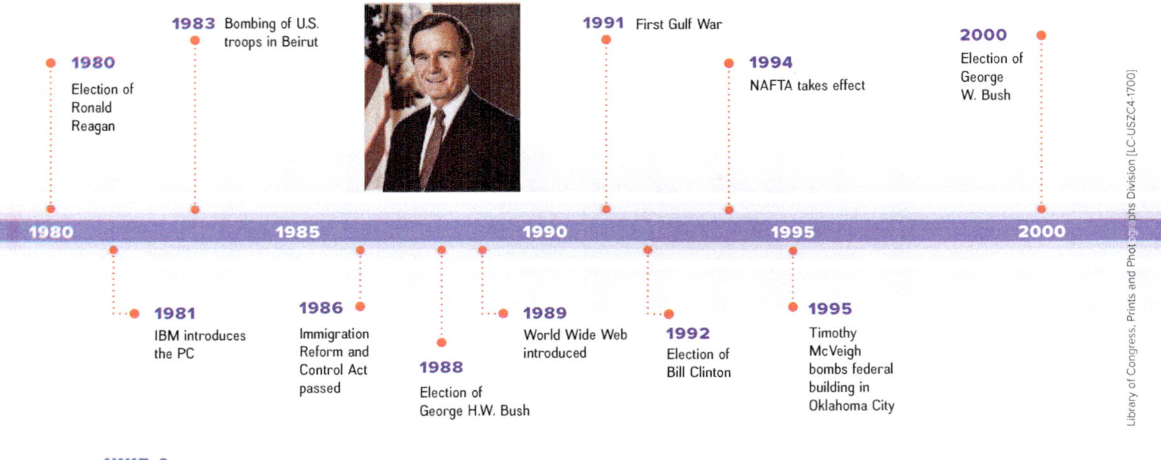

1980 Election of Ronald Reagan
1983 Bombing of U.S. troops in Beirut
1991 First Gulf War
1994 NAFTA takes effect
2000 Election of George W. Bush
1980
1985
1990
1995
2000
1981 IBM introduces the PC
1986 Immigration Reform and Control Act passed
1988 Election of George H.W. Bush
1989 World Wide Web introduced
1992 Election of Bill Clinton
1995 Timothy McVeigh bombs federal building in Oklahoma City

Library of Congress, Prints and Photographs Division [LC-USZC4-1700]

Discussion and Activities

Evaluating Have students examine the time line "Historical Developments: 1980–Present." **Ask:** Based on the time line and what you already know, which events deal with social, economic, diplomatic, or political issues? *(Social: World-Wide Web introduced, death of George Floyd; Diplomatic: First Gulf War, NAFTA, Iraq invasion and withdrawal; Political: Bush, Clinton, Bush, Obama, Trump elections, Trump supporters attack the Capitol;* ***Economic:*** *IBM introduces the PC, World-Wide Web, NAFTA, Affordable Care Act).* Which category seems to be most prevalent? **PCE** **WXT** **SOC** **WOR**

MAKING CONNECTIONS

Unit Nine focuses on the period in United States history from the Reagan Era to the present. The rise of a religious and conservative counter-movement to answer the liberalism of the 1960s and 1970s was the beginning of an ebb and flow of extremes in American politics that would persist into the twenty-first century.

The election of Ronald Reagan in 1980 represented the enshrinement of conservative values into American politics that would last throughout the decade. His economic policies focused on lowered tax rates and deregulation of industry to encourage economic growth. While the decade saw economic growth, the national debt increased and there were substantial cuts made to government social support systems. Reagan confronted the Soviets head-on, and he and Gorbachev came to dominate international relations, particularly nuclear armament. The collapse of the Soviet Union and the end of the Cold War would leave the United States as the dominant world power.

Iraq's invasion of Kuwait brought the United States back to the world stage under the administration of George H.W. Bush. The war was over quickly, but domestic economic issues again allowed for political fluctuation, and Democrat Bill Clinton won the presidency in 1994. His strong advocacy for free-trade agreements helped push the globalization of the economy forward. The advent of new technologies deepened global connections but also increased the disparity between nations and individuals.

George W. Bush won the presidency in the close and contested election of 2000. He soon faced the challenges of leading a nation stunned by terrorist attacks on the World Trade Center and the Pentagon. American society underwent significant changes as new security measures raised concerns about privacy and civil liberties. The ensuing "war against terrorism" and the redefining of America's role in the world significantly reshaped U.S. foreign policy. But in 2008, the financial crisis was preeminent in the minds of most Americans as they elected the first African American president, Barack Obama. Obama and his administration implemented economic stimulus programs and healthcare reforms. Yet many of his initiatives faced serious hurdles or failed to gain enough support in Congress. There was intense partisanship and an increasingly divided populous throughout Obama's second term and leading into the 2016 election.

The election of Donald Trump in 2016 illustrated the extreme partisanship that prevailed throughout the first two decades of the twenty-first century. Trump's rhetoric polarized the nation, with many Americans responding in anger and others with whole-hearted support. Trump and his administration disparaged globalism and withdrew from or renegotiated trade agreements. Foreign policy initiatives centered around "America First" ideologies, and the Trump administration pushed to remove American troops and support around the globe. Domestically, opposition to Trump's ideologies led to increasing tension and protests. The COVID-19 pandemic seemed to increase the divide among Americans as debates over precautions, the role of government, civil liberties, and science polarized society.

The partisanship and polarization continued with the election of Joe Biden in 2020. Trump and his supporters continued to assert victory citing massive voter fraud and other election interference despite the lack of any evidence. The Biden administration faced a divided nation, a pandemic, an unstable economy, and a world that viewed the United States with uncertainty.

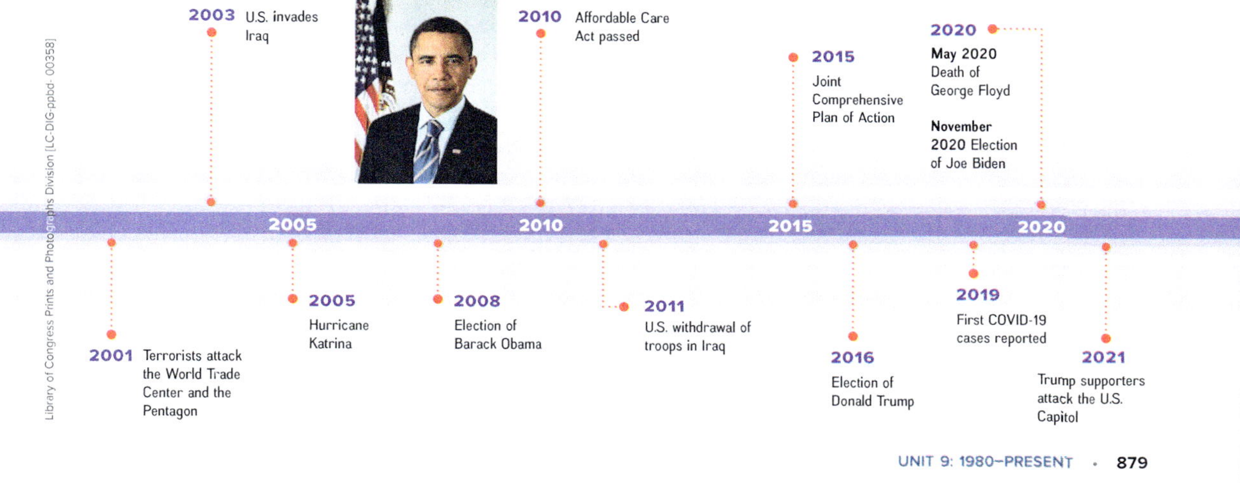

Library of Congress Prints and Photographs Division [LC-DIG-ppbd-00358]

Historical Thinking Skills

Contextualization Have students read the section "Making Connections." Discuss as a class the state of the nation in 1980. *(The impact of Watergate and the liberalism under the Kennedy and Johnson administrations on conservative movements and the political, economic, and social landscape of the 1980s.)* **PCE** **NAT** **ARC** **WXT** **SOC** **WOR**

Go Online Additional Resources

Adaptive Learning with SmartBook A proven adaptive learning program, SmartBook offers an interactive environment that helps students learn faster, study more efficiently, and retain more knowledge.

Assign this resource to differentiate instruction for students and report on year-long progression.

Pacing Guide

Chapter 33 explores key concepts from Period 9: 1980–Present of the AP U.S. History Curriculum Framework. The suggested instruction time for Chapter 33 is 2 days.

Key Concepts

9.1.I Conservative beliefs regarding the need for traditional social values and a reduced role for government advanced in U.S. politics after 1980.

9.3.I The Reagan administration promoted an interventionist foreign policy that continued in later administrations, even after the end of the Cold War.

33 THE AGE OF REAGAN

RONALD AND NANCY REAGAN The president and the first lady greet guests at a White House social event. Nancy Reagan was most visible in her efforts to make the White House, and her husband's presidency, seem more glamorous than those of most recent administrations. But she also played an important, if quiet, policy role in the administration.

CONNECTING CONCEPTS

Chapter Thirty-Three begins by examining the emergence of the New Right in response to significant changes in America's politics, economy, and culture in the 1970s. Conservatives — especially evangelical Christians alarmed at the social changes in the United States since the 1960s — mobilized and organized in the "Sunbelt" and suburbs across the country. An anti-tax revolt also provided a new and potent argument against government programs. These changes played a significant role in the 1980 presidential election with conservative Ronald Reagan defeating the unpopular incumbent, Jimmy Carter.

Reagan dominated American politics in the 1980s by forging a coalition of corporate elites, neo-conservative intellectuals, and populist conservatives from the South and West who distrusted political insiders. His "supply-side" economic policies lowered taxes and reduced regulations on corporations. But they also led to a higher national debt and lower spending on social programs. Internationally, the Reagan Doctrine sought to restore American pride and prestige by actively opposing communism in Grenada and Nicaragua.

After Reagan easily won reelection in 1984, he decided to place his trust in the new Soviet leader Mikhail Gorbachev. Together, the two men signed arms-reduction agreements that facilitated the waning of the Cold War. But Iraq's invasion of Kuwait forced Reagan's successor, George H.W. Bush, to confront Saddam Hussein in the First Gulf War of 1991. An international coalition assembled and, led by the United States, easily defeated the Iraqi Army. After the victory, Bush enjoyed great popularity, but political gridlock and economic recession cost him the 1992 election, which Bill Clinton won.

Discussion and Activities

Evaluating Evidence Have students read the section "Connecting Concepts." Ask students to create a KWL chart listing what they already know about the Reagan administration, what they want to know, and to add information to the chart that they learn throughout chapter. **PCE** **WXT** **SOC** **NAT**

CHAPTER 33
THE AGE OF REAGAN

As you read, you should:

- Analyze the reasons for and consequences of the rise of the New Right.
- Identify how conservative Christian movements organized their constituents and became a major force in politics.
- Evaluate the changing role of the government in the economy during the 1980s.
- Describe the role of internal and external migration to the South and West on the increase in political influence of the regions.
- Explain the factors that led to the decline of the Cold War during the 1980s.

THE RISE OF THE NEW AMERICAN RIGHT

Much of the anxiety in the 1970s was a result of public events that left many men and women shaken and uncertain about their leaders and their government. But much of it was also a result of significant changes in America's economy, society, and culture. Together these changes provided the right with its most important opportunity in generations to seize a position of authority in American life.

THE SUNBELT AND ITS POLITICS

RISE OF THE "SUNBELT"

The most widely discussed demographic phenomenon of the 1970s was the rise of what became known as the "Sunbelt"–a term coined by the political analyst Kevin Phillips. The Sunbelt included the Southeast (including Florida), the Southwest (particularly Texas), and above all, California, which became the nation's most populous state, surpassing New York, in 1964. By 1980, the population of the Sunbelt had risen to exceed that of the older industrial regions of the North and the East.

The rise of the Sunbelt helped produce a change in the political climate. The strong populist traditions in the South and the West were capable of producing progressive politics. But more often in the late twentieth century, they produced a strong opposition to the growth of government and a resentment of the proliferating regulations and restrictions that the liberal state was producing. Many of those regulations and restrictions–environmental laws, land-use restrictions, even the 55-mile-per-hour speed limit created during the energy crisis to force motorists to conserve fuel–affected the West more than any other region.

SAGEBRUSH REBELLION

The so-called Sagebrush Rebellion, which emerged in parts of the West in the late 1970s, mobilized conservative opposition to environmental laws and restrictions on development. It sought to portray the West (which had probably benefited more than any other region from federal investment) as a victim of government control. Its members complained about the large amounts of land the federal government owned in many western states and demanded that the land be opened for development.

SUBURBAN CONSERVATISM

Some of the most conservative communities in America–among them Orange County in southern California–were in suburbs. Many suburbs insulated their residents from contact with diverse groups–through the relative homogeneity of the population, through the transferring of retail and even work space into suburban office parks and shopping malls.

THE POLITICS OF RELIGION

In the 1960s, many social critics had predicted the extinction of religious influence in American life. *Time* magazine had reported such assumptions in 1966 with a celebrated and controversial cover emblazoned with the question "Is God Dead?" But religion in America was far from dead. Indeed, in the 1970s the United States experienced the beginning of a major religious revival, perhaps the most powerful since the Second Great Awakening of the early nineteenth century. It continued in various forms into the early twenty-first century.

Some of the new religious enthusiasm found expression in the rise of various cults and pseudo-faiths: the Church of Scientology; the Unification Church of the Reverend Sun Myung Moon; even the tragic People's Temple, whose members committed mass suicide in their jungle retreat in Guyana in 1978.

EVANGELICAL CHRISTIANITY

But the most important impulse of the religious revival was the growth of evangelical Christianity. Evangelicalism is the basis of many forms of Christian faith, but evangelicals have in common a belief in personal conversion (being "born again") through direct communication with God. Evangelical religion had been the dominant form of Christianity in America through much of its history, and a substantial subculture since the late nineteenth century. In its modern form, it became

Historical Thinking Skills

Contextualization Have students read the section "The Sunbelt and Its Politics." Ask them to discuss in small groups how the Sunbelt grew in influence by the 1980s. *(Migration to the Sunbelt accelerated during and after WWII with the growth of military contractors in the region and the migration of Americans, particularly senior citizens seeking milder climates.)* **MIG** **WXT** **PCE**

Go Online AP Exam Preparation

AP Exam Practice Use the online assessment to help prepare students for the AP Exam. You can assign the ready-made AP-style short answer questions, document-based questions, and multiple-choice questions assessing concepts, themes, and skills from Period 9 and AP style long-essay questions organized in sets of 3 questions from various time periods. You can also create your own tests from available questions. This easy-to-use tool helps you design assessments that meet the needs of different types of learners.

Discussion and Activities

Making Connections After students have read the feature, ask students to discuss as a class their own experiences in malls, and what the status of malls is in their own communities. **SOC** **WXT** **MIG**

PATTERNS OF POPULAR CULTURE

THE MALL

The modern mall is the direct descendant of an earlier retail innovation, the automobile-oriented shopping center, which strove to combine a number of different shops in a single structure, with parking for customers. The first modern shopping center, the Country Club Plaza, opened in Kansas City in 1924. By the mid-1950s, shopping centers—ranging from small "strips" to large integrated complexes—had proliferated throughout the country and were challenging traditional downtown shopping districts, which suffered from lack of parking and from the movement of middle-class residents to the suburbs.

In 1956, the first enclosed, climate-controlled shopping mall—the Southdale Shopping Center—opened in Minneapolis, followed quickly by similar ventures in New York, New Jersey, Illinois, North Carolina, and Tennessee. As the malls spread, they grew larger and more elaborate. By the 1970s, vast "regional malls" were emerging—Tyson's Corner in Fairfax, Virginia; Roosevelt Field on Long Island; the Galleria in Houston, and many others—that drew customers from great distances and dazzled them not only with acres of varied retail space, but also with restaurants, movie theaters, skating rinks, bowling alleys, hotels, video arcades, and large public spaces with fountains, benches, trees, gardens, and concert spaces. "The more needs you fulfill, the longer people stay," one developer observed.

Malls had become self-contained imitations of cities—but in a setting from which many of the troubling and abrasive features of downtowns had been eliminated. Malls were insulated from the elements. They were policed by private security forces, who (unlike real police) could and usually did keep "undesirable" customers off the premises. They were purged of bars, pornography shops, and unsavory businesses. They were off limits to beggars, vagrants, the homeless, and anyone else the managers considered unattractive to their customers. Malls set out to "perfect" urban space, recasting the city as a protected, controlled, and socially homogeneous site attractive to, and in many cases dominated by, white middle-class people.

Some malls also sought to become community centers in sprawling suburban areas that had few real community spaces of their own. A few malls built explicitly civic spaces—meeting halls and conference centers, where community groups could gather. Some published their own newspapers. Many staged concerts, plays, and dances. But civic activities had a difficult time competing with the principal attraction of the malls: consumption.

Malls were designed with women, the principal consumers in most families, mainly in mind. "I wouldn't know how to design a center for a man," one architect said of the complexes he built. They catered to the concerns of mothers about their own and their children's safety, and they offered products of particular interest to them. (Male-oriented stores—men's clothing, sporting goods, hardware stores—were much less visible in most malls than shops marketing women's and children's clothing, jewelry, lingerie, and household goods.)

Malls also became important to teenagers, who flocked to them in the way that earlier generations had flocked to street corners and squares in traditional downtowns. The malls were places for teenagers to meet friends, go to movies, avoid parents, hang out. They were places to buy records, clothes, or personal items. And they were places to work. Low-paying retail jobs, plentiful in malls, were typical first working experiences for many teens.

The proliferation of malls has dismayed many people, who see in them a threat to the sense of community in America. By insulating people from the diversity and conflict of urban life, critics argue, malls divide groups from one another and erode the bonds that make it possible for those groups to understand one another. But malls, like the suburbs they usually serve, also create a kind of community. They are homogeneous and protected, to be sure, but they are also social gathering places in many areas where the alternative is not the rich, diverse life of the downtown but the even more isolated experience of shopping in distant strips—or through catalogs, telephone, and the Internet.

EARLY MALLS In the 1960s most malls, such as Bullock's Fashion Square in Sherman Oaks, CA, were outdoor collections of stores focused largely on shopping.

TODAY'S MALLS Contemporary malls, such as the Grove shopping mall, in Los Angeles, CA, combine shopping with entertainment. By 2014 business in many malls began to decrease owing to online purchasing.

SHOPPING CENTER, NORTHERN VIRGINIA This small shopping center near Washington, D.C., was characteristic of the new "strip malls" that were emerging in the 1950s to serve suburban customers who traveled almost entirely by automobile.

HISTORICAL THINKING SKILLS

1. **Drawing Conclusions** How did the shopping mall change suburban life?
2. **Explaining Historical Developments** Are malls a unifying influence on social life? In what ways are malls divisive?
3. **Making Connections** Originally, malls were designed to cater largely to women, especially mothers. Has the target audience for malls changed? If so, to whom do malls principally cater today?

Answers

Patterns of Popular Culture

1. Possible answer: Malls were self-contained spaces and that largely reflected the homogeneous nature of suburbia.
2. Possible answer: Malls provided a social gathering place and targeted the retail needs of the female suburban consumer. They also could limit access to "undesirables" and avoided many of the issues that plagued downtown areas which created an isolated and homogeneous experience.
3. Student answers will vary. Some students may indicate that malls cater to a more diverse clientele while others may feel they are still focused on specific groups.

increasingly visible during the early 1950s, when evangelicals such as Billy Graham and Pentecostals such as Oral Roberts began to attract huge national (and international) followings for their energetic revivalism.

By the 1970s, more than 70 million Americans described themselves as "born-again" Christians–men and women who had established a "direct personal relationship with Jesus." Christian evangelicals owned their own newspapers, magazines, radio stations, television networks, and later Internet-based forms of communication. They operated their own schools and universities.

For some evangelicals, Christianity formed the basis for a commitment to racial and economic justice and to world peace. For many other evangelicals, the message of the new religion was very different–but no less political. They were alarmed by what they considered the spread of immorality and disorder in American life. They feared the growth of feminism and the threat they believed it posed to the traditional family. Particularly alarming to them were Supreme Court decisions eliminating religious observance from schools and, later, the decision guaranteeing women the right to an abortion.

Despite the historic antagonism between many evangelical Protestants and the Catholic Church, the growing politicization of religion in the 1970s and beyond brought some former rivals together. Catholics were the first major opponents of the Supreme Court's decision legalizing abortion in *Roe v. Wade*, but evangelical Protestants soon joined them in the battle. The rapidly growing Mormon Church, long isolated from both Catholics and traditional Protestants, also became increasingly engaged with the political struggles of other faiths. Mormons were instrumental in the 1982 defeat of the Equal Rights Amendment to the Constitution, which would have guaranteed women the same rights as men. And they too supported the evangelical agenda of opposition to abortion and homosexuality.

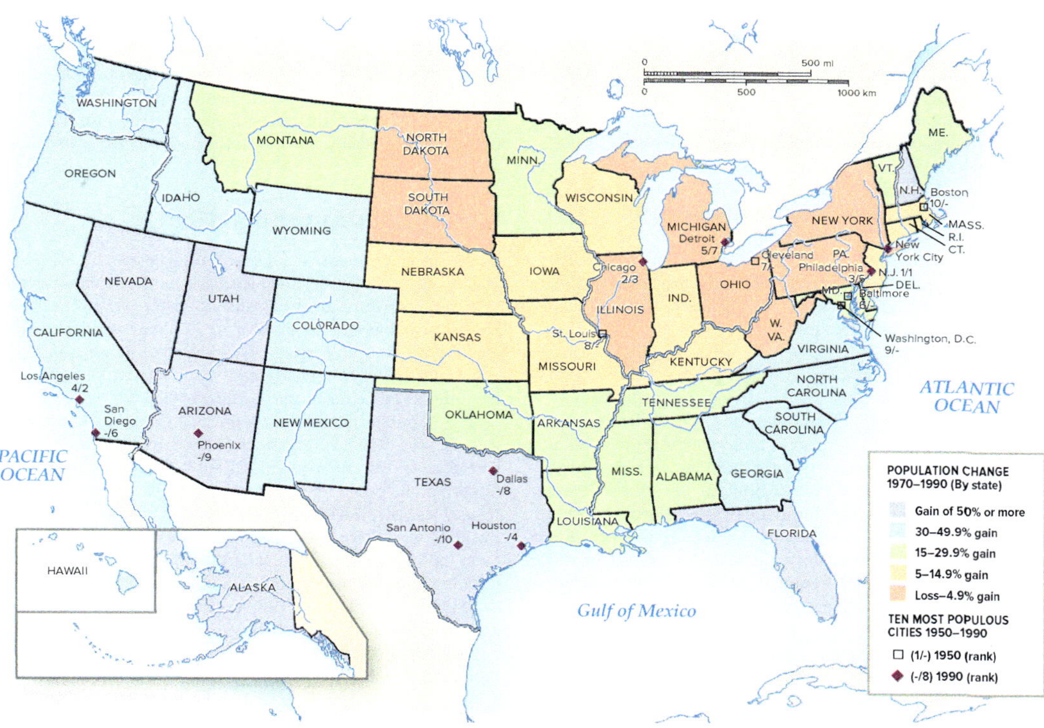

GROWTH OF THE SUNBELT, 1970–1990 One of the most important demographic changes of the last decades of the twentieth century was the shift of population out of traditional population centers in the Northeast and Midwest and toward the states of the so-called Sunbelt—most notably the Southwest and the Pacific Coast. This map gives a dramatic illustration of the changing concentration of population between 1970 and 1990. The orange/brown states are those that lost population, while the purple and blue states are those that made very significant gains (30 percent or more).

What was the impact of this population shift on the politics of the 1980s?

Discussion and Activities

Evaluating Evidence After students have read the section "The Politics of Religion," ask them to discuss in small groups how religion and politics became increasingly intertwined in the 1980s, and if they believe that trend has continued in the present. **PCE** **SOC** **ARC**

Answers

Growth of the Sunbelt, 1970–1990.

The growth of the Sunbelt led to a political re-alignment with increasing power for the Southwest and West with an emphasis on limiting exercise of federal power.

Discussion and Activities

Historical Developments and Argumentation Have students read the section "The New Right." Discuss as a class the factors that enabled the rise of Ronald Reagan in the Republican Party. *(Growing influence of the Sunbelt, particularly Reagan's home state of California, Reagan's communication skills, Reagan's early commitment to the conservative wing of the Republican Party.)* **PCE** **MIG** **SOC**

THE "NEW RIGHT"

Conservative Christians were an important part, but only a part, of what became known as the "New Right"—a diverse but powerful coalition that enjoyed rapid growth in the 1970s and early 1980s. Its origins lay in part in the 1964 presidential election. After Republican senator Barry Goldwater's shattering defeat, Richard Viguerie, a conservative activist and organizer, took a list of 12,000 contributors to the Goldwater campaign and used it to begin a formidable conservative communications and fund-raising organization. Beginning in the 1970s, largely because of these and other organizational advances, conservatives usually found themselves better funded and organized than their opponents. By the late 1970s, there were right-wing think tanks, consulting firms, lobbyists, foundations, and schools.

Another factor in the revival of the right was the emergence of a credible right-wing leadership to replace the defeated conservative hero, Barry Goldwater. Ronald Reagan, a well-known film actor turned political activist, became the hope of the right. As a young man, he had been a liberal and a fervent admirer of Franklin Roosevelt. But he moved decisively to the right after his second marriage, to Nancy Davis, a woman of strong conservative convictions, and after he became embroiled, as president of the Screen Actors Guild, in battles with communists in the union. In the early 1950s, Reagan became a corporate spokesman for General Electric and won a wide following on the right with powerful speeches in defense of individual freedom and private enterprise.

RONALD REAGAN

In 1964, Reagan delivered a memorable television speech on behalf of Goldwater. After Goldwater's defeat, he worked quickly to seize the leadership of the conservative wing of the Republican Party. In 1966, with the support of a group of wealthy conservatives, Reagan won the first of two terms as governor of California.

The presidency of Gerald Ford also played an important role in the rise of the right, by destroying the fragile equilibrium that had enabled the right wing and the moderate wing of the Republican Party to coexist. Ford touched on some of the right's rawest nerves. He appointed as vice president Nelson Rockefeller, the liberal Republican governor of New York and an heir to one of America's great fortunes. This appointment was offensive to many conservatives. Ford proposed an amnesty program for draft resisters, embraced and even extended the Nixon-Kissinger policies of détente, presided over the fall of Vietnam, and agreed to cede the Panama Canal to Panama. When Reagan challenged Ford in the 1976 Republican primaries, the president survived, barely, only by dropping Nelson Rockefeller from the ticket and agreeing to a platform largely written by one of Reagan's allies.

THE TAX REVOLT

Equally important to the success of the New Right was a new and potent conservative issue: the tax revolt. It had its public beginnings in 1978, when Howard Jarvis, a conservative activist in California, launched the first successful major citizens' tax revolt in California with Proposition 13, a referendum question on the state ballot rolling back property tax rates. Similar anti-tax movements soon began in other states and eventually spread to national politics.

PROPOSITION 13

The tax revolt helped the right solve one of its biggest problems. For more than thirty years after the New Deal, Republican conservatives had struggled to halt and even reverse the growth of the federal government. But attacking government programs directly, as right-wing politicians from Robert Taft to Barry Goldwater discovered, was not often the way to attract majority support. Every federal program had a political constituency. The biggest and most expensive programs—Social Security, Medicare, Medicaid, and others—had the broadest support.

In Proposition 13 and similar initiatives, members of the right separated the issue of taxes from the issue of what taxes supported. That helped them achieve some of the most controversial elements of the conservative agenda (eroding the government's ability to expand and launch new programs) without openly antagonizing the millions of voters who supported specific programs. Virtually no one liked to pay taxes, and as the economy weakened, that resentment naturally rose. The right exploited that resentment and, in the process, greatly expanded its constituency.

ATTACKING TAXES

THE CAMPAIGN OF 1980

By the time of the crises in Iran and Afghanistan, Jimmy Carter was in political trouble—his standing in popularity polls lower than that of any president in history. Senator Edward Kennedy, younger brother of John and Robert Kennedy, challenged him in the primaries. And while Carter managed to withstand the confrontation with Kennedy and win his party's nomination, he entered the fall campaign badly weakened.

The Republican Party, in the meantime, rallied enthusiastically behind Ronald Reagan. He linked his campaign to the spreading tax revolt by promising substantial tax cuts. Equally important, he called for restoration of American "strength" and "pride." Reagan clearly benefited from the frustration at Carter's inability to resolve the Iranian hostage crisis. He benefited even more from the accumulated frustrations of more than a decade of domestic and international disappointments.

On election day 1980, the one-year anniversary of the seizure of the hostages in Iran, Reagan swept to victory, winning 51 percent of the vote to 41 percent for Jimmy Carter, and 7 percent for John Anderson—a moderate Republican congressman from Illinois who had mounted an independent campaign. Carter carried only five states and the District of Columbia, for a total of 49 electoral votes to Reagan's 489. The Republican Party won control of the Senate for the first time since 1952 (53 Republicans versus 46 Democrats), and the Democrats retained a majority in the House by 277 to 158.

1980 ELECTION

Historical Thinking Skills

Argumentation Have students read the section "The Tax Revolt." Ask them to create a poster either supporting or opposing Proposition 13 in California. Have students consider what would be persuasive arguments on either side of the issue. **PCE** **WXT**

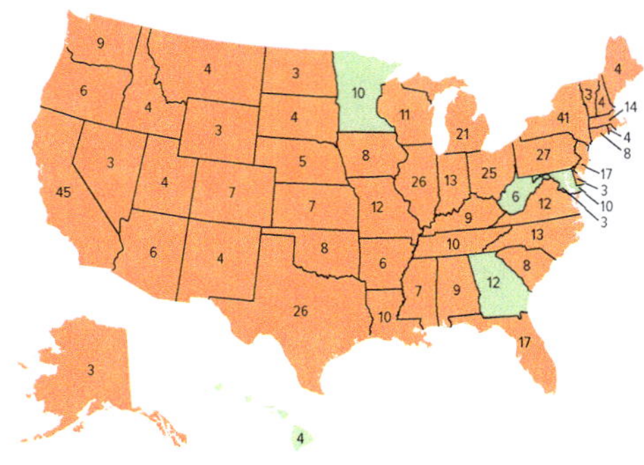

Candidate (Party)	Electoral Vote	Popular Vote (%)
Ronald Reagan (Republican)	489	43,901,812 (50.7)
Jimmy Carter (Democrat)	49	35,483,820 (41.0)
John B. Anderson (Independent)	—	5,719,722 (6.6)
Other candidates (Libertarian)	—	921,299 (1.1)

52.6% of electorate voting

THE ELECTION OF 1980 Although Ronald Reagan won only slightly more than half of the popular vote in the 1980 presidential election, his electoral majority was overwhelming—a reflection to a large degree of the deep unpopularity of President Jimmy Carter in 1980.

What had made Carter so unpopular?

On the day of Reagan's inauguration, the American hostages in Iran were released after their 444-day ordeal. The government of Iran, desperate for funds to support its floundering war against neighboring Iraq, had ordered the hostages freed in return for a release of billions in Iranian assets that the Carter administration had frozen in American banks.

THE "REAGAN REVOLUTION" AT HOME

Ronald Reagan assumed the presidency in January 1981, promising a change in government more fundamental than any since the New Deal of fifty years before. He had only moderate success in redefining public policy. But he succeeded brilliantly in making his own engaging personality the face of American politics in the 1980s.

THE REAGAN COALITION

Reagan owed his election to the widespread disillusionment with Carter and to the crises and disappointments that many voters associated with him. But he owed it as well to the emergence of a powerful coalition of conservative groups.

The Reagan coalition included an influential group of wealthy Americans associated with the corporate and financial world. What united this group was their firm commitment to capitalism and unfettered economic growth; a belief that the market offers the best solutions to most problems; a deep hostility to most government interference in markets. Central to this group's agenda in the 1980s was opposition to what it considered the "redistributive" politics of the federal government (especially its highly progressive tax structure) and hostility to the rise of what it believed were "antibusiness" government regulations. Reagan courted these free-market conservatives carefully and effectively.

CORPORATE ELITES

A second element of the Reagan coalition was even smaller, but also disproportionately influential: a group of intellectuals commonly known as "neo-conservatives," a firm base among "opinion leaders." Some of these people had once been liberals and, before that, socialists. But during the turmoil of the 1960s, they had become alarmed by what they considered to be the dangerous and destructive radicalism that they believed was destabilizing American life. Neo-conservatives were sympathetic to the demands of capitalists, but their principal concern was to reaffirm Western democratic, anticommunist values and commitments. Some neo-conservative intellectuals went on to become important figures in the battle against multiculturalism and "political correctness" within academia.

"NEO-CONSERVATIVES"

These two groups joined in an uneasy alliance in 1980 with the populist New Right. But several things differentiated the New Right from the corporate conservatives and the neo-conservatives. Perhaps the most important was the New Right's fundamental distrust of the "eastern establishment": a suspicion of its motives and goals; a sense that it exercised a dangerous, secret power in American life; a fear of the hidden influence of such establishment institutions and people as the Council on Foreign Relations, the Trilateral Commission, Henry Kissinger, and the Rockefellers.

POPULIST CONSERVATIVES

These populist conservatives expressed the kinds of concerns that outsiders, non-elites, have traditionally voiced in American society: an opposition to centralized power and influence, a fear of living in a world where distant, hostile forces are controlling society and threatening individual freedom and community autonomy. It was a testament to Ronald Reagan's political skills and personal charm that he was able to generate enthusiastic support from these populist conservatives while appealing to elite conservative groups whose concerns were in some ways antithetical to those of the New Right.

REAGAN IN THE WHITE HOUSE

Even many people who disagreed with Reagan's policies found themselves drawn to his attractive and carefully honed public image. Reagan was a master of television, a gifted public speaker, and—in public at least—rugged, fearless, and seemingly impervious to danger or misfortune. He turned seventy weeks after

Historical Thinking Skills

Argumentation After students have read the section "The Campaign of 1980," ask them to write a short speech supporting one of the candidates for president in 1980. Ask for volunteers to deliver their speeches to the class. You may consider holding a mock election. PCE SOC WXT NAT

Answers

The Election of 1980.

Economic stagnation and the Iran Hostage Crisis undermined Carter's support in the 1980 election.

Reasoning Processes

Comparison After students have read the section "Reagan in the White House," ask them to create a Venn Diagram comparing the three groups that made up the Reagan coalition: corporate elites, neo-conservatives, and populist conservatives. Have students discuss in small groups what the most important factors were that held the coalition together. **PCE** **SOC** **WXT**

taking office and was the oldest man ever to serve as U.S. president. But through most of his presidency, he appeared to be vigorous, resilient, even youthful. He spent his many vacations on a California ranch, where he chopped wood and rode horses. When he was wounded in an assassination attempt in 1981, he joked with doctors on his way into surgery and appeared to bounce back from the ordeal with remarkable speed.

Reagan was not much involved in the day-to-day affairs of running the government; he surrounded himself with tough, energetic administrators who insulated him from many of the pressures of the office. At times, the president revealed a startling ignorance about the nature of his own policies. Instead, he used the actions of his subordinates. But Reagan made active use of his office to support his administration's programs by fusing his proposals with a highly nationalistic rhetoric.

"Supply-Side" Economics

Reagan's 1980 campaign for the presidency had promised to restore the economy to health by a bold experiment that became known as "supply-side" economics or, to some, "Reaganomics." Supply-side economics operated from the assumption that the woes of the American economy were in large part a result of excessive taxation, which left inadequate capital available to investors to stimulate growth. The solution, therefore, was to reduce taxes, with particularly generous benefits to corporations and wealthy individuals, in order to encourage new investments. Because a tax cut would reduce government revenues (at least at first), it would also be necessary to reduce government expenses. A goal of the Reagan economic program was a significant reduction of the federal budget.

"REAGANOMICS"

Men and women whom Reagan appointed fanned out through the executive branch of government, reducing the role of government. Secretary of the Interior James Watt, previously a major figure in the Sagebrush Rebellion, opened up public lands and water to development. The Environmental Protection Agency (before its directors were indicted for corruption) relaxed or entirely eliminated enforcement of many environmental laws and regulations. The Civil Rights Division of the Justice Department eased enforcement of civil rights laws. The Department of Transportation slowed implementation of new rules limiting automobile emissions and imposing new safety standards on

DEREGULATION

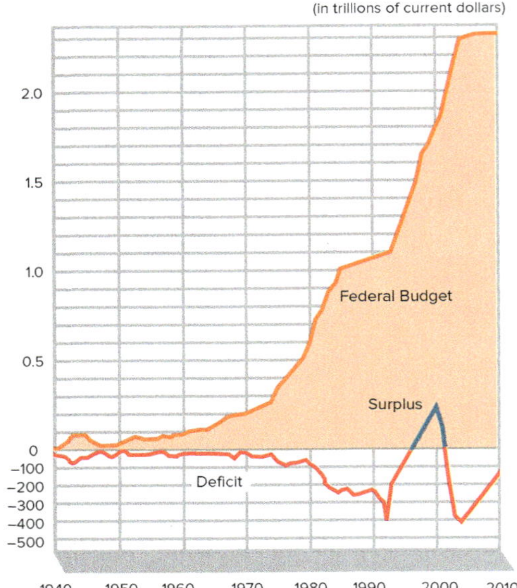

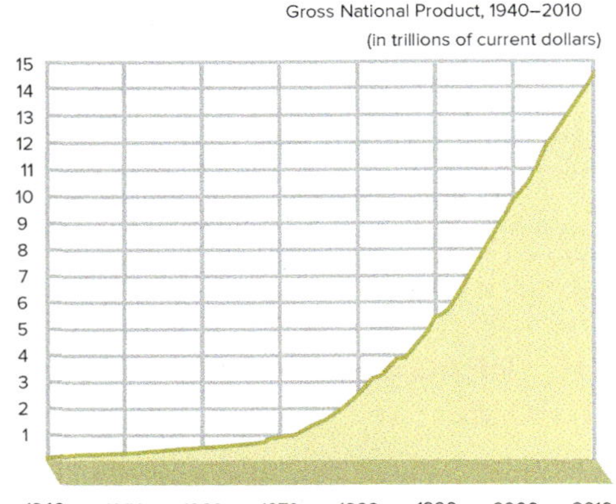

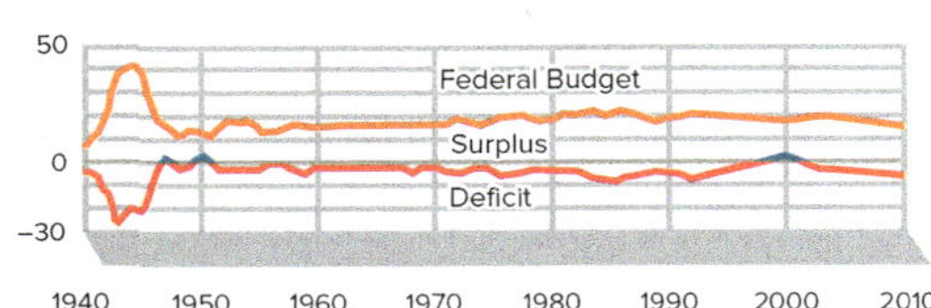

FEDERAL BUDGET SURPLUS/DEFICIT, 1940–2010 These charts help illustrate why the pattern of federal deficits seemed so alarming to Americans in the 1980s, and also why those deficits proved much less damaging to the economy than many economists had predicted. The upper chart shows a dramatic increase in the federal budget from the mid-1960s on. It shows as well a corresponding, and also dramatic, increase in the size of federal deficits. Gross national product (GNP) also increased dramatically, especially in the 1980s and 1990s, as the middle chart shows. When the federal budgets and deficits of these years, shown in the bottom chart, are calculated not in absolute numbers, but as a percentage of GNP, they seem much more stable and much less alarming. After 2000, these deficits rose significantly and became a much larger percentage of GNP.

What factors contributed to the increasing deficits of the 1980s? How were those deficits eliminated in the 1990s?

Answers

Federal Budget Surplus/Deficit, 1940–2010.

The deficits of the 1980s were partly caused by tax cuts and increased federal spending. The surpluses of the 1990s were mainly the result of increased tax collections resulting from the technology boom.

cars and trucks. By getting government "out of the way," Reagan officials promised, they were ensuring economic revival.

By early 1982, the nation had sunk into a severe recession. Unemployment reached 11 percent, its highest level in over forty years. But the economy recovered relatively rapidly. By late 1983, unemployment had fallen to 8.2 percent, and it declined steadily for several years after that. The gross national product had grown 3.6 percent in a year, the largest one-year increase since the mid-1970s. Inflation had fallen below 5 percent. The economy continued to grow, and both inflation and unemployment remained low through most of the decade.

The Fiscal Crisis

The economic revival did little at first to reduce federal budget deficits or to slow the growth in the national debt (the debt the nation accumulates over time as a result of its annual deficits). By the mid-1980s, the sense of a growing fiscal crisis had become one of the central issues in American politics. Having entered office promising a balanced budget within four years, Reagan had record budget deficits and accumulated more debt in his eight years in office than the American government had accumulated in its entire previous history.

SOARING NATIONAL DEBT

The enormous deficits had many causes, some of them stretching back over decades of American public policy decisions. In particular, the budget suffered from enormous increases in the costs of "entitlement" programs (especially Social Security, Medicare, and Medicaid), a result of the aging of the population and dramatic increases in the cost of health care. But some of the causes of the deficit lay in the policies of the Reagan administration. The 1981 tax cuts, the largest in American history to that point, contributed to the deficit. The massive increase in military spending by the Reagan administration added much more to the federal budget than its cuts in domestic spending removed.

WELFARE BENEFITS CUT

Reagan and the World

Reagan encountered a similar combination of triumphs and difficulties in international affairs. Determined to restore American pride and prestige in the world, he argued that the United States should once again become active and assertive

© Richard Falco/BlackStar

POVERTY IN AMERICA The American poverty rate declined sharply beginning in the 1950s and reached a historic low in the late 1970s. But the dramatic increase in income and wealth inequality that began in the mid-1970s gradually pushed the poverty rate upward again. By the mid-1980s, the poverty rate was approaching 15 percent, the highest in twenty years. In the image above, a group of children huddle against a barrier at an emergency center for homeless families in New York City in 1987.

Reasoning Processes

Evaluating Evidence After students have read the section "'Supply-Side Economics,'" ask them to create a chart organizing the successes and failures of Reagan's economic policies. Have students discuss as a class whether they think that supply-side economic policies were successful overall. **PCE** **WXT**

Discussion and Activities

Making Connections Have students read the section "The Fiscal Crisis." Discuss as a class why it was so difficult to control spending on entitlements. *(The more beneficiaries a program has, the more people who will fight to preserve those benefits, and the riskier it becomes for politicians to try to cut the programs.)* **PCE** **WXT**

Reasoning Processes

Comparing and Contrasting After students have read the section "The Reagan Doctrine," ask them to write a short paragraph comparing Reagan's foreign policy with previous presidents' foreign policies. *(Reagan continued a strong anti-communist orientation like most of his predecessors. He sent American troops into pro-communist countries much like Truman did in Korea and Kennedy and Johnson did in Vietnam.)* **WOR** **PCE**

in opposing communism and in supporting friendly governments whatever their internal policies.

Relations with the Soviet Union, which had been steadily deteriorating in the last years of the Carter administration, grew still more chilly in the first years of the Reagan presidency. The president spoke harshly of the Soviet regime (which he once called the "evil empire"), accusing it of sponsoring world terrorism and declaring that any armaments negotiations must be linked to negotiations on Soviet behavior in other areas.

Although the president had long denounced the SALT II arms control treaty as unfavorable to the United States, he continued to honor its provisions. But Reagan remained skeptical about arms control. In fact, the president proposed the most ambitious new military program in many years: the Strategic Defense Initiative (SDI), known to some as "Star Wars." Reagan claimed that SDI, through lasers and satellites, could provide an effective shield against incoming missiles and thus make nuclear war obsolete. The Soviet Union claimed that the new program would elevate the arms race to new and more dangerous levels and insisted that any arms control agreement begin with an American abandonment of SDI.

SDI

The escalation of Cold War tensions and the slowing of arms control initiatives helped produce an important popular movement in Europe and the United States in the 1980s calling for an end to nuclear weapons buildups. In America, the principal goal of the movement was a "nuclear freeze," an agreement between the two superpowers not to expand their atomic arsenals.

The Reagan administration supported opponents of communism anywhere in the world, whether or not they had any direct connection to the Soviet Union. This new policy became known as the Reagan Doctrine, and it meant a new American activism in the developing world. In October 1982, the administration sent American soldiers and marines into the tiny Caribbean island of Grenada to oust an anti-American Marxist regime that showed signs of a relationship with Moscow. In Nicaragua, a pro-American dictatorship had fallen to the revolutionary "Sandinistas" in 1979; the new government had grown increasingly anti-American (and increasingly Marxist) throughout the early 1980s. The Reagan administration supported the so-called contras, a guerrilla movement drawn from several anti-government groups and trying to topple the Sandinista regime.

REAGAN DOCTRINE

In June 1982, the Israeli army launched an invasion of Lebanon in an effort to drive guerrillas of the Palestinian Liberation Organization from the country. An American peacekeeping force entered Beirut to supervise the evacuation of PLO forces from Lebanon. American marines then remained in the city to protect the fragile Lebanese government. As a result, Americans became the targets in 1983 of a terrorist bombing of a U.S. military barracks in Beirut that left 241 marines dead. Rather than become more deeply involved in the Lebanese struggle, Reagan withdrew American forces.

The tragedy in Lebanon was an example of the changing character of Third World struggles: an increasing reliance on terrorism by otherwise powerless groups to advance their political aims. A series of terrorist acts in the 1980s–attacks on airplanes, cruise

TERRORISM

CONTRAS ON PATROL The Reagan administration's support for the Nicaraguan "contras," who opposed the leftist Sandinista regime, was the source of some of its greatest problems. Here, a small band of contras pause in the Nicaraguan jungle to catch their breath. The machine gunner carries an M-60 American weapon.

© Steven Clevenger/Corbis Historical/Getty Images

Reasoning Processes

Continuity and Change Have students examine the image "Contras on Patrol." Ask students to work in small groups to discuss if U.S. involvement in Nicaragua represented a continuity or change from previous American involvement in Latin America. Ask for volunteers to share their findings with the class. *(Students may share continuities in American interventions in Cuba, Haiti, Dominican Republic, El Salvador in the early twentieth century.)* **WOR**

ships, commercial and diplomatic posts; the seizing of American and other Western hostages–alarmed and frightened much of the Western world.

THE ELECTION OF 1984

Reagan approached the campaign of 1984 at the head of a united Republican Party firmly committed to his candidacy. The Democrats followed a more fractious course. Former vice president Walter Mondale, the early front-runner, fought off challenges from Senator Gary Hart of Colorado and the magnetic Jesse Jackson, who had established himself as the nation's most prominent spokesman for minorities and the poor. Mondale brought excitement to the Democratic campaign by selecting a woman, Representative Geraldine Ferraro of New York, to be his running mate and the first female candidate to appear on a national ticket.

In the campaign that fall, Reagan spoke of what he claimed was the remarkable revival of American fortunes and spirits under his leadership. His campaign emphasized such phrases as "It's Morning in America" and "America Is Back." Reagan's victory in 1984 was decisive. He won approximately 59 percent of the vote and carried every state but Mondale's native Minnesota and the District of Columbia. But Reagan was stronger than his party. Democrats gained a seat in the Senate and maintained only slightly reduced control of the House of Representatives.

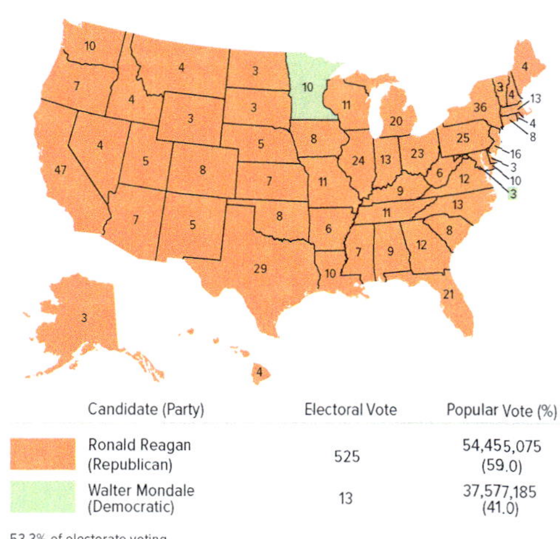

Candidate (Party)	Electoral Vote	Popular Vote (%)
Ronald Reagan (Republican)	525	54,455,075 (59.0)
Walter Mondale (Democratic)	13	37,577,185 (41.0)

53.3% of electorate voting

THE ELECTION OF 1984 In 1984, Ronald Reagan repeated (and slightly expanded) his electoral landslide of 1980 and added to it the popular landslide that had eluded him four years earlier. As this map shows, Mondale succeeded in carrying only his home state of Minnesota and the staunchly Democratic District of Columbia.

What were some of the factors that made Reagan so popular in 1984?

THE "REAGAN DOCTRINE" AND THE COLD WAR

Many factors contributed to the collapse of the Soviet empire. The long, stalemated war in Afghanistan proved at least as disastrous to the Soviet Union as the Vietnam War had been to America. The government in Moscow had failed to address a long-term economic decline in the Soviet republics and the Eastern-bloc nations. Restiveness with the heavy-handed policies of communist police states was growing throughout much of the Soviet empire. But the most visible factor at the time was the emergence of Mikhail Gorbachev, who succeeded to the leadership of the Soviet Union in 1985 and, to the surprise of almost everyone, very quickly became the most revolutionary figure in world politics in several decades.

THE FALL OF THE SOVIET UNION

MIKHAIL GORBACHEV

Gorbachev transformed Soviet politics with two dramatic new initiatives. The first he called *glasnost* (openness): the dismantling of many of the repressive mechanisms that had been conspicuous features of Soviet life for over half a century. The other policy Gorbachev called *perestroika* (reform): an effort to restructure the rigid and unproductive Soviet economy by introducing such elements of capitalism as private ownership and the profit motive.

The severe economic problems at home evidently convinced Gorbachev that the Soviet Union could no longer sustain its extended commitments around the world. As early as 1987, he began reducing Soviet influence in Eastern Europe. And in 1989, in the space of a few months, every communist state in Europe–Poland, Hungary, Czechoslovakia, Bulgaria, Romania, East Germany, Yugoslavia, and Albania–either overthrew its government or forced it to transform itself into a noncommunist (and, in some cases, actively anticommunist) regime.

TIANANMEN SQUARE

The challenges to communism were not successful everywhere. In May 1989, students in China launched a mass movement calling for greater democratization. But in June, hard-line leaders seized control of the government and sent military forces to crush the uprising. The result was a bloody assault on June 3, 1989, in Tiananmen Square in Beijing, in which a still-unknown number of demonstrators died. The assault crushed the democracy movement and restored the hard-liners to power. It did not, however, stop China's efforts to modernize and even Westernize its economy.

Early in 1990, the government of South Africa, long an international pariah for its rigid enforcement of "apartheid" (a system designed to protect white supremacy), began a cautious retreat from its traditional policies. It legalized the chief black party in the nation, the African National Congress (ANC), which had been banned for decades. On February 11, 1990, it released from prison the leader of the ANC, and a revered hero to black South Africans, Nelson Mandela. He had been in jail

Historical Thinking Skills

Argumentation Have students read the section "The Election of 1984." Ask students to create a social media campaign for either Reagan or Mondale for president. Have students discuss as a class why they believe Reagan won so decisively and if there was anything Mondale could have done to win more votes. **PCE** **NAT**

Answers

The Election of 1984.

Reagan was popular due to the recovering economy, and his skills as a communicator.

Historical Thinking Skills

Developing Arguments After students have read the section "The Fall of the Soviet Union," ask them to create a list of factors that led to the collapse. Have students write a thesis statement that makes a historically defensible claim about the most important reason for the fall of the Soviet Union. **WOR** **PCE**

for twenty-seven years. Over the next several years, the South African government repealed its apartheid laws. And in 1994, after national elections in which all South Africans could participate, Nelson Mandela became the first black president of South Africa.

In 1991, communism began to collapse at the site of its birth: the Soviet Union. An unsuccessful coup by hard-line Soviet leaders on August 19 precipitated a dramatic unraveling of communist power. Within days, the coup itself collapsed in the face of resistance from the public and, more important, crucial elements within the military. Mikhail Gorbachev returned to power, but it soon became evident that the legitimacy of both the Communist Party and the central Soviet government had been fatally injured. By the end of August, many of the republics of the Soviet Union had declared independence; the Soviet government was clearly powerless to stop the fragmentation. Gorbachev resigned as leader of the now virtually powerless Communist Party and Soviet government, and the Soviet Union ceased to exist.

DISSOLUTION OF THE USSR

REAGAN AND GORBACHEV

Reagan was skeptical when Gorbachev took power in 1985, but he gradually became convinced that the Soviet leader was sincere in his desire for reform. At a summit meeting with Reagan in Reykjavik, Iceland, in 1986, Gorbachev proposed reducing the nuclear arsenals of both sides by 50 percent or more, although continuing disputes over Reagan's commitment to the SDI program prevented agreements. But in 1988, after Reagan and Gorbachev exchanged cordial visits to each other's capitals, the two superpowers signed a treaty eliminating American and Soviet intermediate-range nuclear forces (INF) from Europe–the most significant arms control agreement of the nuclear age. At about the same time, Gorbachev ended the Soviet Union's long and frustrating military involvement in Afghanistan.

THE FADING OF THE REAGAN REVOLUTION

For a time, the dramatic changes around the world and Reagan's personal popularity deflected attention from a series of political scandals. There were revelations of illegality, corruption, and ethical lapses in the Environmental Protection Agency, the CIA, the Department of Defense, the Department of Labor, the Department of Justice, and the Department of Housing and Urban Development. A more serious scandal emerged within the savings and loan industry, which the Reagan administration had helped deregulate in the early 1980s.

SAVINGS AND LOAN CRISIS

But the most politically damaging scandal of the Reagan years came to light in November 1986, when the White House conceded that it had sold weapons to the revolutionary government of Iran as part of a largely unsuccessful effort to secure the release of several Americans being held hostage by radical Islamic groups in the Middle East. Even more damaging was the revelation that some of the money from the arms deal with Iran had been covertly and illegally funneled into a fund to aid the contras in Nicaragua.

In the months that followed, aggressive reporting and congressional hearings exposed a widespread pattern of illegal covert activities orchestrated by the White House and dedicated to advancing the administration's foreign policy aims. The Iran-contra scandal, as it became known, did serious damage to the Reagan presidency.

IRAN-CONTRA SCANDAL

THE FALL OF THE BERLIN WALL The Berlin Wall is widely considered to have "fallen" on November 9, 1989. Starting on that date and in the days and weeks that followed, people used sledgehammers and picks to tear the wall down, often keeping the broken pieces as souvenirs of this symbolic conclusion of the Cold War.

Discussion and Activities

Analyzing Points of View Have students examine the image "The Fall of the Berlin Wall." Ask them to write a short journal entry from the point of view of a Berliner who was present at the event, or an American high school student watching the event on television describing their reactions to the event. **WOR** **SOC**

THE ELECTION OF 1988

The fraying of the Reagan administration helped the Democrats regain control of the U.S. Senate in 1986 and fueled hopes for a presidential victory in 1988. Even so, several of the most popular figures in the Democratic Party refused to run, and the nomination finally went to a previously little-known figure: Michael Dukakis, a three-term democratic governor of Massachusetts. Dukakis was a flat and somewhat dull campaigner. But Democrats were optimistic about their prospects in 1988, largely because their opponent, Vice President George H. W. Bush, had failed to spark public enthusiasm.

Beginning at the Republican Convention, however, Bush staged a remarkable turnaround by making his campaign a long, relentless attack on Dukakis, tying him to all the unpopular social and cultural stances Americans had come to identify with "liberals." The campaign revealed the new political aggressiveness of the Republican right. Bush won a substantial victory in November: 54 percent of the popular vote to Dukakis's 46 percent, and 426 electoral votes to Dukakis's 112. But the Democrats retained secure majorities in both houses of Congress.

THE FIRST BUSH PRESIDENCY

The broad popularity George H. W. Bush enjoyed during his first three years in office was partly a result of his subdued, unthreatening public image. But it was primarily because of the wonder and excitement with which Americans viewed the dramatic events in the rest of the world. Bush moved cautiously at first in dealing with the changes in the Soviet Union. But like Reagan, he eventually cooperated with Gorbachev and reached a series of significant agreements with the Soviet Union in its waning years. The United States and the Soviet Union moved rapidly toward even more far-reaching arms reduction agreements.

On domestic issues, the Bush administration was less successful. His administration inherited a heavy burden of debt and a federal deficit that had been growing for nearly a decade. The president's pledges to reduce the deficit and simultaneously to promise "no new taxes" were in conflict with one another. Bush faced a Democratic Congress with an agenda very different from his own.

POLITICAL GRIDLOCK

The Congress and the White House managed on occasion to agree on significant measures. They cooperated in producing the plan to salvage the floundering savings and loan industry.

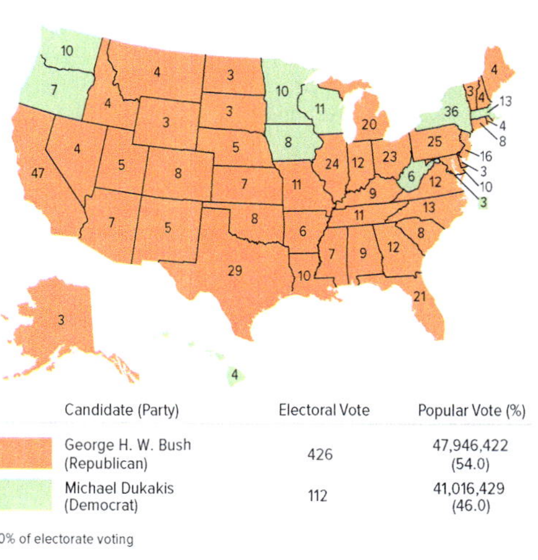

THE ELECTION OF 1988 Democrats had high hopes going into the election of 1988, but Vice President George Bush won a decisive victory over Michael Dukakis, who did only slightly better than Walter Mondale had done four years earlier.

What made it so difficult for a Democrat to challenge the Republicans in 1988 after eight years of a Republican administration?

THE BUSH CAMPAIGN, 1988 Vice President George Bush had never been an effective campaigner, but in 1988 he revived his candidacy with an unabashed attack on his opponent's values and patriotism. Bush missed no chance to surround himself with patriotic symbols, including this red, white, and blue hot-air balloon in Kentucky.

Discussion and Activities

Speculating Have students read the section "The Election of 1980." Ask them to discuss with a partner why they think Reagan's popularity remained fairly high despite the scandals late in his administration. Ask for volunteers to share their findings and discuss as a class. *(The economy continued to grow, many of Reagan's policies remained popular, and many voters did not hold the President directly responsible for the scandals.)* **PCE**

Answers

The Election of 1988.

Reagan's ongoing popularity and the growing economy made it difficult for a Democrat to win election in 1988.

Discussion and Activities

Evaluating Evidence After students have read the section "The First Bush Presidency," ask them to create a T-chart listing successes and failures of the Bush administration. Have students discuss in small groups which they think were greater and why. **WOR** **PCE** **WXT** **SOC**

In 1990, the president bowed to congressional pressure and agreed to a significant tax increase as part of a multiyear "budget package" designed to reduce the deficit—thus violating his own 1988 campaign pledge.

But the most serious domestic problem facing the Bush administration was one for which neither the president nor Congress had any answer: a recession that began late in 1990 and slowly increased its grip on the national economy in 1991 and 1992. Because of the enormous level of debt that corporations (and individuals) had accumulated in the 1980s, the recession caused an unusual number of bankruptcies. It also increased fear and frustration among middle- and working-class Americans and put pressure on the government to address such problems as the rising cost of health care.

1990 RECESSION

THE FIRST GULF WAR

The collapse of the Soviet Union in 1989–1991 had left the United States in the unanticipated position of being the only real superpower in the world. One result was that the United States would reduce its military strength and concentrate its energies and resources on pressing domestic problems. Another was that America would continue to use its power actively, not to fight communism but to defend its regional and economic interests. In 1989, that led the administration to order an invasion of Panama, which overthrew the unpopular military leader Manuel Noriega (under indictment in the United States for drug trafficking) and replaced him with an elected, pro-American regime.

On August 2, 1990, the armed forces of Iraq invaded and quickly overwhelmed their small, oil-rich neighbor, the emirate of Kuwait. Saddam Hussein, the militaristic leader of Iraq, soon announced that he was annexing Kuwait and set out to entrench his forces there. After some initial indecision, the Bush administration agreed to lead other nations in a campaign to force Iraq out of Kuwait—through the pressure of economic sanctions if possible, through military force if necessary. Within a few weeks, Bush had persuaded virtually every important government in the world, including the Soviet Union and almost all the Arab and Islamic states, to join in a United Nations–sanctioned trade embargo of Iraq.

INVASION OF KUWAIT

At the same time, the United States and its allies (including Great Britain, France, Egypt, and Saudi Arabia) began deploying a large military force along the border between Kuwait and Saudi Arabia, a force that ultimately reached 690,000 troops (425,000 of them American). On November 29, the United Nations, at the request of the United States, voted to authorize military action to expel Iraq from Kuwait if Iraq did not leave by January 15, 1991. On January 12, both houses of Congress voted to authorize the use of force against Iraq. And on January 16, American and allied air forces began a massive bombardment of Iraqi forces in Kuwait and of military and industrial installations in Iraq itself.

The allied bombing continued for six weeks. On February 23, allied (primarily American) forces under the command of General Norman Schwarzkopf began a major ground offensive—not primarily against the heavily entrenched Iraqi forces along the Kuwait border, as expected, but to the north of them into Iraq itself. The allied armies encountered almost no resistance and suffered relatively few casualties (141 fatalities). Estimates of Iraqi deaths in the war were 100,000 or more. On February 28, Iraq announced its acceptance of allied terms for a cease-fire, and the brief Persian Gulf War came to an end.

The quick and (for America) relatively painless victory over Iraq was highly popular in the United States. But the tyrannical regime of Saddam Hussein survived, weakened but still ruthless.

BURNING OIL FIELDS With the advance of Coalition forces into Kuwait, the retreating Iraqi military set fire to hundreds of oil wells and other oil-related resources to punish Kuwaiti overproduction and to create smoke screens to block "smart weapons" (guided bombs) and satellites.

Reasoning Processes

Analyzing Visuals Have students examine the image "Burning Oil Fields." Ask them to identify and discuss in small groups the details within the photo that indicate if the image depicts victory or defeat. Groups should be prepared to defend their position based on their discussion. **WOR** **WXT**

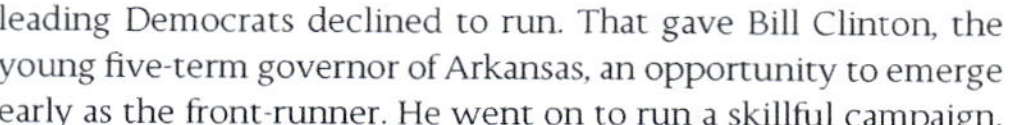

The Gulf War preserved an independent nation and kept an important source of oil from falling into the hands of Iraq. But many Muslims, watching Americans attacking their fellow religionists, became incensed by the U.S. presence in the region. The most conservative and militant Muslims were insulted by the presence of women in the United Nations forces. But even more-moderate Middle East Muslims began to believe that America was a threat to their world. Even before the Gulf War, Middle Eastern terrorists had been targeting Americans in the region. Their determination to threaten America grew significantly in its aftermath.

THE ELECTION OF 1992

President Bush's popularity reached a record high in the immediate aftermath of the Gulf War. But the glow of that victory faded quickly as the recession worsened in late 1991, and as the administration declined to propose any policies for combating it.

BILL CLINTON

Because the early maneuvering for the 1992 presidential election occurred when President Bush's popularity remained high, many leading Democrats declined to run. That gave Bill Clinton, the young five-term governor of Arkansas, an opportunity to emerge early as the front-runner. He went on to run a skillful campaign.

ROSS PEROT

Complicating the campaign was the emergence of Ross Perot, a blunt, forthright Texas billionaire who became an independent candidate by tapping popular resentment of the federal bureaucracy and by promising tough, uncompromising leadership to deal with the fiscal crisis. At several moments in the spring, Perot led both Bush and Clinton in public opinion polls. In July, as Perot began to face hostile scrutiny from the media, he abruptly withdrew from the race. But early in October, he reentered and soon regained much (although never all) of his early support.

Clinton won a clear, but hardly overwhelming, victory over Bush and Perot. He received 43 percent of the vote in the three-way race, to the president's 38 percent and Perot's 19 percent (the best showing for a third-party or independent candidate since Theodore Roosevelt in 1912). Clinton won 370 electoral votes to Bush's 168; Perot won none. Democrats retained control of both houses of Congress.

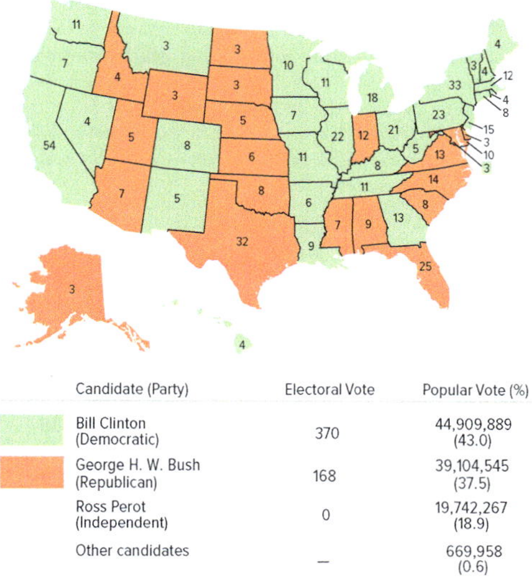

Candidate (Party)	Electoral Vote	Popular Vote (%)
Bill Clinton (Democratic)	370	44,909,889 (43.0)
George H. W. Bush (Republican)	168	39,104,545 (37.5)
Ross Perot (Independent)	0	19,742,267 (18.9)
Other candidates	–	669,958 (0.6)

55.2% of electorate voting

THE ELECTION OF 1992 In the 1992 election, for the first time since 1976, a Democrat captured the White House. And although the third-party candidacy of Ross Perot deprived Bill Clinton of an absolute majority, he nevertheless defeated George Bush by a decisive margin in both the popular and electoral vote.

What factors had eroded President Bush's once-broad popularity by 1992? What explained the strong showing of Ross Perot?

Reasoning Processes

Identifying Cause and Effect After students have read the section "The First Gulf War," ask them to create a list of the causes and effects of the Gulf War. Have students discuss as a class what they believe are the most important causes and effects. **WOR** **PCE** **WXT** **NAT**

Answers

The Election of 1992.

Economic recession and support for tax increases eroded support for President Bush in the 1992 election.

Historical Thinking Skills

Explaining Historical Developments Organize the class into four groups. Assign each group to review one of the following topics: the political effects of the rise of the New Right, the impact of the fall of the Soviet Union on U.S. foreign policy, the economic impact of the Reagan supply-side economic policies, or the impact on society of the increasing involvement of evangelicals in politics. Have each group make a short presentation of their most important conclusions to the rest of the class. **WOR PCE WXT SOC ARC NAT**

Key Terms

Students should be familiar with the key terms and be able to define them in the context of the rise of the New Right in domestic affairs, and the effects of the fall of the Soviet Union on foreign policy. Encourage students to use these terms in performing review exercises and exam practice for this chapter.

CHAPTER 33 REVIEW

CONNECTING THEMES

Chapter Thirty-Three explored the political, economic, and social climate of the United States during the 1980s. The 1970s saw a religious revival and growth of evangelicalism and a migration out of the Northeast and Midwest population centers to the Sunbelt. These changes contributed to the rise of a New Right coalition. This diverse coalition opposed the growth of government, resented government regulation and restrictions, and, fueled by evangelicals, was increasingly concerned about what they perceived as growing immorality and disorder in American society.

The New Right and other conservative groups, including wealthy elites and populist conservatives, united to elect Ronald Reagan in 1980. Reagan supported the idea of supply-side economics that reduced taxes for corporations and wealthy individuals to spur new investments. These tax cuts reduced government revenue and lowered spending on social programs. Deregulation followed with a general reduction in the enforcement of laws and regulations surrounding industry, the environment, and civil rights protections. Reagan's foreign policy focused on supporting opponents of communism anywhere globally and backing pro-U.S. governments regardless of their internal policies. The accompanying increase in military spending raised the already substantial budget deficit and heightened Cold War tensions.

As Cold War tensions eased between the United States and the Soviet Union, Reagan and Gorbachev came to a historic arms control agreement. The eventual collapse of the Soviet Union would leave the United States as the remaining superpower in a post-Cold War world. The U.S. led coalition in Iraq during the First Gulf War in 1991 reinforced the dominant role of the United States in world affairs. However, a new set of challenges arose, domestically and internationally, as the nation moved towards the twenty-first century.

You should consider the following questions as you review the themes for this chapter:

- How did the increasing conservatism alter American identity?
- What were the reasons for and consequences of the geographic and class realignment in the political arena during the 1980s?
- What were the major causes of the rise of the New Right?
- What were the domestic and foreign challenges faced by the Reagan administration?
- What were the major factors in the collapse of the Soviet Union?
- How did the policies of the Reagan era impact domestic and foreign policy in the 1990s?

KEY TERMS

Bill Clinton 893
deregulation 886
evangelical Christianity 881
George H. W. Bush 891
glasnost 889
Iran-contra scandal 890
Mikhail Gorbachev 889
neo-conservatives 885
New Right 884
perestroika 889
Reagan doctrine 888
Reaganomics 886
Ronald Reagan 884
Ross Perot 893
Saddam Hussein 892
Sagebrush Rebellion 881
Sunbelt 881
Strategic Defense Initiative (SDI) 888
Tiananmen Square 850

Go Online **Chapter 33 Content Review**

Assessing Student Understanding Use the online assessment to assess student understanding of concepts and topics within the chapter. You can assign the ready-made Chapter 33 Content Review or create your own from available questions. This easy-to-use tool helps you design assessments that meet the needs of different types of learners.

AP EXAM PRACTICE

Questions assume cumulative content knowledge from this chapter and the previous chapter.

MULTIPLE CHOICE

Use the election graphic on page 889 and your knowledge of U.S. history to answer questions 1-3.

1. Reagan's margin of victory portrayed in the election graphic indicates
   (A) the country remained politically divided through the 1980s.
   (B) the country voted along geographical lines as in the 1968 election.
   (C) the country clearly rejected the policies of Reagan's first term.
   (D) the country demonstrated unusual electoral unity.

2. What movement was central to Reagan's political success?
   (A) the New Right
   (B) the New Left
   (C) secular Americans
   (D) the Women's Movement

3. Many in the political movement that supported Reagan had been motivated by which belief?
   (A) The belief that religion had been too integrated into government policies.
   (B) The belief that the military had expanded too much.
   (C) The belief that rates of taxation were too high.
   (D) The belief that it was necessary to end conflict with the Soviet Union.

SHORT ANSWER

Use your knowledge of U.S. history to answer questions 4 and 5.

4. Use the map on page 883 to answer A, B, and C.
   (A) Briefly describe the historical situation responsible for the demographic shift depicted in the map.
   (B) Briefly explain ONE specific cause that led to the rise of the Sunbelt.
   (C) Briefly explain ONE specific effect that resulted from the rise of the Sunbelt.

5. Answer A, B, and C.
   (A) Briefly describe ONE specific historical similarity between the 1950s and the 1980s.
   (B) Briefly describe ONE specific historical difference between the 1950s and the 1980s.
   (C) Briefly explain ONE effect that resulted from a difference between the 1950s and the 1980s.

LONG ESSAY

Develop a thoughtful and thorough historical argument that answers the question. Begin your essay with a thesis statement, and support it with specific historical evidence and examples.

6. Evaluate the relative importance of causes that gave rise to a conservative movement in the second half of the twentieth century in the United States.

Answers

Multiple Choice

1. D; **2.** A; **3.** C

Short Answer

4A) Possible answer: Beginning in the 1970s, large number of Americans began moving into the South from the Northeast and Midwest.

4B) Possible answer: Jobs moving into the South led to a significant population shift beginning in the 1970s.

4C) Possible answer: The rise in the Sunbelt helped produce a change in the political climate with many in the region having strong opposition to the growth of government and increasing regulations.

5A) Possible answer: Both the 1950s and the 1980s saw the rise of a politically active evangelical movement, which fueled the rise of a conservative political counterculture.

5B) Possible answer: While both decades saw mostly Republican presidencies, the New Deal programs that began under FDR continued throughout the 1950s while the 1980s saw the Reagan Administration cut many social programs.

5C) Possible answer: The cuts in social programs in the 1980s reduced spending in one area but massive increases in military spending added more to the federal budget deficit.

Answers

Long Essay

6. Possible Thesis: The rise of the Sunbelt, evangelicals' strong response to the counterculture of the 1960s, and the pushback of conservative Americans led to the rise of a "New Right" during the 1980s. Specific Historical Evidence: The Watergate crisis brought to the surface a mistrust of government. The rise of the radical 60s counterculture and general social unrest increased anxieties among some Americans about the state of society. The rise of the Sunbelt and the suburbs also contributed to the rise of a conservative movement with largely isolated and homogeneous communities. The rise of the evangelical Christian movement also contributed to the rise of the conservative movement.

Pacing Guide

Chapter 34 explores key concepts from Period 9: 1980–present of the AP U.S. History Curriculum Framework. The suggested instruction time for Chapter 34 is 2 days.

Key Concepts

9.2.I New developments in science and technology enhanced the economy and transformed society, while manufacturing decreased.

9.2.II The U.S. population continued to undergo demographic shifts that had significant cultural and political consequences.

9.3.II Following the attacks of September 11, 2001, U.S. foreign policy focused on fighting terrorism around the world.

34 GLOBALIZATION AND POLARIZATION

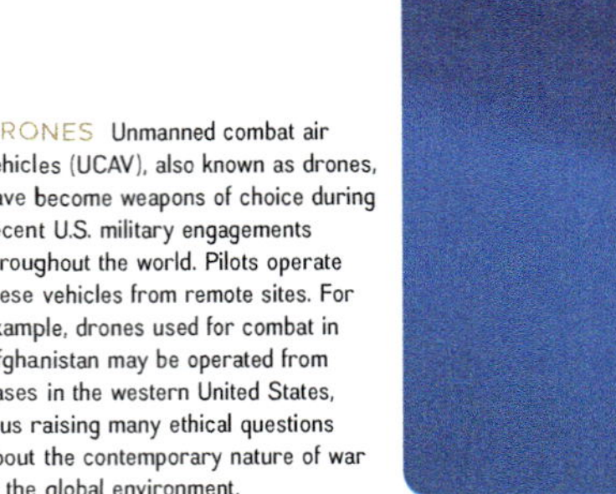

DRONES Unmanned combat air vehicles (UCAV), also known as drones, have become weapons of choice during recent U.S. military engagements throughout the world. Pilots operate these vehicles from remote sites. For example, drones used for combat in Afghanistan may be operated from bases in the western United States, thus raising many ethical questions about the contemporary nature of war in the global environment.

CONNECTING CONCEPTS

Chapter Thirty-Four begins by examining the Clinton presidency and changes during the 1990s. The economy boomed as businesses reduced labor costs and invested in new technologies. Globalization increased but had an uneven impact as some regions and individuals prospered while others struggled, leading to anger and resentment. Despite increasing political partisanship, President Clinton won reelection in 1996, but scandal led to impeachment (though not removal from office) in 1998. Two years later, George W. Bush defeated Al Gore in a close and controversial election.

By the twenty-first century, the American population was larger and older due to decreasing birth rates and increasing life spans. Immigration from countries outside Europe also made the United States more ethnically and racially diverse. Middle-class African Americans achieved economic and educational progress, but African Americans in poor or isolated communities continued to face adversity. Drug use and the AIDS epidemic further strained society while contentious cultural and political battles over feminism and abortion rights erupted.

The terrorist attacks on the World Trade Center and Pentagon in September 2001 shocked Americans and led to wars in Iraq and Afghanistan. The new security measures instituted in the wake of the terrorist attacks raised concerns over government infringement on personal liberties. The federal government's slow response to Hurricane Katrina in 2005 and the financial crisis of 2008 eroded the popularity of President Bush and voters elected Democratic Senator Barack Obama as president in 2008.

As the first African American president, Obama faced high expectations and great challenges—an economic crisis, an unpopular war, and political gridlock. He created a stimulus package to prevent an economic meltdown and provided healthcare to tens of millions. But in a tense era of political polarization, both liberal measures were unpopular with conservatives and libertarians. Although Obama won reelection in 2012, many Americans remained anxious and angry about the state and direction of the nation, leading to the unexpected victory of Donald Trump in 2016.

Discussion and Activities

Making Connections Have students examine the image "Drones." Discuss as a class other ways that drones are utilized in modern society. **WXT** **SOC**

Trump's term in office saw the social and political divide widen. Domestically, tax cuts, the elimination of many environmental regulations, and the reshaping of the federal judiciary gained Trump widespread support among conservatives. The COVID-19 pandemic brought new challenges socially, economically, and politically for the United States and the Trump administration. The politicized response to the pandemic and racial tensions, often strengthened by Trump's comments, led to an increasingly divided society and widespread unrest.

The spread of misinformation that intensified during the pandemic also led Trump's supporters to dispute the 2020 presidential election results. The resulting attack on the U.S. Capitol by Trump's supporters shook the nation. The questioning of the legitimacy of democratic institutions, from the free press to the federal judiciary and the electoral process itself, was unprecedented. When Biden took office in January 2021, he faced many challenges, including a deeply divided nation and an ongoing pandemic.

- Describe the reasons for and consequences of the changes in U.S. foreign policy following the end of the Cold War.
- Evaluate the influence of science and technology on globalization and social interaction.
- Analyze the causes and effects of the inequitable distribution of wealth in American society.
- Describe the political, social, and economic effects of increased immigration from Latin America.
- Analyze the reasons for and consequences of the extreme polarization of political parties and American society.

ECONOMIC BOOM AND BUST

The end of the twentieth and beginning of the twenty-first century have seen remarkable changes in American life. Some developments were a result of the end of the Cold War, some the changing demographics of the United States, and some a product of rapidly evolving technology and culture. But many of these changes were due to the dramatic transformation of the American economy.

FROM "STAGFLATION" TO GROWTH

The roots of the economic growth of the 1980s, 1990s, and early 2000s lay in part in the 1970s, when the United States seemed to be losing its ability to produce long-term prosperity. In the face of the sluggish growth and persistent inflation of the 1970s, however, many American corporations began to alter how they ran their businesses. These changes contributed to the prosperity of the last decades of the twentieth century and the growing inequality that accompanied it. Businesses invested heavily in new technology to make themselves more efficient and productive. Corporations merged with other companies to provide themselves with a more diversified basis for growth. Many enterprises created more energy-efficient plants and offices. Perhaps most importantly, American businesses sought to reduce their labor costs, which were among the highest in the world and which many economists and business leaders believed had made the United States uncompetitive against emerging economies that relied on low-wage workers.

NEW BUSINESS PRACTICES

Businesses cut labor costs in many ways. They took a much harder line against unions. Nonunion companies became more successful in staving off unionization drives. Some companies moved their operations to areas of the country where unions were weak and wages low—the American South and Midwest in particular. And many companies moved much of their production out of the United States, to such nations as Mexico and China, where there were large available pools of low-cost labor.

Digital technology made possible an enormous range of new products and services: computers; the Internet; cellular phones; digital music, videos, and cameras; and many other products. The technology industries created many new jobs and produced new consumer needs and appetites. But they did not create as many jobs as the industrial sectors of the past.

TECHNOLOGY INDUSTRIES

The American economy experienced rapid growth in the last decades of the twentieth century and into the twenty-first. The gross national product (the total of goods and services produced by the United States) almost quadrupled between 1980 and 2000. Inflation was low throughout these decades, never rising above 3 percent in any year. Stock prices soared to unprecedented levels—and with few interruptions—from the mid-1980s to the end of the twentieth century. Economic growth was particularly robust in the last years of the 1990s. From 1994 to 2000, the economy recorded growth in every quarter, something that had never before happened so continuously in peacetime.

Reasoning Processes

Comparison Have students read the section "From 'Stagflation' to Growth." Ask them to create a Venn diagram comparing business practices of late twentieth and early twenty-first century with business practices during the late nineteenth century. **WXT** **PCE**

Go Online AP Exam Preparation

AP Exam Practice Use the online assessment to help prepare students for the AP Exam. You can assign the ready-made AP-style short answer questions, document-based questions, and multiple-choice questions assessing concepts, themes, and skills from Period 9 and AP style long-essay questions organized in sets of 3 questions from various time periods. You can also create your own tests from available questions. This easy-to-use tool helps you design assessments that meet the needs of different types of learners.

Reasoning Processes

Identifying Cause and Effect Have students read the section "2008 Financial Crisis." Ask them to make a T-chart listing causes and effects of the recession. Have students discuss in small groups which causes and effects they believe were the most important. **WXT** **PCE**

2008 Financial Crisis

The economic boom of the 1990s was not sustainable. Financial institutions, using credit instruments developed to make borrowing easier and cheaper, lured millions of people into taking on large and risky mortgages. One such instrument, called an adjustable rate mortgage (ARM), offered homebuyers mortgages with initially low interest rates that would increase in later years. Other mortgages extended credit to people who lacked the financial means to repay the loans. These high-risk loans increased home sales and created a "housing bubble," or a rapid rise in housing prices fueled by high demand. These business practices were made possible with the 1999 repeal of the Glass-Steagall Act, which was passed in 1933 to prevent irresponsible banking practices by mandating layers of government oversight designed to catch fraud or risky investment strategies. Home prices eventually fell, and the market value of properties sank below the value of the mortgages. This left homeowners unable to sell properties when they could no longer afford the mortgage payment, and the default rates on loans increased exponentially. Many of the nation's largest banks had invested heavily in the securities that backed these risky loans. As the housing market collapsed, banks lost vast sums of money.

The Great Recession of 2008, influenced by the loan crisis, also pushed down wages and triggered widespread job layoffs. Many Americans could not meet other financial obligations, such as the repayment of school loans or credit card debt. Less money was also available for investing or economic growth. The increased unemployment rate further accelerated the downward economic spiral.

By mid-September 2008, the financial crisis was acute. Secretary of the Treasury Henry Paulson, supported by other economic leaders, proposed the massive use of federal funds to help bailout the banks that were failing. Both the Bush administration and eventually the Obama administration won congressional support for $750 billion in the form of the Troubled Asset Relief Program (TARP) to shore up the tottering financial institutions. The bailout kept the economy from collapsing, but it remained very weak for several years, and the country experienced exceptionally high unemployment rates.

The Two-Tiered Economy

The increasing abundance of the late twentieth and early twenty-first centuries created enormous new wealth that enriched those talented or lucky enough to profit from the areas of booming growth. The rewards for education–particularly in such areas as science and engineering–increased substantially. However, the benefits of the new economy were less widely shared than those of earlier boom times. Incomes remained flat for most Americans. Poverty in the country had steadily declined in the years after World War II, and by the end of the 1970s, the percentage of people living in poverty had fallen to 12 percent (from 20 percent in preceding decades). In the last 50 years, the poverty rates have fluctuated between 10 and 15 percent with 37 million people living in poverty in 2020.

The Digital Revolution

The new economy that emerged in the late twentieth and early twenty-first centuries was driven by dramatic new scientific and technological discoveries that had profound effects on the way people throughout the world lived. The most visible element of the technological revolution to most Americans was the dramatic growth in the use of computers and other digital electronic devices in almost every area of life.

Among the most significant innovations that contributed to the digital revolution was the development of the microprocessor, first introduced in 1971 by Intel, which represented a notable advance in the technology of integrated circuitry. A micro-processor miniaturized the central processing unit of a computer, making it possible for a small machine to perform calculations that in the past only very large machines could do. Considerable technological innovation was needed before the microprocessor could actually become the basis of what was at first known as a "minicomputer" and then a "personal computer." But in 1977, Apple launched its Apple II personal computer, the first such machine to be widely available to the public. Several years later, IBM entered the personal computer market with the first "PC." IBM had engaged a small software development company, Microsoft, to design an operating system for its new computer. No PC could operate without it. The company and its software debuted in August 1981 and immediately became enormously successful.

Development of the PC

The computer revolution created thousands of new, lucrative businesses, including computer manufacturers, fabricators of silicon chips, and manufacturers of accessories and software.

The Internet

Out of the computer revolution emerged another dramatic source of information and communication: the Internet. The Internet had its beginning in 1963, in the U.S. government's Advanced Research Projects Agency (ARPA), which funneled federal funds into scientific research projects, many of them defense related. ARPA created a linked network of computers that mainly served research labs and universities. Gradually, interest in the system began to spread, and the number of connected computers increased. The network, soon renamed the Internet, was then free to develop independently. It did so rapidly, especially after the invention of technologies that made possible digital mail (e-mail) and the emergence of the personal computer, which vastly increased the number of potential users of the Internet. As late as 1984, fewer than a thousand host computers were connected to the Internet, but by 2020 it had over 4 billion users worldwide.

ARPA

As the amount of information on the Internet increased, without any central direction, new forms of software emerged

Discussion and Activities

Making Connections Have students read the section "The Digital Revolution." Discuss as a class the ways that the digital revolution has impacted their lives at home, at school, and at work. **WXT** **SOC** **ARC**

TWENTY-FOUR HOUR NEWS CYCLE With the increasing popularity of digital communication, news events are reported around the clock and often in real-time. With tablets or smartphones, people can immediately consume and convey information. The inability to control how content and messaging is transmitted and received often causes problems for people and entities using social media and the Internet.

to make it possible for individual users to navigate through the vast number of Internet sites. In 1989, Tim Berners-Lee, a British scientist working at a laboratory in Geneva, introduced the World Wide Web, which individuals could use to publish information on the Internet. The World Wide Web helped establish an orderly system for both the distribution and retrieval of electronic information.

WORLD WIDE WEB

New forms of communication developed rapidly as technologies expanded. LinkedIn, a business-oriented social networking site launched in 2003; YouTube, an Internet video and live-streaming site, launched in 2005; and Facebook and Twitter, two social networking services that became major forums for entertainment and personal and public discourse, emerged in 2006. Many other social media platforms like Instagram, Snapchat, and TikTok quickly followed and became increasingly popular. Together, these websites and mobile applications have revolutionized the ways people interact, exchange personal information, and conduct business. Social media has played a significant role in organizing political and social movements and has become increasingly important in political campaigns. As social media platforms became an effective way to communicate, they also became efficient tools to spread misinformation.

SOCIAL MEDIA

GLOBALIZATION'S PROMISE AND PERILS

The celebration of the beginning of a new millennium on January 1, 2000, was a notable moment as a shared global event. But if the millennium celebrations suggested the bright promise of globalization, other events at the dawn of the new century suggested its dark perils.

GLOBALIZATION OF THE ECONOMY

The globalization of the economy was perhaps the most important economic change of the late twentieth century. The great prosperity of the 1950s and 1960s had rested on the relative insulation of the United States from the pressures of international competition. As late as 1970, international trade still played a relatively minor role in the American economy, which thrived on the basis of the vast domestic market in North America.

The world had intruded on the American economy by the end of the 1970s, and the trend continued into the twenty-first century. Exports rose from just under \$43 billion in 1970 to over \$2.5 trillion in 2019. But imports rose even more dramatically: from just over \$40 billion in 1970 to over \$3.1 trillion in 2019. Most American products now face foreign competition inside the United States. The first American trade imbalance in the postwar era occurred in 1971; only twice since then, in 1973 and 1975, has the balance of trade been

THE GLOBAL ECONOMY Hundreds of shipping containers, virtually all of them from China, stand waiting for delivery at the Yang Ming container terminal in Los Angeles in February 2001. The vast number of containers illustrates the increasing penetration of the American market by overseas manufacturers and the growing interconnections between the U.S. economy and that of the rest of the world.

Historical Thinking Skills

Argumentation After students have read the section "The Internet," ask them to list the ways the Internet has impacted life in the United States. Have students write a thesis statement that makes a historically defensible claim about the most important effect of the Internet. **WXT** **SOC** **ARC** **PCE**

Discussion and Activities

Speculating Have students examine the image "The Global Economy." Ask them to discuss in small groups potential benefits and costs of a highly interconnected global economy. *(Benefits: access to wider variety of inexpensive goods, Costs: potential adverse impact on domestic producers who are unable to match prices, potential disruptions of international supply chains.)* **WOR** **WXT**

Discussion and Activities

Historical Developments and Argumentation After students have read the section "Globalization of the Economy," ask them to discuss in small groups whether it is a problem for the United States to maintain a trade deficit. *(Consumers can benefit by purchasing inexpensive goods from overseas, but producers may be hurt by low-priced foreign competition.)* **WOR** **WXT**

favorable to the United States. Globalization increasingly connects the American economy to that of the world, but it is not without its critics.

Opposing the "New World Order"

In the United States and other industrial nations, opposition to globalization—or what President George H. W. Bush once called "the new world order"—took several forms. Many Americans on both the left and the right opposed the nation's increasingly interventionist foreign policy. Critics on the left charged that the United States was using military action to advance its economic interests in the 1991 Gulf War and in the Iraq War that began in 2003. Critics on the right claimed the nation was swayed by the interests of other nations—as in the humanitarian interventions in Somalia in 1993 and the Balkans in the late 1990s— and was ceding its sovereignty to international organizations.

Critics of Intervention

But the most vigorous opposition to globalization in the West came from an array of groups that saw it as an economic threat. Labor unions insisted that the rapid expansion of free-trade agreements led to the export of jobs from advanced nations to less developed ones. Other groups attacked working conditions in new manufacturing countries on humanitarian grounds, arguing that the global economy was creating new classes of laborers working in horrible conditions for extremely low wages that few Western nations would tolerate. Environmentalists argued that globalization, in exporting industry to low wage countries, also exported industrial pollution and toxic waste to nations that had no effective laws to control them, and contributed significantly to global climate change. Others opposed global economic arrangements by arguing they enriched powerful individuals and empowered multinational corporations while threatening the freedom and autonomy of individuals and communities.

The opponents of globalization mostly agreed the targets of their discontent were not just free-trade agreements but also the multinational institutions that policed and advanced the global economy. Among them were the World Trade Organization (WTO), which monitored the enforcement of the GATT treaties of the 1990s; the International Monetary Fund (IMF), which controlled international credit and exchange rates; and the World Bank, which made money available for development projects in many countries. In 1999, when the leaders of the seven leading industrial nations (and the leader of Russia) gathered for their annual meeting in Seattle, Washington, they were confronted with tens of thousands of protesters. Most of the protesters were peaceful, but some were violent, clashing with police, smashing store windows, and all but paralyzing the city. Later, a smaller but still substantial demonstration disrupted the IMF and the World Bank meetings in Washington, D.C. And in 2001, at a meeting of the same leaders in Genoa, Italy, an estimated 50,000 demonstrators clashed violently with police in a melee that left one protester dead and several hundred injured. Both the World Bank and the IMF have faced criticism for forcing Western economic practices on non-Western nations and instituting policies that aggravate the poverty and debt of developing nations. The IMF has also received criticism for requiring countries to privatize public services and eliminate social services as conditions for receiving loans.

Globalization Protested

PROTESTS IN SEATTLE In this photograph, a WTO protester faces Seattle police in a cloud of tear gas, waiting to be arrested.

Historical Thinking Skills

Argumentation Have students read the section "Opposing the 'New World Order.'" Ask them to create a sign or poster expressing an argument either supporting or attacking the World Trade Organization, the International Monetary Fund, or the World Bank. **WOR** **PCE** **WXT**

AMERICA IN THE WORLD

THE GLOBAL ENVIRONMENTAL MOVEMENT

An international movement for well over a century, environmentalism has grown rapidly throughout the world in the late twentieth and early twenty-first centuries. What began as a series of efforts to preserve wilderness sites and to clean up air and water in particular nations has evolved into a broad effort to deal with problems that affect, and threaten, the entire globe.

Organizations both in the United States and elsewhere have sought to create an international environmental movement. The World Wildlife Fund (WWF) was created in Switzerland in 1961. It eventually attracted more than 5 million supporters in over 90 countries and now claims to be the world's largest independent conservation organization. Greenpeace was founded in Canada in 1971 in opposition to U.S. nuclear testing in Alaska. It too has grown into an international organization, with 2.9 million financial supporters worldwide and a presence in 42 nations. Leading American environmental associations include the Wilderness Society, the Sierra Club, and the National Audubon Society.

Nongovernmental organizations (NGOs) such as Greenpeace and WWF were not the only institutions to recognize environmental concerns. In June 1972, the United Nations held its first Conference on the Human Environment. Representatives of 113 countries attended the conference to discuss issues of global environmental importance—including the role of chlorofluorocarbons (CFCs), a chemical compound used in refrigerants and aerosol sprays, in depleting the ozone layer. After the conference, the UN created the United Nations Environment Programme (UNEP) to help coordinate international efforts for environmentalism and encourage sustainable development in poorer nations around the world.

The world's first "Green" parties—political parties explicitly devoted to environmental concerns (and often also to other issues of social justice)—appeared in 1972, beginning in New Zealand (the Values Party) and Tasmania (the United Tasmania Group). Since then, Green parties have proliferated throughout the world, including the United States. The most powerful Green party to date has been *Die Grüne* in Germany, founded in 1980.

Large-scale ecological catastrophes have often helped galvanize the global environmental movement. Among the more significant of these events was the Bhopal disaster of 1984, in which a gas leak at a Union Carbide pesticide plant in Bhopal, India, resulted in the deaths of an estimated 3,000 to 15,000 people. Two years later, a nuclear reactor accident in the Soviet city of Chernobyl in Ukraine caused 56 direct deaths, with predictions of many thousands more deaths to follow as a result of exposure. The area around Chernobyl is expected to be partially contaminated for 24,000 years, the radioactive half-life of plutonium-239. A less catastrophic nuclear accident at Three Mile Island, Pennsylvania, in 1979 heightened antinuclear sentiment in the United States. In 1989, the oil tanker *Exxon Valdez* ran aground on Bligh Reef in Prince William Sound, Alaska, and spilled approximately 10.9 million gallons of crude oil. Eventually covering thousands of square miles of ocean water (and 1,300 miles of Alaska shoreline) in oil, the spill killed hundreds of thousands of animals instantly and devastated the fragile ecosystem of the Sound. An even greater oil spill occurred in the Gulf of Mexico in 2010 from an explosion in a deep well established by BP. Eleven people died in the explosion, and almost 5 million barrels of petroleum were released into the water.

In developed, industrialized nations, environmental advocacy has largely focused on energy policy, conservation, clean technologies, and changing individual and social attitudes about consumption (as in the recycling movement). In the developing world, however, the growth of environmentalism is often linked to issues of human and democratic rights and freedom from economic exploitation. For example, the Green Belt Movement in Kenya, begun in 1977 by Wangari Maathai, encouraged Kenyan women to plant over 30 million trees across the nation to address the challenges of deforestation, soil erosion, and lack of water. The Green Belt Movement became an important human rights and women's rights organization, focused on reducing poverty and promoting peaceful democratic change through environmental conservation and protection. Maathai won the 2004 Nobel Peace Prize in 2004 and also served as Kenya's assistant minister for Environment and Natural Resources.

The environmental movement has grown even more global in scope, with multilateral environmental treaties and worldwide summits becoming principal strategies of advocates. In 1997, an international effort to reduce global warming by mandating the lowering of greenhouse gas emissions culminated in the Kyoto protocols, which by 2010 had been ratified by 183 nations (with the United States a conspicuous exception). A leading figure in bringing the issue of global warming to widespread attention both in the United States and around the world has been former vice president Al Gore, whose 2006 film, *An Inconvenient Truth*, raised awareness of the threat of global warming. The film won an Academy Award as Best Documentary Feature, and Gore won the 2007 Nobel Peace Prize for his efforts on behalf of the movement he has championed. His co-winner was the International Panel on Climate Change, launched in Switzerland in 1988 and affiliated with the United Nations.

Despite these efforts, carbon levels continued to rise as climate change accelerated. In 2014, China and the United States reached an agreement to fight climate change by reducing carbon emissions. President Obama and President Xi Jinping hoped that two of the largest industrial nations setting emission targets would inspire other nations to set their own carbon emission reduction goals. In 2015, countries met in Paris to create a stronger agreement known as the Paris Agreement. Countries pledged to lower carbon emissions with the intent of limiting global warming to less than 2°C. President Obama ratified the agreement by executive action, bypassing Senate approval. In 2017 President Trump announced that the United States would withdraw from the agreement and officially pulled out in 2020. President Biden, who pledged to make climate change a priority during his presidential campaign, rejoined the agreement in February 2021. Meanwhile, young activists such as Greta Thunberg used social media to bring attention to environmental issues and urge political leaders to protect the environment for future generations.

HISTORICAL THINKING SKILLS

Questions assume cumulative content knowledge from this chapter and previous chapters.

1. **Drawing Conclusions** Why are environmental movements in developing nations often linked to issues of human rights and protection from exploitation by developed nations? How do developed nations threaten the environment of developing nations?
2. **Explaining Historical Developments** How did the 2010 BP explosion and oil spill in the Gulf of Mexico affect the environment? What was the effect on the environmental movement?
3. **Developing Arguments** Environmental organizations include grassroots associations, worldwide NGOs, and national political parties. How do these groups focus attention on environmental issues? Which type of organization do you think would be most successful at reaching its goals? Why?

Discussion and Activities

Making Connections After students have read the feature, discuss as a class the different environmental issues that are of the most concern to them at the local, state, and national level. **WXT** **GEO**

Answers

America in the World

1. Possible answer: In developing nations there are often issues surrounding human rights, poverty, and other concerns that are linked to environmental issues. Developing nations are often industrializing which impacts developing nations due to pollution, carbon emissions, and waste issues.
2. Possible answer: The BP explosion caused widespread and ongoing damage to the environment. It brought attention to the environmental movement due to the scale of the disaster.
3. Student answers will vary. Students may indicate that groups focus attention on different levels, from local to international with varying levels of effectiveness.

Historical Thinking Skills

Contextualization Have students read the section "Defending Orthodoxy." Ask them to discuss in small groups why they think Islamic fundamentalists have expressed hostility toward the United States. *(U.S. support for the Shah of Iran, U.S. support for Israel, the perception that the U.S. interferes in the Middle East to maintain the flow of oil to the West.)* **WOR** **ARC** **SOC**

BP OIL SPILL The photograph shows BP's attempts to extinguish the fire and cap off the oil spill that resulted from an explosion on an offshore drilling platform. The oil leaked for months, and it continues to damage the ecology of the Gulf of Mexico today.

DEFENDING ORTHODOXY

Outside the industrialized West, the impact of globalization created other concerns. Many citizens of non-industrialized nations resented the way the world economy had left them in poverty and, in their view, exploited and oppressed them. The increasing reach of globalization created additional grievances in other regions, particularly the Islamic nations of the Middle East. These grievances were rooted not just in economics but also in religion and culture.

The Iranian Revolution of 1979, in which orthodox Muslims ousted a despotic government whose leaders had embraced many aspects of modern Western culture, was one of the first large and visible manifestations of a phenomenon that would eventually reach across much of the Islamic world and threaten the stability of the globe. In one Islamic nation after another, waves of fundamentalist orthodoxy emerged to defend traditional culture against incursions from the West. Militants in various parts of the world used isolated incidents of violence and mayhem to disrupt Western societies and governments and create fear among their peoples. Such tactics are known to the world as terrorism.

RISE OF ISLAMIC FUNDAMENTALISM

RISE OF TERRORISM

The term "terrorism" was used first during the French Revolution in the 1790s to describe the actions of the radical Jacobins against the French government. The word continued to be used intermittently throughout the nineteenth and early twentieth centuries to describe the use of violence as a form of intimidation against peoples and governments. But the widespread understanding of terrorism as a fact of modern life is largely a product of the end of the twentieth century and the beginning of the twenty-first.

ORIGINS OF TERRORISM

Acts of what we have come to call terrorism have occurred in many parts of the world. Irish revolutionaries engaged in terrorism regularly against the English through much of the twentieth century. Jewish resistance groups used it in Palestine against the British before the creation of Israel, and Palestinians used it against Israelis over several decades. Revolutionary groups in Italy, Germany, Japan, and France have engaged in terrorist acts intermittently over the past several decades.

The United States, too, has experienced terrorism for many years, much of it against American targets abroad. These included the bombing of the Marine barracks in Beirut, Lebanon, in 1983; the explosion that brought down an American airliner over Lockerbie, Scotland, in 1988; the bombing of American embassies in 1998; the assault on the U.S. naval vessel *Cole* in 2000, and other events around the world. Terrorist incidents were relatively rare, but not unknown, within the United States itself before September 11, 2001. Militants on the American left performed various acts of terror in the 1960s and early 1970s. In 1993, a bomb exploded in the parking garage of the World Trade Center in New York City, killing six people and causing structural damage to the towers. Convicted of the crime were several men connected with militant Islamic organizations. In 1995, a van containing explosives blew up in front of a federal building in Oklahoma City, killing 168 people. Timothy McVeigh, a former Marine who had become part of a militant anti-government movement of the American right, was convicted of the crime in 1997 and executed in 2001.

Most Americans, however, considered terrorism a problem that plagued other nations. One of the many results of the terrible events of September 11, 2001, was to jolt the American people out of a sense of complacency. New security measures following 9/11 changed the way Americans traveled. New government regulations altered immigration policies and affected the character of international banking. Warnings of possible terrorist attacks fostered widespread tension and uneasiness.

Discussion and Activities

Evaluating Evidence Have students read the section "Rise of Terrorism." Ask them to create a two column chart listing acts of domestic and foreign terrorism against the United States. Have students discuss as a class which is a greater threat, and what policies the U.S. might implement to deter terrorists. **WOR** **PCE**

A CHANGING SOCIETY

The American population changed dramatically in the late twentieth and early twenty-first centuries. It grew larger, older, and more racially and ethnically diverse.

A SHIFTING POPULATION

Decreasing birth rates and growing life spans contributed to one of the most important characteristics of the American population in the twenty-first century: its increasing agedness. The enormous "baby boom" generation–people born in the first ten years after World War II–drove the median age steadily upward. This growing population of aging Americans contributed to stresses on the Social Security and Medicare systems, including the provisions of the Affordable Care Act introduced by President Obama. It also had important implications for the workforce. The number of people aged 25-54, known statistically as the prime workforce, is growing at a much slower rate than the population aging out of the American workforce in the twenty-first century.

The slowing growth of the native-born population, and the workforce shortages it has helped to create, helped rapidly increase immigration. In 2018, the number of foreign-born residents of the United States was the highest in American history at roughly 14 percent of the total population. These immigrants came from a wider variety of backgrounds than ever before due to the 1965 Immigration Reform Act, which eliminated national origins as a criterion for admission. Immigrants from Latin America and Asia were the largest groups in these years. But other immigrants came in significant numbers from Africa, the Middle East, Russia, and eastern Europe. The growing presence of the foreign-born residents contributed to a significant drop in the percentage of non-Hispanic white residents in the United States–from 90 percent in 1965 to 76 percent in 2019.

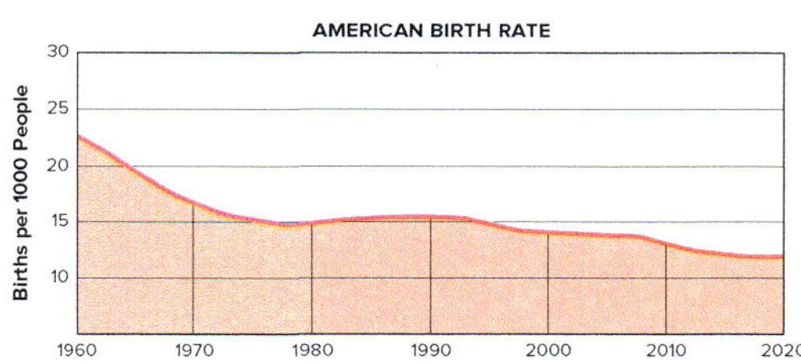

THE AMERICAN BIRTHRATE, 1960–2020 The line graph illustrates the striking change in the pattern of the nation's birthrate from the twenty years after 1940, which produced the great "baby boom." From 1960 onward, the nation's birth rate steadily declined.

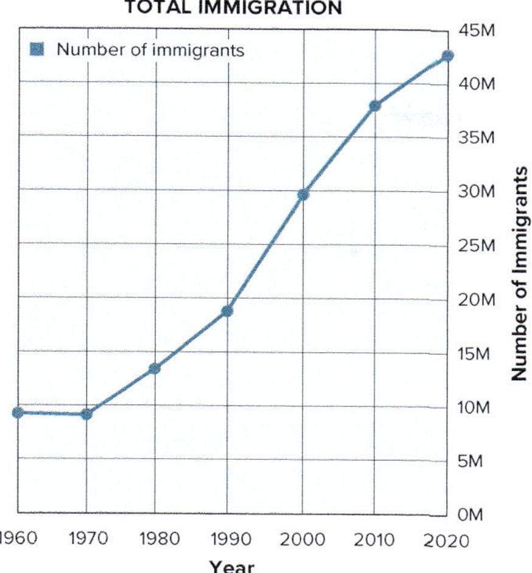

TOTAL IMMIGRATION, 1960–2020 The line graph illustrates the tremendous increase in immigration to the United States in the decades since the Immigration Reform Act of 1965.

AFRICAN AMERICANS IN THE POST-CIVIL RIGHTS ERA

The civil rights movement and resulting legislation brought increased opportunities to some African Americans. Yet, as the industrial economy declined and government services dwindled, there was a growing sense of despair among large groups of African Americans who continued to find themselves barred from upward mobility.

ECONOMIC PROGRESS FOR AFRICAN AMERICANS

For the black middle class, which in the first decade of the twenty-first century constituted over half of the African American population of America, progress was remarkable in the decades after the high point of the civil rights movement. African American families moved into more affluent urban and suburban communities. The percentage of black high-school graduates going on to college was virtually the same as that of white high-school graduates by the early twenty-first century (although a smaller proportion of African Americans than white Americans completed high school). In 2019 the percentage of African Americans twenty-five and older with a bachelor's degree or higher was just over 26 percent, while 40 percent of white Americans attained the same level of education. African Americans also made gains in many professions in which previous generations had been barred or segregated. However, black men and women continue to comprise a low percentage of the white-collar workforce relative to the overall population.

The economic growth and the liberal programs of the 1960s and beyond failed to reach many African Americans. Sometimes

Discussion and Activities

Evaluating Have students read the section "A Shifting Population." Ask them to create a chart listing political, economic, and social challenges presented by demographic shifts in the United States. **PCE** **WXT** **SOC**

Discussion and Activities

Analyzing Continuity and Change Have students read the section "Economic Progress for African Americans." Ask them to discuss in small groups reasons why, in spite of gains, African Americans continue to face challenges economically, socially, and politically. **PCE** **WXT** **SOC**

Discussion and Activities

Making Connections Have students read the section "Public Health Challenges." Discuss as a class the most daunting public health challenges facing the United States today and how those challenges have changed since the 1980s. **PCE** **SOC**

described as the "underclass," as much as a third of nation's African American population were impoverished and living in deteriorating inner-city neighborhoods. As more successful African Americans moved out of the inner cities, the poor were left behind in urban neighborhoods with limited resources. Young African Americans in urban areas were less likely to graduate high school and suffered high rates of unemployment. The family structure also struggled from the dislocations of urban poverty, and there was a large increase in the number of single-parent, female-headed households. In 2020, the percentage of white children who lived with both parents was nearly twice as high as the percentage of black children who lived in such households.

THE "UNDERCLASS"

PUBLIC HEALTH CHALLENGES

Two new and deadly epidemics ravaged many American communities beginning in the 1980s. One was a dramatic increase in drug use, which penetrated nearly every community in the nation. The enormous demand for illegal drugs, particularly for "crack" cocaine in the late 1980s and early 1990s, spawned what was in effect a multibillion-dollar industry. The use of illegal drugs declined significantly among middle-class Americans beginning in the late 1980s, but usage decreased much more slowly in the poor urban neighborhoods where it was doing the most severe damage. By the late 1990s, a new crisis emerged with the abuse of prescription opioids.

While the use of illegal drugs declined in the 1990s, the prescribing of opioids increased. By the late 1990s, what became known as the "opioid crisis" emerged as the abuse of and overdose deaths from prescription opioids rose. To address the issue, controls on prescription opioids tightened, resulting in a rise in the use of heroin and other illegal drugs. The crisis continues as the Center for Disease Control and Prevention estimates at least 500,000 people died from an opioid overdose between 1999 and 2019. The opioid crisis costs the United States close to $80 billion per year in health care, treatment, productivity losses, and enforcement actions by the criminal justice system.

OPIOID CRISIS

The illegal drug epidemic was related to another scourge of the late twentieth century: the epidemic spread of a new and often lethal disease first documented in 1981 and soon named AIDS (acquired immune deficiency syndrome). AIDS is the product of the HIV virus, which is transmitted by the exchange of bodily fluids (blood or semen). The first American victims of AIDS (and for many years, the group among whom cases remained the most numerous) were gay men. But by the late 1980s, as the gay community began to take preventive measures, the most rapid increase in the spread of the disease occurred among heterosexuals, many of them intravenous drug users, who spread the virus by sharing contaminated hypodermic needles.

AIDS EPIDEMIC

Beginning in the mid-1990s, AIDS researchers discovered effective treatments for the disease. The advent of antiretroviral therapy (ARV), a powerful combination of drugs, has allowed people with HIV to live longer, more productive lives. But the drugs remained scarce in less-affluent parts of the world where the epidemic was rampant. The United Nations, many philanthropic organizations, and several governments committed significant funds to fight the AIDS crisis worldwide and to sponsor initiatives to educate the public, prevent HIV infection, provide treatment, and search for a cure.

PARTISANSHIP RESURGENCE

Bill Clinton assumed office in 1993 with a domestic agenda more ambitious than that of any other president in nearly thirty years. But having won the votes of well under half the electorate, he did not have a powerful mandate. The Republican leadership in Congress was highly adversarial and opposed the president with unusual unanimity on many issues.

LAUNCHING THE CLINTON PRESIDENCY

The Clinton administration encountered many missteps in its first months, with several early appointments withdrawn due to controversy. Clinton did push through a budget that marked a significant turn away from the policies of the Reagan-Bush years. It included a substantial tax increase on the wealthiest Americans, a large reduction in many areas of government spending, and a major expansion of tax credits to low-income working people.

Clinton was an advocate of free trade and a proponent of what came to be known as globalism. After much negotiation, he won approval of the North American Free Trade Agreement (or NAFTA), which eliminated most trade barriers among the United States, Canada, and Mexico. Later he won approval of other far-reaching trade agreements negotiated in the General Agreement on Trade and Tariffs (or GATT).

NAFTA

The president's most ambitious initiative was a major reform of the nation's healthcare system. Early in 1993, he appointed a task force chaired by his wife, Hillary Rodham Clinton. He proposed a sweeping reform designed to guarantee coverage to every American and hold down the costs of medical care. Substantial opposition from conservatives and many insurance companies doomed the plan in 1994.

FAILURE OF HEALTHCARE REFORM

REPUBLICAN RESURGENCE

In 1994, for the first time in forty years, Republicans gained control of both houses of Congress and proposed a series of measures to transfer important powers from the federal government to the states. They also proposed dramatic reductions in federal spending, including a major restructuring of the Medicare program.

Discussion and Activities

Analyzing Issues Have students read the section "Launching the Clinton Presidency." Ask them to discuss in small groups why they think that Clinton's health care initiative failed. *(Republican opposition, opposition from many in the insurance and health care industries, fear of consumers losing benefits or access to health care, fear of the high cost of government-provided medical care, accusations about socializing medicine.)* **PCE** **WXT**

CLINTON AND GINGRICH For a time after Republicans won control of both houses of Congress in 1994, some observers suggested that Newt Gingrich was now the most powerful figure in government, and that President Clinton was (as some journalists suggested) irrelevant. But Clinton surprised everyone by working cordially with Gingrich and, in the process, rebuilding his own popularity. They are seen here together in public at a senior center in Claremont, New Hampshire.

John Mottern/© AFP/Getty Images

President Clinton announced his plan to cut taxes and balance the budget. But compromise between the president and the Republicans in Congress became difficult. In November 1995 and again in January 1996, the federal government shut down for several days because agreement could not be reached on a budget. Public opinion turned quickly and powerfully against the Republican leadership and much of its agenda. House Speaker Newt Gingrich quickly became discredited, while President Clinton slowly improved his standing in the polls.

THE ELECTION OF 1996

By 1996, President Clinton was in a commanding position to win reelection. Unopposed for the Democratic nomination, he faced Republican Senator Robert Dole of Kansas, who inspired little enthusiasm even within his own party. Clinton's revival resulted from his adroitness in taking centrist positions that undermined the Republicans and in championing traditional Democratic issues that were broadly popular. But his greatest strength came from the remarkable success of the American economy. Like Reagan in 1984, Clinton could campaign as the champion of peace, prosperity, and national well-being.

CLINTON VS DOLE

As the election approached, Congress passed several important bills, including one that raised the legal minimum wage for the first time in more than a decade. The passage of a welfare reform bill, which President Clinton somewhat reluctantly signed, marked the most important change in aid to the poor since the Social Security Act of 1935. The bill ended the fifty-year federal guarantee of assistance to families with dependent children. It turned most of the responsibility for allocating

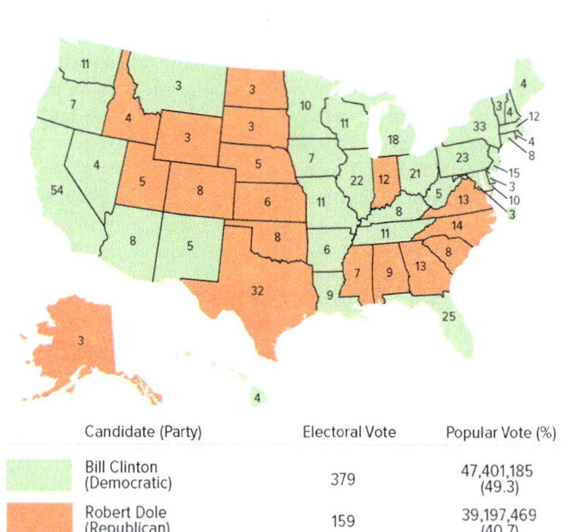

Candidate (Party)	Electoral Vote	Popular Vote (%)
Bill Clinton (Democratic)	379	47,401,185 (49.3)
Robert Dole (Republican)	159	39,197,469 (40.7)
Ross Perot (Reform)	0	8,085,294 (8.4)

49% of electorate voting

THE ELECTION OF 1996 Ross Perot did much less well in 1996 than he had in 1992, and President Clinton came much closer than he had four years earlier to winning a majority of the popular vote. Once again, Clinton defeated his Republican opponent, this time Robert Dole, by a decisive margin in both the popular and electoral vote. After the 1994 Republican landslide in the congressional elections, Bill Clinton had seemed permanently weakened.

What explains Clinton's political revival?

Discussion and Activities

Analyzing Issues After students have read the section "Republican Resurgence," ask them to discuss in small groups the implications of a federal government shutdown. *(Many Federal employees would stop being paid, non-essential agencies like the National Park system would shut down, and small businesses that serve federal agencies/employees would be impacted.)* **PCE** **WXT**

Answers

The Election of 1996.

Clinton's weak Republican opponent and passage of popular legislation like welfare reform contributed to his resurgence.

Historical Thinking Skills

Explaining Historical Developments After students have read the section "The Election of 1996," ask them to discuss in small groups how Clinton managed to win reelection despite opposition from a Republican Congress. *(Voters mostly blamed Republicans for the government shutdown, Clinton was charismatic and an effective communicator, Clinton signed popular legislation like welfare reform prior to the election, the Republicans did not nominate a compelling opponent.)* **PCE**

the greatly reduced federal welfare funds to the states. It also shifted the bulk of welfare benefits away from those without jobs and toward support for low-wage workers.

Clinton's buoyant campaign flagged slightly in the last weeks, but the president nevertheless received just over 49 percent of the popular vote. Clinton won 379 electoral votes to Dole's 159. But other Democrats made only modest gains and failed to regain either house of Congress.

CLINTON TRIUMPHANT AND EMBATTLED

Although Bill Clinton was the first Democratic president to win two terms as president since Franklin Roosevelt, he still faced a Republican Congress. He proposed a modest domestic agenda, consisting of tax cuts and tax credits targeted at middle-class Americans to help them educate their children. He also negotiated a plan for a balanced budget, which passed late in 1997. By the end of 1998, the federal budget had generated its first surplus in thirty years.

BUDGET SURPLUSES

Clinton needed the popularity he had gained from the budget surplus when the most serious crisis of his presidency emerged. In early 1998, the president was charged with having had a sexual relationship with a young White House intern, Monica Lewinsky, and lying about it in a deposition. Those revelations produced a new investigation by Kenneth Starr, a former judge and official in the Reagan Justice Department. Clinton forcefully denied the charges, and the public strongly backed him. His popularity soared to record levels and remained high throughout the year that followed.

MONICA LEWINSKY

The Lewinsky scandal revived again in August 1998, when Lewinsky struck a deal with the independent counsel and testified about her relationship with Clinton. Starr then subpoenaed Clinton himself, who finally admitted that he and Lewinsky had what he called an "improper relationship." A few weeks later, Starr recommended that Congress impeach the president.

The House Judiciary Committee and then, on December 19, 1998, the full House, approved two counts of impeachment: lying to the grand jury and obstructing justice. The matter then moved to the Senate, where a trial of the president–the first since the trial of Andrew Johnson in 1868–began in early January. The trial ended with a decisive acquittal of the president.

IMPEACHMENT

In 1999, the Clinton administration faced a serious foreign policy crisis - once again in the Balkans. A long-simmering conflict between the Serbian government of Yugoslavia and Kosovo separatists erupted into a savage civil war in 1998. In May 1999, NATO forces, dominated and led by the United States, began a bombing campaign against the Serbians. After little more than a week, the leader of Yugoslavia, Slobodan Milosevic, agreed to a cease-fire. Serbian troops withdrew from Kosovo, and NATO peacekeeping forces replaced them. A precarious peace returned to the region.

KOSOVO

Clinton's popularity was higher at the end of his second term than when he first took office. Public approval of Clinton's presidency was consistently among the highest of any postwar president despite the many scandals and setbacks he suffered in the White House.

THE ELECTION OF 2000

The 2000 presidential election was notable not because of the campaign that preceded it, but because of the controversy over its results. Republican George W. Bush– a son of former president George H.W. Bush and a second-term governor of

ELECTION NIGHT, 2000 The electronic billboard in New York City's Times Square, showing network coverage of the presidential contest, reports George Bush the winner of the 2000 presidential race late on election night. A few hours later, the networks retracted their projections because of continuing uncertainty over the results in Florida. Five weeks later, and then only because of the controversial intervention of the Supreme Court, Bush finally emerged the victor.

Discussion and Activities

Evaluating Evidence Have students read the section "Clinton Triumphant and Embattled." Ask them to create a T-chart listing successes and failures of Clinton's second term. Have students discuss with a partner which they think was greater and ask for volunteers to share their answers with the class. **PCE** **WXT** **SOC**

Candidate (Party)	Electoral Vote	Popular Vote (%)
Al Gore (Democratic)	266	51,003,894 (48)
George W. Bush (Republican)	271	50,459,211 (48)

51% of electorate voting

THE ELECTION OF 2000 The 2000 presidential election was one of the closest and most controversial in American history. It also starkly revealed a new pattern of party strength, which had been developing over the previous decade. Democrats swept the Northeast and most of the industrial Midwest and carried all the states of the Pacific Coast. Republicans swept the South, the plains states, and the mountain states (with the exception of New Mexico) and held on to a few traditional Republican strongholds in the Midwest.

Compare the 2000 election map to those of earlier elections, particularly the election of 1896, and analyze how the pattern of party support changed.

Texas—and Vice President Al Gore, a Democrat, easily won the nominations of their parties.

Both men ran cautious, centrist campaigns. Polls showed an exceptionally tight race right up to the end. In the congressional races, Republicans maintained control of the House of Representatives by five seats, while the Senate split evenly between Democrats and Republicans. Gore won the national popular vote in the presidential race by about 540,000 votes out of about 100 million votes cast. But on election night, both candidates remained short of the 270 electoral votes needed for victory because no one could determine who had won Florida's electoral votes. After a mandatory recount over the next two days, Bush led Gore in the state by fewer than 300 votes.

FLORIDA

When a court-ordered deadline arrived, the recount was not yet complete. The Florida secretary of state, a Republican, then certified Bush the winner in Florida by a little more than 500 votes. The Gore campaign contested the results. Late on December 12, 2000, in *Bush v. Gore*, the U.S. Supreme Court issued a controversial 5-4 decision for Bush, and the long election ended.

THE SUPREME COURT'S DECISION

TURBULENT POLITICS

THE SECOND BUSH PRESIDENCY

George W. Bush assumed the presidency in January 2001, burdened by both the controversies surrounding his election and the perception by some that he was ill prepared for the office.

Bush's principal campaign had centered on the promise that he would use the predicted budget surplus to finance a massive tax reduction. He narrowly won passage of the largest tax cut in American history, $1.35 trillion over several years.

BUSH TAX CUTS

Although he campaigned as a moderate adept at building coalitions across party lines, Bush governed as a staunch conservative, relying on the most orthodox members of his party for support. The president's political adviser Karl Rove encouraged the administration to take increasingly conservative positions. Bush appealed to the gun lobby by refusing to support a renewal of the assault weapons ban that Clinton had enacted. He also proposed a constitutional amendment to ban same-sex marriage. The Bush administration was part of a broad and successful effort to mobilize evangelical Christians as an active part of the Republican coalition. But almost from the beginning, the aftermath of the September 11, 2001, attacks dominated both Bush's presidency and the nation's politics.

THE ELECTION OF 2004

The 2004 election pitted President Bush, who was unopposed within his party, against John Kerry, a Democratic senator from

CHANGING POSITIONS The tradition of accusing opponents of changing their public positions for political gain, called flip-flopping, has been a long-time feature of American politics. In the photograph, a supporter of George W. Bush uses her footwear to ridicule his opponent, Senator John Kerry as a flip-flopper on the issue of the war with Iraq.

Historical Thinking Skills

Developing Arguments After students have read the section "The Election of 2000," ask them to write a short paragraph explaining whether the resolution of the election increased or decreased their faith in the electoral process. Remind students to support their argument with specific evidence. **PCE**

Reasoning Processes

Comparison Have students read the section "The Second Bush Presidency." Ask them to discuss in small groups how the actions of President Bush in his first term differed from his campaign promises. Ask students to identify actions of more recent elected officials at the local, state, or national level that have differed from their campaign promises. **PCE**

Discussion and Activities

Analyzing Continuity After students have read the section "The Election of 2004" and examined the map "The Election of 2004," discuss as a class the similarities and differences between the 2004 election and the election of 2000. Have students consider why the "red" and "blue" states in recent presidential elections appear to be so stable. *(Elections may be becoming more about identity than ideology, voters may be migrating to areas where their ideology is in the majority.)* **PCE** **MIG** **NAT**

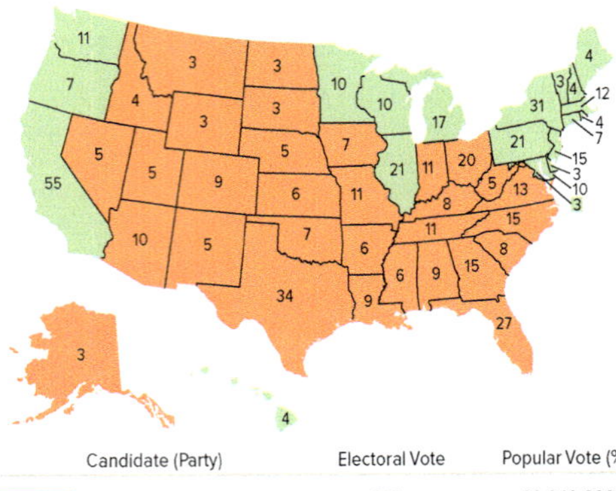

	Candidate (Party)	Electoral Vote	Popular Vote (%)
(orange)	George W. Bush (Republican)	286	62,040,606 (51)
(green)	John F. Kerry (Democratic)	252	59,028,109 (48)

60% of electorate voting

THE ELECTION OF 2004 The 2004 election repeated the pattern established in 2000. The Democratic presidential candidate, John F. Kerry, swept the Northeast, most of the industrial Midwest, and the Pacific Coast. The Republican candidate, President Bush, carried almost everything else. Although Bush's popular and electoral margins were both larger than they had been in 2000, the election was extremely close.

Massachusetts. Throughout the months before the election, voters were again almost evenly divided. The election itself, although very close, was more decisive than the election of 2000. Bush won 51 percent of the popular vote to Kerry's 48 percent.

The War on Terrorism

In the aftermath of September 2001, the United States government launched what President Bush called a "war against terrorism." The attacks on the World Trade Center and the Pentagon, government intelligence indicated, had been planned and orchestrated by Middle Eastern agents of a powerful terrorist network known as al-Qaeda. Its leader, Osama bin Laden—until 2001 little known outside the Arab world—quickly became one of the most notorious figures in the world.

AL-QAEDA

Convinced that the militant "Taliban" government of Afghanistan had sheltered and supported bin Laden and his organization, the United States began a sustained campaign of bombing against the regime and sent in ground troops to help a resistance organization overthrow the Afghan government. Afghanistan's Taliban regime quickly collapsed, and its leaders—along with the al-Qaeda fighters allied with them—fled the capital, Kabul. American and anti-Taliban Afghan troops pursued them into the mountains but failed to capture bin Laden and the other leaders of his organization.

American forces in Afghanistan rounded up several hundred people suspected of connections to the Taliban and

SEPTEMBER 11, 2001 One great American symbol, the Statue of Liberty, stands against a sky filled with the thick smoke from the destruction of another American symbol, New York City's World Trade Center towers, a few hours after terrorists crashed two planes into them.

Discussion and Activities

Analyzing Points of View Have students examine the image "September 11, 2001." Ask them to talk with a parent or older relative about their memories of that day and write a paragraph about the discussion. Ask for volunteers to share their paragraphs and discuss as a class. **WOR** **NAT**

SADDAM HUSSEIN On December 14, 2003, American forces captured Hussein at a farmhouse near Tikrit, Iraq. He was tried and found guilty of crimes against humanity for the death of 148 Iraqi Shi'ites. Hussein was hanged on December 30, 2006.

al-Qaeda. Eventually, they moved these prisoners to a facility at the American Guantánamo Bay Naval Base in Cuba. They were among the first suspected terrorists handled under the new laws created by the federal government to deal with terrorism after September 11, 2001. The Patriot Act of 2001 was the most important of these new laws. The post-September 11 laws and policies made it possible to detain suspected terrorists for months, and in many cases years, without access to lawyers, without facing formal charges, subjected to intensive interrogation and torture. They became examples to many critics of the dangers to basic civil liberties they believed the war on terrorism had created.

The Bush administration argued that detainees in Guantánamo were outside the reach of American law. The Supreme Court dismissed this argument in several rulings. But the administration was slow to comply. Before his election in 2008, Barack Obama promised to close the Guantánamo prison, which had become a symbol to many of unfair treatment. But once in office, President Obama found it difficult to keep this promise because of popular opposition to moving prisoners into facilities in the United States. The status of detainees in Guantánamo continues to be in flux. President Donald Trump signed an executive order in 2018 to keep the detention camp open indefinitely, while President Joe Biden announced in 2021 the intention of his administration to shut down the facility before he leaves office.

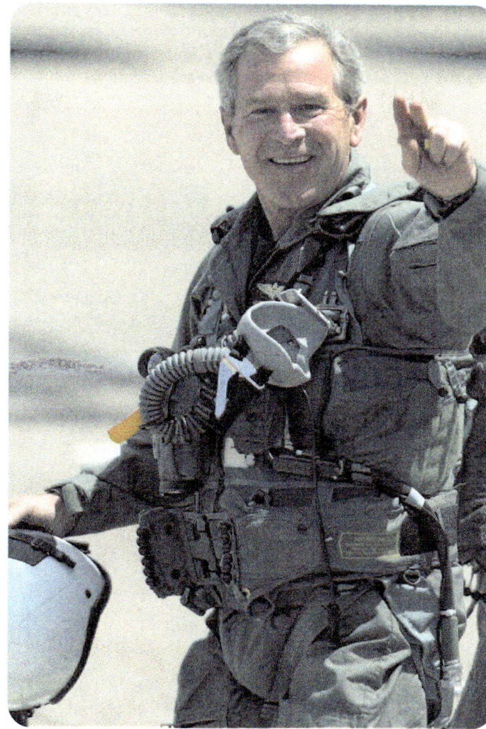

"MISSION ACCOMPLISHED," 2003 President George W. Bush chose the USS *Abraham Lincoln*, an aircraft carrier moored just off the coast of San Diego, for his first major address after the end of formal hostilities in the Iraq War on May 1, 2003. To strengthen his own identification with the military, he flew in on an S-3 Viking that landed on the carrier's deck and appeared before cameras wearing a flight suit and carrying a helmet. Later, dressed in a conventional business suit, he addressed a crowd of service men and women on the deck, standing beneath a large banner reading "Mission Accomplished." Later, as fighting in Iraq continued with no clear end in sight, and as the war became increasingly unpopular, Bush received much criticism and ridicule for what many Americans considered a premature celebration of victory.

THE IRAQ WAR

In his State of the Union address to Congress in January 2002, President Bush spoke of an "axis of evil," which included Iraq, Iran, and North Korea. These nations had anti-American regimes and either possessed or were thought to be trying to acquire nuclear weapons. Although President Bush did not say so at the time, many people around the world interpreted these words to mean that the United States would soon try to topple the government of Saddam Hussein in Iraq.

For over a year, the Bush administration slowly built a public case for invading Iraq. Much of that case rested on two claims. One was that Iraq was supporting terrorist groups that were hostile to the United States. The other, and eventually

Discussion and Activities

Making Connections After students have read the section "The War on Terrorism," discuss as a class the extent the "War on Terrorism" affects them today, and if they believe that the threat of terrorism against the United States has changed since 2001. **WOR PCE NAT**

Historical Thinking Skills

Sourcing and Situation Have students examine the images "Saddam Hussein" and "Mission Accomplished, 2003." Ask them to write a short paragraph explaining the purpose, point of view, intended audience, or historical situation of either photo. **WOR PCE SOC NAT**

Historical Thinking Skills

Evaluating Evidence Have students examine the image "Crises in the Middle East." Ask them to discuss in small groups the successes and failures of U.S. Middle East policy. Have students consider what different approaches might have led to greater peace and stability in the region, if any. **WOR** **PCE** **WXT** **SOC** **NAT**

the more important, was that Iraq either had or was developing what came to be known as "weapons of mass destruction," which included nuclear weapons and agents of chemical and biological warfare. Less central to these arguments was ideal of spreading democracy in the Middle East and the charge that the Hussein government was responsible for major violations of human rights. Except for the last, none of these claims turned out to be accurate.

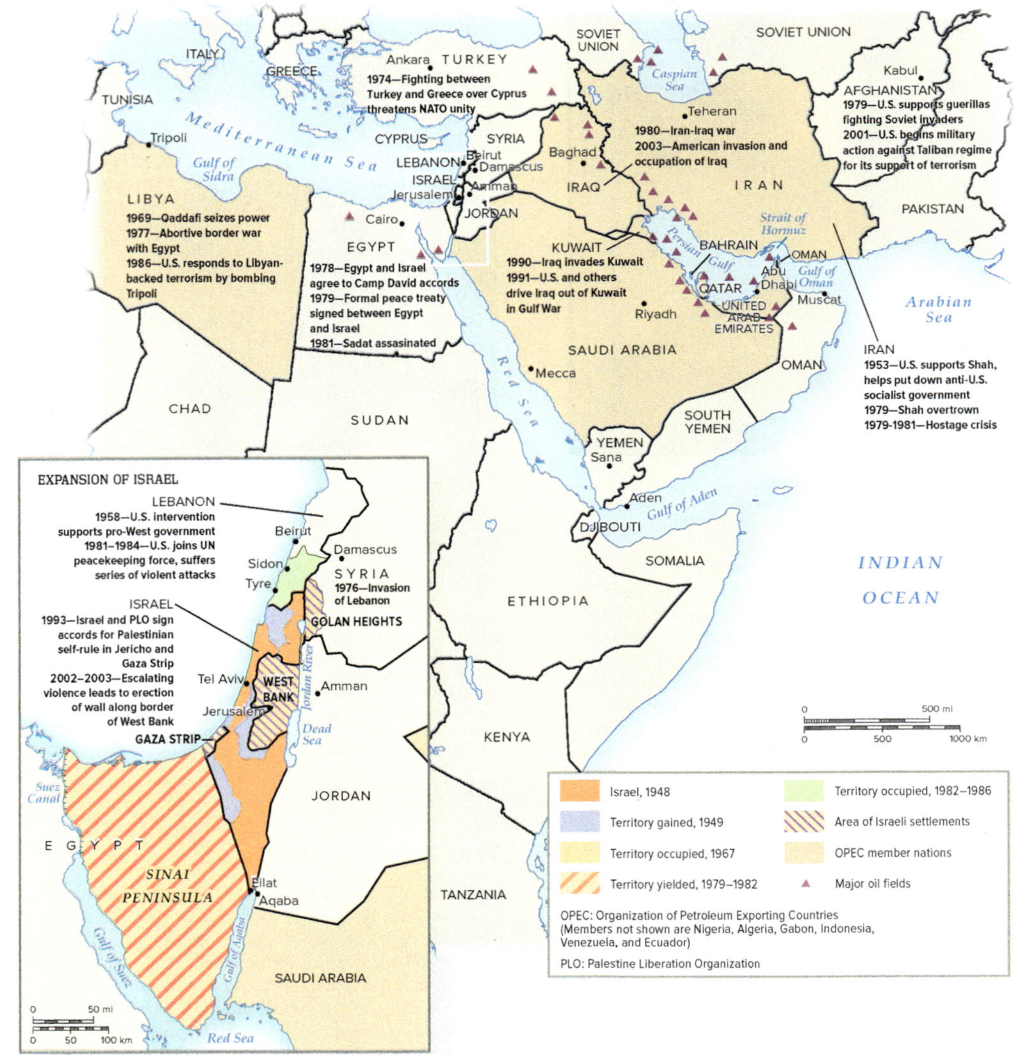

CRISES IN THE MIDDLE EAST The United States has intervened in the Middle East since the end of World War II. The map illustrates the tension among the nations of the region along with the increasing actions taken by the U.S., particularly after 9/11.

Why did the United States have so much at stake in the Middle East?

910 · CHAPTER 34

Answers

Crises in the Middle East.

The United States was focused on the Middle East due to its large reserves of oil and U.S. support for the state of Israel.

In March 2003, American and British troops invaded Iraq and quickly toppled the Hussein regime with scant support from other countries and partial authorization from the United Nations. Hussein went into hiding but was eventually captured in December 2003 and executed in 2006. In May 2003, shortly after the American capture of Baghdad, President Bush made a dramatic appearance on an aircraft carrier off the coast of California and declared victory in the Iraq War.

In fact, the war in Iraq continued for six more years, during which 3,600 soldiers were killed (out of just over 4,200 in total). Support for the war in the United States steadily declined in the first months of the war, especially when it became clear that the "weapons of mass destruction" in Iraq turned out not to exist. Reports of torture of Iraqi prisoners by American soldiers increased the unpopularity of the war.

The invasion of Iraq was the most visible evidence of a basic change in the structure of American foreign policy under the presidency of George W. Bush. Ever since the late 1940s, when the containment policy became the cornerstone of America's role in the world, the United States had worked to maintain stability in the world by containing, but not often directly threatening or attacking, its adversaries. Even after the Cold War ended, the United States continued to demonstrate a reasonable level of constraint, despite its unchallenged military preeminence. In the administrations of George H. W. Bush and Bill Clinton, for example, American leaders worked closely with the United Nations and NATO to achieve U.S. international goals and usually resisted taking unilateral military action.

There had always been those who criticized these constraints. They believed that America should do more than maintain stability and should move actively to topple undemocratic regimes and destroy potential enemies of the United States. In the administration of George W. Bush, these critics took control of American foreign policy and began to reshape it. The legacy of containment was repudiated and replaced by the stance that the United States had the right and the responsibility to spread freedom throughout the world—not just by example, but by military force when necessary.

The Unraveling of the Bush Presidency

For most of the first three years of his presidency, George W. Bush enjoyed broad popularity because of his resolute stance against terrorism. Indeed, his firm position even buoyed his approval ratings during the controversial Iraq War, at least for a while. Bush's domestic policies did little to strengthen him politically, however. The president's tax cuts of 2001 disproportionately benefited wealthy Americans, reflecting the view of White House economists that the best way to ensure growth was to put money into the hands of people most likely to invest. The tax cuts also contributed to the nearly $10 trillion increase in the national debt during the Bush presidency. Also controversial was one of Bush's most significant domestic accomplishments, an education bill known as "No Child Left Behind," which tied federal funding in schools to students' success in taking standardized tests. Some educators and parents favored No Child Left Behind, but many others felt that students spent too many hours in the classroom learning how to take tests rather than think for themselves. By 2004, when the president faced reelection, it was uncertain if he would be returned to office. Senator John Kerry of Massachusetts, a Vietnam veteran who opposed the war in Iraq, mounted a strong attack against the president by criticizing his policies. But harsh assaults on Kerry in return, combined with the mobilization of large numbers of conservatives, helped Bush win a narrow victory.

Bush's second term was a difficult one. The war in Iraq was going badly, and its growing unpopularity added to the rapidly declining approval ratings of the president himself—ratings that by mid-2008 had reached the lowest level of presidential approval in the history of polling.

Hurricane Katrina

Perhaps even more damaging to President Bush was the government's response to a disastrous hurricane, Katrina, which devastated a massive swath of the coastline of the Gulf of Mexico in August 2005 and gravely damaged the city of New Orleans. The federal government's slow response aroused anger throughout the nation, contributing to the loss of the Republican majorities in both houses and leaving Bush with little support. At the same time, scandals in the Justice Department, revelations of illegal violations of civil liberties, and declining economic prospects culminated in the financial crisis of 2008.

The Election of 2008

Both parties began the 2008 campaign with large fields of candidates, but the contest had narrowed considerably by spring. Senator John McCain of Arizona emerged from the early primaries with the Republican nomination assured. Senator Hillary Rodham Clinton of New York (the former First Lady) and Senator Barack Obama of Illinois campaigned aggressively against each other for months. Clinton might have become the first female U.S. president. But Obama's organizational power among young voters and his inspirational messages of hope and change helped him secure primary votes and win the Democratic nomination. He entered the general election with a chance to become the nation's first African American president.

McCain and Obama came into the campaign with very different programs. McCain supported the Iraq War, and Obama did not. Obama wanted national health insurance and McCain did not. McCain wanted additional tax cuts to spur investment, while Obama urged tax increases on the wealthiest Americans. Obama went with experience and name recognition in picking his vice-presidential running mate, Senator Joe Biden of Delaware. McCain chose an almost unknown figure to share his ticket—Governor Sarah Palin of Alaska. Palin soon became the hero of many conservatives in the Republican convention. But her inexperience seemed to damage the

Reasoning Processes

Identifying Cause and Effect After students have read the section "The Iraq War," ask them to create a T-chart listing the causes and effects of the Iraq War. Have students discuss in small groups what they believe to be the most important causes and effects. **WOR** **PCE** **NAT** **WXT**

Discussion and Activities

Historical Evidence and Argumentation Have students read the section "The Unraveling of the Bush Presidency." Ask them to discuss in small groups the successes and failures of President Bush's second term. Have students write a thesis statement that makes a historically defensible claim about whether Bush's time in office was successful or not. **WOR** **PCE** **WXT** **SOC** **NAT**

Reasoning Processes

Comparing and Contrasting After students have read the section "The Election of 2008," ask them to create a Venn diagram comparing the candidates and issues of the presidential elections of 2004 and 2008. Have students discuss in small groups how the elections were similar and different. **PCE**

OBAMANIA Posters of and about Barack Obama were widely visible during the 2008 presidential campaign. In this photograph, a New Yorker walks past one example of the Obama street art that spread through many American cities—and, indeed, through cities around the world. Among the depictions of Obama during the campaign were the work of leading artists, who saw in him a figure of historic significance.

© Chris McGrath/Getty Images

Republican campaign. Before the conventions, Obama was already leading strongly in the polls.

As the nomination campaigns were heating up, a series of financial problems arose in mid-2007. By 2008, the nation was facing its worst financial crisis since the Great Depression. During this crisis, McCain and Obama fought out the last two months of their campaign. Obama benefited from George W. Bush's unpopularity. With the incoming president facing another powerful downturn in the economy, McCain's response seemed to associate him with Bush's policies, increasingly viewed by many Americans as causing the financial meltdown. In contrast, Obama conveyed a message that seemed to signal new and more hopeful possibilities. The race ended in a strong showing for Obama, and on November 4, 2008, he won the popular vote 53 percent to McCain's 46 percent and the electoral vote by an even larger margin.

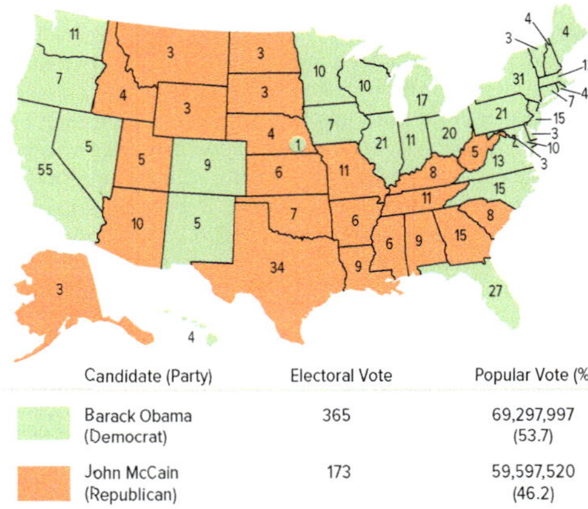

Candidate (Party)	Electoral Vote	Popular Vote (%)
Barack Obama (Democrat)	365	69,297,997 (53.7)
John McCain (Republican)	173	59,597,520 (46.2)

THE ELECTION OF 2008 The election of 2008 broke the pattern of very close divisions between the two parties and instead produced a decisive victory for Barack Obama. For the first time since 1996, Democrats won states in the South and carried most of the "swing states." The election also carried large majorities for the Democrats in both the House and the Senate, only to see the Republicans carry a majority of the House in 2010.

IDENTITY POLITICS

The last years of the George W. Bush administration and those of Barack Obama's presidency were difficult for each man with both losing support over domestic and foreign policy issues.

THE OBAMA PRESIDENCY

Few modern presidents have entered the White House with higher expectations from the nation and even the world, so it was inevitable that many of Obama's supporters would eventually be disappointed. The enormity of the tasks Obama faced–managing the worst economy since the 1930s, one war

Historical Thinking Skills

Evaluating Evidence Have students examine the image "Obamania." Ask them to discuss as a class how Obama was able to defeat Clinton for the Democratic nomination and McCain in the general election. Have students consider which of these tactics or characteristics, if any, they have seen used in recent presidential elections. **PCE** **WXT** **SOC** **NAT**

in Iraq and another in Afghanistan, and a polarized political climate–made his presidency extraordinarily difficult.

At the time of Obama's inauguration, millions of Americans were unemployed. Major companies, especially in the automobile industry, faced bankruptcy. The home mortgage and other financial industries were still on the verge of collapse despite Bush's intervention. Obama set aside his initial aspirations to confront the dangerous reality that the country was on the brink of an economic depression possibly greater in scope and impact than the one of the 1930s.

To shore up the faltering economy, Obama engineered the largest economic stimulus that had ever been introduced up to that point. The Obama stimulus package, announced in 2009, included tax cuts, expanded unemployment benefits, and increased spending on education, infrastructure, police, health care, and job creation. The total funding for all of these programs reached $787 billion. Though controversial and passed by only a slight margin in Congress, most economists agreed that the stimulus measures saved the economy from catastrophe. Still, many critics believed that Obama's stimulus package was a significant waste of money that added considerably to the national debt, while others believed it was not large enough.

STIMULUS PACKAGE

Even in such a precarious economic environment, Obama pressed for the passage of his Patient Protection and Affordable Care Act to realize the dream of many liberals since the 1930s: universal health care. The act urged all Americans to purchase health insurance, making provisions to help those of limited financial means to acquire it. Though the bill finally passed Congress in March 2010 despite threats of filibustering, the Republicans condemned this reform as "socialized medicine." They vowed to repeal it or defeat it through judicial action. Most of the Affordable Care Act benefits did not go into effect until Obama's second term. To the embarrassment of the administration and delight of critics, the rollout of the plan in 2013 experienced significant technical problems when the federal website designed to process new insurance applications failed to work properly.

There were many opponents of "Obamacare"–as many called the Affordable Care Act. Some of Obama's political adversaries were a group of evangelical, conservative, and libertarian Republicans who came to be known as the "Tea Party." Although the Tea Party could not stop passage of the Affordable Care Act, they used their opposition to it to spearhead their overall conservative agenda: deficit reduction, tax reduction, and smaller government. The Tea Party's appeal to wealthy conservatives brought large financial contributions that gave this group a disproportionate political influence that belied its relatively small numbers. With the help of the conservative media, the Tea Party exerted increasing pressure on the Republican Party as a whole. In the 2010 midterm elections, 130 Tea Party-endorsed candidates were sworn in as members of Congress. The Tea Party contributed to the strong polarization of the federal government that resulted in a great deal of legislative gridlock.

TEA PARTY

Obama came into office with an ambitious plan for reshaping America's role in the world. The American combat role in Iraq was diminishing in the last year of the Bush administration, but Obama brought it to an end in 2010. At the same time, he committed significant additional troops to the war in Afghanistan, where Americans had been fighting since 2001.

INTERNATIONAL RELATIONS

With former rival Hillary Clinton as his secretary of state, Obama sought peace between Israel and the Palestinian Authority–an effort that, like all previous ones, was extraordinarily difficult. They sought to improve relations with many nations that the Iraq War had damaged and built new international trade opportunities. In 2009, Obama received the Nobel Peace Prize for his "extraordinary efforts to strengthen international diplomacy and cooperation between peoples." In the fall of 2010, President Obama visited India, China, and South Korea. The administration hoped for progress on trade, but China and South Korea failed to reach agreements with the United States.

The Tea Party wasn't Obama's only critic during his first term–he also faced opposition from the political left. Some Democrats felt that he had moved too far to the right and had unnecessarily compromised core Democratic goals. Many people believed that Obama had failed to deliver on campaign promises, such as closing the Guantánamo prison. Disgruntled critics protested that the president did not punish those financiers whom they held responsible for the global economic crisis. The so-called Occupy Wall Street movement arose as a populist response to increasing economic inequality. Protesters gathering near Wall Street and in other cities across the country used an article by economist Joseph Stiglitz that found that the wealthiest 1 percent of Americans owned over 40 percent of the nation's wealth to animate their position. Economic inequality became an important theme in the presidential election of 2012.

OCCUPY WALL STREET

The impact of money on politics became mainstream news in 2010 with the Supreme Court decision in *Citizens United v. Federal Election Commission*. In this case, the conservative-leaning court ruled that government could not limit campaign-related expenditures from corporations or unions. Critics of the decision, including people sympathetic to the "Occupy" movement, felt that it favored the Republicans because wealthy donors tended to donate to that party. The ability of corporations to donate freely to individual campaigns would change the financing associated with the coming 2012 presidential election; indeed, more money was spent on that election than on any previous election.

While Barack Obama and Joe Biden once again occupied the Democratic ticket, the Republican primaries were tough contests involving a large field of candidates. Businessman and former Massachusetts governor Mitt Romney finally prevailed to win the Republican nomination with his vice-presidential running mate, Representative Paul Ryan of Wisconsin. Considered a moderate Republican, Romney changed his position on a

Discussion and Activities

Comparing and Contrasting After students have read the section "Stimulus Package," ask them to create a Venn diagram comparing Obama's stimulus package with either the New Deal or the Great Society. Ask for volunteers to share their diagram and discuss as a class. **PCE** **WXT**

Historical Thinking Skills

Evaluating Evidence After students have read the section "Tea Party," ask them to discuss in small groups arguments for and against the passage of the Affordable Care Act. Have students consider the most persuasive argument for or against the act and prepare a social media campaign in support of their argument. **PCE** **WXT** **SOC**

Historical Thinking Skills

Developing Arguments After students have read the section "NSA Controversy," ask them to create a script for a campaign commercial supporting either Obama or Romney in the 2012 presidential election. PCE WXT SOC NAT

range of issues, including abortion rights and health care, apparently to appeal to the increasingly conservative nature of his party. Democrats made his changed positions a focus of their campaign.

The key issues of the 2012 election included healthcare reform, immigration reform, the federal budget deficit, and taxation and government spending. The strained economy kept the focus more on domestic than international concerns. Perhaps the most pressing issue was the high unemployment rate– a problem that President Obama had struggled to remedy throughout most of his first term. Despite this lingering problem, Obama outlined his successes and pointed to them as the justification for a second term. He had withdrawn most of the troops from Iraq, as promised. Most dramatically, he had succeeded in overseeing the tracking down and, on May 2, 2011, the killing of al-Qaeda leader Osama bin Laden, the mastermind of the 9/11 attacks.

The head-to-head contest between Romney and Obama at times seemed close. But a generally improving economy, the death of bin Laden, and several political missteps by Romney helped Obama. When voters finally cast their ballots, Obama won 51 percent of the popular vote to Romney's 47 percent, translating into 332 electoral votes for the president and 206 for his rival.

President Obama's second term posed many challenges on both the domestic and international fronts. One event that extended to both realms was the disclosure of many classified documents by computer specialist Edward Snowden. On June 5, 2013, Snowden, a former contractor for the National Security Agency (NSA), released a vast number of classified documents to several media outlets. Many observers viewed this action as the most serious leak since Daniel Ellsworth released the Pentagon Papers in 1971. The released documents showed extensive governmental surveillance of private Internet and telephone data, including the monitoring of the personal phone lines of such foreign leaders as Germany's Chancellor Angela Merkel. Snowden fled the United States, first to China and then to Russia, to avoid criminal charges. Some called Snowden a traitor, others, a heroic champion of civil liberties.

NSA Controversy

During President Obama's second term, one of the most serious international events took place in Syria, a country locked in violent civil war since 2011. Opponents of the Ba'ath government sought the ouster of President Bashar al-Assad and his repressive regime. Assad unleashed the army in response, killing an estimated 120,000 of his own people by September 2013. The displacement of hundreds of thousands of Syrians into neighboring countries threatened to destabilize the region further. Assad's use of chemical weapons triggered a strong condemnation by the United States and its European allies. Working with Russia, a traditional ally of the Assad regime, the United States and Europe brokered a deal to remove the stockpile of chemical weapons from the country. Obama, aware of the national unwillingness for the United States to become involved in another ground war, resisted calls for sending troops to dislodge Assad. In September 2014, the United States and five Arab countries launched airstrikes against Islamic State targets in Syria, and in 2015 Russia entered the conflict. American leaders were suspicious of Russia's involvement, believing that they had aimed their attacks more at anti-Assad rebels. By September 2016, the United States stopped cooperating with Russia's continued bombing of the city of Aleppo, Syria. The Trump administration briefly increased the troops in Syria. But soon after the US effectively withdrew from Syria, the rebels collapsed, Bashar al-Assad consolidated his power, and the refugee crisis spread to Europe.

Obama also focused on the global issue of nuclear security by promoting a nuclear weapons agreement with Iran in 2013. The deal, signed by the United States, Iran, Germany, France, and the United Kingdom, limited Iranian development of weapons-grade plutonium and uranium enrichment. Iran also agreed to allow more inspections of industries and supply chains that could be used in nuclear weapons manufacturing. Iran agreed to this deal to reduce economic sanctions the United States and the United Nations had placed upon it for a variety of reasons, including the 1979 hostage crisis during the Carter administration, terrorist actions in the 1980s, and to weaken Iran's ability to create a nuclear weapons program in the 1990s. These sanctions weakened Iran's economy. But critics of the Obama administration's cooperation in this nuclear deal warned that lifting the sanctions could allow the Iranian government to use its growing economy to resume nuclear weapons development.

Diplomatic Efforts

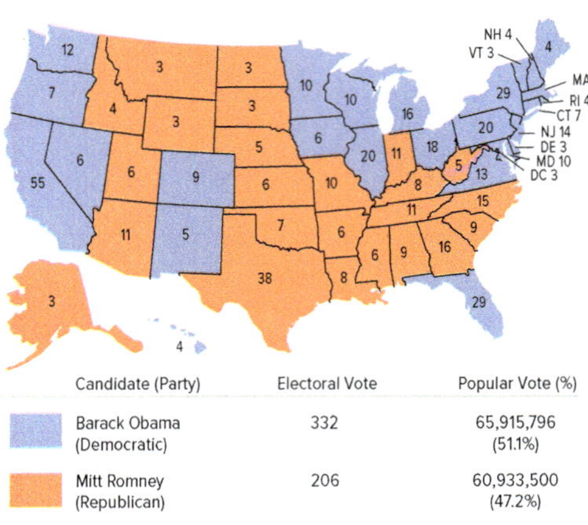

THE ELECTION OF 2012 President Obama and Vice President Biden won a decisive victory over the Republican ticket of Mitt Romney and Paul Ryan.

Reasoning Processes

Continuity and Change Have students examine the map "The Election of 2012." Ask them to compare this map with map of the 2008 election earlier in the chapter. Have students discuss similarities and differences between the maps. Ask them to consider why the maps are similar. *(Indiana and North Carolina flipped from Democratic to Republican. Elections may be becoming more about identity than ideology, voters may be migrating to areas where their ideology is in the majority.)* PCE WXT SOC NAT

In March 2016, the United States restored diplomatic relations with Cuba for the first time since 1959, when the Cuban Revolution established a communist government under the leadership of Fidel Castro. Obama reopened the U.S. embassy in 2015 and, with his family, visited in March 2016, making him the first president to visit Cuba since Calvin Coolidge in 1928.

Obama also sought improvements in the areas of economics and trade, diplomacy, and global stability. Obama joined the Trans-Pacific Partnership (TPP), a multi-national trade agreement between the United States, Canada, and nine other nations in Asia and across the Pacific Ocean region. Obama believed that joining the TPP would increase American exports and help guarantee high-quality jobs for Americans.

The political gridlock of Obama's presidency continued into his second term. Many of his initiatives either encountered serious obstacles or did not come to pass. One initiative, the immigration reform bill, garnered support. On June 27, 2013, the Senate passed the Border Security, Economic Opportunity, and Immigration Modernization Act of 2013 as a comprehensive package of provisions, including a path to US citizenship for undocumented immigrants already in the country. As of spring 2014, the House had not passed the bill owing to powerful conservative Republican opposition.

POLITICAL GRIDLOCK

Another disappointment for President Obama and his supporters involved the failure to enact meaningful gun control measures despite a series of horrific shootings occurring during his terms in office, including the shooting of twenty children and six adults at the Sandy Hook Elementary School in Newtown, Connecticut, on December 14, 2012. Despite the president's promise to exert "whatever power this office holds" to generate gun control reform, Congress resisted enacting any such legislation. The National Rifle Association and the conservative wing of the Republican Party successfully warded off any change on the federal level of the right of Americans to buy and use guns.

OBAMA GRIEVES WITH A NATION President Barack Obama speaks at a memorial service for the 26 people killed on December 16, 2012, by a gunman at the Sandy Hook Elementary School. His subsequent attempts at gun control reform were blocked by the House of Representatives whose majority argued for the right of Americans to keep and bear arms without interference from the government.

The gridlock of the House also dashed any hopes President Obama had of gaining a grand budget deal. The parties remained sharply divided on questions of taxation, budget deficits, and government spending. The midterm election of 2014 resulted in Republicans gaining their largest majority in the House of Representatives since the 1920s. The Republicans also took control of the Senate for the first time since 2007. With Congress back under their control beginning in January 2015, Republicans hoped to advance their legislative agenda ahead of the 2016 presidential election.

Election of 2016

The nominations for president by the major parties in 2016 were significant for several reasons. Hillary Clinton won the Democratic Party nomination, marking the first time a major party had nominated a woman to run for president. Clinton had served as Secretary of State under Obama and as a senator from New York. She was also First Lady of the United States from 1993 to 2001. The Republican nominee, Donald Trump, was the first person nominated by a major party who had not held elective office nor served in the military. Trump was a wealthy businessman and a well-known celebrity, appearing regularly on radio and television since the 1980s.

Trump adopted a controversial and aggressive campaign style where he often interrupted, talked over opponents, and argued with the moderators. He was an active user of Twitter, where he criticized opponents, government policies, and the news media. Trump's style polarized the nation and angered those Americans who saw him as a liar and a bully. But to many others, his style seemed honest and direct compared to typical politicians. Trump claimed that political donors and lobbyists could not influence him the way they influenced other politicians because of his wealth.

While polls predicted Clinton would win the election, Trump prevailed. Clinton won 48 percent of the popular vote to Trump's 46 percent, but Trump won the Electoral College. Additionally, Republicans held onto majorities in the House and the Senate, giving Republicans control of both the executive and legislative branches of the government.

The Trump Presidency

Trump's style did not change upon taking office. He continued to use Twitter to criticize opponents and the media, often launching allegations of "fake news" to discredit news outlets. He also quickly terminated members of his administration if they seemed to be ineffective or disloyal. By the end of his term, he had fired and replaced more cabinet members and White House advisors than any previous president in the same amount of time.

Trump pursued an agenda intent on overturning several Obama era programs and policies. One target was the repeal of

Discussion and Activities

Evaluating Evidence After students have read the section "The Obama Presidency," ask them to create a two column chart listing successes and failures of the Obama administration. Have students share their charts in small groups and try to rank the items they identified in order from most to least important. Ask groups to share their rankings with the class. **PCE** **WXT** **SOC** **NAT**

Reasoning Processes

Continuity and Change Have students read the section "The Election of 2016." Discuss as a class ways in which the Trump campaign was similar to previous presidential campaigns, and ways in which it was different. **PCE** **SOC** **WXT** **NAT**

Reasoning Processes

Continuity and Change After students have read the section "Trade," ask them to discuss as a class how President Trump's policies on taxation and trade were similar to or different from previous Republican presidents. *(Like many Republican presidents, Trump called for reducing income tax rates. Unlike most of them, he called for more trade restrictions including raising tariffs.)* **WOR** **PCE** **WXT**

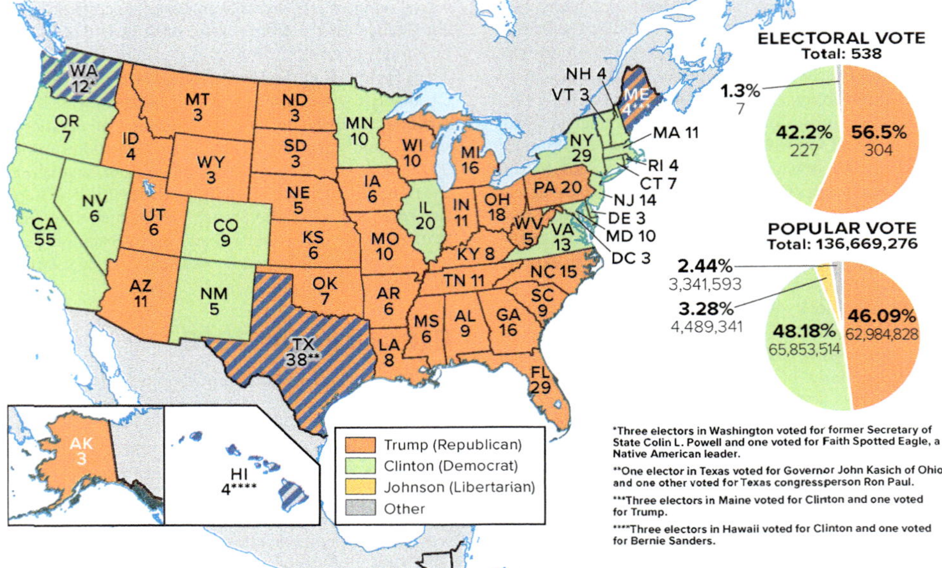

THE ELECTION OF 2016 President Trump and Vice President Pence won the Electoral College but lost the popular vote.

the Affordable Care Act or Obamacare. Despite Republicans controlling both chambers of Congress, Trump was unsuccessful in repealing Obamacare. Republicans were successful, however, in ushering in massive tax cuts and spending cuts to major welfare programs, including Medicare and Medicaid. Trump also flexed his presidential power with several executive orders leading to the rollback and deregulation of industry at the expense of environmental protection. However, one of the most lasting impacts of the Trump administration will be his appointment of three conservative U.S. Supreme Court Justices: Neil Gorsuch, Brett Kavanaugh, and Amy Coney Barrett.

DOMESTIC POLICIES

New tax cuts also became a priority for the Trump administration. Trump had long argued that companies moved factories and jobs to other countries because American corporations paid some of the highest taxes in the world. In late 2017, the Republican-controlled Congress passed the Tax Cuts and Jobs Act, the largest tax code overhaul since Ronald Reagan's tax reforms in 1986. The act reduced income taxes for most Americans, with middle class Americans getting the biggest percentage cut. However, the wealthy gained more in terms of dollars as the act also cut corporate tax rates from among the highest in the world to among the lowest compared to other industrial nations.

Trump also continued the philosophy of "Make America Great Again" or "MAGA," which was a focus of his campaign. Trump argued that the United States had lost its way by supporting globalism. Trump's approach resembled policies before World War II, where opponents of global interdependence were referred to as nationalists, or protectionists, both terms he frequently used. Protectionists believe government should regulate trade and impose tariffs to protect U.S. companies from foreign competition and discourage them from moving their factories and jobs overseas where wages are lower.

TRADE

Upon taking office, Trump withdrew from negotiations on the Trans-Pacific Partnership (TPP) and warned Canada and Mexico that the United States would withdraw from the North American Free Trade Agreement (NAFTA) unless the treaty was renegotiated. He then imposed tariffs on steel and aluminum from Canada and Mexico. Negotiations began soon after, and in late 2018, the three countries signed the United States-Mexico-Canada Agreement (USMCA). Trump likewise sought to pressure China into a new trade deal with additional tariffs on steel, aluminum, and a few other products and then steadily expanded the list of goods when China did not respond. These tariffs led to a trade war, and China imposed tariffs on American cars, airplanes, and soybeans. The trade war eventually led to the U.S.-China Phase One trade deal in early 2020 that set new rules for currency exchange rates, intellectual property, and the transfer of technology along with implementing targets for the goods China would import from the United States.

Discussion and Activities

Speculating Have students examine the map "The Election of 2016." Ask them to think about and share with a partner why they think there was an unusually high number of "rogue electors," or electors who cast votes for a candidate other than the one they were pledged to, in the 2016 election. *(There were likely more rogue electors due to the unconventional divisive nature of Donald Trump as a campaigner and politician.)* **PCE** **SOC**

DEMILITARIZED ZONE President Trump and Kim Jong-Un met at the Demilitarized Zone (DMZ) between North and South Korea in 2019. The 154 mile long and nearly 3-mile-wide DMZ was created as a buffer between North and South Korea at the end of the Korean War.

Handout/Dong-A Ilbo/Getty Images News/Getty Images

Trump often used the phrase "America First" in discussions surrounding efforts to disentangle the nation from what he called the "forever wars" in the Middle East, bring troops home from overseas, and reduce the amount of money the United States spent defending allies in Europe and East Asia. To support this policy, Trump pushed to end the war in Afghanistan. Yet many disagreed, believing the Taliban would continue to support terrorism and might destroy Afghanistan's fragile democracy. When Trump left office, only 2,500 troops remained in Afghanistan, the lowest number since the war began. However, the war between the Taliban and the Afghan government continued, and the U.S. continued airstrikes to support Afghan forces fighting the Taliban. The subsequent withdrawal of American forces in August of 2021 enabled the Taliban to gain power and brought an abrupt and chaotic end to America's longest war.

FOREIGN POLICY

The Trump administration believed Iran was responsible for much of the ongoing violence in the Middle East that kept American troops in the region. In spring 2018, he withdrew from the Iran nuclear deal, imposed sanctions, and shifted to a policy of "maximum pressure." Tensions escalated and came to a head with a U.S. airstrike that killed Iranian general Qasem Soleimani, and Iran retaliated with missiles attacks on Americans stationed on Iraqi bases. Trump rejected further military escalation and instead imposed more sanctions and new negotiations. Although Iran rejected the offer, both countries backed away from war.

In 2017, Trump kept a campaign promise by officially recognizing Jerusalem as Israel's capital and directing the American embassy to be moved to Jerusalem. In 2020, the Trump administration brokered a series of agreements known as the Abraham Accords between Israel and several Arab states that pledged a commitment to normalize relations among the nations.

The United States had long imposed sanctions and worked to keep North Korea isolated to discourage the building of nuclear weapons by the nation. The Trump administration reached out to North Korea's leader, Kim Jung-Un, to broker a deal to dismantle their nuclear program, and Trump became the first president to meet with a North Korean leader. He met Kim Jong-Un three times in 2018 and 2019 but was unable to reach an agreement.

Domestically, Trump capitalized on the concerns of some Americans regarding immigration. Shortly after taking office, Trump signed an order halting refugee admissions and temporarily barring people from several Muslim-majority nations. Likewise, concerns about undocumented immigrants crossing the southern border had been an important platform during Trump's campaign. He promised to build a wall along the border with Mexico to deter unauthorized border crossing from Latin America into the United States. But strong opposition from Democrats in Congress, civil rights groups, environmentalists, and state governments delayed construction and the wall remained mostly unbuilt as of 2021.

TRAVEL BAN AND IMMIGRATION POLICIES

To further deter unauthorized crossings at the southern border, Trump announced a "zero tolerance" policy under which adults were separated from their children and held for trial, and the children were sent to overcrowded facilities or placed with sponsors. The Trump administration also developed a new plan, the Migrant Protection Protocols (MPP), sometimes called the "Remain in Mexico" policy that required all immigrants at the southern border to stay in Mexico pending case hearings.

Trump also opposed the Deferred Action for Childhood Arrivals (DACA) program during his campaign. DACA was a program created by President Obama in 2012 that allowed undocumented immigrants who had arrived as children to remain for two years, subject to renewal. Supporters of DACA believed that undocumented immigrant children had not come of their own choice and were not legally responsible for the circumstances of their arrival in the United States. Once in office, Trump issued an order ending the program, but in 2020 the Supreme Court reversed Trump's order.

Trump's victory in 2016 was so unexpected many people questioned the results. Clinton's win of the popular vote and the small margin of Trump's victory in Wisconsin, Michigan, and Pennsylvania only reinforced doubts about the outcome. News stories about Russia stealing emails led to suggestions that it might have used computer hacking to alter the election results.

ELECTION INTERFERENCE

The FBI continued investigating the Trump campaign after he took office. Trump called it a "witch-hunt" and a "hoax." He repeatedly clashed with FBI Director James Comey over the investigation, and in May 2017, Trump fired Comey. Democrats then called for a Special Counsel to continue the investigation, and former FBI Director Robert Mueller was appointed to investigate Russian election interference. Mueller's investigation took almost two years. His report concluded that Russia had tried to influence the election by hacking the Democratic Party and Clinton campaign, releasing stolen emails, and posting fake

Discussion and Activities

Evaluating After students have read the section "Travel Ban and Immigration Policy," ask them to create a chart of Trump administration policies and identify each as primarily political, social, or economic. **WOR** **PCE** **SOC** **WXT**

Historical Thinking Skills

Explaining Historical Developments Have students examine the image "Demilitarized Zone." Ask them to discuss in small groups the historical situation of the photo. *(The DMZ separates North and South Korea. It is the boundary determined by the cease-fire that ended the Korean War. President Trump was visiting North Korea, the first American president to do so, to promote relations between the countries. There are many concerns in the region and around the world regarding North Korea's nuclear capabilities.)* **WOR**

Historical Thinking Skills

Developing Arguments After students have read the section "Impeachment," ask them to create arguments in favor of or opposed to the impeachment of President Trump. Discuss as a class what students believe were the most compelling arguments. **PCE**

information on Facebook and Twitter to sway voters. Mueller found no evidence that Russia had hacked voting machines or altered actual votes. Nor did he find evidence of a conspiracy between the Trump campaign and the Russian government to influence the election.

Following the Mueller investigation, new allegations of wrongdoing emerged. A whistleblower in the intelligence community filed a complaint about a call between Trump and the president of Ukraine. A few months before the call, stories circulated that Joe Biden, while vice president, had threatened to cut off aid to Ukraine if the country did not fire a prosecutor investigating a company that had hired Biden's son. The whistleblower claimed Trump wanted Ukraine to investigate the story to help Trump win reelection and threatened to withhold military aid if Ukraine refused.

IMPEACHMENT

After an investigation, the House Judiciary committee drafted two articles of impeachment. They charged Trump with abuse of power and obstruction of Congress for refusing to turn over subpoenaed documents. In December 2019, the House voted in favor of the articles, with nearly all Democrats voting in favor and almost all Republicans opposed. Donald Trump became the third president to be impeached. Andrew Johnson was impeached in 1868. Bill Clinton was impeached in 1998. None were convicted by the Senate.

A CONTESTED CULTURE

American culture changed dramatically in the years after World War II. By the 1960s, the roles of women began to change profoundly. The sexual revolution changed traditional American values. American culture also became more diverse, open, and contentious than it had been in the past. As a result, new controversies and issues emerged.

BATTLES OVER FEMINISM AND ABORTION

The "New Right" actively challenged feminism and its achievements. Conservatives had campaigned successfully against the proposed Equal Rights Amendment to the Constitution. They also played a central role in the most divisive issue of the last thirty years: the controversy over abortion rights.

For those who favored allowing women to choose to terminate unwanted pregnancies, the Supreme Court's decision in *Roe v. Wade* (1973) seemed to settle the question. By the 1980s, abortion was the most commonly performed surgical procedure in the country. But at the same time, opposition to abortion was creating a powerful grassroots movement. The right-to-life movement found its most fervent supporters among Catholics, and indeed, the Catholic Church itself lent its institutional authority to the battle against legalized abortion. Religious doctrine also motivated the anti-abortion stance of many Mormons, evangelical Christians, and other groups. The opposition of some other anti-abortion activists had less to do with religion than with their commitment to traditional notions of family and gender relations. To them, abortion was part of a much larger assault by feminists on the role of women as wives and mothers. It was also, some contended, a form of murder. Fetuses, they claimed, were human beings who had a "right to life" from the moment of conception. Although the right-to-life movement was persistent in its demand for a reversal of *Roe v. Wade* or a constitutional amendment banning abortion, it also attacked abortion at its most vulnerable points. Starting in the late 1970s, Congress and many state legislatures began barring the use of public funds to pay for abortions, thus making them almost inaccessible for many poor women in some states. The Reagan and the two Bush administrations imposed further restrictions on federal funding and even on the right of doctors in federally funded clinics to give patients any information on abortion. Extremists in the right-to-life movement began picketing, occupying, and at times bombing abortion clinics. Several anti-abortion activists murdered doctors who performed abortions; other physicians were subject to campaigns of harassment.

"RIGHT-TO-LIFE" MOVEMENT

The changing judicial climate of the late twentieth and early twenty-first centuries mobilized defenders of abortion as never before. They called themselves the "pro-choice" movement because they were defending every woman's right to choose whether and when to bear a child. The pro-choice movement was in many parts of the country at least as strong as, and in some areas much stronger than, the right-to-life movement. With the election of President Clinton in 1992, a supporter of "choice," the immediate threat to *Roe v. Wade* seemed to fade. Abortion rights remained highly vulnerable as the nation vacillated between Republican and Democratic administrations. Serious challenges for the pro-choice movement arose as Donald Trump impeded abortion access through a series of rule changes that restricted the way taxpayer funds flow to foreign and domestic organizations that perform or promote abortions. The confirmation of three conservative justices to the Supreme Court during Trump's presidency has placed the future of *Roe v. Wade* very much in doubt.

"PRO-CHOICE" MOVEMENT

POLITICAL AND SOCIAL MOVEMENTS

The increasing divisiveness of Trump's rhetoric along with his popularity with far-right groups worried many Americans because it suggested there was widespread support for racist and sexist ideologies. This led his opponents to protest and take other actions to push back against society's apparent shift toward values they rejected.

On January 21, 2017, the day after Trump's inauguration, a worldwide protest known as the Women's March took place. Protesters marched in opposition to Trump in response to the statements he made and accusations of harassment that came to light during the presidential campaign. Many wished to raise awareness of far-ranging issues including women's equality,

Historical Thinking Skills

Analyzing Perspectives Have students read the section "Battles Over Feminism and Abortion." Ask them to discuss in small groups the influence of politics on abortion rights. **PCE** **SOC**

WOMEN'S MARCH AND #METOO

sexual assault awareness, immigration reform, healthcare reform, climate change, LGBTQ rights, and racial equality. Over 450,000 people marched in Washington, D.C., and an estimated 3 to 5 million marched in other cities around the United States and the world. The Women's March of 2017 was the largest one-day protest in American history. The accusations against Trump during the campaign and the march drew attention to how some people with power use their position to sexually harass or abuse others. Later in 2017, a movement known as #MeToo gained national attention as many prominent women began to report their stories of harassment and abuse by major figures in the news, sports, entertainment, and financial industries.

SOCIAL JUSTICE

Social justice is the idea that all people should be treated fairly, and that society should not have rules that give advantages to some people at the expense of others. Those concerned with social justice look at the distribution of wealth and power in society and analyze who has privilege or advantages over others.

By the 2010s, some 50 years after the civil rights movement's achievements and despite the election of the nation's first African American president, it was evident that African Americans still had not achieved full equality with white people. Although many African Americans had achieved wealth, power, and success, the black community as a whole still did not have an equal share of the nation's wealth or the same rate of higher education. African Americans also experienced higher rates of arrest and imprisonment and more medical problems. The disparity suggested to activists that there were other types of systemic racism embedded in society.

Activists tried to point out bias, racism, or stereotypes in the nation's symbols, often seeking to remove or alter them. For many, the most prominent symbols that spoke to the nation's history of racism were statues and flags related to the Confederate States of America. The concern with Confederate symbols erupted in 2014 when white supremacist Dylann Roof killed nine African Americans in a church in Charleston, South Carolina. The attack renewed discussion about racism and led to calls and protests across the United States for the removal of Confederate flags and statues of Confederate war heroes.

Six months after Trump's inauguration, white supremacist, neo-Nazi, and Ku Klux Klan groups organized a rally in Charlottesville, Virginia, to protest the city's decision to remove a statue of Confederate General Robert E. Lee. As news of the rally spread, counter-protestors traveled to Charlottesville to march in opposition. Violence erupted, and a white supremacist rammed his car into counter-protesters killing one and wounding 19 others. Both Democrats and Republicans condemned the violence. But President Trump inflamed the situation when he said, "we condemn in the strongest possible terms this egregious display of hatred, bigotry and violence on many sides, on many sides."

In 2012 Trayvon Martin, an African American teen, was shot and killed in Florida on his way home from a nighttime trip to the convenience store. George Zimmerman, a neighbor-

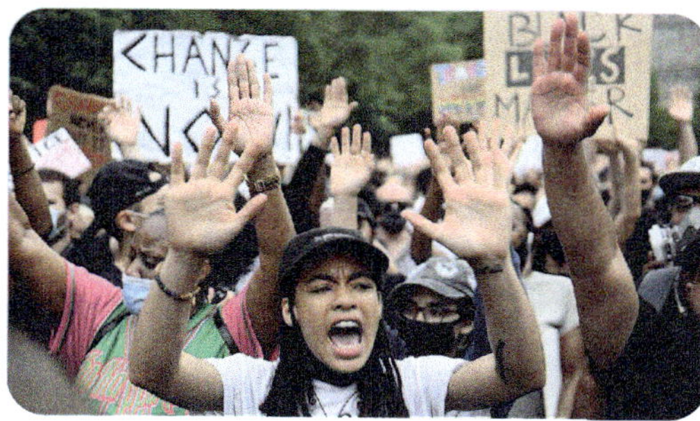

Erik Pendzich/Alamy Stock Photo

SUMMER OF 2020 Following the death of George Floyd in May 2020, protests occurred across the United States and the world to demand equity in the criminal justice system for people of color. In the photograph, people gather and protest as they attend a memorial service to honor the life of George Floyd in New York, June 4, 2020.

BLACK LIVES MATTER

hood watch volunteer, followed Martin and called 911 to report suspicious activity. Zimmerman then shot and killed Martin. The outrage surrounding Martin's death created a social media hashtag that grew into the Black Lives Matter (BLM) movement. In 2014 the shooting death of Michael Brown by police in Ferguson, Missouri, brought the Black Lives Matter movement to national prominence. The movement expanded beyond exposing police violence to bring attention to the economic and social inequality experienced by African Americans in society. In May 2020, George Floyd, an African American man, was killed by Derek Chauvin, a white Minneapolis police officer. Within days of Floyd's death, large demonstrations began in Minneapolis and quickly spread worldwide with over 8,700 Black Lives Matter protests, the vast majority peaceful.

COUNTER-PROTESTERS

In addition to the peaceful demonstrations, riots erupted in many cities. Many mayors and governors enacted curfews to contain the violence, and National Guard troops arrived in many cities. Counter-protesters called for Americans to "Back the Blue" and waved the "Blue Lives Matter" flag created in 2014 after the shooting of two New York police officers. Trump expressed support for the police as well. During his campaign, he criticized Black Lives Matter, and he continued to do so during the protests, blaming the movement for the rioting and violence. With the 2020 election approaching, Trump stressed his commitment to "law and order," a phrase Richard Nixon used during his 1968 campaign to appeal to voters concerned about the violence of the era.

COVID-19

On December 31, 2019, Chinese health officials reported a contagious disease of unknown origin in Wuhan in central China. A week later, they identified a coronavirus as the cause of the disease. The virus was designated Severe Acute Respiratory Syndrome Coronavirus 2, and the illness it caused

Discussion and Activities

Making Connections After students have read the section "Political and Social Movements," discuss as a class the reasons movements advocating for equal rights for women and African Americans are still necessary. PCE SOC NAT

Discussion and Activities

Analyzing Points of View Have students examine the image "Summer of 2020." Ask them to write a journal entry from the point of view of a participant in or observer of the demonstration depicted in the photo. PCE SOC

Discussion and Activities

Making Connections After students have read the feature, ask them to think about whether there is a need for a women's movement today. If so, what should its focus be? If not, why not? Have students share their thoughts with a partner or discuss as a class. **SOC** **WXT**

DEBATING THE PAST

WOMEN'S HISTORY

Historians have long considered the influence of ideas, economic interests, class, and race and ethnicity on the course of history. Women's history challenged them to consider the role of sex and gender as well. Throughout history, many scholars now argue, societies have created distinctive roles for men and women. How those roles have been defined, and the ways in which the roles affect how people and cultures behave, should be central to our understanding of both the past and the present.

In the nineteenth century, women's history generally stressed the unrecognized contributions of women to history—for example, Sarah Hale's 1853 *Record of All Distinguished Women from "the Beginning" till A.D. 1850.* Work of the same sort continued into the twentieth century and, indeed, continues today.

But after 1900, people committed to progressive reform movements began to produce a different kind of women's scholarship, focusing primarily on the ways in which women were victimized by industrialism. Feminist scholars such as Edith Abbott, Margaret Byington, and Katherine Anthony examined the impact of economic change on working-class families, with a special focus on women; and they looked at the often deplorable conditions in which women worked in factories, mills, and other people's homes. Their goal was less to celebrate women's contributions than to direct attention to the oppression of women by harsh working conditions and arouse sentiment for reform.

After the victory of the suffrage movement in 1920, women's history entered a half century of relative inactivity. Women continued to write important histories in many fields, and some—for example, Eleanor Flexner, whose *Century of Struggle* (1959) became a classic history of the suffrage crusade—wrote explicitly about women. Mary Beard, best known for her sweeping historical narratives written in collaboration with her husband, Charles Beard, published *Women as a Force in History* (1964), in which she argued for the historical importance of ordinary women as shapers of society. But such work at first had little impact on the writing of history as a whole.

Along with the rise in modern feminism in the 1960s and 1970s, interest in women's history revived as well. Gerda Lerner, one of the pioneers of the new women's history, once wrote of the impact of feminism on historical studies: "The recognition that we had been denied our history came to many of us as a staggering insight, which altered our consciousness irretrievably." Much of the early work was in the "contributionist" tradition, stressing the way in which women had played more notable roles in major historical events than historians had usually acknowledged. Other work stressed ways in which women had been victimized by their subordination to men and by their powerlessness within the industrial economy.

Increasingly, however, women's history began to question the nature of biological sex and gender itself. Some scholars began to emphasize the artificiality of gender distinctions, arguing that the difference between women and men was socially constructed, superficial, and (in the public world, at least) unimportant. The history of women was, therefore, the history of how men (with the unwitting help of many women) had created and maintained a set of fictions about women's capacities that modern women were now attempting to shatter.

By the early 1980s, some feminists had begun to make a very different argument: that there were basic differences between women and men—not just biological differences, but differences in values, sensibilities, and culture. The feminists of the 1970s and 1980s did not see these differences as evidence of women's incapacities. They saw them, rather, as evidence of an alternative female culture capable of challenging (and improving) the male-dominated world. By the twenty-first century, some historians of women, therefore, began exploring areas of female experience that revealed the special character of women's culture and values: family, housework, motherhood, women's clubs and organizations, female literature, the social lives of working-class women, women's sexuality, and many other subjects that suggested "difference" more than "contributions" or "victimization." Partly in response, some historians began to make the same argument about men—that understanding "masculinity" and its role in shaping men's lives was as important as understanding notions of "femininity" in explaining the history of women.

The notion of gender as a source of social and cultural difference raised a powerful challenge to the way in which scholars view the past. Many historians continue to believe that other categories (race and class in particular) have in fact been more important than gender in shaping the lives of men and women. But, as Joan Scott, a theorist of gender studies, contends, it is not enough simply to expand the existing story to make room for women. Rather, recognizing gender as a central force in the lives of societies calls for a reconceptualization of the past.

HISTORICAL THINKING SKILLS

Questions assume cumulative content knowledge from this chapter and previous chapters.

1. **Identifying Historical Developments** Identify three broad schools of historical interpretation regarding women's history. For each, identify a representative interpretation made by a historian discussed.
2. **Evaluating Evidence** Describe how historical evidence from the time period could be used to support each of the three broad schools of historical interpretation concerning women's history.
3. **Developing Arguments** Analyze the school of thought you find most convincing using evidence from the text in your argument.

Answers

Debating the Past

1. Possible answer: Hale discussed women's contribution to history while Abbot and Byington focused on how women were victimized by business and industry. Flexner and Beard argued that women were "shapers of society." In the 60s and 70s, Lerner and others focused on women's roles and the impact of subordination while historians of the 1980s discussed differences between women's and men's culture.
2. Possible answer: Many progressive reforms of the early twentieth century were led by women, like the settlement house movement. Women took on increasing roles in the workforce and experienced significant changes during both world wars. The modern feminist movement achieved significant workplace progress and increased opportunities for women.
3. Student answers will vary. Student answers should be supported with evidence from the text.

PATTERNS OF POPULAR CULTURE

RAP

The long musical lineage of rap includes elements of the disco and street funk of the 1970s; of the fast-talking jive of black radio DJs in the 1950s; of the onstage patter of Cab Calloway and other African American stars of the first half of the twentieth century. It contains reminders of tap and break dancing—even of the boxing-ring poetry of Muhammad Ali.

Rap's most important element is its words. Rap is as much a form of language as a form of music. It bears a distant resemblance to some traditions of African American pulpit oratory, which also included forms of spoken song. It draws from some of the verbal traditions of urban black street life, including the "dozens"—a ritualized trading of insults particularly popular among young black men.

But rap is also the product of a distinctive place and time: the South Bronx, New York, in the 1970s and 1980s and the hip hop culture that was born there and that soon dominated the appearance and public behavior of many young black males. "Hip hop is how you walk, talk, live, see, act, feel," said one Bronx hip hopper. Some elements of hip hop culture faded, and by the 1990s the most popular element of hip hop culture was rap, which had by then been developing for nearly twenty years.

Beginning in the early 1970s, Bronx DJs began setting up their equipment on neighborhood streets and staging block parties, where they not only played records but also put on shows of their own—performances that featured spoken rhymes, jazzy phrases, and pointed comments about the audience, the neighborhood, and themselves. Gradually, the DJs began to bring "rappers" into shows—young men who developed the DJ style into a much more elaborate form of performance, usually accompanied by dancing. As rap grew more popular in the inner city, record promoters began signing some of its new stars. In 1979, the Sugarhill Gang's "Rapper's Delight" became the first rap single to be played on mainstream commercial radio and the first to become a major hit. In the early 1980s, Run-DMC became the first national rap superstars. From there, rap moved quickly to become one of the most popular and commercially successful forms of popular music. In the 1990s and early 2000s, rap recordings routinely sold millions of copies.

Rap has taken many forms. There have been white rappers (Eminem, House of Pain), female rappers (Missy Elliot, Queen Latifah), even religious rappers and children's rappers. But it has always been primarily a product of the young male culture of the inner city, and some of the most successful rap has conveyed the frustration and anger that these men have felt about their lives—"a voice for the oppressed people," one rap artist said, "that in many other ways don't have a voice." In 1982, the rap group Grandmaster Flash and the Furious Five released a rap called "The Message,"* a searing description of ghetto culture:

> Got a bum education, double-digit inflation
> Can't take the train to the job, there's a strike at the station
> Don't push me, 'cause I'm close to the edge
> I'm tryin' not to lose me head
> It's like a jungle sometime it makes me wonder
> How I keep from going under.

In the late 1980s, the Compton and Watts neighborhoods of Los Angeles—two of the most distressed minority communities in the city—produced their own style, known as West Coast rap, with such groups as Ice Cube, Ice T, Tupac Shakur, and Snoop Doggy Dog. West Coast rap often had a harsh, angry character, and at its extremes (the so-called gangsta' rap), it could be strikingly violent and highly provocative. Scandals erupted over controversial lyrics—Ice T's "Cop Killer," which some critics believed advocated murdering police; and the sexually explicit lyrics of 2 Live Crew and other groups, which critics accused of advocating violence against women.

KANYE WEST Testifying to the continued popularity of rap, Kanye West remains one of the best-selling artists of all time. He has continued his success as an entrepreneur and fashion designer.

But it was not just the lyrics that caused the furor. Rap artists were almost all products of tough inner-city neighborhoods, and the rough-edged styles many took with them into the public eye made many people uncomfortable. Some rappers got caught up in highly publicized trouble with the law. Several—including two of rap's biggest stars, Tupac Shakur and Notorious B.I.G.—were murdered. The business of rap, particularly the confrontational business style of Death Row Records (founded by Dr. Dre, a veteran of the first major West Coast rap group NWA), was a source of public controversy as well.

These controversies at times unfairly dominated the image of rap as a whole. Some rap is angry and cruel, as are many of the realities of the world from which it comes. But much of it is explicitly positive, some of it deliberately gentle. Chuck D and other successful rappers use their music to exhort young black men to avoid drugs and crime, to take responsibility for their children, to get an education. And the form, if not the content, of the original rappers has spread widely through American culture. Rap came to dominate the music charts in America, and its styles made their way onto *Sesame Street* and other children's shows, into television commercials, Hollywood films, and the everyday language of millions of people, young and old, black and white. It became another of the arresting, innovative African American musical traditions that have shaped American culture for more than a century.

*Edward Fletcher, M. Glover, and S. Robinson, "The Message," recorded 1982 by Grand Master Flash & The Furious Five. Reprinted by permission of Sugar Hill Music Publishing Ltd.

HISTORICAL THINKING SKILLS

Questions assume cumulative content knowledge from this chapter and previous chapters.

1. **Identifying** What other African American musical forms have helped shape American popular culture?
2. **Explaining Significance** If rap is so closely associated with the inner-city culture where it originated, what accounts for its widespread popularity and commercial success? What other forms or styles of popular music enjoy a popularity that extends far beyond its cultural origins?
3. **Developing Arguments** Do you think rap's popularity will endure? Why or why not?

Historical Thinking Skills

Sourcing and Situation Have students examine the image "Kanye West." Ask them to write a short paragraph explaining a purpose, point of view, audience, or historical situation for the photo. **WXT SOC ARC**

Answers

Patterns of Popular Culture

1. Possible answer: African American music has significantly contributed to jazz, blues, and rock music. It continues to shape American culture and society today.
2. Possible answer: It provides a message that resonates with many different groups of people.
3. Student answers will vary. Students may indicate that it will continue to be popular as it has evolved over generations to reflect societal issues at every juncture.

Historical Thinking Skills

Evaluating Evidence After students have read the section "COVID-19," ask them to create a chart listing the economic, social, political, and scientific consequences of COVID-19. Have students discuss in small groups the areas they feel COVID-19 had the greatest impact. **PCE** **WXT** **SOC** **NAT**

was named Coronavirus Disease 2019 and quickly became known as COVID-19.

In the weeks following its discovery, the number of COVID-19 cases in China began to climb rapidly. One month after the first reported cases, COVID-19 had spread to 19 countries, with the first case in the United States confirmed in January 2020. President Trump soon established the White House Coronavirus Task Force, which included Dr. Deborah Birx and Dr. Anthony Fauci. The WHO declared COVID-19 a global pandemic in March 2020, and the United States restricted travel to the European Union, Britain, and Ireland.

PANDEMIC RESPONSE

The Task Force recommended Americans not gather in groups greater than ten people and introduced the idea of social distancing. Throughout March 2020, the United States began to shut down. Schools and many businesses closed, which led to widespread layoffs across the nation. For the first time since World War II, Americans experienced widespread shortages of basic supplies as people prepared for the crisis and emptied store shelves of food and goods.

From the beginning, the response to the pandemic was highly politicized. Trump did not trust the media, the Democrats, or government officials not appointed by him. The Democrats, having just attempted to impeach Trump, did not trust his judgment, or look to him for leadership during the crisis. Complicating the policymaking was that the risk of dying from COVID-19 was lower for some Americans than it was for others. This posed a basic civics problem that divided Americans: how to balance the public good against individual rights and how to protect the vulnerable without intruding too much on people's freedom. State governments varied in their responses to the pandemic, but mask mandates generated the most controversy, with the issue polarizing Americans.

To prevent an economic collapse, Congress passed two pieces of legislation. The first was the Families First Coronavirus Relief Act, which provided $104 billion in sick leave and unemployment benefits. The second was the Coronavirus Aid, Relief, and Economic Security Act, or CARES Act, passed on March 27, 2020. In an attempt to produce the medical supplies and equipment needed by the healthcare system, Trump invoked the Defense Production Act (DPA). The DPA, first passed in 1950 to help the nation fight the Korean War, gives the president the authority to order companies to make goods and services needed for national security. Trump used the DPA to order companies to increase the production of medical equipment.

In May 2020, President Trump announced Operation Warp Speed, a program to accelerate the development of vaccines. Under Operation Warp Speed, 6 pharmaceutical companies, including Moderna and Johnson & Johnson, received a share of $10 billion to accelerate research and testing and help scale up their manufacturing. Another company, Pfizer, received $400 million from the German government to develop its "Project Lightspeed" vaccine and $2 billion from Operation Warp Speed to manufacture 100 million doses for Americans. By February 2021, all three vaccines were in use in the United States.

VACCINES

ELECTION OF 2020 AND THE BIDEN PRESIDENCY

To run against Trump, the Democratic Party nominated Joe Biden, a former senator from Delaware and Barack Obama's vice president. Biden made history by choosing Senator Kamala Harris to be his running mate. Harris was the first woman of African American and South Asian descent to run for vice president. Trump and Biden took different approaches when campaigning. Biden spoke to Americans who were very worried about the pandemic or suffering economic losses because of it. He stressed the need to come together and heal the divisiveness of the Trump years. He also promised to address the issues raised by the summer's protests against racial injustice. Trump spoke to Americans who resented the loss of freedom from the pandemic and doubted the necessity of safety measures. He reminded people the economy had done well in his first three years and promised he would restore that growth after the pandemic. He also criticized Black Lives Matter and the subsequent racial unrest, stressing that he supported law and order.

Biden won the popular vote with just over 51 percent to Trump's 47 percent. Biden won the states Clinton had won in 2016, but he also carried the three states in the upper Midwest key to Trump's victory in 2016: Wisconsin, Michigan, and Pennsylvania. Trump had to win one of those states while winning all the states he had won in 2016 to win reelection in 2020. But Biden also narrowly won Arizona, and to the surprise of many people, the state of Georgia, which had not voted for a Democrat since 1992. These victories gave Biden an Electoral College victory of 306 to Trump's 232. Voter analysis showed that African American turnout had rebounded after declining in 2016, and this played an important role in Biden's victories in Georgia, Michigan, and Pennsylvania.

AFTERMATH OF THE ELECTION

Republicans gained seats in the House of Representatives despite Trump's loss, although Democrats kept a slight majority. The Democrats won both Senate seats from Georgia, creating a 50–50 tie in the Senate. This meant the Democrats had gained control because the new vice president, Kamala Harris, would break tie votes.

Election officials faced a challenging situation in 2020 because of the pandemic. Concerns arose that voters would not go to polling stations, and states modified election rules to address the problem. New rules extended early voting, allowed no-excuse absentee voting, allowed people to vote by mail, allowed officials to send mail-in ballots directly to registered voters whether or not they had requested them, and set up drop-off locations where people could deposit their ballots. The new ways of voting, along with the effort both sides made to get their voters to participate, led to the highest percentage of eligible voters turning out since 1900.

CHALLENGES TO THE 2020 ELECTION

Discussion and Activities

Explaining Significance Have students read the introduction to the section "Election of 2020 and the Biden Presidency." Discuss as a class the major issues during the 2020 campaign and have students identify the ones they feel played the largest role in the outcome of the election. **PCE**

Trump began questioning the outcome of the election almost immediately. Unsubstantiated reports of hacked election machines, balloting irregularities, and voter fraud circulated on social media, amplified by Trump and his legal team. Challenges to the election were widespread, with over 50 cases filed by Trump and his legal team, Republican officials, and private individuals and groups. Trump also lobbied state lawmakers and state officials to appoint different electors or refuse to certify election results.

When the lawsuits and lobbying failed, Trump, with the support of most Republicans in Congress, focused on objecting to the Electoral votes when Congress met to count them. If Congress rejects enough Electoral votes so that no one has a majority, the House of Representatives votes by delegation to select the president. If that happened, with a Republican majority in the House, Trump could have had a second term. With this idea in mind, Trump made the fateful decision to ask supporters to rally at the Capitol on the day Congress counted the Electoral votes.

On January 6, 2021, Congress met to count the Electoral votes and certify the winner of the presidential election. As members of Congress gathered for the count, tens of thousands of Trump's supporters gathered for his rally in front of the White House. At the rally, President Trump repeated his claims that he had won the election and that there had been enough fraudulent votes to swing the election to Biden. The examples Trump cited were unsubstantiated, and many were already proven false. Trump urged supporters to march to the Capitol and "peacefully and patriotically make your voices heard."

Attack on the Capitol

Even before he finished his speech, crowds of protestors began gathering outside the U.S. Capitol. As the crowd grew, protestors surged past security barriers, overwhelmed police, broke windows and doors, and entered the Capitol building. Warned that a mob had broken into the building, members of Congress took shelter. The rioters roamed through the Capitol, vandalized offices, and entered the Senate chamber. As they broke into a hallway outside the barricaded House chamber, a Capitol officer fired and killed one of the protestors. Over the next few hours, police and National Guard forces regained control and expelled the rioters. Congress immediately reconvened. At 3:40 a.m., January 7, 2021, Congress completed the count, and Vice President Pence declared that Joe Biden and Kamala Harris would be the next president and vice president of the United States.

For those who had opposed Donald Trump, the attack confirmed their fears that he was an authoritarian. The House of Representatives voted 232-197 to impeach Trump on the charge of incitement of insurrection.

Trump's Second Impeachment

Ten Republicans joined all the Democrats to vote for the impeachment and the second impeachment trial began in the Senate on February 9, 2021. Although a majority of senators voted to convict, the vote of 57 to 43 was 10 votes short of the two-thirds majority needed for conviction.

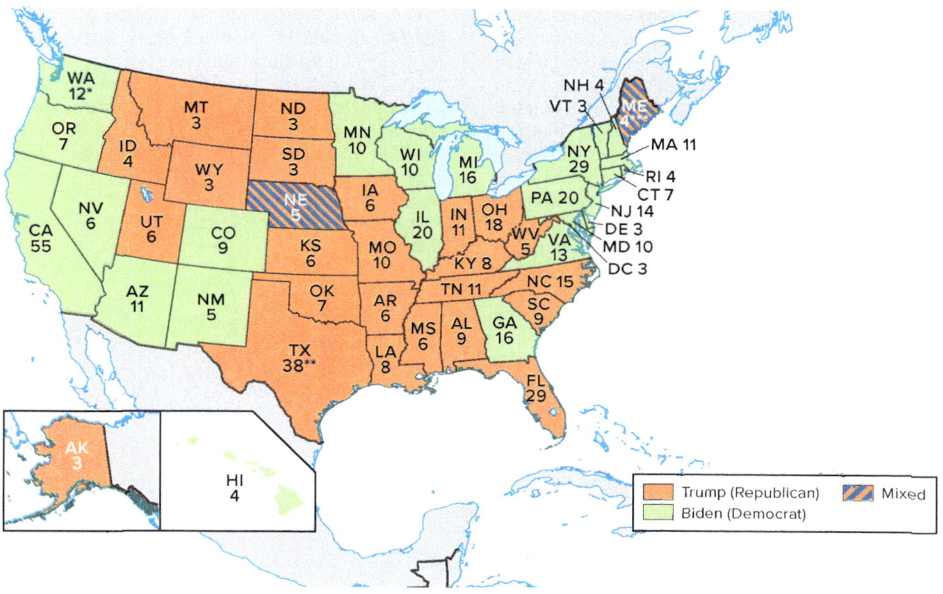

THE ELECTION OF 2020 Democratic candidates Joe Biden and Kamala Harris won a decisive victory over Republican candidates Donald Trump and Mike Pence.

Discussion and Activities

Speculating After students have read the section "Aftermath of the Election," discuss as a class what it might take to restore most Americans' faith in the fairness and integrity of elections. **PCE**

Reasoning Processes

Evaluating Evidence Have students examine the map "The Election of 2020." Ask them to go online to find an electoral map of the 2020 election broken down by county. Have students discuss in small groups what conclusions they can draw from the more detailed map. *(In the county-by-county breakdown, it becomes clearer that Biden carried most major metropolitan areas and had an advantage in most suburban areas, but that Trump dominated in rural areas.)* **PCE** **ARC** **NAT** **SOC** **GEO**

Discussion and Activities

Historical Developments and Argumentation Have students read the section "Biden's Domestic Policies." Have students work in small groups to discuss those policies as a class and evaluate whether the President's initial agenda seemed to focus more on political, economic, social, or foreign policy issues. Ask for volunteers to share their findings with the class and discuss which issues they find most important. **PCE** **SOC** **WXT** **WOR**

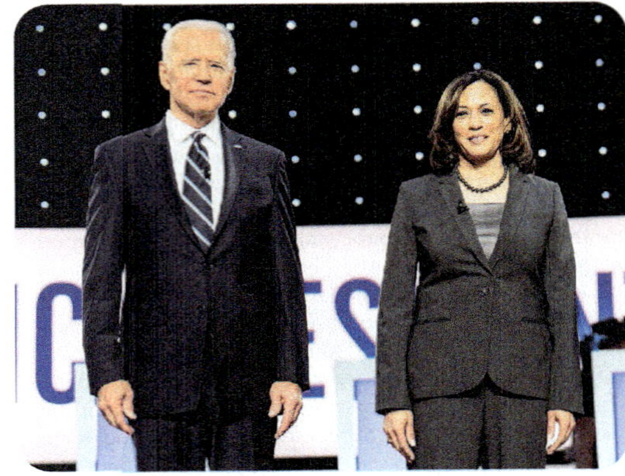

BIDEN AND HARRIS President Joe Biden and Vice President Kamala Harris, pictured here during the Democratic presidential debate in Detroit while both were vying for the Democratic nomination. Kamala Harris, the child of Jamaican and Indian immigrants, made history as the first female vice president.

BIDEN'S DOMESTIC POLICIES

Upon taking office, Biden began repealing many of the Trump era executive orders and policies. Biden rejoined the Paris Climate Agreement, revoked the permit for the Keystone XL pipeline, and issued a series of executive orders to address the impact of COVID-19.

Biden directed the government to improve data collection related to COVID-19 and established a new COVID-19 Pandemic Testing Board to expand testing. He also issued an order requiring all federal workers and people on federal property and all people at airports or traveling on aircraft, trains, ships, or intercity buses to wear masks. Vaccination rates had begun to rise in December 2020, and they continued to increase in early 2021. Biden set a target of 100 million vaccinations by the end of his first 100 days in office. By the end of Biden's 100 days in office, more than 225 million vaccines were administered, but vaccination rates began to fall. Vaccine hesitancy, misinformation, and conspiracy theories spread on social media reduced vaccination rates and contributed to the growing political and social divide.

Biden also issued a series of orders reversing the immigration policies President Trump had implemented. He lifted the travel ban, stopped work on the border wall, ended the "zero tolerance" policy, and reaffirmed support for the DACA program. He also set up a task force to reunite families separated at the border. Biden soon faced a surge in illegal border crossings, many by unaccompanied children, similar to what President Obama and President Trump had faced. By April 2021, the total number of immigrants entering illegally had reached levels not seen since 2001. With detention facilities growing overcrowded, Biden promised his administration he would focus on getting the children processed and moved to sponsors and develop a plan to address the problems in Central America that were causing so many people to come north. Issues persist along the border as more immigrants seek to escape violence, poverty, and the effects of natural disasters and the pandemic.

IMMIGRATION POLICIES

Unemployment and economic issues continued to be a concern, and Congress passed the American Rescue Plan Act, a $1.9 trillion economic aid package in March 2021. The plan extended the increased unemployment benefits provided by the CARES Act into the fall of 2021. It provided cash payments and tax credits to individuals, grants to small businesses, funds to help people cover rent and mortgages, and funds for state, local, and tribal governments to cover budget shortages. It also provided funds to allow schools to address needs and issues related to the pandemic.

ECONOMIC POLICIES

The United States confronted monumental tests after the first two decades of the twenty-first century. As Joe Biden declared in his inaugural address:

"We face an attack on democracy and on truth. A raging virus. Growing inequity. The sting of systemic racism. A climate in crisis. America's role in the world. Any one of these would be enough to challenge us in profound ways. But the fact is we face them all at once, presenting this nation with the gravest of responsibilities."

Whether America could successfully meet these profound challenges was unclear at the end of 2021, but the nation had overcome great crises in the past and could look to history for hope and inspiration.

Discussion and Activities

Analyzing Points of View Have students examine the image "Biden and Harris." Ask them to write a journal entry from the point of view of a spectator at the inauguration of President Biden and Vice President Harris. Have students consider that Biden became the oldest person elected President, and Harris became the first woman of color to be elected Vice President. **PCE** **SOC**

CHAPTER 34 REVIEW

CONNECTING THEMES

Chapter Thirty-Four explored the economic, social, and political climate of the United States from 1990 to the present. The economy moved through a boom-and-bust cycle during the time period. New digital technologies changed American society and created new jobs and industries. A deep recession beginning in 2008 depressed wages and triggered widespread layoffs. The increasing population of older Americans also stressed economic structures as pressure increased on Social Security and Medicare systems. As more Americans aged out of the workplace, immigration increased as laborers were needed in the workforce.

The terrorist attacks in September of 2001 initially united the nation, but the prolonged involvement in the Middle East brought more disagreements both domestically and internationally. The corresponding increase in security measures at home also created tension among Americans who had concerns about personal liberty and privacy. The competing liberal and conservative ideologies throughout the time period helped create a growing divide within the nation. The divisions showed clearly in the extremely close presidential elections of 2000, 2004, 2008, and 2016.

The election of Donald Trump and the COVID-19 pandemic exacerbated societal and political divisions. Americans became more divided as responses to the pandemic became politicized. The attack on the Capitol on January 6, 2021, was a product of the disinformation and extremism that divided the nation. While the attack shook Americans and people around the globe, the election of Biden gave many people hope for a more tempered society and a renewed role for the United States in the world.

You should consider the following questions as you review the themes for this chapter:

- How did both domestic and international issues shape the social, political, and economic climate of the United States at the end of the twentieth and the first decades of the twenty-first century?
- What were the concerns surrounding global climate change and how did this and other factors influence environmental movements in the early twenty-first century?
- What were the reasons for and consequences of the extreme polarization in American politics during the time period?
- What major global events affected America's role in the world during the time period?
- How was American culture transformed through technology and communications at the end of the twentieth and the first decades of the twenty-first century?

KEY TERMS

AIDS 904
Al Gore 907
al-Qaeda 908
Barack Obama 911
Bill Clinton 904
Black Lives Matter (BLM) 919
COVID-19 919
Donald Trump 915
George W. Bush 906
Hillary Rodham Clinton 915
Joe Biden 922
John McCain 911
Kamala Harris 922
Monica Lewinsky 906
"New World Order" 900
Newt Gingrich 905
North American Free Trade Agreement (NAFTA) 904
Osama bin Laden 908
Taliban 908

Discussion and Activities

Making Connections Organize students into four groups. Assign a group to review and research each of the following challenges presently facing the United States: political division, cultural division, economic uncertainty, uncertainty about America's role in the world. Have each group present its findings and debrief as a class by discussing which of these challenges they believe is the most threatening, and what, if anything, can be done about it. Conclude by asking students to discuss what they believe are the greatest opportunities awaiting the United States presently.

Key Terms

Students should be familiar with the key terms and be able to define them in the context of economic instability, the threat of terrorism, the aging of America, and competition between liberal and conservative visions of America's future. Encourage students to use these terms in performing review exercises and exam practice for this chapter.

Go Online Chapter 34 Content Review

Assessing Student Understanding Use the online assessment to assess student understanding of concepts and topics within the chapter. You can assign the ready-made Chapter 34 Content Review or create your own from available questions. This easy-to-use tool helps you design assessments that meet the needs of different types of learners.

CHAPTER 34

GLOBALIZATION AND POLARIZATION

Answers

Multiple Choice

1. C; **2.** C; **3.** D

Short Answer

4A) Possible answer: Following the election of Democrat Bill Clinton, Republicans had to work with the administration to ensure both parties received important input into national politics.

4B) Possible answer: Following the election of Clinton, many Republicans feared that they were going to lose national popularity. Gingrich emerged as a voice for Republican concerns.

4C) Possible answer: A Republican legislative agenda, "Contract with America," emerged during the 1994 congressional election campaign.

5A) Possible answer: Both were leaders of the Republican Party during a significant resurgence of conservative politics in the United States. Both were involved in the entertainment industry before becoming involved in politics.

5B) Possible answer: Reagan was more willing to work with Democrats during his presidency.

5C) Possible answer: Reagan became popular among both political parties and remains a popular American president as well as a touchstone for many in the Republican Party.

AP EXAM PRACTICE

Questions assume cumulative content knowledge from this chapter and the previous chapters.

MULTIPLE CHOICE

Use the photograph on page 909 and your knowledge of U.S. history to answer questions 1-3.

1. The photograph of President George W. Bush reflects which reaction to the terror attacks on September 11, 2001?
   (A) The nation experienced an extraordinary moment of national reflection.
   (B) The nation expressed gratitude to first responders and others who made personal sacrifices to help the victims of the attacks.
   (C) The government launched widely supported military actions to respond to the attacks and prevent further terrorist aggression.
   (D) The nation passed a number of controversial laws which sought to identify domestic threats.

2. Critics of domestic legislation passed in the wake of the terror attacks argued that laws such as the Patriot Act
   (A) were too costly to implement.
   (B) unfairly vilified European Americans.
   (C) infringed upon basic civil liberties.
   (D) threatened the safety of children.

3. What changes to foreign policy were implemented under President George W. Bush after the terrorist attacks of 9/11?
   (A) Foreign policy shifted to focus on defensive wars only.
   (B) Foreign policy shifted to deescalate foreign conflicts.
   (C) Foreign policy shifted away from unilateral actions to focus only on those supported by major allies.
   (D) Foreign policy shifted to promote active intervention in support of pro-U.S. governments.

SHORT ANSWER

Use your knowledge of U.S. history to answer questions 4 and 5.

4. Use the image on page 905 answer A, B, and C.
   (A) Briefly describe ONE specific historical context of politics in the 1990s as depicted in the photo.
   (B) Briefly explain ONE specific cause that led to the rise of the popularity of Newt Gingrich during the 1990s.
   (C) Briefly explain ONE specific effect that resulted from the rise of the popularity of Newt Gingrich during the 1990s

5. Answer A, B, and C.
   (A) Briefly describe ONE specific similarity between President Reagan and President Trump.
   (B) Briefly describe ONE specific difference between President Reagan and President Trump.
   (C) Briefly explain ONE specific effect that is a result of one of the differences you identified.

ESSAY

Develop a thoughtful and thorough historical argument that addresses the statement. Begin your essay with a thesis statement, and support it with specific historical evidence and examples.

6. Evaluate the relative importance of causes that led to political polarization following the 2016 election.

Answers

Long Essay

6. Possible Thesis: The election of the country's first African American president, Barack Obama, gave the country great hope, but at the same time continued to expose the problems the country still faced. However, the social and cultural divides took center stage with the election of 2016. Specific historical evidence: The election of Obama exposed the racist views that some Americans held. Economic and social issues came to dominate the country's politics and divided the country. These divisions were exasperated by divisive rhetoric that grew with the emergence of the COVID-19 pandemic as precautions, lockdowns, and vaccines became deeply politicized.

AP EXAM PRACTICE

As you answer the questions, consider how the historical developments, processes, and individuals in Unit 9 connect to those in previous units.

MULTIPLE CHOICE

Use the image on page 890 and your knowledge of U.S. history to answer questions 1-3.

1. The photograph illustrates the
   (A) military conflict around the end of the Cold War.
   (B) popular support for the dismantling of the Berlin Wall.
   (C) anxiety surrounding the reunion of divided Germany.
   (D) protests aimed at ending the policy of apartheid.

2. The global approach taken by the Reagan administration in fighting the Cold War included
   (A) aiding Afghanistan as they fought the Iraq War throughout the 1980s.
   (B) supporting Contras in Nicaragua as they fought a leftist regime.
   (C) supporting the growth of democracy in South Vietnam.
   (D) brokering a peace process and treaties between Israel and surrounding nations.

3. The Reagan administration became embroiled in controversy as it became publicly acknowledged that arms were illegally sold to
   (A) China.
   (B) the Soviet Union.
   (C) Afghanistan.
   (D) Iran.

Use the graph on page 886 and your knowledge of U.S. history to answer questions 4-6.

4. What impact did the election of Ronald Reagan have on federal spending?
   (A) Reagan reversed the large federal budgets of the Carter administration.
   (B) Reagan kept federal spending steady, neither expanding nor contracting the budget.
   (C) Reagan continued the trend of significantly expanding federal spending.
   (D) Reagan was the last president to oversee an expanding federal budget.

5. What contributed to the expansion of the deficit during the Reagan administration?
   (A) Reagan's insistence on expanding social welfare programs.
   (B) The significant tax cuts passed in 1981 that decreased federal revenues.
   (C) The contraction of the military that left many Americans unemployed.
   (D) The expansion of government regulation on multiple industries.

6. The solution for fiscal challenges that the Reagan administration pursued has been termed
   (A) Keynesian economics.
   (B) supply-side economics.
   (C) demand-side economics.
   (D) command economics.

Use the election graphic on page 915 and your knowledge of U.S. history to answer questions 7 and 8.

7. The election graphic indicates which of the following about the 2000 presidential election?
   (A) The nation was united in its reaction to the 1998 impeachment of President Bill Clinton.
   (B) The nation was significantly divided over several foreign and domestic issues.
   (C) The nation did not want to choose a candidate from the Baby Boom generation.
   (D) The nation was united in the face of looming terror attacks.

8. How did the 2000 election prove controversial after the November voting took place?
   (A) The state of Florida refused to certify an election winner.
   (B) The state of Texas challenged the certified results from other states.
   (C) The Supreme Court issued a controversial decision ending a Florida recount.
   (D) Congress refused to certify the election.

UNIT 9
AP Exam Practice

Discussion and Activities

Making Connections Direct students' attention to the Questions to Consider posed at the beginning of Unit 9:

- What impact did the end of the Cold War have on U.S. domestic and foreign policies?
- What were the major causes and effects of conservative movements during the last 50 years in the United States?
- What were the most important continuities and changes in U.S. foreign policy during the "War on Terror?"

Discuss these questions as a class to review important concepts from the unit. To close the discussion, **ask:** What was the most important development in the United States between 1980 and today?

Answers

Multiple Choice

1. B; **2.** B; **3.** D; **4.** C; **5.** B; **6.** B; **7.** B; **8.** C; **9.** B; **10.** C

Answers

Short Answer

11A) Possible answer: Reagan dominated politics in the 1980s leading a coalition of corporate elites, neo-conservative intellectuals, and populist conservatives from the South and West.

11B) Possible answer: School and mass shootings became politicized around gun control and gun rights debates.

11C) Possible answer: The debate over gun control in the United States continues to divide American society. The NRA has amassed an enormous amount of support for gun rights. The continuing volatility and instability within society drives the anxieties of many Americans, often leading to increased gun purchases. States like Texas have passed laws making acquisition of guns even easier.

Use the graph on page 903 and your knowledge of U.S. history to answer questions 9 and 10.

9. What situations in the United States contributed to the immigration trends seen in the graph?
   (A) Cold War tensions created an atmosphere unwelcoming to immigrants.
   (B) Economic prosperity increased the demand for workers and promise of financial opportunity.
   (C) Social divisions added to anti-immigrant sentiment and a hostile culture.
   (D) The revival of a manufacturing-based economy led to increasing demand for skilled workers.

10. Unlike previous waves of immigration, more recent immigrants to the United States were increasingly from
   (A) Northern and Western Europe.
   (B) Great Britain and Africa.
   (C) Asia and Latin America.
   (D) Ireland and Germany.

SHORT ANSWER

Use the photograph on page 880 and your knowledge of U.S. history to answer question 11.

11. Answer A, B, and C.
   (A) Briefly describe the historical context of the event depicted in the photograph.
   (B) Briefly explain ONE specific cause that led to the polarizing issue of gun rights and gun control in the United States.
   (C) Briefly explain ONE specific effect that resulted from the debate over gun rights and gun control in the United States.

ESSAY

Develop a thoughtful and thorough historical argument that addresses the statement. Begin your essay with a thesis statement, and support it with specific historical evidence and examples.

12. Evaluate the extent that polarization in the United States led to the election of Joe Biden in 2020.

Answers

Long Essay

12. Possible Thesis: The response to the COVID-19 pandemic and increasing polarization of the pandemic response was the most important factor in the election of Biden. Specific Historical Evidence: COVID-19 responses including economic shutdowns, mandatory mask mandates, testing availability, and vaccines became political issues rather than public health issues. As Americans became more frustrated, the polarization increased. This led to dramatic increase in voter turnout at the polls for the 2020 election.

APPENDICES

TOPOGRAPHICAL MAP OF THE UNITED STATES

ANADA
Lake Nipigon
ake of
e Woods
Lake Superior
Lake Michigan
Lake Huron
Lake Ontario
Lake Erie
Lake Champlain
ADIRONDACK MTS.
CENTRAL
PLAINS
OZARK PLATEAU
ALLEGHENY MTS.
APPALACHIAN MOUNTAINS
SHENANDOAH VALLEY
BLUE RIDGE MTS.
ATLANTIC COASTAL PLAIN
Chesapeake Bay
ATLANTIC OCEAN
Gulf of Mexico
Galveston Bay
Lake Okeechobee
BAHAMAS
CUBA
L PLAIN
St. Croix R.
Mississippi R.
Cedar R.
Iowa R.
Des Moines R.
Rock R.
Fox R.
Kankakee R.
Illinois R.
Wabash R.
Missouri R.
Osage R.
Ohio R.
Scioto R.
Kanawha R.
Cumberland R.
Tennessee R.
White R.
Arkansas R.
Ouachita R.
Red R.
Sabine R.
Yazoo R.
Tombigbee R.
Pearl R.
Alabama R.
Chattahoochee R.
Altamaha R.
Savannah R.
Saluda R.
Roanoke R.
James R.
Potomac R.
Susquehanna R.
Allegheny R.
Delaware R.
Hudson R.
Mohawk R.
Connecticut R.
St. Lawrence R.
Kennebeck R.
0 150 300 miles
0 150 300 kilometers
Land Elevation
Feet Meters
Over 13,000 Over 3,000
6,560–13,000 2,000–3,000
3,280–6,560 1,000–2,000
660–3,280 2001–1,000
0–660 0–200
Below sea level Below sea level
ATLANTIC OCEAN
PUERTO RICO
Caribbean Sea
0 50 100 miles
0 50 100 kilometers

UNITED STATES TERRITORIAL EXPANSION, 1783–1898

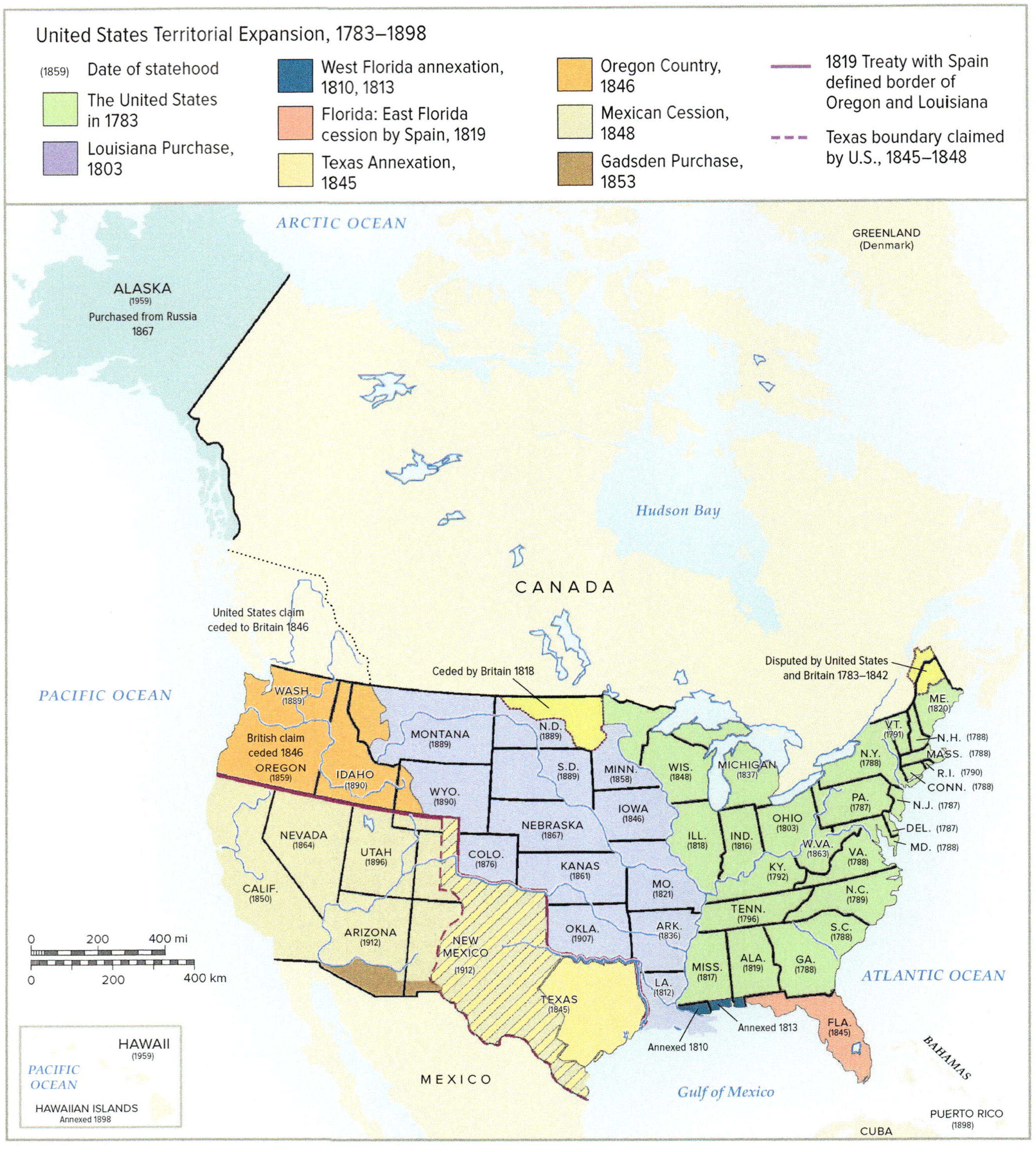
United States Territorial Expansion, 1783–1898
(1859) Date of statehood
The United States in 1783
Louisiana Purchase, 1803
West Florida annexation, 1810, 1813
Florida: East Florida cession by Spain, 1819
Texas Annexation, 1845
Oregon Country, 1846
Mexican Cession, 1848
Gadsden Purchase, 1853
1819 Treaty with Spain defined border of Oregon and Louisiana
Texas boundary claimed by U.S., 1845–1848
ARCTIC OCEAN
GREENLAND (Denmark)
ALASKA (1959) Purchased from Russia 1867
Hudson Bay
CANADA
United States claim ceded to Britain 1846
Ceded by Britain 1818
Disputed by United States and Britain 1783–1842
PACIFIC OCEAN
WASH. (1889)
British claim ceded 1846
OREGON (1859)
IDAHO (1890)
MONTANA (1889)
WYO. (1890)
N.D. (1889)
S.D. (1889)
MINN. (1858)
WIS. (1848)
MICHIGAN (1837)
N.Y. (1788)
VT. (1791)
ME. (1820)
N.H. (1788)
MASS. (1788)
R.I. (1790)
CONN. (1788)
N.J. (1787)
DEL. (1787)
MD. (1788)
PA. (1787)
OHIO (1803)
W.VA. (1863)
VA. (1788)
IND. (1816)
ILL. (1818)
IOWA (1846)
NEBRASKA (1867)
NEVADA (1864)
UTAH (1896)
COLO. (1876)
KANSAS (1861)
MO. (1821)
KY. (1792)
N.C. (1789)
TENN. (1796)
CALIF. (1850)
ARIZONA (1912)
NEW MEXICO (1912)
OKLA. (1907)
ARK. (1836)
S.C. (1788)
MISS. (1817)
ALA. (1819)
GA. (1788)
LA. (1812)
TEXAS (1845)
FLA. (1845)
Annexed 1810
Annexed 1813
ATLANTIC OCEAN
Gulf of Mexico
MEXICO
BAHAMAS
CUBA
PUERTO RICO (1898)
0 200 400 mi
0 200 400 km
HAWAII (1959)
PACIFIC OCEAN
HAWAIIAN ISLANDS Annexed 1898

THE DECLARATION OF INDEPENDENCE

In Congress, July 4, 1776,

The Unanimous Declaration of the Thirteen United States of America

When, in the course of human events, it becomes necessary for one people to dissolve the political bands which have connected them with another, and to assume, among the powers of the earth, the separate and equal station to which the laws of nature and of nature's God entitle them, a decent respect to the opinions of mankind requires that they should declare the causes which impel them to the separation.

We hold these truths to be self-evident, that all men are created equal; that they are endowed by their Creator with certain unalienable rights; that among these, are life, liberty, and the pursuit of happiness. That, to secure these rights, governments are instituted among men, deriving their just powers from the consent of the governed; that, whenever any form of government becomes destructive of these ends, it is the right of the people to alter or to abolish it, and to institute a new government, laying its foundation on such principles, and organizing its powers in such form, as to them shall seem most likely to effect their safety and happiness. Prudence, indeed, will dictate that governments long established, should not be changed for light and transient causes; and, accordingly, all experience hath shown, that mankind are more disposed to suffer, while evils are sufferable, than to right themselves by abolishing the forms to which they are accustomed. But, when a long train of abuses and usurpations, pursuing invariably the same object, evinces a design to reduce them under absolute despotism, it is their right, it is their duty, to throw off such government and to provide new guards for their future security. Such has been the patient sufferance of these colonies, and such is now the necessity which constrains them to alter their former systems of government. The history of the present King of Great Britain is a history of repeated injuries and usurpations, all having, in direct object, the establishment of an absolute tyranny over these States. To prove this, let facts be submitted to a candid world:

He has refused his assent to laws the most wholesome and necessary for the public good.

He has forbidden his governors to pass laws of immediate and pressing importance, unless suspended in their operation till his assent should be obtained; and, when so suspended, he has utterly neglected to attend to them.

He has refused to pass other laws for the accommodation of large districts of people, unless those people would relinquish the right of representation in the legislature; a right inestimable to them, and formidable to tyrants only.

He has called together legislative bodies at places unusual, uncomfortable, and distant from the depository of their public records, for the sole purpose of fatiguing them into compliance with his measures.

He has dissolved representative houses repeatedly for opposing, with manly firmness, his invasions on the rights of the people.

He has refused, for a long time after such dissolutions, to cause others to be elected; whereby the legislative powers, incapable of annihilation, have returned to the people at large for their exercise; the state remaining, in the meantime, exposed to all the danger of invasion from without, and convulsions within.

He has endeavored to prevent the population of these States; for that purpose, obstructing the laws for naturalization of foreigners, refusing to pass others to encourage their migration hither, and raising the conditions of new appropriations of lands.

He has obstructed the administration of justice, by refusing his assent to laws for establishing judiciary powers.

He has made judges dependent on his will alone, for the tenure of their officers, and the amount and payment of their salaries.

He has erected a multitude of new offices, and sent hither swarms of officers to harass our people, and eat out their substance.

He has kept among us, in time of peace, standing armies, without the consent of our legislatures.

He has affected to render the military independent of, and superior to, the civil power.

He has combined, with others, to subject us to a jurisdiction foreign to our Constitution, and unacknowledged by our laws; giving his assent to their acts of pretended legislation:

For quartering large bodies of armed troops among us:

For protecting them by a mock trial, from punishment, for any murders which they should commit on the inhabitants of these States:

For cutting off our trade with all parts of the world:

For imposing taxes on us without our consent:

For depriving us, in many cases, of the benefit of trial by jury:

For transporting us beyond seas to be tried for pretended offences:

For abolishing the free system of English laws in a neighboring province, establishing therein an arbitrary government, and enlarging its boundaries, so as to render it at once an example and fit instrument for introducing the same absolute rule into these colonies:

For taking away our charters, abolishing our most valuable laws, and altering, fundamentally, the powers of our governments:

For suspending our own legislatures, and declaring themselves invested with power to legislate for use in all cases whatsoever.

THE DECLARATION OF INDEPENDENCE • A-5

He has abdicated government here, by declaring us out of his protection, and waging war against us.

He has plundered our seas, ravaged our coasts, burnt our towns, and destroyed the lives of our people.

He is, at this time, transporting large armies of foreign mercenaries to complete the works of death, desolation, and tyranny, already begun, with circumstances of cruelty and perfidy scarcely paralleled in the most barbarous ages, and totally unworthy the head of a civilized nation.

He has constrained our fellow citizens, taken captive on the high seas, to bear arms against their country, to become the executioners of their friends, and brethren, or to fall themselves by their hands.

He has excited domestic insurrections amongst us, and has endeavored to bring on the inhabitants of our frontiers, the merciless Indian savages, whose known rule of warfare is an undistinguished destruction of all ages, sexes, and conditions.

In every stage of these oppressions, we have petitioned for redress, in the most humble terms; our repeated petitions have been answered only by repeated injury. A prince, whose character is thus marked by every act which may define a tyrant, is unfit to be the ruler of a free people.

Nor have we been wanting in attention to our British brethren. We have warned them, from time to time, of attempts made by their legislature to extend an unwarrantable jurisdiction over us. We have reminded them of the circumstances of our emigration and settlement here. We have appealed to their native justice and magnanimity, and we have conjured them, by the ties of our common kindred, to disavow these usurpations, which would inevitably interrupt our connections and correspondence. They, too, have been deaf to the voice of justice and consanguinity. We must, therefore, acquiesce in the necessity, which denounces our separation, and hold them as we hold the rest of mankind, enemies in war, in peace, friends.

We, therefore, the representatives of the United States of America, in general Congress assembled, appealing to the Supreme Judge of the world for the rectitude of our intentions, do, in the name, and by the authority of the good people of these colonies, solemnly publish and declare, that these united colonies are, and of right ought to be, free and independent states: that they are absolved from all allegiance to the British Crown, and that all political connection between them and the state of Great Britain is, and ought to be, totally dissolved; and that, as free and independent states, they have full power to levy war, conclude peace, contract alliances, establish commerce, and to do all other acts and things which independent states may of right do. And, for the support of this declaration, with a firm reliance on the protection of Divine Providence, we mutually pledge to each other our lives, our fortunes, and our sacred honor.

The foregoing Declaration was, by order of Congress, engrossed, and signed by the following members:

John Hancock

New Hampshire
Josiah Bartlett
William Whipple
Matthew Thornton

Massachusetts Bay
Samuel Adams
John Adams
Robert Treat Paine
Elbridge Gerry

Rhode Island
Stephen Hopkins
William Ellery

Connecticut
Robert Sherman
Samuel Huntington
William Williams
Oliver Wolcott

New York
William Floyd
Philip Livingston
Francis Lewis
Lewis Morris

New Jersey
Richard Stockton
John Witherspoon
Francis Hopkinson
John Hart
Abraham Clark

Pennsylvania
Robert Morris
Benjamin Rush
Benjamin Franklin
John Morton
George Clymer
James Smith
George Taylor
James Wilson
George Ross

Delaware
Caesar Rodney
George Read
Thomas McKean

Maryland
Samuel Chase
William Paca
Thomas Stone
Charles Carroll,
of Carrollton

Virginia
George Wythe
Richard Henry Lee
Thomas Jefferson
Benjamin Harrison
Thomas Nelson, Jr.
Francis Lightfoot Lee
Carter Braxton

North Carolina
William Hooper
Joseph Hewes
John Penn

South Carolina
Edward Rutledge
Thomas Heyward, Jr.
Thomas Lynch, Jr.
Arthur Middleton

Georgia
Button Gwinnett
Lyman Hall
George Walton

Resolved, That copies of the Declaration be sent to the several assemblies, conventions, and committees, or councils of safety, and to the several commanding officers of the continental troops; that it be proclaimed in each of the United States, at the head of the army.

A-6 •

THE CONSTITUTION OF THE UNITED STATES OF AMERICA[1]

THE CONSTITUTION OF THE UNITED STATES OF AMERICA

We the People of the United States, in Order to form a more perfect Union, establish Justice, insure domestic Tranquility, provide for the common defence, promote the general Welfare, and secure the Blessings of Liberty to ourselves and our Posterity, do ordain and establish this CONSTITUTION for the United States of America.

ARTICLE I

SECTION 1.

All legislative Powers herein granted shall be vested in a Congress of the United States, which shall consist of a Senate and House of Representatives.

SECTION 2.

The House of Representatives shall be composed of Members chosen every second Year by the People of the several States, and the Electors in each State shall have the Qualifications requisite for Electors of the most numerous Branch of the State Legislature.

No Person shall be a Representative who shall not have attained to the Age of twenty-five Years, and been seven Years a Citizen of the United States, and who shall not, when elected, be an Inhabitant of that State in which he shall be chosen.

[Representatives and direct Taxes[2] shall be apportioned among the several States which may be included within this Union, according to their respective Numbers, which shall be determined by adding to the whole Number of free Persons, including those bound to Service for a Term of Years, and excluding Indians not taxed, three fifths of all other Persons.][3] The actual Enumeration shall be made within three Years after the first Meeting of the Congress of the United States, and within every subsequent Term of ten Years, in such Manner as they shall by Law direct. The Number of Representatives shall not exceed one for every thirty Thousand, but each State shall have at Least one Representative; and until such enumeration shall be made, the State of New Hampshire shall be entitled to chuse three, Massachusetts eight, Rhode-Island and Providence Plantations one, Connecticut five, New York six, New Jersey four, Pennsylvania eight, Delaware one, Maryland six, Virginia ten, North Carolina five, South Carolina five, and Georgia three.

When vacancies happen in the Representation from any State, the Executive Authority thereof shall issue Writs of Election to fill such Vacancies.

The House of Representatives shall chuse their Speaker and other Officers; and shall have the sole Power of Impeachment.

SECTION 3.

The Senate of the United States shall be composed of two Senators from each State, chosen by the Legislature thereof, for six Years; and each Senator shall have one Vote.

Immediately after they shall be assembled in Consequence of the first Election, they shall be divided as equally as may be into three Classes. The Seats of the Senators of the first Class shall be vacated at the Expiration of the second Year, of the second Class at the Expiration of the fourth Year, and of the third Class at the Expiration of the sixth Year, so that one-third may be chosen every second Year; and if Vacancies happen by Resignation, or otherwise, during the Recess of the Legislature of any State, the Executive thereof may make temporary Appointments until the next Meeting of the Legislature, which shall then fill such Vacancies.

No Person shall be a Senator who shall not have attained to the Age of thirty Years, and been nine Years a Citizen of the United States, and who shall not, when elected, be an Inhabitant of that State for which he shall be chosen.

The Vice President of the United States shall be President of the Senate, but shall have no vote, unless they be equally divided.

The Senate shall chuse their other Officers, and also a President pro tempore, in the absence of the Vice President, or when he shall exercise the office of President of the United States.

The Senate shall have the sole Power to try all Impeachments. When sitting for that purpose they shall be on Oath or Affirmation. When the President of the United States is tried, the Chief Justice shall preside: And no person shall be convicted without the Concurrence of two thirds of the Members present.

Judgment in Cases of Impeachment shall not extend further than to removal from Office, and disqualification to hold and enjoy any Office of honor, Trust, or Profit under the United States: but the Party convicted shall nevertheless be liable and subject to Indictment, Trial, Judgment, and Punishment, according to Law.

SECTION 4.

The Times, Places and Manner of holding Elections for Senators and Representatives, shall be prescribed in each State by the Legislature thereof; but the Congress may at any time by Law make or alter such Regulations, except as to the Places of Chusing Senators.

The Congress shall assemble at least once in every Year, and such Meeting shall be on the first Monday in December, unless they shall by Law appoint a different day.

SECTION 5.

Each House shall be the Judge of the Elections, Returns and Qualifications of its own Members, and a Majority of each shall

[1]This version, which follows the original Constitution in capitalization and spelling, was published by the United States Department of the Interior, Office of Education, in 1935.

[2]Altered by the Sixteenth Amendment.

[3]Negated by the Fourteenth Amendment.

THE CONSTITUTION OF THE UNITED STATES OF AMERICA • A-7

constitute a Quorum to do Business; but a smaller number may adjourn from day to day, and may be authorized to compel the Attendance of absent Members, in such Manner, and under such Penalties, as each House may provide.

Each House may determine the Rules of its Proceedings, punish its Members for disorderly Behaviour, and, with the Concurrence of two thirds, expel a Member.

Each House shall keep a Journal of its Proceedings, and from time to time publish the same, excepting such Parts as may in their Judgment require Secrecy; and the Yeas and Nays of the Members of either House on any question shall, at the Desire of one fifth of those Present, be entered on the Journal.

Neither House, during the Session of Congress, shall, without the Consent of the other, adjourn for more than three days, nor to any other Place than that in which the two Houses shall be sitting.

Section 6.

The Senators and Representatives shall receive a Compensation for their Services, to be ascertained by Law, and paid out of the Treasury of the United States. They shall in all Cases, except Treason, Felony, and Breach of the Peace, be privileged from Arrest during their Attendance at the Session of their respective Houses, and in going to and returning from the same; and for any Speech or Debate in either House, they shall not be questioned in any other Place.

No Senator or Representative shall, during the Time for which he was elected, be appointed to any civil Office under the Authority of the United States, which shall have been created, or the Emoluments whereof shall have been increased, during such time; and no Person holding any Office under the United States shall be a Member of either House during his continuance in Office.

Section 7.

All Bills for raising Revenue shall originate in the House of Representatives; but the Senate may propose or concur with Amendments as on other bills.

Every Bill which shall have passed the House of Representatives and the Senate, shall, before it become a Law, be presented to the President of the United States; If he approve he shall sign it, but if not he shall return it, with his Objections, to that House in which it shall have originated, who shall enter the Objections at large on their Journal, and proceed to reconsider it. If after such Reconsideration two thirds of that House shall agree to pass the bill, it shall be sent, together with the objections, to the other House, by which it shall likewise be reconsidered, and if approved by two thirds of that House, it shall become a Law. But in all such Cases the Votes of both Houses shall be determined by Yeas and Nays, and the Names of the Persons voting for and against the Bill shall be entered on the Journal of each House respectively. If any Bill shall not be returned by the President within ten Days (Sundays excepted) after it shall have been presented to him, the Same shall be a Law, in like Manner as if he had signed it, unless the Congress by their Adjournment prevent its Return, in which Case it shall not be a Law.

Every Order, Resolution, or Vote to which the Concurrence of the Senate and House of Representatives may be necessary (except on a question of Adjournment) shall be presented to the President of the United States; and before the Same shall take Effect, shall be approved by him, or being disapproved by him, shall be repassed by two thirds of the Senate and House of Representatives, according to the Rules and Limitations prescribed in the Case of a Bill.

Section 8.

The Congress shall have Power To lay and collect Taxes, Duties, Imposts and Excises, to pay the Debts and provide for the common Defence and general Welfare of the United States; but all Duties, Imposts and Excises shall be uniform throughout the United States;

To borrow money on the credit of the United States;

To regulate Commerce with foreign Nations, and among the several States, and with the Indian Tribes;

To establish an uniform rule of Naturalization, and uniform Laws on the subject of Bankruptcies throughout the United States;

To coin Money, regulate the Value thereof, and of foreign Coin, and fix the Standard of Weights and Measures;

To provide for the Punishment of counterfeiting the Securities and current Coin of the United States;

To establish Post Offices and post Roads;

To promote the Progress of Science and useful Arts, by securing for limited Times to Authors and Inventors the exclusive Right to their respective Writings and Discoveries;

To constitute Tribunals inferior to the Supreme Court;

To define and punish Piracies and Felonies committed on the high Seas, and Offenses against the Law of Nations;

To declare War, grant Letters of Marque and Reprisal, and make Rules concerning Captures on Land and Water;

To raise and support Armies, but no Appropriation of Money to that Use shall be for a longer Term than two Years;

To provide and maintain a Navy;

To make Rules for the Government and Regulation of the land and naval forces;

To provide for calling forth the Militia to execute the Laws of the Union, suppress Insurrections and repel Invasions;

To provide for organizing, arming, and disciplining the Militia, and for governing such Part of them as may be employed in the Service of the United States, reserving to the States respectively, the Appointment of the Officers, and the Authority of training the Militia according to the discipline prescribed by Congress;

To exercise exclusive Legislation in all Cases whatsoever, over such District (not exceeding ten Miles square) as may, by Cession of particular States, and the acceptance of Congress, become the Seat of the Government of the United States, and to exercise like Authority over all Places purchased by the

A-8

Consent of the Legislature of the State in which the Same shall be, for the Erection of Forts, Magazines, Arsenals, Dockyards, and other needful Buildings;–And

To make all Laws which shall be necessary and proper for carrying into Execution for foregoing Powers, and all other Powers vested by this Constitution in the Government of the United States, or in any Department or Officer thereof.

Section 9.

The Migration or Importation of such Persons as any of the States now existing shall think proper to admit, shall not be prohibited by the Congress prior to the Year one thousand eight hundred and eight, but a tax or duty may be imposed on such Importation, not exceeding ten dollars for each Person.

The privilege of the Writ of Habeas Corpus shall not be suspended, unless when in Cases of Rebellion or Invasion the public Safety may require it.

No bill of Attainder or ex post facto Law shall be passed.

No capitation, or other direct, Tax shall be laid unless in Proportion to the Census or Enumeration herein before directed to be taken.

No Tax or Duty shall be laid on Articles exported from any State.

No Preference shall be given by any Regulation of Commerce or Revenue to the Ports of one State over those of another: nor shall Vessels bound to, or from, one State, be obliged to enter, clear, or pay Duties in another.

No Money shall be drawn from the Treasury, but in Consequence of Appropriations made by Law; and a regular Statement and Account of the Receipts and Expenditures of all public Money shall be published from time to time.

No title of Nobility shall be granted by the United States: And no Person holding any Office of Profit or Trust under them, shall, without the Consent of the Congress, accept of any present, Emolument, Office, or title, of any kind whatever, from any King, Prince, or foreign State.

Section 10.

No State shall enter into any Treaty, Alliance, or Confederation; grant Letters of Marque and Reprisal; coin Money; emit Bills of Credit; make any Thing but gold and silver Coin a Tender in Payment of Debts; pass any Bill of Attainder, ex post facto Law, or Law impairing the Obligation of Contracts, or grant any title of Nobility.

No State shall, without the Consent of the Congress, lay any Imposts or Duties on Imports or Exports, except what may be absolutely necessary for executing its inspection Laws; and the net Produce of all Duties and Imposts, laid by any State on Imports or Exports, shall be for the use of the Treasury of the United States; and all such Laws shall be subject to the Revision and Control of the Congress.

No state shall, without the Consent of Congress, lay any duty of Tonnage, keep Troops, or Ships of War in time of Peace, enter into any Agreement or Compact with another State, or with a foreign Power, or engage in War, unless actually invaded, or in such imminent Danger as will not admit of delay.

Article II

Section 1.

The executive Power shall be vested in a President of the United States of America. He shall hold his Office during the Term of four years, and, together with the Vice President, chosen for the same Term, be elected, as follows:

Each State shall appoint, in such Manner as the Legislature thereof may direct, a Number of Electors, equal to the whole Number of Senators and Representatives to which the State may be entitled in the Congress: but no Senator or Representative, or Person holding an Office of Trust or Profit under the United States, shall be appointed an Elector.

[The Electors shall meet in their respective States, and vote by Ballot for two persons, of whom one at least shall not be an Inhabitant of the same State with themselves. And they shall make a List of all the Persons voted for, and of the Number of Votes for each; which List they shall sign and certify, and transmit sealed to the Seat of the Government of the United States, directed to the President of the Senate. The President of the Senate shall, in the Presence of the Senate and House of Representatives, open all the Certificates, and the Votes shall then be counted. The Person having the greatest Number of Votes shall be the President, if such Number be a Majority of the whole Number of Electors appointed; and if there be more than one who have such Majority, and have an equal Number of Votes, then the House of Representatives shall immediately chuse by Ballot one of them for President; and if no Person have a Majority, then from the five highest on the list the said House shall in like Manner chuse the President. But in chusing the President, the Votes shall be taken by States, the Representation from each State having one Vote; a quorum for this Purpose shall consist of a Member or Members from two-thirds of the States, and a Majority of all the States shall be necessary to a Choice. In every Case, after the Choice of the President, the Person having the greatest Number of Votes of the Electors shall be the Vice President. But if there should remain two or more who have equal votes, the Senate shall chuse from them by Ballot the Vice President.][4]

The Congress may determine the Time of chusing the Electors, and the Day on which they shall give their Votes; which Day shall be the same throughout the United States.

No person except a natural-born Citizen, or a Citizen of the United States, at the time of the Adoption of this Constitution, shall be eligible to the Office of President; neither shall any Person be eligible to that Office who shall not have attained to the Age of thirty-five years, and been fourteen Years a Resident within the United States.

In Case of the Removal of the President from Office, or of his Death, Resignation, or Inability to discharge the Powers and Duties of the said Office, the same shall devolve on the Vice

[4]Revised by the Twelfth Amendment.

THE CONSTITUTION OF THE UNITED STATES OF AMERICA • A-9

President, and the Congress may by Law provide for the Case of Removal, Death, Resignation, or Inability, both of the President and Vice President, declaring what Officer shall then act as President, and such Officer shall act accordingly, until the disability be removed, or a President shall be elected.

The President shall, at stated Times, receive for his Services a Compensation, which shall neither be increased nor diminished during the Period for which he shall have been elected, and he shall not receive within that Period any other Emolument from the United States, or any of them.

Before he enter on the execution of his Office, he shall take the following Oath or Affirmation:–"I do solemnly swear (or affirm) that I will faithfully execute the Office of President of the United States, and will, to the best of my Ability, preserve, protect, and defend the Constitution of the United States."

Section 2.

The President shall be Commander in Chief of the Army and Navy of the United States, and of the Militia of the several States, when called into the actual Service of the United States; he may require the Opinion, in writing, of the principal Officer in each of the executive Departments, upon any subject relating to the Duties of their respective Offices, and he shall have Power to Grant Reprieves and Pardons for Offenses against the United States, except in Cases of Impeachment.

He shall have Power, by and with the Advice and Consent of the Senate, to make Treaties, provided two-thirds of the Senators present concur; and he shall nominate, and by and with the Advice and Consent of the Senate, shall appoint Ambassadors, other public Ministers and Consuls, Judges of the supreme Court, and all other Officers of the United States, whose Appointments are not herein otherwise provided for, and which shall be established by Law: but the Congress may by Law vest the Appointment of such inferior Officers, as they think proper, in the President alone, in the Courts of Law, or in the Heads of Departments.

The President shall have Power to fill up all Vacancies that may happen during the Recess of the Senate, by granting Commissions which shall expire at the End of their next Session.

Section 3.

He shall from time to time give to the Congress Information of the State of the Union, and recommend to their Consideration such Measures as he shall judge necessary and expedient; he may, on extraordinary occasions, convene both Houses, or either of them, and in Case of Disagreement between them, with respect to the Time of Adjournment, he may adjourn them to such Time as he shall think proper; he shall receive Ambassadors and other public Ministers; he shall take care that the Laws be faithfully executed, and shall Commission all the Officers of the United States.

Section 4.

The President, Vice President and all civil Officers of the United States, shall be removed from Office on Impeachment for, and Conviction of, Treason, Bribery, or other high Crimes and Misdemeanors.

Article III

Section 1.

The judicial Power of the United States, shall be vested in one supreme Court, and in such inferior Courts as the Congress may from time to time ordain and establish. The Judges, both of the supreme and inferior Courts, shall hold their Offices during good Behaviour, and shall, at stated Times, receive for their Services, a Compensation, which shall not be diminished during their Continuance in Office.

Section 2.

The judicial Power shall extend to all Cases, in Law and Equity, arising under this Constitution, the Laws of the United States, and Treaties made, or which shall be made, under their Authority;–to all Cases affecting ambassadors, other public ministers and consuls;–to all cases of admiralty and maritime Jurisdiction;–to Controversies to which the United States shall be a Party;–to Controversies between two or more States;–between a State and Citizens of another State;[5]–between Citizens of different States–between Citizens of the same State claiming Lands under Grants of different States, and between a State, or the Citizens thereof, and foreign States, Citizens, or Subjects.

In all Cases affecting Ambassadors, other public Ministers and Consuls, and those in which a State shall be Party, the supreme Court shall have original Jurisdiction. In all the other Cases before mentioned, the supreme Court shall have appellate Jurisdiction, both as to Law and Fact, with such Exceptions, and under such Regulations as the Congress shall make.

The trial of all Crimes, except in Cases of Impeachment, shall be by Jury; and such Trial shall be held in the State where the said Crimes shall have been committed; but when not committed within any State, the Trial shall be at such Place or Places as the Congress may by Law have directed.

Section 3.

Treason against the United States, shall consist only in levying War against them, or in adhering to their Enemies, giving them Aid and Comfort. No Person shall be convicted of Treason unless on the Testimony of two Witnesses to the same overt Act, or on Confession in open Court.

The Congress shall have power to declare the Punishment of Treason, but no Attainder of Treason shall work Corruption of Blood, or Forfeiture except during the Life of the Person attained.

Article IV

Section 1.

Full Faith and Credit shall be given in each State to the public Acts, Records, and judicial Proceedings of every State. And the Congress may by general Laws prescribe the Manner in which such Acts, Records and Proceedings shall be proved, and the Effect thereof.

Section 2.

The Citizens of each State shall be entitled to all Privileges and Immunities of Citizens in the several States.

[5]Qualified by the Eleventh Amendment.

A-10 •

A Person charged in any State with Treason, Felony, or other Crime, who shall flee from Justice, and be found in another State, shall on demand of the executive Authority of the State from which he fled, be delivered up, to be removed to the State having Jurisdiction of the crime.

No Person held to Service or Labour in one State, under the Laws thereof, escaping into another, shall, in Consequence of any Law or Regulation therein, be discharged from such Service or Labour, but shall be delivered up on Claim of the Party to whom such Service or Labour may be due.

Section 3.

New States may be admitted by the Congress into this Union; but no new State shall be formed or erected within the Jurisdiction of any other State; nor any State be formed by the Junction of two or more States, or parts of States, without the Consent of the Legislatures of the States concerned as well as of the Congress.

The Congress shall have Power to dispose of and make all needful Rules and Regulations respecting the Territory or other Property belonging to the United States; and nothing in this Constitution shall be so construed as to Prejudice any Claims of the United States, or of any particular State.

Section 4.

The United States shall guarantee to every State in this Union a Republican Form of Government, and shall protect each of them against Invasion; and on Application of the Legislature, or of the Executive (when the Legislature cannot be convened) against domestic violence.

Article V

The Congress, whenever two-thirds of both Houses shall deem it necessary, shall propose Amendments to this Constitution, or, on the Application of the Legislatures of two-thirds of the several States, shall call a Convention for proposing Amendments, which, in either Case, shall be valid to all Intents and Purposes, as part of this Constitution, when ratified by the Legislatures of three-fourths of the several States, or by Conventions in three-fourths thereof, as the one or the other Mode of Ratification may be proposed by the Congress; Provided that no Amendment which may be made prior to the Year One thousand eight hundred and eight shall in any Manner affect the first and fourth Clauses in the Ninth Section of the first Article; and that no State, without its Consent, shall be deprived of its equal Suffrage in the Senate.

Article VI

All Debts contracted and Engagements entered into, before the Adoption of this Constitution, shall be as valid against the United States under this Constitution, as under the Confederation.

This Constitution, and the Laws of the United States which shall be made in Pursuance thereof; and all Treaties made, or which shall be made, under the Authority of the United States, shall be the supreme Law of the Land; and the Judges in every State shall be bound thereby, any Thing in the Constitution or Laws of any State to the Contrary notwithstanding.

The Senators and Representatives before mentioned, and the Members of the several State Legislatures, and all executive and judicial Officers, both of the United States and of the several States, shall be bound by Oath or Affirmation to support this Constitution; but no religious Tests shall ever be required as a qualification to any Office or public Trust under the United States.

Article VII

The Ratification of the Conventions of nine States shall be sufficient for the Establishment of this Constitution between the States so ratifying the same.

Done in convention by the Unanimous Consent of the States present the Seventeenth Day of September in the Year of our Lord one thousand seven hundred and Eighty seven, and of the Independence of the United States of America the Twelfth. In Witness whereof We have hereunto subscribed our Names.[6]

George Washington,
President and deputy from Virginia

New Hampshire
John Langdon
Nicholas Gilman

Massachusetts
Nathaniel Gorham
Rufus King

Connecticut
William Samuel Johnson
Roger Sherman

New York
Alexander Hamilton

Delaware
George Read
Gunning Beford, Jr.
John Dickinson
Richard Bassett
Jacob Broom

New Jersey
William Livingston
David Brearley
William Paterson
Jonathan Dayton

Pennsylvania
Benjamin Franklin
Thomas Mifflin
Robert Morris
George Clymer
Thomas FitzSimons
Jared Ingersoll
James Wilson
Gouverneur Morris

North Carolina
William Blount
Richard Dobbs Spaight
Hugh Williamson

Maryland
James McHenry
Daniel of St. Thomas Jenifer
Daniel Carroll

Virginia
John Blair
James Madison, Jr.

South Carolina
John Rutledge
Charles Cotesworth Pinckney
Charles Pinckney Pierce Butler

Georgia
William Few
Abraham Baldwin

[6]These are the full names of the signers, which in some cases are not the signatures on the document.

THE CONSTITUTION OF THE UNITED STATES OF AMERICA • A-11

Articles in Addition to, and Amendment of, the Constitution of the United States of America, Proposed by Congress, and Ratified by the Legislatures of the Several States, Pursuant to the Fifth Article of the Original Constitution[7]

[Article I]

Congress shall make no law respecting an establishment of religion, or prohibiting the free exercise thereof; or abridging the freedom of speech, or of the press; or the right of the people peaceably to assemble, and to petition the Government for a redress of grievances.

[Article II]

A well regulated Militia, being necessary to the security of a free State, the right of the people to keep and bear Arms shall not be infringed.

[Article III]

No Soldier shall, in time of peace, be quartered in any house, without the consent of the Owner, nor in time of war, but in a manner to be prescribed by law.

[Article IV]

The right of the people to be secure in their persons, houses, papers, and effects, against unreasonable searches and seizures, shall not be violated, and no Warrants shall issue, but upon probable cause, supported by Oath or affirmation, and particularly describing the place to be searched, and the persons or things to be seized.

[Article V]

No person shall be held to answer for a capital or otherwise infamous crime, unless on a presentment or indictment of a Grand Jury, except in cases arising in the land or naval forces, or in the Militia, when in actual service in time of War or public danger; nor shall any person be subject for the same offence to be twice put in jeopardy of life or limb; nor shall be compelled in any criminal case to be a witness against himself, nor be deprived of life, liberty, or property, without due process of law; nor shall private property be taken for public use, without just compensation.

[Article VI]

In all criminal prosecutions, the accused shall enjoy the right to a speedy and public trial, by an impartial jury of the State and district wherein the crime shall have been committed, which district shall have been previously ascertained by law, and to be informed of the nature and cause of the accusation; to be confronted with the witnesses against him; to have compulsory process for obtaining witnesses in his favour, and to have the Assistance of Counsel for his defence.

[Article VII]

In suits at common law, where the value in controversy shall exceed twenty dollars, the right of trial by jury shall be preserved, and no fact tried by a jury, shall be otherwise reexamined in any Court of the United States, than according to the rules of the common law.

[Article VIII]

Excessive bail shall not be required, nor excessive fines imposed, nor cruel and unusual punishments inflicted.

[Article IX]

The enumeration in the Constitution, of certain rights, shall not be construed to deny or disparage others retained by the people.

[Article X]

The powers not delegated to the United States by the Constitution, nor prohibited by it to the States, are reserved to the States respectively, or to the people. [Amendments I-X, in force 1791.]

[Article XI][8]

The Judicial power of the United States shall not be construed to extend to any suit in law or equity, commenced or prosecuted against one of the United States by Citizens of another State, or by Citizens or Subjects of any Foreign State.

[Article XII][9]

The Electors shall meet in their respective States and vote by ballot for President and Vice-President, one of whom, at least, shall not be an inhabitant of the same State with themselves; they shall name in their ballots the person voted for as President, and in distinct ballots the person voted for as Vice-President, and they shall make distinct lists of all persons voted for as President, and of all persons voted for as Vice-President, and of the number of votes for each, which lists they shall sign and certify, and transmit sealed to the seal of the government of the United States, directed to the President of the Senate;—The President of the Senate shall, in the presence of the Senate and House of Representatives, open all the certificates and the votes shall then be counted;—The person having the greatest number of votes for President, shall be the President, if such number be a majority of the whole number of Electors appointed; and if no person have such majority, then from the persons having the highest numbers not exceeding three on the list of those voted for as President, the House of Representatives shall choose immediately, by ballot, the President. But in choosing the President, the votes shall be taken by states, the representation from each state having one vote; a quorum for this purpose shall consist of a member or members from two-thirds of the states, and a major-

[7]This heading appears only in the joint resolution submitting the first ten amendments.

[8]Adopted in 1798.

[9]Adopted in 1804.

A-12

ity of all the states shall be necessary to a choice. And if the House of Representatives shall not choose a President whenever the right of choice shall devolve upon them, before the fourth day of March next following, then the Vice-President shall act as President, as in the case of the death or other constitutional disability of the President.–The person having the greatest number of votes as Vice-President, shall be the Vice-President, if such number be a majority of the whole number of Electors appointed, and if no person have a majority, then from the two highest numbers on the list, the Senate shall choose the Vice-President; a quorum for the purpose shall consist of two-thirds of the whole number of Senators, and a majority of the whole number shall be necessary to a choice. But no person constitutionally ineligible to the office of President shall be eligible to that of Vice-President of the United States.

[Article XIII][10]

Section 1.

Neither slavery nor involuntary servitude, except as a punishment for crime whereof the party shall have been duly convicted, shall exist within the United States, or any place subject to their jurisdiction.

Section 2.

Congress shall have power to enforce this article by appropriate legislation.

[Article XIV][11]

Section 1.

All persons born or naturalized in the United States, and subject to the jurisdiction thereof, are citizens of the United States and of the State wherein they reside. No State shall make or enforce any law which shall abridge the privileges or immunities of citizens of the United States; nor shall any State deprive any person of life, liberty, or property, without due process of law; nor deny to any person within its jurisdiction the equal protection of the laws.

Section 2.

Representatives shall be apportioned among the several States according to their respective numbers, counting the whole number of persons in each State, excluding Indians not taxed. But when the right to vote at any election for the choice of electors for President and Vice-President of the United States, Representatives in Congress, the Executive and Judicial officers of a State, or the members of the Legislature thereof, is denied to any of the male inhabitants of such State, being twenty-one years of age, and citizens of the United States, or in any way abridged, except for participation in rebellion, or other crime, the basis of representation therein shall be reduced in the proportion which the number of such male citizens shall bear to the whole number of male citizens twenty-one years of age in such State.

[10]Adopted in 1865.

[11]Adopted in 1868.

Section 3.

No person shall be a Senator or Representative in Congress, or elector of President and Vice-President, or hold any office, civil or military, under the United States, or under any State, who, having previously taken an oath, as a member of Congress, or as an officer of the United States, or as a member of any State legislature, or as an executive or judicial officer of any State, to support the Constitution of the United States, shall have engaged in insurrection or rebellion against the same, or given aid or comfort to the enemies thereof. But Congress may by a vote of two-thirds of each House, remove such disability.

Section 4.

The validity of the public debt of the United States, authorized by law, including debts incurred for payment of pensions and bounties for services in suppressing insurrection or rebellion, shall not be questioned. But neither the United States nor any State shall assume or pay any debts or obligation incurred in aid of insurrection or rebellion against the United States, or any claim for the loss or emancipation of any slave; but all such debts, obligations, and claims shall be held illegal and void.

Section 5.

The Congress shall have the power to enforce, by appropriate legislation, the provisions of this article.

[Article XV][12]

Section 1.

The right of citizens of the United States to vote shall not be denied or abridged by the United States or by any State on account of race, color, or previous condition of servitude–

Section 2.

The Congress shall have power to enforce this article by appropriate legislation.

[Article XVI][13]

The Congress shall have power to lay and collect taxes on incomes, from whatever source derived, without apportionment among the several States, and without regard to any census or enumeration.

[Article XVII][14]

The Senate of the United States shall be composed of two Senators from each State, elected by the people thereof, for six years; and each Senator shall have one vote. The electors in each State shall have the qualifications requisite for electors of the most numerous branch of the State legislatures.

When vacancies happen in the representation of any State in the Senate, the executive authority of such State shall issue writs of election to fill such vacancies: *Provided*, That the

[12]Adopted in 1870.

[13]Adopted in 1913.

[14]Adopted in 1913.

THE CONSTITUTION OF THE UNITED STATES OF AMERICA • A-13

legislature of any State may empower the executive thereof to make temporary appointments until the people fill the vacancies by election as the legislature may direct.

This amendment shall not be so constructed as to affect the election or term of any Senator chosen before it becomes valid as part of the Constitution.

[Article XVIII][15]

Section 1.
After one year from the ratification of this article the manufacture, sale, or transportation of intoxicating liquors within, the importation thereof into, or the exportation thereof from the United States and all territory subject to the jurisdiction thereof for beverage purposes is hereby prohibited.

Section 2.
The Congress and the several States shall have concurrent power to enforce this article by appropriate legislation.

Section 3.
This article shall be inoperative unless it shall have been ratified as an amendment to the Constitution by the legislatures of the several States, as provided in the Constitution, within seven years from the date of the submission hereof to the States by the Congress.

[Article XIX][16]

The right of citizens of the United States to vote shall not be denied or abridged by the United States or by any State on account of sex.

Congress shall have power to enforce this article by appropriate legislation.

[Article XX][17]

Section 1.
The terms of the President and Vice-President shall end at noon on the 20th day of January, and the terms of Senators and Representatives at noon on the 3d day of January, of the years in which such terms would have ended if this article had not been ratified; and the terms of their successors shall then begin.

Section 2.
The Congress shall assemble at least once in every year, and such meeting shall begin at noon on the 3d day of January, unless they shall by law appoint a different day.

Section 3.
If, at the time fixed for the beginning of the term of the President, the President elect shall have died, the Vice-President elect shall become President. If a President shall not have been chosen before the time fixed for the beginning of his term or if the President elect shall have failed to qualify, then the Vice-President elect shall act as President until a President shall have qualified; and the Congress may by law provide for the case wherein neither a President elect nor a Vice-President elect shall have qualified, declaring who shall then act as President, or the manner in which one who is to act shall be selected, and such person shall act accordingly until a President or Vice-President shall have qualified.

Section 4.
The Congress may by law provide for the case of the death of any of the persons from whom the House of Representatives may choose a President whenever the right of choice shall have developed upon them, and for the case of the death of any of the persons from whom the Senate may choose a Vice-President whenever the right of choice shall have developed upon them.

Section 5.
Sections 1 and 2 shall take effect on the 15th day of October following the ratification of this article.

Section 6.
This article shall be inoperative unless it shall have been ratified as an amendment to the Constitution by the legislatures of three-fourths of the several States within seven years from the date of its submission.

[Article XXI][18]

Section 1.
The eighteenth article of amendment to the Constitution of the United States is hereby repealed.

Section 2.
The transportation or importation into any State, Territory, or possession of the United States for delivery or use therein of intoxicating liquors, in violation of the laws thereof, is hereby prohibited.

Section 3.
This article shall be inoperative unless it shall have been ratified as an amendment to the Constitution by conventions in the several States, as provided in the Constitution, within seven years from the date of the submission hereof to the States by the Congress.

[Article XXII][19]

No person shall be elected to the office of the President more than twice, and no person who has held the office of President, or acted as President, for more than two years of a term to which some other person was elected President shall be elected to the office of the President more than once.

But this Article shall not apply to any person holding the office of President when this Article was proposed by the Congress, and shall not prevent any person who may be hold-

[15]Adopted in 1918.
[16]Adopted in 1920.
[17]Adopted in 1933.
[18]Adopted in 1933.
[19]Adopted in 1961.

A-14 •

ing the office of President, or acting as President, during the term within which this Article becomes operative from holding the office of President or acting as President during the remainder of such term.

This article shall be inoperative unless it shall have been ratified as an amendment to the Constitution by the legislatures of three-fourths of the several states within seven years from the date of its submission to the states by the Congress.

[Article XXIII][20]

Section 1.

The District constituting the seat of Government of the United States shall appoint in such manner as the Congress may direct:

A number of electors of President and Vice-President equal to the whole number of Senators and Representatives in Congress to which the District would be entitled if it were a State, but in no event more than the least populous State; they shall be in addition to those appointed by the States, but they shall be considered, for the purposes of the election of President and Vice-President, to be electors appointed by a State; and they shall meet in the District and perform such duties as provided by the twelfth article of amendment.

Section 2.

The Congress shall have power to enforce this article by appropriate legislation.

[Article XXIV][21]

Section 1.

The right of citizens of the United States to vote in any primary or other election for President or Vice President, for electors for President or Vice President, or for Senator or Representative in Congress, shall not be denied or abridged by the United States or any state by reason of failure to pay any poll tax or other tax.

Section 2.

The Congress shall have the power to enforce this article by appropriate legislation.

[Article XXV][22]

Section 1.

In case of the removal of the President from office or of his death or resignation, the Vice President shall become President.

Section 2.

Whenever there is a vacancy in the office of the Vice President, the President shall nominate a Vice President who shall take office upon confirmation by a majority vote of both Houses of Congress.

[20]Adopted in 1961.

[21]Adopted in 1964.

[22]Adopted in 1967.

Section 3.

Whenever the President transmits to the President Pro Tempore of the Senate and the Speaker of the House of Representatives his written declaration that he is unable to discharge the powers and duties of his office, and until he transmits to them a written declaration to the contrary, such powers and duties shall be discharged by the Vice President as Acting President.

Section 4.

Whenever the Vice President and a majority of either the principal officers of the executive departments or of such other body as Congress may by law provide, transmit to the President Pro Tempore of the Senate and the Speaker of the House of Representatives their written declaration that the President is unable to discharge the powers and duties of his office, the Vice President shall immediately assume the powers and duties of the office as Acting President.

Thereafter, when the President transmits to the President Pro Tempore of the Senate and the Speaker of the House of Representatives his written declaration that no inability exists, he shall resume the powers and duties of his office unless the Vice President and a majority of either the principal officers of the executive departments or of such other body as Congress may by law provide, transmit within four days to the President Pro Tempore of the Senate and the Speaker of the House of Representatives their written declaration that the President is unable to discharge the powers and duties of his office. Thereupon Congress shall decide the issue, assembling within forty-eight hours for that purpose if not in session. If the Congress, within twenty-one days after receipt of the latter written declaration, or, if Congress is not in session, within twenty-one days after Congress is required to assemble, determines by two-thirds vote of both Houses that the President is unable to discharge the powers and duties of his office, the Vice President shall continue to discharge the same as Acting President; otherwise, the President shall resume the powers and duties of his office.

[Article XXVI][23]

Section 1.

The right of citizens of the United States, who are eighteen years of age or older, to vote shall not be denied or abridged by the United States or by any State on account of age.

Section 2.

The Congress shall have power to enforce this article by appropriate legislation.

[Article XXVII][24]

No law varying the compensation for the services of Senators and Representatives shall take effect until an election of Representatives shall have intervened.

[23]Adopted in 1971.

[24]Adopted in 1992.

THE CONSTITUTION OF THE UNITED STATES OF AMERICA • A-15

GLOSSARY OF AP TERMINOLOGY

American republic This political term refers to the United States of America and the idea that it protects individual civil liberties as well as represents the people's will.

African chattel Africans and their descendants were forced to work for masters in the English colonies without political or economic freedoms. Alt: slaves

American System An early 19th century vision of an economically self-sufficient America that would see government funded internal improvements paid for with higher protective tariffs.

Anglicization English political, religious and economic traits would transfer to the New World through trans-Atlantic print culture and Protestant evangelism.

Antebellum A period in American history prior to the Civil War which generally falls between 1800-1860. Alt: early 19th century or first half of 19th century

Assimilation Foreign born immigrants acquire the cultural traits of a society they have migrated to through this process. Alt: Acculturation

Baby boom Following WWII (1945-1965) there was a very large increase in the number of children born in America.

Backcountry culture This frontier American culture combined aspects of both the Eastern seaboard society with the unique aspects of the wilderness.

British Empire By the turn of the 20th century the island of Great Britain and her vast colonial holdings stretched from North and South America to the Pacific ports of China

Bonded labor People, either voluntarily (indentured servants) or involuntarily (slaves), legally tied to working for another person.

Capitalism This economic system is marked by private ownership of factories and resources and is based on free trade and competition whose formal principles were laid down in Adam Smith's *Wealth of Nations* (1776).

Central government This supreme political institution is invested with more power than the smaller regional or state governments that fall under its jurisdiction. Alt: Federal government

Centralized power A concept that refers to one government gathering nearly complete economic and political authority over a society.

Cereal crops Corn, oats and wheat are these types of crops that are grown to feed communities. Alt: Staple crops

Civil War Amendments Added to the Constitution in the five years following the end of the Civil War, the 13th, 14th and 15th amendments gave liberty, "equal protection" under the law and voting rights to the newly freed slaves.

Collective security This concept refers to several countries joining together in a defensive alliance for mutual protection against perceived enemies.

Colonial elites These wealthy individuals tended to be large plantation owners, merchants or shippers.

Colonization The process by which European powers settled their people in the western hemisphere during the 16th and 17th centuries and transplanted their economic, political and cultural features.

Columbian Exchange Plants, animals and material goods were transferred between the Western and Eastern Hemispheres because of the discovery of the New World by Christopher Columbus in 1492.

Conservatism A smaller federal government, low taxes, reduction of government funded social programs, a less regulated capitalist society and an adherence to traditional social mores define the general beliefs of this political philosophy.

Demographic This refers to the characteristics of population patterns and or changes.

Democratic Republicans This political party born in the 1790's followed the beliefs of Thomas Jefferson which included strict interpretation of the United States Constitution and a limited central government. Alt: Jeffersonians

Democrats Generally used in reference to a 20th century political party, this political group believes in broadening the powers of the federal government to regulate business and provide enlarged social programs for the underprivileged.

Dētente, mutual coexistence During this period of relaxed tension between the United States and the Soviet Union in the early 1970's, the Cold War saw a reduction of armaments in the SALT I and ABM Treaties.

Encomienda system During Spanish colonization of the 16th and 17th century, Spain established this plantation-based agriculture system which included forced labor extracted from Native-Americans and later enslaved Africans. Alt: plantations

Enlightenment An intellectual movement that utilized human reason to question commonly accepted beliefs in political and religious practices of the late 17th and 18th century period.

European expansion, imperialism In the second half of the 19th century, European countries took economic and political control over foreign lands in Africa, Asia and the Middle East.

European Romanticism Emphasizing the emotional and intuitive over the rational, this intellectual movement of the early 19th century rejected many precepts of the Enlightenment.

Evangelism This religious concept refers to the spreading of a religious faith through proselytizing by its adherents and generally saw a surge during periods of religious revivalism such as the two Great Awakenings of the 18th and 19th centuries.

Federalism This principle embedded in the United States Constitution outlines the division of power between the state governments and the federal government.

Federalists These proponents of the ratification of the United States Constitution supported a stronger central government over state sovereignty in the late 18th century.

Feudalism Under this economic and cultural arrangement the mass of European population (serfs) exchanged their labor and service for protection provided by the nobles.

Free trade agreement An economic pact that reduces tariffs and economic restrictions between countries and is intended to stimulate economic activity; with the most notable attempt being the North American Free Trade Agreement (NAFTA).

Globalization, economic This growing network of international businesses has interests in many countries and is uniting the worldwide economy.

Great Society Lyndon Johnson's domestic social reform program, known as "The Great Society," featured the passage of Medicare and Medicaid and the addition of a new cabinet agency called the Department of Housing and Urban Development (HUD).

Hereditary privilege This cultural and legal system involves the passing down of property and social standing to one's heirs and thus enables wealthy families to maintain their social supremacy for generations.

Hierarchy Operating as a social class system, it artificially ranks people according to their economic and social standing.

Hispanics This contemporary term denotes someone from Central America with mixed Spanish and indigenous ancestry.

Holding companies These companies exist solely on paper and control the majority of stock in an actual company.

Homogeneous society A society, such as the Puritans of the 17th century, that enforces religious, cultural or racial conformity upon its inhabitants.

Ideology These beliefs or values define a person or a society.

Imperialism expansion of A mid-19th century movement by European countries designed to take over foreign lands for economic resources and markets.

Indentured servants Europeans who contracted out their labor for up to seven years in return for paid passage across the Atlantic to the New World.

Indian People native (indigenous) to North America prior to the arrival of the Europeans in the 16th century. Alt: American Indian, Native American

Intellectual This term tends to be used in regards to history that is conceptual or philosophical in its orientation. Alt: intellectual history

Intermarriage In reference to the mixing of two different ethnic groups through marriage, this term is generally used in reference to the relationships that developed between the Native-Americans and European groups during the colonization period. Alt: miscegenation

Laissez-faire This term refers to the economic concept in which the government does little to regulate big business or in other words keeps its "hands off" of businesses and is usually used in reference to the late 19th century industrialization period.

Latinos From Latin America (Central and South America), these people are linguistically connected (Spanish-speaking) and they are the largest growing minority group in contemporary America.

The Left In reference to the left side of the political spectrum, proponents support a more activist government that works to safeguard consumers against business abuses and provide social programs for the underprivileged.

Liberalism This economic-political ideology promotes more government involvement in the economy to correct social and economic inequalities.

Loyalist This person supported the king and Parliament during the American Revolution.

Maize cultivation Introduced to the Europeans by the Native-American peoples, this agricultural crop was the main staple crop that sustained both societies. Alt: corn

Market economy During the antebellum period, the agricultural interior of the United States (Ohio River Valley) was able to connect to the Northeast through transportation improvements, thus enabling the industrial north to sell its manufactured goods while receiving the raw materials of the Great Lakes Region.

Mercantilism A trade system between a mother country (European nation) and her colonies that uses the colonies both as a source of raw materials and as a market for manufactured goods.

Mexican-Americans Second generation Americans that emigrated from Mexico.

Middle class Based on socio-economic standing, people in this group have annual incomes that are above the poverty line which allows them have disposable income.

Military-industrial complex Businesses that manufacture armaments (planes, guns, ships, etc.) for the US military. Alt: defense industry

Mission settlements As the Spanish settled northward into North America in the 16th century they established Catholic churches (missions) which became the cultural and economic centers for the indigenous people.

Nationalism This cultural belief professes that one's own country is superior to other countries economically, culturally and/or politically. Alt: patriotism

Nativism A belief that a country should be composed of only original settlers (inhabitants) and should restrict emigration by foreigners.

Neoconservatism The resurgence of former conservative ideals following the implementation of the Great Society in the 1960's.

New World This 16th century European concept refers to the newly discovered lands to the west of Europe and across the Atlantic Ocean. Alt: Western Hemisphere

Nullification An antebellum belief that a state had the power to void a federal law if it was deemed oppressive.

Old World This is a reference to Europe and the Mediterranean regions following Columbus' voyage. Alt: Eastern Hemisphere

Partisan A person that supports a specific political ideology and works to actively advance it. Alt: party activist

Patriot A supporter of the independence of the American colonies from Great Britain during the American Revolution.

Peopling This geographic term refers to the movement of people to a particular area, region or country. Alt: Emigration or population shift

Plantation This large Southern farm during the pre-Civil War period employed slaves and grew cash crops such as cotton or tobacco.

Political machines A group of government officials associated with one party or political faction that control the government and who tend to rule in such a way as to favor themselves and their political benefactors.

Pueblo Revolt This 1680 revolt by Indians of the Southwestern part of the contemporary United States successfully removed Spanish control for twelve years.

Republican Party This political party born in the 1850's supports government encouragement of business growth through tax breaks or subsidies and a more conservative ideology in reference to maintaining the status quo.

Republicanism This ideology professes that a government's power is based upon the people's will and that the people's civil liberties should be protected.

The Right In reference to the right side of the political spectrum, proponents support a more limited government role in people's lives to protect individual liberties.

Second party system A political system which arose in the Jacksonian era that entails, it involves two partisan groups competing for the electorate's vote through campaigning for political office.

Shared labor market This concept refers to the sharing of labor between eastern and western hemispheres during the colonial period.

Segregation This cultural and legal term means the separation of public places and schools based on race.

Semisubsistence agriculture In the frontier regions due to terrain or climate the ability to farm was very limited and thus a farmer needed to hunt and gather as well as farm in order to survive.

Settlement houses These privately run organizations in the late 19th and early 20th century operated in urban areas and assisted immigrants with assimilating into the new world by providing education, housing and other vital services. Alt: Hull House Movement

Social justice This cultural belief states that lower socio-economic classes deserve equality in economic, political and social areas.

Social mobility Lower socio-economic groups have the opportunity to move upward in the social class structure.

Social safety net Government programs that aid the poor, indigent, elderly and disabled.

Staple crops Corn, oats and wheat are these types of crops that are grown to feed communities. Alt: Foodstuffs

States' rights These are state powers invested in a state according to the US Constitution and implied in the 10th amendment.

Tariff This is a tax imposed on foreign goods entering a country.

Trusts Usually associated with businesses during the Gilded Age and early 20th century, this term refers to large corporations that monopolize an industry Alt: business oligarchies

Utopianism The belief that society can be perfected and that through the correct application of political, religious or humanitarian precepts human misery can be eradicated.

Whigs A political party born in the 1830's in opposition to Andrew Jackson, it supported a stronger national government as proposed in the American System.

Worldview These perspectives reflect a person's ideas and beliefs concerning people and places that lie outside of their day-to-day lives.

Xenophobia Fear that a foreigner's beliefs or cultural values (communism, anarchy, Catholicism, etc.) will undermine and destroy the traditional fabric of the American society.

Geographic Terms

Asia Traditionally this region includes those countries that touch the Pacific Ocean on the east, the Indian Ocean to the south and the Arctic Ocean to the north and blends into Europe at the eastern edge of the Mediterranean Ocean.

Atlantic Seaboard Stretching from the southern tip of Newfoundland to the Florida Peninsula this geographic term tends to be used during the colonial period and would encompass New England, Middle and upper Southern colonies.

Atlantic World A reference to the African, European and American societies that border the Atlantic Ocean. This body of water touches the shores of Africa, Europe, North and South America.

Backcountry In U.S. history courses, this area is most commonly associated with western frontier Virginia and the Carolinas during the colonial era and the early republic; the focus is usually on conflict with the small-hold farmers of those areas and the coastal elite (i.e. Bacon's rebellion).

Caribbean Situated east of Central America, this area is composed of hundreds of islands from Cuba to the Bahamas that lie between North and South America and which is the land that the Spanish originally inhabited. Alt: West Indies

Central America The panhandle of North America, this geographic region refers to the isthmian countries South of Mexico and north of Columbia.

Great Basin This geographic region stretches between the Rocky Mountains on the eastern border to the Cascade and Sierra Nevada Mountains on the western side.

Great Plains Stretching between the Mississippi River and the Rocky Mountains these flat grasslands are composed of prairies and steppes.

Interior regions Generally used during the colonial period, this geographic terms refers to the middle part of contemporary United States east of the Mississippi River that ranges from the Great Lakes Region in the north to Louisiana.

Latin America This cultural term refers to the countries that stretch from Mexico to the Straits of Magellan.

Lower South This term is used in reference to the seven most southern states that seceded before Fort Sumter was fired upon in April of 1861.

Middle East Centered on the Arabian peninsula, this geographic region is bordered on the north by Turkey, the east by Afghanistan, the south by Yemen and the west by Egypt.

Midwest This region is composed of the twelve states that lie between North Dakota, Ohio and Kansas.

Northeast This region is composed of the nine states between Pennsylvania and Maine.

Northwest Territory South of the Great Lakes, east of the Mississippi and north of the Ohio River this area was the first area to see westward migration in order to find cheap farmland. The settlement of this area in the early 19th century led to the Market Revolution.

Old Northwest This region lies between the Great Lakes in the north, the Ohio River in the south and the Mississippi River on the west.
Alt: Northwest Territory

The Pacific This historical term refers to the islands and archipelagos that stretch between China on the west to California on the east.

The Philippines Consisting of thousands of islands, this Southeast Asian country was taken over by the United States during the Spanish-American War.

Sun Belt Stretching from Virginia to Arizona, this southern region of the United States saw a tremendous growth in population following World War II because of its low tax rate, the invention of air-conditioning, and business-friendly environment.

Tidewater This most commonly refers to coastal areas of Virginia. In U.S. history it is often described as being wealthier, more established and more politically powerful than the backcountry areas (i.e. Bacon's rebellion).

Trans-Appalachian West Generally referred to as the lands west of the Appalachian Mountains which would include the Ohio River Valley and the lands of Kentucky during the late 18th and early 19th century.

Upper South Distinguished for its lower slave percentages than its southern brethren, this region was composed of those states that bordered northern states (Kentucky, Virginia, Delaware, Maryland)

West Indies Those islands that the Spanish, French and English colonized in the 15th and 16th century whose principal cash crop was sugar.

Western Hemisphere North and South America combined.

Terms with Multiple Labels

American Indian also known as Native American

American Revolution also known as Colonial War for Independence, War of Independence, The Revolutionary War

Central government also known as national government

Centralized power also known as federal power

Seven Years' War also known as the French and Indian War

Understanding Dates

Fifteenth century (15th century): 1400–1499

Sixteenth century (16th century): 1500–1599

Seventeenth century (17th century): 1600–1699

Eighteenth century (18th century): 1700–1799

Nineteenth century (19th century): 1800–1899

Twentieth century (20th century): 1900–1999

Twenty-first century (21st century): 2000–2099

Page references followed by b indicate boxes; i, illustrations; m, maps

A

D

F

H

K

L

O

Q

R

U

V

X

Y

Z

AP PRACTICE EXAM

SECTION I

PART A: MULTIPLE CHOICE

Use the image and your knowledge of U.S. history to answer questions 1-3.

1. As illustrated by the image, at the time of European contact many Native American societies
   - (A) used horses to support a primarily nomadic culture.
   - (B) lived in permanent villages supported by agriculture and hunting-gathering economies.
   - (C) formed large scale cities.
   - (D) lived in harmony with no need for defensive structures.

2. When the Spanish encountered such settlements, they generally sought to
   - (A) adapt Spanish culture to the practices of the Native American societies.
   - (B) convert to Native American religious belief systems.
   - (C) force Native Americans into involuntary labor and religious conversions.
   - (D) pressure Native Americans to expand access to the fur trade.

3. In reaction to European demands, many Native Americans
   - (A) sought to defend their political sovereignty and social autonomy.
   - (B) willingly surrendered to European control.
   - (C) allied with other Native American nations to fight off European forces.
   - (D) relocated and retained their independence.

Use the excerpt and your knowledge of U.S. history to answer questions 4-6.

". . .wee must be knitt together, in this worke, as one man. Wee must entertaine each other in brotherly affection. . . . Wee must uphold a familiar commerce together in all meekeness, gentlenes, patience and liberality. Wee must delight in eache other; make other's conditions our owne; rejoice together, mourne together, labour and suffer together, always having before our eyes our commission and community in the worke, as members of y [the] same body. . ."

–John Winthrop, "A Model of Christian Charity," 1630

4. How did the motivations of earlier settlers in North America differ from those of the Puritan settlers?
   - (A) Settlers in the early Chesapeake colonies were largely Dutch merchants who lived in isolated outposts.
   - (B) Settlers in the early Chesapeake colonies were motivated by economic activities such as cultivating tobacco.
   - (C) Settlers in the early New England colonies sought to attract a broad mix of migrants.
   - (D) Settlers in the early Chesapeake colonies were primarily motivated by religious goals.

5. The sentiments expressed in the excerpt were integrated into which political structure in New England?
   - (A) participatory town meetings
   - (B) governorship by appointment of the monarch
   - (C) a legislature dominated by wealthy landowners
   - (D) a single wealthy proprietor designated to make political decisions

6. A resurgence of the religious beliefs expressed in the excerpt was known as
   - (A) the Enlightenment.
   - (B) the Dark Ages.
   - (C) the Great Awakening.
   - (D) the Age of Reason.

Answers

Part A: Multiple Choice

1. B; **2.** C; **3.** A; **4.** B; **5.** C; **6.** C

Use the excerpt and your knowledge of U.S. history to answer questions 7-9.

"Whereas some doubts have arisen whether children got by any Englishman upon a negro woman should be slave or free, Be it &e *[therefore enacted]* that all children born in this country shall be held bond or free, only according to the condition of the mother."

–Virginia Municipal Law, 1662

7. The Virginia law marked a difference between indentured servitude and slavery in that
   (A) the children of enslaved women were also enslaved.
   (B) enslaved people faced harsher legal penalties for crimes committed than indentured servants.
   (C) the children of indentured servants were enslaved.
   (D) indentured servants were not permitted to have children.

8. Colonial Virginia expanded the use of enslaved workers in economic pursuits that centered around
   (A) commercial activities such as shipbuilding.
   (B) production of textiles and steel.
   (C) cultivation of mixed agriculture such as corn and wheat.
   (D) cultivation of cash crops such as tobacco.

9. In response to such strict racial systems, enslaved people
   (A) submitted to the increasingly restrictive system.
   (B) sought political office to reverse such policies.
   (C) engaged in both overt and subtle means of resistance.
   (D) refused to form communities and families.

Use the image and your knowledge of U.S. history to answer questions 10-12.

10. Franklin was compelled to create the image in 1754 because the Americans
    (A) needed to unite to fight alongside the English in the Seven Years' War.
    (B) needed to fight the French in their attempts to take control of Florida.
    (C) needed to unify against English taxation.
    (D) needed to fight the Spanish invasions along the New England coast.

11. The sentiments expressed by the image continued to have importance in the following decades as the English
    (A) sought to draft colonists into their military to continue the fighting.
    (B) ended Salutary Neglect and imposed new taxes to fund the ongoing colonial defense.
    (C) forced North American colonists to expand their use of an enslaved labor force.
    (D) offered colonists representation through a seat in the House of Commons.

12. In an attempt to prevent further conflict, the English
    (A) sought an alliance with the French.
    (B) ended colonial participation in the transatlantic slave trade.
    (C) supported Native American suffrage in colonial elections.
    (D) prohibited further colonial settlement in contested lands west of the Appalachians.

Use the excerpt and your knowledge of U.S. history to answer questions 13-15.

"Be it enacted by the Senate and House of Representatives of the United States of America, in Congress assembled, that from and after the first day of January, one thousand eight hundred and eight, it shall not be lawful to import or bring into the United States, or the territories thereof, from any foreign kingdom, place or country, any negro, mulatto, or person of color, with intent to hold, sell, or dispose of such negro, mulatto, or person of color, as a slave, or to be held to service or labor."

–Act to Prohibit the Importation of Slaves, 1807

13. The legislation made it illegal for Americans to
    (A) participate in the transatlantic slave trade.
    (B) continue to be slaveholders.
    (C) sell enslaved people within the country.
    (D) sell products made by enslaved people.

The Library of Congress (LC-USZC4-5315)

Answers

Part A: Multiple Choice

7. A; **8.** D; **9.** C; **10.** A; **11.** B; **12.** D; **13.** A

14. In what sectors of American life did slavery expand?
   (A) In New England, as the Industrial Revolution expanded the demand for factory workers.
   (B) In the West, as mining industries increased westward migration.
   (C) In the South, as the cotton gin increased the profitability of agriculture.
   (D) In the coastal regions, as enslaved workers were primarily in maritime industries.

15. How did Southern leaders justify the expansion of the institution of slavery?
   (A) They argued that the institution would naturally decrease and eventually end.
   (B) They argued that the institution was an important part of the Southern way of life.
   (C) They argued that the institution was foundational to the principles of the American system.
   (D) They argued that the North required Southern agriculture which necessitated the institution of slavery.

Use the excerpt and your knowledge of U.S. history to answer questions 16–18.

"It gives me pleasure to announce to Congress that the benevolent policy of the Government, steadily pursued for nearly thirty years, in relation to the removal of the Indians beyond the white settlements is approaching to a happy consummation. Two important tribes have accepted the provision made for their removal at the last session of Congress, and it is believed that their example will induce the remaining tribes also to seek the same obvious advantages."

—President Andrew Jackson's Message to Congress, "On Indian Removal," 1830

16. In his address to Congress, Andrew Jackson indicates his willingness to
   (A) embrace the use of federal power to relocate Native American communities.
   (B) punish white settlers for encroaching on Native American lands.
   (C) ask for international assistance to settle the conflicts.
   (D) purchase land to expand the United States.

17. The removal of the Native American nations largely opened up the land for
   (A) the resettlement of European immigrants.
   (B) expansion of Spanish-speaking communities.
   (C) the cultivation of cotton.
   (D) the construction of textile mills.

18. The removal of Native Americans facilitated the later idea that
   (A) the United States should always abide by treaties with Native Americans.
   (B) the United States should punish white settlers who infringe Native American lands.
   (C) the United States had a Manifest Destiny to overspread the continent.
   (D) the United States could settle any dispute with political compromise.

Use the excerpt and your knowledge of U.S. history to answer questions 19–21.

"When, in the course of human events, it becomes necessary for one portion of the family of man to assume among the people of the earth a position different from that which they have hitherto occupied, but one to which the laws of nature and of nature's God entitle them, a decent respect to the opinions of mankind requires that they should declare the causes that impel them to such a course.
We hold these truths to be self-evident; that all men and women are created equal; that they are endowed by their Creator with certain inalienable rights; that among these are life, liberty, and the pursuit of happiness; that to secure these rights governments are instituted, deriving their just powers from the consent of the governed."

—Declaration of Sentiments, Seneca Falls Convention, 1848

19. The Declaration of Sentiments was patterned after what fundamental American document?
   (A) Declaration of Causes
   (B) Declaration of Independence
   (C) Constitution of the United States
   (D) Bill of Rights

20. The Declaration of Sentiments was proclaimed within what historical context?
   (A) increased participation by women in moral and social reform movements
   (B) increased income inequality
   (C) significant conflicts with foreign powers
   (D) increased national participation in the transatlantic slave trade

21. The woman suffrage movement struggled to gain public support as national attention increasingly focused on
   (A) the raising of tariffs.
   (B) legislation limiting immigration.
   (C) foreign conflicts over imperialism.
   (D) the expansion of slavery.

Answers

Part A: Multiple Choice

14. C; **15.** B; **16.** A; **17.** C; **18.** C; **19.** B; **20.** A; **21.** D

Use the image and your knowledge of U.S. history to answer questions 22-24.

–John Brown, 1939 painting by John Steuart Curry

22. Action taken to prevent conflict such as that portrayed in the image included
    (A) increasing limitations placed on the institution of slavery.
    (B) removal of new slave states from the Legislature.
    (C) political compromises such as the Compromise of 1850.
    (D) increasing westward expansion.

23. Renewed conflict over slavery occurred
    (A) as new territories and states entered the Union.
    (B) as new immigrants led to expanding populations in Northern states.
    (C) as economic downturns increased in frequency.
    (D) abolitionists increased campaigns in Southern states.

24. What event sparked the secession of Southern states?
    (A) the Supreme Court decision *Dred Scott v. Sandford*
    (B) the Kansas-Nebraska Act
    (C) Lincoln's victory in the election of 1860
    (D) the Crittenden Compromise

Use the excerpt and your knowledge of U.S. history to answer questions 25-27.

"That on the first day of January . . . all persons held as slaves within any State, or designated part of a State, the people whereof shall then be in rebellion against the United States shall be then, thenceforward, and forever free; and the executive government of the United States, including the military and naval authority thereof, will recognize and maintain the freedom of such persons, and will do no act or acts to repress such persons, or any of them, in any efforts they may make for their actual freedom."

–President Abraham Lincoln,
Emancipation Proclamation, 1862

25. According to President Lincoln, he issued the proclamation due to his motivation to
    (A) see his personal wish to end slavery fulfilled.
    (B) satisfy his political supporters.
    (C) end the rebellion and reunite the country.
    (D) reward his African-American voting base.

26. When Lincoln issued the Emancipation Proclamation, what impact did he hope to achieve?
    (A) limit the use of enslaved soldiers by the Confederates
    (B) prevent European nations from supporting the Confederacy
    (C) encourage Confederate soldiers to resign
    (D) encourage Native American nations to join the Union Army

27. What was the military impact of the final Emancipation Proclamation?
    (A) It allowed the United States to draft immigrant soldiers.
    (B) It authorized loans from foreign powers.
    (C) It created a military strategy for the Union Army.
    (D) It allowed African American men to officially enter the United States military.

28. The Emancipation Proclamation increased international support for the Union from
    (A) politically conscious British workers.
    (B) the German ruling class.
    (C) Cuban textile workers.
    (D) French diplomats.

Use the excerpt and your knowledge of U.S. history to answer questions 29-31.

"All persons born or naturalized in the United States, and subject to the jurisdiction thereof, are citizens of the United States and of the State wherein they reside. No State shall make or enforce any law which shall abridge the privileges or immunities of citizens of the United States; nor shall any State deprive any person of life, liberty, or property, without due process of law; nor deny to any person within its jurisdiction the equal protection of the laws."

–United States Constitution,
Fourteenth Amendment

Answers

Part A: Multiple Choice

22. C; **23.** A; **24.** C; **25.** C; **26.** B; **27.** D; **28.** A

29. The Fourteenth Amendment was passed in reaction to
    (A) the Southern states' threat to secede again.
    (B) the fear that Irish and German was increasing.
    (C) the attempts to prevent African Americans from exercising their citizenship rights.
    (D) the concern that woman suffrage would limit men's political participation.

30. One key question addressed by the post-war Amendments concerned
    (A) the ability to regulate immigration policy.
    (B) the process to immediately achieve woman suffrage.
    (C) the process to legalize secession.
    (D) the relationship between the states and the federal government.

31. One issue related to the Fourteenth Amendment but specifically addressed in the Fifteenth Amendment was
    (A) the rate of income tax.
    (B) the right to vote.
    (C) the responsibility for military service.
    (D) the rampant employment discrimination.

Use the image and your knowledge of U.S. history to answer questions 32-35.

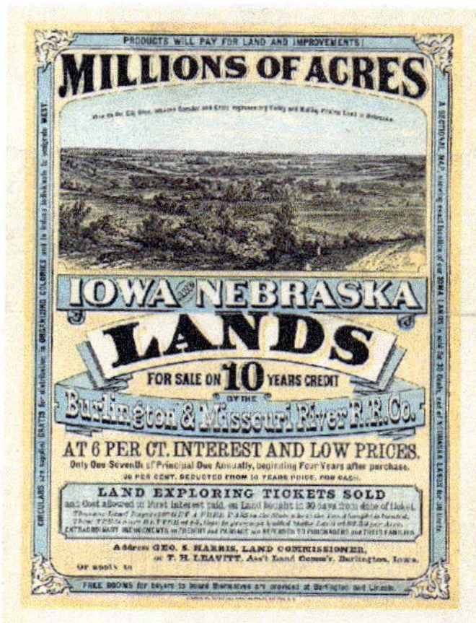

Library of Congress American Memory Collection [rbpe13401300]

32. Advertisements, such as the image, represent the interest in fostering Western settlement by
    (A) immigrant assistance organizations.
    (B) African Americans.
    (C) railroad companies.
    (D) Native American nations.

33. Government policies for Western settlement
    (A) discouraged the westward migration of Americans.
    (B) protected the treaty rights negotiated with Native Americans.
    (C) balanced the interests of farmers and urban residents.
    (D) subsidized the construction of railroads and communication systems.

34. In response to the tensions with railroad companies, the Western farmers
    (A) staged a revolt similar to the Whiskey Rebellion.
    (B) formed local and regional cooperative associations.
    (C) supported the passage of the Fourteenth Amendment.
    (D) developed alternative transportation systems to ship their products.

35. Western settlement, which relied on railroad construction, posed problems for Native Americans including,
    (A) the need to update existing treaties.
    (B) the challenge of assimilating new populations into the Native American culture.
    (C) the decimation of the buffalo population.
    (D) the increase in availability of manufactured goods.

Use the excerpt and your knowledge of U.S. history to answer questions 36-38.

"In conclusion let me add that the southern states owe it to themselves not to pass unfair election laws because it is against the constitution of the United States and each state is under a solemn obligation that every citizen, regardless of color, shall be given the full protection of the laws. No state can make a law that can be so interpreted to mean one thing when applied to the black man and another when applied to a white man, without disregarding the constitution of the United States."

–Booker T. Washington, interview in The Atlanta Constitution, 1900

36. Washington's statement was a reaction to
    (A) economic competition between African Americans and new immigrants.
    (B) conflicts between Native Americans and African Americans moving west.
    (C) violence and discrimination that prevented African Americans from exercising their citizenship rights.
    (D) challenges faced by African American officeholders in the federal government.

Answers

Part A: Multiple Choice

29. C; **30.** D; **31.** B; **32.** C; **33.** D; **34.** B; **35.** C; **36.** C

AP PRACTICE EXAM • E-5

37. African Americans faced increased political and social challenges that was legitimized by
    (A) the Supreme Court decision in *Plessy v. Ferguson*.
    (B) the ratification of the 15th Amendment.
    (C) the passage of the Dawes Act.
    (D) the establishment of settlement houses.

38. In the decades after Reconstruction, some Southern leaders promoted a "New South" in which
    (A) segments of the Southern economy industrialized and diversified.
    (B) the primary agricultural focus would be on tobacco cultivation.
    (C) integrated educational institutions would become the norm.
    (D) the political focus would include actively supporting ratification of the 19th Amendment.

Use the graph and your knowledge of U.S. history to answer questions 39-41.

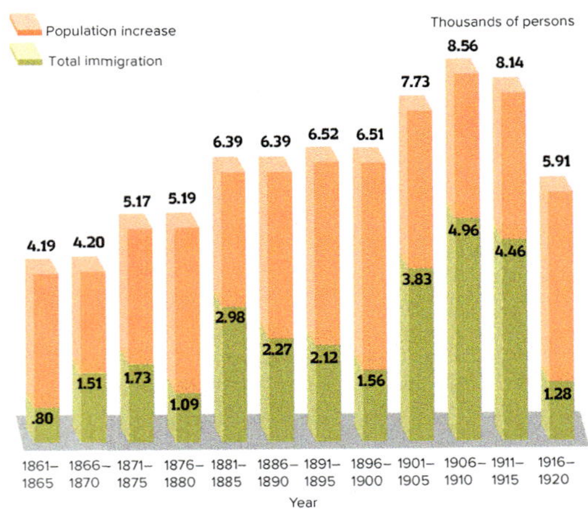

39. The population changes indicated in the chart had what impact on employment and industries?
    (A) Recent immigrants filled all available agricultural jobs.
    (B) Business leaders saw decreased profits as recent immigrants commanded high incomes.
    (C) Industrial workplaces became racially integrated as immigrants refused factory employment.
    (D) The industrial workforce expanded and became increasingly ethnically diverse.

40. Immigration to the United States between 1860 and 1920 was highest among peoples from
    (A) northern and western Europe.
    (B) northern Europe and Latin America.
    (C) Latin America and Asia.
    (D) eastern Europe, central Europe, and Asia.

41. In response to the population changes indicated in the chart, female activists such as Jane Addams
    (A) established Settlement Houses to aid immigrants in assimilation.
    (B) founded migration societies to help immigrants move to the Western territories.
    (C) found employment in government agencies to help relocate immigrants.
    (D) established political parties to advocate for immigration restrictions.

Use the image and your knowledge of U.S. history to answer questions 42-44.

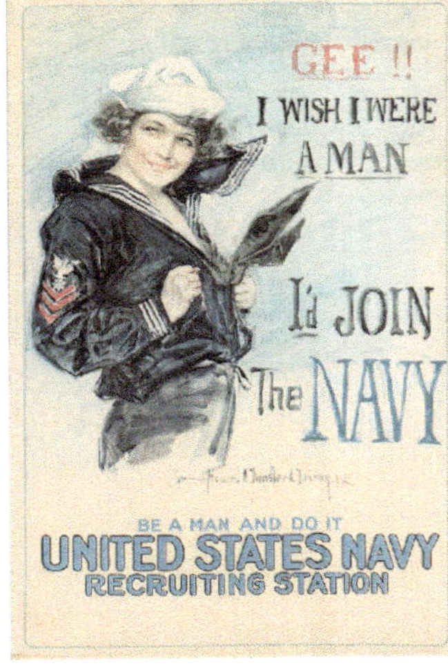

42. What message is the poster trying to convey?
    (A) The cooperation of Americans in rationing and other home front policies.
    (B) The need for Americans to support the war effort through purchasing war bonds.
    (C) The enlistment of American men into the armed forces.
    (D) The support of Americans for policies enforcing neutrality.

Answers

Part A: Multiple Choice

37. A; **38.** A; **39.** D; **40.** D; **41.** A; **42.** C

43. The focus of the American efforts during World War I reflected Woodrow Wilson's call to
(A) protect the safety of the continental United States.
(B) advance democracy around the world.
(C) stop the German advance into Poland.
(D) contain the spread of Communism.

44. The role of women in the war effort during World War I contributed to the passage of
(A) a pay equity act mandating fair compensation for equal employment.
(B) a resolution supporting women's participation in combat roles.
(C) the 19th Amendment guaranteeing women's suffrage.
(D) the Civil Rights Act that banned discrimination based on gender.

Use the excerpt and your knowledge of U.S. history to answer questions 45-47.

"YESTERDAY, December 7, 1941 a date which will live in infamy the United States of America was suddenly and deliberately attacked by naval and air forces of the Empire of Japan. . . . No matter how long it may take us to overcome this premeditated invasion, the American people in their righteous might will win through to absolute victory. I believe that I interpret the will of the Congress and of the people when I assert that we will not only defend ourselves to the uttermost but will make it very certain that this form of treachery shall never again endanger us. . . .
I ask that the Congress declare that since the unprovoked and dastardly attack by Japan on Sunday, December 7, 1941, a state of war has existed between the United States and the Japanese Empire."

—President Franklin D. Roosevelt, 1941

45. President Roosevelt delivered the above speech in response to what event?
(A) German invasion of Poland
(B) Soviet invasion of Poland
(C) Japanese attack on Manchuria
(D) Japanese attack on Pearl Harbor

46. What was the impact of American industry in World War II?
(A) American industries supplied U.S. troops and Allied forces.
(B) American industries failed to support the military during the war.
(C) American industrial leaders refused to integrate factories and failed to meet production demands.
(D) American industrial production fluctuated as business leaders sought to maximize profits.

47. The American military strategy in the Pacific relied heavily on
(A) the use of Allied forces for a ground invasion.
(B) the use of "island hopping" and atomic weapons.
(C) the use of embargos.
(D) the use of guerilla warfare and extensive spy networks.

Use the image and your knowledge of U.S. history to answer questions 48-49.

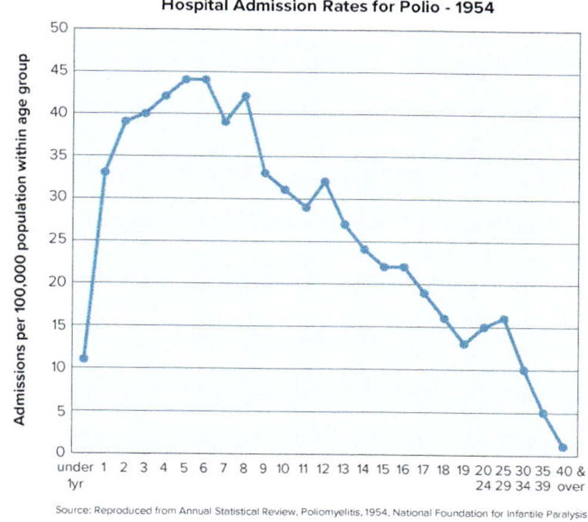

Source: Reproduced from Annual Statistical Review, Poliomyelitis, 1954, National Foundation for Infantile Paralysis.

48. Which of the following most significantly contributed to the public health crisis represented in the chart?
(A) The worsening Cold War diverted resources from domestic problems.
(B) The economy was struggling after the Korean War leading to a lack of health care resources.
(C) The post war baby boom and the large scale movement to suburbs concentrated large populations of young children.
(D) Popular culture and mass media divided Americans and hid the prevalence of the illness.

49. In addition to solving the above health crisis, technological advances in the 1950s also impacted American society through
(A) television and other forms of entertainment shaping an increasingly homogenous culture.
(B) air travel leading to more integrated communities.
(C) accelerated racial integration.
(D) de-escalation of the Cold War.

Answers

Part A: Multiple Choice

43. B; **44.** C; **45.** D; **46.** A; **47.** B; **48.** C; **49.** A

AP PRACTICE EXAM • E-7

Use the excerpt and your knowledge of U.S. history to answer questions 50-52.

"My Fellow Citizens:
For a few minutes I want to speak to you about the serious situation that has arisen in Little Rock. . . . In that city, under the leadership of demagogic extremists, disorderly mobs have deliberately prevented the carrying out of proper orders from a Federal Court. . . . This morning the mob again gathered in front of the Central High School of Little Rock, obviously for the purpose of again preventing the carrying out of the Court's order relating to the admission of Negro children to the school. . . . In accordance with that responsibility, I have today issued an Executive Order directing the use of troops under Federal authority to aid in the execution of the Federal law at Little Rock, Arkansas."

–Address by President Eisenhower, September 25, 1957

50. Schools were ordered to be racially desegregated by
   (A) the Civil Rights Act of 1964.
   (B) the Supreme Court decision *Plessy v. Ferguson*.
   (C) the Supreme Court decision *Brown v. Board of Education of Topeka*.
   (D) the Voting Rights Act of 1965.

51. As evidenced by Eisenhower's address, efforts at exercising legal rights were met with
   (A) resistance that occasionally turned violent.
   (B) little attention from most Americans.
   (C) overwhelming support from all Americans.
   (D) resistance from the legal system.

52. As the modern civil rights movement moved into the 1960s, debates arose over
   (A) the use of the legal system in the face of Supreme Court losses.
   (B) the continuing need for direct activism.
   (C) the efficacy of non-violent tactics.
   (D) the importance of national leadership.

Use the excerpt and your knowledge of U.S. history to answer questions 53-55.

"We welcome change and openness. For we believe that freedom and security go together–that the advance of human liberty can only strengthen the cause of world peace. There is one sign the Soviets can make that would be unmistakable, that would advance dramatically the cause of freedom and peace. General Secretary Gorbachev, if you seek peace–if you seek prosperity for the Soviet Union and Eastern Europe. . . Mr. Gorbachev, open this gate! Mr. Gorbachev, tear down this wall."

–President Ronald Reagan, "Remarks at Brandenburg Gate," Germany, 1987

53. At the time Reagan delivered this speech,
   (A) the Cold War was accelerating due to the recent Soviet invasion of Afghanistan.
   (B) the Soviet Union was disposing of its nuclear arsenal.
   (C) many Americans were concerned about another war with Germany.
   (D) the Soviet Union was attempting to avoid collapse as it faced political and economic challenges.

54. Americans sought a change in foreign policy in the 1980s as
   (A) a series of foreign policy crises in the 1970s lessened public confidence in the government's ability to solve problems.
   (B) the Conservative movement declined.
   (C) the ongoing war in Vietnam soured Americans on the continuation of military engagements.
   (D) Americans sought to disengage from foreign entanglements and soothe Cold War tensions.

55. Reagan's foreign policy approach was complemented by a domestic policy that focused on
   (A) increased movement away from service industry jobs and an expansion of manufacturing.
   (B) support for union membership and an expanded government role in labor conflicts.
   (C) the belief in tax cuts and deregulation of industry.
   (D) an expansion of the social safety net and government spending.

PART B: SHORT ANSWER

You must answer questions 1 and 2. Then choose to answer either question 3 or question 4.

Use the images and your knowledge of U.S. history to answer question 1.

–A twentieth century painting by Jean Ferris depicts the signing of the Mayflower Compact.

Archive PL/Alamy Stock Photo

Answers

Part A: Multiple Choice

50. C; **51.** A; **52.** C; **53.** D; **54.** A; **55.** C

–A nineteenth century engraving depicts the signing of the Mayflower Compact.

1. Answer A, B, and C.
   (A) Briefly describe ONE major difference between the depictions of the signing of the Mayflower Compact.
   (B) Briefly describe ONE major similarity between the depictions of the signing of the Mayflower Compact.
   (C) Briefly explain how ONE specific historical event or development from the period led to the creation of the Mayflower Compact.

Use the image and your knowledge of U.S. history to answer question 2.

2. Answer A, B, and C.
   (A) Briefly describe ONE point of view about the rise of nationalism in the United States from 1816 to 1832.
   (B) Briefly explain ONE specific historical cause that gave way to the rise of nationalism in the United States from 1816 to 1832.
   (C) Briefly explain ONE specific historical effect that resulted from the rise of nationalism in the United States from 1816 to 1832.

3. Use your knowledge of U.S. history to answer A, B, and C.
   (A) Briefly describe ONE specific historical similarity between the 1920s and the 1950s.
   (B) Briefly describe ONE specific historical difference between the 1920s and the 1950s.
   (C) Briefly explain ONE specific effect that resulted from societal tensions within American society from either the 1920s or the 1950s.

4. Use your knowledge of U.S. history to answer A, B, and C.
   (A) Briefly describe ONE specific historic continuity within American foreign policy from 1900 to 1950.
   (B) Briefly describe ONE specific historical change within American foreign policy from 1900 to 1950.
   (C) Briefly explain ONE specific effect of American foreign policy after 1950 that was a direct result of foreign policy changes between 1900 and 1950.

Rubric: Short Answer Question

General Scoring Notes

- Each point is earned separately.
- Students are required to demonstrate historical accuracy within their answers. Student answers may contain minor errors provided they do not detract from the overall quality of their response.
- Student answers should be considered rough drafts. Grammatical errors do not count against the student unless they prevent the demonstration of the knowledge and skills necessary to be awarded points.
- Student answers must include not only applicable terms, but also a description of the relevant characteristics as appropriate to the prompt.
- Student answers must include an explanation of how or why a historical development or event occurred and/or the reasoning for a relationship between historical developments or events.

Answers

Part B: Short Answer

1A) Possible answer: The engraving presents a formal and ceremonial point of view. In contrast, the painting offers a casual interpretation of the event.

1B) Possible answer: Both depictions include women and present the group collaborating while gathered around the compact.

1C) Possible answer: The Pilgrims, having arrived in Massachusetts instead of Virginia, felt the original charter was void and created the compact to establish temporary laws.

2A) Possible answer: Americans experienced a surge of national pride following the War of 1812.

2B) Possible answer: Following the War of 1812, political parties essentially disappeared, leading to a single political party in control of the government.

2C) Possible answer: As part of the surge in nationalism, authors Charles Brockden Brown, William Austin, and Washington Irving all sought to portray a unique American identity and ideology.

3A) Possible answer: Both the 1920s and the 1950s saw a significant rise in evangelicalism that merged with national politics.

3B) Possible answer: The economic prosperity of the 1920s was followed by the Great Depression, but the economic prosperity of the 1950s continued through much of the following decade.

3C) Possible answer: American society experienced rising racial tensions and increasing nativism during both time periods.

4A) Possible answer: The U.S. attempted positions of neutrality in world affairs and professed isolationism during the period.

4B) Possible answer: The U.S. increased its involvement in world affairs after WWII, as evidenced by its role in the United Nations.

4C) Possible answer: The policy of containment resulted from the foreign policy changes after WWII.

Answers

Part A: Document-Based Question

Full rubrics are available online.

Thesis/Claim (0–1 Point)

Scoring Notes: Student responses that earn a point should establish a claim and a line of reasoning. Example: Many causes drove Cold War fears in the U.S. Americans were concerned with the physical and intellectual threat of Soviet infiltration.

Contextualization (0–1 Point)

Scoring Notes: Student responses that earn a point should incorporate relevant historical context. Example: During the early decades of the 20th century, the U.S. was in an existential conflict with Russia. The U.S. did not want to be perceived as soft on communism. Tensions also manifested in an early Red Scare during the 20s, as fears about communism began to take root.

Evidence (0–3 Points)

Scoring Notes: Student responses that earn points incorporate 3–6 documents. Example: Document 5 illustrates the action that can be taken to deal with a nuclear attack by the Soviet Union. Student responses that incorporate evidence beyond the documents receive a point. Example: The threat of nuclear attack by the Soviet Union is also seen in popular culture in films such as *Red Dawn*.

Analysis and Reasoning (0–2 Points)

Scoring Notes: Student responses that incorporate the full analysis of 3 documents and utilizes evidence receives point(s). Example: The nuclear capabilities of the Soviets drove domestic fears. The image in document 5 is from the point of view of the public. It was meant to alleviate fear with a plan of action and implied that the U.S. was prepared for such an attack.

AP PRACTICE EXAM

SECTION II

PART A: DOCUMENT-BASED QUESTION

Use the documents and your knowledge of U.S. history to answer question 1.

Be sure to do the following when writing your answer:

- **Write a historically defensible thesis statement that explicitly addresses all parts of the prompt.**
- **Support your thesis and develop your argument using at least six of the documents.**
- **Include evidence to support, develop, or modify your argument.**
- **Address how at least three of the documents support your argument through: intended audience, purpose, historical context, and/or point of view.**
- **Support your argument with at least one piece of historical evidence outside of the provided documents.**
- **Connect your argument to broader historical events and/or processes that are relevant to the prompt.**

1. Evaluate the relative importance of causes that led to Cold War fears in American society from 1945 to 1965.

Document 1

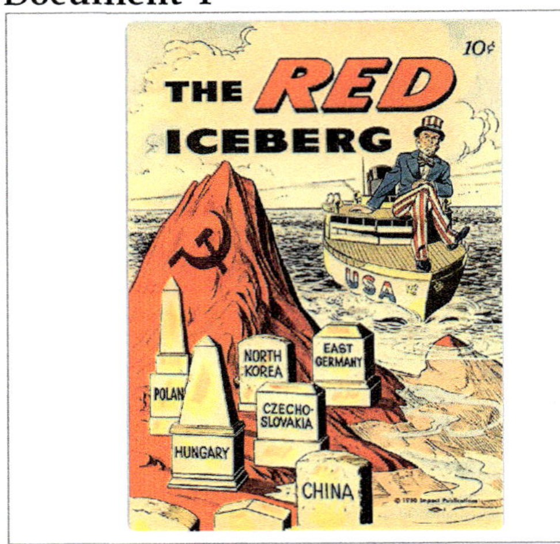

Document 2

"Behind the black portent of the new atomic age lies a hope which, seized upon with faith, can work our salvation. If we fail, then we have damned every man to be the slave of Fear. Let us not deceive ourselves: We must elect World Peace or World Destruction.

Science has torn from nature a secret so vast in its potentialities that our minds cower from the terror it creates. Yet terror is not enough to inhibit the use of the atomic bomb. The terror created by weapons has never stopped man from employing them. For each new weapon a defense has been produced, in time. But now we face a condition in which adequate defense does not exist.

Science, which gave us this dread power, shows that it can be made a giant help to humanity, but science does not show us how to prevent its baleful use. So we have been appointed to obviate that period by finding a meeting of the minds and the hearts of our peoples. Only in the will of mankind lies the answer. . . .

When an adequate system for control of atomic energy, including the renunciation of the bomb as a weapon, has been agreed upon and put into effective operation and condign punishments set up for violations of the rules of control which are to be stigmatized as international crimes, we propose that –

1. Manufacture of atomic bombs shall stop;
2. Existing bombs shall be disposed of pursuant to the terms of the treaty; . . .

Now as to violations: in the agreement, penalties of as serious a nature as the nations may wish and as immediate and certain in their execution as possible, should be fixed for–

1. Illegal possession or use of an atomic bomb;
2. Illegal possession, or separation, of atomic material suitable for use in an atomic bomb;"

–Bernard Baruch to the U.N. Atomic Energy Commission, June 14, 1946

Retro AdArchives/Alamy Stock Photo

Rubric: Document-Based Question

General Scoring Notes

- Each point is earned separately.
- Students are required to demonstrate historical accuracy within their answers. Student answers may contain minor errors provided they do not detract from the overall quality of their response.
- Student answers should be considered rough drafts. Grammatical errors do not count against the student unless they prevent the demonstration of the knowledge and skills necessary to be awarded points.

Document 3

COOPERATION
means prosperity

Document 4

"(Two) We must see that our public is educated to realities of Russian situation. I cannot over-emphasize importance of this. Press cannot do this alone. It must be done mainly by Government, which is necessarily more experienced and better informed on practical problems involved. In this we need not be deterred by fglinness *[sic]* of picture. I am convinced that there would be far less hysterical anti-Sovietism in our country today if realities of this situation were better understood by our people. There is nothing as dangerous or as terrifying as the unknown. It may also be argued that to reveal more information on our difficulties with Russia would reflect unfavorably on Russian-American relations. I feel that if there is any real risk here involved, it is one which we should have courage to face, and sooner the better. But I cannot see what we would be risking. Our stake in this country, even coming on heels of tremendous demonstrations of our friendship for Russian people, is remarkably small. We have here no investments to guard, no actual trade to lose, virtually no citizens to protect, few cultural contacts to preserve. Our only stake lies in what we hope rather than what we have; and I am convinced we have better chance of realizing those hopes if our public is enlightened and if our dealings with Russians are placed entirely on realistic and matter-of-fact basis.

(Three) Much depends on health and vigor of our own society. World communism is like malignant parasite which feeds only on diseased tissue. This is point at which domestic and foreign policies meet. Every courageous and incisive measure to solve internal problems of our own society, to improve self-confidence, discipline, morale and community spirit of our own people, is a diplomatic victory over Moscow. . ."

—George Kennan, U.S. Ambassador,
"Long Telegram," February 22, 1946

Document 5

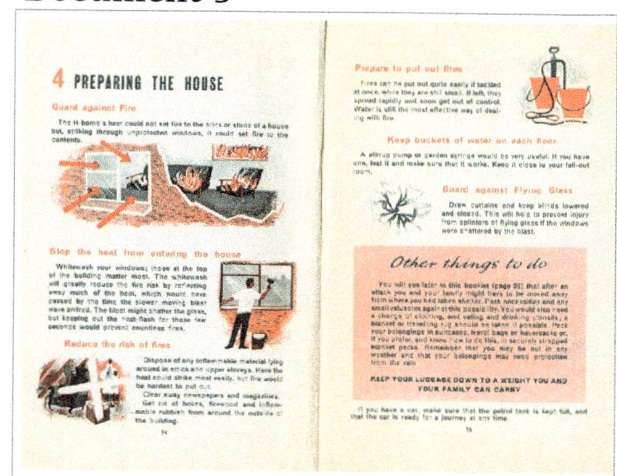

Document 6

"A more rapid build-up of political, economic, and military strength and thereby of confidence in the free world than is now contemplated is the only course which is consistent with progress toward achieving our fundamental purpose. The frustration of the Kremlin design requires the free world to develop a successfully functioning political and economic system and a vigorous political offensive against the Soviet Union. These, in turn, require an adequate military shield under which they can develop. It is necessary to have the military power to deter, if possible, Soviet expansion, and to defeat, if necessary, aggressive Soviet or Soviet-directed actions of a limited or total character. The potential strength of the free world is great; its ability to develop these military capabilities and its will to resist Soviet expansion will be determined by the wisdom and will with which it undertakes to meet its political and economic problems. . . .

The threat to the free world involved in the development of the Soviet Union's atomic and other capabilities will rise steadily and rather rapidly. For the time being, the United States possesses a marked atomic superiority over the Soviet Union which, together with the potential capabilities of the United States and other free countries in other forces and weapons, inhibits aggressive Soviet action. This provides an opportunity for the United States, in cooperation with other free countries, to launch a build-up of strength which will

Answers

Part B: Long Essay

Full rubrics are available online.

2. Thesis/Claim (0–1 Point)
Scoring Notes: Student responses that earn a point should establish a claim and a line of reasoning. Example: The South attempted to diversify its economy but remained largely agricultural.

Contextualization (0–1 Point)
Scoring Notes: Student responses that earn a point should incorporate relevant historical context. Example: The Southern colonies were comprised of tracts of land that were held by small families. This model continued through the Civil War and the Southern economy remained based on agricultural exports.

Evidence (0–2 Points)
Scoring Notes: Student responses that incorporate evidence in support of an argument receives point(s). Example: The South before the Civil War was largely agricultural, providing cotton not only to Northern textile industries, but also to Europe.

Analysis and Reasoning (0–2 Points)
Scoring Notes: Student responses that use historical reasoning and incorporate evidence receives point(s). Example: Despite attempts on the part of Southern business leaders to industrialize, which did occur in select cities, like Atlanta, which became a strong source of iron and steel, the South remained largely agricultural. This led to major disadvantages for the South even into the latter part of the nineteenth century.

Rubric: Long Essay Question

General Scoring Notes

- Each point is earned separately.
- Students are required to demonstrate historical accuracy within their answers. Student answers may contain minor errors provided they do not detract from the overall quality of their response.
- Student answers should be considered rough drafts. Grammatical errors do not count against the student unless they prevent the demonstration of the knowledge and skills necessary to be awarded points.

Answers

Part B: Long Essay

Full rubrics are available online.

3. Thesis/Claim (0–1 Point)
Scoring Notes: Student responses that earn a point should establish a claim and a line of reasoning. Example: Interactions with European colonists had devastating social, cultural, and demographic consequences for Native Americans.

Contextualization (0–1 Point)
Scoring Notes: Student responses that earn a point should incorporate relevant historical context. Example: European nations, in competition with one another for territory and resources, increased exploration in the Americas. As European settlement increased, so did conflict with and consequences for Native Americans.

Evidence (0–2 Points)
Scoring Notes: Student responses that incorporate evidence in support of an argument receives point(s). Example: Native American populations were greatly reduced though the spread of European diseases.

Analysis and Reasoning (0–2 Points)
Scoring Notes: Student responses that use historical reasoning and incorporate evidence receives point(s). Example: Native Americans experienced cultural and social changes due to loss of land and introduction to European weapons and goods.

support a firm policy directed to the frustration of the Kremlin design. The immediate goal of our efforts to build a successfully functioning political and economic system in the free world backed by adequate military strength is to postpone and avert the disastrous situation which, in light of the Soviet Union's probable fission bomb capability and possible thermonuclear bomb capability, might arise in 1954 on a continuation of our present programs."

—excerpt from A Report to the National Security Council, April 14, 1950

Document 7

"A vital element in keeping the peace is our military establishment. Our arms must be mighty, ready for instant action, so that no potential aggressor may be tempted to risk his own destruction. . . . Our military organization today bears little relation to that known by any of my predecessors in peacetime, or indeed by the fighting men of World War II or Korea. . . . Until the latest of our world conflicts, the United States had no armaments industry. American makers of plowshares could, with time and as required, make swords as well. But now we can no longer risk emergency improvisation of national defense; we have been compelled to create a permanent armaments industry of vast proportions. Added to this, three and a half million men and women are directly engaged in the defense establishment. We annually spend on military security more than the net income of all United States corporations. . . . This conjunction of an immense military establishment and a large arms industry is new in the American experience. The total influence-economic, political, even spiritual – is felt in every city, every State house, every office of the Federal government. We recognize the imperative need for this development. Yet we must not fail to comprehend its grave implications. Our toil, resources and livelihood are all involved; so is the very structure of our society. . . . In the councils of government, we must guard against the acquisition of unwarranted influence, whether sought or unsought, by the military-industrial complex. The potential for the disastrous rise of misplaced power exists and will persist. . . . We must never let the weight of this combination endanger our liberties or democratic processes. We should take nothing for granted. Only an alert and knowledgeable citizenry can compel the proper meshing of the huge industrial and military machinery of defense with our peaceful methods and goals, so that security and liberty may prosper together."

—Dwight D. Eisenhower, "Farewell Address," January 17, 1961

PART B: LONG ESSAY

Select ONE of the following questions to answer.

Be sure to do the following when writing your answer:

- **Develop a thoughtful and thorough historically defensible thesis statement with a clear line of reasoning.**
- **Expand your argument using historical reasoning processes, such as compare and contrast, cause and effect, and/or patterns of continuity and change.**
- **Support your argument using specific and appropriate historical evidence.**
- **Evaluate how the prompt is related to a larger historical context.**
- **Include additional evidence to support, develop, or modify your argument.**

2. Evaluate the extent of continuities within the American South from 1820 to 1880.
3. Evaluate the extent that Native Americans were impacted by the migration of and encounters with European colonists from 1491 to 1650.
4. Evaluate the extent that the modern civil rights movement impacted Supreme Court decisions and legislation between 1950 and 1980.

Answers

Part B: Long Essay

4. Thesis/Claim (0–1 Point) Scoring Notes: Student responses that earn a point should establish a claim and a line of reasoning. The modern civil rights movement significantly influenced legislation during the time period. **Contextualization (0–1 Point) Scoring Notes:** Student responses that earn a point should incorporate relevant historical context. The civil rights movement brought attention to a variety of issues, including segregation, discrimination, and voter suppression. **Evidence (0–2 Points) Scoring Notes:** The attention garnered by civil rights activists, particularly in Birmingham, Alabama, helped produce political pressure to pass the Civil Rights Act of 1964. The Warren Court made numerous important decisions including *Brown v. Board of Education* and *Bolling v. Sharpe* regarding public school segregation. **Analysis and Reasoning (0–2 Points) Scoring Notes:** Student responses that use historical reasoning and incorporate evidence receives point(s). Example: The civil rights movement spurred the passage of the Civil Rights Act of 1964; ended segregation on public spaces; and banned employment discrimination based on race, religion, sex, or national origin.